THE FACTS ON FILE
ENCYCLOPEDIA OF
WORD AND
PHRASE
ORIGINS

Third Edition

ROBERT HENDRICKSON

Checkmark Books®
An imprint of Facts On File, Inc.

For my son,

Robert Laurence Hendrickson

––––––––––––––––––

The Facts On File Encyclopedia of Word and Phrase Origins, Third Edition

Copyright © 2004 by Robert Hendrickson

Checkmark Books
An imprint of Facts On File, Inc.
132 West 31st Street
New York NY 10001

Library of Congress Cataloging-in-Publication Data

Hendrickson, Robert, 1933–
The Facts on File encyclopedia of word and phrase origins / Robert Hendrickson—3rd ed.
p. cm.
Includes index.
ISBN 0-8160-4813-4 (hc: acid-free paper) ISBN 0-8160-5992-6 (pbk.)
1. English language—Etymology—Dictionaries. 2. English language—Terms and phrases.
I. Title.

PE1689 H47 2003
422'.03—dc21
2003044948

CONTENTS

Preface to the Third Edition   v

Preface to the Original Edition   vii

Abbreviations for the Most Frequently Cited Authorities   ix

Entries A–Z   1

Index   807

Preface to the Third Edition

This edition of *The Facts On File Encyclopedia of Word and Phrase Origins* contains more than 30 percent more new material than the last revised and expanded edition, making it the largest American collection of its kind. Among new features added to these pages are more words and phrases deriving from classical sources, a larger selection of up-to-date slang origins recording "the living language of the day," and a unique sample of interesting English words and phrases that originated in the 200 or so countries other than the United States and Great Britain where English is spoken as an official language.

A good number of these new entries were suggested by readers who responded to my requests for help in previous editions. Thanks to all of you, especially to Professor Masayoshi Yamada, trustee and professor of linguistics at Japan's Shimane University, for his explanations of the many forms of "Japanized" English words, and to Professor Howard Marblestone of Lafayette College, whose wise counsel and great learning in classical Greek, Latin, and Hebrew saved me from many embarrassing errors.

My correspondent Eric Halsey should also be singled out for his learned contributions. Among many other highly valued contributors are Professor William Matthews of New York's City College; Admiral Edgar Keats; Joseph M. Clark; W. D. Grisson, Sr.; Dr. Frank Young; Vernon A. Johnson; William R. Appel; Hans Thomas; Dr. John B. Dehoff; Professor Barbara Field of Columbia University; Joel Ben Izzy; J. Larry Nederlef; Robin Lawson; Henry Gordon; Barry Zimmerman; Ric Sciacca; Donald A. Yates; Virginia Thorndike; Marion Morgan; Professor Bruce T. Adams; June Holdup; Jack Melb; Barbara Casto; Douglas Campbell; John Otto Olson; Kevin Heneghan; Linda Clifford; Toby J. Sommer; Robert V. Weisser; and Professor Bruce T. Adams.

Many thanks are also due to my editors, Jeff Soloway and Anne Savarese, and to copy editors Jerry Kappes and Michael G. Laraque, who labored so long on this huge project.

To my wife, Marilyn, whose name should really be on the book's cover along with my own, I can only say: "Take the sweetest phrases the world has ever known and make believe I said them all to you."

—R. H.
Peconic, New York

PREFACE TO THE ORIGINAL EDITION

This book is, I believe, the longest collection of word and phrase origins in print.

In any case, I've tried to make all the selections as accurate and entertaining as possible and tried to use words illustrating all of the many ways words and phrases are born (words deriving from the numerous languages and dialects that have enriched English, echoic words, coined words, slang, words from the names of places, people, animals, occupations, leisure activities, mispronunciations, etc.). Yet in the final analysis any selection from such a vast semantic treasure house (the 5–10 million or so general and technical English words) must be highly subjective. Perhaps I have erred in devoting too much space to fascinating but speculative stories about word origins, but I don't think so, for the wildest theories often later turn out to be the correct ones. In any case, while no good tale is omitted merely because it isn't true, where stories are apocryphal or doubtful, they are clearly labeled so. I've tried to include as many plausible theories about the origins of each expression as possible and also attempted to show the first recorded use of a word or phrase wherever possible, something lacking in many word books but a great, sometimes indispensable, help to anyone using the work as a linguistic or historical reference. The only limitations I have imposed are those of importance and interest. Some expressions, no matter how prosaic the stories behind them, have been included because they are commonly used; on the other hand, interesting and unusual expressions have often been treated even if obscure or obsolete. No word or phrase has been eliminated because it might offend someone's sensibilities, and you will find all the famous four-letter words here (and then some!). I consider myself no judge of what is or is not obscene, and such self-appointed lobotomizers of language remind me of Kurt Vonnegut's dictator who eliminated noses in order to eliminate odors. Though there has been a renewed general interest in word origins recently—thanks mainly to magazines like *Verbatim*, the work of Stuart Berg Flexner, Professor Frederic Cassidy's monumental *Dictionary of American Regional English*, or *DARE*, and William Safire's excellent and entertaining syndicated column "On Language"—etymology remains something less than an exact science. Scholars like Professor Gerald Cohen of the University of Missouri-Rolla do devote years and pages enough for a book in scientifically tracking down the origins of a single word, but a great number of the word derivations on record amount to little more than educated guesswork. I agree, however, with the late, great, and "always game" word detective Eric Partridge that even a guess is better than nothing—even if it's just inspired fun, or if it merely stimulates thinking that leads eventually to the expression's true origin.

The debts for a work of this nature and length are so numerous that specific thanks must be confined to the many sources noted in the text, and due to space limitations even these are only a relative handful of the works I have consulted. On a personal note, however, I would like to thank my editor, Gerard Helferich, for all his herculean labors (just toting the manuscript about was a herculean labor), and of course my wife, Marilyn—this book, like every line I write, being as much hers as mine. Nevertheless, despite all the help I've gotten, any errors in these pages result from my own wide-ranging ignorance and are solely my responsibility. They cannot even be blamed on a committee or a computer.

—R. H.

ABBREVIATIONS FOR THE MOST FREQUENTLY CITED AUTHORITIES

BARTLETT—John Bartlett, *Dictionary of Americanisms* (1877)

BARLETT'S QUOTATIONS—John Bartlett, *Familiar Quotations* (1882 and 1955)

BREWER—Rev. Ebenezer Cobham Brewer, *Brewer's Dictionary of Fact and Fable* (1870)

DARE—Frederic Cassidy, ed. *Dictionary of American Regional English*, Vol. 1, 1986; Vol. 2 (1991); Vol. 3 (1996); Vol. 4 (2002)

FARMER AND HENLEY—John S. Farmer and W. E. Henley, *Slang and Its Analogues* (1890–1904)

FOWLER—H. W. Fowler, *Modern English Usage* (1957)

GRANVILLE—Wilfred Granville, *A Dictionary of Sailor's Slang* (1962)

GROSE—Captain Francis Grose, *Dictionary of the Vulgar Tongue* (1785, 1788, 1796, 1811, 1823 editions)

LIGHTER—J. E. Lighter, ed., *Random House Historical Dictionary of American Slang*, Vol. 1 (1994); Vol. 2 (2000)

MATHEWS—Mitford M. Mathews, *A Dictionary of Americanisms* (1951)

MENCKEN—H. L. Mencken, *The American Language* (1936)

O.E.D.—*The Oxford English Dictionary* and Supplements

ONIONS—C. T. Onions, *The Oxford Dictionary of English Etymology* (1966)

PARTRIDGE—Eric Partridge, *A Dictionary of Slang and Unconventional English* (1937; 8th ed., 1984)

PARTRIDGE'S ORIGINS—Eric Partridge, *Origins, A Short Etymological Dictionary of Modern English* (1958)

PEPYS—Henry Wheatley, ed., *The Diary of Samuel Pepys* (1954)

RANDOM HOUSE—*The Random House Dictionary of the English Language* (1966)

ROSTEN—Leo Rosten, *The Joys of Yiddish* (1968)

SHIPLEY—Joseph T. Shipley, *Dictionary of Word Origins* (1967)

SKEAT—W. W. Skeat, *An Etymological Dictionary of the English Language* (1963)

STEVENSON—Burton Stevenson, *Home Book of Quotations* (1947)

STEWART—George R. Stewart, *American Place Names* (1971)

WALSH—W. S. Walsh, *Handbook of Literary Curiosities* (1892)

WEBSTER'S—*Webster's Third New International Dictionary of the English Language* (1981)

WEEKLEY—Ernest Weekley, *Etymological Dictionary of Modern English* (1967)

WENTWORTH AND FLEXNER—Harold Wentworth and Stuart Berg Flexner, *Dictionary of American Slang* (1975)

WESEEN—Maurice H. Weseen, *The Dictionary of American Slang* (1934)

WRIGHT—Joseph Wright, *English Dialect Dictionary* (1900)

Many different works by the same authors, and additional works by other writers, are cited in the text.

To make dictionaries is hard work.

—Dr. Samuel Johnson

A. Like Chinese characters, each letter in our alphabet began with a picture or drawing of an animal, person, or object that eventually became a symbol with little resemblance to the original object depicted. No one is sure what these pictographs represented originally, but scholars have made some educated guesses. *A* probably represented the horns of an ox, drawn first as a *V* with a bar across it like the bar in *A*. This may have been suggested by early plowmen guiding oxen by lines attached to a bar strapped across the animal's horns.

Adulterers were forced to wear the capital letter *A* as a badge when convicted of the crime of adultery under an American law in force from 1639 to 1785. Wrote Nathaniel Hawthorne in his story "Endicott and the Red Cross" (1838): "There was likewise a young woman, with no mean share of beauty, whose doom it was to wear the letter A on the breast of her gown, in the eyes of all the world and her own children . . . Sporting with her infamy, the lost and desperate creature had embroidered the fatal token in scarlet cloth, with golden thread; so that the capital A might have been thought to mean Admirable, or anything rather than Adulteress." Hawthorne, of course, also wrote about the *A* of adultery in his novel *The Scarlet Letter* (1850).

Perhaps only UGH! has been deemed by dime novels and Hollywood to be more representative of American Indian speech than the omission of *a* as an article. Willa Cather made an interesting observation on this American Indian habit (and there is no telling how widespread the habit really was) in *Death Comes for the Archbishop* (1927): " 'Have you a son?' 'One. Baby. Not very long born.' Jacinto usually dropped the article in speaking Spanish, just as he did in speaking English, though the Bishop had noticed that when he did give a noun its article, he used the right one. The customary omission, therefore, seemed a matter of taste, not ignorance. In the Indian conception of language, such attachments were superfluous and unpleasing, perhaps."

aa. *Aa* for rough porous lava, similar to coal clinkers, is an Americanism used chiefly in Hawaii, but it has currency on the mainland, too, especially among geologists, or where there has been recent volcanic activity, mainly because there is no comparable English term to describe the jagged rocks. The word *aa* is first recorded in 1859, but is much older, coming from the Hawaiian *'a'a*, meaning the same, which, in turn comes from the Hawaiian *a*, for "fiery, burning."

AAA. The AAA, standing for *Agricultural Adjustment Administration*, was among the first of the "alphabet agencies" (government agencies, administrations, authorities, offices, etc.) created for relief and recovery in the early days of the New Deal during America's Great Depression. The New Deal itself took its name from Franklin Delano Roosevelt's acceptance speech at the Democratic National Convention on July 2, 1932: "I pledge you, I pledge myself, to a new deal for the American people." Coined by Roosevelt's speech writers, Raymond Moley and Judge Samuel Rosenman, the phrase incorporated elements of Woodrow Wilson's New Freedom and Teddy Roosevelt's Square Deal. Among the many alphabet agencies spawned by the New Deal are the CCC (Civilian Conservation Corps), FCA (Farm Credit Administration), FDIC (Federal Deposit Insurance Corporation), SEC (Securities and Exchange Commission), and the WPA (Works Progress Administration).

A & P. These familiar initials have become the common name of the supermarket chain they were once an abbreviation for. The Great Atlantic *and* Pacific Tea Company began life in 1859 as a partnership between George Huntington Hartford and George Gilman. The new company originally bought tea directly off ships bringing it to America and sold it to consumers, eliminating the middleman. Within 20 years the company became the first American grocery chain.

aardvark; aardwolf. Both these animals dig in the earth for termites and ants, the former somewhat resembling a pig, the latter looking a little like a striped wolf. Thus the Boers in South Africa named them, respectively, the aardvark (from the Dutch *aard*, "earth," plus *vark*, "pig") or "earth pig," and aardwolf, or "earth wolf."

Aaron lily; Aaron's beard; Aaron's rod; Aaron's serpent. Numerous plants are named for the patriarch Aaron. Mention the 133d Psalm of "the beard of Aaron" led to *Aaron's beard* becoming the common name of the rose of Sharon (which in the Bible is really a crocus), icy-leaved toadflax, meadowsweet, *Aaron's-beard* cactus, and the Jerusalem star, among others, in reference to their beard-like flowers. *Aaron's rod* comes from the sacred rod that Aaron placed before the ark in Num. 17:8, a rod that Jehovah caused to bud, blossom, and bear ripe almonds. Many tall-stemmed, flowering plants that resemble rods, such as mullein, goldenrod, and garden orpine, are called *Aaron's rod*, and the term is used in architecture to describe an ornamental moulding entwined with sprouting leaves, a serpent, or scrollwork. *Aaron lily* also honors Aaron, but the name derives from the folk etymology of arum lily. *Aaron's serpent*, denoting a force so powerful as to eliminate all other powers, alludes to the miracle in Exod. 7:11–12, when the Lord commanded that Aaron cast down his rod before Pharaoh: "Then Pharaoh also called the wise men and the sorcerers: now the magicians of Egypt, they also did in like manner with their enchantments. For they cast down every man his rod, and they became serpents, but Aaron's rod swallowed up their rods." Linguists have found that the word *tannen* given in the Exodus sources really means "reptile," but there is little chance that "Aaron's reptile" will replace *Aaron's serpent* in the language.

aarschgnoddle. *See* FARTLEBERRY.

AB; able-bodied seaman. *AB* stands for an *able-bodied seaman*, a first-class sailor who is a skilled seaman and has passed his training as an ordinary seaman. The expression *able-bodied* dates back to 17th-century England, when apprentices or boys formed the other, inexperienced class among the crews on sailing ships.

abacus. Our name for this incredibly efficient instrument, which a skilled person can operate as fast and as accurately as an adding machine, is from the Greek *abax*, meaning a tablet for ciphering. The abacus was invented by the Chinese, but they call the beaded ciphering machine a *suan pan*, which is the source for the Japanese abacus called the *soroban*.

abash. *See* BAH!

abassi. Though of interest primarily to collectors, the abassi is the first of many coins named after famous persons. It is a silver piece worth about 29 cents that was formerly used in Persia, and it honors Shah Abas II.

abbreviations. Unlike ACRONYMS, abbreviations aren't usually pronounced as words, but they do serve the same purpose as time- and space-savers. They have been popular since the earliest times, a good example being SPQR, the abbreviation for *Senatus Populusque Romanus*, the famous insignia of Rome. Most abbreviations merely suggest the whole word they represent to the reader (as Dr.), but many have become almost words themselves: the letters spoken, as in I.Q. for intelligence quotient. A few are even spoken as words, such as *vet* for veterinarian or armed service veteran, *ad* for advertisement, and *ad lib*. There are entire dictionaries devoted to the tens of thousands of abbreviations we use, and a complete list of abbreviations of government agencies can be found in the *United States Government Organization Manual*. Below are a handful of interesting and humorous abbreviations from slang and standard English that illustrate the diverse and complex ways such coinages are formed. Included are *eusystolisms*, "initials used in the interest of delicacy," such as S.O.B:

A.A. Alcoholics Anonymous

ad lib from the Latin *ad libitum*, at one's pleasure; was first a musical term.

C-Note century note, $100.

C.O.D. collect on delivery; has been traced back to 1859.

DTs delirium tremens.

et al. from the Latin *et alia*, "and others."

F.Y.I. For Your Information; ubiquitous on office memos.

G.P. general practitioner.

Ibid. from the Latin *ibidem*, "in the same place."

IHS the abbreviation is simply the first two letters and last letter of the Greek word for Jesus, capitalized and Romanized. It does not stand for *in hoc signo* ("in this sign") or any other phrase.

I.O.U. for "I owe you"; an unusual abbreviation that is based on sound, not sight.

MIG standing for a Russian jet fighter, from the initials of the designers of a series of Russian fighters.

Mrs., Mr. *Mrs.* originally stood for "mistress," when "mistress" meant a married woman, but since a mistress today is something entirely different, *Mrs.* cannot be considered a true abbreviation anymore—there is no full form for the word, unlike for *Mr.* (mister).

P.D.Q. stands for "pretty damn quick," e.g., "You'd better get started P.D.Q." Its origin hasn't been established beyond doubt, although it has been attributed to Dan Maguinnis, a Boston comedian appearing about 1867–1889.

Q.T. an abbreviation for "quiet"; "on the q.t." means stealthily, secretly, e.g., "to meet someone on the q.t." Origin unknown.

Q.V. from the Latin *quod vide*, "which see."

R.S.V.P. stands for the French *répondez s'il vous plait*, "please reply," "the favor of a reply is requested."

UFO Unidentified flying object, the term coined in recent times, although the first sightings of such objects were reported as far back as 1896.

Abderian laughter. Inhabitants of ancient Abdera were known as rural simpletons who foolishly derided people and things they didn't understand. Thus these Thracians saw their name become a synonym for foolish, scoffing laughter or mockery. Though proverbially known for their stupidity, the Abderites included some of the wisest men in Greece, Democritus and Protagoras among them.

abecedarian hymns. *See* ACROSTIC.

Abelia. A plant genus of the honeysuckle family that was named for British physician and plant collector Dr. Clarke Abel, including some 80 ornamental shrubs that are found across the Northern Hemisphere from eastern Asia to Mexico. *Abelis schumannii* is a species of *Abelia* named for Dr. Karl Schumann, a 19th-century German botanist, and is one of the many plants bearing both genus and species human family names.

Abe Lincoln bug. Anti-Lincoln feelings died hard in the South after the Civil War, as the name of this little bug shows. Even as late as 1901 this foul-smelling insect, also known as the harlequin cabbage bug, was commonly called the *Abe-Lincoln bug* in Georgia and other Southern states. *See also* LINCOLNDOM.

Abe Lincoln War. The Civil War was given this name in New England, the only U.S. region where names associating the war with slavery were commonly employed. *The Abolition War, The War of the States,* and *The War to Free the Slaves* were others. *See* CIVIL WAR.

Abert's towhee. A colorful bird of the Southwest named for soldier-naturalist Lt. J. W. Abert (1820–87), who has several other southwestern birds and animals, including *Abert's squirrel,* named in his honor,

abet. *Abet* means to incite, instigate, or encourage someone to act, often wrongfully. The word derives from an old command for a dog to "sic'em" or "go get'em," and owes its life to the "sport" of bearbaiting, which was as popular as cricket in 14th- and 15th-century England. In bearbaiting, a recently trapped bear, starved to make it unnaturally vicious, was chained to a stake or put in a pit, and a pack of dogs was set loose upon it in a fight to the death, which the bear always lost, after inflicting great punishment on the dogs. Spectators who urged the dogs on were said to *abet* them, *abet* here being the contraction of the Old French *abeter,* "to bait, to hound on," which in turn derived from the Norse *beita,* "to cause to bite." Bearbaiting was virtually a Sunday institution in England for 800 years, until it was banned in 1835; Queen Elizabeth I once attended a "Bayting" at which 13 bears were killed.

abeyance. *See* BAH!

abigail. A lady's maid or servant is sometimes called an *abigail,* which means "source of joy" in Hebrew. Several real Abigails contributed their names to the word. The term originates in the Bible (Sam. I:25) when Nabal's wife, Abigail, apologizes for her wealthy husband's selfishness in denying David food for his followers—humbly referring to herself as David's "handmaid" six times in the course of eight short chapters. David must have appreciated this, for when Nabal died he made Abigail one of his wives. The name and occupation were further associated when Francis Beaumont and John Fletcher's *The Scornful Lady,* written about five years after the King James version of the Bible (1611), gave the name Abigail to a spirited "waiting gentlewoman," one of the play's leading characters. *Abigail* was thereafter used by many writers, including Congreve, Swift, Fielding, and Smollett, but only came to be spelled without a capital when popularized by the notoriety of Abigail Hill, one of Queen Anne's ladies-in-waiting from 1704 to 1714.

able-bodied seaman. *See* AB.

Abolition War. *See* ABE LINCOLN WAR.

A-bomb; H-bomb; the bomb. The atomic bomb was first called the *atom bomb* or *A-bomb* within a few months after it was dropped on Hiroshima on August 6, 1945. People were also calling it simply *the bomb* by then. Soon after the far more powerful thermonuclear hydrogen bomb or H-bomb was tested, in 1952, it was commonly called *the bomb,* too. Lighter cites a 1945–48 reference for *A-bomb* as a powerful mixed drink. The nickname of the uranium bomb dropped on Hiroshima was Little Boy, while the plutonium bomb that obliterated Nagasaki three days later was called Fat Man.

Aboriginal Australian words. English words that come to us from Aboriginal Australian include boomerang, kangaroo, dingo, koala, wallaby, wombat, and bellycan (water can).

aborigine. William Hone, in his *Table Book* (1827–28) says that *aborigine* "is explained in every dictionary . . . as a general name for the indigenous inhabitants of a country. In reality, it is the proper name of a peculiar people of Italy, who were not indigenous but were supposed to be a colony of Arcadians." Nevertheless, these people of Latium were thought by some Romans to have been residents of Italy from the beginning, *ab originie,* which gave us the Latin word *aborigines* for the original inhabitants of a country.

aboveboard; under the table. *Aboveboard* means "honest." The expression, first recorded in the late 16th century, derives from card-playing, in which cheating is much more difficult and honesty more likely if all the hands of cards are kept above the board, or table. *Under the table,* a later expression, means dishonest, and refers to cards manipulated under the playing surface.

above ground and moving. Words for someone bemoaning his or her fate: "Don't complain, you're above ground and moving." Origin unknown.

above the salt. *See* SALT.

abracadabra. One of the few words entirely without meaning, this confusing term is still used in a joking way by those making "magic." It was first mentioned in a poem by Quintus Severus Sammonicus in the second century. A cabalistic word intended to suggest infinity, *abracadabra* was believed to be a charm with the power to cure toothaches, fevers, and other ills, especially if written on parchment in a triangular arrangement and suspended from the neck by a linen thread. *Abracadabra* is of unknown origin, though tradition says it is composed of the initials of the Hebrew words *Ab* (Father), *Ben* (Son), and Ruach Acadsch (Holy Spirit). When toothache strikes, inscribe the parchment amulet in the following triangular form:

ABRACADABRA
ABRACADABR
ABRACADAB
ABRACADA
ABRACAD
ABRACA
ABRAC
ABRA
ABR
AB
A

See SHAZAM.

Abraham Lincoln. Old Abe's nicknames include, among others, *Honest Abe, The Railsplitter, The Liberator, The Emancipator, Uncle Abe, Father Abraham, The Chainbreaker,* and *The Giver of Freedom.* He was called many derogatory names, too, notably the sarcastic *Spot Lincoln,* because he had supported the anti–Mexican War resolution in 1847, demanding that President Polk identify the exact spot where Polk claimed Mexico had already started a war on American soil. During the Civil War Lincon was called *Ape* in the South, the word mocking his appearance and playing on *Abe. Tycoon,* in its sense of military leader, was also applied to him at that time.

Abraham Lincoln Brigade. The famous military organization had nothing to do with the American Civil War. It was formed in 1937 to fight fascism in Spain and was composed of some 2,800 volunteers, mostly American Communists.

Abram; Abraham man; Abraham's bosom. *Abram* or *Abraham man,* a synonym for beggar, can be traced to the parable in Luke 16:19–31, where "the beggar [Lazarus] died and was carried into Abraham's bosom." But it may actually derive from the Abraham Ward in England's Bedlam asylum, whose inmates were allowed out on certain days to go begging. *In Abraham's bosom* is an expression for the happy repose of death, deriving from the same source.

Absalom. *See* WOULD GOD I HAD DIED FOR THEE.

absence makes the heart grow fonder; out of sight, out of mind. Whether you believe the first proverb or the contradictory saying *out of sight, out of mind,* the phrase does not come from the poem "Isle of Beauty" by Thomas Haynes Bayly (1797–1839), as Dr. Brewer, Bartlett, and other sources say. Bayly did write "Absence makes the heart grow fonder,/Isle of Beauty, Fare thee well!," but the same phrase was recorded in Francis Davison's "Poetical Rapsody" in 1602. *Out of sight, out of mind* comes from the poem "That Out of Sight" by Arthur Hugh Clough (1819–61):

> That out of sight is out of mind
> Is true of most we leave behind.

the absent are always wrong. The saying is a translation of the old French proverb *Les absents ont toujours tort,* which dates back to the 17th century. The words suggest that it is easy to blame or accuse someone not present to defend himself.

absinthe. This alcoholic drink, not invented until about 1790, is made from various species of wormwood, *Artemisia absinthium,* the plant so named because it was dedicated to Artemis, Greek goddess of the hunt and the moon. Long prized for its aphrodisiac powers, the drink can cause blindness, insanity, and even death. For this reason absinthe was banned in the United States in 1912 and in France three years later. Still, many great writers and artists praised the drink, including Dumas fils, de Maupassant, Anatole France, Verlaine, Rimbaud, Toulouse-Lautrec, Degas, Gauguin, Picasso and Van Gogh—the last artist reportedly drank it in a concoction of five parts water to one part absinthe and one part black ink!

absolute zero. The lowest temperature theoretically possible, which is −459 degrees Farenheit; zero on the Kelvin scale; and −273.15 degrees Celsius. *See* CELSIUS SCALE; FARENHEIT; KELVINATOR.

absolutism tempered by assassination; despotism by dynamite. Count Ernst F. Munster (1766–1839), the German envoy at St. Petersburg, was referring to the Russian Constitution when he said this in 1800, but he claimed that a Russian noble really invented the phrase. Gilbert and Sullivan altered the phrase to *despotism by dynamite.*

absquatulate. A historical Americanism coined in the early 19th century and meaning to depart in a clandestine, surreptitious, or hurried manner, as in "He absquatulated with all the funds." The word is a fanciful classical formation based on *ab* and *squat,* meaning the reverse of "to squat."

absurd. This word for ridiculous, foolish, or irrational comes to us from the world of music, as the original meaning of its Latin ancestor, *absurdus,* was "out of tune or harmony." The Romans, however, used *absurdus* in the figurative sense long before it passed into English. In recent times the term *Theater of the Absurd* has been used to describe the plays of contemporary dramatists that conceptualize the world as absurd, that is, irrational, meaningless, and indecipherable.

abundance. An overflowing of precious water—as in a wave breaking over the shore or perhaps as in a flooding river—suggested this word to the Romans, for *abundance* comes to us from the Latin *abundare* "to overflow, to be plentiful."

abyss. *Abyss* is one of the few English words that derive from Sumerian, the world's first written language, which evolved some 5,000 years ago in the lower Tigris and Euphrates Valley of what is now called Iraq. The word came into English in the late 14th century from the Latin word *abyssus,* meaning "bottomless, the deep," but has been traced ultimately to the primordial sea that the Sumerians called the Abzu. Another word with Sumerian roots is *Eden,* the word for the lost paradise that came into English from a Hebrew word.

academy, academic. *See* GROVES OF ACADEME.

acanthus. *Acanthus* comes from the Greek *a* (without) and *canthos* (cup), indicating that its upside-down flowers can't hold water, have no cups. There are at least two charming stories, neither verifiable, about how the spiny or toothed leaf of the Mediterranean blue-flowered plant *Acanthus mollis* gave the name *acanthus* to the architectural ornament resembling those leaves that is used in the famous Corinthian capital or column. One tale has it that the Greek architect Callimachus placed a basket of flowers on his young daughter's grave, and an acanthus sprang up from it. This touched him so deeply that he invented and introduced a design based on the leaves. Another story, from an early 18th-century book called *The Sentiment of Flowers* tells it this way:

> The architect Callimachus, passing near the tomb of a
> young maiden who had died a few days before the time

appointed for her nuptials, moved by tenderness and pity, approached to scatter some flowers on her tomb. Another tribute to her memory had preceded his. Her nurse had collected the flowers which should have decked her on her wedding day; and, putting them with the marriage veil, in a little basket, had placed it near the grave upon a plant of acanthus, and then covered it with a tile. In the succeeding spring, the leaves of the acanthus grew around the basket: but being stayed in their course by the projecting tile, they recoiled and surmounted its extremities. Callimachus, surprised by this rural decoration, which seemed the work of the Graces in tears, conceived the capital of the Corinthian column; a magnificent ornament still used and admired by the whole civilized world.

Acapulco gold. First recorded in 1967, *Acapulco gold* supposedly means a strong variety of marijuana grown near Acapulco, Mexico. But no one is even sure whether it is really a special variety of marijuana grown there or just any premium pot that dealers ask high prices for. Hawaiian *Maui wowie* is another well-known kind.

accidentally on purpose. Someone who does something *accidentally on purpose* does it purposely and only apparently accidentally—often maliciously, in fact. The expression is not an Americanism, originating in England in the early 1880s before it became popular here.

accolade. In medieval times men were knighted in a ceremony called the *accolata* (from the Latin *ac,* "at," and *collum,* "neck"), named for the hug around the neck received during the ritual, which also included a kiss and a tap of a sword on the shoulder. From *accolata* comes the English word *accolade* for an award or honor.

according to Cocker. *According to Cocker,* an English proverb similar to the five *according* entries following, means very accurate or correct, according to the rules. *According to Cocker* could just as well mean "all wrong"; however, few authorities bother to mention this. The phrase honors Edward Cocker (1631–75), a London engraver who also taught penmanship and arithmetic. Cocker wrote a number of popular books on these subjects, and reputedly authored *Cocker's Arithmetick,* which went through 112 editions, its authority giving rise to the proverb. Then in the late 19th century, documented proof was offered showing that Cocker did not write the famous book at all, that it was a forgery of his editor and publisher, so poorly done in fact that it set back rather than advanced the cause of elementary arithmetic.

according to Fowler. Many disputes about proper English usage are settled with the words, "according to Fowler. . . ." The authority cited is Henry Watson Fowler (1858–1933), author of *A Dictionary of Modern English Usage* (1926). Fowler, a noted classicist and lexicographer, and his brother, F. G. Fowler, collaborated on a number of important books, including a one-volume abridgement of the *Oxford English Dictionary* (1911). But *Modern English Usage* is his alone. The book remains a standard reference work, though some of the old schoolmaster's opinions are debatable. Margaret Nicholson's *A Dictionary of American English Usage, Based on Fowler,* is its American counterpart.

according to Guinness. Arthur Guinness, Son & Co., Ltd., of St James Gate, Brewery, Dublin, has published *The Guinness Book of World Records* since 1955. Many arguments have been settled by this umpire of record performance, which has inspired the contemporary expression *according to Guinness.* Few business firms become factual authorities like the Guinness company, which has brewed its famous stout since 1820, its registered name becoming synonymous with stout itself for over a century.

according to Gunter, etc. Many practical inventions still in use were invented by the English mathematician and astronomer Edmund Gunter nearly four centuries ago. Gunter, a Welshman, was professor of astronomy at London's Gresham College from 1619 until his death five years later when only 45. In his short life he invented Gunter's chain, the 22-yard-long, 100-link chain used by surveyors in England and the United States; Gunter's line, the forerunner of the modern slide rule; the small portable Gunter's quadrant; and Gunter's scale, commonly used by seamen to solve navigation problems. Gunter, among other accomplishments, introduced the words *cosine* and *cotangent* and discovered the variation of the magnetic compass. His genius inspired the phrase *according to Gunter,* once as familiar in America as "according to Hoyle" is today.

according to Hoyle. *A Short Treatise on the Game of Whist* by Englishman Edmond Hoyle, apparently a barrister and minor legal official in Ireland, was published in 1742. This was the first book to systemize the rules of whist and remained the absolute authority for the game until its rules were changed in 1864. The author also wrote *Hoyle's Standard Games,* which extended his range, has been republished hundreds of times, and is available in paperback today. The weight of his authority through these works led to the phrase *according to Hoyle* becoming not only a proverbial synonym for the accuracy of game rules but an idiom for correctness in general. History tells us little about Hoyle, but he enjoyed his eponymous fame for many years, living until 1769, when he died at age 97 or so. Hoyle is responsible for popularizing the term *score* as a record of winning points in games, a relatively recent innovation. "When in doubt, win the trick," is his most memorable phrase.

according to Rafferty's rules. Unlike the five other "according to" entries listed here, this one means according to no rules at all, no holds barred. It is an Australian expression with some international currency that apparently arose from Australian boxing matches, perhaps referring to a roughhouse fighter named Rafferty, although he has not been identified. Partridge, however, suggests that *Rafferty* derives from *refractory,* "obstinately resistant to authority or control."

accumulate. *Accumulate* means literally "to heap up," from the Latin *accumulare.* (We also find the idea in "cumulus" clouds, billowing clouds heaped up in the sky.) One who accumulates wealth piles it up by adding money to the figurative pile.

ace; aces. *Aces* has been American slang for "the best" at least since the first years of the last century, deriving from *aces,*

...he highest cards in poker and other card games. But *ace* for an expert combat flier who has shot down five or more enemy planes appears to have been borrowed from the French *as*, "ace," during World War I. From there *ace* was extended to include an expert at anything. The card name *ace* comes ultimately from the Greek *ás*, one. An *ace* in tennis, badminton, and handball, among other games, is a placement made on a service of the ball, while an *ace* in golf is a hole in one. The trademarked *Ace bandage*, used to bind athletic injuries, uses *ace* meaning "best," too. *Ace* figures in a large number of expressions. *To ace* a test is to receive an A on it, and *ace it* means "to complete anything easily and successfully." *To be aces with* is to be highly regarded ("He's aces with the fans."), and *to ace out* is to cheat or defraud ("He aced me out of my share.") *Easy aces* in auction bridge denotes aces equally divided between opponents; it became the name of a 1940s–1950s radio program featuring a husband and wife team called *The Easy Aces*. Another old *ace* term is *to stand ace high*, to be highly esteemed.

ace in the hole. A stud poker card dealt face down and hidden from the view of the other players is called a hole card. An ace is the highest hole card possible, often making a winning hand for the player holding it. Thus from this poker term came the expression *an ace in the hole* for "any hidden advantage, something held in reserve until it is needed to win." The term probably dates back over a century, and was first recorded in *Collier's Magazine* in 1922: "I got a millionaire for an ace in the hole." *Hole card* is a synonym. *See* AN ACE UP ONE'S SLEEVE.

Aceldama. *See* POTTER'S FIELD.

ace up one's sleeve. Ever since crooked gamblers in the wild and woolly West began concealing aces up their sleeves and slipping them into their hands in card games, we have had the expression *an ace up one's sleeve* for "any tricky, hidden advantage." Although the practice is not a common way to cheat at cards anymore, the phrase lives on.

Achilles' heel. When he was a baby, Achilles' mother, the goddess Thetis, dipped him into the magic waters of the river Styx to coat his body with a magic shield that no weapon could penetrate. However, she held him by the heel, so that this part of his body remained vulnerable. Paris learned of his secret during the Trojan War, shooting an arrow into his heel and killing him. *Achilles' heel* has since come to mean the weak part of anything.

acid test. This expression dates back to frontier days in America, when peddlers determined the gold content of objects by scratching them and applying nitric acid. Since gold, which is chemically inactive, resists acids that corrode other metals, the (nitric) *acid test* distinguished it from copper, iron, or similar substances someone might be trying to palm off on the peddlers. People were so dishonest, or peddlers so paranoid, that the term quickly became part of the language, coming to mean a severe test of reliability.

acknowledge the corn. Much used in the 19th century as a synonym for our "copping a plea," this phrase is said to have arisen when a man was arrested and charged with stealing four horses and the corn (grain) to feed them. "I acknowledge [admit to] the corn," he declared.

Acoma. A Native American tribe of New Mexico and Arizona. The tribe's name means "people of the white rock" in their language, in reference to the pueblos in which they lived. Acoma is also the name of a central New Mexico pueblo that has been called "the oldest continuously inhabited city in the United States." The name is pronounced either *eh-ko-ma* or *ah-ko-ma*.

aconite; monkshood; wolfsbane. Aconite (*Aconitumnapellus*) is a deadly poisonous plant, also known as wolfsbane and monkshood. *Aconite* itself derives from an ancient Greek word meaning "wolfsbane." Ancient legend says the showy perennial herb is of the buttercup family and that it became poisonous from the foam that dropped from the mouth of the monstrous hound Cerberus, who guarded the gates of Hell, when Hercules dragged him up from the nether regions. Some authorities say *aconite* derives from the Greek *akon*, "dart," because it was once used as an arrow poison. *See also* WOLFSBANE.

acorn. *Acorn* is an ancient word deriving from the Old English *aecern*, meaning "fruit" or "berry." Its present form *acorn* is due in large part to folk etymology; people believed that the word *aecern* was made up of "oak" and "corn" because the fruit came from the oak and was a corn or seed of that tree. Thus *aecern* came to be pronounced and spelled "acorn."

acqua tofana. Acqua Tofana, a favorite potion of young wives in 17th-century Italy who wanted to get rid of their rich, elderly, or ineffectual husbands, recalls a woman who peddled her deadly home brew on such a large scale that she has achieved immortality of a kind. Her first name is unknown, but Miss or Mrs. Tofana was either a Greek or Italian lady who died in Naples or Palermo, Sicily about the year 1690. Apparently she died a natural death, although five others headed by an old hag named Spara, who had bought her secret formula, were arrested and hanged in 1659. Tofana's poison was a strong, transparent, and odorless solution of arsenic that she sold in vials labeled *Manna di S. Nicolas di Bari* (the "Manna of St. Nicholas of Bari"), in honor of the miraculous oil that was said to flow from the tomb of the saint. *See* BRUCINE.

acre; wiseacre. The Sumerian *agar* meant a watered field, a word the first farmers in Babylonia formed from their word *a* for water and applied to fertile watered land in the river valleys. *Agar*—related to the Sanskrit *ajras*, an open plain—came into Latin as *ager*, "fertile field," and finally entered English as *acre* or *acras* in the 10th century. The word first meant any unoccupied land but then came to mean the amount of land a yoke of oxen could plow from sunup to sundown. During the reign of Edward I, it was more fairly and accurately defined as a parcel of land 4 rods in width and 40 rods in length (a rod measures 16½ feet). The area remains the same today except that the land does not have to be rectangular, that is, 4×40 rods. In case you want to measure your property another way, in the United States and Great Britain an acre equals 43,560 square feet, or ¹⁄₆₄th of a square mile, or 4.047 square meters. One old story says that Ben Jonson put down a landed aristocrat with "Where you have an acre of land, I have ten acres of wit," and that the gentleman retorted by calling him "Mr. Wiseacre." Acreage doesn't actually figure in this word, however. *Wiseacre* has lost its original meaning, having once been the Dutch *wijssegger*, "a wisesayer, soothsayer, or prophet," apparently an adaptation of the Old High German *wizzago*, with the same meaning. By the time *wijssegger* passed into English as *wiseacre* in the late 16th century, such soothsayers with their know-it-all airs were already regarded as pretentious fools.

acrobat; neurobat. *Acrobat* comes from the Greek *akros*, "aloft," plus *batos*, "climbing or walking," referring of course to the stunts early acrobats performed in the air, which included ropewalking. The greatest of the ancient Greek acrobats were called *neurobats*, from the Greek *neuron*, "sinew." These men performed on sinewy rope that was only as thick as the catgut or plastic used for fishing line today, appearing from the ground as if they were walking on air.

acrolect; basilect; idiolect. The *acrolect* (from the Greek *akros*, "topmost") is the best English spoken, the KING'S ENGLISH, while the *basilect* means the lowest level of poor speech. Another unusual word patterned on *dialect* is *idiolect*, meaning the language or speech of an individual, which always differs slightly from person to person. These words were apparently coined toward the end of the 19th century. *See* DIALECT.

acronym. According to the *Guinness Book of World Records*, there is a Russian acronym of 56 letters. *Guinness* also claims that the longest English acronym is the 22 letter ADCOMSUBORDCOMPHIBSPAC, used in the U.S. Navy to denote the Administrative Command, Amphibious Forces, Pacific Fleet, Subordinate Command, U.S. Naval Forces Eastern Atlantic and Mediterranean, Commander Headquarters Support Activities—itself abbreviated as CSCN/CHSA. Strictly speaking, these are both acronyms, new words formed from the initial letters or syllables of successive words in a phrase. But *acronym* has come to mean any such word that can be easily *pronounced* as a word, and not even Demosthenes could pronounce these abbreviations designed to appeal to the eye rather than to the ear. The term *acronym* derives from the Greek *akros* ("top") and *onym* ("name"); it is a fairly new coinage, although scholars claim to have found early examples of acronyms in Hebrew writings dating back to biblical times. Acronyms came into prominence during World War I with coinages such as AWOL (absent without leave), proliferated during the New Deal with all its "alphabet agencies," and got entirely out of hand during World War II, as can be seen by the two monsters cited above. The good ones appeal to the American preference for brevity and wit in speech. New acronyms are invented every day, but relatively few stand the test of time. A number are apparently happy accidents, but in many cases the long form was invented so that the acronyms could be born. There is no good explanation for why common abbreviations such as G.O.P., F.O.B., and O.P.A. haven't become acronyms, except that they just don't sound right to most ears when pronounced as words. Unfortunately, there isn't room here for interesting place-name acronyms such as Pawn, Oregon, which wasn't named for a pawnshop but comes from the initials of four early residents named Poole, Aberley, Worthington, and Nolen. *See* ABBREVIATIONS.

across the board. Around 1935, racetrack combination tickets naming a horse to win, place, or show—giving a bettor three chances to win—began to be called *across-the-board* bets. Since then, the term has been widely used outside the racetrack to mean "comprehensive, general, all inclusive."

acrostic; telestich; abecedarian hymns. Acrostics can be any composition (poems, puzzles, etc.) in which certain letters of the lines, taken in order, form a word, phrase, or sentence that is the subject of the composition. When the last letters of lines do this, the acrostic is sometimes called a *telestich* (from the Greek *tele*, "far," and *stichos*, "row"). *Acrostic* derives from the Greek *akros*, "top," and *stichos*. The term was first applied to the prophecies of the Greek Erythraean sibyl, which were written on separate pages, the initial letters forming a word when the pages were arranged in order. Another famous early acrostic was made from the Greek for "Jesus Christ, God's Son, Savior": *Iesus Christos, Theou Uios, Soter*. The first letters of each word (and the first two letters of *Christos* and *Theou*) taken in order spell *ichthus*, Greek for "fish," which became a Christian symbol for Jesus. There are even earlier examples of acrostics in the Bible. In Hebrew, for instance, Psalm 119 is an acrostic in which the first letters of each of the 22 stanzas descend in alphabetical order. Such alphabetical acrostics are usually called *abecedarian hymns*, or *abecedarius*, and there are more complicated species of them in which each word in every line begins with the same letter:

> An Austrian army, awfully array'd
> Boldly by battery besieged Belgrade, etc.

action. A good example of how English is changing as it spreads around the world. *Action* in Singapore, where English is an official language (along with Malay and Chinese) means to show off, as in: "That fellow always like to action, walking around with his Rolex over his shirtsleeves."

actuary. An actuary is a highly skilled statistician who calculates and states insurance risks and premiums, but his or her title derives from the Latin for clerk, *actuarius*, for in the Roman army, during Caesar's time, an *actuary* was no more than a payroll clerk.

act your age. Perhaps *act your age!* originated as a reproof to children, but it is directed at both children and adults today, meaning either don't act more immature than you are, or don't try to keep up with the younger generation. The expression originated in the U.S., probably during the late 19th century, as did the synonymous *be your age!*

Adam; human. Adam, the name of the first man in the Bible, is the Hebrew word for man, deriving from *adama*, "earth," just as the Latin *humanus*, "human," is related to the Latin *humus*, "earth." For his sins, according to the Talmud, Adam was evicted from Paradise after only 12 hours. In addition to entries following, his name is represented by *Adam's wine*, or *ale*, a humorous expression for water; *Adamic*, naked, free like Adam; *Adamite*, a human being or descendant of Adam; *the second Adam*, a biblical reference to Christ; *the old Adam in us*, a reference to man's disposition to evil; and I DON'T KNOW HIM FROM ADAM.

adam-and-eve.   This pretty North American woods orchid (*Aplectrum hyemale*), also called puttyroot, apparently takes its name from its two bulbous roots, which are joined together by a small filament about two inches long that suggested Adam and Eve, hand in hand, to some poetic soul. When the plant has three bulbous roots or corms joined together it is called "Adam-and-Eve-and-their-son." The name *adam-and-eve* includes the dogtooth violet, because its plant bears a large and a small flower at the same time, and the common monkshood. It is said that when immersed in water one root or corm of the puttyroot sinks and the other floats—whether it is Adam or Eve who sinks is never told. Folklore also holds that adam-and-eve sewn together and carried in a bag on one's person protects the bearer from evil.

adamant.   Stubbornly unyielding, inflexible, impervious to reason. The word comes ultimately from the Greek *a*, not, plus *damao*, to tame, and originally meant something very hard, such as a diamond or steel. Poet John Milton writes in *Paradise Lost* (1667) of Lucifer dwelling in hell in "adamantine chains and penal fire . . ."

Adamastor.   Vasco da Gama is said to have seen a hideous sea phantom called the "*Adamastor*," the spirit of the stormy Cape of Good Hope, which warned him not to undertake his third voyage to India. Da Gama made the voyage anyway and died soon after reaching his destination. The Adamastor is first mentioned in the epic poem the *Lusiads* by Portuguese adventurer and poet Luis de Camoëns (1524–80), which was translated into English by Sir Richard Burton in 1881. The word *Adamastor* is probably Portuguese in origin, but its exact derivation is unknown.

adamite.   A historical name for any supporter of John Adams, the second president of the United States. Old Parson Weems, George Washington's biographer, wrote a book entitled *The Philanthropist, or a Good Twenty-five Cents Worth of Political Love Powder for Honest Adamites and Jeffersonians*. John Adams, who died in 1826, age 91, died on a July 4th, as did Thomas Jefferson and James Monroe. Adams and Jefferson died on the same July 4th. *See* JEFFERSON BIBLE.

Adam's apple.   Adam never ate an apple, at least not in the biblical account of his transgressions, which refers only to unspecified forbidden fruit on the tree in the Garden of Eden. The forbidden fruit of which the Lord said "Ye shall not eat of the fruit which is in the midst of the garden, neither shall ye touch it, lest ye die" (Gen. 3:3) was probably an apricot or pomegranate, and the Muslims—intending no joke—believe it was a banana. Many fruits and vegetables have been called apples. Even in medieval times, pomegranates were "apples of Carthage"; dates, "finger apples"; and potatoes, "apples of the earth." At any rate, tradition has it that Adam succumbed to Eve's wiles and ate of an apple from which she took the first bite, that a piece stuck in his throat forming the lump we call the *Adam's apple*, and that all of us, particularly males, inherited this mark of his "fall." Modern scientific physiology, as opposed to folk anatomy, explains this projection of the neck, most prominent in adolescents, as being anterior thyroid cartilage of the larynx. But pioneer anatomists honored the superstition in the mid-18th century by calling it *pomum Adami*, or *Adam's apple*. They simply could find no other explanation for this evasive lump in the throat that even seemed to move up and down.

Adam's apple tree.   This particular tree is popularly named for Adam and the entire genus containing it was named by Linnaeus in honor of German botanist Dr. J. T. Tabernaemontanus (d. 1590), a celebrated Heidelberg botanist and physician who—despite the length of his patronym—also has species in two other plant genera commemorating him. Why the folkname *Adam's apple tree*? Clearly still another case of a claim on Eden. I quote from the *Encyclopedia of Gardening* (1838) by J. C. Loudon: "The inhabitants of Ceylon say that Paradise was a place in their country . . . They also point out as the tree which bore the forbidden fruit, the *Devi Ladner* or *Tabernaemontana alternifoxlia* [the species name has since been changed to *coronaria*] . . . In confirmation of the tradition they refer to the beauty of the fruit, and the fine scent of the flowers, both of which are most tempting. The shape of the fruit gives the idea of a piece having been bitten off; and the inhabitants say it was excellent before Eve ate of it, though it is now poisonous." *T. coronaria*, a five-to-eight-foot-high tropical shrub with white fragrant flowers, is also called the East Indian rosebay, crape jasmine, and NERO'S CROWN, after the Roman emperor.

Adam's needle.   Adam and Eve sewed fig leaves together to cover their nakedness (Gen. 3:7). This led to the belief that they used the spines of a plant as a needle. Most often the honor goes to the yucca (*Yucca filamentosa*), native to Mexico and Central America and grown in gardens all over the world.

Adam's profession.   "There is a no ancient gentlemen but gardeners, ditchers, and grave-makers; they hold up Adam's profession," Shakespeare wrote in *Hamlet*. The bard also said "And Adam was a gardener" in *Henry VI, Part III*. Much later, Kipling wrote: "Oh Adam was a gardener, and God who made him sees/That half a proper gardener's work is done upon his knees." The phrase *Adam's profession* was proverbial for gardening long before both poets lived. No one has called it "Eve's profession," even though she picked the first apple. *See also* FIACRE.

adder; auger.   Many English words have changed over the years because of lazy or quick pronunciation—depending on how you look at it. *Adder*, is an example. *Adder* was originally "nadder," but starting in the 14th century its *n* began to become part of the article *a*, making *an adder* out of "a nadder." Much the same happened to the tool, *an auger*, during the same time, the auger having originally been "a nauger."

add insult to injury.   One of the oldest of expressions, this goes back to an early fable of Aesop, in which a bald man tried to kill a fly on his head and missed the fly, smacking himself instead. Said the fly: "You wanted to kill me for a mere touch. What will you do to yourself, now that you have added insult to injury."

addisonian termination.   *See* PREPOSITION.

Addison's disease. British physician Thomas Addison (1793–1860) discovered this glandular disease in 1855, and it was shortly named after him. The chronic, sometimes fatal malady affects the adrenal or suprarenal glands, located above the kidneys. It is said that President John F. Kennedy suffered from and was treated for *Addison's disease*, whose symptoms are often tiredness, weakness, puffiness of the face, and a gradual brownish pigmentation of the skin. British novelist Jane Austen died of Addison's disease.

Adidas. The popular running shoes, famous since marathons became popular in the late 1970s, bear the name of their German inventor and manufacturer *Adi Dassler.*

adieu. *Je vous recommande à Dieu,* "I commend you to God," was in times past said to Frenchmen who were going on a long journey and would not be seen for some time. Eventually the *à Dieu* detached itself (merged to *adieu*) from the phrase and came to mean the same kind of good-bye.

adios. Heard in the U.S. since about 1830, this Spanish word meaning good-bye (literally, "to God") is now widely used throughout the country. It can also mean "get going, vamoose": "You better adios before the law comes."

Adirondacks. The Mohawk Indians contemptuously dubbed a tribe of Algonquin Indians *Adirondack,* meaning "they eat bark," and the tribe's nickname came to be applied to the mountain region in northeastern New York that these Indians inhabited. The insulting name gives us, literally, "they eat bark" chairs, pack baskets, and even grapes, among many other items characteristic of the Adirondacks.

ad lib. Deriving from the Latin *ad libitum,* at will, *ad lib* means to speak words or perform actions not in a script or speech being used. *Ad libitum* is first recorded in 1705.

the Admirable Crichton. The perfect man, the perfect servant. James Crichton, born in 1560, was an English prodigy who while still in his teens earned his Master of Arts degree, mastered over a dozen languages, all the sciences, and achieved some fame as a poet and theologian. The fabled prodigy was also said to be handsome and without peer as a swordsman— "All perfect, finish'd to the fingernail," Tennyson wrote of him. Unfortunately, this ideal man proved either unwise or human enough to steal the heart of a prince's lady while traveling in Italy and was assassinated by three men in the prince's hire. Crichton was only 25 or so when he died. His name, in the form of *The Admirable Crichton,* was long used as a synonym for the perfect man, and when playwright James M. Barrie used it as the name of his butler hero in *The Admirable Crichton* (1902) it became synonymous with a perfect servant.

admiral. Technically, all admirals come from the Arabian desert, for the word can be traced to the title of Abu Bakr, who was called Amir-al-muninin, "commander of the faithful," before he succeeded Muhammad as caliph in A.D. 632. The title Amir, or "commander," became popular soon after, and naval chiefs were designated *Amir-al-ma,* "commander of commanders." Western seamen who came in contact with the Arabs assumed that *Amir-al* was one word, and believed this was a distinguished title. By the early 13th century, officers were calling themselves *amiral,* which merely means "commander of." The *d* was probably added to the word through a common mispronunciation.

Admiral of the Red. An old term for a drunkard, whose face and nose are often red. The expression is a play on the naval term *Admiral of the Red,* one of the three classes of admirals in early times named from the color of their flags. In British naval engagements prior to 1864 the *Admiral of the Red* held the center of the line, while the Admiral of the White held the vanguard and the Admiral of the Blue held the rear.

adobe. An adobe can be a house made of *adobe,* from the Spanish word for sun-dried clay or mud bricks. The term was first recorded in the U.S. in 1759. *Adobe* also means things of Mexican origin, as in the slang expression *adobe dollar,* a Mexican peso. *See* DOUGHBOY.

adolescent. *See* ADULT.

Adonis. During the Adonia, an annual feast held in Greece, women wept eight days over Adonis's death, finally rejoicing in his resurrection. In classic mythology Adonis was the handsome lover of Aphrodite, goddess of love and beauty, and thus any man called an Adonis is among the most handsome of men.

Adonis flower; Adonis garden. The Greek goddess Aphrodite punished the king of Cyprus for his disrespect by making his daughter Myrrha fall in love with him. Discovering this, King Cinyras tried to kill Myrrha, but she was changed into a myrtle, from which the handsome youth Adonis was born. Aphrodite herself fell in love with Adonis; when he was killed by a wild boar while hunting she caused a beautiful red flower to spring from his blood, which had been watered by her tears. Over the centuries, the anemone, the poppy, and the rose have been said to be this Adonis flower. John Gerard's famous *Herball* (1597) was the first source to mention that the plant commonly called "pheasant's eye," of the family Ranunculaceae, was known as the "Adonis." A species of butterfly is also so named. An "Adonis garden" is any worthless or very perishable thing, or a momentary pleasure. Its source was the plots of earth in which quick-growing plants such as wheat, lettuce and fennel were planted during the Adonia, the ancient feast of Adonis celebrating his death and resurrection. Symbolic of the brief life of Adonis and grown around a statue of him, the plants were only tended for eight days, allowed to wither and then thrown into the sea along with little images of Adonis. The next year, of course, seeds were sown again and Adonis was resurrected, a ceremony symbolic of the course of vegetation.

adroit. *See* RIGHT.

adult. The Latin *adolescere* means "to grow up." The past participle of this word, *adultus,* gave us our word *adult* while its present participle, *adolescens,* gave us *adolescent. Adolescent* seems to have first been recorded in 1440, about a century before *adult.*

adultery. Contrary to popular opinion this word is not related to *adult.* It can be traced back to the Latin *adulterare,* "to pollute, to commit adultery," which also gives us the word *adulterate*. Interestingly, the English word *adulterate* once meant to commit adultery, Shakespeare using it in *King John* (1596): "She adulterates hourly with thine Uncle John."

advertising euphemisms. Manufacturers and their ad agencies have originated some ingenious if sometimes silly euphemisms in touting their products. Here is a short collection, to which you may want to add your favorites: *underarm* (armpit); *halitosis* (bad breath); *derriere* (buttocks); *irregularity* (constipation); *foundation garment* (corset); *color-correct hair* (dye hair); *problem days* (menses); *lingerie* (underwear).

Aegean Sea. King Aegeus of Greek mythology gives his name to the Aegean Sea. The king's son Theseus promised to hoist a white sail on his voyage home to Athens from Crete, to signal that he was alive. Theseus neglected to do so and Aegeus, thinking his son had been killed, committed suicide by throwing himself into the sea that came to be named for him.

aegis. *See* UNDER THE UMBRELLA OF.

aeon. An *aeon*, a variant of *eon*, means a very long period of time, or the longest period of geological time, composed of two or more eras. The Irish author and editor George William Russell (1867–1935) used AE, a contraction of the word *aeon*, as both his signature and his pen name. No one knows why—perhaps because he thought his work would live for aeons, which perhaps it will.

aerial. *Aerial*, formed from the Latin word for "airy," wasn't introduced during the age of aviation, nor does it have its origins in circus aerial acts. The word is first recorded by Shakespeare, who may have coined it, in *Othello* (1604).

aerobics. Derived from the Greek for "air" and "life," *aer* and *bios*, aerobic was first used to describe an organism that requires air or free oxygen for survival. Its relatively new usage was first recorded around 1965, when the physical fitness boom began in the United States. In brief, aerobics is any exercise, such as running or swimming, that stimulates and strengthens the heart and lungs, thus improving the body's use of oxygen. It can also refer to a physical fitness program based on such exercises.

aerugo. *See* VERDIGRIS.

affiliate. "Adopted" is the meaning of the Latin *affileatus*, composed of *ad*, "to," and *filius*, "son," from which the word *affiliate* derives. Thus a smaller company affiliated with a larger one could be said to have been adopted by the parent corporation. The word is first recorded by Tobias Smollett in *Gil Blas* (1761).

affluent. After the publication of economist John Kenneth Galbraith's book *The Affluent Society* in 1958, *affluent* came to be commonly used as a synonym for rich or wealthy. *Affluent*, however, had been used for "flowing or abounding in wealth" since the 18th century and for "flowing in abundance" since at least 1413, when the word is first recorded.

afghan. A soft, knitted, or crocheted wool blanket, often with a geometric pattern, that was once made exclusively in Afghanistan. An *Afghan*, capitalized, is a native of Afghanistan, sometimes called an *Afghani*.

Afghan hound. Bred in Afghanistan since at least 3000 B.C., this large, slender, heavy-coated dog, related to the greyhound, was used by the Egyptians for hunting. It is one the few dogs that hunt by sight.

Afghanistan. Afghanistan is named after the biblical King Saul's grandson, Afghana, according to legend, which has traditionally described the Afghanistan people as *Ben-i-Israel*, "Children of Israel." Legend also has it that King Solomon (Sulaiman) settled the country. Whether such stories, and many more, are true or not, they are widely believed, and the country does bear Afghana's name.

aficionado. An ardent, devoted fan of bullfighting or anything else. Ernest Hemingway, who wrote much about bullfighting, said in *The Sun Also Rises* (1926): "Aficion means passion [in Spanish]. An aficionado is one who is passionate about the bull-fights." *See* BULLFIGHT.

afraid of one's shadow. The ancient Greeks used this expression and it probably wasn't original with them. Still very common today, after thousands of years, the workhorse phrase means, of course, to be very fearful for no good reason, to be extremely jittery.

Africa. The Romans may have named this continent *Apricus*, meaning "sunny," which became the English *Africa*. But *Africa*, according to my correspondent Professor Howard Marblestone, "probably derives from the *Afri*, a name centered in the Carthagonian realm . . ."

African American. *African American*, a term many blacks and whites prefer as the name for blacks today, is not of recent origin and wasn't coined in the North, as some people believe. *African American* did become common in the late 1980s but was first used in the American South some 140 years ago. Even before its birth, terms like *Africo-American* (1835), and *Afro-American* (1830s) were used in the names of black churches.

African language words. English words and phrases that possibly came to us from African languages include: banjo, bad mouth, boogie-woogie, to bug, buckra, chigger, cooter, goober, hip, jazz, jitterbug, jukebox, mumbo jumbo, okra, poor Joe (great blue heron), speak softly and carry a big stick, sweet talk, tote, voodoo, yam, and zombie.

African violet. *See* SAINTPAULIA.

Afrikaans words. English words that came to us from Afrikaans (the Taal) include: veldt, trek, commando, wildebeest, and aardvark.

Afro. The bushy hairstyle called the *Afro* became popular in the early 1960s. The term *Afro* originated at the time, along with its synonyms *fro* and *natural*.

afromobile. Confined to Florida, this expression referred to an early-1900s Palm Beach vehicle consisting of a two-seated wicker chair in the front and a bicycle in the back pedaled by a black man. For many years, this taxi for rich white patrons was the only vehicle permitted in the city.

aftermath. The *after mowth*, which later came to be pronounced "aftermath," is the second or later mowing, the crop of grass that springs up after the first hay mowing in early summer when the grass is best for hay. This term was used as early as the 15th century, and within a century *aftermath* was being applied figuratively to anything that results or follows from an event.

after someone with a sharp stick. To be determined to have satisfaction or revenge. John Bartlett called this phrase a common Americanism in 1848 and it is still occasionally heard today.

afterward. The Saxons called the stern of a boat the *aft* and their word *ward* meant "in the direction of." Thus *aftward* meant "toward the rear of a ship," or "behind." Over the years, the word *aftward* changed in spelling to *afterward* and came to mean "behind in time," "later on," or "later."

againbite [agenbite] of inwit. James Joyce revived the expression *agenbite* [againbite] *of inwit* in *Ulysses*. It is a good example of Anglo-Saxon replacements of foreign words, meaning the "remorse of conscience" and originally being the prose translation of a French moral treatise (*The Ayenbite of Ynwit*) made by Dan Michel in 1340.

agate; agate type; aggie. In ancient times colored stones were often found near the Achates River in Sicily. The river gave its name to these pretty stones, or gems, as they were called. Because they were small, the stones gave their name to a small printing type, *agate type*, that is still used widely today. This type is called *ruby* in England but has been *agate type* in America since 1871. The marbles called *aggies* are so named because their coloring resembles agate.

agave. Any of several southwestern plants with tough, spiny, sword-shaped leaves. Named for Agave, daughter of the legendary Cadmus, who introduced the Greek alphabet, the large *Agave* genus includes the remarkable century plant (*Agave americana*), which blooms once and dies (though anytime after 15 years, not after 100 years, as was once believed). Introduced to Europe from America in the 16th century, this big agave is often used there for fences. It is regarded as a religious charm by pilgrims to Mecca, who hang a leaf of it over their doors to ward off evil spirits and indicate that they have made the pilgrimage.

age before beauty. There has been some controversy about this expression, which originated in 19th-century England. One story tells us that Clare Boothe Brokaw, who later became Clare Boothe Luce, had joined the staff of *Vanity Fair* and encountered Dorothy Parker in the lobby one morning. "Age before beauty," said the sharp-tongued Clare, holding the door open. "Pearls before swine," the sharper-tongued Dorothy Parker said, entering first. Clare Boothe Luce later denied this story, and a similar quip was used in one of Alexander Woollcott's pieces, but it has nevertheless become part of the Parker legend. Recalled Mrs. Robert Benchley in a biography of her husband: "I was right there, the time in the Algonquin, when *some little chorus girl* and Dottie were going into the dining room and the girl stepped back and said, 'Age before beauty,' and Dottie said very quickly, 'Pearls before swine.' I was right there when she said it." This last is probably the correct version of the story.

agelast; agelasta. An *agelast*, from the Greek for "not laughing," is a person who never laughs. The term for a non-laughter is first recorded in 1877, but *agelastic*, also meaning a morose, severe person who never laughs, is recorded in English as early as 1626. Rabelais was the first writer to use the word, fashioning it from the Greek. The *agelasta*, coming from the same Greek root for "joyless," is the stone upon which the fatigued Ceres sat when worn down in searching for her daughter Persephone.

agent. The first professional author's agent appears to have been Alexander Pollock Watt, an Englishman who had as his clients Thomas Hardy, Rudyard Kipling, Arthur Conan Doyle, and Bret Harte, among other great writers. Watt published a list of his clients, along with testimonials, in 1893. The firm he founded, A. P. Watt and Sons, is still in business. *Agent* for any person authorized to act on another's behalf dates back to the 16th century and derives from Latin words meaning the same.

Agent Orange. This herbicidal spray, used in Vietnam for purposes of jungle defoliation and crop destruction, has great toxicity, and many former U.S. soldiers claim to have suffered terribly because of it. Tens of thousands of tons of 2,4,5,-T, as it is called more scientifically, were used on over 5 million acres in South Vietnam during the 1960s. The term *Agent Orange* is first recorded in 1970 and derives from the color code stripe on the side of the herbicide's container—to distinguish it from the toxic herbicides Agent Blue, Agent Purple, and Agent White, which had their own appropriately colored stripes.

Age of Anxiety; anxiety neurosis. Though it is possibly more pertinent today, the term *Age of Anxiety* was coined over a half century ago in 1948 by British-born poet W. H. (Wystan Hugh) Auden in his long Pulitzer Prize-winning poem *The Age of Anxiety: A Baroque Ecologue*. The term *anxiety neurosis* is a translation of Freud's *Angstneurose*, which he coined in about 1895. The mild illness is marked by excessive anxiety.

Age of Aquarius. In the early 1960s it was widely believed that the decade was the start of an age when space would be conquered and there would be peace and brotherhood for all. This age was connected with the great constellation Aquarius, hence the name, which was also the title of a popular song from the musical *Hair* (1966), a song not sung much anymore. *See* AGE OF ANXIETY.

Age of Reason. Also called the Age of Enlightenment and the Enlightenment, this term describes the main trend of thought of 18th-century Europe, which put reason and individualism over tradition. Owing much to 17th-century thinkers, the philosophy was championed a hundred years later by Voltaire, Rousseau, and Kant, among many others. Thomas Paine's 1794–95 book attacking the Bible and defending deism was entitled *The Age of Reason. See* FROM THE RIDICULOUS TO THE SUBLIME.

ageratum. "The flower that never grows old" translates the name of this flower, from the Greek *a*, "not," and *geras*, "old age." Actually, the Greeks were probably referring to another flower than our garden annual the *ageratum*, but it seemed a good name for this little, long-lasting, lavender-blue bedding plant, also known as the "everlasting flower."

ages ago. *See* THE GREAT MAJORITY.

aggie. *See* AGATE.

aggie fortis. An Americanism meaning anything very strong to drink. As one old-timer put it ". . . this man's whiskey ain't Red Eye, it ain't Chain Lightnin either, it's regular Aggie forty [sic], and there isn't a man living who can stand a glass and keep his senses." *Aggie fortis* derives from *aqua fortis*, strong water, the Latin name for nitric acid.

agita; agit. *Agita* is an Italian word that has become popular recently in American usage, where it refers to acid indigestion brought on, especially, by stress and anxiety, as in "You're giving me agita with all this trouble." *Agita* derives from the Italian *agitare*, "to agitate," which comes from the Latin *agitare*, "to drive," "to set in motion." The term *agit*, used in prescriptions to mean "shake, stir," hails from the same source.

agit-prop drama. *Agit-prop* plays were commonly performed in the 1930s. They are plays that convey very emphatic social protest, the word *agit-prop* being a combination of *agit*ation and *prop*aganda. The word has its roots in the early U.S.S.R. *Agitpropbyuro*, "Agitation and Propaganda Bureau."

agnostic. Nineteenth-century British scientist Thomas H. Huxley coined the word *agnostic*, one who believes there is no proof of God's existence but does not doubt the possibility that God exists. The anonymous rhyme "I do not know, / it may be so" sums up the position. Huxley, who described himself as "a man without a rag or label to cover himself" coined his label from the Greek *a*, "without, not," and *gnostic*, which is related to the Greek *gnosis*, "knowledge."

agonizing reappraisal. Secretary of State John Foster Dulles coined the phrase *agonizing reappraisal* and used it at a NATO meeting in December 1954. The term was so overworked and applied to so many piddling matters everywhere that it became a cliché, as did "massive retaliation," which the Secretary had coined several months earlier. *Agony* itself derives from the Greek *agonia*, a contest between wrestlers, boxers, or even dramatists that took place at an *agon*, or meeting. The physical or mental struggles of these contestants gave rise to our word *agony. Agony* was first used in English by the translators of the Bible in describing Christ's intense mental suffering or anguish in the Garden of Gethsemane. Thus in the true spirit of the word, any *agonizing reappraisal* would be best made regarding matters of great consequence, if used at all.

agony. The Greek word from which *agony* derives first meant an athletic contest, next came to mean a struggle for victory in an athletic contest, then any struggle, and finally mental struggle or anguish like Christ's in Gethsemane. The idea of physical pain and suffering isn't recorded for *agony* until about the 17th century, but it is hard not to think of an athletic contest when contemplating this meaning. As one writer notes: "You only have to look at a photograph of anybody running the 100-yard dash to understand how it [the athletic contest] came in its English version to have the sense of 'agony.' "

Agony Aunt. *See* MISS LONELYHEARTS.

agree to disagree. To *agree* to *disagree*, to remain friendly while holding differing opinions, is considered an Americanism by many writers. But in 1948 a writer in *Notes and Queries* reported finding the expression in a 1770 sermon of English theologian John Wesley, founder of Methodism. What's more, he found the phrase in quotation marks, suggesting that Wesley hadn't invented it but had heard it elsewhere.

agronomist. Agronomists are today's scientifically trained farmers, taking their name from the Greek *agros*, "field," and *nomis*, "to manage." The word only recently came into the language—in the early 19th century.

Aha! William Safire (in his *New York Times Magazine* column "On Language," 2/17/97) calls this exultant cry of discovery "one of the great, unappreciated and deliciously nuanced words in the English language." First recorded in Chaucer's *The Canterbury Tales* (ca. 1387), the palindronic *Aha!* has, I should add, even become the official scientific name for a genus of sphecid wasp. The genus was so named by Smithsonian Institution researcher Arnold Menke to express his joy on discovering it. When he discovered a second species of *Aha*, Mr. Menke was even happier, naming it *Aha ha*. For still more good news about *Aha!* see Mr. Safire's column and our entries HAH HAH and EUREKA.

ahoy. Sailors had been saying *"ahoy"* for "hello" or "hey" at least a few years prior to 1751, when Tobias Smollett first recorded it in his novel *The Adventures of Peregrine Pickle:* "Ho! the house a hoy." The word is a combination of the interjection *a* and *hoy*, a natural exclamation used to attract attention that is first recorded as a cry for calling hogs and which in nautical language was also spelled "hoay." Incidentally, *ahoy* was suggested by Alexander Graham Bell as the salutation for telephone calls when he invented the telephone, but the term never caught on, phone users opting for "hello" and depriving *ahoy* of a more prominent place in the language.

AIDS. As an acronym for *a*cquired *i*mmune *d*eficiency (or, more currently, immunodeficiency) *s*yndrome, *AIDS* was first recorded in September 1982. It denotes an often fatal disease in which, according to one authority, "infectious or malignant tumors develop as a result of a severe loss of cellular immunity, which is itself caused by earlier infection with a retrovirus (HIV), transmitted in sexual fluids and blood." The epidemic of *AIDS* remained unnamed for more than a year before the U.S. Centers for Disease Control gave a name to it. At one point it was called *K.S.O.I.* (*K*aposi's *S*arcoma and *O*pportunistic

Infection). In Africa it has since 1985 been called *slim*, after the extreme weight loss suffered by people afflicted with the disease.

ain't.   *Ain't*, first recorded in 1706, began life in England as a contraction of "am not" (an't). Once widely used among all classes and quite proper, it became socially unacceptable in the early 19th century, when people began to use it improperly as a contraction for "is not" and "are not" as well as "am not." But "proper" or not, *ain't* is still widely used wherever English is spoken.

ain't got sense enough to poke acorns down a peckerwood hole.   An old rural Americanism said of someone pitifully stupid. A *peckerwood* is a woodpecker but can also mean a poor southern white. *See* CRACKER; POOR WHITE; REDNECK.

ain't hay.   *Hay* has meant a small amount of money in American slang since at least the late 1930s, which is about the same time that this expression is first recorded. Little more is known about the very common *and that ain't hay* for "a lot of money," a saying that I would suspect is older than currently supposed.

ain't never seen no men-folks of no kind do no washing no-how.   A forceful example of the use of the double negative heard in the Ozark mountains. Though considered ignorant today, such double negatives have strong links with Elizabethan England, when the double negative was simply employed as a stronger, more effective negative. Shakespeare, in fact, wrote: "Thou hast spoken no word all this while, nor understood none neither."

ain't no place in heaven, ain't no place in hell.   Nowhere for one to go, limbo. The expression is from an old African-American folk song quoted in William Faulkner's *Sanctuary* (1931): "One day mo'! Ain't no place fer you in heaven! Ain't no place fer you in hell! Ain't no place fer you in white folk's jail! Whar you gwine to?"

air ball.   Today's fans would have trouble deciphering newspaper accounts of 19th-century baseball games. Consider this description of a shortstop catching a pop-up or short fly ball. Wrote a reporter in the *Chicago Times* on July 26, 1867: "Williams hit an air ball which was sugared [caught] by Barnes at short stop." An air ball is what we call a pop fly today.

Airedale terrier.   First called a *"Bingley" terrier* after the Bingley district in Yorkshire, England, the dog's name was officially changed to *Airedale* in 1886 (the Aire River runs through Bingley). *Terrier*, from the Latin *terra* ("earth"), means a dog that "takes to earth," a reference to the terrier digging into burrows for badgers and other prey.

airplane.   *See* FLYING MACHINE.

airtights.   Canned food was called *"airtights"* by cowboys in the American West during the latter part of the 19th century. Canned beef was *meat biscuit* or *beef biscuit.*

aisle.   *Aisle* strictly means a section of a church or auditorium, deriving from the Latin *ala*, "wing," and that is how the word has been used by the British until relatively recently. But Americans have long used *aisle* to mean a passageway in a church, auditorium, or elsewhere, and this usage is becoming universal.

A.K.   A euphemism for *"ass kisser,"* one who curries favor. The term has been widely used for well over 50 years in the New York City area, among other places, especially by children. The same initials are also very common for an *alter kocker,* which means a crotchety old man or "old fart" in Yiddish. *Kocker* in Yiddish literally means "crapper" or "shitter."

akimbo.   *In kene bowe* meant "in a sharp bend" in Middle English. It is believed that *akimbo,* for a hand resting on the hip, comes from the mispronunciation of this phrase, the shape of the arm in this position resembling "a sharp bend."

Alabama.   "The Cotton State," our 22nd, took the name *Alabama* when admitted to the Union in 1819. *Alabama* is from the Choctaw *alba ayamule,* which means "I open the thicket," that is, "I am one who works the land, harvests food from it."

Alabama egg.   *See* HOBO EGG.

alabaster.   The name of this variety of gypsum derives from the Greek *alabastos,* which in turn is said to come from the name of an ancient Egyptian town where it was found. Because the substance is often white and translucent, *alabaster* has also come to mean smooth and white, as in "her alabaster skin."

à la Comanche.   To ride a horse by hanging onto one side, as the Comanches used to do to protect themselves in battle while they fired arrows from under the horse's neck. The technique has been depicted in scores of Western movies.

alamo.   The name of several poplar trees, including the cottonwood; from the Spanish *alamo* meaning the same. The Alamo is also the name of a Franciscan mission in San Antonio, Texas, besieged by 6,000 Mexican troops in 1836 during the Texan war for independence. The siege lasted 13 days and ended with all 187 of the defenders being killed. "Remember the Alamo!" became the Texan battle cry of the war. The most recent use of the Alamo's name is San Antonio's Alamodome sports stadium constructed in 1992 at a cost of $130 million.

Alan Smithee.   Just as "George Spelvin" is used in play or movie credits as the name of an actor playing a part anonymously, "Alan Smithee" is sometimes used as the name for a director or producer who desires anonymity. A recent film jokingly used the pseudonym as part of its title: *An Alan Smithee Film: Burn Hollywood Burn* (1998). *See* GEORGE SPELVIN.

alarm; to arms.   *As armes! As armes!* was the Old French military call when a sentry spotted the enemy coming. This became the English *At arms! At arms!* and finally the more recent *To arms! To arms!* Though these were all signals indicating danger, it was, strangely enough, the Italian expression *all' arme!* meaning the same thing, that passed into English as *allarme* and became the English word *alarm,* "a warning."

alas.   Our *alas*, expressing grief or unhappiness, is recorded as early as 1260. It derives from the Old French *ah, las!*, "oh weary [me]!"

Alaska.   SEWARD'S FOLLY, SEWARD'S ICEBOX, Seward's iceberg, Icebergia, and Walrussia were all epithets for the 600,000 square miles now known as Alaska. All of these denunciations today honor one of the great visionaries of American history, William Henry Seward. Seward's most important work in Andrew Johnson's administration was the purchase of Alaska, then known as Russian America, from the Russians in 1867. Negotiating with Russian Ambassador Baron Stoeckl, the shrewd lawyer managed to talk the Russians down from their asking price of $10 million to $7.2 million, and got them to throw in a profitable fur-trading corporation. The treaty was negotiated and drafted in the course of a single night and because Alaska was purchased almost solely due to his determination—he even managed to have the treaty signed before the House voted the necessary appropriation—it was widely called *"Seward's folly"* by irate politicians and journalists. Seward himself named the new territory Alaska, from the Aleut *A-la-as-ka*, "the great country."

Alas, poor Yorick.   The famous passage from *Hamlet* in which the prince holds the old jester's skull in his hand and reflects on the variety of life is thought by some to be a funeral oration commemorating the most noted of English clowns, Richard Tarleton (d. 1588). A very short, broad man who was one of the Queen's Men, Tarleton was immensely popular in his day for his quick wit, jests, jig-dancing, singing, and comic acting. As a boy Shakespeare may well have known him, and Tarleton may even have carried little Willie on his back on one of his visits to Stratford as a traveling actor: *Alas, poor Yorick! I knew him, Horatio, a fellow of infinite jest, of most excellent fancy. He hath borne me on his back a thousand times; and now, how abhorr'd in my imagination it is! My gorge rises at it. Here hung those lips that I have kiss'd I know not how oft. Where be your gibes now; your gambols, your songs, your flashes of merriment that were wont to set the table on a roar? Not one now to mock your own grinning? Quite chopfall'n? Now get you to my lady's chamber, and tell her, let her paint an inch thick, to this favour she must come: Make her laugh at that.*

Albany beef.   Sturgeon was once so plentiful in New York's Hudson River that it was humorously called *Albany beef.* The term is first recorded in 1791 and was in use through the 19th century; sturgeon caviar was so cheap in those days that it was part of the free lunch served in bars. Cod was similarly called *Cape Cod turkey* in Massachusetts.

albatross.   Probably the subject of more legends than any other sea bird, the albatross takes its name from a corruption of the Portuguese *alcatraz*, meaning "large pelican." Dubbed "gooney birds" because of their clumsy behavior, the big albatrosses—whose wingspans often reach 12 feet, greater than that of any other bird—frequently lumber about the decks of ships, unable to take off after they land because of the cramped space, and actually get as seasick as any landlubber. Another name for them is "mollymawks" or "mollyhawks," from the Dutch *mollemok*, "stupid gulls." Despite their apparent stupidity and stubbornness—nothing can force them to abandon their nesting sites, as the U.S. Navy learned at Midway Island—and their poor flying ability when there is no wind current, albatrosses have managed to thrive. They are also called Cape Hope sheep.

Albion, Perfidious Albione.   No place in England is more than 75 miles from the sea; the sea is the very soul of the nation and is even responsible for its poetical name, Albion, which may derive from the name of the giant son of Neptune, who according to legend founded the country and ruled over it for 44 years. Another story states that the king of Syria's 50 daughters, married on the same day, all murdered their husbands on their wedding night and as a punishment were put to sea in a ship and set adrift. They came ashore in Britain, which was named Albion for the oldest daughter, Alba. *Albion* could also derive from the Latin *albus* (white), describing the white cliffs of Dover, or from the Celtic *alp*, rock or crag, also describing the cliffs. *New Albion* is the name Sir Francis Drake gave to the area north of what is now San Francisco on his voyage of 1579. The term *Perfidious Albione*, an English translation of the French *la perfide Albion*, refers to Britain's alleged deceitful policy toward foreigners. It was apparently coined by French preacher Jacques Bossuet (1627–1704), sometimes called France's greatest orator, but it wasn't much used until Napoleon's military recruitment drive in 1813. Another possible coiner of the term is the marquis de Ximenès (1726–1817).

album.   The Romans called the white tablet on which edicts were written an *album*, from the Latin *albus*, "white." In English *album* came to mean any empty book for entering or storing things, especially photographs, only the wedding album still being traditionally white. A record album, a collection of songs, derives from the same root.

Alcatraz.   The former high-security prison in San Francisco Bay takes its name from the island on which it is situated. *Alcatraz Island* was so named by an early Spanish explorer, who named it after the many pelicans he saw there, *alcatraz* being the Portuguese for pelican. First a Spanish fort and then a U.S. military prison, it was made in 1933 a federal prison for dangerous inmates from other locations. Alcatraz, closed in 1963, was nicknamed *The Rock* after the rocky island on which it stands. Among its many infamous inmates were Al Capone and Machine Gun Kelly, none of whom managed to escape so far as is known.

alchemilla; lady's mantle.   Grown for their silvery leaves, these plants derive their name from the Arabic word *alkemelych*, which refers to their use in the past by alchemists who collected dew from their leaves for operations. They are also called *"lady's mantle,"* after the Virgin Mary, to whom the plant was dedicated.

alcinoo poma dare.   Alcinous, legendary king of Phaeacians on the island of Scheria, who entertained Odysseus, had the most renowned and prolific orchards of ancient time. *Alcinoo poma dare*, to give apples to Alcinous, was long proverbial for to do what is superfluous, as to CARRY COALS TO NEWCASTLE.

alcohol.   One apocryphal tale claims that an Arab named Jabir ibn Hazzan "invented" alcohol in about A.D. 800 when he discovered the process of distilling wine. In trying to find the intoxicating agent in wine he distilled *alkuhl*, which meant "a finely refined spirit." According to the story, the word itself was adopted from the name for an antimony powder used at the time as an eyelid cosmetic (an ancient eye shadow). More sober etymologists will only say that *alcohol* derives from the Arabic *alkuhl*, powdered antimony, or the distillate.

alewife. One early traveler in America, John Josselyn, seems to have thought that this plentiful fish was called the *alewife* because it had "a bigger bellie" than the herring, a belly like a wife who drank a lot of ale. More likely the word is a mispronunciation of some forgotten American Indian word.

Alexander. A cocktail made with creme de cacao, gin or brandy, and sweet cream, said to have been invented by and named for American author Alexander Woollcott in about 1925. "The lethal mixture . . . tasted like cream," actress Helen Hayes once said. "I drank one down and took another and drank it down, and I was blind."

Alexander Hamilton. Sometimes used as a term for one's signature, similar to the use of JOHN HANCOCK or JOHN HENRY. The term, of course, comes from the name of American statesman Alexander Hamilton (1757–1804).

Alexander the Corrector. One of the great censors to be found in these pages (*see* BOWDLERIZE; COMSTOCKERY). Alexander Cruden (1701–1770) believed himself divinely appointed to reform England, suffered periodic attacks of insanity, and was confined in lunatic asylums several times. Cruden compiled a highly regarded *Biblical Concordance*, but would be more valued today for his peculiar form of censorship. He was called "Alexander the Corrector" because he had a penchant for going about London with a sponge and erasing all the "licentious, coarse and profane" graffiti he saw. Cruden was found dead in an attitude of prayer.

Alexandria. Ancient *Alexandria* in the Nile delta was founded in 332 B.C. by Alexander the Great, the king of Macedonia, the *Alexandrine verse* or line of poetry derives from a French poem written about him, and the *Alexandrine rat*, or roof rat, indirectly comes from his name, via the Egyptian city. Great though he was in war and statecraft, Alexander's personal life was a loss. Excluding the Sicilian ruler Dionysius, he is probably the only king to die from overindulging in drink. One story has it that a six-day drinking bout led to his death, while another claims that his wife, Roxana, persuaded him to plunge intoxicated into an ice-cold pool, causing the conqueror of Persia to die of a high fever at the tender age of 33. Robert Graves, however, points out that Alexander may have died from poisoning after a mushroom orgy rather than a drunken one.

alfresco. Now widely used in the United States, *alfresco*, meaning outdoors (as in "We dined alfresco"), is first recorded in 1853 as a borrowing of the Spanish *al fresco*, meaning the same.

alga. Snow in Arctic and Alpine regions that appears red has often been regarded as a supernatural portent of evil. It is actually caused by the presence of large numbers of the minute alga *Protococcus nivalis*. *Alga*, from the Latin *alga*, "seaweed," are simple microscopic flowerless plants, ranging from those that coat ponds with green scum to giant seaweeds 100 feet long.

alibi. "We the jury, find that the accused was *alibi*," was the verdict in one 18th-century criminal trial. This simply meant that the defendant was "elsewhere" when the crime was committed, and therefore innocent. Over the centuries, the Latin *alibi*, for elsewhere, was used so often in the courts in this sense that it entered everyday speech as both the synonym for an accused criminal's "story" and an excuse, often a spurious one, in general.

Alibi Ike. Someone who is always making excuses or inventing alibis is called "Alibi Ike." The designation was invented by Ring Lardner in his short story "Alibi Ike" (1914) as a nickname for outfielder Frank X. Farrell, so named because he had excuses for everything. When Farrell drops an easy fly ball, he claims his glove "wasn't broke in yet"; when questioned about last year's batting average he replies, "I had malaria most of the season"; when he hits a triple he says he "ought to had a home run, only the ball wasn't lively," or "the wind brought it back," or he "tripped on a lump o' dirt roundin' first base"; when he takes a called third strike, he claims he "lost count" or he would have swung at and hit it. The author, who had a "phonographic ear" for American dialect, created a type for all time with Alibi Ike, and the expression became American slang as soon as the story was published. In an introduction to the yarn the incomparable Lardner noted, "The author acknowledges his indebtedness to Chief Justice Taft for some of the slang employed."

Alice; Alice in Wonderland. For over a century Lewis Carroll's *Alice in Wonderland* (1865) has been the most famous and possibly the most widely read children's book. That there is an *Alice* cult even among adults is witnessed by the numerous works of criticism devoted to the book, which has been translated into Latin. The model for the fictional Alice was Alice Liddell, daughter of Dean Henry George Liddell, noted coauthor of *Liddell & Scott's Greek Lexicon*, still the standard Greek-English Dictionary. Carroll, his real name being Charles Lutwidge Dodgson, wrote *Alice* for his friend's daughter, who later became Mrs. Reginald Hargreaves. The author apparently made up the story while on a picnic with Alice and her sisters, actually improvising the classic tale as the group rowed up a river. Incidentally, Carroll is regarded as the greatest 19th-century photographer of children and his best pictures were of Alice Liddell. An *Alice*, in allusion to *Alice in Wonderland*, is sometimes used to refer to a person newly arrived in strange, fantastic surroundings.

Alice blue. Alice blue is one of several colors named for real people. The shade signalizes Alice Roosevelt Longworth, daughter of President Theodore Roosevelt, who favored the pale greenish or grayish blue. Mrs. Longworth is the witty lady who said of Calvin Coolidge: "He looks as if he had been weaned on a pickle." Princess Alice, as she was called, was born on February 12, 1884; her mother, Alice, died from Bright's disease, a kidney inflammation, two days after her birth, on the same day that Theodore Roosevelt's mother died of typhoid fever. On February 17, 1906, Alice married Congressman Nicolas Longworth of Ohio in an elegant East Room wedding in the White House. Mrs. Longworth long remained a leader of Washington society, her name and the color Alice blue rendered familiar by the tune "Alice Blue Gown," which she inspired.

alien corn. *See* CORN.

alive and kicking. Though it is a cliché by now, this expression has an interesting history. Meaning alert and active, *alive and kicking* apparently goes back to the 18th century, when it was first used by London fishmongers in reference to the fresh fish flapping about in their carts.

alkahest. The alkahest was the universal solvent of alchemy that supposedly dissolved anything, the word being coined from Arabic by the Swiss alchemist Theophrastus Bombastus von Hohenheim (1490–1541), who also coined his own pseudonym. This charlatan called himself Paracelsus, from the Greek *para*, "beyond," plus *Celsus*, the name of a prominent first-century physician—thus advertising himself as beyond or better than the much esteemed Celsus!

alkali. Arab chemists in medieval times extracted sodium carbonate from the marine saltwort plant, calling the substance *al-qaliy*, "ashes of salt wort." Later chemists applied the term *alkali*, a transliteration of the Arab word, to all salts with properties similar to sodium carbonate.

Alka-Seltzer. A Miles Laboratory trademark, *Alka-Seltzer*, an antacid taken for the relief of an upset stomach or a headache, was coined from *alkaline*, the opposite of *acid*, and *seltzer* water (from the medicinal mineral water at Neider-*Selters* in Germany). *Seltzer* was suggested by the effervescense of the analgesic preparation.

all aboard! This common train conductor's call is an Americanism, first recorded in 1837, and is nautical in origin. Wrote Joshua T. Smith in his *Journal in America* (1837): "They [the Americans] describe a situation by the compass 'talk of the voyage' of being 'all aboard' & etc.; this doubtless arises from *all* their ancestors having come hither over ocean & having in the voyage acquired nautical language." The call *all aboard!* was used on riverboats here before it was used on trains.

all-American. Walter Chauncey Camp, "the Father of American Football" who formulated many of the game's rules, picked the first all-American football team in 1889 along with Caspar Whitney, a publisher of *This Week's Sport Magazine*. But the idea and designation was Whitney's and he, not Camp, should be credited with introducing *all-American* to the American lexicon of sports and other endeavors. *See* ALL-STAR GAME.

all at sea. Early mariners hugged the coastlines because their navigational aids were crude and inaccurate. But often they were blown far out to sea where they had no landmarks to guide them. The expression *all at sea* described their plight perfectly, as anyone ever caught in rough, open seas will testify, and the term was soon used to describe the condition of any helpless, bewildered person.

all chiefs and no Indians. Many businesses have experienced trouble because they had all chiefs and no Indians, that is, too many officers who want to do nothing but give orders to others. The origin of this common worker's complaint has been traced to about 1940 in Australia, where the expression was first *all chiefs and no Indians, like the University Regiment*. Yet the first half of the expression has an American ring, and one suspects that some determined word sleuth might turn up an earlier printed use in the United States.

all ears. *I'm all ears*, I'm listening attentively, is hardly modern slang, being at least three centuries old. Its first recorded use in this precise form is by Anthony Trollope in 1865. But over two centuries before this Milton wrote in *Comus* (1634): "I was all ear,/And took in strains that might create a soul/Under the ribs of death."

alley-oop. This interjection may have been coined by American soldiers during World War I, for it sounds like the French *allez* ("you go") plus a French pronunciation of the English *up*—hence *allez oop*, "up you go." During the 1920s *allez-oop* (often spelled *alley-oop*) was a common interjection said upon lifting something. The expression became so popular that a caveman comic strip character was named Alley Oop. Soon *alley-oop* became a basketball term for a high pass made to a player near the basket, who then leaps to catch the ball and, in midair, stuffs it in the basket. In the late 1950s, San Francisco 49er quarterback Y. A. Tittle invented a lob pass called the *alley-oop* which was thrown over the heads of defenders to tall, former basketball player R. C. Owens.

all foreign fruit, plants are free from duty. This is the classic example of the importance of proper punctuation. In the 1890s a congressional clerk transcribing a new law was supposed to write: "All foreign fruit-plants are free from duty" but changed the hyphen to a comma and wrote: "All foreign fruit, plants are free from duty." Before Congress could amend his error, the government lost over $2 million in taxes.

all for one and one for all. The motto of the Three Musketeers in Alexandre Dumas's novel *The Three Musketeers* (1844). Still widely read and made into movies, the novel describes the swashbuckling adventures of the immortal trio, Athos, Porthos, and Aramis, mounted guards of the French king, and their friend d'Artagnan, who was based on a musketeer of Louis XIV.

all good Americans go to Paris when they die. *See* MUTUAL ADMIRATION SOCIETY.

all gussied up. A gusset, (probably from the French *gousset*, "pod, or shell of nuts") is a triangular piece of material inserted into a garment to make it more comfortable, and perhaps more fashionable because it fits better. *Gusseted* means to have a gusset or gussets in clothing and may have become corrupted in everyday speech to *gussied*. Someone with many gussets in her dress, many improvements in it, might have been called "all gussied up," which could have come to mean "to be dressed in one's best clothes." This is all guesswork, but it is the best explanation we have for the phrase, which dates back to the 17th century.

all hands and the cook.   *All hands and the cook on deck!* was a cry probably first heard on New England whalers in the early 19th century when everyone aboard was called topside to cut in on a whale, work that had to be done quickly. Fishermen also used the expression, and still do, and it had currency among American cowboys to indicate a dangerous situation—when, for example, even the cook was needed to keep the herd under control.

all hat and no cattle.   A Texan phrase describing someone who acts rich or important but has no substance, such as a person who pretends to be a cattle baron, even dressing the part: "He's all hat and no cattle."

all his bullet holes is in the front of him.   A colorful phrase describing a brave man, not a coward, coined by cowboys in late 19th-century America.

alligator.   The biggest lizard that the Romans knew was about the size of the forearm and was thus named *lacertus* ("forearm"), which eventually came into Spanish use as *lagarto*. When the Spaniards encountered a huge New World saurian that resembled a lizard, they called it *el lagarto*, "the lizard," putting the definite article before the noun as they are accustomed to doing. Englishmen assumed this to be a single word, *elagarto*, which in time became corrupted in speech to *alligator*. This is probably the way the word was born, but much better is an old story about an early explorer sighting the creature and exclaiming, "There's a lagarto!" Less dangerous than the crocodile, the alligator does have a worse "bark": it is one of the few reptiles capable of making a loud sound. *See also* CROCODILE TEARS.

all I know is what I read in the papers.   This saying has become a popular American expression since Oklahoman Will Rogers coined it in his *Letters of a Self-Made Diplomat to His President* (1927). It has various applications but is commonly used to mean "I'm not an expert, just an ordinary person, and what I've told you is true to the best of my knowledge." It implies one may be wrong because one's sources are not infallible.

all in the same boat.   Just more than a century old, this saying means that two or more people are sharing the same risks or living under similar conditions. It may derive from some unknown situation when two or more people were adrift in the same lifeboat, or it may even come from the earlier expression "to stick" or "have an oar in another's boat"; that is, to meddle in someone else's affairs, which dates back to the 16th century.

all is lost save honor.   After Francis I of France was defeated by Spain's Charles V at Pavia, Italy in 1525, captured, and forced to sign a humiliating treaty, he sat down and wrote to his mother. His actual words were not so eloquent, but the most memorable phrase in his letter was translated into English as *All is lost save honor*. Despite the fact that Francis soon lost his honor by breaking the treaty, the sentiments of this patron of Rabelais and creator of Fontainebleau became proverbial.

alliteration.   An old device (older than rhyme) used in poetry, and less commonly in prose, which consists of the repetitions of an initial sound in two or more words of a phrase, line, or sentence. The word derives from the Latin for "repeating and playing upon the same letter." A good example is Tennyson's line, "The moan of doves in immemorial elms / And murmuring of innumerable bees." The device has been much used and much abused. The poet Huchbald, who flourished in the ninth century, wrote the *Eclogue on Baldness*, which he appropriately dedicated to the king of the Franks and Holy Roman Emperor Charles the Bald. The 146-line poem has been called "a reductio ad absurdum of alliteration," every word beginning with the letter *c*. Better known is the 1817 alliterative alphabetic poem by B. Poulter that begins "An Austrian army, awfully arranged / Boldly by battery, besieged Belgrade . . ."

all mouth and no ears.   Proverbial for someone who tries to dominate every discussion, won't listen, won't yield the floor, and has a big mouth. The first recorded use of the term is unclear, but similar sentiments have been expressed by writers since ancient times. Zeno of Citium (ca. 335–ca. 263 B.C.), the founder of the Stoic school, remarked to a pupil who talked in class excessively: "The reason why we have two ears and only one mouth is that we may hear more and talk less."

all my eye and Betty Martin.   This saying may have originated when a British sailor, looking into a church in an Italian port, heard a beggar praying *"An mihi, beate Martine"* ("Ah, grant me, Blessed Martin") and later told his shipmates that this was nonsense that sounded to him like "All my eye and Betty Martin." Most authorities dismiss this theory summarily, especially because *Joe Miller's Jests* included the story, but St. Martin *was* the patron saint of beggars. One etymologist tells us that "no such Latin prayer is to be found in the formulary of the Catholic Church" and another claims to have in his possession "a book of old Italian cosmopolitan life . . . [that] mentions this prayer to St. Francis by beggars." It seems likely that beggars would have recited such a prayer and so the story has some basis in fact, more at least than linguists have been willing to admit. Meanwhile, there is no better identification of "Betty Martin."

all oak and iron bound.   A 19th-century Americanism meaning in the best of health and spirits, as in "He's feeling all oak and iron bound." The comparison is to a well-made barrel. Oak alone is a hard, strong, durable material.

all-overs.   An American southernism that goes back to at least the early 19th century, the *all-overs* describes a general state of nervousness. Something close to it is first recorded in an 1820 song entitled "Oh, What a Row": "I'm seized with an all-overness, I faint, I die!"

all over the ballpark.   Anyone or anything very confused and unfocused can be said to be all over the ballpark. The expression, dating back to the 1850s, is from baseball, where it refers to a pitcher who can't find the plate.

all quiet on the Potomac.   Sylva Clapin explained this phrase in *A New Dictionary of Americanisms* (1902): "A phrase now become famous and used in jest or ironically as indicative of a period of undisturbed rest, quiet enjoyment, or peaceful possession. It originated with Mr. [Simon] Cameron, Secretary of

War during the Rebellion [Civil War], who made such a frequent use of it, in his war collections, that it became at last stereotyped on the nation's mind." E. L. Beers published a poem in *Harper's Weekly* (Nov. 30, 1861) extending the expression: " 'All quiet along the Potomac,' they say, / 'Except now and then, a stray picket / is shot, as he walks on his beat to and fro./ By a rifleman hid in the thicket.' " General George McClellan is also said to have invented the phrase. *See* ALL QUIET ON THE WESTERN FRONT.

all quiet on the western front.   Although it may owe something to the Civil War slogan ALL QUIET ON THE POTOMAC, this phrase became well known in World War I because it was often used in communiqués from the western front, a 600-mile battle line that ran from Switzerland to the English Channel and was in reality far from quiet just with the moans of the wounded and dying. The most famous use of the words is in the title of Erich Maria Remarque's great antiwar novel, *All Quiet on the Western Front* (1929).

all roads lead to Rome.   The ancient Romans built such an excellent system of roads that the saying arose *all roads lead to Rome*, that is, no matter which road one starts a journey on, he will finally reach Rome if he keeps on traveling. The popular saying came to mean that all ways or methods of doing something end in the same result, no one method being better than another.

all shook up.   The Elvis Presley song of this name helped to popularize the expression when he recorded it in 1958, but these words meaning "very excited, disturbed, worried" originated 10 years or so before, probably as slang associated with the rock-and-roll music becoming popular at the time.

allspice.   Allspice, or pimento (*Pimenta dioica*), is the dried, unripe berry of an aromatic 20- to 40-foot tree now found generally in Jamaica and other West Indian islands. It should not be confused with pimientos, the fruits of certain capsicum garden peppers. Allspice has long been regarded, and feared, as an aphrodisiac. Pious Peter the Venerable forbade the monks under his charge at Cluny in 1132 to eat pimiento because it was "provokative to lust." Allspice takes its name from the fact that the berry smells and tastes something like cinnamon, nutmeg, and cloves combined.

all's right with the world!   This saying is frequently misquoted as "all's *well* with the world." The words are from Robert Browning's dramatic poem "Pippa Passes" (1841) and is one of the songs of Pippa, a young girl who passes through town on her yearly holiday. Unknown to her, each of her songs affects and changes the lives of people who hear them, the best-known one filling a murderer with remorse for what he has done:

> The year's at the spring,
> And day's at the morn;
> Morning's at seven;
> The hill-side's dew-pearled;
> The lark's on the wing;
> The snail's on the thorn:
> God's in his heaven—
> All's right with the world!

All-Star Game.   The idea for an All-Star Game between the American and National baseball leagues came from *Chicago Tribune* sports editor Arch Ward in 1933. Under Ward's plan, fans voted for the best players and the winners played each other. In most seasons since then the fans have picked the teams, but balloting is now conducted by the national newspaper *U.S.A. Today*. Babe Ruth hit a home run in the first All-Star Game, or Midsummer Dream Game, as it is sometimes called. The premiere was played in 1933 at Chicago's Comisky Park as a special feature of the Chicago World's Fair. Football's Pro Bowl was called the All-Star game until its name was changed in 1951. *See* ALL-AMERICAN.

all systems go.   All preparations have been made and the operation is ready to start. Widely used today, the expression originated with American ground controllers during the launching of rockets into space in the early 1970s.

all that glitters is not gold.   "Do not hold everything gold that shines like gold," French theologian Alain de Lille wrote as far back as the 12th century. Since then Chaucer, Cervantes, and Shakespeare have all contributed variations on the saying. Its present form originated with English author John Dryden in his *The Hind and the Panther* (1687): "All, as they say, that glitters is not gold."

all that meat and no potatoes.   An exclamation of pleasure and admiration by a man on seeing a woman with an attractive figure, although the term and/or the exclamation might be offensive to many women. *See* POTATO; MEAT AND POTATOES; HOT POTATO.

all the news that's fit to print.   Adolph S. Ochs purchased the *New York Times* in 1896 and raised it to the eminent position it enjoys today. Instead of participating in the YELLOW JOURNALISM of the day, he chose the high road, adopting two slogans to make his intentions clear. One, still used, was the famous "All the news that's fit to print." The other was "It does not soil the breakfast cloth."

all the tea in China.   All the tea in China would be nearly 600,000 tons, according to the 1985 estimates of the United States Department of Agriculture. It may be an Americanism, but this expression denoting a great sum probably is of British origin and over a century old; the trouble is that no one has been able to authoritatively pin it down.

all the traffic will bear.   Partridge's definition of this catchphrase is "The situation, whether financial or other, precludes anything more." Because it literally relates to railroad fares and freights, the expression, which is first recorded in the United States circa 1945, may originally be the cynical words of a railway magnate.

all the world's a stage.   Shakespeare used this phrase in *As You Like It* (1598–1600): "All the world's a stage, / And all the men and women merely players." About 20 years before this, Guillaume de Salluste, seigneur du Bartas (1544–90), wrote in *Divine Weekes and Workes* (1578): "The world's a stage, where God's omnipotence, / His justice, knowledge, love, and providence Do act the parts." Other well-known phrases that the

French poet used before Shakespeare, suggesting that the English bard was familiar with his work, include: *night's black mantle*, for which Shakespeare has *night . . . with thy black mantle* (*Romeo and Juliet*, 1594); *the foure corners of the world*, which Shakespeare has as *the three corners of the world* (*King John*, 1596); *these lovely lamps, these windows of the soul*, which Shakespeare has as *the windows of mine eyes* (*King Richard III*, 1592); and *in the jaws of death*, which Shakespeare has as *out of the jaws of death* (*Twelfth Night*, 1598).

all this for a song.   The phrase, reflecting an often prevalent attitude toward poetry, was spoken by William Cecil, Lord Burleigh, England's Lord Treasurer under Queen Elizabeth, when the Queen ordered him to give 100 pounds to Edmund Spenser as a royal gratuity for writing *The Faerie Queene*. Burleigh was later satirized in Richard Sheridan's *The Critic*, in which he comes onstage but never talks, just nodding because he is much too busy with affairs of state to do more. This inspired the expression *Burleigh's nod* and *as significant as a shake of Burleigh's head.*

all thumbs.   *All thumbs* for a clumsy person, or someone with no dexterity has its roots in an old English saying first recorded in John Heywood's *Proverbs* (1562): "Whan he should get ought, eche fynger a thumbe."

all vines an' no taters.   An Americanism of the 19th century used to describe something or someone very showy but of no substance. "He'll never amount to nothin'. He's all vines and no taters." Probably suggested by sweet potato plants, which produce a lot of vines and, if grown incorrectly, can yield few sweet potatoes.

all washed up.   At the end of a day's work a factory worker usually washes his hands. From this notion of washing hands after finishing a job came the expression *all washed up*, finished with anything, which led to its later meaning of a business failure, finished with everything, or anything that has become obsolete and unfashionable. The expression dates back to the early 1920s.

all wool and a yard wide.   Dating back at least to the late 19th century, this expression may have originated during the Civil War, when SHODDY, cloth made from reprocessed wool and supplied to the Union Army, often literally unraveled on a wearer's back. The phrase has come to mean something or someone of high quality or reliability, as in "He's all wool and a yard wide."

all wool and no shoddy.   Something or someone genuine, trustworthy, pure. SHODDY was a cheap material manufactured during the Civil War.

almanac.

> Early to bed and early to rise
> Makes a man healthy, wealthy and wise.

The above is just one sample of the shrewd maxims and proverbs, almost all of which became part of America's business ethic, that Benjamin Franklin wrote or collected in his *Poor Richard's Almanac*. This was by no means the first almanac issued in America, that distinction belonging to *An Almanack for New England for the Year 1639*, issued by William Peirce, a shipowner who hoped to attract more paying English passengers to the colonies and whose almanac was (except for a broadside) the first work printed in America. *Poor Richard's* was written and published by Franklin at Philadelphia from 1733 to 1758 and no doubt takes its name from the earlier English *Poor Robin's Almanac*, first published in 1663 by Robert ("Robin") and William Winstanley. Almanacs, which take their name from a medieval Latin word for a calendar with astronomical data, were issued as early as 1150, before the invention of printing, and were compendiums of information, jokes, and proverbs.

almighty dollar.   Washington Irving coined the phrase *the almighty dollar* in his sketch called "The Creole Village," first published in 1836: "The almighty dollar, that great object of universal devotion throughout the land, seems to have no genuine devotees in these peculiar villages." But Ben Jonson had used "almighty gold" in a similar sense more than 200 years before him: "that for which all virtue now is sold, / And almost every vice—almighty gold."

almond; Jordan almond.   Almonds, which came out of China, are today the most popular of all nuts worldwide. They especially please the Japanese, who often have English signs reading "Almond" outside shops that would otherwise say "Bakery" or "Confectionery" in their own language. But then this ancient nut (mentioned 73 times in the Old Testament) has been associated with beauty and virility for centuries. Rich in protein, amino acids, magnesium, iron, calcium, and phosphorus, and a good source of vitamins B and E, the almond is also a harbinger of spring and the joyous expectancy of new life and love; in fact, the tree's pale pink blossoms appear about the time that the swallows return to Capistrano. The word *almond* has its roots in *amandola*, the medieval Latin word for the nut. Jordan almonds come from Spain; they have no connection with the country named Jordan, as many people assume. The term "Jordan almond" is simply a corruption of the French *jardin amande*, which translates as "garden almond."

aloha.   Both a greeting and farewell, the Hawaiian *aloha* means, simply and sweetly, "love." It has been called "the world's loveliest greeting or farewell." Hawaii is of course the ALOHA STATE, its unofficial anthem "Aloha Oe" (Farewell to Thee) written by Queen Liliuokalani. *Mi loa aloha* means "I love you" in Hawaiian.

aloha shirt.   Although these colorful Hawaiian shirts with bright prints of hula girls, surfers, pineapples, and other Hawaiian subjects date back to the 1920s, they were made famous by manufacturer Ellery Chun (1909–2000), who first mass-produced them. The shirts were made in small Honolulu tailor shops until Mr. Chun, a native Hawaiian and Yale graduate, manufactured them in quantity and coined their name in 1933. They sold for 95 cents apiece during the Great Depression. *See* ALOHA.

Aloha State.   *See* ALOHA, above, for this nickname for Hawaii, which is also called the Crossroads of the Pacific and the Paradise of the Pacific.

aloof. To *stand aloof* was originally a nautical term meaning "to bear to windward," or luff, which derives from the Dutch *loef*, meaning "windward." Since a ship cannot sail to windward except by keeping the bow of the ship pointed slightly away from the wind, the term took on the general meaning of "to keep away from," "to keep at a distance," "to be reserved or reticent."

alpha and omega. Everything, the most important part. The expression has its origins in the Greek alphabet, where *alpha* and *omega* are the first and last letters respectively, as well as in the biblical phrase (Rev. 1:7): "I am the Alpha and Omega, the beginning and the ending, saith the Lord."

alphabet. *Alphabet*, Brewer notes, is our "only word of more than one syllable compounded solely of the names of letters"—the Greek *alpha (a)* and *beta (b)*. He goes on to say that the English alphabet "will combine into 29 thousand quadrillion combinations [possible words]," that is, 29 followed by 27 zeros (29,000,000,000,000,000,000,000,000,000,000). Others dispute this figure, saying the number of combinations of words possible is "only" 1,906 followed by 25 zeros. In any case, remember that these figures were arrived at by using each of the 26 letters of the alphabet *only once* in each combination or word—and they do not include possible compound words, homonyms, etc.! I'd guess that there are now at least 10 times as many English words as the half million or so recorded in the most complete dictionary, there being over 1 million scientific words for organic and inorganic chemical compounds alone. Of the 65 alphabets now used around the world the Cambodian has the most letters, with 72, and the Rotokas, spoken on Bougainville Island in the South Pacific, has the least, with 11. Among others, the Russian alphabet has 41 letters, the Armenian 38, the Persian 32, the Latin 25, the Greek 24, the French 23, the Hebrew 22, the Italian 20, and the Burmese 19. The German and Dutch alphabets, like the English, have 26 letters. Wrote William Walsh in 1892: "The 26 letters of the English alphabet may be transposed 620,448,401,733,239,439,369,000 times. All the inhabitants of the globe could not in a thousand millions of years write out all the possible transpositions of the 26 letters, even supposing that each wrote 40 pages daily, each page containing 40 different transpositions of the letters."

Alphard, and other star names. Alphard, the only bright star in the constellation Hydra, was named by Bedouin tribesmen traveling through the desert thousands of years ago. The word comes to us from the Arabic *Fard ash-Shuja*, meaning "the lone one in the serpent." Surprisingly, most star names are of Arabic origin. Of 183 star names listed in one study, 125 are Arabic (Vega, Algol, etc.), 14 are Latin (Capella, Spica), 9 are Arabic-Latin combinations (Yed Prior), and three are Persian (Alcor). A good number of Arabic star names were bestowed by tribesmen who named the more prominent stars after camels, sheep, birds, jackals, hyenas, frogs, and other animals, but most were named by Arabian astronomers.

Alps. These mountains in southern Europe take their name directly from the Latin *Alps*, the "high mountains," which is what the ancient Romans called them. The highest peak in the range is Mont Blanc, 15,781 feet.

also-ran. The joy may be in playing, not winning, but *an also-ran* means a loser, someone who competed but didn't come near winning. The term is an Americanism first recorded (as *also ran*) with political reference in 1904, and derives from horse racing. The newspaper racing results once listed win, place, and show horses before listing, under the heading "Also Ran," all other horses that finished out of the money.

aluminum. The English word *aluminum* for the metal is the same or very similar in many languages: Italian, *alluminio*; Spanish, *aluminio*; French, *aluminum*; Dutch, *aluminium*; Danish, *aluminium*; Hungarian, *aluminium*; Polish, *aluminjum*; Indonesian, *aluminium*; Arabic, *alaminyoum*; and Japanese, *aruminyuumu*. The words are so alike simply because British scientist Sir Humphrey Davy named the metal aluminium when he discovered it in 1812, from the Latin *Alumina*, for "a white earth," which he used in his experiments.

always be nice to people on your way up—you may meet them on your way down. Not comic Jimmy Durante but humorist Wilson Mizner invented this catchphrase coined in the 1920s, when Mizner served the Muse in Hollywood and invented dozens of well-known, usually caustic expressions. The phrase is now heard almost everywhere English is spoken.

always do right . . . Mark Twain's advice, given to the Young People's Society of the Greenpoint (Brooklyn) Presbyterian Church in 1901: "Always do right, This will gratify some people, and astonish the rest."

"always scribble, scribble, scribble! eh! Mr. Gibbon?". Henry Digby Beste, in his *Personal and Literary Memorials* (1829), tells the full story of this famous remark made to English historian Edward Gibbon: "The Duke of Gloucester, brother of King George III, permitted Mr. Gibbon to present him with the first volume of *The History of the Decline and Fall of the Roman Empire*. When the second volume of that work appeared, it was quite in order that it should be presented to His Royal Highness in like manner. The prince received the author with much good nature and affability, saying to him, as he laid the quarto on the table, 'Another damn'd thick, square book! Always scribble, scribble, scribble! Eh! Mr. Gibbon?' " This insulting remark about the greatest historical work in English (though Gibbon generally saw history as "little more than the crimes, follies and misfortunes of men") has also been attributed to the duke of Cumberland.

alyo. The unusual term *alyo* has had some currency in baseball, where it means "a cool hand, a player who is not easily disconcerted." *Alyo* was probably first an underworld expression with the same meaning. It apparently derives from the Italian idiom *mangiare aglio*, literally "to eat garlic," but meaning to appear calm and placid while being angry; this idiom is rooted in the Italian folk belief that garlic wards off evil.

alyssum. The Greek word for madness is the chief component of this delicate plant's name, for the Greeks believed it cured madness and named it *alysson*, from *lysa*, "madness," and *a*, "not." The popular garden plant with its clusters of fragrant white or golden flowers is called "madwort" for the same reason. "Wort," from the Old English *wyrt*, "root, plant," means a plant, herb, or vegetable and is usually used in combinations like "madwort."

Alzheimer's disease. Victims of this disease or syndrome affecting the brain cells display common symptoms of senility, such as memory loss, but Alzheimer's disease can strike people in their 40s as well as those of more advanced age. The disease takes its name from German neurologist Alois Alzheimer (1864–1915), who first identified it in about 1900. *See* THE LONG GOODBYE.

A.M.; P.M. A.M. is the abbreviation of the Latin *ante meridiem*, "before noon or midday", not ante meridian, even though *meridian* also means noon. P.M. is the abbreviation of *post meridiem*, "after noon."

amalgam. Although the derivation of *amalgam*, meaning an alloy of metals or a combination of diverse elements, is of obscure origin, Weekley says the "most probable conjecture connects it, via Arabic, with the Greek for "marriage.' " The " 'marriage' of the metals," he notes, "is often referred to in alchemistic jargon."

amalgamationist. "Blending of the two races by amalgamation is just what is needed for the perfection of both," a white Boston clergyman wrote in 1845. Few American abolitionists were proponents of amalgamation, but many were called amalgamationists by proslaveryites in the two decades or so before the Civil War. This Americanism for one who favors a social and genetic mixture of whites and blacks is first recorded in 1838, when Harriet Martineau complained that people were calling her an amalgamationist when she didn't know what the word meant.

amaranth. The Greeks believed this flower never died and gave it the name *amarantos*, "everlasting." It was said to be a symbol of immortality because the flowers keep their deep blood-red color to the last. John Milton wrote in *Paradise Lost*:

> Immortal amarant, a flower which once
> In Paradise, fast by the Tree of Life,
> Began to bloom, but, soon for man's offence
> To heaven removed where first it grew, there grows
> And flowers aloft, shading the Fount of Life . . .

amaretti. A lovesick baker daydreamed so long about his lady while baking a special kind of almond cookie for her that he left the cookie in the oven too long and the light, dry *amaretti* cookie resulted. Such is the legend, that the delicious cookies, often served with wine, take their name from the Italian *amoretti*, "little loves." Actually, they take this name from *amare*, "bitter," because they are made from bitter almonds. *Amaretto* liqueur comes from the same source.

amateur. An amateur player in any sport is one who plays for pleasure or the love of the sport rather than for financial gain or professional reasons. Appropriately, the word derives ultimately from the Latin *amator*, lover. The term was first recorded in English around 1775 and was initially used in reference to sports about 25 years later in a description of gentleman boxing enthusiasts. In the late 19th century, men

vied for the title of "the world's greatest amateur athlete," and one of the leading contenders was New Yorker Foxhall Keene. *See* CHICKEN À LA KING.

Amazon. The first Amazons, from the Greek *a* ("without") plus *mazos* ("breast"), were popularly said to be a tribe of fierce warrior women who cut or burned off their right breasts so as not to impede the drawing of their bows. Amazons have been reported in Africa and South America as well as in Greece. The Amazon River, which had been named Rio Santa Maria de la Mar Dulce by its discoverer, is said to have been rechristened by the Spanish explorer Francisco de Orellana in 1541 after he was attacked by the Tapuyas, a tribe in which he believed women fought alongside men. Most word detectives believe both these stories are examples of folk etymology but offer no alternatives.

ambergris. The *ambergris* Melville described in *Moby-Dick* remains a valuable, important ingredient in perfume making. It is a black waxlike substance, originating in the stomach of a sick sperm whale sometimes found floating in the sea. As the soft secretion ages, it becomes harder and sweet in smell. The French thought it resembled amber, save for its color, and called it *amber gris*, gray amber, which was taken into English as *ambergris*.

ambidextrous. *See* RIGHT.

ambition. Politicians are still among the most ambitious men, but the Romans thought them so much more so than others that they confined their word *ambito* (from *ambi*, "around," and *eo*, "go"), meaning "ardent striving for pomp and power," to politicians alone. In fact it took centuries before *ambition*, the English derivative of *ambito*, took on a more positive meaning and was applied to any person striving for wealth, power, skill, or recognition.

ambulance chaser. It is said that ambulance chasers in days past had cards like the following:

SAMUEL SHARP
THE HONEST LAWYER
CAN GET YOU

$5,000 $10,000
for a leg   for a liver

Ambulance chaser is a thoroughly American term that originally described (and still does) a lawyer who seeks out victims immediately after an accident and tries to persuade them to let him represent them in a suit for damages. The expression probably originated in New York City during the late 1890s, a time when disreputable lawyers frequently commissioned ambulance drivers and policemen to inform them of accidents and sometimes rode with victims to the hospital to proffer their services.

ambush. In the mid-16th century the Old French *embusche* became through mispronunciation the English *ambush*. Appropriately, the French word derived from *embuscher*, "to hide in the woods."

Ameche.   Though not much used anymore, *Ameche* has been American slang for "telephone" since 1939, when actor Don Ameche played the lead role in *The Story of Alexander Graham Bell*, the inventor of the telephone.

amen corner.   A group of fervent believers or ardent followers is called an amen corner, after the similarly named place near the pulpit in churches occupied by those who lead the responsive "amens" to the preacher's prayers. The term may come from the Amen Corner of London's Paternoster Row, but it is an almost exclusively American expression today.

America.   Many writers have assumed that the Italian navigator Amerigo Vespucci (whom Ralph Waldo Emerson called "a thief" and "pickle dealer at Seville") was a con man who never explored the New World and doesn't deserve to be mentioned in the same breath with Christopher Columbus, much less have his name honored in the continent's name. Deeper investigation reveals that Vespucci, born in Florence in 1454, did indeed sail to the New World with the expedition of Alonso de Ojeda in 1499, parting with him even before land was sighted in the West Indies. Vespucci, sailing in his own ship, then discovered and explored the mouth of the Amazon, subsequently sailing along the northern shores of South America. Returning to Spain in 1500, he entered the service of the Portuguese and the following year explored 6,000 miles along the southern coast of South America. He was eventually made Spain's pilot major and died at the age of 58 of malaria contracted on one of his voyages. Vespucci not only explored unknown regions but also invented a system of computing exact longitude and arrived at a figure computing the earth's equatorial circumference only 50 miles short of the correct measurement. It was, however, not his many solid accomplishments but a mistake made by a German mapmaker that led America to be named after him—and this is probably why his reputation suffers even today. Vespucci (who had Latinized his name to Americus Vespucci) wrote many letters about his voyages, including one to the notorious Italian ruler Lorenzo de' Medici in which he described "the New World." But several of his letters were rewritten and sensationalized by an unknown author, who published these forgeries as *Four Voyages* in 1507. One of the forged letters was read by the brilliant young German cartographer Martin Waldseemüller, who was so impressed with the account that he included a map of the New World in an appendix to his book *Cosmographiae Introductio*, boldly labeling the land "America." Wrote Waldseemüller in his Latin text, which also included the forged letter: "By now, since these parts have been more extensively explored and and another 4th part has been discovered by Americus Vespucius (as will appear from what follows); I see no reason why it should not be called Amerigo, after Americus, the discoverer, or indeed America, since both Europe and Asia have a feminine form from the names of women." Waldseemüller's map roughly represented South America and when cartographers finally added North America, they retained the original name; the great geographer Gerhardus Mercator finally gave the name "America" to all of the Western Hemisphere. Vespucci never tried to have the New World named after him or to belittle his friend Columbus, who once called him "a very worthy man." The appellation *America* gained in usage because Columbus refused all his life to admit that he had discovered a new continent, wanting instead to believe that he had come upon an unexplored region in Asia. Spain stubbornly refused to call the New World anything but *Columbia* until the 18th century, but to no avail. Today Columbus is credited for his precedence only in story and song ("Columbia, the Gem of the Ocean"), while Amerigo Vespucci is honored by hundreds of phrases ranging from *American know-how* to *American cheese.*

American.   The first person recorded to have used this term for a citizen of the U.S. or of the earlier British colonies was New England religious leader Cotton Mather in his *Magnolia Christie Americana* (1702).

american.   The Japanese have taken to many things American, but not our coffee, which they find weak. Preferring espresso or other strong brews, they call any weak coffee *american*. This seems to be the case in many countries. In Spanish-speaking places, for example, an espresso mixed with extra water is called a *cafe-americano.*

the American dream.   The American dream is almost impossible to define, meaning as it does so many different things to so many different people. These words go back at least to de Tocqueville's *Democracy in America* (1835) and are usually associated with the dreams of people new to these shores of freedom, material prosperity, and hope for the future.

American English.   There are thousands of Americanisms that are different from English expressions, although these have dwindled with the spread of movies, television, and increased foreign travel. A good example of such differences is found in a story about *tuna fish*. The highest word rate ever paid to a professional author is the $15,000 producer Darryl Zanuck gave American novelist James Jones for correcting a line of dialogue in the film *The Longest Day.* Jones and his wife, Gloria, were sitting on the beach when they changed the line "I can't eat that bloody old box of tunny fish" to "I can't stand this damned old tuna fish." If they had translated *box* they would have substituted *can.*

American Indian language words.   English words that come to us from American Indian languages include: chocolate, tomato, potato, llama, puma, totem, papoose, squaw, caucus, Tammany, mugwump, podunk, chinook, chautauqua, tomahawk, wampum, mackinaw, moccasin, sachem, pot latch, manitou, kayak, hogan, teepee, toboggan, wigwam, igloo, porgy, menhaden, quahog, catalpa, catawba, hickory, pecan, persimmon, pokeweed, scuppernong (grapes), sequoia, squash, tamarack, hominy, hooch, firewater, pone, bayou, pemmican, succotash, cayuse, wapiti, chipmunk, caribou, moose, muskrat, opossum, raccoon, skunk, terrapin, and woodchuck.

Americanism.   In 1781 Dr. John Witherspoon, president of the College of New Jersey (now Princeton), wrote a series of essays on "the general state of the English language in America." He listed a number of "chief improprieties" such as Americans using "mad" for "angry," etc., and coined the word *Americanism* to define them.

America's Cup.   This racing trophy was originally called the Hundred Guinea Cup when it was offered by the British Royal

Yacht Squadron to the winner of an international yacht race around the Isle of Wight. The U.S. schooner *America* won the first race in 1875, defeating 14 British yachts, and the cup, still the greatest prize in yachting, was renamed in her honor. American yachts won the cup in every competition until 1983, when the Australians took it home to Perth, ending the longest winning streak in sport.

America the Beautiful; America. Katherine Lee Bates (1859–1929), was a professor at Wellesley College when she wrote the poem "America the Beautiful" (1893), which was made into the famous patriotic song of the same name. The lyrics have been set to music by 60 different composers. "America," another well-known patriotic song, was written in 1831 by Boston Baptist minister Samuel Frances Smith (1808–95) when he was a seminary student. It is sometimes called "My Country 'Tis of Thee," after its first line. *See* GOD BLESS AMERICA.

Ameslan. *Ameslan* is the acronym for *American Sign Language*, the shorter term being first recorded in 1974. American Sign Language, a system of communication by manual signs used by the deaf, is more efficient than finger spelling and closer to being a natural language. Finger spelling is just "a means of transposing any alphabetized language into a gestural mode."

amethyst. This bluish-violet gem was once regarded as a great charm against drunkenness, leading the ancient Greeks to name the variety of quartz *amethystos*, from *a*, "not," and *methystos*, "drunk." *Amethystos* eventually became our *amethyst*.

AMEX. *See* NYSE.

amicus curiae. Latin for "friend of the courts," *amicus curiae* in law applies to "any person, not a party to the litigation, who volunteers or is invited by the court to give advice on some matter pending before it." Its second word is pronounced "kyoor-ee-eye" and its plural is *amici curiae*.

Amish; Mennonites. The Amish people, located mainly in Pennsylvania, Ohio, Iowa, Indiana, and Canada, are descended from the followers of Jakob Amman, a 17th-century Swiss Mennonite bishop. The Mennonites are an evangelical Protestant sect that practices baptism of believers only, restricts marriage to members of the denomination, and is noted for simplicity of living and plain dress. They, in turn, were named for the religious leader Menno Simons (1496–1556). The Amish still cling to a rural, simple way of life, but many of their young have begun to rebel against seemingly restrictive conventions and to yield to the attractions and conveniences of 20th-century life.

ammonia. While camel riders worshipped at the Egyptian temple of the god Ammon, near Thebes, enterprising men and women extracted urine from the sand where their camels were hitched, later using it for bleaching or whitening clothes. The agent was called "sal ammoniac," salt of Ammon, by the Romans, and when the gas obtained from this salt (NH_3) was first extracted in 1782 it was named *ammonia*.

amn't I. Among others, James Joyce used this expression in *Dubliners*, which contains some of the most eloquent stories ever written; Rumer Godden employed it in *An Episode of Sparrows;* and Rebecca West used it in one of her novels ("I'm just awful, amn't I?"). So, as odd as it may sound to some ears, the locution is preferred to "Aren't I?" and "Ain't I?" by a number of good writers and is widely employed. *Amn't I?* is especially popular in Ireland, the expression dating back at least two centuries there.

amok. *See* RUN AMUCK (OR AMUCK).

among. *Among* comes from the Old English *on*, "in" and *gemang*, "crowd." These terms made up the Old English *on-mang*, "in a crowd," which eventually became *among*.

amortize. You gradually kill a debt (in the sense of resolving it) when you amortize it, for *amortize*, once more generally used than it is today, has its roots in the Latin *mors*, "death." Chaucer wrote: "The goods werkes that men don whil they ben in good lif ben al amortised by synne folwying." The word MORTGAGE comes from the same source.

ampere. *See* MORON.

& (ampersand). The symbol *&* was invented by Marcus Tullius Tiro, who introduced it about 63 B.C. as part of the first system of shorthand of which there is any record. A learned Roman freedman & amanuensis to Cicero, Tiro invented his "Tironian notes" to take down his friend's fluent dictation, but he also used it to write works of his own, including some of the great orator's speeches & even some of Cicero's letters to Tiro! His system was based on the orthographic principle & made abundant use of initials, the *&* sign that was part of it being a contraction for the Latin *et* or "and." Tiro's shorthand system was taught in Roman schools, used to record speeches in the Senate, & saw wide use among businessmen in Europe for almost a thousand years.

amphigory. *Amphigory* derives from the Greek for "circle on both sides" and means a burlesque or parody, usually a kind of nonsense verse that seems to make sense but doesn't. Swinburne's *Nephelidia*, a parody of his own style, is an example. The poem begins:

> From the depth of the dreary decline of the dawn
> Through a notable nimbus of nebulous moonshine,
> Pallid and pink as the palm of the flag flown that
> Flickers with fear of the flies as they float . . .

amscray. *See* PIG LATIN.

Amy Dardin case; Amy's case. An obsolete term for procrastination. Virginia widow Amy Dardin of Mecklenburg County submitted to Congress her claim to be compensated by the federal government for a horse impressed during the American Revolution, sending a bill every year from 1796 to at least 1815; some sources say she kept dunning Congress for 50 years before the procrastinating government paid.

anachronism.

> Cecil B. DeMille
> Was feeling ill
> Because he couldn't put Moses
> In the War of the Roses.

This famous clerihew by Nicholas Bentley, the son of the inventor of the CLERIHEW, comments on filmmakers who don't often get ill about the anachronisms in their epics. If Moses was put in the War of the Roses, or if Cleopatra's barge was depicted as powered by an outboard motor, these would be anachronisms. The word derives from the Greek *ana chronos*, "out of time," to be late, or "back-timing," and means an error in chronology, putting a person, event, or thing in the wrong time period. Some classic examples are Shakespeare's reference to billiards in *Antony and Cleopatra*, to cannon in *King John*, and to turkeys in *Henry IV, Part I*. Famous American anachronisms include George Washington throwing a silver dollar across the Potomac (there were no silver dollars at the time) and the flying of the Stars and Stripes in paintings of major Revolutionary War battles (the flag wasn't used until 1783). Sometimes anachronism is used to describe an institution or a person who lives in the past.

anaconda.   This is one of the few English words, if not the only, that comes to us from Singhalese. *Anaconda* probably derives from the Singhalese *henakandayā*, although this word means "lightning stem" and refers to Ceylon's whip snake, not the large snake we know as the anaconda. Weekley notes that "the mistake may have been due to a confusion of labels in the Leyden museum."

Anacreontic.   Not many names of people have come to mean "amatory, loving, convivial," but this is exactly what happened, many centuries after his death, to the Greek poet Anacreon (ca. 570–ca. 480 B.C.). The poet wrote many love poems and drinking songs, which inspired writers in the 17th century to coin the word *Anacreontic* (sometimes used in the lower case today). *See also* HOBSONIZE; MASOCHISM; SADISM.

anadama bread.   Anadama bread, a Yankee cornmeal recipe, offers one of the most humorous stories connected with any foodstuff. Tradition has it that a Yankee farmer or fisherman, whose wife Anna was too lazy to cook for him, concocted the recipe. On tasting the result of his efforts a neighbor asked him what he called the bread, the crusty Yankee replying, "Anna, damn her!" Another version claims that the husband was a Yankee sea captain who endearingly referred to his wife as "Anna, damn 'er." Anna's bread was much loved by his crew because it was delicious and would not spoil on long sea voyages. The captain is said to have written the following epitaph for his wife: "Anna was a lovely bride,/but Anna, damn'er, up and died."

anagram.   An anagram is the rearrangement of the letters of a word or group of words to make another word or group of words, the word anagram itself deriving from the Greek *ana graphein*, "to write over again." Popular as wordplay since the earliest times, anagrams were possibly invented by the ancient Jews, and the cabalists, constantly looking for "secret mysteries . . . woven in the numbers of letters," always favored them, as did the Greeks and Romans. A famous Latin anagram was an answer made out of the question Pontius Pilate asked in the trial of Jesus. *Quid est veritas?* ("What is truth") was the question, the answer being *Est vir qui adest* ("It is the man who is here"). Though poet John Dryden called anagrams the "torturing of one poor word ten thousand ways," the English are among the best and most accurate anagrammatists. Samuel Butler's novel *Erewhon* derives its title from the word *nowhere*, almost spelled backward, and a tribe in the book is called the Sumarongi, which is *ignoramus* spelled backward. Among the many interchangeable words that can form *anagrams* in English are *evil* and *live*, and *eros* and *rose*, but the longest are two 16-letter pairs: *conservationists* and *conversationists;* and *internationalism* and *interlaminations*. A recent apt anagram suggested by Martin Gardner is *moon starer,* an anagram for *astronomer.*

Ananias.   The word *Ananias*, for a liar, refers to the New Testament's Ananias (Acts 5:1–10), who with his wife, Sapphira, tried to cheat the church at Jerusalem by withholding part of the money he made from a sale of land. Ananias was struck dead after the apostle Peter declared that he had "not lied unto men, but unto God." His wife shared his fate later that day when she maintained his deception and was told of his demise. *Ananias* was popularized by President Theodore Roosevelt, who referred to those he suspected of deceit as members of the Ananias Club, especially members of the working press who published confidential information they had promised not to reveal. Roosevelt did not coin the phrase, but as H. L. Mencken observed, he popularized or originated scores of other expressions, including *walk softly and carry a big stick, to pussyfoot, the strenuous life, one hundred percent American,* and *muckraker,* all of which are still in use today.

an apple a day keeps the doctor away.   A proverb that dates back to the early 19th century, states *Bartlett's.* An apple a day is nutritious and delicious but doesn't provide any immunity against illness, according to the latest scientific studies.

anchor.   The "ch" in this common word, the cause of much trouble to beginning spellers, really has no place there. *Anchor* derives from the Latin *ancora*, meaning the same, which the Romans, in turn, borrowed from the Greek *ankura*. Some Latin writers, however, changed the *ancora* spelling to *anchora*, mistakenly believing that the Greek word was properly spelled *anchura* (because the *k* sound was often spelled *ch* in Greek words). When the word came into English in about 1400, English writers adopted this incorrect Latin spelling and it became the basis for the word *anchor.*

anchor man.   The strongest member of a track team, the runner who runs the last leg in a relay race, has been called the anchor man since the late 19th century. Possibly the term has its roots in the "anchor man" at the end of a tug of war, but there is no proof that this usage came first. In any case, *anchor man* came to be applied to the last swimmer in a relay race, too, and by the 1930s was being used for the strongest member of a radio broadcasting team. With the rise of women in sports and television news broadcasting, the term is increasingly heard as *anchor.*

"Anchor's Aweigh."

> Anchor's aweigh, my boys, anchor's aweigh.
> Farewell to college joys, we sail at break of day!
> Through our last night on shore,
> Drink to the foam,
> Until we meet once more
> Here's wishing you a happy voyage home.

These are the words to "Anchor's Aweigh" that were commonly sung by sailors during World War II. Although they are accepted as the lyrics of the song by almost everyone today, they are far different from the original words to this official marching song of the U.S. Navy, which was composed for the 1906 Army-Navy football game, music by Charles A. Zimmerman and lyrics by Alfred H. Miles. *See* ARMY AIR CORPS.

ancillary. Subordinate clauses in technical business documents such as wills, insurance policies, and legal briefs are often referred to as *ancillary.* The aptness of the word can be seen in its literal meaning of "handmaiden," which derives from the Latin *ancilla,* the diminutive of *anca,* servant.

Andalusia. The region of Andalusia in southern Spain so named for the Vandals who invaded and occupied it some 15 centuries ago. The region was first called Vandalusia, the word dropping the *V* over the centuries.

and don't you forget it! An intensive recorded in England as early as 1898 and adopted in the U.S. soon after, *and don't you forget it!* remains a popular expression often used to reinforce one's anger, especially anger in chastising children. For close to a century experts have inveighed against it as "vulgar and senseless," but it is alive and thriving nonetheless.

Andes mountains. The name for these mountains derives from the Quecha *andi,* meaning "high crest." The similarity of *andi* to the Egyptian *andi* for "high valley," along with the similarity of other Egyptian and Quecha words, has led some observers to suggest that Egyptian explorers may have traveled to South America in ancient times.

and how! Indicating "intensive emphasis of what someone else has just said," *and how!* is a long-popular catchphrase first recorded in 1924. The Americanism possibly derives from the German *und wie!* or the Italian *e come!,* meaning the same thing, and once very common among Americans of German and Italian extraction, respectively.

andirons. Andirons are pairs of metal stands used to hold logs above the floor in a fireplace. One theory holds that the word derives from the Gaulish *andera,* "heifer," cows' heads once commonly used as decorations on the supports.

and pigs have wings! Used sarcastically as one would say *yeah* or *sure,* both expressing disbelief. The British say *and pigs fly!* instead, but their expression *when pigs fly!* means "never."

Andrea Ferrara. Many Scotsmen will know that an Andrea Ferrara is the Scottish broadsword frequently mentioned in Elizabethan literature, and more than a few will proudly claim that the original sword maker was a Scottish drill sergeant named Andrea Ferras or Ferrier. However, it is more likely that the real Andrea Ferrara was a 16th-century Italian sword maker who lived in Belluno and whose correct name was Andrea dei Ferrari, "Andrew of the armorers." How his swords got to Scotland is something of a mystery; either he was an exile, or as Sir Walter Scott suggests in the notes on *Waverley,* he was brought over by James IV or V to instruct the Scots in the manufacture of his blades. In any event, he left us with many references in literature to Andrea Ferraras, Ferraras, and even Andrews, all deriving from his name.

the Andrew. Since at least 1860 *The Andrew* has been British slang for the Royal Navy, and *The Andrew Miller* was used long before that. The expression derives from the name of Andrew Miller, a notorious press-gang leader of Lord Nelson's day who SHANGHAIED many men into the British Navy.

andromeda. Linnaeus named this early-blooming shrub with white blossoms for the mythological maiden Andromeda, daughter of the king of Ethiopia, who was chained to a rock as an offering to a sea monster, but was rescued by Perseus, the son of Zeus. In order to marry the beautiful Andromeda, Perseus had to defeat another suitor who tried to carry her off. He did so by showing his rival the head of the Medusa, which changed him to stone.

Andromeda strain. Any strain of bacteria or other microorganism "whose accidental release from a laboratory might have catastrophic effects because of its unknown biochemical makeup" is called an Andromeda strain. The term comes from American author Michael Crichton's 1971 novel of that title, in which an unknown type of bacteria escapes accidentally from a returning space probe and threatens to contaminate the planet Earth.

and then some! *And then some!* is an Americanism dating back to about 1910. But its roots probably go deeper than this in history, some investigators believing it is an elaboration of the Scots *and some,* meaning "and much more so," which is recorded about two centuries earlier. One British professor claimed he found a parallel expression in the *Aeneid* (Book viii, line 487)!

and thereby hangs a tale. This has been the title of more than one book in modern times, though it is rarely used seriously anymore as a storytelling device. The expression goes back at least to the time of Shakespeare, who used it a number of times, notably in *As You Like It.*

anecdote; anecdotage. We owe the word *anecdote* to Justinian, Byzantine emperor from A.D. 527 to 565, who wrote a book of brief tales about life in his court. These true stories were satirical, scandalous, and sometimes off-color. Justinian—better known for the Justinian legal code—probably didn't intend them for publication, but they were published by Procopius, a secretary to one of Justinian's generals, as a supplement to his history of the times. Procopius entitled the book *Anekdota,* a Greek word meaning "unpublished, secret." The title of the book later became the term *anecdote,* meaning a brief factual story like the ones *Anekdota* contained. *Anecdotage,* "the state of being advanced in age and strongly inclined to tell reminiscent anecdotes," is probably a happy coinage of John Wilkes in about 1835.

anemone.   Also called the windflower, the dainty anemone takes its name from the Greek *anemos*, "wind," and *mone*, "habitation," the Greeks having observed that it often grew in windy places. A Greek legend says that the *anemone* was born after the handsome Greek youth Adonis, beloved by Aphrodite, goddess of love and beauty, was killed in the forest on a wild boar hunt. Aphrodite was so grief-stricken that the gods took pity on her and allowed Adonis to spend each spring with her in the form of a flower, the anemone rising from his blood.

anesthesia.   Here we see a word being born, even to the exact date. Soon after William Thomas Green Morton successfully employed ether in an operation at Boston's Massachusetts General Hospital in 1846, New England poet-physician Oliver Wendell Holmes wrote in a November 21st letter to him: "Every body wants to have a hand in a great discovery. All I will do is give you a hint or two as to names— or the name—to be applied to the state produced and the agent. The state should, I think, be called 'Anaethesia' (which derives from the Greek *anaisthesia*, 'lack of sensation'). This signifies insensibility . . . The adjective will be 'Anaesthetic'." Thus, Holmes clearly coined the term *anaesthesia* (now usually spelled *anesthesia*), even though it had been recorded in a different sense over a century before in England. Holmes also coined the "unsuccessful" word *chrysocracy*, in his novel *Elsie Venner* (1861). As he explained in another letter: "In *Elsie Venner* I made the word *chrysocracy*, thinking it would take its place; but it didn't; *plutocracy*, meaning the same thing, was adopted instead." *See also* BETTER A HASH AT HOME THAN A ROAST WITH STRANGERS.

angel dust.   So called because of its white color, *angel dust*, or PCP (phencyclidine), is used as a narcotic, being mixed with barbiturates or sprinkled on marijuana and smoked. The potent, dangerous depressant goes by many street names, including "white powder," "peace pills," "superjoint," "green tea," "busy bee," "hog elephant," "tranquilizer," and "killer weed"—all first recorded in the early 1970s.

Angeleno.   Anyone residing in Los Angeles, California; this Spanish term dates back to the mid-19th century.

angelica.   According to one story, the Archangel Raphael assured a pious hermit that this plant was a remedy against the plague. This may account for the name *angelica*, which comes from the Latin *herba angelica*, "the angelic root," or "root of the Holy Ghost," and is first recorded in English in 1570. A confection called candied angelica was made from its roots in early times.

angels on horseback.   One of the more colorfully named foods of the world, angels on horseback are oysters rolled in bacon, cooked (often on skewers over a fire) and served on points of toast. They are recorded under this name early in the 20th century, but the name is probably a translation of the earlier French *anges à cheval*.

angel teat.   Down in the holler, in mountain country, moonshiners call particularly good mellow whiskey with a good bouquet angel teat, or angel's teat. The term is first recorded in 1946 but is probably much older.

Angelus; Angelic Hymn; Angelic Doctor.   The Angelus is a Roman Catholic devotion, so named for its initial word. The prayer, which is said three times a day (at 6 A.M., noon, and 6 P.M.) commences at the sound of a bell called the Angelus and begins "Angelus Domini . . . (The Angel of the Lord . . .)." The Angelic Hymn isn't a synonym for the Angelus. It is the hymn beginning "Glory be to God in the highest" that was sung by the angels to the shepherds of Bethlehem after they brought tidings of the birth of Christ the Lord that day. St. Thomas Aquinas (ca. 1225–74) is traditionally called the Angelic Doctor because of the purity of his thought, regarded as the result of more than human intelligence. His schoolmates had called him the "Dumb Ox," and his teacher Albertus Magnus had predicted, "This dumb ox will one day fill the world with his lowing." Followers of the scholastic philosopher are called Thomists.

angle with a silver hook.   An unlucky fisherman who fails to catch anything doesn't want to go home empty-handed. Thus when he buys fish (with silver coin, in past times) to conceal his abject failure, he is said to *angle with a silver hook*.

Anglo.   A term for an English-speaking white person, an Anglo-American, that originated among Spanish speakers in the Southwest in the early 19th century and is now common throughout the United States. Unlike *gringo*, it is not always a derogatory term. *Anglo* can also mean the English language: "He doesn't speak Anglo."

Anglo-Saxon.   Also called *Old English, Anglo-Saxon* is the English language from the mid-fifth to the 12th century. In her libretto for Deems Taylor's opera *The King's Henchman* (1927), which is set in the palace of King Edgar in 10th-century England, American poet Edna St. Vincent Millay tried to use no word that came into English after the Norman Conquest (1066). Her "Anglo-Saxon" libretto began "Wild as the white waves / Rushing and roaring . . ." *See* BURN CANDLE AT BOTH ENDS.

Angora cat; Angora goat.   Angora cats probably originated in Ancyra or Angora, Turkey (now Ankara), where their long, silky hair may have been used like wool. Bred in Angora 2,000 years ago for its hair, sometimes called mohair, the Angora goat is now raised throughout the world.

angstrom.   A unit of length equal to one 10-millionth of a millimeter is known as an angstrom unit, or angstrom. It is used primarily to measure wavelengths of light and was named for Anders Jonas Angstrom (1814–74), Swedish astronomer and physicist, as was the Angstrom crater in the moon. Anders Angstrom taught physics at Uppsala University, his most important research work undertaken in heat conduction and light, and he is considered one of the founders of spectrum analysis. In 1867 he became the first man to examine the spectrum of the aurora borealis; the characteristic bright line in its yellow-green region is often called the *Angstrom line* in his honor.

animal.   The ancient Romans gave the name *animalis*, which derives from *anima*, "having breath or soul," to all living creatures that perceptibly breathed, obviously not including plants because the way plants breathe could not be seen by them. *Animalis* later became the English *animal*.

animal spirits. Novelist Jane Austen (1775–1817) may have coined the term *animal spirits* in its sense of an excess of exuberant energy; vivacity; good humor. In any case, as Weekley notes, the expression is first recorded in this sense in her novel *Pride and Prejudice*, published in 1813, but which she wrote some 15 years earlier.

Annie Oakley. Annie Oakley was the stage name of Ohio-born Phoebe Annie Oakley Mozee (1860–1926), star rifle shot with Buffalo Bill's wild west show. Married at 16, Annie joined Buffalo Bill when 25 and amazed audiences for more than 40 years with her expert marksmanship and trick shooting. Annie once broke 942 glass balls thrown into the air with only 1,000 shots. Her most famous trick was to toss a playing card, usually a five of hearts, into the air and shoot holes through all its pips. The riddled card reminded circus performers of their punched meal tickets, which they began to call Annie Oakleys, and the name was soon transferred to free railroad and press passes, both of which were customarily punched with a hole in the center. Today all complimentary passes, punched or not, are called *Annie Oakleys*, and the expression is also used in yacht racing for a ventilated spinnaker or head sail.

the annual fish. Gobies commonly don't live from one spawning to the next and are often called *the annual fish* for this reason. They aren't the shortest-lived fish, however, this dubious honor going to a species of killifish of Africa and South America that lives about eight months. The Philippine dwarf pygmy goby (*Pandaka pygmaea*) is the world's smallest fish—normally about as long as the word *fish* printed here and so light that it would take 35,000 of them to make an ounce.

Annuit Coeptis. The mottoes on the reverse side of the Great Seal of the U.S. are *Annuit Coeptis* ("He [God] has favored our undertakings") and *Novus Ordo Seclorum* ("a new order of the ages"). These were condensed by William Barton, designer of the Great Seal, from a line in Virgil's *Eclogues* (line 5).

anode. *See* FARAD.

anonymous. Dating back to the late 16th century in English, *anonymous* derives from the Greek *anonymos*, meaning the same. An *anonym* is an anonymous person or a false name. "Anonymous" is surely the world's most prolific author; tens of thousands of books and pamphlets have been published anonymously since the invention of the printing press. Famous anonymous works include Poe's first poems; Richardson's *Pamela*, the first genuine novel in English; Fielding's *Joseph Andrews*; almost all of Jonathan Swift's work; Smollett's *Roderick Random*; all Jane Austen's early works; Gray's "Elegy"; Byron's "Don Juan"; Dryden's "Absalom and Achitophel"; Pope's "Essay on Criticism"; and Tennyson's "In Memoriam." *See* BY A LADY.

another nail in my coffin. *See* COFFIN NAILS.

another Richmond in the field. Henry of Richmond, afterward England's King Henry VII, is honored by this expression, which means that still another, unexpected opponent has shown up to do battle. The phrase is from a speech made by the king in Shakespeare's *Richard III*, though the last line is more famous than the first:

> I think there be six Richmonds in the field;
> Five have I slain today, instead of him—
> A horse! a horse! my kingdom for a horse!

Anstie's limit. Nineteenth-century English physician Edward Anstie advised his patients that more than one-and-a-half ounces of pure alcohol a day, consumed day in and day out, will eventually cause physical damage to the body. Stay under this limit, Anstie said, and drinking won't harm you. One-and-a-half ounces of pure alcohol translates roughly into three one-ounce drinks of 100-proof whiskey, or four beers, or half a bottle of wine. Some experts still agree with Anstie, but most refuse to generalize. Dr. Charles S. Lieber, who specializes in the effects of alcohol on health, does set a "danger level." He says that anything over eight ounces of whiskey a day regularly "is the cause of complications in most individuals. Anyone who drinks above that level is high risk." Judging by this, Anstie's limit is very cautious.

ant cow. A term used for the aphid or plant louse, which excretes honeydew, a sugary substance, and is tended by honeydew-gathering ants. The term was coined in about 1870.

antediluvian. The Latin *ante*, before, and *deluvian*, flood, form the word *antedeluvian*, which literally means "before the flood." Because the flood is the biblical flood escaped by Noah, *antedeluvian* has thus come to mean anything or anyone ancient, or, for that matter, anyone far behind the times—an OLD FOGEY, in language of another era.

antenna. The Romans originally applied *antenna* to a ship's wooden horizontal yard, from which sails were hung. Centuries later, in the 1600s, the word was borrowed to describe the "horns" of various insects, such as the snail. In the early 20th century the term was finally applied to radio and television receptors.

anthology. *Anthology* derives from the Greek word meaning "a collection of flowers"—the first recorded one, in fact, is the Greek *Garland of Meleager* (ca. 90 B.C.). Two of many historically famous ones include the *Anthologia Palatina*, called the *Greek Anthology* (ca. 925), and Palgrave's *Golden Treasury* (1861), the most noted of English anthologies. Tens of thousands of anthologies have been compiled since. Bennett Cerf told the story of a book called *The Ten Commandments* that was to be published for the armed services but was too long. "How about using only five of them," quipped editor Philip Van Doren Stern, "and calling it 'A Treasury of the World's Best Commandments?' "

anthracite coal. Strictly speaking, *anthracite coal*, a hard, nearly pure carbon coal often used for heating, should be called *anthracite*, as *anthracite* comes directly from the Greek *anthrax*, meaning coal. To call it *anthracite coal* is a tautology: that is, *coal coal* or *coal-like coal*.

antibiotic. Dr. Selman Waksman, the discoverer of streptomycin, invented the term *antibiotic* in 1941. He coined it from the Greek *bios*, life, and *anti*, against. Thus an antibiotic is, strictly speaking, "against life"—against that life that seeks to destroy other life. An earlier sense of *antibiotic*, defined as "opposed to a belief in the presence or possibility of life," was recorded in 1860.

anticlimax. Dr. Johnson seems to have invented or at least been the first to record the word *anticlimax*, which he defines as "a sentence in which the last part expresses something lower than the first." Pope used the anticlimax humorously in his line "Men, monkeys, lap-dogs, parrots, perish all." Everyone has a favorite anticlimax, fine examples of which can be found in the *Anthology of Bad Verse* by Wyndham Lewis and C. Lee, but one of the best is the last line of Tennyson's poem "Enoch Arden" (1864), in which Enoch Arden, thought dead at sea, returns home after some years to find his wife happily married, and resolves that she won't know of his return until his death. The poem ends this way:

> So past the strong heroic soul away.
> And when they buried him, the little port
> Had seldom seen a costlier funeral.

antifogmatic. An antifogmatic is any alcoholic drink taken in the morning to brace one against the fog or dampness outside, or taken with that as the excuse. This amusing Americanism is first recorded in 1789.

antimacassar. Macassar oil, a trademarked product originally made in Makassar, Indonesia, was a highly popular men's hair dressing in Victorian times. The oil stained chair backs and housewives used antimacassars, small cloths that they pinned to the backs of armchairs, to protect their fabric.

ant killer. A humorous term for the foot, especially a big foot. The term is an Americanism dating back to the mid-19th century.

antler. When the stag lowers his head to drink, his lower horns are often before his eyes. The Romans noticed this and called the horns the *rammum ante ocularis*, "the branch before the eyes." Shortened to *ante ocular*, this name became *antoillier* in French and eventually *antler* in English.

ants in one's pants. *See* ANTSY.

antsy. Originating in the early 1950s, *antsy* means jittery, restless, nervous. The expression derives from the earlier phrase *to have ants in one's pants*, which dates back to World War II America and is recorded in humorist H. Allen Smith's book *Putty Knife* (1943): "She dilates her nostrils a lot, the way Valentino used to do it in the silent movies to indicate that he had ants in his pants." The quotation shows that *to have ants in one's pants* can suggest lust, but to my knowledge *antsy* never has this sexual meaning.

Antwerp. *Antwerp*, Belgium got its name, legend says, because a giant who lived there used to hack off the hand (*handt*) of any traveler who couldn't or wouldn't pay a toll on entering the area, throwing (*werpen*) each hand into the water. But the city really is so named because it is "the city at the wharf," Antwerp, composed of the Dutch *aan*, "at," and *werf*, "wharf."

anvil chorus. When the opposition, especially in politics, joins collectively in condemning an action or proposal, the criticism is called an anvil chorus. The reference is to the famous "Anvil Chorus" based on the "Gypsy Song" in Giuseppe Verdi's opera *Il Trovatore*, complete with the sound of many loud anvils and cymbals.

anxious seat. Front seats at religious revivalist meetings in the American West during the 19th century were called anxious seats, because their occupants were so eager to be saved.

any man who hates dogs and children can't be all bad. W. C. Fields didn't coin this expression. It was ad-libbed by the admirable Leo Rosten, author of *The Joys of Yiddish*, among many marvelous books, at a Friars Club testimonial banquet given to honor the comedian in 1938, which marked Field's 40th year in show business.

anything for a quiet life. Though Dickens's Sam Weller immortalized this phrase in *The Pickwick Papers*, referring to a man who took a "situation" at a lighthouse, the expression dates back to the 17th century and a play by Thomas Middleton. A variation, dating only to about 1968, is the catchphrase *anything for a quiet wife*.

anyways. Anyway, anyhow, in any case. "Anyways I've got my opinion," Mark Twain wrote in "The Celebrated Jumping Frog of Calaveras County" (1865). The Americanism can also mean to any degree at all: "Is he anyways hurt?"; or at any time: "Come visit anyways from May to October."

A-O.K. An accidental coinage, *A-O.K.* was not used by American astronaut Alan Shepard while making the first suborbital space flight, as was widely reported. The term is actually the result of a mistake by NASA public relations officer Colonel "Shorty" Powers, who thought he heard Shepard say "A-O.K." when the astronaut, in fact, uttered a rousing "O.K." Powers liked the sound of *A-O.K.* so much that he reported it several times to newsmen before he learned of his mistake. By then it was too late, for the term became part of the language practically overnight. Speech purists insist that *A-O.K.* is a repetition, increasing O.K. 50 percent in size, but in spoken communication redundancy is not necessarily bad—in fact, it is often essential to clarity and understanding, especially in emergencies. And in everyday conversation A-O.K. usually means "better than O.K.," "great," "near perfect"—not, repeat *not*, just "all right." *See* O.K.

A-1. *A-1*, for anything excellent, first class, originated with the expression *A-1 at Lloyd's*, referring to the rating of ships in *Lloyd's Register*. Lloyd's of London, the world-famous insurance association, has insured everything from the first airplane to Hollywood sex symbols, but at its inception the company wrote only marine insurance. Lloyd's takes its name from a coffeehouse operated by Edward Lloyd, of whom the earliest record is in 1688 and who died in 1713. For travelers, Lloyd served as a sort of one-man tourist bureau, and there is even evidence that he would fix the press gang who shanghaied men into the naval service—for a price. Virtually nothing else is known about the elusive, enterprising Lloyd except that businessmen willing to insure against sea risks congregated at his coffeehouse on Lombard Street and issued marine policies to shipowners. Here *Lloyd's List*, a paper devoted to shipping news, was published in 1734, making it the oldest London newspaper, except for the *London Gazette*. By 1760 the precursor of *Lloyd's Register of Shipping* had been printed, and only 15 years later the phrase *A-1* was used in its pages to denote the highest class of ship. Charles Dickens first applied *A-1* to people and things in 1837. Lloyd's, now international in scope, eventually moved to the Royal Exchange and finally to its present $15-million head-quarters on Lime Street. It adopted its name legally when incorporated a century ago, not long before writing the first burglary insurance (1889). Lloyd's also wrote the first policy covering loss of profits resulting from fire and pioneered in automobile and worker's compensation insurance. The corporation can issue anything but long-term life insurance. Not actually an insurance company, Lloyd's is a corporate group of some 300 syndicates composed of about 5,500 strictly supervised individual underwriters, each of whom must deposit large sums—about $35,000—as security against default on the risks each accepts. Some interesting Lloyd's policies and losses in its risky history include:

■ A $100,000 "love insurance" policy that provided payment if a certain photographer's model married (she did, after the policy expired).
■ A "happiness policy" that insured against "worry lines" developing on a model's face.
■ Losses paid of $3,019,400 after the Lutine Bell rang over the rostrum announcing the *Titanic* disaster; more than $5.6 million on the sinking of the *Andrea Doria;* $1,463,400 on the 1906 San Francisco earthquake damage; and $110 million on Hurricane Carol in 1954.

apache. An *apache* is a Parisian criminal or ruffian and an *apache dance* is a violent dance originated by the Parisian *apaches.* The word, in this sense, was coined by French newspaper reporter Emile Darsy, who is said to have read of "bloodthirsty Apache Indians" in the works of American authors and thought that their name would aptly fit denizens of the underworld. The Apache Indians, perhaps not deserving this reputation, derive their name from a Zuni word meaning enemy, and the name was applied to many nomadic bands of Indians roaming the southwestern United States. The Apaches called themselves *dene*, an Athabascan word for "human being."

apartheid. Although racial segregation is no longer the law in South Africa, this word for official racial segregation is still applied to any such official policy anywhere and even segregation in general. The word seems to have first been used in English in a 1947 South African newspaper article. *Apartheid* is from Afrikaans, the language of Dutch settlers in South Africa. It is composed of the Dutch *apart*, "separate," and *heid*, equivalent to the English suffix *hood*, literally meaning "separateness" but actually being far more insidious in both meaning and practice.

A-per-se. This common expression for the best, something or someone unbeatable, goes all the way back to Chaucer, who calls Cressida "the floure and A-per-se of Troi and Greek."

aphrodisiac. Anything, including food, drink, drugs, art, and words, that arouses or enhances sexual desire. The word comes from the name of Aphrodite, the Greek goddess of love and beauty, who sprang beauteous from the foam (*áphros*) of the sea that gathered around the severed penis of her father, Uranus, after his son Cronos dethroned and mutilated him. The Cytherean, as she is also called, is probably a goddess of Oriental origin; she bears a strong resemblance to the Asian Astarte. The Romans identified her with Venus. "Goddess born of the blue foam," mother of Eros and Priapus, Aphrodite had as lovers in various legends not only Adonis but also Dionysus, Anchises, and Paris. She was worshipped in two separate forms: as Aphrodite Urania, "the goddess of higher, purer love," and as Aphrodite Pandernos, "the goddess of sensual lust"—a distinction that, significantly, wasn't made until later more repressed times. Fathered by Dionysus or Bacchus, god of wine, Aphrodite's son PRIAPUS is identified with phallic worship. The Cestus, her legendary girdle, is said to have endowed all its wearers with irresistible powers of love.

Api. The French gave this name to the old tasty apple variety that in English is called the "Red Lady." It is named after the legendary Roman gourmet Apicius, who is said to have produced it in his garden by grafting more than 2,000 years ago. *See* APICIUS.

Apicius. Apicius might be called the world's first gourmand and bon vivant as well as the author of the earliest cookbook. His *Of Culinary Matters*, has gone through countless editions since first written about 1,500 years ago. Some historians claim that Apicius was a rich Roman merchant who collected recipes wherever he traveled, others that his name is a nom de plume deriving from the word for "epicure," but most authorities believe that he was the Roman nobleman Marcus Gavius Apicius, who lived under Tiberius in the first century A.D. Whatever his identity, an *Apicius* still brings to mind a chef and gastronome without peer, one who went to such lengths as spraying his garden lettuce with mead in the evening so that it would taste like "green cheesecakes" the next morning, one who concocted *Apician* dishes that remain, in the words of Mark Twain, "as delicious as the less conventional forms of sin."

Apollinaris; Polly. One of the oldest and most famous of bottled spring water, *Apollinaris* has been on the market since the mid-19th century, when German farmer Georg Kreuzberg hit upon a spring while digging an irrigation ditch in his vineyard near Bonn. He named the spring and its water *Apollinaris* after a nearby chapel. The water became so popular in England that it was called by the nickname *Polly*.

Appalachia. The Appalachian Indian tribe gave its name to this mountainous region in the southeastern U.S., though the naming was a mistake. As Roderick Peattie put it in *The Great Smokies and Blue Ridge* (1943): "[The Spanish explorer] De Soto left no memorial or trace, except for the name Appalachian itself (from the Appalachi tribe of Muskhogeans on the Gulf Coast), misapplied by him to the fair mountains he traversed so long ago." It is interesting to note that Washington Irving once suggested (in the *Knickerbocker Magazine*, August 1839) that the name *United States of Appalachia* be substituted for the *United States of America*.

Appaloosa. This hardy breed of white horses with dark spots and white-rimmed eyes was developed by the Nez Percé Indians and named by the Canadian-French voyageurs, who referred to the Indian horses as *à palouse*," "from the grassy plains" (where the Indians lived). In time *à palouse* became *Appaloosa* in English, the word first recorded in 1849. The Appaloosa is sometimes called "the Dalmation of horses."

appeal from Philip drunk to Philip sober. A woman petitioned King Philip of Macedon for justice for her husband and was refused. "I shall appeal against this judgment!" she exclaimed, and Philip—while still in his cups—roared: "Appeal—and to whom will you appeal?" "To Philip sober," the woman replied, and according to Valerius Maximus, who tells the tale, she won her case.

applause. *Applause* derives from the Latin *applaudere*, to applaud or clap. "Applause," said one anonymous actor who apparently didn't get enough applause, "is but a fart, the crude blast of the fickle multitude" (1645). Most actors and producers don't feel that way. In fact, the practice of asking radio and television studio audiences to applaud at various points during a show isn't an annoying modern-day invention. It dates back at least to Roman times, when in Plautus's comedies a character called the Epilogue summed up the play after its conclusion and finally asked the audience for applause. In Plautus's *Amphitryon*, for example, the actor implores the audience: "Now, spectators, for the sake of Jove almighty, give us some loud applause!" The Athenian lawmaker Draco, an avid theatergoer, got too much applause. According to one story, the official, popular despite his draconian laws, was killed by applause there. While he was sitting in the theater at Aegina in about 590 B.C., other spectators hailed him by applauding wildly and throwing their cloaks and caps in tribute. So many landed on Draco that he was smothered. Of all performers past and present, so far as history records, opera tenor Placido Domingo won the most applause from an audience. He needed no help from a claque. After his performance of *Otello* at the Vienna Staatsoper on July 20, 1991, Domingo was applauded for a full one hour and 20 minutes. However, Italian tenor Luciano Pavarotti received more curtain calls than Domingo—165 to Domingo's 101—for his performance in *L'Elisir d'amore* at the Deutsche Opera in Berlin on February 24, 1998. Pavarotti was "only" applauded for one hour and seven minutes. *See* CLAQUE; CLAPTRAP.

apple; apple hawk; apple orchard. *Apple* for a baseball dates back to the early 1920s; before that the ball had been called a "pea," a term heard no more. A good fielder was called an *apple hawk* at the time, this term obsolete now, and the ball park was called an *apple orchard*, an expression still occasionally used. *Apple* itself comes from the Old English *appel* for the fruit. An *apple* can also be a derogatory name given to certain American Indians by other American Indians who believe their values are too much like those of whites; that is, they are, like an apple, red on the outside and white on the inside. This term is based on the American black derisive name *Oreo* for a black person whose values are believed to be too much like those of whites. An Oreo is a trademarked chocolate cookie with creamy white filling.

apple cart. *See* UPSET THE APPLE CART.

Apple Island. A nickname for Tasmania, which is Australia's main apple-growing area. Its inhabitants are often called Apple Islanders, though *Tassies* is more common.

apple-knocker. An abusive term meaning a stupid person, especially a rustic stupid person, that is still used by city dwellers. The term is recorded in this sense in a 1939 *New Yorker* story: "I had a reform-school technique, whereas them other sailors was apple-knockers. They were so dumb they couldn't find their nose with both hands." *Apple-knocker* first meant a fruit picker, deriving from the mistaken urban belief that fruit is harvested by being knocked from trees with long sticks.

the apple never falls far from the tree. Children always share the characteristics of their parents. The mid-19th-century proverb is usually said in a negative sense, emphasizing bad characteristics.

apple of discord. This legendary golden apple was thrown on the table by the god Eris (Discord) at the wedding of Thetis and Peleus, to which all the Greek gods but Eris had been invited. The apple was said to be "for the most beautiful woman" present, and Paris judged between Hera (Juno), Aphrodite (Venus), and Athene (Minerva), who offered him, respectively, bribes of power, sex, and martial glory. He chose Aphrodite, and the vengeance of Hera and Athene supposedly led to the fall of Troy. The *apple of discord* still means the cause of a dispute, or something to be disputed.

apple of one's eye. That which one holds dearest, as in "You're the apple of my eye." The phrase is from the Bible (Deut. 32:10), which says the Lord kept Israel "as the apple of his eye." *Pupillam*, or pupil, is actually the Latin for the "apple" of the phrase, but English translators of the Bible used "apple" because this was the early word for the pupil of the eye, which was thought to be a solid apple-shaped body. Because it is essential to sight, the eye's apple, or pupil, is to be cherished and protected, and *the apple of one's eye* came to mean anything extremely precious. The literal translation of the Hebrew phrase, incidentally, is "You are as the little man in the eye" (one's own reflection in the pupil of another's eye).

apple orchard. *See* APPLE.

apple pandowdy. Imogene Wolcott's *New England Yankee Cookbook* (1939) gives several authentic recipes for this deep-dish apple dessert, noting that the modern version is often called *apple brown Betty*. It has also been called *flummery apple pot-pie*, *apple Jonathan*, *apple Johnny*, and *apple slump*. So much did Harriet Beecher Stowe like the dish that she named her Concord, Massachusetts, house *Apple Slump* in its honor.

apple-pie order. One old story holds that New England housewives were so meticulous and tidy when making their apple pies—carefully cutting thin slices of apples, methodically arranging them in rows inside the pie, making sure that the pinches joining the top and bottom crusts were perfectly even, etc.—that the expression *apple-pie order* arose for prim and precise orderliness. A variant on the yarn has an early American housewife baking seven pies every Monday and arranging them neatly on shelves, one for every day of the week in strict order. Nice stories, but the term *apple-pie order* is probably British in origin, dating back to at least the early 17th century. It may be a corruption of the French *nappes-pliées*, folded linen (neatly folded) or cap-a-pie, "from head to foot." Yet no use of either *nappes-pliées* order or cap-a-pie order appears in English. "Alpha beta order" has also been suggested, but seems unlikely. The true source of the term must still be considered a mystery, the matter far from in apple-pie order.

apple-polisher. The traditional practice of a student giving teacher a bright, shiny apple is the source for this expression for a sycophant, the Americanism being first recorded in 1928. The synonym SYCOPHANT interestingly has its origins in another fruit, figs.

applesauce. The expression *applesauce* for disguised flattery dates to the early 20th century and may derive from "the boarding-house trick of serving plenty of this cheap comestible when richer fare is scanty," according to a magazine of the time. The term also came to mean lies and exaggerations. As a word for a sauce made from stewed, sweetened apples, *applesauce* is an Americanism dating back at least to the mid-18th century. *Applesauce* as a term for insincere flattery may also have been invented by American cartoonist Thomas Aloysius Dorgan (1877–1929), "Tad" having been the most prolific word coiner of his day. No one knows for sure.

apples of paradise. According to tradition, each of the apples in the Garden of Eden had a bite taken from it after Eve took a bite of the forbidden fruit. Over the years *apples of paradise*, referring to the apples in Eden, has come to mean forbidden fruit.

apples of perpetual youth. These were golden apples of Scandinavian mythology that were in the care of Idhunn, daughter of Svald the dwarf. By eating them, the gods preserved their youth.

apples of Sodom. An old legend says that apple trees grown near the Dead Sea, "where Sodom and Gomorrah stood," bear beautiful red fruit that falls to soot and ashes in the mouth. The gallnuts produced on apples by the insect *Cynips insana* are said to be scientific fact behind the legend, but the expression still means anything disappointing.

Appleton layer. English physicist Edward Appleton (1892–1965) discovered this upper region in the ionosphere that is 150 miles from Earth and part of the earlier discovered HEAVISIDE LAYER. Appleton named the region after himself and was knighted for his discovery in 1941. Sir Edward won the Nobel Prize in physics in 1947.

Appomattox. The name for a Virginia river that in turn gave its name to a sleepy town it meandered through in south-central Virginia, a hamlet more properly called *Appomattox*

Court House, where all Confederate dreams died at the end of the Civil War when General Lee surrendered there. *Appomattox* itself later became a synonym for surrender or for victory, or for reconciliation, depending on who pronounced it. But perhaps Carl Sandburg defined the word best in *Abraham Lincoln: The War Years:* "For a vast living host the word Appomattox had magic and beauty. They sang the syllables 'Ap-po-mattox' as a happy little carol of harvest and fields of peace and the sun going down with no shots in the night to follow."

apricot. The Romans called this fruit *praecoquum*, or "early ripe." From there the word entered Arabic as *alburquq* and went into Portuguese as *albricoque*, whence it come into English as *apricock*. By the 18th century the shears of prudery had pruned the word from apri*cock* to apri*cot*.

April. The romantic Romans named *April* after the flower buds that open in this month, basing their *Aprilis* on the Latin *aperia*, meaning "open."

April fool! All Fools' Day, when childish pranks are played and their victims are taunted with cries of *April fool!*, seems to have been brought from France to England in about 1700. But its origins and the reason it is celebrated on April 1 remain unknown. There are several explanations. The oldest says All Fools' Day is a relic of the Roman "Cerealia," held at the beginning of April to honor Ceres, the goddess of agriculture. It seems that Ceres' daughter Proserpina was carried off by Pluto, the king of Hades, and when Ceres heard the echo of her screams, she followed the echo—a fool's errand. Other theories hold that April Fools' Day falls in April because of the tricky weather at the time; because April is the first month of spring, when people are half awake from their winter hibernation and easily hoaxed; and because of the mock trial of Christ held in April. Still another explanation is that New Year's Day fell on March 25 under the old Julian calendar (used until the Gregorian calendar was adopted in 1756) and that people capped a week of festivities with April Fools' Day on April 1. The French call an April Fool a *poisson d'Avril* (an "April fish"), in reference to a newly spawned, naive, and easily caught fish.

apron strings. *See* TIED TO ONE'S MOTHER'S APRON STRING.

aptronyms. American columnist Franklin P. Adams (F.P.A.) coined the term *aptronym*, but writers have used aptronyms—"label names" that fit the nature or occupation of a character—at least since the time of Spenser's allegorical *Faerie Queene* and Bunyan's *Pilgrim's Progress*. It is said that Plato's real name was Aristocles and that he was called Plato ("broad") because of his broad shoulders. Mr. Gradgrind, Mr. Worldly Wiseman, Lord Easy (a careless husband), William Congreve's gossipy character Scandal, Scott's Dr. Dryasdust, and many of Dickens's characters are famous fictional examples of aptronyms.

aquanaut; oceanaut. Based on the Greek *nautes*, sailor, these words were coined in recent times to describe scientist-explorers who work and live at sea for long periods. Jacques Cousteau coined *oceanaut*.

Arabic words. English words that come to us from Arabic include: saffron, mattress, admiral, hazard, cotton, henna, camphor, alembic, alchemy, elixir, alkali, zenith, almanac, azimuth, cipher, gismo, syrup, antimony, alcoran, mosque, sumac, bedouin, rebec, sash, algebra, monsoon, arsenal, assassin, jar, alcohol, apricot, giraffe, hashish, coffee, sirocco, fakir, emir, sherbet, alcove, sofa, harem, gazelle, minaret, zero, albatross, Allah, houri, magazine, genie, ghoul, candy, jehad, safari, tariff, coffee, cafe and, possibly, so long (from *salaam*).

arachnida.   *Arachnida*, the class of spiders (plus scorpions and mites), takes its name from the Lydian maiden Arachne, so skilled at weaving that she challenged Athena, goddess of the household arts, to a contest. Athena won the contest, weaving perfect tapestries that told glorious stories about the gods, while Arachne's excellent but imperfect efforts were unflattering to the gods. The proud Arachne, frightened when Athena tore her impious work to pieces, tried to hang herself, but the goddess interceded, changing her into a spider (from the Greek *arachne*) so that she would forever weave her beautiful designs. Yet she really wants no more of her weaving, legend says, and keeps trying to hang herself—the reason spiders hang on threads from their webs.

Arawak.   This language of the Arawak people of the Lesser Antilles is unique because it developed into a separate "female language." Many years before Columbus landed, fierce South American Caribs had invaded the islands, butchering and eating all the male inhabitants and claiming their women. In retaliation, the women devised a separate female language based on Arawak, refused to speak Carib, and for generations thereafter maintained silence in the presence of all males.

Arbor Day.   "Tree Day" is the exact meaning of *Arbor Day*, for *arbor* is a Latin word for "tree." Arbor Day was first celebrated in 1872, when Nebraskan J. Sterling Morton and his supporters persuaded their state to set aside April 10th for tree planting, to compensate for all the trees Americans had destroyed over the years in clearing the land for settlements. More than a million trees were planted on that first Arbor Day alone, and today the holiday is celebrated in every state.

arborvitae.   The white cedar was named arborvitae, Latin for the "tree of life," by French explorers in Canada during the early 17th century. Champlain's men had observed that Indians drank a medicinal tea made from the bark and needles of the white cedar *(Thuja occidentalis)* and so named the tree because it saved lives.

arcades ambo.   *See* SIX OF ONE AND A HALF-DOZEN OF ANOTHER.

archaeopteryx.   One of the world's most famous fossils, the 150-million-year-old archaeopteryx has the body and teeth of a small dinosaur and the feathered wings of a bird. When found in a German limestone quarry in 1861 it was hailed as a missing evolutionary link between reptiles and birds. Since that time five similar specimens have been found. *Archaeopteryx* is, appropriately, the Greek for "ancient wing."

Archie Bunker.   Among the most recent of eponymous words, an *Archie Bunker* means a bigoted lower-middle-class American. The words recall the bigoted lead character of the long-running television show *All in the Family*.

Archimedean principle.   The Greek mathematician and inventor Archimedes, supposedly born at Syracuse in Sicily in 287 B.C., was both the Albert Einstein and Thomas Edison of his day. He devised the Archimedean drill, pulley, and windlass, and the screw of Archimedes, a machine for raising water, among many other inventions. Archimedes, however, thought little of these ingenious contrivances, even declining to leave written records of most of them. He preferred to be remembered for his great work in mathematics, or for his founding of the science of hydrostatics, which his Archimedean principle made possible. As fate would have it, Archimedes is best remembered for his coining of an expression. One day he was asked to determine the amount of silver an allegedly dishonest goldsmith had used for the king's crown, which was supposed to have been made of pure gold. While pondering the solution to the problem in his bath, he observed that the quantity of water displaced by a body will equal in bulk the bulk of the immersed body (the Archimedean principle). All he had to do then was to weigh an amount of gold equal in weight to the crown, put crown and gold in separate basins of water, and weigh the overflow to determine how much gold the crown really contained. According to one story, he was so overjoyed with his discovery that he forgot his clothes and ran out into the streets naked, astonishing passersby with his shouts of *"Eureka, eureka!"* ("I have found it, I have found it!").

archipelago.   *Archipelago* first referred only to the Aegean Sea, the Italians giving the Aegean this name in the 13th century from their word *arcipelago*, "chief sea." *Archipelago* later came to mean any group of islands.

architecture is frozen music.   Goethe did not coin the above phrase which we owe to the German poet Friedrich von Schelling (1775–1864). Von Schelling used the term several times in his *Philosophy of Art:* "Since it [architecture] is music in space, as it were a frozen music. . . .If architecture in general is frozen music . . ." Soon after, in 1830, Goethe said *Die Baukunst ist eine estarrte Musik*, the form usually quoted today.

Arctic.   *Arctic* for the far north derives from *arctos*, the Greek word for bear. The Greeks referred to the north as *arctos* because the Great Bear constellation (Ursa Major) is the most prominent one in the northern skies.

arena.   The floors of the amphitheaters of ancient Rome had to be covered with absorbent sand because so much blood was spilled in the gladiatorial contests held there. The Latin word for sand is *arena*, and this became the name for the structure itself.

Aretines.   An ancestor of sorts to *The Joy of Sex, Sonnetti Lussuriosi* (1524) was written by Pietro Aretino (1492–1556). The book was a collection of verses and erotic drawings showing positions of sexual intercourse and became an underground favorite in Europe for centuries. Many courtesans were so proud to have slept with Aretino that they called themselves *Aretines*. But others hated the satirist—one critic wrote this mock epitaph:

Here lies the Tuscan poet Aretino
Who evil spoke of everyone but God,
Giving as his excuse, "I never knew him."

are you a man or a mouse?   American slang probably dating back to the early days of the century, *Are you a man or a mouse?* is used to disparage or spur on a timorous person. The reply is often: "A man; my wife's afraid of mice."

Argentina.   The South American country takes its name from the Latin *argentum*, "silver," after the precious metal Spanish explorers found there. Its official name, bestowed in 1816, is *La Republica Argentina*, "The Silver Republic." One legend holds that llamas grazing on Mount Posi in 1545 uprooted shrubs beneath which there was a vein of silver ore. Spanish prospectors noticed the ore, and the mining of silver began.

Argonaut.   While searching for the Golden Fleece, Jason sailed from Greece to Colchis in the galley *Argo*. His 50 companions were thus called *Argonauts* (from the ship's name and the Greek *nautis*, "sailor"), and the word *Argonaut* is now applied to any adventurer on the sea. *See* AQUANAUT.

argosy.   This large ship carrying rich cargo takes its name from the once great Adriatic seaport of Ragusa, the former name of the present-day Dubrovnik, Croatia. Italians called the *Ragusan* vessels *ragusea*, and the English corrupted *ragusea*, in several stages, to *ragusye*, *arragouse*, *aragosa*, and finally *argosy*.

argus-eyed.   In Greek mythology the hundred-eyed Argus was chosen by the jealous Zeus to guard over the nymph Io, even though he had turned his love into an unattractive cow. Apparently he grew jealous of Argus, too, for he had him killed and transferred his eyes to the peacock's tail—which is, according to tradition, why it looks the way it does. Argus managed to live on in name only, *argus-eyed* still meaning vigilant.

argyle.   The original pattern for argyle socks was the traditional green and white pattern of the Scottish Campbell clan of Argyle, or Argyll. The Duke of Argyle, head of the clan, was famous among Highlanders for the posts he erected in his pastures to enable his cows to rub their backs and ease the itching caused by insects. Perhaps the posts were only erected to indicate a trail covered with snow, but nevertheless "God bless the Duke of Argyle!" became a common humorous remark whenever a Scotsman scratched himself. The clan found new popularity when mentioned in several of Sir Walter Scott's novels. Not long after, its tartan was adapted by fabric manufacturers as the *argyle plaid*, and socks knitted in such a pattern were called *argyle socks*. Nowadays, argyle socks are any two or more bright colors, retaining only the diamond-shaped pattern of the original adaptation.

aria.   *Aria*, for an air or melody for a single voice with accompaniment, is an Italian word (*aria*, "air," "music") that entered English in the first half of the 18th century. It is said that three-quarters of our musical terms are Italian in origin, including, to name only a few, *violin, mandolin, pianoforte, orchestra* (from Greek), and *opera*.

Aristarch.   A very pedantic or very severe critic. This eponymous word comes from the name of Aristarchus of Samothrace (ca. 217–145 B.C.), a Greek scholar, critic, and the chief librarian of the Alexandrian library for over 30 years. It is from his editing of Homer's *Iliad* and *Odyssey*, among other great works, that Aristarch won his fame or infamy.

Aristotelian logic.   A number of words are named after Aristotle (384–322 B.C.), the Greek philosopher who was the pupil of Plato and tutor to Alexander the Great. These include *Aristotelianism*, a philosophy emphasizing deduction and investigation of concrete, particular things and situations; *Aristotelian logic*, traditional formal logic; *Aristotle's lantern*, a zoological term so called from a reference by Aristotle to a sea urchin that resembled certain lanterns; and the *Aristotelian* or dramatic *unities*, the necessity for unity of action, time, and place in drama. One of the greatest thinkers of all time, Aristotle's habit of giving his lectures in the *peripatos*, or walking place, of the Athenian Lyceum gave his school of philosophy the name Peripatetic, which yielded the English word *peripatetic*, "walking about or carried on while walking about from place to place."

Arizona.   Our 48th state, admitted to the Union in 1912, is nicknamed "the Grand Canyon State." *Arizona* derives from the Papago Indian word *Arizonac*, "the place of the small spring."

Arizona nightingale.   A humorous Americanism for a braying burro or mule that dates back to the late 19th century.

Arizona strawberries.   American cowboys and lumberjacks used this term as a humorous synonym for beans, also employing the variations *Arkansas strawberries*, *Mexican strawberries*, and *prairie strawberries*. Dried beans *were* pink in color like strawberries. One wit noted that the only way these beans could be digested was for the consumer to break wild horses.

Arizona tenor.   A person suffering from tuberculosis and the coughing that accompanies it; many people with the illness were drawn to the dry Arizona climate.

Arkansas.   Originally spelled *Arkansaw*, our 25th state, nicknamed "the Wonder State," was admitted to the Union in 1925. *Arkansas* is the Sioux word for "land of the south wind people."

Arkansas toothpick.   *See* BOWIE KNIFE.

Arkansawyer.   A nickname for a native of Arkansas, often used by Arkansas residents themselves, because the original spelling of the state's name was Arkansaw. *Arkansawyers* have suffered their share of insults in the language, including *Arkansas asphalt* (a log road); *Arkansas chicken* or *T-bone* (salt pork); *Arkansas fire extinguisher* (a chamberpot); *Arkansas lizard* (any insect louse); *Arkansas travels* (the runs, diarrhea); and *Arkansas wedding cake* (corn bread).

armadillo; Texas turkey.   *Armadillo* is the Spanish diminutive of "the armed one" and is related to words like armor, this obviously in reference to the little porkilotherm's being encased in bony armor and by its habit of rolling itself, when threatened, into an impregnable ball. The Mexican native, which cannot survive north of Texas, was a source of food to Americans during the Great Depression, when it was known as the "Hoover hog" or "Texas turkey." Darwin was fascinated by the little armadillo and its ancient prehistoric predecessor, the glyptodont, which was about the size of a Volkswagen Beetle. A children's poem has it that a peccadillo of the armadillo is that it must be washed with Brillo.

Armageddon. Today *Armageddon* usually refers to a nuclear war that marks the end of the world. It derives from the biblical prophecy that the final battle between good and evil on Judgment Day would be fought on the battlefield of Armageddon (Rev. 16:14–16), which is now Megiddo, near Samaria in Israel. The Hebrew *har Megiddo*, from which *Armageddon* derives, means the *har* or mountain of Megiddo.

armed to the teeth. Some real or imaginary pirate swinging aboard a ship, one hand on a rope, the other hand wielding a cutlass or a pistol, with a knife clamped between his teeth, suggested this expression. The phrase, still used if mostly in a humorous way, seems to have originated in the first half of the 19th century. English politician Richard Cobden used it in 1849, perhaps inspired by an adventure writer of the day.

armoire. These large wardrobes or cupboards started off as places to store weapons, deriving from the Roman *armarium*, "closet," which derives from the Latin *arma*, "arms."

the Army Air Corps. There is no Army Air Corps now, but a lot of people remember when there was and know the words to "The Army Air Corps," written by Robert Crawford, which won first prize in a 1939 Army Air Force competition. It begins: "Off we go into the wild blue yonder, / Climbing high into the sun . . ." *See* ANCHOR'S AWEIGH.

Arnie's army. *See* FRED KARNO'S ARMY.

around the horn. In the days of the tall ships any sailor who had sailed around Cape Horn was entitled to spit to windward; otherwise, it was a serious infraction of nautical rules of conduct. Thus, the permissible practice of spitting to windward was called *around the horn*. Cape Horn isn't so named because it is shaped like a horn. Captain Schouten, the Dutch navigator who first rounded it in 1616, named it after Hoorn, his birthplace in northern Holland.

arrant thief; knight errant. *Arrant* was originally just a variation of *errant*, nomadic or vagabond, the word best known in *knight errant*, a knight who roamed the country performing good deeds. But from its persistent use in expressions such as an *arrant thief*, a thief who roamed the countryside holding up victims, *arrant* came to mean thorough, downright, or out-and-out. Expressions such as *an arrant thief*, *an arrant coward*, etc., have been common since the late 14th century.

arras. This richly woven tapestry with scenes and figures takes its name from the town of Arrasin, in Artois, France, where it was first woven in medieval times. The French call it a *tapisserie*.

arrive. The Latin *ad*, to, plus *ripan*, shore or river bank, are the components of our word *arrive*, which first was a maritime term meaning a ship had reached shore or land. Since medieval times, however, *arrive* has meant to reach anywhere, as in "He finally arrived in Rome."

arrow of Acestes. In Greek legend Acestes, scion of a river god, was an unrivaled archer. Acestes had such great strength that in one contest he shot an arrow hard enough that it caught fire flying through the air. Since then *arrow of Acestes* has come to mean an oratorical point made with fiery brilliance.

arrowroot. The Arawak Indians of the Caribbean Islands called this plant (*Maranta arundinacea*) *aru-aru*, "meal of meals," because they thought it highly nutritious. It would have been more precise for English speakers to name the plant "aru-root" when they learned of it, but the plant was also a valuable medicine used to draw poison from the wounds caused by poisoned arrows. Speakers thus associated "aru" with arrow and folk etymology added *arrowroot* to the dictionaries; the word is recorded as early as 1696.

arroz con pollo. A Mexican chicken and rice dish seasoned with garlic, saffron, paprika, and other spices that was first introduced to the United States in the Southwest but is now known throughout the country. The Spanish name translates simply as "rice with chicken."

ars gratia artis. Latin for "art for art's sake." The expression is famous as the slogan for Metro-Goldwyn-Mayer since 1916, when publicist Howard Dietz introduced it along with the Metro-Goldwyn-Mayer lion. Dietz also invented the MGM slogan "More stars than there are in heaven." The French, however, used a phrase similar to *ars gratis artis* in the early 19th century, their *l'art pour l'art* meaning that art couldn't or shouldn't be in any way useful, could serve no moral or political purpose.

artesian wells. *Artesian wells*, wells whose shafts penetrate through an impervious layer into a water-bearing stratum from which water runs under pressure, take their name from Arteseum, now Artois, in northern France, where such wells were worked as early as the 17th century.

artichoke; Jerusalem artichoke. As the poet Richard Armour observed, the *artichoke* is the one vegetable you have more of when you finish eating it, due to its compact leaves, which are scraped with the teeth and discarded. Often called the *globe* or *French artichoke*, it is the flower bud of a thistle picked before it blooms. At one time it was seriously suggested that the plant was so named because some *artist* had *choked* on the inedible "needles" covering its delicious base, or "heart." Actually *artichoke* has more prosaic and complicated origins. The Arabians called it *al* ("the") *kharshuf*, which became *alcachofa* in Spanish. Northern Italians corrupted the Spanish version to *articiocco* and this entered French as *artichaut*, from which our *artichoke* evolved. It is true that the English *choke* in the word replacing the French *chaut* may have been influenced by the sensation one gets from eating the wrong part of the vegetable. As for the *Jerusalem artichoke*, it neither comes from Jerusalem, is an artichoke, nor tastes anything like an artichoke.

The starchy underground tuber (a good potato substitute) was called *girasole articiocco*, "sunflower artichoke," by northern Italians because it is a member of the sunflower family and resembles a sunflower in leaf and stem. To Englishmen the word *girasole* sounded like *Jerusalem*, and they mistakenly translated the name as *Jerusalem artichoke*.

article.   A derogatory Irish slang term for a person, as in "Shut your hole (mouth), you stupid article." The term has some currency in England.

asafetida bag.   *Asafetida* is a foul-smelling resinous material made from roots of several plants of the parsley family. Its odor was once thought to ward off illness, and it was often placed in small bags that were worn under the clothing of children.

A.S.A.P.   This initialism for *as soon as possible* (as in "Send the check A.S.A.P.") seems to have been coined in the military during the Korean conflict and is first recorded in 1955. It can be pronounced as initials (A.S.A.P.) or as a word (pronounced *a sap*). After about 30 years it spawned the slang A.S.A.F.P. (as soon as fucking possible), first recorded in 1985.

ascham.   This tall narrow locker for arrows takes its name from Roger Ascham, an English scholar who would otherwise not be remembered for his 16th-century treatise on archery.

ascot.   A neck scarf knotted in a special way; so named from the fashionable dress worn at the Ascot races in England. Also called *ascot tie*, the term dates back to the early 1900s. Ascot Week is held every June at Ascot Heath in Berkshire.

as every schoolboy knows.   Jonathan Swift used this expression, which has been traced back as early as 1621. It is generally associated with the British historian Macaulay because of his frequent references to somewhat abstruse subjects as subjects that any public schoolboy should know.

Asiatic hordes.   These words are so distasteful to Orientals that they have officially asked on several occasions to be called Asians instead of Asiatics in all cases, so as to avoid any association with the term *Asiatic hordes*. "Hordes" itself, however, is clearly associated with Asians. The word first described the tent of Batu Khan, Genghis Khan's grandson, who crossed the Volga in 1235 leading the savage Mongol invasion of Europe that left massacred people and leveled cities in its path. Batu's magnificent tent, made mostly of embroidered silk, was called the *sira ordu*, the "silken camp." Conquered Poles called it the *horda* and soon the name "Golden Horde" was applied to both Batu's tent and his army. In time "horde" came to describe any large, savage army, especially in the phrase *Asiatic hordes*.

ask a silly question and you'll get a silly answer.   Still a common expression, the above probably dates to the late 19th century. It possibly evolved from the old proverb "ask no questions and you'll be told no lies."

ask not what your country can do for you; ask what you can do for your country.   The precise wording of this famous phrase, especially the catchy inversion "ask not" can be credited to John F. Kennedy, as it usually is, but the sentiment was hardly original with J.F.K. Wrote Oliver Wendell Holmes, Jr., for just one example: "It is now the moment . . . to recall what our country has done for each of us, and to ask ourselves what we can do for our country in return." After this, in a 1916 speech, future president Warren G. Harding said: "We must have a citizenship less concerned about what the government can do for it and more anxious about what it can do for the nation."

as long as grass grows and water runs.   A promise, meaning "forever," often made to Indian tribes in the American West regarding their rights to their lands and their freedom. But as a writer put it in *Colliers Magazine* (11/30/07): "The white invaders [settlers] pleaded for Statehood, and Statehood forever laid aside the promise to the red man that he should have freedom 'as long as grass grows and water runs.' "

as Maine goes, so goes the nation.   A common political saying since at least 1880, when it was first recorded, meaning that the political party that wins the most votes in the state of Maine in a national election will win nationally. This has often, but not always, been the case. The saying, however, originally referred to New York, being first recorded in 1848 as "As goes Duchess County, so goes the state, and as New York goes, so goes the Union."

as one man.   Unanimously, with one accord. The expression is an ancient one, coming from the Bible (Judges 20:8): "So all the people got them up as one man."

asparagus.   There is a story that *asparagus* takes its name from the Greek *aspharagos*, meaning according to this theory, "as long as one's throat," because diners often swallowed the spears whole. But the meaning of the word *aspharagos* from which our *asparagus* derives is unclear and more likely meant "sprout or shoot" in Greek. *See* QUICKER THAN YOU CAN COOK ASPARAGUS.

Aspasia.   The great Athenian statesman Pericles (ca. 500–429 B.C.) took for his lifelong companion the beautiful and celebrated hetaera Aspasia of Miletus. This accomplished courtesan gave birth to his son Pericles the Younger and over the centuries her name became a literary euphemism for a courtesan. *See* THAIS.

aspen; trembling poplar.   The trembling or quaking poplar, as the aspen is also known, is said to have trembling leaves because it began shaking in shame and horror when Christ's cross was made from its wood. *Populus tremula* and its related species have long, compressed, twisted leafstalks that cause the leaves to tremble in even the slightest wind.

asphodel; Jacob's rod.   The asphodel of the ancients so frequently encountered in poetry is *Asphodeline luta*, a perennial yellow-flowered herb sometimes called Jacob's rod. In ancient times the dead were thought to sustain themselves on the roots of asphodels, and the flowers were often planted on graves. Interestingly, the much better known daffodil bears a name that is a corruption of *asphodel*.

aspic.   A tasty meat jelly, aspic is supposed to have been named for the asp (the same hooded venomous snake that Cleopatra used to kill herself), because French gourmets said it was "cold as an asp." The word came into English late in the 18th century and there is no better explanation for its origin.

aspidistra.   This foliage plant takes its name from the Greek *aspis*, a small round shield in reference to the shape of its stigma. It is often called the cast-iron plant because it withstands all kinds of ill treatment. Widely used in bars, movie houses, and other public places, it is also called the beerplant—because bartenders often water it with beer left on the bar at the end of the evening!

aspirin.   Originally a trademark of the German Bayer Aspirin Company, *aspirin* is now a generic term and needn't be capitalized. The famous analgesic's name was coined by German scientist Charles Witthauer in 1899, *aspirin* being a shortening of the German *Acetylirte Spirsaure* (acetylated spiraeic acid), plus the chemical suffix *in*. By 1915, after many headaches, Bayer had lost its battle for the trademark in court.

assembly line.   The term *assembly line* was first recorded in 1914 in connection with Henry Ford's car company, but the practice in America goes back at least to the 18th century, when muskets were made from several standard parts in one factory. Among automobile manufacturers, Henry Ford is generally credited with the idea for an assembly line, but Ford actually improved upon a method the Olds Motor Vehicle Company, maker of the Oldsmobile, used long before him in 1902, although he did introduce the electric conveyer belt.

ass in a sling.   The *Dictionary of American Slang* says that *to have one's ass in a sling* means "to be or appear to be sad, rejected, or defeated." Originating in the South perhaps a century ago, the now national expression was probably suggested by someone with his arm in a sling, that image being greatly and humorously exaggerated. A good story claims that this *ass* is really a donkey, that the expression comes from a practice of blacksmiths rigging slings for donkeys, or asses, because they can't stand on three feet while being shoed. But the good story isn't a true story. Donkeys *can* stand on three feet, and so far as is known, no blacksmith ever shod a donkey in a sling.

ass-up.   The unusually named small woodpecker of the family Sittidae, found in the eastern United States, is so called because it runs up and down tree trunks with its head held lower than its tail.

as sure as God made little green apples.   Very certain, as in "He'll be there as sure as God made little green apples." First recorded in the mid-19th century, the phrase is sometimes heard with the word *green* deleted.

aster.   This daisy takes its name from the Latin *aster*, "a star," in reference to the shape of its flower. However, when *aster* occurs at the end of other plant names, as in *Cotoneaster*, it doesn't have anything to do with this root but instead indicates inferiority.

asterisk.   *Asterisk*, from the Greek word for "star," can mean "little star" in English, but much more frequently refers to the star that writers use after a word to indicate a footnote at the bottom of the page. Stoddard King wrote about one in "The Writer and the Asterisk" (1913), showing another function of the star:

> A writer owned an Asterisk,
> and kept it in his den,
> Where he wrote tales (which had large sales)
> Of frail and erring men
> And always, when he reached the point
> Where carping censors lurk,
> He called upon the Asterisk
> To do his dirty work.

asteroid.   An *asteroid*, from the Greek *aster*, "star," and *eidos*, "form," is also called a minor planet, being one of the thousands of small planets, the largest less than 500 miles in diameter, that circle the sun mainly between the orbits of Jupiter and Mars. *Asteroid* was coined in 1804 by British astronomer Sir William Herschel, who so named the minor planets. *See* EARTH-LIGHT for a word Herschel's son coined.

as the crow flies.   Meaning, "in a straight line," the expression dates back to at least 1800. *Corvus brachyrhynchos* of North America is a remarkable bird, far too clever for any SCARECROW. These crows are said to hold conventions of 40 to 60 birds in which a leader they will follow is chosen. They can apparently be ruthless, too. Wrote the New England naturalist Alan Devoe: "The most extraordinary rites of a flock are the 'trials' they conduct. When a crow has broken the laws of crowdom, the flock gathers in judgment, parleying sometimes for hours while the offender waits some distance away. Suddenly the discussion ceases; there is a moment of silence. Then the flock either rises in unison and leaves, or dives in a mass upon the offender, pecks out his eyes, and pummels him to death." *See* CROW BAR, CROW'S-FEET, CROW'S NEST, EAT CROW.

as the saying goes.   This common saying has been traced back to George Farquhar's play *The Beaux' Stratagem* (1707), in which the landlord Boniface consistently utters, "As the saying is . . ." before his every phrase. Over the years Boniface's words became *as the saying goes*.

astrology.   *Astrology* means "speaking of the stars" in Greek, and an astrologist is "one who speaks of the stars." The word did not come into English, through Latin, until the late 14th century. Prior to that ASTRONOMY had been used in its place.

astronomy.   *Astronomy* comes from a Greek word meaning "star arranging, or arrangement of the stars," and was first applied to the work of men charting the heavens. It came into English, via Latin, early in the 13th century, meaning at first the whole field of ASTROLOGY, not the modern science of astronomy.

asylum.   *Asylum*, from the Greek *asulon*, refuge, first meant a sanctuary for debtors or criminals, but in the 18th century it came to mean a *lunatic asylum*. After another two centuries that meaning lost favor, *mental hospital* preferred, and now it is mainly heard in sayings such as British prime minister Lloyd

George's "The world is a lunatic asylum run by the lunatics." *Asylum* is used frequently today in *political asylum*, protection and immunity from extradition granted to a political refugee from another country.

AT&T. *American Telephone and* Telegraph, formed in 1885, was called The Long Distance Company until it acquired the Bell Company four years later and began buying local phone companies. Today, as the result of a 1982 antitrust suit, it has divested itself of local phone companies and is back to long distance again (along with some new ventures and the manufacture of phone equipment).

Athanasian wench. Though it's rarely used anymore in everyday speech, this 18th-century slang for "a forward girl, ready to oblige any man that shall ask her" has an amusing origin. It alludes to the ecumenical *Athanasian Creed*, which takes its name from St. Athanasius, an exiled third-century Alexandrian bishop who was a pioneer in scientific theology. The *English Book of Common Prayer* includes the *Athanasian Creed*, and the term *Athanasian wench* arose when some wit pointed out that the familiar first words of the creed read *quicunque vult*, "Whosoever desires . . ."

Athens. According to the myth, when Cecrops founded a great city in Attica, the Greeks offered to name it for the god who gave them the most valuable gift. Poseidon gave them the horse, but Athena stuck her spear in the ground and an olive tree rose from the earth. Because she gave them this greatest gift of all, the city was named in her honor. In any event, the city is assuredly named for the goddess.

athlete. *Athlete* ultimately comes to us from the Greek *athlos*, meaning "prize," which led to the Greek *athlein*, "to contend for a prize," and finally *athletes*, "one who contends for a prize." Entering English early in the 16th century, the word described anyone who competed in the physical activities—running, jumping, boxing, wrestling, etc.—that formed part of the public games in ancient Greece.

athlete's foot. An advertising copywriter coined this term in 1928 when Absorbine Jr., a remedy for this disease often caught in gyms and locker rooms, popularized the euphemism. For over 400 years before that, *athlete's foot* had been called "ringworm." *Jock itch*, the term for a condition caused by the same fungus, was coined in the 1970s.

Atlantic Ocean. The Atlantic may take its name from the fabled kingdom of Atlantis that is said to have existed in its domain, or from the Atlas Mountains in northwest Africa, which the ancients thought overlooked the entire ocean. It is interesting to note that the Atlantic Ocean is widening an inch every year, while the Pacific Ocean is shrinking.

Atlantis; Lemuria; Lyonesse. First mentioned by Plato and said to have existed in the Atlantic Ocean, *Atlantis* was supposed to have been destroyed by an earthquake and sunk beneath the bottom of the sea more than 10,000 years ago, which hasn't stopped legions of adventurers from searching for it over the ages. *Lemuria*, said to be near Madagascar, is another famous lost island in history, as is *Lyonesse*, a mythical country "forty

fathoms down" stretching off England from Lands End to the Scilly Isles.

atlas. In Greek mythology Atlas stood on a mountain peak in what is now Africa holding the heavens apart from the earth. This myth inspired the great geographer Gerardus Mercator (1515–94) to use a drawing of Atlas holding a globe on his shoulders for the cover of a collection of maps he published in the 16th century. The picture was used on so many similar books to follow that *atlas* became synonymous for any book of maps.

at loose ends. There are at least two good explanations for this expression meaning "not knowing what to do with oneself," or to be unemployed. The saying dates back to the middle of the 19th century in England and was originally *to be at loose end*. One theory connects it with a string hanging loose from a garment, the end of it attached to nothing. But Weekley in his *Etymological Dictionary of Modern English* says the phrase suggests "freedom from tether," like a horse out to pasture, out of harness, untied and unemployed.

at low tide. *To be at low tide* or *water* or *the low watermark* is to have financial difficulties, or no money at all, as if one were stranded by the ebbing tide. Nautical slang in origin and dating back to the early 17th century, the expression is Standard English today.

atom. The *atom* takes its name from the Greek *atomos*, undivided or indivisible, being to the Greeks something that could not be cut up or divided anymore. More poetically, the Greek word *atomos* is closely related to the Greek for "the twinkling of an eye," a charming way to express minuteness. *Atom* came into English in the 15th century from the Latin *atomus*, which derives from the Greek word.

atomic bomb. This term was apparently first used in a science fiction story—H. G. Wells's "The World Set Free," written in 1914. Thirty years later it became a reality.

atone. A person who must atone for his sins must find inner unity and become "at one" with himself. That is the origin of the word *atone*; in fact, an obsolete definition of *atone* is "to bring into unity, harmony."

at one fell swoop. The first use of this phrase in English appears to be by Shakespeare in *Macbeth*, where he describes a Hell-Kite killing chickens. But the word *swoop*, referring to a bird of prey pouncing suddenly on its victim, occurs in an earlier reference to a fabled bird of Madagascar that could swoop down and carry off "a horse and his rider, or an elephant." *One fell swoop* means a sudden single strike or blow, fierce and often brutal. The *fell* in the phrase has nothing to do with the verb "fall," as might be suspected, deriving instead from the old English adjective *fell* meaning "fierce, savage, ruthless," which is the basis for the word *felon*. *Swoop* comes from a Scandinavian word that meant to move in a stately manner, to sweep along as with trailing garments.

atropa. *See* BELLADONNA LILY.

atropidae. *Atropidae* are book lice that feed on the bindings and paper of books, eventually destroying them. They are named for *Atropos*, one of the three Fates in Greek mythology, the Fate that finally cut the thread of life. Why were the Atropidae or book lice named for someone who destroyed life? In ancient times the ticking sound they made was said to forebode a death. *Atropos*, the unturning (unbending) fate, takes his name from the Greek *a* (without) and *tropos* (turning).

attest. *See* TESTICLES.

at the end of one's rope. *I'm at the end of my rope* means I've gone as far as I can, I can't do anymore, and suggests the image of an animal tied on a tether. The expression is first recorded, however, in the sense of someone finally checked in wrong-doing, in a 1686 translation of a French work. This suggests that the expression may have been inspired by the sight of a man executed by hanging, dangling at the end of his rope.

attic; attic salt. Both the *attic* in one's house and *attic salt*, pointed wit, came to us from the same source, the Greek word *Attikos*, an Athenian, or citizen of Athens. Salt was a common term for wit and the Athenians were noted for their elegant turns of thought, which inspired the Romans to coin the expression *sal atticus* ("attic salt"). The Athenians had no *attics* in their houses as we know them, but the Attic (Athenian) style of architecture featured decorative walls at the tops of buildings. When storage rooms were built behind such decorative walls centuries later, they were called *attics*, after the walls.

Attila the Hun. *See* HUN.

attorney. *See* LAWYER.

Au; gold. *Au*, an abbreviation of the Latin *aurum*, is the chemical symbol for gold, which is itself one of the four oldest words in English, deriving from the Indo-European substrate word *gol* (the other three are *apple*, from *apal*; *bad*, *bad*; and *tin*, *tin*). Hundreds of expressions, some of them covered in these pages, are based on *gold*, from *all that glitters is not gold* and *good as gold* to *heart of gold* and *gold digger*. Various kinds of real or counterfeit gold include the following:

> *Argental gold, electrum*—an alloy of gold and silver.
> *Colored gold*—gold whose luster is destroyed by nitric acid.
> *Dead gold*—colored gold.
> *Fool's gold*—iron or copper pyrites, sometimes mistaken for gold.
> *Green gold*—gold alloyed with silver.
> *Jeweler's gold*—an alloy containing three parts silver to one of gold.
> *Leprous gold*—lead.
> *Mannheim gold*—an alloy containing copper, tin, and zinc.
> *Mock gold*—an alloy of copper, zinc, and platinum.
> *Red gold*—gold alloyed with copper.
> *Shell gold*—a gold put into shells by miners.
> *Spangle gold*—gold beaten for spangles.
> *White gold*—an alloy of about five parts silver to one of gold.

Aubepine. As a preface to his famous story "Rappaccini's Daughter" Nathaniel Hawthorne originally wrote a paragraph claiming that the tale was written by a Frenchman named Aubepine. Some readers immediately recognized that Aubepine meant "hawthorn" in French and that Hawthorne was actually discussing his own work.

aubergine. Another word for the eggplant, deriving from the French *auberge*, a kind of peach, possibly because the first cultivated eggplants were about the size of a peach. *Aubergine* is also used as an adjective meaning "black" or "dark purple." *See* EGGPLANT.

aubrieta. Few great painters have a genus or species of plants named after them, not even French artist Claude Monet, whose paintings of his exquisite garden at Giverny are indisputable masterpieces. But one small genus of perennials honors Claude Aubriet (1651–1743), the venerable French natural history painter. Its only horticultural species is *Aubrieta deltoidea*, purple rock cress, which comes in many varieties and is often used for rock gardens and edgings. *Aubrieta* is pronounced "au-bree-sha."

Aubry's dog. The dog Dragon's French master, Aubry of Montdidier, was murdered in 1371 by Richard of Macaire. Thereafter, whenever Richard appeared, Dragon attacked him. This excited suspicion of Richard, and he was ordered into judicial combat with the dog. Dragon killed him, and in his last moments Richard confessed the murder of Aubry. An Aubry's dog is thus a very loyal, faithful dog.

auburn. A word that has changed its color. Though it refers to something darker today, *auburn* originally meant whitish, from the Latin *alburnus*, which derives from the Latin *albus*, "white." Somehow over the years *auburn* became confused with the English *brown* and has come to mean golden brown or reddish brown.

auction; augment. When an item is auctioned, bids on it keep going up, of course, until there is no more bidding and the highest bidder makes the purchase. The word *auction*, widely used by the Romans, reflects the process, deriving as it does from the Latin *augere*, to increase, which also gives us *augment*.

auger. *See* ADDER.

auger in. Pilots superstitiously avoid the use of the word *crash*, using many euphemisms, including *buy the farm* and *auger in*. *Auger in* dates back to the day of the prop plane, planes with props resembling an auger as they crashed into the earth.

August; Augustan age. Augustus Caesar stole a day from February to give *August* 31 days—simply because he did not want July, named after his great uncle and adopted father, to be longer than his own name-month. History is made up of such petty jealousies, but Augustus and Julius Caesar really got along very well; there is no evidence of any generation gap. Born Gaius Octavianus, his mother the daughter of Julius Caesar's sister, Augustus was eventually chosen by the Roman ruler as his heir, adopting the name Caesar. Octavius, as he was commonly known, was only 19 at the time of his uncle's assassination in 44 B.C. On returning to Rome from Spain, he found that Caesar had secretly adopted him and willed him all his property. It was then that he changed his name and embarked on a celebrated military career that included the conquest of Egypt. In 29 B.C., already immensely popular among the people, he was chosen first emperor of Rome, and two years later the Senate bestowed upon him the title *Augustus*, or "imperial majesty." Finally, what was the sixth month of the year *(Sextillus)* was renamed "Augustus" in his honor—complete with an extra day at his insistence. *August* wasn't chosen because it was his birth month (September), but because it happened to be his "lucky" month of the year—the one in which he first became a consul, reduced Egypt, put an end to civil wars, received the oath of allegiance from his legions at Janiculum, and scored his greatest military triumphs. Octavius Augustus ruled wisely until his death at the age of 75, his reign marked by great progress and a flowering of literature that is today known as the *Augustan age*.

auld; Auld Lang Syne. *Auld*, as in the song "Auld Lang Syne," simply means "old." *Auld Lang Syne* probably dates back at least before the 18th century, but the famous version rewritten by Scottish poet Robert Burns in 1796 is the one that is known and sung today. *Auld Lang Syne* means "old long since," or times past.

Auld Reeky. "Old Smoky," an old nickname for the Scottish city of Edinburgh, which used to be covered with smoke and soot from factories.

Aunt Edna. The creation of British playwright Terence Rattigan (1911–77) in his *Collected Works* (1953). An *Aunt Edna* is a close relative of the American little old lady from Dubuque—nice but provincial, middle-class, very prudish, and traditional. *See* OLD LADY IN DUBUQUE.

Aunt May. An *Aunt May* is British naval slang for a person generous to sailors. It is aptly named for Mrs. May Hanrahan, the widow of a United States naval captain, who "adopted" 16 British destroyers during World War II and spent almost a quarter of a million dollars on their crews in the form of presents and comforts. *Aunt May* Hanrahan was received by the queen when she visited England after the war and was piped on board the destroyer *Tartar* while a naval band on the jetty played in her honor.

au pair. A young woman, often foreign, who receives room and board and a small salary in return for housework. The term, dating back to 1965, is becoming more common in the United States, especially to describe one who watches children. It is from the French for "on equal footing."

aurora borealis; auroral. *Aurora borealis* means "northern dawn" in Latin and is used to describe the electrical streams of light sometimes seen at night in the northern sky. The phenomenon is so named because the Greek goddess Aurora was said to begin her day's travels before the sun rose. Aurora's name is also remembered in *auroral*, "dawnlike."

auspicious, augur, augury. The Roman auspex was a man appointed to foretell the future by observing the flight of birds, listening to their songs, observing the food they ate, or examining their entrails. The name comes from the Latin *avis*, "bird," and *specere*, "to look at." No important enterprise was begun without the auspex's consulting the birds to see if omens were favorable; favorable omens came to be called *auspicious* ones. In later Roman times the *augur* replaced the auspex as the observer and interpreter of bird signs, his name deriving from the Latin *avis*, "bird," and *garrire*, "to talk or tell." His interpretation was called an augurism, which became the English word *augury*, an omen, while the Latin *inaugurare*, "to install an official after consulting the birds," became our word *inaugurate*.

Aussie. Australians have been called Aussies since about 1895, when the term seems to have been coined by Australians. *Aussie* became popular worldwide during World War I, as did *digger* for an Australian soldier, though this last term may have originated during the Australian gold rush in the 1850s. Australia, of course, has long been called *the land down under* (along with New Zealand). In contrast, Alaska is sometimes jokingly called *the land up over*.

Aussie salute. A humorous term for waving a hand in the air to swat or scare off flies. The words were probably coined by the Australians, who aren't at all a pompous people.

Australia. Captain Matthew Flinders is the second of only two men in history who alone named a continent. The English navigator named Australia in 1803, after sailing completely around it. It had previously been known from the 16th century as *Terra Australis*, "the southern land." For the first person to name a continent see AMERICA and the story of the mapmaker who could be credited with naming both North America and South America—though his map depicted only the area we now know as South America, and he did not realize that he was naming a continent.

Australian crawl. Pacific Island natives probably invented this fastest of all swimming strokes—the one used by all freestyle swimmers today—but it was introduced into Europe (where the breaststroke was the favored stroke) from Australia at the turn of the century, and thus dubbed the *Australian crawl*.

Austrian lip. The British historian Macaulay wrote that Charles II of Spain, last of the Spanish Hapsburgs, had a jaw so malformed that he couldn't chew his food. Another Hapsburg, Emperor Charles V, possessed a lower jaw that protruded so far beyond his upper jaw that he could not speak an intelligible sentence. This inherited genetic defect, one of the most curious in history, is common to all the Hapsburgs, and can be seen in many of their portraits. It was probably inherited through marriage with the Polish princely family of Jagellon and perpetuated by intermarriage among the Hapsburgs themselves. The term *Austrian lip* describes the deformity far better than "severely protruding lower jaw."

autantonym. An *autantonym* (from the Greek for "self" plus "antonym") is a word that has come to mean its opposite. An example is the word *fast*, which in the case of a fast runner means a runner who runs rapidly, but in the case of a *fast* color means a color that doesn't run at all. The word seems to have been coined in the last 50 years or so. Another example of an autantonym is raze/raise.

auteur; cineast(e).   A movie director who displays a unique personal style in his films is often called an *auteur*, from the French for "originator" or "author." A *cinéaste*, on the other hand, is a French word for a devoted movie fan.

auto-da-fé.   A public judgment against someone tried by the Spanish Inquisition was called an *auto-da-fé*, the judgment usually followed by burning condemned heretics at the stake, burning employed because the Catholic church forbade the shedding of blood. *Auto-da-fé* is Portuguese for "act of the faith."

auto-icons.   Jeremy Bentham (1748–1832), the philosopher-author whose clothed skeleton is on display at University College, London, thought that dead people should all be embalmed and used as their own monuments. He called these *auto-icons*. "If a country gentleman have rows of trees leading to his dwelling," he wrote, "the auto-icons of his family might alternate with the trees; copal varnish would protect the face from the effects of rain—caoutchouc the habiliments." But then Bentham also had an unusual "pet"—a teapot.

automatic writing.   *Automatic writing* is writing performed without the will or control of the writer, sometimes without the writer being conscious of the words written. The phenomenon first appeared in mid-19th-century America as a tool of spiritualism, and the writer was sometimes (but not always) hypnotized or drugged and aided by instruments including a planchette, "a little heart-shaped board running on wheels," that was supplemented by a Ouija board containing the alphabet and other signs.

automation.   *Automation* was coined in 1936 by D. S. Harder, a General Motors employee, but it didn't come into popular use until the 1950s. Harder defined *automation* as the "automatic handling of parts between progressive production processes," but it is more commonly defined today as "the technique or system of operating a mechanical or productive device by highly automatic means, as by electronic devices."

automobile.   "[Automobile] being half Greek and half Latin, is so near indecent that we print it with hesitation," a *New York Times* editor wrote in 1899. But *automobile* and *car* are the only survivors of the many names Americans gave to early *horseless carriages*, which included *diamot*, *motor buggy*, and even *stink chariot* (probably the work of an early environmentalist). A French construction of the 1880s, it was broken down to *auto* here by 1899. *See* CAR.

autumn; fall.   *Autumn* is used much more in England, *fall* in America. Both are lovely old words. *Autumn*, from the Latin *autumn* for the season, dates back to the early 14th century. *Fall*, first recorded in 1545, is short for the season of *leaf-fall*. In the 1850s *autumn* was British slang for a hanging through a drop door, the grim joke showing that the British did use *fall* as a synonym for *autumn*.

ave atque vale.   Latin for "hail and farewell." In about 57 B.C. the Roman poet Catullus traveled to Asia and found the tomb of his brother, who had died near Troy. After he performed the ancient Greek burial rites over the grave, there came to him the famous *ave atque vale* lament containing a phrase still common to dozens of languages over 2,000 years after he invented it:

> Dear brother, through many states and seas
> Have I come to this sorrowful sacrifice,
> Bringing you the last gift for the dead . . .
> Accept these offerings wet with fraternal tears;
> And forever, brother, hail and farewell.

Avenging Angel.   A Colt revolver with a portion of its barrel sawed off was called an *Avenging Angel* in the early West. Avenging Angels were used by Brigham Young's Morman followers, one of whom was said to have killed hundreds with his.

average.   *Average* has an unusual rather than average derivation. The word derives from the French *avarie*, a word of Arabic origin that meant "less than total damage to a ship or its cargo." Since average damage was a mean between the extremes of total damage and no damage, the word average ultimately came to take its current meaning.

avocado.   When Montezuma served the *avocado*, or alligator pear, to Cortés and his conquistadores, the Aztecs explained that their *ahucatl* was so named from their word meaning "testicle," not only because the fruit resembled a testicle but because it supposedly excited sexual passion. The Aztecs even drew their guests pictures to illustrate their story, but to the Spaniards *ahucatl* sounded like *avocado*, their word for "advocate," and they named it so when they brought it back to Spain. In Europe the *avocado* became a great favorite, and France's Sun King called it *la bonne poire* (the good pear) because it seemed to get a rise out of his setting libido. Aphrodisiac or not, the fruit remains an important meat substitute in parts of the world today and a delicious dessert in others.

Avogadro's law.   Also called *Avogadro's hypothesis*, this physics law states that "equal volumes of all gases under identical conditions of pressure and temperature contain the same number of molecules." It is named after its creator, Italian physicist Count Amedeo Avogadro (1776–1856), who developed it in 1811. Avogadro, who became a professor at the University of Turin, also has named after him *Avogadro's number*: "the number of molecules in a mole of any substance." A *mole* is the molecular weight of a substance.

avoid extremes.   Common to many languages, *avoid extremes* has been traced back as far as the writings of Pittacus of Mitylene (652–569 B.C.), one of the Seven Wise Men of Greece. Ovid has it "You will go more safely in the middle," and Aristotle, "Moderation in all things."

avoid Latin derivations.   *Avoid Latin derivations; use brief, terse Anglo-Saxon monosyllables* was long a popular admonition to students in college English composition classes. The only Anglo-Saxon word in the anonymous admonition is *Anglo-Saxon*.

Away Down South in Dixie. As the *Star of the West* sped from New York to Fort Sumter in Charleston, South Carolina, just before the start of the Civil War, the Union troops gathered on deck, telling stories and singing. Ironically, their favorite tune turned out to be "Away Down South in Dixie," which songwriter and minstrel David D. Emmett had composed on his violin in 1859 "while looking out at the cold dreary streets of New York City and wishing he were down home in Dixie." This would become the favorite marching song of the Confederates during the Civil War, but it was first sung as a war tune by these Yankees heading South. "In Dixie land I'll take my stand, to live and die in Dixie . . .": one war correspondent reported that these words were heard again and again, over 20 times on the first day alone, as the ship cut through the billowing waves. *See* GOD BLESS AMERICA.

AWOL. This commonly used abbreviation meaning "absent without leave" originated during the Civil War, according to H. L. Mencken (*The American Language*, supplement I, 1945): "[In the Confederate Army] unwarranted absences of short duration were often unpunished and in other cases offenders received such trivial sentences as reprimand by a company officer, digging a stump, carrying a rail for a hour or two, wearing a placard inscribed with the letters AWOL."

axel. In figure skating an *axel* is a graceful jump consisting of one-and-a-half turns in the air, among other qualifications. Having nothing to do with the axle of a wheel, it is named for its inventor, Norwegian skater Axel Paulsen, who perfected it in the late 19th century. It is the only figure-skating jump to take off from a forward position.

Axis; Allies; Axis of Evil. *Axis* and the *Allies* were terms common during World War II, the former referring to the political alliance of Germany, Italy, and Japan, and the latter referring to the allies of the United States and Britain. *Axis* is first recorded in 1936 and *Allies* in 1914, when it was the name of those countries that opposed the Central Powers in Europe during World War I. In recent times, as early as 2001, the phrase *Axis of Evil* was coined by U.S. president George W. Bush's speechwriters David Frum and Mike Gerson to describe the alliance of terrorist organizations and terrorist states around the world. *See* EVIL ONE.

Axis Sally. *See* TOKYO ROSE.

an ax to grind. In the tale "Who'll Turn Grindstones" a man carrying a dull ax compliments a boy on his intelligence and good looks and then asks him if he can borrow his father's grindstone. Flattered, the boy says yes, and then the man proceeds to tell him how strong he looks for his age. The boy falls for all this flattery, and to demonstrate his strength keeps turning the grindstone until the dull ax is as sharp as a razor. Then the man goes off without so much as thanking the boy. The author concludes his story with the observation: "When I see a merchant overpolite to his customers, begging them to taste a little brandy and throwing half his goods on the counter—thinks I, that man has *an axe to grind*." Ben Franklin is frequently credited with this yarn, thought responsible for the expression meaning to flatter a person while seeking a favor from him, but perhaps the credit should go to Charles Miner (1780–1865), who related this incident from his childhood in the columns of the *Wilkes-Barre Gleaner* (1811). The phrase *an ax to grind* has since the publication of his story become widely synonymous for an ulterior motive.

ayuh. Yes; though the word has shades of meaning ranging from the affirmative to the sarcastic. Chiefly heard in Maine, *ayuh* is found throughout New England in variations such as *eyah*, *ayeh*, *eeyuh*, *ehyuh*, *aaay-yuh*, and even *ayup*. A touchstone of New England speech, it possibly derives from the nautical *aye*, "yes," which in turn probably comes from the early English *yie*, "yes." Another theory has *ayuh* coming from the old Scottish-American *aye-yes* meaning the same.

azalea. The ancient Greeks had the erroneous idea that this shrub required a dry, sandy soil and named it after their word for dry, *azalea*. Technically, azaleas are not different from rhododendrons, but they are kept distinct from that genus by gardeners.

Aztec two-step. More commonly known as *Montezuma's revenge*, a term recorded much earlier, the *Aztec two-step* is a humorous designation for diarrhea, usually diarrhea suffered by travelers in Mexico, and refers, of course, to the ancient Aztecs of Mexico. The term is first recorded as the title of a book in 1953 but is probably older.

B

B. Our Capital *B* can be traced back to the Phoenician alphabet; the lower-case *b* derived from the cursive form of the capital. *B* was called *Beth*, "a house," in Hebrew.

baaad. *Bad*, when slowly pronounced *baaad*, has long been black slang for something or someone good, and recently this meaning has come into general usage to a limited extent. The variation is so old that it is found in the American Creole language Gullah three centuries ago, when *baaad* was used by slaves as an expression of admiration for another slave who successfully flaunted "Ole Massa's" rules.

babbitt. Congress deemed the invention of babbitt or babbitt metal so important to the development of the industrial age that it awarded inventor Isaac Babbitt (1799–1862) a $20,000 grant. Babbitt is a soft, silver-white alloy of copper, tin, and antimony used to reduce friction in machine bearings. It was discovered as a result of the inventor's experiments in turning out the first Britannia metal tableware ever produced in America. After the Taunton, Massachusetts goldsmith successfully manufactured Britannia in 1824, he experimented further with the same three metals and ultimately invented babbitt, which he used to line a patented journal box in 1839. The metal proved far better than any other substance used for reducing friction and is still widely used for machine bearings today. *Babbitt soap*, no longer marketed, also bore the inventor's name. Babbitt wasn't the prototype for Sinclair Lewis's ambitious, uncultured, and smugly satisfied American businessman in his novel of the same name, but the character's name was probably suggested by Lewis's early memories of advertisements for the soap.

babble; babel. *Babel*, for a confused turbulent medley of sounds ("a babel of sounds"), or a scene of utter confusion, takes its name from the biblical city of Babel described in Genesis, where as punishment for the people's attempt to build a tower to reach heaven itself, God confused their speech and, where there was previously one universal language, created the many tongues that we know today. *Babel* comes to us from the ancient Assyrian *bab-ili*, "gate of the gods." *Babel* and Babylon are the same city, the latter word passing to us from the Greek *Babulon*. Babylon stands for any corrupt, luxury-loving place of riotous living, owing much of its reputation to the Babylon of the Revelation of St. John the Divine—"Babylon the Great, the Mother of Harlots and Abominations of the Earth." In days past, and in rare instances today, Protestants have called Rome, seat of the Catholic church, "the Woman of Babylon." *Babel* is of no relation to *babble*, a word probably suggested by the sounds made by infants, though the *O.E.D.* says that *babble*'s association with *babel* may have affected some of the former word's meaning. Babel can be pronounced baybel or babble, the latter usually the American pronunciation. One time British playwright Noël Coward corrected singer Elaine Stritch on her pronunciation of the word. "It's bayble, Stritch," he advised. "I've always said babble," she countered. "Everyone says babble. It means mixed-up language, doesn't it? Gibberish. It's where we get babble from." "That's a fabble," Coward said.

Babcock test. Though not as famous as Pasteur, the agricultural chemist Stephen Moulton Babcock played an important role in the development of the modern dairy industry. While chief chemist at the Wisconsin Agricultural Experiment Station in 1890, Babcock invented a process for determining the butterfat content of milk. The Babcock test makes possible rapid, accurate milk grading and helps farmers develop better dairy herds by enabling them to test milk from their stock. Babcock taught for 25 years at the University of Wisconsin, from 1887 to 1913. He died in 1931, at age 88, having spent the last 20 years of his life researching the nature of matter.

babe; baby. *Babe* was once the standard English word for child, deriving from the Middle English *baban*, an imitative nursery word in origin—that is, similar to the cries of an infant. Infant sounds also give us "mamma" and "poppa" and the Latin *mamma*, breast, from which all we mammals take our name. *Baby* is just a diminutive of *babe* and was once used as a word for doll. *Baby* as a term of endearment for a sweetheart, male or female, doesn't seem to go back further than 1901 in America, though it may have arisen a little earlier in fast English sporting circles, and *baby* for a tough guy ("That baby packed some punch") dates back only to the Roaring Twenties. The most famous example of *Babe* as a pet name for a boy is baseball great BABE (George Herman) RUTH (1895–1948). The nickname is often used in the South as a familiar name for a boy or man, especially the youngest of a family. *Babe* as a term for a woman (often an attractive woman) is an Americanism first recorded in 1905. *See* BAMBINO.

babe in the woods.   The old ballad "Children in the Wood" (1595), gives us the still-common expression *a babe in the woods*, for someone easily gulled because he is simple and trustful, inexperienced in life or some aspect of life. The ballad probably predates a tragedy by Robert Harrington on the same theme that was written in about 1601. Both play and ballad tell the story of two children left by their dying father to the care of his wife's brother. The brother, wanting their inheritance, hires two men to kill the children, but one of them repents and kills his companion, abandoning the children in the wood, where they die. The wicked uncle is arrested and dies in jail and the hired killer is sentenced to death. The ballad was vastly popular, and no doubt became a nursery story, too.

Babel.   *See* BABBLE.

babe of love.   *See* LOVE CHILD.

Babe Ruth.   George Herman Ruth wasn't the first athlete to be called Babe, but he is certainly the most famous to bear the name, which was bestowed upon him in 1914 by a Baltimore Orioles coach, who shouted, "Here's Jack's new Babe!" when Ruth (signed by Baltimore owner Jack Dunn) first entered the ballpark. Over his long career, Ruth earned many other nicknames—including *Jidge, Monk, Monkey*, and the *King of Swat*—but history will always remember him as *the Babe*. A variation on this is *Bambino*, the Italian for "baby," which for centuries has meant an image of the infant Jesus in swaddling clothes. No sports records are better known than the legendary *Sultan of Swat's* 60 home runs in one season and 714 throughout his career (though both records have been surpassed), and his "call" of a home run in the 1932 World Series is on every list of "most memorable sports events." There seems no reason to doubt that when all his records are broken, Babe Ruth will still be more famous than those who broke them. Ruth (1895–1948), the poor boy brought up in an orphanage who became the most renowned American athlete of all time, is one of the few people ever to become a folk hero while still alive (Joe Louis is another). Some of the stories about the Bambino bear repeating. For example, he began his baseball career as a catcher for St. Mary's School in Baltimore. He was an outstanding pitcher in the major leagues before switching to the outfield. He led the major leagues in strikeouts in 1923 with 93, being a strikeout king as well as home run king. He once hit a home run that literally went around the world, the ball landing in a freight car that was transported to a ship. And one could go on for pages from memory alone. The New York Yankees star, the Homer of Home Runs, has never been equaled for talent or color. His name will remain a synonym for the ultimate in sluggers even after someone else has hit 120 homers. *See* SULTAN OF SWAT; JOE LOUIS.

babushka.   One of the few Russian words widely used in English, *babushka*, for a woman's scarf, derives from the Russian *baba*, "village woman," plus the diminutive suffix *ushka*—because scarves have long been worn hoodlike by old women in Russia.

baby boom.   According to *New York Times* columnist William Safire, *baby boom*, the sharp increase in the birth rate after World War II, hasn't been traced back further than 1953, when it appeared in a report to President Truman by the Commissioner on Immigration and Naturalization. Attorney Harry Rosenfield wrote the report, but he doesn't claim to have coined the expression. *See* BOOMER.

baby-kisser.   Politicians have been baby-kissing since the first election, but the term doesn't seem to have been used before the U.S. presidential election of 1884. The words were applied to Benjamin Butler, who ran on the independent Greenback-Labor ticket and came in a poor third behind Democrat Grover Cleveland and Republican James Blaine. "As a baby-kisser," a contemporary newspaper observed, "Ben Butler is not a success." One theory has it that the idea for the term appears in the Eatanswill election episode of Dickens's *Pickwick Papers* (1837), although *baby-kisser* doesn't appear there.

Babylon of the West.   An old name for bloody Dodge City, Kansas, a town famous or infamous in the last half of the 19th century for its gunfights, saloons, and "soiled doves" and "Calico Queens" like Molly-be-damned and Cotton Tail. Some historians hold that the first RED LIGHT DISTRICT called by that name was located in Dodge.

Baby Ruth.   The popular candy bar was probably named after BABE RUTH in 1921, when Ruth was already a legendary star. Soon after, Ruth challenged the naming, trying unsuccessfully to patent his own *Babe Ruth Home Run Bar*, and the candymaker then claimed its *Baby Ruth* had been named after President Grover Cleveland's daughter Ruth, widely called Baby Ruth. Since Baby Ruth had died in 1904, 17 years before the candy bar was marketed, such a naming seems highly unlikely. The Baby Ruth candy bar probably was named for Babe Ruth, even though the candymaker doesn't support the story anymore. Ira Berkow's "A Babe Ruth Myth . . ." (*New York Times* 4/7/02) tells the story in greater detail.

baby-sitter.   *Baby-sitter* offers a good example of what is called back-formation of a word. Usually nouns derive from verbs, as *diver* derived from *dive*. In the case of *baby-sitter*, however, this process was reversed. *Baby-sitter* is an Americanism first recorded in 1937, while the verb to *baby-sit* was born from it over 10 years later. The noun has come to mean one who takes care of children or anything else that requires attention.

Baby State.   A nickname for Arizona because it was long the youngest state in the Union, admitted in 1912. It is also known as the Valentine State (it was admitted on St. Valentine's Day), the Grand Canyon State, the Sunset State, the Sandhill State, the Coyote State, and the Apache State.

Bacchus.   *See* APHRODISIAC.

bachelor. It wasn't until relatively recent times that the word *bachelor* was used exclusively for unmarried males. In the past the word was applied without distinction of sex, Ben Jonson using it to mean an unmarried woman in his play *The Magnetic Lady* (1632). *Bachelor* derives ultimately from the medieval Latin *baccalaris*, which became the Old French *bacheler*.

bachelor's buttons. In his *Herbal*, Gerard wrote that "The similitude these flowers have to the jagged cloath buttons anciently worne . . . gave occasion . . . to call them Bachelor's Buttons." But *bachelor's buttons*, a name now applied mainly to *Centaurea cyanus*, or the common cornflower, but also to the red campion, the upright crowfoot, and the white ranunculus, may take their name from the old custom of bachelors carrying the flower in their pockets to determine how they stood with their sweethearts. If the flowers stayed fresh in the pocket, it was a good omen; if they shriveled up "she loves me not." Other colorful names for the cornflower include blue-bottle, blue bonnets, and ragged sailor.

bacitracin. This antibiotic used to treat bacterial skin infections takes its unusual name from *baci*(llus) plus the first four letters of the last name of Margaret *Tracy* (b. 1936), a child in whose tissues *Bacillus subtilis* was found.

back and fill. Hardly any progress is made when you back and fill a sailing ship; that is, when you are tacking the craft while the tide is running with her and the wind is against her. The sails are alternately backed and filled and the ship seems to remain in roughly the same place, going back and then forward. The term was a natural for sailors, and then landlubbers, to apply to any vacillating or irresolute action—to HEM AND HAW.

back-answer. To talk back. Mainly an Irish expression, as in "Don't you back-answer me or you'll get the back of me hand," but it is heard in England as well.

Back Bay. The Back Bay area has been since the mid-19th century a fashionable residential district in Boston, Massachusetts. So much so, in fact, that *Back Bay* has been synonymous almost as long for the culture of Boston.

backbite. This expression was formed from the noun *back* and the verb *bite*, almost certainly as an obvious description of someone slandering another person in his absence, or behind his back. An old chestnut connects the words with the medieval "sport" of bearbaiting, where the bear was fastened to a post by a short chain, some of the dogs that fought him holding him at bay face to face while others attacked him from the back. There are no known old quotations to support this theory, the oldest one recorded (1175) referring to "Cursunge [cursing] backbitunge [backbiting] and fikelunge [deceit]." There is a legend that Diogenes, when asked what beasts "bit sorest," answered: "Of wilde beasts, the Back-biter; of tame, the Flatterer." Wrote Tennyson of the secret calumniator, "Face-flatterers and back-biters are the same."

back east. A term used by westerners referring to the eastern United States; *east* in the expression means anywhere east of the Mississippi River or in the general direction of the East coast. Easterners, in turn, say *out west* in referring to the western U.S.

backfin. The choicest prime crabmeat from the blue crab (*Callinectes sapidus*) comes from the rear or back bony chambers of that esteemed creature. The meat is called *backfin* because it is found in that location near the crab's fins, *not* because the crabmeat comes from the fin, which contains little or no meat at all. The expression dates back over a century and is still common among people who know their crabmeat.

backgammon. Backgammon takes its name from the early English *gamen*, "game," the *back* in the word reflecting the strategy in the game of "sending back" pieces to the board. The game, closely related to checkers, is far older than its English name. "Back game," or backgammon, dates back thousands of years; in fact, a handsomely crafted backgammon board was found in the 5,000-year-old tomb of Babylonian queen Shub-ad.

backhand. One of the oldest technical sports terms, *backhand* for a tennis stroke can be traced to the early 18th century, when Sir John Van Brugh recorded it in his play *The Mistake* (1706). The English playwright used the term figuratively, but there seems no doubt that he borrowed it from the tennis court. One hopes that Van Brugh, also the architect of massive Blenheim Palace, wasn't criticized for his backhand as he was for his buildings. A contemporary mock epitaph of him went:

> Lie heavy on him, O Earth!, for he
> Laid many heavy loads on thee!

backseat driver; backseat necker. Automobiles have introduced many general terms into the language. "Step on the gas," "detour," "hitchhiker," "hit-and-run," "streamlined," and "joyride" are only a few of the automobile expressions that are now widely applied. *Backseat driver*, describing species *Autokibitzer accidentus*, an indomitable breed that does more harm than good on the road (and often occupies the *front* seat next to the driver) has considerably weakened the meaning of "to take a back seat"—that is, to be humble, to take an inconspicuous position in the background. The newer expression, coined in the 1920s, applies to all those who have pinned humility to the mat for their lifetime, particularly critics of the incumbent administration in politics. *Backseat necking*, making love in the backseat of a car, dates to 1922, and "necker's knob," the suicide knob on a car's steering wheel that allows for one-armed driving, was first recorded in the early 1940s.

backslider. Someone who converted to a religion or cause when things were going bad and rarely or never practices it again once times have improved is called a *backslider*. In *Night Comes to the Cumberlands* (1962), Harry M. Caudell tells of a man reporting on the health of a relative he had taken in: "He's a lot better than he was. In fact, he's about well enough to backslide." The word, first recorded in the early 16th century, can also mean to relapse into bad habits or undesireable activities.

back the wrong horse. When we support the wrong person, party or thing, or bet on the loser in any situation, we back the wrong horse. The term is an Americanism taken from the racetrack, and is still widely used although it is a century or more old.

back to square one.   This phrase means to "start all over again" or to "go back to the beginning" of a problem or project in an attempt to solve it. An expression of frustration, it was probably suggested by players of the various board games in which a playing piece is moved off the first square after the drawing of a card or the throw of the dice.

back to the salt mines!   Back to work, especially dreary, unrewarding work, "slave labor." This catch phrase may be several hundred years old. It originated in Russia, where people have been punished for centuries by banishment to Siberia and compulsory labor in the salt mines there. The phrase is, however, first recorded in an 1890s play about Russian exiles in Siberia.

back water.   When a steamboat's paddle wheel is reversed it is said to *back water*, or move backward. The expression came into use with the rise of the steamboat in the early 1800s and was soon being used figuratively to mean "to reverse one's position on a subject, withdraw from a situation, or retract a statement."

bacteria.   *Bacteria* means little sticks, from the Greek *bakterion*, the diminutive of *baktron*, staff or stick, because the first bacteria observed by scientists (in about 1847) looked like little sticks under the microscope.

bad.   Most major dictionaries, including the *O.E.D.*, hold that *bad* derives from the Middle English *badde*, meaning the same, which, in turn, most probably derived as a back formation (altering a word by dropping rear syllables, *e.g.*, "zoo" from "zoological garden") from the Old English *baeddel*, "hermaphrodite," and *baeddling*, "effeminate man" or "sodomite." This would explain why there aren't many early written examples of the word, which is first recorded circa 1300 ("good" is recorded circa 800, with many early examples). By that time *bad* had almost entirely lost its sexual connotation, but it still retains the sense of "evil misbehavior" that was then the dominant attitude about homosexuality—though *bad* of course means many things today, including "of poor quality," "invalid," "spoiled or rotten," "dejected" (feeling bad), and even (in black slang) "good" (especially in the sense of very stylish or sharp). *See* GOOD; BAAAD.

bad ball hitter.   A term of recent vintage, a *bad ball hitter* describes someone who makes bad judgments or evaluations. The Americanism refers to a batter in baseball who often swings at pitches that are not strikes and usually misses. There is no similar term in cricket or tennis. It should be noted that many batters have hit so-called bad-ball pitches for home runs, including career home run record-holder Hank Aaron, who frequently did so.

bad cess to you.   Many of us on hearing the Irish expression *bad cess to you* have assumed that the *cess* in the term is a corruption of the word success. This, however, isn't the case. The expression originated in Ireland, where *cess* meant an

assessment or land tax. The words thus mean "May your taxes be raised."

bad egg; good egg.   Shakespeare used the word *egg* to contemptuously describe a young person in *Macbeth*, when the murderers of Macduff's son cry, "What you egg! Young fry of treachery!" But the expression *bad egg* for a disreputable, thoroughly rotten person doesn't seem to have been coined until the mid-18th century in America, no matter how obvious the analogy might seem. "American criminal Thomas Egg" isn't in any way responsible for the expression; it derives from just the odor of a bad egg itself. *Good egg*, for a "nice guy," came along about 50 years later, probably originating as Oxford University slang.

badger; badger game.   Badger baiting consisted of putting a badger in a barrel or hole and setting dogs on him to "worry him out"; the cruel process was repeated several times until the animal died. The ancient "sport" gave us the phrase *to badger*, to worry or tease, even though the dogs, not the badger, did the badgering. Centuries later *badger* was applied to the *badger game* by American confidence men and women. Commonly the woman member of the team in this con game pretends to fall for her victim and goes to bed with him. While they are having sex, the male member of the team surprises them, playing the part of the outraged husband. The victim is badgered by the "husband," who finally agrees to accept money as compensation for the wrong done him. It is sometimes months before the victim realizes he is being black-mailed, and even then he often keeps on making payments to avoid publicity. Figuratively, the expression *badger game* is used to indicate any deception for personal or political gain.

Badger State.   A nickname for Wisconsin, after pioneers in the state who lived in hillside caves resembling badger burrows and who were called badgers.

bad hair day.   A term that originated in the United States for a day on which it is hard to do anything with one's hair, male or female. The expression dates back to about 1990 and by extension came to mean a day on which nothing seems to go right.

badlands.   A barren, severely eroded region in southwest South Dakota and northwest Nebraska. According to the *Century Magazine* (1882, XXIV), "The term Bad Lands does not apply to the quality of the soil. The Indian name was accurately rendered by the early French voyageurs as *mauvaises terres pour traverser*—'bad lands to cross.' The ground between the buttes is fertile, and the whole region is in excellent cattlerange, the rock formation affording the best possible winter protection." Badlands National Park is in South Dakota.

bad man; badman.   A mainly historical term for an outlaw or professional gunfighter who had killed people. Many were brutes, bullies, and psychopaths, but several who carried the title were men who had killed others in arguments or in self-defense. In *The Great American Outlaw* (1993), Frank Richard Prassel has this to say about the compound word *badman*, as opposed to *bad man*: "Indirectly [John] Wayne gave popular language the very word. His film *The Angel and the Badman*

(1946) fixed the compound in vernacular English with a contradictory meaning. A badman is not necessarily bad; *goodman* has no meaning. Films issued before 1946 consistently divided the term; those made later routinely adopted the compound. For the original it was of no significance; whenever John Wayne played a badman, as he did with some frequency, something was clearly wrong with the law. His mere appearance in the role of a criminal made justification for illegality pointless; it could be assumed."

bad medicine. Among American Indians, bad medicine meant a person's bad luck, his spirits working against him. Cowboys used the term *bad medicine* to describe any very dangerous person, such as a feared gunfighter. *See* MEDICINE.

badminton. The racket game, really the Indian game of *poona* adopted by the British, is named for the eighth Duke of Beaufort's estate, Badminton, in Gloucestershire, where it was introduced in 1783.

badmouth. To speak ill of someone. Probably originating among African-American speakers and possibly deriving from a Vai or Mandingo expression, *to badmouth* was at first employed mostly by southern blacks but is now used nationwide. Its first recorded use in this sense came in 1941 when James Thurber used it in a *Saturday Evening Post* story: "He badmouthed everybody."

the bad place. Hell. Wrote Erskine Caldwell in *Georgia Boy* (1943): "I thought when I come to that I was in the bad place. I sure thought I had been knocked all the way down to there."

bad spot (place) in the road. A very small, seedy town or group of houses, so small it can hardly be considered a town. Usually a road or a highway winds by it. The expression seems to date back to the 1930s.

Baedeker; Fielding guide. A *Baedeker* once referred to a specific guidebook published by the German printer and bookseller Karl Baedeker (1801–59), but the word is now used loosely to mean any travel guide. Baedeker's guides were so authoritative and comprehensive that they were eventually printed in numerous languages and became almost a necessity for travelers of the time. Similar to the contemporary Fielding guides, named for travel writer Temple Hornaday Fielding (b. 1914), the books covered every aspect of travel, from historic questions to cuisine, and started the practice of rating places with one to four stars. *Baedeker* became synonymous for an exhaustive guide, the word adopted in many countries.

bafflegab. *See* GOBBLEDYGOOK.

bagasse. Crushed sugarcane or the beet refuse from sugarmaking that is used as animal feed. The word was borrowed from the Spanish word *bagazo*, meaning the same.

Bagdad on the Hudson. *See* HYPOGLYCEMIA.

bagel; bialy. "Bagels, BEGORRAH!" Macy's bakery once advertised on St. Patrick's Day in our word-rich land. *Bagel* derives from the Middle High German *bouc*, "bracelet," which became the Yiddish *beggel*—the *bagel*, of course, resembling a bracelet in shape. The roll topped with onion flakes called a bialy (plural bialys, not bialies) takes its name from Bialystok, Poland, where it was first made. Bialystok, played by Zero Mostel in *The Producers*, is one of the great comic characters in movie history.

bag lady; old bag; bag. Short for "shopping bag lady," *bag lady* entered the language in the 1960s. It has nothing to do with the term *old bag*, for an ugly woman (which goes back to the 1920s), or BAGMAN, a term for someone (often a policeman) assigned to collect bribe or extortion money, an expression also dating back to the flapper age. *Bag* has many meanings in American slang, including "to be sacked (bagged) from a job"; "a prostitute" (from douche bags being associated with prostitutes); "a condom"; "to arrest"; "a base in baseball"; and "to be drunk" (to have a bag on). But *bag* here refers to the shopping bags, filled with their possessions, that the unfortunate women we call bag ladies carry with them as they wander—from doorway to alley to abandoned car to park bench—through American cities. The *lady* in their name is both ironic and kind.

bagman. In America *bagman* means a racketeer or anyone assigned to collect a bribe, extortion, or kidnapping money. In England, however, a bagman is simply a traveling salesman, a drummer who carries bags of samples. "In former times," one authority tells us, "these commercial travelers used to ride a horse with saddle bags sometimes so large as almost to conceal the rider."

bagnio. A brothel, the word deriving from the Latin for bath. Originally, a *bagnio* was a bath or bathhouse, especially one with hot baths. However, to quote British author Thomas Wright's *A History of Domestic Manners and Sentiments in England During the Middle Ages* (1862), the bathhouses "were soon used to such an extent for illicit intrigues, that the name of a hothouse or bagnio became equivalent to that of a brothel."

bah!; bashful; abeyance, etc. *Bah!* is an interjection indicating scorn, contempt, or disgust, but "ba!" is a natural expression of surprise in any language, a sound uttered by both sheep and men when the jaw drops down. It forms the basis for a number of English words. *Bashful* and *abash* come to us from the French *esbaiss*, which derives from the Latin *ex* plus *ba! Abeyance*, a state of temporary suspension or inactivity, derives from the Latin *badare*, which developed from the elementary sound "ba!" and meant to hold the mouth wide open, to gape—someone "held in abeyance" would stand, jaw dropped, waiting for a decision. The "baying" of hounds, from the Old French *beer* (later *bayer*), to gape, is also related to "ba!", the exclamation of surprise becoming the sound of impatience here.

Bahaism. Bahaism is an Iranian religion with an Oriental mystical quality that specifically reflects the attitudes of the Islamic Shiah sect, emphasizing religious tolerance. Founded by a Shirez merchant who was executed for heresy in 1850, the religion was named for its founder's leading disciple, known as Baha Allah, who gave it a worldwide following. Baha Allah, in turn, means "splendor of God" in Persian. The Bahais have been persecuted in Iran since the fundamentalists took power in 1979.

bah-fong-goo. An Italian slang term popularized by Mario Puzo's *The Godfather* (1969), this curse meaning "fuck you" is often accompanied by the common hand-chopping-the-elbow-joint motion meaning the same. According to the *Random House Dictionary of American Slang*, the curse derives from the Italian *affanculo*, "I fuck you up the ass." *Fungoo* and *boff-on-gool* mean the same.

bahuvrihi. *Heavy-handed* and *redcoat* are examples of this grammatical term first recorded in about 1850. The first half of these compound words is an adjective describing the noun coming after it. The term comes from Sanskrit, the ancient Indo-European language of India. In Sanskrit *bahu* means "much," and *vrihi* means "rice," *bahuvrihi* meaning "much-rice." Thus, one of the examples of the term is also the name of the term.

Bailey bridge. Portable Bailey bridges designed to replace bridges destroyed by retreating forces and to carry much heavier loads than military bridges could previously support, were to a large extent responsible for the Allied victory in World War II, particularly in northwestern Europe. They were invented by Sir Donald Coleman Bailey, an engineer with the British Ministry of Supply, who was knighted in 1945 for his contribution to the war effort. The versatile truss bridges were first used in 1941 and are still employed throughout the world in flood and disaster areas. They consist of some 29 different parts, but are made principally of 10-foot-long, 5-foot-wide prefabricated lattice-steel panels weighing 600 pounds each that are held together by steel pins. Bailey first sketched his bridge on the back of an envelope and he always claimed that his invention was "just part of the job." Field Marshal Montgomery, on the other hand, said, "Without the Bailey bridge we should not have won the war." Bailey died in 1985, at age 83.

bailiff; bailiff wand. Someone authorized to perform legal actions, such as a sheriff's deputy who carries out arrests. The word dates back to at least 1297 in England and derives from the Latin *bajulus*, carrier or manager. English bailiffs have even arrested dead people. When British playwright and politician Richard Brinsley Sheridan died penniless in 1816, a well-dressed man at the wake touched Sheridan on the forehead with his *bailiff's wand* and declared that he was arresting him in the name of the king for a debt of £500. Since the corpse was arrested, the funeral and burial could not go on until Sheridan's friends pulled out their purses and paid the man. *See* BAILIWICK.

bailiwick. The district within which a *bailie* or BAILIFF has jurisdiction. The word has also come to mean a person's best area of skill or authority, as in "I'm not going to interfere—it's your bailiwick."

bait tree. The quick-growing catalpa *(Catalpa bignonioides)* is called the bait tree because its branches provide homes to many caterpillars that can be used as fish bait. It is also known as the Indian bean, bean tree, cigar tree, and smoking bean tree, due to its long pods. *Catalpa* is a North American Indian name for the tree.

baked alaska. Consisting of ice cream mounded on a cake base placed briefly in a hot oven to brown its blanket of meringue, baked alaska is among the most posh of desserts. It was created and named at New York's Delmonico's restaurant in 1876 in honor of the newly purchased Alaskan territory. An informant advises that a blow torch is now commonly used to make it. As my informant notes—nouvelle cuisine indeed!

Bakelite. Employed chiefly as an electric insulator, Bakelite has numerous industrial uses, including the manufacture of phonograph records, machinery, and even buttons, pipe stems, and billiard balls. A heat-resistant, synthetic resin or plastic, valuable as a nonconductor of electricity, it is prepared by the chemical interaction of phenolic substances and aldehydes. Bakelite was invented by Leo Hendrik Baekeland (1863–1944), a Flemish chemistry teacher who migrated to the United States from Ghent, Belgium in 1889. Seven years later he announced the invention of Bakelite, a registered name used by the company.

baker's dozen. Bakers in ancient times were subject to severe penalties for shortweighting their customers; in ancient Egypt, for example, they were sometimes nailed by the ear to the doors of their shops when caught selling light loaves. Thus when the English Parliament passed a law in 1266 subjecting the Company of White Bakers and the Company of Brown Bakers to strict regulations regarding bread weight, the bakers made sure that they complied. Since it was difficult to make loaves of a uniform weight at the time, bakers customarily added a thirteenth loaf, the "in-bread" or "vantage loaf," to each shipment of 12 they sent to a shopkeeper or retailer, thus guaranteeing that there would be no shortchanging or ear-nailing. Most authorities believe this led to the expression *baker's dozen* for 13.

baksheesh. *Baksheesh* is Persian for a tip or present. But the insolent persistent demands of beggars, servants, and officials in the Near East over the years have made baksheesh seem more a claim or demand upon a traveler than a gratuity in many cases, giving the word an unsavory connotation.

balbriggans. Men's white cotton socks are called balbriggans, after Balbriggan, Ireland, a Dublin suburb, where the fabric they are made of was first manufactured in the 19th century.

bald. Bald seems to derive from the Welsh *bal*, white-browed, a white streak or blaze on the brow, but there is some confusion about the word's origins. In any case, the term came to be used of someone partially bald or completely so, like Charles the Bald (823–77), Holy Roman emperor, and other rulers. According to legend, another bald man, the Greek playwright Aeschylus, was killed when an eagle dropped a tortoise on his head, mistaking it for a rock on which it could break open its evening meal.

bald; Old Baldy. A bare mountain top without any trees or vegetation or such a peak sparsely covered with vegetation is called a *bald*. These *balds* are also called *slicks*, both words first recorded in the 1830s. Mountaintops covered with snow have since at least the early 1860s been called *Old Baldy* or *Baldy*.

bald as a coot. Totally or severely bald. The common waterfowl called the coot (of the genus *Fulica*) has a white bill and front shield, which make it appear bald. *See* CRAZY AS A COOT.

bald eagle. This American eagle is so named because the feathers on the head of the adult are white, making it appear bald when seen from a distance. Said to be the most pictured bird in the world, the bald eagle appears on the Great Seal of the United States and on many U.S. coins and paper currency. There was some controversy over its choice for the great seal by the Second Continental Congress because it commonly steals fish from other hawks, but its majestic presence prevailed. It has also been called the bird of freedom, bird of Washington, calumet eagle, gray eagle, brown eagle, nun's eagle, white-headed eagle, and national bird.

balderdash. Nonsense, a senseless jumble of words or ideas. *Balderdash* is still another word for which no one knows the origin. First recorded in the late 16th century, it meant a light frothy liquid, then came to mean incongruous liquids, such as beer and milk mixed together, and finally took its modern meaning. The Danish *balder*, "noise, clatter," has been suggested as its parent, but this derivation is doubtful at best.

bald-headed. An expression used for a hurried action taken without caution or much thinking: "He really went at it bald-headed." As Maximilian Schele de Vere put it in *Americanisms* (1871), the expression probably derives from "the eagerness with which men rush to do a thing without covering the head."

Baldwin. In 1800 Colonel Loammi Baldwin (1740–1807) of Wilmington, Massachusetts, found the seedling that was developed into the much-grown winter apple tree and the fruit that bear his name. He was more noted in his time as a civil enginer and canal builder.

baleboss. This Yiddish expression has no etymological connection with the English word *boss*. To be called a *baleboss* (pronounced bahl-eh-BOHSS) is indeed a compliment, but the term has several meanings. A baleboss, the word deriving from the Hebrew *baal*, "master," and *bayis* "house," can be the head of the household, the owner of a business establishment of any kind, or anyone who assumes authority. A female baleboss is a *baleboosteh*, and she can be the same things as a baleboss, or be the wife of a baleboss, or be an excellent homemaker.

Balfour Declaration. *See* BOB'S YOUR UNCLE.

balk. A balk, deriving from the Old English *balca*, was a ridge between two furrows made in ploughing. Since the balk was an obstacle, the word *balk* came to be applied figuratively to any obstacle, and *to balk* came to mean "to place obstacles in the way of." The baseball term *balk*, an illegal movement by a pitcher when runners are on base, comes from an obsolete meaning of *balk:* "to miss, slip, or fail."

ballast. Ballast, loaded in the belly of a ship to help keep it right side up, probably has its ancestor in a Teutonic word meaning "belly load," but no one is sure, though the word has been used for centuries. Everything from rocks to gold bars has been used for ballast. After unloading its emergency cargo at Corregidor in the Philippines in February 1941, at the beginning of World War II, the submarine U.S.S. *Trout* took on the most valuable ballast in the history of shipping. No other ballast was available, and the *Trout* traveled back to San Francisco loaded with Philippine government gold bars valued at over $9 million at the time.

ballast for his (her) balloon. Apparently, Mrs. Bronson Alcott coined this term for a person who is a down-to-earth or steadying influence on another. Mrs. Alcott did all her life follow wherever her utopian husband led. At least so their daughter Louisa May Alcott claimed in her essay "Transcendental Wild Oats" (1876).

balled up; balls. Dashing through the snow on a horsedrawn sled could be hazardous in days past. One difficulty was the balls of snow or ice that formed in the curve of a horse's shoe and often made a horse slip and fall. When horses did fall, especially a team of them, the resulting confusion and entanglement gave rise to the expression *all balled up*. That is *almost* everybody traces this term for helpless confusion to floundering horses. Mencken suggests a connection with the ejaculation *balls!* (1890), one for which little proof can be found. A second alternative linking the expression to balls of knitting yarn that the cat got at is a possibility, too. *Balls* has been American slang for testicles since the early 1880s, and slang for guts or courage since about 1935.

ballot. In days past, people voted by dropping little balls, or ballots, (from the Italian *ballotta*) into a box or other receptacle. In this ancient method of voting, still used in some clubs today, a white ball signified an affirmative vote and a black ball a negative one. By the 19th century paper was being widely used in place of these balls, but the new form retained the old name.

ballpark figure. An approximation based on an educated guess or a reasonable estimate is a ballpark figure. Only about 25 years old, the American expression obviously comes from baseball, *ballparks* being another name for the stadiums where baseball is played. The phrase probably derives from the 1962 coinage of *in the ballpark* for "something that is within bounds, negotiable, not out of reach"; *out of the ballpark* means just the opposite. Baseball stadiums were first called ballparks around 1900; before then they had been called ball grounds, baseball grounds, ball fields and baseball parks.

ball the jack. To move or work swiftly. Originally an American railroad term ("That train is sure balling the jack.") of the 19th century, *ball the jack* came to mean "to move or work swiftly," as in "When he saw his boss coming he really balled the jack."

ballyhoo. The little village of Ballyhooly in County Cork, Ireland once had a reputation for loudmouthed, violent street debates. "The residents engage in most strenuous debate," the *Congressional Record* of March 1934 advises, "a debate that is without equal in the annals of parliamentary, or ordinary discussion, and from the violence of these debates has sprung forth a word known in the English language as *ballyhoo*." However, this is but part of the possible truth. Ballyhooly did have a reputation for violent arguments that drew crowds, but today *ballyhoo* denotes something far from violent, being glib advertising or the spiel of a carnival barker. Possibly the residents of Ballyhooly, noted for their blarney as well as their violent arguments, lent their village's name to a popular British music-hall song of 1885 that used the refrain *bloody hooly truth* as a phrase for "the whole bloody truth." *Bloodyhooly*, in turn, was later applied to the spiels of carnival barkers and acquired its present meaning.

balm. *See* NO BALM IN GILEAD.

balmy. *Balmy*, in its sense of silly, foolish, eccentric, is the Americanized version of the British *barmy*, and may derive from the name of St. Bartholomew, patron saint of the feebleminded. Most etymologists, however, trace the word to the Old English *barm*, the froth on fermenting beer, which could indeed make one act balmy. Still another theory is that the word derives from the Barming lunatic asylum at Kent in England, meaning that a barmy or balmy person is "one fit only for Barming." This overlooks the fact that the *Oxford English Dictionary* gives the first use of *barmy* as 1535, whereas Barming was established in the early 19th century, but it may be that the popularity of the word was enhanced by the asylum.

baloney. *See* BOLONEY.

balsa rafts. Spanish sailors off South America in the 16th century gave the name *balsa*, meaning "float," to the rafts lashed together with vines that the natives used. They later applied the same name to the tree logs, half the weight of cork, that made the rafts so buoyant. That the rafts make even better boats than the Spaniards expected was demonstrated by Thor Heyerdahl centuries later, when he sailed from South America to Polynesia on a balsa raft.

Baltic Sea. This body of water is named for either the Lithuanian *baltas*, "white," or from the Scandinavian *balta*, "strait." Thus, no one knows for sure whether the Baltic means "the white sea," or "the sea of straits."

Baltimore; Baltimore oriole; Baltimore clipper. An early dictionary tells us that the Baltimore oriole is "so called from the colors of Or (orange) and Sable in the coat of arms belonging to Lord Baltimore." This oriole is not closely related to the orioles of Europe, belonging to the blackbird or meadowlark rather than the crow family. In fact, many American birds with the same names as European species are in reality birds of a different feather. (The American robin, for instance, is really a thrush, and other Old World avian words given new significances include partridge, blackbird, lark, and swallow.) But whatever its true species, the Baltimore oriole definitely takes its name from the Baltimore family, founders of Maryland, the bright colors of the male bird indeed corresponding to the orange and black in their heraldic arms. The city of Baltimore, Maryland also honors the barons Baltimore, as do the early 19th-century Baltimore clippers, more indirectly, the famous ships having been built in the city. The same can be said of baseball's Baltimore Orioles and football's Baltimore Colts. No particular Lord Baltimore has been singled out for the honor. George Calvert, the first baron Baltimore (ca. 1590–1632), prepared the charter for the proposed colony that became Maryland, but died before it could be accepted; the charter

was granted to his son Cecilius, but the second baron Baltimore never even visited the province; and the third baron Baltimore, Cecilius's son Charles, governed the province from 1661 to 1684. A Catholic who ruled quite arbitrarily over his predominantly Protestant subjects, Charles returned to England and never came back, leaving little more than the family name behind.

Baltimore Ravens. Would you believe this football team is named after a poem? It is. The *Baltimore Ravens* honors Edgar Allan Poe's "The Raven," one of the most famous poems in American history, which Poe wrote in 1844 and sold to the *New York Mirror* for 35 bucks. Poe was intimately connected with Baltimore, where he spent his last weeks on earth, dying four days after he'd been found delirious outside a saloon-polling place where he may have been casting ballots for drinks. Few remember that Poe was also an accomplished athlete, possibly the greatest author-athlete in American literary history. He once swam seven and a half miles from Richmond to Warwick, Virginia, against a tide running 2–3 miles an hour. He long-jumped 21 feet while at West Point and was a swift runner. Fully six members of Princeton University's 1899 football team were named Poe, each of them a great-nephew of Edgar Allan Poe. To further honor the writer, the Ravens have named their three mascot ravens *Edgar*, *Allan*, and *Poe*. *See* EDGAR; PRINCETON.

Baltimore Whore. A humorous name given to the B-26 Marauder bomber by U.S. pilots during World War II. The *Baltimore Whore*, made in Baltimore, Maryland, was so called because it was very difficult to fly and was frequently cursed out with such names.

baluster. *See* BANISTER.

The Bambino. Taken from the Italian *bambino*, baby, this is a well-known nickname of American baseball great Babe (George Herman) Ruth (1895–1948), also known as The Sultan of Swat. But *Bambino* has for centuries meant an image of the infant Jesus in swaddling clothes.

bambochades. Genre paintings of rural life, especially rustic drinking scenes treated in an exaggerated or comic manner, are called *bambochades* or *bambociades*, after the nickname of Dutch landscape painter Pieter van Laar (ca. 1600–74). Van Laar, or Laer, worked some 15 years in Italy, where he was nicknamed *Il Bamboccio*, "the cripple." Famous for his landscapes and etchings depicting rustic life—pictures usually in heavy brown tones showing wakes, weddings, and other country scenes—the artist was also called *Michel-Ange des Bambochades*.

bamboo. Linnaeus adopted the Maylay name *bambu* for these giant grasses, giving the name to the plant's genus, which consists of about 120 species and whose name has come to be spelled *bamboo*, probably in error. The tropical bamboos range from 15 to 100 feet in height. An interestingly named bamboo is the Chinese *Buddha's belly bamboo* (*Bambusa ventricosa*). *Bambis oldhamii*, Oldham's bamboo, is grown for the excellent flavor of its shoots. In the U.S. the native bamboo is called a *cane*, including the *sugar cane*, which often forms impenetrable *canebrakes* 15 to 25 feet high in the South.

bamboo curtain. The *bamboo curtain* is a term suggested by the IRON CURTAIN that means a political and economic barrier between China and noncommunist countries. The policy came into effect when Mao Zedong (Tse-tung) cut China off from much of the free world after winning the Communist revolution. The expression may have been invented at *Time* magazine, in which it was first recorded on March 14, 1949: "The Communist bosses of Peiping dropped a bamboo curtain cutting off Peiping from the world." Bamboo, of course, had long been a synonym for things Asian.

bamboozle, bombazine. How did a fabric used for women's mourning clothes since the early 19th century give its name to our word for "to cheat or swindle"? Probably an early confidence game had a female swindler posing as a bereft widow wearing black bombazine, her costume lending its name to the swindle or hoax she and others like her practiced. Jonathan Swift included *bamboozle* in a list of new distasteful slang words, but it survived nevertheless. *Bombazine* itself comes from the Greek *bombux*, "silkworm."

banana. *Banana* derives from the Arabic word *banana*, meaning finger, and even today the individual fruits forming the familiar banana "hand" are called "fingers." The banana tree is really a giant herb with a rhizome instead of roots, and its "trunk" is made up of large leaves, not wood. The fruit was given the scientific name *Musa*, comprising 18 species, by Linnaeus in honor of Antonio Musa, personal physician to the first emperor of Rome. *Musa sapientum*, the most common banana tree species, takes its second name from the Latin word for "wise man," in reference to the Indian sages of old who reposed in its shade and ate of its fruit. Arabian slang and a score of other languages make the fruit a synonym for the male sexual organ, not surprisingly, and "I had a banana with Lady Diana" was British slang for sexual intercourse up until about 1930. "Where the banana grows man is sensual and cruel," Emerson wrote in his *Society and Solitude*, and the Koran says that the forbidden fruit in Paradise was a banana, not an apple. Banana oil, incidentally, is a synthetic—bananas produce no commercial oil—and the banana, like the pear, is one of the few fruits that ripen better off the tree.

banana leaf restaurant. Any Malaysian restaurant featuring cuisine served on large banana leaves.

banana oil. Nonsense, foolishness. An obituary of the syndicated advice columnist Ann Landers (Eppie Lederer, 1918–2002) noted that she never made public expressions of annoyance "much stronger than 'oh banana oil!'"

banco; Mark Banco. *Banco*, meaning bank money on account as distinguished from banknotes or currency, is often used in the international exchange business. Mark Banco was the mark of fixed value employed as an invariable standard in the old Bank of Hamburg in Germany and used by the Hanseatic League. Since all gold and silver deposits were credited in Mark Banco and all banking transactions carried on in Mark Banco, it made no difference how the exchange rate varied from day to day.

Band-Aid. Invented by Robert W. Johnson and George J. Seabury in 1874, the *Band-Aid* was registered by Johnson as a trademark in 1886 when he left Seabury and formed his own business, Johnson & Johnson. Widely used today, the word is a zealously protected trademark and still must be capitalized.

bandanna. A Hindu method of dyeing called *bāndhnu* consisted of knotting pieces of silk and dipping them in dyes so that parts of the silk would retain their original color. The Portuguese, who reached India during the 16th century, brought clothes dyed in this manner back to Europe, where the Hindi *bāndhnu*, corrupted to *bandanna*, soon came to mean a large silk handkerchief, especially one with a background of red with white spots.

bandersnatch. *See* JABBERWOCKY.

bandicoot. A word like this is needed in a time noted for both green thumbs and slick fingers, when thefts of shrubs, flowers, and vegetables right from the ground are occurring more frequently from public places and private residences. *Bandicooting* is an Australian word for the practice of stealing vegetables out of the ground, and a bandicoot is a thief who does this. The word could have a wider application, covering all vegetative thefts. Human bandicoots, like the Australian marsupial they are named for, usually steal root vegetables, leaving their tops protruding from the ground to avoid suspicion for a longer time.

bandwagon. *See* HOP ON THE BANDWAGON.

bandy; bandy-legged. This word for bowlegged (legs shaped something like these parentheses), strangely enough, derives from a comparison of bowlegs with the curved sticks used in the 17th-century Irish game of bandy, the precursor of hockey. No one is sure where the word *bandy* that gave us the game of bandy, bandysticks, and bandy-legged comes from, though earlier it was a tennis term. In playing ancient hockey, the ball was bandied from side to side and fought for, which led to metaphors like "I'm not going to bandy words with you"; that is, "I'm not going to argue, wrangle over nothing."

bang. *See* ONOMATOPOEIA.

bangers and mash. Visitors to Australia sometimes mistake this for an alcoholic drink, but it is simply Australian for a dish of sausage and mashed potatoes. The British also use the term.

bang for the buck. *See* GET MORE BANG FOR THE BUCK.

bangs. A bang-tailed horse is one whose tail is allowed to grow long, and then cut or "banged off" horizontally to form an even tassel-like end. Such fashioning of horses' tails was popular in the late 19th century and when several bang-tailed horses won major races the style attracted wide attention. Apparently, American hairstylists or women themselves named the similar women's hairstyle after the horse-tail style, adding *bangs* to the fashion lexicon. *Bangtail*, incidentally, was also a synonym for a prostitute in 18th- and 19th-century England.

Bang's disease; Brucellosis.   These are names for what is probably the most diversely named disease—it is called, variously, undulant fever, Malta fever, Gibraltar fever, rock fever, Mediterranean fever, and goat fever. Its cause, an infectious bacteria called *Brucella*, was discovered in 1887 when Scottish physician Sir David Bruce (1855–1931) performed an autopsy on a patient who had died of the illness on the island of Malta. Later, Danish veterinarians Bernhard L. F. Bang and V. Stribolt isolated a second strain of *Brucella* and in 1895 found that it caused a disease in cattle, which was called Bang's disease in that scientist's honor. Bang's disease, the name still used for the infection, is thought to have been responsible for the epizootic disease or storms of abortions that commonly occurred in American and European cattle herds in the early 19th century. Scientifically speaking, all diseases caused by *Brucella* bacteria are termed brucellosis. The disease affects not only cattle and goats but swine, chickens, dogs, cats, wild deer, and bison as well. It is usually contracted by humans from contact with infected animals or by ingesting infected milk, and is sometimes fatal. No complete cure is known for infected animals, and the incidence of the disease is said to be on the rise throughout the world.

banister; baluster.   *Banister,* a support for a handrail on a staircase, is a mispronunciation of *baluster,* first recorded in English over three centuries ago. *Baluster* comes from *balaustion,* the Greek name for a specific flower. Because Greek architects used the outlines of these flowers for the shapes of the short pillars supporting handrails, *baluster* came to mean the supports themselves.

banjo.   There are two theories about *banjo*'s origin. One holds that the word derives from a black mispronunciation of *bandore,* an English word of Spanish origin denoting a musical instrument similar to the banjo. The other cites the Angolan Kimbunde-language *mbanza,* which also means a banjo-like instrument. It would be hard to prove or disprove either theory.

bank; bankrupt.   In medieval times Italian moneylenders used a small bench in the marketplace to conduct their business. The Latin word for such a bench, *banca,* is in fact the source for the English word *bank.* These moneylenders, the bankers of their day, were required to break up their benches if they failed in business, and the Latin expression for doing so, *banca rupta,* later became the English word *bankrupt.*

bank holiday.   *Bank holiday* was one of the first of many words and phrases coined during the New Deal in America's Great Depression. President Franklin Delano Roosevelt used it on March 6, 1933, two days after his inauguration. Providing for the reopening of sound banks in a period when most banks had failed and "runs" had abounded, F.D.R. declared a four-day bank holiday while Congress rushed to pass the Emergency Banking Act.

bankrupt.   *See* BANK.

bankrupt worm.   A little parasite roundworm of the genus *Trichostrongylus* is called the bankrupt worm because it often infects cattle herds, sometimes bankrupting those cattlemen whose stock it attacks.

banned in Boston.   In its heyday during the 1920s the phrase *banned in Boston* made a number of books best-sellers throughout the rest of the country. Books were frequently banned in Boston for foolish reasons at the time because the local ultraconservative Watch and Ward Society wielded great power in the city. This is no longer the case, but the expression is still used jokingly.

banquette.   A raised sidewalk, usually made of bricks or planks. The term is mainly used in Louisiana, especially along the coast, and in East Texas. It derives from *banquette,* little bench, and is another French loan word.

to bant; banting.   William Banting (1797–1878) might have made a fortune had he published his booklet on dieting a century later, in our own weight-conscious era. As it turned out, he merely amused Londoners in the mid-1860s, although his name did become a word. Banting was an enormously overweight cabinetmaker and undertaker who couldn't bend to tie his shoelaces and had to walk downstairs backwards to relieve the pressure on his legs. Convinced by his own discomfort, and perhaps from his undertaking activities, that many deaths resulted from overeating, he went on a strict diet, losing 46 pounds and taking 12 inches off his waist. As so many dieters do, he then wrote a book about his experience, setting forth his method of reducing. "Bantingism" called for a meat diet and abstention from practically everything else—beer, butter, sugar, farinaceous foods, and even vegetables. Needless to say, it wasn't popular very long, but Londoners humorously took to calling dieting *banting* and to diet *to bant.*

bantam.   The dwarf fowl called the *bantam* takes its name from Bantam, Java where it was developed, and gives its name to any little, feisty creature.

bantling.   *See* BASTARD.

Bantu.   *See* ESKIMO.

banyan tree.   Here is a tree named for merchants who sold their wares beneath it. The Indian tree, which spreads out by sprouting aerial extensions that grow into the ground to form new trunks, can cover an area large enough to shade thousands of people. Noticing this, Hindu merchants set up naturally shaded marketplaces underneath the trees and the British later named the tree after the merchants, *banions,* who traded there.

banzai.   Before World War II, when the Japanese Navy and those of the Western powers were on good terms, banzai parties, or shore parties, were held where seamen from Japan and other nations mingled. The expression derives from the general Japanese felicitation, *banzai,* which means "May you live forever." During World War II, the once pleasant *banzai* was shouted by Japanese soldiers making bayonet charges.

baobab tree.   So thick is the baobab tree (*Adansonia digitata*)—up to 30 feet across—that several African tribes hollow it out so that families can live inside, much like the mesquite is used in Central America. The baobab is grown as a curiosity in the southernmost United States. Arabian legend holds that it acquired its peculiar shape when the devil plucked it out of the earth and replanted it with branches underground and roots in the air. The origin of the tree's name is obscure but may have something to do with that legend.

baptism of fire.   There is a strange, little-known story behind this common expression. The phrase had been used from antiquity as a synonym for martyrdom, in reference to Christian martyrs burned at the cross. It came to mean any severe ordeal or painful experience, but not until the late 19th century were the words used to describe a soldier's first experience in battle. We even have an exact date for the phrase used in this sense. At the battle of Searbuck during the Franco-Prussian War of 1870, Napoleon III (Louis-Napoleon Bonaparte) ordered that his 14-year-old son and only male heir, Prince Louis Napoleon, be sent into battle and exposed to enemy fire for the first time. The French ironically called this event the child's *baptême de feu,* "baptism of fire." The teenaged prince, who had agreed with his father's order, if that means anything, survived the battle, but went into exile in England with the enigmatic Napoleon III when France was defeated. Later he joined the British army and did die under fire, while fighting the Zulus in Africa, at the age of 22.

BAR.   The *Browning automatic rifle,* or BAR, of World War II fame was invented by John M. Browning (1854–1926) of Ogden, Utah, who designed many famous weapons. The BAR, an air-cooled weapon capable of firing 200–350 rounds per minute, was generally assigned one to a squad. It is said that none of the prolific Browning's designs ever failed. These included the light and heavy Browning machine guns, the .45 caliber pistol, the .50 caliber machine gun, the 37mm aircraft gun, and a number of shotguns and repeating rifles. Browning took out his first patent in 1879, on a breech-loading, single-shot rifle that the Winchester Arms Company purchased. After his entry into the military field, the U.S. Army relied almost exclusively on Browning's automatic weapons.

bar; before the bar.   Shakespeare used the word *bar* for a tavern, this *bar* first recorded in 1572 and taking its name from the bars that were pulled over the serving counter in taverns at closing time. Similar bars or gratings were used in early courts of law, leading to the expression about lawyers practicing *before the bar.*

barani roll.   A barani roll is a difficult one-and-a-half-rotation twist in the air in gymnastics. It has been suggested that the maneuver is named for Austrian physician Robert Barani (1876–1936) who, appropriately, won the 1914 Nobel Prize for his research into the human sense of balance.

Barbados.   The Spanish *barbados,* "bearded," is the source for this country's name. What they had in mind were the many vines hanging from all the trees in the area, vines so dense that they looked like beards.

a Barbara Fritchie.   A courageous, patriotic old woman. The term is from John Greenleaf Whittier's famous poem "Barbara Frietchie," in which a 96-year-old Mrs. Frietchie flaunts the U.S. flag in the face of Confederate troops marching through Frederick, Maryland. The poem was based on a true incident, but Whittier gave credit to the wrong flag waver. The real eponym should have been Mrs. Frietchie's neighbor, Mrs. Mary Quantrell. Mrs. Quantrell in reality was not molested by the Confederates, who raised their hats as they passed, saying, "To you Madam, and not to your flag." Whittier, who got his information from novelist Mrs. E.D.E.N. Southworth, later admitted his mistake.

barbarian; barber.   *Barba* means "beard" in Latin, and when the Romans called hirsute foreigners *barbarians* they were strictly calling them "bearded men," though the word shortly came to mean, rightly or wrongly, "rude, uncivilized people." A barber was, of course, one who cut beards or hair. The barber pole outside barber shops today has its origins in the ancient barber's duties as a surgeon and dentist as well as a hair cutter. It was first the symbol of these medical professions—a blood-smeared white rag. However, *barbarian* may have Greek origins.

barbecue.   Here's an English word that comes from the language of the extinct Haitian Taino tribe. The tribe smoked meat on a framework of sticks called a *barbacoa*—at least the name sounded like that to Spanish pirates who visited Haiti in the mid-17th century. *Barbacoa* came to mean the cooking of the meat itself and passed into English as the American *barbecue.* The Tainos also gave us the word POTATO, which was first their *batata.*

barbed wire.   When in the 1850s farmers began fencing in their land with barbed wire—twisted strands of wire fence with sharp barbs at regular intervals—ranchers tore the fences down so their herds could pass. This led to barbed wire fence wars in the West, notably one that broke out in Texas in 1884, and helped end the reign of the cowboy by the close of the century.

barber.   *See* BARBARIAN.

barberry.   The barberry is an ornamental bush often planted for hedges in place of privet and valued for its flowers, its gorgeous fall foliage, and the striking red berries that often hang on the bush all winter long. Few gardeners would believe that the common spiny barberry (*Berberis vulgaris*) provides fruit that can be eaten in a variety of ways. The English, in fact, once cultivated the handsome bush for its berries, and the Arabs before them grew barberries for their sherbets. The barberry may take its name from *berberys,* the Arabic name for a shell, possibly in reference to the shape of its leaves. The Berbers cultivated it on Africa's Barbary Coast. Some 50 species are widely grown in America.

Barbie doll.   I've heard *Barbie doll* used as American slang for a conformist or a dehumanized person since the late 1960s, though the first recorded use of the term seems to have been in a 1973 issue of *Rolling Stone.* The term derives from the trade name of a very popular blue-eyed blond doll made for little girls. The doll's name, in turn, comes from the name of Barbara Millicent Roberts, daughter of Ruth Handler, who created the doll in 1959–Barbie's birthday is March 9 to be exact. Barbie and her husband Ken became grandparents in 2003.

barcarole. A boating song of the Venetian gondoliers, or a song like it with a slow tempo and sad refrain. The gondoliers are called *barcaroli* after the Italian *barca*, a small boat.

Barcelona. The Spanish city is named after Hamilcar Barca, who founded it in about 230 B.C.

bard; bardolatry. Originally a wandering Celtic minstrel, a *bard* wrote and recited epic and heroic poems, often while playing a harp or lyre. But the Celtic word came to mean any poet or writer, although *The Bard* or *The Bard of Avon* or *The Bard of All Time* are titles reserved for William Shakespeare. There are at least a dozen titles like Shakespeare's, including *The Bard of Twickenham* (Alexander Pope), *The Bard of Ayrshire* (Robert Burns), *The Bard of Prose* (Boccaccio), and *The Bard of Democracy* (Walt Whitman). *Bardolatry* is excessive admiration of Shakespeare. Wrote H. G. Wells in *The Outline of History* (1920): "Bards were once blinded so they would not wander from the tribe. In recent memory a writer describes such a blindman in Rhodesia. The Slav word for bard was blind." Few modern societies place such a value on bards. The greatest blind authors in history are doubtless Homer and Milton, whose stories are well known. Louis Braille, who invented the Braille system of printing, and Helen Keller, the author of 10 books, are also familiar figures. Not so familiar are publisher Joseph Pulitzer, for whom the Pulitzer Prize is named, who went blind at age 40; blind historian William Hickling Prescott, who had secretaries to read source material to him; and blind Argentine writer Jorge Luis Borges. James Thurber was blinded in one eye in a childhood accident and went all but completely blind in his later years, while James Joyce, Charlotte Brontë, and Aldous Huxley all had extremely poor eyesight. *See* SWAN SONG.

bardash. A *bardash* is a male prostitute, or "a catamite," in the definition of the *O.E.D.* First recorded in 1548, the word may be an adaption of the Arabic *bardaj*, "slave." In 1760 a magazine spoke of the practice of "Publikely maintaining bardassaes and concubines." *Berdache* is an alternate spelling.

Barebones's Parliament. The historically important Barebones's Parliament nominated by Cromwell in 1653 wasn't so called because it was a small body, the skeleton of a real parliament. Rather, the assembly, which first met on July 4th of that year, was derisively nicknamed for one of its members. Praise-God Barebones was his name. Barebones, a famous London preacher as well as a leather merchant and man of property, was vociferously opposed to the restoration of the Stuarts. Controversial for his Baptist religious views, Praise-God Barebones's preaching attracted large crowds, the meetings frequently disturbed by riots, and one time a mob stormed his house, Barebones barely escaping with his life. Barebones's Parliament passed a number of reforms, including civil marriage and public registration of births and burials, but was generally unqualified for its task of governing, "more fools than knaves," as someone wrote. Praise-God Barebones, who seems to have taken little part in the debates, long outlived his namesake, dying in 1680, at about 84.

barefaced liar. *Barefaced*, "beardless, with no hair upon the face," may have been coined by Shakespeare in *A Midsummer Night's Dream*, where it is first recorded. Within half a century or so it came to mean bold, audacious, impudent, or shameless, like many boys, who were barefaced. By 1825 we find "the barefacedness of the lie" recorded, and Harriet Beecher Stowe writes of a *barefaced lie* in *Uncle Tom's Cabin*.

barge in. Useful but clumsy flat-bottomed barges, probably named from an early Celtic word for boat, have been common in England since medieval times. These shallow-water craft are often pulled through canals by conventional vessels or by animals on the bank. But accidents involving the unwieldy vessels were frequent; they were constantly bumping into other boats. By the late 19th century, English schoolboys were using the slang term *barge*, "to hustle a person," *to barge about* someone, bump him or move him heavily about. It is this practice, far removed from the water but related to barges, that led to the expression *to barge in*—to clumsily or rudely intercede, to butt in—that originated in the early 1900s.

bark. American pioneers were often excellent marksmen. At a distance of 100 yards or more, for example, an expert could *bark* a squirrel with a rifle shot, that is, hit the limb the squirrel was sitting on, the concussion killing the animal without wounding it. Some marksmen claim they can do this today.

Barkis is willin'. In Charles Dickens's novel *David Copperfield* (1849–50) the eponymous hero takes a message from the carrier Barkis to his (David's) nurse, Clara Peggotty, telling her that Barkis is ready to marry her. The message, "Barkis is willin'," has over the years become proverbial for any willingness or consent.

bark up the wrong tree. Coon dogs, which could be almost any breed of dog or even mongrels in Colonial days, commonly chased raccoons through the underbrush and treed them, barking furiously at the base of the tree until their masters came to shoot the "gone coon." But the crafty nocturnal animal, called a rahaugum by John Smith, often escaped through the branches to another tree in the dark, leaving the dogs barking up the wrong tree, which is the origin of the American phrase. Skilled hunters who could *bark* a squirrel, that is, strike the bark on the lower side of the branch where it sat, killing it by the concussion, have nothing at all to do with the expression. The *bark* of a tree comes to us from the Anglo Saxon *beore*, while a dog's *bark* is related to the Old English *barki*, "windpipe." It's said that dogs in the wild state howl, whine, and growl, but that their barking is an acquired habit—anyway, debarking operations are available to silence dogs whose barks are worse than their bites and dogs that bark at the moon. *Barkable* is an unusual old word. One would take the adjective to be a modern affectation, but it dates back to at least the 13th century, a treatise of the time on estate management advising lords to have "discreet shepherds . . . with good barkable dogs."

barlow knife. Russel Barlow, who has been called "the patron saint of whittlers," invented the barlow knife over 200 years ago and it has been known to Americans under one name or another ever since. The *barlow*, a single-bladed pocket-, pen-, or jackknife, was the pride, joy and bartering power of many an American boy, and is mentioned in the works of Mark Twain,

Joel Chandler Harris, and many other writers. It has also been called the Russel Barlow knife.

Barmecide's feast.   A *Barmecide's feast* is an illusion of plenty, figuratively a poor meal leaving much to the imagination. The expression comes from the "Story of the Barber's Sixth Brother" in the *Arabian Nights*. A rich noble named Barmecide (based on one of a real family of Baghdad princes) served the beggar Schacabac course after course of imaginary dishes, pretending that the empty golden plates he set before his guest constituted a sumptuous feast. Schacabac got the better of the prince, pretending to enjoy each course and finally boxing his host's ears while feigning drunkenness from the illusory wine. So amused was Prince Barmecide that he gave the beggar a real banquet, but his name is remembered for the first, imaginary meal.

barn; barnstorming.   The Old English *bere*, "barley," combined with *ern*, "storage," gives us the word *barn*, which was originally a place to store grain. Only in early America did the *barn* become a joint grain storage place and animal stable, American barns becoming so big that they spawned sayings like *You couldn't hit the broad side of a barn* and *as big as a barn*. Eventually we had car barns, furniture barns, and antique barns. *Barnstorming*, first applied in 1815 to a theatrical troupe's performances in upstate New York barns, has come to mean tours of rural areas by political candidates.

barnacle.   The barnacle takes its name from the barnacle goose, which is so called because of its "bare neck," *barnakylle* in Middle English, for in ancient times people firmly believed that these geese were born from what we now know as *barnacles*. A barnacle's long stalk and rounded body does resemble the neck and body of a goose, and its tentacles, which wave during the feeding process, suggest the wings of an infant bird being born from a shell and straining out to sea. The ubiquitous crustacean takes its scientific names, *Cirripedes*, from the Greek for "feet-like curls of hair," in reference to its tentacles.

barnburner; hunkers.   Barnburners were members of a faction of the Democratic Party in New York State from about 1830–50, so-called because they were so zealous for reform in the party that they would burn the barn (the Democratic Party) to get rid of the (pro-slavery) rats. The Democratic Party majority at the time was called the Hunkers, perhaps from the Low German *hunk*, "home, place of refuge," but possibly because they once packed the state convention and nominated a complete ticket for their faction, "took the whole hunk." *Barnburner* is used by wildcat oil men for a big well, a gusher, a strike that lights up the sky. It is common presently in Michigan, among other states, but probably originated in Pennsylvania toward the end of the 19th century, though I've never seen it recorded.

barnstorming.   *See* BARN.

barnyard epithet.   This widely used euphemism for plain old *bullshit* was coined by a *New York Times* editor as recently as 1970 in reporting the reply of David Dellinger, one of the Chicago Seven tried for conspiracy to disrupt the 1968 Dem-

ocratic National Convention, to a police version of his actions ("Oh, bullshit!").

barrage.   A barrage of artillery is strictly speaking a "barrier," the word deriving from the French *barre*. One can see the logic of this when considering that strategically an artillery barrage is meant primarily to be not an assault but a barrier to any enemy activity. The word in its military sense is first recorded during "the war to end all wars," in 1917.

barrio.   A Spanish word, common in many areas of the U.S., for a Spanish-speaking, often poor, section of a city. The term is first recorded in 1890 and has become common generally over the last 30 years.

barrister.   *See* LAWYER.

barter.   Few, if any, American sports terms derive from the names of great players, no matter how proficient. In baseball a home run is not called a "Babe Ruth," though we may (rarely) say a "Ruthian blast"; a hitting streak is not a "DiMaggio"; nor is a strikeout a "Sandy Koufax." Across the Atlantic this is not the case. *Barter*, for example, is an English cricket term dating back nearly 150 years. It comes from the name of Robert Barter, warden at Winchester College from 1832 to 1861, famed for his half-volley hits. The word is unrelated to the word "barter" meaning to trade, which is of unknown origin, although it may be related to the Old French *barater*, to cheat, exchange.

Bartholomew pig; Bartholomew fair.   Shakespeare called Falstaff a *Bartholomew pig*. This has long been the synonym for a very fat person, after the whole roasted pigs that were traditionally sold at the *Bartholomew Fair* in London. The fair, held on St. Bartholomew's Day (August 24th) from 1133 to 1855, was the center of London life. St. Bartholomew, martyred in Armenia in A. D. 44, has as his symbol a knife, in allusion to the knife with which he was flayed alive.

Bartlett pear; Seckel pear.   The yellow Bartlett grown commercially mostly in Oregon and Washington, where it is less susceptible to blight than in the East, represents 70 percent of the country's 713,000-ton crop and is certainly America's most commonly grown pear. It is a soft European-type fruit, in season from July to November, as opposed to earlier hard Asian varieties like the Seckel, which is named for the Philadelphia farmer who first grew it in America just after the Revolution. The Bartlett was not, in fact, developed by Enoch Bartlett (1779–1860), a merchant in Dorchester, Massachusetts, as is generally believed. Bartlett only promoted the fruit after Captain Thomas Brewer imported the trees from England and grew them on his Roxbury farm. The enterprising Yankee eventually purchased Brewer's farm and distributed the pears under his own name in the early 1800s. They had been long known in Europe as Williams or William Bon Chrétien pears. Bartletts, by any name, are one of the most delicious of the over 3,000 pear species, and pears have been one of man's favorite fruits from as early as 1000 B.C.

Bartlett's.   For many years John Bartlett owned the University Book Store in Cambridge, Massachusetts, where Harvard teachers and students came for assistance in tracking down the source of a quotation. Bartlett's erudition soon made the saying "Ask John Bartlett" a customary one when anyone sought the origins of a phrase, a faith that was justified when Bartlett's *Familiar Quotations*, or *Bartlett's*, appeared in 1855. John Bartlett died in 1905 at age 85, and his book remains a standard reference work today, unequaled by any similar English work except *The Oxford Dictionary of Quotations*. The Bartlett pear doesn't bear the scholar's name.

baseball. The name of America's national pastime is first recorded in 1744 as "base ball" in *The Little Pretty Pocket Book* as a synonym for the British game of rounders, a direct ancestor of the sport. Another early mention of the name is found in Jane Austen's *Northhanger Abbey* (1788) in which the heroine mentions that she played base ball as a child. Around the turn of the century, *base ball* became *baseball* in America.

Basedow's disease. *See* GRAVE'S DISEASE.

bash. Meaning a blow or even a wild party, *bash* seems to have originated in the world of boxing, the first use of the word recorded in the 19th century, when a *basher* was a prizefighter. No one is sure whether the word is a blend of "bang" and "smash," or simply of echoic origin.

bashful. *See* BAH!

basil. Basil was once believed to have been used in making royal perfume, and so the aromatic herb takes its name from the Greek *basilikos*, royal. In ancient times it was thought to have great healing properties. Boccaccio's *Decameron* tells the story of Isabella, who put her murdered lover's head in a pot, planted basil on top, and watered it with her tears.

basilect. *See* ACROLECT.

basilisk. This is another name for the legendary COCKATRICE. The two names seem to have been interchangeable, and the same myths applied to both beasts. Just to look in the basilisk's eyes was enough to kill a person, and the serpent hatched from a cock's egg had breath so fiery that it killed off all vegetation. The basilisk took its name from the Greek *basiliskos*, "little king," in reference to the cock's crest on its head that resembled a crown; the mythical creature had a cock's head, a dragon's tail and bird's wings. The monster's killing glance led to the use of *basilisk* for a wanton woman, who you never looked at while making love, and the term "cockatrice" for a prostitute or whore. Today *basilisk* is the name of a real South American lizard, a harmless two-foot-long creature that has a crest on its head.

Basin State. A nickname for the state of Utah. "The Judge has friends goin' to arrive from New Yawk for a trip across the Basin," wrote Owen Wister in *The Virginian*, 1902.

basketane. *See* CUBANE.

basketball; basket. The game of basketball might be called boxball today if its inventor's intentions had been realized. Canadian James Naismith (1861–1939) invented the game while working at the International YMCA Training School in Spring-field, Massachusetts, in late 1891. Though Naismith gave the game no name, his plan called for hanging an overhead wooden box at each end of the school's gym. Since the school's supply room had no boxes, Naismith agreed to use two half-bushel peach baskets instead. This suggested the name *basket ball* to him, even though the game was first played with a soccer ball, and he used it a month later, in January 1892, in an article for the school magazine describing the game. Soon *basket ball* was contracted to *basketball*. Incidentally, Naismith's peach baskets were not cut open at the end and his players had to climb on a ladder to retrieve each ball sunk in the basket. *Basket* for a score in basketball comes of course from the peach basket first used in the game. But *basket* wasn't the most common name for a score until about 1905—before that a score was most often termed a goal. In fact, the very first score in the first basketball game—made by one William R. Chase—was called a goal. *See* ACCORDING TO HOYLE.

Basque. *Basque*, which derives from the Latin *vasco*, for an inhabitant of Vasconia, a country up on the slopes of the Pyrenees, is spoken in northern Spain and southwestern France, and has been called "the most difficult language in the world to learn," being the remains of a prehistoric cave language that is related to no other language save a tongue spoken in a small area of the Caucasus Mountains. A Spanish proverb says that when God wished to punish the devil he made him study Basque for seven years. The Basques have jealously guarded their ancient customs and traditions, which include the strenuous national game of *jai alai*, now widely played throughout the world. There are some 200,000 Basques in Spain and France and another 250,000 in other countries.

Basque words. English words that come to us from Basque include: *bizarre*, *original* (a word for the American moose), and JAI ALAI.

bass. *Bass*, or *bast*, is the inner bark of the linden or basswood tree. This bark has been used to make everything from cloth to shoes and hats; gardeners use it often for packing and tying up plants.

bastard; bantling. Provençal mule drivers on the road in the Middle Ages used packsaddles called *basts* for beds whenever they checked into an inn or stretched out under a tree. Atop his *bast* (from the Latin *bastum*, "packsaddle") the typical muleteer must have fathered many an illegitimate child, for the expression *fils de bast*, "son of a packsaddle" (a child begotten on a packsaddle bed as opposed to a marriage bed) became an epithet for a natural child and the basis for the Old French word *bastard*. Many other attempts have been made to explain the word—even a happy one tracing it to the Old English word *besteaerd*, "the best disposition"—but "packsaddle child" is clearly right. *Bantling* has a similar derivation, coming from the German *bank*, "bench," and conveying the idea of a child begotten on a bench instead of in the marriage bed. "Born on the wrong side of the blanket" is a euphemism for *bastard* and indicates prudery at work—implying that sex in marriage should be performed in the dark, under the covers.

bat. To call a woman an *old bat* is not to call her an *old battle-ax*, as many people believe. *Bat* is not a shortening of *battle-ax* here, but English slang for a prostitute that goes back to at least 1612. A *bat* was a prostitute who walked the streets; like a bat she usually worked at night or, if she worked during the day, she hid out in dark recesses like a bat. To go *on a bat*, "a binge" or "a drinking spree," is similarly connected with the nocturnal bat—the "nightbird," not the prostitute. Someone who goes on a bat usually stays out all night, often stumbling around, as people thought a bat did in the dark. (The first such *bat* recorded in literature, in 1848, describes the spree taking place at night. In days past the winged, rodent-like bat was called by the colorful name "flitter-mouse.")

bathing machine. These structures were wooden bath houses drawn into the water by horses so that no one on the beach could see bathers in their bathing costumes (though these were certainly modest enough). The term was used in the U.S. as early as the late 18th century and in England even before then.

bathos; pathos. *Pathos*, which derives directly from the Greek word for "suffering," is the quality or power in any of the arts to evoke feelings of tender pity, compassion, or sadness, and gives us pathetic characters in literature such as Ophelia in *Hamlet* or even Dickens's Little Nell. *Bathos* means something quite different and was coined by Alexander Pope from the Greek word *bathos*, "depth" (not related to our English word *bath*), to indicate a descent from the sublime to the depths of the ridiculous. Pope and other writers of the early 18th century, including Swift, Gay, and Arbuthnot, made a sport of parodying contemporary writers. Out of this game of wits came Pope's satire "Bathos, the art of sinking in Poetry" (1727), in which he invented the word because no similar one existed in English to express the idea. "The taste of the Bathos is implanted by Nature itself in the soul of man," he wrote in his essay, and he proceeded to give an example of bathos at its worst:

> And thou, Dalhousie, the great god of war,
> Lieutenant-general to the earl of Mar.

bathukolpian. A rare, rather elegant way to say "big breasted" or "deep bosomed," *bathukopian* is first recorded in 1825. Coined apparently as a euphemism, the word comes from the Greek for "deep" and "breast."

bathysiderodromophobia. There are many people afraid of subways, but few who call themselves *bathysiderodromophobes*, people who fear subways and other things underground. A 20th-century coinage, the word is based upon the Greek *bathys*, "deep."

bathysphere. This reinforced spherical deep-sea chamber in which people are lowered by a cable to study the ocean and marine life was invented and named by American scientist and author William Beebee in 1930. Dr. Beebee later described the coinage exactly: "As the great chamber took shape, we found the need of a definite name. We spoke of it casually and quite incorrectly as tank and cylinder and bell. One day, when I was writing the name of a deep-sea fish—*Bathytroctes*—the appropriateness of the Greek prefix occurred to me; I coined the word *Bathysphere*, and the name has stuck." The Greek prefix *bathy* is so appropriate because it means "deep"; *sphere*, also from the Greek, is self-explanatory.

batiste fabric. One account claims that the popular *batiste fabric* takes its name from the soft linen used in medieval times to wipe holy water off the heads of baptized infants. It is more likely that the word derives from the name of one Jean Baptiste, of Cambrai, a 13th-century French linen weaver about whom little is known beyond his name. Cambric was at the time already a trade name for a linen manufactured at Cambrai, or Kamoric. English merchants needed another word for this new Cambrai product, so they named it after the French weaver but misspelled his name. Today *batiste* is no longer only linen material. Sheer cotton *batiste* is used for lingerie, handkerchiefs, and children's wear, and sheer rayon, silk, and woolen *batistes* are common, too.

Bat Masterson. A fabled gunfighter; after William Barclay "Bat" Masterson (1853–1920), a western lawman who never lost a gun battle. Masterson is one of the few gunfighters who didn't die a violent death. He became a sports writer in New York City and is said to have "died at his desk gripping his pen with the tenacity with which he formerly clung to his six-shooter." Masterson got the nickname "Bat" because while a sheriff in Kansas he often batted down law-breakers with his cane instead of shooting them.

bat out of hell. Since bats are nocturnal creatures that loathe the light, the hellfires of the infernal regions would inspire them to flap like hell to get out of there. That may be the idea behind the expression to move *like a bat out of hell*, extremely fast, which *Partridge* traces to 1908 and which probably goes back to the late 19th century. It was also slang used by R.A.F. pilots since World War I for "to fly extremely fast."

bats in his belfry; batty. Blind bats flapping about in the vast emptiness of someone's head, which suggested a church belltower or belfry to somebody, form the basis of this expression meaning a little crazy in the head, *poco loco in the coco*. Apparently no one told anybody *You've got bats in your belfry* until early in this century, for the first recorded use of the words is 1907. *Bats*, meaning crazy or nuts, seems to derive from the phrase, as does *batty*, meaning the same. The expression holds on mainly because of its alliteration, like the much older BEE IN HIS [HER] BONNET. But the image of bats flapping their wings and squeaking in the dark is a strong one that does suggest craziness.

battalion. A battalion is a large body of military troops, often an army unit with a headquarters and two or more companies of soldiers. The word derives ultimately from the Latin for "battle." But in Japan *battalion* means a zombie, of all things. The word came to mean zombies in Japan after a Japanese distributor in 1985 rather arbitrarily changed the name of the film *The Return of the Living Dead* to *Battalion*. Japanese moviegoers thought that *battalion* referred to the zombies in the picture and began calling all zombies *battalions*.

batten; batten down the hatches. A *batten* is simply a sawed strip of wood. This word gives us the nautical phrase *batten down the hatches*, for battens were once used to fasten canvas over a ship's hatchways during a storm. The phrase probably originated in the early 18th century.

battering ram. Romans of old called this device for battering down the walls of an enemy city an *aries* ("ram"), alluding to the male sheep and its powerful butting horns, and our term *ram* or *battering ram* is just a translation of the Latin. The long log, sometimes hung on chains, was used until the invention of the cannon and has been depicted in hundreds of film epics. It has never to my knowledge been shown in the form of a huge ram's head, although some ancient armies actually constructed it that way.

batting average; batting a thousand. *Batting average* has come to mean one's degree of achievement in any activity, but the term dates back to 1865 when it was used only in baseball. There it is the measure of a player's batting ability that is obtained by dividing the number of base hits made by the number of official times at bat and carrying out the result to three decimal places. *Batting a thousand* is doing something perfectly. No one knows when the common saying came into the general language from baseball, but it is based on the fact that 1.000 is the perfect average in baseball with a base hit every time at bat.

batting eyelids. To bat your eyelids is to flutter them, an American expression that goes back to the late 19th century. It has nothing to do with bats flapping in a cave, someone "gone batty," or even baseball bats. *Batting* in this case comes from the lexicon of falconry in Tudor times. According to a falconry book written in 1615: "Batting, or to bat, is when a Hawke fluttereth with his wings either from the perch or the man's fist, striving, as it were, to fly away." The old word had long been used by sportsmen, and some American with a lot of *Sprachgefühl*, "feeling for language," found a fresh use for it in the 1880s.

battle. One persistent old joke has the Civil War caused by the widespread Southern pronunciation of *battle*. It seems that three high-ranking Northern generals stomped into a Washington, D.C., saloon and shouted, "We want a bottle right away!" A Southern spy overheard them and breathlessly reported to General P. G. T. Beauregard: "Top Union generals say they want a battle right away!" Chivalrous Beauregard obliged, leaving the evening's quadrille in Montgomery and proceeding to Charleston, South Carolina, where he gave them the *bottle* (or *battle*) of Fort Sumter, the first of the war.

Battle Above the Clouds. A poetic name for the Civil War battle of Lookout Mountain, near Chattanooga, Tennessee, on November 25, 1863. The battle was so called because the heavy clouds below the summit obscured the fighting going on above. By the next morning the Stars and Stripes was flying at the summit, and by the end of the day the Union had won Chattanooga. Both sides lost about 10 percent of their large forces.

battle-ax. It took over 600 years for someone to think of this description of a domineering, sharp-tempered wife. Battle-axes were used at least since the Bronze Age, and were so named in the Middle Ages, most of them fearsome weapons that could fell a man with a single blow. Long after the lethal weapons were made obsolete by firearms, they remained a favorite of collectors and were displayed in museums. But it wasn't until the early years of this century that someone, possibly a vaudeville comedian, compared his warring wife to an *old battle-ax*. The expression is still used, often in a humorous, affectionate way. *Old battle-ax*, as slang for a strong man who is disliked and considered mean, has passed out of use.

Battle-born State. A nickname for Nevada, the 36th state, because it was admitted to the Union in 1864 while the Civil War was still being fought.

"Battle Hymn of the Republic." Sung to the tune of "John Brown's Body" (1856) by William Steffe, this was the favorite marching song of Union troops during the Civil War. The words were written by Julia Ward Howe (*see* UNCLE TOM) in December 1861 while she visited Union troops in Virginia, its major theme, according to the writer: "The sacredness of human liberty." *See* GOD BLESS AMERICA.

Battle of Britain. *See* BLITZ.

battle of the giants. *See* WAR OF THE GIANTS.

battle royal. Cockfighting does have a lot to do with this metaphor for a free-for-all, a battle in which more than one contestant is involved, but it probably didn't originate with the now outlawed "sport," as is often stated. The earliest quotations using the phrase support the theory that it derives from medieval jousting tournaments, where it was used to describe two sides fighting, each commanded by a king. Later, the expression became cockpit jargon before passing into standard English. In cockfighting, *battle royal* better describes what we mean by a *battle royal* today. It was an elimination tournament for gamecocks in which only the best fighters survived. A number of cocks, say eight, were thrown in the pit. These eight fought until there were only four left. Then these remaining four were rested and pitted against each other until two survived. The two survivors finally fought for the championship.

battology; battologist. A stammering man named Battos mentioned in the works of the Greek historian Herodotus, "The Father of History," is responsible for the word *battology*, "needless or excessive repetition in speech or writing," The *Oxford English Dictionary* records *battology*'s first use in 1603. It was formed by combining the name of the man Herodotus described, *Battos*, with the Greek *logia*—from *logos*, "word." *Battologist* is a term sometimes applied to boring speakers.

batty. *See* BATS IN HIS BELFRY.

Bavius; Maevius. Virgil sarcastically criticized the two minor Roman poets Bavius and Maevius in his Third Eclogue and Maevius was further criticized by Horace in his Tenth Epode, making their names forever synonyms for inferior poets or poetasters. In 1794 William Gifford wrote a fierce satire called *The Baviad* and followed it two years later with the *Maeviad*. The works attacked the Della Cruscan school of poetry, founded by sentimental young English poets living in Florence at the time. Ironically, the school bore the name of Florence's famous Accademia della Crusca (Academy of Chaff) whose object was purifying the Italian language, sifting away its chaff. By the way, Virgil himself was much criticized in his time; one critic published eight volumes consisting of resemblances between lines in Virgil's poems and earlier Roman poems.

bawdy; bawdy houses. *Bawdy,* "obscene, indecent, or lewd," derives from *bawd,* originally a procurer of either sex, and then either a prostitute or the madam of a brothel. Some scholars link *bawd* with Middle French *baud,* "gay," "dissolute," but the *O.E.D.* marks *bawd* "of uncertain origin." *Bawd* also means a hare in English, but as this use of the word is recorded two centuries after the first, it is hard to show any relationship between the fabled sexual energy of hares and the activities of human bawds. In the 17th century it was customary on Shrove Tuesday for apprentices to beat or frighten bawds on the street or in their bawdy houses.

bawl; bawl out. Dating back to the 15th century, *bawl* for a loud, rough cry probably derives from the Latin for *baulere,* "to bark like a dog." The word was also applied to the sounds of other animals, especially cows and bulls, which supports the theory that to *bawl out* originated as American ranch slang, suggested by the bawling or bellowing of angry bulls.

bayberry. *See* LIGHT ON A BUSH.

Bay City. A nickname for San Francisco since the mid-19th century. Also the proper name of several U.S. cities.

baying. *See* BAH!

bay laurel tree. Because this tree (*Laurus nobilis*), the *tree laurel* of history, was sacred to the god Apollo it was thought to be immune to lightning. According to legend, Apollo fell in love with the beautiful Daphne, daughter of the river diety Peneos, who changed her into a bay laurel tree to protect her when she spurned the god's advances. Apollo vowed that thereafter he would always wear bay laurel leaves and that all who worshipped him should do the same. The legend inspired Tiberius and other Roman emperors to wear wreaths of bay laurel as amulets during thunderstorms. Observation, however, has proved that the bay laurel tree is no more immune to lightning than any other tree. Another ancient superstition holds that the withering of a bay tree is an omen of death. The historian Holinshed noted that in 1399 old bay trees throughout England withered and then inexplicably grew green again. Shakespeare made use of this note in *Richard II:* " 'Tis thought the king is dead. We'll not stay—/The bay-trees in our country are withered." *See* LAURELS.

Bay of Fundy tide. *See* TIDE.

bayonet. Originally a short dagger, the *bayonet* almost certainly takes its name from Bayonne in southwestern France, where it was first made in the early 17th century. The word is first recorded, meaning "dagger," in 1611, and first cited meaning "a dagger attached to a musket" in 1674.

bayou. A marshy, sluggish outlet of a lake or river; any slow-moving body of water. Used chiefly in the lower Mississippi Valley and Gulf States, it probably derives from the Choctaw

bayuk for a river forming part of a DELTA. Louisiana is sometimes called the Bayou State.

Bay State. A nickname for Massachusetts since 1789. It has also been called the Old Bay State and the Old Colony.

bay window. The bay window, devised as early as the 14th century, is so named because in projecting from the house it made the room inside appear to mariners like a little harbor or bay. *Bay window* has been American slang for a "pot belly" since the 1890s.

bazaar. Used for a store or marketplace where many kinds of goods are sold, *bazaar* is one of the few English words that come to us from the Middle East, in this case deriving from the Persian *bazar,* "marketplace."

bazooka. Arkansas musician Bob Burns invented the musical instrument called the *bazooka* in 1905, out of two overlapping pieces of gas pipe that could be used like a trombone. The name he gave it is supposedly from the obsolete slang word *bazoo,* meaning loud talk, with a humorous ending tacked onto it. In 1943 U.S. Army Major Zeb Hastings gave the name of the instrument to the rocket-projectile gun that somewhat resembles it.

BBC English. *See* RECEIVED PRONUNCIATION.

beach glass. Small pieces of glass from broken bottles that are made opaque over time by the movements of tide and sand. They come in as many colors as there are broken-bottle colors on the beach, and some collectors make bracelets, necklaces, and earrings from them. I don't know why no dictionary records this beachcombing treasure. My mother called them *poverty gems* and *poorman's diamonds.* Howard Moss (1922–87) wrote a lovely poem called "Beach Glass," first published, if I remember well, in *The New Yorker,* whose poetry he edited for many years. Also called *sea glass.*

bead. *Bead* derives from the Middle English word *bede,* which meant "a prayer" and in turn came from the Old English *gebel,* meaning the same. Since prayers were often said on a string of small round balls (now called a rosary), the name for "prayer" came to be applied to the balls themselves, the spelling changing to *bead* over the years.

beam me up, Scotty. This has become a very popular humorous expression, often used on bumper stickers as well as in conversation, for "get me out of here, free me from this mess," etc. It originally requested transportation, a frequent order Captain Kirk gave to chief engineer "Scotty" Scott on the television series *Star Trek,* which premiered in 1966. It meant that Scotty should transform Kirk's body into energy. Interplanetary polyglots will be interested to know that a 1996 video game, *Star Trek Klingon,* teaches players the Klingon language. *Beam me up!* in Klingon is *Hljol! See also* KLINGON.

bean; string bean; green bean. Deriving from the Old English *bean,* and possibly akin to the Latin *faba* by a circuitous route, *bean* was long used for the seeds of many plants. "Common beans" (string beans, first recorded in 1759; Lima beans;

wax beans; etc.) are native to the Americas. Napoleon wouldn't eat string beans, afraid that he would choke on the strings, but today's varieties are virtually stringless and thus are often called green beans. As early as 1830, one observer noted: "We do not call it a string bean, because the pod is entirely stringless." Yet *string bean* is still used for the vegetable and Americanisms like *string bean* for a tall, thin person remain in the language. *Bean pole*, another Americanism for a lanky person, takes its name from the tall poles that support climbing bean plants.

Beaneater; Boston baked beans. Since at least the late 19th century, *Beaneater* has been a humorous nickname for a Bostonian, Boston being called *Beantown*. *Boston baked beans* have been regarded as the best of baked beans for a half century longer and are still so thought today. They are made basically with navy beans flavored with molasses and slowly cooked with pork. Baked beans have been the traditional Saturday night supper in New England since early times, the leftover traditionally being part of Sunday breakfast.

beanfeast. No one is sure about *beanfeast*'s derivation. The annual dinner that British employers gave their workers in the 1800s may be so named because beans were served at the feast or because a "bean goose," a goose "with a beak like a horse bean," was part of the fare. On the other hand, *bean* here may come from *bene*, "prayer, solicitation," because charitable collections were made at the feasts.

bear down upon. The nautical practice of *bearing down* on another ship means to sail toward her rapidly from a position upwind. From this naval strategy comes the phrase *to bear down upon*, to put pressure on someone or something, which probably originated late in the 19th century.

beard the lion in his den. In the biblical story young David assures Saul that he can handle the giant Goliath: "Your servant used to keep sheep for his father; and when there came a lion, or a bear, and took a lamb from the flock, I went after him, and smote him and delivered it out of his mouth; and if he arose against me, I caught him by his beard and smote him and killed him." His words became the basis for our expression *beard the lion in his den*, boldly confront a dangerous adversary, though the exact saying was first recorded in Sir Walter Scott's *Marmion* (1808).

bear flag. The white flag with a star and grizzly bear upon it that was adopted by Americans in California in 1846 when they defied Spanish authorities and proclaimed the California Republic. It has since become the California state flag.

a bear for work. In the early 19th century, as Americans pushed on into the wilderness, a number of native expressions arose comparing men with great strength or strong appetites or emotions to bears. *A bear for work* was born at this time, as was CROSS AS A BEAR.

bear paw. A popular pastry made with nuts and raisins that roughly suggests a bear's paw in shape; also called a bear claw. It appears to have originated in California in about 1940.

bear the brunt. *Brunt* is an old word for the main force of an army and the expression to *bear the brunt* has been used since at least the early 1400s in the sense of to take the main force of an enemy attack. Today it means to bear the worst of anything.

beastly drunk. The first recorded use of *beastly drunk* seems to have been by John Bristed in *Anthroplanomenus, being an account of a pedestrian tour through part of the Highlands of Scotland* (1803): "He . . . comes home every morning about two or three o'clock quite beastly drunk." But Jonathan Swift in 1709 wrote of the "beastly sin of drinking to excess." And Thomas Nashe in his *Pierce Pennilesse . . .* (1592) gives descriptions of eight types of drunks, comparing many of them to wild beasts, such as the "Lion drunke [who] flings the pot about the house, calls his hostess whore, breaks the glass windowes with his dagger . . ." Nashe's work may have first suggested the expression, even if he didn't use the exact words.

beast 666.

> Let he who hath understanding
> Reckon the number of the Beast;
> For it is a human number,
> Its number is Six Hundred and Sixty Six.
>
> —Book of Revelations 13:18

No one has been able to identify satisfactorily the Beast alluded to in the Bible. Since each digit in 666 falls short by one of the "sacred number" seven, it has been suggested that 666 therefore symbolizes the Antichrist expected by some Christians to precede the second coming of Christ. Others have tried to prove that 666 is a cryptogram based on the names of various men throughout history. The Hebrew letters of the name Nero Caesar, for example, represent numbers that add up to 666. Nero has always been a favorite candidate for the Beast, but Roman emperor Diocletian, Martin Luther, Muhammad, Napoleon, and many others have been suggested, too. The matter is further complicated by the fact that some ancient authorities say the number given in Revelations is 616.

beast with a belly full of bedsprings. A colorful cowboy term for a wildly bucking horse. The expression seems to have originated in rodeos within the last 50 years or so.

beast-with-two-backs. Shakespeare used this expression for face-to-face sexual intercourse in *Othello*, having Iago say: "I am one sir, that comes to tell you your daughter and the Moor are now making the beast with two backs." The words are often hyphenated today.

beat a dead horse. *See* FLOG (OR BEAT) A DEAD HORSE.

beat a retreat. In early times drums were played when armies retreated from the field. Over the years the drumming and a bugle call came to be the ceremony of retreat at sunset, when day was done and the flag was lowered. *To beat a retreat* now means to retreat or retire from all activities rather than just battlefield withdrawal.

beat around the bush. It's hard not to beat around the bush about the origins of this one. Hunters once hired beaters who "started" birds and other game for them by beating the bush and scaring them out into the open. The simplest explanation for the phrase *to beat around the bush*, to approach a matter very carefully or in a roundabout way, is that these beaters had to take great care when approaching the bush or they would "start" the game too soon for the hunter to get a good shot. But etymologist Ernest Weekley and others believe that the expression, which dates back to at least the early 16th century, is a mixed metaphor. Weekley suggests that the old proverb "I will not beat the bush that another may have the bird" joined with "to around the bush," an early expression used for a hound hesitating when circling the bush—and gave us *beat around the bush*.

beat black and blue. Originally the colors in this phrase, recorded as early as 1300, were *blak* and *bla*, the *blak* for "black," and the *bla*, for "a dark color between black and blue," a livid blackish-blue. These of course are the colors the human body commonly turns when beaten, bruised, or pinched.

beat it! Although most authorities say *beat it!* is American slang first recorded in 1905 for "get out of here, go away!", the expression is much older. The term was used by both Ben Jonson and Shakespeare for "go" and is said to have been coined by Shakespeare. It may be a shortening of "beat the trail" or some similar expression, but no one is sure. *See* SCRAM.

beats; beat generation; beatnik. Novelist Jack Kerouac claimed he invented the word *beat* for Allen Ginsberg's "angel-headed hipsters" of the fifties, and said it meant "beatific, blissfully happy," that "you got the beat," but it probably owes a lot to the early thirties jargon of jazz musicians in which *beat* meant "exhausted, frustrated, played out." In fact, *beat* in this last sense was used generally as far back as 1830. *Beat generation* seems certainly to have been Kerouac's name for the fifties "Lost Generation," though it was first used in John Clellon Holmes's novel *Go!* (1957). Columnist Herb Caen of the *San Francisco Chronicle* coined *beatnik* in 1958. The pejorative though affectionate Yiddish suffix *nik* (as in "nudnik," "no-good-nik," etc.) was probably added to *beat* to make the word, but remember that the Russian sputnik ("fellow traveler of the earth") with its Polish suffix *nik* was launched at the time.

beat the band. Banagher, an Irish town on the Shannon, was in the mid-19th century a notorious "pocket borough" where most residents were employed by the local lord and voted as he directed (were "in his pocket"). It became a standing joke in Parliament at the time to quip "Well, that beats (or bangs) Banagher!" whenever someone mentioned a pocket borough where *every* resident was employed by the local lord. Either via this route, or because of an Irish minstrel named Bannagher who told amazing stories, the saying *that beats Banagher*, for "anything amazing or superior," became an English favorite. It's reasonable to suggest, as Partridge does, that the later phrase *that beats the band*, derived from it. The alliterative expressions do sound alike and "*bang*" (from both the alternate version of the English phrase and Banagher) would suggest "band"—that beats something louder, bigger, better than a great brass band. Attempts to connect *that beats the band* with several real bands have all failed.

beat the devil and carry a rail. To beat someone decisively. The saying derives from the rural custom of having the favorite runner in a race carry a rail as a handicap.

beat the living daylights out of you. To say "I'll let daylight into you!" to an enemy in days past was to threaten that you'd open him up, make a hole in him with a sword, knife, or gun. The expression, in the form of its variant "I'll make daylight shine through you," is recorded in America as early as 1774 and is probably much older. Sayings like "I'll fill him full of holes" replaced the older expression when modern weapons like machine guns made wholesale ventilation easier, but it lived on in the form of *I'll beat the living daylights out of you*—I'll beat you to a pulp, punish you unmercifully. Unlike the old swordsman's words, this makes no sense literally. It is merely the ghost of an imaginative phrase.

beat to the punch. British boxing champion Daniel Mendoza weighed only 160 pounds but defeated many bigger fighters with his speed and agility, which enabled him to throw a punch before his opponents could. Mendoza reigned through the 1790s, when the phrase *beat to the punch* became a common one in boxing circles. It wasn't until about 30 years later, in 1823, that *beat to the punch* began to be used figuratively for "to do what someone else plans to do before he does it." Possibly the first of the "scientific" boxers, Mendoza operated a boxing school where he taught many British gentlemen how to fight. Among many innovative techniques he originated were INFIGHTING, the jab, the hook, and the old one-two.

Beau Brummell. Beau Brummell, born George Bryan Brummel, was more a dandy than a gentleman; it is said that he even refused to tip his hat to ladies, out of fear that he might mess his wig. Brummell's name has indeed been synonymous for a dandy, fop, or fancy dresser for over a century. From his early years at Eton and Oxford the incomparable Beau paid extravagant attention to his dress. There he met the Prince of Wales, later George IV, who became his patron when he left college, commissioning him in his own regiment in 1794. Brummell retired from the service four years later, when he inherited a large fortune, and set up a bachelor apartment in Mayfair, where he held sway as London's arbiter of fashion for almost 20 years. Though he showed good taste and originality in dress, he is remembered for his excesses. Beau Brummell often spent a whole day dressing for a royal ball; his gloves were the work of three glovers—one to fashion the hands, another for the fingers, and a third for the thumb. In 1816 he fled to France to escape his creditors. Here he spent his last 24 years in exile while struggling to survive, imprisoned once for debt and suffering several attacks of paralysis. He died in an asylum for the poor in Caen in 1840, aged 62. He had long before lost all interest in elegant fashion and manners, his dress becoming slovenly and dirty. *See also* BEAU NASH.

beaucoup. Many, a lot, an abundance. A term (from the French *beaucoup*, much) pronounced *boocoo*, that has gained wider use in recent years, as in "He's got boocoo money."

Beaufort scale. The Beaufort scale, a means to measure wind velocity, was devised in 1806 by Sir Francis Beaufort (1774–1857), noted surveyor and hydrologist, who later became a rear admiral and served as hydrographer to the British navy from 1829 to 1855. Beaufort's scale consists of numbers from 0 to 12 that indicate the strength of the wind ranging from "light," force 0, to "hurricane," force 12, or in Beaufort's words, "that which no canvas could withstand." My learned correspondent Eric Halsey points out that the best thing about the scale is that it can be used without instruments. When the tops of the trees begin to stir, for example, the wind is 5 knots.

Beaujolais. Often drunk very young—even as early as mid-November of the year its grapes are harvested—*Beaujolais* is a full-bodied fruity wine that has become very popular in America recently. It takes its name from the Beaujolais region in France, north of Lyon, where it is produced.

Beau Nash. Beau Nash is the only "beautiful person" comparable to BEAU BRUMMELL. Master of Ceremonies at Bath, then England's most fashionable gambling and cultural center, Nash spent much of his long life preening and strutting, riding in a chariot drawn by six gray stallions and attended by laced lackeys. The "King of Bath" died in 1761, aged 87, and the town ordered a full-size statue of him erected in the Pump Room between the smaller busts of Newton and Pope. That Beau Nash, like Brummel, was remembered for his excesses and not his many good works can be seen in Lord Chesterfield's epigram concerning this statue:

> The statue placed these busts between
> Gives satire all its strength;
> Wisdom and Wit are little seen,
> But Folly at full length.

beautiful. *See* BROKEN-HEARTED.

beautiful bodacious Babylon of the West. A colorful old name for Dodge City, Kansas, once a wild and rowdy cowtown on the Santa Fe Trail.

beautiful nuisance. A euphemistic Southern name for the kudzu vine, a scourge in the U.S. South where it was introduced as a valuable forage crop and soil conditioner but became a fast-growing weedy pest in southern gardens. *Kuzu* is the Japanese name for this Asiatic plant (*Pueraria thunbergiana*) of the pea family. The kudzu has had more publicity but the most pernicious weed in the South, and in all America, is the purple nutsedge (*Cyperus rotundas*), which can grow 39 inches long and does far more damage.

beautiful people; flower people. *The beautiful people* for fashionable rich people dates back only to the 1960s, when it was supposedly invented by fashion authority Diana Vreeland, though there is no firm proof of this. The term is probably based on *flower people*, hippies of the time until their bloom faded. Flower people were people who advocated love and peace, so-called because they sometimes offered others flowers as symbols of their beliefs.

beauty is only skin-deep. *Skin-deep*, for "superficial" or "shallow," "penetrating no deeper than the skin," can be traced back to the early 17th century, as can the proverbial *beauty is only skin-deep*, expressing the limitations of beauty. The last expression is first recorded in a poem by Thomas Overbury in about 1613: "All the carnall beauty of my wife,/Is but skin-deep." *Skin-deep*, literally, can range from 1/100th of an inch on the eyelid to 1/5th of an inch on the back.

beaver. Though extinct in England, this aquatic rodent retains its English name, which comes from the Old English *beofor*. Books have been written about the beaver (*Castor fiber*), the largest and most ingenious of North American rodents. Valuable beaver pelts, used largely in felt hats, were a great incitement to the exploration of the New World, and in the early 19th century hundreds of thousands of beavers were killed for their fur. Growing to a length of four feet and a weight of over 80 pounds, beavers are peaceful family animals devoted to their kittens and live in large towns or colonies. Their engineering skills in building dams and lodges are well known, and they have been observed building 1,000-foot-long canals to divert a stream into their pond or to reach a food source (usually the inner bark of trees). Beavers have "more engineering skill than the entire Army Corps of Enginers," claimed one admirer in Civil War times. *See* EAGER BEAVER.

Beaver State. A nickname for Oregon. It has also been called the Sunset State and the Webfoot State, suggested by the term *Webfooters* for residents of the state, which has a 77.2-inch annual rainfall, good weather for (webfooted) ducks. Oregon was once known as the Hard-Case State, this unusual state nickname referring to the many shady characters who came there in the early 19th century.

beaver tail. A round pastry, popular in Canada, made with brown sugar, lemon juice, flour, and other ingredients.

because it's there. The humorous or wry answer of a mountain climber who is asked why he chose to climb a certain mountain. The phrase is often attributed to Sir Edmund Hillary, who climbed Mt. Everest with his guide Tenzing Norgay in 1953, but it was said many years before then by British climber George Leigh Mallory (1886–1924) when asked why he wanted to climb Everest. It is also applied to people other than climbers, meaning generally "a foolish reason for any foolish act."

bechamel. The marquis de Bechamel, it is said, made his money financing various fraudulent deals before turning from crookery to cookery, but the French forgave him everything for the sauce he invented. Louis de Bechamel became steward to Louis XIV, the Sun King, as he liked to call himself, whose motto was, "He who eats well works well." While superintendent of the royal kitchens, Bechamel created many sublime dishes for the dedicated gourmet king, under whom the now proverbial Cordon Bleu school of cookery was established. However, what we call a *bechamel*, a *bechamelle*, or a *Bechamel sauce* today—a cream sauce thickened with flour—bears little resemblance to the original, which was a complicated concoction prepared from egg yolks, cream, and butter blended with an elaborate bouillon made from vegetables, wines, "old hens, and old partridges." This may be for the best, though. "Thank goodness," writes the noted chef Raymond Oliver, "[such recipes] are no longer more than pale ghosts of what they were."

bêche-de-mer.   Bêche-de-mer, a lingua franca known only in the Pacific, is a combination of English and native dialects. The bêche-de-mer was a staple of trade, the natives prizing it for food, and the language takes its name from this sea slug or sea cucumber.

bedbug letter.   According to an old story, a guest at a famous hotel was bitten by a bedbug one night and on returning home wrote a letter of complaint. He received an apologetic letter claiming that this had never happened before; however, the guest's letter was enclosed, with the notation scrawled across the top: "Send him the bedbug letter." Ever since, the expression *bedbug letter* has meant a form letter apologizing for poor service or a defective product.

bed of ice.   A short story I read recently described as a *bed of ice* the water bed a quarrelling couple shared. The expression has a much crueler connotation in history. It seems that for one capricious reason or another Empress Anne of Russia demoted an old noble at her court to court jester and then ordered him to marry an old crone who served her as a chambermaid. At great expense the sadistic Anne had a house of ice built on the frozen Neva River and furnished it entirely with ice. The newlyweds were, amid great fanfare, transported to their home on the back of an elephant, put into their ice bed naked and the house's ice door was moved in place. They did not last until morning.

bed of Procrustes.   Procrustes, sometimes called Damastes or Polypemon in Greek legend, always obliged weary travelers when they came to his house on the road to Eleusis seeking lodging for the night. But the notorious highwayman of Attica makes modern muggers look NAMBY-PAMBY in comparison. He had two sadistic M.O.s. Once he got a short victim inside, he'd lead him to a long bed, tie him up, and stretch him on a rack until he fit it. If the victim was tall, Procrustes would show him to a short bed, restrain him, and lop off his legs so that he fit. Either way his victims died in bed and Procrustes stole their money. From his inhumane hospitality we have the expression to put a person *on the bed of Procrustes*, meaning to force him to one standard of thought or action by arbitrary methods.

bedouin.   A bedouin has come to mean any wandering person or vagabond, and derives from the French word *(Bedouin)* for the nomadic Arab tribes of the Arabian, Syrian, and North African deserts. The French adapted the word from the Arabic *bidwan,* "a dweller in the open lands." The Bedouins of the Arabian desert, about 1 million in number, are nomadic camel breeders who trade their camels with Persian (Iranian) and Syrian traders for food and other goods. Living in groups of up to 100, they are strongly united through blood relationships, a woman generally marrying her father's brother's son.

to bedpost.   An interesting expression that means to hold down a child's shirttail or other garment by placing it under a heavy bedpost that the child can't lift. While they were busy in the kitchen, garden, or elsewhere, mothers a century ago often did this to prevent young ones from wandering off into trouble. Also called *bedpost on a dress tail.*

bedswerver.   In days past this delightful word served as a synonym for an unfaithful spouse (one of *its* synonyms being a *spouse-break*). Shakespeare used the term in *The Winter's Tale.*

bee.   *Spelling bee* is among the last survivors of a large number of *bees* relating to social gatherings (bees being busy, cooperative, social animals) "for performing some task in common." These are American in origin—the first one recorded is a 1769 *spinning bee* in Taunton, Massachusetts, though the term was in use before that. Later came *bees* prefixed by apple, building, candy, checker, chopping, drawing, housecleaning, husking, knitting, logging, paring, picking, political, quilting, raising, sewing, shingle, shooting, shouting, shucking, spinning, squirrel, stone, tailor, and wood. There were even *rattlesnake bees,* where "the venomous reptiles . . . were summarily excised by fire and lethal weapons"; *kissing bees,* parties for young people; *whipping bees,* where toughs beat someone; and *lynching bees.* The affairs, sometimes called "frolics," were often followed by parties.

beech.   *See* BOOK.

Beecher's Bibles.   *Beecher's Bibles* were Sharps repeater rifles that the Reverend Henry Ward Beecher (1813–87), one of America's most famous and controversial preachers, raised money for at his Brooklyn Heights church in New York, and shipped to "Bloody Kansas" in crates labeled "Bibles." Beecher encouraged his parishioners to join the "underground railroad" and even held mock slave auctions at Plymouth Congregational Church to illustrate the evils of slavery. The church, still in use, was called "The Church of the Holy Rifles," and is now a national historic shrine. Beecher once wrote that "the Sharps rifle was a truly moral agency . . . [had] more moral power . . . than a hundred Bibles." The great preacher, brother of Harriet Beecher Stowe, was a complex man whose interests ranged from involvement in antislavery movements to involvement with female members of his congregation. *See* SHARPS RIFLE.

beefcake.   *See* CHEESECAKE.

beefeater.   The popular name of the warders of the Tower of London and the Yeoman of the Guard, all of whom dress in 15th-century uniforms and are perennial tourist attractions. Their name, however, was originally a derogatory term for a well-fed servant, something of a glutton, and three centuries ago the French used it as a contemptuous word for an English soldier.

beef on weck.   Another notable American sandwich, this one from western New York, especially Buffalo. *Beef on weck* is slices of beef piled on a crusty roll topped with caraway seeds and coarse salt. *Weck* is a shortening of the German *Kummelweck* for caraway roll. *See* HERO.

beef Stroganoff; beef Wellington.   Nineteenth-century Russian diplomat Count Paul Stroganoff has the honor of having the well-known *beef Stroganoff* named after him. It is beef sauteed with onions and cooked in a sauce of consommé, sour cream, mushrooms, mustard, and other condiments. *Beef*

Wellington, another popular dish, commemorates Arthur Wellesley, first duke of Wellington, whose name is part of a number of terms, including WELLINGTON boots. *Beef Wellington* combines a choice cut of beef, liver pâté, bacon, brandy, and various condiments, all baked in a golden crust of puffed pastry.

Beehive State. *See* MORMON STATE.

bee in his (her) bonnet.

> Ah! woe is mee,
> woe, woe is mee
> Alack and well-a-day!
> For pity, sir, find out the bee,
> Which bore my love away.
> I'le seek him in your bonnet brave,
> I'le seek him in your eyes.

Robert Herrick's little-known poem "Mad Maid's Song," above, written in 1648, is supposed to be the basis for the expression *to have a bee in one's bonnet*, "to be eccentric, have a screw loose, especially to be obsessed with one idea." If the poem is implying in the last two lines that the mad maid is slightly insane, this is the case. Herrick was probably playing with an older expression, "to have bees in the head or brain," which means the same and dates back to the early 16th century. Bees humming in the head obviously suggested an obsessive idea busy at work there. A bonnet at the time was either a man's or woman's hat.

Beelzbub. The devil or prince of the devils, whose name is mentioned several times in the Bible. Poet John Milton, in *Paradise Lost*, makes him a fallen angel next to Satan in power. Originally a god of the Philistines, he was called *Lord of the Flies* because his statue, believed to be always coated with blood, attracted flies to it.

been down so long it looks like up to me. This expression is the title of a book by the late Richard Fariña and still has currency today. It dates back to the 1960s or before and is akin to several ancient phrases. For example, in 1590 one writer noted: "They verife the olde Proverb, Charles, which is, That such as were never but in Hell, doo thinke that there is no other Heaven."

been there, done that. A recent American phrase, first recorded in 1983, usually said by someone bored to death with something overly familiar to him or her.

beer. *Beer* possibly derives from the Latin *biber*, for "drink." Roman soldiers most likely demanded *biber* in taverns wherever they went in Germany and the tavern owners assumed that this meant the ale in which they specialized. Gradually, the German word for ale became *biber* and then *Bier*, which came into English as *beer*.

beer and skittles. Mainly a British tavern game of ninepin in which a wooden ball or disk is used to knock down the pins, skittles takes its name from the Scandinavian *skutill*, "shuttle." This game, similar to shuffleboard, has been played since the early 17th century in taverns, where *beer and skittles* became an expression for a relaxed, laid-back lifestyle in which people want no more from life, and no less, than their beer and a game of skittles. Life sometimes gives more, of course, and frequently gives less.

beerplants. *See* ASPIDISTRA.

beet; red as a beet. *Beet* comes to us from the Greek *beta*, for a similar plant. *Red as a beet* has probably been used as long as man has used beets. The French *betterave*, "beet," has served as slang for the penis, an analogy not unknown in history, despite the unlikely shape of the modern beet for such—Catullus wrote about a Roman matron who left her husband because the object of her desires "dangled like a limp beet."

beetle. Born to bite, beetles take their name from the Old English word *bitula*, meaning "biter." The species of beetle called *dermestes* derive their name from the Greek words for "skin or leather" and "to eat," meaning what an entomologist-etymologist in the early 19th century observed: that they ate even the hides of dead animals. *Dermestes* are interesting little beetles that PLAY POSSUM when touched. Actually, their larvae do the eating, and they demolish everything on a dead animal. They're so thorough that large museums sometimes keep a colony on hand to clean delicate specimens to the bone instead of risking chemical or mechanical means.

beetle-brained. We don't call someone *beetle-brained* because he acts as though he has a brain about as big as a beetle. The English term, first recorded in 1604, derives from the Old English *betl*, "a hammer," a *betl* or *beetle-brained* person having a head as hard as a hammer head.

beetle-browed. To be beetle-browed is simply to have an overhanging forehead, like the beetle. The word has nothing to do with the Old English word *betl*, for hammer.

beezer. Rarely heard anymore, *beezer* was once popular slang for the nose, slang brought back by U.S. Marines serving in China, where Westerners were called the insulting *ta-bee-tsee*, or "big-nosed ones." *See* CHINESE LANGUAGE CONTRIBUTIONS TO ENGLISH.

before the mast. Seamen on sailing ships in days past always bunked in the forecastle (fo'c'sle), literally "before the mast," which accounts for the title of Richard Henry Dana's classic *Two Years Before the Mast* (1840). But *before the mast* also means to be hauled before the mast, where the captain held court, to be tried for some offense.

beggar; to beg. A *beggar*, as Ernest Weekley pointed out in *The Romance of Words*, is not etymologically one who begs, for in the case of *to beg* the verb evolved from the noun. Many scholars share this opinion. Surprisingly, *beggar* is not of ancient vintage, like "eat" and "drink" and "sleep." The word probably derives from the nickname of the 12th-century Liege priest, Lambert le Begue (Lambert the Stammerer), who founded a Belgian lay order devoted to the religious life and chastity as a reaction against the suffering of the Crusades. Little is known about Lambert le Begue besides the fact that he died in 1177, but his secular order, though it demanded communal living, poverty, and self-denial, was a tolerant and popular one. There were no requirements that his followers take vows or lock themselves in a monastery, and members were allowed to own private property, as well as to leave the order and marry. The nuns of the Beguine order were called *beghinae* in Medieval Latin, and the monks belonging to a male group formed in the Netherlands were similarly called *beghardi*, these Latin formations influenced by the name of their order and by the Old Flemish *beghen*, "to pray." But the brotherhood of *beghardi* or *Beghards*, composed mostly of the tradesmen, was very loosely organized, making it easy for thieves and mendicants to pose as members of the poor and ill-clad group. Imposters traveled the Low Countries claiming to be Beghards and asking for alms, and the group was held in low repute by the end of the 13th century—especially because a large number of the Beghards were militant trade unionists who raised havoc wherever they went, and because many other members had become idle, wandering mendicants like their imitators. The Old French word *begard*, meaning mendicant, was soon formed from either the Medieval Latin *beghardi*, for Beghards, or from the Middle Dutch *beggaert*, meaning the same thing. *Begard*, in turn, became the Anglo-French *begger*, which was transformed into the Middle English *beggare*, or mendicant, with its verb *beggen*, meaning to ask for alms. Eventually we had the English word *beggar* that we use today, the verb *to beg* thus growing out of what the *beggar* did. Other scholars trace *beggar* to the obscure Old English word *bedecian*, which is only related to a Gothic word meaning mendicant and is so rare it has been found only once. But even if this is correct, there is no doubt that the Beghards at least reinforced the idea of *beggar* in people's minds. *See also* BIGOT.

beggar on horseback. "Set a beggar on horseback and he will ride a gallop," Robert Burton observed in his *Anatomy of Melancholy*. But the proverb, meaning there is no one so arrogant as a beggar who has suddenly made his fortune, probably dates back much earlier. It possibly derives from the old English proverb, "Set a beggar on horseback and he'll ride to the devil." This proverb is common to many languages, its German equivalent, for instance, being "Set a beggar on horseback and he'll outride the devil."

begin with b. Whether it is true or not no scientific study has established, but this is a venerable nautical saying regarding the naming of ships. Because ships whose name begin with A supposedly have a greater history of misfortune, *begin with b* has been almost a rule among some sailors and shipowners when naming their vessels.

begonia. Michel Begon (1638–1710) served as a minor navy official at various French ports until a fortunate marriage led to his appointment by Louis XIII as royal commissioner in Santo Domingo, though he wasn't Santo Domingo's governor, as is often claimed. Begon primarily concerned himself with protecting the natives from unscrupulous merchants and attending to their medical needs, but the amateur horticulturist ordered a detailed study of the island's plant life, collecting hundreds of specimens. Among these he found the begonia, now a common house and garden plant, which he took back to France with him and introduced to European botanists. The begonia however, wasn't named for him until 67 years after his death, when it was first brought to England. Begon is remembered for his patronage of science and his public spirit. On the opening of his large private library to the public, for example, friends advised him that he would surely lose numerous books. "I had much rather lose my books," he replied, "than seem to distrust an honest man." The begonia he discovered is a most valuable garden plant because it prefers the shade, where it flowers freely, is available in a large variety of colors, and can be grown for its foliage as well as its beautiful blooms. The *Begonia* genus contains some 1,000 species.

begorrah! *By God!* is the curse this comic Irish euphemism conceals, though practically no one thinks *begorrah!* means that by now. The corruption dates back to at least the late 19th century.

beg the question. *Begging the question* doesn't mean evading the question by giving an indirect answer, as is often assumed. The old phrase, which can be traced back to the 16th century, is the rough equivalent of the logician's *petitio principii* and means "to stack the cards in an argument by assuming something that hasn't been proved before the debate begins." *Beg the question* actually means that someone is acting like a beggar, asking his opponent to concede the argument at the beginning. "O shameless beggar, that craveth no less than the whole controversy to be given him!" an early English author wrote in explaining the term.

beg to advise. The much-used phrase *beg to advise*, so often read in business letters, may be dated but isn't incorrect by any means. Here *advise* doesn't mean "to give advice" but "to give information," information being one of the meanings of *advice*. This is seen in another common business expression: "We would appreciate the benefit of your advice."

behind the eight ball. *See* EIGHT BALL.

behind the scenes. Though the origins of this phrase are theatrical, as you would expect, it goes back to the English theater in the time of Charles I, when elaborate paintings were commonly used for the first time to create atmosphere on the stage. Since these paintings were often landscapes, they were called "scenes." Behind them much of the important action of a play went on—birth, murders, intrigues, and the like—action that wasn't represented on the stage. As early as 1658 we find the playwright John Dryden writing on "Things happening in the Action of the Play, and suppos'd to be done behind the Scenes." It wasn't long before the phrase began to be used figuratively to describe any important action hidden from the ordinary spectator, especially in places of power.

beignet. This square, French-style powdered doughnut without a hole takes its name from the French loanword *beignet*, meaning "fritter." It is popular in New Orleans and other parts of southern Louisiana. Marketed widely today, it is also spelled *bignet* and is sometimes pronounced *ben-ya*.

béisbol. *Béisbol*, or baseball, is so popular in many Spanish-speaking countries that they have borrowed and altered numerous baseball words from American English. These also include *aut!* (out!), *battero* (batter), *al bate* (at bat), *estraik* (strike), and *jonron* (home run).

bel canto. *Bel canto* is virtuoso singing, a vocal technique emphasizing the quality of sound rather than emotion, a style found in some Italian opera. The words are Italian for "beautiful singing." *Bel canto* writing might be writing with more style than substance, though some would say the only substance *is* style.

Belcher scarf; Belcher ring. Jim or Jem Belcher, England's version of Gentleman Jim Corbett, carried and made popular a large pocket handkerchief, its blue background spotted with large white spots with a small dark blue spot in the center of each. Such handkerchiefs or neckerchiefs, often more descriptively called "bird's eye wipes," were named after the boxer, as was the *Belcher ring*, a huge gold affair set with a large stone that was prominent even on Belcher's massive dukes. Jim Belcher, the most celebrated boxer of his time, lost an eye in 1803, thereafter retiring from the ring and owning or operating a pub. He died in 1811, when only 30 years old. Belcher's name, oddly enough, means "fine gentleman" in French. He bore a remarkable resemblance to Napoleon and was in fact billed as the "Napoleon of the Ring."

beldam. Beautiful things deteriorate. So do beautiful words. *Beldam* comes ultimately from the French *belle dame*, beautiful lady. It crossed the Channel and eventually became a polite English term for a grandmother. Then (as the English grew less polite?) it came to mean any old woman at all, and finally, an ugly old woman, a hag.

belfry. This word for a church steeple isn't directly named for the bells hung inside it; in fact, it owes its life to the worship of war, not God. In their desire to conquer their neighbors, German strategists of the Middle Ages built moveable wooden towers ironically called *bergfieds* ("peace" shelters) that they used in their advances on walled cities. Soldiers concealed inside these primitive, "vertical" tanks could protect themselves from enemy archers, and the devices proved so effective that many other European armies adopted them. By the time the English imported the siege tower in about 1500 it was called the *berfrey* and the English built it even taller, so that their own archers could climb to the top and fire arrows into a walled city or castle. But with the invention of new weapons using gunpowder, the wooden *berfreys* became outmoded in offensive military operations and were hauled within the walls of cities to serve as watchtowers. Here they were equipped with bells so that watchmen inside could sound the alarm of an enemy attack. Over the years people constantly associated the word *berfrey* with the word bell and because of this "klang association"—the hearing of one word in the sound of another—they began to pronounce it *belfrey*, substituting an *l* from bell for the *r*; this dissimilation being *belfry's* only etymological connection with the word *bell*. Later, churches were built with bell towers and the name *belfry* was used for them, too.

believe it or not. Robert Ripley's (1893–1949) syndicated newspaper column, books, and television show called *Believe It Or Not* have been with us since 1923 and almost from the beginning made this expression a part of the language. Up until his death in 1975 the late Norbert Pearlroth researched most of the material for the column—not in exotic places but in the New York Public Library.

Belisha beacon. *See* HORE-BELISHA.

belittle. Thomas Jefferson coined the word *belittle* in about 1780 and Noah Webster included it in his 1828 dictionary, but many critics denounced it as an incurably vulgar term, one going so far as to say "It has no visible chance of becoming English . . ." The condemnations went on for almost a century, but needless to say all the belittling of *belittle* failed to ban the word from the language.

belladonna lily. Belladonna means "pretty lady" in Italian and this flower may be so named because its smooth petals resemble a pretty girl's skin, or because Italian women once used the red sap of the plant as a cosmetic or to brighten their eyes. A beautiful shepherdess in the poems of Virgil and Theocritus gives the *belladonna lily* its scientific name *Amaryllis*.

bellarmine. *Bellarmine* is a historical term referring to a glazed stone beer jug designed to ridicule Italian cardinal Roberto Francesco Romolo Bellarmino (1542–1621). Cardinal Bellarmine, as he is better known, distinguished himself as a Jesuit scholar and was a friend of Galileo, but is usually remembered for his persecution of Protestants in Flanders. The Flemish later retaliated by caricaturing him with the large *bellarmine*, which was designed as a burlesque likeness, having a huge belly and a narrow neck. The controversial cardinal was canonized in 1930.

bellibone. In the 16th century a pretty lass was called a *bellibone*, the whimsical word an Anglicization of the French *belle et bonne*, "fair and good."

bell the cat. To bell the cat is to take on a dangerous mission at great personal risk for the benefit of others. Cats, of course, have long been belled to prevent them from killing songbirds. But the expression derives from a wise mouse. It is from an old fable retold in William "Long Will" Langland's alliterative poem "The Vision Concerning Piers Plowman," which was written, as far as is known, between 1360 and 1399. "Piers Plowman" tells of a family of mice who hold a meeting to decide what to do about a cat who has been preventing them from foraging for food. One cunning mouse suggests that a brass bell be hung around the cat's neck so that they could be warned of its approach. Everyone agrees that this ploy is perfect, except for one sage mouse, who steps forward and says, "Excellent idea, but who will bell the cat?"

bellwether. Since Anglo-Saxon times a bellwether has been a castrated male sheep that usually has a bell fastened around its neck and leads the flock. Later the word was applied humorously to a ringleader, the leader of any mob, conspiracy, or the like, and then was used to describe any leader who assumes the forefront of a profession or industry, etc., as in "New York is the bellwether of the publishing industry."

bellyache. *Bellyache* had earlier meant "colic" in England, but in the sense of "to complain" it is an Americanism coined about midway through the 19th century and first recorded in 1881. As with so many coined words, no one knows its clever inventor's name.

bellyache root. The plant scientifically named *Angelica lucida canadensis fortasse* was widely used as a tonic for stomachaches by American colonists. They gave it the popular name *bellyache root* that it still goes by today.

belly cheater; belly robber; belly burglar. *Belly cheater* is an old American cowboy term for a cook, which may date back to the 19th century but is first recorded as U.S. Navy slang in the form of *belly robber*, specifically referring to a commissary steward. The term has also been used for an Army mess sergeant. Another (later) variant is *belly burglar*.

belly laugh. *See* HIGH HAT.

belly-timber; belly-cheer; belly-god. An old English term for food or provisions—timber for the belly—*belly-timber* is recorded as early as 1607 and as late as the mid-19th century, having been used by a number of great writers, including Butler and Smollett. *Belly-cheer*, another delightful word, is perhaps a century older, and refers to food that cheers the belly. A *belly-god* is usually a person who makes a god of his belly, a glutton, though a *belly-god* can be "a god presiding over the appetites": the three belly-gods being Bacchus, Ceres and Venus.

below the belt; Queensberry rules. Boxing enthusiast John Sholto Douglas, the eighth marquis of Queensberry, put boxing on a more humane basis in 1867 when he and lightweight boxer John Graham Chambers drew up a code of 12 rules to govern boxing matches that were generally accepted by 1875 and standard throughout England by 1889. The rules instituted many modern features, including the use of gloves, a limited number of three-minute rounds, the 10-second count for a knockout, and the outlawing of wrestling, gouging, and hitting below the belt line on a boxer's trunk. The Queensberry rules became the basis for all world boxing regulations. The rule that attracted most attention was the one prohibiting hitting below the belt, a practice that had been widely accepted despite the fact that fighters hit in the testicles suffered excruciating pain. *Queensberry rules* mark the first literal use of the expression, and not long after their formation *below the belt* was being used figuratively to describe any dirty, unfair methods.

beluga caviar. *See* CAVIAR.

belvedere. *Belvedere* is Italian for "fine or fair sight." Summer houses commanding a fine view of the garden were beginning to be built on English estates in the 16th century, when the word came into the language from France or Italy.

Ben Day. A New York printer named Benjamin Day (1831–1916) invented the Ben Day process of quick mechanical production of stippling, shading, or tints on line engravings. *Ben Dayed* means produced by the Ben Day photoengraving method. The process, which has been used since about 1879, eliminates the shading of a drawing by hand.

bender. Though most benders, or drunken sprees, take place on land today, the word has nautical origins. Before it came ashore it was a sailor's word for a drinking bout, first recorded in the 19th century.

Bendigo, Australia. The only city ever named for a prizefighter is Bendigo, Australia, which has a population of some 50,000 and is the third largest sheep and cattle market in that country. Bendigo, the site of a famous gold strike in 1851, honors the ring name of English pugilist William Thompson (1811–89), as does the bendigo fur cap popular in the late 19th century. Thompson was born the same year that Fighting Jim BELCHER died. He may have been one of triplets nicknamed Shadrach, Meshac, and Abednego, or his nickname could have stemmed from his evangelical pursuits, but, in any event, in 1835 he signed his first ring challenge "Abed-Nego of Nottingham," and used the nickname Bendigo for the remainder of his career—until he gave up fighting to become a full-time evangelist. Bendigo, Australia had some second thoughts about its eponymous name, changing it to Sandhurst in 1871, but reverted back to the old application in 1891, two years after Thompson's death.

beneath; beneath contempt. Deriving from an Old English word, *beneath* is first recorded in 1205. As for its prepositional use, the *O.E.D.* puts it this way: "The prepositional use of *beneath* seems originally to have been introduced to express the notion of 'lower than' . . . But in the process of time *beneath* was so widely used for *under* that *below* was laid hold of to express the more general idea . . ." *Beneath* has thus become "more or less a literary and slightly archaic equivalent" of both *under* and *below*, and is preferred to these words only in a few phrases, such as *beneath contempt*, below the level or dignity even of contempt, which seems to have first been recorded in the late 19th century.

benedick; benedict. A benedick is strictly a sworn bachelor entrapped in marriage, while *benedict* refers to a bachelor of marriageable age. The former term derives from the name of the character Benedick in Shakespeare's *Much Ado About Nothing* and the latter honors St. Benedict (d. 543), founder of the Benedictine order and a great advocate of celibacy. Benedict originally meant a perennial bachelor sworn to celibacy, and it is probably for this reason that Shakespeare adopted and adapted the name—for its amusing contrast to his Benedick, the young lord who vows at the beginning of *Much Ado About Nothing* to forever remain a bachelor and is finally talked into marriage. Shakespeare may have borrowed his idea from Thomas Kyd's *The Spanish Tragedy*, and the Latin *Benedictus*, "the blessed," probably also influenced his choice of the name. Although there is a distinction between the two words, they are used interchangeably today, meaning not a bachelor anymore, but a newly married man who had been a bachelor for a long time. *Benedict*, as in "a happy *benedict*," is the usual spelling.

Benedict Arnold. QUISLING and a few others have endured, but most traitors have not been included in the dictionaries. *Benedict Arnold* is an exception. The term has been used for over 200 years in America, and is still a common one. Every schoolboy knows the story of how General Benedict Arnold plotted to deliver the garrison at West Point to Major John André, how the plot failed with André's capture and how Arnold fled to the British army. Less familiar are the facts that Arnold was a brilliant soldier and that his treason was provoked by shabby treatment at the hands of superiors several times during the course of the Revolutionary War.

Benedictine; Benedictines.　Many famous drinks treated in these pages—champagne, coffee, chianti, mocha, scotch, seltzer, and Vichy water—are named after places, but the celebrated liqueur Benedictine is named for the monastery of a famous religious brotherhood. The particular monk who concocted the drink was one Don Bernardo Vincelli, a man whom the medieval archbishop of Rouen declared as important to humanity as any saint for his inspiration. Benedictine, one of the oldest liquors in the world, was first made at the Benedictine monastery at Fecamp, France in about 1510. Called Benedictine in honor of the order, its makers dedicated it "to the greater glory of God." Though the monastery was destroyed during the French Revolution, monks managed to save the secret formula, and 50 years later a Frenchman named Le Grand began manufacturing Benedictine, his distillery still standing on the site of the abbey. Le Grand labeled each bottle D.O.M., which are the initials of the order's motto and stand for *Deo optimo maximo*, "for the most good and great God."

benefit of clergy.　Benefit of clergy was until 1827 a procedure in British law whereby a criminal arrested for a felony was exempt from trial in the secular courts if he could recite a passage from the Bible—the passage becoming known as *neck verse*. After reciting the verse, whether he was accused of murder, rape, or burglary (all capital offenses), he would be turned over to an ecclesiastical court, which could not invoke the death penalty for such crimes, and his neck would be saved from the hangman or axman. Originally, this privilege was granted only to the clergy, but as it was based on the biblical injunction, "Touch not my annointed and do my prophet no harm" (1 Chron. 26:22), it was extended to anyone who could read or write, that is, anyone who could *become* an ordained clergyman. This early-day "diplomatic immunity" of course discriminated against the uneducated poor. The *neck verse* that had to be recited was from the first verse of Psalms 51: "Have mercy upon me, O God, according to Thy loving kindness: According unto the multitude of Thy tender mercies blot out my transgressions. . . ." This verse is commonly called the *Miserere* because its opening words in Latin are *Miserere mei Deus*.

benign neglect.　*Benign neglect* was used in reference to a proposed policy of giving fewer welfare benefits to U.S. minorities in the 1970s, but it originated long before this. The term was coined in 1839 by the Earl of Durham and described England's treatment of Canada.

Benjamin.　Probably the least known of American currency notes. The *Benjamin*, a two-dollar bill, honored Judah Philip Benjamin (1811–84), Confederate secretary of war and secretary of state during the Civil War. The brilliant lawyer, statesman, and plantation owner was one of Jefferson Davis's best friends and was known in the North as "the brains of the Confederacy." He escaped to England after the Civil War and carved out another brilliant legal career. Today, *Benjamin*, or *Ben*, is common slang for a $100 bill, named in honor of Ben Franklin, whose pictures is on the bill.

benne.　Another name for sesame seeds. *Sesamum indicum* is said to be the oldest herbaceous plant cultivated for its seeds. *Benne*, as the seeds are called in Africa, or *sim sim*, another African name for them, were brought to America on the first slave ships. They have been used for everything from ink to cattle feed to flour to oil, and are popular ingredient in cookies, crackers, and candies. *Benne* is a Wolof word for the sesame seed. *Sesamum* is the Greek version of the Arabic word for sesame.

benny; benjamin.　Today a benny is usually American slang for an amphetamine tablet, especially Benzedrine, a trademarked name, but it also signifies both a pawnbroker and an overcoat. A pawnbroker became a *benny* because he often makes loans on overcoats, which are sometimes called *bennies* or *benjies*, a shortened form of *benjamins*. The benjamin, at first a certain tight-fitting style of overcoat and then any overcoat at all, probably derives from the biblical Benjamin, in humorous reference to his brother Joseph's coat of many colors (Gen. 37: 3). But some scholars claim that the *benjamin* was created by a mid-19th-century London tailor of that name, the biblical tale rendering the term popular, and Mencken suggests that *benny* for an overcoat may have derived from the Romany *bengru*, "a waistcoat." *Benny* is also slang for a derby.

Ben Trovato.　*Ben Trovato* comes from the Italian phrase *Se non e vero, e ben trovato* ("If it is not true, it is well invented"), so it has often been used humorously as the authority for a good story that really isn't true—*ben trovato*, in other words, has over the years become the quoted scholar Ben Trovato. Every effort has been made to bar Ben Trovato from these pages, but in a work of this size it is impossible to be sure that he hasn't sneaked in somewhere. What can be promised is that if old Benjamin is anywhere on the premises, he'll certainly be spinning a good yarn.

Bering Sea.　*See* SEWARD'S FOLLY.

Berlin blue.　*See* PRUSSIAN BLUE.

berm.　*Berm* is first recorded in 1854, in the sense of "the bank of a canal opposite the towing path." The word derives from the German *Berme*, "a path or strip of ground along a dike," and over the years has come to mean the side or shoulder of a road, especially in the southern U.S.

Bermuda.　Juan de Bermúdez, a Spanish colonist, had been migrating elsewhere late in the 18th century when he was shipwrecked in what is today called the Bermuda Triangle. He and a cargo of pigs wound up on the island that now bears his name.

the berries.　*The berries* has been American talk for "the best, the greatest" since 1902, when it seems to have originated as college slang. *Berry* had been recorded a few years earlier as slang for a dollar and perhaps this use suggested the expression.

berserk.　Old Berserkr ("Bear Skin"), a famous hero in Norse mythology, was a supernatural warrior who fought with feral fury and feared nothing; he even spurned weapons or armor, rushing into battle protected only by the bearskin thrown over his shoulder and clawing and biting his victims to death. His 12 sons bore the same name, and these mad warriors could also turn themselves into wild beasts that neither fire nor armor could kill. Together they terrorized the land. This is the most widely accepted biography of Old Berserkr. Another account says he was a grandson of the eight-handed Starkader and that he got his name not from his bearskin, but from Norsemen calling him *baer-serce*, bare of mail, because he went into battle without armor. At any rate, the legends surrounding Berserkr and his dozen scions became known to the English, who spelled his name Berserkar. Any fierce fighter was soon called a *berserker*, especially one who fought with a fury that seemed almost insane and terrified even his allies. In time *to go berserk* came to mean the violent, furious rage of a madman.

berth. *See* GIVE A WIDE BERTH TO.

Bertillon system. The first modern scientific method for identifying criminals was the Bertillon system, devised by Alphonse Bertillon (1853–1914), French anthropologist and pioneer criminologist. Bertillon developed *Bertillonage*, as the system is also called, when he headed the criminal identification bureau in the Seine prefecture and described it in his book *La Photographie judiciare*. Adopted by France in 1888, the revolutionary method relied on anthropometry—the classification of skeletal and other body measurements, plus the color of hair, eyes, etc., for purposes of comparison. Fingerprints were a late addition to these *Bertillon measurements* and soon supplanted the system itself. The term is still used, though, to describe fingerprints and all anthropometric measurements.

beshame bush. A colorful name for the mimosa (*Mimosa pudica*), or any sensitive plant that closes its leaves when touched. This mimosa plant should not be confused with the mimosa tree.

Bessemer converter, etc. We might almost as fairly call the Bessemer process the Kelly process. This revolutionary method for converting pig or cast iron to steel is named after Englishman Henry Bessemer (1813–98), but it was discovered almost concurrently by American inventor William Kelly (1811–88). Bessemer, the son of a French artist, was already a respected metallurgist and the inventor of a machine used to reduce gold and bronze to powder when he began experimenting to produce better and cheaper iron for cannons during the Crimean War. He started his work about the year 1854, being granted his first patent a year later, and in 1856 discovered the basic principle involved in his process, which he described in his paper, "The Manufacture of Iron Without Fuel." Bessemer's secret was the removal of carbon and other impurities from pig iron by melting it in his *Bessemer converter* and forcing a blast of air through the molten metal. The Bessemer process, much improved today, produced far better steel more cheaply and faster than ever before, tripling English steel production within a few years after its introduction.

best boy. This old term, often puzzling to moviegoers when seen in film credits, simply means the main gaffer, the electrician's chief assistant, on a movie set.

the best fish swim near the bottom. Anything worthwhile takes trouble to obtain. Some tasty fish, such as sole, do swim near the bottom.

the best laid schemes (plans) of mice and men. In his poem *To a Mouse* (ca. 1786) Scottish poet Robert Burns wrote: "The best laid schemes o'mice an'men / Gang aft a-gley." The words have ever since been a common expression for failed plans in both Great Britain and the U.S., often in its original form, often as *the best laid plans of mice and man often go astray*, and often as the abbreviated *the best laid plans of mice and men*.

best of all possible worlds. *See* DOCTOR PANGLOSS.

best-seller. *Best-seller*, for a book that sells many copies, is an Americanism first recorded in 1905. The Sears Roebuck Catalog was probably the "best-seller" of all time, though it was distributed free for more than three-quarters of a century. Over 5 billion copies may be a conservative estimate for its total distribution since 1896. In second place is the Bible.

betel nut. The betel nut is a famous masticatory that people prize for the joy of a stimulating chew, even though it turns their teeth pitch-black. It comes from the areca or betel palm (*Areca catechu*); the tree's fruit, roughly the size of a hen's egg, contains the mottled gray seed or nut. The nuts are boiled, sliced, and dried in the sun until they turn black or dark brown, when they are ready to be wrapped up in betel leaves and chewed. Native to Malaya and southern India, betel nuts are so widely used in Asian nations that it is estimated that $\frac{1}{10}$th of all the people on earth indulge in betel chewing. The introduction of modern chewing gum has cut into this figure slightly, but the betel chewers aren't easily discouraged, not by the copious flow of brick-red saliva caused by chewing the betel nuts, which dye the lips, mouth, and gums, nor by all those black teeth resulting from a betel nut habit. Betel is a true excitant and arouses a great craving in the addict. Legions of devotees—black-toothed, bloody-mouthed, and bad-breathed—can still be seen throughout Asia chomping away and squirting scarlet juice on the walls.

bet one's bottom dollar. To be so sure about something that one will bet all one has on it, the last of one's money, as in "I'll bet my bottom dollar on it." Commonly heard throughout the U.S. today, the expression comes from the American West over a century and a half ago, when poker was often played with silver dollars. Someone completely sure of a hand would push his whole stack of silver dollars, including the one on the bottom, into the pot to cover a bet or a final raise.

better a hash at home than a roast with strangers. A saying coined by New England poet-physician Oliver Wendell Holmes in a letter home while traveling far from Boston. *See* ANESTHESIA.

better half. Originally these words bore no hint of male chauvinism, applying to a husband as well as a wife and meant to be taken seriously. The expression can be traced back to the Roman poet Horace, who called his old friend Maecenas his *better half*. But the term became common in England only about 1570, not long before Sir Philip Sidney began writing his prose romance *Arcadia* (1580). The Puritans had used the phrase to describe the soul, the *better half* of the person, but Sidney popularized its use as a description of either partner in a marriage. For three centuries husbands and wives called their mates *my better half* without any humor intended. It wasn't much more than a century ago that it began to be used jocularly and mainly in reference to a wife.

better mousetrap.   *See* BUILD A BETTER MOUSETRAP.

between a rock and a hard place.   In days past if one was badly in need of money, almost bankrupt, he or she was said to be *between a rock and a hard place*. This expression was probably born in Arizona during a financial panic early in this century, but over the years its meaning changed. It came to mean being in a very tight spot, on the horns of a dilemma in making a hard decision. The words do lend themselves best to this last definition, for wherever one turns in making the decision there is rock or something as hard as or harder than rock.

between grass and hay.   The period between childhood or adolescence and adulthood; the term dates back to the 19th century.

between Scylla and Charybdis.   The *Odyssey* vividly describes Odysseus's passage between Scylla and Charybdis. In Greek mythology Scylla (Skulla) was a beautiful maiden loved by Poseidon, the lord of the sea. But her rival, Amphitrite, fed Scylla magic herbs that transformed her into a monster with 12 dangling feet, six long necks with a head on each, and three rows of teeth. She dwelt in a high cave overlooking the sea (situated, according to tradition, in the Strait of Messina) and from every ship that passed by, each of her terrible mouths reached down and devoured a sailor. On the other side of the narrow channel, beneath an immense wild fig tree, lay a dangerous whirlpool called Charybdis (Charubdis) that sucked in and regorged the sea three times a day. It was Odysseus's fate to sail between Scylla and Charybdis, as it is still the fate of anyone steering a mid-course between equally dangerous perils. Odysseus had mixed luck: he lost his crew and ship, but saved his own life by clinging to the fig tree above Charybdis.

between the cup and the lip there's many a slip.   No one knows where this common phrase originated, though it has been traced back to the 16th century. It means of course that anything can happen between the making of plans and their fulfillment.

between the devil and the deep blue sea.   The Devil didn't inspire this old saying, as many people believe. It is thought to be a nautical expression, as its earliest recorded use in 1621 indicates, the "devil" in it referring not to Satan but to a seam between planks in a wooden ship's deck, specifically the long seam nearest to either side of a ship. This seam was "the devil to get at" and any sailor caulking it in a heavy sea risked falling overboard. The seam that ran around a ship's hull at the waterline, another one difficult and dangerous to get at, was also called "the devil," and these two devils inspired the memorable alliterative phrase *between the devil and the deep blue sea*— someone caught on the horns of a dilemma, caught between difficulties that are equally dangerous. Similarly, "the devil to pay" refers to "paying"—waterproofing with pitch—the devil on a ship. *Pay* here comes from the Latin *picare*, for the process, and the original phrase was "the devil to pay and no hot pitch."

between the lines.   *See* READ BETWEEN THE LINES.

between wind and water.   Any ship struck by a shell or torpedo in an area that is *between wind and water*—that is, damaged in a part of the hull that dips into the water and then rises to the wind when plowing through rough seas—is usually seriously damaged. The expression *between wind and water* has thus been used since the 16th century to signify hazardous damage in a ship and is used metaphorically to mean an unexpected attack on someone.

between you, me, and the bedpost.   This is the earliest of the *between you, me, and . . .* expressions, dating back to about 1830 and meaning "confidentially, between us." Bedposts were of course part of the often curtained four-poster beds of the time. Other expressions with the exact same gossipy meaning include *between you, me, and the barn*, first recorded 20 years later, and BETWEEN YOU, ME, AND THE LAMPPOST, which probably dates to the 1850s and is similar to *you, me, and the gatepost* (of a fence) common at about the same time.

between you, me, and the lamppost.   Dickens used this expression in *Nicholas Nickleby* (1838) and it couldn't be much older, for "lamppost" is first recorded in 1790. But the words probably derive from earlier expressions meaning "in confidence," such as *between you and me* and *between you and me and the gatepost* (or *bedpost*).

Beulah land.   A biblical term (Isaiah 62:4) used for heaven or the promised land; also called Beulah shore.

Bevinism.   British public servant Ernest Bevin, who once served in Winston Churchill's cabinet, was a mangler and mauler of language on par with the Reverend William Spooner, Count Joseph Marrowsky, film producer Samuel Goldwyn, and baseball player and manager Casey Stengel. A typical Bevinism: "If you open this Pandora's box, you will find it full of Trojan horses." *See also* MALAPROPISM; MARROWSKY; SPOONERISM.

beware of and eschew pompous prolixity.   *See* LEGALESE.

Beware of Dog!   This common warning sign has probably been around as long as the dog has been domesticated and humankind has known how to write. An archaeological dig in Italy found such a sign (*Cave canem!*) on a house among ancient Roman ruins, and Petronius Arbiter (d. A.D. 66) records the warning in his *Satyricon*. *See* ONE GOOD TURN.

beware of Greeks bearing gifts.   *See* GREEK.

beyond the pale; put to the pale.   There is no connection between this expression and the word *pale*, "of whitish appearance," which comes from the Latin *pallidus*, "pallid." *Pale* here refers to the Latin *palus*, "a stake or boundary marker driven into the ground with others to fence off a territory under the rule of a certain nation." Pale or picket fences (we call them palings today) were erected all over Europe from Roman times to designate territory belonging to a certain country. Later, the "pale" came to be used figuratively, as in the famous 15th-century "English pale" portion of Ireland that the English dominated before Cromwell conquered the whole island. *Beyond* *the pale* first meant simply to be outside the boundaries or jurisdiction of a nation, but by extension, and with the aid of Kipling's "Beyond the Pale," it came to describe a dismal place to which we assign social outcasts, those regarded as beyond the bounds of moral or social decency. To *put to the pale* often means to defeat someone so badly that he'll be banished from competition with you forever ("Write more poems like this and you'll put Poe to the pale.").

be your age.   *See* ACT YOUR AGE.

bialy.   *See* BAGEL.

Bibb lettuce.   An amateur gardener named John B. Bibb developed Bibb lettuce in his backyard garden in Frankfort, Kentucky, about 1850, and the variety has been an American favorite ever since. Bibb is the most famous and best of what are called butterhead lettuces, having a tight small head of dark green color and a wonderful flavor. Because the variety is inclined to bolt in hot weather, a summer Bibb is now offered by nurserymen for the home garden. Several kinds of lettuce are named after their developers, including blackseeded Simpson, a loose-leaf variety. The vegetable can be traced back to ancient India and Central Asia, but takes its name from the Latin word *lac*, meaning silk, the Romans favoring lettuce for its milky juice and calling it *lactuce*. Bibb is not often found in the market, the most popular sellers in the United States being iceberg lettuce, a heading variety, and loose-leaf Boston lettuce.

Bible.   The following quote succinctly gives the history of the word: "Round about the twelfth century B.C., an Egyptian envoy, Wen-Amon by name, visited the king of the Phoenician town of Byblus . . . Now, Byblus, today the small city of Gebal, was one of the oldest cities of Syria and Palestine. It had been long in close contact with Egypt and, as a trading center, among other articles of import it included papyrus . . . From Byblus the Greeks called papyrus *biblos;* and from the plural *(biblia)* of the diminutive *biblion* is derived our word Bible, properly '[the] books,' " (Stanley Cook, *An Introduction to the Bible*, 1945.) *See* BOOK.

Bible Belt.   H. L. Mencken invented this term to describe parts of the United States where the literal accuracy of the Bible is widely believed, which of course is not limited to the South, despite the first use of the term: "*The Baptist Record*, in Jackson, Mississippi, [is] in the heart of the Bible and Lynching Belt" (*American Mercury*, 1926). More recently the term has been used to refer to any area of religious or moral fervor.

Bibles.   *See* BUG BIBLE.

biblia a-biblia.   "I can read anything which I call a *book*," wrote Charles Lamb. "There are things in that shape which I cannot allow for such. In this catalogue of books which are not books—*biblia a-biblia*—I reckon Court Calendars, Directories, Pocket Books, Draught Boards, bound and lettered on the back, Scientific Treatises, Almanacs, Statutes at Large, the works of Hume, Gibbon, Robertson, Beattie, Soame Jenyns, and generally, all those volumes which 'no gentleman's library should be without.' "

bibliobibuli.   This little-known word was coined by that great lover of language, H. L. Mencken, who defined it thus: "There are people who read too much: The bibliobibuli. I know some who are constantly drunk on books, as other men are drunk on whiskey or religion. They wander through this most diverting and stimulating of worlds in a haze, seeing nothing and hearing nothing." Wrote Anatole France: "We live too much in books and not enough in nature, and we are very much like that simpleton of a Pliny the Younger, who went on studying a Greek author while before his eyes Vesuvius was overwhelming five cities beneath the ashes." *See* BOOKWORM.

bibliopoles and other bibliotypes.   A *bibliopole* is simply a bookdealer, while a *bibliotaph* is one who conceals or hoards books, keeping them under lock and key, and a *biblioclast* is someone who collects and treasures books either for their value or for what's in them, and a *bibliomaniac* is a *bibliophile* gone bonkers, one who loves books to the point of madness. Legend has it that Don Vicente, a Spanish friar and scholar, murdered five or six collectors to steal a rare book, which makes him a *biblioklept* as well as a *bibliomaniac*. Another noted book thief was Innocent X, who, before he became pope, was caught redhanded stealing *L'Histoire du Concile de Trente* from a painter's studio while visiting with a religious party. The future pope was evicted bodily by the painter, and some historians believe that this action caused the ill-feeling toward France that marked the pontifical reign of Innocent X. The ancient Assyrians had curses like this for the library *biblioklept*: "The gods of heaven and earth and the gods of Assyria, may all these curse him with a curse which cannot be relieved, terrible and merciless, as long as he lives, may they let his name, his seed, be carried off from the land, may they put his flesh in a dog's mouth!"

Bic.   Disposable Bic pens have been manufactured by the billions since they were invented by Hungarian Ladislas Biro in 1953, so many used throughout the world that the *Bic* trademark has become synonymous for a pen. Bics are named after the Frenchman (born in Italy) Baron Marcel Bich (pronounced "beek"), who bought the rights to the pen from Biro and manufactured and promoted them, his first factory a leaky shed on a street in Paris. Bich died in 1994, age 79.

Bickerstaff Hoax.   Nearly all of Jonathan Swift's works were published anonymously and he received payment only for *Gulliver's Travels* (£200). In the case of the Bickerstaff Hoax, Swift used the pen name Isaac Bickerstaff. Indignant when an ignorant cobbler named John Partridge, claiming to be an astrologer, published an almanac of astrological predictions, Swift parodied the book under the title "Prediction for the ensuing year by Isaac Bickerstaff." In his parody, he foretold the death of John Partridge on March 29, 1708, and when the day arrived Swift published a letter affirming his prediction and giving an account of Partridge's death. Partridge indignantly protested that he was very much alive, but Swift wrote what he called a "Vindication," *proving* that Partridge was dead. Poor Partridge was doomed to a literary death as a result, especially when other writers perpetuated the joke. So famous did the pseudonym Isaac Bickerstaff become that Richard Steele used it as his pen name in the *Tatler*. Benjamin Franklin later emulated Swift's hoax in America.

bicycle. Englishman J. I. Stassen coined the word *bicycle* in 1869. The two-wheeled vehicles were previously called *veloci-pedes*, among many other names, including the humorous *boneshaker* because of the machine's vibrations on the terrible roads of the time. Early bicycles so scared horses on the road that many towns and cities required bicycle riders to dismount when approaching one. *See* ROADHOG.

bidet. Ben Jonson is the first to record *bidet*, in 1630. A low basinlike bath "used especially in France for bathing one's private parts," the bidet is "bestridden, one squatting to wash." Someone with a sense of humor named the bath after the small horse called a bidet that people had to ride with their legs drawn up to avoid dragging their feet on the ground.

big. No one really knows the origin of this important monosyllabic word. *Big* has been traced to the Middle English *bigge*, meaning the same, but no further than that. It may come from the Scandinavian *bugge*, "an important man," but it could also derive from the Latin *bucca*, in the sense of "inflated cheek," among other possibilities.

the Big Apple. A nickname for New York City since the 1960s, *the Big Apple* was first used in New Orleans. In about 1910 jazz musicians there used it as a loose translation of the Spanish *manzana principal*, the main "apple orchard," the main city block downtown, the place where all the action is.

big as old Cuffey. A historical expression describing someone or something of great size. The eponym is Captain Paul Cuffey, a black ship captain of New Bedford, Massachusetts, who in about 1787 recruited free African Americans to settle in Sierra Leone and transported them there on his ship.

Big Bang theory. The cosmological theory holding that the universe originated with the explosion of a single compact mass, blasting matter in every direction. The term was invented in 1950 by astrophysicist Fred Hoyle (1918–2001), who used it derisively in defending his *steady state theory* (1938). "This big bang theory seemed to be unsatisfactory," he wrote, but over the years the *big bang theory* has become generally more accepted than his own.

Big Ben. Big Ben is not the huge clock in London's Parliament tower, though it is often given this name. The words really describe the huge, deep-toned bell in St. Stephen's Tower that strikes the hours over the British Houses of Parliament. Big Ben, cast from 1856 to 1858, weighs 13½ tons, more than twice the weight of the 6½-ton bell in Philadelphia's Independence Hall. The great bell's first stroke, not the last, marks the hour, four smaller bells in the tower striking the quarter hours on the famed Westminster Chimes. The tower clock, 329 feet high, was designed by lawyer and architect Edmund Grimthorpe (1816–1905), and was named St. Stephen's Tower. This was to be the name of the bell, too, but newspapers took to calling it after Sir Benjamin Hall, Chief Commissioner of Works at the time, and the sobriquet stuck. Big Ben, though a notable achievement in bell founding, is far from being the world's largest bell. Moscow's Tsar Kolokol, a broken and unused giant weighing about 180 tons, is called the "King of Bells."

Big Bertha. On close examination, Big Bertha, the famous cannon that shelled Paris during World War I, is not so complimentary to the woman for whom it was named. *Big Bertha* is a translation of *die dicke Bertha*, "the fat Bertha," a nickname the Germans had for their 42-cm howitzers. They had in mind portly Frau Bertha Krupp von Bohlen und Halbach, whose husband owned the giant Krupp steel and munitions plant at Essen, it being mistakenly believed that the howitzers were manufactured by Krupp, whereas they were actually made at the Skoda works in Austria-Hungary. The Big Bertha aimed at Paris, an even larger gun with a range of 76 miles, began bombarding the city on March 23, 1918, firing every third day for 140 days and killing 256 people in all. On Good Friday of that year alone its shells killed or wounded 156 worshippers in the church of St. Gervais. It was at this time that journalists resurrected the term from the German and began applying it specifically to the Paris gun.

big brass. *See* BRASS.

Big Brother is watching you. *Big Brother* has come to mean a dictator or a dictatorship, a person or a political system that controls people's minds and lives so that there is nothing private and personal anymore. The reference is of course to the character Big Brother in George Orwell's novel *Nineteen Eighty-Four* (1949). *See* BIG WILLIE.

big butter-and-egg man. Speakeasy owner Texas Guinan may have coined this expression for a wealthy big spender during the Roaring Twenties. According to the story, one of her patrons kept buying rounds for the house all evening and showering $50 bills on the chorus girls. Texas asked him to take a bow but he would only identify himself as being in the dairy business, so Texas put the spotlight on him, asking for "a hand for my big butter-and-egg man." In any case, George S. Kaufman used the phrase as the title of a play in 1925, giving it greater currency.

big cheese. A *big cheese*, for "a boss or important person," is an Americanism dating back to about 1890. But it derives from the British expression *the cheese*, meaning "the thing or the correct thing, the best." The British expression, in turn, is a corruption of the Persian or Urdu *chiz* (or *cheez*), "thing," that the British brought back from India in about 1840. A *big cheese* thus has nothing to do with cheese and should properly be "a big chiz."

Big Chill. Recent slang for death or a depressing situation. The expression derives from the title of the popular movie *The Big Chill* (1983), which deals with the death of a member of a close-knit group of friends and their reactions to it.

Big Daddy. An affectionate term for one's grandfather or the paternalistic head of a family, the term made famous by Tennessee Williams as the nickname of the wealthy cotton planter in his play *Cat on a Hot Tin Roof* (1955).

big doolie. Any important person, is sometimes called a *big doolie*, as in this *New York Times* quote from an Olympic gold medal winner: "I got a gold today, so I'm a big doolie." The expression, perhaps half a century old, may have its origin in the older American slang term *dooly*, meaning "dynamite," its origin unknown.

the Big Drink; Big Ditch; Big Water; Big Pond. *The Big Drink*, the first humorous American phrase for the Atlantic, Pacific, or any big body of water, seems to have been coined anonymously in 1844 and was also a name for the Mississippi River, which is more commonly called the Big Ditch of Big Water. Big Ditch, coined in 1825, has also been applied to the Atlantic, but is most commonly associated with the Erie Canal. The *Big Pond*, a humorous term for the Atlantic, stems from about 1840, when it was coined by Canadian humorist Thomas Haliburton.

Big Easy. Possibly this was originally a jazz term referring to the pleasant, easygoing life in New Orleans. No dictionary records the fact, but New Orleans's nickname among its residents is the *Big Easy*, as is noted in the 1987 film of that name. Some authorities believe that Frank Conaway, who wrote the 1970 novel (also called *The Big Easy*) that the movie was based upon, coined the term.

big enchilada. A person who is the boss, the head man or woman, the big shot of any organization. The term is first recorded on one of the Watergate tapes in 1973, the speaker, John Ehrlichman, referring to Attorney General John Mitchell. In a letter from jail to author William Safire, Ehrlichman later claimed he had coined the expression, having "cooked my own enchiladas for years" as part of his "California upbringing." Possibly the term owes something to the phrase *the whole enchilada*—everything, the whole ball of wax—which had been around at least seven years longer, first recorded in 1966. Other foodstuffs associated with bossdom include *big banana*, *big cheese*, *big fish*, *big potato*, and *big vegetable*, among others. An *enchilada*, an American Spanish word, is a tortilla rolled and stuffed with cheese, meat, or beans and served with a hot chili sauce.

big fleas have little fleas. The words, a favorite of President John F. Kennedy's, are found in full in Jonathan Swift's poem "On Poetry" (1733): "Big fleas have little fleas upon their backs to bite them, / and little fleas have lesser fleas, and so on *ad infinitum*." The similar proverbial saying *big fish eat little fish* has been around since the 13th century.

Bigfoot. A huge, hairy, humanoid creature said to inhabit the Pacific Northwest forests, so named because of the size of its alleged footprints, said to be 16 to 17 inches long and 7 inches wide. This abominable snowman of the California mountains is also called Sasquatch, a name recorded in 1925, some 35 years before the name Bigfoot.

big galoot. *See* GALOOT.

the bigger they come, the harder they fall. Boxer Robert "Bob" Fitzsimmons (1862–1917) fought and beat many men bigger and heavier than himself, holding at one time or another the world middleweight, light-heavyweight, and heavyweight championships. Fitzsimmons destroyed "Gentleman Jim" Corbett with his famous "solar plexus punch" and won the admiration of such boxing legends as John L. Sullivan. In 1902, when he was to fight James (Jim) Jeffries in defense of his

heavyweight title, it was pointed out that Jeffries was 50 pounds heavier. "The bigger they come, the harder they fall," Fitzsimmons responded. Unfortunately, despite one of boxing's most memorable bon mots, he lost the fight by a knock-out to Jeffries, who was also 15 years younger. While Fitzsimmons's words were original, both Herodutus and Pindar expressed the same sentiment thousands of years before him. Wrote Pindar:

> It is the lofty pine that by the storm
> Is oftener tossed; towers fall with heavier crash
> Which higher soar.

big gooseberry season. In Victorian times summer was a dull period for the British newspapers. So much space was left for reports of record-size vegetables and fruits grown by one gardener or another that it was nicknamed *the big gooseberry season*.

Big House. The British use this term for the main house in a village, but in the United States it has meant, since about 1913, a prison or penitentiary. The American meaning may, however, come from the mid-19th-century British slang *Big House* for "the workhouse."

Big Hungry. The poor country area around Tuskegee, Alabama, was once commonly called the *Big Hungry*. The famous Tuskegee Institute is located in this area today. Booker T. Washington was the school's first principal, and George Washington Carver taught there.

big kahuna. Originally *kahuna* in Hawaiian meant "a priest or wise man." Then, in the mid-1950s, it also came to mean any expert surfer, and by the 1980s it took on the meaning of "an important person or thing," this last usually in the form of *big kahuna*: "He's the big kahuna around here." The expression is now heard in all the 50 states and in other countries as well.

big league. A term for Major League Baseball (the highest level of organized ball) since the 1890s, *big league* has come to mean the highest level in any field, from art to zoology; its antonym is another baseball term: bush league. *See* BUSH LEAGUE; MAJOR LEAGUE.

Big Muddy. A nickname for the Missouri River dating back a hundred years or so when the West was being settled.

bignonia. A widely distributed woody flowering vine, the bignonia is sometimes confused with the BEGONIA, and the names of the men that the two plants honor are often confused as well. The species are not related, and Abbé Jean-Paul Bignon, court librarian to Louis XIV, did not discover the beautiful bignonia vine bearing his name. The bignonia was named by the French botanist Tournefort about 1700 in honor of the abbé, who had never ventured from Europe.

big nose. A slurname given mainly to Americans and British, among others, by some Chinese, Koreans, and Vietnamese, who apparently believe occidentals have big noses. The term, first recorded in 1952, is said to be a translation of a Chinese expression. During the Korean conflict the U.N. forces, especially Americans, were called *kho-jang-ee*—big noses. Then again, the Koreans may have had a reason not to favor large prominent noses. When the brutal Japanese warlord Toyotomi Hideyoshi invaded Korea in 1592, according to James L. McClain's *Japan: A Modern History* (2002), he and his men hacked off tens of thousands of noses from the faces of Koreans, shipping them back to Kyoto, where he displayed them in a hideous pile for all to see.

bigot. *"Ne, se, bi got!* ('No, by God!')" the Norman lord Rollo is supposed to have shouted indignantly when he was told to kiss the foot or posterior of Charles the Simple as an act of homage, and legend has it that the word *bigot* arose because this phrase of Rollo's was thereafter applied to any obstinate person. But the amusing old story is probably no more than that. Some scholars do suspect, however, that *bigot* stems from the Teutonic oath *bi got,* suggesting that it may have been bestowed as a derogatory nickname upon the Normans, who were regarded as obstinately and intolerantly devoted to their own religion. Nobody knows, but whatever the case, the formation of *bigot* was certainly influenced by the fanatical, intolerant behavior of the Beguine religious order. *See also* BEGGAR.

big shot. Italian general Giuseppe Garibaldi's forces used a 90mm cannon against the Austrians. The big projectile it fired was translated into English by Garibaldi's American followers as the *big shot,* which came to mean a big, important person. Such, at least, is one version of the origin of *big shot,* an Americanism first recorded in 1910, some 30 years after Garibaldi had breathed his last.

Big Sky; Big Sky State. Nicknames for Montana, which is still one of the least populated states.

big sleep. It is believed that this synonym for death was coined by American novelist Raymond Chandler. Chandler used the sometimes capitalized term in his novel *The Big Sleep* (1938), and there is no record of its use before then.

big ticket. Since about 1945 in the U.S. a *big ticket* item has meant an expensive item such as a television set or a fur coat, etc., sold in retail stores.

Big Ugly. There is no more homely named hometown than Big Ugly, West Virginia.

big wheel, etc. *Big wheel,* first recorded in 1941, is the latest in a long line of similar earlier expressions. Of these *bigwig, big shot, big cheese, big gun,* and even *big noise* are still heard, while *big bug, big fish, big dog,* and *big toad in the puddle* are all but dead. The "wheel" in the term could come from the huge wheels in textile mills, or the phrase may derive from the mid-19th-century expression "to roll a big wheel," used by mechanics as a synonym for "to be important or influential."

bigwig. All of Europe's royalty aped France's Louis XIV when he took to wearing long, flowing wigs in his middle years. In England especially, the more important a man was, or imagined himself to be, the bigger the wig he likely would wear. In fact, custom soon dictated that only the nobility, judges, and bishops were permitted to wear the full-length wig still

retained in British courts of law. By then the word *bigwig,* for "an important person," had passed into the language.

Big Willie. Another weapon named after a real person, in this case the first tank to be used in warfare. Officially called the Mark I, the behemoth was invented by Sir William Tritton (1875–1946) and popularly named *Big Willie* in his honor. Tritton was knighted for his invention in 1917, but his tank, first pressed into action a year before on the Somme battlefield, had very little effect on the outcome of World War I. It did, however, mark the beginning of a new kind of land warfare. It is often forgotten that Major W. G. Wilson jointly invented *Big Willie* with Tritton. *See* BIG BERTHA.

bikini. Soon after the two 1946 atomic bomb tests at Bikini Atoll in the Pacific, a French couturier created "L'atome—the world's smallest bathing suit." This was supposed to compare "the effects wrought by a scantily clad woman to the effects of an atomic bomb," as *Webster's* put it. However, French designer Louis Réard outdid L'atome with his Bikini, named after the atoll and "smaller than the smallest bathing suit in the world." *Bikini* caught on, *L'atome* did not. Since then we have had the *string* and the *thong,* even briefer than the bikini, so brief that an American slang synonym for it is *butt floss.*

bilberries. "Pinch the maids as blue as Billberry," Shakespeare wrote in *The Merry Wives of Windsor.* Billberries, or "whortleberries," or "blaeberries," or "whinberries," as they are variously called, are of the same genus as the blueberry. The main difference between the two is that the bilberry (*Vaccinium myrtillus*) is a little plant no more than 18 inches tall that usually produces berries singly, not in clusters as blueberries do. "Nineteen bites to a bilberry," a centuries-old British expression, means to make a major production of an inconsequential act, just as it would be to take 19 bites of a berry no more than one-quarter inch in diameter.

bilge. Now meaning nonsense or filth, *bilge* was originally the dirty water that collected in the bottom of a ship. *Bilge* was first spelled *bulge,* which referred to the fact that the dirty water collected in the bulge, or curve, at the bottom of a straight-sided ship.

bilingual. To be *bilingual* is to be able to speak two languages with facility. The word comes from the Latin *lingua,* tongue, and *bi-,* two, and is first recorded in about 1835. The importance of bilingualism is illustrated by the old South American tale of the cat, mouse, and dog who live in the same house. The cat and the mouse were mortal enemies, of course, but the dog and mouse lived on good terms. So when the mouse heard barking one day, he came out of his hole to greet his canine friend. He was quickly caught by the cat. "You're not supposed to bark!" were the rodent's last words. Replied the cat, licking her chops: "To get along in this life, it is necessary to know more than one language."

bilk. *Bilk* comes from the game of cribbage, where this variant of *balk* means to defraud another player of points by sharp, sly tactics. The term was widely used by the mid 1800s in its current general sense of to cheat or defraud in a clever way.

Bill Daley.   A long lead in a horse race is called a Bill Daley after a 19th-century American jockey instructor of that name. Bill Daley persistently advised his pupils that the best way to win a horse race is to take a long lead and hold on to it.

billiards.   Billiards takes its name from the French word for the cue stick used in the game, a *billard*. The name of the game is first recorded in 1591 and Shakespeare mentions it in *Antony and Cleopatra* (1606): "Let it alone, let's to billiards."

Billies and Charlies.   Collectors will still pay premium prices for genuine *Billies* and *Charlies*, even though they are fake historical objects. They are named for antique dealers William (Billy) Smith and Charles (Charlie) Eaton, who manufactured bogus medieval articles from 1847 to 1858, planting them around London and then "discovering" them in excavations.

billingsgate.   Coarse and abusive language, billingsgate is language similar to that once used by the fishwives in the Billingsgate fish market along the River Thames in London. The area was named for whoever built the gate below the London Bridge leading to the old walled city. But who built Billing's Gate is a matter of controversy. Some historians credit a Mr. Billings (or Billin, or Belin), a builder or famous burgher who owned property thereabouts; others suggest that Billing's Gate was named for an ancient clan called Billings, or for one Belen (Belinus), a legendary monarch, citing a 1658 map that ascribes it to "Belen, ye 23rd Brittish Kinge."

billionaire.   There are no British billionaires, for a billion is a million million there, whereas it is "merely" a thousand million in the U.S. The word *billionaire* was first recorded in 1861. Though stingy with his dimes, John D. Rockefeller was the world's first known billionaire—American style. *See also* MIL-LIONAIRE, TRILLIONAIRE.

bill of lading; bill; check.   *Lading* in this expression simply means "loading." The *bill* part refers not to the modern meaning of bill as a statement of money owed, but to a written, formal, and sealed document. *Bill*, in fact, derived from the Latin *bulla* for seal. Today a bill of lading is "A written receipt given by a carrier for goods accepted for transportation." None are as poetic as the old bills of lading, which ended with the prayer: "And so God bring the good ship to her desired port in safety." Because *bill* meant an "official paper" it came to be applied to paper currency in late 16th-century England. As for the word *check* for a bank check, it originated from a bank draft with a counterfoil. The counterfoil prevented or "checked" forgeries and alterations of the drafts.

billy.   The American policeman's *billy*, or nightstick, seems to have taken its name ultimately from a short crowbar once used by burglars for prying open doors and windows. The crowbar was named in about 1848 after the personal name *Billy*, though not after any specific person, and within 10 years it became the name of the club policemen wear at their sides.

billycan.   Even an aboriginal language has made its contributions to English. *Billycan* or *billy* for any can in which water can be carried and boiled over a fire, derives from the Aboriginal Australian *billa*, "water." The word has limited use in England and America as well as in Australia.

billycock.   *See* BOWLER.

Billy Yank.   The common term for a Union soldier during the Civil War; his Confederate counterpart was called Johnny Reb. These terms were often shortened to *Billy* and *Johnny* and were frequently lowercased. In all wars after the Civil War, up until Vietnam, American soldiers were called Yanks regardless of what section of the country they came from.

biltong.   Animal lovers will not much like this South African word (from the Dutch *bil*, buttock, plus *tong*, tongue, meaning a strip of filet). In South Africa *biltong* is usually strips of air-dried and salted wild game meat. There is shark biltong, ostrich biltong, lion biltong, elephant biltong, and many other types. Elephants culled from the herds in Kruger National Park are often sold to butchers. The meat of "an elephant facing due east" when shot is said to be particularly tasty for some reason, or superstition. *See* JERKEY.

bimbo.   This word for a loose woman who is viewed as just a sex object, was originally applied to men and used to describe a man unimportant or undistinguished. It was first recorded in this sense in 1919, 10 years before it meant a sexually promiscuous woman. No one knows its origin, but one guess is that it derives from the Italian *bimbo*, baby.

Binet-Simon tests.   The first intelligence tests were developed by Alfred Binet (1857–1911), a French psychologist who directed the laboratory of psychology and physiology at the Sorbonne, in conjunction with psychologist Theodore Simon. The initial tests, later extended in age, determined the intelligence quotient of children three to 12, each subject being asked questions adapted to the intelligence of a normal child of his age. The *Binet-Simon tests* have been revised many times since their invention in 1905. Intelligence quotient, or I.Q., on such tests is merely a ratio, expressed as a percentage, of a person's mental age to his actual age, his mental age being the age for which he scores 100 percent on all the questions. The score 150 is generally accepted as genius and below 70 is classified as mental deficiency.

Bing Boys.   All Canadian troops in World War I (the "war to end all wars" that preceded World War II) were called *Bing Boys* after their commander, the British Lord Byng of Vimy (1862–1935). *Bing Boys* became a household name due in large part to newspaper and magazine articles and even a stage play called *The Bing Boys Are Here*.

Bing cherry.   *Bing cherries* are popular dark red, nearly black fruit of the Bigarreau or firm, crisp-fleshed group. The tree was developed in 1875 by a Chinese farmer named Bing in Oregon, where over a quarter of the United States's sweet cherry crop is grown. Other cherry varieties named after their developers include the Luelling, for the man who founded Oregon's cherry industry in 1847, the Lambert, and the Schmidt. Countless varieties honor famous people, such as the "Napoleon," the "Royal Ann," and the "Governor Wood," though none is named for George Washington. Surprisingly, sour cherries outnumber sweets two to one in the United States because they are easier to grow and are more in demand for cooking and canning. Cherries were probably first cultivated in China over 4,000 years ago, so Bing was carrying on a great ethnic tradition.

Bingley terrier. *See* AIREDALE TERRIER.

bingo! Nineteenth-century Christian missionaries introduced the game of bingo to inhabitants in various parts of Africa while they were enthusiastically converting people to their religion. The people associated the Christian concept of heaven, a Christian's final reward, with a player's shout of *bingo!* when he wins a game of bingo—making *bingo!* their word for heaven. *Bingo* is a corruption of *beano*, an early name for the game, and *beano* was patterned on *Keno*, another game of chance, which takes its name from the French *quine* for "five winning numbers."

biological warfare; bioscare. *Biological warfare*, the use of disease and famine as weapons of war, seems to have been coined by *Life* magazine in 1946. *Germ warfare* (1938) and *bacteriological warfare* (1924) are older similar terms, while *bioscare* was invented in 2001 after the World Trade Center disaster to describe the reaction of U.S. citizens to reports of terrorists using anthrax as a deadly weapon.

bird; birdie. *Bird* is one of the most common examples in English of metathesis, the transposition of letters, sounds, or syllables that sometimes occurs as a word develops. *Bird* arose from the Old English (Anglo-Saxon) *brid* meaning the same. For well over half a century, beginning in about 1849, *bird* was American slang for a person or thing of excellence ("He's a perfect bird of a man"), the expression coming into use at about the same time as the still heard use of *bird* for "fellow" or "guy" ("He's a strange old bird"). In the early 1920s, possibly at the Atlantic City Country Club in New Jersey, the popular expression attached itself to golf in the form of *birdie*, which means "one stroke under par for a hole," an excellent performance. Since about 1880 *bird* has been British slang for a girl.

a bird in hand. This proverbial expression can be traced back in English to the early 16th century, when it is rendered as "A byrde yn hande ys better than three yn in the wode," and probably much earlier, counting variations such as "Some bete the bush and some the byrdes take" (1440). Later, Cervantes used it in *Don Quixote* in the full form best known today: "A bird in the hand is worth two in the bush." Actually, the proverb, which is found in German, French, Italian, and several other languages, has its direct ancestor in an ancient saying from Plutarch's *Of Garrulity*, written in about A.D. 100: "He is a fool who lets slip a bird in the hand for a bird in the bush." It is what Weekley calls one of those proverbial expressions "which contain the wisdom of the ages."

bird of ill omen. Birds that appeared to the right of the augur who stood on Rome's Capitoline Hill were considered good luck, and any bird that appeared on his left was said to indicate bad luck. It is from the ceremony of this Roman religious official and fortune-teller that we get the phrase *bird of ill omen*, which is still applied to a bearer of bad news or an unlucky person. Specific birds that have been considered unlucky over the years include the owl, which is said to screech when bad weather (and hence, sickness) is coming, the raven, and the vulture, held to indicate death, as well as the crow and the albatross under certain circumstances.

Bird o' Satan. A colorful name for the blue jay, especially among rural black speakers. In folklore the bird is associated with hell and Satan, perhaps in part for its thievery of bright objects.

bird's nest soup. This most recherché of gourmet soups is definitely made from bird's nests—notably those of swallows of the genus *Collichia*, whose nests are glutinous half-cups composed of the spawn of fish and seaweed bound together by the birds' cementlike saliva. The swiftlings whose nests are used for the soup are mainly found on the island of Borneo, where literally millions live in great systems of limestone caves, their nests of solidified saliva stuck to the walls. The nests of the swifts are thought to be a gourmet aphrodisiac because they are the only nonhuman bird known to make love on the wing. After being collected, the nests are washed in hot water and rubbed with ground nut oil to help remove feathers and dirt. They must be soaked for two hours before they swell and become transparent for use in bird's nest soup. When the soup cooks, the nests fall to pieces, giving the soup its characteristic viscid texture.

Bird Woman. A name given to the Shoshoni Indian woman Sacagawea (pronounced *Sa-cuh-juh-we-uh*), famous guide for the Lewis and Clark expedition in 1805.

birrellism; birreligion. The charm and unobtrusive scholarship displayed by Augustine Birrell (1850–1933) in his *Obiter Dicta* and other works led to the formation of the word *birrellism* for shrewd cursory comments on humankind and life in general. Birrell, a barrister elected to Parliament in 1889, became president of the national board of education and chief secretary for Ireland (1907–16). He is noted for Birrell's Educational Bill of 1906 and the founding of the Roman Catholic National University of Ireland. *Birreligion* indicated the political import of his educational bill.

birthday suit. Anyone parading in his *birthday suit* is stark naked. The phrase, first recorded in 1771 but probably older, simply means that someone is wearing nothing, just what he or she wore at birth.

biscuit. *Biscuits* were cooked a second time to keep them from quickly spoiling at sea. Thus their name derives from the French *biscuit*, "cooked twice."

to bishop. Unlike BURKE, which it resembles, the expression *to bishop* is used only historically today, although the words arose at about the same time and for essentially the same reason. *To bishop* is to murder by drowning. It is named for a Mr. Bishop, who in 1831 so murdered a little boy in Bethnal Green, England in order to sell the child's body to surgeons for dissection, the murderer probably influenced by the earlier work of Burke and Hare.

bistro. When the Russians invaded Paris after Napoleon I's fall in 1815, restaurant owners or their shills would lure them into their places by shouting the Russian word *bystro*, meaning "quick," assuring them that they could eat quickly here at a good price. They used the word so often that it became altered to *bistro*, the common French word for any small unpretentious restaurant where cheap meals could be had, and from there *bistro* soon entered into English. But *bistro* could come from the French *bistoille*, cup of coffee. Or the word may derive from the French *bistouille*, raw spirits, for the cheap liquor served in such establishments. No one is sure.

bitch. Captain Grose defines a bitch as "A she dog, or doggess; the most offensive appellation that can be given to an English woman, even more provoking than that of *whore*, as may be gathered from the regular Billingsgate or St. Giles [woman's] answer [on being called a bitch]: 'I may be a whore but can't be a bitch.' " *Bitch* has meant "a lewd woman" and been applied opprobriously to a woman since about 1400. It has been applied to a man, "less opprobriously and somewhat whimsically," for almost as long. Fielding, for example, calling the landlord "a vast comical bitch" in *Tom Jones*. The word *bitch* derives from the Old English *bicchu*, meaning "a female dog."

bitchbox. *See* MEGAPHONE.

bite moose! An unusual expression heard in British Columbia for *get out of here!, get lost!, go bite a moose!*

bite the bullet. The cartridge used in the 1850s British Enfield rifle had a paper tube, the end of which riflemen had to bite off to expose the powder to the spark. A rifleman doing this had to remain calm when reloading in the midst of a battle, giving rise to the expression *to bite the bullet*, to stand firm while under attack. Another theory, however, has the expression deriving from the bullet patients bit to alleviate pain when they were operated on without aid of an anesthetic.

bite the dust. Every time we hear of still another desperado biting the dust in western films, we are hearing an almost literal translation of a line found in Homer's *Iliad*, written thousands of years ago. American poet William Cullen Bryant translated the words in 1870: ". . . his fellow warriors, many a one, Fall round him to the earth and bite the dust." Earlier, Alexander Pope had eloquently translated the phrase as "bite the bloody sand" and English poet William Cowper had it, literally, as "bite the ground." The idea remains the same in any case: a man falling dead in combat, biting the dust in his last hostile, futile act.

bitin' and gougin'. Ernest Hemingway described this vicious kind of fighting (sometimes seen in the ring today) in one of his late Michigan stories. It was often practiced by frontiersmen and mountaineers, a brutal practice in which ears, noses, and cheeks were bitten off and eyes were actually gouged out of the sockets. Harry M. Caudell wrote of it in *Night Comes to the Cumberlands* (1963): "A story is told of a mountaineer . . . attacked by a large and angry female bear. . . . The monster hugged him in her immense forepaws and undertook to bite away his face. But the mountaineer was determined to die hard.

He seized the end of the bear's nose between his sturdy teeth and plunged his thumbs deep into bruin's eyes. With a roar the bear flung him aside and fled, leaving the tip of her nose in his mouth. The victim later proudly displayed her nose, explaining that 'bars can't stand bitin' and gougin.' Whether true or not, the tale illustrates the vital savagery which the early mountaineers perpetrated so long."

biting remark. A remark capable of wounding, causing pain. The old story says that the tyrant Nearchos ordered Zeno (ca. 335–ca. 263 B.C.), founder of the Stoic school of philosophy, to be pounded to death by sticks in a large bowl-shaped container. After suffering this punishment a short time, Zeno told Nearchos he had something important to say to him and when Nearchos leaned over to hear better, Zeno bit off his ear. Somehow Zeno survived and from this tale, true or false, came the proverb, "A remark more biting than Zeno's," which yielded the expression, *a biting remark*. The *O.E.D.*, however, only traces the word *biting* in this sense back to Chaucer's time. Zeno is also credited by some with the old saw "The reason we have two ears and one mouth is that we may listen more and talk less."

to the bitter end. The first theory here is that death has always been regarded as the bitter end, as in the phrase from Proverbs, "Her end is bitter as wormwood." Poetically, then, any unpleasant final result, utter defeat or death would be the bitter end. But the anchor rope on early sailing vessels was attached to a device called the *bitt*, from which the anchor and anchor rope were paid out into the sea. The portion of the anchor rope nearest the bitt was called the "bitter end." There was no more anchor rope to be paid out after you came to the bitter end, and so you were at the end of your rope. This nautical expression has become widely known and so has at least helped to perpetuate the expression.

bitter pill to swallow; pill-pusher. Figurative bitter pills were being swallowed more than two centuries before Horace Walpole used the expression in 1779. The phrase may have been proverbial ever since apothecaries began making the round little pellet that the Romans called a *pila* (ball) and from which our word *pill* derives. Though many pills were coated with honey and spices (and later sugarcoated), some bitter ingredients could not be masked. The intensely bitter chinchona bark, which contains quinine and was used to treat malaria, is one example. (Chinchona, incidentally, was named for the Condesa Ana de Chinchon, wife of the Spanish viceroy of Peru, who was stricken with a tropical fever in 1639 and cured by chinchona bark.) Bitter pills are also responsible for the expression *an old pill* for a grouchy person, first recorded in about 1880, and *pill-pusher*, early 20th-century slang for a doctor, which has a derogatory connotation but has its roots in old, nonobjectionable British military slang for a doctor, a "pill," that goes back to about 1860.

blab. *Blab*, first recorded by Chaucer, is supposed to be a shortening of the earlier *blabber*. *Blabber* in turn, is said to derive from *blaeberen*, an echoic word that imitates the sound of blabbering. It means, of course, CHATTER, or loose talk, or to chatter, to spill out information.

black arts.   As Weekley points out, this name for conjuring or the art of divination is a mistake, no matter how apt it seems. It was translated into English directly from the Old French *nigromancie*, "divination by means of the dead." But the Old French word itself had been formed in error from the Greco-Latin *necromantia* meaning the same, people confusing the sound-alike words *necro*, "dead," and *niger*, "black"—and associating black with the dark, secret ways of conjuring. The Greeks and others after them believed that they could divine or foretell the future, or discover hidden knowledge in many ways besides the study of corpses, these methods ranging from the study of animal entrails to the study of water.

blackball.   So infamous was the 19th-century Black Ball Steamer Line between Liverpool and New York (the pilfering of its sailors widely known on both sides of the Atlantic and second only to the cruelty of its officers) that the term *blackball* came to mean stealing or pilfering at sea. In its most common use *blackball* means to vote against, to ostracize. When voting by ballot for a candidate proposed for membership in certain social clubs in 18th-century England, club members who accepted the candidate dropped a white ball into the ballot box and those who voted against the candidate dropped in a black ball. The term *blackball* is first recorded in a 1770 letter referring to a lady shunned by polite society.

Black Belt.   Any southern region, especially in Alabama and Mississippi, with rich black soil and a large population of African-Americans. The term dates back to the late 19th century.

blackberry.   The blackberry, a member of the rose family and named for its color, has been valued since ancient times, when the Greeks enjoyed it and believed that it prevented gout. In England blackberries are the most common fruit growing in the wild and proverbially came to represent what is plentiful because they outyield all other bramble fruits: One plant can produce up to five gallons of berries. "Plentiful as blackberries" comes to us from Shakespeare, though what he actually wrote was, "If reasons were as plenty as blackberries, I would give no man a reason upon compulsion." (Henry IV, Part I). A period of cool weather in spring, usually May or June, when blackberries are in bloom, is called a "blackberry winter," and a "blackberry summer" is a period of fine weather in late September or early October. *Blackberry baby* is a century-old American euphemism for an illegitimate child, suggesting that such children are secretly conceived in places like the distant woods where blackberries grow. *See* BOYSENBERRY.

Black Betsy.   Probably the most famous bat in baseball was BABE RUTH's black 44-ounce bat, which he called *Black Betsy* and with which he made baseball history. No one knows for whom he named the large bat, if anyone; in fact, it may have been named *Black Betsy* by its maker, A.G. Spalding & Co. Shoeless Joe Jackson of Black Sox shame used a bat named *Black Betsy* before Ruth did. *See* SAY IT AIN'T SO, JOE.

blackbirder.   A blackbirder was a ship engaged in the African or Polynesian slave trade in the mid-19th century. A *blackbird* was a captive aboard these slavers and *blackbirding* was used to describe such kidnapping or slaving.

black book.   None of the slang dictionaries seem to record it, but a *little black book* has for at least half a century been the name for any Casanova's address book filled with the names, addresses, and especially phone numbers of desirable or compliant companions. But *black book* has far greater historical importance as the synonym for a book containing the names of people liable to censure or punishment, the term used most frequently in the phrase *I'm in his black book*, meaning "in disfavor with someone." The first such black books were compiled by agents of Henry VIII, who listed English monasteries under the pretext that they were sinful but really in order to convince Parliament to dissolve them so that the crown could claim their lands—which Parliament did in 1536. Later, the British universities, the army, and the police began the practice of listing censured people in *black books*, which reinforced the meaning of the term.

black bottom.   Originally a low-lying section of a town inhabited solely by blacks. The dance called the black bottom, which originated among blacks in the South, is not named for this geographical description. *The New Yorker* (October 7, 1926) said the hip-moving dance "was constructed to simulate the movements of a cow mired in black bottom river mud."

Black Daniel; Ichabod.   His black hair and black eyes suggested the nickname *Black Daniel* for the great American statesman, orator, and folk hero Daniel Webster (1782–1852). The name is noted in Stephen Vincent Benét's story "The Devil and Daniel Webster" (1937), which was made into a film. The nickname *Ichabod* was bestowed upon Webster by John Greenleaf Whittier in his poem "Ichabod" (1850), which expresses the Abolitionists' great disappointment with Webster's support of the Compromise of 1850. *Ichabod* means "inglorious" in Hebrew, and Whittier later apologized for the description, praising Webster's noble qualities. *See* GODLIKE DANIEL

Black Death; bubonic plague.   The bubonic plague that started in Constantinople (now Istanbul) and devastated Europe from 1347–51, killing from one-quarter to three-quarters of the population, was called the Black Death because the bodies of plague victims rapidly turned black after death. Over 25 million died of the Black Death, far more than in the 1665 plague of London that Defoe described in his *Journal of the Plague Year* and Samuel Pepys in his *Diary*. Bubonic plague is carried by rat fleas that have become infected by biting diseased rats (and certain squirrels on the West Coast of the U.S.). It is so named because the rod-shaped bacterium, *Pasturella pestis*, responsible for it causes swellings (buboes) of the glands in the groin or armpit.

black dog.   Someone with a case of the *black dog* is suffering from despondency, melancholy, or depression. British statesman Winston Churchill wrote that he was one of the many who have suffered from the condition. Long before him, Dr. Johnson used the words to describe his bouts with the blues. Perhaps the term derives from the old Roman superstition that a black dog with pups is an unlucky omen. Or it may be that its origins can be found in another version of the term that the *OED* says was used in some country places: "*The black dog is on his back.*" Robert Louis Stevenson called this last "a terrifying nursery metaphor." The expression is first recorded in about 1700. *See also* BLACK MONEY.

black eye; a black-eyed beauty. *Black eye* has had two meanings for over three centuries. In one sense it is a mark of beauty, an eye in which the iris is very dark and lustrous—hence our expression *a black-eyed beauty.* In another sense a black eye is of course a discoloration of the flesh around the eye from a blow or contusion. Both expressions were coined toward the beginning of the 17th century.

black-eyed peas. So named for their black hilum, black-eyed peas (*Vigna sinensis*) are simply a variety of cowpeas that originated in India thousands of years ago (though the name "cowpea" originated in colonial America). George Washington grew these peas, which are actually botanically closer to the bean than the pea family. They are often cooked southern style: stewed with a bit of ham or pork fat. Black-eyed peas go by many names in the South, including "crowders," "black bean," "black-eyed bean," "black-eyed susan," "bung belly," "China bean," "cow bean," "cream pea" and even "chain-gang pea" because they are said to be fed to prisoners on chain gangs. *See* PEA.

Black Friday, etc. The first Black Friday in the British financial world fell on May 10, 1886, when certain brokers suspended payments and a widespread panic ensued. America's first Black Friday also came in 1886, when Jay Gould and Jim Fisk tried to bribe public officials in an attempt to corner the gold market; their manipulation failed when the government released gold for sale, but it ruined thousands of investors. With the Panic of 1929, the beginning of America's Great Depression, came Black Wednesday (October 23) when stocks began falling; Black Thursday (October 24), the day the bottom dropped out of the market; and Black Tuesday (October 29), when over 16 million shares were traded. Black Monday was Easter Monday in 1360, a terrible day for the English armies in France, while Black Saturday refers to August 4, 1671, when there was a violent storm in Scotland. History seems to record no Black Sunday. *Black Friday* today usually means the Friday after Thanksgiving, marking the beginning of the Christmas season, when manufacturers and retailers often see their books go from in the red to in the black, giving them a profit for the year.

black frost. Long a name for a severe frost that kills plants, sometimes turning them black or blackish; a *killing frost,* as opposed to a slight or light frost. The average time of the first *black frost* depends primarily upon the area of the country, and some U.S. areas (such as Key West, Florida) have no *black frosts.* A black frost marks the end of the growing season.

black goods; white goods. *Black goods* is a term rarely if ever heard anymore. Back almost a century ago department stores often carried a complete line of coffins and black goods, the contemporary euphemism for the mourning clothes of black crepe worn by members of a bereaved family. *White goods* in retail parlance can mean anything from bedsheets to large appliances.

blackguard. The modern meaning of *blackguard,* a low, contemptible person, may derive from the characteristics of medieval kitchen servants, who were humorously called *blackguards* in allusion to their filthy appearance and the black pots and pans that they guarded when the household retinue moved from place to place. These kitchen workers surely weren't always "rough and worthless knaves," as one source has it, so the theory, accepted by most etymologists, isn't entirely convincing. Perhaps the word really derives from some actual band of soldiers who wore black uniforms and whose vicious crimes are lost to history—unlike those of the contemporary BLACKSHIRTS.

Black Hand. The late 19th-century and 20th-century precursor of the American Mafia. The *Black Hand,* Neopolitan in origin, embraced all crimes but specialized in extortion. Many letters sent to their victims had the imprint of a black hand upon them. *Black Hand* was also the name of the Slav secret society that planned the 1914 assassination of Archduke Franz Ferdinand, which led to World War I.

black hole. The infamous Black Hole of Calcutta gives its name to any black hole or cell in a prison where prisoners are confined as a punishment. The original black hole in this sense was the 18- by 14-foot room into which the French-supported Nawab of Bengal, Siraj Uddaula, thrust 146 British prisoners on the terribly hot night of June 20, 1756. The only ventilation in the room was two small air holes, and by the next morning 123 of the men had died. Robert Clive retook Calcutta the following year and avenged the atrocity, but the story of the Black Hole was never forgotten. Several Indian writers have claimed it was a British hoax, perpetrated to rouse patriotic sentiments, but three witnesses testified to the story and none of the 23 survivors ever denied it. In 1967 Princeton physicist John Wheeler used the term to describe "an object whose gravity is so powerful that it swallows everything around it—even light." Today *black hole* is part of everyday language, used to describe the economy, the deficit, the post office, etc.

black humor. Humor that regards suffering as absurd, not pitiable, or that regards existence as ironically pointless yet comic. The expression was first recorded in 1963, though such humor has always been around; it is said to have been coined by American author Bruce Jay Friedman. Wrote Friedman in *Newsday* (1/1/96) regarding the coinage: "I don't really know if I invented it, or if a publisher came to me and said, 'How about doing an anthology and calling it *Black Humor?*' What I do remember is, they were going to pay me for a chance to read writers like Barthelme, Heller and Pynchon, so it was a terrific deal. Then I had to write an introduction (to *Black Humor,* 1963), so I slapped together some justification for the collection: the stories had a certain edge to them—they often connected with social issues in very bold colors—whatever. The next thing I know, black humor is being taught in college courses and becomes imprinted in the language."

black is beautiful. It has been suggested that this slogan of pride for black Americans since the late 1960s may derive from the Song of Solomon in the Old Testament: "I am black but beautiful." But the "but" in the song casts doubt upon such a derivation.

Black Jack Pershing.   Among the most famous generals of World War I, John J. Pershing (1860–1948) was widely called by the nickname Black Jack. The American general who commanded the American Expeditionary Force in Europe and later became chief of staff wasn't so named for his black hair and dark complexion (as was General John A. Logan [1826–86] during the Civil War), or because he liked to play the card game black jack. Pershing was called Black Jack because he commanded the Tenth U.S. Cavalry, the renowned black regiment that distinguished itself in the Spanish-American War.

blacklist; white list.   The blacklist is centuries old, having originated with a list England's Charles II made of 58 judges and court officers who sentenced his father, Charles I, to death in 1649. When Charles II was restored to the throne in 1660, 13 of these regicides were executed and 25 sentenced to life imprisonment, while the others escaped. The white list is not quite the opposite of a blacklist, usually being a list, often kept by unions, of people suitable for employment.

black magic; voodoo.   Black magic doesn't divine the future as the black arts do; it is rather the casting of magic spells for an evil purpose. *Black magic* is a synonym for *voodoo*, which is found in its purest forms today in the villages of Haiti, where it was encouraged and practiced by the former Haitian dictator "Papa Doc" Duvalier. *Voodoo* was brought to the New World by African slaves as early as the 1600s, and some authorities believe the word derives from the West African *vodun*, a form of the Ashanti *obosum*, "a guardian spirit or fetish." Others say that *voodoo* takes its name from the Waldensians, followers of Peter Waldo or Valdo (d. 1217), who were accused of sorcery and given the name *Vaudois* by the French. French missionaries later remembered these "heretics" when they encountered the witch doctors who preached black magic in the West Indies, this story says. They called the native witch doctors *Vaudois* and the name was soon applied to any witchcraft similar to the magic spells they cast, *Vaudois* being eventually corrupted to *voodoo*. Americans further corrupted *voodoo* to "hoodoo," but use the word in a playful sense.

blackmail.   Sixteenth-century Scottish farmers paid their rent, or mail, to English absentee landlords in the form of white mail, silver money, or black mail, rent in the form of produce or livestock. The term black mail took on a bad connotation only when greedy landlords forced cashless tenants to pay much more in goods than they would have paid in silver. Later, when freebooters along the border demanded payment for free passage and "protection," the poor farmers called this illegal extortion blackmail, too.

Black Maria.   Maria Lee, an imposing black woman, became a national heroine in 1798 when she delivered swivel guns to outfit the little cutters Alexander Hamilton had ordered built to protect American merchant ships on the high seas. Maria was just as reliable when she opened her boardinghouse for sailors in the early 1800s; her place was the cleanest and her guests the best-mannered on the Boston waterfront because even hardened criminals feared her awesome strength. The giant woman aided the police so often that the saying "send for the Black Maria" became common whenever there was trouble with an offender. Fiery Maria sometimes helped escort prisoners to jail, and when the first British police horse vans or paddy wagons were introduced in 1838 they may have been christened Black Marias in her honor. But this tradition has skimpy evidence to support it. Critics point out that the first van was black and that *Maria* (which is pronounced *mar-eye-ah*) could have come from numerous sources.

black money; black dog.   In the early 18th century, counterfeit coins were commonly made of double-washed pewter and looked black or dirty. They were therefore called *black money* or *black dogs*, as readers of historical romances know.

blackout.   In the sense of turning off or concealing lights before an enemy air raid, *blackout* dates back to the London BLITZ at the start of World War II. The term was used before this to mean the extinguishing of all stage lights to signal the end of a scene in a play, to indicate the passing of time, or to mark the end of a vaudeville skit.

black power.   No one is sure of the origins of this slogan urging or demanding political and economic power for African-Americans. CORE, the Congress of Racial Equality, used it as a slogan in the 1960s but it was not new at the time. In his *Simple Takes a Wife* (1953) poet and novelist Langston Hughes wrote: "Black is powerful," which may be the source for the term.

Black Republican.   Long an insulting nickname for a Republican in the South, the term was first used to describe a Republican favoring emancipation of the slaves. It came to be applied to any Republican and is still occasionally heard.

Black Robe.   A historical name given to Jesuit missionaries working among Indians in the West, the name originating with the Indians themselves and referring to the robes the Jesuits wore. They were also called Black Gowns.

Black Sea.   The ancient Greeks never gave a derogatory name to any natural force, good or bad. So they named what we know as the *Black Sea*, the Euxine or "the Hospitable," even though it was noted for its storms and rocky shores. The Turks later named it the *Black Sea* because they were terrified of its dangers and large stretches of open water.

black sheep.   Black sheep were once thought to bear the devil's mark in their wool. The superstition arose in days when dyestuffs were so ineffective and expensive that it wasn't practical to dye the wool of black sheep. Since black sheep were biological rarities, there weren't enough of them to market black wool, and the animals were regarded as practically worthless. Generations of farmers cursing their bad luck for having black sheep in their flocks evolved the term *black sheep*, for any disgrace in a family or community. Wild sheep are usually brownish, and American mountain men called the buff wool of the bighorn *(Ovis canadensis)* its "long underwear."

Blackshirts.   These were first members of the Italian fascist militia, who wore black shirts and were imitated in England and other countries by fascists who wore similar uniforms. The term became much better known as the popular nickname of the elite military unit of the German Nazi party, officially called the *Schutzstaffel* (protection staff), or SS Corps. As its German name implies, the black-shirted SS served as a special protection unit and Hitler's bodyguard.

black-shoe navy. Rear Admiral Edgar Keats, USN (ret.), kindly provides the true origin of this controversial term. "During the 1920s and 30s," Admiral Keats writes, "naval aviators were permitted to wear green cloth uniforms in cold weather and lightweight khaki working uniforms during warm weather, in addition to service dress blue and white. Non-aviators did not have that option. When World War II approached it became apparent that battles could not be won in the tropics by officers constrained to heavy blues or impractical whites, so khaki, but not green, uniforms were made available to all officers. The khaki uniform was changed somewhat with stripes being removed from sleeves and the shoulder boards of whites being substituted. Above all, and fatefully, the orders from Naval Headquarters gave officers the option of continuing to wear the black shoes they had previously worn with the blue uniforms. Aviators, without exception, continued with their brown shoes, but many senior surface ship officers, flag and ship commanders, decreed that in their commands only black shoes would be worn. Thus junior and mid-grade officers on surface ships had no choice but to wear black shoes. In the early years there was hardly a ripple of controversy, but as time wore on the words "brown shoe" came to be used as a substitute for "naval aviator" and "black shoe" came to be a designation for an officer who was not a naval aviator. Some, but not all, may have used the words as epithets, probably because of surface officers' jealousy of the increased pay of aviators. Another explanation may be naval aviators looking down on those not qualified to fly airplanes. The words have over time become identifiers of an intramural split within the naval establishment that, until recently, has had adverse consequences for the overall navy. Had there been far-sighted leadership in the navy in the early years of the war either brown or black shoes would have been ordered for all officers and, with uniforms being truly uniform, these unfortunate words would never have gained currency."

blacksmith. A smith is a craftsman who shapes any metal by hammering, and a blacksmith takes his name from the iron or black-colored metal he works with, not from the soot that gets on his clothes and skin while he works over a fire. His opposite is called a whitesmith, or tinsmith, one who works with tin or white metal. The *Harmonious Blacksmith* is the popular name of a musical composition by Handel; it wasn't really suggested to him by a smithy hammering at his forge.

black widow spider. The little jet-black American spider *Latrodectus mactans* is called a widow because it eats its mate. Spiders, however, are often cannibalistic. Generally, spider venom causes no harm to humans, but the venom of the black widow spider causes pain and can be fatal. A black widow can be identified by a red mark shaped like an hourglass on its underside. *See* SPIDER.

blame game. An expression said to be coined by President Ronald Reagan in a speech given on October 14, 1982: "The pounding economic hangover America is suffering from didn't come about overnight, and there's no single, instant cure. In recent weeks, a lot of people have been playing what I call the 'blame game.' "

blanket. There may have been a Thomas Blanket of Bristol, England who made blankets, setting up "the first loom for their manufacture in 1340." But the word *blanket* comes from the Old French *blankete*, originally a "white wool cloth used for clothing" but meaning the blanket we know today by the mid-14th century. This is not to say that a Thomas Blanket couldn't have adopted the name *blanket* for his product and popularized the word. *See* WET BLANKET.

blanket Indian. A derogatory term commonly used in the 19th century for an Indian thought to be docile and of a low cultural level because he or she wore a blanket instead of dressing like white people. To *wear the blanket* meant that an Indian was "half-civilized."

Blanket Mountain. In order to have a plain target for his compass, 19th-century surveyor Return J. Meigs hung a bright-hued blanket on a 4,609-foot mountain in the Great Smokies range. The mountain, at Elkmont, was soon dubbed *Blanket Mountain*, a name it still holds today.

blanket tossing. *See* TOSS IN A BLANKET.

blankety-blank. An expression some 150 years old that is still heard as a euphemism though the practice that suggested it is fast fading. *Blankety-blank* (as in "You blankety-blank S.O.B.!") derives from the use of printed blank spaces (dashes) to represent what are considered profane words, such as *d---* for *damn*.

blarney. Built by Cormac McCarthy in 1446 and named for a nearby village only a few miles north of Cork, Ireland, Blarney Castle was put under siege by the British in 1602. The story goes that McCarthy Mor, descendant of its builder, refused to surrender the fortress to Queen Elizabeth's Lord President of Munster, Sir George Carew. All Carew got from McCarthy for months were promises that he would eventually surrender. This smooth talk became a joking matter, making Carew the laughingstock of Elizabeth's ministers and *blarney* a byword for cajolery, flattering or wheedling talk. There is today, about 20 feet from the top of the castle wall, a stone inscribed "Cormac McCarthy *fortis me fieri fecit*, A.D. *1446*," which may have been set there to commemorate the verbal defeat of the English by the Irish. This triangular stone is difficult to reach and the legend grew in the 17th century that if you could scale the wall and kiss the blarney stone you would be blessed with all the eloquent persuasive powers of McCarthy Mor, that is, you'd be able to lie with a straight face. The blarney stone that people kiss today is a bit of *blarney* itself—a substitute provided to make things easier for tourists.

blaspheme. To speak impiously or irreverently of sacred things. The word came into English in about 1300, ultimately from the Greek *blasphemos*, blasphemous. It also means to speak evil of, slander, or abuse. The Greeks took blasphemy seriously, to say the least. The Greek author Lucian, "The Blasphemer," is said to have been ripped to pieces by a pack of mad dogs for his impiety.

blast from the past.   Early in the 1960s disc jockey Murray the K (Kaufman) made this phrase popular as his way of introducing a great old song. The expression is now used to describe someone or something that appears from one's past out of the blue, as in "Wow! Seeing him was a blast from the past!"

blazer.   The jacket called the blazer may take its name from the "somewhat striking blue-and-white-striped jerseys" that the captain of Britain's H.M.S. *Blazer* ordered his crew to wear in the 19th century. But others say the jackets were called blazers because they were the "brightest possible blazing scarlet." According to this theory the jackets were first worn by the crew of the *Lady Margaret*, St. John's College, Cambridge, Boat Club in 1889.

blazing star.   A stampede. As described in *Munsey's Magazine* (25, 1901): "The herd . . . burst like a bombshell into the most dangerous of plains mishaps—a 'blazing star.' The solid herd streamed suddenly in all directions, scattered in knots and bunches, and twos and threes, and vanished into the storm and darkness."

blazing ubiquities!   *See* GLITTERING GENERALITIES.

bleachers.   When you sit in the open outfield seats of a baseball stadium on a hot day, the sun seems strong enough to bleach your shirt. That is the humorous idea behind the coining of the word *bleachers* for all such seats in a stadium, the term first recorded in the early 1880s.

bleed white.   *See* PAY THROUGH THE NOSE.

blenker.   An eponymous verb remembering Union general Louis Blenker (1812–63) that first meant the wholesale theft of civilian property by the military and then came to mean any theft at all. General Blenker's troops, having insufficient rations, raided civilian farms in the Shenandoah Valley in April 1862, the division's plundering inspiring a Northern song that went: "His knapsack with chickens was swelling; / He'd Blenkered those dainties, and thought it no wrong . . ."

bless.   As unlikely as it seems, our word *bless* derives from the Old English *blod*, blood. *Blod* yielded the Old English verb *bledsian*, which meant "to make sacred or holy with blood," as when sacrificial blood of animals was used in religious ceremonies. *Bledsian* became *blessen* in Middle English and by Shakespeare's time had become *bless*.

bless the meat and damn the skin.   Part of an old American grace said before a meal: "Bless the meat an' damn the skin, / Throw back your 'eads an' all pitch in."

Blighia Sapida.   *See* CAPTAIN BLIGH.

blimp.   The word wasn't coined, as Mencken's story goes, by two Britishers while they were having "blunch" (or brunch, as it is called in America) at an airport. Nor was the nonrigid dirigible airship so named by its manufacturer, the Goodyear Company in the early years of World War I. It is often reported that Goodyear's first model, the "A limp" (nonrigid), hadn't worked and that their second model, the "B limp," succeeded and kept its name, but Goodyear has denied that they or anyone else had airships with "limp" or type "B" designations. This leaves us with the possibility that the word is an onomatopoeic one, possibly coined by a Lt. Cunningham of the British Royal Navy Air Service in 1915. Cunningham, according to this story, flicked his thumb at one of the airships while on an inspection tour and "an odd noise echoed off the taut fabric. . . .[He] orally imitated the sound his thumb had drummed out of the airship bag: 'Blimp!' Those nearby saw and heard this unusual interlude in the inspection, and its account quickly spread."

blind as a one-eyed mule in a root cellar.   Unable to see or to understand, completely blind to sight or reason. The American expression is probably from the mid-19th century.

blind eye.   *See* TURN A BLIND EYE.

blind leading the blind.   This phrase describing the ignorance of both leaders and followers is biblical in origin, from Matt. 15:14, where Jesus says of the Pharisees: "They be blind leaders of the blind. And if the blind lead the blind, both shall fall into the ditch."

blindman's buff.   This old children's game is sometimes called "blindman's bluff," which makes no sense at all. *Blindman's buff* is actually right, the *buff* coming from the buff, or slap on the backside, other players would give the blindfolded player when he tried to grab them to make somebody else the "blindman."

blind pig; blind tiger.   No doubt these names for "speakeasies serving illegal liquor during Prohibition" owe much of their popularity to the fact that people believed the rotgut served therein would get you blind drunk. The names, however, may have more interesting origins. *Blind pig* is traditionally said to derive from the nickname of a band of soldiers called the Public Guard serving in Richmond, Virginia, in about 1858. Their militia hats had the initials P.G. on them, the sobriquet arising because "P.G. is a pig without an *i*, and a pig without an *eye* is a blind pig." One would have to assume that the soldiers were much disliked and were drunk a lot of the time—and the saloons they drank in named after them—to accept this theory, which has law officers being called "pigs" long before the sixties, as indeed they were. The theory seems all the more unlikely when it is known that *blind pig* is recorded as early as 1840, 18 years before the Richmond Public Guard was formed. *Blind tiger* (1857) possibly takes its name from the saloons in faro gambling establishments a century ago, the game of faro commonly known as "tiger." But it is just as good a guess to say that both names were suggested because cheap whiskey got people *blind drunk*.

blindside.   For centuries *blind side* has meant the obscured part of one's field of vision. In the early 1970s, the word became a verb in professional football meaning to tackle or block an opponent from the blind side. Soon the verb was taken up generally to describe an attack on anyone who is unprepared or taken by surprise.

Blind Tom.   Baseball fans began calling umpires Blind Toms at about the turn of the century and the expression is still occasionally heard for the boys in blue. One theory has the often affectionate term originating with Old Blind Tom, a popular black musician in the post-Civil War era.

blintz.   Another delicious ethnic food that has become popular nationwide, thanks largely to its appearance in the frozen food sections of supermarkets. Ultimately *blintz* comes from the Ukranian *blints,* "pancake," which became the Yiddish *blintzeh* and was then shortened to *blintz.* A blintz in Jewish cookery is a thin pancake folded or rolled around a filling of cheese, potatoes, fruit, etc., fried or baked, and often served with sour cream. The word is also spelled *blintze.*

blister.   Everything has a name if you look hard enough. If you've ever wondered what those delicious bubbles commonly seen on baked pizza dough, or in the cheese on pizza itself, are called, your wondering is over. Proud pizza makers, or pizzamen as they like to call themselves, advise me that in New York, among other areas, they are known as *blisters.* I have found no printed use of the word.

the Blitz.   Short for *Blitzkrieg* (literally "lightning war"), specifically the German Luftwaffe's bombing raids on London and other British cities between September 1940 and May 1941 that attempted to terrorize England into surrender. According to the *New York Times* (Oct. 7, 2000), more than 40,000 civilians, 5,000 children among them, were killed in these World War II air raids, in what was also known, in Winston Churchill's words, as the Battle of Britain. The word *blitz* is also a verb meaning to bomb or to destroy.

blizzard.   In its meaning of a severe snowstorm *blizzard* seems to be an Americanism dating back to about 1835. Its direct ancestor is probably the English dialect word *blisser,* meaning the same, but could be the German *blitz,* "lightning, flash." Before *blizzard* meant a storm in America it meant a violent blow of the fist or a crushing remark.

blockhead.   Since the 14th century, when hats began to replace hoods as the most popular headwear, head-shaped blocks of oak have been standard equipment in the shops of hatmakers. By the time of Henry VIII these *blockheads,* used to shape hats and wigs, had already been compared to simpletons, stupid people whose heads contain no more brains than a block of wood. "Your wit will not so soon out as another man's will," Shakespeare wrote in *Coriolanus,* " 'tis strongly wedged up in a blockhead."

block of stock.   People have been buying *blocks* of stock, a large number of shares in a company, on the stock market since the late 19th century. In fact, a humorous anonymous poem about a block of stock appeared in Carolyn Wells's *A Whimsey Anthology* (1906):

> He bought a little block of stock
> The day he went to town;
> And in the nature of such things,
> That
> Stock
> Went

> Right
> Straight
> Down!

bloke.   Word origins can be lost very quickly. *Bloke,* for a "man," "chap," or "guy" (in America) entered the language only in 1839 or so, but no one has been able to establish its ancestors. Suggestions are that it came from the Hindustani *loke* for "man," introduced by the Gypsies into England; that it derives from an old Irish tinker's cry; and that it is from the Dutch *blok,* for "fool." The Celtic *ploc,* "a large, bull-headed person," reinforced by *plocach,* "a strong, coarse person," has its supporters, too. However, the evidence doesn't prove any of these theories. *Bloke* has been in fairly common humorous usage in America since late in the 19th century, as in "he's a nice bloke."

Blondenfreude.   A recent front-page story in the *New York Times* (5/23/02) about a prominent personality claims that "*Blondenfreude,* the glee felt when a rich, powerful, and fair-haired business woman stumbles, is the guilty pleasure of the age." This is the earliest mention I can find of the word, which is clearly patterned on the German SCHADENFREUDE. Perhaps it was coined by the article's authors, Alessandra Stanley and Constance L. Hays.

Blondin.   Blondin was the stage name of one of the greatest tightrope walkers of all time, the Frenchman Jean François Gravelet (1824–97). The Inimitable Blondin, whose name became a synonym for a star acrobat or tightrope walker, began his career at a mere five years of age and performed many great feats thereafter. The first man to cross Niagara Falls on a tightrope, on June 30, 1859, he later made the crossing while pushing a wheelbarrow, twirling an umbrella, and with another man on his back. The rope was 1,100 feet long, only three inches thick, and was suspended 160 feet above the falls. *Blondin* is still used occasionally to describe an accomplished acrobat or nimble person.

blood diamonds.   This recent term has nothing to do with the color of diamonds. It refers to the diamonds of Africa, which rebels of various countries fight for and use to finance their operations, much blood being spilled in wars over the gems.

bloodhound.   The breed of dog called the *bloodhound* was known in Italy as early as the third century. This dog's name has nothing to do with its following the blood trail of an animal or person. The bloodhound was so named because it was one of the first of the "blooded," or purebred, breeds. Its main modern use, however, is in trailing criminals or finding lost persons. *See* HOUND.

the bloodiest battle of World War I.   *See* THEY SHALL NOT PASS!

blood is a big expense.   Another saying from the movie *The Godfather* (1972). This time a rival gangster proposes a truce. "I don't like violence, Tom," he explains. "I'm a businessman. Blood is a big expense."

blood is thicker than water. This was the reply of U.S. commodore Josiah Tattnall on the Peiho River, China, in 1859, when he went to the aid of the British against the Chinese and was told this step would violate U.S. neutrality. But Tattnall didn't invent the phrase, which is recorded in German as far back as the 12th century. Tattnall was referring, of course, to the close ties between the Americans and British. It is interesting to note that blood has a specific gravity of 1.06—only slightly thicker than water, which has a specific gravity of 1.00!

the Bloodless War. *See* TO HAVE THE LUCK OF HIRAM SMITH.

blood money. The expression can mean money paid to a hired killer; money obtained ruthlessly from someone; money paid to an informer; money earned at the cost of another's life; and even money paid to the family of a slain person. It is an old term for old practices, the words appearing in the 1535 Coverdale Bible (Matt. 27).

bloody. Partridge's *Word, Words, Words!* has a 2,000-word essay on *bloody*, which has been an objectionable adjective in Britain since the early 1800s, though it had been respectable enough for a century before. Meaning "very," it may have become objectionable because it suggested menstruation, or suggested the profanity "By'r Lady"—many plausible and implausible suggestions have been made. But Partridge believed that "the idea of blood suffices" to explain the squeamishness. *Bloody* is often inserted for emphasis within words, as in *abso-bloody-lutely*.

bloody back. A contemptuous name Americans gave the British red-coats during the Revolutionary War. A newspaper of the day recorded the taunts of one group: "The Mob still increased, and were outrageous . . . calling out 'Come, you Rascals, you bloody Backs, you Lobster Scoundrels; fire if you dare!' "

bloody hand of Ulster. *See* RED (BLOODY) HAND OF ULSTER.

Bloody Mary. It is said, without much proof being offered, that this cocktail made from vodka and tomato juice takes its name from Mary I or Mary Tudor (1516–58), queen of England, who was nicknamed Bloody Mary. Not because she drank the concoctions (for one thing tomatoes were unknown in England at the time), but because she had some 300 of her subjects put to death during her reign, including a former queen and the archbishop of Canterbury.

bloomers. Bloomers take their name from early feminist Amelia Jenks Bloomer (1818–94), who did not invent them as is often stated. Bloomers were originally billowing Turkish pantaloons, bound with elastic around the ankles and covered by a short skirt and loose-fitting tunic, a kind of pants suit of the 19th century. They were designed and first worn in 1850 by Mrs. Elizabeth Smith Miller, daughter of the wealthy abolitionist, Gerrit Smith, but Mrs. Bloomer defended the masculine pantaloons with the same vehemence as their detractors and it is her name that they immortalize. Editor of *The Lily*, the house organ of a temperance society, Mrs. Bloomer was an ardent feminist who demanded that the word "obey" be omitted from the marriage vows when she wed. She wore Mrs. Miller's new costume on lecture platforms across the country, insisting that fashionable hoopskirts were both cumbersome and unsanitary, picking up dust and mud on the then largely unpaved American streets. When preachers banned women wearing bloomers from church, threatening excommunication and pointing out that the Bible forbids a woman donning anything that pertains to a man (Deut. 22:5), she reminded her religious critics that Genesis made no distinction between the fig leaves of Adam and Eve. Mrs. Bloomer even inspired a troop of Bloomer Girls to sail to England, where they were generally met with laughter or indignation. Her proselytizing, coupled with the fact that the pantaloons "bloomed out" so, made the appellation *bloomers* stick in the public mind.

Bloomsbury group. This literary term has nothing to do with James Joyce's Leopold Bloom or a country place where flowers profusely bloom. The term Bloomsbury group referred to a coterie of writers, and artists who resided in London's Bloomsbury district in the first few decades of the 20th century. Their ranks included Virginia and Leonard Woolf, Lytton Strachey, John Maynard Keynes, E. M. Forster, Clive Bell, Roger Fry, and Duncan Grant. While not constituting a "school," they strongly influenced literature and art criticism.

Bloomsday. Bloomsday, originated by James Joyce-o-phile and bookstore owner Enrico Adelman, celebrates each year the June 16, 1904, day of Leopold Bloom's odyssey through Dublin in Joyce's *Ulysses*. A marathon public reading by actors is held at Mr. Adelman's New York bookstore every Bloomsday and lasts from 8:00 A.M. until Molly Bloom says, "yes I said yes I will Yes" some 40 hours later.

blossom; flower. In Anglo-Saxon times the word for flower was *blossom*, this changing after the Normans conquered England in 1066 and their *fleur* became the English *flower*. However, both words have the same common ancestor—the ancient Indo-European *blo*, which eventually yielded both *blossom* and *flower*. The Old English verb *blow*, to bloom, is still alive and well today in the compound forms *full-blown* (full flowered) and *over-blown* (faded and wilted, past the prime).

blow a fuse. Meaning to explode in anger, this expression, first recorded in 1945, was probably suggested by *to have a short fuse*. The *fuse* here, however, is the one in a house's fuse box controlling the electricity.

blowhard. *See* BLOW HIS (HER) OWN HORN.

blow his mind. This was originally an expression employed by drug users, comparing the effect of a drug on the mind to an explosive that blows something up. From this 1960s usage the words came to mean "to experience, or cause someone to experience, great mental excitement."

blow his (her) own horn. The term *blowhard*, for "a braggart," can be traced back to the American West in about 1855. To *blow your own horn*, or "to promote yourself," derives from a much older expression, *to blow your own trumpet*, which goes as far back as 1576. Such "hornblowing" may have its origins in medieval times, when heralds blew their trumpets to announce the arrival of royalty but commoners such as street vendors had to blow their own horns.

blow his top. For several centuries *blow* has been used in the sense of a violent explosion of temper, and for just as long *top* has meant the top of the head. Yet somehow the expression to *blow one's top* didn't enter the language until about the time of the Great Depression. There have been attempts to link it with the top of a volcano erupting, but the phrase seems to have come down the road to general speech via the off-trail slang of jazz musicians. Mencken alludes to its "blushful" sexual origin, but doesn't explain further, probably meaning ejaculation of the male organ.

blow off steam. The diesels that have replaced steam engines have robbed us of the literal basis for this metaphor, but it's still widely used. To *blow off* or *let off steam* is to have an emotional outburst, a psychological safety valve. This is reflected in the origins of the term, which goes back to the 1830s. Early steam locomotives had no safety valves and when steam pressure built too high in an engine, the engineer had to pull a hand lever to blow off steam to prevent an explosion. The angry-looking engine blowing off steam to save itself quickly suggested the colorful metaphor.

blowth. In the past people often called the blossoming of trees a *blowing*, a colorful term that means a tree's buds were exploding or blowing outward to make its flowers. This suggested the word *blowth* for blossoming in general, as in "There's a good blowth on my fruit trees."

blow the whistle. This phrase means to inform on someone or something. The expression, of recent vintage, was inspired by the whistles blown by basketball or football officials after a foul has been committed.

blucher boots. This half boot has evolved into today's basic, low-cut men's shoes. Originally laced low boots or high shoes, *bluchers* were named for Gebhard Leberecht von Blücher (1742–1819), a Prussian field marshal who fought with Wellington against Napoleon at Waterloo. Field Marshal von Blücher did not design but sponsored the boots in 1810, considering them better footwear for his troops. Another word commemorating him was the British slang expression *Blucher*, for a cab allowed to take passengers to London stations only after all others had been hired—in allusion to the fact that the old man had arrived at Waterloo too late to be of much help!

bludgeon. One guess is that *bludgeon* for a heavy club or to hit with a heavy club, may be related to the word *blood*, which certainly sounds like the first part of the word and certainly describes a possible result of being hit with such a club. But this is only a theory, there's no proof to back it up. We only know for sure that *bludgeon* is first recorded in 1730.

blue; blue movies; blue laws. A series of off-color French books called *La Bibliothèque Bleu* contributed to the coining of the word *blue* for obscene, as in pornographic *blue movies*, as did the customary blue dress of prostitutes in the early 19th century when the books were written. *Blue laws*, which might repress *blue movies*, has an entirely different derivation. The term usually means Never-On-Sunday moral laws and may take its name from a nonexistent Connecticut "blue book" rumored to contain fanatical laws. The vengeful rumor was spread by the Reverend Samuel Peters, an American Tory who returned to England after the Revolution. Peters claimed that the fictitious blue-bound book contained laws prohibiting such activities as kissing one's wife on Sunday.

bluebacks. Paper money used by the Confederates during the Civil War; also called *graybacks*. "During the Civil War . . . the original Blue Backs of the Confederacy (so-called in opposition to Green Backs of the Union) soon became known as Shucks, a name sufficiently significant of their evil repute . . . ," Maximillian Schele De Vere wrote in *Americanisms* (1871). Over a billion dollars' worth of bluebacks and graybacks were issued by the South during the Civil War; the bills were worth about 1.7 cents in gold for each Confederate dollar by the end of the hostilities. *See* GREENBACKS.

Bluebeard. Many of the most famous fairy tales, including "Sleeping Beauty," "Red Riding Hood," "Puss in Boots" and "Cinderella," were collected by Charles Perrault and published in his *Contes du Temps* (1697). Among them was "Barbe Bleue" ("Blue Beard"), in which a sadistic indigo-bearded wife killer is foiled when his last wife, Fatima, discovers the bodies of her predecessors in a secret, locked room and is saved from death herself by her brothers' arrival in the nick of time. According to local tradition in Brittany, the real Bluebeard upon whom the story is based was the monstrous Frenchman General Gilles de Retz, the marquis de Laval, who murdered six of his seven wives and was burned at the stake for his crimes in 1440. But similar stories are common to many languages and other candidates have been nominated as well. A Bluebeard has come to mean a man who murders women he has married, and a number of contemporary wife killers, especially the Frenchman Henri Desire Landru, have been called "The Modern Bluebeard."

blueberry. The blueberry, like the BLACKBERRY, is of course named for the color of its berries. Blueberries have been a favorite food for centuries and are among the most widely distributed fruits. Early colonists gathered the "blues," "whortleberries," and "bilberries," and made good use of them as the Indians had done since prehistoric times. But more than any other fruit, cultivated blueberries are children of the 20th century. It was in the early 1900s that Elizabeth C. White of Whitesbog, New Jersey (one of several pioneer women fruit growers), offered local prizes for highbush blueberries bearing the largest fruits. Hearing of her work, Dr. Frederick V. Coville, a U.S. Department of Agriculture plant breeder, began to work in cooperation with her starting in 1909, and crossed many wild plants she or her contestants had selected from the Pine Barrens of New Jersey, an area with an acid, sandy, but fertile soil. By the time Coville died in 1937 there were 30 large-fruited, named highbush varieties where there had been none, and today there are myriad varieties that have been selected from hundreds of thousands of fruited hybrid seedlings. From its status as a lowly fruit often confused with the huckleberry (even though, unlike the bony-seeded huckleberry, its 50 to 75 seeds are small and barely noticeable when eaten), White and Coville had elevated the blueberry to a position where it became the basis for an entirely new agricultural industry. *Vaccinium corymbosum*, the highbush or swamp blueberry, had gone through a revolution rather than an evolution and became a mass-produced fruit in less than 25 years. *See* BILBERRIES; RAB-BIT-EYE.

blue blood; blue-brick. The warriors of Islam who were called the Moors (or, more poetically, the lyrical name black-amoors) ruled over most of Spain for five centuries. Toward the end of their rule the Spanish aristocrats of Castile began to distinguish themselves from these darker-skinned people by adopting the name *sangre azul*, "blue blood," to describe themselves. The expression simply refers to the fact that these nobles had lighter complexions than the Moors and that the veins in their skin showed up a vivid blue. Pure Castilians became known as blue bloods and the term was borrowed to describe European noblemen of other countries. Today, the British make use of the expression in an interesting way. Universities with the highest prestige and pedigrees, like Cambridge and Oxford, are called blue-brick universities.

bluebonnet. The blue-flowered lupine, *Lupinus sub-carnosis*, the official state flower of Texas. Due to extensive seeding, great masses of these flowers bloom along the roadsides in spring. They are also called buffalo clover.

blue-chip stocks. The most valuable counters in poker are the blue chips. Since the early 1900s Wall Street, borrowing the expression from another world of gambling, has called secure, relatively high-yielding stocks "blue-chip stocks." Among the earliest terms for worthless or speculative stocks is "cats and dogs," first recorded in 1879.

bluegrass. Whether *Poa pratensis* or bluegrass was brought here from Europe or was here long before the first white settlers came is a matter of opinion among laymen if not scientists. The late John Ciardi discussed the question in *Good Words to You* (1987):

> "Various Kentucky historians . . . including Dr. Eslie Asbury, surgeon, raconteur, and well-known breeder of race horses, insist that the bluegrass was there when the first white settlers reached Kentucky . . . I have driven across Kentucky many times, even on the Bluegrass Highway, without seeing any but green grass. A number of natives have assured me that I have seen only cropped pastures, and that the blueness of the bluegrass becomes visible only when the grass is allowed to go to seed, the seed covering having a distinctly blue cast . . . Others have added that the blueness of bluegrass is visible only when the sun is low and a soft wind tosses the grass . . . I choose to agree with Dr. Asbury, who attributes the blueness (in season) to the small blue flowers this grass bears. Even in season, they are not commonly visible because the grass is usually cropped."

Another theory holds that bluegrass takes its name from a pest grass that settlers on the Atlantic coast so named because its leaves were distinctly bluish in color. When these settlers moved into what is now Kentucky they found a grass, of about the same size and shape as the bluegrass previously discovered, and gave it the same name, which we still use today. *See* BLUEGRASS STATE.

Bluegrass State. A nickname for Kentucky since Civil War days (*see* BLUEGRASS). Kentucky has also been called the Hemp State, the Rock-Ribbed State, and the Dark and Bloody Ground (the translation of an Indian name for ground on which bloody battles between Indian tribes were fought).

blue hen's chicken. One who is a good fighter, because blue hens are said to breed the best fighting cocks; the term also means someone high-spirited, aggressive, quick-tempered or high-class and was applied to soldiers from Delaware during the Revolutionary War, resulting in the nickname *blue hen's chicken* for a native of Delaware.

Blue Hen State. A nickname for Delaware (*see* BLUE HEN'S CHICKENS). Delaware has also been called the Diamond State, Uncle Sam's Pocket Handkerchief (due to its small size), and New Sweden, after the 1638 settlement of Swedes there in *Nye Sverige*.

blue jeans. In the late 16th century the cotton cloth used to make jeans was called *Genoa fustian* after Genoa, Italy, where it was first woven. *Genoa* was shortened to *Gene* and then *Jean* by Englishmen, fustian was dropped, and the men's work pants made from the material were called blue jeans for their color—all this centuries before they reached their present popularity.

blue laws. *See* BLUE.

blue lights. *Blue lights* became an Americanism for traitors during the War of 1812 when on December 12, 1813 pro-British Americans flashed blue lights to British ships off the coast as a signal that Commodore Stephen Decatur's two frigates would soon be sailing from their New London, Connecticut harbor. Acting on this information, the British blockaded the port.

blue moon. *See* ONCE IN A BLUE MOON.

blue movies. *See* BLUE.

bluenose. The term *bluenose* to describe a person of rigid puritanical habits was first applied to lumbermen and fishermen of northern New England and referred to the color of their noses, the blue induced by long exposure to cold weather. Only later was the word applied to the aristocratic inhabitants of Boston's Back Bay area in the sense that we know it today, possibly in alluding to their apparently "frigid" manner. *Bluenose* is also used as an opprobrious nickname for Nova Scotians, but there the word probably derives from the name of a popular Nova Scotian potato.

blue-nose certificate. The blue-nose certificate was an illuminated diploma once awarded aboard British vessels to those who had crossed a meridian north of the Arctic Circle, the "blue-nose" referring, of course to the cold. The certificate is no longer awarded.

blue-pencil. To alter, abridge, correct, or delete, as an editor does with a manuscript requiring anything from first aid to intensive care. The term, dating back to the late 19th century, was suggested by the pencil with blue lead often used by editors to edit manuscripts.

blue peter. On ships ready to leave port, a signal flag called the blue peter is raised to call all crew members aboard and to notify everyone in port that all money claims must be settled because the ship is departing. The flag is blue with a white square in the center. Why the *peter* in the term? It may be a corruption of the French *partir*, "to depart," while most consider it to be a telescoping of the word *repeater*. The flag may have originally been used as a "repeater flag," a signal hoisted to indicate that a message from another ship hadn't been read and should be repeated.

blue ribbon; cordon bleu. Britain's highest order of knighthood is the Most Noble Order of the Garter, which has as its badge a dark blue velvet ribbon edged with gold that is worn below the left knee. Inscribed on the ribbon in gold is the motto *Honi soit qui mal y pense* (Shame to him who thinks evil of it). Popular legend says that these words and the name of the order result from the gallantry of King Edward III—the king was dancing with the countess of Salisbury at a royal ball and when she lost her garter, he retrieved it and slipped it on his own leg to save her embarrassment, uttering the famous words. In any case, Edward III instituted the award in about 1344 and the blue ribbon awarded with it came to symbolize the highest honor in any field of endeavor. The French *cordon bleu* (blue ribbon), a decoration suspended on a blue ribbon, also influenced the term's meaning. Under the Bourbons it was the highest order of knighthood in France and was later used to honor great chefs.

blues; blue devils. *Blues*, for a state of depression or despair, is probably a shortening of the 18th-century expression *blue devils*, or low spirits. Surprisingly, Washington Irving first used the term in *Salmagundi* as far back as 1807: "[He] concluded his harangue with a sigh, and I saw that he was still under the influence of a whole legion of the blues." Later *blue devils* became the hallucinations associated with the D.T.s, or delirium tremens, and a *blue devil* is now drug users' slang for sodium amytal, suggested by the color of the capsule and the narcotic's effects. *Blue devils*, *blue*, *blue-eyed*, and *blue around the gills* all have meant drunk in one way or another, possibly because blue is the color of approaching death and they are all associated with the SEVEN STAGES OF DRUNKENNESS. This would also explain the linking of blues with depression. *The blues*, toward the end of the 19th century, gave their name to the melancholy jazz music called the blues, deriving in part from sad black prison and funeral songs of slavery and oppression.

blue-sky laws. These are American state laws regulating the sale of securities, especially laws designed to inhibit the promotion of fraudulent stocks. Kansas, in 1912, enacted the first law so described by the press as protection against unscrupulous land promoters. Behind the words is the idea that suckers will buy even the blue sky from con artists or that "blue-sky" land or securities lack substance, like cloudless blue skies.

bluestockings. Only one of the original bluestockings wore homely blue stockings, and he was a man, a Mr. Benjamin Stillingfleet. The group was founded by Mrs. Elizabeth Montagu in about 1750 as a kind of literary salon based on Parisian models. Leading intellectuals of the era gave talks at Mrs. Montagu's London home and conventional evenings of card-playing were replaced by intellectual discussions. All of the club members dressed simply as a reaction against the ostentatious evening clothes of the time, but only the one male member wore blue-gray tradesman's hose in place of gentlemen's black silk hose. Nevertheless, a contemporary wit twisted the fact and called all these intellectual ladies bluestockings, the word coming to mean a dowdy, affected literary lady, even though Mrs. Montagu was a beautiful woman and an author whose work was highly praised by Dr. Johnson. These early feminists were held in contempt by "proper ladies" of the time, but male chauvinists were most vehement about them. "A bluestocking," said Rousseau, "is a woman who will remain a spinster as long as there are sensible men on earth."

blue streak. *See* TALK A BLUE STREAK.

blue-water sailor. This is a complimentary term for a sailor who customarily sails in the "deep (blue) sea" as opposed to safer coastal waters; it probably dates back to the mid-18th century.

bluff. Mathew's *A Dictionary of Americanisms* records *bluff*, origin unknown, as the term for a riverbank as early as 1687, referring to a "Bluffe" in South Carolina. According to Stuart Berg Flexner, in *I Hear America Talking* (1976), this is a historical curiosity, the very first of what would be a long list of Americanisms that the British termed "barbarous." In poker to bluff is to deceive an opponent about the strength of one's hand by betting heavily on it. This *bluff* probably derives from the German *bluffen*, "to frighten by menacing conduct." Early names for poker, recorded in 1838, were bluff and brag. From poker also comes the expression *to call one's bluff*.

Bluff City. A nickname for both Memphis, Tennessee, and Hannibal, Missouri. Both cities are located on bluffs overhanging water.

blunderbuss. The Dutch gave the name *dunderbluss* ("thunder tube") to this short musket with a wide bore and expanded muzzle, which they used to scatter shots at close range. But the English, who adopted it in the 17th century, soon learned that it was an erratic weapon, changed its name to *blunderbuss*, and applied the word to "a blundering, stupid person" as well.

blunt. One of the few words meaning money in general that derives from the name of a person. *Blunt*, which means cash, possibly comes from the name of John Blunt, chairman of the British South Sea Company, who was a very rich man indeed. *Blunt* in this sense has been used by many writers, including Dickens in *Oliver Twist*. The obsolete historical term led to the expressions *in blunt* and *out of blunt*, to be rich or poor. A *blunt* is also a cigar stuffed with marijuana, the term named after the Phillies Blunt trademarked brand of cigar and first recorded in 1988. *See* OSCAR ASCHE.

blurb. Humorist Gelett Burgess invented *blurb* in 1907 with the publication of his *Are You a Bromide?* Burgess's publisher, B. W. Huebsch, later told the story: "It is the custom of publishers to present copies of a conspicuous current book to booksellers attending the annual dinner of their trade association, and as this little book was in its heyday when the meeting took place, I gave it to 500 guests. These copies were differentiated from the regular edition by the addition of a comic bookplate drawn by the author and by a special jacket which he devised. It was the common practice to print the picture of a damsel—languishing, heroic, coquettish . . . on the jacket of every novel, so Burgess lifted from a Lydia Pinkham or toothpowder advertisement the portrait of a sickly sweet young woman, painted in some gleaming teeth, and otherwise enhanced her pulchritude, and placed her in the center of the jacket. His accompanying text was some nonsense about 'Miss Belinda Blurb,' and thus the term supplied a real need and became a fixture in our language."

blushing thigh of the aroused nymph.   The French gave this sensuous, poetic name *(la cuisse de nymphe ému)* to a double pink alba rose developed in France in 1797. According to rosarian Stephen Scanniello *(see* YELLOW ROSE OF TEXAS*)*, the name was too daring for English gardeners who imported the lovely fragrant rose, so they bowdlerized it to "Great Maiden's Blush."

BMX.   Cross-country bicycle racing is called BMX, as is the cross-country bicycle itself. BMX stands for *bicycle moto cross, moto* coming from the French for "motorcycle" and *cross* (X) from the English "cross-country."

B.O.   Lifebuoy Health Soap, better known as Lifebuoy, ran its first "Lifebuoy stops B———O———" advertisements (with a two-note foghorn warning accompanying the "B.O.") on the radio in 1933. Since then B.O. has become synonymous with *bad* body odor, though it is of course an abbreviation of *body odor,* which isn't necessarily bad.

Boanerges.   Any loud orator or preacher. The Hebrew *Boanerges* means "sons of thunder" and was the surname Jesus gave to his disciples the brothers James and John, sons of Zebedu. These disciples were rebuked by Jesus when, after the Samaritans failed to receive their master, they suggested: "Lord, wilt thou that we bid fire to come down from heaven and consume them." The story is told in Mark 3:17 and Luke 9:54.

boat; ship; craft.   A *boat,* deriving from the Old Norse *beit* or *bato,* is any small marine craft, while a SHIP is any large ocean-going vessel, and a *craft,* from the Old English *craeft,* means all boats and ships of any size.

boat names.   *See* SHIP NAMES.

bob.   It has been suggested that this British slang word for a shilling, familiar to all English-speaking peoples, may come from the name of Sir Robert (Bob) Walpole (1676–1745). The first Earl of Walpole was intimately connected with money in his posts as army paymaster, first commissioner of the treasury, chancellor of the Exchequer, and finally as England's Prime Minister. But the word *bob* isn't recorded until about 1810, some 65 years after Walpole's death, so the derivation remains uncertain.

bobadil.   Ben Jonson's play *Every Man in His Humor* (1598) gave us the character Captain Bobadill, an old soldier who gravely boasts of his conquests and is proved as vain and cowardly as he is boastful. From the old soldier's name we have the word *bobadil,* "a braggart who pretends to great prowess." Johnson patterned his character on Boabdil, a late 15th-century Moorish king of Granada. King Boabdil was noted for the same characteristics as the fictional captain.

bobbasheely.   "You and Sweet Thing bobbasheely on back to the hotel now," William Faulkner has a character say in *The Reivers* (1962). *Bobbasheely* means "to walk in no great rush but to move on," "to saunter." It can also mean a very close friend—in fact, it is said to derive from a Choctaw Indian word for "my brother."

bobbitt.   One night in 1993 while he slept, John Wayne Bobbitt's wife, Lorena, cut off his penis with a kitchen knife, allegedly in revenge for acts of rape and abuse. Surgeons reattached his penis, but Bobbitt's name would never wholly be his own again. People began using *bobbitt* to mean the act of a woman amputating a husband's or a lover's penis, especially in revenge, and this most extreme of eponymous words became part of the vocabulary of millions, thanks to news stories about the dismemberment, reattachment, and trial that followed. *See* JOHN THOMAS.

bobble.   An Americanism meaning a mistake or error. The word, first recorded in 1805, is commonly used today for a mishandled chance in baseball.

bobby; peelers; robert.   *Bobby* is among the most familiar of eponymous words, despite the fact that "copper" or "cop" is more often used today to describe an English policeman. The well-known word honors Sir Robert Peel, British Home Secretary (1828–30) when the Metropolitan Police Act remodeled London's police force. Peel, whose wealthy father bought him his seat in Parliament, as was customary in those days, first won fame as chief secretary for Ireland, where he was nicknamed "Orange Peel" for his support of the Protestant "orangemen." It was at this time that he established the Irish constabulary under The Peace Preservation Act (1814), and his policemen were soon called "Peel's Bloody Gang" and then *peelers. Peelers* remained the name for both Irish and London police for many years, *bobby* and *robert* not being recorded in print until about 1851.

bob house.   According to *Yankee Magazine* (January 1974), this is a little hut built on a frozen lake for fishing. The fishermen fish through holes cut through the wooden floor and through the ice.

bob ruly.   American pioneers called a burned out area a *bob ruly,* which leads some to think that the term might have been named after a notorious firebug of old. But *bob ruly,* first recorded in 1848, though older, is just how the French words *bois brulé,* "burned woods," sounded to American ears.

Bob's your uncle.   Americans mainly know this expression from films. It means "that's it" "that'll be all right" "you've got it right," "there you go," "there you are." The term dates back only to the 1880s, but no one has been able to identify without doubt the real "Bob" in the phrase, if indeed there was one. It may, however, be derived from the promotion in 1885 of Arthur

J. Balfour (1848–1930) to chief secretary for Ireland by his uncle the marquess of Salisbury, who had just appointed him to another position the year before. Balfour is better remembered for the Balfour Declaration of 1917, in which as British foreign secretary he favored a Jewish homeland in Palestine.

bobtailed flush or straight. A bobtailed flush or straight in poker is a three-card flush or straight, one that is worthless because poker rules require five-card flushes or straights. The term apparently originated in the West in the mid-19th century, modeled on the short-cut tails of bobtailed horses.

bocaccio. A fish named after the great Italian poet, storyteller, and diplomat Giovanni Boccaccio (1313–75). The American rockfish has a big mouth and the poet was said to be something of a gossip. Or it may be simply that this famous person's name combined nicely with the Spanish *bocacha* for "bigmouth," yielding *bocaccio* (with three c's, not four).

boccie. An Italian game of lawn bowling played on a dirt court shorter and narrower than a bowling green, boccie takes its name from the Italian *boccia*, "ball." It is often played in city parks today. *See* SPALDING.

bock beer; lager beer. Beer drinkers who favor the strong, dark Bavarian lager beer called bock, which is usually brewed in the autumn and aged through the winter, may be surprised to learn that it takes its name from the German word for buck, or male goat—"because of its great strength making its consumers prance and tumble like these animals." *Bock beer* comes from the German *Eimbockbier*, "buck beer from Eimbeck" in Lower Saxony, Germany. A lager beer is a beer that, like bock beer, has been "bedded down" in a storehouse for aging, *lager* simply meaning the German for "bed or resting place."

bodacious. *Bodacious* dates back to at least the early 1840s, but it is said to have been popularized by the Snuffy Smith comic strip about American hillbillys. *Bodacious* can mean remarkable, enormous, strong, and prodigious, as well as insolent, or even big-breasted. It is possibly a blend of *bold* and *audacious*.

bodega. *Bodega* is Spanish for "storehouse." Originally indicating a small Hispanic grocery store, often selling a large variety of items, including wine, the word is now often used to refer to any small grocery store. There are thousands of bodegas in the United States today.

bodkin. *Bodkin's* origin is uncertain, but it may derive from an unknown Celtic word, or be the corruption of a Gaelic word for "little dagger." A *bodkin* was once a stiletto worn by ladies in their up-swept hair and this is probably the weapon Shakespeare refers to in the famous passage from *Hamlet:* "When he himself might his quietus make with a bare bodkin." *See* QUIETUS.

Bodleian Library. England's Bodleian Library at Oxford is among the greatest libraries in the world. Its name honors founder Sir Thomas Bodley (1545–1613), who devoted nearly 20 years of his life to developing the library. The Bodleian is entitled under the national Copyright Act to receive on demand a copy of every book published in the United Kingdom. Thomas

Bodley, a Protestant exile who returned to England from Geneva when Elizabeth I ascended the throne, served in Parliament and as a diplomat in several European countries before retiring from public life in 1596. He began to restore the old Oxford library two years later and left most of his fortune to it as an endowment.

bodock; Osage orange. *Bodock* is another name for the Osage orange tree (*Maclura pomifera*). It is so called because the Indians used its wood for making bows and the French thus called it the *bois d'arc* ("bowwood") tree, which became corrupted in English to *bodock*. It is called the *Osage orange* because it grew in Osage Indian country and has large, rough-skinned greenish fruits somewhat suggestive of an orange, but inedible. The spiny-branched tree is often used for hedges and called the Osage thorn. It is first recorded, in 1804, by the Lewis and Clark expedition, as the Osage Apple.

Boeotians. This is among the oldest of the many words dishonoring an entire people. Meaning ignorant, dull, and lacking in refinement, *Boeotian* recalls the inhabitants of Boeotia, a farming district in ancient Greece, whom the urbane Athenians found thick and stupid, with no understanding of art or literature. In truth, as Homer and other knowledgeable Greeks noted, the region produced Pindar and Plutarch as well as country bumpkins. *Boeotian* is also used in terms like "Boeotian ears," ears unable to appreciate good music or poetry.

Boer War. Actually there were two of them, in 1880–81 and in 1899–1902. The first Boer War saw the Duch and Huguenot Boer settlers in South Africa rebelling against British rule and winning an independent republic controlled by the British. In the second Boer War, blame is divided between Britain's imperialist designs and the refusal of the Boers to give equal rights to British immigrants. After the British won the second Boer War, the Boer republics of the Orange Free State and Transvaal became part of the Republic of South Africa. The word *Boer* is from the Dutch *boer* meaning agriculturist, though some writers claim it means "peasant."

bog. *Bog* is the Russian word for God. In 1930 1 million copies of a school textbook containing a poem by Nekrasov with the word *Bog* in it were printed by the Soviet government. Then someone discovered, to the horror of the Kremlin, that *Bog* was spelled with a capital letter throughout the poem. Reducing *Bog* to *bog* required resetting type in 16 pages of each of the million books printed, but the change was made, despite the expense, so that "the books reached the Soviet children uncontaminated." Despite the past efforts of Soviet censors the Russian language remains rich in references to God, such expressions as "God knows," "God save us," "Oh, my God," and "Praise God" being quite common. "Communism is gone," one anonymous wit said recently, "but God remains."

bogart. *See* DON'T BOGART THAT JOINT.

bogey. *Bogey*, a word for "an imaginary or real thing that causes fear or worry," may be just a dialectical form of the old word *bug*, "ghost or specter," and it gives us both the *bogeyman* used to scare children and the golf term *bogey*, one stroke over par, which arose from a popular 1890 song called "Coloney

Bogey." This latter term at first meant "par" in England, because Colonel Bogey's name was adopted by golfers to signify a fictitious gentleman who could play a course or hole in the lowest number of strokes that a good golfer could play it in. American golfers, satisfied with "par" to express the British meaning of *bogey*, made Colonel Bogey something of a duffer.

bogus. Most theories about the word *bogus*, meaning "fake or spurious," relate it to some form of bogey, in its sense of an imaginary or false thing. One version claims the word can be traced to May 1827 when the Painesville, Ohio, *Telegraph* ran a story about a gang of counterfeiters whose fake coins were so perfect that they were compared to the work of some supernatural bogeyman. Another says the word comes from the name of a device called a bogus, used for counterfeiting coins in the same state in the same year, connecting this machine with "tantra-bogus," an old Vermont term for bogeyman. Complicating matters is the fact that the first use of *bogus* isn't recorded until 1838. Although it is certainly possible that the word was in use 10 years or so before it appeared in print, another derivation traces it to a counterfeiter who was operating at exactly the time *bogus* was first recorded. "The word *bogus*," according to a *Boston Courier* of 1857, "is a corruption of the name Borghese, a man who, 20 years ago, did a tremendous business in supplying the Great West of America with counterfeit bills on fictitious banks. The western people came to shortening the name Borghese to *bogus*, and his bills were universally styled 'bogus currency.'" However, there is still another theory that suggests a direct passage from *boghus*, a gypsy word for counterfeit coin. More than one of these speculations has to be bogus.

bohemian. *Bohemian* was first used as a synonym for a gypsy or vagabond during the Middle Ages, people mistakenly believing that the gypsy tribes entered the West via the ancient kingdom of Bohemia. *Bohemian* became synonymous with a poor writer or artist with French novelist Henri Murger's stories in *Scènes de la vie de bohème* (1848), his book providing the basis for Puccini's opera *La Bohème*. The English novelist William Makepeace Thackeray made the word a synonym for a nonconforming artist in *Vanity Fair* (1848) when he wrote of his headstrong heroine Becky Sharp: "She was of a wild, roving nature, inherited from her father and mother, who were both Bohemian by taste and circumstance."

bohunkus. A humorous term for the buttocks. It may derive from *bohunk*, a derogatory term for any eastern European, which in turn comes from *Bohemian* and *Hung*arian. *See also* HONKIE.

Bolivia; boliviano; bolivar. Commemorative of Simon Bolívar (1783–1830), the legendary South American revolutionary, soldier, and statesman, are the *bolívar* monetary unit of Venezuela and the *boliviano* of Bolivia. Simon Bolívar, the Liberator, led Venezuela's revolution against Spain and founded Greater Colombia (then a union consisting of Venezuela, Ecuador, and New Granada, the present-day Colombia). He is one of the few men in history to have a country named after him in his lifetime and probably the only one to create and give that same country its constitution. Bolivia, or Upper Peru as it was then known, was first named República Bolívar in the great soldier and statesman's honor.

bollard. A thick, low cylindrical post that combined with other bollards can stop out-of-control cars from crashing into pedestrian areas and is also employed in blocking cars from roads, lawns, etc. The word first described the black posts found on ships and docks used for tying hausers. *Bollard* derives from *bole*, Middle English for a tree trunk, and is first recorded in about 1835–40.

bollixed up. Messed up, mixed up, spoiled, thrown into confusion. The expression, only traced to the 1930s, is thought to derive from *bollocks*, testicles, which comes from the Old English *bealluc*, meaning the same.

boll weevil. *Weevil* comes from the Old English *wifel*, "beetle," and *boll*, first spelled *bowl*, refers to the pod of the cotton plant, which the beetle attacks. In Enterprise, Alabama there is a monument to a boll weevil—erected at the turn of the century after the beetle so devastated the cotton crop in the area that farmers were forced to plant peanuts, and as a result became more prosperous than they ever had been as cotton growers. *See also* GULL.

Bollywood. English and Hindi are the official languages of India. Among the many English words coined there is *Bollywood*, a nickname for the busy motion picture industry in Bombay. The blend word, first recorded about 1970, is patterned on HOLLYWOOD and was meant to suggest Bombay's initial slavish imitation of Tinseltown.

bolo. Paul Bolo, a French traitor popularly known as Bolo Pasha, faced a firing squad in 1917, having been convicted of treason the previous year. *Bolo*, though now generally a historical term, saw extensive use during World War I in describing a traitor, fifth columnist, or spy, someone working underground for the enemy. Bolo's treason consisted principally of spreading pacifist propaganda financed by the Germans.

bolo alert. *Bolo* is a recent acronym used by law enforcement agencies, including the FBI, to mean *be on the look out for*, in reference to the whereabouts and intentions of a terrorist or any criminal. A bolo is also a long single-edged machete. *See* BOLO above.

boloney. Al Smith, governor of New York and unsuccessful presidential candidate in 1928, helped popularize this expression with his remark "No matter how you slice it, it's still baloney." But *boloney* for "bunk" dates back to at least the early 20th century, bologna sausage having been pronounced *boloney* as early as the 1870s, when there was a popular song "I Ate the Boloney." There are those who say that *boloney* for "bunk" has nothing to do with bologna sausage, however, tracing it to a corruption of the Spanish *pelone*, "testicles," and claiming that this meant "nonsense" or "bunk" just as "balls," "all balls," and "nerts" did. The word is also spelled *baloney*.

bolshevik; menshevik. Synonymous today for an agitator or radical reformer, *bolshevik* originally signified the left wing of the Russian Social Democratic Party, the designation evolving from a party congress in 1903 when the majority (Bolshevik), accepted the views of Vladimir Lenin. The vote was close (25–23), and behind the tactical issues involved lay great differences—such as the minority belief that revolution in Russia should be gradual in contrast to Lenin's insistence that there be an immediate overthrow of the czarist regime. In 1917, the Bolsheviks again gained a small majority in the Socialist party congress, though not in Russia itself, and simultaneously overthrew the existing Russian government. Ironically, it was Lenin's view that the Bolsheviks (the majority party) should be composed of a small select minority rather than the masses. "Bolshie," for an agitator, is simply a corruption of *bolshevik*. The Mensheviks (from the Russian *menshevik*) were the members of the minority in the Russian Socialist party, who favored a more gradual transition to communism.

bolt from the blue. *See* TALK A BLUE STREAK.

bomb. *Bomb*, in reference to theatrical productions, has completely opposite meanings in England and America. When a play bombs in America it is a complete flop—a *bomb*. When a play bombs in England it is a great success—a *bomb*. The British use seems to be built on the explosive force of a real bomb, while the American usage is based upon the destruction a bomb creates. The word *bomb* derives ultimately from the Latin *bombus*, "a booming sound."

the Bomb. The term refers to any nuclear bomb, unique from other bombs because of its great destructive power. *The Bomb* was first recorded in 1945 and is also heard in the phrase *Ban the Bomb*, which nuclear arms protestors probably invented in 1960.

bombast. Bombast was cotton used as a padding or stuffing for clothes in days past, the word deriving from the word *bombyx*, for "silkworm or silk," which was applied to cotton as well. Just as stuffing or padding in clothing was called bombast so was padded, stuffed, inflated, grandiose speech—this figurative use of *bombast* being first recorded in 1589, not long after the word was first used in its literal sense. Write off as entertaining but untrue the old story that *bombast* for inflated speech on trivial subjects comes from the real name of the egotistical Swiss physician, alchemist, and writer Paracelsus (1493?–1541)—Theophrastus Bombastus von Hohenheim.

bombazine. *See* BAMBOOZLE.

bonanza. *Bonanza*, for a rich body of gold or silver ore in a mine, or any rich strike, began life as a Spanish word meaning "fair weather at sea." Miners in California probably learned the word from seamen, who also used it to mean prosperity in general, and applied *bonanza* to any rich vein of ore.

Bonaparte's gull; Zenadia bird. Bonaparte's gull, one of only two black-headed species in the United States, was described scientifically for the first time in Prince Charles-Lucien Bonaparte's *American Ornithology*. Bonaparte, Napoleon's nephew, resided in this country from 1824 to 1833. The gull bearing the naturalist's name breeds hundreds of miles from the sea, becoming a seabird in winter, and inland bird-watchers consider it a harbinger of spring. *Zenadia*, the scientific designation for several species of wild doves and pigeons, is named for Bonaparte's wife, Princess Zénaïde.

bon-bon. *Bon-bon* means "good, good" in French and the name was probably given to candies by children, "originating in the nursery," according to the *O.E.D.* The term is first recorded in Thomas Moore's satirical poem "The Fudge Family in Paris" (1818): "The land of Cocaigne . . . / Where for hail they have bon-bons, and claret for rain."

bond. *See* STOCKS AND BONDS.

bond paper. In the early 1800s a Boston, Massachusetts paper mill made a desirable all-rag paper that was widely used for printing bonds, bank notes, and legal documents. People began to call it *bond paper* when ordering it, and the expression soon was applied to any high-quality paper.

bone; bone up on. Bones were once used to polish shoes, and some scholars have attempted to link such bones to the expression *to bone up on* a subject, to study it hard and thoroughly, especially for an exam. One would then "polish up" his knowledge, presumably, but bones probably have nothing to do with this term. It was first used in the 1860s by collegians, and they apparently first spelled the *bone* in the phrase *Bohn*, probably referring to the Bohn translations of the classics, or "trots," that they used in studying. British scholar Henry George Bohn (1796–1884) was the author and publisher of many books, including the "Classical Library."

bonehead play; pulling a boner. The original *bonehead play* was made on September 9, 1908 by Fred Merkle, New York Giants first baseman. It was the last of the ninth, two out, and the Giants had Moose McCormick on third and Merkle on first. The next man up singled to center and McCormick scored the winning run, but Merkle ran into the dugout instead of touching second base. Johnny Evers of the Cubs got the ball and stepped on second, forcing out Merkle. The winning run was nullified and the game not counted in the standings. Merkle's play became all the more important later in the season when the Cubs and Giants finished tied for first place and the Cubs won the pennant in a playoff game. Though *boneheaded* had been used in the sense of "stupid" a few years earlier, it was a sportswriter's use of *bonehead play* in reference to Merkle's blunder that introduced the phrase to the language, along with the related *to pull a boner*.

bone, hide, and hair. Everything, every part of. For the term's origin *see* NEITHER HIDE NOR HAIR.

boner. *See* BONEHEAD PLAY.

bone to pick. It has been suggested that this expression arose from "an old Sicilian custom" where the father of the bride gave "the bridegroom a bone to pick clean as a symbol of the difficult task of marriage that he was undertaking." If such a custom exists, it has nothing to do with the phrase, which in modern usage means to have an argument to settle with someone. The expression, though its meaning has varied over the years, is some four centuries old and was probably suggested by two dogs fighting over a single bone tossed between them—*a bone of contention*—or by a dog preoccupied with a bone, which suggested the phrase's original meaning of "to mull over something." The idea is conveyed in several earlier phrases common to English and other languages.

bonfire.   Dr. Johnson believes *bonfire* was a hybrid word derived the French *bon*, good, and the English *fire*, reasoning that this fit the definition of *bonfire* as a fire made for a "cause of triumph or exaltation." But most experts believe the word comes from *bone* plus *fire* and originally described a fire made from bones. The word is first attested in English as *bane* (bone) *fire* in 1475 and its earliest known ancestor is the Latin *ignis ossium*, fire of bones.

bongo.   The reddish brown forest antelope of tropical Africa may have been named from the people of the Sudan, noted for their reddish brown skin color. Or according to another theory, these people were named after the antelope. In any case *bongo* is a Bantu word of uncertain meaning.

boniface.   Innkeepers are called bonifaces after Will Boniface, a character in George Farquhar's comedy *The Beaux' Stratagem* (1707). Will Boniface is the landlord of an inn in Lichfield, a pleasant old man of 85 with a comic tongue who loves his ale. *See* LADY BOUNTIFUL.

bonkers.   Most Americans know this British slang word for silly, stupid, or crazy. Many use it, and some act it. Partridge claims the word, about 1920, first meant "slightly drunk, light-headed," but has no explanation for its origin except that it arose in the navy. Perhaps the word has something to do with getting bonked (hit) in the head. Other Brit favorites for *crazy* include *crackers, dotty, loopy,* and *certified.*

bonne-bouche.   An English term since the 18th century, *bonne-bouche* means "a dainty or tasty mouthful or morsel." It comes from the French *bonne-bouche* (*bonne*, "good," plus *bouche*, "mouth"), which means "a pleasing taste in the mouth" in that language. French for a dainty morsel would be *morceau qui fait ou donne bonne bouche.*

bonnet.   Back in the 14th century, when the word is first recorded, a bonnet wasn't a woman's hat but a brimless man's hat, its name deriving from the Old French *bonnet.* ("Off goes his bonnet to an Oyster-wench," Shakespeare wrote in *Richard III.*) It was over a century before *bonnet* meant a headdress exclusively for women.

bonnet squash.   This common vegetable sponge (*Luffa cylindrica*) was so named in the American South because women made bonnets out of its fibrous matter. Wrote Joel Chandler Harris in *On the Plantation* (1892): "The girls made their hats of rye and wheat straw, and some very pretty bonnets were made of the fibrous substance that grew in the vegetable patch known as the bonnet squash." These inedible squashes are also called "dishcloth gourds" and "loofah." They are widely sold as sponges.

Bonnie Blue flag.   The Civil War secession flag of South Carolina, which had a blue field and a single star; also the name of a popular secessionist song. It was at a state convention at Jackson, Mississippi, when that state voted to secede from the Union, that the famous patriotic song of the South was inspired by an immense blue silk banner with a single star that someone carried through the crowd. According to one old story, Arkansas comedian Harry Macarthy witnessed the scene and began writing the song's lyrics, which he finished when the rest of the southern states seceded.

bonus.   Those who have received a bonus for an outstanding piece of work will understand the derivation of the word, for *bonus* derives from the Latin *bonum*, "a good thing." According to the best conjecture, the term originated as a pun on the classical Latin word early in the 17th century among London stock market traders.

boo.   "Boo is a corruption of *Boh*, the name of a terrible Gothic general whose gross brutalities struck terror among his enemies," swears one old source. "It was early used to conjure fear among stubborn children." I like this story as well as the next person, but there is no proof for it. Unfortunately, the *boo!* used to startle someone, first recorded in about 1430, is probably just a loud startling sound—Latin had a similar exclamation, *bo-are!* The *O.E.D.* claims that the *boo* used to express disapproval, as in *booing*, is a sound imitating the lowing of oxen. It is first recorded in about 1800. In *Listening to America* (1982), Stuart Berg Flexner notes that "*boo* may have been used much earlier in the theater and elsewhere, but before the 1880s [in baseball] it was considered just a roaring sound and not a word." Thus, *boo* dates back to the early 19th century, but *to boo* did not mean "to show disapproval" until it was first used that way in connection with baseball.

boob tube.   *See* COUCH POTATO.

booby; booby trap; booby hatch.   *Booby*, for "a dunce, a nincompoop," is recorded in English as far back as 1599, probably deriving from the Spanish *bobo*, "a fool," which in turn, may come from the Latin *balbus*, "stammering." It explains later expressions such as *booby prize* (ca. 1900), "a prize of little value given to the loser of a game," and *booby trap* (ca. 1850), "a trap set for fools." The last originally described practical jokes played by English schoolboys (balancing a pail of water atop a door that a *booby* would open, etc.), but in World War I *booby traps* became lethal explosive devices, killing wise men and poets as well as fools. *Booby hatch*, for an insane asylum, may have its beginnings in the "booby hatch," a police wagon used to carry criminals to jail. This term can be traced back to 1776 and certainly some of the criminals confined (for a short time, anyway) in booby hatches were deranged. Further, a "booby-hutch" was a police cell in the late 19th century—before some unknown American wit coined *booby hatch*. The term may have been suggested, however, simply from the idea of boobies confined and crammed under a hatch in some snake pit of an early insane asylum.

boodle.   The Dutch in the New World called a bundle of paper money or a sack of gold a *boedal*, which served as the term for any property, goods, or effects. The word's spelling gradually became *boodle* and it was used as underworld slang for counterfeit money and graft or bribery money, later becoming slang for a large bundle of money or money in general, with no implication of dishonesty.

boohoo. *Boohoo*, first recorded in 1525, originally expressed weeping or laughter. (Thackeray wrote that one of his characters "burst into a boohoo of laughter.") The imitative word is today applied only to crying. American humorist Thomas Haliburton made a verb of the word, *to boohoo*, to weep noisily, in 1837.

boojum tree. Perhaps the only tree to be named after a fictional character. This deciduous tree *(Idria columnaris)* of Baja, California, with a thick, tapering trunk and spiny branches, has since about 1960 been popularly named for the imaginary character the *boojum* in Lewis Carroll's nonsense poem *The Hunting of the Snark* (1867). In fact, Carroll (Charles Lutwidge Dodgson) insisted that his poem "sprang from one line of verse—one solitary line—'For the Snark *was* a Boojum, you see,'" which came to him while he was out walking one day. Asked what the poem meant, he replied, "I have but one answer, 'I don't know.'" *See* CHORTLE; SEQUOIA.

book; folio; bible; bibliography; volume; code. Smooth-skinned beech trees have always been the favorite of lovers carving their names or initials inside a heart. The outer bark of the beech and slabs of its thin, inner bark were also the first writing materials used by Anglo-Saxon scribes. Saxons called the beech the *boc* and also applied this name to their bound writings made from slabs of beech, the word becoming *book* after many centuries of spelling changes. Numerous terms for things related to writing come from the names of raw material. Folio, now a book of the largest size, is from the Latin word *folium*, "a tree leaf," which also gives us the word *foliage*. *Bible* and related words, such as *bibliography*, derive from the Greek *biblos*, "the inner bark of papyrus." *Volume* is from the Latin *volumen*, which meant "a roll of papyrus manuscript"; and *code*, for a system of laws, etc., is from the Latin *codex*, "the trunk of a tree," from which wooden tablets were made to write codes upon.

book burner. The term *book burner*, meaning "self-appointed censor" and worse, didn't arrive until 1933 when thousands of pro-Nazi students ended a torchlight parade at the University of Berlin by burning a pile of 20,000 books while Nazi propaganda minister Joseph Göbbels proclaimed: "The soul of the German people can express itself. These flames . . . illuminate the . . . end of an old era and light up the new." But the first mass *book burners* in American history were, oddly enough, the anti-mail-order small merchants at the turn of the century who burned mail-order catalogs to censor not the free expression of ideas, but free enterprise. Local merchants persuaded or arm-twisted people into tossing their catalogs into a bonfire in the public square every Saturday night. Prizes of up to 50 dollars were offered to those who brought in the greatest number of catalogs to be burned. This practice seemingly descended to its nadir in a small Montana town where a movie theater gave free admission or 10 cents to any child who turned over a catalog to town authorities for public burning. Yet the Montana orgy of destruction was repeated in other states, all in the name of insuring a continuance of "freedom of opportunity in America." The world's worst book burner was probably China's first emperor, Shi Huang Ti (259–210 B.C.). Shi, who

buried alive 460 scholars in the process, burned all the books in his kingdom, except for one copy of each deposited in the royal library, which he planned to destroy before his death, reasoning that if all records were destroyed history would begin with him. For generations after, the Chinese expressed their hatred of Shi by "befouling his grave."

book club. America's first book club was the Book-of-the-Month Club, founded in April 1926 by Harry Scherman with Robert Haas as president. Its distinguished panel of judges consisted of Dorothy Canfield, Heywood Broun, Henry Seidel Canby, William Allen White, and Christopher Morley, and they chose as the first book-of-the-month Sylvia Townsend Warner's *Lolly Willowes, or the Loving Huntsman* (Viking) to be distributed to 4,750 members. Within 20 years the club had revolutionized the publishing industry and 25 similar clubs were distributing 75 million books, over one-sixth of all American book sales. Customarily, members receive a free book or books upon joining a book club and a free book with every two or three books purchased. Book club editions are often, but not always, printed on cheaper paper. While the clubs have been criticized for inculcating a mediocrity of taste, they have offered many excellent books to their members and there is no doubt that they bring books to areas without bookstores. Ancestors of the book clubs were the circulating libraries of the 19th century, which supplied popular novels to readers for a small subscription price. These libraries often forced publishers to conform to their puritanical standards and made good writing all the more difficult. George Gissing's *New Grub Street* (1891) treats the subject in detail.

Booker Prize. The prestigious British literary prize for British or Commonwealth citizens is well known in the United States, but few know the term's origin, even believing "Booker" is synonymous with "book." The $50,000 award actually takes its name from the Booker McConnell firm, which has given it annually since 1968. Its American counterpart is the National Book Award or the PULITZER PRIZE.

book in breeches. The great English historian Thomas Babington Macaulay was a walking library who had filled his head with learning ever since he began reading at age three. He was a "book in breeches," the Reverend Sydney Smith (1771–1845) said, but Smith had some reservations about his loquacity. "Yes, I agree, he is certainly more agreeable since his return from India," Smith said of the historian. "His enemies might perhaps have said before (though I never did so) that he talked rather too much; but now he has occasional flashes of silence that make his conversation perfectly delightful." But then everyone had a bad word for Macaulay. "His conversation was a procession of one," said Florence Nightingale of him. "Macaulay is well for a while, but one wouldn't want to live under Niagara," said Carlyle. "I wish I was as cocksure of anything as Tom Macaulay is of everything," Viscount Melbourne said. Sydney Smith added that the historian "not only overflowed with learning, but stood in the slop."

bookworm. Bookworms are literally the larvae or adults of various insects, moths, and beetles that live in and feed upon the pages and bindings of books. No single species can properly be called the bookworm, but the little beetle *anolium*, silverfishes (order *Thysanura*) and book lice (order *Psocoptera*) are widely known by the name. The human of the bookworm species also lives in and feeds upon the pages of books, but doesn't usually destroy them. Human bookworms have been scorned since before Ben Jonson wrote of a "whoreson book-worm." Authors especially are fools to be contemptuous of bookworms, but from Elizabethan times to the present few scriveners have had anything good to say about them. As for insect bookworms, a 19th-century journal called *The Bookworm* had this to say about them: "Bookworms are now almost exclusively known in the secondary and derivative meaning of the word as porers over dry books; but there was a time when the real worms were as ubiquitous as our cockroaches. They would start at the first or last page and tunnel circular holes through the volume, and were cursed by librarians as *bestia audax* and *pestes chartarium*. There were several kings of these little plagues. One was a sort of death-watch, with dark-brown hard skin; another had a white body with little brown spots on its head. Those that had legs were the larvae of moths, and those without legs were grubs that turned into beetles. They were dignified, like other disagreeable things, with fine Latin names, which we spare our readers. All of them had strong jaws and very healthy appetites; but we are happy to find that their digestive powers, vigorous as they were, quail before the materials of our modern books. China clay, plaster of Paris, and other unwholesome ailments have conquered the *pestes chartarium*. They sigh and shrivel up. Peace to the memory, for it is now hardly more than a memory, of the *bestia audax*."

boomer.   Someone who was born during the prolific post–World War II baby boom, a sharp increase in the birth rate that lasted from about 1947 through 1961. *Boomer* is of course short for *baby boomer*, which is first found in print in a 1974 *Time* magazine article. In 1941 *Life* magazine used the term *baby boom*, but it did not refer to the post–World War II boom. In Australia a boomer is a large, full-grown kangaroo. *See* BABYBOOM; GENERATION X.

boomerang.   *Boomerang* is another loan word from Australia's aboriginals (like *kangaroo*, *dingo*, *koala*, and *wombat*). Captain Cook noticed the native weapon on his voyages to Australia but did not record its name, which is first mentioned in 1798 in an account of aboriginal weapons.

boondocks.   *Bundok* is the word for "mountain" in Tagalog, the Indonesian language of the Philippines. But during the U.S. occupation there, American soldiers extended its meaning to include any rough back country with wild terrain difficult for troops to penetrate, corrupting the word to *boondocks* in the process. After World War II, Marines brought *boondocks* home with them and it became the name for difficult terrain on the fringes of training camps, where recruits were often taken on long bivouacs. These remote areas naturally suggested the "sticks," rural areas where there is similarly little to do but work and be bored, and *boondocks* began to be applied to them as well. The word is most frequently heard in the expression *out in the boondocks*, way out in the sticks.

boondoggles.   One dictionary defines boondoggles as: "Useless, wasteful tasks, 'make-work' projects that are often performed by recipients of a government dole." The word was employed in 1929 by Scoutmaster Robert Link of Rochester, New York, who applied it to the braided leather lanyards made and worn around the neck as a decoration by Boy Scouts. Under the New Deal during the Great Depression, the term was transferred to the relief work for the unemployed that some people, not out of work themselves, thought was as useless as making lanyards, and soon *boondoggling* meant to do any work of no practical value merely to keep or look busy. Before Scoutmaster Link applied *boondoggle* to lanyards it had been a word for a belt, knife sheath, or other product of simple manual skill, and in Scottish dialect it means a marble that you get as a gift, without winning it. The yarn about *boondoggle* being suggested by Daniel Boone idly whittling sticks to throw to his dog does convey the sense of the word, but is just another spurious tale.

booster.   Sinclair Lewis's Babbitt was a booster who wore a Booster Club button in his lapel. But Lewis didn't invent the term in his novel. This term for an enthusiastic, often puerile supporter or promoter of a person, team, cause, etc., was born in the American Southwest in about 1890, quickly spreading throughout the country, and has its roots in the verb to boost.

boot camp.   U.S. sailors serving during the Spanish-American War wore leggings called *boots*, which came to mean "a navy (or marine) recruit." These recruits trained in what were called boot camps.

Boot Hill.   Now a joking name for any cemetery, the term was first applied to any small cemetery where men who died in gunfights, with their boots on, were buried. The first such is said to have been in Deadwood, South Dakota; the Mount Moriah cemetery there is now a big tourist attraction.

bootlegger.   Bootleggers got the name because they smuggled illegal whiskey in the legs of their tall boots. The word originated in about 1850, at least 70 years before Prohibition. Today a *bootleg* is a football ploy in which the quarterback fakes a handoff and hides the ball on his hip, running with it himself.

boots and saddles!   Most Americans are familiar with the old western song "Give Me My Boots and My Saddle," but this familiar cavalry call has nothing to do with boots and saddles, as one might suspect. It derives from the old French cavalry command *Boute selle!* ("Put saddle!"), which the British corrupted to *boot and saddle* and which American cavalrymen further corrupted to *boots and saddles!*

booty.   (Frequently pronounced boody). Originally meaning a woman's sexual organs and sexual intercourse, this term has come to mean "buttocks." It is widely used in this sense today, even in the names of tanning parlors, such as "Tan Your Booty," not to mention popular songs.

B.O. Plenty; Bathless Groggins.   These are the names of comic strip characters who rarely washed, if ever, and whose names became synonymous for anyone who pays no attention to bodily cleanliness. B.O. Plenty, his prenom influenced by B.O. above, was a character in cartoonist Chester Gould's Dick Tracy comic strip in the 1940s; he eventually married Gravel

Gerty, who looked as bad as he did. *Bathless Groggins*, always scratching himself, appeared in his own, earlier strip.

booze. Mr. E. G. or E. S. Booze of either Philadelphia or Kentucky, circa 1840, was a distiller who sold his *booze* under his own name, the bottles often made in the shape of log cabins. But *booze* probably has its roots in the Middle English verb *bousen*, "to drink deeply," which comes from an earlier German word. However, the English use *booze* only for beer and ale and there is no doubt that the labels on our Mr. Booze's bottles influenced the American use of the word for hard liquor and strengthened its general use. Today booze most often signifies cheap, even rotgut whiskey.

bora. Bulgarian has contributed only a few words to English. One may be *bora*, for the fierce north wind of the Black Sea that can blow up to 70 miles an hour an create 12-foot waves. *Bora* may, however, derive from the Latin *boreas*, north wind.

borax. The real source for the term *borax*, for "cheap furniture, or any cheap and inferior merchandise," is probably not a Yiddish expression used by Jewish immigrants on New York's Lower East Side in the late 19th century, as many sources contend, but the premiums for cheap furniture offered by early manufacturers of borax soap.

Bordeaux. The largest of France's great wine areas, the province of Gironde, surrounds the port city of Bordeaux, after which the elegant red and white wines made there are named.

bored. British actor George Sanders committed suicide, leaving behind a note saying that he had been bored by it all. Another worldly Englishman, the poet Lord Byron, used the word *bored* for "wearied, suffering from ennui," in *Don Juan* (1823), in which he wrote:

> Society is now one polished horde
> Formed of two mighty tribes, the bores and the bored.

Bored is first recorded in 1768, apparently being a figurative use of *to bore*, "to pierce, make a hole through," although the French *bourrer*, "to stuff or pad," has also been suggested.

bore for the hollow horn. An expression popular in days past. It was explained in *Dialect Notes*, v. 5, 1919. "A hole is bored in the horn of a cow (having a hollow horn) with a gimlet. This custom gave rise to the epithet applied to people who behaved foolishly (suggesting a hollow head): 'He ought to be bored for the hollow horn.'"

Borgia; nepotism. Whether any Borgia was ever a poisoner is a matter of dispute, but Lucrezia and Cesare Borgia, children of Pope Alexander VI (1431–1503), were reputed to indulge in such activities. Tradition has it that the Borgias employed some secret deadly poison to eliminate their enemies. Historians have never been able to substantiate this, but a GLASS OF WINE WITH THE BORGIAS has long been proverbial for a great but risky honor, and *Borgia* is still a synonym for a poisoner. There is no doubt that the Borgias were murderers, the family generally a pretty unsavory lot. They are also responsible for the word *nepotism*, this directly from the Latin *nepos*, "a descendant, especially a nephew," coined when Pope Alexander VI filled important church offices with his relations. Among the many family appointments Rodrigo Borgia made were the installing of his son Cesare as an archbishop when the boy was only 16, and the bestowing of a cardinal's hat on his young nephew, Giovanni.

bork. Hardly a year after conservative judge Robert H. Bork's nomination to the Supreme Court was defeated in 1989 the verb *to bork*, to attack someone's nomination in an extreme media campaign, was being used to describe such actions against other nominees and candidates, conservative or liberal. Only time can tell if the word will fade from common usage and become a historical relic.

born-again Christian. This term for a Christian who has found a renewed commitment to Christ has long been known to evangelists, but came into prominence when U.S. presidential candidate Jimmy Carter described himself as a "born-again Christian." The phrase's source is John 3:3 and 3:7: "Jesus answered and said . . . Except a man be born again, he cannot see the kingdom of God . . . Marvel not that I said unto thee, ye must be born again."

born in the middle of the week and looking both ways for Sunday. A colorful expression dating back to the 19th century that describes someone extremely cross-eyed.

born on the wrong side of the blanket. *See* BASTARD.

born on the wrong side of the tracks. *See* WRONG SIDE OF THE TRACKS.

born to the purple. From earliest times purple has been the color of kings, especially Tyrian purple, a color yielded by a species of Murex shellfish. But the expression *born to the purple*, or "born of royal parentage," doesn't have its origins in the purple robes of royalty. It really derives from an ancient Byzantine custom that dictated that the empress give birth to her royal child in a lavishly appointed special chamber called the *Porphyra*, whose walls were lined with royal purple porphyry. The Greeks had a word for such a royal birth, *porphyrogenitus* (from *porphyra*, "purple," and *gennetos*, "born"), which translates directly as "born in the purple." Today the expression is *born to the purple*, and it is used to describe anyone of exalted birth, not necessarily royalty, or anyone born rich.

born with the gift of laughter and a sense that the world was mad. These words became famous not because they are from Shakespeare, Milton, or any of the great classical writers of antiquity, but because they were inscribed as a hoax over a door in the Hall of Graduate Studies at Yale University. The line is from novelist Rafael Sabatini's rousing *Scaramouche*, beloved to generations of romantics, and the full quote, referring to the hero, is "Born with the gift of laughter and the sense that the world was mad, and that was his only patrimony." The words apparently were written on Yale's hallowed walls as the result of a hoax. At least the building's architect, John Donald Tuttle, confessed in a letter to *The New Yorker* (December 8, 1934) that collegiate Gothic repelled him. It is, he wrote, "a type of architecture that had been designed expressly . . . to enable yeomen to pour molten lead through slots on their enemies below. As a propitiatory gift to my gods . . . and to make them forget by appealing to their senses of humor, I carved the inscription over the door." Yale authorities apparently didn't enjoy the joke. After employing medievalists, classical scholars, and Egyptologists to find the source of the quotation, only to learn it was from a mere adventure novelist, they planted the ivy that hides the words today.

born with two strikes against him.   It is uncertain when this expression was coined, but it clearly has its roots in baseball as an analogy to a batter only one strike away from striking out and thus failing completely. The words are usually said of someone born with great disadvantages, or of someone with incredibly bad luck.

borracho.   *Borracho* is a word borrowed from Spanish meaning "drunk" or "a drunk person." It has been commonly used in English for 20 years, though no major dictionaries admit it to their pages.

borrow.   *Borrow* was originally a noun deriving from the Anglo-Saxon *borg* and meaning "a pledge of security." This use of the word became obsolete in England by Spenser's time, but early on *borrow* became a verb meaning "to give security for, to take on pledge." Security is no longer essential in a borrowing transaction, but the idea that what is loaned is the property of the lender and must be returned is still preserved.

bosey; googly.   *Bosey* is a cricketing term familiar to Australians but not much used anymore in England, where it originated. The term honors the English bowler, B. J. T. Bosanquet, who popularized the technique known elsewhere as the *googly* when he toured Australia in 1903–04. The googly is, according to the *Oxford English Dictionary*, "an off-break ball bowled with leg-break action." There is no popularly known technique in American baseball, basketball, or football named after its player-inventor, so B. J. T. Bosanquet is somewhat unique in the world of sports.

bosh.   Meaning "stuff and nonsense," *bosh* came into English from the Turkish word *bosh* for "nothing, empty, worthless." The novelist James Morier introduced the word in a book about Turkish life published in 1834.

bos'n; boatswain.   *Bos'n* is a corruption of *boatswain*, the boy ("swain") who took care of the ship's dinghy and summoned its crew. The boatswain didn't get his whistle until sometime in the 15th century and wasn't called a *bos'n* for 200 years more.

bosom bread.   A historical term for the large flat loaves of bread that black hands working the Mississippi steamboats in the 19th century often carried inside their shirt fronts for snacks throughout the day. They needed such fuel, as these longshoremen expended more energy than almost any other workers at the time.

boss.   Early Americans, independent and democratic, never liked the word "master" with all its aristocratic associations. Late in the 18th century they adopted the Dutch word *baas* meaning the same thing, and were soon spelling it *boss*. By as early as 1838 *boss* had achieved common usage and writers as prominent as James Fenimore Cooper were condemning it as a barbaric vulgarization of the language. Some people think that *boss* as an adjective meaning the best, the greatest, is recent teenage slang, but the word has been used in the same sense since the mid-19th century. The usage of *baas* (boss) as a form of address from a black to a white man is dead in Namibia, where it has been banned by law, and it is fast dying in South Africa.

Boston.   A historical term once used by Indians of the Northwest for any white American, as opposed to the foreign English, French, and so forth. These Bostons were also called Bostonians by the Indians and were so named because so many settlers came from New England or had connections with that great hub of commerce.

Boston Brahmin.   A Brahmin is a worshipper of the Hindu god Brahma, the creator of the universe. The Brahmin's status as a member of the highest caste in Hinduism inspired the Americanism *Boston Brahmin* for an aristocratic, upper class, conservative Bostonian; the term was first recorded in January 1861 by Oliver Wendell Holmes in his novel *Elsie Venner* as "the Brahmin caste of New England." Holmes found the Boston Brahmins a "harmless, inoffensive, untitled aristocracy . . . which has grown to be a caste by the repetition of the same influences generation after generation" so that it has acquired a distinct character and organization. In November 1947 the *Atlantic Monthly* noted: "The Brahmins do not think of themselves as Brahmins: the word is antique as the wooden cod hanging in the State House." Antique or not the term is still widely used, usually in a humorous way. *Brahmin caste* is a synonym.

Boston Braves.   A National League baseball team that was named after the New York City Tammany Hall political machine. Tammany politicians had invested in the club in 1912 and since members of the political club were called "braves," in honor of the Indian chief for whom Tammany was named, the name was applied to players on the baseball team. The Braves moved from Boston to Milwaukee in 1953 and later moved on to Atlanta. *See* DODGERS.

Boston fern.   *See* BRAMLEY'S SEEDLING.

Boston Pops.   Members of the Boston Symphony orchestra, founded in 1881 and one of America's oldest symphony orchestras, make up the Boston Pops, which plays more *popular* light music rather than classical music. They usually perform at summer concerts.

Boston Tea Party.   The first act of violence in the disputes leading to the Revolutionary War, occurring on December 16, 1773 when members of the Sons of Liberty, incensed by the tax on tea, boarded British ships and dumped 342 chests of tea into Boston Harbor.

Boswell; boswellize.   "I have a notion," Somerset Maugham once observed, "that it is pleasanter to read Boswell's record of the conversations than it ever was to listen to Dr. Johnson." *Boswell*, after the ultimate in biographers, honors James Boswell (1740–95), whose *The Life of Samuel Johnson* (1791) is the prototype of biographies. Boswell, born in Scotland, met Dr. Johnson only after numerous rebuffs but became both friend and admirer of the great English man of letters. Over a relatively short period, he recorded in detail Johnson's words and activities. "That Boswell was a vain, intemperate man of dubious morals is of no matter to history," writes one biographer. "He shines in the reflected glory of his great portrait." To *boswellize* means to write biography in the same detailed, intimate and faithful manner as "Bozzy" did.

botanomancy. Botanomancy is divination by leaves. The most popular method was to write sentences on leaves as possible answers to a question. The leaves were then left outside exposed to the wind, and those that weren't blown away were supposed to compose the answer. The practice and word date back to at least the early 17th century. *Botanomancy's* earliest renowned practitioner was the Cumaean Sibyl.

Botany Bay. Captain James Cook named Botany Bay after the many new botanical specimens he found there on his voyage to Australia in 1770. Later, the inlet's name came to be wrongly applied to a convict settlement at Sydney, and even to the whole of Australia.

both ends against the middle. *See* PLAY BOTH ENDS AGAINST THE MIDDLE.

bottom dollar. *See* BET ONE'S BOTTOM DOLLAR.

Bottomley's Own. Surely the only army named for a writer. In 1916 author Horace Bottomley wrote an article for *John Bull* revealing that too many British armies were "rotting in England" instead of fighting the Great War. The 12th London regiment had been encamped at home for a long time and was quickly dispatched to the front, soon becoming known as *Bottomley's Own*.

botulism. Why, you ask, does the Latin word for sausage, *botulus*, give us the English word *botulism*, first recorded in 1878, for "a form of food poisoning"? The answer is that the earliest cases of such food poisoning through improperly stored food involved canned sausages.

bougainvillaea. The largest island in the Solomon group, two Pacific straits, and a brilliantly flowering South American vine are all named after the French navigator and adventurer Louis-Antoine de Bougainville (1729–1811). Bougainville commanded a French expedition around the world in 1766–69, "discovering" the Solomon Islands and Tahiti. Naturalists in his party named the woody climbing vine family, of which there are about a dozen known species, *Bougainvillaea* in his honor. Bougainville's descriptions of the natives he encountered on his voyages helped popularize Rousseau's theories on the morality of man in his natural state, especially as concerns sexual freedom. He fought for America during the Revolution, and in his later years Napoleon I made him a senator, count of the empire, and member of the Legion of Honor. The plant named after him is often cultivated in greenhouses, can be raised outdoors in the southern parts of the United States, and is regarded as the handsomest of tropical vines.

boughten goods. Once common as a participal adjective in the U.S., *boughten* is rarely heard any more, though it is listed in the *O.E.D.* as poetic dialect and an Americanism. *Boughten goods* is sometimes used today as a pseudo-rustic term meaning "manufactured or store bought things that are valued above familiar, homemade ones."

bought the farm. As late as the Vietnam War, soldiers killed in action were said to have *bought the farm*. The expression was inspired by the draftees's dream to go home—in many cases to a peaceful farm, or perhaps to buy a farm—in any case, to settle down somewhere far away from the army and war. "Well, he finally did buy the farm," a friend could say on hearing of the death of such a man, and the expression was used so often that *bought the farm* became an ironic synonym for death. The phrase dates to World War II or earlier. Here's another guess at its origin: When a farmer takes a bank mortgage there is a life insurance claim that is built into the payment, so that when the farmer dies the farm becomes the property of his estate; hence, he has finally bought the farm.

bouillabaisse. A French invention made of fish and shellfish, *bouillabaisse* derives from Provençal words meaning "boil it, then lower the heat." It has a worldwide reputation. In Greece it is called *psaro*, in Italy it is *zuppa di pesce*, and in Belgium it's *Ghentsche waterzoaie*. In his *Gastronomy of France* chef Raymond Oliver tells the legend of the spurned lover who invented *rouille*, the hot pimento sauce that makes *bouillabaisse* so passionate a potage. This poor sailor sat on the Martigues quay, sadly watching his perfidious beloved sail off with a rich Greek shipowner (they've always been around) when she added humiliation to heartbreak by tossing him the liver of a *racasse*, or scorpion fish, that the yacht's cook had been cleaning on deck. "There, that's for you!" she cried scornfully. But the sailor treasured even the scraps from her hands, and crushing the liver with garlic and oil, he cooked it with pimento and— marvelous to relate—from the moment he first tasted it he found *all* women lovely. "As *rouille* increases *bouillabaisse's* erotic proportion a hundredfold," Oliver concludes, "the perfidious girl was forgotten on the spot. Once more, a fairy tale with a happy ending."

Boulangism; boulangerite. General Georges-Ernest-Jean-Marie Boulanger (1837–91) won the admiration of all France for his exploits during the Franco-Prussian War. That he was a handsome man who looked impressive astride a horse in parades didn't hurt his image, either. In 1886 Boulanger was made minister of war and insisted that he was the man to retrieve the lost glories of France with doctrines of militarism and reprisal against Germany. For a short time a wave of political frenzy called *boulangisme* swept over France, but the movement came to nothing, the general in reality no Napoleon and his backers largely reactionary elements. Boulanger eventually went into exile, ending his life in a suburb of Brussels as a suicide.

boulevard. Stroll down a boulevard and you are literally strolling down a military rampart or bulwark. The first boulevard was a wide promenade made from the old defensive walls encircling Paris. This was called *le boulevard* after the abandoned ramparts it followed, and was soon applied to any similar broad street.

bouncer; checker-out.   The American *bouncer*, for "a person who acts as a guard in a disco, nightclub, brothel, or bar, someone who bounces out unruly people," dates back to Civil War days. *Checker-out* is the British term for the same, but it seems to have been coined later, in about 1880.

bourbon.   *Bourbon whiskey* takes its name from Bourbon County, Kentucky, named for France's Bourbon kings, and home of the first still that produced it. The word *Bourbon* for a political reactionary also derives from France's Bourbon kings, a dynasty that reigned for over 200 years beginning in 1589, and of whom it was said that they "forgot nothing and learned nothing." *The Dictionary of Americanisms* gives its first use for a political diehard as 1876.

Bourbon Street.   Another storied American street, this one named for the French Bourbon kings (see BOURBON above). In *Love and Money* (1954), Erskine Caldwell called the noted New Orleans street "that Southern gentleman's skid row."

the Bourse.   The world's first stock exchange, in Belgium, originated in the 14th century. Few people are aware that it takes its name from the Van der Buerse family in Bruges, at whose house early traders congregated.

boutique.   Though it has been used for over 700 years in France for a small retail shop, *boutique* only became widely known in the 1950s in the sense of a small shop selling very fashionable merchandise. It is so used now all over the world.

bouts rhymes.   *See* YESTERYEAR.

Bovarian.   *See* MADAME BOVARY.

Bovril; vril.   The well-known trade name *Bovril* for a concentrated essence of beef has an unusual ancestry. *Bovril* is composed of the Latin *bovis*, ox, and *vril*, which is an invented literary word. The British novelist Edward George Bulwer-Lytton (1803–73) coined the word *vril* in his novel *The Coming Race* (1871), describing it as an "electric fluid called Vril, which was capable of being raised and disciplined into the mightiest agency of all forms of matter." This seemed perfect for the manufacturer of the beef essence in 1887, and he quickly adopted it as the last half of his product's name. It has been suggested, too, that *vril* has a linguistic connection with *virility*—all the better as far as the company was concerned.

Bowditch.   A name for the navigation handbook *American Practical Navigator*, prepared by American navigator, astronomer, and mathematician Nathaniel Bowditch (1773–1838) in 1802 and published in a series of editions ever since. Nathaniel Bowditch left school in Salem, Massachussetts, at age 10 and went to sea, where he studied navigation, correcting some 8,000 errors in the leading guide of his time. So respected was Bowditch and his work on navigation that ships of all nations flew their flags at half-mast when he died.

bowdlerize.   His inability to stand the sight of human blood and suffering forced Dr. Thomas Bowdler to abandon his medical practice in London, but this weakness apparently did not apply where vendors of words were concerned. Bowdler so thoroughly purged both Shakespeare and Gibbon that they would have screamed in pain from the bloodletting had they been alive—to *bowdlerize* became a synonym for "to radically expurgate or prudishly censor." Thomas Bowdler, the most renowned of self-appointed literary censors, was born at Ashley, near Bath, England on July 11, 1754. After he retired from medicine, a considerable inheritance enabled him to travel about Europe, where he wrote accounts of the Grand Tour that seem to have offended or pleased no one. Though he came from a religious family, Bowdler never earned the "Reverend Doctor" title often applied to him, and his early years are conspicuous for the lack of any real accomplishments, unless one counts membership in organizations like the Society for the Suppression of Vice. Only when he was middle-aged did he retire to the Isle of Wight and begin to sharpen his rusty scalpel on the Bard of Avon's bones. His *Family Shakespeare* was finally published in 1818. In justifying this 10-volume edition, Bowdler explained on the title page that "nothing is added to the text; but those expressions are omitted which cannot with propriety be read aloud in a family," adding later that he had also expunged "Whatever is unfit to be read by a gentleman in a company of ladies." He would probably have turned his scalpel to other great authors if death had not excised him in 1825. About 10 years later Bowdler's name was first used as a verb, the official definition then being "to expurgate by omitting or modifying words or passages considered indelicate or offensive." Today the word means "prudish, ridiculous censorship."

bowels of compassion.   Though not a common expression anymore, these words are frequently encountered in literature. The phrase itself is given in the King James Bible (I John 3: 17), and Shakespeare, Congreve, and other great writers all made use of the ancient idea that the bowels are the seat of misery or compassion in the body—just as the liver was supposed to be the location of courage; the heart of affection and learning *(learn by heart);* the head of understanding; and the spleen of passion. The blunt word *bowel* comes from the Latin *botellus*, little sausage or pudding, a diminutive of the Latin word for sausage, *botulus*. Aside from the expression the *bowels of the earth*, it is heard today mainly in medieval references or in the entreaties of parents toilet-training children. Certainly it isn't associated with compassion anymore, so once-current expressions such as *the bowels of compassion, the bowels of pity, the bowels of Christ*, and *child of my bowels* have all but died.

bowie knife; Arkansas toothpick.   One writer defines the *bowie* (pronounced "boo-ie") *knife* as "the principal instrument of nonsurgical phlebotomy in the American Southwest." Sad to say, this lethal instrument was not invented by the legendary Colonel James Bowie (1796–1836), friend of Davy Crockett and hero at the Alamo. According to testimony by a daughter of Rezin Pleasant Bowie, the colonel's older brother, it was her father who invented the knife in about 1827, though Jim Bowie did make it famous in a duel that year at Natchez, Mississippi, in which six men were killed and 15 wounded. The common long-bladed hunting knife was originally made at Rezin Bowie's direction by a Louisiana blacksmith, who ground a large file to razor sharpness and attached a guard between the blade and handle to protect the user's hand. After he killed one man with it in the Natchez duel, Colonel Bowie is said to have sent his knife to a Philadelphia blacksmith, who marketed copies of it under his name. Its double-edged blade was 10 to 15 inches long, and curved to a point. Once called an Arkansas toothpick, it was even carried by some congressmen.

bowing.   *Bowing*, to show someone respect, derives from an Old English word meaning the same, and the custom is recorded as far back as *Beowulf*. While Westerners commonly bend the neck and uncover the head when bowing, people in several other cultures uncover the feet to show their respect. As Brewer explains, this is because "with us the chief act of investiture is crowning or placing a cap on the head; but in the East it is putting on the slippers."

bowler; billycock.   The same hat by different names, each probably named for a different person. Its shape can be traced back to the helmet worn by the ancient Greeks, but the billycock, a round, soft felt hat with a wide brim, most likely first graced the head of William Coke, a rich British landowner, in 1850. It is said to have been designed at "Billy" Coke's request by a hatter named Beaulieu because Mr. Coke's tall riding hat was frequently parted from his head by tree branches when he rode to the hounds. There is little doubt about the origin of *billycock* then, and *bowler* may derive from the name of the hatter, M. Beaulieu. The only trouble is that some authorities credit a London hatter named William Bowler, quoting a newspaper item tracing his "invention" to 1868. Still others say *bowler* is simply named for the hat's "bowl shape" or from the fact that it is round, stiff-brimmed, and can be bowled along.

bowl game; bowl.   The first football bowl game ever recorded was the 1916 Pasadena Bowl (which was a year later renamed the Rose Bowl). *Bowl*, however, had been a synonym for a football stadium since 1914, when the Yale University stadium was first called the Yale Bowl.

bowling.   Pins and balls for a sport similar to bowling were found some years ago in an Egyptian tomb dating to 5200 B.C. Bowling was long banned in England, along with football and other games, because kegling diverted men from practicing sports more valuable to a country often at war, such as archery and swordsmanship. Several English monarchs did like to bowl, though; in fact, Henry VIII built his own alley at Whitehall. The Dutch brought bowling to America, and Bowling Green in New York's financial district is so named because the sport was taught there.

bowl over.   Apparently this term, meaning to surprise greatly, is not from bowling, nor is it an Americanism. Logan Pearsall Smith's *Words and Idioms* (1925) claims it derives from a cricket term describing the bowler throwing the ball to the batsman. First used in England, the expression crossed the Atlantic by the end of the 19th century.

box.   *See* TO BE IN A BOX.

box and cox.   This old expression came to mind after I read a report that poor immigrants in Central Islip, New York, are renting beds in private residences for $300 a month, these "hot beds" (so called because the sheets are always warm) rented for night and day shifts of 12 hours. This practice of alternate privileges has been called box and cox since 1847, when English playwright John Maddison Morton's one-act farce of the same name made the expression popular. In the play Mrs. Bouncer, a landlady, rents the same room to Box, who works nights, and Cox, who works days. When one of them arrives home out of turn, the fun begins. The author's father, Thomas Morton, also contributed a word to the language. *See* MRS. GRUNDY.

Boxer Rebellion.   The Chinese anti-foreigner movement early in the 20th century originated with a Shantung secret society known as the I-Ho-Chuan, which the British thought meant "righteous, uniting fists" (it actually meant "righteous harmony band"). So the British, or "foreign devils," as they were called, punned upon members of what they thought were the "fists" and called them Boxers, dubbing their uprising the Boxer Rebellion.

boxes.   Opera houses were the first theaters to feature the partially enclosed rooms that came to be called boxes. While opera houses still have boxes encircling the auditorium, most other theaters have abandoned them because of their poor view of the stage. Once, however, they were the only desirable choice for those who came to the theater to be seen as much as to see. Some boxes held as many as 20 people, and they were often equipped with blinds that could be pulled down to give occupants complete privacy when, for one reason or another, they didn't care to watch the play. As early as Shakespearean times rich patrons were allowed to buy seats onstage in English theaters, usually to the dismay of the actors, who objected to fops proudly displaying their new clothes and chattering endlessly, paying no attention to the play.

boxing.   Scholars have declared the name of this sport to be "of uncertain origin," suggesting that it may derive from Middle English *box*, a blow, or *boxen*, beat. Others say that *boxing* comes from the boxlike shape of a prizefighting ring. The sport seems always to have had its grudge matches and prefight staredowns. Postfight imbroglios weren't unknown in the ancient Olympic games. In one case, a boxer arrived too late to fight, put on his gloves, ran after the winner, and began punching him, crowned as he was with his wreath of wild olive. The champion finally hid among the judges. *See* BANTAMWEIGHT; BEAT TO THE PUNCH; BELCHER; BELOW THE BELT; BENDEGO; BRAINS KNOCKED OUT; BRODERICK; BROWN BOMBER; BUCKHORSE; CAULIFLOWER EAR; CESTUS; DO A BRODIE; DOWN AND OUT; HANG IN THERE; HAPPY AS LARRY; HEAVYWEIGHT; INFIGHTING; KILLER INSTINCT; KNOCK DOWN, DRAG OUT FIGHT; JACK DEMPSEY; JACK JOHNSON; JOE LOUIS; LEAD WITH YOUR CHIN; MUTT AND JEFF; NOBLE SCIENCE; ON THE ROPES; PALOOKA; PLUG UGLY; PUT ON THE GLOVES; PUNCH DRUNK; PUNCHING BAG; PUT UP YOUR DUKES; REAL MCCOY; ROLL WITH THE PUNCHES; THROW IN THE TOWEL; SAVED BY THE BELL; SEEING STARS; STRAIGHT FROM THE SHOULDER; WE WUZ ROBBED; ZIGGED WHEN I SHOULD HAVE ZAGGED.

box office.   Most likely *box office* derives from the theater office that sold box seats to customers. But an old story insists that the expression originated in Elizabethan times, when theater admission was collected by passing a box attached to a long stick among the audience.

box score.   From its original baseball use to describe a condensed statistical record of a game that includes the performances of both teams and all the players, *box score* has taken on the extended meaning of a record of results in any area, as in the box score of an elected political figure or corporate administrator. Similar summaries of baseball games were printed in newspapers as early as 1853, but the term *box score* isn't recorded until the turn of the century, so named because these summaries were usually printed in boxed-off sections on the sports pages of a newspaper.

box the compass.   Mariners who boxed the compass literally named all 32 points of the compass, from north through east and back to north. One describes a complete turn in doing so, however, which is why, in the early 19th century, the expression *to box the compass* began to be used figuratively for a complete or full turn.

boy.   The *O.E.D.* traces *boy*, which came into the language in the late Middle English period, to the Old French *abuie*, "fettered or chained," which suggests that the word originally meant a slave. Other sources, however, suggest the Frisian *boi*, "young gentleman," the German man's proper name *Boia*, and the Old Norse, *bofi*, "rascal," among other choices. Nobody really knows. Male American Indians, black slaves, and white indentured servants who were little more than slaves, were all called boy in America before the Civil War, and black men were commonly called the same for more than a century after. The term is insulting, however, not because *boy* here means a male child. This *boy* is a word dating back to the 13th century that originally meant a low menial servant, deriving from the Latin *boiae*, "fetters."

boycott.   Captain Charles Cunningham Boycott (1823–97) lived to see his name immortalized as a synonym for a refusal to deal with a person or business firm, the word current not only in English but in French, German, Dutch, Russian, and a number of Asiatic languages as well. Boycott, a stubborn British soldier turned farmer, had been hired to manage the Earl of Erne's estates at Lough Mask House in Connaught, County Mayo, Ireland. Absentee landlords like the earl owned most of the land in Ireland at the time and were evicting poverty-stricken tenant farmers who could not pay their rents. The fiery Irish leader Charles Stewart Parnell had already formed his National Land League, agitating for land reform by these "English usurpers." In September 1880, Parnell addressed tenants near Connaught, advocating that anyone working a farm from which a man had been evicted, or any landlord refusing to accept his new, reduced rent scales, should be ostracized "by isolating him . . . as if he were a leper of old . . . by leaving him strictly alone. . . ." When Captain Boycott harshly refused to accept more reasonable lower rents and tried to evict one farmer, Boycott's tenants forced his workers to leave him; organized marauders destroyed his property; his fences were torn down and cattle driven into his fields; he was refused service in all local stores; his mail went undelivered; he was jeered in the streets and hanged in effigy; and his life was repeatedly threatened. So successful had been the famous "ex-communication" against him that it was commonly called a boycott in the papers within two months.

the boys.   *The boys,* for "political hangers-on," has a long history in America, dating back to at least 1832. It is often spelled *b'hoy,* the Irish pronunciation. *See* BOY.

boysenberry.   Americans have always been pie makers without peer, thanks to sugar resources close by, an abundance of native fruit, and a willingness to experiment. The blackberry, long regarded as a nuisance and called a bramble or brambleberry in England, is a case in point. Many varieties of blackberries have been developed here, long before anyone paid attention to the family *Rubus* in Europe. Among them is the boysenberry, a prolific, trailing variety that is a cross between the BLACKBERRY, RASPBERRY, and LOGANBERRY, another eponymous berry. The boysenberry, a dark wine-red fruit that tastes something like a raspberry, was developed by California botanist Rudolf Boysen in the early 1900s. Single plants commonly produce two quarts of the large ¾-inch round, 1½-inch-long fruit.

boys of the bulldog breed.   Pugnacious Englishmen, often sailors, are called boys of the bulldog breed. The words come from the popular 19th-century song "Sons of the Sea, All British Born."

bozo.   A word of southwestern origin with Spanish antecedents that means fellow or man but has come to have a derogatory connotation. It possibly derives from the Spanish *mozo* (young man). As one champion of this theory explained: "With the word '*bo* (for hobo) in mind, and a cold in the head, what more simple than to change *mozo* (pronounced with the Mexican *s,* not the Spanish *th*) into *bozo?*"

bozzonga.   I haven't found this word meaning "ass" or "behind" in any dictionary, slang or otherwise, but it was definitely used by tennis star Billie Jean King in September 1973. "I hate sitting around on my bozzonga," she told a television interviewer at the time, referring to her need to play. Maybe Billie Jean invented the word.

bra.   The brassiere, which Roman matrons wore in the form of leather straps beneath the breasts and which euphemizers have called "breast shields" and "cup forms," probably takes its name from the French *bras,* "arm." The name was first coined in about 1914. However, in a punning hoax, one source claims that its inventor in modern times was Otto Titzling, who designed a bra for a hefty opera singer named Swanhilda Olafsen in 1912. Titzling failed to patent his invention, but Mary Phelps Jacobs (a descendant of Robert Fulton of steamboat fame), who had independently invented a similar device, did so, filing for a patent application for a brassiere in February 1914. The same source credits dress designer Phillippe de Brassière, who glamorized the "chest halters" and sold them under his name beginning circa 1929, popularizing *brassiere* and hence *bra.*

bracero.   Any Mexican laborer in the U.S. Formerly meaning a Mexican migrant picker legally admitted to the U.S., the word derives from the Spanish *bracero,* "a person with strong arms."

bradbury. One of the few men to have bank notes named for them, even in slang, was Sir John Bradbury, whose signature as Secretary of the Treasury from 1914–19 was on the British one-pound note, which was widely called a bradbury.

Bradley. According to Gary Jennings in *Personalities of Language* (1965): "All of the few Chickahominy Indians still existing in Virginia are surnamed Bradley. This commemorates either the popularity or the fecundity of an early English colonist, a runaway indentured servant, who joined and married into the tribe."

braggadocio. You will look high and low in Italian dictionaries for this word, to no avail. For it was invented by Edmund Spenser (1552–99) in *The Faerie Queene*. Spenser gave the name Braggadochio to a loud-mouthed braggart in his poem who was finally revealed as a coward, and may have based his character on the duc d'Alençon, a suitor of Queen Elizabeth. The word came to mean "any braggart," and finally "empty or loud boasting."

Brahma. A famous western cattle breed first imported from India, its place of origin, by South Carolinian Dr. James Bolton Davis in 1849. *See* BOSTON BRAHMIN.

Brahmin. *See* BOSTON BRAHMIN.

braille. When only three years old, Louis Braille was blinded by an awl driven into his eye while he was playing in his father's leather-working shop. Total blindness extended to both eyes, but young Louis attended the village school in Coupvray outside of Paris, where he learned his alphabet by feeling twigs in the shape of letters, and then the *Institution Nationale des Jeunes Aveugles*, where he learned to read from three huge 400-pound books engraved with large embossed letters. This last method had been invented by Valentin Hauy, Father and Apostle of the Blind, the Institute's founder, but it could not be easily written by the blind and was thus inadequate. At about the time that Louis Braille was made a junior instructor at the Institute, French army officer Captain Charles Barbier introduced his "night writing," a system of 12 raised dots and dashes that fingers could "read," enabling brief orders like one dot for advance, or two dots for retreat to be written with a simple instrument and understood in total darkness. Barbier demonstrated his invention at the Institute and it fired young Braille's imagination. When only 15 he began work on the improved system that bears his name. Louis Braille, highly regarded as an organist and composer in his own right, also invented a braille musical notation, but braille was not officially adopted at the Institute where he taught until 1854, two years after his death. Tradition has it that a blind organist performing at a fashionable salon told her audience that she owed everything to Louis Braille, who had died unheralded of tuberculosis in 1852 when only 42 years old, and that her touching story finally led to universal recognition of his system.

brains knocked out. *To have one's brains knocked out* is not a modern Americanism for "to be badly beaten in a fight." It dates all the way back to the late 16th century and the first British bare-knuckle "fistfights," as boxing matches were called at the time. *See* BELOW THE BELT.

brains of the Confederacy. *See* BENJAMIN.

brain trust. James M. Kieran of the *New York Times* called the group of experts surrounding presidential candidate Franklin Delano Roosevelt the brains trust in his 1932 dispatches, the term having previously been used in sarcastic reference to the first American general staff in 1901, not at all in the same sense. Headline writers quickly chopped off the cumbersome *s*, and by the time Roosevelt became president his larger group of experts was called the brain trust. Brain trust now is applied to trusted business as well as government advisers.

brainwashing. *Brainwashing* was coined during the Korean War, when a number of American prisoners of war violated military codes after being captured, imprisoned, interrogated, and tortured by the North Koreans and Chinese. The vivid term is not an Americanism, however, being a direct translation of the Mandarin Chinese *hsi*, "to wash," and *nao*, "brain." *See* CHINESE LANGUAGE CONTRIBUTIONS TO ENGLISH.

Bramley's seedling. Bramley's seedling is a delicious English apple, notable not only because it was discovered by a butcher named Bramley of Southwell, Nottinghamshire in his garden, but because it is a "sport," or mutation. Most mutations, or changes in genes, occur in seedlings, but the Bramley was the result of a bud mutation, a variation in which only part of a plant is affected. Thus the first Bramley as well as the first Golden Delicious apple, and the first New Dawn Rose, among others, developed on one branch of a plant bearing an entirely different race. The Boston fern, which originated in a shipment of ferns sent from Philadelphia to Boston in 1894, is another well-known mutation, but the most famous bud sport is the nectarine.

branch water. A branch is a tributary stream, or any stream that isn't a large river. Branch water is pure, natural water that comes from such a stream or creek, as in "I'll have a bourbon and branch water."

brand. *Brand*, though commonly used in the U.S. for over a century, is not of American origin. It is an Old English word meaning "torch" that is related to the word *burn*. The ancient Egyptians marked their cows with brands thousands of years ago.

brand-new. *Brand-new* has nothing to do with the brand name of a product. It is rather associated with the word *brand* that is cognate with "fire," as in firebrand. The product would thus be fresh from the anvil, or as Shakespeare put it in *Twelfth Night*, "fire-new."

brand of villain. Up until the early 19th century, when the practice ended, British criminals were branded with large letters indicating their crimes. Murderers or manslayers were branded with an *M* on the thumb or back of the right hand, while thieves got a *T* on the left hand; rogues, usually kidnappers, had an *R* branded on their shoulders; and felons were marked with an *F* on the cheek. In early times the English also branded people convicted for brawling in church (*F* for felon), and blaspheming *(B)*. Some of these brands were used in colonial America, too, and we had one of our own, the *A* or Scarlet

Letter that was sewn on the dress of an adulteress. English criminals often pleaded BENEFIT OF CLERGY and were released to a church court, where they automatically received lighter penalties. But even if they did so, they were frequently branded before the secular court let them go. Branded criminals were thus a familiar sight on the streets of London and other large cities, and it was their presence that suggested the old expression *he had the brand of villain in his looks.*

brandy. *Brandy* is a shortening of *brandywine*, which comes from the Dutch *brandewijn*. *Brandewijn*, in turn, derives from the Dutch *branden*, "burn" and *wijn*, "wine," translating as "burned (or distilled) wine." The word is first recorded in the early 17th century.

brass; brazen. As the ancient word for an alloy of copper with tin or zinc, *brass* is of unknown origin; it comes directly from the Anglo-Saxon *braes*, not found in any other language, though it may have some relation to the Danish *brase*, "to fire"—as in the firing and hardening of metal. The metal brass does give us several other easily explained words, though. *Brass* meaning "shameless impudence" goes back to Elizabethan times and is explained by the 1642 quotations cited by the *O.E.D.*: "His face is of brasse, which may be said either ever or never to blush." *Brazen*, "shamelessly impudent, as bold as brass," is simply from the English word *braze*, "to make hard like brass." The word *brass*, used to describe anyone in authority, is a shortening of the British *brass hat*, for "a high-ranking military officer," a term used before the turn of the century and referring to the oak leaves, commonly thought to be brass, that adorned the brim of a British officer's cap. This term was adopted by U.S. soldiers in World War I, was streamlined to *brass* (or *top brass, big brass, heavy brass*, etc.) in World War II and was then applied to high-ranking civilian officials, executives, and influential people in general, none of whom had "scrambled eggs" (gold braid) on their hats.

brass ankle. This often derogatory name for a person of mixed race was first recorded in 1930, according to *The Random House Historical Dictionary of American Slang*. However, the words are probably considerably older. One possible explanation has the term deriving from Portuguese settlers in South Carolina who intermarried with local blacks. These racially mixed people then tended to marry within their own group. Noted for the brass anklets they liked to wear and their dark skin, they came to be known as brass ankles or black ankles.

brass tacks. There are no brass tacks, only brass-headed ones, used because they rust less easily. The American expression, which has been traced back only to 1903, though it may have been common before then, has several possible origins. Brass-headed tacks were used in upholstering chairs, especially at the foundations of the chairs, and in taking a chair apart to reupholster it from the bottom up, craftsmen might have said they were getting down to business, to the root of the matter, getting down to the brass tacks. There is no solid evidence for this theory, however, just as there is none for the country-store hypothesis. Merchants in country stores, it's said, hammered brass-headed tacks at intervals into their fabric department counters to indicate lengths of a yard, a half-yard and a quarter-yard. After a customer selected the cloth she wanted, the

merchant would say, "All right, now we'll get down to brass tacks—I'll measure it up for you." This certainly was a practice in country stores and a common one at about the time the expression is first recorded.

brawl. Did the British dance called the brawl, a kind of cotillion popular into the 19th century in which many dancers held hands and moved closer together, have anything to do with our slang expression *brawl*, for "a party"? Some etymologists believe that it is the origin of the word, but others believe the clamor or disturbance of *brawl* in the sense of "an argument" is responsible.

brazen. *See* BRASS.

Brazen Guts. Didymus of Alexandria (ca. 65 B.C.–A.D. 10) was nicknamed Chalkenteros (Brazen Guts or Bronze Guts) by his Greek contemporaries because of his enormous literary output. Didymus actually wrote a stunning 3,500 to 4,000 books over his 45-year lifespan—assuming that he started writing when age 18, that's roughly 148 books a year, 12 or so a month, about three a week—according to Lionel Casson's *Libraries in the Ancient World* (2000). No other author comes close, not even Lope de Vega with his 1,500 plays (*see* ES LOPE). Yet only fragments of Brazen Gut's "vast and varied work" survive.

Brazil. The country of Brazil was named for the wood called brazilwood, not the other way around. Brazilwood is a red-colored wood used as a dye source that takes its name from the Spanish *brasa*, "red coal or ember," and was used in Europe centuries before what is now Brazil was discovered. Because so many similar dye-wood trees were found there, Portuguese explorers named the country *terra de Brasil*, "land of red dye-wood," which later became *Brazil*.

bread. As a synonym for money, *bread* is an underworld term, first recorded in 1935 but not widely used until the late 1950s. Several English proverbs equating *bread* with one's livelihood, such as *taking the bread out of someone's mouth*, could have suggested the coinage, or, more likely, it may have been suggested by the common term *dough* for money.

bread and circuses. *Bread and circuses* is a translation of a line by the Roman poet Juvenal that refers to the practice in ancient Rome of government feeding the people and providing them with entertainment to prevent rebellion. The term means the same today.

bread crumbs; fork in the beam. Naval discipline was much harder to take a century or so ago. For instance, when a British senior officer used the expression *Bread crumbs!* at that time, it was a signal that junior midshipmen in their mess were not allowed to hear what was going to be said next and actually had to stuff their ears with bread until the senior officers finished speaking. Similarly, when a senior officer placed a fork in the beam (above his head), it meant that he wanted privacy, and all junior midshipmen had to leave the mess. *See* FORK.

breadfruit. Breadfruit (*Artocarpus incisa*), which grows wild on trees on South Pacific islands, was so named because English seamen who sampled the fruit in the 17th century believed its soft white pulp resembled fresh baked bread—although it tastes something like sweet potato. *See* CAPTAIN BLIGH.

breadline. In *The Dictionary of Americanisms, breadline* is said to have been first recorded in 1900, but no specific account of its origin offered. However, in his fascinating book *Here at the New Yorker,* Brendan Gill attributes the expression to the Fleischmann family from whose yeast fortune rose the *New Yorker* magazine. The family ran the Vienna Model Bakery in New York City during the late 1870s: "In order to call attention to the freshness of Fleischmann's bread and also, it appears, because of an innate generosity, Lewis [Fleischmann] made a practice of giving away at 11 every evening whatever amount of bread had not been sold during the day. The poor lined up to receive it at the bakery door; hence our word 'breadline.' " The term had its widest use during the Great Depression 50 years later.

breadwinner; bread. *Breadwinner* is one of the few words still retaining the meaning of the Anglo-Saxon word *winnan,* "to toil," that gives us the word "win"—a breadwinner being one who toils to obtain bread. As slang for money, *bread* dates back to about 1935 and may derive from the Cockney rhyming slang "bread and honey," for money.

break. When a criminal went to trial or left prison in the late 19th century his friends often took up collections called breaks to raise money for a lawyer or to help give him a fresh start. These breaks possibly took their name from collections performers had made since medieval times during pauses, or "breaks," in their acts, but there is no solid proof of this. The collections for criminals may have given rise to the expression "to get a break," meaning "to have some good luck." Perhaps collection breaks were held long before the first recorded mention of them. Or "to get a break" might come from a break in pool or billiards, where once a player breaks the racked balls he has a chance to make a long, successful run.

break a leg! *Break a leg!* means "good luck" in theatrical circles, probably *not* because the great Sarah Bernhardt "had but one leg and it would be good luck to be like her." No one is sure, but one theory has the expression deriving, possibly through Yiddish, from a German expression meaning "May you break your neck and your leg," for which I can find no satisfactory explanation. It may also have something to do with wishing someone a "big break," that is, good luck leading to success. Or bad luck like breaking a leg may simply be wished because actors, a superstitious lot, have long believed that wishing them good luck guarantees something terrible will happen. *See* THE SCOTTISH PLAY.

break the ice. Ice skaters might test the ice in a rink, but would never break it, and so have nothing to do with this expression meaning to be the first to try something, or to break a silence or uneasiness when people meet, etc. The allusion is probably either to ice being sold for the first time in America, in the 1830s, when *to break the ice* came to mean to introduce something, or to a ship breaking ice in its path so that it could proceed on its journey. There is no proof for either guess.

Breathalyzer. This trademarked portable device that scientifically measures alcohol in the blood, helping to enforce drunk driving laws, was invented by Robert F. Borkenstein (1912–2002) in 1953. Previously, he had helped invent the harder-to-use Drunkometer, among the first of such instruments. For his Breathalyser Borkenstein was elected by the National Safety Council in 1988 to its Safety and Health Hall of Fame International.

breed a scab on one's nose. American cowboys have used this expression for a century as a warning to a man who is stirring up trouble, looking for a punch in the nose: "Keep talking like that and you'll breed a scab on your nose."

breeze. John Hawkins and his men heard the Spanish word *breza,* for the northeast trade winds, on their voyage along the Spanish Main in the mid-16th century. They introduced the word to English, where it became the lovely refreshing *breeze,* which within 50 years was used in the sense that we employ it today.

brevity is the soul of wit. "Since brevity is the soul of wit, and tediousness the limbs and outward flourishes, I will be brief," Polonius says in *Hamlet.* But Shakespeare did not mean *wit* in the sense of a witty remark when he wrote this. He used *wit* here in its older meaning of "wisdom," and what Polonius is really saying is that wise men know how to put things succinctly—which the Bard knew was a dramatically ironic thing for a windy chap like Polonius to say. The newer meaning of *wit* was known in Shakespeare's time; he himself used it in *Much Ado About Nothing:* "They never meet but there's a skirmish of wit between them." Yet "brevity is the soul of wit" meant "brevity is the soul of wisdom" for many years before it took on its present, universal meaning. Swinburne's "An Epigram" (1802) is both witty and wise:

> What is an Epigram? A dwarfish whole,
> Its body brevity, and wit its soul.

Brevoortia Ida-Maia. *The floral firecracker,* as this plant is popularly called, shows how oddly things sometimes get their names. Ida May, the daughter of a 19th-century California stagecoach driver, had noticed the bulbous plant many times in her travels and pointed it out to Alphonso Wood, a naturalist always interested in collecting botanical specimens. Wood named the single plant, a member of the lily family *Brevoortia Ida-Maia,* its prenomen in honor of his fellow American naturalist J. C. Brevoort, and its patronym in gratitude to the observant little girl who had brought the scarlet-flowered perennial to his attention.

Brewster chair. A spindle chair named after William Brewster (1566–1644), elder of the Pilgrim Church, who was the sole leader of the Pilgrims, 1620–29.

Briadism. *See* HYPNOTISM.

a Briareus of languages. Briareus was a mythological giant with 50 heads and 100 hands, but the phrase *Briareus of languages* first honored Cardinal Giuseppe Caspar Mezzofanti (1774–1849), chief keeper of the Vatican library. The term is used to describe an accomplished linguist, having been invented by the English poet Byron, who called the cardinal "a walking polyglot; a monster of languages; a Briareus of parts of speech." Mezzofanti, we are told, learned Latin and Greek fluently while listening to an old priest giving lessons to students next door to the shop where he had been an apprentice to a carpenter. He eventually mastered 39 languages, from Albanian to Wallachian, speaking these as well as he did his native tongue. All in all, he could speak 60 languages and 72 dialects fluently and could translate 114 languages. Among these were such exotics as Bimbarra, Geez, Kurdish, Tonkinese, and Chippewa.

bribe. A bribe, a sinister thing today, was originally, in 14th-century France, alms that one gave a beggar. Because beggars began to *demand* such alms the word came to mean "to extort or steal" when it reached England a century or so later. Within a century or so a *bribe* came to mean, instead of an extortion, "a voluntary inducement to get someone to do something for the giver," an ironic change that has carried over into the word's meaning today.

brick of a man. A good, solid, substantial person that you can rely upon. The expression is said to have originated with King Lycurgus of Sparta, who was questioned about the absence of defensive walls around his city. "There are Sparta's walls," he replied, pointing at his soldiers, "and every man is a brick."

bridegroom. The *groom* in *bridegroom* is of no relation to the "groom" who takes care of horses. *Groom* here is a corruption of the Old English *guma*, "man." *Guma* became *grome* in Middle English and this word was associated with *grome*, "a lad," finally becoming part of *bridegroom*, first recorded in the early 16th century.

Bride of the Sea. Early in the 11th century, the wedding of the doge of Venice to the Adriatic symbolized the sea power of Venice. Every year the doge, in his state barge, the *Bucentaur*, sailed into the Adriatic on Ascension Day and dropped a wedding ring into the sea. This practice, still part of the annual ceremony called the *Sposalizo del Mar*, is responsible for Venice's historical name "The Bride of the Sea."

brides of the multitude. A colorful euphemism for prostitutes used in the early West, though the expression may not have been coined there.

bridewell. In England, as readers of English history and fiction know, a bridewell is a house of correction, jail or prison. All the bridewells take their name from the original Bridewell, an ancient house of correction in London that remained in operation until 1863.

bridge. Bridge is a card game derived from whist that first became popular in the 1880s. Its name is of obscure origin. Since it was earlier called *biritch*, some scholars believe the word derives ultimately from the Turkish *bir*, "one," plus *iic*, "three," referring to one hand of cards in the game being exposed while the other three are concealed. Bridge was possibly introduced to Europe from the Near East, but there is no record of a Turkish game with a name anything like *bir iic*.

brie. The delicious cheese is named for Brie, an agricultural district in France noted for its cheese and other dairy products.

brier. The brier from which pipes are made has no connection with the thorny bush called the brier. Rather, pipes are made from the roots of the tree heath, which was called *bruyer* in Old English; this name was corrupted to *brier* over the centuries. The tree heath *(Erica arborea)* is a small tree 10–20 feet high with long, fragrant flowers. It is popular in southern Europe. A "brierpatch child" or "brierpatch kid" is a term for an illegitimate child. This Americanism dates back at least a century. *See* CABBAGE.

brig. *Brig*, for "a prison on a ship," is an Americanism first recorded in 1852. One theory has it that pirates called "brigands" sailed on "brigandines" or "brigantines," small, two-masted sailing vessels, the name of which was soon shortened to *brig*. Since the brigands were criminals and were often in jail, the name of the type of ship they sailed supposedly became associated with jail cells.

bright and early. This common expression, meaning "very early in the morning," isn't as old as one would suspect, being an Americanism that is first recorded by Washington Irving in his *Adventures of Captain Bonneville, U.S.A.* (1837).

bright-eyed and bushy-tailed. *Bright-eyed* is obvious, and the *bushy-tailed* here is a reference to the tail of a cat, which fluffs up when the animal becomes excited. The expression means cheerful and lively, and it dates back to the 19th century.

Bright's disease. One of the scores of maladies named for medical researchers is Bright's disease, after English Dr. Richard Bright (1780–1858), whose findings determined the nature of the kidney affliction. Other names in the same morbid category include Basedow's disease, a swelling of the thyroid gland, for German Dr. Karl von Basedow (1799–1854); Hodgkin's a disease of the lymphatic glands, after English Dr. Thomas Hodgkin (1798–1866); Lindau's, a brain disease, for Arvid Lindau, a Swedish pathologist; *Paget's*, a disease of the breast, after Sir James Paget (1814–99); Pott's, a tuberculosis infection, after English surgeon Percivall Pott (1714–88); Riggs pyorrhea for American dentist John M. Riggs (1810–85); Jacksonian epilepsy, after English Dr. John Hughlings Jackson (1835–1911); and Vincent's infection, trench mouth, for French Dr. Jean Hyacinthe Vincent (1862–1950). All also go by far, far longer medical names.

brightwork. Metal fixtures of a ship that are kept bright by hand polishing are called brightwork. The term is an Americanism, first recorded in 1841, but probably older.

Brillat-Savarin. "The destiny of nations depends on the manner wherein they take their food." "A dessert course without cheese is like a beautiful woman with one eye." "Animals feed: man eats; only a man of wit knows how to dine." Anthelme Brillat-Savarin, author of these and many other well-known aphorisms on *la cuisine*, was 70 when he published his *Physiologie du goût (Physiology of Taste)* in 1825, his celebrated book 30 years in the making. He was to die the following year but not before he had given the world the most trenchant discussion of food and its effects on trenchermen ever written. The greatest of French bon vivants had been born, appropriately enough, in the town of Belley—"Belley is its name and Belley is its nature," someone wrote over a century later. He became the town's mayor after the French Revolution but had to emigrate to America during the Reign of Terror, living in Connecticut for a few years. Portly and gregarious, the sage of Belley remained a bachelor all his life—perhaps too devoted to food and women ever to marry, possibly because he loved his cousin, the society beauty Madame Récamier. A lawyer who wrote on political economy and law, and penned a few licentious tales as well, he is remembered above all for his bible of gastronomy. "Tell me what you eat and I will tell you what you are," he once declared. Though he was something of an eccentric—he often carried dead birds around in his pockets until they became "high" enough for cooking—Brillat-Savarin's reputation has not suffered for his eccentricities, his name long synonymous with supreme authority on cooking. The greatest of gourmets also has the savarin, a yeast cake soaked in a rum- or kirsch-flavored syrup, named for him, and there are countless restaurants and a brand of coffee using the last half of his hyphenated name, as well as two classic garnishes, both made in part with truffles, the most extravagant of gourmet foods. Brillat was actually Anthelme's real name—he took on the hyphen and Savarin when his great aunt left him her entire fortune on the condition that he add her name to his, Mademoiselle Savarin wanting a little immortality and getting more than she bargained for. Love of food, in fact, seemed to run in the Brillat family. Anthelme's youngest sister, Pierrette, for instance, died at the dinner table. She was almost 100 and her last words are among the most unusual in history: "And now, girl, bring me the dessert." *Physiologie du goût*, incidentally, had to be printed at the author's expense. And when Brillat-Savarin's brother later sold the rights to a publisher, he got only $120—after throwing in a genuine Stradivarius as well.

brilliant diamond. This isn't a diamond that sparkles brilliantly, but a diamond cut in a specific way, a perfect brilliant diamond having 58 facets. The term has been used since the late 17th century, when the Venetian diamond cutter Vincenzo Peruzzi invented the technique.

Brinell hardness, etc. A Brinell machine or tester determines the hardness of a metal, especially steel, by forcing a hard steel or tungsten carbide ball into it under a fixed hydraulic pressure. By dividing the force applied by the indenter into the surface area of the indentation made, the metal's Brinell number is obtained, this indicating its relative *Brinell hardness* on the scale. The machine and method were devised by the Swedish engineer, Johann August Brinell (1849–1925), who first demonstrated his famous invention at the Paris International Exposition of 1900.

bring down the house. A performer who brings down the house is so good that the theater seems to vibrate from all the applause he receives and it even seems as if the building will collapse. The common expression is from the British theater and is first recorded in 1754. At least once the house nearly did come down on an audience. During an early performance of Christopher Marlowe's *The Tragicall History of Dr. Faustus*, the story of a man who sold his soul to the devil, timbers in the Theater Playhouse suddenly began to crack. Many in the audience thought the building was on the verge of collapse—some attributing this to supernatural causes—and alarmed patrons hurried from the premises. It turned out to be a false alarm, but no one ever established the cause of cracking timbers.

bring home the bacon. An English custom initiated in 1111 and lasting until late in the 18th century provided that any married couple who swore that they hadn't quarreled for over a year, or had not at any time wished themselves "single again"—and could prove this to the satisfaction of a mock jury sometimes composed of six bachelors and six maidens—was entitled to the Dunmow Flitch, a side of bacon awarded at the church of Dunmow in Essex County. The expression to *bring home the bacon*, "to win the prize," isn't recorded until 1925, but bacon was used as a word for "prize" centuries before, and most scholars believe that the Dunmow Flitch is responsible for the usage. This custom, along with the popular American one of awarding the pig to the winner of "greased-pig" events at county fairs, gives us the phrase, which now means to support a family by working.

bring me the winner. The French dramatist Georges Feydeau (1862–1921) is apparently the originator of the old restaurant joke about the lobster with one claw. A waiter supposedly brought such a specimen to his table, explaining that lobsters often fought in the tanks and were mutilated in this way. "Take this one away then," Feydeau said, "and bring me the winner."

bristlecone pine. Called the "oldest living things on earth," some gnarled, twisted bristlecone pines *(Pinus aristata)* in California's White Mountains are more than 5,000 years old. Named for the bristle-like prickles at the end of its cones, this slow-growing tree also goes by the names Jack pine, cattail pine, and foxtail pine, the last two names alluding to the tufts at the ends of its twigs.

Bristol. This city in Connecticut takes its name from its sister city in England. Bristol, England, in turn, got its name from the peculiar habit its residents had of tacking an "l" onto words ending in a vowel. This local dialectical eccentricity, which persists there to this day, changed the seaport's name from Bristowe to Bristol.

Bristols. British rhyming slang made the slang *titties* (for breasts) into *Bristol Cities* (because they come in pairs), later dropped the second word, as is frequently the case in rhyming slang, and made *Bristol* plural so that *Bristols* became slang for female breasts. *See* CHARLEY; BRISTOL.

bro; bra. The use of *bro* for *brother* dates back to 1666 in England, 300 years before American blacks began using the word. As for the Jamaican and South African black slang *bra*, it can be used to mean "brother" or as the equivalent of "Mr." applied to any man.

broad. *Broad* has meant both a promiscuous woman and any young woman since the 1920s, though it is generally used today, when it is used, to mean a young woman—not necessarily a promiscuous one, but not someone toward whom much respect is shown. The Americanism may derive from *bawd*, but was more likely suggested by broad breasts and buttocks.

Broadway; B'way. By the mid-19th century most New York playhouses were located on Broadway or nearby, but the name *Broadway* wasn't used to attract customers until 1800, when *The Black Crook*, a strange hybrid of ballet and melodrama, was produced. This extravaganza ran over a year on Broadway and toured for more than 20 years, advertising itself as "the original Broadway production." After that the name *Broadway* was commonly used both in describing a successful touring company and in attracting visitors to New York as well. *The Black Crook* also did much to further burlesque, employing a long line of chorus girls in flesh-colored tights, which proved sensational at the time. Broadway is, of course, the best-known street in New York City, though rivaled in fame by Wall Street, Park Avenue, and Fifth Avenue. According to the *Dictionary of Americanisms*, the first recorded use of the name *Broadway* for the street was 1673; before then it had been called High Street. Originally an Indian trail, it now runs 17 miles through Manhattan and four miles through the Bronx. It has been called the longest street in the world, but doesn't come close, the record being held by Toronto's 1,178.3-mile-long Yonge Street. Columnist Walter Winchell may have coined the popular spelling *B'way*. *See* GREAT WHITE WAY.

brobdingnagian. A big word that means "giant" or "huge," and honors a race of fictional giants. The Brobdingnagians were the giants who inhabited the island of Brobdingnag in Jonathan Swift's *Gulliver's Travels* (1726). Men were "odious little vermin" to the Brobdingnagians. *See* LILLIPUTIAN.

brocard; Brocard's circle and ellipse. Brocard was the French name for Burchard, an 11th-century bishop of Worms. Bishop Brocard published a collection of canons, *Regulae Ecclesiasticae*, celebrated for its short, sententious sentences, and a *brocard* soon came to mean both a brief maxim or proverb in philosophy or law and a pointed jibe or biting speech. *Brocard's circle* and *Brocard's ellipse* are mathematical terms named for French mathematician Henri Brocard (1845–1922).

broccoli. Roman farmers, who must have been more poetic than their contemporary counterparts, are said to have called *broccoli* "the five green fingers of Jupiter." The word has a more prosaic derivation, however, coming from the Latin *bracchium*, "a strong arm or branch," in reference to its shape. According to Pliny the Elder, Drusus, the eldest son of Emperor Tiberius ate so much broccoli that his urine turned bright green! *See* I SAY IT'S SPINACH AND I SAY THE HELL WITH IT.

broderick. His tactics wouldn't be officially approved today, but Johnny (The Boffer) Broderick is still remembered as a tough New York City cop who relied on his fists as much as his police revolver. Known as the world's toughest cop, Detective Broderick worked "the Broadway beat," dealing out punishment with his fists on the spot so often that *to broderick* became a synonym for "to clobber." Broderick once flattened the hoodlum Jack (Legs) Diamond, and he knocked out and captured Francis (Two-Gun) Crowley before Crowley could find the courage to shoot. Another time he battered two men molesting a woman, threw them through a plate-glass window

and then arrested them for malicious destruction of property. In fact, Bellevue Hospital used him as an exhibit to show how much punishment the human hand could take. Broderick, an image of sartorial splendor, was used as a bodyguard by many celebrities, including Franklin Roosevelt and Jack Dempsey. Dempsey confessed that the detective was the only man he wouldn't care to fight outside the ring. This graduate of New York's gashouse district was immortalized by Damon Runyon as Johnny Brannigan and played by Edward G. Robinson in *Bullets or Ballots*. By the time he retired in 1947, after 25 years on the force, Broderick had won eight medals for heroism. Broadway gamblers once gave 9–5 odds that he would be killed on any given day, but he died in his bed in 1966, 72 years old.

brodie. *See* DO A BRODIE.

brogue. One theory holds that the *brogue* long associated with the Irish derives from the Gaelic *barrog*, for "a wrestling hold"—Irish tongues were held by tradition and couldn't speak any other way. A rival theory says that *brogue* comes from the heavy brogans (from the Gaelic *brog*, "shoe") worn by Irish peasants, who usually spoke with what we now call a brogue.

brokenhearted. Brokenhearted lovers weren't the inspiration for this word. It was coined in 1526 by William Tyndale, English translator of the Bible, who was later strangled and burned at the stake for heresy. The word first occurs in Luke 4:18: "To heale the broken harted," and was preceded by such formations as "broken-minded," "broken-backed," and "broken-winded." Tyndale is also said to have coined the word *beautiful*, in his translation of the Bible (in Mat. 23:27).

a broken reed. Someone untrustworthy, undependable, not to be relied upon. The phrase is from the Bible (Isa. 36:6): "Lo, thou trusteth the staff of this broken reed. . . ."

broker. Brokers today are associated with stocks or real estate, but all brokers were originally *brokieres*, or men who opened up wine casks (usually to bottle and sell the wine inside). This Old French word came to be transferred to wine salesmen, or brokers, and finally to one who sold anything at all. Wall Street brokers who work on the floor (or in the pit) of the exchange are called floor brokers; they were once called two-dollar brokers because they received a fee of two dollars per transaction.

broker than the Ten Commandments. A humorous expression from the 1930s, during the Great Depression. Wrote Henry Roth in *From Bondage* (1996), a novel set in that period: "Listen Bud, I'm flat broke. I'm broker'n the Ten Commandments."

bronco. A name (from the Spanish for rough and wild) given to small, half-wild American horses descended from steeds that escaped from early Spanish settlements. Any wild, unbroken horse is also called a bronco or bronc.

the Bronx. The Bronx, one of New York City's five boroughs, takes its name from Jonas Bronck, a Dane who first settled the area for the Dutch West India Company in 1641. Points of interest in the celebrated borough are the Bronx Zoo and Botanic Gardens, the Edgar Allan Poe cottage, and Yankee Stadium, "the house that Ruth built." The Bronx River runs from Westchester County through the Bronx and into the East River. The *Bronx cocktail* was named in honor of the borough, or invented there in about 1919. Long associated with baseball, the razz, or raspberry, called the Bronx cheer wasn't born at Yankee Stadium, home of baseball's New York Yankees. It may derive from the Spanish word *branca*, "a rude shout," or have originated at the National Theater in the Bronx. We know for certain only that the term was first recorded in 1929. *See* RASPBERRY.

Bronx Bombers. This nickname for the New York Yankees, who make their home in THE BRONX, first appeared in the *New York Post* in 1936. Baseball historian Paul Dickson says the name became popular when heavyweight champion Joe Louis was known as the Brown Bomber. *See* JOE LOUIS.

bronze. Many scholars trace the word *bronze* to the late Latin *brundisium*, "brass from Brundisium," Brundisium being the modern Adriatic city of Brindisi. But since that city doesn't produce exceptional brass or bronze, the derivation is doubtful. Another possible source is the Persian *birindj*, "alloy." In any case, *bronze* is a fairly modern word, first recorded in 1721.

Brooklyn. A borough of New York City almost as well known as Manhattan. Officially it is designated King's County, but no one calls it that. In 1645 the area was named Breuckelen after an ancient village in the Netherlands. Over the years this changed to Brockland, Brocklin, Brookline, and finally Brooklyn.

Brooklynese. Betty Boop, Popeye the Sailor Man, and Bugs Bunny all speak Brooklynese. *Brooklynese* is a synonym for the worst of New York speech, coined about 1945. It is an extreme form of New York talk that had its golden age 60 or so years ago and has been heard less ever since. Someone long ago defined *Brooklynese* as what you have a bad case of if you recite the sentence "There were thirty purple birds sitting on a curb, burping and chirping and eating dirty worms, brother," as "Dere were toity poiple boids sittin onna coib, boipin and choipin an eatin doity woims, brudda."

broom. British housewives in early times used the besom, "a handful of twigs with the leaves attached," to sweep their homes. Because these "besoms" were often made of twigs from the broom shrub they came to be called brooms by about the year 1000. "Besom," however, remained the name for a sweeping implement well into the 19th century. Brooms were often placed across the door of a house to ward off witches, for even though witches were believed to ride on brooms, it was thought that a witch had to count every straw in a broom placed across a door before she could open it.

broomstick marriage. Broomstick marriages were common in remote districts of England, Scotland, and the southern U.S. in the 18th century. In order to avoid paying clerical fees and waiting for the preacher to ride by, rural folk devised a ceremony that was regarded as perfectly legal and binding in many communities—all the prospective bride and groom had to do was jump over a broomstick held by two people who knew them and they were declared man and wife. It has been suggested that the broomstick has something to do with "witches riding on their broomsticks to their unholy pleasures," but no one really knows why the superstition developed. At first *broomstick marriage* meant only a rural marriage, but its meaning deteriorated over the years as laws grew more uniform and it is now regarded as a mock marriage or a common-law marriage.

brothel. Prostitutes in the 15th century were called brothels, from the Old English *breothan*, "to go to ruin." *Brothel houses* soon meant houses of prostitutes, or whorehouses, the word shortened to *brothel* by the late 1700s.

brother, can you spare a dime? A popular song published in 1932 had these words as its title and they quickly became the common plea of panhandlers throughout America during the Great Depression.

Brother Jonathan. Brother Jonathan was originally Connecticut governor and minister Jonathan Trumbull (1710–85), one of the few colonial governors to stand up for the rights of the colonists. The redoubtable Trumbull was a trusted friend and adviser of George Washington, and an unsupported story has it that General Washington, when he needed ammunition and none of his officers could solve the problem, declared, "We must consult Brother Jonathan on this." Trumbull came up with a solution and Washington's remark became proverbial in time. Washington did rank Trumbull "the first among patriots," and the term *Brother Jonathan* for an American first appeared in print in 1816. Some debunkers point out, however, that Jonathan was a very common American name at the time and that the British had used *Brother Jonathan* in allusion to the Puritans as early as the 17th century.

brother's keeper. *See* MARK OF CAIN.

brougham. The brougham, a four-wheeled carriage for two or four passengers, honors Henry Peter Brougham, Baron Brougham and Vaux (1778–1868). This name for a one-horse carriage with an open driver's seat and a closed, low-slung passenger cab behind also designated the first tall electric automobiles, as well as an early gasoline-powered limousine with the driver's seat unenclosed. The brougham was named after Lord Brougham in about 1850, because of his design for the "garden chair on wheels," similar to the old "growler" horse cab. The amazing Lord Brougham, born in Edinburgh, Scotland, was among the most versatile of men—a noted lawyer, orator, politician, statesman, scientist, writer, publisher, abolitionist, reformer, and one of the great wits of his day. In his later years the many-faceted genius built a cottage in Cannes, and his presence there was directly responsible for the French town's great vogue as an international resort.

browbeat. A browbeaten person is literally "someone who is beaten or put down by the knitted or wrinkled brow and frown of somebody else." *To browbeat*, "to belittle someone with sternness, arrogance, or insolence," is first recorded in 1581.

brown. *See* AUBURN.

brown as a berry.   The first expression was used by Chaucer in 1386: "His palfrey [small saddle horse] was as broune as is a bery." Though most berries aren't brown, the reference is possibly to brown berries like those of the juniper or cedar.

the Brown Bomber.   *See* JOE LOUIS.

brown-eyed peas.   These are black-eyed peas with a brown rather than black spot where they were attached to the pod. They also go by the name "brown-eyed crowder peas." Regardless, they always taste just like black-eyed peas. *See* BLACK-EYED PEAS.

Brownie.   The cheap simple Kodak camera called a Brownie is not named after its inventor, Charles Brownell. Kodak's founder, George Eastman, chose it himself in about 1900 from the little creatures called *Brownies* in the stories of Canadian children's book author and artist Palmer Cox. The Brownie camera, he reasoned, was helpful and efficient like the Brownies, and it could be operated by a child.

brownie.   This friendly country goblin of Scottish folklore helps with household chores at night when all the house is asleep. In Celtic legend, however, the brownies were "tall dark fellows." It was a long series of popular illustrated books by Quebec-born U.S. author and artist Palmer Cox (1840–1924) that made the brownies a race of good-natured elves. The first of the series was *The Brownies: Their Book* (1887).

browsing.   We associate *browsing* mainly with bookstores today, but the word, from the French *broust*, "young bud or shoot," originally meant the feeding of animals such as cattle, deer, and goats on the leaves and shoots of trees and bushes; *to browse* was recorded as early as 1542 in this sense. Shakespeare seems to have been the first to use the word figuratively, in *Cymbeline*, but Charles Lamb first used it in its modern sense in his largely autobiographical *Essays of Elia* (1823): "He browsed at will upon that fair and wholesome pasturage [a good library]."

brucellosis.   *See* BANG'S DISEASE.

brucine.   Another poison named for a real person, but this time not for someone who used it for nefarious purposes. Brucine is a bitter, poisonous vegetable alkaloid found in seeds of various *Strychnos* species, especially *Nux vomica*. It resembles strychnine, though it isn't as powerful and it is rapidly eliminated from the body. *Brucine*, used in the denaturing of alcohol, was named for the apparently innocent Scottish traveler and explorer, James Bruce (1730–94), who merely discovered it. *See* ACQUA TOFANA.

bruin.   Bears have been called bruins ever since medieval times, when the bear in the folk tale *Reynard the Fox* was named Bruin. The tale is Dutch in origin and *bruin* is the Dutch word for "brown." The Swiss capital, Bern, takes its name from the German word for bear.

brumby.   An Australian wild horse is often called a brumby, or brumbie. The word possibly derives from the name of Major William Brumby, an early 19th-century settler from England whose descendants still live in Australia. Major Brumby was a noted breeder of horses, but much of his stock escaped and ran wild. *Brumby* may come, however, from the Aborigine *booramby*, meaning "wild."

brummagem.   Counterfeit or cheap merchandise is called brummagem, after the city of Birmingham, England, which was often pronounced *Brummagem* locally in the 17th century. The city had a reputation as a manufacturing center of cheap trinkets and a place where counterfeit coins were made.

brunch.   *Brunch* is a dictionary-accepted word for a meal. Brunch came into the language back in 1895, when it was introduced in *Hunter's Weekly*, a British publication, to describe a combined breakfast and luncheon. It had probably been a collegiate coinage a little earlier. *Lupper*, a midafternoon meal eaten instead of lunch and supper, is a new portmanteau word "struggling to be born," according to William Sherk in *500 Years of New Words* (1983). *Dunch* and *blupper* are two possible substitutes for *lupper*, suggested by readers of Marian Burros's "De Gustibus" column in the *New York Times*.

Brunswick stew.   A stew of squirrel meat, lima beans, and green corn seasoned with salt and pepper and said to have been invented by a cook in Brunswick County, Virginia, over 100 years ago.

brushfire.   Two uses of the word *brush* probably suggested this recent coinage for a relatively small, localized war, an expression first recorded about 30 years ago. *Brushfire*, the term invented by early emigrants on the western frontier, was a fire in the brush, or scrubby areas where shrubs and small trees grew, a fire relatively easy to control compared with a forest fire. More than a century later the word *brush* became slang for uncivilized regions of any kind. Since they took place in what many considered "uncivilized" areas and were presumably easy to contain, local wars in far-off places became known as brushfire wars in the mid-1950s. *Brushfire* has also been used as an adjective for other things limited in scope, area, or importance, as in a *brushfire labor dispute*.

brussels sprout.   Unknown in America until about 1800, this relatively "new" vegetable is named for the capital of Belgium, where it was developed or improved upon early in the 16th century.

Brutus; Et tu Brute?   Marcus Junius Brutus (ca. 85–42 B.C.) was, of course, the principal assassin of Julius Caesar and *a Brutus* is any treacherous person, especially a former friend. *Et tu Brute* ("You too, Brutus?"), Caesar's last words when he glimpsed his friend, is among the most familiar of quotations. History holds two opinions of Brutus. One claims that he conspired with Cassius to save the republic from Caesar's tyranny. The other suggests that his reputation as a moneylender and his friendship with the self-seeking Cassius prove that his motives were far more crass. Two years after he took part in Caesar's assassination, Brutus committed suicide, following a battle at Philippi that the republicans lost to Mark Antony and Octavian (later Augustus Caesar). A brutus, without the capital, is both a rough, cropped wig and a bronze variety of chrysanthemum, the origin of these terms unknown.

Bubba.   *Bubba*, chiefly among blacks in the American South, is a term of address meaning "brother" and is used by friends as well as relatives. But reference works generally fail to note that the word is also commonly used to mean a white southerner. An essay in the *New York Times* by Molly Ivins put it this way: "In theory, the battle for Southern voters revolves around the stereotypical white Southerner, usually known as 'Bubba,' who is partial to country music and conservative politics. But as Presidential politics move into the states of the Confederacy, the biggest question about Bubba may not be how he will vote but how to find him." *Bubba* is also a nickname in the press for former president William Jefferson Clinton, "the man from Hope (Arkansas)."

bubblegum machine.   Since the mid-1960s this has been the name for a police car with a flashing revolving red light on the roof. Also called a *bubbletop* and a *gumball*. Recently, other emergency vehicles have adopted the mechanism but not the name.

bubby; bubee.   Both Bartlett and *Webster's* state that *bubby*, a familiar name for "a little boy," is a corruption of "brother," claiming it as an Americanism first recorded in about 1848. More likely, it is from the German *bube*, "little boy." *Bubee*, a Yiddish term of endearment that can be addressed to a child or any loved one, appears to have a separate etymology. It derives from the Yiddish *bubeleh*, meaning the same, which probably comes from the Russian *baba*, "little grandmother," and the Hebrew *buba*, "little doll."

bubby bush.   The strawberry shrub (*Calycanthus floridus* or *glaucus*) is possibly named the "bubby bush" because its blossoms resemble a woman's breasts, sometimes called "bubbies." However, according to Thomas Anburey in his *Travels Through the Interior Parts of America* (1791), the word derives "from a custom that the [American] women have of putting this flower down their bosums . . . till it has lost all its grateful perfume." The plant is also called the bubby, bubby blossom, bubby flower, bubby shrub, and sweet bubbies.

bubkes.   Usually pronounced "bub-kiss," this Yiddish word, widely heard in America, comes from the Russian for "beans" and means nothing or very little, a small amount, something trivial: "You know what I got for the job? Bubkes!"

bubonic plague.   *See* BLACK DEATH.

buccaneer.   *Buccaneer* was the name applied to themselves by the sea raiders roaming the Caribbean. The word derives from the *boucanes*, or little dome-shaped smokehouses, on Hispaniola Island, where strips of boar meat and beef were smoked dry over a slow fire. The men who smoked *viande boucanee*, or "jerky," and sold it in bundles of a hundred for six pieces of eight were called *boucaniers*, "smokers of meat." Pirates in the area so often bought this dried meat from the *boucaniers*—it was perfect food to carry in the days before refrigeration—that they began to be called *boucaniers* or *buccaneers*, too.

Bucephala.   *See* PERITAS AND BUCEPHALA.

buck; pass the buck.   The American slang word for a dollar may have its origins in animal skins that were classified as "bucks" and "does." The bucks, larger and more valuable than does (some 500,000 of them were traded every year in 18th-century America), could have become a part of early American business terminology (ca. 1800) and later become slang for a dollar. But *buck's* origin could just as well be in poker. A marker called a *buck* (perhaps after a buck horn knife made from a deer's anthers) was placed next to a poker player in the game's heyday, during the late 19th century, to remind him that it was his turn to deal next. When silver dollars were used as the markers, they could have taken the name *buck* for their own. Although markers called *bucks* may or may not have given us the slang term for a dollar, they are almost certainly responsible for the expression *to pass the buck*, "to evade responsibility"—just as poker players passed on the responsibility for the deal when they passed the buck. Buck is also a derogatory term for an Indian man that dates back to the early 19th century. *Buck warrior* and *buck aborigine* were synonymous, though they are rarely, if ever, used anymore.

buckaroo.   *Buckaroo*, for "a cowboy," is a corruption of the Spanish *vaquero*, meaning the same. The first recorded quotation using the word, in a letter from Texas, shows the mispronunciation of *vaquero* by Americans: "These rancheros are surrounded by peons and *bakharas* or herdsmen." The mispronunciation "bakhara" was further corrupted to "buckhara," "buckayro," and finally *buckaroo*. *Buckaroo* has probably lasted because it is a good descriptive word, suggesting a cowboy on a bucking horse. It inspired well over 50 other American slang words ending in "-aroo" or "-eroo." *Stinkaroo*, a bad play or movie, still has wide currency, as does *the old switcheroo*, the act of substituting one thing for another. Others not so familiar anymore are *antsaroo*, ants in his pants; *jugaroo*, a jail; and *ziparoo*, energy.

bucket letter.   During the largely ineffective administration of President John Quincy Adams, a series of anonymous letters were sent to the president by David Holt of Georgia, writing under the pseudonym Edward Bucket. These letters, widely published, became familiar to many Americans, and for a number of years a *bucket letter* became the name for any anonymous letter. Such a letter was also called a "bucket."

bucket shop.   Before it became the term for "an illegal brokerage house that cheats its customers," *bucket shop* was the designation for "an unsavory bar where patrons could buy beer by the buckets." However, in 1882, the Chicago Board of Trade prohibited grain transactions of less than 5,000 bushels. Illegitimate brokerage houses began trading in smaller lots and whenever larger, legitimate houses dealt illegally in smaller lots they sent down for a "bucketful" to the bucket shops.

buckeye.   American pioneers in what is now Ohio so named this horse chestnut tree because its dark-brown nut resembles the eye of a buck deer "when the shell first cracks and exposes it to sight." A useful tree whose soft wood, cut into long shavings, even made ladies' hats and whose very roots were made into a soap, the buckeye (*Aesculus glabra*) eventually gave its name to all the natives of the BUCKEYE STATE. The nuts, or buckeye beans, of the tree were carried as good-luck charms and thought to ward off piles, rheumatism, and chills, among other maladies.

Buckeye State.   A nickname for Ohio, after the buckeye tree (*see* BUCKEYE). Like Virginia, Ohio has also been called the Mother of Presidents (Presidents Grant, Hayes, Garfield, Benjamin Harrison, McKinley, Taft, and Harding all hailed from Ohio). In the early 1800s Ohio was called the Yankee State because so many of its settlers were from New England.

buckhorse.   If you gave him a few shillings, the English fighter John Smith, who went by the ring name of *Buckhorse*, would let you punch him on the side of the head as hard as you could. The well-known boxer saw his nickname become slang for "a punch or a blow" beginning about 1850; that is, if he saw anything but stars after a while.

buckle down to work.   To buckle oneself, when English knighthood flowered, meant to fasten one's armor, to buckle the straps securely in their holders, to prepare for battle. Soon the expression was used figuratively, meaning "to apply oneself resolutely to any task": "Everie man . . . must buckle himself to a painful kind of life" (1574). The word *buckle* itself comes from the Latin *buccula*, a diminutive of "cheek," which originally was used to describe the strap holder or clamp on Roman battle helmets that rested near the cheek.

buckra.   A Gullah term from the African Elik word *mbakara* (white leader or man), which can be a derogatory term for any white person or mean "white boss" or "poor white person."

buckwheat.   The grain of buckwheat resembles the seed of the beech tree, so the Dutch called it *bockweit*, or "beech wheat." From *bockweit* came the English *buckwheat*, which is used in Europe mainly for animal feed ("A grain which in England is commonly fed to horses," Dr. Johnson notes characteristically in his *Dictionary*, "but in Scotland supports the people."), but is used in America to make *buckwheat pancakes* and was the name of one of the most popular characters in the "Our Gang" film comedies.

Buddhism.   Buddha, "the Enlightened One," was the title given to Prince Siddhartha (ca. 563–ca. 485), the Hindu prince who founded Buddhism in the sixth century B.C. It had been prophesied on his conception that the prince would renounce the world upon seeing a sick man, an old man, and a corpse, which human misery he saw while riding through the royal park one day when he was 29 years old. Prince Siddhartha left his wife and child, and after six years of solitude and contemplation, during which he devoted himself to the severest asceticism, living on seeds, grass, and even dung, he emerged as the Buddha, preaching a religion based on salvation by suffering. Existence, he proclaimed, was evil, and desire was the cause of sorrow. Nirvana the absorption into the supreme spirit, was the reward obtained by the suppression of desire. Gautama Buddha (Gautama is from his clan name, and he is called Sakyammuni Buddha from his tribal name) spent all his life as a wanderer, preaching his doctrine from the time he attained enlightenment under a Bo tree at Buddh Gaya in northern India until his death 45 years later. Buddha, or the Enlightened,

derives from the Sanskrit *bodhati*, "he awakens." It is estimated that Buddhism has about 140 million followers today.

buddy.   Most experts believe this word arose from a children's mispronunciation of *brother*, children frequently having trouble with the letter *r* in that word and pronouncing it buddy. From its use as a substitute for brother, *buddy* was extended to mean a close friend as well.

budgerigar.   This ancient word is the aboriginal name for a favorite Australian parrot or cockatoo. *Budgerigar's* origins may be lost in time, but some experts have theorized that it comes from the aboriginal *budgeri*, good, and *gar*, cockatoo.

budget.   Originally, a budget was a leather bag or wallet, deriving from the French *bougette*, wallet. The word's meaning may have been extended to cover a statement of financial requirements when the British Chancellor of the Exchequer, in appearing before Parliament, began the custom of carrying papers containing his annual statement of estimated revenues and expenses in a leather bag and "opening the budget" for the year. Another theory claims that in 1733 Sir Robert Walpole introduced an unpopular excise duties bill and a political pamphleteer compared him to "a mounte-bank at a fair opening his budget of crank medicines," the word *budget* from then on becoming linked with government financial requirements.

Budweiser.   Though one of America's most popular beers, Budweiser, or Bud, as it is often abbreviated, is German in origin. The brand of beer is not named for an American brewmaster, as many people suppose, but takes its name from the German village of Budweis, where a visiting St. Louis businessman "discovered" it.

Buenos Aires.   Few American cities today could honestly take the name of this city, for the Spanish *Buenos Aires* means "good air" in English. Buenos Aires was so named over a century ago for the bracing air in the major seaport and capital of Argentina. *See* MALARIA.

buff; in the buff.   So many buffalo hides were taken in the 19th century that buff coats made of them became very fashionable, the undyed yellowish coats giving us the word *buff*; the verb *buff*, "to polish," entered the language from the strips of buffalo hide that were used to bring metals like bronze to a high polish. Even the word *buff* for an avid devotee of some activity or subject owes its life to *buffalo*. Buffalo robes were the winter gear of firemen in the middle of the 19th century. The amateur firefighters who rushed to blazes emulated the professionals by wearing buffcoats made of buffalo skins and were called buffs as a result. The expression *in the buff*, "in the nude," derives from the soft yellow buff skins made from buffalo hides, which looked something like bare human skin tanned by the sun. Buff is also one of the most unusual acronym nicknames. According to Frederick Forsyth in *The Fist of God* (1993): "The B-52 Stratofortress [bomber] is not called the Buff because it is painted a tan or dun-brown color. The word is not even a derivation of the first two syllables of its number—*Bee-Fifty-two*. It just stands for Big Ugly Fat Fucker." Buffs dropped 40 percent of the entire bomb tonnage during the Gulf War. Each plane can carry 51 750-pound bombs.

buffalo. Most people believe that *buffalo* is a misnomer, a name applied with zoological inexactitude to the American bison. Cortes described the creature as "a rare Mexican bull, with crooked shoulders, a hump on its back like a camel and with hair like a lion," but later explorers thought it was the Asian or African water buffalo and called it after the Spanish *bufalo*, already used in Europe as the name for those animals. Actually the water buffalo and the American buffalo both belong to the bison family, so the real mistake of early explorers was in calling the native American animal simply *buffalo* and not qualifying it with a name such as *prairie buffalo*.

Buffalo Bill. Colonel William Frederick Cody (1846–1917), the peerless horseman and sharpshooter who became the original Buffalo Bill, earned his nickname as a market hunter for buffalo (bison) hides and as a contractor supplying buffalo meat to workers building the Union Pacific Railroad in 1867. To his glory then, and shame now, he killed 4,280 buffalo in one year, mostly for their hides and tongues. It is hard to separate truth from fiction in Cody's life, his fame owing much to the dime novels that made him a celebrity in the late 19th century. Buffalo Bill was a herder, a Pony Express rider, a scout and cavalryman for the U.S. Army in the Civil War, and an Indian fighter who is said to have killed the Cheyenne chief Yellowhand single-handedly. He was a member of the Nebraska state legislature. His Wild West Show, which he organized in 1883, toured the United States and Europe, bringing him great personal fame, yet financial problems caused this legendary American hero to die in poverty and relative obscurity. Today his name conjures up visions of "sportsmen" picking off buffalo from the platforms of moving trains, abundant buffalo meat rotting on the plains, and the destruction of the great herds. Thanks to early conservationists, some 20,000 American bison survive today, protected on government ranges.

buffalo chips. Dried buffalo dung. Louis L'Amour describes their gathering and use by wagon team women in his novel *Comstock Lode* (1981): "There was a space of wagon-tongue lashed there and a sheet of canvas . . . 'What's that for?' 'Buffalo chips,' a bystander said. 'The women folks walk behind the wagon and pick up buffalo chips and toss them onto that canvas. They're the only fuel you are likely to find.'" American resourcefulness at its most fundamental.

buffalo soldier. An American Indian name for African-American soldiers stationed in the West. One explanation of the name is given by F. M. A. Roe in *Army Letters* (1872): "The officers say the negroes make good soldiers and fight like fiends . . . The Indians call them 'buffalo soldiers,' because their wooly heads are so much like the matted cushion that is between the horns of the buffalo." *The Encyclopedia of African-American Heritage* (2000) states "The name is said to have originated with the Plains Indians, who likened the soldier's bravery to that of the buffalo, and because the soldiers' curly black hair was reminiscent of a buffalo mane."

bug; insect. The word *bug* originally had nothing to do with insects, possibly deriving from the Welsh *bwg*, "a specter or a ghost." How *bug* came to mean *insect* (insect is short for the Latin *animal insectum*, an "animal notched near the middle")

no one knows, but perhaps the beetles and other insects first called *bugs* terrified some people, suggesting supernatural creatures. Another possible source is the West African word *baga-baga*, "insect," which the English may have encountered in the slave trade. *Bug* is first recorded in 1642. Some etymologists trace the *bug* in "don't bug me" to the West African *bugu*, "annoy." This may be so, but if the term did come to America with slavery, there should be earlier references to it than we have, *bug* only being recorded in this sense since the early 1950s. *Bug* for "annoy" may also have derived in some roundabout way from one of the many other slang uses of *bug*, including an obsessed person, a trick, or even *bugging* a person's telephone calls surreptitiously. It could also derive from BUGGER for sodomy, or from BOGEY. *Bug* in the sense of a defect ("This new model car has a lot of *bugs* in it") does not derive from the moths that supposedly plagued the first U.S. experimental computers in the 1940s, as the old story goes. Used long before then, *bug* is most likely a form of bogey, in this case, "a real thing that causes worry." The bug used to wiretap a telephone or a room may have its origin in bogey, being "a device that causes worry, even terror." But the term has its origins in the underworld and could be a shortened form of *burglar alarm*—back in the '20s advertisements used to say that premises protected with burglar alarms were *bugged*. In racing terminology, a *bug* means the weight allowance granted to a horse because the jockey riding him is an apprentice; the apprentice jockey himself is also called a bug. This term comes from the asterisk appearing on racing forms next to the weight of a horse granted such an allowance. In printing jargon an asterisk, being small, was called a bug, and the term was adopted by horseplayers.

The Bug Bible. Numerous editions of the Bible have been named for their translators or patrons, the most famous being the *King James* or *Authorized Version*, which was prepared by a group of British scholars working at the command of King James I from 1604 to 1611. James commissioned this version mainly because other Bibles of the time had marginal notes questioning the divine right of kings. *Coverdale's Bible, Crammer's Bible, Cromwell's Bible, Matthew's Bible, Matthew Parker's Bible, Taverner's Bible, Tyndale's Bible,* and *Wycliffe's Bible* are all famous in history. *Coverdale's Bible* is sometimes known as *The Bug Bible* because it reads "Thou shalt not need to be afraid for any bugs by night" in a passage from *Psalms*, using "bugs" instead of "terror" in the sentence. Other amusing instances of printer's errors occur in *The Wicked Bible* (1805), where the seventh commandment reads "Thou shalt commit adultery"; the *Unrighteous Bible*, which says that "the unrighteous shall inherit the Kingdom of God"; and *The Sin On Bible*, which in the book of *John* reads "sin on more" instead of "sin no more." There is even a *Vegetarian Bible* and one with no references to sex. *See also* GUTENBERG BIBLE.

bug-eater. A humorous, derisive nickname for a Nebraskan. The name comes either from some Nebraskans's impoverished appearance in times past, or from parts of the state being overrun by locusts; suggestions were even made at one time to make food of the locusts, one farmer writing a cookbook with the theme "If you can't beat 'em, eat 'em." According to *Notes* *and Queries*, June 15, 1883: "Several Nebraskan entomologists and journalists actually got up a dinner at which locusts were served in various styles."

bugger. *Bugger* in British English never means a child, as it does in American expressions like "he's just a little bugger." A *bugger* in England is only a sodomite and *to bugger* is to sodomize—in fact, use of the word in print was actionable in England for many years. *Bugger* in this sense, which is American slang as well, derives, down a tortuous path, from the Medieval Latin *Bulgarus*, meaning "both a Bulgarian and a sodomite." The word first referred to a Bulgarian and then to the Bulgarian Albigenses or Bulgarian Heretics, an 11th-century religious sect whose monks and nuns were believed to practice sodomy. Some historians claim that the charge of sodomy against these heretic dissenters was a libel invented with the approval of the Church. They had already been banished from Bulgaria, were living in the south of France, and the trumped-up story caused the French to oust or exterminate them, too.

buggy. The horse carriage *buggy* is thought to derive from the old meaning of *bug*—"a specter or a ghost," often called a BOGEY. It seems that the light carriages were called "bogies" (which later became *buggie*) because they were so fast that they scared people out of their wits.

Bughouse Square. A popular name since the 1920s for the famous Chicago landmark Washington Square, where street corner orators and preachers hold forth. *Bughouse* can mean "insane" or "crazy," and many speakers past have seemed so. This name seems to have hobo origins.

bug juice. *Bug juice*, for "cheap liquor," is a century-old term that takes its name from the tobacco-colored secretion of grasshoppers.

bugle. The rude ancestor of this musical instrument was made from the horn of a young bull or bullock, a *buculus*, in early Roman times. *Buculus* passed into French and English as *bugle* and the *bugle horn*, or *bugle*, remained the name for the instrument well after it was no longer made from a bull's horn.

bug out; swanning. *To bug out*, "to retreat hastily," is an expression that dates back to the time of the Korean War, when it was first used by teenagers and then in the United Nations "police action" to indicate a military retreat. Since retreats are generally the result of fear, the expression is another one that probably derives in a roundabout way from "bugaboo" or "bogey." Incidentally, the migrating habits of the swan inspired the word *swanning*, "going purposefully anywhere without a purpose," which meant the same thing that *bugging out* did during the Korean War. Today *bug out* is also slang for "freak out" or "flip out."

build a better mousetrap. Ralph Waldo Emerson is often credited with "If you build a better mousetrap the world will beat a path to your door," mainly because a book entitled *Borrowings* by Sarah S. B. Yule and Mary Keene, published in 1889, reported that he had said it in a speech. But many scholars believe that Emerson was too wise to believe that the world would always seek out the best, and nothing concerning a mousetrap can be found in any of Emerson's published writings.

build (or set) a fire under. Ornery mules may be responsible for the expression to set a fire under, or "to stir someone to action or movement": southern farmers, it is said, sometimes built fires under their mules to get the beasts to move when they were standing with four legs spread and refusing to budge despite every other tactic. Palmer Clark, research librarian at the Van Noy Library in Fort Belvoir, Virginia, advises that relatives of hers in the "chuggy huggy hills of Tennessee" were familiar with the practice. "Aunt Clellie," Mrs. Clark writes, "said when she was a young girl, loads of cedar were transported to Murfreesboro from Hall's Hill Pike. She distinctly remembered that her brother-in-law . . . literally and actually built fires under the mules who hauled the cedar to get them going [this about 1921 or 1922 in middle Tennessee]."

bull; phallus. *Bull*, for "the male of any bovine animal," is first recorded in about 1200 and derives from the Old English *bula*, "bull." The word is akin to the Greek *phallos*, "phallus," which comes from an Indo-European root meaning "to swell up." *Bull* as an opprobrious Americanism for a policeman, or prison guard, came into the language in 1893 from the Spanish Gypsy *bul*, policeman.

bull! *Bull!*, in the sense of "a lie, an exaggeration, an incredible concocted story," was first recorded in 1911 and is not a euphemism for the euphemistic "booshwah" (which derives from the French *bois de vache*, "cow's wood" or "dried dung"). It has nothing to do with a papal bull either or, for that matter, with Irish bulls (ludicrous incongruities such as "It's grand to be alone, especially if your swateheart is wid you"). No one can say for sure just how the expression originated. *Bull!* may have passed into English via the French *boule*, meaning "fraud." Or it could come from a "cock and bull story," an expression that dates back to at least the early 17th century. Another explanation is that it's simply a shortening of *bullshit*, which was first recorded in 1928, but it was probably around long before that. Still another has it deriving from the American expression "I wouldn't trust him as far as I could throw [fling] a bull," dating back to the 1830s. The papal *bull* comes from the Latin *bulla* for the heavy leaden seal attached to papal edicts, while the term *Irish bull* may derive from either the Middle English *bull*, to cheat, or the Old French *boule*, fraud.

bulldog. This breed of dog takes its name from the so-called sport it was bred for, not because it bears any resemblance to a bull. Bulldogs were bred centuries ago for bull-baiting "contests" held in England until they were outlawed by Parliament in 1835. A bull was chained to a stake in the center of the arena and then whipped into a frenzy when dogs were loosed upon it. The dogs had to be able to get by the bull's horns, seize its nose, and hang on tenaciously. Therefore, they were bred to be strong, savage, courageous animals with a low center of gravity and an undershot jaw. These bulldogs were often killed, but the bull could *never* win: if it killed several bulldogs, more were set upon it. Because of its courage and tenacity the bulldog became a symbol of England. Over the years much of the savage aggressiveness has been bred out of the animal. *See* PIT BULL.

bulldog edition. In the 1890s several New York City newspapers brought out early-morning editions that came to be called bulldog editions, possibly because the newspapers "fought like bulldogs" among themselves in their circulation wars.

bulldogging. "One of the men . . . reached well over the animal's back to get a slack of the loose hide next the belly, lifted strongly, and tripped. This is called 'bulldogging.' " So did an early writer describe the way cowboys wrestled steers to the ground in the American West. They often, however, leaped from their horses and twisted the cow's neck, flipping it over. Neither method suggests the way bulldogs fought bulls when such cruel contests were held in England—for the bulldog seized the bull's nose in its mouth. Esse F. O'Brien's *The First Bulldogger* (1961) therefore suggests that a black cowboy named Bill Pickett is responsible for the word—Pickett would sink his teeth into a bull's nose while wrestling it to the ground, his method being responsible for the name of the more conventional method!

bulldozer. The earth-moving bulldozer takes its name from a band of political terrorists. After the Civil War, a group of Louisiana vigilantes, who brutally prevented freed slaves from voting freely, were termed "bulldozers," the word first printed in an 1876 newspaper account of their activities. It is not certain whether they were whites forcing blacks to vote Democratic, Republican Negroes forcing their brothers *not* to vote Democratic, or groups of both. Neither is the exact origin of their name clear—it probably came from *bulldose*, to mete out a "dose of the bull" with the long heavy bullwhip often made from the animal's penis. *Bulldozer* was soon used for "a revolver" and to describe anyone resembling the original terrorist bullies. Later the huge earth-moving machine, which brutally pushes everything in its path aside, became a natural candidate for the designation. Few people realize that when someone is called a *bulldozer* today he is being named not for the machine, but for the vigilantes so much like him. *See also* DERRICK; MONKEY WRENCH.

bullfight. Ernest Hemingway commented on this term in *The Sun Also Rises* (1926): "He [the matador] was very bashful about his English . . . Bull-fight he was suspicious of. I explained that bull-fight in Spanish was the *lidia* [fighting] of a *toro* . . . There is no Spanish word for bull-fight." In English *bullfight* dates back to about 1745. *See* AFICIONADO.

bullhorn. *See* MEGAPHONE.

bull in a china shop. Back in 1936 bandleader Fred Waring lost a bet to actor Paul Douglas and had to lead a bull through Plummer's China Shop in New York City. Waring agreed to make good any damage the bull might do, but Ferdinand walked up and down the aisles with aristocratic grace, whereas his leader knocked over a table of china. Obviously bulls aren't as clumsy and reckless in delicate situations as the old saying holds, but the expression has been common in English since before 1834, when Frederick Marryat used it in his novel *Jacob Faithful.*

bullion. Meaning gold or silver in the mass, or in bars or ingot form, *bullion* derives from the French *bouillir*, "to boil," referring to the boiling or melting of the metal before it is made into bars or ingots. The word is first recorded in the 14th century.

bull pen. Early in this century the imposing Bull Durham Tobacco signs behind outfield fences in American baseball parks pictured a big brightly colored bull, proclaiming that any batter whose home run hit the bull would get $50 and two bags of Bull Durham. Pitchers usually warmed up near these Bull Durham signs, which may be why warm-up areas for relief pitchers are called *bull pens* today, although the word could have derived from the word *bull pen* that had meant a stockade for prisoners since 1809. Or perhaps the two meanings reinforced each other.

bull's-eye. There are many plausible ways to explain this term, all of them based on a bull's eye, which is about the same size as the small black spot at the dead center of a target. Bull's-eye targets were not used in ancient archery contests, as is commonly thought, but were introduced to England as targets in rifle and handgun competition. Perhaps the bull's-eyes in them were simply named for their resemblance to a bull's eye. But it is possible that bull's-eyes take their name from a British coin called the bull's-eye, which was worth a crown, or five shillings. This coin was in circulation in the early 1800s, about the time bull's-eye targets were introduced, and it would seem more logical to name the flat target centers after flat coins than after the round eye of a bull. As for the coin, it was so named in the late 17th century, possibly because the one-crown piece was often bet on the outcome of a bull-baiting contest; when one put money "on the bull's eye" one was betting on the bull, just as today we are said to put a bet on a horse's nose.

bullshit. Utter nonsense, a flagrant, outrageous lie. This American expletive is first recorded in 1914 but is almost certainly a century or more older. Common euphemisms for it include bull, bushwa, and BS. Flinging, slinging, and throwing the bull is done by a bullshit artist—and much less commonly, a Spanish athlete. "I enclose a prize sample of bullshit," James Joyce wrote in a 1914 letter to Ezra Pound. *See* SHIT.

bum; on the bum. No self-respecting hobo, or tramp, would allow himself to be called a bum, for the word has degenerated from its original meaning of "a vagabond" over a century ago, and today usually stands for a "moneyless, prideless, filthy, hopeless derelict and habitual drunkard." One working definition to distinguish between the three classes of vagabonds is that "a hobo will work, a tramp won't, a bum can't." *Bum* was first recorded in 1855, and during the Civil War was used to describe a foraging soldier. It appears to derive from two words: the German *bummer*, "a high-spirited, irresponsible person," and the old English word *bum*, which has for over four centuries been slang for both "a drunk" and "the buttocks." By the turn of the century a *bum* was the pitiable creature described above instead of a romantic vagabond singing the song of the open road. The term is also used today to describe any no-good person and has a score more uses, including terms like *tennis bum* and *ski bum*. *On the bum* is an American expression dating back to San Francisco Gold Rush days, when it simply meant living the life of a hobo. Later humorist George Ade used the slang term to mean someone not feeling well, and from this use derives our expression *on the bum* for something that isn't working well. *Bum* for a drunken loafer or vagrant is first recorded in reference to men who lost their fortunes in the California gold rush. To *bum*, to borrow or panhandle money, comes from the practice of bums begging in the streets. *Bum*, for "the buttocks" is a very old word dating from Middle English; only within the past two centuries has it become a vulgar expression. *Bum* now is apparently not an abbreviation of "bottom" but an echoic word. A long-suppressed nursery rhyme goes:

> Piss a bed
> Bailey Butt,
> Your Bum is so heavy
> You can't get up!

bumashka. *Bumashka*, a pejorative form of *bumage*, "paper," is the Russian term for GOBBLEDYGOOK or "officialese." Much of this existed in the Soviet Union, as in America, one government directive calling for "the mobilization of personnel for the removal of dust."

bumboat. In the early 17th century, bumboats (also called dirtboats) were scavengers' boats used to remove filth from ships anchored in the Thames. Their name ultimately derives from the medieval *bum*, for "buttocks," a word of echoic origin imitative of "the sound of breaking wind." The bumboats' crews used to sell fresh vegetables to the ships in the harbor, so these craft came to be known as "any boat employed to carry provisions, vegetables, and small merchandise for sale to ships, either in port or lying at a distance from shore."

bumf. A word, British in origin, for what Americans more frequently call GOBBLEDYEGOOK. *Bumf* is a shortening of *bum fodder*, "toilet paper," and refers to the reams of directives issued by government agencies. The *bum* in *bum fodder* refers of course to the buttocks.

Bummers. A Southern nickname for Union general William Tecumseh Sherman's soldiers as they made their way plundering and burning across Georgia in Sherman's fabled March to the Sea during the Civil War. They were also called "scabs," "huns," "scavengers," "hateful," "despised," "fiends," "red-handed devils," and "human fungi." But *Bummer* became the only word more anathema to Southerners than that hated word *Yankee*. After looting a town named Barnwell, the Bummers set it on fire and jokingly renamed it Burnwell. *See* SHERMAN'S HAIRPINS.

bummie. Shepherds give this name to a lamb that has lost its mother, or whose mother has deserted it, and which has to be raised by humans or by another ewe tricked into believing the lamb is her own. Also called a bummer, a bum, and a lappie.

bump. The prevailing theory is that *bump* was first an onomatopoeic word meaning "a knock or blow," the swelling or protuberance arising from the knocking or bumping becoming known as a *bump* as well. The trouble is that the *bump* for "a swelling" is the first recorded of the two words, by Shakespeare in *Romeo and Juliet* (1592): "It had upon its brow a bumpe as big as a young Cockrel's stone [testicle] . . ." Being *bumped* from

a list, such as an airline passenger list, is a fairly recent and widespread Americanism. *Bump* also refers to a gesture that was probably born in the 1970s. Sometimes called the *fist bump*, it is fast replacing *high-five* and *low-five* among young people. Some trace its origins to professional basketball, where the great "Earl the Pearl" Monroe was a pioneer bumper. Others claim characters in *The Superfriends*, a 1973 cartoon show, first used the bump. There are several possible ancestors, too, including the punch to the muscle of the upper arm popular in the 1950s. In any case, *bump* means "a light bumping of fists" and is not an aggressive gesture.

bumper crop. *Bumper*, in the sense of "something large," is only heard today in the expression *a bumper crop*, one that is extraordinarily abundant, as in "We had a bumper crop of tomatoes."

bump off. The underworld slang for to kill or murder may have its origins in the relatively genteel world of British boating. The theory is that *bump off* derives from a rule in boat racing that disqualified any shell that was bumped by the boat behind it. This elimination regulation was familiar to gamblers betting on the races, proponents argue, and the term passed into the lexicon of the British underworld. Neither the *Oxford English Dictionary* nor the late British slang authority Eric Partridge support this theory, simply citing *bump off* as an Americanism first recorded in 1910.

bump on a log. "Ye ain't goin to set there like a bump on a log 'thout sayin' a word to pay fer yer vittles, air ye?" This recorded use of the above American expression, from Kate Douglas Wiggins's *The Bird's Christmas Carol* (1899), uses the words as they are still used today and best defines them. The metaphor is a good one, for a log is stolid and stupid, and a bump on a log seems all the more so. Also, sitting next to someone who is *like a bump on a log*, who just sits silently without being able to make conversation, is as uncomfortable as sitting on a bump on a log.

bundling. In the late 1700s many tracts pro and con were written about the custom of bundling, which was all the rage in America at the time. When bundling, courting couples would lie in the same bed partly or fully clothed, sometimes with a special bundling board between them. Often the bundling board was breached or hurdled and the couples groped in the dark for additional ways to keep warm, and that is where the controversy came in. In his *Classical Dictionary of the Vulgar Tongue*, Grose defined *bundling* as "A man and woman lying on the same bed with their clothes on; an expedient practiced in America on a scarcity of beds, where, on such occasions, husbands and parents frequently permitted travelers to 'bundle' with their wives and daughters." But there was more to the practice than the scarcity of beds or the lack of heat, as Washington Irving noted in his *History of New York*. Irving cited those "cunning and ingenious" Yankees who permitted young couples to bundle due to their "strict adherence to the good old pithy maxim about 'buying a pig in a poke.'" On the other hand, one old gentleman, explaining the custom to his grandson late in the 19th century, emphasized the practicality of bundling and denied any wrongdoing on the part of the participants.

"What is the use of sitting up all night and burning out fire and lights, when you could just as well get under cover and keep warm?" he said. "Why, damn it, there wasn't half as many bastards then as there are now!" In any event, bundling was with us from the beginning in America and came close to being a universal custom from 1700 to 1780.

bungalow.   In India a *bangala* is a one-story thatched or tiled house surrounded by a verandah. Its name literally means "of Bengal," where such dwellings are common. The British in India borrowed the word, which changed to *bungalow* over the years, applying it to any cottage of one story. In America a bungalow usually has one-and-a-half stories and a gabled roof, among other characteristics, but the word is also used here loosely to mean any small dwelling.

bungay.   For reasons unclear, the old town of Bungay in Suffolk, England, is associated with stupidity, perhaps because *Bungay* sounds like "bungle." In any case, the British have long called any stupid play in whist, such as when one leads with the highest scoring card, a bungay.

bung-o!   A British toast that lives on in Hemingway's *The Sun Also Rises* (1926), if nowhere else. Hemingway characters, notably Lady Brett, use the word several times, Brett shortly before she makes her famous remark, "You know it makes one feel rather good deciding not to be a bitch."

bunk.   The Missouri Compromise was being hotly debated the morning of February 25, 1820 when long-winded Congressman Felix Walker of Buncombe County, North Carolina rose on the floor of the House of Representatives and insisted that he be heard before a vote was taken. "Old Oil Jug," as his fellow congressmen called him after his well-lubricated vocal cords, did not address himself to the monumental question of the extension of slavery; his interminable oration actually had little to do with anything and important members began interrupting him with cries of "Question, Question!" On being asked what purpose his speech served, Walker calmy remarked, "You're not hurting my feelings, gentlemen. I am not speaking for your ears. I am only talking for Buncombe." Old Oil Jug apparently had written his speech some time before and believed he would ingratiate himself with the voters back home if he delivered it in the midst of a great debate, but the strategy didn't work, judging by the fact that he lost the next election. Yet his reply, "I am talking for Buncombe," was widely published in newspapers covering the debate and became a synonym for talking nonsense. Eventually, *Buncombe* became *bunkum* and it finally took the shortened form of *bunk* (in the 1850s), meaning not only "bombastic political talk," but "any empty, inflated speech obviously meant to fool people."

bunko.   Any swindler or cheat, from the Spanish *banca* (a game of chance at cards). The term originated in the U.S., Herbert Asbury advising in *Sucker's Progress* (1938): "Eight-Dice Cloth was introduced into San Francisco by a crooked gambler who made various changes in the method of play and christened it Banco. After a few years this was corrupted into Bunco, sometimes spelled Bunko, and in time Bunco came to be a general term applied to all swindling and confidence games."

bunny.   *Bunny*, as in the *Easter bunny* or a *Playboy bunny*, has its origins in the Scottish dialect word *bun*, which according to some scholars, originally meant just the tail of a rabbit or a squirrel. By 1690 *bun* had been extended to *bunny* and had become the pet name for a rabbit.

Bunsen burner; bunsenite.   Robert Wilhelm Bunsen (1811–99) invented the Bunsen burner that is standard equipment in every chemistry laboratory. This laboratory burner, which mixes gas with air to produce a hot smokeless flame, wasn't the only scientific contribution the German chemist made. He discovered, with Gustav Kirchhoff, the elements cesium and rubidium, and shared with Henry Roscoe the discovery of the reciprocity law, doing much original work in spectrum analysis. The Heidelberg professor also has bunsenite, a nickel monoxide, named in his honor.

bunt.   The bunt in baseball, used mostly by a batter as a sacrifice play to advance another runner into better scoring position, is probably a corruption of the word *butt*, which sounds like *bunt* when spoken through the nose. Hitters butt at the ball with the bat when they bunt. *Bunt* dates back to at least 1872, when the strategy's first use is recorded by a player named Pearce on the Brooklyn Atlantics.

Buntlinism.   Ned Buntline was the pen name of Edward Z. C. Judson (1823–86), an adventurer, trapper and soldier in the Far West whose life pales even those of the heroes of the more than 400 dime novels he wrote. This founder of the Know-Nothing party, rioter and accused murderer gave William Cody the name Buffalo Bill and featured him in a series of dime novels. His rowdy, jingoistic political doctrine inspired the term *Buntlinism*.

buoy; buoyant.   Pronounced "boy" in England and by many sailors and some landlubbers in America (as in Lifebuoy soap), the word *buoy* (also pronounced "boo-i") has no etymological connection with "boy." *Buoy* comes from the Old French *boye* meaning "chained," in reference to the chain that holds a buoy in place. However, the chain is invisible to anyone looking at a *buoy* and *buoys* came, ironically enough, to suggest lightness and freedom (the opposite of being chained) to onlookers, giving us the words *buoyant* and *buoyancy*. This was perhaps because of the floating action of the buoy itself.

Burbank; Burbank plum; Burbank potato.   There has been muted controversy over whether the plant breeder Luther Burbank (1849–1926) was a "plant wizard" or something of a failure. Burbank was born in Lancaster, Massachusetts, and there developed the Burbank potato, his most important achievement, while just a boy experimenting with seeds in his mother's garden. At 26 he moved to Santa Rosa, California, using the $150 he made from the sale of his potato to pay for the journey. It was in Santa Rosa, his "chosen spot of the earth," that he bred almost all the varieties of fruit, vegetables, and ornamentals for which he became famous. These included at least 66 new fruits, 12 new bush fruits, seven tree nuts, and nine vegetables, of which a number, notably the Burbank plum, bear his name. He once grew half a million strawberry plants to obtain one prize plant. However, according to Dr. W. L. Howard (University of California Agricultural Experiment Station Bulletin, 1945), only a few of the several hundred varieties developed by Burbank have stood the test of time. The patient Burbank was not the first American plant breeder—Thomas Jefferson, George Washington Carver, and Charles Hovey, originator of the Hovey strawberry, came long before him. Burbank was strongly influenced by Darwin's *The Variation of Animals and Plants Under Domestication*. His credo can be summed up in his statement "I shall be contented if, because of me, there shall be better fruits and fairer flowers." Burbank did have a sense of humor, unlike some of his critics. The renowned horticulturist was working in his experimental garden one day when approached by an obnoxious neighbor:

"Well, what on earth are you working on now?"
   the man asked.
"I'm trying to cross an eggplant and milkweed,"
   Burbank replied.
"What in heaven do you expect to get from that?"
   asked the neighbor.
"Custard pie," said Burbank calmly.

The city of Burbank, California was named for the famous plant breeder.

burbs; suburb.   For better or worse, *burbs* has been American slang for *suburbs* for the last decade or so. I record it here mainly because I haven't seen it in any dictionary. *Suburbs* wasn't used much in America until about 1940, though the word dates back to 14th-century England, where it meant residential areas outside a town or city, deriving from the Latin *suburbium*, formed from *sub*, "near," and *urbs*, "city."

burdock.   *Burdock* (of the genus *Arctium*), or *gobo*, as it is also called, has been recommended as a marvelous aphrodisiac by several ancient writers, but it is generally considered a garden weed today, one of the 50 worst weeds of all time. It's that little plant whose prickly burrs commonly stick to clothing. There's obviously nothing stimulating about eating the burrs or about rolling around in a field of burdock.

burgoo.   The rich southern American stew called *burgoo* probably takes its name from a similar stew that American seamen used to make, which, in turn, may derive its name from the Arabic *burghul*, "bruised grain." The word, however, is first recorded out West as *burgou*, in 1837, and may be a corruption of "barbecue." Someone has noted about *burgoo:* "No two people tell the same story about its origin and no two people will give you the same recipe."

burgoynade.   "Gentleman Johnny" Burgoyne hardly deserved his fate. General John Burgoyne (1722–92), an accomplished dramatist as well as a soldier, commanded the British forces that came down from Canada to capture New York's Fort Ticonderoga during the Revolutionary War. It was his intention to join with Howe's army farther downstate, but due to a delay on Howe's part, excellent American tactics, and enemy forces three times the strength of his own, he was forced to surrender after the battle of Saratoga. English Tories condemned him for his alleged use of savage Indians, and his name in the form of *burgoynade* came to mean the capture of a notable person, particularly a general or high-ranking officer.

burgundy.   Burgundy wines are usually red wines made from grapes from the French province of Burgundy, especially the area between Dijon and Chalons. The province, in turn, takes its name from the Medieval Latin *Burgundia*, land of the Burgunds (a German tribe). When one thinks of burgundy, one often remembers James Thurber's famous put-down in a caption to a *New Yorker* cartoon depicting a wine-snob saying to another: "It's a naive domestic Burgundy without any breeding, but I think you'll be amused by its presumption."

burial of an ass.   This is a biblical term meaning no burial at all, burial with the body thrown on a refuse heap. The expression is from Jeremiah 22:9: "He shall be buried with the burial of an ass, drawn and cast forth beyond the gates of Jerusalem."

Buridan's ass.   Buridan's ass is "a hypothetical beast that stands exactly between two haystacks in every respect equal and starves to death because there is no reason why it should eat from one rather than the other." The argument is a sophism, false because it ignores the fact that random choice remains when choice based on knowledge is impossible. Aristotle knew that the argument was specious when he drew the analogy in his *De Caelo* ("On the Heavens"), where he used it to criticize a theory of an earlier writer. However, the French scholastic philosopher Jean Buridan (ca. 1295–1356) accepted it as a philosophical principle when he wrote a commentary on Aristotle's work. Buridan used a dog dying of hunger between two equally tempting dishes of food to illustrate the will's paralysis when confronted with two equal choices and his philosophical sophism should really be called Buridan's dog. How *Buridan's dog* became *Buridan's ass* remains something of a mystery. Aristotle used a *man* standing between food and drink in his analogy, so there is no help there. What probably happened was that Buridan's opponents substituted the ass, long a symbol of stupidity, for the dog in Buridan's analogy in order to deride his doctrine. Other myths about the rector of the University of Paris, as false as *Buridan's ass*, insist that he founded Vienna University and was the lover of Joan of Navarre and/ or Margaret of Burgundy, both queens of France.

buried; buried in booze.   *Buried*, and sometimes *buried in booze*, was popular slang for "dead drunk" in the 1920s during Prohibition, when the ingredients in BOOZE could kill more quickly.

burka.   It was compulsory for all Muslim women to wear this loose garment when the Taliban ruled in Afghanistan. It covers the whole body, its only opening being a slit for the eyes, even this covered by pieces of cotton-mesh. It has been called a "head-to-toe shroud."

burke.   The best-known of eponymous murderers and among the most unwise, William Burke (1792–1829) was an Irish laborer who emigrated to Scotland in 1817. There he eventually opened a used-clothing store in Edinburgh and, far more important, rented a room from William Hare, a fellow Irishman and owner of a boardinghouse catering to vagrants and elderly pensioners. It was in 1827 that Burke and Hare embarked upon their career. One of Hare's lodgers—an old man named Donald—had died owing him four pounds, and the landlord convinced Burke that they had stumbled upon an easy source of income. Ripping the cover off the coffin in which parish authorities had sealed Donald, the pair hid his body in a bed and filled the coffin with tanner's bark, resealing it and later selling the cadaver for seven pounds 10 shillings to Dr. Robert Knox, who ran an anatomy school in Surgeon's Square.

Burke and Hare soon expanded their operation. Another boarder lingered too long at death's door and they helped him through, smothering the man with a pillow and selling his body to Knox for 10 pounds. Hare and his wife, and Burke and his mistress, Helen McDougal, proceeded to dispatch from 14 to 28 more unfortunates in similar fashion, receiving up to 14 pounds for each body. They were careful to smother their victims, leaving no marks of violence, so that it would appear that they were merely grave robbers. Whenever the boarding-house supply ran low, they lured victims there, usually choosing old hags, drunks, and prostitutes, whom they often plied with drink. If a candidate offered too much resistance to being smothered by a pillow, Burke would pin him down while Hare smothered him, holding his hands over the victim's nose and mouth. But the murderers eventually got careless.

First they killed Mary Peterson, a voluptuous 18-year-old, so free with her body that it was quickly recognized by Knox's young medical students, who even preserved it before dissection as a perfect example of female pulchritude. Then they did in "Daft Jamie" Wilson, a familiar, good-natured imbecile who made his living running errands on the streets of Edinburgh. Finally, the suspicions of neighbors aroused, police caught them with the body of a missing woman named Mary Dougherty. Hare turned state's evidence at the ensuing trial, which began on Christmas Eve; he and his wife were freed, and Helen McDougal was discharged for lack of evidence. Burke for some reason foolishly refused to give state's evidence. He was convicted and hanged a month later on January 28, 1829, before a crowd of some 30,000.

The word the murderer contributed to the language was even heard as he stood on the scaffold in the Grassmarket, spectators exhorting the executioner with cries of "Burke him, Burke him!" (*i.e.*, don't hang him but smother or strangle him to death). The crowd wanted to *burke* Hare, the real brains behind the operation, despite his immunity, but he escaped them and is believed to have died of natural causes many years later in England, where he lived under an assumed name.

Burke's Peerage.   Like DEBRETT'S PEERAGE before it, *Burke's Peerage* has often been called the "studbook" of the British aristocracy. Originally published in 1826, it was fully titled *A Genealogical and Heraldic History of the Peerage and Baronetage of the United Kingdom*, and has been issued annually since 1847. The famous reference book, the first alphabetical guide to the British aristocracy, was the inspiration of John Burke (1787–1848), an English genealogist whose family hailed from Tipperary. Burke's son Sir John Bernard, a genealogist and barrister, assisted him in the compilation, and began its annual re-editing. John Burke also published *Burke's Landed Gentry* (1833–38), another work well known by those interested in tracing lost ancestors.

Burleigh's nod.   *See* ALL THIS FOR A SONG; CECIL'S FEAST.

burlesque.   The American burlesque in which stripteasers performed owes something to traditional burlesque, which is comedy employing satire or caricature (the word *burlesque* in fact deriving from the Italian *burla*, ridicule). But burlesque derived more directly from the minstrel show and variety theater. American burlesque, rarely produced today, featured often raunchy dialect and slapstick comedians, song and dance acts, and scantily dressed chorus girls as well as bump-and-grind strippers. It operated in circuits distinct from vaudeville after the turn of the 20th century, mainly in the Columbia and Empire Circuits, and grew more daring until police raids inspired by laws proposed by New York mayor La Guardia led to the closing of the famed Minsky burlesque houses and others during the Great Depression. The best-known and most artistic stripper of the golden era was Gypsy Rose Lee (born Rose Louise Hovick), who began her show business career as a child song-and-dance act and wrote mystery novels after her burlesque days ended. Fanny Brice, Bobby Clark, Phil Silvers, and Abbott and Costello were among the many great talents who worked in burlesque. *See* ECDYSICST; VAUDEVILLE.

burning ears; itching ears.   Pliny writes: "When our ears do glow and tingle, some do talk of us in our absence." This superstition probably goes back before the ancient Romans and is recorded early in English, Shakespeare writing of "fire in mine ears." *To have itching ears*, "to enjoy hearing gossip," is perhaps even older, the words recorded in the Bible (2 Tim. 3:3).

burning the midnight oil; it smells of the lamp.

> Wee spend our mid-day sweat, or mid-night oyle;
> Wee tyre the night in thought; the day in toyle.

I've read that this saying is of American origin, but it obviously isn't, judging by the above poem by Francis Quarles, English author and later "chronologer to the City of London," who first recorded the expression in the mid-17th century. Oils of many types were of course widely used for lamps long before American petroleum made low-priced lamplight available. The words mean "to sit up late at night working," especially in the pursuit of learning. *It smells of the lamp* (Latin, *olet lucernam*) is an equally old saying, referring to literary work that is overworked and tired from too much burning of the midnight oil. Of authors who consistently burned the midnight oil, Honoré de Balzac is the best example. Like Pliny the Elder before him, Balzac liked to begin work at midnight and write for 18 hours at a stretch. He did this for weeks on end and was so meticulous a craftsman that he often completely rewrote his novels in proof.

burn one's fingers.   To be harmed by meddling with something. Several sources suggest that the allusion here is to taking chestnuts from the fire. But there is no evidence for this in the first recorded use of the phrase in a 1710 book of English proverbs: "The busiebody burns his own fingers."

burn or hang in effigy.   I've found effigies washed up on New York City beaches several times—once two small plastic dolls bound together face-to-face with the names of lovers taped on their foreheads and hundreds of pins stuck in their bodies; on another occasion, an unhusked coconut that represented the head of a real person and had a message carved on it, urging her death. This handiwork of members of local voodoo cults shows that the practice of executing, burning, or hanging people in effigy still exists, as it has since prehistory. It means, of course, "to vent one's wrath on a facsimile or copy of a hated person in the hope of insulting him or actually harming him." Apparently, no one gave a name to the practice until the 17th century, when the phrase *in effigy* is first recorded in a beautiful sermon of John Donne (1617): "In those that are damned before, we are damned in Effigie." *Effigy* itself, for "a likeness or image," is from the Latin *effigies*, meaning the same, and was first written *effigies* until this was mistaken for a plural and the *s* that should be in the word was dropped. The practice of hanging people in effigy to disgrace them publicly dates back long before the French Revolution, when it was customary for the public executioners to hang an effigy of a criminal if the criminal himself couldn't be found.

Burnside carbine; Burnside hat. *See* SIDEBURNS.

burn the candle at both ends.

> My candle burns at both ends;
> It will not last the night;
> But ah, my foes, and oh, my friends—
> It gives a lovely light!
>
> —Edna St. Vincent Millay,
> "First Fig" (1920)

These are the words I remember when I hear the above expression; Millay's bright brief candle shows how even an old hackneyed phrase can be transmuted into poetry. The phrase goes back to the early 17th century in English and is much older, for it was translated then from the French *Bruloient la chandelle par less deux bouts*. Originally the expression meant to waste material wealth; that is, to use the candle wastefully. Then it took on its more common modern meaning of wasting one's strength, as when someone goes from his day job to one he holds at night, or works for a worthy cause every moment of his spare time, or even does too much partying after work.

burn your bridges behind you. This expression may have originally been "burn your boats behind you," which originated with the Romans. Roman generals, including Caesar, often did burn all their boats after invading an alien land to impress upon their legions the fact that there could be no retreat. Later, bridges were burned for the same reason and the phrase to *burn your bridges behind you* came to mean, figuratively, to take a stand from which no withdrawal is feasible. *See* ANGLO-SAXON.

burrito. A tortilla wrapped around meat, beans, cheese, or other fillings. *Burrito* is Spanish for "little burro." The word was originally confined to the U.S. Southwest but is used nationwide now with the spreading popularity of Mexican food.

burro. A donkey, from the Spanish meaning the same; used mostly in the U.S., rarely in England.

bury the hatchet.

> Buried was the bloody hatchet;
> Buried was the dreadful war-club . . .
> There was peace among the nations.

Longfellow wrote this in *Hiawatha* (1855), but the expression *bury the hatchet*, "to settle all differences, to let bygones be bygones," goes back much further. Recorded as early as 1794, it stems from an old Indian custom. Crude stone axes, or hatchets, were long the most important weapon of northeastern American Indians. Such ceremony was attached to these tomahawks that when peace was made between two tribes, it was customary to take the tomahawks of both chiefs and bury them. When hostilities broke out again, the hatchets were dug up again as a declaration of war. The earliest record of this practice is found in the letters of American author Samuel Sewall, dated 1680: "Meeting with the Sachem they came to an agreement and buried two axes in the ground . . . which ceremony to them is more significant and binding than all the Articles of Peace, the hatchet being a principal weapon."

busboy. The waiter's assistant in restaurants, who clears dishes off tables and other tasks, takes his name from the *bus*, a "hand-pushed four-wheeled vehicle used typically for carrying dishes in restaurants." The term dates back to the late 19th century.

busby. *Busby*, once a large 18th-century bushy wig, is now the name for the plumed fur cap comprising part of the full-dress uniform of the British Hussars and Royal Home Artillery. It has long been thought to derive from the name of the noted schoolmaster and disciplinarian, Dr. Richard Busby (1606–95). Dr. Busby, headmaster of Westminster School, had among his pupils such greats as Dryden, Locke, and Prior, and once boasted that he at one time or another birched 16 of the bishops then in office with his "little rod." As far as is known, however, the good doctor did not wear a frizzled wig. Perhaps his hair naturally stood on end, suggesting the wig when it came into vogue, or possibly there was another Busby thus far unknown to history.

bush league. The Dutch *bosch*, "woods or forest," gave us our word early on for *bush*, "wilderness." By 1909 American baseball fans were calling the minor leagues the bush leagues, because they were out in the wilderness, away from the cities where professional teams played. *Bush league* and then *bush* soon came to mean anything amateur.

bushwacker. The first bushwackers weren't soldiers who hid in the woods or thickets carrying on guerrilla warfare. These bushwackers didn't appear until the Civil War, almost 50 years after the first bushwackers got their name from pulling their boats up parts of the Mississippi by grasping bushes along the bank. In more recent time *bushwacking* has also come to mean making one's way through unbroken forest, off the trail, by pushing bushes aside or breaking them.

business. *Business* derives from an Anglo-Saxon word, *bisigian*, which means "to worry, to fatigue, to occupy." All the earliest recorded uses of the word *business*, dating back to about 950, are to express anxiety, distress, and uneasiness, the word eventually coming to mean "a pursuit, occupation, or employment," its modern sense, only in about 1400.

business tomorrow. After the Spartans seized Thebes, Archias commanded the garrison in that Greek city. The enemy plotted to kill him, but were discovered, their plot revealed in a letter sent to Archias. Archias, however, was enjoying himself at that moment. He put the letter aside, remarking, "Business tomorrow." He was assassinated before the sun rose the next day.

busker. A *busker* is a street musician or other entertainer who performs on the street, in malls, at subway stations, or wherever one can entertain and solicit money for one's performances. *Busk*, in the sense of "to entertain," is first recorded in 1851, when *busking* was defined as "going into public houses [pubs] and playing and singing and dancing." The term is becoming quite common in large U.S. cities. No one is sure of *busk*'s origin, but it may derive from the French *brusquer*, "to seek."

buskin; sock; put on the buskin. *Buskin* for the high thick-soled boot (*cothurnus*), worn by actors to make them appear taller in ancient Greek tragedy, has been part of many languages since the 16th century, but its origin has never been established, and no one has been able to trace it back beyond the Middle Dutch *broseken*. Comic Greek actors wore a low shoe called the *sock*. Thus, *sock* is used allusively to denote comedy, and *to put on the buskins* means to write tragedy.

busman's holiday. An old story has a London bus driver spending his days off riding the bus he regularly drives, his peculiarity resulting in the expression *busman's holiday*, for "spending one's spare time doing what one regularly does for a living." But the story cannot be authenticated and the phrase, which is first recorded in 1921 but is probably 10 years or so older, must still be marked "origin unknown."

bust a gusset. To laugh hard or very heartily, as in "I like to bust a gusset laughing." *Gusset* refers to a piece of material added to a garment to make it fit more comfortably or roomier. To bust one, a person would have to laugh as hard or even harder than in *busting a gut* or *splitting a side*.

busted, by gosh! *See* PIKES PEAK OR BUST.

busy as a beaver. *See* BEAVER; EAGER BEAVER.

busy as a bee. "For aye as busy as bees been they," Chaucer wrote in *Canterbury Tales* (1387), the first recorded mention of the phrase. But bees must have been noticed busily collecting nectar since prehistoric days and no doubt the expression was used long before Chaucer's time. *Bee*, in fact, is a word found in all languages with Indo-European origins. That bees are busy there is no doubt—one pound of honey results from the visiting of some 10 million flowers where bees collect nectar, which they change to honey in their bodies.

busy as a one-armed paperhanger. This phrase is often attributed to cartoonist T(homas) A(loysius) Dorgan (1877–1929), but may have originated with O. Henry, who wrote in

a 1908 story: "Busy as a one-armed man with a nettle rash pasting on wall-paper."

Busy Lizzie. *See* TOUCH-ME-NOT.

Butch Cassidy. A fabled gunfighter; after the alias of George LeRoy Parker (1866–1909?), who once worked as a cattle butcher and later led a gang called the Wild Bunch, one of whose members was the Sundance Kid (Harry Longabaugh). Legend holds that he was killed in a gunfight with Bolivian troops, but his sister claimed that he visited her long after his alleged death.

butcher. There is a story of a 13th-century queen of France wedding a butcher, so esteemed was the trade at the time. Our word *butcher* does come to us from the French *bocher*, which derives from *boc*, "goat," all butchers originally having been slaughterers of goats before bloodying their hands with other animals.

butcher's dog. *See* LIE LIKE A BUTCHER'S DOG.

butler. *Butler* originally referred to a male servant in charge of wine and liquors, the word entering English in about 1250. It came from the French *bouteillier*, "bottle bearer," which in turn derives from the French *bouteille*, "bottle." Today, a butler is the chief male servant in a household.

butte. A French word, adopted by early explorers in the West, meaning an isolated hill or mountain rising abruptly above the surrounding land.

buttercup. Centuries ago English dairy farmers believed that if their cows ate the little yellow flowers that commonly grew in the meadows, the butter they yielded would be colored the same rich yellow. Experience seemed to prove that this was true and so the flowers were named buttercups. Actually, the field buttercup (*Ranunculus acris*) did improve the quality of Bossy's output, because the flower grows only on good pasture and thus provides good feed. The flower's scientific genus name, *Ranunculus*, is Latin for "a little frog," in allusion to the meadow habitat of the wildflower.

butterfingers. Although the word *butterfingers*—used for someone who drops things or can't hold on to anything, as if his fingers were coated with slippery butter—has been traced back to early-17th-century England, its popularity in America stems from its use as a baseball term for a fielder who drops the ball. The baseball usage is first recorded in 1888 and *butterfingers* was being generally and widely used shortly thereafter.

butterflies; butterfly kisses. The nervous butterflies that we sometimes feel in our stomachs are a fluttering sensation, which accounts for this Americanism, first recorded in the classic W. C. Fields movie *The Bank Dick* (1940). Similarly, the light soft fluttering of one's eyelashes against a loved one's cheek is called a "butterfly kiss," this expression dating back at least to late 19th-century England. *See* BUTTERFLY; FLOAT LIKE A BUTTERFLY.

butterfly. The Dutch early called the butterfly the *boterschijte*, which translates as butter excrement, or butter shit. They supposedly called it this because the insect leaves streaks of its yellowish excrement wherever it lands. There we have one theory about the origin of *butterfly*. A second explanation claims that the Dutch believed a little witch with wings frequently stole their butter, and therefore named the insect the *butter fly*. But though these are amusing theories, the butterfly was probably so named simply because the most common English species (the brimstone) is a butter-yellow color. Anyhow, why would anyone want such a wonderful creature to be associated with those other derivations?

butterfly pea. A woody perennial vine of the pea family, the butterfly pea (*Clitoria mariana*) has pale blue flowers that appear as if upside down, the standard (the upper, broad and usually erect petal of a pea flower) much larger than the rest of the flowers. It takes its popular name from its imagined resemblance to a butterfly. One gardening guide says "the origin of [the genus name] *clitoria* is unprintable"; fortunately, it is not too difficult to figure out. *See* AVOCADO; PEA.

butter up. In the sense of bestowing fulsome flattery upon someone this phrase dates all the way back to Congreve's *Way of the World* (1700): "The squire that's buttered still is sure to be undone." It is probably a translation of the French *cirer*, which means the same.

butter wouldn't melt in her mouth. Men have been saying this about demure women since the early 16th century; in fact, Heywood listed it as a proverb in 1536: the lady so prim and proper, so cold, that is, that even a piece of soft butter wouldn't melt in her mouth. In *Pendennis* Thackeray used the expression with reference to a girl who "smiles and languishes," but today it isn't usually employed in the sense of suspiciously amiable. In fact, the phrase once had a longer form: "She looks like butter wouldn't melt in her mouth, but cheese won't choke her," *i.e.*, she's really not fastidious at all, but in fact rather earthy.

buttinsky. Someone who interrupts conversations or intrudes in matters not concerning him is said to *butt in*. Most authorities believe the "-sky" ending a play on Russian and Polish names ending in "-sky," *buttinsky* a punning word formed toward the turn of the century when there were plenty of "greenhorn" immigrants among these ethnic groups who had to ask a lot of questions in order to survive. At any rate, the term was soon used to describe all buttinskies and still is.

buttock broker. *Buttock broker* is a humorous term for a matchmaker or marriage broker, first recorded in the late 17th century. Used in slang speech until the early 19th century, it also meant the madame of a brothel, equally adept at getting buttocks together.

Buttondownhemd. A button-down shirt. One of well over a thousand English words adopted or adapted by the Germans, this one combining German and English. Others include *der Clown*, *der Toaster*, *der Computer*, *der Swimming pool*, *das Apartment*, *der Hobby*, *die Cocktail Party*, *der Drink*, *der Boss*, *das Baby*, *die Chips* (french fries), *der Teenager*, and *das Rock and Roll*.

buttonhole. "Barricade your door against the button-holding world!" a British magazine warned its readers over a century ago. *Button-holding*, "grabbing a man by the top button of his coat and holding on with all the strength of the boring until you sell him one thing or another," was so common in the early 19th century that *button-holder* was defined in many dictionaries as "one who takes hold of a man's coat by the button so as to detain him in conversation." People must have been button-holding and wearying people in France, too, at the time, for the French had a similar phrase. In those days men's coats had buttons all the way up to the neck, including one on the lapel that could be buttoned in cold weather. When fashion decreed that upper buttons be eliminated, button-holders didn't suddenly reform. Instead, they began grabbing people by the buttonholes designers (for no good reason) left on the lapels and the phrase became *to buttonhole*. According to Robert Caro's *Master of the Senate* (2002), Lyndon Johnson perfected the "buttonhole" technique, sometimes holding a man so hard by the buttonhole in his lapel that the buttonhole ripped.

buy; purchase. Both *buy* and *purchase* mean "to acquire by payment of money." But *purchase* is a more formal, highfalutin word applying to grand transactions, such as the Louisiana Purchase. Only a very pompous person indeed would say he was going to purchase an ice-cream cone or a bar of candy.

buying back the nut. Troupes of actors in days gone by often traveled by wagon to the theaters where they performed. Innkeepers would rent them rooms on credit if they would leave or deposit the nut holding one of the wheels to the wagons. When the troupe was paid for its performance, they would pay the bill and receive the essential wheel nut in return. This came to be called *buying back the nut*, a term purely of historical interest today.

buzkashi. The word is not in any English dictionary but had its 15 minutes of fame during the war in Afghanistan. Buzkashi is a furious game dating back to the horsemen of Genghis Khan, in which riders fight in a free-for-all for the carcass of a goat or calf that must be deposited in a circle on the ground by the winner. Before this, the riders must lean to the ground from their horses, avoiding flashing hooves and often holding their own horse's reins in their teeth while they try to lift the 150-pound carcasses. Their reward is the honor of victory and money contributed by the spectators.

buzz. *See* ONOMATOPOEIA.

buzzard. A New World vulture of the family Cathartidae, especially the turkey vulture. The word is also used to describe a cantankerous or contemptible person, usually in the form *old buzzard*.

buzzword. A buzzword, the term dating back to about 1965, is a word or phrase that sounds authoritative or technical and is in vogue in a particular profession or field of study. Such words are often GOBBLEDYGOOK. According to the *Washington Post*, Philip Broughton, a veteran employee of the United States Public Health Service, invented the "Systematic Buzz Phrase Projector," a surefire way to fashion such language should you want to use it for purposes of obfuscation. A writer just thinks of any three-digit number at random and selects the corresponding "buzzwords" from three columns of such words that Broughton provides. The number 257, for example, yields "systematized logistical projection," a phrase that can be used in almost any report. "No one will have the remotest idea of what you're talking about," says Broughton. "But the important thing is that they're not about to admit it." Author Gershon Legman has a similar four-column system of phrases called FARK (Folklore Article Reconstruction Kit) which he claims will enable any "Folklore Ph.D." to devise "40,000 new and meaningful, well-balanced, and grammatically acceptable sentences packed with Folklore terms." Choosing, for example, the numbers 7, 4, 8, and 2 from Legman's columns, the writer gets: "Based on my own fieldwork in Guatemala/initiation of basic charismatic subculture development/recognizes the importance of other disciplines, while taking into account/the anticipated epistemological repercussions."

B.V.D.s.   There is no doubt about the origin of *B.V.D.s.* The initials do not derive from the words "Boys Ventilated Drawers" or any such humorous phrase. *B.V.D.s* comes from the initials of the three men (Bradley, Voorhies, and Day) who founded, in 1876, the company that makes them. *B.V.D.* is a trademark and cannot be legally used to describe the product of any other company, though it is often used, unlawfully, as a generic term for underwear. *Beeveedees* is a variant spelling that is recorded in print as early as 1915.

bwana.   The journalist Henry Morton Stanley of Stanley and Livingstone fame first recorded the Swahili *bwana* in 1878. *Bwana* is a title of respect translating as "father of sons," but meaning "sir, Mr., boss, or master." Often applied exclusively to white men in the past, it is today a common form of address to both Africans and whites in many African countries. *See* DOCTOR LIVINGSTONE, I PRESUME.

by a hairbreadth.   *See* HAIRBREADTH ESCAPE.

by a Lady.   *By a Lady* has the distinction of being the world's most common pseudonym or anonym, aside from *Anonymous.* There are about 1,000 literary works in England alone whose authors are identified as *By a Lady.*

by and large.   *By and large* originated in the days of sailing ships, roughly meaning "to sail a ship to the wind and off it." These instructions to a helmsman were not precise, and so the 17th-century nautical term came to indicate imprecise generalities in everyday English and to mean "generally speaking," "on the whole"—especially when the speaker or writer is telling the substantial truth, despite minor exceptions. Literal-minded linguists object to the expression because *by and large* really describes a more complex marine operation than is indicated in the above definition.

Byerly Turk; Darley Arabian; Godolphin Barb.   The names of the three Oriental horses from whom, without exception, all modern Thoroughbred racehorses descend through the male line. *Byerly Turk*, first of the founding fathers, was the charger of English Captain Byerly at the Battle of the Boyne (1690). Little is known about him except that he was a Turkish

stallion purchased abroad a few years before. *Darley Arabian*, most celebrated of the three sires, was sent from Syria to Richard Darley of Yorkshire by his son Thomas in 1704; he was a certified Arabian stallion. *Godolphin Barb* or *Arabian*, called "the mysterious Frenchman," was brought to England from France in 1730 by Edward Coke and later sold or given to the Earl of Godolphin.

by exclamations.   These old exclamations aren't much used anymore, but are a pleasure to hear. They include, among hundreds: By gum! By Godfrey! By fire! By guess and by God! By gum and by gosh! By guess and by gory! By gum and by golly! By the green horn spoon! By the livin' law! By the Old Lord Harry! By the prophet's nippers! By the snakes of Babylon! By chowder! By crackie! By Crimmins! By dad! By gary! By ginger! By gory! By gravey! By hen! By the holy smut! By hokey! By Joe Beeswax! By Jove! By King! By scissors! By swan! and By zounds!

by George.   Ben Jonson (and presumably his contemporaries) used the mild oath *by St. George!* as far back as 1598, but it wasn't until the late 19th century that the expression began to be shortened to *by George!* St. George has been the patron saint of England since the institution of the Order of the Garter. A historical character about whom little is really known, the patron saint of soldiers was perhaps a soldier in the Roman army who was martyred for the faith in Asia Minor. In legend he is said to have slain a dragon that fed on villagers at Silene, Libya, rescuing the Princess Sabra from its clutches. This tale of course became a Christian allegory for good triumphing over evil. The name George has its roots in the Greek *Georgos*, "a farmer," literally a worker of the earth. The word comes from the Greek *ge*, "the earth," and *legon*, "a work," which also gives us Virgil's *Georgics*, an "agricultural poem" about the land and the men working it.

by Godfrey!   An early U.S. euphemism for "by God!"

by guess and by God.   To do something randomly, without much careful planning, is to do it "by guess and by God." The planner hopes that God will see his strategy through, no matter how poor the planning.

by hook or by crook.   Used by John Wycliffe in 1380 and now standard English, this expression has a dozen explanations that can't be proved or disproved. The most widely accepted theory traces *by hook or by crook* to the forests of medieval England, which belonged to the King and were off limits to all commoners except those gathering firewood. Ancient law restricted these peasant gatherers to dead wood on the ground or dead branches that they could reach with a shepherd's crook and cut off with a reaper's billhook. The story does explain the phrase meaning "by any means possible," but leaves something to be desired regarding the foul means suggested by *crook.* One widely accepted version traces the expression to 1100, when a charcoal burner named Purkiss found the body of William Rufus, King of England, who had been slain by an archer in Hampshire's New Forest. Purkiss carted the king's body to Winchester and was rewarded with permission to gather all the wood in the forest that he needed for his charcoal burners— provided he took only wood that he could reach *by hook or* *crook.* Almost 900 years have passed and the Purkiss family (now spelled Purkess) still live in the New Forest, which is the largest surviving medieval forest in England thanks to such *hook and crook conservation laws,* if I may coin a phrase.

bylaw. A law or rule, or a secondary law or rule. The *by* in the word, however, has nothing to do with "secondary" as many people believe. *By* here comes from the Old Norse *by* in the names of English places, such as Whitby, where Scandanavian invaders settled. The word, which itself may be Old Norse, is first recorded in 1283, in the sense of a body of regulations of a village or town.

by my troth, I care not; a man can die but once; we owe God a death . . . and let it go which way it will he that died this year is quit the next. British Captain E. E. Dorman-Smith, later a general, wrote these words out for Ernest Hemingway in the Italian hospital where he was recovering from his wounds during World War I. Hemingway later put the words into the mouth of the white hunter Robert Wilson in "The Short Happy Life of Francis Macomber." There Wilson comments upon the little-known phrase: "Worst one can do is kill you. How does it go? Shakespeare. Damned good. See if I can remember. Oh, damned good. Used to quote it to myself at one time. Let's see . . . Damned fine, eh?" The words are originally from Shakespeare's *Henry IV.* In his anthology *Men at War* (1942) Hemingway wrote that they had become "a permanent talisman" for him.

Byronic. George Gordon, Lord Byron (1788–1824), contributed to the creation of the *Byronic* hero with deeds as much as poems. Byron's slight lameness, his good looks (which were likened to the Apollo Belvedere), his myriad and often sensational romantic entanglements, his wanderings on the Continent and his devotion to the cause of Greek freedom, were among many factors that made the English poet the perfect model for the wildly romantic yet despairing and melancholy heroes of his poems. Byron's poetry was the most popular of his day, at home and especially abroad, despite its criticism on what today might be considered ridiculous moral grounds. No English poet but Shakespeare had greater influence on European literature, and all Byron's major works, such as *Childe Harold's Pilgrimage* and *Don Juan,* have stood the test of time. The poet was haunted in his lifetime by the charge that he committed incest with his half-sister, Mrs. Augusta Leigh. His tempestuous life, the panache and bravura of this poet ("His eyes the open portals of the sun—things of light and for light," in Coleridge's words; "The only man to whom I could apply the word beautiful," according to another contemporary) were more romantic than any of his poems. Byron died in Missolonghi, Greece, of malarial fever when only 35. His heart is buried there, where he had sought a soldier's grave in the name of Greek freedom. His body lies buried in England in a small village church, the authorities having refused his burial in the Poet's Corner of Westminster Abbey.

by the numbers. To do something by the numbers is to do it mechanically, in precise order. The expression dates back to World War I, when soldiers were taught a complex task by breaking the task into a number of steps, often performed as the numbers were called out.

by the skin of the teeth. Many phrases from the Book of Job in the Old Testament are proverbial in English: "Naked I came from my mother's womb, and naked I shall return"; "The Lord gave, and the Lord hath taken away"; "Man is born unto trouble. . . ." The scholars who prepared the Geneva Bible in 1560 were the first to render Job's reply to Bildad that he had barely escaped with his life as "I have escaped with the skinne of my teethe," and their poetic translation was retained by the editors of the King James version of the Bible (Job 19:20). The full King James quotation is: "My bone cleaveth to my skin and to my flesh, and I am escaped with the skin of my teeth." Despite objections that the teeth have no skin, centuries of Bible reading have given the expression a permanent place in the language as the description of a close escape, though it has been altered a hairbreadth to *by the skin of the teeth.* Thornton Wilder's play *The Skin of Our Teeth* (1942) won a Pulitzer Prize in 1943.

by-two coffee shop. Any shop in the south of India where two customers can share a cup of coffee between them, one-half a cup each. Such economical shops are the Starbucks of the poor and/or struggling.

C

C. The letter *C* is probably the highly modified form of an ancient sign for a camel. One of the strangest stories attached to any letter is told about it. It seems that an Admiral George Cockburn led the incendiaries who demolished the *National Intelligencer* when the British burned Washington during the War of 1812. This gentlemanly incendiary ordered his men to melt down all the *C*s in the newspaper office, "so that later they can't abuse my name." A lowercase *c.* (with a period) signifies more than 30 things including "carat," "cent," "centimeter," and "about" (for example, ca. 1776), deriving in the last case from the Latin *circa*, about. *C.* can abbreviate at least 10 things when capitalized, including "Centigrade," "Catholic," and "College." After the clef sign on sheet music, the C is not an initial standing for "common" 4/4 time, but stands for an incomplete circle, a symbol representing what was once considered "imperfect time." A circle, symbolizing the Trinity, was used in the early days of written music to indicate "perfect time," three beats to the bar.

C; Secret Service. Ian Fleming gave the name M to the head of the British Secret Service (MI6) in his James Bond novels. But the only real-life head of the British espionage agency to go by an initial was the colorful John Cumming of World War I, who wrote in green ink and insisted on being called "C." The term *Secret Service* itself is recorded as far back as 1737, in the reign of George II.

cab. The word *cabriolet*, for a type of light horse-drawn carriage, has been all but forgotten save for its use in abbreviated form for what is just as well known as a TAXI. *Cab* has been used in this sense since the early 1800s when cabriolets were available for hire in London. When motorcars could be hired *cab* was quickly applied to them.

cabal. This word, for a group of conspirators, has for many years been popularly regarded as the most famous acronym in English. Tradition has it that the word was formed from the initials of certain members of King Charles II's infamous ministry in the years 1667–73. *C*lifford, *A*shley (Shaftesbury), *B*uckingham, *A*rlington, and *L*auderdale were only five among a number of Charles's ministers who plotted often diametrically opposed secret intrigues. They rarely met all together, although they did constitute the Privy Council foreign committee. The infamous five did, however, secretly sign the Treaty of Alliance with France in 1672, without Parliament's approval, forcing the nation into war with Holland. After this shameful episode, their enemies were quick to point out that their initials formed the word *cabal*, but this does not say that *cabal* originated with the acrostic ministry. *Cabal*, for a society of intriguers, had previously been introduced into English from the Latin *cabbala*, which derives, in turn, from the Hebrew *qabbalah*. The qubbalah were doctrines said to be originally received from Moses, enabling their possessors to unlock secrets of magical power. During the Middle Ages, the secret meetings of cabbala groups claiming knowledge of such doctrines gave rise to the English word *cabal*. *Cabal* did, however, take on a new political significance and popularity in English with the machinations of Clifford and the others. The historian Macaulay writes, for example, that "These ministers were called the Cabal, and they soon made the appellation so infamous that it has never since their time been used except as a term of reproach."

cabbage. Ask for a head of cabbage and you are repeating yourself, for *cabbage* means "head," the name of the vegetable deriving from the Old French *caboce*, "swollen head." *Caboce* itself comes from the Old French *boce*, "a swelling," the *ca* in the word very likely suggested by the Latin *caput*, meaning "head." Cabbage, probably the most ancient of vegetables, has been cultivated for more than 4,000 years. In Greek mythology it is said to have sprung from sweat on the head of Jupiter. The Greeks also believed that eating it cured baldness.

cabbage head. Describing a fool as a *cabbage head* dates back to the late 17th century and is best explained by the old music-hall lyrics: "I ought to call him a cabbage head, / He is so very green . . ."

cabbages and kings. This expression meaning "odds and ends," "anything and everything," was used by O. Henry as the title for his first book of stories. It comes from Lewis Carroll's *Through the Looking Glass:*

> "The time has come," the Walrus said,
> "To talk of many things:
> Of shoes and ships—and sealing wax—
> Of cabbages—and kings—
> And why the sea is boiling hot—
> And whether pigs have wings."

cablegram; telegram. First used in 1868, the word *cablegram* initially met with some resistance, scholars condemning it as a hybrid derived from Latin ("cable") and Greek ("gram"). Use the all-Greek *calogram* instead of the New York City–born monster, they suggested, but few agreed and the coinage proved durable. Something of the same happened with the earlier coinage *telegram*, which we know was invented by a friend of a man who wrote a letter to the *Albany Evening Journal* on April 6, 1852, asking that it be adopted in place of the clumsy "telegraphic dispatch" used at the time. Grammarians pointed out that *telegram* was not properly formed from its Greek elements and suggested "telegraphemie" instead, but the "barbaric new Yankee word" won out in the test of time. Such improperly formed words are of course common in English and there is a liberal supply of hybrids like *cablegram*, including such common words as because, dentist, grateful, starvation, talkative, and parliament.

caboose. Before it became "the last car on a train," a caboose, from the Dutch *kombius*, was a seaman's term for a ship's galley. The word went West in America to become the name for the cook wagon on the range and then became the car on a train carrying provisions.

caca. Though it appears to be simply the imitation of an infant's sounds, *caca*, for "excrement or a bowel movement," has an aristocratic Roman ancestor. The word derives from the Latin *cacare*, "to defecate."

ca' canny. This Scots expression for "go easily, don't exert yourself" is used by trade unions in Scotland when they want to bring pressure on their employers without going on strike. It amounts, in effect, to what Americans would call a *slowdown*.

cacao tree. The drink called "cocoa" is made from the cocoa beans of the South American cacao tree, *cocoa* being simply a variant spelling of *cacao*. Chocolate is also made from the beans, taking its name from the Nahuatl (Aztec) word *xocoatl*, "food made from the cacao." For many years the cacao tree was confused with the coco tree because a printing error in Samuel Johnson's great dictionary (1755) listed the two trees together under the *cocoa* entry. *See* COCONUT.

cackle. *See* CHUCKLE; ONOMATOPOEIA.

cackleberry. A humorous American designation for eggs, dating back a century or so. It is said to have originated in early logging camps.

caconym. A *caconym*, deriving from the Green *caco*, "bad, evil," and *onoma*, "name," is a bad or undesirable name. Many *caconyms* were given to people in German-speaking countries during the early 19th century, when all citizens were required to take surnames and village clerks often assigned objectionable ones unless bribes were given. An apocryphal story is told of two men who paid such bribes. "You can't imagine how much it cost to have the *m* put in my name," said Herr Schmeiss." (*Schmeiss* means "fling" in German, while *Scheiss* means "shit.") "You can't imagine how much I paid to have the *m* taken out of my name," replied his friend, Herr Schutz. (*Schutz* means "protection" in German, while *Schmutz* is "filth.")

cactus. *See* CARNEGIEA.

cadaver. In the seventh century the scholar St. Isadore of Seville taught his students that the word *cadaver* was an acronym of the Latin *caro data vermibus* (flesh given to worms), this one of the earliest examples of folk etymology. *Cadaver*, a dead body or corpse, actually comes from a Latin word spelled, pronounced, and meaning the same—nowhere near as good a story as the worms crawl in, the worms crawl out . . . tale. Isadore had hundreds more stories in his 20-part encyclopedia *Books of Origins or Etymologies.*

caddy; cadet. According to legend, Mary Queen of Scots was the first woman golfer, so avid a player, in fact, that she continued playing her round when she was informed of her husband's murder one day in 1567. An old story also claims that Mary introduced the word *cadet* (from the Gascon *capdet*, "little chief") into English from French. *Cadet* first meant the youngest son of a noble, and by 1630 meant a young no-good who had taken to the streets—its spelling changed to *caddy*. By the mid-18th century a *caddy* came to mean a young porter on the streets and finally, a century later, a young porter who carried golf clubs. Independently, the word *cadet* for the youngest son of a nobleman came to mean a student at a military academy, because the youngest sons of nobles usually became soldiers.

Cadillac. *Cadillac*, which is of course a trade name, has long been to expensive automobiles what FORD has been to low-priced cars. Ironically, the Detroit Automobile Company, formed by Henry Ford in 1899, was the forerunner of the Cadillac Company, Cadillac later being absorbed by General Motors. The Cadillac, in the United States and elsewhere, has become a symbol of success to some, vulgar pretension to others, and is a synonym for an expensive car to all. It bears the name of Antoine de la Mothe Cadillac (1658–1730), a minor nobleman and French colonial governor who, in 1701, founded Detroit as an important post for French control of the fur trade. Cadillac also established a trading post in what is now Cadillac, Michigan, on Lake Cadillac. Unlike the car bearing his name, the Frenchman seems to have been popular with no one. Neither Indians nor settlers could get along with him at Fort Pontchartrain (present-day Detroit), and his later governorship of the vast Louisiana Territory (1711–16) met with similar hostility. Cadillac, recalled to France, died in his native Gascony.

Cadmean letters; Cadmean victory. Myth is often a reflection of fact, and the 16 letters of the old Greek alphabet said to be introduced to the Boeotians by the mythological hero Cadmus from Phoenicia really do derive from Phoenician script. It is uncertain whether there was an actual Cadmus, a prototype for the hero who introduced the Cadmean letters. A *Cadmean victory* refers to the same mythological warrior. It derives from the story that Cadmus killed a dragon and sowed the dragon's teeth. Armed warriors sprang up and he set them fighting by throwing a stone among them; only five warriors survived, and these became the ancestors of the noble family of Thebes. A Cadmean victory, in remembrance of these five surviving stalwarts, became proverbial for a victory achieved where the victors can hardly be distinguished from the vanquished.

cadre. *Cadre* are trained or key men, generally in the military, who instruct and supervise untrained troops. Thought to be the "skeleton" or foundation of an outfit, they appropriately take their name from the French *cadre*, "frame." The word didn't come into English until the mid-19th century.

Caesar cipher. In his secret communications Caesar simply wrote down the third letter following the one he meant (thus in English today the letter *A* would be *D* and the word *dog* would be *GRJ*). Though this elementary cipher or substitution code was used long before him, cryptologists still call it the *Caesar cipher*. His successor, Augustus Caesar, made the process even simpler, merely substituting the letter immediately following the one he meant, which enabled him to write in code as quickly as he could in normal letters.

Caesarian section. According to Pliny the Elder, the first of the Caesars was brought into the world by the *Caesarian section* operation named in his honor. However, Julius Caesar probably wasn't extracted from his mother's womb by this incision through the abdominal walls, though the operation was commonly practiced on dead mothers in early times. Caesar, whose mother, Julia, lived many years after his death, probably has his name confused with the operation because it became mandatory under the *lex Caesarum* ("law of the Caesars," the codified Roman law of the time), just as it had been under the previous *lex regia* ("royal law"), that every woman dying in advanced pregnancy be so treated in an effort to save the baby. It is also possible that *Caesarian section* simply comes from the Latin *caesus*, past participle of the verb *caedere*, "to cut."

Caesar salad. This popular salad was not named after Julius Caesar nor any of his family. It seems to have been invented in the late 1920s by Caesar Gardini, a restaurant owner in Tijuana, Mexico, but there are several contenders for the honor.

Caesar's mushroom. *Amanita caesaria* or Caesar's mushroom, honoring Julius Caesar, happens to be one species of the deadly *Amanita* genus that is edible, but more than a few "experts" have been poisoned thinking that they had distinguished this delicacy from its deadly relatives. Every summer brings scores of deaths from mushroom poisoning. Hippocrates referred to cases of mushroom poisoning in his day, and Horace warned the ancients to beware of all fungi, no matter how appetizing the appearance. One of the first recorded cases of mushroom poisoning occurred in the family of the Greek poet Euripides, who lost his wife, two sons and a daughter when they partook of a deadly *Amanita* species. Pope Clement VII, the Emperor Jovian, Emperor Charles VI, Czar Alexander I,

the wife of Czar Alexis, and the Emperor Claudius (his niece and wife Agrippina poisoned his *boleti*) are among historical figures who lost their lives in the same way. Many species of *Amanita* are lethal even when eaten in minuscule amounts, and *Amanita verna*, the destroying angel, is easily confused with *Amanita caesaria* and the several other edible species. *See* MUSHROOM.

cafeteria. A relatively young Americanism, *cafeteria* was probably introduced in 1893 at the Chicago World's Fair. It derives, however, from the Spanish *cafetería*, meaning the same.

cager. This early term for a basketball player still has some currency today. The word derives from the net-enclosed gyms the game was played in that prevented the ball from getting into the crowd and prevented zealous spectators from getting onto the court. *See* BASKETBALL.

cahoots. To be in partnership, often shady partnership, with. There are two theories about *cahoots*. First, that the word derives from the French *cahute*, "cabin," suggesting that the two in cahoots shared a cabin together. Or, second, more probably, that *cahoots* derives from the French *cahorte*, "a gang."

Ça ira. Benjamin Franklin is said to have invented this French phrase when he was asked in 1776, while ambassador to France, how the American Revolution was going and replied, *Ça ira*, "things will work out." In 1790 the phrase became the refrain of the popular song "Carillon national" of the French Revolution.

Cajun. A group of people of French Catholic ancestory who were expelled from Acadia in the late 18th century and settled in Louisiana and Maine. The word, deriving from *Acadian*, is also applied to any of their characteristics, such as the French dialect they speak. Also *Cajan*.

cakes and ale. Long before it became the title of Somerset Maugham's novel, *Cakes and Ale* meant "fun or pleasant activity," as in "life isn't all cakes and ale." Shakespeare may have invented the expression, for he first recorded it in *Twelfth Night* (1600): "Dost thou think, because thou art virtuous, there shall be no more cakes and ale?"

calabash. Since the mid-19th century a *calabash* has meant an empty-headed person, someone with nobody home upstairs, in U.S. slang. *Calabash* in this sense derives from the gourd of the same name, which comes from the Arabic *qar 'ah yābisah*, "empty gourd." Sherlock Holmes's famous pipe, readers may recall, was made from a hollowed-out calabash gourd.

calaboose. Any jail, but usually a small one in a small town. The word derives from the Spanish *calaboza* (dungeon).

Calamity Jane. Those who tried to outshoot Calamity Jane (Martha Jane Canary Burke, 1852–1903) brought calamity upon themselves. The legendary markswoman's nom de guerre came to mean a woman who predicts or suffers calamity. It also describes the queen of spades (long associated with death) in poker.

calculate.   The abacus, or counting board, was borrowed by the Romans from the Greeks, who called it an *abax*. Although today it contains wooden beads strung on wire, it was first divided into compartments, with pebbles moved from compartment to compartment as the reckoning progressed. Thus, from the Latin name for these abacus pebbles, *calculus*, comes our word for mathematical reckoning, *calculate*.

Calendar Islands.   The Calendar Islands in Maine's Casco Bay are among the most appropriately named of island groups—there are exactly 365 of them.

calepin.   I don't know of any synonym for a polyglot dictionary, one in many languages, save the unusual *calepin*. The word comes from the name of Italian Augustine friar Ambrosio Calepino, who in 1502 published a famous Latin dictionary that went through many editions and was *the* Latin dictionary of the day. Apparently this Latin dictionary of Calepino's was published in an "octoglot" edition, which led to the man's name being employed as it is. Anyway, *calepin* was used for "a polyglot dictionary, a dictionary, or any book of authority or reference" until well into the 18th century, and has had limited use since.

Calhounery.   John C. Calhoun (1782–1850), the preeminent spokesman of the South and a giant intellect of his day, is remembered in historical dictionaries by this word, first recorded in 1837. *Calhounery*, despite the nice ring to it, was not of his making. It is a historical term once used to describe causes such as stuffing ballet boxes, permitting illegal votes to be cast, and so forth—all practices not of the vice president but of his supporters, who were called *Calhounites* or *Calhounists*.

Caliban.   A brute; an ugly, degraded, beastlike man. The original was created by Shakespeare in *The Tempest* (1611), in which Caliban is the deformed semi-human son of a demon and the witch Sycorax. A slave of Prospero, the misshapen monster speaks poetic language still fascinating today. His name may be a variant of *Cariban*, a Carib, or could have been formed by metathesis from the Spanish CANNIBAL. At one point in the play he cries, "All the infections that the sun sucks up / From bogs, fens, flats, on Prosper fall and make him / By inch-meal a disease!"

calico.   The cotton cloth is named after the Indian city of Calicut (now Kozhikode), from where it was first exported in 1498, when Vasco da Gama took it back to Portugal.

California.   Lexicographers aren't positive about the origin of *California*, but the state may be named after a woman named Calafia in an old Spanish romance, Calafia ruling over an island called California. On the other hand, other etymologists insist that *California* is a Catalan word meaning "hot oven"—a story that's not good for the tourist trade.

California blanket.   A humorous term for layers of newspapers used as blankets. The Americanism dates back to the early 1900s, when it was apparently invented by hoboes in California.

California breakfast.   A derogatory expression that, according to a January 1962 *Western Folklore* article, means "a cigarette and an orange."

California collar.   A joking term given to the hangman's noose when vigilante justice ruled in early California.

California fever.   The desire to go to California, the term first recorded not when gold was discovered but after explorer J. C. Frémont journeyed there in 1844.

California prayer book.   A joking term for playing cards, popular in gold-rush days.

California widow.   The common ancestor of American golf widows, football widows, baseball widows, fishing widows, and computer widows, to name but a few species. *California widow* dates back to the 1850 gold rush in California, when women throughout the U.S. lost their husbands for a year or forever while the men tried their luck or pursued their fantasies in the gold fields. One such widow advertised in a San Francisco newspaper: "Husband Wanted—Whereas my husband has lately left my bed and board without provocation on my part, I hereby advertise for a suitable person to *fill the vacancy*." It should be noted that the term *American widow* preceded all those noted above; it was used in England to describe a woman whose husband had left home to seek a fortune in America. *See* GRASS WIDOW; GOLF WIDOW.

call a spade a spade.   To be straightforward and call things by their right names, to avoid euphemisms or beating around the bush. The words are from the garden, not from the game of poker. So old is this expression that it wasn't original with Plutarch, who used it back in the first century when writing about Philip of Macedon, Alexander the Great's father. The saying has been credited to the Greek comic poet Menander, who described the life of ancient Athens so faithfully that he inspired a critic to exclaim, "O Menander and Life, which of you imitated the other?" If this is so, to "call a spade a spade" goes back to at least 300 B.C., and the faithful Menander could have been quoting a much older Greek proverb. The expression was introduced into English by Protestant reformer John Knox, who translated it from the Latin of Erasmus as: "I have learned to call wickedness by its own terms: A fig, a fig, and a spade a spade." Erasmus had taken the phrase from Lucian, a Greek writer of the second century and translated it as "to call a fig a fig and a boat a boat," which is possible because the Greek words for boat and garden spade were very similar.

call his bluff.   This widely used phrase certainly originated in American poker games of the early 19th century, bluffing being an integral part of poker, and *to call* meaning to match a bet. Some etymologists trace *bluff* itself back to the Low German *bluffen*, "to frighten by menacing conduct," which became the Dutch *buffen*, "to make a trick at cards," but *bluff* is first recorded in an 1838 account of an American poker game.

calligraphy.   The word comes from the Greek for "beautiful writing." In its sense of small handwriting the historical Hemingway of calligraphy is Peter Bales (1547–ca. 1610), who is also said to be one of the inventors of shorthand. Diarist John

Evelyn tells us that the dexterous Bales wrote "the Lord's Prayer, The Creed, Decalogue, with two short prayers in Latin, his own name, motto, day of the month, year of the Lord, and reign of the Queen, to whom he presented it at Hampton Court, all of it written within the circle of a single penny, incased in a ring and borders of gold, and covered with a crystal, so accurately wrought as to be plainly legible, to the great admiration of her majesty . . ." However, several later calligraphers bettered Bales's record. According to *The Guinness Book of World Records* (1998), "During the mid 1950s Horace Dall of Luton, England built a pantograph—which reduces movement—fitted with a diamond stylus, with which he engraved writing small enough to fit 140 Bibles to one square inch."

callipygian. According to Sir Thomas Browne, *callipygian* refers to "women largely composed from behind." This is a term of admiration (unlike STEATOPYGOUS), deriving from the Greek roots for "beauty" and "buttocks." The *Callipygian Venus* is a famous classical statue of Venus with substantial, nicely shaped buttocks.

call the turn. Someone who *calls the turn* guesses correctly how an affair or transaction will turn out. The expression doesn't derive from "turn out," however, but comes to us instead from the card game FARO, a very popular game in 19th-century America. One who *calls the turn* in faro, that is, guesses correctly what the last three cards turned over will be, wins at high odds from the bank.

calumny; libel; slander. The Romans branded false accusers with a *K* on the forehead, this standing for their word *kalumnia*, which became *calumnia* when they gave the *c* the *k* sound and for the most part stopped using the *k*. Our word *calumny*, a false accusation deliberately intended to hurt another's reputation, comes directly from the Latin *calumnia*, which means the same. Shakespeare and Shelley believed that only the dead knew not calumny, the bard writing in *Hamlet:* "Be thou chaste as ice, as pure as snow, thou shalt not escape calumny." A false accuser, the slanderer who spreads calumnies, is called a calumniator, and those who are the victims of calumniatory charges are the calumniated. "Calumny," said Queen Elizabeth I, "will not fasten on me forever." Libel is written or printed calumny, and slander is legally calumny by oral utterance. For example, Whistler's paintings were slandered by English critic John Ruskin, but Ruskin was only sued for libel when he published such statements as "I . . . never expected to hear a coxcomb ask two hundred guineas for flinging a pot of paint in the public's face." Whistler won his case, but was awarded only a farthing, a coin then worth less than one cent.

Calvary. *See* GOLGATHA.

Calvary clover. Legend holds that the common trefoil Calvary clover *(Medicago echinus)* sprang up in the foot-steps of Pontius Pilate when he went to Christ's cross at Calvary or Golgotha. Each of the plant's three leaves has a carmine spot in the center, the leaves roughly form a cross in the daytime, and in flowering season the plant bears a little yellow flower resembling a crown of thorns.

Calvinism; Calvinist. The system of theological thought called *Calvinism* was founded by French Protestant reformer John Calvin, or Cauvin (1509–64). Calvinist beliefs, held in much modified form today in Presbyterian and Reformed churches, were formulated as the Five Points in 1618. These are, briefly: 1) Original Sin, man's natural inability to exercise free will since Adam's fall; 2) Predestination; 3) Irresistible grace; 4) Perseverance of the saints or elect; and 5) Particular redemption. *Calvinism* has overwhelmingly been regarded as a bleak, forbidding theology.

Cambridge flag. A popular name for the first flag of the American Continental Army at the start of the Revolutionary War. Its official name was the Grand Union flag (because it had been patterned on the British Grand Union flag with its red and white stripes and crosses), but it was popularly called the Cambridge flag because it was first flown near Boston and Cambridge, Massachusetts.

camellia. One of the most beautiful flowering plants, the evergreen camellia is named for George Joseph Kamel (1661–1706), a Moravian Jesuit missionary and amateur botanist who wrote extensive accounts of the shrub, which he found in the Philippine Islands in the late 17th century. Kamel, who called himself Camellus, the Latinized form of his name, operated a pharmacy for the poor in Manila, planting an herb garden to supply it. He published reports of the plants he grew in the Royal Society of London's *Philosophical Transactions*, and some authorities believe that Kamel sent the first specimens of the shiny-leaved camellia back to Europe. In any event, he was the first to describe the shrub, a relative of the tea plant, and the great Swedish botanist Linnaeus read his accounts in *Transactions* and named the plant camellia after him. Camellias are used extensively as garden shrubs in southern areas of the United States and England. Their wax-like, long-lasting flowers are white, red, or pink.

camelopard. *See* GIRAFFE.

Camelot. The legendary spot where King Arthur held court in British fable, which has come to mean any ideal place. The real Camelot has been located in Somerset near Winchester, in Wales, and in Scotland, among other places.

camel's hair. A German artist named Kemul may have given his name to camel's hair artists' brushes because he invented them, but there is no evidence to support the theory that *camel's hair* is a corruption of *Kemul's hair.* In any case, the name *camel's hair* is a misnomer: the artists' brushes are made from long tail hairs taken from squirrel species inhabiting cold areas such as Siberia. Most likely the brushes were erroneously named because people thought they were made from the fine hair of the two-humped Bactrian camel when the brushes were introduced in the 18th century. Camel hair, longer than sheep's wool and as fine as silk, had been used in Europe since the early 14th century for cloth, scarves, and other items.

Camera. *See* COMRADE.

Cameroon. This African country has an unusual name, one that derives from the Portuguese word for shrimp—*camarão*.

Not because it is a small country, but due to the abundance of the crustaceans off its shores.

Camille.   In *la Dame aux camélias* (1848), better known on the stage and screen as *Camille*, Alexandre Dumas fils wrote about Marguerite Gautier, a courtesan who wore no flower other than the camellia—a white camellia for 25 days of the month and a red camellia the other five days. One of the world's most endearing fictional creations, Marguerite was based on a real-life Parisian courtesan, or prostitute, Marie Duplessis, the mistress of many wealthy aristocrats and Dumas's lover for a time. Marie, who used the camellia as a trademark, died of tuberculosis at the age of 23, and Dumas immortalized her in his book, her name becoming a symbol for anyone like her.

camino real.   A term from Spanish meaning "royal road" and once used in the Southwest for a main public highway built by the state. It also referred to several specific roads leading from Mexico into California and New Mexico.

camouflage.   In Parisian slang, prior to World War I, *camoufler* meant "to disguise." After 1914 the term was "naturalized with remarkable rapidity" by the English as *camouflage* and applied to anything disguised from the enemy, whether a varicolored battleship or a convoy of trucks.

Camp David.   The U.S. presidential retreat was named by President Dwight D. Eisenhower after his grandson, David Eisenhower. Previously the retreat in the beautiful verdant Catoctin Mountains of Maryland was named Shangri-La by President Franklin Roosevelt after the refuge in James Hilton's 1933 novel *Lost Horizon*.

Canaan.   "A good land and a large . . . flowing with milk and honey," *Canaan* is the biblical name for Palestine, where blood has been flowing in our time. The land was named in the Old Testament after Canaan, the fourth son of Ham. It is also known as the Promised Land, promised by God to Abraham for his obedience (Ex. 12:25).

Canada.   *Canada* actually appears to be an American Indian word, but several amusing stories are told regarding its origin. One has an Indian chief telling French explorer Jacques Cartier that his little village was named *Kana da* and Cartier thinking the name applied to the whole vast region. Another story has a Spanish explorer climbing a tree to sight what prominent geographic features lay to the north. "Aca nada (Nothing's there)," he called down to his comrades, who took to calling the region *Acanada*, which was soon corrupted to *Canada*.

canapé.   *Canopy*, for a covering hung on poles over a bed or throne, derives from the Latin *canapeum*, meaning a mosquito net. The tasty *canapé* appetizer consisting of a cracker spread with cheese, paté, etc., seems to have been named after this bed canopy—probably because people felt the appetizer resembled a bed canopy in shape.

canard.   *Canard* means "duck" in French, and the word *canard*, for "a ridiculously false story," comes from the French expression *vendre un canard à moitié*, literally, "to sell half a duck." The expression means to make a fool out of a buyer, or

anyone else, with a false story. Tellers of "half-ducks," or *canards*, were known in France three centuries ago, and the word probably gained a firmer foothold with a hoax played by a Frenchman named Cornelessin, who, testing the gullibility of the public, published a story that he had 30 ducks, one of which he killed and threw to the other 29, who ate it. He then cut up a second, then a third, until the 29th duck was eaten by the survivor—an excellent, bull, duck, or *canard* story.

canary; sing like a canary.   How did dogs give their name to canaries? It happened that in about 40 B.C. Juba, the native chief of Mauritania, explored a group of islands far off the coast of his kingdom and named the largest of them Canaria, or "Island of Dogs," because of the wild dogs inhabiting it. Later visitors called the whole island group the Canary Islands, and when the grayish-green songbird of the island was tamed and exported in the 16th century, it became widely known as "the bird from the Canary Islands," which was inevitably shortened to *canary*. Informants, or stool pigeons, are sometimes said by police to *sing like a canary* when they reveal everything they know, the expression dating back to the late 19th century.

Canberra.   The Australian capital's name is said by some to be an Aboriginal place-name that means "woman's breasts," after a pair of prominent hills in the area.

cancan.   University scholars in Paris often prefaced their erudite arguments about anything and everything with the Latin word *quamquam*, "although . . ." This ridiculous habit grew so common that the word soon meant "a piece of nonsense," *quamquam* coming to be pronounced *concon*. Carousing French students of the 1830s, punning bawdily on the sound of *concon*, then made it the name of the high-kicking, skirt-lifting dance of Parisian cafés. So goes the most interesting story of the origin of *cancan*. Other experts say it is simply a repetitive French compound based on *can*, without further elaboration.

cancel.   Medieval scribes crossed out errors on parchment by drawing lines obliquely across the words. They called such criss-crosses *cancelli*, "lattices," because they resembled such structures, and the word *cancelli* for such cross-outs eventually gave us the English *cancel*.

candidate.   Pure or not, political candidates take their name from the Latin *candidus*, white, symbolizing purity. In ancient times a Roman *candidatus* dressed in a white toga when he appeared at the forum to seek election to the magistracy.

can do.   *See* NO CAN DO.

candy.   We know that candy of various kinds has been around for at least 4,000 years and that there are at least 2,000 varieties of it available today. It was probably the Greeks who brought the word *candy* into the language. It seems that a favorite of the troops of Alexander the Great was a Persian delicacy called *kand*—a sweet reed garnished with honey, spices, and coloring. The word *candy* itself either came to us from this *kand* that Alexander's men brought home to Greece, or from the old Arab word for sugar, *quand*.

candytuft. These colorful flowers have nothing at all to do with candy, which they do not taste like or look like. *Candy* here is simply a variation on *Candia*, a city in Crete, where candytuft (*Iberis umbellata*) was originally found over a century ago.

cane; canebreak. *See* BAMBOO.

canfield. Lonely people playing solitaire can at least have the company of Richard C. Canfield (1855–1941), for this American gambler invented the world's most popular game of solitaire one summer toward the end of the 19th century during breaks from the gaming tables at the fashionable resort of Saratoga Springs, New York. Canfield based his new game, named *canfield* after himself, on the solitaire game called klondike, which gold miners in Alaska had invented a few decades before.

canicular days. *See* DOG DAYS.

canned music; canned laughter. O. Henry coined the expression *canned music*, prerecorded music, in a 1904 story. "The Latin races . . . are peculiarly adapted to be victims of the phonograph," advises one of his characters. Replies another character: "Then we'll export canned music to the Latins." The term is based on canned tins of food, and it led to later expressions like *canned speeches* and the *canned laughter* used for radio and television shows. *See* KNOW ONE'S CANS.

cannel coal. This is not "channel coal." Found in Kentucky and Indiana, *cannel coal* is "a brightly burning coal rich in hydrogen that burns well in open fireplaces" and is becoming popular again as fireplaces become more common. Because it gives off a lot of light compared with other coals, it was first called "candle coal," the name eventually corrupted to *cannel*.

cannibal. When Columbus encountered the Caribs upon landing in the Lesser Antilles on his second voyage in 1493, these natives told him their name was Canibales. This word was merely a dialect form of *Caribs* and these people were Caribs themselves, but the Spanish thereafter called the whole Carib tribe Canibales. Because some of these fierce warriors ate human flesh, within a century their name was used in Europe as a synonym for man-eaters, and *cannibalism* was substituted for the classical *anthropophagy*. The word was probably also influenced by the Spanish word *canino*, meaning "canine" or "voracious." Columbus, incidentally, thought he had landed in Asia and that the Canibales were subjects of the Great Khan, or Cham, another doubtful but possible influence on the word's formation. *See* CARIBBEAN SEA.

cannoli. To be good, this Italian pastry has to be crispy when filled with its mixture of ricotta cheese, cream, candied fruits, and other ingredients. It shouldn't be filled hours before, which makes its shell soggy. The cannoli has become a popular "international food" today. The pastry is named from the Italian *cannolo* for "tube," being tubular in shape. However, *cannoli* is never used in the singular form, although one such pastry should technically be a *cannolo*.

canoe; paddle your own canoe. Abraham Lincoln's frequent use of the phrase *paddle your own canoe* did much to make it popular, but Captain Frederick Marryat, that unflattering critic of American manners, seems to have been the first to have used the expression in its figurative sense, "be independent," in his novel *The Settlers in Canada* (1844). *Canoe* probably derives from the Arawak word *canoa*, for "a small boat carved from a tree trunk," which Columbus recorded in his diary and introduced into Spanish.

canoe birch. The birchbark canoes of American Indian fame were made from the birch species *Betula papyrifera*, which is the most widespread birch in the world. This canoe birch is also called "white birch," "silver birch," and "paper birch" and is very common in eastern North America.

can of worms. Any source of complex problems or troubles, usually unpredictable. The Americanism is first recorded in 1927 and is chiefly heard in the form of *don't open that can of worms. Can* here refers to an unopened can of food with worms or maggots inside.

canoodle. Hugging, snuggling, kissing, petting between a man and woman or boy and girl. The Americanism dates back to the mid-19th century and is still used in a humorous sense today, probably because the word itself sounds funny.

canopy. *See* CANAPÉ.

cant. *Cant*, for "a whining manner of speech or pious hypocritical talk," surely derives from the Latin *cantare*, "to sing or chant." Yet some evidence indicates that the word's meaning may have been influenced by the unpopularity of a Scottish preacher named Andrew Cant (1590–1663). In fact, the *Spectator* tried to trace *cant* to the Reverend Cant in an article written in 1711, observing that he talked "in the pulpit in such a dialect that it's said he was understood by none but his own Congregation, and not by all of them." Most dictionaries do not recognize the connection between the preacher's name and *cant*—the usual explanation being that the word evolved from the Latin *cantare*, in reference to the whining speech of beggars. But there seems to be enough evidence to indicate that Reverend Andrew Cant's unpopularity at least strengthened the word's meaning.

Cantab; Cantabrigian. *Cantabrigian* has been since about 1645 a synonym for a resident of Cambridge, England, deriving from the Latin *Cantabrigia* for "Cambridge." Hence the word has long meant Cambridge or Harvard (in Cambridge, Massachusetts) students who are more commonly called *Cantabs*, even this shortened form dating back to early 18th-century England.

can't abide one. *Abide* means to endure, stand, or tolerate, usually in the negative sense, as in "I can't abide him." Mark Twain used this expression, which is now common nationally and has been considered standard American English since at least 1930.

cantaloupe. The melon called a cantaloupe in the United States is not a cantaloupe. The cantaloupe, a variety of muskmelon, is named for Cantalupo, the Pope's country seat near Rome, where the melon was first bred in Italy from an Armenian variety. True cantaloupes are only grown in Europe. The "cantaloupe" grown in the United States is really the netted or nutmeg muskmelon, which originated in Persia (Iran). Muskmelons were introduced to America by Columbus, who brought seeds to Hispaniola on his second voyage; the many delicious varieties of muskmelon include the honeydew, Persian, casaba, and banana melons.

cantankerous. Oliver Goldsmith coined this word for "contrary or ill-natured" in *She Stoops to Conquer* (1773). Or rather, he fashioned it from an earlier, now obsolete word, *cantecker*, meaning a quarrelsome, disputatious person.

Can't anyone here play this game? Casey Stengel, legendary manager of the New York Mets (and the New York Yankees previously), uttered this plaintive cry when one of his players committed two errors to lose an extra-inning game during the 1962 season. The hapless Mets finished last that year, 62½ games out of first place, losing more games than any other 20th-century team. Writer Jimmy Breslin called the Mets "a team . . . for losers, just like nearly everybody else in life." Since Stengel said them, the words have been widely used outside of baseball as a humorous admonition to anyone who can't do a job right.

can't cut the mustard; can't cut (hack) it. Whatever the origins of *can't cut the mustard*, and they are about as clear as mustard, the expression *too old to cut the mustard* is always applied to men today and conveys the idea of sexual inability. *Can't cut the mustard*, however, means not to be able to handle any job for any reason, not just because of old age. Preceding the derivation of *too old to cut the mustard* by about a half a century, it derives from the expression *to be the mustard*. "Mustard" was slang for the "genuine article" or "main attraction" at the time. Perhaps someone cutting up to show that he was *the mustard*, or the greatest, was said *to cut the mustard* and the phrase later came to mean to be able to fill the bill or do the important or main job. In any case, O. Henry first used the words in this sense in his story "Heart of the West" (1907) when he wrote: "I looked around and found a proposition that exactly cut the mustard." Today *can't cut the mustard* is usually *can't cut it* or *can't hack it*. A recent variant on *too old to cut the mustard* is *if you can't cut the mustard, you can lick the jar*.

canteen. *Canteen*, like CANTINA, derives from the Italian *cantina* for "wine cellar." The word is often associated with U.S.O. canteens, free clubs for lonely servicemen during World War II, but it also means a small portable water bottle that soldiers carry in the field.

canter. Originally the canter—the gait of a horse between a trot and a gallop—was called a Canterbury gallop, because it was thought to be the traditional pace of pilgrims riding to the Canterbury shrine in England.

Canterbury bells. Pilgrims to Canterbury in Chaucer's time thought that the bellflowers (*Campanula medium*) they saw along the road resembled the little bells on their horses and called the flowers Canterbury bells. Campanula itself is the Latin word for "bell."

can't hold a candle to. *See* HOLD A CANDLE TO.

cantina. A Spanish term for a bar or saloon in southwestern states, where cantinas with colorful names like "The Spring of Golden Dreams" were once common.

can't make head nor tail of it. "I can't understand this, it's totally confusing." The saying, born in a rural world some three centuries ago, is applied today mainly to stories or explanations, though someone will occasionally say he or she *can't make head nor tail of* an object. It is sometimes heard as *I can't make head or tails of it*, this variation possibly suggested by coin flipping.

can't walk and chew gum at the same time. Is unusually stupid. We have it on the authority of John Kenneth Galbraith that President Lyndon Johnson said Congressman Gerald Ford "can't fart and chew gum at the same time," which may be an old expression common in Johnson's home state of Texas. In any case, by the time Ford became president after Richard Nixon's resignation, the words had been laundered to *can't walk and chew gum at the same time*.

Canuck. *Canuck* as a derogatory name for a French Canadian has been around since about 1865, with both Canadians and Americans using it. It may be from CANADA and CHINOOK, but it may also be from *Canada* plus the Algonquin Indian ending *-uck*.

canvasback duck. Courtiers in the 17th century wore doublets that covered them from shoulders to waist. These were made of leather or other expensive materials, but some impecunious gallants couldn't afford such fine garments and had to settle for doublets made of leather in the front and cheaper canvas in the back. These "canvas back" garments later inspired the name *canvasback* for the North American duck with whitish back feathers.

canyon. Used mostly in the U.S. for a very deep valley or gorge with steep sides, sometimes with water flowing at the bottom; the word derives from the Spanish *canon* (a large tube or funnel).

Capability Brown. "Your estate holds great capabilities" the great English landscape gardener and architect Lancelot Brown (1715–83) often told prospective employers. His words earned the founder of modern English landscape gardening many commissions and the nickname "Capability."

capador. Edna Ferber defined this Spanish word in *Giant* (1952): " 'He's the capador. He castrates the males and that makes them steers. And [as an additional duty] he nicks a piece off the end of the left ear of male and female and sticks it in his pocket, and he marks the right ear with a hole and a slit, for identification. At the end of the day he adds up, and the number of pieces of ear in his pocket shows the number of calves we've branded . . . [As for] the testicles of the castrated calves, [the vaqueros] roast them on the coals, they burst open and they eat them as you'd eat a roast oyster . . . very tasty . . . the vaqueros think they make you potent and strong as a bull.' "

Cape Cod turkey. New Englanders have called baked cod-fish Cape Cod turkey for many years, at least since the mid-19th century, just as melted cheese has been called WELSH RABBIT the world over.

Cape Horn. *See* AROUND THE HORN.

Cape of Good Hope. The stormy southern tip of South Africa, which was so named because it seemed to be on the way to India and all its riches. When the inexperienced explorer Vasco da Gama rounded it in 1497, he reached India and opened up a new trade route to the world, bringing back a rich cargo of spices.

Cape of Good Hope; Greenland. Early Portuguese explorers named this treacherous area off the southern tip of Africa the "Cape of Storms." But King John II of Portugal changed the name to "Cape of Good Hope" to encourage exploration of the area! Earlier the Vikings had played the same public relations game when naming Greenland, which is hardly green.

capital. Our word *capital*, for "wealth," comes to us from the Latin *caput*, "head," dating to days when a person's wealth was reckoned in the number of head of cattle that he owned.

the Capital of the World; the Second City of the World. Former New York City mayor Rudolf Giuliani has in recent years used this sobriquet for New York. But he didn't invent it. The name was given to the city in 1939 when the World's Fair was held there and became popular again when the United Nations made New York its home. In 1898, when a reorganization of the city took in Brooklyn and other parts, New York City became known as the Second City of the World, London being the First City. In recent times Chicago has commonly been called the Second City among American cities.

capital punishment. The word *capital* derives from the Latin *caput*, "head," and capital crimes in English law were at first crimes for which the offender literally lost his head, had it chopped off on the block. (The first recorded use of the word *capital* shows this: "To have capytal sentence & be beheaded," 1483). *Capital punishment* was used about a century later, by which time commoners sentenced to death were hanged and only nobles were allowed to have their heads chopped off. "Capital (or deadly) punishment is done sundry wayes," observed the first writer employing the term. The death penalty, of course, goes back to prehistoric times. It was originally used only to appease an offended diety because of a grave religious offense, but also came to be imposed for murder and many other crimes. Among the ancient Hebrews adultery, bestiality, blasphemy, cursing father or mother, idolatry, incest, rape, sabbath-breaking, unchastity, and witchcraft were all punishable by death. The Romans punished by death crimes such as forgery by slaves, corruption, sodomy, and seduction, and in 18th-century England more than 200 crimes, most of them against property, called for capital punishment. Since the 19th century, crimes punished by death have been reduced greatly in number throughout the world and many countries have now abolished capital punishment.

capitol. A building in which a state legislature meets, or, when capitalized, the building where the U.S. Congress meets. The name comes from ancient Rome's Capitoline hill, on the summit of which was erected the great temple of the city's guardian, Jupiter Optimas Maximus. In A.D. 340 the Capitol was saved from the Gauls when the sacred geese kept there awakened its defenders, who repulsed a night attack.

cappuccino. This Italian espresso coffee mixed with steamed milk or cream is so called because its color resembles the color of the habits worn by the CAPUCHIN monks.

capsule wisdom. No one has identified the inspired genius who invented small medicine capsules that dissolve in the stomach so that the terrible-tasting stuff inside never touches the tongue. From their shape these capsules seem to have been patterned on plant seeds, pods, or capsules, which take their name from the Latin *capsula*, a small box or case. The medicines were mass-produced by the middle of the 19th century, and the first recorded use of their name is in 1875. The little capsules, a clever idea themselves, became so common that soon after they were compared to anything short and concise, as in *capsule wisdom*, "a wise, pithy saying."

Captain Bligh. *Captain Bligh*, commemorating the captain of *Mutiny on the Bounty* fame, is still used to describe a cruel, cold-hearted task-master. Captain William Bligh is also remembered by the ackee fruit, which looks and tastes like scrambled eggs when properly prepared, but can be poisonous when over- or under-ripe. The ackee tree's botanical name is *Blighia sapida*, after the man who introduced it, along with breadfruit. Bligh was called "Breadfruit Bligh" for his discovery of that fruit's virtues and was in fact bringing specimens of the breadfruit tree from Tahiti to the West Indies in 1789 when his mutinous crew foiled his plans. The lesson of *Bounty* apparently taught him little or nothing, for his harsh methods and terrible temper aroused a second mutiny, the Rum Rebellion, while he served as governor of New South Wales. Bligh, a brave and able officer, retired from the Navy a vice admiral. He died in 1817, at age 63. *See also* BREADFRUIT.

captain cook. Captain James Cook and his men introduced the domesticated pig to New Zealand. Many of these animals escaped into the wild and multiplied; there were soon so many that settlers took to calling the wild pigs *captain cooks*, after the great explorer.

Captain Half-Ass. Blackbeard, Diabolito, Long Knife, Captain Buzzard, Gentleman Harry, Big John, Black Bart, and Calico Jack—these are only a few of the many pirates who chose to live under colorful pseudonyms that they invented or had bestowed upon them. The pirate with the oddest *nom de guerre*, however, must be the 18th-century French pirate whose pseudonym translates as Captain Half-Ass, an appellation about which history remains silent.

captain of the heads. A jocular Navy term for the enlisted man responsible for keeping the lavatories, or *heads*, neat and clean. Wrote one proud mother to a friend: "My son is doing very well in the Navy. In only six months he's been promoted to Captain of the Heads!" Heads are so called because they were originally in the bow, or head, of a ship.

Capuchin. The order of Capuchin monks, established in 1520, came into being when Franciscan friar Matteo di Bascio insisted that the habit worn by the Franciscans wasn't the one that St. Francis had worn. He stubbornly fashioned himself a sharp-pointed pyramidal hood *(capuche)*, let his beard grow, and went barefoot; the pope granted him permission eight years later to wear this costume and form a separate order that would preach to the poor. The new offshoot of Franciscans came to be named for the headdress its monks still wear, and it wasn't long before a woman's combined cloak and hood was dubbed a *capuchin* after the monks' cowl. The tropical *Capuchin monkey* and *Capuchin pigeon* are named for the Capuchin's costume— the monkey's black hair and appearance resembling the monastic cowl, and the pigeon having a hoodlike tuft of black feathers.

caput. In medieval times, during bubonic plague epidemics, German burial squads counted each corpse as a head, from the Latin *caput*, "head," the term used so often that the German *kaputt* came to mean anything "broken, wrecked, unserviceable, finished." This is probably the origin of the English slang term *caput*, used in both England and America for "all gone, no more, done for."

capybara. The South American capybara *(Hydrochoecrus)* looks like a rat from out of a low-budget science-fiction movie, certainly taking the prize as the world's largest rodent (up to 174 pounds and 4½ feet long). The animal bears its ages-old Tupi Indian name. Though as large as a pig, the gentle vegetarian, also called the *carpincho* or *water hog*, would rather hide than fight and makes its home in tall grasses along riverbanks. Unfortunately, it has many cunning enemies that it cannot always escape despite its swimming abilities. Its predators include the cougar, the jaguar, and man, all of whom hunt the giant rodent for food.

car. The word *car* comes from a Celtic word that sounded like *karra* to Julius Caesar, who gave the name to his chariots. *Karra* later was Latinized to *carra*. Surprisingly the word *car* appears first around 1300; *carriage* evolved from it, then *horseless carriage*, and, finally, back to *car* again as a shortened form. *See* AUTOMOBILE.

caramba! A Spanish exclamation of admiration or annoyance, as in "Caramba! Look at that girl!" The word entered the American vocabulary through Mexico, though few dictionaries record it.

carbine. The carbine, a short, light rifle, probably takes its name from the Medieval Latin *Calabrinus*, meaning "a Calabrian." Calabria in southern Italy was noted for its light horsemen or skirmishers, and the first such weapons were either used or manufactured there. "Carabins," as the weapons were called in 16th-century England, were originally "large pistols . . . having barrels 3 ft. long." They were much shorter and less cumbersome than muskets, however, and were employed by light cavalry troops. By the early 17th century *carbine* was being spelled in its present form, although it took many years for the weapon to develop into the short, light rifle that we know today.

cardigan. "It is magnificent but it is not war," was Maréchal Bosquet's memorable remark on the Charge of the Light Brigade, famous in history and in Tennyson's poem of the same name. The charge at Balaclava during the Crimean War was led by James Thomas Brudenell (1797–1868), the seventh earl of Cardigan. Cardigan, a foolish, vain, violent-tempered man, somewhat redeemed himself by his great personal courage. Cardigan's troops were the most precisely drilled and splendidly dressed of British soldiers, their commander invariably surpassing them in the last respect. The knitted woolen vest he wore to protect himself against the Crimean winter was named in his honor during his fleeting moments of fame, but today the cardigan is a collarless, buttoned sweater or jacket with a round or V-neck, bearing little resemblance to the original.

cardinal. Certain Roman Catholic bishops were called cardinals, from the Latin *cardo* ("hinge"), because the election of the pope "hinged" on them. The handsome red bird we know as the cardinal was so called because of the Roman Catholic cardinal's bright red hat. This name for the North American grosbeak was first recorded in 1802.

the cards beat all the players. The philosophy that fate or luck is all, despite our efforts. It is not certain with whom the saying originates, but Ralph Waldo Emerson was familiar with it, meditating on the words in his essay "Nominalist and Realist" (1844): "For though gamesters say that the cards beat all the players, though they were never so skillful, yet in the contest we are now considering the players are also the game, and share the powers of the cards."

careen. Careening a ship means to ground her at high tide, and when the tide has receded to heel her over on her side. This is sometimes done with small vessels so their bottoms can be scraped, caulked, or otherwise repaired. The word is first recorded in the late 16th century and derives from the French *carene*, "keel," which comes from the Latin *carina*, "keel." A ship is also said to *careen* when she inclines to one side or heels over when sailing on a wind. From this nautical expression comes our term for any leaning, swaying, or tipping to one side of something that is in motion, such as, "The car careened around the corner."

Carême. "The king of cooks and the cook of kings" was born in Paris on June 8, 1784, in his own words one of 25 children "of one of the poorest families in France." Marie-Antoine Carême worked from the time he was seven as a kitchen scullion. In his teens he was accepted as an apprentice chef and after much study under many masters went on to found *la grande cuisine française*, classic French cooking as we still know it today. Carême's creations reflected his considerable artistic abilities, his pastries often looking more like sculpture than food. His supreme taste and meticulous standards illustrated in his many books, as well as his 48-course dinners, made French cuisine sovereign throughout Europe. Among other notables, Carême cooked for Talleyrand, the future George IV of England, Czar Alexander I, Lord Castlereagh, Baron Rothschild (the world's richest man), and France's Louis XVIII, who granted him the right to call himself "Carême of Paris." But his motto was "One master: Talleyrand. One mistress: Cooking." Monarch of the entire culinary empire, his name today symbolizes a great chef. He died on January 12, 1833 while sampling a *quenelle* of sole prepared by a student in his cooking school. Someone wrote that he had died "burnt out by the flame of his genius and the heat of his ovens."

Caribbean Sea.   The Caribs of the South American coast were far more adventurous and warlike than those of the larger islands such as Cuba, and it is from these expert mariners—they were one of the few New World peoples to use sails—that the Caribbean Sea takes its name. *See* ARAWAK; CANNIBAL.

carnap.   A term based on *kidnap* that in Philippine English means to steal a car. English and Tagalog are the official languages in the Philippines.

carnation.   The word *carnation*, meaning "fleshlike," was first the name of a fleshlike color developed by artists in the 15th century, derived from the Latin *carnis*, "flesh." Soon a gillyflower of this color was developed and took the same name for its pinkish color. The carnation (*Dianthus caryophyllus*) has retained its name even though it is available in many other shades; in fact, it is also popularly called a "pink." Carnations with two or three stripes of contrasting colors in the petals are called "bizarres," while those with only one color are called "flakes." A carnation played a part in the attempted rescue of Marie-Antoinette from the guillotine on August 28, 1793. On that day the royalist noble chevalier de Rougeville visited her in her cell and left a carnation in which a tiny note was hidden telling the French queen of a plan to save her. The plot failed, and Marie was executed when her guard refused to go along with a bribe attempt, but the "affair of the carnation" lives on in history.

Carnegiea.   One of the world's richest men, Andrew Carnegie (1835–1919), gives his name to the largest cactus in the world, *Carnegiea gigantea*, or the saguaro. One *Carnegiea* specimen found near Madrona, New Mexico in 1950 had candelabra-like branches rising to 53 feet. *Carnegiea* had been named for Carnegie a half century before in gratitude for his help in financing Tucson's Desert Laboratory. The millionaire, whose family emigrated to America from Scotland when he was a youth, rose from rags to riches, starting as a bobbin boy in a cotton factory at $1.20 a week and becoming a multimillionaire with his Carnegie Steel Company, which was merged with the United States Steel Corporation when he retired in 1901 to live on his estate in Scotland. Carnegie believed that it was a disgrace to die rich. He became one of the greatest individual philanthropists in history, his benefactions totaling about $350 million.

carnival.   The word *carnival* is associated with fasting. Carnival was first the whole season leading up to Mardi Gras, the word deriving from the Latin *carne vale*, "flesh, farewell," signifying that the revelry will soon be over and the lean days of Lent will be upon us.

carol.   Our English word for a song, as in a *Christmas carol*, derives from the French word *carole*, meaning "ring." This refers to the early carollers dancing around in a ring as they sang.

Carolina rice.   Some sources say that the first rice successfully grown in South Carolina was introduced into Charleston in 1694 by a Dutch brig out of Madagascar, while others hold that Yankee shipmaster Captain John Thurber presented a packet of Madagascar rice to one of the early settlers on pulling into Charleston harbor late in the 1680s. According to the latter story, the settler planted the rice rather than dining on it, and after it sprouted, he gave seed to his friends, who in turn raised rice on their fertile land. Charleston and the Carolina low country soon became the "Rice Coast," rice fortunes building Charleston and marking the beginning of a plantocracy considered by many to be the New World aristocracy. The Madagascar rice raised there was being called Carolina rice or golden rice by 1787.

carotid artery.   The ancients knew that if you pressed the arteries leading to the head long enough, unconsciousness would result. Thus they named these arteries *karotides*, from the Greek *karoun*, to stupefy. *Karotide* later became *carotid* in English.

carouse.   An ancient Roman goblet used by the Germans was made in the shape of a crouching lion, with the belly as the bowl so that a drinker couldn't put it down until he finished his wine. This led to the German toast *Gar aus!*, meaning "Completely out!" or "Drink fully!" when drinkers lifted their goblets. Over the centuries *Gar aus* eventually became *garouse* and finally *carouse* in English, meaning to engage in a drunken revel or to drink deeply and frequently.

carpe diem.   Latin for "seize the day," enjoy the present instead of worrying about the future. The well-known phrase *seize the day* is the title of a 1956 novella by American Nobel laureate Saul Bellow.

carpetbagger.   In Victorian times luggage made from red carpets became an institution and was so popular among embezzling bankers as a place to stash their loot that the embezzlers themselves were dubbed *carpetbaggers*. After the American Civil War carpetbags were used by most of the unscrupulous northern political adventurers, often poor whites, who packed their few worldly possessions in them to satisfy state property residence requirements and moved to the South to take advantage of the newly enfranchised blacks and to win power and fortune by controlling elections. These greedy, unprincipled men, carrying their red carpetbags, and the previous association of the bags with men who milked banks as these men were milking the South, gave birth to their name, *carpetbaggers*, as well as to the name *Carpetbag Era* in American history.

carpet knight.   In days of old, when knighthood was in flower, *carpet knight* was a contemptuous term for a knight who fought all his battles in a lady's bed or on her carpet, one who stayed home from the wars. The expression, first recorded in 1576, came over the years to mean someone who avoids practical work.

carrot. From the Latin *carota* for the vegetable, which derives from the Greek *karoton*. When carrots were first brought to England, women liked to use the plant's fern-like leaves as hair decorations, but didn't much care for them as food. The ancient Greeks extolled them as "love medicine" and called them *philtron*.

carry a torch. No one is sure of the origin of this expression meaning to love someone unrequitedly, the phrase dating back to the 1930s. Some writers suggest the source of the words is Venus, the Roman goddess of love, who often carried a torch, while others say the expression was coined by Broadway cabaret singer Tommy Lyman.

carry coals to Newcastle. England's Newcastle-upon-Tyne was the first coal port in the world, the initial charter granted to the town for the digging of coal given by Henry III in 1239. The fact that no one in his right mind would import coal into this coal-mining county gave rise in the 19th century to the expression *to carry coals to Newcastle*, "to do something superfluous, to take something where it is already plentiful."

Carry Nation. Any intemperate temperance agitator. Carry Nation (1846–1911), convinced that she was divinely appointed to bring about the downfall of the saloon, embarked upon her career in Kansas in 1899, chopping her way through the United States and Europe with her "hatchetings" or "hatchetations." Her temperance lectures were not as interesting as her spectacular destruction of saloon interiors with her trusty ax, but the title of her autobiography, *The Use and Need of the Life of Carry A. Nation* (1904), is a classic. The much ridiculed schoolteacher seemed to believe that she was made for martyrdom; she even enjoyed her frequent stays in jail.

carry the ball. The person in charge *carries the ball* and has been doing so since the 1920s, when the football term began to be used figuratively by Americans.

carte blanche. *Cartes blanches* is the plural, if anyone dares use it. The phrase simply means "white paper" in French and originated as a military term referring to unconditional surrender—a defeated government signing a blank sheet of paper on which the victor could write whatever terms he pleased. The phrase has been commonly used in English since the beginning of the 18th century, soon after which the expression took on its fuller meaning, by extension, of unconditional authority, total discretionary power.

Cartesian. *Cartesian* refers to the philosophy of René Descartes (1596–1650) and his followers, deriving from *Cartesius*, the Latinized form of his name. The French philosopher was an eminent mathematician who based the starting point of his philosophy on the famous phrase *Cogito, ergo sum* ("I think, therefore I am"). His influence on science, philosophy, and literature has been immense, for he was among the first to rely on the rule of reason, rejecting all philosophical tradition. *Cartesian* also means "the explanation of philosophical problems by mathematics." Descartes spent much of his life in Holland, dying in Sweden, where he had been invited by Queen Christiana. His major work is *Discours de la Méthode* (1637). I remember reading somewhere that Descartes was fascinated all his life by women with a squint, which means absolutely nothing but might be of encouragement to some readers.

Carthage must be destroyed! When Rome destroyed Carthage she became the great power in the ancient world. That she destroyed Carthage is due in large part to the eloquent orator Cato, who inspired the Romans by using *Carthage must be destroyed! ("Cartago delenda est!")* as the final words in every speech he made in the Roman Senate.

Carthaginian peace. A destructive peace settlement, one like the severe Punic War treaties that the Romans imposed on the Carthaginians.

Carvel. In 1934 Thomas Andreas Carvelas, a Yonkers, New York, resident, invented a machine for making soft, frozen custard ice cream, which he sold from a truck, competing with such rivals as the Good Humor man. Carvelas later legally changed his name to Tom Carvel and sold franchises that made the Carvel name a household word for soft ice cream by the 1960s.

Carvel's ring. Captain Grose, in his *Dictionary of the Vulgar Tongue* (1785), relates the anecdote explaining why *Carvel's ring* means "a woman's private parts or the *pudendum muliebre*": "Ham Carvel, a jealous old doctor, being in bed with his wife, dreamed that the Devil gave him a ring, which, so long as he had it on his finger, would prevent his being made a cuckould: waking he found he had got his finger the Lord knows where." Rabelais also told this story.

Carver chair. A type of chair with three vertical and three horizontal spindles named for John Carver (1576–1621), first governor of the Plymouth Colony, who first owned one so designed. Carver, a rich man, is considered to be the chief figure in arranging the Pilgrim migration to America and chose the site at Plymouth for the colony.

caryatid; atlas. Caryatids are draped or partially clad female figures used in place of columns or pillars as supports, especially in classical architecture. They take their name from the maidens of Caryae (Latin for Karyai, a town in Laconia, Greece). The Karyatids, or maidens of Karyai, danced in temples at the festival of Artemis and occasionally assumed the poses represented in the statues. Some accounts say that their figures were first used by the Greeks as a reminder of Karyai's disgrace, for the Karyatids had supported the Persians at the battle of Thermopylae (480 b.c.). An atlas, the male counterpart of a caryatid, takes its name from the Titan who supported the Earth on his shoulders.

casaba. A variety of winter melon with a wrinkled skin and sweet, juicy green flesh. It is named after Kassaba (now Turgutlo), Turkey, where it was first grown about 1885. Also called "casaba melon" and "cassaba."

Casablanca. When Warner Bros. warned the Marx Brothers not to use the name "Casablanca" in their film *A Night in Casablanca* because (the studio claimed) this would infringe upon the title of Warner's movie *Casablanca*, Groucho Marx wrote the company the following letter now in the Groucho collection of the Library of Congress. Jack Warner, who regarded actors as "bums" and writers as "schmucks with Underwoods," was not amused. "Apparently there is more than one way of conquering a city and holding it as your own," Groucho wrote. "For example, up to the time that we contemplated making a picture, I had no idea that the city of Casablanca belonged to Warner Bros. However, it was only a few days after our announcement appeared that we received a long ominous document warning us not to use the name 'Casablanca.' It seems in 1471, Ferdinand Balboa Warner, the great-great-grandfather of Harry and Jack, while looking for a shortcut to the city of Burbank, had stumbled on the shores of Africa and, raising his alpenstock, which he later turned in for a hundred shares of the common, he named it Casablanca. I just can't understand your attitude. Even if they plan on releasing the picture, I am sure that the average movie fan could learn to distinguish between Ingrid Bergman and Harpo. I don't know whether I could, but I certainly would like to try. You claim you own Casablanca and that no one else can use that name without your permission. What about Warner Brothers—do you own that too? You probably have the right to use the name Warner, but what about Brothers? Professionally, we were brothers long before you were. Even before us, there had been other brothers—the Smith Brothers, the Brothers Karamazov, Dan Brothers, an outfielder with Detroit and 'Brother, can you spare a dime?' This was originally 'Brothers, can you spare a dime,' but this was spreading a dime pretty thin. The younger Warner Brother calls himself Jack. Does he claim that, too? It's not an original name—it was used long before he was born. Offhand, I can think of two Jacks—there was Jack of 'Jack and the Beanstalk' and Jack the Ripper, who cut quite a figure in his day . . ." And so the letter went on à la Groucho. Needless to say, *A Night in Casablanca* remained *A Night in Casablanca*.

Casanova. Giovanni Jacopo Casanova de Seingalt's famous memoirs run to some 1.5 million words and take us only through his 49th year. It is said that his autobiography should be trusted in the main as a portrait of the 18th century, but not in the details, yet it seems relatively tame today and the details are not as licentious or racy as they once appeared. It is often forgotten that the Italian adventurer was a man of many talents: in turn, journalist, raconteur, soldier, gambler, gastronome, preacher, abbe, philosopher, violinist, alchemist, businessman, diplomat, spy, and so on. Casanova is of course best remembered as a great lover, his name equaled only by DON JUAN as a synonym for a promiscuous womanizer.

case. Criminals case or survey a place in order to get useful information to enable them to rob it. This underworld expression dates back to early 20th-century America and has been adopted by the British and Australians.

Casey at the bat.

Oh! somewhere in this favored land the sun is
  shining bright,
The band is playing somewhere, and somewhere
  hearts are light;
And somewhere men are laughing, and
  somewhere children shout,
But there is no joy in Mudville—mighty Casey
  has struck out.

This mock-heroic poem by Ernest Laurence Thayer (1863–1940) was first published in the *San Francisco Examiner* on June 3, 1888, and *Casey at the Bat* has been popular ever since. Its initial popularity was due as much to the actor De Wolf Hopper, who included the 13 stanza poem in his repertoire, as it was to the poet, a former editor of the *Harvard Lampoon*. Everyone knows that there was no joy in Mudville when the mighty Casey struck out, but few are aware that Thayer patterned his fabled slugger on a real player, Daniel Maurice Casey, who was still posing for newspaper photographers 50 years after the poem's initial publication. Dan Casey, a native of Binghamton, New York, holds no records worthy of recording—not even as a strikeout king. He was a pitcher and an outfielder for Detroit and Philadelphia, but his career was overshadowed by the exploits of his elder brother, Dennis, an outfielder for Baltimore and New York. Casey died in 1943, when he was 78, in Washington, D.C. As for Thayer, he was paid only five dollars for his poem, which De Wolf Hopper recited over 5,000 times.

Casey Jones. Engineer John Luther Jones, who died in a wreck of the Chicago and New Orleans Limited on March 18, 1900, probably inspired the perennially popular folk ballad, "Casey Jones." The song's authorship is unknown and it may have been adapted from a ballad about a black railroad fireman. There are numerous versions of both music and lyrics, the folk song based on the tradition that "there's many a man killed on the railroad and laid in his lonesome grave." Casey Jones's story was dramatized in Robert Ardrey's *Casey Jones* (1938).

cash; hard cash. *Cash* is a back-formation from *cashier*, the keeper of any money box, or *caisse* as the French called it. The word came into English in about 1600. *Hard cash* means actual currency without any checks among it and got its name because it first meant only hard metal money.

cashier. *Cashier* is recorded as far back as 1596, as "a person who handles financial transactions." The term derives from the French *caisse*, meaning "money box."

cash in one's chips. *See* CHIP IN.

cash on the barrelhead. Though there is no proof of it, the origins of this expression most likely lie in the makeshift saloons on the American frontier over a century ago, which were often no more than a room in a log cabin with a barrel serving as both booze container and counter. No credit was extended, and any customer who wanted a smack of tarantula juice, or any rotgut likely to make him brave enough not to want to pay, was required to put down cash on the barrelhead, or counter.

cash register. The term *cash register* was devised by the machine's inventor—Dayton, Ohio restaurant owner James J. Ritty—who called it the "Cash Register and Indicator" in his patent filed March 26, 1879. Ritty invented the machine to help prevent his cashiers from stealing and, in fact, called it the Incorruptible Cashier. Unfortunately, he sold out his company after two years, discouraged by slow sales, never really cashing in on what would prove to be a billion-dollar invention.

casino. *Casino* means "little house" in Italian, the diminutive of the Italian *casa*, "house," which comes from the Latin *casa* meaning the same. The word was first used for a country house and then for a building or room in a building where one could dance or gamble. This last meaning, first recorded in 1851, gave us our words for a gambling establishment and the card game called casino.

Cassandra. Any prophet of doom, woman or man, is called a *Cassandra* after Cassandra, King Priam of Troy's daughter, who had been given the gift of prophecy by the god Apollo and frequently warned her people of impending disaster. Her prophecies always went unheeded because she spurned the advances of Apollo, and she met a violent end after her father declared her mad.

cassava. *See* MANIOC.

castanet. The first castanets were made of ivory or very hard wood, but the Spanish dancers who invented this musical instrument saw their resemblance to two chestnuts and gave them the Spanish name for that nut.

Castilloa elastica. This tree species—commonly called the ule or Mexican rubber tree—is not by any means the most important source of rubber today, but is a historical curiosity, having yielded the heavy black rubber balls Columbus was amazed to see natives playing with on his second voyage to South America—the first recorded observation of rubber by a European. The tree *C. elastica* is a species of the *Castilloa* genus of the mulberry family, and is named for Spanish botanist Juan Castillo y Lopez. Like Columbus, later explorers were astounded by the resilient balls made from the tree's vegetable gum, remarking that they rebounded so much that they "seemed alive," but rubber wasn't brought into commercial use in Europe until three centuries after its discovery. The tree *Hevea brasiliensis*, yielding high-grade Para, is by far the most important rubber source today. *Castilloa elastica*, however, still yields a good quality Caucho rubber, the large tree being particularly valuable when Para rubber is high priced. *See* RUBBER.

cast-iron plant. *See* ASPIDISTRA.

Castle Garden. *See* ELLIS ISLAND.

castles in the air. Boswell's famous remark that he was the first man to live in a castle in the air was charming self-analysis, and Bulwer-Lytton's observation that such castles are cheap to build but expensive to maintain is profound. However, the expression came into English long before both writers from the French *un chateau en Espagne* ("a castle in Spain") in about 1400, which later became *castles in the air*. French dreamers had been building castles in far off Spain or *Albanie* or *Asie* since the 11th century, when a poem called "The Roumant of the Rose" introduced the French phrase into English:

> Thou shalt make castels thanne in Spayne,
> And dream of Ioye [jfoy] all but in vayne.

cast pearls before swine. This is a familiar biblical injunction, from Matt. 7:6: "Give not that which is holy unto the dogs, neither cast ye your pearls before swine, lest they trample them under their feet, and turn again and rend you." John

Wyclif, commenting on the passage in 1380, added that "men should not give holy things to hounds," a phrase that has been used much more sparingly.

Castroism. *See* MAOISM.

catamaran. Today's *catamaran*, a vessel with two hulls held side by side some distance apart by a frame above them, bears only a slight resemblance to the rafts formed by a number of logs tied side by side at some distance apart that the British first saw in India late in the 17th century. But the Tamil *kattamaran*, "tied wood," for the rafts served well as a name for "two boats tied together at a distance apart" and finally for the vessel now called a *catamaran*. How *catamaran* became a synonym for a quarrelsome woman is anybody's guess. The term seems to have originated in America, *catamaran* possibly having been confused with "catamount," a bad-tempered cat also known as the cougar.

cat and mouse. Surprisingly enough, suffragettes arrested in England in about 1913 inspired the first popular use of this expression. The suffragettes often went on hunger strikes when imprisoned, and the government retaliated by passing the "Prisoners' Temporary Discharge for Ill-Health Act," which said that prisoners could be set free while fasting but were liable for rearrest when they recovered from their fasts to serve the remainder of their sentences. Critics compared the government's action to a big cat cruelly playing with a little mouse and dubbed the legislation "The Cat and Mouse Act." From the act, which wasn't particularly successful, came the popularization of *to play cat and mouse with*, though the expression may have been used long before this.

Catawaba. Catawaba, an oral language with no written form, lost its last speaker early in 1996 with the death of Red Thunder Cloud. It is said that Red Thunder Cloud prayed in Catawba every night and that with his final prayer the language died. According to Carl Teeter, emeritus professor of linguistics at Harvard University, "There were once about 500 [American Indian] languages in North America. About a hundred are still spoken and half of them are spoken by older people." *See also* AMERICAN INDIAN LANGUAGE WORDS; CATAWBA GRAPES; SEQUOIA.

Catawba grapes; Concord. A light reddish variety of grape grown in the eastern United States, the Catawba was developed by John Adlum in his vineyard near Georgetown in 1829, its dominant parent being the northern fox grape. It was named three years later for the Catawba Indians of the Carolinas, or for the Catawba River, which takes its name from the Indian tribe. The Catawba, long a traditional favorite, contains some vinifera blood and is one of the best grapes for white domestic wines. By 1860, nine-tenths of all grapes grown east of the Rockies were Catawbas, but they were thereafter replaced by the Concord, perfected in 1850, as the leading American variety. *See also* CATAWBA.

catbird; catbird seat. The slate-colored North American thrush (*Dumetella carolinensis*) has been called the *catbird* since the early 18th century because "its ordinary cry of alarm . . . somewhat resembles the mew of a cat." The name is also given to several Australian birds with similar cries. *To be in the catbird* *seat*, to be sitting pretty, is a southern Americanism dating back to the 19th century but popularized nationally by Brooklyn Dodger baseball announcer Red Barber, who used it frequently, and James Thurber's story "The Catbird Seat." *See also* TEARING UP THE PEA PATCH.

catboat. *Catboat* remains a double etymological mystery. No one knows why the name *cat* was given in the late 17th century to "a large vessel formerly used in the English coal trade and capable of carrying some 600 tons." Neither is it known why this name was later transferred to the small single-masted pleasure sailboat known as a catboat today. Perhaps the two boats were named independently, the reason for the former's name anybody's guess, and the *cat* sailboat so named because it is small and moves quickly and quietly, like a cat.

catcalls. Though this word, first recorded in 1659, is inspired by the nocturnal cry, or "waul," of the cat, catcalls are actually "human whistles expressing disapproval." A catcall was apparently first "a squeaking instrument, a kind of whistle used especially in British music halls to express impatience or disapprobation." It then came to mean a shrill shrieking whistle people made in imitation of the instrument and used for the same purposes. In America, however, such shrill whistles (though in this case not called catcalls) can be expressions of approval of a performance.

catch a crab. When an oarsman *catches a crab* he of course doesn't literally catch one on his oar. The expression, dating back to the 19th century, means that the oarsman has slowed down the speed of the boat either by missing the water on a stroke, or, more commonly, by making a poor, awkward stroke that doesn't completely clear the water when completed.

catch on the rebound. This metaphor has been used for close to a century, and it means to capture the heart of someone after he or she has been rejected by another person. It has a sports origin and could refer to a rebound in basketball, a baseball rebounding off an outfield wall, or even a rebounding hockey puck.

catchpenny. Back in 1824 London printer James Catnach sold at one penny each the "last speech by the condemned murderers" of a merchant named Weare. After the sheet sold out in a day, Catnach realized he had a good thing, and he headlined another penny paper WE ARE ALIVE AGAIN but ran the first two words together so that the banner read WEARE ALIVE AGAIN. Buyers of the Catnach penny paper punned on his name after discovering the cheap trick, referring to his paper as *catchpenny*, which soon came to mean any low-priced, fraudulent item. This is a good story, one of the best and earliest examples of folk etymology. However, the fault in this ingenious yarn lies in the fact that *catchpenny* was used in the same sense, "any flimflam that might catch a penny," 65 years before the very real Catnach ploy.

catchphrase. *Catchphrase* means simply a phrase that catches one's attention, especially a clever expression that lasts long enough to become a slogan. There are thousands if not millions of them, including advertising catchphrases (*Coke is it*) and political catchphrases ("Read my lips, no new taxes"), among many other groupings.

catch-22. Joseph Heller's novel *Catch-22* gave us this expression for an "insoluble dilemma, a double bind." In the novel, American pilots, forced to fly an excessive number of dangerous missions, could not be relieved of duty unless they were diagnosed insane. On the other hand, the same regulations stipulated that a pilot who refused to fly, so that he wouldn't be killed, could not be insane because he was thinking too clearly. There was no way out. By the way, Heller's *Catch-22* was originally titled *Catch-18*, the title changed at the last minute because Leon Uris's novel *Mila-18* came out just before Heller's book was to be published. Save for this we would be saying *catch-18*.

catchword. Catchwords are expressions caught up and repeated for effect. Because catchwords are often used by political parties, the term has become a contemptuous one, applied to insincere, misleading statements. *Catchword*, however, has an honorable history. Books were once printed with the word that began the first line on the next page directly under the last line of the preceding page. Such words, designed to catch the reader's attention and make him turn to the next page, were called *catchwords*. Then the term began to be applied to the last word, or cue, in an actor's speech and finally to any expression that catches the attention.

caterpillar. A caterpillar is a *chatepelos*, a "hairy cat," in French and it is from this word that we originally got our word for the "wyrm among fruite," as the English once called the creature. But the meaning and spelling of *caterpillar* were strengthened and changed by two old English words. "To pill" meant "to strip or plunder," as in "pillage," which came to be associated with the little worm stripping the bark off trees, and a glutton was a "cater," which the creature most certainly is. Thus the caterpillar became a "greedy pillager" as well as a "hairy cat," both good descriptions of its mien and manner.

catgut. Stray cats aren't killed to get it, as some people believe. *Catgut* is a misnomer, actually being the intestines of sheep, and sometimes horses and mules, used to make the tough cords that violins and tennis rackets are strung with (when nylon isn't employed). Probably the word *catgut* was originally *kitgut*, the word *kit* meaning a small fiddle as well as a kitten, but the English word *catlings*, "small strings for musical instruments," contributed to the confusion, too. The toughest and best catgut comes from the intestines of lean, poorly fed animals. "Roman strings," the best catgut strings for musical instruments, are made in Italy. Catgut is also used for hanging clock weights and for sutures in surgery.

a cat has nine lives. Recorded in 1546, this old English saying surely goes back well before the 16th century. Cats were regarded as tenacious of life because of their careful, suspicious nature and because they are supple animals that can survive long falls, though not from the top of a skyscraper as some people believe.

Cathedral of Commerce. In 1919 the Reverend Dr. S. Parker Cadman christened New York's Gothic-style Woolworth

Building, with its silvery lacework, the *Cathedral of Commerce*. Later, visiting British statesman Arthur Balfour observed: "What shall I say of a city that builds the most beautiful cathedral in the world and calls it an office building." Woolworth's 50-story "Skyqueen," modeled after London's House of Parliament, was then the world's tallest skyscraper, at 792 feet, but was proportioned so gracefully by architect Cass Gilbert that it is still regarded as one of the most majestic buildings in the City of Towers. Frank Woolworth's office inside is a replica of the Empire Room of Napoleon Bonaparte's palace in Comiègne. But amid all the superlatives about the building, too myriad to catalog here, perhaps the most amazing is that it was built without a mortgage and without a single dollar's indebtedness. Frank Woolworth just shelled out $13.5 million in cold cash—unique in the history of great buildings in the United States or anywhere else for that matter.

Catherine wheel. The Christian martyr St. Catherine of Alexandria is said to have confessed her faith to Roman Emperor Maximinus and rebuked him for the worship of false gods. After she converted his wife and the Roman general who escorted her to prison, Maximinus ordered her broken on the wheel, but the spiked wheel was shattered to pieces by her touch. This virgin of royal descent was then put to death by the ax, and tradition has it that her body was carried by angels to Mount Sinai where Justinian I built a famous monastery in her honor. St. Catherine is known as the patron saint of wheelwrights and mechanics, and her name day is November 25. The Catherine wheel, fireworks in the shape of a wheel rotated by the explosions; the circular, spoked Catherine wheel window; and Catherine wheels, lateral somersaults, all derive from her name.

cathode. *See* FARAD.

cathouse; cat wagon. *Cat* was slang for a prostitute as far back as 1401, when a poem of the day warned men to "beware of cats' tails." Though the term associating the cat and commercial sex is obsolete, the connotation hangs on in the word *cathouse*, for "a bordello, crib, fancy house, whorehouse, or sporting house." A cathouse is usually a cheap bordello, and even cheaper cat wagons pulled by horses brought harlots thataway when the West was being won. It's anybody's guess whether the cathouses take their name in some obscure way from the old word for harlot or were named independently after the sexual qualities usually attributed to cats.

cat ice. Thin, dangerous ice that would not support the weight of a (light-footed) cat. Dating back to late 19th-century America, the phrase has the same figurative meaning as thin ice, as in, "You're skating on cat ice taking a position like that."

Catiline; Catilinarian. Catiline's conspiracy (64 B.C.) gives us the term *Catiline* for a conspirator or plotter against the government. Lucius Sergius Catiline (ca. 108–62 B.C.), already guilty of at least one murder and extortion, had plotted with other nobles to kill the consuls, plunder the treasury, and set Rome on fire, but Cicero's eloquent *Catilinarian oration* alerted the public, foiling the conspirators. Catiline, sentenced to death, attempted to escape but was defeated in battle by Antonius and slain near Pistoria. Catiline represented himself as a democrat who would cancel all debts and outlaw all wealthy citizens. Ironically, Julius Caesar, the victim of assassins himself 20 years later, was probably a party to the planned assassinations.

cat in the meal. Something hidden or sinister. The expression comes from a story in the once-popular Webster's "Blue-Backed Speller" a century ago and is still used today.

catlinite. A clay stone of pale grayish-red to dark red, *catlinite* honors American painter and writer George Catlin (1796–1872). Catlin, a self-taught artist, is remembered for his primitive but authentic paintings of Indian life. An impresario, too, he displayed troupes of Indians in the East and Europe long before Buffalo Bill or Barnum. Early used by American Indians for making pipes, catlinite is commonly called pipe rock.

cat on a hot tin roof. Best known today as the title of Tennessee Williams's famous play, the expression has been in wide use in America since the turn of the 19th century. *Like a cat on a hot tin roof* derives from a similar British phrase, *like a cat on hot bricks*, which was first recorded about 1880 and also means someone ill at ease, uncomfortable, not at home in a place or situation.

cat-o'-nine-tails. Some black humorist probably coined the name for this terrible scourge—because it scratched the back like a cat—but the fact that the first Egyptian scourges were made of thongs of cat hide may have had something to do with the word's origin. The nine tails of the scourge, similar to the "nine lives" of a cat, could also have suggested the name. Scourging criminal offenders with a whip is a punishment as old as history. There are cases in medieval England of prisoners receiving 60,000 stripes from whips with three lashes and 20 knots in each tail. But the cat-o'-nine-tails, composed of one 18-inch handle with nine tails and three or more knots on each tail, only dates back to about 1670. Men were flayed alive with this scourge, which people believed was more holy, and thus effective, because its nine tails were a "trinity of trinities" ($3 \times 3 = 9$).

cats and dogs. *See* BLUE-CHIP STOCKS.

cat's cradle. Word detectives have given this one up as a bad job. The first mention of the child's game is in a little-known book called *The Light of Nature Pursued* (1768), in which the author attempts to explain it: "An ingenious play they call cat's cradle; one ties the two ends of a packthread together, and then winds it about his fingers, another with both hands takes it off perhaps in the shape of a gridiron, the first takes it again from him in another form, and so on alternately changing the packthread into a multitude of figures whose names I forget, it being so many years since I played it myself." Some say that suggestions that the game's name is a corruption of *cratch-cradle*, the manger cradle in which Christ was born, are not founded in facts. The story I was told when a boy had it that the first figure in the game resembled a *cratch*, a medieval English word for a hayrack, while the last figure resembled a cradle. Supposedly the game was first called *cratch-cradle* and this was changed to *cat's cradle* in later years when the hay cratch was no longer used or familiar to people—not because cats had anything to do with the game but because the word *cat* sounded something like *cratch*. Moreover, before its meaning as a hay-rack, *cratch* was a verb meaning "to seize, snatch, grab"—so maybe the cratching, or grabbing, of the string became the cat in the name. Then again perhaps I, too, should give this one up.

cat's-paw. A cat's-paw is light air during a calm that moves as silently as a cat and causes ripples on the water, indicating a coming storm. The term is recorded as early as 1769. Captain Frederick Marryat wrote in *Jacob Faithful* (1834): "Cat's paws of wind, as they call them, flew across the water here and there, ruffling its smooth surface." In the old folktale a monkey tricks a cat into using its paw to pull chestnuts from a fire, the monkey getting the nuts and the cat getting a burnt paw. From the tale comes our expression *cat's-paw*, for "a dupe."

catsup. *See* KETCHUP.

"The Cat's Waltz." This Chopin composition is so named because when Chopin was composing his Waltz No. 3 in F Major, his cat scrambled across the keys of his piano and he tried to reproduce the same sounds in his piece. *See also* KREUTZER SONATA.

cattail pine. *See* BRISTLECONE PINE.

cat the anchor. *Catting the anchor* simply means to keep the anchor clear of the ship by hanging it outside the vessel on a piece of timber called the cathead. The term dates back to at least the early 19th century.

cattle; chattel. Capitalists and cows have much in common, *cattle* being a corruption of the Latin *capitale*, "capital or principal holdings," a word that medieval English peasants found hard to pronounce and altered to *catel* and finally *cattle*. Because the principal holdings of peasants were often livestock, especially cows, cattle came to mean what it does today, while the medieval French *chatel*, another corruption of the Latin *capitale*, entered English as *chattel*, our legal term for all personal property.

cattle call. Alfred Hitchcock infamously called actors "cattle," and the term is still used in Hollywood. So is *cattle call*, first recorded in 1952, an open casting call or audition of many actors for one part or more parts. A cattle call for models is called a "go-see." The use of *cattle* as a derogatory term for people dates back to at least 1673, when it is first recorded in this sense. The theatrical use of the term may have originated with actors who thought they were treated like cattle.

cattle singer. An interesting Americanism explained by Edna Ferber in *Cimarron* (1930):

> . . . Shanghai Wiley, up from Texas, was the most famous cattle singer in the whole Southwest. . . . Possessed of a remarkably high sweet tenor voice . . . he had been known to quiet a whole herd of restless cattle on the verge of a mad stampede. It was an art he had learned when a cowboy on the range. Many cowboys had it, but none possessed the magic soothing quality of Shanghai's voice. It was reputed to have in it the sorcery of the superhuman. It was told of him that in a milling herd, their nostrils

distended, their flanks heaving, he had been seen to leap from the back of one maddened steer to another, traveling that moving mass that was like a shifting sea, singing to them in his magic tenor, stopping them just as they were about to plunge into the Rio Grande.

cattleya. This most popular of florist's orchids has nothing to do with cattle, having been named for William Cattley (d. 1832), English amateur botanist and botany patron. The *Cattleya* genus includes some 40 species, though over 300 hybridized forms are known. *Cattleya labiata*, with its 200 or so named varieties, is the most commonly cultivated orchid in America—the showy magenta-purple-lipped, yellow-throated "florist's orchid"—although the enormous orchid family contains perhaps 500 genera and 15,000 species. The *Cattleyea fly* and the *Cattley guava*, a subtropical fruit, also commemorate the English plant lover.

Caucasian. When the German anthropologist Johann Blumenbach divided mankind into the Caucasian, Mongolian, Ethiopian, American, and Malayan races in 1795, he chose a skull from the Caucasus, in what is now the Soviet Union, as the perfect type in his collection. He also claimed that the Caucasus area was the home of the hypothetical race known as "Indo-Europeans," to whom many languages can be traced. Blumenbach's theories proved unscientific and tinged with racism. In *Webster's New 20th Century Dictionary* the word he coined is now given "in default of a better" and as "one of the main ethnic divisions of the human race: [including] the Mediterranean, Alpine, and Nordic subdivisions, and is loosely called the white race."

caucus. In American politics party leaders hold caucuses, off-the-record meetings, to select leaders and form policy. These leaders are in one sense counselors or advisers, and it is probably the Algonquin Indian word *caucauasu*, meaning "counselor or adviser," that gives us the Americanism *caucus*, first recorded in 1773.

caught between the hammer and the anvil. To be surrounded by powerful enemy forces. The allusion is to the blacksmith's hammer and anvil, but the expression was first heard by most Americans from the lips of General Tommy R. Franks, regional commander of American forces in the war against terrorism (2001), who referred to Al-Queda forces trapped on the battlefield in Afghanistan.

caught flat-flooted. Americans have only used this expression, meaning "to be caught unprepared," since about 1910. However, it has been traced to the reign of Queen Anne in England, where it was first applied to horses left at the line after the start of a horse race. These horses weren't dancing forward on their toes, but had all four feet flat on the ground. In fact, the term *flat-footed* for someone with little or no hollow in the sole and a low instep, was first used to describe animals afflicted with the condition, especially horses with flat hooves and soles near the ground. Later *caught flat-footed* must have been a good description for a runner not on his toes and left at the mark when a footrace began, and it was eventually generalized to mean anyone asleep at the switch.

caught red-handed. *To be taken with red hand* in ancient times was to be caught in the act, like a murderer, his hands red with his victim's blood. The use of *red hand* in this sense goes back to 15th-century Scotland and Scottish law. Scott's *Ivanhoe* has the first recorded use of *taken red-handed* for someone apprehended in the act of committing a crime. Not long after, the expression became more common as *caught red-handed.*

caught with his pants down. Partridge has managed to trace this expression only to 1920, to England, where it was, of course, *caught with one's trousers down.* But possibly the phrase is much older and was kept out of print for prudish reasons until the '20s. Two explanations are given for its origins: that it refers to a man caught with a lady *in medias res* by her husband; or that it arose when a hostile Indian came upon a frontiersman answering the call of nature in the woods without his rifle at his side. The phrase *in medias res,* into the middle of things, was coined by Horace.

cauliflower. Cultivated for some 2,000 years, cauliflower takes its name from the Latin *caulis,* "cabbage," and *floris,* "flower." Its delicate flavor led Mark Twain to call it "cabbage with a college education." It is a relative youngster, however, when compared with cabbage, which has been grown for more than 4,000 years. *See* CABBAGE.

cauliflower ear. The white, gnarled scar tissue that forms on an ear repeatedly injured by boxing gloves gives that deformed ear the look of a head of cauliflower. The term has been around for a century or so and is even used by doctors to describe the condition.

caustic; cauterize. *See* HOLOCAUST.

cavalry steak. An old army name for the meat of mules and horses. "Army veterinarians who under ordinary circumstances were supposed to care for the health of the pack mules and horses had instead [during the Baatan retreat in World War II] been overseeing their slaughter for 'cavalry steak.' " (Hampton Sides, *Ghost Soldiers,* 2001).

cave!; Five-O; shote! In Britain *cave!* (pronounced in two syllables) has traditionally been used by schoolboy lookouts to warn others in a group that a master (teacher), policeman, or any adult is approaching and they'd better clear out or stop what they are doing. *Cave* is Latin for "beware," and *Cave Canem* signs in ancient Rome meant *Beware of Dog.* In the U.S. the warning would be CHICKEE! or CHEESE IT, or *Five-O* (after the police drama Hawaii Five-O). The Scottish equivalent is *shote!*

caveman. Fred Flintstone didn't inspire this term for a man, sometimes crude and brutal, but often attractive, who has a rough primitive manner, especially toward women. The word, used in this sense, comes from the title of John Corbin's *The Cave Man* (1907), a romantic novel that was a best-seller in its day. Outside of U.S. slang, *caveman* means a cave dweller of the Stone Age, the word used in that sense since about 1860.

caviar. *Caviar* derives from the Persian *khavyar,* salted sturgeon eggs. The Russians call the fish eggs *ikra,* not caviar, and it is from a select sturgeon species called the beluga that the highly regarded Beluga caviar comes. Actually, the most prized caviar of all is that made from selected golden sterlet's eggs of the *Acipenser ruthenus* species, produced by sterlets "with a particularly happy frame of mind." While dispelling myths about caviar, we should mention that *malossol* isn't a quality name like Beluga; it is just less salty caviar, and you can buy Beluga malossol, Sevruga malossol, et cetera.

caviar to the general. "I heard thee speak me a speech once," Hamlet says to the players at Elsinore, "but it was never acted . . . ; for the play, I remember, pleased not the million, 'twas caviar to the general." When Shakespeare says "general" here, he means the general public, the generality, the masses as they were later called, not the general of an army. The play he refers to (which was actually pretty bad, judging by the fragments presented) is, like caviar, for the tastes of only the most discriminating people; others would find it repugnant because they haven't acquired fine tastes. The rather snobbish remark is still commonplace in describing something for which one has to acquire a taste.

cavy. *See* UNCLE!

cayenne pepper. *Cayenne* is an English word contributed by the Tupi language of Brazil. It derives from the Tupi *quiynha,* meaning "capsicum," *quiynha* deriving from the name of the island (now called Cayenne) where the pepper is ground.

cayuse. Characters in westerns sometimes use the word *cayuse* to describe a horse of little value, but *cayuse,* strictly, is a name for Indian ponies, a breed that western pioneers knew as *kiyuse* and which were rarely properly tamed by white men. The cayuse takes its name from the Cayuse Indians of Oregon and Washington, who bred the small horse. In 1847, blaming whites for a smallpox epidemic, the tribe attacked and killed 14 missionaries near the present city of Walla Walla, Washington. Subdued and put on a reservation in 1855, their ranks decimated by disease, they died as a people, with no full-blooded Cayuse Indian surviving today.

CC. A song that became a slang nickname for a city. In 1975 George Clinton entitled a song *Chocolate City,* referring to Washington, D.C., and its large African-American population. Soon after, the initials CC from the song's title became slang for D.C.

CC; copycat. CC, for copycat, is the name of the first kitten ever cloned, born on December 22, 2001, at Texas A&M. She is the genetically identical copy of a two-year-old cat named Rainbow and developed inside Allie, her surrogate mother. CC is the sixth animal to be cloned around the world, the first being a sheep named Dolly.

CCCP. There isn't a "Communist" behind any of these "C's". The common abbreviation stands for *Soiuz Sovetskikh Sotsialisticheskikh Respublik,* the former Union of Soviet Socialist Republics, written as CCCP in English because in the Russian alphabet *c* is equivalent to our *s* and *p* to our *r.*

Cecil's fast. In an attempt to improve the fish trade in England, Queen Elizabeth's longtime minister William Cecil, baron Burghley, had legislation passed requiring Englishmen to eat fish and no meat on certain days of the week. Beef-eating and mutton-eating Britons didn't much like the idea and dubbed all fish dinners *Cecil's fasts*. Possibly the idea remained distasteful to Englishmen for over two centuries, because in the early 1800s, cold hash patties were being called Cecils—another substitute for "real" meat.

celery. Celery is the *selinon* mentioned by Homer in the *Odyssey*, but the word comes to us directly from the French *céléri*, a derivation from the Greek word for the vegetable. Celery has been cultivated for centuries and its wild form, smallage, has been gathered in its native Mediterranean home for thousands of years. The Greeks held bitter smallage in high esteem and awarded stalks of it to winners of athletic contests.

cellar. *Cellar*, for "the lowest position in league rank for a baseball team" is first recorded in a *New York Times* headline of July 9, 1922: "Red Sox Are Up Again. Leave Cellar to Athletics by Taking Final of Series, 4 to 1." Thus the Philadelphia Athletics were the first baseball team to be in the cellar. Cellar, for "an underground room or basement," dates back to the 14th century and derives from the Latin *cella*, "cell."

cellophane. *Cellophane* is a good example of a trademark name that became a generic term. The transparent, waterproof, paperlike substance commonly used to wrap products was a trademark up until 1915, when the courts ruled that it had been used too often generically to be protected anymore. Much the same happened to the word *celluloid*, the first synthetic plastic. *Cellophane* derives from *cell*ulose, the main constituent of plant tissue, and the French dia*phane*, "transparent." *See* ASPIRIN.

Celsius scale. The centigrade thermometer is often called the Celsius thermometer in honor of the eminent Swedish astronomer who invented the Celsius scale. Anders Celsius (1701–44) first suggested his improvement of the Fahrenheit scale before the Swedish Academy of Sciences in 1742, proposing the more obvious gradation between 0 and 100. Today the mercury thermometer patterned on this scale is widely used in Europe for meteorological and all other temperatures. Celsius also founded the observatory at Uppsala, where he was a professor, and made and collected many observations of the aurora borealis. Boiling water measures 212 degrees on the Fahrenheit scale and 100 degrees on the *Celsius* or centigrade scale; water freezes at 0 degrees centigrade and 32 degrees Fahrenheit. *See* F; OLD PHILADELPHIA LADY.

Celtic words. English words that come to us from Celtic include: bin, crag, curse, the color dun and possibly ass (perhaps a Celtic contraction of the Latin *asinus*). Whiskey, clan, glen, heather, shillelagh, claymore, slogan, dirk, brogue, wraith, bog, plaid, and bard are Celtic, too, but are modern borrowings from the Irish and Scots. Celtic words also survive in British place names, such as the Avon ("water"), Dover ("black") and YORK. *See* TOR.

cemetery. With all the talk about the euphemisms used by today's "morticians" it is often forgotten that *cemetery* is a euphemism coined by early Christian writers from the Greek

word for dormitory, a place where one sleeps. *Cemetery* is first recorded in English in 1387, over a century after *burial ground* (ca. 1250). *Graveyard* isn't recorded until the early 19th century.

cent. *Cent* is an Americanism introduced during the Revolution by Gouverneur Morris to replace the British word "penny." Though both words are still used today, *cent*, deriving from the Latin *centum* for "one-hundredth," (of a dollar) is more common than PENNY.

Centennial State. Colorado has had the nickname Centennial State since it was admitted into the Union in 1876. It has also been called the Switzerland of America (New Hampshire, New Jersey, West Virginia and Maine also claim this title) the Silver State (Nevada claims this one, too) and the Treasure State (Montana is its competitor here).

cento. The Roman poet Virgil (70–19 B.C.) was so popular in ancient times that an artificial poem called the *cento*, a "patchwork" or "crazy quilt" poem, was made by putting together bits of lines of his poetry. Much later, Virgil's epic poem, *The Aeneid*, became so venerated that it was used to foretell the future. A page, selected by opening a volume at random, supposedly could predict what was to come.

centurion. The Roman noncommissioned officer was named a centurion because he was in charge of a *century*, originally a hundred legionaries, or ordinary soldiers of the Roman legion (consisting of 3,000–6,000 soldiers).

century plant. *See* AGAVE.

Cerberus. The many-headed dog of Greek mythology who guards the entrance of the infernal regions. Cerberus (pronounced *Sir-burr-rus*) has been represented with from three to 100 heads, with snakes for hair and the tail of a serpent. Described by Lucretius, Horace, Ovid, and Virgil, among other great Latin poets, the huge and fearsome guardian of the gates of the Underworld gives his name to any formidable and often surly guard or gatekeeper, animal or human. Cerberus was not infallible: Hercules dragged him back to Earth in his legendary 12th labor and Orpheus lulled him to sleep with his lyre. The myth of the watchdog of Hell has its roots in the ancient Egyptian custom of guarding graves with dogs. *See* GIVE A SOP TO CERBERUS.

cereal. Gardeners have prayed to many garden deities through the ages. After a drought ruined crops in 496 B.C., Roman priests insisted that a new goddess named Ceres be worshipped and prayed to for rain. When the drought ended, Ceres became protector of the crops and the first grains harvested each year were sacrificed to her and called *cerealis*, meaning "of Ceres." From *cerealis* came the English word *cereal*, which honors the goddess every morning on millions of breakfast tables. Ceres' Greek counterpart was Demeter, the goddess of fruit, crops, and vegetables.

cestus. *Cestus* refers to a leather belt covered with metal spikes and studs that was wrapped around the fists of Greek gladiators when they stood toe-to-toe in arenas and fought to the death. The greatest cestus "boxer" was Theagenes of Thasos, said to have maimed or killed all 1,425 of his opponents.

cha.   *See* TEA.

Chablis.   Though its name has been widely appropriated in other wine producing countries, true Chablis, a dry white Burgundy, is produced near the town of Chablis, southeast of Paris, and made only of Chardonnay grapes.

cha cha.   This dance should properly be called the cha cha cha, as it takes its name from the sound of its musical accompaniment. In fact, it is called the cha cha cha in Cuba, where it originated, and people dancing it call out *cha cha cha*, not *cha cha*.

chachalaca.   Native Americans named the turkeylike bird chachalaca in imitation of the loud, harsh cackling cry it makes, the bird's name being *chachalacametl* in Nahuatl. Common in Texas, the bird's scientific name is *Ortalis vetula macalli*.

chad.   A relatively new word, made famous during the 2000 presidential election, but dating back to about the late 1960s, for (of all things!) the bits of cardboard remnants that are punched out from computer ballot cards or from any paper on which a paper punch is used. "What the city is trying to avoid," the *Los Angeles Times* (5/19/81) reported "is a repeat of April's Great Chad Chore, when more than 40,000 ballots had to be recounted because their chads—the punched-out portions—failed to break loose." *Chad* may derive from the mining term *chat* meaning bits of white gravel-like rock, a by-product of lead mining, that are sometimes used to surface roads. A recent synonym for *chads* is "confetti." A *pregnant chad* is a chad with a "dimple" on it, made by the stylus pushing too lightly against it.

chain lightning.   Lightning bolts that appear to move very quickly in wavy and zigzag lines. The term is an Americanism coined in about 1825.

chaise lounge.   The French called it a *chaise longue*, or "long chair," but Americans, on importing it from France, assumed that the *longue* in the term was French for "lounge." *Chaise lounge* it has remained ever since, despite all the efforts of purists.

Champ.   A fabled water creature said to reside in Lake Champlain; the American counterpart of the Loch Ness Monster. Explorer Samuel de Champlain first sighted the creature in 1609, describing it as a "barrell thick monster . . . [with a] horseshaped head." Descriptions have varied since.

champagne.   As defined by French law only sparkling wine produced from grapes grown in the French province of Champagne can, strictly speaking, be called champagne. It must be fermented in the bottle and varies from *brut*, the driest, to sweeter *doux* champagnes. Champagne has been called "the wine of love," "the wine of the gods," "the devil's wine," "the laugh of a pretty girl," "the only wine that leaves a woman beautiful after drinking it," and "the barometer of happiness." It is of course produced all over the world today and is still "the wine of wines," the most celebrated of all festive drinks. DOM PÉRIGNON is said to have cried out when he first tasted his historic version of it, "Come quickly, I am tasting stars!"

champ at the bit.   An expression that has been used figuratively since the late 17th century to describe someone impatient or anxious while waiting—like a horse ready to run, champing at the bit in its mouth and stomping the ground. Both *champ* and *chomp* mean "to bite upon or grind," *chomp* probably deriving from the earlier *champ* for reasons unknown.

champion.   Knights of old fought for their honor on a field, *campus* in Latin. A knight was thus called a *campion*, a fighter in the field, this word becoming *champion* in English. *Champion* came to have its present meaning of one who wins first place, or one who is clearly superior because a knight remained in the field only if he won or was superior.

Chanukah.   A Jewish festival of eight days that usually falls in December commemorating the rededication of the Temple of Jerusalem by the Maccabees after the victory over the Syrian Antiochus IV. The festival is characterized by the lighting of the MENORAH on each of the festival nights, the giving of small cash gifts (*Chanukah gelt*) and games such as one played with a four-sided top, or *dreidel*. *Chanukah* is the Hebrew word for "a dedicating." It is also spelled Hanukkah and is called "The Festival of Lights" and "The Feast of Dedication."

Chaos chaos.   Linnaeus discovered and christened this microscopic animal in 1775. It has since been identified only 50 times. The Swedish founder of scientific nomenclature gave the one-celled animal its name because of the chaos it creates. The voracious *Chaos chaos* never fails to attack and destroy all smaller protozoa it encounters.

chap.   The word *chapman*, for "a wandering peddler," lives in the language long after the last chapman has passed from the scene. For the British term *chap*, "fellow or man," as in "he's a good old chap," is simply an abbreviation of *chapman*—a good chapman, or *chap*, became in time a good fellow. The old English word *chop*, "to barter," gave us both *chapman* and *cheap*.

chaparral.   Any dense growth of shrubs or small trees, a tangle, a thicket. The Spanish word is used mainly in the Southwest but has national use due to its use in western stories and movies.

chapel; chaplain.   St. Martin of Tours converted to Christianity as a young pagan soldier in the Roman army under Constantine. According to Butler's *Lives of the Saints*, "In a very hard winter, during a severe frost, he met at the gate of the city a poor man almost naked, begging alms of them that passed by. Martin, seeing those that went before take no notice of this miserable creature . . . had nothing but his clothes. So drawing his sword, he cut his cloak into two pieces, gave one to the beggar and wrapped himself in the other half." That night Martin saw a vision of Christ "dressed in that half of the garment he had given away" and decided to enter into the religious life. He eventually became bishop of Tours and was credited with many cures and miracles. After his death in about A.D. 400, Martin became patron saint of the Frankish kings, who preserved the remaining half of his cloak, or *cappella*, as a relic. It was enshrined in a chest in "a special sanctuary," which also came to be known as a *cappella*, and the soldiers who watched over it, or carried it into battle and from place to place, were called *cappellani*. These two words, in French *chapelle* and *chapelain*, are the source of the English *chapel* and *chaplain*, the former deriving initially from St. Martin's cape and the latter from the soldiers who guarded it in its sanctuary.

chaperone.   The *chaperone* was originally a hood or mantle worn by priests and others in medieval France, the word itself meaning "little mantle." It was later adopted as a fashion by English ladies, but it wasn't until the 18th century that *chaperone* meant a married woman who shelters or protects a young woman, much as the hood protects the face.

chaps.   The leather leggings worn by cowboys take their name from the CHAPARRAL (the dense growth of tangled shrubs and thickets) that chaps are designed to protect against.

chard.   *See* SWISS CHARD.

Charing Cross.   In 1290 Edward I erected a cross to the memory of his beloved Queen Eleanor (*chère reine*, his "dear queen") in the center of the ancient village of Charin, midway between London and Westminster. He chose the spot because it was there that her coffin rested for the last time before her burial in Westminster. The Puritans destroyed the original cross in 1647 (it stood on the south side of Trafalgar Square, on the site now occupied by an equestrian statue of Charles I), but a new one was erected in 1865 in the courtyard of what is now called Charing Cross Station.

charity begins at home.   An ancient saying, *charity begins at home* was probably old when the Roman author Terence expressed the idea in a comic play: *Proximus sum egomet mihi.* Similar words are first recorded in English late in the 14th century.

charlatan.   *Charlatan* can be traced to the Italian *ciarlatano*, for "a quack," but a notorious quack dentist may have helped it along. A. M. Latan, it is said, was a 19th-century Frenchman who dressed in a long-robed exotic costume and often toured Paris in a magnificent dispensary car, a horn player heralding his approach. Spectators would cry out *"Voila le char de Latan"* ("There is Latan's car"), the words *le char de latan* popularizing *charlatan*. Most likely Latan was an assumed name, chosen to accompany his *char*, but the mischievous Frenchman probably strengthened the meaning of a word that had been used in English since the early 17th century.

Charles's Wain.   Much legend surrounds Charlemagne, Charles the Great (742–814 A.D.), king of the Franks and founder of the Holy Roman Empire. Charlemagne is said to have been eight feet tall and so strong that he could bend three horseshoes at once. He had four wives and five mistresses who among them presented him with 50 children. Charles the Great was also associated, probably erroneously, with the legendary King Arthur. The constellation now better known as the Big Dipper, the Plough, Ursa Major, or the Great Bear was at one time called Arthur's Wain because it resembled a wain, or wagon of old, the stars in the handle of the Dipper being the wagon's shaft. Since there was a legendary association between Charles the Great and King Arthur, the star cluster called Arthur's Wain eventually became known as Charles's Wain, too.

Charleston.   This peppy dance, symbolic of the Roaring Twenties, takes its name from Charleston, South Carolina, where it was probably first introduced as a variation of an earlier dance originated by American blacks. The word is first recorded in 1925.

Charley; Charlie; charlies.   Long before English policemen were dubbed bobbies, London night watchmen were called Charleys, or Charlies. The obsolete designation is believed to derive from the name of Charles I, who extended and improved the London night watch in order to curb street offenses in 1640, or from his son the lascivious Charles II. Charles I, beheaded by Cromwell in 1649, also wore a short, triangular beard called a Charlie that is now known as a VANDYKE. The slang *charlies*, for a woman's breasts, one etymologist suggests, derives from "the opulent charms displayed by the mistresses of Charles II"—*charlies* was probably originally *charlie's* because they were "playthings belonging to the king." *Charley* was also the term for a fox used by the English for almost a century, beginning in the late 1700s. The eponym here is brilliant British politician and Foreign Secretary Charles James Fox (1749–1806), who constantly outfoxed the opposition. *See* BOBBY; CHARLEY HORSE.

charley horse.   Back in 1946 the *Journal of the American Medical Association* published an article entitled "Treatment of the Charley Horse," rather than "Treatment of Injury to Quadriceps Femoris." This would indicate that *charley horse* has been a part of formal English for at least 50 years. But did this term for "a leg cramp" arise from a lame horse named Charley that pulled a roller across the infield in the Chicago White Sox ballpark in the 1890s? That's the old story, and there was such a horse, but the expression may have been printed several years before his baseball days, in 1888, to describe a ballplayer's stiffness or lameness. Another derivation that seems likely but hasn't been proved traces *charley horse* to the constables, or Charleys, of 17th-century England. According to this theory, *Charleys*, for "local police," survived in America through the 19th century and because aching legs were an occupational disease among Charleys, ballplayers suffering such maladies were compared to the coppers and said to be "weary from riding Charley's horse." *See* CHARLEY.

Charley More.   "Charley More—the fair (or square) thing" was the legend on the huge tavern sign of a Maltese publican about 1840. His name became synonymous with fair or straight dealing, and *Charley More* became a British term for one who is honest and upright.

Charley Noble.   Commander, captain, or ship's cook Charles Noble (ca. 1840) demanded that the cowl of the copper funnel of his galley stove always be kept brightly polished. So obsessed was he with the idea that galley funnels were dubbed *Charley Nobles* in his honor. *See* GRABLE-BODIED SEAMAN.

Charlie Dunns.   Custom-made cowboy boots worn by many celebrities, including Gene Autry, Slim Pickens, Arnold Palmer, and Harry Belafonte, costing up to $3,000 and fashioned of leather and exotic skins like ostrich. The boots were made in Austin, Texas by Charlie Dunn, whose father, grandfather, and great-grandfather before him were Texas bootmakers. Mr. Dunn, who died in 1993 at 95, is also remembered by the popular country-western song "Charlie Dunn," first recorded in the 1970s.

charlotte russe; apple charlotte.   Marie-Antoine Carême, the greatest chef of his day, created a lavish pastry that he called the apple charlotte, after England's Princess Charlotte, George IV's only daughter. The master chef apparently could not forget Charlotte, for while serving Czar Alexander in Russia, he created a jellied custard set in a crown of ladyfingers that he named the charlotte russe in her honor. Carême's creations were so valued that it is said that they were stolen from the table at the court of George IV—not to be relished at home, but to be sold in the market at high prices. *See* CARÊME.

Charon's toll.   *See* RIVER STYX.

Charterhouse.   Charterhouse, the venerable London public school and hospital, was, in the 14th century, the site of a religious house of the Carthusian monks. When one Thomas Sutton died in 1611, he endowed a hospital, chapel, and school on this property, which had come into his possession that same year. All three institutions were called *Charterhouse* as was the Carthusian monastery before them, the word deriving from the early English spelling (Chartrouse) of the French *maison Chartreuse*, "Carthusian house." The school moved to Surrey in 1872, but the hospital, or almshouse, still stands on its old site. Many of the Charterhouse buildings were destroyed in World War II. *See* CHARTREUSE LIQUEUR.

Chartreuse liqueur.   A cordial that takes its name from a monastery of the Carthusian monks. La Grande Chartreuse, the mother house of the Carthusian order, was founded by St. Bruno of Cologne in 1084 near Grenoble, France, the monastery taking its name from nearby Carthusia, after which the Carthusians had been named. Early in the 17th century the Maréchal d'Estrées gave the monks a recipe for a liqueur made from fragrant herbs and brandy; the Carthusians called the liqueur Chartreuse. They began to manufacture and sell it on a large scale only when they returned to La Grande Chartreuse after their expulsion during the French Revolution, using the revenues to rebuild and maintain their devastated monastery. Les Chartreux, as the French call the Carthusians, were again expelled from France in 1903, their distillery and trademark being sold and an imitation Chartreuse marketed by a commercial firm. Cognoscenti hold that only the liqueur made by the monks is worthy of the name, claiming that Chartreuse owes its distinctive flavor to the still-secret formula that employs angelica root and other herbs of the Grenoble region. The Carthusians were allowed to return to Grenoble in 1938, and now sell their liqueur under the *Les Pères Chartreux* trademark. The best Chartreuse is a pale apple-green, hence the name of the color chartreuse. See CHARTERHOUSE.

chaste tree.   *See* VITEX.

chat; chatter; chatterbox.   *Chat*, like BLAB, is a truncated form of an earlier word, *chatter*, which is supposed to be an echoic word imitative of the sound of birds chirping. *Chatter* is first recorded in about 1225, *chat*, for "to talk idly," about three centuries later. *Chatterbox* is an Americanism first recorded in 1814.

Chateaubriand.   One old story tells us that Brillat-Savarin dined in Paris with the vicomte François-Auguste-René-de Chateaubriand on the night that an anonymous restaurant proprietor invented steak Chateaubriand in his honor. The occasion, according to this version, was the publication of the French romantic's *la Génie du christianisme*, and the succulent tenderloin was encased between two flank steaks, symbolizing Christ and the thieves. The outer steaks, seared black, were discarded, leaving the tenderloin rare and juicy. More likely, steak Chateaubriand was invented and named by the novelist's chef, Montmirel, and served for the first time at the French embassy in London. *See also* BRILLAT-SAVARIN.

chattel.   *See* CATTLE.

chatterbox.   *See* CHAT.

chauffeur.   The first chauffeurs known to the world were members of a band of brigands led by Jean l'Ecorcheur (Jack the Scorcher), a bandit leader who took advantage of the chaos created by the French Revolution to terrorize the French countryside in the late 18th century. Jack's gang would force their way into homes and demand that all hidden valuables be surrendered, tying up those householders who refused and roasting their bare feet in the fire until they capitulated. They thus came to be known as *chauffeurs*, "firemen," their nickname deriving from the French *chauffer*, "to heat or stoke." Many years after its application to Jack the Scorcher and his *chauffeurs*, the word was logically applied to steamship stokers, locomotive firemen, and, finally, to the stokers required to tend early powered automobiles. These last stokers often operated someone else's car, and the word was retained when chauffeurs no longer needed to be firemen in addition to drivers.

Chautauqua.   Chautauqua, New York, which takes its name from a Seneca Indian word possibly meaning "one has taken out fish there," was the home of a Methodist summer colony where various cultural activities were offered beginning in 1874. Lectures there came to be called *Chautauquas* and by the end of the century lecturers giving lectures in towns and cities across the country were calling them *Chautauquas* no matter where they were held.

chauvinism.   Nicolas Chauvin of Rochefort was a genuine hero, wounded 17 times in service of the French Grande Armée and retiring only when so scarred that he could no longer lift a sword. How then did his name become associated with excessive nationalism or superpatriotism? Chauvin actually was left with little after his war service. For his wounds and valor he received a medal, a ceremonial saber, and a pension of about 40 dollars a year. Instead of growing bitter, the old soldier turned in the opposite direction, for, after all, his sacrifices had to mean something. Chauvin became an idolator of the Little Corporal; even after Waterloo and Napoleon's exile, he spoke of little but his hero's infallibility and the glory of France. The veteran became a laughingstock in his village, but he would have escaped national attention if dramatists Charles and Jean Cogniard hadn't heard of him and used him as a character in their comedy *La Cocarde tricolore* (1831). The play truthfully represented Chauvin as an almost idolatrous worshipper of Napoleon and was followed by at least four more comedies by other authors caricaturing the old soldier. As a result the French word *chauvinisme*, or "chauvinism," became synonymous with fanatical, unreasoning patriotism and all that such blind, bellicose worship of national prowess implies. The closest English synonym is JINGOISM, while the Germans use *Hurrapatriotismus.*

chaw stick; chew stick.   The ancient chew stick or chaw stick is the branches and twigs of the *Gouauia domingenia* tree. These were and are still used in the West Indies for cleansing the teeth and sweetening the breath, just as the roots of the cola tree, called chew stick, are used in Sierra Leone.

cheap as a Sardinian.   Many groups of people have been unfairly characterized as cheap, but the Sardinians do not carry this stigma. The phrase *cheap as a Sardinian* refers not to penny-pinching Sardinians but to the fact that the Romans under Tiberius Gracchus auctioned off great numbers of Sardinian prisoners in Rome for whatever price they could get, no matter how cheap.

cheap John.   For well over a century *cheap John* has meant inferior goods, a person who deals in them, and, by extension, any cheap person. There is even a chain of stores called Cheap Johns today. "None of your cheap-John turn-outs for me. I'm here to have a good time, and money ain't any object," wrote Mark Twain in *Roughing It* (1872).

cheapskate; a good skate.   Revolutionary War soldiers liked to sing the Scottish song "Maggie Lauder," the chorus of which chided a *blatherskate*, a gabby person full of nonsense or hot air. The song is a very old one, dating back to the 17th century, and the word blatherskate is older still, formed from *bladder*, an obsolete English word for an inflated pretentious man, a windbag, and a contemptuous use of the word *skate*, referring to the common food fish. Why the skate was chosen for the humorous word isn't clear, perhaps because it was believed to inflate itself like a blowfish, or possibly just because it was common. In any case, "Maggie Lauder" made *blatherskate* popular in America and later, in the 19th century, when Americans invented their native word *cheapskate*, for a tightwad, they borrowed the *skate* from it. This is a more roundabout explanation than the theory that the *skate* in *cheapskate* comes from a British slang word for chap, but it seems more logical, as *skate* in the sense of *chap* never had much currency in the U.S., except in the term *good skate*, meaning a good person.

cheat.   In feudal times *escheators* were officers of the king's exchequer appointed to receive dues and taxes and handle estates that might possibly revert to the crown because of failure of descendants to qualify as heirs. The escheators did so many people out of money unscrupulously that their name was inherited by future generations in the form of *cheat*.

check.   *See* BILL; CHECKMARK.

✔ (checkmark).   As far back as the 17th century teachers were for some unknown reason using the checkmark (✔) to mean "correct." The word *check* is much older, deriving ultimately from the Persian *shah*, for "king," which became the *check* in the game of chess and, from its use in the game, was widely transferred to other meanings in English. *See* CHECKMATE.

checkmate; chess.   Chess was already an ancient game when the Persians introduced it to the Arabs. The Arabs retained the Persian word *shah* for the king, the most important piece in the game, and when the *shah* (pronounced "shag" by the Arabs) was maneuvered into a helpless position, ending play, they exclaimed *shah mat*, "[your] king is dead." Soon after the Arabs introduced chess into Spain in the eighth century this expression became *xague mate*, from which derived the French *eschec mate* and finally the English *checkmate*. For many years *checkmate* was restricted to chess, but by the 14th century Chaucer and other writers were using it in the figurative sense of "to thwart, defeat, or frustrate." Our word *chess* comes from a shortening of the French *eschis*, the plural of *eschec*, so the game's name really means "kings." By a similar process the king in the game, the *shah* that became the French *eschec*, is also the source of every use of the word *check* in English, from bank checks to security checks. *See also* CHECKMARK.

cheddar.   Originally a cheese made in the village of Cheddar in England's Somerset County, *cheddar* today refers to "a wide variety of hard, crumbly cheeses ranging in flavor from mild to sharp and in color from yellow to orange." The word is first recorded in 1666, but the cheese probably was made long before then.

cheechako.   A newcomer, tenderfoot, or greenhorn in Alaska and northern Canada. The term comes from Chinook jargon and is often spelled cheehako and cheechaco. First recorded in about 1895, the word (in the form of *chechaquo*) is used to describe the main character in Jack London's famous short story "To Build a Fire" (1908).

cheek by cheek; cheek by jowl.   *Cheek by cheek*, recorded over six centuries ago, implies closeness, intimacy. *Cheek by jowl* is just a variation invented some two centuries later, substituting the French *jowl*, "cheek," for the second cheek in the phrase.

cheerio; cheers.   *Cheerio* means good-bye or good health. Used as a toast and when parting among the British, the word was first recorded in 1910 as *cheero*, which is rarely heard today. The British also use *cheers* as a toast, as do Americans, and the British and Irish say *cheers* as a synonym for "thanks" when acknowledging a small favor.

cheerleader.   The young men and women who lead formal cheers at sports events began to be called cheerleaders in the early years of this century. The first to officially bear the name seem to have been those who cheered Amos Stagg's University of Chicago Maroons, a football powerhouse at the time.

cheer up; cheer up—the worst is yet to come.   The British have been using the expression *cheer up* since at least 1597. It took over three centuries but an Americanism finally managed to cheerfully deflate these encouraging words, with *cheer up— the worst is yet to come*, first recorded in 1920.

cheese.   Clifton Fadiman wrote that cheese is "milk's leap to immortality." The word *cheese* itself comes from the Latin *caseus* for the food, whose origin dates back several thousand years before Christ. One legend claims that cheese was discovered by a traveling merchant named Kanana. When he started on one long trip, Kanana put his supply of milk in a pouch made of a sheep's stomach. The heat and shaking of the pouch on the journey, plus the rennet in the lining of the stomach, caused the curds in the milk to separate from the whey, and when he sat down to eat his lunch, Kanana found delicious cheese. In any case, there are thousands of cheeses produced today. Most are named for the regions where they were born. Some important examples are Roquefort and Camembert, from France; Cheddar and Cheshire, from England; Edam from Holland; Muenster from Germany; Swiss from Switzerland; and Limburger from Limburg, Belgium. It would be impossible to list them all. In fact, France alone has enough varieties to fill a volume. French President Charles de Gaulle once remarked, "How can you govern a nation which has 246 kinds of cheese?"

cheesecake; beefcake.   The old story is that in 1912 *New York Journal* photographer James Kane was developing a picture of an actress that included "more of herself than either he or she expected." As he looked at it, he searched for the greatest superlative he knew of to express his delight and exclaimed, "That's real cheesecake!" The word soon became synonymous with photographs of delectable models. In the 1970s, *beefcake* became the male equivalent.

cheese it, the cops!   If you've ever wondered why *cheese it* means "stop it," or "watch it," Partridge has an answer for you. He suggests that the term, first recorded in England in 1812, is a mispronunciation of "cease it."

chelae.   You may have eaten them many times, but you probably don't know their name. They are chelae, the large pincerlike claws of the lobster and other crustaceans, which are named from the Greek *chelé* for "claw." They are usually banded at the market for good reason: among many other cases, one lobster chela nearly amputated a child's finger, and another one reached up and snapped in half a Maine lobsterman's pipe!

chenangoe.   Upstate New York farms in Chenango County supplied many of the longshoremen who worked the New York waterfront in the late 19th century. So many, in fact, that *chenangoe* became a term for any longshoreman who loads cargo from railroad barges to ships. Before this the chenangoe had been a popular variety of potato.

cheri.   A nice story has it that *cheri* for a charming, adorable, often young woman, may come to us from Rose Cheri, the stage name of a French actress who appeared in Paris from 1840 to 1860. "She was a singularly pure woman," writes J. Redding Ware in *Passing English* (1909), "and an angelic actress. The word [first became] used by upper class men in society . . .

to describe the nature of their mistresses." But nice story or naughty there is no absolute proof of the Rose Cheri derivative, and the word may simply come from the French *chère*, meaning "dear," "sweetheart."

cherish a serpent in his bosom.   An ancient Greek legend tells of a man who found a frozen serpent that he put beneath his shirt against his breast, only to have the snake, revived by the warmth of his bosom, bite and kill him. The story, adapted by Shakespeare, became the basis of the saying *to cherish* (or *nurse*) *a serpent in his bosom*, "to show kindness to someone who proves ungrateful."

Cherokee.   The name of this Indian tribe is a mystery, their name perhaps stolen from them like their land. "The word *Cherokee* itself has no meaning in the Indian language," writes Michael Frome in *Strangers in High Places* (1966). "It may have had its origin in the time of the [Fernando] de Soto expedition (1540) with the word Achelaque, modified in stages to spell Cherokee, until not even their name remained to them." *See* TRAIL OF TEARS.

cheroot.   Originally only a thick stubby cigar with open untapered ends, *cheroot* has also come to mean any small cigar. It is one of the few words English has taken from the Indian and Ceylon Tamil language, deriving from the Tamil *curuttu*, roll (of tobacco leaf).

cherry.   *Cherries* in English first meant *one cherry*, the word deriving from the French *cerise* (which came from the Latin *cerasus*) for the fruit. *Cerise* became *cherries*, but the *s* in *cherries* was dropped, because it made the singular word sound like a plural, and the result was *cherrie* or *cherry*.

Cheshire cat.   *See* GRIN LIKE A CHESHIRE CAT.

chess.   *See* CHECKMATE.

chesterfield.   *Chesterfieldian* usually means writings on dress and manners, referring to Philip Dormer Stanhope, the fourth earl of Chesterfield (1694–1773), whose posthumous "Letter to His Son" and "Letter to His Godson" are models of their kind. Lord Chesterfield, whose last words were "Give Dayrolles [a visitor] a chair," did not intend his letters for publication. Dr. Johnson described them as teaching "the morals of a whore and the manners of a dancing master"—but then the Great Cham was hardly an unprejudiced judge, Chesterfield having neglected the plan for his great *English Dictionary*, which resulted in Johnson's famous letter rejecting his support when it was finished. The witty "Letters" of the statesman and diplomat were meant to be filled with worldly knowledge and thus reflected the morality of the age. The large overstuffed chesterfield couch and the man's velvet-collared overcoat with concealed buttons called a chesterfield were introduced in the 19th century. Both may have been named in honor of Philip Stanhope, but it is more likely that they commemorate a later earl of Chesterfield, who may even have invented them. Just which earl no one seems to know.

chestnut.   No one is sure about the antecedents of *chestnut*. The word may derive from the name of Castana in Asia Minor, a city near which chestnuts grew, or from the Armenian *kaskene*, meaning "chestnut."

Chevrolet. Swiss engineer Louis Chevrolet worked for U.S. car manufacturer William Durant as a racing driver. When Durant opened his new automobile company, he named it the Chevrolet Motor Company after Chevrolet because, he explained, his driver's name "had a musical sound and the romance of foreign origin."

chew the fat (rag). One guess is that this expression was originally a nautical one: Sailors working their jaws on the tough salt pork rationed out when supplies ran low constantly grumbled about their poor fare while literally chewing the fat. *Chewing the rag* also had a grouchy connotation when first recorded in print at about the same time, in 1885. There are a few stories relating these words to actual rag chewing (men chewing pieces of rags when out of tobacco and grousing about it, etc.), but more than likely the expression has its roots in the English verb *to rag*, "to scold," its origin unknown. Both phrases are probably much older than their first appearance in print, and both are used more often today to mean a talkfest between friends than the act of complaining.

chew up the scenery. To overact or ham it up. Originally only a theatrical expression, these words can be traced to their inventor, Dorothy Parker, who used them first in a 1930 theater review: "More glutton than artist . . . he commences to chew up the scenery."

Cheyenne. No one is certain about it, but the name of this North American Indian tribe of the Algonquian linguistic family, now found in Montana and Oklahoma, may derive from the French feminine for dog, *chienne*. French traders in Minnesota may have so named them because the tribe, like many Indian tribes, ate dog meat.

Cheyne-Stokes breathing. A medical term for gasping breathing that ceases for up to a minute, continues, and keeps alternating between gasping and breathlessness until death comes. As he lay on his deathbed, British poet A. E. Housman (1859–1936) remembered a passage from Arnold Bennett's novel *Clayhanger* describing this "death breathing" named for William Cheyne and William Stokes, the physicians who first described it. This may have been his *last* terrible memory, for he remembered it when he began the same "death breathing." But then maybe he realized the joke of it all and DIED GENTLY LAUGHING.

Chianti. The Chianti mountains in Tuscany, where this wine is produced, give their name to the best-known of Italian reds, their squat flasks traditionally wrapped in straw.

chiasmus. A *chiasmus* is "a reversal in the order of words in two otherwise parallel phrases," as in Shakespeare's "Suit the action to the word, the word to the action" (*Hamlet*); or "This man I thought had been a Lord among wits; but, I, find, he is only a wit among Lords" (Dr. Johnson of Lord Chesterfield). These quotes are from among the hundreds in Dr. Mardy Grothe's *Never Let a Fool Kiss You or a Kiss Fool You* (1999), the title of which is also a chiasmus.

Chicago. The Windy City unfortunately derives its name from an Indian word that means "place of the bad smell," "place of skunk smells," or "skunktown." There is only a slight chance that the Indian word means "wild onion place," as has been suggested.

Chicago fire. The only plant named after a great fire, this midwestern bush (*Kochia scoparia*) with bright red foliage takes its unusual name from the Chicago fire of 1871, which raged for three days and took several hundred lives. It is also called "firebush," "burning bush," "summer cypress," and "Kochia bush," after the German botanist W. D. J. Koch, for whom the brilliant Eurasian genus is named. The Chinese make brushes from the bushy plant, which is grown as an ornamental here.

chicanery. *Chicanery*, the use of mean, petty subterfuge, especially legal dodges and quibbles, came into English through a French word meaning the same. It seems originally to have derived from the Persian *chaugan*, for the crooked stick used in polo. The stick's name somehow came to mean a dispute in polo and other games, then took on the meaning of a sharp, crooked practice in those games and in general.

Chicano. An American of Mexican descent. One explanation claims this word is a contraction of the Spanish for "I am not a boy." Another suggests it comes from the ending of the word *Mexicano*, which the Aztecs pronounced "Meshicano," this eventually shortened to *shicano* and then *chicano*.

chichi. Slang for the female breasts as sexual objects, *chichi* or *chi-chi* can also mean anything sexually stimulating. The term arose after World War II during the U.S. occupation of Japan and derives from *chisai chichi*, a corruption of the Japanese words meaning "little breasts." The expression had widespread use in Korea.

chickaree. A name in many parts of the U.S. for the red squirrel, the appellation deriving from the cry the red squirrel makes.

chickee. 1) An American term for someone who serves as a lookout in a crime such as a burglary. "You guys go in, I'll play (or lay) chickee." 2) A cry made by a criminal or schoolboy lookout meaning stop what you're doing and get out of there, as in "Chickee, the cops!" Both uses date back to at least the 1930s, and the word is often spelled chickie. *See* CAVE; CHEEZIT.

chicken. A game teenagers have played since at least the late 1940s in which two drivers (often with passengers) drive their cars directly at each other at high speed, the loser, or chicken, the one who first swerves out of the way. It can also be played by driving at telephone poles, etc., to see how narrowly a driver can avoid hitting them, and by racing another car toward a cliff, as famously depicted in the film *Rebel Without a Cause*, starring James Dean. The game takes its name from *to chicken out*, to back away in fear, CHICKEN-HEARTED or *chicken* as a slang synonym for a coward. The expression has often been used figuratively, as in the words of military expert Stephen Philip Cohen (12/23/01): "The Indians are playing chicken. They're counting on the United States to jerk the steering wheel so the

Pakistanis do swerve out of the path of an onrushing Indian vehicle."

chicken à la King. Chicken à la King, diced pieces of chicken in a sherry cream sauce, is now available canned, frozen, and even in Army mess halls, a long way from the éclat tables where it was served in the late 19th century. The dish was not invented for a king, as is popularly believed, yet it's hard to pinpoint just whom chicken à la King does honor. Some say that New Yorker Foxhall Keene, self-proclaimed "world's greatest amateur athlete," suggested the concoction to a chef at Delmonico's. Of the numerous stories surrounding the dish's creation the most reliable seems to be that of the famous Claridge's Hotel in London. Claridge's claimed that the dish was invented by its chef to honor J. R. Keene, whose horse had won the Grand Prix in 1881. Perhaps J.R. passed on the recipe to his son, the peerless Foxhall. At any rate, the Keenes did not hold public interest long enough, and the *Keene* in *Chicken à la Keene* eventually became *King*.

chicken feed. Chickens were fed grain too poor for any other use by American pioneers, and these pieces of poor-quality grain had to be small so the chickens could swallow them. This obviously suggested the contemptuous term *chicken feed* for small change (pennies, nickels, and dimes) to riverboat gamblers fleecing small-town suckers. The first in-print mention of the expression is in *Colonel [Davy] Crockett's Exploits* (1836): "I stood looking on, seeing him pick up chicken feed from the green horns." By extension, *chicken feed* has come to mean any small or insignificant amount of money, and even (rarely today) misleading information deliberately supplied or leaked by a government to spies employed by another government.

chickenhearted; chicken-livered. Not nearly a new expression, *chickenhearted* is first recorded in a 1681 poem by John Dryden: "Where 'tis agreed by bullies chickenhearted/ To fight the ladies first, and then be parted." *Chicken-heart*, for a heart, or courage, as weak as a chicken's, is first attested in 1602. *Chicken-livered* is a variant of the term, first recorded in America in 1857.

a chicken in every pot. Often attributed to Herbert Hoover, this synonym for prosperity was, indeed, a Republican campaign slogan during the election of 1932—a ridiculous one that helped the Democrats more than the Republicans, with the Great Depression gripping the land. The words can actually be traced to Henry IV of France and his vow on being crowned king in 1589: "If God grants me the usual length of life, I hope to make France so prosperous that every peasant will have a chicken in his pot on Sunday." Assassinated in 1610 when only 57, Henry wasn't able to provide such prosperity.

chicken-livered. *See* CHICKENHEARTED.

chicken Marengo. Napoleon's chef invented chicken Marengo at the Battle of Marengo in Lombardy during the Italian campaign, the quite exact date being two o'clock in the afternoon of June 14, 1800. Having no butter on hand, the resourceful but anonymous chef sautéed the chicken in the local olive oil, adding the sauce consisting of tomatoes, herbs, mushrooms, and white wine.

the chicken or the egg? An abbreviation of the old puzzle, "Which came first, the chicken or the egg?" The answer seems to be that each thing is necessary to the other. People have been asking this question since at least the time of Macrobius in about A.D. 400, the Latin author using it in his *Saturnalia* or *Feast of Saturn* at that time: *Ovumme prius fuerit aut gallina?*

chicken pulling. A game of Mexican origin played by U.S. cowboys that consisted of burying a live chicken in soft ground up to its neck, the players riding by at a gallop and attempting to pick the chicken out of the ground, usually breaking its neck in the process. The game, also called pulling the chicken, fortunately isn't played much anymore, if at all.

chicken ranch. Unlike most sexual euphemisms, this synonym for "a brothel" takes its name from a real place. The original Chicken Ranch was a bordello in Gilbert, Texas, early in this century, so named because poor farmer clients often paid for their visits with chickens. It is celebrated in the play *The Best Little Whorehouse in Texas.*

chickens come home to roost. Malcolm X stirred up a hornet's nest when he said this about John F. Kennedy after the president was assassinated, possibly alluding to alleged C.I.A. attempts on Fidel Castro's life. But the saying is an old one, dating back to at least 1810 in the form of "Curses are like young chickens; they always come home to roost," which appears to have been the invention of English poet laureate Robert Southey as the motto of his poem "The Curse of Kehama." The idea, of course, is that every curse or evil act returns to its originator as chickens return to their roost at night.

chicken scratch; crow tracks. These are Americanisms for illegible handwriting. *Chicken scratch* is first recorded in 1956 but is probably much older, while *crow tracks* dates back to at least 1875. Variations are *hen tracks* and *turkey tracks*.

chickenshit. Petty rules, especially in the Army, probably had been called chickenshit before the first recorded use of the expression in this sense in the 1930s. The early Canadian term *chickenshit* for "information from a superior officer" may be the source for the term.

chickens today, feathers tomorrow. Well-off one day, impoverished the next. The saying probably dates back to at least the 1930s, when people were still plucking chickens that many still raised in their yards.

chicken Tetrazzini. Luisa Tetrazzini, the Italian-born diva whose role of Lucia di Lammermoor made her famous to opera lovers throughout the world early in this century, counted this dish as her favorite. Chicken Tetrazzini is diced chicken in cream sauce flavored with sherry and baked in a casserole with thin spaghetti, cheese, and mushrooms. According to those who saw her, Madame Tetrazzini shared a problem common to most opera stars, looking as if she had dined many times on the highly caloric dish. The coloratura soprano made her debut in

Florence in 1895 and ended her concert career in 1931, after starring in Spain, Portugal, Russia, England, America, and many other countries. She died in 1941, aged 69.

chickenweed. This name is given to common ragwort, a bane of gardeners, because its seed used to be mixed with chicken feed as a remedy for various maladies of chickens. Other plants named after chickens include the "chicken grape" of the South, valued for its fragrance, the common "hen and chicks" and "chicken on the wing" (the fringed polygala), so called because of the shape of its flower.

chick pea. *Chick pea* came into English in the 16th century from the French *pois chiche* for the vegetable and was originally called the *chiche pea*, until people began to confuse the word *chiche* with *chick*. *Cicer arietium* is also known as the *chick bean*. The word has nothing to do with the *chick* of *chicken*, as is often claimed.

Chic Sales. Outhouses have been called Chic Sales, Chic Sale or Chick Sales since the 1920s after American vaudevillian Chick Sale, who had a comedy routine about building an outhouse and wrote a book about his "specialty."

chief cook and bottle washer. A humorous expression meaning someone who does a lot of menial work, or any person in charge of many things. The expression is first recorded as far back as 1840 and is usually said in a spirit of fun.

chigger. Both mites and fleas are called chiggers, the name deriving from the African *jigger*, for "a blood-sucking mite." In fact, even in this country *jigger* is sometimes used. *Chigger* came to mean a flea as well as a mite because it was confused with the West Indian *chigoe*, for "a flea," somewhere along the line.

Chihuahua. A very small breed of dog native to Mexico, especially the state of Chihuahua. They can weigh as little as one pound or as much as six pounds and are considered to be the world's smallest dog. *See* IRISH WOLFHOUND.

child. "A boy or a child, I wonder?" Shakespeare wrote in *The Winter's Tale* (1610). In fact, as Ernest Weekley pointed out in *An Etymological Dictionary of Modern English (1921)*, "my child in Shakespeare never refers to *son*," for *child* originally meant a female infant in Anglo-Saxon, as it did in Middle English and in English dialect. *See* BOX; INFANT.

Childe ballad. American ballads are generally classified in three groups: Childe ballads, broadside ballads, and native American ballads. Childe ballads are not about children but refer to the 305 early songs collected by Harvard English professor Francis James Childe (1825–96) in the late 19th century. Of Childe's *English and Scottish Popular Ballads*, half the songs were brought to America by English settlers; they are considered the best of American ballads, and are still sung today, although many have undergone great transformations through the years.

children and chicken must always be pickin'. Both are always hungry and ready to eat, testing everything for food.

The saying, first recorded in 1682 as an old proverb, uses *chicken* as a plural, one of the few cases in English where this still occurs. William Carew Hazlitt (1834–1913) included this wise observation in his *English Proverbs and Proverbial Phrases Collected From the Most Authentic Sources* (1882). Hazlitt was the grandson of the more famous William Hazlitt (1778–1830), said to be the first English writer to make a living as a critic.

children's death. The terrible common name of this plant (*Cicuta maculata*) reflects the fact that children have died after mistaking its root for an edible carrot and eating it. It is also called "children's bane," "musquash root," "beaver poison," "spotted cowbane" and, most frequently, "water hemlock." A member of the carrot family with feathery leaves, its roots contain a deadly alkaloid. It thrives on pond edges and in bogs.

chili. Short for the Spanish *chili con carne*, a thick meat stew, sometimes including beans, spiced with chilies.

chili pepper. The pungent pods of *Capsicum annuum longum* and several other species are named after the Nahuatl *chilli*, meaning the same. *Chilli*, in turn, derives from a Nahuatl word meaning "sharp" or "pointed," because it is so pungent or biting to the tongue. Both "hot" and "sweet" varieties of garden peppers belong to the *Capsicum* genus native to tropical America. They are no relation to the condiment pepper, which is made from the berries of a climbing shrub of the *Piper* genus. Hottest of the hot chili peppers is the *habanero* variety, which is said to cause slight, temporary deafness—so you don't hear your screams when you eat them, some people believe. *See also* CAYENNE PEPPER; PEPPER.

chime in. When someone butts into a conversation he can interrupt with words of agreement or disagreement, but a person who intrudes by chiming in usually echoes the words of the last speaker. The term is often labeled slang in this sense but is really standard English now, common since Byron used it in the early 19th century. It has its origins in the harmonious chimes or bells in church towers, a music known since before the 14th century wherein a simple melody is struck and the other bells repeat it many times. As a musical term, meaning to join in harmoniously or in unison, the expression has been used since the late 19th century.

chimpanzee. *Chimpanzee*, from the Bantu *chimpanzee*, meaning "mock man," entered the English lexicon in 1738 when British explorers shipped the first of such animals to England from Angola. The highly intelligent ape more closely resembles man than any of the other anthropoids. British zoologist Jane Goodall, who spent years in Africa studying chimps, says they don't "have a language that can be compared with ours, but they do have a tremendous variety of calls, each one induced by a different emotion." Studies of chimps raised in captivity show that they use a vocabulary of about two dozen "words" or utterances. One chimp, Viki, raised from birth by Keith and Cathy Hayes in Florida, after three years learned to speak three human words (papa, mamma, and cup), none of them very well—at the same age when a human child knows 200 or more words. *See* DOLPHIN; PARROT.

China; sinologist.   China was not the name of the country that ancient Romans in Persia heard about from Chinese traders. The country is so named by mistake, because when asked where they came from, the Chinese would diplomatically give the name of the ruling dynasty at the time, the *Ch'in*, instead of the name of their country, *Chung-kuo*, "the Middle Kingdom" or "Central Country." *Ch'in* was Latinized by the Romans as *Sina*, which became the English *China*, as well as the basis for words like *sinologist*. The term *china* (lowercased here) refers to the fine porcelain brought to Europe from the Far East as early as the 16th century.

Chinaman's chance.   The Chinese immigrants who built so many miles of American railroads often tried to make their fortune by working old claims and streams abandoned by white prospectors during the California gold rush of 1849. They had an extremely poor chance of finding any gold in such abandoned claims, and thus *a Chinaman's chance* came to mean "no chance at all." The poor lot of Chinese in a segregated society probably reinforced the phrase, for the Chinese had as poor a chance on the railroads and other places as they did in the gold fields.

chin chin.   Relatively few Americans have been greeted by anyone using this expression, but it is an oriental English greeting often encountered in literature since the early 19th century. There is no connection here with the lower jaw, the word for which derives from the old English *cin*. *Chin chin* is just a corruption of the Chinese salutation *ts'ing ts'ing*.

Chinese home run.   Because Chinese immigrants were forced to work for little pay in a segregated society, their name came to mean "cheap" in American slang and formed the basis of a number of expressions. *Chinese home run* is the only one of these that still has much currency. It describes a cheap home run, one that just makes it over the fence. No one is sure who coined the phrase. It either arose in some ballpark on the West Coast at the turn of the century and was brought East by the cartoonist "Tad" Dorgan (who is also responsible for the words YES-MAN and HOT DOG), or it originated in a baseball park with a fence a relatively short distance from home, possibly the old 239-foot right-field fence in Philadelphia's Shibe Park, or the short right-field fence in New York's old Polo Grounds.

Chinese language contributions to English.   One out of every four people in the world speaks Chinese, "the world's first language." A good number of English words have Chinese ancestors. Among these are: BEEZER for a nose (from the Chinese *ta-bee-tsu* for Westerners, "the great-nosed ones"); BRAINWASHING (originally a Korean conflict term that is a direct translation of the Chinese *hsi nao*, "to wash the brain"); CHOP-CHOP ("hurry," from pidgin English); CHOP SUEY; CHOW; chow mein; fantan; GUNG HO; JOSS; KOWTOW; LONG TIME NO SEE; MAH-JONGG (although the Cantonese Chinese word really means "house sparrow"); NO CAN DO (from pidgin English); tong; and typhoon. The Chinese have a proverb *cat gone, old rat comes out* that is much older than our centuries-old *when the cat's away the mice will play*. Even the insulting, abusive word *Chink* for a Chinese person is said to be a mispronunciation of the Chinese word *Chung-kuo* for "China." *See also* CHINAMAN'S CHANCE; PIDGIN ENGLISH.

Chink.   *See* CHINESE LANGUAGE CONTRIBUTIONS TO ENGLISH.

Chinook; Chinook wind.   Chinook, an important pidgin language, enabled 18th- and 19th-century American farmers and traders, French trappers, and even visiting Russian seal hunters to converse with Indians in the Pacific Northwest. Chinook jargon was used for more than 100 years. Named for the Chinook Indians, who had large settlements along the Columbia River, this lingua franca combined various Chinook dialects, other Indian languages, English, French, and probably Russian. Chinook wind, so called by early settlers because it blew from the direction of the Chinook Indian camps, designates a dry wind blowing from the west or north over the Rocky Mountains—warm in winter and cool in summer—while a wet Chinook is a warm, moist wind blowing from sea to land in Washington and Oregon.

Chinook State.   *See* EVERGREEN STATE.

chintzy.   *Chintzy* is American slang for "cheap," or "poorly made," or even "stingy," dating back to about the 1940s. But it comes from the plural of the Hindu word *chint*, for "a glazed cotton fabric with flowery designs" first made in India. The British mistook the plural of the word, *chints*, for the singular, applying it to the cloth and eventually spelling it *chintz*. Regarded as a cheap material in America, *chintz* finally gave us the word *chintzy*.

chin whiskers.   A beard, a term that was apparently coined in California in gold-rush days.

chip in; blue-chip, etc.   Poker chips are the basis of a number of English expressions. *To chip in*, "to share expenses," derives from the practice of each player putting up his ante of chips at the start of the card game and chipping in with each bet. *To cash in one's chips*, or *hand*, that is, "to die," comes from the end of a poker game, when players turn in their chips to the cashier for money. *In the chips*, "affluent," refers to having a lot of poker chips, and *the chips are down*, signifying a situation of urgency, means literally that all bets are in the pot, the hand is over and the cards now have to be shown to determine the winning hand. All of these expressions date back to the 19th century, when poker became our national card game. So does a *blue-chip stock*, a high-priced common stock that pays high dividends consistently over a long period, which derives from poker's highest-valued blue chips.

chipmunk.   This small striped squirrel-like rodent takes its name from the way it descends trees. *Chipmunk* comes from the Chippewa Indian *atchitamon*, meaning "head first."

chip off the old block.   A son or daughter who strongly resembles his or her father or mother. The phrase, recorded in the 1600s, was originally British, but is now widely used and refers to the chip off a block of wood. A variation on the expression is found in a remark of Eugene O'Neill's father, James, who gave up a promising career for the financial security of playing only the leading role in *The Count of Monte Cristo*, which he played over 5,000 times. "A chip off the old block, eh?" his son Eugene said to him soon after he, too, had chosen the theater as a career. "Say, rather, a slice off the old ham," James O'Neill replied.

chip on one's shoulder.   In 1830 the *Long Island Telegraph* in Hempstead, New York reported that "When two churlish boys were determined to fight, a *chip* would be placed on the shoulder of one, and the other demanded to knock it off at his peril." From this New York State boyhood custom, first recorded above, comes the expression *to have a chip on one's shoulder*, "to be sullen or angry, looking for a fight." The phrase itself isn't recorded until 1934, but is probably much older.

Chippendale.   Thomas Chippendale (ca. 1718–79) worked primarily in the French rococo, Chinese, and Gothic styles, sometimes combining them without incongruous results. Setting up his factory in London in 1749, he later published *The Gentleman and Cabinet Maker's Directory* (1754), in which he illustrated some 160 designs. Chippendale almost invariably managed to combine comfort, grace, and solidity in his wide variety of furniture, which is highly valued today. So many of his designs were slavishly copied during the latter half of the 18th century that it has always been difficult to identify his own work, dealers generally using the term *Chippendale* to designate a large variety of furniture in his style.

chippy.   Most sources say *chippy*, first recorded in the late 1880s, comes from *chip*, "to chirp," as a streetwalker might do when a prospective client walked by. But it's hard to believe that prostitutes commonly chirped at men. More likely, this name for a whore derives from the *chips* prostitutes were paid with by clients in Mexican-American whorehouses (*chippy houses*) in the western United States. The customers purchased chips from the madam, paid the women with them and the women cashed them in for their percentage.

chips are down.   *See* CHIP IN.

Chisholm Trail.   In the spring of 1866 Jesse Chisholm (ca. 1806–68), a halfbreed Cherokee Indian trader and government agent, drove his wagon loaded with buffalo hides through the Oklahoma territory to Wichita, Kansas. The wheels cut deep into the prairie, providing rut marks for a route that was to become the most important and famous of all western cattle trails, extending from San Antonio, Texas to Abilene and other Kansas railheads. The trail was used for more than 20 years after the Civil War, and 450,000 Texas longhorns were driven up it in 1872 alone. Remnants of the trail, celebrated in folklore and cowboy ballads such as "The Old Chisholm Trail," still remain along the Santa Fe Railroad line.

chit.   *Chit*, for "an I.O.U." or "a voucher of money owed for food or drink," derives from the Hindustani *citthi*, "a short note." In British colonial India, Hindu civil servants seem to have been in the habit of writing an inordinate amount of *citthis* about every conceivable matter. The British found this practice time-consuming and inefficient, criticizing it so often that the word *citthi* eventually became the easier to pronounce *chitty* and then *chit* in their vocabulary. They used *chit-coolies* as a term for Indian messengers, and soon they used *chit* for the notes they signed for drinks and food at their clubs. The *chit* that means a young, often insignificant person or a child ("a

chit of a girl") goes back much further in time. Found in Wycliffe, it refers to the young of an animal and probably derives from *kitten* or *kit*.

chivalry; shovelry; the Great Entrencher.   The *chivalry* means a group of knights or gallant gentlemen. The word derives ultimately from the Latin word *caballus* for a horse, knights and gentlemen usually being the only ones who could afford to own horses. It is often forgotten that in the American South up until the Civil War the wealthy ruling class was frequently called *the chivalry*, sometimes in a joking way or sarcastically. In the North Robert E. Lee's forces were called the *shovelry* toward the end of the war, because all they seemed to do was dig in deeper. Lee himself was called "The Great Entrencher" by his own troops.

cho cho.   One of the few Basque words that has entered American English. *Cho cho* means a young child or boy and is sometimes used by non-Basque speakers in parts of the West.

chockablock.   Originally a nautical term meaning "no more slack can be taken on rope," *chockablock* came to mean "completely full" ashore. *Chockfull*, which has more currency countrywide, comes from the same source, dating back to the 14th century.

chocolate.   *See* CACAO TREE.

chocolate mousse.   One theory has it that this dessert was invented by French artist Henri de Toulouse-Lautrec a century ago. Lautrec gave it the witty name *chocolate mayonnaise*, but this was changed to chocolate *mousse*, ("foam," "lather") over the years.

Choctaw.   *Choctaw*, a fancy step in ice-skating, and southern slang for unintelligible speech, is from the Choctaw Indian tribe of southern Mississippi. The Choctaws, named from the Spanish *chato* ("flattened") for their practice of flattening the heads of male infants, fought against the British during the American Revolution and aided the United States in later years against the Creeks. They ceded their lands to the government in 1832, the majority moving to reservations in what is now Oklahoma. *See* LUTZ.

choke'em.   A colorful popular name in the western United States for dodder, a plant of the genus *Cuscuta*, because of its parasitic effect on host plants: it literally chokes or smothers them to death. Few plants can match dodder's colorful derogatory names. The sprawling, yellow, threadlike plants are also called "beggarweed," "devil's guts," "hairybird," "hellweed," "robber vine," "strangle-weed," "tangle-gut," "love-in-a-tangle," and "witch shoelaces."

choke pear; chokecherry.   Because of its rough, astringent taste, which could make a person choke, this fruit was called a choke pear. Later the term was applied, figuratively, to anything that stopped someone from speaking, such as biting sarcasm or an unanswerable argument. The wild black cherry is sometimes called the *chokecherry* for similar reasons, and there is a berry called the *chokeberry*. *See* CHOKE-PEAR; PEARS OF AGONY.

choke-pear; pears of agony.   The choke-pear, whose name also became the synonym for "a severe reproof" in the 16th century, has to be among the most perverse instruments of torture man has invented. Named after the indigestible pear called a CHOKE PEAR, it was "of iron, shaped like a pear" and originally "used in Holland" by robbers. According to an early source: "This iron pear they forced into the mouths of persons from whom they intended to extort money; and of turning a key, certain interior springs thrust forth a number of points, in all directions, which so enlarged it, that it could not be taken from the mouth: and the iron, being case-hardened, could not be filed; the only methods of getting rid of it were either by cutting the mouth, or advertising a reward for the key. These pears were also called pears of agony."

chop-chop.   Noticing how fast the Chinese ate with chopsticks, 19th-century traders in China adopted the "chop" from the word *chopsticks* and invented the pidgin English expression *chop chop*—"quick, fast, or make it snappy." The word *chopsticks* itself is a corruption of the Chinese name for the eating implements, *k'wai-tse*, which means "the quick or nimble ones." *See* LONG TIME NO SEE.

chopsticks.   *See* CHOP-CHOP.

chop suey.   Chop suey isn't native to China; in fact, most accounts of its origin say that the dish was invented in America. The widely accepted theory, advanced by Herbert Asbury in his *Gangs of New York* (1928), makes the tasty melange the brainchild of a San Francisco dishwasher, though the Chinese dishwasher is sometimes promoted to a "cook in a California gold mining camp." I've traced the term's invention, however, to 1896, when it was concocted in New York by Chinese ambassador Li Hung-chang's chef, who tried to devise a dish appealing to both American and Chinese tastes. Since the ambassador had three chefs, it's hard to say which one invented chop suey. The name has nothing to do with the English word "chop," deriving instead from the Cantonese dialect *shap sui*, which means "pieces of mixed bits," *sui* being the Chinese for "bits." The chef who invented it took leftover pieces of pork and chicken and cooked them together with bean sprouts, green peppers, mushrooms, and seasonings in a gravy, serving it with rice and soy sauce.

chortle.   Author Lewis Carroll coined *chortle*, "to chuckle gleefully," in *Through the Looking Glass* (1871)—the word a blend of "snort" and "chuckle."

chouse.   The word *chouse*, "to cheat or swindle," is thought to derive from the Turkish *chaush*, for "an official messenger." How the messenger became a swindler is an interesting story. It seems that in 1609 the English adventurer Sir Robert Shirley, who had been barred from his homeland, sent a Turkish messenger to England to transact business with Turkish and Persian merchants there. The messenger *choused* the merchants of 4,000 pounds and disappeared, the notoriety of his swindle leading to the coining of the word. However, this derivation is not certain because there are no contemporary records of the swindle.

chow.   *Ch'ao*, the Mandarin Chinese for "to fry or cook," probably gives us the word *chow*, an Americanism first recorded in the 1850s in California, where there were many Chinese laborers and cooks working on the railroads. *See* CHOW CHOW.

chow chow.   Chow chow, or chow, a medium-sized, generally red, black, or brown nonsporting dog of Chinese breed, may derive its name from *chow*, a pidgin word for food, or from *chow-chow*, the Chinese mixed-fruit preserve. Another theory, which seems more plausible, is that it is simply from the Chinese *Chou*, this being the name of the ancient Chinese race that formed the Chou dynasty, which ruled from about 1122 to 256 B.C., and which brought China's first "golden age." The chow is noted for its sturdy build, large head, and deep-set eyes. Probably originally bred in northern China, it can be traced back as early as 150 B.C.

chowder.   *Chowder* derives from the French *chaudière*, stew pot, the word brought to the New World by Breton fishermen who settled the Maritime Provinces of Canada. The soup called a clam chowder is made with milk, vegetables, and clams in Maine and Massachusetts, this being the famous New England clam chowder. But in Rhode Island and as far away as New York, it often is made with water, vegetables, tomatoes, and clams, this called Manhattan clam chowder. The two schools are not at all tolerant of each other. One Maine legislator, in fact, introduced a bill making it *illegal* to add tomatoes to chowder within the state of Maine, the penalty being that the offender dig up a barrel of clams at high tide.

chowderhead.   According to one theory, neither clam chowder nor any other chowder has anything to do with this expression, used to mean a dolt or a stupid, clumsy person. *Chowderhead*, this theory holds, is a mispronunciation of *cholterhead*, which dates back to the 16th century and is derived from the older term *jolthead*. Unfortunately, we're all a bunch of chowderheads when it comes to the origins of *jolthead*.

Christ bird.   According to ancient legend, the robin is called the "Christ bird" because its breast was stained red by Christ's blood when the bird tried to comfort him on the cross.

Christian.   The first known usage of *Christians*, for "followers of Christ," is recorded in the Bible, Acts 11:25–26: "So Barnabus went to Tarsus to look for Saul; and when he had found him, he brought him to Antioch. For a whole year they met with the church, and taught a large company of people; and in Antioch the disciples were for the first time called Christians." The word *Christ* is from the Greek *Christos*, "the anointed one." *See* BUDDHISM; JEW.

Christian name.   A term often used by Christians for a given or first name. Here the word *Christian* represents not the name of the religion, as most people believe, but *christen* or *christened name*, the name given at a christening. Over the years, folk etymology made *christened name* into *Christian name*.

Christmas.   *Christmas* simply means Christ's mass. The Christian holiday celebrates Christ's birth, but there are no trustworthy records of the real date—August 28, May 20, April 19 or 20, November 17, and March 28 having all been suggested by scholars as more accurate than December 25. In northern Europe, Christmas was originally a pagan feast celebrating the winter solstice, a time when ancient peoples built great bonfires to give the winter sun god strength and to receive him. The early church fathers wisely chose a day near the winter solstice as the date to celebrate Christ's birth, the return of light becoming associated with the hope of the world in the birth of the savior.

Christmas card.   The idea for the Christmas card was conceived in 1843 by Sir Henry Cole, the Englishman who drew the sketch for the world's first postage stamp, the Penny Black. Cole suggested the idea to Royal Academician John Horsley, who designed the card, which depicted three generations of a family toasting the season with wine. About 1,000 of the cards sold that first year, a figure that would rise to billions.

Christmas tree.   The Christmas tree is an ancient German custom, though Germans call the small decorated firs or spruces they use a *Weihnachtsbaum*, or "holy-night tree." German settlers brought the custom to America, where English-speaking settlers dubbed it the Christmas tree as early as 1838, the first recorded use of the term. Americans thought the trees idolatrous at first, but soon realized the German immigrants weren't worshipping the tree and adopted the custom themselves.

christy.   Also called a christiania, the christy is a quick turn in skiing, so named for the capital of Norway, Christiania (now Oslo), where it was invented.

Christy minstrels.   Folk music fans may be surprised to learn that the name of this popular group honors an early American songwriter and that the term *Christy minstrels* is a synonym for Negro minstrel-type groups. Edwin Christy (1815–62) popularized his songs through his black-face troupe, which toured America and England and was widely imitated up until the beginning of this century. Christy wasn't the first to perform in blackface, but his group brought the minstrel show to perfection. His name had such great drawing power that it was assumed by the man who led the troupe when Christy retired.

chrononhotonthologos.   The longest words ever delivered on stage were: "Aldiborontiphoscophornio! Where left you Chrononhotonthologos?" which begins Henry Carey's farce *Chrononhotonthologos, the Most Tragical Tragedy That Ever Was Tragedized by Any Company of Tragedians* (1734). Chrononhotonthologos was the King of Queerummania, and his name is now used (though seldom, if ever, verbally) for any bombastic person delivering an inflated address. Aldiborontiphoscophornio was a courier in the play. Carey, who wrote the popular song "Sally in My Alley," may have written the words and music to the British anthem, "God Save the King."

chrysanthemum.   These fall flowers are of many colors today, but when the ancient Greeks grew them they were mostly gold-colored; hence their name *chrysanthemum* from the Greek *chrysos anthemon*, gold flowers. In the city of Himeji, Japan locals consider the chrysanthemum unlucky and refuse to grow the flower or display it. This stems from a legend about a servant girl named Chrysanthemum Blossom (O-Kiku) who threw herself into a well and drowned upon discovering that

one of 10 golden plates it was her duty to safeguard had disappeared. According to the story, Chrysanthemum Blossom's spirit returned every night to the castle where she had lived to count the plates, screaming each time she reached the count of nine. So persistent were her visits and so fiendish her screams that the inhabitants of the castle were forced to desert it. In most of Japan, of course, the chrysanthemum is a much-prized symbol of the nation. The largest fireworks in the world, more than 2,000 feet in diameter, are made in Japan and explode into the shape of a chrysanthemum. The chrysanthemum's botanical name has recently been changed to *Dendranthema x grandiflora*. But people will still be calling the flowers "mums" for years to come.

chrysocracy.   A word that didn't make it, even though the venerable Oliver Wendell Holmes coined it in his popular novel *Elsie Venner* (1861). Holmes later wrote in a letter: "In 'Elsie Venner' I made the word *chrysocracy*, thinking it would take its place; but it didn't; *plutocracy*, meaning the same thing, was adopted instead. *See* ANESTHESIA.

chubby.   For nearly 400 years now overweight people have been called chubby after the thick, fat, and roundcheeked fish named the chub, a type of carp common in England and northern Europe. The American fish called the chub is not the same fish at all.

chuck; chuck wagon.   Food or provisions in general; a meal. The term is an Americanism first used in about 1840 and probably derives from the cut of meat (beef) called chuck. The first chuck wagon was made from a surplus Civil War army wagon in 1867 by rancher Charles Goodnight. By the 1880s the term was common for a wagon carrying provisions and equipment for cooking, the Studebaker Company by then manufacturing them for $75 to $100.

chucker-out.   *See* BOUNCER.

chuckle; cackle.   The *O.E.D.* says *chuckle* is an echoic word like *cackle*, both perhaps suggested by sounds chickens make. *Chuckle* provides a problem, however, because it meant "to laugh vehemently or convulsively" when first recorded in 1598, and such laughter, to my ear, hardly sounds anything like a chicken. The soft, suppressed laughter that is *chuckle*'s meaning today does fit such origins, though. *See* ONOMATOPOEIA.

chum.   *Chum*, for "close friend or pal," came into English only in the late 17th century, probably from British university slang. It possibly is a shortening and slight alteration of *chambermate* (roommate), but there are no quotations to prove this. *Chum*, for "fishing bait," possibly comes from a Scottish dialect word meaning "food"; in any case, it derives from a different source from the *chum* meaning "pal."

chump.   *See* SAP.

Chunnel.   The name for the railroad tunnel under the English Channel from England to France, which was not built for many years, mainly because of British fears of invasion from Europe through it. It was finally opened to the public in 1994. *Chunnel* is a combination of *ch*annel and *tunnel*. When uncapitalized it can be used as the name for any underwater tunnel.

Churchillian. Often accompanying elegant oratory or prose, great wit, and statesmanship, and even a large cigar, this familiar adjective commemorates British prime minister Sir Winston Leonard Spencer Churchill (1874–1965). "On the 30th of November at Blenheim Palace, the Lady Randolph Churchill, prematurely, of a son," read the one line notice in the *London Times* announcing his birth, but Churchill's life was to fill volumes. Soldier, journalist, writer, and statesman, his brilliant public career included service as home secretary of state for war, and chancellor of the exchequer. Yet all his life, he felt, was merely a preparation for his crucial prime ministership during World War II. Some have gone so far as to say that England would not have survived the Blitz of 1940–41 without his leadership. Great Churchillian words and phrases include the much quoted, "I have nothing to offer but blood, toil, tears and sweat"; "Never in the field of human conflict was so much owed by so many to so few"; "The soft underbelly of the Axis"; the "iron curtain"; and his words on the fall of France: "Let us therefore brace ourselves to our duties, and so bear ourselves that if the British Empire and its Commonwealth last for a thousand years, men will still say: 'This was their finest hour!'" On April 9, 1963, Winston Churchill was paid the unique honor of being proclaimed a citizen of the United States.

churl. *See* EARL.

churrigueresque. This man's name itself is elaborate, suggesting the style it represents. Extravagant overornate architecture, especially that of 17th- and 18th-century Spain, is called *churrigueresque*, after Spanish architect and sculptor José Churriguera (1650–1725). Churriguera, a native of Salamanca, was an architect of the baroque school whose important works include the great catafalque for Queen Maria Louisa (1688), the palace of Don Juan de Goyeneche, and a portal of the Church of Santo Gayetano. Spanish baroque, with its free lines and vast profusion of detailed ornament, is named for him because he and his two sons were the most successful practitioners of this Renaissance form. *Churrigueresque* strongly influenced the Spanish colonial style in the southwestern part of Spain and in Mexico.

chutzpa. *Chutzpa*, or *chutzpah*, derives from a Hebrew word meaning "insolence, audacity." Signifying impudence, gall, brazen nerve, incredible cheek, and unmitigated audacity in Yiddish and in American slang, it more often today indicates an admirable quality in a person—guts bordering on the heroic. Leo Rosten gives the classic definition of *chutzpa* in *The Joys of Yiddish:* "that quality enshrined in a man who, having killed his mother and father, throws himself on the mercy of the court because he is an orphan." (No one knows if this ever happened, but a 19th-century anecdote does mention such a man.)

ciao! *Ciao* (pronounced "chow") is an Italian word for "hello" or "good-bye" used frequently in the U.S. over the past 20 years or so. *Ciao!* derives from the Italian *schiavo*, "I am your slave," according to one inventive wordsmith. Another source says *ciao!* is an adaptation of the Swiss-German *Tschau* used by Italians vacationing at Swiss ski resorts.

Cibola. Coronado, among other early Spanish explorers, searched in vain for a fabled land of great wealth in the U.S. Southwest called "Cibola," or the "Seven Cities of Cibola," which later proved to be an area in western New Mexico inhabited by the Zuri Indians, who had no great material wealth. The name, which derives from a native term for buffalo, was once suggested as a state name for the territory that became Colorado.

Cicero; cicerone; Ciceronian. If you travel in Italy, any guide you hire will be called a *cicerone*, these guides often being well versed about the places of interest and objects they point out. The Italians invoke the name of Marcus Tullius Cicero (100–43 B.C.) for this word because the eloquent statesman, orator, and writer epitomized the knowledge and style they expected of their *cicerones*. The story, from Plutarch, is that Cicero got his name from the Latin *cicer* ("a wart"), due to the "flat excrescence on the tip of his nose." Cicero is also honored by *Ciceronian*, pertaining to his clear, forceful, and melodious oratorial or prose style, and *Cicero*, a unit of print similar to a pica. Today, *cicerone* has come to mean a guide in any country.

cider. That cider was originally hard cider—that is, a fermented alcoholic drink—is witnessed by the derivation of the word, which came into English, via French (*cidre*), from the Latin word *sicera*, which comes from the Hebrew *shekar*, "strong drink." General William Henry Harrison of "Old Tippecanoe and Tyler, too" fame (he was called Tippecanoe because he won a battle against Indians at Tippecanoe River), was also known as the "log cabin and hard cider candidate" when he defeated Martin Van Buren for the presidency in 1840. As a campaign song put it:

> Let Van from his cooler of silver wine drink
> And lounge on his silken settee.
> Our man on a log-cabin bench can recline;
> Content with hard cider is he!

See POLITICAL SLOGANS; SLOGAN.

cigarette. *See* COFFIN NAILS.

cigarette punch. A powerful, bone-breaking uppercut to the jaw of someone who has relaxed and begun to open his mouth after being offered a cigarette. Invented by the Cockney career criminal Ronnie Kray (1934–95), who, along with his twin brother, Reggie (d. 2000), ran London's underworld from about 1955 to 1970, heading a crime family called the Firm. The Firm is also a nickname for the American CIA, which is usually called the Company.

cimarron. This big-horned sheep ultimately takes its name from a plant. The Latin *cyma*, meaning the spring shoots of any plant, yielded the Spanish *cima*, mountain peak or summit. This became the Spanish *cimaron*, meaning any wild, unruly solitary creature, probably because such animals roamed the mountains. In American English, however, *cimarron* is mainly used for the bighorn or mountain sheep (*Ovis canadensis*), the word first recorded in 1840. In *Western Words* (1944), Ramon Adams points out that Mexicans and some Americans in the West use *cimarron* "for an animal, horse, bovine or even human, which, deserted by all its friends, runs alone and has little to do with the rest of its kind." Literally, it signifies one who flees from civilization and becomes a fugitive or wild person.

Cimmerian darkness; Crimea. The ancient Cimmerians were believed to live in total darkness in a land where the sun never shone—hence the expression *Cimmerian darkness*, often "the darkness of ignorance." Homer used the term *Cimmerian darkness* in the *Odyssey*. These wandering nomads also gave their name to the *Crimea* because they lived on the shores of the Black Sea.

Cinc. A new term, from the war on terrorism, meaning commander in chief, as in "The Cinc—General Tommy R. Franks, the commander of the war in Afghanistan—relies on his commanders on the ground to make those assessments" (*N.Y. Times*, 3/14/02).

cinch. A strong belly band used on horse saddles with a ring on each end to which a strap running from the saddle is secured. *Cinch*, from the Spanish *cincha* (saddle girth), came to mean a firm hold or tight grip and then became an American term for something sure and easy, as in "It's a cinch."

cinchona; quinine. About 1639 the condesa Ana de Chinchón, wife of the conde de Chinchón (ca. 1590–1647), Spanish viceroy of Peru, was stricken with a persistent tropical fever. After European doctors failed to restore her health, she was cured by taking the powdered bark of a native evergreen tree that Peruvian Indians brought her. The condesa and her husband collected the dried bark, which contained quinine, and sent it back to Spain. There the miracle bark was at first called "Countess bark" or "Peruvian bark," but when Linnaeus named the genus of trees and shrubs yielding it in the condesa's honor, he misspelled her name. What should have been the "Chinchona tree" became known to history as the *Cinchona tree*. Today the native South American *Cinchona* is widely grown throughout the world, notably in Java and India. The *quinine* extracted from its bark derives its name from *quinaquina*, its Peruvian Indian name.

Cincinnati. Cincinnati, Ohio, takes its name from the Society of the *Cincinnati*, honoring the Roman statesman Cincinnatus, which former Revolutionary officers in the area founded in 1783.

Cincinnatus. In the early days of the republic George Washington was called the Cincinnatus of America, after the hero of that name who in about 458 B.C. came out of retirement on his farm to lead the Roman army to victory. Returning to the plow, Cincinnatus again served as dictator many years later to successfully avert a civil war. Like Lucius Quinctius Cincinnatus, Washington was a simple, dignified man. *See* CINCINNATI.

CINCUS; FIB. No doubt the most embarrassing acronym in naval history was CINCUS (pronounced "sink us"), which stood for the *C*ommander *in* *c*hief of the *U*nited *S*tates Navy before World War II, but was dropped from use following Pearl Harbor. Another amusing nautical acronym is FIB, standing for the *F*isherman's *I*nformation *B*ureau of Chicago.

cineaste. *See* AUTEUR.

cinema verité. Documentary filmmaking in which the camera records events without directional control. The technique was introduced in France from one developed by Russian filmmaker Dziga Vertov (1896–1954). It can also mean any film using this technique or a simulation of it.

cinnamon. Cinnamon was called *Kinnamomon* by the Greeks, who may have adapted the word from an earlier Semitic one. The bark of the tropical cinnamon tree (*Cinnamonum zeylamium*) yields cinnamon, which has been used as a spice for thousands of years. Most of it comes from Malaya and Indonesia, and the Arabs, seeking to keep their monopoly on trading it, concocted some incredible tales about its harvesting. The Greek historian Herodotus repeated this story:

> What they say is that the dry sticks . . . are brought by large birds which carry them to their nests, made of mud, on mountain precipices which no man can climb, and that the method the Arabians have invented for getting hold of them is to cut up the bodies of dead oxen, or donkeys, or other animals, into very large joints which they carry to the spot in question and leave on the ground near the nests. They then retire to a safe distance and the birds fly down and carry off the joints of meat to their nests, which, not being strong enough to bear the weight, break, and fall to the ground. Then the men come along and pick up the cinnamon, which is . . . exported to other countries.

cinque ports. From the 13th to the 17th century and even later the British crown granted special privileges to the ports of Hastings, Sandwich, Dover, Romaney, and Hythe, because they provided men and ships for the defense of the English Channel. The ports of Rye and Winchelsea were later added, but the favored ports were still called cinque ports, from the Latin *quinque*, "five."

Circassian. *Circassian beauty* refers to the legendary charms of the Circassian women, inhabitants of a region in the northeast Caucasus once known as Circassia, where fathers often sold their beautiful daughters to Turkish merchants for the harems of Eastern monarchs. No degradation was implied; the women considered their sale an honor. The Circassians had a number of unusual customs: any young man who purchased a bride was required to come with friends, fully armed, and carry her off from her father's house; a younger brother had to rise from his seat whenever an elder brother entered the room and remain silent whenever he spoke; a murderer could escape punishment by rearing the newborn child of his victim until his or her education was completed; and any man pursued by enemies had sanctuary after he touched the hand of a woman, so long as he remained under her roof. Russia finally subjugated these proud, warlike Muslims in 1864, after which many of them migrated to Turkish territory. Today Circassia forms part of the Russian federation.

Circe. A dangerous, irresistibly fascinating woman, like the sorceress and enchantress Circe, who in *The Odyssey* turned the companions of Odysseus into swine by means of a magic potion. Odysseus himself was protected by the herb moly, given him by Hermes, and after a year passed persuaded Circe to restore his companions to human beings and let them all leave her island of Aeaea. Circe, whose name derives from the Greek *kirkos*, falcon, bore Odysseus a son, Telegonus, and years later

Telegonus unwittingly slayed his father while he was searching for Odysseus in Ithaca. Circe, the daughter of Helios, the sun god in Greek mythology, lived on with the wild animals on her island.

circus. A traffic circle in British cities that is called a circle in the U.S. The most famous one in Britain is London's Piccadilly Circus. New York's Columbus Circle is an American counterpart. Both are open circle areas where several roads merge.

circus; charity circus. The expression *charity circus* for a circus that donates part of its proceeds to charity dates back to famous American circus owner and clown Dan Rice, who helped popularize his circus by donating part of the proceeds in the 1850s and gave performances for the Union cause during the Civil War. Circuses in America go back to at least 1785, however, and circuses were popular in Roman times, the word *circus* itself deriving from the Latin *circus* for ring. A *three ring circus* is thus, strictly speaking, "a three ring ring."

cisatlantic. *Cisatlantic* is the opposite of *transatlantic*, *cis* being the Latin prefix for "on this side of," while *trans* means "on the other side of."

City of the Saints. Salt Lake City, Utah, home of the Mormon Church, or Church of Jesus Christ of Latter-day Saints.

civet. Civet cats are raised commercially in Ethiopia for the civet excretion used in making perfume. Wild male civets are captured, caged, and well cared for because they constitute about a fifth of each villager's income. Typically, a stick is inserted into the cage. The civet grabs it with his teeth, and then the animal's rear legs are held by a worker while the oil is removed from an external sac in the genital area. Ethiopia exports a ton or so of rare civet every year. *Civet* comes ultimately from the Arabic *zabad*, meaning civet perfume. For centuries its excretion has been considered an aphrodisiac as well as a perfume agent. Wrote Shakespeare in *King Lear* (1604–5): "Give me an ounce of civet, good apothecary, to sweeten my imagination."

Civil War. The northern name for what some southerners called the War, the Revolution, the War of Independence, the Second War of Independence, the Second War of Secession, the Confederate War, the Glorious Cause, the War Between the States, the Unpleasantness, the Second American Revolution, the War for Constitutional Liberty, the War for Nationality, the War for Separation, the War for Southern Freedom, the War for Southern Independence, the War for Southern Nationality, the War for Southern Rights, the War for States' Rights, the War of the North and South, the War of the Sixties, the War to Suppress Yankee Arrogance, the Yankee Invasion, the Late Unpleasantness, and Mr. Lincoln's War. All of these terms, including *Civil War*, were first recorded in 1861. *See* ABE LINCOLN WAR.

clam chowder. By New England definition clam chowder is a dish made with clams, vegetables and *milk*—never with a tomato base. Manhattan clam chowder, however, is *always* made with tomatoes. This great American gastronomic controversy became national news in February 1939 when Assemblyman James Seeder introduced a bill into the Maine legislature making the use of tomatoes in clam chowder illegal. The punishment his unenacted bill specified: Make any offender harvest two bushels of clams at high tide. *See* CHOWDER.

clam up. *Clam up* is an Americanism for "to become silent, refuse to disclose information," dating back to 1916 and referring to the difficulty of opening the "lips" of the clam. *Clam*, for "mouth," has been common in America since the early 19th century. *Close as a clam*, describing a stingy person, is an older expression that probably originated in England. *See* HAPPY AS A CLAM AT HIGH TIDE.

the clap. The Old French *clapoire* ("bulge," "venereal sore"), which comes from the Old French *clapier* ("brothel"), gives us the word *clap* for gonorrhea. Partridge advises that the word was standard English from its introduction in the 16th century until Victorian times, noting, interestingly enough, that "They sing, they dance, clean shoes, or cure a clap" (in the poem "London") is "almost the sole instance in Dr. Johnson's work of a monosyllabic sentence."

claptrap. *Claptrap*, first recorded in 1727, initially meant a playwright's trick or device to catch applause, "a trap to catch a clap by way of applause from the spectators at a play," as the first person to define the term put it. The word finally came to mean pretentious, insincere, or empty language.

claque. Playwrights have had an advantage over most authors in the past because they or their backers could hire a claque, a body of people to applaud their work. The French, who originated the system in 1820 or so, had it down to a science. Claqueurs were divided into:

Commissaires—memorized the play and pointed out its literary merits.
Rieurs—hired to laugh at the jokes.
Pleureurs—women hired to cry when appropriate.
Chatouilleurs—kept the audience in good spirits.
Bisseurs—hired to cry *"bis!,"* "encore!"

Clarence. *See* SAILOR KING.

claret. Though it hasn't been heard much since the 1930s, when radio fight announcers popularized it, *claret* is one of the oldest boxing terms. Used to describe the blood drawn in a boxing match, it is named after red claret wine; the term is recorded in the description of a boxing match held in 1604.

Clarkia; Lewisia. Captain William Clark (1770–1838) is best known for his leadership with Meriwether Lewis of the Lewis and Clark Expedition to find an overland route to the Pacific, their party being the first to cross the continent within the limits of the United States. But the Army officer and veteran Indian fighter had an avid interest in natural history, describing many plants in his journals covering the 1803–07 expedition. The showy *Clarkia* genus, native to California, was named in his honor. Clark, the youngest brother of the famous frontier military leader, George Rogers Clark, was appointed superintendent of Indian affairs when his expedition returned. Clark's partner Captain Meriwether Lewis has *Lewisia*, a genus of 12 species of low-growing perennial flowers widely grown in the rock garden, named in his honor. Lewis, who had been Thomas Jefferson's secretary, was appointed governor of the newly acquired Louisiana Territory after the expedition. He died suddenly in 1808, only 35 years old, his death shrouded in mystery. He had been traveling to Washington to prepare the expedition journals when he died alone in an inn near Nashville, Tennessee. Suicide, or more probably murder, has been suggested as the cause of his death.

class. *See* UPPER CLASS.

classic; classical. The Roman author of *Attic Nights*, Aulus Gellius (ca. 123–ca. 165) is said to have invented the terms *classic* and *classical*, by which he meant "art of the first class." More likely, the terms have their origins in the Roman five classes of citizens, of which the highest class were termed *classici*. Later, during the Renaissance, the best authors, thought to be Greek and Latin, were called *classici auctores* (classic authors) and their works were called *classics*. Today *classic* can mean 1) first class 2) ancient 3) typical (as in "She has a classic case of flu.")

clatter. *See* ONOMATOPOEIA.

clavicle. *Clavicle*, or collarbone, derives from the Latin *clavicula*, meaning "little key." According to Littré's *Dictionnaire de la langue française* (1863–77) "because it was compared to the key of a vault, or, as others think, because its form is that of the ancient bolts."

clay-eater. One who eats clay for its nutritional content, especially a poor white or black. "He was a little, dried up withered atomy—a jaundiced sand-lapper or clay-eater from the Wassamasaw county," William Gilmore Simms wrote in *The Scout* (1854). The term has often been used disparagingly, along with terms like *poor white*, *hillbilly*, and *redneck*. *Clay-eating, also called dirt-eating, is still practiced in parts of the South, especially in the South Carolina and Georgia low country.*

clay pigeon. George Ligowsky of Cincinnati, Ohio, was in spirit an early conservationist who deplored the practice of using live birds in target shooting. One afternoon while watching boys skipping flat stones over the surface of a pond, he got the idea of making a clay target that could be released and shot at in place of pigeons or other birds. Ligowsky patented his invention in 1881, calling them flying targets, but because they usually took the place of pigeons, they quickly came to be called clay pigeons. Since then, for obvious reasons, *clay pigeons* has also become widespread American slang for an easy target, someone who is easily duped, a sucker.

clean as a whistle. One possibility is that the old simile describes the whistling sound of a sword as it swishes through the air to decapitate someone, and an early 19th-century quotation does suggest this connection: "A first rate shot . . . [his] head taken off as clean as a whistle." The expression is proverbial, at least since the 18th century, when Robert Burns used a variation on it. More likely the basic idea suggests the clear,

pure sound a whistle makes, or the slippery smooth surface of a willow stick debarked to make a whistle. But there is also a chance that the phrase may have originally been *as clean as a whittle*, referring to a piece of smooth wood after it is whittled.

a clean bill of health. Used generally today this term has its origin in the document issued to a ship showing that the port it left was suffering from no epidemic or infection at the time of departure. Its antonym is *a foul bill of health*, both expressions dating back to the 18th century.

clean heart. Pure. An English translation of a word from a local language in Kenya, where English is the official language along with Swahili.

cleanliness is next to godliness. Writers have variously assumed that this proverb originated with the American Puritans, that Benjamin Franklin created it in *Poor Richard's Almanac*, or that it is from the Bible. The truth is that it can be traced back to writings of Phinehas ben Yair, an ancient rabbi, and is found in the Talmud in this form: "The doctrines of religion are resolved into carefulness; carefulness into vigorousness; vigorousness into guiltlessness; guiltlessness into abstemiousness; abstemiousness into cleanliness; cleanliness into godliness." In this quotation "cleanliness" is literally next to "godliness." The first written record of the expression in English is by John Wesley, the founder of Methodism, who in a 1778 sermon wrote "Cleanliness is indeed next to godliness" and put the words in quotes as if to indicate that he had borrowed or slightly changed them from another source. Wesley said, "I look upon all the world as my parish." His "Rule of Conduct" was:

> Do all the good you can,
> By all the means you can,
> In all the ways you can,
> In all the places you can,
> At all the times you can,
> To all the people you can,
> As long as ever you can.

clean one's plow. To beat someone severely in a fight, as in "He better watch it or I'll clean his plow!" Said to derive from the way farmers clean their plows by dragging them through gravel. The phrase, first recorded in 1919, has several synonyms, including *clean one's clock*, *clean one's canyon*, and *clean one's greens*.

cleanse the Augean stables. This means a formidable if not impossible task. It was one of the 12 tasks of Hercules, hero of Greek mythology, given to him by Eurysteus before he could gain immortality. Hercules managed to clean the stables of King Augeus in one day, even though they contained 3,000 oxen, by turning the course of two rivers through the stalls.

clean sweep. Though it is often used in sports for the winning of every game in a series, this expression may be of nautical origin. It could refer to a huge wave from a typhoon or the like sweeping everything off the deck of a ship, even permanent structures. It's possible, however, that a storm or tornado causing the same destruction on land may have suggested the words. A third choice would be someone sweeping out a room or house with a broom.

clean up. In the early 19th century, American farmers used the expression *to clean up* as a synonym for gathering the harvest, stripping all the grain from a field. However, this doesn't appear to be the source when the expression means "to make an exceptional financial success," a "big haul." In this sense *clean up* came into the language after the gold strikes toward the end of the 19th century. It apparently derives from the mining term *clean-up*, which describes the process of separating gold from the gravel and rock that collected in the sluices or at the stamping mill.

cleanup spot. The term CLEAN UP above apparently gives us the expression *cleanup spot* for "the fourth position in a baseball team's batting order." The batter in the cleanup spot is always a long-ball hitter who is expected to empty, or clean up, the bases of any teammates, that is, to bring them all home with a long hit.

a clear and present danger; Every idea is an incitement; The Great Dissenter. In the 1919 case *Schenk v. United States* the U.S. Supreme Court, in a unanimous decision written by Justice Oliver Wendell Holmes, held that speech must present "a clear and present danger" to be considered criminal. Later, in 1925, Holmes dissented from the majority in the *Gitlow v. New York* case, in which Benjamin Gitlow, during the Red Scare, published a communist manifesto. Wrote Holmes: "It is said that this manifesto is more than a theory, that it was an incitement. Every idea is an incitement." For these and many other liberal opinions Holmes became known as The Great Dissenter, his memorable phrases becoming part of the language.

clear the decks. Make everything ready, especially before a great activity such as a fight. The expression goes back to the 18th century or earlier, when it was a naval command ordering seamen to prepare the ship for a battle.

clematis. The clematis is a woody twining vine, which led the Greeks to name it *klematis* from their word *klema* or "vine branch." The species *Clematis virginiana* is popularly called "old man's beard" because its seed pods have feathery appendages. The *Clematis* genus contains some of the most beautiful of climbing plants and there are thousands of varieties available.

Cleopatra. Cleopatra was only 38 when she died in 30 B.C., but in her short life she became one of the great romantic heroines of all time, her name still synonymous with feminine allurement and charm. At the age of 17, the Queen of the Nile married her younger brother, as was the custom, and led a revolt against Ptolemy XIII when he deprived her of her royal authority. Inducing Julius Caesar to fight a war to place her on the throne, she became his mistress, living openly in Rome with him after she poisoned her second younger sibling-husband. Caesar's assassination marked her return to Egypt with their son, Caesarion. There, in 41 B.C., Mark Antony fell under her spell and gave up his wife for her. Cleopatra hoped that Antony would restore her former powers. However, Octavian (later Emperor Augustus) declared war on them, vowing to destroy the two lovers, and defeated Antony at Actium. Cleopatra coldly accepted Octavian's proposal to assassinate Antony and persuaded him to commit suicide so that "they

might die together." Antony took his life by falling on his sword, believing that Cleopatra had already died, but "the serpent of the old Nile" was unable to win over Octavian, despite her treachery. She ended her own life by putting an asp to her breast. Her three sons by Antony were allowed to live, but Caesarion was put to death soon after.

Cleopatra's Needles. *Cleopatra's Needles* is a misnomer. The two originally pink obelisks—one 68½ feet tall standing on the Thames embankment, and the other 69½ feet tall in New York's Central Park—really have nothing at all to do with the Queen of the Nile. Hieroglyphics on the needles show that Pharaoh Thutmose III erected them centuries before Cleopatra. Originally raised at Heliopolis in 1475 B.C., the obelisks were moved to Alexandria under Augustus in about 14 B.C., where they adorned the Caesareum. In 1878 and 1880, respectively, Ismail Pasha made gifts of them to England and the United States, and it is said that they have suffered more from erosion in their present locations over the last 90-odd years than they did over thousands of years in Egypt. The formerly rose-red syenite granite obelisks were probably named for Cleopatra because they stood outside the Caesareum, honoring her dictator lover.

Cleopatra's nose. "If the nose of Cleopatra had been shorter the whole face of the earth would have been changed," wrote the French philosopher Blaise Pascal (1623–62) in his famous *Pensées*. His proverbial observation refers to the effects of Cleopatra's charms on Caesar and Mark Antony, but a different nose length, at least a moderately different one, would probably have made little difference to history. For Cleopatra's allure did not depend on her physical beauty; most sources, in fact, indicate that she wasn't a beautiful woman at all. What she was was an accomplished, artful lover, and the "salad days" that Shakespeare has her admit to—when she was young and loved unskillfully, like a salad, green and cold—were distant memories long before she had married at 17.

Cleopatra's pearl. *Cleopatra's pearl* concerns a sumptuous banquet Cleopatra gave for Antony. Her lover, the legend tells us, expressed astonishment at the costly meal, and she promptly removed a pearl earring, dropped it in a cup of vinegar and let it dissolve, saying, "My draft to Antony shall far exceed it." Vinegar cannot dissolve a pearl, however, and anything strong enough to do so wouldn't have conveniently been on Cleopatra's table—unless the wileful woman planted it there, in which case it is just as possible that she used a fake pearl.

clerical collar. Also called the *Roman collar* and the *reversed collar*, the clerical collar is a stiff narrow white collar fastened at the back and worn by some clerics. The term is first recorded in the mid-19th century. *See* CLERK.

clerihew.

> Sir Humphry Davy
> Abominated gravy
> He lived in the odium
> Of having discovered sodium.

This was the first *clerihew* written by Edmund Clerihew Bentley (1875–1956). The English detective-story writer composed it while only a schoolboy, according to his schoolmate G. K. Chesterton, "when he sat listening to a chemical exposition, with his rather bored air and a blank sheet of blotting paper before him." Bentley, one of the few people to have a word honoring his middle name, could in Chesterton's words "write clear and unadulterated nonsense with . . . serious simplicity." *See* GEORGIAN.

clerk. Clerks were originally scholars; the word *clerk* is simply a slurred pronunciation of the word *cleric*, which in medieval times meant a member of a religious order, all of whom were regarded as scholars because they could read and write. When education became more widespread, the term *clerk* gradually lost its scholarly connotation and assumed the meaning it has today, surviving in its old sense in legal circles, where, for example, a clerk to a Supreme Court Justice is still considered a scholar.

Cleveland. Cleveland, Ohio was laid out in 1796 by General Moses Cleaveland and was later named for him. Still later, a descendant of the general, Grover Cleveland, became president.

Cleveland Indians. There has been controversy recently over whether sports teams should be given Indian names, which has been a practice for over a century. One of the oldest was the name *Cleveland Indians*, the winning entry in a 1915 newspaper contest to rename the team. (It was formerly known as the Naps, in honor of star second baseman Napoleon Lajoie, who had just retired.) The team's new name honored Louis Sockalexis, a Penonscot Indian from Old Town, Maine, who had played college ball at Holy Cross and Notre Dame before signing with Cleveland in 1897 to become the first American Indian to play in the majors. After an excellent rookie year in which he batted .338 and was known for his power hitting and strong throwing arm, Sockalexis apparently succumbed to the pressures of his situation, which included loud war whoops from the fans when he came to bat. He began drinking heavily, and his playing deteriorated until he was dropped from the club in 1899. Although he played only 94 games, he remains the only person after whom an existing major league baseball team was named. Football's Kansas City Chiefs were named after the mayor of Kansas City, who was instrumental in bringing the franchise from Dallas to Missouri and was popularly nicknamed "the Chief." Other teams bearing "Indian" related designations include football's Washington Redskins and basketball's Golden State Warriors. Baseball's Atlanta Braves took the name of their predecessor, the Boston Braves, who were named not for any American Indians but for the emblem (an Indian brave) of New York City's Tammany Hall political machine—members of which had invested in the team. *See* INDIAN.

clicketing. In days past, people had more names for natural things than we can imagine today. *Clicketing*—not slang, but standard English—means "the copulation of foxes" and has been used in this sense since the late 16th century or before. This is perhaps a distinct word from *clicket*, meaning "to chatter," the first recorded use of it explaining: "When a bytche foxe goeth on clycqueting . . . she cryeth with a hollow voyce like unto the howling of a madde dogge . . ." The term is also applied to the wolf.

client. In ancient Rome a *client* (Latin for "learning") was a plebeian under the patronage of a patrician who was called his patron, the client performing certain services for the patron in exchange for the patron's protection of his life and interests. Hundreds of years later, in the 15th century, the word's meaning changed to describe a person who employs the services of a legal adviser or a person who employs the services of any professional businessman.

cliff dwellers. Prehistoric people of the Southwest who were ancestors of the Pueblo Indians and were named Cliff Dwellers because they built their homes in caves or on the ledges of cliffs. The name is now humorously applied to residents of tall apartment houses in large cities.

Cliffs Notes. These scholastic study guides to literary classics such as *Moby Dick* and *Wuthering Heights*, used by generations of students since 1958, were published by and named after Clifton Keith Hillegass (1918–2001). Though popular with students, they are not much loved by educators, several universities having banned their sale on campus. A *New York Times* obituary of Hillegass noted that "the phrase 'Cliff Notes' has entered the language as a shorthand for shortcut, often used in a way that implies a lack of nuance or thorough understanding." But the publisher never intended the guides to be used as "cheat sheets" by students who never read original texts. Until he sold his firm in 1998 for $14 million, he sold over 50 million copies of 220 titles.

climate. The ancient Greeks thought that the earth sloped toward the North Pole from the equator and for this reason named any particular part or region of the earth *klima*, "slope." Since they also believed that the earth's slope accounted for the varied weather in these different regions, they called the weather of a specific region its *clima*, which evolved into the English *climate*.

climb a sour apple tree. First recorded in the early 1900s but probably older, *go climb a sour apple tree* means "go to blazes, go to hell." It is an Americanism that is still occasionally heard.

clink. *Clink*, which is still heard humorously as the term for a jail, dates back at least to 1515, when a writer noted, "Then art thou clapped in the . . . Clinke." One theory has the word deriving from "a noted jail in the borough of Southwark." Milton is among the distinguished writers to have used the term. *To kiss the clink* was an expression, now virtually obsolete, meaning to be imprisoned.

clipped ears. Though the term isn't recorded in *A Dictionary of Americanisms*, Australians who migrated to the California gold fields in 1849 were often called *clipped ears*, because a certain number of them had been criminals who had suffered the punishment of ear clipping in Australia.

clipper ship; Flying Clipper. The origin of the *clipper* in *clipper ship* is not definitely known, but we may owe the expression to Cleopatra. The first authentic clipper ship was the *Ann McKim*, built in Baltimore in 1832, but an early French ship of this type was christened *Cleopatra-cum-Antonio*. The French ship's name, some scholars say, was shortened in usage to *Clipster* and then to *Clipper*, the last becoming the designation for all vessels of this class. Other authorities contend that rude clippers were being built before the War of 1812 and were known as Baltimore clippers because they clipped the the surface of the sea as they sped over the waves. Still another source holds that the expression *going at a clip* resulted in the word; and some investigators even claim that *clipper* is an invention of either Robert Burns or Percy Bysshe Shelley. But the French developed the principle for this type of ship in the 18th century, long before the Baltimore clippers, and as the *Cleopatra-cum-Antonio* dates from that period, the Cleopatra theory has much to say for it. *Clipper ship* was later applied to transoceanic flying boats, the famed Flying Clippers.

clodhopper; country bumpkin; hayseed; hick; rube. *Clodhopper*, before it became a word for "shoes," was an old 17th-century English term for a farmer or rural dweller who hopped over clods of dirt in the fields. *Country bumpkin*, from the Dutch *boomkin*, "little tree," became common in England a century later. *Rube* (from "Rustic Rueben"), *hick* (a pet name for "Richard") and *hayseed* are 19th-century Americanisms.

close as a clam. *See* CLAM UP.

clothes make the man. Apparently *clothes make the man* is an "alteration" of Shakespeare's "The apparel oft proclaims the man," which the Bard puts into the mouth of Polonius in *Hamlet*.

Cloud Cuckoo Land. Unrelated to life, an imaginary state of affairs. The reference is to the imaginary city built in the air in Aristophanes' comedy *The Birds* (414 B.C.).

clover. Rather than the other way around, as one might expect, the clover of the *Trifolium* genus takes its name from the suit of clubs at cards, which was *claver* in Old English. The four-leaf clover has, of course, long been a symbol of luck, having one more leaf than clovers usually do (this tradition was first recorded in about 1840), but there have been several authenticated cases of people finding *14*-leaf clovers. Someone who is "in clover" is well nourished, rich, and happy. This American metaphor, first recorded in 1847, has its source in the protein-rich clover species used here for fattening cattle. *See* LIKE PIGS IN CLOVER.

clue. Tracing *clue*, or *clew*, back in time we find that it first meant (in about 1393) "a ball of yarn or thread." Two centuries passed and *clues*, balls of thread, began to be used to guide people "threading" their way out of garden labyrinths or mazes. This soon led to the use of the word *clue* for something that "points the way, indicates a solution, or puts one on the track of a discovery or solving a mystery."

C.M.G. A British term that has some use in the U.S. It is the initials for *Call Me God* and is used derisively for any vain self-important person who is a V.I.P. to himself or herself: "Here comes C.M.G."

coach. The little village of Kocs in northwestern Hungary is responsible for the word *coach* in all its senses of the word "carriage" and for academic and athletic *coaches* as well. In the 15th century an unknown carriage maker in Kocs devised a larger, more comfortable carriage than any known at the time. It was called a *Koczi szeter*, a "wagon of Kocs," which was shortened to *kocsi*. Copied all over Europe in the next century it eventually became a *coche* and then a *coach* in English. From the name of the English horse-drawn coach came all stage-coaches, motor coaches, and finally air coaches. *Coach*, for "an instructor," arose as college slang—a coach was a figurative carriage whose coaching would "carry" you through exams. The same idea was applied to athletic coaches, who were, however, known as *coachers* up until the late 1880s, when they became *coaches*.

coast is clear. When this expression was first recorded in 1531 it described a ship that had safely cleared the coast in England. Later Shakespeare used the expression similarly in *Henry VI*, but the phrase's nefarious connotation suggests that it may at one time have had some reference to smuggling as well.

cobbler should stick to his last; ultracrepederian. Alexander the Great's favorite artist, Apelles, corrected his drawing of a man's sandal latchet in one of his paintings when a cobbler criticized it. But when the shoemaker went on to criticize the way Apelles had drawn the man's legs, the artist admonished him: *Ne sutor ultra crepidam*, "The cobbler should stick to his last [the metal foot-model on which shoes are shaped]." Apelles' words give us not only the familiar expression but the term *ultracrepederian*, meaning "criticism ranging beyond the critic's range of knowledge." Its first recorded use is by Hazlitt in an 1819 letter to critic William Gifford, who had savaged Keat's "Endymion" in the *Quarterly Review*.

cobra. The deadly snake was so named by one of Vasco da Gama's men when the Portuguese explorer landed in India in 1498. Because the snake (whose name was *nag* in Hindi) had a head shaped like a hood, this unknown person called it a *cobra de capello* a "hooded snake." Over time its name was shortened to *cobra*, which simply means "snake" in Portuguese.

cobwebs; spiderweb. Dating back to at least 1300, *cobweb* is older than *spiderweb* by about 200 years. *Cob* is a form of *cop*, a Middle English word for spider. Strangely enough, although *cobweb* is of older ancestry than *spiderweb*, *cob* or *cop* was only rarely used as a separate word for *spider*. It is a back formation from *cobweb*, which means that we have to look elsewhere for the origin of *cobweb*. Possibly the answer may be found in an earlier use of *cob* or *cop* for "head." *Cobweb* may have been suggested by people walking into spiderwebs and brushing their heads *(cobs)* in the webs.

Coca-Cola. *See* COKE.

cock. The word *cock*, for "the penis or male sexual organ," is included in the great *O.E.D.*, which traces it to the earlier term *cock*, for "the spout or short pipe serving as a channel for passing liquids through . . ." *Cock* for the penis is, however, recorded earlier than the *O.E.D.*'s date of 1730, being first found in Beaumont and Fletcher's comedy *The Custom of the Country* (ca. 1619). *Cock* for a rooster is recorded much earlier, in ca. 897, its origin unknown, although it is earlier *cocc* in Old

English. In the U.S. South *cock* is a name for the female sexual organ rather than the penis, as is the case in the rest of the country. "She's a good piece of cock," is a rather common expression. Several authorities, including Hugh Rawson's *Dictionary of Euphemisms*, make note of this.

cockadau.　Vietnamese slang from the Vietnam War, meaning to kill. "VC (Viet Cong) number ten, cockadau beaucoup G.I." *Beaucoup* here means "many" and is military slang dating back at least to the mid-19th century.

cock-a-doodle-doo.　English speakers might think that the use of our centuries-old echoic word for the sound of the crowing of a rooster would be universal, but only the "k" sound in the word is common to most languages, their echoic words for the cock's crowing being quite different. German, for example, uses *kikiriki*; Italian, *chicchirichi*; French, *cocorico*; Spanish, *quiquiriqui*; Russian, *kikareku*; Rumanian, *cucuriqu*; Vietnamese, *cuc-cu*; Japanese, *kokekkoko*; and Arabic, *ko-ko*. The same is true for many echoic words. *See* MEOW.

cockamamie.　*Cockamamie* means something worthless or trifling, even absurd or strange; a *cockamamie* excuse or story is an implausible, ridiculous one. The word may be a corruption of *decalcomania* ("a cheap picture or design on specially prepared paper that is transferred to china, wood, etc."), a word youngsters on New York's Lower East Side early in the century found tiring to pronounce and impossible to spell.

cock and bull story.　This long, rambling, unlikely yarn, like the similar CANARD, takes its name from the barnyard. The phrase first appeared in about 1600 and has been constantly used ever since; even in classics like Laurence Sterne's *Tristram Shandy* (1767), one of our most imaginative and whimsical novels, where the words end the book: " 'L———d' said my mother, 'what is this story all about.' '———A COCK and a BULL,' said Yorick—'and one of the best of its kind, I ever heard.' " The expression *cock and bull story* hasn't been traced to the specific fable where it originated, but it arose in all probability from a fantastic tale about a cock and bull who talked to each other in human language. Since people knew that such a conversation was impossible, they most likely labeled any incredible yarns *cock and bull stories*. The French have used the expression *coq-à-l'âne*—literally "cock to the donkey"—in the same sense as *cock and bull* for almost four centuries, too. But it is also the term for a satirical verse genre that ridicules the follies and vices of society, deriving in this sense from the old French proverbial expression *c'est bien sauté du coq à l'âne*, which signifies incoherent speech or writing.

cock a snook.　A British expression, with some U.S. currency, for defiantly thumbing one's nose at somebody. Precisely it means to place the thumb on the nose and spread out the fingers (which is why it is also called "Queen Anne's fan"). *Snook* is of unknown origin.

cockatoo.　A crested parrot native to Australia and other places, *cockatoo* derives from Malay *kakatua*, which is said to be an imitation of a common sound the bird makes. Thousands of cockatoos are non-natives in cages all over the world. *See* COCK-A-DOODLE-DOO.

cockatrice; ichneumon.　Thanks to Pliny and other incredulous observers, people were terrified of this fantastic monster with the wings of a bird, the tail of a dragon, and the crested head of a cock until well into the 17th century. Said to be born of a cock's egg, the monster was, according to one old description, about "a foot long, with black and yellow skin and fiery red eyes," but others described it as much larger. It could be killed only by the crowing of a cock and so travelers often carried roosters with them to Africa or wherever they feared a cockatrice might be encountered. Otherwise, just a glance from the fabulous creature's eye could kill them, with only the crafty weasel immune to its "death rays." The cockatrice takes its name from the Greek *ichneumon*, which means "a tracker." This was translated into the Latin *calcatrix*, "a tracker," and *calcatrix* was ultimately corrupted to the English *cockatrice*. The mythical creature was called "a tracker" by the Greeks because they believed that it tracked down and devoured the eggs and young of the crocodile. In this respect it was probably given the characteristics of the real Egyptian *ichneumon*, an animal that does hunt down and devour crocodile eggs.

cocker spaniel.　The dog is not so named because it's "cocky," but because it was bred for hunting and retrieving wood*cock*, among other small game birds or, possibly, from the way the dog *cocks* its long, drooping ears. *Spaniel* simply means "Spanish dog," deriving from the Old French *Chien epagneul*, which was shortened to *espagnol*, "Spanish," and became *spaniel* in English. The spaniel may have been a breed developed in Spain, or perhaps the breed's silky hair and soft, soulful eyes suggested the appearance of the Spaniards, though there is no hard evidence of this. *Spaniel* has served as a verb and adjective, a symbol of affectionate humility, as well as a noun. Shakespeare has Antony speak of the "hearts that spaniel'd me at heels, to whom I gave their wishes."

cockles.　*See* WARM THE COCKLES OF ONE'S HEART.

cockney.　*Cockney* literally means a "cock's egg," deriving from the Middle English *cokeney*. The word first meant a foolish child or a foolish person who did not know a good egg from a cock's egg or cockney (a small egg with no yolk). Country people next applied the term to city people in general, then to Londoners and finally to London East Enders, people born within sound of the bells of St. Mary-le Bow (Bow Bells) in London who share a characteristic accent called *Cockney*. *See* GEORDIE.

cockpit; cockpit of Europe.　Belgium has long been known as the cockpit of Europe because so many important European battles have been fought there, from the battle of Oudenarde in 1708, to Waterloo in 1815, and the many battles fought there during World Wars I and II. *Cockpit* is of course an allusion to the arena where gamecocks are set to fight, which also gave its name to the space in fighter planes where the pilot sits.

cockroach.　Captain John Smith must have had a lot of trouble with cockroaches, judging by his description of the nocturnal household pest in his *The generall historie of Virginia, New England and the Summer Isles* (1624). Smith described the insect as "A certaine India Bug, called by the Spaniards a

Cacarootch, the which creeping into Chests they wat and defile with their ill-scented dung." His rendition of the Spanish *cucaracha* as *cacarootch* started the long and involved process whereby the name for the bug became *cockroach* in English. The most famous literary cockroach is undoubtedly American humorist Don Marquis's Archy, who wrote modern free verse because he couldn't work the typewriter shift key—along with his friend Mehitabel the Cat, he is immortalized in *archy and mehitabel* (1927) and a number of sequels. It was once thought that the smell of the cockroach apple, a Jamaican plant, would kill cockroaches.

cocksure.   Since the word *cocksure* first meant secure, safe, and certain—not dogmatic and self-confident, as it does today—it probably didn't originally have anything to do with the pompous, strutting rooster usually associated with it. But no one is cocksure about *cocksure*'s origins, which go back almost five centuries. In its now obsolete sense of lecherous, *cocksure* is much younger, so that eliminates a likely source and a better story. A real possibility is that the word was just a euphemism for *God sure!*—since *cock* was often a euphemism for God in oaths. Or it may have first meant the security of God, as in the following quote from Foxe's *Book of Martyrs* (1563): "Who so dwelleth under . . . the help of the Lord, shall be cock-sure for evermore." Shakespeare uses the word as if it derives from the sureness of the cock on the firelock of a gun, a cock that keeps the gun from going off, and the *O.E.D.* suggests as a source the cock, or tap, on a barrel of whiskey, which secured the liquor inside, preventing its escape. The Welsh word *coc*, "cog," has also been nominated—*cocksure* would thus mean "as sure as cogs fit into one another." So has the Irish *coc*, "manifest," and the Old English *cock*, for "the notch of a bow"—an arrow would have to be set *cocksure* to hit its target. No matter which is correct, it's almost certain that the idea of the strutting aplomb of a barnyard cock and the phallic associations of the word contributed to its later meaning of "pert and cocky."

cocktail.   There are well over 50 theories as to the word *cocktail*'s origin, H. L. Mencken alone presenting seven plausible ones in his *American Language*. These include a derivation from the French *coquetier*, "an egg cup," in which the drink was supposedly first served in 1800; from *coquetel*, "a mixed drink of the French Revolution period"; from the English *cock-ale*, "fed to fighting cocks"; from *cocktailings*, "the last of several liquors mixed together"; and from a toast to that cock that after a cockfight had the most feathers left in its tail. Just as reliable as any of these guesses is the old folktale that Aztec King Axolotl VIII's daughter Octel or Xochitl concocted the first cocktail; or, in another version, that an Aztec noble sent his emperor a drink made of cactus juice by his daughter, the emperor enjoying it so much that he married the girl and called the drink by her name—again Octel or Xochitl. According to this story, General Scott's soldiers are supposed to have brought the drink back to America centuries later. Suffice it to say that the origin of the word, first printed in 1806, is really unknown.

cocktail party.   Cocktail parties have been traced back as far as ancient Athens, where you could drop by a neighbor's early in the evening with your own goatskin of wine and be treated to a variety of "provocatives to drinking" that included caviar, oysters, shrimp, cheese, and even marinated octopus and roasted grasshoppers. The literary cocktail party is a creature of recent times, possibly evolving from the literary dinner parties so popular in the 19th century. Sherwood Anderson died of peritonitis and its complications after swallowing a toothpick with an hors d'oeuvre at a cocktail party.

coconut; copra.   Safe in its buoyant, waterproof pod, the coconut sailed the high seas from southern Asia in prehistoric times and was propagated and cultivated throughout tropical regions. But it wasn't given its present name until the late 15th century, when Portuguese explorers came upon it in the Indian Ocean islands and fancied that the little indentations at the base of the nut looked like eyes. Thinking that these three "eyes" gave the nut the look of a grinning face, they named it the *coconut*, *coco* being the Portuguese word for "a grinning face." The nut deserves a better appellation, having been "the fruit of life" for ages, providing people with food, drink, oil, medicines, fuel, and even bowls, not to mention the many uses of the 60- to 100-foot tree it grows on. Copra, important to the plot of many a South Sea tale, is the dried meat of coconuts that oil is pressed from, and *coconut* itself is slang for "a head," which takes the word back to its origins. *Copra* derives from the Hindu *Rhopra* for coconut.

coconut crab; robber crab.   The large robber crab or coconut crab (Birgus latro) of the Pacific islands is closely related to hermit crabs, but has given up carrying a portable dwelling and developed a permanent hard-plated shell. Called the *coconut crab* because it climbs palm trees to get the fruit, it is named the *robber crab* for an entirely different reason. After chasing another crab, *Cardisoma*, into its hole in the ground, the robber crab threatens to enter. When *Cardisoma* thrusts out its big claw to guard the entrance, the robber crab seizes it, twists it off, and scuttles off to enjoy a gourmet feast.

cod; you can't cod me.   Experts have suggested that *cod* might derive from an old Danish word for "bag" (because it was said to be a "bag fish," in reference to its shape), but its origin must be marked unknown due to lack of evidence, even though the word has been with us at least since the 14th century. The North Atlantic cod (*Gadus morrhua*), reaching a length of up to three feet and a weight of up to 50 pounds, has long been one of the most important fish of commerce (*see* CODFISH ARISTOCRACY). It is called the *sacred cod* because it is said to be the fish that Christ multiplied and fed to the multitude. According to one early-19th-century writer: "Even today the marks of His thumbs and forefingers are plainly visible on the codfish. His Satanic majesty stood by and said he, too, could multiply fish and feed multitudes. Reaching for one of the fish it wriggled and slid down his red-hot fingers, burning two black stripes down its side and thus clearly differentiating the haddock from the sacred cod. These markings, in actual practice, do distinguish one fish from another." *You can't cod me* means "You can't get a rise out of me, you won't make me rise to the bait like a codfish."

code.   *See* BOOK.

Code of Hammurabi.   *See* EYE FOR AN EYE.

code pricing.   Still practiced on occasion, but rarely used anymore, code pricing was common in early American country stores. It gave a storekeeper an added advantage when bargaining with a customer because he could tell what every piece of merchandise cost without the customer's knowing. A merchant, for instance, might make the letters in NOW BE SHARP represent 1 2 3 4 5 6 7 8 9 10 (an N would equal the numeral 1, an O the numeral 2, a W the numeral 3, and so on). Every trusted clerk would be given this equation, and if a piece of merchandise was marked, say, NWW on the back, anyone with the formula would know its cost was $1.33.

codfish aristocracy.

> Of all the fish that swim or swish
> In ocean's deep autocracy,
> There's none possesses such haughtiness
> As the codfish aristocracy.
>
> —Wallace Irwin

It's hard to think of any group haughtier than the Cabots and Lowells (who spoke only to God, according to another old poem), but the Boston nouveau riche who made their money from the codfishing industry in the late 18th and early 19th century apparently gave a grand imitation of them. At any rate, they were disliked enough to inspire the derogatory expression *codfish aristocracy,* for "any pretentious, newly rich person."

codger.   An old codger is generally a nuisance or an eccentric old man, but can also be a term of affection akin to "old chap" or "old fellow." No dictionary honors the derivation, but both definitions may have been strengthened by the existence of a club called The Ancient Society of Cogers in London in the 1860s. The Cogers came onto the scene half a century after *codger* was first used in its whimsical sense, but they were well known, all prominent writers and artists. The debating club derived its name from the word "cognition" and these thinking men, "ancient" at least by title, met at the Barley Mow Tavern on Fleet Street. (The tavern is now named The Cogers in their honor, though they moved to the Cock Tavern in 1921.) Codger probably comes from the Scottish *cadger,* for "a wandering peddler or beggar," but it is not hard to imagine the Cogers' influence on the word. "Ancient . . . Cogers" could easily have become *old codgers,* meant either affectionately or derisively.

codpiece.   The *cod* in the word originally meant "the bag enveloping the testicles, the scrotum." In the 15th century the *codpiece* was introduced as a simple leather bagged appendage attached to the front of breeches, the word first recorded in 1460. But within a century the appendage became a spectacular ornament, brightly colored and often the size of a small melon. In *The Unfashionable Human Body,* Bernard Rudofsky claims that the codpiece died as a fashion in the 17th century because the male genitals "seem too unsubstantial to warrant display." This may be the case, because men often used the codpiece as a kind of pocket, storing things like money and bonbons in it. Robert Herrick wrote of a thieving dinner guest in *Hesperides* (1648): "If the servants search, they may decry in his wide codpiece, dinner being done, Two napkins cramm'd up, and a silver spoone."

codswallop.   I came across *codswallop* in a newspaper account about a scientist's charge that a rare and extremely important bird fossil (the ARCHAEOPTERYX, pronounced "arky-opterix") in the British Museum was a fake. The account quoted several British Museum curators on the charge: "It's rubbish," one official said. "Absolutely ludicrous," added another. "Codswallop," echoed a third. *Codswallop?* Does it mean to flop about like a cod, in reference to the scandalmonger's tongue. *Wallop* does mean in one sense "to flop about." Or does it stand for "cod's beer," meaning the charge is an awful concoction? (*Wallop* is British slang for beer.) To tell the truth I don't know. And neither does the *O.E.D.,* Mencken, Flexner, Partridge, and all those other high-flying etymology birds. Hawkeyed William Safire, however, noted in his *New York Times Magazine* column that James McDonald's *Wordly Wise* (1984) mentions a 19th-century "inventor called Hiram Codd [who] patented a new type of bottle with a glass marble in its neck. Mineral waters were sold in such bottles, and, *wallop* being a slang term for fizzy ale, the contents became known as *Codd's Wallop.*" And if this explanation doesn't satisfy you, either, perhaps *codswallop,* as Mr. Safire also points out, derives in some way from the British slang *cod,* meaning "to horse around."

coelacanth.   For many years no one believed that the coelacanth still existed. This prehistoric link between sea and land creatures (some scientists think that the stumps connecting its fins to its body were the beginning of legs) was thought to have become extinct some 70 million years ago, according to researchers who had studied its plentiful fossil remains. After evolving 200 million years before the first dinosaur appeared on Earth and thriving for millions of years, they said, it had died out or evolved into a lizardlike form that crawled ashore. Then in late 1938 a strange fish was netted by a South African trawler off the southeast coast of Africa. Five feet long and weighing 125 pounds, it was steel-blue in color and had large scales and stumpy fins. In the four hours that it lived, the fish snapped its sharp teeth at any hand that came near its gaping jaws. Fishermen had never seen a specimen like it, nor had scientists, who named it after the Greek words for "hollow spined." Obviously some coelacanths hadn't died or crawled up onto land and still remained in the sea. But it took a full 14 years before a fisherman working in the Indian Ocean hauled in another of the "monsters." Since then, at least 10 more specimens have been found of the fish that brought animal life to land, perhaps the greatest biological discovery of the 20th century. The story certainly goes to prove that no one really knows what goes on in the great depths of the sea where the coelacanth lives, that despite the intense cold, pressure, and darkness, creatures can survive there—"monsters" perhaps more incredible than "the fish that couldn't be." The coelacanth's scientific name (*Yatimeria Chaluminae Smith*) derives from the name of Marjorie Courtney Yatimer, director of the East London Museum in 1938; The Chalumna River in South Africa, where the fish was first discovered; and the name of prominent South African fish biologist Dr. J. L. B. Smith.

Coeur d'Alene.   It is said that the Skitswish Indians of northern Idaho took the name *Coeur d'Alene* (French for "awl-heart") after some unknown chief of the tribe used the words to describe the size of a dishonest white trader's heart, which he compared to the small point of an awl.

coffee.   *Coffee* was introduced to England from Turkey, where it was called *qahwah*, pronounced *kahveh*, a word that apparently first meant some kind of wine and derived from a verb meaning "to have no appetite." The word came to England, perhaps from the Italian *caffè*, in about 1600. At first coffee's reputation wasn't good, one early English traveler warning that it "intoxicated the brain." It has had widely varying reviews since.

coffee break.   *See* ELEVENSES.

coffin nails.   *Coffin nails* has been American slang for cigarettes since the 1880s, at least 20 years before cigarettes were called weeds and 40 years before they were called butts. *Another nail in my coffin*, said by a person lighting a cigarette, has been a catchphrase since about 1910, when it was first recorded in Australia. Cigarette itself is first recorded in England in 1842, though these "little cigars" had been smoked for at least two centuries before then.

cognac.   The town of Cognac in southwestern France gives its name to this high-quality brandy, produced by the old pot-still method and aged two to five years or more in oak barrels.

coin.   Our coin takes its name from the wedge-shaped die once used to make pieces of metal money. The French *coign*, deriving from the Latin *cuneus* and meaning wedge, was given first to the die and then to the money made on the die. *Coign* later passed into English as *coin*. *Coin* came to be a general word for money in early times because most money was in the form of coins.

Coke; cola.   Coke, or Coca-Cola (both registered trademarks), was invented by Atlanta, Georgia, druggist Dr. John S. Pemberton in 1886, and is so named because its original ingredients were derived from coca leaves and cola nuts. *Coke* is also slang for *cocaine* and for this reason the Coca-Cola Company long avoided use of this name—especially because, up until 1909, Coca-Cola did contain minute amounts of cocaine. While the Supreme Court declared *Coca-Cola* and *Coke* exclusive trademarks, *cola* was ruled a generic word that anyone could use. Coca-Cola's slogans "The pause that refreshes" and "Coke is it" are also well known. In 1985 a Mr. Frederick Koch (pronounced "Coke") of Guilford, Vermont, got tired of people pronouncing his last name "Kotch" and changed it to Coke-Is-It. Coca-Cola objected to the use of its trademark, but finally reached a settlement with Mr. Coke-Is-It, letting him keep his new name. For the record, the actual coiner of the name Coca-Cola was Pemberton's bookkeeper, Frank M. Robinson, who invented it in 1893. In those early days Coca-Cola was advertised as the "Esteemed Brain Tonic and Intellectual Beverage."

Coke upon Littleton.   This expression suggests the shades or subtleties of law and honors British legal experts Edward Coke (1552–1664) and Thomas Littleton (1407–81).

cola.   *See* COKE.

Cold Arse.   One of the most distinctively named places in the nation: an island near Port Clyde, Maine, said to be so called after the fundament of a fisherman who was marooned there one freezing night.

cold blood.   Early physiologists believed that the blood actually boiled within the body when a person grew excited and that it grew cold when someone was calm or detached. While the term *in hot blood* suggested by the belief is no longer heard (*hot-blooded* is), *in cold blood* remains as common as it was back in the late 16th century. Generally it is used today to describe a deliberate act of murder, as in Truman Capote's "fact-fiction" *In Cold Blood*. Mankind has always regarded calculated killing in cold blood as something less than human. Trollope summed up the idea in describing one of his characters: "But then Aylmer was a cold-blooded man—more like a fish than a man."

cold burning.   *Cold burning?* Yes. In the late 18th to early 19th century *cold burning* was a British navy and army punishment for minor offenses in which ice-cold water ("so cold that it burns") was poured down a man's upraised arm so that it came out "at his breeches-knees." According to one explanation: "The prisoner is set against the wall, with the arm which is to be burned tied as high above his head as possible. The executioner then ascends a stool, and having a bottle of cold water, pours it slowly down the sleeve of the delinquent, patting him, and leading the water gently down him till it runs out at his breeches-knees."

cold enough to freeze the balls off a brass monkey.   Here and in Australia the saying is as above; in Canada it is often the euphemistic *freeze the ears off a brass monkey*. Partridge indicates this is a late-19th-century Australian saying for very, very cold indeed, but I have heard others claim it for America and Ireland. Some say the "monkey" here is not the brass image of a monkey but a rack called the "monkey" used on wooden naval ships in the days of sail to hold cannonballs in place, to keep them from rolling all over the deck. But no one as yet has proved the existence of any rack called a "monkey," one made of brass or anything else. And how cold weather could cause cannonballs to spill from a rack also remains to be explained.

cold feet.   The old Italian expression *avegh minga frecc i pee* literally means "to have cold feet" and the proverb in a figurative sense of "to be without money" was used by Ben Jonson in his play *Volpone*. Professor Kenneth McKenzie pointed this out in an article in *Modern Language Notes* (Vol. XXVII, 1912) and also explained how a phrase meaning "to be without money" could come to mean "to lose one's nerve." In card-playing, he wrote, a player "as a pretext for quitting a game in which he has lost money, [might] say that his feet are cold, [and] the expression might come to mean in general 'to recede from a difficult position,' or more specifically, 'to have cold feet.'" This may be true, but if it is, it didn't happen in Ben Jonson's time, to the best of our knowledge. *Cold feet* in the sense of "fear," originated as an American expression in the early 1890s. It could, however, have journeyed here with Italian immigrants, as the Italian proverb was still used in Lombardy at the time. Otherwise the expression must be marked "of unknown origin" and perhaps refers to the association of fright with cold—chattering teeth, shivers, and chills, etc.

cold fish.   An emotionally cold, impassive person, either a man or a woman. The expression, first recorded in the early

1920s in the U.S., can also mean a sexually cold or frigid person.

cold shoulder. "Cold shoulders" have been turned to so many passionate advances that this expression is usually thought to be connected with women spurning unacceptable men. But it seems that the phrase has no romantic origins. In the early 19th century, when the phrase was first recorded by Sir Walter Scott, it was the custom of hostesses to serve hot meat to a welcome visitor and to bring out a cold shoulder of mutton to someone who had overstayed his welcome or wasn't particularly welcome in the first place. That this is the source of *cold shoulder* can best be seen in the Victorian slang *to give the cold shoulder of mutton*, meaning the same thing.

cold war. *Cold war*, for a situation where two nations aren't actually at war but are doing everything they can to damage each other short of war, is first recorded in 1947, when Walter Lippmann's *The Cold War*, a study of American-Soviet relations, was published.

coleslaw; hot slaw. The word is *coleslaw*, not *cold slaw*, and isn't so named because the dish is served cold. An Americanism of Dutch origin, *coleslaw* derives from the Dutch *koolsla*, composed of *kool*, "cabbage," plus *sla*, "salad." First recorded in 1792, it must be older, as Dutch farmers on Long Island cultivated the first cabbage in America long before this. Though there is no *cold slaw*, there is a *hot slaw*, the word for this dish first recorded in 1870.

collage. The device of using pieces of newspaper in paintings was much used by the Cubists, who called the technique *collage*. But Matisse and many other artists before them built pictures partly or wholly of pieces of paper, cloth, and similar materials. The word *collage* comes from the French *coller*, "to stick."

collards. Although they are associated with southern cooking in the United States, collards, which take their name from the Anglo-Saxon *coleworts*, "cabbage plants," probably originated in Asia Minor. One of the most primitive members of the cabbage family, they were grown by the ancient Greeks. The Romans brought them to England.

collateral damage. Originally military jargon, *collateral damage* has become widely used since the Gulf War (1991), especially in the war against terrorism (2001). It strictly means damage to a civilian area near a target by bombs or missiles that did not hit the exact target. It is now a euphemism for civilian deaths caused unintentionally by these same weapons.

collective bargaining. Beatrice Webb of the FABIANS first suggested this term in 1891. In America *collective bargaining* came to mean, after the 1935 Wagner Act, "the process by which wages and working conditions are negotiated and agreed upon by a union with an employer for all the employees that the union collectively represents."

colleen. A young Irish girl. The word derives from the Irish Gaelic *cailin*, meaning the same, which in turn comes from Old Irish. Gaelic, incidentally, is still spoken by anywhere from 40,000 to 600,000 people in Ireland, depending on whose estimate you accept. A marriageable Irish girl is called a "colleen bawn."

collie. Though they are generally white and brown today, *collies* were originally black medium-sized shepherd's dogs when bred in 17th-century Scotland. They may have taken their name from their black color, being first called *coalies*, then *collies*. But the dogs could also have been named after the common Scottish name Colin, which in pastoral verse denotes "a shepherd."

a collision at sea can ruin your entire day. Thucydides, Greek statesman, sailor, and adventurer of the fourth century B.C., was a cool customer, judging by this remark he made after his boat was rammed by another; it has since been repeated by other blasé boatmen. During the cold war era, a popular bumper sticker read: "A nuclear bomb can ruin your whole day."

colly birds. If you've ever wondered what the gift of "colly birds" was on the fourth day of Christmas in the traditional song "The Twelve Days of Christmas," wonder no more: *colly bird* is simply an old name for a blackbird, *colly* a dialect word for soot or coal dust that derives from English *col*, coal.

collywobbles. No relation to colly birds above, *collywobbles* seems to have been suggested by *colic* and *wobble*. It means a rumbling upset stomach, a bellyache, cramps, or even a feeling of fear and is first recorded in 1823. Often but not always called the collywobbles, as in "He had a good case of the collywobbles."

cologne. A scent that almost takes its name from a woman. The Roman emperor Claudius established a colony in what was then Oppidum Ubiorum in 50 A.D., renaming the place Colonia Agrippina ("colony of Agrippina") after his wife, Nero's mother, who had been born there. This cumbersome name was later modified by the French to *Cologne*, which grew into the beautiful German cathedral city that we know today. When centuries later a resident Italian chemist, Johann Maria Farina, invented a perfume made with alcohol and aromatic citrus oils, it was named *eau de cologne* or *cologne water*, for the city where he had settled in 1709. "Agrippina" had been lost over the years and only a fragment of her *colonia* remained, but the perfume was unknowingly and obliquely named for her.

colon. *See* COMMA.

colonel. An honorary title in the American South, as are major and general, since the 18th century. William Faulkner explained it this way: "Jefferson, Mississippi, the whole South for that matter, was still full at that time of men called General or Colonel or Major because their fathers or grandfathers had been generals or colonels or majors or maybe just privates, in Confederate armies, or who had contributed to the campaign funds of successful state governors" (*The Town*, 1957). The unofficial title of respect is also used in an ironic or joking sense. The confusing pronunciation of *colonel* is due to several errors. *Colonel* comes from the Italian *colonello*, which meant "the officer who led 'a little column' of soldiers at the head of a regiment." This became the French *colonelle*, meaning the same. So far, so good. But the French word became corrupted to *coronel* in Spanish through faulty pronunciation and was introduced into England in this form. Until the 17th century the word was spelled and pronounced *coronel*, and then its spelling was changed to the current *colonel*. Yet despite the efforts of teachers and pronouncing dictionaries, people refused to pronounce the word *colonel*. Early habits were too great to overcome and they continued to pronounce it like *coronel*, the experts finally giving up and accepting this as the standard pronunciation.

colophon.   Originally, this word, derived from the Greek *kolophon*, meaning "summit" or "finish," was the "finishing touch" at the end of a book, a bibliographical note on the last page giving the printer, date, place, and so on. Today the word has two meanings—the original one, which has been expanded to include design and typographic information, and a new one, referring to the publisher's trademark or logo, which often appears on the title page of the book. The great Italian printer Aldus Manutius established the custom of the publisher's colophon; his was a dolphin, symbolizing speed, and an anchor, symbolizing stability. A compulsive worker, he hung this inscription over the door of his study: "Whoever thou art, Thou art earnestly requested by Aldus to state thy business briefly, and to take thy departure promptly . . . For this is a place of work." *See* ITALIC.

Colorado.   Colorado was the Colorado Territory before it was admitted to the Union in 1876 as our 38th state. "The Centennial State" takes its name Colorado from the Spanish *colorado*, "red land," or "red earth."

Colorado potato beetle.   A yellow, black-striped beetle *(Leptinotarsa decemlineata)* very harmful to potatoes, which was originally confined to Colorado and vicinity before potatoes began to be extensively cultivated in the United States.

color-blind.   *See* DALTONISM.

Colosseum.   Its size had nothing to do with the name of the Roman arena called the Colosseum, which gives its name to all coliseums. The original Colosseum took its name for a colossal statue of Nero that stood near it, the statue placed there after the dissolute emperor's palace had been destroyed, when Rome burned. *See* THEATER.

colporteur.   Today's book salesmen follow an honorable calling, one that dates back hundreds of years to when their kind carried Bibles and other books in a basket or pack hanging from their necks by a strap. For this reason they were, and sometimes still are, called *colporteurs*, from the French *col*, "neck," and *porter*, "to carry." Typical of these was Old Parson Weems, noted for his charming fabrication of George Washington chopping down the cherry tree, not to mention his bold Homeric yarns about Ben Franklin and General Francis "the Swamp Fox" Marion.

colt.   When Samuel Colt (1814–62) ran away to sea from his home in Hartford, Connecticut at 16, he spent his lonely nights on deck whittling a wooden model of the Colt revolver that was to make him famous. Young Colt had several metal models made of his gun upon arriving home and patented his invention. He built his armory into the largest in the world, his use of interchangeable parts and the production line making him one of the richest men in America. As for the Colt, the first pistol that could be effectively employed by a man on horseback, it played a more important part in the conquest of the West than any other weapon, the famed "six-shooter" becoming so popular that its name became a generic term for revolver. *Colt* for a young horse comes from the Old English *colt* meaning the same.

Columbia; columbium.   Although AMERICA was named for someone else, Columbus did win fame on the globe in the name for Colombia, South America, the U.S. District of Columbia, and a number of towns and cities. *Columbus* itself has for centuries meant an intrepid discoverer or explorer; Columbus Day (October 12) commemorates the discovery of America; and Columbia is the feminine symbol for America from which the element columbium is named. Christopher Columbus—Cristoforo Colombo in his native Italian and Christóbal Colón in Spanish—arrived in America in 1492, a familiar story that needs no repeating here. He may have come ashore in the Bahamas on an island he named San Salvador and which is now called Cat or Watlings Island, but his landing site is disputed by historians. A sailor named Rodrigo de Triana first sighted the New World.

Columbia the Gem of the Ocean.   English actors David T. Shaw and Thomas A. Becket are said to have written this patriotic song for an 1843 benefit performance in America. But it has also been claimed that they first wrote it in England as "Britannia the Pride of the Ocean," later changing it for American consumption. *See* GOD BLESS AMERICA.

columbine.   In medieval times people thought the inverted white flower on this plant bore a resemblance to five doves or pigeons clustered together and it was given the name columbine from the Latin *columba*, "dove." There are 60 known species of the genus *Aquilegia* comprising columbines, and the flowers' horned nectaries were once symbols of cuckoldry.

Columbus's egg.   Washington Irving told this proverbial tale in his *History of . . . Christopher Columbus*. It relates a classic squelch supposedly made by Columbus at a banquet given by Cardinal Mendoza shortly after the explorer had returned from his first voyage:

> A shallow courtier present, impatient of the honors paid to Columbus, abruptly asked him whether he thought that in case he had not discovered the Indies, there were not other men in Spain who would have been capable of the enterprise. To this Columbus made no immediate reply, but taking an egg, invited the company to make it stand on end. Every one attempted it, but in vain. Whereupon he struck it upon the table so as to break the end and left it standing on the broken part; illustrating in his simple manner that when he had once shown the way to the New World nothing was easier than to follow it.

Although Irving had the tale on good authority, it may really apply to an earlier historical figure, an Italian architect named Filippo Brunelleschi.

Coma Berenices; varnish; vernis martin.   Berenice's hair, or *coma Berenices*, is the lock of a woman's hair that became a constellation. It was made famous by the five surviving lines of the poem *The Lock of Berenice* by the Greek poet Callimachus, which is said to be based on a true story. Berenice was married to Ptolemy III, king of Egypt, and when he invaded Syria in 236 B.C. to avenge the murder of his sister, she dedicated a lock of her hair to the gods as an offering for his safe return. The hair mysteriously disappeared, but the court astronomer, Conon of Samos, perhaps to assuage her, pretended to discover that it had been carried to heaven and transformed into a constellation of the Northern Hemisphere, which has been known ever since as Coma Berenices. (A coma is the hazy envelope around a comet, and the word *comet* itself derives from the Greek and Latin words for hair, alluding to a fancied resemblance between the tails of comets and hair blowing in the wind.) Ptolemy returned from the wars safely, but soon after his death in 221 B.C. the fabled Berenice was murdered at the instigation of her son. Later the Greeks named the town of Berenike in Libya for Berenice. Here a paint industry thrived and one new coating was called Berenice, its color said to resemble the amber hair of the queen. This paint was called *bernix* in medieval Latin, but the Italians corrupted its name to *vernice*, which became *vernis* in French and *varnish* in English—the chances being that the floor under your feet has something of the color of Berenice's hair. *Vernis martin*, or Martin varnish, a finish for furniture, is twice eponymous, being also named for the brothers Martin, 18th-century French craftsmen who invented it in imitation of Chinese lacquer.

comanchero.   An old Spanish term for a man of Mexican-Indian origin; comancheros were often traders between the Indians and the Mexicans or whites.

Comanche yell.   A blood-curdling yell used by Comanche Indians in battle; said by some to be the basis for the REBEL YELL.

come a cropper.   To fall head over heels, to fail, or be struck by some misfortune. This is a British expression that originally meant only to fall head over heels from a horse, to fall to the ground completely, neck and crop, but it most likely refers to the crop, or back, of a horse—when a horse falls neck and crop, it falls completely, all together in one heap.

Comédie-Française.   The French national theater, famous for its extensive repertoire of classical French drama, is also called the Théâtre-Français and La Maison de Molière, but it is best known as the Comédie-Française. Celebrated as "the glory of the French theater" by more than one critic, it was founded in 1680 and before the end of the decade moved into a playhouse built for it in an indoor tennis court, whose layout, with its boxes for spectators, was easily converted to a theater. Since 1770, it has remained at the site of what was the Palais Royal Theater, which is now called the Comédie-Française. The acting company is a cooperative society, each actor holding from one-quarter to one full share (depending on the actor's experience or importance) once he or she is admitted to the company. Admission comes after the actor successfully performs a role of his or her choosing and serves a salaried probationary period of up to several years. At that point the actor becomes a full member, sharing in the company's profits, and is entitled to a pension after twenty years' service. The head of the company, called the *doyen*, is its oldest member.

come down like a ton of bricks on someone.   To be very severe with someone, to come down hard on him. This Americanism dates back to the 19th century and sounds much better than the British *come down like a thousand bricks on him*. But it has been pointed out that the British expression is more technically accurate, in that bricks aren't sold or measured by the ton.

comedy.   The word *comedy* may derive from the Greek word *kome* for "village," because the first comic thespians were scorned in the cities and had to wander about rural villages to give performances. This was Aristotle's belief, but others say *comedy* comes from Greek *komas*, meaning "revel," because it first was performed by revelers at festivals.

come hell or high water.   The ancestor of this common expression is apparently BETWEEN THE DEVIL AND THE DEEP BLUE SEA. Between hell and high water seems to have been a 20th-century variation on (or deviation from) the earlier phrase. Then the variation took on a life of its own in the expression *come hell or high water*, meaning "no matter what," as in "Come hell or high water, I'll finish it!"

come in with one's five eggs.   *See* PUT IN ONE'S TWO CENTS' WORTH.

come off it.   Stop your nonsense, cut it out, don't give me that. Originally the phrase was *come off*, first recorded in the late 19th century. *Come off it* seems to have first found print in Ernest Hemingway's *The Sun Also Rises* (1926), when Hemingway put the words in the mouth of Lady Brett Ashley.

come out of here, you damned old reb.   *See* IN THE NAME OF . . .

come out the little end of the horn.   That prolific Canadian word coiner Thomas Haliburton (see *Index*) may have invented this expression meaning to end in failure, in allusion to the pointed end of the cornucopia or horn of plenty. At least Haliburton used it in his *The Clockmaker; or, The Sayings and Doings of Samual Slick, of Slickville* (1837–1840): "Can you wonder that people who also keep such an unprofitable stock, come out of the small end of the horn in the long run?"

come see.   A lovely expression from the Gullah dialect of the American South that means a delicate child, one who has come to see this world and decide whether or not it wishes to stay, which is to say its life may be very brief.

come to a head.   When we wait for something to come to a head, wait for it to come to maturity, we are doing what farmers have long done in waiting for cabbage leaves to come together and form a head. The expression is an old one from the farm, probably dating back centuries.

come up and see me sometime.   The still much-imitated words of actress Mae West to her leading man Cary Grant in the 1933 film *She Done Him Wrong.* Her actual words, however, were, "Why don't you come up some time and see me?" Another memorable Mae West line is her "Beulah, peel me a grape!" to her maid in the movie *I'm No Angel* (1933).

come up for air.   The allusion here can't be to a scuba diver or suited diver, who usually have plenty of air, but it might refer to pearl or sponge divers, who must surface periodically to breathe fresh air. The words are often humorously said to a person so immersed in something (reading, writing, etc.) that he or she ignores everything and everybody else, to a point where it might not be healthy.

comeuppance.   Whether this expression is an Americanism or not is the subject of some dispute; it is first recorded in America in 1859 and in England some 20 years later, if that proves anything. *Comeuppance* means "just desserts" or "merited punishment," and has several dialect versions in different areas, including *comings* and *come-uppings,* the British once using *come-uppings* for a flogging. Possibly the expression *come up,* "to present oneself for judgment before a tribunal," fathered the phrase.

come up to scratch.   Deaths and maimings were so frequent in the lawless early days of boxing that one rule had to be established if there were to be enough boxers alive to please the crowd. A line was scratched in the center of the ring (in the ground or on the canvas) and a fighter who couldn't "come up to scratch" when the bell sounded for a new round was considered physically unable to fight any longer. This early version of the technical knockout probably led to use of *to come up to scratch* as a figurative expression for fulfilling or meeting requirements of any nature. *Scratch,* however, was the term for a starting point or boundary in cricket, shooting matches, horse racing, and cockfighting as well as boxing, so the expression could have originated in one of these sports, especially from cockfighting, where a cock that doesn't come up to scratch and fight is considered an inferior specimen.

comfort me with apples.   The phrase is from the Bible, the Song of Solomon II, 5: "Stay me with flagons [bottles of wine], comfort me with apples: for I am sick of love." Paulus Silentiarius, a sixth-century Greek poet, noted a certain deficiency in comforting anyone with apples. "If, my pet," he wrote, "you gave me these two apples as tokens of your breasts I bless you for your great kindness. But if your gift does not go beyond the apples, you wrong me by refusing to quench the fierce fire you lit." His words may have inspired another phrase, *to go beyond the apples,* but if they did, I've been unable to prove that saying's existence.

coming apart at the seams; seamless.   *Seam,* an Anglo-Saxon word, has been used figuratively since at least the 12th century. Chaucer wrote of "the semes of freenshippe," Shakespeare of "the rough seames of the waters," and Ben Jonson of "poor seam-rent fellows." Similarly, *coming apart at the seams* describes someone suffering from a mental or physical breakdown. On the other hand, *seamless* means something perfectly consistent. *See* SEAMY SIDE.

comma; colon; period.   Before they became common terms used for punctuation, these words were the names of elements of sentence structure. A comma was a short phrase or clause, a colon a long phrase, and a period two or more colons. *Period,* for example, was recorded as early as 1533 for a sentence of several clauses, almost a century before it meant the point or character that marks the end of such a sentence. Has anyone written a book about periods, those at the end of sentences? I don't know, but an entire book (Hendrik Hertzberg's *One Million,* 1980) is filled with dots, which might loosely be considered periods. Periods are not always the last thing in a sentence; for example, a sentence ending with a quoted word must have its period inside the quotation marks. Christopher Marlowe wrote of all poetry distilled into "one poem's period," but the period's great lover in literary history was Russian author Isaac Babel. Babel, murdered by Soviet secret police in 1939, wrote: "No iron can stab the heart with such force as a period put just at the right place." In Scandinavian author Gustav Wiel's novel *Knagsted* (1902), one of his eponymous character's creations is a full-length book collection of Danish writers' commas. The most costly grammatical error in history occurred when the U.S. space probe *Mariner 1,* bound for Venus, headed off course and had to be destroyed at a cost of $18.5 million. The rocket responded erratically because an anonymous flight computer programmer left out a comma from *Mariner's* computer program. See HYPHEN; PUNCTUATION.

commander in chief of the navy.   *See* CONTINENTAL NAVY.

commando.   This term was adapted by the British during World War II when they established their specially trained commando units to raid enemy territory. It derives, however, from the Portuguese word for "small commands that raided native villages in South Africa," a word the Boers borrowed when they used similar tactics to wipe out thousands of bushmen in their villages.

commerce.   *See* MERCHANT.

commercial.   An American term for a radio or TV ad. The term was first recorded on a 1923 *Eveready Flashlight Hour* radio show. According to one ad executive, ad agencies today air 300,000 commercials a year. The highest price ever paid for a commercial was the $1.3 million paid for a 30-second spot by Pepsi Cola during Super Bowl XXXI in 1997.

Common.   Short for the Boston Common (the last word always singular), a public park in Boston once used in common by all the people for grazing their cattle. Robert E. Parker wrote in *Spenser's Boston* (1994): "Hayshakers from New York and Los Angeles are always looking ignorant by saying . . . Boston Commons, and generally disgracing themselves in front of us Bostonion sophisticates."

common.   When in 1948 Henry Wallace campaigned with the slogan that this was "the century of the common man," many southerners had trouble understanding at first, for *common* is often a term of contempt in the South, far more than in the rest of the United States. It can also be a complimentary term for an unassuming, friendly person, as in "He's a real common man."

the commonest English words. According to a count made by the *World Almanac* (1950) of 240,000 words from books, magazines, and newspapers, the 12 most commonly used written English words are: 1) *the* 2) *of* 3) *and* 4) *to* 5) *a* 6) *in* 7) *that* 8) *is* 9) *I* 10) *it* 11) *for* 12) *as*. This is seconded by a *Guinness Book of World Records* study (1998), which adds that the commonest word used in conversations is *I*. But the *American Heritage Word Frequency Book* (1971) doesn't agree, listing the 12 most commonly written words as: *the, of, and, a, to, in, is, you, that, it, be,* and *for*—in that order. Stuart Berg Flexner, in *I Hear America Talking* (1976), says that the four most common *spoken* English words are *I, you* (these two account for 10 percent of all "informal conversation"), *the,* and *a*. The rest of his top 50 spoken words (in no special order) are: *he, she, it, we, they, me, him, her, them, what, an, on, to, of, in, for, with, out, from, over, and, about, now, just, that, not, this, is, get, was, will, have, don't, do, are, want, can, would, go, think, say, be, see, know, tell,* and *thing*. Flexner points out that 10 basic words account for 25 percent of all English speech, 50 simple words account for about 60 percent, and just 1,500–2,000 words account for 99 percent of all we say. Seventy words make up 50 percent of our written language. Amazing statistics, considering that the English language contains about 800,000 words (including technical terms). Today the average American uses something like 2,000 words in everyday speech, while extremely learned persons use as many as 60,000 of the 800,000 or so words in English, which has the largest vocabulary of any language. Shakespeare possessed a large vocabulary for his or any time, using 22,000 different words in his plays, only 6,000 having been used in the entire Old Testament.

commonwealth. Officially, Massachusetts is not a U.S. state, but a commonwealth, as are Virginia, Maryland, Pennsylvania, and Kentucky. Technically, Rhode Island is not exactly a state, either; its official title is the State of Rhode Island and Providence Plantations.

commute. The verb *to commute* developed as a back formation from the noun *commutation* at about the time of the Civil War—Americans were commuting to work on the train even at that early date. *Commute* later became the word for a railroad ticket, a shortening of "commutation ticket." *Commute* has its roots in the Latin *commutare,* to change, thus someone commuting is changing from one place to another.

compadre. A Spanish term for a godfather or very close friend that has long been used in the American West for one's partner or close friend and which has wide use throughout the country from its frequent use in cowboy novels and movies. *Comadre* is the female version.

company. A business company, in the strictest sense of the word, is a group of people who sit down and share bread together. For *company* derives from the Latin *con* "together," and *panin,* "bread." The idea is that a company consists of friends so close that they sit at the same table sharing any bread they have.

company store. *See* TOMMYROT.

comparisons are odious. The correct word in the proverb is *odious,* not *odorous,* and the prolific poet and monk John Lydgate was the first to put the idea on paper, in 1430: "Odyous of olde have been comparisons,/And of comparisons engendyrd is haterede." Cervantes, Donne, Swift, and Hazlitt are other great writers who used the proverb, and Shakespeare had Dogberry give his variation on the expression, *comparisons are odorous,* in *Much Ado About Nothing*. Lydgate's version was printed some 40 years before that of John Fortescue, to whom *Bartlett's* credits the phrase.

comparison shopper. Comparison shoppers had their heyday from the 1920s to the 1960s. They originated, however, in the early 20th century price wars of department stores and were at first simply a clerk whom a buyer would send across the street to get an idea of his competitor's prices. Then comparison departments were formed, the average New York department store employing four or five professional shoppers, "the eyes and ears of the store," to study the stock, prices, and customers of rival stores and report back to their employers. This was essential to stores like Macy's with its long-standing policy of selling all merchandise at 6 percent below the prices of other stores. Macy's comparison shoppers were so wily that they sometimes wore disguises.

compass cactus. Western settlers in the U.S. gave this name to the barrel cactus (*Echinocactus*) because it almost always leans southwest, and they could tell directions by it.

compass plant; polar plant; pilotweed.

> Look at this vigorous plant that lifts its head from the meadow,
> See how its leaves are turned to the north, as true as the magnet;
> This is the compass flower, that the finger of God has planted
> Here in the houseless wild, to direct the traveler's journey
> Over the sea-like, pathless, limitless waste of the desert.
>
> —Longfellow, *Evangeline* (1847)

A huge coarse-stemmed plant six to eight feet tall with flowers like the sunflower, the compass plant (*Silphium laciniatum*) was much valued by pioneers on the great western plains because its leaves show polarity, always pointing north and south. For this reason it was called not only the compass plant, but polar plant and pilotweed as well.

complected. The journals of the Lewis and Clark expedition in 1806 contain the first recorded use of the word *complected* for being of a particular facial complexion. The word is used throughout the U.S., as in "She is dark complected and he is rather light complected."

compound. English merchants in the Orient during the 18th century often built enclosed trading stations to protect themselves and their goods from thieves. They called these stockaded enclosures compounds, from the Malay *kampong,* "enclosure." This *compound* is no relation to the chemist's *compound,* which derives from the Latin *componere,* "put together."

comptonia. Henry Compton, bishop of London, was a collector of rare and exotic plants. The prelate, an anti-papal leader during the Revolution of 1688, had many admirers in England, even after his death in 1713 at the age of 81. One of these was the great naturalist Sir Joseph Banks, who traveled to Newfoundland and Labrador in 1766 to collect native plants and accompanied Captain Cook on his first voyage two years later for the same purpose. Banks expressed his admiration for the plant-loving divine by naming the comptonia bush *(Comptonia peregrina)* after him. The *Comptonia* is a single shrub, sometimes called sweet bush or sweet fern. Native to eastern North America, it is highly aromatic, with fernlike leaves and green, rather inconspicuous flowers.

comptroller.   There is really no good reason for this word. It is pronounced the same as *controller* and means the same, except that it looks a bit more elegant than its counterpart. Probably influenced in spelling by the French *compte,* "account," *comptroller* means the official in a business firm who controls funds, just as *controller* does.

computer.   *Computer,* for a person who computes, goes back to the mid-17th century. The word was not applied to the machine we call the *computer* until 1944, when it was so used in a *London Times* story. Though there have been a number of mechanical computers over the years, the first electronic computer, using 18,000 radio tubes, was built in 1946 by three scientists at The University of Pennsylvania—Dr. John W. Manchly, J. Presper Eckert, Jr., and J. G. Brainerd. Their ENIAC—*Electronic Numerical Integrator And Computer*—cost $400,000 and had to be housed in a 30-foot by 50-foot room.

comrade; camera.   Three centuries and more ago Spanish soldiers resided in separate chambers called *camaradas,* two or more to the room, instead of barracks. Soldiers who shared the same chambers came to call themselves *comaradas,* which in time became the English word *comrade.* The Italian word *camera* is similar to the Spanish *camarado,* and also means "room." From the *camera oscura* ("dark room") used for projecting and viewing outdoor scenes through a lens or pinhole, we get our word *camera.*

comstockery.   About 160 tons of books, stereotyped plates, magazines, and pictures were destroyed by Anthony Comstock (1844–1915), founder of the New York Society for the Suppression of Vice, in his long career as a self-appointed crusader against immorality in literature. Comstock, who inspired Boston's Watch and Ward Society, headed a YMCA campaign against obscene literature in 1873, the same year in which he came to national prominence by founding his society and securing federal passage of the so-called Comstock Laws to exclude objectionable matter from the mails. Appointed special agent of the Post Office Department and chief special agent for the Society, Comstock had the power of an inquisitor, and *comstockery* became a synonym for narrowminded, bigoted, and self-righteous moral censorship. The crusader particularly objected to George Bernard Shaw's play, *Mrs. Warren's Profession,* and Shaw coined the word, making good clean fun of the censor's name.

Comstock lode.   A Nevada sheepherder and prospector named Henry Tompkins Paige Comstock first laid claim to the Comstock lode that bears his name. In 1859, Old Pancake, as he was known, had taken possession of a cabin belonging to other prospectors who had discovered the lode but had died tragically before filing their claim. Comstock filed his claim, but he later sold all his rights for a pittance and the Virginia City mine became the world's richest known silver deposit, producing $20 million to $30 million annually at its peak and making great fortunes for many a "silver king." Virginia City mushroomed to 40,000 inhabitants and anyone associated with the mines, hopeful prospector or millionaire, was called a comstocker.

con; con game; con man.   Just after the Civil War, one of the most common frauds in America was the sale of fake gold mine stock in the West. Sometimes gold would be salted in played-out "mines" to fool "marks," but the swindlers who worked the scheme usually settled for a small score from a great number of investors and never bothered about tricking up a real mine. Investors were often reluctant to advance funds without examining the property, however, and the swindlers asked their victims to make a small investment in advance "just as a gesture of confidence," deposits that they quickly absconded with. The trick was soon dubbed the *confidence game,* and, in time, its fast-moving practitioners became known as *con men.* Reinforcing the word is the idea that victims of a con game are bamboozled into confidence that they're going to make a killing. To con, in this sense, has nothing to do with the older English verb *to con,* to study or commit to memory, which derives from the Middle English *cunnen,* "to try." *Con games* were practiced, of course, long before this word for them was coined. On the American continent, for example, Mayan swindlers painstakingly drilled small holes in cocoa beans, emptied out their precious powder and refilled them with dirt before selling them to Europeans.

concatenation; concatenated sins.   *Concatenation* simply means a chain, the word deriving from the Latin *catena,* "chain." One early (1688) felicitous writer described two lovers as "the most affectionate couple since the concatenation of Adam and Eve," while John Donne wrote of "concatenated sins."

conceive.   *Conceive,* ultimately from the Latin *concipere,* to take fully, to take in, can mean "to hold or form an opinion," or "to become pregnant." Both uses are illustrated in a story about 18th-century British author and politician Joseph Addison, who once gave a speech in the House of Commons beginning: "Mr. Speaker, I conceive—I conceive, sire—sir, I conceive—" At this point he was interrupted by a member who quipped: "The right honorable secretary of state has conceived thrice and brought forth nothing." *See* PROPOSITION.

conch.   Pronounced "conk," this is an often derogatory term for a white resident of the Florida Keys, though *conchs* in the past also lived along the south coast of Florida and in North Carolina. The term dates back to the early 19th century when white native Bahamians were called conchs because they were skilled in diving for the large shellfish called the conch *(Strombus alatus),* an important item in their diet. The descendants of a band of Cockney Englishmen called the Eleutherian Adventurers who migrated from London to Bermuda in about 1649 in search of religious and political freedom, these Bahamians came to the Florida Keys from Eleuthera in the 19th century. One persistent old story has the conchs able to dive fathoms in search of their quarry. According to the *New York Weekly Tribune*, May 1, 1852, "Nearly half of all residents [of Key West] are natives of the Bahama Islands. They are called Conchmen or Conchs by reason of their skill in diving for conchs, which they are said to locate underwater and crack open with their teeth!"

conchie; CO. *Conchie* was sometimes disparaging slang for a conscientious objector during World War I and World War II, that is, someone exempted from military service on grounds of conscience. *Conchie* (KON-chee) is first recorded in 1917 in England and a year later in the U.S.; *conscientious objector* had been used in the late 19th century to mean someone who objected to vaccination. *CO* was another term for a conscientious objector, as were *conchy* and *conshie*. In Australia, *conchie* means a person who is too conscientious and works too hard, often trying to impress someone. In Britain those who wanted CO status had to be questioned by a government panel. According to Robert Graves in *Goodbye to All That*, when the author Lytton Strachey was asked what he'd do if he saw a German soldier trying to ravish his sister, he replied, "I would try to get between them."

conclave. This word, now applied to any secret or confidential meeting, once meant only the assembly of cardinals that meets to elect the pope of the Roman Catholic Church. *Conclave* itself comes from the Latin *conclave* (*con*, with, and *clave*, key), "a room or place with key" and was initially used to describe the small cells or apartments of the Vatican given to each member of the College of Cardinals at the assembly, which was established by Pope Gregory X in 1274.

Concord grape. *See* CATAWBA GRAPES.

concrete boat; marble boat. According to legend, the relics of the Apostle St. James were miraculously transported from Jerusalem in a "marble boat" with sails—and a huge stone used to be exhibited as this boat at Padron on the Spanish coast. It is definitely no legend that "concrete boats" were built in the U.S. during World War I to help conserve steel. These reinforced concrete ships performed well but weren't kept in operation after the war.

concubine. An old English word recorded in the 13th century for a woman who cohabits with a man she isn't married to, or a woman who is kept in a harem. The word ultimately derives from the Latin *con*, with, plus *cubare*, to lie down, hence a woman who lies down with (a man).

condign punishment. Just a fancy way of saying an appropriate punishment, a punishment that fits the crime. *Condign* (pronounced kun-dine) is from the Latin *condignus*, "altogether worthy." The phrase *condign punishment* has been commonly used since it originated in the Tudor Acts of Parliament, and the two words have become so inseparably yoked that *condign* is rarely used in any other way. Thomas De Quincey complained about this back in 1859, but it did no good: "Capriciously ... the word *condign* is only used in connection with the word *punishment*. These and other words, if unlocked from their absurd imprisonment, would become extensively useful. We

should say, for example, 'condign honors,' 'condign reward,' 'condign treatment'. . . ."

condom. *Condom* derives from either of two real names. Proksch in his *Prevention of Venereal Diseases* traces *condom* to a London doctor in the court of Charles II named Dr. Conton and insists that the contraceptives should thus be called "contons." Dr. Conton's invention is said to have been made from lamb intestines, dried and well oiled to make them soft and pliable. They immediately became popular, and Casanova is on record as buying a dozen, though he called them "English caps." It was only in 1826, Proksch claims, that a papal bull by Leo XIII damned Conton's discovery, "because it hindered the arrangement of providence." Dr. Conton probably did improve upon the *condom*, but an equally reliable source traces the word derivation to a Colonel Condum of Britain's Royal Guards. This authority notes that the colonel devised the "French letter" early in the mid-17th century to protect his troops from the French. (The French, chauvinistic, too, called *condoms* "English letters.") In 1667 three English courtiers—Rochester, Roscommon, and Dorset—even wrote a pamphlet entitled *A Panegyric Upon Condom*, extolling their countryman's invention. An excellent monograph on the origin of *condom* is William E. Kruck's *Looking for Dr. Condom* (University of Alabama Press, 1982).

condominium. *Condominium*, meaning "an apartment owned by tenants rather than rented" (although the owners do pay a monthly maintenance charge), is composed of the Latin *con*, "together," and *dominion*, "property." The word has been used for the joint control of a territory by two states since the early 18th century, but its newer usage dates back only to the late 1950s.

Conestoga wagons; stogy. The heavy, covered, broadwheeled Conestoga wagons that carried American pioneers westward, crossing many a waving sea of grass like "prairie schooners," were named for the Conestoga Valley in Pennsylvania, where they were first made in about 1750. But as Mencken points out, *Conestoga Valley* derives in turn from the name of a long-extinct band of Iroquois Indians. So little has been done for the Indian that we should honor him where we can. The wagons, pulled by their six-horse teams, also supplied the West with manufactured goods and brought back raw materials, some carrying up to eight tons of freight. *Stogy*, a cheap cigar today, was coined by the Conestoga teamsters—either after the Conestoga Valley tobacco that they rolled into thin, unbound cigars for their long trips or after the wagons themselves.

Coney Island; coney. The *Coney* in *Coney Island* should really be pronounced to rhyme with *honey* or *money*. The word derives from *cony* (or *coney* or *cuny*), meaning the adult long-earred rabbit (*Lepus cunicula*) after which the Brooklyn, New York community was named. However, *cony*, pronounced *cunny*, became a term for the female genitals in British slang, and proper Victorians stopped using the word, substituting *rabbit*, which previously had meant only the young of the cony species. The only trouble remaining was that *cony* appeared throughout the King James Bible, which had to be read aloud during church services. Proper Victorians solved this problem by changing the pronunciation of cony to *coney* (rhymes with *boney*), which it remains to this day in *Coney Island* as well as the Bible.

Confederate money. A term that means "money not worth the paper it is printed on," referring to the worthless banknotes of the Confederacy after the Civil War. At that time, according to Margaret Mitchell in *Gone With the Wind* (1936), an anonymous poem entitled "Lines on the Back of a Confederate Note" was circulated in the South, sometimes written by hand on pieces of paper pasted to the backs of the "useless" Confederate notes:

> Representing nothing on God's Earth now
> And naught in the waters below it—
> As the pledge of a nation that's passed away
> Keep it, dear friend, and show it.
>
> Show it to those who will lend an ear
> To the tale this trifle will tell
> Of Liberty, born of patriot's dream,
> Of a storm-cradled nation that fell.

See also BLUEBACKS.

confession magazines. Confession magazines, which have been with us now for over 65 years, are an American invention that were an outgrowth of long soul-searching letters sent to physical culture crusader Bernard MacFadden's *Physical Culture* magazine in 1919. MacFadden's first confession book was *True Story*, the great-grandmother of the genre, which currently has a circulation of 5 million, but there are scores of other confessions on the newsstands today. The first stories dealt with sweet young things who were so wicked that they dared to elope against their parents' wishes, etc., while contemporary tales have virtually no taboo themes, ranging from well-written confessions about incest to stories such as "My Bride Is a Man" (where Julie was Jules before her sex-change operation). The yarns, which earn five to 10 cents a word, aren't all written by readers. Professional writers turn out a large number, perhaps the majority of them, though some magazines do require an author to sign a release saying his or her story is based on a true experience.

Confucius say; kung-fu. Historians tell us that there is little positive evidence of the Chinese philosopher's life, but it is said that the Chinese K'ung clan, descendants of Confucius, numbers over 50,000 today and that Confucius's burial place outside Kufow is still a place of homage. Confucius is the Latinized form of the philosopher's name, K'ung Fu-tzu ("philosopher," or "master," K'ung), which may be the origin of the oriental martial art kung-fu, though no hard evidence supports this theory. Born around 551 B.C. of a poor but noble family, Confucius taught and held a number of government posts. By his death at about 72, the philosopher had attracted some 3,000 disciples who helped spread his ethical teachings, which were based primarily on his "golden rule": "What you do not like when done to yourself do not do to others."

confused flower beetle. This little fellow is so named not because he is frequently confused, but because scientists often have trouble identifying him. The confused flower beetle (*Tribolium confusum*), it seems, looks remarkably like the red flower beetle (*Tribolium castaneum*). *See* BEETLE.

congregation. The use of the term *flock* as a synonym for a church's congregation has an etymological as well as poetic basis, for *congregation* derives from the Latin *congregare*, to flock together, suggesting birds rather than lambs or sheep, however. Daniel Defoe's verse satire *The True-Born Englishman* (1710), which sold some 80,000 copies on the streets, had this to say on the subject:

> Whenever God erects a house of prayer
> The devil always builds a chapel there;
> And 'twill be found upon examination,
> The latter has the larger congregation.

congressane. *See* CORTISONE.

Congressional Medal of Honor. *See* MEDAL OF HONOR.

Congreve rocket. This is the proper name of the rocket used in 1814 during the British bombardment of Fort McHenry that inspired Francis Scott Key to write his poem "The Star-Spangled Banner," which later became the U.S. national anthem. Before "the rocket's red glare" at Fort McHenry it had been used as early as 1806. The rocket was invented by Sir William Congreve (1772–1828), who named it after himself.

conjure bag. A collection of magic charms tied in a ball and kept in a small bag, used to ward off evil spirits or gain control over someone; also called a conjure ball and kungu. "The conjurer's bag of the Africans . . . is called 'waiter' or 'kunger' by blacks, and is supposed to have the power to charm away evil spirits, and do all manner of miraculously good things for its wearers," Edmund Kirks wrote in *My Southern Friends* (1863).

Conjurer John. "Solomon's seal," a member of the lily family, was dubbed "Conjurer John" because the plant was considered a powerful charm in conjuring. It is also called "Big John the Conjurer" and "Big John the Conqueror." In the southern United States it has been used to induce spells in voodoo ceremonies.

conk. A once popular hairstyle worn by African-Americans that straightens and waves curly hair. It probably takes its name from the slang *conk* for head and/or from the commercial preparation Congolene used to so fashion hair. The term is used widely throughout the United States, but its point of origin is unknown. It is also called a process. *See also* CONK OUT.

conker. This name for the horse chestnut is used mainly in England, but the English game called "conkers" is sometimes played by children in the United States. In the game, a horse chestnut is hollowed out with a penknife and is knotted to one end of a length of string. The children then swing their strings, trying to break each other's conkers. The game may have first been called "conqueror," which was corrupted to *conker*, which in turn gave its name to the horse chestnut used in the game. It could, however, derive from the French *conque*, a "shell," for the game was originally played with small shells instead of horse chestnuts.

conk out. Partridge suggests that this aviation term for "the stalling of an engine," which is also applied to "someone who falls asleep, passes out, or dies," stems from the words "to be conquered," an ingenious theory, while the *O.E.D.* says it may come from a Russian word meaning "to stall." The word seems to have been coined by World War I military aviators and may just be imitative of the "conking" sound a motor makes when it stalls. Another theory is that *conk out* derives from the *conk* that means "a blow on the head," which has been common in England and America since about 1870. *Conk* in this sense is a direct ancestor of the British slang word *conk*, for the head itself, known in England since the early 19th century: a blow on the *conk* was probably dubbed a *conk* because the blow was associated with the head *(conk)* and sometimes sounded like a "conk" as well. *Conk* for the head, in turn, is probably a variant spelling of the Latin word *concha*, "the head," the same word that gives us the *conch* (pronounced "conk") *shell.*

Connecticut. "The Nutmeg State," the fifth to enter the Union, in 1788, takes its name from the Mohegan Indian *quinnitukqut*, "at the long tidal river," in reference to the state's location on what is now the Connecticut River.

Connecticut warbler. This bird is not seen much in Connecticut and New England. It is so named because the first specimen was collected in Connecticut, through which the bird was migrating. It is mainly found in south-central Canada and northern Minnesota, Wisconsin, and Michigan.

connect the dots. To make a coherent picture out of a mass of information. The phrase seems to have been suggested by children's coloring books in which the kids consecutively connect a series of numbered dots and then color the resulting picture. The game dates back even before that to a game popular with children in the late 19th century. In the controversy about possible warnings of the 9/11 terrorist attack, government agencies were accused of failing to connect the dots, that is, not putting the information they had together and preventing the tragedy.

conniption fit. The English dialect word *canapshus*, meaning "ill-tempered, captious," is the ancestor of the Americanism *conniption*, for "a fit of rage or anger." A person can go into conniptions, have a conniption fit, or go into a fit of conniptions—all mean the same. The expression is first recorded in 1833: "Ant Keziah fell down in a conniption fit."

considerable. Considerably; noticeably; much; a nonstandard usage common in the U.S. that actually dates back to 14th-century England. As in, "I'm feeling considerable better now."

consigliore. A term that became familiar to millions of Americans through Mario Puzo's *The Godfather* (1969) and the movies made from it. Puzo defined the word in the book: "The Consigliori was also what his name implied [*consigliore* in Italian means adviser]. He was counselor to the Don, his right hand man, his auxiliary brain." Since that time *Consigliore*, often capitalized, has become in popular speech any person in an important advisory position.

consistency is the hobgoblin of little minds. It is hard to understand how Ralph Waldo Emerson, as reasonable and

consistent as anyone and certainly no little mind, could have written this until you look at what he really wrote in his essay "Self-Reliance" (1841). There is quite a difference in the qualification he makes: A *foolish* consistency is the hobgoblin of little minds, adored by little statesmen and philosophers and divines."

conspicuous by one's absence. Someone or something not present in a place where he, she, or it should be. The Roman historian Tacitus (ca. A.D. 56–120) seems to have coined this term (or the germ of it) in his *Annals* when he wrote of the funeral procession of Junia, the sister of Brutus and widow of Cassius: "The effigies of twenty highly distinguished families headed the procession. But Cassius and Brutus were the most gloriously conspicuous—precisely because their statues were not to be seen." Brutus and Cassius, of course, were the leaders of the conspirators who assassinated Julius Caesar, both of them later committing suicide.

conspiracy of silence. I can find no earlier use of this term than that of popular Victorian poet Sir Lewis Morris (1833–1907), who complained that no one reviewed his work. Approaching Oscar Wilde, he said, "Oscar, there's a conspiracy of silence against me. What shall I do?" Advised Oscar: "Join it."

constable. *Constable*, for "a police officer," comes from the late Latin *comes stabuli*—any count, or officer, of the stable, or "master of the horse," under the Theodosian Code in about A.D. 438. In England the word first meant the chief officer of the court or of the nation's military forces.

Constellation. Though there is some question about its authenticity (some historians say it was broken up in 1854 and an entirely new ship built in its place), the *Constellation*, launched in 1797, is still called the oldest American warship afloat and honored as a national shrine in its Baltimore Harbor slip. It was renowned in its time for its valiant battle against the French *Insurgente* in 1799. "We would put any man to death on this ship for looking pale," said a combative officer of its combative crew.

contemplate one's navel. The first recorded mention of this expression is in Robert A. Vaughan's *Hours With the Mystics* (1860): "They call these mystics Navel contemplators." Vaughan's mystics were meditating or reflecting on inner spiritual matters, but over the years the phrase *to contemplate one's navel* took on the additional meaning of excessive self-absorption, what is also called "navel-gazing." The best example history offers of navel (or umbilicus, or belly button) gazing is that *Guinness Book of Records* record holder who for over a period of 15 years has collected some 5½ ounces of lint (fluff) from his navel, his goal being enough lint to someday make a pillow. Now that is really contemplating one's navel. *See* PROUD BELOW THE NAVEL.

contempt. Disparaging disdain for something regarded as base or unworthy. The word, first recorded in 1393, comes to us from *contemptus*, the past participle of the Latin word for to despise. Writing to Mademoiselle Quinault, Voltaire was the first to point out what has become almost a literary maxim:

"The only reward to be expected for the cultivation of literature is contempt if one fails and hatred if one succeeds."

Continental navy. America had a Colonial Navy until 1631, but this was replaced by the 53-ship Continental navy in 1776 after the break with Great Britain and the Revolutionary War. Commodore Esek Hopkins was appointed its commander in chief (the only time a navy head has held that title aside from presidents). The Continental Navy became the U.S. Navy in 1794.

controller. *See* COMPTROLLER.

conversation; criminal conversation. As early as 1511 *conversation* was used as a synonym for sexual intercourse, Shakespeare employing it this way in *Richard III* (1594). *Conversation* derives from the Latin *conversari* "to turn oneself about, to move to and fro, pass one's life, dwell, live somewhere, keep company with." It was used in these senses long before it came to mean "to communicate by speech or writing" in the late 16th century. *Converse* no longer means to have sexual intercourse, but *criminal conversation*, used at least since the late 18th century, and often abbreviated to *crim. con.*, is still a legal term for adultery.

cooker. The usual British name for a kitchen stove. It is safe to say that the term is never used (except by Brits) in the U.S., where *stove* and *range* are the common terms. *See* RUMFORD STOVE.

cook his (her) goose. The Mad King of Sweden, Eric XIV, was supposedly so enraged because residents of a medieval town he had attacked hung out a goose, a symbol of stupidity, to "slyghte his forces" that he told the residents "[I will] cook your goose" and proceeded to burn the town to the ground. This story is generally disregarded, because Mad King Eric supposedly avenged his insult in about 1560 and the expression *cook his goose*—"to put an end to, ruin"—isn't recorded until 1851. Attempts have been made to relate the phrase to the old Greek fable of the goose that laid the golden eggs. The peasant couple to whom that goose belonged, you'll remember, killed it (and perhaps cooked it later) because they were eager to get at the golden eggs within its body, which turned out to be undeveloped in any case. The first recorded use of the phrase *cook his goose* is in a London street ballad condemning "Papal Aggression" when Pope Pius IX tried to strengthen the power of the Catholic church in England with his appointment of Nicholas Wiseman as English cardinal:

> If they come here we'll cook their goose,
> The Pope and Cardinal Wiseman.

cookin' with gas. Efficient gas ranges were common in the U.S. before World War I, models including the 1912 Lindemann with four burners, a broiler, and an oven for $57. But the expression *cookin' with gas*, to perform excellently, doesn't seem to have been commonly used until the 1940s, although it is said examples of it are found in 1930s jive talk. The same is true of the synonym *to cook on the front burner* ("Brother, you're cookin' on the front burner").

Cook's tour. *Cook's tours* were invented by English travel agent and former missionary Thomas Cook, who founded the venerable Thomas Cook & Son travel agency in 1841. His first tour was a railroad excursion to a temperance convention, for which he charged a shilling a head. Cook's first grand tour of Europe, which he organized in 1856, was more expensive, and its excellent organization, along with the high quality of tours to follow, made *Cook's tour* the byword for any complete, well-organized travel tour. So reliable was the agency that the British government hired it to convey General Gordon and his troopers to the Sudan in 1884, making it probably the only travel agency ever to accommodate an army.

cool. *Everything is cool. That's cool. Real cool. Cool, man. Cool.* Truly, *cool* has become among the most used or overused workhorse words in the language and its use seems in no way to be abating, though some people believe the "cool" invasion "sucks" (often *cool's* overused antonym). No one is sure where *cool* as a term of approval comes from. It could derive ultimately from the British English *cool* meaning impudent or insolent. According to this theory, the impudent meaning, first recorded in 1825, became extended to mean clever or shrewd by the time of World War I. This in turn probably yielded the black English *cool* for great, excellent, superlative, which arose during the early years of the Great Depression and has become more common ever since. *Cool* meaning to be under control, dispassionate, as in *play it cool, cool it, lose one's cool, supercool, cool out, cool hand,* and even the old saying COOL AS A CUCUMBER, is a workhorse of a different color. It appears to ultimately date back to the year 1000, when it meant to cool down, be unemotional, and is found in the works of Chaucer and Shakespeare, among other great writers.

cool as a cucumber. It took scientists with thermometers until 1970 to find out what has been folk knowledge for centuries—that cucumbers are indeed cool, so much so that the inside of a field cucumber on a warm day registers about 20 degrees cooler than the outside air. The belief is ancient, but was first put on paper by Francis Beaumont and John Fletcher in their play *Cupid's Revenge* (1610), when they referred to certain women "as cold as cucumbers." The metaphor describes anyone self-possessed and unemotional. *Cucumber*, which derives from the Latin *cucumir*, was considered "bookish" and commonly pronounced *cowcumber* in England in the early 19th century, the way Sara Gamp said it in Dickens's *Martin Chuzzlewit*. Roman emperor Tiberius is said to have enjoyed the "fruits" so much that he ordered them served to him every day, even though they had to be grown in greenhouses out of season.

coolie. Coolies did not originally come from China. The word for an unskilled laborer almost certainly derives from the name of the aboriginal Kuli or Koli tribe of Gujerat, an Indian province. Ironically, coolie labor emigration came about mainly as the result of the outlawing of slavery in British colonies in 1834. Cheap labor was needed, and obtained, primarily from India and China in the form of natives hired under five-year contracts that were enforceable by prison terms. Conditions were often intolerable for these coolies, of whom the *Kulis* were apparently the first, their home on the northern Indian coast making it easy to recruit them. Many thousands of them died on the long voyages aboard coolie ships, which were often as inhuman as African slave ships. Another possible source for the word *coolie* is the Urdu or Tamil *kuli*—both words meaning "hireling"—but most writers support the Indian tribe theory.

coon.   This racial slur against a black person may have nothing to do with the animal called a raccoon, or coon, which derives from an American Indian word. *Coon* here possibly comes from the last syllable of the Portuguese *barracoos*, which is pronounced *coon* and meant "buildings especially constructed to hold slaves for sale."

a coon's age.   Meaning "a very long time," *a coon's age* is an Americanism recorded in 1843 and probably related to the old English expression "in a crow's age," meaning the same. The American term is an improvement, if only because the raccoon usually lives longer—up to 13 years in the wild—than the crow.

cooper.   Dr. Kenneth Cooper, an American physician, wrote a book on aerobic exercise, including jogging, that was a worldwide bestseller in the 1960s. No word honors him in the U.S. for the many lives he saved, but in Brazil the word *cooper* means to go jogging. *See* AEROBICS.

Cooper's Droop.   *Cooper's Droop* provides another name linked forever with female breasts (*see* CHARLEY). Honoring 19th-century British surgeon Sir Pastor Cooper, *Cooper's Droop* contradicts the current case for nonsupport, or wearing no bra. It seems that Cooper discovered that going without a support, or without a firm enough one, can stretch Cooper's ligaments, which attach the breasts to the body, causing the breasts to sag—a condition for which there is no recuperative exercise.

to coot; old coot.   Applied to tortoises, the obsolete verb *coot* meant "to copulate." Recorded in 1667, its origin is unknown, but it is responsible for the name of two amorous American turtles commonly called the cooter (*Chrysemys concinna*). The first recorded use of the word: "The Tortoises . . . coot for fourteen daies together." The Americanism *old coot* for a foolish or crotchety old man comes from the name of the coot, a North American rail of the genus *Fulica* noted for its laugh-like cry.

cooties.   Our slang word *cooties*, for "body lice," derives from the Malayan-Polynesian *kutu*, "louse," which British sailors became familiar with (both word and nit) in the early years of this century.

coot stew.   A few generations ago people actually enjoyed this dish. Wrote one feisty Yankee world traveler in the late 19th century: "Frederick's pressed duck at the Tour d'Argent isn't bad, but it can't hold a candle to coot stew." There is a real recipe for coot stew, but the anonymous old Maine recipe for it is more famous: "Place the bird in a kettle of water with a red building brick free of mortar and blemishes. Parboil that coot and brick together for three hours. Pour off the water, fill the kettle, and again parboil three hours. Once more throw off the water, refill the kettle, and this time let the coot and brick simmer together overnight. In the morning throw away the coot and eat the brick."

cop.   Many authorities say that the word *cop* for a police officer has nothing to do with copper buttons or shields, tracing it back to the verb *cop*, which was recorded in the sense of "to catch or capture" in early 18th-century England. But a more colorful derivation is offered by Herbert Asbury in *The Gangs of New York*. Asbury traces the term to the early days of the old Bowery Theatre in New York. "For many years," he writes, "it was one of the foremost theaters on the continent; its boards creaked beneath the tread of some of the greatest players of the time. It was then the largest playhouse in the city, with a seating capacity of 3,000, and was the first to be equipped with gas [lighting]. The structure was burned three times between 1826 and 1838, and again caught fire some fifteen years before the Civil War, when the police, recently uniformed by order of Mayor Harper, appeared on the scene in all the glory of their new suits and glistening brass buttons. They ordered the spectators to make way for the firemen, but the Bowery gangsters jeered and laughed at them as liveries lackeys, and refused to do their bidding. The thugs attacked with great ferocity when someone howled that the policemen were trying to imitate the English bobbies, and many were injured before they were subdued. So much ill-feeling arose because of this and similar incidents that the uniforms were called in, and for several years the police appeared on the street with no other insignia than a star-shaped copper shield, whence came the name *coppers* and *cop*." *See* BOBBY.

copacetic.   The word is also spelled *copesetic*, leading Partridge to suggest that this slang for "excellent, all right," or "all safe or clear," as he defines it, is a combination of *cope* and *antiseptic*. But the expression is American and was largely confined to black speech when first recorded in the 1920s. Luther Bill "Bojangles" Robinson may have invented *copacetic*, and the great tap dancer certainly did popularize it in his routines, giving the word wide currency. Robinson claimed he coined it when he was a shoeshine boy in Richmond. But a number of southerners have testified that they heard the expression used by parents or grandparents long before this. Another theory holds that *copecetic* is from a Yiddish word meaning the same. It's also spelled *kopasetic* and *kopesetic*.

Copenhagen.   In 1807 the British destroyed the Danish fleet in a surprise attack off Copenhagen. As a result, all surprise attacks came to be called Copenhagens after the site of the original battle.

Copernican; Copernican theory.   Early in the 16th century the Copernican theory established that all the planets, including the earth, revolve in orbits around the sun, in opposition to the older Ptolemaic theory (*see* PTOLEMAIC SYSTEM) that the sun and planets move around the earth. It immortalizes Copernicus (1473–1543), the Latinized form of the surname of Mikolaj Koppernigk, whose work revolutionized astronomy, changing man's entire outlook on the universe and influencing a profound change on the inner man as well. The great astronomer, born in Prussian Poland, made his living as a physician and canon of the cathedral of Frauenburg. He completed his theory as early as 1530, when he circulated in manuscript a brief popular account of it, but *De Revolutionibus Orbium Coelestium* wasn't published until 13 years later, when he lay on his deathbed. Though the work was dedicated to Pope Paul III, it was placed on the church's index of forbidden books. *Copernican* also means revolutionary, in reference to the new system's impact on the world. *See* FLATEARTHERS.

copper. *Copper*, first recorded in English in about 1000, comes from the Low Latin *cuprum*, "metal of Cyprus," the island of Cyprus having an exceptional wealth in copper in ancient times.

copperhead. Northerners sympathetic to the southern cause during the Civil War were called *copperheads* after the poisonous "sneak snake" of that name that strikes without warning and is so named for its copper color. The term was coined by a *New York Tribune* editorial writer on July 20, 1861, and is still used today to denote "an enemy sympathizer."

copra. *See* COCONUT.

Coptic words. The Coptic language, now extinct, was superseded by Arabic, but it was the ancient Egyptian language most spoken in early Christian times. Two English words that come to us from Coptic are *oasis* and *ebony*.

coquette. This French word adopted into English signifies a flirt, a woman who makes teasing sexual or romantic overtures. In an etymological sense the word is oddly inappropriate, for it derives from the French *coquet*, a *man* who strutted about and was as promiscuous as a barnyard *coq* (cock) or rooster. *Coquette* is just the diminutive of *coquet* and literally means a woman who is a "little cock."

coral. Its ancestor an old Greek word, *coral* first meant the beautiful red coral of the Red Sea and the Mediterranean. It was then extended to mean coral of all colors. In ancient times red coral was a highly prized precious gem and was believed to be a charm against shipwreck, lightning, whirlwinds, and shipboard fire. The Romans hung it in necklaces around the necks of infants to "preserve and fasten their teeth."

cord of wood. Stacks of firewood were once measured with cords of rope, this practice giving us the term *cord of wood* for "a pile of split logs stacked eight feet long and four feet high and wide." The expression was used, indicating the same dimensions, as early as 1616.

cordon bleu. *See* BLUE RIBBON.

corduroy. Plebeian cotton forms the basis for the ribbed cloth we know as *corduroy* today, but the fabric was once woven from regal silk. The word had generally been thought to derive from the French *corde du Roi* ("cord of the King"), no one venturing to say which Gallic king first wore the material. But no such word has ever been used by the French, *velours à côtes* being their name for corduroy. Thus it has been suggested that the fabric had its origins in England, the *O.E.D.* pointing out that an 1807 French list of cloths used the English words "king's cordes." The surname Corderey or Corderoy is one possibility, from its first manufacturer's name, or it may be that some enterprising merchant, relying on snob appeal in advertising, christened the product "cord of the king," using the French

corde du Roi for even greater distinction. The word was first used for a cloth in 1787.

core. *Core* for the central part of something—anything from an apple to a doctrine—probably derives from the Latin word *cor*, meaning "heart." Words like the French *coeur* and the Spanish *corazon* for "heart" suggest this, though the English word has not been traced back to the original Latin. *Core* was first recorded in 1398.

coreopsis. No one calls it the "bedbug plant," but this beautiful long-blooming member of the daisy family has seeds that look like little bedbugs, which inspired gardeners of old to name it *coreopsis* from the Greek *koris*, "bug," and *opsis*, "appearance."

corn; maize. When in Keats's "Ode to a Nightingale" a homesick Ruth stands "in tears amid the alien corn" (the phrase is Keats's own and not from the King James Bible), she is standing in a field of wheat or rye, any grain but New World corn. The English have always used the word corn to describe all grains used for food and never specifically for the grain that built the Mayan and Incan empires. Corn derives from the Old Teutonic *kurnom*, which is akin to *granum*, the Latin word for grain. *Kurnom* eventually became the Old Saxon *korn* and then *corn* in Old English. The semantic confusion arose when English settlers in America named corn on the cob "Indian corn" soon after Squanto brought ears to the starving Puritan colony in Massachusetts; the settlers then dropped the cumbrous qualifying adjective "Indian" over the years.

The British call our "corn" *maize*, a word that derives from the Spanish *maiz*, which has its origins in *mahiz*, a Caribbean Indian tribe's name for the plant. But while "corn" is the most valuable food plant native to the New World and has a fascinating history and manifold uses (employed in more than 600 products, it may even have been used as a binding for this book), it is still little known in Europe. This is perhaps because most corn loses some 90 percent of its sugar content an hour after harvesting and can't survive a transatlantic voyage without losing practically all its taste, though today there are new varieties that hold their sugar much longer.

corn coffee. A substitute coffee made from parched corn and other ingredients. In 1844, an American traveler wrote: "The supper consisted of coffee made of burnt acorns and maize . . . He advised us to drink some of this corn coffee." The traveler didn't like it very much.

corn dodger. Usually a fried or baked corn bread cake, though it can be boiled. In fact, one theory has it that the name *dodger* for this southern treat comes from the boiling water moving them around in the pot.

corned beef. There is of course no corn in corned beef. The *corned* here is for the corns, or grains, of salt used in preparing this "salted beef."

Cornelian cherry. The berries of several dogwood species are edible, but those of the Cornelian cherry (*Cornus mas*) have the longest history as a food. Called "cornet plums" in England, this tree's scarlet berries were once used to make preserves, tarts, and drinks, and were even packed in brine to be used like olives. In addition, the Cornelian cherry has exceedingly hard wood that gives more heat than most firewoods, and is said to have been used to build the Trojan horse. Its bark yields the red dye used for the traditional Turkish fez, and the berries of a dwarf form of it *(Cornus sericea)* were believed by the Scottish Highlanders to create appetite, inspiring them to name the plant *Lus-a-chraois*, Gaelic for "plant of gluttony." Like all species of dogwood, the Cornelian cherry's bark is rich in tannin and has been used medicinally (just as the bark of the flowering dogwood, *Cornus florida*, was used as a substitute for quinine). Virgil in the *Aeneid* tells how Aeneas, landing in Thrace, pulls up several Cornelian cherry bushes and finds their roots dripping blood. Groans come from the hole and a voice cries out that his murdered kinsman Polydorus is buried there. Aeneas then performs funeral rites so that the spirit of Polydorus can rest in peace. *See* DOGWOOD TREE.

corner the market.   This term arose in U.S. financial circles toward the middle of the 19th century. Used generally today, it originally meant only to buy "one kind of stock or commodity, thereby driving potential buyers and sellers into a corner because they have no option but to yield to the price demands of those controlling the stock."

Corn Husker's State.   This is the popular nickname for Nebraska, deriving from the nickname of the University of Nebraska football team. But a 1895 Nebraska law made it officially the Tree Planters State. It has also been called the Beef State, the Antelope State, and the Black Water State (from the dark color of its rivers). Its humorous nickname the Bugeater's State dates back to the 19th century, when Nebraskans were called bugeaters because of widespread poverty in the state.

corn in Egypt.   An expression that has come to mean anything that can be purchased relatively cheaply in abundance. The Bible is the origin of the expression (Gen. 42:2): "And he said, behold, I have heard that there is corn in Egypt; get you down hither, and buy us from thence; that we may live, and not die."

corn pone.   *Corn pone* is a famous southern American cornmeal cake or bread, defined by *Bartlett* in 1859 as "a superior type of corn bread, made with milk and eggs and cooked in a pan." It is often called "corn bread." *Cornpone* has also come to be a derogatory term for someone or something rural and unsophisticated: "That's a cornpone story." The word *pone* comes from the Powhatan Indian word *apan*, something baked.

corny.   *Corny*, for something old-fashioned, unsophisticated, and unsubtle, what is often called "tacky" in today's slang, has its origin in America's Corn Belt. Comedians playing to unsophisticated "corn-fed" audiences in the Midwest gave them the corn-fed humor they wanted, so much so that corn came to be known as "what farmers feed pigs and comedians feed farmers." Soon *corn-fed humor* became simply *corny jokes*, the phrase possibly helped along by the Italian word *carne* "cheap meat," being applied to the "cheap jokes" the comedians told. *Corny* eventually was used to describe anything old-fashioned, full of clichés, or mawkishly sentimental.

coroner.   Shakespeare called a *coroner* a *crowner*, which is nearer to the word's meaning of a "crown officer" (from the Latin *corona*, "crown"). Coroners, or crowners, collected the Crown revenues in Saxon days, and did not assume their official Crown duties of looking over corpses and holding inquests on suspicious deaths until the 18th century.

Corporal Violet; Little Corporal.   Napoleon Bonaparte, the Little Corporal, who stood barely 5'2", was nicknamed Corporal Violet by his followers after he was banished to Elba and boasted that he would return with the violets. His followers used the question "Do you like violets?" to identify each other.

corporation.   *Corporation* can be either singular or plural, depending on whether the writer regards it as an entity or has in mind the individual stockholders. Corporations generally use the plural in their communications ("Write for our catalogue," etc.), but it is equally correct to say "Sears have issued their catalog," or "Sears has issued its catalog." Many great writers have mixed a singular verb and a plural pronoun, as in the second example, including the framers of the Constitution. Tertullian, one of the fathers of the Christian church, coined the word *corporation* in A.D. 190 from the Latin *corporare*, "to make into a body," using it in ecclesiastical law. By the 17th century the word began to take on the meaning that it has today.

corpus delicti.   *Corpus delicti*, first recorded in 1832, is *not* the corpse in a murder case, as is commonly thought. The term, translating from the Latin as "the body of the offense," refers to the basic element of a crime, which in a murder would be the death of the murdered person.

corral.   *Corral* has for well over a century had many more meanings than simply an enclosure for animals. In a letter to the *New York Tribune* in 1867, a rancher in the Montana Territory put it this way: "If a man is embarrassed in any way, he is 'corraled.' Indians 'corral' men on the plains; storms 'corral' tourists. The criminal is 'corraled' in prison, the gambler 'corrals' the [gold] dust of the miner."

correspondence.   *Correspondence*, from the Latin *correspondenta*, can be an exchange of letters and, in our time, e-mail. It can also mean similarity or analogy, and agreement or conformity. English clergyman and wit Sydney Smith (1771–1845) once wrote to a correspondent: "Correspondences are like small-clothes [knee britches] before the invention of suspenders: It is impossible to keep them up." But consider that from 1961 until his bedridden wife died in 1985 Uichi Noda wrote her 1,307 long letters during his travels. This world record for correspondence was published in 25 books totaling 12,404 pages.

corridors of power.   This expression was first a name for the British Whitehall ministries and the senior civil servants who run them, those top people who can make important decisions. Now *corridors of power* has come to be used all over the world. The term was popularized by C. P. Snow's novel *Corridors of Power* (1964), but Snow himself had employed it years before in his novel *Homecomings* (1959). No one seems to know who coined it.

corsair. *Corsair*, which came into English in the late 16th century, was a Spanish word for someone between a pirate and a privateer, while "sea robbers" and "sea rovers" were German and Dutch inventions, also carelessly applied. At any rate, very few of these thieves of the sea were not the *hostes humani generi*, "enemies of the human race," that the Roman orator Cicero called all pirates centuries ago—though it is important to note that almost all pirates euphemistically called themselves PRIVATEERS.

corsned. This unusual word means "an ordeal by bread." In medieval times guilt was sometimes determined by making the accused swallow an ounce of bread or cheese consecrated by a priest—if the accused choked on the bread he was considered guilty. Blackstone explained in his *Commentaries* that people believed that the Almighty would "cause convulsions and paleness and [the bread would] find no passage if the man was really guilty, but might turn to health and nourishment if he was innocent." The practice is recorded as early as the 10th century and the word *corsned* derives from the Old English *cor*, "trial," and *snaed*, "piece."

cortisone. Recognizing that the scientific name 17α dihydroxy-4-pregnene-3,11,20-trione would never do, Dr. Edward C. Kendall, one of the pioneers in using that drug, cut out a lot of the letters and came up with *corsone*. But his colleague at the Mayo Clinic, Dr. Philip S. Hench, thought that the prominence of *cor*, Latin for heart, might suggest that the drug had some use in treating heart disease. He accordingly inserted a *ti* in *corsone* to make it *cortisone*. The new word was appearing in dictionaries by 1949.

corvette. Originally *corvettes* were cumbersome, ponderous freighters, "old baskets" that took their name from the Latin *corbis*, "basket." Over the years, as the design changed, they became swift, streamlined armored cruisers.

Cosa Nostra. The Italian words mean "our thing," and the mob has adopted them as another name for the Mafia. Wrote Mario Puzo in *The Godfather* (1969): " 'Sonna cosa nostra,' Don Corleone said, 'These are our own affairs. We will manage our world for ourselves because it is our world, *cosa nostra*.' "

cosine. *See* ACCORDING TO GUNTER.

cosmonaut. *See* COSMOPOLITAN.

cosmopolitan; cosmonaut. Socrates, Diogenes, and Alexander the Great all claimed to be "citizens of the world," which in Greek is *kosmopolitis*, the root of our word *cosmopolitan*. Today we apply *cosmopolitan* to a man at home anywhere, the word's latest relative being *cosmonaut*, the Russian space pilot.

Cossack. The Cossacks, quartered in 11 communities throughout Russia, were 4 million strong before the country's revolution. In return for certain privileges their men were all required to give military service for 20 years, from age 18. These cruel, fearless fighters and expert horsemen, constituting an elite Russian cavalry, were used by the czars to suppress revolution and were much feared by the people. *Cossack* is still often used to describe a brutal or brave warrior. The Cossacks

were descended from serfs who had fled their masters in the 15th to 17th century and settled on the border steppes, their name coming from the Russian *Kayaki*, "wanderers." In World War II they were used as cavalry by the Soviet Union. *See* GUSSUK.

costermonger. An old rare British term familiar to Americans through their reading. *Costermonger* means a pushcart vendor of fruits and vegetables, but was originally, in the 16th century, an apple-seller, hawking large ribbed cooking apples called *castards* that are not grown today. *Monger* means a trader or dealer, deriving from the Old English *mangian*, to trade. Today supermarkets are far more common than costermongers in Britain.

cot. At first a *cot* was a light-framed Indian bed strung with ropes, and named by British traders from the Hindi word for the bed, *khat*, in the early 17th century. In time *cot* was applied to any narrow bed and even, in England but not the U.S., to a child's crib.

cotangent. *See* ACCORDING TO GUNTER.

Cotterel's salad. Hanged for rape in the early 18th century, Sir James Cotterel had no chance to see his name immortalized in this historical pun. As the baronet was hanged for rape and rape is also the name of a rather hot salad green, *Cotterel's salad* became the synonym for a hemp rope, like the one that burned his neck.

cotton gin. *See* ENGINE.

cotton-pickin'. Despicable, wretched, damned; now sometimes used in a humorous sense. The term has its roots in the inferior status of poor farmers and field hands in the southern United States and dates back to the 19th century. The word is often heard in the expression "Get your cotton-pickin' hands off me!"

Cotton State. A nickname for Alabama, which is also called the Lizard State, and the Yellow Hammer State (after the beautiful yellow-hammer woodpecker, or after the yellowish home-dyed uniforms of Alabama Confederate soldiers).

cotton to. Cotton clings readily to many surfaces, and clung to the machines, clothing, and hair of the English weavers who worked with it in the 16th century. This clinging quality of cotton probably suggested the expression *cotton to*, "to like or be attracted to a person or thing." Although an earlier phrase used the word in essentially the same sense, its first recorded use by itself is in an old English play (1605): "John a Nokes and John a Style and I cannot cotton." Early technical processes of cloth manufacturing may have been responsible for the idea, as the *O.E.D.* points out, but it all amounts to the same thing—cotton sticking to something. No one has offered any proof that the expression derives from *kowtow*, or the French *côté*, "side," or from the obsolete slang *to cotton*, "to perform coition."

cottonwood blossom. In the Old West, an outlaw hanged from the limb of any tree was called a cottonwood blossom after the common cottonwood tree (*Populus balsamifera*), which was often used as a gallows tree. This use of the cottonwood led to the saying *have the cottonwood on him*, meaning to have the advantage over someone. Among the most unusual American desserts of pioneer days was cottonwood ice cream, a sweet, pulpy white mass scraped in the spring from the inner bark of the cottonwood.

couch potato. A phrase from a pun. *Couch potato* means a lazy, inactive person who does little else in leisure time save lie on the couch watching TV. As for the punning derivation of *couch potato*, first came the slang term *boob tube* for television, recorded in 1963. Someone who watched too much of the boob tube was shortly after dubbed a "boob-tuber." *Boob tuber* suggested the potato, a plant tuber, to Tom Iacino of Pasadena, California, in 1976, and he invented the term *couch potato*, which he registered as a trademark eight years later. Soon after his inventive punning, Iacino and some friends formed a club called the Couch Potatoes, which appeared in the 1979 Pasadena Doo Dah Parade, in which they lay on couches watching TV while their float was pulled through the streets. Little remained but for cartoonist Robert Armstrong to draw the familiar image of a couch potato—a potato sprawled out on a couch watching TV—for his book *Dr. Spudd's Etiquette for the Couch Potato* (1982).

Couéism. "Every day, in every way, I am getting better and better." The bowlegged man who repeated this famous psychotherapeutic formula too often and became merely knock-kneed is a myth, but Emile Coué (1857–1926) is not. The French pharmacist and hypnotist turned psychotherapist established a free clinic in Nancy in 1910. Here he put into practice his system of therapeutics, based primarily on his theory that, by means of autosuggestion, ideas that cause illness may be eliminated from the will. This power of the imagination over the will was best expressed in his formula, and Coué claimed to have effected organic changes. He lectured widely abroad and his healing methods became well known in the United States and England during the 1920s.

cough; whooping cough. *Cough* was defined by Dr. Johnson as "a convulsion of the lungs, vellicated by some sharp serosity!" First recorded in about 1325 it is of echoic origin, "representing various sounds and actions made with the breath," as are many words, including *whoop*. Thus *whooping cough* is an echoic term.

cough up. Four centuries ago *to cough up* meant to disclose. It did not take on its present meaning of "to pay up or hand over" until the end of the 19th century, probably originating in this sense as American criminal slang. One theory is that underworld suspects tried to bribe police officers with money instead of coughing up information about crimes, and that *cough up* then came to mean "pay up."

couldn't hit the broad side of a barn. Said of someone with very bad aim, usually with a gun. The expression, and variations on it, dates from the early 1900s.

couldn't hit the ground if he (she) fell. Said of a clumsy person, or even someone inept at any venture.

coulee. A deep ravine or gulch with sloping sides, formed by running water, that is often dry in summer; it can also be a small valley or a small stream. The word derives from the French *couler* (to flow). Grand Coulee Dam is at the end of the deep, dry canyon called Grand Coulee that is cut by the Columbia River in the state of Washington.

coulomb. Charles-Augustin de Coulomb (1736–1806), a French military engineer who became a physicist when bad health forced his retirement from the army, did much work on electricity and magnetism. He designed his torsion balance for measuring the force of magnetic and electric attraction in 1777, while still an army engineer, but didn't publish his findings until about 10 years later, finding that Michel had invented the same system independently. Bearing his name are Coulomb's law of magnetism; the coulomb, a unit for measuring the quantity of an electrical current; and the coulometer, which is more often called a voltameter. *See* VOLT.

countdown. Ninety-nine people in a hundred would say that the countdown, counting backwards for rocket launches, was invented at Cape Canaveral. But the technique was conceived and the word coined by film director Fritz Lang in his science-fiction classic *The Lady in the Moon*, to give the rocket launching in his realistic movie greater suspense. Persecuted by the Nazis, Lang fled Germany in the 1930s, but his countdown invention was used in early German rocket experiments leading to the V-2 and brought to America by German scientists who had worked on the early rockets.

counterpoint. Originally, *counterpoint* was the Latin musical term *punctus contra punctus*, "note against note." This means "melody against melody or simultaneous independent melodic lines," and was shortened to *counterpunctus*, which became the English *counterpoint* with its general as well as musical meaning. The word is first recorded in the early 16th century.

count noses. This expression meaning to count the number of people in an audience may come from the old practice of horse dealers counting horses by the nose, or may go back to the Danes, who invaded Ireland in the ninth century and took a census by counting noses.

country bumpkin. *See* CLODHOPPER.

country mile. Any long distance; a widely used Americanism that apparently originated a century ago in some rural area. Also called a country block. In baseball we often hear the expression "He hit the ball a country mile."

country pay. Trading in early American country stores was often conducted by barter, or country pay, as it was called, with customers exchanging corn, wheat, rye, and flax, or articles of household manufacture like blankets and baskets for goods on the merchant's shelves. Homemade Indian brooms, maple syrup, aphrodisiac ginseng (sold in China), barrel staves, dried fruits, the potash and charcoal left when forests were burned down to clear land, even Indian wampum—all these and a hundred other things were used as country pay.

count your chickens.   See DON'T COUNT YOUR CHICKENS BEFORE THEY'RE HATCHED.

the course of true love never did run smooth.   Another coinage or borrowing by Shakespeare, this one from *A Midsummer Night's Dream*, not *Romeo and Juliet*.

couvade.   The custom among some American Indian tribes in which a father-to-be retires to bed and simulates childbirth. He believes that by doing this he prevents his regular daily exertions from harming the child, that he is magically assisting in the birth of the child, and that the act is "a symbolic assertion of identification of father and child." *Couvade* is from the French *couver*, "to hatch," which comes from the Latin *cubare*, "to lie down."

Coventry blue.   See SEND TO COVENTRY.

cover girl.   A term popularized by the Conover modeling agency, but dating back to the late 19th century, when it was suggested by the GIBSON GIRLS, who graced so many magazine covers. In fact, the term was originally *magazine cover girl*.

cowabunga!   *Cowabunga!* has recently come to be used as a general cry of delight, due to the popularization of it by the cartoon character Bart Simpson of television fame. An earlier TV character, Cowboy Bob on the *Howdy Doody* show, used the expression in the 1950s. *Cowabunga!* is still shouted by Australian surfers at the beginning of a good ride or wave.

coward.   *Coward* derives ultimately from the French *coue*, "tail," and was possibly first suggested to hunters by the white tail of a frightened animal, such as a hare or deer, seen when it turns and runs. In any case, *coue* became the French *coart*, which came into English as *coward*. "The cowards never started and the weak died on the way," was a popular saying about those who made their way West on the Oregon Trail beginning in 1843.

cowboy.   A term first applied to members of Tory bands in New York state who rustled cows, but by the mid-19th century, it came to mean a man who herds and tends cattle on a ranch, most of his work done on horseback. Because of Hollywood westerns, *cowboy* has also taken on the meaning of any reckless person, such as a speeding automobile driver. Ironically, in recent times the word has been applied as much to handlers of sheep as to handlers of cattle.

cowboy boots; cowboy hats; cowboy shirts.   Cowboys never called them this, at least not until the term was invented in the East in about 1912. Cowboys just called them *boots* or *cowhides* until then. In about 1860, however, cowboys did begin to wear boots with higher heels and pointed toes that better fit the stirrups. Edna Ferber describes a fancy pair in *Cimarron* (1930): "The gay tops were of shiny leather, and alternating around them was the figure of a dancing girl with flaring skirts, and a poker hand of cards which she learned was a royal flush, all handsomely embossed on the patent leather cuffs of the boots." Similarly, cowboys simply called their hats *hats*, and there were many kinds of them, all with wide brims to keep the weather off their faces. *Cowboy hat* was coined in the East in about 1900. Real cowboys didn't wear fancy bright-colored shirts until recently, either; the term *cowboy shirt* isn't recorded until about 1930 when such shirts were popularized by cowboy movie star Tom Mix. See CHARLIE DUNNS; JUSTINS.

Cowboy President.   A nickname given to President Theodore Roosevelt, who was a North Dakota ranchman from 1884–86 and remained interested in cowboy life.

cowboy saddle.   The original name of the common western saddle, first recorded in the 1870s. Vaqueros developed this saddle with a high pommel and cantle from the war saddle of the Spanish conquistadores.

cowboys and Indians.   No one knows exactly when children started playing cowboys and Indians in the 19th century (or possibly earlier), but the first recorded use of this name for the game has been traced to 1887.

cowgirl.   When it was first recorded in 1884, *cowgirl* meant a female rancher or a rancher's daughter; it later came to mean a cowpuncher as well.

cowlick.   This word for "a tuft of hair that refuses to lie down" is British in origin. It almost certainly comes from a comparison with the projecting ridge of hairs on a cow's hide, licked into that shape by the animal. The word is first recorded in 1598.

cowpoke; cowpuncher.   Cowpokes and cowpunchers were originally cowboys who poked cattle onto railroad cars with long poles. The terms, first recorded in 1880, were soon applied to all cowboys.

cow pony.   This cowboy horse used to work cattle weighs 700–900 pounds and is 12–14 hands high. The name is first recorded in 1874. It is also called a cow horse.

cowslip.   This pretty flower takes its name from the droppings, or slips, of cattle, because it grew best and thickest in English pastures where cattle grazed. The ancient word dates back to at least A.D. 1000.

Coxey's Army.   Over his long life—he died in 1951, aged 97—Jacob Sechler Coxey lived through everything from the Civil War to the atomic bomb. His Coxey's Army was one of the first and best remembered groups to march on Washington, D.C., to demand change of some kind. Coxey's followers were a band of unemployed workers who presented Congress with a "petition in boots" the year following the Panic of 1893. It was their leader's plan to have Congress authorize money for public construction, which would provide employment, an idea that would be implemented during the Great Depression in the 1930s. But his highly publicized march from Massillon, Ohio on Easter Sunday failed to accomplish its purpose. The 100 men who started never swelled to 100,000 as he had predicted, and only about 500 reached Washington on May Day to protest their situation. "The Commonweal of Christ" came to an anticlimactic end when its leaders were arrested for walking on the Capitol lawn.

coxswain. Several centuries ago a *coxswain* was the *swain* ("boy servant") in charge of the small cock, or cockboat, that was kept aboard for the ship's captain and used to row him to and from the ship. But with the passing of time the *coxswain* became the helmsman of any boat, regardless of size.

coyote. Its name deriving from the Nahuatl *coyotl*, meaning the same, the coyote (*Canis latrans*) is a canid distinguished from the wolf by its smaller size, slender build, large ears and narrow muzzle. *Coyote* is also used today to mean a contemptible person, a liar, or a cheat. In its most recent usage it describes a person who smuggles Mexicans across the U.S. border. Other names for the coyote include the prairie wolf, medicine wolf, and brush wolf.

Coyote State. A nickname for South Dakota, after the prairie wolf (*Canis latrans*) resident there. South Dakota has also been called the Artesian State, the Sunshine State, the Blizzard State and the Land of Plenty.

CQD; Mayday. One of the telegraph symbols for requesting aid was CQD (*CQ*, the general call alerting other ships that a message follows, and the *D* standing for "danger"). But these letters, proposed after the *Titanic* sank in 1912, proved unsatisfactory for technical reasons and the easy-to-remember dashes and dots that coincidentally spell out SOS were retained. *Mayday*, not SOS, is the *oral* radio signal for requesting aid and probably derives from the French *m'aidez*, "help me." See SOS.

crabby. Jacob Grimm contended that the German word *Krabbe*, from which our *crabby* ultimately derives, meaning "a cross, ill-tempered person," owes its origin to the crab, "because these animals are malicious and do not easily let go of what they have." But another authority has it that the primary reference here is "to the crooked or wayward gait of the crustacean, and the contradictory, perverse and fractious disposition which this expresses."

cracked; crack-brained. *Cracked* has meant "crazy" in English since at least the 16th century and was indeed Standard English until about 1830, when it was labeled slang. But the expression is much older than this, for a character in Aristophanes's (ca. 448–ca. 388 B.C.) *The Frogs* is said to be *cracked*. A variant is *crack-brained*, first recorded in 1557.

cracker. A poor white person, especially one from Georgia (the Cracker State), so called, perhaps, from their use of cracked corn. Originally the expression was *corncracker*, someone who cracks corn to make grits or cornmeal. At one time (1766), *cracker* meant "a liar," but when, after the Civil War, many people in the South became too poor to buy cornmeal and had to make their own, *cracker* came to mean a backwoodsman and then a poor white, generally a person living in the southern states of Georgia and Florida. Others say that cracker was originally applied to Florida cowboys and derived from their cracking their whips as they herded cattle. In any case, the term is generally an offensive one and is now regarded as a racial epithet that is a violation under the Florida Hate Crimes Act. Many people, however, are proud to call themselves *Georgia crackers*, *Florida crackers*, etc., just so long as they're doing the calling.

cracker-barrel philosopher. One small-town Missouri storekeeper in 1829 sold a line of books that included Homer, Herodotus, Josephus, Shakespeare, Cervantes, Milton, Defoe, Bunyan, Smollett, Hume, Fielding, and Scott. A town's most educated man aside from the schoolteacher and the preacher, the country storekeeper was usually the local crackerbox philosopher, and he and others of his breed often sat around on the large cracker barrels in general stores philosophizing on all the issues of the day. Such wise rustics were probably called cracker-barrel philosophers at the time, though the term isn't recorded until 1938 in a *Time* magazine piece.

crackerberry. No, this berry doesn't taste like or resemble a cracker. *Crackerberry* is simply another name for the common huckleberry (*Gaylussacia baccata*), also called "cracker" and "black snap," because its seeds crack or snap between biting teeth.

crackle. *See* ONOMATOPOEIA.

Cradle of American Liberty. A nickname for Massachusetts, where the Revolutionary War began. However, Boston is called the *Cradle of the Revolution* as well as the *City of Nations*. Faneuil Hall in Boston is also called the *Cradle of Liberty*.

Cradle of the Confederacy. A nickname given to Montgomery, Alabama, where the seceded southern states met on February 4, 1861, to form the Confederate States of America.

crag. *See* HOG.

cranberry. This berry grows wild in the marshlands favored by cranes, which leads some experts to trace it to the Low German word *kraanbere*. However, since the word is recorded in America as early as 1647—a time when it is unlikely that Low German terms would have much currency here—it could be that Americans coined the word independently, noting themselves that the berry grew where cranes lived.

crap; crapper. Poor Thomas Crapper, whose name is about as close as anyone would normally want to get to the fourth most expurgated word in the English language, was an Englishman who developed and manufactured the modern toilet bowl, which U.S. soldiers in World War I saw and used everywhere, bringing the name *crapper* home with them to America. The story of his life, of "the power behind the throne," has recently been published under the title *Flushed with Pride*. It is apparently not a put-on, although it has the ring of a classic hoax. Crapper's name, of course, is only a lucky or unlucky coincidence. It does not give us the word *crap* from the Dutch, *krappe*, "scraps," which through the ages has been applied to offal or excrement. Crap is now most often used metaphorically to mean "nonsense or lying," as in "That's a lot of crap."

craps. Dice have been found in ancient Egyptian tombs and in the ruins of Babylon, but the game of dice as we know it today dates to the early 19th century and may owe its name, craps, to a Frenchman. Johnny Crapaud was the sobriquet of French gambler Bernard Marigny, who introduced dice to New Orleans in about 1800 (*Crapaud* being slang for any Frenchman, owing to the belief that three *crapauds*, or toads, were the ancient arms of France). High-roller Marigny became associated with the game, which was named *Johnny Crapaud's game* after his nickname, this eventually shortened to *craps*. It is said that Marigny even named the present Burgundy Street "Craps Street" in honor of his favorite pastime.

crash. *Crash* in the sense of to *crash a party* is an Americanism that derives from *gate-crasher*, an American expression that originated in about 1920. The latter term has its roots in the idea of a person forcing his way through a gate into a sporting event. *Gate-crashing* is not much heard of anymore, but *crashing* and *party-crashing* are commonly used.

Crassus. *Crassus* describes "a rich man of unbounded avarice and ambition." Marcus Licinius Crassus (ca. 115–53 B.C.), Roman "real estate dealer," military leader, and statesman, personified these qualities. It is said that crafty Crassus made his fortune by forming his own fire-fighting company and forcing the sale of houses on fire by letting them burn until he could buy cheap—holding off his fire brigade until the sale was consummated. Other ploys of his included buying property at nominal prices confiscated from those outlawed by Sulla, under whom he served; by slave trafficking; and by usury. Thus he became the richest man in Rome and a force to be reckoned with in the corrupt politics of the day. Crassus suppressed the slave uprising of Spartacus in 71 B.C. and was elected consul with Pompey the following year, both men joining with Caesar in forming Rome's First Triumvirate 10 years later. In this last capacity Crassus encouraged the infamous Cataline conspiracy. Finally, his ambitions outran his ability. Lusting for military glory, he launched a campaign against the Parthians in Syria. However, his army was routed by Parthian archers at Carrhae in one of the most notable examples of military stupidity in history. Crassus was captured by the Parthians and put to death; one story has it that they poured molten silver down his throat.

crate. Americans began using *crate* for a beat-up old car, or even boat or plane, in about 1920. However, the term dates back before that to 1917, when Partridge says it was first applied in the R.A.F. to old planes. The old biplanes would seem to resemble a wooden crate more than any car would and this is probably the word's source. *Old crate* is more common than *crate* today.

cravat. The modern *cravat*, another word for "necktie," was originally a huge colorful linen or muslin scarf edged with lace and worn knotted loosely around the neck. The scarves were introduced into France by mercenaries enlisted in the royal Croatian regiment during the Thirty Years War (1618–48). French men and women, impressed by such sartorial splendor, adopted the scarves, tying them with long flowing ends and calling them *cravats*, after the French word (*Cravate*), for "Croatian." Croatia was part of Austria at the time.

crawler. A relatively recent term for news information that moves across the television screen (sometimes continuously) while another program is going on. First recorded in 1967 as *crawl*, it is also called a *worm* or a *snake* today.

crayfish. The crayfish, not a fish but a crustacean, takes its name from an error of pronunciation. *Crayfish*'s source was the Old High German *kreliz*, "edible crustacean," which became *crevice* in Middle English. But the last part of *crevice* began to be pronounced "fish" and by the late 16th century the word was being pronounced and spelled *crayfish*. *Crawfish* is a synonym, as is *crawdad* in the American South.

crazy as a bedbug. That great Yankee homespun humorist Seba Smith (1792–1868) may have coined *crazy as a bedbug* in the series of letters by "Major Jack Downing" that he published in his newspaper, *The Portland Courier*, in 1832: "Nabby ran about from house to house like a crazy bedbug." *Crazy as a bedbug* means completely crazy. It may be that bedbugs scoot about crazily at times, or that their victims jump out of bed and run around crazily when bitten by them. The word *bedbug*, incidentally, is also an American invention.

crazy as a coot. As far back as the 18th century the coot's stupid facial expressions and clownish behavior inspired the expression *silly as a coot, stupid as a coot,* and *crazy as a coot.* "During the breeding season *Fulica americana* acts especially odd, breaking water, flapping wings, sitting on their tails, slashing at one another with taloned feet and thrusting with their bills," one expert explains. *See* BALD AS A COOT.

crazy as a loon; loony. The common loon (*Gavia immer*) is noted for what one expert calls its "mirthless laughter, a high, far-crying, liquid tremolo that sets your spine atingle." This water bird's name may come from the Dutch *loen*. The loon has nothing to do with the word *loony*, for "crazy," which is a shortening of *lunatic*, but it does give us the expression *crazy as a loon*.

crazy bone. *See* FUNNY BONE.

crazy like a fox. The fox is, of course, traditionally regarded as sly and crafty. Its reputation for cunning led to the Americanism *crazy like a fox*, which is first recorded in 1908 and is used to describe someone who seems to be a fool but is putting on an act and is really exceedingly clever.

credenza. In the Middle Ages servants of the nobility were expected to taste a master's food and wine before serving him, to help prevent their employer from being poisoned. This of course gave confidence or trust (*credenza* in Italian) to the master, and since the food or wine to be served at table was placed on the sideboard before being tested, the sideboard itself came to be called a credenza.

credibility gap. A lack of public confidence in the truth of claims or statements made by the government, large corporations, politicians, or other individuals. The term originated during the Vietnam War, when there was widespread distrust of the veracity of official government statements. No one is sure who coined it.

credit. According to J. P. Morgan, loans are made safe by character rather than collateral. This idea is reflected in the word *credit*, which derives from the Latin *credo*, meaning "I believe," which indicates that the person giving credit "believes" in the person to whom he gives it. The word, in its financial sense, was first recorded in 1542.

creepmouse. "Here comes a little mouse/creeping up to baby's house" is the rhyme often used in this familiar game played with infants. Most common in the South under the name *creepmouse*, the game is played everywhere, the idea "to tickle babies to make them laugh by moving the fingers rapidly on their bodies as if a mouse was running over them." The name *creepmouse* is first recorded in 1899.

creosote. *Creosote* was coined in the early 19th century from Greek words that the word's inventor thought meant "flesh saving"; though the Greek meant something else entirely, *creosote* has never been abandoned. Creosote, an oily liquid with a burning taste and penetrating odor, is obtained by the distillation of wood tar, and it is a "flesh saver" because of its early use as a preservative of meat and fish. (Now, when used at all, it is to preserve wood.) The evergreen Creosote bush (*Larrea tridentata*), which has a strong odor of creosote, is now regarded as the world's oldest known living plant; a specimen found in 1985 in the Mojave Desert is believed to be 11,700 years old, making it far older than the previous record holder, a 5,000-year-old bristlecone pine.

crêpe suzette. When or where crêpes suzette were invented in France remains a mystery, but the dessert pancake must have been named for someone's favorite Susy, *Suzette* being the French diminutive for the proper name Suzanne. The thin, rolled pancakes, or *crêpes*, are generally heated in an orange-flavored liqueur sauce and flambéed at the table, making the blazing dessert one of the more spectacular glories of the French cuisine. One theory has the dish created by San Francisco chef Henri Charpentier, but it was more likely invented by a chef known only as M. Joseph at the Restaurant Marivaux in Paris and named in honor of actress Suzanne Reichenberg.

Crescent City. A nickname for New Orleans, because, according to Joseph Ingraham in *The South-West* (1835), "it is built around the segment of a circle formed by a graceful curve of the Mississippi River."

cress. *See* WATERCRESS.

crestfallen. A term from the ancient "sport" of cockfighting, *crestfallen* refers to a defeated bird that stands waiting for the death blow with crest fallen to its beak, no longer erect and proud. Shakespeare appears to have been the first writer to apply the term to humans, in *Henry VI* (1593). *See* SHOW THE WHITE FEATHER.

cretan. Ever since the semilegendary prophet and poet Epimenides wrote that "the cretans are always liars, evil beasts . . ." *cretan* has meant a liar. Ironically, Epimenides came from Crete. Epimenides is said to have as a boy fallen into a sleep prolonged for 57 years and afterward to have lived a long life—which sounds a lot like a lie itself. A Cretan, capitalized, is an inhabitant of the island of Crete.

cretin. Our pejorative *cretin*, for "an idiot," began as a kindly word. In the Middle Ages many deformed people with a low mentality lived in the Alpine regions, their condition resulting from a thyroid condition now known as myxedema, which was possibly caused by a deficiency of iodine in their drinking water.

These unfortunates were called *Chrétiens*, "Christians," by the Swiss because the word distinguished human beings like these people from brutes and they believed these childlike innocents were incapable of actual sin. But the kindly word went into French as *cretin*, meaning "idiot," and retained the same meaning when it passed into English.

cretonne. About 1865 the French village of Creton in Normandy began making the heavy cotton material called "cretonne" in its honor. The material, with its colorful printed designs, is used mainly for slipcovers and draperies.

crib. Recent slang use of *crib* for "apartment" isn't new at all; *crib* has been used in this sense since the early 19th century and not long after became slang for either a bed or a small room in a brothel big enough to contain just a bed. *Cribbing* from *crib sheets* on an examination, a kind of euphemism among students for cheating, has its origins in the use of *to crib* for "to pilfer or take furtively," common since about 1740. The reasoning behind this last was probably the idea that cribs or wicker baskets were used by thieves to hide stolen articles. It is said that thieves in London carried baskets in which to stash stolen goods and that they were hard to spot because most women in the marketplaces carried the same baskets.

cribbage. The brilliant Cavalier poet and playwright Sir John Suckling (1609–41) is probably the only poet ever to invent a popular card game. According to his contemporary John Aubrey's *Lives* (first published 1813), Suckling, the greatest gallant and gamester of his day, invented and named the game of cribbage in about 1630. He named the game for the set of cards in it called the crib. The only other author I can think of who invented a card game is American novelist Frank Harris. His pornographic game, called *Dirty Banshee*, came complete with playing cards depicting satyrs and goddesses engaged in sexual acts. It was never sold to the public.

cricket; it's not cricket. In 1622 villagers in Boxgrove, England, near the cathedral city of Chichester, were prosecuted for playing the game of cricket on a Sunday, and replied that "It's not cricket!" This is reportedly the first use of the expression and, clearly, if these villagers did say it, they were just trying to get out of paying a fine. In any case, over the years, perhaps after the villagers paid their fine, the phrase *it's not cricket* came to mean it's unfair, it's "not playing the game." I can find no proof of the story except in the one source that gives it and the earliest I can trace the expression to is 1900, though it is foreshadowed in 1867. *Cricket* itself is of unknown origin, possibly coming from the Old English *cric*, "a staff," for the bat used in the game. John Gunther in *Inside Europe* (1943) writes of the British national game of cricket "and the ritualistic attitude to fair play that it has proclaimed."

Crillon. "The bravest of the brave," as he was called by Henry IV, is still remembered more than four centuries after his birth, by the famed Paris *hôtel* named in his honor. Louis Balbis de Berton de Crillon (1541 or 1543–1615) was a French soldier who joined the army when only 14, distinguised himself in many battles, was wounded numerous times, and became one of the greatest captains of the 16th century. It is said that in his old age Crillon was listening to the story of the crucifixion in church one day and, unable to bear the outrages Christ had suffered any longer, leaped to his feet, drawing his sword and crying out, "Where were you then, Crillon?"

Crimea. *See* CIMMERIAN DARKNESS.

criminal conversation. *See* CONVERSATION.

crimson. The kermes, or scarlet grain insect, which takes its name, ultimately, from the Sanskrit *krmi*, "worm," gives its name to the red dye called *crimson* that is made from it, the word familiar in England since the 15th century.

Crippen. *Crippen* is used to describe any man wild and unkempt in appearance, but is more common for a doctor-murderer, of which there have unfortunately been too many. Dr. Hawley Harvey Crippen, English murderer, killed his wife, Cora, and was hanged for his crime on November 23, 1910. Captain Kendall of *The Montrose* transmitted a message on July 22 of that year leading to Crippen's capture, marking the murderer the first to be caught by wireless telegraph. Dr. Crippen, born in Michigan in 1861, received his medical education in London and settled there in 1896 with his wife, who had previously appeared unsuccessfully in opera and on the music hall stage as Belle Elmore. Crippen fell in love with his secretary and on New Year's Eve, 1909, poisoned his wife, dissected the body and, after destroying what he could by fire, interred the remains in the cellar. He and Ethel le Neve, who disguised herself as a boy, eventually fled England, but on the boat crossing the Atlantic Captain Kendall recognized them from their pictures and wired the police to come aboard when *The Montrose* reached Canadian waters.

crisis. *Crisis*, strictly speaking, means "the ability to judge," deriving from the Greek *krinein*, "to decide or determine." In ancient times physicians believed that "the humours of the body ebbed and flowed like the tides of the sea." *Brewer* notes that Hippocrates called these tidal days *critical days* and called the tide itself a *crisis*, "because it was on these days that the physician could determine whether the disorder was taking a good or bad turn." From this original use the word *crisis* took on its present meaning of "a turning point."

Crispin. A word often found in literature for "a shoemaker," but rarely used in everyday speech, *Crispin* commemorates the legendary brothers Crispin and Crispinian, patron saints of shoemakers and all leather workers, noble Romans who left Rome for Gaul in A.D. 303 to preach Christianity, supporting themselves by their craft. They made many converts and survived several attempts by Emperor Maximian to put them to death, but were finally beheaded. The martyrs also have St. Crispin's lance, humorous for "a shoemaker's awl," named after them. St. Crispin's Day is October 25.

criss-cross. Criss-cross sounds like a mere reduplication of sounds similar to zigzag, or ding-dong, but when we call a series of crossing lines criss-cross we are really saying Christ-cross, "the cross of Christ." In the old 16th-century hornbook primer—originally one vellum sheet slotted into a wainscot board frame and protected by a thin transparent front covering of horn—only the alphabet, a few numbers, a little spelling, and the Lord's Prayer were taught. Most teachers at the time were trained for the ministry and so there was a close connection between education and religion. Thus the alphabet printed on the sheet's top line was preceded by a small cross that was referred to as the Christ-cross, or Christ's cross. Soon the alphabet row came to be called Christ-cross row, this eventually becoming *criss-cross* row due to the duplicative tendency of tongues, or perhaps because the word was pronounced slurred, like "Christmas" or "Christian." Eventually *criss-cross* alone was applied to any pattern of crossing lines similar to the cross at the beginning of criss-cross row.

critic. *Critic*, referring to someone who passes judgment on something, was first recorded by Shakespeare in *Love's Labour's Lost* (1588), but we don't know if the bard coined the word, which is based ultimately on a Greek word meaning the same. Shakespeare is said to have been the first to record over 1,700 words.

critical list. Someone in critical condition medically has abnormal, unstable vital signs and other unfavorable signs such as loss of appetite and unconsciousness. Such a person is put on the "critical list" in a hospital, and this is reported to callers or visitors seeking the patient's condition. The British call the same list by the somewhat less ominous term *danger list*. "He's better now, he's off the critical (danger) list."

critters. Though western movies have long favored this corruption of "creatures" to mean horses or cattle, *critters* has been used in this sense by Americans since at least 1782, when the term is first recorded.

Croatan. A person of mixed Indian, white, and black ancestry living mainly in North Carolina. The name is objectionable to many of these people, who, however, at first asked to be called Croatan Indians after Sir Walter Raleigh's lost colony of Croatan off North Carolina. They consider the name "Cro" given to them by blacks and whites in the area even more offensive.

crocodile tears. Crocodiles can't shed real tears, but the myth arose in early times that the creature moaned and cried to attract the sympathetic and helpful, and then snatched and ate its saviors while "wepynge" ("weeping"), as British adventurer and nature faker Sir John Maundeville, the first to record the legend, put it in about 1400. The story was repeated in *Hakluyt's Voyages* (1600) and by many other writers including Shakespeare, and these hypocritical *crocodile's tears* became a term for any feigned sorrow. The crocodile takes its name from the Greek *kroke*, "gravel," and *crilos*, "worm," the newly hatched animal resembling to early observers an oversized worm emerging from gravel on the banks of the Nile. In Africa the crocodile is sometimes called "the animal that kills while it is smiling."

crocus. The showy solitary flower known as the crocus, one of the first flowers of spring, takes its name from the Greek word for saffron. The stamens of *Crocus sativus*, the autumn crocus, one of the 80 or so species of crocus, have indeed been used to make saffron since prehistoric times. It takes some 225,000 hand-picked stamens to produce just one pound of saffron, making it one of the world's costliest spices. A crocus sack or gunnysack, a sack made of coarse material such as burlap, is so named because crocuses, or saffron, was first shipped in sacks made of this material. Hall of Fame sportscaster Red Barber (1907–92) sometimes used the Americanism *tied up in a crocus sack* for a game that was sewed up, a sure win for one team. *See* SAFFRON.

Croesus.   When we say, as the ancient Greeks did, that a man is as rich as Croesus, we are invoking the name of the last king of Lydia (560–546 B.C.). As a result of his conquests and trade, King Croesus was regarded by the Greeks as the wealthiest man on earth, his riches proverbial even at that time. Croesus probably minted the first gold and silver coins. Although he had subjugated the Ionian cities of Asia Minor, he was friendly to the Greeks, making spectacular offerings to their oracles. According to a legendary story told by Herodotus, the Athenian Solon once advised Croesus that no man could be deemed happy, despite his riches, until he finished his life happily. Later, after Croesus had been defeated by Cyrus the Great and condemned to be burned alive, he supposedly cried out Solon's name three times from the pyre. Cyrus, moved by his explanation and perhaps reflecting on his own fate, is said to have spared his captive's life and they became great friends. The tale, however, is chronologically impossible and only one of a number of legends concerning this very real MIDAS.

croissant.   Croissants were first made by the Viennese in 1689 to celebrate the lifting of the siege of Vienna by the Turks. The Viennese called the rich crescent-shaped rolls *Hörnchen,* "a crescent-shaped object," but today the French *croissant,* a translation of *Hörnchen,* is their most common name throughout the world.

Cromwell; a Cromwellian.   His name was once pronounced "Crumwell," hence the historic Royalist toast, "God send this crumb well down!" Royalists had every reason to wish no good to this brilliant military leader and forceful statesman. A devout Puritan and member of Parliament who vigorously supported the Roundheads, Oliver Cromwell (1599–1658) eventually led his new model army to victory over Charles I's forces in battle, had the king executed in 1649, and abolished the monarchy. In 1653 he became England's Lord Protector, rejecting the offer of the crown but accepting what was an undisguised dictatorship. He who had established the Commonwealth and began his career as an opponent of absolutism had become an abolutist himself. To this day, his name is a synonym for *dictator.* Cromwell died a natural death, naming his ineffectual son, Richard, as Lord Protector on his deathbed. He was buried in Westminster Abbey, but when the Royalists regained power in 1660, his body was exhumed, hanged from a gallows, and beheaded. Such was their revenge on the man who had said of Charles I, "I tell you we will cut off his head with the crown upon it." *See also* OLIVER.

crony.   *Crony* began its life as college slang for a long-time "chum." That college wits at Cambridge coined it from the Greek *chronios,* "long-standing," is evidenced by its spelling in the first recorded use of the term, which we find in Samuel Pepys's *Diary* in 1665: "Jack Coles, my old schoolfellow . . . who was a great *chrony* of mine."

crooked as a barrel of snakes; crooked as a dog's hind leg.   Someone very dishonest or sly is *crooked as a barrel of snakes,*

this Americanism dating back to the 19th century. The Americanism *crooked as a dog's hind leg* means the same and was first recorded at about the same time.

crooked as a bull's pizzle.   An old American expression from pioneer days in the 1800s. *Pizzle* means, of course, a penis.

crooked as Crawley.   Crawley Brook in England's Bedfordshire runs into the Ouse River. It runs so crookedly, however, that it takes a boat 80 miles to go a straight distance of 18 miles, which led to the old saying *as crooked as Crawley*—very crooked indeed.

croon.   A popular singer who croons doesn't need much vocal equipment; he or she sings softly, sadly, uses the voice as little as possible. So *croon* has come to mean "to sing in a melancholy way," a meaning far removed from its original one. Croon first meant "to utter a continued, loud, deep sound; to bellow as a bull, roar; to boom as a bell." Bulls crooned to the hills in old poems, and crooning was associated with hearty, virile singers by Burns and other poets. It was only by misuse through the years that the word changed in meaning from a roar to a lamentation and then to the singing we call crooning today, which approaches the bellowing of a bull only when the amplifiers are turned way up.

crop.   A crop was originally the top or head of a plant; these were gathered during the harvest, of course, and came to be the general name for what was collected, the crop.

crops.   *See* ROUNDHEADS.

croquet.   Croquet was made famous on expansive, immaculate English estate lawns in the mid-19th century, but the sport's origins go back to France. There it was first played with a crooked stick called a *croche* (similar to a hockey stick) which eventually gave its name to the English game.

cross as a bear.   "Major Smalleye war as made as a beaten b'ar," wrote Robert Bird in *Nick of the Woods* (1837). The still common Americanism for "quite cross or mad" goes back at least a decade earlier and is probably even older. *See a* BEAR FOR WORK.

crossing the bar.   *To cross the bar* can mean to die or to cross from one side to another, over a bar or sandbar that separates the two. In this sense the phrase may derive from Lord Tennyson's poem "Crossing the Bar," which he wished to be published as the last poem in any collection of his work. The four-stanza poem—with the last lines "I hope to see my Pilot face to face / When I have crost the bar"—was written in October 1889, three years before the poet's death, as he crossed the Solent, the channel between the Isle of Wight and England's mainland. The celebrated poem took only a few moments to write, Tennyson jotting down the 16 lines (almost unchanged in the final version) on an old envelope.

crossing the line.   Anyone who crosses the line has sailed across the international date line, an occasion that in days past was celebrated with an initiation ceremony for those who were crossing for the first time. The custom, still practiced to a limited extent, called for a sailor, dressed as King Neptune, and his court to seize novices and lather and shave them, among other antics.

crossing the Rubicon.   The Rubicon, a river in Italy, marked the boundary between Roman Italy and Gaul, which was governed by Julius Caesar. When Caesar crossed the Rubicon in 49 B.C. he had invaded the Roman Republic and there was no going back. Thus the expression *crossing the Rubicon* became synonymous over the years with "taking an irreversible step."

cross of gold.   It was the gold standard, "the standard of monetary value solely in terms of gold, the single standard," that William Jennings Bryan, an advocate of the silver standard, referred to when he made his famous Cross of Gold speech at the National Democratic Convention in Chicago in 1896: "You [the rich and powerful] shall not crucify mankind upon a cross of gold." On the gold standard since 1834, the U.S. legally adopted it in 1900, then abandoned it in 1933.

crowbait.   This term for an old, decrepit horse is an Americanism first recorded out West in 1884. But it has its ancestor in the English *crow meat,* applied to both humans and horses, which was used back in the 16th century.

crow bar.   This iron or steel bar used for prying is named for the resemblance of its forked end to either a crow's foot, beak, or tail—no one seems to be sure which. The term dates back to about 1825, but for four centuries before this, *crow* had been used for the tool, Shakespeare so calling it in his *Comedy of Errors. See* AS THE CROW FLIES.

crowder.   A variety of black-eyed pea that grows crowded together in the pod; in his diary, George Washington records growing them, and they are widely grown today.

crowherd; crow-keeper; scarecrow.   We've heard of sheepherds (shepherds) and cow-herds, but *crow-herds?* Crowherds, it seems, were boys or old men equipped with makeshift bows and employed to keep crows off planted fields. They were apparently first called crow-keepers, this term mentioned in Shakespeare's *King Lear:* "That fellow handles his bow like a crow-keeper . . ." A crow-keeper could also be called a scarecrow, a word first recorded as applying to humans hired to scare off crows (1553) and applied to "a straw dummy dressed like a man" about a half century later.

crown of thorns.   To wear a crown of thorns means to suffer from a terrible burden, such as pain, anxiety, or guilt. The reference is to the crown of thorns placed on Christ's head to mock him before his crucifixion (Matt. 27:29). There are also two creatures, a prickly spurge plant and a spiny starfish, called the "crown of thorns." Dorothy Parker, summoned to appear before the House Un-American Activities Committee in 1952, had her own crown of thorns. She spent the evening before the dread day in a Washington, D.C., bar. There a loudmouth annoyed her, voicing his disapproval. Miss Parker rose and stared at him icily. "With the crown of thorns I'm wearing," she said as she turned and left, "why should I be bothered by a prick like you?"

Crows.   The name, bestowed by themselves, of a tribe of Sioux Indians; they were known to dance a "crow dance" wearing a "crow belt," which was a long bustle or tail made of crow feathers.

crow's-feet.   There is nothing new about this expression meaning "the wrinkles formed by age or anxiety about the corners of the eyes," according to the *Oxford English Dictionary.* These wrinkles have been thought to resemble imprints of the feet of crows at least since Chaucer's time. *See* AS THE CROW FLIES.

crow's nest.   Now a word for any lookout station, this was of course first a naval term referring to the highest lookout point aloft. It is said to have originated with the ravens carried in cages aboard Norse vessels; the cages were hoisted aloft when land was thought to be nearby and the birds were released, the ship following their direction to shore. In any case, *crow's nest* is first attested in 1604, as a fort built high on a hill. It wasn't recorded in its present nautical sense until the early 19th century.

crow tracks.   *See* CHICKEN SCRATCH.

cru.   A *cru,* its plural *crus,* is a vineyard or a region producing wine in France and also means a grade of wine, such as *premier cru.* The term, heard increasingly in the U.S. today, derives from the French *croitre,* to grow.

crucial.   In the sense of decisive, or of supreme importance, *crucial* comes from Francis Bacon's phrase *instantia crucis,* Latin for being present at the cross, which he used metaphorically for coming to a crossroads signpost or guidepost where a traveler has to continue one way or another. Isaac Newton and Robert Boyle later patterned their *experimentum crucis,* crucial experiment, on Bacon's phrase.

crud.   An Americanism dating back to the early 1920s in army use, *crud* doesn't come directly from the Middle English *crudd,* for "coagulated solids of milk, or curds," even though Shakespeare used the word *crudy* in this sense. It probably derives from the mispronunciation of the word *curdled* as *cruddled,* anything curdled or cruddled being undesirable crud. The word first described semen sticking to the body or clothes after sexual intercourse, and was probably so named for this, but is now used mainly as a synonym for feces, or, even more commonly, for "anything dirty, inferior, worthless, ugly, or disgusting."

cruise.   *Cruise* is from the Dutch *kruisen,* to cross or traverse. Today it mainly means to sail about on a pleasure trip, but since 1674 it has also meant to look in a public place for a sexual partner, which is mostly said of a prostitute.

crummy.   Hoboes begging for food on the road often received bread and other baked goods that were so stale they were literally crummy, had begun to turn to crumbs. *Crummy* is recorded in this sense in the early 1900s and within 25 years or so meant "anything cheap or inferior."

cry all the way to the bank. Usually said by or of someone who may not be a critical or professional success but nevertheless makes lots of money. The origin of the saying is unknown, but it is often attributed to the popular American pianist Liberace, who frequently used it.

crying bird. Limpkins (*Aramus guarauna*) are often called crying birds in America because the usual cry of this noisy bird "possesses a quality of unutterable sadness," according to one ornithologist.

crying out loud. Probably coined in the 1920s, *for crying out loud* is a still common American euphemism that backs away from *for Christ's sake* just when it seems you are going to say it.

crying towel. *See* GET OUT THE CRYING TOWEL.

cry one's eyes out. To cry long and uncontrollably, as if one's eyes would flood out of their sockets. Cervantes may have coined this expression, which is first recorded in *Don Quixote* (1604). There Sancho begs his master not to make him witness the Don's acts of penance: "Good sir, as you love me, don't let me stay to see you naked; 'twill grieve me so to the heart that I shall cry my eyes out."

cry over spilt milk. Canadian humorist Thomas C. Haliburton, whose Down East humor strongly influenced American literature, had a friend say this to his famous character Sam Slick, a shrewd Yankee peddler, in *The Clockmaker; or the Sayings and Doings of Samuel Slick of Slickville* (1836). "What's done, Sam, can't be helped, there is no use cryin' over spilt milk" were the exact words. This is the first use of the expression in print, though to *cry over spilt milk* seems homely enough to be of much older origin. It expresses, of course, the folly of vain regret, meaning "to grieve over something beyond saving," something you can't do anything about. Haliburton, a Canadian jurist, later returned to England and became a member of Parliament.

crystal. *Crystal* derives from the Greek word for ice and, indeed, was an early English synonym for ice. When the first quartz crystals were observed by the ancients, they were thought to be merely ice crystals petrified by some natural process over the ages and were thus given the same name. We still retain the old meaning of crystal as "ice" in the fortune-teller's *crystal ball*, which isn't at all like crystal as we know it but does resemble a ball of ice.

cry uncle. *See* UNCLE!

Cuba libre. During the Cuban War of Independence in 1896 rebels drank a refreshing energizing drink of sugar and cold water that they called a *Cuba libre*, or "free Cuba." Later some anonymous bartender added rum to the drink, which is now made of rum, cola, and lime juice.

cubane; basketane; squaric acid. Whimsical scientists named these molecules because of their shapes. In cubane the six carbon atoms are arranged in the form of a cube; basketane's molecular shape suggests a basket; and in squaric acid the atoms are arranged in a square.

Cuban sandwich. A name, generally confined to Florida, for a submarine or hero sandwich. The sandwich, often grilled, seems to have been introduced in the early 1970s.

cubbyhole. The *cub* or *cubby* in this term has nothing to do with bear cubs who live in a hole or den. *Cub* is a word still used in rural England for any small shelter, from a rabbit hutch to a chicken coop. Possibly first altered to *cubbyhole* by children in reference to a small hiding place, it came to mean "any small, snug place."

cuckold. Instead of building its own nest, the cuckoo eats other birds' eggs and lays its eggs in their place. The cuckoo eggs are then hatched by the sparrow, wagtail, yellowhammer, or whatever. For this reason the bird's name became the basis for the derisive word *cuckold*, "a husband whose wife has been unfaithful," a term that dates back more than a century before Chaucer's time. How cuckold came to be applied to the husband instead of the adulterer isn't clear, though Dr. Johnson believed that "it was usual to alarm the husband at the approach of an adulteress by calling out 'cuckoo,' which by mistake was applied in time to the person warned." *See* CUCKOO.

cuckold hazel. *See* WITCH HAZEL.

cuckoo. The cuckoo was so named for the one-note song it repeats over and over. Why it became a symbol for stupidity in the 16th century isn't really known. Perhaps it got this reputation because it lays its eggs in other birds' nests, though many would consider this clever. Or we may owe this meaning of *cuckoo* to the folktale "Wise Men of Gotham," in which the villagers tried to prolong summer by fencing in the cuckoo so that it wouldn't fly off. *See* CUCKOLD; ONOMATOPOEIA.

cuckoo nest. *See* SNAKE PIT.

cucumber. *See* COOL AS A CUCUMBER.

cue. In the 16th century the Latin *quando*, "when," was abbreviated as *Q* on actors' copies of play scripts as a direction telling an actor when to begin speaking his part. *Q* was read and pronounced *cue*, the abbreviation becoming a word when it was finally written *cue* as well. No play manuscripts with *Q*'s on them survive, but several 16th- and 17th-century writers tell this story and it seems likely, especially since *cue* is first recorded as *q*, in 1553: ". . . a man's *q* in a play."

cueball. A bald man, usually completely bald, is called a *cueball* after the round white cue ball used in the game of pool. This unflattering term is an American one dating back to World War II. *See* CUE STICK.

cue stick. The long, tapering pool and billiard cue stick or cue ultimately derives from the Latin *cauda* for "tail," which went through many changes in many languages before becoming *coe* and then our *cue*. *See* BILLIARDS.

cul-de-sac. In French *cul-de-sac* (from *cul*, "bottom or anus," and *sac*, "bag") means the bottom of the bag or sack. First used as an anatomical term, *cul-de-sac* was by the early 19th century a military term for the position of an army hemmed in on all sides with no chance of escape, and then came to mean "a dead-end street," one from which there is no exit save the entrance.

Cullinan diamond. Most famous of the precious stones bearing someone's name is the 3,106 metric carat (over 1¼ lbs.) diamond found in South Africa's Premier Mine in 1905. The stone, the largest diamond ever unearthed, was named after the mine's discoverer-director, Sir Thomas Major Cullinan. Presented to England's King Edward VII in 1907, it was cut into a number of specimens worth collectively over a million pounds. The Star of Africa made from it is, at 530.2 metric carats, the largest cut diamond in the world.

cumshaw. *Cumshaw*, for "a tip or gratuity," came into the language early in the 19th century from the Chinese Amoy dialect. The Chinese words it derives from were a traditional beggar's phrase that has a literal meaning of "grateful thanks."

cunt. *Cunt*, for the female sexual organ or vagina, dates back (as *cunte*) to Middle English, deriving from a Teutonic word corresponding to the Latin *cunnus*, which is related to the Latin *cuneus*, "a wedge." While the *O.E.D.* records COCK and *prick*, it doesn't include *cunt*. Partridge calling this "an injustice to women." The word has been avoided in public speech since the 15th century and considered obscene since about the 17th century, though it has recently been included in dictionaries and is commonly printed in other works.

Cupid; cupidity. *Cupidity* doesn't derive from the name of Cupid, the Roman god of love and the son of Venus, the goddess of love. Rather both terms derive from the Latin *cupere*, to desire. Cupidity is eager or excessive desire to possess something.

cuppa char. *See* TEA.

cur. This word, for a mean mongrel or worthless dog, is associated with the growling of such dogs. Used by Spenser in the *The Faerie Queene* (1589), *cur* is an old word that derives from the Scandinavian *kurra*, "to snarl or grumble."

curare. This well-known deadly poison, with which South American natives sometimes tipped their arrows, takes its name from the *wrari* of the Brazilian Tupi Indians. In Tupi it translates as the poetically apt "he to whom it comes always falls."

curate's egg. *See* LIKE THE CURATE'S EGG.

curbstone broker. *See* NYSE.

curfew. Domestic fires left unextinguished at night caused many devastating fires in medieval times. Therefore laws made it mandatory to cover fires at night, church bells ringing at the hour (usually 8 or 9 o'clock) that this was to be done. The French for "cover fire," *couvre feu* passed into English as *curfew* and the word later was applied to all regulations banning people from the streets at certain hours.

curie. Several words honor the husband and wife co-discoverers of radium, whose work laid the foundation for much later research in nuclear physics. The Curie point—the temperature at which the magnetic properties of a substance change—had been named for Pierre Curie (1859–1906) before he married Manya Sklodowska in 1895. He and Madame Curie, who came from Poland to study at the Sorbonne, worked together to extract from pitchblende the twin radioactive elements polonium and radium in 1898, the former being named for Mme. Curie's native country. Marie Curie's name has become more widely known than her husband's; it was she who first suspected the presence of new elements in pitchblende, and she was a pioneer woman scientist as well. But the curie or curiegram—a unit of measurement for radioactivity—was named for *both* scientists in 1910, as was the radioactive element curium when discovered by Glenn Seaborg and his co-workers at the University of California in 1945. Both Curies shared a NOBEL PRIZE in 1903 for their discovery of radioactivity; Madame Curie received a second Nobel Prize, in 1911, for the discovery of radium. Their daughter, Irène Joliot-Curie, shared a Nobel Prize in chemistry with her husband in 1935. *See* POLONIUM.

curlicism. John Arbuthnot remarked that English publisher Edmund Curll's inaccurate biographies were "one of the new terrors of death," but Curll was more notorious for the obscene books he published, these including *The Memories of John Ker of Kersland* (1728), *The Nun in Her Smock*, a book on flagellation, and other inspirational works. Today "the unspeakable Curll" might be a rich man, but in his time he was fined, put in the pillory, and imprisoned for his efforts. Among the greats who lampooned him were Jonathan Swift and Alexander Pope, who described him as "a fly in amber." No one has identified the anonymous wit who coined the word *curlicism*, "literary indecency," from his name.

curmudgeon. A resentful, bad-tempered person. To his embarrassment, Dr. Johnson in his great dictionary defined *curmudgeon* as "a vicious manner of pronouncing *coeur mechant*," these last words being French for "heart" and "evil." The truth is that no one knows the origin of *curmudgeon*, just that the word is first recorded in 1577. *See* PASTERN.

currants. Currants may taste nothing like them, but they take their name indirectly from grapes. In the early 14th century the chief place of export for the small seedless raisins made from grapes was Corinth, Greece. As Corinth was pronounced *Corauntz* in Anglo-French at the time, these dried raisins were called "raisins of Corauntz." Later, the tart berries of the genus *Ribes* were given the same appellation because their plant clusters looked like the dried grapes or raisins of Corauntz. *Corauntz* was eventually corrupted to *currants* and this became the tasty fruit's name. Wrote early-17th-century poet Richard Hughes:

> Puddings should be
> Full of currants for me:
> Boiled in a pail
> Tied in the tail

Of an old bleached shirt;
So hot that they hurt.

The most famous dish made from red and white currants has to be the seedless *currant jelly* once laboriously made by professional "seeders," who used goose feathers to delicately pick out the currant seeds without damaging the berries. A currant preserve used to be a gourmet delicacy made only in Bar-le-Duc, France, on the banks of the Meuse. Ever since 1559, when Mary Stuart, later Mary Queen of Scots, was given a jar of the rare substance, it was presented to every visiting chief of state. But a decade ago its last manufacturer went out of business, and the gastronomical rarity apparently is no more.

currency; coins named after people. *Currency*, a synonym for paper money, applied to coins when the term was first used in late 17th-century England, there being no paper money at the time. It was so named because it was the current medium of exchange. The first European to sight the Pacific Ocean, Vasco Núñez de Balboa (1475–1519), has the balboa, Panama's main monetary unit, named after him. Similarly, the cordoba, Nicaragua's principal monetary unit, honors Francisco de Córdoba (1475–1526), who explored Nicaragua for Spain. The most renowned explorer of all, Christopher Columbus (1451–1506), who is called Cristóbal Colón in Spanish, has the colón, the basic monetary unit of Costa Rica and El Savador, named in his honor. Two other heroes who have money named after them are the Honduran Indian chief Lempira, who valiantly resisted the Spanish conquest and is honored by Honduras's principal monetary unit, the lempiro, and Simon Bolívar, the Liberator, for whom both the country of Bolivia and its main monetary unit, the bolivar, were named. Up until the 1978 Iranian revolution, a gold coin called the pahlavi honored Reza Shah Pahlavi (1877–1944), longtime ruler of Iran. Similarly, the albertin of the Austrian Netherlands honored Archduke Albert, and the alfonso of Spain, Spanish king Alfonso.

current. In the sense of a large body of water moving in a certain direction, *current* derives from a Latin word meaning "running." There are some 30 major currents. The world's greatest current is the West Wind Drift Current, which flows at one point at the rate of 95 billion cubic feet per second and ranges from 185 to 1,240 miles. The strongest current is in British Columbia's Nokwakto Rapids, which travel up to 18.4 mph. An unlikely story says Aristotle drowned himself because he could not explain the current off the island of Euboea in the Aegean. Scientists are still mystified by the current and can't explain why it reverses its direction some 14 times a day. *See* GULF STREAM.

curry favor. These words are literally meaningless. What does currying, or brushing, favor have to do with bootlicking, or ingratiating oneself by flattery? The expression shows that a mistake repeated often enough can become standard usage. *Favor* here is a corruption of *Fauvel*. Fauvel was a fallow-colored or chestnut horse in the early 14th-century satirical poem *Roman de Fauvel*. The equine hero of this popular French allegory symbolized cunning duplicity; thus cunning people who resorted to insincere flattery in order to gain someone's favor were said to curry Fauvel, to groom or brush the rascally fallow-colored horse so that he would look kindly on them and perhaps impart to them his powers of duplicity. *Fauvel* came to be spelled *favel* in English. But because *favel* sounded like *favor* to Englishmen and because the idea of gaining someone's favor is the essence of the phrase, the proverbial expression became *curry favor*.

curse. The word *curse* goes back to the Old English *curs* for the same, while the expression *curse word* for a profane or obscene word is first recorded in about 1870. Though it hasn't made the *Guinness Book of World Records*, the oldest curse yet found is: "If you do not obey this decree, may a donkey copulate with you!" According to Reinheld Aman, editor of *Maledicta*, this is found in documents of the Egyptian 23rd Dynasty (749–21 B.C.). "The curse" is still used for "menstruation" among a large number of American women. How old the expression is hasn't been established, but it is first recorded in John Dos Passos's *42nd Parallel* (1930): "She was afraid her period was coming on. She'd only had the curse a few times yet." Variations are Eve's curse and the curse of Eve.

curse of Adam. The book of Genesis tells the story of God driving a disobedient Adam and Eve from the Garden of Eden and cursing the Earth with troublesome thorns and thistles as well as plants that produced good and plentiful food. This and "In the sweat of thy face shalt thou eat bread," the need to work hard for a living, constitute the "curse of Adam." God's judgment on Cain after he killed his brother, Abel, is the "curse of Cain," that he always be on the move, "a fugitive and a vagabond . . . upon the earth."

curse of Scotland. The nine of diamonds playing card. The name may have been suggested by the card's resemblance to the coat of arms of the Earl of Stair, who was hated in Scotland as a Judas for helping bring about the union with England in 1707. However, there are many other possible derivations for this expression first recorded in the early 18th century.

curse of the Bambino. A curse against the Boston Red Sox's winning baseball's World Series said to be in effect since Red Sox owner Harry Frazee sold Ruth to the New York Yankees in 1920.

curtain lecture. This is a reproof or lecture given in private or secret. *Curtain lectures* date back to the 18th century, when beds were often curtained and within the privacy of them wives often scolded or lectured their husbands, or vice versa.

curtain speech; curtain call. *Curtain speech* refers to the final speech of an act or scene in a play, or at the end of the play. It is also a brief speech by an actor, author, or producer, etc., after the end of a play in front of the closed curtain. *Curtain call* refers to the appearance of the performers or a single performer at the close of a play or opera in response to audience applause, as in "She took three curtain calls."

Curzon line. The Curzon line separating Russia and Poland was suggested in 1919 by the British Conservative politician, statesman, and writer George Nathaniel Curzon, first marquess of Kedleston (1859–1925). Lord Curzon, secretary of foreign affairs at the time, served in many capacities for the British government. As viceroy of India from 1899 to 1905 and chancellor of Oxford University from 1907 to 1915, he became noted for his aloof regal manner, which was the butt of many jokes. Behind the facade was a witty, modest, friendly man whose sheer willpower overcame serious physical weakness (a curvature of the spine). Curzon failed in his ambition to become the British prime minister in 1923, when Stanley Baldwin was chosen over him. It is said that he died of overwork. The Curzon line was adopted as Poland's eastern frontier after World War II, having been confirmed at Yalta in 1945. By the way, the diplomat wasn't at all like the rhyme composed about him at Balliol College in the late 1870s: "My name is George Nathaniel Curzon,/I am a most superior person."

cush-cush. This South American relative of the yam is also called the yampee. *Diosorea trifida,* which grows in the wild, is valued for its edible orange-colored tubers, but no one seems to know how it got the unusual name cush-cush.

Cushing's syndrome. A disease caused by the malfunction of the adrenal glands; its symptoms include obesity and high blood pressure. It was named after American brain surgeon Harvey Williams Cushing (1869–1939). Cushing, a leading medical writer as well, was also honored with a Pulitzer Prize in 1925 for his biography of Sir William Osler. *See* OSLERIZE.

cushlamachree. *Cushlamachree* is one of the few native locutions that Irish immigrants retained after being in America awhile. The expression is a corruption of the Gaelic *cuisle me chroidhe,* "vein of my heart."

cushy. Comfortable, undemanding, as in "She's got a cushy job." Here we have two good choices, neither of them certain. One theory says the word is simply a shortening of *cushion* with a *y* attached. Another traces the word, first recorded in 1916, to the Hindi *khuush,* pleasant, which British soldiers in India heard and added a *y* to.

cuspidor. James Joyce felt that *cuspidor* was the most euphonious word in English. The large receptable for spit (especially from chewing tobacco) certainly doesn't inspire any pretty pictures to complement its sound, but it was commonly used wherever tobacco was chewed in the 18th and 19th centuries. The word derives from the Portuguese *cuspidor,* spitter, which comes from the Latin *conspuere,* to spit upon. It is also called a "spittoon."

Custer's Last Stand; Custer Battle; Custer Tragedy. Names for the battle of Little Bighorn in Montana on June 26, 1876, when a large force of Sioux wiped out U.S. forces serving under General George Armstrong Custer (1839–76).

customer. *Customer* first meant one who acquired ownership of a house after long use or possession, the word deriving from the Latin *custodia,* "guarding or keeping." *Customer* also meant a common prostitute in the early 17th century and was used by Shakespeare twice in this sense. By the end of the 15th century it took on its meaning of "one who frequents any place for the sake of purchasing." In this sense, it probably derived from the long-standing satisfied tenant who became an owner, the first customers giving all their business and allegiance to one merchant in early times.

the customer is always right. American retailer H. Gordon Selfridge (1856–1947) coined this slogan when he opened his huge department store, Selfridge's, in London. Before this, while working for Marshall Field & Co. in Chicago, he coined the expression "——— shopping days until Christmas."

cut. To cut someone, "to refuse to recognize someone socially, to shun him," was originally Cambridge slang, dating back to the 18th century. As one contemporary observer put it: "There are several species of the *cut* . . . The *cut direct* is to start across the street at the approach of the obnoxious person in order to avoid him. The *cut indirect* is to look the other way and pass without appearing to observe him. The *cut sublime* is to admire the top of King's College Chapel, or the beauty of the passing clouds, till he is out of sight. The *cut infernal* is to analyze the arrangement of your shoe-strings, for the same purpose."

cut a Dido. *See* CUTTING UP.

cut and dried. The allusion is probably not to ready-cut timber, as *Brewer* says, but to the cut-and-dried herbs that were sold in the herbalists' shops of 17th-century England. Used as remedies, herbs were more effective cut and dried than they were fresh picked, and herbalists stocked great quantities of them. The phrase came to mean "far from fresh, hackneyed," its first recorded use in this sense being in a 1710 letter to a preacher whose sermon was described as "cut and dry'd." The words also came to mean "clear cut." By the time Swift used the phrase for hackneyed literary style in his poem "Betty the Grizette" (1730), it was already fairly hackneyed itself:

> Sets of phrases, cut and dry,
> Ever more thy tongue supply.

cut a wide (big) swath. This Americanism, meaning "to make a big pompous show, to appear important," dates back to the early 19th century or before. "Gracious me! How he was strutting up the sidewalk—didn't he cut a swath!" exclaimed one writer in 1843. The term is a farming one, a *swath* being "the amount of grass or any crop cut down with one sweep of a scythe."

cute. First recorded in 1731 as a shortening of *acute,* in its sense of "keenly discerning or shrewd," *cute* over the next century somehow acquired its present meaning of attractive or pretty. Today the word is also used to mean contrived or overly precious.

cut it. *See* CAN'T CUT THE MUSTARD.

cut neither nails nor hair at sea. An old superstition, which goes back at least to the ancient Romans, has it that the cuttings of nails and hair were votive offerings to Persephone, queen of Hades. Therefore, Neptune, ruler of the sea, would be jealous and show his displeasure if sailors cut their nails or hair because he would believe his subjects were making offerings to another god and wreck their ship or drown them.

cut-nose woman. American Indian women of certain tribes whose noses were cut off because of their adultery. "He reckoned he . . . would . . . never have to cut Teal Eye's nose off . . . the way a Piegan did when he found his woman had lain in secret with another man. It was a sight, the squaws you saw with no end to their noses. Cut-nose women, they were called," wrote A. B. Guthrie Jr. in *The Big Sky* (1947).

cut off your nose to spite your face. "Henry IV well knew that to destroy Paris would be, as they say, to cut off his own nose in taking spite on his own face," Gédéon Tallemant des Réaux wrote this in his *Historiettes* (ca. 1658), and the fact that he wrote "as they say" indicates that the expression is even more venerable. There may have been an old story about someone angrily cutting off a portion of the long, unattractive nose nature had cursed him with and succeeding only in spiting his face, but, if so, it is lost in time. The expression has survived so long and is still so frequently used simply because it is the most graphic, homeliest, and most grimly humorous of all sayings describing someone injuring himself through pique or anger.

cut of his jib. The cut of a jib, or foresail, of a ship indicates her character to a sailor and *jib* means "face" in sailor's slang. Thus *don't like the cut of his jib*, which probably dates to a century ago, translates as "I'm suspicious of him; I don't like the expression on his face."

cut one's eyeteeth; wisdom teeth. The eyeteeth are those directly under the eye, the long, pointed canines that are cut at 14 to 20 months for the first set and at 11 to 12 years of age for the second set. To *cut one's eyeteeth* means "to acquire wisdom and become worldly," because the permanent set is acquired when a child is passing into young adulthood. It is usually said in the negative, as in *he hasn't cut his eyeteeth yet*. The expression was used by Haliburton's Sam Slick in 1837 and Emerson after him, but is British in origin, dating back to the early 1700s, when it was *to have one's eyeteeth*. *Eyeteeth* commonly referred to the canine teeth of dogs and other animals long before this, so the phrase may have been suggested by the fact that fighting dogs were considered dangerous to handle when they developed their eyeteeth. Actually, the words better describe the emergence from infancy or childhood than they do the acquiring of wisdom. If wisdom does come with age, *to cut one's wisdom teeth* is more appropriate, for these are cut at the ages of 17 to 25 and up to age 50! These molars have been known as *dentes sapientiae*, "teeth of wisdom," since the time of Hippocrates.

cut one's foot. To *cut one's foot* means to step in cow dung. The euphemism, traced back to the Appalachians, was first recorded in 1899 and still has some currency in rural areas today. A variation is *to cut one's foot on a Chinese razor*.

cut the Gordian knot. The workman Gordius of old was chosen king of Phrygia when he fulfilled an oracle's prophecy that the first man to approach the temple of Jupiter driving a wagon would rule the land. King Gordius dedicated his wagon to the god and tied it to a temple beam with a knot of cornel bark so baffling that another oracle declared that the man who untied it would become lord of all Asia. Enter Alexander the Great, whose hopes lie in that direction. "Well then it is thus I perform the task," says the Conqueror, drawing his sword,

and he simply cuts the knot in two. The whole tale is improbable, scholars say, although Gordium, ancient Phrygia's capital, had been named for Gordius, the father of King Midas. But a Gordian knot remains an intricate problem and *to cut the Gordian knot* still means "to solve a baffling problem by a single bold and incisive act."

cut the mustard. *See* CAN'T CUT THE MUSTARD.

cut the painter. A painter is the rope by which a ship's boat can be tied to the vessel, a buoy, or a dock, and the word ultimately derives from the Latin *pendere*, "to hang." Thus *to cut the painter*, a phrase much used in the 19th century, came to mean "to sever all connection with something."

cut the tail off the dog. To make a long story short, to cut to the chase, as in "Well, to cut the tail off the dog, she finally divorced him."

cutting horses. Edna Ferber described the breed in *Giant* (1952): " 'They're what we call cutting horses. They're used to cut out certain animals from the herd . . . You don't have to touch the reins half the time. Just sway your body and your horse will turn your weight this way or that.'

cutting up; cut a Dido. To *cut a Dido*, or play a prank, though an almost obsolete expression, may be the origin of the more common phrase *cutting up*. The original cutup could be Dido, the legendary princess who founded and became queen of Carthage. The daughter of a Tyrian king, Dido married her uncle and upon his murder by her brother Pygmalion sailed to the African coast with his treasure. There she purchased land from a native chieftain, with the provision that all the ground she could cover with an oxhide would be hers. She then cut the hide into thin strips long enough to enclose a space that became the fort of Carthage. In a later myth, Virgil's *Aeneid*, Dido is the lover of Aeneas and commits suicide upon her own funeral pyre when he abandons her at the command of Jupiter. It's a shame to spoil a good story, but the legend of Dido probably arose because the fortress protecting Carthage was named *Bozra*. *Bozra* meant "fortress" in Phoenician but sounded like the Greek *byrsa* (oxhide) and most likely the tale was fabricated by some ancient Greek seeking to explain a fort named Oxhide.

cut to the quick. The QUICK in this sense is the most sensitive or tender flesh in the body, such as the flesh under the fingernails. The word derives from the Anglo-Saxon *cwicu*, "alive or living," as do the adverb and adjective *quick*. *Cut to the quick* means to cut through the skin to sensitive, tender living tissue and, figuratively, to hurt someone deeply. It has been used both ways (by Shakespeare, Dryden, Swift, Defoe) since the early 16th century, sometimes in the form of *galled*, *touched*, or *stung to the quick*. Other instances of *quick* used in the sense of "living" are the biblical phrase the *quick and the dead* ("the living and the dead"), the phrase *quick with child* ("pregnant with living child"), and QUICKSILVER.

cutty; Cutty Sark. *Cutty* means anything short in Scottish English, a short person, a short-tempered person, etc. *Cutty Sark* is the name of a famous 19th century British tea clipper that took its name from Robert Burns's poem "Tam O'Shanter," in which a young witch wearing only a "cutty sark" (a short shift or nightgown) chases a Scottish farmer.

cut up (or split) the melon. This means to divide the spoils or profits of any kind, each person getting a slice of the tasty melon, or profits. Surprisingly, it is a relatively recent term, dating back only to 1906 or so, when it arose as Wall Street jargon for the distribution of extra, unexpected dividends to stockholders.

c.v. Short for *curriculum vitae*, generally called a résumé. "He asked me to send my c.v." The term *c.v.* has currency in the U.S. chiefly among academics.

cyclamen; sowbread. Here is a plant named for the shape of its bulbous roots, *cyclamen* deriving from the Greek *kyklos*, "circle." *Sowbread*, the plant's common name, referred to the fact that its fleshy roots were once fed to pigs.

cyclone. In December 1789 great storm waves claimed 20,000 lives in Coringa, India. Writing about the disaster 49 years later, British East India company official Henry Piddington coined the word *cyclone* for such a storm. Piddington thought he was using the Greek word for "the coil of a snake" in his coinage, "this expressing sufficiently the tendency to circular motion in these meteors," but he actually used the Greek for "circle," or "moving in a wide, whirling manner."

cymling. A stupid person is called a cymling head after the small, round variety of melon or squash called the cymling (*Cucurbita pepo melopepo*). In the U.S. the melon is often called a "simling," which better shows its origins—its name derives from its shape resembling the fruitcake called a simnel cake. Other names for the cymling are the scallop squash and the pattycake squash.

Cymru. The Welsh name for Wales, pronounced Kim-rue. The Cymry (pronounced Kim-ree) are the Welsh people.

cynic. Disciples of the Greek philosopher Antisthenes (born ca. 440 B.C.), especially his later followers such as Diogenes, were nicknamed *kunikos* (*cynikos*), "doglike" or "snarlers," for their insolent, currish manners. Antisthenes and his pupils believed that independent virtue formed the sole basis for happiness, scorning freedom, honor, art, learning, health, riches—life itself. Insolently self-righteous, this small but influential band of ascetics derided all social customs, even sleeping in kennel-like quarters. From their churlishness and rude manners we probably have our word *cynic*, meaning "a surly, sarcastic person who believes that only selfishness motivates human behavior." It is possible, however, that this nickname is only a coincidence and that *cynic* derives from *Cynosarges* ("white dog"), the Greek gymnasium outside Athens where Antisthenes taught; or perhaps each word contributed to the other. (The gymnasium was supposedly named for a white dog that carried off part of a victim being offered to the gods.)

cynosure. Someone or something at the center of attention, such as a beautiful woman ("She was the cynosure of all eyes").

Cynosure derives from *kunosoura*, "dog's tail," the name the ancient Greeks gave to the constellation Ursa Minor, whose tail contains the North Star. Since navigators from earliest times used the North Star to guide them and were constantly observing it, *cynosure* came to mean anything that attracts attention.

cypress. An old legend tells of Cyparissus, a young friend of Apollo who died of grief because he killed Apollo's favorite stag. Cyparissus was transformed by the god into a cypress tree. Once cut, the cypress never grows again, which probably led to its being dedicated to Pluto, the king of the infernal regions in Roman mythology. For this reason the beautiful *Cupressus funebris* was often planted in cemeteries along the Mediterranean, and its wood was used to make coffins. The Romans placed a branch of cypress in front of their houses when a friend died, and the Turks customarily plant a cypress on the graves of loved ones. Cypress wood can last for hundreds of years. According to one story, the cypress gates of St. Peter's Church in Rome lasted from the time of Constantine to that of Pope Eugene III—more than 1,110 years—with no decay.

Cyprus. *Cyprus* was an important source of copper in ancient times, so much so that the country takes its name from the Greek word for copper.

Cyrano de Bergerac. The most famous proboscis in history. Anyone with a prodigious nose is likely to be called a Cyrano de Bergerac after the eponymous hero of Edmond Rostand's play of the same name (1897). Rostand's hero was based on the very real Savinien Cyrano de Bergerac (1619–55), who had a nose as long as his fictional counterpart's and whose exploits were even more remarkable. The historical Cyrano was a brave soldier, great lover, and eloquent, influential writer of comedies and tragedies. This swaggering swordsman fought countless duels with those foolish enough to insult or even mention his nose, and his duel single-handedly against 100 enemies while serving as an officer in the Guards is a well-documented fact. Cyrano's exploits became legend long before Rostand fictionalized him. Surprisingly, he did not perish on the wrong end of a sword. Cyrano died as a result of a wound caused by a falling beam or stone while staying at the home of a friend.

czar; tsar; tsarina; etc. When Julius Caesar died, his proper name was adopted by the Roman emperors, beginning with Augustus, and retained until the fall of the Holy Roman Empire. The title later came to be adopted by various European countries with minor changes in spelling. *Czar* or *tsar* can be traced to the old Slavic word *cesare*, deriving from "Caesar" and introduced into Russia in the 15th century as a title. The word, first spelled *tsear*, was applied to all Russian rulers after Ivan the Terrible assumed it officially to describe his rule as king of Poland. The Russian tsar was considered to be appointed by God as head of church and state, his authority unlimited by laws of any kind; his wife was called the tsarina, his son the tsarevitch, and his daughter the tsarevna. Today *czar* is often used for "any tyrannical despot with absolute power," a czarist being anyone who believes in such a system of government. Spelling of the word varies in both British and American dictionaries—neither form is accepted by all authorities in either country.

D

D. The letter *D* can be traced back to the ancient Phoenician and Hebrew alphabets, where it also had the shape of a rude archway or door (in Hebrew it is called *daleth*, "a door"). *See* DELTA.

d (for pence). Why is the British written abbreviation for pence or pennies *d* and for the pound *L*? The abbreviations actually go back to Roman times in Britain when the Latin *denarius*, "penny," was shortened to *d* and *libra*, "pound," was shortened to *l*.

D (River). This river, usually called the D, flowing into the Pacific Ocean from Devil's Lake in Lincoln City, Oregon, is the shortest-named body of water anywhere. For the longest-named body of water *see* LAKE WEBSTER.

Da. A widely used Irish term meaning a father, grandfather, or any respected elderly man. *Da* is the title of an award-winning play later made into a motion picture.

dachshund. This low-to-the-ground, sausage-shaped dog dates back at least to the early Egyptians, but it took its name from the German *Dachs*, "badger," plus *Hund*, "hound," "badger hound." The breed was originally used in Germany for hunting badgers.

Dada. An artistic and literary movement founded in Switzerland in 1916 that flouted conventional values and advocated works marked by nonsense and incongruity. The child's word *dada* for a plaything admirably suited the group's purpose and was adopted, according to the old story, by one member randomly opening a dictionary and pointing randomly to the word. According to the tale, artist Tristan Tzara made the selection and (surely one of the most exact descriptions of the coining of a word) he made it at 6:00 P.M., February 8, 1916, at the Terrace Cafe in Zurich.

Daedal, Daedalist. *See* LABYRINTH.

daffodil. No one knows why people began to call the flower asphodel, which carpeted Elysium, an affodill, in the 15th century. But the mispronunciation stuck and eventually *affodill* was corrupted further to *daffodil*, which remains the flower's name today. The best explanation, according to the *O.E.D.*, is that the change was "due to childish or playful distortions, as in *Ted* for *Edward* or *tante* for *aunt*..." *Daffodil* and *narcissus*, though there are differences between them, are often used interchangeably for *daffodil*. The narcissus takes its name from the mythological youth who was so enamored of his own reflection that after long gazing at it he was changed into the flower. The "dainty daffodil," the "lamp of beauty," is perhaps English lyric poetry's favorite flower next to roses and rosebuds, from Herrick's "Fair daffodils, we weep to see/You haste away so soon"; to Wordsworth's host "of golden daffodils;/Beside the lake, beneath the trees,/Fluttering and dancing in the breeze.../Continuous as the stars that shine.../Tossing their heads in sprightly dance..." *See also* NARCISSUS.

dago; wop; guinea. *Dago* is an offensive word that may derive from the name of a saint. Mencken traces this disparaging term to 1832, when it was used in Louisiana to describe a Spaniard, not an Italian. But *dago* is a corruption of the very common Spanish name Diego, or alludes to St. Diego, Spain's patron saint, or both. *Diego* was used in Elizabethan times for a "swarthy" Spanish or Portuguese seaman. As recently as the beginning of this century the word also meant the Italian language, as well as a professor or student of Italian. The pejorative term is not heard as often today as its derivative, *dago red*, "any cheap wine." *Dago* may also come from "day come, day go," a term reputedly used by early Italian laborers in expressing their patient philosophy. Far more offensive is *wop*, which arose toward the end of the 19th century. This ugly word comes from a relatively innocuous one, the Neapolitan *guappo*, a term used by immigrant laborers signifying a showy, pretentious person. Similarly, the offensive *guinea* may have originally referred to Italian laborers working for the equivalent of a guinea a day.

daguerreotype. *See* DIORAMA.

dahlia. Over 14,000 named varieties of dahlias have been cultivated and crossed from the single plant that the German naturalist, Baron Alexander von Humboldt, discovered in Mexico in 1789. Sent to Spain in that year, the specimen was named there by the head of Madrid's Botanic Garden, Professor Cavanilles. But Cavanilles named the plant for a fellow professor, ignoring Humboldt. Thus the entire *Dahlia* genus honors the Swedish botanist and pupil of Linnaeus, Anders Dahl (1751–89), who had died at about the time the flower was discovered. The first single-flowered dahlia bore little resemblance to the giant, colorful, double-flowered species so important in gardens today. There was, incidentally, a time in the 19th century when dahlia roots were touted as an excellent substitute for potatoes. They were easy to grow and unsusceptible to blight, said their advocates, but unfortunately no one seemed to like the way they tasted.

daily bread. The essentials, the food or money needed in order to live. The common term is from the Lord's Prayer (Matt. 6:9): "… Give us this day our daily bread."

daisy; fresh as a daisy; up-see-daisy. *Daisy* still sounds like the Old English word for the flower, "day's eye," or "eye of the day." *Bellis perennis* was so named in allusion to its appearance and because it closes its ray in the evening to conceal the flower's yellow disk, and opens it again in the morning. *Fresh as a daisy* is first recorded in Captain Frederick Marryat's *Peter Simple* (1833), but there is no telling if he coined the phrase. The daisy takes its scientific name *Bellis* from a Roman legend about Belides, one of the Dryads. Vortumnus, the god of orchards, beheld and admired Belides dancing in the fields and pursued her. Wishing to escape him, she was changed into the little flower called *bellis* by the Romans. *Up-see-daisy*, a variation on the earlier *up-a-daisy*, is a playful term said when lifting a small child up into the air, often by the arms. The "daisy" could refer to the little child, pretty or delicate as a flower plucked from the earth, although the *Oxford English Dictionary* prosaically suggests that the word is patterned on "lack-a-daisy" and "lack-a-day." In any case, the term is first recorded in Jonathan Swift's *Journal to Stella* (1721): "Come stand away, let me rise … So-up-a-dazy." Other variations include "oop-a-daisy," "up-see-day," "up-see-daddy" and "up-a-deedies."

daisy cutter. A 15,000-pound U.S. bomb that explodes just above the ground. The euphemistic name was first heard during the war on terrorism in 2001.

Dallia blackfish. A tasty fish named in honor of William Healey Dall (1845–1927), an authority on marine life for the Smithsonian Institution. Dall wrote one of the first books on Alaska's immense resources, and the edible blackfish of Alaska called the Dallia, a species of the genus *Dalliidae*, does honor to his pioneer work in the territory.

dalmatian. The spotted coach dog and fire dog of the past originated in Dalmatia on what is now Croatia's Adriatic Sea coast.

daltonism. So determined was British scientist John Dalton (1766–1844) to solve the mystery of color blindness that he willed his eyes for study after his death. His pioneering paper, "Extraordinary Facts Relating to the Vision of Colours" (1794), is the earliest account of the problem, based on observations of himself, his brother, and other similarly afflicted persons. As a result of his descriptions, *daltonism* became a synonym for color blindness, especially the inability to distinguish between the colors red and green. One of the great pioneers in science, the industrious Dalton also kept a meteorological diary in which he entered 200,000 observations over 57 years. This diary both resulted in a remarkable book on weather conditions (*Meteorological Observations and Essays*, 1793) and contained the germs of his atomic theory, Dalton's major scientific contribution and the basis of modern chemistry.

dam. *Dam* for the female or mother of a horse, sheep, or other animals is simply a shortening of the word *dame*. It is first recorded in 1330.

damask rose. Brought to England as a present for Henry VIII by his physician in about 1540, the famous damask rose is named for the Syrian city of Damascus. Long used in making attar of roses, *Rosa damascena* was then only pink in color, which led poets to write of fair ladies with damask complexions. *See* ROSE. It is generally thought that Damascus is the oldest city in the world, dating back more than 2,000 years before Christ. It was while traveling to Damascus that Saul (St. Paul) became a convert to Christianity, giving us the expression *the road to Damascus* for any sudden personal conversion.

Dame Partington. English politician and author Sydney Smith alluded to the legendary Dame Partington in an 1831 speech condemning the opposition of the House of Lords to reform measures. Dame Partington had tried to mop up the Atlantic Ocean, which was flooding her cottage in Devon. Thanks to Smith, her name became synonymous for "anyone futilely trying to hold back progress or natural forces."

Damien's bed of steel. "Such was the end," wrote an eyewitness, "of that poor unfortunate who it may well be believed suffered the greatest tortures that a human being has ever been called on to endure." He was referring to the public execution of Robert-François Damien (1715–57), the madman who tried to assassinate France's Louis XV and inflicted a slight knife wound on the monarch. Early that morning Damien had been racked and wounded deeply with glowing forceps, his torturers pouring molten lead, boiling oil, pitch, and sulphur into his open wounds. His screams never ceased and the stench pervaded the entire court, but many of the thousands who turned out to witness the "spectacle" applauded the prisoner's agonies. Damien's limbs were finally ripped off one by one in the Place de Greve, the man suffering longer because four wild horses couldn't pull him apart and two more had to found. Until nine o'clock at night the pathetic creature stayed alive, and it is said that his black hair turned completely white, that his rump still twitched up until the moment what was left of him was burned at the stake. Damien's bed of steel has become a symbol for the barbaric, sadistic cruelty he suffered.

damn. Though it is first recorded in the 16th century *damn* is a much older oath than that. It derives ultimately from the Latin *damnare*, to condemn. As mild an oath and commonly used as it is, *damn* is still often considered an objectionable word in many quarters.

Damnation Alley.   An alley in Boston so named because it was wide enough for only one oxcart, so that whenever two teamsters met going in opposite directions the air was blue with *damns* and much stronger curses.

damned if you do, damned if you don't.   Early American evangelist Lorenzo Dow (d. 1834) coined these words while condemning other preachers who "make the Bible clash and contradict itself, by preaching somewhat like this: 'You can and you can't—You shall and you shan't—You will and you won't—And you will be damned if you do—And you will be damned if you don't.' "

Damn the torpedoes! Full speed ahead!   *See* TORPEDO.

damn with faint praise.   Alexander Pope invented this phrase when satirizing the scholar and author Joseph Addison as Atticus in 1723. The full paradox is seldom quoted anymore but Pope wrote that "Atticus" would:

> Damn with faint praise, assent with civil leer,
> And, without sneering, teach the rest to sneer.

Damn Yankee.   *See* PEDDLER.

Damon and Pythias (Phinotias).   Two ancient Greeks of the early fourth century whose names became proverbial for devoted friends. In the Greek version of the legend, Phinotias (Pythias) was condemned to death by the tyrant Dionysus. Damon offered himself as a hostage so that his friend could make a last visit home. True to his word, Phinotias returned, but Damon insisted that his own head be put on the block, so impressing the monarch that he freed both the philosophers and begged to be allowed to join their brotherhood. The phrase should therefore be Phinotias and Damon, but when Richard Edwards wrote his play *Damon and Pythias* in 1564, he turned the tale around, using the corruption *Pythias* instead of *Phinotias*, and it was from this source that the story became popular.

Damson plum.   *See* PLUM.

dance hall hostess.   Western dance halls like Dodge City's *Variety* were often combined saloons, gambling houses, and brothels. By the 1870s, *dance hall hostess* became a euphemism for prostitutes like the Variety's Squirrel-Tooth Colie, Big Nose Kate, and Hambone Jane.

dandelion.   "Lion's tooth"—referring to the plant's indented leaf—was the old English name for this flower, but apparently some language snob gave it the French name *dent de lion* in the 16th century. Since the French *dent de* was pronounced *dan de*, the word soon became *dandelion*. Another theory is that the dandelion's name derives not from its indented leaves, but from its huge, white, toothlike root. In modern French the dandelion is called *pissenlit*, or "wet-the-bed," from the belief that eating dandelion greens at dinner results in nocturnal bedwetting. "If you can't beat 'em, eat 'em" is a phrase that has been applied over the years to the gardener's perennial battle against weeds,

most recently by Dr. James Duke, a botanist at the U.S. Department of Agriculture. Dr. Duke, quoted in Anne Raver's gardening column in the *New York Times*, made the remark specifically in reference to dandelions, which make a dandy salad and wine, among other comestibles. But the words have been applied to garden insects as well. The best example is a little book by English farmer V. M. Holt entitled *Why Not Eat Insects* (1885). "The insects eat up every blessed green thing that do grow and us farmers starve," Holt reasoned. "Well, eat *them* and grow fat." He then proceeded to give a series of appropriate recipes, including "Fried soles with woodlouse sauce," "curried cockchafers," "fricasse of chicken with chrysalids," "boiled neck of mutton with wireworm sauce," "cauliflowers garnished with caterpillars," and "moths on toast." Nutritionists today say that insects could be a useful protein supplement to the human diet. Locusts, for example, are said to be about 75 percent protein and 20 percent fat, as well as being rich in some vitamins.

dander.   *See* GET ONE'S DANDER UP.

Daniel Boone.   "A good gun, a good horse, and a good wife," in that order, were the ingredients for Daniel Boone's prescription for happiness. The American pioneer's name has long been synonymous with a frontiersman, an intrepid explorer or hunter, and a resourceful backwoodsman. Boone's accomplishments have been exaggerated in popular accounts, but there is no doubt that his explorations opened the way for millions. Born near Reading, Pennsylvania, the great folk hero moved to North Carolina with his Quaker family in his early years. After serving under British General Braddock as a wagoner, he explored Florida, and fought as a lieutenant colonel of militia during the American Revolution, among many other activities. But his major contribution was the blazing of the famous Wilderness Road, which he and a band of 30 men forged in March, 1775, to found Boonesboro on the Kentucky River. Daniel and his wife, Rebecca, figure in more frontier lore than any other pioneers, and he has been commemorated in numerous place names. Boone was 86 when he died in 1820, a legend in his own time.

a Daniel in the lion's den.   Someone who braves great danger out of faith and courage. The Old Testament prophet Daniel, of the Book of Daniel, prayed to God in violation of King Darius's order and was sealed in a den of lions. When the king went to the door the next morning, he found the seals unbroken and Daniel very much alive. "O king live for ever," Daniel told him. "My God hath sent his angel, and hath shut the lions' mouths, and they have not hurt me. . . ."

Danish pastry.   Often shortened to *Danish*, this sweet buttery pastry made with raised dough was named not after a country but for the Danish baker, who made them at Gertner's restaurant in Manhattan a century ago. The Danes in Denmark used the expression *Vienna bread* at the time, as they still do.

D'Annunzio.   A synonym for a great lover and adventurer. Gabriele D'Annunzio's prose style was admired by James Joyce, and his play *Le Martyre de Saint Sebastien* was set to music by Claude Debussy, but the Italian poet, playwright, and novelist, who died in 1938, age 75, is better remembered today for his sexual and military adventures than for his lyric writings. D'Annunzio's whole life was onstage. His spectacular exploits by sea and air were widely reported in the press when he fought for the Allies during World War I. He is the only playwright (if not director) ever to become an actual dictator—for two years beginning in 1919, when he and his small volunteer force occupied the city of Fiume. His sexual adventures were legion, making Casanova look like an amateur. Stating that "a good soldier is prepared for anything," D'Annunzio carried condoms into battle in Napoleon's snuffbox, which he had won as a prize of war. There are legends that he rode to the hounds in the raw with a naked lady at the front of his saddle, nonchalantly strode nude into the dining room of an illustrious hotel, slept on a pillow filled with locks of hair from his conquests, served wine from a carafe made from the skull of a virgin who had committed suicide because of him, and used strychnine as an aphrodisiac. Once he boasted that he had eaten a roasted baby. D'Annunzio, whose most famous affair was with the great actress Eleonora Duse (about whom he wrote a callous tell-all biography), publicly boasted that he was "hated by a thousand husbands." It is said that but for his often "swinish behavior," he would have won the 1926 Nobel Prize in literature. *See* CASANOVA.

danse macabre. *See* MACABRE.

darb. Not much heard anymore, *darb* was common in the 1920s and 1930s for someone or something excellent, superior. It is said to have derived from the name of Ruby Darb, a voluptuous Oklahoma showgirl after whom many oilmen named new gushers.

darbies. *Darbies* is a British expression for handcuffs, but the word, oddly enough, derives from the name of a usurer. It seems that a shrewd 16th-century lawyer and moneylender named Derby drew up an ironclad bond that left no loopholes for debtors to escape through. This contract, used extensively by usurers, came to be called father Derbie's bands. Because they were also impossible to "unlock" it wasn't long before all manacles were known as *derbies*, too, the word often pronounced *darbies. Darbies* is first recorded in 1576, and no other plausible explanation has been offered for its derivation.

Darby and Joan.

> Old Darby, with Joan by his side,
>   You're often regarded with wonder:
> He's dropsical, she is sore-eyed,
>   Yet they're never happy asunder.

This verse was printed in the *Gentleman's Magazine* in 1735 under the title of "The Joys of Love Never Forgot: a song." The ballad, whose anonymous author may have been poet Henry Woodfall, praises, in a number of stanzas, Darby and Joan, whose names have come to stand for any mutually affectionate and contented old married couple. The poet, if he did write the verse, probably patterned his pair on John and Joan Darby who lived in Bartholomew Close, London. Woodfall had served an apprenticeship under John Darby, a printer, who, with his wife, was widely known for his good works and faithfulness.

dark. Said of any theater that is closed, or in which no performances are being given, as in, "The theaters in the city are dark on Sundays." The term apparently dates back to the turn of the 19th century.

the dark and bloody ground. *See* KENTUCKY.

dark horse. A wonderful story is told about a swift, coal-black horse named Dusky Pete who belonged to Tennessean Sam Flyn. Sam made an easy living riding his horse from town to town and entering him in local races, which Dusty Pete, who looked like a lame plug, always won handily, Sam collecting his bets and going on to his next conquest. But the story is fable as far as scholars are concerned. *Dark horse* was first recorded in England, not America, in about 1830. Benjamin Disraeli used it in his *The Young Duke* (1831) as a racing term indicating more than the color of the horse: "A dark horse, which had never been thought of, rushed past the grand stand in sweeping triumph." Given Disraeli's widespread popularity as a novelist and public figure, it wasn't very long before the term was introduced in American politics to describe a candidate about whom little is known or who wins unexpectedly. The Democratic Convention of 1844 produced the first political *dark horse* in James Polk, who went on to become president, and the term was in wide use by 1865.

dark meat; white meat. These were originally American euphemisms for the leg and the breast, respectively, of turkey and other fowl, *leg* and *breast* being embarrassing words in Victorian times. The words are still frequently used, but descriptively now and not euphemistically.

Darley Arabian. *See* BYERLY TURK.

Darlingtonia. When an insect enters the pitcher-shaped leaves of the curious California pitcher plant, *Darlingtonia*, it is trapped by down-pointing hairs, which allow it to crawl in but not out. Then it is drowned in liquid from the leaves, and, according to some scientists, ultimately is eaten or digested by the plant. Not a particularly wholesome thing to have named after one, but the single specie's scientific name honors William Darlington (1782–1863), an American botanist who wrote several biographies of famous botanists and published *American Weeds and Useful Plants* (1859). The naming was done by a fellow botanist, John Torrey, there being no record of bad feelings between the two men. *Darlingtonia* is sometimes sold as *Chrysamphora californica* and is not the only insectivorous plant. These include the famous Venus's flytrap, bladderwort, sundew, butterwort, and pitcher plants belonging to the genus *Sarracenia*, all varying in the ways they capture their prey.

darn. *Darnation* is recorded as a euphemism for *damnation* as early as 1798, with *darn* recorded not long after. Some early scholars held that *darn* derived from *derne*, the Middle English word for secret, while others claimed it was an aphetic form of *eternal*, with the *er* pronounced as in the British *clerk (clark)*.

d'Artagnan. Memoirs attributed to Charles de Batz-Castelmore d'Artagnan (ca. 1623–73) were used by the novelist Alexander Dumas père in his fictional series beginning with *The Three Musketeers*. In real life Gascon d'Artagnan did serve in the king's musketeers, but he wasn't a *comte*, as he called himself, claiming the title without right. About all that can be verified about the man is that he captained the contingent that arrested the powerful French superintendent of finances Nicolas Fouquet in 1661, became a brigadier general nine years later, and was fatally wounded at the siege of Maastricht. Yet d'Artagnan will always be remembered for the heroic adventures Dumas and his collaborator Maquet adapted or created from his story.

darts.   *Dart* for a pointed missile or spear is first recorded in 1314, deriving from the French *dart* meaning the same. The indoor game called darts, in which small darts are thrown at a target, isn't recorded in England until 1901, though this game, so popular in British pubs, must be much older.

Darwinian.   "A hairy quadruped, furnished with a tail and pointed ears, probably arboreal in habits." So Charles Robert Darwin (1809–82) described our common ancestor in *The Descent of Man* (1871), which didn't sound at all like Adam or Eve. The epochal theory of evolution was formulated by Darwin in his *On the Origin of the Species by Means of Natural Selection* (1859), *The Descent of Man*, and other works. Evidence gathered during a five-year cruise to South America and the Galapagos Islands as a naturalist aboard the *Beagle* (1831–36) enabled Darwin to confirm organic evolution, and to propose his theory of natural selection, which he explained 20 years later. Darwin deduced that all species descended from a few primal ancestors and that favorable variations within a species better enabled it to survive—*the survival of the fittest*, as Herbert Spencer called the process. Special development and natural selection, he explained, not special creations, accounted for the diversity of species on earth. The Darwinian theory is widely known and accepted today, but provoked a storm of controversy in the 19th century in both religious and scientific circles.

dash; dash it!   The dash (—) has probably been used as a euphemism to suggest words not in favor at least since the invention of the printing press. In fact, the euphemistic curse dash it! is a euphemism based on d—m, a printed form of *damn*. Sometimes the dash is used by itself, but it most often is accompanied by a letter or two. D. H. Lawrence, in principle as opposed to the euphemistic use of the dash as any person, used it this way in his satirical poem "My Naughty Book" (1930), which begins:

> They say I wrote a naughty book
> With perfectly awful things in it,
> putting in all the impossible words
> like b—— and f—- and sh—.

The book he refers to is *Lady Chatterley's Lover* (1928), not a dash in it. The dash that ends Laurence Sterne's *A Sentemental Journey* (1768) has the distinction of being the first (and perhaps only) dash to end a novel and the only dash that is listed in a dictionary (Farmer and Henley's *Slang and Its Analogues*, 1890). The novel ends: ". . . so that, when I stretched out my hand, I caught hold of the fille-de-chambre's ————."

date.   Date palms from the Mediterranean area were introduced to America by Spanish missionaries in the early 1700s. The fruit of this palm takes its name from the Latin *dactylus*,

"finger," as people in ancient times believed it resembled the human finger. The date has been called "the candy that grows on trees" because about half its weight is sugar. Thousands of acres of date trees grow in California's Coachella Valley. Their large bunches of fruit are wrapped in heavy paper to protect them from insects and moisture, and helicopters periodically hover over the groves to fan away dampness. A merely "average" date palm produces about 100 pounds of fruit a year. In times past, dates were cheaper than grain in some regions, and the tree was said to have 360 uses, ranging from fermented drinks made from its sap to the "cabbage" consisting of the new foliage sprouting from its crown. *See* PHOENIX TREE.

Datsun.   The Japanese car, first made in 1913 by the forerunner of Nissan Motors, was originally named Dat, after the initials of its three owners, Messrs. *D*en, *A*yoyama, and *T*akeuchi. Later *Dat* was changed to *Datson*, the *son* meant to suggest "the son of Dat." But the Japanese pronunciation of *son* sounded too much like the Japanese word for "loss," something no business would want to suggest, and in 1932 the name was changed to Datsun.

davenport.   In American *davenport* generally means a large, often convertible sofa, while in England it is a small desk or escritoire. The British meaning came first and nobody is sure where the word derives from. *Webster's* attributes it to its original 19th-century manufacturer, another source to "a Captain Davenport who first commissioned it," and a third to "some now forgotten craftsman." The word, for a desk, was first recorded in 1853 and most likely honors an English furniture maker of ca. 1820–40. The sofa may have been devised by another manufacturer of the same name.

David and Goliath.   *See* GOLIATH.

Davis Cup.   While still an undergraduate at Harvard in 1900, American statesman and sportsman Dwight Filley Davis (1879–1945) donated a silver cup to be presented as a national trophy to that country winning an international championship contest in lawn tennis. The cup still bears his name.

Davisdom.   *See* LINCOLNDOM.

davit.   Since the 14th century *davit* has meant a cranelike device used for supporting, raising, and lowering boats and anchors from a ship. Formerly called a David, the device is thought to take its name from the proper name David. Several tools at the time were called Davids and they may or may not have been named for a specific person or persons.

Davite.   *See* DAVY LAMP.

davy; I'll take my davy of it.   In England *davy* has been used for *affidavit* since at least 1764, which gives us the common extension *I'll take my davy of it*: I'll vouch that it's true.

Davy Crockett.   David (Davy) Crockett, as the song goes, was "a son of the wild frontier" from his earliest years. Born in 1786 in Limestone, Tennessee, Davy was hired out to a passing cattle driver by his Irish immigrant father when only 12; he wandered the frontier until he turned 15, before finally returning home. He became a colonel in the Tennessee militia under Andrew Jackson during the Creek War, and after serving as a justice of the peace and state legislator, acted on a humorous suggestion that he run for Congress in 1827. Much to his surprise, he won the election. Crockett served two terms in Congress, and was noted in Washington for his backwoods dress and shrewd native humor, though many of the comments often attributed to him are largely apocryphal. His motto was "Be sure you are right, then go ahead." When defeated for reelection in 1835—mainly because he opposed Jacksonian banking and Indian policies—he moved to Texas, where he joined the Texas war for independence from Mexico. On March 6, 1836, Colonel Crockett was killed with the defenders of the Alamo. The folk hero's famous autobiography, *A Narrative of the Life of David Crockett of the State of Tennessee* (1834), was probably dictated, but is written in his robust style, complete with many examples of the tall tale.

Davy Jones's locker.   Since at least 1750 *gone to Davy Jones's locker* has been used by sailors to indicate death, especially death by drowning, but no one has yet fathomed the origins of the phrase. In *The Adventures of Peregrine Pickle* (1751) Tobias Smollett wrote: "I'll be damned if it was not Davy Jones himself. I know him by his saucer eyes, his three rows of teeth and tail, and the blue smoke that came out of his nostrils." This same Davy Jones, according to mythology of sailors is the fiend that presides over all the evil spirits of the deep, and is often seen in various shapes, perching among the rigging on the eve of hurricanes, shipwrecks, and other disasters to which seafaring life is exposed, warning the devoted wretch of death and woe. The original Davy Jones may have been the 16th-century owner of an English pub, commemorated in the ballad "Jones Ale is Newe," who stored his ale in a mysterious locker for some reason much feared by seamen. Or *Jones* could be a corruption of Jonah, the unlucky biblical character swallowed by a whale, and *Davy* the Anglicization of the West Indian word *duppy*, meaning "a malevolent ghost or devil." A third, more plausible explanation proposes the Jonah above for *Jones*, but derives *Davy* from St. David, the partron saint of Wales often invoked by Welsh sailors. Jonah was indeed considered bad luck to the sailors aboard the vessel on which he was attempting to flee God's wrath and the phrase was first recorded in Captain Francis Grose's *Classical Dictionary of the Vulgar Tongue* (1785) as *David Jones' Locker*, which lends still more support to the Welsh patron saint theory. The *locker* in the phrase probably refers to an ordinary seaman's chest, not the old pub owner's mysterious locker.

Davy lamp; Davy Medal; davite.   Sir Humphry Davy, who "abominated gravy" (*see* CLERIHEW), invented the *Davy lamp* and has the mineral ore *davite* named in his honor. The great English chemist (1778–1829) invented the safety lamp for miners in 1816; largely outmoded today, it is a flame enclosed in a fine-meshed wire cage that prevents high heat from escaping and has saved thousands of lives that would have been lost due to the igniting of explosive gases. Like Madame Curie, the largely self-educated genius refused to take out a patent for his discovery. Among his myriad scientific achievements were his electrical theory of chemical affinity, said to be 100 years before its time; the discovery of the anesthetic effect of "laughing gas"; the isolation of the alkali metals potassium and sodium; the

isolation of calcium, barium, strontium, magnesium, and boron; and the discovery that chlorine is an element. Davy was presented with an expensive silver dinner service by grateful coal mine owners for his invention of the Davy lamp. In his will he decreed that it be melted down and sold, interest from the proceeds to be used to establish the *Davy Medal* of the Royal Society, "given annually for the most important discovery in chemistry made in Europe or Anglo-America."

day clean.   There are many colorful poetic terms for dawn in English, including daylight, daybreak, and dayspring. One of the most unusual is *day clean*, often heard in the Bahamas: "He start at day clean for the job."

a day late, a dollar short.   An old saying describing someone or something that just misses being successful. The term dates back at least a century.

daymare.   On first coming across the word, you might think it a recent coinage by some whimsical writer tuned into the times. But *daymare*, patterned after NIGHTMARE and referring to a similar condition occurring during wakefulness, goes back to at least the early 18th century. It was probably invented by English author Matthew Green in his poem "The Spleen" (1737), which praised the contemplative life as a cure for boredom:

> The daymare Spleen,
> by whose false pleas
> Men prove suicides in ease . . .

Coleridge confessed that he had daymares, an English medical writer called daymares "attacks of imperfect catalepsy," and James Russell Lowell implored:

> Help me to tame these wild day-mares
> That sudden on me unawares.

day of infamy.   "Yesterday, December 7, 1941, a date which will live in world history, the United States was simultaneously and deliberately attacked by naval and air forces of the Empire of Japan." So began the first draft of Franklin Delano Roosevelt's historic Pearl Harbor speech, which he wrote himself. In the second draft FDR substituted the infinitely better "infamy" for "world history" and "suddenly" for "simultaneously," making a sentence that will live in world history.

days of wine and roses.   *See* GONE WITH THE WIND.

D-day.   June 6, 1944, the day Allied forces invaded France during World War II. D-day does not mean Designated Day, as is commonly believed. The *D* in the term is a redundancy, simply standing for "day"; thus *D-day* literally means *Day Day*. According to *Time magazine* (June 12, 1944): ". . . so far as the U.S. Army can determine, the first use of D for Day, H for Hour was in Field Order No. 8, of the first Army A.E.F., issued on Sept. 20, 1918 [during World War I], which read, 'The First Army will attack at H-Hour on D-Day with the object of forcing the evacuation of the St. Mihiel Salient.' "

dead as a dodo; dodo.   The hapless dodo left behind as its epitaph both its common name, which has become a synonym for stupidity and extinction, and its scientific name *Didus ineptus*, which says about the same for it. Barely a century after it was discovered by man on the islands of Reunion and Mauritius, east of Madagascar, the heavy, flightless bird became extinct. Dodoes were not only big (larger than a swan), but they were barely able to run, and the colonists who settled the islands, along with their pigs, found them delicious. By the early 18th century gone was the short-winged bird that seemed "to have been invented for the sole purpose of becoming extinct," leaving behind only its sad story and a synonym for something utterly gone or a hopelessly dumb person. *Dodo* is a corruption of the Portuguese *dondo*, silly.

dead as a doornail. Since ordinary nails aren't used in making doors, perhaps the "nail" in this phrase, which can be traced all the way back to 1350, was a small metal plate nailed on a door that visitors pounded with the knockers attached to it when announcing their arrival. Life would eventually be pounded out of the "nail" in that way. Then again the "nail" could be the heavy-handed decorative nails outer doors were studded with, though why these doornails would be regarded as any "deader" than, say, coffin nails is a mystery. It has even been suggested that since nails weren't ordinarily used for doors, the phrase means "dead as something that never existed." Anyway, people are still getting good mileage out of the expression, as did Langland in *Piers Plowman*, Shakespeare more than once, and Dickens in *A Christmas Carol*. *Dumb as a doornail* and *deaf as a doornail* are variations on the phrase that appeared after its coining.

deadbeat. Though *deadbeat* meant an exhausted, almost dead person at the beginning of the 19th century, by about 1863 it had become American slang for "a hobo or sponger riding the rails." The idea of hoboes not paying their way, riding trains free, inspired the present prevailing use of *deadbeat* for "someone who doesn't pay his debts."

deadbolt lock. A lock bolt moved into position by the turning of a knob or a key rather than by spring action. The British use the expression *mortise lock*, which has some currency in America, and *dead lock*.

dead cat on the line. Field workers for the *Dictionary of American Regional English* found 21 people who used this expression, meaning "there's something suspicious, something wrong"—but not one of them could explain it. When William Safire asked readers of his nationally syndicated word column for help, an old man in Louisiana scrawled a letter explaining that the expression has its roots in fishing for catfish, when trotlines with many hooks on them are set in the water. The lines are checked every day, so if a fisherman checks a neighbor's line and there's a dead catfish (cat) on the line he knows there's something wrong, something suspicious or fishy is going on.

dead-end (street); Dead End Kids. *Dead end* refers to a CUL-DE-SAC, a street with no exit except the way one came in. The term has also come to mean no hope of progress, advancement, etc. The Dead End Kids were a movie gang of young, often lovable hoodlums featured in a series of films beginning with *Dead End* (1937), originally a Broadway play featuring, among others, Leo Gorcey and Huntz Hall. They

lived and hung out at the end of a dead-end street on the East Side waterfront, where there were luxury apartments as well as tenements.

deadhead. A spectator who doesn't pay at the theater or at sports events, or one who rides free in a train or other public conveyance. Formed from the noun *deadhead*, the verb *to deadhead* means to drive an empty train, truck, or the like, one with no passengers or freight, on a return trip to a terminal. Most authorities agree that the term derives from railroad use. Conductors on passenger trains possibly counted heads to be sure every early passenger had paid and deducted from their total passengers, or heads, those who had free passes—the first *deadheads*. The gardening term to *deadhead*, to pull off spent blooms, is unrelated to the above; in this case the dead blooms are the dead "heads." In recent years the followers of the rock group The Grateful Dead were widely known as *deadheads*.

dead heat. Any contest—from an election to a horse race—that ends in a tie is called a dead heat. The expression was first used in British horseracing in the 1790s. As used here, *heat* means "a single course of a race," while *dead* suggests that the horses are "dead even," or completely even. A dead heat is a rarity in this age of electronic timing.

Dead Letter Office. A place where undeliverable letters (no return address, etc.) go. The U.S. Postal Service has long had no office of that name, changing it in 1994 to the Mail Recovery Center. But *Dead Letter Office* will live on in poem and story, especially in Herman Melville's "Bartleby the Scrivener" (1856), which suggests that Bartleby was a clerk in the Dead Letter Office, where its strange atmosphere may have affected his strange attitude toward life. Some critics hold that the neglect of Melville's novels led him to regard his work as "dead letters."

deadline. This expression has its origin in the infamous Confederate prison camp at Andersonville during the Civil War. There the deadline was a line marked 17 feet from the camp fence. Any prisoner who crossed that line was shot dead by the guards. It seems that newspaper reporters and editors were the first to use the word in its present sense of a time when a task must be finished. They applied it to the time when a story had to be completed; if the story wasn't in by that time, it was in effect killed or dead for that edition.

deadlock; wedlock. Though it wasn't applied to stalemates at political conventions until 1888 in America, *deadlock* was first used as a term for a complete standstill in Richard Sheridan's play *The Critic* (1779), which also gave us the word PUFFERY. *Deadlock*, for "a springless lock that opens with a key" came later. The *O.E.D.* suggests that the expression simply employs the word *dead* in its sense of obsolete, complete. Others have offered, without proof, the theory that *deadlock* comes from the ancient sport of wrestling, where a deadlock hold is one that keeps an opponent immobile indefinitely without forcing him to submit. *Holy deadlock* as a term for marriage comes from the title of A. P. Herbert's novel *Holy Deadlock* (1934), but the idea is anticipated by Byron's "A wedlock and a padlock mean the same." The *lock* in *wedlock*, however, is not a lock, deriving instead from *lac*, "a gift."

deadly nevergreen.   *The deadly nevergreen* has been a humorous term for the gallows in England since the late 18th century, because the gallows bears no leaves but "bears fruit all the year round."

deadly nightshade.   *See* BELLADONNA LILY.

dead man's flower.   A name heard in Canada and the U.S. for the beautiful spirea (*Spiraea latifola*). The name derives from the old folk belief that if a child picked this common white flower his or her father would die.

deadman's hand.   James Butler "Wild Bill" Hickok, only 39, had come to Deadwood, Dakota Territory, in 1876 to make a stake for the bride he had just taken, but lawless elements, fearing his appointment as town marshall, hired gunman Jack McCall to assassinate him, giving McCall 300 dollars and all the cheap whiskey he needed for courage. Wild Bill was playing cards in the No. 10 saloon (his back to the open door for only the second time in his days of gunfighting) when McCall sneaked in and shot him in the back of the head, the bullet passing through his brain and striking the cardplayer across the table from him in the arm. Hickok's last hand, which he held tight in a death grip, was aces and eights, which has ever since been called the deadman's hand. McCall, freed by a packed miner's court, was later convicted by a federal court, his plea of "double jeopardy" disregarded on the ground that the miner's court had no jurisdiction. He was later hanged for his crime.

deadman's vine.   Deadman's vine, also called ayahuasco, was used by Columbian Indians in religious rituals. A sip of the brew they made from this vine sends one into a deathlike coma. The woody vine is scientifically named *Banisteriopsis caapi* and today its bark is the source of the hallucinogenic alkaloid harmine.

dead men.   There is nothing new about this term for "empty beer or liquor bottles," which originated well before 1700, not in World War I, as has been suggested. It referred to the empty pots or bottles on the tables of English taverns when drinking bouts were held. Swift used the expression in his *Polite Conversations* (1738) and may give a clue to the word's origin: "Let him carry off the dead Men [the empty bottles], as we say in the army." In the army, where life is cheap, it would be appropriate to call bottles without any spirits dead men, after the spiritless bodies of the battlefield. In fact, the term is sometimes dead marines and dead soldiers today, these phrases dating back to World War I. *Dead soldiers* and *dead men* are also applied to empty beer cans, canned beer having been introduced by Coors in 1935.

dead men don't talk.   A saying common in the Wild West, perhaps from the Spanish saying *los muertos no hablan* with the same meaning.

deadpan.   *Pan* has been used since at least the early 19th century to mean "the face," possibly because the face is "broad, shallow and often open," as *Webster's* suggests, but just as likely because *pan* meant "the skull or head" as far back as the early 14th century and was used by Chaucer, among many much-read writers. (The word is still used in *brainpan*.) *Deadpan*, a

contemporary expression for an expressionless poker face, especially applied to comedians with a dry delivery, is just a combination of *pan* with *dead*, "unanimated." It has nothing to do with Elizabeth Barrett Browning's poem about the "great dead Pan," the god of Greek mythology who, legend says, died when Christ was crucified.

dead presidents.   Slang for paper money of any denomination, as all the presidents pictured on U.S. currency are dead because U.S. law forbids any living person's likeness on currency. The term was first recorded in New York's Harlem in 1944 and now is used throughout the country.

dead ringer.   *See* RINGER.

Dead Sea.   The Dead Sea, actually a salt lake in Palestine, is 51 miles long and 11 miles wide, falls to a depth of about 1,300 feet and is 26 percent salt, as opposed to about 3 or 4 percent in most oceans. Because its limpid blue-green water supports practically no life, the Romans named it the Mare Mortum, or Dead Sea.

Dead Sea fruit.   In days past the apple of Sodom was thought to grow along the Dead Sea, the mythical fruit beautiful to behold but turning to ashes when touched. From this belief arose the expression *Dead Sea fruit* for something promising that turns out to be worthless, the phrase first recorded in 1868 as the title of a novel but probably older.

Deadwood Dick.   *Deadwood Dick* became proverbial through many late 19th-century dime novels, especially those written by Edward L. Wheeler, and long stood for a fearless Indian scout and outlaw fighter. The prototype for Wheeler's westerns was Richard W. Clarke (1845–1930), who had been nicknamed Deadwood Dick long before his fictional exploits. Clarke, an Englishman attracted to the Black Hills by the gold diggings, won fame as both an Indian fighter and an express guard for gold shipped from the mines in and around Deadwood, South Dakota. Many of the Deadwood Dick myths have been debunked, but he was certainly a real character. Clarke lies in a mountain grave near Deadwood.

deaf as an adder.   The ancients believed that a serpent could protect itself against the music of snake charmers by holding one ear against the ground and sticking its tail in the other ear. This belief led to the expression *deaf as an adder*, first recorded in the biblical book of Psalms.

deaf ear.   *See* TURN A DEAF EAR.

dealing from the bottom of the deck; deal me out.   Both of these expressions passed into general use from the American poker tables of the early 19th century. *Dealing from the bottom of the deck*, like a crooked gambler, means to take unfair or illegal advantage of someone, while *deal me out*, meaning "I don't want to play this hand," or "I don't want to participate this time," or, as Sam Goldwyn reputedly said, "Include me out."

dean.   Most of us know the word *dean* as the title of a head of a faculty or school in a university. But *dean* can also mean the head of a cathedral chapter and the senior member of any group, as in "He's the dean of reporters in Washington." Originally, *dean* (from the Greek *déka*, ten) meant a group of 10, not one person.

dear. In times past a "dear of corn" meant a scarcity of corn, for *dear* is related to the word *dearth* meaning "scarcity" and was once used as its synonym. Over the years *dear* came to mean expensive because something scarce, if needed, is bid for competitively until its price rises.

Dear John letter. No one has identified the original jilted John, if there was one, but this term for a letter to a soldier saying that his wife or sweetheart is leaving him for another dates back to World War II. It is often abbreviated to a *Dear John* and can be used for a similar letter to any man distant from the woman writing it. *See* THAT'S ALL SHE WROTE.

dear me! This is among the most interesting of interjections, which usually haven't much of a story behind them. *Dear me!* is thought to derive from the Italian *Dio me salvi!*—"God save, or spare, me!"

death and taxes. *See* SNUG AS A BUG IN A RUG.

death camas. The poisonous plant *Zigadenus venenosus*, whose root can be deadly; also called crow poison, poison camas and white camas, among other names.

death he makes no promise. An old Bahamian folk saying meaning death strikes at any time with no warning; you never know when or where it will come and he'll never tell you.

death's head moth. A hawk moth (*Acherontia atropos*) with markings resembling a skull on the back of the thorax. Its scientific name *Acherontia* means "woeful river of Hell" and *atropos* means "the Fate who cuts the thread of life." The moth is an image in much English verse, including Keats's poem "Ode on Melancholy":

> No, no, go not to Lethe, neither twist
> Wolf's bane, tight-rooted, for its poisonous wine.
> Nor let the beetle, nor the death-moth be
> Your mournful Psyche.

See A THING OF BEAUTY.

deathwatch beetle. When the little beetle *Anobinidae tesellatum* clicked or tapped, according to an old superstition, death would come to someone in the house. The beetle was therefore named the *deathwatch*. The sound of the deathwatch is really the beetle's mating call, which it makes by raising itself on its hind legs and beating its head rapidly against wood.

debauch. To debauch someone was originally to entice him away from duty or the service of his master. According to one theory, corrupt friends persuaded workers in small French shops known as *bauches* to go off on sprees, that is, enticed them from the *bauche*, or *debauched* them. The word passed into English in the early 16th century as *debauch*, coming to mean any excessive indulgence in sensual pleasure.

debonair. In the medieval French sport of falconry, many distinct strains of hawks were developed for hunting. But long-winged "noble" falcons (usually females, because males were too difficult to train) were the most prized. Such birds were said to be proud and haughty and were called *de bonne air* (of good air). The word was used so often by sportsmen that by the 17th century it came to mean any cultured or well-groomed person and it eventually passed over into English as *debonair*.

Debrett's Peerage. Another guide to the British aristocracy, *Debrett's Peerage* was published in 1802 as a peerage of England, Scotland, and Ireland, making it the first compilation of its kind. Its publisher, John Debrett, who died 20 years later, also published a *Baronetage of England* (1808). In England *to be in Debrett* means "to be of noble birth." *See also* BURKE'S PEERAGE, a term more familiar to Americans.

debt. *Debt* actually derives from the French *dette*, meaning the same, and should rightly be spelled without a *b*. However, clerical scholars in medieval times assumed that the word derived from the Latin *debita* and changed the spelling accordingly, saddling future generations with their learned error.

debunk. Meaning to strip of false or exaggerated claims, *debunk* was coined from the word BUNK by American novelist William Woodward (1874–1950), who, indeed, wrote a lot of debunking books and introduced *debunk* in one of them entitled *Bunk*.

debut. *Debut*, from the French *début* and meaning "from the mark," was originally a gaming term in French signifying the opening move in a game, similar to the English "your move" in chess, or "your play" in cards. From the old gambling term came the French verb *debuter*, "to lead off in a game," which in time was extended into "to make one's first appearance," this last being the word's only meaning ever since *debut* was first recorded in one of Lord Chesterfield's letters in 1752.

decapitation. I've only been able to trace this military term as far back as the beginning of the second Iraq War (Operation Iraqi Freedom) in 2003. It means to kill someone with missiles from a long distance, often by hitting the building or even room in which he is quartered or visiting—sometimes literally blowing his head off.

December. *See* SEPTEMBER.

December is thirteen months long. A humorous saying originating with Canadians that refers to Canada's long, severe winters, especially in northern Canada.

decent; indecent. Our English word *decent* comes from the Latin *decent*, the present participle of *decere*, to be fitting, which is similar to the word's usual present-day meaning, "to be free from indelicacy, modest, to be respectable." People in the mountain areas of the American South still don't frequently use the word *decent*. H. L. Mencken explained this taboo, regarding the South, in *The American Language* (1919): "Fifty years ago the word *decent* was indecent ... no Southern woman was supposed to have any notion of the difference between *decent* and *indecent*. *See* COMMON.

decibel.   "Watson, come here; I want you." These were the undramatic words spoken by inventor Alexander Graham Bell to his lab assistant on March 10, 1876, the first complete sentence conveyed over the telephone. Bell was a Scottish immigrant who in 1871 came to the United States, where he lectured to teachers of the deaf on his father's visible speech method and opened his own school of vocal physiology in Boston. In the course of work on his harmonic telegraph, he invented the first practical telephone, an idea he had conceived as early as 1865. Later inventions included the first practical phonograph record, the audiometer, and a telephonic probe for locating bullets in the human body. The Bell Telephone Company was formed in July, 1877. The inventor died in 1922, aged 75. *Bel*, a unit of measuring the loudness of electrical signals, and *decibel*, 1/10 of a *bel*, both honor his name.

deciduous; evergreen.   Trees that keep their leaves all year long are called evergreen, while those that lose their leaves in fall are called deciduous. *Evergreen* is of course self-explanatory, while *deciduous* derives from the Latin *deciduus*, "falling down."

decimate.   After any mutiny in the Roman army, or any cowardice, the standard punishment was to take one man by lot out of each of the 10-man squads and have his fellow squad members kill him. From this disciplinary measure came the word *decimare* (from the Latin *decem*, 10, meaning "to kill one in 10") that became the English *decimate*. *Decimate* strictly means to reduce a military force by 1/10, but through careless usage has come to mean to destroy a large part of any population, even to obliterate it.

decrepit.   "Very old, at the pittes (pit's) brink," instructs a 16th-century Latin dictionary in defining this word. *Decrepit* means more specifically, "weak, worn out, broken by age, illness or hard use." It comes from Latin *decrepitus*, meaning the same, which comes ultimately from Latin *crepare*, "to creak," which those of us decrepit, or on our way there, often do.

deep-six.   *Deep-six* is an old nautical term meaning "to drown," the *six* meaning "six fathoms down." It has recently taken on the meaning of "to kill a person or thing," as in "we're going to deep-six that project."

Deep Throat.   The code name of the still unrevealed source who gave *Washington Post* reporter Robert Woodward information about the 1972 Watergate break-in. *Deep Throat* was borrowed by Woodward and fellow reporter Carl Bernstein from the well-known pornographic film of that name. *Deep Throat* has become a synonym for any secret source, just as *Watergate* (the Watergate office-apartment complex in Washington, D.C., which housed the headquarters of the Democratic National Committee) has for any Waterloo of a scandal. *Gemstone*, the secret code name for the Watergate break-in, has been all but forgotten. The pornographic movie *Deep Throat* (1972) made over a half-billion dollars, but Linda Lovelace, the pseudonym of the woman who starred in it, wasn't paid a cent. Linda Lovelace claimed that her husband at the time forced her to appear in the film, holding a gun at her back, and that the movie depicted her rape. Her story is told in her autobiography, *Out of Bondage*, published a few years before she died in an auto accident in 2002, age 53. *See* SMOKING GUN.

deer.   In *King Lear* Shakespeare writes of "rats and mice and such small deer." This reflects the fact that in Old English *deor*, from which *deer* derives, meant any wild animal. Only in relatively modern times has deer come to mean only the species we identify it with today. *See also* REINDEER.

defalcate.   *Defalcate* may have originally been a gardening term, deriving as it does from the Latin *de*, "off," and *falx*, "sickle." Translating as "to cut off with a sickle," the word's meaning was extended to "take away," especially in the sense of taking away or embezzling money.

defenestration.   Here is a nonce word that lasted. On May 21, 1618 three Catholic members of the Bohemian National Council were thrown out of a window of the castle of Prague by Protestant insurgents. Though the Catholic members landed in the moat and weren't badly injured, this incident marked the beginning of the Thirty Years War that spread throughout Europe. The incident became known as the Defenestration of Prague, the word *defenestration* coined to describe it from the Latin *de*, "from," and *fenestra*, "window." *Defenestration* has since meant "the act of throwing a person out a window."

deipnosophist.   Anyone seeking a big word meaning "a master of the art of dining" need look no further. The word derives from an early work entitled *Deipnosophistai*, which might be best translated as *Gastronomes at Dinner*, written by the Greek writer Athenaios of Naucratis in about A.D. 200. *Deipnosophist*, first recorded in 1656, is formed from the Greek *deipnon*, "dinner," plus *sophistes*, "learned person." The word is first recorded in the late 15th century.

déjà vu.   These are the French words for "already seen," which were adopted by psychologists at the beginning of the 20th century as the name for the illusion of having already experienced something actually being experienced for the first time. Since then this term has come to mean an impression of having experienced or seen something before, as in "Brooklyn fans followed the Yankees wins with a definite sense of déjà vu."

Delaware.   Mencken points out that the map of this country is "besprinkled with place names from at least half a hundred languages, living and dead." Of the eight classes he lists as their sources, "surnames" comes first. *Delaware* falls into this category, being the first alphabetically of American states that take their names from the names of individuals. The Diamond State commemorates English soldier Thomas West, Baron De La Warr (1577–1618), who in 1609 was appointed the first governor of Virginia by the Virginia Company. Delaware Bay was named for Lord De La Warr by Sir Samuel Argall, who discovered it when the governor sent him on an expedition to locate supplies for the starving settlers at Jamestown; both Delaware and the Delaware Indians derive their names from this body of water. De La Warr had been appointed governor of Virginia for life, but died on his second trip from England to the colony and was buried at sea.

delft.   A style of glazed pottery, generally opaque white and blue, that was originally made in the city of Delft in the western Netherlands. The Delft potters began making tableware, called delftware, in the early 1700s and later shortened its name to delft. Today the pottery is made in Delft and many other places.

Delilah. A Delilah, from the name of the biblical courtesan, signifies both a temptress and a seductive wife or mistress who turns to treachery. Delilah in the biblical story (Judg. 16:4–20) had been bribed by the Philistines to learn the source of Samson's strength. Samson lied to her three times, but on her fourth attempt she learned that his power lay in his long hair, had his head shaved while he slept upon her knees, and betrayed him to his enemies. Little is told of Delilah except that she was a "woman in the valley of Sorek." After she collects "eleven hundred pieces of silver" for her tonsorial treachery, she is heard from no more.

delirium. In Latin *lera* means the ridge left by ploughing, so the verb *de-lerare* means to make an irregular ridge when ploughing. A *delirus* was one who couldn't make a straight furrow and thus came to mean "a crazy, disoriented person whose mind wandered from the matter at hand." The state of such a person was called *delirium*, which is still our word for the condition today. *See also* PREVARICATION.

delphinium. The dolphin has a home out of water in our gardens, at least in the form of the perennial *delphinium*, which the Greeks named "little dolphin" (*delfinium*) because they thought the flower's nectary looked like the marine mammal. There are about 200 species of delphiniums, all of which have a poisonous juice in their foliage. *See* LARKSPUR.

delta. The Greek letter for D, *delta* was drawn in the form of a triangle: △. *Delta* was thus applied to the area of the mouths of the Nile, which was of a triangular shape. It has since been applied to similar formations of other rivers. The Mississippi Delta, by the way, is not, strictly speaking, a delta. Far from the sea, it is simply a flood plain.

demagogue. In ancient times the word *demagogue*, from the Greek *demagogos*, "popular leader," simply meant a leader of the common people or great popular orator. It wasn't until the 17th century that the word acquired its present pejorative connotation of a popular leader who gains power by means of impassioned pleas to the emotions and prejudices of the people.

dem bums. This nickname for the Brooklyn Dodgers, beloved of memory, was given to them by an irate fan seated behind home plate at a home game in Ebbets Field during the Great Depression. Particularly incensed at one error he shouted, "Ya bum, ya, yez bums, yez!" and his words, reported by a baseball writer, stuck as an endearing nickname for the team. It was in 1900 that the team was named the Dodgers, after all Brooklynites, who were called trolley dodgers by Manhattanites, contemptuous of all the trolleys in the borough. *See* DODGERS.

demijohn. The shape of a portly lady is suggested by the demijohn, which is narrow at the neck and round in the body. For this reason some etymologists trace the word, first recorded in 1769, to the French *Dame Jeanne*, "Lady Jane," theorizing that the large glass bottle was named for some forgotten French housewife whose bulging figure it resembled, or for such portly women in general. The theory that *demijohn* is a corruption of *Damaghan*, a Persian town where glassware was manufactured, is not generally accepted. A demijohn generally holds five gallons and is usually encased in wickerwork. *See also* BELLARMINE.

democracy. *See* ENCYCLOPEDIA.

demoralize. *Demoralize* has the distinction of being the only word coined by the great American dictionary maker Noah Webster. Webster invented the word in 1794 when writing of the French Revolution and the bad effects such civil wars had on the morals of the people involved. He did not borrow it from the French word *demoraliser*, as many people thought, but made it by simply placing the common prefix *de* on the English word *moralize*.

Demosthenic. There are legends that the great Greek orator Demosthenes was a stammerer, that he could not pronounce the letter *p*, that he overcame his impediment by practicing with pebbles in his mouth against the sound of the surf, or by declaiming as he ran uphill. According to still another tradition, Demosthenes also mastered language by copying Thucydides' direct and graphic *History of the Peloponnesian War* eight times. Whatever the truth of these stories—and there is little doubt that Demosthenes did have some speech defect as a boy—the Greek statesman ranks as the greatest orator of all time, surpassing even Cicero, who patterned himself on the Athenian. Demosthenes (ca. 383–322 B.C.) is particularly noted for his denunciations of Philip of Macedonia (*see* PHILIPPIC), which roused his countrymen to the danger of the subjugation of Greece. The word *Demosthenic* refers to his oratory and also means eloquent, patriotic speech, for his two most constant themes were the greatness of Athens and the need to preserve her traditions.

Dennis the Menace. A name given to any mischievous but good-hearted overactive, mostly good-intentioned child, after the freckled-faced cartoon character Dennis the Menace drawn by cartoonist Hank Ketcham (1920–2001). Hank Ketcham drew his creation from 1950 to 1994, when he retired and a team of artists took over his strip, which now appears in over 1,000 newspapers in 48 countries and 19 languages. According to Mr. Ketcham, the cartoon character Dennis was named after the cartoonist's four-year-old son. The real-life Dennis wrecked his bedroom while he was supposed to be napping one afternoon, leading his mother to shout, "Your son is a menace!"

den of thieves. *Den* is recorded as "the lair or habitation of a wild beast" at least as far back as *Beowulf*, written sometime in the 10th century. By the 18th century the word began to be used for a secret hiding place of thieves or the like, Daniel Defoe first recording the expression *den of thieves* in *Robinson Crusoe* (1719).

dénouement. The resolution of a play or any literary work following its climax is called a dénouement. The word came into English intact as the French *dénouement*, meaning "untying of the knot," being first recorded by Lord Chesterfield in one of his letters.

dentist. *Dentist* is an elegant borrowing from the French, who formed the word from their word *dent* for tooth. Before the mid-18th century, dentists were often called tooth-drawers in England. Noted the *Edinburgh Chronicle* of September 15, 1759: "*Dentist* figures now in our newspapers, and may do well for a French *puffer* [an advertising writer]; but we fancy Rutter [a local dentist at the time] is content being called a tooth-drawer."

deoch-an-doris. One of the few Gaelic expressions that is widely known today, at least among the Irish, Scottish, and British to a lesser extent. It means a farewell drink. From the Gaelic for "drink at the door," it is also called *doch-an-dorach*. The ancient Roman counterpart to the term is *a parting cup.* See STIRRUP CUP.

deodand. *Deodand* itself derives from the Latin *Deodandum*, something "given to God." Under the law of *deodand* any automobile that hit and killed a pedestrian would be sold and the proceeds given to the church. This custom was abolished in England in 1846, but previously any personal chattel—such as a bull that killed a man—was forfeited by the owner and sold for some pious purpose. It was reasoned that, as a person meeting such an accidental death had died without extreme unction, the money could be used to pay for masses for him.

department store. The term *department store* isn't recorded until 1887, when a New York establishment advertised itself as H.H. Heyn's Department Store, though the idea of separate departments in stores can be found in print at least 40 years earlier, when an article in *Hunt's Merchandising Magazine* told of "tubes connecting with each department of a store, from the garret to the cellar, so that if a person in a department . . . wishes to communicate with the employer, he can do so without leaving his station."

dephlogisticated air. See PHLOGISTON.

derby. *Derby* is the American name for a version of the dome-shaped felt hat that the English call a bowler. The man it honors also has the English Derby at Epsom Downs and the Kentucky Derby at Churchill Downs named for him. The 12th earl of Derby, Edward Stanley (d. 1834), came from a family that traced its origins to William the Conqueror. He had a great interest in horse racing but little in his wife—a mutual feeling—and so devoted most of his time to the improvement of the breed. Races had long been held at Epsom Downs, but in 1780 the earl started a series of annual contests for three-year-olds, the races named in his honor because he both suggested them and was such a convivial host each season at The Oaks, a house near the course that had belonged to his uncle General "Johnny" Burgoyne. The Derby became so popular that almost a century later, in 1875, the Kentucky Derby adopted part of its name. After the Civil War, American spectators at the "Blue Ribbon of the Turf" noticed that English sportsmen often wore odd-shaped bowler hats. A few were brought back home, where it is said that a Connecticut manufacturer made a stiff felt, narrow-brimmed version that an unknown New York store clerk sold as "hats like the English wear at the Derby." In any event, *derby* became the American term for bowler, the most popular headwear for men up until the 1920s.

derelict. Deriving from the Latin *derelictus*, "to forsake wholly, abandon," *derelict* at first meant any piece of property abandoned by its owner, being first recorded in 1649. Within 10 years, however, the word was applied to abandoned ships and it came to be used mainly in this sense over the years.

der Führer. See FÜHRER.

derrick. The large crane for lifting heavy objects that we call the *derrick* takes its name from English executioner Godfrey Derrick. Derrick was responsible for some 3,000 hangings and beheadings in his long career as public executioner, which extended into the reign of James I. His name was most likely applied to the gallows itself and then to the crane which resembled the gallows, though the comparison might have been made between his and the crane's great strength or huge stature. Ironically, Derrick, a convicted rapist, had been pardoned by Robert Devereux, earl of Essex, his commander in a military expedition, when he agreed to become executioner at the infamous Tyburn Prison just outside London. The young and handsome Essex, long a favorite of Queen Elizabeth, was later condemned for treason and sentenced to be executed at Tyburn in 1601. By an odd twist of fate, Derrick became his executioner, though as a headsman, for even then nobles were exempt from hanging. See DICK; DIRK.

derringer. This is the small but deadly large-bored gun that in real life has been the choice of a large variety of villains, including assassin John Wilkes Booth. The pistol is named for Philadelphia gunsmith Henry Deringer, who invented it in 1835. Posterity cheated Deringer a bit, though, for the stubby gun came to be spelled with a double *r.*

Deseret. A place-name used in the Utah Territory by the Mormons in 1850. The word is a coined one from the *Book of Mormon* and means "honeybee," a symbol of hard work and cooperation. What is now Utah was called the State of Deseret, and Salt Lake City was called Deseret.

Deseret alphabet. Members of the Mormon church from all over the world came to settle in what is now Utah when Brigham Young led the Mormons there across the desert. Many of them spoke no English, and Young and other church leaders felt they needed a better alphabet to teach them the language. Forsaking the standard English alphabet, which has only 26 letters to represent the approximately 43 sounds in English, they developed what they called the Deseret alphabet, which had a letter for each sound. Despite all their efforts, however, the alphabet never became popular and all efforts to promote it were abandoned after Young's death in 1877. See DESERET.

desert rat. *Neotoma desertorum*, a rat found in desert areas and often called the desert brush rat. It is one of many animals and plants named for the deserts where they are found, including the desert ant, desert gray fox, desert oak and desert willow. A desert rat is also a person, often a hermit-like prospector, who has lived in the desert for many years.

Desert Rats. The nickname of British soldiers in World War II's North African campaign; they are said to have been so named by their enemy, the Italian dictator Mussolini. The nickname was especially associated with the 7th Armoured Division, whose division sign was the jerboa. The jerboa, really a jumping or hopping mouse, is well-equipped for the desert, hibernating for five months and getting by without drinking any water all year.

despot. The original Greek *despotes*, the source of *despot*, simply means "master," not a tyrannical master or ruler. But over the centuries the title was bestowed upon many kings, emperors, and bishops who were tyrannical, and by the time of the French Revolution the word came to mean an absolute, tyrannical ruler.

despotism by dynamite. *See* ABSOLUTISM TEMPERED BY ASSASSINATION.

dessert. *See* JUST DESERTS.

destroyer. This relatively light, fast, naval combat ship was first called the *torpedo boat destroyer* after what was then its primary mission. The first U.S. destroyer was the 273-ton USS *Farragut*, named after U.S. admiral David Farragut, a Civil War hero.

Destroying Angel. A historical term for a member of an alleged secret militant Mormon organization. Also called the Destroying Band and Mormon Destroying Angels. The group was said, in Mark Twain's words, "to conduct permanent disappearances of obnoxious citizens."

desultory. Circus riders in ancient Rome jumped from one horse to another during their acts, which led to their being called *desultors*, or leapers, from the Latin *salire*, "to leap." They were soon compared to people who fitfully jump from one idea to another in conversation, which resulted in the word *desultorious*, "to be inconsistent, beside the point," the ancestor of our English word *desultory*.

deuce. *Deuce* for "the devil" may have its origin in the hairy demon of Celtic mythology called the Dus. Other suggestions are the Old German *deurse*, "a giant," the Latin expletive *Deus!*, "My god!," or the two, or deuce, which is an unlucky throw (snake eyes) in a dice game. Congreve first recorded the expression *the deuce take me!*, in 1694. *Deuce* for the number "two" comes from the Latin *duos*, two.

deus ex machina. Some unlikely event that extricates one from a difficult situation, usually in a play or other work of fiction, is called a deus ex machina, which literally means "a god [let down upon the stage] from a machine." In ancient Greek drama a god was often lowered onto the stage by a pulley system to help the hero out of trouble, this practice giving rise to the expression. Euripides used the device widely, while Sophocles and Aeschylus avoided it—as almost all writers avoid it today. Much later Bertolt Brecht parodied the practice

at the end of *The Threepenny Opera* when Mack the Knife is saved from hanging by Queen Victoria's proclamation.

devil. *Devil* has a more complicated history than the old story that it is a contraction of "do-evil." It is a translation of the Hebrew "Satan" in the Old Testament, where it meant "adversary." When the Old Testament was translated into Greek, its translators chose the word *diabolos* to convey the meaning of "adversary," *diabalos* coming from the Greek verb *diaballian* "to slander or accuse." *Diabolos* thus meant "accuser," and the devil, whose name derives from *diabolos* via the Old English *deofol* is "the slanderer or accuser of the soul."

devil dances in his pocket. Someone who is broke, penniless. This early 15th- to 19th-century expression derives from an old belief that the cross on ancient coins prevented the devil from entering one's pockets.

devil dogs. The Germans in World War I called the U.S. Marines of the 4th Brigade *Teufelhunden*, or *devil dogs*, because they were such fierce fighters. The name stuck as a nickname for marines. So did the Marine slogan *Retreat, hell!*, a shortening of the reply Marine captain Lloyd Williams gave a Frenchman when asked to fall back at the Battle of Belleau Wood: *Retreat, hell! We just got here!*

devil's advocate. Deriving from the Latin *Advocatus Diaboli*, the *devil's advocate* was first an official appointed by the Roman Catholic church, his job to argue the case against a person's canonization, or recognition as a holy person. From this the term came to mean anyone who argues against an idea to test it.

devil's darning needle. Thoreau and other New Englanders called the dragonfly the *devil's darning needle* and *devil's needle* because of its big eerie eyes, which are far out of proportion to its long, needlelike body. But the two colorful expressions yielded to the shorter *darning needle* over the years. Another colorful Americanism was *devil's riding horse* for the praying mantis. It was also called the devil's horse, cheval du diable, devil's mare, devil's rear horse, and devil's war-horse.

Devil's Island. Devil's Island, the former French penal colony off the coast of French Guiana, isn't so named because it was like hell for prisoners sent there, or because the climate was as hot as hell. The island, one of the three Safety Islands, takes its name from the dangerous turbulent waters surrounding it, the major reason why escape from it was so difficult.

Devil's paintbrush. The strangest but most apt name for a gun ever coined. The MAXIM MACHINE GUN was dubbed the "Devil's paintbrush" because it spewed out bullets so fast that the earth, grass, trees, and anybody on them were drenched or touched scarlet red. *Devil's paintbrush* is also a popular name for hawkweed (*Pilosella aurantiaca*), a troublesome weed that bears brilliantly colored flowers ranging from yellow to orange-red that are exceptionally beautiful in meadow masses.

devil's picture book. A colorful, little-known term for "playing cards" that was used by the Puritans, who considered it sinful to play cards or even have a deck of cards in the house.

In fact, it wasn't until the mid 19th century that playing cards were deemed permissible in devout New England homes. Long before this, however, 16th-century clergymen issued playing cards bearing scriptural passages and Cardinal Mazarin taught France's Sun King history, geography, and other subjects by printing instructive text on "educational" playing cards. We take our 52-card deck from the French, but there is a 56-card deck (Italian), a 32-card deck (German) and many others around the world. Playing cards are called pasteboards because they were made of pasteboard for centuries, the paste making them opaque so that they couldn't be seen through. It was only after 1850 that designs on the backs of cards were used, for early gamblers had felt that plain white backs couldn't be so easily marked as decorative ones.

devil's walking stick.   *See* HERCULES' CLUB.

devil to pay.   *See* BETWEEN THE DEVIL AND THE DEEP BLUE SEA.

dewar flask.   The dewar flask, the original thermos bottle, is named for its inventor, Sir James Dewar (1842–1923), a Scottish chemist and physicist who devised the vacuum-jacketed vessel in 1892 for the storage of liquid gases at low temperatures. The thermos takes its name from the company that adapted Dewar's invention commercially. Originally a trademark, the word is now spelled without a capital in most dictionaries.

dewberry.   Dewberries, which are trailing blackberries similar to boysenberries, are a native American fruit, although they are cultivated today by gardeners in other parts of the world. Not that there aren't native European varieties of dewberries as well. In Europe the dewberry can be traced back to the 16th century, when Shakespeare praised it. Its name, in fact, may be a corruption of "dove berry," which it has been called for centuries in Germany, but it has long been associated with "dew" in English usage.

Dewey Decimal system.   The father of American library science, Melvil Dewey (1851–1931), first proposed his famous Dewey Decimal system in 1876 while serving as acting librarian at Amherst College. It is now used by some 85 percent of all libraries. The classification scheme, invented when he was in his early twenties, divides the entire field of knowledge into nine main classes (from 000 to 999), a second set of numbers following a decimal point indicating the special subject of a book within its main class. A man of fantastic energy and originality, Dewey later became chief librarian at Columbia College (1883–88), where he founded, in 1887, the first American school of library science. As director of the New York State Library (1889–1906), he reorganized the state library, making it one of the most efficient in the nation, and originated the system of traveling libraries. Dewey also helped found the American Library Association, the New York State Association, and the *Library Journal*. He crusaded for simplified spelling and use of the metric system, among many other causes.

dewitt.   To dewitt, or brutally lynch, is chiefly a historical expression today. The brothers DeWitt—Jan (b. 1625) and Cornelius (b. 1623)—were Dutch statesmen opposed to the war policies of their monarch when the French invaded the Netherlands in 1672. Jan DeWitt, King William III's major opponent and a wise, eloquent statesman, was arrested that same year and tortured in the Gevangenpoort at The Hague. When his brother Cornelius came to visit him in jail, an incensed chauvinistic mob gathered and broke into the prison, hacking the two men to pieces and hanging their limbs and parts on lampposts. For many years after, *to dewitt* meant to perform such grisly lynchings or mob murders, one of the few such verbs in English deriving from someone's name.

dewlap.   The lap, or fold, of skin hanging loosely from the throat of certain dogs, cattle, and other animals, including humans, may be so named because someone humorously observed that such folds "brushed the dew of the grass." However, no one is sure about the origins of this old word, which is first recorded early in the 14th century.

dextrous.   *See* RIGHT.

dey.   Gone are the days of the deys. *Dey* (pronounced day) was up until 1830 the title for a governor of Algiers, as well as a title for rulers of Tunis and Tripoli. The word derives from the Turkish *dayi*, which means a maternal uncle. Caroline of Brunswick, wife of King George IV, enjoyed a notorious affair with the dey of Algiers. Lord Norbury, England's chief justice, remarked, "She was as happy as the dey is long."

D4D.   *See* K- CORPS.

dharna.   This Indian word means "persistence." Those practicing *dharna* in India have in fact been known to seek justice by sitting at the door of someone who owes them money, and fasting to death.

dialect.   *Dialect* is first recorded in 1577, deriving from the Latin *dialectus*, "way of speaking," and is defined as "one of the varieties of a language arising from local peculiarities of vocabulary, pronunciation and idiom." It is often forgotten that dialects sometimes become languages. Italian, Spanish, Portuguese, French, and Rumanian, for example, began life as regional dialects of Latin.

Diamond Jim.   The nickname of the legendary James Brady (1856–1917), a millionaire speculator who rose from a bell boy to one of America's richest men and certainly its greatest eater. The gargantuan Diamond Jim, whose postmortem revealed a stomach six times the size of a normal person, used to eat as a typical dinner: two or three dozen oysters, six or so large crabs, two bowls of turtle soup, seven or eight lobsters, two portions of turtle meat, a huge sirloin steak, assorted vegetables (for a balanced diet), a bulging platter of pastries, and a two-pound box of candy—all washed down with several gallons of orange juice (he abhorred alcohol). It was, in fact, at such a feast in New York City that Brady, bedecked with diamonds, proposed to zaftig Lillian Russell. Diamond Jim supposedly plunked an open valise containing a million dollars on the table, carefully spread out a napkin on the floor, knelt down, and promised the actress, "This is all yours if you'll marry me." Miss Russell simply shook her head and calmly ordered more Beluga caviar.

diamonds of the dustheap. Virginia Woolf (1882–1940) apparently coined this phrase. After reading her previous year's diary she wrote: "I . . . am much struck by the rather haphazard gallop at which it swings along. . . . Still, if it were not written rather faster than the fastest typewriting, if I stopped and took thought, it would never be written at all. The advantage of the method is that it sweeps up accidentally severed stray matters which I should exclude if I hesitated, but which are the diamonds of the dustheap."

Diana's tree. This is not a plant but an amalgam of crystallized silver obtained from mercury in a solution of silver. It is so called because to alchemists silver was represented by Diana, the Roman nature goddess. The substance is also known as philosopher's tree.

diaper. Baby's diaper has no relation to the town of Ypres in France, as has been suggested. The word probably comes from the French *diapre*, "a white cloth variegated with flowers," which, in turn, derives from the Greek *dia*, "through," and *aspros*, "white" or "white in places." First used to mean such a cloth in 1350, *diaper* wasn't used for a baby's "clout" or napkin until the 19th century. In fact, in Britain the term has never been applied in this way.

dicing. An expression from auto racing meaning "to jockey for position on the track." The term originated in England in the 1950s, and has its origins in the old melodramatic expression *dicing with death*, taking great chances.

dick; dirk. Partridge suggests that *dick*, as a common slang synonym for penis, comes indirectly from the English hangman Godfrey Derrick's name (*see* DERRICK). It seems that among the dreaded hangman's victims were many sneak thieves and picklocks, who often carried short daggers. These came to be called dirks after Derrick (which is a Dutch name identified with Dirk). The dagger called the dirk then gave its name, in the form of *dick*, to the penis.

dickens; Dickensian. The expression *what the dickens* has nothing to do with author Charles Dickens's name, as is often believed, *the dickens* in this case probably being an old euphemism for *devil*. Dickensian is another, greater story. As a noun Dickensian refers to novelist Charles John Huffam Dickens (1812–70) and his works, while as an adjective it describes the energy and living presence of his characters, the tremendous vitality and richness of the world he created. Dickens did exaggerate his characters, but no one before or after has been able to exaggerate just like him. The people he created in his 14 novels and many shorter works are better known worldwide than those of any English author save Shakespeare. Micawber, Pickwick, David Copperfield, Steerforth, Oliver Twist, Scrooge, Tiny Tim, Sarah Gamp, Uriah Heep, Gradgrind, the Artful Dodger, Fagin, Little Nell—and so many others—have become words in themselves as well as names, escaping the books that contained them. Dickens, the son of an improvident government clerk—elements of him are found in both Micawber and Dorrit—had to go to work in a blacking factory at the age of 12 when his father was imprisoned for debt. He had little formal schooling and, after being apprenticed to a lawyer, served as a parliamentary reporter for newspapers. Following the success of *Sketches by Boz* (his pen name) and *Pickwick Papers* in 1836, his fame was assured, and books like *Oliver Twist*, the semiautobiographical *David Copperfield*, and *Hard Times*, with their descriptions of the brutality of industrial society, made him one of the world's most influential novelists. Dickens toured America twice, his unflattering *American Notes* the result of his first visit. His more complex works such as *Bleak House, Great Expectations, Our Mutual Friend, Little Dorrit*, and *Hard Times* have been acclaimed by critics as Dickens's greatest novels, but his early books, *A Tale of Two Cities* and his Christmas stories have remained just as popular over the years. *A Christmas Carol*, as G. K. Chesterton pointed out, did much to revive the true spirit of Christmas throughout the world. Dickens died suddenly and prematurely at the age of 58, probably of overwork, but his wildly comic, grotesque, and tearfully pathetic characters lived on. As Chesterton wrote in his brilliant essay on the novelist, "There can be no question of the importance of Dickens as a human event in history . . . a naked flame of mere natural genius, breaking out in a man without culture, without tradition, without help from historic religions or philosophies or from the great foreign schools; and revealing a light that never was on sea or land, if only in the long fantastic shadows that it threw from common things." Dickens's grave is in the Poets' Corner of Westminster Abbey.

dicker. Deriving from *decem*, "10," *decuria* was the Latin word for the bundle of 10 animal hides that Caesar's legions made a unit of trade in Britain and elsewhere. This word eventually was corrupted to *dicker*. On the frontier in America the haggling and petty bargaining over dickers of pelts became the meaning of the word itself.

Dick Smith. *Dick Smith* or *Dick Smither* refers to a solitary, selfish, cheap man with short arms and deep pockets, who would never order a round for other drinkers at a bar, though he'd always accept a free drink. The eponymous expression, first recorded in 1876 in the *Congressional Record*, may be based on a real Michigan lumberjack of that name. A quiet, unsociable baseball player named Dick Smith is another possibility, as is Richard Penn Smith (1799–1854), a Philadelphia playwright who introduced romantic tragedy in the U.S. and was indebted to the work of several French and English playwrights as models for his own work.

Dick test. Like the more famous CURIES, Drs. George Frederick and Gladys H. Dick form a famous husband and wife scientific team. In 1923 they isolated the streptococcus that causes scarlet fever. The following year the Dicks devised the test used to determine an individual's susceptibility to the disease and developed a serum providing immunity. In the Dick test scarlet fever toxins are injected into the arm; if the individual is not immune, the skin reddens around the injection. George Frederick Dick (b. 1881) was professor of clinical medicine at Rush Memorial College when he and his wife made their discoveries. He served as chairman of the department of medicine at the University of Chicago Medical School from 1933 to 1945.

diddle. In its sense of to cheat or deceive *diddle* derives from the name of the main character in James Kenny's farce *Raising the Wind* (1803). Jeremy Diddler continually borrows small sums from other people and fails to pay them back. Since the late 19th century *diddle* has been slang for to fornicate, making Mr. Diddler perhaps the only eponymous person in literature so honored. *Diddle* can mean "nothing," as in "He doesn't know diddle about it."

diddledees.   An unusual Americanism meaning pine needles. It has been suggested that since diddledees are sometimes used as kindling, they take their name from the diddledee tree or shrub of the Falkland Islands, which is also used for fuel. The term could have been brought to America by whalers a century or so ago. In various regions of the U.S., pine needles are also called needles, spills, pins, twinkles, straws, tags, and shats.

didn't lay a finger on.   These words seem so obvious for "didn't touch, didn't harm in the slightest way" that one would think the expression is of ancient origin. But the *O.E.D.* has only traced the first recorded use of the common phrase back to England in 1865.

dieffenbachia.   *See* MOTHER-IN-LAW PLANT.

die for the want of lobster sauce.   Vatel, the chef of the French prince de Condé, is said to have killed himself because the lobsters (or fish) he needed for a sauce he was preparing for Louis XIV didn't arrive on time. Thus, *to die for the want of lobster sauce* is said of someone who suffers greatly because of some small disappointment.

diehard.   The British won the battle of Albuera on May 16, 1811, and although the battle is generally considered a strategic mistake it provided the éspirit de corps that aided Wellington in future battles against Napoleon's superior forces. The victory was due in large part to the heroic action of the famous British 57th Foot commanded by Colonel William Inglis. His regiment, part of a thin line of 1,800 redcoats, occupied an important strategic position in the small Spanish village and had been pinned down by deadly French fire. "Die hard, fifty-seventh, die hard!" Inglis cried out from where he lay wounded. His men responded. Of 579 troops, 438 were killed or wounded and the regiment passed into legend as the *Die Hards*. Later their nickname was used to describe ultraconservative political groups or individuals refusing to change with the times, many of them far less honorable than the 57th.

die laughing.   Shakespeare, in *The Taming of the Shrew* (ca. 1592), was apparently the originator of this expression, or at least the first to record it: "Went they not quickly, I should die with laughing." Several cases are recorded of people actually dying of laughter while watching a stage comedy. More ironic was the death of the ancient soothsayer Calchas, who died of laughter on learning that he had just outlived the predicted hour of his death.

to die like a dog.   *See* DOG'S LIFE.

Diervilla.   *See* WEIGELA.

diesel.   German mechanical engineer Dr. Rudolph Diesel developed the heavy-duty internal combustion engine bearing his name from 1892–97 at the Krupp factory in Essen and spent the rest of his life perfecting it and manufacturing *diesel engines* at a factory he founded in Augsburg. Today it is employed in locomotives, ships, generators, cars, trucks, submarines, and much heavy equipment. Diesel became rich and famous as a result of his invention, yet he may have ended a suicide in 1913, when he was only 55. It is possible that he fell overboard while crossing the English Channel on a mail steamer on the night of September 30, but his hat and overcoat were found by the rail, suggesting that he had jumped.

different drummer.   *See* HEAR A DIFFERENT DRUMMER.

dig.   *Dig*, for "understand," is first recorded in about 1935, which is not to say that it couldn't have been in use much earlier. No one knows how the Americanism came to be, but there are two contending theories: (1) the Celtic *twig*, "to understand," is the word's ancestor, and (2) the West African *degu* yielded *dig*. *Dig* for an insulting remark, a *dirty dig*, goes back to the turn of the century and may derive from the *dig* meaning a poke or jab.

digger.   *See* AUSSIE.

Digger Indian.   A small Paiute tribe near St. George, Utah, was apparently the first Indian tribe to be called Diggers, because they practiced agriculture instead of hunting for food. The name is said to be an English translation of their Indian name. Later, *Diggers* was applied to all agricultural tribes and eventually the name became a derogatory one for any Indian.

digging one's grave with a knife and fork.   This humorous expression for gluttony was first recorded in England during the late 19th century and is still occasionally heard there and in America in these weight-conscious days.

digit.   Roman numerals first represented human fingers, so the numbers one to nine were called *digitis* after the Latin *digitus*, "finger."

digital film restoration.   By one estimate, almost half the movies made before 1950 have been lost because they were improperly stored, and many more have deteriorated to some degree. Digital film restoration can do nothing about the former films but can vastly improve those that are flawed. The process involves converting each frame of a movie into a digital image, which is then displayed on a computer screen and repaired by an artist using a digital pen and tablet; the repaired frame is finally recorded back onto the film. The process can also be used to correct mistakes made in the original filming; for example, the artists restoring Walt Disney's *Fantasia* added an animal's foot missing in the original, and director George Lucas added new creatures to scenes of the *Star Wars* trilogy. "With digital, if you can think it, you can do it," one restoration expert says. "If you want to take Humphrey Bogart out and put Brad Pitt in you can do it." Entire pictures can be virtually made over. The biggest, if not the only, problem in this complicated process is the $1 million to $5 million it costs to digitally restore a film.

digitalis. The flower *digitalis*, long known as a heart stimulant, is so named because a human finger, or *digit*, fits snugly into one of its deep-throated bells.

dilapidated. In a state of ruin, deterioration, disrepair. The word derives from Latin *dilapidare*, to throw or scatter stones, which was what invaders often did to demolish buildings and walls in medieval times.

dildo. Several derivations have been suggested for this instrument of sexual pleasure, which the French call a *consolateur*: 1) a corruption of the Italian *deletto*, "delight"; 2) a corruption of the English *diddle*; 3) the cylindrical dildo tree or bush, which grows 10 feet or so straight up. The *O.E.D.* says only that the word is of obscure origin and offers an earlier date (1610) for its use for a phallus than its use for a plant.

dilly. In its meaning of "some outstanding thing or person," *dilly* is first recorded in the early 1930s. But it was used as an adjective in America before then and probably has a long history, deriving either from the 17th-century English *dilling*, "darling," or from the first four letters of *delightful*.

dime. *Dymes*—the word's origin from the Latin *decema*, "a 10th part"—were originally the tithe, or 10th, of one's income paid as a tax to the church by temporal rulers. Chaucer so used the word in 1362 and it was not employed in its present sense—for a U.S. coin representing ¹⁄₁₀ of a dollar—until 1786.

dime novel. *See* PENNY DREADFUL.

dimity. This durable cotton cloth woven with raised patterns isn't so named after Damietta, Egypt, as is often claimed. It takes its name from the Greek *di-mitos*, "double-thread."

dimples. Englishman William Taylor is credited with manufacturing the first golf ball with dimples (that is, a meshlike surface made up of small depressions) in 1908. The dimples enable the ball to carry farther and, in case you haven't counted, there are 360 of them on a modern golf ball. *See* PAR FOR THE COURSE.

dine. Meaning to eat, possibly to eat well or to eat "seriously" (not to eat a sandwich, for example), *to dine* originally meant "to eat dinner, the principal meal of the day." In this respect the word is a contradiction, deriving as it does from the Latin *disjunare*, "to breakfast, to eat the *first* meal of the day."

dine with Duke Humphrey. It was popularly believed in days of yore that Humphrey, duke of Gloucester (1391–1447), a man noted for his hospitality, was buried in London's old St. Paul's Cathedral. For many years after his death those poor who remained in the cathedral during dinner hours, or those debtors afraid to leave the sanctuary for fear of imprisonment, were said to be dining with Duke Humphrey. Although the good duke had actually been buried at St. Albans, the expression *to dine with Duke Humphrey* remained linked with St. Paul's and came to mean to go without any dinner at all. It is now solely a literary expression, often found in the novels of Dickens and other great English authors.

dingbat; dingus, etc. *Dingbat*, a favorite expression of Archie Bunker's, is American in origin, going back to at least 1861, when it meant "anything that can be thrown with force or dashed violently at another object," according to Farmer's *Americanisms* (1899). The word possibly derives from *bat*, "a piece of wood or metal," and *ding*, "to throw." But *dingbat* came to be used in describing anything of which the proper name is unknown to or forgotten by a speaker, much as we more frequently use such meaningless words as *thingamabob* (an extension of the word *thing* that goes back to the late 17th century), *thingamajig*, *dingus*, *doohickey*, *whatsit*, and other infixes. A father describing how to assemble a complicated piece of equipment, such as a child's toy, might say: "You put this *thingamajig* into this *doohickey* and tighten this *doodad* and this *thingamabob*; then you take this *dingus* over here near this *gismo* and attach it to this *hickeymadoodle* so that it barely touches the *thingamadoodle* there near the *whatchamacallit*—then you have to grease it up with this *jeesalamsylborax* or the damn *dingbat* won't work!" *Dingbat* has also served over the years as a slang term for "a gadget, money, buns or biscuits, a woman, and a hobo or bum." But Archie Bunker's contemptuous use of the word for a "nut," an ineffectual, bumbling fool (that is, anyone he doesn't agree with), may come directly from the Australian *dingbats*, meaning "eccentric or mad." *Dingbats* are also the small marks and printers' decorations used in publishing.

dinghy. Small boats carried on larger vessels take the name *dinghy* from the Hindi *dingi*, "little boat." In the late 18th century British mariners noticed small native rowboats called *dingis* in Indian waters and brought the word for the boat home with them, changing its spelling a bit.

dingo. *Dingo* (*Canis dingo*) refers to an Australian wild dog with a reddish brown or yellowish brown coat. The word was taken into English in the late 18th century from the Aboriginal language of southeast Australia, where it was *dingu*. Since then *dingo* has come to mean an informer or a coward in Australian slang.

dink. A recent term dating back to the 1980s for either the male or female of a married couple with two incomes but no children. The word comes from the first initials of *double income, no kids*. *Dink* is also a derogatory term for a Vietnamese, among other meanings.

dinosaur. A word coined in 1841 by British scientist Sir Richard Owen (1804–92) long after the great beast roamed the earth, at about the time its fossil bones were beginning to be assembled and studied. Owen made the word from the Greek *deinos*, fearsome, plus *sauros*, lizard.

Diogenes; Diogenes crab; Diogenic. He is said to have walked the streets of Athens with a lantern in broad daylight searching for an honest man, thus expressing his contempt for his generation. His home was a narrow, open earthenware tub or barrel that he trundled about with him. On seeing a child drinking from cupped hands, he threw away his only worldly possession, a wooden bowl. On being asked by Alexander the Great if the emperor could oblige him in any way, he replied, "Yes, by standing out of my sunshine." More lore surrounds Diogenes of Sinope (ca. 412–322 B.C.), a relatively minor philosopher, than many a more deserving thinker. Diogenes the Cynic held that the virtuous life was the simple life and advocated a return to such ways; he considered self-control, the lack of all pleasure, and even pain and hunger essential to achieving goodness. The Greeks nicknamed him "dog" for what they considered his shameful ways (*see* CYNIC), but Diogenes considered himself a governor of men; in fact, he once told pirates who had captured him that he would like to be sold to a man who needed a master. Diogenes died on the same day as Alexander the Great, who had said, admiringly, "If I were not Alexander, I would be Diogenes." Today a Diogenes or a diogenic person is a cynical, churlish, but independent one, while a West Indian hermit crab bears the philosopher's name because it lives in empty shells reminiscent of his tub.

diorama; photography.   Invented in 1822 by Louis Daguerre (1787–1851), who later invented the daguerreotype, the first permanent photographic process that really worked, the diorama is a scene, often in miniature, reproduced in three dimensions. The French inventor probably patterned the word on *panorama*, which comes from the Greek *(h)orama*, view. The word photography was coined from Daguerre's *photo*genic drawing process plus his helio*graphic* system.

Dioscorea.   While many genera and species of flowers and fruits are named for people, the yam is the only major vegetable, excluding vegetable varieties, to take even its scientific name from a real person. The yam's botanical name is *Dioscorea batatas*; the genus, containing many species, was named by Linnaeus for Pedanius Dioscorides, or, more correctly, Dioscurides, a first-century physician and an early father of botany. A surgeon in Nero's Roman army, Dioscorides gathered information about 600 medicinal plants and other remedies of the period, which he recorded in his *De Materia Medica*, translated in 1934 as the *Greek Herbal of Dioscorides*. Dioscorides' work remained standard for centuries and he is considered to be the first man to establish medical botany as an applied science. *Dioscorea batatas*, the yam, is often incorrectly called a sweet potato, to which it is no relation, despite the similarity in appearance and taste.

diploma; diplomat.   Diplomas were originally official documents that were folded in two and sealed, taking their name from the Greek *diploma*, "a letter folded double." Though mainly a document given to graduates today, they were at first government documents and the government officials who carried these diplomas were called diplomats.

diplomacy.   British author and politician Edmund Burke introduced this word to English from the French *diplomatie* (pronounced *diplomacy*) in his *Letters on a Regicide Peace* (1795–97). *See* ELECTIONEERING.

dirge.   In medieval times the memorial song at funeral services for the dead was based upon the eighth verse of the fifth Psalm, which in English is "Guide, O Lord, my God, my way in Thy sight." The song was sung in Latin, however, where the line is *"Dirige, Domine, Deus meus, in conspectu tuo viam meam."* The first word of the song in Latin was heard so often through the years that it became, slightly altered, *dirge*, the name of such a funeral song.

dirt-eater.   One who eats dirt or clay for its nutritional content, especially a southern poor white or black person. Dirt-eating, or clay-eating, is still practiced, especially in South Carolina and Georgia low country among poor farmers and sharecroppers. It has a long history. The German explorer Alexander von Humbolt described geophagists or dirt-eaters called the Ottomaques of the Orinoco, who fed "on a fat, unctuous earth . . . tinged with a little oxide of iron." Similar practices have flourished in many lands: the Aleppo fed a kind of fuller's earth called Byloon to pregnant women and sickly girls; the Javanese ate little balls of reddish clay called Ampo if they wished "to become thin and graceful"; the Swedes enjoyed a hearty "mountain meal" called *bergmehl*, sometimes mixed with flour; and workmen in the European Kiffhausen stone quarries spread a very fine clay called "steinbutter" on their bread. Geophagists usually suffer from mineral deficiencies which the soil helps remedy.

Dirty Banshee.   *See* CRIBBAGE.

dirty dig.   *See* DIG.

dirty dog.   *See* GO TO THE DOGS.

dirty dozens.   *See* THE DOZENS.

dirty linen; dirty laundry.   *See* DON'T WASH YOUR DIRTY LINEN IN PUBLIC.

dirty little secret.   Something embarrassing that must be concealed. The phrase, much used today, was invented by British author D. H. Lawrence (1885–1930) in his essay "Pornography and Obscenity" (1928).

dirty rat.   Jimmy Cagney is supposed to have snarled this epithet in one of his gangster movies, but no one has established which one. The expression, meaning a disgusting, treacherous person, may date back to the late 19th century. In any case, there is really no truth in the saying a *dirty rat*, for the rat is soiled only by human dirt; it is naturally quite a clean animal, loves water, and delights in bathing in it. One researcher meticulously observed the daily ritual of a wild rat rising: "Eyes open. Rises and stretches. Licks hands; washes face; washes behind ears and continues to lick hands at intervals. Licks fur of back, flanks, abdomen. Licks hind toes, scratches with them, licks scratches . . . scratches flank and belly . . . Licks genitals . . . Licks tail while held in hands . . . Licks hind legs while held in hands . . ." Some dirty rat!

Dirty Thirties.   The 1930s, when terrible dust storms afflicted the Great Plains of the U.S., causing many deaths and great financial loss. *See* DUST BOWL.

dis.   The word *dis*, here, has nothing to do with Dis, the ruler of the Roman Hell. This *dis* (as in "She dissed him," or "He was dissing her") means *disrespect*, deriving from its first syllable. Rap performers seem first to have used the word, which was initially recorded as recently as 1982 and is now widely used.

discount. The French practiced discounting as early as 1500, calling the practice *déscompte* because it first involved "selling by the count" rather than knocking down prices. For example, a buyer was charged for only nine items when buying 10, the 10th item set aside from the count and given to him free—a practice that would better be called the premium technique. By the time *déscompte* spread to England in the early 17th century, however, its name transformed to *discounting*, it meant the reduction in price that discounting is today.

discretion is the better part of valor. Shakespeare probably coined this old saw, in *Henry IV, Part I*. But what he wrote exactly was "The better part of valor is discretion."

discus. The ancient Greek word *diskos*—which derived from the Greek *dikein*, to throw—meant a flat, round stone or metal object thrown in athletic contests. *Diskos* passed into Latin, and finally into English as *discus*, retaining the same meaning. Because of its round shape, the discus gave us the words DISH, *disk*—as in *floppy disk*—and even *desk*, which originally meant a round table.

dish. The round, flat quoit that the Romans called the *discus* probably gives us the word *dish* for "a plate." Apparently, German soldiers jokingly called their mess tins *diskaz*, after the *discus* and *diskaz* passed into English as *dish*. *Dish* is not an Americanism for "a pretty or sexy girl," as many slang dictionaries claim. Shakespeare called Cleopatra Antony's *dish* in *Antony and Cleopatra* (1606), when Enobarbus remarked of Antony: "He will to his Egyptian dish again." *Dish* also means gossip, as in "Don't read Liz Smith's memoir for dish." (*Newsweek* 9/25/00) The term is probably from the verb *dish out*, to gossip, or from *dish out the dirt*, both of which are first recorded in 1926.

dismal. Two days of every month on medieval calendars were designated "evil days," *dies mali* in Latin. These days were thought to be evil and unlucky because Egyptian astronomers had pronounced them so centuries before. We have since learned not to place much stock in Egyptian astronomers or medieval calendars, but *dies mali* is still with us in the form of *dismal*, which has come to mean gloomy, dreary, dull, or lacking in merit.

Dismal Swamp. A large swampy area of about 600 square miles extending from southeastern Virginia into northwestern North Carolina. It is also called "the Dismal," and its residents are called "Dismalites." *Dismal* serves, too, as the name of any American swamp, all of which are lonely, forbidding places.

Disneyan. Among Walt Disney's 39 awards from the Academy of Motion Picture Sciences, and his more than 800 awards and decorations for his work from other sources, there is one that honors him "for creating a new art form in which good was spread throughout the world." It is on this creation that his fame rests secure. Walter Elias Disney (1901–66) did not invent the animated cartoon but brought it to perfection and created characters that have become a permanent part of American folklore (*see* MICKEY MOUSE). His many full-length animated motion pictures (*Snow White and the Seven Dwarfs, Bambi, Fantasia, Dumbo, Pinocchio, Cinderella, Alice in Wonderland, Robin Hood, Peter Pan,* and so on) set a standard for all others. Disney's Mickey Mouse film *Steamboat Willie* was the first animated sound cartoon and he is credited with the invention of the storyboard and other innovative cartoon techniques. On another less creative level, the artist has been invidiously called "the Henry Ford of the entertainment industry" for his Disneyland in California and the Disney World in Florida. Like Henry Ford—and Disney films were his favorites—Disney's was a typical American success story: humble beginnings (although his family traces its origins to England's noble D'Isney clan), hard work, and hardships of every description. Even the success marred by crass commercialism in later years is not unfamiliar. Yet the genius triumphs in the end. Disney's characters remain, in the words of British artist David Low, "the most significant figures in graphic art since Leonardo."

distance lends enhancement to the view. *See* FEW AND FAR BETWEEN.

district attorney. A cowboy stew containing cheap or unmentionable ingredients, such as sweetbreads, guts, and kidneys. It is so named because of the cowboy's hatred of legal authorities. Also called county attorney and son-of-a-bitch stew.

dithyramb. A Greek choral lyric said to have been invented, in literary form, by the semilegendary poet Arion. The poet made a fortune in Italy and was returning to Corinth when he was robbed by sailors and thrown overboard. But his assailants allowed him to sing a song before throwing him to his death, and a dolphin, charmed by the song, carried him safely to land.

ditto; ditto marks. *Ditto* means "the same as above," "the same as came before." The word derives from the Latin *dictus*, "having been said," which is the past participle of the Latin *dicere*, to tell. *Dictus* became *ditto* in the Italian Tuscan dialect and later passed into English in the 17th century. The word can also mean a duplicate or a copy. *Ditto marks* are small marks (") used to indicate that a word written above is to be repeated.

divan. *Divan* has an involved but logical history. Originating as a Persian word meaning "a brochure," it came to mean, in order: "a collection of poems"; "a register"; "a military pay book"; "an account book"; "a room in which an account book was kept"; "an account office or custom house"; "a court"; "a great hall"; and, finally, by 1597, "the chief piece of furniture in a great hall"!

a Dives. Dives is not named in current versions of the Bible, but he is the rich man mentioned in the parable told by Jesus in Luke 16:19–31, and his name has become proverbial for a wealthy, often insensitive person.

÷ (division sign). British mathematician John Pell (1611–85), who taught mathematics at Cambridge and Amsterdam, invented the division sign ÷ that we still use today. *See* AMPERSAND.

Dixie; Dixieland. It sounds incredible, but the first *Dixieland* or *Dixie* may have been in New York City. Some etymologists lean to the following derivation of the word given by the *Charlestown Courier* of June 11, 1885: "When slavery existed in

New York, one Dixie owned a large tract of land on Manhattan Island, and a large number of slaves. The increase of the slaves and of the abolition sentiment caused an emigration of the slaves to more thorough and secure slave sections, and the Negroes who were thus sent off (many being born there) naturally looked back to their old houses, where they had lived in clover, with feelings of regret, as they could not imagine any place like Dixie's. Hence it became synonymous with an ideal location combining ease, comfort, and material happiness of every description." Although no slave "lived in clover," the explanation seems somewhat less doubtful than other theories about Dixie—that it derives from the 18th-century Mason Dixon line, or that the word comes from the French-Creole word *dix*, meaning "10," which was prominently printed on the back of 10-dollar notes issued by a New Orleans bank before the Civil War. *See* AWAY DOWN SOUTH IN DIXIE.

Dixie cup.   The American Water Supply Company's vending machines sold a drink of water in a disposable paper cup for one cent beginning in 1906, the cup possibly called a *Dixie cup* because it was so reliable—like the old 10-dollar bills issued in Louisiana prior to the Civil War (*see* DIXIE). In years to come the Dixie cup was frequently applied to ice cream sold in a small cup as opposed to Popsicles, or ice-cream pops, and cones.

DNA.   The DNA we have been hearing so much about as evidence of guilt or innocence in murder trials is (very roughly) a nucleic acid that carries the genetic information in the cell. Its scientific name is the longest word in the English language. According to the *Guinness Book of World Records* the longest of all words is "the systematic name for deoxyribonucleic acid (DNA), which contains 16,569 nucleotide residues and is thus 207,000 letters long."

do a Brodie.   As a result of his famous leap off the Brooklyn Bridge, Steve Brodie's name became a byword—in the form of to *do (or pull) a Brodie*—for "taking a great chance, even taking a suicidal leap." Brodie made his jump from the Manhattan side of the Brooklyn Bridge on July 23, 1886, to win a $200 barroom bet. Eluding guards on the bridge, the 23-year-old daredevil climbed to the lowest cable and plummeted 135 feet into the water below, where friends were waiting to retrieve him in a rowboat. He was arrested for endangering his life and reprimanded by a judge, but that didn't stop him from making future leaps off other bridges. Some say that Brodie never jumped at all, an unproved theory, and many at the time belittled his claim. It is said that Brodie once angered boxer Jim Corbett's father by predicting that John L. Sullivan would knock his son out. "So you're the fellow who jumped over the Brooklyn Bridge," the elder Corbett said when the two met for the first time. "No, I jumped *off* of it," Brodie corrected him. "Oh," replied Corbett, "I thought you jumped *over* it. Any damn fool can jump off it."

do a number on.   When this voguish slang expression first appeared in the late 1960s, it simply meant "to deceive." It derives, in this sense, from the old vaudeville days, when acts were called numbers because they were numbered on theater programs. The meaning evolved from an act to a pretense and then to an outright deception. Recently, however, the meaning has been softened and extended and *to do a number on* often means only "to affect," though still usually in a devious way.

Doberman pinscher.   Louis Dobermann, a German breeder of Apolda in Thuringia probably helped develop the ferocious, medium-sized guard dog we know as the *Doberman pinscher.* Dobermans were originally bred from *pinscher* hunting dogs to be used as herders for livestock. About all that is known about the breed is that it was developed by Dobermann in about 1890, its origins before that being a mystery. The short-haired, fearless dog is generally black or rust in color, and proud of bearing. The male stands 24 to 27 inches, weighing 60 to 75 pounds. Dobermans are used extensively by the military and as guards for department stores and other commercial establishments. Their ferocity is fabled, and there are tales of them holding onto a gunman's arm after being shot to death. *See* ROTTWEILER.

Doctor Fell; Fell types.

> I do not love thee, Dr. Fell,
> The reason why I cannot tell;
> But this alone I know full well,
> I do not love thee Dr. Fell.

Dr. John Fell's classes at Oxford must have been something to see. The English divine (1625–86) was quite a permissive teacher for his day, initiating many educational reforms and even allowing classroom debates, which often ended in fistfights. Fell, a dean of Christ Church, Oxford, and bishop of Oxford, is also noted for the *Fell* (printing) *types* he collected for the university press and for the extensive building program he began at the university. Yet his name is used to describe someone disliked for no apparent reason. He owes his unjust fate to Thomas Brown (1663–1704), once his student at Christ Church and later an author and translator. Dean Fell had threatened to expel Brown for some offense if he could not translate a Martial couplet. The resulting jingle above bore little resemblance to the 33d epigram, but Dr. Fell, to his credit, good-naturedly accepted the paraphrase. As for Tom Brown, he never wrote anything else that was remembered.

Doctor Jekyll and Mr. Hyde.   In Robert Louis Stevenson's novel *The Strange Case of Dr. Jekyll and Mr. Hyde* (1886), Dr. Jekyll, a physician, discovers a drug that creates in him a personality that absorbs all his evil instincts. This personality, which he calls Mr. Hyde, is repulsive in appearance and gradually gains control of him until he finally commits a horrible murder. Jekyll can rid himself of Hyde only by committing suicide. Stevenson, who wrote the novel in three days locked in his study after he had had a dream about the story, based the main character on an Edinburgh cabinetmaker and deacon named William Brodie (1741–88), who was a "double being," by day a respected businessman and by night the leader of a gang of burglars. Brodie was finally hanged for his crimes, but Stevenson, who was raised in Edinburgh, knew his story well and in fact wrote a play entitled *Deacon Brodie, or The Double Life* when he was only 15. This was the germ of the idea for the later work.

Doctor Livingstone, I presume!   The phrase is still used in a humorous sense, as it was several generations ago. It recalls, of course, the very British greeting of journalist Sir Henry Morton Stanley when after a long, arduous journey—only 700 miles in 236 days—he found the ailing Scottish missionary-explorer David Livingstone on the island of Ujiji in the heart of Africa. The star reporter had completed one of the greatest manhunts of all time. Deserted by his bearers, plagued by disease and warring tribes, he was probably too tired and overwhelmed to think of anything else to say. Stanley (1841–1904) had been sent to Africa by the *New York Herald* to locate the famous explorer, Livingstone, feared dead or swallowed up by the Dark Continent. Born John Rowlands in Denbigh, Wales, Stanley assumed the name of his adoptive father when he emigrated to America as a youth. He later became a noted explorer in his own right. Dr. Livingstone died, aged 60, a year after the reporter left him in 1873. His body was shipped back to England and buried in Westminster Abbey.

Doctor My-book. British surgeon Dr. John Abernethy (1764–1831) wrote a number of books on medicine, the best known of which was *Surgical observations on the constitutional Origin and Treatment of Local Diseases* (1809). Very popular with his patients, he got the name Dr. My-book because like many an author he invariably told his patients, "Read my book," whenever a medical question came up.

Doctor Pangloss. Any incurable optimist is called a *Dr. Pangloss* after the pedantic old tutor of the same name in Voltaire's *Candide, or the Optimist* (1759), which was an attack against Rousseau's philosophy. Dr. Pangloss remained optimistic to the end, despite all his misfortunes, believing "all is for the best in this best of all possible worlds."

doctrinaire. This word for a pedantic theorist is taken from the nickname of Pierre Paul Royer-Collard (1763–1845), whose political party, in turn named the "Doctrinaires" in his honor, made it their business "to preach a doctrine and an orthodoxy." Royer-Collard's party arose in France in 1815 after the second restoration of Louis XVIII. Moderate royalists, he and his colleagues desired a king who would govern liberally, accepting the results of the French Revolution, and were noted for the rigidity of their arguments. Unattuned to political realities, the "Doctrinaires" were destroyed by a reactionary Charles X in 1830. Before being applied as a nickname to Royer-Collard the word had been the popular name for a religious order founded in 1592. Today *doctrinaire* is used contemptuously to describe an inflexible theorist, as distinguished from one who tries to accomplish something within the existing political system.

Dodgers. The incomparable Brooklyn Dodgers, who became comparable after their move to Los Angeles, were called the Dodgers because Manhattanites contemptuously referred to all Brooklynites as "trolley dodgers" at the turn of the century, the bustling borough being famed for its numerous trolleys, especially in the central Borough Hall area. Attempts were made to change the name to the Superbas, the Kings, and the Robins, all to no avail. Some baseball team names just seem to catch on while others don't. The Boston Bees, for example, were named by a distinguished committee of baseball writers from a choice of 1,300 names, but people stubbornly called them the Braves, a name they retained after they moved to Milwaukee. The Cincinnati Reds tried to become known as

the Redlegs to avoid identification with communism, but their name remains the Reds. *See also* DEM BUMS.

dodo. *See* DEAD AS A DODO.

Does a bear shit in the woods? Absolutely, certainly, as in "Can I do it? Does a bear shit in the woods?" One euphemism for this humorous expression is "Does a bear sneeze in the woods?" Another: "Does a bear crap in the woods?" The expression dates back at least to the 1920s and is widely heard today, especially among men.

Does Macy's tell Gimbels? Gimbels department store has long gone out of business, but this expression is still commonly heard. The by now proverbial words arose from a friendly, well-publicized, and well-advertised retailing war between the two giant New York department stores. The expression possibly originated as a publicity gag, perhaps as a line in an Eddie Cantor comedy skit when a stooge asked Cantor to reveal some dark secret and the comedian replied, "Does Macy's tell Gimbels?" Actually, Macy's often told Gimbels and vice versa. One time Gimbels ran an ad calling attention to Macy's fabulous annual flower show, heading it: "Does Gimbels tell Macy's? No, Gimbels tells the world!" On another occasion, in 1955, both stores posted signs on their buildings directing shoppers to the other's store. The Gimbels-Macy's rivalry was further publicized in the film *Miracle on 34th Street*, in which Macy's directs customers to Gimbels when it doesn't have a particular item in stock.

doesn't hold water. For over 300 years this expression has meant that something doesn't pass a test, fails, is not sound. It possibly derives from a prospective buyer testing a water pitcher by filling it with water. If it leaked, it didn't hold water, it failed the test and wasn't bought.

doesn't know beans. Boston, home of the "bean eaters," "home of the bean and the cod," may be behind the phrase. Walsh, in his *Handbook of Literary Curiosities* (1892), says that the American expression originated as a sly dig at Boston's pretensions to culture, a hint that Bostonians knew that Boston baked beans were good to eat, that they were made from small white "pea beans"—even if Bostonians knew nothing else. It may also be that the American phrase is a negative rendering of the British saying "he knows how many beans make five"—that is, he is no fool, he's well informed—an expression that probably originated in the days when children learned to count by using beans. But *he doesn't know beans*, "he don't know from nothing," possibly has a much simpler origin that either of these theories. It probably refers to the fact that beans are little things of no great worth, as in the expression "not worth a row (or hill) of beans."

dog. First recorded in 1050 but probably born before then, *dog* is an early example of a "native" invented English word not borrowed from any other tongue. Before its introduction, the Teutonic *hund* had been the Old English word for the canine. Then *dog* (*docga*) first appeared in English as the name for a now unknown breed of powerful *hunds*, the word *dog* eventually passing into other Continental languages. Some famous dogs in history include: Argos, the dog of Ulysses;

Buddy, President Bill Clinton's dog; CERBERUS, guard of Hades; Checkers, President Richard Nixon's dog, the subject of his famous Checkers speech; Diamond, Isaac Newton's dog; Fala, President Franklin Roosevelt's dog; Flush, Elizabeth Barrett Browning's dog; Lassie, of movie and TV fame; Pete the Pup, a star of the *Our Gang* pix; Pluto, Mickey Mouse's dog; Rin Tin Tin, the first great canine movie star; Rufus, Winston Churchill's dog; Sandy, Little Orphan Annie's dog; Snoopy, Charlie Brown's dog; Toto, Dorothy's dog in *The Wizard of Oz*. *Dog* is commonly heard today, mostly in black English, as a synonym for *man*, as in "Yo, dog, where you goin'?" Before this, again in black English, it meant a brutal or treacherous person, especially a male, while in sports talk it meant an unaggressive, spiritless boxer. Long before, American mountain men used *dog* as an affectionate form of address for one another, much as youngsters do today.

dog days. Mad dogs don't give us this name for the hot, close days of July and August, though perhaps the prevalence of mad dogs at that time of year has kept the phrase *dog days* alive. The expression originated in Roman times as *canicularis dies*, "days of the dog," and was an astronomical expression referring to the dog star Sirius, or possibly Procyon. The Romans linked the rising of the Dog Star, the most brilliant star in the constellation, *Canis Major*, with the sultry summer heat, believing that the star added to the extreme heat of the sun. "Canicular days," of course, have nothing to do with heat from the Dog Star, but the ancient expression remains popular after more than 20 centuries.

dog eat dog. According to the *Dictionary of Americanisms*, this is a phrase from the American frontier first recorded in 1834. It means ruthless competition with no holds barred; everyone for himself or herself; tit for tat. British poet Thomas Gray in an 1858 letter quoted a saying meaning exactly the opposite: "I cannot promise any special instruction and shall take no fee. 'Dog does not eat dog' is the saying, you know." Whether these two sayings arose independently or have something to do with each other hasn't been firmly established.

doggerel. *See* PIG LATIN.

doggone. There are two top choices for the origins of this mild, still popular word. An Americanism first recorded in 1826, it may be simply an alteration of goddamn, a "fantastic perversion" Weekley called it. Or it could come from the Scotch *dagone*, meaning "gone to the dogs." *See* GADZOOKS.

dog grass. Said to be eaten by dogs when they have lost their appetite, *dog grass* is another name for the very troublesome, weedy "quack grass," "witch grass" or "couch grass" (*Agropyron repens*). The plant acts as an emetic and purgative, illustrating the fact that even the most pernicious garden plants have their uses.

dogie. The American cowboy has been shouting "git along, little dogie" for more than a century, but no one knows where the word *dogie*, for "a motherless calf," comes from. Maybe it derives from "dough-guts," referring to the bloated bellies of such calves, perhaps *dogie* is a clipped form of the Spanish *adobe*, ("mud"), possibly the cows were so small that they were playfully

called "doggies" and the pronunciation changed. Since some American cowboys were black there is also the possibility that the Bambara *dogo*, "small, short," is the source, or the Afro-Creole *dogi*, meaning the same. Your guess is as good as any etymologist's.

dog it. To dog it is to loaf on the job, to shirk one's responsibilities and evade work. This common expression goes back to about 1920 and may come from baseball, where it means to play in this lackadaisical manner. One theory suggests it originated when an infielder lifted his leg, as a dog might, as a hard-hit grounder came to him, but the reference may simply be to the expression *a lazy dog* or *lazy as a dog*.

dog latin. *See* PIG LATIN.

dogmerd. British novelist Anthony Burgess apparently invented this new word in the 1980s, employing the English *dog* and the French *merde* (for "excrement"). It is a word more adult than all other euphemisms we have for good old Anglo-Saxon expressions, and yet it conveys the nose-squinching reaction one has to stepping in the stuff. The word *merd* for excrement has of course been used in English for centuries, first recorded in 1477 and employed by Ben Jonson and Richard Burton, among other great writers.

do-gooder. When this term was first recorded in 1654, it simply meant someone who does good, or a reformer. However, by the 1920s in the U.S. it began to take on the derogatory sense of a bleeding heart or naive idealist, and today it has only that meaning.

dog robber. Sometimes heard as a derogatory term for a baseball umpire, *dog robber* has military origins. It was used in the mid-19th century to describe an Army officer's orderly, who ate in the officers' mess and was contemptuously said to rob the dogs of the table scraps there. Later the contemptuous words were applied to umpires.

dog rose. The wild, hardy dog rose (*Rosa canina*, called *cynorrodon* by Pliny) is said to have been so named because the Romans thought that eating the flower cured the rabid bites of wild dogs. But then the Romans also believed that shortening a dog's tail was a preventative for rabies, and the Greeks thought that dogs could cure many diseases by licking patients. Today the dog rose is more realistically valued for the high vitamin-C content of its "hips."

dogs famous in history. *See* DOG.

dog's letter. *See* R.

dog's life; to go to the dogs; die like a dog; dirty dog. Dogs aren't the prized, often pampered pets in other countries that they are in America. In the East they are often considered pariahs, scavengers of the streets, and the Chinese, Koreans, and Japanese, among other Asians, commonly eat them. Englishmen of earlier times used dogs primarily for hunting and kept them outside or in a rude shelter, not generally as house pets. The dogs were fed table scraps there wasn't any further use for, and these they had to fight over. It didn't seem ideal, a dog's life, and Englishmen of the 16th century began to compare anyone who had become impoverished, who was going to utter ruin naturally or morally, to their maltreated canines. *To lead a dog's life* was to be bothered every moment, never to be left in peace; *to go to the dogs* was to become just like the helpless animals; and *to die like a dog* was to come to a miserable, shameful end. There were many other similar phrases that arose before the dogs had their day in England and America, including *throw it to the dogs*, "to throw something away that's worthless"; and of course *a dirty dog*, "a morally reprehensible or filthy person."

dog soldiers.   Dog soldiers were originally members of a Cheyenne warrior society, the word often applied loosely to any Cheyenne or Indian warrior. The origin of the name is unknown. Later *dog soldiers* came to mean outlawed members of certain Western Indian tribes who banded together.

dog tags.   The metal identification tags worn by soldiers were not dubbed dog tags until World War I, when they were so called because they resembled a license tag on a dog's collar. Identification tags became required in the Army in 1906, but men had worn them on their own initiative since the Civil War. Two are worn so that, in the event of death, one can be buried with the body and the other kept as a record. The Army is now experimenting with an embedded microchip dog tag that can hold up to 12,000 characters—an individual's vital medical data and personnel file as well as his service number, blood type, and religion.

dog towns.   *See* TRY IT OUT ON THE DOG.

dogwatch.   The dogwatch at sea is the period between 4:00 and 6:00 P.M. (the first dogwatch) or the period between 6:00 and 8:00 P.M. (the second dogwatch). The other watches aboard ship are:

    12:00 to 4:00 P.M.—afternoon watch
    8:00 P.M. to midnight—first night watch
    12:00 to 4:00 A.M.—middle watch
    4:00 to 8:00 A.M.—morning watch
    8:00 A.M. to noon—forenoon watch

The dogwatches are only two hours each, so that the same men aren't always on duty at the same time each afternoon. Some experts say *dogwatch* is a corruption of *dodge watch*, and others associate *dogwatch* with the fitful sleep of sailors called dog sleep, because it is a stressful watch. But no one really knows the origin of this term, which was first recorded in 1700.

dogwood.   *See* ZEP.

dogwood tree.   This common tree has a mysterious name. John C. Loudon wrote in *The Hardy Trees and Shrubs of Britain* (1838) that the beautiful tree "is called Dogwood because a decoction of its leaves was used to wash dogs, to free them from vermin." This may be true, but no evidence has been found to support the theory. The popular ornamental *(Cornus florida)* was in early times called the "dogger tree," the "dogge berie tree," the "hounder tree" and the "hounde berie tree" as well as the dogwood, so it surely has some connection with dogs. Another possibility is that it was named the "dogberry

tree" because its dark-purple berries resembled the berries of another, unknown tree that was used as a medicine for dogs, and that *dogberry* became *dogwood* in time. No link between the tree's wood and dogs has been found; we only know that in the past its wood was used to make toothpicks and that its crushed bark was thrown into the water to intoxicate fish and make them easy to catch by hand. John Ciardi proposes in *A Second Browser's Dictionary* (1983) that "Dog is a simple corruption of OE *dagge*, spit, skewer, because the wood of the European dogwood, being hard and smooth-grained, was commonly used for spitting meat." *See* CORNELIAN CHERRY.

dogwood winter.   Similar to BLACKBERRY *winter*. In 1907 an issue of *American Folk-lore* reported this explanation by a contributor: " 'Don't you know what dogwood winter is?' demanded the man from Hickory, North Carolina. 'There is always a spell of it in May, when the dogwood tree is in bloom. For several days there is cold, disagreeable, cloudy weather, and often a touch of frost.' "

doily.   It is probable that a London linen draper named Doily, Doiley, Doylet, or Doyly sold and perhaps invented the first doily napkins. Eustace Budgell, a cousin of British essayist Joseph Addison, uses the first spelling in the January 24, 1712, number of *The Spectator*, noting, "The famous Doily is still fresh in everyone's memory, who raised a Fortune by finding out Materials for such Stuffs as might at once be cheap and genteel . . . [a] frugal method of gratifying our pride . . ."

doing a land-office business.   Before the Civil War, the U.S. government established land offices for the allotment of government-owned land in western territories just opened to settlers. These agencies registered applicants, and the rush of citizens lining up on mornings long before the office opened made the expression *doing a land-office business*, "a tremendous amount of business," part of the language by at least 1853. Adding to the queues were prospectors filing mining claims, which were also handled by land offices. After several decades the phrase was applied figuratively to a great business in something other than land, even, in one case I remember, to a land-office business in fish.

do it while standing on one foot.   This Americanism means to do something easily and quickly, to encapsulate or describe it with little effort, as in "She explained her theory to reporters while standing on one foot."

doldrums.   The doldrums has come to mean any area where a ship is likely to be becalmed, especially that area near the equator between the northeast and southeast trade winds. *Doldrums*, first recorded in 1811, probably derives from the words *dull* and *tantrum*, as if the dullness of such an area could drive one to tantrums. The phrase *in the doldrums* means "down in the dumps," much like mariners felt when they weren't moving anywhere. *See* MONSOON.

the dole.   Since 1911, when the National Insurance Act became law, the British have used *the dole* (from Old English *dal*, share, and a later meaning of a charitable contribution) to mean a state unemployment benefit: "He lives on the dole." Americans usually call such state payments "unemployment checks," "welfare," or "family assistance," among other things, but *dole* does have limited usage in the U.S., most often in a disparaging way.

Dole's beard.   A name in Hawaii for Spanish moss *(Tillandsia usneodides)* that is named after Sanford Dole, "the grand old man of Hawaii." The Pineapple King had a long gray beard that reminded people of Spanish moss hanging from a tree. The moss is also called Mr. Dole.

doll.   *Doll* was originally a nickname for Dorothy. In the 16th century it became a popular name for a mistress or loose woman, such as Shakespeare's Doll Tearsheet, and a century later, perhaps because such women were considered "playthings," became the name for a child's toy representing a human being.

dollar.   The word *dollar* can be traced to the name of a saint. The most likely candidate is St. Joachim, father of the Blessed Virgin, for whom the small mining town Sankt ("Saint") Joachimsthal in Bohemia had been named. It happened that the town and valley, or *thal*, belonged to a vast estate containing a rich silver mine from which one-ounce coins were minted. These silver coins, with a picture of St. Joachim on the face, were at first called *Joachimsthalers* ("of the valley of Joachim"). But the cumbersome name was soon shortened to *thalers*, pronounced *dahlers* in northern German dialect. The name eventually got to England as *daller* and by the end of the 17th century *dollar* was the accepted term applied to any foreign coin, especially Spanish pieces of eight. When the newly formed United States adopted its monetary system in 1785, it completely broke with England and "resolved that the money unit of the U.S.A. be one dollar (Spanish)." The first silver dollars were coined here in 1792, and greenback dollars as we know them were first printed during the Civil War.

dollar-a-year man.   Someone who serves the federal government for patriotic rather than financial reasons is called a *dollar-a-year man*. The term came into use during World War I when such volunteers were paid a dollar a year because one dollar was the "valuable consideration" needed to make their contracts binding.

dollar bugs.   A nickname for the whirligig beetle, because an old story holds that if you catch one in your hand you'll find a dollar in it. The bugs are called lucky bugs for the same reason.

$ (dollar sign). $—the dollar sign—probably doesn't derive from the figure "8" on Spanish "pieces of eight," the usual explanation. The dollar sign was most likely modified from the twisted Pillars of Hercules stamped with a scroll around them on the pieces of eight. It may, however, result from a combination of the two symbols, or a corruption of the Spanish *Ps*, the contraction for "peso." Anyway, if George Washington threw a silver dollar across the Potomac or Delaware, it must have been a foreign coin—for, as noted, American silver dollars weren't minted at the time.

Dolly; cloning.   Dolly is the name of the famous sheep (died on February 14, 2003) Scottish scientist Ian Wilmut and his coworkers cloned from another sheep, creating a genetically identical individual from body cells. The word *clone*, first recorded in 1903, derives from the Greek *klon*, twig or slip, and originally referred to plant propagation. William Safire wrote in his *New York Times* op-ed column (7/16/01) that Dr. Wilmut "is an informed opponent of human replication; he knows how many of his attempts to clone a sheep failed, and believes similar attempts with humans would be horrifying."

dolphin.   The *dolphin*, its name derived from the Latin *delphin*, for "the cetaceous mammal," has long been regarded as "man's best finned friend." *Dolphinet* is an old word for a female dolphin. Wrote Spenser: "The Lyon chose his mate, the Turtle Dove Her deare, the Dolphin his own Dolphinet." In recent experiments dolphins have been taught to understand 25 words arranged in sentences. *See* CHIMPANZEE; DORADO; PARROT.

domino effect.   The domino effect is the political theory holding that if one country or region is taken over by a neighbor, especially a Communist one, the nearby nations will fall one after another. Also called the domino theory, the term was coined in about 1960 and true or not, was especially applied to Vietnam and the rest of Southeast Asia. It is based on the way a row of dominoes falls when stood upright on the board or table in a common entertainment. The game takes its name from a likening of the pieces once used in it—then black backs and ivory faces—to "domino hoods" worn by priests in medieval times. Another possibility would be the likeness of the double-one domino to the *domino*, the small black eye mask with two holes for the eyes.

Dom Pérignon.   Dom Pierre Pérignon (1638–1715), the man who put the bubbles into CHAMPAGNE and after whom Moët et Chandon named its most famous vintage some years ago, was a blind man who renounced the world when only 15 and joined the Benedictine order. Cellarmaster of the monastery near Epernay, France, Dom Pérignon eventually found that corks tightly drawn in his bottles would not be forced out, as would rags, and would retain naturally expanding gases, allowing for the so-called second fermentation in the bottle that is essential for any true sparkling champagne. Although unproved, the old story certainly rates a toast, if only as an excuse for another glass.

donate.   The verb *donate* is a back formation from the noun *donation*. An Americanism recorded as early as 1795, it is firmly established today, but at first met with vociferous opposition, having been placed on William Cullen Bryant's *Index Expurgatorius* and denounced as "pretentious and magniloquent vulgarism" by a British writer as late as 1935.

Don Juan.   Of the names most frequently applied to libertines and lovers—Casanova, Don Juan, Cyrano, Valentino, Romeo, and Lothario—only the last is completely fictional. Don Juan, though immortalized in Byron's incomplete cantos, Mozart's Don Giovanni, and the myths and literature of many countries, is supposedly based on the 14th-century Spanish nobleman Don Juan Tenorio. That this original Don Juan had 2,594 mistresses, according to the valet's figures in Mozart's opera, is doubtful if not impossible, but the aristocratic libertine's conquests were legion. His last was the daughter of Seville's commandant. While attempting to ravish young Dona Anna, the legendary lover was surprised by her father, whom he dispatched in a duel. But local Franciscan monks decided that this was one debauchery too many and lured Don Juan to their monastery, where he was killed with his boots on. The monks, to conceal their crime, claimed that he had been carried off to hell by a statue of the commandant on the grounds, and thus the legend of Don Juan had its basis in fact.

donkey's years.   A very long time. The words may be a punning allusion to the long length of a donkey's ears and the fact that donkeys do often live to a great old age. The expression is first recorded in 1916 but may be older. *See* YONKS.

Donnelly.   A fighter so powerful that any staggering punch came to be named after him. In this case the eponym is Irish boxer Daniel Donnelly (1788–1820), heralded in his time but little known today. *See* BRODERICK; BELCHER; BENDIGO.

Donner Pass; Donner Lake.   The scene of one of the most gruesome tragedies in western history is named for the two Donner families who were part of a California-bound wagon train of emigrants that set out across the plains from Illinois in 1846. The Donner party, beset by great hardships, paused to recoup their strength at what is now *Donner Lake* in eastern California's Sierra Nevada, only to be trapped by early snows that October. All passes were blocked deep with snow and every attempt to get out failed. Forty of the 87 members of the party, which included 39 children, starved to death during the winter, and the survivors, driven mad by hunger, resorted to cannibalism before expeditions from the Sacramento Valley rescued them in April. The Donner party's gruesome yet heroic adventures have figured in much native literature. California's Donner State Historic Monument commemorates the event; the Donner Pass is traversed by U.S. Highway 40 today.

donnybrook.   Too much flowing *usquebaugh* and too many flailing shillelaghs made the Donnybrook Fair a dangerous place to visit in old Ireland. The two-week-long fair, held in August every year since King John licensed it in 1204, was the scene of so many wild free-for-alls that the town's name became a synonym for any knock-'em-down-drag-'em-out brawl involving a group of people. By 1885 things had gotten so bad that they were too much for even those legendary Irishmen who love a good fight and the fair was finally closed. Donnybrook is now a relatively peaceful suburb about a mile and a half from Dublin.

Do-Nothing Congress.   *See* USELESS PARLIAMENT.

don't bogart that joint; Bogard.   In his films Humphrey Bogart often left cigarettes dangling from his mouth without smoking them. This led to the counterculture expression *Don't bogart that joint*; that is, "don't take so long with, don't hog, that stick of marijuana; smoke and pass it on to the next person." The term became widely used after appearing in a song in the film *Easy Rider.* Among those who practice the long-standing, widespread habit of communally smoking marijuana cigarettes, *bogarting* is considered both selfish and a waste of the expensive weed. Bogart's name, in the form of *Bogard,* also became inner-city slang for "to act tough or in a forceful manner" in the 1950s, deriving from the tough-guy heroes Bogart portrayed.

don't change horses in midstream.   The phrase, possibly suggested to Abraham Lincoln by an old Dutch farmer he knew, is recorded almost a quarter of a century before Lincoln said it. But Lincoln immortalized the expression when he accepted his nomination for the presidency in 1864. Waving aside any suggestions that the honor was a personal one, he told the Republicans that he was sure they hadn't decided he was "the greatest or the best man in America, but rather, . . . have concluded it is not best to swap horses while crossing the river, and have further concluded that I am not so poor a horse that they might not make a botch of it in trying to swap." Over the years "the river," which was of course the Civil War, was abbreviated to "midstream" and the saying *don't change horses in midstream* came to mean "don't change leaders in a crisis."

don't come the acid.   Don't play the wise guy, don't give me any of your wise "acid" (vitriolic) answers. The phrase is British in origin with some American use.

don't count on rain [when it's needed] 'til it's floatin' chips up around your belly button.   *Chips* in this Texas saying refer to cow manure chips from the pasture.

don't count your chickens before they're hatched.   Don't count on profits before you have them in hand. "I woulde not have him to counte his chickens so soone before they be hatcht," is the first recorded use of this expression, in 1579. Perhaps the idea behind the words goes all the way back to Aesop's fable of the woman who brings eggs to market, announcing that she will buy a goose with the money she gets for her eggs, that with her profits from the goose she will buy a cow, and so on—but in the excitement of all her anticipations kicks over her basket and breaks her eggs. *Don't count your chickens before they're hatched* is also used as the moral of Aesop's tale "The Milkmaid and Her Pail."

don't even think about it.   A stern warning to someone who might be about to do something, as in "She gave them a look that said, *don't even think about it.*" The expression, widely heard today, possibly originated in the 1980s, as is witnessed in New York City Mayor Ed Koch's "Don't even think about parking here" signs of the day.

don't fence me in.   Give me freedom, elbow room—an expression and a song often associated with the American West. Originally *don't fence me in* was a line in a poem written by Bob Fletcher, a westerner. Cole Porter bought the rights to the poem, revised the lyrics, and wrote the music for the song, which wasn't used until a decade later, in the film *Hollywood Canteen* (1944). The next year it was featured in the Roy Rogers's movie *Don't Fence Me In.* "Meanwhile, in a sad irony," Frank Richard Prassel notes in *The Great American Outlaw* (1993), "Porter had been left crippled by a riding accident."

don't get your bowels in an uproar.   Calm down, cool it. Said to someone who is acting unreasonably angry or excited. The expression, still commonly heard, isn't a new one, dating back a century or more. It may be a euphemism for the expression *don't get your balls in an uproar.*

don't get your knickers in a twist. A British slang expression first recorded in 1980 that is fairly common in America today. It means "don't get excited, confused, amazed, worried." KNICKERS, as many if not most Americans know, are women's underwear in England and Ireland.

don't give a rap. Counterfeiters took advantage of the scarcity of copper coins in the early 18th century and began flooding Ireland with bogus halfpence. These worthless coins became known as raps and inspired the expression *not worth a rap*, "of no value at all," and *I don't give a rap*, "don't care in the slightest."

don't give holy things to hounds. *See* CAST PEARLS BEFORE SWINE.

Don't give up the ship! A mortally wounded Captain James Laurence, in command of the frigate U.S.S. *Chesapeake*, may really have said, "Tell the men to fire faster and not to give up the ship until she sinks" during the famous sea battle off Boston in the War of 1812—no one is sure of his exact words—but whatever his order, the British won the battle.

don't go to the bad for the shadow of an ass. Though little heard today, this expression, meaning "don't fight over foolish things," has a long history. Demosthenes told the story of a young Athenian traveler who rented an ass or donkey. When he took shelter from the sun at midday under the shadow of the beast its owner appeared and claimed the shadow for his own, saying he had rented the ass to the traveler but not its shadow. The two fought and fought over the shadow, then took the matter to the law courts, where both men were ruined because the suit lasted so long.

don't hurry, Hopkins. A Mr. Hopkins, late of Kentucky, once returned a promissory note to a creditor along with instructions that "The said Hopkins is not to be hurried in paying the above." Since that day in the middle of the 19th century, it is claimed, said Hopkins has been remembered by the admonition *Don't hurry, Hopkins*, an ironic reproof to deadbeats late in paying their bills or persons slow in anything else. But the phrase was used in England almost a century before with just the opposite humorous meaning, implying "don't be too hasty." In this sense it derived from a Mr. Hopkins, or Hopkin, "that came to jail over night, and was hanged the next morning."

don't know him from Adam. Many have observed that only a fool wouldn't know someone from Adam, since Adam had no navel and wore only a fig leaf. But the old proverb persists. *I wouldn't know him from Adam's off ox* is possibly an attempted improvement on the original expression, *off ox* referring to the yoked ox farthest away from the driver—the one even less familiar than the near ox, and surely less distinguishable than old Adam.

don't let money burn a hole in your pocket. Dating back to the early 16th century, this advice has often been given to children in recent times. It means "don't be so eager to spend your money, don't feel like it is burning a hole in your pocket to get out and be spent."

don't like the cut of his jib. *See* CUT OF HIS JIB.

don't look a gift horse in the mouth. The age of a horse can be roughly determined by examining its teeth. That people knew this long before A.D. 400 is witnessed by the appearance of the above expression in the writings of St. Jerome, who called it a familiar proverb at the time. *Don't look a gift horse in the mouth*, an injunction to accept presents gracefully without trying to find something wrong with them or determine how much they're worth, is literally reproduced in German, French, and other languages, though its first English use is *don't look a given horse in the mouth*.

don't look back, something might be gaining on you. Sage advice from baseball great Leroy "Satchel" Paige, who would have been one of the greatest pitchers in the major leagues if the color barrier had been broken earlier. Paige's five additional rules were: 1) avoid fried meats which angry up the blood; 2) if your stomach disputes you, lie down and pacify it with cool thoughts; 3) keep your juices flowing by jangling around gently as you move; 4) go very gently on the vices, such as carrying on in society—the social ramble ain't restful; and 5) avoid running at all times.

don't make two bites of a cherry. The expression is an old one warning against dividing things too small to be divided, against prolonging for two days jobs that should take only one. It may have some connection with polite European courtiers three centuries ago who acted so daintily in public that they always took two bites to eat a cherry.

don't poke one's nose into it. Don't pry into something that is not your concern, as in "Don't poke your nose in my business." This term has been used for over four centuries, the American version often substituting *stick* for *poke*.

don't sell the steak, sell the sizzle. *See* SALMON.

don't stick your neck out. Chickens, for some reason still known only to chickens, usually stretch out their necks when put on the chopping block, making it all the easier for the butcher to chop their heads off. Probably our expression, a warning to someone not to expose himself to danger or criticism when this can be avoided, which is American slang from the late 19th century, originated from the bloody barnyard image. Lynchings have also been suggested, but lynched men rarely stick their necks out for the noose.

don't take any wooden nickels. First recorded in about 1915, this expression was originally a warning from friends and relatives to rubes leaving the sticks in the great migration from rural areas to the big cities at the turn of the century. It was a humorous adjuration meaning beware of those city slickers, for no real wooden nickels were ever counterfeited—they would have cost more to make than they'd have been worth. Ironically, country boys were the ones who possibly *did* succeed in passing off wooden objects as the real thing. Yankee peddlers as early as 1825 allegedly sold wooden nutmegs, which cost manufacturers a quarter of a cent apiece, mixed in with lots of real nutmegs worth four cents each.

don't wash your dirty linen in public. Anthony Trollope didn't coin this phrase in *The Last Chronicle of Barset* (1867). What the hardworking novelist did was turn around the old French proverb *Il faut laver son linge sale en famille*, "One should wash one's dirty linen in private." Both sayings mean the same: don't expose family quarrels or skeletons in public, keep discreditable things within the house where they in all decency belong. The "dirty linen" is considered discreditable to the person who washes it as well as his family and is usually exposed out of anger at a relative.

don't write it if you can say it; don't say it if you can grunt it. Advice TV news commentator Chris Matthews heard an old political pro give to an aspiring politician. Heard on NBC-TV on January 18, 2002.

doodlebug. An American word probably dating back to California at the beginning of the 20th century for any divining rod said to be able to locate oil and other minerals. The term is usually applied to the bogus divining rods of con men. The word was also used during World War II to describe the German flying bomb or V-1, and previously was the name of a tiger beetle or its larva.

doofus. Originally American slang of the late 1950s meaning "a fool, a dope, a jerk," or any combination of the three. Some writers claim the word is an alteration of *goofus* for the same, while others say it is of Yiddish or German origin. Australians would call a doofus a "donk."

doolally. Nuts, crazy, bonkers. British troops in India during the 19th century waited in the town of Deolali for troopships to take them home after their enlistments expired. Deolali, which they pronounced Doolally, became the scene of so much abberant behavior and illness among soldiers with too much time on their hands that the town's name became synonymous with their crazy behavior, which was also called "doolally fever."

dooley. Another name for a sweet potato and yam in the American South, possibly named after someone who developed a superior variety—which makes that individual one of the few people to have a vegetable named after him or her. *Dooley* also refers to an outdoor toilet building in parts of the South, apparently named after a contractor who built such public structures for the federal government during the Great Depression. *See* CHIC SALES.

Doolittle do'd it! In World War II days Red Skelton's "mean widdle kid" used to say "I do'd it!" on the comic's radio show. A news story borrowed Skelton's words on April 18, 1942, when Lt. Colonel James "Jimmy" Doolittle and his men took off from the carrier *Hornet* and made the first air attack on the Japanese mainland, greatly uplifting American morale in those dark days. "*Doolittle do'd it!*" became a popular catchphrase throughout America.

doornail. *See* DEAD AS A DOORNAIL.

doo-wop. A 1950s singing style in which back-up singers of a group chant rhythmically in the background while the lead singer carries the song. This rhythm-and-blues style is named after the nonsense word *doowop* that the backup singers often chant repetitively, though other nonsense words like *sh-boom* and *sh-bop* are also used.

a doozy. Something special, outstanding, as in "That's a doozy of a coat you've got," or, in the negative, "That's a doozy of a cut you've got." An Americanism first recorded in the early 1900s, it may be an alteration of *daisy*, influenced by the last name of the great Italian actress Eleanora Duse (1859–1924), who was indeed *a doozy* of a thespian.

dope; dopey. *Dope* for drugs is an Americanism of Dutch origin, deriving from the Dutch *doop*, "sauce or gravy." It is only since the late 1890s that stupid people have been called dopes, or dopey (like Dopey of *Snow White and the Seven Dwarfs*), as if they were under the influence of dope. The word was first recorded as *doop*, or "gravy," in 1807 by Washington Irving. It then came to mean any preparation containing unknown substances (1872), and then drugs (1895), possibly because these were mysterious unknown substances to most people. How *dope* came to mean information, or knowledge, a usage first recorded in 1901, is anybody's guess. Maybe knowing the dope, or "inside information," first alluded to knowing what was inside preparations whose constituents were unknown to most people. "Gimme a dope" still means "Give me a Coca-Cola" in the South, especially among teenagers, and dates back to the 19th century when the fabled soft drink was touted as a tonic and contained a minute amount of cocaine. Coca-Cola's inventor, druggist John S. Pemberton, brewed the drink in his backyard and knew it was done when he smelled the cooked cocaine—no reactions in the man or among his neighbors are reported.

dorado. The *dorado (Coryphaena hippuras)* is for reasons unknown sometimes called the DOLPHIN, but this game fish is no relation to the friendly mammal. The fabled "dolphin" of sports fishermen has been clocked at 40 miles an hour while chasing flying fishes. Among the most majestic of fish, old male dorados have a high, narrow crest heightening the forehead. All dorados are beautifully colored—marked with blues, purples, golds, and bright yellows. When taken from the water, pink and green flushes run over their sides. Byron and many another poet has celebrated the beauty of the dorado's colors when it is dying. The splendid creature's name appropriately comes from the Latin *deaurare*, to gild.

dord. *See* GHOST WORD.

do, re, mi, fa, so, la, ti, do. The work of Italian musician and singing teacher Guido d'Arezzo, born toward the end of the 10th century, forms the basis of the modern system of musical notation. In about 1040 this inspired genius devised the Guido scale, or Artinian syllables, that still sing his praises. The names he gave to the musical notes of the scale are still used today in modified form (do, re, mi, fa, sol, la). The Benedictine monk based them on six lines of a Latin hymn to St. John the Baptist, which happened to form the scale. Over the years the final syllable *ti* was added to the scale and two centuries ago the syllable *do* joined it in English. *Solfeggio* is the English word, taken from the Italian, to describe the musical exercise sung with Guido's scale.

dormouse.   A member of the rodent family that the Romans raised for food, the little, six-inch-long dormouse *(Glis glis)* resembles a small squirrel in looks and habits. Its name—about five centuries old—is something of a mystery, but many etymologists believe the creature is named for its appearance of sleepiness, that dormouse derives from the Swedish *dorsk,* "sleepy," or the Latin *dormire,* "to sleep." In fact, the dormouse, which Alice had such a hard time keeping awake at the Mad Hatter's tea party, is one of the legendary "seven sleepers" of the animal world, along with the ground squirrel, marmot, hedgehog, badger, bat, and bear. A hibernating dormouse—coiled up with its forefeet tucked under its chin, its hind feet clenched in front of its face, and its tail curled over its face—can be rolled across a table like a wheel and won't come awake. The savage garden dormouse will immediately devour any dormouse that begins its winter sleep before the others, even its own mother.

dornick.   An unusual Irish word that came to America with immigrants in the 19th century and is still used by farmers in the lower northern U.S. Deriving ultimately from Irish Gaelic *dornog,* it means a round stone small enough to be thrown from a field in the process of being cleared.

Dorothy Perkins's rose.   Ranking with Peace and Crimson Glory as the best known of American roses, the Dorothy Perkins is a pink rambler introduced by the famous Jackson & Perkins Nursery of Newark, New York, in 1901. It is a small, cluster-flowering type, and though ramblers have bowed in popularity to larger-flowered varieties, it remains a sentimental favorite much mentioned in literature. The rose was named for the wife of the firm's co-owner.

d'Orsay pump; dossy; Quai d'Orsay.   The last of the dandies, Count d'Orsay, Alfred Guillaume Gabriel (1801–52), designed the innovative *d'Orsay pump* that became the model for women's footwear. Like his contemporary Beau Brummel, d'Orsay, the son of a distinguished French general, was an *arbiter elegantarium* of English society, and the slang term *dossy,* for "elegant or smart," may also derive from his name. The man's shoe he devised in 1838 fit more snugly than any pump before it, due to its low-cut sides and V-shaped top, and was soon adopted by women. D'Orsay, an ex-soldier who came to London from France in 1821, won fame as a painter, sculptor, diarist, and wit, being "the most perfect gentleman of his day." Named for d'Orsay's famous father is the *Quai d'Orsay*—that quay along the south bank of the Seine in Paris that has become synonymous with the French Foreign Office, Department of Foreign Affairs, and other government offices located there.

do-si-do.   The square dance call, sometimes *dozy dozy,* instructs partners to circle back to back and, appropriately, comes from the French *dos-à-dos,* "back to back."

doss.   A British word hardly used by Americans in conversation but encountered fairly frequently in literature. It means 1) a bed, 2) to sleep outside as homeless people do, and 3) something that is easy, not very difficult. *Doss house* refers to what Americans would call a *flop house,* and *to doss about* means "to goof off."

do the needful.   This is an English expression used only in India up to this time. It means "to do what is proper," "to do what is right," "to do the right thing," as the African-American phrase instructs.

do time.   To serve a prison sentence. The expression was first recorded in 1865. A cautionary rhyme among criminals goes: "If you can't do the time, don't do the crime."

dot the i's and cross the t's.   Be meticulous, make sure the smallest details are covered, just as these letters must be dotted and crossed to be correctly written. The expression dates back to the mid-19th century and is still common today.

double cross.   *Double cross* came into use only in about 1870, apparently as an English racing term describing the common practice of winning a race after promising to arrange a *cross,* to lose it. *Cross,* for "a prearranged swindle or fix," dates back to the early 19th century and was used by Thackeray in *Vanity Fair* to describe a fixed horse race. The adjective *double* here is meant in its sense of "duplicity," so *double cross* really means "dishonesty about dishonesty"; in fact, the earlier expression "to put on the double double" meant the same as *double-cross.*

double-dealer.   Card playing gives us this term for a cheat. The word is hardly a new one, dating back to before 1547, when William Baldwin wrote in *A Treatise of Moral Philosophie:* "God . . . abhorreth . . . hypocrites and double dealers."

double entendre.   *Double entendre,* "double meaning" (one often of doubtful propriety), is a French term that came into English in the 17th century. While the French expression for the same is *double entente* today, it was *double entendre* when the term was adopted.

doubleheader.   A railroad train pulled by two locomotives was called a doubleheader in the 1870s. Though there were baseball doubleheaders—two games played in succession on the same day—as early as 1882, the term doesn't seem to have been used in baseball until the end of the century. It could have derived from the railroad usage but there is no absolute proof of this.

double in brass.   To be versatile, to be able to do more than one thing well, or to hold two jobs in order to make more money. In its earliest recorded use, the American expression meant to play in a circus act and perform in a circus band as well. It was very common for a circus performer in the 1880s to play in the brass band when not performing as a clown, acrobat, or equestrian, and it is still sometimes the practice in small one-ring circuses. So *to double in brass* became circus talk of the day, was adopted by actors to describe an actor playing two parts in the same play, and then passed into general use.

double negatives.   Though considered ungrammatical, double negatives such as, "I ain't seen nobody" are common in both American and British English. Americans in various regions also use triple negatives ("I ain't got nary none"), quadruple negatives ("That boy ain't never done nothin' nohow"), and even quintuple negatives ("I ain't never seen no men of no kind do no washin'). In fact, there is nothing new about multiple negatives, which were standard in English through the time of Shakespeare.

double play. Baseball's double play, a play in which two putouts are made, is recorded as early as 1858, but it was often called a force play up until the 1870s. It has since become a term Americans use when referring to any two accomplishments made at the same time.

double-talk. Purposely confusing talk, sometimes humorous, often meant to cheat a customer or evade a question. *Double-talk* is first recorded in the mid-1930s. For a humorous example, here's an excerpt from the Federal Writer's Project *New York Panorama* (1938):

> Observe in this sample of Mr. Hymie Caplin's double talk the creation of gibberish having a distinctly disturbing "sensible sound," and the ingenuity with which it is woven into the entire melody line: "Well, take now you're in a restaurant. So you say to the waiter, 'Gimme the chicken and vegetables but portostat with the chicken with the fustates on it.' So he says 'What?' and you say 'You know, the portostat, and moonsign the sarina on the top with the vegetables.' "

The same source explains that this "humorously conceived system of language corruption" is meant to seduce or rib the unknowing listener into believing that he is "either deaf, ignorant, or ready for a lifetime run in the part of Napoleon." Also called *talking on the double*, the "language" hasn't nearly the number of speakers that it had a half-century ago.

double tap. Recent slang, unrecorded, among detectives for two gunshots to the head, a technique often used by contract killers to make sure their victims are dead.

doublethink. A coinage of British author George Orwell in *Nineteen-Eighty-four* (1949), *doublethink*, as the author explained in his novel, meant "the power of holding two contradictory beliefs in one's mind simultaneously, and accepting both of them." Orwell's book, a warning about the possible coming of the ultimate police state, contributed many words and phrases, including its title, to the language. NEWSPEAK (a language of the dictatorship that narrows the range of free thought), *Thought Police* and BIG BROTHER IS WATCHING YOU are among them.

doubting Thomas. History's first doubting Thomas was St. Thomas, one of the 12 apostles. Because he doubted the resurrection of Christ (John 20:24–29) and questioned Christ in an earlier passage in the Bible (John 14:5) early readers of the Scriptures gave his name to any faithless doubter. Thomas, however, reformed when the resurrected Christ let him touch the wounds he suffered on the cross and admonished him, "Blessed are those who have not seen and yet believe." Tradition has it that later, when no longer a doubter, Thomas went on a mission to India where a king gave him a large sum to build a magnificent palace. He spent the money on food for the poor instead, "erecting a superb palace in Heaven," and so became the patron saint of masons and architects.

doughboy. This word for a U.S. Army infantryman may have originated from the term *adobe*, which Spaniards in the Southwest called military personnel, though this is only one of several possible explanations for the term. *See* ADOBE.

doughnuts. American doughnuts go back to the time of the Pilgrims, who learned to make these "nuts" of fried sweet dough in Holland before coming to the New World. It is to the Pennsylvania Dutch that we owe the hole in the middle of the doughnut, or sinker, as the doughnut is sometimes called.

Douglas fir. Only the giant sequoias and redwoods of California among North American trees exceed the Douglas fir in height and massiveness. The coniferous evergreens grow to heights of 300 feet and reach 12 feet in diameter, yielding more lumber than any other American species. The Douglas fir, or Douglas spruce, as it is sometimes called, was named for its discoverer, David Douglas (1798–1834), who came here from Scotland in 1823 to study American plants and to collect specimens for the Royal Horticultural Society. The former gardener at Glasgow's botanical gardens collected more than 200 plants and seeds then unknown in Europe. His 11-year journal became historically valuable because he was one of the first travelers in the Pacific Northwest. The Douglas fir, which he first observed in 1825, is botanically of the pine family, and yields a hard, strong wood of great commercial importance. Douglas died a strange death: In 1834 he extended his travels to the Hawaiian Islands, where he was killed by a wild bull.

Doulton. Like Wedgwood, Doulton is one of the most honored names in art pottery. Invented some time after 1815 by John Doulton, who was influenced by Italian pottery techniques, Doulton is still manufactured today. After John Doulton died, the pottery was made by his descendants, especially Sir Henry Doulton (1820–97). Sir Henry, who first produced stoneware drainpipes, apparently named the decorative pottery after himself. *See* ODE ON A GRECIAN URN.

Dover's powder. An early pain-relieving medicine containing opium, sugar, milk, and other ingredients that was invented by and named after English Dr. Thomas Dover (1660–1742), who also won fame as a pirate or privateer. It was the accomplished Dr. Dover who while returning to England on a captured Spanish man-of-war rescued the marooned Alexander Selkirk from the Juan Fernandez Islands, providing novelist Daniel Defoe with the theme of *Robinson Crusoe*. *See* ROBINSON CRUSOE.

dove's dung. During a famine in Samaria, the Bible tells us (2 Kings 6:25) "an ass's head" was sold for fourscore pieces of silver and a quantity of "dove's dung" for five pieces of silver. This implies that dove's dung was eaten by the Samarians, surely one of the most disgusting substances ever used as food. It is said that the Hebrew for "lentils" and "locust pods" might easily be mistaken for "ass's head" and "dove's dung," but many modern versions of the Bible still translate the words as the latter. The expression might have been used for dramatic impact, but people have eaten some strange foods throughout history, including rats, cats, dogs, all manner of insects, and other people.

do we eat it, or did we eat it? Probably an army saying when some mysterious dish, such as "mystery meat," appeared on the serving line. *Mystery meat*, however, in the form of *mystery*, is an older term, first recorded in the late 19th century. It is usually a hash or sausage of questionable origins.

Dow Jones. Short for the *Dow Jones Industrial Average*, the Dow Jones is the average daily price of selected industrial stocks. It was first published in 1884, five years before its founders, Charles Henry Dow and Edward D. Jones, began to publish the *Wall Street Journal*. In 1909 their company was acquired by Walker Barron, of *Barron's Financial Weekly*.

down. A completed play has been called a down in football since the late 19th century, *Walter Camp's Book of College Sports* (1893) explaining that it was so named because a tackled ball carrier cried "down" when he was stopped by the opposite side and could go no farther. This got the other side off his back.

down and dirty. In stud poker the last cards are dealt face down, often followed by the dealer's remark "Down and dirty," which the cards are for some of the players. From this practice came the expression *down and dirty*, meaning nasty, low, vicious and deceptive: "These are down and dirty times."

down and out. Another boxing expression which, like *down for the count*, has been used since the turn of the century. Figuratively, it can mean anything from death to abject poverty, as it does in the title of George Orwell's *Down and Out in Paris and London* (1933) as well as the movie *Down and Out in Beverly Hills*. See DOWN FOR THE COUNT.

down at the heels. See WELL-HEELED.

down bucket. An unusual greeting heard in Marblehead, Massachusetts, when one sees a friend. One theory has it that the words originated in the old days as a warning when chamber pots were being lowered from windows to the street. The reply to the greeting "Down bucket!" is usually "Up for air!"

downeaster. In the late 19th century *downeaster* was used to mean a fast, fully rigged sailing ship built in Maine or New England. Today it is a name for a resident of Maine or New England.

down for the count. A fighter who is "down for the count" is knocked out, unable to get up by the count of 10. In the 1920s these words began to take on the extended use of totally defeated, unable to go on, doomed to fail miserably.

Downing Street; Downing College; a George Downing. Like its French counterpart, the Quai d'Orsay, England's No. 10 Downing Street is another famous diplomatic address deriving from a family name. *Downing Street* is used figuratively to mean the British foreign office or government in power, No. 10 Downing Street having been the official residence of almost all British prime ministers since George II gave the house to Sir Robert Walpole for that purpose in 1735. The street in London, which also contains the British foreign and colonial offices, is named for soldier and diplomat Sir George Downing (ca. 1624–84). Downing, a nephew of Massachusetts's governor John Winthrop, was graduated in the first class at Harvard, but returned to England, where he performed the difficult trick of

serving under both Cromwell and then Charles II. A talented but selfish man, his character is said to have been "marked by treachery, servitude, and ingratitude." In his own time *a George Downing* was proverbial for "a false man who betrayed his trust." Downing College, Cambridge, derived its name later from his generous grandson, but Downing Street was on the king's property and named for the statesman during Charles II's reign. The facade of No. 10 Downing is the same as it was in 1735. Who's at No. 11? The Chancellor of the Exchequer. The government whip's office is No. 12. See D'ORSAY PUMP.

down in the dumps; dump. Someone *down in the dumps* may momentarily feel ready to be hauled off to the *garbage dump*, but the *dumps* in the expression derives from the Dutch *domp*, "mental haze or dullness," or from the German *dumpf*, "close, heavy, oppressive, gloomy." The *dump* in *garbage dump* has an entirely different origin and is an old echoic word like *bump* and *thump*, common to many languages—from garbage being thrown down heavily and making this sound. *Garbage dump* gets its name from this, as does *dumping stock* on the market, or *dumping* ("accepting a bribe to lose") a basketball game. In the 1811 edition of his *Dictionary of the Vulgar Tongue* (edited and revised by someone else) Captain Francis Grose writes that *down in the dumps* is "jocularly said to be derived from Dumpos, a king of Egypt, who died of melancholy." Note that the key word here is "jocularly," for despite reputed citations over the centuries, this is not the origin of the old expression.

down my alley. An alley in baseball is the imaginary line between each outfield, between right field and center field and between left field and center field. The term *right down my alley* refers to any task suitable to one's talents, and may refer to a baseball player getting easy hits down the alley. It is also possible that the expression derives from the alley that is the center of home plate. When a pitcher throws one right down the alley, a batter considers it an easy pitch to hit.

down on one's uppers. The *upper* in this phrase, meaning to be in bad financial condition, is the upper part of a shoe. Anyone stepping down on his uppers then would be someone very needy indeed.

Down syndrome. This congenital disorder caused by the presence of an extra 21st chromosome is named after British physician John L. H. Down (1828–96), among the first who studied the condition. Those affected with Down syndrome are mildly to severely mentally retarded, are usually short, and have a flat facial profile. The genetic disorder is also called *Down's syndrome, trisomy-21,* and *mongolism*. The latter term is rarely used anymore; in fact, its hurtful racial connotations were the main reason scientists named the disease after Dr. Down about 1960.

down the hatch! This toast originated in the 18th-century British navy, the mouth compared to the hatches, or openings, leading to various parts of a ship. *Hatch* comes from the Old English *haecc*, grating or hatch. It is unrelated to the verb *hatch*, to incubate, which derives from the Greek *hecken*, meaning the same.

down to a gnat's eyebrow. Exactly, precisely, as in "He planned it down to a gnat's eyebrow." The term *gnat's eyebrow* is first recorded in 1930; before that *gnat's heel* was used to mean the same.

down to the wire. For over a century *wire* has been synonymous with the finish line in horse racing, because of the wire stretched across the track that the horses passed under at the end of a race. The *Oxford English Dictionary* records the term from William McPaul's *Ike Glidden* (1902): "The conquering colt swept under the wire for a nose ahead of the trotter." But Mitford Mathew's *A Dictionary of Americanisms* cites an earlier, 1887 U.S. newspaper usage of *wire*, claiming it as an Americanism. *A Dictionary of Americanisms* goes on to date *down to the wire* as an expression first recorded in 1950 in the newspaper account of a baseball game. Widely used as slang now for "to the very last moment or the very end," it is also heard as *to go to the wire.*

Down Under. *See* AUSSIE.

downwinder. A term applied to people in the Southwest "who claim they were harmed by wind-carried radioactive fallout resulting from open-air testing of atomic bombs in the 1950s and early 1960s," according to a *New York Times* article of December 29, 1993.

the dozens. The art of hurling invective at one's enemies is an ancient one (*see* LOGOMACHY), and American slaves probably brought the verbal exchange called *the dozens* or *dirty dozens* with them from Africa, basing it on the Tuareg and Galla game of two opponents cursing one another until one man lost his temper and began fighting with his hands instead of his mouth; he was considered the loser. Alive and thriving today among blacks, the game takes its name not from dozen, "12," but probably from the Americanism *bulldoze,* which meant "to bullwhip someone," especially a slave, the insults likened to whiplashes. *See* BULLDOZER.

Dr. Everybody knows that *Dr.* is an abbreviation for "doctor"—and it has been for about four centuries. Few are aware, though, that *Dr.* is also an abbreviation for "debtor"—in bookkeeping jargon.

draconian. "The Draconian Code is written in blood," one Greek orator declared, and Plutarch observed that under Draco's code "for nearly all crimes there is the penalty of death." They referred to the severe laws—now largely lost—codified and promulgated by the Athenian legislator Draco about 621 B.C. Draco was the first to collect Athens's unwritten laws, but his assignment wasn't to modify them and he is therefore not really responsible for their proverbial harshness. The written Draconian Code proved valuable because it substituted public justice for vendettas and made it impossible for magistrates to side openly with the nobility. Its severity may have been exaggerated by future generations. Draco's laws, except for those dealing with homicide, were abolished or ameliorated by the wise Solon 30 years later, but they were so harsh, or thought to be so harsh, that the word *draconian* remains a synonym for "severe" and *draconian laws* still means any code

of laws or set of rules calling for ironhanded punishment of violators.

draftee. First recorded in an 1866 Civil War memoir, *draftee* was surely used before this during the war, probably as soon as the Confederate Conscription Act of 1862 and the Union Draft Law of 1863 were passed. In the North single men 20 to 45 and married men 20 to 35 were drafted, while the South conscripted all men 18 to 35. Most men volunteered, however; only about 2 percent of the Union Army consisting of draftees. During World War II *draftee* and other *ee*-ending words (such as *trainee, enlistee, escapee,* and *amputee*) were widely used. *Draft* in the sense of "conscript" comes from the "to draw or pull" meaning of the verb *to draft.*

dragonflies of the deep. *See* FLYING FISH.

dragon's blood. A colorful name given to the red resinous exhudation of certain palm trees that was once used as an astringent in medicines and is now employed as a coloring for varnishes. A cheap Rhine wine is also called dragon's blood, taking its name from the German myth about Siegfried bathing in the blood of a dragon to make himself immune from injury.

dramaticule. A word coined by Irish playwright Samuel Beckett meaning very short dramatic stage pieces. Beckett wrote one of these little plays, entitled *Come and Go,* that had three female characters and a text of just 120 words.

Drambuie. Bonnie Prince Charlie (Charles Edward Stuart, 1720–80), the Young Pretender to the British throne, led the 1745 Jacobite uprising and had to flee Scotland when it was suppressed. The Young Chevalier, as he was also called, made a gift of the secret recipe for his royal liqueur to John Mackinnon, who had helped him escape, as the old story goes. Bonnie Prince Charlie's recipe wasn't made commercially by the Mackinnon clan for nearly another century and a half, but it quickly became popular worldwide when it was. It had been named by the Mackinnons from the Gaelic *dram,* drink, and *buidheach,* pleasing or satisfying.

drat it! Charles Dickens, among other great writers, used the word *drat* as a mild expletive. *Drat* was first recorded in the early 19th century as a contraction of "God rot"; thus *drat it!* means "God rot it!"

draw a blank. To search hard but fail to find out about something. The reference is to the losing ticket in a lottery in which people buy numbered tickets to win prizes; a blank ticket wins nothing. The expression dates back to the late 19th century.

drawers. Drawers, "women's or men's underwear," were originally made something like women's pantyhose, their name bestowed on them back in the 16th century when they were drawn on over the feet and legs.

draw in one's horns. *Horns* here refers to the horns of the land snail, which draws in its horns and remains in its shell when threatened with danger, or when weather conditions aren't favorable. The snail's actions do suggest someone who draws in his horns, that is, draws away from a situation and takes no action while reconsidering the matter. The expression is first recorded in the early 1300s and clearly indicates that the land snail is its source.

draw lots of water.   An old nautical term for a ship in the water loaded down with cargo; on land the expression came to mean an important person, one who carries a lot of weight, as in "He draws lots of water up in Albany."

drawn and quartered.   *See* HANGED, DRAWN, AND QUARTERED.

drawn teeth.   *See* PULLED TEETH.

draw the line.   When we say "This is where I draw the line," we are of course laying down a definite limit beyond which we refuse to go. Several attempts have been made to trace actual sources of the figurative "line" in the phrase. One says that it referred to tennis, a sport almost as popular as cricket in England by the 18th century. When tennis was introduced from France four centuries before, according to this story, there were no exact dimensions for the court and players drew lines beyond which they agreed the ball couldn't be hit. Another explanation says that the line was cut by a plowhorse across a field to indicate the boundary of a farmer's holding in 16th-century England. No examples of the figurative expression *to draw the line* have been found recorded before 1793, but either theory could be right. The phrase could also derive from early prizefights, where a line was drawn in the ring that neither fighter could cross. For a famous American use of *drawing the line, see* TEDDY BEAR.

draw to an inside straight.   An inside straight is a very difficult straight to draw for in poker, so difficult, in fact, that the expression *draw to an inside straight* has become American slang for building up hope for something that has little chance of happening.

dray; drey.   *Dray,* sometimes still spelled in its obsolete form *drey,* refers to a squirrel's nest, but I have also seen the word used as a collective noun for squirrels ("A dray of bushy-tails darted across the lawn."). More specifically, according to Richard E. Mallery's estimable *Nuts About Squirrels* (2000), a "dray" is a squirrel's nest of "bundled leaf structures that protect them from weather conditions." First recorded in 1607, the word *dray's* origin is unknown, and it is not included in any of the major dictionaries, nor any reference book I checked excepting Mallery's fine work. *See* SQUIRREL.

dreadnought.   With her 10 12-inch guns, 11-inch armor belt, and 21.6-knot speed, the 17,940-ton British battleship *Dreadnought* outclassed any battleship on the seas and made all others virtually obsolete. Before *Dreadnought's* 1906 debut, battleships commonly had four 12-inch guns and a number of smaller ones. The British built the *Dreadnought* in just four months, but it was three years before Germany could produce a comparable ship. The *Dreadnought* marked a turning point in naval military history, and her name became synonymous for any big ship of comparable size. By 1916 Britain had 29 dreadnoughts, enabling her to defeat Germany in the Battle of Jutland. Indeed, by that time Britain had super-dreadnoughts

like the 27,000-ton *Warspite* with her eight 15-inch guns and 13-inch armor-belt, and the original *Dreadnought* did not even see service at Jutland.

dress down.   To severely reprimand or censure someone, as in "He gave him a good dressing down." This was probably originally a mining term describing the breaking and crushing of various ores into a powdery form.

Dr. Feelgood.   A term dating back to at least the early 1960s for an unprincipled physician who injects any paying patients with drugs such as amphetamines (speed) to give them a high. Dr. Feelgoods also prescribe pills containing amphetamines to people addicted to them—again, if they can pay the price. *Feelgood* can also be used singly today, as in "They dropped a few feelgood bombs, but really accomplished nothing."

dribs and drabs.   Small, irregular amounts, as in "He was paid in dribs and drabs." The expression isn't recorded earlier than 1942, but it clearly derives from *drib,* a back formation from *dribble* that is first recorded in 1862 and means "a drop, a small amount."

drink like a fish.   Fish don't intentionally drink water. Most of the water they appear to be drinking while swimming along is actually passing through their gills to supply them with oxygen. But they certainly do *seem* to be drinking continually, many swimming with their mouths open. That is why what has been called an "idiotism" (like "cold as hell") has been a common synonym for drinking excessively, especially alcohol, since at least the early 17th century.

drink off dead Nelson.   To drink alcohol copiously and indiscriminately. Lord Horatio Nelson, England's greatest naval hero, was killed at the battle of Trafalgar in 1805, and his body was brought back to England for burial. The fabled hero became the subject of many legends, including one claiming that his body was brought home preserved in rum. This led to the British slang expression *Nelson's blood* for rum and the Canadian expression recorded here, used mainly in Newfoundland.

drive-in.   The first U.S. drive-in movie opened in Camden, New Jersey, on June 6, 1933, admission to this 400-car site costing 25 cents for the double feature. Richard M. Hollingshead, Jr., had used the term *drive-in* a month earlier when he patented the system. Within about 25 years there were more than 4,000 U.S. drive-ins. Very few are left today.

drive one's ducks to a poor market.   To manage something poorly, or to associate with the wrong people, associates, or friends who lead you in the wrong direction. Also *drive one's goose to a poor market.*

drive round the bend.   *See* GO ROUND THE BEND.

droit du seigneur.   *Droit du seigneur,* French for "the lord's right," is also called "the right of the first night" in English. It is said to have been a custom in medieval Europe, permitting the lord of a manor to have sexual relations with all brides of his vassals on their wedding nights. The story is part of folklore and literature in many countries and often finds its way into history books, but there is little evidence that such a custom really existed. A suspect 1392 French document mentions such a law and that is the only "proof" we have of it in history.

drongo.   The racehorse Drongo, which had been named after an Australian bird, is said rarely to have won a race. This caused Australians at the track to curse him roundly and use his name to describe a fool or any lazy, stupid, useless person.

drop a dime.   To make a phone call to police detectives informing on someone. *Dime dropper* refers to a *rat*, a *snitch*, a *stool pigeon*, among other choice terms. The term, still in use, dates back to the 1960s, when a phone call cost a dime.

drop dead; drop-dead beautiful.   As an insult roughly meaning go to hell! this expression dates back to the early 1930s when it was originally *why don't you drop dead!* The expression has its equivalents in several languages. *Drop dead* has achieved some respectability today in its meaning of "unusually striking," as in "That's a drop-dead dress."

Drop dead as a curse isn't recorded until its mention in a 1908 book about baseball, but it is probably 10 years or so older. *Drop-dead beautiful*, awesomely beautiful, gorgeous, etc. seems to have been coined by a magazine editor or writer about 1970. It has since been appended to gowns and a multitude of things. It was reported recently that someone involved in an argument told his opponent to drop dead and that person did so—that instant.

drop in the bucket.   Another biblical phrase, meaning very little compared with the whole. It is from Isa. 40:15: "Behold, the nations are as a drop in the bucket, and are counted as the small dust of the balance."

drop of a hat.   No one has offered a convincing explanation for this very common American expression, and both *Webster's* and the *O.E.D.* ignore it entirely. It has been suggested that it is Irish in origin and that since the words are most often heard in the form of "he's ready to fight at the drop of a hat" the phrase parallels challenges like "roll up your sleeves," "take off your coat," and other expressions used at the start of a fistfight. Another possible explanation lies in the duels with guns, knives, whips, or fists so common in the 19th century. The referee who judged these duels usually dropped a handkerchief or hat as a signal for the fight to begin. The expression seems to have originated in the West and was first recorded in 1887.

drown the shamrock.   *See* SHAMROCK.

drug on the market.   We use this expression for "something not in demand, something unsalable because the market is glutted or the woods are full of them." But since the phrase's first appearance in 1661 no one has figured out just what it means. What drug is referred to? Is it possibly items of trade like the tea and spices that were sometimes called drugs in the past, and, if so, when in early times were markets ever glutted with such rare commodities? Or is *drug* here just a pronunciation of *dreg* in certain English dialects? Take your choice, but the theory that apparently has the most supporters claims that the drug here is from the French word *drogue*, meaning "rub-

bish." The word *drug* has been used in this sense, as when Robinson Crusoe, discovering coins in a wreck, cried out: "O Drug! what art thou good for?"

drugstore.   *Drugstore* is an Americanism for the appellations "chemist's shop," "apothecary," and "pharmacy," used in England. But before they were called drugstores here, pharmacies were called druggist shops (1786) and druggist stores (1817). *Drugstore* is first recorded in 1818 and *drugstore cowboy* in 1925, the latter being a man who lounges around public places trying to impress young women by showing off.

drumhead court-martial.   In days past, battlefield courts-martial trying soldiers for desertion, cowardice, and similar offenses, were held around a large drumhead (animal skin stretched upon a drum) that served as a table. The brief courts-martial, which usually resulted in immediate death sentences, were thus called drumhead courts-martial, this term first recorded in 1835.

Drummond light.   *See* LIMELIGHT.

drumstick.   The drumstick of a turkey or other fowl is so called because it resembles a drumstick in shape. But the word is a euphemism of British origin, invented as a substitute for "leg," which the Victorians found offensive enough to call a "limb."

drunk as a lord.   Both *drunk as a lord* and *drunk as a beggar* were coined in the mid 17th century, but only the former expression survives today—perhaps because most drunks like to consider themselves lords rather than beggars. Three hundred years ago there were no class restrictions on drinking in England and anyone could buy enough gin to get drunk on for a penny.

as drunk as David's sow.   Very drunk, "beastly drunk." The wife of David Lloyd, "a Welchman who kept an alehouse at Hereford" became known to history as David's sow early in the 17th century. "David," according to one old story, "had a living sow, which was greatly resorted to by the curious; he had also a wife much addicted to drink . . . One day David's wife having taken a cup too much, and being fearful of the consequences [David's wrath], turned out the six-legged sow and lay down to sleep herself sober in the stye. A company coming to see the sow, David ushered them into the stye, exclaiming, 'There is a sow for you! Did any of you ever see such another?,' all the while supposing that the sow had really been there. To which some of the company, seeing the state the woman was in, replied, it was the drunkenest sow they had ever beheld; whence the woman was ever after called *David's sow*."

drunken forest.   An expression used to describe a full-grown forest in which many trees are as twisted as miniature bonsai and others tilt in different directions, the scene suggesting drunken people. The condition is often caused by landslides.

drunkometer.   *See* BREATHALYZER.

Drury Lane Theatre.   This long-famous street and theatre in London get their name from the Drury House, which once stood just south of the present lane. The house was built by English statesman and soldier Sir William Drury (1527–79) during the reign of Henry VIII. There have been four Drury Lane Theatres, including the present one; the first was originally a cockpit that was converted into a theater under James I. All the great English actors, from Booth and Garrick on, have performed at one or another Drury Lane.

druthers.   *If I had my druthers* means "if I were free to choose." It is based whimsically on *I'd ruther,* an American dialect form of *I'd rather,* which dates back to the 19th century.

dry goods.   *Dry goods stores* ("drapist's shops" in England) may take their name from stores run by New England merchants, many of whom were shipowners and direct importers in Colonial times. Two chief imports were rum and bolts of calico, which were traditionally carried on opposite sides of the store—a wet-goods side containing the rum and a dry-goods side holding the calico. "Wet goods" disappeared from the language, but stores that sell fabric are still called *dry goods stores.*

the dry salvages.   A small but well-known group of rocks, with a beacon, off the coast of Cape Ann, Massachusetts, *Salvages* here rhymes with *assuages,* perhaps because "the dry salvages" is a corruption of *les trios sauvages.* "The Dry Salvages" is the title of a poem by T. S. Eliot.

dubok.   Fans of espionage novels will recognize this word as the synonym for a drop, or a safe place where other espionage activities can be carried out. It comes from the Russian word for oak tree.

Dubuque, Iowa.   *See* OLD LADY IN DUBUQUE.

duck and cover.   An exercise used in schools during the early years of the cold war, when students were taught to protect themselves from a nuclear attack by ducking under their desks and covering their heads with their hands.

duck in a noose.   A phrase that figured as a sidelight in the sniper killings case that terrified the Washington, D.C., area for three weeks in the fall of 2002. The sniper wanted the chief of police of Montgomery County to repeat this phrase, which he had mentioned in a phone call, and Chief Moose did as he requested at a late-night news conference. What the sniper meant by the phrase was revealed in a Cherokee folk tale, "The Rabbit, the Otter and Duck Hunting." In the tale, according to Celestine Bohlin writing in the *New York Times* (10/24/02), "a boastful rabbit is challenged by an otter to capture a duck. The rabbit manages to slip a noose around the neck of a duck, which then takes off, with the rabbit hanging on for dear life. The duck flies higher and higher, and finally the rabbit loses its grip and falls into an old sycamore tree where it is trapped . . ." Obviously, the sniper regarded himself as the escaping duck who couldn't be caught, and the police as the hapless rabbit that would never catch him.

duct tape.   Duct tape was developed for the army during World War II as a seal for the cracks in ammunition boxes. It was first called *duck tape* because water rolled off it like water off a duck's back. After the war, the tape, which has many applications, was used by plumbers to seal ducts and came to be known as *duct tape.* In early 2003, the government recommended the tape as an aid against terrorist bomb attacks, to prevent shattering of windows, etc. Critics said the tape was of little or no help.

dude ranch.   At first a term for tourist ranches in the West but now used to describe such places everywhere, from the Catskills to the Texas Panhandle.

duff.   Depending on where one is in the U.S., *duff* can mean the buttocks; the decaying leaves on a forest floor; to work hard; and a New England pudding made from flour, water, and raisins or other fruit. In Australia the word means to steal cattle by changing their brand.

duffel bag.   A duffel bag is a large canvas bag for carrying clothes or gear. Originally it was made of a woolen fabric called duffel, which was so named because it came from Duffel, Belgium.

duffer.   A *duffer,* for "a bad golf player" is a British expression that dates back to the early 1840s. It probably comes from the Scottish *duffar,* for "a dull or stupid person."

duh.   An exclamation now widely used in the U.S. to make fun of someone after that person has spoken, indicating that he or she has said or done something stupid or obvious. The expression dates back to the early 1940s and may have been introduced or popularized by ventriloquist Edgar Bergen's dummy Mortimer Snerd, a rustic moron who constantly had the word put in his mouth.

dukes.   *See* PUT UP YOUR DUKES.

dull as ditchwater.   Uninteresting people and tedious undertakings have been called *dull as ditchwater* for over two centuries. The allusion is to the dull muddy color of water in ditches, which were much commoner in days past. *Dull as dishwater* is a later variant.

dumbcane.   *See* MOTHER-IN-LAW PLANT.

Dumb Dora.   U.S. cartoonist T. A. ("TAD") Dorgan (1877–1929) contributed this term for "a scatterbrained young woman" to the language. *Dumb Dora* was originally the name of a dizzy cartoon character he invented.

dumb down.   Though it has become more popular recently, the verb *dumb down* dates back to the early 1930s, when it was used to describe radio or motion picture scripts that are oversimplified, dumbed down so that they will be understood by a large number of listeners. Today the practice and the word isn't applied only to radio, covering everything from textbooks to television.

dumb ox. When he was a young monk in Germany (ca. 1250) other members of his Dominican order thought St. Thomas Aquinas was stupid—perhaps because they weren't intelligent enough to understand what he said. They dubbed him the *Dumb Ox*, which has become synonymous for "a stupid person." *Lummox*, an Americanism first recorded in 1825, apparently derives from *dumb ox*, perhaps combined with *lumbering* or another word suggesting clumsiness. *See* DUNCE.

dumb ship; lightship. Lightships are simply floating lighthouses that warn other ships of danger and serve as aids in navigation, usually in places too distant from shore to erect a permanent structure. Almost all are dumb ships, unable to navigate themselves, and the first of them seems to have been anchored near the Thames estuary in 1732. The best-known American lightship is probably the dumb ship situated off Nantucket, which sank in 1935 after the liner *Olympic* rammed it. Today lighted buoys, which provide the same service, are more commonly used than lightships.

dumbwaiter. In America the term *dumbwaiter* is used to describe a small, usually hand-operated elevator used to carry food and drink. The British, however, use the word to mean what Americans call a LAZY SUSAN.

dumdum bullet. This particularly hideous bullet—it expands on impact, creating an ugly wound—is named for the Dum-Dum arsenal in Bengal, India, where the British made it to stop the charges of "fanatical tribesmen." *Dumdum*, or soft-nose, bullets were outlawed by many world powers under an international declaration made in 1899, but that has not entirely stopped them from being used since.

dummy's plant. The common name for the *planta del mudo*, dummy's plant is a Venezuelan herb that when chewed supposedly renders its user totally unable to speak for two days. *See* MOTHER-IN-LAW PLANT.

dump. *See* DOWN IN THE DUMPS.

dumpy. *Dumpy*, for "a short fat person," is thought to be related to *dump* in its sense of melancholy (*see* DOWN IN THE DUMPS), but no one knows exactly how. Perhaps because such people appeared melancholy, perhaps from the German adjective *dumpf*, which means "heavy" in another sense.

dun. "Send Dun after him," creditors would say when a person was slow to pay his debts. According to the old story, they referred to Joe Dun, a London bailiff during the reign of Henry VIII who had proved himself particularly efficient in collecting from defrauding debtors. But most authorities trace *dun* to various words meaning din or thundering noise, sometimes connecting this with the drum that town criers pounded when they shouted out the names of debtors. Though only a few Celtic words survive in English, and most of these must be marked "doubtful," philologists do think that a word similar to *dun*, for the dull brown color, was spoken by the Celts 2,000 years ago.

Duncan Phyfe. Duncan Phyfe's furniture workshop stood on the site of the present Hudson Terminal Building in New York City. The Scottish-born master craftsman had arrived in New York in 1783 at the age of 15 and later opened his own shop, changing his name from Fife to Phyfe. Duncan Phyfe and Sons employed more than 100 artisans at its height of popularity, but the master craftsman's best work was done in the early period up until 1820, when he evolved his own style, using the creations of Sheraton, Hepplewhite, and the Adam brothers as models. This work has become known as the Duncan Phyfe style, characterized by excellent proportions, graceful, curving lines, and beautifully carved ornamentation.

dunce. Ironically, one of the most brilliant scholars and philosophers of the Middle Ages is the source for the word *dunce*. Little is known about John Duns Scotus outside of his new theology. He was probably born in 1265 in Scotland, most likely died while still a young man, aged 43 or so, and his middle name is presumably a place name, either from the village of Duns, Scotland, Dunse in Berwickshire, or Dunston in Northumberland. The "Subtle Doctor," as he was called, apparently taught at Oxford and the University of Paris, but again there is no hard evidence available. Duns Scotus did found a school of philosophy that attracted numerous followers. A Franciscan, he successfully opposed the teachings of St. Thomas Aquinas and the Dominicans, challenging the harmony of faith and reason, and insisted on the doctrine of the Immaculate Conception, for which he was known as the Marian Doctor. After his death—tradition has it that he died in Cologne, buried alive—Duns Scotus remained a great influence on scholastic thought. His works were studied in all the great universities throughout Europe and his followers, called Scotists, reigned supreme. However, these same Dunsmen sabotaged his reputation some 200 years later. During the Renaissance, blindly resistant to change, "the old barking curs" raged from the pulpit against the new learning, being scorned and ridiculed as hairsplitters and stupid obstructionists. *Dunsmen* became *dunses* and finally *dunces*, "blockheads incapable of learning or scholarship." Exactly the opposite of the precise, learned mind of the man who started it all. *See* DUMB OX.

dunderhead. *Dunderhead* for a dunce or blockhead, may come from the Dutch *donderbol*, cannonball, the head of a dunce thus compared to a thick iron ball. However, the origin of the word, first recorded in 1625, is obscure.

dundrearies. Long silky whiskers drooping in strands from both cheeks were high fashion during the 1860s and after. They are named for Lord Dundreary, the witless indolent chief character who sported such whiskers in English dramatist Tom Taylor's play *Our American Cousin* (1858). Abraham Lincoln was watching the play at Ford's Theatre on the night he was assassinated.

dungarees. *Dungarees* isn't used as much as *jeans* or *Levi's* for these coarse blue cloth pants today, but the word is still frequently heard. The name derives from what Partridge calls the "disreputable Bombay suburb" where the cloth used for the pants was first made and exported to England early in the 1830s.

dungeon. *Dungeon* apparently derives from the Latin *domnio*, "the lord's tower," and was used to mean "castle" in 14th-century England. But the word also meant "the keep of a castle" and "a prison cell under the castle" at the time. Over the course of a few more centuries, however, *dungeon* came to retain only this last meaning, having changed from a high tower to a room beneath the ground.

duodenum. This word for the first part of the small intestine is the Latin for "12 fingerbreadths [inches] long," the measurement early physicians and anatomists gave the organ. The term is recorded as early as 1398.

duotrigintillion. *See* GOOGOL.

dupe. Because its cry sounds like "up up," the south European bird *Upupa epops* was called the *upup* or *upupa* by the Romans. The bird, about the size of a large thrush and noted for its long, curved beak, variegated plumage, and beautiful orange erectile crest in the male, became known in French as the *huppe* and in English as the *hoopoe*, or *hoop*. The French considered it to be an especially stupid bird because it laid its eggs most anywhere without a nest (in a hole in a wall, tree, or bank, etc.). They commonly said that any fool had the head of a *huppe*, *tête d'huppe*. *D'huppe* in the expression eventually became *duppe* and passed into English in the late 17th century as *dupe*, a person who is easily fooled or deceived.

the duration. *For the duration* means without a fixed time limit for as long as is necessary or may be. The phrase originally referred to the duration of World War II.

durian. The durian fruit takes its name from the Malasian *duri*, thorn. This lopsided, hard-shelled green fruit of the *Durio zibethinus* tree, volleyball-sized and covered with spines on its outer pod, is widely believed to be an aphrodisiac in Malaya, Thailand, Indonesia, and the Philippines. An old Malay saying has it that "When the durians fall, the sarongs rise." The *emperor fruit* or *king fruit* or *queen fruit* is thought to be so rich in protein that pregnant women are advised to eat it only in moderate amounts for fear that they might produce a child "too large to come out." The durian, which comes in over 100 varieties, is so well regarded in Asia that the ownership of just one tree (they often reach 80 feet high) can make a person prosperous. One 16th-century traveler claimed that the durian "surpasses in flavor all the fruits of the world." The only trouble with the durian is that it literally stinks. Addicts say that it is no more objectionable than Gorgonzola or Camembert cheese, but most non-Asians consider it among the foulest-smelling foods in the world; one gourmet wrote, "to say it smells like rotten garlicky cheese is generous." British author Anthony Burgess has compared eating durian to eating vanilla custard in a latrine. Airlines refuse to carry durians even in sealed containers, and Asian hotel rooms literally have to be fumigated after durian feasts. One husband is reported to have chased his wife out of bed, making her eat her prize specimen on their hotel fire escape.

dust bowl. Severe dust storms beginning in 1934 destroyed crops and dried the soil in the southern High Plains of the United States, largely because this land in Kansas, Colorado, Oklahoma, New Mexico, and Texas had been poorly farmed for years. The Great Depression, drought, and the dust forced large numbers of people to migrate from the area, which was first called the *dust bowl* in a story written by Associated Press reporter Robert Geiger in April 1935. The dust storms lasted almost a decade and dust from them blew as far as 300 miles out into the Atlantic, where it coated ships. *See also* OKIES, DIRTY THIRTIES.

dust bunny; slut's wool. The term *dust bunny* for any ball of dust found under the bed and in other places difficult to reach is only about 50 years old. The British, passing judgment in this case, would call a dust bunny "slut's wool," condemning the person who let such dust accumulate. Synonyms are HOUSE WOOL and HOUSE MOSS.

dust devil. A dust devil is a small whirlwind common in dry regions and made visible by the dust it picks up from the ground. The term originated in the American West in about 1890. F. M. Parker described desert dust devils in his novel *Skinner* (1981): "The strong wind blew out of the northwest, sweeping the hotter air of the desert toward the mountain. Heated unevenly by the baking sunlight on the white earth of the bottom of the long-gone lake, the wind in places lost its smooth southeast flow and began to eddy and swirl. The swirls grew and pirouetted like invisible dancers and then, as their strength grew, birthed giant dust devils that dizzily spun white dust around and upward in vortices of counter clockwise-whirling turbulent pools of air four to five hundred feet deep. The ghostly columns, like giant dancing worms, wiggled and zig-zagged along to the southwest with the wind."

Dutch; Dutch courage, etc. The Dutch people have been so offended by the English language over the past three centuries that in 1934 their government decided to drop the word *Dutch* and use *Netherlands* whenever possible. But the stratagem didn't succeed in stopping up the dike. *Dutch* remains what one dictionary calls "an epithet of inferiority." In both England and America a torrent of verbal abuse has descended upon the Dutch. It all began with the bitter hostilities between England and Holland in the 17th century, when the Dutch colonial empire threatened to usurp Britain's own. Two major wars were fought over this naval and trade rivalry and a flood of invective was loosed upon the Dutch that has barely subsided over the years. To complicate matters, the name *Dutchman*, from the German *Deutsch*, has been applied to Germanic peoples (for instance the Pennsylvania Dutch), such contacts and two world wars adding still more derogatory expressions to the list. Below is a short dictionary of abusive terms using the word. Though it runs to some 60 expressions, surely a complete list would more than triple this amount. All of these terms but a few are derogatory. If only in the subtlest way, each makes the Dutch either cheap, cowardly, stubborn, deceitful, or worse, all a far cry from the traditional picture of Hans Brinker, bright tulips, and gently turning windmills:

double-Dutch—double talk; gibberish; also an American play-language and a jump-rope game.
Dutch act—suicide, probably referring to a supposed German morbidity, rather than a cheap Dutch way to end it all.
Dutch auction—an auction starting off with inflated prices.

Dutch bargain—one clinched over liquor; a one-sided bargain.

Dutch bond—an economical brickwork bond of alternate courses of stretchers and headers.

Dutch brig—cells on board a ship.

Dutch build—a thickly built person.

Dutch by injection—describing an Englishman living with a Dutch woman.

Dutch cap—a prophylactic or pessary.

Dutch cheese—cottage cheese; a bald-headed person.

Dutch clinker—a long, narrow, hard yellowish brick made in Holland.

Dutch clover—white clover, *Trifolium repens*.

Dutch comfort—consolation ("Thank God it wasn't any worse").

Dutch concert—a great uproar; everyone playing a different tune.

Dutch courage—courage inspired by booze, the Dutch once said to be heavy drinkers. "The Dutch their wine and all their brandy lose, / Disarmed of that from which their courage flows . . ." (Edmund Walles, 1665).

Dutch cupboard—a buffet with open upper shelves.

Dutch defense—a surrender, no defense at all.

Dutch door—a two-section door that opens at the top or bottom.

Dutch foot—a furniture foot.

Dutch gold—an originally Dutch alloy of copper and zinc used for cheap imitation gold leaf.

Dutch kiss—sexually intimate kissing.

Dutch lap—an economical shingling method.

Dutch luck—undeserved luck.

Dutch lunch—an individual portion of cold cuts; probably an American expression referring to the Pennsylvania Dutch.

Dutchman—a hard lump in brown sugar.

Dutchman's anchor—a nautical expression that derives from an old tale of a Dutch sea captain who lost his ship because he forgot to bring along his anchor. The story gives us this term, meaning anything important that has been forgotten.

Dutchman's-breeches—the popular plant *Dicentra cucullaria*, the flowers resembling baggy breeches; patches of blue in a stormy sky, in allusion to patches on a Dutchman's trousers, or because there is just enough blue to make a cheap pair of pants for a Dutchman.

Dutchman's drink—the last one in the bottle.

Dutchman's headache—drunkenness.

Dutchman's land or *cape*—illusory land on the horizon.

Dutchman's log—a piece of wood used in an economical navigation method, the practical method itself.

Dutchman's-pipe—a climbing vine, *Aristolochia dorior*, whose calyx resembles a tobacco pipe.

Dutch medley—everyone playing a different tune.

Dutch nightingale—a frog.

Dutch oven—economical heavy kettle or brick oven.

Dutch palate—a coarse, unrefined palate.

Dutch pennants—untidy ropes hanging from aloft on a ship.

Dutch pink—blood.

Dutch praise—condemnation.

Dutch pump—a nautical punishment.

Dutch reckoning—pure guesswork, or a lump account that would be cheaper if itemized.

Dutch red—a highly smoked herring.

Dutch route—American slang for *Dutch act* above.

Dutch straight—a poker hand.

Dutch treat—a meal or entertainment where each pays his own way. Pennsylvania Dutch.

Dutch two hundred—a bowling score of 200 made with alternate strikes and spares.

Dutch uncle—an unsparingly frank and critical person, an Americanism probably referring to the Germans.

Dutch wife—the pillow of an Englishman in the tropics who takes no native mistress; or a framework used in beds to support the legs.

High Dutch—High German.

His Dutch is up—he's angry.

I'm a Dutchman if I do—Never! From the days when "Dutchman" was synonymous with everything false.

in Dutch—in trouble; in jail; this may refer to the early New York Dutch but probably refers to the Germans.

it's all Dutch to me—it's all Greek to me, an American expression.

Low Dutch—Low German.

my old Dutch—my wife, but possibly from the word *duchess*.

Pennsylvania Dutch—German emigrants in Pennsylvania; their language.

that beats the Dutch—that beats the devil, deriving from an American song of the Revolution.

to Dutch—to harden or clean by placing in hot sand; to run away, desert.

The Netherlands has in its long history been known as *Belgica* (to the Romans), *Holland*, *The Seven Provinces*, and *The Low Countries*. In 1999 Jon Spruijt wrote a book, *Total Dutch*, listing more than a thousand Dutch words and expressions used in various languages. Some are far from being exclusively Dutch. A *Dutch treat*, for instance, is *going Catalan* in Spain; *going Rome* in Italy; and *going Swiss* in France.

Dutch words in English. Dutch and other Low German languages (Frisian, Flemish, and Plattdeutsch) have contributed a great many words to English. These include: date, dotard, bowsprit, golf, gin, uproar, wagon, bounce, snatch, huckster, tackle (fishing), boy, booze, wainscot, hobble, splint, kit, mart, hop (plant), spool, rack, sled, excise, buoy, hoist, hose (stockings), bulwark, boor, loiter, snap, groove, luck, placard, brandy, stoker, smuggle, sloop, cruise, walrus, jib, yawl, knapsack, furlough, blunderbuss, sketch, stipple, decoy, slur, hanger, snort, snuff, hustle, snow, and mangle. Many Dutch words became part of American English. These include: bush, hook (of land), boss, patroon, Yankee, sawbuck, stoop (porch), hay, barrack, boodle, dingus, dope, dumb, logy, poppycock, Santa Claus, snoop, spook, skate, coleslaw, cruller, cookie, pit (of fruit), pot cheese, waffle span (of horses), sleigh, caboose, scow, bedspan, bedspread, cuspidor, keelboat, landscape, and a good scout.

duxelles sauce. A *duxelles* today is a purée of mushrooms and onions, the tasty sauce once made from a much more elaborate recipe. It was named for the marquis d'Uxelles, employer of the too often ignored chef François Pierre de la Varenne. Varenne's *Le Cuisinier Français* (1651) is a landmark of French cuisine, and his rare pastry book *Le Patissier Français* has been called the most expensive cookbook in the world. The chef is said to have been trained by those Florentine cooks brought to France by Marie de' Medici, second wife of Henry IV. It is often claimed that these Italians taught the French the art of cooking, but Varenne's cuisine was much more delicate and imaginative than that of his masters; and if anyone can be called the founder of classical French cuisine he deserves the honor. Varenne did not name the *duxelles* after his employer; this was done at a later date when it became customary to honor a man's name in a recipe.

D.V.   When someone writes or says, "I'll be home next week, D.V.," he is saying "I'll be home next week, God willing," *D.V.* being an abbreviation of the Latin *deo volente*. First recorded in 1873, the term appeared in church publications before that, and is still heard occasionally.

dyed in the wool.   *See* SPOILS SYSTEM.

dynamite.   Swedish inventor Alfred Nobel invented this explosive and the word for it. Nobel constructed *dynamite* from the Greek *dunamis*, "power," and the Swedish suffix *it*. His *dynamit* almost immediately came into English as *dynamite*. *See* NOBEL PRIZE.

dyvour.   This synonym for "a bankrupt" is an old Scottish term. Dyvours were once compelled by law to wear a half-yellow, half-brown shirt along with a particolored cap and hose.

E

E. *E* is the most commonly used letter in English. It is followed in order of use by: *t, a, i, s, o, n, h, r, d, l, u, c, m, f, w, y, p, g, b, v, k, j, q, x,* and *z.* The most common initial letter is *t.* Called *he* in Hebrew, the letter *E* was representative of the Phoenician and Hebrew sign for "a window."

eager beaver. Referring, of course, to the industrious beaver, this near-rhyming expression is a Canadian Army one that isn't recorded before 1940, although it obviously derives from such phrases as "as busy as a beaver," which dates back to the early 18th century. Unlike the early expression, however, *eager beaver* is usually applied derisively to someone who is overly industrious, zealous, gung ho in his work, one who tries to impress his superiors by his diligence and becomes obnoxious to his associates as a result. *See* BEAVER.

eagle shits on Friday. At least since the years of the Great Depression, U.S. workingmen have used this phrase meaning "payday is Friday," and the term may date back to the Spanish-American War. The eagle, of course, is the one on the U.S. dollar. A euphemism for the expression is *the eagle screams on Friday.*

eaglestones. These lumps of ironstone, often the size of small eggs, are so called because the ancient Greeks believed that an eagle's eggs wouldn't hatch unless the bird deposited an eaglestone in her nest. Nobody knows how the myth originated, but the Greeks called the ironstones *aetites,* which translates into the English *eaglestone.*

ear. Though ears of corn grow on the side of the corn plant and might suggest the ears that are organs of hearing, the two words are historically unrelated. The *ear* used for hearing comes to us from the Latin *aurus,* meaning the same, while the *ear* of corn comes from the Latin *aucus,* husk. Even traced back to their ultimate roots, the two words have different etymological origins. Their similarity is purely coincidental.

ear biter. Government jobs weren't always so safe, secure, and uneventful, as this obsolete term shows. In 1845 a special agent of the U.S. Post Office bit off the ear of an opponent in a fight. For some time afterward all post office special agents were facetiously called *ear biters* as a result.

earl. Any *earl,* third in rank among the British peerage, below a duke and a marquess, takes his name from the Old English *eorl,* "a man of position," as opposed to a *ceorl,* or *churl,* "a freeman of the lowest rank." A *churl* is today a peasant, a rude, surly person, and a miser.

early to bed, early to rise . . . *See* SNUG AS A BUG IN A RUG.

earmark. Back in the 16th century English farmers began to notch their own identifying marks in the ears of their sheep and cattle to prevent them from being stolen. This practice didn't always work, for many thieves were adept at altering earmarks, but the animal earmark was so common that it soon gave its name to any kind of identifying mark and, figuratively, to something, such as money, marked or set aside for some special purpose. Incidentally, thieves who altered an *earmark* ran the risk of being sent to prison where *they* would be earmarked—slitting the ears of pilloried criminals, earmarking them, was as common as nose-slitting or earmarking animals in those days.

ears have walls. *See* WALLS HAVE EARS.

earthlight. *Earthlight* is not light on the earth; it is light reflected from the earth to the moon and back that is visible on the dark side of the moon. British astronomer John Herschel seems to have coined the word in 1833. *See* ASTEROID, for a word his father coined.

the earth moved. "Did the earth move for you?" These joking words said to one's lover after sex were apparently invented or popularized by Ernest Hemingway in *For Whom The Bell Tolls* (1940) when he has Maria say to Robert Jordan, " 'Did the earth never move for thee before?' 'Never,' he said truly." *For Whom The Bell Tolls* itself comes from a sermon by John Donne: "No man is an *Iland* intire of it selfe; every man is a peece of the *Continent* . . . And therefore never send to know for whom the *bell* tolls; It tolls for *thee*."

ear to the ground.   Rámon Adams wrote in *Western Words* (1944) that old plainsmen often placed a silk neckerchief on the ground and thus could hear the sounds of men and horses miles away. Even if plainsmen and American Indians didn't hear distant hoofbeats by putting their ears to the ground, so many writers of Westerns have attributed this skill to them that the practice has become well known. The phrase is first recorded in 1900 in the *Congressional Record*, meaning to use caution, to go slowly and listen frequently. Since then someone with *an ear to the ground* has become someone trying to determine signs of the future, trying to find out what's coming.

earwig.   The nocturnal earwig *(Forficula auricularia)* is a common garden pest, but it won't wiggle or wriggle into people's ears and then drill its way into the brain with the aid of its large pincers. Yet it was exactly this popular superstition that gave the *earwig*, or *ear-wiggle*, its name over a thousand years ago. One English writer even instructed: "If an earwig begotten into your eare . . . spit into the same, and it will come forth anon. . . ." Good trick if you can do it. To *earwig* someone is to fill his mind with prejudices by insinuations, by whispering into his ear and wriggling into his confidence.

easel.   The three-legged frame used to hold a painting while the artist works on it suggested a donkey to 17th-century Dutch painters because it somewhat resembled one and because it carried a burden. So they named this piece of equipment an *ezel*, Dutch for "donkey," the word becoming *easel* in English, as use of the device increased. The idea seems to be a widespread one, however, as the French call an *easel* a *chevalet*, a wooden "horse."

Easter.   The pagan festival held at the vernal equinox to honor Eastre, the goddess of dawn, was called Eastre in Old English. Since the Christian festival celebrating Christ's resurrection fell at about the same time, the pagan name was borrowed for it when Christianity was introduced to England, the name later being changed slightly to *Easter*.

Easter Island.   Over 2,300 miles west of Chile and some 1,200 miles east of its closest inhabited neighbor, lonely Easter Island is so named because it was discovered by Europeans on Easter Sunday in 1722.

Easter Rising.   *See* A TERRIBLE BEAUTY IS BORN.

easy as rolling off a log; logrolling.   No one seems to know the origin of the first expression, which dates back to Colonial times. One ingenious theory suggests that colonists searching for home sites in the wilderness would leave their toddlers seated on dry logs temporarily while they explored the area and that the round-bottomed children often rolled off the logs, not knowing how to keep their balance. The metaphor could just as likely have derived from colonists rolling logs off toward a building site, across a meadow or down a hill. Logs can be quite heavy, though, and difficult to move, which explains the origins of *logrolling*. When an early settler in the West was building a log cabin, his neighbors helped him roll the heavy logs to the home site, or helped him clear the land of felled trees, with the understanding that he would do the same for them if need be. Eventually the frontier expression *logrolling* came to describe this mutual "backscratching," passing into politics by 1838 as the practice of one lawmaker voting for a bill sponsored by another if his colleague reciprocates and votes for a bill sponsored by him—the political deal, "help me roll this one, I'll help you roll that one past the opposition."

easy as taking candy from a baby.   An expression meaning "anything very easy to do," which probably doesn't date back much before the 1930s. Neither does *easy as ABC* or *easy as shooting fish in a barrel*, among other similar sayings, all of which seem to have been inspired by the old Americanism EASY AS ROLLING OFF A LOG.

easy does it.   *See* TAKE IT EASY.

easy rider.   Popularized by the film *Easy Rider*, this term for a sexually satisfying male lover originated among southern blacks. William Faulkner in *Soldier's Pay* (1926) quotes a line from an old blues song: "Oh, oh, I wonder where my easy rider's gone."

easy street; to live on easy street.   To be well-off financially or to be rich, to live in comfortable circumstances. The earliest known reference to this expression is in 1897. A little later in 1901 it was used by American author George V. Hobart in his novel *It's Up To You*, where he describes a prosperous young man who had it made and could "walk up and down Easy Street." *On easy street* could, however, have some relation to the old English expression an *easy road*, "a road that can be traveled without discomfort or difficulty," an expression that was used figuratively by Shakespeare.

eat crow.   During an armistice toward the end of the War of 1812, an American soldier out hunting crossed the Niagara River past British lines. Finding no better game, he shot a crow, but a British officer heard the shot and surprised him. The Britisher tricked the Yankee out of the rifle with which he shot so well. He then turned the gun on the American, demanding that he take a bite out of the crow he had shot as a punishment for violating British territory. The American complied, but when the officer returned his weapon and told him to leave, he covered the Englishman and forced him to eat the rest of the crow. That is the origin of the expression *to eat crow*, "to be forced to do something extremely disagreeable," as related in an 1888 issue of the *Atlanta Constitution*. Although *to eat crow* is possibly a much older expression, the saying first appeared in print in 1877 and the story may well be true—nothing better has been suggested. The concept behind *to eat crow* is that crows are not good eating, but the flesh of young ones was once esteemed and I have it on the authority of the Remington Arms Co. that even old crows aren't so bad if you simply "skin the bird, salt and cut it into pieces, parboil till tender and then fry with butter and onions." I'll eat crow if someone conclusively proves that the recipe isn't authentic.

eat dog for another.   Various American Indian tribes ate dog meat, and at least one was called *the Dogeaters* by their enemies. When white men sat at Indian councils where dog meat was served, those who didn't relish the comestible could, without offending their host, put a silver dollar on the dish and pass it along, the next man taking the dollar and eating the dog. From this practice arose the American political expression *to eat dog for another.*

eat, drink, and be merry, for tomorrow we die.   Brewer tells us that this was "a traditional saying of the Egyptians, who, at their banquets, exhibited a skeleton to the guests to remind them of the brevity of life." *Eat, drink, and be merry* itself, however, appears in Eccles. 8:15: "A man hath no better thing under the sun than to eat, drink and be merry."

eat humble pie.   Here is an expression probably born as a pun. The *humble* in this pie has nothing to do etymologically with the word *humble*, "lowly," which is from the Latin *humilis*, "low or slight." Umbles or numbles (from the Latin *lumbulus*, "little loin") were the innards—the heart, liver, and entrails—of deer and were often made into a pie. Sir Walter Scott called this dish "the best," and an old recipe for it (1475) instructed "For to serve a Lord"—but some thought it fit only for servants. When the lord of a manor and his guests dined on venison, the menials ate umble pie made from the innards of the deer. Anyone who ate umble pie was therefore in a position of inferiority—he or she was humbled—and some anonymous punster in the time of William the Conqueror, realizing this, changed *umble pie* to *humble pie*, the pun all the more effective because in several British dialects, especially the Cockney, the *h* is silent and *humble* is pronounced *umble* anyway. So the play upon words gave us the common expression *to eat humble pie*, meaning to suffer humiliation, to apologize, or to abase oneself.

eatin' a green 'simmon.   The *'simmon* in this 19th-century Americanism is a persimmon, which takes its name from the Cree *pasiminan* (dried fruit). Although the fruit is delicious when thoroughly ripe, a green unripe persimmon is so sour it could make you whistle, which led to the expression *he looks like he's been eatin' a green 'simmon.* On the other hand, ripe persimmons suggested *walking off with the persimmons* (walking off with the prize), which also dates back to the 1850s.

eat one's hat.   This is an asseveration, as the *O.E.D.* so neatly puts it, "stating one's readiness to do this if an event of which one is certain should not occur." A woman named Miss E. E. Money first recorded the phrase, in 1887, and it is sometimes given as *I'll eat Rowley's hat.* One persistent folk etymology has the *hat* here being "a food made of eggs, veal, dates, saffron, salt, and spices" that no one else seems to have heard of.

eat one's words.   "God eateth not his word when he hath once spoken" is the first recorded use of this expression meaning "to retreat in a humiliating way"—in a 1571 religious work. There are several instances of people literally eating their words, the earliest occurring in 1370 when the pope sent two delegates to Bernabo Visconti bearing a rolled parchment, informing him that he had been excommunicated. Infuriated, Visconti arrested the delegates and made them eat the parchment, words, leaden seal, and all. I doubt that this suggested *to eat one's own's words*, but it is a good story.

eat something with one toe in the fire.   A colorful backwoods expression meaning that something tastes so good one could enjoy eating it even while in extreme pain. "Mmmmmm, this is so good I could eat it with one toe in the fire."

eat the Yank way.   To Brits, who have long called Americans Yanks, this phrase means to hold the fork in the right hand, as Americans generally do.

eavesdropper.   The eaves of a house is simply the edge of the roof that overhangs the side. (*Eaves* is both singular and plural, there being no word *eave*.) In ancient times, English law forbade the building of a house less than two feet from another person's property, because rainwater dropping off the eaves might injure a neighbor's land. So the space beneath the eaves of a house and about two feet out came to be called the *eavesdrip* or *eavesdrop*. Later, in the 15th century, persons standing in this space near a window trying to overhear conversations inside a house were called *eavesdroppers*, and it was from their name that the verb *to eavesdrop* was formed. One 16th-century English writer warned of "eavesdroppers with pen and ink outside the walls," and the great jurist Sir William Blackstone called "eavesdroppers" a "common nuisance."

eavestrough.   What are usually called gutters in America are for the most part called *eavestroughs* in Canada, though younger Canadians are increasingly using the American term. Both are the names for a trough fixed on the eaves for draining rainwater from a roof. *Rainspout* and *spouting* are still other names for the same thing.

ebb tide.   *See* TIDE.

Ecce Homo.   In Latin *Ecce Homo* means "Behold the man." The words were said by Pontius Pilate to the people after he brought forth Jesus wearing the crown of thorns and purple robe, as told in John 19:5. *Ecce Homo* is also the name of the many paintings of Christ crowned with thorns and bound by ropes, some of them masterpieces by the likes of Titian, Van Dyck, and Rembrandt.

eccentric.   *Eccentric* derives from the Latin *ex centrum*, "out of center, deviating from the center," the word originally an astronomical term and used this way early in the 16th century. Not for almost another 200 years was *eccentric* applied to odd, whimsical people who deviated from the center. (The eccentricity of the earth's orbit is 0.017, should anyone have need to know.)

ecdysiast; stripteaser.   Stripteaser Georgia Sothern, or her press agent, wrote H. L. Mencken in 1940 asking him to coin a "more palatable word" to describe her profession. The Sage of Baltimore, who had hatched other neologisms (*i.e.,* "booti-cian" for a bootlegger), gallantly responded, suggesting that "strip-teasing be related in some way or other to the zoological phenomenon of molting." Among his specific recommendations were lizards, called the Geckonidae (not very appetizing, either), and *ecdysiast*, which comes from *ecdysis*, the scientific term for "molting." Miss Sothern adopted the last, and it was publicized universally; born to the world was a new word and a new union called the Society of Ecdysiasts, Parade, and Specialty Dancers.

But not every artfully unclad body was happy with Mencken's invention. Said the Queen of Strippers, Gypsy Rose Lee: " 'Ecdysiast,' he calls me! Why the man is an intellectual slob. He has been reading *books. Dictionaries.* We don't wear feathers and molt them off. . . . What does he know about stripping?' " Most would agree that *stripteaser* is far more revealing. *Striptease*, first recorded in 1938, and *stripping* seem to have been coined within the last 65 years or so, but the word *stripping* for a woman removing her clothes to sexually stimulate men goes back at least 400 years. "Be sure that they be lewd, drunken, stripping whores," says a character in Thomas Otway's comedy, *The Soldier's Fortune* (1581). Joseph Addison wrote in *The Guardian* (1713): "At a late meeting of the stripping ladies . . . it was resolved for the future to lay the modesty price aside." Synonymous for *stripteaser* are *peeler* and *shucker. See* G-STRING; BURLESQUE.

echo.　The Greek nymph Echo chattered with Hera in order to distract her from the pursuit of Zeus. Hera punished her by depriving her of all speech save the ability to repeat the words of others, giving her heartache—she lost her love, Narcissus—but giving us the word *echo.* Over time Echo died of grief, withering away, with only her voice, the echo, remaining. The Roman poet Ovid probably invented this tale for his *Metamorphoses*, Book III.

economist.　*Economist* is a lofty occupational title but has its roots in a very common calling—housekeeping—deriving from the Greek *oikonomia*, meaning "house management." An economist was a household manager in England at least after 1580, when we find the first known use of the word; the term did not acquire its present meaning until the 18th century. The old meaning of the word is retained in the home economics courses still taught in schools.

Ecuador.　The Spanish named this South American country after the equator, which passes through it.

Eddyism.　*Eddyism*, a synonym for Christian Science, honors its founder, Mary Baker Eddy (1821–1910). Though she lived to be nearly 90, Mrs. Eddy was plagued all her life by illness and unhappiness. Married three times, her first marriage was ended by her husband's death and the second by divorce. A serious accident in 1866 turned her to the Bible. The story in Matthew of Jesus healing the paralyzed man brought her the spiritual enlightenment she attributed to her discovery of Christian Science. "The Bible was my textbook," she once wrote. "It answered my questions as to how I was healed, but the Scriptures had to me a new meaning . . . I apprehended for the first time . . . Jesus' teaching and demonstration, and the Principle and rule of spiritual Science and metaphysical healing—in a word, Christian Science." Before this, however, Mrs. Eddy had been treated by Phineas P. Quimby, a faith healer of Portland, Maine, and his influence may be reflected in her work. An indefatigable worker, she remained the leader of the movement until her death. In 1908 she established the famous international newspaper, *The Christian Science Monitor.*

edelweiss.　The edelweiss (*Leontopodium alpinum*), well known in song and picture (the little Alpine flower is featured in many Swiss designs), takes its name from the German *edel,* "noble," and *weiss,* "white," or "pure." An Italian liqueur named edelweiss is flavored with extracts of this Alpine flower.

Eden.　*See* ABYSS.

Edgar.　The Edgar is a small bust of Edgar Allan Poe presented annually to the best writers of detective stories by the Mystery Writers of America. Edgars are awarded in several categories, such as best novel and best short story. Poe himself once won a prize for his "Gold Bug" (1843), the code in the story developing from his interest in cryptography. Though he did invent the detective story in his "Murders in the Rue Morgue," "The Purloined Letter," and "The Mystery of Marie Roget," the writer is best remembered for his poetry and horror tales. Among his greatest stories are "The Fall of the House of Usher," "The Black Cat," "The Pit and the Pendulum," and "The Tell-Tale Heart." He died at 40, perhaps addicted to drugs, having spent his last days stumbling into Baltimore polling places and casting ballots in exchange for drinks. "Three-fifths genius and two-fifths sheer fudge," was James Russell Lowell's facile opinion of Poe, but Yeats declared him "always and for all lands a great lyric poet." *See* BALTIMORE RAVENS.

edgy.　*Edgy* for nervous or irritable is an Americanism first recorded as late as 1931. However, it derives from the expression *on edge*, which has been common since the beginning of the century. No doubt the latter is patterned on someone on the edge of a precipice, close to falling. The *mulligrubs, jimjams, shakes, fantods,* and *willies* are all earlier synonyms.

Edison; Edison effect.　When Thomas Alva Edison died in 1931, aged 84, the *New York Times* devoted four and a half full pages to his obituary, calling him the greatest benefactor of humanity in modern times. His name is a synonym for inventor and his more than 1,300 United States and foreign patents establish him as probably the world's greatest genius in the practical application of scientific principles. Born in Milan, Ohio, reared in Port Huron, Michigan, Edison had been interested in science since childhood—so curious in fact, that he once fed another boy a large dose of Seidlitz powders to see if the gas generated would enable him to fly. He had less than three months of formal schooling, was educated by his schoolteacher mother, and at 12 became a newspaper boy on the Grand Trunk Railway—his hearing became impaired at that time by a cuff on the ear from a railroad conductor. Edison's first successful invention was an improved stock ticker, which he proceeded to manufacture. He then devoted his full time to the "invention business." The Wizard of Menlo Park—where one of his first shops was located—soon had a new laboratory in West Orange, New Jersey, where he could "build anything from a lady's watch to a locomotive." A list of only his most noted inventions is still almost unbelieveable. These included assisting in the invention of the typewriter; invention of the carbon telephone transmitter; the first commercially practical electric light; an entire complex system, complete with many inventions, for the distribution of electricity for light and power, which resulted in the first central electric light power plant in the world in New York City; an electric automobile; the first full-sized electric motor; electric railway signals; station-to-station wireless telegraphy; an efficient alkaline storage battery;

the magnetic ore separator; paraffin paper; an improved Portland cement; the Dictaphone; a mimeograph machine; the phonograph; the fluoroscope; and a motion-picture machine called the kinetoscope, from which developed the modern motion picture. Many of his inventions spawned giant modern industries—the electric light, his telephone transmitter, the phonograph, and the motion-picture camera being only four such discoveries. Ironically, the Edison effect, one of the few discoveries named for him, was not exploited by the inventor. It is the principle of the radio vacuum tube that made radio and television possible. The Edison base of light sockets also bears the immortal inventor's name, as does a town in central New Jersey. One of his five children, Charles Edison, served as that state's governor.

editorial. *Editorial* is an Americanism for what the British call a *leader* or *lead article*, that is, an article expressing the views of the editor or publisher of a periodical. The word is first recorded in 1830 and still hasn't caught on in England.

Edna St. Vincent Millay. Here is a great poet who took her name from a hospital, in part. Edna St. Vincent Millay (1872–1950) was named after New York's St. Vincent's Hospital by her mother, who was grateful to the hospital for saving her brother's life. Mrs. Millay's brother, Charles Buzzell, had been trapped in a cargo ship's hold without food and water for nine days on a voyage from New Orleans to New York. Doctors at St. Vincent's said he couldn't live but pulled him through, and when her daughter was born, Mrs. Millay named Edna after the famous hospital, or after the saint for whom the hospital was named. The story was confirmed recently in a letter to the *New York Times* by Edna St. Vincent Millay's daughter, who observed, "Had it been Doctor's Hospital or Lenox Hill she [her grandmother] would have reconsidered—they wouldn't scan."

Edsel. Named in 1957 for Edsel Ford, founder Henry's son, the Ford Motor Company's Edsel was, and is still, so ridiculed, unjustly, for its defects that its name became almost a synonym for a car that doesn't work. But the car failed because of the 1957 recession, not because of its poor design or quality. Edsel Ford, to his greater and probably longer-lasting fame, also has the Edsel Ford Range in Antarctica named for him. *See* UTOPIAN TURTLETOP.

education. *See* ENCYCLOPEDIA.

Edwardian. *See* TEDDY BOYS.

eelgrass. A word commony used in the eastern U.S. for the marine grass *Zostera marina*, where eels are found. Eeelgrass is called "grass-wrack" in Europe.

eena, meena, mina, mo; eeny, meeny, miny, mo. Look in the *O.E.D.*, *Webster's Second*, Mathews's *Dictionary of Americanisms*, Partridge's *Dictionary of Slang*, Brewer's *Dictionary of Phrase and Fable*—look anywhere, in any etymological reference work—and still you will not find the "counting out" expression *eena, meena, mina, mo*, or *eeny, meeny, miny, mo*, as it is perhaps more often said. Yet this is a very familiar phrase in both the United States and Britain, used at one time or another by almost all children and frequently employed by adults. It is, of course, part of a counting-out expression used in children's games to determine who will be "it" among a group of players. The full rhyme, probably dating back to the 19th century, was originally the insensitive (at best): "Eena, meena, mina, mo,/ Catch a nigger by the toe,/ If he hollers, let him go,/ Eena meena, mina, mo." Sometimes the fourth line is "My mother says I should pick this here one," and, happily, the second line is much more frequently today "Catch a tiger by the toe." The rhyme is said, of course, with the counter pointing at each player in rotation with each word, the player who is last pointed at being "it." One tradition has it that counting-out rhymes are relics of formulas Druid priests used to choose human sacrifices. Another source says these are old Welsh words for one, two, three, four.

effigy. *See* BURN OR HANG IN EFFIGY.

effing. *Effing* or *effen* has been a euphemism for *fucking* in America since at least the early 1960s, though it is first recorded in a *New York Times Magazine* article by Anthony Burgess in 1972: "I have already had several abusive phone calls, telling me to eff-off back to effing Russia, you effing, corksacking limey effer."

egghead. Usually a term of mild contempt or derision applied to intellectuals, *egghead* was first used in its present sense to describe candidate Adlai Stevenson and his advisers during the 1952 presidential campaign. Though the physical description better fit Stevenson's opponent, General Dwight D. Eisenhower, the term echoed the popular misconception that all intellectuals have high brows and heads shaped like eggs, the same kind of heads cartoonists give to "superior beings" from outer space. The continued popularity of the expression seems to suggest, sadly enough, that though these heads be admittedly full of brains, they are alien to the "common person." But *egghead* is often used humorously, even endearingly, and may yet become a word with no stigma attached to it. *See* HIGHBROW.

eggnog. Eggnog is an American invention, the word first recorded at the time of the Revolutionary War. Made of eggs, milk, sugar, spices, and rum or other spirits, it takes its name from the eggs in it and *nog* for "strong ale."

egg on. The expression *to egg on* has nothing to do with hen's eggs or any kind of eggs. Neither does it derive from Norman invaders pricking Anglo-Saxon prisoners in the buttocks with their *ecgs* ("the points of their spears") when urging them to move faster, as one old story claims. *To egg on* is just a form of the obsolete English verb "to edge": to incite, provoke, encourage, urge on, push someone nearer to the edge. To *egg* someone meant the same as *to edge* someone and was used that way until about 1566, when the expression was first lengthened and became *to egg on*.

egg phrases (a dozen more, ungraded).

> *as alike as eggs*—"We are almost as like as eggs"—Shakespeare, *The Winter's Tale*, 1611.
> *break an egg in someone's pocket*—to spoil someone's plan, 1734.
> *crush in the egg*—to crush at the very beginning, as in crushing rebellion, 1689.

eggshell blond—a bald man—Australian slang, 1945.

find a hair upon an egg—to make a picky criticism—"Critics that spend their eyes to find a hair upon an egg" (1606).

have eggs on the spit—to have business in hand, 1598.

in egg and bird—in youth and maturity, 1711.

put all your eggs in one basket—to risk all on a single venture—" 'Tis the part of a wise man to keep himself today for tomorrow, and not venture all his eggs in one basket," Cervantes, *Don Quixote*, 1605. "Put all your eggs in one basket and WATCH THAT BASKET," Mark Twain, *Pudd'nhead Wilson*, 1894.

take eggs for money—to be fooled with something worthless, 1611.

teach one's grandmother to suck eggs—to lecture one's elders or betters—dates from about 1700 and was originally *to teach one's dame to grope* (handle) *ducks* (1590).

turn up the eggs of the eyes—the whites of the eyes—"The eggs of their eyes were at their highest elevation" (1635).

walk on eggs—to walk warily, 1734.

eggplant. Eggplant of course, takes its common name from its supposed resemblance to a large egg in shape. The vegetable is generally known as the aubergine to the English. Its early reputation varied in Europe, where it was thought to induce insanity and was called the "mad apple," but where it was also considered to be an aphrodisiac and, like the tomato, was dubbed the "apple of love." Native to India, the fruits range in size and in color from purple-black to white. The name *eggplant* is first recorded in 1767 in England, where the first cultivated eggplants were indeed white and shaped like eggs. An earlier folk name for the fruit was "Guinea squash." Vineland, New Jersey, advertises itself as the "Eggplant Capital of the World," and at its annual *Eggplant Festival* serves many eggplant dishes, including an eggplant wine. *See* AUBERGINE.

eggplant Imam Baildi. A favorite Turkish dish featured in several cookbooks which translates as "the eggplant the imam (a Moslem priest or leader) fainted over." According to the old story, an elderly imam married the daughter of a wealthy oil merchant, who brought as her dowry 12 huge man-sized jars of the world's finest olive oil. A famed cook, his bride prepared him a delicious eggplant dish a few days after the wedding. So pleased was he that he ordered her to prepare the dish every day for dinner. For 12 days all went well, but on the 13th day no eggplant graced the table. When the furious imam demanded to know why, his bride explained: "Dear husband, you shall have to purchase me more oil, as I have used all that I brought with me from my father." This financial shock proved too much for the elderly imam who straightaway fainted.

eggs benedict. Oscar of the Waldorf once confirmed the story that *eggs benedict* was invented by a man suffering from a hangover. It seems that early one morning in 1894, Samuel Benedict, a prominent New York socialite, tread softly into the old Waldorf-Astoria Hotel after a night of partying—his head hurt that much. But he had what he thought was the perfect cure for his splitting headache—a breakfast of poached eggs served on buttered toast and topped with bacon and hollandaise sauce. Oscar, the maitre d'hotel, thought this combination excellent, but substituted an English muffin for the toast and ham for the bacon, naming the dish in Benedict's honor. Whether the cure worked or not isn't recorded, and another version of the tale claims that the dish was created between Oscar and New Yorker Mrs. Le Grand Benedict.

egregious. This word, deriving from the Latin *ex gregis*, "out of the flock," originally meant outstandingly good or outstandingly bad. It was used this way for 300 years, until about the mid 19th century, but for the last hundred years it has meant only "outstandingly bad." No one knows the reason for the change.

egri bikaver. This distinctive red wine of Hungary takes its first name from Eger, a leading Hungarian wine center. Its second name, *bikaver*, means "bull's blood," so it is literally the "bull's blood of Eger."

Egypt of the West. President Lincoln coined this term in an 1862 message to Congress. It was a name for the interior area of the United States between the Alleghenies and the Rocky Mountains.

eh? This expression is considered typical of Canadian speech and is often noted by U.S. visitors to Canada. It means approximately "Isn't it?" and is used at the end of a sentence, as in "Nice day we have, eh?"

Eiffel Tower. At the time it was erected in the Champ-de-Mars for the Paris Universal Exposition of 1889, the Eiffel Tower, standing 984.25 feet high, ranked as the world's tallest structure. The structural iron tower had been designed by French engineer Alexandre Gustave Eiffel (1832–1923), the earliest and foremost builder of iron structures in France and a pioneer in the science of aerodynamics with his *Resistance of Air* (1913). The tower, with three platforms at different heights, reached by stairs and elevators, has since become as much a symbol of France as the fleur-de-lis. The interior structure of the Statue of Liberty, presented to the United States by France in 1884 and a symbol of America, was also designed by Eiffel, although the statue itself was created by F. A. Bartholdi.

eight ball. In a version of rotation sometimes called Kelly pool, players must sink all 15 balls in numerical order, except for the black eight ball, which must be pocketed last. Furthermore, if a player hits the eight ball with the cue ball prematurely, he loses points. Thus anyone who makes a shot and finds the cue ball behind or very close to the eight ball is in a difficult position, for unless he makes a difficult cushion shot, he'll probably hit the eight ball when he shoots and be penalized. From this hazardous position in Kelly pool came the expression meaning to be "in an unfortunate position with little or no hope of winning, to be up the creek, out of luck." It seems to be black poolroom slang from about 1920. The later *eight ball* for a maladjusted or inefficient person derives from the phrase (such a person is always *behind the eight ball*), with some help from the armed services "Section 8" discharge for mental instability in World War II.

Eighteen-hundred-and-freeze to death. A humorous name for the year of 1817, when an unusually cold winter in

New England was followed by a cold spring, and the weather continued to be so unseasonable that many crops failed. Some sources put the years as 1816–17 and include the summer of 1816 as a very cold one when crops failed.

eight-hour day; five-day week.   Henry Ford brought attention to the *eight-hour day* and *five-day week* for workers in 1926 when he instituted them at the Ford Motor Company plant in Detroit. However, a small number of workers had worked such hours before this, and the former term is recorded a quarter-century earlier.

eighty-six.   To murder someone or put an end to something, as in "Eighty-six him, I don't want to see him again." The expression derives from restaurant waiter slang term *eighty-six*, which, among other things, means to "deny an unwelcome customer service" or to "cancel an order" ("Eighty-six the eggs!"), or which directs the cashier's attention to a customer trying to leave a lunchroom without paying his check. The code word has been used in restaurants and bars since the 1920s, but the extended uses of *eighty-six* have only been around for half as long. Its origin is unknown. *Eighty-seven and a half* is slang used by waiters to indicate that an attractive woman is approaching.

Einstein; einsteinium.   Albert Einstein (1879–1955) was unquestionably one of the greatest thinkers of all time, and *Einstein* is still widely used as a synonym for a genius. *Einsteinium*, a man-made radioactive element, was named for the physicist in 1953 by its American discoverer, Albert Ghiorso, who formed it in the laboratory after it had been detected among the debris of the first H-bomb explosion the year before. Einstein's genius wasn't apparent in his early years. Born in Ulm, Germany, he had been regarded as a dullard and even "slow, perhaps retarded" in his first years at school there. The same opinion may have been shared by his parents, for he did not learn to walk until a relatively late age, nor begin to talk until he was past three. Einstein was graduated from the Polytechnic Institute of Zurich and took employment with the Swiss Patent Office, devoting all his spare time to pure science. In 1905, at 26, his genius suddenly, inexplicably, burst into full bloom with three discoveries in theoretical physics that included his revolutionary theory of relativity, which reshaped the modern world. He was awarded the Nobel Prize in 1921—but not specifically for his theory, which few understood at the time.

Einstein's theory of relativity.   Albert Einstein published his theory of relativity, which reshaped the modern world, in a 1905 issue of *Annelen der Physik*. After he finished the 30-page article, "On the Electrodynamics of Bodies in Motion," he was so physically and mentally exhausted that he had to go to bed for a full two weeks. *See* EINSTEIN; TWO PERCENT TO GLORY.

Eisenhower jacket; I like Ike.   One of the most popular presidents in American history, Dwight David Eisenhower (1890–1969) was elected to a second term of office in 1956 by a landslide. Graduated from West Point in 1915, the Texas-born soldier later became General Douglas MacArthur's aide in the Philippines. "General Ike," or "Ike," as he was known to G.I.s, was appointed commander of the Allied armies in World War II, and was noted for his success as both a strategist and a diplomat who fashioned his command into a smoothly functioning machine. At this time the *Eisenhower jacket*, a waistlength woolen jacket once worn as part of the service uniform, was named in his honor. He is also remembered by his presidential campaign slogan *I like Ike*.

Elberta peach.   *See* PEACH.

elbow; elbow bender; elbow grease; elbowroom, etc.   *Elbow grease* has been a term of "hard manual labor" since before 1639, *B.E.'s Dictionary of the Canting Crew* (ca. 1698) calling it "A derisory term for Sweat." The old joke that *elbow grease* is the best brand of furniture polish was probably common centuries ago, too, in some form. The phrase was known in France from early times as well *(huile de bras)*. *Elbowroom*, for plenty of room to move around so that people are not rubbing elbows, dates back to early-16th-century England, but it didn't become popular here until British General John Burgoyne boasted in the 1770s that he'd find plenty of elbow room in America. *Elbow bender*, for "a habitual drinker," someone who does little more than bend the elbow to lift a glass to his mouth, is also of ancient vintage in both languages. *Out at the elbows*, shabby, "down at the heels," has aged equally well, Shakespeare using it in *Measure For Measure*: "He cannot [speak], Sir; he's out at Elbows." *Elbowing*, "jostling," is another elbow term going back to Shakespeare's time, and the Elizabethans used the term *elbonic* for "a rude, awkward verse or sentence that seemed to be pushing with the elbow." *Elbow* is from the Anglo-Saxon *el*, "length of arm," plus *bow*, "bend."

elderberry.   He who cultivates the elderberry, says an old proverb, will live until an old age and die in his own bed. Amazing properties have long been attributed to the wine and other products made from *Sambucus nigra*. Said 17th-century English herbalist John Evelyn: "If the medicinal properties of the [elderberry] leaves, bark, berries, etc., were thoroughly known I cannot tell what our countrymen could ail for what he would not find a remedy, from every hedge, either for sickness or wounds."

elder tree.   *See* JUDAS.

El Dorado.   A mythical land filled with gold, jewels, and other great riches. El Dorado, "the gilded one," was in the original 16th-century story an Indian chieftain in what is now Colombia, who was coated with gold dust during festivals and thought so little of it that he washed it off in a lake. Explorers from many European countries tried to find him, to no avail, and the yarn grew more fantastic with each telling, El Dorado becoming a country filled with riches, often spelled as one word—*Eldorado*.

Eleanor blue.   Like ALICE BLUE, this color is named for a Roosevelt, in this case, Anna Eleanor Roosevelt (1884–1962), whose dresses popularized the dark blue shade while she was "first lady of the world." Eleanor Roosevelt married her distant cousin Franklin Delano Roosevelt in 1905, two weeks after her uncle, Theodore Roosevelt, had been inaugurated as president. When F.D.R. was stricken with polio, she encouraged him to overcome his handicap and return to politics. He became the only man ever to be elected to the presidency four times, breaking the two-term tradition, and from 1933 to 1945, when he died, Eleanor was by far the most active first lady in American history. Among many activities, she wrote the syndicated newspaper column "My Day" and traveled extensively abroad on good-will missions. Outspoken on all important issues, she remained active even after her husband's death, serving as a delegate to the U.N. general assembly and chairman of the U.S. Commission on Human Rights. Orphaned at 10 and starved for love and affection in her childhood, Mrs. Roosevelt nevertheless became one of the most compassionate human beings of modern times, always an enemy of prejudice and poverty despite her aristocratic origins.

electioneering.   The art or practice of managing elections. The term appears to have been invented and first used by the great British author and politician Edmund Burke in 1790 in his *Reflections on the Revolution in France. See* DIPLOMACY.

electricity.   English scientist William Gilbert published his researches on magnetism in 1600, writing in Latin and using the Latinized word for amber, *electricus*, because he had rubbed amber in his experiments to attract light substances. Gilbert himself later translated *electricus* into English as *electric* and gave the name *electricity* to the entity through which he had effected magnetism.

electrocute; electric chair.   There was no need for a word meaning "put to death by electricity" before Thomas Edison began using electricity to light cities beginning about 1875. But many workers lost their lives in Edison's great endeavor, and such a word did become necessary. From numerous new coinages Americans came to prefer *electrocute*, an invented word (source unknown) formed from the Greek *electro* and the *cute* in the word *execute. Electrocute* also came to mean "to execute a criminal with electricity," after the electric chair was invented in 1889 and murderer William Kemmler was put to death in one at New York's Auburn State Prison. *See* ELECTRICITY.

elegantiae arbiter.   *See* GREAT MAJORITY.

elementary, my dear Watson.   *See* SHERLOCK HOLMES.

elephant bird.   You won't find *elephant bird* in any dictionary, but there is such a term. *Elephant bird* refers to what Afghans call a turkey, because of its great size. Afghan Zahis Shah told the *New York Times* (11/25/01): "This is my bird. When I run out of money I take one and come to the city and sell it at the bazaar. I heard last night . . . that in America there is a harvest festival and they eat this bird. We call it elephant bird." *See* TURKEY.

elevenses.   The British term for what Americans would call a "coffee break," the British traditionally enjoying their late-morning tea or coffee and snack at about 11 o'clock. *Elevenses* dates back to the 18th century, while *coffee break* has been around only since about 1940. Each usually takes about 10 to 20 minutes. *See* COFFEE; TEA.

11th Commandment.   All sorts of commandments have been added to the original 10 by cynics, including "Thou shall not be found out." However, the practice seems to have started with Cervantes when he wrote in *Don Quixote* (1605) that the 11th commandment was, "Mind your own business."

11th hour.   This expression, meaning "the latest possible time, with not a moment to spare," comes from the Bible, where Jesus used it in the parable of the laborers (Matt. 20:1–16). *The 11th hour,* as the parable shows, referred not to the hour before midnight but to the last hour of sunlight, for in Jesus' day hours were counted from dawn to dusk, with the 12th hour bringing darkness. The parable says that it is never too late to earn the right to enter the kingdom of heaven: "For the kingdom of heaven is like unto a householder, which went out early in the morning to hire laborers into his vineyard. And when he had agreed with the laborers for a penny a day, he sent them into his vineyard . . . And about the eleventh hour he went out and found others standing idle, and saith unto them, Why stand ye here all the day idle. They say unto him, Because no man hath hired us. He saith unto them, Go ye also into the vineyard; and whatsoever is right, that shall ye receive." And when evening came, all the laborers, those who arrived both early and at the 11th hour, received the same penny for their wages.

elevetrich.   *See* HUNT ELEVETRICH.

elfin.   The English poet Edmund Spenser invented *elfin*, "of an elfish nature, like an elf," in *The Faerie Queene* (1589), where he writes about an "elfin knight." Some say the word was suggested to Spenser by the phrase *elvene land,* "land of elves," or the proper name Elphin in the Arthurian romances.

Elizabethan Age.   The era when Queen Elizabeth of England reigned (1558–1603) was a vital one of great accomplishments in literature, poetry, drama, architecture, exploration, commerce, and many other areas. *Elizabethan* is used as an adjective to describe both the Elizabethan spirit—adventurous, vivid, eloquent, artistically brilliant, and generous, among numerous admirable qualities—and its counterparts today. Shakespeare, Edmund Spenser, Francis Bacon, Francis Drake, and Walter Raleigh were only a few of the giant figures produced in the 45-year period that Elizabeth ruled. Though "Good Queen Bess" was certainly vain, capricious, and jealous—for example, she had put to death her cousin Mary Queen of Scots and their favorite, the earl of Essex—her personal courage and sense of responsibility made the last of the Tudors one of England's greatest rulers and probably the greatest queen in history. The only daughter of Henry VIII and his second wife, Anne Boleyn, who was beheaded for alleged adultery, Elizabeth was an intelligent, well-educated woman whose court became the center of England's cultural life as it had never been before and has never been since. "There will never be a queen," she once told Parliament, "sit in my seat with more zeal to my country and care to my subjects. And though you have had and may have princes more mighty and wise sitting in this seat, yet you never had or shall have any that will be more careful and loving." She died in 1603, having lived a biblical three score and 10.

elk.   *See* LAMB.

Ellis Island; Castle Garden. Ellis Island was the United States's chief immigration station from 1892 until 1943. Previously Castle Garden, an old Dutch fort that had been converted into a noted opera house and amusement hall, had processed immigrants from 1855 to 1892 in Battery Park at the southern tip of Manhattan. Located in upper New York Bay, Ellis Island originally occupied three acres but was built up with landfill to 27.5 acres to accommodate the millions of people arriving there. During its use as an immigration center from 1892 to 1943, the Ellis Island facilities processed 16 million immigrants, roughly 70 percent of all immigrants to the United States in that period. People arriving there were screened for various undesirable factors such as contagious illnesses or mental deficiency before being granted entry to the United States. When the government began screening prospective immigrants in their native countries, Ellis Island fell into disuse. The government offered it for sale in the 1950s but could not find an adequate buyer, and the island eventually became a national monument under the care of the National Park Service. In 1998, most of Ellis Island officially became part of New Jersey after many years of legal debate over whether it actually belonged to that state or New York. Ellis Island was once called "Oyster Island" because of the abundant oysters in its waters. It was also called the "Isle of Tears," after the many people who were rejected at the center. *See* STEERAGE.

Elmer. Many given names derive from the last names of famous persons. *Elmer,* which has come upon bad times recently, is the most surprising of them. *Elmer* was even more popular than Washington as a given name during the Revolution. Its origins have long been forgotten by most, but *Elmer* may have originally honored the brothers Ebenezer and Jonathan Elmer, Revolutionary War patriots from New Jersey—"pamphleteers, organizers of Revolutionary militia, surgeons, and officers in command of troops throughout the Revolution, members of Congress and fierce debators of a hundred stirring issues of their times." Some experts disagree with the derivation, but no better explanation has been given. Said a *New York Herald Tribune* editorial on January 18, 1935: "The name Elmer . . . has such an honorable genealogy that it is time for America's countless Elmers to stand up for it."

Elmira, New York. A local legend tells us that Elmira, New York, was named for a little girl whose mother called her home so frequently and stridently ("Elmira! Elmira!") that people in the neighborhood named the town after the child.

El Niño. Warming of the ocean off South America's west coast that occurs every four to 12 years and affects weather over the Pacific Ocean. It was observed by Peruvian fishermen 300 years ago and named in honor of the Christ child, (*niño* meaning boy in Spanish) because it first occurs around Christmastime.

Elysian Fields; Elysium. Greek mythology has the Elysian Fields or Elysium as the place where those favored by the gods will blissfully enjoy their life after death. It was also called the "Islands (or Fields) of the Blessed" and may have been suggested by tales ancient Greek mariners told of reaching islands off Africa's west coast. In later years heroes and patriots were said to occupy the Elysian Fields. The Champs Élysées (Elysian Fields) is Paris's wide main boulevard.

Emancipation Proclamation. All slaves in those territories still in rebellion against the Union were freed by President Abraham Lincoln's Emancipation Proclamation on January 1, 1863: "All persons held as slaves within said designated States, and parts of States, are, and henceforward shall be free." The provisions for the freed slaves permitted all former slaves to serve in the Union armed services. The proclamation did not affect slaves in slave states loyal to the Union or conquered states, but future legislation and, finally, the Thirteenth Amendment to the Constitution ended all slavery everywhere in the U.S. *See* JUNETEENTH.

embarrassment of riches. A great amount of wealth, or anything, almost too much to have and certainly too much to conveniently use. The expression apparently came into English from the French *embarras de richesse,* meaning the same, which seems to have originated as the title of a 1753 play by the Abbé d'Allainvail. *Embarras de richesse* is also much used in English.

embedding. A U.S. policy permitting accredited war correspondents to live and travel with the military, often in combat situations. Embedded reporters have been permitted since the beginning of the second Iraq War (Operation Iraqi Freedom) in 2003.

embezzler. *Embezzle* derives from the French word *embeseiller,* meaning "to make away with, cause to disappear, fraudulently destroy." One theory has it that this word was formed from the French *bezel,* "a chisel," and referred to the practice of con men shaving small bits off gold and silver coins, passing off the shaved coins at face value, and melting down the shavings into bullion. *Bezelers,* who used the *bezel,* were these first embezzlers, according to this theory.

emcee. *See* M.C.

Emerald Isle. Doctor William Drennan claimed that in 1795 he invented the term *Emerald Isle* for Ireland, obviously because the island is so brilliantly green. The expression is first recorded in Drennan's poem *Erin,* which contains the lines:

> Arm of Erin! Prove strong, but be gentle as brave,
> And, uplifted to strike, still be ready to save,
> Nor one feeling of vengeance presume to defile
> The cause or the men of the Emerald Isle.

Emigration Road. A nickname for the Oregon Trail, which brought so many settlers West and was called by a traveler in 1862 "the best and longest natural highway in the world."

éminence grise. Père Joseph (François Le Clerc du Tremblay, b. 1577) was a Capuchin monk who became French cardinal Richelieu's personal secretary in 1612. Richelieu was the chief minister of France's Louis XIII and both men were powers behind the throne. Père Joseph came to be called *l'éminence grise,* the gray eminence, not because of his gray hair but because of his gray Capuchin habit, which distinguished him from the red-robed Cardinal Richelieu, who was called *l'éminence rouge*, the red eminence. These names were used derisively by their opponents but with the passage of time—not until the 1920s, so far as is known—Père Joseph's nickname came to mean any eminent old person, such as an elder statesman, probably because the *gray* in *gray* eminence was associated with gray hair. It also means a person who wields unofficial power, often surreptitiously through another person.

Emma Chisit?   How much is it? An example of *Strine*, a comic Australian pronunciation whose name (Strine) is a joke made by collapsing the four syllables of the word *Australian* into one.

Emmanuel.   The name of Jesus Christ, especially as the Messiah, as given in Matt. 1:23: "Behold, a virgin shall be with child, and shall bring forth a son, and they shall call his name Emmanuel, which being interpreted is, God with us." This had also been prophesied earlier in the Old Testament Isaiah: 7:14: "Behold, a virgin shall conceive, and bear a son, and shall call his name Emmanuel."

Emmenthaler.   The classic "Swiss" cheese laced with holes, *Emmenthal*, or *Emmenthaler*, is formed in huge wheels weighing up to 145 pounds. It is named for Switzerland's Emma Valley, where it is made.

Emmys.   *Emmys* refer to any of several statuettes awarded annually for excellence in television programming, productions, or performance. No one is sure of the origin of the name, which may be an alteration (influenced by the name "Emmy") of *immy*, which, in turn, could be an alteration of *image orthicon*. An image orthicon is a sensitive television camera pickup tube. On the other hand, it could have been named for some now unknown Emmy. The Emmy Awards were instituted in 1948 by the Academy of Television Arts and Sciences. All in all there are some 40 categories in which Emmys are given. *See* OBIE.

emolument.   This fancy word for salary or reward comes from Latin *molere*, to grind, the *emolument* (in the form of the Latin *emolumentum*) originally being the payment a miller got for grinding corn. *Molere* also gives us the word for grinding our molar teeth.

emperor fruit.   *See* DURIAN.

emperor's new clothes.   One of the few stories whose title has become a popular expression, in this case a byword for human vanity. The masterpiece is "The Emperor's New Clothes," a well-known fairy tale Hans Christian Andersen wrote in 1837. Andersen submitted his immortal *Fairy Tales* to every publisher in Copenhagen. All of them turned him down, and he was forced to publish the book himself.

Empire State.   A nickname for New York State, possibly because George Washington called New York "the seat of Empire" in 1784. The EMPIRE STATE BUILDING, formerly the tallest building on earth, is named for it. New York was also once called "The Gateway to the West."

Empire State Building.   It isn't widely known that the Empire State Building was jokingly called the "Empty State Building" because many of its floors were not rented for some 15 years after its completion in 1931. It takes its official name from New York State's sobriquet, the Empire State, which George Washington inspired when in discussing the 13 original states he referred to New York State as "the seat of the Empire." Until 1972 the Empire State Building was the tallest building in the world at 1,250 feet. It was surpassed as New York's tallest building by the TWIN TOWERS of the World Trade Center at 1,350 feet, until those great buildings were destroyed by terrorists in 2001. Today the Empire State Building is the second tallest building in the U.S., bested by Chicago's Sears Tower at 1,454 feet. The tallest building in the world is the Petronas Towers (1,483 feet) in Kuala Lumpur, Malaysia. The Empire State Building was featured unforgettably in the movie classic *King Kong* (1933), and in 1945 a B-25 crashed into its side in an accident similar to the terrorist act that destroyed the Twin Towers, though with much less loss of life.

Empire style.   Whenever you hear the term *Empire style* for furniture or fashions of any kind, the term doesn't refer to the Roman Empire or the British Empire. *Empire style* takes its name from Napoleon's first empire of France and refers to fashions inspired by styles developed there in the early 19th century.

emporium.   Since the 16th century, *emporium* has been used to describe principal centers of trade, the word deriving from the Greek *emporion*, a place where merchants come together, the Greek for merchant being *emporos*, which was formed from the prefix *em*, "in," and *poros*, "travel"—the first merchants being traveling salesmen. Early on we had the words *emporial*, pertaining to an emporium, and *emporentic*, of or pertaining to trade, both now obsolete, but *emporium* wasn't applied to a single store until well into the 19th century. Today the latter meaning has almost entirely replaced the former, and though it is considered grandiloquent by some, *emporium* is frequently used for a large store selling a great variety of articles and having a luxurious air.

Empress Eugénie hat.   A number of fashions that held sway in the 19th century commemorate the French Empress Eugénie, wife of Napoleon III. This beautiful, elegant, and charming woman, the undisputed leader of French fashion, which led the world then as now, was especially celebrated for her smart hats. She sometimes wore five different specimens in a day, one of her favorites being a small model with the brim turned up on the side and often decorated with ostrich plumes, named the *Empress Eugénie* in her honor. Born Eugenía Maria de Montijo de Guzmán, the empress was the daughter of a Spanish grandee and a Scottish noblewoman. Prince Louis Napoleon at first offered to make her his mistress, but she intrigued to become his wife and prevailed. Their marriage was celebrated in 1853 at Notre Dame. "The Spanish Woman" seemed too conservative in politics to be popular with the French at the time, but strongly influenced Napoleon, often efficiently governing the empire as regent in his absence. When the Second Empire fell in 1871, she fled to England with her husband, where she died almost half a century later in 1920, 94 years old and a legend in her time.

Empress of Desserts.   A nickname for the French apple properly called the Calville. This difficult-to-grow apple is so delicious that in the days of the Sun King it was believed to be the tempting apple that grew in the Garden of Eden.

Emu War.   *See* WAR OF THE STRAY DOG.

encomium.   High praise or a eulogy is called an *encomium*, from the Greek *enkomion*, meaning a eulogy or a panegyric honoring a victor in the Bacchic games, which was sung in a procession moving from *kome* to *kome* ("village to village").

encore.   *Encore* is not what the French call out in the concert hall for "repeat it, do it again," as many people believe; the French use *bis bis* for this. But since the early 18th century the word has been used in this sense in English, possibly because *encore* does mean "another" (*encore une tasse*, "another cup") and "once again" (*encore une fois*) in some French phrases.

encyclopedia.   Statesman-scholar Sir Thomas Elyot (1499?–1546), whose translations helped popularize the Greek classics in England, coined the word *encyclopedia* from the Greek *en kyklos*, "in a circle," and *paedia*, "teaching of children," the two words possibly suggesting to him "some kind of universal classroom or round table," as someone has suggested. Elyot also naturalized the Greek *democratia* into *democracy* and was the first to use *education* (Latin *educare*, "to raise a child") in its modern sense.

end of his rope.   An executed murderer dangling at the end of a rope didn't inspire this old saying for someone who has outrun fortune, exhausted all his resources. It derives from an earlier phrase *at the end of his tether*, which refers to an animal who has come to the end of the rope he is tied to and can graze no more. The exact words aren't recorded in English until 1809, but similar expressions are recorded as early as the 16th century, and Locke used something similar in *Human Understanding*. The expression GIVE HIM ENOUGH ROPE TO HANG HIMSELF probably did reinforce the stronger meaning of the phrase.

end up as a yard sale.   A very recent expression largely confined to skiers but which may find more general usage. The phrase is explained in a *New York Times* story (1/6/02): "After about three days, most reasonably athletic people can learn to [snow] board without winding up as a yard sale—the term for skiers who wipe out in operatic fashion."

engine; engineer.   The *gin* in Eli Whitney's *cotton gin* is no more than another word for *engine*, an old word that dates back to the 13th century as the synonym for a mechanical contrivance or device. *Engine* itself has a more interesting history. It is from the Latin *ingenium*, "the powers inborn," the same word that gives us *ingenious*. In English it first meant "native talent, mother wit, genius," Chaucer noting three qualities of the mind: "Memorie, engin and intellect." By extension *engine* came to mean "trickery or device," and Shakespeare used it this way when he wrote in *Othello* that men's lures and promises are "engines of lust." But as more complicated machines were developed the word came to mean the "products of engine or wit," the name for the power transferred to its product, and it is only in this sense that it is used today. An *engineer* was first a wit, one who might have invented a phrase, or even a tricky political plot. Only later was the name applied to constructors of military engines (Shakespeare writing in *Hamlet*, "For 'tis sport to have the enginer hoist with his own petard") and in this sense applied to anyone who operated an engine, like a railroad engineer. The only engineers to whom the title applied in early times, however, were military engineers, who constructed military engines and works intended to serve military purposes. It wasn't until the mid-18th century that the title was used for those who designed and constructed public works such as roads, bridges, and tunnels—these men called *civil engineers* to distinguish them from their military counterparts.

England.   The four tribes that invaded Britain from western Germany and the Jutland (Danish) peninsula after the Romans left in 410 A.D. were called the Saxons, the Frisians, the Jutes, and the Angles. The Angles, last to arrive, in A.D. 547, eventually acquired dominance and by the year 1000 the country as a whole became known as *Englaland*, land of the Angles (the shift of the *A* in *Angle* to the *E* in *England* known technically as a front mutation). The land's language, however, was known as *Englisc* 300 years earlier. *See* ENGLISH.

England expects every man will do his duty.   These were Lord Nelson's famous words to his men at Trafalgar on October 21, 1805. A British member of Parliament has written that the officialese or gobbledygook so common in government services everywhere today would express the same sentiment this way: "England anticipates that, as regards the current emergency, personnel will face up to the issues and exercise appropriately the functions allocated to their respective occupational groups." It should be noted that Nelson's famous sentence was first reported as "Say to the fleet, England expects that every man will do his duty." Nelson's flag lieutenant, Captain Pasco, suggested that it be changed to the above.

English.   As the designation for a language *English* is first recorded in about A.D. 1000. At the time English contained perhaps 30,000 words. Today the most complete dictionary (*Webster's Second International*) contains some 650,000 words, but there are probably 5 million to 10 million English words if all scientific and technical terms were included. (We should also remember that there are a vast number of personal names in English. In *The Mountain of Names* (1985), Alex Shoumatoff reports that an estimated 69–110 billion names have been bestowed since humans first made their appearance in the world and that 6–7 billion names of the dead are believed to be extinct!). In any case, the average English-speaking person has a vocabulary of about 3,000 words, while a very well-educated or well-read person might have a vocabulary of 60,000 words. Shakespeare used 19,000 to 25,000 different words to write his plays. *English* for, roughly, the spin on a ball in billiards or baseball, doesn't stem from any derogatory American reference to the affectedness or tricky ways of Englishmen, as has often been proposed. It was probably suggested by *body English*, the way the body gestures or "speaks" when words cannot be found to express an action. The English call this spin "side," the term used in billiards long before its use in baseball.

English letters.   *See* CONDOM.

English sparrow.　People have compared the destructive English sparrow to the rat because of the damage it does in eating tree buds and grain. The bird is so named because eight pairs of them were brought from England to Brooklyn in 1850 and freed in an attempt to rid the area of a caterpillar pest called the inchworm. The birds thrived, ultimately proved more of a liability than an asset, and are now ubiquitous pests throughout the country.

enlightenment.　*See* AGE OF REASON.

Enoch Arden.　Enoch Arden, Philip Ray, and Annie Lee grow up together in a little seaport town. Though both boys love Annie, Enoch wins her hand and they live together happily until Enoch sails aboard the merchantman *Good Fortune* to make his fortune. Shipwrecked for 10 years on a deserted island, Enoch is finally rescued. Annie, meanwhile has been reduced to poverty and Philip asks her to marry him, certain that Enoch is dead. Enoch is brokenhearted when he returns after the 10 years and witnesses, unknown to them, Annie and Philip's happiness, but he vows never to let them know of his return until after his death, sacrificing his happiness for theirs. Such is the plot of Alfred, Lord Tennyson's long poem "Enoch Arden," which he based on the true story of a sailor thought drowned at sea who returned home after several years to find that his wife had remarried. A similar case was reported after the *Arctic* went down in 1854; a New Orleans merchant named Fleury was believed drowned and his young widow remarried. The "widow" had three children by her new marriage and lived happily until a letter arrived from Fleury six years later. A whaler just setting out on a long voyage had rescued him and when the whaler was also wrecked, Fleury was rescued by still another whaler starting out on a long voyage, thus accounting for the many years he had spent at sea. An *Enoch Arden* has come to mean that rare creature who truly loves someone better than himself.

Enough already!　A widespread expression, influenced by Yiddish, meaning "stop doing that, that's enough, stop talking," etc. *All right already* is a variation, both terms first recorded in the early 20th century.

enough to make the angels weep.　Something so foolish that it causes one to lose all hope. Shakespeare appears to have invented the expression in *Measure for Measure* (1604): ". . . man,/ Drest in a little brief authority,/ . . . Plays such fantastic tricks before high heaven/ As make the angels weep."

ensign.　No ensigns served in the early American navy, for ensign only became the lowest commissioned rank in 1862. *Ensign* simply means "banner," and the first ensigns were British army officers who led a group of men under a flag.

entangling alliances.　George Washington didn't invent this political expression often attributed to him, even if he was against alliances with other countries that could entangle or ensnare the U.S. The words are Thomas Jefferson's, from his inaugural address in 1801: ". . . honest friendship with all nations—entangling alliances with none. . . ."

entertain.　The word's meaning "to hold the attention of, to divert, amuse" reflects its Latin origins, from Latin *inter* and *tenere*, to hold. Possibly the most embarrassing modern-day typographical error came in 1915 when an unknown *Washington Post* editor or typesetter somehow dropped *tain* from the word 'entertaining.' In the resulting news story it was noted that President Wilson had taken his fiancée Edith Galt to the theater the previous night and, rather than watching the play, "spent most of his time 'entering' [instead of 'entertaining'] Mrs. Galt."

enter the lists.　This phrase means "to compete or join in the game." *Lists* in the old expression is not a listing of names, but the borders of a field in medieval times when armed horsemen fought each other for the sport of it.

entire horse.　*Entire* is used to indicate any ungelded animal, including uncastrated stallions. The expression seems to be a Victorian one first recorded in 1881, when a sportsman wrote. "He bought two young bay entires . . ."

entropy.　This term in thermodynamics is generally used today to express the doctrine of inevitable social decline and degeneration. It is said to have been coined about 1865 by the German scientist Rudolf Clausius from the Greek prefix *en*, in, into, within; and the Greek *trope*, transformation.

environment.　Thomas Carlyle invented the word *environment* (from the English *environ*) in its modern meaning of "the aggregate of external circumstances, conditions, and things that affect the existence and development of an individual, organism, or group." The word, first recorded in 1827, is his rendering of the German *Umgebung*, meaning the same, which had apparently been coined by Goethe.

eon.　*See* AEON.

epicure.　"The fountain and root of every good is the pleasure of the stomach," is a quotation attributed to Epicurus by the Greek writer Athenaeus five centuries after the philosopher's death. Nothing could be further from the spirit of Epicurus. The Greek philosopher (341–270 B.C.) did not teach that mere sensual pleasure is man's reason for being. He argued, rather, that while pleasure constitutes the happiness of life, pleasure means peace of mind and freedom from want and pain, which can be achieved only through noble thoughts, self-control, and moderation. Though this generous, brave man regarded virtue as having no value in itself, the real harm in his philosophy lay in the fact that it was an escapist one—permitting, for example, no marriage, children, or participation in public life. Later students of his garden school in Athens—which lasted over 200 years—distorted his teachings completely, using them as an excuse for selfish hedonism and heedless indulgence. Seizing upon his idea of pleasure, they magnified it so that epicure became one entirely devoted to gluttony, debauchery, and every wanton sensual pleasure imaginable. It took centuries before the word acquired its present meaning of "gourmet or connoisseur," one with refined tastes and knowledge of food and drink, and even today's epicure is still far removed from the simple serene philosophy of Epicurus.

epiphany.   Epiphany is the Christian "Little Christmas," January 6, commemorating the manifestation or appearance of Christ to the gentiles, as represented by the Magi. The word, first recorded as far back as 1310, comes to us from a Greek word meaning "to manifest or appear" and originally referred to the gods of the Greeks making sudden appearances. Today *epiphany* can mean a sudden insight into the reality or meaning of something as well as an appearance.

epitaph.   The earliest epitaphs—the word is from the Greek term for "writing on a tomb"—are found on Egyptian sarcophagi. One of the best-known of early valedictions is that of the Assyrian king Ashurbanipal, a poem said to have been left beside his burial mound at Nineveh in the seventh century B.C. (*see* SARDANAPALIAN). The famous epitaph on Shakespeare's tomb is doggerel and may be unworthy of the Bard, but he could well have written it:

> Good friend, for Jesus' sake forbear
> To dig the dust enclosed here,
> Blest be the man that spares these stones,
> And curst be he that moves my bones.

There have been many bitter epitaphs by and about wives and husbands. English poet John Donne's famous lines on his wife are often cited as a mock epitaph but they are not. According to the story, which is often distorted, Donne's father-in-law, Sir George More, was so enraged when his daughter married without his consent that he turned the couple out of his house and caused Donne to lose his position as secretary to the lord keeper of the great seal. While considering all that had happened when he moved into his new house, Donne scratched on a pane of glass:

> John Donne.
> Anne Donne.
> Undone.

epithalamium.   Deriving from Greek for "at the bridal chamber," *epithalamium* refers to a love song or poem in honor of a bride and bridegroom sung outside the bride's room on her wedding night. The word is first recorded about 1580. "The Song of Solomon" or "Song of Songs" is said to be an epithalamium, and memorable epithalamia were also written by Spenser, Donne, Ben Jonson, Herrick, Marvell, and Dryden, among other poets.

epizootic.   Deriving from the Greek *epi*, "upon or among," and *zoo*, "animal," epizootic diseases include rabies and hoof-and-mouth disease. The Great Epizootic (the word can be either a noun or adjective) of 1872 claimed almost a quarter of America's horses (some 4 million) and left the nation's business without the power it needed to function for three months—most power at the time being horsepower. Scientists never isolated the virus that caused the epizootic, and it ended its ravages only when cold weather killed the mosquitoes that transmitted the deadly virus. By that time the financial losses suffered had helped bring on the Panic of 1873. To a nation wholly dependent on horsepower, the epizootic was indeed a tragedy. In cities across the country homes went without heat, fires blazed unfought, garbage wasn't collected, deliveries halted, public transportation ceased, stores closed, and unem-

ployment soared. Racetracks closed their gates, and at least one great American thoroughbred, Pocohontas, fell to the disease. In several cities unemployed men were even harnessed to carts and trolleys in place of horses.

E Pluribus Unum.   The motto on the obverse side of the Great Seal of the United States may come from an expression found on the title page of the British *Gentlemen's Magazine*, widely circulated in America for several decades after 1731. The title page of the magazine's first volume shows a hand holding a bouquet over the epigraph *E Pluribus Unum*. The Latin words mean, in this case, "From many, one," and are as fitting for a bouquet of flowers as they are for a nation composed of many former colonies. Other possibilities, however, include a line in Virgil's poem "Moretum," which deals with the making of a salad and reads *color est e pluribus unus*, probably the first use of the phrase in any form, and an essay by Richard Steele in *The Spectator* (August 20, 1711), which opens with the Latin phrase *Exempta juvat spiris e pluribus unus* ("Better one thorn plucked than all remain"). The Continental Congress ordered the President of Congress to have a seal in 1776 and *E Pluribus Unum* appeared on the first seal, as well as on many early coins. Congress adopted the motto in 1781 and it still appears on U.S. coins as well as on the Great Seal.

Epsom salts.   Epsom salts, whose composition is essentially the same as that of seawater, derive their name from the mineral springs in Epsom, England, where the natural hydrated magnesium sulphate baths attracted many people searching for good health.

Equality State.   Wyoming is called the Equality State because its Territorial Legislature was the first to grant women the vote, in 1863. For the same reason it is called the Suffrage State.

equalizer.   Inventors Daniel B. Wesson and Horace Smith founded the Smith & Wesson Arms Company at Springfield, Massachusetts, three years after they published the first firearms magazine in 1854. Their Smith & Wesson pistols replaced the Colt to a large extent and have been famous ever since. It is said that the term *equalizer* derives from a remark made by Chicago gangster Tim Smith, who died in a gangland killing on June 26, 1928. "Smith and Wesson made all men equal," this non-related Smith is supposed to have said.

era.   *See* AEON.

ergonomics.   Said to have been coined about 1950 by Englishman K. F. H. Murrell from Greek *ergon*, work, to describe the science of equipment design, especially for the workplace, to increase worker efficiency and maximize production. The field is also called "human engineering." Engineer Alphonse Chapanis (1917–2002) was a leading American exponent of the science and examined it at length in his autobiography, *The Chapanis Chronicles* (1999). One story described his meeting in a showroom with Chrysler chairman Lyman A. Townsend: "I was looking at a sporty model that had a steering column with a sharply pointed tip extending an inch or two beyond the steering wheel. Townsend asked me what I thought about it. My exact, or very nearly exact, words were: 'Mr. Townsend, do you know what you've designed here? You've designed a spear aimed at the driver's heart.' I also remember distinctly his cynical reply, 'Doc, it'll sell.' "

Erlenmeyer flask. Emil Erlenmeyer put his name in mothballs for posterity when he devised the first formula for naphthalene, used in making them. The German organic chemist also invented the cone-shaped, flat-bottomed *Erlenmeyer flask* made from thin glass and commonly used in chemistry laboratories. Erlenmeyer, who taught at Heidelberg, conducted many important experiments in his long, fruitful career. He died in 1909, aged 84.

ermine. The lovely fur takes its name from a rat, *ermine* deriving from the Latin for the Old World weasel, *Armenius mus*, "the Armenian rat"—so called because it was thought to come from Armenia.

erosion. *Rodere*, the Latin for "to gnaw," gives us both the *rodent* and the word *erosion*, which is common to most languages today. *Erosion* was first used in medieval times to describe acid eating through metals, and in the 19th century was applied to the gnawing action of water upon land.

erotic. Of or concerning sexual love. The word comes from the name of Eros, the young, handsome Greek god of love, whose mother is Aphrodite and who carries a golden bow and arrows that stir up sensual passion whenever he shoots someone with them. The Romans called Eros Cupid and his mother Venus. Not even the mighty god Zeus could survive Eros's shafts, though some stories say his golden arrows awakened the highest virtuous love and his lead arrows inspired sex. *See* VENUS DE MILO; APHRODISIAC.

erotolabia. Words such as *cherry*, *nuts*, *tart*, *dish*, et al., used alternatively to express gastronomical or sexual meanings. The language is rich with gastronomical metaphors and allusions such as *cheek*, TOMATO, *piece*, CHEESECAKE, *beefcake*, *dumpling*, *tidbit*, *delicious morsel*, *feast your eyes upon her*, etc.—there are enough for their own book.

to err is human. The old proverb dates back to at least the 14th century in its Latin form: *humanum et errare*. Long before this, the Greek dramatist Sophocles wrote in his tragedy *Antigone* (?441 B.C.) "To err from the right path is common to mankind." Sometimes the proverb is heard as "to err is human, to forgive divine," which seems to have been coined by English poet Alexander Pope in his "Essay on Criticism" (1711).

ersatz. Something ersatz is an imitation or a substitute. A German word that came into English in about 1870, *ersatz* derives from the German *ersetzen*, to replace.

Esau's mess of pottage. There are two versions of the proverbial story in the Bible. In one (Gen. 25:27–34) Esau sells his birthright to his twin brother Jacob for a mess of red pottage, while in the other (Gen. 27) Jacob conspires with his mother Rebekah to cheat his older twin out of his paternal blessing. Historians believe that the stories symbolize conflicts between the Edomites, led by the eponymous Edom or Esau, and the Israeli tribe headed by Jacob. The Edomites were probably wandering hunters, as represented by Esau in both stories, and the Israelites more civilized pastoral nomads. The phrase is generally used today without Esau's name (*mess of pottage*). Incidentally, the "mess" was most likely tempting. Arabians still prepare lentils in what is thought to be a similar way, blending onions and rice with them and simmering the concoction in sesame seed oil—a delectable dish, it is said.

escalator. *Escalator* does not derive from the (imaginary) French word *escalateur*, as an old persistent story has it. Though it is no longer a trademark, *escalator* was coined as such by the Otis Elevator Company in 1900, but lost its exclusivity over the years. The moving stairway was first exhibited by the New York City company at the Paris exposition in 1900, which may account for the erroneous *escalateur* theory.

escape. The Latin word *excappare* (from *ex*, "out of," and *cappa*, "cloak") means "to slip out of one's cloak," and is the ancestor of our word *escape*, although the Greeks had a similar word meaning literally "to get out of one's clothes." The idea behind these words is probably someone slipping out of a cloak or coat held by a robber or jailer, and escaping, leaving the villain or keeper with the cloak in his hands. An *escape* in gardening terminology is any cultivated plant, such as phlox, daylily or lily of the valley, that runs wild and propagates itself without further cultivation.

eschscholtzia. A very popular American plant that is almost always more likely to be called the "California poppy" or the "yellow poppy" by gardeners than its forbiddingly long proper name. The species was named after German botanist J. F. von Eschscholtz in 1816, after he found it while hunting for plants in California.

Escoffier sauce; Escoffier garnish. If one man had to be chosen to epitomize modern gastronomy it would have to be Auguste Escoffier (1847–1935). Escoffier, made a member of the French Legion of Honor in 1920, was renowned as a chef and restaurateur, operating, with César Ritz, the Ritz in Paris, London's Savoy, and the Grand Hotel in Monte Carlo. Author of a number of books on the art of cooking, Escoffier invented both the basic sauce and the chopped, carmelized almond topping for peach melba that bear his name.

Es de Lope. Perhaps only Ernest Hemingway and William Faulkner of today's writers could claim styles so unique that their work is easily recognized without being identified. Neither of them, however, had a style so recognizable and beloved that a popular expression was dedicated to it. Only the Spanish playwright Félix Lope de Vega y Carpio (1563–1635) can claim this honor. The prolific author, who penned some 2,000 dramas, wrote in a graceful, flowing style at once so elegant, earthy, and effortless—so perfect, most people thought—that it gave rise to the common expression *Es de Lope* ("It is Lope's"), said whenever a line or two of his was heard. Lope de Vega's brilliant, prodigious output inspired Cervantes to call him the *monstruo de la naturaleza* (the "monster of nature").

Eskimo. *Eskimo* is an Algonquian word meaning "eaters of raw flesh." The Eskimos do not recognize it. They proudly call themselves Inuit, "the People," or "the human beings."

Bantu, Navaho, and *Ainu* also translate as "the People" or "all the People," as do the names of many indigenous groups.

Eskimo Pie.   Invented in 1919 and originally called an "I Scream Bar," this still-popular chocolate-covered ice-cream bar was manufactured in 1921 by Russell Stover (for whom the well-known chocolate-covered candies are named) and given the trade name Eskimo Pie.

Esperanto.   Over the past seven centuries scores of artificial universal languages have been invented. The French philosopher Descartes devised one in 1629; there is another called Sobresol, based on the notes of the musical scale; and a third, Timerio, is written solely in numerals (*i.e.,* 1–80–17—"I love you"). Esperanto is far better known than any other such invention. It takes its name from the pseudonym chosen by its inventor, Lazarus Zamenhof, when he wrote his first book on the subject, *Linguo Internacia de la Doktoro Esperanto.* Dr. Lazarus Ludwig Zamenhof (1859–1917), the "Doctor Hopeful" of the title, was a Warsaw oculist who believed that a world language would promote peace and understanding. He launched his system in 1887, and today the movement has some 8 million supporters, with from half a million to a million people capable of speaking Esperanto fluently. Advocates claim that the language—based primarily on words common to the major tongues, with a Latin-type grammar—is much easier to learn than any other and can be mastered in a relatively short time. Esperanto is now taught in over 750 schools in 40 countries around the world, has textbooks for study in 54 languages, has been used in more than 8,600 books, and is the subject of some 145 periodicals.

Esperanto II and others.   *Esperanto II, Ido,* and *Nov Esperanto* are simpler offshoots of Esperanto—indeed, the word *Ido* is the Esperanto word for "offspring." All in all, some 700 artificial languages have been invented. Notable ones besides those already mentioned include Basic English, invented by linguists I. A. Richards and C. K. Ogden, which has a vocabulary of only 850 words but is rather unwieldy ("winged machine for flight" is the phrase for "airplane"); Novial, invented in 1928 by Danish philologist Otto Jespersen; Latino Sine Flexions, which derives from classical Latin; Interlingua, developed over a period of 25 years by the International Auxiliary Language Association; the Gibson Code, another language that uses numbers instead of words; Monling, which employs only monosyllabic words; and Lincos, a truly universal language composed of scientific symbols that is translatable into the binary code and could be transmitted to any place in the universe! Still other artificial languages, should you want to find out more about them, are Mandolingo, Volapuk, Idiom Neutral (simplified Volapuk), Veriparl, Bopal, Dil, Balta, Ro, Neo, Loglan, Arulo, Suma, Latinesce, Gloro, Universal, Interglossa, Nordlinn, Lanque Bleue, and Romanal.

esquire.   Esquire is mainly used in American English today as a title of respect after an attorney's name, a usage applied to both male and female lawyers in recent times. In British English, however, the title is commonly used after the name of any man. *Esquire* began life as the title given to a knight's personal attendant, one training to be a knight himself. Such attendants carried the knight's shield, hence their name, from the Old French *esquier,* shield bearer.

-ess (feminine termination).   Unlike most feminists today Mrs. Sara Josepha Hale thought that the *-ess* or feminine termination in words, declining steadily since Chaucer's day, should be revived in many cases or carried much further. So in 1867 the editor of *Godey's Lady's Book* recommended the following words: actress, adventuress, arbitress, authoress, citizeness, doctress, governess, huntress, instructress, monitress, murderess, negress, paintress, poetress, postmistress, preceptress, professoress, sculptress, shepherdess, songstress, sorceress, stewardess, tailoress, teacheress, tormentress, traitress, victress, waitress. Of these only *actress, waitress,* and *governess* are commonly used today. *Songstress, sorceress* (historical), and *stewardess* (despite *flight attendant*) still have some currency, but the rest are rarely, if ever, heard. I have never heard anyone called a *teacheress* or a *victress,* a female victor—and many feminists today would feel that a woman called any of these terms would qualify as a *victress.*

essay.   Montaigne's *Essais,* published in France in 1580, were the first in history to bear the name *essay* for a literary composition, while Bacon's *Essays Dedicated to Prince Henry* (1597) were the first in English to use the name. "To write treatises," Bacon explained, "requireth leisure in the writer and leisure in the reader . . . which is the cause which hath made me choose to write certain brief notes . . . which I have called essays. The word is late, but the thing is ancient." There are three words for short essays, none of which is used very much, if at all, anymore: "essaykin," "essaylet," and "essayette."

essence.   *Essence* derives from the Latin word *essentia,* thought to be a translation of the Greek phrase for "What is it?" It means what a thing basically is, its primary kind of being, the word first recorded in 1576.

Essenes; Essenian; Essenic.   According to unsubstantiated traditions, both Jesus and John the Baptist were originally Essenes, a sect of pre-Christian Jews that emphasized ascetic self-discipline, communal property, ceremonial purity, and baptism. The Essenes dressed in white, strictly obeyed the Sabbath, ate no meat, and drank only water. They led a monastic life, shunning marriage and wealth, and similarly ascetic persons are sometimes called Essenes or Essenic today. Little accurate historical information is available about the Essenes, but since the discovery of the Dead Sea Scrolls in Qumràn, thought to be the Essenian homeland, there has been renewed interest in the group.

Esso; Exxon.   The Esso Oil Co. coined its name from the first letters (*SO*) of the *Standard Oil* Co., the trust formed by John D. Rockefeller in 1888. The name *Exxon* was born when the courts in 1973 ordered Standard Oil to use a name other than *Esso* in several states. Employing computer technology, the company chose *Exxon* from out of 10,000 other choices, essentially because it was easily recognized and remembered. Today Exxon Mobil is the world's largest oil company.

E.T.   *See* EXTRATERRESTRIAL.

et. When American hillfolks say *et* for *ate*, they are following a precedent that goes back to the 1300s (when English author Richard Rolle wrote that "men and wimmen et and drank") and are pronouncing the word close to its accepted British pronunciation.

etaoin shrdlu. I've never heard anyone say this (it's pronounced *et i oy-in shurdloo*), but it is sometimes used by writers to indicate confusion or mistakes. It is a printer's mark, dating back to the late 1950s. *Etaoin shrdlu* are the letters on the first two vertical rows of keys at the left of the keyboard of a Linotype machine. Those letters are used as a temporary marking slug or to indicate that an earlier mistake in the line necessitates resetting. Sometimes, however, *etaoin shrdlu* is inadvertently cast and printed.

ethnic cleansing. The most terrible euphemism coined since the Final Solution of the Nazis, *ethnic cleansing*, first recorded in 1991, less than 50 years after Hitler, refers to genocide or mass murder of one religious or ethnic group by another. It is a translation of the Serbo-Croat word meaning the same. Under a policy of ethnic cleansing, in the fighting between Bosnian Serbs and Bosnian Muslims, thousands were killed or expelled from scores of towns and villages. *See* LINGUISTIC CLEANSING; HOLOCAUST.

ethnophaulism. A term for ethnic slurs, *ethnophaulism* was coined (from the Greek *phaulos*, "ugly") by A. A. Rodack in the subtitle of his authoritative *Dictionary of International Slurs* (1944). Such insults—usually cheap humor—have been known since the earliest times and still prevail. The Irish call the English names, the English insult the French, the French defame the Germans, and so on ad infinitum, or ad nauseam.

et tu Brute. *See* BRUTUS.

euchre. *Euchre*, to cheat or to swindle, comes from the American card game of euchre, which was very popular in the West in the early 19th century. Gamblers cheated at the game so frequently that its name became synonymous with their chicanery.

Euclidian. The Greek mathematician Euclid's *Elements*, written in the third century B.C., was a collection of theorems and problems that formed the basis for geometry. So famous were Euclid's mathematical works—the *Elements* alone consisted of 13 "books"—that they completely overshadowed his life; almost nothing is known about the man himself. The mathematician probably received his training from pupils of Plato in Athens, and it is certain that he founded a school in Alexandria about 306 B.C. Euclid is said to have told Ptolemy that "there is no royal road to geometry" when the ruler asked if there wasn't an easier way to learn it. Much of his *Elements* owes a great debt to the work of earlier mathematicians.

eudaemonia. *The Eudaemonic Pie*, a recent book by Thomas A. Bass, brings this rare but useful word to mind. It means, according to one dictionary definition, "a state of felicity or bliss obtained by a life lived in accordance with reason," and was apparently coined by Aristotle in that sense, deriving from the Greek word for happiness. *Eudaemonia* also means, quite simply, plain old uncomplicated "happiness."

euhemeristic. *Euhemeristic* is an adjective applied to attempts to interpret myths, especially primitive religious myths, on a historical basis. The Greek writer Euhemerus is responsible for the word, it being this mythmaker's theory that the gods popularly worshipped in the fourth century B.C. had all originally been kings and heroes. In his philosophical romance *Sacred History* Euhemerus depicted the gods thus, insisting that they had merely been deified by their subjects or admirers. The writer claimed that he had discovered an inscribed gold pillar confirming his theory in a temple on an island in the Indian Ocean.

eunuch. A little consciousness-raising for eunuchs! At one time eunuchs were "keepers or guardians of the bed," hence their name, which derives from the Greek *eune*, "bed," and *echo*, "keep." Today the term refers to any castrated human male and is used figuratively to describe a man with no courage, strength, or backbone, a weak, powerless, spineless person. Strictly speaking, however, all of our uses of *eunuch* are wrong, for eunuchs were never what most people still think them to be. Eunuchs were *not* deficient in courage and intellect. From earliest times throughout the world they took charge of harems or were the chamberlains of royal households and their confidential position often enabled them to rise to stations of great power. Neither were eunuchs always castrated. And even when they were castrated, in certain cases—if the castration took place after puberty and only the testicles were removed—they were still capable of sexual intercourse, some ladies of ancient Rome preferring them as both natural birth control devices and lovers best at prolonging the sex act. Among famous eunuchs in history were the Italian *castrati*, young boys who were castrated so that they could be trained as adult soprano singers, and the *Skopski*, a Russian religious sect whose members castrated themselves as an act of salvation and numbered over 5,000 before the Russian government prosecuted them in 1874.

euphemism. *See* GUEVARISM.

euphonious. Greek *euphonos*, sweet-voiced, gives us this word for pleasing to the ear or an agreeable sound, especially in a word's phonetic quality. *Euphonious* dates back to about 1765, and since then many authors have nominated their choice for the most beautiful (euphonious) English word, even when realizing that such a choice is so subjective as to mean nothing. Carl Sandburg, I believe, chose *Monongahela*, which rolls like a long river off the tongue, while James Joyce felt that *cuspidor* was the most euphonious word in the language. *M* words such as *melody* and *murmuring* are great favorites among many people, as are *lullaby*, *golden*, *silver moon*, *cellar door*, and *dawn*. As his favorite French word Baudelaire chose *hemorroides* (hemorrhoids). A poll taken by the National Association of Teachers of Speech gave the ten worst-sounding English words as *cacophony*, *crunch*, *flatulent*, *gripe*, *jazz*, *phlegmatic*, *plump*, *plutocrat*, *sap*, and *treachery*. Another favorite is *diarrhea*.

euphuism. *See* GUEVARISM.

eureka. When Archimedes discovered the principle of buoyancy in his bathtub while determining by specific gravity the proportion of base metal in Hiero's golden crown, he supposedly ran naked through the streets of Syracuse shouting *"Eureka, Eureka!"* ("I have found it! I have found it!") Since the 16th century the term has been used allusively as an exulting cry of discovery. Plutarch tells the story about Archimedes, and it could be true, for the Greeks commonly exercised in the nude, though a naked man running through the streets would probably have been considered immoral.

euro. The single currency of the European Union that in 2002 replaced the national currencies of 12 countries in the union, all but Britain and Sweden. The introduction of euro notes of various value has been so smooth that the old currencies have already been vanquished. The word *euro* (from *European*) was coined in 1971, when first recorded in print.

eusystolism. *See* ABBREVIATIONS.

even a worm will turn. Even the weakest, most groveling person, the lowest of the low, will resist if pushed beyond a certain limit. Cervantes coined the expression in *Don Quixote* (1605–15), the full quotation being: "Even a worm when trod upon, will turn again." *See* WORM.

even keel. The expression *to get things on an even keel*, "to make things move smoothly," dates back to at least the early 19th century. It, of course, derives from the nautical term *an even keel*, which one early writer defined this way: "A ship is said to swim on an even keel when she draws the same quantity of water abaft as forward."

even steven. Contrary to some accounts, there was never a gentleman named Steven who matched his wife blow for blow. The term apparently stems from a far less equitable character in Jonathan Swift's *Journal to Stella* (1713): " 'Now we are even,' quoth Steven, when he gave his wife six blows to one." Stella was Swift's name for Esther Johnson, and his *Journal* letters to her described his daily life in London. Their relationship was a complicated one. Swift, 14 years Stella's senior, taught her to read and write, loved her all his life, and when he died was buried beside her, but the two lovers probably never married.

Everest. *See* MOUNT EVEREST.

evergreen. *See* DECIDUOUS.

Evergreen State. A nickname for Washington state, after its abundance of evergreen forests. Washington is also called the Chinook State in honor of the Indian tribe once numerous there. *See* CHINOOK.

everlasting flower. *See* AGERATUM.

every day, in every way, I am getting better and better. *See* COUÉISM.

every dog has his day. Cervantes apparently deserves credit for this proverb, which is given in *Don Quixote* (1605–15). Two centuries later, English author George Borrow wrote: "Youth will be served, every dog has his day, and mine has been a fine one." No one has been able to trace the proverb to the Himalayan valleys north of India, where all dogs literally do have a day. *Dog's Day* in the region is called *Khich Mavas* by the Kashmiris and *Swana Boli* by the Nepalese. It is a day when humans pay reverence to dogs as their brothers and sisters among living things. Choice food is set out for the dogs; even the mangiest strays get flower garlands hung around their necks and the Nepalese dogs wear the red spot of Hindu holiness imprinted on their foreheads. The following day things get back to normal until the next Dog's Day and the dogs lead a dog's life, 364 days of curses, kicks, and stonings from humans who consider them unclean and contemptible.

every hair a rope yarn. An old nautical term for a rugged seaman. The complete quotation is "Begotten in the galley and born under a gun, every hair a rope yarn, every tooth a marlinspike, every finger a fishhook, and all his heart's blood good Stockholm tar."

every inch a man, etc. In every way. *Every inch* phrases are nothing new, having been popular ever since Shakespeare used one in *King Lear* (1606):

> *Gloucester:* Is't not the king.
> *Lear:* Ay, every inch a king.

Everyman. The term *Everyman* means "every man and woman." It derives from the central character of the 15th-century morality play *Everyman*, of unknown origin, which is still read and performed today.

every man has his price. Some cynic other than Sir Robert Walpole coined this phrase. The British prime minister said something entirely different and referred only to corrupt members of Parliament, according to William Coxe in his *Memoirs of Sir Robert Walpole* (1798). Wrote Coxe of Sir Robert: "Flowery oratory he despised. He ascribed to the interested view of themselves or their relatives the declarations of pretended patriots, of whom he said, 'All those men have their price.' "

every man jack. Everybody without exception, even the most insignificant. This apparently isn't a nautical phrase; at least it is first recorded by Dickens in *Barnaby Rudge* (1840). Dickens may have coined the precise phrase, but Shakespeare used a similar term in the same sense in *Cymbeline:* "Every Jack-slave hath his belly full of fighting."

everyone to his own taste. Sometimes this late 16th-century proverbial saying is heard as *everyone to his taste, each to his own taste*, or even *to each his own*. The Latin version translates as *concerning tastes there can be no disputing*. Among other foreign counterparts are *Ten men, ten colors* (Japanese); *Every person is free in his opinions* (Arabic); and *Every baron has his own special fantasy* (Russian).

everyone to their liking, as the old woman said when she kissed her cow. An old saying that dates back to 16th-century England, when it appeared as, "Every man as he loveth, quoth the good man, when he kyst his coowe."

everything's all tiggerty-boo. The American *O.K.* is generally replacing *right-o* in England, but *right-o* is still heard, as is its synonym *tiggerty-boo*, especially in the above expression. The *tiggerty* here (sometimes pronounced *tickerty*) is from the Hindustani *teega* and is said to have been introduced to Britain by Lord Mountbatten.

every which way. In every way, in all directions. The first recorded use of this Americanism, in 1824, says it was originally an "odd phrase" taught by slaves to the children of Virginia gentry.

Eve's curse. *See* CURSE.

Eve's date. Since we have mentioned ADAM'S APPLE, it's only fair to devote a few lines to *Eve's date (Yucca baccata)*. Found in Mexico and the southwestern United States, this little-known fruit can be eaten out of hand. The dark-purple Eve's date probably takes its name from its shape, like a stubby banana; it is tempting and sweet in taste but leaves a slight bitterness in the mouth.

Eve-teasing. In India, where English is an official language (along with Hindi), *Eve-teaser* refers to someone who teases and harasses young women, an offense that is punishable by a fine and/or jail time.

Evil One; Evil Empire; Evil Man Number One. The first is a term coined by President George W. Bush, or his speechwriter, for the terrorist Osama bin Laden after the destruction of the World Trade Center on September 11, 2001. The younger Bush probably knew that the Iraqis had called his father, President George Bush, "Evil Man Number One." Previous to this, beginning in 1983, President Ronald Reagan called the Soviet Union "The Evil Empire." Long before both Bushes and Reagan, poet John Milton used *The Evil One* as a name for the Devil in *Paradise Lost* (1667). *See* AXIS OF EVIL.

evil-starred. *See* MOONLIT.

Excalibur. King Arthur's famous sword, which Arthur pulled from a stone in which it had been fixed by magic, proving him "the right born king of all England." Excalibur is so called from the name of a sword famous in Irish legend: *Caledvevlch* or *Caladbolg*, meaning "hardbelly," that is, voracious, capable of consuming anything.

excelsior. *Excelsior*, or "wood shavings," derives from New York State's Latin motto *Excelsior*, "Yet higher, ever higher." The word was originally a trademark of the New York-based Excelsior Mattress Company, which borrowed *Excelsior* for its name from the State's Great Seal in 1868 and also applied it to the wood shavings used to stuff its mattresses.

! (exclamation mark). Like *&*, *!* goes by a number of names. In America it's usually called an exclamation mark or point, but the British call it, more simply, an exclamation, and sometime note or point of exclamation. Anyone using the older rhetorical terms *ecphonesis* ("the outcry") or *epiphonema* for the grammatical interjection rates an *!* of surprise, which is called a note of admiration, or, depending on your taste, a note of detestation.

Shakespeare used the phrase *note of admiration* (!) effectively in *The Winter's Tale*: "The changes I perceived in the King and Camillo were very Notes of admiration." But sometimes writers slashed pages with scores of them following words and phrases intended to be uttered with an intonation of exclamation or surprise, leading Swift to write that a reader should skip over sentences with notes of admiration at the end. For that matter the exclamation has had few friends throughout history. Dr. Johnson defined it as "a note by which a pathetical sentence is marked thus!" While Spenser said, "The lowest form of language is the exclamation, by which an entire idea is vaguely conveyed through a single sound." But the powerful points do have their uses in small doses—showing strong emotions or emphasizing commands or warnings. They seem to have been invented by the Italians and came into English use about four centuries ago. Tradition says that the mark derives from the Latin *io* (exclamation of joy), written vertically as ɸ, which became ! in time.

excruciating. This interesting word should not be used lightly when describing pain. It comes from the Latin *crucifigere*, "to crucify," and reflects the fact that the Romans thought that crucifixion was the most painful of all ways of execution.

excuse-me-people. Derogatory black slang in South Africa for educated black professionals or white-collar workers who, despite their fine manners, are contemptuously regarded by some as being aloof and conceited, not in touch with the problems of the people. Also called "uscuse me."

Exeter's daughter. *See* RACK ONE'S BRAINS.

Ex-Lax. Possibly the best-known laxative on the American market, Ex-Lax was originally called "Bo-Bo" (short for bonbon) by its Hungarian inventor, who introduced it in New York in 1905 and so named it after its chocolate composition and flavor (though some would never agree that it tastes like bonbons). No one is sure why its name was changed to Ex-Lax, but *ex* does mean "excellent" and *lax* does suggest "laxative"—excellent laxative.

expedite. An old story that no one has been able to prove or disprove holds that the Latin word *expedire*, the ancestor of *expedite*, derives from the name of St. Expeditus, a soldier in the Roman Army before being martyred at Melitene, Armenia, in the fourth century. St. Expeditus, it seems, was the advocate of *urgent* causes. The *O.E.D.* merely says that the Latin word *expedire* means "to free a person's feet (ped) from fetters, to help forward, to dispatch, send off."

expletive deleted. *Expletive deleted* has quickly become a euphemism to use in place of a curse, especially for four-letter words. The phrase originated in the 1970s after Watergate, deriving of course from the transcripts of President Nixon's White House tapes in which many curses are rendered as "expletive deleted."

extra innings. A baseball game that goes into *extra innings*, a term first recorded in 1885, goes beyond the normal time played (nine innings). To *go into extra innings* is said of any activity that lasts longer than usual or that takes a long time, as in "We went into extra innings on that job." The British phrase *to have a good innings* means to perform something well, but comes from the game of cricket, where innings (the singular would be *inning* in baseball) is the time during which a team or player is batting.

extras.   People who appear in stage and movie crowd scenes or background scenes have been called "extras" since 1772 on the English stage. These actors have no lines as bit players do. As early as 1912 the Italian film *Quo Vadis* had a cast of thousands—most of them extras—for verisimilitude. Extras have been around since the earliest days of movies, but never so many as played in *Gandhi*, which won the Academy Award as best picture in 1982. In the funeral scene of *Gandhi* close to 300,000 extras appeared.

extraterrestrial; E.T.   H. G. Wells first recorded, and perhaps invented, *extraterrestrial* as an adjective at the turn of the century. Meaning "outside the limits of the earth," the word was first used as a noun by American author L. Sprague de Camp in the May 1939 issue of *Astounding Science Fiction*, the author inventing the abbreviation *e.t.* in the same article. *E.T.* has since become the name of the extraterrestrial being in the popular film *E.T.* Wells, or someone before him, may have patterned *extraterrestrial* on *extraterritorial*, which dates back to at least 1665.

extreme remedies are very appropriate for extreme diseases.   An aphorism from the Greek physician Hippocrates' book of *Aphorisms* (ca. 380 B.C.). *See* HIPPOCRATIC OATH.

extrovert.   *See* JUNGIAN.

eyeballs in, eyeballs out.   Test pilots in the 1960s coined this term to describe the physical effect of acceleration on the person being accelerated. For example, the acceleration experienced by an astronaut at lift-off is *eyeballs in*, while the expression of an astronaut when the retrorockets fire is *eyeballs out*.

eye for an eye.   These words did not originate in the Old Testament, as most people believe. They come from the legal code of Hammurabi, the sixth king of the first Babylonian Amorite dynasty, which was found carved upon an eight-foot diorite column dating back to about 1750 B.C. The exact words on the column are "If a man destroy the eye of another man, they shall destroy his eye." This later became the biblical *an eye for an eye*.

eyeless in Gaza.   *See* GAUZE; SAMSON.

eyeteeth.   *See* CUT ONE'S EYETEETH.

F

F. *F* was the sixth letter in the Phoenician and Latin alphabets, as it is in ours. In both Phoenician and Hebrew its character was a peg. An *F* branded on a person's left cheek in medieval times signified that he was a felon. *F.*, following temperatures, has become the shortest and one of the most widely used eponymous symbols. In 1714 Gabriel Daniel Fahrenheit perfected and manufactured the first practical mercury-in-glass thermometer, and invented the scale for measuring temperature that is named after him. Galileo had developed a faulty air-thermoscope long before this, and there were numerous contact thermometers employing alcohol in 1654, but Fahrenheit's was the first fairly precise instrument of its kind. Even at that, his thermometric scale has had to be revised since he invented it—his thermometer being inaccurate enough for him to regard 96 degrees as the temperature of a healthy man. Today only two of his fixed reference points—32 degrees and 212 degrees, the freezing and boiling points of water under standard atmospheric pressure—are still used on the Fahrenheit scale. The inventor, a German born in Danzig, Poland, lived most of his life in Holland and England after being orphaned at 15. He was elected to Britain's Royal Society before his death in 1736 when only 50 years old. *See* CELSIUS SCALE.

Faber and Faber. The famous British publishing firm of Faber and Faber (T. S. Eliot was an editor there) was established in 1929, and only one Faber owned it: Geoffrey Faber (1887–1961). It is said that the second fictional Faber was something of a joke suggested by British poet Walter de la Mare but was a high compliment to Geoffrey Faber as well. Use another Faber in the firm's name, de la Mare said, "because you can't have too much of a good thing."

Fabian tactics. Such delaying tactics are named after Quintus Fabius Maximus, the Roman dictator who over a 10-year period defeated Hannibal's superior Carthaginian army. His strategy was to avoid open engagements and employ his troops only in harassing raids and skirmishes in the hills, where Hannibal's cavalry was ineffective. Marches, countermarches, and other hit-and-run tactics were among the "masterly inactivities" devised by this cool, unemotional man to gradually erode Hannibal's forces, despite the objections of the subjects who had elected him dictator. After his victory in the Second Punic War, in 209 B.C., he earned the agnomen, or official nickname, of "Cunctator," the "slow-goer" or "delayer," for his wariness. England's socialist Fabian Society, founded in 1884, adopted Fabius Cunctator's name upon rejecting Marxist revolutionary theory and decided to accomplish "the reorganization of society" without violence, "by stealing inches, not by grasping leagues," this giving the word a new, political significance. Fabian policy is thus patient, long-range planning.

face. According to one police detective (*New York Times*, 3/15/92) *face* has taken on a new meaning in recent times: "He's a guy who looks like a mobster's supposed to look . . . They [the mob] send him to scare the hell out of someone, like 'Go send a face.' "

face-off. In hockey a face-off is initiated when the puck is dropped by the official at the start of a game or period or to resume play. The puck is dropped between the sticks of two players, who stand face to face ready to hit it. Whether this act inspired the general term for any open confrontation (as first recorded in about 1895) is unknown, but it certainly has given the term wider currency today. *See* HOCKEY PUCK.

the face that launched a thousand ships. *See* GROVES OF ACADEME.

face the music. Though not listed by Mathews, this appears to be an Americanism first recorded in 1850. Meaning "to face up to the consequences of one's actions" it may have originally been army slang, alluding to the "Rogue's March" being played when an offender was drummed out of the service.

fad. A persistent old story holds that *fad*, a temporary fashion, derives from the initials of *for a d*ay, but there is no proof of this. Most authorities believe that the word, first recorded in 1834, comes from the English dialect *fad*, "to busy oneself with trifles," which may be a contraction of the *faddle* in *fiddle faddle*, "trifling talk or trivial matters"—but there is no real proof of this theory either.

fade-out; fade-in. These are movie terms that have come to be widely used outside the film industry. *Fade-out* refers to a gradual decrease in the visibility of a scene from full exposure to complete black. *Fade-in* refers to a gradual increase in the visibility of a scene from black to full exposure.

Fahrenheit scale. *See* F.

fag. *Fag* is a British slang term for a cigarette that is well known in the U.S. through song and story, but is rarely heard anymore. The word is still used here as an offensive term for a male homosexual. The British uses of *fag* for a young schoolboy forced to work for an older student, or *fagged* for tired, worn out, are not common in America.

fail-safe. The fail-safe system, intended to help prevent nuclear war, was developed by the Strategic Air Command of the U.S. Air Force in the 1950s. Under the fail-safe procedure a bomber had to return home without dropping its bombs if specific orders to drop the bombs weren't received. Thus a failure to receive such a radio message would be a failure on the safe side that wouldn't accidentally trigger a nuclear war. The term *fail-safe* is now used to describe any precautionary system.

fairbanks. Movie actor Douglas Fairbanks, Jr., was said to take great pleasure in the company of royalty. Picking up on this, contract bridge players dubbed a hand chock full of kings and queens a *fairbanks*.

fair dinkum; hard dinkum. *Fair dinkum* means "true, real, genuine," as in "That's fair dinkum, mate," the Australian expression probably deriving from an obsolete word meaning the same. *Hard dinkum* means "hard work." Australian troops used the word *dinkums* so often in World War I that they were nicknamed "Dinkums."

fairy rings. Fairies dancing on the spot were once thought to cause the dead or withered circles of grass often found on lawns. The fairy rings are, sad to say, caused by more prosaic fungi below the surface that envelop the grass roots and prevent them from obtaining water. The term is first recorded in 1598 when Ben Jonson used it in his satirical play *Every Man in his Humour*, in which Shakespeare acted at its first performance at the Globe Theatre. *See also* FASCINATE.

Faito! This is a Japanese borrowing and alteration of the English word *fight*. The Japanese mostly use it at sporting events, in the sense of "Fight! Go for it! Go! Go! Go!"

falderol. First used as a meaningless refrain in Scottish songs (as in Browning's line Fol-di-rol-di-rido-liddle-iddle-o!) *falderol* or *folderol*, recorded early in the 18th century, came within a century or so to mean "nonsense, empty talk or ideas."

fall. *See* AUTUMN.

fall guy. In American professional wrestling during the 1890s, just like today, many of the bouts were fixed, with a loser picked beforehand. This may have resulted in the term *fall guy* being applied to the loser, the wrestler who took a fall, the words later coming to mean any person who takes the blame for the actions of others. But there is no proof of this theory. The earliest quotation using the term *fall guy*, in 1904, links it to the underworld, and even before that in 1893 *fall* is recorded as a criminal arrest or conviction, making the wrestling connection seem unlikely.

fall in love. "So fare I—falling into love's dance;" wrote a man smitten back in 1423, the first recorded use of the expression. It took over a century more for *falling in love* to detach itself from *falling into love's dance*, but since then the phrase has been indispensable, suggesting so simply and well the dizzy loss of control of the love-struck.

false front. Gay Nineties merchants often built the facades of their stores in such a way as to give the appearance of greater size, which they thought appropriate in an era of great prosperity. But in time these false fronts became the symbol of pretense or sham that the expression means today.

family hour. In recent times this expression has been used to describe the television time slot between 6:00 P.M. and 7:00 P.M. during which programs are supposed to be free of violence and sex, though this seems at best improbable considering that most news programs are aired at this time.

famine food. Food that people wouldn't normally eat but were forced to consume because nothing else was available. The Irish coined the name during the terrible potato famine of the 19th century, when they ate foods like mussels to ward off hunger and starvation. Mussels, of course, are a gourmet food today. The same could be said of the lobster, which early Americans disdained and called a *bug* (still a term used by Maine lobster fishermen). In fact, our ancestors raked up all the windrows of lobsters storm-swept on our shores and used them for fertilizer. *See* LOBSTER; BUG.

fan. *See* FANS.

fancy footwork. Originally a term from American boxing describing the footwork of a skillful boxer in the ring, fancy footwork has come to mean any clever evasion or maneuver. It probably dates back to the early 1900s, when there were a lot of fast, clever boxers around.

fancy-shmancy. Something so fancy that it is pretentious. A blending of Yiddish and English (Yinglish), the Yiddish in this case being the *shm* that is often prefixed to a word in a funny, mocking way. Other examples are *Santa-Shmanta* and *Oedipus-Schedipus*.

fanfare; fanfaron. A fanfare, an "ostentatious display or flourish," was originally a flourish or short air played by trumpets when important people, or self-important people, arrived. In this sense it derived from the Spanish *fanfarria*, meaning "bluster, haughtiness," haughty people often demanding that heralding trumpets be played when they came upon the scene.

Another word deriving from the Spanish *fanfarria* is *fanfaron*, for a braggart.

Fannie Mae. *See* GINNIE MAE.

fanny. This euphemism may be an unknown personification, the diminutive of the feminine name Frances, or it may have a more objectionable history than the word it replaces. For Partridge suggests that the euphemism for "backside" comes from the eponymous heroine of John Cleland's hardly euphemistic novel *Fanny Hill* (1749). The term in this sense is originally an American one, however, probably deriving from the English slang use of Cleland's *Fanny* for "the female pudenda." Or else Americans were reading *Fanny Hill* long before it was legally permissible to do so. Cleland's classic of brothel life, which he wrote to escape debtor's prison, has already been made into a movie, had had vast sales in paperback and, judging by recent examples, may indeed finally prove euphemistic for its genre. Another etymologist feels that *fanny* may come from the obsolete expression *fancy vulva;* still another source traces the word to a pun on *fundament* (which became *fun,* then *fan,* then *fanny*), and *Webster's* derives it from "the fanciful euphemism 'Aunt Fanny' for the buttocks."

Fanny Heath raspberry; Lloyd George raspberry. Raspberries have not been cultivated for nearly as long as apples, peaches, and pears. Called a brambleberry and considered a nuisance in England, it was not until about 1830 that the delicate, delicious fruit began to be developed in America. The *Fanny Heath* variety is a tribute to a determined pioneer woman who immigrated to North Dakota in 1881. This young bride had been told that she could never grow anything on the barren alkaline soil surrounding her house, but 40 years later her homestead was an Eden of flowers, fruits, and vegetables. After her death in 1931, the black raspberry she developed was named in her honor. A red raspberry variety honoring a famous person is the *Lloyd George,* named after British prime minister David Lloyd George (1863–1945), who led Britain to victory in World War I and dominated British politics in the first quarter of this century.

fans. *Fans* for enthusiasts or devotees, is a shortening of *fanatics,* the Americanism first recorded in 1889. Fans were originally sports enthusiasts, but soon the word was applied to the devoted followers of thespians as well.

farad; faraday. Born into extreme poverty, he had virtually no formal education and is said to have possessed a very poor memory, yet Michael Faraday (1791–1867) became probably the world's greatest experimental genius in the physical sciences. As both a physicist and chemist Faraday became one of the immortals of science—discovering the principle of the electric motor, developing the first dynamo, formulating the laws of electrolysis, producing the first stainless steel, and discovering benzene and butylene, among many other brilliant accomplishments. His discovery of electromagnetic induction alone provided the basis for our modern electrified world and produced his "field concept," which in turn was the basis a century later of Einstein's revolutionary theory of relativity. The *farad* named for the scientist is an electromagnetic unit, while a *faraday* is a unit of electricity used in electrolysis. Faraday invented the electrical terms "anode" and "cathode."

farce. French theatrical programs used to be stuffed, or completed, with brief broad comedies based on swift action and surprising situations—which gave us the word for such broad comedies, *farce,* from the French *farcir,* "to stuff." The word is first recorded sometime in the 15th century in connection with religious dramas.

farewell-to-spring. A pretty name for a pretty flower (*Godetia amoena*) with satiny petals that blooms in early July. It is named botanically for Swiss botanist Charles H. Godet.

fare-you-well. It seems much older, but this expression is an Americanism that has been traced back to 1775. It means: 1) a state of perfection, to the last point, as in "His book is documented to a fare-you-well"; 2) the maximum effect, as in "She played each scene to a fare-you-well." Still heard occasionally as *fare-thee-well.*

far from the madding crowd. A common expression meaning to be in a peaceful place. The phrase is often said to come from the title of British novelist and poet Thomas Hardy's novel *Far from the Madding Crowd* (1874). However, Hardy took the title from a line of Thomas Gray's poem "Elegy Written in a Country Churchyard" (1750), the full line being, "Far from the madding crowd's ignoble strife." Gray's poem contains several of the best-known phrases in English literature, including "full many a flower is born to blush unseen," "some mute inglorious Milton," "the pomp of power," "the brook that babbles by," "the peep of dawn," and "along the cool sequester'd vale of life." *Madding* in the poem means acting madly, insanely, not acting maddeningly. *See* PATHS OF GLORY; PEEP OF DAWN.

farm. The Anglo-Saxon *feorm,* which meant both food and hospitality, is the ultimate source of the word *farm.* By the Middle Ages *feorm* had changed to *ferme,* which became the word for the food tenants paid their landlords as rent. Eventually the name for this rent was applied to the land that had produced it, the *ferme* or *farm,* as it was later called.

farm out. Branch Rickey, then with the St. Louis Cardinals, founded baseball's first farm system in 1918, buying stock in minor league teams on which he cultivated new players for the Cardinals. These clubs became widely known as farm teams and the major league players sent down to them from the parent club for more seasoning (or forever) were said to be farmed out. (The expression had been used for the sale of a major leaguer to the minors 15 years or so before this.) The term is now also used to mean assigning work to another person by financial agreement.

farm (plant) to the walls of the barn. To plant a crop extensively, using all or almost all available land on a farm. A variant is *farm right up to the walls of the barn.* By extension the old U.S. phrase means to employ all the resources one has at one's disposal.

faro. Faro, which is now a card game principally played in gambling houses, derives its name from *pharaoh,* but so far as we know, from no particular king except the king of spades. The game came to England from France or Italy and little more is known about it than that. The French version was named *pharaon* (pharaoh), but this was altered to *faro* as it grew popular among the English. It is assumed that at a certain stage in the game's history, a likeness of an Egyptian pharaoh appeared either on all the cards, or, more likely, on the king of spades. *See also* IN HOCK.

farrago of nonsense. *Farrago*, from the Latin *farrago*, is "a mixed fodder for cattle," and figuratively means "a confused mixture, a hodgepodge." Since the 17th century the word has been used in expressions such as a *farrago of doubts, cant, fears, nonsense,* etc.

Far Rockaway. *See* XANTHOS.

fartleberry; aarschgnoddle. These two words may never be seen together again, unless, perhaps, in some thesaurus of slang. It is remarkable that these are two words with the same meaning: "[Small globules] of excrement stuck on the anal hair," according to Eric Partridge in his *A Dictionary of Slang and Unconventional English* (1961). Partridge defines *fartleberry,* which he dates to the 18th or 19th century. *Aarschgnoddle* is a Pennsylvania Dutch synonym about which I know nothing more, except that Bill Bryson, in his delightful *Made in America* (1994), says in listing the Pennsylvania Dutch term "no, I cannot think why they might need such a word."

fascinate. Ben Jonson first recorded the word *fascinate* in his play *Every Man in his Humour* (1598), which had in the cast Shakespeare, who would fascinate the world forever. The word derives from the Latin *fascinum,* "a spell," and meant in Jonson's time "to literally case a spell by means of the evil eye," not taking on its present meaning, "to be irresistibly attractive," for another half century. *See also* FAIRY RINGS.

fast as Ladas. This literary reference is rarely heard today but should be remembered, for Alexander the Great's courier Ladas was said to run so fast that he never left a footprint. Other legendary runners include Queen Camilla of the Volsci, who, according to Virgil in the *Aeneid,* could run over water without getting her feet wet; and the Greek Iphicles, who, the Greek poet Hesiod says, could run over standing corn (wheat) without bending the ears. The Greek god Hermes (Mercury to the Romans) was swifter than all of them and was represented with wings on his sandals.

fastest man alive. *See* FOUR-MINUTE MILE.

fast food. McDonald's isn't responsible for this term, which dates back to the early 1940s, but fast food chains have popularized the expression throughout the world. It refers of course to quickly prepared and served foods, relatively inexpensive and often relatively tasteless.

fast one. *See* PULL A FAST ONE.

fast shuffle. A fast shuffle by a crooked cardplayer often results in a deck stacked to that player's advantage. This has happened so often in card games that the expression *a fast shuffle* has come to mean a dishonest dealing in any enterprise.

Fata Morgana. Mirages of houses, ships, and mirror images, often seen in the water as well as in the air, and often doubled—inverted above each other—have frequently been reported in the Strait of Messina and other places. They are named Fata Morgana after Morgan le Fay, a sorceress in Arthurian legend, the words *Fata Morgana* being an Italian translation of Morgan le Fay.

fat cat. *Fat cat* for a rich contributor to political compaign funds was coined by *Baltimore Sun* writer Frank R. Kent in his 1928 book *Political Behavior.* Today it also means any rich, secure person.

Father Christmas. The preferred British name for the American name SANTA CLAUS. Americans never use *Father Christmas,* though the British sometimes favor *Santa Claus.* Both figures have white beards and wear red suits trimmed with white fur, but in Britain *Father Christmas* has more cachet.

Father Damien. *Father Damien,* the religious name of Joseph De Veuster (1840–89), is often used to describe "a selfless, heroic man of God." Damien de Veuster, a Belgian Catholic missionary of the Society of the Sacred Heart of Jesus and Mary, was sent to the Hawaiian Islands in 1863 to replace his ailing brother, and was ordained as a priest the following year. He volunteered to be the first resident chaplain for the leper colony on Molokai 10 years later. For many years the courageous priest labored almost single-handedly to improve the condition of the 700 lepers there, contracting leprosy himself but remaining in the colony among his people until he died.

Father Mathew. A Capuchin priest and Irish social worker, Father Mathew took a pledge of total abstinence from alcohol in 1838 and through his campaigning in Ireland, England, and America, gained a tremendous following, coming to be known as "the Apostle of Temperance." His name became proverbial for a temperance reformer, his good work rewarded by a pension Queen Victoria bestowed upon him. Father Mathew was 66 when he died in 1856.

Father of American Football. While serving as a member of the Intercollegiate Football Rules Committee for 48 years, Walter Chauncey Camp (1859–1925) was responsible for so many rules governing American football that he can truly be said to have laid the foundations for the modern game. The Yale coach was being called the Father of American Football by 1920, five years before his death at one of the committee meetings.

Father of Angling. English author Izaak Walton (1593–1683) earned this title with his book on the joys of fishing, *The Compleat Angler, or the Contemplative Man's Recreation* (1653). The most quoted advice in his much-quoted work: "Thus use your frog . . . Put your hook through his mouth, and out at his gills . . . and in so doing use him as though you loved him."

Father of Baseball. This is the name given to 1) Henry Chadwick, a British-born author whose writings strongly influenced the game, though he held that it evolved from the British game of rounders; 2) Abner Doubleday, erroneously thought to have "invented" baseball (an honor even he denied); and 3) to American Alexander Cartwright who may have "invented" the modern game.

Father of Bibliography. The Swiss scholar Konrad von Gesner (1516–1565) wrote important medical, natural history, and philological works. In his *Bibliotheca Universalis* he strove to catalog all known Greek, Hebrew, and Latin writings. He finished all but one volume of a proposed 21 and earned for posterity the title *Father of Bibliography*.

Father of His Country. Every schoolchild knows that George Washington is called the Father of His Country. The title was first bestowed upon Washington in 1779 by Francis Baily, an American soldier of German descent from Pennsylvania. Baily printed a calendar in that year with a picture on the cover of the general above the German words *Des Landes Vater* (Father of His Country). Baily apparently knew that the epithet dated back to about 68 B.C., when Quintus Catullus, in a speech before the Roman senate, called his friend Marcus Tullius Cicero "the father of his country." Cicero, a Roman consul, was regarded as a great patriot for putting down the Cataline conspiracy.

Father of Waters. A nickname for the Mississippi River that may derive from an Indian name, *Meact-Chassipi* (the ancient father of the rivers), a word the French corrupted into *Mississippi*. For another possible derivation of Mississippi, see the entry MISSISSIPPI. The river is also called the father of floods.

Father's Day. *Father's Day* isn't recorded in print until 1943, 35 years after MOTHER'S DAY. Celebrated on the third Sunday in June, it was the idea of Mrs. John Bruce Dodd of Spokane, Washington. The day was proclaimed by the governor of Washington in 1910 but wasn't widely observed until about 1935.

fathom. A fathom is now a nautical measure of six feet, but it was once defined by an act of Parliament as "the length of a man's arms around the object of his affections." The word derives from the Old English *faethm*, meaning "the embracing arms."

Fat Man. *See* A-BOMB.

Fatso; Ratso. *Fatso* as the nickname for a fat person is an Americanism dating back to the Great Depression years, which were hardly fat years. The word is first recorded in a Damon Runyon tale and later gained in popularity when it became the name of a button-popping character in the comic strip *Smilin' Jack*. It may have suggested *Ratso* for an unkempt unsavory person, most notably the character Ratso Rizzo in the film *Midnight Cowboy*.

fatted calf. *See* KILL THE FATTED CALF.

fatten the kitty. *See* SWEETEN THE KITTY.

fatwa. An Arabic word meaning an edict given by a Muslim religious authority, the ruling often a death sentence. The word, also spelled fatwah, became well-known internationally in 1989 when Iran's religious leader Ayatollah Khomeini called for the death of novelist Salmon Rushdie for writing *The Satanic Verses* (1988), a novel many Muslims thought blasphemous. Though this fatwa was cancelled 10 years later, the word is still used, often loosely.

faubourg. A synonym for *suburb*. This French word was borrowed and used in Scotland and England as early as the 15th century. Now, however, *suburb* is the preferred word almost everywhere but in New Orleans, a city whose French heritage has encouraged its use since the early 19th century. Though the word is obsolete today in the sense of a suburb, it is still heard in the names of New Orleans quarters or districts such as Faubourg Sainte Marie.

Faulknenian. Resembling the writing style of U.S. author William Faulkner (1897–1962), often in reference to Faulkner's long, convoluted, often sparsely punctuated sentences. *See* NO ACCOUNT.

fauna. Linnaeus first used *fauna* as a term for "animals" in his 1746 book *Fauna Suica*, a companion volume to his *Flora Suica* (1745). The great naturalist took fauna from the name of a Roman rural goddess.

fava bean. The fava bean takes its name from *faba*, the Latin word for "bean." It is often called the broad bean, horse bean, or Windsor bean. Since antiquity this widely grown legume has been known to cause favism in people of African and Mediterranean origin with a certain enzyme deficiency, fava-bean poisoning sometimes proving fatal.

F.B.I. Its abbreviation was being used almost as soon as the Federal Bureau of Investigation was named in 1935. The first recorded use of the initials, however, came a year later, in 1936, when it was used in an article describing "Baby Face" Nelson shooting it out with an FBI agent. Today F.B.I. or FBI is usually used instead of the longer name. The bureau is also called the *Feds*, which was the name the *Confeds* (Confederates) used for federal U.S. troops during the Civil War. *See* G-MEN.

feague. In times long past, fortunately, horse trainers would insert ginger or even a live eel, it is said, into a horse's anus to liven him up and make him "carry his tail well" when he was to be shown to prospective buyers. This was called feaguing a horse. The expression, coming to mean "encouraging or spiriting him up," was used well into the 19th century. The origin of *feague* is unknown though it may derive from the German *fegen*, to polish.

fearnought. Heavy woolen clothing worn by sailors was called fearnought in the 19th century. Men wearing clothing made of fearnought needed to "fear nought" from the weather.

featherbedding. "What do you want, feather beds?" management supposedly snapped when Rock Island Railroad freight crews complained that their caboose bunks were too hard. This has been cited as the origin of the term *featherbedding*, for "unions forcing employers to hire more men than necessary for a job." It is certain, however, only that the expression was first recorded during a labor dispute in 1943.

featherbed lane. Any bad, unpaved, rutted road. According to an old unlikely story, George Washington had housewives pave a road with featherbeds (bedcovers) so that the Redcoats wouldn't hear his troops marching by at night—this giving rise to the term.

feather in his cap. American Indians of various tribes often wore feathers to show their past bravery in wars. This custom led to the Americanism *a feather in his cap*, "an honor or an accomplishment of which a person can be proud."

feather into. To shoot someone, physically do someone harm, or do something with great vigor. The commonly used Ozarkian term dates back to early England, when it strictly meant to shoot someone with the arrow from a longbow so forcefully that the feather on the end of the arrow entered the person's body. The words can also mean to attack, as in "He feathered into the whole bunch of them."

feather one's nest. Birds commonly use their breast down to make a soft, comfortable lining for their nests when they will be hatching eggs for a long period. This practice gave rise, in the early 16th century, to the expression *to feather one's nest*, "to accumulate wealth for one's comfort in the future."

featherweight. *See* LIGHTWEIGHT.

February. February is named for Februaria, the name Juno was given as goddess of fertility. February had been the month when the festival of Lupercalia was held and youths roamed the streets supposedly making barren women fruitful by striking them with magic thongs called *februa*, fashioned from the hides of goats sacrificed to Februaria. By the way, February originally had 29 days, but the Romans took one from it to give to July, so that July, named after Julius Caesar, wouldn't be inferior to August, named after Augustus Caesar.

fecalemia. Medical school students in relatively recent times invented this term for "cowardice." The mocking word was made from *fecal*, "feces," and *emia*, "of the blood," literally meaning "shit in the blood."

fedora. This common man's felt hat was named for a Russian princess. Fedora Romanoff was the leading character in Victorien Sardou's 1882 play *Fedora*, the part written for Sarah Bernhardt, the greatest actress of her day. In its American production, however, Fanny Davenport played the lead role and had a great success. The name of the character she played became known throughout the country and a hat manufacturer cashed in on its popularity by naming one of the soft felt hats he made after it. *See also* TRILBY HAT.

Feds. *See* F.B.I; G-MEN.

fed up. To be disgusted with something, wanting no more of it. The phrase has been attributed to the practice of force-feeding geese for FOIE GRAS, but it isn't found in print until 1882. It more likely is a figurative use of the English term to *feed up*, to fatten cattle for the market, which was first recorded in 1630. *Fed up to the eyeballs* is a variant. A popular army saying is *fed up, fucked up, and far from home*. The phrase *fed up to the back teeth* is a British exaggeration dating back to about 1910.

fee. The Anglo-Saxons used cattle for trading, these cattle called *feoh*, like all farm animals. Eventually *feoh* came to mean "payments of any kind." Altered to *fee*, the term finally was used for any public or private charges as well.

feeding frenzy. Wild, unseemly attention from the media toward someone in the news has aptly been called a feeding frenzy since the 1980s. Feeding frenzies of sharks, which suggested the expression, were so named 30 years or so before this and describe a pack of sharks surrounding and attacking a large wounded fish or whale.

feed the fishes. This old expression has two meanings. In Sicilian criminal circles it means that someone has been murdered, whether his body has been literally weighted down and thrown into the water or not. The expression was used in Mario Puzo's *The Godfather*, when a large fish is delivered to the Godfather's family and someone explains that this is an old Sicilian message from their enemies meaning one of their henchmen "feeds the fishes." In a more humorous vein, dating back over a century, *feed the fishes* means that someone has become seasick and vomited over the ship's rail into the water.

fee-faw-fum. The famous words of the giant in the old fairy tales "Jack and the Beanstalk" and "Jack the Giant-Killer" are "Fee-faw-fum, I smell the blood of a British man." Shakespeare, however, uses *Fie, foh, and fum*, while many Americans remember hearing *Fee-fie-foe-fum* when the story was read to them.

feel one's oats. Someone feeling his oats or full of oats is in high spirits, full of pep, so full of himself that he may even be showing off a bit. The allusion is to lively horses fed on oats and the expression is American, first recorded in 1843 by Canadian Thomas Haliburton, the humorist whose Sam Slick gave us "cry over spilt milk" and other expressions. Men, women, and children can feel their oats, but only young men are said to sow their wild oats.

feet of clay. The phrase comes from the Old Testament (Dan. 2:31–32). There the Hebrew captain Daniel interprets a dream for Nebuchadnezzar, founder of the new Babylonian Empire. Nebuchadnezzar had dreamed of a giant idol with golden head, silver arms and chest, brass thighs and body, and iron legs. Only the feet of this image, compounded of iron and potter's clay, weren't made wholly of metal. Daniel told Nebuchadnezzar that the clay feet of the figure made it vulnerable, that it prophesied the breaking apart of his empire. Over the years readers of the Bible were struck with the phrase *feet of clay* in the story and it was used centuries ago to describe an unexpected flaw or vulnerable point in the character of a hero or any admired person.

feijoa. The delicious guava (*Feijoa sellowiana*) is native to South America and grown in Florida and California for its highly esteemed white-fleshed fruit. The small tree, introduced into southern Europe in 1890, is named Feijoa for Spanish naturalist J. da Silva Feijo. A member of the myrtle family, it is a small genus noted only for the pineapple guava, which is often called "feijoa." Closely related to the true guava, its fruit is used widely for jam and jelly. The oblong fruit, about two inches long and a dull green marked with crimson, has a delicate pineapple flavor that literally melts in the mouth.

feisty.   Oddly enough, the Old English word *fist*, meaning to break wind, or a foul odor, gave us our word *feisty* for a touchy, quarrelsome person, or someone with a lot of spirit or spunk. By at least the late 1600s *fisting* in the form of a *fisting hound* was used in England as a contemptuous term for a small dog. *Feisting hound*, a variant form of *fisting hound*, came to be the name of any small mongrel dog in the southern U.S., such dogs soon being called *feists*. Because these small dogs were often lively and temperamental, their name suggested the adjective *feisty* and by the end of the 19th century this adjective was applied to people who acted like them.

fella.   In Australian pidgin English *fella* can mean a person or any thing. When Australian Aborigines say *big stone fella*, for example, they mean a mountain, while a *big fella water* is a lake.

fellowfeel.   As a synonym for empathy, the ability to get inside the other fellow's skin and feel like him, *fellowfeel* was commonly used from the 17th through the 19th century. The word is a back-formation from *fellowfeeling*, a rendering of the Latin *compassio*.

fellow traveler.   Used since the 1930s to describe a sympathizer with a cause, though not one who identifies himself with that cause. The term is said to have been coined by Russian communist leader Leon Trotsky as *sputnik*, which was translated into English as "fellow traveller." *See* SPUTNIK.

Fell types.   *See* I DO NOT LOVE THEE, DR. FELL.

fell with a dead thud.   *See* SPALDING.

female.   The word *female* is not related to the word *male*, as many people believe. It ultimately derives from the Latin *femella*, which means a girl or young woman. *Male* for a man comes from another Latin word, *mas*, which became *masaulus* and then *masclus* in Latin and finally *masle* and then *male* in French, from which it came into English as *male*.

♀ (female) and ♂ (male).   Perhaps you've wondered about the derivation of these standard scientific symbols for female and male. The female symbol is the representation of a hand mirror and is associated with Aphrodite, the Greek goddess of beauty; it also serves as the symbol of the planet Venus (the Roman equivalent of Aphrodite). The male symbol represents the shield and spear of Mars, the Roman god of war; it serves also as the symbol of the planet Mars. *See also* HOMO SAPIENS.

female language.   *See* ARAWAK.

fence-mending.   Secretary of the Treasury John Sherman, later to author the Sherman Anti-Trust Act, decided to run for the Senate in 1879, knowing that he would shortly lose his Cabinet post because President Rutherford B. Hayes wouldn't be running for reelection. When he visited his Ohio farm, he told reporters "I have come back to mend my fences" and reporters assumed he meant political fences, not the ones around the farm. Soon after, *fence-mending* came to mean "trying to gather political support at home by making personal contacts," and "patching up disagreements," the last its most common use today.

fender-bender.   A minor automobile accident on the road or in a parking lot in which not much damage is done to the cars involved or their passengers. The term was probably coined, author unknown, in the early 1960s or late 1950s.

fennel.   *Finocchio* or *fennel* can be traced to the Latin word *feniculum*, meaning "product of the meadow." "Florence fennel," a sweet variety, is often called "finocchio." Anciently held to be an aphrodisiac, fennel was also emblematic of flattery, was thought to clear the eyesight, and was said to be the favorite food of serpents. "To eat conger and fennel" (two supposed aphrodisiacs) was held to be especially stimulating. *See* MARATHON.

fermium.   Fermium, like einsteinium, is an artificially produced radioactive element first detected by American physicist Albert Ghiorso in the debris of the first H-bomb explosion. Element 100 was named for Enrico Fermi (1901–54), "the father of the atomic bomb," the year after his death. Professor Fermi, Italian born, left Italy in 1936 to receive the Nobel Prize for his theory of radioactive substances known as Fermi statistics. Opposed to Mussolini's anti-Semitic policies, he did not return, immigrating to America and becoming a citizen of the United States. Fermi directed the scientific team that produced the historic self-sustained nuclear chain reaction at the University of Chicago in 1942, and worked on the development of the atomic bomb at Los Alamos, New Mexico. *See also* EINSTEIN.

ferret.   This domesticated polecat has been much used over the centuries to drive rats and rabbits from their burrows, thus giving us expressions like *to ferret out the facts*. The animal, however, takes its name from the Latin *fur*, "thief," probably because it had a bad reputation for killing and stealing domestic fowl.

Ferris wheel.   Not even Little Egypt, the first belly dancer to perform in America, outdrew the Ferris wheel at the World's Columbian Exposition held in Chicago in 1893. The ride was the work of George Washington Gale Ferris (1859–96), a Galesburg, Illinois, railroad and bridge engineer. A giant steel structure weighing over 1,200 tons, the first Ferris wheel stood 140 feet high and measured 250 feet in diameter, with 36 cars at its rims capable of carrying 1,440 riders. The chief wonder of the "World's Fair" had been built on the tension spoke principle, the large power-driven vertical wheel revolving on a stationary axis and rotating between two pyramids. So great was the wheel's success that imitations soon became standard at all amusement parks worthy of the name.

fertilizer. The first recorded mention of the word *fertilizer* came in 1661 when an English writer noted that "Saint-foime [Saint-foin] or Holy-hay [*Onobrychis sativa*, a member of the pea family, also called Holy Clover] . . . [is] a great Fertilizer of Barren-ground." Fertilizers, however, have been known since time immemorial. The word *fertile*, from which *fertilizer* derives, comes from the Latin *ferre*, "to bear." While animal and plant fertilizers date far back in history, chemical fertilizers weren't developed until the first half of the 19th century.

ferule. *Ferula communis*, or the giant fennel, is a plant that became famous as a switch or stick used in classrooms on disobedient students. This member of the fennel family, which takes its name from the Latin for "stick," grows up to 8 to 12 feet high and was grown by the Romans both for its handsome yellow flowers and for the dried pith of its stems, which provided excellent tinder for starting fires. But by the 16th century the pliable stalks of the plant were being used as schoolroom switches, their name slightly changed to *ferule*. Eventually *ferule* was applied to "a sort of flat ruler, widened at the inflicting end into a shape resembling a pear . . . with a . . . hole in the middle, to raise blisters."

fescennine. Long ago a school of poets in Fescennia, Etruria, was famous or infamous for a style of scurrilous, obscene poetry. Such poetry anywhere came to be called fescennine verse, and *fescenninity* a word for scurrility in general.

fetus. *Fetus* is the etymologically correct spelling of this word for "the young of viviparous animals," not *foetus*, as the word derives from the Latin *fetus*, "offspring." The word is first recorded in English as *fetus*, in 1398.

few and far between. Scottish poet Thomas Campbell's poem "The Pleasures of Hope" (1799) contains this line, as well as "distance lends enhancement to the view." *Few and far between* is "Like angel-visits, few and far between" in the poem and is adapted from Robert Blair's "Like angels' visits, short and far between." *See also* IBERIA'S PILOT.

fey. *Fey* usually means "being in unnaturally high spirits, or unreal, enchanted," as in "elves and other fey creatures." In times past someone who suddenly acted so lighthearted was thought to be on the point of death, *fey* deriving from the Anglo-Saxon *faege*, "on the verge of death." *Fey* has recently become a derogatory synonym for effeminate, perhaps from being associated with *fairy*.

Feydeauesque. French playwright Georges Feydeau (1862–1921) was so noted for his bedroom farces that his name, in the form of *Feydeauesque*, has become a synonym for them. It is said that one of Feydeau's early farces was almost booed off the stage on opening night, and a friend spotted the playwright himself standing in the aisle, joining in the hissing and catcalls. "Have you gone crazy?" his friend asked him. "No, this way I can't hear them," Feydeau replied, "and it doesn't hurt so much."

Feynman diagram. This physics graph was designed by and named after physicist Richard Phillips Feynman, who shared a Nobel Prize in 1965 for his work in quantum electrodynamics.

Feynman helped develop the atom bomb in the early 1940s and wrote several books on his experiences. One time he visited his hometown of Far Rockaway, New York, to take a look at his high school records. Afterward he told his wife that according to his file, his IQ was only 124, "just above average." His wife later recalled that he was nonetheless delighted with the results of his investigation: "He said to win a Nobel Prize was no big deal. But to win it with an IQ of 124—*that* was something." *See* NOBEL PRIZE.

fez. This well-known traditional Arab red hat with a flat top and black tassel was first made in Fes, Morocco (spelled Fez by the Europeans), where the berries yielding the red dye for it grew abundantly. The hat is brimless, so that Muslims wearing it can touch their heads to the ground when praying.

Ff. Personal names beginning with a double *f* in English, such as Ffoulkes or Ffrench, originated as mistakes when the medieval or Old English capital *F*, which in script appears to be two small entwined *f*'s, was transferred to print as two lowercase *f*'s. No word in English should really begin with two *f*'s.

F.F.V. An abbreviation for First Families of (or in) Virginia. The term is an old one, dating back at least to the early 19th century.

fiacre. Fiacres are small horsedrawn cabs that take their name from an old town house called the Hôtel de St. Fiacre in Paris, where they were first rented out from a stand in 1648. The hotel, in turn, took its name from an image of St. Fiacre that hung outside it. St. Fiacre, who can be invoked as the patron saint of both gardeners and cab drivers, was an Irish priest who founded a monastery with a hospital and extensive gardens near Paris in about A.D. 615. Legend has it that his Bishop granted him as much land as he could turn over in a night and that the ground miraculously opened at the touch of his spade. It is also St. Fiacre's fate to be invoked for perhaps the most unpleasant assortment of diseases that any saint is responsible for—including diarrhea, venereal diseases, and even warts on the knees of horses. But this saint was the first man to restore people to mental health by hard work in the garden, by what psychiatrists now call hortotherapy, and he is thus best remembered as the patron saint of gardeners. His monastery eventually grew into the village of St. Fiacre, and his day is August 30, appropriate for the harvest. French gardeners have observed his anniversary for generations, attending services in the flower-decked chapels dedicated to him.

fiasco. Our word for "a total, foolish failure" derives from the Italian *fiasco*, "bottle," but no one seems to know why. First recorded in England as a theatrical term in the late 19th century, the word may have something to do with a bottle breaking—either accidentally or as part of the plot—in some forgotten Italian play. Perhaps also a brand of wine in some bottles was flat or sour—a complete failure or fiasco—or imperfect bottles made by glassblowers were called *fiascos*. There is no proof for any theory.

fiat money. Fiat money is currency that is convertible into coin or specie. *Fiat* derives from the Latin for "let it be done."

fiddle. The word fiddle comes from the Anglo-Saxon *fithele*, which may have derived from the Latin *vitula* that gives us violin. In any event, no musical instrument is involved in as many common English expressions as the fiddle, which is usually called the violin today but, surprisingly, still retains its homely name among a number of prominent musicians. With the exception of FIT AS A FIDDLE, a metaphor that goes back at least to the early 17th century and shows the great pride with which the English regarded their well-made fiddles, these expressions generally reflect a Puritanical scorn of fun and gaiety, the notion that hard work is the only important thing in life. They include "fiddlesticks," "fiddling around," "to play second fiddle," "drunk as a fiddle," "to play the fiddler," "fiddle-faddle," and many others.

fiddle-dee-dee! An exclamation indicating that something is nonsense, made famous by Margaret Mitchell's heroine Scarlett O'Hara in *Gone With the Wind* (1936): "She said 'fiddle-dee-dee!' many times . . . and vowed that she'd never believe anything any man told her." *Fiddle-dee-dee* was popular long before Scarlett, being a corruption of the Italian *fedido* (by the faith of God).

fiddlehead ferns. These delicious greens, the young furled heads of various fern species, taste something like a combination of asparagus, broccoli, and artichokes and are so named because their delicate fronds resemble the head of a fiddle. Legend has it that when Adam and Eve were banished from the Garden of Eden, the Archangel Gabriel guarded the gate through which they left to earn their bread by the sweat of their brows in the wilderness. Stepping aside to let them pass, Gabriel brushed a wing against a boulder and a feather dropped to the ground. The feather took root and grew into the fiddlehead fern, which has ever since been sacred to the archangel.

fiddler crab. The fiddler crab (*Uca pugilator*) takes its American name from the one greatly enlarged claw in the male of the species, which to someone two centuries ago suggested a fiddle. I've found no collective name for a group of these small, aggressive, burrowing crabs, but perhaps an "orchestra of fiddlers" would do.

Fiddler's Green. Since the 19th century, British sailors have called the traditional heaven of mariners Fiddler's Green, "a place of unlimited rum and tobacco."

fiddle while Rome burns. The origin of this old expression is an incident described by the Roman historian Suetonius, who said that Nero set fire to Rome in A.D 64 because he wanted to see what Troy had looked like when it burned centuries before. Suetonius added that Nero regarded the blaze with cynical detachment, singing his own composition "The Sack of Ilium" and playing the harp while flames consumed the city. Tacitus, a more reliable historian and one who, unlike Suetonius, lived in Nero's time, says that the last of the Caesars was at his villa at Antium 50 miles away when Rome burned. However, it could be that Nero climbed the tower of Maecenas on the third day of the fire and recited Priam's lament over the burning of Troy to musical accompaniment, as other accounts say. The tyrant did rebuild Rome in a much improved way, but he blamed the fire on the Christians to save his own skin and persecuted them with such fury that these first martyrs regarded him as an Antichrist (he is possibly the fantastic beast referred to as 666 in Rev. 13:11–18).

field. The Anglo-Saxons called any place that had been cleared of trees a *feld*, which by the 15th century or so became *field* and meant "open land" as opposed to woodland. *Feld* is probably related to the Old English word *felde*, "earth."

field corn. Corn that is raised as feed for livestock is called *field corn*, even though all corn is, of course, grown in fields. Before the 19th century, when *sweet corn* was developed, what is now called field corn served as both fodder for animals and human consumption (when the ears were picked young and tender). As the late John Ciardi pointed out, "fodder corn" would be a less absurd name for field corn, but language is not always a matter of logic.

field day. *See* HAVE A FIELD DAY.

Fielding guide. *See* BAEDEKER.

fiend. The Anglo-Saxon ancestor of *fiend, feond*, simply meant "enemy." However, one meaning of *enemy* was "Satan" and *fiend* took on this stronger meaning, too, over the years, finally being used to describe any diabolically cruel or wicked person.

15 minutes of fame. Thirty-five years ago, in 1968, Andy Warhol proclaimed, "In the future everybody will be famous for fifteen minutes." The leader of the pop art movement died 15 *years* ago and he is still world famous, as are his words.

fifth column. During the Spanish civil war (1936–39), a group of sympathizers within Madrid worked secretly to help Francisco Franco's Falangist rebels overthrow the Loyalist Republic and establish his dictatorship. These sympathizers were first called the *fifth column* in 1936 by Lt. General Queipo de Llano, a Falangist propagandist who broadcast the following in an attempt to demoralize Loyalist forces in Madrid: "We have four columns on the battlefield against you and a fifth column inside your ranks." When a little later that year the Falangist commander General Emilio Mola was leading four columns of Fascist troops on Loyalist Madrid from various directions, he said essentially the same thing, and so the term has often been credited to him. *Fifth column* is a direct translation of the Spanish *quinta columba* and has come to mean "any group of secret agents or traitors at work within a country." The expression gained wide currency because Ernest Hemingway used it as the title of a 1940 play about espionage in the Spanish civil war.

fifth wheel. Looking at the fifth wheel of wagons and carriages many people thought it had no function, but this wheel, or circular plate, which was attached to the upper side of the front axle and never touched the ground, supported the vehicle's body when it made a turn. Ignorance prevailed, however, and the expression *fifth wheel* came to mean "a useless or needless person or thing in any enterprise."

fifty-fifty. *Fifty-fifty*—50 percent for one party, 50 percent for the other—is still a common Americanism for "equally divided." An expression that one would guess is much older, it is first recorded in a 1913 *Saturday Evening Post* article, though it may date back to the late 19th century or earlier.

the 51st state. A name President John F. Kennedy bestowed upon *Meet the Press*, so great has been its influence on American politics. The show first aired in 1947 and has been broadcast every week since then, with a panel of newsmen interviewing guests.

54-40 or fight. James Polk won election to the American presidency in 1844 with this slogan, which referred to the ousting of the British from the whole of the Columbia River country up to latitude 54 degrees 40 minutes N. After his election Polk discarded the slogan and settled the Oregon question without going to war. The sarcastic Whig slogan "Who is James K. Polk?" inspired the myth that Polk was a political nonentity and weak president. In truth, he was one of the hardest-working of all presidents, attained almost all his stated aims, and added more territory to the U.S. than any president except Jefferson.

57 varieties. *See* HEINZ'S 57 VARIETIES.

fig. When someone says "I don't care a fig," she isn't referring to the delicious fruit (whether she knows it or not), but to the ancient "Spanish fig," a contemptuous gesture made by thrusting the thumb forth from between the first two fingers. The insult is said to be an invitation to "kiss my ass." The fig takes its English name from the Latin *ficus*, "fig," which became the Provencal *figa*. It figures in a number of phrases of its own. English, for example, features it in various expressions from the euphemistic *fig you* to far worse, and in French *faire la figue* means "to give the obscene finger gesture." The exclamation, *Frig you* has nothing to do with the "fig you" etymology, however, probably deriving from the Old English *frigan*, to love. The distinguished etymologist Laurence Urdang points out in *The Whole Ball of Wax* (1988) that the natural shape of the fig has much to do with its sexual implications: "When one encounters fresh figs growing or even in a market, it becomes clear why their visual appearance has given rise to so many translinguistic metaphors: Not to mince words, a pair of fresh figs closely resembles in size and configuration, a pair of testicles. Pressed together, they resemble the external parts of the female genitalia." "Nothing is sweeter than figs," Aristophanes wrote. Figs are mentioned in the biblical story of the Garden of Eden, and it was under a Nepal species of fig tree called the Bo that Buddha's revelations came to him. The ancient Egyptians trained apes to gather figs from trees. According to the biblical story (Gen. 3:7), after the Fall, Adam and Eve covered their nakedness with fig leaves (or leaves of the banyan tree). It wasn't until the era of Victorian prudery, however, that statues in museums were covered with fig leaves. *Fig Sunday* is an old name for Palm Sunday, when figs used to be eaten to commemorate the blasting of the barren fig tree by Jesus when he entered Jerusalem. The Persian king Xerxes boasted that he would invade Greece, thoroughly thrash all the Greek armies, and then feast on the famous fat figs of Attica. Ever since he was soundly defeated by the Greeks in 480 B.C. at the battle of Salamis, *Attic figs* has meant wishful thinking. *See* JUDAS; SYCOPHANT.

fight fire with fire. An Americanism, possibly deriving from the use of backfires to help extinguish great prairie and forest fires in the early West. Settlers would set fire to a circle or strip of land in the path of a blaze but at a good distance from it, then extinguish it and leave a barren patch so that the advancing fire would have nothing to feed on and so would burn itself out. Fighting fire with fire could be a dangerous practice, for the backfire might get out of control itself, so the expression came to mean "any desperate measure involving great risk."

fight like Kilkenny cats. During the Irish rebellion or revolution of 1798, Hessian mercenaries stationed in Kilkenny amused themselves by tying two cats by their tails and throwing them over a clothesline to fight to the death. Just before an officer interrupted their banned "sport" unexpectedly one day, a quick-thinking trooper reportedly cut off the two tails and let the cats escape, telling the colonel that the soldiers had nothing to do with the fight—the two cats had just devoured each other except for the tails. The above tale may have inspired the expression *to fight like Kilkenny cats*, to fight bitterly until the end. But another story has it that two Kilkenny cats fought so ferociously in a sandpit that they devoured each other except for their tails. And still another yarn has a thousand fabled Kilkenny cats fighting an all-night battle with a thousand cats selected by "sportsmen" from all over Ireland, the tough Kilkenny cats killing them all. Most authorities go along with Jonathan Swift, who, more conservatively, prefers the explanation that *cats* in the phrase refers to men. It seems that in the 17th century residents of Englishtown and Irishtown in Kilkenny—which was bisected by a stream—were constantly fighting over boundary lines and were compared to battling cats. But nobody has offered convincing proof for any of these stories.

fight the good fight. *See* KEEP THE FAITH, BABY!

figurehead. Ship figureheads are carved figures or busts attached below the bowsprit directly over the cutwater. They have great ornamental value, but no function whatsoever and the ships would sail just as well without them. The carvings do inspire pride and confidence among seamen, however, and lend prestige to ships. Thus, *figurehead* has been used for at least a century to describe "a person who normally heads an organization, who lends his good name to it, but has no real duties in it."

filbert. About the only connection between St. Filbert and filbert nuts is that the saint's feast day falls on August 22, the height of the nut-harvesting season. This was enough reason, however, for Norman gatherers to name the nuts *philberts* in his honor. St. Philibert, his name *Filuberht* in Old High German, was a Benedictine who founded the Abbey of Jumieges in 684. What Americans call filberts after him are actually hazelnuts. Filberts are confined botanically to two European nut varieties—about 250 million pounds of them bearing the saint's name each year. *Gilbert Filbert* was British slang for a very fashionable man about town early in this century, deriving from the popular song "Gilbert the Filbert, Colonel of the Nuts." *Cracked in the filbert* meant "eccentric or crazy."

filch. Thieves in the 16th century used a rod and line with a hook on it to steal goods from vendors' stalls. This device, called a filch, gave rise to our word for "to steal in a furtive manner," to snatch.

filibuster. Deriving from the Dutch *vribuiter*, "freebooter or pirate," *filibuster* was originally used in American English to describe gun-runners in Central America, men who engaged in war with a country with whom their own country was at peace. Over the years the word came to mean "obstruction of legislation in the U.S. Senate by prolonged speechmaking," after a congressman described one such obstruction as "filibustering against the U.S."

fill the bill. Theatrical companies in the 19th century advertised mainly on posters and handbills that were distributed in towns by advance men several weeks before a show came to town. The name of the troupe's star performer was featured on these bills in large letters, to the exclusion of the rest of the company—he or she *filled the bill*, was the show's star. Soon the vivid image behind this theatrical expression meaning "to star" came to encompass a more complex, broader thought, and by 1860 *to fill the bill* meant "to be very competent, effective, to do all that is desired, expected, or required."

filthy lucre. *Lucre*, in the form of *lucrum*, is a Latin word that means "profit or wager." The term *filthy lucre* comes to us from the letters of St. Paul to his followers, Timothy and Titus. In these letters the apostle denounced religious leaders who were greedy lovers of money and taught Christianity for dishonorable gain. But when William Tyndale translated the New Testament from Greek to English in 1525, he mistranslated Paul's figurative expression "dishonorable gain" as "filthy lucre." Paul's words didn't mean "dirty money," but the phrase was retained by the authors of the great King James Version of the Bible in 1611 and soon entered English as a term for money in general, no matter how honorably earned.

fin. The Yiddish word *finnif* is probably the ancestor of our slang for a five-dollar bill. *Finnif* meant a five-pound note in mid-19th-century England. Shortened to *fin* in England, it became American underworld slang by the 1920s. The Yiddish word, in turn, derives from the German *funf*, or "five." The *fin* of a fish comes from the Old English *finn* meaning the same.

finagle; finagle factor. A 1939 contribution to *Modern Language Notes* quoted in the *Dictionary of American Regional English* suggests that *finagle*, meaning to get something by guile or trickery, to wangle or scheme, may come from the name of the "German proponent of mnemonics" Gregor von Feinaigle (1765?–1819), "who lectured (and was often ridiculed in England and France. . . .)" Another possible eponym is a German mesmerist and whist expert of the Regency (1812–20) named Feinagel, who apparently cheated at cards. Or perhaps Feinaigle and Feinagel are the same man. Most authorities say the origin of *finagle* (rhymes with *bagel* or *Hegel*) is uncertain, or that it is a variant of *fainaigue*, an English dialect word meaning "to

shirk work, cheat at cards, to renege on a debt." The earliest recorded date for *finagle* (in the form of *finagler*) is 1922. *Finagle factor*, according to the *New Dictionary of American Slang*, refers to "the putative mathematical constant by which a wrong answer is multiplied to get a right answer." It is also called *Fink's factor*, and no particular Fink seems to be involved.

the final condensation. The founder, publisher, and editor of the *Reader's Digest*, De Witt Wallace, suggested this mock epitaph for himself.

finalize. *Finalize*, despite the objections of many critics, is recognized by most dictionaries and has been current in both American and British English for about half a century in both formal and casual writing. Such formations as *neutralize*, *minimize*, and *generalize* don't seem to bother people, but *finalize* rankles many, perhaps because most critics believe it is a pretentious bureaucratic synonym for "to complete." But it has a meaning different from "complete." It means "to put into a final form a set of conclusions that has been agreed upon roughly through a preceding series of discussions or actions."

Final Solution. A translation of German *endgultige Losung*, these words were a euphemism for the Nazi program for annihilating all Jews in Europe during the Third Reich. This mass murder policy, the Nazi answer to "the Jewish Question" or "the Jewish Problem," apparently began in 1941, and the mass extermination, with the introduction of gas chambers and crematoriums, might have succeeded if the war hadn't ended when it did. *See* HOLOCAUST; ETHNIC CLEANSING.

find the devil's golden tooth. A once-common saying that refers to a story about the pirate Captain Kidd, who was believed to have stolen the devil's eyetooth, which gave one the power of changing all metals into gold.

fine as silk. *See* QUICKER THAN HELL CAN SCORCH A FEATHER.

fine fettle. The expression *in fine fettle*, "in excellent condition," isn't recorded until 1890, but expressions like *in poor fettle*, *in good fettle*, etc., were common long before this. *Fettle* here probably comes from the belts or girdles, called *fettles*, that ancient warriors bound themselves with before going into battle; when their fettles were on they were "in good condition, ready for battle."

fine kettle of fish. A *kiddle* or *kiddle net* is a basket set in the sluice ways of dams to catch fish, a device well known from the time of the Plantagenets. Royal officials had the perquisite to trap fish in kiddles, but poachers often raided the traps of fish, frequently destroying the kiddles in the process. Possibly an official came upon a destroyed trap and exclaimed, "That's a pretty kiddle of fish!" or something similar, meaning "a pretty sorry state of affairs!" and the phrase was born. Repeated over the years, *kiddle* was corrupted in everyday speech to *kettle*, giving us the expression as we know it today.

fine words butter no parsnips. *See* PARSNIP.

f'ing. *See* EFFING.

finger in the pie. This expression, recorded in 1659, has nothing to do with being meddlesome, as has been suggested. It means simply "to have something to do with, to have a part in something." "Lusatia . . . must needs, forsooth, have her Finger in the Pye" is the first attested use of the words.

finger man. *See* POINT THE FINGER.

fingerpointing. In its sense of accusing someone, frequently unfairly, the expression is said to date back to 1941, when *Social Focus* magazine said northern states shouldn't be *fingerpointing* at lynchings in southern states when they had their own race riots.

fingers were made before forks. An old expression dating back several centuries, *fingers were made before forks* is still used as an excuse when someone is chastised for eating with ones fingers. Forks are a relatively new culinary innovation, dating back to 14th-century Italy.

fink. The original *fink* may have been either a Pinkerton man or a cop named Albert Fink, who worked for railroads in the American South. Mencken prefers the former explanation, tracing the term to the 1892 Homestead steel strike when Pinkerton men were hired as strikebreakers, these brutal "Pinks" becoming *finks* in time, the word synonymous with the earlier "scab" or the British "blackleg." Finks were anathema to the early labor movement, but the word is now used to describe not only "a strikebreaker but any treacherous, contemptible person or a police informer." Mr. Albert Fink could just as well have inspired the term in similar fashion. The German-born Fink, according to a reliable source, long headed a staff of detectives with the Louisville and Nashville Railroad and then switched to the New York Trunk Line Association in about 1875. He was not involved in railroad labor disputes, but his operatives probably policed rates charged on the lines and some of them were likely planted spies who came to be known as *finks*. This gives the word more a management than a labor flavor, but it is possible that *fink* gained currency in this way before being adopted by union men. It is at least as plausible as the transformation of "Pinks" to finks. *Ratfink* is a stronger variant of *fink* that originated in the U.S. within the last 30 years or so. *See* PINKERTON.

finnan haddie. Finnan haddie, or smoked haddock, was originally a Scottish dish. It is named after the haddock cured around Findon or Findhorn, a small fishing village near Aberdeen, Scotland. Today it is also made in the U.S., among other countries.

Finnegan's Wake. A little-known American-Irish song entitled "Finnegans Wake" gave James Joyce the title for his famous novel. It was a song of Irish immigrant laborers in New York City and the lyrics go on to tell how Finnegan falls and is pronounced dead, only to revive when he gets hold of the whiskey bottle passed around at his wake. According to Padraic Colum, "James Joyce found in this song a comic statement of universal mythology—the Fall of Man, the Partaking of the Water of Life, the Renewal of Existence—and used it for the title of his last and enigmatic book."

Finnish words in English. This remarkably constant language, which has changed little over the centuries and in which letters of the alphabet can be pronounced only one way, has only contributed a few words to English, the best known of these being *sauna*.

fire. First recorded in 1871, *fire out* meant "to throw out or eject a person from a place." Thirteen years later the term, shortened to *fire*, was first recorded as a synonym for "dismissing an employee." Both terms have their origins in the firing, or discharging, of a gun.

fireboy. To call a man a *boy* today is often to insult him, but in the 19th century compound words commonly used *boy*, as in *fireboy* for a fireman, and no one took offense. About the only common such compound still surviving is COWBOY.

firebug. *Firebug* derives from those bugs who have enthusiasms often amounting to manias. That this is an old American expression is evidenced by the fact that Oliver Wendell Holmes used it figuratively, writing of "political firebugs" in his book *The Poet at the Breakfast Table* (1872). That is the first recorded use of the term, which generally means "a pyromaniac, someone mentally unbalanced who lights fires for his pleasure." But people with a mania for anything have been called bugs in America since at least the early 19th century; we have had our slavery bugs, those who wished to see slavery extended into the West, and we still have our money bugs, whose sole interest is money.

firecracker. Firecrackers were called crackers in England, because of the sound they make when ignited, long before they became known as firecrackers here because a distinction had to be made between them and the "crackers" Americans eat, which are called "biscuits" in England.

fire-eater. An often violent, always uncompromising believer. The expression has its roots in the southern cause before and during the Civil War, the term dating back to the 1840s. Anonymous doggerel of the day described the fire-eaters:

> Down in a small Palmetto State the curious ones may find
> A ripping, tearing gentleman, of an uncommon kind,
> A staggering, swaggering sort of chap who takes his whisky straight
> And frequently condemns his eyes to that ultimate vengeance which a clergyman of high-standing has assured must be a sinner's fate;
> This South Carolina gentleman, one of the present time.

fire-fishing. An unusual sport practiced by the voyageurs and others after them, *fire-fishing* consisted of building a platform of fire on the bow of a canoe, the reflection of which would reveal any fish at the bottom of the deepest water. It is also called *torch fishing*. *Fire-hunting* was a method of hunting employed by some Native American tribes whereby the woods were set on fire, usually in autumn, and the animals in it were killed as they tried to escape the flames. Some colonists later adopted this "sport."

firewater. A traveler in North America in 1817 reported that "[the Indian chiefs] called the whiskey fire water." An accurate description of whiskey's taste going down, especially the whiskey Indians were traded, *firewater* is probably a translation of the Algonquian Indian *scoutiouabou*, meaning the same.

first catch your hare.   Writers still attribute these humorous directions to a recipe in Mrs. Hannah Glasse's *Art of Cooking Made Plain and Easy* (1747). What the lady really wrote was "Take your hare when it is cased and make a pudding . . ." To "case" a hare is to skin it. The joke, which is all the phrase was, is first recorded in Thackeray's *Rose and Ring* (1855), and he used the words as if his readers would be familiar with them.

first edition.   A book's entire run of copies from the same plates, no matter how many printings, is a first edition. A book's original press run, or first printing, is a first issue or first impression. The terms go back to 19th-century England.

first fruits.   John Wycliffe mentions *first fruits* in the first translation into English of the whole Bible (1382), specifically in Num. 18:12 with reference to the custom of making offerings to the Lord of the first fruits gathered in a season. Over two centuries passed before the expression was used figuratively to mean "the first products of one's efforts," as in the *first fruits of our labor.*

the first hundred years are the hardest.   Hollywood writer and cynical wit Wilson Mizner and America's greatest word inventor T. A. Dorgan vie for the authorship of this humorous saying about life in general. Dorgan seems the more likely candidate, considering his creation of such American masterpieces, among many others, as *dumbbell, dumbhead, Dumb Dora, nobody home upstairs* (dumb), *applesauce* (for insincere flattery), *drugstore cowboy, lounge lizard, chin music* (pointless talk), *the once-over, the cat's meow, the cat's pajamas, flat tire, you said it, for crying out loud, see what the boys in the backroom will have,* and *the only place you'll find sympathy is in the dictionary.* See 23 SKIDDO; HOT DOG.

first in war, first in peace, first in the hearts of his countrymen.   A 2002 poll by the American Council of Trustees and Alumni revealed that only 42 percent of all students at America's top 55 universities could identify George Washington as the man described by this phrase. Its author was intrepid Henry Lee (1756–1818), who included it in *Resolutions Presented to the House of Representatives on the Death of Washington* (December 26, 1799). Lee, called Lighthorse Henry Lee, served as an officer under Washington in the Revolutionary War. Southern Civil War leader Robert E. Lee was his son. *See* WASHINGTON.

First Lady.   The first First Lady of (or in) the land was Dolley Madison, according to one old story, but most writers say the honorary title dates from the mid-19th century, long after Dolley served as Thomas Jefferson's and later her husband, James Madison's, official hostess. The first mention of *First Lady* is in British correspondent William Russell's *My Diary North and South* (1863): "The gentleman . . . has some charming little pieces of gossip about the first Lady in the Land [then Mary Todd Lincoln]." Dolley Madison did, however, die in 1849, so there might be some connection between her and the title. The term is also used, usually uncapitalized, for a prom-

inent woman in any profession, as in "She's the first lady of the American theater." An old joke makes *First Lady* a synonym for spare ribs, because Eve was made from Adam's spare rib. Jacqueline Kennedy is the only First Lady who didn't want to be called *First Lady.* She said it sounded like the name of a saddle horse.

first name.   *See* SURNAME.

First Nations.   Canadians use *First Nations* as a synonym for the U.S. term NATIVE AMERICAN, although they are also partial to *First Canadians.* Both terms were coined in the 1970s.

first rate, etc.   From Elizabethan times up until the 19th century, British warships were rated by the number of guns they carried and the weight of those guns, rather than by the weight of the ships themselves. Six rates, or categories, were applied, a mighty first-rate ship being the highest. Before long these technical navy terms were being used to describe degrees of excellence generally.

first string; second string.   Archers in medieval times are responsible for these terms, so common on athletic fields today in describing first and second teams. An archer was only as good as the bowstring on the stout, five-foot English longbow, and in competitions a marksman always carried two—a *first-string* to be used as his best and a second to be held in reserve lest the other should break. This led to the popular Elizabethan saying *two strings to his bow,* meaning to carry something in reserve in case of accident, which fathered our *first string* and *second string.*

first water.   Arab diamond traders graded gems as first water, second water, and third water—diamonds of the first water being perfect, flawless ones. ("Water" here signified the transparency of a diamond and may be the translation of an Arabic word for luster.) Europeans used the Arab grading system for more than 300 years, and even when it was discarded in the mid-19th century the expression *of the first water* remained in English as a synonym for unsurpassed perfection in anything.

fiscal.   In ancient Rome merchants used a small basket called a *fiscus,* so named because it was made of rush or reeds (fiscus), to carry money from one place to another. From these little baskets, so common in Rome, the public treasury was named the *fisc,* and over the centuries anything to do with money matters came to be called fiscal.

fish-and-chips.   An originally British dish consisting of fish fried in batter and served with French fries (chips). The delectable dish is no longer served wrapped in newspaper, as it was traditionally. Cod used to be the fish most used by the British in their *fish n' chips,* but haddock and hake are probably more common today. There is now at least one fish n' chips fast food chain.

fisherman's joke.   *Scherzo del pescatore* means *a fisherman's joke.* It is a fried Italian dish of small squid, or calamari, which are usually eaten by popping them in the mouth. One of the squid, however, has a sac filled with hot red pepper.

fishfall; frogfall.   Fishfalls, or a rain of fish falling from the sky, have occurred fairly often throughout the world, and the word was first recorded over a century ago. They are probably due to high winds or the waterspouts that suck up fish and water and release them miles away. Similarly, frogfalls are also common phenomena, and falls of snails, mussels, shrimp, crabs, and even alligators have been widely reported. *See* RAINING CATS AND DOGS.

fish in troubled waters.   *To fish in troubled waters*, meaning "to take advantage of another's marital troubles and gain something for yourself," refers to the fact that fish bite best in rough waters, as all good fishermen know. The expression probably dates back to the 19th century, its origin unknown.

fish names from land animals.   Many fish are named after land animals, including such terms as *alligator fish, bird fish, boar fish, cat fish, dog fish, elephant fish, frog fish, goat fish, goose fish, hawk fish, horse fish, leopard fish, lizard fish, parrot fish, porcupine fish, rabbit fish, robin fish, squirrel fish, tiger fish, toad fish, unicorn fish, viper fish, wolf fish,* and *zebra fish.*

fish or cut bait.   These words, associated with politics since the late 19th century, demand that someone "take a definite stand, take action instead of procrastinating, or else stop trying and give somebody else a chance to act." Someone in a choice fishing spot on land or aboard a ship was possibly told to stop fooling around, to either drop his line in the water and fish, or cut the bait from his line and let another fisherman take his place.

fish out of water.   Older by at least several hundred years than the dates cited in the *O.E.D.* and the *Oxford Dictionary of Quotations*, this expression may even have originated with the fourth-century Greek patriarch St. Athanasius. Its earliest recorded use, however, is by English theologian and religious reformer John Wycliffe in his *English Works* (ca. 1380): "And how thei weren out of ther cloistre as fish is withouten water." The metaphor, as widely used as ever today, describes "anyone floundering in an element or environment to which he is unaccustomed and in which he is practically helpless."

fish royal.   In the United Kingdom the *fish royal* are the sturgeon, whale, dolphin and porpoise, if caught within three miles of the coast. Only the sturgeon among these is a fish, but ancient law makes them all the property of the Crown.

fit as a fiddle.   Someone or something that is fit as a fiddle is, of course, in great shape. The common expression is about 400 years old, first recorded in 1616 in England, but that is all we know about its etymology. Perhaps a fiddle was considered fit because musicians almost always treated their instruments, the source of their livelihood, with tender, loving care.

five-and-ten.   A name still occasionally heard for stores like F. W. Woolworth, long after it was possible to buy anything there for a nickel or a dime. Five-and-tens, or five-and-ten-cent stores, flourished from the mid-19th to the mid-20th century in America, with Woolworth's (founded by Frank Woolworth in 1879 as a five-cent store) being the most notable chain. Such stores are even remembered in popular song lyrics, including "I found my million-dollar baby in a five-and-ten-cent store," and "and if that diamond ring don't shine, poppa's gonna take you to the five-and-dime."

five-day week.   *See* EIGHT-HOUR DAY.

fix.   *Fix*, for the dishonest prearranging of games, races, or other sports events, is an Americanism first recorded in 1881 to describe tampering with a horse to prevent it from winning a race. It may be a shortened version of an earlier term with the same meaning, *fix up*.

fizzle.   The first English meaning of the word *fizzle* was, as the *Oxford English Dictionary* put it, "to break wind," that is, to fart. By the mid-19th century, however, the word took on the meaning of "to hiss," the word probably first used in this sense to describe the hissing of fireworks. Similarly, *to fizzle out*, "to fail or die out," seems to have derived from the sound of fireworks falling to earth.

fjord; fjeld.   *Fjord* and the seldom encountered *fjeld* are the only two words in English beginning with *fj*. Both are Norwegian in origin. The latter, pronounced *fyeld*, means an elevated rocky plateau virtually without vegetation, and the former, pronounced (and sometimes spelled) *fiord*, is a long narrow arm of the sea running up between high banks or cliffs, as on Norway's coast.

flabbergasted.   Astounded or utterly confused. A relatively new word, *flabbergast* is first recorded in a British magazine article called "On New Words" in 1772. It is possibly a combination of *flabby* and *aghast*, but neither the source of the word nor its inventor is known.

flack.   This term has been used since the mid-1940s for "advertising copy," ever since the similarity between rapid gunfire and exaggerated advertising copy or publicity writing was first noticed. *Flack* probably derives from the World War II acronym *flak* (from the German *Flieger abwehr Kanonen*, "aircraft defense gun"). A *flack* can also mean a public relations person today.

flake.   *Flake* has meant "a packet of cocaine" since the 1920s, but it first appeared in its meaning of an odd, eccentric person, often a colorful, likable eccentric, in the 1950s, probably in baseball. It possibly referred originally to "offbeat San Francisco outfielder Jackie Brandt, from whose mind, it was said, things seemed to flake off and disappear," according to Tim Considine, writing in the *New York Times Magazine* and quoted in Paul Dickson's *The Dickson Baseball Dictionary* (1989). Then again, the *flake* of eccentricity could derive from association with the narcotics sense of the word. Stuart Berg Flexner's *Listening to America* (1982) says *flake* appeared "in professional football in the early 1970s, especially when referring to John Don Looney (who couldn't, after all, be called merely a looney . . .), who attacked tackling dummies in anger and seldom heeded signs . . ." In any case, consistent sports use of the word made it common American slang.

flamingo.   This long-legged pink wading bird is named for the people of Flanders, the *Flemings*, as they were called.

Flemings were widely known for their lively personalities, their flushed complexions, and their love of bright, gay clothing. Spaniard explorers in the New World thought it was a great joke naming the bird the *flamingo*, which means "a Fleming" in Spanish and became the English *flamingo* in time.

Flanders poppies. In England the artificial red flowers sold on Remembrance Day for the benefit of war veterans are called Flanders poppies. A 1915 poem by John McCrae called "In Flanders Fields" seems to have been the first to connect this flower with the dead of World War I:

> If ye break faith with us who die
> We shall not sleep, though poppies grow
> In Flanders fields.

flapper. The word *flapper* didn't originate in the JAZZ AGE. *Flapper* was originally a British expression meaning a young girl, first recorded in 1888. This word may have derived from the flapping of the pigtails such young girls often wore, but, on the other hand, it could come from *flap*, a loose woman, which was used as far back as the early 17th century. Another possibility is the late 18th-century British *flapper* meaning a duck too young to fly. By 1915 Americans may have finally adopted one or another of these British words to describe the wild, flighty, unconventional, pleasure-loving young women of the Roaring Twenties who boldly smoked cigarettes; drank from a flask; wore short dresses, no corsets, and stockings rolled beneath the knees; had bobbed hair; loved to dance with their "sheiks"; and were also called *jazz babies, hot mamas,* and *whoopee mamas.* Or the scandalous American *flapper* could descend from the British *flapper* that was used in the late 19th century to mean a very young, immoral teenager, especially one who had been trained for vice. "They all want flappers," a sedate British actress complained in 1927, "and I can't flap." Another possible origin of the word is the flapping sound of unbuckled galoshes American girls favored as a fashion fad in the 1920s. The *New Dictionary of American Slang* (1986) suggests "the idea of an unfledged bird *flapping* its wings as dancers did when dancing the Charleston." Take your choice.

flash in the pan. Old flintlock muskets had a pan, or depression, that held the priming powder. The guns fired after the trigger was pulled and sparks produced by the steel hammer striking a flint ignited the powder, which exploded the main charge. That is, the guns *sometimes* fired. Flintlocks, used since the 17th century, were unreliable weapons and frequently didn't work. Often the powder just flared or flashed up in the pan, failing to explode the main charge because the charge was wet or because the touchhole linking the two was clogged. Flintlocks "hanging fire" like this were common enough to make the term a *flash in the pan* a natural figure of speech for "any short-lived brilliance yielding no results in the long run" and, long after the old flintlocks were relegated to museums, it is still used to describe a person who fails to live up to his early promise.

flashy. Nineteenth-century Flash men from outside the village of Flash in England's Derbyshire were squatters, who, like some gypsies, traveled from county fair to county fair in the district doing no good. Their slang dialect, called Flash talk, and their distinctive clothing, often bright and showy, made

them quite conspicuous. The word *flashy*, used to describe conspicuous dressers, among many showy, ostentatious things, could well have been applied to anyone like them, for the word came into use at a time when they were the cause of much trouble. On the other hand, some investigators say the word simply derives from "a sudden flame" or "a lightning flash."

flat. While many Americans are familiar with the British word *flat* for a suite of rooms, it is seldom used in the U.S. except in the old expression *cold-water flat* (one that has no running hot water). Almost all Americans would call a flat an apartment. Recent British slang for *flat* is *squat*.

flatboats; store boats; keelboats; Kentucky arks. Adam Gimbel, founder of the Gimbels department store chain, among other pioneer American merchants, often fitted out flatboats with shelves and counters, stocked them with goods, and floated downriver to sell his wares on the banks of towns too small to have permanent stores. Such early American store boats stocked everything from groceries to dry goods, liquor, and gun powder. Many flew calico flags, and many at the end of each spring trip were taken apart and sold for lumber. Sometimes the merchants used KEELBOATS instead of flatboats. Intense rivalry between crews of these two types of riverboats led to bitter fights that made the boats unwelcome in some towns, but both were of great importance in developing the American West.

flatearthers. Some people still refuse to accept that the Earth is a sphere and rotates around the sun. One such group is the International Flat Earth Research Society in Lancaster, California. Founded in 1888, this society of flatearthers has 1,600 members accepting its tenets: that the Earth is flat, that the Sun and planets revolve around the Earth, and that the theory about the Earth being a sphere is a gigantic hoax. Says the society's president, Charles J. Johnson: "Ever since Copernicus, the new religion-science, they call it—has been trying to fool the people with their notion that the earth is a ball. . . . They got most people to accept the hoax, but not us." *See* COPERNICAN THEORY.

flat-hatter. A hotshot pilot who flies much too low while showing off. An old story dating back to the 1920s traces the expression to a man wearing a straw hat flattened by a plane flown by such a pilot. But there is no proof of this derivation.

flathead. A name for members of a tribe of Salishan Indians of Montana and members of the Chinook Indian tribe; the name derives from their supposed practice of flattening their children's heads at birth. The word was extended to mean a simpleton or a fool among settlers.

flatlanders. *See* HILLBILLY.

flattop. Though the *Langley*, a converted coal ship commissioned in 1922, was America's first aircraft carrier, no one thought of calling any aircraft carrier a *flattop* until World War II, when the United States built 150 carriers.

flaybottomist; bum brusher. Here is a jocular synonym for a schoolteacher in the days of "spare the rod and spoil the child." The term for a schoolmaster originated in the mid-18th century and lasted for some 200 years. *Bum brusher* was a synonym.

fleabitten. *Fleabitten* has since the late 16th century been a *color* as well as a condition. It describes a dog, horse, or other animal with a light coat flecked with red, the reddish flecks reminiscent of the bites of fleas on human skin.

flea market. These bargain markets have nothing to do with fleas. *Flea market* has been an American expression as far back as Dutch colonial days when there was a very real Vallie (Valley) Market at the valley, or foot, of Maiden Lane in downtown Manhattan. The Vallie Market came to be abbreviated to *Vlie Market* and this was soon being pronounced *Flea Market*. Today there is a flea market (*marché aux puces*) area in Paris.

fledgling nation. *Fledgling nation* usually means a newly formed, poor nation that the United States has taken under its wing. The euphemism was probably coined by Eleanor Roosevelt after World War II.

Fleet Street. Fleet Street in London has been synonymous with journalism since the end of the 18th century, when the first newspaper was published there. The street takes its name not from fleet reporters writing stories while type is being set, but for the Fleet River that ran alongside it.

Flemish. When rope is flemished it is coiled down concentrically in the direction of the sun, or like the coil of a watch spring, beginning in the center. *Flemish* also once meant "to force or score the planks." The terms seem to have arisen in the early 19th century and take their name from Flemish sailors, considered to be neat seamen and who may have coiled their rope like this.

flesh and blood. The phrase has two meanings, both dating back a millennium ago. The younger means one's kin: mother, father, children, siblings, etc., while the older means humankind, any individual, a living, breathing being, not something abstract or robotic.

fleshpots. The word is commonly used to mean, metaphorically, luxurious living or places offering unrestrained pleasure. In this sense *fleshpots* goes back to a biblical passage, Exodus 16:3: "And the children of Israel said unto them Would to God we had died by the hand of the Lord in the land of Egypt, when we sat by the flesh pots, and when we did eat bread to the full."

flesh-spades; flesh-tailor. In *Tom Jones* (1749) Fielding writes about "The injury done to the beauty of her husband by the 'flesh-spades' of Mrs. Honour." The humorous term *flesh-spade* for fingernails, those digging tools protruding from our fingers, may have been invented by the British novelist, but there is no proof of this. *Flesh-tailor* was a 17th-century term for a surgeon, used by John Ford in his play *'Tis Pity She's a Whore* (1633).

Fleshy School of Poetry. The poet and painter Dante Gabriel Rossetti was viciously attacked from a moral point of view by the poet Robert Buchanan in an article in the *Contemporary Review* called "The Fleshy School of Poetry." Published in October 1871 under the pseudonym Thomas Maitland, the article accused Rossetti, Swinburne, William Morris, and several others of being decadent, morally irresponsible, and obsessed with the sensual and carnal. The piece created great controversy, Swinburne replying at length to the charges in his *Under the Microscope* (1872), and Rossetti, who got the brunt of the criticism, never really recovering from it. His tendency toward gloomy brooding increased, he avoided people, overused narcotics, and became paranoid enough for friends to fear for his sanity. Rossetti died in 1882 at age 54. *See* SNARK.

fletcherize. The author of *Glutton or Epicure* (1899) advocated cutting out regular meals and eating only when really hungry, consuming very small amounts of food at one time, and chewing each tiny mouthful vigorously and thoroughly before swallowing. Horace Fletcher (1849–1919), a Lawrence, Massachusetts businessman turned nutritionist, believed that this regimen—which he had followed from the time he went on a diet and lost 65 pounds at age 40—would promote better digestion and health as excellent as his own. *Fletcherism*, described more fully in a later book of that name, swept the country; thousands attended Fletcher's lectures and followed his instructions to the letter. As a result of the health fad, the word *fletcherize*, "to masticate food thoroughly," became a common expression that still remains in the dictionaries. Fletcher had really borrowed his idea of 32 chews to the bite from British prime minister Gladstone, who "made it a rule, to give every tooth of mine a chance," and who claimed he owed much of his success in life to this rule. Slogans like "Nature will castigate those who don't masticate" won Fletcher many famous converts, including John D. Rockefeller, Thomas Edison, William James, and the cadets at West Point.

fleur-de-lis; iris. *Fleur-de-lis*, or lily flower, is the French name for the iris, which is so named because its striking colors reminded the Greeks of Iris, goddess of the rainbow. The French symbol of empire since the 12th century, the *fleur-de-lis* was chosen by the 14th-century Italian navigator Flavio Gioja to mark the north point of the compass in honor of the King of Naples, who was of French descent.

flibbertigibbety. Silly restless actions are called *flibbertigibbety* after Flibbertigibbet, one of the five fiends who possessed "poor Tom" in Shakespeare's *King Lear*. Shakespeare borrowed the character and his name from an earlier work.

Flickertail State. An old nickname for North Dakota, because of its many flickertail squirrels.

floater. In medical slang a *floater* can refer to a corpse found floating in water. It is also a speck, dot, or string that seems to be floating across the eye just outside the line of vision that is caused by cell fragments in the vitreous humor registering on the retina. In recent slang a floater can mean an employee of a firm who "floats" from department to department.

float like a butterfly, sting like a bee. Words describing Muhammad Ali's boxing technique. His trainer and friend Bundini Brown coined the phrase when Ali was still Cassius Clay in the 1960s. One of Ali's major opponents in his fights was Joe Frazier, whom he taunted whenever he could, calling him an "ugly old bear," among other choice insults. Today Frazier calls him the Butterfly. *See* BUTTERFLY.

flog (or beat) a dead horse.   Though he supported the measure, British politician and orator John Bright thought the Reform Bill of 1867, which called for more democratic representation, would never be passed by Parliament. Trying to rouse Parliament from its apathy on the issue, he said in a speech, would be like trying to *flog a dead horse* to make it pull a load. This is the first recorded use of the expression, which is still common for "trying to revive interest in an apparently hopeless issue." Bright's silver tongue is also responsible for "England is the mother of Parliament," and "Force is not a remedy," among other memorable quotations. He was wrong about the Reform Bill of 1867, however. Parliament "carried" it, as the British say.

floorwalker.   "Dandified ushers," the first department store floorwalkers were called, and in the 1890s that was often exactly what they were. Dressed in either a black frock or a cutaway coat, with gray-striped trousers, a very high collar, and a rose in the buttonhole, the floorwalker was usually a spiffy, or smarmy, exceedingly polite living directory, who pompously patrolled the aisles, the arbiter elegantiarum of conduct and store etiquette. Charlie Chaplin knew the type well and portrayed one in his film *The Floorwalker.* Today floorwalkers are more often called *floor managers,* their main job still the supervision of sales personnel and assistance of customers.

floozie.   "Flat-Foot Floogy with the Floy Floy," a popular song in 1945, spelled *floozie* differently, but it meant the same. A floosie, floogy, flugie, or even faloosie is a gaudily dressed, dumb, disrespectable, frequently high-spirited woman, often a prostitute. If the word derives from *Flossie,* a nickname for Florence, no one has proved it, and the word was first recorded in the form of *flugie* at the turn of the century. Hollywood's HAYS CODE banned *floozie,* along with *red-hot mamma* and other words, but the term got a breath of new life with the song mentioned above, which describes a floozie with what it seems is a kind of venereal disease, the floy floy. This American slang, as a British writer observes, is "picturesque" and should be retained for its "blousy flowery atmosphere" suggesting "good spirits, gaudy flowered dresses, and bad but delightful perfume."

floral firecracker.   *See* BREVOORTIA IDA-MAIA.

Florida.   "The Sunshine State" was the Florida Territory before being admitted to the Union as the 27th state in 1845. *Florida* means "land of flowers" in Spanish, Ponce de Leon naming it in 1513 with "flowery Easter" in mind.

Florida room.   A term used in Florida and other states for a living room with large windows to catch the sun; also called a sun room.

flotsam and jetsam.   *Flotsam,* from the Old French *floter* (Latin *fluere*), "to float," means the contents or parts of a wreck found floating on the sea, and belonged to the Crown. *Jetsam,* which could be claimed by the lord of the manor, derives from the French *jeter* (Latin *jacere*), "to throw out," and means cargo or equipment purposely thrown overboard, or jettisoned, in order to lighten a ship in an emergency. Jetsam was considered flotsam only if it was found between the high and low waterlines, because no one could tell whether it had been jettisoned there or had floated there.

flour.   *See* FLOWER.

flourish.   An old euphemism for the sex act used by Virginia tobacco planter, author, and colonial official William Byrd, who kept a secret diary in shorthand as an avocation, never intending for it to be published. He had no inhibitions about married love, judging by his entry for July 30, 1710: "In the afternoon my wife and I had a little quarrel which I reconciled with a flourish. Then she read a sermon in Dr. Tillitson to me. It is to be observed that the flourish was performed on the billiard table."

flower; flour.   In Anglo-Saxon times the word for flower was *blossom;* this changed after the Normans conquered England in 1066, and their *fleur* became the English *flower.* However, all three words have the same common ancestor—the ancient Indo-European *blo,* which eventually yielded both *blossom* and *flower. Flour,* the finely ground meal of any grain, is just a specialized use of the word *flower.* In fact, *flower* and *flour* were used interchangeably until the 19th century, as in Milton's *Paradise Lost,* where we find the line "O flours that never will in other climate grow." In French *fleur de farine* is the flower or finest part of the grain meal. Still used today and one of the longest-lived modern-day slogans, the phrase *say it with flowers* was coined for the Society of American Florists in 1917 by plantsman Patrick F. O'Keefe (1872–1934). *Cut flowers* is an old term for flowers cut from the garden for bouquets or display. A visitor once asked George Bernard Shaw why he kept no vases of cut flowers. "I thought you were so fond of flowers," he said. "So I am," Shaw retorted. "I'm very fond of children too. But I don't cut off their heads and stick them in pots all over the house." According to tradition, Saint Elizabeth of Hungary gave so much food to the poor that her own household didn't eat well. Her husband suspected this and when he saw her leaving the house one day with her apron full of something, he demanded to know what she carried. "Only flowers, my lord," Elizabeth said, and God saved her from her lie by changing the loaves of bread in her apron to flowers. *See* BLOSSOM.

flower people.   *See* BEAUTIFUL PEOPLE.

Flowery Kingdom.   The most ancient name of China, a translation of *Hua Kuo.* One theory has it that the Chinese first resided in barren central Asia and named their new country *flowery* in contrast to their grim desert home. But *Hua Kuo* may have been meant in one of the words other meanings of glorious, distinguished, and polished, with no reference to flowers at all.

floy floy.   *See* FLOOZIE.

flummery.   Flattery, meaningless deceptive language. The word, dating back to the 1840s, comes from *flummery,* the name of a soft paplike food fit for infants, which in turn derives from Welsh *llymru* meaning the same.

flunky. *Flunky*, also spelled *flunkey*, was originally a very nice Scots word, probably deriving from *flanker*, "one who stands at a person's flank or side." *Flunky* was simply the word for a servant or footman, but by the 19th century it took on its contemptuous meaning of a lackey, a slavish, obedient servant who will always do his master's bidding.

fly a kite; kiting. *Go fly a kite!* means "get lost, don't bother me, go do something somewhere else." To *fly a kite* is another story. This is Irish, not American, slang dating back to the early 19th century and means "to raise money on a fraudulent note or to cash a check without having the funds in the bank to cover it." The expression possibly derives from an older Irish phrase, *to raise the wind*, "to borrow money," but in any event it suggests an action far removed from down-to-earth reality and honesty. *To fly a kite* isn't heard much anymore, the expression *kiting* being used in its place. Someone *kites* a check when he overdraws his account and quickly cashes another check somewhere else, depositing this cash in the bank to cover the original shortage. The *kiting* can go on for sometime, with new obligations incurred again and again to discharge old ones—a kite soaring farther and farther away from firm ground.

fly below the radar. To avoid detection. "He flew below the radar for a long time, but the police finally got him." The term has its origin among fliers in World War II.

fly-by-night. *Fly-by-night* was originally an ancient term of reproach to an old woman, signifying she is a witch, according to Grose's *Dictionary of the Vulgar Tongue*. From a witch flying about at night on a broom, the term was applied, at the beginning of the 19th century, to anyone who flies hurriedly from a recent activity, usually a business activity and usually at night—someone who is a swindler and whose activities are fraudulent. The first fly-by-night operator recorded in English makes his appearance in Thomas Love Peacock's novel *Maid Marian* (1822), a parody of the Robin Hood legend in which a character refers to Maid Marian and the outlaw: "Would you have her married to an old fly-by-night that accident made an earl and nature a deer-stealer?" *Fly-by-night* has also been, in British slang, a prostitute and a prostitute's vagina.

flying clippers. *See* CLIPPER SHIP.

Flying Dutchman. The legend of the *Flying Dutchman* trying to round the Cape of Good Hope against strong winds and never succeeding, then trying to make Cape Horn and failing there too, has been the most famous of maritime ghost stories for over 300 years. The cursed spectral ship sailing back and forth on its endless voyage, its ancient white-haired crew crying for help while hauling at her sails, inspired Samuel Taylor Coleridge to write his classic "The Rime of the Ancient Mariner." The real *Flying Dutchman* is supposed to have set sail in 1660.

flying fish. The name generally given to fishes of the *Exocoetidae* family. These are the fish Kipling wrote about: "On the road to Mandalay / Where the flying fishes play." However,

they aren't playing in their leaps out of the water; they are trying to escape hunters like the dorados that are pursuing them. Vibrating their tail fins at a rate of 50 beats a second, these "dragonflies of the deep" build up momentum; with both pairs of "wings" spread they soon become airborne and glide over the waves at a speed of up to 40 miles an hour. They can cover the length of three football fields, jumping as high as 45 feet into the air. They hit the water tail first, scull again to regain propulsion, and then fly another 25 feet or so, taking about 45 seconds to cover one-quarter of a mile in the course of 10 or so leaps.

flying machine. The Wright brothers, Orville and Wilbur, liked to call their epochal invention a *flying machine*, never an *airplane*, *aeroplane*, *aerial ship*, or *aerial machine*. The term *flying machine* is recorded as far back as 1730. The name of the Wright's plane, which on December 17, 1903, near Kitty Hawk, North Carolina, made the first powered flight in a heavier-than-air craft, was the *Wright Flyer*, an appellation they chose in honor of something so down-to-earth as a bicycle brand these bicycle shop owners (and high school dropouts) made and sold back in their Dayton, Ohio, store. A place with a *hawk* in it would be a wonderful location for the world's first airplane flight, but the Wright flight actually took place not in Kitty Hawk, as is usually said, but on Kill Devil Hill, a place close by.

flying saucer. U.S. pilot Kenneth Arnold is said to have been the first earthling to sight a flying saucer, in June 1947, near Mount Ranier in Washington State. Arnold has also been credited with naming the dish-shaped object many believed to have come from outer space. But unidentified flying objects have been reported since at least 1878 in America, when a Texas *Daily News* story told of a flying object "about the size of a large saucer" that some pedestrian had spotted directly over and far above his head. In any case, there have been thousands of sightings since Arnold's, but no landing so far as we know. *See* U.F.O.

fly in the ointment. "Dead flies cause the ointment of the apothecary to send forth a stinking savour; so doth a little folly him that is in reputation for wisdom and honour." The unknown author of the biblical book of Ecclesiastes (a Greek rendering of the Hebrew word *Koheleth*, "preacher") wrote this sometime in the third century B.C. Like many other vivid figures of speech in the 21st book of the Old Testament ("Vanity of vanities, saith the preacher; all is vanity . . ." "For everything there is a season . . ." "He who digs a pit will fall into it . . ." etc.), these words from the first verse of the 10th chapter became proverbial when translated into English. For five centuries now a *fly in the ointment* has meant a small defect that spoils something valuable or is a source of annoyance.

fly off the handle. Axes in American pioneer days were frequently handmade, frontiersmen whittling their own handles and attaching axe-heads shipped from back East. Because they were often crudely fitted to the helve, these axe-heads often flew off the handle while woodsmen were chopping down trees or preparing firewood, sometimes injuring the axeman or people nearby. The sudden flying of the head off the axe, and the trouble this caused, naturally suggested a sudden wild outburst of anger, the loss of self-control, or the losing of one's head that the expression *to fly off the handle* describes. The expression is first recorded in John Neal's novel *Brother Jonathan; or the New Englanders* (1825) as *off the handle*, but isn't known in its full form until 1844, when it was used in still another of Thomas Haliburton's "Sam Slick" tales. *See* FEEL ONE'S OATS.

fly the flag at half mast.   To mourn someone. The naval practice of flying a ship's flag halfway up the main mast as a sign of respect for a sailor killed in battle dates back at least 400 years. The custom soon spread to military installations, public places, and even homes with flagpoles.

flyting.   *See* LOGOMACHY; RAP MUSIC.

fly-up-the-creek.   We don't hear this expression today, but it is recorded as early as 1845 as the nickname for a resident of Florida. Floridians were so called because *fly-up-the-creek* is a popular name of the small green heron common in the state. Walt Whitman used the expression in this sense and it later meant "a giddy capricious person."

F.M.C.; F.W.C.   There were a good number of freed and escaped slaves in America long before the Civil War. By 1840 the terms *F.M.C.*, for "free man of color," and *F.W.C.*, for "free woman of color," are recorded, and blacks for many years proudly affixed the terms after their names.

fo'c'sle.   *See* FORECASTLE.

focus.   In Latin the word *focus* means fireplace or hearth. The word was probably first employed outside of its Latin literal use as "the burning point of a lens or mirror," in optics, and then came to mean any central point. The German astronomer Johannes Kepler first recorded the word in this sense in 1604.

fofarraw.   Tawdry baubles and trinkets, or clothes, as in "He traded his furs for all that fofarraw." The word probably derives from the Spanish *fanfarron* (braggart). It is also spelled foofarar.

Foggy Bottom.   This derogatory name for the U.S. State Department in Washington, D.C., is said to have been coined by Washington *Post* columnist Edward Folliard in the early 1940s. Previously *Foggy Bottom* was a marshy area of the Potomac River where the State Department is now located. This (and the foggy GOBBLEDYGOOK of official State Department papers) accounts for the persistence of the disparaging name.

fohn.   The famous dry spring wind, varying from warm to hot, that blows along and down the valleys on the northern side of the Alps, melting snow in its path. Its name derives from the Latin *Favonius* for the West Wind.

foie gras; stuffed as a goose; fed up.   *Foie gras* literally means "fat liver" in French. Despite its unappetizing name, it has been considered a royal dish from earliest times, the most desirable and expensive of all the patés. The making of foie gras is nothing to be talked about while eating it. Traditionally, a goose was tied down firmly so that it could move only its neck, and six times a day "crammers" used their middle fingers to push into the throats of these geese a thick paste made of buckwheat flour, chestnut flour, and stewed maize. Today the process is hardly more humane. When about six months old, those birds fated for foie gras are crammed into wooden cages along with plentiful food and water. There they would eventually eat themselves to death by suffocation if their keepers did not slaughter them and remove their swollen livers after about six weeks. At that time they're so fat they can barely move, having gorged themselves on over 70 pounds of food. It is said that the term FED UP derives from this cruel practice, though there is no hard evidence of the derivation. *Stuffed as a goose* might more likely derive from the sight of a stuffed goose on a Christmas dinner table.

folio.   *See* BOOK.

folklore.   British antiquary William John Thoms, the founder of *Notes and Queries*, coined this word in the *Athenaeum* (August 1846). In an article therein entitled "Folk Lore" he wrote: "What we in England designate as Popular Antiquities, or Popular Literature . . . would be more aptly described by a good Saxon compound, Folk-Lore—the Lore of the People . . ."

folk-maal.   Norwegian philologist Ivar Andreas Aasen (1813–96) is the only person known to have created a national language. The author had collected all of his country's difficult regional speech for the books he had written on Norwegian dialects. Out of these he fashioned a popular language, or *folk-maal*, which replaced the Dano-Norwegian his countrymen had previously used, to enable all the nation's different dialect users to understand each other. Aasen has been hailed as having "an isolated place in history as the one man who has invented or at least selected and constructed a [national] language." In order to do this, he not only constructed the new composite language, but also wrote poems and plays in the folk-maal to help popularize it. *See* SEQUOIA.

follow one's nose.   To go straight forward, or, figuratively, to be guided by instinct. Shakespeare used the term, first recorded in 1591, in *King Lear* (1605).

fond.   If you were fond of someone several centuries ago, you would have been "foolishly affectionate or doting." In fact, *fond* originally meant "foolish." But over the years the word has changed in meaning and now to be fond of someone means to have a strong liking for that person.

fontange.   Through the ages women's hair has been tortured into shapes of full sails, bird nests with fledglings in them, and even windmills, but no style has ever topped the fontange created by Louis XIV's beautiful red-haired mistress. In the brief time that they were lovers "The Sun King" made Marie Angelique de Scorraille de Roussilles, duchesse de Fontanges, a territory in France. She died all too soon in 1681, when only 20, but a year before her death the lovely young woman introduced what was probably the most extravagant, expensive hairdo in the history of coiffures. Called a fontange after her, this pile of style rose to heights of two feet and more above the wearer's head, including feathers, bows, and a large assortment of jeweled ornaments in the gummed-linen circular bands that held them in place. So great a nuisance did fontanges become that Louis XIV had to issue a royal decree abolishing them in 1699. To the duchess's further shame, the hairdo was dubbed a "commode" in England, and *fontange* itself was adopted as a polite word for a commode, the piece of furniture having come into use in the late 17th century and serving as a toilet among other uses.

fool. The Latin word *follis*, which literally meant "bellows" but came to mean a "windbag," gives us our word *fool*—foolishness and tongue-wagging being equated early on.

fool killer. A character of folklore who kills fools. Wrote Stephen Vincent Benét in *Tales Before Midnight* (1939): "Whenever he heard of the death of somebody he didn't like, he'd say, 'Well, the Fool-Killer's come for so-and-so,' and sort of smack his lips."

foolscap. A size of drawing or printing paper measuring 13½ × 17 inches that is so named because the watermark of a fool's or jester's cap was formerly used on such paper. One old story holds that in 1653 Cromwell invented the design to replace the royal crown used on the paper, but the fool's cap design dates back to at least 1540.

fool's gold. A term coined in the American West around 1875 for iron or copper pyrites, which are sometimes mistaken for gold; used figuratively to mean anything that deceives a person. " 'That's fool's gold. See how green those flakes look in the light? Real gold don't do that,' " wrote Anke Kristke in *Women of the West* (1990).

the fool's tax. No reference consulted lists this term, but the *New York Times* cites it in an editorial (8/29/01): "Lotteries have collectively taken the name 'the fool's tax' because the odds of winning are so small . . . [Powerball, for example, offers odds of one in 80 million] . . . In New York State, as many as one in every eleven players is a compulsive gambler feeding an addiction."

football. The American game of football has been traced back to a wild and bloody game related to the Roman game of harpastum, which had been known in England since the Roman conquest of A.D. 43. It was essentially a free-for-all in which a pack of young men (sometimes numbering in the hundreds) would try to kick, push, and butt an air-filled bladder into a rival group's area often a mile or more away. First the game was called kicking the bladder (a leather ball made by the local shoemaker), then during the Danish invasion, kicking the Dane's head, though skulls probably weren't used. The game wasn't played on a field with boundaries until the 12th century, when the name *fut balle* was first given to it. The sport was often banned but never successfully, and it eventually evolved into rugby football, which became the American sport of football. *See also* FOOTBALL PLAYER; RUGBY.

football player. Though Shakespeare did not use the modern spelling, the term *football player* is first recorded in his *King Lear* (1605): "I'll not be stricken, my Lord." "Nor tripped, neither, you base futball player." *See* FOOTBALL.

footnote. Used mostly in scholarly works to list a source or make a minor or related comment on the main text of a work,

footnotes are so called because they are usually placed at the bottom of a page. Often called *bottom notes* in the early 19th century, when they were apparently used extensively for the first time, they are indicated in the text by superior numbers. Many readers would agree with John Barrymore, who said: "A footnote is like running downstairs to answer the doorbell on the first night of marriage." When historian Sir John Newle published his excellent biography *Queen Elizabeth* (1975) without footnotes, an Oxford don told historian Eileen Power that this indicated Newle had sold the pass—that is, traded scholarship for popularity. "I don't know about selling the pass," Power rejoined, "but he has sold 20,000 copies."

forbidden fruit. An ancient phrase that has its origins in Gen. 3:3, although the exact words are not found there: "But of the fruit of the tree which is in the midst of the garden, God hath said, Ye shall not eat of it, neither shall ye touch it, lest ye die." Figuratively, *forbidden fruit* is usually used to describe a tempting but forbidden person or thing.

for crying out loud. An Americanism first recorded in 1924, but probably dating back earlier, *for crying out loud* is what is called a "minced oath," a euphemism that may have originated when someone started to say "For Christ's sake!" but got only as far as the first syllable of the second word, realized the curse was inappropriate in the circumstances, and changed the offensive word to "crying." It's hard to believe that this common expression was consciously invented by someone. But it has been traced to American cartoonist and prolific word coiner Thomas Aloysius (TAD) Dorgan (1877–1929).

Ford. John Dillinger, the first "public enemy number one," once wrote Henry Ford extolling the performance of his car as a getaway vehicle. That curious incident shows just how widespread was the Ford's really incalculable influence on society, both good and bad. Henry Ford's motor cars, though not the first invented, put America and the world on wheels, his assembly-line and mass-production methods marking the beginning of modern industry, and his "Five Dollar Day" heralding a new era for labor. Ford (1863–1947), born on a farm near Detroit, Michigan, founded the Ford Motor Company in 1903. First came his two-cylinder Model A and then in 1909 the immortal Model T, the Tin Lizzie, the flivver, America's monument to love, available in any color so long as it was black. Fifteen million of these cars were built over almost 20 years—a record that lasted until the Volkswagen broke it in 1972—and any cheap, dependable car became known as a ford. The word is usually capitalized now, but Ford still remains a symbol of American mechanical ingenuity. Though he was often controversial and foolish in his public life, no one has ever doubted the inventor's genius. He is honored today by both the motor company bearing his name and the philanthropic Ford Foundation. *See also* CADILLAC.

Ford's Theatre. The national landmark in Washington, D.C., was a Baptist church before theatrical manager John Thompson Ford converted it to a playhouse in 1861 and named it after himself. Only a year later it burned to the ground in a mysterious fire. Ford rebuilt it in brick the following year, only to see it become the most famous—or infamous—American theater on April 14, 1865, when Abraham Lincoln was assassinated there. The theater was then purchased by the U.S. government and converted into an office building. But the jinx continued in 1890, when part of the building collapsed, killing 22 government workers. Since it reopened as the restored Ford's Theatre in 1965, there have been no further incidents.

fore! This golfing term meaning "watch out" hasn't been with us for much more than a century, being first recorded in 1878, though the game of golf is much older. Deriving from the word *before!*, "in front of," it probably was coined when the harder golf ball came into use at that time.

forecastle (fo'c'sle). By the 14th century the forward part of many large ships had an area that was raised and protected like a castle, from which the captain could overlook the decks of an enemy ship. Today the forecastle is simply "that part of the upper deck forward of the foremast or, in merchant ships, the forward part of the vessel under the deck, where the sailors live." *Forecastle* is almost always spelled and pronounced *fo'c'sle* (fo'ksl).

Forest City. At least three American cities share this nickname because of the many trees in their vicinity. These include Portland, Maine; Savannah, Georgia; and Cleveland, Ohio.

the forest primeval. A phrase from Henry Wadsworth Longfellow's narrative poem *Evangeline* (1847), once taught in almost every American high school:

> This is the forest primeval. The murmuring pines and
>   the hemlocks . . .
> Stand like Druids of old, with voices sad and prophetic.

forget it! As an expression of annoyance or anger meaning "never mind," *forget it!* has been popular since before 1912, when the Americanism, in the form of *aw, forget it*, was discussed in a scholarly work on slang. The term enjoyed a resurgence of popularity in the hippie 1960s.

forget-me-not. We have it on the authority of the little volume *Drops from Flora's Cup* (1845) that this flower (*Myosotis palustris*), also called the "mouse ear" due to the resemblance of its small leaves to the ears of a mouse, received its more popular name in the following way: In an age when ladies were ladies and gentlemen were gentlemen, sometimes to a fault, an engaged lady and gentleman were walking on the banks of the Danube when the lady spied a flower floating on the water. Knowing that she was sad to see the pretty flower lost, the gentleman waded into the water to retrieve it. But he stepped in over his head and couldn't get back to shore. With a last desperate effort he threw the flower at her feet, exclaimed "forget me not," and drowned. The flower's name since that time has been the same. The tale is not recorded elsewhere, so far as I know.

forgotten man. Franklin Roosevelt popularized this phrase when running for president in 1932, applying it to all those suffering during the Great Depression whom government had done little to help. The term was invented, however, by Yale professor William G. Sumner, who in 1883 applied it to the American workingman, the decent, average American citizen.

Forgotten War; police action; conflict; 38th parallel. *Forgotten War* is a tag for the war, or conflict, in Korea, which began on June 25, 1950, and cost 33,629 American lives before the July 1953 cease-fire. Korea is called the "Forgotten War" because it is often ignored, coming as it does after World War II and before Vietnam. It should be added that neither the United States nor its UN allies ever declared war in Korea (President Truman called the fighting a *police action*), and 50 years later, the war still hasn't technically ended, both South Korea and North Korea maintaining troops along the 38th parallel border. According to *Time Goes To War* (2002): "Even this demarcation between the two [sides] had been hastily—almost randomly—selected by two young U.S. officers working with a student atlas late at night in the closing days of World War II." *See* MANSEI!

for he's a jolly good fellow. Only "Happy Birthday," written in 1893, has been sung more frequently than the popular "For He's a Jolly Good Fellow," according to the *Guinness Book of World Records*. "Jolly Good Fellow," however, is much older. It was originally the French song "Malbrouk," which dates back to at least 1781.

fork. The dinner-table fork takes its name from the farmer's pitchfork. The first such eating instrument was brought to England in the mid-15th century and named for the big fork it resembled in miniature. The pitchfork called a fork is recorded in England more than 400 years earlier.

forlorn hope. This expression is one of the best, or worst, examples of folk etymology recorded anywhere. The Dutch called a small squad of volunteer soldiers assigned to an extremely perilous mission a *verloren hoop*, "a lost troop." Such a squad of doomed death-defiers was called *enfants perdus* ("lost children") by the French, *verloren Kinder* by the Germans, and in modern times might be described as *shock troops* or *point men* in the U.S. Army, or *kamikaze*, "suicide pilots," by the Japanese. Though *verloren* does not mean "forlorn" and *hoop* does not mean "hope," the Dutch words sound like these English words, and *verloren hoop* was spelled *forlorn hope* by the Englishmen. The expression was first applied to similar bands of English soldiers picked to lead attacks, but by 1641 *forlorn hope's* common meaning of any undertaking almost surely doomed to failure, any vain expectation, was established. The poor chances of success and high casualties suffered by forlorn hope squads are mainly responsible for the expression's staying power, but the pathos and word music of "forlorn"—alliterative and suggesting "forgotten," "forsaken"—were helpful, too.

to form a firing squad in a circle. Said of any group that does great harm to itself, shoots itself in its collective foot. I had never heard this expression until the 2001 New York City mayoral election, when former Mayor David Dinkens told an interviewer, "The Democratic party tends to form a firing squad in a circle," that is, often eliminates or badly wounds itself by its infighting. I've been unable to find the expression recorded elsewhere.

for my next trick . . . These words, "followed by a pause," says lexicographer Tom McArthur, "are especially said by someone who has just botched something." The expression derives from the patter of stage magicians in the 1930s and is a good example of a catchphrase that has become a lasting idiom of the language.

fornication. *Fornication* was one of the words Noah Webster tried to BOWDLERIZE from the Bible in 1833. He substituted *lewdness* for it, but *fornication* remained popular in love and language. The word comes from the Latin *fornix*, for "an arch or vault." Since brothels in ancient Rome were often in caves or under arches (not always: they were sometimes even located in baker's ovens), *fornix* became the Latin for a brothel, which eventually gave us the English word *fornicate*. *Fornicate* strictly means "voluntary sexual intercourse between unmarried men and women," but it more generally means the four-letter word nobody wants to print.

for openers. *See* JUST FOR OPENERS.

forsythia. These handsome yellow-flowered shrubs, their bloom the first obvious sign of spring in many places, were named for William Forsyth (1737–1804), a Scottish gardener and horticulturist who became superintendent of the royal gardens at St. James and Kensington in London. Forsyth introduced many unusual ornamental plants to England and may have personally brought the forsythia from China. Also the inventor of a plaster that stimulates new growth in dying diseased trees, he received formal thanks from Parliament for this contribution. The *Forsythia* genus is especially valuable to gardeners because it is easy to propagate, is virtually carefree, and does well in partial shade. Incidentally, most people in the U.S. pronounce the plant's name *for-sith-ia*, though it should strictly be pronounced *for-sigh-thia* since Forsyth pronounced his name *For-sigh-th*.

fortnight. *See* SE'NNIGHT.

fortune cookies. The cookie with a fortune inside was invented in 1918 by David Jung, a contemporary Chinese immigrant who had established Los Angeles's Hong Kong Noodle Company. Jung got the idea after noting how bored customers got while waiting for their orders in Chinese restaurants. He employed a Presbyterian minister (the first fortune cookie author!) to write condensations of biblical messages and later hired Marie Raine, the wife of one of his salesmen, who became the Shakespeare of fortune cookies, writing thousands of classic fortunes such as "Your feet shall walk upon a plush carpet of contentment." The Hong Kong Noodle Company is still in business, as are hundreds of other fortune cookie "publishers." Notable ones include Misfortune Cookies of Los Angeles: "Look forward to love and marriage, but not with the same person." Today fortune cookies are of course served at the end of a meal.

fortunella. *Fortunella*, or the kumquat, is the only genus of well-known fruit trees to be named for a living person, and no more deserving eponym could be found than Robert Fortune (1813–80), Scottish botanist and traveler. Few men have equaled Fortune as a plant hunter. The author of *Three Years' Wanderings in the Northern Provinces of China* (1847) and other botanical books began traveling in the Orient for the Royal Horticultural Society in 1842. A former employee in the Society's English gardens, his express orders were to collect flora and he brought many beautiful plants back to Europe, including the kumquat, tree peonies, the Japanese anemone, and a number of chrysanthemums. Fortune also introduced the tea plant into India for the East India Company, founding its cultivation there. The tallest species of *Fortunella* is only 10 feet high, the smallest a bush of about three feet, and the kumquat fruit is orange-like but smaller, having three to seven cells, or sections, as opposed to eight to 15 in the orange. The kumquat, which is eaten fresh or preserved, has been crossed with other citrus fruits into a number of strange hybrids, such as the citrangequat and limequat.

40 acres and a mule. A promise, with no basis in fact, made by dishonest politicians to newly freed slaves after the Civil War. Each freed slave, they said, would receive 40 acres of land and a mule to work it with. "When we were children we used to ridicule the slogan 'forty acres and a mule' as a stupid deception used by the Yankees to get the black men to vote for the Republicans," wrote Katherine Lumpking in *The Making of a Southerner* (1947). *See also* HOLD THE FORT.

40 miles of bad road. The old expression from the American West describes any very ugly or unattractive person or place, as in "She looks like 40 miles of bad road and he looks 10 miles longer."

49er. A person who went to California in 1849 during the gold rush, or someone in favor of the use of the 49th parallel of latitude as a compromise boundary line in the Oregon boundary dispute with Great Britain.

40 rod lightning. Whiskey in the early West could literally kill a man and was thus given colorful names, none more vivid than *40 rod lightning*—which likened it to a rifle or shot that could kill a man at 40 yards.

40-shilling word. In days long past, Jamaicans could be fined 40 shillings if they uttered a "dirty word" in public (and a good deal more if they issued a string of obscenities). This led to the term *40-shilling word* for any indecent expression.

40 winks. Why 40 winks for a short nap? One story suggests that the Thirty-nine Articles, the articles of faith that Church of England clergy have been required to accept since 1571, are responsible for the phrase. It seems that a writer in *Punch* (November 16, 1872) quipped: "If a . . . man, after reading through the Thirty-nine Articles were to take forty winks . . ." and that his joke about the long and often tedious articles led to the expression for a short nap. But this isn't possible unless the writer was repeating a very old joke indeed, for *40 winks* is recorded in print as early as the middle 1820s, George Eliot using it in 1866. More likely the 40 follows the old tradition of using 40 to designate an indefinite number, as in Shakespeare's "I could beat forty of them," Ali Baba and the Forty Thieves, and many other instances.

for whom the bell tolls. *See* EARTH MOVED.

Fosbury Flop. American high jumper Dick Fosbury (b. 1947) won a gold medal and broke the world record for the high jump in the Mexico City 1968 Olympics using this unorthodox headfirst-over-the-bar technique. Ira Berkow in the *New York Times* (3/23/02) described a meeting with him many years later: "At first glance, it was remarkable to see Dick Fosbury enter the Manhattan hotel restaurant Friday perpendicular to the ground, rather than horizontal. If you've never seen Dick Fosbury before, all you have to go on are the old photos of him soaring over the high-jump bar headfirst, like a falcon in flight except upside down, with that inspired, innovative technique that would be laughed about but widely imitated to this day and that would come to be known as the Fosbury Flop." Fosbury began working on the technique in high school.

fossick.   Nineteenth-century Australian miners apparently coined this word meaning to search for gold by reworking waste piles of rock called *washings*, or to undermine another person's diggings. The word seems to derive from *fuss*, or a dialect word for a fussy person. Over time it came to mean to rummage or to search around for anything, as in "I was fossicking among some old papers and found a letter from her." Chiefly heard in Australia, the word has some currency in England and the U.S.

fo-ti-tieng.   Legend has it that the Chinese herbalist Li Chung-yun was 256 years old when he died in 1933, just after marrying for the 24th time. Moreover, he had all of his own hair and teeth and looked about 50. Whether the story is true or not is highly debatable (one writer says that "it is a matter of record with the Chinese government that Li was born in 1677"), but there is no doubt that the venerable vegetarian heartily recommended fo-ti-tieng for those who desired a long active life marked with sexual vigor. Several scientists, including the French biochemist Jules Lepine, have found an alkaloid in the leaves and seeds of this low-growing plant of the pennywort family *(Hydrocotyle asiatica minor)* that they claim has a rejuvenating effect on the nerves, brain cells, and endocrine glands. The Indian sage Nanddo Narian, then 107 himself, informed his faithful that fo-ti-tieng (which means "the elixir of long life" in Chinese) contained "a missing ingredient in man's diet without which we can never control disease and decay." Others have claimed that one-half teaspoon of the herb in a cup of hot water will remove wrinkles and increase sexual energy, and larger doses will act as an aphrodisiac. So off to the jungle marches of the Asian tropics, where the herb is found! And remember, too, Li Chang-yun's more general (and better) advice: "Keep a quiet heart, sit calmly like a tortise, walk sprightly like a pigeon, and sleep soundly like a dog." Also, said the sage, eat only food that grows above the ground, with the exception of ginseng root. *See* GINSENG.

foul ball.   A ball hit outside of the fair playing area in baseball has been called a foul ball since the 1860s. By the 1920s the term was being used generally for any useless, inadequate or contemptible person, and specifically for an inferior boxer, a palooka. The great American word inventor and cartoonist T. A. Dorgan is said to be the first person to use the expression in this extended sense. More recently *foul ball* has been used to mean an outsider. *See* PALOOKA.

foul play.   Shakespeare may have invented the term *foul play*. At least he used it first in print, in *King John*, where Salisbury

says "It is apparent foul play," when suspecting (wrongly) that Hubert has killed the young Prince Arthur. *Play* is a strange word to associate with murder, rape, and other crimes, even if the term originated in some gambling den, as has been suggested.

founder.   When a ship founders it fills with water and goes to the bottom. And *bottom* is the key to the ancestry of the word *founder*, which comes from the Latin *fundus*, meaning "bottom."

fountain pen.   The first fountain pens weren't made in late-19th-century America, as many people believe. There is an account of one dating back to 1657 and in 1712 the term *fountain pen* is first recorded in an advertisement in a Welsh almanac.

fourdrinier.   The brothers Fourdrinier, Henry and Sealy, invented the fourdrinier machine that makes most of the paper we use. In 1807 they patented the first practical machine for converting wood pulp into paper, but labored 30 years in perfecting it, aided only by a partial grant from Parliament. The English papermakers revolutionized the industry with their fourdrinier, which is today a huge automatic machine working on the same basic principle but bearing little resemblance to the original.

fourflusher.   A flush in poker is five cards all of the same suit, the hand taking its name either from a flush, or flight, of birds, or more likely, from the Latin *flux*, "a copious flow." A four-card flush is worthless, but in open-handed poker, if four cards of the same suit are face up on the table a player is in an excellent position to bluff, nobody knowing whether he has a fifth card of the same suit as his concealed "hole" card. Gamblers in the American West at the turn of the century bluffed so often with such four-card or bobtail flushes that the term *fourflusher* spread from the gambling tables into politer society, where it came to signify anyone who bluffs or pretends, especially someone who pretends to be more than he is while living on money borrowed from others.

Four Horsemen.   "Outlined against a blue-gray October sky, the Four Horsemen rode again. In dramatic lore they are known as Famine, Pestilence, Destruction and Death. These are only aliases. Their real names are Stuhldreher, Miller, Crowley and Layden." This was the opening of sportswriter Grantland Rice's coverage of Notre Dame's 13–7 defeat of Army at New York City's Polo Grounds on October 18, 1924, that immortalized the Notre Dame backfield. Notre Dame student publicist George Strickler seems to have suggested the name to Rice after seeing Rudolph Valentino's movie *The Four Horsemen of the Apocalypse. The Seven Mules*, for Notre Dame's line, was first suggested by Notre Dame center Adam Walsh in 1924, when, piqued by all the attention given to the backfield, he told the press: "We are just the seven mules. We do all the work so that these four fellows can gallop into fame." The expression *Four Horsemen* is a shortening of *the four horsemen of the apocalypse*, who are mentioned in the biblical book of *Revelation*, the four horsemen there being Conquest, Slaughter, Famine, and Death. Just the day before Notre Dame's backfield was dubbed *The Four Horsemen*, "Granny" Rice invented the name

The Galloping Ghost for Illinois star running back Red Grange. *See* RETIRING A NUMBER.

the Four Hundred. Society columnist Ward McAllister coined this term in 1889, when he claimed only 400 people formed New York City's high society. The old story says "400" was chosen because Mrs. Astor's ballroom held only that number, but the truth is that she often invited twice that many people to parties held there. *See* FOUR MILLION.

Fourierism. Fourierism, or utopian socialism, has inspired at least 41 experimental communities around the world at one time or another, all of them failures. Developed and introduced by François-Marie-Charles Fourier (1772–1837), a French merchant reacting against his commercial background, the system advocates dividing the world into phalanxes of 1,620 people. Each phalanx would live in a common building, or phalanstery, with separate apartments. One common language, a federal world government, and the encouragement of talent and industry were among other features of this very elaborate scheme, its ultimate goal being a systematic agricultural society. Fourier made a number of converts in France and wasn't dismayed when the only community established in his lifetime failed. His disciples later brought his doctrine to America, where several Fourier communities were established, none of them remaining today.

four-leaf clover. *See* CLOVER.

four-letter man. *Four-letter man* for "an excellent athlete" originated in college sports and originally meant someone who earned a letter in football, baseball, basketball, and track. Since its first use in early 20th-century America it has also come to be slang for a stupid person, from the four letters of *dumb*, and a contemptible person, from the four letters of *shit*. Amos Alonso Stagg, longtime football coach at the University of Chicago, was the first to award monograms of the first letter of a school's name to athletes and these monograms were being called letters by 1916. Stagg himself was called "the grand old man of football."

four-letter word. *The* four-letter word, as it is called, is *YHWH*, which in the Bible is the name of God. Many pious Jews will neither speak nor write this sacred name. Since this "ineffable name" was too sacred to use, the scribes added to it the vowels of the word *Adonai* (Hebrew for Lord), indicating that readers should say "*Adonai*," not "YHWH." *Yahweh* is a form of it that probably is its pronunciation, and *Jehovah* is a modern reconstruction of the name. It is the oldest four-letter word under taboo in history. In Greek it is rendered as *Tetragrammaton.*

Four Million. The title of O. Henry's (William Sydney Porter) collection of 25 New York short stories, which includes "The Gift of the Magi." Wrote the author in a preface explaining the title: "Not very long ago some one invented the assertion that there were only 'Four Hundred' people in New York City who were really worth noticing. But a wiser man has arisen—the census taker—and his larger estimate of human interest has been preferred." *See* FOUR HUNDRED.

four-minute mile. Today high school runners run sub-four-minute miles, but for at least most of the 20th century, such a time was thought by many experts to be an almost impossible barrier to break. Others kept on trying and finally, in 1954 at Oxford, British Dr. Roger Bannister (b. 1929) achieved this holy grail of runners with a time of three minutes 59.4 seconds. Bannister's record stood for 25 years before Sebastian Coe broke it in 1979. Today Algerian runner Noureddine Morceli holds the record with a 1993 time of three minutes 44.39 seconds. "The fastest man alive," however, is a title reserved for the 100-meter dash world record holder—today Tim Montgomery of the United States, whose 2002 time is 9.78 seconds (about 27 miles per hour).

fourscore and seven. The words *fourscore and seven* are from American president Abraham Lincoln's classic Gettysburg Address, delivered on November 19, 1863, dedicating the National Cemetery at Gettysburg, Pennsylvania, where a great and bloody battle of the Civil War had been fought. The two-minute or so speech famously began: "Fourscore and seven years ago our fathers brought forth upon this continent a new nation, conceived in liberty and dedicated to the proposition that men are created equal." It ended: "We here highly resolve that these dead shall not have died in vain—that this nation, under God, shall have a new birth of freedom—and that government of the people, by the people, for the people, shall not perish from the earth." It is one of the most famous and most quoted speeches, or prose poems, in history and used the words *under God* long before the Pledge of Allegiance to the flag (June 1954). *See* THREE SCORE AND TEN.

fourteen hundred. This obsolete phrase is a good example of secret language used in a profession. For many years, starting in about 1870, the London Stock Exchange had only 1,399 members. To ensure secrecy in the Exchange, the catchphrase *fourteen hundred!* was cried as a warning whenever a stranger came onto the floor.

Fourth Estate. This term for the press is said to have been coined by British statesman Edmund Burke (1729–97), who reputedly said of the Reporters' Gallery in the House of Commons: "Yonder sits the Fourth Estate, more important than them all." The other three estates of the realm are the Crown, the House of Lords, and the House of Commons. Unfortunately, no record exists of the Burke observation, and some historians believe the words should be credited to Lord Macaulay, who wrote in an 1843 essay: "The gallery in which the reporters sit has become a fourth estate of the realm."

four-word epithet. *See* LES SOMMOBICHES.

fox fire. A fungi-caused phosphorescent glow on decayed wood, often turquoise in color. The term is not an Americanism, as has been claimed, first recorded in England in 1483.

foxglove. "Fairy glove" and "finger-flower" are two other popular names for the handsome foxglove (*Digitalis purpurea*), which takes its scientific name from the Latin *digitus*, "finger." The flower's tubular blossoms resemble a finger or the empty finger of a glove, but no one knows where the *fox* in the popular designation comes from, though it could be a corruption of *folks'* (folks' glove). The ground leaves of the plant are used to make the heart medicine digitalis.

fox grape. *The Theatre of Plants* (1640) by John Parkinson informs us that "The Foxe Grape . . . is white, but smelleth and tasteth like unto a Foxe," which is presumably why the American grape is so named. There are two species of wild fox grapes, the northern (*Vitis labrusca*, which is the source of the cultivated Concord grape and other varieties) and the southern (*Vitis rotundifolia*, which is the source of the scuppernong). The wine term *foxy* refers to the pungent fruity flavor of Concord wine and other wines made from native American grapes, these wines reminiscent of jelly or jam to many people. *See* NORTHERN FOX GRAPE.

foxhound. The American foxhound (usually a black, white, and tan combination) is a variation of the English foxhound, both of them used in packs for fox hunting. It is one of the few dog breeds developed in the U.S. (another being the Boston terrier). George Washington helped develop and owned a good many foxhounds. *See* HOUND; IN AT THE KILL; TALLYHO.

fox hunt. British wit Oscar Wilde defined a fox hunt as "The unspeakable in full pursuit of the uneatable." Whenever an Englishman goes after foxes, he goes on a "fox hunt." A hunting expedition on which small game such as birds and rabbits are shot is called a "shoot."

foxtail pine. *See* BRISTLECONE PINE.

fox-trot. One story has it that actor Harry Fox's original trotting type of dance was a show-stopper in a 1913 Broadway hit musical. The show's producers realized the dance had promotional value and hired the noted social dancing teacher Oscar Duryea to modify it and introduce it as the *Fox Trot* to the public. This he did and the fox-trot has been America's most popular slow dance ever since. The story does jibe with the fact that the term is first recorded as *Fox* (with a capital *F*) *trot* in an RCA Victor Catalog in 1915.

fragging. *Fragging* came into the language during the Vietnam War. Meaning the intentional wounding or killing of an officer by his own troops, it takes its name from the fragmentation grenades sometimes used to accomplish this.

franc. This French unit of currency honors "John the Good" (1319–64), King John II of France. Captured by the British after the battle of Poitiers, John was freed in 1360 so that he could return to France and raise a ransom of 3 million gold crowns. He failed to do this, but in trying he ordered a new gold coin struck that was equivalent in value to the livre. John was pictured on horseback upon the coin's face, the Latin legend beneath his effigy reading, *Johannes Dei gracia Francorum rex,* "John, by the grace of God King of the Franks." It is from this coin, and a similar one honoring his successor Charles V, that the word *franc* derived. John, though he debased the currency, proved to be a man of honor. He returned to England when one of the hostages held for him escaped.

France; frank; etc. Late in the sixth century the warlike Francs conquered Gaul, giving their name to France and the French. The Gauls had named these Germanic tribes after the Latin *Franci,* the name the Romans bestowed upon the fearless warriors for the javelins they carried. Soon *Franc* itself, *Frank* in English, came to mean "free"—for the barbaric tribes reduced the Gauls to virtual slavery and were the only truly free nobles in the land. This meaning eventually led to such English words as *franking privilege,* free use of the public mails, but the Frank influence does not end there. Similarly, our *frank,* for "straightforward, or candid," derives from the Franks' blunt integrity in dealing with others—they were so powerful that there was no need for subterfuge. *See also* FRANKFURTER.

frangible booster. This space-age term describes a booster rocket with a casing of material that fragments easily so that there will be no large pieces to create a hazard if the rocket is destroyed in flight. *Frangible,* meaning breakable, comes from the Latin *frangere,* to break.

frangipane. The marquis Muzio Frangipani, a general under Louis XIV, is said to have invented the pastry cake filled with cream, sugar, and almonds called frangipane or frangipani. The name is also applied to the fragrant but ugly *Plumeria rubra* tree or shrub, and to a perfume either originally prepared from or imitating the odor of its flowers. The perfume is usually associated with the name of its otherwise unknown inventor—possibly a Frangipani relative or the marquis himself. An alternate suggestion is that both pastry and perfume may have been introduced by an earlier member of the Italian Frangipani family, a relative who came to France with Catherine de Médicis a century before the marquis. Considering Catherine's many contributions to French cooking, this is not unlikely.

frankenfood. Genetically engineered fruits and vegetables, such as new strains of corn and tomatoes. The expression takes its name from the idealistic German scientist Baron Frankenstein in Mary Shelly's novel *Frankenstein, or the Modern Prometheus* (1818). Frankenstein, of course, engineered a monster who later turned upon his creator. *Frankenfood* was coined by Paul Lewis, a Boston College English professor, the word first appearing in print in a letter he wrote to the *New York Times* on June 28, 1992. According to Anne H. Soukhanov in *Word Watch* (1995), Lewis "coined *Frankenfood* in the second week of June 1992," a few weeks before his *Times* letter. His letter read in part: "Ever since Mary Shelley's baron rolled his improved human out of the lab, scientists have been bringing such good things to life. If they want to sell us Frankenfood, perhaps it's time to gather the villagers, light some torches, and head to the castle." *See* FRANKENSTEIN.

Frankenscience. Modeled on Victor Frankenstein, like FRANKENFOOD, *Frankenscience* may be the coinage of William Safire, who used the young word in his *New York Times* July 5, 2001, column: "In a prime-time speech, he [President Bush] should announce his support of embryonic stem cell research and the careful oversight called for by scientists and doctors who are disinclined to play God. At the same time, he should convene a White House conference on bioethics; that would focus world attention on both the opportunities in genetic exploration and America's awareness of the real dangers of the slippery slope to Frankenscience."

Frankenstein. Frankenstein is the name of the young scientist who created a soulless monster out of graveyard corpses in Mary Wollstonecraft Shelley's novel by that title published in 1818. Frankenstein's monster is the proper name of the creature, not Frankenstein. Contrary to popular notion, Dr. Frankenstein's monster does have a name. The good doctor, played by Boris Karloff, named him Adam in the 1931 film *Frankenstein*. Because many other movies about the monster give him no name, the name Adam has been all but forgotten. Dr. Frankenstein's first name, incidentally, was Victor. Frankenstein's monster has been portrayed in 117 movies around the world, making him the second most portrayed horror movie character in film history—Count Dracula is in first place by a large margin.

frankfurter; frank. The frankfurter is named after Frankfurt, Germany, where it was first made centuries ago. Frankfurt itself was so named because it was the "ford of the Franks," the place from which the Franks set out on their raids. The frankfurter seems to have been introduced to the U.S. in St. Louis in about 1880 by Antoine Feuchtwanger, an immigrant from Frankfurt. *Frank* for *frankfurter* isn't recorded until the 1920s. Franks are also called HOT DOGS and New York tube steaks. *See* FRANCE; HAMBURGER.

Frankie Bailey's. Only movie star Betty Grable's "million-dollar legs" can compare with the gams of American performer Frankie Bailey, who was the toast of the town in the Gay Nineties. Miss Bailey's shapely stems were so celebrated that *Frankie Bailey's* became the term for any sexy, pleasing pair of legs. *See* GRABLE-BODIED SEAMAN.

Franklin conductor; Franklin stove; etc. Benjamin Franklin (1706–90), one of the broadest and most creative minds of his time—statesman, scientist, writer, printer, and inventor— devised the *Franklin stove*, a great improvement over its predecessors, in 1743. This portable, coal-burning iron fireplace had a pipe connecting it to the chimney, producing heat cheaply and relatively efficiently. Franklin's other inventions include *Franklin's bifocals*, and his famous experiment with a kite during a thunderstorm in 1762 led to his development of the *Franklin lightning rod*. Every branch of science held his interest, but Franklin's contributions to mankind did not end here. Among many civic achievements, he founded America's first circulating library, set up Philadelphia's first fire company, established what is now the University of Pennsylvania, organized the American Philosophical Society, wrote and published *Poor Richard's Almanack*—which sold 10,000 copies a year—and published the *Pennsylvania Gazette*, the most widely circulated newspaper in colonial America. The *Franklin tree*, or *Franklinia*, is also named after Benjamin Franklin. This species has an unusual history— introduced into cultivation from the wild in 1770 by American's first botanist, John Bartram, no one has been able to find it in its wild state since.

Franklin's gull. *Franklin's gull*, the only bird ever to have a monument erected to it, is intimately connected with English and American history. The black-headed gull was named in honor of Sir John Franklin (1786–1847), the English explorer who died in discovering the Northwest Passage that so many other mariners had striven to find. The story of his expedition and his wife's later attempts to find him is one of the most interesting in maritime history. *Franklin's gull (Laridae pipixcan)* has the same upland-breeding and seashore-wintering habits as the BONAPARTE'S GULL. *See also* GULL.

Frankly my dear, I don't give a damn. *See* GIVE A DAMN.

Fred Karno's army; Arnie's army. British music-hall performer Fred Karno (1866–1941) led a troupe of slapstick comedians in the early 1900s, Charlie Chaplin and Stan Laurel often performing with him. So popular was the erratic, disorganized troupe that the term *Fred Karno's army* came to be applied during World War I to any company of green, untrained recruits. *Arnie's army* is a name given by sportswriters to the many loyal fans who followed U.S. golfer Arnold Palmer (b. 1939), winner of four Master's championships, as he played his way around the golf course.

Fredonia. In 1827 a group of adventurers tried to set up a Texan republic called Fredonia; the name Fredonia had been invented in about 1800 by Dr. Samuel Latham Mitchell as a term for the United States, "a land where things are freely done," and was borrowed by the unsuccessful adventurers. Fredonia, incidentally, was the name of Groucho Marx's homeland in the film *Duck Soup*.

free lance. A free lance, for a self-employed person, is a term with an unsavory history. The original free lances were medieval Italian (*condottiere*) and French (*compagnies grandes*) knights, free men who would sell their skills with the lance to any master, whether his cause was good or bad. However, the name *free lance* for these knights was invented by Sir Walter Scott in *Ivanhoe* (1820). *Free lance* doesn't seem to have been applied to writers until about 60 years later.

freesia. There is some question about the naming of this fragrant and beautiful genus of South African herbs. Comprising three species but scores of horticultural forms, freesias grow from a bulblike corm, belonging to the iris family and bearing typically white or yellow flowers at the end of their stems. They are generally raised in greenhouses and are a popular florist's flower. Some authorities, including *Webster's Biographical Dictionary*, say the genus was named for E. M. Fries (1794–1878), a Swedish botanist; others cite F. H. T. Freese, a pupil of Professor Klatt, the christener of the genus.

free soil, free speech, free labor, free men. This was the slogan of the American Free-soil Party during the election of 1848. The slogan referred to the party's opposition to the extension of slavery into any of the territories newly acquired from Mexico. With former President Martin Van Buren as its candidate, the Free-soilers polled nearly 300,000 votes and were a decisive factor in the victory of the Whigs over the Democrats. In 1854 the Free-soil Party was absorbed into the new Republican Party.

freewheeling. A freewheeling person is one who moves about freely, independently, one who might even be irresponsible, or someone who isn't governed by rules and regulations. The term comes from bicycling in the old days before the coaster brake was invented, when cyclists coasted, freewheeling down the hills. The term *freewheeler* for a bicycle is first recorded in 1889.

French. The prejudice that anything French is wicked, sexual, and decadent has let Frenchmen in for more than their fair share of abuse in English. Many such expressions date back to 1730–1820, the height of Anglo-French enmity, but some are current and others go back even further. FRENCH LEAVE and FRENCH DISEASE are covered in entries following; for *French letter* or *French cap* see CONDOM. At one time *French by injection*, like its Dutch counterpart, meant any English woman living with a Frenchman. *French kiss* for the lingual "soul kiss"; *French fare*, overelaborate politeness; *French postcards*, "dirty" prints; and *pardon my French* for "excuse my strong language" are all familiar expressions. By no means are such phrases confined to English, either. In Prussia, for example, lice are called *Franzosen*. The French, however, have done their share of international name-calling, too. Their word for a louse is *espagnol* (Spanish), for a flea *espagnole* (Spanish woman), and for a creditor they once said *un anglais* (an Englishman). The French phrase for a dirty trick is a *Chinese trick*, their red tape is *chinoiserie*, their expression for our *that's Greek to me* is *that's Hebrew to me*; our *Dutch courage* is their *German happiness*, and our *Dutch treat* is their *going Swiss*. As recently as the early '60s they introduced *la vice anglaise* as a synonym for homosexuality. On the whole English reflects admiration for the French exceeding any animosity. There are some 100 words prefixed with *French* and most of them recognize French expertise. Among the most common are French cuffs, French heel, French twist, French cleaning, French roof, French doors and windows, French kiss, French telephone, French harp, French horn, French cuisine, French dressing, French endive, French bread, French ice cream, French pancake, French pastry, French toast, French fried and French fries.

the French disease. SYPHILIS has been blamed on nearly every country and continent, always by residents of other countries and continents. For Poles, it was *the German sickness;* the Russians blamed it on the Poles; to the Dutch it was the *Spanish Pox;* and carried to India, China, and Japan it was there branded *the Portuguese disease.* But the French have been blamed far more than most nations, mainly because they have long been widely associated with anything sexual. When in 1496 an Italian wrote that "the French disease is a new plague . . . contracted by lying together," the phrase was quickly adopted throughout Europe. In later years syphilis became *French pox, French marbles, the French goods, the French gout, the French sickness,* and *a Frenchman.* Furthermore, *French crown* long meant baldness produced by syphilis, *to be Frenchified* meant to be venereally infected, and *a French pig* was a venereal sore. As for the French, they steadfastly refused to call the disease anything but the *Italian* or *the Naples disease.*

French fried potatoes. Many youngsters think McDonald's invented them, but they were conceived in Belgium toward the middle of the 19th century. From there the Belgian fries spread in popularity to France, and the method of deep frying them soon imported to America, where they are still known under the misnomer *French fries.*

Frenchified. Since the late 16th century *Frenchified* has been a contemptuous term for having French manners or qualities. Ben Jonson, the first to record the word, wrote of "Monsieur Fastidious Brisk, otherwise called the fresh Frenchified courtier." The phrase once also meant "to be infected with the venereal disease," this usage recorded as early as 1655.

French leave. The French are noted for their politeness—witness the expression *French fare* (See FRENCH), overelaborate manners, which makes it all the more clear that the pejorative *French leave* was invidiously coined. In 18th-century French society it was the custom to depart from a dinner or ball without formally bidding the hostess or guests goodbye. Such a surreptitious departure was dubbed *a French leave* by the decorous English, but the voluble French always pinned the custom on their self-conscious cousins, calling it taking *English leave (s'en aller* [or *filer*] *a l'anglaise).* *French leave* is also widely used for a soldier who has gone A.W.O.L. or "over the hill." In all cases it means someone who has slipped out before his absence is noticed.

French toast. In America *French toast* refers to sliced bread soaked in a mixture of eggs and milk before frying the dish golden brown. In England the popular breakfast dish is simply sliced bread fried in bacon fat or butter. The French themselves make it the same way Americans do, calling it *pain perdu* ("lost bread") since the bread is "lost" in the other ingriedents.

French words in English. French words came into English by the thousands after the Norman Conquest in 1066, and many had entered the language long before then. It would take a volume to list these basic contributions, but here is a brief sample of just those words that have come into American English: crappie (fish), gopher, pumpkin, cache, carry-all, pirogue, portage, voyageur, brioche, chowder, jambalaya, [pie] à la mode, praline, cent, dime, mill, bayou, butte, chute, crevasse, flume, levee, prairie, rapids, [Indian] brave, Cajun, calumet, Canuck, lacrosse, lagniappe, parlay, picayune, rotisserie, sashay, bureau, depot, shanty.

fresh as a daisy. *See* DAISY.

fret. Tracing *fret* back to Middle English we find that the word, related to the German *fressaen*, primarily meant "voracious eating by animals." Today *fret* means only to worry, its new sense probably arising from the idea that worry eats into one, as in the expression "What's eating you?"

Freudian. No other contemporary thinker has influenced 20th-century intellectual thought more profoundly than Dr. Sigmund Freud (1856–1939), the founder of psychoanalysis. His Freudian theories, though often modified and even discarded over the years, emphasize the importance of the unconscious, infantile sexuality, and the role of sexuality in the development of neuroses, while Freudian methods, such as free association, are methods for treating mental disorders. A Freudian slip is popularly a slip of the tongue revealing a repressed subconscious thought or desire. The Austrian physician and psychoanalyst met with extreme hostility when he published *The Interpretation of Dreams* in 1900, but his views became increasingly accepted. *See* SLIP OF THE TONGUE.

Friar's Club. This theatrical fraternity, founded in 1904, has been headed by such prominent abbots as George M. Cohan, Georgie Jessel, Milton Berle, Joe E. Lewis, and Frank Sinatra. The Friars, based in a clubhouse on East 55th Street in New York City, is noted for its "roasts" of celebrities—facetious tributes at a banquet in which the celebrity is both praised and good-naturedly insulted in speeches by friends.

Friday. The Scandinavian goddess of love Freya was deserted by her husband Odin, or Wotan, god of war, wisdom, agriculture, and poetry, because she paid too much attention to a life of luxury and not enough to him. Odin may have forgotten her, but history didn't, the Old English for her name becoming the basis for our *Friday: Fria daeg,* or *Freya's day.* WEDNESDAY is named for Wotan.

Friday's child. *See* MONDAY'S CHILD.

Friday the 13th. Friday is considered unlucky by some because it was the day of Christ's crucifixion, while 13 is so considered because the Last Supper was attended by Christ and his 12 disciples. But these widely believed superstitions actually go back much further in time. Today few if any buildings have a 13th floor, and many sailors object to leaving port on a Friday the 13th. In the theater the widespread Friday the 13th bad luck tradition applies only to opening nights. According to theatrical tradition, a show should never open on Friday the 13th. The reasons behind the tradition, if there are any, are unknown.

fried chicken. *See* SOUTHERN FRIED CHICKEN.

frig. *See* FIG.

Frisbee. *Frisbee* is the trademarked name for a plastic, concave disk used in catching games between two or more players, who spin the disk off into the air with a flick of the wrist. The disk and name are said to have been inspired by a similar game played by Yale students, who tossed about disposable metal pie tins that came from pies made by the Frisbie Pie Company of Bridgeport, Connecticut. The modern plastic Frisbee, however, is said to have been invented by William Morrison, who sold it to the Wham-O Manufacturing Company in 1955 and whose name is on the patent. Then Ed Headrick (1924–2002), head of research at Wham-O, further improved the product, changing its name from the *Pluto Platter* to *Frisbee,* a name that Wham-O says does not derive from the pie company name, despite the similarity, coming instead from a once-popular comic strip called "Mr. Frisbie." It is estimated that about 4 million people play Frisbee; no one knows how many dogs play. Just before his death Mr. Headrick told a reporter that "Frisbyterians," loyal Frisbee enthusiasts, don't go to purgatory when they die: "We just land up on the roof and lay there." *See* HULA-HOOP.

frogfall. *See* FISHFALL.

frog in the throat. It has been suggested that this term for a hoarse throat has its origins in the medieval practice of inserting a live frog into a patient's mouth head first, so that the frog could draw the patient's infection into its own body when it inhaled. However, the expression isn't recorded until the nineteenth century, which makes such a derivation suspect. *Frog* was once a common name for thrush, the mouth and throat infection, and this may have something to do with a *frog in the throat.*

Frogmore stew. A dish made not of frogs but of seafood; originally made on Frogmore, one of the Sea Islands off South Carolina, which is often pronounced *Frogmow* by Southerners.

from A to izzard. Chiefly British in usage and rare today, *from A to izzard* means *from A to Z,* ALPHA AND OMEGA, from beginning to end. *Izzard* here may be a 1597 dialect variation of *zed (z),* according to the *O.E.D.*

from away. Used to describe anyone residing in Maine who doesn't hail from the state. The expression is also heard on the North Fork of Long Island, New York, and can mean a summer visitor as well.

from China to Peru. Throughout the world, this literary phrase still has currency, though seldom in speech. It is from these lines in Samuel Johnson's *On the Vanity of Human Wishes* (1749): "Let observation with extended view/ Survey mankind from China to Peru."

from Dan to Beersheba. The Bible (Judges 20:1) tells of the ancient Israelites assembling from Dan in the north to Beersheba in the south to fight the Benjamites (members of the tribe of Benjamin). This meant all over the world, or everywhere to the Israelites of the day, and so the phrase *from Dan to Beersheba,* mentioned several times in the Old Testament, came to mean the same. *See* JOHN O'GROAT'S HOUSE.

from Fort Kearney west, he was feared a great, great deal more than the Almighty. A saying about the notorious American desperado "Captain" J. A. Slade. Wrote Mark Twain of these words in *Roughing It* (1872): "For compactness, simplicity and vigor of expression, I will back that sentence against anything in literature."

from hell, Hull, and Halifax, Good Lord deliver us. British vagabonds and beggars often recited this famous prayer in the early 17th century and after. *Hell* was to be avoided for obvious reasons, the town of *Hull* demanded hard labor for any "charity" given, and *Halifax* had a celebrated Gibbet Law that provided for the execution of prisoners *and then* a trial to determine whether they were guilty or not!

from John O'Groat's to the Land's End. *See* JOHN O'GROAT'S HOUSE.

from scratch. *See* START FROM SCRATCH.

from soup to nuts. An American expression for "everything," apparently coined in the late 1920s and obviously based on the menu of a sumptuous meal or banquet at which everything from a first course of soup to a last course of nuts is served. *In the soup* is an Americanism meaning "in trouble."

from the sublime to the ridiculous. This very common expression most often means from one extreme to the other, or from the noble to the ignoble. Sometimes it is heard, erroneously, as *from the ridiculous to the sublime.* The phrase has been traced to English and American patriot Tom Paine, who wrote in *The Age of Reason* (1794–95): "The sublime and the ridiculous are often so nearly related that it is difficult to class them separately, and one step above the ridiculous makes the sublime again." Paine spent 11 months in prison in between the writing of the first two parts of his great book.

from the word go. From the start, the beginning, the very first. This lasting expression is first recorded in the autobiography *The Life and Adventures of Colonel David Crockett of West Tennessee* (1833): "I was plaguy well pleased with her from the word go."

front runner. *Front runner* appears to be a relatively recent addition to the language, dating back only 60 years or so. It means a person leading in any competition, especially in a political race, and derives from either track and field or horse racing.

frozen words. An old story from the Texas Panhandle tells of a winter so cold that spoken words froze in the air, fell entangled on the ground, and had to be fried up in a skillet before the letters would reform and any sense could be made of them. The idea is an ancient one, used by Rabelais and familiar to the Greek dramatist Antiphanes, who is said to have used it in praising the work of Plato: "As the cold of certain cities is so intense that it freezes the very words we utter, which remain congealed till the heat of summer thaws them, so the mind of youth is so thoughtless that the wisdom of Plato lies there frozen, as it were, till it is thawed by the refined judgement of mature age."

frozen Yankee Doodle. A famous saying from brilliant American conversationalist Thomas Gold Appleton about the Boston Art Museum, torn down in 1908. Appleton said that if architecture was frozen music, this building was "frozen Yankee Doodle." *See* YANKEE DOODLE; ARCHITECTURE IS FROZEN MUSIC; MUTUAL ADMIRATION SOCIETY.

fruit parlor. This English-language borrowing, which is widely used in Japan, means "ice cream parlor." The definition doesn't seem so strange on realizing that the parlors there are named for the fruit used as toppings for ice-cream sundaes, etc.

fry. *Fry* is mostly used today for the spawn of salmon and other fishes, but, as the still common *small fry* shows, it was once a common term for human children as well. In fact, *fry* was used to describe children before it was applied to other species.

fubar. A euphemistic army acronym made up of the initials of "*f*ucked *u*p *b*eyond *a*ll *r*ecognition"—that is, completely screwed up, botched up, confused. The term, probably suggested by the earlier *snafu* ("*s*ituation *n*ormal, *a*ll *f*ucked *u*p") arose during World War II.

fuchsia; Fuchsian group; fuchsin. *Fuchsia*, for a vivid bluish or purplish red, takes its name from the ornamental fuchsia shrubs that honor German physician and botanist Leonhard Fuchs (1501–66). These principally Mexican and South American shrubs, which are of the evening primrose family and can have purple, red, yellow, or white flowers, were named for Fuchs in 1703 by the French botanist Charles Plumier. Dr. Fuchs was noted for his treatment of the "English sweating sickness," a plague that had spread to Europe. He became professor of medicine at the University of Tubingen in 1535, remaining there until his death over three decades later. His herbal *De historia stirpium* (1530) was widely known, this compendium of medicinal and edible plants probably the main reason why the genus *Fuchsia* was named in his honor. The genus contains some 100 species, with *fuchsia* shrubs being only one of its many widely cultivated plants. *Fuchsin*, or *fuchsine*, is a purplish red aniline dye, and *Fuchsian group* is a mathematical term that derives from the name of I. L. Fuchs (1833–1902), an eminent German mathematician.

fuck. Originally a quite acceptable word, *fuck* was recorded in an English dictionary as early as John Florio's *A World of Words* (1598). The word doesn't derive from the police blotter entry "[booked] for *u*nlawful *c*arnal *k*nowledge," as some people still believe. Our word for the act of sexual connection may remotely come from the Latin for the same, *futuere*, but most probably is from the Old German *ficken/fucken*, "to strike or penetrate," which had the slang meaning "to copulate." As *Partridge* points out, the German word is almost certainly related to the Latin words for *pugilist*, *puncture*, and *prick*, through the root *pug*, which goes back to prehistoric times. Before *fuck* came into English in the late 15th century—its first recorded use is in 1503—*swyve* was the verb most commonly used for *fucking*. *Fuck* began to become more rare in print in the 18th century when human experience began to be disguised behind a "veil of decency," and the last dictionary it was recorded in up until recent times is Francis Grose's *Dictionary of the Vulgar Tongue* (1785), in the form of *f**k*. The great *O.E.D.* banned it, just as it banned *cunt* (but not *prick*, for some reason), and this made the word's acceptance all the harder. Though great writers like D. H. Lawrence, James Joyce, and Henry Miller tried to restore *fuck* to its proper place in print, it wasn't until 1960 that Grove Press in America won a court case that permitted publishers to print *fuck* legally for the first time in centuries. The book containing the word was D. H. Lawrence's *Lady Chatterley's Lover*, written in 1928.

fuck-you lizard; gecko. FUCK-YOU LIZARD is another designation, decidedly unscientific, for *Gekko gecko*, the tropical tokay gecko lizard that G.I.s encountered in Vietnam. The croaking of this gecko's call resembles the English "Fuck you, fuck you," hence the name, first recorded in 1933. Green troops in Vietnam were sometimes told that the gecko's call was the enemy taunting them. Strange as it may seem, the word *gecko* itself takes its name from a Malay word imitative of the lizard's call. U.S. prisoners in the Japanese Cabanatum P.O.W. camp in the Philippines during World War II also heard the gecko's peculiar cry. Wrote Hampton Sides in *Ghost Soldiers* (2001): "Geckos were draped all about the barracks, sated from the night's mosquitoes, occasionally calling out in their distinctive two-note chirp that prisoners swore sounded like "Fuck you! Fuck you!" A small annoyance next to all the horrors they experienced but just what the fickle finger of fate had done.

fudge. Isaac D'Israeli, father of the British prime minister, had an interesting story about the word *fudge*, for "lies or nonsense," in his *Curiosities of Literature* (1791): "There was sir, in our time one Captain Fudge, commander of a merchantman, who upon his return from a voyage, how illfrought soever his ship was, always brought home a good cargo of lies, so much that now aboard ship the sailors, when they hear a great lie told, cry out 'You fudge it!' A notorious liar named Captain Fudge, called "Lying Fudge," did live in 17th-century England. His name, possibly in combination with the German word *futch*, "no good," may well be the source of the word *fudge*. Where the word *fudge* for candy comes from no one seems to know, though it probably dates back to the 19th century.

fugu. The Japanese fugu, also called the puffer fish, hosts a deadly poison in its ovaries and liver if prepared the wrong way and kills an estimated 300 people a year. An ounce of this deadly tetrodotoxin is theoretically enough to fatally poison 56,000 diners. Only a trained fugu chef (who must take a rigid government examination which only 30 percent of all candidates succeed in passing) is permitted by law to prepare fugu. Yet the Japanese continue to consume their national love dish at the rate of about 10,000 tons a year. Since amateur chefs persist in preparing the fish and there is no known antidote for its poison, this amounts to a kind of culinary Russian roulette. One well-known Japanese love poem relates how "Last night he and I ate fugu. / Today I carry his coffin."

fuhgeddaboutit. The New York pronunciation of the expression *forget about it* has thanks to the movies (see *Mickey Blue Eyes*) and television (see *The Sopranos*) become well known all over the world. It is usually the equivalent of "don't mention it, it's no trouble at all," "no problem," etc., in response to a "thank you." But it can also mean "no way!," "I won't even consider it," etc.

führer; Hitler; Schicklgruber. Before Adolf Hitler preached his doctrines of the "master race" and The Thousand Year Reich, *Führer* was simply a German word for "leader." But Nazi blood purges, millions dead in gas chambers and concentration camps, towns like Lidice wiped off the map, and planned world conquest made both his name and title symbols for terror, horror, and evil, synonyms for a mad tyrant or megalomaniac. *Der Führer* was the title Hitler chose when he combined the offices of president and chancellor in 1934. Hitler is said to have committed suicide in his Berlin bunker in 1945, aged 56, but legends persist that he still lives, which indeed he does, if only symbolically. *Schicklgruber* is another word often used to describe someone like him, but contrary to widespread belief, it was not his legal name—Hitler's father, Alois, an illegitimate child, bore his mother's name, Schicklgruber, for a time, but changed it to Hitler, his father's name, before Adolf was born. A *Hitler* or a *Mr.* or *Mrs. Hitler* is a blustering, domineering person.

Fulbright scholarship. A Fulbright is a scholarship grant provided under the U.S. Congress Fulbright Act (1946), which was introduced by Senator James William Fulbright (1905–

1995) and has been awarded to a large number of now prominent Americans.

full as a tick. Ticks gorge themselves with the blood of humans and animals, often transmitting diseases such as Lyme disease. This bloating suggested a person filling himself with liquor and gave birth to the term *full as a tick* for someone very drunk. The expression is said to have originated in Australia about a century ago, but it has been common in America for many years.

full court press. In basketball a very aggressive, close-guarding defense all over the court is called a full court press. The expression, dating back 50 or so years, is now also used to mean maximum pressure applied in any situation.

Fuller Brush man. Alfred C. Fuller, founder of the Fuller Brush Company, liked to quote the boosterism " 'American' terminates in 'I can' and 'Dough' begins with 'Do,' " which he may have invented. Fuller, who built his door-to-door business into a $130 million enterprise, died in 1973, aged 88. At one point his ubiquitous Fuller Brush men and Fullerettes (female salesmen) called on 85 of every 100 American homes, even made home deliveries by dog sled in Alaska. These modern-day peddlers weren't welcome everywhere—some communities still have laws against any door-to-door salesmen calling without a specific invitation—but for the most part they were American favorites. Disney's big bad wolf in the *Three Little Pigs* film disguised himself as a Fuller Brush man, Red Skelton played the lead in the movie *The Fuller Brush Man*, and Lucille Ball starred in *The Fuller Brush Girl*. Fuller Brush men were the subject of about as many off-color jokes as the traveling salesman and the farmer's daughter.

full many a flower is born to blush unseen. *See* FAR FROM THE MADDING CROWD.

full monty. The success of a 1997 British movie of the same name about a group of neophyte male strippers made this expression popular throughout the English-speaking world. It means the full amount expected or possible, the works, everything; unfortunately its origin is unknown. It has been suggested that its eponym was Field Marshal Bernard "Monty" Montgomery (1887–1976), who liked to have a full British breakfast wherever he was soldiering; others cite a three-piece suit sold by early 20th-century tailor Montague Burton; and still others champion the Spanish card game monte.

full nelson. The name for this wrestling hold didn't come into use until the 19th century, when it was named either for some celebrated grappler who excelled at the pressure hold, or for Nelson, a town in Lancashire, England, once famous for its wrestling matches. The town of Nelson changed its name from Marston in the 19th century, calling itself after the popular Lord Nelson Inn there, which in turn honored England's great naval hero.

full of beans, etc. The phrase is used like *full of baloney, full of soup*, and worse, but it usually means someone who is full of energy, high-spirited, lively—sometimes in a foolish or silly way. Some say it is a horsey expression, like *full of oats*, going back to the days when horses were fed "horse beans" raised for fodder. The saying, however, is a British one from about 1870 and may derive from an earlier phrase, *full of bread*. Beans, a high-protein food, certainly should make one lively; in fact, they have long been regarded as an aphrodisiac. As an old English ballad, "The Love Bean," put it:

> My love hung limp beneath the leaf
>   (O bitter, bitter shame!)
> My heavy heart was full of grief
>   Until my lady came.
> She brought a tasty dish to me,
>   (O swollen pod and springing
>   seed!)
> My love sprang out right eagerly
>   To serve me in my need.

The gas that beans inspire also has something to do with the expression; as the word *prunes*, substituted in the phrase for *beans* some seventy years later, would indicate, both beans and prunes having a laxative effect. In fact, beans were primarily regarded as an aphrodisiac by the ancients because the eructations they caused were thought to produce prodigious erections. But the U.S. Department of Agriculture has recently developed a "gas-less variety," "a clean bean" seed guaranteed not to cause social distress at the dinner table or elsewhere. So bean eaters can now be as full of beans as ever and much less obnoxious, though maybe not as sexy.

full of oats. *See* FEEL ONE'S OATS.

Fun City. A well-known nickname for New York City said to have originated in 1966 with Mayor John V. Lindsay (1921–2001) on his first day in office when a reporter asked if he was happy he'd been elected. "I still think it's a fun city," Lindsay replied. Author Dick Schapp first capitalized the name in his *Herald Tribune* column "What's New in Fun City." *See* BIG APPLE.

funk; funky. *Funk*, for "fear of panic," still has its best explanation in the Flemish phrase *in de fonck siin*, "in a state of panic." Yet this literally means "to be in the smoke" and no one has been able to explain the connection between smoke and panic. Possibly smoke was associated with a panic-stricken person trying to find a way out through the smoke of a fire, or with the smoke of hell fire. The word owes part of its long popularity to its similarity to the most famous of four-letter words beginning with *f*. Since its introduction to England in the early 18th century it has also come to mean a dejected mood, especially in the phrase *in a blue funk*, "blue" intensifying the phrase by suggesting "the blues." If there is an eponymous Funk somewhere, he or she would be glad to know that *funky*, which derives from *funk*, means good jazz with an earthy blues-based character. This *funky* is popular recent slang for anything very good or beautiful (clothes, hairstyle, etc.), but it can also mean something cheap or no good, depending on the context.

funkia. This widely cultivated plantain lily or hosta is named after a real person, the German botanist C. H. Funkia. Funkia is one of the few plants that is doubly eponymous, for its alternate name, *hosta*, honors Austrian botanists Nicholaus and Joseph Host. The plant, valued in the garden for its shade

tolerance, is also known as the "niobe." Its genus name is *Hosta*, and there are at least 14 species.

funny bone.

> They have pull'd you down flat on your back,
> And they smack, and they thwack,
> Till your "funny bones" crack,
> As if you were stretched on the rack,
>   At each thwack!
> Good lack! what a savage attack!

Reverend Richard Harris Barham, well known for his punning, wrote the above in *The Ingoldsby Legends* (1840) and it is the first mention of the expression *funny bone* in literature. The funny bone—Americans called it the *crazy bone* in the past—is technically the medial condyle of the humerus, that is, the enlarged knob on the end of the bone of the upper arm, which lies below the ulnar nerve. The unpadded nerve hits the humerus as if against an anvil when we strike it on something, causing sharp, tingling pain. Nothing is very funny about this—it inspires cursing rather than laughter. But Barham or some punster before him probably saw the pun *humorous* in the *humerus* bone and dubbed it the funny bone, adding one of the few puns that have become phrases to the language.

furlong. In medieval times a furlong—from the Old English *furh*, "furrow," and *lang*, "long"—was the length of an ideal furrow in a plowed field, which was one-eighth of a Roman mile. Though the length of furrows and other land measurements changed over the centuries, a furlang, changed slightly to furlong, remained the same eighth of a mile, or 220 yards, and became a measurement used primarily in horse racing.

furphy. Any baseless report, a latrine rumor, is in Australian military slang called a *furphy* and honors, or dishonors, one of two possible candidates: either the firm of Furphy & Co., whose name appeared on World War I latrine buckets supplied to the Australian forces; or a contractor named Furphy who supplied rubbish carts to Melbourne army camps about 1915.

fuss and feathers. Nonsense over nothing at all. The expression dates back to the 19th century, a time when *Old Fuss and Feathers* was the nickname of U.S. general Winfield Scott, a very vain man, all 300 pounds of him. Scott, a genuine American hero and a general from the War of 1812 through the Civil War, was said to love himself, food, and wine—in that order. Dressed to the nines in his splendid self-designed gold-braided uniform and plumed hat, he was "almost a parade by himself" as he waddled down the street. As a contemporary put it: "What a wonderful mixture of gasconade, ostentation, fuss, feathers, bluster and genuine soldierly talent and courage is this same Winfield Scott." *See* GREAT SCOTT!

fustian. *Fustian* first referred to a coarse cloth material made of cotton and flax in Fostat, a suburb of Cairo. By the 16th century it came to mean inflated, turgid, pompous, or bombastic language. For example, in *Epistle to Arbuthnot* (1735), Alexander Pope wrote: "And he, whose fustian's so sublimely bad, / It is not poetry, but prose run mad."

futz around.   To fool around, play around, as in "Don't futz around with the papers." *Futz* here may be a euphemism for "fuck," or could derive from *putz,* or from a Yiddish word. It is first recorded in James T. Farrell's *Young Lonigan* (1932).

fuzz.   Most etymologists have given up as a lost cause the derivation of *fuzz* for the police or a police officer, but here are a few suggestions for the Americanism's origin. *Fuzz,* which apparently was born in the early 1920s, may contemptuously refer to "fuzzy" lint or hair on the uniforms of police officers. It may also have originally been black slang for the hairy body of a white person, although no such usage has been documented. The *New Dictionary of American Slang* (1986) says it was first black slang for "man with the fuzzy balls," meaning a white man. *Fuzz* has to be marked "Origin Unknown."

F.W.C.   *See* F.M.C.

G

G. According to the old Phoenician alphabet, *G* represented the outline of a camel's head and neck.

gabfest. *Gabfest* is an Americanism, which like all *fest* words (*e.g.*, talkfest, funfest) half derives from the annual family *fest* (from the German *Fest*, "festival") held by the German-American Turner family beginning in the mid-19th century. The *Turner fest* was the model for *gabfest*, first recorded in 1897, but *gab* had been used in England for "to talk fluently, very well, or too much." *Gab* may be an old Norse word, or may be onomatopoeic like *gabble*, and has been used since at least 1670. *Gift of gab* ("He's got a gift of gab"), the ability to talk well or convincingly, dates back to 1681 in England, while *gabby*, too, is British, first recorded in 1719.

Gabriel's hounds. Gabriel's hounds are wild geese, so called centuries ago because their sound in flight is like a pack of hounds in full cry. Legend has it that they are the souls of unbaptized children wandering in space until the Judgment Day. *Gabriel* here refers to one of the biblical archangels.

gadget. *Gadget*, as it is usually employed, is a relatively new word, dating only to 1886 and possibly deriving from the French *gachette* for "a little mechanical thing." Its latest and most ironic use (ca. 1970) is a widely used synonym for an atomic bomb, especially among scientists who make the monsters.

gadolinite; gadolinium. In 1794 Finnish chemist Johann Gadolin analyzed a black mineral found in rare-earth elements at Ytterly, near Stockholm, Sweden. The mineral, from which he extracted the oxide yttria, was named *gadolinite* in his honor eight years later. Gadolin (1760–1852) also has the metallic chemical element *gadolinium* to commemorate him. It was discovered in 1880 by the Swiss chemist J. C. G. de Marignac, being one of several elements extracted from *gadolinite*. Marignac did not name the new element for Gadolin until six years after his discovery.

gadzooks! Ernest Weekley traces this mild oath to *God's hooks*, that is, the nails used to crucify Christ. Originating in the mid-17th century, the expletive has not been used seriously for a hundred years now, but it is still heard humorously. *See* GODDAM.

Gaelic words in English. Gaelic, still spoken by about 600,000 people in Ireland and Scotland, has contributed a number of words to English, including: bard, bog, glen, slogan, blarney, shillelagh, shamrock, colleen, brogue, galore (all Irish Gaelic); and clan, loch, and ptarmigan (Scots Gaelic).

gaff; stand the gaff. To stand the gaff means to endure goading or kidding by someone, but its roots extend to the Provençal word *gaf*, for "a boathook." *Gaff*, for "a hoax or trick" possibly derives from the idea of "hooking some poor fish," from the time when a large fishhook was referred to as a gaff.

gaffer. *Gaffer* means an old man, so *an old gaffer* is somewhat redundant, but that is how the expression is mostly used. *Gaffer* is thought to be a contraction of either *grandfather* or *godfather*, and is believed to be much older than its first recorded use at the end of the 16th century. *An old gammer*, for "an old woman," derives from either *grandmother* or *godmother* and is rarely heard outside rural England. A *gaffer* is also the chief lighting technician on a movie or TV set.

gaga. Someone cuckoo, off his rocker, mentally unbalanced. It has been suggested that *gaga* is of French origin, the word deriving from the name of the French artist Paul Gauguin, who gave up banking to become a painter at the age of 35 and experienced considerable mental anguish toward the end of his life. The word seems inappropriate, however, to express Gauguin's tortured genius and would be a cruel and stupid coining if true. Alternatives are the theories that *gaga* derives from the French *gateux*, "an old man feeble-minded and no longer able to control his body," or that it is in imitation of an idiot's laugh. The phrase has been artist's slang, which would support the Gauguin theory, but according to the *gateux* theory, *gaga* originated in the theatrical world about 1875, eight years before Gauguin (1848–1903) became a painter.

gag rules. Gag rules restrict or prevent discussion on a particular subject by a legislative body. The term is an Americanism first recorded in 1810, though gag tactics were used as early as 1798 in Congress to try to restrict freedom of the press.

Gainsborough hat. Paintings have inspired a number of fashions, but no artist has been more influential than English portrait painter and landscapist Thomas Gainsborough in this regard. The Gainsborough is a wide-brimmed, large hat, turned up at the side, similar to those included in many of his portraits. Gainsborough (1727–88) did not invent the plumed velvet or taffeta hat, but painted it so well that it has been revived several times by designers, as have a number of the gracious fashions he depicted.

galah. An Australian Aboriginal language gives us this name for the Australian cockatoo (*Kakatoe roseicapilla*) with its rose-colored underside. Because the bird's incessant raucous call makes it seem foolishly talkative, Australians have made its name a synonym for *fool*, as in "He made a galah of himself."

Galahad. The term is not much used anymore, except in jest, but a true gentleman is still sometimes called a Galahad, after the noble knight Sir Galahad of Arthurian legend. The noblest knight of all, Galahad was the son of Lancelot.

galatea. Here is a cotton fabric named for a ship. *Galatea*, often used to make children's sailor suits in the past, honors H.M.S. *Galatea*, a mighty British warship of the 1860s. The *Galatea*, in turn, took her name from the sea nymph Galatea of Greek mythology.

galaxy. The Greek *galaxis*, "circle of milk," a reference to the Milky Way, gives us our word *galaxy*, first recorded in about 1398.

galenical. A medicinal preparation composed mainly of herbal or vegetable matter is called a galenical. Opium, for example, would be among such drugs. The term honors Claudius Galen (ca. A.D. 129–99), who is known in history as the "prince of physicians." This Greek doctor and philosopher served as personal physician to Roman emperor Marcus Aurelius, and his writings were the most influential in medicine for a thousand years.

gallium. French chemist Paul-Emil Lecoq de Boisbaudran named this element after *Gallia*, the Latin name for present-day France, on discovering it, in 1874. Some etymologists suspect that the scientist may have been crowing a bit, however, as *le coq* means "rooster" in French and "rooster" is *gallus* in Latin.

galliwampus. A mythical monster of Texas, once described by O. Henry as "a mammal with fins on its back and 18 toes on its feet."

Gallup Poll. The Gallup Poll is the best known, though not the first, public-opinion poll. It was originated by Dr. George Horace Gallup (b. 1901), a professor of journalism at Northwestern University. Gallup developed his technique about 1933, basing it on carefully phrased questions and scientifically selected samples. He became prominent nationally by predicting the outcome of the 1936 American presidential election, when many other pollsters failed. His poll, operating both at home and abroad, has proved remarkably accurate but is far from infallible. In the 1948 national elections, for example, Gallup chose the late Governor Thomas E. Dewey over incumbent President Truman.

galoot. Often used in the form of *big galoot*, this word signifies a clumsy, ignorant, loutish person. Apparently sailor's slang for a soldier or landlubber, *galoot* is first recorded in the early 19th century but little else is known about its derivation.

galore. *Galore*, meaning "abundant," "plenty," "enough," derives from Irish Gaelic *go leor*, which has the same meaning. The British have used *galore* for at least four centuries, while Americans have been quite familiar with the word at least since Ian Fleming's James Bond 007 series, with its enticing character Pussy Galore. *Casino Royale*, Fleming's first Bond book, appeared in 1953.

galumph. *See* JABBERWOCKY.

galvanic; galvanism, etc. These words enshrine Luigi Galvani (1737–98), a brilliant physiologist at Italy's University of Bologna—although galvanism originally proved less than brilliant. Galvani's experiments began in about 1771. No one knows if his observant wife Lucia pointed out the first galvanic reaction, or if the professor had been preparing frog legs for her dinner—the tale has numerous versions—but one evening Galvani did notice that the skinned leg of a frog he was dissecting twitched when he touched it with a scalpel. After experimenting for about 20 years, Galvani wrote a paper concluding that the reaction had been produced by "animal electricity." Actually, the original frog's leg had twitched because his scalpel had touched the brass conductor of a nearby electrical machine, the charged knife shocking its muscles involuntarily "into life" with a current of electricity. Alessandro Volta quickly pointed out that the contact of two different metals really produced the electricity, but controversy raged between his and Galvani's supporters for years. Despite his monumental mistake, Galvani's name was lionized in numerous scientific terms indicating the use of direct current. Technically, we speak of *galvanizing* as shocking with an electric current, or *galvanizing* metal as giving it a protective zinc coating, while *galvanic* refers to electricity produced by chemical action. Yet the words have much broader nontechnical meanings when they imply arousal or stimulation, as when we say someone is *galvanized* into action by a *galvanic* happening—shocked into an excited response like Galvani's frog. *See* VOLT.

gam. No one knows the origins of this word for a sailor's bull session, or a chat, or conference, although it appears to have been first recorded as a sociable visit between two whaleships at sea. Herman Melville used and defined the word in *Moby Dick* (1850), which owed much to whaling chronicles of the day. Melville defined the word as: "A social gathering of two (or more) whale-ships, generally on a cruising-ground; when, after exchanging hails, they exchange visits by boats' crews; the two captains remaining for a time on board of one ship, and the two chief mates on the other." *Gam* was later used ashore, as in "I had a long gam with John yesterday," and the author a year or so ago heard it employed to describe two police patrol cars in Connecticut "gamming at the side of the road." Some etymologists suggest that the word *gam* for a pod of whales is the source, while others opt for the obsolete English word *gammon*, animated talk or chatter.

Gamalielese. Not many eponymous words derive from the middle names of people, but H. L. Mencken coined this one from President Warren Harding's middle name, Gamaliel. The word *Gamalielese* refers to the fractured language of Warren Gamaliel Harding, a man Mencken thought was a serial killer of English.

gamble away the sun before sunrise. This saying about gold and riches might be considered the first American proverb, though it isn't recorded in *Bartlett's* or any other book of quotations. The expression surely is old enough, dating back to 1533, when Pizarro conquered Cuzco, the capital of the Inca Empire, and stripped the Peruvian metropolis of gold and silver. One cavalryman got as his share of the booty a splendid golden image of the sun "which raised on a plate of burnished gold spread over the walls in a recess of the great temple" and which was so beautifully crafted that he did not have it melted down into coins, as was the usual practice. But the horseman came to symbolize the vice of gambling. That same night, before the sun had set on another day, he lost the fabulous golden image of the sun at cards or dice, and his comrades coined the saying *Juega el Sol antes que amanezca:* "He gambles (or plays) away the sun before sunrise," which crossed the ocean from America on Pizarro's gold-laden galleons and became proverbial in Spain.

gambrel roof. A type of roof named after a horse's leg. It is more specifically a ridged roof with two slopes on each side, with the lower side having the steeper pitch. John Bartlett's *Americanisms* (1848) says the roof is "so called from its resemblance to the hind leg of a horse which by farriers is termed the gambrel."

game. A game person is one who displays great courage and has the spirit of a gamecock (a cock bred and trained for cockfighting). *Gamecock* is first recorded in 1677 in the saying "Young lovers, like gamecocks, are made bolder by being kept without light," but cockfighting was brought to England by the Romans centuries before this. In the 12th century it was so popular that English schoolmasters permitted students to stage cockfighting contests, as long as all the birds killed were given to the teacher. The courage of these fighting birds was much admired and it is the likely reason that courageous people were called game long before the expression was first recorded in 1727.

game as Ned Kelly. It cost nearly half a million dollars to finally capture Australia's Kelly gang, even though the band was only four in number. Ned Kelly (1854–80), the son of a transported Belfast convict and a convicted horse thief himself, took to the hills with his brother Daniel when the latter was charged with horse stealing. Joined by two other desperados, the brothers held up towns and robbed banks for two years

until the police finally caught up with them. Ned Kelly became something of a folk hero, and the great deprivations he suffered led to the phrase *as game as Ned Kelly.* When the gang was traced at last to a wooden shanty hideout, police riddled it with bullets, burned the shack down and found Ned Kelly alive and dressed in a suit of armor. He was tried, convicted, and hanged for his crimes, without the iron suit.

the game is up. The Roman comic playwright Terence used essentially the same expression over 2,000 years ago, and the words may go back to the Greeks, considering the Romans' assimilative temperament. It means "all is over," "the plot can't succeed," "there's no longer any chance of winning." The expression *the jig is up*, referring always to a dishonest activity being over, is an Americanism first recorded in 1777. No one is sure of the origin of *jig*, though it may be from the dance called a jig or from an obsolete use of *jig* meaning "trick."

game leg. A game leg is a bad leg, the *game* here probably from the English dialect *gam* or *gammy*, both meaning crooked. The expression isn't recorded until late in the 18th century.

the game of the arrow. American artist George Catlin recorded this favorite (though little known) amusement of the Plains Indians: "The young men . . . assemble on the prairie [and] . . . step forward in turn, shooting their arrows into the air, endeavoring to see who can get the greatest number flying in the air at one time, thrown from the same bow."

game plan. Since the late 1950s *game plan* has meant the specific strategy a football team plans to use in a game. The term took on broader usage in politics and business after President Richard Nixon, an avid football fan, adopted it as a favorite expression in the 1970s.

gamesmanship. British author Stephen Potter coined this word in his 1947 book *The Theory and Practice of Gamesmanship, or The Art of Winning Games Without Actually Cheating. Gamesmanship* means "the use of dubious or seemingly improper methods that are not strictly illegal" and is almost an antonym of *sportsmanship*, upon which Potter probably based it.

the game's not worth the candle. In days past, card games were often played by candlelight at night. No doubt some of these nocturnal games were disparaged by high-stakes gamblers as penny ante games not worth playing in, or not worth the cost of the candle to play by, and this inspired the common expression *the game's not worth the candle.*

gammer. *See* GAFFER.

gammon and spinach. The expression *gammon and spinach* for "nonsense, humbug" is not as familiar today as it was in Dickens's time, when he used it in *David Copperfield:* "What a world of gammon and spinnage it is, though, ain't it!" The phrase, most likely an elaboration of the slang word *gammon*, which meant nonsense or a ridiculous story, is probably patterned on the older phrase *gammon and patter*, the language of London underworld thieves. The nonsense part of it was possibly reinforced by the old nursery rhyme "A Frog He Would

A-wooing Go" (1600) heard by millions: "With a rowley powley gammon and spinach/ Heigh ho! says Anthony Rowley."

gamp; brolly. *Gamp* is a term for an umbrella, especially an untidy one, in England, but is rarely, if ever, used in the U.S. The word comes to us from Charles Dickens's *The Life and Adventures of Martin Chuzzlewit* (1843–44), in which the garrulous and disreputable nurse Sarah Gamp always carries a bulky cotton umbrella. Her name is sometimes used for a midwife as well. *Brolly*, first recorded in 1873, is more commonly British slang for an umbrella today.

gams. In the U.S., since about 1900, *gams* has referred only to women's legs. But before then, in England, *gamb* meant any leg, especially a bare leg, and long prior to that *gamb* meant the leg of an animal, deriving from the late Latin *gamba*, "hoof or hock," from the Greek *kampi*, "bend, curve."

gandy dancer. There are several theories about this term for a railroad construction worker, which is immortalized in the song "The Gandy Dancer's Ball." One says *gandy dancer* is an American hobo term for fellow tramps who helped build the transcontinental railroad. Another claims the expression comes from the gander-like movements of these men as they worked, while a third and most probable theory opts for Chicago's Gandy Manufacturing Co., which made prominently marked track-laying tools used by the workers.

gangplank; gangboard; gangway. Whether it's called a *gangplank* or *gangboard*, the plank connecting a ship to land takes its name from the Old English *gang*, a way of passage, because it was a way of going on or off a ship. In time, *gangway* became a synonym.

gaol. Americans spell the word *jail*, though both words are pronounced the same in the U.S. and Great Britain. Other British spellings include *cheque* (check), *manoeuvre* (maneuver), *tyre* (tire), and *kerb* (curb).

garage. A garage originally was a place to moor a boat, not park a car. *Garage* is an early-19th-century French word meaning "a place where one docks." The French began to use *garage* for "a place to keep a vehicle in" when the automobile became popular early in the 20th century and the English soon borrowed the word from them.

Garand rifle. In the early 1930s, Canadian-born John Cantius Garand invented the semiautomatic *Garand*, which works on the principle of expanding gas, while employed as a civilian ordnance engineer at the U.S. Armory in Springfield, Massachusetts. The famous M-1 was adopted in 1936 as the official U.S. Army rifle. The .30-caliber, eight-shot, clip-loading weapon proved to be a great improvement on the old standard Springfield, firing up to four times as many shots, or 100 rounds per minute, and contributed greatly to the Allied victory in World War II. Garand was never paid a cent in royalties for his invention, and never earned more than $12,000 a year in his 34-year service with the U.S. Ordnance Corps.

garbage. There are several possibilities here. Wrong as usual, folk etymology has it that *garbage* derives from the Latin *gerbe*, "green stuff," reflecting the nobility's scorn for vegetables in centuries past. Another possibility is the French *gerbe*, "wheat, hay and other vegetative matter chopped up together for horse fodder." *Garbage* may also derive from the Italian *garbuglio*, for "confused intrigue," hence confusion, a mess—the intrigue part appropriate for our modern-day *garbologists*, people who apparently first appeared in the 1970s to make their living by poking through the garbage of celebrities and others at the top of the heap and learning their deep, dark, dirty secrets.

garbled. The Arabic *gharbala* means to sift something or purify it. The word became *garble* in English and by the 17th century came to mean to sift information selectively so that it is distorted or muddled. Soon the meaning of distorted was discarded and today *garbled* only means muddled, mixed up, unclear. One would suspect that the sound of *garbled* itself contributed to this final transformation.

garden. *Gardins* or *jardins* were originally fruit and vegetable plots that monks in medieval France enclosed, or guarded, to keep cattle and other animals away from their plants. By the early 14th century the word *gardin* was being used in England, but it wasn't spelled *garden* for another 100 years or so.

garden bed; bed of roses. The term *garden bed* probably owes its origin to the beds we sleep in, like the shape or purpose of the garden bed. However, the word *bed* itself may come from a Teutonic word meaning "a dugout place, a lair," and the term *garden bed* could have come directly from there. English-speaking people have been using the expression since at least A.D. 1000. The expression *to bed out* plants is recorded as early as 1671 in a gardening manual but is probably much older. Shakespeare used the old phrase *bed of roses*, and it may have been popular centuries before him. It seems to have first been employed by the poet Robert Herrick and means a situation of luxurious ease, a highly agreeable position of comfort or pleasure. A variant seldom heard anymore is *a bed of flowers*.

gardenia. "Mr. Miller has called it Basteria. But if you will please to follow my advice, I would call it Gardenia, from our worthy friend Dr. Alexander Garden of S. Carolina." "If Dr. Garden will send me a new genus, I shall be truly happy to name it after him, Gardenia." These quotations from an exchange of letters between a friend of Linnaeus and the great botanist himself, 1757–58, reveal the politicking that is sometimes involved even in naming something. Linnaeus did honor his promise to their mutual friend and two years later dedicated a newly discovered tropical shrub to Garden, even though the amateur botanist did not discover the beautiful, sweet-smelling *gardenia*. Dr. Alexander Garden (ca. 1730–91), a Scottish-American physician, resided in Charleston, South Carolina, where he practiced medicine and also devoted much of his time to collecting plant and animal specimens, discovering the Congo eel and a number of snakes and herbs. Garden carried on an extensive correspondence with Linnaeus and many other European naturalists, probably as much out of loneliness as for intellectual stimulation. An ardent Tory, he returned to England during the Revolutionary War, resuming his practice in London and becoming vice-president of the Royal Society. Dr. Garden was by all accounts a difficult, headstrong man. When his granddaughter was named Gardenia Garden in his honor, he still refused to see her. After all, her father had fought against the British!

Garden of Eden.   Ths most famous garden of all. Located, it is said, at El Mezey near Damascus, where the waters of the Tege and Barrady divide into four streams that are said to be the four streams of Moses mentioned in Genesis. But, on second thought, many places have been called the original Garden of Eden, among them Persia (Iran); Armenia; Chaldea; Basra; southern Iraq; Israel; Egypt; East Africa; Java; Ceylon; China; Lemuria; the Seychelles Islands; Sweden; and, yes, Mars, by Brinsley Le Poer Trench in his book *The Sky People*. In the late 19th century, Galesville, Wisconsin, was proposed as the site of the biblical garden, and in recent times Baptist minister Elvy E. Calloway has claimed the honor for Bristol, Florida, offering as "proof," among other evidence, the fact that Bristol, on the banks of the Apalachicola River, is the only place in the U.S. where gopher wood (the Torrey tree) grows, Noah having made his ark of gopher wood. In the 17th century a Swedish professor even wrote a book attempting to prove that the fabled garden had been located in the Land of the Midnight Sun. At Al-Qurna in Iraq, the site of so much recent bloodshed, there is a sign that stands outside a little enclosure around a tree, reading: "On this holy spot where the Tigris meets the Euphrates this holy tree of our father Abraham grew symbolizing the Garden of Eden on earth. Abraham prayed here two thousand years B.C." A Garden of Eden is sometimes termed a "Garden of Paradise," as it is in Ceylon. There, Ceylonese point to the Adam's apple tree (*Tabernaemontana coronaria*) when claiming their country as the original Eden. The small tree or shrub bears an attractive fruit with a shape suggesting that a piece has been bitten off, and the Ceylonese say that it was delicious before Eve and Adam ate of it, though it became poisonous after their "fall." *See* ADAM'S APPLE TREE.

Garden of the Gods.   An area near Colorado Springs, Colorado, noted for over a century for its great natural beauty.

Garden State.   A nickname for New Jersey, which has had an abundance of nicknames, including the Jersey Blue State, New Spain, the Clam State, and even, strangely, the Switzerland of America (which mountainous New Hampshire has also been called). In the late 19th century New Jersey was known as the Mosquito State, though its mosquitos are no match for Alaska's.

gargantuan.   Broad, coarse exuberant humor and sharp satire mark the *Rabelaisian* spirit or style. The word honors the prodigious French humanist and humorist François Rabelais (ca. 1490–1553), who "drank deep as any man," of life as well as wine. Rabelais, whose voracious appetites would have sufficed for any two ordinary men, started out as a Benedictine monk, later turning physician, but his reputation rests on his ribald writing, a paean to the good life—love, drink, food—a satire on the bigotry and blindness of Church, state, and pedant. Gross and noble at the same time, marked by vast scholarship, his masterpieces are *Pantagruel* (1533) and *Gargantua* (1535). The last book, though Gargantua had been a figure in French folklore, gives us the word *gargantuan*—"enormous, gigantic"—from the giant prince of prodigious appetite, who was 11 months in the womb, as an infant needed the milk of 17,913 cows, combed his hair with a 900-foot-long comb, once ate six

pilgrims in a salad, and lived for several centuries. Pantagruel, Gargantua's son, is just as famous and classic a character.

Garibaldi shirt; Garibaldi fish.   In the crowning achievement of his eventful life, Giuseppe Garibaldi, commanding his 1,000 Redshirt volunteers, conquered Sicily, crossed back to the Italian mainland and expelled King Francis II from Naples. One year later in 1861, Italy was united under King Victor Emmanuel II and Garibaldi became an international hero. Both a woman's loose, high-necked blouse with full sleeves—similar to those worn by his followers—and a currant biscuit were named for him, as well as an edible, brilliant orange fish (*Hypsypopa rubicundus*) discovered off the southern California coast by Italian-American fishermen.

garlic.   Owing to its resemblance to the leek, garlic, the herb that "makes men drink and wink and stink," takes its name from the Old English *garleac: gar*, "spear," and *leac*, "leek." The Romans believed garlic contained magical powers and hung it over their doors to ward off witches, just as some people wear cloves around their necks to protect themselves against colds, diseases, and even vampires. *Pilgarlic* is an interesting word once used to mean a "baldheaded man." It takes its name from the early English *pyllyd garleke*, "peeled garlic," for someone whose head resembles a shiny peeled garlic bulb. Since many bald-headed men were old and pitiful, the word came to take on the meaning of a person regarded with mild contempt or pity, an old fool or someone in a bad way. *See* ONION.

garnet.   *See* POMEGRANATE.

Garret election.   Presumably, there are no more bawdy Garret elections *anywhere*, but such popular ceremonies were held near Wandsworth, London in the 18th century. There in the borough of Garret, a small hamlet consisting of "a few struggling cottages," the ludicrous "election" was held with the opening of every new parliament, the only voting qualification being "open-air coition in or near Garret." According to an account of the time: "The ceremony consists of a mock election of two members to represent the borough of Garret. The qualification of a voter is having enjoyed a woman in the open air within that district. The candidates are commonly fellows of low humour who dress themselves up in a ridiculous manner. As this brings a prodigious concourse of people to Wandsworth, the publicans of that place jointly contribute to the expenses, which is sometimes considerable." Similar elections might prove the answer to voter apathy in the U.S.

Garrison finish.   Holding Montana back from the pack until they came into the homestretch, "Snapper" Garrison suddenly stood high in the stirrups, bending low over the horse's mane in his famous "Yankee seat" and whipped the mount toward the finish line, moving up with a rush and winning the 1882 Suburban Handicap by a nose. This race made jockey Edward H. Garrison an American turf hero. Garrison, who died in 1931, aged 70, used his new technique many times over his long career, winning many of his races in the last furlong, and the Garrison finish became so well-known that it was applied to any close horse race, finally becoming synonymous with all last-minute efforts—in sports, politics, or any other field.

garryowen. In rugby a garryowen is a high punt the offensive team uses to gain ground when the forwards are rushing downfield. It takes its name from the Irish rugby club Garryowen, well known for using the tactic. *Garry Owen* is also the name of a martial song and the name of General George Armstrong Custer's horse.

garum; titmuck. It is hard to find anything good to say about the legendary Roman sauce garum, but the ancient Romans loved it. Their garum was made from the putrified guts of fish, blended with fish blood and gills in an open tub, salted heavily, then exposed to the sun, where they were stirred occasionally until the whole mess fermented and herbs were added. At the legendary banquet of the Roman merchant Trimalchio, statuettes of four satyrs in the corners of the room poured vile-smelling garum sauce over fish molded to appear almost alive, to make it seem as if they were swimming in a jelly sea. The only thing comparable to it available today is titmuck, an Eskimo salmon delicacy that ripens in a hole filled with dirt and grass until it decays.

gas; gasoline. Though it is also the abbreviation of *gasoline*, *gas* is the older of the two words. *Gasoline* made its debut in the late 19th century when scientists coined it (from *gas* plus the Latin *oleum*, "oil," and *ine*) to describe the colorless liquid obtained by the fractional distillation of petroleum. *Gas* itself was coined nearly three centuries earlier by Dutch physician and chemist Jean Baptiste van Helmont (1577–1644). Van Helmont thought that he had discovered an occult principle contained in all bodies and named his discovery *gas* from the German *chaos*, "chaos." He had little understanding of the nature of gases, and no one knows exactly what sense of the word *chaos* he had in mind when he coined *gas* from it. But despite all this chaos, he was *cooking with gas*, for his invention has become part of almost every language.

gasconade. The Gascon inhabitants of Gascony, France, a region and former province near the Spanish border, have traditionally been regarded by other Frenchmen as flamboyantly boastful, a poor people except in bravery and bragging. This tradition can be seen in Dumas's *The Three Musketeers*, where brave, boastful d'Artagnan is the model of a Gascon. Many old French *contes* illustrated Gascon braggadocio. One tells of a Gascon being asked how he liked the great Louvre in Paris. "Pretty well," the braggart replies, "It reminds me of the back part of my father's stables." Such stories and the sentiments that inspire them led to the coining of *gasconade*, "extravagant boasting or swashbuckling braggadocio," a word that became universal because it described so many people other than Gascons.

gasper. *Gasper* is British slang for a cigarette, for obvious reasons. Although the term isn't common in the U.S., an excellent novel by Frank Freudberg about the cigarette industry is entitled *Gasp!*

gat. *See* GATLING GUN.

Gate City. A nickname now or in the past for several cities, including Atlanta and Louisville, because they are each situated at the entrance to a region. Atlanta is also called the Gate City of the South.

gate crashing. *See* CRASH.

Gateway to the West. An old nickname for Pittsburgh, Pennsylvania; also called Gate City of the West.

gathering nuts in May. Since there are no nuts to be gathered in May, the old children's song that goes, "Here we go gathering nuts in May" seems to make no sense—and indeed, it may have been intended as a nonsense song. But the *nuts* in the phrase has been explained as being *knots* of May, that is, bunches of flowers. In Elizabethan England Elizabeth herself gathered knots of May in the meadows, one author tells us, and this is a plausible explanation, even though there are no recorded quotations supporting the use of *knots* for flowers, except possibly the English knot gardens of herbs.

Gatling gun. The Gatling gun won fame as the best of the 11 mostly eponymous Civil War machine guns (including the Ripley; the Ager "Coffee Mill"; the Claxon; the Gorgas; and the Williams, which, when used by the Confederates on May 3, 1862, became the first machine gun to be fired in warfare). Designed by Doctor Richard Jordan Gatling (1818–1903), a North Carolina physician and inventor, the Gatling was perfected by 1862 but adopted by Union forces too late to be used in more than a few battles. Mounted on wheels, it had a cluster of 5 to 10 barrels that revolved around a central shaft. The gunner, by turning a hand crank, controlled the rate of fire, up to 350 rounds per minute. Despite the weapon's late introduction, the Gatling's effective range of 2,000 yards had a strong psychological effect on the Confederacy; adopted by many nations after the Civil War, it remained in use until about 1900. Although the weapon is of only historical importance today, as the precursor of the modern machine gun, another word deriving from it has wide currency. *Gat*, a slang term for a small gun, apparently arose as a humorous exaggeration. By 1880, however, fictional characters were talking of having gatlins under their coats and it wasn't long before *gatlin*, or *gatling*, was shortened to *gat*.

gaucho. Since the early 18th century *gaucho* has meant a cowboy of the South American pampas, often a *mestizo* of mixed Spanish and Indian ancestry and always a skilled horseman and soldier with an independent spirt and a wanderlust. The gauchos have been in decline for over a century and so have the *payadors*, the singing minstrels of the plains, much of the plains now being farmed. Gauchos may take their name from Quechua Indian *wahcha*, "a vagabond or poor person," but Arawak *cachu*, "comrade," is a possibility, too.

Gaullist. A Frenchman practicing right-wing nationalistic politics in France is often called a Gaullist, the term known in France and throughout the world. The word of course honors Charles André Joseph Marie de Gaulle (1890–1970), the tall, imposing first president of France from 1958–69. General de Gaulle, a great patriot who had led the Free French during World War II, did not become active in French politics until he was almost 70. He once remarked while in office, "I myself have become a Gaullist only little by little."

gauntlet. *See* THROW DOWN THE GAUNTLET.

gauss. Known as "the prince of mathematicians," and possibly the greatest mathematical genius of all time, Karl Friedrich Gauss (1777–1855) was a German prodigy who when only 10 discovered independently how to sum up complex arithmetic series. He did much important work in his field before turning 21, including a proof of the fundamental theorem of algebra, but did not confine himself to mathematics. Of his many important contributions in topology, physics, and astronomy—he headed the Gottingen Observatory—one of the most valuable is his founding of the mathematical theory of electricity. Thus the gauss, a unit of intensity of the magnetic field, pays honor to his name.

gauze. *Eyeless in Gaza* and the *Gaza Strip* are phrases well known to readers of the Bible and history, but few people know that the city of Gaza on the Mediterranean Sea gives its name to the light filmy fabric called *gauze*, which was first manufactured there.

gay. Some commentators have argued that *gay*, used to describe a homosexual, makes obsolete older, more traditional uses of the word, and that, besides, homosexuals are as morose as anybody else. But no one can legislate word usage, and what the language at the time needs, it takes. *Gay* came into use in the 1950s, possibly originating from the older (ca. 1935) term *gaycat*, for "a homosexual boy." In addition to suggesting gaiety, *gay* has also had strong links with "affectation, dissipation, and immoral life" for over three centuries.

gay Lothario. Lothario's boastful speech from Nicholas Rowe's tragedy in blank verse *The Fair Penitent* (1703) explains why his name became a synonym for a libertine or seducer. Lothario isn't by any means a model lover, for Calista, the fair penitent, stabs herself after being seduced by him. Wounded in a duel, he dies claiming: "In Love I Triumphed: Those joys are lodg'd beyond the reach of Fate . . ." Rowe apparently stole the plot for his play from Massinger and Field's *Fatal Dowery* (1632), shortening it and modifying the ending, and borrowed Lothario's name and character from William D'Avenant's tragedy *The Cruel Brothers* (1630), though Lothario is also the name of characters in Cervantes's *Don Quixote* and Goethe's *Wilhelm Meister*. Rowe's play, a favorite of Dr. Johnson's, was extremely popular for over a century, the legendary David Garrick playing the lead for a time, and made "the haughty, gallant, gay Lothario" proverbial. Lothario's philosophy might be summed up in his lines: "The driving storm of Passion will have way, and I must yield before it."

Gay Nineties. *See* NAUGHTY NINETIES.

gazebo. A gazebo is a garden structure of Dutch origin that was originally built of stone or brick. It is now a small, wooden-roofed building that is screened on all sides and set apart from the house to provide an attractive view of the garden. The word's origin is uncertain. One unproved theory holds that this word for a garden lookout or belvedere is a humorous invention of some 18th-century wit, who modeled it on the word *gaze*, pretending that gaze was a Latin word (it is of unknown origin), which would make gazebo the future form "I shall see" of that hypothetical verb. Nor has anyone proved that the word is from some obscure Chinese source, as its brief first-recorded use in 1752 in an architectural book suggests to some etymologists: "The Elevation of a Chinese tower of Gazeba."

gazette. Newspapers were first called *gazettas* in 16th-century Venice, where they were so named because one could be bought with a Venetian coin of small value called a *gazeta*. By 1605 we find Ben Jonson using the word in English, though it wasn't spelled in its present form for another 75 years or so.

gazumping. A term coined in Britain that is often heard in the U.S. and Australia as well. The word, when used in relation to real estate transactions, refers to the practice of a seller refusing to honor an agreement with a buyer and selling his property to someone else for more money. No one knows with certainty the origin of *gazumping*, which was first recorded in 1928, referring to swindling in general.

gear. 1980s slang for clothes, replacing "threads," "vines," etc., in the inner city, the word *gear* derives from the common term for military or outdoor equipment, including clothing, and was either introduced by Vietnam veterans or associated with the Army-Navy "surplus stores" where the young often buy clothing that sets styles. French designer Jean-Charles de Castelbajac had even introduced the *Gear Look* for the not so young with money, "rough-hewn outdoorsy materials translated into high fashion." *Gear* was standard English for the female and male sexual organs from the 16th to the 19th century.

gee! An American euphemism for "Jesus!" *gee!* dates back to only 1895. Its antecedents are *jewillikin* (1851); *gee whillikins!* (1857); *gee whiz!* (1895); *gee whitaker!* (1895); and *holy gee!* Since then we have had *jeez!* (1900); *jeepers!* (1920s); and *jeepers creepers!* (1934). *See also* JIMINY CRICKET.

gee and haw. Cries meaning "turn right" and "turn left" respectively, used when working mules, horses, and oxen. These old terms date back to 17th-century England, and their derivations are unknown.

gee-gee. This term for a poor or mediocre racehorse isn't an Americanism. It can be traced back to England over 150 years ago and derives from the turning command *gee* given to a workhorse pulling a wagon. A racehorse called a *gee-gee* is thus compared to a common workhorse. *Gee* alone was also English slang for a horse.

geek. The carnival "wild man," usually an alcoholic, who bit off the heads of chickens; any person who has sunk to the lowest depths of degradation, or who is odd and ridiculous. The word is a variation on the English word *geck* for a fool, which dates back to the 16th century and was used by Shakespeare among other great writers.

geezer. *See* OLD GEEZER.

gefilte fish. Hot or cold it is delicious, but the Jewish delicacy, made with many ingredients and traditionally served on Friday nights, is *not* a separate species of fish. Gefilte fish is a kind of fish loaf made of various ground fish, eggs, onions, pepper, salt, and sometimes sugar—every good cook having her or his secret recipe. The "stuffed fish." is more properly called *gefilte fisch* in Yiddish. *See* SLEEPS AT THE BOTTOM OF THE OCEAN.

Geiger counter.   The Geiger counter is sometimes called the Geiger-Muller counter, for both German physicist Hans Geiger (1882–1945) and the scientist who helped him improve upon it in 1927. Actually it might better be named the *Geiger-Rutherford-Muller counter,* because the New Zealand–born British physicist Ernest Rutherford had invented the device, with Geiger, 15 years earlier. The clicking electronic counter, which measures nuclear radiation, is owned by many hopeful prospectors today and widely used as a safety device; it is also employed in medicine to locate malignancies. Geiger designed other types of counters as well.

gelati.   Italian *gelati* have become more popular in America over the past 10 years. *Gelato* is the Italian for ice cream, and the delicacy, which is folded rather than churned when made, has a much higher butter-fat content than any other kind of ice cream.

gelt; mazuma; shekels.   The first slang term for money given here owes its currency to Yiddish. *Gelt* derives from the German *Geld,* "money," and has been common here since the mid 19th century, in England since 1698. *Mazuma,* usually a more humorous term, possibly derives from the Hebrew *mezumman* "the ready necessary," or money. For some strange reason *mazuma* was first recorded (1907) in a book about Kansas, of all places. The *shekel,* the first money mentioned in the Bible (Gen. 33:12–16), was a silver coin weighing about two-thirds of an ounce, common in ancient times. In the plural it has come to mean money in general, since at least the mid-19th century.

Gem of the Mountains.   A nickname for Idaho, often erroneously said to be a translation of the state's name (*see* IDAHO). Idaho has also been called the Gem State and Little Ida. Residents of Idaho are called Idahoans or Idahovans.

Gene Autry.   Gene Autry, Oklahoma; is named after the popular singer and film star of the 1940s and 1950s. It is perhaps the only American city named after a movie star, unless one counts Tarzan, Texas.

generation.   *Generation* derives ultimately from Latin *genus,* birth. There is no definite period of years for a generation; it is the average interval of time between the birth of parents and the birth of their children. A generation is a period of more than 50 years in the Old Testament. Today a generation is generally considered to be 30 to 33 years in length, about three generations to a century.

Generation X.   The generation born roughly between 1960 and 1975, one which has often been described as another directionless, disaffected LOST GENERATION. The term became popular with the publication of Douglas Coupland's novel *Generation X: Tales for an Accelerated Culture* in 1991, but had actually been coined 27 years earlier as the title of a book by Charles Hamblett and Jane Deverson entitled *Generation X.*

Generation Xers are often called "Xers" and "slackers," the latter from a 1991 film of that name. *See* BABY BOOM.

genius award.   A name invented by the media for the MacArthur Fellowships, which are grants given annually by the MacArthur Foundation. The awards are given in many disciplines, from astrophysics to writing, valued at about $500,000, distributed over five years. Some 25 "geniuses" are chosen each year from candidates nominated by various authorities, whose identity is kept secret.

genius does what it must.   *See* TALENT DOES WHAT IT CAN.

genocide.   Acts intended to destroy national, ethnic, racial, or religious groups are called *genocide,* the word based on the Greek *genos,* "race," and the Latin *cadere,* "to kill." The word was invented by Professor Raphael Lemkin of Duke University and used in the official indictment of Nazi criminals in 1945; three years later the United Nations made genocide a crime against international law.

gentian.   Among the loveliest wild flowers, the fringed gentian, has been immortalized by Bryant and other poets, and the large *Gentiana* genus to which it belongs, containing some 400 species, provides us with many valued alpine plants for the rock garden. *Gentians* take their name from the powerful monarch Gentius, who reigned as king of Illyria about 180–167 B.C. and who was first to experience the medicinal value of gentians, according to Pliny and Dioscorides. Since early times the roots and rhizome of the European yellow gentian (*Gentiana lutea*) have been used to dilate wounds, as a bitter tonic and counterpoison, and in curing diseases. Certain alcoholic beverages are made from the plant, too. The beautiful flowers, predominantly blue, despite *Gentians lutea,* are generally found at high altitudes. Difficult to cultivate, they are nevertheless extensively grown in the home garden. *Gentianaceae,* the *Gentian* family, consisting of 800 species and 30 genera, also bears the Illyrian king's name.

Gentlemen, get in your cars.   Words traditionally said to drivers at the start of the Indianapolis 500, America's premier race-car event. An extremely dangerous race, it inspired one sportswriter to change the words to "Gentlemen, get in your coffins." (I am unsure of the identity of the writer [the *New York Times*'s Ira Berkow?]. Perhaps some reader could be of help). Another famous phrase from Indianapolis is "Gentlemen, start your engines."

Gentlemen prefer blondes.   *Gentlemen Prefer Blondes* (1925) was the title of the Anita Loos (1893–1981) novel, but the words in the text were, "Gentlemen always seem to remember blondes." Her famous book, made into a play and movie, had such diverse admirers as James Joyce, George Santayana, Mussolini, and Churchill, and was written as a spoof of her good friend Mencken's taste for "dumb blondes." Loos herself was a brunette and wrote a sequel to her book, *But Gentlemen Marry Brunettes* (1926), among over a hundred books and screenplays, including her script for D. W. Griffith's masterpiece *Intolerance.* She considered Hollywood a "mink-lined rut," and, as for men, "always believed in the old adage, 'Leave them while you're looking good.' "

gentoo. *Gentoo*, for prostitute, is a South African word that may come from a disparaging Hindi term for a Hindu who speaks Teluga rather than Hindi. But it possibly derives from the name of the *Gentoo*, a ship transporting female servants to Africa that was wrecked on the South African coast. The women were saved but lost all their belongings and were forced to work as prostitutes in gentoo houses to support themselves. *Gentoo*, first recorded in 1638, also means a heathen.

geoduck. The geoduck clam (*Panope generosa*) of the Pacific Coast and elsewhere is pronounced "qweduc" by *Webster's* and "gooeyduck" by its diggers. This enormous intertidal clam takes its name from the Nisqualli *geoduck*, "dig deep." The clam indolently suns itself on warm days, its huge neck so prominent emerging from the sand, the *West Coast Cookbook* (1952) tells us, "that ladies of an earlier day stayed at a discreet distance when their men went hunting them . . . the hunt of the reclining geoduck, it was hinted, not being quite nice." The geoduck is hard to catch. As soon as the huge clam senses danger, it begins digging furiously into the sand and one has to dig all the faster; two people are usually required to beat the clam at its game.

geography. *Ge*, the Greek word for earth, is the basis for many words, including *geography, geology, geometry, geocentric, geodetic*, and even *Gaea*, the Greek goddess of the earth, who sprang from primordial Chaos, produced Uranus, and then married him and was the mother of Cronus, the Titans, the Cyclopes, and the Hundred-headed Giants, who gave us such words as *chronology* and *titanic*.

Geordie. A dialect spoken in northeastern England. Some authorities say it derives from the regional pronunciation of the name George (Geordie), but others give an assist to the name of George Stephanson, the famous local resident who constructed the world's first practical steam engine in 1814 and has ever since been associated with the area. The region is often called "Geordieland." *See* COCKNEY.

George. Though it may have originated 30 years or so earlier, *George* for anything good, O.K., or excellent ("that's real George") was most popular during the 1950s. No one knows if there was a real George behind the expression (certainly not George Washington, whose first name is slang for a dollar bill because of his picture on it, and surely not either of the two other U.S. presidents named George). Perhaps *George* here derives from the name of the French cardinal Georges d'Amboise of LET GEORGE DO IT.

George Spelvin; Harry Selby; Walter Plinge. Playwright Winchell Smith's 1906 dramatization of George Barr McCutcheon's *Brewster's Millions*, a perennial favorite, included among its cast members a "George Spelvin." This was a second fictitious name given in the playbill to a member of the cast who played two parts. Since that day "George Spelvin" has had the same theatrical use. Though Smith's play widely popularized the name, it had been used in this way as early as 1886 in Charles A. Gardiner's *Karl the Peddler*. It has since been given to dolls substituted for infants, to animals, and even to dead bodies in movies and play credits, having been used well over 10,000 times in Broadway productions alone. At one time, a club of Broadway actors was called the Spelvin Club. "Harry Selby" is another fictitious name used in the same way but far less frequently. In England "Walter Plinge" is similarly employed. One version of this story claims that the fictitious Walter Plinge was a genial bartender working at a pub near the Lyceum Theatre about 1900. His policy of easy credit endeared him to the players, who immortalized his name in print. *See* ALAN SMITHEE.

georgette. Whether she invented it or not isn't known, but the finespun fabric *georgette* honors Madame Georgette de la Plante, a celebrated Parisian dressmaker and modiste of the late 19th century. The formerly trademarked sheer silk crepe is used primarily for blouses and gowns. It is sometimes called *crêpe georgette*.

Georgia. Georgia is named for George II of England (1683–1760). Discovered by Hernando de Soto in 1540, it became the last of the 13 original colonies in 1732 when a British charter was granted for the establishment of "the Colony of Georgia in America." George II, a methodical man who "took the greatest pleasure in counting his money piece by piece, and . . . never forgot a date," wasn't a particularly popular monarch. Historians straining for something interesting to say about him seem only to be able to tell us that he was the last British sovereign to command an army in the field—at the battle of Dettingen (June 27, 1743) in the War of the Austrian Succession.

Georgian. Anything to do with the reign of the British monarch George III (1738–1820), who was king for 60 years, from 1760 until his death. This would include Georgian poetry, Georgian architecture, Georgian literature, Georgian furniture, etc. George III was not a popular king and was more than a bit unbalanced (it was said that he "lost America and then lost his wits."). Wrote Edmund Clerihew Bentley in a CLERIHEW about the monarch: "George the Third / Ought never to have occurred / One can only wonder / At so grotesque a blunder." *See* PEACOCK.

geranium. The beaked seed pods of these flowers resembled the head and beak of a crane, the Greeks thought, and so they named the plant for the crane, *geranos* in Greek. This family of flowers, containing about 250 species, does not include the very popular common garden geranium (*Pelargonium*) so widely grown today, which was mistaken for it over the years and so shares its name. *Pelargonium*, however, is from the Greek for "stork," an allusion to the shape of its fruit.

germ. The Latin word *germen*, "sprout," is the ultimate root of *germ*. Long before it meant the seed of a disease, a usage first recorded in 1803, *germ* meant "any portion of a living thing, animal or vegetable, that is capable of development into a likeness of that from which it sprang." Hence the name *wheat germ* for the tiny living protoplasm in the wheat kernel.

German measles; German shepherd; etc. During both World Wars anything *German* was anathema to her enemies. As Mencken points out, Bismarck herring became *Eisenhower herring*, sauerkraut, *liberty cabbage*, and German measles even became *liberty measles. German measles*, or rubella, is a milder virus disease than measles, though particularly dangerous to the offspring of pregnant women who are exposed to it; the *German* may be spurious in that sense, but the disease could be so named because it was first identified by Dr. Friedrich Hoffmann, a German physician, in 1740. Similarly, *German silver* was initially made at Hildburghausen, Germany, although the fact that it is a silvery alloy, a fake silver compound of copper, nickel, and zinc, may have influenced its name. Typical of words using the national adjective is the now ubiquitous *German shepherd* guard dog. *See* MEASLY; ROTTWEILER.

German words in English.   English is of course structurally Germanic and is considered a Germanic language because of its Anglo-Saxon roots, but many words from Germanic languages have come into English at a later time in history, from the Middle Ages up until the present. A brief sample of these include: junker, lobby, carouse, plunder, saber, zinc, hamster, cobalt, shale, quartz, feldspar, gneiss, nickel, meerschaum, waltz, zigzag, iceberg, poodle, spitz, dachshund, zither, leitmotiv, yodel, protein, paraffin, ohm, poltergeist, rucksack, semester, kindergarten, seminar, poker, and bum. Words in American English of German origin include the following: fresh (impudent), bub, hex, hausfrau, loafer, nix, ouch, phooey, wunderkind, spiel, Kris Kringle, Christmas tree, semester, seminar, noodle, sauerkraut, pretzel, lager beer, bock beer, frankfurter, hamburger, liverwurst, sauerbraten, pumpernickel, schnitzel, delicatessen, snits, wienerwurst, zweiback, stollen, dunk, bake oven, and how!, cookbook, ecology, gabfest, check (restaurant tab), hold on, hoodlum, klutz, loafer, rifle, scram, slim chance, shyster, gesundheit, schnapps, standpoint, wisenheimer, wanderlust.

Geronimo!   Chiricahua Apache leader Geronimo is said to have made a daring leap on horseback to escape U.S. cavalry pursuers at Medicine Bluffs, Oklahoma. As he leaped to freedom down a steep cliff and into a river below he supposedly cried out his name in defiance of the troopers. There is no mention of this incident in the great warrior and prophet's autobiography, which he dictated to a white writer before his death under military confinement at Fort Sill, Oklahoma, in 1909. But by that time Geronimo was an old man, well over 70, and had converted to the Dutch Reformed Church; little remained of the brave leader who in protecting his people's land against white settlers had terrorized the American Southwest and northern Mexico with cunning, brutal raids and whose actions became western legend. The cry *Geronimo!* is part of that legend and was adopted as the battle cry of American paratroopers leaping from their planes in World War II. The 82nd Airborne at Fort Bragg, North Carolina first used it, taking it either from the oral legend about Geronimo or from the popular movie featuring the Indian warrior, showing near the paratrooper training center at the time.

gerrymander.   Above editor Benjamin Russell's desk in the offices of the *Centinel*, a Massachusetts Federalist newspaper, hung the serpentine-shaped map of a new Essex County senatorial district that began at Salisbury and included Amesbury, Haverhill, Methuen, Andover, Middleton, Danvers, Lynnfield, Salem, Marblehead, Lynn, and Chelsea. This political monster was part of a general reshaping of voting districts that the Democratic-Republican-controlled state legislature had enacted with the approval of incumbent Governor Elbridge Gerry. The

arbitrary redistricting would have happily enabled the Jeffersonians to concentrate Federalist power in a few districts and remain in the majority after the then yearly gubernatorial elections of 1812, and was of course opposed by the Federalists. So when the celebrated painter Gilbert Stuart visited the *Centinel* offices one day before the elections, editor Russel indignantly pointed to the monstrous map on the wall, inspiring Stuart to take a crayon and add head, wings, and claws to the already lizard-shaped district. "That will do for a salamander," the artist said when he had finished. "A *Gerry*-mander, you mean," Russell replied, and a name for the political creature was born, *gerrymander* coming into use as a verb within a year.

Gestapo.   *Gestapo* is a contraction formed from *Geheime Staats Polizei*, the NAZI secret state police agency that was formally declared a criminal organization at the Nuremberg trials. Founded in 1933 by Hermann Göring, it came under Heinrich Himmler's control as part of the S.S. the following year. The group's ruthless methods of capture, torture, and extermination, the fact that it was responsible for all concentration camps, and its exemption from any control by the courts made it the symbol for brutal, sadistic repression that it is today.

get a break.   There are several explanations for this expression meaning "to have some good luck," but no one is certain of its origins. It has been suggested that *to get a break* might come from a *break* in pool. When a player breaks the racked balls in a pool game a good number may be pocketed, putting that player in a good position to make a long, successful run.

get a horse!   A phrase from the early age of the automobile in the U.S. when motor cars were often mired in ditches or chugged slowly down the street, and people, especially children, would shout "get a horse!" to the motorists manning them. The phrase is not obsolete as some writers have it. I have heard it directed at runners or joggers several times in the last few years—mostly by children.

get a rise out of someone.   These words first applied to fish rising to the bait. Writers on the art of angling popularized the word *rise* in this sense 300 years ago, and the metaphor from fly-fishing became standard English. Just as the fish rises to the bait and is caught, the person who *rises* to the lure of a practical joke becomes the butt of it. From its original meaning of raising a laugh at someone's expense, the expression has been extended to include the idea of attracting attention in general—getting a rise out of a sales prospect, etc.

get by the short hairs.   It is widely assumed that the *short hairs* here are the pubic hairs, and *short hairs* is, in fact, slang for the hair around the genitals. George P. Burnham first used the expression in the form "get where the hair is short" in his *Memoirs of the United States Secret Service* (1872), and some department of dirty tricks no doubt invented it. But to get complete mastery over a person by grabbing his or her pubic hair would be difficult, to say the least, even if he were naked. So would holding someone by the short hairs at the nape of the neck, another explanation. Maybe the relatively short hairs of the beard provide a logical answer, and there is a much earlier expression *to take by the beard* that means about the same thing.

get in one's hair. Shakespeare wrote "Thou art ever in my beard," but it took almost another three centuries before someone invented "You get in my hair." That someone is anonymous, but the expression describing somebody or something persistently annoying a person is of American origin. The phrase is first recorded in an Oregon newspaper in 1851 and no explanation is given for it. The obvious explanation is that the original comparison was to lice, or "cooties," getting in the hair and irritating the scalp, but the possibilities are limitless.

get more bang for the buck. These words, frequently heard today, have nothing to do with sex and ladies of the night, as has been suggested, although *bang* is slang for copulate. The expression means to get more value for your money and was apparently coined by President Dwight Eisenhower's defense secretary, Charles E. Wilson, in applauding a policy aiming for "more basic [national] security at less cost." Wilson's words were more exactly, "a bigger bang for the buck," and *bang* here means "firepower," not sex. More details can be found in William Safire's *The New Language of Politicians* (1968).

get off the dime. To get started, take some action, as in "You'd better get off the dime while you still have time." Originally a term used by floor managers in 1930s dance halls, telling dancers to move from an often stationary position. Ten cents was the cost of a dance.

get one's ashes hauled. To be sexually satisfied, as in the old black folk blues, "Well, you see that spider climbin' up the wall,/ Goin' up there to get her ashes hauled."

get one's back up. Once upon a Tom someone noticed the hair standing up on a cat's humped back and coined this expression. No one knows exactly when the aggressive arching of an angry cat's back suggested this phrase for humans aroused into anger, but it's surprising that the phrase seems no more than two centuries old, for an angry cat with its back arched high is an impressive sight, and a common one wherever there are felines wild or domestic. Cats were introduced to Europe long before the Crusades and became valued pets, despite their aloofness, when they demonstrated a proficiency at rat killing at least equal to the ferret's, and they proved far more prolific and easier to keep.

get one's dander up. Many of the early Yankee humorists—Seba Smith, Charles Davis, Thomas Haliburton—used this Americanism for "to get angry," and it is found in the *Life of Davy Crockett*. It is one of those expressions with a handful of plausible explanations. The most amusing is that the *dander* in the phrase is an English dialect form of *dandruff* that was used in the Victorian era; someone with his dander up, according to this theory, would be wrathfully tearing up his hair by the fistful, dandruff flying in the process. Another likely source is the West Indian *dander*, for a ferment used in the preparation of molasses, which would suggest a rising ferment of anger. The Dutch *donder*, "thunder," has also been nominated, for it is used in the Dutch phrase *op donderon*, "to burst into a sudden rage." And then there is the farfetched theory that *dander* is a telescoped form of "damned anger." And if these aren't enough, we have the possibilities that *dander* comes from an English

dialect word for "anger"; from the Scots *danders*, for "hot embers"; and from the Romany *dander*, "to bite."

get one's ducks in a row. American bowling alleys were the first to introduce duck pins, short slender bowling pins unlike the rotund pins that the English used. Pin boys who set up these pins (before the advent of automatic bowling machines) had the job of getting their ducks in a row. Soon the expression *I've got my ducks in a row* was being used by anyone who had completed any arrangements.

get one's Ebenezer up. *See* THAT GETS ME.

get one's goat. High-strung racehorses often have goats as stablemates, on the theory that the goats have a calming effect on the thoroughbreds. But the horses grow attached to their companions and become upset if they are removed, throwing off their performance on the track. It is said that 19th-century gamblers capitalized on that fact by stealing on the preceding day the goat of a horse they wanted to lose a race and that this practice gave us the phrase *to get one's goat*—they got the horse's goat and he became upset or angry. It's as good an explanation as any, but isn't supported by much evidence. Jack London was the first to record the expression, in his novel *Smoke Bellew* (1912), though its usage there has nothing to do with racing. Attempts have also been made to connect the goat in the phrase with the *scapegoat* of Hebrew tradition; with the word *goad*, "to anger, irritate"; and to an old French phrase *prendre la chèvre*, literally meaning "to take the goat," which dates back to the 16th century and certainly took a long time making the journey to America if it is the source of our expression.

get one's Indian up. *See* THAT GETS ME.

get one's Irish up. *See* THAT GETS ME.

get one's monkey up. Monkeys have quick tempers, though they calm down sooner than humans, which suggested the phrase *to get one's monkey up*, "to become angry," an expression that is British in origin, and is first recorded in a popular 1853 song.

get outta here!; get outta town! Both expressions are common replies to an absurd claim or the like. "I'm making 20,000 a week," someone might say, and the reply would be, "Get outta here!" or "Get the hell outta here!" or "Get up outta here!" or "Get outta town!" or just "Get out!"

get out the crying towel. Originally a military expression, probably dating back to about the beginning of World War II, *get out the crying towel* is a sarcastic reply to a chronic complainer who consistently bemoans his often minor misfortunes, meaning that he is complaining too much and should desist.

get thee to a nunnery. Shakespeare gives these words to Hamlet, when he spurns Ophelia's advances. The prince is telling her to go to a whorehouse, for which *nunnery* was Elizabethan slang.

get (catch) the gold ring. To win a big prize of some kind. Though the phrase has been reinforced by the gold ring of merry-go-rounds in modern times, it dates back to the days when knighthood was in flower. At the time tournament jousters vied to pick up a small ring with their lances, trying to win the ring.

get the hook.   A defunct journal named *The Actor's Fan Bulletin* (1931) gave the first use of the phrase: "At Miner's Bowery Theatre in New York were presented the first amateur nights in burlesque. Here the aspirants for footlight fame were given the opportunity to show their goods. The audience was at liberty to give full expression to their approval or dislike to the offerings of the contestants for the prizes. One Friday night, in October 1903, at Miner's Bowery, a particularly bad amateur was inflicting upon a patient audience an impossible tenor solo. Despite howls, groans and cat-calls, the artist persisted in staying on, when Tom Miner, who was running the show, chanced to see a large old-fashioned crook-handled cane which had been used by one of the Negro impersonators. Quickly, he had Charles Guthinger, the stage manager, lash it to a long pole. With this, he stepped to the wings without getting into sight of the audience, deftly slipped the hook around the neck of the singer and yanked him off the stage before he knew what happened. The next amateur was giving an imitation when a small boy yelled, 'Get the hook!' The audience roared and the actor fled in dismay." Many later stars including Fanny Brice, Joe Cook, and George White endured the ordeal of the hook. *See* GIVE THE HOOK.

get the man, not the ball!   A recent ugly expression urging fooball players to rough up a quarterback or anyone else involved in a play. Used not only by spectators at pro games but by the parents of Little Leaguers or the like as they cheer their sons on to glory.

getting the upper hand.   It would seem on first thought that this expression derives from the way kids choose sides with a bat in sandlot baseball. Two players, usually the best two by general agreement, participate in the choosing. One puts a hand around the bat near the fat end, then the other puts a hand around the bat just above his hand. This goes on, hand over hand, until the bottom of the bat is reached and there is no room for another hand. The last hand on the bat wins the contest (although the loser does have the chance to delicately grasp with his fingertips whatever little wood is left and twist it around his head, winning if he can hold on to the bat while doing this three times). The winner, in any case, gets to choose first for the first player on his team and the picks are made in rotation thereafter. Perhaps this sandlot choosing popularized the expression *getting the upper hand*, "getting the best of someone," but the phrase apparently was used long before the age of sandlot baseball. It probably derives from an English game of chance that has been traced back to the 15th century and was played in the same way as the sandlot choosing contest.

get to first base.   To make love that progresses no further than innocent kissing, or not to progress very far in any endeavor, as in "He couldn't get to first base learning Greek." The allusion is to baseball, and the expression dates back to the early 20th century.

Gettysburg Address.   *See* FOURSCORE AND SEVEN.

get up on the wrong side of the bed.   The wrong side of the bed is the left side, according to a superstition that goes back to the time of the Romans. People have been saying other people *got up on the wrong side of the bed*, "awoke surly or grouchy," for well over three centuries now, usually not knowing the real meaning of what they are saying, but the equally old expression *got up left foot forward* tells the story. The supposedly sinister nature of the left is reflected in many English superstitions and expressions, such as the belief that it is unlucky to put on your left shoe first, or to walk into a house left foot first. The Romans, especially Augustus Caesar, were very careful that they got up on the *right* side of the bed, but there is no evidence that they were less grouchy than anyone else.

geyser.   All spouting hot springs called *geysers* take their name from the Geysir, a particular hot spring in Iceland that the English learned about in the mid-18th century. *Geysir* itself derives from the Old Norse *geysa*, "to gush."

ghetto.   *Ghettos* are now generally areas in which racial minorities are forced to live through economic necessity, though the word has been applied loosely to areas where higher-income groups live as well, even in such terms as *middle-class ghetto*. But originally a ghetto was an area where Jews in western Europe were cruelly forced to live by law. The practice dates much earlier, but the word derives from the Venetian Jewish quarter in Italy.

ghost dance.   An Indian ceremonial religious dance. Writes Grand Forman in *The Last Trek of the Indians* (1946): "The Ghost dance was a ceremonial religious dance connected with the Messiah doctrine which originated among the Paviotso in Nevada in 1888 and spread rapidly among other tribes until it numbered among its adherents nearly all the Indians of the interior basin from the Missouri River to beyond the Rockies."

ghost town.   Though there have been abandoned towns and deserted villages since the earliest days of civilization, the term *ghost town* describing them did not come into use until the settlement of the American West. Such towns, empty or in ruins, suggesting places where only ghosts could live, were usually in regions where gold or silver deposits were mined out or that the railroad passed by, causing people to move off to more prosperous places. The term appears to have been first recorded around 1870.

the ghost walks.   It's payday and all the salaries will be paid; said to have originally been a 19th-century British theatrical expression. A company doing *Hamlet* hadn't been paid for a month or so. When during a performance Hamlet exclaimed "Perchance 'twill walk again," the actor playing the ghost answered from the wings, "No, I'll be damned if the ghost walks any more until our salaries are paid." That night the salaries were finally paid.

ghost word.   Ghost words are words that never existed until someone mistook an error for a word or invented a word for a special occasion. An example of the latter, also called a nonce word, is Lewis Carroll's *jabberwocky*, invented for the nonce (for a single use in his book *Through the Looking Glass*). Many nonce words have become full members of the language. Ghost words—the term was invented by etymologist Walter William Skeat—are usually spurious terms, the result of errors made by authors, typists, editors, and printers, and they hardly ever become part of the language. An example of a lasting ghost word is *dord* (meaning density) which can be found in the 1934 *Merriam-Webster Dictionary*, second edition. *Dord* began life as an error made in transcribing a card that read: "D or d, meaning a capital D or small d—for 'density.' " Eliminated from future Merriam-Webster dictionaries, this ghost word lives on in the 1934 edition.

ghost writer. This term for someone who writes a book, article, etc. for another person who is named as the author of it, only dates back to the late 1890s. However, the practice dates back much earlier. Caesar's secretary, for example, may have coined the immortal VENI, VIDI, VICI ("I came, I saw, I conquered,") and Seneca may well have written the Emperor Nero's speeches. Mark Twain wrote most of Ulysses S. Grant's autobiography and Archibald MacLeish and Robert Sherwood wrote speeches for Franklin Delano Roosevelt. Alexander Dumas *père* kept a stable of ghost writers to churn out formula novels, paying them with little more than food and wine. There is even a story about a ghost writer who ghosted a novel and later was hired to ghost a review of the book he had ghosted. He reviewed it glowingly, of course.

giants in the earth. See THERE WERE GIANTS IN THE EARTH IN THOSE DAYS.

gibberish. Geber, or, more properly, Jabir ibn Hazyan (*Jabir* is the Arabic for *Geber*) was an eighth-century Arabian alchemist who wrote his formulas in seemingly unintelligible jargon and anagrams in order to avoid the death penalty for sorcery. For this reason Dr. Johnson, Grose, and other prominent word detectives believed that *gibberish*, "nonsense or words without meaning," derives from his name. Geber could not have written all the 2,000 books attributed to him, but he was a prolific writer, respected enough for many medieval scientists to cite him as an authority, and for one 14th-century Spanish alchemist to go so far as to adopt his name. Today many authorities speculate that *gibberish* is imitative of the sound of nonsense, an echoic word like "jabber," "gabble," "giggle," and "gurgle," and at most was only influenced by Geber's name. *Gibberish* does not derive from the verb *gibber*, which it preceded in use, and has no roots in "gypsy jabber," as has been claimed.

gibbon. Is this long-armed ape really named after a man? Possibly, if it's true that the naming was the practical joke of an eminent naturalist. Several respected etymologists believe that this is the case. Apparently the French naturalist Buffon first named the Indian ape in his *Natural History* (1749–1804). The witty Buffon may have been aware that the tombs of the English Gybbon family in Kent, "dating from about 1700, are surmounted by an ape's head, the family crest." A less inspired derivation suggests that *gibbon* comes from an Indian dialect, but there is no abundant evidence for either theory.

Gibraltar. *Rock of Gibraltar* signifies any impregnable stronghold. Gibraltar was called Calpe in ancient times, and forms the renowned Pillars of Hercules with Abyla on the opposite coast; but when the Saracen conqueror Tarik captured it from the Visigoths and built a castle there in A.D. 710, it was named Jebel el Tarik, "the mountain of Tarik," in his honor. *Gibraltar* is simply an English corruption of the longer name. The island, a rocky promontory on Spain's southern coast, acquired a further reputation for impregnability when the British captured it in 1704, made the island a fort and naval base, and successfully repelled several attempted invasions in future years. Gibraltar remains in British hands today, despite recent demonstrations for its return to Spain. Strategically important because it commands the only entrance to the Mediterranean from the west, the island is honeycombed with natural and man-made caves used by the military. It is also an important tourist center, a major attraction being the Barbary apes that live there.

Gibson cocktail; Gibson girl. A bartender at the New York Players Club is supposed to have run out of olives and garnished artist Charles Dana Gibson's martini with a pearl onion instead, giving us the *Gibson cocktail*. Gibson was no stranger to such honors. The popular American artist's Gibson girls appeared on the covers of national magazines in the period 1896 to about 1920 as frequently as Norman Rockwell's work has in more recent times. His pen-and-ink drawings typically depicted slender, wasp-waisted beauties clad in sweeping skirts, shirtwaists, and large hats. The well-bred Gibson girls, widely imitated, were the ideals of young men and women alike up until about the end of World War I, when their vogue ended, but their creator remained active until his death in 1944.

gibus. A gibus is the folding opera hat invented by Paris hatmaker Antoine Gibus in 1837. This cloth top hat with collapsible crown proved ideal for gentlemen attending the opera, who could fold it flat and put it out of the way, the patented gimmick making a considerable fortune for its inventor and his heirs. By now almost a relic of the past, the gibus is rarely used today.

giddy. The Greek word that gives us *giddy*, first recorded in about 1000, translates as "possessed by a god." *Giddy*, however, started off meaning mad, insane, and foolish, in English, and today generally means frivolous and lighthearted, flighty, though it sometimes means to be dizzy or affected with vertigo.

Gideon Bible. In 1910 one very proper Bostonian sought an injunction to prevent the Gideon Society from distributing the Bible—"on the ground that it is an obscene and immoral publication." But not even crackpots have deterred the organization of traveling salesmen from their goal of placing a Gideon Bible in every hotel room and Pullman car in America. The Gideon Society, formally the Christian Commercial Young Men's Association of America, was founded in Boscobel, Wisconsin in 1899 and is now based in Chicago. Its name derives from that of the biblical Gideon, a judge of Israel who became a warrior and ingeniously delivered Israel from the Midianites, giving his country 40 years of peace (Judg. 6:11–7:25).

gift horse. See DON'T LOOK A GIFT HORSE IN THE MOUTH.

gift of gab. Someone with the gift of gab is a very good talker or speaker, though sometimes a braggart, too. This common expression would best be given as "the gift of the gab," for the word *gab* was originally Gaelic *gob*, meaning "mouth," the expression originally "the gift of the gob," the gift of the mouth.

gigaton. A word born with the hydrogen bomb, a gigaton is a measure of energy equal to 1 billion tons of T.N.T. *Giga* means "1 billion times," deriving from the Greek *gigas*, "giant." A kiloton, from the Greek for "1,000," is a measure of energy equal to 1,000 tons of T.N.T.

GIGO (garbage in, garbage out). This U.S. catchphrase was coined back in the 1960s when computers were first widely used for data processing. The phrase is now common among computer people wherever English is spoken and is, in fact, so well known that it is pronounced "GIGO" (with a long *i*).

Gila. A name, from the Gila River in Arizona, attached to a number of animals, including the Gila bat, Gila chipmunk, Gila monster, Gila trout, and Gila woodpecker.

gilbert. Physician to Queen Elizabeth I, and author of the first scientific book published in England, William Gilbert, or Gylberde, (ca. 1544–1603) was the most distinguished scientist of his day. His work on magnetism—he was the first European to accurately describe the behavior of magnets and the earth's magnetism—led to the gilbert, a unit of magnetic force, being named in his honor. Gilbert first used the terms *electricity*, *electrical force*, and *magnetic pole* in English, and introduced the Copernican theory to his countrymen.

Gilbert and Sullivan; Gilbertian. These two terms are used to describe light-hearted, fanciful wit similar to that of the many comic operas by Sir William Schwenck Gilbert (1836–1911) and Sir Arthur Seymour Sullivan (1842–1900). Notable examples are *The Mikado* (1885), *The Pirates of Penzance* (1879), and *H.M.S. Pinafore* (1878). Gilbert, the librettist, and Sullivan, the composer, collaborated for 25 years before a quarrel ended a perfect partnership peerlessly combining social satire with grand opera. Sullivan is also known as the author of many songs and hymns, including "Onward, Christian Soldiers." Gilbert died a hero's death, of heart failure, while trying to save a drowning girl. He was 75 years old at the time.

Gilbert filbert. *See* FILBERT.

Gilderoy's kite. *See* HUNG HIGHER THAN GILDEROY'S KITE.

gild the lily. Everybody knows that this expression is wrong and hackneyed as well, but it is still used to describe something superfluous, and I'd bet that it comes to mind first as *gild the lily* even to most of those fastidious few who correctly say *paint the lily*. The fault lies, of course, in confusing what Shakespeare really wrote in *King John*, when the Earl of Salisbury makes his protest against the king's second coronation.

> Therefore, to be possessed with double pomp,
> To guard a title that was rich before,
> To gild refined gold, to paint the lily,
> To throw a perfume on the violet,
> To smooth the ice, or add another hue
> Unto the rainbow, or with taper-light
> To seek the beauteous eye of heaven to garnish
> Is wasteful, and ridiculous excess.

Since *to gild* comes first in the pertinent line and it is just as ridiculous to gild a lily as to paint one, the phrase was often remembered as *to gild the lily*. Perhaps the old phrase to *gild the pill* also helped create the confusion. It meant to coat a bitter pill with sugar and gave *gild* wide currency as a word meaning "to cover over, to paint" (*not* to paint with gold necessarily). As for King John, he was far from "ridiculous." The unscrupulous king, who had unjustly seized the throne after the death of his brother Richard in 1199, wanted a second coronation because like any shrewd politician he knew that the awe-inspiring spectacle would win him more support among his subjects.

gillie suit. A camouflage uniform made by attaching dry grass and other vegetation to one's clothing, allowing a soldier or a hunter to blend in with the environment. Sometimes used by snipers today, gillie suits were first worn by Scottish shepherds to surprise thieves stealing from their flocks. These shepherds were often young lads, "gillies" or "gillys" in Scotch Gaelic.

gimlet. A "healthy" cocktail invented by a naval officer. Anyway, it was a lot healthier than drinking gin neat, which is exactly why Sir. T. O. Gimlette devised the *gimlet* that commemorates him. Gimlette, a British naval surgeon from 1879 to 1917, believed that drinking straight gin harmed the health and impaired the efficiency of naval officers, so he introduced a cocktail that diluted the gin with lime juice. Today the gimlet is made with gin or vodka, sweetened lime juice, and sometimes soda water.

gimme a dope. *Gimme a dope* still means "give me a Coca-Cola" in the southern U.S., especially among teenagers. This isn't recent slang, but dates back to the late 19th century, when the fabled soft drink was touted as a tonic and contained a minute amount of cocaine. *See* COKE.

gimmie. A slang pronunciation of "give it to me," *gimmie* describes a putt of less than 18 inches or so that is so easy that it is conceded to a player in a friendly amateur game of golf. The expression is a recent one, probably only dating back 50 years or so. *See* DIMPLES; SMILEY.

gin and it. A term more familiar with the British than Americans, the gin and it is a type of martini, a drink made of gin and vermouth. The *it* is short for *Italian* vermouth. The drink seems to have been invented in the last 35 years.

gin and tonic. *Tonic*, deriving from the Latin *tonicus*, had only the meaning of "pertaining to tension" when first used in the 17th century. But the word took on the meaning of a medicine that restored the tension or tone of the body, and the first tonic drinks weren't far behind. When people began adding alcohol to such drinks in the 19th century or thereabouts, tonics became the mixers that are today used in concoctions like gin and tonic, enough of which can destroy the tone of the body.

gingham. Originally all gingham cloth may have been striped, for the origin of this word, which came into English from French in the 18th century, is probably the Malay *gingam*, "striped."

Ginnie Mae. Despite talk of an eponym behind this term, this is really simply a nickname for the Government National Mortgage Association, fashioned from its initials, GNMA. There are a number of similar nicknames, such as the *Fannie Mae*, for the Federal National Mortgage Association, and *Sally Mae*, for the Savings and Loan Mortgage Association.

gin rickey. Rickeys can be made of any liquor, carbonated water, and lime juice, but the most famous drink in the family is the gin rickey, invented in about 1895 and named after "a distinguished Washington guzzler of the period," according to H. L. Mencken. Just which Washington Colonel Rickey was so honored is a matter of dispute, however. Several theories have been recorded by Mencken in his *American Language, Supplement 1*, and other sources, but none is generally accepted.

ginseng. Ginseng, which can cost up to $32 an ounce or $512 a pound for a piece of "heaven grade root," has surpassed the cost of even the truffle as a reputed aphrodisiac. In the past it has been sold at $300 an ounce or $4,800 a pound, which is probably the all-time record for a food. One Chinese emperor reputedly paid $10,000 for a perfect man-figure ginseng root, or at least so the story goes. Similarly, it's said that Chairman Mao drank a ginseng tea made from $100-an-ounce ginseng root at least three times a week. At any rate, the herb still sells briskly in Asian markets for $200 a pound and despite the protests of modern pharmacologists, lovers throughout the world cling to the mystique of its so-called super powers. Lovers have been fascinated by the "Man Plant" for more than 5,500 years. The most potent ginseng roots are said to be shaped like a man's body (in fact, the plant takes its name from the Chinese *jen shen*, "man herb") and supposedly even better results are obtained when the root is dug up at midnight during a full moon. The Chinese call ginseng, or *goo-lai-san*, the "elixir of life," "the herb that fills the heart with hilarity," and the "medicine of medicines." An American species of ginseng *(Panax quinquefolium)* is grown and gathered in this country, especially in the Ozarks and Appalachia. Diggers can earn $33 to $44 per pound of dried root, and our largest domestic dealer exports some 70,000 pounds of the herb annually. Such profits are nothing new, however; it is a matter of record that the first American ship to reach China in 1784, Major Samuel Shaw's *Emperor of China*, carried a cargo of the ginseng so dear to Chinese lovers. *See* MANDRAKE.

Giotto's O. Tradition holds that the great Italian artist Giotto di Bondone was a shepherd boy when discovered by the Florentine painter Giovanni Cimabue. While serving his apprenticeship to Cimabue, he was approached by a messenger of the pope, who had been sent all over Italy to find artists to work on a new church. Giotto was asked to submit a drawing that could be shown to the pope as evidence of his talent and with a single flourish of his brush he drew a perfect circle on a panel, Giotto's O being proof enough for the pope.

G.I. party. No celebration at all, but since World War II the name for a compulsory cleaning of a barracks by its G.I. residents. The complete cleaning includes floors, walls, ceilings, and latrines and in basic training generally takes place every week before Saturday inspection. Often the inspections are white-glove inspections, during which any dust that shows up on the inspecting officer's white gloves is cause for the G.I.s to be punished with loss of weekend passes.

gippy tummy. The word *gippy* in this British euphemism for diarrhea is a corruption of *Egyptian*, and the complaint was probably so named by visitors to the Middle East, where the drinking water can be treacherous. *See* AZTEC TWO-STEP.

giraffe. The camelopard is not a mythical monster, but a very real animal, though you might not have believed it existed if you hadn't seen it in a jungle or zoo. The ancient Greeks came across the beast on the African plain and called it *kamelopardalis*, believing it to be a cross between the camel—because of its height—and the leopard—because of its spots. It was called the camelopard in English for many years, beginning in at least 1398, until its present designation began to be used in the late 16th century: *giraffe* (from the Arabic word for the animal). The giraffe, the world's tallest quadruped, at up to 20 feet (so tall that newborn calves come to life with a jolt, falling six feet to the ground), also has the highest blood pressure of any animal (an average 260/160, as opposed to 120/80 in humans) to compensate for the pull of gravity while it is supplying blood to a brain 10 feet above the heart.

gird one's loins. A good wife, says the Bible (Prov. 31:17), "girds her loins with strength and makes her arms strong." That is, she prepares for action, usually hard physical work. The expression *gird one's loins* came into the language directly from this biblical phrase, though today it can refer to mental as well as physical labor. Workers preparing for strenuous jobs used to tuck or gird the skirts of their long garments into the girdles or belts about their loins so that they could move more freely and not worry about soiling their clothes—much as men roll up their sleeves today. *Gird*, incidentally, is either *girded* or *girt* in the past or past participle, so "He girt up his loins" is correct. Today the expression is usually the shorter *gird one's loins*.

girl. The origin of *girl*, first recorded in 1290, is obscure. Among many suggestions as to its ancestor are the Anglo-Saxon *gyrlgyden*, "virgin goddess"; the Anglo-Irish *girlun;* and the Irish *cailin* or *colleen*. It may also come from the Low German *göre*, "a young person" and, indeed, in some Scottish dialects *girl* means either a young male or female. A synonym probably just as old as girl is *gay girl (gaye girle)* for a young woman. *See* BOY.

girl Friday. *See* MAN FRIDAY.

gismo. Did this word come from the Arabic *shu ismo*, meaning a gadget, as at least one philologist suggests? The theory is that American soldiers were introduced to the expression in Morocco during World War II, and the theory has not been proved or disproved. A gismo, or gizmo, of course, is a thingamajig.

give a damn. The above was originally "I don't give a *dam*," the expression probably brought back to England from India by military men in the mid 18th century. A *dam* was an Indian coin of little value. *I don't give a damn* is first recorded in America in the 1890s. Its most famous use was in *Gone With the Wind* (1939), when Rhett Butler tells Scarlett O'Hara: "Frankly, my dear, I don't give a damn."

give a deaf ear.   *See* TURN A DEAF EAR.

give a leg up.   To give a leg up is to help someone climb up, as in mounting a horse, or, figuratively, to help someone over any difficulty. "The wall is very low, sir," Dickens wrote in *Pickwick Papers* (1837), the first recorded use of the phrase, "and your servant will give you a leg up."

give a man luck and throw him in the sea.   A man with luck will survive anything says this old saying, which brings to mind Jonah, who was thrown into the sea and swallowed by a whale, only to escape, and Arion, who was thrown into the sea and brought to shore by a dolphin.

give and take.   The expression *give and take* is first recorded (1769) in British horse racing as "a prize for a race in which the horses which exceed a standard height carry more, and those which fall short of it less, than the standard weight." By 1816 we find the phrase being used on and off the track for making allowances or concessions, the practice of compromise. In an interesting study of the words *give* and *take*, researchers found that over a given period among an observed group *give* was used 2,184 times, while *take* was used 7,008 times.

give a sop to Cerberus.   The sibyl who conducted Aeneas through the Inferno in Greek mythology lulled Cerberus, the watchdog of Hell, into a deep sleep with a drugged cake seasoned with poppies and honey. Over the centuries this story gave rise to the saying *give a sop to Cerberus*, to give a bribe to somebody, especially a troublesome or formidable person, such as a politician. The sop that came to replace the drugged cake in the legend is a piece of bread or any tasty morsel, and, indeed, *sop* itself is a synonym for a bribe today. Brewer tells us that "when persons died the Greeks and Romans used to put a cake in their hands as a sop to Cerberus, to allow them to pass without molestation." *See* CERBERUS.

give a whaling to.   Many etymologists believe this phrase should be *give a waling to*, as a wale is a mark raised on the flesh by the blow of a stick or whip. But the key word in the phrase has been spelled with an *h* ever since it first appeared, two centuries ago. This suggests that a whaling, "a terrible beating," was one given with a whalebone whip, though the wales it raised may have contributed to the phrase, making it more vivid. Riding whips were commonly made of whalebone in the 18th and 19th centuries and were used to beat more than horses. Whalebone, incidentally, is a misnomer: It's not made from the bones of a whale but from a substance found in the whale's upper jaw.

give a wide berth to.   Berth, its origin unknown, has since the 17th century meant working or operating room for a ship. *Giving good berth* to a ship, the earliest version of this nautical expression, meant to avoid or keep far away from her, which is what *give a wide berth to* means today, in reference to ships or anything else.

give a wigging.   Mark the origin uncertain for this expression, meaning to "give a severe rebuke, reprimand, or angry tongue lashing to someone." But the term, first recorded in 1813, may derive from the wigs that British justices wear, or there may be a connection with the BIGWIGS of the day.

give 'em hell.   Harry S Truman and his supporters didn't originate this Americanism during the Presidential election of 1948. The expression has been traced back to the early 19th century and has military origins. In 1851 it was recorded in *Harper's Magazine:* "At daybreak old Rily shouted, 'Forward and give them h-ll!' " Four years earlier, during the Battle of Buena Vista in the Mexican War, General Zachary Taylor had exhorted his men to "Give 'em hell!" after the enemy launched a fierce attack. *See also* HARRY S TRUMAN.

give her the gun; jump the gun.   *Give her the gun* means to accelerate a car, plane, boat, or any machine. Originally it was an RAF term for "open the throttle wide," dating to about 1920 and referring to the noise generated by a wide-open airplane motor. *Jump the gun*, on the other hand, is an expression about 50 years old that derives from both foot racing and hunting. An anxious runner often jumps the gun, that is, starts before the starter fires his pistol in a track event, and a startled pheasant will frequently take flight before a hunter can fire his gun, both situations responsible for our figurative use of the phrase—to begin something before preparations for it are complete.

give him an inch and he'll take a mile.   The expression may someday become "give him a millimeter and he'll take a meter," or something similar. It has already been put this way humorously and might someday be standard English. This shouldn't be surprising, since the expression was originally *give him an inch and he'll take an ell*, a very old proverb that goes back before the 16th century. An *ell*, the word deriving from the Anglo-Saxon *eln*, "the forearm to the tip of the middle finger," varied in length from 27 to 48 inches, depending on in which country you were measuring forearms (the English had it at 45 inches). No matter what the measurement, past or present, the expression means the same—give him a small concession and he'll take great liberties.

give him enough rope to hang himself.   Originally *give him enough rope to hang himself* took the form of *give him enough of rope*, recorded in about 1659 and meaning to allow someone free scope or action enough to embarrass himself. The image behind this is an animal tied up on a long rope, but within another 30 years we have the crude beginnings of *give him enough rope to hang himself*, when a critic of poet John Dryden said, "Give our Commentator but Rope and he hangs himself." Executions by hanging no doubt suggested the stronger version.

give him Jesse.   Still heard infrequently, *give him Jesse* means "give him hell." A 19th-century expression of obscure origins, it has been credited to the 1856 presidential campaign slogan of General John C. Frémont, "Give them Jessie!", which referred to his wife Jessie. But *Jesse* was used earlier than this and probably stems from the biblical "rod out of the stem of Jesse" mentioned in *Isaiah*.

give it up. In the last few years *give it up!* has become a common synonym for soliciting applause for a performer, as in "Come on, give it up! Give it up for Britney Spears!" The expression is equivalent to "Let's hear it for . . . !" or "A big round of applause for . . . !" In street language the phrase also means "Give me all your money, all your valuables—or else!" It is most often said during a holdup, at the same time a gun or knife is pressed against one's back. Neither term is recorded in any slang dictionary. In recent Black English *give it up!* urges a woman to have sex.

give me liberty or give me death. The full quotation from Patrick Henry in the 1775 Virginia provincial convention was supposedly, "Is life so dear, or peace so sweet, as to be purchased at the price of chains and slavery? Forbid it, Almighty God! I know not what course others may take, but as for me, give me liberty or give me death." The last seven words constitute the first quotation millions of American schoolchildren have learned over the past two centuries, but there is no record that Patrick Henry ever spoke them, and they may have been invented by Henry's biographer William Wirt 41 years later. The whole matter is discussed in Bill Bryson's *Made In America* (1994), which makes reference to learned papers on the subject.

given name. *See* SURNAME.

give short shrift to someone. To treat someone curtly, swiftly, and unsympathetically. *Short shrift* was originally, in the 16th century, the few minutes given a condemned man to make his confession to a priest before he was executed, *shrift* meaning "a confession."

give someone a cold deck. When a crooked gambler substitutes a new or "cold" deck for the used "warm" pack in a card game, the new deck is often stacked to his advantage. This practice led to the century-old expression *to give someone a cold deck* or to shamelessly swindle a person.

give someone the bird. To hiss or boo someone, especially an actor; to ridicule; to give the raspberry, the Bronx cheer, the finger (meaning "fuck you"); to fire an employee. The first definition goes back to the early 19th century, and *bird* refers to the goose, which hisses a lot. In fact, *to give the goose*, meaning the same, is the ancestor of *to give the bird*. The first published American use of the phrase is credited to Eugene O'Neill, who wrote in *The Hairy Ape* (1921): "Give him the boid, fellers—the raspberry." *See* BIRD; THE BRONX

give someone the gate. *Giving someone the gate*, "firing him, showing him the door," has been American slang since at least 1921, when it first appeared in print. There is some precedent for it, however, in the old English phrase *to give or grant the gate to*, that is, to let someone pass through the castle gate and out to the road, which the *O.E.D.* traces back to 1440. The American term is of course negative, but ironic use of the earlier *give the gate to* could have inspired it.

give the hook. Amateurs competing in early vaudeville talent nights were sometimes difficult to coax off the stage no matter how unfavorably the audience reacted to their performances. In order to prevent egg and tomato damage to the theater, all obstinate hams were yanked offstage and into the wings before the audience got violent. The instrument used was a long pole with a hook on the end, which inspired the expression *to give the hook*. Today the phrase is used to describe anyone fired for incompetence. *See* GET THE HOOK.

give the slip. Probably originally an expression used at sea in the 17th century or earlier, describing an anchored ship quickly getting out of trouble by slipping her cable or anchor line. The expression came ashore soon after and has since been associated with criminals giving the police the slip.

give up the ghost. The belief that the ghost, or soul, is an alter ego independent of the body, a spirit that departs the body when we die, is behind this phrase. The words are recorded in the Bible (Job 14:10): "Man dieth, and wasteth away; yea, man giveth up the ghost, and where is he?" That is the majestic King James Version speaking. The Revised Standard Version of the Bible cuts out the words as if they had no history, substituting: "But man dies, and is laid low; man breathes his last, and where is he?" *Ghost* comes from the Old Teutonic root *gaistjam*, "to terrify," and so was always associated with something frightening. English printer William Caxton was the first to add the *h* to *ghost*, in error, and this spelling didn't become standard English until about 1600.

give up the ship. *See* DON'T GIVE UP THE SHIP.

gladhander. Indiana humorist George Ade is supposed to have invented *gladhander*, for a demonstrative, even overfriendly person in his *Artie* (1896): "She meets me at the door, puts out the glad hand and . . ." *See* PANHANDLER; TIGHTWAD.

gladiator. These were originally prisoners of war, condemned criminals, slaves, and even volunteers who fought each other at public shows in ancient Rome. Sometimes women were among the combatants and, indeed, fought each other in the arena. Gladiators take their name from the Latin *gladius*, sword, which many of them used as weapons. Today their name is given to anyone, including a boxer, who engages in a fight or controversy.

gladiolus. Gladiolus used to be called sword lilies. Long before this the Romans named the flower *gladiolus*, "little sword," from the Latin *gladius*, "sword," because their long brilliant spikes of flowers, or the shapes of their leaves, resembled the swords Roman gladiators used in the arena. The Chinese call the gladiolus the "sword orchid."

Gladstone bag; Gladstone wines. At least one writer claims that English statesman and orator William Ewart Gladstone (1809–98) never carried the Gladstone bag named after him. Neither did the four-time prime minister *invent* the light, hinged leather bag, but he did do much traveling in his long public career and the flexible bag was made with the convenience of travelers in mind. Gladstone's name was given to certain cheap clarets—*Gladstone wines*—because he lowered the customs duty on French wines while chancellor of the exchequer in 1860. A two-seated, four-wheeled carriage also paid him honor. Gladstone has been rated as the most inspiring and among the five greatest of British prime ministers, but his private life sometimes provoked comment. Until he was well past 75, for example, he made it his habit to walk the streets of London at night trying to persuade prostitutes to convert to a different way of life. When the prime minister left office for the last time, he was 85 years old.

glare ice. A term used mostly in the northeastern U.S. for a sheet of smooth, very slippery ice, which is also called "a glare of ice." It is probably called "glare" because of its intense shining.

glass of wine with the Borgias. It was rumored that Lucretia and Cesare Borgia, the children of Pope Alexander VI, used some secret deadly poison to eliminate their enemies. One never knew whether he was an enemy of the Borgias, so *to have a glass of wine with the Borgias,* or *to dine with the Borgias* has been proverbial for a great but risky honor since the 16th century. Historians haven't been able to substantiate whether any Borgia was a poisoner, but there is no doubt that some of the Borgias were murderers, the family being a pretty unsavory lot. Sir Max Beerbohm gave the proverb his attention in his *Hosts and Guests:* "I maintain that though you would often in the 15th century have heard the snobbish Roman say, in a would-be off-hand tone, 'I am dining with the Borgias tonight,' no Roman was ever able to say, 'I dined last night with the Borgias.' "

glass slippers. There is no record of anyone really wearing glass slippers, though millions of readers and viewers of *Cinderella* over four centuries have believed otherwise. Some scholars believe that when French poet Charles Perrault wrote his collection of eight fairy tales *Histoires ou contes de temps passé, avec des moralités* (stories or tales of olden times, with morals) in 1697, giving classic form to folktales like *Cinderella, Puss in Boots,* and *Little Red Ridinghood,* he misread *pantoufles en vair,* or squirrel-fur slippers, in the Cinderella tale for *pantoufles en verre,* glass slippers—making a charming slip, or slipper.

glitch. This scientific word, meaning a sudden change in the rotation period of a neutron star, has its roots in the Yiddish *glitch,* "a slip," which, in turn, comes from the German *glitschen,* "slip." Apparently a scientist familiar with Yiddish is responsible for the coining, but he remains nameless. Today the term is most used in computerese for a mechanical malfunction, or for any problem or emergency due to a defective or broken machine.

glitterati. This word isn't as young and glistening as you might think, the term for rich celebrities dating back to before 1940. It is said to be a blend of *glitter* and *literati* and often appears in gossip columns and on TV.

glittering generalities. American attorney Rufus Choate (1799–1859) coined this term for clichés, empty words, and platitudes in a letter to a friend about the Declaration of Independence: "the glittering and sounding generalities of natural rights which make up the Declaration of Independence." Less well-known, but truer, is Ralph Waldo Emerson's remark when he heard of Choate's coinage: "Glittering generalities! They are blazing ubiquities!"

glitz. A combination of *glitter* and *ritz* that means either ostentatious glitter or sophistication and is first recorded in 1977, according to the *OED.* The word *ritz* comes from the name of restaurateur César Ritz. See RITZY.

gloaming. A poetic word for twilight, the time of day after the sun has set and before it is deeply dark. The word dates back at least to A.D. 1000, but the *OED* states its literary use is "comparatively recent from Scottish writers." *Glow* is apparently the root of the word.

Gloomy Gus. A person who is always gloomy, sad, pessimistic, as in "He's a real Gloomy Gus." The expression is still heard today, although it dates back to 1904, when it was introduced as the name of a character in Frank Opper's comic strip *Happy Hooligan.* Gloomy Gus's British counterpart is Dismal Jimmy, whose 19th-century origins are elusive.

glory hole. A large, open surface mining pit; so named either because of a previous 19th-century nautical usage or because such a hole, usually funnel-shaped, resembles in shape a morning glory flower.

glossary; gloss over. The two senses of *gloss* constitute one of the 700 or so sets of homonyms in English, words that are spelled the same but have different meanings. The earlier *gloss,* from the Greek *glossa* which meant "tongue," then "word," and finally "explanation of the word," came to be used in the sense of *language* and gave us both the term *to gloss,* "to explain, or translate a text," and *glossary,* alphabetical wordbook or "collection of explanations" (*glosses*) sometimes printed in the backs of books to explain difficult words or passages. The Middle High German *glos,* "shun," had nothing to do with language, but yielded our word *gloss,* for "superficial luster." However, the words were often confused by early writers and influenced each other, *to gloss over* coming to mean "to excuse or explain something away, to provide a false or superficial appearance or explanation." Possibly, too, the idea of careless or lazy scholars changing the meaning of difficult passages in classical works by making incorrect, superficial *glosses* or marginal comments reinforced the meaning of *to gloss over.*

Gluckist. *Gluckist* refers to a supporter of German composer Christoph Willibald Gluck (1714–87), who in the 1770s was feuding with his rival the Italian composer Piccini and his "Piccinists." The Gluckists can be said to have triumphed in this musical war if one considers that Gluck's operas are still staged today and Piccini's aren't even championed by a few Piccinists.

G-man. In about 1932 the name *G-man* originated in the underworld for special agents of the Department of Justice, Division of Investigation, who had been organized since 1908. Criminals meant government men when they coined *G-men,* which the newspapers and the movies quickly adopted. *Feds, Dee Jays* and *Whiskers* (for Uncle Sam's Agents) were other names G-men were called by, the last two designations obsolete today. See F.B.I.

gnu. There are hundreds of thousands of these large antelopes in Africa, where they are also called "horned horses," but elsewhere they are mainly encountered in crossword puzzles. Their unusual name is a corruption of the even more unusual and difficult to pronounce *ngu* that Bushmen call the animal. They are also called *wildebeests*.

go all the way. A euphemism for having sexual intercourse that originated with the FLAPPERS and the sheiks of the Roaring Twenties and is still in use today. *See* JAZZ AGE.

goatee. The style of chin whiskers cut in the form of a tuft like that of a he-goat apparently became popular in mid-19th-century America, when the word *goatee* is first recorded. *Goatee* simply means "little goat" and the Americanism is first recorded in 1842 as *goaty*. *Billygoat beard* or *billygoat whiskers* means the same and is first recorded in the mid-1880s.

goat meat. An American euphemism for venison, deer hunted and killed out of the legal hunting season. There are several synonyms, including *goat mutton*.

goatsucker. This nocturnal bird *(Caprimulgus europaeus)*, also known as the nightjar because its calls "jar the night," is called the *goatsucker* in Greek, Latin, French, German, Spanish, and several other languages besides English, its name reflecting the widespread belief that it attacks and sucks the udders of goats for food. Aristotle was among the first to note the legend, writing that "flying to the udders of she goats, it sucked them and so it gets its name. They say that the udder withers when it has sucked it and that the goat goes blind." Even this bird's scientific name, *Caprimulgus*, honors the story, deriving from the Latin *caper*, "goat," and *mulgere*, "to milk." The short-billed, wide-mouthed bird actually feeds on insects it captures in the air.

gob. The U.S. Navy banned the use of *gob* for a sailor in the early 1920s, claiming it was undignified. Like most such COMSTOCKERY, the ban on *gob* failed, but the navy might have been right about its lack of dignity, considering the word's possible origins. *Gob*, first recorded in 1909, probably comes either from *gobble*, an allusion to the way many sailors reputedly ate, or from the word *gob*, for "spit," in reference to English coast guardsmen who were called *gobbies* in the past because they were in the habit of expectorating so much. Little better is the suggestion that the word is from the Irish *gob*, "mouth," as in the expression *shut your gob*. Sailors might then have been compared to "big mouths" or something similar.

go bananas. Go crazy, go wild, act unreasonably. The expression is fairly recent, 50 or so years old as far as is known. It may derive from the saying *to go ape*, bananas being associated with apes, or the phrase may have been suggested by an excited troop of apes or monkeys feeding on bananas.

gobbledygook. *Gobbledygook* means obscure, verbose, bureaucratic language characterized by circumlocution and jargon, and usually refers to the meaningless officialese turned out by government agencies. The late Representative Maury Maverick coined the word in 1944 when he was chairman of the Smaller War Plant Committee in Congress. Maverick had just attended a meeting of the committee, at which phrases such as "cause an investigation to be made with a view to ascertaining" were rife. He wrote a memo condemning such officialese and labeled it *gobbledygook*, later explaining that he was thinking of the gobbling of turkeys while they strutted pompously. BAFFLEGAB, JARGANTUAN, PUDDER, and PENTAGONESE are all synonyms. George Orwell's "translation" of Lord Nelson's immortal phrase "England expects every man to do his duty" is a good example of gobbledygook: "England anticipates that, as regards the current emergency, personnel will face up to the issues, and exercise appropriately the functions allocated to their respective occupational groups." *See also* MAVERICK.

gobshite. To the Irish *gobshite* refers to a worthless contemptible fool, someone not worth a gob of spit or a heap of the word's latter component. In the U.S. *gobshite* has served as the much milder term for a navy seaman and for a wad of chewed tobacco.

go by the board. This expression, originating in England, literally means to go overboard, to fall down past the board, or side of a ship, into the sea. Since the mid-18th century it has also figuratively meant to be utterly lost, as in the first recorded use of the expression: "Every instinct and feeling of humanity goes by the board."

go-by-the-ground; go-by-the-wall. A little person, man or woman, has been jocularly called a *go-by-the-ground* in England since the 18th century, though today the term is heard only in English dialect. A *go-by-the-wall* meant a creeping, helpless person, or a coward.

God, I wish I'd said that. *See* TELL YOU WHAT I'M GONNA DO.

"God Bless America." American composer Irving Berlin, who emigrated with his parents from Russia to the U.S. when five years old, wrote the unofficial American national anthem while serving in the army during World War I at Camp Upton in Yaphank, a Long Island, New York, farm town. Berlin wrote the song for the benefit musical revue *Yip, Yip, Yaphank*, which was performed entirely by soldiers, but he felt the lyrics were too solemn for the show and filed it away. In 1938, when singer Kate Smith requested a song for her popular radio program, he suggested "God Bless America," and it became an American classic before World War II to the present-day war on terrorism. Berlin, who died in 1989 at 101, donated all the song's millions in royalties to the Boy Scouts. The seldom sung first verse of the song goes: "While the storm clouds gather, far across the sea/Let us swear allegiance to a land that's free/Let us all be grateful for a land so fair/As we raise our voices in solemn prayer." *See* AMERICA THE BEAUTIFUL, AMERICA; STARS AND STRIPES, STAR-SPANGLED BANNER; COLUMBIA THE GEM OF THE OCEAN; BATTLE HYMN OF THE REPUBLIC; AWAY DOWN SOUTH IN DIXIE; YANKEE DOODLE DANDY; OVER THERE; SOUSAPHONE.

God bless you. The custom of saying *God bless you* after someone sneezes supposedly arose with St. Gregory the Great, who said it to people during a plague in which sneezing was often a symptom. The custom has been widespread throughout the world since ancient times, though notably among the Greeks and the Romans, who exclaimed *Absit omen!* Another theory claims that Satan can't enter a sneezer's body when this blessing is offered.

goddam.   English-speaking people have been quick on the draw with curses since earliest times. So often did the English in medieval times take the Lord's name in vain, for example, that the French called them *goddams*. Later, in the American Southeast, Indians gave the Anglos the same name for the same reason. Cape Cod fishermen of Portuguese descent often bestowed nicknames on each other and used the nicknames so consistently that they virtually replaced the surnames of the families concerned after several generations. One family, for example, became known as the Codfishes, another as the Rats. The most extreme example recorded is the Goddams. Captain Joseph Captiva explained this oddest of surnames to Alice Douglas Kelly of the Federal Writer's Project and she recorded it in *Living Lore* (1938): "That's cause the old lady she couldn't speak English so good and she'd call the children when they was little: 'You come here, goddam,' 'Don't you do that, goddam.' So they call 'em the 'Goddams.' " Many readers have heard comedian Bill Cosby's routine in which the child thinks his name is "Damnit" because his father so often summons him with a "Commere, damnit!"—there's truth behind every good fiction! *See also* LES SOMMOBICHES.

godfather.   Since the late 1960s, when Mario Puzo's *The Godfather* (1969) was published, soon to become the basis for one of the most popular movies of all time, *godfather* has meant the don or head of a Mafia family or unit. Wrote Puzo: "Don Vito Corleone was a man to whom everybody came for help, and never were they disappointed . . . His reward? Friendship, the respectful title of 'Don,' and sometimes the more affectionate salutation of 'Godfather.' "

God finally caught his eye.   Waiters were American author George S. Kaufman's pet hate; he believed they were actually trained to exasperate him and other customers. His many remarks about the breed culminated with his long-lasting mock epitaph for a dead waiter: "God finally caught his eye."

God heals and the doctor takes the fee.   Benjamin Franklin's improved version of the old proverb "God restoreth health and the physician hath the thanks."

Godlike Daniel.   Few if any American politicians have been so idolized as bold blackmaned New England statesman Daniel Webster, who was in his lifetime called *Godlike Daniel* or the *Godlike*. Noted the *Whig* magazine back in 1850: "Black Dan, alias the Godlike, as he had been cognomened by his especial admirers, is a sort of intellectual hippopotamus." A century later, Senator Webster even defeated the devil in Stephen Vincent Benét's short story "The Devil and Daniel Webster" (1937), which later became a play and movie. *See* BLACK DANIEL.

Godolphin Barb.   *See* BYERLY TURK.

go down like a sack of spuds.   This recent expression, very common in Australia, means "to lose very badly," especially in a sporting event.

go (drive) round the bend.   To lose control of oneself for a short or long time, to go mad, crazy. Originating in Britain during World War II, this phrase may have been suggested by a speeding car taking a sharp turn and going out of control.

"God save the Queen" (King).   The saying is found in the Old Testament, was used in the British navy, and by the 17th century became the basis for what is now the British national anthem (perhaps written by Dr. John Bull). The melody of "God Save the Queen" (King) has been appropriated for patriotic songs by 19 other countries, including Germany and the U.S. No one has used the words more memorably than English author John Stubbs (ca. 1541–90), who attacked Queen Elizabeth in his pamphlet THE DISCOURSE OF A GAPING GULF WHERE INTO ENGLAND IS LIKELY TO BE SWALLOWED BY ANOTHER FRENCH MARRIAGE. His pamphlet was burned in a public bonfire, and the author's right hand was hacked off with a meat cleaver at the same time. Stubbs is said to have immediately raised his hat with his left hand and cried, "God save the Queen!"

God should be allowed to just watch the game.   The great entertainer Yogi Berra is supposed to have made this remark from behind the plate after watching Chicago White Sox batter Minnie Minoso appeal for divine intervention by drawing a cross in the dust on home plate. The story has become sports legend, but syndicated columnist William Safire recently contacted the former Yankee catcher and Yogi denied he ever said it. Yogiisms Yogi hasn't denied include "I've been playing 18 years and you can observe a lot by watching" (on his managerial abilities); "He can run anytime he wants—I'm giving him the red light" (on giving a player permission to steal a base); and the much-quoted "It ain't over till it's over."

God's little acre.   The phrase is best known as the title of Erskine Caldwell's 1933 novel of that name. But it is also a piece of land from which all crops are given to the church. Sometimes called God's acre.

God's nightgown!   An exclamation of exasperation or surprise made famous by Margaret Mitchell's heroine Scarlett O'Hara, who used it several times in *Gone With the Wind* (1936). I can't find the words recorded elsewhere, so they may be the novelist's coinage.

God speed the plough; Plough Monday.   *God speed the plough*, "a wish for success or prosperity," was originally a phrase in a 15th-century song sung by ploughmen on Plough Monday, the first Monday after Twelfth Day, which is the end of the Christmas holidays, when farm laborers returned to the plough. On this day ploughmen customarily went from door to door dressed in white and drawing a plough, soliciting "plough money" to spend in celebration. British playwright Thomas Morton wrote a play, *Speed the Plough* (1798), which introduced the character MRS. GRUNDY. American playwright David Mamet wrote a play, *Speed-The-Plow* (1988), excoriating Hollywood.

God's seal pup.   Jesus Christ is called not the "lamb of God," but "God's seal pup" in the Eskimo Bible. These are the same doe-eyed harp seal pups that human seal hunters savagely club to death off the coast of Newfoundland so that they can be turned into sealskin coats. The little white seal pups can do nothing to defend themselves against the spiked clubs, and their mothers look on helplessly. Often the pups are skinned before they are dead.

God tempers the wind to the shorn lamb. Since lambs are never shorn, Laurence Sterne's phrase, from his *Sentimental Journey* (1782), seems to make little sense. Sterne coined it from an earlier, less poetic expression—invented some 140 years before—that said *To a close-shorn sheep, God gives wind by measure.* But George Herbert, its author, got it in turn from a French saying in Henri Estienne's *Premices* (1594), which said *God regulates the cold to the shorn lamb.* Poetry usually triumphs.

God wills it! No ancient phrase spilled more blood than *God wills it! (Deus volt!)*, words uttered by Pope Urban II that launched the Christian Crusades to deliver the Holy Land from the Muslims. The Holy Land, conquered at great cost in human lives, could not be held.

God writes straight with crooked lines. God's ways are mysterious and indecipherable by humankind, we are incapable of understanding his actions. No one seems sure just when this proverb originated, some crediting St. Augustine (A.D. 354–430).

go fly a kite. Get out of here, go away, stop bothering me, go to hell, get lost. Still heard, though not so often as it once was. The expression may be older but is first recorded in a 1928 number of the *Saturday Evening Post.*

go for a song. To be sold or bought cheaply, for almost nothing at all. The expression was possibly inspired by the phrase ALL THIS FOR A SONG, in the sense that the song was a mere trifle. More likely, however, the expression refers to the small cost of old ballad sheets, or the small coins thrown to street singers.

go for the jugular. Quickly go for the kill, show no mercy whatsoever. The expression originated with Massachusetts lawyer and U.S. senator Rufus Choate. Remarked Choate in describing President John Quincy Adams: "He has . . . an instinct for the jugular and carotid artery, as unerring as that of any carnivorous animal."

go for the long ball. This contemporary American slang means to take a big risk for a big gain. It does not come from baseball but from football, referring to long desperate passes made in the last minutes of a game.

go from Dan to Beersheba. To go everywhere, from one end to the other. The phrase is recorded in the Bible (Judges 20:1) and refers to Dan, the northernmost city, and Beersheba, the southernmost city of ancient Palestine.

go-go funds. In the late 1960s go-go dancers inspired the name for these "exciting" mutual investment funds, which were "very attractive" to investors. Mutual funds themselves date back to early 19th-century Belgium.

going by shank's mare. This means to go somewhere by walking, to use "Walker's bus," and as far as is known no horseless Mr. Shank is responsible for the 200-year-old phrase, which is probably Scottish in origin. Neither is there any proof that the expression refers to King Edward I, nicknamed "Long Shanks" because whenever he rode a pony his long legs reached to the ground. The *shank* is the leg, or that part of the leg below the knee, and a mare is usually slower than a stallion. Going by *marrow-bone stage*, a play on the once-real Marylebone (pronounced "Marrybun") stage in London, means the same.

going fishing. A baseball term, dating back at least to the 1930s, for a batter who swings at bad pitches out of the strike zone that he should take as balls, usually pitches high and outside. *Fishing trip* is a synonym.

going like 60. In 1860 a terrible drought in the Missouri and Arkansas valleys devastated that part of the country, lasting more than a year. Some tracers of lost word origins believe that the memory of the drought was so vivid that people began linking the year 1860 with extremes of any kind. But the drought could only have reinforced and possibly accelerated the meaning of the popular expression *going like 60*, for it was used by James Russell Lowell in his *Biglow Papers* in 1848 ("Though like sixty all along I fumed an' fussed") and was recorded in an early 1860 slang dictionary as "[to go] at a good rate, briskly." Perhaps 60 is used simply to express a large number, as an abbreviation of "like 60 miles an hour," or something similar. "Forty" was used in this way at least since Shakespeare's *Coriolanus* (1607), and in *Uncle Tom's Cabin* (1852) a character says: "I has principles and I stick to them like forty."

going 19 to the dozen. Still heard occasionally today to describe someone who can't cease talking, a motormouth. The expression dates back to the early days of steam, when steam engines powered pumps in the mines. A steam engine going 19 to the dozen was pumping 1,900 gallons of water for every 12 bushels of coal it used for fuel.

going postal. Patterned on *going crazy, going bonkers*, and, especially, *going ballistic*, this expression has been around since the late 1980s. It first meant the sudden explosive attack by a postal worker on coworkers in the workplace. According to Anne H. Soukhanov in *Word Watch* (1995): "This expression takes its cues from Patrick Henry Sherrill's attack on an Edmund, Oklahoma, post office in 1986, in which fourteen people were killed and six wounded, followed in subsequent years by several other such incidents." Today the expression is used much more loosely to mean "totally stressed out," "almost losing it," etc.

go in off the deep end. These words suggest someone leaping off a diving board at the deep end of a swimming pool and finding the water was over his or her head. When first used, as military slang in England during World War I, the expression simply meant to get very excited, as if finding yourself in deep water. Then the words came to mean "passionate" as well. A British novelist wrote: "In her set the word adultery was not often mentioned. One went in off the deep end about somebody . . ." U.S. use of the expression is often similar, but Americans also apply it to other situations. Someone who displays a terrible temper, or one who is so reckless as to go into a situation over one's head, or even someone who is crazy is said to have "gone off the deep end."

go into extra innings; good innings. A baseball game that goes into extra innings goes beyond the normal time played (nine innings). *Go into extra innings*, a phrase I've heard recently but which is recorded nowhere, means to live a long life, as when someone says, "He's over 80, he's already gone into extra innings."

golconda. Any source of great wealth is *a golconda*. The term owes its life to the town of Golconda in India, which the British in the 16th century thought was the site of extensive diamond mines. Though the area actually was a diamond-cutting center without mines, the term lasted in the language.

gold. Gold is one of the four oldest words in English, deriving from the Indo-European substrate word *gol* (the other three are *apple*, from *apal; bad, bad*; and *tin, tin*). Hundreds of expressions, some of them covered in these pages, are based on *gold*, from *all that glitters is not gold* and *good as gold* to *heart of gold* and *gold digger*.

goldbacks. *See* GREENBACKS.

goldbrick. Con men working Western mining properties toward the end of the 19th century sometimes sold gullible investors lead or iron bricks coated with gold paint, representing them as the real thing. One Patrick Burke of St. Louis is recorded as having paid $3,700 for such a "gold" brick in 1887. This all-too-common confidence scheme gave the name *goldbrick* to any swindle or fakery. Later, soldiers picked up the expression and used the phrase *to goldbrick* in its present meaning of avoiding work or shirking duty. The phrase is first recorded in 1914 in this sense, applied to army lieutenants appointed from civilian life.

gold-bug. In Edgar Allan Poe's celebrated cryptological tale "The Gold-Bug" (1843), a poor southern gentleman captures a rare "golden scarab beetle" that helps him locate the buried treasure of Captain Kidd. According to several authorities, the "gold-bug" of the story is based upon the brilliantly colored goldsmith beetle (*Cotalpha lanigere*), also called the "horn beetle."

gold digger. Long before *gold digger* meant a mercenary woman, a use first recorded in 1915, it signified a miner in California gold fields such as Jackass Gulf, Puke Ravine, Greenhorn Canyon, and Rattlesnake Bar. In fact, the term *gold digger*, for a miner, is recorded in 1830 during America's first gold rush, which took place in northern Georgia. It was gold diggers of the most mercenary kind that a humorous Western song referred to in one of its verses:

> The miners came in '49
> The whores in '51
> And when they got together
> They produced the native son.

Golden Bible. The Book of Mormon, which is said to have been translated by Joseph Smith from an original that was engraved on golden plates; the term is first recorded in 1830, before the Mormons came to Utah and built the temple there.

golden calf. *See* WORSHIP THE GOLDEN CALF.

golden floor. A Victorian term for the floor of heaven, where all good folk go. When British poet A. E. Housman (1859–1936) lay dying, a friend tried to cheer him up by telling him a risqué tale. "Yes, that's a good one," Housman said when he finished, "and tomorrow I'll be telling it on the Golden Floor."

Golden Gate. The strait at the entrance to San Francisco Bay from the Pacific Ocean; also a name for the Golden Gate Bridge spanning the strait, a 4,200-foot bridge that connects northern California with the San Francisco Peninsula. The bridge is not golden-colored but named after the Golden Gate Strait, which was discovered by Sir Francis Drake in 1579.

golden handshake. Though frequently used in the U.S., this business term was coined about 1960 by British newspaper editor Frederick Ellis. It is a generous severance payment made to an executive as compensation for dismissal or early retirement. One recent payment was so large that it was called a "24-caret golden handshake." *See* GOLDEN PARACHUTE.

golden horde. This was the name given to the Mongolian Tartars who invaded Russia in the 13th century and established an empire there under Bator, a grandson of Genghis Khan, that lasted two centuries. They were so called because the color of their skin appeared golden to their adversaries. *Hordes* has always been a favorite word of Europeans for Asian armies. *See* ASIATIC HORDES.

golden parachute. A contract guaranteeing a company executive very generous benefits, including severance pay, if one loses a job because the company is sold or merged. The American term is first recorded in 1981 but is actually an offshoot of the earlier British GOLDEN HANDSHAKE, which dates back to 1960 and means essentially the same, except that the golden parachute is contractual.

golden rule. Usually phrased "Do unto others as you would have them do unto you," the *golden rule* is based upon the biblical injunction from the Sermon on the Mount (Matt. 7: 12): "whatsoever ye would that men should do to you, do ye even so unto them." *Golden rule* has also come to mean any guiding principle. The ethical golden rule has many negative variations, from William Blake's epigram: "He has observed the golden rule,/ Till he's become the golden fool," to Edward Noyes Wescott's: "Do unto the other feller/ the way he'd like to do/ unto you an' do it first" (*David Harum*, 1898). Wrote George Bernard Shaw in *Maxims for Revolutionists* (1903): "Do not do unto others would they should do unto you. Their tastes may be different"; and "The golden rule is that there is no golden rule." An anonymous contemporary golden rule advises: "He who has the gold rules." It should be added that Confucius wrote, "What you do not want done to yourself, do not do to others," fully five centuries before Jesus gave the Sermon on the Mount. British theologian Isaac Watts (1674–1748) was the first person to directly call this precept the Golden Rule, in an essay he wrote in 1725. *See* RECIPROCITY.

Golden State.   A nickname for California since Gold Rush days a century and a half ago. It has also been called El Dorado and the Bear State, after its grizzly bears.

golden wedding anniversary.   The 50th wedding anniversary of two living partners is called the golden anniversary because of the German medieval custom of presenting one's wife with a wreath of gold. This idea, elaborated upon over the years, led to the giving of anniversary gifts ranging from cotton to gold and diamonds.

gold of Tolosa.   Ill-gotten gains that will never leave one prosperous. The Roman consul Caepio looted the temple of Apollo at Tolosa of all the gold and treasure belonging to the Cimbrians. Not only were the gold and treasure stolen from him shortly after, but he was defeated on the battlefield by the Cimbrians, who killed 112,000 of his men.

Goldwynism.   "Include me out," "In two words: impossible," and "We have passed a lot of water since then" (for "a lot of water has passed under the bridge") are but three legendary Goldwynisms. An American film pioneer, Samuel Goldwyn has long been considered a modern "Mr. Malaprop," unrivaled for his fractured English. Goldwyn, born in Warsaw, Poland, on August 27, 1882, founded Goldwyn Pictures Corporation, which became part of Metro-Goldwyn-Mayer in 1924, and later turned independent producer. He died in 1974. No doubt many of the thousands of Goldwynisms attributed to him— word manglings, mixed metaphors, malapropisms, grammatical blunders, and the like—were invented by press agents, writers, friends, and enemies. But genuine or not, they became part of the legend surrounding the man. *See* MALAPROPISM.

golem.   The legendary golem is a huge supernatural creature made of clay who is brought to life by magic and fights against persecution of the Jews. The word ultimately derives from Hebrew *golem* for "a shapeless man."

golf.   One guess is that the name of this sport, first recorded in 1425, comes from the Dutch word *kolf* for the club used in the game. This seems to suggest that the sport had its origins in Holland, but the first records of the game are from Scotland, although early on the Scots did import their best-quality golf balls from Dutch makers. According to another theory *golf* may have come from the Scottish *goulf,* "to strike or cuff." Games roughly similar to golf were played as far back as Roman times, but modern-day golf can be traced to Scotland's St. Andrews course, which was built in 1552, where, two centuries later, the Thirteen Articles laying down the rules of the sport were established.

golf links.   All golf courses were originally built on ridges of virtually flat land along the seashore. They were called *links* from the Old English *hlinc,* for "ridge of land."

golf widow.   A woman whose husband frequently leaves her alone at home while he plays golf is called a *golf widow.* The game is much older but the term doesn't seem to have been recorded until around 1915. *Football widow* and *baseball widow* are related terms heard today.

golgotha.   A cemetery; a place of martyrdom; a place of torment or anguish. The reference is to the crucifixtion of Jesus as told in the Bible (John 19:17–18): "And he bearing His cross went forth into a place called the place of the skull, which is called in the Hebrew Golgotha: where they crucified him." Golgotha is located outside Jerusalem and may be the site where the Church of the Holy Sepulchre stands. It may have originally been an execution place for criminals whose bodies were picked bare by animals. The Greek word *Calvaria* is the equivalent of *Golgotha* and gives us the word *Calvary,* meaning the same.

Goliath.   The original Goliath stood between 9 feet 9 inches and 11 feet 3 inches tall, depending on how you value the "6 cubits and a span" given as his height in the Bible. Nevertheless, the stripling David slew him with a stone from his sling (I Sam. 17:49–51) and defeated the Philistines. A *David and Goliath* contest is one between a great and a small man. Not to take anything away from David, but Goliath was a stripling compared to the giant Og (16 feet 2½ inches) and other biblical big men. All such claims, however, are most likely based on our ignorance of ancient measurement units.

gondolas.   The little American gondolas of the Revolutionary War take their name from the Italian double-ended boats used on the Grand Canal in Venice, but there the resemblance ends. The Continental gondolas were rigged with sails and fitted with guns.

gone for a Burton.   A euphemism, typically British, for "dead" that was commonly used in the R.A.F. during World War II. Many R.A.F. pilots fell "in the drink" to their deaths and it was easier for fellow pilots to deal with their deaths by saying that they had gone for a drink of the popular Burton's ale. *See also* GO WEST.

gone goose.   No connection has been made between this American expression and the much older phrase COOK HIS GOOSE. Apparently, the Americanism dates only from about 1830, and there is no story about a goose in a helpless, hopeless state to explain it. Probably *a gone goose, a gone beaver, a gone chick,* and similar expressions all derive from the earlier *a gone coon,* which, according to one of several legends, goes back to the Revolutionary War. It seems that an American had disguised himself in raccoon skins and climbed a tree to spy on the British. But an enemy soldier discovered him that night while coon hunting and took aim, ready to shoot the biggest coon he had ever seen, when the spy cried out, "Don't shoot—I'll come down! I know I'm a gone coon!" According to the legend, the British soldier was so terrified to hear an "animal" talk that he dropped his gun and ran. The tale need not be true for it to have popularized the expression *a gone coon,* and other animals could have been substituted for the coon by storytellers in different areas of the country.

gone today, here tomorrow.   This twist on the old saw "here today, gone tomorrow" is attributed to the publisher

Alfred Knopf (1892–1984). He was talking about book returns from bookstores.

gone to pot.   Marijuana isn't even a contender here. Neither is there reason to believe that *gone to pot* has its origins in cremation; that is, in the placing of human ashes in an urn or pot. Neither has it any connection with drunkards dissipating in wine pots. Most authorities agree that this expression for being ruined, disintegrated, which dates back before Elizabethan times, was inspired by pieces of meat being chopped up and going into the pot for a stew. They were usually inferior cuts of meat, this stew meat, the kind rich men trimmed off a joint in old England and gave to the servants for their stew pot. "Going to the pot" suggested going down in the world, because a mere stew didn't compare to more savory ways of preparing meat. When you went to the stew pot, like a piece of meat, your identity was destroyed, you literally disintegrated. Nevertheless, the old story persists that a tailor who lived near a cemetery in a small European town dropped a stone in a pot for every funeral that passed by. When he himself died, a wag quipped that he too had *gone to pot*.

gone where the woodbine twineth.   Woodbine is a honeysuckle *(Lonicera periclymenum)* that was often planted on graves in years past. An 1870 song written as a tribute to those who died in the bloody Civil War went: "Then go where the woodbine twineth,/ When spring is bright and fair,/ And to the soldier's resting place/ Some little tribute bear." From this song by Septimus Winner the expression *gone where the woodbine twineth* came to mean someone who had died, or even someone who had gone someplace from which he would never return.

gone with the wind.   Margaret Mitchell's immensely popular novel *Gone With the Wind* (1936) made this expression popular in our time, but the title comes from English poet Ernest Dowson's love poem "Non Sum Qualis Eram" written in 1896 and containing the line "I have forgot much, Cynara, gone with the wind." Mitchell's novel about the Civil War won a Pulitzer Prize, and in 1939 the film version won the Academy Award for best picture. Dowson also wrote "Vitae Summa Brevis," which gave the language the beautiful line, "They are not long, the days of wine and roses: / out of a misty dream / Our path emerges for a while, then closes / Within a dream."

Gongorism.   It is only fair to say that the arrows that were transferred into "flying asps" and the birds that became "feathered zithers" were part of a larger plan. Luis de Gongora y Argote (1561–1627) wrote in a twisted, torturous style in his later years, his syntax deliberately distorted in order to highlight words and create an unreal world. But he inspired many imitators, who inspired many critics and, unfortunately, his name is now a synonym for a deliberately obscure, meaningless, and affected ornamental style. The Spanish poet after whom *Gongorism* is named was essentially a lyric poet in his early years; his work was much admired by Cervantes, though no poem of his was published in his lifetime. Readers have discovered that his baroque Gongorisms, a great influence on modern poetry, are far from meaningless, as difficult as the long poems like *Soledades* are to read. Gongora, who adopted his mother's name, was a priest as well as a poet and dramatist. Toward the end of his life he turned back from cultivated obscurity to a simple, unaffected style.

goo.   *Burgoo* is a New England term for a thick stew that traveled West with the pioneers. It may have suggested the Americanism *goo* for a thick, wet, sticky substance and by extension any sentimental drivel. *Goo* is first recorded, however, in about 1915.

goober.   *Goober,* for "peanut," was not coined in the southern U.S. It originated in Africa as the Bantu *nguba,* for "peanut," and was brought to the America South by African slaves in about 1834. Long a southern dialect term, it has achieved wider currency over the past 70 years. *Pindal,* another word for peanut, comes from the Kongo *npinda.*

good.   *Good,* first recorded circa A.D. 800, derives from the Old English *god,* which is akin to earlier words basically meaning "suitable," so that, according to the *O.E.D.* "the original sense of *good* would be 'fitting' . . ." Thus, unlike BAD, *good* has its roots in "the suitable, the fitting, the natural."

goodbye.   *Goodbye* derives from the words *God be with you,* its first recorded use in a 1573 letter. Earlier forms of *God be with you* were *God be wy you, godbwye, god bwy ye* and *good-b'wy.* Why then is *good* instead of *god* in the current expression? Probably because, most etymologists agree, the new word's formation was influenced by the expression *good day.*

good egg.   *See* BAD EGG.

good enough Morgan.   On September 12, 1826, the day his book revealing secrets of the Masons was to be published, William Morgan disappeared, never to be seen again. It was charged that Masons had kidnapped, killed, and buried him, but that charge was disproved. "Now that we have proven that the body found at Oak Orchard is that of Timothy Monroe, what will you do for a Morgan?" Masons chided their political opposition. "That is a good enough Morgan for us until you bring back the one you carried off," replied the opposition. After such answers, a *good enough Morgan* became a political expression meaning any political scheme or device that can be temporarily used to influence voters. Morgan was never found, but the expression lived on in America's political lexicon for at least a century.

good evening, ladies and germs.   *See* I'LL TELL YOU WHAT I'M GONNA DO!

good fences make good neighbors.   The proverbial expression originated in the mid-17th century, but in the U.S. it has become associated with poet Robert Frost, who used it in "Mending Wall" (1914), which also gives us, "Something there is that doesn't love a wall."

good field, no hit.   This baseball catchphrase is sometimes applied jokingly to other things, to anyone who does one thing better than another, who is good in one field and not another. The expression dates back to 1924 when coach Miguel "Mike" Gonzales scouted Dodger player Moe Berg for the St. Louis Cardinals. Observing Berg at Brooklyn's Clearwater, Florida training camp that spring, Gonzales wired his boss the four-word evaluation: "Good field, no hit." The Cardinals didn't offer a contract, but the scholarly Berg, who spoke seven languages, including Chinese and Japanese, became an American spy during World War II, spying on German atomic scientists.

good for you! An American expression of approval or congratulations since at least 1861. It is equivalent to *well done!* or *well said!* Sometimes the variation *good on you!* is used.

Good Gray Poet. We Americans haven't bestowed affectionate sobriquets on many of our poets, but Walt Whitman (1819–92), surely our greatest poet, is an exception. Whitman was given the name Good Gray Poet by William Douglas O'Connor, who used the words as the title of his 1866 book, which was written in defense of his friend Whitman when the poet was fired from his clerkship in the Indian Bureau of the Department of the Interior on the grounds that his poetry collection *Leaves of Grass* was immoral. Much later, Whitman wrote the preface for his friend's *Three Tales*, which was published posthumously in 1892 and included a story called "The Carpenter," a Christ-like portrait of the poet. In his old age, with his full flowing gray beard, Whitman seemed more the Good Gray Poet than ever.

good holding ground. A place where one can stay even when conditions are bad, originally a nautical term referring to a place offshore where an anchor can catch and hold fast even when the sea is rough and the wind is blowing hard.

good honk. Correspondent Madolin Johnson Wells advises that her mother often used this old-fashioned expression when startled or upset, as in "Good honk (pronounced "good haohonk"), Lon, what've you done?" In rare cases of extreme emphasis, Mrs. Wells writes, her mother would say, " 'Great honks!' which conjured images of a strange bird or a mythical god." American playwright Meredith Willson used the phrase "Great honks!" for the same purpose in his hit play *The Music Man.*

good morning, damn you. Louisa May Alcott related the story of this unlikely phrase in "Transcendental Wild Oats," a short story based on her father, Bronson Alcott's, idealistic but short-lived Fruitlands community: "One youth [a member of the community] believing that language was of little consequence if the spirit was only right, startled newcomers by blandly greeting them with 'Good morning, damn you,' and other remarks of an equally mixed order." No one seems to have objected.

goodnighting. Students of the old West may be aware that bulls on long cattle drives often suffered from chaffing of the testicles, which frequently swelled so large that the animal sickened and died. The remedy was to cut off the testicle bag, push the testicles up into the body and sew the cut—a process that enabled the bulls to travel well and did not impair their breeding. This remedy was called goodnighting, after cattleman Charles Goodnight, who invented it, and is surely among the most unusual of words named after people.

good ole boy. Though it is used nationally now, a *good ole boy* is still generally a white southern male exemplifying the masculine ideals of the region; any amiable southerner, provided he likes guns, hunting, fishing, drinking, football, and women, in roughly that order; or a loyal southerner, rich or poor, devoted to all things southern. The term had popular use in the mid-1960s. Said the late Billy Carter, President Jimmy Carter's brother, of the good ole boy: "A good ole boy . . . is somebody that rides around in a pickup truck . . . and drinks beer and throws 'em out the window." (*Redneck Power: The Wit and Wisdom of Billy Carter,* 1977.) Perhaps older than *good ole boy* is the little-heard *good ole rebel,* which derives from a song entitled "Good Old Rebel" written by Innes Randolph in the 1870s: "I am a good old rebel—/ Yes, that's just what I am—/ And for this land of freedom/ I do not give a damn. I'm glad I fit agin 'em/ And I only wish we'd won;/ And I don't ax no pardon/ For anything I've done."

good riddance to bad rubbish. *Riddance* refers to the act of cleaning away something undesirable and *good riddance* signifies a welcome relief from something, this last expression first recorded in 1783 as *a good riddance!,* a saying common in the U.S. today. The much stronger and rarer *good riddance to bad rubbish!* might be said to or of some worthless person who is leaving a place or a group of people, someone everyone is glad to be rid of. This alliterative phrase appears to be an Americanism but apparently hasn't been recorded anywhere, though it has been used in America for at least a century.

good Samaritan. The good Samaritan is nameless in the biblical story (Luke 10:30–85) told by Christ; he is only referred to as "a Samaritan" and Christ tells how he helped a man who had been assaulted and left half dead by robbers, how he cared for the stranger and paid for his room in an inn after two holy men passed him without helping. This anonymous man of Samaria, a district of ancient Palestine, the northern kingdom of the Hebrews, became over the centuries the good Samaritan, lending his name to the countless kind, helpful, philanthropic people who do good for others with no thought of worldly gain. The Samaritans are also a religious community who claim that they are descendants of the 10 tribes of Israel and that their religion contains the true undiluted teachings of Moses. These Samaritans, who broke with the Jews in about 458 B.C. but are said to observe the Torah even more scrupulously than orthodox Jews, are now represented by a few families living in Jordan. There are also 650 Samaritans in Israel, half living on Mount Gerizim, overlooking Nablus, and the others residing in Holon, near Tel Aviv. They all speak an ancient Hebrew dialect.

good scout. A *good scout,* "a regular person, a good fellow," is probably much older than its first recorded date of 1912. The *scout* here most likely comes from the Dutch *schout,* "a sort of combination town mayor-sheriff"—not the English word *scout,* which derives ultimately from a Latin word for "to listen," *ascultare.*

good skate. *See* CHEAPSKATE.

good sport. The expression *good sport,* for one who plays fair and accepts victory or defeat amicably, is something of a redundancy, for *sport* itself has meant such a person since the end of the 19th century, when the expression *be a sport* was popular in England.

good-time Charlie; good-time girl. *Good-time Charlie* refers to an affable, sociable, convivial man, the term perhaps coined by that great American word inventor T. A. Dorgan (*see* HOT DOG), who first used it in 1927, probably before anyone else. Not long after this, in 1928, the term *good-time girl* is first recorded. It usually describes a convivial young woman who is looking to have a good time, to play, anything for a laugh, much the same as a good-time Charlie.

good times. *See* PLAY THE MARKET.

good to the last drop. This slogan for Maxwell House coffee, coined in 1960, is a good example of advertising slogans that have come into general use, and means "thoroughly or completely good or enjoyable." Another example is Ivory soap's *99 and 44/100ths % pure*, which, though coined in 1925 and no longer used in the company's ads, still persists in the language. Similar slogans have enjoyed popular use, even if only comic, for over a century, like the old patent medicine *Pink pills for pale people*, coined in the mid-19th century and still used, though rarely, today. Another example is Alka-Seltzer's more recent *I can't believe I ate the whole thing . . .*

good wine needs no bush. Dating back some 2,000 years to ancient Rome, this expression refers to the vine leaves or ivy (honoring Bacchus) frequently depicted on signs outside Roman wine shops or taverns. The Romans continued this custom when they occupied England, where the saying arose that *a good wine needs no bush*, that is, it isn't necessary to advertise a good wine with a bush outside the tavern—its good quality will soon make it known to everyone anyway. Today the words mean generally that "excellent things speak for themselves."

goody. A historical polite form of address for a "goodwife," a good woman of humble means in the early American colonies and well before then in England. *Goody* can also refer to a piece of candy or cake, while *goody-goody* refers to a smug, often officious, self-righteous person.

goof off; goofy. *Goofing off*, "wasting time," originated in the U.S. armed forces during World War II. It implies shirking like a silly or goofy person, a *goof*, which word derives from the English dialect word *goff*, "a simpleton," first recorded in 1570.

googly. *See* BOSEY.

googol; googolplex. A nine-year-old child invented *googol*—a word for the number one followed by 100 zeroes, or 10 to the 100th power (10^{100}), which is frequently used in mathematics. Distinguished American mathematician Dr. Edward Kasner asked his nephew to make up a name for the big number and the boy replied *googol*. Possibly the word was suggested by childish sounds like *goo*, *coo*, etc., or possibly the comic strip *Barney Google* had something to do with it. A googol can also be called 10 duotrigintillion, if you want to go to the trouble.

Dr. Kasner, who died in 1955, is also, along with his nephew, responsible for the term *googolplex*. This is 10 raised to the power of a googol, or one followed by a googol zeroes. Using *googolplex* as shorthand for this finite number certainly saves a lot of time, for as Kasner wrote, "there would not be enough room to write it, if you went to the farthest star, touring all the nebulae, and putting down zeroes every inch of the way."

gook. *Gook* is among the most universal of derogatory words, in that it has been applied by Americans, Englishmen, Canadians, and Australians to practically every nationality group but Americans, Englishmen, Canadians, and Australians. Most commonly it is used as a nickname for Filipinos, Pacific islanders, Japanese, Chinese, Vietnamese, and Koreans. The word probably derives from *goo-goo* and *gu-gu*, military names for a Filipino during the Spanish-American War. The Korean *kuk* (pronounced *kook*), used to convey the idea of nationality (as in *Chungkuk:* "China"), probably reinforced the word during the Korean War. So did the later slang use of *gook* (pronounced like "book"), which means "slime or dirt" and is a blend word formed from *goo* and *muck*.

goolies. Though rarely heard in America today, *goolies* is fairly common British slang for the testicles. First recorded in 1929, it derives from Hindi *goli*, "ball," "bullet," and originally came from Sanskrit. Gershon Legman wrote in *No Laughing Matter* (1969): "Well, pop it again—you've got me by the goolies!"

goon. Alice the Goon, a big stupid creature who appeared in E. C. Segar's comic strip "Popeye, the Thimble Theatre" in the late 1930s, gave her name to both stupid people called goons and the big stupid thugs called goons. Segar (1894–1938) may have fashioned the name from the 1895 slang term *goony*, for "a simpleton," but he could also have blended *gorilla* and *baboon* or even *goof* and *baboon*.

goondaism. Pakistan has been much in the news recently, focusing attention on the Pakistani language, which has given the world English hybrids like this synonym for hooliganism. *Goondaism* is from the English word *goon* and a local language word.

gooney bird. *See* ALBATROSS.

goop. A bad-mannered, inconsiderate person; a sticky, wet substance; something messy and unpleasant to handle. Another of the many words coined by American humorist Gelett Burgess, this one in *Goops and How to Be Them* (1900). Burgess may have used the word *goo*, first printed in the U.S. (ca. 1910) to build *goop*. *See* BLURB.

to goose. Mencken characterized *to goose* as "one of the most mysterious of American verbs . . ." No other language employs this term for "to jab sharply with the thumb in the anus, with the intention of startling or stimulating," which is only about 60 years old and has taken on the additional meaning of goading someone into action. There are many theories about the word's etymology. Most experts lean to the explanation that pugnacious geese "sometimes attack human beings, and especially children, by biting their fundaments." Since they are also said "to attack women by striking at the pudenda," the sexual associations are obvious. Others say that goose breeders examine their birds' rear parts for eggs before turning them out from the pens each day, and that thrusts of a similar nature are the only way to distinguish between male and female geese in certain varieties— either practice could have inspired the expression. *To goose* could also be a euphemism for *to roger*, 18th-century British slang for to have sexual intercourse, since Roger, like Dobbin for a horse, was a conventional English folk name for a goose. Finally, there is the suggestion that *to goose* is named from a poolroom receptacle called "the goose" that jokers frequently jabbed into the fundament of a pool player just as he was about to make a shot.

gooseberry. How the *gooseberry* got its name is a puzzle to historians and etymologists. One theory claims that "goose-berry" is a mispronunciation of "gorge berry," an early name for the fruit; a nice theory, except that *gooseberry* was used before *gorgeberry*, according to what records there are. For similar reasons, most word detectives do not believe that goose-berry is a corruption of *groseille*, the French name for the fruit, or the Dutch *kruishes*, which means "cross berry." Perhaps a better explanation is that *gooseberry* is a corruption of the German *Jansbeeren* (*John's berry*, so named because it ripens during the feast of St. John), which corrupted into the German *Gansberren* and was translated into English as *gooseberry* because *gans* means "goose" in German. That, in fact, is the only thing linking geese with the berry or plant—the goose doesn't like berries, isn't even averse to them, just ignores them entirely. Neither were gooseberries customarily served with roast goose, as is sometimes stated. The consensus is that *gooseberry* does come from some unknown association with the goose, plant names associated with animals often being inexplicable. There is even a theory that holds, simply put, that the goose gave its name to a fool or simpleton (as in *a silly goose*) and that the green berry (suggesting a "greenhorn" or fool) became known as a *goose* (or fool) *berry*.

gooseberry fool. Probably the most famous dish made from gooseberries is gooseberry fool, a dessert made of the fruit stewed or scalded, crushed, and mixed with milk, cream, or custard. Some say the *fool* in the dish is a corruption of the French verb *fouler*, "to crush," but this derivation seems to be inconsistent with the use of the word. More probably the dish is simply named after other, older fruit trifles, the use of *fool* in its name in the sense of "foolish or silly" being suggested by "trifle." In any case, gooseberry fool has been an English favorite since at least 1700. So widely known is the dish that a plant is named after it, the English calling the willow herb *Epilobrium hirsutum* gooseberry fool because its leaves smell like the dessert!

goose egg. *See* LAY AN EGG.

goose pimples; horripilation. When geese are plucked, the thousands of tiny muscles that pull their feathers erect to form a natural insulation system continue to contract in the cold. The contracted muscles look like bumpy, pimply skin on a bare bird and as far back as the 17th century suggested the bumps on human skin caused by cold or fear. At first this condition was called *gooseflesh* or *goose skin*, or "creeping of the flesh." A

fancier name is *horripilation*, "erection of the hair on the skin by contraction of the cutaneous muscles caused by cold, fear, or other emotion." This word effectively suggests fear and derives from the Latin *horrere*, "to bristle or shudder," which gives us the word *horror*. It is first recorded in 1623.

goosestep. The military goosestep is in modern times most associated with German troops during World War II and has unpleasant connotations, to say the least. However, the "elementary drill in which the recruit is taught to balance his body on either leg alternately, and swing the other backwards and forwards" dates back to the end of the 18th century. Apparently there were many who didn't much like it then, hence the contemptuous name *goosestep*. Wrote an observer in 1806: "The balance or goose-step introduced for this practice excites a fever of disgust." By 1900 *goosestep* came to mean the slow, stiff-legged march step now associated with the Nazis.

go out on a limb. To go out on a limb is to take a chance, to make a chancy prediction, as in "I'll go out on a limb and say he'll win in a landslide." The expression is an Americanism dating back to the later 19th century; the word *limb* is of course a tree limb.

go over big. To become a big success, a great hit. Apparently the expression is from the world of entertainment. Its first mention in print suggests this: "A comedy that 'goes over big' and is very funny is often referred to as a 'wow.' " (*American Speech* 10/21/27).

go over the top. Millions of men met their death going over the top in World War I. The expression means to climb out "over the top of one's trench" and attack the enemy over the open ground (top) between the trenches. *Over the top* has been used figuratively since the end of the Great War to mean to do something excessive, or even dangerous, as in "His story is interesting but goes a little over the top near the end."

go peddle your papers. Far more common today than 50 years ago, this American expression has a variety of meanings depending on the situation it is used in, including go away, get lost, be a good guy and leave, go away before you get hurt, mind your own business, leave us alone, etc.

G.O.P.; G.O.M. G.O.P stands for *Grand Old Party*, the official nickname of the U.S. Republican Party. First used in 1887, when it also meant "get out and push" (your own horse or car), it was probably suggested by *G.O.M.*, which the English called their *Grand Old Man*, Prime Minister Gladstone.

gopher. *Gopher* is probably theatrical in origin, dating back to the 1940s. The word is a corruption of the words *go for* and describes an errand runner, hired to do menial chores—to go for coffee and doughnuts or whatever else the boss and other higher-ups can't acquire from a sedentary position. A *gopher* can also be a zealous salesman, from "go for broke." The burrowing animal called the gopher has nothing to do with the expression.

Gopher State. The most popular nickname for Minnesota, though it prefers the North Star State and the motto *L'Étoilei* *du Nord* is on its state shield. It has also been called the Bread and Butter State, the Bread Basket of the Nation, the Wheat State, the Cream and Pitcher of the Nation, and the Playground of the Nation.

go quick plant. An old American name for rhubarb, probably because of its laxative effect. Seldom heard anymore, the name dates back to at least the early 19th century.

Gordian knot. *See* CUT THE GORDIAN KNOT.

Gordon Bennett! James Gordon Bennett (1841–1918), the son of the founder of the *New York Herald*, was an eccentric who ran the paper well but had little or no regard for money. Once he gave a train guard a $14,000 tip. Another time he threw a batch of money into a roaring fireplace to watch it burn but became angry and flung the bills back into the flames when a young man tried to salvage them. When he found someone seated at his favorite table in a Monte Carlo restaurant, he bought the place for $40,000, evicted the diners, sat down to eat—and when he left gave the restaurant back to its original owners as a tip. Bennett had a thing for restaurants. As he strolled through them to his reserved table, he liked to yank tablecloths off all the tables in his way. He'd then hand the headwaiter a large wad of cash to distribute to the disturbed and stained diners. He did this so often that the expression *Gordon Bennett!* became (and remains, in England) a cry of anyone soiled by a clumsy waiter.

Gordon setter. In contrast to the red-coated Irish setter, bred at about the same time, the Gordon setter is a brilliant black and tan. The breed originated in Scotland, partially developed by Alexander, the second duke of Gordon (1743–1847), a Scottish breeder and sportsman who also served in the House of Lords and wrote a number of folk ballads. The long-haired Irish and Gordon setters, extensively used by sportsmen for game pointing, both descend from the English setter, developed some three centuries before them.

gorgon. A terribly ugly person, especially a woman. The three snaky-headed Gorgons of classical Greek mythology, the best known of whom is Medusa, were so hideous that they turned to stone all humans who met their gaze.

Gorgonzola cheese. The village of Gorgonzola in northern Italy first made this mottled, strong-flavored, semisoft cow cheese that bears its name. Over the years other places in and out of Italy have copied the Gorgonzola recipe, leaving the little village without a monopoly but still with a pride in craftsmanship.

gorilla. Tough, hairy men aren't named after the gorilla, as most people believe. Such men actually gave their name to the ape. Originally, *Gorillai* seems to have been the name of a hairy African tribe known to the Greeks in about 500 B.C. This word came into English as *gorilla*, which first meant a hairy aboriginal person. Then in 1847 the American missionary and naturalist Dr. Thomas S. Savage observed the largest of the anthropoid apes in West Africa, naming them *gorillas* in an article published in the Boston *Journal of Natural History*. For other instances of animals named after men *see* BOOBY, BRUMBY, CAPUCHIN, CAYUSE, CHOW, FLAMINGO, GIBBON, GUPPY, HALCYON, HUSKY, MAVERICK, MOLLY, PETRELS, SHARK, and SHRIMP.

go someone one better. A common American expression today, *to go someone one better* means to exceed the performance of someone else. It began life as a poker term (which it still is) in the early 19th century, meaning to raise the bet one more chip over someone who has bet before you.

gospel bird. Southern fried chicken, almost universally known today, is probably an African invention, the chicken fried in deep fat introduced to America by blacks brought here as slaves. Gospel bird is almost certainly a black invention, chicken so called because the bird is so often served at southern Sunday dinners, especially when the preacher is coming. The humorous item is first recorded in 1902, though it must surely be older. *Kentucky fried chicken* is a synonym for *southern fried chicken*, the former term a trademark of the popular chain of restaurants that coined it.

gossamer. *See* ST. MARTIN'S DAY.

gossip. A *gossip*, the word a corruption of *god-sib*, "related to God," was originally a sponsor of a child at a baptism; Shakespeare used the term in this sense in *Two Gentlemen of Verona*. There was so much chatter at christenings, as at funerals, that the word came to mean "a tattler or newsmonger."

gotch-eared; gotch-eyed. An animal such as a horse or donkey with clipped, drooping ears is called "gotch-eared, *gotch* deriving from the Spanish *gaucho*, "turned downwind." A "gotch-eyed" person is someone with eyes looking in different directions.

Gotham. Washington Irving first called New York Gotham in his *Salmagundi Papers* (1807), because its residents reminded him of the legendary inhabitants of the English town of Gotham. An old tale has it that these villagers had discouraged King John from building a castle in their town, and taxing them for it, by feigning madness—trying to drown fish, sweep the moon's reflection off the waters, etc. This legend led to more stories about the villagers, collected in a book called *Merrie Tales of the Mad Men of Gotham*, and Irving, reading of these alternately wise and foolish people, thought that they resembled New Yorkers.

go the extra mile. To make a supreme effort, exceed what is asked or expected of one. The phrase probably has its roots in the Bible (Matt. 5:41): "And whosoever shall compel thee to go a mile, go with him twain."

Gothic. After overthrowing Rome in the fifth century, the Gothic tribesmen, an east German people, dominated much of Europe for the next 300 years. Not much is known of them, and their architecture was certainly not Gothic, but Renaissance architects nevertheless bestowed their names on all buildings characteristic of the Middle Ages, considering such structures crude and barbaric, suitable for the Goths. The 12th-to-16th-century building style, characterized by the pointed arch, as well as *Gothic art*, *Gothic type*, and myriad other things, was thereby named for a people who had nothing to do with it.

go to bat for someone.   *Going to bat for someone* means to defend, support, or take up the cause of that person. This common American phrase is from baseball and was first recorded in 1916, although it was probably used earlier. The British use bats for cricket, but the phrase is not common in England.

go to hell in a handbasket.   A handbasket is a small basket with a handle, which is carried by hand and is often used for shopping, a good example being the plastic handbaskets supplied by some supermarkets. The word *handbasket* (hand-basket) is first recorded about 1485, but no one has established when the expression *go to hell in a handbasket* came into the language. It means to degenerate quickly and decisively, as in "This company has gone to hell in a handbasket." Anyone who could fit in a small handbasket for the journey to hell would certainly have deteriorated very rapidly and decisively. A southern U.S. variation on the phrase is *go to hell in a bucket:* "Neither of us could figure it out, all we know for certain was that the marriage of Rose and Dave began to go to hell in a bucket . . ." (Calder Willingham, *Rambling Rose,* 1972).

go to poodic.   George Stewart in *Names on the Land* (1945) cites this Indian name for a point of land on the Maine coast. It translates as "Go jump in the bay!"

go to the devil.   The Devil Tavern was one of the most famous taverns in London, standing in Fleet Street and taking its name from its sign, which showed the devil tweaking St. Dunstan's nose. The tavern was a favorite hangout for lawyers, and 17th-century wits spread the story that whenever a lawyer was wanted and couldn't be found in his offices, his clerk would tell the client to "go to the Devil." This has been suggested as the source of the above phrase, but is not to be believed. To *go to the devil,* "to go to ruin or hell," dates back to at least 1384, and there are many examples of its use through the centuries. William Caxton, for example, wrote: "Let them go to a hundred thousand devils!"

go to the dogs.   *See* DOG'S LIFE.

go to the mat.   The mat in wrestling is the padded canvas covering the whole floor of a wrestling ring to protect the athletes from injury. The sight of wrestlers contending on it suggested the general phrase *go to the mat,* "to struggle mightily in a determined, unyielding way," as in "The President is going to the mat with Congress over that bill."

go to the wall.   A traveler set upon by robbers in medieval times tried to protect his back against the wall of a street or country lane so that he didn't have to worry about anyone running him through from the rear while he defended himself with his sword. But *to go to the wall* nevertheless suggested serious difficulties, for someone in such a position still had to fight off attackers from three sides. So the phrase came to describe anyone in serious straits, anyone up against it, down to his last resources, physical or financial. The expression *driven to the wall* and *up against the wall* derive, just as early, from the same situation.

go troppo.   Australians like to use this expression meaning "to go crazy," "to become mentally disturbed." *Troppo* may be a shortening of *tropical,* perhaps in reference to someone stranded on a tropical island with no companionship.

got to see a man about a dog.   An excuse to use the bathroom. Widely heard today, the expression probably originated in England toward the middle of the 19th century. The man originally referred to in the excuse may have been a bookmarker who took bets on dog races.

gourmet.   The first gourmet was a *groumet,* "a horse groom." The word changed to *gourmet* in French and was applied to grooms and any minor servants in a household. Among these servants were boys who tasted wine, and such wine tasters, or *gourmets,* were given the same name when they worked as assistants in wine shops. Eventually the wine-shop *gourmets* became connoisseurs of fine wines and food in general, giving us the *gourmet* we know today. The word is not recorded in English until 1820.

gout.   Regarded today as a form of arthritis, *gout* derives from the Latin *gutta,* "drop," because it was once believed that drops of bad blood or acrid matter dropped from the bloodstream into the joints and caused the painful swellings associated with the disease. The word came into English via the French *goutte* in about 1290.

the government is best which governs least.   *See* SUMMER SOLDIER AND SUNSHINE PATRIOT.

government of the people, by the people, for the people. *See* FOURSCORE AND SEVEN.

go west; occident.   An unknown poet may have independently coined the phrase *to go west,* "to die," in the trenches of World War I. The expression was common then, possibly suggested by the setting of the sun in the west. But the phrase is much older. In America, Indian legend had it that a dying man had gone to meet the setting sun, and, later, when explorers and prospectors didn't return from dangerous country west of the Mississippi, they were said to have gone west. In 16th-century England the phrase was used of criminals going to be hung at Tyburn, which is west of London, and an early 14th-century English poem with the refrain "his world is but a vanity" had the lines: "Women and many a willful man,/ As wind and water are gone west." The idea behind the expression is even older. The Egyptians spoke of the west as the home of departed spirits, and among the Greeks the association of death with the west was proverbial, as in *Ulysses:*

> My purpose holds
> To sail beyond the sunset, and the paths
> Of all the western stars, until I die.

Even our word *Occident,* for "the west," is associated with death. It comes from the Latin *occidens,* "the place where the sun died at the end of each day," which is from the verb *occidere,* "to die."

go west, young man, go west.   In America *go west* came to stand for new life and hope instead of death (*see* GO WEST) with the expansion of the frontier. There is some controversy about who said *go west, young man* first, however. Horace Greeley used the expression in an editorial in his *New York Tribune:* "Go west, young man, and grow with the country." Later, as the phrase grew in popularity, Greeley said that his inspiration was John Babsone Lane Soule, who wrote "Go West, young man" in an 1851 article in the *Terre Haute Express.* Greeley even reprinted Soule's article from the Indiana newspaper to give credit where it was due, but several writers insisted that Greeley had given them identical advice before Soule had written the piece. William S. Verity said that the great editor had coined the expression a full year before Soule.

go whistle for it.   One story claims that this saying arose as a perversion of the old nautical superstition that one could raise the wind for a becalmed ship by whistling (the basis of the "magic" was that air would come from the sky just as air came from your mouth). But another tale, also unproved, attributes the words to the whistle tankards once used in British pubs, drinkers blowing a whistle on the side of each when they wanted a refill. Thus both possible sources imply the opposite of the phrase's meaning "You'll never get it from me, you won't get it at all."

go whole hog.   Probably the expression *to go the whole hog,* or *to go whole hog,* "to go the limit, all the way," has its origins in William Cowper's poem "The Love of the World Reproved; or Hypocrisy Detected" (1779). Cowper told a story about pious but hungry Muhammadans who were ordered by Muhammad not to eat a certain unspecified part of the pig. Unable to determine what part, they began to experiment:

> But for one piece they thought it hard
> From the whole hog to be debar'd;
> And set their wit at work to find
> What joint the prophet had in mind . . .
> Thus, conscience freed from every clog,
> Mohometans eat up the hog . . .
> With sophistry their sauce they
>   sweeten,
> Til quite from tail to snout 'tis eaten.

goy.   *Goy* is a Yiddish word for a gentile, and can be completely innocent or disparaging, depending on who is using it and how it is used—just as *Jew* can be either, depending on the circumstance. Leo Rosten notes that the word itself is not derogatory and discusses it at length in his *The Joys of Yiddish,* one of the best and brightest word books of this or any other time. *Goy* derives from the Hebrew *goy,* nation, and dates back at least to the 19th century.

Grable-bodied seamen.   Movie actress Betty Grable, her "million-dollar legs" insured by Lloyds of London, was the pin-up girl par excellence during World War II. British sailors used the term *Grable-bodied seamen* to describe long-stemmed lovelies in the Wrens (Women's Royal Naval Service) who fit the description. *See* FRANKIE BAILEY'S; FANNY; CHARLEY.

grace under pressure.   This phrase is often attributed to American president John F. Kennedy, but it was really author Ernest Hemingway's coinage and credo. JFK borrowed the expression from Hemingway.

graft.   This American term for dishonest earnings, usually of politicians, isn't recorded until 1859. Its origins are unclear, but the word may derive from the British slang *graft,* for "any kind of work, especially illicit work," which, in turn, may come from the British *graer,* "to dig," influenced, Partridge says, by the gardening *graft.* The gardening *graft* derives, ultimately, from the Greek word *grapheion,* "a bone or wood pencil-like instrument used for writing on wax tablets." Someone in early times possibly thought that a *grapheion* resembled a twig for grafting.

Graham crackers, etc.   Young Presbyterian minister Sylvester Graham (1794–1851) became so ardent a temperance advocate that he not only traveled far and wide to lecture on the demon rum, but invented a vegetable diet that he was sure would cure those suffering from the evils of drink. Graham soon extended his mission to include changing America's sinful eating habits. Meats and fats, he said, led to sexual excesses and mustard and catsup could cause insanity, but Graham mainly urged the substitution of homemade unsifted whole wheat flour for white flour. Modern science has affirmed his belief that refining flour robs it of vitamins and minerals, and most of his regimen, including vegetables and fruits in the diet, fresh air while sleeping, moderate eating, and abundant exercise, is now widely accepted. His memorials are the *Graham flour, Graham bread,* and *Graham crackers* that his followers ate and dedicated to him.

grain of salt.   *See* TAKE WITH A GRAIN OF SALT.

Gramont's memory.   The name is often spelled *Grammont* due to its misspelling in the *Mémoires du comte de Grammont.* A *Gramont's memory,* a convenient one, derives from a tale told about the count and Lady Elizabeth Hamilton. While visiting England in 1663, the sharp-tongued Gramont is said to have grossly insulted and refused to apologize to La Belle Hamilton, whose brothers followed him as he prepared to leave the country, drew their swords, and asked if he hadn't forgotten something. "True, true," he replied, unruffled. "I promised to marry your sister." This he did. Only the year before his marriage, Philibert, comte de Gramont, had been exiled from Paris for attempting to rival King Louis XIV in a love affair. The French diplomat's memoirs, a masterpiece of their kind, vividly describe the licentious court of England's Charles II. They were written by Gramont's brother-in-law, Anthony Hamilton, from materials supplied by the count. So sharp-tongued was Philibert that one writer describes the immense feeling of relief expressed by the French court when, in 1707, it was announced that he had died. Even at 87 he was still a threat to anyone who crossed him.

grand.   *Grand* for a thousand dollars is American slang that dates back to at least 1900, and is probably so named because it is "a grand sum of money." *Grand* was abbreviated to a *G* or a *G-note* within 20 years or so. An older term for a thousand dollars is a *thou,* first recorded in 1869 and still used; a newer term meaning the same is *a big one,* which seems to have been coined about 50 years ago, about the time that *large* for a thousand dollars is first recorded.

grandbaby. A common term for a grandchild that dates back to at least 1916; heard recently (1991) from a southern woman in the Empire State Building in New York City, of all places: "I got three grandbabies down home." *Grand boy* is a male grandbaby.

grand climacteric. As far back as 1653, people have been writing about the grand or great climacteric. This is a superstition involving the age 63 (a number that is the product of the "magic numbers" 7 and 9) and holding that if you survived that dangerous year you would live to a ripe old age. The word *climacteric* itself, which also refers to the female menopause, derives from a Greek word meaning "a critical period."

grandfather clause. A clause used by some southern states in their constitutions after 1890, in which they disenfranchised blacks by stipulating that new literacy and property qualifications for voting applied only to those whose ancestors did not have the right to vote before 1867. Since no blacks could vote or had ancestors who could vote before that time, this meant that no blacks were permitted to vote.

grandfather clock. A pendulum floor clock with a case as tall as or taller than a person. This is possibly the only English word that came into the language from a song: American songwriter Henry Clay Work's "Grandfather's Clock," written in 1875. Work's song became so popular that people began calling 0all such clocks grandfather's clocks, grandfather clocks, and grandfathers. The first stanza of the song goes:

> My grandfather's clock was too large for the shelf,
>   So it stood ninety years on the floor;
> It was taller by half than the old man himself,
>   Though it weighed not a pennyweight more.
> It was bought on the morn of the day he was
>   born
>   And was always his treasure and pride.
> But it stopped short—never to go again—
>   When the old man died.

Grand Guignol. Violent, sensational plays were the staple of the Théâtre du Grand Guignol in Paris up until recent times, these short plays giving us the name *Grand Guignol* for such works, or the staging of them. The theater took its name, ultimately, from the French *guignol*, "puppet or marionette," in relation to the violence and brutality of Punch-and-Judy shows.

grandma. Two humorous stories from the Ozarks: *To grandma* there means "to cut down and steal timber from someone else's property," perhaps because an anonymous thief who stole timber explained that he got it from his "grandma's" place. Another theory has this unusual word deriving from an old story or joke about a man accused of stealing another's timber and finally admitting that "Grandmaw might have taken a few sticks."

Grand Marnier. The famous orange liqueur was devised by French industrialist Marnier Lapostolle in the 1890s. According to an old story, Lapostolle asked hotelier Cesar Ritz what he should call his liqueur. "Why Monsieur, call it after yourself, *Le Grand Marnier!*" Ritz replied.

grandmother story. This old American Indian expression is explained in Grant Foreman's book *The Last Trek of the Indians* (1946): "The absentee Shawnee cherished a prophetic tradition generally known as the 'grandmother story' as told by a Shawnee woman, having reference to certain present and eternal judgments that would be visited upon the unfortunate head of any Indian who laid aside the blanket to adopt the white man's dress."

Grand Old Flag. The original title of "You're a Grand Old Flag" (1906) was "You're a Grand Old Rag." George M. Cohan changed it when critics protested that he was profaning the Stars and Stripes. Cohan (he pronounced his name Cohen) wrote his famous song "Harrigan" in honor of his friend, vaudeville performer, Ed Harrigan, of Harrigan and Hart fame.

Grand Old Man of Football. Amos Alonzo Stagg (1862–1965), "the Grand Old Man of Football," began coaching the University of Chicago football team in 1892 (after two years with the Springfield YMCA), switched over to the College of the Pacific in 1934 when he was 72, and coached there until he was 98! The five-foot-four-inch Stagg was a divinity school graduate and a firm believer that football encouraged clean living and built character. It is unlikely anyone will ever break his record of 75 years of active coaching, and only Walter Camp can match his contributions to football. The coach, who never retired, gave football many things, including the huddle, the single and double wingback, the shift, the man in motion, the end around or end run, the tackling dummy, and letters awarded to athletes. Stagg was 81 when named college coach of the year in 1943, so there really is hope for all coaches. *See* FATHER OF AMERICAN FOOTBALL.

grand panjandrum. *See* NO SOAP!

grand slam. In bridge a grand slam is the taking of all 13 tricks in a deal and the phrase dates back to about 1895 in that sense. By 1940 it became baseball's home run hit with the bases loaded—the sport's ultimate home run. In general use, a grand slam is the ultimate of anything.

grandstanding. *See* PLAY TO THE GRANDSTAND.

Grand Tetons. French voyageurs early named these mountains in northwestern Wyoming the Grand Tetons, the "big breasts," because of their resemblance to a woman's breasts. For the same reason the rounded hillocks or mounds west of the Mississippi are called *mamelle*, from the French *mamelle*, for "a woman's breast."

grangerize. Reverend James Granger (1723–76) himself clipped some 14,000 engraved portraits from other books to use as possible illustrations for his *Biographical History of England*. Some of the books he pillaged were rare ones, and to make matters worse, he suggested in his preface that private collections like his might prove valuable someday. This resulted in a fad called *grangerizing*, or extra-illustration, with thousands of people mutilating fine books and stuffing pictures and other material into Granger's book. Editions following the 1769 *Biographical History . . . adapted to a Methodical Catalogue of Engraved British Heads* provided blank pages for the insertion of these extra illustrations; the book eventually increased to six volumes from its original two. Sets of Granger illustrated with up to 3,000 engravings were compiled, and so many early English books were ravaged that *to grangerize* came to mean the mutilation that remains the bane of librarians today.

The Granite State.   A nickname for New Hampshire. The state's granite industry, storytellers say, was established as a result of locals drilling for salt. In 1827 citizens drilled hole after hole searching for the precious condiment, only to give it up as a bad job upon striking layer after layer of granite. Soon after, they decided to mine the granite.

granny knot.   A poorly tied knot that often comes loose, one that looks like it might have been tied by someone's granny. Though it is a nautical term referring to a landlubber's knot, *granny knot* is heard on land as well today, in every place where seamen have introduced it.

grant (give) no quarter.   *To grant (give) no quarter* originally meant to spare no life of an enemy in your power, but it has come to mean "to be unmerciful." The expression has its origin in its opposite, *to grant quarter*, which may derive from an ancient agreement between the warring Spaniards and Dutch that the ransom of a soldier be a quarter of his pay. More likely the words have their origin in the old custom of a victor providing his captives temporary housing. *Quarters* (from the Latin *quadrus*, "square"), for "a residence or a place where an army lodges," is recorded as early as 1591.

grape; grapefruit; wineberry.   Grapefruit *(Citrus paradisi)* resemble grapes only in that they grow in clusters on their trees, but that was sufficient reason to bestow the name upon them, early explorers in Barbados thought. *Grapes* themselves look nothing like their namesakes. Grapes were named for the *grape*, or grapple, the small hook that the French used to harvest them. The English called grapes *wineberries* until they imported the French word toward the end of the 11th century.

grapes of wrath; wrath of grapes.   The words *grapes of wrath* are from Julia Ward Howe's "Battle Hymn of the Republic" (1862), which was often sung by Union soldiers in the Civil War: "Mine eyes have seen the glory of the coming of the Lord; / He is trampling out the vintage where the grapes of wrath are stored. . . ." The words are also the title of John Steinbeck's novel (1938) and the movie made from it (1939). The term *wrath of grapes* is a recent humorous phrase for a hangover.

the grapevine.   Some 15 years after Samuel Morse transmitted his famous "what hath God wrought" message, a long telegraph line was strung from Virginia City to Placerville, California, so crudely strung, it's said, that people jokingly compared the line with a sagging grapevine. I can find no record of this, but, in any case, grapevines were associated with telegraph lines somewhere along the line, for by the time of the Civil War a report *by grapevine telegraph* was common slang for a rumor. The idea behind the expression is probably not rumors sent over real telegraph lines, but the telegraphic speed with which rumormongers can transmit canards with their own rude mouth-to-mouth telegraph system.

graphite.   *See* LEAD.

grass.   All the words in the sentence *Grass grows green* come from one source, the Teutonic *gro*, which in turn derives from the Aryan *ghra*, to grow. Our word *graze* also ultimately comes from this source. Grasses are worldwide in distribution and a listing of them would fill a large book. It has been noted that the grass family supports the temperate and tropical world, containing as it does wheat, corn, rice, rye, barley, oats, and sugarcane. But most people think of lawns or meadows when they think of grass, as is witnessed by common American sayings such as "don't let the grass grow under your feet"—don't be lazy, be active and energetic. Such grass is probably one of the few plants that almost everyone can identify, though not the many varieties of it. Home lawns made of grass covered about 23 million acres across the U.S. in 1995.

grasshopper.   The very appropriate name for this common insect is more colorful in other languages. The Italian name for the grasshopper is *cavalletta*, "little mare," while the Spanish call it *saltamontes*, "jump mountains." For some reason the Germans call it *die Heuschrecke*, "the terrible hay-thing." In Greek mythology the sound of the grasshopper is said to be the voice of the handsome Tithonus, who married Aurora, the goddess of dawn. Aurora asked Zeus to grant her husband immortality, which the great god did, but she neglected to ask Zeus to keep him forever young. Time passed and the handsome Tithonus fell victim to its ravages, while Aurora remained young and beautiful. She eventually took pity on her old doddering husband and turned him into a grasshopper, locking him in a palace room. Tithonus has since been heard every evening at his palace window crying for his lost Aurora. *Knee-high to a toad*, first recorded in 1814, was the original of the Americanism *knee-high to a grasshopper*, which came on the scene some 37 years later. *Knee-high to a grasshopper* is generally used in comparisons, emphasizing youth, smallness, or remoteness in time. There are some 120,000 varieties of grasshoppers, and to be literally knee-high, or tibiahigh, to a grasshopper a person would have to range from one millimeter tall to little more than an inch tall. *See* GULL.

grasshopper battle.   A historical term for a battle fought in 1873 between the Shawnee and Delaware Indians, supposedly started by an argument among children over the ownership of a pet grasshopper.

grass roots.   "A little classic of the poetic imagination," the *New York Times* once called this phrase, but whose "poetic imagination" we don't know. In 1935, when the Republican Party was seeking a broader base of support among the voters, John Hamilton of Topeka, Kansas used the words in describing the "new" G.O.P. No one has traced the phrase back further in print, but one respected etymologist has testified that he heard the expression back in rural Ohio in about 1885. A term dear to politicians, it simply means to get down to basic facts or underlying principles, its appeal becoming more nostalgic as more concrete replaces grass. *Grass roots* itself, for "basics, fundamentals," has been traced to 1932 when used, appropriately enough, to describe the candidacy of Oklahoma Governor William H. ("Alfalfa Bill") Murray for the Democratic presidential nomination. It, too, probably stems from the prairie farms of the West.

grass widow. The old story that this synonym for a divorcée derives from *veuve de grace*, "a divorcée or widow by courtesy or grace of the Pope," has no basis in fact—for one thing, *grace widow* is nowhere recorded in English. Just as unlikely is the theory that the phrase originated with the custom of British officers in India sending their wives on vacation to the cool grassy hills during intensely hot summers, where, separated from their husbands, they were humorously referred to as *grass widows*. There is also a yarn that "forty-niners" in America "put their wives out to grass," boarding them with neighbors until they returned from prospecting. The most plausible explanation of this old English expression, which dates back to at least the early 16th century, is that it formerly meant an unmarried mother and just changed in meaning over the years. "Grass" probably referred to the grass in which the grass widow's child might have been begotten, outside of the proper marriage bed, and "widow" to the woman's unmarried state. We find the same parallel in many languages, including our current slang *a roll in the hay*; the German *Strohwiteve*, "straw widow"; and the Middle Low German *graswedeue*, an obsolete word for a woman with an illegitimate child. One joke has it that a *grass widow* is a forlorn middle-class matron whose husband spends all his spare time playing golf.

Grauman's Chinese Theater. Since 1927 scores of movie stars have left imprints of their feet and hands in cement outside Grauman's Chinese Theater in Los Angeles; the first was Hollywood actress Norma Talmadge. A good number of stars, however, left more imaginative imprints for posterity. Jimmy "The Schnoz" Durante, for example, impressed his impressive nose in the forecourt sidewalk, and comedian Joe E. Brown left a likeness of his huge mouth, while Betty Grable laid down one of her "million-dollar legs" and Mickey Mouse left his paw prints. The hoofprints of cowboy star Gene Autry's faithful horse, Champion, and Roy Rogers's Trigger are also enshrined outside Grauman's, as is Al Jolson's right knee, which he knelt on white singing "Mammy." So are matinee idol John Barrymore's profile and actor Monty Woolley's beard. The theater, now owned by the Mann Theaters Corporation, has no plans to discontinue this tradition begun in the first year it was built.

Graves's disease; Basedow's disease. These are one and the same disease, an enlargement of the thyroid gland, also called exophthalmic goiter that is visible as a swelling at the front of the throat and is often associated with iodine deficiency. It bears the name of Irish physician Robert Graves (1796–1853), who first discovered it in 1835, and German physician Karl von Basedow (1799–1854), who discovered it five years later in more detail, unaware that Graves had gotten there before him.

graveyard. *See* CEMETERY.

graveyard stew. During the Great Depression we ate toasted bread and milk, sweetened with a lot of sugar when no one was looking, for too many meals. There were complaints about this *graveyard stew* or *soup*—so named because it was often fed to old people with no teeth or because a steady diet of it might send you to the grave—but it doesn't seem that bad anymore.

gravy train. In the 1920s, railroad men invented the expression to *ride the gravy train* to describe a run on which there was good pay and little work. The words were quickly adopted into general speech, meaning to have an easy job that pays well, or, more commonly, to be prosperous. *Gravy*, however, had been slang for easy money since the early 1900s.

grayback. Any huge Atlantic Ocean wave that isn't breaking is called a *grayback* by Newfoundlanders. *See* GREENBACKS.

gray eminence. *See* ÉMINENCE GRISE.

greased. Grunt (infantryman) lingo in Vietnam for being killed. "They used a hard vocabulary to contain the terrible softness," Tim O'Brien wrote in "The Things They Carried" (1987). "*Offed, lit up, zapped while zipping* [killed by a sniper just after urinating]. It wasn't cruelty, just stage presence." *See* ZAP.

greased lightning. Lightning is fast enough, striking before it can be heard, but *greased lightning!* Why, this is the kind of American exaggeration for emphasis that British grammarians sneered about all through the 19th century. Americans surely are a hyperbolic people, but the trouble here is that *like greased lightning*, "faster than anything," is a British expression, despite some disclaimers. At least it first appeared in the *Boston, Lincoln, and Louth Herald* of January 15, 1833. The hyperbole is of course not meant to be taken seriously. No more than the everyday expressions *as old as the hills, a million thanks, I haven't seen you for ages*, or even Shakespeare's famous poetic device in *Macbeth*:

> No; this my hand will rather
> The multitudinous seas incarnadine,
> Making the green one red.

grease one's palm. *To grease one's palm* was originally *to grease one's hand*, an expression first recorded by the poet John Skelton in 1526. From such early times, *to grease one's hand, palm*, or *fist*, or simply *to grease*, has meant to bribe or tip. There is an identical old expression in French, *graisser la patte*, and the idea behind the expression is the same as that behind greasing the wheels, making things run smoothly—greasing the hand or palm of a person will make his hand work more smoothly for you.

greaser. A derogatory offensive name for Mexicans and Mexican-Americans first recorded in 1836 in what is now Texas. *Greaserdom* is a derogatory historical name for New Mexico. An unlikely explanation says that *greaser* derives from men hired by Mexican freighters to run alongside their wagons and grease the wooden axles.

greasy luck. Whalemen "trying out" oil from whale blubber on the decks of whaleships in the 19th century invented this expression, meaning "good luck." The decks became very greasy or slippery at such times, and this was considered lucky because it meant a more prosperous voyage. Well-wishers often wished whaleman "greasy luck" when they embarked on a voyage. In Britain today *greasy* is still a synonym for slippery.

Great American Desert.   The idea of a Great American Desert in the West discouraged many people from settling in the region, which they thought was uninhabitable. The term *Great American Desert* was used in newspapers and geographies as early as 1834. Before this, the area, which is part of the Great Plains, was called the *Great Desert*, this term recorded 50 years earlier.

The Great American Mudhole; the Capital of Miserable Huts.   Humorous nicknames for the U.S. capital, Washington, D.C., in the early years after its founding. *See* WASHINGTON.

The Great American Novel.   This term sprang up toward the end of the 19th century. Frank Norris wrote: "The Great American Novel is not extinct like the Dodo, but mythical like the Hippogriff . . . the thing to be looked for is not the Great American Novelist, but the Great Novelist who shall also be American." Observed Jack London a little later: "I'd rather win a water-fight in a swimming pool, or remain astride a horse that is trying to get out from under me, than write the great American novel."

Great Carbuncle.   Nathaniel Hawthorne described the Great Carbuncle in "Sketches From Memory" (1835): "There are few legends more poetical than that of the 'Great Carbuncle' of the White Mountains. The belief was communicated to the English settlers, and is hardly yet extinct, that a gem, of such immense size as to be seen shining miles away, hangs from a rock over a clear, deep lake, high up among the hills. They who had once beheld its splendor, were enthralled with an unutterable yearning to possess it. But a spirit guarded that inestimable jewel, and bewildered the adventurer with a dark mist from the enchanted lake. Thus, life was worn away in the vain search for an unearthly treasure, till at length the deluded one went up the mountain, still sanguine as in youth, but returned no more. On this theme, methinks, I could frame a tale with a deep moral." Hawthorne did later write "The Great Carbuncle" (1837), noting that the tale was based on an "Indian tradition."

The Great Commoner.   This nickname was applied to a number of American political leaders with a populist bent after it was first given to Henry Clay in the early 1840s—among them: Thaddeus Stevens, William Jennings Bryan, and Thomas Jefferson.

Great Communicator.   A name in praise of Ronald Wilson Reagan (b. 1911), celebrated for his skills in dealing with people. The former movies and television star served as U.S. president from 1981–89.

Great Dissenter.   *See* CLEAR AND PRESENT DANGER.

Great Divide.   A name used since about 1860 for the continental divide of North America; the Rocky Mountains.

greatest man that ever touched shoe leather.   An extravagant Irish compliment for someone much loved and respected.

greatest show on earth.   *See* THERE'S A SUCKER BORN EVERY MINUTE.

Great Father.   A Native American name for the president of the United States. Dee Brown in *Bury My Heart at Wounded Knee* (1970) quotes Spotted Tail of the Brule Sioux as saying, "This war . . . was brought upon us by the children of the Great Father. . . ." *Great White Father* means the same and is also used as a humorous title today. *See* GREAT KNIVES.

great fleas have lesser fleas.   All of us, no matter how great, have our troubles, our enemies who prey on us. The expression has its roots in Jonathan Swift's volume of satirical advice to a poet, *On Poetry, a Rhapsody* (1733), with its lines: "Hobbes clearly proves that every creature/Lives in a state of war by nature;/ So naturalists observe a flea/ Has smaller fleas that on him prey,/ And these have smaller still to bite 'em/ And so proceed *ad infinitum*."

great hulking man.   *Hulk* has its origins in the ancient Greek *holkas*, "a trading vessel," originally a towed ship, the word akin to the Greek *helkein*, "to drag," because such ships were towed or dragged behind. The English word first meant a large sailing ship, then became the hull of a ship, and today means the body of an abandoned ship. Shakespeare was the first to record *hulk* as the synonym for a big unwieldy person and this comparison to a large unwieldy ship remains in the language today, both in the names of wrestlers ("The Hulk") and other big people called *hulks* and the expression *a great hulking man*.

Great John L.   After well over a century, the name of swashbuckling John Lawrence Sullivan (1858–1918) remains synonymous for a great fighter, up there with Jack Dempsey, Jack Johnson, Joe Louis, Sugar Ray Robinson, and Mohammed Ali. Reigning as the bare-knuckle heavyweight champion of the world from 1882 until he retired in 1896, he lost only to Gentleman Jim Corbett (in an 1892 bout fighting with gloves under the Queensberry rules). Nobody ever beat Sullivan with bare knuckles, although Jack Kilrain once took him 75 rounds. After he retired, Sullivan became, to everyone's great surprise, a temperature advocate. The Great John L. was also called the Boston Strongboy, the Boston Hercules, Boston's Pet, Boston's Pride and Joy, the Boston Miracle, the Young Boston Giant, Boston's Goliath, and Boston's Philanthropic Prizefighter, among many more nicknames.

Great Knives; great medicine; Great Spirit.   Several Native American terms for great things. *Great Knives* referred to U.S. soldiers, in reference to their bayonettes; *great medicine* meant anything especially effective; explorers Lewis and Clark noted that whatever is mysterious or unintelligible (to the Indians) is called "great medicine"; and *Great Spirit* refers to the chief deity in the religion of many North American Indian tribes. *See* GREAT FATHER.

great majority.   A humorous British term, with some American use, for the dead, as in "Even there among the great majority you can bet he's a voice of dissent." The term was coined by British poet Edward Young, who joined the great majority in 1765, when he was 82, but Young apparently got the idea from the vivacious first-century Roman satirist and *elegantiae arbiter* (arbiter of taste) Petronius, who in his *Satyricon*, among his many great works, wrote *Abiit ad plures*, "he's gone to join the majority." Petronius also coined or first recorded the common expression *ages ago* (*olim oliorum*) and the famous phrase *the studied felicity of Horace*. He took his own life in A.D. 65, when he felt he had fallen out of favor with the emperor Nero.

Great Profile. Sobriquet for actor John Barrymore (1882–1942) of the theater's "royal family." Known for his chiseled, matinee-idol good looks, he had great success on stage in such roles as Hamlet, then appeared in many films before declining into alcohol abuse. One of his last movies was *The Great Profile* (1940), in which he parodied his own reputation.

Great Revival. The religious revival begun in Kentucky and Tennessee near the beginning of the 19th century. According to Everett Dick in *The Dixie Frontier* (1948): "The Great Revival of 1800 and its attendant institution, the camp-meeting, were pure products of the frontier of the Old Southwest."

Great Scott! Old Fuss-and-Feathers, General Winfield Scott, a brigadier general at only 28, was well known for his arrogant swagger, and his opponents may have jeeringly dubbed him "Great Scott" with this in mind. On the other hand, the hero of the Mexican War and the Whig candidate for president in 1852 wasn't the only Scottophile in the country—his many supporters may have named him "Great Scott" in admiration of his great dignity. At any rate, the exclamation *Great Scott!* hasn't been traced back before Old Fuss-and-Feathers' day and he could certainly have been responsible for the expression in one way or another. That the term is just a euphemism for "Great God!," a play on the German *Gott*, is a simpler but not necessarily truer explanation.

Great Smokies. The Great Smokies area takes its name from the Cherokee name for the mountains, which translates as "The Place of Blue Smoke." The mountain range, on the North Carolina-Tennessee border, is apparently the only American range with *great* attached to its name. Also called the Great Smokey Mountains, Smokey Mountains, and, most poetically, Land of the Sky.

The Great Unknown; the Great Magician of the North. Few authors would appreciate such a designation, but Sir Walter Scott (1771–1832) was known as "The Great Unknown" because for 13 years, beginning with his first novel, *Waverley* (1814), he published 26 novels anonymously or as "by the author of *Waverley*." Scott's publishing partner, James Ballantyne, coined the nickname for him after Scott decided he did not want the novels confused with his well-known poetry. He was also called "The Great Magician (or Wizard) of the North" because of his magical works.

the great unwashed. In 1901 the *Congressional Record* noted that "the Democratic Party has long been known as the 'great unwashed.' " By then the epithet was at least 50 years old. *The great unwashed* is still heard today occasionally in reference to what the speaker believes are "the lower classes," but is not applied to the Democrats. In the late 18th century the British had called the rabble of the French Revolution the great unwashed.

Great White Fleet. The United States decided to show the world its naval power in 1907 and sent 16 battleships and four destroyers on a world cruise. Because all these ships were painted white, they were popularly called the *White Fleet* or *Great White Fleet*.

Great White Hope. *See* JACK JOHNSON.

Great White North. A nickname for Canada that is known internationally. *See* DECEMBER IS THIRTEEN MONTHS LONG.

The Great White Way. This nickname for the Manhattan theatrical or entertainment district, a reference to all the lights there, was coined by Albert Bigelow Paine, best known today as Mark Twain's first biographer, and used as the title of his novel *The Great White Way* (1901), which is about the Antarctic, not Broadway.

Greek. The Greeks are the subject of many proverbs still heard. *Beware of Greeks bearing gifts* dates to a line in Virgil, "I fear the Greeks especially when they bring gifts," and refers to the fabled wooden horse containing soldiers that the Greeks gave to the Trojans. *Greek trust* was to the Romans no trust at all; and *when Greek meets Greek then comes the tug of war* commemorates the resistance of the ancient Greek cities to the Macedonian kings Philip and Alexander the Great. Putting something off *until the Greek calends* is to never do it, for the Greeks, unlike the Romans, had no term like "calends" for the first days of their months. To *play the Greek* is to live a luxurious life, while the modern expression *when Greek meets Greek, they open a restaurant* at least admits that Greeks are enterprising. Then there's *it's all Greek to me*; and the slang term *Grecian bend*, a posture bent forward from the waist much affected in the late 19th century; and the straight-lined *Grecian profile*, among other expressions. To many, Grecian itself is the term "for all civilized and subtle thoughts and feelings," the Grecians "swelling o'er with arts," as Shakespeare wrote. Lastly, there's *Greek fire*, the mysterious ancient naval weapon that burned when wet and was so effective against wooden ships from A.D. 700 to 900, which is said to have been invented by the Greek Callimachus. No one knows its constituents, but it is thought to have been composed of sulphur, naphtha, and pitch. Water helped Greek fire spread and it could be extinguished only with wine.

Greek and Roman proverbs. The words of ancient Greek and Roman writers have lasted for thousands of years, many of them becoming proverbial in English and other languages. Here are just a few such proverbs:

"God loves to help him who strives to help himself."—Aeschylus, *Seven Against Thebes*
"None love the messenger who brings bad news."—Sophocles, *Antigone*
"Leave no stone unturned."—Euripides, *Heracleidae*
"I laughed till I cried."—Aristophanes, *The Frogs*
"Old age is but a second childhood."—Aristophanes, *The Frogs*
"Conscience makes cowards of us all."—Menander, unidentified fragment

"You knew not how to live in clover."—Menander, *The Girl From Samos*

"Whom the gods love, die young."—Menander, unidentified fragment

"Nothing in excess."—Terence, *Andria*

"In the bloom of youth."—Terence, *Andria*

Greek words in English.   Classical Greek and Latin borrowings possibly account for a majority of English words. Many Greek words have come into English, often through Latin and other languages. These include: ANTHOLOGY, *barometer*, BIBLE, *catastrophe*, *cheer*, CYCLONE, *elastic*, HOI POLLOI, IDIOT, *magic*, *tactics*, and TANTALIZE.

green.   The word *green* (deriving from the Old English *grene*) has long signified the color of youth ("ripe in years but green in heart") and the color of envy or jealousy (the "green-eyed monster" in Shakespeare's *Othello*). Green is also the color that means to proceed, as in *green light*, and it has been recruited recently as the color of environmentalists and political parties espousing environmentalism. These meanings are not the same in many other languages; in fact, Americans do not use many meanings of *green* found in other languages. In French, for example, *to be green to someone* means "to bear that person a grudge"; *to get a green reply* means a "tart reply"; *green tale* refers to a spicy story; *green language* signifies slang. In Spanish, a *green old man* refers to an old reprobate, and *giving oneself a green* means "to take time off from work." It should be noted that Germans are not green with envy but "yellow with envy"; they use the expression *beaten green and blue*, not *beaten black and blue*; and when they feel sick or nauseated, they say "get green and yellow before the eyes."

Greenacre!   *Greenacre!*, a word popular in the 19th century, is a good example of true gallows humor. The rope broke when they hanged James Greenacre at Newgate Prison in 1837 and he had to be strung up again. However, little sympathy was shown for the murderer, who had hacked up his victim and buried sections of the body under various London landmarks. Stevedores, in fact, promptly adopted the killer's name to indicate the falling of cargo. Whenever rope slings broke while goods were being loaded or unloaded, the cry *Greenacre!* went up along the docks.

greenbacks.   Union troops in the Civil War named U.S. Treasury legal-tender banknotes *greenbacks* for the obvious reason that the backs of the bills were green. Over a half-billion dollars' worth of them were issued. The Confederacy issued more than a billion dollars' worth of "bluebacks" and "graybacks," which were worthless because they had no gold or silver behind them. "Goldbacks" (1873) and "Yellowbacks" (1902) were other colorful U.S. banknotes.

green bean.   *See* BEAN.

Green Berets.   Another name for the U.S. Special Forces, which are the core of the American Special Operations Community. These elite troops are named for the dashing green berets they wear as part of their uniform and are thought to number over 10,000. They are trained mainly at the U.S. Army

John F. Kennedy Special Warfare Center and School at Fort Bragg, North Carolina ("The Schoolhouse"), especially in guerrilla fighting. The first Green Berets were advisers to the South Vietnamese army in the early 1960s. *Green Beanies* is a derogatory or humorous term for the Green Berets.

Green Book.   The *Green Book*, with its 6,000 entries, is "The Social List of Washington, D.C.," encompassing "socially acceptable" Washington and official Washington, there being quite a distinction between the two. It was begun by Helen Ray Hagner in 1930 and is run by her granddaughter today. To get in it one has to be recommended by two people already there and approved by an anonymous board of governors. The book also serves as an arbiter of protocol.

green-eyed monster.   Why since the 16th century has the color green been associated with jealousy? It has been suggested that oriental jade ground into powder and used as a love potion by jealous suitors to win their loved ones has something to do with it, but that seems a farfetched explanation. Shakespeare was the first to use the expression *green-eyed monster*, in *Othello*, where Iago says: "O, beware, my lord, of jealousy;/ It is the green-eyed monster which doth mock/ The meat it feeds on." Clearly the reference here is to cats toying with their victims before killing and eating them, so the first green-eyed monster is a cat. However, before this, in *The Merchant of Venice*, Shakespeare wrote of *green-eyed jealousy* without any reference to a feline. We must mark the ultimate origin "unknown."

green Friday; green death; green around the gills.   The first is a humorous name for the day after Thanksgiving, which always falls on a Thursday, because people who ate too much feel overstuffed and perhaps a bit nauseated. *Green death* is student slang for diarrhea brought on by eating college cafeteria food. Several other "green" expressions, including *green around the gills*, are also associated with nausea.

greenfront.   A term heard in Maine for a liquor store, which all have green fronts in that state. *See* PACKAGE-GOODS STORE.

greengage plum.   Greengage plums are actually yellow with a tinge of green. The renowned plum, which has two eponymous names, was brought from Italy to France about 1500, where it was named and is still called the Reine-Claude, after Claudia, *la bonne reine*, queen to Francis I from their marriage in 1514 until his death. In about 1725 Sir William Gage, an amateur botanist, imported a number of plum trees from a monastery in France, all of which were labeled except the Reine-Claude. A gardener at Hengrave Hall in Suffolk named the unknown variety Green Gage in honor of his employer and the Reine-Claude has been the greengage in England ever since. The blue and purple gage were developed from their illustrious ancestor on the fertile grounds of Gage's estate, probably much to the delight of his eight children.

greenhorn.   Authorities reason, without any proof, that *greenhorn* was first the name for a young ox, one with young, or "green," horns. Because young oxen were inexperienced and untrained as farm work animals, they were undesirable, and their name became attached to raw army recruits by the 16th century and finally to any raw, inexperienced person. *Greenhorn* is also remembered as a derogatory term for newly arrived immigrants in turn-of-the-century America.

greenhouse effect. Not a new term, *greenhouse effect*, despite its current importance, dates back to 1929, when it was first recorded. It wasn't until the 1980s that the effect began to concern the public, and it has been a common term ever since. The effect occurs in greenhouses when the sun's radiant heat passes through the greenhouse glass and is trapped inside, warming the plants there. The term *greenhouse effect* compares the effect in a greenhouse to the effect on Earth's atmosphere, in which carbon dioxide and other gases—increasing each year by the burning of fossil fuels—trap Earth's surface radiation, causing global warming.

Greenland. *See* CAPE OF GOOD HOPE.

greenmail. Patterned on *blackmail*, which it strictly is, *greenmail* was coined on Wall Street in 1983, *green* suggested by the color of U.S. currency. When one company buys enough shares in another to threaten a takeover, the "greenmail" company is forced to buy the shares back at a higher price to avoid that possibility. *See* BLACKMAIL.

Green Mountain State. A nickname for Vermont first recorded in 1838 but suggested by *Green Mountain Boy*, a Vermont inhabitant, which goes back to 1772 when a militia of Green Mountain Boys was organized to protect the state's boundary lines.

greenroom. This lounge in the theater where performers rest when they aren't on stage, or where people who are to appear on TV wait before they go on, probably takes its name from such a room in London's Drury Lane Theatre, which just happened to be painted green sometime in the late 17th century. Most authorities reject the old story that the room was painted green to soothe the actors' eyes. The long-lived English actor Charles Macklin, famous for his portrayal of Shylock in *The Merchant of Venice*, killed fellow player Adam Hallam, one of a large family of English actors, in the greenroom at the Drury Lane Theatre in 1735. Macklin, an extremely jealous and quarrelsome man, wanted to wear a wig Hallam had chosen for a play both men were appearing in. The Wild Irishman, as he was called, got away with the murder and went his tempestuous way, celebrated as a great lover, boxer, card player, distance walker, and drinker, expending more energy offstage than on.

green thumb. No one, it seemed, knew why the Italian monk Fra Antonio could make plants grow so well in the cloister garden. But one day an elderly monk watching Fra Antonio observed that he had a green thumb on his right hand, which made him an excellent gardener—the green thumb, no doubt, colored by the plants he had been handling. This is a nice little story, but so far as we know the term *green thumb* doesn't go back to medieval times. In fact, it is first recorded in 1925 by Dean Middleton, a BBC broadcaster and garden-book author. It is probable that Middleton merely popularized the phrase, which many people remembered hearing around 1910 and is probably a generation older.

Greenwich time. A borough of London, at latitude 51 degrees 28' 38" No., and longitude 0 degrees 0' 0", Greenwich was long the place where the world's time was officially measured, specifically at the Royal Observatory there. At a meeting in Washington, D.C. in 1884 most nations agreed to the place. In 1985, however, a decision was made to dismantle the historic Greenwich clock.

Gregg system. *Gregg*, the most widely used shorthand writing in the world and by far the most popular in the United States, was invented by John Robert Gregg (1864–1948), an Irishman who explained Gregg in *The Phonetic Handwriting* (1888) and emigrated to introduce it in America. Once called "Light-Line Phonography," it is an improvement on the earlier phonetic PITMAN and is much easier to write.

Gregorian calendar. While an improvement on its predecessors, the inaccurate JULIAN CALENDAR resulted in the calendar year gradually losing on the actual solar year, or the time it takes the earth to travel around the sun. By the 16th century, for example, the first day of spring came on March 11, instead of March 21. As this interfered with seasonal church celebrations, Pope Gregory XIII introduced a modified calendar in 1582. He decreed that the day after October 4 in that year would be October 15, making up for the lost days in this way and ensuring that they would not be lost again by ruling that century years would no longer be leap years unless divisable by 400. Pope Gregory himself probably did not devise the "new style" calendar, but it was named in his honor. Immediately accepted in Catholic countries, the Gregorian calendar wasn't adopted in England or America until 1752—when the calendar gained 12 days overnight. Imperfect itself, it is nevertheless used today throughout most of the world.

Gregorian tree. The English so valued one hangman, Gregory Brandon, that they granted him a coat of arms for his gruesomely efficient work on the scaffold. Gregory, whose son succeeded him as public executioner and beheaded Charles I in 1649, lived to see his name become a synonym for the gallows in the form of *Gregorian tree*.

grenade. *See* POMEGRANATE.

Gresham's Law. Though the tendency of bad money to drive good money out of circulation is known as *Gresham's Law*, it was formulated as an economic principle long before Sir Thomas Gresham (ca. 1519–79). Gresham, a London merchant and founder of what is now the Royal Exchange, noted that the more valuable of two similar coins would be hoarded, but Copernicus and others had already made similar observations. Unaware that he had not formulated the principle, the economist H. D. MacLeod named the law for Gresham in 1857.

Gretna Green. A place where quick lawful marriages are performed, especially for eloping couples. The village of Gretna Green in Scotland, just across the border from England, was such a place for over a century, before Scotland changed its marriage laws in 1856. Up until then even Gretna Green's village blacksmith could perform marriages.

greyhound. Noted for its great long-legged speed and keen sight, the greyhound breed of dog isn't usually grey. The word *grey* in its name has nothing to do with color, deriving ultimately from Old Norse *grey*, which means "bitch," *hound* coming from Old English *hound*, "dog." The dog's name is first recorded about A.D. 1000. Today its name adorns any swift ocean liner and Greyhound buses. Greyhounds, still used for hunting, are generally used in dog racing.

gribble. *Linnoria lignorum*, better known as the gribble (its name possibly a diminutive of *grub*), is a small crustacean resembling a wood louse that bores its own distinctive holes in ships and piers, though it hasn't done as much damage as the SHIPWORM over the years. The gribble's work, unlike the ship-worm's, is visible on the surface of the structure it attacks, because it burrows in the superficial layers of wood. Because its handiwork is visible, gribble damage is usually caught before it goes too far, though this is not always the case. In 1838, for example, the docks at Plymouth, England, were almost completely destroyed by gribbles.

gridiron. *Gridiron* is a football term inspired by Walter Camp, the FATHER OF AMERICAN FOOTBALL, when his rules for the game made it necessary to mark the football field with horizontal white lines at five-yard intervals. This arrangement suggested to fans that the word *gridiron* derived from *griddle* plus *iron*, for the bars running across the field did make it resemble an iron griddle or grate. But in fact *gridiron* was originally the name for a metal barrel griddle and comes from the Middle English *gredire*, "griddle," which in turn developed from the Old French *gridel*.

griffin. The griffin, half lion and half eagle, was an enormous aerial monster of antiquity that fed living humans to its young. It took its name from the Greek *grypos*, "hooked," because of its large hooked beak. The griffin was known to the Sumerians, under the name *chumbaba*, as early as 3000 B.C.

grigri; grisgris; greegree. A charm or a magical formula used to bring bad luck to a rival; the terms derive from an African word recorded as early as 1557.

Grimm's Law. The brothers Grimm are not only noted for their collected fairy tales, which are known worldwide. Both Jacob Grimm (1785–1863) and William Grimm (1786–1859) were respected philologists. Jacob was one of the great founders of comparative philology, interested mainly in the relationship between the various Germanic languages. He also invented the UMLAUT.

Grinch. A nasty, miserly, Scrooge-like person. Taken from the name of the character in the popular children's book *How the Grinch Stole Christmas* by Dr. Seuss (Theodor Seuss Geisel, 1904–94).

gringo. Many scholars trace this disparaging term for an American to the Spanish *gringo*, "gibberish," which is a corruption of the Spanish word *Griego*, "a Greek." *Gringo*, by this theory, would be related to the old saying "It's all Greek to me," indicating that the Yankees were strange and unfamiliar in their ways to the Mexicans who so named them. But we haven't exhausted all the conjectures by any means. Another etymologist boldly claims "green coat" as the base for *gringo*, and a second theory says that the first two words of the Robert Burns lyric "Green grow the rashes O," a song sung by American soldiers in the Mexican War, is the origin of the contemptuous word—somehow one can't imagine battle-hardened veterans riding along singing: "Green grow the rashes O/ The happiest hours that ere I spent/ Were spent among the lasses O!" If the "gibberish" theory is to be challenged, the most likely contender is Major Samuel Ringgold, a brilliant strategist dreaded by the Mexicans during the Mexican War until he was killed at the Battle of Palo Alto in 1846. Ringgold's name, pronounced with a trilled *r* and without the last two letters as it normally would be by a Mexican, might yet prove the correct source for the word.

grin like a Cheshire cat. The pseudonymous British satirist Peter Pindar (John Wolcot) first used this expression for a broad smile in the late 18th century, but Lewis Carroll popularized it in *Alice's Adventures in Wonderland* (1865)—the Cheshire cat in the story gradually faded from Alice's view, its grin the last part of it to vanish. No satisfactory explanation of the allusion has been made. *To grin like a Cheshire cat* probably goes back much further than Pindar, and the source could be Cheshire cheeses that were at one time molded in the form of a cat—supposedly, the cat was grinning because the former palatine of Cheshire once had regal privileges in England, paying no taxes to the crown, etc. Another story relates the expression to the attempts of an ignorant sign painter to represent a lion rampant on the signs of many Cheshire inns—his lions supposedly looked more like grinning cats. The most unlikely yarn credits an eponymous forest warden of Cheshire named Caterling. In the reign of Richard III, it's said, this Cheshire Caterling stamped out poaching, was responsible for over 100 poachers being hanged, and was present "grinning from ear to ear" at each of these executions. *To grin like a Cheshire Catling* became proverbial and was later shortened *to grin like a Cheshire cat*. Another fanciful story makes the same Catling the "cat" of the nursery rhyme "Hi Diddle Diddle, the Cat and the Fiddle."

grip. A general movie crewman who helps shift scenery, operates cranes and dollies, etc., or a stagehand in the theater who works on the stage floor. *Key grip* refers to the head grip. Grips are probably so named for their strong grips (their strength) in handling the heavy equipment on movie sets. *See* BEST BOY.

grist for the mill. One might think that this 17th-century proverbial saying would be little used today, when many people don't even know that *grist* refers to grain ground to make flour. But *grist for the mill* is commonly heard to denote anything profitable or useful, material that a person can change into something valuable.

grizzly bear. This fearsome bear has also been called the *silvertop*, because the ends of its hair are silver gray; the *mule bear*, because early prospectors thought it found their mules especially tasty; and *Moccasin Joe*, because its footprints somewhat resemble those of a man wearing moccasins. Indians in California called the bears *Josmites*, "the killers," a word still preserved in the name of the Yosemite Valley and Yosemite

National Park. The great beasts were given the name *grizzly*, however, because of their grayish color, not from the word *grisly* meaning horrible or terrible.

grocer. Grocers in medieval times were so named from the Latin *grossus*, "large," because they sold only in large quantities. England's Company of Grocers, an association incorporated in 1344, were wholesale dealers in spice and foreign produce.

grog. Mount Vernon was named after Vice Admiral Sir Edward Vernon by George Washington's half-brother Laurence, who served under "Old Grog" when he led six little ships to the West Indies and captured heavily fortified Portobello during the WAR OF JENKINS' EAR (1739). This action made Vernon England's hero of the hour, Parliament voting him formal thanks and street pageants being held on his birthday to celebrate his humbling of the Spaniards. But the arrogant former war hawk MP never won popularity with his men. Old Grog had been nicknamed for the impressive grogram cloak he wore on deck in all kinds of weather, the coarse taffeta material symbolizing his tough and irascible nature. Then, in August 1740, the stern disciplinarian issued an order that made his name a malediction. In order to curb drunken brawling aboard ships in his command, and to save money, he declared that all rum rations would henceforth be diluted with water. Incensed old sea dogs cursed Vernon roundly, for half a pint of rum mixed with a quart of water seemed weak stuff indeed to anyone on a raw rum liquid diet. Furthermore, the rationed bilge was divided into two issues, served six hours apart. His men soon defiantly dubbed the adulterated rum Grog, using the nickname they had bestowed upon the admiral. Vernon's order served its purpose and "three water rum" became the official ration for all enlisted personnel in the Royal Navy, but *grog* quickly took on the wider meaning of any cheap, diluted drink. *See* BOOZE.

Grolier binding. Rich, ornate book bindings are called *Grolier bindings*, after Jean Grolier, vicomte d'Aguisy (1479–1565), who was not a bookbinder or printer but a prominent French bibliophile. Grolier collected books and had them bound by the best artisans of his day, each book bearing the inscription *Groliere et Amicorum*. All the books in his library, sold in 1675, are world-famous collector's items. The Grolier Club, which has published many books and catalogs of its exhibitions, was founded in New York City (1884) "for the study and promotion of the arts pertaining to the production of books."

groovy; in the groove. *In the groove* has lasted longer than most slang expressions, possibly because of a popular song of the same name. The phrase, meaning "exciting, satisfying, or functioning smoothly," isn't heard much anymore, nor is its offspring, *groovy*. But from the '30s to the '50s it was all the rage, was even translated into Latin: *in canaliculo*. The allusion is to the quality of music reproduced when a good phonograph needle traverses the grooves of a record without jumping out. Oddly enough, an older English expression *groovy*, dating back to the late 19th century, means just about the opposite—to be in a rut, like a cart stuck in the grooves of a muddy road.

grotesque. In the 16th century, excavated chambers, or *grotte*, in ancient Roman buildings revealed murals on the walls depicting figures that were unnaturally distorted or comically exaggerated. These figures were called *grotesca*, after the *grotte* they were found in, *grotesca* eventually becoming the English *grotesque*, for any similar figure.

ground floor; first floor; to get in on the ground floor. In Britain and other countries, *ground floor* refers to the street-level floor of a building, while *first floor* refers to the next floor up. In America these would be called the first and second floors, respectively. However, *ground floor* is used in America as a synonym for the lobby of a building. To *get in on the ground floor* means "to be among the first" to invest in a business, stock, etc., that shows promise of being profitable.

groundhog; woodchuck. American settlers named the marmot, or woodchuck (*Arctomys monax*), the groundhog, perhaps because this member of the squirrel family seems hoggish in the way he burrows through the ground. Or, possibly, *groundhog* is a translation of the Dutch *aardvark* made by Dutch settlers in America, even though the South African aardvark, or earth hog, is a larger burrowing animal than the groundhog. The groundhog isn't a hog then, but his other American name, woodchuck, is no more accurate, for he doesn't chuck wood, either, a fact even the old tongue twister implies: "How much wood would a woodchuck chuck if a woodchuck could chuck wood?" "Woodchuck" has no connection with wood at all, simply deriving from the Cree Indian word *wuchuk* or *otchock* for another animal, the fisher, or pekan, which early settlers corrupted finally to "woodchuck" and applied through mistaken identity to the groundhog.

Groundhog Day. February 2, when the groundhog is supposed to come out of his hole to evaluate the weather. If he sees his shadow winter will last six weeks more; if he doesn't, there will be an early spring.

ground zero. Nuclear bombs are detonated before hitting the ground, and *ground zero* (or hypocenter) refers to the area directly below their explosion. The term dates back to the early 1940s and the first A-BOMB tests, but now also applies to the area around any huge explosion, fire, etc., such as the World Trade Center destruction on September 11, 2001. *Ground zero*, loosely used, means the "most elementary or beginning level," as in "Let's start at ground zero."

groupie. Originally describing a very young girl who followed rock 'n' roll groups on concert tours, worshipping them in an idolatrous fashion, this word has since the early 1960s come to mean a young woman who makes herself available for sexual intercourse with a member of a rock group or other celebrity. A groupie can also be a young girl constantly on the make. The groupie's counterpart in sports is sometimes called a BIMBO.

groves of academe. According to legend, the Athenian hero Academus helped Castor and Pollux rescue their little sister Helen when she was kidnapped by the Athenian Prince Theseus. Academus revealed Helen's hiding place, and she was spared marriage with Theseus, growing up to become the famous "face that launched a thousand ships," in reference to her later abduction by Paris, which caused the Trojan War. As a reward for his help the Spartans gave an olive grove on the outskirts of Athens to Academus, the place later becoming a public park called the Grove of Academus in his honor. Much later, around 387 B.C., the philosopher Plato had a house and garden adjoining this park and opened a school of philosophy there. He walked and talked with his students in the peaceful olive grove for the rest of his life, was buried near the grove, and his peripatetic successors taught there as well, so his school of philosophy became known as the Academia, after the olive grove honoring the eponymous hero Academus. Renaissance scholars later adopted the name *académe*, or "academy," for an institution devoted to learning, from the learning of philosophy to the learning of war, and it is from the word *academy* that our word *academic* derives. Possibly the most famous of academies is the French Académie française founded in 1635, but this literary school has its detractors, too, having been called the *"hôtel des invalides de la littérature."* American author Mary McCarthy (1912–89) wrote the satirical novel *The Groves of Academe* (1952).

grow like Topsy.   "Never was born, never had no father, nor mother, not nothin' . . . I 'spect I growed," the slave child Topsy replies when Aunt Ophelia, a white woman from the North, questions her about her family. The scene in Harriet Beecher Stowe's antislavery novel *Uncle Tom's Cabin, or Life Among the Lowly* (1852), the most popular book of its day, had great impact, especially in dramatic versions of the novel, and inspired the saying *to grow like Topsy*, describing any unplanned, often sudden growth. Little Eva's companion, like Uncle Tom and the brutal, drunken planter Simon Legree, has become part of the language, and Mrs. Stowe's book, despite its faults, has spawned more new words than any other American novel.

Grub Street hack.

> Here lies poor Ned Purdom, from misery freed,
> Who long was a bookseller's hack;
> He led such a damnable life in this world,
> I don't think he'd wish to come back.
>
> —Oliver Goldsmith

Grub Street in London was known a century before Dr. Johnson's lifetime as the stamping ground of (depending on your perspective) needy writers or literary *hacks* (from *hackney*, "a horse or carriage anyone could hire"). When compiling his famous *Dictionary of the English Language* (1755) the Great Cham defined Grub Street as "much inhabited by writers of small histories, dictionaries and temporary poems, whence any mean production is called grubstreet." The term lasted even after the street name disappeared, probably because it suggests writers grubbing (from the Middle English *grobben*, "to dig") for money for grub (as Johnson himself was forced to do) and often producing cheap works in the process. Grub Street has been called Milton Street since 1830—not in honor of the great poet John Milton, but after a landlord who owned most of the houses on the street at the time.

grue.   Grues are grisly little comic poems with sadistic content and trick last lines. They are sometimes called Little Willies in honor of the "hero" of so many, but the name *grue*, coined by Robert Louis Stevenson from "gruesome," is more appro-

priate. Though their content is never worse than the daily news, most grues are anonymous:

> Willie poisoned father's tea;
> Father died in agony.
> Mother looked extremely vexed;
> "Really, Will," she said, "what next?"

grueling.   No matter how you cook it, *grueling*, meaning exhausting or punishing, has something to do with *gruel*, a light, cooked, thin cereal usually made of oatmeal. There's no doubt that the word derives from the expression *to get*, or *take*, *one's gruel*, first recorded in the late 18th century. Why eating oatmeal came to be associated with a punishment is open to question. The traditional story is that *to get one's gruel* is an allusion to Medici poisonings. The Medici family, which directed the destiny of Florence from the 15th century to 1737 and produced two queens of France, did much good and evil, ranging from patronage of the arts to political tortures and poisonings. In fact, they were so prone to dispose of each other by assassination that their genealogy is highly complicated. Catherine de Médicis (1519–89), queen of France, was particularly infamous for political assassinations, especially for her part in the attempted assassination of Admiral Coligny and the St. Bartholomew's Day Massacre (1572) in which 30,000 Protestants were killed. She was also rumored to give poisoned drink to her enemies under the guise of friendship, usually serving it in a thin drink of gruel. It wouldn't be unreasonable to assume that Catherine's alleged poisonings inspired the expression *to get one's gruel*, except that the words aren't recorded until some 200 years after her death. The Medici family is a more likely candidate, but most word sleuths now believe the poisonings have nothing to do with the phrase. Partridge suggests that it comes from an earlier nautical expression, *to serve out the grog*, "to mete out punishment," making it comparable to humorous expressions such as *settle one's hash* and *cook one's goose*.

grunt.   *Grunt*, as in "He grunts and groans," is an onomatopoeic word that imitates the sound of grunting. The use of *grunt* for an American infantryman, who does a lot of grunting and groaning, probably dates back no further than the late 1950s and did not become common for "dogfaces" until the Vietnam War. One story has Marine Corps pilots coining the term.

G-string.   Stripteasers, who sometimes call this a "gadget," aren't responsible for the word. *G-string* is an Americanism first used to describe an Indian's loincloth or breechclout in the 19th century. It could be that some fiddler in the West compared the heaviest of violin strings, the G string, to the length of sinew or gut that Indians tied around their waists to hold up their breechclouts. But even the heaviest of violin strings wouldn't really do the job. Perhaps the g is just a euphemistic shortening of "groin," an indecent word at the time. The burlesque G-string is of course far smaller than the Indian variety and must have seemed even skimpier a century ago, considering the Brunhildian builds of yesterday's ecdysiasts. One burlesque company of the day proudly advertised "two tons of women" and had only 20 strippers. *See also* ECDYSIAST.

G.T.T.   A historical term common in the 19th century standing for "Gone to Texas," apparently derived from *G.T.T.* signs that emigrants hung on the doors of their homes and businesses when they went west. Soon these initials came to be entered by lawmen in their record books when a wanted man couldn't be located. Finally, they became a designation for any disreputable man.

guano.   A rich, natural manure composed mostly of the excrement of seabirds found on small islands near the Peruvian coast, guano takes its name ultimately from the Quechua Indian *wanu*, meaning "dung," for fertilizer or fuel. Beds of guano on these rocky islands are sometimes as deep as 60 feet. The word *guano* has also come to mean any similar natural fertilizer, and in the southern United States also means commercial chemical fertilizer.

the Guard dies but never surrenders.   History courses teach us that General Pierre Cambronne, the commander of Napoleon's Imperial Guard at Waterloo, made the above reply to a British surrender demand. What Cambronne really said was "Shit! The Guard never surrenders!" The polite French call this episode *le mot de Cambronne*, "the word of Cambronne."

gubmint catchum fella.   An amusing Australian pidgin term for a policeman. "Gubmint catchum fella brother belong me" means "That policeman is my friend." Other interesting pidgin expressions, from among thousands, include these Melanesian Pidgin terms: *finish altogether* (die) and *long way bit bit* (very far). *See* BECHE-DE-MER; PIDGIN LANGUAGE.

guerrilla.   *Guerrilla* means a "little war" in Spanish, the word first becoming popular when Napoleon Bonaparte invaded Spain in 1808. The Spanish peasants took up arms and Napoleon, used to fighting trained armies, couldn't cope with these small units of men that seemed to be everywhere and yet could rarely be found. The Spanish peasants, with English help, eventually expelled Napoleon, and ever since then *guerrilla army* has meant small bands of men fighting in unconventional ways.

Guevarism; euphuism.   Spanish writer and moralist Antonio de Guevara (ca. 1480–1545) has been regarded as the father of *euphuism*, for which his name is equivalent. But *euphuism*, an ornate, artificial writing or speaking style characterized by alliteration, eloquence, and high-flown phrases, was coined more than a century after his death. *Euphuism* takes its name from *Euphues: the Anatomy of Wit* (1579) by John Lyly, who displayed such a style in his book in an attempt to "soften" the English language, Euphues being the name of the main character in his romance. Guevara may have been among Lyly's inspirations, for the Spanish author's *The Golden Book of Marcus Aurelius* (1535) and other works were translated early into English.

guillotine.   Dr. Joseph Ignace Guillotin (1738–1814) did not invent the *guillotine*, did not die by the *guillotine*, and all his life futilely tried to detach his name from the height reducer. The confusion began on October 10, 1789, when the eminent Parisian physician, a member of the National Assembly during the French Revolution, the Revolution, suggested that a "mer-ciful" beheading device replace the clumsy sword and degrading rope then used by French executioners. Dr. Guillotin remained in the public's mind for his eloquent speech and one of many popular songs about the new machine claimed that he had invented it. Not much time passed before "La Louisette" (this name honoring its real inventor, Dr. Antoine Louis) lost out to *La machine Guillotine*, *Madame Guillotine*, and then *guillotine* itself. After his death, Guillotin's children petitioned the French government to change the name of the *guillotine*, but won only permission to change their own names. *See* TERRORIST.

Guinea.   The area on the African west coast and the countries there called *Guinea* may take their name from a misunderstanding. One story claims that the first Portuguese seafarers to land in the area asked local tribesmen the name of the coast. The residents thought they were pointing at a group of women nearby and answered *guiné*, their word for women, which became the name of the area. In any case, the name of the country first appears in Portuguese as *Guine*. *See also* DAGO; INDRI; KANGAROO; LLAMA; LUZON; NOME; PAGO PAGO; SIERRA LEONE; WOP; YUCATAN.

guinea hen.   The ancestor of today's tasty *guinea hen* hailed from Guinea in western Africa, unlike the GUINEA, PIG.

guinea pig.   The South American rodent isn't a pig and doesn't hail from Guinea in West Africa. Native to Brazil, the guinea pig takes its first name from the fact that it was first brought to Europe on the *Guinea-men* slave ships that sailed from Guinea to South America to deliver their human cargo and to fill their holds with whatever cargo was available for the return trip to Europe. How the creature came to be called a pig is anybody's guess.

Gulf Stream.   An old yarn has it that the redoubtable Benjamin Franklin—who discovered so many other things—introduced sailors to the use of the Gulf Stream in the westward crossing of the Atlantic. This familiar story claims that when Franklin was deputy postmaster for the colonies in 1770 the British treasury asked him why British postal packets took two weeks or so longer to reach New York than merchantmen did in sailing from London to Boston and to Providence, Rhode Island. Franklin, so the tale goes, consulted his cousin, Captain Timothy Folger, a Nantucket whaleman of long experience, who quickly told him of the influence of the Gulf Stream, advising him that the postal packets commanded by Britishers always bucked the Gulf Stream, whereas the merchantmen, commanded by Rhode Islanders, had long since been taught by American whalemen that one did not resist the Gulf Stream in its eastward flow. Actually, British explorer William Dampier had written about the Gulf Stream in his *Discoveries on the Trade Winds* a century earlier, and British mariners were quite familiar with it. The real explanation for the delay of the mail packets was their notoriously laggard captains, who took their own sweet time—there being no bonus for speed—and often trusted their ships to inexperienced mates. Franklin did talk to his cousin and had him draw a crude chart of the Gulf Stream, which Franklin later published. He and his cousin probably were responsible for speeding up the mail service back in 1770—if only by embarrassing the British captains—but they certainly didn't *discover* the Gulf Stream. *See* CURRENT; FRANKLIN.

Gulf War syndrome. The major U.S. and Allied casualties in the Gulf War of 1991 were those who fell victim to this nerve disorder, which resulted in symptoms such as hair loss, fatigue, and dizzy spells. The cause may have been nerve gas, pesticides, or other chemical agents. The syndrome, which has affected hundreds of veterans, is also called "Desert Storm syndrome," after the Gulf War land campaign.

gull. The *gull*, the only bird ever to have a monument erected to it, is intimately connected with American agricultural history. All gulls take their name from the Breton *guylan*, for the bird, which derives from the Breton *gwela*, "to weep," in reference to the bird's cry. In 1848 an invasion of grasshoppers threatened starvation for the Mormon settlers near the Great Salt Lake and it was checked only by the appearance of flocks of gulls, which devoured the crickets and saved the crops after all other means had failed. The Sea Gull Monument on Temple Square in Salt Lake City is dedicated to the species, "in grateful remembrance of the mercy of God to the Mormon pioneers." In a similar 1947 incident, gulls destroyed a plague of caterpillars in Scotland. *See also* BOLL WEEVIL.

Gullah. The American dialect called Gullah, with some 5,000 African terms in it, takes its name either from *Ngola* ("Angola") or from the West African Gola tribe. It is spoken on the Sea Islands and along the South Carolina-Georgia coast.

gully-washer. An Americanism meaning a heavy rain. One old story has it that in the Ashland *Virginia Herald-Progress* someone advertised: "Wanted: One good rain. No 10-minute gully-washers need apply."

gumbo filé. William Read, in *Louisiana-French Cooking* (1931), explains the origins of this term: "Gumbo [is now] applied to other kinds of gumbo thickened with a powder prepared from sassafrass leaves. This powder goes by the name of *filé*, the past participle of French *filer*, 'to twist'; hence *gumbo filé* signifies properly, 'ropy or stringy gumbo.'"

the Gum Nebula. The name of this star, which may have shone as bright as the full moon 11,000 years ago, has nothing whatever to do with chewing gum. It is named for Australian astronomer Colin Gum, its discoverer in 1950.

Gump. This word meaning a fool, a stupid person is recorded in James Russell Lowell's *The Biglow Papers* (1866), and accounts for the last name of the early comic strip character Andy Gump, as well as the last name of the eponymous hero of the 1994 film *Forrest Gump*.

gumption. Born as a Scottish word, first recorded in 1719 and meaning "common sense, mother wit, shrewdness," gumption, changed in meaning after emigrating to America, coming to mean determination, spirit, courage. Perhaps the hard cider called gumption, known here during the early 19th century, and possibly before, gave the word this sense because of the spirit and courage it gave to those who drank it.

gumshoe. *Gumshoe* refers to a private investigator or private eye, this expression dating back to the early 20th century. The American-English term can also mean a police detective or plainclothes officer and derives from "gumshoes," rubber-soled shoes or sneakers, which one can walk stealthily on. *See* PLIMSOLLS.

gum up the works. The expression *gum up the works* possibly derives from our national gum-chewing habit. The phrase became popular at the turn of the century and may refer to youngsters who went into the woods on gumming expeditions and got covered hair to foot with tree resin, which their parents had to work for hours to remove. But clogged machines in factories were referred to as *gummed up* as early as 1889, in reference to gummy substances such as inspissated oil clogging or stiffening them. It seems more likely that our expression for throwing a project into confusion derives from clogged machines (or works) than from youngsters daubed with gum.

gun. *Gun* doesn't derive from the echo of its sound, as has been suggested. *Gunnr* and *hildr* meant "war" and "battle" in Icelandic, so the Scandinavian female name Gunhildr was a favorite among missile-throwers in the Middle Ages as a pet name for their ballistic devices. It is also possible that some anonymous soldier named a specific ballista Gunhildr for his sweetheart, the name gaining currency in this way. Whatever the case, we find *Gundhildr* recorded before 1309 in England, where it was shortened to *gunne*, and then *gun*, the last designation transferred to firearms after the cannon was invented. A "large ballista called Lady Gunhilda," a mechanized catapult used to hurl huge stones and balls of fire at troops, is listed in a weapons inventory made at Windsor Castle in 1330. This particular ballista, its name derived from the Scandinavian, must have been around for a number of years and may even have been the particular Gunhilda abbreviated to *gunne* some years before.

gunboat diplomacy. Not until 1927 is there a printed reference to *gunboat diplomacy*, which might translate as "getting one's way by force," but the expression may date back to 1841, when American ships exacted trade concessions from the Chinese by sending gunboats to Canton, after the British had done the same in the First Opium War. *Gunboat* itself dates back to 1793. The expression has, however, long been associated with President Theodore Roosevelt's Latin American policy.

gunch. There are words for everything if you look hard enough. A *gunch* is an attempt to influence the roll of the ball in a pinball machine game by jostling the machine. *Gunching* and *nudging* have long been common among pinball players and pinball games have been around since the 1880s.

gung ho. *Gung ho* means "work together" in Chinese, but after Carlson's Raiders, the 2nd Marine Raider Division commanded by Lt. Colonel Evans F. Carlson, a veteran of the China campaign, adopted the expression as their slogan in World War II, it took on a different meaning. Carlson's Raiders were a remarkably brave, loyal, and enthusiastic band, so *gung ho* came to describe these qualities. Yet when noncombat marines and soldiers displayed the same enthusiasm in picayune matters such as white-glove inspections, *gung ho* was disparagingly applied to them, resulting in its present meaning of overzealousness.

gunkhole; gunk.   A gunkhole is a deep mudhole. One theory has it that the word *gunk* here is old Scottish meaning "to hoax or fool" and that *gunkhole* is used to mean a mudhole because "some fool once thought he could walk in mud and it let him down." But one guess is as good as another for the origins of these early Americanisms. *Gunk* refers to any thick or sticky substance ("He cleaned the gunk off it"). Originally the word was the trademark of a degreasing solvent, patented by a U.S. company in 1932.

gun moll.   This term arose from the mistaken belief that the female accomplices of criminals carried their guns for them. The *gun* in the term does not refer to a firearm but derives from the Yiddish *goniff*, "a thief," and *moll* is 18th-century slang for a woman. A gun moll in the 1920s was originally a female pickpocket, before newspaper reporters mistakenly took to calling any racketeer's girl a gun moll.

gunnysack.   Still another word that was brought back from India by the British, *gunnysack* derives from the Hindi *goni*, for the coarse hemp fabric from which the sacks are fashioned.

gunsel.   *Gunsel*, for "a cheap thief or criminal," is another word reinforced by "gun" in the mind but which really has nothing to do with any weapon. *Gunsel* derives from either the German *ganzel* or the Yiddish *gantzel*, both meaning a gosling. At the beginning of this century prisoners and hoboes called young, inexperienced boys, especially homosexuals, *gunsels*. From constant underworld use, where it later meant a sly, sneaky person, it was adopted generally as a term for a "run-of-the mob," usually second-rate criminal. *Cannon*, for a male pickpocket, has a similar roundabout derivation. As far back as 1840 a pickpocket was called a *gun*, from the Yiddish *goniff*, "thief"; *cannon* was simply an elegant variation on this word adopted by criminals in about 1910. Thus the popular belief that a male pickpocket is so named because he carries a gun or cannon is all wrong—in fact, pickpockets don't usually carry guns.

Gunter's chain.   *See* ACCORDING TO GUNTER.

gun-toter.   This isn't a true historical term for a gunfighter, having been first recorded in a western movie in 1925.

guppy.   The guppy, or "rainbow fish" (*Lebistes reticulatus*), is also called the millions fish. It takes its name from R. J. Lechmere Guppy, once president of the Scientific Association of Trinidad, who presented the British Museum with specimens of the species in the late 19th century. A namesake of the guppy is the little guppy submarine, developed toward the end of World War II, but the sub's name is also an acronym, the first four letters standing for "greater underwater propulsion power."

guru.   The word is used lightly today, but it comes from Sanskrit meaning "weighty," someone with gravitas, an elder, a respected teacher. From meaning strictly a Hindu spiritual teacher, *guru* has "progressed" to "guru of wrestling," "stock-market guru," "plumbing guru," etc.

gusset.   *See* ALL GUSSIED UP.

gussuk.   *Gussuk* is an Inuit word for a white man, heard in Alaska. It is said to have been patterned on the Russian word COSSACK back in the days when the Russians ruled "SEWARD'S FOLLY"

Gutenberg Bible.   The first printed Bible, long erroneously thought to be the first book to be printed from movable type in the Western world, is named for Johannes Gutenberg (ca. 1398–1468), the German printer generally believed to be the inventor of movable type. Few great men of relatively modern times have left such meager records of their lives as Gutenberg. No likeness exists of him, and his life is veiled in obscurity. Gutenberg may have adopted his mother's maiden name, for his father's surname appears to have been Gensfleisch. It is known that the goldsmith Johann Fust loaned the printer money to establish his press in Mainz, which Gutenberg lost to him in 1455 when he failed to repay the loan. But no book extant bears Gutenberg's name as its printer and though he is still regarded as a likely candidate, he may not have invented printing in the West or even printed the *Gutenberg Bible* (1450).

guts.   *Guts* has been an Americanism for courage since about 1880 and is still much heard, though *balls* is used more among men. *Grit*, *spunk*, and *gumption* are early synonyms rarely heard today.

gutter.   *See* EAVESTROUGH.

guv.   The British once commonly used *governor* (pronounced "guv'nor"), as in "Need a lift, guv?" which one might hear from a cab driver. *Sir* is more usual today.

guy.   American expressions often vary greatly in meaning from their identical British cousins. *A regular guy* to many Englishmen means "a thoroughly grotesque person," not "a decent chap" at all. The difference is not as pronounced as in the past, but the American meaning still has a strange ring to British ears. For the English, *guy* owes its origin to the grotesque effigies of Guy Fawkes, a leader of the infamous Gunpowder Plot, which are carried through the streets of England and burnt in bonfires on November 5, Guy Fawkes Day. All of the festivities through the years probably mellowed the meaning of the word to include both good and bad guys. But only in America, far removed from the Gunpowder Plot in distance as well as time, is *guy* widely used for any "chap" or "fellow," no ridicule intended. In England to this day a *guy* remains a ridiculous-looking person. Since the 1970s *guys* in America has been used in referring to women as well as men, especially in mixed groups of men and women (i.e., "Do you guys want to come over?"). American playwright Eugene O'Neill was the first person to record this last use of *guy*, in a 1927 letter to a friend; it became widely used by both men and women within the next 10 years or so.

guyascutus.   Early Americans invented this humorous historical term, which describes a cow with short legs on one side so that it could better walk around the steep Vermont hills. The pronunciation is generally "guy-as-cut-as."

guyot. A guyot is a flat-topped submarine mountain or seamount rising above the deep-sea floor. It is named after American geologist Arnold Guyot (1807–84).

gwine. Going, going to, as in "I'm gwine call them boys." The word is actually a pronunciation the American South's early aristocrats borrowed from upper-class British speech. Also heard as "guyne," "gine," "guin."

gymnast; gymnasium; gymnite. Greek athletes were required to train in the nude to allow their bodies maximum freedom of movement. The famous Olympic track meets were run in the nude, wrestlers competed naked, and all exercises were performed without clothes. Thus the Greek word *gymnazo*, "to train naked," gives us the words *gymnast* (literally someone in the nude exercising), and *gymnasium*, a place where naked exercises are done. The ancient Greeks considered the physical training of boys and young men as essential as mental training, and one of the best gymnasiums in Athens was in Plato's Academy. An amusing sidelight on all this nudity is the mineral *gymnite*, a hydrated silicate of magnesium, so named because it is found at Bare Hills, Maryland.

gyp. According to the popular etymology, *to gyp*, "to cheat," derives from the name of the much maligned gypsies, who got their name because 16th-century Englishmen erroneously assumed that they hailed from Egypt. The *O.E.D.*, however, doesn't dishonor the Romany people, deriving gyp from *gee-up*, which meant "to treat roughly" in some localities of England. The *gippo* theory also saves face for the gypsies. A *gippo*, later shortened to *gyp*, was a short jacket worn by the valets of Oxford undergraduates in the 17th century. The word *gyp* this theory holds, was eventually applied to the servants themselves, who were often cheats and thieves.

H

H. *H* can be traced back, through the Roman and Greek alphabets, to the Phoenician alphabet, where the letter was called Heth and represented a fence, having two crossbars instead of one: The reason Dr. Johnson made his famous remark "I'd rather dine with Jack Ketch [the public hangman] than Jack Wilkes" is seldom told. John Wilkes had written a comic review of Johnson's *Dictionary* in which he addressed the great man's pronouncement that "The letter 'h' seldom, perhaps never, begins any but the first syllable." Wilkes wrote: "The author of this observation must be a man of quick apprehension and of a most comprehensive genius," going on in the same fashion for several paragraphs. Johnson never forgave him.

haberdasher. A 17th-century source derives *haberdasher*, a dealer in men's furnishings such as shirts and ties, from the German *Hab' Ihr das?*, "Have you that?," which such shopkeepers asked when waiting on a customer. Another possibility is the Old French *hapirtus*, "a fur dealer," for haberdashers did originally carry fur hats along with other small wares and notions. We only know surely that *haberdasher* has been part of the language for almost seven centuries.

hack. *See* GRUB STREET HACK.

hack it. *See* CAN'T CUT THE MUSTARD.

hackle. A hackle was originally an instrument used to work flax. Then the word was applied to the raised feathers of angry cock-fighting fowls, which looked like they had been rumpled with a hackle, this usage dating back to at least 1450. Some two centuries later (no one is sure exactly when), the first artificial fishing lures used two bright hackles from a gamecock as the legs of the artificial flies to be tied to the hook. Soon after *hackle* became the name of the artificial lure itself.

Hadassah. The benevolent Jewish women's organization takes its name from the Hebrew name of Queen Esther, mentioned in the Old Testament, Esther 2:7.

haggard. Here is a word that comes from the 3,000-year-old sport of falconry. A *haggard* bird is one trapped as an adult and very difficult to train, unlike a bird captured when a nestling. By the 14th century the word came to mean a wild, intractable person. Then it took on the meaning of a terrified, anxious, or exhausted, expression on a human face. This finally resulted in the meaning of *haggard* we use today, gaunt, drawn, wasted, or exhausted.

ha-ha. Here is an exclamation that became a word, one of the most peculiar of derivations. A *ha-ha* is "an obstacle interrupting one's way sharply and disagreeably, a ditch behind an opening in a wall at the bottom of an alley or walk." It is used in English gardens as a boundary that doesn't interrupt the view from inside, and can't be seen from the outside until you come very close to it; it is in effect a sunken fence, the inner side of the ditch perpendicular and faced with stone, while the outer side is turfed and sloping. When these ditches, or fosses, were first used extensively in the 17th century, etymologists tell us, people out for a stroll in the country were frequently surprised to find a sudden check to their walk. Their exclamations of "ha-ha!," "ah-hah!," or "hah-hah!" in expressing their surprise became the name of the ditch or sunken fence.

Haigspeak. The press coined this eponymous word after Secretary of State Alexander Haig (who served 1981–82). In his conferences with the press Haig used such complicated confusing terms as "a comprehensive pressurized capability."

"Hail Columbia." In 1798, when war with France threatened, this song by Joseph Hopkinson was introduced by the American actor Gilbert Fox as an appeal to patriotism. Hopkinson was later to serve in Congress. "Hail Columbia" became very popular and even served as a euphemistic curse (*hail* substituting for *hell*) over a period of time.

Hail fellow well met. The exclamation of welcome or greeting, *hail*, goes back over a thousand years, as in the Anglo-Saxon expression *wes hal*, "may you be in good health." *Hail fellow well met*, for "a jovial, convivial person, a good mixer," is one of the longest phrases treated as a descriptive word in English and is recorded in print as early as 1550. No doubt it is older still and it possibly originated as a greeting: "Hail, fellow! Well met!" Today the exclamation *Well met!* is sometimes, though rarely, used to mean "Glad I met you!"

"Hail to the Chief."   Verses from Sir Walter Scott's poem "Lady of the Lake" (1810), including "Hail to the Chief who in triumph advances!" were put to music in about 1820 by composer James Sanderson (1769–1841) and became the march traditionally played to honor the president of the United States, especially at official events.

hairbreadth escape.   A very narrow escape; just how narrow is shown by the old English formal unit of measurement called the hairbreadth, the 48th part of an inch, or 12th part of a line. The measurement is said to have been used by the Jews in ancient times. *Hairbreadth*, the breadth or diameter of a hair, is recorded as early as the 15th century, but Shakespeare appears to have coined the phrase *hairbreadth escape* in *Othello*, where his leading character speaks of the "hair-breadth 'scapes" he has experienced throughout his life. *Hairbreadth* is often corrupted to *hair'sbreadth* in everyday speech and has indeed been said this way since the 16th century. Every *hair'sbreadth Harry*, anyone who is always having narrow escapes, honors an old comic strip hero of that name.

hair in the butter.   A very delicate or sensitive situation. This Americanism dating from the early 20th century refers to the difficulty of removing a single hair from a piece of butter. Wrote Molly Ivins in *Molly Ivins Can't Say That, Can She?* (1991): "The Great Iranian Arms Caper is not only hair in the butter, I'd say someone's thrown a skunk in the churchhouse as well."

hair of the dog that bit you.   Like cures like, *similia similibus curantur*, the Romans believed, like many ancient peoples before them, and they commonly bound hairs of a dog that had bitten someone to that person's wound in order to make it heal better—even if the dog was rabid. The treatment was recommended for centuries by serious medical books, about the only change until medieval times being that *burnt* hair of the dog that bit you was prescribed. By then it was also believed that the best cure for a hangover was a drink of the same poison that "stifflicated" you the night before, and the old proverb *a hair of the dog that bit you* applied to this practice. The first mention of the phrase in reference to hangovers is in John Heywood's *Proverbs* (1546): "I pray thee leat me and my fellow have a heare of the dog that bote us last night—and bitten were we both to the braine aright."

hair-raising.   This Americanism came into the language too late, about 1910, for it to be associated with Indians or Indian hunters taking scalps. There is no evidence that horrible accounts of Indians or whites "lifting or raising hair" inspired the synonym for "frightening." Most likely the term is a streamlining of the old expression *to make one's hair stand on end*.

hairy.   *Hairy*, as slang for unpleasant or rough, seems to be of Army origin, from about 1935, when a *hairy patrol* was an unpleasant one that met with resistance. Its origin is unknown, but the word may have something to do with *to make one's hair stand on end* and "scary." Another possibility, a longshot, is the English expression *hairy at the heel*, common in the late 19th century. A horse with hair about the heels or fetlocks was an underbred one, so the expression was used figuratively for an ill-bred, bad-mannered, thoroughly unpleasant person, as was *hairy*.

hairy money.   Hairy money—money with hair on it? Yes. Hairy money was a term for beaver pelts in the American fur trade. The skins were worth a lot of money and even used as a medium of exchange.

hairy quadruped.   There have been many variations on Charles Darwin's description of humankind's common ancestor in *The Descent of Man* (1871), but his words were: "A hairy quadruped, furnished with a tail and pointed ears, probably arboreal in habits."

halcyon days.   A storm killed her mortal husband and the heartbroken goddess Alcyone, daughter of Aeolus, the wind god of Greek legend, drowned herself in the sea. Punishing the suicide, the angry gods turned both Alcyone and her husband Ceyx into birds later known as *halcyons*, or kingfishers as we call them today. Yet the goddess' father took pity on the couple and decreed that during the halcyon's breeding season, the seven days before and the seven days after the shortest day of the year, the sea would always be perfectly calm and unruffled. Thus, during the 14 days, at about the time of the winter solstice, the halcyons could sit on their nests, which floated securely on the tranquil water, borne by currents across the world, hatching their eggs. This legend was widely believed through Roman times, when Alcyone's name became Halcyone, and well into the 15th century. The halcyon days had an actual place on ancient calendars, and the legend inspired much poetry. Eventually, the legend turned the phrase *halcyon days* into not only windless days of peace and calm but any time of peace, serenity, and rejoicing.

haler.   This small Czechoslovakian coin was first minted in the German town of Hall, Swabia, West Germany, from which it takes its name.

half-back.   A new term, rarely recorded, for northern Americans, usually retired, who relocate in Florida, find it too hot in the summer but don't want to return to northern winters and so go halfway back, to settle in North Carolina.

half-baked.   Anything or anyone raw, incomplete, or not thoroughgoing has been called *half-baked* since at least the early 17th century, the allusion being to undercooked baked goods. Some say, however, that the expression *half-baked* as applied to half-witted, uncultured persons is of American origin. This seems unlikely, for although the term is first recorded here in the mid-19th century, an old Cornish proverb cited in 1868 defines a fool as "only half-baked; put in with the bread and taken out with the cakes."

half-breed.   An offensive term for the offspring of an American Indian and a white person; first recorded in 1760, though later much used in the West. It is now used as offensive slang for the offspring of parents of different racial origin.

half-seas over. *Half-seas over* indicates a person quite drunk but not yet under the table. British in origin and dating back to the late 17th century, the phrase probably originated in the resemblance of a drunk's stagger to that of a man walking on the deck of a storm-battered ship, one side heeled over in the sea. Or perhaps the expression is a corruption of *op-zee-zober* ("oversea beer"), a strong, heady beer imported from Holland in the 17th century. The earlier phrase *halfway across the sea* for a drunk suggests the former theory, however.

half-wit. Humorists take note that *half-wit* was first used in English to mean an ineffectual writer of humor, "a dealer in poor witicisms," someone who wasn't funny half the time. Wrote John Dryden in *All For Love* (1678), the first recorded use of the term: "Halfwits are fleas;/ so little and so light,/ We scarce could know they live,/ but that they bite." It wasn't until nearly a century had passed (1755) that *half-wit* was applied to anyone who hasn't all his wits.

half woman and half rainwater. An old American saying descriptive of someone, usually a man, who is soft or effete; unlike a "macho man," rainwater is soft, not hard.

halibut. Five hundred years ago every flatfish from the flounder to the skate was called a butt, even the largest of the flounders, *Hippoglossus hippoglossus*. The most esteemed was *Hippoglossus*, which was only eaten on Church holy days and became known as the holy butt. This fish is no longer reserved for holy days, of course, but it is still known as the halibut, or "holy flounder."

hallelujah. According to an Italian folktale the word *hallelujah* was born when three Roman legionnaires—a Roman, a Piedmontese from northern Italy, and a German—were guarding Christ's body in the sepulchre after His crucifixion. When Christ rose from the dead the Roman exclaimed *Ha!*, the Piedmont man cried *L'e lii!* ("It's him!"), and the German shouted *Ja!*—which gave us *Hallelujah*. But, as good as the story is, *hallelujah* derives from the Hebrew *hallelu-yah*, "praise ye Yahweh."

Halley's comet. Halley's comet, the first comet whose return was accurately predicted, was observed by English astronomer Edmund Halley in 1692, when he correctly estimated its reappearance in 1758, 16 years after his death, as it turned out. Halley based his calculations on Newton's theory; a long-time friend of the great scientist, he had paid for the initial printing of Newton's *Principia*, collaborating on the section dealing with comets. Over his 86-year lifetime Halley made a number of important discoveries, which resulted in his appointment as astronomer royal in 1720. The comet that blazons his name across the sky last appeared in 1986. Mark Twain was born when Halley's Comet appeared in 1835 and died—as he had predicted—when it appeared again in 1910. "It will be the greatest disappointment of my life if I don't go out with Halley's Comet," he had written. "The Almighty has said, no doubt: 'Now here are two unaccountable freaks; they came in together, they must go out together.' "

hallmark. *Hallmarks*, "marks of excellence on products," owe their origin to the official stamp of the Goldsmiths' Company of London, which in 1300 was ordered by Edward I to stamp all gold and silver with such a mark to indicate its purity. They were called hallmarks because the stamping was done at Goldsmith's Hall in London.

ham. Actors prefer to think that this word derives from the old theatrical use of ham fat to remove blackface makeup—actors were thus called hamfatters, or hams. Many scholars lean to this theory, but *ham* in the sense of an amateur actor or a 10th-rate actor who outrageously overplays his scenes has enough folk etymologies to make a one-act play. Since none really seems capable of absolute proof, I'll simply list three: 1) Ham derives from the Cockney slang *hamateur*, for "amateur actor." (Unlikely, as the term *ham* in this sense is American from about 1880.) 2) The word structure of *amateur* itself suggested *ham*. (A good possibility, but why did it wait so long to suggest itself?) 3) It comes from the role of *Hamlet*, which actors frequently misperformed. (Another good possibility, but, if so, *ham* should have been with us since Shakespeare's time.) *Ham* for one of the rear quarters of a hog, or its meat, derives from Old English *hamm* for the bend of the knee.

Hamal. The name of the star *Hamal* in the constellation *Aries* (the ram) is an example of a word that comes to us from ancient Sumerian, which flourished over 5,000 years ago and dates back even further than that. *Hamal* derives from the Arabic *al-Hamal*, "the full-grown lamb," which is a modified form of the Sumerian *mul LULIM*, which means "the constellation of the lamb." Thus fragments of the Sumerian survive, as they do in the names of a few other stars.

hamburger. Most authorities say that the hamburger first appeared in the U.S. in 1884 under the name of *Hamburg steak*, after the place of its origin, Hamburg, Germany. But the town of Hamburg, New York persistently claims that America's favorite quick food was invented there in the summer of 1885 and named for the burger's birthplace. According to this tale, its inventors were Charles and Frank Menches from Ohio, vendors who ran out of pork at their concession at the Erie County Fair. Since the first recorded use of *hamburger* seems to have been in 1902, according to the *O.E.D.*, Hamburg, New York could be the source. *White Castles, McDonalds* and *Wimpeyburgers* (for the Popeye comic-strip character who ate prodigious amounts of them) are synonyms for hamburgers. *See* FRNAKFURTER.

Hamiltonianism. U.S. founding father and statesman Alexander Hamilton (1757–1804), in his essentially conservative political philosophy, advocated a strong central government and protective tariffs. A *Hamiltonian* is one who supports this doctrine of *Hamiltonianism*, the word loosely describing a level-headed political conservative.

hamlet. The English term *ham*, for "a small village," survives in place names like *Shoreham, Oakham,* and *Hamton*. *Hamlet*, for a small village, is simply a diminutive of *ham*, and has been part of the language since medieval times.

Hamlet-like. Someone who cannot make up his mind is often called Hamlet-like, after Shakespeare's tragic character. The expression is used too loosely, however, and should be reserved for those indecisive because—like Hamlet—they are faced with impossibly difficult choices.

hammer and tongs. "To go at it *hammer and tongs*" means to literally or figuratively fight with all one's resources with no hold barred, with might and main. The blacksmith has become a rarity and a curiosity, but this 17th-century expression alluding to his art lives on. It refers of course to the brawny smitty taking red-hot metal from the forge with his long-handled pincers, or tongs, and vigorously beating it into shape on the anvil with his hammer.

hamster. The name for this little seven-inch-long rodent (*Cricetus cricetus*) derives ultimately from Middle High German or possibly from Old Saxon *hamstra*. Hamsters are today even more popular than guinea pigs as pets. Of the several hamster species common to Europe and Asia, the best known is the golden hamster, a gentle, docile rodent that is much valued for laboratory research work. The golden hamster, with its deep golden color, has the shortest gestation period of any nonmarsupial mammal, females giving birth in an incredible 16 days. Just how widely this hamster has been studied by scientists is attested to by the 3,000 articles about it cited in the *Bibliography of the Golden Hamster* by R. Kittel (1966). The millions of golden hamsters being bred today all descend from one hamster male and three females found by a scholar, I. Aharoni, in 1930. Professor Aharoni came across a brief reference in ancient Hebrew writings to a special kind of "Syrian mouse" appearing "in Chaleb which was brought into Assyria and into the land of the Hittites." Determining that Chaleb is today Aleppo in northern Syria, the professor traveled there from his home in what was then called Palestine and found the "Syrian mice" that have since become known to millions as golden hamsters.

hamstring. The part of the leg behind the knee was once called the ham in English and the tendons there were given the name *ham string*, a designation still used today. To cut the hamstrings was to cripple or disable someone, which gives us the expression *to hamstring* "to cripple, or destroy the activity or efficiency of," an expression first recorded by John Milton in 1641.

to handbag. An interesting recent expression meaning "to treat a person or idea ruthlessly or insensitively," especially for a woman politician to do so. The term, recorded in the *OED*, refers to former British prime minister Margaret Thatcher (who held office 1977–90) and the handbag she carried, which became "an often-noted symbol of her swaggering power when she was prime minister," according to one news article. The word, first recorded in 1982, also suggests the handbag being used as a weapon against opponents.

handball. The name of this popular sport can be traced back to 15th-century England, but it originated in Ireland over four centuries earlier and was known as the game of fives for the five fingers of the hands used in it. Handball became popular in America in about 1882, when it is said to have been introduced by Irish immigrant Phil Casey in Brooklyn, New York.

handbook. Dr. Richard French, the philologist who first suggested the great *Oxford English Dictionary* in 1857, called *handbook* "an ugly unnecessary word . . . scarcely . . . ten or fifteen years old," a very poor substitute for the Latin "manual." Actually, the handy *handbook* had reentered the language after a long absence. It dated back to the Anglo-Saxon *handboc*, used before Alfred the Great. Besides its standard English meaning, a *handbook* is American slang for a place where bets are made away from the racetrack, which gives us the terms *bookie* and *bookmaker*, both first recorded in the 1880s. *Handbook* was suggested by the small concealable notebooks that bookies carry for secrecy and convenience. In England, a bookmaker is called a turf accountant or commission agent.

handicap. A word first used in horse racing (1754) and then in golf (since the 1870s), *handicap* may derive from an old English game called "hand in cap," which was a drawing before a horse race. According to this theory, "hand in cap" was shortened to *handicap* in speech and came to mean an attempt to predict the winner of a horse race or other contest by comparing the past performances of all the contestants.

hand in glove. To be hand-in glove with someone is to be very close indeed, as close or intimate as a glove is to a hand. We know the expression dates back to at least the late 17th century, when it was *hand and glove*. It wasn't until 1891, however, that *hand in glove* is recorded. Jonathan Swift called *hand and glove* a cliché in *Polite Conversation* (1738).

Handkerchief Moody. The nickname of eccentric Maine pastor Joseph Moody (1700–53), who for 20 years preached with his back to his congregation. Moody wore a crepe mask when in public. Upon his death it was revealed that he had once accidentally killed a man and was ashamed to be seen. Nathaniel Hawthorne based his short story "The Minister's Black Veil" (1836) on Moody.

hand of glory. This is an example of a new custom or superstition created by an etymological error. *A hand of glory* was originally a charm made of a mandrake root, which was believed, among other things, to double one's money when put beside it overnight. *Hand of glory* was a translation of the French *main de gloire*, meaning exactly the same, but the French expression was a corruption "by popular etymology" of what had originally been the Old French for *mandragore*, "mandrake." Thus, when the term came into English early in the 18th century, people couldn't help but think that the charm consisted of a human hand. This led to a completely new superstition due to the deformation of the word. By 1816 we find a writer explaining that *the hand of glory* "is a hand cut off from a dead man, as has been hanged for murther, and dried very nice in the smoke of juniper wood." Such charms made from the hands of executed criminals were said to help one sleep, that is, lull one into a dead sleep, among other things.

hand over fist. Seamen reached the rigging on old sailing ships by climbing hand over hand up a thick rope—a skill sailors prided themselves on—and when sails were hoisted, the same hand over hand technique prevailed, just as it did when ropes or even fish were hauled in. American seamen in the 19th century changed this expression to the more descriptive *hand over fist*, which shows one fist clenching a rope and a loose hand passing over it to make another fist on the rope, etc. The rapid ascent on the ropes and the act of hauling in nets soon suggested someone rising rapidly in the business world and hauling in money, which is what we still mean when we say someone is making money *hand over fist*.

handsome is as handsome does.   Perhaps this is an old proverb that Chaucer suggested in "The Wife of Bath's Tale," part of *The Canterbury Tales* (ca. 1387). There Chaucer wrote: ". . . he is gentil that dooth gentil dedis [deeds]." Anyway, some four centuries later, in *The Vicar of Wakefield* (1766), Oliver Goldsmith first used the expression in close to its modern form: "She would answer, 'They are as heaven made them—handsome enough, if they be good enough; for handsome is that handsome does.' " By the early 20th century the phrase had become *handsome is as handsome does* in American English and was often used as a motto under pictures of male graduates in college yearbooks. The words aren't often heard today and when they are, they are always applied to men. Originally, the expression was said of both men and women. The cynical Frances Grose, for example, wrote in *A Dictionary of the Vulgar Tongue* (1796) that it was "A proverb cited by ugly women." A recent variation on the saying is the famous line from the film *Forest Gump* (1994), "Stupid is as stupid does."

hands up!   Nathaniel Hawthorne's son, Julian, seems to be the first writer to record the expression *hands up!*, in an 1887 novel, but he meant the words for schoolchildren, not outlaws: "Hands up—every soul of you. Hands up, those who have the right answer!" There appears to be no certainty as to who first used the words to mean "a robber's, policeman's, etc., order to preclude resistance," as the *OED* states. The *OED* dates the first use of *hands-upper* ("one who surrenders with his hands held up") to 1902, giving a number of references. However, the surrender order itself isn't dealt with. Because the Americanism *holdup*, "robbery," is recorded in 1878, someone must have said "hold your hands up" or "hands up" before then.

hand to mouth.   One of the earliest uses of this phrase best explains it: "Hungry folkes that are fed from hand to mouth." The expression arose in the 16th century, when famines in which thousands of people starved to death were frequent for the first time in England, usually occurring with the failure of grain crops. People living under such conditions had no choice but to cram a piece of bread into their mouths as soon as they got it in their hands, so great was their hunger; there was no thought or possibility of saving for the future. Later, a *hand to mouth existence* came to describe a life of poverty in general, and even a thriftless, improvident life.

handy-andy.   A handyman, named after the eponymous hero of *Handy Andy* (1842), a humorous novel by the Irish painter, novelist, and songwriter Samuel Lover (1797–1868).

handyman.   *Handy*, "ready or clever with the hands, dextrous," dates back to the early 17th century, but the term *handyman*, for a person useful for all kinds of odd jobs, doesn't

appear in print for almost 200 years more. *Handywright* is an older synonym rarely, if ever, used today.

hang by a thin thread.   The flatterer Damocles annoyed Dionysus the Elder of Syracuse with his constant references to the ruler's great power and consequent happiness. Deciding to teach the sycophant the real perils of power, he invited Damocles to a magnificent banquet, surrounding him with luxuries only a king could afford. Damocles enjoyed the feast until he happened to glance up and see a sharp sword suspended by a single thin thread pointing directly at his head, after which he lay there afraid to eat, speak, or move. The moral was "Uneasy lies the head that wears a crown"—that there are always threats of danger, fears, and worries that prevent the powerful from fully enjoying their power, the sword of Damocles symbolizing these fears. From this fifth-century story, recounted by both Cicero and Horace, comes our expression *to hang by a thin thread*, to be subject to imminent danger.

hangdog look.   It's said that hunting dogs living in the great English country houses of the past, eating scraps tossed from the table and sleeping as close to the fire as they could get, were kept orderly by special handlers who broke up dogfights, whipped their charges, and even hanged incorrigible dogs. Shakespeare, no dog lover, does refer to the hanging of dogs five times in his plays, but I've been unable to find any reliable record of actual cases of a dog hanging, though there are other cases of animals tried and executed by law (*see* E. P. Evans, *The Criminal Prosecution and Capital Punishment of Animals*, 1906). Nevertheless, since the late 17th century anyone with a cringing, abject appearance, or a base, sneaky demeanor has been said to have a hangdog look. Whether real or the product of someone's imagination, the allusion was originally to a despicable, degraded person fit only to hang a dog, or to be hanged like a dog. Nowadays a *hangdog look* has almost entirely lost its meaning of contemptible and sneaky and generally describes someone browbeaten, defeated, intimidated, or abject—someone who looks a little like a bloodhound.

hanged, drawn, and quartered.   At first this punishment for high treason and other crimes in England was called drawn, hanged, and quartered—that is, the criminal sentenced to death was drawn (dragged) through the streets behind a horse to the gallows, hanged, and then his head was cut off and his body torn into four pieces, often by horses. In the 15th century a further barbaric penalty was added and drawn, hanged, and quartered became hanged, drawn, and quartered. In this case the victim was hanged and drawn (eviscerated) before he was torn to pieces. Often he was only partially hanged, his body cut down, and his "bowels burnt before his face." There was even a legal term in Latin for the perversion: *detrahatur* ("drawn, dragged"), *suspendatur* ("hanged"), *devellatur* ("disemboweled"), *decolletur et decapitetur* ("beheaded and quartered").

hanged high as Haman.   The biblical Haman, King Ahasuerus's counselor, built a "fifty cubits high" gallows on which he planned to hang Mordecai and other Jews. But Esther turned the king against him and he was hanged on his own gallows, giving Ahasuerus pleasure, Mordecai great relief, and posterity the expression *hanged high as Haman*, "destroyed by one's own machinations."

hanging around.   This expression meaning to idle or loiter about is possibly the ancestor of *hangout*, a place for hanging around, and today's popular phrase *hanging out*, idling about. *The Dictionary of American Slang* gives its origin as the late 19th century, but it is definitely older than this, since Oliver Wendell Holmes uses it as an Americanism in his novel *Elsie Venner* (1861), putting it in quotes.

hanging breathless on.   A very common phrase that comes from Henry Wadsworth Longfellow's poem "The Building of the Ship" (1849):

> Sail on, O Ship of State!
> Sail on, O Union, strong and great!
> Humanity with all its fears
> With all the hopes of future years,
> Is hanging breathless on thy fate!

Hanging Garden of Babylon.   There are, of course, thousands of outstanding gardens throughout the world. Among the most famous was the Hanging Gardens of Babylon, one of the Seven Wonders of the World. The Hanging Gardens were supposedly built by the biblical King Nebuchadnezzar to please his wife, Amytis, who had grown tired of northern Babylon's flat plains and longed for scenery that would remind her of her native home in the Median hills. Should you want to cultivate the same, build a square garden, 400 feet each way, rising in a series of terraces from an adequate river and provide it with enough fertile soil to hold even great trees. Vague directions, but the plans have been lost over the years.

hanging out.   *See* HANGING AROUND.

hang in there.   This common Americanism, meaning "to refuse to give up" and "to stick with it," originally hails from the world of boxing, where managers exhorted exhausted fighters to finish a round or a bout, even to hang on to the ropes. In recent years the expression has come to be used as common parting words to someone in trouble, or in fact to anyone, since everyone in this life is usually up against the ropes in one way or another. Similarly, a frequent answer from anyone asked how he or she is: "I'm hanging in there."

hang it up.   American slang since about the 1920s for "to quit work or retire," *hang it up* is a shortened term for the baseball expression *to hang up one's spikes* ("One more season and I'll hang up my spikes") meaning the same. A less frequent variation among men is *hang up one's jockstrap*, a phrase of more recent vintage. *See also* JOCK.

hangman's wages.

> For half of thirteen-pence ha' penny wages
> I would have cleared all the town cages . . .
>
> —The Hangman's Last Will and
> Testament

This term is referred to occasionally in English literature from the late 17th to early 19th century. It means 13 pence and a halfpenny, which was the execution fee (a Scottish mark) set by James I—one shilling for the work and three halfpence for the rope. The nobility were expected to give the executioner up to 10 pounds for beheading them. As time went on, of course, hangmen and headsmen raised their prices like everyone else.

hangnail.   The Anglo-Saxon word *angnaegl* meant "a painful corn on the foot," deriving from *ang*, "pain," and *naegel*, "nail," a hard corn resembling the head of a nail. Later, its meaning was extended to include a painful corn on the finger as well, or anywhere on the skin for that matter. This word, eventually pronounced *angnail*, appropriately defined a painful corn, but through mispronunciation an "h" was added to it. *Hangnail* served only as the term for a painful corn or swelling until someone in the early 17th century realized that it perfectly described the small strip of skin that sometimes tears away and hangs down from the fingernail, causing considerable pain. The mispronunciation that was superfluous in the old meaning of the word has become essential to the new meaning.

hang on by the eyelashes.   As late as this expression came into the language—it is traced by Partridge to 1860—we still don't know who or what is responsible for it. Two centuries earlier something hung by the eyelids was something in a state of suspense, but the other phrase, used literally or figuratively, means to hang on precariously, to be barely able to hang on to the most meager of holds. As with the much older expression *hang on by the skin of one's teeth*, no real situation inspired the imaginative description.

hang one's head.   *See* SWORD OF DAMOCLES.

hang out your shingle.   To become a doctor or lawyer, among other professions. The Americanism comes from pioneer days, when doctors did use shingles for their signs.

Hangtown fry.   Placerville, California, used to be nicknamed Hangtown because a good number of men were hanged there—or so the story goes. *Hangtown fry* refers to an omelet made of eggs, fried oysters, bacon, and onions that was invented during the gold rush in Placerville, or Hangtown.

hang up one's spikes; hang up the gloves.   Strictly speaking, the phrase *hang up one's spikes* means "to retire" from professional baseball, football, or any sport in which spiked shoes are worn, as in "Slugger Mark McGwire has decided to hang up his spikes." However, the expression is used lightly for to retire from anything. The term was first recorded in 1942, the same year boxing's *hang up the gloves* made its initial appearance.

hanky-panky.   A synonym for trickery, *hanky-panky* may have been coined, with the help of reduplication, from the magician's handkerchief, or *hanky*, under which so many things have mysteriously appeared and disappeared through clever sleight of hand. Probably related to *hocus pocus*, it is first recorded in *Punch* (1841).

Hansard.   What the *Congressional Record* is to the United States Congress, the Hansard is to the British Houses of Parliament. A Hansard is the official printed report of proceedings in Parliament, the name in honor of Luke Hansard (1752–1828) and his family after him, private printers who published the reports from 1774 until 1889. Today the proceedings are recorded by the government, but the reports still bear the printing firm's name.

Hansen's disease.   The scientific name, sometimes used euphemistically, often given to leprosy. Norwegian doctor Armauer Gerhard Henrik Hansen (1841–1912) discovered the bacillus *(Hansen's bacillus)* that causes leprosy and his name soon came to be used as a synonym for the disease itself.

hansom.   If Joseph Aloysius Hansom invented the hansom cab, once the most popular of horse-drawn carriages—"the gondolas of London," as Disraeli called them—he certainly gained nothing from his invention. Most word authorities vouch for Hansom, but one source claims that Edward Bird invented the vehicle, presenting the idea gratis to his brother-in-law, Edward Welch, a partner in Hansom's Birmingham architectural firm. Hansom (1803–82) was an English architect specializing in churches and public buildings. He did patent the cab—possibly as Bird's Patent Safety Cab—but the financial arrangement he made upon selling his patent rights proved disastrous. Promised 10,000 pounds, Hansom received, according to conflicting accounts, either nothing or a mere 300 pounds for his patent. *Hansom cabs,* however, made millions for their manufacturers. The low, two-wheeled covered carriage, with the driver's seat above it in the back, was noted for its maneuverability and safety features as well as its privacy and unobstructed view for passengers. Soon after its appearance in 1834, it became the most popular cab in London and around the world. The last hansom disappeared from London in 1944, but a few are still available for hire in New York's Central Park.

hapa haoli.   In Hawaii this term means a person who is half white. *Hapa* here is the English word *half* assimilated phonologically into Hawaiian, with *l* dropped, *f* replaced by *p*, and the first vowel added. *Haoli* (pronounced HOW-lee) means white.

happi awaa.   The Japanese borrowing and alteration of the English words *happy hour,* a time that is now known around the world. It means, just as it does in the U.S., the late afternoon or early evening time when bars offer drinks at reduced prices.

happy as a clam at high tide.   Clams are usually dug at low tide, so a clam might be happy indeed at high tide. This expression is an Americanism, first noted in 1834.

happy as a colt in clover.   Novelist and historian Shelby Foote (b. 1916) says he first heard this expression when he was a boy some 80 years ago. It means to be very content and happy and seems to be one of those phrases that hasn't been recorded up until now.

happy as Larry.   Australians who use this phrase often say it originated with famous fighter Larry Foley (d. 1917), who was happy in and out of the ring, a kind of clown prince of boxing—a nice thing to be remembered for.

"Happy Birthday to You."   Most people are surprised to learn that "Happy Birthday to You" is still (until the year 2010) a copyrighted song that earns over $1.2 million dollars a year. Ranked as the world's most frequently sung song in the *Guinness*

Book of World Records, it was written in 1893 by Patty Smith Hill (d. 1946) and Mildred J. Hill (d. 1916) as part of their *Song Stories for the Kindergarten.* Originally entitled "Good Morning to All," it took its present name from the first line of its second stanza.

happy hunting grounds.   Perhaps American Indians invented this synonym for heaven, but it seems more like the work of an author like Washington Irving, who first recorded it in one of his books (1837).

happy landin' with Landon.   The Republicans coined this campaign slogan for Alfred M. Landon in 1936, when he ran against Franklin D. Roosevelt for president. It was more like a crash landing than a "happy landin'," Landon suffering one of the most devastating defeats in American political history.

happy pills.   A term from the late 1950s for tranquilizers and stimulants, uppers and downers, some of which are dispensed by DR. FEELGOODS. Recently I heard the words *happy pills* described as painkillers by a patient in a doctor's office: "I just want him to give me some happy pills for the pain."

happy trails.   This farewell has been popular for many years, thanks in part to the song "Happy Trails" sung by many country singers, including Roy Rogers. "Happy trails, Hans," the hero (Bruce Willis) says to the villain in the movie *Diehard 2* (1991) as he dispatches him.

happy warrior.   Since the beginning of the 19th century *happy warrior* has meant someone cheerfully undeterred by opposition of any kind. Capitalized, it was a nickname for Alfred (Al) E. Smith, governor of New York and an unsuccessful presidential candidate in 1928.

hara-kiri.   The word isn't spelled *harikiri* or *hari kari* and doesn't mean "happy dispatch," as many people believe. Formed from the Japanese *hara,* "belly," and *kiri,* "to cut," *hara-kiri* literally means "belly cutting." It is, of course, the Japanese method of suicide by disemboweling, practiced especially when honor is lost, and is said to have been first turned to by Tametomo, brother of ex-Emperor Sutoku, in the 12th century, after he suffered a devastating military defeat. *Hara kiri,* which Mencken also gives as the name of a cocktail, was one of the first Japanese words to come into English, introduced shortly after *tycoon* in 1856. *Hara-kiri* is seldom used by the Japanese, who find it vulgar and offensive, the proper term is *seppuku.*

harass.   Though it means inflicting any kind of unpleasantness today, to *harass* originally had a much stronger meaning, as its derivation shows. *Harass* derives from the Old French verb *harer,* meaning "to set a dog on," and came into English early in the 17th century.

harbinger of spring.   The robins flying north or the swallows returning to Capistrano are harbingers: messengers who announce that spring is coming. It's hard to imagine this expression having its roots in war, but it does. *Harbinger* derives from the Old High German *hari,* "an army," and *bergan,* "to lodge." In English it was first spelt *herbergeour* and meant one who provides or obtains lodgings for the military. Later the word changed in meaning, describing someone sent ahead to obtain lodging for a party of travelers, and finally it came to mean someone who goes forth in advance to announce the coming of travelers or things—like the swallow, robin, and other harbingers of spring.

hardball. *See* PLAY HARDBALL.

hard-boiled. Tough, strict, unsentimental. The comparison is to a hard-boiled egg, a term that dates back to early 18th-century England. The American tough-guy use of the word dates from the late 19th or early 20th century. American writers seem to like the expression; Mark Twain, Eugene O'Neill, Theodore Dreiser, Maxwell Anderson, Raymond Chandler, and Ernest Hemingway are among the many writers who have used it. Wrote Hemingway, a tough guy who knew the score, in *The Sun Also Rises* (1926): "It's awfully easy to be hard-boiled about everything in the daytime, but at night it is another thing."

Hard-Core State. *See* BEAVER STATE.

hard hat. *Hard hat* used to be a designation for a man who wore a derby hat, especially Eastern bankers and businessmen during the 1880s. A century later, in the late 1960s, it came to mean a construction worker, because of the metal or plastic safety helmets such workers wear. Because these hard hats often clashed with antiwar demonstrators during the early 1970s and supported the war in Vietnam, the term *hard hat* also came to mean a political conservative.

hard-on; heart-on; horny. The taboo slang term for an erection is often slurred in speech out of embarrassment, so that it is difficult to tell if the first word is pronounced *hard* or *heart*. Both words are actually used interchangeably in the expression, *hard* obviously referring to the erect penis and *heart* perhaps referring to the shape of the glans of the *membrum virile*. The term goes back only to about 1860 and was preceded in use by the expression *to have the horn*, which gives us the slang *horny*: lustful, sexually aroused.

hard-shelled Baptist. Often called simply a "hardshell," but in both cases a strict Baptist who proclaims hellfire. Such a Baptist can be a member of the Primitive Baptist Church or an Old-School (Antimissionary) Baptist, a Baptist who judges everyone very strictly by his beliefs and rules, even himself in many cases. "What I don't like about hardshells, they think everybody but them is goin' t' hell—even the dead little babies," wrote Carl Carmer in *Stars Fell on Alabama* (1934).

hardtack. A century ago, *tack* meant food of any kind. Sailors took to calling hard biscuit—biscuit that was hard and lasted through long voyages in rough weather—*hard tack*, or what we'd more often call *dog biscuits* today.

hard up. When the weather was bad at sea *Hard up the helm!* was the order given and the tiller had to be put up as far as possible to the windward in order to turn the ship's head into the wind. These words came to mean "to weather the storm as best you can" and then took on the meaning of being short of money or some other necessity—that is, the condition of someone weathering a "storm."

harem. Used by the Greeks before any Arabian, and called a *gynaeceum* by them, *harem* does take its name from the Arabian *harim*, "sacred or forbidden place." *Harem* first meant the section of a house in which the wives and concubines of a Muslim lived and then was applied to the women themselves.

harlot. William the Conqueror, known in history as the Bastard, was the result of a union between Arlette or Herleva, the attractive daughter of the tanner Falbert of Falaise, and Robert le Diable, duke of Normandy—perhaps even, as the old tale says, when Robert the Devil came cantering by, saw Arlette kneeling naked washing her clothes and dismounted from his horse. But Arlette's name doesn't give us the word *harlot*, which was born long before her illegitimate son and most probably derives from the old German *hari*, "army," and *lot*, "loiterer," meaning "an army camp follower." *Harlot* first signified a person of low birth and applied to both men and women before taking on its present meaning of a female prostitute.

harmattan. *See* MONSOON; WINDS.

harmonica. *See* STORMONTER.

harp. Long synonymous with an Irishman, this derogatory expression stems from the use of the harp as the national symbol of Ireland. One of many legends about the word's origin says that an early King David of Ireland took the harp of the psalmist as his badge. Another story says the Irish were so called because in days past they were often gamblers who flipped coins, calling "harp!" for tails because the shilling had a harp engraved on one side. The musical instrument called a harp takes its name from the Old English *hearpe* meaning the same. *See also* DAGO; KIKE; WASP; WELSH.

Harpers Ferry, West Virginia. This beautiful little town in easternmost West Virginia on the bluffs at the confluence of the Potomac and Shenandoah Rivers is famous in American history because the old fanatic abolitionist John Brown was captured and hanged there just before the Civil War. The town takes its name from one Robert Harper, who established a ferry at the site in 1747.

harridan. The French *haridelle* means a worn-out wreck of a horse. From this word comes the English *harridan*, "a haggard, disreputable old woman, a vicious or violent old hag."

harrier. Harriers were a breed of small hounds developed to hunt hares long before the word was used as a synonym for cross-country runners. The application of the word to human runners arose out of a game called "hounds and hares" or the "paper chase," in which one team of runners (the hares) would run through the woods leaving a trail of paper scraps that the other team (the hounds) would follow, trying to catch the hares before they reached the finish line. The name *harrier* was soon given to the "hounds" and finally it became a synonym for all cross-country runners. *See* PAPER CHASE.

Harriet Lane. *Harriet Lane* is a merchant-marine term for Australian canned meat, because it supposedly resembled the chopped-up body of the girl murdered by a man named Wainwright in about 1875.

Harry S Truman.   The S in the American president's name has been the subject of a word story for over half a century now. This middle initial has no period after it. According to an April 12, 1945 Associated Press dispatch, "[It] is just an initial—it has no name significance. It represents a compromise by his parents. One of his grandfathers had the first name of Solomon; the other Shippe. Not wanting to play favorites, the President's parents decided on the S."

Hart, Schaffner and Marx.   An anonymous poker player, perhaps someone dressed in one of this American clothing manufacturer's suits (jacket off, shirtsleeves rolled up), probably coined the term *Hart, Schaffner and Marx* for a hand containing three jacks. In any case, the term has become an amusing, little-known part of the game's vocabulary.

Harvard beets.   Harvard beets, often called pickled beets, are made from sliced beets cooked in sugar, cornstarch, vinegar, and water. There is no record that the dish was invented at Harvard University, but it is said that the unknown chef noticed the resemblance in the color of the deep red beets to the crimson jersies of the then vaunted Harvard football team. Harvard, the first institution of higher learning in North America, bears the name of John Harvard (1607–38), an English minister who lived for a time in Charlestown, Massachusetts, and later willed the fledgling university half his estate and his library of over 400 books. Cambridge, Massachusetts, where Harvard is located, was named for England's Cambridge University.

harvest; aftermath; defalcation; threshold; tribulation. The harvest was so important in ancient times that the word *haerfest*, or *harvest*, became the Old English term for autumn as well as for the gathering in of crops. This usage prevailed well into the 10th century, when *harvest* began to be used exclusively to mean the gathering in of wheat (called "corn" in England) and finally crops in general. The German word for autumn is still *Herbst*, which is related to the English *harvest*. *Harvest* is cognate with the Latin *carpere*, to pick. A number of English words have their roots in the harvest, words that most people would not expect to have a botanical heritage. In Roman times, for example, harvested grain was ground with a heavy roller called the *tribulum*. Being ground under and pressed out by this machine soon suggested the word *tribulation* to those who felt that they were under similar pressure. The Anglo-Saxons had a harvest ceremony called the threscan in which people stamped on piles of dry wheat, separating the grain from the stalks. This action resembled the stamping of feet when people cleaned their shoes against the sills of wood or stone that marked the doorways of houses and soon the sill came to be called the threshold of a house. Misappropriation of money or funds by an official trustee or fiduciary is called defalcation. This word has its roots in the Latin *falculus*, sickle, which yielded the verb *falcare*, to cut. The Latin *de*, down, plus *falcare*, means to cut down. Someone guilty of defalcation thus cuts down someone else's possessions as a farmer might cut down grain with a sickle when he harvests it. The after mowth, which later came to be pronounced *aftermath*, is the second or

later mowing, the harvest of grass that springs up after the first hay mowing in early summer when the grass is best for hay.

Harvey Smith.   Here is a man whose name means "the finger," or, anyway, two fingers, meaning the same. Harvey Smith, a well-known British show-jumper, saw his name become better known after he "was alleged to have raised two fingers" at the judge of a 1971 competition. A *Harvey Smith* came to mean "the obscene gesture" in English, and still does, though, of course, the gesture dates back much further than Mr. Smith, and will almost certainly last longer than this probably apocryphal eponymous word. Harvey Smith, for his part, claimed that he simply made a V for victory sign.

hash.   Horne Tooke's *Diversions of Purley* (1786) derived *hash* from the Persian *ash*, or stew. An ingenious derivation, but completely wrong, as *hash* comes from the French *hacher*, "to cut up," which also gives us the word *hatchet*. As a noun meaning the common meat dish, *hash* is first recorded in Samuel Pepys's *Diary* (13 Jan. 1663): "I had . . . at first course a hash of rabbits, a lamb."

hassayampa.   *DARE* traces this Western word for someone given to exaggeration, or a liar, back to 1901 and says it derives from the name of the Hassayampa River in Arizona, the river's name in turn, probably coming from a Yuma Indian word. The term was first applied to old prospectors with wondrous but untruthful stories. Why was the river associated with liars and lying? According to the *Dictionary of American Folklore*: "There was a popular legend that anyone who drank of the Hassayampa River . . . would never again tell the truth."

hassle.   Some etymologists believe *hassle*—a fight, or trouble—is a blend of *harass* and *hustle*; others say *haggle* and *tussle*; while still others opt for *haggle* and *wrestle*. On the other hand, *hassle* may derive from the southern American dialect word *hassle*, meaning "to breathe heavily." All that is certain is that the word is first recorded in 1945. The hassle about *hassle*'s origins goes on.

hasta la vista, baby.   This phrase has become a well-known U.S. cliché since Arnold Schwarzenegger uttered it in his film *Terminator 2* (1980). It means "goodbye," *adios* in Spanish, Schwarzenegger uttering it as he dispatched a victim. Other less hackneyed Spanish terms for goodbye include *hasta luego* and *hasta mañana* (see you tomorrow).

hasty pudding.   John Bartlett in his *Dictionary of Americanisms* (1850) defines this as "Indian meal stirred into boiling water until it becomes a thick batter or pudding . . . eaten with milk, butter, and sugar or molasses." It is mentioned in a verse of the Revolutionary War song *Yankee Doodle*: "Father and I went down to camp,/ Along wi' Captain Goodin,/ And there we see the men and boys,/ As thick as hasty puddin'." But its most famous mention is in Joel Barlow's mock-epic *The Hasty Pudding* (1793), which the poet wrote in a Savoyard inn in France when he was served a dish of boiled Indian meal that reminded him of Connecticut. Part of it goes:

> Thy name is Hasty Pudding! thus our sires
> Were wont to greet thee fuming from their fires;

And while they argued in thy just defence,
With logic clear they thus explain'd the sense:
"In *haste* the boiling caldron o'er the blaze
Receives and cooks the ready-powder'd maize;
In *haste* 'tis serv'd; and then in equal *haste*,
With cooling milk, we make the sweet repast."
Such is thy name, significant and clear,
A name, a sound to every Yankee dear.

Hasty Pudding Club. The oldest American theatrical social club and perhaps the best-known is Harvard's Hasty Pudding Club, founded in 1795 and named after Joel Barlow's mock-epic poem "The Hasty Pudding." Over the years its theatricals have featured as performers and writers such notables as Oliver Wendell Holmes, William Randolph Hearst, Franklin Delano Roosevelt, and Robert Sherwood.

Hatfield-McCoy feud. *See* RAZORBACK.

hat trick. British cricket bowlers in the 19th century were awarded a new hat, or the proceeds of a collection made by passing a hat, when they bowled down three wickets with three successful balls. This practice is the origin of the American phrase *hat trick*, used for a jockey who has three consecutive winners, a hockey or soccer player who scores three goals in one game and, less often, a baseball player who hits for the cycle (that is, a batter who hits a single, double, triple, and home run in one game).

haul over the coals. Heresy in medieval times was determined not by a jury trial but by ordeal by fire. Accused persons were hauled or dragged over the coals of a slow fire and those who burned to death were considered guilty of departing from the teachings of the church; those who survived were pronounced innocent. From this and similar barbarous practices in 15th- and 16th-century England, comes the expression *to haul over the coals*, for "a severe reprimand or censure."

Haussmannization. *Haussmannization* is frequently heard today in connection with the blight and plight of cities around the world. To *Haussmannize* means to remodel a city along beautiful lines and celebrates Baron Georges Eugène Haussman (1809–91), who administered a face-lifting to Paris, starting in the middle of the 19th century. While prefect of Paris, Haussmann completely remodeled the city. He laid out the Bois de Boulogne and other parks; constructed new streets and widened old ones; instituted a new water supply and sewer system; created wide, open spaces and vistas; and built new bridges, railroad stations, and numerous public buildings. These and many other improvements required expenses and loans that resulted in a public debt of hundreds of millions and eventually led to Haussmann's dismissal in 1870, 17 years after he had begun his plan. Interestingly, Haussmann was trained not as an architect but as a financier. The Boulevard Haussmann also bears his name.

have a bear by the tail. This is another of those colorful expressions (*see* A BEAR FOR WORK) that arose in America during the first half of the 19th century. *To have a bear by the tail* is to be in a bad situation—you're in trouble whether you hold on or let go!

have a burr in (under) his saddle. An old Western expression still said of someone who is extremely irritated or agitated, even impatient.

have a field day. Beginning in the mid-18th century the British army held field days featuring military exercises and display. The term soon was applied to outdoor gatherings such as picnics, and then to field days at schools devoted to outdoor sports and athletic contests in which winning was not as important as having a good time. From these last field days came the expression to *have a field day* meaning to indulge oneself freely and successfully, to go all out, as in "the papers will have a field day with this story."

have a good (nice) day. As William Safire points out in *On Language* (1980), Chaucer used the expression "Fare well, have a good day" in "The Knight's Tale" of the *Canterbury Tales* (1387). It is still common today, with the variation *have a nice day* probably even more prevalent since about 1970. Writers have railed against both banal expressions, but they are harmless enough and usually said with good feeling.

have an oar in another's boat. *See* ALL IN THE SAME BOAT.

have at one's fingertips. To have thorough familiarity or knowledge of a subject. The phrase isn't recorded until 1870 in America, but it is obviously an elaboration of the much earlier *to have at one's fingers' ends*, which is recorded in England in 1553 as a familiar saying.

have fishhooks in one's pocket. To be very cheap. First recorded in 1913, the Americanism may have originated much earlier with Long Island, New York, sea captain Samuel Mulford. Mulford lined his pockets with fishhooks to foil pickpockets when he visited London before the American Revolution. His ploy worked.

havelock. Sir Henry Havelock (1795–1857) was rarely in fashion—it took him 23 years to be promoted to captain, for example—but this most British of British soldiers did eventually do well. Havelock, an evangelist as well as a soldier, served over 34 years with the British Army in India, taking only one leave home in all that time. Known as "the Saint" to his men for his habit of trying to convert everyone under his command to temperance and moderate ways, he was indeed among the fussiest and most tiresome of men. But as to his military ability and bravery there is no doubt. Havelock led his troops to many victories during the Sepoy Rebellion (1857) and is remembered for his recapture of Cawnpore and his stand at Lucknow until reinforcements arrived. The general died of dysentery brought on by the arduous Lucknow defense. The *havelock*, or covering, that he had devised for his "Ironsides" brigade wasn't his invention; similar helmet coverings had been used since the Crusades. This trademark of the French Foreign Legion in films was fashioned of white linen, hanging halfway down the back and protecting the neck from the sun.

have one's heart in one's throat. To be very anxious, tense, frightened. Dating back four centuries, the expression was first *have one's heart in one's mouth*, and it is sometimes still heard that way. *My heart was a lump in my throat* is also used today.

have one's innings. *Inning* has its roots in British cricket where *innings* (always spelled with an s but considered singular) means a time at bat for a batsman, because that player is "in" at bat while the opposition team is "out" on the field. It is from the cricket *innings*, not baseball's borrowing of it, that we get the expression *to have one's innings*, one's opportunity or chance or one's time at bat, as it were. Other expressions stemming from cricket include *to keep one's end up*, *to catch up*, and *to bowl over*. See also BOWL OVER; CRICKET.

have one's number on it. The widely accepted belief in the American military that the bullet, grenade, shell, or bomb that kills one is marked by fate with one's number. *Number* could refer to one's serial number; American soldiers all wore identity tags or DOG TAGS at the time the expression was first recorded during World War I.

have other fish to fry. To be busy, usually with something important, so that one can't do anything else at the moment. The old American phrase is still heard today, often with variations, as in this example from the television series *The West Wing* (7/25/01): "I've got a bigger fish to fry."

haves and have-nots. The *haves* and *have-nots* are the rich and poor of any society. The term is not of recent vintage as one might expect. In fact, Cervantes may have invented it in *Don Quixote* (1605–15) where he has Sancho Panza say: "There are only two families in the world, the haves [*el tenor*] and the have-nots [*el no tenor*]." See also QUIXOTIC.

have someone's number. To know someone's weaknesses, to have great insight into someone's thoughts and actions. There seems to be no widely accepted explanation of the word *number* in the phrase, the telephone having been invented long after the expression's first recorded use in 1853.

have the edge. A player to the left of the dealer in 19th-century American poker games often had the right to continue in the game or drop out. This was called *to have the age*, and the poker term began to be used outside the game, as when Mark Twain in a 1907 magazine article wrote, "How could I talk when he was talking? He 'held the age,' as the poker-clergy say." Soon the *age* in the expression became *edge*, due to the similarity in pronunciation and the aptness of *edge* in the phrase, and *to have the edge* came to mean to have any advantage.

have the goods on. The goods here are stolen goods, those found by the police on a criminal and almost assuring his conviction. The phrase dates back only to the early 1900s, and "goods" may have referred specifically to bogus money made by counterfeiters before it was applied to stolen goods in general. Soon after its introduction, the expression was being used generally for "to have knowledge giving one a hold over another."

have the inside track. This phrase means "to have an advantageous position in any competitive situation." The expression is from American track and field and dates back to the mid-19th century. The inside track or lane on a race course is the shortest and the runner positioned in it has the least distance to run (which is why many races have staggered starts).

have the luck of Hiram Smith. Few, if any, soldiers have been as unlucky as Hiram Smith, who fought in the Aroostook War of 1836–39, a war between New Brunswick and Maine over land near the Aroostook River on the U.S.-Canadian border. When New Brunswick sent loggers into the area, Maine authorities recruited a force to eject them. There were several clashes between 1838 and 1839 before an agreement was reached by General Winfield Scott's troops, the conflict known as the "Bloodless War." However, one person was killed in the war—luckless Hiram Smith, the only person to die in the entire war, whose luck was at least as bad as any soldier before or since.

have the world by the tail. When they say this in Texas, as they have for a century, it means they have everything going exceedingly well for them. When they have the world by the tail on a downward pull, things are even better.

have words with someone. These words, denoting a verbal altercation, go back at least five centuries, though in a slightly different form. We find the expression was first *at words* (1462). After that, various phrases such as *to fall at words with*, *to have hard words with*, *high words with*, and *sharp words with* have all served to express the same idea.

haw. The fruit of the Old World or English hawthorn (*Crataegus monogyna*), which can be red or yellow, is called "haw" or "hall." These names are also used for hawthorns themselves. In the language of flowers, hawthorn is the symbol of "good hope" because it is a spring flowering tree that shows winter is over. Commonly called the "thornapple" for its thorny trucks, which make impenetrable barriers, the hawthorn's lovely flowers were used to crown Athenian girls at weddings, and the Romans placed leaves of the hawthorn on the cradles of newborn infants to ward off evil spirits. In China, the fruit or haws of the Asiatic hawthorn is considered a delicacy.

Hawaii. Hawaii is from *Owykee* or *Hawaeki*, which means "homeland" in the native language. Our 50th state, admitted to the Union in 1959, was previously known as the Sandwich Islands (see SANDWICH) and is nicknamed "the Aloha State" (see ALOHA).

Hawaiian words in English. Hawaiian and South Sea Island languages such as Tongan and Tahitian have contributed a number of words to English, including tattoo, taboo, lei, atoll, muumuu, poi, ukelele, and sarong (a borrowing from the Malay language).

hawk. *Hawk* for an eager advocate of war didn't come into the language during the Vietnam War, as is often believed. Thomas Jefferson coined the term *war hawks* in 1798 to describe Federalists crying for war with France, and the modern term *hawk* was first given to those of John F. Kennedy's advisers who during the Cuban Missile Crisis of 1962 wanted the president to get tougher with Cuba and the Soviet Union.

Hawkeye State. A nickname for Iowa dating back to at least 1839, when *Hawkeye* described an Iowan. Candidates for the original Hawkeye after whom Iowans were named include a great Indian chief; newspaper editor James Gardiner Edwards, known as "Old Hawkeye"; and Natty Bumppo, hero of James

Fenimore Cooper's *The Last of the Mohicans* (1826), whose nickname was Hawkeye.

hawkweed. *See* KING DEVIL WEEDS.

hay is for horses. One of the earliest and most enduring of catch phrases, *hay is for horses* is a retort to someone who cries out *hey!* It is first recorded in Jonathan Swift's *Polite Conversations* (1738):

> Neverout: Hay, Madam did you call me?
> Miss: Hay! Why; hay is for horses.

Hayism. "Acidosis," Dr. William Howard Hay advised in his book *Health Via Food* (1933), causes almost all bodily ills. Therefore, since proteins need acid for their digesting and carbohydrates require alkaline conditions, such foods should not be eaten in combination—no milk with your potatoes or vice versa—for "no human stomach can be expected to be acid and alkaline at the same time." Hays ignored the fact that most foods contain mixtures of proteins and carbohydrates. Like most food fads his regimen had its loyal, even fanatical followers. Hayism, incidentally, recommended frequent fasting—which is said to cause acidity or acidosis.

haymaker. "Gentleman Jim" Corbett used this colorful expression for a heavy, swinging blow, usually a knockout, in his autobiography *The Roar of the Crowd* (1925). It originated a decade or so earlier, in about 1910, and was popularized by radio boxing announcers. The term probably derives from the slang expression *to make hay*, "to take full advantage of one's opportunities," and *the hay*, "sleep or unconsciousness." The idea of a worker swinging a scythe while haymaking is also suggested.

Hays Code. Long the moral code of the American film industry, the *Hays Code* commemorates Will Harrison Hays (1879–1954). "Czar" of the movies, Hays served as first president of the Motion Picture Producers and Distributors of America from 1922 to 1945. A former chairman of the Republican National Committee and postmaster general under Harding, he helped formulate the so-called *Hays Code* in 1934 and zealously administered it from what was dubbed the Hays Office.

hayseed. *See* CLODHOPPER.

haywire. A fairly recent autobiography entitled *Haywire* shows that this Americanism still has a long life ahead of it, even though its rural origins are remote from most Americans now. Someone or something gone haywire is confused, out of order, deranged, crazy. The expression is first recorded toward the beginning of the century and was suggested by the baling wire, or haywire, that farmers and ranchers used to tie bales of hay. When a bale of hay was opened with a hatchet to feed livestock this thin sharpened wire would spring out and whirl about a farmer, the sharp ends frequently cutting him or snagging in his clothing. Old haywire lying around—and there was of course much of it—also wound about the legs of horses and other livestock, hopelessly tangling them up. Finally, farmers used old haywire to make temporary repairs on everything from machinery to fences and houses—temporary repairs that were often never made permanent and gave their places a disorderly look. All of these associations, from the crazy leaping of the wire to the tangling up of livestock and the disorder created by haywire, contributed to the coining of the colorful expression, which probably dates back to the 19th century, though first recorded in 1910.

hazard. *Hazard* has come to mean "random chance," or "an unavoidable danger or risk, or something causing danger, peril or risk." But the word originally meant a dice game, a usage it still has today. This is clearly seen in the word's ancient ancestor, the Arabic *al*, "the," and *zahr*, "die." Because the cast of the dice is uncertain or risky, the word came into Spanish as *azar*, "an unexpected accident," this becoming the French *hasard*, which became the English *hazard*.

H-bomb. *See* A-BOMB.

H.D. *See* IMAGIST.

he. *See* SHE.

head. Heads, "latrines," are so called because they were originally in the bow, or head, of a ship. Our word *head* for the upper part of the body joined to the trunk by the neck comes from the Old English *heáfod* for the same.

headache! A warning to "watch it!," "heads up!" used by loggers, oilmen, and other workers in the U.S. over the past 70 years or so because a heavy object is overhead or coming down: "Be careful or you'll get a headache," that is, get hit on the head.

headline. Newspaper headlines are an American invention that came into frequent use during the Civil War, but the earliest known example blared forth from the front page of the Tory *New York Gazette* and the *Weekly Mercury* on October 20, 1777. Fortunately for the United States the headline was all wrong:

> Glorious News from the Southward. Washington
> Knocked up—The Bloodiest Battle in America—
> 6,000 of his Men Gone—100 Wagons to Carry
> the Wounded—General Howe is at present in
> Germantown—Washington 30 Miles Back in a
> Shattered Condition—Their Stoutest Frigate
> Taken and One Deserted—They are Tired—And
> Talk of Finishing the Campaigne.

head nor tail. *See* CAN'T MAKE HEAD NOR RAIL OF IT.

head over heels. As you might suspect, *head over heels*, for "a state of helplessness" ("He's head over heels in love with her") was originally *heels over head*. For nearly 500 years it was used that way, until in the late 18th century it was popularly corrupted to its present topsy-turvy form. The allusion is probably to a somersault. There is no proof that the phrase is a translation of Catullus's *per caputque pedesque*, "over head and heels," or that it alludes to the practice of hanging criminals by the heels as a warning in medieval times—though anyone so hanged would certainly have been helpless.

head peace. A colorful expression heard in Ireland for quiet, rest, as in "Play outside and give me some head peace."

He ain't heavy, Father, he's my brother. The famous inscription, said to a priest, that appears on a statue at Omaha Boys Town. The statue shows an older boy helping a younger boy by lifting him up.

heap. Very, a lot; said to be a feature of American Indian speech in early times. According to *Blackwood's Magazine* (LXiii, 1848): "An Indian is always a 'heap' hungry or thirsty—loves a 'heap'—is a 'heap' brave—in fact, 'heap' is tantamount to very much."

hear a different drummer. The expression is from Henry David Thoreau's *Walden* (1850): "If a man does not keep pace with his companions, perhaps it is because he hears a different drummer. Let him step to the music which he hears, however measured or far away." A variation is *march to a different drummer*.

hear, hear! The well-known British cry of affirmation or support often heard in Parliament. It was originally "Hear him! Hear him!," a cry directed at the opposition when they tried to drown out a speaker by humming in unison. The "him" in the phrase was eventually dropped for the sake of brevity.

Hear, O Israel, the Lord our God, the Lord is One. The first line of the most common of Jewish prayers, the *Shema*, whose origin is Deut. 6:4–7. The prayer is recited several times daily and as a final affirmation of faith when a person is dying.

heart-burial. Up until relatively recent times heart-burial, the burial of the heart apart from the rest of the body, was commonly practiced. The heart of British poet Thomas Hardy, for example, was willed to be buried in Stinsford, England, his birthplace, after the rest of his body was cremated in Dorchester. All went according to plan until a cat belonging to the poet's sister snatched the heart off her kitchen table and disappeared into the woods with it.

heart of oak. The solid inner part of an oak tree, which was traditionally used as the timber to build sailing ships. A popular British sea song called "Heart of Oak" (1757) had the lyrics "Heart of oak are our ships, / Heart of oak are our men. . . ."

heart of stone. English scholar John Wyclif was the first to use the term *herte of stoon*, recorded from his writings four years after his death in 1388. Since then the words have been used by many writers, including Dickens, so many, in fact, that they have become a cliché.

heart on one's sleeve. *See* WEAR ONE'S HEART ON ONE'S SLEEVE.

hearts-a-bustin'-with-love. A colorful old American name for the burning bush (*Euonymus americanus*), which has seed pods that burst open to reveal many scarlet seeds. It also goes by the names hearts-a-bustin', strawberry bush, swamp dogwood, arrowwood, and spindle bush.

hearts and flowers. A synonym for sentimentality that was first the title of a popular 1910 American song. Overuse of the song as background music played by violinists in sentimental dramas led to its title becoming synonymous with the overly sentimental. People began playing imaginary violins while humming "Hearts and Flowers" whenever they heard a sad story. Soon the song itself was forgotten and only the phrase and the mock playing of violins remained.

Heath Robinson contraption. William Heath Robinson (1872–1944) drew cartoons of complicated and impractical but clever and humorous machines or devices like Rube Goldberg contraptions. These were featured in *Punch* and other prominent British publications, his name becoming attached to the devices just as Rube Goldberg's did.

heavens to Betsy! No one has been able to uncover the origins of this old common exclamation of surprise, joy, or even annoyance. Etymologist Charles Earle Funk tried hardest, devoting several pages to the expression in his 1955 book of the same name. "Possibly the phrase was known in Revolutionary War days," he writes, "but I doubt it. Nor do I think, as some friends have suggested, that it pertained in any way to the maker of the first American flag, Betsy Ross. It is much more likely to have been derived in some way from the frontiersman's rifle or gun which, for unknown reasons, he always fondly called Betsy. However, despite exhaustive search, I am reluctantly forced to resort to the familiar lexicographical locution, 'Source unknown.' "

Heaving Day. See LIFTING MONDAY.

Heaviside layer. Increasing deafness forced Oliver Heaviside (1850–1925) to retire from his post with the British Great Northern Telegraph Company when he was only 24. The mathematical physicist and electrician devoted the remainder of his long life to theoretical investigations into electricity. In 1902 he suggested that a conducting layer of ionized gas exists in the upper atmosphere that conducts, reflects, and refracts radio waves. This Heaviside layer, about 60 miles above us, reflects radio waves back to earth, and enables reception around the globe. Because Edison's former assistant Arthur Edwin Kennelly (1861–1939) postulated the same theory shortly before the British scientist, the stratum is also called the *Kennelly-Heaviside layer*. Today it is more generally known as the ionosphere. *See* APPLETON LAYER.

heavy brass. *See* BRASS.

heavy hitter. A batter who consistently hits the ball hard, a power hitter, has been called a heavy hitter in baseball since at least the first recording of the term in 1887. By extension the term has come to apply to anyone powerful in any profession or undertaking, giving us *political heavy hitters, literary heavy hitters*, etc.

heavyweight. A boxer who is a heavyweight fights in the heaviest competitive class, which is now over 175 pounds. The term has been applied to fighters in that approximate division since about 1850 although formal weight classes in boxing weren't instituted until the Queensberry rules in 1872. In the

United States the boxing use of *heavyweight*, combined with an earlier (1840s) use of *heavy* for wealthy or important, led to the expression *heavyweight* for any person, company, or other entity that is very powerful, influential, or important. *See also* LIGHTWEIGHT.

Hebrew words in English.   Among the many Hebrew words that came into English, sometimes through other languages, are: amen, hosanna, manna, rabbi, Sabbath, Satan, seraphim, cherubim, sapphire, babble, behemoth, leviathan, cabal, shibboleth, jubilee, kosher, shekel, Torah, kibbutz, and hallelujah. See also YIDDISH.

heck.   Contrary to popular legend, Mark Twain didn't invent *heck* as a euphemism for "hell" to please his prudish wife. The word goes back to Lancashire dialect several centuries ago, deriving from *(h)eck!*, an expression of surprise, or possibly from the Lancashire oath *go to ecky* meaning "go to hell."

heckle.   To *heckle* recorded as early as the 13th century, originally meant to disentangle and straighten flax fibers by drawing them through an iron comb. Since the fibers were disturbed by the comb, *heckle* also came to mean to annoy or harass someone, especially a public speaker.

hectic.   *Hectic*, which derives ultimately from the Greek *hektikos*, meaning habitual, was first used in English in medicine, to describe a fluctuating fever. By the late 19th century it took on the meaning of intense or feverish activity, or confusion that it mainly conveys today.

hector.   Why did Hector, Troy's mightiest, bravest defender in Homer's *Iliad*, become a blustering, domineering bully? His name, symbolic for a gallant warrior in early English literature, today means not only a bully, but to bully, torment, or treat insolently. The change seems to have taken place toward the end of the 17th century when a gang of young bullies, who considered themselves paragons of valiant courage, adopted the honorable name "Hectors." This ruffian band insulted passersby, broke windows, and became notorious for their bullying, terrorizing the streets of London. It is probably from their name that *hector* and *to hector* derive, rather than from that of the exalted magnanimous Hector, noble in victory and in defeat. Some scholars point out, however, that Hector was represented in medieval drama as boastful and domineering, possibly from the notion that any hero is swashbuckling and blustering.

hedge.   *Hedge*, in the form of *hegge*, is recorded in English as early as 785, referring to rows of bushes or trees, such as privet or hawthorn, planted in a line to form a boundary. In time the word *hedge* came to mean a safeguard and by the 16th century writers were using the word as a verb, meaning to protect oneself with qualifications, to avoid committing oneself. Shakespeare was the first to record the expression, in *The Merry Wives of Windsor*.

hedge word.   A good story about these common disclaimers of responsibility concerns Mark Twain and his first job as a reporter. Twain was told by his editor never to state anything he couldn't verify by personal knowledge. After covering a gala social event, he hedged his bets by turning in the following story: "A woman giving the name of Mrs. James Jones, who is reported to be one of the society leaders of the city, is said to have given what purported to be a party yesterday to a number of alleged ladies. The hostess claims to be the wife of a reputed attorney." The use of such disclaimers does *not* automatically confer immunity from prosecution for libel, as the law punishes *publication* of a libel, which, legally, means "making public."

heebie jeebies.   Cartoonist Billie DeBeck (1890–1942), who invented "hotsy totsy," "hot mama," and other slang expressions, is credited by Mencken with this coinage, for "a feeling of nervousness, fright, or worry"—the willies or jitters. What he based the rhyming compound on, outside of a sheer joy of sound, is hard to say. One guess is that it is a "reduplicated perversion" of "creepy" or "the creeps." More likely DeBeck took the expression from the name of a dance called the Heebie-Jeebies popular in the 1920s, a dance that inspired a popular song titled "Heebie Jeebies" (1926). The dance, of American Indian ancestry, is said "to represent the incantations made by Red Indian witch doctors before a sacrifice."

heeler.   In the early days of Texas dogs were trained to catch and herd cattle. Often of the bulldog breed, they were called *heelers* because they typically caught the heel of the cow in their jaws.

he (she) found the hole.   Said of someone very unlucky or stupid. The expression is a shortening of an old one-line joke: "He's a guy that drowned in a river that was only six inches deep on the average—he found the hole."

hegira.   Any flight, often a political one, to a more desirable place than where one is, is called a hegira. It is so called from the flight of Muhammad from Mecca to Medina in A.D. 622 to escape persecution by wealthy traders, a date regarded as the beginning of the religion of Islam.

He has a leak that will send him to hell.   A nineteenth-century American expression, nautical in origin, describing someone or something with a fatal flaw.

he hath slept in a bed of saffron.   This old Latin expression refers to the supposed exhilarating effects of saffron, meaning "he has a very light heart." As an old poem puts it:

> With genial joy to warm his soul,
> Helen mixed saffron in the bowl.

One of the most expensive spices, saffron is made from the dried stigmas of crocuses.

Heimlich maneuver.   U.S. physician Henry J. Heimlich (b. 1920) will be long remembered for this emergency rescue procedure used on someone choking on a foreign object. Dr. Heimlich invented the procedure in 1970, and it has since saved thousands of lives.

heinie.   Our word for the buttocks has nothing to do with the offensive slang word for a World War I German soldier, which derives from the common German name Heinrich (Henry). *Heinie* here is an alteration of *hinder*, which comes from *hind*, the back or rear, the posterior. See HINEY.

Heinz hound.   A humorous name for a mongrel dog. From the name of the Heinz Company, which long advertised HEINZ's 57 VARIETIES of canned food (see below). Also called a "Heinz dog" and a "Heinz."

Heinz's 57 varieties.   The original Mr. Heinz, forebear of the millionaire senator, adapted his company's famous slogan from a New York City billboard ad he saw featuring "21 Styles of Shoes." Heinz actually had 60 varieties at the time he coined the slogan in 1892, but he thought an odd number sounded better. The company used its "57" slogan until 1969.

Heisman Trophy.   The Heisman Memorial Trophy has been called the ultima Thule for undergraduate football players, being awarded annually since 1935 to the best of their breed in the country. It is named for John W. Heisman, former Georgia Tech coach. Called "Shut the Gates of Mercy" Heisman, the coach was a great mentor, though not noted for being a gentleman on the playing field. On one occasion he allowed his team to rack up an incredible 222 points against an opponent. Notable Heisman Trophy winners include Tom Harmon of Michigan (1940), Paul Hornung of Notre Dame (1956), and O. J. Simpson of Southern California (1968). Jay Berwanger of the University of Chicago won the initial award in 1935.

he is not being executed, he is being shot.   The death penalty had been abolished in Soviet Russia when Admiral Aleksie Shchastny was sentenced to be shot. Spectators in the court that day in 1918 began to stir when the state prosecutor explained: "What are you worrying about? Executions have been abolished. But he is not being executed; he is being shot." This most extreme of euphemisms is recorded in Aleksandr I. Solzhenitsyn's *Gulag Archipelago* (1974).

he kept us out of war.   The political slogan *he kept us out of war* has been used in two American presidential campaigns. The Democrats used it in 1916 to help return Woodrow Wilson to the White House, only to have Wilson ask Congress to declare war on Germany a year later, "to make the world safe for democracy." In 1956 the Republicans used it to sell Dwight D. Eisenhower as a peacemaker in Korea, though it took a backseat to the very popular "I like Ike." *See* EISENHOWER JACKET.

helicopter; whirlybird; chopper.   The helicopter was named before it was invented. *Helicopter* came into the language about 1885 from the French *hélicoptère* as the name of a purely theoretical heavier than air craft capable of horizontal and vertical flight. Such an aircraft, like the airplane itself, had been sketched by Leonardo da Vinci four centuries earlier. After many experiments by many inventors, Russian-born U.S. aeronautical engineer Igor I. Sikorsky (1889–1972) and Germany's Henrich K. I. Focke designed the first successful modern helicopters in 1937–41. By the time of the Korean conflict (1950) helicopters were called "whirlybirds" and, more commonly, "choppers," even though the slang word *chopper* also means a tommy gun, a motorcycle, the penis, and even death itself, "to get the big chopper." A rare humorous synonym for the helicopter is *heligoflipter*; while the earliest name (1926) for a helicopter pilot, *helicopterist*, is almost never heard anymore, *jockey* or *chopper jockey* often being the terms for the people who fly the choppers. *See* Jolly.

heliotrope.   Many plant leaves and flowers turn toward the sun. The ancient Greeks noticed that this fragrant vanilla-scented perennial flower (*Heliotropium arborescems*), often called "cherry pie," did so and called it the *heliotrope*, from the Greek *heleo*, "sun," and *trepo*, "turning to go into it." Another fragrant flower sometimes called heliotrope, and also called "cherry pie" for its blossoms, is common valerian (Valerian officinalis), probably named for the Roman Emperor Valerianus. A Greek legend says the god Apollo loved the ocean nymph Clytie but abandoned her for her sister, whereafter she died of sorrow. A remorseful Apollo changed the dead Clytie into a living flower that always turns toward the sun.

Helius.   *See* ISLAND OF THE SUN.

hell.   *Hell* is a colorful name for thick tangles of rhododendron or laurel so vast that people become lost in them. These huge thickets are also called "laurel hells," and they are most common in southern mountain areas, where this term seems to have been coined.

hell afloat.   Usually old hulks no good for sailing anymore, British prison ships were the concentration camps of the Revolutionary War. It has been estimated that they took the lives of more American fighting men (11,000 to 15,000) during the Revolution than enemy rifles did. Such ships were often dubbed *hell afloat* by the prisoners, whatever the ship's real name.

hell for leather.   After pondering various theories about the origin of *hell for leather*, several scholars have determined that it is a British expression first recorded by Rudolph Kipling in *The Story of the Gadsbys* and used again by him in *Many Inventions* and *Barrack Room Ballads*. Kipling may have invented this phrase meaning "to travel at great breakneck speed" by horse or by vehicle, or it may have been an army expression he adopted. It clearly suggests a rider (trooper or civilian) riding at full speed and beating against the leather saddle he rides on. However, the great scholar Ernest Weekley in his *Etymological Dictionary of Modern English* (1921) throws doubt upon this derivation. "My memory of it [the phrase *hell for leather*] goes back nearly fifty years," he writes. "Can it [hell for leather] be for *all of a lather* [the foam in a racing horse's mouth] with secondary allusion to *leather* in [the] sporting sense of skin as affected by riding?" This may true be, and I would certainly trust Weekley's memory of the expression first being used about 1870, some 20 years before Kipling employed it. A variation in the U.S. is *hell-bent for leather*; the word *leather* suggested by the hard use of a leather whip while riding a horse at a very fast pace.

Hell Gate.   Before this famous narrow passage in New York's East River was blasted, thousands of vessels were wrecked against the rocks in its strong conflicting currents. Dutch mariners in early New York probably named it so, calling it Hel Gat, though some etymologists have suggested that the name derives from Dutch for "whirling gut."

hello.   *Hello*, one of the most frequently used words in everyday speech, isn't recorded until 1883 or thereabouts. But in the form of *hallow*, its earliest ancestor, the word dates back to at least 1340 and was used by Chaucer. *Hallow* probably derives from the Old French *hallo-er* "to pursue crying or shouting."

Hello came into fashion with the invention of the telephone late in the 19th century, replacing the earlier variant *hullo*. *Hello girl*, once used for a telephone operator, is an Americanism first recorded by Mark Twain in *A Connecticut Yankee in King Arthur's Court*.

hello? Over the past 20 years or so HELLO has taken on the additional meaning of a kind of derisive question inquiring whether someone is at home upstairs (in his or her head) for proposing a silly or dumb idea, often in conversation. Pronounced hel-*lo*, the new expression is frequently written with a question mark. *Duh* is similarly used.

hell on wheels. Union Pacific Railroad construction gangs in the 1860s lived in boxcars that were pulled along as the line progressed. Traveling and living with these hard-drinking, often violent men were gamblers, prostitutes, and other unsavory characters. The wild congregation assembled in the boxcars suggested the population of hell to settlers, and the transient town was called *hell-on-wheels*, a colorful term soon applied to any violent, vicious person or lawless place.

to hell or Connaught. During the Commonwealth, under Oliver Cromwell, the native Irish were dispossessed of their land in the other provinces and ordered to settle in Connaught or be put to death. This led to the phrase common throughout Ireland, or wherever Irishmen emigrated, of *to hell or Connaught*.

hell or high water. *See* COME HELL OR HIGH WATER.

hello the house. For over a century this has been a common greeting upon approaching a house in the American West. A variation is *hello in the house*. The expression probably has British roots.

Hell's Angels. The best-known, if not the first, of the motorcycle gangs came into prominence in the 1950s in the San Francisco Bay area. *Hell's Angels* founders were descendants of the OKIES of the Great Depression.

Hell's bells! The more colorful curse *hell's bells and buckets of blood!* was the original of the imprecation, which probably originated at sea during the late 19th century, under what circumstances no one knows.

hell's half acre. A 19th-century term for a low saloon, a dive, or for a small or distant place, especially one that is disreputable or crime-ridden.

hell's kitchen. As that part of hell where the fires are hottest, hell's kitchen would be unpleasant indeed, which is why it came to mean any very unpleasant, disreputable place. The expression is first recorded in Davy Crockett's *An Account of Col. Crockett's Tour to the North and Down East* (1834). By 1879 it was being used as a name for an infamous district on New York City's West Side, which Mitford Mathews tells us was "once regarded as the home of thieves and gunmen." The Stovepipe was part of it, and nearby were the tenements of Poverty Gap.

hell with the fires out. An old colorful expression describing the southwestern desert in the U.S. especially in the hottest months.

helot. The original helots, slaves or serfs, were inhabitants of the town of Helos in Laconia, enslaved by the Spartans in ancient times. The Spartans actually ranked their helots midway between citizens and slaves, but certainly treated them like flunkeys. As an object lesson to Spartan youth that drunkenness is evil, helots were often forced to drink more than they could handle and then exhibited in the public square.

helpmeet. *Helpmeet*, "a companion or helper, a wife or husband," is the source of the more familiar *helpmate*, meaning the same. *Helpmeet* is a misreading of the biblical Gen. 2:18, which refers to "a help meet for him," *meet* in this sense actually meaning "suitable" (a "suitable help").

hem and haw. As an expression for hesitancy, to *hem and haw* isn't recorded until 1786. But it is found centuries earlier in similar expressions such as *to hem and hawk, hem and ha*, and *hum and ha*, which Shakespeare used. These are all sounds made in clearing the throat when we are about to speak. When a speaker constantly makes them without speaking he is usually hesitating out of uncertainty, which suggested the phrase. Said the first writer to record the idea in 1469: "He wold have gotyn it aweye by humys and by hays but I would not so be answered."

henpecked. The pecking order among hens, according to the famous study made by biologist W. C. Allee, has a definite prestige pattern: Hens, like many humans, male and female, freely peck at other hens below their rank and submit to pecking from those above them. Although hens rarely peck at roosters in the barnyard, where the rooster is the cock of the walk, it was widely believed in the 17th century that they often pulled feathers from young roosters below them in the pecking order. This led to the comparison of domineering wives to aggressive hens. Samuel Butler defined the term first, Dryden complained that he was henpecked, and Steele called Socrates "the undoubted head of the Sect of the Hen-pecked." There was even a noun *henpeck*, for a wife who domineered her husband, and Byron, in *Don Juan*, wrote his celebrated couplet: "But—oh! ye lords of ladies intellectual, / Inform us truly, have they not hen-peck'd you all."

henry. Scientist Joseph Henry's career constitutes a series of famous firsts and foremosts. The U.S. Weather Bureau was created as a result of his meteorological work while first director of the Smithsonian Institution, and Henry was the first "weatherman" to make forecasts from collected scientific data. Not only a brilliant administrator who initially planned the Smithsonian's scope and activities, Henry has been acknowledged as the leading physicist of his day. His researches on sound gave America the best fog signaling service among maritime nations, he stimulated geologic and geographical exploration, and his influence on the character of science, especially concerning the free publication of scientific results, was exceeded by no contemporary. Before becoming secretary of the Smithsonian in 1846, Henry taught physics at Princeton, where he built the first electromagnetic motor (1829) and devised the first practical telegraph (1830–31). It is not for the theory of electromagnetic induction that the henry, the measurement unit of induction, is named in his honor. This theory is credited to the English scientist Faraday, although Henry's experiments may have preceded his, and it is for his theory of producing induced current (1832) that the International Congress of Electricians gave the celebrated American's name to the standard electrical unit in 1893. He died in 1876 at the age of 81.

Henry Higgins. Henry Higgins, the professor-phonetician who teaches Cockney flower-seller Eliza Doolittle standard English in George Bernard Shaw's *Pygmalion* (1913), has become the name for any knowing, exacting, sometimes dictatorial and thoughtless teacher of speech. Shaw took the title of his play, one of his most popular, from the Greek legend of Pygmalion, a sculptor and king who fell in love with the statue he carved of his ideal woman. Aphrodite granted his prayer that it come to life so he could marry it. In 1957 the long-running musical *My Fair Lady* was made from the play. David Jones (1881–1967), head of the phonetics department at University College, London, always insisted that he was the prototype for Shaw's Henry Higgins. Jones claimed that Shaw in gratitude had a free box reserved for him for any production of the play as long as the author lived. He said Shaw chose the name Higgins after glimpsing a sign reading Jones and Higgins over a London shop, Shaw calling the character Higgins because he obviously couldn't use Jones. More likely, according to most writers, Shaw based Higgins on the pioneering scholar Henry Sweet (1845–1912).

Henry rifle. The Henry rifle has been called the grandfather of repeating arms. Invented by Benjamin Tyler Henry (1821–98), one of the Henry family of gunsmiths, the weapon was tested under fire by Union forces in the Civil War. The breech-loading, lever-action rifle never became popular as a military weapon but saw some use on the frontier and is featured in many a western. Henry may also have worked on the Martini-Henry rifle adopted by the British army in 1889. This was basically an improvement on the Martini, invented by Swiss mechanical engineer Frederic de Martini (1832–97), but another Henry, a Scottish gunsmith, possibly deserves the credit for it.

hepatica. These charming little wildflowers have three-lobed leaves that resemble the human liver. Noticing this, someone in medieval times named them from the Greek *hepatikos*, "of the liver."

Hepplewhite style. Nothing is known about the British furniture designer George Hepplewhite except that he operated a fashionable cabinetmaking shop in the parish of St. Gile's, Cripplegate, London, died in 1786, and willed his business to his wife, Alice. But his furniture was widely imitated in England and the United States, resulting in a style often eloquent and graceful. It has been assumed that the original Hepplewhite styles were delicate and soundly constructed. The cabinetmaker invented or popularized the shield-back chair and the "spider leg" for chairs, tables, and sideboards, and was among the first to inlay much of his furniture with exotic woods. Hepplewhite's small pieces, such as inlaid knife boxes, fire screens, and tea caddies, are highly valued by collectors. His *The Cabinet-Maker and Upholsterer's Guide*, published by his wife in 1788, inspired a host of imitators at home and abroad.

herba sacra. Vervain *(Verbena officinalis)*, the *herba sacra* or "divine weed" of the Romans, who believed that, among other things, it cured the bites of rabid animals, arrested the progress of snakebite, cured the plague and scrofula, reconciled enemies, and warded off witches. The Romans so esteemed vervain that they held annual feasts called Verbenalia in its honor. Ambassadors in ancient times wore vervain as a badge of good faith.

herb of grace. Rue is called the herb of grace because it is the symbol of repentance, owing to its extreme bitterness. Shakespeare used the expression in *Richard II*, and there are many old records telling of the use of rue in ceremonies of exorcism.

herb Robert. A common herb *(Geranium robertianum)* said to be named after Robert, duke of Normandy, or Saint Robert, and first recorded in the 14th century. It has fernlike, strong-scented leaves and pink to reddish purple flowers. Also called *red shanks* for its red stems, its plural is *herbs Robert.*

herculean task. A herculean task may not require great strength, even though the expression derives from the name of the mythical Greek superman, Hercules. Such a task is a difficult or dangerous one and refers to the fabled 12 labors of Hercules that he performed while overcoming great difficulties.

Hercules' club. The club carried by the mythological strongman Hercules was hewn from a thick wild olive branch, but somehow *Aralia spinosa*, a small, spring-trunked ornamental tree of the ginseng family, came to be known as Hercules' club. The prickly plant, which also goes by the names *angelica tree* and *devil's walkingstick*, has a medicinal bark and root, and hedges of Hercules' club form a strong impenetrable barrier. Creating some confusion, however, is the fact that *Zanthoxylum clava-herculis*, commonly known as the "prickly ash" and the "toothache tree," is also called Hercules' club. *See* APPLE.

to herd. *See* LIKE HERDING CATS.

herd's grass. *See* TIMOTHY GRASS.

here lies one whose name was writ in water. English poet John Keats (1795–1821) did not invent his own epitaph (above) as is often said. While he lay dying in Rome, listening to the falling water in a fountain outside his room, he remembered words from the play *Philastes, or Love Lies A-bleeding*, written by Beaumont and Fletcher in 1611. "All your better deeds / Shall be in water writ," one of the characters says. Keats mused upon this sentiment, and a week or so before he died told his friend the painter Joseph Severn that he wanted no epitaph or even name upon his grave, just this line, "Here lies one whose name was writ in water." On a lighter note, Robert Ross (1869–1918), remembered today as one of Oscar Wilde's most loyal friends, led a short, stormy life filled with trouble. Toward the end, he was asked what he would have as the words on his gravestone, and Ross, quickly adapting Keat's famous epitaph, replied "Here lies one whose name is writ in hot water."

here's lookin' at you, kid. This has become a toast from a man to a woman the whole world over. It was first made by Humphrey Bogart to Ingrid Bergman in the movie *Casablanca*, which has given us at least a dozen more great lines.

here's mud in your eye. This toast was originally made in the muddy trenches of World War I, or in the cafes where English and American soldiers spent their leaves trying to forget them.

here's to swimmin' with bowlegged wimmin. Is this a humorous nautical toast? Possibly. It is given by old salt Captain Quint in the movie version of Peter Benchley's *Jaws* (1974).

here today, gone tomorrow. Something or someone passing with time, transient. Often said humorously and sometimes shortened to *here today*. The phrase dates back to the late 19th century. American publisher Alfred Knopf (1892–1984) turned the words around. He was talking about book returns from bookstores one day when he observed, "GONE TODAY, HERE TOMORROW."

Hermannia. *See* MAHERNIA.

hermaphrodite. One who has the reproductive organs and many of the secondary sex characteristics of both sexes; and by extension, anything that is a combination of disparate elements. The word derives from Hermaphroditus of Greek mythology, the son of Hermes (a personification of the male principle) and Aphrodite (Hermes' female counterpart). In the Greek myth Hermaphroditus became united in one body with the young and beautiful nympth Salmacis, the nymph of the fountain in which he bathed.

hermetically sealed. Mystic philosophers in the third century claimed that their magical secrets had been dictated to them by Hermes Trismegistus, his name meaning "Hermes thrice greatest [three times as great as the original Greek god Hermes]," and that this Hermes was really the Egyptian god of wisdom, Thoth. The wisdom of Hermes Trismegistus became the basis for the 42 *Hermetic Books* containing secrets for alchemists, and one formula in these books told how to seal a container so that no air could get in. Today we don't claim to seal bottles, cans, and jars by any "magical" method, but all such airtight containers are called *hermetic* or *hermetically sealed* in Hermes' honor.

Hermia. *See* HERNIA.

hermit's derby. This is an interesting British expression, with limited American use, for "an upset victory." Hermit was the long shot that won the English derby at Epsom Downs in 1868, his victory all the more memorable because the marquis of Hastings lost his entire fortune betting on the favorite—to the great pleasure of Hermit's owner, Henry Chaplin, whose fiancee had eloped with Lord Hastings not long before the race. *See also* LONG SHOT.

hernia. The protrusion of an organ through an opening in its surrounding walls, especially the abdominal walls. The word comes ultimately from Latin for a rupture, which is akin to Latin *hira*, gut. In writing an article about Shakespeare's *Midsummer Night's Dream*, British author J. C. Squire (1884–1958) found that Hermia (the name of the young heroine in the play) was spelled Hernia in the proofs of the article. He let the mistake stand, inserting an asterisk and the note: "I cannot bring myself to interfere with my printer's first fine careless rupture."

heroin. Formerly a trade name, heroin was discovered around 1897 by Professor Paul Dresser, chief of the research department of Germany's Elberfeld Farben Fabriken. It was named from the Greek *heros*, "hero," apparently "because of the inflation of the personality consequent on taking the drug," because it made a user feel like a hero, for a short while.

Hero of New Orleans; Old Hickory. Hero of New Orleans was the nickname of General Andrew Jackson, referring to his victory over the British at New Orleans in 1815. He was also called Old Hickory because of his toughness (as tough as hickory wood) during the war, and Old Mad Jackson by his political enemies after he became president. *See* JACKSONIAN.

hero sandwich; poor boy. New York City's Italian hero sandwiches, the term first recorded in the 1920s, are named for their heroic size, not for Charles Lindbergh or any specific hero of the Roaring Twenties. Hero sandwiches are surely among the most numerous-named things in English. Synonyms include such terms as *hoagies* (in Philadelphia), *submarines* or *subs* (in Pittsburgh and elsewhere), *torpedos* (Los Angeles), *wedgies* (Rhode Island), *wedges* (New York State), *bombers* (New York State), *Garibaldis* (Wisconsin), *Cuban sandwiches* (Miami), *Italian sandwiches* (Maine), *Italians* (Midwest), *grinders* (New England), *spuckies* (pronounced "spookies"; Boston), *rockets* (New York State), *zeps* or *zeppelins* (several states), and *poor boys* (New Orleans), though this last one is made with French instead of Italian bread and can feature oysters. *Blimpie* is a trade name for a similar sandwich, and *Dagwood* refers to any huge sandwich—after "Blondie" comic strip character Dagwood Bumstead's midnight snack creations. That's 20 in all—and there must be more!

hertz. Radio waves take their scientific name, *hertzian waves*, from German scientist Heinrich Hertz (1857–94), whose interest in electromagnetic theory led to the discovery of the electromagnetic waves. Hertz also has the unit of frequency called the "hertz" named after him.

he's a poet but don't know it. The rhyme in this expression has kept it alive for nearly three centuries. The catchphrase dates back to at least 1700, when it was first directed at people who rhyme words accidentally in conversation.

he's gone, and with him what a world is dead. *See* TONGUE.

he's got short arms and long pockets. Heard by the author on one occasion in Connecticut as a description of someone very cheap, whose arms don't reach the deep pockets where he keeps his money.

Hessian. As an American epithet *Hessian* can be traced back to the Revolutionary War, when the British employed 30,000 Hessian mercenaries and their name, justly or not, came to mean any boorish, uncouth person of low moral character. The Hessians came from the former Grand Duchy of Hesse in Germany. Their name is also found in the high-tasseled Hessian boots fashionable in early 19th-century England; Hessian cloth, a strong, coarse jute or hemp cloth originally made in Hesse; Hessian, for any mercenary; and the Hessian fly so destructive to wheat, which was erroneously believed to have been brought to America by the Hessian soldiers.

heterosexual. *See* HOMOSEXUAL.

hewers of wood and drawers of water. *Hewers of wood . . .* describes people who aren't particularly clever, those who depend more on physical labor for their livelihood. The old expression is from the Bible (Josh. 9:21).

he who fights and runs away, lives to fight another day. The Athenian orator Demosthenes when a young man fought in the infantry against the Macedonians at the battle of Chaeronea. The Athenians were overwhelmed, losing 3,000 men, and Demosthenes deserted the battlefield. When he was called a coward, however, he replied, "The man who runs away may fight again," which is the original of this saying. *See* DEMOSTHENIC.

hex. An evil spell, or to create an evil spell. The word is an Americanism from the Pennsylvania Dutch, German immigrants who settled in Pennsylvania in the late 17th century. The first recorded use of *hex*, from the German *hexen*, to practice witchcraft, is in 1830.

hey! The exclamation *hey!*, to attract attention, first attested in about 1225, but probably as old as English, has its counterparts in all languages. In ancient times the Romans used *eho!*, and the Greeks before them cried out *eia!*

hi! Possibly the most common greeting in the U.S. It is a variant of *hey!* and became popular as a greeting about 1880. For five centuries before then, however, the British had used *hi!* as a cry to attract someone's attention, as *hey!* is in America today.

hiccup. No matter how it is spelled, the word is pronounced *hiccup.* Why is hard to say. Only in the 17th century did people begin to use *hiccup*, closely allied to the Danish *hicke* and the Dutch *hikke.* The *hic* in this echoic word is fine, but any connoisseur of hiccups would agree that a *cup* is rarely if ever heard in a hiccough.

hick. *See* CLODHOPPER.

hickery dickery dock. Some authorities call this familiar phrase an "onomatoplasm," an attempt to capture a sound (in this case that of a ticking clock) in words. However, it has been argued in the *Oxford Dictionary of Nursery Rhymes* that "the shepherds of Westmorland once used *Hevera* for 'eight,' *Devera* for 'nine' and *Dick* for '10.' "

hickory. *Pawcohiccora* was the name American Indians near Jamestown, Virginia gave to the milky liquor they obtained from nuts from a tree that abounded in the area. Colonists called the milky liquor and nuts *hiccora*, or *hickory*, abandoning the first part of the Indian word, and eventually applied the word *hickory* to the useful tree the nuts came from, which supplied them with a stony, tough wood good for many purposes.

hidebound. Cramped, constricted people, those who are rigidly opinioned, have been called *hidebound* since the 16th century. The word derives from a term applied to emaciated cattle in days before veterinary science had made many advances. Feeding and care of cattle was so poor in England at the time that by winter the animals were often thin and diseased and had lost the fatty tissue under the skin. As a result their skin clung tightly to their bones, they moved stiffly, and their hides couldn't be removed from their backbone or ribs when they died. Their physical condition naturally suggested the inelastic, constipated minds of some people.

hide your light under a bushel. Early translations of the Bible introduced the above phrase from Matt. 5:14–15 into English. Jesus, after urging his disciples to be "the light of the world," added that "A city that is set on a hill cannot be hid. Neither do men light a candle and put it under a bushel, but on a candlestick." The *bushel* in the phrase is a bushelbasket, not today's loosely made type, which lets some light through, but a sturdy earthenware or wood container. Thus *to hide your light under a bushel* was to unduly conceal your abilities so no one could see them, to be excessively modest.

Hi Diddle Diddle. *See* GRIN LIKE A CHESHIRE CAT.

hieroglyphics. From the Greek words for "sacred pictograph." The limitations of hieroglyphics or "picture writing," the precursor of alphabets, can be seen in the old story about Darius the Great, king of Persia. He received a hieroglyphic message from his enemies the Scythians; they sent him a live mouse, frog, bird, and arrows instead of pictures of these things. Darius interpreted this to mean they would surrender come morning—the arrows, he thought, meant they would give up their arms, mouse and frog represented surrender of the land and water, and the bird meant the Scythians would soon fly away from the field of battle. Accordingly, Darius went to bed without preparing his troops for attack and the Scythians raided his camp that night and overwhelmed his armies. They then explained *their* interpretation of the live hieroglyphics: the bird meant the Persians would never escape the Scythians unless they could literally fly, the mouse and frog meant that the only other way they could escape would be to turn themselves into mice and burrow through the ground or into frogs and hide out in the swamps, and the arrows meant they would never escape the infallible Scythian weapons.

Higgins boat. A naval landing craft greatly responsible for the success of D-Day, the invasion of Nazi-occupied France during World War II. Officially, it was designated the LCVP (*l*anding *c*raft, *v*ehicle, and *p*ersonnel). Its popular name honors its inventor and manufacturer Andrew Higgins, described by General Eisenhower as "the man who won the war for us." More Americans were carried ashore in Higgins boats during World War II than in all other landing crafts combined.

higgledy-piggledy. As an adjective *higgledy-piggledy* means "jumbled, topsy turvey," as in "They were thrown higgledy-piggledy into a large pile." The word is an old rhyming compound of uncertain origin that dates back to the late 1500s and may possibly have something to do with pigs being herded together.

highball. Long drinks were first called highballs in the 1890s, and were so named because they came in tall glasses and all glasses were called "balls" in bartender's slang. There is some reason to believe that the common, much older, railroad term *to highball* helped keep the drink *highball* in the public mind. *To highball* means to travel at top speed. In the early days of railroading a large metal ball hanging from two crossarms at the approach to railroad stations signaled locomotive engineers as to how they should proceed. A lowered ball meant come to a full stop and a ball raised to the top of the mast, a high ball, meant to proceed full speed ahead.

highbinder. A highbinder can be a swindler and cheat, especially a confidence man, or a gangster or rowdy. The word, first used in its latter meaning, derives from a gang of ruffians called the *Highbinders* that plagued New York City about 1806. Later their name was applied (in the lower case) to members of American-Chinese secret societies believed to be employed in blackmail and assassination.

highbrow; supercilious. Dr. Franz Joseph Gall (1758–1828), founder of the "science" of phrenology, gave support to the old folk notion that people with big foreheads have more brains. Gall's lifelong studies purportedly showed that the bigger a person's forehead was, the higher his brow, the smarter he would be. This theory was widely accepted through the 19th century, until phrenology was discredited by scientists, and the belief led to the expression *highbrow* for an intellectual, which is first recorded in 1875. The term is often used disparagingly and is the source of the similar terms *lowbrow* and *middlebrow*. *Highbrowed* people can be supercilious, meaning disdainful, and this word has a connection with the brow, too. *Supercilious* is from the Latin *supercilium*, "eyebrow," and the Latin suffix *-osus*, "full of." Thus a supercilious person is literally one "full of eyebrow," an etymology that goes well with the image of someone lifting the eyebrow slightly in disdain. *New York Sun* reporter Will Irvin popularized *highbrow*, and its opposite *lowbrow*, in 1902, basing his creation on the wrongful notion that people with high foreheads have bigger brains and are more intelligent and intellectual than those with low foreheads. At first the term was complimentary, but *highbrow* came to be at best a neutral word used to describe such things as *highbrow books*, and at worst sank as low as *lowbrow*, being used by lowbrows and other anti-intellectuals to describe supercilious intellectuals or psuedo-intellectuals. *Life* magazine coined the term *middlebrow* in the mid-1940s. *See also* EGGHEAD.

high dudgeon. *Dudgeon* is a feeling of anger, resentment, or offense, so *high dudgeon*, which dates back over a century, means great anger or resentment. S. J. Perelman's *in a low dudgeon* is a decided improvement on the timeworn phrase. No one seems to know where *dudgeon* itself comes from. An Italian word meaning "to overshadow" has been suggested, implying that someone who cuts off another's sunlight provokes anger. This is an idea that at least goes back to Diogenes the Cynic, who on being asked by Alexander the Great if the emperor could oblige him in any way, replied: "Yes, by standing out of my sunlight." But *dudgeon* has also been linked to a much earlier word for "the handle of a dagger." By this theory, which isn't documented or widely accepted, an insulted man reached for his dagger handle, or *dudgeon*, in anger. By extension the dagger handle became the dagger, and the dagger, or *dudgeon*, was used to describe the anger that led to its use.

the higher I go, the crookeder it gets. Words spoken by the Godfather (played by Al Pacino) to his sister, Connie, in the movie *Godfather III*. I can find no earlier use of the expression.

higher order. *See* UPPER CLASS.

highfalutin. Pretentious, pompous. The Americanism, dating back at least to 1839, may be a variation on *high-flown*. Ernest Weekley, in *An Etymogical Dictionary of Modern English* (1921), wants to know if "this type of oratory is due to Red Indian influence" on Americans, though he does admit "we [British] can do a little in the same line. . . ." As an example of highfalutin American language he cites one of Dickens's portrayals of American stereotypes in *Martin Chuzzlewit* (1843–44): "He is a true born child of this free hemisphere! Verdant as the mountains of our country; bright and flowing as our mineral licks; unspoiled by withering conventionalities as air our broad and boundless perearers! Rough he may be. So air our buffalers. But he is a child of natur' and child of freedom; and his boastful answer to the despot and the tyrant is that his bright home is in the settin' sun."

high five. *High-fiving* is a celebratory gesture where two participants raise their hands over their heads and slap each other's hands. The high five is often seen after a good play in sports, and indeed, University of Louisville basketball players Wiley Brown, Daryl Cleveland, and Derek Smith claimed to have invented it in 1979 during preseason practice as an odd, attention-getting gesture of triumph. However, hand slapping is also a way of greeting, especially among African-Americans. *The New Dictionary of American Slang* (1986) says the high five is "Chiefly used by and adopted from athletes, who themselves adopted the style from black colleagues." *See* BUMP.

high-handed. In the Bible (Num. 23:3) the direct ancestor of this phrase means "triumphantly." It is used in describing the departure of the Israelites from Egyptian bondage: ". . . on the morrow after the passover the children of Israel went out *with a high hand* in the sight of all the Egyptians." The description does suggest a certain amount of arrogance, however, and it is probably from this passage that *high-handed* came, with the passage of time, to mean arrogant or overbearing.

high hat. Jack Conway, a former baseball player and vaude-villian who became editor of the show business newspaper *Variety*, coined the expression *high hat*, for "a snob," in 1924. It suggests an affected rich or nouveau riche man in a high silk hat and tails strolling about town with his nose almost as high as his hat, and it gave birth to the expression *to high hat*, to snub or act patronizingly. The prolific Conway—Walter Winchell called him "my tutor of slanguage"—died in 1928. *Belly laugh, pushover, to click* (succeed), *baloney* (bunk), *S.A.* (sex appeal), *payoff*, and *palooka* are among his other memorable coinages.

high horse. In the royal pageants of Medieval England nobles and others of high rank customarily rode "high horses," great chargers a hand or so taller than the average mount. Riding such a high horse naturally came to be equated with superiority and the arrogance superiority often breeds. *To ride the high horse* came to mean to affect arrogance or superiority, and this phrase gave us the still common *to get up on one's high horse*, to scorn what we consider "beneath us." *See* TELL HIM (HER) WHERE TO GET OFF.

high jinks. *High jinks*, a somewhat dated expression for fun and pranks, was originally the name of an ancient drinking game played with dice, and the antics of the players gave birth to the phrase. Sir Walter Scott describes the game in his novel *Guy Mannering* (1815): "Most frequently the dice were thrown by the company, and those upon whom the lot fell were obliged to assume and maintain for a time a certain fictitious character or to repeat a certain number of fescennine [obscene] verses in a particular order. If they departed from the character assigned . . . they incurred forfeits, which were compounded for by swallowing an additional bumper, or by paying a small sum toward the reckoning."

high jump. The track and field term *high jump* has been used recently as slang meaning death, suggesting someone trying to jump high enough to reach heaven.

highlight; high spot. The *high light* or *high lights* of a painting, the brightest parts of a subject, which are focal points in the composition, was a technical term, well-known to artists in the early 17th century. These focal points of highest light intensity became familiar in photography, too, and by the beginning of this century the expression *high light* began to be used frequently for any bright, prominent, or outstanding feature of any occasion, subject, or situation. The much newer American expression *high spot* (1928), meaning the same and deriving from *spotlight*, doesn't seem to be used as often.

high muckey-muck; mogul. A high muckey-muck, or muck-a-muck, is someone in a position of authority, especially an overbearing person in such a position. *Muckey-muck* may be a childish play on the word *muckle*, "great," or is possibly a corruption of *Great Mogul*. The Great Mogul (mogul itself being a corruption of *mogol*) was originally the emperor of Delhi, and eventually his title was used to describe any big shot.

high noon. Many people associate this term for a peak or pinnacle, or a crisis or confrontation, with the classic western movie *High Noon*, though it is in fact first recorded in 14th-century England.

high on (off) the hog. Well aware that the best cuts of meat on a hog—the hams, pork chops, bacon, tenderloin, and spare ribs—are high up on a hog's sides, American southerners used the expression *eating high on the hog*, "good eating," as opposed to *eating low on the hog*—eating the pig's feet, knuckles, jowls, and sow belly, well known today as "soul food." By extension, *living high on* (or *off*) *the hog* came to mean living prosperously.

high plains drifter. A person, often an outlaw, who rode the high plains from place to place in the early West in order to be aware of possible enemies around him.

high seas. *High* in the term *high seas* means "chief" or "principal." The high seas, or the "main," are the open seas—those waters beyond any territorial limit that belong to no one nation.

High Street. *See* MAIN STREET.

hightail it. Mustangs, rabbits, and other animals raise their tails high and flee quickly when they sense danger. Trappers in the American West noticed this, over a century ago, probably while hunting wild horses, and invented the expression *to hightail it*, to make a fast getaway.

high tea. Americans are often curious about the meaning of the British expression *high tea*, having no real equivalent for the phrase. High tea is simply a light evening meal, often served at about six o'clock in place of supper, that includes cooked dishes as well as tea, scones, etc.

hijack. Back in Prohibition days, the story goes, criminals who robbed trucks of their loads of whiskey commanded their drivers to "Stick 'em up high, Jack!" or "Up high, Jack!" From their command they were called *highjackers*, then *hijackers*, and the word *hijack* became part of the language. Another explanation is that the crooks pretended to be friends of the drivers, calling out "Hi, Jack!"

hillbilly. Despite TV sitcoms like *The Beverly Hillbillies*, the word *hillbilly* is a derogatory name for hill people or highlanders, a designation, insulting at best, that has in the past provoked fights to the death. *Hillbilly* is first recorded in 1900 and usually implies laziness, ignorance, and stupidity. Highlanders don't mind being called "hillbillies" by other mountain folk, but they do object to flatlanders or "furriners" using the term.

the hills are closing in on him. He's going mad. This expression, heard in America, England, New Zealand, Australia, and Canada, originated with United Nations troops during the Korean War, or Conflict. Korea of course has many forbidding hills and mountains.

himself. The Irish frequently use *himself* instead of the personel pronoun *he*, and the word can also mean the master of the house or anybody of importance. Humorously it is used to describe someone who *thinks* he is important, as in "Will himself be wanting his tea served in the silver or gold cup?"

hiney; Heinie. *Hiney* is a name, deriving from hindparts, that is often but not always used when speaking to a child, as a term for the buttocks, backside, or ass. Sometimes spelled *heinie*, it should not be confused with *Heinie*, the name for a German soldier since World War I that derives from the common German name Heinrich. In 1904 *Heinie* is also recorded in the U.S. for any German, making it an Americanism. Other derogatory names for German soldiers, and sometimes Germans in general, are *Jerry, Boche, Sauerkraut,* and *Kraut.*

hip. There was supposedly a cool cat named Joe Hep who tended bar in Chicago during the 1890s and it was from this aware, all-knowing, disaffiliated man that we get the word *hep,* of which *hip* is a variant. Most scholars don't go along with this theory, dividing their loyalties between the opium smoker's term for smoking opium, *on the hip* (opium smokers often reclined on one side while smoking), or the West African *hipi,* "to be aware," or the African Walof *hipicat* (hence *hepcat,* too) meaning "one who has his eyes wide open." All we really know is that *hep* was recorded first in 1903 and has by now been almost totally replaced by its variant *hip,* which gave us the word *hippy* in the 1960s.

hip! hip! hurrah! The old story here can be taken for what it's worth, which isn't much. *Hip,* we're told, derives from the initials of the Latin words *Hiersolyma est perdita,* "Jerusalem is destroyed." German knights, not a very bright bunch, were supposed to have known this and shouted *hip, hip!* when they hunted Jews in the persecutions of the Middle Ages. *Hurrah!* by the same strained imagining, is said to be a corruption of the Slavonic word for Paradise *(hu-raj).* Therefore, if you ever shout *hip! hip! hurrah!* you are supposedly shouting: "Jerusalem is destroyed [the infidels are destroyed] and we are on the road to Paradise!" There is not the slightest proof for any of this, and the phrase, which doesn't date back earlier than the late 18th century, almost certainly comes to us from the exclamation *hip, hip, hip!* earlier used in toasts and cheers, and *huzza,* an imitative sound expressing joy and enthusiasm.

hipper-dipper. A *hipper-dipper* is slang for a fixed prizefight, the term dating back to the 1940s. The unusual word is of uncertain origin, but may derive from "hipper," slang for a small swimming pool, in the sense that someone takes a "dive" in it.

hippie. A much younger opposite of the *hippie (hippy)* in the HIP entry above. *Hippie* here means a *highly intelligent person pursuing intelligent endeavors.*

Hippocratic Oath. The original version of the *Hippocratic Oath,* which in altered form is still administered to medical school students upon graduation, begins with an invocation to the gods: "I swear by Apollo the physician . . ." All forms of the oath memorialize Hippocrates (ca. 460–377 B.C.), "The Father of Medicine," but not a line of it was written by the Greek physician and surgeon, it being rather the body of Greek medical thought and practice of his day. The words do, however, embody Hippocrates' ideals. Believed to have been born on the island of Cos off the coast of Asia Minor, the son of a physician who claimed descent from the Greek god of medicine, Hippocrates apparently studied medicine with his father and philosophy under the famed Democritus. He separated medicine from superstition, and his acute observations have been used in medical teaching for centuries. Hippocrates was at least 85 when he died, and some estimates put his age at 110. *See* EXTREME REMEDIES ARE VERY APPROPRIATE FOR EXTREME DISEASES; LIFE IS SHORT; TIME HEALS ALL WOUNDS.

hippodrama. A century ago the Hollywood term *horse opera* for a western had another meaning when horses acted in hippodramas on the stage, just as they do in the opera *Aida* and movies today. Some of the most spectacular equestrian performances included:

- Horses that danced on stage in horse ballets *(balleto a cavallo)* or performed in elaborate battle scenes. One critic said they were "trampling Shakespeare" out of existence.
- A sturdy horse that in the German play *Die Rauber in den Abruzzen* (1830) carried the hero up a pile of rocks onstage to the window of a house, while a ferocious dog attacked the villain downstage.
- A talented horse in an 1833 French play that, according to a viewer, "fired a pistol and then walked all about as if it was lame—and at last it lay down . . . and died—with its four legs in the air!"

hippopotamus. The ancient Greeks thought the *hippopotamus* looked like a horse and, since it spent so much time in the water, called it "river horse," from the Greek *hippos,* "horse," and *potamos,* "river." British historian Thomas Macaulay wrote: "I have seen the Hippo both asleep and awake, and I can assure you that, asleep or awake, he is the ugliest of the Works of God."

hippopotomontrosesquipedalianism. This word (I won't repeat it out of pity for the typesetter) is the term for "the practice of using long words." Composed of 32 letters itself, it is far longer than its synonym *sesquipedalian words,* from Horace's *sesquipedalia verba,* words a foot and a half long. The Greeks, too, had a word for mile-long words: *amaxiaia remata,* "words large enough for a wagon."

hirquitalliency. James Crichton, the Admirable Crichton, took a prince's lady to bed, according to Sir Thomas Urquhart in his *The Discovery of a Most Exquisite Jewel* (1652), the love scene described by Urquhart with majestic euphemisms:

> . . . the visuriency of either, by ushering the tacturiency of both, made the attraction of both consequent to the inspection of either: here it was that Passion was active, and Action passive: they both being overcome by each other, and each the conqueror. To speak of her *hirquitalliency* at the *elevation* of the *pole* of his Microcosm, or of his luxuriousness to erect a *gnomon* on her *horizontal* dial, will perhaps be held by some to be expressions full of obsceneness, and offensive to the purity of chaste ears.

Not today, Sir Thomas. The italics and spellings are Urquhart's as is the opinion that the Admirable Crichton was killed IN MEDIAS RES by the jealous prince. So is the word *hirquitalliency,* which the author apparently coined for the occasion from the

Latin *hirquitallire*. The nonce word, meaning to acquire a strong voice (like an infant's), is apparently found nowhere else in literature. *Visuriency*, another nonce word, means "the desire of seeing."

his elevenses are up.   Canadians are familiar with this expression, which hails from Newfoundland. It means a person is dying, because in some old people the two muscles in the back of the neck protrude like two bones resembling the numeral 11.

hisn.

> Him as prigs what isn't hisn
> When he's cotch'd he goes to prison.

The old proverbial adage is proof that *hisn* isn't a backwoods Americanism. *Hisn* has a long and respectable lineage, dating back to the early 15th century and used by Richardson in *hisn* novel *Clarissa*. Nowhere, however, is the word properly used in place of *his* today.

his name is mud.   Dr. Samuel Alexander Mudd (1833–83), a Maryland physician and Confederate sympathizer, set the broken left leg of Lincoln's assassin, John Wilkes Booth, who escaped from Ford's Theater by leaping to the stage from President Lincoln's box, breaking his leg when he landed. Dr. Mudd had nothing to do with the assassination or any escape plot, but in the hysteria of the moment he was sentenced to life imprisonment, though President Andrew Johnson pardoned him in 1869. Mudd's name (robbed of a *d*) has ever since been associated by many with the phrase *his name is mud*, and most undeservedly so. In the first place, this is a British phrase, not an Americanism. Second, according to Eric Partridge's highly respected *Dictionary of Slang and Unconventional English* (1961 ed.), *his name is mud* is first recorded in 1823 England, 10 years before Mudd was born, and is probably a few years older. The 1823 quotation Partridge gives is: " 'And his name is mud!' ejaculated upon the conclusion of a silly oration. . . ." Partridge's definition of the phrase is the same as most American definitions: "one has been badly defeated, one is in utter disgrace." Rather than being inspired by poor Dr. Mudd, the expression was almost certainly suggested by the universal dislike or even loathing of plain old mud, which has never been exactly popular with humankind.

hiss.   We find *hiss* as "a sound uttered in disapproval or scorn" (said to derive from the hissing sound made by geese) first recorded in the *O.E.D.* in the review of a 1602 play. Many years later, British author Charles Lamb saw his first play hissed off the stage and actually joined in the hissing so that he wouldn't be recognized as the author by the violent audience. Lamb, however, had the last word about the hissing, writing: "Mercy on us, that God should give his favorite children, men, mouths to speak with, discourse rationality, to promise smoothly, to flatter agreeably, to encourage warmly, to counsel wisely; to sing with, drink with, and to kiss with; and that they should turn them into mouths of adders, bears, wolves, hyenas, and whistle like tempests, and emit breath through them like distillations of aspic poison, to asperse and vilify the innocent labour of their fellow creatures who are desirous to please them. God be pleased to make the breath stink and the teeth rot out

of them all therefore!" Another time a loud *hiss* came forth from somewhere in the audience while Lamb was delivering a lecture. After a brief silence, Lamb, showing no emotion, simply said: "There are only three things that hiss—a goose, a snake, and a fool. Come forth and be identified."

histrionic.   Etruscan actors from the Roman province of Etruria, who were called *istri*, give us our word *histrionics*: of or relating to actors and acting or excessively emotional, affected. The Romans called these provincial actors *istriones*, and from this Latin word came the English word *histrionics*.

Hitchcock chairs.   Hitchcock chairs were so well made that they have become collector's items even though they were originally mass-produced in 1818. Lambert H. Hitchcock (1795–1852) established a factory in Barkhamsted, Connecticut, where some 100 employees turned out his product. Hitchcock chairs came in a variety of designs and sizes, but were characterized by strong legs, curved-top backs, and seats (initially rush-bottomed) that were wider in front than in the back. The chair maker won such renown that Barkhamsted renamed itself Hitchcocksville in his honor, although the town changed its name again to Riverton in 1866. The sturdy chairs, all identified by Hitchcock's signature stenciled on the back edge of the seat, include the first rocking chair designed and made as such—i.e., not made by just adding rockers to a regular chair.

Hitchcock ending.   An often ironic, surprise ending characteristic of the 53 films, numerous TV plays, short-story anthologies, and magazine stories directed, sponsored, collected, and published by Alfred Joseph Hitchcock. Hitchcock's films have received high critical praise as well as a great popular following. The English director, born in London in 1899, began his career as a scenario writer, becoming an art director and production manager before starting to direct films in 1925. His many suspenseful thrillers, objects of a cult for their brilliant camera technique, include *The Lodger, Blackmail, The 39 Steps, The Lady Vanishes, Rebecca, Suspicion, Foreign Correspondent, Shadow of a Doubt, Life-boat, Spellbound, Rope, Strangers on a Train, North by Northwest, Psycho,* and *The Birds*.

hitch your wagon to a star.   Set your goals high, aim high. These oft-quoted words were written by American philosopher Ralph Waldo Emerson in his essay "Civilization" in *Society and Solitude* (1810).

hit 'em where they ain't.   Wee Willie Keeler, inventor of baseball's hit-and-run play with New York Giants manager John McGraw, contributed this expression to the language in 1897 when asked by a reporter how such a little man could have such a high batting average. (Keeler was 5'4" and weighed 140 pounds.) "Simple," Keeler advised, "I keep my eyes clear and I *hit 'em where they ain't*." William Henry Keeler had a lifetime average of .345 over a 19-year career and collected 2,962 hits; he was elected to baseball's Hall of Fame in 1939. His *hit 'em where they ain't* is sometimes used outside of baseball for doing something unexpectedly, though I can find no dictionary that records the usage.

hit man.   Partridge recorded this synonym for a hired killer or assassin in 1963, but it must be older, as *hitter* is recorded four years earlier and *to hit* for "to kill or assassinate" goes back to 1942. At least one source credits mobster Louis "Lepke" Buchalter with coining *hit* "as a euphemism for contract murder." The term *hit woman* seems to have come in with women's lib in about 1974, and *hit list* for a list of people to be assassinated dates back to at least 1976.

hit on all six. In the early days of motor cars this phrase was *hitting on all fours*, referring of course to the four cylinders of automobiles and meaning that all the pistons in the cylinders were hitting, or firing, perfectly. With bigger cars came the expression *hitting on all six*, and though engines got even bigger, the expression never exceeded this number. Most sources have the expression as *hitting on all six* today, but mostly I've heard it as *hitting on all sixes* to describe any good performance.

hit the jackpot. The "progressive jack pot" in draw poker has been explained as follows: "If a pot is not opened on the first deal, the opening hand for the next deal increases from jacks or better [to open], to queens or better . . . on the second deal . . . from queens, or better, to kings, or better . . ." Since the players bet on each hand until someone can open, the pot can grow larger than usual, which led to large pots in poker being called jackpots. From poker the word passed into general usage, first recorded in a nonpoker use in 1884 and subsequently employed in phrases like *to hit the jackpot*, "to have great luck," first attested in 1944, but probably older.

hit the nail on the head. Although the allusion is obvious here, no one knows who invented the expression. John Stanbridge's *Vulgaria* (1520) has "Thou hyttest the nayle on the head" and English poet John Skelton used it a little later, but the phrase was probably proverbial before then. One suggestion is that it derives from the Roman saying *acu rem tangere*, "you have touched the thing with a needle," which refers to the custom of probing sores. To be *off the nail* was slang over a century ago for being slightly drunk.

hit the wall. Though it is ignored in all dictionaries, so far as I know, this expression was born in the mid-1970s, when marathon running became popular in the United States. The *wall* is a point in a 26-mile 385-yard marathon run (usually at the 18-to-20 mile mark) when a runner seems to lose everything physically, hits up against a wall, so to speak, and can go no farther—at least not at his or her customary pace. It can be a terrible feeling, especially if one hasn't trained properly for the marathon, but most runners pull themselves over the wall and go on to finish. Figuratively, the phrase is now used to describe any situation in life that stops a person's progress and seems to make it impossible to go on.

Hobbesian. English philosopher Thomas Hobbes (1588–1679) wrote in his chief work, *The Leviathan* (1651), that man is a naturally selfish creature whose life is "solitary, poor, nasty, brutish, and short." Therefore, he argued, an absolute monarchy, a leviathan or strong man is needed to control man's natural "condition of war of everyone against everyone." This has become generally known as the Hobbesian philosophy, or Hobbesism.

hobby; hobbyhorse. *Hobby* first meant only a small Irish horse, or pony, in English, the word first recorded in 1375. By the late 16th century the toy *hobbyhorse*, also called a *hobby*, had been invented and within another century people were comparing their favorite occupations for amusement to the riding of such toy horses, which they had found so pleasurable in their youth. These favorite pastimes were first called *hobbyhorses*, the word not shortened to *hobby* until the early 19th century. *Hobbyhorse* is sometimes used as a synonym for a rocking horse today.

hobnob. To hobnob with someone is to be very close friends with him. The word is formed from *hob*, "give," and *nob*, "take," which derive from the Anglo-Saxon *hab* and *nab*, meaning the same. To hobnob involves giving and taking, as has always been the way with true friends.

hobo. True hoboes claim that they will work whereas tramps and bums will not, and, indeed, the first hoboes, in the 1890s and early 1900s, were often migrating workers who carried their IWW union cards. The word *hobo* is of uncertain origin. Perhaps it derives from a once common greeting of vagabonds to each other: "Ho! Bo" (*Ho!* a form of "Hi!" and *Bo* meaning "guy or brother"). This seems to be the most popular explanation, but wandering *ho*meward *bo*und Civil War veterans have also been suggested, as have *hoe boys* who left the farm and were on the road. The word is first recorded in the American Pacific Northwest, about 1889.

hobo egg. An egg made by cutting a round center out of a piece of bread, putting the bread in a hot greased pan, dropping the egg into the center without breaking the yolk, and frying the whole until done (sometimes turning it over). Called a "hobo egg" because in the Great Depression era hoboes on the road were said to make it over their fires; called an "Alabama egg" for no reason I've been able to find. Years ago I thought I invented the dish as dinner for my kids, who called it "an egg in the hole in the bread." Actually, I did invent it, but others did, too. I can only add that it is as delicious as the egg sandwiches Ernest Hemingway describes in his short story "The Battler."

Hoboken. For no good reason this New Jersey city across the river from New York (and Frank Sinatra's birthplace) has been the butt of jokes for over a century, just the mention of its name getting a laugh. Hackensack and Secaucus (once noted for its pig farms) have had much the same trouble.

hobsonize. Lieutenant Richmond Pearson Hobson (1870–1937) won fame during the Spanish-American War, stepping into the national limelight when he tried to sink the collier *Merrimac* and block Santiago harbor. The young naval engineer was honored with parades and dinners wherever he went when he returned to the United States in August 1898. His good looks and popularity led to his name becoming a verb meaning *to kiss*: women often flung their arms around him and showered him with kisses when he appeared in public. Though *hobsonize* is an obsolete expression today, it remains in historical dictionaries as one of the most curious of linguistic curiosities.

Hobson-Jobson.   The substitution of native English words, unrelated in meaning, for foreign ones, especially oriental expressions, is called *Hobson-Jobsonism*. Hobson and Jobson were applied to the Muslim processional chant "Ya Hassan! Ya Hussein!" by British soldiers in 19th-century India because these traditional English surnames sounded something like the repeated exclamations of the parading Muhammadans (*Hodge* was the first of the English names, but it became *Hobson* by reduplication). The Hassan and Hussein of the chant are the grandsons of Muhammad, their names still honored at the festival of Murarram. The term *Hobson-Jobson*, for "a kind of pidgin language," was popularized with the publication of a book of the same name by the English Sanskrit scholar Arthur Coke Burnell in 1886.

Hobson's choice.   This expression has lasted for over three centuries, even though it derived from the name of an obscure English carrier and innkeeper, Tobias or Thomas Hobson. For some 50 years Hobson drove his stage 60 miles from Cambridge to London, often at breakneck speeds, and kept some 40 horses on the side to rent to students at Cambridge University. Hobson, a humane man who realized that "the scholars rid hard," put his mounts on a strict rotation basis so that the best and most often chosen horses would not be ruined. When you rented a horse from Hobson, you rented the horse nearest the livery stable door, the one best rested, no matter what your preference or how many horses were available. Hence, *Hobson's choice* is no choice at all.

Ho Chi Minh's revenge.   Another, later variation on MONTEZUMA'S REVENGE. Here diarrhea is named after the Vietnamese leader Ho Chi Minh (1890–1969) by G.I.s serving in the Vietnam War (1954–75). After the war, Saigon, South Vietnam's capital, was renamed Ho Chi Minh City.

hock.   *Hock*, for any white Rhine wine, is simply an abbreviation of *Hockamore*, which is what the English called *Hochheimer*, a fine white wine made in Hochheim on the River Main in Germany. In commerce the name *hock* became extended to all white Rhine wines, fine or not. *See also* IN HOCK.

hockey puck.   A hockey puck is a fool, a lamebrain, a blockhead, a numskull or any of a hundred similar adjectives—in short, an inert someone who can offer no resistance to the blows of life or someone who is knocked around like a puck by a stick in the game of hockey. The term seems to have been coined by insult comedian Don Rickles in the early 1970s.

hocus-pocus; hoax.   "I will speake of one man . . ." wrote Thomas Ady in *A Candle in the Dark* (1656), "that went about in King James his time . . . who called himself, The Kings Majesties most excellent Hocus Pocus, and so was called because that at the playing of every trick, he used to say, *Hocus Pocus, tontus talontus, vade celeriter jubio*, a dark composure of words, to blinde the eyes of the beholders, to master his trick pass the more currantly without discovery." Whether this juggler's assumed name became the basis for our *hocus-pocus*, "deception or trickery," no one really knows. Ochus Bochus, "a wizard and demon of Northern Mythology," or "a 17th-century magician," whose identity has been established in neither case, has also been nominated. Neither is there proof positive that *hocus-pocus* is a blasphemous Scandinavian corruption of the first words of the consecration in the Catholic Mass, *Hoc est corpus (filii)*, "This is the body [of the Son of God]." Many scholars lean to this last theory, pointing out that *hokus-pokus-fileokus* is still unwittingly used in Norway and Sweden, just as *hocus-pocus-dominocus* (for *hoc est corpus Domini*, "this is the body of the Lord"), is an expression common in children's play in America. (I remember the possibly euphemistic *hocus-pocus-minniocus*.) Perhaps the word does originally come from the perversion of the sacramental blessing, reinforced by the nickname that the ancient juggler assumed from his diverting pseudo-Latin patter, and further strengthened by the names of other successful jugglers and magicians named after him. We do know that many Tudor conjurors famous for their legerdemain were called Hocus Pocus or Hokas Pocas after their predecessor and that Master Hocus Pocus became a symbol of illusion and deceit. From *hocus-pocus* came, in all probability, the words *hoax*, "a trick"—*hoax* is merely *hocus* said quickly—and *hokum*, which is a blend of *hocus-pocus* and "bunkum" or "bunk."

hodgepodge.   A mixture of many things, a conglomeration, a confused mess. The word, used since the late 15th century, derives from the French *hocher*, "to shake together," and *pot*, "pot," which yielded the French word *hochepot* for a stew made of many ingredients. *Hochepot* became *hotchpotch* and, finally, *hodgepodge* in English.

Hodgkin's disease.   *See* BRIGHT'S DISEASE.

hoecake.   It seems unlikely that the cakes of coarse cornmeal called *hoecakes* are so named because they were baked on hoes, for the hoe was a valuable tool on the frontier and baking bread on one would damage and eventually destroy it. More likely the cake takes its name from the Indian *nokehick*, for "coarse cornmeal," which the earliest settlers pronounced *nocake*. These settlers called the cake baked from this meal *nocake*, too, but the name changed to *hoecake* over the years, perhaps because this was close in sound to *nocake* and people thought that *nocake* couldn't possibly be the name for a cake that did exist! All this aside, however, the Japanese *sukiyaki* does mean "shovel-broil," the dish made by Japanese peasants on their shovels.

hoe one's own row.   Unlike LONG ROW TO HOE this expression means to be independent, to paddle one's own canoe. It is also an agricultural phrase, dating back to the 18th century, when farm workers, unaided by machinery, did hoe their own rows. The saying first appeared in print after John Tyler became president on William Henry Harrison's death in 1841, when it became apparent that Tyler wouldn't follow Harrison's policies, but would "hoe his own row."

hog.   Few English words that were used by the Britons remain. *Hog* is such a native word, deriving from the British *hukk*, probably first referring to a pig of a certain age, such as a yearling, and then coming to mean pigs in general. "Crag" and "tor" are other words the Britons used.

hogan; Hogan's goat, etc.   Goats don't eat tin cans (they eat the paper labels off them), but they do stink. For this reason, and no other, anything said to be like *Hogan's goat* (a play, a book, or whatever) is something that is very bad, that really stinks. *Hogan* is just a common name affixed to this Americanism that dates back to the turn of the century—no real Hogan has anything to do with it. "Hogan's brickyard," for a rough-hewn baseball diamond—one usually in a vacant lot—is a similar expression, but *Hogan*, a variety of cotton, is named for its 19th-century developer, William Hogan. The Navaho Indian *hogan* is a dwelling constructed of earth and branches, usually built with the entrance facing east. Wrote Willa Cather in *Death Comes for the Archbishop* (1927): "The Navajo hogans, among the sand and willows. None of the pueblos would at that time admit glass windows into their dwellings. The reflection of the sun on the glazing was to them ugly and unnatural—even dangerous."

Hog and Hominy State.   A old nickname for Tennessee.

Hogarthian.   His paintings uncompromisingly realistic in style, his name came to indicate the same, but English painter William Hogarth (1697–1764) wasn't above fantastic flights of the imagination. Once when an ugly client refused to pay for a realistically ugly portrait, Hogarth threatened to add a tail and other appendages to his likeness and dedicate it to "Mr. Hare, the famous wildbeast man." His client paid on condition that the portrait be destroyed. Hogarth's great ability as a painter was overshadowed by his consummate skill as a caricaturist, which he used in his engravings to expose the hypocrisy and degeneration of English society. Among his numerous satiric works the most celebrated are *The Rake's Progress*, the *Marriage à la Mode* series, *Gin Lane*, and *Four Stages of Cruelty*, all noted for their frank humor and realistic attention to detail. It has been said that Hogarth, despite his great skills, was less a painter than an author, "a humorist and satirist upon canvas." Yet he was capable of painting such masterpieces as the *Shrimp Girl* and *Captain Coram*.

hogging moment; sagging moment.   Any time a ship is out of the water at both ends and waterborne amidships is known by the term *hogging moment*, an expression dating back two centuries, as does the opposite moment of stress, the "sagging moment."

hog latin.   *See* PIG LATIN.

hogwash.   Anything worthless, nonsensical, or false and insincere. The *wash* in the term refers to garbage or swill, *hogwash* being the swill fed to hogs. The word has been used in its general sense since the 18th century.

hog wild.   To become wildly excited or irrational due to excitement, anger, or even happiness. The Americanism probably originated in the mid 19th century, though it isn't recorded until about 50 years later. It obviously refers to the way hogs become wildly excited when aroused and is just as obviously another phrase from the farm, still hanging in there long after most Americans began buying their bacon wrapped in cellophane.

hoi polloi.   *Hoi polloi* means the masses, the crowd, deriving from the Greek *hoi pol'oi* "the many." It shouldn't be written as *the hoi polloi*, which is equivalent to saying "the the many,"

though great writers like Dryden have made this usage acceptable. *Hoi polloi* is often erroneously associated with snobs because of its resemblance to HOITY-TOITY, "haughty or snobbish," another English word that dates back more than three centuries.

hoist with his own petard.   The petard of medieval times wasn't a derrick, but a kind of rude hand grenade or mine that invaders would fasten to castle walls or gates. It took its name, oddly enough, from the French *peter*, "to break wind." Metal and bell-shaped, it contained an explosive charge that was fired by a slow-burning fuse, but it was often poorly constructed and went off prematurely, blowing up the man who lit it as well as the castle wall. Such a man was said to be *hoist* (lifted or heaved) *by his own petard. See* DERRICK.

hoity-toity.   A pretentious upper-class Frenchman a few centuries ago often took the opportunity to literally look down from his *haut toit*, or "high roof," on the lower classes, his *haut toit* becoming through mispronunciation the English *hoity-toity*, "haughty, pretentious." Or so goes one theory on *hoity-toity's* origins. The *O.E.D.* claims the word is a rhyming compound based on *hoit*, "to romp," now obsolete. By this theory *hoity-toity*, first recorded as meaning giddy behavior (1668), came to mean haughty by 1830—possibly because the same socialites who were *hoity-toity*, "silly," were haughty as well.

hold a candle to.   It was common in the 16th century and later for servants holding candles to guide their masters along the poorly lighted streets of English cities. Theaters also employed candle-holders called link-boys in the days before gas lighting. These were among the most menial of jobs, but some poor wights failed at them for not knowing the roads or the layout of a theater, and they were said to be *not worthy to hold a candle to anyone*. This expression soon came to be used in the sense of comparing the abilities of two people, *he can't hold a candle to you*, meaning "he's greatly inferior to you."

hold at bay.   Surprisingly, scholars haven't been able to connect this expression with hunting dogs that ran down big game like stags and held them at bay by barking, or baying, until the hunters arrived. Perhaps the baying of big-throated hounds bred for this purpose in medieval times did reinforce the expression; but *hold at bay*, to hold at a standstill, to keep someone on the defensive, derives from the French phrase *tener a bay*, which means "to hold in a state of suspense, to hold in abeyance." The French expression, in turn, comes from the Italian *tenere a bada*, meaning the same. *Bada* in the latter phrase indicates the state of suspense or expectation, deriving from the Latin *badare*, "to open the mouth." So although the idea of dogs baying at a trapped stag conveys the idea behind the expression perfectly, it literally means to hold agape, or to hold with mouth open.

Holden Caulfield.   The fictional character created by J. D. Salinger in *The Catcher in the Rye* (1951) was named in an unusual way. The author happened to be passing a movie theater and looked up at the marquee to see the names William Holden and Joan Caulfield starring in *Dear Ruth*. He focused on the last names, which were featured in large letters, and the two names seemed a natural for the name of the teenager in the book he was writing.

holding the bag. *See* LEFT HOLDING THE BAG.

hold one's feet to the fire. This Americanism dates back to the 19th century and means to force someone to do something. It may have originated somewhere on the frontier, although the form of torture is surely much older.

hold one's tongue. To keep quiet, keep a secret. According to Matt. 26:23, in one version of the Bible, "Jesus held his tongue." There is a story about the tongue featuring 18th-century Viennese writer and cleric Zacharias Werner. Werner gave a sermon on "that tiny piece of flesh, the most dangerous appurtenance of a man's body." On and on he graphically expounded to a blushed and blanched congregation—including several ladies who fainted in the aisles—about all the evils this tiny piece of flesh had caused. Finally, Werner concluded, his voice rising to a shout: "Shall I show you that tiny piece of flesh?" Not a breath could be heard until he cried: "Ladies and gentleman, behold the source of our sins!" Smiling at last, he stuck out his tongue.

hold the fort. Union General William Tecumseh Sherman is said to have invented this expression in 1864, when he wired the words to General Corse. Since the Civil War the words have not been used literally and have come to mean to take charge of any post or position, giving the job, temporary as it may be, your best efforts. It is sometimes heard as *hold down the fort*. General Sherman also suggested the phrase *40 acres and a mule* when, in a field order of 1865, he authorized that "Every family shall have a plot of not more than forty acres of tillable ground." Southern blacks took this to mean that all shareholders' plantations would at the end of the war be divided up into 40-acre plots that would be distributed to their slaves along with a mule to work them. The mule in the phrase was probably suggested by the old expression *three acres and a cow*, a common promise of British politicians.

hold your horses. Harness racing at American country fairs about a century and a half ago probably inspired the expression *hold your horses*. The amateur drivers, frequently young and inexperienced, often started their charges before a race had begun, leading the starter and the spectators to shout "Hold your horses!" By the 1840s the expression was being used to urge human patience in general.

hole. Often used in place names, such as Jackson Hole, Wyoming, usually to mean a deep valley, a place surrounded by mountains.

holistic. Though the word hardly fits in with that country's policy of apartheid, South African prime minister General Jan C. Smuts coined this term from the Greek for "whole" in his book *Holism and Evolution* (1926). Smuts wrote that "The whole-making, holistic tendency . . . operating in and through particular wholes, is seen at all stages of existence . . . There is a synthesis which makes the elements or parts act as one, or holistically." Thus *holism* is defined as "the theory that whole entities, as fundamental components of reality, have an existence other than as the mere sum of their parts."

holly. The Romans used *holly* as a decoration in their wild festival of Saturnalia before the early Christians in Rome adopted it for Christmas. Related to the word *holy*, *holly* derives ultimately from the Anglo-Saxon *holen*, for the holly tree.

hollyhock. The old favorite garden flower wasn't introduced to England by the Crusaders and named after the Holy Land as legend has it. *Holly hock* is a corruption of *holy hock*, which the plant was first called. *Hock* is an old name for "mallow," and the plant probably became *holy* because it had been known as *St. Cuthbert's cole* at one time. St. Cuthbert, who lived in the seventh century and also has an eider duck named for him, was of course holy and had his retreat on Holy Island (the Isle of Farne) off the English coast as well. He lived in a hermit's cell on the island, where the mallow grew in marshes, and pilgrimages were made there as early as the ninth century.

Hollywood. There is no proof for the tale that the film capital of the world, laid out in 1887, was first called Holywood by its pious founders, this corrupted to Hollywood as the town corrupted. Hollywood may have been named for the native California holly or toyon (*Heteromeles arbutifolia*), a large shrub that isn't a true holly but whose scarlet berries, borne from Christmas to Easter, suggest the holly and are much used for Christmas ornaments. Most probably, however, Tinseltown takes its name from the name of a ranch in the area owned by Mr. and Mrs. Harry Henderson, or from a hamlet named Hollywood in 1887 by the Wilcox family, who farmed in the area. It is hard to find anyone with many kind words for Hollywood. "It's hard to tell where Hollywood ends and the DTs begin," said W. C. Fields. "Hollywood's a trip through a sewer in a glass-bottomed boat," said Wilson Mizner. "Hollywood impresses me as being ten million dollars worth of intricate and highly ingenious machinery functioning elaborately to put skin on baloney," observed drama critic George Jean Nathan. Said comedian Fred Allen: "All the sincerity in Hollywood can be put into a gnat's navel and you'd still have room for three caraway seeds and an agent's heart."

Hollywoodese. A term referring to the hyped-up speech of movie people. "Hollywood talks and thinks in superlatives," Leo Rosten wrote 60 years ago in *The Movie Colony*. "Movie people do not 'like' things; they are 'mad' about them. They do not dislike things; they 'loathe' or 'detest' them. . . . The revealing story is told of two movie producers meeting on the street; 'How's your picture doing?' asked the first. 'Excellent.' 'Only excellent? That's too bad!' "

Holocaust. *The Holocaust* refers to the slaughter of over 6 million Jews, in Nazi concentration camps, many murdered in cyanide gas showers, their bodies desecrated and burned in bake ovens. The word has been used in the sense of a great slaughter or massacre, usually by fire, for over three centuries, one writer noting that France's Louis XII "made a *holocaust* of 1,300 people in a church." *Holocaust* is also used today to describe a great fire, such as the firebomb raids of World War II, or Hiroshima and Nagasaki. A *holocaust* was originally a sacrifice completely consumed by fire, a burnt offering to the pagan gods, the word deriving from the Greek *holokaustos*, "burnt whole." *Kaustos*, "burnt," is also the basis of the English words *cauterize* and *caustic* (used literally of *caustic lime*, which burns, and figuratively of *caustic words* that "burn" their recipients).

Holofernes. The name of several historical figures real and fictional. The earliest (the book of Judith in the Apocrypha) is the Babylonian general of Nebuchadnezzar who was decapitated by the comely Judith after he let his guard down and got drunk when she promised to sleep with him. Judith holding Holofernes's head is the subject of a number of gory Renaissance paintings. Her action saved her city. Holofernes is also the name of the great doctor of theology Tubal Holofernes, who taught the young Gargantua in Rabalais's *Gargantua* (1534); it is also the pedantic schoolmaster's name in Shakespeare's *Love's Labour's Lost* (1595). Shakespeare is thought to have ridiculed the learned John Florio (1553–1625), the son of an Italian Protestant refugee and well known as a lexicographer and translator, the Bard inventing Holofernes as an imperfect anagram of Florio's full name.

holy deadlock. *See* DEADPAN.

Holy Rifles. *See* BEECHER'S BIBLES.

holy roller. A term common in America for a member of any religious sect whose services are often characterized by ecstatic movements that may include rolling on the ground or floor; the word is also applied to any overbearingly religious person. A *holy tone* or *holy whine* refers to the speaking of Primitive Baptist preachers, who sound an audible "ah" at the end of each pause for breath.

holystone. Soft sandstone, often used to scrub the decks of ships, is called *holystone* because it is full of holes. First it was spelled *holeystone*, losing the "e," it's said, because sailors who used it knew no ease ("e's") and had to kneel as if in prayer (a holy attitude) when scrubbing the decks.

homage. When we pay homage to someone we are acknowledging our respect for him. This is what peasants were required by law to do in a medieval ceremony called *homage* (from the French *homme*, "man"), which demanded that a vassal kneel before his lord on the feudal estate and swear allegiance that he would ever be his man. From the ceremony comes our word *homage*, first recorded in 1390 in anything like its modern sense.

homburg. The *homburg* hat, a soft felt TRILBY HAT, was first made at Homburg in Prussia. It was introduced to England by King Edward VII, who often enjoyed the hot springs in Homburg.

home court advantage. An expression from basketball that has become part of the American lexicon, *home court advantage* means the psychological advantage one has in familiar surroundings, where one knows the terrain better and has a sympathetic audience.

home, James, and don't spare the horses. Passengers in autos still use this phrase humorously to friends when given lifts home. *Horses* here has nothing to do with engine horsepower, however. The old expression, dating back perhaps to the 17th century, was once a common command of English nobility to their private coachmen.

Homeric laughter; Homer sometimes nods. *Homeric laughter* is hearty, lusty laughter like that of the Gods in the greatest of epic poems. No one really knows who wrote the *Iliad* and *Odyssey*. Some authorities doubt that there was even a poet Homer, pointing out that the name means "one who puts together"; instead, they ascribe his work to a number of authors. But modern scholars tend to support the traditional story that the author was the blind Greek Homer, who lived in the eighth century B.C., wandered from city to city writing his poems, and whose life remains a blank historically. *Homer sometimes nods* is another expression associated with the author, meaning that the best authors can make mistakes. This phrase comes from Horace's "Ars Poetica": "Sometimes even good old Homer nods."

home run. The term *home run* in baseball was first recorded in 1856 and, as Stuart Berg Flexner pointed out in *Listening to America*, it "couldn't have appeared much sooner because it wasn't until the late 1840s and early 50s that *home* was used in games to mean the place one tried to reach in order to win or score . . ." A home run was also called a *home* at the time, but *homer* isn't recorded until 1891. It should be noted that *home run* was a cricket term before it was used in baseball. Because it is the ultimate hit in baseball, a *home run* has come to mean a great accomplishment in any field.

Homestead State. An old nickname for Oklahoma because so much of the state was settled by homesteaders under the Congressional Homestead Act of 1862.

home, sweet home. "Home, Sweet Home," its words written by John Howard Payne in 1823, may have used the melody of an old Italian folk song that Englishman Henry Bishop adapted when he wrote the music. Payne received 250 pounds from an English producer for the words and other material, the song first sung in a popular British opera of the time. Legend says that the author wrote the song while homesick in Paris. The Payne family cottage in East Hampton, Long Island, New York is a national landmark today.

homey. Originally black English for a friend or anyone from your hometown or neighborhood. Short for *homeboy*, the term now has some general usage. *Homeboy* is first recorded at the end of the 19th century and *homey* during World War II.

hominy. Hominy isn't a vegetable, as so many believe, but the inner part of corn (maize) that has been soaked to remove the hull. The word derives from the Algonquin Indian *rockhominy* for the dish.

homo sapiens. Carolus Linnaeus (1707–78), the great Swedish botanist and methodical classifier of things animal, vegetable, and mineral, gave the name *homo sapiens*, "thinking man," to the human species. Before this the Latin *homo*, "man," had been similarly used, Shakespeare writing in *Henry IV, Part II*: "Homo is a common name to all men." Linnaeus also first used the Mars (♂) and Venus (♀) symbols as symbols for male and female.

homosexual; heterosexual. *Homosexual* does not derive from the Latin word *homo*, for "man," as *homo sapiens* does. It comes from the Greek *homos*, meaning "the same," like many other English words, including *homogenized* and *homonym*. Therefore, contrary to popular belief, it can be applied to females as well as males. Its antonym, *heterosexual*, comes from the Greek *heteros*, "other." The use of *heterosexual* as a noun, meaning a heterosexual person, not as an adjective, was rare up until the 1960s, but the term dates back to the late 19th century, when it was first recorded in a paper of Sigmund Freud. *Homosexual* as a noun is first recorded at about the same time (1912).

honcho. This word for boss or big boss is Japanese in origin, deriving from the Japanese army designation *hancho* for a squad leader. American soldiers stationed in Japan and Korea after World War II picked up the word and brought it back home, where it is still widely used.

Honda. The Japanese car, now among the two or three best-selling automobiles in the U.S., bears the name of Soichirio Honda, an engineer who founded the Honda Motor Company in 1948. Honda made motorcycles before it made cars, at first installing surplus World War II engines on bicycles.

Honest Abe. The most common nickname for Abraham Lincoln, inspired by the "every schoolboy knows" stories of his honesty. *The Rail Splitter* is another well-known Lincoln nickname, from his splitting fence rails as a young man in Illinois. Least known is his derogatory nickname *Spot Lincoln*, because as a congressman he had questioned President Polk's story that Mexico started the Mexican War on U.S. soil, Lincoln demanding that the spot where this had happened be identified. In the South Lincoln was often called *Old Abe* and his enemies also called him the *Ape* (based on *Abe* and his aspect), as well as the *Baboon*. Blacks often called Lincoln *Uncle Abe* and his White House staff affectionately called him the *Tycoon*, the first use in America of this Japanese term for a military leader. Lincoln, of course, is also known as the *Liberator*, the *Emancipator* and the *Great Emancipator*, for his freeing of 4 million slaves. His wife was known as the *She-Wolf* and, rarely, *Mrs. President*; many of her contemporaries thought her bad-tempered and meddling.

honest Injun. A pledge of faith (meaning "it's true," "I swear it"), an American equivalent to the British expression *honor bright*. The first printed reference to this Americanism, which is sometimes considered offensive today, appeared in an 1851 issue of the San Francisco publication *Pioneer*: "Instead of simply asking you if it is true, he will invariably nod his head interrogatively, and almost pathetically address you with the solemn adjuration, 'Honest Indian'?" Whether the reference to Indian honesty was originally sarcastic or admiring, the phrase is certainly not sarcastic anymore. An expression common in Mark Twain's stories, *honest Injun* is still heard, if infrequently.

honey. Several dictionaries of slang call *honey*, as a personal term of endearment for a lover, an Americanism originating in the 1880s. But among the Greek betrothal rings in the British Museum's collection is a gold ring from the fourth century B.C. engraved inside with the Greek word *meli*, "honey."

honey buckets. A truck used to empty cesspools. In the Far East American G.I.s gave the name to carts that collected wastes from outhouses to spread on the fields as fertilizer.

honeydew melon. *Honeydew* is a popular shortening of "honeydew melon" *(Cucumis Melo inodorus)*, a variety developed around 1915 and so named because of its sweetness. Honeydew can also either be the sweet material that exudes from the leaves of certain plants in hot weather or a sugary material secreted by aphids and other insects. In either case, it gets its name from its sweetness coupled with its dewlike appearance. Spenser wrote of it in *The Faerie Queene:*

> Some framed faire lookes, glancing like evening
>   lights,
> Others sweet words, dropping like honey dew.

honey hole. A huge hole dug outside coal towns to hold the excrement from the town's privies. During the Great Depression one group of miners held a mock-burial in a "honey hole" of President Herbert Hoover, on whom they blamed the bad times. A wooden slab prominently displayed his mock-epitaph:

> HERE LIES HOOVER,
> DAMN HIS SOUL,
> BURIED IN A HONEY HOLE.
> LET HIM LIE HERE TILL
>   THE END,
> POOR MAN'S ENEMY,
> RICH MAN'S FRIEND.

honey, I forgot to duck. President Ronald Reagan's words to his wife, Nancy, after would-be assassin John W. Hinckley, Jr., shot him with a handgun in March 1981, just 70 days into his first term. This has to be the presidential assassination attempt with the most remarkable bon mots. Mr. Reagan joked, "Who's minding the store?" to his top aides as he was wheeled into surgery. Nancy Reagan leaned over the gurney and told the president, "I brought your jelly beans, darling," holding onto a jar of her husband's favorite candy. Later, she dropped the jelly beans when during a news conference Secretary of State Alexander M. Haig, Jr., presumptuously announced, "I am in control, here at the White House." *See* HAIGSPEAK.

honeysuckle. This plant was named in error in ancient times, when it was thought erroneously that bees extracted honey from the plant. The name is applied to several other plants but mainly the more than 180 species of woody vines and shrubs belonging to the *Lonicera* genus, named for 16th-century German botanist Adam Lonitzer.

honk. The word *honk* is imitative in origin, deriving from the sound Canadian geese make *k-honk, k-honk*—when flying in their large V-shaped groups; the Indians, in fact, called these big birds *cohonks*, and we call them *honkers* today. The word was much later applied to the sound of horns on early automobiles and soon after was being widely used as a verb.

honkie; bohunk.   *Bohunk*, a low expression for a Polish- or Hungarian-American, arose at the turn of the century, and is probably a blend of *Bohemian* and *Hungarian* (both Poles and Hungarians were called Bohemians). *Bohunks* were also called *hunkies*, and black workers in the Chicago meat-packing plants probably pronounced this as *honkie*, soon applying it as a derisive term not just for their Polish and Hungarian co-workers but for all whites.

honky-tonk.   The first printed use of this word for a cheap dance hall featuring gambling or burlesque shows, in a February 1894 Oklahoma newspaper, described a *honk-a-tonk* "well attended by ball-heads, bachelors and leading citizens." No one is sure how the word originated. The British attribute it to America, calling *honky-tonk* "Negro slang," while one American authority claims it is from the English dialect word *bonk*, "to idle about." Either way *honky-tonk* is a reduplication, with *tonk* repeating the sound of *honk*. ". . . It was nothing for a man to be drug out of them dead," testified a jazz musician of an early *honky-tonk*.

honorificabilitudinitatibus.   The making of long words was a popular game in Elizabethan England and *honorificabilitudinity*, meaning "honorableness," was one of the most absurd ones made. Shakespeare made fun of this word by stretching it out still longer in *Love's Labour's Lost*, using its original Latin ablative plural when he has Costard the clown say to the servant Moth: "I marvel thy master hath not eaten thee for a word, for thou art not so long by the head as *honorificabilitudinitatibus*." This is the word, incidentally, that to some "proves" Bacon was the author of all plays attributed to Shakespeare. For its rearranged letters form the Latin sentence *Hi ludi F. Baconis nati tuiti orbi*, which says, translated: "These plays born of F. Bacon, are preserved for the world." The word, however, is found as early as 1460.

hooch.   The American soldiers who first occupied Alaska in 1867 were forbidden any liquor, but the long Alaskan nights were cold. They apparently made do with crude firewater, a brew made in their own rude stills from yeast, flour, and sugar or molasses. This BOOZE has been blamed on a local Indian tribe called the *Hoochen* by slightly *chauvinistic* (or *groggy*) etymologists, but these Alaskan natives only happened to live nearby—they were in reality the Hutsnuwu, Tlingit Indians, a name easy to mispronounce, and probably had no part in brewing the potent *hoochino* that the soldiers named after them. The brew's name remained *hoochino* or *hoochinoo* until the Klondike gold rush in 1897, when more of it was needed more often, in a hurry, and it was shortened to *hooch*. Being firewater, *hooch* was splendidly accurate to describe the bathtub concoctions made during Prohibition. The name caught on and is still with us, though more in a comic sense for all liquor. *Hootch* is a variant spelling. A *hooch* to those among U.N. troops in Korea, 1951–54, was a temporary shelter, but there the word derives from the Japanese *uchi*, "house."

hood.   Though its origin is unknown, this word for a cheap crook certainly doesn't come from Robin Hood's name. Dating back only to the early 1900s, it is almost surely a contraction of *hoodlum*, which may derive from the Bavarian German *hodalum*, a "scamp."

hoodwink.   Blindman's buff was known as the "hoodwinke game" in Elizabethan times. Players would *hoodwink*, or blindfold, a player who would then grope around to find the others. From the game came the expression *to hoodwink* someone, "to deceive or trick a person, to leave him groping about for his money."

hoo-ha!   Leo Rosten in *The Joys of Yiddish* gives 13 uses for the expression *hoo-ha!*, popularized by comedian Arnold Stang during radio days. But *hoo-ha!* (rhymes with Poo Bah) is mainly used to express envy, admiration, or scorn, as in (for the latter): "Some friend. Hoo-ha!" *Hoo-ha* means "uproar" or "hullabaloo."

hooiaioia.   *Hooiaioia* is the Hawaiian word for "certified." It has the distinction of having the most consecutive vowels, eight, of all the words in the world. The English leader is *queueing*, with five.

hooker.   *Hooker*, for "a prostitute," may derive from the name of the small vessels called hookers that traded between British ports and the Hook of Holland in the 19th century. Prostitutes, it was said, would wait at the Hook for sailors from the hookers and lure them to their rooms. Another theory is that U.S. Civil War general Joseph Hooker, a fiery, opinionated man, didn't believe that his men should dissipate their energies in the Washington, D.C., red-light district, putting the area off-limits. His troops, it seemed, counterattacked by dubbing all prostitutes *hookers*. Still another theory traces *hooker* to the way a prostitute "hooked" prospective customers by linking arms with them. Finally, a fourth guess holds that the large number of brothels in New York City's Corlear's Hook district in the 1850s gave rise to this name for a prostitute. There is no firm proof for any one of these possible derivations for the origin of *hooker*, first recorded in North Carolina in 1845, but the arm-linking theory seems the best to me. Comedian Bob Hope wrote a humorous book about his "lifelong love affair with golf" entitled *Confessions of a Hooker* (1985). In this case *hooker* refers to a golfer who frequently hits the ball to the left if a right-handed player, or to the right if a left-hander.

Hookey Walker!   Dickens used the variation *Walker!* in *A Christmas Carol*, but most Victorian writers wrote *Hookey Walker!* as a synonym for *incredible!* or *Nonsense!* on hearing a tall story. Several writers have suggested a hawk-nosed liar named John Walker as the source, but the origin of the expression is really unknown.

hook, line, and sinker.   Any extremely gullible person who swallows a fantastic yarn *hook, line, and sinker* is like a hungry fish who gulps down not only the fisherman's baited hook but the entire tackle. This Americanism has been traced back to the age of Davy Crockett, when tall tales hooked many a fish hungry for belief. But a 16th-century British expression, to *swallow a gudgeon* (a small bait fish), conveyed the same idea.

hooligan.   A proper name is the origin for this word for a violent roughneck, a fact conclusively established when British etymologist Eric Partridge brought to light Clarence Rook's *Hooligan Nights* (1899) in his *Dictionary of Slang*. Excerpts from Rook's sociologically valuable work follow: "There was, but a few years ago a man called Patrick Hooligan, who walked to and fro among his fellow men, robbing them and occasionally bashing them . . . It is . . . certain that he lived in Irish Court, that he was employed as a chucker-out [bouncer] at various resorts in the neighborhood. Moreover, he could do more than his share of tea-leafing [stealing] . . . being handy with his fingers . . . Finally, one day he had a difference with a constable, put his light out . . . He was . . . given a lifer. But he had not been in gaol long before he had to go into hospital, where he died . . . The man must have had a forceful personality . . . a fascination, which elevated him into a type. It was doubtless the combination of skill and strength, a certain exuberance of lawlessness, an utter absence of scruple in his dealings, which marked him out as a leader among men . . . He left a great tradition . . . He established a cult." This man called Hooligan made the Lamb and Flag pub in the Southwark section of London his headquarters, attracting a gang of followers around him. The entire rowdy Hooligan family, the nucleus of his gang—their real name was probably Houlihan—"enlivened the drab monotony of Southwark," as another observer put it. The entry "Hooligan gang" is found on many police blotters in the late 1890s. *Hooligan* has also been used as a synonym for a prison guard, screw, or hack.

hoosegow; jug. *Hoosegow* is a western word of the 1860s that derives from Spanish *juzgado,* "a court or tribunal," which to Mexicans means a jail and was borrowed in this sense by American cowboys. Our slang word *jug* for a jail probably also comes from *juzgado* and was recorded a half century or so earlier.

Hoosier. A nickname for a native of Indiana, which is called the Hoosier State. *Hoosier* probably derives from the English dialect word *hoozer* for anything large. In America the altered word *hoosier* came to mean a big person, a burly frontiersman, and the like, until in about 1826 we find it applied to natives of Indiana, once a frontier state. Hoosier humorist James Whitcomb Riley, tongue in cheek, offered the following theory: "The real origin is found in the pugnacious habits of the early Indiana settlers. They were very vicious fighters, and not only gouged and scratched, but frequently bit off noses and ears. This was so ordinary an affair that a settler coming in to a bar on a morning after a fight, and seeing an ear on the floor, would merely push it aside with is foot and carelessly ask, *Who's year?*"

hootchie-kootchie. The Turkish belly dance that many of us "have no stomach for," as Beatrice Lillie once said. This name for the "mildly lascivious" dance—"not as sensuous as actual bumps and grinds since the hips are swayed rather than the pelvis rotated," we're told—has no source in an oriental name, unless it comes from the Bengal state of Cooch Behar. The best guess is that *hootchie-kootchie* derives from the English dialect words *hotch,* "to shake," and *couch* (pronounced cooch), "to protrude." But this fails to explain why the dance was first recorded as the *cootchie-coot* in the 1890s. Dancer Little Egypt (Catherine Deviene) made a fortune and got herself arrested several times by dancing the hootchie-kootchie in the nude at the 1893 Chicago World's Fair and a number of private parties. A lowdown *hootchie-kootcher,* like Danny Kaye's Minnie the Moocher, is a *hootchie-kootchie* dancer.

hootenanny. A hootenanny has since the 1950s been best known as a folk song concert or a lively gathering featuring musical entertainment. But the word can also be a derogatory epithet ("You're nothin' but a fat hootenanny") and what is more commonly called a WHATCHAMACALLIT, a THINGAMABOB, or a DINGBAT.

Hooterville. *See* PODUNK.

hoot-owl trail. The night trail, the trail of crime and wrongdoing; an expression from the American West over a century ago that is a little-used historical curiosity today.

Hoover hog. *See* ARMADILLO.

Hooverize, etc. Before becoming the 31st president of the United States Herbert Clark Hoover (1874–1964) had a distinguished career as an engineer and administrator, popularizing scientific management among businessmen and inspiring the building on the Colorado River of Boulder (now Hoover) Dam, for example. Hoover first came to national attention as the head of various European relief agencies and as U.S. Food Administrator during World War I. In the latter capacity he met the food crisis by ending farm hoarding of crops, curbing speculation, and urging Americans to live by "the gospel of the clean plate" and to institute "wheatless and meatless" days. It was only a few days after these suggestions that the term *to Hooverize* began to appear in newspapers around the country, and housewives soon adopted the phrase when discussing ways to stretch food. Later, when Hoover was president during the Great Depression, more than a few derogatory terms bearing his name were invented. Shoes with hobs in them were Hoover shoes, and Hoover blankets were newspapers bums slept under. The Hoover cart was a southern mule-drawn wagon made from the rear axle and chassis of a discarded automobile, and a Hooverville was a collection of shacks housing the unemployed at the edges of cities throughout the country. Later Hoover Commissions under both Truman and Eisenhower studied the reorganization of the executive branch of government and suggested many improvements that were adopted. The Hoover vacuum cleaner—*hoover* long a synonym for vacuum cleaner—is named for the man who founded the Hoover company in the 1920s. *See also* ARMADILLO.

hop on the bandwagon. Barnum and earlier showmen perfected the American bandwagon—a brass band perched atop a brightly decked dray pulled by a team of horses—but politicians quickly adopted it for national and local election campaigns. It wasn't, however, until the handsome silver-throated champion of silver, William Jennings Bryan, ran for president for a second time in 1901 that the expression to *hop on the bandwagon,* "to rush to join a popular movement," entered the language. The phrase remembers local politicians and ward heelers hopping up on Bryan's bandwagons as they banged and rolled through town, to show the support for their candidate and help create enthusiasm for him.

hopping John. So far as is known, no real John's name is honored by this old favorite southern American dish. Hopping John is made of black-eyed peas, rice, bacon or ham or pork knuckles, and red pepper or other hot seasoning. It is traditionally served on New Year's Day because of the superstition that black-eyed peas eaten then bring good luck for the coming year.

hopscotch. The Scots didn't invent the ancient children's game, and the *scotch* in its name had nothing to do with them; either, deriving from the lines that are hopped in the game, these being *scotched*, or scored, in the ground. In fact, the game was once called hop-score.

Horatio Alger story. Ironically, none of the heroes Horatio Alger, Jr. (1834–99) created in his novels ever became rich. His poor but honest characters struggled to get ahead against overwhelming odds and always succeeded in improving their lot, even found fame and glory (at least one became a senator), but great monetary rewards never came to Ragged Dick and company. Nevertheless *Horatio Alger story* became synonymous with a rags-to-riches story. Alger's books, of little interest to anyone but historians and nostalgia buffs today, served a real need in his time. Dull and unimaginative, as filled with preachments as his pages might be, his philosophy of hard work and clean living influenced three generations of Americans. In recent time historians have claimed that this author of moralistic books for children was a pederast obsessed with young boys.

horde. *See* ASIATIC HORDES.

Hore-Belisha. These black-and-white striped posts topped with yellow globes honor Lord Leslie Hore-Belisha, British minister of transport, 1934–37, who introduced them to indicate pedestrian crossings. A colorful, controversial figure, Hore-Belisha instituted a campaign to halt "mass murder" on the highways, and the beacons were a warning to drivers that pedestrians had the right-of-way at approaching intersections. Not overly modest, Lord Leslie seems to have named the lights after himself. The British statesman, born in 1895, fought in World War I as a major, was a member of Parliament, and served as head of the British War Office at the beginning of World War II. The beacons are often called *Hore-Belishas*.

hormone. British scientist Dr. E. H. Sterling coined the word *hormone* from a Greek root meaning "to set in motion," in a 1905 article he wrote for the *Lancet* about such "chemical messengers." A hormone can be defined as "a substance formed in one organ and carried by the blood-stream to another organ, which it stimulates [sets in motion]."

horns of a dilemma. *Lemma*, in Greek, means a thing taken for granted, deriving from *lampanien*, "to take." Affixing the Greek *di*, "two," we have *dilemma*, two things taken for granted. Therefore, in logic, a dilemma is an argument that forces a person to choose one of two things taken for granted, both of which may be untrue and unacceptable (*e.g.*, "Do you still beat your wife?"). Philosophers in the Middle Ages also called each *lemma* of a *double lemma* a horn, because it was so easy to get caught on the sharp point of each, even coining the Latin expression *argumentum cornutum*, "a horned argument." Since both terms meant the same, they were eventually wedded in the phrase *to be caught on the horns of a dilemma*, to be unable to make up one's mind about which course of action to choose.

hornswoggle. *Hornswoggle*, "to bamboozle or cheat," is one of the few extravagant American phrases of the early 19th century surviving today. It is described as "a fanciful formation" by Mathews and first attested in 1829 in Kentucky, but no one knows who coined it. It may be related to the English dialect word *connyfogle*, "to deceive in order to win a woman's sexual favors," which is rooted in the English slang *cunny* for vagina.

horsefeathers! As a euphemism for "horseshit!" this word has been around at least since 1925. It may or may not be related to the term *horsefeathers* once used in carpentry, these horsefeathers being the feathering strips used in roofing and siding houses. Because they are big feathering strips, they may have been called horse feathers (like HORSERADISH, etc.), but how these horse feathers came to be a euphemism for "horseshit!" is not clear—unless it came easily to some roofer's tongue when he had half-said "horseshit!" and a lady abruptly appeared upon the scene. On the other hand, *horse-feathers* may have first been a synonym for "nonsense," originating with a saying such as, "That's nonsense, that's like saying horses have feathers!"

horse latitudes. The horse latitudes, regions of calm found at 30 degrees north and south latitudes, may be so named because sailing ships carrying horses to America became becalmed and had to throw horses overboard in order to lighten the vessels and to take advantage of any slight breeze that did blow up. However, the name may simply be a translation of *golfo de las yeguas*, "gulf of the mares," which was the Spanish name for the ocean between Spain and the Canary Islands and compares the supposed fickleness of mares with the fickle winds in these latitudes.

horselaugh. A *horselaugh* is a loud, coarse, vulgar laugh, a guffaw. The word probably alludes to the loud neigh of a lusty horse, but an obscure pun on the word *horse* has also been suggested as a source. The expression has been common since Pope used it in 1710.

horse of a different color. Cut into the chalk downs of Berkshire, England, is the enormous crude outline of a galloping white horse covering some two acres. The figure possibly dates back to Saxon times, when a white horse was the emblem of Saxons invading Britain, and over the ages local residents have kept it clear of overgrowth. It is thought that this might be the source of the expression *a horse of a different color*, something of a different nature from what is under consideration, for the White Horse of Berkshire changes from green to white periodically when the locals clear grass and weeds from its outline. The expression may, however, come from races in medieval tournaments, where armored knights were distinguished by the color of their horses. A favored knight might have lost a race, leading one of his supporters to say "That's a horse of a different color" as the winner crossed the finish line. But both explanations are conjectures. The phrase is first recorded in Shakespeare's *Twelfth Night*, Shakespeare using the expression as if it were quite familiar to his audience.

horse opera. Any cheap western movie, dating back to the first motion pictures featuring a lot of horses and gunplay in the early years of the 20 century. *See* SPAGHETTI WESTERN.

horsepower. A car's horsepower is actually about one and a half times the power of a horse. Seeking a way to indicate the power exerted by his steam engine, inventor James Watt calculated that a strong dray horse averaged 22,000 foot-pounds per minute working at a gin on an eight-hour-a-day basis. Increasing this by 50 percent, Watt got 33,000 foot-pounds, which has ever since been one horse-power: "The standard theoretical unit of rate of work, equal to the raising of 33,000 pounds one foot high in one minute."

horseradish. There is apparently no truth to old tales that the fiery horseradish (*Armoracia lapathifolia*) is so named because it was once used to cure horses of colds, or because it made a good seasoning for horse meat. *Horse* is used as an adjective before a number of plants to indicate a large, strong, or coarse kind. Others include the horse-cucumber, horsemint, and horseplum. The horseradish is of course hotter, and has a much larger root and leaves than the ordinary radish. However, many plants are named after the horse because they were used to feed or train horses or because they resemble the animal. The horsebean is used as horse feed; horse-bane was supposed to cause palsy in horses; the horse-eye bean was thought to resemble a horse's eye; and the pods of horse-vetch are shaped like horseshoes. The horse chestnut, Gerade says in his famous *Herbal* (1597), bears its name because "people of the East countries do with the fruit thereof cure their horses of the cough . . . and such like diseases." But the horse chestnut is big, too, and when a slip is cut off the tree "obliquely close to the joint, it presents a miniature of a horse's hock and foot, shoe and nails." Incidentally, Samuel Pepys in his *Diary* mentions a *horseradish ale*, ale flavored with horseradish, which must have been hot indeed.

horse sense. *Horse sense* for good plain common sense comes from the American West, about 1850, inspired by the cowboys' trusty intelligent little cow ponies, trained even to do a good deal of cattle-herding work without directions from their riders (as noted in *The Nation*, August 18, 1870).

horses famous in history. There are surely hundreds, but I've limited my choices to a dozen: Black Bess—English outlaw Dick Turpin's horse; Black Nell—Wild Bill Hickok; BUCEPHALUS; Copenhagen—duke of Wellington; Incitatus—EMPEROR CALIGULA; Man-O-War—race horse; Pegasus—Perseus; Rosinante—Don Quixote; Silver—Lone Ranger; Traveller—Robert E. Lee; Trigger—Roy Rogers. And finally, the only talking horse in the stable: TV's Mr. Ed, who was watched by tens of millions in a 1960s sitcom, the horse "actor" who portrayed him dying in 1973 and Sherman Allman, his singing voice, dying in 2002. The songs Mr. Allman wrote and sang included "The Pretty Little Filly With the Pony Tail" and "The Empty Feedbag Blues." Mr. Ed's talking voice was provided by Alan Lane.

horses for courses. A mostly British expression urging someone to stick to the thing he knows best, *horses for courses* comes from the horse racing world, where it is widely assumed that some horses race better on certain courses than on others. In 1898 a British writer noted, in the first recorded use of the expression: "A familiar phrase on the turf is 'horses for courses.' "

horseshoe crab. See LIVING FOSSIL OF THE SEA.

horseshoes. A game that can be traced back to the ancient Greeks, horseshoes is said to have originated with soldiers taking old horseshoes they had removed from their horses and tossing them for distance. These contests evolved into the game of horseshoes played by throwing horseshoes as close as possible to a stake driven into the ground 30 or 40 feet away. The name for the game, however, doesn't seem to be recorded until the beginning of the 19th century. See LUCKY HORSESHOES.

horsmandering. This old word would serve well today in describing the efforts of the many public officials, even corrupt ones, who write books about their experiences. Meaning just that, *horsmandering* comes from the name of an 18th-century American judge who was "one of the first public servants to use his records of a public experience as the basis of a full-length book."

Hosackia. Few people know that New York City's Rockefeller Center was once the site of the famous Elgin Gardens, one of the first botanic gardens in America. The Elgin Gardens were established by Dr. David Hosack (1769–1835) who subsequently deeded them to Columbia University, long the landlord of Radio City. Hosack, a professor at Columbia, is remembered as the physician who attended Alexander Hamilton after his fatal duel with Aaron Burr. He served on the first faculty of Columbia's College of Physicians and Surgeons, and helped found Bellevue Hospital as well as founding and serving as first president of the now defunct Rutgers Medical College. Hosack wrote a number of medical and botanical books, including a biography of Casper Wistar (*see* WISTERIA). *Hosackia*, a genus of over 50 species of perennial herbs of the pea family, is named for him. Its most cultivated species is *H. gracilis*, "witch's teeth," a rock-garden plant about 12 inches high with pretty rose-pink flowers borne in small umbels.

hostages to fortune. Francis Bacon (1561–1626) coined this phrase in the first sentence of his essay "Of Marriage and Single Life." "He that hath wife and children hath given hostages to fortune; for they are impediments to great enterprises, either of virtue or of mischief." This simply means that we will behave and hesitate to take risks if we have loved ones, because they will suffer if we don't—they will pay for our sins.

hot as hell. The expression is heard so frequently that it's surprising that a compressed word such as *hotshell* hasn't evolved; it is certainly not slang anymore and is surely colloquial if not standard English by now. *Hot as hell* and *hot as hades* have been traced back only to the 18th century, but the idea is doubtlessly much, much older in one form or another. *Hell* is mentioned 21 times in the New Testament alone under various names (Hades, Gehenna, Hell, and Tartarus), and it was always thought to be hot in the nether regions. Internal heat in the form of hot springs and volcanoes and the fact that the temperature of the earth goes up as one digs deeper, no doubt gave early man the idea of a fiery underground hell. *See* DRINK LIKE A FISH.

hotbed. *Hotbed*, a gardener's term for a glass-covered bed of soil heated by decaying manure or electrical cables in which seedlings are raised early in spring, has since the 18th century been used to mean a place favoring rapid growth of something disliked or unwanted. At that time one writer called theater "the devil's hotbed." The gardening term "hothouse," an artificially heated greenhouse for the cultivation of tender plants, also does double duty, meaning "overprotected, artificial, or unnaturally delicate," as in "He grew up in a hothouse environment."

hot-blooded; cold-blooded.   One would guess such a basic term as hot-blooded, for "passionate or excitable," would go back to early English. But the term appears to have been coined by Shakespeare. Wrote the Swan of Avon, in *The Merry Wives of Windsor* (1598): "Now the hot-blooded gods assist me." Shakespeare had earlier coined, or at least first recorded, the antonym *cold-blooded*, in *King John* (1595): "Thou cold-blooded slave, hast thou not spoken like thunder on my side?"

hotcha.   The Spanish word *muchacha*, for "a girl," may be the source of this expression of delight, pleasure, or approval over seeing someone sexually attractive. *Hotcha*, a favorite of Jimmy Durante, isn't used much anymore and could simply be an elaboration of *Ah-hah!* rather than a corruption of the Spanish exclamation for "What a girl!" It doesn't have anything to do with *cha*, the Cantonese word for tea that the British occasionally use.

hot cross bun.   A sweet bun filled with raisins and marked on the top with a white cross of frosting. Such Lenten buns date back to 16th-century England.

hot dog.   According to concessionaire Harry Stevens, who first served grilled franks on a split roll in about 1900, the franks were dubbed hot dogs by that prolific word inventor sports cartoonist T. A. Dorgan after he sampled them. "TAD" possibly had in mind the fact that many people believed frankfurters were made from dog meat at the time, and no doubt heard Stevens' vendors crying out "Get your red hots!" on cold days. Dorgan even drew the hot dog as a dachshund on a roll, leading the indignant Coney Island Chamber of Commerce to ban the use of the term *hot dog* by concessionaires there (they could be called only *Coney Islands, red hots* and *frankfurters*). *Hot dog!* became an ejaculation of approval by 1906, one that is still heard occasionally; *hot diggity dog!* was invented during the Roaring Twenties. Dorgan at least popularized the term *hot dog*, which may have been around since the late 1880s. *See* FRANKFURTER. In fact, *hot dog* for a frankfurter is recorded in the college newspaper *The Yale Record* in 1895 in a humorous poem about someone who "bites the dog" when it's placed inside a bun.

hotfoot.   U.S. author Damon Runyon was the first to record and define the practical joke called a *hotfoot*, in a 1937 story. Wrote Runyon: "The way you give a hotfoot is to sneak up behind some guy, stick a paper match in his shoe between the sole and the upper . . . and then light the match." This is usually done while the practical joker's confederate distracts the victim. The word is not related to *hotfoot* meaning "rapidly, with speed," as in "Let's hotfoot it out of here."

hot pillow joint.   *See* NO-TEL MOTEL.

hot potato.   *Hot potato* can mean a "delicate situation," something to be handled with great care. It is said to derive from the phrase *drop someone* (or *something*) *like a hot potato* and was first recorded in 1950. Over 70 years older, however, is *hot potato* for an energetic person or for a sexy woman, the last sometimes called a *hot patootie*, which was apparently an American invention during World War I. *See* POTATO; MEAT AND POTATOES; ALL THAT MEAT AND NO POTATOES.

hotshot.   *Hotshot* refers to an aggressive, often flamboyant or vain, highly successful person, such as a hotshot lawyer or a hotshot athlete. The word was recorded as far back as 1600 in the sense of a reckless, hot-tempered troublemaker, this definition giving rise to the present one. The *OED* states the early "reckless" definition was suggested by a person who "shoots with a firearm 'hotly' or eagerly." Others claim its ancestor was a piece of shot hot from firing, or made hot to spread flames among enemy land or sea forces.

hot slaw.   *See* COLESLAW.

Hotspur.   A person with a terrible temper noted for extreme behavior is known as a *Hotspur*. The word remembers Sir Henry Percy (1364–1403), who led a revolt against English king Henry IV, which resulted in Hotspur's death at the Battle of Shrewsbury. Hotspur's name, however, would probably have never entered the language if Shakespeare did not immortalize him in *Henry IV, Part I*, two centuries later.

Hottentot.   The Khoikhoi were a proud tribe, and their native name meant "men among men," but they had the misfortune to be the first Africans to come in contact with the Dutch settlers of the Cape of Good Hope, eventually losing most of their land and now numbering less than 20,000. Even their name was taken from them and they became the *Hottentot* tribe, a word that means gibberish in English, describes a stupid, depraved person as well, and is sometimes used as an ugly slang word for a black person. *Hottentot* is the name that Boers gave to this South African tribe closely allied to the Bushmen. The Dutch and other Europeans, imposing their own values on another civilization, had long thought the pastoral people small and stupid; hence Hottentot's second meaning. As for *Hottentot* meaning "gibberish," the Khoikhoi dialect is full of harsh, staccato clicks and clacks and kissing sounds, unique in that it is spoken by breathing in rather than out. These noises made by the tongue (similar to the way we say "tsk tsk") sounded like so much stammering or clucking to Dutch ears. The Boers therefore named the people after what the language sounded like to them, calling them *Hottentots* from the Dutch *hateren en tateren*, to "stammer and stutter," and it wasn't long before *hottentot* was applied to any gibberish at all.

hotter than a fresh-fucked fox in a forest fire.   This alliterative humorous phrase has been used frequently since 1950, when it was first recorded, according to John Ciardi's *Browser's Dictionary* (1980). It means very hot indeed and is used in reference to the climate as well as in its sexual sense.

hotter than a two-dollar pistol.   An old Americanism meaning very hot, an allusion to cheap 19th-century pistols that got hot when fired.

a hot time in the old town tonight. "A Hot Time in the Old Town Tonight," by Theodore Metz, was the rallying song of Teddy Roosevelt's Rough Riders during the Spanish-American War and was so popular with all the troops that the enemy thought it was our national anthem!

hot toddy. Today this drink, often used as a folk remedy to ward off colds, is made of brandy mixed with hot water, sugar, and spices. Originally, however, it was a drink called *tari*, made from the fermented sap of the palmyra tree, which the British encountered in India and brought home, changed in name and content, and called the *toddy*.

hotto dogu. The Japanese borrowing and alteration of the English term *hot dog*. A hamburger is a *hambaga* in Japan, a Coke is a *koka-cora*.

The Hot Water War. The unusually named war is officially called *Fries's Rebellion*. It took place in 1799 in eastern Pennsylvania, when a direct federal property tax on houses was imposed. When federal agents, precursors of the IRS, came to take house measurements for tax purposes, houseowners poured hot water on them. The leader of the rebellion, John Fries (ca. 1750–1818), was captured by federal troops when his hiding place was betrayed by his dog. Sentenced to death, he was later pardoned by President John Adams.

Houdini. Someone who *pulls a Houdini* performs an amazing disappearing act or escape, and *a Houdini* is anyone with seemingly magical powers in any field. The expressions lionize Eric or Ehrich Weiss (1875–1926), an American magician who adopted the stage name Harry Houdini. Houdini named himself after Jean Eugène Robert Houdin (1805–71), a celebrated French magician noted for the fact that he did not attribute his feats to supernatural powers. Harry Houdini became world-famous for his escapes from "impossible traps" such as locks, handcuffs, and straitjackets while suspended high in the air, or chained in chests submerged under water—all tricks, it is said, that can be explained today. A magician's magician who invented many magic tricks, he exposed numerous spiritualists and other fraudulent performers. Houdini also wrote a number of books and left his extensive magic library to the Library of Congress, where there is now a Houdini Room. The supreme magician has become the object of almost cult-like worship among fellow necromancers. Once he claimed that if anyone could break the shackles of death and contact the living from the grave, he could. Since his death—"He was fifty-two when he died, his life like a deck of cards"—followers have periodically held seances where he is buried in Glendale, New York in Machpelah Cemetery, a granite bust of the magician staring down at them. He has inspired a Houdini Hall of Fame at Niagara Falls, New York, and a worldwide research committee has been formed to determine whether the "Handcuff King" was really born in Budapest, Hungary on March 24, 1874, or in Appleton, Wisconsin on April 6, 1874.

hound dog. *Hound dog* refers to a dog bred for hunting, but it can be a derogatory term for a mongrel or even a person, as in Elvis Presley's "You Ain't Nothin' But a Hound Dog," which, incidentally, was a remake of an old blues standard. *See* THAT DOG DON'T HUNT.

hound someone. *Hound* derives from the common Teutonic *hund*, related to "hunt," and may be related to the Teutonic verb *hinpan*, "to seize," in reference to big hunting dogs that actually seized their prey. Eventually, however, the designation *hound* was reserved for hunting dogs that followed their quarry by scent. There were many breeds of these from early times, but all were noted for their tenacity as well as for their keen sense of smell. Hounds would follow a trail for hours, doubling back to find a scent if they lost it. By the late 16th century their grim persistence had suggested the expression *to hound someone*, to relentlessly pursue someone with the determination of a hound.

household words. Shakespeare may have invented this workhorse phrase, for it is first recorded in his *Henry V:* "... then shall our name,/ Familier in their mouths as household words ..." More likely, the Bard was repeating an already common expression.

houseleek. An attractive succulent that often grows on the roofs of thatched cottages in England, the houseleek or "roof houseleek" *(Sempervivum tectorum)* was originally planted on house roofs because it was believed to ward off lightning, fever, and evil spirits. The emperor Charlemagne decreed that each of his subjects must grow the houseleek on his roof. Wrote Thomas Hill in the early-16th-century *Natural and Artificial Conclusions:* "If the houseleek or syngreen do grow on the housetop, the same house is never stricken with lightning ..." The plant is also called "Jove's beard" and "Juniper's beard." It is no relation to the onionlike vegetable called a LEEK.

house names. In *Memories of My Boyhood Days* (1923) New Englander Joseph Farnum writes of the "unique, catchy, original and forcefully cute titles ..." given to many old houses by "a hardy farmer and fisherman people of days long agone." He remembers, among many others, house names like *Takitezie, In and Out, Bigenough, Nonetoobig, House of Lords, Seldomin, Thimble Castle,* and *Waldorf Astoria, Jr.* Today vacation homes often are given such names.

house that Ruth built. A familiar name for Yankee Stadium in the Bronx, New York, the house that Ruth built was constructed in 1923 to hold the huge crowds that came out in large part to see baseball immortal George Herman ("Babe") Ruth. Previous to this the Yankees played in the nearby Polo Grounds, which remained the home of the National League New York Giants until it was torn down years later. (Yankee Stadium was completely reconstructed in 1976.) *See also* BRONX.

houstonize. On April 13, 1832, Sam Houston, the soldier and political leader who became president of the Republic of Texas, fought and gave a beating to Congressman William Stanberry. As a result, *houstonize* became a synonym, but now only a historical curiosity, for "to beat someone up, especially a congressman." Sam Houston's name is better honored, of course, by the city of Houston, Texas.

House with Lungs. Thornton Wilder referred to the Wyckoff House near the ocean in Newport, Rhode Island when he wrote in *Theophilus North* (1937): "There's a house that the famous Italian architect, Dr. Lorenzo Latta, has called the most beautiful house in New England—and the healthiest. Built in the nineteenth century, too. He called it 'The House That Breathes' 'The House With Lungs.' "

houyhnhnms.   These are the intelligent breed of horses that Jonathan Swift created in *Gulliver's Travels* (1726). Swift said he coined their name from the characteristic whinny of a horse as it sounded to him. The talking horses, endowed with reason, ruled over the brutish Yahoos, another word coined by Swift in the book. *Gulliver's Travels* also gives us *brobdingnagian*, for any immense thing, after the giants Gulliver encounters in the country of Brobdingnag, and *lilliputian*, after Lilliput, a country of tiny people. *Houyhnhnms* is pronounced "whinims."

how!   Some etymologists believe the *how!* used by western Indians as a salutation is an abbreviation of "How do you do?" It could just as well derive from the Sioux *hao* or the Omaha *haw*, these ejaculations used in a variety of ways, signifying "come on" and "let us begin" as well as "hello."

Howardism; Tiny Thompson.   Pithy, witty one-line (sometimes a bit more or a bit less) reviews of movies by *New York Times* film critic Howard Thompson (1919–2002), who likened their composition to writing on the head of a pin. The mini-reviews, written oven a 20-year or so period beginning in the mid-1960s, included *The Pride and the Passion* with Cary Grant, Sophia Loren, and Frank Sinatra: "Sophia looks fine, Cary uneasy, Frank starved"; *Paint Your Wagon* starring Clint Eastwood: "Clint sings like a moose"; *Bikini Beach* with Frankie Avalon and Annette Funicello: "You're only young once. With them, be glad of it."

Howard Libbey Tree.   The redwood, native to the coast of California and a few miles into Oregon, is probably the tallest tree in the world, and towering above all other redwoods is the specimen called the *Howard Libbey* or *Tall Tree* growing along Redwood Creek in California's Redwood National Park. Standing 367.8 feet tall, the Tall Tree may be the tallest tree of all time, although there are unconfirmed reports that an Australian eucalyptus felled in 1868 reached 464 feet. It was first named the *Howard Libbey* after the president of the Arcata Redwood Company, on whose land it was located until Congress established the park.

how are they crawlin'?   Fish "run" for fishermen, but lobsters "crawl." A lobsterman wanting to know how good the lobstering is in a certain area will ask, "How are they crawlin'?"

how are you suffering?   A common greeting in the English-speaking southern African country of Zambia to anyone who has recently suffered a great loss or misfortune, such as a death in the family.

how come?   *Bartlett's* (1848) says *how come?* is "Doubtless an English phrase, brought over by the original settlers . . . the meaning . . . [being] How did what you tell me happen? How came it?" Others opt for the Dutch *hockum*, "why?," which the "original settlers" heard in New Amsterdam.

How do I love thee? Let me count the ways.   The famous line above, from Elizabeth Barrett Browning's *Sonnets from the*

Portuguese, is one of the best known in English poetry, but up until recently no one thought to actually count the ways Miss Barrett loved Mr. Browning in Sonnet XLIII. Author Randy Cohen did so and published the results in *New York* magazine, finding that she loved him "nine ways—unless 'with the breath,/ Smiles, tears, of all my life' is considered to be three separate ways, in which case she loved him a total of eleven ways." *Sonnets from the Portuguese* was written for Robert Browning and published, reportedly, only because Browning felt: "I dared not keep to myself the finest Sonnets written in any language since Shakespeare's." There is, of course, no Portuguese model for the sonnets and they were probably called *Sonnets from the Portuguese* because Browning's pet name for his wife was "my little Portuguese."

How do you like them apples?   An American expression that means "what do you think of that?" *How do you like them apples?* was first recorded in 1941 and is still heard; "*How do you like them grapes?* came on the scene 15 years earlier and may be obsolete today.

howdy.   Generally regarded as an expression born in the American West, *howdy*, a contraction of "how do you do?," began life as a southern expression and was taken West by Confederate Civil War veterans. It is first recorded in 1840.

how the other half lives.   This expression for "how people belonging to another class live" usually refers to the rich today, but it originally referred to the poor. The words derive from the title of social reformer Jacob Riis's book *How the Other Half Lives* (1890), describing the lives of New York City poor people.

How there, bonnie lass?   A common greeting, meaning, "How are you, dear?" used in the working-class dialect called GEORDIE of northern England and Scotland.

Howzit my bru?   A common South African English greeting meaning, "How's it going, buddy?", "What's up, mate?"

hoyden.   Most scholars think that this word for a boisterous, bold, carefree girl comes from Dutch *heiden*, meaning "heathen" or "boor." Another theory, however, has the word related to German *Heide* for "heath," suggesting that someone from the wild heath would be a wild person with much vitality but little culture.

The Hub.   A nickname for Boston. The name possibly originated from all the roads leading into the city like spokes to the hub of a wheel. However, in *The Autocrat of the Breakfast Table* (1858) Oliver Wendell Homes writes of a young man who told him he had heard that "Boston State-House is the hub of the solar system." Holmes replied that to the residents of every other town or city, "the axis of the earth sticks out visibly through the center of each." He concluded that "Boston is just like other places of its size—only, perhaps, considering its excellent fish market, paid fire-department, superior monthly publications, and correct habit of spelling the English language, it has some right to look down on the mob of cities . . ."

hubba-hubba.   "A delirious delight in language making," Mencken calls the coining of *hubba-hubba.* The expression was ubiquitous during World War II, made famous by a leering Bob Hope, the linguistic equivalent of a wolf whistle that was uttered lasciviously when an attractive woman walked past a group of men. Sexual but highly complimentary, it was often *hubba hubba hubba*, the third awesome *hubba* thrown in for added emphasis if body language warranted it. Anyway, we're told that the term originated with "flyboys," U.S. airmen who got it from Chinese airmen being trained at a Florida air base early in World War II. Supposedly it is a corruption of the familiar Chinese greeting *how-pu-how*. A second theory, wholly unpalatable, traces the expression to *Hubba*, "a cry given to warn fishermen of the approach of pilchards."

Hubbard squash. The tasty squash was bred and first grown over a century ago by Mrs. Elyabeth Hubbard, a Massachussetts gardener. Soon after, it was named in her honor.

Hubble Space Telescope. This space observatory, designed for use in orbit around the Earth, was named after U.S. astronomer Edwin Powell Hubble (1889–1953), a pioneer in extragalactic research who discovered in 1929 the expansion of the universe. Hubble also has Hubble's law and Hubble's constant named after him.

hubbub. An ancient Irish war cry may be responsible for this word, meaning an uproar of confused sound from a crowd of voices. The *O.E.D.* suggested as a source the cry of *abu! abu!* repeated again and again by hordes of warriors running into battle. The word has been spelled many ways. In its first recorded use (1555) it was an "yrishe (Irish) whobub." In *The Present State of Ireland* (1596) Edmund Spenser wrote: "They come running with a terrible yell and *hubbabowe*, as if heaven and earth would have gone together, which is the very image of the Irish *hubbabowe*, which theyr kerne [soldiers] used at theyr first encounter." Shakespeare called a *hubbub* a *Whoo-bub* in his *The Winter's Tale*.

huckleberry. The first American settlers noticed the wild huckleberry, comparing it with the English bilberry, and first calling it a *hurtleberry* or *hirtleberry*, from which its present name derives. Huckleberries were so little, plentiful, and common a fruit that a *huckleberry* became early 19th-century slang for a small amount or a person of no consequence, both of these expressions probably inspiring Mark Twain to name his hero Huckleberry Finn. The berry was also used in the colloquial phrase *as thick as huckleberries*, very thick, and *to get the huckleberry*, to be laughed at or ridiculed, a predecessor of sorts of the raspberry (razz), or Bronx Cheer. *To be a huckleberry to someone's persimmon* meant, in 19th-century frontier vernacular, to be nothing in comparison with someone else. Huckleberries, which are not a true berry but a drupe fruit, belong to the *Gaylussacia* genus, which was so named in honor of French chemist Joseph-Louis Gay-Lussac (1778–1850). *See also* BRONX.

huddle. The football huddle may have been invented and named by Herb McCracken (1900–95) when coach of the Lafayette College football team in 1924. According to Coach McCracken's *New York Times* obituary (3/25/95): "Aware that Penn State had memorized its offensive signals, he ordered his players not to start each down at the line of scrimmage. Instead, he told them to gather behind the line to learn the next play

in secret, and the *huddle* was invented." But some sources credit Amos Alonzo Stagg with earlier inventing the huddle while coaching at the University of Chicago. Still others credit coach Bob Zuppke of the University of Illinois in the early 1920s, and Zuppke certainly did make the huddle a standard part of the game. There are other claimants, too, and there is not sufficient evidence to crown any one of them.

Hudson River. A river originating in New York's Adirondack Mountains and flowing about 315 miles south to New York Bay at New York City. It was first sighted by Giovanni da Verrazano in 1524. The Hudson is named for Henry Hudson, English explorer for hire who in 1609 sailed for the Dutch East India Company on the *Half Moon*, trying to find a new route to the Indies and exploring the river that now bears his name. His name was not Hendrick Hudson as is widely believed. The confusion probably resulted because Dutch explorer Hendrick Christiaensen was the first to sail the river after him and made numerous voyages to the Hudson from 1610 to 1616, when he was killed by an Indian near Albany.

hue and cry. For at least 600 years, up until the 19th century, *hue and cry* was the legal name in England for the outcry of someone who had been robbed, someone calling "with horn and with voice" for others to join in the chase after the thief. *Hue* is from the Old French *huer*, "to shout," and may have meant in ancient times the sound of a horn as well, while the cry was probably "Stop thief!" or something similar. In any case, the clamor that attended such chases (any man who refused to join in could be punished under the law) led to *hue and cry* becoming a synonym for any public clamor, protest, or alarm.

huh. *See* UH, OH.

hula hoop. Another of the great toy fads of the 20th century (see FRISBEE), the hula hoop was invented about 1956 by an Australian toymaker, who based the plastic hoop on a wooden exercise hoop of gymnastic classes. Marketed by the U.S. Wham-O toy company, as the Frisbee was, the hula hoop sold up to 40 million in 1958, mostly to teenagers who gyrated them on their hips in and out of school until the fad ended.

hula-hula. The Hawaiian name for this pantomime story-dance is simply *hula*, the dance noted for its highly styled hand imagery, which uses many of the over 700,000 "distinctive movements of the hands, arms, fingers and face by which information can be transferred without speech." During World War II, Japanese soldiers posing as Filipinos often tried to penetrate Allied lines in the Philippines. Suspects were given *hula-hula* to pronounce and the Japanese infiltrators who, unlike the Filipinos, had trouble with their *l*'s, invariably pronounced it "hura-hura," sealing their fate. *See* SHIBBOLETH.

Huli stomach. This Hawaiian term for an upset stomach derives from the name of a jealous, evil-eyed monster called the Huli, who is said to turn the stomachs of babies upside down, causing them to suffer from colic.

hulk. *See* GREAT HULKING MAN.

hullabaloo. *See* HURLY-BURLY.

hull down over the horizon. Sailors have long—no one knows how long—used this phrase to describe the phenomenon of the masts of an approaching ship appearing before her hull does. The phenomenon itself is one way observant people proved to themselves that the world was round and not flat long before Magellan's men circumnavigated the globe in 1522.

hully-gully. The *New York Times* once described the "dignified" hully-gully disco dance as "like Wyatt Earp drawing his guns, Dean Martin downing drinks..." Deriving from the twist in the 1960s, the dance may be so called because some of its gestures are similar to gestures used in the southern children's guessing game hull-gull.

human. *See* ADAM.

humble pie. *See* EAT HUMBLE PIE.

humbug. *Humbug*, a fraud or hoax, has long outlived those purists who so vehemently attacked the word when it entered the language from underworld slang in the 1750s. No one is sure just where *humbug* came from. Several authorities suggest the Irish *uim bog*, "soft copper," referring to the debased money with which James II flooded England from the Dublin mint. But *bug* in its slang sense had meant to cheat or "sting" before *humbug* was coined, and in former times people expressed approbation, perhaps even false encouragement, by humming. Then again, since the original meaning of bug is "bogey," a humbug may first have been a really harmless bug that hums and frightens us. Dickens's Scrooge with his "Bah, humbug!" gave the word great popularity worldwide, as did P. T. Barnum, "the Prince of Humbug."

humdinger. Someone or something excellent, attractive, wonderful, hot-stuff, as in "She's a real humdinger!" The expression, dating back to 1888, is a combination of the earlier *dinger*, something excellent, said to be first recorded in 1809, and *hummer*, also meaning the same, which also goes back to 1888.

humdrum. Maybe the *drum* got in the word just because it rhymed with the monotonous *hum*, but *humdrum* does suggest both the monotony of a humming bee or other insect and a monotonous drumbeat. Anyway, *humdrum* sounds like the boredom it imitates, meaning routine, monotonous, and dull. The term has been around since the early 16th century. Addison in *The Spectator* (1711) told his readers about "The *Hum-Drum Club*... made up of very honest Gentlemen of peaceful Despositions, that used to sit together, smoke their pipes and say nothing till Mid-night." A later writer, fed up with the humdrumishness of the world, said it was made up of "hum-drums and jog-trots." *Humdudgeon* means an imaginary illness, "nothing... but low spirits."

humility; humility bird. Two birds—the wilet (*Symphemia semipalmata*) and the snipe (*Gallinago gallinago*)—are called the humility bird, both because of their bowing movements. *See* EAT HUMBLE PIE.

hummingbird. These beautiful little American birds, some of which weigh less than a penny, take their name from the humming sound their wings make when they hover over a flower. The "flying jewels" were so admired in early times that American Indians often dried and pressed them for use as earrings.

hummums. *Hummums* is standard English for a Turkish bath, a corruption of the Arabic *hammam*, meaning the same. The word came into the language in the late 17th century and soon became, in the form of *hummum*, British slang for a brothel, because so many Turkish baths were corrupted into brothels.

humongous. *Humongous* got a lot of play in the 1980s as a term for a huge, monstrous person, often wrestlers standing 6'8" or so and weighing about 300 pounds. The word is often used humorously and though its origin is obscure it seems to be based, consciously or subconsciously, on words like huge, monstrous, and mountainous.

Humuhumumkunukun-a-puaa. No true fish can "talk," so far as is known, but this fish is one of several that does make a grunting sound. In fact, this Hawaiian name of this trigger fish translates as "fish that grunts like a pig." It may also be the longest-named of any fish.

humus. The word *humus*, the dark organic material in soils familiar to all good gardeners, comes from *humus*, the Latin for "ground" or "soil." Less apparent is the derivation of the word *humble*, which also comes from *humus*, via the Latin adjective *humilis*, "on the ground."

Hun. A common name for Germans during World War I, the so-called Great War. It equated the German soldier with the barbaric tribe of Huns led by Attila in the fourth century. Ironically, the Germans themselves created the designation after their emperor Wilhelm II in 1900 urged his soldiers embarking for China to give no quarter, to act "just as the Huns [did] a thousand years ago."

a hundred of these days. *A hundred of these days* is a birthday wish commonly expressed by Italians and sometimes by Italian-Americans. Italians, however, attach less attention to birthdays than to a person's name day, the feast day of the patron saint after whom a person is named.

hundreds and thousands. Very small pieces of confits or candy used as the topping on small cakes. The term was first recorded about 1830.

hundred thousand dollar bill. The $100,000 gold certificate, bearing President Woodrow Wilson's likeness, is the highest denomination ever issued in the U.S., or anywhere in the world for that matter. Used for official government transactions and never put into general circulation, $100,000 bills were issued in 1934. Twelve remain in Federal Reserve Banks. The highest currency in general circulation is the $10,000 bill, discontinued in 1944, of which perhaps 500 remain in the hands of fortunate people.

Hundred Years War; Hundred Hours War. The first was a series of wars between England and France over claims to the French Crown beginning in 1337 and ending in 1453, a little more than a century. *Hundred Hours War* is a humorous name for the Gulf War of January and February in 1991 against Iraq. It took just about 100 hours for the U.S. and U.N. allies to win and force the withdrawal of Iraqui troops from Kuwait.

Hungarian. *See* OGRE.

Hungarian words in English. Hungarian is not an Indo-European language like most European tongues, but it has contributed a few words to the English lexicon, including paprika, goulash, and coach.

hunger. An ancient word deriving from the Old English *hungor.* There are few synonyms for hunger in English. By way of contrast, Otto Jespersen tells us in *The Growth and Structure of the English Language* that the Araucanian Indians speak a tongue "that distinguishes nicely between a great many shades of hunger."

hung higher than Gilderoy's kite. Patrick Mac Gregor, a handsome highwayman regarded as something of a Robin Hood in folklore, was nicknamed "Gilderoy" for his red hair (from the Scottish dialect words *Gillie roy,* "a red-headed lad"). The daring Gilderoy, who boasted that he had robbed old Cardinal Richelieu in the presence of the king and picked Cromwell's pocket, made the mistake of hanging a much-hated judge. A bad tactical error, for the judge who sentenced the outlaw after his capture in 1636 was a hanging judge who didn't want to encourage the hanging of hanging judges. He sentenced Gilderoy to be hanged far higher than his four confederates, "high aboon the rest" as the old ballad goes. Gilderoy's gallows stretched 30 feet into the Edinburgh sky, and he was left hanging there for weeks as a warning. No *kite,* or "body," had ever been hung higher than Gilderoy's, it was said by the thousands who saw him, and since that sad June day to be *hung higher than Gilderoy's kite* has signified the most severe punishment possible.

hunk. *See* PIECE.

hunky-dory. No one is certain about it, but a product called Hunkidori, a breath freshener introduced in 1868, may have given us the American expression *everything is hunky-dory,* or O.K. We do know for sure that *hunky-dory* is first recorded the same year that Hunkidori was introduced. The old tale that the word comes from the name of a pleasure street in Yokohama much frequented by American sailors seems to be spurious. According to Carl Whittke in *Tambo and Bones* (1930): " 'Josiphus Orange Blossom,' a popular song . . . in reference to Civil War days, contained the phrases 'red hot hunky dory contraband.' The Christy's [a minstrel group] made the song so popular that the American people adopted 'hunky-dory' as part of their vocabulary." Still another theory has the expression deriving in 1866 from *hunk,* a New York dialect word for "home base," which in turn derives from Dutch *honk,* "good."

hunt elevetrich. To be led on a fool's mission. A Pennsylvania Dutch term several centuries old that is equivalent to hunting an imaginary snipe. No such bird as the elevetrich exists, of course, and the naive hunter who is led out in the woods to shoot one is usually abandoned there, left wandering the woods, burlap bag in hand.

hunting pink. The famous English *hunting pink* jacket is scarlet, not pink. Moreover, it never was pink, taking its name instead from the London tailor named Pink who designed it for fox hunting in the 18th century.

hurly-burly; hullabaloo. The famous "When the Hurleyburley's done, When the Battaile's lost, and wonne," of *Macbeth's* witches seems to support the old story that *hurly-burly,* an uproar or noisy disturbance, derives from the excitement of burly men hurling spears in battle. But no proof of this exists. Neither does *hurly-burly* appear to have derived from *hullabaloo,* the Irish word for wailing at funerals, which now means any loud noise or uproar. The word may just be imitative of the howling of the wind—*burly* chosen to reduplicate *hurly* simply for the rhyme.

hurrah! *See* HIP! HIP! HURRAH!

Hurrah Henry. A boisterous, foolish, rich, or upper-middle-class society man. U.S. short story writer Damon Runyon first recorded the term in 1936 as *Hurray Henry,* but since about 15 years later the alteration *Hooray Henry* has been more common in England, where the derogatory expression is heard far more often than in the U.S.

hurricane. A hurricane, the word deriving from the Spanish *huracan,* was first a violent tropical cyclonic storm of the western North Atlantic, but it eventually came to mean a violent storm in general. A hurricane is called a *hurricane* in the Caribbean Sea, but a *cyclone* in the Indian Ocean, and a *typhoon* in the China Sea.

hush-hush operation. *Hush!* an exclamatory demand for silence, has been recorded as far back as 1350 and is still heard, especially in libraries and other public places, though somewhat old-fashioned. *Hush-hush* didn't come into the language until World War I to describe something top secret or confidential, such as a hush-hush operation or a hush-hush investigation. In fact, the first printed reference to the term is found in 1916 when someone wrote of "hush-hush tanks" being developed by the British.

hush money. One would expect this term for a bribe for silence, to keep a person quiet about something, to be a fairly recent term judging by its common media use. But it dates back to the early 1700s. A 1726 quotation from *The Memoirs of Jonathan Wild* told of the eponymous hero, a thief himself, expecting to get a reward from a criminal of a pair of gloves "by way of hush."

hush puppy. These cakes of deep-fried cornmeal batter, very popular in the South, have been traced back only to the time of World War I; at least the name isn't recorded before then. The most common explanation for the odd name is that hunters tossed bits of the cakes to their dogs, telling them to "*hush, puppy.*" A perhaps more authentic version notes that the cakes were first made in Florida, where people often fried fish outdoors in large pans, attracting dogs who would whine and bark.

To quiet the dogs, the cook would fry up some cornmeal cakes and throw them to the dogs, shouting, "Hush, puppies!" *Hush puppies* for soft shoes or slippers seem to have been so named by the first company to manufacture them, in the 1960s.

husk. An ear of corn wrapped in its husk can be thought of as content and cozy in its little house, for the word *husk* is simply a shortening of the Dutch *huisken*, meaning "little house." The name was first applied to the shells of various nuts and finally to corn (maize) when it was discovered in America.

husking bee. In a husking bee, the term used in America since at least 1693, neighbors got together to help husk corn. A young man who found an ear of red corn got a kiss from the girl of his choice, a custom originated by the Iroquois Indians, though an Iroquois youth got more than a kiss in the Indian fertility rite. There were also apple bees in the early days of America. The *bee* in the terms may refer to busy, laboring bees in a hive, but more probably it derives from the Yorkshire dialect, where the word *bean* meant a "day," similar gatherings having been held on special days in Yorkshire, England. *See also* BEE.

husky. Any man called husky, "stocky and muscular," is actually being compared to a sled dog—specifically, to a husky, or Eskimo dog, a strong breed capable of pulling great loads and covering 60 miles a day. *Husky* is used loosely for any arctic dog, but the breed is a recognized one. An unusual animal that yelps or howls like a wolf, although not closely related to the wolf, the husky normally feeds on fish and sleeps without shelter in the snow. Its name is a corruption of either the Tinneh Indian *uskimi*, "an Eskimo"; *Esky*, English slang for Eskimo; or the word *Eskimo* itself. Early explorers in the far north named the dog after the natives who bred it, and the dog's name was later applied to trappers who exhibited the breed's vigor, endurance, and stocky build.

Hussite. A follower of the reformist religious teachings of John Huss (1369?–1415) also known as Jan Hus, a Czech priest whose ideas strongly influenced Martin Luther. Because he attacked the abuses of the clergy and championed John Wycliffe's translation of the Bible, Huss was excommunicated and burnt at the stake.

hussy. *Hussy*, a bold or lewd woman, was originally no more than another word for housewife, simply a phonetic reduction of the earlier term, which was first pronounced *hussif*. Justly or not, housewives were associated so often with impudence, boldness, or lewdness that the word *hussy* began to be used as early as the 17th century to describe bold and lewd women, possibly to provide a distinction in the language between most housewives and such women. Over the years *hussy* became more degraded, until we find Henry Fielding writing in *Tom Jones* (1749): "Hussy . . . I will make such a saucy trollop as yourself know that I am not a proper subject of your discourse."

hustings. *See* TAKE TO THE HUSTINGS.

hyacinth. According to Greek legend, Hyancinthus was a handsome Spartan youth beloved by both the gods Apollo and Zephyrus, the West Wind. Jealous Zephyrus caused Apollo to kill Hyacinthus by making a heavy disc he had thrown while playing quoits go astray and strike the boy on the head. Although grief-stricken Apollo could not restore the youth's life, he made a beautiful new flower spring from the red earth and named it the hyacinth.

hybrid. The offspring of a tame sow and a wild boar was called a *hybrida* by the Romans, and this Latin word came into English in the early 17th century to describe such animal offspring. *Hybrid* wasn't applied to plants until almost 200 years later. A hybrid is, strictly speaking, the offspring of a cross-fertilization between parents differing in one or more genes, and a great many, possibly the majority, of cultivated plants have resulted from either natural or artificial hybridization.

hydrangea. The Greeks of old thought this plant's seed capsule looked like a "water cup" and named it from the Greek *hydr*, "water," and *angos*, "seed" or "capsule." Long one of the most commonly grown shrubs in America, the hydrangea consists of some 80 species, usually with large, showy pink, white or blue blooms.

hydrophobia skunk. An American name for the spotted skunk (*Spilogale putorius*) because of the belief that its bite causes hydrophobia (rabies) in humans.

hydroplane. Almost as soon as the airplane became a reality in the early 20th century, inventors began experimenting with seaplanes with floats that were able to take off from and land on the sea. These were called *hydroplanes*, and some of the first examples were built in France. But the name created some confusion, and still does, for it had, since 1870, also been used for a light, high-powered boat designed to plane over the water at high speeds. Invented by English pastor Charles Meade Ramus in the mid 19th century, the hydroplane boat did not become a reality until about the same time as the seaplane. It is often called the sea sled or hydrofoil today.

hygiene. *Hygiene* derives from the name of *Hygeia*, the Greek goddess of health, who was the daughter of Aesculapius, the god of medicine. Legend has it that Aesculapius once appeared in Rome during a plague in the form of a serpent; thus Hygeia's symbol is a serpent drinking from a cup in her hand.

hymen; hymn. *Hymen*, for the vaginal membrane, may derive either from the Greek *humen*, "membrane," or from the name of the Greek *Hyman* (Latin *Hymen*), "the god of marriage." The god could have taken his name from the membrane or the membrane may have been named for him. Our word *hymn* is related to *hymen*, coming from the related *hymnos*, "wedding song."

Hypatia. *Hypatia* refers to a woman philosopher, often a beautiful one. The original Hypatia (d. 415) was an Alexandrian Neoplatonic philosopher, an astronomer, and a mathematician, the daughter of famed mathematician Theon. This philosopher of renowned learning, elegance, and beauty drew great crowds at her lectures and wrote an unknown number of books, none of which survive. According to one story, she remained a virgin even after she married. Another tale claims that a young man propositioned her and the beautiful Hypatia hiked up her dress, telling him, "This symbol of unclean generation is what you are in love with, and not anything beautiful." Her barbarous murder is said to have been encouraged by archbishop St. Cyril of Alexandria, a personel enemy of the prefect, who was believed to be Hypatia's lover. She met her end when a band of fanatic monks and a murderous crowd of infuriated Christians, hating her philosophy, "pulled her from her carriage, dragged her into a church, stripped her of her garments, battered her to death with tiles, tore her corpse to pieces, and burned the remains in a savage orgy." British novelist Charles Kingsley wrote of her life in his historical novel *Hypatia, or New Foes With Old Faces* (1851).

hype; hyperbole.   Although there lived in the fourth century B.C. an Athenian demagogue named Hyperbolus given to exaggerated statements, his name does not give us the word *hyperbole*, or *hype*, as it is abbreviated today. *Hyperbole* derives from the Greek *hyper*, "over," plus *bole*, "throw," which conveys the idea of excess or exaggeration. Hyperbolus was just appropriately named.

hyphen.   A short line (-) connecting the parts of a compound word. The term has been used since at least the end of the 16th century and derives ultimately from the Greek word for the same, though the Greeks used a different sign than a short line. In the 1890s a congressional clerk was supposed to write: "All foreign fruit-plants are free from duty" in transcribing a recently passed bill. However, he changed the hyphen to a comma and wrote: "All foreign fruit, plants are free from duty." Before Congress could correct his error with a new law, the government had lost over $2 million in taxes. *See* COMMA.

hyphenated Americans.   Starting as contemptuous slang in the late 19th century, *hyphenated American* meant any naturalized citizen who regarded himself as both American and of the country from which he came (Irish-American, German-American, etc.). Today, the term is not generally contemptuous and refers to one's ancestry and to racial and religious groups as well.

hypnotism.   The word *hypnotism* was invented by Scottish Dr. James Briad (ca.1795–1860), who experimented with MESMERISM. Briad wanted to describe the sleeplike state of his subjects and coined the term *neurohypnotism* from the name of Hypnos, the Greek god of sleep, this unwieldy word soon shortened to *hypnotism*. Hypnotism was also called *Briadism* in Briad's time, but that term isn't often heard today.

hypochondriac.   *Hypochondriac*, for a person morbidly anxious about his health, comes from the Greek *hypo*, "below, under," and *chondros*, "rib cartilages." This is puzzling until one learns that "under" the "rib cartilages" lies the upper abdomen, once thought to be the seat of melancholy. *Hypochondriac* is first recorded in its modern sense midway through the 17th century.

hypocrite.   The Greek *Hypokrites* originally described an actor on the stage, but came to mean any pretender or liar. It is recorded in English late in the 13th century, for a person pretending to beliefs or feelings he doesn't really have.

hypoglycemia.   An abnormally low level of glucose in the blood, the opposite of diabetes. American author O. Henry, a life-long alcoholic, suffered from hypoglycemia, his classic summary of the condition being, "I was born eight drinks below par." During the long period he lived in his beloved Baghdad on the Hudson, his name for New York City, he claimed he drank an average daily two quarts of whiskey, which never prevented him from writing 50 to 65 stories a year. *See* O. HENRY.

hysteria.   Early physicians decided 1) that women are more liable to emotional disturbances than men, and 2) that this was because of the malfunctioning of an organ men didn't have, the womb. This mistaken notion gave us the word *hysteria*, from the Greek *hysterikós* "of the womb."

I

I. The letter *I* comes from the stylized drawing of the Phoenician alphabet and is thought to have been based on a picture of the human finger. People at first did not have to remember to dot their *i*'s. The dot on the *i* wasn't added to the letter until the 11th century, when scribes introduced it to distinguish two *i*'s coming together (as in *filii*) from the letter *u*. Up until the 19th century the written and printed *i* and *j* were interchangeable and dictionaries didn't treat them as separate letters. Our word *I* is a shortening of the much older *ik*. The vowel in this word was originally pronounced like the *i* in *his*. *See* IOTA; TITTLE.

I am become death. *See* IT WORKED.

I am going to sleep in their camp tonight or in hell. *See* SHERIDAN'S RIDE.

I am going to telephone Hitler (Je vais téléphoner à Hitler). A euphemism members of the French Resistance used during World War II when they excused themselves to go to the toilet.

Iberia's pilot. Columbus was not called this in his own day. This little-known name for the great navigator is first recorded in the poem "Pleasures of Hope" (1799), by Scottish poet Thomas Campbell. *See also* FEW AND FAR BETWEEN.

I cannot tell a lie (Pa). The folktale of George Washington cutting down the cherry tree and admitting it to his father ("I cannot tell a lie, Pa") is one of the most persistent in American history. It is first recorded in the Reverend Mason L. Weems's *Life of Washington* (1800), told to him by an old lady who had spent much time with the family. No one has ever *disproved* this story, though there is some evidence that it was current as a country tale before Parson Weems printed it. Weems's book went through over 40 editions, and millions of Americans were raised on the story, including Abraham Lincoln, who borrowed a copy of the book, and when it was damaged by a sudden rain had to work three days to pay its owner for it. All we can say with certainty is that like most folklore the tale was exaggerated over the years: a tree stripped of bark becoming the chopped-down tree, "I can't tell a lie, Pa," becoming "Father, I cannot tell a lie."

I can't believe I ate the whole thing. *See* GOOD TO THE LAST DROP.

ice bear; winter bear. *Ice bear* is a name that Eskimos give to a monstrous grizzly bear they fear even more than the polar bear. In the course of roaming about the country, these grizzlies sometimes take a dip in the water and roll in the snow, their fur becoming thickly coated with ice. From time immemorial the Eskimos have feared this deadly "winter bear," for the thick ice serves as a shield that breaks arrows shot at it and has been known to stop bullets.

Icebergia. *See* ALASKA.

iceblink. Seamen gave the name *iceblink* to a luminous sky caused by light reflected from ice. The term is first recorded late in the 18th century and was shortly applied as well to the huge ice cliffs of Greenland.

icebound. *Icebound* means to be held "fast by ice," hemmed in, frozen in, as a ship might be. Figuratively, the word has been used to describe a cold, reserved person unable to care or show emotion. *Icebound* is the title of a 1922 Pulitizer Prize–winning play by Owen Davis about the tight-lipped, icebound Jordan family.

ice storm. Anyone who has ever walked in one knows the beauty of this winter storm in which rain freezes on and bejewels all it touches, though often causing trees or limbs to break and fall. Robert P. Tristan Coffin wrote that walking in one is like "living inside a diamond with all the walls cut and polished so they flame."

ichor. *Ichor* (rhyming with "liquor") is in classical mythology "the ethereal fluid that flows in the veins of the gods" in place of blood. From such lofty heights *ichor* fell to become the

English name for the blood of animals, little used today, and, finally, the water discharged from a wound or ulcer!

iconoclast. A debunker, one who attacks cherished beliefs, is called an iconoclast. The word dates from the time of Byzantine emperor Leo III, who in 726 began a program of destroying icons, or images, in churches because he believed his people actually worshipped the icons, not the religious figures they represented. The monks fanatically opposed Leo and called him, among other things, an *iconoclast*, "image breaker," the first recorded use of the word.

I could not love thee, Dear, so much, Loved I not Honour more. *See* STONE WALLS DO NOT A PRISON MAKE.

Idaho. *Idaho* may be the only state name that is a complete fraud—at any rate, its name may mean nothing at all. Many sources derive the word *Idaho* from a Shoshonean Indian word meaning "gem of the mountain," but the Idaho State Historical Society claims that there never was any such Indian word and that *Idaho* and its translation was the phony creation of a mining lobbyist who suggested it to Congress as the name for the territory we now know as Colorado. Congress rejected the name, but it caught on among gold prospectors along the Columbia River, and when it was proposed in 1863 as the name for what we know today as Idaho, Congress approved it and the Idaho Territory was born. The origin of the word may be Shoshonean, however, though it does not mean "gem of the mountain" or "Behold! The sun is coming down the mountain," as another writer suggested. Idaho residents, in fact, ought to forget about the real Shoshone word that *Idaho* may have derived from, for that word would be *Idahi*, a Kiowa curse for the Comanches that translates roughly as "eaters of feces," "performers of unnatural acts," "sources of foul odors," etc.

Idaho baked potato. Very few potatoes are named and known for their place of origin. Strangely enough, this well-known name was made famous by a New York department store "taster." William Titon, better known as Titon the Taster, worked 60 years for Macy's and was the store's final authority on all groceries, wines, and liquors. Among other accomplishments, Titon discovered the Idaho potato in 1926 while buying apples for Macy's and promoted it until the spud's name became synonymous with baked potato, for which Idaho's governor wrote a letter of thanks to the store.

idiolect. *See* ACROLECT.

idiot. When Horace Walpole dubbed Oliver Goldsmith "The Inspired Idiot," he wasn't aware that the ancient Greeks had often termed prose writers idiots. But *idiots*, the Greek word for *idiot* (from *idios*, private), first meant a private person, someone who kept to himself, often not active in the affairs of state; only later did it come to mean uneducated or ignorant. Although the Greek expression *a poet or an idiot* calls a prose writer an "idiot," it contrasts not the intelligence but the medium of the two callings, the poet a public person who often, in fact, read his or her works at public festivals. In more recent times novelist Georges Simenon said that Count Keyserling once called him an "imbecile de genie." Today *idiot* usually means a "foolish person" or, scientifically, someone with a mental age no higher than that of a child of three or four years of age.

I disapprove of what you say, but I will defend to the death your right to say it. Voltaire didn't say it. In her book *The Friends of Voltaire* (1906), E. Beatrice Hall, using the pen name S. G. Tallentyre, proposed this well-known quotation on freedom of speech as a paraphrase on a thought in Voltaire's *Essay on Tolerance:* "Think for yourself and let others enjoy the privilege to do so too."

I do not choose to run. Said to be the words of President Calvin "Silent Cal" Coolidge when reporters were questioning him about whether he would run for re-election. Coolidge, in fact, said nothing at all. He passed out sheets of paper with the words written on them—"I do not choose to run for President in 1928."

I do not love thee, Dr. Fell. *See* DOCTOR FELL.

I don't give a damn. *See* GIVE A DAMN.

I'd rather dine with Jack Ketch. *See* H.

I'd sooner vote for the devil. Among the most famous of political ripostes, this put-down has been attributed to several politicians, but it originated with British MP John Wilkes. "I'd sooner vote for the devil than John Wilkes," a constituent once told him. "And what if your friend is not running," Wilkes replied.

If his IQ slips any lower, we'll have to water him twice a day. Said of someone exceedingly stupid. Columnist and Texan Molly Ivins says it in her *Molly Ivins Can't Say That, Can She?* (1992) and either invented it or is passing it along. She was referring, of course, to a politician.

If I can't dance, it's not my revolution. The expression originated with American anarchist Emma Goldman (1869–1940) in the early 1900s, after her lover and fellow anarchist, Alexander Berkman, berated her one night for dancing wildly in a radical hangout.

If I live to be a hundred, I hope I never see you again. This old cliché was used by Marlene Dietrich in one of her 1930s movies. It is probably much older and is still heard today.

If it bleeds, it leads. Recent instruction for tabloid broadcasting and newspaper journalists, referring to the need for emphasizing bloody sensational stories in their coverage of the news, specifically leading off the first page or the program with such stories. Such coverage is, however, older than the tabloids themselves.

If it is not true, it is well-invented. *See* BEN TROVATO.

If Jesus were alive today, he would be at the Super Bowl. According to *Time* magazine (January 21, 1982) Protestant clergyman and author Norman Vincent Peale, a football fan, made this remark in referring to the 1981 Super Bowl. It has been much quoted since, though rarely if ever used seriously.

if life spare.   A common Jamaican English expression that means "God willing," "if God spares me," a promise to do something if one doesn't die before one can: "I'll see you tomorrow if life spare." Also heard as "if life save."

If the mountain will not come to Muhammad, Muhammad must go to the mountain.   The saying arises from the time when Muhammad, founder of the Muslim religion and prophet of its God Allah, brought his message to the Arabs, and they demanded miraculous proof of his claims. He ordered Mount Safa to move, and when it failed to do so, explained that God had been merciful—for if the mountain had moved it would have fallen on and destroyed them all. Muhammad then went to the mountain and gave thanks to God. The proverb is used to indicate that it is wise to bow before the inevitable after failing to get one's way. *See* MUHAMMADANISM.

If you ain't the lead horse, the scenery never changes.   A humorous American expression I've only found in Thomas McGuane's *Keep the Change* (1989): "My old man used to say, 'If you ain't the lead horse, the scenery never changes.' Now it looks like I might lose the place. I need to get out front with that lead horse."

If you can't lick 'em, join 'em.   This Americanism probably dates back to the late 19th or early 20th century. Cynical and pragmatic, it comes from the political precincts, as one would expect.

If you can't say something nice, don't say anything at all.   This self-explanatory expression, popularized by the movie *Bambi*, has been in use for at least a century and a half in the U.S. It's good advice as a general rule, but you wouldn't want to apply it to someone like Hitler, Stalin, or Mussolini, who people said made the trains run on time.

If you can't stand the heat, get out of the kitchen.   The aphorism is usually attributed to President HARRY S TRUMAN but there is some evidence that he got it from his military adviser General Harry Vaughn, who got it from who knows where. It has also been suggested, with no proof, that what the salty Truman really liked to say was "If you can't stand the stink get out of the shithouse."

If you don't like the weather, just wait a minute.   A saying referring to the mercurial nature of New England weather attributed to Mark Twain, who despite his many years in the region, never got used to the weather.

If you need anything, just whistle.   When Humphrey Bogart died and was cremated in 1957, his wife, Lauren Bacall, placed a small gold whistle in the urn with his ashes. Inscribed on the whistle is a variation on the famous line she delivered to Bogey in their first film together, *To Have and Have Not:* "If you need anything, just whistle." Her exact words had been, "If you need me, just whistle," but no one remembers it that way.

if you peel that onion a little farther.   An American expression, its exact origin unknown, meaning "as you examine something a little closer" it begins to take on a new appearance or meaning, as in. "On its surface the tax bill seems to help the poor, but if you peel that onion a little farther, you begin to find that's not the case at all." An onion, of course, has many layers.

If you've got the money, honey, I've got the time.   There is a popular song of this title, but the expression has its roots in the *any day you 'ave the money, I 'ave the time,* an approach said to have been much used by prostitutes and "enthusiastic near-amateurs" in London toward the beginning of the century.

If you want God to laugh, tell him your plans.   A Spanish proverb quoted in the Mexican film *Amores Perros* (2001).

If you want peace, prepare for war.   Whether this advice remains good in our nuclear age is debatable, but there is no denying that this is an ancient phrase. It is a translation of the Roman proverb: *Si vis pacem, para bellum.*

ignoramus.   Up until the 17th century *ignoramus* was just the Latin plural for "We don't know" and was written by grand juries across the backs of indictments if they thought there wasn't enough evidence in a case for the accused to be prosecuted. *Ignoramus* took on its present meaning in 1615, when George Ruggle wrote a play entitled *Ignoramus*, after the name of its main character, a lawyer who didn't know anything about the law. Soon this ignorant fictional lawyer's name was being applied to any ignorant person, lawyer or not. *See* IGNORE.

ignorance is bliss.

> Yet ah! why should they know their fate?
> Since sorrow never comes too late,
> And happiness too swiftly flies
> Thought would destroy their paradise.
> No more; where ignorance is bliss,
>   Tis folly to be wise.

English poet Thomas Gray wrote the above in his *Ode on a Distant Prospect of Eton College* (1742), and unintentionally added a proverb to the language. It has been observed that Gray didn't mean it is better to be ignorant than wise at all times, the popular usage given to his words, for he makes an important qualification by using the word *where*. But a reading of the whole poem shows that he did mean it is better for man to be blissfully ignorant of his fate.

ignore.   *Ignore*, in the sense of "pay no attention," was a word scorned by pedants well into the 19th century. It apparently derives from the old law term *ignoramus*. Indictments not to be sent to court were marked *ignoramus*, "not found," on the back by the grand jury. They were thus given no attention by the court, or *ignored*. *See* IGNORAMUS.

I gotta million of 'em.   Often said by a comedian, or any joke-teller, after telling a gag. The words are associated with American comedian Jimmy Durante (1893–1980) and thus may date back to the early 1900s, when the beloved "Schnozzola" appeared in vaudeville. Durante ended all his radio shows with the still mysterious, raspy words, "Good night, Mrs. Calabash, wherever you are."

I have but one answer, "I don't know."   *See* BOOJUM TREE.

I have lost a day.   According to the Roman historian Suetonius in his *Life of Titus*, the Roman emperor uttered these words at the end of a day when he had done no good to anyone. Titus, who reigned from A.D. 79 to 81, is known as the conqueror of Jerusalem and as the lover of Berenice, daughter of the Jewish king Herod, their ill-fated romance the subject of Racine's tragedy *Bérénice*.

I have not yet begun to fight.   *See* SIR, I HAVE NOT YET BEGUN TO FIGHT.

IHS.   This well-known abbreviation, used as a symbol or monogram, is simply the first two letters and the last letter of the Greek word for Jesus, capitalized and Romanized. It does not stand for *in hoc signo* ("in this sign") or any other phrase.

I laughed till I cried.   *See* SECOND CHILDHOOD.

an Iliad of woes.   This old expression was used in a similar form by the ancient Greeks. It refers, of course, to the myriad human woes mentioned in Homer's *Iliad*, which ignores virtually no calamity that can befall humankind.

I like Ike.   *See* EISENHOWER JACKET; HE KEPT US OUT OF WAR.

ilk.   *Of that ilk* means of the same class or kind, *ilk* coming from the Old English *ilca*, meaning "same." The expression has been traced back to about A.D. 800.

I'll be there with bells on.   Early-18th-century Conestoga wagons usually arrived at their destination with bronze bells ringing, giving rise to this Americanism. These same Conestogas are responsible for traffic moving on the right side of the road in the U.S. rather than on the left as in Britain. According to one authority, the Conestogas were "best guided from the left and so afforded a clear view ahead only when driven from the right side of the road. Drivers of other vehicles found it not only wise not to argue but convenient to follow in the ruts made by the heavy wagons and habit soon became law." *See* STOGY.

I'll drink all the blood that is spilled between North and South.   A common quip heard among Southern "fireaters" just before the Civil War, a war in which 620,000 men were killed, the casualties exceeding America's losses in all other wars.

illeist.   The word for the habit of referring to oneself excessively in the third person singular is *illeism*. A nonce word modeled on the Latin *ille* ("he") and *egoism*, it was apparently invented by Coleridge, or at least he is the first author recorded to have used this coining for "a consummate egoist" (in about 1809). Using *he* does sound better than employing the royal *we*, and even a little better than constantly using *I*, for which Victor Hugo was called "a walking personal pronoun."

Illinois.   This central "Prairie State" is named for the Illinois Indians, as the French called the confederation of six Indian tribes in the area. Frenchmen were the first Europeans to enter Illinois territory, in 1673. They changed the Indian name *Hileni* or *Ileni*, meaning "man," to *Illin*, adding their *ois* plural. Since the Indian plural is *uk*, *Illinois* might be *Illinuk* today if they hadn't done so. The Illinois group is almost extinct today, numbering between 200 and 300, compared to an estimated 8,000 in the 17th century.

Illinois Baboon.   A derogatory name given to Abraham Lincoln by his detractors, sometimes shortened to *the Baboon* and sometimes changed to *Illinois Gorilla* and *Gorilla*.

I'll tell you what I'm gonna do!   A saying that became famous nationwide after its use by Sid Stone playing a pitchman on comedian Milton Berle's *Texaco Star Theater*. Stone rolled up his sleeves and played a street hustler on a segment of the television show every Tuesday night from 1948 to 1954. However, the very similar *I'll tell you what* goes back to Shakespeare, both phrases meaning roughly, "I'll tell you something, or I'll make a deal with you." Milton Berle (1909–2002), television's first star, introduced a number of popular expressions on his show, including the nonsensical "what the hey!"; "good evening, ladies and germs"; "I swear I'll kwill (kill) you"; and "God, I wish I'd said that, and don't worry, I will." As for jokes, Berle said he knew 200,000. "Uncle Miltie's" program was immensely popular. In his autobiography the comedian wrote: "In Detroit, an investigation took place when the water levels took a drastic drop in the reservoirs on Tuesday nights between 9 and 9:05. It turned out that everybody waited until the end of the Texaco Star Theater before going to the bathroom."

I loved the sweat of his body and the dust of his feet more than any other man.   The poetic words of an old woman in the Ozarks recalling the extent of her love for her husband, who had died many years before.

I love everything that's old.   The expression refers to the preference of Squire Hardcastle in Oliver Goldsmith's *She Stoops to Conquer* (1773), who "loves everything that's old: old friends, old times, old manners, old books, old wine."

I ♡ New York.   Mary Wells Lawrence of the Wells Lawrence Green advertising agency coined the ubiquitous tourism slogan for New York City. Ms. Lawrence, the first woman to own a major ad agency, also invented the famous Alka Seltza "Plop Plop" jingle, among many other ads.

"I'm a Cranky Old Yank in a Clanky Old Tank on the Streets of Yokahama with My Honolulu Mama Doin' Those Beat-O, Flat-On-My-Seat-O, Hirohito Blues."   Possibly the world's longest song title, composed by U.S. songwriter Hoagy Carmichael (1899–1981).

I'm a curly-tailed wolf with a pink ass and this is my night to howl.   A humorous oath heard among drinkers of potent moonshines and recorded by students of American Mountain dialect.

imaginary biographies.   This term is used to describe biographies of people who do not exist. In William Beckford's *Biographical Memoirs of Extraordinary Painters* (1824) we find biographies of imaginary artists such as Og of Bason. *Appleton's Cyclopedia of American Biography*, first published in 1886, for many years contained 84 biographies of nonexistent persons sent in by an unknown correspondent; it wasn't until 1936 that they were all weeded out. Noel Coward did a bit of the same in his *Terribly Intimate Portraits* (1922), giving us imaginary biographies of people like Jabey Puffwater and E. Maxwell Snurge. Later, he pulled similar stunts in *Spangled Uniform* and *Chelsea Buns*. Many critics have been fooled by phony books and poems, but the only instance I've come across of a critic writing imaginary book reviews is Gerald Johnson, who, according to Martin Gardner, reviewed "six imaginary books . . . perceptively" in the *New York Times* on January 2, 1949. Gardner adds that many whimsical authors—Rabelais, Huysmans, and James Branch Cabell (with his "distinguished German scholar" Gottfried Johannes Biilg)—liked to "refer to the books of non-existent authors." Jorge Luis Borges has done the same in recent times.

imagist.   A poet who employs free verse and the patterns and rhythms of common speech; or one of a specific group of such poets in England, France, and America from 1909–17. American poet Ezra Pound is said to have coined the name while reading his friend Hilda Doolittle's poems in the tearoom of the British Museum one day in 1912. According to Robert Wernik's "The Strange and Inscrutable Case of Ezra Pound" (*Smithsonian Magazine*, 12/95), Pound told Doolittle her poems were excellent: "[He] took out one of his sharp red pencils and shortened a few lines, changed a few adjectives and signed at the bottom 'H.D., Imagiste,' with one stroke creating a new school of poetry and conferring upon Doolittle the name under which she appears in the anthologies."

Ima Hogg.   Perhaps this is the best known of humorous American names, for Ima Hogg's father was the governor of Texas and she was a prominent socialite. It is not necessarily the best humorous real American name, for we have hundreds of gems like the following to choose from: Virgin Muse, Fairy Guy, Lance Amorous, Etta Turnipseed, Fannie Bottom, Arsie Phalla, and Dill L. Pickle (who was a pickle salesman). There was even someone named La Void.

I'm all right, Jack.   First recorded in the late 19th century, *I'm all right, Jack* was originally British naval slang employing the *Jack* of JACK TAR and a shortening of the lustier "Fuck you, I'm all right, Jack," common in the military at the time.

I'm from Missouri.   During the Civil War, an officer of the Northern army fell upon a body of Confederate troops commanded by a Missourian. The Northerner demanded a surrender, saying he had so many thousand men in his unit. The Confederate commander, game to the core, said he didn't believe the Northerner's boast of numerical superiority and appended the now famous expression, "I'm from Missouri; you'll have to show me." Dr. Walter B. Stevens recorded this proud derivation of the phrase in *A Colonial History of Missouri* (1921), but other authorities support the following derogatory origin: Miners from the lead district of southwest Missouri had

been imported to work the mines in Leadville, Colorado, sometime after the Civil War. They were unfamiliar with the mining procedures in Leadville and fellow workers regarded them as slow to learn, their pit bosses constantly using the expression, "He's from Missouri; you'll have to show him." Residents of the "Show Me" state obviously favor the former theory, in which "I'm from Mizorra" is a badge of distinction, signifying native skepticism and shrewdness.

Immelmann turn.   Sergeant York, Eddie Rickenbacker, Black Jack Pershing, the Red Baron . . . not many men are remembered of the millions who fought and the millions who died in "the war to end all wars." But World War I German ace Max Immelmann (1890–1916) is one of them, if only because he is the eponym behind the eponymous term *Immelmann turn*, or *Immelmann*, a maneuver he developed (consisting of a half loop and a roll) that enabled him to take evasive action in such a way that his plane quickly secured an offensive position. Immelmann won many of his 15 victories with his turn, as did other aces of the two world wars. He died at age 26 like the Red Baron, when his plane broke apart in midair, perhaps as a result of his acrobatic tactic. *See* RED BARON.

immolate.   *Immolate* means to sacrifice by fire or other means, but it derives from the Latin *immolare*, "to sprinkle with meal." This is because the ancient Romans sprinkled wine and pieces of the sacred cake, made from meal, on the heads of humans to be sacrificed to the gods.

imp.   A graft or shoot was called an *impian* by the Anglo-Saxons and this word, shortened to *imp*, later came to mean an offspring or a child. At first *imp* meant any child, but the word is now almost always applied to a mischievous child.

impala.   The name of this large South African antelope (*Aepyceros melampus*) was taken directly from Zulu *impala* meaning the same. The word was first recorded in English as far back as 1801.

impatiens.   *See* NOLI ME TANGERE.

imperial beard.   Louis Napoleon (1808–73), nephew of Napoleon Bonaparte, staged a coup d'état in 1851 that made him emperor the following year. As Napoleon III, the despot reigned until his empire was overthrown 20 years later and he retired to England. While emperor, Napoleon sported a small, pointed tuft of hair under the lower lip that was named an imperial beard in his honor.

impressionism.   A painting by Claude Monet entitled *Impression-Sunset* is responsible for the name of the school of art called impressionism. French critic Louis Leroy coined the term in a review he wrote on April 25, 1874, ridiculing Monet's painting and others of an experimental nature that he had seen exhibited at a photographer's studio in Paris. Meaning to be sarcastic, he entitled his review *L'Exposition des Impressionists*. Soon the term caught on, losing its pejorative sense.

improvisator.   An improvisator is someone who composes, acts, sings, etc., on the spur of the moment, without preparation. The word derives from the Italian *improvvisatore*, which originally referred only to a person who extemporized verse. Petrarch is supposed to have introduced the game of inventing poems on the spot for a particular occasion and to have received a laurel crown for extemporizing in verse. Others among many famous for this talent were Italian poet Angelo Mazza (1741–1817), reputedly best of all; Francisco Gianni (1759–1822), whom Napoleon made imperial poet to celebrate his victories in verse; English poet Thomas Hood, author of "The Bridge of Sighs"; William Cowper; and Alexandre Dumas père.

in a bad box.   *Box* here means "predicament." The old saying may have been invented by Mason Locke Weems in his *The Drunkard's Looking Glass* (1818), the same Parson Weems who may have invented the story of George Washington and the cherry tree in a biography of the first U.S. president. Others of what the good parson called his "good books" were *Hymen's Recruiting Sergent* and *God's Revenge Against Adultery*. *See* I CANNOT TELL A LIE.

in a hole.   The expression *in a hole*, "in debt or some other kind of trouble," can be traced to gambling houses of the mid 19th century where the proprietors took a certain percentage of each hand for the house. This money, according to a gambling book of the time, was put in the "hole," which was "a slot cut in the middle of the poker table, leading to a locked drawer underneath, and all checks deposited therein are the property of the keeper of the place." When one had put more money into the poker table hole than was in his pocket, he was *in a hole*.

in a New York minute.   A very short time, instantly. "He did it in a New York minute." A popular expression that was first recorded in print in 1967, though William Safire, in *Coming to Terms* (1980), quotes an informant who says his father, who died in 1929, age 69, often used the expression.

in a nutshell; the Iliad in a nutshell; Iliad.   One writer recently called the first expression a cliché that is rarely heard anymore, but the cliché must be a useful one, for in just two weeks since I read his pronouncement I've heard the expression five times, once in the title of Stephen Hawking's book *The Universe in a Nutshell* (2002). *In a nutshell* has a long, distinguished history dating back to Cicero, who claimed in the first century B.C. that someone actually copied all 24 books of Homer's epic poem *The Iliad* in a handwriting minuscule enough to fit in a walnut shell (a feat that has since been repeated several times). The phrase *the Iliad in a nutshell* later came to be *in a nutshell*, meaning "very small," of great brevity, a condensation beyond the wildest dreams of the *Reader's Digest*. Wrote Shakespeare in *Hamlet* (1601): "Oh God! I could be bounded in a nutshell, and count myself a king of infinite space, were it not that I have had bad dreams." *The Iliad* takes its name from *Ilion*, another name for the city of Troy, *Ilion* honoring its legendary founder, *Ilus*.

in a pig's eye.   A fiery emphatic denial meaning "never," "not a chance," "like hell," as in "In a pig's eye you could beat me." Variations on the well-known Americanism include *in a pig's ass* and *in a pig's ear*.

in a pretty pickle.   *In de pikel zitten*, a Dutch phrase going back at least four centuries, literally means to sit in the salt solution used for preserving pickles. This saying apparently suggested the expression to be *in a pretty pickle*, an uncomfortable or sorry plight—like someone sitting in such a bath. Our word *pickle* comes from the Dutch. A sour pickle is perhaps the last thing anyone would expect to be named after a man, but at least one source claims that the word *pickle* derives from the name of William Beukel or Bukelz, a 14th-century Dutchman who supposedly first pickled fish, inventing the process by which we shrink and sour cucumbers. This pickled-herring theory may be a RED HERRING, however. All the big dictionaries follow the *O.E.D.'s* lead in tracing pickle to the Medieval Dutch word *pekel*, whose origin is ultimately unknown.

in at the kill.   If you consider fox hunting a sport—Oscar Wilde said a fox hunt consisted of "the unspeakable in full pursuit of the inedible"—this expression can be considered a sporting phrase. *In at the kill* means "participating in the finish of something, especially something satisfying and vindictive," and originated in the upper-crust British world of the hunt sometime during the 1800s. *See also* TALLYHO.

inaugurate.   *See* AUSPICIOUS.

inauspicious.   It has been remarked that "no other word ever had such a premiere as *inauspicious*," which made its debut in Shakespeare's *Romeo and Juliet*, Romeo crying:

> Here, here, will I remain . . .
> And shake the yoke of inauspicious stars
> From this world-wearied flesh.

Shakespeare probably invented *inauspicious*, as he did *auspicious* (in *The Tempest*), meaning favorable, conducive to success. Its roots are in the Latin *auspex*, a corruption of *avispex*, for the Roman birdwatcher who deduced omens from the flight of birds.

in a word.   Brief, shortly. Shakespeare may have coined this phrase, for he is the first to record it, in *Two Gentlemen of Verona* (1591): "And in a word . . . he is compleat in feature and in mind."

in cahoots with.   *Cahoots* apparently derives from the French *cahute*, cabin, and is first recorded in about 1820. American fur trappers on the frontier probably borrowed the word from French trappers there. Trappers living together in a *cahute* or *cahoot* were often partners, giving rise to the expression *in cahoots with*.

Incas.   The Peruvian Indians of South America did not call themselves the Incas, as the Spanish did. Inca in their language meant lord, king, or ruler, a "man of the royal blood" or a king's relative, not any one of their people. The king himself was sometimes called the *Capa Inca*, or "sole lord."

incorporated; Inc.   No one seems to know what corporation first abbreviated *incorporated* to *Inc.* after its name. *Incorporated* means to be united in one body, *incorporate* and *incorporated* having been used in the sense of legal or formal business corporations since the 15th century.

incubate; incubus. *See* NIGHTMARE.

incunabula. The word *incunabula* (the singular form is *incunabulum*) is used to signify books produced in the infancy of printing from movable type, usually those printed before 1500. Caxton's edition of *The Canterbury Tales*, printed in 1478, is a famous incunabulum. The Germans coined the name *incunabula* for these early books in the 19th century, using the Latin word for swaddling clothes and cradle.

indaba. A word used in South African English for a meeting or a conference, as in "The indaba was held in Capetown." The word, which comes from the Zulu language, also means a problem or a concern, as in "It's not our indaba."

indenture. *Indenture* strictly means "a document with serrated edges," deriving from the Latin *dens*, "tooth," and referring to the once common practice of cutting a document into halves with serrated edges—one half to each party of agreement—so that the document could be authenticated by fitting the edges together. The word's legal meaning today is "a contract in which two parties bind themselves to an exchange of services and observances." *Indentured servitude*, sometimes called "white slavery" and banned under the U.S. Constitution, bound a person to service to another for a period of time, usually seven years, and could amount to virtual slavery. A number of noted early Americans were once indentured servants.

index finger. The second finger of the human hand was called the *towcher* (toucher) in Middle English because it is so frequently used for touching objects. Today it is called the *index finger* because it is the finger used most for pointing. *Index* means "informer" or "that which informs" in Latin. *See also* THUMB.

Index Librorum Prohibitorum. Often abbreviated to the *Index*, this list of books forbidden by the Catholic church is practically a synonym for censorship. Established by the Holy Office in 1559, the *Index* mostly condemned books for doctrinal or moral reasons. Pope Paul VI ended publication of the *Index* in 1966, making a paperback book that had once banned as many as 5,000 books no more than a "moral guide" without force of church law, though the Vatican can still issue warnings about books that might be "dangerous" to the faithful. No American novelist has ever been listed in the *Index*. Among prominent writers who did make the list are: Boccaccio, Galileo, Bacon, Milton, Locke, Gibbon, Defoe, Descartes, Montaigne, Spinoza, Rousseau, Kant, Stendhal, Hugo, Casanova, Balzac, Dumas, Flaubert, Gide, Sartre, and Moravia. *See also* BOWDLERIZE; COMSTOCKERY.

India ink. In France *India ink* is called *China ink* as it rightly should be, for it was invented in China and first traded there. *India ink* it is in America and England, as it has been since 1665, when the dark black ink is mentioned in Samuel Pepys's famous *Diary*.

Indian. At least one writer has speculated that *Indian* may have been suggested to Columbus as a name for the Taino people he encountered because they were so friendly, peaceful, and gentle, *una gente in Dios*, a people of God. But there is no proof of this, most etymologists believing these people were mistakenly named by Columbus because he thought he had reached the Indies of Asia, the first but not the worst mistake immigrants made regarding the native Americans. *See* CLEVELAND INDIANS.

Indiana. Indiana's name denotes that it was the domain of Indians. Before it became our 21st state in 1816 the Hoosier State had been called the Indian Territory.

Indiana accolade. The common action of banging the cue on the floor in a vertical position to applaud a good shot in a game of pool is called an Indiana accolade, possibly because an unknown Indiana player first "applauded" the shot of a rival this way.

Indian book. This interesting use of the word *book* is recorded in Carlisle S. Abbott's *Recollections of a California Pioneer* (1917): "Upon reaching the summit of the mountain we came to an Indian book which must have been hundreds of years old, for it was now thirty feet in diameter and nearly five feet high in the center." Such "Indian books" were accumulations of natural objects like sticks and stones left on a trail by passing Indians to inform their friends that they had come this way. *See* BOOK.

Indian bread. Pioneers called the strip of fatty meat extending from the shoulder along the backbone of the buffalo Indian bread because the Indians favored it. As one writer put it: "When scalded in hot grease to seal it, then smoked, it became a 'tit-bit' the buffalo hunter used as bread. When eaten with lean or dried meat it made an excellent sandwich."

Indian corn. *See* CORN.

Indian giver. Tradition holds that American Indians took back their gifts when they didn't get equally valuable ones in return. Some Indians were no doubt *Indian givers;* others, however, got insulted if they received *more* than they gave. Instances of Indians *Indian-giving* are hard to come by, and even the *Handbook of American Indians* (1901), published by the Smithsonian Institution, defines the practice as an "alleged custom." Perhaps the expression is explained by the fact that *Indian* was once widely used as a synonym for bogus or false. Many of the nearly 500 terms prefixed with *Indian* unfairly impugn the Indian's honesty or intelligence—even *honest Injun* was originally meant sarcastically, and *Indian summer* means a false summer.

Indian head penny. A favorite of coin collectors, the Indian head penny was issued by the U.S. Government from 1859 to 1909. The "Indian" depicted on the coin is not really an Indian; the figure was modeled by Sara Longacre, the daughter of a U.S. mint official. Mint officials have on several occasions used relatives and friends to model for figures on coins. The wife of noted American poet Wallace Stevens, for example, posed for the goddess of Liberty on the Liberty half-dollar. *See also* CENT, PENNY.

Indian paintbrush. *Castilleja linariaefolia*, a plant of the figwort family that is the state flower of Wyoming; also a name given to other plants of the genus.

Indian post office. Indians in the American West often piled sticks and stones in a mound to indicate that they had been at a certain point and would return there in a certain number of days, depending on the number of rocks and sticks piled there. Cowboys called such a mound an Indian post office because messages could be left there.

Indians don't count. An offensive boast of gunmen in the early Southwest, who supposedly kept a count of all but Indians and Mexicans that they killed. Also heard was *Mexicans don't count.*

Indian whiskey. Cheap rotgut often sold to Indians by cynical traders as good liquor. E. C. Abbott and Helene Huntington Smith in *We Pointed Them North* (1939) tell a story about early western traders making it from the following recipe: "Take one barrel of Missouri River water, and two gallons of alcohol. Then you add two gallons of strychnine to make them crazy—because strychnine is the greatest stimulant in the world + three bars of tobacco to make them sick—because an Indian wouldn't figure it was whiskey unless it made him sick + five bars of soap to give it a head, and half pound of red pepper, and then you put in some sage brush and boil it until it's brown. Strain this into a barrel and you've got your Indian whiskey." Also called Indian liquor.

Indian words in English. It is estimated that nearly a thousand basic English words derive from words in Hindu, Sanskrit, and Romany, all Indian languages. Some of these are: panther, ginger, pepper, sandal, guru, pundit, nabob, punch (drink), chintz, mongoose, dungaree, cot, bungalow, juggernaut, tom-tom, mugger, bandana, jute, sari, chit, myna, jingle, shampoo, puttee, cashmere, thus, pajamas, gazelle, dumdum, loot, dinghy, polo, chutney, zen (through Japan), and loot.

indigo. *Indigo* derives from Greek *indikon*, Indian, because the plant, which produces a blue dye, was an important crop in India. The dye plant was also much valued in the Carolina Low Country. Introduced there in the early 18th century, it did more to enrich the South Carolinian plantocracy than New World gold did for the Spaniards.

indri. The little short-tailed lemur of Madagascar was so named a century ago when a French naturalist and his Madagascan guide were identifying animals in the jungle. The guide saw a lemur and cried "Indry! Indry!" This actually meant "Look! Look!," but the naturalist recorded it as the animal's native name and the lemur has been called the *indri (Indri indri)* ever since. *See also* KANGAROO.

(the) industry. There are about a thousand kidnappings in Colombia annually, on the order of three a day, the proceeds from ransoms more than some legitimate businesses make. Therefore Colombians have adopted the English word *industry* to mean kidnapping.

I need it like I need a hole in the head. Popularized by comedians, this phrase became common in the late 1940s and is still frequently heard. It means "I don't need that at all, I'm better off without it."

I never missed one in my heart. Veteran major-league baseball umpire Bill Klem, who retired in 1941, said this to assure his admirers and detractors that he had never made a call, right or wrong, that he didn't believe was right. The expression is now used by people in and out of sports as a profession of sincerity.

I never shot a man who didn't need it. A saying repeated in a number of westerns but actually said first by outlaw Clay Allison, who is also remembered for pulling a dentist's tooth at gunpoint after the dentist pulled the wrong tooth in his mouth.

infant; infantry. First recorded by John Wycliffe in 1382 *infant* comes from the Latin *infans*, "unable to speak." It once meant a "childe" or "a young knight, a youth of gentle birth" as well as a baby. Thus we have the word *infantry* for foot soldiers, "soldiers too young and inexperienced to serve in the cavalry."

inferiority complex. Carl Jung established the psychoanalytical term *complex* in a 1907 work, but it had been coined by his colleague A. L. S. Neisser a year before. *Complex* means in this sense "a system of interrelated, emotion-charged ideas, feelings, memories, and impulses that is usually repressed and that gives rise to abnormal or pathological behavior." *Inferiority complex* became a psychiatric term at about the same time and came generally to mean "lack of self esteem, lack of confidence."

infernal machine. President John Tyler once had White House ushers defuse a package that he thought to be "an infernal machine," or bomb, but that turned out to conceal a mere cake. *Infernal machine* has been synonymous for a bomb concealed as some harmless object since at least 1810, and in the form of *infernal apparatus* is recorded in 1769. The *infernal* in the phrase derives from the Latin *infernalis*, "of the realms below, or hell."

infighting. Infighting is a style of fighting at close quarters developed by 160-pound British champion David Mendoza; the term was first recorded in 1816. Since about 1848 *infighting* has also meant fighting among rivals within a group, the expression most often heard as *political infighting*.

inflation. The word *inflation*, used in relation to inflated prices and money, is first recorded in 1838, during the Panic of 1837, which actually lasted three years. President Martin Van Buren did nothing to alleviate the panic or the bread riots that it brought, enabling William Henry Harrison to defeat him in his 1840 bid for reelection.

influenza. *Influenza* first entered the language about 1743, when an outbreak of "a contagious distemper" was reported in Rome. This was called "the Influenza" because it was believed to have been evilly "influenced" by the stars, and such occult *influenzas* were said to cause plagues and pestilences as well.

The Italian word for influence, anglicized in pronunciation, became the English specific name.

in for a penny, in for a pound; pennywise and pound foolish. Since the British have not adopted the Euro as their currency like most nations in the Common Market, these expressions may be around for centuries to come. Both date back to the mid-17th century and are familiar to Americans as well as to the British. *In for a penny, in for a pound* means "to be committed" to a course once you have embarked upon it. *Pennywise and pound foolish* is obvious. Other expressions that need no explanation in Britain or the U.S. include: *a penny for your thoughts, a bad penny; not have one penny to rub against another; a penny saved is a penny earned;* and *take care of the pence and the pounds will take care of themselves.* The word *pound* comes from the Latin *pondus,* while *penny* derives from Old English *pening.*

infracaninophile. A person who favors the underdog. Coined by American author Christopher Morley (1890–1957) to describe such a person, though the construction of the humorous nonce word from Latin may be slightly wrong. *See* UNDERDOG.

infra dig. This is short for the Latin *infra dignitatem,* "beneath one's dignity," and means something not befitting one's position, station, character, or talent.

in full sail. An admiring term for a remarkably endowed woman that is heard in coastal areas, especially in New England and most commonly in Maine: "There she goes in full sail!"

In German a young lady has no sex, but a turnip has. Mark Twain said this and he was referring to the fact that while vegetable names are given a gender in the German language, the words *Madchen,* for "girl," and *Weib,* for "wife," "female," and "woman," are not feminine but, curiously, neuter.

ingle; inglebrook. *Ingle* refers to an open fire in a fireplace, or the fireplace itself, the word deriving from Scottish Gaelic *aingeal,* "fire, light," and first recorded in the early 16th century. *Inglebrook,* recorded about 1765, is a corner or nook beside an open fireplace.

in God we trust. *Mind Your Business* was the first motto used on a U.S. coin. *In God We Trust,* the motto now found on all American coins large enough to hold it, was authorized by two Congressional acts of 1865. It was used on the eagle (the $10 gold piece), the double eagle (the $20 gold piece), the half eagle (the $5 gold piece), the silver dollar, the half dollar, and the quarter—and still appears on those latter three coins. This motto inspired the humorous slogan *In God We Trusted, In Kansas We Busted* that settlers in Kansas, bankrupt by the severe droughts from 1887 to 1891, painted on their old covered wagons when they returned East.

in hock. In the game of faro, much played in 19th-century America, the last card in the box was called the *hocketty card* (from a word of unknown origin), this card later said *to be in hock,* as was any player who bet on the last card. This was a bad bet, most often a losing one, so that *to be in hock* soon meant "to owe money." Pawnshops were a convenient place to get money to pay debts, so they became known as *hock shops,* and *to be in hock* soon meant to have some or all one's valuable possessions in a hock shop or, generally, to be in very bad financial shape.

In Hoover we trusted, now we are busted. Herbert Hoover won the U.S. Presidency in 1928 with his party's slogans A CHICKEN IN EVERY POT and RUM, ROMANISM AND REBELLION, the latter a reference to his opponent Al Smith's Catholicism. He lost the presidency in 1932, in the midst of the Great Depression, Franklin D. Roosevelt's supporters calling for "New Deal" and chanting *in Hoover we trusted, now we are busted. See* HOOVERIZE.

in hospital. "He's been in hospital since Sunday last," the British would say, dropping the article from *in the hospital.* On the other hand, Americans always say "in the hospital," retaining the article.

ink; red ink; red numbers. *Ink* itself is from Greek *enkauston,* "burned in," which the Romans used to describe the royal purple ink used by Roman emperors. *Red ink,* dating back to about 1925, means a business loss ("He went into the red ink") or a financial deficit, though during Prohibition it meant home-brewed wine. *Red numbers,* on the other hand, is a golf term that means to be under par by one or more strokes, as in "He's in the red numbers," something every golfer aspires to.

in like Flynn. Chicago's "Boss" Flynn's machine never lost an election and was always "in office," inspiring the expression *in like Flynn,* meaning "to have it made." The popularity of movie actor Errol Flynn and his amorous activities helped popularize the phrase in the early 1940s.

in limbo. Something or someone *in limbo* is in an intermediate state or in oblivion. The term derives from the place called Limbo in Roman Catholic theology that is located on the border of Hell, a place where souls reside that cannot enter into Heaven. The Roman Catholic church no longer teaches this doctrine.

in Macy's window. A synonym for the ultimate in public exposure: "If we do that we might as well be in Macy's window." Traditional window displays date back to the early 1880s when the use of plate glass on a wide scale made display windows a standard feature of department stores. Macy's display windows in New York were long the most prominent among them, especially those in their flagship store on West 34th Street, "The World's Largest Store" with over 2.2 million square feet of floor space. In fact, Macy's old 14th Street store in Manhattan was famous for its Christmas displays as far back as the mid-1800s, featuring a collection of toys revolving on a belt.

in medias res. Latin for "in the middle of things," a term often used as a euphemism for "in the midst of sexual intercourse." There is an old story, for example, about the poet son of an Arabian prince who was "caught *in medias res* with the wife of a court officer, who skewered them on the same sword."

in mufti.   In civilian clothes, in contrast with military or other uniforms, or as worn by someone who usually wears a uniform. Any military person, priest, judge, etc., can be said to be *in mufti*. The term apparently derives from the title of Arabian legal advisers called mufti, who were often military men acting as judges.

innings.   *See* HAVE ONE'S INNINGS.

innocuous desuetude.   President Grover Cleveland coined this phrase and first used it in a message to Congress on March 1, 1886. It means "harmless disuse" and describes a law, custom, or anything else long disregarded, something on the junk pile. Said President Cleveland: "After an existence of nearly twenty years of almost innocuous desuetude, these laws are brought forth." Later, Cleveland explained that he thought such sesquipedalian words (*i.e.,* words a foot-and-a-half long) "would please the Western taxpayer," give them something for their money.

inoculate.   *Inoculate* derives from the Latin *inoculare,* "to graft by budding," "implant." The word was first recorded in this sense at the beginning of the 15th century and wasn't used in the medical sense of inoculation, to plant a disease agent or antigen in a person to stimulate disease resistance, until 1722. *See* GRAFT.

in one ear and out the other.   Only slightly changed over the past four centuries, this expression, said of things that make no impression on the mind, dates back to at least 1583, when an annoyed preacher said that his sermon "goes in one ear and out the other." Almost two centuries earlier, in about 1400, the expression is used in the poem "Romaunt of the Rose" in the form of "out at oon er / That in at that other."

insane asylums.   People haven't usually been kind in naming hospitals for the insane (though there have been several euphemisms such as *insane asylum, insane hospital, sanitarium, mental hospital,* and the names of prominent mental hospitals like *Bedlam* and *Creedmore*). Starting with *madhouse* (1687), the synonyms have been mainly derogatory, including *nut house, crazy house, booby hatch, funny house, funny farm, snake pit, cuckoo-nest,* and *puzzle factory.*

insane root.   Banquo says to the witches in *Macbeth:*

> Were such things here as we do speak about?
> Or have we eaten the insane root
> That takes the reason prisoner?

Either henbane (*Hyoscyamus niger*) or poison hemlock (*Conium maculatum*), the hemlock that killed Socrates, is the *insane root* of the ancients that was supposed to deprive anyone who ingested it of his senses.

insect.   *See* BUG.

inseminate.   Our word for "to impregnate," *inseminate* first meant to sow or implant seed into the ground. It was first recorded in English in this sense in 1623, and is derived from the Latin *seminare,* "to sow" or "to plant."

inside track.   *See* HAVE THE INSIDE TRACK.

in state.   In Nigeria, where English is an official language, *in state* means to be pregnant, as in "She is in state five months now." There might be confusion with the last two words of the phrase *to lie in state,* to be exhibited with honor before burial, and *to lie in,* to be confined in childbirth.

insult.   The Latin *insultare,* to jump or trample upon, yielded the English word *insult,* to disrespect, dishonor, desecrate, in the mid-16th century. It is said that the Latin word originally meant to contemptuously leap on the body of a foe killed or felled in battle.

intelligentsia.   Another Russian borrowing. The Latin *intelligere* (*inter,* "between" + *legere,* "to choose"), "to perceive or understand," is the ultimate basis of our word *intelligentsia* for the "intellectual elite," but the word comes to us through the Russian *intelligentsiya,* taken from the Latin. It came into English in the 1920s.

interloper.   The Russia Company, operated by Englishmen, had a virtual monopoly on Russian trade in the late 16th century, but Spanish traders bribed czarist officials in trying to break the monopoly, and the English in propagandizing against them coined the word *interloper* to describe the trespassers, building it from the Latin *inter,* "between," and the English *lope,* "to run."

international.   Eccentric English philosopher Jeremy Bentham coined the much used word *international* in 1780. He is also responsible for *maximize* and *minimize,* and thus the ancestor of a lot of less desirable advertising words ending in "ize."

the Internationale.   The song of revolutionaries the world over today, the "Internationale" was first sung in France, in 1871. It was not the anthem of the French Revolution, as many people believe. *See* MARSEILLAISE.

interrobang.   This is the very newest of punctuation marks, devised by an American typecasting company in the 1970s. A combination question mark and exclamation point, it is used after an expression that could be both a question and exclamation, such as "Where's the fire?!" Resembling an exclamation point superimposed on a question mark, it takes its name from the *interro* in *interrogation* and the printers' slang *bang* for an exclamation point.

interview.   Media interviews can be traced back to 1859, at about the time of John Brown's raid on Harper's Ferry. At this time abolitionist Gerrit Smith gave an interview to a *New York Herald* reporter who remained anonymous. Other sources, however, claim that journalist Anne Royall invented the form in an 1825 story about President John Quincy Adams.

intestinal fortitude.   The head coach of Ohio State University's football team, Dr. John W. Wilce, is said to have invented this word for "guts" in 1915 as "a protest against the lurid language of the gridiron and locker room," *guts* then being considered "improper for drawing-room conversation." They don't make coaches like Dr. Wilce anymore, nor locker rooms so mild.

In Texas the cattle come first, then the men, then the horses and last the women. An old Texas saying quoted by Edna Ferber in *Giant* (1952).

in the arms of Morpheus. *See* MORPHINE.

in the bag. It's usually assumed that this metaphor derives from hunting, where it refers to birds and other small game already safely in the game bag. *Bag* has been used as an abbreviation for *game bag* since at least the 15th century, but the expression *in the bag* is first recorded in 1925. William Bancroft Miller, writing in *Verbatim* (February 1977), offers another explanation, attributing the phrase to cockfighting: "Until comparatively recent years, it was common to transport game chickens to the scene of battle in cloth bags rather than in the comfortable and elaborate carrying cases now in vogue, and the roosters were not removed until the fight was about to begin. A cocker, confident of the prowess of his feathered warrior, would say that victory was *in the bag* for him." Neither theory is supported by quotations and neither explains the sinister implication these words often have, for the expression frequently means "rigged" or "fixed."

in the ballpark. *See* BALLPARK FIGURE.

in the chips. *See* CHIP IN.

in the clutch. A baseball player who performs well in a critical moment of a game has been called a clutch player or clutch hitter for over half a century now. The derivation of the term is unclear but the expression is widely used today outside of sports as well. Someone who performs well in any important or crucial situation is said to be dependable or reliable in the clutch.

In the country (land) of the blind, the one-eyed man is king. This old English proverb has been traced back to the early 1500s, and may be older.

in the doghouse. The expression *in the doghouse*, "out of favor or undergoing punishment," isn't of ancient origin but is an Americanism first recorded toward the end of the 19th century. Possibly the term originated during the African slave trade, when sailors locked the hatches at night, to prevent slaves from escaping, and slept on deck in tiny sleeping cubicles called "doghouses." There is no evidence, however, to support this theory, or any other for that matter.

in the driver's seat. Figuratively, this means to be in control of a situation; usually it implies complete control, too, although of course, no one in any driver's seat has that, considering the vehicle itself, the road, other drivers, and the power natural or supernatural that propels the vehicle. Surprisingly, the expression isn't a modern one, dating back at least 400 years, when the driver drove horses or oxen rather than an automobile.

in the hole. *See* ON DECK.

in the name of the Great Jehovah and the Continental Congress. The traditional words attributed to Ethan Allen when he demanded the surrender of Fort Ticonderoga by the British commander during the Revolutionary War. There is another, better story, however. According to John Pell in *Ethan Allen* (1929): "Professor James D. Butler, of Madison, Wisconsin, has informed me that his grandfather Israel Harris was present and had often told him that Ethan Allen's real language was, 'Come out of here, you damned old rat.' "

in the nick. To Americans *in the nick of time* means "just in time, not a minute too early." One theory holds that the word *nick* here refers to the notches made in a tally, a piece of wood used for reckoning. This doesn't, however, explain other uses of *nick*. In Britain, for example, *in the nick* means to be "in the pink, in good shape," while Australians use *nick* to mean "nude," as in "She posed in the nick."

in the ozone. A phrase probably invented within the last 25 years, *in the ozone* is synonymous with *way out, far out*. The ozonosphere or ozone layer is a region in the upper atmosphere far from Earth.

in the pink. Brewer says *in the pink* for "in the best of health" refers to the flower called the PINK, as in the old saying *the pink of perfection*, which dates back at least to the 18th century. More likely, *in the pink*, first recorded in 1905 as *in the pink of condition*, refers to "the healthy pink of firm flesh." *See also* HUNTING PINK.

in the red. An American term that since the early 1900s has meant "to do business at a loss for a certain period." The term derives from the practice of accountants using red ink to enter debits in a firm's books. *In the black* means operating at a profit.

in there pitching. People who try hard and keep working are *in there pitching*. The baseball-derived term suggests a workhorse pitcher doing his best, allowing a hit or walk or run here and there but diligently getting the job done. Interestingly, the expression is not recorded until the Great Depression, when everyone had to be *in there pitching* to survive. The word *pitcher* in baseball was first recorded in 1854.

in the tub. *See* TAKE A BATH.

in the wings; proscenium. The unseen backstage part on both sides of the stage of a proscenium theater is called the wings. The expression *in the wings* has come to mean someone waiting in the wings, like an actor ready to go onstage, someone available on short notice, as in "At least one presidential candidate is waiting in the wings." *Proscenium* refers to the arch that separates a stage from the auditorium and was once a term for the stage itself.

Into each life some rain must fall. All of us have a little trouble from time to time. The phrase, from Henry Wadsworth Longfellow's poem "The Rainy Day" (1842), is often heard as "Into each life a little rain must fall."

intoxicated. There are more synonyms for *intoxicated* in *Webster's Collegiate Thesaurus* than for any other entry in the book, 46 of them in all. *Intoxicate*, ironically enough, comes from a Greek word meaning poison—*toxikon*, the poison into which war arrows were dipped. Then in the Middle Ages, the Latin *toxicum* became a general term for any poison. This resulted in the English *toxic*, "poisonous," our *intoxicate*, meaning "to poison," becoming limited to the temporarily "poisonous" effects of too much liquor. Which is something to remember the next time someone quips, "Name your own poison."

intransigent.   *Los Intransigentes* was the nickname of a Spanish political party that tried to introduce a form of communism into Spain in 1873, five years after Queen Isabella II had been deposed and the country was without a sovereign. This splinter group, the left wing of a party favoring a republic, called themselves "the volunteers of liberty," but they were dubbed *Intransigentes* (*in*, the Latin for "not," and *transigo*, Latin for "to come to an agreement") because they stubbornly refused to compromise in any way with other political viewpoints. A dictator outlawed the party the following year, and in 1875 Isabella's son Alfonso restored the monarchy, but *Los Intransigentes* lived on. Their name quickly came into English as *Intransigeant*, and then *intransigent*, meaning "any unyielding, inflexible person or doctrine."

introvert.   *See* JUNGIAN.

in two shakes of a lamb's tail.   A lamb can shake its tail twice quite rapidly, apparently more quickly than many animals can shake their tails once, which explains this Americanism, meaning "in hardly any time at all." The expression dates back to the early 1800s and no one knows who coined it. Possibly it is a humorous extension of the older British phrase *in two shakes*, meaning the same, and probably alluding to the quick shaking of a dice box.

Inuit words in English.   There are only about 80,000 speakers of Inuit, but even this little-spoken language has contributed words to the English lexicon, including *kayak*, *igloo*, and *makluk* (a large bearded seal).

invented words.   When Gelett Burgess published his *Burgess Unabridged: A New Dictionary of Words You Have Always Needed* (1914), he offered scores of new words he had invented, none of which caught on and survive today. In fact, the only two of the hundred or so words Burgess coined over his long writing career that we still use are BROMIDE and BLURB. Hundreds of new words are invented every year, but few last more than months. One good example is Mark Twain, who, besides a number of winners, coined these losers, none of which is widely used today: *disenthusem*, *humanbeingship*, *jumbulacious*, *mental telegraphy*, *perhapser*, *psychologizer*, *Shakesperiod*, *soda sequester*, *type girl*, *uncledom*, and *vinegarishly*.

Inverness.   Sherlock Holmes wore one of these warm overcoat-cape combinations, which were named for the Highlands town of Inverness, Scotland, where they were apparently invented one bone-chilling winter in the 1850s. The cape is removable from the coat or cloak.

investigate.   *Investigate* comes from the Latin *investigare*, to track, as when a Roman hunter tracked game. By the 16th century Englishmen were using the word in its present sense of to track down anything, to examine systematically, to observe or inquire.

Io; Europa; Ganymede; Callisto.   These four objects or satellites that endlessly circle the planet Jupiter (the Roman *Jove*) weren't named by Galileo, who discovered them, but by a rival astronomer, Simon Marius, who falsely claimed the discovery. Marius named them after the four objects of the god Jove's sexual desire, even writing a poem to make it easy for all to remember the names: "Io, Europa, the boy Ganymede, and likewise Callisto,/ Aroused to excess the lust of Jove."

iodine.   This common antiseptic is, oddly enough, named after the violet. *Iodine* derives from the Greek word *iodes*, "like a violet," which in turn comes from the Greek *ion*, "violet." The iodine we commonly use is rust-colored, but when heated it forms a dense violet-colored vapor.

I only regret that I have but one life to give for my country.   Supposedly the last words that American spy Nathan Hale said on the gallows before he was hanged by the British. According to the recently discovered diary of British officer Captain Frederick Mackenzie, what he really said was, "It is the duty of every good officer to obey any orders given him by his commander-in-chief." Hale was executed on September 22, 1776. British author Joseph Addison's play *Cato* (1713) has the words "What pity it is that we can die but once to serve our country."

ionosphere.   *See* HEAVISIDE LAYER.

iota.   The *i* or *iota* is the smallest letter in the Greek alphabet, so when we say *not one iota* we are saying "not the smallest amount." The expression is found in Matt. 5:18, with *jot*, a synonym for *iota*, being used. *See* TITTLE.

IOU.   The term *IOU*, for a signed document acknowledging a debt, is an old expression dating back to at least the early 17th century. In 1618 a writer described "fellows" who: "play tricks with their Creditors, who in stead of payments, write I O U, and so scoffe many an honest man out of his goods." *IOU*, of course, stands for "I Owe You."

Iowa.   Nicknamed the *Hawkeye State* (after a resident sharp-eyed Indian chief), our 29th state, which entered the Union in 1846, is so called from the name of the Sioux *Ioways* or *Aiouez*, meaning "sleepy ones." The tribe, however, didn't consider themselves lazy, calling themselves the *Pahoja*, "gray snow." A rival tribe had named them "the sleepy ones."

ipecac.   Ipecac is a medicine made to induce vomiting that is prepared from the roots of the ipecac shrub of tropical America. It is one of the few English words that come from the Tupi Indian language, deriving from the Tupi *ipeh*, low, *kae*, leaves, and *quene*, vomit.

ipicles.   *See* FAST AS LADAS.

IQ. The abbreviation *IQ* for intellience quotience has become widely known since it was first used about 1920. Loosely speaking, it is an intelligence test score obtained by dividing mental age by chronological age and multiplying by 100. So widely known is the term, in fact, that at least one country, Thailand, had adopted the English *IQ* into its language as a word meaning smart or clever, as in "He's IQ."

Iran. *See* IRELAND.

Ireland. The English, no slouches at ethnic slurs, dubbed the urinary organs *Ireland* as far back as the 16th century, the term recorded in Shakespeare's *Comedy of Errors.* A writer on British slavery later explained that the denigration was deserved because Ireland's wet climate made her "The Urinal of the Planets." (For a similar Irish slur on an Englishman, *see* TWISS.) *Ireland* is perhaps the only word left in English that derives from the language of the Iberians, the first inhabitants of the British Isles—so the name of the country might well be the earliest surviving word spoken on British shores. The Iberians probably gave their tribal name to the island of *Iveriu*, which over the years was shortened to *Eiri*, this finally anglicized to *Ireland.* The Iberians, however, may also have named Britain itself. One cannot call either of these words "native" words, though, for the Iberians came to the British Isles from somewhere else in Europe. One scholar, taking *Ireland* or *Erin* back to its ultimate ancestor, says the name comes from the Indo-European *ariyan,* "noble." *Iran* derives from the same source. *See* DOG.

the Ireland hoax. While working as a clerk in a lawyer's office, William Henry Ireland (1777–1835) discovered blank Elizabethan parchments and used them and a faded brown ink he concocted to forge a number of documents purporting to be in the handwriting of William Shakespeare. Ireland, only 17 at the time, claimed that he received the documents from an old "gentleman of fortune" who "had many old papers which had descended to him from his ancestors" but wanted to remain anonymous. When Ireland's father, an engraver and bookseller, pronounced the first documents authentic and notified scholars of the find, his forger-son proceeded to turn out scores of Shakespeare documents, including letters to the Earl of Southampton, a "Profession of Protestant Faith," and even a love letter to Anne Hathaway enclosing a lock of hair. The young man published his findings in book form and exhibited them, charging admission and gulling people like Pitt, Burke, Boswell, and the Prince of Wales. Ireland's masterworks, however, were two new "Shakespeare" plays: *Vortigern and Rowena* and *Henry II.* Playwright Richard Sheridan actually purchased *Vortigern* for £300 and half of any royalties, producing it at Drury Lane on April 2, 1796. By this time many people had sensed that Ireland's "discoveries" were forgeries, and the play proved it. A complete fiasco, it was treated as a joke by the actors and practically hooted off the stage by the audience, never to be played again. Its failure and an exposé by Shakespearean scholar Edmund Malone at the end of the year prompted Ireland to confess his forgeries in print. The only punishment he received was the condemnation of literary critics, and he went on to write several forgettable novels.

iris. Iris, the Greek goddess of the rainbow, gives her name to the colored portion of the eye called the iris and the iris flower, which has varieties in all the colors of the rainbow. Orrisroot is a powder used in perfumes and other products that is made from the roots of certain irises.

Irish. No one would think that those with "the gift of tongues" could be bested when it came to the English language. But the Irish have been done more harm than ever they inflicted. In fact, many expressions bearing their name seem too good to have been coined by anyone but an Irishman himself, as indeed some undoubtably were. The English began this verbal war on the Hibernians with expressions like *Irish mail,* a sack of potatoes; *Irish draperies,* cobwebs; *Irish lantern,* the moon; *Irish wedding,* the emptying of a cesspool; *Irish hurricane,* a flat sea; *Irish battleship,* a barge; *Irish bull,* any obvious contradiction in terms; and *Irish blunder,* which Swift defined as "to take the noise of brass for thunder." But when the Irish emigrated to America, the other immigrants, old and new, did worse by them, appropriating some ancient expressions and adding some new ones. *Irish evidence* here was perjury; an *Irish beauty,* a girl with two black eyes; an *Irish diamond,* a rock; an *Irish spoon,* a spade; an *Irish apple,* a potato; an *Irish bouquet,* a brickbat; an *Irish promotion,* a demotion; an *Irish dividend,* an assessment; *Irish confetti,* bricks; and an *Irishman's dinner,* a fast. It all was enough for them to *get their Irish up,* which they occasionally did, though it didn't hurt as much as the common No Irish Need Apply signs. Somehow all the favorable coinings didn't help matters much. These include *Irish daisy, Irish potato, Irish moss, Irish setter, Irish stew, Irish terrier, Irish wolfhound* and, of course, *Irish whiskey* and *Irish coffee. See* GAELIC WORDS IN ENGLISH.

Irish pennants. Nautical slang often reflects hostility toward particular groups of people. This is the case with *Irish pennants,* which originated as British naval slang for untidy ropes hanging from the rigging aloft. In another age, when the Dutch were England's major foes on the high seas, *Dutch pennants* meant the same thing.

Irish wolfhound. The tallest of all dogs is also one of the oldest, having been used by the Celts for hunting wolves at least as early as 273 B.C. These large, powerful dogs have a rough shaggy coat and stand up to 32 inches at the shoulder, more than the heftier Great Dane (which was probably bred from it). The smallest of dogs is the CHIHUAHUA. *See* SALUKI.

iron curtain. Winston Churchill did not invent this expression, as is commonly believed. Many pages have been devoted to tracking down its originator, but the first person known to use the phrase in a political sense was Queen Elizabeth of Belgium, who said in 1914: "Between [Germany] and me there is now a bloody iron curtain which has descended forever." Before this, H. G. Wells referred to a man held incommunicado by the police as "held behind an iron curtain" in his story "The Food of the Gods" (1904). After Belgium's Queen Elizabeth, several military writers used *iron curtain* with reference to a curtain of artillery fire. Then, in 1945, Nazi propaganda minister Joseph Göbbels employed the phrase in the same sense as Churchill would use it eight months later, with reference to Russia, and so did German statesman Count Schwerin von

Krosigk. The expression refers of course to the impenetrable secrecy with which happenings in the Soviet Union and countries occupied by it were concealed from the world, the image that inspired the saying probably being the iron fireproof curtains long used in European theaters. Five months before Churchill made his famous Iron Curtain speech on March 5, 1946, at Westminster College in Fulton, Missouri ("From Stettin in the Baltic to Trieste in the Adriatic, an iron curtain has descended across the continent . . ."), his countryman Sir St. Vincent Troubridge, a former British staff officer of SHAEF, had written an article in the *Sunday Empire News* headed "An Iron Curtain Across Europe." *See* BAMBOO CURTAIN.

iron man. *See* LOU GEHRIG'S DISEASE.

iron men and wooden ships. Old salts used to say this of the old days: "When I went to sea there were iron men and wooden ships; now there are iron ships and wooden men." The phrase probably dates back to the 18th century.

irons in the fire. *See* SECOND CHILDHOOD.

Iroquois. These Indians often ended their speeches with "Hiroquoue!"—meaning "I have spoken with strong emotion!" To the ears of French explorers in North America this sounded like *Iroquois*, the name they gave to the Indian tribe.

Irrepressible Conflict. A name for the American Civil War coined by Secretary of State William Seward in 1858.

isabel; isabelline. Traditionally, this lady's soiled underwear gives her name to the brownish-yellow or grayish color *isabel*. The full story is rarely told. Archduchess Isabella of Austria was the daughter of Spain's Philip II and his fourth wife, Anne of Austria, daughter of Austrian ruler Maximilian II. In 1598 King Philip married Isabella to Austrian Archduke Albert, and as part of a plan to reconquer the United Provinces, handed over the whole of the Netherlands to the newly married couple as a sovereign state. Philip died that same year, but his war continued, which is where Isabella's underwear makes its contribution to history. Supposedly, Isabella vowed never to remove her underwear, even for washing, until husband Albert took the city of Ostend by siege. But Ostend's Flemish defenders had little sympathy for either Isabella or Albert. They held out for three years, playing a glorious role in the Dutch struggle for independence. Ostend was in ruins and 40,000 Spanish lives had been lost before the Belgian port city surrendered in 1604. After three years Isabella's underwear certainly must have been *isabelline*, and she might have worn it even longer, for we are told that Albert did not win Ostend at all. General Ambrogio Spinola captured the city. Perhaps this led to jokes about why Albert and Isabella had no children, but, at any rate, the couple ruled wisely after a 12-year truce was effected in 1609, the war resuming again at the truce's expiration. Albert died in 1621 and Isabella 13 years later. Some authorities, such as the *Oxford English Dictionary*, flatly reject the dirty-underwear hypothesis, while others, like *Webster's*, admit it with a cautious "It is said," and with still others it washes well.

I say! This British exclamation of surprise or astonishment is thought to be typical of Englishmen by most Americans but is considered rather old-fashioned in England, though it is still heard there. The expression probably dates back before the late 18th century.

I say it's spinach and I say the hell with it. E. B. White wrote the caption that became this catchphrase, for a 1928 Carl Rose cartoon in the *New Yorker* showing a spoiled little girl who rejects her mother's offer of broccoli with these words— which have come to mean, "When I'm indulging my prejudices I don't want to be confused with facts." The phrase's abbreviated form, *spinach*, however, means the same as boloney, malarkey, bull, etc.

Is everybody happy? Some will remember this catchphrase as the cry of American song and dance man Ted Lewis working the audience, meaning "Is everybody satisfied with the show?" The words certainly go back long before 1905, when the American song "Is Everybody Happy?" appeared. According to Partridge, "it has been the traditional cry of the red-nosed comedian [bidding for] the raucous chorus [of affirmation] guaranteed to come rolling back at him from the stalls . . ."

Ishmael. An *Ishmael* is an outcast, which is one reason why Herman Melville gave the name to his narrator in *Moby Dick*. Ishmael was the son of Abraham and Hagar; he and his mother were banished to the wilderness by Sarah, where an angel predicted that he would forever be at odds with society (Gen. 21:9–21). The Muslims, however, do not share this biblical tradition, considering Ishmael their progenitor.

I should have stood in bed. This still-heard expression was coined by fight manager Joe Jacobs after he left his sickbed to watch the 1935 World Series (*see* WE WUZ ROBBED). *Stood* for stayed is first recorded in a Dorothy Parker short story "Yussel the Muscle" (1939) and dates back farther than that. *I should have stood in bed* was used as the title of a 1941 song and a 1942 play was entitled *They Should Have Stood in Bed*. "I Should Have Stood in My Neighborhood" was a 1943 song.

isinglass. *Isinglass*, derived from the Dutch *huizenblas*, "sturgeon's bladder," is a semitransparent substance made from that fish's bladder. Isinglass is still employed in cooking as a form of gelatin used as a thickening agent, though it was once much more popular.

Island of the Sun. A poetic name for Sicily in ancient mythology. Here Helius the Sun god (the Roman Sol) kept his oxen. In his light-giving chariot pulled by white horses Helius climbed the vault of Heaven, descending every evening in the west. Sicily was also called Trinacria by the ancients.

Islands of the Blessed. *See* ELYSIAN FIELDS.

Isle of Rhodes; Colossus of Rhodes. The Greek island of Rhodes in the Aegean Sea off the southwest coast of Turkey is called *Rhodos* in Greek. It takes its name from the *erods* (snakes) on the island. The Colossus of Rhodes was one of the SEVEN WONDERS OF THE WORLD. It was a great bronze statue of Apollo that stood at the entrance to the Isle of Rhodes harbor.

Isle of Tears. *See* ELLIS ISLAND.

islets (islands) of Langerhans. German anatomist Paul Langerhans (1847–88) may be the only person to have a group of small islands named after him. However, these islets are endocrine cells throughout the pancreas that secrete insulin and glucagon, the malfunction of which causes diabetes. Dr. Langerhans was, in 1869, the first to describe the cells.

I smell a rat. No one can say with irrefragable certainty how this expression originated, but the allusion may be to a cat smelling a rat while being unable to see it. Terriers and other rat-hunting dogs could also be the inspiration. The expression dates back to about 1780, but long before that *to smell* was used figuratively for "to suspect or discern intuitively," as when Shakespeare writes "Do you smell a fault?" in *King Lear*. St. Hilarion, the Syrian hermit who died about 371, could allegedly tell a person's vices or virtues simply by smelling his person or clothing. Some people really have been able to smell a rat. One legendary underground worker for the New York City Transit Authority was renowned for smelling out dead rats, the odor of which has ruined many a business. John "Smelly" Kelly, also known as "Sniffy," patrolled the New York City subway system for years, his uncanny sense of smell enabling him to detect everything from gas leaks to the decomposing corpses of poisoned rats that crawled into the walls of stores adjoining the subway. Smelly Kelly was one of those rare people who could say with certainty, "I smell a rat."

I swan. People who say *I swan!* in historical novels are merely saying "I swear!" The old expression derives from British dialect and is a corruption of either "I'se warrant!" or "I'se warn you!"

I swear I'll kwill you. *See* I'LL TELL YOU WHAT I'M GONNA DO.

it. The little workhorse pronoun *it* derives from the Anglo-Saxon *hit*, neuter gender of "he." Though *it* is used to describe anything sexless, among other things, *it* also means sex appeal in slang usage. Clara Bow was Hollywood's *It girl*, but the first use of *it* to represent sex appeal was in Rudyard Kipling's *Mrs. Bathurst* (1904) when he writes: "'Tisn't beauty, so to speak, nor good talk necessarily. It's just It. Some women'll stay in a man's memory if they once walked down a street." The expression became very popular in the late 1920s when Clara Bow starred in the 1926 movie version of Elinor Glyn's novel *It*. As the *It girl* Miss Bow was one of a long line of types loved by American men, including the *Gibson girl*, the *Ziegfeld girl*, the *Vamp* (Theda Bara), the FLAPPER, the *oomph girl*, the *sweater girl*, the *pinup girl*, the *Playmate*, and the *Bunny*. *It* may be somewhat euphemistic as well, as it is used in slang as a synonym for a chamber pot and the male and female sexual organs. Calling the unlucky player who does all the work *you're it* in a game of tag or hide-and-go-seek dates back to about 1888. In modern slang this *it* has also become someone who is appointed to do a certain job, usually an undesirable one, in an office or elsewhere. In Britain and the U.S. it has become shorthand or short tongue for Italian vermouth, as in "I'll have a gin and it." *See also* ITS.

Italian. There has been much controversy recently about the use of the word *Mafia*, which recalls prohibition days in Chicago, when *Italian* was used so frequently in describing gunmen that newspapers bowed to Italian objections and, iron-ically, began to use *Sicilian* instead. In reality, Italians have been abused as much as any group in the country, but the adjective *Italian* is attached to few derogatory expressions. Aside from the *Italian malady* (*see* FRENCH DISEASE), an ancient synonym for syphilis used no more, it is hard to think of even one popular expression defaming the name. *Italian aster, Italian clover, Italian honeysuckle*—all innocent terms describing innocuous things. Compared with groups like the Dutch and Irish, the Italians have indeed fared well, linguistically. Sometimes home gardeners curse *Italian ryegrass*, not realizing that it is an annual grass that won't come up the next year, but that's about the extent of *Italian's* infamy. *See* DAGO for a different story.

Italian words in English. The contributions of Italian to English are vast, including three-quarters of our musical terms. Examples are: alarm, million, ducat, florin, brigand, bark (ship), tunny (fish), race, nuncio, artisan, doge, magnifico, mountebank, umbrella, gondola, carnival, mustachio, attack, cavalier, musket, squadron, battalion, citadel, bankrupt, contraband, carat, cornice, pedestal, piazza, stucco, portico, grotto, balcony, corridor, sentinel, catacomb, dado, concert, madrigal, viol da gamba, fugue, pastel, fresco, volcano, sonnet, stanza, canto, caprice, regatta, lagoon, balloon, muslin, mercantile, risk, opera, serenade, sonata, spinet, largo, piano, intaglio, profile, vista, miniature, cartoon, chiaroscuro, burlesque, ghetto, incognito, broccoli, sketch, casino, mafia, vendetta, malaria, influenza, bronze, area, lava, braccia, travertine, mezzanine, figurine, soprano, trombone, viola, cantata, trio, concerto, aria, violin, quartet, finale, andante, adagio, crescendo, tempo, bravo, piccolo, prima donna, sextet, scherzo, contrapuntal, fiasco, imbroglio, tirade. Italian words that have entered American English include: spaghetti, pasta, lasagne, tortoni, spumoni, antipasto, minestrone, Chianti, provolone, and many other food and drink terms. AMERICA itself, named after Amerigo Vespucci, could also be said to be an Italian word, as could the District of Columbia, from Columbus's name. *See also* DAGO; SPIC; WOP.

italic type. *Italic type*, in which the first two words of this sentence are printed, was invented about 1500 by the noted Italian printer Aldus Manutius, the Latin name of Teobaldo Mannucci. There is a tradition that the printer modeled his invention on the fine Italian hand of the poet Petrarch, but the Italian hand, a beautiful cursive style, had been widely used for copying manuscripts since its development by scholars in the 12th century. In fact, it was so well known that *a fine Italian hand* had already become an ironic synonym for the scheming Machiavellian politics of assassination by stiletto for which Italian nobles were notorious. Manutius, also a classical scholar, had his type cast by Francesco Griffi of Bologna and in 1501 first used it to publish an edition of Virgil, dedicating the book to his native Italy. Because of that Aldine Press dedication, the new slanting style—the first type that wasn't upright—came to be known as *Italicus*, which means "Italian" or "italic." Today words are *italicized* in print mainly to give them emphasis, and to indicate titles and foreign-language words. This is not the case in the King James or Authorized Version of the Bible, however, a fact that creates confusion for many people. Words italicized in the Bible should not be emphasized in reading, for they merely indicate that the original translators, who considered the text sacred, arbitrarily supplied a word not existing in the text in order to make its meaning clearer—similar to the way bracketed words are used within quotes today.

itch. Itching of various bodily parts has been thought to indicate different cravings for centuries. An itching foot, for example, purportedly means a craving for travel, and itching lips mean a craving for a kiss, or that you're about to be kissed. In *Julius Caesar* Shakespeare used an itching palm as a synonym for the readiness to take a bribe, making Brutus say to Cassius "... you yourself/Are much condemned to have an itching palm." Shakespeare was the first to record the words, but long before him an itching palm probably signified a craving for money or was taken as an omen that a person was about to receive money from an unexpected source. An *itch* has been synonymous for sexual desire since 1660. *See also* SEVEN-YEAR ITCH.

itching ears. *See* BURNING EARS.

itchy trigger finger. To have an itchy trigger finger is to be quick on the trigger, to be quick to act, itching to go, impetuous or even alert. The American expression was first recorded in 1903 as *to have trigger itch*. Within 30 years or so it took its present form.

it doesn't go on all fours. Unlike similar Madison Avenue expressions, this saying, meaning "something isn't quite right," goes back to the ancient Latin proverb *Omnis comparatio claudicat*, which literally means "every simile limps," but which British historian Thomas Babington Macaulay translated as "No simile can go on all fours."

It is harder for a rich man to enter the kingdom of heaven than for a camel to go through the eye of a needle. There may be some sense in this last part of this ancient proverb. In ancient Middle Eastern walled towns the rear gate was called the Needle's Eye, after its narrow rise and pointed top. A camel could pass through this Needle's Eye, though with extreme difficulty, by kneeling down. It has been suggested that this is the source of the expression, an equivalent of which is found in the Koran ("The impious shall find the ages of heaven shut; nor shall he enter till a camel shall pass through the eye of a needle").

it might have been. It is said that American poet John Greenleaf Whittier (1807–92) penned his famous couplet because he never married, having devoted his life to several careers:

> Of all sad words of tongue and pen
> The saddest are these: It might have been.

it rains on the just and unjust alike; scholium. The phrase above can be traced to the biblical (Matt. 5:45): "He ... sendeth rain on the just and on the unjust ..." A *scholium* on the verse by Charles, Baron Bowen (1835–94) has it a little differently:

> The rain it raineth on the just
> And also on the unjust fella:
> But chiefly on the just, because
> The unjust steals the just's
> umbrella!

Scholium means "an explanatory note or comment," deriving from the Greek for "school" and first recorded in the early 16th century.

I trust it's nothing trivial. In his *City Editor* (1934), Stanley Walker wrote of another city editor, Charles E. Chapin, who was widely respected for his professionalism but generally hated for his cold-hearted efficient methods. Chapin fired 108 men when city editor of the *Evening World*. When *World* reporter Irvin S. Cobb heard he was ill one day, he remarked, "I trust it's nothing trivial." Chapin died in 1930 in Sing Sing prison, where he was sent after killing his wife.

its. There is a tale of literary ratiocination involving this little word. Before the 17th century *its* wasn't used to indicate the possessive case, *it* and *his* serving this purpose (e.g., "For love and devocion toward God also hath *it* infancie ..."; "Learning hath his infancy ..."). When he was only 16, English poet Thomas Chatterton (1752–70) wrote a number of poems purporting to be the work of an imaginary 15th-century monk, Thomas Rowley. These poems were published after the destitute, despairing Chatterton committed suicide by drinking arsenic, and they were hailed as works of poetic genius. But critic Thomas Tyrwbitt later revealed that the poems were forgeries, finding, among other errors, that one of Chatterton's lines read: "Life and its goods I scorn." *See also* IT.

It's a great life if you don't weaken. Often said derisively or ironically after something has gone wrong. Probably an Americanism, the phrase dates back to World War I and is commonly heard today.

It's all in a day's work. Usually said by someone ironically, after performing a difficult task. The expression was common back in the 18th century, but no one knows who coined it.

It's all over but the shouting. Victory is certain. The expression seems to have appeared in print for the first time in 1842, when a Welsh sportswriter used it, but it may have its roots in local elections settled by voice vote in rural England. These elections, associated with great noise, came to be called "shoutings." There is no proof of this, but perhaps some candidate or observer of the day was so sure of the outcome of a "shouting," so certain of victory, that he remarked "It's all over but the shouting" and the phrase passed into popular usage.

It's all worth it, including the final crash. According to the film *White Hunter, Black Heart* (1994), this is a mantra among pilots, particularly bush pilots in Africa. It could date back 50 years or more.

It's a naive domestic burgundy without any breeding but I think you'll be amused by its presumptions. This originated as the caption under a James Thurber drawing of a pretentious oenologist offering a glass to a friend. It is an expression that has been used jokingly by many a host pretending to be a "wine expert" while dispensing a $3.99 special.

It's a new ball game. Since about 1940 Americans have been using this catchphrase to mean "What's past is past, we start over from here." Though it could have come from several sports, the saying almost certainly has its origins in baseball and sounds like something a baseball announcer may have spontaneously invented. The expression is often "It's a whole new ball game."

It's chess, not checkers. It's complicated, with no easy answer to a question, chess being a much more difficult game than checkers. This relatively recent phrase is an Americanism that has been used by government officials answering the questions of reporters at press conferences.

It's Greek to me. I don't understand any of it; it's totally confusing. The linguist Charles Berlitz, grandson of Maximilian Berlitz, founder of the famed Berlitz language schools, has noted that the Italians say, "You're speaking Turkish"; the Polish say, "I'm hearing a Turkish sermon"; the Russians say, "That's Chinese grammar"; the Spanish say, "That's Chinese to me"; and the Germans say, "That seems like Spanish to me."

It's how you played the game. Sportswriter Grantland Rice, who coined the term the FOUR HORSEMEN to describe Notre Dame's famous backfield in an account of a Notre Dame–Army game ("Outlined against a blue-gray October sky, the Four Horsemen rode again . . .") is also responsible for *it's how you played the game*. The much-loved writer, who died in 1954 at the age of 73, first used the expression in a poem he published in one of his "The Sportlight" columns:

> When the One Great Scorer comes
> To mark against your name,
> He writes—not that you won or lost—
> But how you played the game.

It smells of the lamp. *See* BURNING THE MIDNIGHT OIL.

It's naughty but it's nice. A catchphrase that isn't heard much anymore, the expression refers to sexual intercourse. It comes from the song "It's Naughty But It's Nice" popularized by U.S. singer Minnie Schult in the 1890s.

It's not cricket. *See* CRICKET.

It's not over till the fat lady sings. Things are never over until they're over. The expression is a contraction of the older "The opera's never over till the fat lady sings."

It's not the size of the dog in the fight, it's the size of the fight in the dog. An old Texas proverb that is still frequently heard.

It's not what it's cracked up to be. *To crack* was standard English for "to boast or brag" until about 1700. Today this sense of the word is only found in the expression above, which can refer to a person as well as a thing. Davy Crockett was the first to use the phrase when he wrote in 1835 that "Martin Van Buren is not the man he's cracked up to be," an opinion of the president that history has affirmed.

It's the only ballgame in town. *See* THAT'S THE BALLGAME.

It's the pits. Grape pits, orange pits, etc. contributed nothing to this relatively recent derogatory slang expression, which describes something of the worst order, though you might suspect that the bitter, unpalatable pits of a fruit would logically have something to do with the term. *It's the pits* was originally junkie talk from "Needle Parks" across the country, the armpits being among the last and most painful places a drug addict can shoot dope when the rest of his body is pocked and diseased, the blood vessels collapsed.

It worked; I am become death. Physicist Robert Oppenheimer recalled that after he and his brother watched the explosion of the first atomic bomb at Los Alamos on July 16, 1945, he "remembered the line from the Hindu scripture, the *Bhagavad Gita*: 'I am become death, the destroyer of worlds.' " However, according to Greg Herken's *Brotherhood of the Bomb* (2001), Oppenheimer's brother says these words came some time after the fact. What Oppenheimer really said at the moment was, "It worked!"

I vant to be alone. Aside from some GOLDWYNISMS, this may be the single most famous quotation to come out of Hollywood, partly because it is a sentiment uncharacteristic of most film stars. Too bad that Greta Garbo didn't say it. The legendary actress has made it clear for history that what she really said was: "I want to be *let* alone."

I've got to see a man about a dog. A euphemism for "I've got to go to the bathroom" that people use to excuse themselves, often abruptly. In its sense of "to urinate" the expression is British in origin, dating back to 1867. In the U.S. it was first recorded in 1942, when it meant to go for a drink: "[Got to] go see a dog—a dog about a man or a man about a dog." But this American term for getting a drink is much older in the expression *to go see a man*, recorded in an 1867 baseball magazine: ". . . the rest of our nine having gone to see a man there was nobody to take the bat."

Ivory soap. Probably the only soap named from the Bible. In 1879, one of Proctor & Gamble's executives was inspired in his coinage by Psalm *45:* "All the garments smell of myrrh, and aloes, and cassia, out of the ivory palaces, whereby they have made thee glad."

ivory tower. In the *Song of Solomon* the poet sings that his beloved's neck is "as a tower of ivory," but the phrase in its modern sense has nothing else to do with biblical poetry. French literary critic Charles-Augustin Sainte-Beuve used *un tour d'ivoire* in 1837 to charge that romantic poet Alfred de Vigny evaded the responsibilities of life by retiring to an *ivory tower*. Whether the charge was justified or not, the image did evoke someone sitting cool and elegantly detached, above it all and looking down on life. The phrase has become a cliché, especially when applied to scholars or intellectuals. It is seldom used anymore in a kind sense, that is, to indicate a place of refuge from the world's strivings and posturings.

ivy. The ivy of the Greeks bore golden berries and was probably not the plant we call ivy today. Thought to prevent drunkenness, it was also given as a wreath to the winners of athletic contests. *Hedera helix*, the common English ivy so widely cultivated in temperate climates, is regarded as a symbol of everlasting life because it remains green in all seasons.

Ivy League. The colleges referred to as the *Ivy League* are Harvard, Yale, Princeton, Dartmouth, Cornell, Brown, Columbia, and the University of Pennsylvania. They are all "old-line institutions," with thick-vined, aged ivy covering their walls, and the designation at first applied specifically to their football teams. Sportswriter Caswell Adams coined the term in the mid-thirties. At the time Fordham University's football team was among the best in the East. A fellow journalist compared Columbia and Princeton to Fordham, and Adams replied, "Oh they're just Ivy League," recalling later that he said this "with complete humorous disparagement in mind."

I Want You! The words on the most famous recruiting poster of World War I, which showed Uncle Sam looking out and pointing at the viewer. It was by American artist and writer James Montgomery Flagg (1877–1960).

I would like my roses to see you. *See* THE LAST ROSE OF SUMMER.

I wouldn't know him from Adam's off ox. *See* ADAM.

IWW. The initials of the "Wobblies," a labor organization important in the early years of this century, do not stand for International Workers of the World, as many people think. The organization was the Industrial Workers of the World.

ixnay. *See* PIG LATIN.

Izvestia. *See* PRAVDA.

J

J. The letter *j*, along with *v*, came into the language in post-Shakespearean times, about 1630, making it one of the two youngest letters in the English alphabet. Before this it had shared its form with *i*.

jabberwocky. In its 28 lines Lewis Carroll's immortal nonsense poem "Jabberwocky" has contributed at least four new words of common usage to the English language, more than any other poem by far. *Jabberwocky* itself means "nonsense or gibberish"; a "bandersnatch" is an imaginary wild fierce animal or a person who is a menace or a nuisance; "galumph" (from *gallop* + *triumphant*) means to move heavily or clumsily; and "chortle" (from *chuckle* + *snort*) means to chuckle or utter with glee. Cases could also be made for *frabjous, frumious, slithy,* and other words in the poem, though these haven't yet been admitted to most dictionaries.

jack. *Jack*, for money in general, is an Americanism first recorded in 1859, but the expression is probably older, possibly deriving from the expression *to make one's jack*, "to succeed in one's endeavors," first attested in 1778. This expression, in turn, may come from the British slang *jack*, for "a farthing and a counter used at gaming tables," which dates back to about 1700.

jackanapes. Applied to any pretentious upstart who apes his betters, the word *jackanapes* probably comes from the nickname of William de la Pole, duke of Suffolk. *Jack* was a common name for a tame male ape in England at the time (attached to the word, as it was to *jackrabbit, jackass,* and others), and Suffolk's coat of arms bore the clog and chain of a trained monkey. When, in 1450, the duke was arrested and beheaded at sea off Dover for alleged treason against Henry VI, he was derisively styled "the Ape-clogge" and later won the nickname Jack Napes, or Jacknapes. The ending might mean "of Naples," the source of apes brought to England in the early 15th century, but there is little doubt that the word earned its popularity and present meaning through Suffolk's nickname, which was even recorded in a satirical song of the day.

Jack and Jill. Jack and Jill / went up the hill / to fetch a pail of water / Jack fell down and broke his crown / and Jill came tumbling after. The most familiar of nursery rhymes has several most unfamiliar explanations. One has Jack and Jill being Hjuki and Bil of an older Scandinavian rhyme. Another has Jack and Jill as Empson and Dudley, the executed ministers of Henry VIII. A third explanation describes Jack and Jill as young lovers, with Jill, not Jack, being the one who "broke her crown," that is, lost her virginity at the top of the hill.

Jack Armstrong, the all-American boy. Jack Armstrong, and Frank Meriwell before him, seem to have no counterpart today on the airwaves, unless television's Hardy Boys qualify. "Jack Armstrong, the All-American Boy" was presented afternoons, right after school, by "Wheaties—Breakfast of Champions," during the thirties and early forties. No more than an animated ideal, he often inspired cynical jokes, but the name of this Wheaties-eating hero certainly became part of the language, frequently as a kind of sarcastic description for someone too square or goody-goody, in the language of the time. I had thought Jack's name might have been suggested by the real-life bully Jack Armstrong, who lost that legendary wrestling match with young Abe Lincoln and later became his friend. But it appears that General Mills (Wheaties) executive Sammy Gale had roomed with a real Jack Armstrong in college and decided to use his name for the program's hero because it seemed to convey "all-American virtues of courage, a sense of humor, and the championing of ideals." Jack Lawrence Armstrong, the real Jack Armstrong, the son of a retired British Army officer, moved to the U.S. from Canada at the age of four and later received a civil engineering degree from the University of Minnesota. He was a much-decorated army air force officer during World War II and later served on the Atomic Energy Commission and worked for the Apollo and Gemini space programs. He died in 1985, aged 74.

the jackass express; jackass mail. Any stagecoach pulled by mules in the early American West was called *the jackass express. Jackass mail* was the name used for the mail that was carried on the jackass express.

Jack Dempsey. The Amazonian fish named after the former world heavyweight champion is described as a "very aggressive species," although "the fighting between males . . . is ritualized."

Jack Frost. *Jack Frost* has been the personification of frost or cold weather since at least 1826, when the term is first recorded in a British sporting magazine.

jackfruit. The enormous edible fruit of this tropical tree in the mulberry family often weighs up to 70 pounds. The fruit of *Artocarpus integrifolia* is perhaps the largest tree fruit known, far larger than that of its close relative the breadfruit tree (made famous by Captain Bligh). *See* BLIGHIA SAPIDA.

Jack Horner. "He put in his thumb and pulled out a plum / And said, 'What a good boy am I!' " The Jack Horner of the nursery rhyme is supposed to have been, in reality, steward to the abbot of Glastonbury at the time that the monasteries were being dissolved in England. Jack somehow obtained deeds to the Manor of Mells in the area, either by subterfuge or, as the popular story states, when he found the papers hidden in a pie he was delivering from the abbot to Henry VIII. By this account, he lifted the crust, put in his thumb, and pulled out the "plum," becoming owner of the property himself. This may be the only nursery rhyme based on fact. In any event, the real Jack Horner's descendants have owned the manor for generations.

Jack-in-the-pulpit. The upright spadix of *Arisaema triphyllum* is arched over by a green or striped spathe, which to early American settlers made it look like a man (Jack) standing in a pulpit, resulting in the common name *Jack-in-the-pulpit*. In parts of Great Britain it is known, perhaps more aptly, as "priest's pintle," the latter word meaning "penis."

Jack Johnson. John Arthur (Jack) Johnson, his memory recently revived by the play *The Great White Hope*, loudly proclaimed that he reigned as the first black world heavyweight champion in 1908 when he KO'd Englishman Tommy Burns—though his title claim was disputed and not settled until he demolished Jim Jeffries, the original great white hope, in 1910. Johnson held the title until 1915, when giant Jess Willard knocked him out in 26 rounds in Havana, Cuba. The American fighter had often been called the "Big Smoke" in the United States, "smoke" being common slang at the time for Negro. For this reason, and because he was so powerful a man, the German 5.9 howitzer, its shell, and its shell burst were named after Johnson. A formidable weapon, whose shells emitted thick black smoke upon exploding, the Jack Johnson saw action against the Allies during World War I, when Johnson's name was prominent in the news for his fights and love affairs. Johnson, in fact, had fled to Europe in 1913 after being convicted of violating the Mann Act, unjustly or not. The great boxer died in 1946, aged 68.

Jack Ketch. Jack Ketch, appointed public executioner in 1663, was generally regarded as a clumsy, barbaric bungler who had taken several strokes to sever William, Lord Russell's head after he moved slightly when the axe was falling. He later apologized for his clumsiness, explaining that Russell did not "dispose himself as was most suitable" and that he had been disturbed while taking aim. No one believed him though, and his name became a mark of execration long before he died in 1683—"There stands Jack Kitch, the son of a bitch" went one contemporary rhyme. Of all the public executioners who hung commoners and beheaded nobles his name would be remembered longest, given, as Macaulay wrote, "to all who have succeeded him in his odious office." *See also* H.

jackknife. The ubiquitous American jackknife may take its name from the earlier Scottish *jocktilig*, a clasp knife named for its original manufacturer, Frenchman Jacques de Liège. A respected Scottish historian traced the word to this source in 1776, but modern scholars have been unable to confirm his derivation. *See* PENKNIFE.

Jack of all trades and master of none. The eloquent term for *a Jack of all trades and master of none* is a *sciolist*, which is Latin for "smatterer," and means someone having a smattering of knowledge, a little learning. *Jack of all trades and master of none* extends the little learning to a lot of things. The expression is first recorded in 1618 as *Jack of all trades* and seems to have been a complimentary term for someone who could do any kind of work. But within a century the work of *Jack of all trades* was being disparaged as not expert enough (specialization becoming more important every year) and by at least 1878 the derogatory expression *Jack of all trades and master of none* was being used.

jackpot. *See* HIT THE JACKPOT.

jackrabbit. An abbreviation of *jackass rabbit*, the large hare of North America so named because of its long jackass-like ears and legs. *Jackass-rabbit* is first recorded in 1847 by a traveler in the West: "[We] started a number of hares (called Jackass rabbits) and had no little amusement in witnessing some animated runs." Within 15 years the same hares were being called jackrabbits. They were also called mule rabbits.

Jack Robinson. *As quick as you can say Jack Robinson* has no connection with Jackie Robinson, the first black major league baseball player, though he was quick enough to beat out many a bunt and steal many a base. Notable attempts have been made to trace this 18th-century British phrase, all unsuccessful. One popular explanation, first advanced by Grose, is that the saying has its origin in the habit a certain Jack Robinson had of paying extraordinarily quick visits to his friends, the gentleman leaving even before his name could be announced. But *Jack Robinson* was probably used in the phrase simply because it is a very common name in England and is easy to pronounce.

Jack Russell terrier. English country parson John Russell (1795–1883) was an avid foxhunter who rode to the hounds in his native Devon until he died at the age of 87. Though Oscar Wilde would have taken exception (*see* IN AT THE KILL), most everyone liked Jack Russell or "The Sporting Parson" and a famous strain of hunting terrier was named in his honor.

Jackson Haines. The well-known sitting-spin of figure skating is called the Jackson Haines, after American skater Jackson Haines (1840–79), a former dancer, who is largely responsible for creating modern figure skating by applying dance techniques to the sport.

Jackson Hole, Wyoming. *See* HOLE.

Jacksonian democracy, etc. Jacksonism is the term for the political principles and policies advocated by Andrew Jackson, seventh president of the United States, and his followers. Old Hickory, so called because he was as tough as hickory wood, commanded troops in the War of 1812. Elected to the presidency in 1829, General Jackson served two terms, espousing a widespread Jacksonian democracy while vigorously opposing nullification and the national Bank of the United States. His famous "kitchen Cabinet," the first of its kind, was simply a group of intimate advisers, and by adopting the "spoils system," the granting of political jobs and favors to loyal supporters, he established a well-knit Democratic Party but intensified evils that were not removed until the Civil Service came into being half a century later. Jackson Day, January 8, is a legal holiday in Louisiana, celebrating his victory at the Battle of New Orleans in 1815. Jackson boots, crackers (firecrackers), hats, jackets, and trousers were all named after the hero, who died in 1845, aged 78. Today almost 100 places in the nation bear his name. Jacksonia was the name of a new Southern state suggested by the Tennessee senate in 1841 that was to include parts of Tennessee, Kentucky, and Mississippi. The proposal came to naught.

Jacksonian epilepsy. *See* BRIGHT'S DISEASE.

Jackson, Mississippi. One of the four U.S. state capitals named after presidents. The others are Lincoln, Nebraska, for Abraham Lincoln; Madison, Wisconsin, for James Madison; and Jefferson City, Missouri, for Thomas Jefferson. *See* MONROVIA.

jackstraw. A worthless person, a man of straw. Jack Straw was the name or nickname of a leader of the Peasants Revolt, Wat Tyler's rebellion of 1381. This revolt against English king Richard II mainly protested restrictions on pay increases to laborers and repudiated higher poll taxes. Richard agreed to the peasants' demands, but the revolt was suppressed and his promises unfulfilled when Tyler was slain by the mayor of London at a meeting held between the two men. In the original march on London to petition the king Tyler and his followers burned and wrecked much property, incurring the wrath of many. The protestor called Jack Straw must have been particularly hated, for his name soon took its present meaning.

Jack Tar. One story has it that the name Jack Tar, for "a sailor," arose in the 17th century, when sailors wore canvas breeches often spotted with tar from work done on ships. According to another tale, sailors in Lord Nelson's navy wore overalls and broad-brimmed hats made of the tar-impregnated tarpaulin cloth commonly used aboard ship. The hats, and the sailors who wore them, were called *tarpaulins*, which was finally shortened to *tar*.

Jack the Ripper. After 82 years, Jack the Ripper's name remains the most familiar of all murderers; no other single criminal has been so exhaustively examined in literature and on stage and screen. The Ripper murdered and disemboweled at least five and possibly nine or more prostitutes in London's East End in 1888, in one of the most gruesome, gory serial killings in British or any other history. "Saucy Jack" was never captured in the foggy night streets of Whitechapel or Spitalfields, and his pseudonym was derived from his signatures on the bizarre, mocking notes he reputedly sent to the police. (Sept. 30th: "Double event this time. Number one squealed a bit—could not finish straight off—had no time to get the ears for police.") "Bloody Jack" was described as a man of medium height who wore a deerstalker cap, sported a small mustache and "talked like a gentleman." For almost a century writers have speculated on the Ripper's real identity, naming literally hundreds of "suspects," including even Prime Minister Gladstone and Albert Victor Christian Edward, duke of Clarence and Avondale, Queen Victoria's grandson and heir to the throne of England.

Jacobian; Jacobite. These two words are often confused. *Jacobian* refers to the reign or time of James I (1556–1625), Scottish king of Great Britain from 1603 until his death. *Jacobite* refers to a supporter of James II (grandson of James I), who ruled as king of Great Britain for a brief three years ending in 1688. Forced to abdicate, James II died in exile in 1701, age 68. Jacobites continued to try placing a Scottish (Stuart) king on the throne, failing with James Francis Edward Stuart, "The Old Pretender," and finally with his son, "Bonny Prince Charlie," whose forces were defeated at the Battle of Culloden in 1746.

Jacobin. During the French Revolution the Société des Jacobins, a radical club or society active beginning in 1789, was responsible for many extreme measures, including the bloody Reign of Terror in which thousands were killed. Though it began as a liberal organization, its name in the form of *Jacobin* came to mean any extreme political radical, as it does today. The Jacobins, only 3,000 strong, managed to control the French Revolution until their leader Robespierre's death in 1794, when they went underground. Five years later the group was finally suppressed.

Jacob's ladder. A Jacob's ladder is a ship's wood-runged rope or chain ladder primarily used to let people ascend from or descend to smaller boats alongside. The name is also given to a steep flight of steps up a cliff, an herb or flower in the shape of a ladder, and a burglar's ladder. All take their name from the ladder seen by the biblical patriarch Jacob in a vision (Gen. 28:12–13), the ladder in the dream symbolizing the hopes of Jacob for his descendants.

Jacob's rod. *See* ASPHODEL.

Jacquard loom. This early automated machine (controlled by punched cards) could weave patterns in many fabrics. Napoleon quickly purchased the loom for the state and declared it public property, rewarding Joseph Marie Jacquard (1752–1834), a former Lyons weaver, with a 3,000-franc yearly pension and a royalty on each machine sold. Jacquard improved on his creation in 1806, adapting several features of a similar invention. Though he hadn't foreseen the widespread unemployment caused by the loom, his belief that it would greatly increase output was more than justified; the Jacquard loom revolutionized the textile industry, and created a new era in manufacturing.

Jacuzzi. A trademark name for a whirlpool bath of swirling comforting water that was invented by Candito Jacuzzi (1903–86) and which he first called the "Roman bath." The American inventor made the bath to help his son, who suffered from rheumatoid arthritis.

jade. Spaniards in medieval times believed that this gem helped cure kidney ailments. They called it *piedra de ifada*, "stone of the side," which became shortened and corrupted in English to *jade*. The *jade* for an old horse or a worthless woman, and the adjective *jaded* derive from another unknown word, of Middle English origin.

jaegers. Though *jaegers* can be any of several rapacious seabirds, in England they are also woolen underwear. The underwear is named for Dr. Gustav Jaeger, whose Dr. Jaeger's Sanitary Woolen System Co. Ltd. manufactured and marketed the various undergarments he designed, beginning about 1890. Americans are familiar with the term through *The Bishop's Jaegers* (1932), a novel by Thorne Smith, creator of the inhibited banker Cosmo Topper, and his ectoplasmic friends.

Jaffa orange. Other similar oranges use the name, but strictly speaking, Jaffa oranges are a sweet almost seedless type of orange grown in or near Jaffa, an ancient biblical port that is now part of Tel Aviv–Jaffa in Israel. In ancient times the port was called Joppa.

jag on. To be drunk, as in "He had a jag on." *Jag* here is a 19th-century Americanism for a heavy load of something, such as a wagon full of wood or hay. Figuratively then, someone who has a jag on, carrying a heavy load, more than he or she can handle, is loaded.

jai alai. The name for this court game is Basque in origin, formed from the Basque *jai*, "festival," and *alai*, "joyous," indicating that people have always had a good time playing *jai alai*. Other English words that come from the Basque include *bizarre* and *orignal*, a mostly Canadian word for the American moose.

Jaislaak! A euphemism for *Jesus* heard in South African English. It is an exclamation of surprise, disbelief, etc., as in "Jaislaak, how did you get here so fast?!"

jalapeño. A hot green or orange-red pepper (*Capsicum annuum*) used in Mexican cooking and well known in the U.S.

jalopy. Here's one whose origins etymologists don't even venture a guess upon. It means, of course, a beaten-up old car or (rarely) airplane (usually called a *crate*). Should you want to investigate, the word seems to have surfaced first in Chicago in about 1924 and was sometimes spelled *jaloppi*. Possibly it derived from the slang of a foreign language. *Rattletrap* and *heap* are synonyms of about the same age.

jalousie. First called *jealousies* in 16th-century England, *jalousies*, their name taken from the French for jealousy, were originally blinds or shutters with wooden horizontal slats that admitted air and light but "jealously guarded" one's privacy. Today they are also made of glass.

Jamestown Ships. These small ships—the *Susan Constant*, 100 tons; the *Godspeed*, 40 tons; and the *Discovery*, 20 tons are called the Jamestown Ships because they brought Captain John Smith and English colonists to Jamestown, Virginia, in 1607 to form the first English settlement in America. Exact replicas of these ships can be seen today at Festival Park in Jamestown, which has been called "the birthplace of the United States."

Jamie Duff. A professional mourner. There is a story that this Scottish nickname for a mourner at a funeral comes from the name of one James Duff, an odd character who attended many funerals in the mid 19th century because "he enjoyed the ride in the mourning coach." More likely the term is from the name of an old firm that supplied mourners for a price.

Jane or Jane's. Often cited as an authority in arguments about warships, *Jane* or *Jane's* generally refers to the prime reference on the world's navies, *Jane's Fighting Ships*, an illustrated book published periodically in England for almost a century and founded by Fred T. Jane. A volume on airplanes is also published by Jane's.

janissary. A collective bodyguard or household guard is called a janissary after the sultan of Turkey's *yeni-tshari*, or "new army," originally recruited by the Sultan Orchan in his reign from 1329–59. To strengthen the then feeble military, Orchan at first ordered every fifth Christian youth to be surrendered by his parents to the service of the sultan, given instruction in Muhammadanism, and specially trained in the arts of warfare. The *yenitshari*, the word corrupted into the English *janissary* in the process of passing through several languages, became the flower of the newly independent kingdom's standing army. Its reputation for courage and discipline was highly respected and the fur-capped corps received many privileges, soon making compulsory recruitment no longer necessary. But by the 19th century the "new army" numbered some 135,000 and had begun actively defying the government. In 1826 specially trained Muslim troops were employed to abolish them, and a brutal massacre that year resulted in the death of almost every janissary.

January. Because it was the gateway of the new year, January was named for the Roman god Janus, keeper of the gates of heaven, who had two faces, one at the back to look at the old year and one at the front to view the new year. The Roman *Januarius* became *Januarie* in English and then *January*. Janus is also remembered in the word "Janus-faced," for "a two-faced person," a deceiver or double-dealer.

Janus-faced. *See* JANUARY.

Japanese words in English. Among Japanese words that have enriched English over the centuries are: kimono, karate, judo, tycoon, kamikaze, sukiyaki, samurai, hara-kiri, haiku, kabuki, geisha, sake, tsunami, and Nisei. rickshaw, banzai, Rimona, soybean, jujitsu

jape. *Jape*, possibly from the French *japer*, "to bark like a dog," combined in English with the French *gaber*, "to mock or deride," meant to trick or deceive, or to joke, when first recorded in the 14th century. Then, strangely enough, it lost this sense and came to mean "to seduce a woman" or "to have carnal intercourse with a woman." Labeled an obscene word by the 16th century, *jape* was rarely used in print. Only 300 years later, in the 19th century, did it resurface with its original meaning, a *jape* becoming a joke or trick again.

jargantuan. *See* GOBBLEDYGOOK.

jargon. *Jargon*, or *jargoun*, meant "a twittering sound" or "meaningless chatter" in Medieval French. It later came to mean the argot or special vocabulary of a trade or profession, because such vocabularies were unintelligible to the outsider. Many trades have their own jargon, which facilitates things for the initiated.

jasmine. The jasmine vine with its fragrant flowers is native to Eurasia and Africa and was introduced into England in 1548. It takes its name from the Persian *yasmin* for the plant. According to a legend recounted in the rare 18th-century book *The Sentiment of Flowers:*

> This beautiful plant grew in Hampton Court garden [England] at the end of the 17th century; but, being lost there, was known only in Europe in the garden of the Grand Duke of Tuscany, at Pisa. From a jealous and selfish anxiety that he should continue to be the sole possessor of a plant so charming and rare, he [the duke] strictly charged his gardener not to give a single sprig, or even a flower, to any person. The gardener might have been faithful if he had not loved; but being attached to a fair, though portionless damsel, he presented her with a bouquet on her birthday; and in order to render it more acceptable, ornamented it with a sprig of jasmine. The young maiden, to preserve the freshness of this pretty stranger, placed it in the earth, where it remained green until the return of spring, when it budded forth and was covered with flowers. She had profited by her lover's lessons, and now cultivated her highly prized jasmine with care, for which she was amply rewarded by its rapid growth. The poverty of the lovers had been a bar to their union; now, however, she had amassed a little fortune by the sale of the cuttings from the plant which love had given her, and bestowed it, with her hand, upon the gardener of her heart. The young girls of Tuscany, in remembrance of this adventure, always deck themselves, on their wedding day, with a nosegay of jasmine; and they have a proverb: "she who is worthy to wear a nosegay of jasmine is as good as a fortune to her husband."

jaunty. Every jaunty person, "one who swaggers about cocksurely," takes the adjective describing him from the jaunty, or master-at-arms, aboard British naval ships who supervised floggings. This jaunty in turn took his name from a mispronunciation of the French *gendarme*, or "policeman."

java. *Java*, for "coffee," originated as slang among American tramps in the late 19th century. It is obviously an allusion to the coffee-producing island.

jaw; jaw-jaw. To jaw is to talk incessantly about little of any worth, of any purpose. This expression for idle conversation is recorded as far back as 1748 in Tobias Smollett's novel *Roderick Random*. *Jaw-jaw*, however, though it means the same, is a

creation of British prime minister Winston Churchill, who said in a White House speech (June 26, 1954): "To jaw-jaw is always better than to war-war."

jawbone of an ass. The phrase is from the Bible, Judges 14: 16: "With the jawbone of an ass . . . have I slain a thousand men." *Jawbone* has come to be associated with talking or jawing. On a rare occasion Oscar Wilde was bested after he told a Boston audience: "You're Philistines who have invaded the sacred sanctum of Art." Replied someone in the balcony: "And you're driving us forth with the jawbone of an ass."

jaws of death. Shakespeare is often credited with the coining of this phrase, in *Twelfth Night* ("Out of the jaws of death"), but it appears earlier in *Divine Weekes and Workes* (1578) by Guillaume de Salluste du Bartas. Shakespeare must have read the man for he precedes the Bard with a number of "Shakespearean" phrases, including *The world's a stage*, *Night's black mantle*, and *the four corners of the world*.

Jaws of Life. Suggested by JAWS OF DEATH, this is the name of a trademark hydraulic tool rescuer used to quickly pry or cut open vehicles involved in auto accidents to free people trapped inside them. The heavy duty apparatus was invented and is made in the U.S.

jay. While some writers suggest that the name of this common bird is of origins unknown, it probably derives, via Old French, from the Latin *gaius*, for the bird, and *gaius* probably comes from the Latin proper name Gaius. A number of birds are named after very common proper names, including *jackdaw* and *robin*. *Jay* is recorded in English as early as 1310.

Jay Hawk. This word for a Kansan may come from the nickname of a "Doc" Jennison, who led a regiment of Kansas Free State men in the years preceding the Civil War. It is said that abolitionist Jennison, "a frolicsome immigrant from New York State," was called Gay Yorker, and that the name was naturally applied to his band as well. Even the pro-slavers, at least Quantrill's raiders, were eventually called Jayhawkers in Kansas, as were all residents of the Jayhawk State in time. The transformation from *Gay Yorker* to *Jayhawker* does seem unlikely, though, and can at best be regarded as doubtful. Since *Jayhawker* was also 19th-century slang for a bandit, I would hazard that the word has something to do with the quarrelsome, thieving blue jay and the warlike hawk. Or perhaps there really was a rapacious jay hawk bird, as someone has suggested but nobody has ever confirmed.

Jayhawker State. A nickname for Kansas (*see* JAY HAWK). Kansas has also been called the Battleground of Freedom (in Civil War times), the Garden State (a title it shares with New Jersey), the Garden of the West (Illinois also claims this one), the Grasshopper State (after grasshopper invasions there), the Cyclone State, the Sunflower State (after the state flower), the Squatter State, the Central State, the Dust Bowl State (*see* DUST BOWL) and, best of all, the Navel of the Nation.

jaywalker. *Jaywalker*, which is far more succinct than "a pedestrian who crosses the streets in disregard of traffic signals," was one of the abundant expressions (*backseat driver, joyride, step* *on the gas*, etc.) made necessary by the automobile. First recorded in 1917, the word incorporates the then-current slang term *jay*, for a stupid, inexperienced "hick." *Jay* itself probably either derives from the "*j*" in the slang term *jughead*, or is a reference to the blue jay, a bird once commonly identified with rural areas.

jazz.   Enough men to form a good jazz group are credited with lending their names to the word. One popular choice is a dancing slave on a plantation near New Orleans, in about 1825—Jasper reputedly was often stirred into a fast step by cries of "Come on, Jazz!" Another is Mr. *Razz*, a band conductor in New Orleans in 1904. Charles, or *Chaz*, Washington, "an eminent ragtime drummer of Vicksburg, Mississippi circa 1895," is a third candidate. A variation on the first and last choices seems to be Charles Alexander, who, according to an early source, "down in Vicksburg around 1910, became world famous through the song asking everyone to 'come on and hear Alexander's Ragtime Band.' Alexander's first name was Charles, always abbreviated Chas. and pronounced Chazz; at the hot moments they called, 'Come on, Jazz!', whence the *jazz* music." Few scholars accept any of these etymologies, but no better theory has been offered. Attempts to trace the word *jazz* to an African word meaning hurry have failed, and it is doubtful that it derives from either the *chasse* dance step; the Arab *Jazib*, "one who allures"; the African *jaiza*, "the sound of distant drums"; or the Hindu *jazba*, "ardent desire." To complicate matters further, *jazz* was first a verb for sexual intercourse, as it still is today in slang.

Jazz Age.   A coinage of F. Scott Fitzgerald for the era of the 1920s in America, a time dominated by youth and jazz music and marked by frenetic hedonism as well as great achievement. Also known as the Roaring Twenties and the Boom, this extravagant era, often treating life as a great party, was depicted in the caricatures of John Held and described in Fitzgerald's classic fiction: *Tales of the Jazz Age* (1922), the first use of the phrase *Jazz Age*; his masterpiece, *The Great Gatsby* (1925); *Flappers and Philosophers* (1920); and his first novel, *This Side of Paradise* (1920). Of the Jazz Age Fitzgerald wrote: "It was an age of miracles, it was an age of art, it was an age of excess, and it was an age of satire." See LOST GENERATION.

jeans.   See BLUE JEANS.

jeep.   Eugene the Jeep, a character in Elzie Crisler (E.C.) Segar's widely syndicated comic-strip "Popeye," had supernatural powers and could do just about anything. Introduced in 1936, the mythical little animal was well known by World War II when Willis-Overland began manufacturing their versatile, open, 1¼-ton, four-wheel-drive vehicles for the armed forces. No one knows for certain, but the vehicle was probably named a *jeep* by U.S. servicemen from the sound of the army term GP (general purpose), this reinforced by the popularity of Eugene the Jeep and the "jeep" noise that he constantly made. In any event, *jeep* was "in the air at the time," as Mencken says, used as the name for many contrivances, and the official army name for the vehicle—"half-ton-four-by-four command-reconnaissance car"—was definitely in need of improvement. A *peep* was the term invented to distinguish the new half-ton truck from the jeep, but it never really caught on. Wrote famed

World War I correspondent Ernie Pyle: "The jeep does everything. . . . It is faithful as a dog, strong as a mule, agile as a goat."

Jeez; Jeepers.   See GEE!

Jeff Davis necktie.   See SHERMAN HAIRPIN.

Jeffdom.   See LINCOLNDOM.

Jefferson.   A proposed name for the territory that became the state of Colorado, which before the Civil War was part of what was called the Jefferson Territory, in honor of Thomas Jefferson. Also a name proposed for the territory that became the state of Montana, which was also part of what had been called the Jefferson Territory.

Jefferson Bible; Jeffersonian.   The Jefferson Bible, or Jefferson's Bible, is a collection of Jesus' teaching compiled from the New Testament by Thomas Jefferson and published at various times under his name. The author of the Declaration of Independence, founding father, and third president of the United States led an almost incredibly active life, but history best remembers Jefferson for his idealistic championship of democracy and *Jeffersonian* has become synonymous with "democratic." The expression *Jeffersonian simplicity* honors his dislike of pomp and ceremony in political and social matters. Jefferson was 83 when he died on July 4, 1826—the 50th anniversary of the Declaration of Independence and the same day on which his friend and fellow patriot John Adams died. Some 44 towns and counties bear his name.

Jefferson City, Missouri.   Named after Thomas Jefferson, this is one of the four U.S. state capitals named after presidents. The others are Lincoln, Nebraska, for Abraham Lincoln; Madison, Wisconsin, for James Madison; and Jackson, Mississippi, for Andrew Jackson. See MONROVIA.

Jehovah.   The ancient Hebrews considered YHVH (a name for God in Hebrew and the sacred tetragrammaton meaning "I exist") so holy that they never pronounced it and disguised it in the form of *Jehovah*, adding vowels from *Adonai*, another word for God, to suggest that anyone reading it should say *Adonai* instead of YHVH. During the Renaissance the vowels and consonants added to YHVH were mistaken for part of the name itself, and *Jehovah* was pronounced "Jehovah" or "Yahwe." See SEVEN NAMES OF GOD.

Jehovah's Witnesses.   A religious movement first called the Russellites after its founder, American Charles T. Russell (1852–1916). In 1931 this fundamentalist group, which recognized the authority of Jehovah-God alone, took the name Jehovah's Witnesses. The Jehovah's Witnesses believe in Christ as the perfect man but not divine; they refuse to salute any national flag, to perform military service, or to receive blood transfusions. Their organ, *The Watch Tower*, sold relentlessly door-to-door, has as its motto: *Millions Now Living Will Never Die*.

Jehu.   See JEZEBEL.

jell; It didn't jell. *Jell* is an Americanism meaning "to congeal or jelly" and may have been invented by Louisa May Alcott in her book *Little Women* (1869), where it is first recorded. The expression *it didn't jell,* "it didn't work, it failed," is first recorded in 1949.

Jell-O. The trademark name of this dessert, made of gelatin, sugar, and fruit flavoring, was coined by Mary Wait, the wife of its inventor, cough medicine maker Pearl B. Wait of LeRoy, New York, in 1897. By 1929, Jell-O and Postum cereal were the nucleus of the huge General Foods Corporation.

jelly. Jellies were originally frozen desserts, this reflected by the Latin word *gelata,* meaning "frozen," that is the ancestor of our *jelly,* which is first recorded in 1393. The Romans made their jellies by boiling animal bones. After cooking they set the liquid in a cool place where it solidified, the process suggesting freezing to them.

jellyfish. *See* SPINELESS AS A JELLYFISH.

Jenny Haniver. Seamen once fashioned strange figures from dried skates, rays, or mantas they had caught, and gullible landlubbers often bought these "mermaids" and "dragons," believing them to be real. Beginning in the 13th century, sailors turned out such Jenny Hanivers, many specimens lasting for 600 years or more, but their name remains a mystery. The surname may be a corruption of Antwerp, a bustling seaport of the time, but it is just as possible that some anonymous sailor bestowed the name of his sweetheart or another real woman on the lifelike mummies.

Jenny kissed me. Poet Leigh Hunt had been ill for several weeks during an influenza epidemic that had taken many lives, when he suddenly recovered and unexpectedly visited his friend Jane ("Jenny") Welsh Carlyle. Mrs. Carlyle impulsively jumped up and kissed him as he came in the door. This inspired Hunt's famous verse:

> Jenny kissed me when we met,
> Jumping from the chair she sat in;
> Time, you thief, who love to get
> Sweets into your list, put that in:
> Say I'm weary, say I'm sad.
> Say that health and wealth have missed me,
> Say I'm growing old, but add,
> Jenny kissed me.

Jenny Lind. One of the less sensational P. T. Barnum attractions was Jenny Lind. The incomparable showman brought his *Swedish Nightingale* to America in 1850 for a concert tour, the golden-voiced operatic soprano giving 95 concerts in 19 cities and grossing some $712,000—with over half a million being Barnum's share. Jenny Lind, at the height of her powers, became the most famous singer of her time, due in large part to Barnum's hoopla. Her name and nickname are only rarely heard today, but were once commonly used to describe a gifted singer, and many fashions of the day, including a carriage, were named after her. There were rumors that Barnum and the singer were romantically involved, but she married composer Otto Goldschmidt in 1852, the couple later living in England. She died in 1887, aged 67.

jeopardy. *Jeu parti* was originally a French chess term meaning "a divided play or game." It thus came to mean "an uncertain chance, uncertainty" and entered English in this sense, spelled *jeuparti,* early in the 13th century. By the end of that century it had attained its present meaning of "risk of loss; peril, danger," but its spelling is not recorded as *jeopardy* until 1597.

jeremiad. A lengthy tale of woe or complaint that takes its name from Jeremiah, the major Hebrew prophet of the Old Testament—Lamentations and Jeremiah. Jeremiah's long and sorrowful complaints were a protest against the sins of his countrymen and their captivity, his tirades and dire prophecies rarely equaled in history. Strangely enough, Jeremiah, who lived in the sixth century B.C., is also thought to be the author of several of the *Psalms. See also* NO BALM IN GILEAD.

jerk. Though *jerk* has been since the 1940s harmless, everyday slang for a fool, the word originally meant "a masturbator," in the form of *a jerk off,* this expression having meant to masturbate since at least 1590.

jerkwater town. If you've ever traveled on a railroad line where trains are all steam-powered—and some still exist around the world—you'll know that this expression, first recorded in 1896, has nothing to do with "jerks" who live in small, or jerkwater, towns. Steam engines often make stops in small stations for no other reason than to obtain water, the fireman jerking a cord attached to a long spigot extending from the water tower to fill the engine's water tender. Similar practices, universal in the early days of railroading, gave rise to the Americanism *jerkwater town,* for any small, out-of-the-way place where no train stopped except to "jerk water."

jerky. *Jerky,* first recorded in 1850, is dried and smoked strips of dried beef. Much used by travelers in the West, *jerky* is simply the Anglicization of the Spanish *charqui* for dried meat, and the Spanish word was often used instead of *jerky. Charqui,* in turn, comes from the Incan *echarqui* for dried meat. *See* BILTONG.

jeroboam; rehoboam. Jeroboam reigned as the first of the kings of Israel, "a mighty man of valor," who "did sin and make Israel to sin" (I Kings 14:16). Which may be why the oversized wine bottle, holding from eight to 12 quarts, was named after him by some scholarly wit at the beginning of the 19th century. The bottle is certainly "mighty" enough, anyway, and its contents can surely cause "sin." The rehoboam, two jeroboams, is named after Solomon's son, who was at least wise enough to carry on his father's marital policies: Rehoboam had 18 wives, plus 60 concubines. *Jeroboam* also describes the large bowl or goblet better known as the "jorum," the latter name in allusion to another biblical king who brought King David "vessels of silver, and vessels of gold, and vessels of brass" (II Sam. 8:10).

jerrican. The Germans developed this four-and-a-half-gallon gas container for the Afrika Korps during World War II. But the British stole the idea, naming the can the *jerrican,* after the jerries, or Germans.

Jerries. During World War I *Jerry* was perhaps the most offensive of the derogatory names given the Germans by Allied soldiers, these names including *Boche* (from the French for "blockhead"); *Kraut* (from sauerkraut); *Heinie* (from the German name Heinrich); and *Hun* (after the ancient barbarous warriors). But over the years *Jerry* came to be the mildest of such words, once its origins were forgotten: German soldiers were called *Jerries* by the British because their helmets resembled the chamber pots the British called jerries, which took their name from the slang *jeroboam,* for a chamber pot. *See* JEROBOAM.

jerry-built.   The cheap, flimsy constructs of a Mr. Jerry of the Jerry Bros. of Liverpool may have inspired the word *jerry-built. Jerry-built* could also be connected with the trembling, crumbling walls of Jericho; the prophet Jeremiah, because he foretold decay; the word *jelly,* symbolizing the instability of such structures; or the Gypsy word *gerry,* for "excrement." Still another theory suggests a corruption of *jerry-mast,* a name sailors and shipbuilders gave to makeshift wooden masts midway through the 19th century. Jerry-masts or rigs derive their name from the French *jour,* "day," indicating their temporary nature.

Jersey.   Jersey, the largest of England's Channel Islands, was named for the Caesars, having been called Caesarea when the Romans ruled over it, *Jersey* being simply a corruption of *Caesarea.* In the eighth century B.C., *ey,* the suffix of the word *Jersey,* meant "an island," so therefore Jersey is "the island of Caesar," or "Caesar's island." Little evidence of the Roman occupation remains in Jersey or any of the islands in the English Channel. The Romans added the island to their empire after the Gauls had ruled there and, more than 1,500 years later the only evidence of their occupation is traces of Roman buildings found in Alderney. *Jersey* also refers to a breed of cattle, raised on Jersey and noted for yielding milk with high butterfat content. Close-fitting knitted sweaters and skirts, or similar women's garments, are called jerseys because they were first made from jersey cloth, machine-woven fabrics of wool, etc., manufactured on the island of Jersey. *See* CAESARIAN SECTION.

Jerusalem.   The name of the ancient holy city and capital of Israel derives from Hebrew, meaning "city of peace," an ironic designation today.

Jerusalem artichoke.   *See* ARTICHOKE.

Jerusalem cherry.   Despite its common name, this plant (*Solanum pseudo-capsicum*) is not a cherry and does not grow in or near Jerusalem. A popular greenhouse plant grown for its scarlet, globe-shaped fruits, it is native to Brazil. The name *Jerusalem* is attached to a number of plants not native to that area, including the Jerusalem cowslip, Jerusalem oak, Jerusalem sage, Jerusalem thorn, and Jerusalem artichoke. It seems that, except in the last case, *Jerusalem* was bestowed simply as a vague name for a distant foreign place the plant was thought to hail from. *See* ARTICHOKE.

Jesse James.   Jesse Woodson James became a kind of American Robin Hood in his own brief lifetime. A member of the Confederate Quantrill gang in his youth, he and his brother Frank later led the most notorious band of robbers in the country's history. The gang's daring bank and train robberies caused many deaths, but James was regarded as a hero by a public that hated foreclosing banks and greedy railroads. In 1882, changing his name to Thomas Howard, Jesse went into hiding at St. Joseph, Missouri. There, six months later, Robert Ford, "the dirty little coward that shot Mr. Howard," killed him for a reward. Jesse James was only 35 when he died. He is still a folk hero, commemorated in a popular ballad, folktales, movies, novels, and at least one play. Besides being slang for a criminal, a *Jesse James* is a truckman's name for a police magistrate and has been applied by baseball players to umpires.

Jesse tree.   There is no such tree growing in nature. The Jesse tree is a vine with many branches, tracing the ancestry of Christ that is called "rod out of the stem of Jesse" in the Bible and is represented in church stained-glass Jesse windows, Jesse often represented in reclining position with the vine rising out of his loins.

Jesus bug; sea strider.   While the Earth is host to over 1 million classified species of insects, only one insect lives in the ocean: *Halobates,* or the sea strider. *Halobates* can walk on the waves without getting seasick, but anchors its eggs to albatross or booby feathers. Known also as the Jesus bug because it walks on water, the variegated blue and black inch-long insect is supported by the surface tension of the water, each of its six feet resting in a minute depression as the insect speedily rows itself along, using its stiff-haired middle pair of legs as oars, its front pair for support, and its rear pair for steering. The bugs are attracted to light, and solid sheets containing thousands of immature specimens are often found off the Galapagos. A single bird's feather has been found to contain 25,000 *Halobates* eggs. No one knows what they feed on or where they find shelter to survive storms or tropical downpours, because when their backs get wet, they become waterlogged and sink.

jet black.   The adjective comes from the mineral called *jet,* which is indeed velvet-black. The mineral, in turn, is named for Gagas, a town in ancient Lycaea, where it was discovered. *Gagas* ultimately was corrupted to *jet* in French before entering English.

jetsam.   *See* FLOTSAM AND JETSAM.

Jew.   *Jew* comes from the German *Jude,* which is a shortened form of *Yehuda,* the name of the Jewish Commonwealth in the period of the Second Temple. Since the Commonwealth's name derived from the name of Jacob's son Yehuda (Judah), both *Jew* and *Jewish* ultimately derive from this proper name. *Jew* is first recorded in English in 1275, in the form of *Gyu. See* BUDDHISM; CHRISTIAN; HOLOCAUST; MOSAIC.

Jezebel.   Jezebel "painted her eyes, and adorned her head, and looked out the window" when Jehu entered Jezreel. But Jehu, not to be tempted, promptly cried out, "Throw her down," and appropriately enough, three eunuchs responded. Jezebel's defenestration was complemented with her body being trampled by horses and eaten by dogs in one of the bloodiest of vengeful Old Testament passages (2 Kings 9:30–37). What had she done? The wicked ways of this worshipper of Baal were said to have brought evil upon the kingdom of Israel. So much so that *Jezebel* is still used figuratively for "a woman who flaunts loose morals," "a harridan," "a shameless bitch," or "a bold-faced prostitute." Jezebel was the wanton wife of the wicked King

Ahab and daughter of the King of Tyre. *Jehu* is an old expression for "an intrepid coachman." The son of Jehoshaphat (of *jumping Jehoshaphat!* fame) "rode in a chariot" when he went to war, the Bible tells us, a hot rodder that "driveth furiously."

jibber the kibber. In the late 18th century, *jibber the kibber* meant to fool seamen and wreck ships "by fixing a candle and lantern round the neck of a horse, one of whose fore feet is tied up; this at night has the appearance of another ship's light, and the deceived ship cracks into rocks or a [sand] bar." There seems to be no relation to a ship's *jib* in the phrase. In fact, the most anyone can make of the expression is that *jibber* means to confuse, deriving from the verb *to jibber*, to talk confusedly. *See* MOONLIGHTING.

jicama. The large, turnip-shaped root of the tropical American legume *Pachyrhizus erosus* eaten as a side dish and in salads. The plant ultimately takes its name from the Nahuatl *xicamatl*.

jiffy. Right away, a very short time. *Jiffy* may be a misspelling of *gliff*, an earlier term for a glimpse or a glance, but no one is sure. The word is first recorded in the late 1700s.

jigger. Our word for the small 1½-ounce shot glass used to measure whiskey probably derives from CHIGGER, for "tiny mites and fleas."

the jig is up. The expression suggests that the dance is over, and that the time has come to pay the fiddler. However, its derivation is more complicated. *Jig* is a very old term for a lively dance, but in Elizabethan times the word became slang for a practical joke or a trick. *The jig is up*—meaning your trick or game is finished, has been exposed, we're onto you now—derives from this obsolete slang word, not the *jig* that is still a gay and lively dance. *See* THE GAME IS UP.

jilleroo; jockeroo. A young woman who works on an Australian sheep ranch in the Outback is called a "jillaroo"; her male counterpart on the ranch is a jockeroo. Use of the words has spread to the rest of Australia.

Jim Crow. Blackface minstrel Thomas D. Rice, "the father of American minstrelsy," introduced the song "Jim Crow" in 1828, claiming to have patterned it on the song and dance of an old field hand named Jim Crow he had observed in Kentucky. Rice's routine, part of a skit called "The Rifle," became so familiar here and on tour in England that a few years later a British antislavery book was titled *The History of Jim Crow*. It is from this book and similar uses of *Jim Crow* to signify a black that the discriminatory laws and practices take their name, though the first Jim Crow laws weren't enacted until 1875 in Tennessee.

Jim Dandy. No particular Jim Dandy seems to be the eponym behind the century-old term *Jim Dandy*, which is still heard for someone or something that is especially fine or admirable. *The Dictionary of Americanisms* traces the term back to January 1887. Etymologist Gerald Cohen has cited a published sports usage of it some six months later in a New York Giants game, indicating a possible baseball origin. Certainly baseball helped popularize the phrase.

Jiminy Cricket. Pinocchio's friend, whether Walt Disney knew it or not, bears a name that is a euphemism for *Jesus Christ*. An old one, too, the *Jiminy* portion dating back to 1664, when it was recorded as *Gemini*, probably deriving from the Latin *Jesu domini*. The mild exclamation of surprise *Jimmy!*, still heard occasionally, has the same origin, of course. *See also* GEE!

jim-kay. An historical term meaning to stuff with food to a dangerous point. According to one story, a family kept a pet pig that they named James K. Polk, after the U.S. President, and fed James (or Jim) K. so much that he burst apart. Thus the President's name became the basis for this odd addition to America's political lexicon.

Jimmy Valentine. O. Henry's story, "A Retrieved Reformation," turned into the play *Alias Jimmy Valentine* (1909), popularizing the term *Jimmy Valentine*, for a safecracker Jimmy Valentine, the story's main character, a master YEGG or safecracker, was said to be based on a character O. Henry met while serving time for embezzlement.

jimsonweed. *Jamestown-weed* was the original name of *jimsonweed*, or the thorn apple, a plant that can be deadly poisonous when its foliage is wilted. *Datura stramonium* was named *Jamestown-weed* because it was first noticed growing in America near Jamestown, Virginia, where the Indians smoked it like tobacco; in fact, soldiers among the insurgents in Bacon's Rebellion of 1675 are said to have eaten this weed when defeated and driven into the wilderness, many almost dying of it. Over the years *Jamestown-weed* was slurred to *jimsonweed* in pronunciation and by the 19th century was the common name for the plant.

jinete; jennet. The Zenetes, a North African Berber tribe, were such skilled horsemen and horse trainers that anyone who trains colts to the saddle is called a *jinete* in their honor. They also give their name to the *jennet*, a small Spanish horse and a female ass or donkey.

jingoism.

> We don't want to fight, yet by Jingo
>   if we do
> We've got the ships, we've got the men,
>   and the money, too

This refrain from the British music hall song "The Great MacDermott" (1878), urging Great Britain to fight the Russians and prevent them from taking Constantinople, gives us the expression *jingoism*, for "bellicose chauvinism or excessive patriotism." *Jingo* is a euphemism for "by Jesus" that dates back to the late 17th century. The British fleet did scare off the Russians from Constantinople.

jinx. Baseball Hall of Famer Christy Mathewson was among the first to use the word in print when he wrote in his *Pitching in a Pinch* (1912): "A jinx is something which brings bad luck to a ballplayer." Big Six didn't know that the word may owe its life to a bird called the jynx, which was used to cast charms and spells. The *jynx*, known in America as the wrynecked woodpecker or wryneck, takes its name from the Greek *iynx* for the bird. In the Middle Ages this rara avis, with its grotesque, twisted neck, its odd breeding and feeding habits, its harsh, strident cries during migration and its near silence the rest of the time, was thought to have occult powers. Jynx feathers were used to make love philters and black-magic charms, the bird's name itself coming to mean a charm or spell, especially a black-magic spell, on a selected victim. It's easy to see how the slang term *jinx* arose from *jynx*, but the long flight of the jynx from medieval times to the printed page circa 1912 is not easily explained. That's why the *O.E.D.* and Mencken don't attempt to give the origin of *jinx*. *Webster's* admits the *jynx* version, however, as does the *Random House Dictionary* and other sources. Partridge traces *jinx* to the old Scottish word *jink*, "to make a sudden turn," "the implication being [that jinxes] are all *twisters.*"

jipijapa.   The name for the Panama hat in South America, after the plant such hats are made from. A playful name, pronounced "heepy-hoppa," that should have wider currency in English. *See* PANAMA HAT.

jitterbug.   *Jitter Bug* was first recorded in 1934 as the title of a song by American bandleader Cab Callaway and two collaborators. Calloway probably coined the words, which originally meant a jittery or nervous person, the song's lyrics describing a "jitter bug" as someone who drinks regularly and thus "has the jitters ev'ry morning." Within a few years *jitterbug* began to take on its main meaning of dancing too fast to whirling swing music, *jitterbug* referring to any dancer who does so.

jix.   Among the most interesting of acronyms is the eponymous *jix*, a word coined from the letters of a person's name. *Jix* was a synonym for "prudish interference" popular in England during the late twenties and early thirties. Journalists nicknamed British home secretary Sir William Joynson-Hicks "Jix" and the word only passed out of use with his death in 1932.

jo.   *Jo*, as in "John Anderson, my jo," means beloved one, darling, or sweetheart in Scotland. The word is simply a variant of the word "joy" and dates to the 16th century or before.

job.   First recorded in about 1627, but probably used long before this colloquially, *job*, for "a piece of work," may derive from the earlier word *job*, meaning "a small piece, a lump." The earlier *job*, in turn, may derive from *gob*, for "a lump," which has its roots in the Old French *gober. The New Dictionary of American Slang* (1986) gives the origin of *job*, for a "crime or criminal project," as "underworld from middle 1800s." But it may be much older than this and may not be from the underworld at all. I've come across it in an early poem by English poet William Cowper (1731–1800), "Pity for Poor Africans," in the stanza:

> A youngster at school, more sedate than the
>   rest,
> Had once his integrity put to the test;
> His comrades had plotted an orchard to rob,
> And asked him to go and assist in the job.

jobbing house; job lots; job printer.   *Jobbing house*, referring to a firm buying goods to sell in bulk to retailers, came into the language about 1870. *Job lots* refers to larger, often assorted, quantities of goods sold or handled as a single transaction. *Job Lots* is now often used as a name for stores that sell a miscellaneous quantity of goods, a quantity of odds and ends. *Job printer* is a printer who does varied work.

Job's comforter; patience of Job.   A *Job's comforter* is someone who in meaning to comfort you adds to your sorrows, especially by advising that you brought your troubles upon yourself. "Miserable comforters are ye all," Job told the three friends who came to console him in his misery, the scolding lectures they delivered to him now known as *Jobations*. The Book of Job in the Old Testament is one of the world's greatest writings, questioning the existence of justice and moral order in the universe, its magnificent poetry more appropriate with each passing year. Job's myriad misfortunes—his stock stolen, his sons, daughter, and servants slain, his body afflicted with "loathsome sores"—and his patience with these afflictions by which Satan is said to have tested him, led to the expression *the patience of Job*, great patience, indeed.

Job's tears.   In the Philippines, the annual grass Job's-tears (*Coix lacryma-jobi*) is the source of the nourishing cereal food *adlay*. The tear-shaped seeds are found on the white or dirty-white female flower clusters, and inside each tear are the edible kernels that have long been used in the Far East for grain. Grown in western nations as an ornamental, the 3- to 6-foot-high, sword-shaped grass is named Job's-tears after the biblical Job, whose great misfortunes were borne with proverbial patience, but who must have shed many tears.

jock; jockstrap.   Beginning in the late 1960s *jock* meant a big brainless college football player, but within a decade it covered any athlete at all, although the athlete does not necessarily have to be big or dumb—*jock* is a kinder word today. No one knows if the term is directly related to the racing *jockey* or to the *jockstraps* most athletes wear, though the latter derivation seems more plausible. *Jockstrap* takes its name from the centuries-old English slang *jock*, for "penis," which derived from the common nickname Jock for John.

jodhpurs.   The horseback-riding pants were brought back to England in the 19th century from the district of Jodhpur in northwest India, where riders had been wearing them for many years.

joe.   *Joe* may have become slang for coffee, as in a *cuppa joe*, because of the great consumption of it by G.I. Joes during World War II, according to Mark Pendergast in his fascinating book *Uncommon Grounds: The History of Coffee and How It Transformed Our World* (1999). This seems unlikely, as the term is first recorded in 1930 as tramp and underworld slang. Another interesting theory is that the word derives from Stephen Foster's song "Old Black Joe" (1850), a perennial favorite like so many of his songs ("Oh! Susanna," "Swanee," "My Old Kentucky Home," "Camptown Races," "Jeanie with the Light Brown Hair," among others). But no matter how appealing, there is no firm evidence for any of these theories.

Joe Echoes. People who were called *Echoes* in late-19th-century and early-20th-century America (Joe Echoes, Johnny Echoes, Eddie Echoes, etc.) weren't called that because they echoed other people's words. Those bearing this common nickname, usually the offspring of poor, recent immigrants, often echoed *themselves*, in sentences like "I betcha ya can't do it, I betcha," or "I tell ya it's mine, I tell ya!"

Joe Louis. Joe Louis, perhaps the greatest of all heavyweight fighters, came to be nicknamed the *Brown Bomber* for his blockbusting right and the color of his skin. Joe Louis Barrow, born on May 13, 1914, in Lafayette, Alabama, was the son of a sharecropper who died when Joe was four. The family moved to Detroit where Joe helped support them when he was only 16 by taking odd jobs that included work as a sparring partner in a local gym. This led to a boxing career that finally saw him take the heavyweight title from Jim Braddock in 1937. He defended his title more often than any other champion in ring history, and only Jack Dempsey outpolled him in the Associated Press survey of 1950 in which sportswriters picked the best boxers of the century. Louis lost three times in a career interrupted by service in World War II, once (before he became champion) to Max Schmeling, whom he knocked out in a rematch, and then to Rocky Marciano and Ezzard Charles, after he had retired as undefeated heavyweight champion but was attempting a comeback. His ring record included 64 KOs, eight decisions, and one win by default. A *Joe Louis* is synonymous for the utmost in a fighter, a heavyweight without peer.

Joe Miller. The English comic actor and barfly Joseph or Josias Miller (1684–1738), a favorite at the Drury Lane Theatre in parts such as Hamlet's first gravedigger, was an illiterate; he reportedly married his wife only to have someone to read his parts to him. When Miller died leaving his family in poverty, his friend playwright John Mottley gathered a collection of jokes attributed to Miller—and there were many, either because he was famed for his wit, or because it was something of a joke to credit this "grave and taciturn" actor with any joke making its rounds of the pubs. The proceeds of the 72-page book went to Miller's family, and being the only joke book extant for many years it went into numerous editions over the next two centuries. Because the jokes were widely quoted and imitated on the stage so long, any stale joke came to be called a *Joe Miller*.

Joe-Pye weed. A weed, according to the old saying, is only an uncultivated flower. Sometimes even more. The *Joe-Pye weed*, for instance, may have been named for an Indian medicine man of that name because he "cured typhus fever with it, by copious perspiration." This tall, common plant, with clusters of pinkish flowers, might well be the only weed ever dedicated to a real person. Records from 1787 reveal the existence of a Josephy Pye, or Shawquaathquat, who was possibly a descendant of the original Salem, Massachusetts healer, but the colonial Joe Pye has not yet been unequivocally identified.

Joe Sixpack. A name at least since 1977 for the "ordinary" working man, a beer drinker who is satisfied with his sixpack (six cans of beer packed together) at the end of the day. Joe Sixpack has lots of synonyms, including *Joe Blow, Joe Average,* *Joe Citizen, Joe Q. Citizen, Joe Doakes, Joe Lunchpail,* and just plain *Joe*. See JOHN AND JANE DOE.

Joey. A coin named after a real person is the Joey, a fourpence piece honoring Joseph Hume, M.P. for Kilkenny, who in 1835 recommended that groats be coined for the sake of paying short cab fares and other small transactions. American circus performers coined the word *Joey* for a circus performer in honor of English actor Joseph Grimaldi (1779–1837). An infant of one year when he made his London debut at the Drury Lane Theatre, Grimaldi performed for almost half a century in England. Starting his career as a dancer, he later became internationally famous as the first of modern clowns, one of the best known and beloved performers of his time. Grimaldi, the London-born son of an Italian actor, had no equal in pantomime and his much-acclaimed portrayal of a clown in *Mother Goose* has been revived many times over the years.

jog. To run at a slow though usually jolting pace. First recorded in this sense in 1948 in reference to track athletes training or warming up for a race, the word became commonly used with the beginning of the running-for-fitness craze of the 1960s, which was largely inspired by Dr. Kenneth Cooper's book on aerobic exercise.

John; Johnny; Stage-door Johnny; Sugar Daddy. *John* refers to a prostitute's male customer, John being a common man's name. The word, widely used today, was first recorded in 1908, though it could be older. *John* or *Johnny* is also another term for a rich man who keeps a woman, a "sugar daddy." *Stage-door Johnny* goes back a few years earlier, describing a young or old man who waits at theater doors hoping to pick up chorus girls.

John; John Thomas. The common first name John derives from the Hebrew *Yohanan*, "God is gracious." It is the most popular of all U.S. and European first names, appearing in various languages as John, Jean, Juan, Johann, Joao, Johannus, Hans, Giovanni, Yan, Yannis, and Yahya—not to mention feminine versions such as Jean and Joan. The origins of "John Thomas," long a slang expression for the penis, and "john," a modern synonym for a toilet and a prostitute's client, will probably never be established beyond a doubt. But a British tradition, running counter to all known facts, derives the expression from the name of a real man of prodigious dimensions. According to this story, the expression "John Thomas" dates to the Middle Ages, about 1400. At the time there lived in a Wiltshire village a farmer named John Thomas, whose outlandishly large member constantly attracted the attention of people even when safely concealed beneath his codpiece. But John Thomas succumbed to the sin of pride. Confusing astonishment with praise, he took to exhibiting himself to anyone who happened by. Young John was finally tried, hanged, drawn, and quartered—except for the real offender, that is. Puritans being then as they are still, John Thomas's enormous penis was preserved in an economy-size pickle jar and Barnums of the time toured the countryside exhibiting dead what he had been executed for exhibiting alive. And so, according to the tale, the expression *John Thomas* became part of the language. The trouble is that no etymologist has traced the expression back further than 1840. All we have is the legend and the expression *John Thomas*, which, interestingly enough, D. H. Lawrence first used as the title for *Lady Chatterley's Lover*. In about 1650 the expression, broken down to *john*, became the common name for a toilet. Then again it may all be a phallic fallacy.

John and Jane Doe.　*John Doe* is the oldest and most common of names for the average American, *Jane Doe* not heard nearly as much. *John Doe* was being used in England as a substitute name on legal documents by the 14th century and soon became a name for the common man, while *Jane Doe* was first recorded as his female counterpart in the late 1930s. *Joe Doakes* (1926), *Joe Citizen* (1932), *Joe Average* (1936), *John Q. Public* (1937), *Joe Lunchpail* (1965), and JOE SIXPACK (1977) are other favorites, though hardly as widely used. These are all neutral terms. For derogatory names describing the average man we have *Joe Blow*, dating back to 1867 and still heard frequently, *Joe Zilch* (1925), and *Joe Schmo* (1950)—all of them treating the common man as a foolish nobody or worse. The British term for the average man is *Joe Bloggs*.

John B.　*See* STETSON.

John Bull.　Dr. John Arbuthnot (1667–1735), Queen Anne's physician, wrote a collection of pamphlets anonymously published in 1712 and entitled *The History of John Bull*. Though he did not invent the term *John Bull*, he made it famous as a personification of England, its plump red-faced English farmers dressed in a top hat and high boots. Dr. Arbuthnot described his character as "an honest plain-dealing fellow . . . very apt to quarrel with his best friends . . . if they pretend to govern him . . . a boon companion with his bottle. . . ." Among the other characters in the work is Lewis Baboon, the French king Louis XIV, a strange choice of names for a work meant to champion the end of war with France. Philip of Spain fared no better, dubbed Lord Strutt.

John Dory.　The John Dory, or St. Peter's cock (*Zeus faber*), a flat, highly valued European food fish, had its religious name long before its humorous one. *John Dory* is most likely a humorous designation for some real or imaginary person, perhaps the notorious privateer of that name active in the 16th century, and the subject of a popular song of the time. Like the haddock, which also has a dark black spot on each side, the golden-yellow John Dory has the reputation of being the fish from which the apostle Peter extracted money. In France, it still bears the name St. Peter's cock; its oval spots are said to be the finger marks left when Peter held the fish to take the coin from its mouth.

John Hancock.　If John Hancock had done nothing else, he would be remembered for his big, bold, belligerent signature, the first on the Declaration of Independence, writ "so big no Britisher would have to use his spectacles to read it." "King John" Hancock (1737–93), also known as the King of Smugglers, was a Revolutionary patriot who led local merchants in protesting the Stamp Act, heading as he did the largest mercantile firm in Boston. Immensely popular in his own lifetime, he became a major general of militia, a member and president of the Continental Congress, and, except for one term, was elected annually as governor of Massachusetts from 1780 until his death. His name, as everyone knows, is commonly used to mean a signature or as a synonym for *name* itself. *See* JOHN HENRY.

John Henry.　Like *John Hancock* above, this is a synonym for a signature or name, but we don't know how the term arose. There is probably no connection here with the black folk hero John Henry, who outdrove a steam drill with his hammer. *John Henry* originated in the American West as cowboy slang and that's all anyone has been able to establish about it.

johnnycake.　"New England corn pone" someone has dubbed this flat corn bread once cooked on a board over an open fire. Most scholars agree that no cook named Johnny had a hand in inventing the bread. *Johnnycake* is usually traced to *Shawnee cakes* made by the Shawnee Indians, who by Colonial times were long familiar with corn and its many uses in cooking. Not everyone agrees, though, and one popular theory holds that *johnnycake* is a corruption of *journey-cake*, which is what early travelers called the long-lasting corn breads that they carried in their saddlebags. However, *johnnycake* is recorded before *journeycake* in the form of *jonikin*, "thin, waferlike sheets, toasted on a board . . . eaten at breakfast with butter"; *jonikin* is still used for griddle cakes on the eastern shore of Maryland. The word apparently progressed from *Shawnee cake* to *jonnikin* and *johnnycake*, and then to *journeycake*. Probably when people no longer needed to carry the cakes on journeys, johnnycake became popular again.

Johnny Canuck.　The Canadian cartoon character who represents Canada, much as UNCLE SAM represents the U.S. and JOHN BULL represents England. The word *Canuck*, deriving from *Canada*, is chiefly used by Canadians to mean a Canadian and is often considered derogatory when used by foreigners.

Johnny-come-lately.　Back in the early 1800s, British sailors called any new or inexperienced hand Johnny Newcomer. American sailors apparently adopted the expression, changing it to Johnny Comelately. The first recorded mention of the term—in an 1839 novel set on the high seas—uses it in this form in referring to a young recruit. The expression soon came to describe newcomers in all walks of life, changing a little more to the familiar *Johnny-come-lately*.

Johnny Reb.　*See* BILLY YANK.

Johnny Town-Mouse.　Many fictional characters have been based on real people, and many animal fictional characters, such as MOBY-DICK, have been based on real-life animals. But Beatrix Potter (1866–1943), the British author of *The Tale of Peter Rabbit* and other books, based an animal on a real human being. Johnny Town-Mouse, in her illustrated book of the same name, is based on her friend Dr. George Parson; her description of Johnny Town-Mouse adopts Parson's facial features and even the long golf bag he used.

John O'Groat's house.　*From John O'Groat's [house] to the Land's End* is a colloquial expression for from one end of Britain to the other. The house in question once stood on the northeastern coast of Scotland, having been built by John de Groat, who settled there with his two brothers from Holland in about 1500. The brothers' descendants eventually grew to eight families and quarrels began over the matter of precedency when they met each year at John O'Groat's. Old John solved this problem neatly by building an eight-sided room with a door to each side and an eight-sided table, so that each family would be at the "head of the table." A small green knoll in the vicinity of Duncansby Head is said to be the site of the house. It is not the northernmost point of Scotland, as is often claimed.

John Roberts. This is an amusing historical expression for a huge tankard of ale. In 1886 John Roberts, a Member of Parliament, sponsored the Sunday Closing Act for Wales, the law closing all pubs on Sundays. Confirmed drinkers took revenge by giving the name John Roberts to a large tankard that they filled on Saturday night with enough beer to last them through Sunday.

Johnson Box. The Johnson Box has been described as "an enticing paragraph in direct-mail advertising, just before a letter's salutation, that efficiently and pleasingly synthesized the sales pitch to follow." It was developed by direct-mail pioneer Frank H. Johnson (1911–2001), who said it was suggested to him by the colorful chapter summaries preceding chapters in 19th-century novels.

Johnsonese; Johnsonian. Dr. Johnson, as the great English man of letters Samuel Johnson is usually called, remains most famous for his monumental *Dictionary* published in 1755 and the immortal *Life of Samuel Johnson* written by James Boswell, generally considered the greatest English biography. A man of enormous energies who would have done even more were it not for the debilitating scrofula and often dire poverty that plagued him all his days, Johnson was revered as a moralist and a brilliant conversationalist. His *Dictionary* was the first to introduce examples of word usages by prominent authors, and along with his *Lives of the English Poets* (brilliant but essentially one-sided appraisals), it is still read today. Anecdotes about Johnson abound, but appropriate here is his reply to the lady who asked him why in his dictionary he defined *pastern* (part of a horse's foot) as the *knee* of a horse. "Sheer ignorance, Madam!" he explained. The two words that do Johnson honor reveal opposite sides of the Great Cham. *Johnsonian* refers to the good common sense reflected in his writings and conversation, while *Johnsonese* remembers the rambling polysyllabic style into which he would often slip—the very opposite of pithy *Johnsonian* phraseology. Partridge notes a third term honoring Johnson in his *Dictionary of Slang*: "Doctor Johnson, *the membrum virile*: literary: ca 1790–1880. Perhaps because there was no one that Dr. Johnson was not prepared to stand up to." Dr. Johnson died in 1784, aged 73. *See also* ROSWELL.

John Wayne. The term *John Wayne* (the movie name of Marion Morrison, 1909–79) can mean a "heroic person" or a "reckless, daring showy person," due to Wayne's star movie roles and his off-camera political views. No one knows how long any of these will last, but *John Wayne* has become the word for about 10 other things, including a John Wayne bar, an Army-field-ration candy bar; a John Wayne cookie or cracker, also Army field rations; a John Wayne hat, a bush hat; and John Wayne High School, after those who quit school to join the army. To John Wayne is to attack someone forcefully with little or no consideration.

John Wesley Hardin. A fabled gunfighter. After John Wesley Hardin (1853–95), killer of some 40 men, the first when he was only 12. Hardin, famous for his *quick cross draw* (crossing his arms to opposite sides and pulling his guns from his vest pockets) died when he was shot in the back of the head while playing cards. *See* WILD BILL HICKOK.

joint. "I have smoked opium . . . in every joint in America" (1883), is the first recorded use of the word *joint* for "a place." Joints are possibly so named because people join together in them. Marijuana cigarette joints are, similarly, often smoked jointly by two or more people. Another interesting theory holds that *joint* was first applied to Chinese opium dens, and took its name from the bamboo walls in such places, bamboo having prominent joints.

jolly boat. There is nothing particularly jolly about the jolly boat, a small craft usually hoisted at a ship's stern. The name of this little workboat, used mostly in harbors, is simply a misspelling of the Dutch *jolle*, meaning a small yawl.

jolly good; jolly good show; jolly good fellow. *Jolly good* in British English means "very good, extremely good," and the expression *jolly good show* is said to someone who has performed very well. Less dated than these expressions is *jolly good fellow*, which is frequently used on both sides of the ocean in the well-known song sung after a toast to a very popular person:

> For he's a jolly good fellow
> That nobody can deny.

The British version substitutes "And say so all of us" for "That nobody can deny."

Jolly Roger. French buccaneers may have flown a flag called the *joli rouge* ("pretty red") and this term may have been corrupted to "Jolly Roger" by English pirates when they transferred it to their black flag. *Jolly Roger* could, however, derive from the 17th-century English word *roger*, meaning "rogue or devil." Or it may come from the widely used Tamil title Ali Raja, meaning "king of the sea"—English pirates at first pronouncing "Ali Raja" as "Ally Roger," then "Olly Roger" and, finally, "Jolly Roger."

a Jonah. *A Jonah* means a bringer of bad luck who spoils the plans of others. The phrase is so popular that it has even become a verb, as in "Don't *jonah* me!" The biblical Jonah sailed to Tarshish instead of preaching against the evils of Nineveh as the Lord bade him. But the Lord sent a mighty storm to punish him for fleeing, so "that the ship was like to be broken," the frightened sailors aboard deciding that he was an evil influence, a loser, bad luck. "And they said . . . Come, and let us cast lots, that we may know for whose cause this evil is upon us. So they cast lots, and the lot fell upon Jonah" (Jon. 1:7). After they jettisoned Jonah, calm returned to the seas, but Jonah, of course, was swallowed by a giant fish (possibly a whale) and after three days and nights was "vomited out upon dry land," whereupon he did what he was supposed to have done in the first place.

Jonathan apple. The Jonathan apple, named after Jonathan Hasbrouck, an American judge who died in 1846, is fifth in order of commercial importance in America. It is a late fall-ripening apple, bright red and often yellow-striped, its round fruit mildly acid and the trees bearing it very prolific. The Jonathan, grown mainly in the Northwest, is but one of numerous apple varieties commending their growers or other notables. The Gravenstein, Grimes Golden, Macoun, and Stayman are only a few others that come to mind. *See also* MICHA ROOD'S APPLE.

a Jones. A Jones is a habit, especially drug addiction, the term arising in the drug culture among heroin users and passing into black slang as well. Whether there was any specific eponymous Jones, man or woman, whose name is behind the word is not known; most likely it is just a use of the common family name Jones. The expression was first recorded about 1962 but is probably older. Claude Brown in *Manchild in the Promised Land* (1965) gave the following use: "Yeah, baby, that's the way it is, I've got a Jones."

jonquil. It is good that we no longer pronounce the name of this pretty flower the way it should be pronounced. "Junkwill" is the proper pronunciation if we consider the word's Latin ancestor *juncus*, meaning "rush" (from its long, rush-like leaves). But in the 19th century the jonquil (*Narcissus jonquilla*) began to be pronounced "John-quill," which sounds much better.

Jordan almond. *See* ALMOND.

jorum. *See* JEROBOAM.

Joseph coat. "Now Joseph was handsome and good looking. And after a time his master's wife cast her eyes upon Joseph, and said, 'Lie with me.' " Joseph refused but Potiphar's wife persisted. ". . . One day, when he went into the house to do his work and none of the men of the house was there in the house, she caught him by his garment, saying 'Lie with me.' " Again Joseph abstained, this time fleeing from her and leaving his upper coat limp in her hand. Mrs. Potiphar proceeded to frame Joseph for attempted rape and her husband, captain of the pharaoh's guard, had him flung into prison, though all went well with our hero "because the Lord was with him." It is from this story, recorded in Genesis 37 and 39, and the "coat of many colors" that Joseph's father made him, that the name of the woman's long riding coat, the *joseph*, derives. The name was probably applied by the 18th-century tailor who designed the short riding coat, later given to the women's long coat and a cloaklike one worn by men.

josh. The best guess is that the Americanism *josh*, for "to kid" or "fool around," is a merging of *joke* and *bosh*. The pseudonym of an American writer may have something to do with the word, though. Henry Wheeler Shaw (1818–85) wrote his deliberately misspelled crackerbox philosophy under the pen name Josh Billings. Employing dialect, ridiculous spellings, deformed grammar, monstrous logic, puns, malapropisms, and anticlimax, he became one of the most popular literary comedians of his time. The expression *to josh* was used about 18 years before Josh Billings began writing in 1863, but his salty aphorisms probably strengthened its meaning and gave the term wider currency.

Joshua tree. *Yucca brevifolia*, a twisted, treelike plant that grows only in the Mojave Desert and is named after the biblical Joshua's spear, because of its blade-like leaves.

joss. *Joss* is pidgin English for a Chinese house idol or cult image, while a *joss house* is a Chinese temple, and a *joss stick* is an incense stick burned before an idol. It seems that early Portuguese explorers, on asking the Chinese what they called such idols, were invariably answered with the Portuguese name for God, *Deos*, which sounded like *joss* to them.

jot. *See* IOTA.

joual. A French dialect heard in Quebec and Maine which takes its name from a regional pronunciation of *cheval*, horse. *Joual*, also spelled *jooal*, borrows many words from English and has its own grammar. It is perhaps the least known dialect speech in the U.S.

joule. Though he made his living as the owner of a large brewery, James Prescott Joule (1818–89) had devoted himself to scientific research since inventing an electromagnetic engine as a youth. In 1840, the English physicist formulated Joule's Law of conservation of energy, the first law of thermodynamics. That same year he was the first to determine the mechanical equivalent of heat and the heat equivalents of electrical energy, the unit of work or energy called the *joule* later named in honor of the measurements he made. Only 22 when he had these valuable discoveries to his credit, Joule went on to perform other important research, becoming one of the first to broach the kinetic theory of gases.

journal. Deriving from the Latin *dies*, "day," the English *journal* doesn't contain a single letter belonging to its ultimate ancestor. The Latin *dies* was the basis for the Latin *diurnus*, which became the Italian *giornale*, "journal," and the French *journal*, meaning the same, and then passed into English as *journal* in about 1590.

journalism and strong drink. *See* TAKE TO JOURNALISM AND STRONG DRINK.

jovial. *Jovial* derives from the Latin *jovialis*, of or pertaining to Jupiter or Jove, the Romans' highest deity. In its sense of a hearty, merry person, qualities the planet Jupiter was said to impart, *jovial* is said to have been coined or first used by British author Gabriel Harvey in about 1590. At least Thomas Nash claimed that Harvey invented the word, along with *conscious*, *extensively*, *idiom*, *notoriety*, and *rascality*—all of which Nash abhorred and said would not last. There are, in fact, no earlier citations for any of these words than the year Nash cites.

joy o' the mountain. This colorful name is given to trailing arbutus in the mountains of the American South. Trailing arbutus (of the *Epigaea* genus) is probably the most fragrant of all wildflowers. The evergreen plant is difficult to cultivate in home gardens, but thrives in the wild.

Judas; Judas goat; etc. On Holy Saturday in Corfu the people still throw crockery into the streets, enacting their traditional stoning of Judas Iscariot. Thousands of years have passed, but Christ's betrayer remains the most infamous traitor of all time, his name recorded in many expressions, including *Judas* or *Judas Iscariot*, meaning any treacherous person who turns against a friend for some reward, as Judas did for 30 pieces of silver; *Judas kiss*, outward courtesy clothing deceit, alluding to the way Judas identified Jesus to the high priests in the Garden of Gethsemane; *Judas tree*, any of the several *circis* species, whose purple flowers suggest dark blood and upon which, tradition says, the traitor hanged himself after his act of betrayal; and *Judas goat*, the stockyard goat that leads unsuspecting animals to slaughter.

judo. *Judo* means "the gentle way" in Japanese. It is a modern variation of the ancient sport of *jujitsu*, first played by samurai. *Judo* was invented around 1882 by Japanese educator Jigoro Kano, who was appalled with the violence used by many of his countrymen practicing ju-jitsu. Kano outlawed many dangerous moves of the older sport, including foot strikes, and developed several new moves. The sport quickly caught on in Japan and other countries, including the United States, where Teddy Roosevelt became a devotee.

jugged hare. *Jugged hare* is not an inebriated rabbit, but a young hare (genus *Lepus*) prepared in an earthenware pot or jug, its sauce sometimes thickened with the animal's blood. This classic English dish, along with German *Hasenfeffer*, is the most famous of hare dishes worldwide. The Spanish have a proverb, *vender gato por liebre*, to sell a cat for a hare, an expression that originated when Spanish hostels palmed off cat as hare and which is remembered by those Spanish markets that even today display hare paws intact to prove it isn't some Tom from the back alleys.

jug; jughead. Ernest Benzon, a wealthy playboy, was dubbed "Jubilee Juggins" because he foolishly squandered his entire fortune—a quarter of a million pounds—within two years after beginning to bet at the track during Queen Victoria's Jubilee in 1887. One source claims that the nickname "Silly Juggins" also attached itself to him, and perhaps we do refer to young Jubilee when we use that term. *Juggins*, however, was synonymous with simpleton long before Jubilee Juggins. Possibly it is a rhyming variation of *muggins*, which derives from an unknown personal name and means the same. Or *juggins* may be a diminutive of *Jug*, a 16th-century pet name for Judith, Jane, or Joan. Jugs, Judiths, Janes, or Joans were often maidservants or barmaids at the time, and most servants of the day were considered dull and stupid, at least by their masters. The word *jug*, for "a pitcher," could also come from these maidservant Jugs, who often handled them, but the Greek word *keramos*, "potter's earth," is another possibility. Most authorities regard these etymologies as incapable of proof, yet it is likely that all these words—and thus *jughead*—make fun of a personal name. *Jug*, in fact, may have arisen from some squat Joan or Jug's resemblance to a drinking vessel of similar shape. *See also* HOOSEGOW.

the juice ain't worth the squeeze. The juice here is orange juice, not liquor, and the saying means it's not worth doing, the effort isn't worth the result. Reported by a Maryland correspondent.

jukebox. A juke house or juke is a house of ill repute, a whorehouse, taking its name from the black dialect called Gullah spoken on the islands off the coast of South Carolina, Georgia, and Florida. The Gullah word *juke*, or *jook*, in turn, apparently derives from the Wolof West African word *dzug* or *dzog*, meaning "to misconduct oneself, to lead a disorderly life." *Juke* naturally came to be associated with anything connected with a *juke house*, even the early *jook* or *juke organs*, coin-operated music boxes that sounded like *hurdy-gurdies* and were often found in *juke houses*. When coin-operated phonographs became very popular in the early 1940s they were called *jukeboxes* after their early counterparts, so the name of this ubiquitous electrically operated machine can be ascribed to a West African tribe.

Jukes and Kallikaks. Their names happen to be fictitious, but the Jukes and the Kallikaks are real families whose histories showed early 20th-century sociologists that heredity, rather than environment, was the cause of feeblemindedness as well as the poverty and crime often resulting from it. The Jukes were a New York family given their pseudonym by Richard L. Dugsdale, a prison sociologist who traced the clan back several generations after finding its members in various state prisons. Tracing the family to a backwoodsman named Max, who had married two of his own sisters, Dugsdale uncovered a fantastic record of criminal activity, disease, and poverty. Of the 709 descendants on whom he obtained precise information, he established that 140 Jukes had been in prison, 280 had been paupers, and that the Jukes family in 75 years had cost New York State $1,308,000. The Kallikaks, another real though pseudonymous family, were studied in New Jersey and revealed the same pattern of a high incidence of crime, disease, and delinquency, the two names soon linked together by writers on the subject. *Kallikak* combines the Greek *kallos*, "beauty," and *kakos*, "ugly, bad."

Julian calendar; etc. You can clip precious time from your age if you immigrate to Addis Ababa, the capital of Ethiopia, where the Julian calendar is still used locally. The "slow" Julian calendar, instituted by Gaius Julius Caesar, was corrected and replaced by the GREGORIAN CALENDAR in 1582, although it continued to be used in England until the middle 18th century, when it was proclaimed in 1752, that Wednesday, September 2, would be followed by Thursday, September 14. Inaccurate, but a great reform at the time, the Julian calendar had been introduced in 46 B.C. It established the year as 365¼ days, with a leap year of 366 days every fourth year. Caesar's calendar divided the months into the number of days they presently contain, except for *August*, which Augustus Caesar insisted have 31 days when it was later named in his honor, not wanting Julius's *July* to contain more days than his month. The *Julian day* also pertains to Julius Caesar. It is a chronological reckoning used by astronomers enabling every day since the beginning of the *Julian era* (fixed at January 1, 4713 B.C.) to be numbered consecutively, thus avoiding complications due to months and years of unequal length. The Julian day was devised by Joseph Scaliger in the same year as the Gregorian calendar.

julienne. One celebrated word sleuth seems to feel sure that *julienne,* when applied to a clear soup garnished with vegetables cut into thin strips, comes from the French *potage à la julienne,* the name bestowed by the chef of the Comte de Julienne. The *Oxford English Dictionary* is not so sure, citing "the French Jules or Julien, personal name," and another big dictionary, sweeping any male chauvinism aside, gives us "French, special use of Julienne woman's name." *Webster's* brings our French male chef to America, without a master, and has *julienne* named "after Julien, a French caterer of Boston," as do several American writers on food. While the controversy simmers, people will go on enjoying the soup, and all kinds of other foods cut into julienne strips.

Juliet. *See* ROMEO AND JULIET.

Juliet cap. Actresses playing Juliet in Shakespeare's *Romeo and Juliet* were the first to wear the little mesh cap decorated with pearls that women in later times adopted for dressy occasions and called the Juliet cap.

July. Mark Antony named the seventh month of the year in honor of Julius Caesar because it was the month he was born in. Up until about 1800, *July* was pronounced like the girl's name Julie in English, rhyming with "newly." In the southern United States, the word is still generally accented on the first syllable.

jumbo. P. T. Barnum purchased the fabled elephant Jumbo from the London Zoological Society in 1881 for "The Barnum and Bailey Greatest Show on Earth." Jumbo, captured by a hunting party in 1869, was one of the largest elephants ever seen in West Africa; the natives called the six-and-a-half-ton beast by the Swahili word *jumbo,* meaning "chief." He became a great favorite in the London Zoo, giving rides to thousands of children, and his sale to the American showman caused quite an uproar. Within six weeks the incomparable P.T. had reaped $336,000 from the $30,000 investment, and he made Jumbo's name a synonym for "huge" throughout America and the world. *See* THICK AS JESSE.

jumper. Only in recent times has the jumper become a woman's garment. Originally it was a coarse canvas shirt reaching to the hips that was worn by sailors. The word derives from *jump,* for a short coat men wore in the 18th century.

jumping bean; jumping cactus. The seed of certain Mexican plants of the genus *Sapium* and *Sebastiana* that jump or move about because of the movements of a moth larva inside the seed. *Jumping bean* and *Mexican jumping bean* are Americanisms first recorded in about 1885. *Jumping cactus,* which entered the language at about the same time, refers to the cholla cactus of the Southwest, so named because when the loose stems on the ground are touched the entire plant may move, and/or because it aggressively shoots its needles at people who come too close.

jumping Jehoshaphat! *See* JEZEBEL.

jump the gun. *See* GIVE HER THE GUN.

June. One of ancient Rome's leading class, the Junius family, had June named in its honor, the naming probably influenced by the fact that the festival of Juno, goddess of the moon, fell on the first of that month.

Juneteenth. June 19, in honor of the emancipation date of blacks in Texas, where the holiday is celebrated annually by many African-Americans.

Jungian. Jungian psychology differs from FREUDIAN essentially in that it maintains that the libido, or energy, derives not from sexual instinct but from the will to live. Carl Gustav Jung (1875–1961), an early disciple of Freud, broke with the master over what he considered an excessive emphasis on sex as a cause of neurotic disorders and a regulator of human conduct. He became a world-renowned figure, postulating the existence of two unconscious influences on the mind—the personal unconscious, containing an individual's own experience, and the collective or racial unconscious, holding the accumulated memories of generations past. The Swiss psychiatrist divided mankind into *introverts* and *extroverts,* using those or similar terms for the first time. Among many other innovations, he invented the *word-association test.*

jungle. Another word that the British brought back from India, *jungle* began life as the Hindi *jangal.* In Hindi it first meant "a desert"; then it took on the meaning of "uncultivated land"; and finally, it came to mean "land wild with trees and other uncultivated growth."

jungle gym. *See* MONKEY BARS.

junk. "Junk" was the best pronunciation 18th-century British mariners could make of the rude little Javanese sailing boat called a *djong. Junk,* therefore, became the name for the small boat and possibly the word for the things scattered about any ship that seemed as untidy as the *djongs* appeared, though the origin of *junk* in this last respect isn't certain.

junket. "The term *junket* in America is generally applied to a trip taken by an American official at the expense of the government he serves so nobly and unselfishly," noted a *Detroit Free Press* writer in 1886. The Americanism had been used similarly by Washington Irving in 1809. Our *junket* comes from the British *junket,* for "a banquet," which may derive from the old Norman word *jonquette,* meaning a reed basket in which fish and other things were carried, or "in which sweet cream cheese was brought into town for sale." *Jonquette,* in turn, comes from the Latin *juncus,* "a reed."

Junoesque. Said of any queenly, attractive, often large-breasted woman, after the majestic goddess Juno, wife of Jupiter in Roman mythology.

Jurassic. Wrote James Truslow Adams in *The Epic of America* (1938): "In what is known as the Jurassic period in the geological history of the earth, there suddenly developed in the course of animal evolution a vast number of huge reptiles." The world has recently become more aware of this phenomenon with the release of the movie *Jurassic Park* (1993), based on a novel of that name by Michael Crichton. The geological term takes its name from the *Jura* mountains separating France from Switzerland and means "characterized by large quantities of granular limestone," as these mountains are.

just a heartbeat away from the presidency. Presidential candidate Adlai Stevenson coined this phrase in a campaign speech on October 23, 1952. He was referring to Republican vice presidential nominee Richard Nixon, "the young man who asks you to set him one heartbeat from the presidency of the United States."

just as leave. When someone says "I'd just as leave stay home as go to that party," he or she should properly use *lief*, meaning "gladly or willingly," not *leave*, in the phrase. However, people have used *leave* incorrectly for so long that *lief* is slowly but surely becoming obsolete in the expression. Nevertheless, *just as lief*, or *had as lief* can be traced back almost a thousand years.

just deserts. The expression, meaning something deserved or merited, has nothing to do with the word *dessert*, a sweet course served at the end of a meal, which comes from the French *desservir*, in its sense of "to merit by service." The word *desert* for a wasteland derives from the Latin *deserere* "to leave uninhabited."

just for openers. Originally a poker term dating back to the early 19th century and strictly meaning someone's first bet in a game, *just for openers* quickly extended to many other realms, especially the world of business, where it is still frequently used to mean someone's first action or first offer.

Justins. Cowboys began to wear fancy boots by the end of the 19th century, some handtooled leather ones costing them two months' pay, about $50. The most famous of these were made by Fort Worth bootmaker Joseph Justin and called Justins in his honor. The term is still in use today.

just in the nick of time. Up until the 18th century, both time and transactions were commonly recorded by scoring notches, or nicks, on a stick called a TALLY. These nicks account for the *nick* in the common expression *just in the nick of time*, "not a second too soon."

just like Jell-o on springs. Famously said by Jack Lemmon of Marilyn Monroe walking away in the film *Some Like It Hot* (1959), and since used to describe other sexy women. *Jelly*, not JELL-O, had earlier described this love-potion motion in the popular song lyric "I wish I could shimmy like my sister Kate, / She shakes like jelly on a plate . . ."

Just So Stories. These stories for children about how the leopard got his spots, the camel his hump, the elephant his trunk, etc., were published in 1902 by Rudyard Kipling, who became the first English writer to win the Nobel Prize five years later. The imaginative stories, among the author's best work, got their title, *Just So Stories*, because Kipling's daughter Elsie didn't care about how unscientific they were; the little girl wanted to hear her father's tales over and over, with no scientific explanation added, "just so."

just under the wire. This phrase means to barely make the limit or meet the deadline. The expression is from horse racing, where the imaginary "wire" is the finish line and a horse just under the wire is one who beats out another horse by a nose to finish in the money.

Juvenalian. Savagely satirical, like the verse satires of Juvenal (ca. 60–ca. 140), the greatest Roman satirist, whose style was imitated by John Dryden, Dr. Johnson, Alexander Pope, and, especially, Jonathan Swift, among many. Juvenal wrote 16 satires attacking the vices, abuses, and fatuities of Roman life, satires marred by an excessive hatred of the rich and the condemnation of all women. But though kindly humor is absent in his pages and his unsparing pessimisim fills all of them, his vigorous, ironic, terse style make him one of the world's greatest writers of satire.

K

K. Representing the Greek *kappa* and the Hebrew *kaph* before it, the letter *K* was used by the Romans for the *K* sound in place of the *C*, which they abandoned. Roman libelers, for example, were branded on the forehead with a *K*, for *kalumnia*, "calumny."

K (for a strikeout). The practice of using the letter *K* for a strikeout dates as far back as 1861, according to Joseph L. Reichler of the baseball commissioner's office. In those days, when a hitter struck out, it was said that "he struck." Letters were used for scoring, as they are today: *E* for an error, *S* for a sacrifice, etc. Since the letter S could not also be used for "struck," the last letter, *K*, of the word "struck" was used, and it has remained the symbol for a strikeout. Henry Chadwick, the newspaperman credited with inventing the box score, invented these symbols, the term *K* used at the time "for a player who missed the ball in three swings." It is first recorded in about 1880.

kabloona. A Canadian word meaning a white person, a European. Used chiefly in Arctic Canada, it was first recorded about 1765 and derives from the Inuit *qablunaaq*, which does not mean "person with big eyebrows" as it is often translated, but comes from the Inuit *gava*, "south," suggesting a person who comes from the south.

kachina doll. A Hopi Indian doll. Carved from cottonwood root in the shape of a kachina, an ancestral spirit, it is used as a household decoration or given as a gift to a child.

kaffeeklatsch. This expression is used, mainly among housewives, as a synonym for the more popular "coffee break." *Klatsch* is German for "a good gossip or gabfest," one held over *kaffee*, or "coffee."

kaffir. Long a derogatory term used by whites to describe blacks in Africa, *kaffir* derives from the time when Arab slavers first came to the east coast of Africa. The slavers called the people there *qafirs*, "unbelievers," because they had not yet accepted Islam, and *qafir* became the pejorative *kaffir*.

Kafkaesque. Franz Kafka's three novels (*The Castle, The Trial,* and the unfinished *Amerika*) and his short stories are characterized by the surreal distortion and sense of impending doom in a nightmarishly impersonal world that define this word. Kafka, an Austrian born in Prague, died of tuberculosis in 1924 when only age 40. Believing that he had failed in his life's work, the author's last request was for his friend Max Brod to burn all his papers and unpublished manuscripts. Brod refused to do this, rationalizing that Kafka did not really want it done or he would not have asked someone he must have known would never do such a thing. Instead, Brod published Kafka's immensely influential writings. First recorded in *The New Yorker* in 1947, the adjective *Kafkaesque* is frequently heard today.

kaiser. Like CZAR, *kaiser* too derives from the surname of Gaius Julius Caesar, being merely the German word for caesar. *Kaiser* was the title of the emperor of the Holy Roman Empire and the emperors of Germany and Austria. The word has less of a stigma attached to it than czar. Another title for a ruler often attributed to Caesar is *shah*. *Shah*, however, actually derives from a Sanskrit word, meaning "dominion."

Kalashnikov. Mikhail Kalashnikov invented the Kalashnikov automatic assault rifle, often called the AK-47, while recuperating from his wounds during World War II. Later, the weapon was modified and became known as the AKM. For his invention Kalashnikov was made a hero of socialist labor by the former Soviet Union. His rifle is still widely used throughout the world.

kale. *Kale* is 20th-century American slang for money, as well as a vegetable. The word derives from the Middle English *cale*, a variant of *cole*, for "cabbage." American settlers called this primitive member of the cabbage family *colewarts*.

Kal-el. Superman is an alias or nom de querre in the fight against evil. The comic book hero's real name is Kal-el, bestowed upon him by his parents when he was born on the planet Krypton before it exploded. *See* SUPERMAN.

ka me, ka thee.   An expression dating back to at least the early 16th century that means "I'll help you if you help me," "You scratch my back, I'll scratch yours." No one is sure where the word *ka* comes from, but it could be a corruption of *claw*, which fits in nicely with the "scratch" definition.

Kamerad, Kamerad!   *Kamerad* doesn't mean "I surrender" in German, as many people believe. It is German for "comrade." German soldiers who used *Kamerad, Kamerad!* in surrendering during World Wars I and II were appealing to the mercy of "comrade" human beings. The expression, however, has taken on the meaning of "I surrender" in English.

kamikaze.   Toward the end of World War II improved defenses and better U.S. aircraft made it difficult for Japanese planes to get close to U.S. ships and bomb or strafe them. Kamikaze planes on suicidal missions were employed as a last resort. The planes, heavily loaded with explosives, were flown in mass formations and crashed into enemy ships. Scores of ships were sunk or disabled by this suicidal tactic. The planes and their pilots took their names from the *kamikaze*, or "wind of the gods" of 1281 that had wrecked a Mongol fleet invading Japan.

Kandahar.   This city in southern Afghanistan, important in the 9/11 war, was conquered by Alexander the Great in 329 B.C. It was shortly after named in his honor, Kandahar, a variation on his name.

kangaroo.   The great English explorer Captain James Cook asked a native of the Australian Endeavor River tribe for the name of a strange marsupial Cook had spotted. The native answered, "kangaroo," or "I don't know." Cook assumed that this was what the native called the animal, which is how *kangaroo* (or "I don't know") got in the dictionaries. At least that is the derivation several etymologists suggest, there being no better theory, though the story isn't mentioned in any official account of Cook's voyages. The *O.E.D.* says the story "lacks confirmation" but can find no similar word in any Australian language. *See also* INDRI; LLAMA; LUZON; NOME; YUCATAN.

kangaroo court.   While this expression may have originated in Australia, it was first recorded in America during the California gold rush. Perhaps Australian "49ers" did bring it with them to the gold fields. According to this story, the source for the term is kangaroos in Australia's back country, who when out of spear range sat staring dumbly at men for long periods of time before leaping off for the horizon; their staring was thought to be similar to the dumb stares of jurors sitting on a mock jury, and their leaping away suggesting the quick decisions of such an extralegal court. But there are no quotations supporting the use of *kangaroo court* in Australia at any time. The expression could have been coined in America, in fact, based on the several uses of the word *kangaroo* in England for anything unusual or eccentric. Another guess is that Americans familiar with the kangaroo's jumping habits, or Australians here with gold fever, invented *kangaroo court* as a humorous term for courts that tried "claim-jumpers," miners who seized the mining claims of others.

kan pei!   Thousands of war veterans, among others, know *kan pei* as a Japanese, Korean, and Chinese drinking toast. It translates as "dry cup," and a person making the toast often downs his drink to the last drop and holds his empty glass upside down over his head to show that the glass is drained dry.

Kansas.   The Sunflower State, admitted to the Union in 1861 as our 34th state, takes its name from the name of a Sioux tribe meaning "people of the south wind." It had previously been called the Kansas Territory.

kaolin.   The fine white clay used for ceramics and many other products takes its name from Gaoling Mountain in southeastern China, from where it was first exported to Europe.

kaput.   In the old French gambling game of piquet, *capot* meant not to win a single trick. *Capot* became the German *kaputt*, with the same meaning, which over a long period of time was extended to mean "having been destroyed, wrecked, or incapacitated," just as some players would be after not winning a single trick in a game. By the end of the 19th century *kaputt* had entered English as *kaput*.

karaoke.   The Japanese invented this form of entertainment and the name for it in the late 1970s. Karaoke, frequently offered by bars and clubs, consists of people taking turns singing songs into a microphone over prerecorded tracks that contain music but not the words to the songs. The entertainment has spread worldwide, and many people have karaoke machines in their homes. The word is composed of the Japanese *kara*, "empty," and *oke*, an abbreviation of *okesutora*, a Japanese rendering of the English *orchestra*. Literally it means "empty orchestra."

karate.   Born in China and refined in Japan, karate is the ancient art of defending oneself against an armed attacker by striking sensitive areas on the attacker's body with the hands, elbows, knees, or feet. Centuries later the sport of karate based on this method of self-defense was introduced. Modern karate owes much to Japanese karate master Funakoshi Gichin, who taught the art and indeed gave it the name *karate*, from the Japanese *kara*, "empty," and *te*, "hands." *Shotokan karate* (named after Funakoshi's nickname, Shoto) is the most popular form of karate today.

Katy-bar-the-door.   Watch out, take precautions, big trouble is coming, as in "When that hurricane hits, it's liable to be Katy-bar-the-door." The Americanism, a century or so old, probably was coined in the Wild West.

katydid.   John Bartram, America's first great botanist, first recorded *katydid* (or a word similar to it) in 1751 as the name of the large, green arboreal insect of the locust family known scientifically as *Microcentrum rhombifolium*. The word is of imitative origin, the chattering noise the insect makes sounding like "Katy did! Katy did!"

kayak.   Traditionally an Eskimo canoe with a skin cover over its light framework, but today any small boat resembling it, no matter what materials are used. The word, first recorded in the mid-18th century, comes from the Inuit *qayaq*.

keelboat. "These boats were long and narrow, sharp at the bow and stern, and of light draft. They were provided with running boards, extending from bow to stern, on each side of the boat," a writer noted in the *American Pioneer* (1843). *Keelboats*, also called *keels* at the time, were first recorded in the language in 1785 and the word derives from the *kiel boot* (meaning the same thing) of early Dutch settlers. *Keelboatmen* were among the roughest of men on the frontier.

keelhauling; keelraking. *Keelhauling* today means merely a tongue-lashing from a superior, hardly a punishment compared to the original keelhauling used as a discipline for Dutch sailors in the 16th century. Erring Dutch sailors, and later seamen in many other navies, were keelhauled by being tied to the yardarm, weighted down, and then hauled by a rope under the vessel from side to side. Sometimes they suffered an even more dreaded punishment, being keelraked, or hauled under the ship from stem to stern.

keel over. To *keel* a boat is to roll her over on her keel; that is, to turn up the keel—the bottom of the boat—wrong side uppermost. This nautical practice and term led to the Americanism *to keel over*, first recorded in 1832, which meant "to turn a man or beast over on his back, to upset or capsize."

keep a stiff upper lip. *See* STIFF UPPER LIP.

keep a straight face. To refrain from laughing. One story has this expression deriving from Irish peat diggers, who have to make their spade thrusts perfectly vertical when digging out peat (thus keeping a straight spade face—"face" here the working side of the implement). I can find no proof of this and the words more likely were suggested by someone trying to keep his face from squinching up in laughter. The phrase is first recorded in an 1897 issue of the *Spectator*: "The story is one which few people, to use an expressive vulgarism, will be able to read 'with a straight face.' "

keeping up with the Joneses. According to his own account, cartoonist Arthur R. ("Pop") Momand lived in a community where many people tried to keep up with the Joneses. Momand and his wife resided in Cedarhurst, New York, one of Long Island's Five Towns, where the average income is still among America's highest. Living "far beyond our means in our endeavor to keep up with the well-to-do class," the Momands were wise enough to quit the scene and move to Manhattan, where they rented a cheap apartment and "Pop" Momand used his Cedarhurst experience to create his once immensely popular *Keeping Up with the Joneses* comic strip, launched in 1913. Momand first thought of calling the strip "Keeping Up with the Smiths," but "finally decided on *Keeping Up with the Joneses* as being more euphonious." His creation ran in American newspapers for over 28 years and appeared in book, movie, and musical-comedy form, giving the expression *keeping up with the Joneses* the wide currency that made it a part of everyday language.

keep it under your hat. Keep something under your hat and it is kept to yourself, it remains a secret to anyone but you. Unlike "blockhead," which goes back to the first hats, the expression is of surprisingly recent origin, having been first recorded in a similar form in 1909 and recorded in its present form in P. G. Wodehouse's *The Inimitable Jeeves* (1923).

keep one's end up. *See* HAVE ONE'S INNINGS.

keep on truckin'. Keep going, keep moving, don't quit. Etymologist Joseph T. Shipley wrote that the expression "comes from the great marathon dance contests that were a part of our 1930s scene, when all the partners clung to one another, half-asleep, but on and on moving around the dance hall through the night, like the great trucks that go endlessly across our continent through the dark hours, as they 'keep on truckin' for the prize." This scene was brilliantly depicted in the movie *They Shoot Horses, Don't They?* (1969).

keep the ball rolling. The election of 1840, which pitted President Martin Van Buren running for reelection against "Tippecanoe and Tyler, too"—General William Henry Harrison, legendary hero who fought against the Indians at Tippecanoe, and Virginian John Tyler—brought with it the first modern political campaign. Some historians believe that the election gave us the expression *keep the ball rolling* as well as the word *O.K.* One popular advertising stunt that helped Harrison win was "to keep the ball rolling" for the "log cabin and hard cider candidate." Ten-foot "victory-balls," made of tin and leather and imprinted with the candidate's name, were rolled from city to city for as far as 300 miles. These victory balls did popularize the expression *keep the ball rolling*, keep interest from flagging, but the saying undoubtedly dates back to the late 18th century. Of British origin, it alludes either to the game of bandy, a form of hockey where the puck is a small ball, or the game of rugby. In either sport there is no interest in the game if the ball is not rolling. The first form of the expression was *keep the ball up*. *See* BANDY; O.K.

Keep the faith, baby! This expression was common among Civil Rights workers in the 1960s and became a popular slang expression meaning "don't give up." It is much older than this, however, and has its origins in the Bible (2 Tim. 4:7): "I have fought the good fight. I have finished my course. I have kept the faith." FIGHT THE GOOD FIGHT has also been a popular expression through the ages.

keep your eye on the ball. Many sports could have spawned the American expression meaning "be closely attentive." Baseball, tennis, golf, and basketball are all candidates, but the saying seems to have derived from the exhortations of college football coaches to their charges at the turn of the century. *To be on the ball*, to be vitally alert or in the know, is apparently an offshoot of this phrase, even though in baseball it has been said of a pitcher who has a wide variety of effective pitches.

keep your eyes peeled. To keep your eyes peeled for something is to keep them wide open, to keep a sharp lookout. The earliest known form of the frontier expression, recorded in 1833, was to *keep your eyes skinned* (presumably meaning with the lids drawn back): "I wish I may be shot if I don't think you had better keep your eyes skinned so that you can look powerful sharp . . ."

keep your fingers crossed. Making the sign of the cross has long been thought to be effective in averting evil, but the use of crossed fingers as a symbol of the cross is American in origin, probably originating as a superstition among blacks in the 17th century. The practice was also thought to bring good luck and resulted in the expression to *keep your fingers crossed,* as well as the belief among schoolchildren and others that a lie told with the fingers (or toes, or legs, etc.) crossed "doesn't count."

keep your pants on. Don't be impatient. This old expression could derive from a sexual situation, or it may, more likely, simply be an extension of KEEP YOUR SHIRT ON. No one is sure.

keep your pecker up. These words shouldn't be X-rated; *pecker* here refers not to the penis, as many people believe, but to the lip. *Pecker* has been slang for lip, corresponding as it does to the beak, or pecker, of a bird, since the middle of the 19th century, when we first find this expression meaning "screw up your courage, keep a stiff upper lip." (*Pecker,* for the male organ, has been slang only since the late 19th century.) The first recorded use of the phrase is impeccably British: "Keep up your pecker, old fellow" (1853). A more specific explanation is that it refers to a gamecock's bill, the bird's bill or pecker sinking lower toward the ground as he grows more tired and near defeat.

keep your shirt on. The stiff, starched shirts worn by American men back in the mid-19th century when this expression originated weren't made for a man to fight in. Therefore, men often removed their shirts when enraged and ready to fight, a practice that is reflected in the older British expression *to get one's shirt out,* "to lose one's temper." *Keep your shirt on* was a natural admonition from someone who didn't want to fight and realized that an argument could be settled if both parties kept calm and collected. *Keep your hair on* and *keep your back hair up* are earlier related expressions for "don't get excited."

keep your stick on the ice! Perhaps no other people love the sport of ice hockey more than Canadians do. *Keep your stick on the ice* is their way of saying: Pay attention!

Kelley Blue Book. The standard guide in the U.S. for dealers and the courts in determining the value of all used cars of all makes and model years. It was developed by Sidney "Buster" Kelley (1909–2001) of the Kelley Kar Company, which from the end of World War I to the end of World War II was the biggest used car business in the world. The Blue Book was first published in 1926.

Kelly pool. This is a variety of pool in which each player draws a number; while trying to sink the balls in numerical order, the players must pocket their numbered balls as well. It is said to be named either for an unknown Irishman surnamed Kelly, or in honor of Ireland, where it was invented.

kelpie. Wives of Scottish fishermen believed that a black horse with red eyes called the kelpie rose from the sea to warn them of forthcoming maritime disasters. Kelpie would then descend into the deep until it could be of help again. Yet another Scottish legend has it that an equine water spirit called the kelpie delighted in drowning travelers.

Kelvinator; Kelvin scale. Barely 10 years old when he entered Glasgow University, William Thomson was appointed a full professor of natural philosophy there when only 22. The Scottish mathematician and physicist early became one of the greatest scientists of his or any other era and toward the end of his career was created first Baron Kelvin of Larga. In his long lifetime Lord Kelvin made fundamental theoretical contributions in numerous scientific fields including thermodynamics, electricity, solar radiation, and cosmology. He also personally supervised the laying of the transatlantic cable in 1866, initiated the determination of electrical standards, and invented many useful instruments—among them the modern compass, a deep-sea sounding apparatus, an electric bridge, a standard balance, the mirror galvanometer, the siphon recorder, and a variety of instruments for electrical engineers. This great, good, and kind man invented the absolute or Kelvin temperature scale, which has the advantage of expressing any temperature in a positive number, and the British Kelvinator, or refrigerator, was named in his honor in 1914 when theories he had advanced made the appliance possible. Lord Kelvin retired from Glasgow University after teaching there half a century, but three years later matriculated as a student in order to maintain his connection with the university—thus making him, at 75, the oldest genius ever to go back to school. He died in 1907, aged 83.

Kemble pipe. In 1678 Titus Oates fabricated a story about a Jesuit papist plot that would assassinate England's Charles II, among other Protestants, and put the Catholic duke of York on the throne. As a result, many Catholics were persecuted, and some 35 died by mob violence or by legal hanging. Among the latter was William Kemble, who calmly smoked his pipe and chatted pleasantly all the way to the gallows. The liar Oates was merely, though severely, flogged and imprisoned until he was pardoned and pensioned by William III. All poor Kemble got out of the affair was the naming in his honor of a large pipe like the one he smoked.

Kenilworth ivy. A European creeping vine (*Cymbalaria muralis*) with small pale purple flowers that was named after Kenilworth Castle in central England, where it grows on the castle walls. It is also called coliseum ivy.

kenning. A *kenning* is a poetic phrase used in place of or in addition to the usual name of a person or thing. It is used to introduce color or suggest associations without distracting from the essential statement made. The word for these compound metaphors comes from the *Old Norse* phrase *kenna eitt vio,* "to express or describe one thing in terms of another." For example, the sea in Old English was called "swan's road" (*swansrad*), or "whale's path"; a boat was a "wave traveler" or "foamy necked"; darkness was "the helmet of night"; the queen was "peace weaver"; and a sword was "hammer leaving."

Kensington Hay. A name for the affected accent of residents of London's Kensington borough, who often pronounce *mother* "mothah" and *high* as "hay" (as in *Kensington Hay Street*). The term was first recorded in the early 1900s.

Kentucky. The Blue Grass State was admitted to the Union in 1792 as our 15th state, formerly having been Kentucky County, Virginia. It takes its name from the Iroquois *Kentake*, "meadowland." Historically Kentucky was called "the dark and bloody ground" because it was an Indian no-man's-land used by several tribes as a burial and hunting ground.

Kentucky burgoo. A celebrated stew made of chicken or small game, and corn, tomatoes, and onions; traditionally served on Derby Day. *See* KENTUCKY DERBY.

Kentucky colonel. Someone upon whom the honorary title of Colonel is bestowed in Kentucky, though no one takes the title very seriously.

Kentucky Derby. A horse race for three-year-olds held annually since 1875 on the first Saturday in May at Churchill Downs in Louisville, Kentucky; it was named after the English Derby at Epsom Downs, first held in 1780. *See* DERBY.

Kentucky fried chicken. *See* GOSPEL BIRD.

Kentucky rifle. Famous in American history as the rifle of the pioneers, the long, extremely accurate Kentucky rifle is recorded by this name as early as 1838. The flint-lock muzzle-loader should, however, be called the Pennsylvania rifle, for it was first made in that state by Swiss gunsmiths in the 1730s and perfected there. "The British bayonet was no match for the Kentucky rifle," wrote one early chronicler.

Kentucky right turn. According to William Safire's "On Language" column in the *New York Times* (January 27, 1991), this is a humorous term meaning "the maneuver performed when a driver, about to turn right, first swings to the left."

kept woman. No invention of modern times, this term for a mistress dates back at least five centuries, when it was first recorded in 1560: "Others kept harlots and lived dishonestly."

ketchup. Is it *ketchup, catsup, catchup,* or *kitchup?* Since the word derives from the Chinese Amoy dialect *ke-tsiap,* "pickled fish-brine or sauce," which became the Malay *kechap,* the first spelling is perhaps the best. The original condiment that Dutch traders imported from the Orient appears to have been either a fish sauce similar to the Roman *garum* or a sauce made from special mushrooms salted for preservation. Englishmen added a "t" to the Malay word, changed the "a" to "u" and began making ketchup themselves, using ingredients like mushrooms, walnuts, cucumbers, and oysters. It wasn't until American seamen added tomatoes from Mexico or the Spanish West Indies to the condiment that tomato ketchup was born. But the spelling and pronunciation "catsup" have strong literary precedents, as witness Dean Swift's: "And for our home-bred British cheer,/ Botargo [fish roe relish], catsup and cabiar [caviar]." (1730). *Catchup* has an earlier citation (1690) than either of the other spellings, predating *ketchup* by some 20 years. *Ketjap,* the Dutch word for the sauce, and *kitchup* have also been used in English. Anyway, a red tide of half a billion bottles of ketchup, catsup, catchup, or kitchup is slopped on everything from Big Macs to vanilla ice cream(!) in America each year.

Kewpie doll. In 1909 the American author and magazine illustrator Rose Cecil O'Neill (1874–1944) published a poem in *Ladies' Home Journal* that she illustrated with cupid-like imps. The imps proved so popular that she invented a doll called Kewpie (the name is a form of *cupid*), which she patented and made a fortune with, in the process adding the term *Kewpie doll* to the language.

key lime pie. Named for the tart limes of the Florida Keys, this delicious pie has been part of the Conch cuisine there for well over a century.

Keynesian. Keynesian economic theory advocates government monetary and fiscal programs designed to increase employment and stimulate business activity. The word comes from the name of British economist John Maynard Keynes (1883–1946), whose full employment theory was set forth in his *Treatise On Money* and his *The General Theory of Employment, Interest and Money.* Keynes's work revolutionized economic thinking and made him one of the leading economists of his time. He also belonged to London's intellectual BLOOMSBURY group, which included Virginia Woolf and E. M. Forster among its members.

Keystone State. A nickname for Pennsylvania since at least 1803, when it was first recorded. Pennsylvania also has been called the Quaker State, the Steel State, and the Oil State. Keystone was chosen because Pennsylvania was the keystone of the arch that the original 13 colonies loosely formed.

Key West. This southernmost area of Florida and the U.S. takes its English name from Spanish Cayo-Hueso, a small rocky islet to the west.

khaki. The *khaki* cloth used for soldiers' warm-weather uniforms, which are called *khakis,* owes its name to its color. *Khaki,* twilled cloth originally made in India, means "dust-colored or dusty," deriving from the Persian *khak,* "earth."

kibitzer. It seems that German card players of the 16th century found meddlesome onlookers just as annoying as card players do today. The constant gratuitous "advice" of these chatterers reminded them of the kiebitz (the lapwing, or plover) whose shrill cries frightened game away from approaching hunters. Thus all kibitzers are named for this troublesome bird, our peewit, which inspired the German word *kiebitzen,* "to look over the shoulder of a card player." A play called *The Kibbitzer* (1929), which made Edward G. Robinson famous, contributed and the popularity of *kibitzer.*

kibosh. The Gaelic *cie bas,* pronounced "kibosh," means "cap of death" and seems to offer the most logical explanation for the expression *to put the kibosh on* something, "to put an end to it, to dispose of it." But another theory has the expression as Yiddish in origin, deriving either from the German *keibe,* "carrion," or from the Yiddish word *kibosh,* meaning 18 pence. Regarding the latter, it's said that bidders at small auctions *put the kibosh on* other bidders, forced them out, by jumping their bids to 18 pence. Dickens first recorded the phrase in his *Sketches by Boz* (1836). Two women are fighting in the East End of London and a young playboy shouts to one of them, "Hooroar, put the kye-bosk on her, Mary!"

kick against the pricks.   This expression is from Greek literature. Meaning "to show opposition to those in power," it refers to cattle kicking because they are being driven by someone pricking them with a sharp stick.

Kickapoo joy juice.   A humorous term for any cheap liquor, *Kickapoo joy juice* remembers the Algonquin Kickapoo Indian tribe formerly resident in Pennsylvania, Ohio, and Wisconsin, but now living in Oklahoma and numbering about 800. The Kickapoos weren't notorious drinkers; their name just seemed right for the alliterative phrase. Before the Civil War a *Kickapoo ranger* meant a violent pro-slaver in Kansas. American cartoonist Al Capp gave the expression *Kickapoo joy juice* wide currency in his comic strip "Li'l Abner."

kick it up a notch.   Make something, especially a recipe, a little more intense, better, more flavorful, hotter, etc. The expression is used frequently by Emeril Lagasse, host of the *Emeril Live* television cooking show when he prepares a recipe. It may have its origins in cooking, possibly deriving from a cook turning up the heat a notch on an oven's thermostat.

kickoff.   Today, to kick off an event means to start it. The phrase has obviously been influenced by American football, where the kickoff begins the game, but it more likely comes from soccer, in which there is a similar kickoff. *Kickoff* is first recorded in 1855, long before the first American football game.

kicks; get a kick out of.   Cole Porter's "I Get a Kick Out of You" isn't the source of this expression, though nowhere are the words put to better use. The phrase goes back to the turn of the century and was first used to describe the effects of liquor or drugs, not love. The case for drugs is strong, for the related expression *to get a charge out* of something derives from addicts' use of *charge* for the injection of a narcotic. *Kicks,* anything that gives one a thrill or satisfaction, comes from the same source as the phrase.

kickshaws.   Tidbits of food, trifles of small value. The word, spelled *kickshaws,* was used by Shakespeare in *Henry IV, Part II,* but had formerly been spelled *kickhose.* The confusion is understandable when we realize that the word is merely a corruption of the French *quelque chose,* "something," which comes from the Latin *qualis causa,* "of what kind."

kick the bucket.   A suicide who stands on a pail, slips a noose around his neck and kicks the pail, or bucket, out from under him would be the logical choice for the origin of this old slang term meaning to die. However, some etymologists say the phrase comes from an entirely different source. Slaughtered hogs, their throats slit, used to be hung by their heels, which were tied to a wooden block and the rope then thrown over a pulley that hoisted the animals up. Because hoisting the block was similar to raising a bucket from a well, the wooden block came to be called a "bucket," and the dying struggles of the hogs kicking against this "bucket" supposedly gave birth to

the phrase. There are other theories, however, and this old expression—it may date back to the 16th century—must be marked "of uncertain origin."

kid.   *Kid* is an adaptation of the Old Norse *kio,* also meaning the young of a goat, and seems to have come into the language in about 1200. The word was applied to the young of certain other animals not long after, but isn't recorded for a young child until 1599, as low slang, though it is now standard English. Since *kid* can mean a child or a young goat, *to kid* came to mean to hoax in early-19th-century England, to make a child or goat of someone.

kid-glove orange.   The mandarin orange or tangerine, so called because you can break the skin and peel it without using a knife or staining the fingers.

kidney bean.   The haricot bean takes its name from the French *haricot,* which derived from the Nahuatl Indian *ayacotl* for the bean; it is better known as the *kidney bean* for its shape, resembling a kidney.

kike.   One respected authority offers the surprising theory that this vulgar, offensive term of hostility and contempt, often used by anti-Semites, offends not only persons of Jewish descent but the Italians and Irish as well. The *Random House Dictionary of the English Language* suggests that it is "apparently modeled on *hike,* Italian, itself modeled on *Mike,* Irishman, short for Michael." In other words, the deliberately disparaging term painfully illustrates the transfer of prejudice from one newly arrived immigrant group to the next. This view runs counter to the prevailing theory, however. Mencken and others, including *Webster's,* believe that the word "derived from the 'ki' or 'ky' endings of the surnames of many Slavic Jews." Neither theory offers absolute proof. *See* DAGO; HARP; WASP; WELSH.

Kilkenny cats.   *See* FIGHT LIKE KILKENNY CATS.

killed with (by) kindness.   Shakespeare recorded this expression first in *The Taming of the Shrew* (1596) and Thomas Heywood later wrote a play *A Woman Killed with Kindness* (1603). The words, meaning to destroy or harm by excessive kindness, may be much older. There is a story that the Athenian lawmaker Draco, a popular man despite the stern DRACONIAN laws he imposed, was literally killed with kindness. While he was sitting in the theater at Aegina in about 590 B.C., other spectators hailed him by throwing their cloaks and caps in tribute. So many landed on Draco that he smothered to death.

killer instinct.   It is said that when former heavyweight champion Jack Dempsey fought, all he thought of was killing his opponent. In any case, the expression *killer instinct* seems to have been coined in the 1920s after Dempsey's beatings of Jess Willard, Georges Carpentier, and Luis Firpo. From boxing the term was extended to all areas of life, though no major dictionary records this very common expression.

killer ship.   A killer ship is a ship of any size on which "death has been caused by her sea behavior"; for example, if someone falls overboard or to the deck from aloft; if there is a fatal accident aboard of any kind; or if she rams another ship and causes death. The expression dates back to at least the 19th century.

killer whale; orca.   The killer whale (*Orcinus orca*) is technically a dolphin, but its relative the dolphin is its favorite food. Orca, as it is also called, has been dubbed the king of the sea and is certainly the sea's king of ferocity. Killer whales will leap out of the water onto Arctic ice to catch seals and walruses, and packs of them often attack and kill huge whales many times their size. Among the most intelligent of all marine animals, they are just as greedy and vicious. The creatures have been known and feared since earliest times and take their scientific name from the Latin *orca*, meaning the same.

killie.   The *killie*, often caught by children in shallow water, is a minnow-like fish of several species often used as hook bait for bigger fish. The word is short for *killfish*, which comes from the Dutch *kille*, "channel or stream," plus *visch* or fish, and is first recorded in 1814. *See* MINNOW.

killing fields.   The term is used today for any place where a horrific mass execution has taken place, often of civilians during or just after a war. *Killing fields* was first recorded in the *New York Times* in 1983 in reference to Pol Pot's murderous Khmer Rouge killing of 3 million Cambodians a decade earlier. A year later, the graphic film *The Killing Fields* gave the phrase a permanent place in the language of war.

killing no murder.   The phrase, holding that assassination can sometimes be condoned, was originally the title of a pamphlet urging the killing of Oliver Cromwell (1599–1658). Written in 1657 by Royalist Edward Sexby (d. 1658) the pamphlet is ironically dedicated to Cromwell: "The true father of your country; for while you live we can call nothing ours, and it is from your death that we hope for our inheritances." Sexby tried to kill Cromwell, narrowly failed, and was imprisoned in the Tower of London, where he died.

kill the fatted calf.   When the Prodigal Son returns home in the biblical story (Luke 15:23) his father prepares a great feast for him saying: "Bring hither the fatted calf and kill it." The story gives us the old expression *to kill the fatted calf*, to make a sumptuous feast to welcome someone.

kill the ump.   Umpires were often the targets of rocks, soda bottles, and tomatoes in the early days of baseball, and were frequently assaulted on and off the field by players and fans. Things got so bad that it was suggested that umpires be put in protective cages suspended over the field. As the following little ditty written in 1886 illustrates, fans of the day, much as now, claimed that umpires couldn't see a foot in front of them: "Breathes there a fan with soul so dead,/ Who never to the ump hath said:/ Yer blind, you bum!" This charge so infuriated National League president Thomas Lynch, a former umpire, that in 1911 he had a committee of oculists test the vision of all the umpires in the league. The committee reported that every umpire had 20-20 vision or better. Was *kill the ump* ever more than an idle threat? Several minor league umpires did indeed lose their lives on the diamond over close calls. And in 1911 one Patrick Casey, a convicted murderer at Nevada State Penitentiary, was granted the customary last request. Casey

wanted to umpire a baseball game before he died and so a game was arranged on the prison grounds and he was named umpire. When the game ended, he was executed.

Kilroy was here.   No catchphrase has ever rivaled Kilroy since it appeared on walls and every other available surface during World War II. It was first presumed that Kilroy was fictional; one graffiti expert even insisted that *Kilroy* represented an Oedipal fantasy, combining "kill" with "roi" (the French word for "king"). But word sleuths found that James J. Kilroy, a politician and an inspector in a Quincy, Massachusetts shipyard, coined the slogan. Kilroy chalked the words on ships and crates of equipment to indicate that he had inspected them. From Quincy the phrase traveled on ships and crates all over the world, copied by GIs wherever it went, and Kilroy, who died in Boston in 1962 at the age of 60, became the most widely "published" man since Shakespeare. James Kilroy wrote this about the coinage in the *New York Times Magazine* (Jan. 12, 1947): "On December 5, 1941, I started to work for Bethlehem Steel Company, Fore River Ship Yard, Quincy, Mass., as a rate setter (inspector) . . . I was getting sick of being accused of not looking the jobs over and one day, as I came through the manhole of a tank I had just surveyed, I angrily marked with yellow crayon on the tank top, where the tester could see it, 'KILROY WAS HERE.' "

kimchee.   Korea's traditional kimchee is a very spicy fermented mixture of cabbage, onions, and often fish, highly seasoned with horseradish, garlic, ginger, and red pepper. There are several kinds, the most celebrated being kakutaki kimchee. The dish is often prepared in November and buried in the ground in large earthen jars to preserve it throughout the cold months. South Korean troops fighting in Vietnam had to be supplied with kimchee to bolster their morale, for a Korean meal without it is virtually unthinkable—there is even a Korean proverb saying, "We can live a whole year without meat, but without kimchee we can hardly live a week." Many foreigners, however, find that kimchee burns their palates and complain that it has a strong, unpleasant odor.

Kim's game.   A parlor game in which the memory capacity of the players is tested. A number of objects are quickly shown to the participants, and they try to remember as many as they can, writing down the answers. The game is similar to one the eponymous hero plays in Rudyard Kipling's novel *Kim* (1901), generally considered his masterpiece.

kindergarten.   That young children should be taught according to their natural instincts, by stimulating and creating interest, is an accepted view today in educational circles. But when Friedrich Wilhelm August Froebel (1782–1852) put such ideas into practice in the world's first kindergarten ("children's garden"), which he founded in Blankenburg, Germany in 1837, his "Froebel teaching methods" met with wide disapproval. The German schoolmaster and former forester nevertheless remained convinced that preschool education was essential, devoting his life to establishing kindergartens and training teachers for them. Pleasant surroundings, the use of play, the study of nature, and the importance of the family were stressed in these schools. Froebel's *The Education of Man* (1826) set forth his views, which were strongly influenced by an unhappy childhood both at home and in school.

Kinderhook. Old Kinderhook, the nickname of President Martin Van Buren, is the basis for the universal expression O.K. Old Kinderhook's birthplace, Kinderhook, New York, in turn, takes its name from children. When Henry Hudson anchored the *Half Moon* near this hook of land, he was greeted by Indian children, *Kinder* in German and Dutch. *See also* O.K.

kind-hearted. Miles Coverdale, who translated the Bible from German and Latin versions in 1535, coined the term *kind-hearted:* "O give thanks therefore unto the Lord; for he is kind harted." Coverdale in the same year also invented *noonday,* for the middle of the day. He had as a precedent the earlier "noontime."

kinesics (body language). This modern branch of linguistic science studies body motion as related to speech, taking its name from the Greek *kinein,* "to move." There are said to be over 700,000 distinct movements of the arms, hands, fingers, and face "by which information can be transferred without speech." The term *body language* was introduced in the 1970s.

King Bomba. *King Bomba* is an expression rarely used today, but might well be revived. The original King Bomba was Ferdinand II (1810–59) of Naples, who reigned from 1830–59. At one point in his reactionary reign the treacherous monarch held 40,000 political prisoners. He was called King Bomba for his ruthless bombardment of Sicilian cities in 1848, in which much damage was done, many atrocities committed, and many innocent people hurt. King Bombas, whatever their motives, have been all too common.

King Cole. The "merry old soul" of nursery rhyme fame is in British tradition a king of the third century. The monarch is mentioned in *Historia Regum Britannica* (1508) by Geoffrey of Monmouth, who says nothing about him calling for his pipe, bowl, or fiddlers three, and whose veracity, in fact, has been questioned. Old King Cole may also have been the grandfather of the Emperor Constantine. The city of Colchester doesn't derive from his name, as is often stated, but is probably named from the Latin *colonia.*

King Cotton. A term once much used to personify the economic supremacy of cotton in the South. Wrote R. H. Stoddard in his poem "King Cotton" (1861): "Ye slaves of curs forgotten/ Hats off to great King Cotton!"

king devil weeds. In the late 19th century several European yellow-flowered hawkweeds of the genus *Hieracium* were inadvertently introduced into northeastern North America. Although showy and handsome, they became such troublesome weeds that they were rechristened "king devil weeds." The two worst species of them, orange hawkweed and mouse-eared (yellow-flowered) hawkweed, are regarded by experts as among the 50 worst garden weeds, but they are beautiful to behold when flowering en masse in a meadow. They are called hawkweed because juice from their stems applied to the eyes was once thought to give humans the fabled sight of hawks.

king fruit. *See* DURIAN.

King Kong. Slang for a big, monsterlike man, or for a powerful cheap wine, after the eponymous apelike beast in the movie *King Kong.* But King Kong of Skull Island was not really 50 feet tall and 60 feet broad, as RKO publicists claimed. Kong was created by genius model maker Willis H. O'Brien, who used six different models of the gorilla in the 1933 movie, which was first called *The Beast,* then *The Eighth Wonder.* Each of these miniature models, 18 inches high, had moving parts that enabled the gorilla to be filmed performing various scenes. When Kong scales the Empire State Building with actress Fay Wray in hand, for example, an 18-inch model of the beast holds a six-inch model of Miss Wray as he ascends the clearly phallic symbol. For close-ups, however, O'Brien did create a giant King Kong head 18 feet high, which was covered with hair from the skins of 80 bears, according to a studio PR release. Its eyes were about a foot long, its nose two feet long, and its six-foot-long mouth was big enough to hide several men inside. These hidden technicians operated controls that could move Kong's eyes, mouth, and neck. Later, in 1976, a remake of *King Kong* featured a 40-foot-high model of Kong (built at a cost of $24 million) that required 20 technicians to operate. However, the film was a financial flop, even though it won an Academy Award for visual effects

King of Dullness. After Shakespearian scholar Lewis Theobald (1688–1744) exposed Alexander Pope's errors as an editor of Shakespeare, the great poet retaliated by making him the King of Dullness in his *Dunciad* (1728). In the final edition of the satire, however, Pope enthroned Poet Laureate Colley Cibber (1671–1757) as king of Dullness, and Cibber has been stuck with his monarchy and monicker ever since. A rather rude, vain man with more talent for acting than writing, Cibber nevertheless was made poet laureate in 1730. Pope disliked his work, his appointment as laureate, and his literary criticism of Pope. *See also* NAMBY-PAMBY.

king of papers. A name often given to The Japanese *gampi,* a lustrous, vellumlike paper made from the wild thyme shrub. It was long made by Eishiro Abe, who lived well into his 90s and was designated a Japanese national treasure for his art. He made over 176 different kinds of paper by hand, using a complicated process that includes pressing and drying for a night and a day.

King of the High C's. A nickname for the Italian tenor Luciano Pavarotti (b. 1935) for his unmatched ability early in his career to hit high notes. Pavarotti is responsible for a renewed interest in opera in the U.S. His notable operatic roles include Radames in *Aida,* the duke of Mantua in *Rigoletto,* and notably Calat in *Turandot,* featuring his signature aria "Nessun Dorma."

King of the Planets. Jupiter, so named because it is the largest of the planets. Jupiter honors the supreme god of Roman mythology, who was called Jupiter or Jove and corresponded to the Greek god Zeus. The other planets are Mercury, Venus, Earth, Mars, Saturn, Uranus, Neptune, and Pluto.

King Ranch.   The biggest of the cattle ranches. Started in 1851 by Irish immigrant Richard King who by the end of the 19th century owned over 1 million acres on the Texas Gulf Coast. Today the King Ranch is over 1.25 million acres, half the area of Delaware. At one time a Texas ranch called XIT (after its brand) covered 3 million acres.

Kings County; Queens County; Richmond.   Since we have covered New York and the Bronx, it's only fair that the origins of New York City's remaining three counties, or boroughs, be touched upon here. Kings County, better known as Brooklyn, is named for England's king Charles II; Queens County honors Catherine of Braganza, Charles's queen; and Richmond, better known as Staten Island, is named for King Charles's son, the duke of Richmond. Since New York County, or Manhattan, was named for King Charles's brother James, duke of York, that leaves only the BRONX of New York City's four boroughs that isn't named for Charles II's royal family.

King's English.   Several English kings didn't speak English, but this term has nevertheless meant "proper English, English as it should be spoken," since the mid-16th century. It was used by Shakespeare in *The Merry Wives of Windsor* (1600) and three centuries earlier Chaucer wrote "God save the king, that is lord of this language."

king's evil.   *The king's evil* is an old name, sometimes encountered in literature, for scrofula. Scrofula, a constitutional disorder of a tubercular nature, characterized by swelling of the lymphatic glands in the neck, was believed to be susceptible to cure by the royal touch. France's Louis IX is thought to be the first king to employ the practice, which soon spread to England, where Macaulay records that Charles II touched 92,107 persons during his reign. The practice ended with Queen Anne, Dr. Johnson being one of the last persons to be "touched" by royal hands in 1712.

King's peace.   *See* QUEEN'S (OR KING'S) PEACE.

king's ransom.   Just how much is a king's ransom? When Richard the Lion-Hearted was kidnapped by Duke Leopold of Austria while returning from the Third Crusade, he was ransomed for nearly $5 million in today's dollars, a sum that almost bankrupted England when added to the cost of the Crusade. How far back this expression for "a large sum" goes is anybody's guess. We only know that the first recorded mention of it dates from about 1470. Marlowe used the term in his masterpiece *Faust* (ca. 1590).

King Tut.   Egyptian King Tutankhamen's tomb was discovered in 1922 by George E. S. M. Herbert, earl of Carnarvon, and Howard Carter in the valley of the tombs of the kings at Karnak. Tutankhamen, heretic king of the XVIII dynasty in the 14th century B.C., lay swathed in a gold sarcophagus surrounded by a fortune in jewels, furniture, and other relics that threw much light on Egyptian history. His difficult name was condensed to *King Tut* and his immense wealth caught the public's imagination. *Don't act like King Tut* or *he think's he's King Tut* became expressions applicable to any person pretending to be much more than he was, acting as if the world should pay him homage as it did King Tutankhamen.

King Tut's Golden Typewriter.   The most imaginative of Canadian newspaper editor Charles Langdon Clarke's ingenious hoaxes—which included "the unearthing of the whale that swallowed Jonah"—was the story he printed in 1922 after KING TUT was discovered. KING TUT'S GOLDEN TYPEWRITER, Clarke headlined the tale, and he went on to describe the instrument, never bothering to explain how a typewriter could possibly type hieroglyphics. The story seemed so authentic (even though the typewriter was discovered in the 19th century) that rival newspapers picked up on it before Clarke admitted to the hoax.

Kinkaider.   American Congressman Moses Kinkaid (1854–1922) saw his Kinkaid Act granting homesteads to Nebraska settlers passed into law in 1904. The homesteaders who settled these 640-acre grants under the provisions of the act were called Kinkaiders by the newspapers of the day and his name passed from the pages of the *Congressional Record* to the dictionaries.

kinnikinnik.   Deriving from a similar but unrecorded word "in the Cree or Chippewa dialects of Algonquian" that means literally "what is mixed," *kinnikinnik* was first a nontobacco mix of dried sumac leaves, ground dogwood bark, and other ingredients that the Indians and early American settlers used. Later tobacco was often added to the mixture. *Kinnikinnik* is also the longest palindromic word in English and can have 12 letters when spelled *kinnik-kinnik*, as it sometimes is.

Kirby pickle.   The Kirby pickle familiar to gardeners is a name applied generally to all pickling cucumbers and definitely is named in honor of a man. It bears the name of the developer of a once-popular pickling cucumber called the *Kirby*—Norvel E. Kirby of Philadelphia's I. N. Simon & Son seed company, now out of business. Simon introduced the Kirby in 1920 and it remained popular until the mid-1930s, when more disease-resistant types replaced it. Its name remained, however, as a designation for all pickling cucumbers.

kirk; the Auld Kirk.   *Kirk* can mean a church in Scots. It is also the name, mainly British, of the official Church of Scotland (Presbyterian), and can be used as a verb meaning to attend church. The Auld Kirk is an informal name for the Church of Scotland.

Kismet; Kiss me, Hardy.   *Kismet* comes from Persian *quismat*, meaning "division, portion, lot," which in turn derives from Arabic *quismah*, meaning the same. One's lot or portion is one's fate or fortune, and this became the meaning of the word when it came into English as *kismet* at the beginning of the 19th century. Some writers believe that Lord Nelson said, "Kismet, Hardy" (not "Kiss me, Hardy") to Captain Thomas Hardy as Nelson lay dying after the Battle of Trafalgar, meaning it was his fate to die after his great victory. Other authorities, including Partridge, find this theory improbable.

kiss.   *See* A VELARIC INGRESSIVE BILABIAL STOP.

kiss-cow.   This unusual term, probably obsolete, can be traced back to early 19th-century England, where a *kiss-cow* was someone who would suffer any indignity for a consideration, a sycophant who would "kiss the cow for the milk."

kissing bug. There are several species of venomous blood-sucking Hemiptera of the family Reduviidae called kissing bugs, these assassin bugs inflicting sharp bites on the lips that cause painful sores. There was, in fact, a great kissing-bug scare for two or three months in the U.S. in 1899, with many people bitten by such bugs while they slept. The insect seems to have inspired the punning *kissing bug* for a person who kisses a lot. This is an American expression, not Canadian as Partridge claims, first recorded in the late 1890s, and perhaps first applied to naval hero Richmond "Kissing Bug" Hobson, who was showered with kisses by so many women that his name, in the form of HOBSONIZE, took on the meaning "to kiss." Hobson, however, was always the *kissee* (first recorded in England in 1827), not the kisser.

kissing-comfit. This name was long ago given to the candied root of the sea holly (*Eryngium maritimum*) because it is used as a lozenge to sweeten the breath and was once popular with young lovers.

kissing cousin. *Kissing cousins* is a southern Americanism that dates back before the Civil War. The term first implied a distant blood relationship, but today more often means a very close friend who is considered family. It still is used in its original sense of a relative far removed enough to permit marriage, "an eighth cousin" in the North.

kiss-me-quick. In New England and the southeastern part of the U.S. a kiss-me or a kiss-me-quick was a ridge or depression in a roadway, one that caused a carriage to jolt and possibly throw a girl into her young man's arms. The usage is recorded as late as 1945 in the Southeast and may still be used there to a limited extent. *See* WHAM, BAM (THANK YE, M'AM).

kiss-me-quick-before-mother-sees-me. The kiss-me-quick-before-mother-sees-me was a bonnet young women wore in the mid-18th century, a small hat set far back on the head that was considered daring for the day. It was also called a *kiss-me-quick*.

kiss-my-arse latitudes. *Kiss-my-arse latitudes* is used mostly in the British merchant marine for the "home stretch," when a ship is close to port and the crew cares about nothing but getting ashore and tends to ignore orders—especially if the crew has been paid.

kiss of death. Mafiosi did not invent this expression with their custom of kissing someone full on the mouth to indicate he will soon be killed. The term's probable origin is in the kiss of betrayal Judas gave to Christ. The expression has been commonly used in the U.S. since at least the 1920s.

kiss of life; kiss of death. American English hasn't anything as colorful as the British term *kiss of life* for mouth-to-mouth resuscitation. The lifesaving method's name is based on *kiss of death*, which originally referred to the kiss Judas gave Jesus in the garden of Gethsemane and now refers to any traitorous action.

kit and caboodle. *See* WHOLE KIT AND CABOODLE.

kit-cat. Though pastry cook Christopher (Kit) Catt—or Cat or Catling—created little mutton pies, he nevertheless travels in the company of Titians of the art world. Kit Catt's mutton delights were called kit-cats and some leading Whigs of the early 18th century enjoyed them so much that they formed a club on his pastry shop premises in London. However, when Sir Godfrey Kneller was commissioned to paint 42 portraits of the Kit-Cat Club's prominent members, who included Steele, Addison, Congreve, and Walpole, a problem soon presented itself. The rooms were so low in height that Kneller had to restrict his portraits to three-quarter size, each canvas measuring exactly 28 by 36 inches. Such canvases were called kit-cats, after the club in which they hung and the term is still used for any portrait of these dimensions representing less than half the length of the sitter but including the hands.

kith and kin. Though it dates back to the 14th century or earlier, this expression is still heard today. It means acquaintances and relatives, *kith* being Middle English for acquaintances, friends, or neighbors.

kiting. *See* FLY A KITE.

kitsch. *Kitsch* derives from the German *kitschen*, "to throw together a work of art," which dates back to the 19th century. The Viennese novelist Hermann Broch has been credited with adding the noun *Kitsch* to the vocabulary of literature, in its sense of "art or literature judged to have little or no aesthetic value, especially when produced to satisfy popular taste." The Czech novelist Milan Kundera adds that "Kitsch translates the stupidity of conventional ideas into the language of beauty and feeling."

kitty. Willard Espy offers the following humorous explanation for *kitty*, the pot to which poker players contribute, in *Thou Improper, Thou Uncommon Noun* (1978): "[The name] Catherine turned to Kate, and Kate to Kitty. Some Kittys were no better than they should be, and Kitty became one of the many epithets applied to prostitutes. Spirited Johns—not yet lowercased for a prostitute's customer—used to amuse themselves by tossing coins into the laps of Kittys, as poker players today throw their antes or bets into a kitty in the hope of getting a winning hand. The sequence cannot be proved—no one will talk—but it seems plausible." *See* JOHN; NO BETTER THAN SHE SHOULD BE.

Kitty Hawk. *See* FLYING MACHINE.

Kiwanis. Upper Michigan Indians used the term *keewanis* to mean "make oneself known" or "to express oneself." When a Detroit club promoting good fellowship and civic interests was founded in 1915, a local historian suggested that this Indian word be used for the club name. Feeling that "self-expression" suited the purpose of the club, which of course later became a national organization, members adopted the name with its spelling slightly changed to *Kiwanis*.

kiwi. *Kiwi*, like MAKO, is an English word that comes to us from the Maori language used by the Polynesian natives of New Zealand. *Kiwi-kiwi* is the Maori word for the flightless bird called a *kiwi* (*Apteryx australis*), which is often termed an *apteryx* in crossword puzzles. *Kiwi* is also slang for a non-flying member of the Royal Air Force and Australian slang for a New Zealander. *Kiwi* fruit *(Actinidae sinensis)*, also known as the Chinese gooseberry and *Yangtao*, is native to China but called *kiwi* because most of the fruit sold in American and British markets is grown in New Zealand.

klaxon. *Klaxon* was coined in 1908 from the Greek *klazein*, "to make a noise," by the inventor who patented the first electrically operated horn on an automobile. When the patent expired, this trademark passed into the dictionaries without a capital as a word for any horn.

klieg eyes; klieg light. Hollywood movie stars adopted the dark glasses that became their trademark because of the intense *klieg light* introduced to stage and studio early in this century. These bright incandescent lights, rich in ultraviolet rays, caused a form of conjunctivitis marked by burning of the eyeballs, redness, tearing, and photophobia that was common to all who worked under the arcs. In order to protect their *klieg eyes* the stars, as well as lesser lights, took to wearing "shades," and have traditionally done so ever since. The *klieg light* was the invention of the German-born brothers Kliegl, John H. (1869–1959) and Anton T. (1872–1927), who immigrated to the United States and in 1897 established the firm of Kliegl Brothers, pioneering in the development of lighting equipment and scenic effects for the stage and early motion pictures. The light they invented was first called the *Kliegl light*, which proved too difficult to pronounce, their real name modified like those of many of the actors who worked with them.

Klingon. Etymologists have missed including this word in any straight or slang dictionary I've seen. The word has been used to describe a brutal, barbaric, warlike person for some 30 years now, ever since the term was invented for the TV series *Star Trek*. Therein the Klingons are debased warlike beings from the planet Klingon, who look no better than they act. *See also* BEAM ME UP, SCOTTY.

Klondike. The Canadian Klondike gold rush in the early 20th century brought with it boom times when many great fortunes were made. For Canadians and Alaskans a period when everyone is doing very well financially is termed a *Klondike*, as in "It's a real Klondike here this year." *See* CANFIELD.

klutz. Widely used in the U.S. since about 1918, *klutz* was originally a Yiddish term, deriving from the German *Klotz* for "a log or block of wood." It describes a clumsy, graceless person; a bungler, a fool. *Klutz*, however, can also refer to an intelligent person who is badly coordinated. *To klutz* means "to botch up or bungle."

KMIT. When foreign reporters questioned him about the name of a new ministry the Bolsheviks formed after the Russian Revolution Leon Trotsky told them it was named KMIT. Newspapers all over the world called the agency by these initials until someone found out what they stood for. Trotsky had been playing a contemptuous joke on the reporters and their capitalist employers. KMIT stood for the Yiddish *kuss mir im tuches*, "kiss my ass."

knapsack. *Knapsacks* were originally small sacks that German soldiers carried containing their rations, the word deriving from the German *knappen*, "to eat."

knee-high to a grasshopper. *Knee-high to a toad*, first recorded in 1814, was the original of this Americanism, and *knee-high to a mosquito* as well as *knee-high to a frog* appeared before *knee-high to a grasshopper* came on the scene some 37 years later. But *knee-high to a grasshopper* has outlasted all the others, including the later *knee-high to a duck*. *See also* GRASSHOPPER.

knee jerk. Used to indicate an automatic, unthinking response to anything, *knee jerk* (as in *knee-jerk liberal*) is one of those relatively few terms that can be traced back to its exact origins. In 1948, the distinguished etymologist Sir Ernest Gowers proudly gave us the expression's medical roots: "Some 70 years ago a promising young neurologist made a discovery that necessitated the addition of a new word to the English vocabulary. He insisted that this should be 'knee jerk,' and 'knee jerk' it has remained, in spite of the effort of 'patellar reflex' to dislodge it. He was my father; so perhaps I have inherited a prejudice in favor of homemade words." Sir Ernest's contention seems to be borne out by the *O.E.D.*, which gives as 1878 the first recorded use of the term, in Sir Michael Foster's *Textbook of Physiology*: "Striking the tendon below the patella gives rise to a sudden extension of the leg known as the 'knee-jerk.' " The first figurative use of the term isn't known, but it seems to have been soon after the phrase's coining.

knew him when. American poet and journalist Arthur Guiterman (1871–1943) popularized this expression, meaning "I knew him before he became rich or prominent," in a parody he wrote of Whittier's lines (in *Maud Muller*) "of all sad words of tongue or pen,/ The saddest are these: 'It might have been.' " Wrote Guiterman, in *A Poet's Proverbs* (1924): "Of all cold words of tongue or pen,/ The worst are these, 'I knew him when.' "

knickers. In England women's *panties* are called *knickers*, which take their name from a man. When in 1809 Washington Irving burlesqued a pompous guidebook of his day with his two-volume history of New York, he decided to capitalize on the name of Harmon Knickerbocker, head of Albany's old, prominent Knickerbocker family, and chose the pseudonym Diedrich Knickerbocker. Soon Irving's humorous work became known as *Knickerbocker's History of New York*, but it wasn't until English caricaturist George Cruikshank illustrated a later edition in the 1850s that the Knickerbocker family name was bestowed on the loose-fitting, blousy knee breeches still worn today. In that English edition Cruikshank depicted the alleged author and his fellow Dutch burghers wearing voluminous breeches buckled just below the knee. His drawings of this style that the early Dutch had worn were widely copied for boys' knee pants, baggy golf trousers four inches longer, and even women's silk bloomers—all dubbed *knickerbockers*, after the family Irving had immortalized. *See* DON'T GET YOUR KNICKERS IN A TWIST.

knight errant. *See* ARRANT THIEF.

Knights of the Bath. The order is so named because those inducted into it had to take a bath before their initiation, though the last knight to go through this purification ceremony did so at Charles II's coronation in 1661. It is one of the nine Orders of Knighthood of the British Empire. These, in order of precedence, are Knight of the Garter; Thistle; St. Patrick; Bath; Star of India; St. Michael; St. George; Indian Empire; Royal Victorian Order; and British Empire. Knights of the Bath are divided into Grand Cross of Bath (G.C.B., the first class); Knight Commander of the Bath (K.C.B., the second class); and Companion of the Bath (C.B., the third class). George I of England revived this ancient knightly order in 1725.

K-9 Corps. The army's K-9 Corps, organized during World War II, was originally called D4D, an acronym for "Dogs for Defense." But the much cleverer and more memorable *K-9 Corps*, a pun on "canine," quickly replaced the former term.

knish. A widely popular dish from Jewish cookery, consisting of dough stuffed with potato, cheese, or meat, etc., and baked or fried. The Yiddish word probably comes from the Ukrainian or Polish *knysh*, which, in turn, is of Turkish origin. Leo Rosten in *The Joys of Yiddish* (1968) also gives *knish* as a "vulgarism" for the vagina, and the American poet A. D. Fiske used "Anne Knish" as a pseudonym in *Spectra* (1916), a poetry collection he wrote with Harold Witter Bynner spoofing poetry of the day.

knock down, drag out (fight). This expression for a rough, anything-goes fight is first recorded in 1827 British boxing circles, before there were many rules governing prizefighting. Today it is used figuratively for any all-out fight.

knocked into a cocked hat. To *knock someone into a cocked hat* means to beat him badly in a game of skill. The expression derives from the old game of ninepins, where three pins were arranged in the form of a triangle (like a three-pointed cocked hat). When all pins but these three were knocked down, the set was said to be knocked into a cocked hat.

knock (throw) for a loop. To hit someone or something very hard, to defeat, to astonish or upset. This Americanism has been traced back to the early 1920s. Loop may have originally referred to the loop maneuver made by an airplane, but that is only a guess. The expression has several colorful variations, including *knock for a row of ashcans, knock for a row of milk cans, knock for a row of Chinese pagodas,* and, best of all, *knock for a row of tall red totem poles.*

knock galley west. No one has been able to explain why a ship's galley or the compass point west have anything to do with this expression meaning "to knock into smithereens." They may not. The words may be a corruption of the English dialect term *collyweston,* which in turn derived from the town of Colly Weston in Northamptonshire, a town reportedly given to excessive violence. Colly Weston itself may have been named for a local, violent troublemaker named Colly Weston. All speculative maybes once again.

knock it off. Some authorities believe that these words meaning to stop work or any activity derive from a standard order

in the days when galleys were rowed to the rhythm of mallets on a block. *Knock off* in those days was the signal to rest.

knock-kneed. *Knock-kneed,* having knees that knock together in walking, the opposite of bandy-legged, is, surprisingly, not an ancient term. At least it isn't recorded until 1807, in the statement that "children . . . from bad nursing become knock-kneed." *See also* BANDY.

knock, knock! First recorded in about 1936, this appears to have originally been an American catchphrase used by someone about to tell a dirty story. Then it came into use by someone entering a room without knocking. Perhaps it is from the old schoolboy joke "Knock! Knock! Who's there? Grandpa. Whaddya want . . ." But one writer claims it may come from the Porter's scene in *Macbeth* (Act II. Scene iii): "Knock, knock, knock! Who's there . . . Knock, knock! Who's there, in the other devil's name . . . Knock, knock, knock! Who's there? . . . Knock, knock! Never at quiet! . . ."

knock on wood. Why do we say *knock on wood* and tap wood or our heads after declaring that some calamity has never happened to us? The superstition is an old one and has many possible explanations, none sure. It may be of pagan origin, deriving from the practice of rapping on trees to ask protection from friendly spirits who were believed to reside inside. Or it could be a Christian superstition similar to touching wooden crucifixes or rosary beads. One theory even holds that the practice comes from games like hide-and-seek in which players who succeed in touching wood are safe from capture. A last, farfetched possibility is that the superstition is linked to a verse in the sixth chapter of Galatians: "God forbid that I should glory save in the cross of our Lord Jesus Christ." You will be forgiven any vainglorious boast, according to this story, if you quickly recall the wooden cross Christ carried.

knock out of the box. To cause a pitcher to be removed from the game by the successful hitting of the opposing baseball team. Today there is no such box to be knocked out of, the pitcher pitching from the pitcher's mound. In baseball's early days, in the mid-19th century, pitchers stood in a marked box that they had to throw from, hence the expression. The term was first recorded in 1891 and is today used outside of baseball to mean "to defeat or eliminate."

knock them in the aisles. *See* LAY THEM IN THE AISLES.

knock the spots off. The origins of this Americanism for "to defeat decisively" are not clear, but some word sleuths believe it is from the world of boxing, reasoning that the expression is first recorded in a sports story and—admittedly reaching on this one—speculating that the spots in question were freckles figuratively knocked off the face of a badly beaten fighter. However, the expression could have its roots in the sharpshooting of 19th-century American marksmen, who could shoot the pips (or spots) out of a playing card nailed to a tree a considerable distance away.

knock up. In England *to knock up* has been standard English for "to arouse by knocking at the door" or "to visit" since at least 1663, when Samuel Pepys, in his *Diary*, recorded constables knocking him up. In American slang, however, *to knock up* has since about 1920 meant to make a woman pregnant, usually outside of marriage.

knots. Knots measure the speed of a ship at sea, each knot equaling a nautical mile (6,076 feet), which is slightly longer than a land-measured mile (5,280 feet). Since six nautical (geographical) miles are about equal to seven statute (land) English miles, a ship making 12 knots is actually traveling 14 land miles. A ship's speed came to be measured in *knots* because the log line thrown overboard to record distance was marked off by knots and had been used to measure a ship's speed since early times. In its nautical sense *knot* is first recorded in 1633.

know a hawk from a handsaw. Shakespeare made this phrase immortal in *Hamlet*, but its origins may never be established. The expression means "to be smart, to know one thing from another" and is usually employed negatively today: *he doesn't know a hawk from a handsaw. Handsaw* in the phrase is said to be a corruption of *hernshaw*, a heron (thus it is literally "I know a hawk from a heron"), but there is no proof of this. The expression is quoted nowhere before Shakespeare and he could have been referring to the handsaw carpenters use, as he did in another play. Similarly, *hawk* here could refer to the tool called a hawk, which has long been used by plasterers.

know beans. *See* DOESN'T KNOW BEANS.

know-how. An Americanism coined about 1830 that means "knowledge of how to do something, expertise." It was first recorded in an 1859 issue of *Spirit of the Times* featuring a story in which one character tells another to charge "fifty cents for the killing" (of livestock) "and fifty cents for the know-how."

know like a book. "Complete understanding" is the meaning of *to know like a book*, and the Americanism obviously dates from times when there were few books in most homes. Those that were present, like the Bible, were often committed to memory, hence the familiar expression. *To know one's book*, a British saying, means something different—"to know one's best interest, to have made up one's mind." *To speak by the book*, is to speak meticulously, and *to speak* or *talk like a book* is to speak with great precision, usually pedantically.

know-nothing. Pledged to complete silence about their organization, members of New York's Order of the Star-Spangled Banner told anyone who inquired about their secret society: "I know nothing about it." Thus as early as 1850 they were called Know-Nothings. Later, when they merged with other groups into the national American Party in 1856, this stock reply became "I know nothing in our principles contrary to the Constitution." A strange statement for a party that was anti-Catholic, whose members vowed to vote only for native Americans, and which supported a 25-year residence requirement for citizenship, among other reactionary principles. The Know-Nothings achieved considerable success in local contests, but fared badly in the 1856 national elections, even with ex-President Millard Fillmore as their candidate and they ceased to be a political power after 1860. However, their name lives on as a synonym for any reactionary political group or individual that appeals to base emotions. Other political parties have fared just as badly over the years and one wonders which modern party will go the way of the Doctrinaires, the Intransigents, and the Know-Nothings. *See* DOCTRINAIRE; INTRANSIGENT.

know one's cans. Cowboys on the range in the 19th century were usually starved for reading matter and often read the labels on the cook's tin cans, learning them by heart. A tenderfoot could always be distinguished because he didn't know his cans. The expression isn't recorded in the *Dictionary of Americanisms* but is given in Ray Allen Billington's *America's Frontier Culture* (1977). Wrote Edna Ferber in *Cimmaron* (1930): "The back and the side doors of the dwelling . . . littered with the empty tin cans that mark any new American settlement, and especially one whose drought is relieved by the thirst-quenching coolness of tinned tomatoes and peaches. Perhaps the canned tomato, as much as anything else, made possible the settling of the vast West and Southwest."

know one's onions. Onions aren't widely known by variety, though the Vidalia and Hawaiian varieties are among several that are well known. Therefore, to speak of someone "who knows his apples," a later variant on the above phrase, would be more appropriate, as there are hundreds of apple varieties. *Know one's onions* was first recorded in 1922 and means to be astute in one's field. An old joke has the esteemed lexicographer C. T. Onions, a longtime editor of the *Oxford English Dictionary*, as the eponym behind the phrase.

know the ropes. Though common in horse-racing circles, these words are almost surely of nautical birth, referring to the complex system of lines on full-rigged sailing ships that bewildered recruits had to master before they became seasoned seamen. Dana used the term in *Two Years Before the Mast* (1840), indicating that it was an old expression he'd heard.

know thy opportunity. *See* SEVEN SAGES OF GREECE.

know thyself. *See* SEVEN SAGES OF GREECE.

know what's what. Wrote Samuel Butler in *Hudibras* (1663): "He knew what's what, and that's as high/ As metaphysic wit can fly." To know what is what is still to be a shrewd person, to know what is going on. The phrase is thought to derive from the old question in logic *Quid est quid?* "what is what," one which someone would have to be very shrewd to answer.

know which side one's bread is buttered on. This useful phrase dates back close to 500 years. It was first recorded in John Heywood's *Proverbs and Epigrams* (1562) in the form, "I know on which side my bread is buttered." Both early and later versions mean the same: "I know what's in my own best interest."

knuckle down. Marble players may have been responsible for this expression, which dates back to 17th-century England. One rule in the game provides that a player must shoot directly from the spot where his marble lands, which requires that he put his knuckles on the ground, or "knuckle down." Since marbles was a popular pastime with adults as well as children at the time, *knuckle down* possibly came to express earnest application to any job. However, the bones of the spinal column were also known as "knuckles" in the 17th century, and the expression may therefore derive from the act of "putting one's back into a task."

knuckle under.

> He that flinches his Glass, and to Drink is not able.
> Let him quarrel no more, but knock under the
> table.

This anonymous verse, from the late 17th century, suggests that our expression to *knuckle under,* or "to admit defeat," derives from an earlier British phrase, *to knock under.* People in taverns apparently rapped on the under side of the table when beaten in an argument. But another equally reasonable theory connects the term with an ancient form of submission to one's conqueror. As a token of submission a person fell to his knees. Since *knuckles* in Anglo-Saxon and Medieval English meant the knee joints as well as the joints of the fingers, this would account for the phrase.

Kodak. After inventing this camera in 1888, George Eastman claimed that he intentionally set out to coin a short, easy-to-remember name for it that could not be stolen. He chose *k* as the first and last letters in the word because *k* was the first letter in his mother's family name. The rest of the word came by experimenting with other letters in combination with the two ks, though some have suggested that he might have had Alaska's Kodiak Island in mind.

Koh-i-Noo. *See* MOUNTAIN OF LIGHT.

konpyutaa. The Japanese borrowing and alteration of the English word *computer,* one of the many computer terms borrowed from English. As with all Japanized terms, the English expression can be written in the katakana alphabet or written directly in Roman letters.

kook. A relatively new word for a strange or crazy person that dates back to the early 1950s, when it was apparently fashioned in Hollywood from the much earlier CUCKOO. "Kookie" was the name of a popular TV series actor of the time. Today both *kook* and *kooky* are heard more frequently than *cuckoo.*

Korean conflict; Korean emergency. *See* POLICE ACTION.

kosher. In *The Joys of Yiddish* (1968) Leo Rosten calls *kosher* "the most resourceful Yiddish word in the English language" and gives 10 meanings for it, ranging from its original meaning of "fit to eat, because ritually clean according to Jewish dietary laws," to "legitimate, legal and lawful," as in "Are you sure this deal is kosher?" Probably the most widely used of Yiddish words in English (excepting names for things, such as *matzo, bagel,* etc.) *kosher* derives from the Hebrew *kasher,* "fit, proper, permissible." *See* YIDDISH WORDS IN ENGLISH.

kowtow. The Chinese *k'-o-t'ou,* which we spell *kowtow* (rhymes with "know how"), means "knock your head"—that is, to kneel and bow before a superior by touching the floor with your forehead. The Mandarins required the *k'-o-t'ou* of their

"inferiors," and adventurers in China at the turn of the century brought back the word if not the practice. To *kowtow* to someone has come to mean to show obsequious behavior, everything but banging one's head on the floor.

K.P. K.P. became the abbreviation for *k*itchen *p*olice, those soldiers selected to peel potatoes, wash pots and pans, clean grease traps etc., in World War I, not World War II, as is commonly believed. The verb *police,* meaning "to clean up an area," is first recorded in 1893, and may be a corruption of *polish.*

K-rations. You may have wondered what the "K" stands for in this well-known term for emergency army field rations containing a nutritional meal. The "K" isn't some mystery nutrient. It honors the American physiologist, Ancel Keys (b. 1904), who invented K-rations.

***Kreutzer* Sonata.** Beethoven dedicated his famous violin sonata (op. 47) to violinist and fellow-composer Rodolphe Kreutzer in 1803 and it has since been universally known as the *Kreutzer* Sonata. The musician, a Frenchman of German extraction, was professor of violin at the Paris Conservatoire and conductor at Vienna's Imperial Theater. A prolific composer with some 40 operas, numerous concertos and sonatas, and 40 unsurpassed études for the violin to his credit, Kreutzer died in 1831, aged 65. Tolstoy's novella, *The Kreutzer Sonata* (1890), takes its title from the Beethoven work.

Kris Kringle. After nearly a century and a half this synonym for Santa Claus is still heard, even though the words have nothing at all to do with Santa. The term originated in America in about 1830 and was spelled *Krisskring'l* before taking its present form. *Krisskring'l* stemmed from a misunderstanding of the word *Christkindlein* used by German immigrants, its meaning not "Santa Claus" but "the Child in the Manger," or "the little Christ child."

krummkake. Relatively few Scandinavian words have directly entered American English. An example is *krummkake,* a large, light, and very thin cookie made in an appliance similar to a waffle iron. The hot thin cookie is rolled around a cone-shaped tube until it hardens and is then filled with whipped cream. Krummkakes are known nationally today due to their inclusion in many cookbooks. This name has nothing to do with *crumbs,* deriving from the Norwegian *krumkake,* meaning the same.

kudzu. *See* BEAUTIFUL NUISANCE.

Ku Klux Klan. A secret organization that arose in the South after the Civil War to preserve white supremacy. From 1865 to 1877 the name was often applied to all secret political organizations with the same purpose. The term derives from the Greek *kyklos,* circle, plus *klan,* a variant spelling of *clan.* Since 1915 the Klan's official name has been the Knights of the Ku Klux Klan and the organization has directed its words and actions against Jews, Catholics, and the foreign-born as well as African-Americans. An old story holds that the name of the organization is based on the sound of rifle-bolt being operated.

kulak. Millions of kulaks were exterminated by the Communists in the years following the 1917 Russian Revolution because these small farmers refused to collectivize their farms. These farmers had been named *kulaks* before the revolution from the Russian for "fist," because they were said to be "tightfisted," cheap employers who took advantage of farm workers.

kumquat. The Chinese dialect *gamgwat*, "gold citrus fruit," is the origin of the name of this shrub of the genus *Fortunella*, which yields golden citrus fruits, with sweet rinds and an acid pulp, that are used chiefly for preserves. *See* FORTUNELLA.

kung-fu. *See* CONFUCIUS SAY.

kunzite. One of the few precious stones named after a person, this transparent, lilac-colored gem takes its name from George Frederick Kunz (1856–1932), an American authority on gems and jewelry who worked many years for Tiffany & Co. in New York City and wrote several books on the subject, often serving as a government expert. Kunzite is a varity of the mineral spodumine, which occurs in prismatic crystals. *See* TIFFANY GLASS.

kvetch. To complain, gripe: "She's always kvetching about something." Formerly the Yiddish word mainly meant to squeeze or push out, from the German *quetschen*, "to squeeze," but it has been heard mostly in the above sense since about 1965.

Kwanzaa. A word coined in 1966 by Dr. Maulana Ron Karenga, who invented the holiday, which takes place from December 26 to January 1. *Kwanzaa* derives from Kiswoahili *matunda ya kwanzaa*, "first fruits," and is based on African harvest festivals. The secular holiday celebrates the African-American cultural heritage.

L

L. Our twelfth letter has been traced to the early Phoenician and Hebrew alphabets, where it was drawn as an oxgoad or *lamed.*

£. The symbol for the British pound comes from the Latin word *libra,* just as our *lb.* for pound does. *Libra* in this case is part of the Latin phrase *libra pondere,* which means a pound by weight.

labanotation. This little-known word describes an important notation system that amounts to a graphic shorthand for dance, enabling a choreographer to delineate every possible movement of the human body individually or in ensemble. Introduced by its creator Rudolph Laban in his book *Kinetographie Laban* (1928), *labanotation* was the first practical method capable of scoring the various complex movements and positions of an entire ballet or musical comedy. Unlike the old numbered-footprint plans familiar to us all, the Laban system amounts to a complete break with tradition. It dispenses entirely with the musical five-line horizontal staff, using a three-line vertical staff that is divided in the center. Code symbols on each side of the line indicate foot and leg movements, while symbols in parallel columns outside the lines pertain to all other body gestures. Every slight movement from toe to head can be noted, as well as their direction, timing, and force, and by grouping together the staffs for individual dancers an entire work can be "or-chestrated." Laban did for the dance what Guido d'Arezzo did for musical notation almost a thousand years before him. Prior to his system dancers had to rely on their memories of per-formers who had appeared in classical ballets, but now almost exact revivals can be given and ballet composers can finally adequately copyright their creations. Born in Pressburg (Bra-tislava) on December 15, 1879, the German dance teacher and choreographer died in London on July 1, 1958.

labor. Adam Smith in *The Wealth of Nations* (1776) was the first person to use the word *labor* in its modern sense of work done to supply material wants. Before that, the word had the same meaning as its parent, the Latin *labor,* which means toil, distress, and trouble.

labor of love. *A labor of love,* a work undertaken for the love or liking of it more than for any compensation, has been a common English expression since the 17th century, and it is much older, deriving from the biblical "Your worke of faith and labour of love" (1 Thess. i,3).

Labrador. The peninsula of northeastern Canada and the Labrador retriever dog take their names from Lavrador of Terceira, who in 1498 piloted John Cabot's ship to the area.

labyrinth. Though there were mazes before his, the Laby-rinth, "double-headed axe," of Greek legend built by the artif-icer Daedalus to confine the man-bull Minotaur may give us our word *labyrinth.* The only way out of this maze was through the help of a skein of thread. Later, the king of Crete imprisoned Daedalus and his son Icarus in the Labyrinth. Daedalus made wings for them and they escaped, but Icarus flew too close to the sun, melting the wax binding the feathers to his wings, and fell to his death. The story also gives us the words *daedal,* anything cleverly made, and *daedalist,* for an air pioneer.

Lachryma Christi. *Lacrima Christi* is an Italian wine, its Latin name meaning "tears of Christ." *See* LIEBFRAUMILCH.

lackadaisical. A lackadaisical person, a lethargic, listless, lazy person, was originally someone given to sighing "lackaday, lackaday," a shortening of *alack-a-day* ("woe is the day"). Laur-ence Sterne may have coined *lackadaisical* from the earlier *lackaday;* anyway, he first recorded the word in his *Sentimental Journey* (1768).

lackey. Military commanders of the Moors were called *al-kaid,* "chief," but when the Spanish captured these commanders and their men in regaining control of Spain during the Middle Ages, they enslaved them and made them servants. From their once proud name, corrupted to *alcayo* in Spanish, came our English word for the lowest of servants.

lackluster. *Lackluster* originally referred only to a lack of luster or brightness in the eyes; in fact, we don't find it to describe anything else lackluster until Dickens's time. The word was invented or first recorded by Shakespeare in 1600: "... looking on it with lack-lustre eye, he says ..."

laconic. "If we enter Laconia, we will raze it to the ground," an Athenian herald (or Philip of Macedon) is said to have announced to the Laconians. "If," was the reply he received from the sententious Spartan magistrates. The Lacadaemonians were all supposed to be so parsimonious with words, and were noted in the ancient world not only for their stoic Spartan lifestyle but also for their short, brusque, and pithy way of speaking and writing, which was appropriate for their outward lack of emotion. Not only in Sparta, the capital, but throughout the country youths were taught modesty and conciseness of speech, taught so well that the word *laconic* comes to us by way of Latin from the Greek *Lakonikos*, meaning "like a Laconian." A *laconic* person is generally one who expresses much without wasting words, who is terse, to the point, and usually undemonstrative.

la cover girl. A French borrowing of the American English term *cover girl* (a beautiful or attractive young woman whose photograph often appears on magazine covers). One of the hundreds of such borrowings used by the French despite the protests of language purists.

lacrosse. Lacrosse is probably the only sport whose name has religious significance. When French priest Pierre de Charlevoix saw Algonquin Indians playing their game of *baggataway* in 1705, he thought that the webbed sticks they used resembled a bishop's cross and called the game lacrosse, which eventually supplanted the Indian name. While playing lacrosse "to celebrate George III's birthday" on June 4, 1763, Ojibwa and Sac Indians propelled the ball over the walls of Fort Michillimackinac and rushed in on the pretext of retrieving it, seizing weapons hidden by their squaws and massacring the garrison.

lad; lass. Many authorities cite the Middle English *ladde*, "serving man," as the source for *lad*, "boy or young man." Others, however, suggest the Anglo-Saxon proper man's name *Ladda* as the word's ancestor. *Lass* may be a truncated form of *laddesse*, the feminine of *ladde*, but it could derive from the Swedish *losk kona*, "an unmarried woman."

Ladas. See FAST AS LADAS.

la-di-dah. Used to describe a very affected person or a very affected action. Sometimes heard as *la-ti-dah*, the expression, according to Eric Partridge, dates back to the mid 19th century and was popularized by a British music hall song of 1880 with the line: "He wears a penny flower in his coat, La-di-da!"

Ladies and gentlemen. *Ladies and gentlemen*, as a form of address to a mixed audience, used to be the reverse: It was traditional to say "gentlemen and ladies." The change, putting ladies first, came in early America and first took place in the North, not in the chivalrous South.

ladies of the line. We have all heard of the self-explanatory *ladies of the night*, for prostitutes, but why *ladies of the line?* The expression comes to us from the American West, where prostitutes did business in tents and jerry-built shacks stretched out in lines at the outskirts of towns, mining camps, or railroad yards.

ladies of the night. This American euphemism for prostitutes was popular in the 1870s and is still used today. Interesting collective nouns for such ladies include: *a horde of hookers, a jam of tarts, a wiggle of whores, a flourish of strumpets, an essay of Trollope's, an anthology of pros.* See BRIDES OF THE MULTITUDE.

Ladik; Ladikiyeh; Latakia. Every mother should have a boy like Seleucus, founder of the Syrian dynasty. The emperor is said to have named *five* cities after his mother Laodice in the middle of the third century B.C. This able Macedonian general of Alexander the Great tried hard to build his kingdom in the way that Alexander built his, founding Greek colonies governed along Persian lines wherever he could. Three of the at least five cities Seleucus Nicator named for his mother remain standing today, their names now pronounced *Ladik, Ladikiyeh*, and *Latakia*. Latakia, a seaport of Syria opposite the island of Cyprus, is the most prominent of these and is noted for its Latakia tobacco. (For the story of a city Seleucus Nicator's *grandson* named after *his* Laodice, his wife in this case, *see* LAODICIAN.)

lady. *See* LORD.

ladybird. *See* LADYBUG.

Lady Bountiful. British playwright George Farquhar (1678–1707) wrote his last and best play, *The Beaux' Stratagem*, on his deathbed with the help of a small gift of 20 guineas from an actor friend. A former actor himself who quit the stage after accidentally wounding an opponent in a dueling scene, Farquhar maintained his cheerful disposition to the end and left behind a genial realistic comedy when he died in poverty at the age of 29. Lady Bountiful, a wealthy character in his play, has come to represent any benevolent lady who contributes much of her wealth to a community (*see* BONIFACE). The expression is today used mostly satirically, as in "She's always playing Lady Bountiful."

ladybug; ladybird. In *ladybug, lady* refers to "Our Lady," the Virgin Mary, in whose honor the beneficial insect was named—not to the erroneous belief that all ladybugs are female. These brightly colored beetles of the family *Coccinellidae*, which feed on aphids and other destructive garden pests, are known in England as *ladybirds*, due to a British aversion to the word *bug*, which is strongly associated there with buggery, or sodomy. Some American southerners favor the British word, which is why Claudia Taylor Johnson, our former first lady, bears this familiar southern nickname.

lady chapel. *See* LADY'S-MANTLE.

lady fern. *See* LADY'S-MANTLE.

Lady Godiva. Strategically arranging her long golden tresses, Lady Godiva rode through Coventry, relieving herself of her clothes and inhibitions in order to relieve her people of oppressive taxation. According to the traditional story, Lady Godiva (ca. 1040–ca. 1080) had jokingly agreed to ride naked through the crowded streets at high noon if her husband, Leofric, earl of Mercia and lord of Coventry, and one of the most powerful nobles in England, would lift burdensome taxes he had imposed on the townspeople. At least Leofric *thought* she was joking. To the delight of his twice-blessed tenants, the earl had to keep his promise when his wife took him at his word. He removed the levy almost as soon as she had removed her clothes and displayed herself in the marketplace. *Lady Godiva*, a title more humorously applied to any undraped woman, was apparently the benefactress of several religious houses in the reign of Edward the Confessor, and founded the Benedictine monastery at Coventry. Her real name was Godgifu, and her legendary ride, as famous as and more interesting than that of Paul Revere, was first recorded in *Flores historiarum* by Roger of Wendover (d. 1237), who quoted from an earlier writer. *See also* PEEPING TOM.

lady-killer. People have been humorously calling men "credited with a dangerous power over women" *lady-killers* since the early 19th century, though such *lady-killing* has been with us much longer.

lady of pleasure. James Shirley's play *The Lady of Pleasure* (1635) may have suggested this term for a prostitute, but the lady in the play was not a shady lady. Shirley's play was about "the cure of a wife's desire for a life of fashionable folly by her husband's feigning to engage in gambling and intrigue." Nevertheless, *lady of pleasure* took its present meaning not long after the play was produced.

lady's-mantle; lady chapel; lady fern. A *lady's-mantle (Alchemilla)* is a flowering plant whose large, serrated, and many-lobed leaves resemble "the mantle of Our Lady," and a *lady chapel* is a chapel attached to a large church and dedicated to the Blessed Virgin. The delicate *lady fern (Athyrium filix-femina)* does not refer to the Virgin Mary, as is commonly believed, taking its name from the legend that possession of its seeds could render a woman invisible.

Lady with the Lamp. Florence Nightingale, the greatest of war nurses, is generally considered to be the founder of modern nursing. Born in the Italian city for which she was named, "the Lady with the Lamp" spent her childhood in England. At 17, she is said to have heard the voice of God calling her to service, and several years afterward she decided that she was meant to be a nurse. Despite the objections of her wealthy parents, she embarked upon a career in public health, in spite of the fact that nursing at the time was a disreputable profession filled with prostitutes and worse. World fame came to her when she and 38 other nurses offered their services to the British army in the Crimean War (1854). Overcoming the initial suspicion of the troops, sometimes working as long as 20 hours a day, she became venerated as the *Lady with the Lamp* because she unfailingly made rounds of the wards each night to check on her patients. When the Lady with the Lamp died on August 13, 1910, aged 90, she was buried in the family plot in a small country churchyard in Hampshire, in a private service in which six British soldiers carried her coffin to the grave. The name *Lady with the Lamp* for Florence Nightingale was coined by Henry Wadsworth Longfellow in his poem "Santa Filomina" (1858), in which he referred to her as "A Lady with a lamp."

Laelia. These tropical American orchids, comprising about 35 species and prized for their showy flowers, may be named for Gaius Laelius, a Roman statesman and general who died about 165 B.C., or for his son Gaius Laelius, a Roman consul nicknamed Sapiens, the wise. Both father and son were soldiers and excellent orators, the father the best friend of Scipio Africanus Major, and the son famous for his friendship with Scipio Africanus Minor. The younger Laelius was also a close friend of Cicero, who wrote that he and Scipio used to like to go on holidays to the seaside, "where they became incredibly childish and used to collect shells and pebbles on the beach." Sapiens probably had a hand in writing the plays of Terence; his wide learning was admired throughout Rome. Another candidate English botanist John Lindley may have had in mind when he named *Laelia*, was a vestal virgin of that name, in allusion to the delicacy of the flowers. The vestal virgins, six in number, were daughters of the best Roman families, trained in youth to serve the goddess of hearth and home in her temple in Rome, where they prepared sacrifices and tended a perpetual sacred fire. Their vows included obedience and chastity, and after serving Vesta for 30 years they were allowed to leave the temple and marry, which they seldom did in practice. The virgins were influential, even having the power to pardon criminals, but if they broke the vows of chastity the penalty was a public funeral followed by burial while they were still alive. Needless to say, most remained vestal virgins.

laff box; laugh track. *See* TELEPROMPTER.

lagan; findals. These two terms aren't nearly as popular today as FLOTSAM AND JETSAM, but they have as long a history. *Lagan* refers to jetsam lying at the bottom of the sea but which is usually marked with a buoy in order to be found again by the ship's owner. *Findals* refer to *any* goods found in the sea, including an abandoned ship or derelict.

lager beer. *See* BOCK BEER.

lagniappe. *Lagniappe*, a "bonus gift" often given by merchants to customers, derives from the American Indian *yapa*, "a present to a customer," which came into Spanish first as *la napa*, "the gift." Pronounced *lanyap*, the word has also been used in Louisiana to mean small-scale bribery.

lah. In Singapore, where English is one of three official languages (along with Malay and Chinese), *lah* is an expression similar to American English *like* or *you know*. Whereas an American might say, "She's, like, very tall," a Singaporean speaking English might say, "She's, lah, very tall." *Lah* is said to come from a Chinese dialect, but its use is considered to be a sure way to identify a Singaporean or a Malaysian.

laissez faire. The 18th-century Physiocratic school of French economists were free-traders who wanted all custom duties abolished. Their motto "*laissez faire, laissez passer*" ("Let us alone, let us have free circulation for our goods") later became the term for the principle of noninterference by government in commercial affairs, for allowing things to look after themselves.

Lake Hubbs. Marine scientist Dr. Carl L. Hubbs has more marine namesakes than anyone in history. Besides the lake above, 22 species of fish, one genus and one species of lichen, one bird, one whale, one crab, two insects, two mollusks, three species of algae, and a research institute are named after this scientist. In addition, a minnow and a lantern fish are named *Lauri*, for his wife.

Lake Itasca. Lake Itasca, the source of the Mississippi River, was originally named Lake Veritas Caput, "the true source," by one of the explorers who found it. But his companion thought this Latin name too long and cut it in half, to *Lake Itasca*.

Lake Webster. The body of water with the longest name is located near Webster, Massachusetts, and is called Lake Webster by almost everyone. However, its official, Indian-derived name is composed of 43 letters and 14 syllables, translating into English as "You fish on your side; we fish on our side; nobody fish in the middle." Should anyone want to try pronouncing it, the lake is called Chargoggagoggmanchaugagoggchaubunagungamaug. *See* D (RIVER).

La La Land. A humorous name for Los Angeles (L.A.), California, since the early 1980s. In lower case to be living in la la land means to be far removed from reality.

lallapalooza. *See* LOLLAPALOOZA.

Lamanite. The name given to American Indians in the *Book of Mormon*, which represents them as descendants of the Jewish prophet Laman, who is said to have led them to America from Jerusalem in 600 B.C.

Lamarckism. The chevalier de Lamarck, Jean-Baptiste-Pierre-Antoine de Monet (1744–1829) proposed a theory of evolution holding that species evolve by inheriting traits acquired through the use or disuse of body parts, this concept known as the inheritance of acquired characteristics. His theory in some ways anticipated Darwin's in 1859. Lamarck, who was France's royal botanist and custodian of the Jardin des Plantes, wrote many natural history books. He died in poverty, his eyesight gone and his work discredited. *See* DARWINIAN.

lamb. Somehow the Greek *elaphos*, for "deer," is the basis for our words *elk* and *lamb*, two animals with little else in common. No one has satisfactorily explained this linguistic curiosity, but apparently the Greek word for deer, or one of its derivatives, was mistakenly thought to mean lamb somewhere along the way.

lambert. The son of a poor tailor and largely self-educated, Johann Heinrich Lambert nevertheless managed to win fame as a physicist, philosopher, mathematician, and astronomer. The German scientist, though he died of consumption in 1777 when only 49, made important discoveries in many fields. In mathematics Lambert proved the irrationality of pi and developed several trigonometry concepts, while in philosophy his *Neues Organon* (1764) pointed out the importance of beginning with experience and using analytical methods to prove or disprove theories. Lambert also made valuable contributions in electrical magnetism, mapmaking, and meteorology; several theorems in astronomy bear his name. It is for his work in physics on the measurement of light intensity and absorption that his name is honored in the dictionaries, the *lambert* being the unit of brightness in the metric system.

Lamb of God. *See* GOD'S SEAL PUP.

lame duck. Before the adoption of the 20th Amendment to the Constitution in 1930, any president or congressman who was defeated for election in November elections still held office until the following March 4. These elected officials were called lame ducks because they were mostly ineffectual, although they could help pass legislation embarrassing to an incoming administration. The "Lame Duck Amendment" eliminated them, but lame-duck appointments to diplomatic posts, etc., can still be made by a defeated, outgoing president. No one is sure where the term *lame duck* comes from. It originated about 125 years ago and may have been suggested by the British *lame duck*, "a person who has lost all his money, who has been financially crippled on the stock exchange." On the other hand it could be native born, a qualification of the American phrase *a dead duck*, an outgoing congressman being not quite dead yet, merely "lamed" until March 4 of the following year.

lampoon. The French *lampons*, "let us drink," is said to be the source of our *lampoon*, for a sharp or scurrilous satire ridiculing someone or something. The source suggests the coarseness and crudity of the form, which dates only from the 17th century and is used more in graphic caricature than in prose or verse—although there are notable examples in literature, including Pope's attack on Hervey in *Epistle to Arbuthnot*. Libel laws today make it much more difficult for a writer to really lampoon someone.

landlubber. Six centuries ago *lubber* meant "a clumsy lout," a word sailors originally applied to green seamen who didn't know a sail from a rudder. Eventually the term was lengthened to *landlubber* and applied to all nonsailors.

land-office business. Prior to the Civil War, the U.S. government established "land offices" for the allotment of government-owned land in western territories just opened to settlers. These offices registered applicants, and the rush of citizens lining up mornings long before the office opened made the expression *doing a land-office business*, "a tremendous amount of business," part of the language by at least 1853. Adding to the queues were prospectors filing mining claims, which were also handled by land offices. After several decades the phrase was applied figuratively to a great business in something other than land, even, in one case I remember, to a land-office business in fish.

land of Nod. Jonathan Swift, as fond of puns as the next man and better at them than most, is responsible for this expression meaning "the land of sleep." In his *Polite Conversation* (1738) Swift wrote that he was "going into the land of Nod," that is, going to sleep. The *land of Nod*, which suggests the nodding of a sleepy head, was a pun on the "land of Nod" or "land of wandering," the place where Cain was exiled after he slew Abel (Gen. 4:16).

Land of the Golden Hills. A name given by Chinese prospectors to California at the time of the gold rush of 1849.

Land of the Long White Cloud. A translation of the poetic native Maori name for New Zealand.

Land of the Midnight Sun. Norway is generally called The Land of the Midnight Sun, but strictly speaking many areas in high latitudes above the Arctic Circle deserve the name. During the summer in these places the sun never descends below the horizon within the day and does indeed shine at midnight.

Land sakes alive! Not many people use this old-fashioned euphemistic exclamation of surprise anymore, but many have heard their parents or grandparents say it. Often the phrase was *land sakes!*, *lands sake alive!*, *sakes alive!*, *my lands!*, *good land!*, *land!*, *Lordy!*, *land o' Goshen!*, and *good land a mercy!*

the land up over. *See* AUSSIE.

lang hame. A Scottish expression meaning the "long home," that is, one's grave in the earth, where he or she will reside for a long time. *Lang* is the typical pronunciation and spelling of *long*.

langley. In 1896 Samuel Pierpont Langley, already a celebrated physician and astronomer, constructed and flew the first heavier-than-air model plane. This pilotless steam-driven model traveled a distance of 4,200 feet over the Potomac River and though it included no provision for takeoff or landing, convinced many aviation pioneers that powered mechanical flight was possible. The government appropriated $50,000 for the inventor to build a full-size craft, powered by a 50-horsepower gasoline engine, which failed in two 1903 test flights. This subjected Langley to great ridicule, but the fault was in the launching apparatus, and the plane was reconstructed and flown successfully in 1914, seven years after Langley's death. Samuel Pierpont Langley (1834–1906) had a rich and varied career in science. *Langley Field* in Virginia pays tribute to his pioneering aviation work, and his accomplishments in physics are honored by the word *langley*, a measurement unit of solar radiation.

Langtry fever. America was seized by what was called *Langtry fever* in 1882 when the violet-eyed English actress Lillie Langtry first appeared on the American stage. Huge crowds turned out everywhere to see the beautiful Jersey Lily, who was better known for her liaison with the prince of Wales than for her acting ability. The daughter of a clergyman, she married a wealthy aristocrat and became one of the first English society women to act on the stage.

language. The word *language*, first recorded in about 1290, has its roots in the Latin *lingua*, "tongue." At least 2,796 different languages are spoken on earth, these divided into about 60 families, with Chinese having the most speakers (1 billion) and English the second most (300 million, with an additional 200 million speaking it as a second language). Besides our 2,796 languages on this planet there are some 8,000 dialects or language variants.

language barrier. "He [his language] erects a barrier between himself and his reader," a literary critic wrote in the late 18th century. But Oscar Wilde's quip about British and American English is the earliest mention I can find of the common phrase above. "We and the Americans have much in common," he observed, "but there is always the language barrier."

language of flowers. Many flowers and plants symbolize traditional ideas, such as the red rose for love and beauty and the snowdrop for hope (because its blooming indicates that spring will soon be here). The largest collection I've found of such symbolisms is found in a rare little book called *Drops From Flora's Cup* written by Mary M. Griffin in 1845. Here are a handful of over 300 symbolic flowers the book covers.

Allyssum—Worth beyond beauty
Amaryllus—Beautiful but timid
Birch tree—Grace
Blue bell—Constancy
Crocus—Youthful gladness
Cypress—Mourning
Daisy—Innocence
Honeysuckle—Bonds of love
Ivy—Friendship
Laurel—Glory
Mulberry tree—Wisdom
Olive branch—Peace
Primrose—Early youth
Rose, yellow—Infidelity
Violet—Modesty
Yew—Sorrow
Zinnia—Absence

Laodician. The word *Laodician*—usually meaning someone lukewarm or indifferent in religion or politics—derives from the name of a Syrian city. Its ruins can be seen today close to the Gonjele station on the Anatolian railway. Little is known of *Laodicea's* history, but it was one of the earliest homes of Christianity. Yet the Church of Laodicea grew lazy and indifferent, leading to its chastisement in the Bible. This biblical rebuke led to the word *Laodicean* being applied to all people indifferent to religion, with a Laodicean attitude remaining a major problem to churches today. Ultimately the word came to mean a person unconcerned about politics or even life itself. The city of Laodicea seems to have been named by Antiochus I after his wife Laodice.

Lapageria. French Empress Josephine, Napoleon Bonaparte's first wife, was born Marie Josèphe Rose Tascher de La Pagerie. A Creole of French extraction, she had been married to Viscount Alexandre de Beauharnais, who was guillotined after the French Revolution, Josephine escaping the blade herself only because of powerful friendships. The empress brought Napoleon much happiness, including two children from her first marriage—Eugène, later viceroy of Italy, and Hortense, who became queen of Holland—but her numerous love affairs caused him to consider divorce several times. On one occasion, it is said, the glass cracked over the picture of Josephine that Napoleon always carried. The emperor turned pale and declared, "My wife is either sick or unfaithful";—his latter premonition proved true. In any case, Napoleon finally did have his marriage with Josephine annulled in 1809 on the alleged grounds of sterility, and the emperor married Marie Louise of Austria. Josephine lived out her life in retirement at her private retreat, La Malmaison, near Paris, and the emperor continued to consult her on important matters, always having valued her keen mind. She died in 1814, aged 51. An avid botanist as well as an ardent lover (her garden at Malmaison contained the greatest collection of roses in the world), the beautiful Josephine has the monotypic genus *Lapageria*, containing only one species, named for her. This showy Chilean vine of the lily family is among the most attractive climbing vines, its flowers rose-colored, trumpet-shaped, and, unlike Josephine, usually solitary.

La Pasionaria. A nickname, meaning "passion flower" in Spanish, given to the communist Spanish civil war leader Dolores Ibarruri (1895–1975), who was especially famous for broadcasting the slogan *No pasarán* (they shall not pass) from Madrid on July 19, 1936. Strong, passionate women like her are sometimes called La Pasionaria.

Lapp words in English. Even a little-known language like the Lappish spoken by Laplanders has contributed a few words to our English vocabulary, these including lemming and tundra.

larboard. *See* STARBOARD.

large as life. We owe this popular phrase to one of Thomas C. Haliburton's Sam Slick tales, *The Clockmaker* (1837), in which Sam Slick of Slicksville says of another character: "He marched up and down afore the street door like a peacock, as large as life and twice as natural." Sam's words became a popular catchphrase in America and still survive in both the original and abbreviated versions.

lariat. Deriving from the Spanish *la reata* (the rope), this term for a long-noosed rope used to catch cattle and horses is first recorded in 1831 in the American West.

lark. A frolic, an escapade, a merry carefree adventure; or something very easy, as in "That test was a lark." The word probably doesn't come from the vigorous, cheerful actions of the bird called a lark, as is often stated. *Lark* more likely derives from the Saxon *lac*, meaning "sport."

larkspur. The lark is noted among birds for its long, straight rear claw or spur. Since the spur-shaped flower of the larkspur resembles the claw, it was given the bird's name. Larkspurs, of which there are some 200 species, are just as commonly called delphinium. *See also* DELPHINIUM.

Larousse. The famous series of *Dictionnaires Larousse* commemorates the French grammarian and lexicographer Pierre-Athanase Larousse (1817–75). In 1852 Larousse helped found the publishing house that bears his name. He later compiled the 15-volume dictionary and encyclopedia *Grand dictionnaire universel du XIXᵉ siècle* (1866–76).

larrikin. A chiefly Australian term for a young street hoodlum, one who doesn't usually intend to do serious harm. The word is said to derive from Larry, a pet name for Lawrence,

but no one knows why. It might also come from *larrup*, "to beat or thrash."

larva. One meaning of *larva* in Latin is "a mask." Linnaeus first used the term as the scientific (yet poetic) term for a caterpillar because, as one writer puts it, "such a creature wears a disguise, the future insect is not recognizable in the present grub, its form a 'mask' which will one day be cast off." *See also* PUPA.

lasagna. *Lasagna*, often made of wide noodles, cheese, and meat, among other ingredients, is a hearty, delicious Italian dish with a rather disgusting name. Somehow far back in time the Greek word for chamber pot (*lasanon*) became the Latin word for a cooking pot (*lasagna*) and over the years the lasagna gave its name to the common noodle dish cooked in it.

laser. *See* RADAR.

lass. *See* LAD.

last-ditch effort. A fight to the very end. The expression may have been coined by English bishop Gilbert Burnet in his *History of My Own Time* (1715), at least the *last ditch* part of it. Burnet wrote: "There was a sure way never to see [Holland] lost, and that was to die in the last ditch." He was referring to soldiers dying while defending the last ditch of an entrenchment.

Last Frontier State. A nickname for Alaska, which is also called the Sourdough State, the North Star State, the 49th State, the Great Land State, and the Land Up Over (suggested by Australia's nickname, the Land Down Under).

Lasthenia. Among the students who attended the philosopher Plato's lectures at the Academy in Athens was a woman named Lasthenia, who stole in by disguising herself as a man. Little more is known of her, but centuries later her story inspired the naturalist Cassini to name the plant genus *Lasthenia*, for Plato's woman pupil. The small genus contains but three species, two native to California and the other to Chile. All are tender annual herbs, and their showy flowers are yellow on long, often nodding, peduncles.

last infirmity of noble minds. That infirmity is the desire for fame, according to the proverb, being the last vice an otherwise noble person retains as he grows old. Though Milton said this in his elegy *Lycidas* (1637) on the death of his old friend Edward King, the poem "Sir John van Olden Barnevalt" called glory "that last infirmity of noble minds" 16 years before. An amazed Swinburne was sure that this was "the most inexplicable coincidence in the whole range of literature," but the idea was simply in the air at the time and can be traced back even earlier. Incidentally, both Bartlett and the *Oxford Dictionary of Quotations* still credit the words to Milton.

last leaf. Said of an aged person, the last of his or her generation. Oliver Wendell Holmes invented the expression in his 1831 poem "The Last Leaf," honoring Revolutionary War hero Major Thomas Melville, who had participated in the Boston Tea Party.

last licks. Since at least 1883, *last licks* has meant a team's last three outs in baseball, its last chance to win the game. It has since come to mean anyone's last try at anything. To *put in one's best licks* means to make a winning effort and, although this term dates back to the 1700s and is of unclear origin, the baseball connection has kept it alive.

last of the Mohicans. The Mohicans live—contrary to James Fenimore Cooper's famous story, we have not seen the last of them. Cooper adopted the name of the Algonquian-speaking tribe for the second of his "Leatherstocking Tales," and the title *The Last of the Mohicans* became an expression still used to indicate the last of any group with a certain identity. But the Mohicans—at least mixed-blood remnants of the tribe—still survive near Norwich, Connecticut and in Stockbridge, Indiana. The Mohicans, or Mahicans, were a powerful group in the past, occupying both banks of the upper Hudson in New York, while another branch, the Mohigans, lived in eastern Connecticut. While settlement and war with the Mohawks pushed them out of these areas—Dutch guns supplied to their enemies hastening their dispersal—and they almost entirely lost their identity. Probably some 800 survive today. The tribe owns a profitable gambling casino on its Connecticut reservation.

last rose of summer. Although he measured six-foot-six and 260 pounds, my grandfather was something of a courtly romantic and always rather grandly presented my grandmother with the last rose of the season, calling it "the last rose of summer." This may have been a widespread custom at the time and centuries ago, for the phrase *the last rose of summer* can be traced back to Irish poet and songwriter Thomas Moore's *Irish Melodies* (1807), where it begins a short song: "Tis the last rose of summer / Left blooming alone; / All her lovely companions / Are faded and gone." These words also give us the term *last rose* for the final flowering of anything, but anything written on the rose has to end on a romantic note, and no one ever sounded more romantic than British playwright Richard Brinsley Sheridan (1751–1816), who once said to a beautiful young woman, "Won't you come into my garden? I would like my roses to see you." *See* ROSE.

last straw. *See* THE STRAW THAT BROKE THE CAMEL'S BACK.

last word. Since the end of the 19th century *the last word* has meant the ultimate in fashions. The expression, however, had been used in its literal sense three centuries before this.

last words. The first record we have of *last words*, for the final utterances of a dying man, is the title of a book, *The Last Words of a Dying Penitent*, published in 1672, but the expression is probably much older.

latchkey children. Children whose parents both work and who have to let themselves into their homes after school with a key. The term is older than one would think, dating back at least to World War II in America. At that time many mothers worked in defense industries and many fathers served in the armed forces.

lateen. A triangular sail, common on sailing vessels in the Mediterranean. It is named after the Romans who used such sails, from the Latin *vela latina*, Latin (Roman) sails.

later. Good-bye. An economical form of *see you later on* that some sources date back to the speech of jazz musicians in the 1920s. Widely used today, as in "Later, man," it is also heard as *lates, laters,* and *late*.

lather. *See* WORK INTO A LATHER.

Latin. We find the word *Latin*, for the language of the Romans, first recorded in about 950. Latin was a second language to cultivated Englishmen for over four centuries, from about 1400–1800, and it was then a supreme insult to call someone a "Latinless dolt." According to Trevelyan, grammar school boys were permitted to speak nothing but Latin even out of school and "a spy aptly named *lupus* was sometimes paid to report whether they used English words while at play—if they did, they were flogged."

Latin words in English. Though many Latin words and phrases are the basis for words in the English lexicon, very few can be traced directly back to the Roman occupation of Britain, which lasted almost 400 years, A.D. 43–410. Strangely enough, there are more ruins than there are words attesting to the Roman stay, the latter including port, portal, mountain, and the *cester* (from the Latin *castra*, camp) that forms part of place names such as *Winchester* and *Manchester*. Latin words form about half of the English vocabulary, but the great majority came into the language during and after the Renaissance.

laugh and the world laughs with you. After Ella Wheeler Wilcox (1850–1919) published her poem "Solitude" in 1883, John A. Joyce claimed that he had written it 20 years earlier. Mrs. Wilcox offered $5,000 for any printed version of the poem dated earlier than her own and none was ever produced. Joyce, however, had the last word when he died in 1915, aged 72. The most famous lines from the poem are attributed to him on his gravestone in Oak Hill Cemetery, Washington, D.C.; they have become proverbial:

> Laugh and the world laughs with you
> Weep and you weep alone.

laugher. A game in any sport in which one side wins by a huge margin is called a laugher, because such a lopsided victory is a laughing matter (at least to the winning team). The expression may have originated in baseball.

Laughing Philosopher. Democritus of Abdera lived to a ripe old age in the fifth century B.C., very possibly because of his disposition. Juvenal, at any rate, wrote that the Greek philosopher always laughed at the follies of mankind. This distinguished him from the melancholy and aloof Heraclitus, who lived at about the same time and was called the Weeping Philosopher because man's follies made him sad. *See* WEEPING PHILOSOPHER.

laugh up one's sleeve. It might seem impossible today to hide one's laughter in one's clothing, but it was possible to do so when wearing the large billowy shirtsleeves of four centuries ago. People at the time often smiled or laughed into their sleeves to conceal their amusement or contempt, and this led to the expression *to laugh up one's sleeve*, "to laugh inwardly," usually derisively. *See* UP ONE'S SLEEVE.

launch. Deriving from French, with its first recorded nautical use in about 1400, *to launch* did not first mean to break a bottle of champagne against a vessel and slide it into the water. Animal blood was used long before champagne as a sacrifice to the sea gods, red wine later substituted for the blood, and finally more precious champagne substituted for the red wine.

Laura.

> It was the day when the sun's heavy rays
>   Grew pale in the pity of his suffering Lord
> When I fell captive, lady, to the gaze
>   Of your fair eyes, fast bound in love's strong
>   cord.

The Laura of Petrarch's immortal love poems was no figment of the poet's imagination. According to tradition, the poet laureate of Rome wrote his poems for Laura, the daughter of Audibert de Noves and the wife of Count Hugues de Sade, an ancestor of the French nobleman who gave us SADISM. Petrarch never revealed the real Laura's identity, guarding his secret jealously, but he wrote that he saw her for the first time in the church of St. Clara at Avignon on April 6, 1327, and that his first sight of her inspired him to become a poet. In the 18th century the Abbé de Sade identified her as the wife of Hugues de Sade; she bore the old man 11 children before dying of the plague in 1348 when she was only 40. But this identification is not certain. It is known only that Laura was a married woman who accepted Petrarch's devotion but refused all intimate relations. Their platonic love inspired the long series of poems that are among the most beautiful amorous verse in literature, the most famous being the sonnet in praise of their first meeting quoted above. The Italians call this collection of lyrics the *Canzoniere* and it is titled *Rime in Vita e Morte di Madonna Laura*. Petrarch died long after his Laura (whoever she was), in 1374 in his 70th year.

laurels. Laurels or bay leaves have symbolized victory since the winners at the Pythian games in ancient Greece were crowned with wreaths of laurel. The usage is still common in such expressions as "win the laurels," "to rest on one's laurels," and "to look to one's laurels." Contrary to popular belief, the Greeks did not give wreaths of leaves from the bay laurel tree to Olympic game victors; they were awarded wreaths made of wild olives. (Winners of the Nemean games were given wreaths of green parsley, and Isthmian game victors received wreaths of dry parsley or green pine needles.) In any case, "winning the laurels" or "crowned with bays" has come to mean a reward of victory. Laurel is a symbol of peace, too, and of excellence in all the arts. The bay laurel tree *(Laurus nobilis)* grows up to 60 feet in Greece but is most popular in the United States grown in tubs and kept pruned to a desired shape. *See also* POET LAUREATE.

lava. *Lava* is not a Samoan word, as I read in one place. The word derives from the Latin *labes*, "a sliding down," in reference to the molten rock that flows from a volcano down a mountain. It is first recorded in 1750.

Laval. After the liberation of France, Pierre Laval was tried for treason, sentenced to death, and executed on October 15, 1945. The French politician, born in 1883, held many national offices before becoming premier of the collaborationist Vichy government in 1942. Believing that Germany would win World War II, he was instrumental in organizing a policy of collaboration with the Nazis within occupied France. Under Nazi pressure Laval instituted a rule of terror, authorizing a French fascist militia and agreeing to send forced labor to Germany. His name became a hated one, synonymous with traitor, though he claimed at his trial that his motives were patriotic. Laval fled to Spain when France fell to the Allies, was expelled, and finally surrendered himself. After his conviction, he tried to commit suicide, but was saved for the firing squad.

lavalava. Unlike LAVA, *lavalava* is a Samoan word, meaning clothing. A piece of printed cloth worn as a skirt or loincloth, it is the principal garment of both sexes in Polynesia.

lavaliere. Louis XIV, the Sun King, had a voracious appetite for women as well as food. Françoise-Louise de La Baume Le Blanc, whom he later made Madame la duchesse de La Vallière, was only his first *maîtresse en titre*, or official mistress to the king. Louise, an innocent girl, never asked for anything, and it was only toward the end of their affair in 1667 that Louis made her a duchess, granting her the estate of Vaujours. Long before that she had become famous throughout Europe for her great beauty and the glamorous fashions she introduced. One of these, called the *lavallière* in her honor, was the ornamental jeweled pendant, usually worn on a chain around the neck, that we know as the *lavaliere*. Today the small TV microphone that hangs on a cord from the neck is also called a *lavaliere*, taking its name from the pendant necklace that honors the famous beauty.

lavender. In Medieval Latin the name for the lavender plant *(Lavandula spica)* is *livendula*, from *livere*, "to make bluish." However, the plant was long used for scenting linen, and it was associated with *lavare*, "to wash," which was probably combined with the former name to give it the name *lavender*. *See also* LAY OUT IN LAVENDER.

law and order. This slogan was employed long before present times in America, notably by Rhode Island's Law and Order Party, which opposed Dorr's rebellion in 1844.

lawn. Americans alone spent some 8.4 *billion* on their lawns in 1995. The lawns we maniacally manicure today take their name from the obsolete word *laund*, which is a borrowing from Old French *lande*, "moor," and was first recorded in the early 14th century. *Laund* meant merely "a woodland glade" and its first definition in 1548 described a "place void of trees." *Lawn* is simply a variant spelling of that word, but it isn't until the early 18th century that we find *lawn* used to mean a plot of GRASS kept closely mowed, usually by gardeners with scythes or by grazing animals. However, Chinese emperors had lawns as far back as 157 B.C., and the Maya and Aztec royalty made lawns, as did the ancient Romans, who used sheep to maintain them. Writing in the *Smithsonian* magazine (June 1991), Richard Wolkomir remarks on our passion for lawns despite the backbreaking and mindbending troubles they cause us: "Grassophilia has deep roots. A former Smithsonian ecologist, John H. Falk, once studied people's terrain preferences. He found that, whether they live in the United States, Africa, or India, the great majority prefer grassy savannas over all other landscapes, even if they've never seen a savanna. He had theorized that grasslands were the early human's preferred habitat and that preference seems to be genetically ingrained in man today."

lawnmower. The word *lawnmower* isn't recorded until 1875, while *lawn sprinkler* made its appearance 19 years later. However, the lawn mower was invented in around 1830 by English textile plant foreman Edwin Budding, who patterned his invention on factory machinery used at the time to shear the nap of woven cloth to a uniform height. Close to a century passed before retired American Army colonel Edwin George in 1919 invented the first motorized lawnmower, using the gasoline engine from the family washing machine for his invention. Then came the riding or riden lawnmower upon which all adults look ridiculous, though some people take them seriously—especially the 40 or so people who compete in the Twelve-Mile Riding Lawn Mower Race held in Twelve-Mile, Indiana, on July 4 of every year, the winner usually breaking 45 minutes. Such people might be called "mownomaniacs." *Mownomaniac* is a new word for someone obsessed with caring for, and especially mowing, his or her lawn. Mownomaniacs have been around for about a century and a half now (there were few lawns as we know them before 1850).

law of the jungle. Some people; by words and actions, insist that we still live by the *law of the jungle*, that is, like animals not governed by the rules of civilization. The term probably dates back to the late 19th century. *Law of the prairie*, a similar U.S. term, is first recorded in 1823.

lawrencium. While a physics professor at the University of California in 1930, Ernest Orlando Lawrence invented and built the first atom-smashing cyclotron, for which he was awarded the Nobel Prize nine years later. The physicist also played a prominent role in the development of the atomic bomb while director of the radiation laboratory at Berkeley, California, conducting research into the separation of U-235. Lawrence died in 1958, aged 57. In 1961 Albert Ghiorso, Almon Lash, and Robert Latimer created a new synthetic radioactive element at the laboratory dedicated to its former director. Lawrencium, its atomic number 103, is believed to be a "dinosaur element" that first formed when the world was born and decayed out of existence within a few weeks.

Lawsonia. Linnaeus probably named *Lawsonia inermis*, the mignonette tree and the source of the dye henna, for John Lawson, a traveler in North Carolina said to have been burned alive by Indians. Lawson came to America from England in 1700 and traveled about a thousand miles through unexplored territory, recording his observations of native flora and fauna in his *A New Voyage to Carolina* (1709). A founder of Bath and New Bern, North Carolina, he was appointed the state's surveyor general in 1708, but was captured and put to death in the Tuscarora uprising three years later. Whether Linnaeus related red men and death by fire to the red dyestuff taken from the eastern tree's leaves is unknown, though not impossible. At least one authority, however, claims that the Swedish botanist named the plant for a Dr. Isaac Lawson, a Scottish botanist who published an account of a voyage to Carolina in 1709.

lawyer; attorney; barrister; solicitor. In America, *lawyer* or *attorney* describes anyone who does any kind of legal work, whereas in England a *barrister* is an attorney who does trial work and a *solicitor* one who does general legal work. Attorney in its legal sense dates back to about 1330, lawyer to 1377, solicitor to 1527, and barrister to 1545. *Advocate* and *counsellor* are also words used for a lawyer. All of these terms have finer distinctions in England than in the U.S. There are probably as many derogatory expressions for lawyer as there are honored ones, ranging from *ambulance chaser* to *mob mouthpiece*.

lay an egg. Comedians and other entertainers complain that they *laid an egg*, that their act "bombed," utterly failed, but the phrase originated in the sports world, not in show business. Stranger still, the expression comes from the sport of cricket, England's national game. *Duck's egg* was British slang for "no score" in cricket for many years, and in about 1860 the expression *achieved a duck's egg* was used to describe a team that hadn't scored and had only large oval zeroes shaped like duck's eggs on the scoreboard. Ten years later the phrase became the more expressive *laid a duck's egg* and this came into American baseball slang as *laid a goose egg*. In baseball the expression for "zero" soon became just *goose eggs*, and it still is, but early vaudevillians adopted the expression "they killed the goose that laid the rotten eggs" and changed it to *laid an egg*.

lay out in lavender. The aromatic lavender plant has been cultivated for centuries. Its many uses include the use of its branches to beat just-washed clothes. In allusion to this, *lay out in lavender* first meant to give someone a physical beating, to knock someone down or unconscious. In time, however, the phrase came to mean to give someone a verbal beating or to chastise, as in "If I debate him, I'll lay him out in lavender. *See also* LAVENDER.

lay them in the aisles. Theatrical slang for "to have a sensational success," to *lay* (or *knock*) *them in the aisles* may derive partly from the expression *to knock 'em cold*, which has its origins in boxing. Both expressions date from only about the 1920s. British listeners would have trouble making sense of the phrase, because until fairly recently they have used *aisle* for a section of a theater, not a passageway. Since the word is from the Latin *ala*, "a wing"—this corrupted to *aisle* over the years possibly because of some confusion with *isle*—their use of the word is more proper.

lazar. *Lazar* has almost dropped out of use as a word for a diseased beggar or leper, but *lazarone* still describes a beggar of Naples. Both words are named for Lazarus, the only character in all his parables to whom Christ gave a proper name. During the Middle Ages *lazar* was the name given to those suffering from leprosy and other diseases, outcasts who were allowed to do nothing but beg. A *lazaretto*, or *lazar-house*, is a hospital for such persons, taking its name from *lazar* plus (*N*)*azaretto*, the popular name of a hospital in Venice managed by the Church of Santa Maria di Nazaret. The name Lazarus comes from the Hebrew *Eleazar*, meaning "God-aided," or "God will help." *See also* LAZARUS.

Lazarus.   Strictly speaking a *Lazarus* is someone risen from the dead, but the word is used allusively in many ways. It recalls the brother of Mary and Martha of Bethany, whom Jesus raised from the dead after he had been in his tomb four days (John 11:38–44). One authority notes that "in the fourth century the house and tomb of Lazarus were shown to pilgrims, and the gospel narrative . . . may be based on the story told to first-century visitors to Palestine." *See also* LAZAR.

lazy as Lawrence.   What does a Roman judge do with a saint of a man who when told to bring forth the treasures of his church comes forward with all its poor people? The Romans under Emperor Valerian did not appreciate St. Lawrence's philosophy, and this deacon to Pope Sixtus II (later St. Sixtus) soon followed his bishop to a martyr's death in 258. The Romans burnt him alive on a gridiron over a slow fire, and legend has it that he addressed his torturers ironically with the words "I am roasted enough on this side, turn me round, and eat." Over the years the legend has become more British and St. Lawrence's words are now "Turn me around, for this side is quite done," which is supposed to signify that the martyr was too lazy to move in the flames. More probably the expression *lazy as Lawrence* refers to the heat of St. Lawrence Day, August 10. In fact, the speech over the fire probably comes from a much older story told by Socrates and others about the Phrygian martyrs.

lazy as Ludlam's dog.   Tradition tells us that old Mrs. Ludlam, an English sorceress, had a dog who lived with her for many years in her cottage in Surrey near Farnham. So lazy was her dog that when strangers approached he always lay down or leaned up against a wall to bark, or didn't bother to bark at all. There are several versions of the tale, all of them responsible for the proverbial as *lazy as Ludlam's dog*.

lazybird.   The cowbird *(Molothrus ater)* is called the lazybird in America because the female of the species lays her eggs in the nests of other birds instead of building her own. The term is probably an old one, though first recorded in 1917.

lazy Susan.   The British call our *lazy Susan* a dumbwaiter, which the revolving servitor was called in America until relatively recently. It is said that the first use of the term dates back to about 75 years ago when the device was named after some servant it replaced, Susan being a common name for servants at the time. But the earliest quotation that has been found for *lazy Susan* is in 1934, and it could be the creation of some unheralded advertising copywriter. Therefore, *lazy* may not mean a lazy servant at all, referring instead to a hostess too lazy to pass the snacks around, or to the ease with which guests can rotate the device on the spindle and bring the sections containing different foods directly in front of them.

lb.   *Lb.*, as an abbreviation for *pound* comes from the Latin word *libra*, just as the symbol for the British pound Sterling does. *Libra* in this case is part of the Latin phrase *libra pondere*, a pound by weight.

l'chayim.   *L'chayim* is the Yiddish drinking toast equivalent to the English "To your health," the words translating as "to life." It derives from similar Hebrew words meaning the same, and is pronounced *l-khy-im*.

LCI.   *See* LSD.

LCT.   *See* LSD.

lead a dog's life.   *See* GO TO THE DOGS.

lead by the nose.   The allusion here is to animals like oxen, horses, and asses who from early times were led around by bit and bridle or by a rope attached to a ring hanging from the septum of the nose. Even wild animals like bears and lions were led around Roman arenas by a rope attached to a ring in the nose. Therefore, someone who leads another by the nose dominates him or holds him under submission. The idea is found in the Bible (Isa. 37:29): "Because thy rage against me, and thy tumult is come up into mine ears, therefore will I put my hook in thy nose, and thy bridle in thy lips, and I will turn thee back by the way which thou camest."

lead down the garden path.   The origin of this common expression remains a mystery. Not recorded in print until 1926, it may be the creation of the novelist Ethel Mannin, in whose book, *Sounding Brass*, it first appeared, but this seems unlikely. In the book *to lead down the garden* (path) means "to seduce," but the expression's common meaning is "to deceive in any way." The *garden path* suggests that the deception is done in a pleasant way, so that the victim suspects nothing.

lead pencil; graphite.   Pencils are not made of lead but of a mixture of graphite and clay. Bad habits are hard to break, however, and people have been calling graphite pencils "lead pencils" since the 16th century, when they were first mistaken as such. *Graphite* itself derives frim the Greek word for "to write." *See* PENCIL.

lead-pipe cinch.   A CINCH, borrowed from the Spanish *cincha*, is a saddle-girth used on horses or a girth used on pack mules. Because a well-fastened cinch holds the saddle securely so that it won't slip off, about a century ago the word *cinch* became a natural synonym for something sure and easy. Cinches, however, are usually made of leather, canvas, or braided horsehair, not lead pipe. So the expression *a lead-pipe cinch* is something of a mystery. One guess is that the phrase is from the underworld. Criminals using lead-pipe blackjacks, according to this theory, found it a cinch to dispatch their victims and a cinch to dispose of the "blackjack" should police near the scene of the crime stop them and frisk them for weapons.

lead with your chin.   The allusion here is to boxing, where if he doesn't protect himself with a right- or left-handed lead, but sticks his chin out, leads with his chin, a fighter is exposing himself to a knockout blow. *Leading with your chin* or "sticking your chin out" has been slang for taking a big chance since the 1920s, while "taking it on the chin" has meant to suffer severe failure since about the same time. The expression *take it* as in "He can really take it," that is, "he can deal with adversity well," is probably a descendant of *take it on the chin*.

lean over backwards. Judicial reforms in 18th-century England brought the appointment of many judges sensitive to the civil rights of accused persons, in marked contrast to older judges notorious for favoring or "leaning" toward the crown. The new justices were said to *lean over backwards* toward the accused and away from the crown or prosecution, in judging cases. In order to prove how honest, fair, and disinterested they were, despite their connections with the government, they went beyond the normal and expected. *Fall over backwards* means the same and *two inches beyond upright* is a synonym for "excessive rectitude" that should be heard more than it is.

learn by heart. The ancient Greeks believed that the heart, the most noticeable internal organ, was the seat of intelligence and memory as well as emotion. This belief was passed on down the ages and became the basis for the English expression *learn by heart*, which is used by Chaucer (1374) and must have been proverbial long before that. "To record" reminds us again of this ancient belief in the heart as the seat of the mind. When writing wasn't a simple act, things had to be memorized; thus we have the word *record*, formed from the Latin *re*, "again," and *cor*, "heart," which means exactly the same as *to learn by heart*. *See* BOWELS OF COMPASSION; LILY-LIVERED.

least said, soonest mended. *See* LITTLE SAID IS SOON AMENDED.

leatherneck. "Many sailors maintain that *leatherneck* originally referred to the dark leathery appearance of a dirty and long-unwashed neck," wrote George Stimpson in *Book About a Thousand Things* (1946). "It may be a myth, but according to Navy tradition mariners in the early days were dirty of person. In sailor slang, washing without removing the undershirt and jumper is called a leatherneck or 'Marine wash.' When a sailor washes, according to the sailor, he usually strips to the waist and washes his face, neck and arms, but when a marine washes he does so after the fashion of civilians, that is, he merely takes off his coat and rolls up the sleeves of his shirt to the elbows and washes his hands to the wrist and face to the neck." Stimpson's yarn is the best, but there are other theories, some more likely. One is that the Marines were simply named "leathernecks" for the black leather stock at the neck of the uniforms that they began wearing in 1804.

leave in the lurch. *Lourche*, or "lurch," was an old French dicing game resembling backgammon, popular in the 16th century. Any player who incurred a lurch in the game was left helplessly behind the goal, so far behind his opponent that he couldn't possibly win, which led to the figurative meaning of leaving someone in a helpless plight. The expression persists in English despite the fact that no one plays the old dicing game anymore, possibly because *lurch* describes a similar losing position in the game of cribbage.

leave in the soup. To leave someone in the lurch or in trouble. The expression is an Americanism first recorded in 1889 in connection with some South Dakota con man who skipped town with a lot of money, leaving many investors in trouble.

leave no stone unturned. So familiar is this saying that no one has trouble understanding Ogden Nash's pun, "When I throw rocks at seabirds, I leave no tern unstoned." It was advice that the Delphic oracle gave when the Theban general Polycrates asked how he could find treasure that the defeated Persians had hidden somewhere on the field after the battle of Plataea in 479 B.C. "Move all things," the Delphic oracle said, and Polycrates did so, finally locating the horde. The expression has meant "to show great industry" in English since the mid 16th century, probably first as a variation of the earlier *leave no straw unturned*, in reference to the straw-covered floors typical of the time.

Leave them while you're looking good. *See* GENTLEMEN PREFER BLONDES.

leave well enough alone; don't fix it if it's not broke; Melbourne. The sense of these two common expressions can be found in LET SLEEPING DOGS LIE, which is over 700 years old. *Why not let it alone* was the motto of British prime minister Lord William Lamb Melbourne in the early 19th century, and *don't fix it if it's not broke* is a relatively recent term. Lord Melbourne has the capital of Victoria, Australia, named after him. Originally called Dootigala, it was renamed for the prime minister in 1837, 10 years after it was settled.

Leblang. New York ticket agent Joseph Leblang sold reduced-price tickets to Broadway shows in the 1920s. He was so noted for this that his name became an eponymous word meaning to sell same, or meaning the tickets themselves (Leblangs).

ledger. In medieval times ledgers were large breviaries (books of daily prayers, readings, etc.) used in English churches, their name deriving from the Old English dialect *liggen*, "to lie," because they were books that lay in one place at all times, being too heavy to carry like other books. By the mid 16th century the same name was given to large record books used by businessmen that were also too heavy to move from place to place, and soon *ledger* was applied to any business record book.

leech; leechcraft. *Leechcraft* was the Anglo-Saxon word for the practice of medicine. Only a relatively few doctors are leeches today, but in Anglo-Saxon times doctors were called leeches, the term probably deriving from an Old English word meaning "to heal." One theory holds that the bloodthirsty worms called leeches were named after the doctors called leeches, because the doctors so often employed the worms in trying to cure people. A second theory has it that the bloodsucking worm's name derives from another similar Old English word that was confused with the Old English word for doctor and was eventually pronounced and spelled the same. *To leech* began to be used figuratively in the late 18th century, meaning "to cling to and feed upon and drain" (the way the worm does), a *leech* becoming a person who does this. In the 19th century *to stick to someone* (or *something*) *like a leech* became proverbial and Tennyson wrote of a world swarming with literary leeches.

leek. The national emblem of Wales takes its name from the Old English *leac*, for this member of the onion family; but the plant is native to central Asia and many peoples have had different names for it—Nero was nicknamed "Porrophagus" because he ate so many leeks, believing that they improved his singing voice. The leek has only recently been identified as the fabled store-henge that the Greeks considered a love potion.

Leeuwenhoek's little animals. Antonie van Leeuwenhoek (1632–1723), a former Dutch linen maker who designed a very powerful single-lens microscope, changed the course of science with his observations of the "animalcules" in a drop of pond water and his observations helped disprove the doctrine of spontaneous generation (that eels are generated from sand, grubs from wheat, and so on), making *Leeuwenhoek's little animals* a phrase that has lived for centuries.

left-handed compliment. The expression *left-handed compliment*, "a thinly disguised insult that poses as praise," apparently has its origins in the practice of morganatic marriage widely prevalent among German royalty in the Middle Ages and even practiced in modern times—Archduke Francis Ferdinand and his wife, who were both killed in the assassination that set off World War I, were married morganatically. These were usually marriages between royalty and commoners, the commoner agreeing that she would have no claim to her royal husband's title or property, nor would any children of the marriage—all she received was a *morning gift* (from the Latin *morganaticum*) on the morning after the marriage was consummated. In the special wedding ceremony held for these marriages, common up to the 17th century, the groom gave the bride his left hand instead of his right and thus morganatic marriages came to be known as *left-handed marriages*. Since they were a thinly disguised insult, it is possible that they later lent their name to the deceptive *left-handed compliment*. *See* RIGHT.

left-handed monkey wrench. There is no such tool, but green workers on a job are sometimes told to find one as a joke. The same applies to a "left-handed screwdriver" or "hammer." The terms are Americanisms, probably dating back to the early 20th century but possibly much older.

left holding the bag. To be left responsible for something, to be the fall guy or scapegoat after the others involved in a crooked scheme have protected themselves from prosecution or absconded. The term is an old Americanism dating back to 1760 or earlier, and Thomas Jefferson used it. The British use the phrases *left holding the can* and *left holding the baby*. *Left holding the bag* is recorded in Royall Tyler's *The Contrast* (1787), the first stage comedy written by an American. In the play Jonathan, the trusty Yankee retainer of the serious-minded American Revolutionary War officer Colonel Manley, is a servant full of homespun shrewdness. After referring to Shay's Rebellion, a 1786 revolt of Massachusetts farmers against high land taxes, Jonathan says: "General Shay has sneaked off and given us the bag to hold."

left sittin' on air way up in the sky. Thrown from a horse; the last line from an old folk song about a cowboy trying to break a horse and failing:

> When my stirrups I lose and also my hat,
> And I starts pullin' leather as blind as a bat,
> And he makes one more jump, he is headed up high
> Leaves me settin' on air way up in the sky.

legalese. When Charles A. Beardsley, then president of the American Bar Association, kidded his fellow lawyers with the famous words "Beware of and eschew pompous prolixity," he was campaigning against what philosopher Jeremy Bentham called "literary garbage," legal talk that has nothing to do with communication. "Legalese" consists principally of long-windedness, stilted phrases such as "Know all men by these presents," redundancies including "separate and apart" or "aid and abet," such quaintisms as "herewith and heretofore," and foreign-language phrases that could easily be translated into plain English: e.g., *caveat emptor* ("let the buyer beware") or *amicus curiae* ("friend of the court"). Despite the efforts of Beardsley and many others, the situation has not improved much over the last millennium. Some, like Sir Thomas More, have believed that it never will. More, a lawyer himself, explained that lawyers are "people whose profession is to disguise matters."

legend. The Medieval Latin word *legenda*, from the Latin *legere*, to read, meant "something to be read," especially something about the lives of saints. Often these biographies were filled with incredible stories, which led to legenda's meaning of "unlikely story or myth," a meaning that was retained when the word passed into English as *legend*.

legend in one's lifetime. It is possible that Florence Nightingale may be the first person so described, in Lytton Strachey's *Eminent Victorians* (1918): "She was a legend in her lifetime, and she knew it . . ." In the same book Strachey described the great nurse as a *living legend*, the first recorded use of that cliché. A variation is *a legend in her own time* and a cynical variation on that is the modern *a legend in her own mind*. *See also* LADY WITH THE LAMP.

leghorns. These prolific egg layers are a breed of chickens originally bred in Livorno, Italy, which the English, never good at pronouncing foreign words, called Leghorn. Highly regarded straw hats called leghorns are also made in Livorno.

Legionaires' disease. During a 1976 convention held by the American Legion in a Philadelphia hotel, hundreds of legionaires came down with a type of pneumonia no one had known before. Twenty-nine men died from *Legionella pneumophilia*, or Legionaires' disease, which was found to be thriving in the hotel's air-conditioning unit.

le gouter. An old tradition among Parisians similar to English afternoon tea. At *le gouter* (luh-goo-tay), a little after four o'clock and before six, cafes and tea parlors serve a great variety of rich pastries along with hot chocolate and coffee for a late afternoon snack that will hold hunger off until dinner begins at about nine.

lemon. Lemons were probably initially grown in the Middle East, for *lemon* is first recorded as the Persian and Arabic word *limun*, which became the Old French *limon*. *Limon* passed into

English when the French exported the fruit to England, and by the mid-17th century the fruit was being called the lemon there. *Lemon*, meaning something defective or inferior, derives from the sour taste of a lemon and is apparently an Americanism dating back to the turn of the century, as is *lemonade* (a drink the British call "lemon squash"). *See* ZEST. Slot machines with pictures of lemons may have suggested the term *lemon* for anything of inferior quality. One lemon on a machine and the slot machine player loses, which would not endear lemons to any player. The slot machine was invented at the end of the 19th century, just a few years before *lemon* was being used in this sense.

lemonade.   As mentioned briefly above, *lemonade* is an Americanism for a drink made of lemon juice, water, and sugar, always served cold, usually with ice. To the British, Australians, and New Zealanders, however, *lemonade* means "clear soda pop," often with a lemon flavor, such as the trademarked Sprite or 7-Up.

Lemon Fair River.   This river's name is the subject of several stories. One claims it derives from the old English phrase *lemon fair*, meaning "mistress fair." Another says an Indian massacre occurred on the stream's banks, and the massacre was called the "lamentable affair," which over the years was corrupted to *lemon fair*. George R. Stuart, in *Names on the Land* (1945), states "the most likely explanation is that the strange name is only a Vermonter's attempt to render *Les Monts Verts* (The Green Mountains)."

lemon sole.   Sour lemons have nothing to do with *lemon sole*, except that lemon juice might be squeezed on the fish before eating. The term is an established redundancy; when we say *lemon sole* we are saying "sole sole," for the *lemon* part is a corruption of the French *limande*, for "sole." The sole was so named because its shape was thought to resemble the sole of the foot.

le mot Cambronne.   *See* THE GUARD DIES BUT NEVER SURRENDERS!

lemur.   The great Swedish botanist Linnaeus named this aboreal primate after the ancient Roman *lemures*, frightening specters of the dead, so naming them because of their ghostly appearance (pale face and black eyes) and their nocturnal habits.

Lena Blackburne Rubbing Mud.   Perhaps the only mud named after a person. Lena "Slats" Blackburne managed the Chicago White Sox in the 1920s and 1930s. He found a Delaware River mud close by his New Jersey home that seemed better than other muds umpires rubbed on baseballs to make new balls less slippery and easier to grip when introduced in a game. His mud was in fact so good that it was packaged commercially as Lena Blackburne Rubbing Mud and eventually became the official mud of the American and National Leagues.

Leningrad; Leninism.   N. Lenin was the pseudonym Vladimir Ilyich Ulyanov adopted toward the end of 1901, variants such as V. I. Lenin coming into use a little later as his revolutionary activities in Russia became more prominent. He is thus known in history as Nikolai Lenin or Vladimir Ilyich Lenin, his real name rarely used. Only 54 when he died in 1924, he must still be regarded as one of the most effective political leaders of all time, though not "mankind's greatest genius," as *The Great Soviet Encyclopedia* calls him. But Lenin's name is legendary in the communist world, his body embalmed in a tomb in Moscow's Red Square that was once a shrine to Soviet citizens. The former capital city of St. Petersburg was named Leningrad for him in 1924. *Leninism* refers to the particular communistic principles based upon Marxism propounded by the founder of the modern Soviet state, which are collected in his 22-volume life and works. Leninism's central point is the creation of the dictatorship of the proletariat, or working class. Since 1991, with the overthrow of communism in Russia, Leningrad's name has officially been changed back to St. Petersburg.

lentil; lens.   Lentils are the beans that made the mess of pottage that the Bible implies Esau traded his brother for (though Scripture nowhere mentions the phrase "a mess of pottage"); they take their name from the Latin word for the bean, which also gives us the word *lens*, a double convex lens resembling a lentil bean in shape.

leonine contract.   Aesop's fable about the lion who hunted with several other animals has the lion claiming all the spoils of the hunt. One-quarter of the spoils he claimed as king of beasts; a second quarter because he was braver than any other animal; a third for his mate and cubs; "and as for the fourth, let him who will dispute it with me." Another version of the tale has the lion saying the last share belongs to everyone, "But touch it if you dare!" In any event, from "The Lion and His Fellow-Hunters" derives our term a *leonine contract*, "a completely one-sided agreement," and a *lion's share*, "the largest portion of anything."

a leopard doesn't change its spots.   Leopards are so named because they were once thought not to be a separate species but a cross between the lion (*leo*) and the *pard*, a Tibetan wildcat or panther. Like the creature's name, the saying *a leopard doesn't change his spots* also goes back to ancient times. It is an allusion to the pessimistic rhetorical question found in Jer. 13:23: "Can the Ethiopian change his skin or the leopard his spots? Then also you can do good who are accustomed to evil." *See* GIRAFFE.

leotards.   We owe this word to 19th-century French aerialist Jules Léotard, who claimed in his *Mémoires* to have invented the outfit still worn by circus performers. Originally the costume was a one-piece elastic garment, snug-fitting and low at the neck and sleeveless. Leotard, born to the circus—when he was a baby, his aerialist parents would hang him upside down from a trapeze bar to stop his crying—intended his costume for men, not women. "Do you want to be adored by the ladies?" he exhorts his male readers in his *Mémoires*. "[Then] put on a more natural arb, which does not hide your best features!" Léotard, billed as "The Daring Young Man On The Flying Trapeze," died of smallpox in 1870 when only 28.

leprechaun.   These Irish elves, who figure in many a legend, take their name, first recorded in 1604, from the Old Irish *lu*, meaning "small," and the Old Irish *corp*, "body." The last part of the word, however, was borrowed from the Latin *corpus* for body, this an excellent example of church Latin's influence on the Irish language.

lesbian. Lesbos, a Greek island in the Aegean Sea off the west coast of Turkey, was a center of civilization in the seventh and sixth centuries B.C. There Sappho, the most famous poetess of her time, taught the arts of poetry to a select group of young women. The legend has never been proved but the romantic ardor of some of Sappho's lyrical poems probably accounts for the tradition that she and her followers engaged in homosexual love, female homosexuality being named for the *Lesbians*, or residents of Lesbos. The word *Lesbian* (with a capital) designates any inhabitant of the island, which is noted for its rich soil as well as its sardine and sponge fisheries. Here Epicurus and Aristotle once lived and the philosopher Theophrastus was born. Sapphism, from Sappho's name, is a synonym for lesbianism. The poetess, according to legend, threw herself into the sea when spurned by the handsome youth Phaon, but the story is generally regarded as pure invention. Sappho may have married and had a son. Her simple, passionate verse, characterized by matchless lyricism and vivid use of words, originally formed nine books, but only fragments of these are extant today. The "Tenth Muse," as she was known, used the four-line verse form now called sapphics in her honor, and is in fact noted for her careful control over meter. *See* SAPPHO.

lese majesty. An offense against the sovereign power in a state, especially a ruler, or even an attack against any belief or institution revered by large numbers of people is called *lese majesty* (or *lèse-majesté*), which comes from the Latin *laesa majestas* (injured majesty) by way of the Medieval French. The term is first recorded in 1430.

le shake hand. A French borrowing and alteration of the English word *handshake*. The French language newspaper *Le Monde* recently reported a study claiming that every 166th word in the French vocabulary is English.

lespedeza. Japan or bush clover, sometimes called the hoop-coop plant but widely known as lespedeza, is believed to have been brought to America in the early 19th century with a cargo of tea unloaded at Charleston or Savannah. The plant became an escape that was first identified at Monticello, Georgia in 1846, and this initial collected specimen is now preserved at Harvard's Gray Herbarium. A member of the pea family, *lespedeza* has become a very important crop not only for hay and forage but for improving poor soils—it has been shown that corn and cotton crops can be increased 10 to 30 percent by turning under a crop of lespedeza previous to their planting. The slender plant grows to a height of about 18 inches, its leaves divided into three leaflets on many branched stems. The genus *Lespedeza*, however, contains 125 species, of which Japanese clover (*Lespedeza striata*) is only one. Many of these species are native to America and it was to them that the botanist Michaux referred when he named the genus in 1803. *Lespedeza* was named in honor of V. M. de Zespedes, Spanish governor of East Florida in 1795, whose name Michaux misread as Lespedez.

less is more. British poet Robert Browning (1812–89) may have invented this phrase, which is first recorded in his poem "Andrea del Sarto" (1855). The words have since been applied to writing, acting, architecture etc., deemed good because it is lean and spare, unadorned, as in, for example, Hemingway's best prose.

les sommobiches. A name the French gave all American soldiers during World War I, because so many of them constantly used the expression *son of a bitch*. The latter term is hardly an Americanism, however: *The four-word epithet*, as it has been called, was first recorded in 1688 and is probably centuries older in forms like *bitch-sone*. Son of a bitch, or S.O.B., is so common for a despicable person that it is sometimes even applied to a woman. *See also* GODDAM.

let George do it. We say this satirically today when there is work to be avoided, but France's Louis XII was serious when he said, "Let George do it." He referred to his brilliant adviser Cardinal Georges d'Amboise (1460–1510) and entrusted important affairs of state to him so often that the phrase "let Georges do it; he's the man of the age" became proverbial, eventually losing its *s* and becoming "let George do it" and bestowing more glory on the cardinal than his magnificent tomb in the Rouen Cathedral. Louis's minister of state, a prodigy who became a bishop when only 14, was truly "the man of the age," a Renaissance man who excelled in everything he did, from literature to science.

lethal; lethargy. The *waters of Lethe* refers to the River Lethe, one of the rivers of Hades in Greek mythology. The dead were required to taste these waters in order to forget the past and find oblivion. From the myth derive our words *lethal* and *lethargy*.

let her rip. Letting things go at full speed was called *let-her-rip-itiveness* in mid-19th-century America. The Americanism derives from another American expression, *let her rip*, which apparently first referred to railroad locomotives. Americans were always obsessed with speed. Wrote one early train traveler out West: "Git up more steam—this ain't a funeral! Let her rip!"

let sleeping dogs lie. Chaucer seems to have expressed this idea first in *Troilus and Criseyde* (1374), though he put it in the reverse form: "It is nought good a slepyng hound to wake." For at least 400 years the saying remained basically the same, until in the 19th century it became the familiar *let sleeping dogs lie*, "leave well enough alone."

let's put some lipstick on this pig and sell it. Said to be a recent exhortation of a brokerage firm to its brokers, urging them to make a worthless dog or pig of a stock appear to be an attractive investment.

Let's roll! Inspirational words that may prove as immortal as *Remember the Alamo! Remember Pearl Harbor*, and other patriotic American war slogans. The words were originally used by airline passenger Todd Beamer to rally fellow passengers against terrorists who had hijacked United Airlines Flight 93 on the beginning of the 9/11 terrorist attacks. All 40 passengers and the crew died when the plane crashed in Pennsylvania, but much greater loss of life in the Washington, D.C., area was prevented. President George W. Bush has since used the phrase in various speeches.

let's see the color of your money. When this saying originated in the early 18th century paper money wasn't in general use, so it couldn't allude to the inferior color of counterfeit money, as has been suggested. So-called red money (gold) and white money (silver) was in existence, however. Probably the expression was born when someone selling something refused to discuss the matter until the prospective buyer proved that the more valuable red money, not white, was jingling in his purse or pocket.

Let's slip out of these clothes and into a dry martini. A by-now almost proverbial quip by author and wit Robert Benchley. Benchley was known to drink; in fact, he was known to drink more and to be able to hold more than anyone in his circle. "What do you drink so much for?" F. Scott Fitzgerald, of all people, once lectured him. "Don't you know alcohol is slow poison?" "So who's in a hurry?" Benchley replied. Another time he observed, "Drinking makes such fools of people, and people are such fools to begin with, that it's compounding a felony."

letter. The first private letter written in English dates from about 1392 (before then letters had been written in French), and manuals for letter writers abound from about that date on. *Letter*, for "a missive," is first recorded in about 1225. The word derives from the Latin *littera*, "a letter of the alphabet."

letter (sports). The practice of awarding college varsity athletes letters, or monograms of the first letter of the college's name, began with the great University of Chicago football coach Amos Alonzo Stagg, in the early 1900s.

letter carrier. An old term for a postman still commonly used in northern California; occasionally heard in metropolitan New York and other areas as well.

let the cat out of the bag. *Let the cat out of the bag* may have originally referred to the master-at-arms aboard a British naval ship taking the cat-o'-nine-tails from its blood-red carrying bag before a seaman was flogged. The connection between this and an untimely revelation is a tenuous one, but no better explanation has been offered so far.

let the dead bury their dead. Don't worry about things over and done with, forget what happened in the past. The expression comes from the Bible (Matt. 8:22): "But Jesus said, Follow me, and let the dead bury their dead."

Let them eat cake. Marie Antoinette may have said this in referring to the Paris proletariat after they pleaded for bread in 1770, but she did not invent the famous retort. Rousseau's *Confessions*, written two or three years before the remark is attributed to her, told of a "great princess" who said the same thing to her peasants at least 15 years before Marie Antoinette was born. Some claim that the thoughtless remark was circulated to discredit Marie, while others say she repeated it herself, and she was certainly capable of such a "little joke." The French phrase is *Qu'ils mangent de la brioche* and may mean "they"

should eat the outer crust (*brioche*) of the bread, the "stale" part as opposed to the soft inside part.

lettuce. *Lettuce* probably takes its name from a form of the Latin *lactuca*, "milky juice." The Roman gourmet Apicius watered the lettuce in his garden with mead every evening so that it would taste like "green cheese cakes" when he picked it mornings.

lettuce bird. A popular name for the goldfinch (*Astraglinus tistis tistis*) is "lettuce bird" because lettuce seed is among its favorite foods. A good way to draw this attractive yellow bird to the garden is to let some lettuce plants bolt, blossom and bear seed. Because of its musical abilities the goldfinch is also called the "wild canary."

let your hair down. I can't find an old quotation to support the theory, but this expression may have originated in the days of Louis XIV, when elaborate hairstyles such as the FONTANGE, a pile of style that rose two feet and more above the wearer's head, were popular among Frenchwomen. These styles were such a nuisance that several were actually banned by the Sun King. Certainly none permitted informality or intimacy, and only when a woman let down her hair at night in privacy did she relax any and shed at least one inhibition.

Levi's. The word *Levi's* has become more popular in the eastern United States recently as a synonym for jeans, denims, or DUNGAREES—probably due to the bright-colored styles that Levi Strauss and Company are manufacturing today. The trademarked name has been around since the gold rush days, though, when a pioneer San Francisco overall manufacturer began making them. Levi Strauss reinforced his heavy blue denims with copper rivets at strain points such as the corners of pockets, this innovation making his product especially valuable to miners, who often loaded their pockets with ore samples. Within a few years the pants were widely known throughout the West, where the name Levi's has always been more common than any other for tight-fitting, heavy blue denims.

lewd. Beginning with its original meaning of lay (as in *layman*), *lewd* has had seven different meanings through the years: unlettered, low, bungling, vile, lawless, and licentious. Today only the last meaning is much used and it is first recorded in 1712, for the biblical "lewd fellows of the baser sort" (Acts 17: 5) refers to lawless fellows, not lascivious ones. No one knows why, although the word is in good company with those many words in English that begin with an "*l*" and have something to do with sexual debauchery. They have a rather revolting, loathsome pronunciation; you sort of squinch up your nose and sneer when saying them: leer, lecherous, loose, libidinous, lustful, even luxury. Probably the pronunciation does not have a lot to do with the prevailing meaning. But like many words associated with sex, *lewd* is undergoing a change today. It is being used more playfully, with less high-mindedness, and may have an eighth meaning in another century or so. We already have the precedent of Shakespeare calling Falstaff an old lewdster, and Falstaff, after all, was eminently likable, no one you would squinch up your nose at.

Lewisia. *See* CLARKIA.

lexicographer. Dr. Johnson, working on his great dictionary, invented a definition almost as well known as the word itself— "Lexicographer: A writer of dictionaries, a harmless drudge." The word, from the Greek meaning the same, is first recorded a century earlier.

L 5. My correspondent Eric Halsey advises that L 5 "is the designation of one of the Lagrange points in the Earth's orbit where it would be advantageous to place a self-sustaining human space colony." The L 5 Society advocates the establishment of such a colony.

L'Hara. According to one interesting account, uncorroborated here, this was the name for the police in the Spanish-speaking New York City barrio during the 1930s and 1940s. It seems that many of the Irish New York cops at the time were named O'Hara, which, in the distorted form of *L'Hara*, became the eponym for police in general.

Lhasa apso terrier. The "forbidden city" of Lhasa in Tibet gave its name to this long-haired terrier bred as far back as the 12th century.

libertine. Early in the 16th century a group of European freethinkers dubbed themselves the Libertines, a word that had previously meant "a freed slave." Because they believed that there was no sin, and acted accordingly, these Libertines saw their name become a synonym for any morally or sexually unrestrained person, a rake, or a profligate.

liberty, equality, fraternity! The motto of the French Fifth Republic today, these words were originally the motto of Revolutionary France. Napoleon, an imperialist, employed them most effectively.

Liberty Tree (Elm); Liberty Hall; Liberty Stump. A tree that grew in Boston from which effigies of unpopular people were hanged during the protests over the Stamp Act in 1765. The ground under the tree became known as Liberty Hall. In 1775 the British cut the venerable elm down, and for a time it became known as the Liberty Stump. Soon after Liberty Trees were being planted all over the country, some say in almost every American town. Most of them died from the disease that struck elms early in the 20th century.

library. *Library* derives from the Latin *liber*, "book," but the first library known with certainty to have existed was a collection of clay tablets in Babylonia in about the 21st century B.C. The first private library in ancient Greece was probably that of Aristotle in about 334 B.C. The dramatist Euripides was also said to have a large library, as did Plato and Samos, and later Mark Antony is supposed to have given the vast 200,000-volume library of the kings of Pergamum as a present to Cleopatra. Tradition ascribes the formation of the first public library at Athens to the beneficent tyrant Pisistratus in 540 B.C., but the earliest public library still existing today is the Vatican Library in Rome, founded in 1450. A public library was opened in Boston as early as 1653, and Benjamin Franklin proposed the Library Company of Philadelphia in 1731. The purchase of Thomas Jefferson's library of 6,457 books formed the nucleus of the U.S. Library of Congress after the original holdings of the national library in Washington, D.C., were destroyed by fire in 1814. Created by Congress in 1800, the library is now the world's largest, with 35 acres of floor space containing some 100 million items, including over 17 million books. By law the library on Capitol Hill must be given two copies of every book registered for copyright in the United States, and over 60,000 are published in America annually. *See also* BODLEIAN LIBRARY.

lickety split. Bartlett's *Dictionary of Americanisms* (1859) defines *lickety split* as "very fast, headlong; synonymous with the equally elegant phrase 'full chisel.' " Today *lickety split* is only heard infrequently and it is folksy rather than "elegant." The *lick* in the phrase is probably associated with speed because of the rapidity with which the tongue moves in the mouth, and *split* is perhaps associated with "split second." The Puritans used the phrase, but it wasn't very popular until the mid-19th century. *Lickety cut, lickety switch, lickety click, lickety liver,* and *lickety brindle* were variations on the expression.

lick into shape.

> Beres ben brought forth al fowle and transformyd and after that by lyckynge of the fader and moder they ben brought in to theyr kyndely shap.
> —The pylgremage of the sowle, 1400

For at least 10 centuries people believed that bear cubs were born just formless masses of grotesque flesh and that both Mama and Poppa Bear took turns literally licking them into shape. No one debunked this legend for so long because bears usually keep their cubs hidden for a month or so after their birth, and any debunker who ventured into a bear den in search of evidence probably didn't come out to do his debunking. So the story was widely believed—by Pliny, Montaigne, Shakespeare—up until and even after the discovery of America. By the time the marvelous tale was disproved the expression *lick into shape*, "make ready, make presentable," had gained a permanent place in the language.

lido. *Lido* for a spit of land enclosing a lagoon, or a bathing beach or a public, open-air swimming pool takes its name from the famous Lido resort in Venice, which is on such a spit of land.

Liebfraumilch. The German white wine's name translates as "milk of the Blessed Mother," referring to the Virgin Mary. The name originally applied only to wines made near the Liebfraukirch in Worms. *See* LACRIMA CHRISTI.

Liechtenstein. Liechtenstein is one of the few countries named after a family. It is a principality created in 1719 by uniting the barony of Schellenburg and the country of Vaduy, both of which had been purchased by the Austrian family of Liechtenstein.

lief. *See* JUST AS LEAVE.

lie like a butcher's dog. Grose, in the 1788 edition of his *Classical Dictionary of the Vulgar Tongue*, tells us this was "a simile often applied to married men," who, "like the butcher's dog" would often "lie by the beef without touching it." The humorous expression for involuntary sexual abstinence didn't last until Victorian times, when it might have achieved wider currency.

lie like a tombstone.   Used to describe a great liar; the comparison is with the tombstones of old, whose inscriptions often exaggerated the good qualities of those who lay beneath them.

the lie of the pipe dream.   Although one of the most famous phrases in American literature, *the lie of the pipe dream* is seldom, if ever, collected. It is from Eugene O'Neill's play *The Iceman Cometh* (1946), which takes place in Harry Hope's saloon, where O'Neill's guilt-ridden characters cling to pipe dreams about their lives, illusions that the salesman Hickey shatters for them. One character, the anarchist Larry Slade, decides that they can't live without their illusions, that "the lie of the pipe dream is what gives life" to people like themselves. *See* PIPE DREAM.

life is just a bowl of cherries.   Attempts have been made to link this expression with a much older one, *life is but a cherry-fair*. However, the older phrase, from the early 17th century, means life is all too short and fleeting, as short as the annual English fairs held in orchards where cherries were sold each spring. Evanescence is not the spirit of *life is just a bowl of cherries*—which means life is joyous, wonderful, and which seems to have originally been the title of a popular song of the late 19th century.

life is short, but the art is long.   The full aphorism by the Greek physician Hippocrates is "Life is short, but the art is long, the opportunity fleeting, the experiment perilous, the judgment difficult." A variation in the translation by Chaucer is "The life is so short, the craft so long to learn." *See* HIPPO-CRATIC OATH.

life of Riley.   In a comic song written by Pat Rooney of the "Dancing Rooneys" in the 1880s and performed by him on the vaudeville circuit, the song's hero, Riley, tells of what he'd do if he "struck it rich." He promises New York will "swim in wine when the White House and Capitol are mine." Many word ferrets believe that the phrase *the life of Riley* derives from the Rooney song, though Mencken champions the tune "The Best in the House Is None Too Good for Reilly," written by Lawlor and Blake toward the turn of the century. Yet the Hoosier poet James Whitcomb Riley (1849–1916) may just lend his name in some way to the saying. Riley's simple, sentimental poems depicting the lives of barefoot boys loafing and living a life of ease in the summer were immensely popular at the time the phrase came into use.

Lifting Monday; Lifting Tuesday.   Easter Monday was called Lifting Monday, or Heaving Day, in the English counties of Shropshire, Cheshire, and Lancashire because of an ancient custom that allowed men to lift up and kiss any woman met in the street that day. On Lifting Tuesday women could do the same to men. "Lifting or heaving differs a little in different places," one writer explained. "In some parts the person is laid horizontally, in others placed in a sitting position on the bearers' hands. Usually, when the lifting or heaving is within doors, a chair is produced." According to another observer, "the woman's heaving-day was the most amusing," with the women trying to lift and heave the men, but the custom, recorded as late as the 1870s, caused too many disturbances and was abandoned before the end of the 19th century.

lift yourself up by the bootstraps.   Riding boots and many other long boots have inside, near the top, loops or straps that make it easier to pull on a tight-fitting boot. When yanking on these straps it feels as if you are laboriously lifting yourself upward instead of putting on a boot, and no doubt such struggles inspired the saying to *lift yourself up by the bootstraps*, to raise yourself in the world exclusively through your own efforts. Such bootstraps, and even specialized boot hooks to pull them with, date back to Cromwellian times, but when the expression was invented is a mystery. It hasn't been traced back before 1944, although it is almost certainly much older. In 1941 Robert A. Heinlein published a story in *Astounding Science Fiction* called "By His Bootstraps."

liger.   *See* TIGON.

light a fire under.   *See* BUILD A FIRE UNDER.

light colonel.   Army slang going back 60 years or more, a *light colonel* is a pun on Lt. (Lieutenant) Colonel and indicates that Lt. Colonel is a lower and less weighty rank than full colonel.

lightning never strikes twice.   Not only does lightning strike twice in the same place, it is *more likely* to strike in the same place than not, simply because the tree or whatever else serves as the conductor for the first strike is the highest, most attractive point in the area. Nevertheless, the old superstition has been around for centuries and is often used in the expression *lightning never strikes twice*, meaning that anything, either bad or good, that happened once won't happen again. The ancients held that persons struck dead by lightning were incorruptible and they honored them, but many used various charms to protect themselves against lightning, which kills about 150 people a year in the U.S.

lightning pilot.   A pilot on the Mississippi River in the 19th century who was lightning quick, who got all the speed possible from his ship, was called a lightning pilot. The term was used by Mark Twain and many other contemporary writers.

light on a bush.   Folk poetry for the berries of the bayberry bush (*Myrica pensylvanica*), the phrase *light on a bush* originated among American pioneers in the 17th century. The waxy berries were of course used to make candles; in fact, in Colonial times September 15 was known as Bayberry Day, "a time when old and young sallied forth with pail and basket, each eager to secure his share in the gift of nature."

lightweight.   British boxers who weighed under 154 pounds were called *lightweights* as early as 1850, although the American lightweight division today is 127–135 pounds. Before that, in the 1730s, *lightweight* had been used in English horse racing to refer to lightweight gentleman riders. Both of these terms were the inspiration for the general expression *lightweight* meaning an unimportant or inconsequential person, which is first recorded in 1882. *See* HEAVYWEIGHT.

like a house on fire.   Although log cabins weren't the homes of the earliest American settlers—Swedes settling in Delaware introduced them in 1638—they became a common sight on the western frontier in the 18th and 19th centuries. As practical as they were, these rude wooden structures were tinderboxes once they caught fire. So fast did they burn to the ground that pioneers began to compare the speed of a fast horse to a log cabin burning to the ground, saying he could go *like a house on fire*. By 1809 Washington Irving, under the pseudonym Diedrich Knickerbocker, had given the expression wide currency in his *History of New York from the Beginning of the World to the End of the Dutch Dynasty*, the first great book of comic literature by an American. The phrase soon came to mean "very quickly or energetically."

like a shot out of hell.   When the last half of this phrase was coined is a mystery, but *like a shot* dates back to 1809. Dickens later employed the expression, and it became widely used for "fast, very quickly," like a bullet fired from a gun.

like Grand Central Station.   Very crowded, packed, hectic. In use since the early 1900s, the phrase refers to New York's Grand Central Terminal, where trains arrive and depart for many destinations, and the busy Grand Central subway stop in the terminal.

like herding cats.   A clever recent expression that isn't recorded in any dictionary. It means a "difficult, almost impossible job," as in "Making people pay such a tax will be like herding cats." The cat is an animal that is highly independent and unlikely to be forced into anything. The verb *to herd* is frequently used in the expression *ride herd on* (cattle), which dates back to the turn of the 19th century in the West and means to closely supervise something. *To herd* can also mean "to oversee" convicts or laborers, and even in some regions to take care of children: "Will you herd the baby for me?" or "She was herding the kids."

like it or lump it.   Be happy with it or just put up with it against your will, resign yourself to it. *Lump it* could come from the word *lump*, which once meant to gulp down a bitter medicine. The expression dates back to 1791, according to the *Dictionary of Americanisms*.

like lemmings.   It may not be true that lemmings commit mass suicide by marching into the sea. The Norway lemming (*Lemmus lemmus*), resembling a cross between a rat and a miniature rabbit, is an incredibly prolific creature, females giving birth to three litters every 11 months, with up to 12 babies per litter. Young from each litter can conceive when only 19 days old, which means that females from the first and second litters are able to reproduce within the year. Scientists have recently theorized that the extraordinary lemming population explosions that occur irregularly in periods from five to 10 years are triggered by a super hormone that appears in new spring shoots of grass. This stimulative substance, when nibbled in small doses by the lemmings, apparently increases litter size and hastens maturation. When the lemming population explodes, the fabled lemming migration begins, the basic drive apparently the need to find a suitable nesting area. The pernicious lemmings begin their migration by coming down from the Scandinavian mountains, thousands of them proceeding in a straight line, a few feet separating each. They eat little on the way but destroy everything in their path. The landscape is carpeted with them, and they frequently interrupt rail and highway traffic. Onward the line of lemmings forges, largely male because pregnant females settle down along the way in suitable habitats. The line of lemmings traces a furrow in the earth, stripping it of vegetation while making a low whistling sound. Nothing stops it. It may go around impassable obstacles such as rocks, but will immediately form into a single straight line again. The lemmings resist any attempt to stop them, defending themselves against dogs and even men. The living line avoids human habitations but gnaws through haystacks, levels farmlands, and scoots between the legs of people at times, relentlessly marching on. When they come to water, the lemmings, good swimmers, continue on their course, thousands of them plunging in and trying to make it to the opposite shore, often climbing over boats rather than be diverted from their straight line. The line doesn't steer away from wide rivers and (apparently believing they can reach the other side) even plunges into the ocean on reaching the coast, where the exhausted lemmings, always struggling to stay alive, drown or are swallowed up by fish and seabirds. Those females who remain behind in suitable habitats make their way back to the mountains, so this amazing mass behavior is not suicidal, as many people believe. "The false idea that lemmings have a death wish conforms to some evident need in rhetoric," columnist Philip Howard wrote not long ago in the *Times* of London. "It is all bunkum. Lemmings just don't do what they are supposed to do. The only animal that regularly commits mass suicide is *Homo sapiens*. But evidently we have a need for some vivid metaphor from nature to illustrate the human propensity to self-destruction. The poor bleeding lemming has been adapted as a cliché to fit the description."

like pigs in clover.   To be completely content, very happy. The first mention of the Americanism was a brief poem in the *Boston Gazette* (Jan. 7, 1813): "Canadians! Then in droves come over, / And live henceforth like pigs in clover." In Britain *pigs in clover* describes wealthy people behaving badly, but I've never heard or seen the words used that way in the U.S. See CLOVER.

like rats deserting a sinking ship.   Brewer tells us that "it was an old superstition that rats deserted a ship before she set out on a voyage that was to end in her loss." However, the expression probably comes from a 1579 proverb claiming that rats desert a falling *house*. Any sensible rat would do either if it could, but the expression still describes a selfish, cowardly desertion.

like the curate's egg.   Something satisfactory in some ways but not in others: "The play was rather like the curate's egg." The expression originated with a story in the British magazine *Punch* (November 9, 1895) in which a timid curate had been served a bad egg while dining at the home of an important parishioner. He is asked how the egg tastes and, not wishing to offend his host, says that parts of it are excellent.

like trying to find flea shit in a pile of pepper.   The phrase is used by a U.S. senator in the movie *J.F.K.* (1991), but I'm sure it's older. It means "almost impossible to find," harder by far than finding a needle in a haystack.

like trying to nail jello to a tree. Theodore Roosevelt seems to have invented the idea behind this metaphor, if not the exact words, in a July 2, 1915 letter to William Roscoe Thayer, in which he described the difficulty of negotiating with Colombia regarding the Panama Canal. His exact words were: "You could no more make an agreement with them than you could nail currant jelly to a wall—and the failure to nail currant jelly to a wall is not due to the nail; it is due to the currant jelly."

Likker'll make you not know your momma. A Gullah dialect proverb that dates back to at least the 18th century and probably earlier. It may, in fact, be an adaptation of an African proverb brought to America by South Carolina slaves. *See* SPEAK SOFTLY AND CARRY A BIG STICK.

lilacs. There are lilacs white, blue, pink, red, and purple, in many variations, but the word *lilac* means "blue." *Lilac* began as the Persian word *nilak*, "bluish," for the flower, passed into Arabic as *laylak*, and became *lilac* in Spanish, whence it came into English in the same form.

Lillian Russell. Beautiful and flamboyant Lillian Russell was the toast of the town almost from the night she made her debut at New York's Tony Pastor's Opera House in burlesques of Gilbert & Sullivan comic operas. Only 18 at the time, the singer and actress was fresh from Clinton, Iowa, where she had been born Helen Louise Leonard in 1861. For the next 30 years Lillian Russell's beauty and talent for light opera brought her fame and fortune unsurpassed by any contemporary performer. Success included her own company, a collection of male admirers that has probably never been matched since, and a number of sumptuous apartments and houses, such as her summer home in then fashionable Far Rockaway, New York, where she entertained lavishly. Among several things named for her were the Lillian Russell dessert, half a cantaloupe filled with a scoop of ice cream, and the town of Lillian Russell in central Kansas, which today has a population of about 6,200.

lilliputian. The Lilliputians of the island of Lilliput in Jonathan Swift's satiric novel *Gulliver's Travels* (1726) are little people averaging six inches tall. Thus *lilliputian*, which suggests "little" in sound as well, has come to mean tiny or diminutive. *See* BROBDINGNAGIAN.

lily-livered. The liver, the largest gland in our bodies, was once believed to be the seat of passion. It was also believed that the liver of a coward contained no blood, not as much "as you find in the foot of a flea," since a coward wasn't capable of passionate violence. Hence the expression *white-livered* and *lily-livered* for cowardly. Shakespeare wrote of cowards with "livers white as milk" and later came lusty expressions such as "a lily-livered, action-taking knave." *See* LEARN BY HEART; BOWELS OF COMPASSION.

Lily Marleen. One of the few songs or poems whose real-life origins are known. This song, called "the most beautiful love song of all time" by John Steinbeck, was written in the early years of World War I by German officer cadet and poet Hans Leip. He took the woman's name in the title from a girl he loved back home named Lili, a grocer's daughter, and a green-eyed beauty named Marleen whom he'd met in a Berlin art gallery. The poem was not published for another 20 years and only became popular in 1939 when Berlin composer Norbert Schultze set it to music and singer Lale Andersen recorded it. The whole story of the song, which became popular the world over, is told in Carlton Jackson's book *The Great Lili* (1995). *See also* JENNY KISSED ME.

lima beans. Named for Lima, Peru by early European explorers who found them there, tender lima beans are often called butter beans in the U.S. The succotash made from them (and corn) derives from the Narraganset Indian *msquatash*, literally "fragments." The lima bean's botanical name *Phaseolus* is said to derive from the resemblance between the bean's pod and a special type of ship that originated at Phaselis, a town in Pamphylia.

limb. In the early 19th century "leg" was considered an indelicate word in America and *limb* (from the Anglo-Saxon *lim*, meaning the same) served as a euphemism for it. English novelist Captain Frederick Marryat described a visit to a young ladies' seminary in 1837: "On being ushered into the reception room, conceive my astonishment at beholding a square *pianoforte* with four limbs. However, that the ladies who visited their daughters might feel in its full force the extreme delicacy of the mistress of the establishment, and her care to preserve in their utmost purity the ideas of the young ladies under her charge, she had dressed all these four limbs in modest little trousers with frills at the bottom of them!"

limburger; Limburger cheese. Limburger cheese was introduced to America by German immigrants in the 19th century and was soon well known for its pungent smell. The soft cheese takes its name from the Limburg province of Belgium (not Holland) where it is made. Its strong smell and flavor long ago made Limburger cheese the butt of many comedians' and cartoonists' jokes. And since the cheese from Belgium's Limburg province was popularly thought to come from Germany, *Limburger* also became a derogatory term for a German during World War I.

lime; limey. Limes have been cultivated for thousands of years and take their name ultimately from the Persian *liman* for the fruit. As far back as 1795, lime juice was issued in the British navy as an antisorbutic, to protect against scurvy. After about 50 years, Americans and Australians began calling English ships and sailors "lime-juicers," and later "limeys." The term "limey" was eventually applied to all Englishmen, and today the designation and the story behind it are widely known. Originally a contemptuous term and an international slur, *limey* is now considered a rather affectionate designation.

limelight. Royal Engineer Thomas Drummond (1797–1840), a Scottish inventor, devised the Drummond light as an aid in murky weather while assisting in a land survey of Great Britain, and soon after adapted it for use in lighthouses. Drummond, who later became secretary of state for Ireland, utilized calcium oxide, or lime, which had been isolated by Sir Humphry

Davy and gives off an intense white light when heated. The Drummond light wasn't used on the stage as a spotlight or called limelight until after the inventor's death in 1840, when the expression *in the limelight*, "in the full glare of public attention," naturally arose from it. Limelights have long been replaced by arc and KLIEG LIGHTS, but the phrase *in the limelight* still survives.

limericks.   Poet Edward Lear's (1812–88) nonsense verses were labeled *learics* by M. Russell, a Jesuit wit of the day, the new word a play on the poet's name, on the fact that what he wrote weren't dignified lyrics, and on the leering grins some such verses even then produced. It wasn't until 52 years after Lear's book was published that the one-stanza poems, by now immensely popular, were dubbed *limericks*. One theory has it that the name arose then because a popular contemporary song had a chorus that went, "We'll all come up, come up to Limerick." It seems that there was also a party game played at the time in which each guest would invent and recite a learic, the whole group singing the chorus about "coming up to Limerick" between recitations. This may be true, but it is just as likely that the *learic* became the *limerick* because people believed that the verses were invented in Ireland, the land of poetry.

limousine.   Originally any closed car, the limousine takes its name from a hood of that name worn by Limousins, inhabitants of the French province of Limousin. In recent times *limo* is increasingly being used in place of limousine, and very long custom-made limos are called stretch limos.

Lincolndom; Davisdom; Jeffdom.   Southerners used *Lincolndom* as a humorous designation for the North during the Civil War, the term first recorded in 1861 and referring, of course, to President Abraham Lincoln. On the other side of the lines, the South was called Davisdom, (and, more rarely, Jeffdom), after Jefferson Davis, president of the Confederacy, these words being coined a few months before *Lincolndom*. See *also* FRANKLIN CONDUCTOR, JACKSONIAN DEMOCRACY.

Lincoln gimlet.   *See* SHERMAN HAIRPINS.

Lincolnian, etc.   It is surprising that only some 25 place names in the United States honor our 16th president, little more than half those commemorating Jefferson and less than one-third of those named for Andrew Jackson. But this can be explained by early bitterness toward Lincoln in the South. For none of his countrymen, not even Washington, has become a folk hero and giant in American tradition equal to Lincoln, and he is certainly more loved and respected the world over than any other American. His story, from his birth in a Kentucky log cabin to the Emancipation Proclamation, the immortal Gettysburg Address, and the assassination by John Wilkes Booth, is so widely known in its smallest details that it is, rather than history or myth, a living part of the American legend from generation to generation, making Lincoln a father image to us all. *Lincolnite* designated a supporter of President Lincoln during the Civil War. *Lincolniana* is any material, such as writing, anecdotes, or objects, pertaining to Honest Abe, the Rail Splitter, or The Great Emancipator, while *Lincolnian* pertains to his

character or political principles. Lincoln's birthday, February 12, is a legal holiday in many states. *See* HONETS ABE.

Lincoln, Nebraska.   Named after Abraham Lincoln, this is one of the four U.S. state capitals named after presidents. The others are Madison, Wisconsin, for James Madison; Jefferson City, Missouri, for Thomas Jefferson; and Jackson, Mississippi, for Andrew Jackson. *See* MONROVIA.

Lincoln shingles.   Hardbread, also dubbed sheet-iron crackers, was called Lincoln shingles by U.S. troops on the frontier. The term is first recorded in Captain Eugene F. Ware's *The Indian War of 1874*, but must date back to Civil War times, given the use of Abraham Lincoln's name. A synonym was *teeth dullers*.

Lindau's disease.   *See* BRIGHT'S DISEASE.

linden tree.   The handsome linden, or lime, or basswood tree (*Tilia*) is of interest here because it gave its name to the greatest of botanists and the greatest of name-givers. The story is best told by the American botanist L. H. Bailey in his classic but unfortunately out-of-print treatise *How Plants Get Their Names*, 1933: "Carl Linnaeus was born in southern Sweden in 1707. His father, Nils Ingermarsson, took a Latin surname when he began his school and university career to become a scholar and eventually a churchman, adapting it from a certain famous lind, the lime-tree or linden. It was custom in those days for persons to choose a Latin name or to Latinize the patronymic. The family of the cousins of Linnaeus chose the name Tiliander from the same tree, *Tilia* being Latin for the lindens. Another branch of the family became Lindelius. The particular lind tree, it is written, 'had acquired a sanctity amongst the neighbors, who firmly believed that ill-fortune surely befell those who took even a twig from the grand and stately tree.' Even the fallen twigs were dangerous to remove, and they were heaped about the base of the tree. It had perished by 1823. To the people the name Linnaeus was rendered *Linné*, the accent preserving the essential pronunciation of the word. Linnaeus, for his part, wrote that 'Linnaeus or Linné are the same to me; one is Latin, the other Swedish.' His great Latin books were written naturally under the name Linnaeus, and thus is he mostly known to naturalists. In later life a patent of nobility was granted him and he was then Carl von Linné. We find him signing himself as Carolus Linnaeus Smolander, his province or nation being Smoland and Carolus being the Latin form of Carl or Charles; also as Carl Linnaeus, Carl Linné, and Carl v. Linné. This much is by way of preface to explain the forms in which the name of this marvellous man appear." *See* LINNAEAN SYSTEM.

Lindy.   Even today's astronauts returning from the moon did not receive the hero worship heaped upon Charles Augustus Lindbergh when he made the first solo flight across the Atlantic on May 20–21, 1927, in his *Spirit of St. Louis*. Lindbergh was awarded the Congressional Medal of Honor for his 33½-hour nonstop flight from New York to Paris, promoted to colonel in the Air Force, and received the French Cross of the Legion of Honor, the English Royal Air Force Cross, and the American Distinguished Flying Cross among hundreds of national and international honors. There had never been such adulation and perhaps there never will be again—in June 1927 alone, it is reported, Lindbergh received 3,500,000 letters, 14,000 parcels, and 100,000 telegrams. The Hero, the Lone Eagle, Lucky Lindy, the Flying Fool symbolized the beginning of a new technical age that in itself made great personal heroism less likely. Lindbergh's unprecedented fame even resulted in the lindy or lindy hop, a jitterbug dance very popular up until the mid-1950s, being named in his honor. His name made headlines again in 1932 with the tragic kidnapping and killing of his infant son, for which Bruno Richard Hauptmann was found guilty and which led to the Lindbergh Law passed by Congress in 1934. The law made all kidnappings across state lines and the use of the mails for ransom communications federal offenses.

line-of-battle ship. In the days of sail, a line-of-battle ship, as opposed to other vessels such as frigates, was a capital ship fit to take part in a major battle. "Line of battle" simply referred to the formation of ships in a naval engagement.

lingua franca. A lingua franca is any hybrid language, a combination of various tongues. Pidgin English and Bêche-de-Mer or beach-la-mar, are two such trade languages in the Pacific, but the earliest one recorded is lingua franca itself, meaning "the Frankish tongue" in Italian. Lingua franca arose along the Mediterranean, a medley, or babble, of Italian, French, Spanish, Greek, Turkish, and Arabic common to many seamen in the ninth century or earlier. A Frank was any West European at the time, for the tribe ruled over most of Europe. The language enabled Muslims to conduct business dealings with Europeans, and Mediterranean traders still find it very useful in the Levant.

linguine. Linguine is thin, flat pasta, so thin that it reminded some poetic person centuries ago of "little tongues," which is what *linguine* means in Italian. *See also* VERMICELLI.

linguistic cleansing. An invention of Canadian author Mordecai Richler (1931–2001) apparently based on the far more chilling euphemistic ETHNIC CLEANSING. In coining the term Mr. Richler wrote, "In 1977, shortly after the separatist Parti Quebecois, then in office, brought in the French Language Charter, we were subjected to a degree of linguistic cleansing. [The word *hamburger*] was adjudged an impurity imposed on Quebecois pure laine by their colonial masters in the foreign capital of Ottawa. So it was ruled that it should be immediately replaced by hambourgeois, which was what we were supposed to ask for if we suffered a Gros Mac attack."

lining one's pockets. Despite all the other foppish British Beaus before and after Beau Brummell, only Brummell's name lives on as a synonym for a dandy or fancy dresser. Beau Brummell, aided by the patronage of the Prince of Wales, later George IV, was the *arbiter eleganitarum* of London fashion for almost 20 years, a man noted for his excesses as well as his good taste; he often spent an entire day dressing for an affair, had all his gloves made by three glovers—one to fashion the hands, another for the fingers, and a third for the thumb, etc. So valued was his patronage that one tailor presented him with a coat whose pockets were lined with money, which gave rise to the expression *lining one's pockets*, for "bribery or graft."

links. The Old English *hlinc*, "rising ground," is the ancestor of our links for a golf course; the first course called a links was located at Leith, Scotland in the late 16th century. The most famous poem about golf links
is American poet Sarah N. Cleghorn's quatrain:

> The golf links lie so near the mill
> That almost every day
> The laboring children can look out
> And see the men at play.

Linnaea. Named for its flowers in pairs at the end of slender, upright stalks, the twinflower was scientifically called "Linnaea" by Linnaeus himself. The great botanist apparently chose this humble genus, consisting of two species, out of modesty, describing the twinflower as "a plant of Lapland, lowly, insignificant, disregarded, flowering but a brief space—from Linnaeus who resembles it." *See* LINDEN TREE; LINNAEAN SYSTEM.

Linnaean system. Linnaeus, most famous of all naturalists, not only dubbed us *Homo sapiens*, but chose the names for far more things than any other person in history, classifying literally thousands of plants, animals, and minerals. Carl von Linné—*Carolus Linnaeus* is the Latin form of his name—showed an early love of flowers that earned him the nickname "the little botanist" when he was only eight years old. The son of a Lutheran minister who cultivated his interest in nature, he became an assistant professor of botany at Uppsala University, then studied medicine in Holland, where in 1735 he wrote his *Systema Naturae*. Linnaeus was only 28 at the time, and his masterpiece was followed by *Genera Plantarum* in 1737 and *Species Plantarum* 16 years later. These books marked the beginning of taxonomy, a system of scientific nomenclature that would be elaborated in more than 180 works. The Linnaean system the naturalist developed divided the kingdoms of animals, vegetables, and minerals into classes, orders, genera, species, and varieties, according to various characteristics. It adopted binominal nomenclature, giving two Latin names—genus and species—to each organism. In this two-name system all closely related species bear the same genus name, e.g. *Panthera* (Latin for "cat") *leo* is the lion, and *Panthera tigris* is the tiger. The system Linnaeus invented provided scientists with an exact tool for the identification of organisms and is standard today, although many old popular names for plants and animals linger on. Further it recognized all organisms as part of a grand scheme, a unique concept at the time. Linnaeus continued to practice medicine and headed the botany department at Uppsala, naming thousands of plants that he collected and classifying hundreds more that professional and amateur botanists sent him from all over the world. He named some plants for their characteristics alone, some for prominent people and others for their discoverers, but in almost every case the designation he applied remains intact. Linnaeus was 71 when he died at Uppsala in the cathedral in which he is buried. His garden at the university, where he grew many of his plants, is still visited by pilgrims from all over the world. *See also* LINNAEA; LINDEN TREE.

lionize. To *lionize* a person can mean to show him sights worthy of him, the term taking its name from the old practice of showing visiting dignitaries the lions that used to be kept at the Tower of London menagerie, a major tourist attraction until it was abolished at the beginning of the 19th century. An earlier use of the word, however, is to *lionize* a person by making a fuss over him, by making him feel like a lion. Both expressions date back to the early 1800s.

lion's share. *Lion's share* refers to the whole of or the largest portion of anything. It derives from one of Aesop's fables, in which a lion, hunting with several lesser beasts, insisted that the spoils be divided in four parts: one for his share; a second for his greater courage; a third for his family; "and as for the fourth let who will dispute it with me." *See* LEONINE CONTRACT.

lipogram. If anyone has ever discovered the value of lipograms, except as exercises in verbal ingenuity, she or he ain't telling. A lipogram is "a written work composed of words chosen so as to avoid the use of specific alphabetical characters," and the first practitioner of lipography is said to have been the Greek lyric poet Lasus, born in Achaia in about 548 B.C. The next great poet to write a letterless poem was Lasus's pupil Pindar, who wrote *Ode minus Segma* late in the fifth century B.C. The Greek *Odyssey of Tryphiodorus*, however, outdoes both Lasus and Pindar. It consists of 26 books, with no *a* in the first book, no *b* in the second, no *c* in the third, and so on. (Someone said of the work that it would have been better if the author left out the other letters, too.) Spanish playwright Félix Lope de Vega y Carpio (1562–1635) wrote each of his five novels without using one of the vowels, but Lope de Vega is far better known for the 2,200 plays tradition says he completed (close to 500 survive). Another famous European lipogram is Ronden's *Pièce sans A* (1816). This was perhaps influenced by German poet Gottlob Burmann (1737–1805), who wrote some 130 poems without employing the letter *r* and for 17 years omitted *r* from his daily conversation, never speaking his own name, which he hated anyway. James Thurber wrote a story about a country where the letter *o* was illegal, but the best-known American book without a certain letter is Ernest Vincent Wright's *Gadsby* (1939), which has no *e*'s in it. The author, a California musician, pried the *e* off his typewriter keyboard to restrain himself and typed a 267-page, 50,000-word epic using no word containing that most common of vowels.

liquor will make you not know your mother. *See* LIKKER'LL MAKE YOU NOT KNOW YOUR MAMA.

Listerine. A trademark that is practically synonymous today with "mouthwash," *Listerine* takes its name from Joseph Lister, first Baron Lister (1827–1912), famous for founding antiseptic surgery. Basing his methods on Pasteur's theory that bacteria cause infection, Lister in 1865 used a mixture containing carbolic acid as a germicide and invented methods of applying it to wounds and incisions, such procedures greatly reducing postoperative fatalities from infection. Lord Lister, who became president of the Royal Society, tried unsuccessfully to disassociate his name from Listerine when the product was first marketed, much preferring to see himself commemorated by the Lister Institute of Preventive Medicine in London, of which he was a founder. Lister is also credited with inventing the forceps, a serrated surgical saw called the lister, and many other surgical instruments.

lists. *See* ENTER THE LISTS.

Literary Emporium. Boston used to be known as America's Literary Emporium, due to the comparatively large number of literati and publishing houses there in the early 19th century. British actor Edmund Kean coined the term in one of his speeches from the stage when on a tour of America.

litterbug. *Litterbug*, meaning someone who habitually litters, is an anonymous coinage, probably based on firebug, dating back to the end of World War II. It owes its popularity to the Lakes and Hills Garden Club of Mount Dora, Florida, which used the slogan "Don't be a litterbug!" in a 1950 roadside cleanup campaign.

Little. An American qualifier sometimes attached to first names where the son has the same first name as the father. "In some parts of the world Little Joe would be called Joseph Twine II, but in Texas he's called Little Joe, to distinguish him from his father, Big Joe," Larry McMurtry observed in *Cadillac Jack* (1982).

a little bird told me. One scholar suggests that this familiar saying may have originated with the similar-sounding Dutch expression *Er lif t'el baerd*, which means "I should betray another." More likely the idea behind the phrase is in the noiseless flight of a bird, reinforced by a biblical passage from Eccles. 10:20: "Curse not the kind, no not in thy thought, . . . for a bird of the air shall carry the voice, and that which hath wings shall tell the matter." Used by Shakespeare and Swift, the expression dates back to at least the 16th century.

Little Boy. *See* A-BOMB.

Little Church around the Corner. Several New York City churches refused to hold funeral services for eminent comedian George Holland (1791–1870) on the grounds that he was an actor. Fellow comedian Joseph Jefferson kept up the search and finally found another church where the pompous minister again refused Holland burial services, but told Jefferson, "there is a little church around the corner where they do this sort of thing." The funeral was finally held there, at 1 East 29th Street in the Protestant Episcopal Church of the Transfiguration, which soon became known as the Little Church around the Corner and is still the scene of many theatrical funerals and weddings.

little drops of water make the mighty ocean. The saying comes from the poem "Little Things" (1845) by Julia A. Fletcher Carney, the first two lines of which read: "Little drops of water, little grains of sand, / Make the mighty ocean and the pleasant land." Colorful equivalents in other languages include: A hair from here and a hair from there finally make a beard (Arabic); Little by little the bird makes his nest (French); Drop by drop the sea is filled (Italian); Grains of sand pile up to make a hill (Japanese); and Dripping water hollows a stone (German).

Little Englander. An isolationist who is against Great Britain becoming part of any European Union. The term has been used, however, for over a century and at first described an anti-imperialist.

Little Jack Horner. *See* JACK HORNER.

Little Lord Fauntleroy. The hero of the novel of the same name written by Frances Hodgson Burnett in 1886 gives us the expression *a little Lord Fauntleroy*, for a sissyish boy or man. *Fauntleroy* clothes are frilly velvety ones like those worn by the little lord.

littleneck clams. Littleneck clams don't have little necks, but hailed originally from either Little Neck Bay, Long Island, New York, or Little Neck Bay, Ipswich, Massachusetts. No one knows which for sure.

little old lady in Dubuque. *See* OLD LADY IN DUBUQUE.

Little Rhody. A nickname for Rhode Island first recorded in 1851. Rhode Island is also called the Plantation State, in reference to its official name, the State of Rhode Island and Providence Plantation. Its nickname the Lively Experiment State comes from its 1663 charter, which promised to ". . . hold forth a *lively experiment* . . . with a full liberty in religious concernment."

little said is soon amended. This proverbial phrase, also *least said, soonest mended*, possibly derives from a rhyme Oliver Goldsmith may have written for John Newberry's edition of *Mother Goose's Melody* . . . in 1760:

> There was a little man,
> Who wooed a little maid,
> And he said, little Maid, will you wed, wed, wed?
> I have little more to say,
> So will you aye or nay,
> For the least said is soonest men-ded, ded, ded.

little wee bit lassockie. Fully four words indicating smallness are employed in this Scottish English expression meaning a "little lass," first recorded in 1810. The last word in the expression is sometimes *lassock*.

Little Willies. *See* GRUE.

lit up like a Christmas tree. Brightly and brilliantly colorful. I've been unable to locate a source for the phrase, which might date back to Victorian times. The best I can do is cite F. Scott Fitzgerald's *The Great Gatsby* (1925): "[Gatsby's parties were illuminated by] enough colored lights to make a Christmas tree of Gatsby's enormous garden."

live all the days of your life. "May you live all the days of your life," Jonathan Swift wrote in *Polite Conversation* (1738). Similar instructions that have become proverbial, or almost so, include, live for the moment; you only live once; live and let live; enjoy yourself, it's later than you think; you can't take it with you, and carpe diem.

Live and let live. Apparently this well-known phrase was originally a Dutch proverb—at least an English writer claimed it was in 1622, when the words first appeared in English. It is still widely used.

Live by the sword, die by the sword. This old proverb, dating back to the 17th century, has its roots in the Bible, (Matt. 26:52): "All they that take the sword shall perish with the sword."

live cash; live. Some Canadians, especially those from Newfoundland, often use the term *live cash* for money real or actual, such as a bankroll of bills: "You have any live cash?" *Live* alone is applied to things homemade, including "live bread" or "live jam."

living fossil of the sea. A name often given to the common HORSESHOE CRAB (*Limulus polyphemus*), which is really no crab but a distant relative of the spider. Horseshoe crabs, or king crabs, are called living fossils because they have barely altered their appearance in 200 million years—these anthropods looked the same millions of years before the first of the giant dinosaurs lumbered over the land. They probably haven't changed much because their large shell, which resembles a horseshoe, protects them so well, making it unnecessary for them to develop any further.

living from hand to mouth. Those of us who do so have just enough money to feed ourselves and our families, with maybe enough money to pay the rent. The expression dates back to early 18th-century England.

living in the lap of luxury. To live without wanting for anything, as if a maternal figure, symbolized by a lap, provided for one's every need. The expression is first found in Lord Byron's poetic drama *Werner* (1822): "Rash, new to life, and rear'd in luxury's lap."

living legend. *See* LEGEND IN ONE'S LIFETIME.

living off the fat of the land. To be living a life in which one has the best of everything, especially foods. The expression is based on a verse from the Bible (Gen. 45:18): "Ye shall eat the fat of the land."

living stones of the church. The congregation, the individual worshippers who attend the church. The old term probably first referred to the Roman Catholic church.

llama. "*¿Como se llama?*" ("What is it called?") Spanish invaders asked South American Indians when they first encountered this unfamiliar animal. Not knowing what the Spanish were saying, the Indians repeated the Spanish word *llama*. The Spanish thought this was the name of the animal and dubbed it the *llama*, whose name therefore means "name." So goes the old story about the origin of *llama*. The O.E.D. and others claim that it probably comes from "a Peruvian word." *See* INDRI; KANGAROO; LUZON; NOME; YUCATAN.

llano. A Spanish term, first recorded in 1605, for arid, treeless prairies like the vast *Llano Estacado* (Staked Plain), a high dry plateau of 40,000 square miles in western Texas and New Mexico.

Lloyd's of London. *See* A–1.

L.L. Whisky. Any superior whisky. The words honor the duke of Richmond, who was Britain's *L*ord *L*ieutenant from 1807 to 1813 and had the initials of his title marked on a cask of his favorite whisky.

lo.

> Hope springs eternal in the human breast;
> Man never is, but always to be blessed.
> The soul, uneasy, and confined from home,
> Rests and expatiates in a life to come.
> Lo, the poor Indian! whose untutored mind
> Sees God in clouds, or hears him in the wind;
> His soul proud sciences never taught to stray.
> For as the solar walk, or milky way;
> Yet simple nature to his hope has giv'n,
> Behind the cloud-topped hill, an humbler heav'n.

Alexander Pope's well-known words *Lo, the poor Indian* in the above lines from his *Essay on Criticism* (1711) inspired the term *Lo*, for an American Indian. The word isn't recorded in this sense until 1871, but must be considerably older. "Is it no longer a matter of astonishment," someone wrote in 1873, "that the Lo's are passing so rapidly from the face of the earth?"

loaded for bear. Ready for anything, well prepared, heavily armed. "Loaded for b-ar," as the expression was often pronounced, probably goes back to American pioneers hunting in the forests where they had to carry guns loaded with ammunition powerful enough to kill a bear, the most dangerous beast they might encounter. The phrase was first recorded, however, in 1875. Today it can also mean "very drunk."

loaded to the gills; loaded to the guards. Anyone *loaded to the gills* DRINK LIKE A FISH or has drunk alcohol "like a fish drinks water" and is obviously drunk. Sailors use a younger version of the old expression when they say *loaded to the guards*. The "guards" here are part of the PLIMSOLL MARKS on vessels, lines beyond which it is dangerous to load a ship.

loafer. Loafer, for "a lazy do-nothing, an idler, or lounger," is apparently an Americanism, first recorded in 1830, deriving from the German *Landlaufer*, "vagabond." Other possible ancestors are the English dialect word *louper*, "vagabond," the expression *to loup the tether*, "to wander," and the Dutch *loof*, "weary." The verb *to loaf* is apparently a back-formation from the noun. *Loafer* has been the name for a slip-on shoe without laces in the U.S. since the 1940s.

lobbying. Although it is an Americanism that isn't recorded until 1808, a lobby, a group trying to influence the government to promote its own special interests, seems to derive ultimately from the large entrance hall to the British House of Commons that was called the Lobby as early as the 17th century. In the Lobby people could talk to members of Parliament and many tried to influence MPs there.

Lobelia. Linnaeus named over a thousand plants, including hundreds that have come to be household words. Many of the botanist's namings honored people. Indeed, by labeling species as well as genera, the Swedish botanist sometimes commended two people with the same plant. This is the case with *Lobelia dormanna*, the water lobelia.

Linnaeus named the plant's family *Lobeliaceae* and its genus *Lobelia* after Matthias de l'Obel, or Lobel (1538–1616), a distinguished Flemish botanist and physician who lived a century before Linnaeus. But he called *L. dortmanna*, one of its three hundred species, after an obscure druggest named Dortmann whom he met while studying in Holland. Nothing is known about Dortmann, but Lobel had been both physician and botanist to England's learned King James I. A native of Lille, Lobel tried to classify plants according to their leaf formations long before Linnaeus and wrote several of the earliest botanical books. The *Lobeliaceae* family commemorating him contains 24 genera and over 700 species, some of which are trees and shrubs, but its *Lobelia* genus consists of about 300 species of annual or perennial herbs widely grown for their mainly blue, red, yellow, or white flowers. The species *Lobelia inflata* was used by American Indians like tobacco, has a tobacco-like odor, and was also employed as the base for a popular home remedy, though it is considered poisonous in quantity. Another species, *Lobelia syphilitica*, the blue syphilis, was used by the Indians to treat syphilis; it was even introduced into Europe centuries ago for this purpose.

loblolly pine. *Loblolly* is first recorded in 1597 in Gerarde's *Herbal* as a thick gruel or stew. It is probably an onomatopoeic word, one writer noting that "it describes a semi-liquid state" and "itself shakes in pronunciation like jelly, which is most nearly what it describes." In America settlers began to apply *loblolly* to miry muddy places and called *Pinus taeda*, a long-leaved southern pine, the loblolly pine because it commonly grew in such swampy places. The name is first recorded in about 1730. There is also a *loblolly bay (Gorclonia lasianthus)* and in 19th-century America a mudhole was humorously called a *loblolly*.

lobster. Lobsters are, in fact, a kind of bug. The word *lobster* itself is a melding of two foreign words: the Latin *locasta*, meaning "locust," and the Anglo-Saxon *lappe*, which means "spider." "Real" lobster is not the freshwater lobster that the French call *écrevisse*, or crawfish, the small European crustacean with no claws; or even the warm-water spiny lobster from which lobster tails are obtained and labeled *langosta* or *langouste* in some restaurants. The true lobsters number among their ranks only *Homarus americanus*, often called Maine, or North Atlantic, lobsters; the smaller blue lobster of Europe, *H. vulgaris*; *Nephrops norvegicus*, the orange Norwegian lobster, variously called lady lobster, scampi, or prawn; and *H. capensis*.

lobster à l'américaine. *Homard à l'américaine*, as the French call it, is uncooked lobster meat sautéed in oil and served with a rich tomato and white wine sauce. It may have been invented by the chef M. Reculet during the siege of Paris (1870–71) and named in honor of some customer from across the Atlantic. A second explanation holds that the dish originated in Brittany's Armorique, and that its present name is simply a misspelling of *homard à l'armoriquaine*.

lobster Newburg. The most famous of lobster dishes, lobster Newburg, should have blazoned the name of Benjamin J.

Wenberg (1835–85), a late 19th-century shipping magnate, across the pages of menus everywhere, but gastronomical lore has it that he was foolish enough to displease the great restaurateur Lorenzo Delmonico. It's said that Wenberg discovered the dish in South America and described it glowingly to Delmonico's owner. Lorenzo, instructing his chef to prepare the shelled lobster in its rich sauce of sherry, thick cream, and egg yolks, served the dish to his wealthy patron and named it *lobster Wenberg* in his honor. It remained thus on Delmonico's menu for almost a month, until one evening when Wenberg got drunk, started a fight in the posh restaurant's dining room and was evicted. Soon after, the dish appeared on an enraged Lorenzo's menu as *lobster Newburg*, probably in honor of the city on the Hudson.

lobster shift. *Lobster shift*, for the newspaper shift commencing at four in the morning, is said to have originated at the defunct *New York Journal-American* early in this century. The newspaper's plant was near the East Side docks and workers on this shift came to work at about the same time lobstermen were putting out to sea in their boats.

lobster Thermidor. Creamy lobster Thermidor may have been invented by a French chef in honor of Napoleon. But some culinary experts contend that this classic fare was named for Victorian Sardou's play *Thermidor* and first served to the public on the evening of January 24, 1874, at the once famous Chez Maire restaurant. According to this account, the controversial drama closed after one performance, but the toothsome dish remained a long-running hit.

locate. Probably the earliest of all American back formations, the verb *to locate* derives from the noun *location*. It is recorded by a traveler in 1652 and counted among its early users Ben Franklin and George Washington, who apparently didn't care that some considered it a "vulgarism."

Lochinvar. The brave hero of a Sir Walter Scott ballad in *Marmion* (1808), who steals his love, the bride of a "dastard," from a bridal feast, sweeps her up on his horse, and rides away with her: "So faithful in love, and so dauntless in war, / There never was a knight like the young Lochinvar!" *Dastard*, ultimately from Old Norse, means "a sneaking miserable coward."

loch; Loch Ness monster; Champ. The familiar word *loch* for a lake or an arm of the sea similar to a fjord can be traced back to Old Irish hundreds of years ago. A small lake is called a *lochen*. The 24-mile-long Loch Ness in Scotland is probably the most famous loch, thanks to the fabled Loch Ness monster, a huge marine creature reportedly sighted as far back as the sixth century but never authenticated. Naturalist Sir Peter Scott named the monster *Nessiteras rhombopteryx* ("The diamond-finned Ness Monster"), giving it scientific status for a short while, but this turned out to be a prank, the words being an anagram of "monster hoax by Sir Peter S." "Nessie" has also been dubbed the Great Orm (from Scandinavian *sjo-orm*, "sea serpent"); the Worm; Loathly Worm; Eaeh Uesge (water horse); Water Bull; Hippotatam; Beiste; and the Water Kelpie. America's counterpart of "Nessie" is Champ, a sea monster said to live in New York's Lake Champlain.

lock and load. An order in the military to load one's rifle with a round of ammunition and then lock the weapon in the safety position. The expression was originally *load and lock*, as it logically should be, and was first recorded at the beginning of World War II. Figuratively the words mean "get ready for any action."

locker room talk. This term refers to the vulgar, lewd, or obscene language men (and maybe even women) are thought to speak in locker rooms, although some locker rooms are more staid than others. It's a good guess that the expression doesn't go back beyond the 1940s, but no one knows for sure.

lock horns. Possibly New Englanders who witnessed moose fiercely battling over a female, their massive horns locked together, invented this expression for "a violent clash." There is no evidence of this in the first American literary use of the phrase in 1839, however. When Swinburne used the phrase in 1865, he spoke of a heifer and her mate locking horns, which could also be the source of the expression.

lock, stock, and barrel. The firing mechanism, or lock (by which the charge is exploded); the stock (to which the lock and barrel are attached); and the barrel (the tube through which bullets are discharged) are the three components of a firearm that make up the whole gun. Thus the expression *lock, stock, and barrel* means the whole works, the whole of anything. The saying is an Americanism first recorded in Thomas Haliburton's Sam Slick stories (1843), but likely goes back to the muskets of the American Revolution. However, the expression might also be rooted in the *lock* on a country store's door, the *stock*, or goods, inside, and even the *barrel* on which business was often transacted.

lock the barn door after the horse is stolen. The venerable rustic aphorism for "taking a precaution too late" hangs in there; it is still heard in cities that haven't seen a barn for half a century. Back in England in the 1300s we would have recognized the expression, its first literary use being in John Gower's *Confessio amantis* (1390): "For whan the grete Stiede Is stole, thanne he taketh hiede, and maketh the stable dore fast."

loco. A Spanish word meaning crazy that became common in the West and finally all the United States, the language needing as many words for "crazy" as it can get.

locoweed. Various plants of the genera *Astragalus* and *Oxytropis* native to the southwestern United States are called "locoweed" (from the Spanish *loco*, "insane") because when eaten by horses, cattle, and sheep they cause irregular behavior, including weakness, impaired vision, and paralysis. In the West a person who acts crazy is sometimes said to be "locoed," that is, crazed as if from eating locoweed.

loganberry. California Judge James Harvey Logan (1841–1921), who had been a Missouri schoolteacher before working his way west as the driver of an ox team, developed the loganberry in his experimental home orchard at Santa Cruz. Logan, formerly Santa Cruz district attorney, was serving on the superior court bench in 1880 when he raised the new berry from seed, breeding several generations of plants to do so. Though a respected amateur horticulturist, he never adequately explained how the berry was developed. One account claims that the loganberry originated "from self-grown seeds of the Aughinbaugh [a wild blackberry], the other parent supposed to be a raspberry of the Red Antwerp type." Several experts believe that it is a variety of the western dewberry, or a hybrid of that species, crossed with the red raspberry. The dispute may never be resolved, but experiments in England have produced a plant similar to the loganberry by crossing certain blackberries and red raspberries. In any case, there is no doubt that the purplish-red loganberry is shaped like a blackberry, colored like a raspberry, and combines the flavor of both—or that it was first grown by Judge Logan and named for him. Its scientific name is *Rubus loganbuccus* and the trailing blackberry-like plant is grown commercially in large quantities, especially in California, Oregon, Washington, and other places having fairly mild winters.

log cabin. The first log cabins in America were built by Swedish settlers in Delaware in about 1638. English settlers, who had never seen such structures in England, soon followed the Swedes' example and named the little log houses log cabins.

loggerheads. To be at loggerheads—"engaged in a violent quarrel, or a dispute"—seems to refer to medieval naval battles during which sailors bashed each other with murderous instruments called loggerheads. These loggerheads were long-handled devices with a solid ball of iron on the end that was heated and used to melt pitch or tar, which could be flung at the enemy. The loggerheads themselves apparently made for handy lethal weapons *after* the boiling pitch was used up, and mariners from opposing ships probably engaged each other with them, being at loggerheads. *Loggerhead* also has an earlier meaning of "an ignorant blockhead, a knucklehead," and this idea of stupidity most likely contributed to the popularity of a phrase that suggests that the people at loggerheads in the dispute are headstrong and unwilling to compromise. The expression is first recorded in 1685.

logomachy; flyting. *Logomachy*, from a Greek word meaning "word contest," is "fighting about words," often about verbal subtleties. However, it can be loosely used to mean fighting with words, actual "combats of curses," the most colorful example of these being the poets who led pre-Islamic Arabs into combat, hurling curses at the enemy (warfare and the arts were specialized even then). But a better word for word fighting is *flyting*. Flytings (from the Old English *flyte*, "to contend or jeer") were contests held principally by 16th-century Scottish poets in which two persons "assailed each other alternately with tirades of abusive verse." Following is one of 32 stanzas directed at Scotland's James V by his former tutor, Sir David Lindsay. Bear in mind that this vitriolic diatribe *lost* the flyting.

> Purse-peeler, hen-stealer, cat-killer, no I qyell thee;
> Rubiator, fornicator by nature, foul befal thee.
> Tyke-sticker, poisoner Vicar, Pot-licker, I mon paz
> thee.
> Jock blunt, dead Runt, I shall punt when I slay thee.

See THE DOZENS.

logorrhea. *Logorrhea*, apparently patterned on *diarrhea*, comes from the Greek *logos*, "word," plus *rhein*, "flow," "stream." It is first recorded as a psychological term in 1904: "Logorrhea refers to the excessive flow of words, a common symptom in cases of mania." As with many similar terms the word came to be loosely used and can now describe any bigmouth who talks too much.

logrolling. "You scratch my back and I'll scratch yours" was the idea behind this term, which was invented by American pioneers on the western frontier. Settlers clearing land and building their log cabins could always count on neighbors for help in rolling down logs, with the tacit understanding they'd do the same for their neighbors whenever asked. The good neighborly expression, with its associations of rum, food, and fiddling, became tainted when politicians in many fields adopted it. Legislators are still well known for logrolling with representatives from other states; that is, one congressman will support the pet project of another if he assists in passing a bill furthering the interests of the first. *Literary logrollers* form mutual admiration societies, favorably reviewing each other's books in order to promote sales and reputations. Commenting on one instance of such a practice, A. E. Housman said there had been nothing like it since the passage in Milton where sin gave birth to death.

Lolita. A Lolita has in the last 25 years become the word for a nymphet or adolescent nymphomaniac. Capitalized still, the term derives from the name of the main character in Vladimir Nabokov's novel *Lolita* (1955).

lollapalooza. An extraordinary person or thing; an exceptional example of something. The French expression *allez-fusil*, "Forward the musket!," became common in Ireland after French troops landed at Killala in 1798. County Mayo residents pronounced it "ally foozee" and coined a new word from it meaning "sturdy fellow." Mencken, among others, believes that our *lollapalooza*, which is also spelled *lallapalooza*, comes from this word. Surprisingly few words came to American English from the eloquent Irish, the list almost limited to *banshee, bog, lollapalooza, paddy wagon, shamrock, shanty, shebang, shenanigans, shillelagh, smithareens, whisky,* and possibly *speakeasy*. Phrases, as these pages show, are another story.

lollipop. Is the lollipop named after a racehorse? The story goes that in the early 1900s one George Smith, a Connecticut candy manufacturer, "put together the candy and the stick" and named it in honor of Lolly Pop, the era's most famous racehorse, the name "lollipop" then becoming an exclusive trade name used by the Bradley-Smith company of New Haven. It is true that candy on a stick wasn't known in America before about 1908 and neither was the word *lollipop*. Smith may have invented the confection (there are no other claimants) and he may even have named his candy on a stick after the horse in question. But the word *lollipop*, for a piece of sucking candy that dissolves easily in the mouth (*not* one, however, that is attached to a stick) was widely used in England as early as the late 18th century. It apparently derives from the English dialect word *lolly*, used in northern England to mean "tongue," plus the word *pop*, in reference to the sound children made when sucking the candy. Somehow the lollipop remained unknown to Americans until the candy on a stick was invented in the early 20th century, but this is not to say that the racehorse Lolly Pop couldn't have been named for the earlier British term.

lollipop woman (man). A colorful British name for a school crossing guard. Named after the round red and white STOP sign mounted on a stick that such guards carry and use to stop cars when children are crossing the street.

lolly. Although almost no Americans use the word, many know that *lolly* is somewhat dated British slang for money, thanks perhaps to British crime films. Few know, however, that *lolly* can also refer to an ice or a steak or candy in Britain. In Australia *lolly water* means "soft drink." *See* LOLLIPOP.

lollygagging. The *Dictionary of Americanisms* quotes an indignant citizen in the year of our Lord 1868 on "the lascivious lolly-gagging lumps of licenteousness who disgrace the common decencies of life by their love-sick fawnings at our public dances." This is the first recorded use of *lollygagging*, which means "to fool around, dawdle, waste time" and can mean "lovemaking," though this last is no waste of time and my dear old grandmother never used the word in such a way to me.

Lombard Street. The name of this London street, where many banks and other financial institutions are located, is sometimes used to mean the financial community in general, the way Americans would use WALL STREET. Lombard Street itself is named after the Italian bankers, moneylenders, goldsmiths, and pawnbrokers who first did business there in the 13th century. *Lombard* today can mean "banker" or "moneylender." "All Lombarad Street to [against] a China Orange" is an old proverb meaning very long, almost impossible odds. The winding Lombard Street in San Francisco is called "The Crookedest Street in The World." *See* LUMBER; PAWNSHOP; BOURSE.

London. *London*, loosely translated, meant "the wild place," being so named by Celts who found a harbor in the Thames there near two desolate gravel hills, calling the area *lond*, "wild."

lonely. Shakespeare coined *lonely*, or first recorded it, from *lone* plus *ly*, in *Coriolanus* (1608): "I go alone Like to a lonely Dragon . . ." The word *loneliness* had been invented before this and may also have suggested *lonely* to him.

Lone Ranger. The fictional masked rider of the plains who with his "faithful Indian companion Tonto" and his "great horse Silver" was a champion of justice to a generation of devoted followers on radio, in the movies, and on TV. This enduring symbol of the imaginary West was born in 1933 on Detroit radio station WXYZ. He shot pure silver bullets, never shot to kill and at the end of each program always shouted a hearty "Hi-ho, Silver!"

lone star flag. This name was usually applied to the flag of the Texas Republic but referred to the flags of several southern states in Civil War times, including the flags of Virginia, South Carolina, and Louisiana.

Lone Star State. A nickname for Texas, after the single star on its state flag. Texas has also been called the Beef State, the Jumbo State, the Banner State, and the Blizzard State.

longboat. In the days of sail longboats were so named because they were the largest boats carried by ships. Up to 40 feet long, they were up to eight feet abeam and were built to hold great weights.

long good-bye. A poignant name for ALZHEIMERS DISEASE, a common form of dementia characterized by memory lapses, loss of mobile ability, and an inability to remember anybody or anything. Patients cannot recognize themselves or people near and dear to them and often live a long time, "the long good-bye," before they succumb to the disease. The term is a recent one that has been used by several public figures (including Nancy Reagan on *60 Minutes*, 9/24/02) and apparently isn't included in any dictionary.

long green. The first U.S. greenback dollars were printed in 1863 and this term came into use soon after. *Long green* means "a lot of money," suggesting green bills laid in a long line, end to end.

long in the tooth. That horses' gums recede and their teeth appear longer as they grow older, owing to their constant grinding of their food, is the idea behind this ancient folk phrase, which means one is getting on in years.

long row to hoe. Rows in American home gardens today, usually a dozen feet or so in length, can't compare to the long rows of corn, beans, and other crops on early American farms. These rows, which often stretched out of sight, had to be weeded by hand at the time and approaching one with hoe in hand was dispiriting, to say the least. The expression a *long row to hoe* was probably well established for any time-consuming, tedious task many years before Davy Crockett first recorded it in 1835. It is still heard in a day when mechanized equipment has replaced hoes on farms, perhaps because, according to a recent poll, some 100 million Americans consider themselves vegetable gardeners.

longshoreman. The longshoreman, who helps load and unload ships, takes his name from a contraction of "along-shore-man," while the synonym *stevedore* is from the Spanish *estibodor*, "one who packs things." A *shenango* is a specialized longshoreman, one who handles cargo on railroad barges. His name derives from the county of Chenango in upstate New York, from which many such workers were once recruited.

long shot. From the time of William the Conqueror, archery was encouraged by English rulers and every adult male was required to own a longbow. With a six-foot English longbow made of seasoned heart of red yew, which was so valued at the time that it was protected as a war material, a skilled archer could shoot as far as 400 yards. In village archery contests every man strove to set a village record with the most accurate, longest shot. Thus *long shot* may have entered general speech as a synonym for any unusual or improbable feat, from a long archery shot that hit the mark dead center to a horse that won a race against great odds. *See also* NOT BY A LONG SHOT.

long time, no see.   The expression may date back only to the early 1920s, when it was first recorded as American slang. Other greetings common at the same time are *How's tricks?*, and *What do you say?* But according to another theory, *long time no see* came into the language from PIDGIN ENGLISH, brought home from the Far East by U.S. and British sailors in the early 1900s along with other expressions such as CHOP-CHOP for "hurry" and NO CAN DO. *Long time no see* is said to be a direct translation into pidgin of a Chinese expression meaning the same. *See also* CHINESE LANGUAGE CONTRIBUTIONS TO ENGLISH.

Lonsdale belt.   An important British boxing belt awarded to a fighter who wins a British title three times in a row. It is named after the earl of Lonsdale, Hugh Cecil Lowther, who was a good enough boxer to serve as sparring partner for American world heavyweight champion John L. Sullivan. Lord Lonsdale died in 1944 at the age of 87. He attributed his long life to "good living," which included riding to the hounds until a week or so before his death and drinking white burgundy for breakfast every day.

loo.   *Loo*, a slang word for "toilet" and British in origin, may be a mispronunciation of *le lieu*, French for "the place." But no one is sure. It could also be a shortening of *gardy loo!* a warning cry housewives made when they emptied chamber pails out the windows into the street, *gardy loo* being a corruption of the French *gardez l'eau*, "watch out for the water." A man traditionally walks on the outside of a woman in the street because chamber pots were emptied out the window in Elizabethan times; in those days a man was expected to take the greater risk of walking near the curb and protecting his lady by shielding her with his body as well. Among men walking together without women brutal fights were fought over who would "take the wall." *See* JOHN; TWISS.

look before you leap.   The old saying is often said to be from Samuel Butler's *Hudibras* (1663): "And look before you ere you leap; / For as you sow, ye are like to reap." But John Heywood's collection of proverbs (1562) clearly takes precedence with *look ere you leape*. There are a good number of counterparts in other languages: *Turn the tongue seven times, then speak* (French); *Have an umbrella before getting wet* (Japanese); *Before you drink the soup, blow on it* (Arabic); *First weigh (the consequences), then dare* (German); *If you don't know the ford, don't cross the stream* (Russian); *Be careful bending your head, you may break it* (Italian).

look like death warmed over.   The phrase describes someone who appears very ill and pale, as in "You look like death warmed over, were you out all night?" The expression, which frequently refers to someone hung over, was first recorded in 1939 and is British in origin, although they say, "Look (or feel) like death warmed up."

look one way and row another.   *Look one way and row another* means "to be aimed at one thing, but in reality to be seeking or striving for something quite different," like an oarsman rowing a boat toward land while his eyes are fixed on the open sea. The expression is a well-known one that John Bunyan used or coined in *The Pilgrim's Progress* (1678), a work which has been translated into over 100 languages.

looks like she swallowed a watermelon seed.   A humorous way American mountain folk describe a pregnant woman. The expression dates back to the early 19th Century.

looney tunes.   Looney Tunes was originally the name of a Warner Brothers cartoon series that first appeared in 1930, taking its name of course from *looney*, which comes from lunatic. In recent times, *looney tunes* has been used by law enforcement authorities to mean a crazed subject and has had increased general usage in the same sense. President Reagan referred to terrorists and their supporters as looney tunes. It was street slang long before this, however.

loony.   *See* CRAZY AS A LOON.

Loop.   Well known as Chicago's business, shopping, and theatrical center, the Loop was named after the elevated railroad, built in 1897, whose tracks "loop" the district.

loophole.   Medieval castles and other fortifications were often built with narrow windows that widened inward but were no more than vertical slits on the outside. Enemy archers found these defensive positions difficult targets, but archers behind the windows had ample room to fire on attackers. Called *loopholes* from the old word *loop* for "a narrow window," these windows became obsolete when the invention of gunpowder made castles and city walls unimportant in warfare, but the word came to represent an outlet or way to escape, a purpose loopholes had never really served. By the 17th century, writers were using *loophole* to signify a narrow way out and today we associate the word with a clever, tricky way out of a situation, especially in regard to evading a law.

loose lips sink ships.   World War II posters urged sailors and others not to talk about war-related matters, for "The slip of a lip may sink a ship," "Slipped lips sink ships," and "Idle gossip sinks ships." The most memorable of such slogans was "Loose lips sink ships." Another was "Don't talk chum/chew Topp's gum."

loosestrife.   One credulous author wrote that the Romans put loosestrife flowers under the yokes of oxen to keep the animals from fighting with each other. Many people believed similar myths about loosestrife (*Lysimachia*) in ancient times, this belief stemming from the fact that the plant's name was derived from the Greek *lusi*, from *luein*, "to loose," and *mache*, "strife." Actually, loosestrife was named *lusimachon* by the Greeks from the name of one of Alexander the Great's generals, Lysimachus, who supposedly discovered it.

loot.   *Loot*, wrote Rudyard Kipling, is really "the thing that makes the boys get up and shoot." The word derives from the Hindi *lut*, meaning the same, which the British found plenty of in India.

lord; lady.   Each of these dignified words (though today we have terms like *baglady*) has its roots in a loaf of bread. The lord, or head of a household, was the *loaf-protector*; the Old English for this term, hlaf-weard (loaf-ward) or *hlaford*, eventually yielding the word *lord*. Similarly, the lord's wife, or mistress of the house, eventually took the name *lady* from the

Old English *hlafdige*, "loaf-kneader," or maker of the loaf of bread.

Lord Hawhaw. A *Lord Hawhaw* is especially one who makes propaganda for the enemy. William Joyce (1906–46) earned the sobriquet for his mocking broadcasts from Berlin during World War II. The American-born British fascist is examined at some length in Rebecca West's brilliant *The Meaning of Treason* (1947). Joyce was captured after the war, adjudged a British subject because he held a passport, and hanged for his crimes.

Lord Muck. If someone calls you Lord Muck in Britain, he is calling you a pretentious braggart and show-off. This slang expression dates back to 1890, according to Partridge. I can find no documentation of American use of the words.

Lorelei. The *Lorelei*, rising 433 feet high on the right bank of the Rhine River near St. Goar, is a rock cliff noted for its strange echo. Centuries ago the legend grew that the steep cliff was the home of a young maiden who had leaped into the Rhine and drowned in despair over a faithless lover. She was transformed into a siren whose song lured sailors to death in the dangerous Rhine narrows. Those who saw her lost their sight or reason, and those who heard her were condemned to wander with her forever.

Los Angeles. *Los Angeles* is a shortening of the California city's original name: *El Pueblo de Nuestra Señora la Reina de los Angeles de Porcinúncula* ("The town of Our Lady Queen of the Angels of Porcinúncula"). It is more often called *L.A.* Call it "L.A." and it loses 54 letters.

lose one's head; lose it. The first expression probably gave birth to the current *lose it*, meaning "to lose one's sanity" for a time or permanently. *To lose one's head* means essentially the same, "to lose one's rationality," and dates back to a similar French phrase of the early 19th century.

lose one's shirt. *Lose one's shirt* used to mean to be very angry, giving us the present-day *keep your shirt on*, "keep cool, be calm." Only in this century did the expression come to mean to lose everything. It has many antecedents that convey the same idea, including *He'd give you the shirt off his back*, his last possession, and *not a shirt to his back*, meaning someone penniless and propertyless, with nothing at all. Chaucer, in "The Whf of Bathes Tale," wrote of someone he admired though "had he nought a schert."

losing face. The Chinese have a phrase for losing one's dignity before others, and *tiu lien* was simply translated into *to lose face* by English traders there in the late 19th century. These same English, however, invented the phrase *to save face*, "to maintain one's dignity," using the Chinese model.

lossie. In South Africa *lossie* refers to a fast woman or floozie, with which the word rhymes. *Loss* in Afrikaans means a "loose" or promiscuous woman. *See* FLOOZIE.

lost cause. The cause of the South in the Civil War; first recorded as the title of a book in 1866, a year after the South lost the war. It is still used humorously today.

the Lost Generation. "*Une génération perdue*," remarked Monsieur Pernollet, owner of the Hôtel de Pernollet in Belley. He was speaking to Gertrude Stein and pointing at a young mechanic repairing her car. Young men like the mechanic, Monsieur Pernollet said, had gone to war, had not been educated properly in their formative years, and were thus "a lost generation." Stein remembered Pernollet's phrase and applied it to Ernest Hemingway and his friends. Hemingway quoted her in *The Sun Also Rises* (1926) and the words became the label for an entire literary generation. *See* GENERATION X; BABY BOOM.

lost in the world. A current saying I've heard discrediting someone who is pathetically helpless, childlike, bewildered, unable to deal with reality much of the time, sometimes mentally ill. Perhaps there is a connection with LOST GENERATION after World War I, or with homeless people living on the streets today, but I can find no evidence of either origin.

lotus-eater. A daydreamer, someone who leads an indolent, dreamy life of ease indifferent to the busy world, is sometimes called a *lotus-eater*. In the *Odyssey* Homer writes that the Lotus-eaters, or Lotophagi, were a people who lived on the northeast African coast and ate what later Greek writers identified as the fruit of the shrub *Zizyphus lotus*, which made them dream all day, forget friends and family, and lose all desire of ever returning to their homes. Any traveler who ate the sweet fruit or drank a wine made from it wanted only to live in Lotus-Land. *Lotus*, however, is a name given to many plants. The Chinese make a lotus seed dessert called *pinh tan lian tye*, reputed to be an aphrodisiac, and the delicious sugarberry or hackberry (*Celtis australis*), grown in the northern U.S., has been called the fabled food of the Lotus-eaters. Even jujubes, long a favorite candy, were once thought to be flavored with lotus fruit.

loudhailer. *See* MEGAPHONE.

loud-mouth soup. *See* MARTINI.

loudspeaker. *See* MEGAPHONE.

Lou Gehrig's disease. The fatal paralytic disease amyotrophic lateral sclerosis has had this name since Yankee first baseman Lou Gehrig died of it in 1941. Known as the Iron Man, the Iron Horse, and the Crown Prince (to Babe Ruth) of Swat, Gehrig played in 2,130 consecutive games for the Yankees before the disease took its toll, a record that lasted until 1995.

Louisette. *See* GUILLOTINE.

Louis heel. There is no doubt that France's Louis XIV, called *le Roi Soleil*, the Sun King, because he adopted the rising sun as his personal emblem, was a vain and haughty man who surrounded himself with pomp and ceremony. *Le Grand Monarque* is characterized by the apocryphal remark attributed to him, *L'état, c'est moi*, "the state is I." He is therefore a likely candidate for the inventor of the high Louis heel. Because Louis was a short man, the story goes, he ordered his shoemaker to add cork to his shoe heels to make him taller and kept having more and more cork added to them, his loyal court aping the style. The tale is a good one, but probably isn't true. Most likely Louis's grandson, Louis XV, is responsible for the Louis heel, which became the imposing carved French heel on men's shoes that was ultimately copied by women. The heel, which is only medium today, once reached such ridiculous heights that court ladies had to use balancing sticks to navigate.

Louisiana. The Creole or Pelican State was named Louisiana in 1682 by the French explorer Robert de La Salle as a homage to the Sun King, France's Louis XIV, applying the designation to the entire Mississippi Valley. The Louisiana Purchase, engineered by President Jefferson because he believed Napoleon might close the Mississippi to United States commerce, brought the 1-million-square-mile area under American ownership in 1803 for a mere $15 million. In the history of this country only SEWARD'S FOLLY and possibly MANHATTAN Island were shrewder real estate deals. The purchase included part or all of 11 states—Arkansas, Colorado, Iowa, Kansas, Louisiana, Missouri, Montana, Nevada, North Dakota, South Dakota, and Wyoming. Mencken notes there was a child named Louisiana Purchase to commemorate the event—but then the boy's sister bore the name Missouri Compromise.

Louis styles. Four decorative and architectural styles are named after French monarchs reigning when the styles were in vogue: *Louis Treize style*, for Louis XIII (1610–13): a period characterized by a gradual transition from the rich free forms of the Renaissance to classicism in both architecture and furniture; *Louis Quatorze style*, after Louis XIV (1643–1715): massive baroque designs that emphasized formality and dignity rather than comfort dominated here; *Louis Quinze style*, for Louis XV (1750–74): fantasy, lightness, elegance, and comfort are the main themes of this rococo period, most interior decoration obsessed with a love of curved lines that was almost bizarre; *Louis Seize style*, after Louis XVI (1774–93): here occurred a reaction against the excessive designs of the *Louis Quinze* style, a return to straight lines, and the classic ideal in ornamental details. All of these styles had one thing in common: They emphasized richness and luxury, which is why they were swept out with the French Revolution.

Louisville; Louisville Slugger. Louisville, the largest city in Kentucky, was named for France's Louis XVI in 1780 in recognition of the assistance he had given America during the Revolutionary War. Home of Fort Knox, the Kentucky Derby, the mint julep, many bourbon distilleries, and the only inland United States Coast Guard station, Louisville also houses the famous Hillerich & Bradley's baseball bat factory, where the renowned Louisville Slugger has been made since 1884. The bat is of course named after the city named after a king. Louisville Sluggers are made from prime white ash, one mature tree is needed to make 60 bats, and more than 6 million are turned out each year. Some 2 percent of the annual production goes to professional ballplayers, these fashioned from specifications noted in a 50,000-card file covering the bat preferences of ballplayers past and present.

lounge. Longinus, according to the apocryphal gospel of Nicodemus (7:8), was the Roman soldier who pierced the crucified Christ's side with a spear. Later, tradition tells us, the soldier converted to Christianity and in medieval times was honored as a saint. Contemporary mystery plays may have depicted Longinus, or Longis, as he was also called, as a tall, lazy lout leaning on his spear—at least in the centurion phase of his life. It has been suggested that *to lounge* could have derived from the posture of Longis, *lounges* and *lounge lizards* following after the verb. The theory isn't likely to be confirmed, but *Webster's* and other authorities do give *longis*, the Old French for "an awkward, drowsy person," as the source for the word.

lounge room; sitting room; living room; sitkamer. Australians invite you into the "lounge room" if you visit their homes, while Britons ask you to come into the "sitting room." Both would be inviting you into what both Americans and Canadians call the "living room." If you were in South Africa, however, you'd be asked into the "sitkamer" (composed of *sit* plus *kamer*, Afrikaans for chamber).

love. A person who fails to score in tennis might be said to be playing for the love of the game. According to this theory, which is widely supported, *love*, for "zero in tennis," comes from the expression "play for the money or play for love [nothing]." The idea here is similar to that behind the word *amateur*, which comes from the Latin *amare*, "to love," and strictly speaking means a person who loves a game or subject. But there is another explanation for the term *love* in tennis, an expression used since at least 1742. *Love*, for *goose egg*, or "nothing," may have been born when the English imported the game of tennis from France. Because a zero resembles an egg, the French used the expression *l'oeuf*, "egg," for "no score." English players, in mispronouncing the French expression, may have gradually changed it to *love*.

love affair. Shakespeare may have invented the term *love affair*. We find no use of the words earlier than in *Two Gentlemen of Verona* (1591), where the Bard writes: "I'll . . . confer at large all that may concern thy love affairs."

love apples. Why tomatoes were dubbed "love apples" is a matter of some dispute. First cultivated by the Mayans and called the *xtomatl*, the tomato was named the *pomi del peru* and *mala peruviane* when Cortés brought it to Europe from America. That tomatoes hailed from exotic climes and were a scarlet, shapely fruit undoubtedly helped, but the designation *love apple* owes just as much to semantics as sexuality. All Spaniards at the time were called Moors, and one story has it that an Italian gentleman told a visiting Frenchman that the tomatoes he had been served were *Pomi dei Moro* ("Moor's apples"), which to his guest sounded like *pommes d'amour*, or apples of love. However, another version claims that "apples of love" derives in a similar roundabout way from the Italian *pomo d'oro*, "golden apple," and a third tale confides that courtly Sir Walter Raleigh presented a tomato to Queen Elizabeth, coyly advising her that it was "an apple of love." In any case, the tomato quickly gained a reputation as a wicked aphrodisiac, and justly or not, it has held this distinction ever since. "These Apples of Love . . . yield very little nourishment to the body and the same naught and corrupt," the English traveler John Girard wrote in his 16th-century gardening guide. In Germany the tomato's common name is still *Liebesapfel*, or "love apple," and the expression *hot tomato*, for "a sexy woman," is common to many languages.

lovebird. The West African parrot *Agapornis pullarius* was apparently the first bird to be called the lovebird because of the remarkable affection it shows for its mate. This usage is recorded in the late 1500s, over three centuries passing before *lovebirds* is recorded as applying to humans (as an Americanism in the 1930s). But the phrase *like a pair of lovebirds* was common before this and one doubts that human lovebirds weren't so called much earlier.

love child; love brat. *Love child*, for "a child born out of wedlock," isn't a euphemism from Victorian times, as is often said. The kind words date back at least to 1805, when recorded by a writer referring to *love child*'s use in another locality. Before this Pope used the similar *babe of love* in the *Dunciad* (1728): "Two babes of love close clinging to her waist." *Love brat*, a nastier variant, is recorded earlier than either expression, sometime in the 17th century.

love day. The ancient custom of settling disputes on legally appointed special days called love days is one that might well be revived. The custom is so old that the words are a translation of the Medieval Latin *dies amoris*. Shakespeare mentioned such love days in *Titus Andronicus* and the words also came to mean "a day devoted to love-making" in the 16th century, "when bonny maides doe meete with Swaines in the valley . . ."

lovee. We tend to associate nonce words like *lovee* with modern comics. "Amos and Andy," for instance, were consistently coining things like the *hitter* and the *hittee*, the *kisser* and the *kissee*, etc. But *lovee*, in the sense of the one loved by a lover, a recipient of love, dates back at least to the mid 18th century when Samuel Richardson used it in his novel *Sir Charles Grandison* (1735): "The Lover and the Lovee make generally the happiest couple."

love is blind. Shakespeare possibly coined this now proverbial phrase. At least it is first recorded in *The Merchant of Venice* (1596):

> But love is blind, and lovers cannot see
> The pretty follies that themselves commit.

Lovelace. Another lover to join our eponymous list of Lotharios, Don Juans, Casanovas, etc., *Lovelace*, however, usually refers to a selfish foppish lover, one who lives to seduce young women. The word comes from the name of the handsome rake Robert Lovelace, a character in Samuel Richardson's million-word epistolary novel *Clarissa* (1748–49). The heartless Lovelace stops at nothing to have Clarissa and eventually rapes her, which leads to her death.

love lay. A love lay is a love song, the term dating back to the 14th century. A lay, from the Old French *lai*, "song," was originally a short narrative or lyrical poem intended to be sung, but has come to include historical narrative poems (ballads) such as Scott's *The Lay of the Last Minstrel*.

lovelihead. A rare word, meaning "loveliness," *lovelihead* has its origins in a line by Ben Jonson: "Those Sweet and Sacred fires Of Love betweene you and your Lovelyhead"—in his poem "Underwoods" (1633).

lovelock. Courtiers in the time of Queen Elizabeth I wore lovelocks, which were long locks of hair hanging in front of the shoulders that were curled and decorated with ribbons. Later, *lovelocks* came to mean a small curl plastered to the temples. The man's version was called a bellrope.

lovelorn. No Mr. Lonelyhearts invented the word *lovelorn*, for "someone forlorn or pining for love." John Milton coined the word in *Comus, A Masque* (1634), a pastoral entertainment in which a character says to another: "Where the love-lorn Nightingale Nightly to thee her sad Song mourneth well." Milton also coined *all-conquering*, *earth-shaking*, and SMOOTH-SHAVEN.

love me, love my dog. What the phrase means is "if you want to love me, you'll have to take me faults and all." Almost 900 years ago St. Bernard (1091–1153), famous abbot of the monastery of Clairvaux, said this in Latin: "*Qui me amat, amat et canem meum.*" Despite the canine association, he is not St. Bernard de Menthon (923–1008), who founded the Alpine shelter now called the Hospice of the Great St. Bernard and after whom the ST. BERNARD *dog* is named.

love money. Romantic couples used to break coins in two, each lover keeping a half as a remembrance or pledge of fidelity. The broken coins were called love money and the custom is recorded in Roman times.

love nest. Considering that LOVEBIRDS goes back several centuries, it is hard to believe that *love nest*, for "an apartment where two lovers meet, usually clandestinely," dates only to the beginning of this century. But it is, so far as is known, an Americanism first recorded in 1900.

love tap; love pat. People were probably calling gentle taps indicating love *love taps* long before Mark Twain used the expression in *A Connecticut Yankee in King Arthur's Court* (1889). But Twain's is the first recorded use of the expression, which may have been suggested by the earlier *love pat*, recorded in 1876.

love tooth. *Love tooth*, similar to *sweet tooth*, once meant an inclination for love, a liking of love. "I am nowe old," wrote John Lyly in *Euphues* (1580), "yet still have I in my head a 'love tooth.' "

lovey-dovey. *Lovey-dovey* is often cited as an Americanism, but it is recorded first in England in 1769 as a term of affection: "The domestic Lovies and Dovies." By 1819 we find recorded: "My dearest love—lovey, dovey!" *Dovey*, of course, stands for "little dove."

lowbrow. A word invented in 1902 by a *New York Sun* reporter to describe anti-intellectuals. *See* HIGHBROW.

lower class; lower order. *See* UPPER CLASS.

lower the boom. *Lower the boom* can mean to hit someone hard, as in "Clancy lowered the boom," or to ask someone for a loan. The idea behind the American expression, which probably dates back to the late 19th century, is that of a cargo-loading boom hitting someone.

lox; gox. There is, in addition to the illustrious *lox* (from the Scandinavian *lax*, salmon) of *bagel and lox* fame, a word *lox* used in space research terminology. *Lox* here means *liquid oxygen*, the term used in *lox tank*, *lox unit*, etc., and as a verb meaning to load the tanks of a rocket vehicle with liquid oxygen. This *lox* came into use in the 1960s and is the antonym of *gox*, gaseous *oxygen*.

LSD; LCI; LCT. Many people are confused by these acronyms for World War II landing ships. The *LSD* (*Landing Ship Dock*) was a large ship used for repairs. The smaller troop carriers were called LCIs (*Landing Craft Infantry*), and LCTs (*Landing Craft Tank*).

L7. One rarely hears or sees this late-fifties Hollywood slang for "a square" anymore, perhaps because while it is clever visually, it has no ear appeal. *L7* means square, "not with it" according to bandleader Artie Shaw, because "if you form an L and a 7 with your finger, that's what you get."

lubber. Any clumsy, stupid person. Although it is widely used throughout the U.S., the expression is an old one dating back to fifteenth-century England. It is most often heard in LANDLUBBER, a sailor's derogatory term for someone unfamiliar with ships or the sea that is just recorded in 1690.

lucifer. Like *Vesuvius* and *Promethean*, *lucifer* was a colorful name for "matches" in the 19th century. The words' origins are obvious except in the case of *lucifer*, which doesn't derive from the name of the devil, as one would suspect, but from the morning star, the "Light-Bringer," *lucem ferre*. *Lucifer* is also the only one of the three to still have some currency, in the song "Pack Up Your Troubles In Your Old Kit Bag": "strike up a lucifer to light your fag."

lucky bugs. See DOLLAR BUGS.

lucky dad. In Scottish English *lucky dad* refers to a father who has become a grandfather.

lucky fluke. A *fluke*, in the sense of lucky things that happen to someone, is possibly from the dialect word *flack*, "a blow." The word *fluke* here seems to come from billiards, where a fluke means aiming at one thing and hitting another, a lucky blow that is to your benefit. *Lucky* is redundant here, but is usually yoked to *fluke* in the phrase. The expression dates back to the 19th century.

lucky horseshoe. Legend says that St. Dunstan, a blacksmith who later became archbishop of Canterbury, outwitted the devil when he asked St. Dunstan to shoe his cloven foot. Recognizing Satan, St. Dunstan tied him up and subjected him to great pain while he shoed him, making the devil promise before he released him that he would never enter a place where a horseshoe was nailed (open end up so that the luck won't run out) above the door. Another explanation for the lucky horseshoe, put forth by two respected scholars, is that it was originally a symbol of fertility because it roughly resembled the vulva. England's naval hero Lord Nelson believed in the lucky horseshoe and had one nailed to the mast of his flagship *Victory*. He lost his life beneath it at Trafalgar. *See* HORSESHOES; NELSON'S BLOOD.

Lucky Pierre. *Lucky Pierre* refers to a man who shares a bed with two women, to put it delicately. The term has its origins in an old dirty joke, or jokebook, the age and content of which are unknown. Just when I was about to give up finding any recent use of the words, a play entitled *Lucky Pierre or L.P.* opened Off-Broadway (11/02), L.P. being a synonym for Lucky Pierre. Lucky Pierre can also mean a man or woman in the middle between two men. The term is first recorded in 1943.

Lucullus will sup with Lucullus. Lucius Licinius Lucullus (ca. 119–57 B.C.), a celebrated Roman general and consul who drove Mithridates' fleet from the Mediterranean, among other military successes, had been relieved of his office by Pompey in 67 B.C. But he had amassed a fortune and retired into the elegant leisure for which he has become famous, spending huge sums on public displays and on his estates. Horace tells us he lavishly entertained the artists, poets, and philosophers with whom he surrounded himself, and that his feasts were famous throughout Rome. The gourmand even had files of menus listed according to cost, serving the most expensive ones to his most important guests, and it is said that on one occasion an unparalleled dinner cost him the equivalent of more than $8,000. Another time, Plutarch says, he ordered his cook to prepare a particularly magnificent meal and was reminded that he was dining alone that night. "Lucullus will sup tonight with Lucullus," he replied, or "Today Lucullus is host to Lucullus." These sayings are now used to indicate a luxurious meal enjoyed by a gourmet who dines alone. The Roman general's military prowess is almost forgotten, but the adjective from his name lives on as a synonym for "gastronomically splendid" and a sumptuous and extravagant meal is still called a Lucullan feast or banquet.

lucus a non lucendo. An etymological contradiction, an absurd conclusion or explanation. The Latin words literally mean "grove from not giving light," that is, a grove (*lucus*) is so called because it doesn't shine (*lucere*). The Roman grammarian Honoratus Maurus Servius invented the term to illustrate how words are falsely derived from those having a contrary sense (for example, deriving *ludus*, Latin for "school," from *ludere*, Latin for "to play." Addison gave another example in the *Spectator*: "One Tryphiodorus . . . composed an Epick Poem . . . of four and twenty books, having entirely banished the letter A [Alpha] from his first book, which was called *Alpha* [as *Lucus a non Lucendo*] because there was not an *Alpha* in it."

"Lucy in the Sky with Diamonds." The famous Beatles song isn't about LSD, despite the LSD initials running down the original record cover. John Lennon's son had drawn a picture of what he called "Lucy in the sky with diamonds," which inspired his father to write the song and use the title. The cover was just coincidence. The initials usually stand for lysergic acid diethylamide 25, or acid, as it is called, a potent hallucinogen.

Lucy Stoner. Use of the "Ms." form of address for a woman today recalls the all-but-forgotten *Lucy Stoners* active earlier in this century. A woman who refused to change her maiden name upon marriage was often called a Lucy Stoner. The term recalls American feminist Lucy Stone (1818–93), who deserves far greater recognition than she has received. On graduation from Oberlin, the only college accepting women at the time, Lucy Stone was 29, and she plunged headlong into the woman suffrage and antislavery causes. Her important work included helping to form the National Woman's Association, of which she was president for three years, and the founding of the *Women's Journal*, the association's official publication for nearly 50 years. An eloquent speaker for women's rights, Lucy Stone became well-known throughout the U.S. In 1855 she married Dr. Henry Brown Blackwell, an antislavery worker, but as a matter of principle she refused to take his name, and she and her husband issued a joint protest against the inequalities in the marriage law. Lucy Stone would never answer to any but her maiden name all her married life, and the Lucy Stone League later emulated her, defending the right of all married women to do so.

Luddite. The masked bands of workers who made night raids on English factories from 1811 to 1816 were protesting layoffs, low wages, and poor-quality goods, all caused by the large-scale introduction of textile machines to replace handicraft. The riots began in Nottingham and spread throughout England, the raiders directing their rage against the machines and systematically destroying them. Led by a "General" or "King Ludd"—named for a probably mythical Ned Ludd, said to have destroyed stocking frames in a Leicestershire factory 30 years earlier—the rioters soon became known as Luddites. Increasing prosperity in the country, combined with even more repressive measures, finally put them down. But not the memory of them. Today a Luddite is anyone who fears and would eliminate automation—not only for the unemployment it creates, but for its effect on the quality of life and for the human destruction that the machinery of war might cause. In our rebellion against an impersonal society, the word is used much more sympathetically than before. Indeed, some serious observers believe that the Luddites were right.

luff. *See* ALOOF.

lulus. The lulus we hear most about today are those taken by state legislators, who have been known to abuse them. A lulu, in this respect, is any tax-free item in an official expense account that is regarded as "in lieu of" part of a salary. The term is a recent one, dating back only 20 years or so, and apparently derives from the word "lieu." If it does, *lulu* is one of the simplest of reduplications, that is, new words formed from the repetition of elements in an older word. Like *mama* and *papa*, it contains one basic sound that is repeated. But some authorities think that *lulu* is just a special use of the earlier term *lulu*, for "any remarkable or outstanding person or thing." The earlier word has been traced back to 1886, and since it was often used to describe an attractive woman ("She's a real lulu") it is thought to derive from the common girl's name Lulu, often a nickname for Louise. *Lulu*, or LOO, is a British euphemism for toilet.

lumber. Our story begins with the Longobardi, or long beards, a Germanic tribe that in about 568 invaded Italy, where their name became *Lombardi* in Italian, and settled the region now called Lombardy. The merchants of Lombardy, who gradually migrated to the area from all parts of Italy, eventually won fame or infamy as bankers, moneylenders, and pawnbrokers. In time, the moneymen and their lombards, or pawnshops, radiated out from Milan and other parts of Lombardy to greener pastures. But *Lombard* came to be pronounced *Lumbard*, or *Lumber* in English. London's Lombard Street had its Lombard shops (pawnshops), and these had their Lombard rooms, storage rooms—all pronounced "lumber," too. Over the years the Lumber rooms on the street grew filled with unredeemed pledges on loans—large crates, cumbersome furniture, and other odds and ends that are still called lumber today. At this point, however, the word *lumber* was put to a new use. There are several explanations for the change, which is recorded as early as 1662. One is that American homesteaders in clearing their land for farming, left many discarded trees lying around, this clutter, or lumber, later cut or split into the wooden planks we know as lumber today. The word *lumber* for "to walk clumsily or heavily" does not derive from the Longbeards, coming directly from the Middle English verb *lomeren* meaning the same thing. *See* LOMBARD STREET.

luminarias. Pueblo peoples in New Mexico build bonfires called luminarias outside their houses during the Christmas season, a custom deriving from the Mexican Christmas custom of setting votive candles called *luminarias* (Spanish for lamp or lantern) in sand inside small paper bags, often colorfully designed, through which light shines. The custom has spread in recent times throughout the Southwest, where neighborhoods are filled with luminarias lining driveways, sidewalks, and rooftops. Luminarias are also called *farolitos*.

lummox. *See* DUMB OX.

lunatic. Lunatics are literally "moonstruck persons," the word deriving from the Latin *luna*, "moon." At least since Roman times it has been popularly believed that the mind is affected by the moon and that "lunatics grow more and more frenzied as the moon increases to full." Recorded in English as early as 1290, *lunatic* is no longer used medically. "The lunatic, the lover and the poet," wrote Shakespeare in *A Midsummer Night's Dream*, "are of imagination all compact." *See* LOONEY TUNES.

lurch. *See* LEAVE IN THE LURCH.

lush. Near Drury Lane Theatre in London was the Harp Tavern, where a club of hard drinkers called The City of Lushington had been founded in 1750. Lushington's had a chairman, the "Lord Mayor," and four "aldermen," who presided over the wards of Poverty, Lunacy, Suicide, and Jupiter (the supreme Roman god who presided over all human affairs). The club members, we are told, "were wont to turn night into day," and by example their convivial fraternity may have given us another word for a sot, or habitual drunk. *Lush*, at least as a generic term for beer or drink, first appeared in about 1790, long after The City of Lushington's formation, and it could very well be a contraction of the club's name. For in years to come a number of phrases employed the name Lushington. *Alderman Lushington is concerned*, 1810, meant "somebody drunk"; *to deal with Lushington*, 1820, meant "to drink too much," as did *Lushington is his master*, 1825; and by 1840 *a Lushington* meant "a drunkard." Even before this a *lush cove* had become a slang term for a drunkard, and *lush* itself both a verb for "to drink" and an adjective meaning tipsy. By the end of the 19th century we finally find *lush* alone being applied to any habitual drunk, as it is to this day.

Lusitania. This famous British liner was named for the Roman province of Lusitania in the Iberian Peninsula, which its name from the area's warlike tribes, called the Lusitani. She became one of the most famous ships in history because her sinking by a German submarine set America on the path into World War I; many Americans were among the 1,195 people on the *Lusitania* when she went down off Old Head of Kinsale in 1915. Most historians believe the tragedy was the fault of both a brutal submarine commander and the pigheaded skipper of the *Lusitania*, who refused to stay away from dangerous waters or even to speed through them. Some historians have also maintained that the *Lusitania* was surreptitiously carrying munitions.

Lutetia; Lutece. *See* PARIS.

Lutheran. Pertaining to the works of German theologian Martin Luther (1493–1546) or the Lutheran church. Luther, the German leader of the Protestant Reformation, was a prodigy who began his studies at age five as well as a talented musician who wrote several Lutheran hymns, including the well-known "Away in a Manger." He may have said, "The devil should not have all the best tunes," but this saying has been attributed to several people. His most famous words are from his speech at the Diet of Worms in 1521, in which he said, "I can do no other" ("Ich kaan nicht anders") or "This and this alone can I do." The couplet "Who loves not woman, wine, and song / Remains a fool his whole life long" has also been attributed to him, without any proof. *See* BEAST 666; MEALY-MOUTHED; PAPIST; WHY SHOULD THE DEVIL HAVE ALL THE GOOD TIMES.

lutz; flutz. In 1918 Viennese figure skater Alois Lutz developed the lutz jump, in which a skater jumps from the back outer edge of one skate and makes a full rotation in the air in the opposite direction of the skating curve, landing on the back outer edge of the opposite skate. By the time of the Salt Lake Winter Games of the 2002 Olympics, the word *flutz* had been anonymously coined, probably by a coach or judge, to describe a poorly executed lutz, specifically one made by a skater who takes off on the wrong edge of his or her skate. *Flutz* is a combination of *flip* and *lutz*, the flip being the jump that most closely resembled the lutz. *See* CHOCTAW.

Luzon. When anchored in the Philippines, Magellan's men supposedly asked an old fisherman the name of the place nearest them. "*Luzon?*" the fisherman replied in Tagalog, meaning "What did you say?" But the sailors thought he meant the place was called *Luzon*, which remains the Philippine island's name to this day. Though quite possibly folk etymology, the story bears repeating, both for its entertainment value and for want of a better derivation. *See also* INDRI; LLAMA; KANGAROO; NOME; YUCATAN.

lycanthrope. *See* WOLF MAN.

Lycoris. Mark Antony is mainly remembered for his fatal romantic entanglement with Cleopatra, and it is often forgotten that he led a riotous life while a youth, having had four wives—Fadia, Antonia, Fulvia, and Octavia—before he committed suicide for his Egyptian queen. One of his outside interests was Lycoris, a Roman actress who became his mistress. Centuries later the English botanist Herbert named the six lovely fragrant flowers of the *Lycoris* genus after this beautiful woman. The amaryllis-like *Lycoris* grow from a bulb and are lilac-pink or pink, the flower cluster a loose umbel. Native to China, Japan, and central Asia, they are generally grown in greenhouses in the United States and England.

lyddite. *See* SHIMOSE.

Lyme disease. Lyme disease is named after the Connecticut town where it was first recognized in the 1970s. The minuscule tick *Ixodes dammini* harbors the spirochetes of the disabling disease. The ticks are carried to humans by deer and white-footed mice that leave them on grass and foliage.

lynch. Our word for extralegal hanging definitely comes from the name of a man, but just who was the real Judge Lynch? At least a dozen men have been suggested as candidates for the dubious distinction. Scholarly opinion leans toward Virginia's Captain William Lynch (1742–1820), who was brought to light by Edgar Allan Poe in an editorial on "lynching" that he wrote in 1836 when he edited the *Southern Literary Messenger*. Poe claimed that the "lynch law" originated in 1780 when Captain Lynch and his followers organized to rid Pittsylvania County of a band of ruffians threatening the neighborhood. Poe even affixed a compact drawn up by Lynch and his men to the editorial. William Lynch's identity was further verified by Richard Venables, an old resident of the county, in the May 1859 issue of *Harper's Magazine*. But without evidence of any actual hanging there was still room for doubt. Finally, additional proof was found in the diary of the famous surveyor Andrew Ellicott, who visited Captain Lynch in 1811 and gained his friendship. William Lynch related how his lynch-men, as they were called, were sworn to secrecy and loyalty to the band. On receiving information accusing someone of a crime, the accused was seized and questioned before a court of sorts. If he did not confess immediately, he was horsewhipped until he did, and sometimes hanged whether he confessed or not.

M

M.   *M* in the Phoenician alphabet represented the wavy appearance of water and was, in fact, called *mem*, "water," in Hebrew. In medieval times an *M* was branded on the brawn (fleshy part) of the left thumb of a person convicted of manslaughter. *M* is always pronounced in English, except in Greek words such as "mnemonics." In Roman numerals the capital letter *M* stands for 1,000 (Latin, *mille*).

macabre; danse macabre.   *Macabre*, "gruesome, ghastly, or grim," comes directly from the *danse macabre*, or dance of death, which probably originated with a 14th-century German morality play eventually known throughout Europe. Death debates all his victims in this drama, winning his arguments with young and old, rich and poor, wise and foolish—and a weird dance ends the play as he leads his victims offstage. The dance of death survived in many allegorical paintings, sculptures, and tapestries, notably the engravings by Hans Holbein (1538), its popularity due to the overpowering awareness of death during the Hundred Years' War and the Black Death, a plague that wiped out two-thirds of Europe's population. *La danse macabre* is believed by most scholars to have been suggested by and received its name from the dance of the seven martyred Maccabee brothers recounted in 2 Maccabees, an apocryphal book of the Old Testament. The Medieval Latin *chorea Machabaeorum* became corrupted to *danse macabre* in French, the adjective *macabre* not appearing in English until the end of the 19th century.

Macabre style.   A book-binding style made for France's Henry III after the princesse de Cleves died, a style that used tears, skulls and bones tooled in silver to express the king's grief. A number of books could qualify as macabre in the binding, though not of the macabre style. In France, for example, a publisher with a weird sense of humor produced an edition of Rousseau's *Social Contract* bound in the skins of aristocrats guillotined during the French Revolution. Sold at auction in New York in early 1978 was a 21-volume series about animals by French author Maurice Hammonneau. The author hunted down each animal described and used the appropriate animal skin to bind each volume. Included was a book

on human beings, no explanation being given about the source of that one.

macadam; tarmac.   Perhaps the smooth, perfectly drained miniature stone roads that John Loudon McAdam (1756–1836) built in his father's garden as a child inspired the first macadam roads, but his system seems to have been the improved version of an older French model. McAdam, a Scotsman whose name is also spelt Macadam and MacAdam, began experimenting in road-building at his own expense at Ayrshire and then at Falmouth, where he had moved in 1798, and his persistent efforts finally got him appointed as surveyor for all Bristol roads in 1815. McAdam had discovered that an expensive French roadbuilding method invented 20 years before his first experiments offered the best solution to the problem of drainage. The roads he began to build were layers of small, sharp-angled, broken stones placed over a drained, gently sloping roadbed, each layer compacted by the traffic that passed over it, and with water running off into ditches on each side. McAdam's roads revolutionized transportation, gradually replacing the common dirt road, and in 1827 he was made general surveyor for all highways in England. But his method was improved just as surely as he had improved on the French method. Subsequently his stone layers were crushed into the earth with heavy rollers and their surface coated with a bituminous covering, and these blacktop roads came to be called macadam or tarmac (a shortening of "tar" and "macadam") roads.

macadamia.   *Macadamia*, a genus of Australian trees often called the Queensland nut and valued for its edible seeds, is not named for the roadbuilder John McAdam. It honors a Doctor John Macadam, secretary of the Victoria Philosophical Institute.

macaronic verse.   This is verse where the poet mixes words of his own language with those of another language, forcing his native words to fit the grammar of the foreign tongue, his intention almost always comic or nonsensical. The form seems to have been popularized in 1517 by Italian poet Teofilo Folengo, who called it the literary equivalent of macaroni (which is of course commonplace and a mixture of a number of ingredients). The Germans call it *Nudelverse* (noodle verse). *See* SPAGHETTI.

macguffin. Alfred Hitchcock defined the word *macguffin* while talking about his film *Notorious* (1946): "So the question arose, in designing the story for the film, what were the Germans up to down in Rio, what were they doing there? And I thought of the idea that they were collecting samples of uranium 235 from which the future atom bomb would be made. So the producer said, 'Oh, that's a bit far-fetched—what atom bombs?' I said, 'Well, both sides are looking for it . . . [but] if you don't like uranium 235, let's make it industrial diamonds. But it makes no difference, it's what we call the "macguffin" ' . . . The *macguffin* is the thing the spies are after, but the audience *doesn't care*. It could be the plans of a fort, the secret plans of an airplane engine."

machete. A large, heavy knife often used for cutting brush and as a weapon. *Machete* is a word borrowed from Spanish in early 19th-century America. It is also the name of a tarpon of the Pacific Ocean, after the resemblance of the tarpon's shape to a machete.

Machiavellian; Old Nick. A politician whose last name is a synonym for political immorality. Niccolò Machiavelli first conceived the idea of military conscription. Not a man to be much loved in an age where honor is given great lip service, Machiavelli still wasn't all that bad. Through his famous book *The Prince*, Niccolò di Bernardo Machiavelli (1469–1527) has become known as the father of political science. But this remarkable work is remembered mainly for its insistence that while his subjects are bound by conventional moral obligations, a ruler may use any means necessary to maintain power, no matter how unscrupulous. Thus *Machiavellian* has come to mean cynical political scheming, generally brilliant and always characterized by deceit and bad faith. The legend of this thin-lipped, sarcastic, hyperactive man gave rise in later years to the theory that his first name was the basis for *Old Nick*, a synonym for the devil. No one really knows how *Old Nick* originated, but the Niccolò origin is wrong. The rumor stems from Samuel Butler's humorous identification in *Hudibras*: "Nick Machiavel had ne'er a trick/(Though he gives name to our Old Nick)."

machine politics. Volunteer firemen in the early 19th century learned to work smoothly as a team on the levers of water-pumping machines, and perhaps, as one investigator suggests, their well-organized political associations suggested the term *machine politics* for this reason. Aaron Burr, who converted New York's patriotic Tammany Society into the political Tammany Hall we know today, is often credited with inventing the phrase, but then so are Nathaniel Hawthorne and even the duke of Wellington. The use of *machine* in a political sense, however, doesn't seem to have been recorded until 1865.

Mach number; Mach angle. Mach number is the ratio of the speed of a body to the speed of sound in air. Almost exclusively used to measure flight speed, it has only become common in the last few decades, as increased aircraft speeds have made old mph measurements too cumbersome. Mach 1, for instance, is the speed of sound, 762 miles per hour at sea level, while Mach 2 is twice the speed of sound. The word derives from the name of German scientist Ernst Mach (1838–1916), who died 31 years before Captain Charles Yeager first broke the sound barrier over Edwards Air Force Base in Muroc, California. (On October 14, 1947 Chuck Yeager flew his Bell X-I rocket plane at Mach 1.015.) Because of Mach's investigations into the supersonic speed of projectiles and the shock waves produced at these speeds both the measurement unit and the Mach angle, the angle a shock wave makes with the direction of flight, were named in his honor.

mackerel. *Mackerel* derives from the French *maquereau*, which is of unknown origin. One unproved story has the French word for the fish deriving from the French for "panderer" or "pimp," which is the same *maquereau*. According to this theory, the fish is so named because it is popularly believed to lead female shads to their mates every spring!

Mackinaw blanket; Mackinaw coat. John S. Farmer, in *Americanisms Old and New* (1889) first gave the origins of this term common in America since about 1830: "A superior kind of blanket which derived its distinctive name from the island of Mackinaw, formerly one of the chief posts at which Indian tribes received their grants from the government. A provision of one of the Indian treaties was that part of the payment made to the redskins should be in these superior blankets, and from that fact the name *Mackinaw Blankets* or *Mackinaws* simply was derived." A *Mackinaw coat* is a coat made from a Mackinaw blanket, or from any blanket.

mackintosh. *See* RUBBER.

Madame Bovary. Gustave Flaubert and his publisher were charged with "immorality" when his great novel *Madame Bovary* appeared in magazine form in 1856, but both were acquitted and the book was published a year later. The fictional Madame Bovary is based in part on Louise Colet (1810–76), a French poet and novelist with whom Flaubert carried on an affair for some nine years, beginning in 1846. The real Madame Bovary lived in Paris with her husband, Hippolyte Colet, and her affair with Flaubert was the author's only serious liaison. It is hard to see where Flaubert could have gained his amazing insights into feminine psychology except by his intimate observations of this woman. Louise Colet's story is told in her novel *Lui: roman contemporain* (1859). A *Madame Bovary* has come to mean a woman with an inflated, glamorized opinion of herself. *Bovarism*, a rare word that should have greater currency, means, to quote Aldous Huxley, "the power granted to man to conceive himself as other than he is," *bovaric* and *bovarize* deriving from it. Whether Louise Colet shared these qualities with Madame Bovary is debatable, but her name is linked with the words.

mad as a hatter. Lewis Carroll's Mad Hatter in *Alice in Wonderland* (1865) isn't responsible for this phrase. *Mad as a hatter*, "crazy, completely demented," was used by Thackeray in *Pendennis* (1849) and by that prolific American phrasemaker Thomas Haliburton in *The Clockmaker* (1837), almost 30 years before Carroll. Several explanations for the expression have been advanced. One holds that the term was originally *mad as an adder* (an adder being a venomous viper whose bite was once thought to cause insanity) and that British mispronunciation corrupted *adder* to *atter* and then *hatter*. The curious metaphor is best explained by hatmaking itself, though. The mercuric nitrate long used in making felt hats often poisoned hatters, the effects of this mercurial compound causing men who worked with it for years to be afflicted with uncontrollably twitching muscles, a lurching gait, incoherent speech, and confused minds.

mad as a march hare.   Erasmus used the expression *mad as a marsh hare*, claiming that "hares are wilder in the marshes from the absence of hedges and cover." But Chaucer had the phrase *mad as a hare* before him, and *march hare* seems to have preceded *marsh hare* in use. Buck hares are wild frolickers in March, their breeding season, which has made them a synonym for lunacy for centuries. Lewis Carroll gave the expression new life with his creation of the March Hare in *Alice in Wonderland.*

mad as a wet hen.   Hens don't become very upset from getting wet, so this old expression isn't a particularly apt one. An Americanism that dates back to the early 19th century, it was apparently based on the false assumption that a hen, being exclusively a land animal, unlike, say, the duck, would go beserk if caught in the rain or doused with water. Better was the old expression *wet hen* for "a prostitute."

madcap scheme.   Today a *madcap scheme* is a rash, reckless, wildly impulsive scheme, while a *madcap* is a person with the same characteristics. But in times past a madcap was simply a crazy person, the word deriving from *mad* for "crazy" and *cap* as a synonym for "head." This term, used by Shakespeare, is first recorded by his detractor Robert Greene, in 1589.

made in Japan English.   The Japanese have borrowed and altered thousands of English words to which they have given new meanings. One example of this is the words *image* and *up*, which they have combined into the Japanese word *imejiappu* and given the meaning "improving one's image." The Japanese call constructions like this "made in Japan English."

Madeira.   The Portugese islands of Madeira off the west coast of North Africa give this fortified wine its name. Madeira is said to have originally had its unique taste because of the rolling motions of the ships that carried it on the long sea voyages to Europe.

madeleine.   These small, rich, shell-shaped cakes are doubtless the most famous pastry in all literature. They are said to be named for their inventor, Madeleine Paulmier, a 19th-century pastry cook of Commeray, France, though André Simon and other gastronomes credit their invention to "one Avice, chief pastry cook to the prince de Talleyrand." At any rate, Madeleine Paulmier and the anonymous Madeleine, for whom Avice may have named the cakes, both take their given names from Mary Magdalene. It was on a visit to his mother that Marcel Proust was served the scalloped *petite madeleine*, "so richly sensuous under its severe religious folds," whose taste brought back the flood of memories resulting in his 16-volume masterpiece *À la recherche du temps perdu*. One cynic has called Proust's work "the tale of a man who fell in love with a cookie." Proust's fragile madeleine, made with flour, butter, sugar, and eggs, "the same weight of each," flavored with lemon rind and

baked in a small but deep scallop-shaped mold, has no relation to the English sponge bun bearing the same name.

Madison, Wisconsin.   Named after James Madison, this is one of the four U.S. state capitals named after presidents. The others are Lincoln, Nebraska, for Abraham Lincoln; Jefferson City, Missouri, for Thomas Jefferson; and Jackson, Mississippi, for Andrew Jackson. *See* MONROVIA.

Mad Mullah.   This is not the sobriquet of any Afghanistan mullah involved in the recent war against terrorism. It belongs to Mohammed bin Abdullah, who claimed he was the messiah of all Muslims and made war on all Somaliland tribes allied with the British for some 20 years until he died in 1921.

Mad Prince.   An old name for Hamlet, the complex central figure of Shakespeare's play. George Jones, a British actor who immigrated to the United States in 1838 and changed his name to Count Johannes, for some reason became obsessed with the role of Hamlet. As the years passed, he played the role more and more, until it was the only part he would accept. But the count unfortunately got worse, not better, with each performance. Soon audiences began booing him; he was hooted and jeered off the stage. Jones, probably insane to begin with, grew so mad that he took to gibbering insanely on the stage. Finally, no producer would have him, even as a curiosity, and he was forced to retire. The mad actor, one early critic said, had become too mad to play the Mad Prince.

madras.   Generally *madras* refers to a fine cotton cloth with a plaid, striped, or checked pattern, although it can be a striped silk or rayon cloth, or even a bright colored silk cloth worn as a turban. In any case, it is a cloth originally made in Madras, India, during the 17th century, when the British East India Company founded the seaport city.

madstone.   Any hard substance extracted from the digestive system of an animal (such as a hair ball in a deer's stomach) and used to treat the bites of mad dogs was called a madstone by Americans in the 19th century. Thousands of people believed that they were cured of snakebites, bee stings, spider stings, and other bites by madstones. Abraham Lincoln, in fact, had his son treated for dog bite with a madstone applied to his wound.

madwort.   *See* ALYSSUM.

maelstrom.   Undoubtedly the best-known whirlpool in the world, the Maelstrom is found in the waters of the Lofoten Islands off Norway's west coast. *Maelstrom* is a Norwegian word deriving from the Dutch *malen* ("to grind or whirl"), and *strom* ("stream")—hence "grinding stream." A legend surrounding the Maelstrom has it that two magic millstones aboard a vessel sailing this passage ground out so much salt that the ship foundered, but the millstones still continued to grind away underwater, making the surrounding waters "forever turbulent and salty." First used to describe this Norwegian phenomenon alone, the word since has come to mean all large whirlpools the world over and widespread turmoil in general.

Maevius.   *See* BAVIUS.

Mae West. This inflatable life jacket was introduced at the beginning of World War II and named for one of the world's most famous sex symbols because it "bulged in the right places." Mae West (1893–1980) starred on Broadway until two of her plays, *Sex* and *Pleasure Man* were closed by the police in 1928. Migrating to Hollywood, she won fame as "Diamond Lil," the "Screen's Bad Girl," and the "Siren of the Screen." Her name, *Webster's* advises, is also given to a twin-turreted tank, a malfunctioning parachute with a two-lobed appearance, and a bulging sail.

magazine. "This Consideration has induced several Gentlemen to promote a Monthly collection to treasure up, as in a Magazine, the most remarkable Pieces on the Subjects above-mention'd," explained the editor of *Gentleman's Magazine* (1731), the first publication to be called a magazine. The word *magazine* itself, however, is from the Arabic *makhzan*, "storehouse," and has been used in that sense in English since the 16th century.

magenta. This red-purple dye was synthesized by French chemists in 1859, just after Napoleon had defeated the Austrians at Magenta in Italy. The reddish dye and its color were named in honor of the battle, because there was so much blood spilled there. Magenta, the place, had been named for a would-be emperor of Rome, General Maxentius, who in 306 had established a camp there called Castra Maxentia, "Maxentius's camp," which came to be called simply Magenta.

magic flower. No one knows the name of the magic flower of Greek myth that Flora gave to the goddess Juno to make her pregnant. According to the myth, Juno was jealous about the birth of the goddess Athena without a mother and was determined to have a child by herself. (Athena's father, Zeus, had swallowed his pregnant wife Metis, because he feared she would give birth to a son stronger than himself; Athena sprang from the head of her father when the god Prometheus split his head open with an axe.) Flora's magic flower enabled Juno to have a child without a father, and she gave birth to Mars, who was a god of vegetation sacred to farmers, and later became the god of war.

magic lantern. The first magic lanterns were rude optical instruments employing a lens to cast a magnified image of a transparent picture drawn on glass onto a wall in a dark room. Such devices were known in Europe by the mid-17th century, but the first one called a *magic lantern* was the brainchild of a Danish inventor who exhibited it in France in 1665, the French dubbing the machine a *lanterne magique*.

Maginot line. André Maginot (1877–1932) barely escaped with his life in World War I when he was severely wounded during the defense of Verdun, but it was contaminated oysters that finally caused his death from typhoid. Decorated with the Cross of the Legion of Honor and the Médaille Militaire, the former sergeant, who had enlisted as a private despite the fact that he was French undersecretary of war in 1913, returned to government service and eventually became minister of defense. Determined that France would never be invaded again, he and his generals proceeded to plan and have built a fortified wall along the eastern border from Switzerland to Belgium, a wall that extended 314 kilometers at $2 million per mile. The *Maginot line*, complete with self-sufficient forts dug seven floors deep into the earth, was meant to warn against surprise attacks from Germany in Alsace and Lorraine, but only engendered a false sense of security in France (which became known as the *Maginot mentality*), even though the wall was never extended to the coast. Maginot's death spared him from seeing his defenses easily bypassed by the Germans in World War II when they entered France through Belgium. The line's impregnability was never tested, but it could easily have been blasted by bombs, battered by tanks, or circumvented by paratroopers if it had been finished. The fault lay not so much with Maginot as with a war-weary country almost wanting to be lulled into a sense of false security. *See* SIEGFRIED LINE.

Magna Carta. The Magna Carta is the "great charter" of English liberty that the nobles extorted from King John in 1215. It was intended to guard against abuses of power by the Crown, including the guarantee that no subject be kept in prison without trial and judgment by his peers.

magnet. *Magnet* derives from a Greek word meaning "the stone of Magnesia," Magnesia being an ancient city of Asia Minor where the iron-attracting ore was first found. *Magnesia*, as in *milk of magnesia*, a mild cathartic made from magnesium salts, is also named for the city.

magnolia. Like Matthias de L'Obel, for whom Linnaeus named the *Lobelia*, Pierre Magnol (1638–1715) was a French physician and botanist who published a book classifying plants. Professor of botany at Montpelier University, Magnol had somehow obtained an education despite the fact that he had been denied entrance to French colleges because he was a Protestant. Through his courses in botany his name became celebrated, and Linnaeus honored him further by applying it to the beautiful magnolia tree upon devising his own monumental system of classification. The magnolia had been introduced into Europe from Japan in about 1709, but wasn't named for the professor until after his death. Linnaeus owed much to Magnol, who originated the system of family classification of plants, and picked a large plant family to honor him—Magnoliaceae, including 10 genera and over 100 species. The magnolia family, native to Southeast Asia and the southeastern United States, contains some of the most beautiful garden shrubs and trees. Its lemon-scented fragrance was once used by the Chinese to season rice. The tree's huge, showy flowers, sometimes 10 inches across, are commonly white, yellow, rose, or purple, appearing with or before the first leaves of spring, and the magnolia grows to heights of up to 100 feet. Leaves of one species, the southern umbrella tree, are often two feet long, and the attractive leaves of *Magnolia grandiflora* are used to fashion funeral wreaths.

Magnolia State. A nickname for Mississippi, which was first called the Mudcat State after the large catfish (mudcats) in its waters. It has also been called the Eagle State (probably from the eagle on its state emblem), the Border-Eagle State, the Ground-hog State, the Mud-Waddler State, and the Bayou State.

Magyar. *Magyar,* the language of the Hungarians, is unrelated to English, not stemming from the Indo-European family like most European languages and belonging to a group that includes Finnish, Estonian, and Samoyed. Aside from meaning the Hungarian language, *Magyar* means "an individual of the Mongoloid race, now forming, numerically and politically, the predominant section of the inhabitants of Hungary." Magyar words that have come into English include hussar, vampire, goulash, paprika, and coach—from the Hungarian town of Kocs, where horse carriages were made.

Mahabharata; Ramayana. One of the longest poems in the world is the *Mahabharata,* which tells the story of the descendants of the Hindu King Bharata. *Mahabharata* means "the great Bharata," and the poem's 110,000 couplets, or 220,000 lines, make it four times longer than the Bible and eight times longer than Homer's *Iliad* and *Odyssey* combined. The Indian poem is really the combined work of many generations of writers, written between the years 400 B.C. and 150 B.C. Though its main theme is the war between descendants of Kuru and Pandu, it is a vast repository of philosophy and legend. The *Ramayana,* named after the god Rama, is another great Indian epic poem, containing 24,000 stanzas in seven books as we know it today. Still another claimant for the longest poem is *The Mathnawi of Jalaluddin Rumi*—at 257,000 lines.

Mahernia; Hermannia. One of the most unusual words, the plant genus *Mahernia* is an anagram of *Hermannia,* another genus to which it is closely allied. Linnaeus must have been in a playful mood when he coined the word from *Hermannia,* which he had also named. Linnaeus named *Hermannia* for Paul Hermann (1646–95), a professor of botany at the University of Leyden, who is surely the only man to be honored by two genera in this odd way. *Hermannia* is a large genus, including some 80 species of ornamental, greenhouse evergreen shrubs, their flowers usually yellow. The closely related anagram genus, *Mahernia,* includes about 30 species, which are pretty greenhouse herbs or small undershrubs of which the yellow, fragrant honeybell (*M. verticillata*) is most notable. Both genera are native to South Africa. *See also* MHO; QUISQUALIS.

mah-jongg. *See* CHINESE LANGUAGE CONTRIBUTIONS TO ENGLISH.

mahogany. No one knows where this foremost of all cabinet woods originated or where the word *mahogany* came from. Some say the source of the word may be a non-Carib language of the West Indies, while others say it is perhaps of Mayan origin. The strong durable wood comes mainly from two species of trees of the genus *Swietenia:* the West Indies mahogany (*Swietenia mahagoni*), and the Honduras mahogany of Central and South America (*Swietenia macrophylla*). Lumber from these valuable trees has been used by the Spanish since at least 1514, but the word *mahogany* wasn't recorded until over a century later. *Mahogany* also means a reddish-brown color like the tree's.

mahout. An elephant keeper and driver, usually in India. The word rhymes with *boot* and comes from a Hindi word meaning "elephant driver." It was noted by the English in the mid-17th century.

Maidenhead. Legend has it that the English town of Maidenhead is so named because the severed head of one of 11,000 virgins martyred in Cologne, Germany is buried there. Actually, only one virgin, known as Undecimilla, was beheaded in Cologne centuries ago and later elevated to sainthood. But in transcribing her saint's day to the Roman Catholic Church calendar a scribe erred, indicating in shorthand Latin that on her day, *Undecem militia Virg. Mart.,* "eleven thousands of virgins were martyred." And not even Undecimilla is buried in Maidenhead. She has nothing to do with the town's name, which is a corruption of the town's older name, Maydenhythe, a "dock midway" between two other towns.

Maid of Arts. This was a name briefly experimented with in the 19th century for a woman who received a Bachelor of Arts degree from a college or university. At the time it was felt only men should receive a degree called a *Bachelor* of Arts. By the same reasoning *Maid of Science* and *Maid of Philosophy* also had their brief day.

mailbox; pillarbox. The streetcorner mailbox or pillarbox, as the Brits call it, was invented and named by British novelist Anthony Trollope (1815–82) about 1858 (not by author Tobias Smollett, as is sometimes said). The American name *mailbox* for the collection box wasn't recorded until 1872. Trollope, a Post Office official, wrote over 50 novels in addition to holding his job, rising at 5:30 every morning to write for 2½ hours before going to work.

mailed fist. The term *mailed fist* means "aggressive military might" and though it refers to the mail armor of the medieval knight, who even wore steel gloves, it came into use only in relatively recent times. The phrase derives from an order Kaiser Wilhelm II of Germany gave to his brother, Prince Henry of Prussia, when he sent him to China in 1897 at the head of forces that were to restore order after two German missionaries had been killed. "If any man dares impugn our right," the Kaiser declared, "smite him with your mailed fist!"

Maine. Maximillian Schele De Vere in *Americanisms* (1871) says that the name *Maine* may have been chosen for the Pine Tree State "in compliment to the Queen of England, who had inherited a province of the same name in France." According to George R. Stewart in *Names on the Land* (1945):

> In a New England charter of 1620 the lawyers wrote "the country of the Maine Land," words which suggest a general description rather than a name. Two years later, however, a charter was granted to two old sea-dogs of the Royal Navy, Sir Ferdinando Georges and Captain John Mason, and in it the word had certainly ceased to be a description. Dated on August 10, 1622, the charter declared that "all that part of the mainland" the grantees "intend to name the Province of Maine." Some have thought that this name arose because of the greater number of islands off that northern coast, which made men have more reason to speak of "the main." Others have tried to connect it with the Province, or County, of Maine in France. But again, *main* as equaling *chief* or *important* would have been of good omen, if a little boastful. Moreover, about 1611 Captain Mason had served in the Orkneys, and must have known the name as used there.

main liner. The main line of the Pennsylvania Railroad bordered an exclusive suburban area just northwest of Philadelphia. Hence the expression *main liner*, for "a wealthy, socially prominent person, a member of the upper crust." The expression isn't heard as much anymore as the other *mainliner*, "a drug addict who takes his narcotics by intravenous injection."

Main Street. *Main Street* is the typically American designation for the principal thoroughfare in a town, while the British synonym is High Street (the *high* denoting importance, not elevation). In early Colonial days, along the East Coast, there were High Streets, some surviving today, but *high* came to suggest elevation in America as the pioneers moved inland toward the mountains.

Maintenon. Born in 1635 in a French prison where her father was being held as a counterfeiter, Françoise d'Aubigné's life seemed no better as she grew to young womanhood. She married the famous comic poet Paul Scarron while still a girl of 16, serving mainly as his nurse until his death in 1660. Several years later she finally got a break of sorts when the King's mistress, Madame de Montespan, interceded with Louis XIV to put her in charge of their illegitimate children. Gradually she supplanted de Montespan in the Sun King's esteem, and in time he made her the Marquise de Maintenon. Madame de Maintenon became Louis's *maîtresse en titre* when Montespan left the court and was even a great favorite of Queen Marie-Thérèse, who died in her arms in 1683. Two years later Louis married his older, official mistress in a secret ceremony. Maintenon's influence on court life was considerable, though it has probably been exaggerated as concerns matters of state. Madame de Maintenon was no slouch as a gourmet, and her name is remembered in *lamb chops à la Maintenon* and other creations, in addition to being a synonym for "a mistress." She died in 1719, four years after Louis. *See* LAVALIERE; MONTESPAN; POMPADOUR.

maize. *See* CORN.

major league. The baseball terms *major league* and *minor league* date back to 1882, when the National League was called the major league and the American Association (not today's American League) was called the minor league. Later these two leagues merged and the unified teams became known as the major leagues, any league below them being called a minor league. Today, of course, the major leagues are composed of the American and National Leagues, each with two divisions. Because the major leagues are the highest level of professional baseball, the term *major league* has generally come to mean the best of anything. *Big league*, a synonym, also comes from baseball, where it was used as early as 1899.

makari. *Makari* are poets, from the rare word *makar* (a variant of "maker"), an archaic Scottish term for poet.

make a clean breast of it. "That man of peace . . . hath been entrusted with King's breasts," someone wrote of an early diplomat. *Breast* has been a synonym for the heart since ancient times and, like the organ it houses, was long thought to be the seat of consciousness, the repository of all private thoughts, emotions, and secrets. To memorize something was to *know it on breast* as well as *learn it by heart* and a person burdened by guilt had a *stained breast*. These expressions are obsolete now, but the phrase *to make a clean breast*, "to make a full confession or disclosure," has remained part of the language since the early 18th century. One suspects that it is much older, going back to days "when men had breasts like lions" and ceremonial heart burials like Robert Bruce's were common in England.

make a long story short; short and sweet. One would think the common advice *make a long story short* would be proverbial, but it is first found in print in Robert Bagot's novel *Passport* (1905). On the other hand, *short and sweet*, "brief and pleasant," *is* proverbial, one writer in 1539 calling it "an English proverb."

make a mountain out of a molehill. In his "Ode to a Fly" the ancient Greek satirist Lucian conveyed this same idea, "to give something much greater importance than it deserves." His "to make an elephant out of a fly" remains a French and German proverb to this day, but for some unknown reason the expression never passed directly into English. Instead, the elephant became a "mountain" and the fly a "molehill." Foxe's *Book of Martyrs* (1570) first recorded "makeying mountaines of Molehils."

make a scene. The display involved in *making a scene*, "making a disturbance, usually in public," suggests that the expression is theatrical in origin. Strong emotions often portrayed in short scenes of stage plays probably are responsible for the phrase. In fact, the first literary use of the idea is in Samuel Foote's farce *The Liar* (1762), where one of the characters says, "We parted this moment. Such a scene!"

make bricks without straw. Trying to do anything without the proper tools or materials is said to be *making bricks without straw*. The expression goes back to biblical times and is found in Exodus, it being necessary to make bricks with chopped straw to prevent them from shrinking and cracking as they dry.

make ends meet. This phrase seems to be merely a shortening of *to make both ends of the year meet*, meaning the same—"to live within one's income." Smolett first recorded the saying in his picaresque novel *The Adventures of Roderick Random* (1748).

make fur fly. The cruel "sport" of trapping raccoons and setting dogs on them to see how long the coons could last may have suggested this expression to American pioneers. Certainly the air was filled with fur during such fights. By at least 1825 the saying meant "to attack violently." In the autobiographical *A Narrative of the Life of David Crockett, of the State of Tennessee* (1834) we read: "I knew very well that I was in the devil of a hobble, for my father had been taking a few horns, and was in a good condition to make the fur fly."

make good. To succeed, prosper, or fulfill a promise, as in "He made good on his word." This Americanism was born as a poker term, which is explained in the manual *Poker: How to Play It* (1882): "When all who wish to play has gone in, the person putting the ante . . . can play like the others by 'making good'—that is, putting up in addition to the ante as much more as will make him equal in stake to the rest." By the turn of the 19th century the poker term was being used figuratively.

make hay while the sun shines. Sun is the best and cheapest way to dry grass for fodder, and this proverb thus reminds us to take full advantage of any opportunity before it passes. "When the sunne shinth make hay," John Heywood wrote in his *All the Proverbes in the English Tongue* (1546), and the saying has been a common one ever since.

make him an offer he can't refuse. Used jokingly today, but popularized by the film version of Mario Puzo's *The Godfather* (1972), in which the GODFATHER, played by Marlon Brando, uses it as a veiled threat. One of his confidants tells him that a certain Hollywood producer will never give his godson an important part in a movie he is making. "I'm gonna make him an offer he can't refuse," is the godfather's exact answer, implying the potential of violence to the producer. That violence turns out to be decapitating the producer's prize racehorse and placing the horse's head in the bed where he is sleeping. The phrase is used several times in the *Godfather* movies.

make love. *Make love* began life centuries ago as a synonym for to court; those who were making love were simply courting. No one at the time would have associated the words with their relatively recent sense of having sexual intercourse.

Make me a child again just for tonight. The familiar words are from the poem "Rock Me to Sleep" (1860) by Elizabeth Chase Akers (1832–1911): "Backward turn backward, O Time, in your flight, / Make me a child again just for tonight."

make my day. This expression is first attested in Florence Barclay's 1909 novel *The Rosary*, where a character says: "I knew I wanted her; knew her presence made my day and her absence meant chill night . . ." *Make*, however, had been used as a verb meaning "to secure the success of" (as in *Clothes make the man*), since the 16th century. Today *go ahead, make my day* has come to mean "give me the chance to do what I'd like to do—to hurt you badly!" The expression was popularized by the Clint Eastwood character Dirty Harry (a tough police detective) in the movie *Sudden Impact.*

make no bones about it. Someone who talks frankly or straight from the shoulder about a subject *makes no bones about it.* Possibly the phrase refers to "not making much" of the dice or bones when rolling them in a dice game, but the theory seems farfetched. The allusion is probably to a person making no fuss or objection about eating soup or stew if there are bones in it. (*I can't swallow that, I can't stomach that,* and *That sticks in my craw* are other expressions in which acceptability is related to terms of eating.) *Make no bones about it* is an ancient saying; Nicholas Udall's translation of Erasmus's *Paraphrase of Luke* in 1548 relates that Abraham, when commanded to sacrifice Isaac, "made no bones about it . . . but went to offer up his son."

make one's gorge rise. Hunting falcons are fierce, gluttonous creatures that store the food they eat in a pouch called the crop, or gorge. Their trainers in medieval times noticed that they frequently overate and vomited part of their food, which came to be called gorge, after the pouch it came from. To *make one's gorge rise* therefore became a synonym for "to make some-one sick." The saying at first indicated extreme disgust and later expressed strong resentment, so that today the phrase means to make a person violently angry.

make one's hair stand on end. Surprisingly, this metaphor isn't recorded before 1530, in a French phrase, but the idea behind it is found in the Bible (Job 4: 14–15): "Fear came upon me and trembling . . . the hair of my flesh stood up." The hair on cats, humans, and other animals can stand on end and become rigid with fear; the tiny muscles controlling this reaction are so effective that even baldheaded men feel a prickling of the scalp from sudden terror. An English clergyman at an execution in the early 19th century observed the following: "When the executioner put the cords on the criminal's wrists, his hair, though long and lanky . . . rose gradually and stood perfectly upright, and so remained for sometime, and then fell gradually down again."

make one's mouth water. In his *The Decades of the Newe Worlde or West India* (1555) historian Richard Eden wrote: "These Craftie foxes . . . espying their enemies afarre of, beganne to swalowe theyr spittle as their moths watered for greediness of theyr pray." No one knows who invented the phrase *to make one's mouth water,* "to salivate in anticipation, to look forward to something eagerly," yet it is interesting that this first known use of the expression had reference not to any gourmet food as we know it today but to human meat that West Indian cannibals spotted in the distance.

make the feathers fly. To badly beat an opponent in a fight. This Americanism is first recorded in John Neal's romantic novel *Brother Jonathan* (1825): "If my New York master only had hold o' him; he'd make the feathers fly."

make the grade. A train that makes the grade is one that manages to surmount a steep grade, or slope. Probably someone coined the expression which means "to win despite great obstacles," after a long, heavy effort laboring up a steep hill. But the phrase, which has been traced to only about 1930, may derive from milk making the grade, "reaching a proper standard" and being good enough to be labeled Grade A.

make the horn. The Greek hunter Actaeon came upon Artemis bathing and, either because he saw her naked or because he had boasted that he was a better hunter than she, the goddess of wildlife (she is called Diana in Roman mythology) changed him into a stag and he was torn to pieces by his own hounds. Because he had had horns at least for a short time—Actaeon's name became a synonym for a man with an unfaithful wife. In fact, *to actaeon,* now obsolete, was once a verb meaning "to cuckold." No one really knows why horns are a symbol of cuckoldry, but one guess is that stags, which are of course horned, have their harems taken from them in the rutting season by stronger males. At any rate, making the horn—thrusting out a fist with the first and last fingers extended—has been a gesture of contempt, implying a person is a cuckold, since Roman times.

make things hum. Since at least the early 18th century, humming, suggesting the blending of many human voices or the activity of busy bees, has been used to express a condition of busy activity. Two hundred years later the expression *to make things hum* was invented in America. Possibly the hum of machines in New England textile factories was the inspiration for the phrase, in reference to the fabled Yankee mechanics who made things hum again when the machines broke down.

make waves.   Team players in any sport usually don't make waves, that is, they don't make trouble, and this expression might come from the sport of sculling, in which all of the rowers' strokes must be smooth and uniform, not choppy. But the phrase possibly comes from an old joke about a person who arrives in hell and hears thousands of lovely serene voices singing, though he can't make out the words. Amazed at such peace and tranquility in the nether regions, he approaches closer only to find the chorus of hell standing up to their chins in a sea of excrement, singing endlessly to each other, softly, serenely, carefully, "Don't make waves, don't make waves." Which is a far better story than the sculling one, anyway.

make whoopee.   *Whoopee* has been an American exclamation of joy or approval since about 1860. However, it was apparently newspaper columnist Walter Winchell who coined the expression *making whoopee*, for "wild merrymaking," the expression then made very familiar by the popular song "Making Whoopee" (1930).

mako shark.   A New Zealand Indian fisherman named Mooris is said to have hunted this shark for its long center tooth, hunted it so well in his canoe that the shark was named for him. It may, however, be named for the Maori of New Zealand, who also hunted it in canoes. The mako shark *(Isurus oxyrinchus)*, also called the mackerel shark, is found in both the Pacific and the Atlantic—not to mention seafood restaurants. *See* KIWI.

Malagasy words in English.   Malagasy, the Malayo-Polynesian language of Madagascar, has contributed several words to English, including bantam and kapok.

malakoff.   Malakoff, or Malakhov, a fortified hill overlooking Sevastopol from the east, was the scene of one of the most publicized battles of the Crimean War. After a long siege, the French finally stormed Malakoff and took it on September 8, 1855. The historic hill is supposed to be named for a drunken Russian sailor who set up a liquor shop on the heights after being fired from his job in the Sevastopol shipyards. Houses and finally fortifications were built around him and he ultimately won more fame than most of his more sober contemporaries. At one time a crinoline also honored the man's name and today the reformed drunkard is remembered by *malakoff*, a form of four-handed dominoes, by *malakoff*, a small French cream cheese as well as the name of a rich almond-flavored charlotte dessert—all of which commemorate the battle fought on his famous hill.

malamute.   This blue-eyed Arctic dog, descended from the wolf, is named for the Eskimo tribe called the Malemuit, who originally bred these sled dogs.

malapropism.   "Then, sir, she should have a supercillious knowledge in accounts;—and as she grew up, I would have her instructed in geometry, that she might know something of the contagious countries . . . and likewise that she might reprehearend the true meaning of what she is saying." The preceding is a speech of Mrs. Malaprop in the first act of Richard Brinsley Sheridan's *The Rivals*. Mrs. Malaprop is the name of an affected talkative woman in the play, the aunt of the heroine, Lydia Languish. Sheridan coined her name from the French *mal à propos*, "unsuitable, out of place," for he had her ludicrously misuse many "high sounding" words out of her ignorance and vanity, just as Shakespeare had Dogberry do in *Much Ado About Nothing* and had Mistress Quickly do in *Henry IV, Parts I & II*. Sheridan's *The Rivals* was produced in London in 1775, when he was only 24. Mrs. Malaprop's name soon became a synonym for the misuse of words, especially by those who are trying to sound important. *See* GOLDWYNISM; SLIPSLOP.

malaria.   *Malaria* derives from the Italian for "bad air." The disease was long associated with Rome, where the marshes around the city were a breeding ground for the mosquitoes that spread malaria until they were drained in 1939. Malaria was also called the *summer vapors, the fever,* and *Roman fever.* In his short story "Daisy Miller" (1878), Henry James called it the "villainous miasma."

malarkey.   Baloney, bunk, nonsense. Perhaps some Irishman named Malarkey was so noted for his B.S. that it was named for him, but there is no proof that this is so. More likely, though also not certainly, the word was invented by that prolific word-coiner American cartoonist T. A. Dorgan, TAD having first used it as *Milarkey*, in 1922.

Malay, Tamil, and Telegue words in English.   These Dravidian languages give us a number of English words, including calico, mango, copra, curry, coolie, pariah, junk, atoll, teak, ketchup, bamboo, gong, orangutang, fetish, caste, anaconda, catamaran, and mulligatawny.

male.   *See* FEMALE.

male-female names.   According to Mario Pei's *What's in a Word* (1968), many American names can be both female and male. Such names include Pearl, Marion, Leslie, Beverly, Kim, Francis, and many others. Such namings are more common in the South than elsewhere.

mall.   *See* SHOPPING MALL.

Malpighian.   His name is not well known outside scientific textbooks, but the Italian physiologist Marcello Malpighi (1628–94) deserves recognition as the founder of microscopic anatomy, the discoverer of the movement of blood through the capillaries, which completed the theory of circulation formulated by William Harvey, and for his pioneer work in the study of plant and animal tissues. Malpighi, a professor of medicine at Messina University, later served as private physician to Pope Innocent XII. He was one of the first men to use the microscope to study animal and vegetable tissue and the first to attempt an anatomical description of the brain with this instrument. He is commemorated by several words, including the Malpighiaceae family of ornamental tropical plants. The technical terms of

Malpighian corpuscle, Malpighian layer, Malpighian tube, and *Malpighian tuft* recall his important work in anatomy.

malted milk.   *Malted milk,* used today for the popular soda fountain drink made of malt, milk, ice cream, and syrup, was once a trademark for a baby food. In 1881 James and William Horlick patented a dried extract of wheat, malted barley, and whole milk "For infants, Invalids, the Aged, and Travelers." The investors coined the trademark Malted Milk, which they enjoyed for many years until it was infringed upon and was eventually applied to the ubiquitous fountain drink.

Malthusian.   Thomas Robert Malthus (1766–1834), an English curate, published his *An Essay on the Principle of Population As It Affects the Future Improvement of Society* in 1798, and his name almost immediately aroused a storm of controversy throughout the world. His essay contained what came to be called the Malthusian theory: that population increases faster, geometrically, than the means of subsistence, which increases arithmetically. According to this theory, population would always outstrip food supply unless checked by natural controls such as war, disease, or famine. Malthus later revised and refined his pessimistic outlook, including a control that he called "moral restraint"—late marriage and sexual abstinence. Most of the economist's predictions haven't been borne out, but his analysis remains correct in many respects and the Malthusian principle still operates in parts of the world where the birthrate has not dropped through birth-control practices. A Malthusian is one who accepts the pioneer demographer's theory, or, more generally, an advocate of birth control. It is interesting to note that Charles Darwin was struck by the phrase "struggle for existence" when reading Malthus's *Essay,* the words stimulating him "to find the key to biological change in the process of natural selection."

mama; mammal.   *See* BABE.

mamalese.   I haven't seen this synonym for baby talk anywhere save in Austin Bunn's *New York Times Magazine* article "Terribly Smart" (3/24/02), and perhaps the author coined it: "The Baby Einstein video series, which immerses 'learning enabled' babies in English, Spanish, Japanese, Hebrew, German, Russian and French long before mamalese, was purchased by Disney. . . ."

mamelle.   *See* GRAND TETONS.

mammon; the mammon of unrighteousness.   *Mammon* became the personification of greed or a passion for money, the god of this world, only in medieval times. In the Bible the word (from the Syriac *mamuna*) means riches or gain, as in "Ye cannot serve God and mammon" (Matt. 6:24) or "The mammon of unrighteousness" (Luke 16:9). In Ben Jonson's *The Alchemist* (1610), Sir Epicure Mammon is a worldly sensualist, a greedy, voluptuous knight who is conned by the alchemist.

mammoth.   *Mammoth* means something of great or enormous size, but the word was first applied to a large hairy elephant of the genus *Mammuthus,* sometimes called the woolly mammoth, when skeletons of *Mammuthus primigenius* were found in Siberia in 1706. The creature's name in Russian was *mamant,* which became the English *mammoth* and was eventually applied to anything of huge size.

mammy.   *Mammy* is an Irish term meaning mother, and *mam* is a British regionalism that means the same. *Mammy* was once commonly used in the American South to mean a black woman hired to care for white children but is considered by many to be a derogatory expression today.

mamser; momser.   Some Hebrew words have been standard in English for centuries. *Mamser,* for example, first recorded in 1562, was frequently used to mean "bastard" during the Middle Ages, and people were familiar with the word from its use in Deut. 23:3. *Mamser* became obsolete by the late 19th century, but is still heard in the Yiddish *momser,* meaning the same and a half-dozen other things, including: an untrustworthy man, a difficult man, and impudent man, a detestable man, a scalawag, and even a clever, quick fellow.

man.   *See* WOMAN.

man about town.   This expression has been popular since the mid 17th century, for "a fashionable person who is often seen at public and private functions." *Girl about town,* invented at about the same time, is rarely, if ever, used anymore.

manager.   Managers were originally horse trainers, the word *manage* deriving from the Italian *maneggiare,* meaning "to train horses." But not long after *manage* was introduced in England the word came to be applied to the military, meaning to handle weapons as well as horses and then to conduct a war. By the late 16th century it had assumed its current meaning.

Man alive!   An exclamation expressing anger, disappointment, amazement, or excitement, *man alive!* was first recorded in England in 1829, according to Partridge. Today *Man!* is more commonly heard, as is *Man oh man!*

mañana.   The Spanish word for tomorrow or sometime in the future. The *land* or *kingdom of mañana* was once a common American term used to mean a place where time was often disregarded, a land of postponement, and often applied to Mexico.

man bites dog.   "If a dog bites a man," editors used to instruct cub reporters, "that's an ordinary occurrence. But when a man bites a dog, that's *news.*" The inspiration for both the advice and the saying *man bites dog* can be traced back to Oliver Goldsmith's poem "Elegy on the Death of a Mad Dog" (1757), about a dog that "went mad and bit a man," which concludes with the lines:

> The man recover'd of the bite,
> The dog it was that died.

According to Partridge, this touching poem passed into folklore in a number of versions, possibly including a funny one where a man *did* bite a dog, finally illustrating the journalistic advice.

mandarin orange.   This fruit either takes its name from the orange, flowing robes of Chinese mandarin officials or from the superiority implied in the title "mandarin." The word is first recorded in an 1816 botanical treatise.

man doesn't get his hands out of the tar by becoming second mate.   During the age of sail only the *first* mate was exempted from the dirty work of sticking his hands into the tar bucket for tarring the rigging. Hence this British expression, which probably originated in the 18th century, is used colloquially to indicate that responsibilities don't end with promotion.

mandrake.   The "magical" mandrake (which, incidentally, gave its name to the old comic book hero Mandrake the Magician) was at first known as the "mandragora," because its root uncannily resembles a miniature man, and it was as magical and awe-inspiring as a dragon. But in medieval times the word for dragon was *drake*, so the plant became known as "mandrake." Like ginseng roots, and even peony roots to some extent, the roots of the mandrake were associated with many fantastic beliefs. One claimed they were an aphrodisiac (especially if shaped like a woman), another held that they caused barrenness in women and yet another claimed they could cure any illness. Many people believed that mandrake would shriek like a human being when uprooted and that a person should not touch the roots when pulling them up. To avoid the latter, a dog was actually tied to the plant to tug it out of the ground.

man for breakfast.   Lawlessness often went unpunished in the American West and people reading their morning newspapers had their *man for breakfast*, or murder, every day. The expression persisted from the late 19th century well into the 20th century.

man Friday; girl Friday.   The cheerful, hardworking companion of Robinson Crusoe in the 1719 novel of that title by Daniel Defoe gives his name to both *man Friday*, "a male general helper," and his modern-day female counterpart. *Girl Friday* is more often *gal Friday* today. All of these expressions can now be considered demeaning.

Manglish.   A combination of Malay and English words, or mangled English usage by Malaysians, is sometimes called Manglish. An example of the latter is "My wife, she got no patience one." ("My wife has no patience.").

mango.   The mango is one of the most important of tropical fruits. Mango varieties number in the hundreds. Some of the notable dessert mangoes are the Alphonse of Bombay, the Ferdandin of Goa and the Kimayuddin of South India. The delectable fruit, whose name derives from the Portuguese *manga*, taken from its Malayan name, or from the Chinese *man-guoh*, meaning hair-fruit, is grown in the American South, but these varieties can't be compared to tropical ones in taste. One Indian poet described mangoes as "sealed jars of paradisical honey"; the Buddha was given a grove of them so that he could sit in the shade and meditate; and a Hindu god, Subramanya, renounced the world because he couldn't obtain a mango he desired. The mango isn't a difficult fruit to eat once you get the hang of cutting the pulp away from its large central seed, but it might be better to eat it in a bathtub to avoid the explosion of juice that is common to novices. The nutritious

mango tastes something like a peach, but the comparison is wholly inadequate. An attractive bright yellow and red fruit, it hangs like a pendulum from its long stem. A building in Angkor that dates to A.D. 961 bears the following quotation under one of its most beautiful female figures: "Drawn by the flower of its glory to the fruit of the beauty of the mango tree of her body . . . the eye of man could nevermore tear itself away."

man-hands.   Hands that are large or unfeminine. The term is used to describe a beautiful woman whose overly masculine hands are her only flaw: "She's gorgeous except for those man-hands of hers." Said to be coined on the television series *Seinfeld*.

Manhattan; Manhattanization.   Since 1898 *Manhattan* has been the name of New York's central borough, and has always been a synonym for New York City itself. From the Manhattan Indians, indirectly, we also have the *Manhattan cocktail*, made with whiskey, sweet vermouth, and bitters, first mixed about 1890; *Manhattan clam chowder*, made with tomatoes, unlike the traditional New England milk clam chowder; and *Manhattan Project*, the code name for the project that developed the first atomic bomb. *Manhattanization* is a word that seems to have originated only recently. In the 1971 fall elections, San Francisco residents were urged to vote for an amendment halting the construction of tall buildings to avoid the Manhattanization of San Francisco.

Manhattan clam chowder.   *See* CHOWDER.

Manichean.   The Persian prophet Manes (ca. A.D. 216–276) considered himself a successor to Zoroaster, Buddha, and Jesus, sent into a darkening world to restore light. Zoroastrian priests saw to it that he was banished from Persia. Wandering widely, he spread his new religion (Manicheism) throughout the Roman Empire and as far off as India. However, when he returned to Persia, he was flayed to death or crucified—history is unclear. Manicheism, however, was a major religion in the Orient for over a thousand years and remained an influence on other religions into the 13th century.

manifest destiny.   The 19th-century belief or doctrine that it was the divine destiny of the United States to expand its territory over the whole of North America. An 1845 editorial by John L. O'Sullivan supporting the U.S. annexation of Texas was the first to use the term: "[It is] our manifest destiny to overspread the continent allotted by Providence for the free development of our yearly multiplying millions."

man in the gray flannel suit.   *The man in the gray flannel suit* remains a synonym for a conformist corporation man, although dress styles have changed considerably in the business world since Sloan Wilson coined the phrase in his novel *The Man in the Gray Flannel Suit* (1957).

man in the street; man of the cars.   The "ordinary" or "average" person. The first term is recorded in 1831, when British statesman Charles Greville refers to it as a racing term in his diary. A similar 19th-century American phrase was *man of the cars*, referring to the streetcars of the time.

manioc.   A starch food similar to the potato, tropical manioc is the nutritious tuberous root of the cassava plant that is usually prepared boiled but is also used as a bread flour and for tapioca. *Manioc* derives from the Tupi Indian name for the root, *manioca*. It has a reputation as an aphrodisiac—like a thousand other foods.

man is a wolf to man.   Both *Bartlett's* and *The Oxford Dictionary of Quotations* attribute this expression, in a slightly different form, to Bartolomeo Vanzetti in his eloquent last speech to the Massachusetts court trying him and Nicola Sacco on charges of robbery and murder in 1927. But the expression is much, much older, dating, back at least to the Roman playwright Plautus in his *Asimaria*. In 1577 a British author wrote: "Lyons doo not one encounter another, the Serpent stingeth no Serpent: but Man is a Woolfe to Man." The expression was afterward used by many writers, including Cowper.

Manitoba.   The Canadian province Manitoba is named for God, or Manitou, the Great Spirit of the Algonquins.

manniporchia.   Curiously, only in northern Maryland does this word, deriving from the Greek *mania a potu*, (craziness from drink) mean the D.T.'s. (delirium tremens). If anyone knows why, I haven't been able to find that person, in print or in person.

man of few words.   Shakespeare wrote that "men of few words are the best men." This expression for a laconic, taciturn person who is often "a man of action" was born several centuries before the Bard, however, being first recorded in about 1450.

man of letters.   First attested in English in 1645, *man of letters* may come from the French *homme de lettres*. Originally the term meant "a scholar, a man of learning," but today it is mostly applied to authors, critics, or literary scholars.

man of men.   *A man of men* or *a man among men* means an excellent man, the kind one encounters once or twice in a lifetime, if at all. Christopher Marlowe first recorded the term in 1594, and Shakespeare, the writer of writers, used it not long after.

man of straw; straw man.   A man made of straw would certainly be one without a heart or conscience, so that this expression is apt for "an unscrupulous person who will do anything for gain." However, the words may refer to real "straw men," who in the past loitered near English courts with a straw in one of their shoes—this indicating that they would be willing to give false testimony or swear to anything in court for enough money.

man of Sumter.   General P. G. T. Beauregard (1818–93) is known as *the man of Sumter* in American history because he headed the forces that bombarded Fort Sumter, South Carolina on April 12, 1861 to begin the Civil War. His troops called him "Old Borey" or "Peter."

man of the cloth.   It wasn't until the 17th century that *man of the cloth* was applied to a clergyman of any faith. Until then the term had meant anyone wearing any uniform in his work.

man of the Revolution.   The patriot called the man of the Revolution in American history isn't George Washington, as one might suspect. Samuel Adams has the honor "because of the leading part he played in bringing about the War of Independence."

man on the horse.   We know that this expression meaning "the person in authority or in charge" is an Americanism, but it is first recorded in England. In 1887 a British newspaper writer noted: "The man on the horse . . . to use the picturesque American phrase, is not now Lord Salisbury." No doubt the expression dates back at least 20 years earlier, perhaps to Civil War days.

man proposes, God disposes.   This universal proverb has its roots in Proverbs 16:9: "A man's heart deviseth his way: but the Lord directeth his steps." The words are proverbial in Hebrew, Greek, Latin, English (since at least the 15th century), and many other languages.

mansard.   This type of roof, unlike the conventional peaked shape, has a double, almost vertical, slope on each side, with the upper part almost flat. *Mansard* refers to the roof and the high room under it, both designed by Nicolas-François Mansart (1598–1666), a French architect of the Renaissance who is generally known as François Mansard. The roof he devised allows for high-ceilinged attics and was widely adopted by Victorian architects. Mansard's great Church of Val-de-Grâce, Paris, is said to have influenced Christopher Wren's plan for London's St. Paul's Cathedral. One of the most influential architects of his time, his pure classical designs have been an inspiration to others for centuries. Mansart, the son of a carpenter to the king, was chosen to design the Louvre, but refused to allow his design to be altered during construction, and so the Italian Bertini replaced him. His nephew Jules Hardouin-Mansart designed the magnificent Hall of Mirrors at the Palace of Versailles, the Hôtel des Invalides (which houses Napoleon's tomb), and the Place Vendôme, among other architectural masterpieces. One reason the mansard roof was so popular was taxes, writes my correspondent Eric Halsey: "There was a stiff tax on buildings higher than 6 stories, and the mansard roof allowed the addition of one, two, or three additional floors that officially counted as attic space."

mansei!   The Korean equivalent of Japanese BANZAI. The word was shouted in the charges that the North Koreans made against American and U.N. forces during the Korean conflict. *See* THE FORGOTTEN WAR; KAMIKAZE.

manticore.   The manticore, a vampiric, man-eating monster of ancient times, takes its name from the Persian *martya*, "man," and *xvar*, "to eat." The mythical monster is first mentioned by the Greek physician Ktesias in the 5th century B.C. It was usually represented as a monster the size of a horse with the body and claws of a lion, but it was depicted in many ways, sometimes with the head of a man and the breasts of a woman.

Mantuan Swan.   *See* SWAN SONG.

manufacture.   Mass-produced products that are *manufactured* on assembly lines in the world's factories would be made by hand if we took the word's meaning literally. For *manufacture* derives from the Latin *manu*, "by hand," and *factura*, "a making," from which our word *factory* also derives.

manure. *Manure* originally meant "to work by hand," to do manual labor, especially to work the soil by manual labor, deriving from the Old French verb *manouvrer*, meaning the same. The English verb yielded the noun *manuere*, which at first meant "the action of cultivating the soil" and was extended to include the dung put into the soil when a euphemism was wanted for "dung."

the man who broke the bank at Monte Carlo. Fabled in story and song is the man behind this phrase, Englishman Joseph Hobson Jagger, who in 1886 noticed that one of the roulette wheels at Monte Carlo wasn't functioning properly and bet on numbers that were appearing more often than they should have in mathematical probability. Jagger won more than 2 million francs in one week and became world famous.

man will prevail. People often look for the source of these words but fail to find it because the words are only part of the quotation. The full quote is "I believe that man will not only endure, but prevail," and it is from William Faulkner's acceptance speech when he won the 1950 Nobel Prize in literature. Faulkner's work largely celebrates those who endure, including the old black servant Dilsey (in *The Sound and The Fury*), whose great strength counterpoints the weak, disintegrating family she serves.

man without a country. Contrary to what many people have believed since grade school, Edward Everett Hale's famous story "The Man Without a Country" is fictional. Only the name of the main character is real. In the story Lt. Philip Nolan cries out, "Damn the United States! I wish I may never hear of the United States again!" and is of course sentenced to sail the seas all his life on a Navy ship without ever hearing his country's name again. Nothing like this ever happened to the real Philip Nolan, an adventurer whose career Hale used as background. Hale later regretted using the man's name and wrote a book called *Philip Nolan's Friends* (1876), "to repair my fault, and to recall to memory a brave man," as he put it.

man works from sun to sun, but woman's work is never done. An old American proverb that dates back to life on the farm two centuries ago.

many a fight is lost (left) in bed. An adage that probably dates back, in one form or another, to the earliest days of professional boxing but is rarely recorded in any dictionary. It advises that a fighter, or any athlete, who engages in sex the night before or close to a fight weakens himself and endangers his chance of winning. Athletes in many sports are divided on this. Muhammad Ali, for example, said he didn't believe it, while other fighters and trainers have endorsed the advice. A good marathon runner told me thinking of sex inspired him onward.

many happy returns. Up until the 19th century this was a New Year's Day and even April Fools' Day greeting as well as the birthday greeting that it exclusively is today. What the words wish, of course, is that the happy day returns again many times, not the hope that one will get many "returns," or birthday presents, as some children think.

many small potatoes and few in a hill. New Englanders, especially Mainers, use this expression for something or somebody of small consequence. It dates back about a century.

Maoism. A name given to the Chinese brand of communism, that is, communism adapted to the special needs of China. The term remembers Mao Tse-tung, who dominated communist politics from the outbreak of the revolution until his death in 1976 at 82 and was a virtual dictator in his later years. Collections of his sayings (such as "Engage in no battle you are not sure of winning") have sold hundreds of millions of copies in Chinese. Similarly, *Castroism*, after Cuban revolutionary Fidel Castro (b. 1927), whose forces overthrew the Fulgencio Batista regime in 1959, describes Cuban communist political and economic principles.

Maori words in English. Maori has contributed several words to the English language, including kiwi and mako.

maple-head. Eponymous words and phrases often derive from the names of obscure people. This unusual old term from the Ozarks means "a very small head." It is said to celebrate a pioneer family named Maple noted for their small heads. *See* BOBBIT.

maple syrup; maple sugar. "There can't be a remedy better for fortifying the stomach" than maple sugar, a pioneer wrote in 1705. Maple sugar, boiled from maple syrup and the only sugar the first settlers had, has a long history that dates from the time American pioneers learned how to make it from the Indians. The same, of course, applies to maple syrup, another maple-tree product Americans are still familiar with, but there were also maple-derived products like maple water, maple vinegar, maple molasses, maple wax, maple beer, and even maple wine.

maquiladora city. Cities in Mexico on the U.S. border that have maquiladora programs set up by the Mexican government. Under these programs, parts are shipped by, say, an American manufacturer in El Paso to a company in the nearby Mexican city of Juárez that assembles the parts, the finished products exported back to the United States duty free except for the value added in Mexico. The idea was born in about 1964. *Maquiladora* derives from the Spanish *maquila* (the portion received by a miller for milling someone's grain).

marathon. This grueling 26-mile, 385-yard footrace honors a peerless runner but is named after a prosaic vegetable. It recalls the historic battle of Marathon. *Marathon* means "field of fennel" in Greek, the word deriving from the Greek *marathon*, a fennel plant. In 490 B.C. on the great plain of Marathon covered with this yellow-flowered plant, 20,000 invading Persians tried to establish a beachhead and defeat the armies of the Greek city states before launching an assault on Athens itself. Led by General Datis, the Persians were under the orders of King Darius to enslave Athens and "bring the slaves into his presence." Legend has it that the Greek soldier Pheidippides, a champion of the old Olympic games and the best runner in Greece, was dispatched from Athens to Sparta to announce the arrival of the invading Persians at Marathon and seek a promise of help. Pheidippides covered the distance of 150 miles over mountain trails in two days, only to find that the Spartans were unwilling to send help until after the conclusion of an ongoing religious festival. He then ran back to join his forces in the defense of Athens. Although the bronze-clad Greeks were outnumbered two to one, their commander, Miltiades, employed revolutionary tactics to defeat the Persians on the marshy plain near Marathon village. Another story has Pheidippides (or another runner) racing 22 or 23 miles to Athens from Marathon to announce that the Greeks had won, his dying words, "Greetings! We win!" The standard marathon distance today was set in 1896, the distance from London's Windsor Castle to the stadium where the Olympic games were held. *See* FENNEL.

Marcel wave; marcelling. Every hairdresser might wish to have the success Marcel Grateau had with his curling iron. In 1875, when only 23, this Frenchman invented marcelling, a process that makes soft, continuous waves in the hair. The Marcel wave became so popular with Parisian women, and women everywhere, that Marcel Grateau made a fortune and was able to retire before turning 30. He lived a long life of luxury in an elegant chateau, and just before his death in 1936, aged 84, France's hairdressers held a week-long celebration honoring him and his contribution to their craft.

March. When spring came in days of old the Romans apparently thought it was a better time to make war than love. Anyway, they named the month, then the first month of the new year, for Mars, the god of war, perhaps in the hope that he would help them in their spring campaigns.

Marco Milione. As everyone knows who has seen or read Eugene O'Neill's play *Marco Millions* (1928), this is the name Italians gave to Marco Polo (ca. 1254–ca. 1324) and his many wonderful travel tales of China and the court of Kublai Khan, among other colorful places. His fellow Venetians also called him *Il Milione*, "the million." The name recalls the millions of wonders and riches he discovered.

Marconigram. See WIRELESS.

Mardi Gras. *Mardi Gras*, literally "fat Tuesday" in French, takes its name from the fat ox *(boeuf gras)* paraded through Parisian streets in ancient times by mock priests at the head of the carnival procession on the day before the beginning of Lent. The fat ox was a reminder of the abstinence from meat during the coming Lenten season of fasting and prayer. Called Shrove Tuesday in England, and previously Pancake Tuesday because pancakes were traditionally served on the day before Ash Wednesday, the festival of Mardi Gras may have its origins in the old Roman fertility festival of Lupercalia once held at the same time of the year.

Marenisco, Michigan. Another unusual place name, *Marenisco*, Michigan, was coined from the first syllables of the *four* names of its first woman settler: *Ma*ry *Re*lief *Ni*les *Sco*tt.

margarine. The Latin *margarita*, "pearl," is the ancestor of *margarine*, which, before dyes were commonly added, was a white, pearl-like substance extracted from hog's lard. *Oleomargarine* (from the Latin *oleum*, "oil," plus *margarine*) was coined first, in 1854, by the French chemist Marcellin Berthelot, and shortened to *margarine* in the U.S. by 1873.

marigold. There are several genera whose flowers are called marigold; the chief ones are *Tagetes*, which includes among its 30 species the French and African marigolds, and *Calendula*, a genus that counts the popular pot marigold among its 20 species. The pot marigold was found in the Holy Land by the early Crusaders and brought back to Europe, where it was probably named after the Virgin Mary and the color gold, being called "Mary's gold" or "Marygold" before it became *marigold*. Linnaeus gave the pot marigold its scientific designation, *Calendula officinalis*, but he merely used a name that had been given to the plant centuries before. The herbalist Gerard remarks that the name *Calendula* was bestowed upon the plant because it supposedly bloomed regularly "in the calends" or first days of almost every month (*calends* mean the first of the Roman month). *Calendula officianalis* differs from the so-called French and African species *(Tagetes)* mainly because its leaves are not strong-smelling. But the flowers of the *Tagetes* genus, also herbs, do resemble the pot marigold, so early American settlers gave them the same name. *Tagetes* possibly honors the Etruscan god Tages, though this is not certain. All flowers of the genus are native from North Mexico to the Argentine.

marijuana. *Cannabis sativa* goes by some 200 names in practically every language throughout the world, including pot, grass, seed, weed, tea, dope, reefers, joints, and Texas tea. But the hemp plant's crushed leaves, flowers, and, sometimes, twigs, are best known as marijuana. The word comes from the Spanish prenomens Maria and Juana, translating as Maryjane, and no one knows why. The Chinese used *Cannabis* at least 5,000 years ago, and George Washington is said to have grown it at Mount Vernon—for the rope produced from the hemp. One hundred years ago, according to the National Institute of Mental Health, "extracts of *Cannabis* were as commonly used for medicinal purposes in the United States as aspirin today."

marina. *Marina*, from the Italian *marina* meaning the same, refers to a harbor or boat basin used primarily for small ships such as private yachts and speedboats. The word was recorded as early as 1795, but it wasn't until after World War II that it became commonly used. Today thousands of marinas serve boat owners. Some are small basins mooring 50 boats, while others hold 100 times that many.

marine. The term *marine* for a type of soldier didn't originate with the U.S. Marines but dates back to the early 17th century when the word (from the Latin *marinus*, "of the sea") was used in England to describe specially trained soldiers serving on British warships.

Marinism. Il Cavaliere Marino, as the pompous Neapolitan poet Giambattista Marino (1569–1625) was called, headed the *seicento* school of Italian literature, which became noted for its flamboyance and bad taste. Poems like his 45,000-line *Adone* show brilliant mastery of technique but were intended to dazzle the reader at any cost, their extravagance leading to his name standing for any florid, bombastic style, pages full of sound but signifying nothing. Marino, or Marini, had his trouble with censors, too. His satirical works were not appreciated by his satirized patrons, and he was forced to leave Italy, taking refuge in Paris for eight years before he could return home safely.

marivaudage.   Important advances in the development of the novel were made by French writer Pierre Carlet de Chamblain de Marivaux (1688–1763), who is undeserving of his fate at the hands of the dictionaries. *Marivaudage*, however, means an affected, overstrained style, as exemplified by the witty bantering of lovers in his two unfinished novels and 30 plays. Marivaux's subtle, graceful works are mostly excellent psychological studies of middle-class psychology and led a contemporary to remark that his characters not only tell each other and the reader everything they have thought, but everything that they would like to persuade themselves that they have thought. *Marivaudage* has also been described as "the metaphysics of love making." The author was much admired in his own time, though not by Voltaire, whose work he criticized, and it is said that Madame de Pompadour secretly provided him with a large pension.

marjoram.   Marjoram is any of several mints, including sweet marjoram and pet marjoram. The old saying *as a pig loves marjoram* (that is, not at all) is still heard occasionally. *Marjoram* is an alteration of the Latin *amaracus* for the herb.

Mark Antony's wig.   Cleopatra reputedly gave the virile but balding Mark Antony a wig made of her pubic hairs, and Mark Antony's wig was later brought back to Rome. According to the old story, this wig was worn by many Roman emperors on "revel evenings" and finally presented to the pope by Constantine in 328. The papal treasures supposedly included a sporran of pubic hair that the queen of Sheba had lost to Solomon in a riddling contest, and this was allegedly added to the wig and presented to England's licentious Charles II by Pope Clement X as part of an attempt to convert his kingdom to Catholicism. Charles, it is said, added pubic hairs plucked from his mistresses before he tired of plucking and gave the wig to the earl of Moray, who donated it to his club of ribald rakehells called the Ancient and Most Puisant Order of the Beggar's Benison and Merryland. There the head of the order wore the wig at all ceremonies, and initiates were required to augment it with pubic hairs of their wives or mistresses. Mark Antony's wig was last heard of when some members of the order reportedly absconded with it in 1775 and formed a new group called The Wig Club. *See* CLEOPATRA'S PEARL.

market.   The Latin word *mercari*, "to trade," altered to *markatte* and finally *market*, came to be applied, by the 12th century, to the place where the trading occurred. The word may possibly have been used 300 to 400 years before that.

mark of Cain.   The *mark of Cain* is not described in the Bible, which simply says in Gen. 4:15: "And the Lord put a mark on Cain . . ." The mark was not made to identify Cain as a murderer, but to warn the world that Cain was condemned to be forever "a fugitive and a vagabond . . . in the earth," *i.e.*, that it was forbidden to kill him. Cain, the first born of Adam and Eve, and the first biblical murderer, through jealousy slew his brother Abel, and lied to the Lord that he did not know his whereabouts ("I know not: Am I my brother's keeper?"). The curse of Cain refers to the legend that he was never to die or reach home again. Why Cain's hair (or Judas Iscariot's) is traditionally represented as reddish yellow, or *Cain-colored*, remains a mystery. Cain and Judas were usually depicted with such hair and beards in ancient tapestries, but not necessarily because their acts suggested murder or the shedding of blood. The term probably has as much to do with yellow being the traditional color used to depict jealousy and betrayal.

mark time.   First mention of the military parade ground term *to mark time* is in a British Army manual *Regulations for the Instruction of the Cavalry* (1833). "On the word 'mark time,' " the manual says, "marching is continued without gaining any ground." Naturally the process of marking time suggested any action that fills time but doesn't lead to progress, and not long after its first military use the phrase was used as a metaphor for just that.

mark twain.   *Mark twain!* means "mark two fathoms (12 feet) deep" and was called out when riverboat leadsmen sounded the river with weighted line. It is well known that former riverboat pilot Samuel Langhorne Clemens took his pen name Mark Twain from the leadsman's call *mark twain!*

marmalade.   Though made today of oranges and lemons, the conserve called marmalade takes its name from the Latin *melimelum* or "honey apple," which was some variety of apple grafted on quince stock. The Latin for "honey apple" became the Portuguese word for "quince," and the first marmalades recorded, in the early 16th century, were made of quinces and brought to England from Portugal. But over the centuries there have been plum, cherry, apple, and even date marmalades as well. "Natural marmalade" is the fruit of the marmalade tree (*Lucuma mammosa*).

maroon; marooned.   Black people who lived in the distant forests of Dutch Guiana (now Suriname) and the West Indies were often runaway slaves who had found their freedom there. They were called *marroons*, French for "runaway black slaves," a term first recorded in 1666. Because they lived in the wilderness their name came to mean "to be lost in the wilds," and soon after began to be used to describe someone stranded (marooned) on an island.

marrow.   *Marrow* is a British term that is sometimes used in America. It means "a long, green squash," and has its origins in the use of *marrow* as the term for the pulp of a fruit, which dates back to at least the 10th century. Squash was often called marrow-squash in 18th-century America.

Marrowsky.   SPOONERISMS, the unintentional shifting of sounds at the beginnings of words (for example, "It is customary to kiss the bride" becomes "It is kisstomary to cuss the bride"), were first called marrowskis, a name said to derive from the name of Polish count Joseph Boruwlaski, who suffered the same affliction as Reverend Spooner. The word is first recorded in 1863 and soon after intentional marrowskis became the basis for a kind of slang called marrowsky language. Metathesis, the process of shifting letters or sounds, is responsible for a number of English words, including *dirt*, which was earlier *drit*.

marsala.   Italy's best-known fortified wine, with its molasses-like flavor, takes its name from Marsala, the town on Sicily's west coast where it is made.

Marseillaise.   First entitled "War Song for the Rhine Army," the French national anthem is called "the Marseillaise" because it was sung with great spirit by soldiers from Marseilles while advancing on the Tuileries on August 10, 1792. The song was actually written by a royalist army officer, not a revolutionary—Captain Claude Joseph Rouget de Lisle—who wrote it as a marching song. *See* THE INTERNATIONALE.

marsh; marsh gas.   *Marsh* derives from the Middle English *mershe*, which comes from the Old English *mersc*. Marshes, often a transition between water and land, generally contain grasses, sedges, cattails, and rushes, as well as methane gas, often called "marsh gas" or "swamp gas," resulting from the decomposition of organic matter. Salt marshes, composed of Spartina grasses, are far more productive than wheat or hay fields, producing up to 10 tons of organic material per acre, compared to four tons produced by an acre of hay and two tons produced by an acre of wheat. Several studies have estimated the following average yearly values per acre of marsh: $100 in commercial and sports fisheries by-products; $630 in aquaculture potential, such as the harvesting of oysters; $2,500 in tertiary waste treatment potential, the marsh's capability for removal of phosphorus, nitrogen, and sulphur, compared with the cost of equivalent treatment by man-made facilities; and $4,100 in life-support value, the marsh's ability to absorb carbon dioxide, produce oxygen, support waterfowl and other animals, and protect cities and beaches from the damaging effects of storms. That's $7,330 an acre, compared to the $107 yield-per-acre figure for an acre of corn.

marshal; Marshall Plan.   The German *marahscalc*, meaning "servant in charge of the mares," became *maréchal* in French and *marshal* in English, having been adopted by the French as the title for a high-ranking general of armies when cavalry became important in warfare as early as the fifth century. Though never used in the American military, it is said that *marshal* was being considered for the one rank above four-star general during World War II. It didn't sound right with the name of the man selected for the job, however, and instead of being made Marshal Marshall, George Catlett Marshall was named General of the Armies Marshall. As Secretary of State, General Marshall later proposed the broad European Recovery Plan aiding Europe after the war, the plan popularly named the Marshall Plan in his honor.

Martha.   St. Martha is the patron saint of housewives, and a Martha is a woman somewhat too devoted to her domestic duties. Both references are to the New Testament Martha, the sister of Mary and Lazarus, who, unlike Mary, was preoccupied with her household duties. Though Martha, encumbered with her duties and mildly rebuked by Jesus, represents the active as opposed to the contemplative life, she is later said to have become a missionary in Gaul. St. Martha (her feast day is July 29) is traditionally represented in a plain housedress, a bunch of keys hanging from her belt, and a ladle in her hand. The dragon pictured with her is the fearsome Tarasque, which legend tells us she slew at Aix en Provence while it ravaged Marseilles. Active she certainly was.

Martha's Vineyard.   Possibly discovered by Leif Eriksson in the 11th century, Martha's Vineyard, an island about five miles off Massachusetts's southeast coast, was once an important center for whaling and fishing. The Indians called the island Noe-pe, "Amid the Waters," while the Norsemen named it Staumey, "Isle of Currents." It was christened Martin's Vineyard by English navigator Bartholomew Gosnold in 1602, apparently for no reason in particular. After a century it took the name *Martha's Vineyard*, probably because its name was confused with that of a little neighboring island to the southeast called Martha's Vineyard that had also been named by Gosnold. That little island is now called No Man's Land, after an Indian named Tequenoman.

Martian canals.   The myth of artificial canals on Mars is no longer believed by many people, after recent space explorations. In any case, the search by astronomers for life on Mars in years past was probably inspired by a linguistic accident. When in 1877 the astronomer Giovanni Virginio Schiaparelli observed faint lines on Mars through the telescope he called them *canali*, Italian for "channels." *Canali* was erroneously translated into English as *canals*, "carrying with it a strong connotation of being man-made, which *canali* does not."

Martin drunk.   *See* ST. MARTIN'S DAY.

martinet.   Colonel Martinet, the strict disciplinarian from whose name the term *martinet* originated, was "accidentally" killed by his own troops while leading an assault at the siege of Duisberg in 1672. Jean Martinet, sometimes called the marquis de Martinet, had been a lieutenant colonel of the king's regiment of foot and inspector general of infantry in the army of France's Louis XIV. The Grand Monarch, then only 22, and his brilliant 19-year-old war minister the marquis de Louvois had formed a model standing army in 1660, replacing the old system where the state hired entire units for its army—a regiment, for example, being in the employ of its colonel and a company in the pay of its captain. But these old units had to be molded together into an efficient, homogeneous group and Colonel Martinet's exacting work with the Sun King's own Royal Regiment made him just the man for the job. As inspector general, Martinet was assigned the task of designing all drill systems for the new army and training its infantrymen to fight as a unit in battle. His methods, several of them named for him, were later copied by many European countries. In the process, however, his strict and tedious drills made Martinet's name synonymous with not only sharp military efficiency but stern spit-and-polish discipline inflicted by a goose-stepping stickler for details, who insists that his men carry out his rigid orders as if they were puppets. Today his name is applied to excessively severe soldiers and civilians alike. *See also* MARTINS.

martingale.   Residents of the town of Martigues in Provence, France once wore economical breeches with a strap belt. Some authorities think that these *chausses à la martingale* give us the word for the part of a harness used to keep down a horse's head, as well as part of the rigging of a ship. Other etymologists discount *Martingalo*, "an inhabitant of Martigues," and trace the word to the Spanish *almartaga*, "a rein or harness." How the reckless *martingale*—a betting system in which the stakes are doubled or raised even higher after each loss—derived from either the stingy *Martingalos* or a harness is anybody's guess.

martini.　H. L. Mencken traced the martini to 1899 and traces the cocktail's name from the Martini and Rossi firm, maker of a popular vermouth. Others say the drink originated with a now forgotten Italian or Spanish bartender named Martini. The dry martini is made, according to the classic recipe, by drinking a little vermouth, exhaling into the interior of a cocktail glass and filling it with gin—after you drink it, you'll forget that you forgot the olive. Mencken also mentions the *martini sandwich*, a dry martini between two glasses of beer, which he says "is favored by many American linguists." Novelist George V. Higgins called the martini "loud-mouth soup."

martins.　St. Martin gives his name to the small bluish black swallows called *martins* that begin to migrate southward from France and England at about the time of *St. Martin's Day* and return again in March, the Martian month. The martin was first called the *martinet* in France. Numerous martins occur all over the world, including the American purple martin, a bird valued by farmers because it eats harmful insects and drives away hawks and crows.

Martin varnish.　*See* COMA BENENICES.

martyr.　*Martyr* ultimately derives from the Greek word for "witness" and was applied as a designation of honor by early Christians to those who accepted the penalty of death rather than renounce their faith. But by the 14th century the word was being generally and even sarcastically used. The expression *a martyr to science*, one who loses his life through his devotion to science, seems to have been first applied to Claude-Louis, Comte Berthollet (1748–1822), who died trying to determine the effects of carbolic acid on the human body.

Marx Brothers.　The stage names of the famous family comedy team originated during its early vaudeville days. Groucho was named for the money pouch called a "grouch" that he carried for the act; Chico for the chicks he always chased; Gummo after the rubber boots he wore; Harpo for the harp he played; and Zeppo, it is said, after a trained monkey that once appeared on the same bill as the Marx Brothers.

Marxian.　After the German economist and revolutionary socialist Karl Marx (1818–83). Marx was a founder of the First International Workingmen's Association, but his most important contributions to history by far were the *Communist Manifesto* (1848), which he wrote with Friedrich Engels, and the enormously influential *Das Kapital* (1867). The dialectical materialism set forth in this last work has come to be known as Marxism, and a Marxist, depending on one's political inclinations, is either one favoring Marxian economic teachings or one who is economically doctrinaire and extremist.

mary.　In the Melanesian pidgin jargon of the southern Pacific the word *mary* means "a woman," as in "That fella him catch'm money belong mary." (That man took the woman's money.) Melanesian pidgin is also called Neo-Melanesian and *beche-de-mer*. Other examples of this pidgin include *long way big bit* (very far), *sing-sing* (a song or dance), *pigeon* (a bird of any kind), *finish altogether* (die), *belly* (any part of the body below the neck), and *gammon* (to lie). There are hundreds more. *See* PIDGIN ENGLISH; PIDGIN LANGUAGE.

Mary had a little lamb.

> Mary had a little lamb,
> 　Its fleece was white as snow
> And everywhere that Mary went
> 　The lamb was sure to go;
> He followed her to school one day,
> 　That was against the rule;
> It made the children laugh and play
> 　To see a lamb in school . . .

There seems to be no doubt that the Mary and little lamb in the well-known nursery rhyme were real, but there is some uncertainty about who wrote the poem. Sara Josepha Hale first published the 24-line verse over her initials in the September 1830 issue of *Juvenile Miscellany*. Over the years it became known that it was based on the true experiences of 11-year-old Mary Sawyer, who had a pet lamb that followed her to the schoolhouse at Redstone Hill in Boston one day in 1817. In fact, Mary Sawyer a half century later confirmed the story during a campaign to save the famous Old South Church of Boston from being torn down.

Maryland.　A popular but incorrect belief has it that *Maryland* was named for the Virgin Mary because it was originally settled by Catholics. The Old Line State actually bears the name of Henrietta Maria (1609–69), wife of England's King Charles I and daughter of France's Henry IV. When Maryland was settled under Lord Calvert in 1632 as a haven for persecuted Catholics, Henrietta Maria was a natural selection for its name, and in the original Latin charter the area is called *Terra Mariae*. It seems that Maryland was to be named for King Charles at first, but he already had the Carolinas named after him and suggested "Mariana," as a name honoring his queen. This was rejected by Lord Baltimore because it was the name of a Jesuit who had written against the monarchy and *Terra Mariae* was adopted instead. Maryland, one of the 13 original colonies, bears the name "Old Line State" because of the bravery of her soldiers—men of the line—during the Revolutionary War.

marzipan.　A confection made of almond paste and sugar molded in various forms. One sweet fable tells of a cook of 16th-century Brandenberg, Germany, named Franz Marzip, who is said to have invented marzipan for his physician employer. Other sources say that Oriental rulers had enjoyed the confection for centuries and that the crusaders brought it back to Europe in the shape of a coin of the time called a *marchpane* (which later became *marzipan*). In any case, Lubbeck, Germany is called "the world's marzipan capital" today, famous for its *Holstentors*, cuisine's most celebrated marzipan.

mascot.　*Mascots*, animals that are adopted as good luck symbols for sports teams, take their name from the French word *mascotte*, meaning "good luck charm." The word is first recorded in English in 1881 at about the time the French opera *La Mascotte* was being performed in Europe.

masher.   The first *mashers* may have been not men but Gypsy women who flirted with men. This may be the case if the word for a man who makes passes at women in public places comes from the Gypsy expression *masherava*, "to allure, entice with the eye." *Masher* could, however, derive from the standard English sense of *mash*, "to crush, pound, smash." *Mash* in the lewd sense is first recorded in America in 1860, *masher* in 1875.

mashie.   Golf's number 5 iron may take its (now rarely heard) name from the way unskilled golfers "mashed" a ball with it, or it may have resembled some Scottish kitchen utensil used to mash potatoes when the club was introduced in 1888. But more likely it derives from the French word for club, *massue*.

masochism.   A masochist derives sexual pleasure from having pain inflicted on himself, but, as with SADISM, the use of the term has broadened now to include pleasure derived from self-denial and from suffering in general. The word is taken from the name of Leopold von Sacher-Masoch (1835–95), an Austrian novelist whose characters dwelt lovingly on the sexual pleasure of pain, just as he did. A prolific, talented novelist who had published several scholarly histories and had once been a professional actor, Sacher-Masoch became a leading literary figure of his time. But he finally suffered a complete breakdown before turning 50, and his second wife committed him to an asylum after he tried to kill her on several occasions. In a fitting ending to his bizarre life, his wife officially announced that he had died, even mourning him, 10 years before his actual death in confinement. The pre-Freudian psychiatrist Richard Krafft-Ebing probably first used Sacher-Masoch's name to describe his ailment, recording *masochism* in 1893.

Mason-Dixon line.   Although Dixie wasn't named for the Mason-Dixon line, the latter term has come to be used as a figure of speech for an imaginary dividing line between North and South. The Mason-Dixon line has an interesting history. Originally the 244-mile boundary set between Pennsylvania and Maryland in 1763–67 by English surveyors Charles Mason and Jeremiah Dixon, it was extended six years later to include the southern boundary of Pennsylvania and Virginia. The line had been established by English courts to settle a territorial dispute between the Penns of Pennsylvania and the Calverts of Maryland, but the use of *Mason-Dixon line* in Congressional debates during the Missouri Compromise (1819–20) gave the expression wide currency as a dividing line between free and slave states. After the Civil War the term was retained as the boundary between North and South, especially as a demarcation line of customs and philosophy. Its existence probably did influence the popularity of the word DIXIE.

mason jar.   With the renewed interest in vegetable gardening and fresh, healthy foods that are raised for taste and not ease of shipping, the mason jar, used for home canning, is coming into prominence again. The wide-mouthed glass jars with either glass or metal screw tops were named for their inventor, New Yorker John Mason, who patented them in 1857.

massa.   This American term for "master," long used by slaves, could derive from the English "master," or from the West African *masam*, "chief," or it could be a blend of both. No one knows for sure.

Massachusetts.   "Place of the big hill" is the English translation of the Algonquian *Massachusetts*. The Bay State was admitted to the Union in 1788 as our sixth state and had been called the Massachusetts Bay Colony before then. It is now officially called the Commonwealth of Massachusetts.

massage.   *See* MATZO.

Massholes; foreigner.   A century ago many more rivalries and much more name-calling existed between states. The name-calling, at least, hasn't ended. Novelist Richard Russo, for example, notes in his fine *Empire Falls* (2001) that summer visitors to Maine from Massachusetts are locally called "Massholes," a memorable derogatory regionalism I can find in no other source. It sounds like a coinage typical of Mainers, who also call people from out of state "foreigners" and might call someone a "grasshole" for working too hard on his lawn.

massive retaliation.   *See* AGONIZING REAPPRAISAL.

the mass of men lead lives of quiet desperation.   Henry David Thoreau wrote this in the first essay of *Walden* (1854). More fully he wrote: "The mass of men lead lives of quiet desperation. What is called resignation is confirmed desperation . . ."

masterpiece.   Long before *masterpiece* became associated with the fine arts during the Renaissance, it meant the perfect piece of work that an apprentice under the English guild system had to make before he was recognized as a master. After he had served his apprenticeship and was able to make a piece worthy of a master, a masterpiece, he became a master himself and was no longer required to work under supervision.

mastic; masticate.   Mastic, the chewing gum discovered by Columbus in Santo Domingo, is an exudation obtained from the lentisk, or mastic shrub (*Pistacia lenticus*), cultivated mainly on the Mediterranean island of Chios. The resin, found in the lentisk's bark, speedily exudes when the bark is cut, hardening into oval tears the size of peas that are transparent and of a pale yellow or faint greenish tinge that darkens slowly with age. Mastic's primary use since ancient times has been as a masticatory to sweeten the breath and preserve the teeth and gums. People throughout southeastern Europe and the Near East have used it for this purpose, and Dioscorides, the great Greek physician and botanist of the first century, refers to mastic's curative powers in his *De Materia Medica*. In fact, mastic goes so far back in history that it may have constituted the Greek word *mastichon*, "to chew," which is the root of the English word *masticate*. Today a chewing gum made with mastic and beeswax is still enjoyed by many Greeks and Middle Easterners.

Mata Hari.   Behind the patina of the pseudonym *Mata Hari* ("Eye of the Dawn") is a rather prosaic Dutch name. Margaretha Geertruida Zelle (1876–1917) used *Mata Hari* as both her stage name and *nom de guerre* when she chose to become a spy for the Germans before World War I. Acclaimed throughout Europe for her interpretations of naked Indonesian dances, she met many men in high places, including German officials in Berlin who recruited her as a spy in 1907. During World War I, her dancing was the rage of Paris and she became intimate with top Allied officers, who confided military secrets to her. Mata Hari, who slept with literally hundreds, thrived on the deceit of espionage, but she was eventually betrayed to the French secret service by another German agent, Captain Walther Wilhelm Canaris, later to become head of the German secret service in World War II. Her trial was the most publicized of the many espionage trials held during the war, and her name become synonymous with a glamorous female spy and femme fatale. She was convicted by a French court-martial and executed by a firing squad.

mate.   This word for buddy, chum, comrade, pal, or partner dates back to the late 14th century in England and is still common there. It has, however, become a hallmark of Australian speech. The Aussies even apply *mate* to people thay barely know, while Americans rarely use the word except as a synonym for a spouse. *Matey* in both Australian and British English means very friendly: "They've been matey now for a year or so."

matinee idol.   This term for a star isn't heard nearly so much today as it was 50 years ago. It refers to the matinee (afternoon) performances of plays and films, when many women were present in the audience, some of whom idolized certain actors. *Matinee*, a French word deriving ultimately from the French for "morning," was first recorded in English in 1848 by the English novelist William Makepeace Thackeray. RUDOLPH VALENTINO was probably the most famous matinee idol. Though he was an Irishman with "an incurable Irish brogue" and had played in Dublin and London before sailing for America, the handsome actor John Henry (1738–94) has often been called "America's First Matinee Idol" (even though there were no matinees in his day). Henry did so well acting and producing that he could afford his own coach for transit, a rarity among the thespians of his time, but he tried to avoid ostentation by having the words THIS OR THESE painted on the coach under a picture of two crutches. The coach was necessary, he explained to his detractors, because gout had crippled him and he would have to walk on crutches if he didn't ride. Henry was possibly the first American actor involved in a sex scandal. After his first wife was lost at sea, he lived for some time with her sister, by whom he had a child, but abandoned her to marry still another of his departed wife's sisters. When his star faded in America, he sailed back to Ireland but died of a heart attack in passage; his new wife went insane over her loss and died a year later. *See* STAR.

mattress.   In medieval times Arabs often slept on plush cushions thrown on the floor. The Arabic word *matrah*, "the place where something is thrown," came to mean a cushion or mat in Arabic and eventually passed into English as *materas*, the ancestor of our word *mattress*, when the Crusaders brought this custom of sleeping on cushions home to Europe.

matzo.   This unleavened bread in the form of large, square corrugated crackers takes its name from the Hebrew-Arabic *massah*, "to touch, handle, squeeze," in reference to making the bread. *Matzo* thus has the same root as "massage."

maudlin.   Christ exorcised Mary Magdalene of evil spirits, and *Magdalene* has become a synonym for a reformed prostitute. However, in classical paintings and old folk plays, based on the Bible stories relating to her, Mary was often shown with eyes red and swollen, disheveled and weeping endlessly for her sins. Her name—pronounced *maudlin*, just as Oxford's Magdalene College is pronounced today—was applied by the British, with their mistrust of easy emotion, to the excessive, tearful sentimentality that is often associated with drunkenness. In fact, the fifth stage of drunkenness in Thomas Nashe's analysis of intoxication presents us with the "maudlin drunk," and *maudle*, "to talk in a drunken way," comes from this use of the word. But it should be added that biblical scholars cannot agree on the identity of Mary Magdalene. The Mary of Magdala who was the first witness to the Resurrection may not have been the Mary who washed Christ's feet with her tears, wiped them with "the hairs of her head," and whom Christ forgave because "she loved much." Legend, however, combines the three Marys figuring in Christ's ministry into one.

Maundy Thursday.   The day before Good Friday. *Maundy Thursday* takes its name from Christ's "new commandment" beginning *Mandatum novum do vobis*, "I give unto you" (John 13:34), with which the ceremony of the washing of the feet is initiated. The ceremony commemorates Christ washing the feet of his disciples on Holy Thursday.

Mauser.   The original Mauser, and subsequent improved models, were used by the German army for many years following the rifle's introduction in 1871. Its inventors were Peter Paul Mauser (1838–1914) and his older brother Wilhelm (1834–82), the younger Mauser also inventing the Mauser magazine rifle in 1897.

mausoleum.   Queen Artemisia of Caria was so grief-stricken when her husband, King Mausolus, died in 353 B.C. that she collected his ashes and mixed a portion of them with her daily drink until she died of inconsolable sorrow three years later. But she had ordered a sepulchral monument erected to her husband's memory in the Carian capital of Halicarnassus that became one of the Seven Wonders of the World. Built on a base of about 230 × 250 feet and towering over 100 feet high, the tomb of Mausolus (or more correctly Maussollus) wasn't completed until after Artemisia's own death, in 350 B.C. Caria, located in what is now southwest Turkey, attracted the greatest Greek architects to work on the vast white marble edifice, which was richly decorated with the sculpture of Scopas and Praxiteles and included statues of Mausolus and his queen. Nothing quite like this ornate super tomb had ever been seen before, and the Greeks called it a *Mausoleion* after the dead king, *Mausoleum*, the Latin form of this word, becoming our *mausoleum*. The imposing structure stood for almost 1,800 years before it crumbled in an earthquake in 1375. The Crusaders who occupied Halicarnassus in the 15th century used much of its marble to build a castle, but in 1859 Sir Charles Newton brought some of the structure's remains, including the statue of Mausolus, to the British Museum.

mauve.   British scientist William Perkin discovered the color mauve in 1856 while experimenting with the coal tar component aniline in an attempt to produce clear quinine. Mauve, "a moderate grayish violet to moderate reddish purple," was so named by Perkin after the French name of the mallow plant—he just happened to like the word *mauve*, which sounded quite sophisticated to an 18-year-old. The color became widely popular after Queen Victoria wore it to a royal wedding. *The Mauve Decade* (1926) by Thomas Beer is a study of American life during the last part of the 19th century.

maverick.   Texas lawyer Samuel Augustus Maverick (1803–70) reluctantly became a rancher in 1845 when he acquired a herd of cattle in payment for a debt. Maverick, a hero who was imprisoned twice in the war for independence from Mexico, eventually moved his cattle to the Conquistar Ranch on the Matagorda Peninsula, 50 miles from San Antonio. But he was too involved in other activities to prove much of a rancher. When in 1855 he sold out to A. Toutant de Beauregard, their contract included all the unbranded cattle on the ranch. Since careless hired hands had failed to brand any of Maverick's calves, Beauregard's cowboys claimed every unbranded animal they came upon as a *Maverick*. So, apparently, did some of Maverick's neighbors. Though Sam Maverick never owned another cow, his name soon meant any unbranded stock, and later any person who holds himself apart from the herd, a nonconformist. All of the standard sources give Texan Sam Maverick as the eponym behind this word. But John Gould, in *Maine Lingo* (1975), credits a Sam Maverick who "was already settled on an island in the harbor when the Puritans came in 1630 to establish Boston." Therefore, he "became the only Bostonian permitted to vote without church affiliation" and was considered a "oddball," a "stray," his fame spreading through New England. Gould claims the "use of *maverick* for an unmarked log in a Maine river preceded the meaning of an unbranded calf on the western plain by many years." A good story that may be true, but no specific, dated sources or quotations are given, although Gould says his Maverick "is mentioned often in early Boston records." Could this be a rare, perhaps unprecedented case of two eponyms independently becoming the same word?

mawkish.   *Mawkish* originally meant having a sickly, nauseating or insipid flavor, but also means "characterized by sickly sentimentality, feebly emotional." Whatever the meaning, anything mawkish is being compared to a maggot, the word deriving from the obsolete English *mawk*, maggot, which comes from a Scandinavian word meaning the same.

Maxim gun; Maxim silencer.   Sir Hiram Stevens Maxim, inventor of the first automatic machine gun, also invented a better mousetrap, an automatic fire sprinkler, a gas meter, a delayed-action fuse, a smokeless powder, a heavier-than-air flying machine, an inhalator for bronchitis, and sundry other items. The world did beat a path to his door, for his arms company merged with the Vickers firm in 1896 to become the giant Vickers Armstrong Ltd. and he was knighted for his accomplishments. Sir Hiram (1840–1916) was born in Maine, but became a naturalized British subject in 1881, after serving as chief engineer for America's first electric power company. The Maxim machine gun, invented in 1883, is a single-barreled, recoil-operated weapon that fires some 10 rounds a second, the first modern machine gun in that the recoil from one cartridge was used to both expel the empty shells and reload the weapon. But what has turned out to be the greatest of the Maxim inventions is the Maxim silencer devised by Hiram's son Hiram Percy Maxim (1869–1936), who remained an American and who invented the Maxim automobile as well. Maxim silencers were weapon attachments originally developed only to make the explosion of firearms practically noiseless. But they were soon perfected to eliminate noise from many modern machines. Thanks to the silencer, noise pollution is much less than it would be, the invention prolonging lives rather than making it easier to take them. *See* DEVIL'S PAINTBRUSH.

maximize.   *See* INTERNATIONAL.

Maxwell; Maxwell's equations; Maxwell's law.   For no logical reason, the brilliant Scottish physicist James Clerk Maxwell (1831–79) was better known in his lifetime than he is today. Despite his relatively brief career, Maxwell ranks as one of the greatest theoretical physicists of all time. His most important work was in the field of electricity, where he advanced the theory that light and electricity might be the same in their ultimate nature, and his theory of electromagnetism, published in 1873 in his *Treatise on Electricity and Magnetism*, has been called "one of the most splendid monuments ever raised by the genius of a single individual." Maxwell began his scientific career when a boy of 15. After teaching at Scottish colleges, he was appointed the first professor of experimental physics at Cambridge, directing the organization of the renowned Cavendish Laboratory. Maxwell's law and Maxwell's equations arise from his electromagnetic theory, but he is more widely honored by the *maxwell*, the unit of magnetic flux named in his honor.

May.   The merry month of May may have been named for Maia, the goddess of spring, or to honor the Maiores, the Roman senate in early times. No one is sure, but the Latin *Maius* for the month became our *May*. The Romans, incidentally, thought May was an unlucky month for marriages, for their feast in honor of Bona Dea, the goddess of chastity, was held in the month of May.

Mayan.   *See* NAHUATL.

Mayday.   *See* CQD.

Mayflower Compact.   The former wine ship that transported the early settlers to America took its name from the mayflower, another name for the blossom of the hawthorn tree. In the *Mayflower Compact*, signed by the 51 adult passengers aboard ship, all agreed to stay together where they landed, choose their own leader, and abide by majority rule, this being the rude beginning of American democracy.

mayonnaise.   Port Mahon gave its name to *mayonnaise*. The story is that the duc de Richelieu attacked the Spanish island of Minorca and drove out the British for a while in 1756. But Richelieu was ravenously hungry after the battle. The

Frenchman stormed the nearest kitchen ashore, tossed all the food he could find into one pot and blended it all together. This apocryphal tale got back to Paris, where chefs concocted a dressing of blended-together ingredients that they named *Mahonnaise* in honor of Richelieu's victory at Port Mahon.

may your shadow never grow less.   An expression of Eastern origin, dating back in English at least to the 19th century and meaning "may your health and prosperity always continue." According to Brewer: "Fable has it that when those studying the Black Arts had made certain progress they were chased through a subterranean hell by the devil. If he caught only their shadow, or part of it, they became first-rate magicians, but lost either all or part of their shadow. This would make the expression mean, May you escape wholly and entirely from the clutches of the foul fiend." More likely the expression is just a colorful way of saying "May you never waste away."

Mazda.   Ahura Mazda, the Persian god of light, has lent his name to the lamps and light bulbs of the General Electric Company since 1910, when G.E. borrowed it and registered it as a trademark. According to Persian belief, Ahura Mazda created all the 486,000 good stars—the lucky stars that people are born under as opposed to the like number of evil stars. Today *Mazda* is also the name of a Japanese auto.

mazel tov.   Widely known Yiddish words in the U.S. Although the literal meaning of the Hebrew words is "good luck," the expression *mazel tov* means "congratulations" or "best wishes" on one's success or good fortune. It is not said to a person when wishing him luck, *mazel* alone being used for that purpose.

mazuma.   *See* GELT.

M.C.; emcee.   In this case the initials became the word. *M.C.*, an abbreviation of *Master of Ceremonies*, came first. This began to be used as a verb in the early 1940s and was spelled *emcee*. The term *femcee*, for a female *emcee*, never caught on.

McCarthyism.   *McCarthyism* was coined by author Max Lerner and introduced for the first time in his newspaper column on April 5, 1950. The word notes the witch-hunting practices and disregard of civil liberties that his critics accused Senator Joseph McCarthy (1905–57) of using and inspiring during the "Red" scare in the early 1950s. The Wisconsin senator, a great patriot to his supporters, first charged the Democratic administration with allowing communist infiltration of the State Department. After taking on other government departments, he finally met his match when he attacked the army for alleged security lapses. The army, in turn, accused him of seeking special privileges, and while McCarthy was acquitted by the Senate of this charge, he was censured by a vote of 67–22 for his insolent behavior toward Senate committees. Earlier, the McCarthy hearings were televised and his countenance and repeated "Point of order, Mr. Chairman, point of order" became familiar throughout America. His low tactics ruined the lives of many innocent people.

McDonald's.   In recent times the trademark name of the American fast-food restaurant has become almost as well-known as O.K. and the trademark COKE, mainly because McDonald's has franchises throughout the world. Often McDonald's is a synonym for a hamburger. The Japanese have borrowed the name from English and altered it slightly to *Makudonarudo*. The original McDonald's (which no longer exists) was on E Street in San Bernardino, California. The original McDonald brothers sold all but three of their stores to Ray Kroc. These three, now owned by the "Pep Boys" (Manny, Moe, and Jack), are the world's only legal non-Kroc McDonald's.

McGuffey's reader.   More than 123 million copies of McGuffey's readers have been sold since they were first published in 1836, and as many as 30,000 copies were sold as recently as 1960. The school readers, noted for their moral lessons and selections from great English writers, have had a profound effect on the shaping of the American mind. They were the work of educator and linguist William Holmes McGuffey (1800–73). McGuffey, reared on the Ohio frontier, was possessed of a phenomenal memory that enabled him to become a teacher at the age of 13. After graduating from Washington and Jefferson College in 1826, he became in turn a professor of languages at Miami University in Ohio and president of both Cincinnati College and Ohio University. He later served as a professor at Woodward College, Cincinnati, and the University of Virginia, and was a founder of the Ohio public school system. The educator's initial book was published under the title *McGuffey's First Eclectic Reader*. Five more were to follow, the last being issued in 1857.

McIntosh.   Like many fruit varieties, the McIntosh apple was discovered accidentally. It is named after John McIntosh, an Ontario farmer, who found the late red apple in 1796 while clearing woodland in Dunclas County and was so impressed by it that he began to cultivate the variety. Today the Early McIntosh, one of the best early red apples, bears the same name, as does the Sweet McIntosh, regarded by many as the sweetest of all red varieties. The original McIntosh is still grown, however, a self-sterile type with whitish-yellow flesh and a superb though slightly acid taste. McIntosh apples account for some 10 percent of apples grown in this country, but they constitute about 75 percent of the New England harvest and 50 percent of the New York State crop. Most connoisseurs rate them superior in taste to the Red and Golden Delicious apples that have become the dominant American varieties. *See* MICAH ROOD'S APPLE.

McMansion; McJob.   *McMansion* is a derogatory term first heard in 2000 for a large, very expensive house with no originality of design, one that looks like all the other "mansions" in the area. *Mc* is an allusion to the MCDONALD's fast-food restaurant chain, which has also given us the term *McJob*, coined in the 1980s for any low-paying, unstimulating job.

McNaughton Rules.   Assassin Daniel McNaughton shot and killed British prime minister Robert Peel's private secretary, Edmund Drummond, in 1843, mistaking the Peel look-alike for Sir Robert. McNaughton, an illegitimate, illiterate Scotsman, was tried and acquitted by reason of insanity, the court ruling that a person who is unaware of doing wrong could be considered insane and not responsible for his actions. This McNaughton ruling, though changed considerably over the years, is still used in a general sense today.

mealy-mouthed. *Mealy-mouthed* for someone who doesn't speak directly or simply on an issue may derive from the German expression *Mehl im Maule behalten,* "to carry meal in the mouth, be indirect in speech." In any case, it is first recorded in the works of Martin Luther, who wasn't at all mealy-mouthed.

meander. *Meander,* "to wind in and out, to wander aimlessly," comes from the ancient name of the crooked Menderes River in Phrygia, now in western Turkey. The river, noted for its wandering course, is still called the Menderes, which became *Maiandros* in Greek, the Greek word eventually yielding *meander,* which came into English late in the 16th century via French.

meaner than a junkyard dog with 14 sucking pups. The meanest, that is, a vicious dog that not only guards a junkyard but a big litter of her pups as well. The expression is mainly heard in the American South.

meanwhile, back at the ranch. An expression that originated as a movie caption in the silent film era at the beginning of the century, these words are used humorously today when someone wants to get back to a story after going off on a tangent.

measly. Measles has generally been considered an insignificant disease, despite the fact that a form of the measles used to kill many and can lead to serious birth defects if contracted by a pregnant woman. Hence our word *measly,* "insignificant or worthless," coined sometime in the middle of the 19th century.

meat. *Meat* in Middle English meant food in general. The word became confined to the flesh of animals when there was a large increase in flesh eating and *meat* by the 17th century lost its meaning of food in general.

meat and potatoes. Over the years *meat and potatoes* has come to mean "the simple fundamentals" because a meat course and potato course are so often principal parts of a meal. *Meat and drink* means food in general. See POTATO.

Medal of Honor. The United States' highest military decoration, awarded to a serviceman who distinguishes himself beyond the call of duty, this blue-ribboned gold star was established by Congress in 1862 as an award for Union heroes in the Civil War.

meddlesome Matty. A meddlesome Matty is a woman who is always poking her nose in others' business, or anyone who constantly fidgets with someone else's belongings. The expression derives from the character in the eponymous poem "Meddlesome Matty" (1804) written by Ann Taylor of "Twinkle, twinkle, little star" fame.

median strip. The most common term in America for the grassy strip or area separating opposite sides of a highway.

Among other terms used to describe this strip are a *meridian* (in the Midwest), a *medial strip* (Pennsylvania), *neutral ground* (Louisiana), a *mall* (upstate New York), and a *divider* (New York City area).

Medicean. Immensely wealthy Florentine banker Giovanni di Bicci de' Medici (1360–1429) founded Italy's powerful Medici family. The Medicis ruled in Florence from the 15th to the 18th century, their influence felt throughout Italy, especially since the family produced three popes—Leo X, Leo XI, and Clement VII. Catherine de' Medici became queen of France, as did Marie de' Medici. A genealogical table of the Medici would yield a score of figures who greatly influenced their times, but this family did so much, both good and evil—ranging from patronage of the arts to political poisonings and tortures—that their name came to mean a variety of things. *Medicean,* then, is simply "pertaining to the Medici," its meaning depending on the way it is used, or to which Medici it refers.

medicine. Maurice B. Gordon nicely explained this word, as Indians used it, in *Aesculapius Comes to the Colonies* (1949): "The word 'medicine' itself is a good example of the American Indian's dualism of theology and medicine . . . He employed the term not only for a drug or herb but also for some supernatural agency which may be invoked to cure disease or even insure the success of an undertaking."

Mediterranean Sea. Formed from the Latin *medi,* "middle," and *terraneus,* "earth," the *Mediterranean* means "the sea in the middle of the earth," which, indeed, the ancients believed it to be.

Medusa; medusae. It is because of their labyrinths of poisonous tentacles that the free-swimmer stages of all jellyfish are called "medusae," after the writhing serpentine tresses of the Medusa of Greek mythology, one of the Gorgon's heads that turned to stone anything that met its gaze. It is just possible that the Medusa itself was conceived by some ancient mariner who had encountered a particularly formidable pelagic specimen. At any rate, it has long been known that the poisons of certain jellyfish are very virulent and have inflicted fatal injuries to humans. *See* SPINELESS AS A JELLYFISH.

Meenagorp. Translated from Irish, this well-known mountain in county Tyrone, Ireland, means "mountain of corpses," perhaps after a bloody ancient battle there.

meerschaum. A mineral resembling white clay that is used mostly for making tobacco pipes, *meerschaum* is German for "sea foam." About as heavy as water, frothy pieces of it sometimes float to shore. Ancients, coming upon it, erroneously thought it was a kind of petrified sea foam, giving it its name. Because meerschaum is absorbent, tobacco pipes made of it become brown with use. In mineralogy it is called "sepiolite."

megabucks. This synonym for "big money" is first recorded in 1946, deriving from the Greek *megas,* "large, powerful," and probably reinforced by the constant use of *mega* in *megabombs,* etc.

Megan's Law. In 1994 seven-year-old Megan Kanka was murdered by a previously convicted child molester who lived near her New Jersey home. Public outrage led to a state law allowing police to notify residents if a convicted sex offender moves into the neighborhood. Two years later, a federal court made such notification mandatory.

megaphone; loudspeaker; bullhorn; loudhailer; bitchbox. *Megaphone*, the word first recorded in 1878, refers to a cone-shaped device that greatly magnifies sound, is used outside, and is not electronic; while *loudspeaker* (invented about 1880) refers to an electronic device that magnifies sound in a room or a hall, etc.; and *bullhorn*, first recorded in 1950, refers to a high-powered, cone-shaped, electrical loudspeaker for outdoor use. In Britain and Australia each of these devices would be called a "loudhailer," a term unknown in the U.S. Since World War II *bitchbox* has been U.S. slang for the loudspeaker of a public address system in a military compound, over which authorities always seem to be bitching about something to the troops.

Megillah. One of the Hebrew scrolls in synagogues read on certain Jewish holy days. They include the Song of Solomon, Ruth, Lamentations, Ecclesiastes, and the Book of Esther, which is read in synagogue during the festival of Purim. Since a Megillah is long and detailed, *the whole megillah* became a Yiddish phrase, now used by many Gentiles, meaning a long-winded story or a long, tedious explanation. A *big megillah* means the same. *Megillah* itself derives from Hebrew for "scroll."

melba toast; peach melba. Melba toast, according to the traditional story, originated as several pieces of burnt toast served to the Australian opera star Dame Nellie Melba at the Savoy in London. The prima donna had been on a diet, ordered toast, and enjoyed the crisp, crunchy, overtoasted slices that were served to her by mistake. The maitre d' named them in her honor and put melba toast on the menu. Whether the story is true or not, thin crispy melba toast honors Dame Nellie, as does the peach melba, which the French chef Escoffier concocted for her. Nellie Melba was the stage name adapted from the city of Melbourne by Helen Porter Mitchell (1861–1931), who became a Dame of the British Empire in 1918. The world-famous soprano made her debut in *Rigoletto* in Brussels (1887) and went on to star at London's Covent Garden, the Paris Opera, La Scala, and New York's Metropolitan among numerous opera houses. Unlike many opera stars, Nellie Melba did not study singing until she was over 21 years old, although she had previously been trained as a pianist.

Melbourne. *See* LEAVE WELL ENOUGH ALONE.

meltdown. No more serious accident can happen in a nuclear power plant than a meltdown. The term, first recorded in the 1960s, signifies a condition where the reactor core (the assembly of the fuel elements) burns through or melts into the ground below the nuclear power station, releasing highly dangerous radiation.

melting pot. In his play about immigration entitled *The Melting Pot* (1908) English author Israel Zangwill wrote: "America is God's Crucible, the great Melting Pot where all the races of Europe are melting and re-forming!" Though Zangwill didn't stew blacks and Asians in his pot, the phrase quickly came to include everybody in America, "a homogeneous melting pot of heterogeneous individuals," as someone said. The term, by the way, doesn't refer to the loss of ethnic identity but to the breaking down of racial and national prejudices.

Melungeon. Though you won't find it in many dictionaries, *Melungeon* is the name of a people of mixed white, black, and American Indian ancestry living in eastern Tennessee and western North Carolina.

Memphis. The southern city, famous for Beale Street, the W. C. Handy museum, and Elvis Presley's Graceland home, was founded by Andrew Jackson in 1819. It was named after its storied sister city, which was the capital of the Old Kingdom of ancient Egypt from ca. 3400 to ca. 2445 B.C., at the apex of the Nile delta 12 miles above Cairo.

memsahib; sahib. Indians used to address British women as *memsahib* in the days when the sun never set on the Empire. The word is simply a feminine form of the Urdu *sahib*, "sir or master," *mem* representing the English "ma'am." The respectful title is first recorded in 1857, *sahib* attested to as far back as 1696. The terms are still used in India, but aren't exclusively applied to the British anymore.

men. Among the most amusing of the many words adopted by the Thais that were borrowed from English but have been given different meanings than they have in English. In this case the Thai *men* is a shortening of *menstruate*.

mendelevium. All attempts to classify the elements had failed before Dmitri Ivanovich Mendeleyev (1834–1907) invented his own system in 1869–71. The Russian chemist's *Periodic Law of the Chemical Elements* arranged the elements in order of increasing atomic weight, making it easy to check the now commonplace tables in the vertical columns, and provided spaces into which undiscovered elements would probably fit. Mendeleyev taught organic chemistry at the University of St. Petersburg. Known as one of the greatest teachers of his time, his *Principles of Chemistry* (1869) was a standard textbook. The artificially produced radioactive element *mendelevium* was named in Mendeleyev's honor in 1955 when four American scientists—Glenn Seaborg, Bernard Harvey, Gregory Choppin, and S. G. Thompson—formed it in the laboratory by bombarding the element EINSTEINIUM with alpha particles.

Mendel's law. Mendel's law is the theory of heredity formulated by the Austrian Augustinian abbot and botanist Gregor Johann Mendel (1822–84). Mendel's painstakingly careful experiments, crossing different strains of peas in his monastery garden at Brunn, led to Mendel's law, reported in 1865, stating that characteristics of the parents of crossbred offspring reappear in successive generations in certain proportions and according to fixed laws. His *Mendelian* laws were neglected until long after his death, when Hugo de Vries and others independently rediscovered his findings in about 1900. They soon became the foundation for the modern study of heredity. Mendel was not uneducated as is sometimes inferred, having studied natural science at the University of Vienna from 1851 to 1853.

menhaden. This abundant oily fish has a name related to its use. Caught in great numbers by American Indians and buried in their corn fields, it bears an Algonquian name meaning "fertilizer." It is also called the mosbunker, the bunker, the marshbunker, and by some 30 more popular names (see the *American Naturalist* XII, 1878, pp. 735–39 for a listing). In 1949 *Brevoortia tyrannus* was called "America's No. 1 fish . . . yielding some $10 million worth of oil, meal, and dry scrap last year."

Ménière's disease. According to the *Family Medical Guide* (1976), this disease of the inner ear "is characterized by attacks that commence suddenly with violent dizziness, ringing in the ear, vomiting, a reeling sensation and unsteadiness of body equilibrium so severe that if the person does not lie down, he would fall to the floor. . . ." Bouts may last from a half hour to several weeks. The disease is named after French physician and otologist Prosper Ménière (1799–1862), who first described it. English author Jonathan Swift is thought to have suffered all his life from Ménière's disease or syndrome, long before it was so named. Although he tried many nostrums to improve his condition, including long walks of up to 38 miles, Swift became toward the end of his life "like the ruin of a great empire," as Thackeray put it. Swift came to have so little use for life that as his customary farewell to friends he would say, "Good night, I hope I never see you again."

Mennonites. *See* AMISH.

menorah. 1) A nine-branched candelabrum lit on the Jewish holiday of CHANUKAH, the Feast of Lights. 2) A candelabrum with seven branches used in the biblical tabernacle. 3) A candelabrum with any number of branches used in modern synagogues.

Men seldom make passes / at girls who wear glasses. Author Dorothy Parker's celebrated couplet was originally published in her friend Franklin Pierce Adams's "The Conning Tower" column under the title "News Item." One of the great wits of all time, Parker had the sharpest tongue of anyone at New York's celebrated Algonquin Round Table, a luncheon group that met at the Algonquin Hotel in the 1920s and included Adams, Robert Benchley, Heywood Broun, George S. Kaufman, Alexander Woollcott, and others from time to time. Later, an anonymous wit qualified Parker's famous couplet, writing: "Whether men will make passes at girls who wear glasses / Depends quite a bit on the shape of the chassis."

mentor. Mentor, in Greek mythology, was the friend of Odysseus and took charge of his household when the hero of Homer's *Odyssey* went off to war. When problems arose Pallas Athene descended from heaven to inhabit Mentor's body and, through him, to give good advice to Odysseus's son Telemachus. *Mentor* has since meant an adviser, teacher, or coach.

men with beards. May Lamberton Becker explains the expression in her *Golden Tales* (1981): "Joseph Palmer [a member of Bronson Alcott's short-lived Fruitlands community] jailed (in 1843) for wearing a beard . . . At eighty-four he died and was buried under a stone at North Leominster that gives his name and age, his portrait with the offending decoration, and the words 'Persecuted for Wearing the Beard.' Even Emerson, it seems, was not without a slight sense of superiority to the unshaved; he classified certain reformers as *men with beards*. They were not tolerated in business or the professions in the [1840s]; curiously enough, by the seventies public sentiment had swung in precisely the opposite direction."

meow. *Meow* has been the English echoic word for the sound of a cat for centuries. The word is similar to those in many languages (German *miaw*, Italian *miao*, French *miaou*), but the Japanese hear the sound slightly differently as *nya nya*, and in Arabic our *meow* is *nau-nau*. *See also* COCK-A-DOODLE-DO.

Mercator's projection. Gerardus Mercator, his name being the Latinized form of Gerhard Kremer, devised Mercator's projection in 1568. His famous cylindrical chart gave all meridians as straight lines at right angles to the parallels of latitude, and is the basis of mapmaking today. Mercator, born in 1512, was a Flemish geographer and mathematician whose accurate maps and globes revolutionized mapmaking and freed geographers from "the tyranny of Ptolemy," the earlier astronomer and geographer, who had underestimated the earth's size.

Mercedes-Benz. The Mercedes-Benz auto isn't named after two men who designed it, as most people believe. Emil Jellinik, an Austrian, manufactured the car in 1886, and he named it for his daughter, Mercedes. When the Daimler company later merged with Jellinik's Benz automotive works, the name assumed its present form.

mercerize. A mercer is a dealer in textiles, but the old word has nothing to do with the method for treating cotton textiles called mercerization. The process was invented by John Mercer (1791–1866), an English calico printer who discovered it in 1850. Mercerizing involves treating material under tension with a caustic soda solution and then acid to neutralize the alkali used. This shrinks, strengthens, and gives a permanent silky luster to the yarn or fabric, also making it easier to dye. Mercer's method wasn't widely successful until long after he died, the breakthrough coming in 1895 when the 25 percent shrinkage was virtually eliminated by treating the material under tension, the one factor he had overlooked. The inventor had named his process "sodaizing," but the hundreds of millions of yards of material and thread annually produced by the method are called mercerized in tribute to his pioneering work.

merchant. The swift Roman god Mercury, for whom MERCURY is named, was the god of business. Thus from his name come the words *merchant*, *merchandise*, *mercer*, *commerce*, and *commercial*, among others.

merchants of death. *Merchants of death* is applied to any group of manufacturers or businessmen who make money from war and even promote wars in various ways so that they can make money. This is another term from the title of a book—*The Merchants of Death* (1920) by H. C. Engelbrecht and F. D. Hanighan, which argues that munition makers were among the major causes of World War I.

mercury; mercurial. Mercury, with his winged hat and sandals, was the fastest and busiest of the Roman gods, as our old saying *quick as Mercury* reflects. For the same reason the liquid metal *mercury* was named for him, because it flowed quickly from place to place. The planet *Mercury*, also named for the god; gives us the word *mercurial*, "rapid, unpredictable changes in mood," astrologers in ancient times believing that because Mercury was the planet closest to the sun those born under its influence were most subject to such shifting moods. *See* MER-CHANT; FAST AS LADAS.

meretricious.   The Latin root of *meretricious*, meaning "taw-dry, gaudy, deceitful," is *meretrix*, "whore." The English word first meant "pertaining to a prostitute," taking on its later meanings because prostitutes often dressed gaudily and were deceitful.

Meriden audience.   A humorous theatrical term for a very small audience. It is said to have originated with a performance of Countess Helena Modjeska's traveling troupe, starring Julia Marlowe, in Meriden, Connecticut, in 1888. Miss Marlowe played to an audience of two, the local mayor and a little boy.

mermaid.   Mermaids, whose name derived from the Latin *mer* ("sea"), date back long before history was written. In Geek mythology the 50 daughters of Nereus, the god of the sea, were beautiful mermaids who rode the waves on the backs of dolphins, and any sailor lucky enough to catch one could demand that the mermaid predict the future as a price for letting her go.

mermaid's purses; mermaid's glove.   The horny skate, ray, and shark egg cases often washed up on the beach by wave action are popularly called *mermaid's purses*. A *mermaid's glove* is a British sponge (*Halichondria palmata*) whose branches re-semble human fingers.

Merry Andrew.   Henry VIII's personal physician, Dr. An-drew Borde or Boorde (ca. 1490–1549), has been regarded by some as the original *Merry Andrew*, at least since Thomas Hearne designated him so in the preface to his *Benedictine Abbas Petroburgensis* in 1735. Borde did have a reputation for a sala-cious wit and a bedside manner that mixed facetiousness with healing, but to call the eccentric doctor a buffoon or clown would be stretching the evidence too far. He did not author a contemporary joke book, as is sometimes alleged, but he was a man known for his vast learning as well as his reputation for enjoying a good joke. The *Oxford English Dictionary* notes Hearne's statement, and like most authorities dismisses it, claim-ing that the author based his identification on little evidence or even intrinsic probability. The expression did arise in Borde's time, but probably from the generic name for men servants or serving men, "Andrew" being commonly bestowed on servants in those days. The first *Merry Andrew* was most likely such a servant, the cognomen later being applied to any conjurer's assistant who engaged in buffoonery to help make the magician's hands quicker than the eye.

merrythought.   *Merrythought*, first recorded in 1607, is a charming synonym for the wishbone in the breast of a fowl, taking its name from the tradition of two persons pulling on the bone until it breaks, the one who holds the longer piece getting any wish he has made.

merry widow.   Late in the 19th century Merry Widow was a U.S. trade name for a brand of condoms. Within 30 years or so, however, *merry widow* had become a synonym for any kind of condom and remained so until the firm making Merry Widows went out of business in the 1940s. The product pre-ceded Franz Lehar's operetta of that title, which was first produced in 1905. *Merry* does figure in several British slang expressions, all obsolete, including *merry-legs*, a harlot; *merry-maker*, the penis; *merry bout*, sexual intercourse; *merry bit*, a willing wench; and, merriest of all, a *merry-arsed Christian*, a whore.

mervousness.   A short-lived political word and only an amus-ing historical footnote today, *mervousness* is a blend of *Merv* and *nervousness*. The duke of Argyll coined it in the early 1880s when the British government worried nervously about Russia having designs upon the area of Merv in Turkestan. In fact, the British mervousness was warranted, for the Russians grabbed Merv in late 1883.

mescal button.   A dried, buttonlike top of a mescal of the genus *Lophophora*, long used as a hallucinogen by certain south-western Indians during religious ceremonies. The word, first recorded in 1885, is ultimately from the Nahuatl *mexcalli*, for "an intoxicant distilled from agave."

meshugge.   A Yiddish term for "crazy" that derives from the Hebrew word meaning the same. *Meshugge*, pronounced to rhyme with "Paducah," can be used literally or in a lighter vein. The derivation *meshuggener* for a crazy man has also become fairly common in English, as has the adjective *meshug-geneh* ("That's a meshuggeneh idea").

mesmerize.   Franz Anton Mesmer doesn't entirely deserve his centuries-old reputation as a charlatan. Though he wasn't aware of the fact, Dr. Mesmer was one of the first to treat patients by hypnosis, and his motives generally seem to have been beyond reproach. The Austrian physician, garbed in the flowing, brightly colored robes of an astrologer and waving a magic wand, would arrange his patients in a circle, have them join hands in the dimly lit room and then pass from one to another, fixing his eyes upon, touching, and speaking to each in turn while soft music played in the background. Apparently he never did understand that the supernatural had nothing to do with his success, that his hypnotic powers accomplished this. Many physicians supported his claims but when Louis XVI appointed a scientific commission—which included Benjamin Franklin—to investigate his practice, they labeled him an im-postor. A man born before his time, the hypnotist died in obscurity in Switzerland in 1815, aged 82. Freud and others would profit from his work, but he would mainly be remem-bered as a quack occult healer. Mesmerism was used for hyp-notism before the latter word was coined, but today is employed mostly in the sense of spellbinding, enthralling by some mys-terious power, in fact, swaying a group or an individual by some strange personal magnetism.

Mesmerizer Creek, Texas.   Over a century ago a settler on the banks of this Texas town actually tried to domesticate American bison by hypnosis, his colorful ways inspiring the colorful place name *Mesmerizer Creek*.

Mesopotamia.   Mesopotamia, an ancient region of southwest Asia in modern-day Iraq, was the home of many early civilizations, including Babylonia. To the English speaker the word suggests *mess, pot,* or something of that order, yet there is a nice story about it: The British actor George Whitefield's voice was so masterly that "he could make men either laugh or cry just by pronouncing the word Mesopotamia."

mesquite.   A spiny, shrublike tree of the Southwest (*Prosopis juliflora* or *glandulosa)* that often forms dense thickets; or the wood of such a tree, used for barbecuing at least since the Indians used it in cooking buffalo meat. *Mesquite* derives from the Nahuatl *mizquitl* meaning the same.

message to Garcia.   In his inspirational *A Message to Garcia* (1899), Elbert Hubbard dramatized the true adventure of Lt. Andrew Summers Rowan, U.S. Bureau of Naval Intelligence, who during the Spanish-American War was sent by the U.S. chief of staff to communicate with General Calixto García, leader of the Cuban insurgent forces. No one knew just where the elusive García might be, but Rowan made his way through the Spanish blockade in a small boat, landing near Turquino Peak on April 24, 1898, where he contacted local patriots, who directed him to García far inland, and returned to Washington with information regarding the insurgent forces. The brave and resourceful Rowan became a hero, but Hubbard transformed him into an almost Arthurian figure and it was his essay that made *carry a message to Garcia* a byword.

Messalina; messaline.   The notoriously cruel, greedy, and venal Valeria Messalina managed to cuckold her weak-minded husband Emperor Claudius I so many times that even in corrupt Rome her name became proverbial for a lascivious, unfaithful woman. One of the profligate empress's favorite tricks was to make love to men and learn about their real estate holdings, later condemn them to death for treason, and then confiscate their property. But she went too far when she eliminated the freedman Polybius. Shortly afterward, in her husband's absence, the empress forced her current lover, a handsome youth named Gaius Silius, to divorce his wife and marry her in a public ceremony. The freedman Narcissus, alarmed at Polybius's fate, took this opportunity to inform Claudius of her treachery and he ordered his third wife put to death. She was either killed in the gardens of Lucullus, which she had obtained by confiscation, or forced to commit suicide there with her paramour. She was only 26 when she died in A.D. 48. No one knows why, but the fabric messaline, a thin, soft silk with a tweed or satin weave, also pays the empress homage.

Messerschmitt.   This was the most famous German fighter of World War II and the main support of the Luftwaffe. The aircraft, technically the ME-109 and ME-110 pursuit planes, were designed by German aircraft engineer and manufacturer Wilhelm or Willy Messerschmitt (b. 1898). Messerschmitt built his first plane when he was 18 and owned his own factory by 1923, his early experience in gliding leading to his interest in power-driven aircraft. Besides the renowned fighter he built a remarkable twin jet, the ME-262. The inventor had been awarded the Lilienthal prize for aviation research in 1937, but was declared a minor offender in the postwar trials of Nazis.

mess of pottage.   *See* LENTILS.

mestizo.   A man of mixed Spanish or European and American Indian ancestry; from a Spanish word meaning "of mixed race." *Mestiza* is the feminine form. *See* GAUCHO.

me Tarzan, you Jane.   *See* TARZAN.

metathesis.   *See* BIRD.

method acting.   *See* STANISLAVSKI'S METHOD.

method in one's madness.   Used to describe someone who acts crazy or erratic in order to further his aims, the old expression seems to have originated with Shakespeare. At least its earliest ancestor is first recorded by the Bard in *Hamlet:* "Though this be madness, yet there is method in it."

Methodist.   The evangelical Protestant religion was founded on the principles of the brothers John and Charles Wesley in England in the early 18th century. It was named after Charles Wesley's Oxford "Holy Club" (especially Wesley himself among them), who were noted for their "methodical" ways. Charles certainly was methodical enough to write over 6,500 hymns, the popular *Hark! The Herald Angels Sing* among them.

Methusaleh tree.   *See* BRISTLECONE PINE.

Mexican jumping bean.   *See* JUMPING BEAN.

Mexican standoff.   A stalemate, a confrontation that neither side can win. Originally an American cowboy expression describing a gun battle with no clear winner, the words date back to the mid-19th century. It is often used to describe a pitching duel in baseball today.

Mexico.   *Mexico* derives from the Aztec name of great war god Mextli.

mezuzah.   *Mezuzah* is from Hebrew for "doorpost." It is a small scroll, inscribed on one side with biblical passages (Deut. 6:4–9 and Deut. 11:13–21) and on the other with the word *Shaddoi,* a name for God, that is inserted in a small tube and attached by some Jews to the doorjamb of the home. An Orthodox Jew touches his lips and then the mezuzah on leaving or entering the house or apartment.

mho.   It is safe to make the earthshaking claim that this is the only word deriving from a man's name spelled backwards. This unusual crossword puzzle and Scrabble word means just the opposite of the OHM; mho is the electrical unit of conduction, while the ohm is the electrical unit of resistance. The inverted word, whose plural is *mhos,* was coined by Lord Kelvin and of course honors physicist Georg Simon Ohm, just as the ohm does. In fact, the *mho* is often called a reciprocal ohm. *See* MAHERNIA; QUISQUALIS.

MIA.   This abbreviation for "missing in action" didn't originate during the Vietnam War, as many believe. The initials were used in military parlance at least during the Korean conflict and probably further back, though they did pass into general use in the Vietnam era.

Micah Rood's apple. An apple with streaks of red running through the white flesh. The tale is that on a spring day in 1693 a jewelry peddler visited old Micah Rood's farm at Franklin, Pennsylvania. Shortly afterward the peddler was found murdered under an apple tree in Rood's orchard, but his jewelry was never recovered and the farmer never was convicted of the crime. According to legend, though, all the apples harvested from the tree that autumn had streaks of blood inside. Rood died of fright after seeing them, the "damned" spot or streaks called "Micah Rood's curse" from that day on. When recounting this one, don't ruin a good story by quibbling that apples with red running through the flesh were common before Rood's time, that they are simply a "sport," like the famous golden delicious variety and many others. There seems to be no record of a farmer named Micah Rood, but two other peddlers were involved in sensational murders at the time he was allegedly murdered; perhaps these cases inspired the story. *See* MCINTOSH.

Micawberish attitude. An attitude that is very optimistic, often to a fault. Named after Mr. Wilkins Micawber, a character in Charles Dickens's *David Copperfield* (1849–50), the novel Dickens liked best. Micawber, poor but always hopeful, the eternal optimist, does become an esteemed magistrate in Australia. "An optimist," wrote J. H. Cabell, "proclaims that we live in the best of all possible worlds; and the pessimist fears this is true."

Michigan. Our 26th state, admitted to the Union in 1837, takes its name from *Michigaman*, both the name of an Indian tribe and a place, translating as "great water." The Wolverine State had first been the Michigan Territory. The Indians thought it "the first batch of earth the Great Spirit made."

Mickey Finn. This term, for "a powdered knockout drug or purgative slipped into a drink to render its drinker unconscious or otherwise helpless," seems to have originated in Chicago in the late 19th century and has been attributed to a gangland figure named Mickey Finn, remembered for his sleight of hand but nothing else. The original Mickey Finn is said to have been a laxative commonly used for horses. Possibly some unknown bartender named Mickey actually administered it, but one guess is as good as another here.

Mickey Mouse. Mickey Mouse only began to lose popularity when he was streamlined for later films, his tail cut off and his bare chest covered, among other "modernizations." He looked as if he had come off an assembly line of drawing boards, and this commercial slickness was reflected in phrases like *Mickey Mouse music*. In the armed forces during World War II and the Korean conflict *Mickey Mouse* meant anything childish or silly, such as white-glove inspections. "Mickey Mouse movie" was a humorous term G.I.'s gave the frightening films servicemen were shown that gruesomely detailed the effects of gonorrhea and syphilis and that caused many men to swear off sex—for a few days. Mickey Mouse was of course invented by the late Walt Disney (1901–66) in 1923. Disney called his creation Mortimer Mouse at first, but changed the name when his wife suggested Mickey Mouse instead. The cartoonist was Mickey's

voice in the early Mickey Mouse cartoons. In Disney's words, "He was my firstborn and the means by which I ultimately achieved all the other things I ever did—from Snow White to Disneyland." *See also* DISNEYAN.

Mickey Mouse rules. One theory holds that World War II U.S. Navy Military Indoctrination Centers, or M.I.C.'s, where undisciplined sailors were restrained, gave their initials to this expression for petty rules. The term has been around since early in World War II and probably can be explained by the fact that such rules seem silly and childish, like MICKEY MOUSE cartoons. Mickey Mouse was better honored when his name became the password chosen by intelligence officers in planning the greatest invasion in the history of warfare—Normandy, 1944. Mickey Mouse diagrams were maps made for plotting positions of convoys and bombarding forces at Normandy.

microcosm. *Microcosm* derives from the Greek for "little world," the Greeks applying the word to man, whom they considered as the world in miniature. The term is now used for anything regarded as a world in miniature. Its opposite is *macrocosm*.

microscope. The term was first recorded by Galileo's friend Francisco Stelluti. Galileo himself referred to the instrument as the *occhiolino* (little eye). *See* TELESCOPE.

Midas; Midas touch. Just as the title pharaoh was bestowed upon all Egyptian rulers, Midas was the title of the kings of Phrygia, an ancient kingdom in what is now central Turkey, but the Midas who became the basis for the Midas legends has never been positively identified. In legend King Midas is the father of Gordius. Several tales are told of him in Greek mythology, the most famous of these making his name proverbial. This story had King Midas befriending Silenus, the Greek god of wine and fertility, a jolly old man, often drunk but gifted with great powers of song and prophecy. Midas led Silenus to Dionysus, his pupil and boon companion, and this grateful god of fertility and wine rewarded him by promising to fulfill any wish he might make. King Midas told Dionysus that he wished everything he touched would turn to gold, and his wish was granted. But Midas got much more than he bargained for— even his food and drink turned to gold, and he nearly starved to death before the greedy king's appetite for gold decreased and he asked the god to lift the spell. Dionysus commanded him to bath in the Pactolus River, which washed him clean of his cursed power and has ever since had gold-bearing sands. From this original morality tale, on which there have been many embellishments, we have the *Midas touch*, referring to anyone who effortlessly makes money from every project he undertakes.

Middle America. Capital columnist Joseph Kraft (1925–86) coined *Middle America* in the mid-1960s as a term for "the middle-class America whose views were often overlooked by the opinion-molders on the two coasts," according to one of his editors.

middle class. See UPPER CLASS.

middle finger. This name for the third finger on the human hand (if you include the thumb as a finger) has an obvious origin. Centuries ago it was called the *long man* because it is, also obviously, the longest of the fingers. *See* THUMB.

middle of the road. Toward the end of the 19th century this term came into use to describe political parties or factions of political parties that took a cautious, moderate position between extremes supported by their opponents. Highways at the time were often unpaved, with untended roads whose left and right sides were well below the grade of the middle. After a heavy rain cautious travelers stayed in the middle of the road, which may have suggested the political phrase.

middle passage. *See* TRIANGULAR TRADE.

midnight ride of Paul Revere. A literary reference to the ride of Paul Revere from Charlestown to Lexington and Concord to warn Americans of the approach of British troops at the beginning of the Revolutionary War. It comes from Henry Wadsworth Longfellow's poem *Paul Revere's Ride* (1861).

midshipman fish. Native to mainland America, the midshipman fish (*Porichthys notatus*) has golden spots on each side like the brass buttons on a midshipman's coat. Familiar along the Pacific coast, the luminescent midshipman is also called the talking fish, the grunter, the grunt, and the singing fish. The sound it makes when disturbed—made by vibrating its air bladder—is actually similar to the croak of a tree frog.

midsummer dream game. *See* ALL-STAR.

midsummer madness. Something completely mad, unreasonable, or foolish. Shakespeare is the first to record this expression, in *Twelfth Night* (1600). In the Bard's day midsummer was believed to be a time when madness was common.

midsummer men. The orpine (*Sedum telephium*), also known as live-forever, is called midsummer men because it used to be potted and hung in the house to tell young women if their sweethearts were true—the plant's leaves supposedly bending to the right if they were faithful, to the left if they were false.

midway. *Midway* for the central area of a carnival, fair, or any exposition comes directly from the Midway Plaisance at the World Columbian Exposition held in 1893 in Chicago. At this location stood the first FERRIS WHEEL and other great attractions.

MI5, MI6. Frequently encountered in spy novels, these are official British intelligence organizations. MI5 is supposed to protect domestic military and political secrets, while MI6 is responsible for discovering foreign military and political secrets. Both services work with Scotland Yard's Special Branch. The letters *MI* stand for *M*(ilitary) *I*(ntelligence), and the numbers stand for Section 5 or Section 6.

MIG. All Russian fighter planes called by the acronym MIG honor the original aircraft's inventors, designers *Mi*(koyan) and *G*(urevitch). It is sometimes written *MiG* and *Mig*.

might as well be hung (hanged) for a sheep as a lamb. In former times thieves were sentenced to death when caught stealing either a sheep or a lamb, which led to this originally British expression that dates back to at least the early 19th century and means if the punishment is the same for either action one might as well commit the worse (and more profitable) one.

mighty small potatoes and few to a hill. This old Americanism is heard more often today in its abbreviated form *small potatoes*. Both expressions mean someone or something of little consequence, insignificant, and were first recorded in 1831. A variation is *small potatoes and few in a hill*.

migraine headache. Migraine comes from the Greek *hemikrania*, "half the skull," this extremely severe type of headache usually confined to one side of the head. The word seems to have been a fashionable one when Horace Walpole first recorded it in a 1777 letter to a friend.

a Mike Fink. In days past, a *Mike Fink* was used to mean "a rough and ready hero given to exaggeration about his exploits." Mike Fink was a real American frontier hero (ca. 1770–1822), a river boatman and Indian fighter whose tall tales contributed greatly to the American folklore of exaggeration, a fact supported by the 12 or more different accounts of his death.

mile. The Latin *mille*, "one thousand," is the ancestor of our word *mile*, which is 5,280 feet, because it once referred to 1,000 paces of the Roman legion's formal parade step, left foot and then right foot, each pace equalling 5.2 feet.

milestone; milepost. *Milestone* refers to a surveyor's mark (often a concrete post) set to mark distances by miles, each milestone marking a mile. The Americanism dates back to about 1740 and has also come to mean a notable point in the life of a person, a nation, etc. *Milepost* is used in the same ways, but refers to a post made of wood.

a mile wide, a foot deep, too thick to drink, and too thin to plow. This colorful description of the muddy, shallow Platte River in Nebraska was first recorded over a century ago. It was also used to describe the Powder River. *See* POWDER RIVER.

milk. *Milk* has been used for more than 400 years to mean to dishonestly extract money from someone until there is nothing or very little left, as in "She milked him of everything he had." It literally refers to the milking of animals. To milk a mine is to extract all or large portions of the ore from it after selling the mine.

milk of human kindness. Shakespeare invented this expression for gentleness in *Macbeth* (1606), when he has Lady Macbeth say to her husband, "Yet do I fear thy nature; / It is too full of the milk of human kindness . . ."

milkshake. In most of America a milkshake is a thick sweet drink made of milk, syrup, and ice cream. An exception is Rhode Island where such a drink is called a cabinet, after the wooden cabinet in which the mixer used to be encased; a *milkshake* in Rhode Island is just milk and syrup shaken up together. In northern New England the drink most Americans call a *milkshake* is often called a *velvet* or a *frappé.*

milk the bull, ram. To take on a foolish, impossible task, as the bull or ram has no milk, one being a male cow and the other a male sheep. The expression is a streamlining of the 17th-century proverb "Whilst the one milks the ram, the other holds under the sieve."

mill. To *mill about* is to move aimlessly in a circle. First recorded by Kipling in 1874, the expression is related to the circular motion of mill wheels. *See* PUT THROUGH THE MILL.

Millerite. *See* SEVENTH DAY ADVENTISTS.

milliard. *Milliard* is the British word for the American English "billion" or one thousand million. This term is also used in Russia and Germany. The American English *trillion* is equivalent to the British English *billion. Milliard,* from the French *milliard,* which comes from the French *mille,* "thousand," is first recorded in 1793. Wrote Byron in *Don Juan:* "I'll bet you millions, milliards." *See* BILLIONAIRE.

milliner. One of the great fashion centers of the world in the early 16th century, Milan, Italy set styles for all Europe. Milan gloves, Milan hats, Milan point lace, Milan ribbons, Milan needles, and even Milan jewelry were among the many items exported to England from the Paris of its day. Shopkeepers who sold these imported articles, only some of them merchants from Milan, were naturally named Milaners, but the English pronounced and spelled the word *Milliners,* which eventually lost its capital. The small shops, run primarily by men at first, did often specialize in making and selling ladies' hats, but the use of *milliner* exclusively for a designer or a seller of women's headgear is fairly recent.

millionaire. Fur and real estate tycoon John Jacob Astor (1763–1848) was probably the first American to be called a millionaire, for the word entered English from the French *millionnaire* in about 1820, but there were Americans who accumulated millions before him, the first probably being the Virginia planter and banker Robert "King" Carter, who owned more than 300,000 acres in the late 17th century *See also* BILLIONAIRE; MILLIARD; MULTIMILLIONAIRE; MYRIAD; TRILLIONAIRE.

million-dollar wound. A war wound, suffered in combat or self-inflicted, that is bad enough to send a soldier home or at least behind the lines out of the combat zone. The term *million-dollar wound* dates back to World War II, while the practice of self-inflicted wounds is as old as the "art of war." In the American Civil War, for example, minor self-inflicted wounds were common, and the reaction to them was often harsh. One Union soldier at Cold Harbor shot himself in the foot. Sure by the powder burn that the wound was self-inflicted, a surgeon chloroformed the soldier and sawed off his leg. "I shall never forget the look of horror that fastened on his face when he found his leg was cut off," an observer wrote.

millions for defense, not one cent for tribute. *See* XYZ AFFAIR.

Milquetoast. Timorous men are still called *Caspar Milquetoasts,* or *Milquetoasts,* even though the cartoon character of that name, created by H. T. Webster as "The Timid Soul" in the 1930s, has long ceased to appear in the Sunday comics.

mimosa. *Mimosa* is from the Greek "to mimic," in allusion to the sensitive collapse of the leaves in some species of this tree, which were thought to be mimicking the motions of animals at one time. The mimosa's reaction to shock or cloudy weather is one of the strangest cases of physiological response among plants, its leaflets folding up face to face at the slightest irritation and its leaves collapsing entirely if the shock is sufficient.

mimulus. These showy flowers were once thought to resemble a monkey's face and were thus named from the Greek *mimo,* "face." Other names for them are *monkey flower* and the *cardinal monkey flower.* One species, *Mimulus moschatus,* is called *monkey musk,* but actually has no smell at all. Experts are at a loss to explain why the flower mysteriously lost its perfume at the end of the 19th century.

mind (memory) like a steel trap. *See* SMART AS A STEEL TRAP.

mind your own business. *See* 11TH COMMANDMENT.

mind your p's and q's. Be very careful, precise. We have been using this expression since at least the late 18th century without any definite proof of where it comes from, and we still don't know. Not that there is any want of theories. Of the top 10 contenders, three are listed here:

- The obvious explanation is that English children learning to write the alphabet were told to mind their *p*'s and *q*'s, to be careful not to reverse the loops on the letters and make *p*'s look like *q*'s and vice versa. Why wasn't the admonition mind your *b*'s and *d*'s, though?
- A similar theory holds that apprentice printers were told to mind their p's and q's, to be very careful in picking out type, especially since a typesetter has to read letters upside down. The trouble with this theory is that the reverse of a *p* isn't a *q* but a *d.*
- Word delvers always come up with a good barroom story whenever it's possible to work one in, and a third explanation has British tavernkeepers minding their *p*'s and *q*'s when figuring up the monthly beer bill—being careful, that is, not to confuse pints and quarts.

miniature. *Miniature* doesn't derive from the Latin *minor* or *minimus,* "small," as seems the case. It comes from *minium,* a Latin borrowing from Basque. *Minium* (from the Basque *arminea*) means "red lead, vermilion," Basque Spain being a major source of red lead in ancient times. Miniature first meant "a manuscript containing letters illuminated with red vermilion." The word was then erroneously applied to small portraits, because it was confused with the Latin *minimus,* and later came to describe anything small.

miniature golf.   *See* TOM THUMB GOLF.

minimize.   *See* INTERNATIONAL.

miniskirt.   Though it is associated with the 1960s, the miniskirt has been worn by women in all decades since, with increasing general approval as the years passed and prudishness capitulated to sexual power. Said to be the creation of French designer André Courrèges, the very short skirt was first called a "miniskirt" about 1964.

minister.   The first meaning of *minister* in English was "a servant or attendant," the word deriving ultimately from the Latin *minister* meaning the same. *Ministers* waited on table or worked in the kitchen. *Minister,* for "a clergyman," possibly owes its life to the fact that such men were "servants of God."

Minister's Rib Factory.   A name people jokingly gave to Mount Holyoke Seminary (which later became Mount Holyoke College) "because the South Hadley, Massachusetts, school turned out so many wives for ministers and missionaries," according to Imogene Wolcott in *The New England Yankee Cookbook* (1939).

mink-lined rut.   *See* GENTLEMEN PREFER BLONDES.

minnesinger.   *Minnesinger* refers to a German lyric poet in the troubadour tradition. These poets and singers flourished from the 12th through the 15th century, but their name wasn't coined until the early 19th century, from the German *minne,* love, plus *singer.*

Minnesota.   No one is sure exactly what *Minnesota* means, for the Sioux word translates as either "sky-blue water" or "cloudy water." The Gopher State had been called the Minnesota Territory before being admitted to the Union in 1858 as our 32nd state.

minnie ball.   French Army Capt. Claude Étienne Minié (1814–79) invented the minnie or minié ball bullet that became famous around the world and was extensively used in the American Civil War. Minié's invention came in 1849, designed for the Minié rifle, but more important, something of a final answer in the search for an ideal bullet. The elongated bullet, one of the first of its shape, was more accurate and could be loaded faster than any shell before it. Experts thought it to be the ultimate in ballistic ingenuity and it was certainly the first step in the development of the modern bullet. With it a soldier could fire *two* aimed shots a minute!

minniebush.   Often planted in rock gardens, this small shrub of the heath family is so named not because it's a little bush, as some people believe, but because it honors the Scottish surgeon and botanist Archibald Menzies (1754–1842).

minnow.   The name of this little fish is often used to describe anything small, but it is (at three to four inches) many times the size of gobies (*see* ANNUAL FISH). Minnows are of the order *Cypriniformes.* They can be differentiated from the similar KILLIE by the placement and shape of their fins—the minnow's caudal fin is always forked. The so-called topminnow is therefore not a minnow at all, but one of the many killie species.

minor league.   *See* MAJOR LEAGUE.

mint.   *Mint* derives from the name of the Greek nymph Minthe, who was transformed into the herb by Proserpine, the jealous wife of Pluto, god of the underworld. Wild mint (*Mentha sativa*) has been chewed since earliest times and is often regarded as an aphrodisiac. Aristotle forbade the chewing of mint by Alexander the Great's soldiers because he felt it aroused them erotically and sapped their desire to fight. (For a mint where money is made, *see* MONEY.)

mint julep.   An alcoholic drink, associated with Kentucky since the early 19th century, made with bourbon, sugar, and finely cracked ice and garnished with sprigs of mint, all served in a tall, frosted glass. *Julep* comes ultimately from the Persian *gul,* rose, and *ab,* water, indicating that it was originally some kind of rose water drink.

minx.   *Minx* has nothing to do with *minks,* except that a minx may wear a mink. *Minx* refers to an impudent or saucy, flirtatious girl or woman. The word may come from Low German *minsk,* hussy, but some authorities mark its origin unknown. In any case *minx* has been part of the language since the 16th century, when it first meant a pet dog. In *Othello* (1604) Shakespeare used it as we often do today: "Damn her, lewd minx! O, damn her!"

miracle fruit.   When chewed together, the berrylike fruits of the African shrub *Synsepalum dulcificum* and *Thaumatococcus daniellii* make sour substances taste sweet. For this reason they are called the "miracle fruit," "miracle berry," "miraculous fruit," and "serendipity berry." Another African shrub, *Dioscoreophyllum cumminsii,* goes by the same names for the same reason.

mirage.   *Mirage,* ultimately from the Latin *mirare,* to look or wonder at, refers to an optical illusion, something without substance or reality. Most often mirages occur in the desert, as hundreds of cartoons depicting illusory oases have shown, but American humorist George Ade used the word differently. One afternoon he was sitting with a little girl at a friend's house. "Mr. Ade," she said, looking up from her storybook, "does *m-i-r-a-g-e* spell *marriage?*" "Yes, my child," Ade softly replied.

Miranda.   *See* URANUS.

mirandize.   To advise anyone taken into custody by the police that he or she has a right to remain silent and to have legal counsel. The U.S. Supreme Court made this ruling in 1966, when plaintiff Ernesto A. Miranda brought the case to court in *Miranda v. Arizona. Mirandize* itself has become commonly used, as in, one detective to another: "Did you mirandize him when you picked him up?"

miscegenation.   This term is not often heard anymore. It refers to marriage or cohabitation between a man and woman of different races. The term derives from the Latin words for "to mix" and "race" and is said to have been coined in a pamphlet entitled *Miscegenation: The Theory of the Blending of the Races, Applied to the American White Man and Negro*, published anonymously by New York journalist David Goodman Croly (1829–1889) in 1863.

miserere. *See* BENEFIT OF CLERGY.

mish-mosh. A confusing mess, a hodgepodge. In *The Joys of Yiddish*, Leo Rosten reports that Groucho Marx once told a politician, "You'll never get votes in the Bronx if you go on saying *mish-mash* instead of *mish-mosh*." *Mish-mash* is indeed the most common pronunciation in the U.S., but the *O.E.D.*, tracing the word back to 1585, spells it *mish-mosh*. No one is sure, but the word may come from the German *Mischmasch* or the Danish *misk-mask*, both meaning about the same.

Miss America. The winner of the annual national beauty contest held in the U.S. every year since 1921, though it wasn't called the Miss America contest until the following year. The winner is crowned as the most beautiful young woman in the nation. *Miss America* is also used to describe any pretty American girl. Since the Miss America contest debuted, there have been many spinoffs, including a Mrs. America, Miss Universe, and Miss World contest.

missionary position. The face-to-face position, man atop woman, that Christian missionaries allegedly taught converts (who were ignorant of the position) was the only proper way to have sex. I've been unable to ascertain whether missionaries taught or advocated this practice, and the expression was first recorded only as recently as about 1965—one would expect that the first references to this would be much older. The term's slang antonym, *dogways*, was first recorded in the late 19th century in England, according to Partridge, while in the U.S. *The Random House Historical Dictionary of American Slang* dates *dog fashion* to 1900.

a miss is as good as a mile. Charlemagne's faithful warriors Amis and Amile shared many things in common, even their martyrdom—but they aren't the inspiration for this old saying. The expression is really meaningless until you study its original form: "An inch in a miss is as good as an ell." In the 19th century the phrase was shortened by Sir Walter Scott, who also substituted the alliterative *mile* for "ell."

Mississippi. The Chippewa called the river for which the state is named the *mice sipi*, the "big river," which white men spelled *Mississippi*. The Magnolia State was admitted to the Union in 1817 as our 20th state.

Miss Lonelyhearts. A disparaging name for a newspaper columnist, usually a woman, who gives advice to the lost and lovelorn, typically in answer to their letters. The term is kept alive in American author Nathaniel West's masterpiece *Miss Lonelyhearts* (1933) in which a male writer takes on the job of the columnist. The British call a Miss Lonelyhearts an Agony Aunt or, rarely, an Agony Uncle, but these expressions haven't much currency in the U.S. *Agony column*, common in Britain

and the U.S., dates back to the mid-19th century, when it was a column in which people advertised for missing persons.

miss lucy. A South African fish (*Chrysoblephus gibberups*) that is also called the "red stumpnose" and several other names. Wrote one newspaper editor: "I like the name miss lucy. Maybe in the days of the early fishermen there was a colorful character ashore known . . . as Miss Lucy and this fish was named after her."

Missouri. *Missouri* is either from the name of a Sioux tribe, "people of the big canoes," living in the region, or from an Algonquian word adapted by the French meaning "muddy water," in reference to the Missouri River. The Show Me State was admitted to the Union in 1821 as our 24th state, having previously been the Missouri Territory.

miss the boat. To miss a chance or opportunity because one is too late, as a person might be for a ship set to sail at a specific time. This American expression dates back to the early 1900s. *Miss the bus* or *train* are variations on the phrase.

mistletoe. Kissing under the mistletoe might not seem so romantic to those who know one possible origin of this word. According to some authorities, *mistletoe* derives from the Old English word *mistiltan; tan* means "twig" and *mistil* means "dung." It seems that in olden times people thought mistletoe shoots sprang from bird droppings. Another theory is that *mistil* means "bird-lime" and refers to a sticky substance long used to catch birds that was made by boiling mistletoe twigs. Mistletoe, known to be poisonous, was used in connection with human sacrifices by the Druids, which is why the early Christian church forbade its use in church decoration. Kissing under the mistletoe is an English custom dating back to the early 17th century. Few people know that each kiss requires the plucking of a berry from the mistletoe and that the kissing is finished when the last berry is picked. The berries should not be eaten: They are poisonous.

mistral. A violent, cold, and dry northern wind that blows toward southern France and closeby regions. The word, dating back to the late 16th century, comes ultimately from the Latin *magister*, master.

Mistress of the Night. Not a fabled courtesan but a flower. The tuberose (*Polianthes tuberose*) in the ancient "language of flowers" signifies "the pleasures of love." Because the strongest fragrance of their highly fragrant white flowers is released after sundown, it is called the "Mistress of the Night."

mithridatize. Mithridates VI trusted no one. Coming to the throne when only 11, this king of Pontus, an area in Asia Minor along the Black Sea, eventually murdered his mother, his sons, and the sister he had married in order to retain power, and once killed all his concubines to prevent his harem from falling into enemy hands. All his days he had guarded himself against poisoning by accustoming his body to small amounts of poison, rendering himself immune by gradually increasing these daily doses. Then, weary of his son's treachery, he decided to commit suicide and found that he had *mithridatized* himself far too well. No poison in any amount worked, for he had total immunity.

Instead, he had to have a mercenary or slave stab him to death. Such is the story, anyway, that the credulous Pliny the Elder tells us about Mithridates, King of Pontus (120–63 B.C.), betrayed by the very poisons he himself had so often used to kill. A *mithridate* is the antidote to all poisons that Pliny claims Mithridates had developed. It contained 72 ingredients, none of them given by the historian. *See* TAKE WITH A GRAIN OF SALT.

miz. In the U.S. South, *Miz*, meaning "Mrs.," has long been a title of respect for a married woman. In Britain, however, *miz* means depressed, down, a shortening of *miserable*. A British detective novel might well be titled *The Case of the Miz. Ms.*, for MS. is also commonly used there.

mnemonics. *See* MUSES.

moaningestfullest. American mountain folk like to use comparative and superlative suffixes, which can be attached to any part of speech, as in "He was the moaningestfullest hound I ever did see." *Beautifulest, curiousest,* and *workingest* are also good examples.

mob. Englishmen often criticize Americans for their laziness in shortening words like *fanatic* to *fan*, but they were doing the same thing long before. Early in the 17th century some British Latin scholars introduced the phrase *mobile vulgus*, "movable (or fickle) crowd," for an excited or fickle crowd. People shortened this to one word, *mobile*, which they pronounced "mobilly," and then further abbreviated it to *mob*. Language purists were quite indignant. "This Humour of speaking not more than we need . . . has so miserably curtailed some of our words," Addison complained, citing *mob* as a new vulgarism. "I have done my utmost for some years past to stop the progress of 'mob' . . . ," Steele wrote in the *Tatler*, "but have been plainly borne down by numbers, and betrayed by those who promised to assist me." *Mob*, of course, survived all its critics. Said Swift of the word in *Polite Conversation*, "Abbreviations exquisitely refined: as *Pozz* for 'positively,' *Mobb* for 'Mobile.' "

Moby-Dick. Mocha Dick, the stout gentleman of the latitudes, the prodigious terror whale of the Pacific, the redoubtable white sperm whale that fought and won over 100 sea battles against overwhelming odds—such was the reputation in the extravagant language of the time of the whale Herman Melville immortalized as Moby-Dick. Melville probably first read about Mocha Dick in a piece by Jeremiah N. Reynolds in the May 1839 *Knickerbocker Magazine;* undoubtedly, though, he heard of him long before in the forecastles of ships he sailed on. The last mention in history of Mocha Dick is dated August 1859, when off the Brazilian banks he is said to have been taken by a Swedish whaler. He had already become legend when Herman Melville wrote *Moby-Dick* in 1850—Melville changing his prenomen to Moby probably to suggest his amazing mobility and to avoid association with the color mocha for his white whale. The whale had been named Mocha Dick not for his color, but after the conical-peaked Mocha Island off the coast of Chile. *See* MOCHA.

mocha. The Arabian Red Sea port of Mocha gave its name to the variety of coffee called mocha sometime in the early 15th century, when it was a leading exporter of coffee beans. It was only when chocolate was flavored with mocha coffee centuries later that *mocha* became the word for a chocolate brown color. Today the city of Mocha is in Yemen and is called Mukka. *See* MOBY-DICK.

(a) modest man with much to be modest about. A famous insult by which Winston Churchill summed up Clement Attlee, the British prime minister who came after him in 1946. *See* CHURCHILLIAN.

mogul. *See* HIGH MUCKEY-MUCK.

Mohammedanism. *See* MUHAMMADANISM.

Mohawks. The Mohawk Indians were one of the smallest tribes of the Iroquois League of Five Nations, but were probably the most fierce and aggressive. In fact, *Mohawk* comes from *Mohowawok*, "man-eaters," a name given the tribe by their enemies, the Narragansett. Living along the Mohawk River in New York State from Schenectady to Utica, the Mohawks sided with the British during the Revolution, but the British did not honor their name in English, *Mohawk* or *Mohock* being used as early as 1711 to indicate one of a class of aristocratic ruffians who infested the streets of London. These *Mohocks* were said to have mauled passers-by "in the same cruel manner which the Mohawks . . . were supposed to do," being in Swift's words: "a race of rakes . . . that play the devil about the town every night, slit people's noses, and beat them."

mohole. One of the few people to have a hole in the ground named for him is Yugoslav geologist Andrija Mohorovičić. The first two letters of his name, *Mo*, plus *hole*, give us the word *mohole*, a hole bored through the Earth's crust for geological study.

mojo. An African-based word from the U.S. Gullah dialect that means "magical powers" or power of any type and is heard throughout the country today among both blacks and whites. Gullah in its purest form is spoken by African Americans on the Sea Islands off the Georgia–South Carolina coast.

mokusatsu. If the Japanese word *mokusatsu* hadn't been misinterpreted, World War II might have ended sooner, atomic power might never have been used in warfare, and tens of thousands of lives might have been saved. *Mokusatsu* has two meanings: (1) to ignore, and (2) to refrain from comment. As historian Stuart Chase has written, "The release of a press statement using the second meaning in July 1945 might have ended the war then. The Emperor was ready to end it, and had the power to do so. The cabinet was preparing to accede to the Potsdam ultimatum of the Allies—surrender or be crushed—but wanted a little more time to discuss the terms. A press release was prepared announcing a policy of *mokusatsu*, with the 'no comment' implication. But it got on the foreign wires with the 'ignore' implication through a mix-up in translation: 'The cabinet ignores the demand to surrender.' To recall the release would have entailed an unthinkable loss of face. Had the intended meaning been publicized, the cabinet might have backed up the Emperor's decision to surrender." Instead, there came Hiroshima and Nagasaki.

mole.   John le Carré did not originate the term *mole*, for "an undercover agent in the enemy camp," we are told by retired intelligence officer Walter L. Pforzheimer. According to a news feature in the *New York Times* (Feb. 7, 1984), Mr. Pforzheimer's extensive library of spy literature contains a rare Elizabethan manuscript that proves the term was coined by Francis Bacon. The sense behind the term, of course, is that a mole burrows underground and sleeps there for long periods.

moll.   *See* GUN MOLL.

molly.   Of the many tropical fish kept in millions of home aquariums only guppies are more popular than *mollies*, but few enthusiasts know that the fish takes its feminine name from a man. Count François N. Mollien (1758–1850) wasn't a tropical fish collector—the hobby dates back only to about 1860—but a French financial genius who served several governments. Mollien was often consulted by Napoleon, who unfortunately refused to accept his advice against instituting his ill-fated "continental system." The tropical freshwater fish genus *Mollienesia* was irregularly named in Mollien's honor and since then all *mollies* with their female nickname bear this man's abbreviated surname.

mollymawk.   *See* ALBATROSS.

Molotov cocktail.   This "cocktail for Molotov" was so named by the Finns while fighting the Russians in 1940. The Russians were dropping bombs on Helsinki at the time, but Russian statesman Vyacheslav Mikhailovich Molotov (1890–1986) claimed that they were only dropping food and drink to their comrades. This equation of food and drink with bombs quickly resulted in the black-humorous term *Molotov breadbasket* for an incendiary bomb and then *Molotov cocktail* for a gasoline-filled bottle with a slow burning wick that is ignited before the crude incendiary is thrown; when the bottle hits the ground it bursts and the ignited gasoline spreads over its target. The weapon had first been used by the Chinese against Japanese tanks in 1937. Molotov was Soviet premier at the time the Finns derisively named the "cocktail" after him. He had only the year before negotiated the infamous Russo-German nonaggression pact, which is sometimes called the Molotov-Ribbentrop pact but is best known as the Pact of Steel. Molotov, a communist from his early youth, changed his name from Skriabin to escape the Czarist police. (*Molotov* comes from *molot*, Russian for "hammer.") He rose quickly in the party hierarchy, serving in many capacities. In 1940 the city of Perm was renamed Molotov in his honor, but the wily diplomat later fell into disfavor, being sharply attacked by Khrushchev at the 22nd Party Congress in 1961, and was expelled from the Communist Party, to which he was readmitted in 1984.

molting.   Molting is a process associated with growth that involves shedding an outer covering, such as feathers, skin, or shell, the word deriving ultimately from the Latin *mutare*, to change. A vivid example of molting is seen in the lobster's shedding its hard inelastic shell. After feeding rapaciously, the crustacean lies on its side, and the membrane joining its body and tail splits across the back. Curling up into a V-shape, the lobster then begins working itself out of its suit of armor. It pulls its entire body through the narrow slit, including its claws, which must be drawn through openings only a 10th their size. The whole process takes from five to 20 minutes. With yet another skeleton of its old life behind it, the reincarnated creature crawls into a secure burrow until it grows heavier and its jellylike armor calcifies. It must do this 10 times in its first year alone.

moly.   According to Homer, the Greek god Hermes gave the mythical herb moly to Ulysses as an antidote against the sorceries of Circe. A number of plants bear the name *moly* today, but none has been identified as the moly of legend.

mom and pop stores.   Mom and pop stores are an old American institution; there were, for example, thousands of candy stores run by a husband and wife team in New York City from the 1920s through the 1950s. But the term *mom and pop store* is first recorded in 1962. It is occasionally used today to describe any small business with a few employees.

moment.   *Moment* has always been used to mean a portion of time too brief to be taken into account, an instant. But as the name of a definite measure of time it has varied throughout the years. Today *moment* specifically means a minute, 60 seconds, while, according to one old English time unit, a moment took 1½ minutes and in medieval times a moment was either ¹⁄₄₀ or ¹⁄₅₀ of a minute. Rabbinical reckoning makes a moment precisely 1/1.080 hour. In 1767 a writer described a clock with three hands, "one for the hours, one for the minutes, and a third for the moments."

momser.   *See* MAMSER.

Momus.   Momus, the Greek god of ridicule, was banished from heaven for his censures upon the gods—he once blamed Zeus for not having put a window in the breast of a man that Zeus had made. His name has been used in English for a faultfinder or captious critic since at least the 16th century.

monadnock.   Any mountain or rocky mass that has not eroded greatly over the ages and stands isolated in a plain. The term takes its name from a similar mountain—New Hampshire's Mount Monadnock.

Mona Lisa smile; Gioconda smile.   The *Mona* of *Mona Lisa* is short for Madonna or Milady. Leonardo da Vinci worked over a period of four years on his celebrated portrait of Madonna Lisa, who may have been the wife of the Florentine gentleman Francesco Giocondo. Little is really known about the portrait, among the most beautiful in the world, which was completed in 1506 and is still famous for the enigmatic smile that the sitter wears, which has generally been regarded as subtly sensual, a smile of feminine mystery expressing some secret pleasure or emotion. Leonardo is said to have had music played during Madonna Lisa's sitting so that the strange rapt expression wouldn't fade from her face, but this is only one of the many legends attached to the painting, as is the story that Leonardo was in love with the lady. The painting was sold to Francis I for 4,000 gold florins and has remained a treasure of the Louvre ever since, except for a brief period when it was stolen and returned to Italy. The Mona Lisa smile is sometimes called the Gioconda smile, and the enigmatic Madonna's husband is sometimes identified as Zanobi del Giocondo of Naples rather than Florence.

monastery. Why, when a number of monks share the house called a "monastery," does the word for that house derive from Greek *monazien*, to live alone? No one is sure, but possibly the word, first recorded in the early 15th century, was suggested by early Christian monks such as St. Anthony and St. Paul, who lived alone as hermits in Egypt. St. Paul is said to have been 113 when he died in the third century, and his grave outside his cave is said to have been dug by two lions.

Monday. Monday was called *Monandaeg*, "the day of the moon," by the ancient Anglo-Saxons.

Monday-morning quarterback. Someone who plans strategies or criticizes the actions of others with the benefit of hindsight and not in the heat of battle is a Monday-morning quarterback. The Americanism is from football, dating back to the early 1940s, and originally referred to the fervid fan who tells anyone who will listen on Monday morning just what the quarterback in Saturday's or Sunday's game should have done.

Monday's child, etc. An old anonymous English rhyme, dating back about 150 years, says Monday's child (a child born on a Monday) is fair of face. The rest of the rhyme goes:

> Tuesday's child is full of grace,
> Wednesday's child is full of woe,
> Thursday's child has far to go,
> Friday's child is loving and giving,
> Saturday's child works hard for his living,
> But a child that is born on the Sabbath day,
> Is fair and wise and good and gay.

Mondrian. The nonobjective paintings of Dutch artist Pieter Cornelis Mondriaan, or Piet Mondrian (1872–1944), have had a tremendous influence on 20th-century design and architecture as well as painting. His abstract geometric designs, such as *Broadway Boogie Woogie*, which hangs in New York's Museum of Modern Art, are concerned with the geometric order underlying nature. Mondrian's dislike of curved lines and use of only primary colors developed, starting in about 1910, when he came under the sway of the French cubists; he is regarded as one of the purest nonobjective painters. The artist's work influenced the German Bauhaus movement, which insisted on modern, functional design in industry, architecture, and interior decoration. In the mid-1960s, various Mondrian fashions in women's suits and dresses were named after his style, the connection often tenuous.

money. In Roman mythology Juno was the wife of Jupiter and queen of the heavens, the goddess whose prime responsibility, among many, was to warn people of dangers. The Romans were so grateful that she had warned them of the Gallic invasion in 344 B.C. that Lucius Furius built a temple to Juno Moneta, as she was called (her last name deriving from the Latin word *moneo*, "warn"), on the Capitoline Hill. Later, the first Roman mint was attached to the temple and Juno Moneta became the goddess and guardian of finance. The coins minted there were called *moneta*, after the goddess, and the word became *moneai*

in French, which later became our *money*. The word *mint*, a place where money is made, also derives from *moneta* via the old English *mynot*. *See also* MINT.

money bags. *See* PLAY THE MARKET.

money doesn't stink. Roman emperor Vespasian (A.D. 9–79) supposedly quipped *pecunia non olet*, "money doesn't stink," when criticized for taxing the public urinals in Rome, these later dubbed VESPASIENNES after this frugal successor to Nero.

money is the root of all evil. According to the biblical passage from which the expression derives, Paul wrote to Timothy in 1 Tim. 6:10: "For the *love* of money is the root of all evil." Not the same thing at all.

money makes money. People have known for ages that money makes money, that the wealthy among us are often more successful in financial matters because they have more capital. The saying dates back to the late 1500s and may be older.

money talks. Now a folk saying rather than slang, *money talks* means that wealth is power, or money buys anything. Though it is probably older, no one has been able to trace the phrase back before 1910. J. D. Salinger used it in *Catcher in the Rye* (1950): "In New York, boy, money really talks—I'm not kidding."

monger. *See* WARMONGER.

mongoose. The Marathi name *mangus* for this Indian animal is the basis of our word *mongoose*. The *gus* in *mangus* sounded like *goose* to British ears, even though the mongoose is not even remotely related to the goose.

moniker; monicker. A person's moniker is his or her name or nickname or alias. The word dates back to mid-19th-century England. It could be simply an alteration of *monogram*, but there are many theories about its origins. One involved theory says that hoboes called themselves "the monkery" and that because monks assume new names on taking their vows, *moniker* (as an alteration of *monkery*) became hobo slang for an assumed name.

Monitor; Merrimack; Virginia. Though the Civil War battle of the *Monitor* and *Merrimack*, the first ironclad action at sea, is a familiar one, there is usually some confusion about the name of the Southern vessel. Actually, she was launched as the *Merrimack* in 1855 at the Boston Navy Yard and was originally a wooden steam frigate. She was then seized by the Confederacy in 1861, encased while in dry dock with double layered railroad iron, renamed the *Virginia*, and then launched again in 1862. After that time she was called both the *Merrimack* and the *Virginia*, even though only the last name was correct. In fact, she was most often referred to as the *Merrimac* (without the terminal *k*) over the years, a spelling that is totally unjustified. A nickname for the *Monitor* was the *tin can on a shingle*. She was the forerunner of today's battleship.

monkey. *Monkey* may derive from a proper name. In one Low German version of the *Reynard the Fox* fable, published in about 1580, Moneke is the son of Martin the Ape. Moneke either took his name from the German surname Moneke, which has many variants, or from the Italian *monna*, "a female ape." However, it is certain that the name for monkey persisted due to the popularity of *Reynard the Fox* and the little moneke that the tale included.

monkey bars.   A large three-dimensional playground structure consisting of hotizontal and vertical bars (usually steel) that children can climb and swing on. Originally monkey bars were called "*jungle gyms*," formerly a one-word trademark, but though several sources date *monkey bars* to 1950–55, this term certainly was used at least as far back as the late 1930s, when I swung on monkey bars playing Tarzan.

monkey language.   *See* TARZAN.

monkey's fist.   *Monkey* is generally nautical talk for anything small. A *monkey's fist*, dating back at least to the 19th century, is thus the nautical term for the knot or weight at the end of a heaving line that makes it easier to throw.

monkeyshines; monkey business.   "You may have barefooted boys cutting up 'monkeyshines' on trees with entire safety to themselves," observes one of the earliest writers to use *monkeyshines*, monkey-like antics, which is first recorded in 1828. *Monkey business* was recorded a little earlier, at the beginning of the century, both words suggested by the increasing number of monkeys imported by America's growing circuses and zoos.

monkey suit.   Organ grinders used to dress their simian employees in bright-colored little coats and pants that looked ridiculous on them. Feeling that a tuxedo made him look much the same, some anonymous wit dubbed his tux a monkey suit, back a century or so ago.

monkey's wedding.   Not many Zulu words have come into the English language, but South African English includes the phrase *monkey's wedding*, rain and sunshine coming at the same time, which is said to be the translation of a Zulu expression meaning the same. No one knows, however, what a monkey's wedding has to do with mixed rain and sunshine. Perhaps there is a fable explaining the phrase, but no one has found it.

monkey wrench.   One would think that the monkey wrench was so named because the wrench's sliding jaws reminded someone of a monkey's chewing apparatus. This may be the case, but there is some reason to believe that the tool was named after its inventor. One source suggests that this mechanical wizard was London blacksmith Charles Moncke, but the British do not commonly call the tool a monkey wrench, using instead the term *adjustable spanner wrench*, or just *spanner*, so this theory is suspect. A more likely explanation turned up some years ago in a collection of clippings on word origins collected by a Boston doctor. One article from the *Boston Transcript*, appearing in the winter of 1932–33, attributed the wrench's invention to a Yankee mechanic by the name of Monk employed by Bemis & Call of Springfield, Massachusetts. Monk supposedly invented the movable jaw for a wrench in 1856 and although it was given another name at first, workers in his shop were soon calling it monkey wrench. The tale has not been confirmed, but the 1856 date coincides with the first use of the word in the *Oxford English Dictionary* (1858). None of the standard dictionaries make an attempt to trace the word's origin, not even to say that the wrench resembles a monkey's jaw, just as a crane resembles a crane's neck.

monkshood.   *See* ACONITE.

monosyllable.   *See* VENERABLE MONOSYLLABLE.

Monroe Doctrine.   Something else named for our fifth U.S. president, James Monroe (1758–1831). Monroe Doctrine was the name others gave to his speech before Congress on December 2, 1823, in which he warned European powers not to interfere in affairs of the American continent. *See* ADAMITE.

Monrovia.   Monrovia, the seaport capital of Liberia, was named for U.S. president James Monroe in 1822 when the American Colonization Society founded it as a haven for ex-slaves from the United States. Mencken quotes a Liberian diplomat who says that the descendants of these American slaves, now Liberia's ruling class, "prefer to be called . . . Monrovian Liberians to distinguish themselves from the natives of the hinterland, who are generally called by their tribal names." Monrovia is the only world capital, except Washington, D.C., that is named for an American president.

Monsieur and Madame Veto.   *See* VETO.

monsoon.   1) The seasonal prevailing wind of the Indian Ocean and southern Asia, blowing from the southwest in summer (the wet monsoon), and from the northeast in winter (the dry monsoon). 2) The season of heavy rain caused by the wet monsoon winds. The word *monsoon* comes ultimately from the Arabic word *mawsim*, season. *See* DOLDRUMS; CHINOOK WINDS

Montana.   Montana, previously the Montana Territory, takes its name from the Spanish word for "mountainous." The Treasure State was admitted to the Union in 1889 as our 41st state.

monte.   A card game of Mexican origin that first became popular in the Southwest. Today, three-card monte is an always crooked "game of chance" practiced by card swindlers on street corners throughout the U.S.

Monterey Jack.   A mild American cheddar cheese said to have been named about 1945 after its inventor, David Jack, and Monterey County, California.

Montespan.   Another of Louis XIV's favorites whose name became synonymous with "mistress." Françoise Athénaïs de Pardaillan, the marquise de Montespan, was the daughter of a nobleman, Gabriel de Rochechouart, duc de Mortemart. While serving as maid of honor to Louis's queen Marie-Thérèse in 1663 she married the marquis de Montespan. The Sun King's first mistress, La Vallière, introduced Madame de Montespan to him, which she eventually regretted, as the beautiful and brilliant woman replaced her in the king's affections. La Vallière was cruelly discarded and Montespan became Louis's mistress, bearing him seven children, all of whom were later legitimized by the crown, in addition to the two she bore her husband. In the end, however, Montespan lost out to Madame de Maintenon, her companion and the governess of her children, suffering the same fate as her predecessor. But Montespan did not give up so easily. When Louis's affections showed signs of ebbing and he turned to Madame de Maintenon in about 1673, Montespan tried resorting to magic, consulting the infamous sorceress La Voison. She even tried to poison the Sun King's food, but Louis had such fond memories of her that the assassination attempt was hushed up. In 1691, she retired to a convent with a large pension from the king, and she died 16 years later, aged 66. *See* LAVALIERE; MAINTENON; POMPADOUR.

Montessori method.   Italian physician and educator Maria Montessori (1870–1952), Italy's first female doctor of medicine, became interested in the education of mentally handicapped children and opened a school for them in 1907 in the slums of Rome. This led to her method of educating all children by stressing development of a child's own natural abilities and initiative, often in play rather than by formal teaching methods. Her child-centered approach led to her book *The Montessori Method* (1909) and the development of hundreds of Montessori schools throughout the world.

Montezuma's revenge.   A euphemism for diarrhea, the words apparently dating back to about 1940 and named after the Aztec emperor who lost his empire to the conquistadors. Usually caused by impure water, the debilitating illness also goes by the names the Curse of Montezuma, the Mexican two-step or fox trot, the Aztec hop, and the Mexican toothache. In other parts of the world it is known as the Tokyo trots, the Rangoon runs, and the Delhi belly. *See* AZTECT TWO-STEP.

month of Sundays.   A very long time, as in "It's taken me a month of Sundays to finish this." The expression, still heard, is a holdover from another era, when Sundays were considered long days because Christians weren't permitted to do much on them besides observe the day religiously, an obligation often enforced by laws. The expression dates back to Victorian times in England. *See* BLUE.

mooch.   *Mooch* was first recorded in an 1857 British slang dictionary, meaning "to go about sponging on your friends." This led to the current American meaning of "to borrow, usually with no intention of paying back, to freeload or beg," as in "He's always mooching cigarettes off me." But in British English the original meaning of *mooch* has changed, and the word now means "to walk about slowly and carelessly without any purpose," or to hang out, a meaning not heard in America. "Minnie the Moocher" (telling of a low-down hoochie-coocher) is a 1931 song by Cab Calloway, which became his theme song.

Moog synthesizer.   This computer-like musical instrument, able to duplicate the sounds of 12 instruments simultaneously, was named in the 1960s for its American inventor, Robert Moog.

mooncussers.   Mooncussers were so called because they cussed the moon and the light that it brought, which robbed them of their livelihood. During the early 19th century, these lowlifes lured merchant ships to shore on dark nights by waving lanterns that were mistaken for the lights of other vessels. When ships were destroyed on the rocks, their cargo was collected as salvage. Inhabitants of the "backshore" of Cape Cod were called mooncussers by American sailors. Though these people were not often accused of luring ships to their destruction, they did salvage wrecks off the cape. An old story tells of a man running up to a cape church door one stormy Sunday morning and shouting "Wreck ashore!": "The minister called out authoritatively, 'Keep your seats until I have pronounced the benediction,' in the meantime making his way down the aisle as rapidly as his dignity permitted. Pausing at the door, he gave the blessing, adding, 'And now, my friends, let's all start fair.' "

Moon Hoax.   Quite a few Americans have walked on the moon by now and none has seen evidence of life there, but in 1835, according to *New York Sun* reporter Richard Adams Locke, the eminent British astronomer Sir John Herschel trained a new, powerful telescope on the moon and observed some 15 species of animals, including what seemed to be a race of winged men. Locke's article, supposedly reprinted from the actually defunct Edinburgh *Journal of Science*, raised the circulation of Locke's newspaper from 2,500 to 20,000, and inspired one ladies' club to raise money to send missionaries to the moon. The book that the *Sun* reporter wrote based on the article sold over 60,000 copies, and was studied assiduously by a scientific delegation from Yale. Locke finally admitted his hoax the following year, calling it a satire on absurd scientific speculations that had gotten out of hand. His friend Poe, who never believed a word of the story, nevertheless admitted that it had anticipated most of his own "Hans Pfall," which was the reason he left that story unfinished.

Moonies.   A name given to the followers of Sun Myung Moon (b. 1920), founder of the controversial Unification Church, which has often been charged with the brainwashing of converts and unscrupulous fund-raising methods. An avowed anticommunist, Moon emigrated to the U.S. after the Korean War and became a successful businessman before founding his church.

the Moon is made of green cheese.   Often credited to Sir Thomas More and Rabelais, this proverb actually dates back to at least the early 15th century. Even then it was assumed that anyone who believed the moon was made of green cheese, or "cream cheese," as one writer put it, was a complete fool. Originally the expression was *The moone is made of a green cheese.* Green cheese wasn't a cheese green in color, but a new cheese that hadn't aged properly yet and resembled the full moon in shape.

moonlighting.   *Moonlighting* has taken on the meaning of working at a second job after one's regular job, especially by public servants such as policemen, who are sometimes prohibited from doing so. But the word dates back to at least the late 19th century when, in England and Ireland, it meant "the performance at night of an illicit action," especially an expedition to steal or harm another's property.

moonlit.   *Moonlit* is an adjective one might have guessed had been invented by a young romantic poet, and so it was. Tennyson coined the word in his *Arabian Nights* (1830), when he was only 21: "The sloping of the moon-lit sward . . ." The British poet laureate, successor to Wordsworth, also invented *evil-starred*, in "Locksely Hall," 1842.

moonshine.   Liquor made illicitly by individuals with no distilling license; in this sense, *moonshine* dates back to the late 19th century. The name reflects the fact that the liquor was made surreptitiously, at night under the light of the moon. It was first used in this sense in America, although the British previously used the term to mean any smuggled liquor. Colorful synonyms are angel teat, Kentucky fire, squirrel whiskey, swamps dew, white lightning, and white mule.

moon shot; moon ball.   *Moon shot* refers to a rocket launching aimed at sending a spacecraft to the Moon, the term first recorded in 1958, before the U.S. made a successful moon shot. In baseball *moon shot* or *moon ball* is a long, lofty home run hit far up toward the Moon. Paul Dickson, in *The Dickson Baseball Dictionary* (1989), calls *moon shot* "a space age term," adding that "it took on new meaning in 1986 when a statistician determined that slugger Mike Schmidt hit best under a full moon."

moose.   Early American Indians noticed that the creature we call a moose ate tender bark that it ripped off trees. They named the herbivore *mus*, meaning "to tear away," this Algonquian word becoming the English word *moose*.

moot point.   A moot point is either a question that is debatable or a point that is purely hypothetical. The Anglo-Saxon words *mot*, "to meet," and *gemot*, "a meeting," are the parents of the term. In ancient times a moot was an assembly of the people, usually a court where important questions were settled by means of the public assembly. Debates on important issues were common in such courts, giving the word *moot* its present meanings. Moot courts, where hypothetical cases are discussed by law students for practice, originated at the London law colleges called the Inns of Court in the 16th century, and these moot courts reinforced the current meaning of *moot point*.

mop-up operation.   Along with *concentration camp*, another horror of modern warfare, this military term traces back to the Boer War, when the British cleared the last traces of the enemy from territory they had just won—the way a housewife mops up something spilled on the floor. The word *mop* probably comes from the Latin *mappa*, "cloth," which also gives us the word *map*. Mop fairs, or hiring fairs, were held in England over two centuries ago, with domestics gathering on the fairgrounds ready to be inspected by potential employers.

mora.   Deriving from the Italian *mora*, of unknown origin, *mora* or *morra* is a game in which one player guesses the number of fingers held up simultaneously by another player. The ancient Romans called the game *micare digitis* and a Chinese version is called *chai mei*. The game, explains one writer, "consists in showing the fingers to the other across the table, and mentioning a number at the same moment; as if one opens out two fingers, and mentions the number four, the other instantly shows six fingers, and mentions that number—if he errs in giving the complement of 10, he pays a forfeit by

drinking a cup." A similar game called "love" was recorded in England about a century earlier (1585), a player in this version holding up a certain number of fingers and the other player, eyes closed, trying to guess that number. The old game was played by Rabelais and, no doubt, Shakespeare.

mordido.   Graft, a bribe. In *Texas* (1985) James Michener wrote: "[It's] the most useful word on the border. Means *little bite*. And sometimes not so little. It's the oil that makes Mexico run. Payola. Graft."

more than one way to skin a cat.   *There are more ways of killing a cat than choking it with cream* was the older form of this British expression. This implied that the method under discussion was rather foolish, since cats like cream and wouldn't likely choke to death on it. But the saying evolved until it took on its present meaning—that there are more ways than one of accomplishing an undertaking. The expression shouldn't be confused with the American saying *skinning the cat*, which describes the maneuver where a child, hanging from a tree branch, draws up his legs through his arms and over the branch and pulls himself into a sitting position atop the branch.

morganatic marriage.   *See* LEFT-HANDED COMPLIMENT.

Morgan horse.   Justin Morgan is the only American horse ever to sire a distinctive breed. A bay stallion foaled in about 1793, he belonged to Justin Morgan (1747–98), a Vermont schoolteacher. The horse bearing Morgan's name was probably a blend of Thoroughbred and Arabian with other elements, fairly small at 14 hands high and 800 pounds. Morgan, an aspiring musician, bought his colt in Massachusetts, naming him Figure and training him so well that he won trotting races against much larger Thoroughbreds. Eventually, Figure came to be called after his master. After his owner died, Justin Morgan was bought and sold many times in the 28 years of his life. One of those unusual horses whose dominant traits persist despite centuries of inbreeding, his individual characteristics remain essentially unchanged in the Morgan breed of horses he sired. Morgans are still compact, virile horses noted for their intelligence, docility, and longevity, many of them active when 30 years of age or more. Heavy-shouldered, with a short neck but delicate head, they are noted for their airy carriage and naturally pure gait and speed. Morgans were long the favorite breed for American trotters until the Hambletonian strain replaced them.

Mormon.   The name of members of the Church of Jesus Christ of Latter-day Saints, which is centered in Salt Lake City, Utah. *Mormon* derives from the name of the fourth-century prophet said to be the author of writings found by Joseph Smith and published in 1830 as the *Book of Mormon*. "Mormon Church" is a common but unofficial name for the Church of Jesus Christ of Latter-day Saints.

Mormon City.   An old name for Salt Lake City, Utah.

Mormon crickets.   Early Mormon settlers knew of no way to fight the wingless locustid (*Analrus simplex*) and were left to rely on their prayers. (*See* GULL). The Mormon cricket remains a formidable problem in Utah today, destroying over $25 million in crops in 2001. These "eating machines" will eat anything, even themselves, according to the U.S. Agriculture Department. They have been plaguing Utah farmers for over a century and a half, and there is no end in sight.

Mormon State. A popular nickname for Utah, which was of course settled by Mormons. Utah calls itself the Beehive State and its state seal depicts a beehive and bees representing the industry of its people. It is also called the Deseret State (*deseret* is a word in the *Book of Mormon* signifying a honeybee), the Land of the Mormons, the Land of the Saints, and the Salt Lake State. *See* UTAH.

Mornay sauce. French Protestant leader Philippe de Mornay (1549–1623) invented *sauce Mornay* for King Henry IV. Made with fish broth, the white sauce is enriched with Parmesan and Gruyere cheese and butter. Popularly known as the Protestant Pope, Mornay was Henry's right-hand man until the king converted to Catholicism and the Seigneur Duplessis-Mornay fell out of favor. After Henry's assassination, Louis XIII finally retired Mornay as governor of Saumur because of his opposition to the government's rapprochement with Catholic Spain. Mornay's spiritual writings and organizing abilities strongly influenced the development of a Protestant party in France.

morning glory. Because the morning glory only opens its flowers in the morning, it has been used as a synonym for a person who begins something brilliantly but does not fulfill his or her promise. The expression dates back almost a century in American sports. This honeysuckle (*Ipomoea purpurea*) takes its genus name from the Greek for "worm" and "similar," in allusion to its twining habit.

moron; amp. It is often noted that *moron*, as a scientific designation for a feebleminded person, was the only word ever voted into the language. It was adopted in 1910 by the American Association for the Study of the Feeble Minded from the name of a foolish character in Molière's play *La Princesse d'Élide*. This claim overlooks the fact that the unit of electric current called an *ampere*, or *amp*, was adopted at the International Electrical Congress held in Paris 29 years earlier. The ampere, the unit by which the strength and rate of flow of an electric current can be measured, was named for the brilliant French scientist André-Marie Ampère (1775–1836). His name also gives us such technical terms as *amperehour, Ampère's law, ampereturn,* and *amperometric titration.*

morpheme. A *morpheme*, from the Greek *morphema*, "unit of form," is the smallest part of speech that conveys a meaning. In the word *dogs*, for instance, *dog* is one morpheme, while *s*, indicating plurality, is another.

morphine. The narcotic drug takes its name from the Roman poet Ovid's name for the god of dreams, Morpheus, who is the son of Hypnos, the god of sleep. His name, in turn, is based on the Greek *morphe*, form, with allusion to the forms or shapes seen in dreams. To be IN THE ARMS OF MORPHEUS is to be asleep.

Morris chair. Something of a Renaissance man was English poet, artist, and pamphleteer William Morris (1834–96). His collected works fill 24 volumes, and it would take a good many volumes to do justice to his full life. In addition to his poetry and art, Morris found time to help establish Britain's Socialist Party and can be counted an architect, interior decorator, master craftsman, novelist, translator, editor, publisher, and printer as well. In 1861 he founded a company to reform Victorian tastes by producing wallpaper, furniture, stained glass, metalware, and other decorations. Thus began the arts and crafts movement in Britain, which emphasized naturalness and purity of color in objects produced by hand. Among the furniture made by the company was the Morris chair, a large easy chair with an adjustable back and removable cushions.

Morris dance. The Morris dance, originally a "Moorish dance," derived from the ancient military dances of the Moors. Introduced into England from Spain by John of Gaunt in about 1350, its name in French was *danse mauresque* and in Flemish *mooriske dans*. But the dance, which used the tabor as an accompaniment, eventually assumed a very British flavor. It was usually performed by groups of five men and a boy—the five miming Robin Hood, Little John, Friar Tuck, Allan-a-Dale, and other characters from the Robin Hood stories, while the boy played Maid Marian. Generally danced on May Day and in various processions and pageants, the fantastic spectacular was banned by the Puritans but was later revived. It has been revived recently with the renewed interest in folk dancing.

Morrison shelter; Morrison mousetrap. A portable World War II bomb shelter or air-raid shelter. The British indoor shelter was made of steel and shaped like a table. Two or three people could fit under it, and it was commonly used as a table when not employed during an air raid. It is named after British home secretary Herbert S. Morrison (1888–1965), who possibly did not like the shelter's slang name: "Morrison mousetrap."

Morse code. "What hath God wrought?" were the famous words sent in Morse code by its inventor on May 24, 1844. Samuel Finley Breese Morse (1791–1872) had begun experimenting with his electric telegraph 12 years earlier, and Congress later granted the penniless inventor $30,000 to build the experimental line from Washington to Baltimore over which he sent his historic message. The Morse code he invented in conjunction with his telegraph was first called the Morse alphabet and is of course a system of dots and dashes representing letters, figures, and punctuation, the dash in the system equaling three times the length of the dot in time. Morse didn't start out as a scientist. After graduation from Yale, he studied in England and began a career in art, earning a reputation as a portrait painter. Though his interest in electricity began during his college days, he was unaware that a number of telegraphs had been independently invented before 1830. Morse was forced to defend his invention in various patent suits, but emerged a victorious and very wealthy man.

mortal coil. Shakespeare, of course, made this term famous in *Hamlet*, but many who use the phrase have some vague idea that the *coil* in it is a synonym for the globe or sphere. This is not so, the *coil* here deriving from Elizabethan slang for turmoil or bustle.

mortarboard. The caps worn with their gowns by high school and college graduates in America were apparently named by some anonymous mid-19th-century wit who thought they resembled the square boards masons still use for holding mortar. The cap began life as ecclesiastical headgear in the 17th century and wasn't worn by university students until the early 1800s or thereabouts.

mortgage. English jurist Sir Edward Coke explained in the early 17th century why the Old French expression *mortgage* meant "dead pledge," taking its name from *mort*, "dead," and *gage*, "pledge": "It seemeth that the cause why it is called mortgage is, for that it is doubtful whether the Feoffer will pay at the day limited such summe or not & if he doth not pay, then the land which is put in pledge upon condition for the payment of the money, is taken from him for ever, and so dead to him upon condition, & c. And if he doth pay the money, then the pledge is dead as to the Tenant . . ."

mosaic. The two words *mosaic*, "a design or picture made from small pieces of stone or other material," and *Mosaic*, referring to the prophet Moses, are unrelated. In fact, the strict Jewish and Muhammadan interpretations of the Ten Commandments Moses brought down from Mount Sinai hold that the second Commandment forbids the making of any likeness of anything, so the capital letter in *Mosaic* is an important distinguisher. The word for the design *mosaic* comes to us via French and Latin from the Greek *Mousa* ("a Muse"), *mosaic* work being associated with the Muses in ancient Greece. *See* MOSES' CRADLE.

moscato. Everything is not swell with muscatel. *Moscato*, or *muscatel*, is a rich, sweet wine. According to Bill Bryson's excellent *Mother Tongue* (1990), its name in Italian means "wine with flies in it." *Mosca* means "*fly*" in Italian.

Moses' cradle; Mosaic code. A Moses' cradle is a shallow wicker bassinet, its name deriving from the basket made of bullrushes that Moses' mother hid him in when oppressed Israelites were ordered to kill all their male children (Exod. 2:1–5) Pharaoh's daughter found the child, named him Moses, "Because I drew him out of the water," and let his mother nurse him. As a young man, Moses, who grew up in the splendor of the court, killed an Egyptian oppressing a Jew and fled into the wilderness, but at the age of 80 he was called by God, through a voice from a burning bush, to return to Egypt and free the Hebrews. Pharaoh refused God's demand until 10 plagues were sent and Moses then led his people to Mount Sinai. For 40 years after he led them through the wilderness, drawing up religious and ethical rules known as the Mosaic code during this time. The first five books of the Bible, the Hebrew Torah or the Pentateuch, are regarded as Moses' work. After viewing Canaan from Mount Nebo, he died alone at 120, his people compelled to wander in the wilderness until one generation had passed away because they had rebelled against crossing into the Promised Land. *See* MOSAIC.

mosey. According to *Webster's* and most authorities the Spanish *vamos*, "let's go," became *vamoose* in American English, which begot the slang word *mosey*, "to stroll or saunter about leisurely." But it is possible, one theory holds, that the word instead takes its name "from the slouching manner of wandering Jewish peddlers in the West, many of whom were called Moses, Mose, or Mosey." Neither explanation seems ideal, but nothing better has been offered.

mossback. A very conservative person, a reactionary. The term is said to have been coined to describe draft-dodging southerners who hid out in the swamps so long that moss grew on their backs. These mossybacks weren't forgotten after the Civil War, for by the early 1880s their derogatory name began to be used as an epithet for extremely conservative political factions.

the most unkindest cut of all. "This was the most unkindest cut of all," Shakespeare had Antony say in *Julius Caesar*. This most famous of literary double superlatives wasn't the only such "grammatical crudity" he used. The double superlative and double comparative ("more larger") were considered excellent devices for emphasis, by Elizabethan writers. So were multiple negatives like the Bard's "Thou hast spoken no word all this while—nor understood none either."

motel. Most sources credit West Coast motor lodge owner Oscar T. Tomerlin with coining the word *motel* in 1930, Tomerlin welding it together from *motor hotel*, which he had previously called his place. But in her book *Palaces of the Public, A History of American Hotels* (1983) Doris E. King says that the word originated in 1925 with a San Luis Obispo, California establishment that offered a garage with its roadside cottages and called itself a *Mot-el Inn*. *See* NO-TEL MOTEL.

moth-eaten. People have been using this expression for at least 600 years to describe something eaten by moths or old. However, it isn't adult moths, but moth larvae that destroy clothing that isn't stored properly. The moths we see fluttering around in the closet don't eat clothing, and some species eat nothing at all during their brief adult lives.

Mother Carey's chickens. *Mother Carey's chickens* is a mystery because no real Mother Carey has ever been found. But many etymologists uphold Brewer's theory that the phrase is a corruption of the Latin *Mater Cara* ("Dear Mother"), another name for the Virgin Mary. However, in the absence of evidence, Ernest Weekley's conclusion in *The Romance of Words* still seems best: "Mother Carey's chickens, probably a nautical corruption of some old Spanish or Italian name; but, in spite of ingenious guesses, this lady's genealogy remains as obscure as that of Davey Jones or the Jolly Roger." The sea birds are also called PETRELS.

Mother Goose. The famous book of nursery rhymes often called *Mother Goose's Melodies* is said to have been printed in Boston in 1719 by Thomas Fleet, from verses his mother-in-law, Mrs. Elizabeth Goose, created or remembered and repeated. There is no doubt that Mrs. Goose (1665–1757) existed. She was born Elizabeth Foster in Charlestown, Massachusetts, and at the age of 27 married Isaac Goose (formerly Vergoose) of Boston, inheriting 10 stepchildren and bearing six children of her own. One of her daughters married the printer Fleet, who had a shop on Pudding Lane in Boston. At this point the facts become unclear, yielding, at any rate, many a good story.

mother-in-law plant.   A common name for *Dieffenbachia seguline*, which itself honors 19th-century German botanist J. F. Diefenbach. *Dieffenbachia* is called the "mother-in-law plant" and "dumbcane" because an irritating enzyme in the leaves of this houseplant causes swelling of the tongue and temporary speechlessness should they be chewed. But no one should wish Dieffenbachia poisoning on a mother-in-law or anybody else; it is a dangerous, painful condition requiring prompt medical care.

mother lode.   In contemporary speech, *mother lode* is used as a synonym for "jackpot." Its literal meaning since the 1880s is a principal vein of ore in a mine; also, capitalized, the Mother Lode of the Sierra Nevada, a great California quartz vein running from Mariposa to Amador.

mother of all; Mother of Parliaments; mother of all bombs. The phrase *mother of all* was overused at the time of the Persian Gulf war (1991) and is less often heard today. It was employed in constructions like *the mother of all guns, the mother of all wars, the mother of all ships*, etc. *Mother*, of course, has been used figuratively for centuries for the utmost or origin of anything, as in *Mother of Parliaments*, a British expression coined by John Bright in 1865. The *moab* is a fearsome U.S. bomb developed at the time of the second Iraq War (Operation Iraqi Freedom) but not used in combat. The acronym stands for *mother of all bombs*.

Mother of States.   Usually applied to Virginia, because it was the first state settled by the English, this nickname has also occasionally been given to Connecticut.

Mother's Day; Mothering Sunday   Founded by Julia Ward Howe, the American poet who wrote "The Battle Hymn of the Republic," shortly after she returned to Boston from Europe on a crusade for world peace in 1872. Howe called for June 2 to be set aside for "Mothers' Peace Day" and beginning with Boston, many cities and states adopted the tradition before President Woodrow Wilson authorized Mother's Day as a national holiday in 1915. Today it is celebrated on the second Sunday in May. Father's Day, the third Sunday in June, is set aside to honor fathers.

The original Mother's Day was what the British call Mothering Sunday, the fourth Sunday in Lent, also known as Laetare Sunday or Mid-Lent Sunday. Children since the 19th century have customarily given presents to their mothers on this day, hence its name. But the first Mother's Day was celebrated in the U.S. in 1908, when Congress resolved that the second Sunday in May be recognized as the national day to honor mothers. Mother's Day is widely accepted in Britain today, but the British also celebrate Mothering Sunday.

Mother Shipton.   A female NOSTRADAMUS, Mother Shipton is a legendary figure in English literature who is supposed to have foretold the death of Cromwell and the great London fire of 1666, among other accurate predictions. According to the *Life of Mother Shipton*, written by Richard Head in 1667, more than a century after her death, her real name was Ursula Shipton and she lived in Knaresborough, Yorkshire, from 1488–1561.

Born Ursula Southill or Southiel, her peasant mother was regarded as a witch by villagers, and Ursula appears to have been so ugly that she was called the "Devil's child," though not so ugly as to prevent a builder named Tobias Shipton from marrying her. Virtually nothing is known about her life, all the "facts" at best traditions, but Mother Shipton's prophecies, like Mother Nixon's, had a phenomenal hold on the minds of rural folk until as late as 1881. In that year the rumor that she had predicted the end of the world caused people to flee their homes and pray in the fields and churches all night. It developed that this prediction, along with others foretelling the coming of the steam engine, telegraph, telephone, and other modern inventions arose out of a forgery of the early *Life* by Charles Hindley, in which he added many "predictions" that had already come to pass.

motive-hunting of a motiveless malignity.   Thus did Samuel Taylor Coleridge (1772–1834) describe the villain Iago's soliloquy in Shakespeare's *Othello* (at the end of act one, scene three), which shows Iago trying to rationalize the hostility he feels. The full quote of the famous phrase is "Iago's soliloquy, the motive-hunting of a motiveless malignity—how awful it is!" The observation is from Coleridge's *Lectures on Shakespeare and Milton* (1811–12). In that same work he coined his homely definitions of prose and poetry: "Prose—words in their best order; poetry, the best words in their best order."

Motown.   A much-used nickname for Detroit, Michigan, a shortening of *Motor Town*, referring to all the cars made in America's automobile capital. Since the 1950s *Motown* has also described the upbeat, pop-influenced music made by such black artists as Stevie Wonder, the Supremes, and Marvin Gaye that was first produced on records by the black-owned Tamla Motown label in Detroit. This music is often called the "Motown sound."

mountain lion.   The North American panther or cougar. The name originated in the Colorado Rocky Mountains over a century ago.

mountain man.   Men, much celebrated in song and story, who had great skills for living off the land in the mountains. Usually a guide, trapper, or trader in the Far West before the region was settled.

Mountain of Light.   A translation of the Persian *Koh-i-Noor*, the name of the 106-carat diamond that is one of Britain's Crown jewels and has been kept in the Tower of London since it was given to Queen Victoria with the annexation of the Punjab in 1849. Every queen of England has since worn it at least once.

mountain oysters.   *See* PRAIRIE OYSTERS.

Mount Bote.   In his *Strangers in High Places* (1966) Michael Frome tells a story about how this mountain in the Great Smokies got its name through a mispronunciation: "In the 1850s a road was built from Cades Cove to the Spence Field on Thunderhead Mountain. Since there were no engineers to lay out the route, it was left to the decision of the builders, some of whom were Cherokee, as to which ridge the road should follow. As each Indian was asked his opinion, he reportedly pointed to the westernmost ridge and said 'Bote' to indicate how he voted. There being no V sound in the Cherokee language 'Bote' was a near as they could frame the word; thereafter it was Bote Mountain, while the other ridge, the loser, became Defeat Ridge." *See* GREAT SMOKIES.

mountebank. Quacks often sold their nostrums at medieval fairs by mounting a bench and giving their pitch—so often that they were given the name *mountebanks*, from the Italian *montambanco*, "mount on bench."

Mount Everest. The highest mountain in the world (29,028 feet), in the central Himalaya mountains on the border of Tibet and Nepal, takes its name from Sir George Everest (1790–1866), the British surveyor-general of India from 1830–43. Sir George never reached the top of the mountain, however. Not until 1953 did climber Edmund Hillary (later knighted for his accomplishment) and the Sherpa guide Tenzing Norgay become the first men to reach the summit.

Mount Rushmore. The colossal busts of Presidents Washington, Jefferson, Lincoln, and Theodore Roosevelt are carved on the face of the Mount Rushmore National Memorial in South Dakota, but the mountain itself is named for an obscure New York lawyer who was sent to the area by businessmen eager to know if mineral rights would be a good investment there. Young Charles Rushmore, traveling all over the Black Hills, was well liked by miners thereabouts, and one story has it that when a stranger inquired about the name of a local hill, a worker jokingly replied, "Why that's Mount Rushmore." The name stuck. The story, which may be apocryphal, is from a letter to the *New York Times Book Review* (12/22/02).

Mount Vernon. *See* GROG.

mourning dove. The American bird gets its name from both its often incessant mournful cry and its dull grayish blue plummage. It is also called the turtledove, wild dove, old-field dove, and Carolina dove or pigeon.

mourning tree. Once cut, the cypress never grows again, which probably led to its being dedicated to Pluto, the king of the infernal regions in Roman mythology. For this reason the beautiful *Cupressus funebris* was often planted in cemeteries along the Mediterranean and its wood was used to make coffins, the tree often referred to as the *mourning tree.*

mousse. *See* CHOCOLATE MOUSSE.

mouth-watering. Cavemen 100,000 years ago surely felt their mouths watering over the smell and sight of meat roasting in their fires, but this expression somehow wasn't recorded until 1555 in English. Soon after, this term for appetizing came to be used figuratively as well as literally.

movie; film. The most popular name for American motion pictures is *movies*, a word first recorded in 1906. At first the motion picture industry regarded this term as undignified, but by the 1930s all opposition had faded. Many designations were used before *movies*, including *motion pictures* (1891), *picture show* (1896), and *moving pictures* (1898). *Films, cinema,* and *flicks* are also heard though these are primarily British variations. The word *film* itself was not recorded until 1905. *See* MOVING PICTURES; ROMAN NOIR.

moving picture. This synonym for a movie, film, flick, motion picture, etc., has a longer history than one would think. The term dates back to the early 18th century, when it was first used to describe picture books flipped quickly to give the effect of motion. These flip books, known since ancient times and still common today, suggested other devices called moving pictures and the term was finally applied to the cinema two centuries later.

moxie. The rather bitter, tart, unsweetened flavor of Moxie, a popular New England soft drink, or tonic, as soda pop is often called in the area, has been suggested as the reason it yielded the slang word *moxie*, for "courage, nerve, or guts." Or maybe, Moxie braced up a lot of people, giving them courage. These are only guesses, but the tonic, a favorite since at least 1927, is definitely responsible for *a lot of moxie* and other phrases, which, however, aren't recorded until about 1939. But Moxie was originally made in 1884 as a patent medicine nerve tonic said to cure "brain and nervous exhaustion, loss of manhood, softening of the brain, and mental imbecility." This goes far in explaining *moxie*, "nerve or courage," if earlier uses for the term could be found. In any event, Moxie's Lowell, Massachusetts makers fizzed up their product toward the turn of the century when the government began cracking down on their health claims and Moxie became America's first mass-market soft drink, the company even selling their product in "Moxiemobiles," car-shaped bottles.

Mr.; Mrs. Because it was originally an abbreviation of *mistress* (wife), a word that has completely changed its meaning since then, *Mrs.* can no longer be spelled out in full form and is considered a word in itself—unlike *Mr.* which can be written out as *Mister.*

Mr. Charlie. Originally a slave term for a boss or overseer, *Mr. Charlie* is now black slang for a white man or white people in general. Also heard as *Charlie, Charles, Chuck.*

Mr. Clean. Someone very clean, untouched by scandal or corruption; someone obsessively clean. The eponymn here is the liquid cleaner Mr. Clean introduced in the late 1950s. The Mr. Clean pictured on the bottle and in ads was a bald muscular man who inspired a rash of bad jokes ("He found his wife on the floor with Mr. Clean").

Mr. Micawber. A *Mr. Micawber* is an incurable optimist and to be *micawberish* is to be incurably cheerful and optimistic. The words honor Mr. Wilkins Micawber of Dickens's *David Copperfield*, one of the immortal author's immortal characters. Mr. Micawber fails at every scheme he tries, but remains certain that "something will turn up," and is always optimistic and cheerful. No fool, he is an honest, able man and his optimism does prevail, for he finally emigrates to Australia and becomes a magistrate.

Mrs. Grundy.

> They eat, and drink, and scheme, and plod,
>   And go to sleep on Sunday—
> And many are afraid of God—
>   And more of Mrs. Grundy.

These lines from Frederick Locker-Lampson's poem "The Jester" (1857) were inspired by a character in British playwright Thomas Morton's comedy *Speed the Plough*, first staged at London's Covent Garden in 1800. Actually Mrs. Grundy is something less than a character, for she never appears on stage and is never described physically. She is the epitome of propriety, the narrow-minded, straitlaced neighbor of Farmer Ashfield and Dame Ashfield, his wife, who is obsessed with Mrs. Grundy's opinion of things. "What will Mrs. Grundy say? What will Mrs. Grundy think?" is on Dame Ashfield's lips so often that the words became proverbial for "What will that straitlaced neighbor say? What will the neighbors think?" and Mrs. Grundy herself became a symbol of prudish propriety or social convention. Dickens's Mrs. Harris, the mythical friend of Sara Gamp in *Martin Chuzzlewit* (1843) is a similar character. *See* BOX AND COX.

Mrs. O'Leary's cow.   Mrs. Patrick O'Leary's cow has had more abuse heaped upon it than any cow in history, for something it didn't do. Mrs. O'Leary was supposed to have been milking her cow on the morning of October 8, 1871, when bossie kicked over a kerosene lamp in the barn and started the great Chicago fire that killed 250 people and caused some $300 million in property damage before it was contained. No one knows how the fire really started (perhaps by spontaneous combustion in the O'Leary's haymow), but in 1924, two years before his death, Chicago newspaper reporter Michael Ahern admitted that he had invented the tale to make his stories about the blaze more colorful.

Mrs. President.   *See* HONEST ABE.

Mr. Watson, come here: I want you.   This was the first complete sentence transmitted over the telephone, by American inventor Alexander Graham Bell to his assistant Thomas A. Watson on March 10, 1876. *See* AHOY; TELEPHONE; TELEGRAPH.

Mr. W. H.   Shakespeare's sonnets, published in 1609 by Thomas Thorpe but dating back to the 1590s, were dedicated to "Mr. W. H., the onlie begetter of these insuing sonnets." Who W. H. is remains a mystery after almost four centuries. There are numerous candidates, four favorites among them: 1) Henry Wriothesley, third earl of Southhampton, to whom Shakespeare had dedicated *Venus and Adonis* (1593) and *The Rape of Lucrece* (1594); 2) William Herbert, the third earl of Pembroke, to whom the *First Folio* was dedicated; 3) Sir William Harvey, the earl of Southampton's stepfather; and 4) an anonymous friend of publisher Thorpe who procured the manuscript for the publisher. Also in contention are a mistress who betrayed Shakespeare with a friend; a dark beauty the Bard loved; and a rival poet. Oscar Wilde's *The Portrait of Mr. W. H.* is an amusing attempt to establish W. H.'s identity.

Ms.   This widely used title for a woman (pronounced "Miz") only dates back to 1950, no mention of it found anywhere before the following note in the scholarly journal *Word Study* (October 1950), which explains its origins and reveals its inventor: "An old problem, with a suggested solution, is discussed by Roy F. Bailey of the Bailey-Krehbiel Newspaper Service in Norton, Kansas. Mr. Bailey believes that we should have a word with which to address a woman whether she is married or single. Many women sign their names without indicating their marital condition. Many firms, when they are unable to discover what the condition is, write 'Miss.' Mr. Bailey suggests 'Ms' to stand for either *Miss* or *Mistress* and as an equivalent of 'Mr.' "

much ado about nothing.   Shakespeare contributed this common saying to the language, making it the title of his popular comedy *Much Ado About Nothing* (1598–9), which used as its chief source a novella by Italian writer Matteo Bandello. There are many equivalents in other languages of this expression, including *A great vineyard and few grapes* (Portuguese); *Much smoke but a small roast* (Spanish); and *Much bleating, little wool* (German).

mucilage.   *See* NOSE.

muckluk telegraph.   In Canada *muckluk telegraph* is a humorous term for word of mouth. *Muckluk* alone means "warm, sturdy boots" made from seal fur that Eskimos wear, or a similar boot. The term derives from the Inuit for "large seal."

muckraker.   Teddy Roosevelt used the expression *man with the muckrake*, taken from *Pilgrims Progress*, as a derogatory term for those who indiscriminately and irresponsibly charged others with corruption. Lincoln Steffens and other reformers, however, gladly wore the epithet *muckraker* as a badge of honor.

mucus.   *See* NOSE.

mud.   *See* HIS NAME IS MUD.

muff.   Not much used today, a muff is a thick tubular case for the hands that is covered with fur and used mostly by women to keep their hands warm. Around the turn of the century, the word was first used to describe a baseball player who misses an easy catch, one who makes a play as if his hands were in a muff.

mug; mugging; mugger.   Mugging seems first to have been New York City slang for what was called "yoking" in other parts of the country, that is, robbery committed by two holdup men, one clasping the victim around the neck from behind while the other ransacks his pockets. The term either derives from the "mugs" who commit such crimes or from the expression on the victim's face as he is brutally yoked, which can appear as if he is mugging, grimacing, or making a funny face. The term is now well-known throughout the country. As often as not the *mugger* acts alone today, and *mugging* has become a synonym for holding someone up. The spelling "mugg" seems to be yielding to *mug*. The word *mug*, for "a grimace" was introduced to England by the Gypsies and may derive from the Sanskrit word *mukka*, "face." *Mug* was used as slang for "face" in Britain as early as 1840. *Mug* for a heavy cup may come from the Swedish *mugg* meaning the same.

mugwump.   The term for great chief in Algonquin Indian dialect sounded like "mugquomp" to settlers in what is now the northeastern U.S. and soon came to mean any pompous "big shot," its spelling altered to a simpler *mugwump*. A century later *mugwump* took on another meaning in politics when regular Republicans attached it to those Republicans who bolted the party to support Democrat Grover Cleveland, instead of the corrupt James Blaine. Since then any party member who doesn't accept the party leadership and supports the opposition is called a mugwump.

Muhammadanism.   Muhammad (or Mohammed, or Mahomet) "the praiseworthy," was the title given to the founder of the Muslim religion, his original name having been Kotham or Halabi. The prophet of the Arabs was born after his father's death in about A.D. 570, grew up as an orphan in Mecca, and died in Medina in 632. A camel driver at 25, he married his employer, a rich widow 15 years his senior, who became the first of his 10 wives. Muhammad was 40 when he felt he had been called to be a prophet and began receiving messages he believed were from God, who commanded him to relay them to his countrymen. He called the monotheistic religion he preached Islam, not Muhammadanism, its keystone being that "There is no God but Allah and Muhammad is his prophet." *See* IF THE MOUNTAIN WILL NOT COME TO MUHAMMAD.

mujahedeen.   So often has this word been heard in the war against terrorism (2001) that it will almost certainly be used figuratively before long. *Mujahedeen* is Arabic for "warriors of the Holy War" and refers to the fundamentalist Muslims throughout the world fighting such a war, or *jihad*. These holy warriors are usually guerrillas or terrorists today. According to William Safire's *On Language* column in the *New York Times* (11/9/01), *mujahedeen* isn't recorded in English until 1922. The word isn't listed in any major English dictionary. Its singular form is *mujahid*, and among several alternative spellings of *mujahedeen*, all correct, is *mujahidin*.

mulberry.   Legend has it that the mulberry takes its botanical name, *Morus* from the Greek *morus*, meaning "a fool." According to the *Hortus Anglicus*, this derivation is related to the fact that it "can't be fooled," that the tree "is reputed to be the wisest of all flowers as it never buds till the cold weather is past and gone." As for the word *mulberry* itself, which should properly be *morberry*, it more prosaically derives from the Latin *morus*, which became *mure* in French. The English called the berry the "mureberry" at first, but this was difficult to pronounce (too many *r*'s) and was eventually corrupted to *mulberry* in everyday speech. An ancient legend recounted in Ovid's *Metamorphoses* tells how mulberries became red. Pyramus, a Babylonian youth, loved Thisbe, the girl next door, and when their parents forbade them to marry, they exchanged their vows through an opening in the wall between their two houses. Thisbe agreed to meet her lover at the foot of a white mulberry tree near the tomb of Ninus outside the city walls. But on reaching their trysting place she was frightened by a lion and dropped her veil when she fled deep into a cave. The lion, its mouth red from another kill, ripped the veil, covering it with blood, and when Pyramus arrived and found the bloody veil, he thought that Thisbe had been killed and devoured by the beast. Throwing himself on his sword, he committed suicide

just as Thisbe emerged from the cave. Distraught at the sight of her dying lover, Thisbe, too, fell upon his sword and committed suicide, the blood of young love mingling and flowing to the roots of the white mulberry, which thereafter bore only red fruit.

mulberry mania.   Much has been written about international tulipomania, but almost none of our history books mentions our American mulberry mania of the 1830s. This was a craze for planting the Philippine white mulberry variety *Morus multicaulis* ("many stemmed") with the expectation of making great profits in the silk industry. The leaves of these trees, used by the Chinese in sericulture and even tried by the British under James I, were said to be superior to all others for silkworm feeding, and millions of them were planted in the "multicaulis fever" that ensued. Although Ben Franklin had tried to establish a silk industry in Philadelphia, the fever really began in Connecticut, where the seven Cheney brothers founded America's first silk mill at South Manchester in 1838, after having experimented with silk culture for five years. One year, from 300 mulberry trees laid horizontally in the ground, there sprang 3,700 shoots, or enough to feed 6,000 silkworms. This meant bushels of cocoons and yards of much-wanted silk. Many farmers followed the Cheneys' example, and across America books and articles were published about raising mulberry trees. Silk societies were formed and bounties offered. Prices escalated crazily. In 1838 two-and-a-half-foot cuttings sky rocketed from $25 to $500 per hundred. In Pennsylvania alone as much as $300,000 changed hands for mulberry trees in a week, and trees were frequently resold by speculators at great profits. But by 1840 mulberry trees glutted the market, and were valued at only five cents each. When speculation collapsed and the so-called "golden-rooted trees" were uprooted from plantations in 1839, disgruntled investors coined a new word, *multicaulished*, meaning "run out," "good for nothing," "disliked." *See* TULIP.

mule; no pride of ancestry, no hope of posterity.   The long-eared, short-maned mule takes its name from Latin *mulus* meaning the same. Mules are said to have "no pride of ancestry, no hope of posterity" because they are sterile beasts of burden, being the offspring of a male donkey and a female horse. Maybe the mule has a posterity of sorts in expressions like *stubborn as a mule* and the old term *mule* for a smuggler or person who delivers contraband, especially drugs.

mule bear.   *See* GRIZZLY.

mule deer.   A small, 3½-foot-high deer (*Odocoileus hemionus*) of North America. So called because of its long, mulelike ears. Also known as the burro deer.

mule rabbit.   *See* JACKRABBIT.

muller.   Our murderer wore a low-crowned felt hat pulled down over his face in an attempt to disguise himself. But his scheme didn't work. Mr. Muller was arrested and convicted of murder, the publicity attending his hat making it more famous than the killer himself. Not only was Muller the prototype for countless real and fictional villains with large-brimmed hats pulled down over their eyes, but his name came to mean "a deerstalker hat" in England from about 1855 to 1885, a muller probably being the only hat in history that was named for a murderer.

mulligan. When you're allowed to take a *mulligan* in golf—a free shot not counted against the score after your first one goes bad—you may not be emulating some duffer of days gone by. *Mulligan* probably comes from the brand name of a once-popular sauce that was standard in barrooms. This potent seasoning of water and hot pepper seeds was sometimes mixed with beer, and jokers swore that it ate out your liver, stomach, and finally your *heart*—just what happens when you accept too many *mulligans* on the golf course. On the other hand, there are those who say that *mulligan* derives from the name of Canadian David Mulligan, who in the late 1920s was allowed an extra shot by his friends in appreciation for driving his friends over rough roads every week for their foursome at the St. Lambert Country Club near Montreal.

mulligan stew. Mulligan stew is made of meat and vegetables—whatever is available or can be begged or stolen. It is an American term, honoring an Irishman whose first name has been lost but who may have made a tasty Irish stew. Mulligan, popular among American tramps, is also called slumgullion, or slum, the term coming into use during the American gold rush when slumgullion was originally the muddy residue remaining after sluicing gravel.

mulligrubs. The *O.E.D.* calls *mulligrubs*, "a state of depression," a "gross arbitrary formation," and lets it go at that. The word is from British dialect, first recorded in 1599, and is possibly a corruption of "moldy grubs." Besides meaning *the blue devils* it can mean a stomachache. A variant is the obsolete *mubblefubbles*.

mullion. There are indeed "millions of mullions" in modern skyscrapers, for a mullion is the slender vertical member separating windows. The word is an alteration of the synonymous *monial*, and is first recorded in 1567.

mull over. To study, ponder, think about carefully, ruminate; as in "She mulled over the proposal." The term possibly comes from Middle English *mull* meaning "to moisten, crumble, soften, pulverize." It does not come from *mull* meaning "to spice and heat wine," origin unknown, or *mull*, a soft thin muslin, from a Hindi word.

multimillionaire. *Multimillionaire* was first applied to John Jacob Astor, soon after his death in 1848, aged 85. Astor had made his money in fur and New York City real estate, "the richest man in America" amassing a fortune of well over $75 million—which made a person a lot richer back then than it does today. *See also* BILLIONAIRE; MILLIONAIRE; MILLIARD; MYRIAD; TRILLIONAIRE.

multiplication, division, and silence. A historical expression no longer much used that gives the qualities most needed by a machine politician, who had to *multiply* the sources of graft, *divide* it among his flunkies, and *keep quiet* about it all. New York's "Boss" Tweed (1823–76) may have invented the phrase when asked what qualities he looked for when selecting his henchmen.

mum. *Mum* came into the news recently with the death of Britain's beloved Queen Mum, or Queen Mother, in 2002 at the age of 101. *Mum* is a short form of *mother* rarely heard in the U.S. *Mummy* is also mostly used by the British. The U.S. equivalent is *mom* or *mommy*. Queen Mother becomes the title of the king's consort after her husband, the king's, death and one of her children succeeds to the throne. *Mum* meaning silent, as in *mum's the word*, dates back to the 14th century, but its origin is unknown.

mumbo jumbo. Mama Dyumbo was really more a male chauvinist god than anything else. The English explorer Mungo Park writes in his *Travels in the Interior of Africa* that Mama Dyumbo was the spirit protecting the villages of the Khassonke, a Mandingo African tribe on the Senegal. His name literally means "ancestor with a pompon," or wearing a tuft on his hat. Mama Dyumbo was mostly a ploy used by crafty husbands to silence their noisy wives. He was called upon when a man thought one of his wives talked too much, causing dissension in his house. The husband or a confederate disguised himself as Mama Dyumbo and seized the troublemaker, frightening her with his mask, tufted headdress, and the hideous noises he made. He'd then tie the offender to a tree and "whip her silent" amid the jeers of onlookers. (The custom recalls the ducking stool procedure employed in America.) Mungo Park dubbed the bogey employed in this ritual "Mandingo," but he became known as Mumbo Jumbo, a corruption of *Mama Dyumbo*. Because the god bewildered offending women, *mumbo jumbo* came to mean confusing talk, nonsense, and meaningless ceremony, or even technical jargon that could just as well be put into plain English.

mummichog; mummachog. American names for barred killifish. They derive from the Narragansett Indians' word *Moamitteaug*, "a little sort of fish," which was first recorded in 1787 as "Mummy Chog."

mummy. The Egyptians preserved the corpses of their dead in elaborate ways, concluding the process by wrapping a corpse in bandages and waterproofing the bandages with a waxy pitch that their Persian conquerors called *mum*. This word became *mummia* in Arabic and, over a thousand years later, changed to *mummy* in English, coming to mean not only the waxy pitch covering the bandages but the preserved body itself.

mum's the word. All sorts of theories have been offered for the origins of this term for "Keep quiet, don't tell a soul," but it probably resulted from the humming *mum* sound made when one speaks through closed lips. The expression probably dates back to Shakespeare's day and he used a word something like it.

Munchausen. Baron Munchausen once shot a stag with a cherry stone and afterwards found the stag with a cherry tree growing out of its head. At least so Rudolph Erich Raspe wrote in his *Baron Munchausen's Narrative of his Marvellous Travels and Campaigns in Russia* (1785). Raspe was a German librarian who fled to England to escape the consequences of a jewel theft he had committed and wrote the very successful book to restore his resources. But he did base his character and many of his adventures on an actual Karl Friedrich Hieronymus, Freiherr von Munchausen (1720–97), a German officer who served in the Russian cavalry against the Turks and was known to grossly exaggerate his experiences. Thanks to Raspe's further exaggerations of his escapades in his one-shilling book, and many additions afterward in editions fathered by other authors, the real baron's name soon meant both a fantastic liar and a marvelous, classic lie.

munchkin.　Munchkins were once only the little people who lived in Oz, a land invented by L. Frank Baum in *The Wonderful Wizard of Oz* (1900). But with the great popularity of the book and the motion picture made from it, the word became a synonym for any little person, especially a small, adorable child.

mung bean; bean sprouts.　The Asian mung bean takes its name from the Tamil *mungu* meaning the same. These are the beans that are easiest to sprout, taking barely three days, and are used for Chinese *bean sprouts*.

Murcott Honey orange.　*See* ORANGE.

Murder, Inc.　Spelled this way, but always pronounced "Murder Incorporated." This enforcement agency of the organized crime syndicate during the 1930s is believed responsible for between 400 and 500 deaths. Murder, Inc., was controlled by top crime bosses such as Meyer Lansky, Lucky Luciano, and Frank Costello and led by Lord High Executioner Albert Anastasia, a notoriously violent killer. The group provided the mob with a ready pool of paid assassins to be used around the country. Killings were considered strictly business and carried out to protect the interests of the growing syndicate. Members of the group headquartered at Midnight Rose's, a 24-hour candy store in Brownsville, Brooklyn, where they traded tips on killing techniques and waited for assignments. Most prominent among the assassins was Pittsburgh Phil Strauss, target of 58 murder investigations but believed responsible for twice that many deaths. In 1940 law enforcement authorities arrested a number of mob members, including Abe Reles, a Murder, Inc., lieutenant. Reles, fearing others would talk to the police before him, turned informer to save himself, providing details on hundreds of murders and sending many of his colleagues to the electric chair. Before completing his testimony against the highest-ranking mob bosses, Reles fell to his death from the window of a Coney Island hotel where he was under police protection. He was thereafter called "the canary who couldn't fly."

murder the language.　This common saying, applied to inept writing, may have been suggested by a reference that the *OED* dates back to about 1644 ("Hopkins and Sternhold murder the Psalmes"). John Hopkins (d. 1549) and Thomas Sternhold (d. 1570) were joint versifiers of the Psalms, whose work was ridiculed by John Dryden and especially in an epigram by Lord Rochester entitled "Spoken Extempore to a County clerk after Having Heard Him Sing Psalms":

> Sternhold and Hopkins had great qualms
> When they translated David's psalms
> 　　To make the heart feel glad;
> But it had been poor David's fate
> To hear thee sing, and then translate,
> 　　By God! 'twould have made him mad.

Novelist Henry Fielding, also a British justice of the peace, wrote an article for the satirical journal *The Champion*, demanding that English poet laureate and playwright Colley Cibber (1671–1757) be tried for murder of the English language. Fielding was apparently getting even with Cibber, who had called him "a broken wit."

murder will out.　"Mordre wol out, that see we day by day," Chaucer wrote in "The Nun's Priest's Tale." Before this we find a similar phrase, *Murder cannot be hid*, used with the same meaning: Your sins will find you out, your sinful secret will be revealed.

Murmansk run.　During World War II *a Murmansk run* became a synonym for a dangerous sea voyage because hundreds of cargo ships were sunk by Nazi subs and planes while crossing the North Atlantic to the ice-free Russian port of Murmansk.

murmur.　*See* ONOMATOPOEIA.

murphy.　A murphy is a confidence game, originating in America, in which the victim is let in on "a good thing" and asked to put up evidence of his good faith in the form of cash. When he supplies the required amount, the con man pleads that he must leave quickly on business, but will return shortly, depositing the envelope containing the cash with his victim. Only when the mark opens the envelope later does he realize that paper cut to size has been substituted for his money. There are endless variations on the game, including the trick where a prostitute collects from a customer first and then goes out the back door. No one has identified the Murphy who first used this ruse to murphy someone. The same holds true for the *murphy* that stands for an Irish or white potato, named so because Murphy is a very common Irish name and potatoes, the English believed, were the staple food of the Irish diet. *Donovan*, another common Irish name, is also used by the English as slang for a white potato.

Murphy bed.　A Murphy bed is a space-saving bed that can be folded or swung into a closet or cabinet; it is named after American inventor William Lawrence Murphy (1876–1950).

Murphy's Law.　Who the illustrious Mr. Murphy was remains anybody's guess, but some swear that he formulated two other laws besides the immortal "If anything can go wrong it will." The other two are "Everything will take longer than you think it will" and "Nothing is as easy as it looks." It is said that Murphy was killed by a car driven by an Englishman just arrived in the U.S. while taking a stroll down a country road and carefully walking on the left-hand side of the road to face the approaching traffic. *O'Toole's Commentary on Murphy's Law*, a law in itself, says basically that "Murphy was an optimist."

Musa.　*See* BANANA.

muscle.　*See* MUSSEL.

muscular Christianity.　This expression has nothing to do with the spread of Christianity by force, as some people think. An anonymous admirer so named Charles Kingsley's brand of religion in the middle of the 19th century; the reverend taught that Christianity should be hearty and strong-minded in order to help one "fight the battle of life bravely and manfully." Reverend Kingsley himself found the term "painful if not offensive," but it didn't need his approval. Dickens's amiable canon Mr. Crisparkle in the unfinished *The Mystery of Edwin Drood* is a good example of the type in literature. Kingsley, an advocate of social reform, is famous for his novels *Westward Ho!* and *Water Babies.*

Muses. The nine Muses were the children of Zeus and Mnemosyne (a personification of memory who was one of the six Titans, a daughter of Heaven and Earth). Originally they were goddesses of memory, but Pindar writes that the celestials implored Zeus to create the Muses to sing the great deeds of the gods. It was traditional for authors, especially epic poets, to invoke a particular Muse to help in the act of creation, the appeal for inspiration usually coming near the beginning of a work (as in the *Iliad*, the *Odyssey*, and *Paradise Lost*). While relatively few writers today believe in external forces inspiring them, or the "storm of association," as Wordsworth called it, most depend on inspiration from within rather than the divine afflatus (as William Faulkner said of the Muses and inspiration: "No one ever told me where to find it"). Nevertheless, if one's inner inspiration fails, here are the nine Muses all ready for invoking:

Calliope (her name, pronounced Ka-lie'o-pee, does not rhyme with *rope*, although the musical instrument named after her can; the name means "beautiful voice"). The chief Muse, usually associated with epic poetry, poetic inspiration, and eloquence, she has as her emblems a pen and a scroll of parchment.

Clio (Klie'o; means "to tell of"); Muse of history and heroic exploits, who is often represented like Calliope. The British author Joseph Addison used the name Clio as a pseudonym.

Euterpe (Yoo-ter'-pee; means "to delight well"). Muse of music and lyric poetry, patron of flute players, joy, and pleasure, her symbol is the double flute, which she invented.

Thalia (Tha-lie'a; means "blooming"). Muse of gaity, comedy, and pastoral life, depicted wearing a comic mask and garland of ivy while holding a shepherd's crook and a tambourine.

Melpomene (Mel-pom'i-nee; means "to sing"). Muse of tragedy, song and harmony, "the mournfullest Muse" is shown wearing a tragic mask, sword, and garland of grape leaves.

Terpsichore (Terp-sik'o-ree; means "dance-liking"). Muse of dancing, choral song, and lyric poetry, usually depicted seated and holding a lyre.

Erato (Er'a-toe; from the Greek *eros*, love). Muse of erotic and love poetry, miming, and geometry, shown holding a stringed instrument such as a lyre.

Polyhymnia (Pol'ee-hym'nee-uh; means many hymns). Muse of the chant and inspired hymn and said to be the inventor of the lyre, she is depicted as grave in countenance and wrapped in long, flowing robes.

Urania (Yoo-ray'nee-uh; from *uranus*, sky). Muse of astronomy and celestial phenomena, whose name means "the heavenly one" and whom Milton made the spirit of the loftiest poetry, she is often shown pointing with a wand or staff at a celestial globe she holds in her hand.

Mnemosyne, the mother of the Muses, gave her name to *mnemonics*, the art or science of memory training. Calliope gave hers to an organ composed of steam whistles. *Terpsichorean* means anything pertaining to dance, and *euterpean* is anything having to do with music. The Muses collectively are responsible for *museum*, which literally means the home of the Muses. *See also* 10TH MUSE.

museum. *See* MUSES.

Mush! French trappers in the Northwest used to urge on the dogs pulling their sleds across the snow with *marchons!*: "let's go!, hurry up!" This was corrupted to *mush on!* in English and by 1862 had become *mush!* "Dog French," one writer called it.

mushroom. When Englishmen in the 15th century tried to pronounce the French word for this succulent fungus, *mousseron*, it came out "muscheron," which over the years became "mushroom," this pronunciation probably to some extent influenced by the common English words *mush* and *room*. All in all, they may have been better off with their native name for the edible fungus: *toad's hat.* "Toad's hat" is no longer heard, but *toadstool* is of course still the name for inedible, poisonous mushrooms. The French word *mousseron*, from which mushroom sprang up, is generally accepted as a derivative of *mousse*, "moss," upon which mushrooms grow. Cities that sprang up rapidly, that seemed to spring up like mushrooms overnight, were called *mushrooms* in England as early as 1787. Within another century the name became a verb meaning to spread out, being first applied to bullets that expand and flatten, then to fires, and then to anything that grows rapidly. The fungus called a *mushroom* takes its name from the Latin *mussirio* meaning the same.

mushroom cloud. This image for the explosion of an atomic bomb was first used by *New York Times* reporter William L. Laurence in reporting the initial test of the bomb on July 16, 1945, near Alamogordo, New Mexico. Laurence called the cloud a "supramundane mushroom:" "At first it was a giant column that soon took the form of a supramundane mushroom. For a fleeting instant it took the form of the Statue of Liberty magnified many times."

music of the spheres.

> Forward and backward rapt and whirled are
> According to the music of the spheres.
>
> —Sir John Davies, *Orchestra* (1596)

Pythagoras taught that the spheres, or planets, made harmonious sounds as they moved through space and Plato said that on each planet there sat a siren singing a sweet song that harmonized with the songs of all the other planets. Even further back, in biblical times, the Book of Job relates that "the morning stars sang together." The reasoning behind the belief is that "planets move at different rates of motion . . . and must make sounds in their motion according to their different rates," but "as all things in nature are harmoniously made, the different sounds must harmonize." At any rate, Chaucer, Milton, and Shakespeare all believed this theory and gave expression to it in poetry, although the phrase *music of the spheres* didn't find its way into the spoken language until the end of the 18th century.

musk. *Musk* refers to a pungent substance from the sex glands of the 20-inch-high musk deer that roams the Himalayan and Atlas ranges. The best quality comes from Tibet, where hunters take it from the golf-ball-size scent glands beneath the animal's stomach. Male musk deer secrete the strong-smelling musk to attract females, which may have inspired humans to think of it as an aphrodisiac. It is primarily used in perfumery—a pound of the stuff commanding five times the price of gold. Legend has it that Cleopatra wore perfume made from musk and that the Queen of Sheba wore it to drive King Solomon wild.

mussel. Both the muscles in our bodies and the mussels in the sea take their name from the common house mouse. The early Romans rather whimsically thought that body muscles, appearing and disappearing as men competed in athletic games and then rested, resembled tiny mice appearing and disappearing at play. Similarly, little dark-colored mice were also thought to resemble the dark-colored marine bivalves the Romans liked to serve at their banquets. Thus, both the muscle and the mussel were named *musculus*, or "little mouse." The marine mussel's name is spelled differently today only because this makes it easier to distinguish it from *muscle*.

mustache; ah, your father's mustache; curse be upon your mustache. *Mustache* was originally a French word, borrowed by the English at about the time of the Renaissance. *Ah, your father's (or fadder's) mustache!* was a popular rejoinder among kids in the 1940s to 1950s and may date back much further. It means "Sez you!" or "That's what you think!" *Curse be upon your mustache* is not from any comedy routine. Apparently, it is an old "derogatory Arab epithet," according to a *New York Times* story (3/6/03) by Jane Perlez, reporting from Qatar. There, at a conference of Muslim countries, Iraqi delegate Izzat Ibrahim told the Kuwaiti delegate Muhammed Salah al-Salem al-Sabah to "shut up, you monkey," adding for good measure, "Curse be upon your mustache, you traitor!" The Kuwaiti's response was nowhere near as colorful. He called the Iraqi a hypocrite.

mustang. A small wild horse of the Southwest plains descended from horses introduced to the New World by the Spanish. The word derives from the Spanish word *mestengo* (stray beast).

mustard. Mustard takes its name from the *must* or "new wine" that was first used in mixing the paste, which is made from various plants of the *Brassica* genus, including, chiefly, *Brassica nigra*, "black mustard," and *Brassica hirta*, "white mustard." Frederick the Great believed mustard did so much for his masculinity that he invented a drink made with powdered mustard, champagne, and coffee. The history of hot mustard as an aphrodisiac is a long one. Rabelais, for example, writes that his lusty Demisemiquaver friars "began their meal with cheese, ending it with mustard and lettuce, as Martial tell us the ancients did. As each received a dishful of mustard after dinner, they made good the old proverb: Mustard after dinner / is good for saint and sinner."

mustard gas. The first gas used in World War I. The oily volatile liquid blistered the skin, damaged the lungs, and often caused blindness or death. Introduced by the Germans in 1915, it was named "mustard gas" after its mustardlike odor and the taste it left on the tongue. It is scientifically called dichlorodiethyl sulfide.

muti. A Zulu word used throughout South Africa that means "medicine." "That muti the doctor prescribed is too strong for me."

mutt. *Mutt*, for a "mongrel," has a long pedigree and was first a contemptuous term for a common, stupid man. As early as 1508 *mutton* was a Scottish word for a dumb man; by the 18th century *muttonheaded* was being used in England; and by the early 1900s Americans were calling commonplace stupid men *mutts* before applying the word to commonplace mongrel dogs. Every dog is of course a mutt, if you go back far enough in its ancestry.

Mutt and Jeff. We use this expression frequently to compare two friends or a loving couple, one short and one tall. The term is from the comic strip "Mutt and Jeff" created by Henry Conway (Bud) Fisher in 1907, but the little guy is named after former heavyweight champion James J. Jeffries. It happened when artist Fisher had Augustus Mutt, the tall, chinless member of the duo, visit a sanitarium in an early strip; there Mutt met a pleasant little inmate who fancied himself the boxing great Jim Jeffries. Mutt dubbed him Jeff for this reason. Jeffries (1875–1953) was one of the few heavyweight champions to retire undefeated, but just as Joe Louis was KO'd when he made a comeback so was Jeffries—by Jack Johnson in 1910. *See* MUTT.

mutton dressed as lamb. An old expression describing old (or middle-aged) people trying to look or dress as if they were younger or richer. The allusion may be to a butcher dressing meat. The words seem to be 18th-century British in origin, like *muttonhood*, which meant "adulthood" a century ago and *lamb*, which meant a "virgin."

mutual admiration society. An Americanism that was first recorded in Oliver Wendell Holmes's *Autocrat of the Breakfast Table* (1858) but was coined by Thomas Gold Appleton, Longfellow's brother-in-law. The *OED* defines the phrase as "a satiric designation for a coterie of persons who are accused of overestimating each other's merits," though it also can be used in a lighthearted, humorous way, as between two friends. Called "the first (best) conversationalist in America" by Emerson, the rich, worldly Appleton was according to Van Wyck Brooks in *New England: Indian Summer* (1940) "the only man who could ride over Holmes and Lowell and talk them down." He also coined the humorous *all good Americans go to Paris when they die*, which is often attributed to Holmes or Oscar Wilde. Holmes, in fact, quoted the remark in *The Autocrat of the Breakfast Table.* *See* FROZEN YANKEE DOODLE; ALL GOOD AMERICANS GO TO PARIS WHEN THEY DIE.

muumuu. Missionaries in Hawaii didn't approve of nudity and provided local women with Mother Hubbard dresses to cover themselves. These shapeless dresses lacked a yoke, appearing as if they were cut off at the neck, and the women called them muumuus, from the Hawaiian word for "cut off."

Adapted somewhat over the years, made more colorful for one thing, the muumuu became the typical Hawaiian dress and in time became popular worldwide as a loose-hanging housedress.

Muzak. This trademarked name has been around since the late 1930s, when, so the story goes, it was coined as a blend of *mus*ic and the popular Kod*ak*. Since then Muzak has been the light, serene music piped into elevators, restaurants, stores, and even offices and factories. The word is often used disparagingly for light or overly sentimental music.

my back teeth are floating. "I have to urinate—badly." This U.S. expression, still heard, originated in the early 1900s and is used in England as well.

Mycenae. The ancient city of Mycenae in southern Greece, where important ruins are found today, possibly takes its name from *mykes*, mushrooms. One legend tells that Perseus, son of the god Zeus, being hot and thirsty, picked a mushroom and drank the water flowing from it, expressing his gratitude by naming the city in its honor. While all sources do not accept this story, most say Perseus founded the city.

my country right or wrong. *See* OUR COUNTRY RIGHT OR WRONG.

"My Country 'Tis of Thee." *See* AMERICA THE BEAUTIFUL; AMERICA.

my foot! An American expression of extreme disagreement or strong skepticism about something another person has said. First recorded as *your foot!* in the Roaring Twenties, it is almost always heard as *my foot!* today.

my friends. The first use of these common political introductory words is often credited to Franklin D. Roosevelt, but he borrowed the introduction from another politician and Abraham Lincoln used it long before that. It probably goes back ages, shown by Shakespeare's use of "Friends, Romans, countrymen . . ." in *Julius Caesar* (1599).

my lips are sealed. I'll keep it a secret, I won't tell a soul. This has been traced to British Prime Minister Stanley Baldwin in 1936–37. Baldwin vowed confidentiality several times when asked about the abdication of King Edward VIII. "My lips are sealed," he said on one occasion, "I am bound to keep silence." Whether or not he invented the expression is unknown, but this is the first record of it. *See* LOOSE LIPS SINK SHIPS.

myna bird. *See* PARROT.

myriad. Before MILLION was introduced in about the 12th century the largest number word was *myriad*, which derives from a Greek word meaning countless, infinite, and was then Greek for 10,000. One ancient eclessiastical historian wrote of "a hundred and ten myriads" (1,100,000) slain and starved to death over a certain period, and Archimedes wrote of *the myriads of myriads of myriads* of poppy seeds in the world. Today *myriad* is used chiefly to mean countless or innumerable.

myrmidons of the law. When the inhabitants of the island of Aegina were wiped out by a plague, the Greek god Zeus rewarded his son Aeacus, the island's leader, by creating new human beings from ants to repeople the place. According to Greek legend, these people were called Myrmidons, after the tribe of ants *(Myrmax)*. The Myrmidons later followed Achilles to the Trojan War, in which they were noted for their faithful obedience and brutality. Their name is applied to officers of the law—policemen, sheriffs, etc.—who carry out any order unthinkingly and without scruples.

myrrh. "A bundle of myrrh is my well-beloved unto me; he shall lie all night betwixt my breasts," says the Song of Solomon. Unfortunately, the aromatic herb sweet cicely *(Myrrhis odorata)* that is common to Europe is not the fabled myrrh of the Bible. The word *myrrh* comes from the Greek name for perfume, but the biblical myrrh, which is still used to make incense and perfumes, was probably obtained from the spiny shrub *Commiphora myrrha*. Myrrh's age-old reputation is shown in the classical myth of Myrrh, a daughter of King Cinyras, whom the gods changed into a myrrh tree for having incestuous relations with her father. (Their child Adonis was born from the split trunk of the tree.) Frankincense has a similar reputation and is also still used in incense and perfumes. This biblical aromatic generally comes from the Asian and African species *Boswellia carteri*.

myrtle. Myrtle takes its name from *myrtos*, the Greek word for the plant. Myrtle crowns were awarded to victors of the Greek Olympic games, and the plant has been a symbol of strength and love since ancient times. The Romans offered myrtle to Priapus as tokens of their gratitude for success in sexual affairs. The ancient Britons dedicated the plant to their goddess of love, always including myrtle in bridal bouquets and often planting myrtles near the homes of newlyweds. Mentioned in Petronius's *Satyricon*, myrtle berries, leaves, and flowers were used in many love potions, and the plant's aromatic leaves and flowers have long been employed in perfumery. There are more than 100 species of myrtle from both the Old and New Worlds. In Greek mythology, Phaedra, the wife of Theseus, fell in love with her stepson Hippolytus, but he rejected her advances. While awaiting his return one day she sat under a myrtle shrub *(Myrtus communis)* and wiled away the time by piercing its leaves with a hairpin. This is why, according to legend, the leaves of the myrtle reveal many little punctures when viewed under a strong light. Phaedra hanged herself after falsely accusing Hippolytus as her seducer. Theseus then banished Hippolytus and caused his son's death. Myrtle, which originated in western Asia, is believed by the Arabs to be one of the three things (along with a date seed and a grain of wheat) that Adam took with him when he was cast out of Paradise. According to Roman mythology, Venus wore a garland of myrtle when she rose from the sea, and when satyrs tried to watch her bathing in the nude she hid behind a myrtle bush.

myself am Hell. This expression is from English poet John Milton's *Paradise Lost* (1667) and is fully, "Which way I fly is Hell; myself am Hell." In the same poem Milton wrote, "The mind is its own place, and in itself, can make a heaven of hell, a hell of heaven." Earlier, in *Religio Medici* (1642), Sir Thomas

Browne wrote, "The heart of man is the place the devils dwell in: I feel sometimes a hell within myself."

mystery meat. *See* DO WE EAT IT, OR DID WE EAT IT?

mystique de la merde. The literal meaning of this French phrase is "the mystique of shit," but the term, first recorded in 1956, refers to a preoccupation, mostly of writers and artists, with the coarser, seamier side of life.

myth. *Myth* derives from the Greek word *mythos*, which simply meant a tale or story. Over the ages the word came to mean a story about the gods or demons, and, much later, any fanciful story with supernatural elements.

N

N. The letter *N* was originally a wavy line ($\curlywedge$) in Egyptian hieroglyphs and meant "the sea" or "a fish." In Phoenician the letter was called *nun*, "fish."

nabob. The *nawabs* who governed provinces in India from the early 16th century through the Raj were Moguls who owed allegiance to the Mogul emperors of India but grew so wealthy and powerful that they kept all tributes from the people and made their offices hereditary. Europeans, noting the immense wealth and power of these men, took to calling any wealthy, powerful man a nabob, which is merely a corruption of *nawab*.

Nabokov's Pug. Just to indicate the thousands of specialized eponymous words that can't be included here, we might mention the butterfly *Nabokov's Pug*. It is named for the Russian-born author and lepidopterist Vladimir Nabokov (1899–1977), who, most specifically, discovered *Eupithecia nabokovi Mc-Donough* "on a picture window of [publisher] James Laughlin's Alta Lodge in Utah" in 1943. The prose stylist, author of *Mary, Invitation to a Beheading, Lolita, Pale Fire*, and other novels, emigrated from Russia shortly after the revolution, residing in the United States and Europe. Once a Harvard research fellow in lepidopterology, a number of his discoveries are named for him. The word *butterfly*, incidentally, may be a SPOONERISM for "flutter-by."

Naboth's vineyard. Any property that so excites a person's greed that he or she will do anything to obtain it. The expression has its roots in the biblical story (1 Kings 21) of King Ahab having Naboth murdered and seizing his property after Naboth refused to sell him his magnificent vineyard.

naff. A British expression with some American usage, if only because some Brits tell photographers and reporters to naff off, get lost, beat it, fuck off. The term's origins are unclear, but *naff* may derive from *naf*, English slang for the vagina. *Naf*, in turn, derives from a reverse spelling of the first three letters of *fanny*, British slang synonym for the vagina.

nag. *Nag* meaning "to scold" came into English from the Swedish and Norwegian *nagga*, to gnaw at or to irritate (as in "a nagging pain"). This *nag* is no relation to *nag* meaning an old worn-out horse, which probably entered English from a Low German word meaning the same.

Nahuatl. The language of the Aztecs that is cited as a source of many words treated in these pages. Nahuatl is far from a dead language and is spoken in many interior regions in Mexico. For that matter, the Mayan language lives on in Guatemala and other Central American countries. According to Mario Pei's *What's in a Word* (1968): "In South America, Quichua, the tongue of the Incas, is still used almost exclusively by some six million natives in a broad band from Ecuador, across Peru and Bolivia to northern Argentina." Perhaps one day centuries hence, when the rest of the world has worn itself out, these patient, once-great civilizations will rise again.

nail a lie to the counter. Early country store proprietors often protected themselves against the many types of bogus money in circulation by keeping a copy of *Day's New York Bank Note List and Counterfeit Detector* (1826) on the shelf by the cashbox. They have also been said to have nailed all counterfeit coins they had accepted to the counter as an aide against clerks being cheated in the future and as a warning to would-be sharpies trying to pass bad money in the store. Some say that this practice was the inspiration for the Americanism *to nail a lie to the counter*, "to expose anything false."

nail one's colors to the mast. Crews on warships in the days of sail often nailed their ship's flag or colors to the mast to signify that they would never surrender and would fight to the last man. From this practice came the expression *to nail one's colors to the mast*, to make one's principles or position clear and stick to them no matter what.

naked bear. *Hush or the naked bear will get you!* was an expression mothers stilled their crying children with a century ago. First recorded in 1818, the words refer to an American Indian legend of "a very ferocious kind of bear, which they say once existed, but was totally destroyed by their ancestors." Longfellow mentions the naked bear in one of his poems.

naked boy.   "Naked boy" and "naked lady" are folk names for the meadow saffron or autumn crocus (*Colchicum autumnale*), on which the flowers appear before the leaves. More poetically, the meadow saffron is called "the leafless orphan of the year" because the flowers are destitute or orphaned of leaves.

Naked Fanny.   An obsolete but amusing historical term from the Vietnam War, when U.S. fliers nicknamed the Royal Thailand Air Force Base, *Nakhon Phanom*, Naked Fanny because that's what the Thai words sounded like to American ears.

naked truth.   According to an old Roman fable, when Truth went swimming in the river, Falsehood stole Truth's clothes. Truth went naked rather than put on the clothes Falsehood had left behind. Such is the origin of *nuda veritas* or the "naked truth," which can be traced back as far as the writings of Horace.

namby-pamby.   Poor Ambrose Philips (ca. 1675–1749) had the bad luck to accidentally tread on Alexander Pope, easily the most venomous and malicious of the great English poets. Politics and envy had more to do with Philips's misfortune than insipid versifying, for he was a Whig and Pope a Tory, and in 1713 the Whig *Guardian* praised the Whig pastoral poet as the only worthy successor of Spenser. This inane criticism enraged "the Wasp of Twickenham" and initiated a quarrel between the two poets that Samuel Johnson described as a "perpetual reciprocation of malevolence." Pope's friend, poet, and composer Henry Carey soon joined in the fray. Carey, rumored author of the words and music of the British anthem "God Save the King," satirized Ambrose in the same book that included his popular song, "Sally in Our Alley," parodying Philips's juvenile poems and writing: "So the nurses get by heart Namby-pamby's little verses." The author of *Chrononhotonthologos*, a burlesque that he characterized as "the Most Tragical Tragedy that was ever Tragedized by any Company of Tragedians," even entitled his parody of Philips *Namby-Pamby*—taking the *amby* in each word from the diminutive of Ambrose and the alliterative *P* in the last word from *Philips*. Pope, ready for the kill, seized upon the contemptuous nickname and included it in the edition of his enormously popular poem "The Dunciad," which appeared in 1733. The phrase immediately caught the public fancy and much to his distress, Ambrose Philips saw his name come to stand for not only feeble, insipidly sentimental writing, but a wishy-washy, weakly indecisive person as well. Philips, incidentally, is the author of the well-known palindrome "Lewd did I live, evil I did dwel." *See* PALINDROME.

name.   *See* HIS NAME IS MUD.

names for both sexes.   Linguist Mario Pei says in *What's in a Word* (1968) that in the American South a greater number of first names can be both female and male than in any other area of the country. Such names include Pearl, Marion, Leslie, Beverly, Kim, and Dana. Although these names are all used for both males and females in other sections as well, they are so used with more frequency in the South.

Nantucket.   There is a hoary tale, probably untrue, that an old seaman owned an island group off Massachusetts. To his oldest daughter he gave his most productive island, which he named Martha's Vineyard; to his next, he gave the island closest to home, Elizabeth's Island; and to his last daughter, Nan, he just offered what remained, and Nan-tuck-it. No one is sure of *Nantucket*'s real derivation.

Nantucket sleigh-ride.   This old expression refers to a whaleboat fastened to a whale, which runs off furiously, towing the boat behind it. Such Nantucket sleigh-rides, often lasting for miles, are described in Herman Melville's *Moby-Dick* (1850) and other great books of the sea.

Napoleon.   Emperor Napoleon exacted heavy tolls on those he defeated, which is why this 19th-century card game is named for him. In five-card Napoleon the winner collects chips from each of the other players.

napoleon pastries.   These were not named for Napoleon. A traditional story says the emperor carried napoleons in his breast pocket when retreating from Moscow, a tale that persists despite the fact that *napoleon* in this case is simply a corruption of *napolitain*, because the pastries were first made in Naples, Italy.

narcissus; narcotic.   Like Hyacinthus (*see* HYACINTH), Narcissus was a handsome youth of Greek mythology. The nymph ECHO wished that he would fall in love with himself after he spurned her love. When Narcissus chanced to see his own reflection in a still pool, that is just what he did, and he drowned while gazing at his own image. After his death, the gods changed his body into the beautiful flower that has been called a narcissus ever since. Narcissus's name is also remembered in *narcissism* and in *narcotic*, named after the narcissus because some narcissus varieties contain substances that induce sleep. *See also* DAFFODILL.

narwhal.   The arctic narwhal, a whale that grows up to 20 feet long and has an eight-foot-long tusk, takes its name from the Scandinavian *nar*, "ghost" or "corpse" (for its white color) and *whal*, the Scandinavian word for whale. The narwhal is probably responsible for the legend of the unicorn so widely believed in medieval times. This "unicorn of the sea" uses its long tusk, or left incisor tooth, which grows outward in a counterclockwise spiral, to battle other narwhals. Only the male of the species has the tusk, employing it during the mating season when fighting over females.

nassau.   In a golf game, a nassau is an 18-hole match in which one point is given to each of the players having the lowest scores for the first nine holes, the second nine holes, and the entire round. The scoring and betting system is not named for the seaport capital of Nassau in the Bahamas, as is often said. It is actually named after the Nassau County Golf Course at Glen Cove in Nassau County, Long Island, New York, where it was developed in 1901 by players who didn't want to lose by embarrassingly high scores.

nasturtium.   "Nosetwister" is the translation of the two Latin words, *nasus* and *torqueo*, that make up this word. The name *nasturtium* was given by the Romans to watercress (*Nasturtium* *officinale*) because of its pungency; "it received its name from tormenting the nose," Pliny said, and the English called it *nosesmart*. In the 16th century *nasturtium* was applied to the showy orange-colored flowers we call by that name today, which were also known as Indian cress. The flower is today considered part of the genus *Tropaeolum*, its scientific name no longer *Nasturtium Indicum*, but it is still popularly called *nasturtium*, while watercress never is.

nasty.   A word used at least since the early 15th century, *nasty*'s history is obscure, but it possibly comes from the Aryan *niz'd* for "bird's nest," from which our word *nest* may also derive. According to this theory early Teutons noticed that birds fouled their nests and called anything foul and stinking *nesty* or *nasty*. The *O.E.D.* notes that "the original force of the word has been greatly . . . toned down."

national pastime.   Baseball was becoming a truly national game in about 1856, when the expression is first recorded, but at that time the term really meant baseball as played by a new code of rules introduced by the New York Knickerbocker Ball Club in 1845. As the game grew even more popular, people assumed that the expression *the national game* implied that baseball was the nation's favorite sport, and they used it this way; the variation *the national pastime* was introduced in the 1920s.

nation of shopkeepers.   Napoleon applied this term contemptuously to the English, but he didn't invent it. Apparently he read it in Adam Smith's *Wealth of Nations* (1776) or quoted the phrase of a contemporary. Smith wrote in full: "To found a great empire for the sole purpose of raising up a people of customers, may at first sight appear a project altogether unfit for a nation of shopkeepers; but extremely fit for a nation that is governed by shopkeepers." Thirteen years before him Josiah Tucker, dean of Gloucester, had written in his *Tract Against Going to War for the Sake of Trade:* "A Shop-keeper will never get the more Custom by beating his Customers; and what is true of a Shop-keeper, is true of a Shop-keeping nation."

Native American.   In the last decade *Native American* has been much used as a synonym for Indian, American Indian, or Amerindian. It is preferred by some, though far from all, "aboriginal people of the Western Hemisphere." *Indian* itself is of course a misnomer used since Columbus, believing he had found India on his first voyage, applied the name to the people he found living in the Americas. A Native American, however, can be anyone born in America, and the first people known to have settled in America weren't Native Americans, they were Asians who crossed the Bering Strait sometime during the late glacial epoch. The term *Native American* was first applied not to Amerindians but to white Anglo-Saxon Protestants in about 1837 when the Native American Association was formed as an anti-Catholic and antiforeign movement. Thus, though the term *Native American* does avoid offensive stereotypes associated with the word "Indian" throughout American history, it has a certain negative connotation of its own. *See* FIRST NATIONS.

Native American place-names.   "*Mississippi*," Walt Whitman wrote, "the word winds with chutes—it rolls a stream three thousand miles long. . . . *Monongahela*; it rolls with venison richness upon the palate." Thousands of charming place names deriving from American Indian languages adorn the map of the United States. These include, to mention just a few of the most notable, Chicago, Niagara, Allegheny, Saratoga, Susquehanna, Potomac, Tallahassee, Manhattan, and Tacoma. Fully 24 of the 50 states bear American Indian names.

Nattier blue.   Painter Jean-Marc Nattier (1685–1766) was famous for his portraits of the court of France's Louis XV, and for the soft shade of blue he used in them. It took a few centuries after his death, but this color became very fashionable in textiles and was named after him.

naught; naughty.   *Naughty* has come to mean bad in a minor way, somewhat improper or indecent, mischievous, as in "a naughty child." But in Middle English it was a much stronger word meaning wicked or immoral, deriving from the Old English *nauiht*, which meant "nothing" and also gave us the word *naught* for zero. Dr. Johnson silenced two spinsters who complimented him for the omission of "naughty words" in his great dictionary with the comment: "What! my dears! then you have been looking for them!"

naughty; Naughty Nineties.   The Naughty Nineties, which some called the Gay Nineties, refers to the 1890s, a period when the puritanical ways of the Victorian age were fading and more permissive behavior became acceptable. *Naughty Nineties*, however, isn't recorded in print until 1925.

Naumachia.   Roman emperors held "sea battles" on land in the Naumachia (from the Greek for "sea battle"), a flooded amphitheater Augustus built on the right bank of the Tiber River. The combatants in the two opposing fleets, who were usually prisoners or criminals, fought to the death unless spared by the emperor. As many as 24 triremes fought in these bloody contests.

nausea.   The Greek *naus* means ship, and the ancient Greeks fashioned their word for seasickness, *nausia*, from it. In time *nausia*, which gave us the English word *nausea*, came to mean any stomach disturbance similar to seasickness.

Navaho.   White settlers bestowed the name *Navaho* upon this Indian tribe, which called itself the Diné, or "people." *Navaho* comes from *tewa navaho*, "great planted fields," a term other Indians used in referring enviously to the great land holdings of the wealthy, powerful Diné tribe.

navel-gazing.   *See* CONTEMPLATE ONE'S NAVEL.

Navel of the Nation.   *See* JAYHAWKER STATE.

navel orange.   The first navel orange was a "bud-sport" that originated for reasons unknown from the bud of an otherwise normal orange tree in a monastery garden in Bahia, Brazil, from where it was imported into the U.S. in 1870. This sweet, usually seedless orange takes its name from the depression in its rind resembling a human navel, which contains an aborted ovary that appears as a small secondary fruit within the fruit.

Many other varieties, however, exhibit this characteristic at times. *See* DON'T KNOW HIM FROM ADAM.

navvy. This manual laborer or ditchdigger takes his name from the esteemed *navigator. Navvy* for such an occupation may have been suggested, in about 1825, by a joke about British canal diggers being directors or navigators of ships (the ships could only sail in the directions they dug). Brewer, however, has it this way: "Canals were thought of as lines of inland navigation, and a tavern built by the side of a canal was called a 'Navigation Inn'. Hence it happened that the men employed in excavating canals were called 'navigators,' shortened into navvies." *See also* WORK LIKE A NAVVY.

navy. The color navy blue made its debut in the Royal Navy in 1857, when for the first time an act of Parliament required English sailors to wear identical uniforms. This outfit included a blue jacket, which inspired the name of the color navy blue, or just navy, shortly after it became standard issue. Today any navy blue or navy clothing takes its name from the color of that first navy blue jacket.

Nazi. A Nazi has come to mean any brutal dictatorial person, the word deriving, of course, from Adolf Hilter's National Socialist party, which came to power in 1933 and ruled Germany through World War II. The German *Na*tional *So*zialist yields *Nazi.*

N.B. This is the abbreviation used for the Latin *nota bene,* "note well, take notice," often used in literary and scholarly works. Voltaire told of how a commentator on Lucretius by the name of Creech noted on his manuscript: "N.B. Must hang myself when I have finished." According to Voltaire, "He kept his word, that he might have the pleasure [of committing suicide] like Lucretius. Had he written upon Ovid, he would have lived longer."

Neanderthal; Neandertal. This is among the most ironic of etymologies. It is seldom noted (no English dictionary records the derivation) that *Neanderthal,* for "a primitive backward person," is named after a gentle poet—and a learned, pious churchman to boot! The early forms of *Homo sapiens* called *Neanderthals* were so named because the first skeletons of them recognized as a distinct group of archaic humans was found in the Neander Valley (the Neander Thal) near Dusseldorf, Germany in 1856. But the Neander Valley had been named for the German poet and hymn writer Joachim C. Neander (1650–80), a schoolmaster who wrote the beautiful hymn on the glory of God in creation, "Lo Heaven and Earth and Sea and Air!" There is further irony in the fact that the poet's great-grandfather's name had been Neuman, the great-grandfather changing this to Neander in the 16th century at a time when Germany was undergoing a rebirth of learning and many were translating their names into Greek. Thus, traced to its ultimate source, *Neanderthal,* which today means a primitive and brutal man, translates as "the man from the valley of the new man [the man of the future]"!

neatsfoot oil. Neatsfoot oil doesn't keep anything neat, but it does help preserve leather. Our common word *neat* has no place here, where *neat* is simply an old word for cattle and *neatsfoot oil* refers to an oil made from the feet of neet (cattle).

Nebraska. Nebraska, previously the Territory of Nebraska, takes its name from the Omaha Indian *ni-bthaska,* "river in the flatness," for the Platte River. The Cornhusker State was admitted to the Union in 1867 as our 37th state.

necessary. A euphemism, originating in 17th-century England, for a privy or outhouse. In the U.S. it was also known by the term *necessary house.*

necessity mess. An American dish made of thinly sliced potatoes and onions fried in the grease of salt pork. Also called "very poor man's dinner."

neck and neck. Since the late 18th or early 19th century, this British turf term for a close horse race has been commonly used to describe any race or contest that is virtually tied or even.

necklace. One of the newer horrors of execution, *necklace* refers to a tire filled with gasoline that is placed around the neck of someone thought to be a police informer and set on fire. The gruesome practice was introduced by young black activists in 1985 in South Africa, where Nobel laureate Bishop Desmond Tutu once saved the life of a man about to be necklaced.

neck verse. *See* BENEFIT OF CLERGY.

need it yesterday. Business talk since about the 1950s meaning "to want something," such as a report or study, immediately, with no delay at all. An employee might say to his boss about a recent assignment, "When do you want it done?" and his boss would reply, "I need it yesterday."

negotiate. Those who negotiate are often worried and under a strain. This is reflected in the origin of the word *negotiate,* which derives from the Latin *negotium,* composed of *neg,* "not," and *otium,* "ease," or "not at ease." The word is first recorded in the 16th century.

negus. History tells us little about Col. Francis Negus except that he lived in Queen Anne's reign and concocted the first negus known to be devised by man. A negus is brewed by mixing wine, usually port or sherry, with hot water, sugar, lemon juice, and spices such as nutmeg. Walpole and other writers have praised the hot drink, which warms a body up but can be perilously potent. Colonel Negus died in 1732 and 10 years later people were commonly calling his bequest by his name.

neighbor. Broken down, this word means "near dweller," ultimately from the Germanic *nehwiz,* near, and *buram,* dweller or farmer, which came into Old English as *neahgebur. Neighbor's* later meaning of a fellow human did not come until much later.

Neilsen Ratings; Q rating. Neilsen ratings are a survey conducted by the A. C. Neilsen Company since about 1960 to measure television viewership of various programs. The ratings are based on meters placed in TV sets and viewer diaries of a preselected sample of viewers. A. C. Nielsen had been measuring radio audiences since 1922. The ratings, especially the Sweeps, taken in the months of February, May, July, and November, determine what the networks charge sponsors. The Q rating is a poll that tries to measure the familiarity of actors, products, etc., to the television viewing audience. It is named for its devisor, the TVQ/Marketing Evaluations Co. *See* GALLUP POLL.

neither fish, flesh, nor fowl.   An expression that dates back at least to the 17th century, meaning "neither one thing nor the other," suitable to neither the clergy, who eat fish, nor the generality, who eat flesh, nor the poor, who must eat fowl. A variation is *neither fish nor fowl not good red herring.*

neither here nor there.   Irrelevant, immaterial, as in: "That's neither here nor there; let's get back to the subject at hand." The phrase derives from *neither so nor so* (neither this nor that), an English expression that has been traced back to 1783.

neither hide nor hair.   *In hide and hair,* meaning "completely, wholly, every part," goes back to Chaucerian times, but its opposite, *neither hide nor hair,* is a 19th-century Americanism, probably arising on the frontier. A hungry predator devouring his prey "hide and hair" has been suggested as the source of the first metaphor, but that is hard to swallow for man or beast. Anyway, the reverse phrase means "nothing whatsoever" and its earliest record is in an 1858 book by Timothy Titcomb, the pseudonym of the American writer Josiah G. Holland, who founded *Scribner's Magazine:* "I haven't seen hide nor hair of the piece ever since." *See* BONE, HIDE, AND HAIR.

nekton.   *See* PLANKTON.

Nelly Bly.   American journalist Elizabeth Cochrane Seaman (1867–1922) adopted the pen name Nelly Bly from a song by Stephen Foster. She is said to have taken it when an editor insisted that she use a pseudonym and an office boy happened to walk by whistling the tune. One of the first female reporters, Nelly Bly began her career when only 18. Her forte became exposés, such as her account in *Ten Days in a Madhouse* (1887) of the horrible conditions on New York's Blackwell's Island, where she was an inmate for 10 days after feigning insanity. In 1889 the *New York World* sponsored her famous trip around the globe, which she completed in the record time of 72 days, six hours, and 11 minutes and which brought her international fame far exceeding that of any woman of her day. Flowers, trains, and racehorses were named for Nelly Bly and songs were written in her honor.

nelson.   *See* FULL NELSON.

Nelson's blood.   After Lord Horatio Nelson, Britain's greatest naval hero, was killed at the battle of Trafalgar in 1805 by a sniper firing from the top of the French ship *Redoubtable,* his body was brought back to England to be buried in St. Paul's Cathedral. The fabled hero became the subject of many legends, including one that his body was brought home pickled in rum. Needless to say, it wasn't long before British sailors were calling rum Nelson's blood.

nematode.   Beginning gardeners might be puzzled by the term *nematode-resistant* affixed to many plants, especially tomatoes. A nematode is simply a small, microscopic worm that attacks the roots of plants and often causes great damage. The word is a learned borrowing from the Greek word for "thread" applied to threadlike things such as these unsegmented worms. Some plants have a better ability to repel these worms than others and are called nematode-resistant.

nemesis.   Nemesis was the Greek goddess of justice or revenge, her name deriving from the Greek for vengeance; thus *nemesis* means anyone who avenges or punishes. Shakespeare used the term in *Henry VI, Part I,* but it is first recorded a few years earlier in 1576. The word also means an opponent or rival one cannot best or overcome.

nene.   Hawaii's official state bird, also called the Hawaiian goose (*Nesochen sandvicensis*). The official name of the barred, gray-brown wild goose is pronounced "neigh-neigh."

nepotism.   Deriving directly from the Latin *nepos,* "a descendant, especially a nephew," *nepotism* was coined when Pope Alexander VI (1431–1501), the most notorious of political popes, filled important church offices with his relations. Among the many family appointments the Spaniard Rodrigo Borgia made to consolidate his political power were the installing of his son Cesare as an archbishop when the boy was only 16 and the bestowing of a cardinal's hat on his young nephew Giovanni. Alexander's detractors were so many and so widespead that the new term soon entered all the languages of Europe, referring not only to politics but to business and any other place where such favoritism was practiced.

Neptune.   Neptune, the Roman god of water, is usually represented as a stately old man carrying a trident and sitting astride a dolphin or huge sea horse called a hippocampus. The ruler or king of the sea, his name is used for the sea itself. Poseidon was the god of the sea in Greek mythology, his wife Amphitrite, the goddess of the sea. Other sea gods include Triton, their son; Nereus, his hair seaweed green, who lives with his wife Doris at the bottom of the Mediterranean; Portunus, the protector of harbors; and Oceanus, god of the ocean. There were also 50 nereids, daughters of Nereus, and the oceanids, daughters of Oceanus.

nerd.   The storyteller-artist Dr. Seuss (the pen name of the late Theodor Seuss Geisel) apparently invented the word *nerd* in his children's book *If I Ran the Zoo* (1950): "And then, just to show them, I'll sail to Ka-Troo And Bring Back an It-Kutch a Preep and a Proo a Nerkle a Nerd and a Seersucker, too!" The nerd is pictured by Dr. Seuss as a thin, cross, humanoid creature. His word and illustration were picked up by small kids and within 10 years became a term for a socially inept, though often intelligent, person.

Nero; nero's crown; coliseum.   Cruel, vindictive, dissolute, profligate, treacherous, tyrannical, murderous—it would take a far longer string of adjectives to describe Nero, the last of the Caesars. A Nero is a bloody-minded tyrant for reasons apparent to any high school history student and it is enough to say here that the memory of Nero Claudius Caesar Drusus Germanicus, born Lucius Domitius Ahenobarbus, was publicly execrated when he died. Among the Roman emperor's countless victims were the rightful heir to the throne, Britannicus (Nero poisoned him); his own mother, Agrippa (Nero had her killed by his soldiers after failing to drown her); his first wife, Octavia; his pregnant second wife, Poppaea (Nero is said to have kicked her to death); the son of his benefactor Lucan; and a woman who refused to marry him. Nero may well have set fire to Rome in A.D. 64 because he wanted to see what Troy looked like when it burned, although there is no trustworthy proof of the story. And that Nero fiddled while Rome burned is essentially true, though he probably sang and played the harp, not the fiddle, while regarding the spectacle with cynical detachment. The tyrant rebuilt Rome, including a grandiose "Golden House" for himself, blamed the blaze on the Christians and persecuted them with such fury that they regarded him as the Antichrist. With such a record it's hard to understand why anyone would name a beautiful flowering plant after him, but someone did. Nero's crown (*Tabernaemontana coronaria*) is named for the bloody-minded, spindle-shanked, pot-bellied tyrant. Better to call the fragrant shrub "crape jasmine" or "Indian rose bay." Nero is also remembered in *nero antico*, a black marble found in the Roman ruins and later used for ornamental purposes; and in *Neroinize*, "to rule, oppress, or make depraved in the manner of Nero." The word *coliseum* also owes something to him. An 11-foot-high statue, or colossus, of him by Zenodorus stood near where the emperor Vespasian built the huge amphitheater called the Colosseum, the amphitheater taking its name from Nero's colossus and giving its name to *coliseum*. *See* ADAM'S APPLE TREE.

Nero of the North. In 1520, at Stockholm, King Christian II of Denmark, Norway, and Sweden (1481–1559) massacred some 100 Swedish nobility. Soon after this the despot became known as the Nero of the North, and the Swedes and Norwegians rose up against him, the Swedes raising Gustavus I to the throne. At home in Denmark, Christian became hated for such acts as putting the mother of his mistress in charge of the nation's finances. Also called Christian the Cruel, he wound up spending the last 24 years of his life in jail. *See* NERO.

nervous Nellie. Any very cautious, worried person, often fearful and jittery. Sometimes capitalized, the expression is said to come from the nickname of Frank Billings Kellogg (1856–1937), U.S. secretary of state, who won the Nobel Peace Prize in 1929 largely for his successful negotiating of the 1927 Kellogg-Briand Pact, sometimes called the Pact of Paris, which condemned "recourse to war for the solution of international controversies." Briand was Aristide Briand, foreign minister of France, one of the 62 nations that ultimately ratified the agreement, which failed to provide enforcement measures. The name *Nervous Nellie* seems to have attached itself to Kellogg when he served as a U.S. senator from Minnesota (1917–23), but he was always a nervous man.

nescience. Though *nescience* (from the Latin *nesciens*, "ignorant") can be a synonym for ignorance, some writers make an important and useful distinction between the words. While ignorance is "not knowing something one should reasonably be expected to know," *nescience* means "not knowing something one cannot be reasonably expected to know."

nesselrode. A mixture of preserved fruits and nuts used over desserts, *nesselrode* is believed to have been invented by the Russian statesman Count Karl Robert Nesselrode (1780–1867).

Nessiteras rhombopteryx. *Nessiteras rhombopteryx* was suggested by British naturalist Sir Peter Scott as the scientific name for the fabled Loch Ness Monster, which many have claimed, without much proof, to have seen rising from the depths of Loch Ness in Scotland. Believers rejoiced that a noted scientist was on their side, until it was found that *Nessiteras rhombopteryx* is an anagram of "Monster hoax by Sir Peter S."

nest egg. People saved nest eggs as early as the 17th century. The expression relates to the pottery eggs once put in hens' nests to induce the hens to lay their own eggs. Persons who start saving a nest egg put a little money (like a porcelain egg) aside, which encourages them to save more.

nester. A squatter, homesteader, or farmer who settled in cattle country. The name may derive from the patches of brush such settlers stacked around their first vegetable patches to protect them, which looked like bird nests to cattlemen.

Nestor. There may have been a real King Nestor behind the character the poet Homer describes both in the *Iliad* and the *Odyssey*. Nestor, in Homeric legend, was the youngest of Neleus's 12 sons and the king of Pylos in Greece. At about 70, he was the oldest and most experienced of the Greek chieftains besieging Troy, being represented as a wise and indulgent prince who lived so long that he ruled over three generations of subjects. Nestor counseled moderation among the quarreling Greek leaders. Full of wise advice and stories of his exploits in days gone by, his wisdom was revered and much sought after despite his prolixness. But the fact that Nestor talked too much was redeemed by the fact that he had a lot to talk about. He had been, for example, the only person spared when Hercules took Pylos. His name is frequently used today to describe a wise old man, and *Nestor* does not imply that the sage is garrulous.

neurobat. *See* ACROBAT.

Nevada. The Spanish for "snowed upon" or "snowy" is the basis for *Nevada*. The Silver State, which had first been part of the Washoe Territory, was admitted to the Union in 1864 as our 36th state.

never give a sucker an even break. *See* THERE'S A SUCKER BORN EVERY MINUTE.

never grab with both hands, just grab with one. A cynical contemporary maxim instructing a person not to be too greedy and grasping, but not to be too altruistic either, especially in business dealings.

nevermore. Edgar Allan Poe was not the first or last to "quoth" the word, symbol of darkest doubts, in his poem "The Raven" (1845). Here is a sample from William Faulkner's *Absalom, Absalom* (1936): "Quentin didn't answer. He lay still and rigid on his back . . . breathing hard hot slow, his eyes wide open upon the window, thinking 'Nevermore Nevermore Nevermore.' "

never-never land.   Today *never-never land* usually signifies an unreal, imaginary, or ideal condition or place, as in "the never-never land of the movies." Originally, however, it was Australian slang for an isolated, sparsely settled region and was first applied to all of Australia and then to the remote Australian outback of Western Queensland and central Australia. This region was probably called *never-never land*, or *country*, because those who visited there vowed "never, never" to return. Sir James Barrie first gave the meaning of an imaginary place to *Never Land* in his play *Peter Pan*, having Peter teach the Darling children to fly away to the wonderful realm of a child's imagination. Today the British sometimes call installment plans "never-never plans," because one's ownership of the goods bought on such plans lies far in the distance in never-never land.

never speak ill (or bad) of the dead.   Also heard as *never speak evil of the dead*, this expression wasn't recorded in English until the 16th century, but in Latin it dates back to the sixth century B.C., when it appeared as *say nothing of the dead but what is good*. This ancient belief and saying is believed to have been uttered by the Spartan ephor (magistrate) Chilon, one of the SEVEN SAGES OF GREECE.

never up, never in.   Its sexual implications have helped this golfing expression last since the early 1920s as a catchphrase of pessimism. It means, literally, never up near the hole with the first putt, never in the hole with the second putt. Or else it means "don't leave it short," if you don't putt hard enough to reach the hole it can't go in.

New Deal.   *New Deal* comes from Franklin Delano Roosevelt's acceptance speech at the Democratic National Convention on July 2, 1932: "I pledge you, I pledge myself, to a new deal for the American people." Coined by Roosevelt's speechwriters, Raymond Moley and Judge Samuel Rosenman, the phrase incorporated elements of Woodrow Wilson's New Freedom and Teddy Roosevelt's Square Deal.

New England.   Captain John Smith thought that the area called New England in North America greatly resembled England. He was the first to record the name, on a map he made in 1616: "That part we call New England . . . betwixt the degree 41. and 45."

New England boiled dinner.   Meat, often corned beef, boiled with vegetables such as potatoes, carrots, turnips, and onions.

New England clam chowder.   *See* CHOWDER.

New England conscience.   This expression is often illustrated with a story about William Ellery of Rhode Island, signer of the Declaration of Independence. When Ellery was a collector of customs in 1790, his grandson dropped into the office. Casually taking a sheet of paper off his grandfather's desk to write a letter, he felt Ellery's hand restraining him. "My boy," the old man said, "if you want paper, I'll give you some, but this is Government paper." However, a cynical definition of *New England Conscience* advises that having one doesn't keep you from doing anything, it just keeps you from enjoying it.

New England weather.   An old term for very varied, unpredictable weather. Mark Twain had this to say about it at a dinner of the New England Society in 1876: "There is a sumptuous variety about the New England weather that compels the stranger's admiration—and regret. The weather is always doing something there; always attending strictly to business; always getting up new designs and trying them out on people to see how they will go. But it gets through more business in Spring than in any other season. In the Spring I have counted one hundred and thirty-six different kinds of weather inside of twenty-four hours."

Newgate Calendar.   Often used today as a synonym for a who's who of crime and notorious criminals everywhere, the Newgate Calendar was begun in 1773 as a biographical record of the most notorious criminals confined at England's famed Newgate Prison. Newgate Calendar was long the pseudonym for the reviewer or reviewers of crime books for the *New York Times Book Review*.

New Hampshire.   When Captain John Mason was granted the land including this state in 1622 he named it after his homeland—England's Hampshire County. The Granite State was admitted to the Union in 1788 as our ninth state.

New Jersey.   Though it doesn't look like it at first glance, the state's name is another that has to be credited to the Caesars. *New Jersey* was named after *Jersey*, the largest of England's Channel Islands, in honor of Sir George Carteret, who had been governor of the Isle of Jersey and successfully defended it against Cromwell's forces. In 1664 Charles II had granted all lands between the Delaware River and Connecticut to his brother, the duke of York, who in turn granted the New Jersey portion to Carteret and Lord Berkeley. England's Isle of Jersey (a corruption of *Caesaria*) had been named for the Caesars when the Romans added it to their possessions, and so *New Jersey* also bears the immortal name. The relationship can be best seen in New Jersey's official Latin name, *Nova Caesaria*.

New Mexico.   Spanish explorers from Mexico named this area Nuevo Mexico, "New Mexico," in 1562. The Land of Enchantment became our 47th state in 1912, previously having been called the New Mexico Territory.

new potatoes.   Small, often thin-skinned red potatoes, so called because they are often the first of the season. They are also called "salad potatoes," because they are frequently used in potato salad, and "salt potatoes," because they are boiled in salted water. Another interesting potato term, not often heard anymore, is the 19th-century expression *shadow potatoes* for potato chips.

news.

News is conveyed by letter, word or mouth
And comes to us from North, East, West and
    South.

Contrary to the old rhyme above, which helped popularize the myth, the word *news* wasn't coined from the first letters of the major points of the compass. The word was originally spelled *newes* and derives from the Old English word *niwes*, meaning "new." The legend possibly originated with old newspapers printing a replica of the globe with compass points on their masthead. But the word is much older than the earliest newspapers.

newspeak. *See* DOUBLETHINK.

Newton's apple. Everyone knows the story about Sir Isaac Newton sitting under an apple tree pondering the question of gravitation when an apple fell on his head and inspired the train of thought that led to his law of universal gravitation. But the particulars are usually omitted in this tale. According to Voltaire, who first told the story, and got it from Newton's niece, Mrs. Conduit, the apple fell in his mother's garden at Woolsthorpe, where he was visiting her in 1666. Even the name of the apple is known—it was a red cooking variety called the Flower of Kent. (If you want to sample it, plant the same tree Newton sat under—grafted scions of the tree have been taken over the years since 1666 and are available from English nurseries.) The apple that bopped Newton must have inspired a long train of thought, for the law of universal gravitation didn't come to fruition for nearly 20 years. Such charming stories have become part of the Newton legend, whether reliable or not. Perhaps the greatest figure in the history of science, Newton could still say of himself: "I do not know what I may appear to the world, but to myself I seem to have been only a boy playing on the sea-shore, and diverting myself in now and then finding a smoother pebble or a prettier shell than ordinary, whilst the great ocean of truth lay all undiscovered before me."

New York. New York is named for James, duke of York and Albany, who in 1664 was granted the patent to all lands between the Delaware River and Connecticut by his older brother, King Charles II. The duke gave away the Jersey portion, but held on to what was then the Dutch colony of New Netherlands. York became the patron of Col. Richard Nicholls, who that same year set sail for the New World, captured New Amsterdam from the Dutch and named both the city of New Amsterdam (New York City) and the colony of New Netherlands (New York State) after the duke. New York State's capital, Albany, is also named for the duke of York and Albany. *See* YORK; PUT UP YOUR DUKES.

next year in Jerusalem. Jerusalem belongs to the Jews again, so these words are no longer a wish or a promise. But the ritual declaration *Next year in Jerusalem!* had been made by Jews at Passover for over 2,000 years, ever since Jerusalem was lost to the Romans.

Nez Percé. French traders named this Indian tribe they encountered in Idaho the *Nez Percé* (pierced nose), though there is no evidence that these Native Americans practiced nose piercing. Why they were so named remains a mystery.

n.g.; n.n. The expression *n.g.* has been an abbreviation for "no good" since at least 1839 in America, and it meant "no go," "completely unacceptable," some five years before this.

The term *n.n.* is a British one dating back to the beginning of this century and means "a necessary nuisance," especially a husband.

niacin. The valuable vitamin, surprisingly enough, takes its name from *nicotinic ac*id, plus the suffix *in*. In fact, it was at first called *nicotinic acid*, but that name's association with tobacco necessitated the new coining in the early 1940s.

Nicaragua. The Indian chief Nicaro, who reigned in the country before the Spanish conquered it, gives his name to Nicaragua.

nice guy. *Nice* has undergone a complete change in meaning since it came into English late in the 13th century. Deriving from the Latin *nescius*, "ignorant," *nice* originally meant foolish, or simpleminded, and came to mean "wanton or ill-mannered" before another century had passed. By the early 1400s *nice* was being used for "extravagant dress," but before the century was out "extravagant dress" (as is so often the case in the world of fashion) had changed to "fashionable dress" and by Shakespeare's time *nice* meant "fastidious or refined." It took another 100 years or so before "refined" yielded to "agreeably delightful," this definition first recorded in 1769.

nice guys finish last. This cynical proverb has been attributed by *Bartlett's* to former Brooklyn Dodger manager Leo Durocher, who wrote a book using it as the title. Back in the 1940s Leo was sitting on the bench before a game with the New York Giants and saw opposing manager Mel Ott across the field. "Look at Ott," he said to a group of sportswriters. "He's such a nice guy and they'll finish last for him." One of the writers probably coined the phrase *nice guys finish last* from this remark, but the credit still goes to The Lip.

nice Nelly. Someone so prudish he or she is ridiculous. American humorist Franklin Pierce Adams (he usually signed his work with his initials FPA) is responsible for this term. A prudish woman called Nice Nelly was a character in his newspaper column "The Conning Tower" and her name passed into the language from there. *See also* OLD LADY IN DUBUQUE.

nice night for the sow to have pigs. Heard in the midwestern U.S. to describe a very bright moonlit night. A pig is a young swine, often called a hog when it reaches 120 pounds.

nice work if you can get it. Common in the U.S. since at least the late 1930s, this phrase—which means "a favorable or agreeable arrangement"—is in Noel Coward's *Peace in Our Time* (1947). A musical comedy song of the same title popularized the expression in America (in *A Damsel in Distress*, 1937).

nickel. *Nickel* has stood for a U.S. five-cent piece since 1881, but has never been the official designation for the coin. The coin is so called because it is made partly of nickel. Before *nickel* was applied to the five-cent piece it was the name for a U.S. nickel penny authorized in 1857 and a nickel three-cent piece. A *nickel* is also a Canadian English term, from Newfoundland, that means a movie, as in, "We saw a great nickel." It is so called after a well-known movie theater named the Nickel (a nickelodian) in St. John's, Newfoundland.

nickel curve. In baseball a nickel curve is a curve that doesn't break much. The term has been traced to William Arthur (Candy) Cummings (1848–1924), a Hall of Famer who is credited with inventing the curveball over 120 years ago. Cummings's curve was inspired by the half clam shells that he skimmed across a Brooklyn beach as a youngster, but he perfected it by experimenting with a baseball that cost a nickel.

nickname. *Nickname,* first recorded in 1440, derives from an earlier Old English *ekename,* meaning "an extra name." Sloppy pronunciation of the words eventually turned an *ekename* into a *nekename* and finally a *nickname.*

nick of time. *See* JUST IN THE NICK OF TIME.

nicotine. $C_{10}H_{14}N_2$, as the nicotine staining my fingers is scientifically described, is named for Jean Nicot, lord of Villemain (ca. 1530–1600), French ambassador to Lisbon in 1560 when Portuguese explorers were first bringing back tobacco seeds from the new continent of America. Nicot was given a tobacco plant from Florida, cultivated what is said to be the first tobacco raised in Europe, and sent the fruits of his harvest to France's queen mother Catherine de Médicis and other notables. After introducing what Catherine called *the ambassador's powder* (snuff) into France, the enterprising Nicot proceeded to grow a tobacco crop that he brought back to Paris and built a tidy fortune on. The *American powder* became so popular that the tobacco plant itself was called *nicotina,* after Nicot, and Linnaeus later officially named the whole *Nicotiana* genus of the nightshade family in his honor, this group including the tobacco plant most commonly cultivated today, the species *Nicotiana rustica. Nicotine,* the oily liquid found in tobacco leaves, wasn't so named until 1818, when it was first isolated. It is one of the most physiologically active drugs known, producing most of the observed effects of smoking. The alkaloid is poisonous to bugs as well as humans, and is used as an insecticide in agriculture.

Nietzschean. The philosophy of Friedrich Wilhelm Nietzsche, much distorted by the Nazis and other "supermen," did however champion the "morals of master men," especially in the philosopher's famous four-part work *Thus Spake Zarathustra* (1883–91). The son of a German pastor, Nietzsche was acidly antagonistic to humble and compassionate Christianity—a slave morality born of resentment, he thought. The philosopher denied the values of beauty, truth, and goodness and asserted that man is perfectible through the will to power. Nietzsche did not claim that the Germans were a master race, as Nazi propagandists insisted; his Nietzschean doctrine of the *Ubermensch,* or dominant man, above good or evil, applied to no particular nationality. *Ubermensch,* incidentally, means "overman" or "beyondman" in German, not "superman." George Bernard Shaw coined the latter word from Nietzsche's term when he wrote *Man and Superman* in 1903. Nietzsche, rejected and reviled by his contemporaries, died insane at the age of 56 in 1891, 11 years after suffering a physical and mental collapse that prevented him from doing more work. It is interesting to note that the philosopher criticized anti-Semitism and many other tendencies that led to Nazism. Few other men have had so strong an influence on 20th-century thought. *See* SUPERMAN.

nifty. *Nifty* for "smart, stylish, fine, or clever" may have originated as American theatrical slang. It is first recorded in an 1865 poem by Bret Harte, the author claiming that the word derived from *magnificent.* Another possible source is the older *snifty,* "having a pleasant smell."

nigger; N-word. When used by a white person to describe a black or African-American person, this is probably the most offensive, hateful, hurtful term in the language today. Like *Negro,* the word derives ultimately from the Latin *niger,* black. It is not an Americanism, the first recorded use of *nigger* being in a 1786 poem by Robert Burns, although variations on it, including *negar, neger,* and *niger,* are recorded two centuries before then. Though African Americans do commonly use the word in different ways among themselves ("That nigger's got luck you wouldn't believe"), blacks rarely if ever do so in the presence of whites. Since the O. J. Simpson murder trial in 1995, when evidence of its use by a detective-witness was introduced, it often has been euphemistically called the *N-word. Nigger* has also been an offensive derogatory term applied to Indians as well as blacks up until recent times. In fact, the objectionable word was applied to themselves by white mountain men in the early West. Once commonly used expressions such as *a nigger in the woodpile* (concealed but important information, a "catch" in a situation) are rarely heard today. So sensitive are people black and white to the use of *nigger* that the word *niggardly* (miserly), which sounds like but is no relation to it etymologically, is often avoided. There is no character named "Nigger Jim" in Mark Twain's *Adventures of Huckleberry Finn,* as is so often said. The runaway slave in Twain's novel is named Jim, just Jim; nowhere in the book is his name anything else. For an in-depth study of the abominable n-word see African-American scholar Randall Kennedy's *Nigger* (2002).

nightcap. A drink, usually alcoholic, before going to bed, to help one sleep better. The term was coined two centuries ago when people wore nightcaps to keep their heads warm in those days of primitive heating. The bedtime drink came to be associated with and named after the practice of putting on a nightcap just before retiring.

nightmare. Bad dreams in Roman times were attributed to demons called the *incubus* and *succubus.* The incubus (from the Latin *incubare,* "to lie on," which also gives us the word *incubate*) was said to consort with women in their sleep. This explained the heaviness or suffocation a woman might feel during a bad dream. The superstition was so widely believed in the Middle Ages that any woman who gave birth to a "witch" was supposed to have been visited by a male demon. The female counterpart of the incubus was the succubus (from the Latin *suc* or *sub,* "under," and *cubare* "to lie"), who slid beneath a male sleeper. In the Dark Ages, there were laws against these demons whose existence was recognized by both church and state. Soon they became known as the "night hag," "the riding of the witches," and the *nightmare* as well. The *nightmare,* however, had nothing to do with a female horse, taking its name from *night,* plus the Anglo-Saxon *mare,* meaning "incubus." *Nightmare* eventually replaced the older Latin word *incubus,* which is now used to describe an oppressive load. Although the word wasn't born from a horse, it caught the popular imagination because of the graphic picture it suggested of a terrible horse bearing sleepers off on a frightening ride.

night of the long knives.   On the night of June 29, 1934 Hitler and his allies killed or had imprisoned a number of Nazi party members he wanted out of the way. Since then a *night of the long knives* has meant "a time when an act of great disloyalty is done," especially when several people form a conspiracy to do it.

night soil.   Because cesspools used to be cleaned during the night in the 18th century, their contents were called *night soil* and the cleaners "night men." That the contents were sometimes added as fertilizer to soil at night could account for the *soil* in the expression.

nihilism.   Meaning total rejection of established laws and institutions, and denial of all real existence, *nihilism* was coined from the Latin *nihil*, "nothing," by Russian novelist Ivan Turgenev to name and describe the principles of a Russian revolutionary group in the late 19th century.

nimby.   An American acronym that has been common since the late 1980s. It appears to have been coined by American scientist Walter Rodger and means "*not in my back yard*," referring to objection by residents to the establishment in their neighborhoods of dangerous, unsightly, or other undesirable projects, such as shelters for the homeless, prisons, landfills, and incinerators. The people often don't mind if such projects are built elsewhere.

niminy-piminy.   Affectedly delicate or refined. Apparently the rhyming compound was coined by (General) John (Gentleman Johnny) Burgoyne in his *The Heiress* (1786), when Lady Emily instructs the vulgar Miss Alscrip stand in front of a mirror and keep pronouncing *mimini-pimini* to give a pretty form to the lips. In *Little Dorrit* (1855–57) Dickens had Amy do the same with *papa, potatoes, poultry, prunes,* and *prism*.

Nimrod.   In the Bible Nimrod is the son of Cush and the founder of Babel. He may have been an Assyrian king who built the city of Nineveh, the capital of the Assyrian empire. According to Scripture, Nimrod was "a mighty hunter before the Lord" (Gen. 10:8–10), and historians tell us that the Assyrian kings were noted for their prowess in hunting. Aramaic translations of the Old Testament say "that mighty hunter before the Lord" means "sinful hunter of the sons of men," which accounts for Pope's and Milton's description of Nimrod as "a mighty hunter, and his prey was man." But a *Nimrod* is more generally the nickname for a great, daring, and skillful hunter, or even sportsman. In recent slang it means a stupid person or a jerk, probably after a cartoon in which Bugs Bunny calls hunter Elmer Fudd "poor little Nimrod."

nincompoop.   Dr. Johnson suggested that *nincompoop*, "a fool or blockhead," came from the Latin *non compos mentis*, "of unsound mind," but the earliest forms of the word, first recorded in about 1676, are *nicimpoop* and *nickumpoo*, making this unlikely. The word is probably "a fanciful formation," as the *O.E.D.* puts it, of obscure origin.

nine.   *Nine* is obviously a synonym for a baseball team because that's the number of players on a team. But the first recorded use of the word *nine* in this sense is in the name of a team called the New York Nine, which played against the New York Knickerbockers Ball Club in 1846. Thus the term *nine* may derive from the name of a specific team.

nine days' wonder; 90-day wonders.   Minor marvels, things that cause great sensations for a short time and then pass into limbo, have probably been called *nine days' wonder,* or something very similar, since Roman times. Kittens, puppies, and other young animals have their eyes closed for a number of days after birth and then open them and see the light—just as astonished people eventually "open their eyes" and see astonishing things in their true perspective. This is probably the reasoning behind the expression, *nine* being used because it has always been regarded as a mystical number and might have been thought to be the number of days young animals keep their eyes closed. Robert Burton gave us a proverb that seems to confirm this theory: "A wonder lasts but nine days, and then the puppy's eyes are open." In both World Wars and the Korean Conflict, the nickname *90-day wonders,* an offshoot of the earlier phrase, was given to young, sometimes zealous second lieutenants who were trained for only three months in Officer Candidate School (OCS).

9/11 war.   It seems safe to say that the war resulting from the terrorist attack on the World Trade Center in New York on September 11, 2001, will always be remembered by most Americans as the 9/11 war. The only real rival for this designation is the *war on terrorism*. *See* LET'S ROLL; REMEMBER.

nine months winter and three months late in the fall.   An old one-liner describing, often accurately, New England weather. The saying dates back well over a century.

19th hole.   Mencken calls *the 19th hole* "the one American contribution to the argot of golf." While this isn't quite true (*par, birdie, eagle, chip,* and *sudden death* are among U.S.-invented golf terms) the expression has been with us at least since the early 1920s and means "a convivial gathering place," such as a locker room or bar, after a game of golf.

the 98-cent man.   For many years it was estimated that the value of a human life, in chemical terms, was 98 cents, leading to the expression *the 98-cent man.* Inflation has changed this figure in recent times. Today the chemical elements in the body—5 pounds of calcium, 1½ pounds of phosphorus, 9 ounces of potassium, 6 ounces of sulfur, about 1 ounce of magnesium, and less than an ounce each of iron, copper, and iodine—are worth about $8.37.

99.44 percent pure.   This bit of advertising hype for IVORY SOAP is often used jokingly to describe anything pure. The *New York Times* (5/22/94) reported that: "A Procter & Gamble archivist, Edward Rider, says that although the soap's history is shrouded in myth, the best source for the number is an analysis done Dec. 14, 1882, by a New York City chemist, W. M. Habirshaw, who found the soap to be 72.53 percent 'fatty anhydrides,' 9.28 percent 'soda combined' and 17.63 percent 'water by difference.' " If you add up the numbers you get

99.44 percent. And the first known ad to use this figure appeared a week later.

ninny. *Ninny,* for "a fool or simpleton," is probably an abbreviation or pet form of *innocent,* it being only a short step from "adorably innocent" to "foolishly simple." The word is first recorded in 1592 and an early synonym, used by Rabelais, was *ninny-whoop.* Thus it predates NINCOMPOOP.

ninth wave. A nautical superstition of old holds that waves become progressively higher until the ninth wave (some say the 10th) and that then the progression begins all over again. While waves sometimes form larger ones when they meet, there is no fixed interval when a large one can be predicted.

Niobe of nations. Byron called Rome or Italy the *Niobe of nations* because of her lost empire. Niobe in Greek mythology lost all her 14 children when she taunted Leto because she had only two offspring. Leto commanded her two children—Apollo and Diana—to avenge the insult and cause the death of all Niobe's sons and daughters. Inconsolable, Niobe "wept herself to death and was changed into a stone from which ran water."

nip and tuck. *Nip and tuck* pretty much means "neck and neck," but the latter phrase suggests, say, two runners racing at the same speed with neither one ahead of the other, while *nip and tuck* describes a close race where the lead alternates. The earliest recorded form of the expression is found in James K. Paulding's *Westward Ho!* (1832): "There we were at rip and tuck, up one tree and down another." Maybe the *rip* originally came from "let 'er rip" and later became *nip* because of the expression "to nip someone out," to barely beat him, while the *tuck* was simply an old slang word for "vim and vigor." Other guesses at the phrase's origins are even wilder.

nip in the bud. To obtain larger peonies or tomatoes, to get larger flowers or fruit of any kind, gardeners have long pinched off excessive blossoms on plants, nipped them early in the bud to channel all a plant's strength into a few remaining buds, which will then yield large flowers or fruit. No fruit comes from a nipped-off bud, of course, and so the gardening term *to nip in the bud* became proverbial in Elizabethan times for calling a halt to something before it has a chance to develop, especially in regard to bad habits or plans with little chance of success.

a nip of whiskey. A *nipperkin* (possibly from the Dutch *nypelkin*) was a small container holding a half pint or less of liquor, usually wine or ale, the term being first recorded in 1694. *Nipperkin* was shortened to *nip* within a century or so and came to mean even less, no more than a shot glass full of spirits.

Nissen hut. *See* QUONSET HUT.

nitpicker. "She can wel pyke out lyce and nitis," William Caxton, the first English printer, wrote in a book of fables he translated from the French and published in 1484. But it took centuries before a nitpicker, "one who picks lice eggs [nits] from one's body or clothes," changed in meaning to one who looks for and finds small errors (as small as nits), a pedant. I'd

guess that the expression is an Americanism dating to the late 19th century.

nitty-gritty. Getting down to the nitty-gritty is getting down to basic elements. Though first recorded in the 1960s the expression is probably older; the nitty-gritty of the phrase may be gritlike nits (small lice) that are difficult to remove from the hair or scalp.

nitwit. This Americanism, first recorded in 1926, may be a combination of the German *nicht,* "not," and the English *wit*—*nichtwit,* "not with wits, without wits"—corrupted in speech to *nitwit.* Another theory has *nitwit* deriving from "a scornful English imitation" of Dutchmen who answered questions asked in English with the Dutch expression *Ik niet wiet,* "I don't know." This, however, would date *nitwit* to Dutch days in New York and there are thus far no examples of the word's use that far back.

nix. *Nix* is probably a British borrowing from the German *nichts,* "nothing." Meaning "nothing" or "no," it dates back to the late 18th century, when it is recorded as *nichts* in British slang, the word being spelt *nix* by 1812 at the latest. The expression *nix on that,* "nothing doing," is an Americanism first recorded in 1902. The famous *Variety* headline STIX NIX HIX PIX widely popularized *nix* in America.

Nixon's the one! This political slogan was turned against Richard Nixon in 1968 when he ran for the presidency—the button with the slogan was sometimes worn by pregnant women (Democrats, of course). In any case, Nixon won, perhaps more because of his slogan "Let's Get America Going Again."

n.n *See* N.G.

no-account. No-good, worthless, good-for-nothing, sometimes *no-count* in the South and other regions. Nobel Prize winner William Faulkner (1897–1962), one of America's greatest authors, was known as Count No Count to his neighbors in Oxford, Mississippi, during his early writing days. No one thought he would amount to much, this strange, seemingly lazy, rather seedy little man dressed in greasy khakis and a tweed sports jacket that had seen better days. The rumor spread that an intellectual friend, lawyer Phil Stone, must really be writing the stories that Faulkner to which signed his own name. *See* FAULKNERIAN.

Noah's Ark. It's safe to say that everyone over the age of six is familiar with the biblical story of Noah's Ark. However, few people are aware of this description in the files of the Atlantic Mutual Insurance Company, which has one of the world's largest archives on marine disasters:

> Noah's Ark. Built in 2448 B.C. Gopher wood pitched within and without. Length, 300 cubits; width, 50 cubits; height, 30 cubits. Three decks. Cattle carrier. Owner: Noah and Sons. Last reported stranded Mount Ararat.

Noah's Brig. *Noah's Brig,* a tiny rockbound island in the Hudson River, is named for one Captain Noah, an 18th-century captain of a fleet of rafts who had the misfortune of encountering the island under adverse conditions one night. Noah sighted "a dark object floating the waters," which looked like a brig under sail. "Brig ahoy!" he cried, but no answer came. "Brig ahoy!" he shouted. "Answer or I'll run you down!" There was still no reply and Captain Noah stubbornly held his course. Then a crash—wood crunched on rock: Noah had mistaken two trees on the island for masts with sails set.

no balm in Gilead.   "Is there no balm in Gilead; is there no physician there?" Jeremiah laments in the King James Version of the Bible. His words, from Jer. 8:22, give us the common expression meaning there is no consolation, no remedy. *Balm* is simply a shortening of *balsam*, a resinous gum long noted for its healing and soothing properties. But the Hebrew word *tsori*, rendered as *balm* in the King James Version, really means resin, probably the resin yielded by the mastic tree, another ingredient in many ancient remedies. So Jeremiah should literally be saying "Is there no resin in Gilead?" or "Is there no mastic in Gilead?" Not knowing exactly what substance Jeremiah referred to caused early translators of the Bible a lot of trouble. John Wycliffe and others used the word *gumme* or *resin* in the phrase, and in the so-called Bishops' Bible (1568) the translators had Jeremiah say "Is there no treacle in Gilead?" The bishops who did this translation were using treacle in its early sense of a salve, but later generations knew the substance as molasses or any sickeningly sweet substance and humorously referred to the Bishops' Bible as the Treacle Bible. *See* JEREMIAD.

Nobel Prize.   "The day when two army corps will be able to destroy each other in one second," Alfred Nobel predicted, "all civilized nations will recoil away from war in horror and disband their armies." The Swedish inventor of dynamite proved to be wrong in his prophecy, which may have been a rationalization for his invention, but the $9 million he left in his will to set up the Nobel Prize Foundation has greatly aided the cause of peace. Nobel Prizes are awarded to persons, irrespective of nationality, who have done outstanding work in the five fields Nobel considered most important to the benefit of mankind: physics, chemistry, medicine and physiology, literature, and peace. The prizes, given in Stockholm and Oslo on December 10th of each year in which awards are made, consist of varying amounts of money, a diploma, and a gold medal. The first ceremony was held in 1901. *See* DYNAMITE; FEYNMAN DIAGRAM.

no better than she should be.   An early-18th-century translation by Peter Motteux of *Don Quixote* is the first to record this classic understatement, meaning "an immoral woman." Whether it was coined at this time no one knows.

noble experiment.   President Herbert Hoover did not coin the expression *noble experiment* for Prohibition, nor even repeat the words. While seeking the presidency in 1928, Hoover answered a question about prohibition in a questionnaire Idaho senator William E. Borah sent to several candidates. What Hoover actually replied in part was: "Our country has deliberately undertaken a great social and economic experiment, noble in motive and far-reaching in purpose."

noble science.   A euphemism for "boxing" dating back to the 19th century, when aristocrats like the poet Lord Byron took boxing lessons from pugilists and the ability to box was requisite for a nobleman. Boxing was also dubbed "the manly art of self-defense" at the time.

noblesse oblige.   *Noblesse* has been used as a synonym for nobility in English since it was borrowed from the French in the early 14th century. However, *noblesse oblige*, the French for "nobility obliges," seems to be a recent coinage of the last 50 years or so. It generally means the obligation of the nobility, or the rich, to help others worse off than they.

nobody home!   Knocking themselves on the head, people sometimes say *Nobody home!* or *Nobody's home upstairs!* after forgetting something or after making a foolish statement. This is not contemporary slang, but dates back to the 1700s and an epigram of Alexander Pope's called "The Empty House":

> You beat your pate, and fancy wit will come:
> Knock as you please, there's nobody at home.

A more modern equivalent is "The lights are on, but nobody's home."

nobody loves Goliath.   A saying of the seven-foot-tall Philadelphia Warrior basketball star Wilton "Wilt the Stilt" Chamberlain (1936–1999), whose play dominated the NBA for many years. Called the greatest offensive player in basketball history, Chamberlain was also known as The Dipper, because he dipped so many shots into the basket from above. On March 2, 1962, against the New York Knicks, he scored 100 points, the most ever scored in a single pro game.

nobody's land.   Another name for NO-MAN'S-LAND especially in the military during World War I.

no can do; can do.   The negative phrase, and its opposite, are not contemporary expressions, as many people believe. They date back about a century and a half to England, where they probably originated in the Royal Navy.

no comment.   This common expression used by people hounded by reporters is an Americanism dating back no earlier than the beginning of the century. The original journalists given "no comments" may have been Hollywood gossip columnists in the 1920s.

no dice.   *No dice*, for "no" or "absolutely not," derives from the game of dice, where *no dice* means "a throw that doesn't count." *No dice* can also mean "worthless and completely unsuccessful," all of these meanings apparently dating back to the late 1920s in the U.S.

no good deed goes unpunished.   *See* ONE GOOD TURN DESERVES ANOTHER.

no great shakes.   That monument of noncomputerized scholarship, the great *Oxford English Dictionary*, suggests that this expression alludes to the shaking of dice. Someone who is *no great shakes* is nothing extraordinary, like a gambler who shakes the dice and throws a low point—no sevens or elevens. Considering its first recorded use, the expression must have been known as early as the 17th century. Lord Broughton, recalling an 1816 art show in his *Recollections of a Long Life* (1865), wrote: "W. said that a piece of sculpture there was '*nullae magnae quassationes*,' and the others laughed heartily." The others, proficient linguists, got the joke immediately when they translated the Latin for *no great shakes*. Another suggestion is that the expression derives from the provincial word *shake*, "to brag"—according to this highly improbable theory someone who is *no great shakes* would be nothing to brag about.

no hits, no runs, no errors.   Dating back to at least the 1930s and deriving from literal use in reports of baseball games, *no hits, no runs, no errors* has come to mean either complete failure (like the team shut out with no hits, no runs, no errors), perfection (like the pitcher who pitches a perfect game with no hits, no runs, no errors), and even something uneventful or without hitches (as in a game where there were no hits, no runs, no errors).

no holds barred.   The expression *no holds barred*, meaning "no limits or reservations, free and uninhibited," was surely suggested by a wrestling contest in which all holds are allowed, but not by an officiated match in which there are rules and regulations. It probably dates back to the 19th century.

nohow.   Anyhow. An Americanism dating back to the early 19th century. In one of Solomon Franklin Smith's books set in the Southwest in the 1850s, he tells of a woman who was offered condolences on the death of her husband. "Warn't of much account, no how!" she replied.

no ifs, ans or buts about it.   In British usage *ifs and ans* describe wishful thinking, as in the old jingle:

> If ifs and ans
> Were pots and pans
> Where would be the tinker?

Ans in this case is the plural of the old *an*, meaning "if." But the American expression *there'll be no ifs, ans, or buts about it* means something entirely different. *An* here is an old form of *and*. The saying is a strong negative meaning there will be absolutely no argument about something. A child might say, as children do, "I'll mow the lawn if there's no game this afternoon and Johnny can't come over, but not if it's too hot, Dad," and his Dad might reply, as fathers do, "You'll mow the lawn, period. There'll be no ifs, ans, or buts about it!"

noisette.   The hardy, widely grown garden rose named the *noisette*, a cross of the moss rose and the China rose, originated in America in about 1816. It was named after an early cultivator (not the originator) of the hybrid, Philippe Noisette of Charleston, South Carolina. It is less often called the Champney rose, for its discoverer, John Champney of Charleston.

noisome.   Many people on first encountering this word believe it means "noisy," but *noisome* has no connection with the word *noise*. Noisome, which means "offensive or disgusting, noxious," was formed from the Middle English *noy*, harm or annoyance," and the suffix *some*, in the sense of "characterized by some quality."

no ka de.   A good example of one of the ways English words are used in Japan. Foreign borrowings (not only, but mostly, English, and including technical terms) total about 100,000 words, fully one-third of the Japanese vocabulary. *No ka de* is the Japanizing of the English words *no car day*. In Japan it is the day of the month when certain drivers are not allowed to use their cars. To help curb air pollution every driver is assigned a certain "no car day."

noli me tangere.   *Noli me tangere*, "touch me not," are the words Christ spoke to Mary Magdalene after His resurrection. The impatiens (*Impatiens holotii* and other species) are called *noli me tangere* and *touch me not* because their seed pods burst and scatter their seeds when touched. They are also called snapweed, and Busy Lizzie in reference to their frequent blooming. *Impatiens* is from the Latin for impatience, in allusion to the bursting of the seed pods.

no love lost.   This has been called "an ambiguous phrase" that meant both "they have no love for each other" and "their affection for each other was mutual" when it was first recorded in the late 17th century. Today, however, these words always mean "they dislike each other, have no love for each other."

no-man's-land.   World War I created many a *no-man's-land*, but isn't responsible for the phrase. *No-man's-land* was first used in the early 14th century for the unowned wasteland outside the north wall of London that was used as an execution site for criminals. For many years no one wanted to own this land where criminals were beheaded, hanged, or impaled, their rotting bodies left on display as a warning to lawbreakers. The place became known as *no-man's-land* because no one claimed it, and the expression was soon applied figuratively to other places. About 400 years later *no-man's-land* was applied to the little-used place on a ship's forecastle where blocks, ropes, and tackle were stored. The term was first used in its military sense of the area between hostile entrenched lines in about 1900 and became famous in this sense during World War I. The dead could be seen in these *no-man's-lands* just as they had been seen in the original six centuries before. "A wilderness of dead bodies," the writer who first used the military term called it. In a letter to his mother British poet Wilfred Owen, killed in the war, wrote: "No Man's land is pockmarked like the body of foulest disease and its odour is the breath of cancer . . . No Man's Land under snow is like the face of the moon, chaotic, crater-ridden, uninhabitable, awful, the abode of madness." In another letter he spoke of "Hideous landscapes, vile noises . . . everything unnatural, broken, blasted; the distortion of the dead, whose unburiable bodies sit outside the dug-outs all day, all night, the most execrable sights on earth."

nom de guerre.   "A name of war," just another term for a pseudonym, usually for outlaws, pirates, war lords, and the like. Blackbird, Diabolito, Long Knife, Captain Buzzard, Gentleman Harry, Big John, Black Bart, and Calico Jack—these are only a few of the many pirates who chose to live under colorful pseudonyms or names of war that they invented or had bestowed upon them.

Nome.   The Alaskan seaport, according to one persistent story, was dubbed *Nome* after a British naval cartographer aboard the *Herald* working on a map of Alaska noted a cape without a name and wrote "Name?" above it. In London the printer misread "Name?" as *Nome* and so the cape was named. Later, Cape Nome's moniker was transferred to the port near it, which had been called Anvil City. No other plausible explanation has been given for Nome's name. *See also* INDRI; KANGAROO; LLAMA; LUZON; YUCATAN.

no more chance than a kerosene cat in hell with gasoline drawers on. A southern expression meaning "absolutely no chance at all" and dating back to the 1920s.

No more free lunch! When he was elected in 1934, New York's reform mayor Fiorello La Guardia invented the slogan "No More Free Lunch!" (No more graft). The words are a translation of the Italian "E finite la cuccagna!" said to have been shouted by the Little Flower while he angrily shook his fist at City Hall.

no more Hoares to Paris. In the days before World War II, British diplomat Sir Samuel Hoare made rather disadvantageous arrangements with the French in Paris and King George V quipped famously to his foreign secretary: "[Send] No more coals to Newcastle; no more Hoares to Paris." Sending *coals to Newcastle* means doing something superfluous, as Newcastle was a great coal-mining center—which adequately explains the rest of the quip.

no more use for them than Meader's teeth. A saying, only historical now, that derives from the old story about a man named Nick Meader, who at about the time of the War of 1812 borrowed a hammer to knock out all his teeth, claiming, "I have no need of them, for I can get nothing to eat."

nonce word. *See* GHOST WORD.

none-so-pretties. A folk name, two centuries old, for the flowers more commonly called pansies today.

no news is good news. This is not a recent saying, as one might think. A slight variation on it dates back to at least the reign of England's King James I, who in 1616 wrote to one of his ministers and asked him not to write back unless he had a favorable answer, advising him that "no news is better than evil news."

nong-nong. One of the few words that have entered English from an Aboriginal language, *nong-nong* is heard primarily in Australia, meaning "a complete fool, a silly person." Such a person is also called a "nong."

no-no. *See* YEAH, YEAH.

nonpareil. *See* HUNDREDS AND THOUSANDS.

noodling. A way to catch catfish by using one's bare fingers as both bait and hook. The technique, common in the South, can be painful, as catfish have sharp teeth.

no oil painting. A man or woman whose appearance isn't handsome or beautiful is said to be "no oil painting," as in

"She's no oil painting, but everyone likes her." An oil portrait of someone usually does all it can to make the sitter attractive. *See* WARTS AND ALL.

noon. Why does *noon* derive from the Latin *nono*, meaning "nine"? Noon actually first meant the ninth hour of the day—counted from sunrise, which comes at 6 A.M. on the average. *Noon* was thus at 3 P.M., halfway between midday and sunset, or the middle of the afternoon. Early in the 13th century the meaning of noon began to change from 3 P.M., or the middle of the afternoon, to 12 o'clock, or the middle of the day itself, possibly because it was a handy word to apply to the time when the midday meal was eaten.

noonday. *See* KIND-HEARTED.

no one knows the luck of a lousy calf. An old American saying meaning no one knows the fate of an unpromising person, he or she may succeed beyond all expectations. Usually said of children considered "unpromising" by adults.

no-pan. In Japanese bars and nightclubs, topless and bottomless waitresses abound. The Japanese have taken to calling the latter "no-pan," a word they made by shortening the English expression *no-panties*.

Nordic. This is a word that has been much distorted in modern times, especially by Nazi propagandists, who used it, like *Aryan*, to describe a vastly superior blond, blue-eyed "race" (Nietzsche's "blond beast" type) inhabiting Germany. Actually the Nordic type properly describes Scandinavians. The word derives from the Latin *nordicus*, "northern." According to Walter Theimer, in *The Penguin Political Dictionary* (1949): "There is a Nordic type, making up about 70 percent of the population in Scandinavia, less than 20 percent in Germany, Holland and Great Britain, and less than 15 percent in the United States . . . The existence of a common Nordic-primitive people has never been proved."

no rest for the weary. Frequently said half in jest by someone laboring too hard, this expression was probably suggested by the older phrase *no peace for the wicked*, which is from the biblical "There is no peace, saith the Lord, unto the wicked." (Isa. 48:22).

Norfolk Howard. There are many notable name changes in history. One of the most famous among them would have to be the change made by Italian Cardinal Grugno in 1009, which began the custom of popes taking a new name on accession. The cardinal had an excellent reason for adopting the name Sergius IV; Grugno means "swine snout" in Italian. Usually people do have good reasons for legally changing their names—like C. J. Crook who changed his name to C. J. Noble. This type far outnumbers the logically unaccountable changes like W. Jones to W. Smith (1798). Sometimes even the most logical name changes backfire, though. On June 26, 1862, Joshua Bug of Norfolk, tired of his "base" name, took an ad in the *London Times* announcing that he would henceforth be known as Norfolk Howard, this being one of England's most aristocratic names. His countrymen soon foiled the poor man's grandiose plans for metamorphosis, however, displaying the British sense of humor so many say doesn't exist and adopting *Norfolk Howard* as a slang synonym for "bedbug." *See* OFFICIAL MONSTER RAVING LOONY PARTY; ZIPPITY-DOO-DAH.

no room to swing a cat. This phrase probably has something to do with the old "sport" of swinging cats by the tails as targets for archers. The expression goes back at least to the mid-1600s, and CAT-O'-NINE-TAILS isn't recorded until about 1670, which makes it unlikely that the phrase originated with some sea captain having no room to punish a rebellious sailor with a "cat." The only other plausible explanation is that *cat* in this case refers to a sailor's hammock or *cot*, there being little room on olden ships to swing one, but there are no quotations to support this theory.

Norskie. This mildly derogatory term for a Norwegian-American is mainly heard in the Northwest, as it has been for over a century. *See* SCANDAHOOVIAN.

North Carolina; South Carolina. Both states really honor three kings—deriving from the Latin *Carolus*, meaning "Charles." Originally dedicated to France's Charles XI in the 16th century, the territory now comprising North and South Carolina was next named for England's Charles I. Charles I granted the patent for the Carolinas to Sir Robert Heath in 1629, Heath calling the territory Carolana in his honor. This it remained until 1663, when Charles II granted a new patent and the colony was called Carolina in *his* honor.

North Dakota; South Dakota. These states are named for the Dakota tribes in the area, *Dakota* meaning roughly, "allies" from *da*, "to think of as," and *koda*, "friend." (For other friendly Indians, *see* TEXAS.)

northeast, southwest, northwest, southeast. In parts of Kansas settled along the geographical grids suggested by Thomas Jefferson, the appropriate burners on gas and electrical stoves are still called northeast, southeast, northwest, southwest. Nowhere else is this nomenclature used.

northern fox grape. A wild grape ranging from New England to Illinois and south to Georgia that is so named because it supposedly "smelleth and tasteth like unto a foxe." It is the source of the Concord and other cultivated grape varieties.

North Star State. *See* GOPHER STATE.

Norway rat. The common but infamous brown house rat is called the *Norway rat* in the United States because it was introduced here from Norway, apparently deserting Norwegian ships trading at U.S. ports three centuries ago.

no sabe. Don't know, don't understand. The Spanish phrase has been common in the U.S. since the mid-19th century and is often pronounced *no savvy*.

nose; mucus. Our word *nose* derives directly from the Anglo-Saxon *nosu*, but can be traced back to the Anglo-Saxon *nasa*, which meant "dual or double" and is the tap root for *nosu*, the nose having two nostrils. The nose's mucus, from the Latin *mucus*, "slime from the nose," gives us the word *mucilage* for glue, which someone thought resembled it.

no-see-ems. Thoreau cites this Penobscot Indian term for small biting insects in *The Maine Woods* (1864). Today northwestern loggers use the similar term *no-see-um* for the *punkie*, a minute, almost invisible fly or midge of the family Chironomedae that has a terrific bite. *No-see-um* apparently comes from Chinook jargon or a pidgin English once spoken between loggers and Indians.

nosegay. A bunch of sweet-smelling flowers has been called a *nosegay* since at least the early 15th century. *Nosegay* has survived because it reminds us of how the nose delights in or is made gay by the smell of flowers, but the charming, playful *tussie-mussie*, or *tuzzy-muzzy*, for the same (as well as a gold or silver representation of a bunch of flowers) is extinct now. *Posy*, for a bunch of flowers or flower-like words, is little heard, but lives on in the language forever thanks to Marlowe's "Passionate Shepherd," who rhymed: "I will make thee beds of roses/ And a thousand fragrant posies."

nose out of joint. Sometimes this expression is used wrongly as a general description of a conceited person. The only connection here is that it really means to humiliate a conceited person, as well as to supplant a person in another's affections, and to upset someone's plans. Recorded as early as the 16th century, the phrase suggests the altering of a nose that is always confidently stuck up in the air, the downfall of vanity. Samuel Pepys wrote that the marriage of Charles II to Catherine of Braganza, "a very fine and handsome lady," would put his mistress Madame Castlemaine's "nose out of joynt." Actually having one's nose out of joint is a very painful condition.

nose writing. Aldous Huxley often wrote with his nose, though he produced none of his masterpieces this way. "A little *nose writing*," he notes in *The Art of Seeing*, "will result in a perceptible temporary improvement of defective vision." Huxley's eyesight was so bad that he learned Braille to relieve his eyes; he often read at night in bed, hands and book under the covers. A follower of Dr. William Bates, the author practiced the ophthalmologist's exercises for improving eyesight. Any myopic writer or reader who wants to try need not dip his nose in ink. Simply fix your eyes on the end of your nose and move your head as if you were writing a word, sentence, or anecdote.

Nosey Parker. Matthew Parker, who became Archbishop of Canterbury in 1559, acquired a reputation for poking his nose into other people's business. Actually, he was an intelligent, if somewhat overzealous, churchman of marked Protestant persuasion who introduced many administrative and ceremonial reforms into the Anglican Church. His reputation is largely undeserved, but Catholics and Puritans alike resented his good works, taking advantage of his rather long nose and dubbing him *Nosey Parker*, which has meant an unduly inquisitive person ever since. Parker had been chaplain to Anne Boleyn and Henry VIII before becoming archbishop. A scholar of some note, he died in 1575 aged 71. The above, at least, is the most popular folk etymology for *Nosey Parker*. But other candidates have been proposed Richard Parker, leader of the Sheerness Mutiny in

1797, is one strong contender. This Parker poked his nose so deeply into what the military thought their exclusive bailiwick that he wound up hanged from the yardarm of H.M.S. *Sandwich* on July 30 of that year.

nosh.   To nosh is to snack or eat between meals, while a nosh is a snack. A Yiddish contribution to English first recorded in about 1955, *nosh* is ultimately from the German *naschen*, "to eat on the sly."

no skin off my back.   Originally *no skin off my nose* was the form of this Americanism, which dates back 75 years or so. It means "it is no concern to me, not my business, doesn't hurt me one bit." Perhaps *nose* better fits the phrase than *back*—if you don't stick your nose into someone else's business, you won't get it punched.

no slow fuckin'!   Work faster, no malingering. A guard says to chain gang convicts in the movie *J.F.K.* (1991): "Move it along. No slow fuckin'."

no soap!   In 1775 young actor and author Samuel Foote (1720–77) composed the following speech when pompous fellow actor Charles Macklin boasted that he could repeat anything after hearing it once: "So she went into the garden to cut a cabbage leaf to make an apple pie; and at the same time, a great she-bear coming up the street pops its head into the shop—What! no soap! So he died; and she very impudently married the barber; and there were present the picaninnies and the Jobilies, and the Garyuloes, and the grand Panjandrum himself, with the little round button at top." "Old Macklin" (he lived to be 100) gave up in disgust, unable to memorize this nonsense, but the mnemonic exercise gave the language both the phrase *no soap!*, for the failure of some mission or plea, and *grand Panjandrum*, which was first used as a derogatory term by Edward FitzGerald in his translation of the *Rubáiyát*, when he applied it to a self-important local official. Foote, disliked by Dr. Johnson, once announced that he was going to do an imitation of the Great Cham on the stage. Johnson sent word that he had ordered a new oak cudgel and would be present that evening to correct any faults in the impersonation with it. Foote canceled the show.

nostalgia.   One source claims that philosopher Johannes Hofer coined *nostalgia* in 1668, but the *Oxford English Dictionary* only traces the word back to 1780. *Nostalgia* means a wistful desire to return to one's home or homeland, to a former time or place in one's life. It is made up of the Greek *nostos*, "a return home," and *algos*, "pain." In a *New York Times* (5/19/01) article Edward Rothstein writes that Hofer, a Swiss doctor, invented the word "to describe the lingering malady that afflicted Swiss soldiers away from home . . . Soldiers would be severely overcome with nostalgia when drinking and hearing Alpine folk melodies; the prescribed cures included leeches, opium and a return to the Alps. In 1733 the Russian Army apparently found an effective method for preventing the illness in the first place. Anyone who exhibited any symptoms would be buried alive." *Nostalgie de la boue* ("mud nostalgia") refers to nostalgia for degradation, the expression invented by 19th-century French dramatist Emile Augin in one of his plays.

Nostradamus.   *The Centuries* of Nostradamus, a book of rhymed prophecies, was published in 1555. The French doctor and astrologer gained a reputation as a seer when some of his predictions came true and as a result he won an appointment as personal physician to Charles IX. His real name was Michel de Nostredame, and his book, divided into centuries, was drawn from the whole body of medieval prophetic literature. Nostradamus was 63 when he died in 1566. The papal court condemned his prophecies in 1781, but they have enjoyed wide attention since on a number of occasions, one generation or another applying them to contemporary situations. Detractors claim that the prophecies are so ambiguously worded that they could mean anything, and when *Nostradamus* is used for a seer or prophet it is generally employed in a contemptuous sense. *See* MOTHER SHIPTON.

not a dry seat in the house.   The drama critic's cliché *there wasn't a dry eye in the house*, to describe a moving play, suggested this humorous expression, which has been fairly common in England since about 1930 for a play or movie so funny that the audience was helpless with laughter—in fact, wet their pants laughing.

not all there.   *See* PLAY WITHOUT A FULL DECK.

not by a long shot.   Whether it was suggested by a difficult long shot attempted in archery or shooting isn't known, but the expression *a long shot* first arose in British racing circles some 128 years ago as a bet laid at large odds, a bold wager. *Not by a long shot* therefore means hopelessly out of reckoning. Attempts have been made to derive the saying from the slightly earlier *not by a long chalk*, which comes from the use of chalk for reckoning points in tavern games. But *not by a long chalk* means "not by much," so it seems that the phrase derives from either archery or shooting.

not by bread alone.   This ancient expression, meaning that a person's spirit must be cared for as well as his body, comes from the Bible (Deut. 8:3): "Man doth not live by bread alone, but by every word that proceedeth out of the mouth of the Lord doth man live."

not dry behind the ears.   Used to describe someone totally innocent, or very naive, the old expression refers to newborn animals and the small depressions behind their ears that are the last places to become dry after birth. The similar phrase *wet behind the ears* is also heard today.

No-tel Motel.   Over the last decade or so "hot pillow joints" (the pillows are still warm from the last occupants when you get the room, so rapid is the turnover) have sprung up all over America. These swingers' motels usually offer rooms with porno films on closed-circuit TV, water beds, mirrored ceilings, etc. They often advertise on billboards ("Special Two-Hour Rates $11.95 Only") and are of course usually places of sexual assignation for businessmen and housewives, which is why they have been humorously dubbed *No-tel Motels*. *See also* MOTEL.

not for love or money.   Not at any price or by any means. The phrase is recorded as early as A.D. 971 and has been commonly used ever since, almost always in this negative form. Swift used it in his *Journal to Stella* (1712).

nothing in excess.   *See* SEVEN SAGES OF GREECE.

nothing is certain but death and taxes.   The widely quoted saying is attributed to Benjamin Franklin, who wrote in an 1789 letter: ". . . in this world nothing is certain but death and taxes."

nothing on the ball.   A baseball pitcher who is pitching poorly (giving up hits) is said to have *nothing on the ball*, the expression dating back to at least 1912, when it is first recorded. Conversely, a pitcher with *something* or *a lot on the ball* is pitching well. The first expression is used generally to describe someone who is incompetent, while the latter means someone who has the ability to succeed.

nothing to fear but fear itself.   Franklin D. Roosevelt is often cited as the originator of "The only thing we have to fear is fear itself" in his first inaugural address, when the country was at the bottom of the Great Depression. F.D.R., however, had many ghostwriters past to help him:

- "The only thing I am afraid of is fear."
  —Duke of Wellington
- "Nothing is so much to be feared as fear."—Thoreau
- "Nothing is terrible except fear itself."
  —Francis Bacon
- "The thing of which I have most fear is fear."
  —Montaigne
- "Be not afraid of sudden fear."—Proverbs 3:25

no tickee, no washee.   People have always had a hard time getting their wash back from the laundry without having the receipt for it. This expression was common among Chinese laundrymen starting in the late 19th century or earlier and is still occasionally heard. The words have taken on the new, wider meaning of "no credit without collateral."

not in the same league with.   Not nearly comparable with, nowhere near as good as someone or something else. This American expression comes from baseball, in which someone in the major leagues is generally a far better player than someone in the minor leagues. The British use the phrase *not in the same street with* to mean the same thing. Said San Francisco Giant's first baseman J. T. Snow recently (4/3/02) of his teammate home run king Barry Bonds: "The guy's in another league. . . . I think the rest of us feel like we're Little Leaguers. . . . He does things others can't do."

not so hot.   *Not so hot* is often denoted as an American slang expression dating back to the Roaring Twenties, but Shakespeare used and possibly invented this expression meaning "not very good."

not the only pebble on the beach.   *See* YOU'RE NOT THE ONLY PEBBLE ON THE BEACH.

not to be sneezed at.   At the beginning of the 19th century the expression *to sneeze at* meant to consider something un-important or boring. "It's the sort of thing a young fellow of my expectations ought to sneeze at," said the first writer who used the saying in print. This is guesswork, but the expression may have been suggested by the habit of snuff-taking common among the upper classes at the time. Snuff, also called "sneeze," was a mixture of tobacco, a little pepper, and other ingredients, snuffed into the nostrils to induce a hearty sneeze, which was considered exhilarating. Since a gentleman bored with a conversation might resort to snuff-taking and sneezing, perhaps the phrase *to sneeze at* and its opposite *not to be sneezed at* arose from the practice.

not to care a straw.   Not to care at all. The straw that is left after grain has been separated from a crop is worth very little compared with the grain, and a single straw has almost no value. People have known this since earliest times, which is why *not to care a straw* is probably much older than even its earliest recorded use in 1290. Among other great English writers, Chaucer and Shakespeare used the phrase or one of its variations such as *not to care two straws*, or *not to care three straws*.

not to get the bat off one's shoulder.   These words mean not to get a chance, as in, "He had big plans for the company but was fired before he could get the bat off his shoulder." The common expression, first recorded in the 1920s, is obviously from baseball, referring to a batter who takes a strike without even swinging at the ball.

not tonight, Josephine.   Napoleon Bonaparte is often credited with this phrase, which means "We shall not have sex tonight, dear" and has been around since the late 1800s. *See also* NAPOLEON.

not to turn a hair.   Not to show any signs of distress, to be unruffled, unaffected by exertion or any agitation. This is a "horsey" term from the stables, where the first sign of distress in a horse is sweating, which roughens the animal's coat, his hair remaining smooth and glossy as long as he keeps cool. Jane Austen first recorded the expression in *Northanger Abbey* (1797), writing of a horse: ". . . he had not turned a hair till we came to Walcot church."

not to worry.   *Not to worry*, "don't worry, there isn't anything to worry about," became very popular in the late 1950s, but probably dates back earlier as British army slang. Some scholars trace it to the Italian *non tormentarsi* and others suggest a Maltese connection, but *not to worry* is more likely simply a shortening of the British "You are not to worry."

not what it's cracked up to be.   Martin Van Buren, not a very popular president, though he gave us the expression O.K., was once disparaged by Davy Crockett, who said he "is not the man he is cracked up to be." The expression, meaning "not what he is generally believed to be," is apparently an Americanism dating back to the 1830s, but it may have British roots that go back much further, for *cracked* here has the old meaning of to boast or brag, a usage that dates back to at least the 16th century.

not worth a continental.   Before the U.S. Constitution was adopted, the Continental Congress had no power of taxation to raise revenue. The Congress issued bills of credit called continentals, the dollar bills of the time, printing bills with a face value of more than $250 million though there was virtually no bullion or specie in the treasury with which to redeem them. To make matters worse, the British and Tories circulated immense amounts of counterfeit continentals, selling them for the price of the paper they were printed on and sending the fake currency out of New York City by the cartload with persons going into other colonies. By 1790 continental dollars were worth so little that it took 40 paper dollars to buy a dollar in silver and the expression *not worth a continental*—worthless—had become part of the language.

not worth a Hannah Cook.   Worthless, of no account, as in "He's not worth a Hannah Cook." The expression originally was nautical, but no one has identified a real no-account Hannah Cook behind the phrase. It may be folk etymology for *hand* or *cook*, hands and cooks aboard ships making less money than other seamen and thus having lower status.

not worth a rap.   This *rap* isn't a knock, as many people believe. The rap in the phrase was a half-penny circulated in Ireland in 1721; worth very little, it gave rise to our expression *not worth a rap*, "worth nothing at all."

not worth a red cent.   American pennies—once made with more copper, and thus redder—were formerly called reds, which is what a Californian describing a card game in 1849 meant when he observed, "Silver is not plenty . . . on the tables and anybody can . . . bet a red on any card he chuses." This accounts for the expression *not worth a red cent*, which has roots in the British "not worth a brass farthing" and which remains a good descriptive phrase because the penny still has enough copper in it to appear reddish.

not worth a row (hill) of beans.   The meaning behind this phrase is that beans have little value compared with other crops because they are so easy to grow and prolific. *Not worth a bean* is one of the oldest expressions in English, recorded as early as the 13th century and colloquial since at least 1400. The *hill* in *not worth a hill of beans*, in the American version of the English expression, was a common term a century ago when the saying was born. It means not an actual hill, but a group of bean plants planted close together in a circle. Because most people now plant beans in straight rows and the meaning of hills is unclear to many, the phrase is usually *not worth a row of beans* today.

not worth a tinker's damn (dam).   There are numerous old expressions, some dating back over 400 years, indicating the profanity of tinkers in general. The tinker, who takes his name from "tink," the sound of a hammer on metal, is remembered by *to swear like a tinker* and *not worth a tinker's curse*, among other sayings. Obviously he threw "damns" around so casually that they became meaningless, worthless, giving us the expression *not worth a tinker's damn*. There have been attempts, however, to link the phrase to the little temporary "dams" tinkers fashioned to hold solder in place when they repaired pots and pans.

not worth his salt.   *See* SALT.

not written in stone.   An expression usually heard in the negative, telling the listener that some plan is not absolutely certain or required, not very difficult to change. It may refer to the two stone tablets engraved with the Ten Commandments delivered to Moses on Mount Sinai (Ex. 20: 1–17), or might refer to the finality of a gravestone, among other possibilities. Variations are the expressions *not set in stone; not carved in stone; not set in tablets of stone;* and *not carved in tablets of stone.*

Nova under snow on a sled.   One of the most colorful diner expressions, translating as "Nova Scotia smoked salmon or lox smothered with cream cheese on an English muffin or bagel."

November.   *See* SEPTEMBER.

now Barabbas was a publisher.   These lines are often attributed to Lord Byron. Byron supposedly received a lavish copy of the Bible from publisher John Murray in gratitude for a favor, only to return it with *thief* changed to *publisher* in John 18:40. English poet Thomas Campbell (1777–1844) had earlier made a similar quip after Napoleon had had German publisher Johann Pal put to death for printing subversive pamphlets. At an authors' dinner, Campbell proposed this toast: "To Napoleon. [Voices of protest] I agree with you that Napoleon is a tyrant, a monster, the sworn foe of our nation. But, gentlemen—he once shot a publisher!"

Now I lay me down to sleep. . . .   The first line of a prayer known to millions of Americans through its inclusion for centuries in the *New England Primer*, though the first verse of the prayer is the *Enchiridion Leonis* (1160). The full prayer goes:

> Now I lay me down to sleep,
> I pray the Lord my soul to keep
> If I should die before I wake,
> I pray the Lord my soul to take.

Ernest Hemingway used part of the first line as the title for his short story "Now I Lay Me," in which the wounded narrator (based on the author) feared that "if I ever shut my eyes in the dark and let myself go, my soul would go out of my body . . . and [I] said my prayers over and over and tried to pray for all the people I had ever known."

now-now girl.   In the southern African republic of Zimbabwe, where English is the official language, there are many English usages common only to that country. *Now-now girl* in Zimbabwe, for example, refers to a pretty, up-to-date, modern, and stylish young woman.

nudge.   *See* GUNCH.

nudnik; Phudnick.   A *nudnik* is a man "whose purpose in life is to bore the rest of humanity," according to poet Morris Rosenfeld's essay on the subject. *Nudnik*, indeed, derives from the Russian *nudna*, for "a bore." Leo Rosten's *The Joys of Yiddish* says the recently coined *Phudnik* is "a nudnik with a Ph.D."

nuke.   *Nuke* is relatively new American slang for a nuclear weapon, being first recorded in 1964 in a *Time* magazine article, which discussed the possibility of using nuclear bombs to dig a new canal in Panama. *Nuke* as a verb, "to attack with nuclear weapons," is first recorded in a July 4, 1970 *New Yorker* interview with Eugene V. Rostow.

number. *Number* derives from the Latin *numerare*, meaning the same. It is often forgotten that the word *number*, in addition to its common uses, can also refer to poems (poetry), verses, or metrical feet in a poem. Shakespeare, for example, uses number to mean poems in his 17th Sonnet:

> If I could write the beauty of your eyes
> And in fresh numbers number all your grace.

See also RETIRING A NUMBER.

(one's) number is up. One is about to die; one has been caught in some criminal activity. This phrase may derive from the British and American military expression *lose the number of one's mess*, meaning one has been killed. But the first (British) printed mention of the term in 1806 associates it with a lottery, which suggests that one's death is a matter of luck, like a number coming up in a lottery.

number one; number ten. *Number one*, in the sense of "best, excellent, first-rate," dates back to early 19th-century America, soldiers later carrying it overseas to Asia, where it entered the vocabulary of pidgin English. *Number ten*, on the other hand, was first recorded during the Korean conflict in 1953. It means "worst" or "bad" and was often used in the stronger expression *number hucken (fucking) ten*. In the same war *number sixty-nine* (the number deriving from the name of the sex act) was stronger still. The inflationary expression *number ten thousand*, or *number ten thou*, was pidgin in Vietnam, though I heard it in Korea (ca. 1952). *Number one* can also mean "oneself," this sense recorded earlier than any of the other phrases, in 1704. *Number one* and *number two* can be euphemisms for the acts of urination and defecation, first recorded in the 1930s but probably much older.

number, please. Telephone operators had been advised by Thomas Edison to greet callers with AHOY instead of *hello*, but operators fell into the habit of opening with a curt "What number?" However, according to Stuart Berg Flexner's *Listening to America* (1982), by 1895 the city manager of the Chicago Telephone Company, one J. W. Thompson, issued the following instructions to the company's chief operator in a memorandum: "In answering calls the query 'Number Please?' spoken in a pleasant tone of voice and with rising inflection must be invariably employed." Within 10 years all of the Bell System followed suit.

Number (No.) 10 Downing Street. *See* PRIME MINISTER; DOWNING STREET.

numps. The *OED* says this word of obscure origin is obsolete, but since it was used recently on a TV program (in which a character found *numps* in a dictionary for a word game he was playing) it cannot truly be caught in the cobwebs of antiquity. *Numps*, always used in a humorous way, means "a foolish, silly person." It was first recorded in Francis Beaumont's most successful play, *The Knight of the Burning Pestle* (ca. 1607), a comedy that owes much to Cervantes's *Don Quixote*. It is also spelled *nump* and *numph*. Beaumont was once thought to have written the play with his longtime collaborator, John Fletcher, but now it is known to be his alone. This is the same writing team of whom biographer John Aubrey wrote in *Brief Lives*: "There was a wonderful consimility of fancy. They lived together not far from the playhouse, had one wench between them, the same clothes and cloak, & C."

nut. Due to the round shape of many nuts, *nut* has long been slang for "head," which led to the expression, *he's off his nut* meaning "he's crazy," which in turn gave us *nuts* for "crazy" and *nut house*, meaning "insane asylum." The word *nut* can be used for a sum of money, and figures in many other expressions as well, including *a hard nut to crack* (a tough problem to solve) and *from soup to nuts*, meaning "complete." To give someone a brief summary of something is *to put it in a nutshell* and obviously refers to the small size of a nutshell. The phrase has been with us at least since Pliny reported that the *Iliad* had been copied in so small a handwriting by a contemporary of his that the whole work fit in a walnut shell. This feat has been duplicated several times over the years. Since there are no nuts to be gathered in May, the old children's song with the words, "Here we go gathering nuts in May" seems to make no sense—and indeed, it may have been intended as a nonsense song. But "the nuts" in the phrase has been explained as being "knots" of May, that is, bunches of flowers. In Elizabethan England, Queen Elizabeth herself gathered knots of May in the meadows, one author tells us, and this is a plausible explanation even though there are no recorded quotations supporting the use of *knots* for "flowers," except possibly the English *knot garden* of herbs.

Nutmeg State. A nickname for Connecticut (*see* DON'T TAKE ANY WOODEN NICKELS). Also called the Wooden Nutmeg State, the Land of the Wooden Nutmegs, the Blue Law State (*see* BLUE LAWS), the Mother of States, the Constitution State, the Brownstone State, the Freestone State, and the Land of Steady Habits.

Nuts! When Brigadier General Anthony McAuliffe, known as Old Crock to his troops, was asked to surrender Bastogne during the Battle of the Bulge in World War II, his 101st Airborne outnumbered four to one, he reportedly replied "Nuts!" to the German officer who awaited a reply. There are those who believe that McAuliffe, a tough airborne officer, after all, said something much stronger—"Shit!," to be exact—but no proof has been offered. In any case, he meant "Go to hell!" and *Nuts!* has become immortal. *See also* THE GUARD DIES BUT NEVER SURRENDERS!

nut tree. The southwestern pine tree (*Pinus edulis*), so named for its edible nutlike seeds, which are also called piñon nuts.

nylon. Though it was first mass-produced during World War II and hurt our enemy Japan's silk industry, *nylon* is not an acronym of "*Now You Lousy Nips*," as the old story goes. Formerly a trademark, *nylon* is an arbitrary name with no meaning, though the symbols NY in its chemical formula may have suggested the word. There also could have been a link with the earlier ray*on* or even with cott*on*. In any case, the Du Pont company coined the word in 1938. The most popular use of the word has been in women's nylon stockings. Somehow the English word *nylon* has taken on a disreputable meaning among Serbo-Croatians, as Bill Bryson asserts in *The Mother Tongue* (1990), "so that a *nylon hotel* is a brothel." *See* RAYON.

NYSE; AMEX.   *NYSE* is the abbreviation for the *New York Stock Exchange*, which was originally named the New York Stock and Exchange Board (1817), taking its present name in 1863. The American Stock Exchange (AMEX), which took its present name in 1963, was formed as the New York Curb Exchange in 1842, because it was composed of curbstone brokers who were not members of any exchange and conducted business outside on the curb.

O.   Of all 26 letters in the alphabet *O* has, perhaps, the most interesting and best-documented story. The oldest of letters began as a pictograph common to many languages describing the human eyeball within its protected socket; some drawings of it in ancient alphabets even give it a dot in the center for a pupil. In time the socket and pupil were eliminated from the pictograph and we find it in North Semitic as a plain, full circle that was called "the eye." From there it passed into the Greek alphabet. Unlike any other letter, it has undergone no other major structural change in over 2,700 years. In Anglo-Saxon O's name was *oedel*, "home." It later became probably the only English letter to have a poem written about it by a philosopher (Dr. William Whewell). *O* is also the commonest single-letter surname, there being 13 in the Brussels telephone directory alone. But there is no evidence of an O residing in the Japanese town of O. *See also* GIOTTO's O.

O'.   The *O'* common in Irish names such as O'Connor, O'Reilly, etc., derives from the Gaelic *ogha* or the Irish *oa*, both meaning "a descendant." Denis O'Connor strictly means "Denis, a descendant of Connor." According to a good story, in the past the O was taken away from the name of any family that didn't wholly support the Irish Republican cause, leaving us with Connors instead of O'Connors, etc. Much as it appeals to the storyteller in me, I can find no proof of the practice. In Gaelic, women prefix the family name with *Ni*, not O. Playwright Richard Brinsley Sheridan once remarked to his son Tom that their family was descended from the kings of Ireland and that their rightful name was O'Sheridan. His poet son replied to the brilliant but ever-impoverished playwright: "Yes, that is true, for we owe everybody."

oaf.   *Oaf* is a corruption of the Old Norse *alfr*, which became *aulf* and *ouph* in Old English and was recorded as *oaf* by 1625. An *alfr* was a child supposedly left by fairies in exchange for a child they had stolen, the changeling held to be an idiot, an abnormal child worse than the stolen one. *Oaf* softened in meaning over the years until it came to refer to a clumsy, foolish, or stupid person, most commonly used in the expression *a big oaf*.

oak.   Oaks, venerated by the Druids, were regarded as sacred to the god of thunder in ancient times because the trees were believed to be more likely to be struck by lightning than any other kind of tree. The origins of the oak's name are lost in history; the word was first recorded in the sixth century, but it is undoubtedly much older. One oak still standing in England is said to be 1,600 years old. In case you've ever wondered, a large oak has about 250,000 leaves, so if you have four on your property, you have a million leaves to admire and rake up every fall. "Charles's oak" is a historically famous old oak that grew near Boscobel House in England. When Charles II fled the Parliamentary army after the Battle of Worcester on September 3, 1651, he climbed down into the hollow tree and hid there with a colonel of the royal guard until it was safe to proceed; his supporters lowered food and drink to him. If the oak leafs out in spring before the ash tree, it will be a good, abundant year, according to the old proverb: "Oak before ash, in for a splash; Ash before oak, in for a soak." But if the ash leafs out before the oak, there will be flooding in the summer and a poor fall harvest. An oak winter is a cold spell in the spring that occurs after small leaves have appeared on the oak trees.

oarfish.   Often mistaken as a "sea monster," the very real oarfish (*Regaleus glesno*) is really a gentle creature that doesn't even bite, feeding instead by slurping up little animals with its small mouth. However, it isn't hard to understand how the oarfish might be taken for a sea serpent. The narrow fish—about as wide as a ribbon—is a silverfish color and has what appears to be a bright crimson mane (actually its dorsal fin), with trailing pectoral fins that give it its name. It grows up to 50 feet long. Weaving through the surface waters, it could easily be mistaken for a sea serpent from a distance. The oarfish, which doesn't ever use its oarlike pectoral fins, really spends more time trying to evade pursuers than chasing prey like any self-respecting sea serpent. To escape sharks and other true monsters, it lets predators bite off a section of its manelike tail or dorsal fin and escapes while its enemy is chewing on it. This may or may not be an intentional defense mechanism, but the shorter oarfish seems to function just as well as when it was a few feet longer. *See* LOCH.

obeah. An old term of African origin for a form of belief involving sorcery. According to *Harper's Magazine* (March, 1972) "Obeah is a kind of witchcraft, and is practiced by 'obeah men' by putting horsehair, fowl's feet, fish's bones, coneyskins, and other stuff into a pot, and burying the pot in the ground or near the house of the person against whom the necromancy is to be employed."

O-be-joyful. A humorous American historical term for hard liquor dating back to the 1860s.

Oberammergau Passion Play. *See* PASSION PLAY.

Oberon. *See* URANUS.

obese. *Obese* means very fat indeed, but the word comes from the Latin *obesus*, which is, ironically, the past participle of *obdere*, "to gnaw, to eat away, to thin." It is first recorded in the early 17th century.

Obies. Since 1955 the New York weekly *Village Voice* has presented Off-Broadway awards, popularly called Obies, honoring the best Off-Broadway productions. A different panel of judges each year is picked to select the best play, playwright, actor, director, composer, designer, etc. Other annual awards for outstanding Off-Broadway achievement include the Lucille Lortel awards. *See* TONY.

oblate spheroid. A scientific description of planet Earth, which isn't a perfect ball or sphere but is slightly flattened on the top and bottom.

obscene. According to one theory, *obscene* originally meant "off the stage" in ancient Greek drama, deriving from the Latin *ob*, "against," and *scaena*, "stage." What was kept off the stage in Greek drama was violence (always reported by messenger), not sex, of which there was plenty in comedies and satyr plays complete with actors fitted with huge artificial phalluses. Obscenity wasn't associated with sex until the word made its appearance in England toward the end of the 17th century. However, *obscene* is of obscure origin, and another theory, less likely, derives the word from the Latin *caenum*, "mud." Shakespeare was the first to use *obscene* in the sense of offensive to the senses, that is, disgusting, filthy, foul, etc., in *Richard II*: ". . . so heinous, black obscene a deed." The Bard probably based the word on the French *obscene*, meaning the same, which came from the Latin *obscenus*. Within five years or so, *obscene* was being used to mean "indecent and lewd" as well.

obsidian. Obsidian is a glasslike rock of volcanic origin formed by the rapid cooling of lava on the earth's surface. Usually it is a bright, glossy black, but some examples are gray, green, brown, or red, ranging from opaque to translucent. Usually sharp-edged, the rock was often used for arrowheads and other weapons by the ancients. Pliny the Elder tells us in his *Natural History* that obsidian was named for its discoverer Obsius, who first found it in Ethiopia. In early editions of his work Pliny's *obsianus*, for the mineral, was misprinted as *obsidianus*, this explaining the mysterious "d" in the word.

Occam's razor. Occam's razor, the philosophic principle of economy or parsimony, holds that universal essences should not be unnecessarily multiplied, which means simply that a scientific explanation should contain only those elements absolutely necessary. The axiom is named for William of Occam (ca. 1280–1349), an English philosopher and Franciscan who was a pupil of Duns Scotus and who dissected every question as with a razor. Occam became general of the Franciscan order and his philosophy helped pave the way for pragmatic Renaissance science. He and his followers held that the existence of God and immortality are not capable of philosophical proof and must be accepted on faith alone. His name comes from the town of Ockham in Surrey, where he was probably born. "The Invinceable Doctor," as he was called, so formidable was he in debate, he opposed Pope John XXII over a question of monastic poverty, which led to his imprisonment and excommunication.

occasional verse (prose). Verse written for a particular occasion is called "occasional verse," it is not verse written occasionally (once in a while). Such poems can be light or serious. Celebrated examples include Milton's *Lycidas* (1637); Tennyson's *Charge of the Light Brigade* (1854); Yeats's *Easter 1916*; and Auden's *September 1st 1939*. England's poet laureate is expected to write some occasional verse.

Occident. *See* GO WEST.

occupy.

> All you that in your beds do lie
> Turn to your wives and occupy,
> And when that you have done your best
> Turn arse to arse, and take your rest.

The old song, quoted in John S. Farmer's *Vocabula Amatoria* (1890), shows that *to occupy* was once a synonym for cohabitation. In fact, as Joseph Shipley points out in an article in *Maledicta* (to which I owe most of the information in this entry) the word *occupy* in all its senses became increasingly rare throughout the 17th and 18th centuries, when the verb took on this meaning. People ceased to use it, even Shakespeare commenting on this in *Henry IV, Part II:* "A Captaine? Gods light, those villains will rake the word as advises as the word occupy, which was an excellent good word before it was ill sorted." Luckily, *occupy* survived the puritanical onslaught. Other words haven't. The "cock," for example, is now almost always the "rooster," the "ass" is the "donkey," "haycocks" are "haystacks," "weathercocks" are "weather vanes," and "apricocks" are "apricots." Old Bronson Allcox even changed his name to Alcott, so that the author of *Little Women* isn't known as Louisa May Allcox.

ocean. *Ocean* came into English later than SEA, being first recorded in about 1290. The word ultimately comes from a Greek expression meaning "the great stream or river," which became the Latin *oceanus*. The Greeks personified this water encompassing the disk of the earth as Oceanus, "the god of the great primeval water." In early times, when only the eastern hemisphere was known, the ocean was "the Great Outer Sea of boundless extent everywhere surrounding the land, as opposed to inland sea."

oceanaut. *See* AQUANAUT.

October. *See* SEPTEMBER.

octopus. Octopuses "walk" on eight arms, not eight legs, so they should *not* really be named from the Greek *oktopous*, eight-footed. Apparently, the ancient Greeks reasoned that since the beast walked on the eight appendages, they should be called feet, not arms. In the Polynesian kingdom of Tonga, fishermen caught their octopus by using a lure fashioned into the shape of a rat. The Tongans believed that the rat was the octopus's worst enemy, their legend having it that an octopus once gave a drowning rat a ride to shore, whereupon the ungrateful rat alighted and called out: "O octopus, feel of your head; see what I have left there."

od; odic force. Though only an odd term today, od was once supposed to stream from female fingertips, "burning blue." It was a natural force said to pervade all nature, especially manifesting itself in persons of sensitive temperament, and the odic force was a basic force underlying many natural activities—including magnetism and chemical reactions. The word was an arbitrary coinage of German scientist Baron von Reichenbach, who proposed the odic theory in 1850.

oddwoman; oddsman. The Scottish oddwoman, common during the 16th century, was a female arbiter or umpire who helped settle disputes and was chosen by both parties to the conflict. Her male counterpart was called the oddsman. Both took their names from the term *odd man*, the third or fifth man on a committee of arbitrators, the one who in the event of a tie vote cast the deciding ballot.

ode on a Grecian urn.

> Thou still unravished bride of quietness,
> Thou foster-child of Silence and slow Time . . .

No one would argue that Keats's poem isn't among the most beautiful and best known of all time, but the vase that he wrote about might be called kitsch today. The story begins with the great English potter Josiah Wedgwood (1730–95), who achieved his fame despite the fact that a childhood illness had caused the amputation of his right leg, barring him from using the potter's wheel. Wedgwood, the grandfather of Charles Dickens, was already renowned as a potter when he began to make the ubiquitous blue and white vases that still bear his name. These he copied from the famous "Grecian" Portland vase that Sir William Hamilton, husband of Lord Nelson's great love, Emma, purchased when he served as ambassador to Naples, and sold to the Duchess of Portland, for whom it is named, before she donated it to the British Museum in 1784. The Portland vase, however, wasn't a Greek vase as everybody thought, but a Roman imitation from the time of Augustus. The vase that John Keats saw and that inspired him to write his poem was probably a Wedgwood copy of a Roman copy of a Greek vase—a doubly fake Grecian urn:

> Beauty is truth, truth beauty—that is all
> Ye know on earth and all ye need to know.

O'Donohue's white horses. Every seventh May Day, the Irish chieftain O'Donohue returns to the Lakes of Killarney riding his great white steed, gliding over the waters to sweet unearthly music, a host of fairies preceding him and strewing his path with spring flowers. Foaming waves on a windy day are thus known as *O'Donohue's white horses*. Legend has it that more than one beautiful young girl believed so strongly in O'Donohue that she threw herself into the water so that he would carry her off to be his bride.

odor of sanctity; odor of iniquity. In medieval times people believed that the bodies of saints or holy people gave off a sweet fragrance after death, an odor of sanctity; and that the bodies of evil people smelled to high heaven, an odor of iniquity. The followers of Emanuel Swedenborg, called the Swedenborgians, later attributed the delightful fragrance to the angels present at a saintly person's deathbed. At any rate, the odor of iniquity never took on a figurative meaning, but an odor of sanctity came to mean "a reputation for holiness."

odyssey. Any long, pioneering voyage or journey filled with adventures, usually to many places and peoples. It is so named after Homer's *Odyssey*, the epic poem that takes his Greek hero, Odysseus, on 10 years of wandering before he comes home to Ithaca. Odysseus's Latin name is Ulysses. Among his many adventures he fought bravely in the Trojan War and conceived the immortal scheme of the TROJAN HORSE. James Joyce said the theme of the *Odyssey* was "greater, more human than *Hamlet*, *Don Quixote*, *Dante*, [and] *Faust*" and based his great novel *Ulysses* upon it. *See* HOMERIC LAUGHTER.

oersted. The Danish physicist and chemist Hans Christian Oersted (1777–1851) founded the science of electro-magnetism when he discovered that direct electric current causes a magnetic needle to take a position at right angles to the wire carrying it. This basic fact of electromagnetic induction was the starting point for all future work in the field. Unlike many scientific discoveries, the Copenhagen professor's attracted immediate and widespread attention when he published a Latin monograph describing it in July 1820, about a year later. The scientist's name in Danish is actually Orsted, but has become anglicized to Oersted. The *oersted* honoring him is a unit of magnetic field intensity.

oesophagus. When Mark Twain wrote his satire on Sherlock Holmes's stories called "A Double-Barrelled Detective Story," he began the tale as follows:

> It was a crisp and spicy morning in early October. The lilacs and laburnums, lit with the glory-fires of autumn, hung burning and flashing in the upper air, a fairy bridge provided by kind Nature for the wingless wild things that have their homes in the tree-tops and would visit together; the larch and the pomegranate flung their purple and yellow flames in brilliant broad splashes along the slanting sweep of the woodland; the sensuous fragrance of innumerable deciduous flowers rose upon the swooning atmosphere; far in the empty sky a solitary oesophagus slept upon motionless wing; everywhere brooded stillness, serenity, and the peace of God.

The "solitary oesophagus" in the passage was solitary all right, for it never existed outside of Twain's teeming imagination. He had of course invented the bird—which know-it-alls were quick to describe to friends—and later remarked that few readers ever questioned him about it.

of. An auxiliary verb is a "helping verb" (*have, be, may, do, shall, can, must,* etc.) that is combined with other verbs. But the preposition *of* can be an auxiliary verb, too, at least in American vernacular. Some say the humorist Ring Lardner was the first to recognize this in his characters' conversational speech. One critic goes so far as to say that "until Lardner wrote *You Know Me, Al* (1916) no one ever considered *of* to be an auxiliary verb. *Who would of thought of it* but the man with the phonographic ear for American speech."

ofay. *See* PIG LATIN.

off base. Someone off base in today's slang is wrong or badly mistaken. The term refers to a runner in baseball taking a lead so far off the base that he is caught and tagged out. *See* OFF ONE'S BASE.

Official Monster Raving Loony Party. An Englishman named Screaming Lord Sutch (1941–99) founded this political party in the 1960s, and it has to have the most unusual name of any political party in history. Screaming Lord Sutch himself legally changed his name from David Sutch in the 1970s. He and his party never won an election, out of the record-holding 40 in which Sutch and his cohorts ran. Dressed in his trademark top hat and gold lamé jacket, Screaming Lord Sutch campaigned under the banner of "Vote For Insanity—You Know It Makes Sense," offering such proposals as cheap electricity powered by joggers put to work running on treadmills instead of in the street. He threatened to change his party's name to the Raving Sensible Party because by comparison with Margaret Thatcher's ministers, his followers weren't loony at all. *See* NORFORK HOWARD; ZIPPITY DO-DAH.

off one's base. To be off one's base is to be crazy, mentally unbalanced. Americans have been using this slang term since at least 1912. It has its origins in baseball, suggesting a base runner blithely hanging far off base without any thought of being picked off. *See* OFF BASE.

off the cuff. *See* ON THE CUFF.

off the wall. Many sports, including handball, squash, and racquetball, could be the source of this recent expression meaning "crazy, eccentric, highly unusual, outrageous"—as balls often bounce erratically off walls in all of these games. On the other hand, the term may be related to the earlier expression *bounce off the walls*, referring to the behavior of psychotic patients in mental hospitals.

of the same kidney. Of the same sort, or disposition. This expression was British slang in the early 18th century, its use deplored by Jonathan Swift along with words like banter and bamboozle. All have since become standard English. The expression has its origins in the ancient belief that the kidneys were "the seat of the affections" and thus largely determined one's personality or temperament.

o-grab-me acts. The Embargo Act of 1807, and acts of following years, restricted American ship departures to prevent hostilities on the seas. But since it hurt our British and French enemies less than American shipowners (the policy having the reverse effect than the one intend), shipowners began spelling *embargo* backward and called the acts the *o-grab-me acts.*

ogre. The Magyars were a fearsome Asian people who invaded Europe in about A.D. 900 and eventually settled in what is now Hungary. In fact, another name for them was Uigurs or Ugrians, which, with the addition over the years of an initial *H*, an *n*, and an *a* became *Hungarians*. But because these savage invaders were so feared, Uigur also became *ogre*, which is still the word for "a terrible man-eating monster" in many languages. At least so goes the apocryphal story most often told about *ogre*'s origin, which, unfortunately, is historically unfounded. *Ogre* was in fact coined by French author Charles Perrault in his *Contes* (1697) as the name for a race of hideous man-eating giants, Perrault possibly constructing the word from the name of *Orcus*, the god of Hades. *Ogre* has come to mean a man likened to such a monster in appearance or character.

Oh! Calcutta! Kenneth Tynan's erotic review *Oh! Calcutta!* (1969), famous for featuring nude actors and actresses at a time when this wasn't done, has nothing to do with Calcutta, India. The title is from the French "*Oh, quel cul t'as,*" which translates roughly as, "Oh, what an ass you have." Dada artist Marcel Du-champ once added a mustache and the legend LHOOQ to a copy he made of *The Mona Lisa*. Read aloud in French these letters sound like *Elle au cul*, or "she has a hot ass."

Oh, Diamond, Diamond . . . There is a legend that Sir Isaac Newton's little dog Diamond knocked over a candle on his master's desk and started a fire that destroyed records of many years of research and scientific experiments. On seeing the disaster, Newton is said to have exclaimed, "Oh, Diamond, Diamond, thou little knowest the damage thou hast done!" *See also* NEWTON'S APPLE.

Oh Henry! According to the official story about the name of this popular candy bar, the Oh Henry! was named after a fresh-mouthed boy who teased the girls on the production line at the candy factory where it was made. Reacting to his taunts or jokes, the girls would so often cry out "Oh, Henry!" that the manufacturer adopted the name. *See* BABY RUTH.

O. Henry ending. An immensely prolific author, O. Henry wrote tales characterized by ironic, surprise endings, "twists," "stingers," or "snappers" which while they aren't supposed to be fashionable anymore are still widely used by authors and known as O. Henry endings. O. Henry was the pen name of American writer William Sydney Porter. While working as a bank teller in Austin, Texas, Porter was indicted for the embezzlement (really mismanagement) of a small amount of money and fled the country to South America. On returning to his dying wife, he was imprisoned for three years and adopted the pseudonym O. Henry to conceal his real identity when he began writing and selling the stories that would make him famous. Released from prison he pursued his literary career in New York, where he published at least 15 books of short stories, including such perennial favorites as the "Gift of the Magi," before he died when only 48. O. Henry suffered from hypoglycemia, the opposite of diabetes, his classic summary of the condition being "I was born eight drinks below par." His famous last words, quoting a popular song, could have ended one of his stories: "Turn up the lights, I don't want to go home in the dark." *See* HYPOGLYCEMIA.

Ohio. In Iroquois *Oheo* means "beautiful water," referring to the Ohio River for which this state is named. The Buckeye State (so called for its buckeye or horse chestnut trees) was admitted to the Union in 1803 as our 17th state.

Ohm; Ohm's Law. Unlike his contemporary Oersted, German scientist Georg Simon Ohm (1787–1854) was so poorly treated by fellow scientists that he protested by resigning his post as professor of mathematics at the Jesuit's college in Cologne. In 1827 the physicist had published a pamphlet including what is now known as Ohm's Law. His study of electric currents eventually became the basic law of current electricity, but was coldly received at the time. Ohm may have thought of becoming a locksmith like several generations of his family before him, but despite his humiliations he hung in there. About 10 years later, the importance of his work began to be realized and in 1841 he was awarded the Copley medal of the British Royal Society. It is said that none of Ohm's work before or after his pamphlet is of the first order, this perhaps a reason for his initial rejection. He does appear to have been something of a scientific politician, having sent copies of his first book to all the monarchs of Germany in order to obtain his first teaching position. It was in 1893 that the International Electrical Congress adopted his name for the *ohm*, a unit of electrical resistance. *See also* MHO.

Oh Rinehart! It has been established that this historical expression honors James Brice Gordon Rinehart, Harvard class of 1900. In *Three Centuries of Harvard* (1936), historian Samuel Eliot Morison explained the cry: "*Oh Rinehart* began after a student of the name had been repeatedly shouted to by noisy friends. In the course of time it has become a sort of Harvard battle-cry, and the word is now used to describe any yard uproar, in which the calling of Mr. Rinehart's undying name is an inevitable feature."

oil of angels. A British expression that has some American currency, *the oil of angels* means money or gold, particularly money used as a bribe. The *angel* here refers to a 15th-century coin bearing the visage of Michael the Archangel. As Robert Greene wrote in 1592: "The palms of their hands so hot that they cannot be cooled unless they be rubbed with the oil of angels."

O.K. Many word authorities believe that *O.K.* comes from the nickname of Martin Van Buren (1782–1862), who rose from potboy in a tavern to president of the United States. A colorful character (as vice president he presided over the Senate with dueling pistols on his desk), Van Buren was elected president in 1836. He became an eponym, however, during the campaign of 1840, when he ran for reelection in a tight race against "Tippecanoe and Tyler, too," General William Henry Harrison, legendary hero who fought against the Indians at Tippecanoe, and Virginian John Tyler. The election of 1840 brought with it the first modern political campaign—mostly to President Van Buren's disadvantage. One popular advertising stunt was "to keep the ball rolling for Harrison"—10-foot "victory balls," made of tin and leather and imprinted with the candidate's name, were rolled from city to city for as far as 300 miles. Harrison's followers, trying to identify Van Buren with the aristocracy, christened the general the "log cabin and hard cider candidate," and tagged Van Buren "Little Van the Used Up Man," "King Martin the First," "The Enchanter," "The Red Fox," "The Kinderhook Fox," "Little Magician," and several other of the derogatory nicknames he had earned over the years. But "Old Kinderhook," a title bestowed upon the president from the name of his birthplace in Kinderhook, N.Y., sounded better to his supporters, better even than "the Sage, Magician, or Wizard of Kinderhook." In order to stem the tide, a group in New York formed the Democratic O.K. Club, taking their initials from "Old Kinderhook." These mystifying initials, appealing to man's love of being on the inside of events, became a sort of rallying cry for the Democrats. One contemporary newspaper account reported "how about 500 stout, strapping men" of the O.K. Club marched to break up a rival Whig meeting where "they passed the word O.K. . . . from mouth to mouth, a cheer was given, and they rushed into the hall like a torrent." The mysterious battle cry spread rapidly and soon acquired the meaning "all right, all correct," probably because "Old Kinderhook" or O.K. was all right, all correct to his supporters. But neither mystification, ruffians, nor new words did Van Buren any good, because voters remembered the panic of 1837, and Harrison defeated him in his bid for reelection. Not that victory was any blessing to Harrison; the old general contracted pneumonia on the day of his inauguration and died shortly thereafter. Scores of interesting theories had been offered on the origin of *O.K.* before Columbia Professor Allen Walker Read supposedly laid the ghost to rest with his *Saturday Review* article (July 19, 1941), tracing the word to the president who was O.K. Most etymologists accept Read's explanation but fail to mention an important qualification. Read established an earlier date than the campaign of 1840 for the first use of *O.K.* He showed that the expression was used in the Boston *Morning Post*, March 23, 1839, in the same sense—all correct—by editor Charles Gordon Greene but claims that the word got a second *independent* start in the 1840 campaign and really owes its popularity to Old Kinderhook's candidacy. No earlier reliable date than Read's for the use of *O.K.* has been found, and so the matter is apparently settled for all time—although other scholars have recently come up with entirely different explanations that etymologists are still debating. It will prove difficult, however, to take the credit for *O.K.* away from President Van Buren. The word honoring his name is undoubtedly the best known of American expressions. International in use and what H. L. Mencken calls "the most shining and successful Americanism ever invented," *O.K.* does service as almost any part of speech. Surprisingly, the effort to give it an antonym (*nokay*) has failed, but the expression *A-O.K.* has gained currency from space flights, and the older *oke-doke*, from an abbreviation of one of its forms, *okey*, is still heard in everyday speech. *O.K.* is used more often than *salud* in Spain, has displaced English *right-o*, and is spelled *o-ke* in the Djabo dialect of Liberia. The most universally used of all eponyms in any language since World War II, it is inscribed almost everywhere, from the town of Okay, Oklahoma, to the pieces of equipment marked with *O.K.*s that are possibly on the Moon. However, the useful little word may become even smaller and more useful. To this writer it sounds like *k* with more frequency every year, and perhaps someday that will be the spelling.

O.K. by me.   In use for at least half a century or so this expression is a Yiddish one given wider currency by the media. The *by me* in the phrase comes from the Yiddish *bei mir.*

Okies.   The migrant farm workers of the Great Depression called the Okies took their name from Oklahoma, where many of them originally lived before they left the Dust Bowl and began their journey west searching in vain for a golden land. They were of course immortalized in John Steinbeck's *The Grapes of Wrath.*

Oklahoma.   Oklahoma takes its name from a Choctaw word meaning "red people," for the Indians who lived in the region. The Sooner State (so called after those "sooners" who "jumped the gun sooner" and grabbed choice land there before they legally should have) was admitted to the Union in 1907 as our 46th state.

okra.   Okra was so valuable in ancient Angola that tribes made "sharp knife" raids into neighbors' fields to steal the vegetable, killing anyone who stood in their way. *Okra* derives ultimately from the Tshi *nkruman.* The Arabs held it to be a rare delicacy fit for weddings and other special occasions, naming it *uehka,* which means "a gift." Okra is sometimes called ladyfingers in England, this name being suggested by the shape of the pods.

old age is a shipwreck.   Overhead recently in a health club. If it isn't a proverbial saying, it should be, but I have no evidence of this. Walt Whitman's poem "The Dismantled Ship" tells of "An old, dismantled, gray and batter'd ship, disabled, done,/ After free voyages to all the seas of earth . . . /Lies rusting, mouldering." Writers have long used *shipwreck* figuratively. John Udall, for example, wrote in *A demonstration of the truth of that discipline which Christe hath prescribed* (1588): ". . . hee haue made shipwreck of a good conscience" (meaning he has suffered the loss of his good conscience).

old as Methuselah.   *As old as Methuselah,* "incredibly old," refers to the grandfather of Noah, who the Bible tells us lived to be 969 before he perished in the year of the Deluge. The patriarch is the oldest person mentioned in the Scriptures and is the son of Enoch, descended from Seth, son of Adam. This primeval ancestor of mankind is mentioned in Luke 3:37 as well as Genesis. To recap Methuselah's longevity: "Thus all the days of Methuselah were nine hundred and sixty-nine years; and he died" (Gen. 5:21–28).

old as the hills.   This old phrase for someone very old may have its origins in a similar biblical expression (Job 15:7): "Art thou the first man that was born?, or wast thou made before the hills?"

Old Blighty.   Old Blighty became popular as an endearing name for England during World War I, but it can be traced to Englishmen in India some years before this, *blighty* itself deriving from the Hindustani *bilati,* "a distant country."

Old Brains.   Only one person in American history has the honor of being called Old Brains and he probably didn't deserve it. Union General Henry Wager Halleck (1815–72) was a fortifications expert and able organizer, but the prestige he enjoyed for the victories of U.S. Grant and others under his command were unwarranted—he wasn't the "old brains" behind them, as many believed, contributing little to Union strategy.

old chestnut.   English playwright William Dimond's melodrama *The Broken Sword* (1816) is all but forgotten, along with its characters, plot, and dialogue, and the author himself isn't remembered in most guides to literature. Yet Dimond had found immortality of sorts in the expression *an old chestnut,* "a stale joke or story," which probably derives from an incident in his play. *The Broken Sword*'s principal character is crusty old Captain Xavier, who is forever spinning the same yarns about his highly unlikely experiences. He begins to tell the following one to Pablo, another comic character:

> *Captain Xavier:* I entered the woods of Golloway, when suddenly from the thick boughs of a cork tree—
> *Pablo:* A chestnut, Captain, a chestnut!
> *Captain Xavier:* Bah, I tell you it was a cork tree.
> *Pablo:* A chestnut; I guess I ought to know, for haven't I heard you tell this story twenty-seven times?

Fame didn't come immediately. The lines lay at rest in Dimond's play for almost 70 years before American actor William Warren, Jr. repeated them at a stage testimonial dinner in Boston, after hearing another speaker tell a stale joke. Other actors present adopted Warren's *chestnut,* elaborated on it, and it became the timeworn *old chestnut.*

old coot.   *See* COOT, TO.

old crate.   *See* CRATE.

Old Dominion State.   A nickname for Virginia and the oldest of state nicknames, dating back to 1778 when first recorded. Virginia has also been called the Cavalier State, the Mother of Presidents, and Mother of States.

Old English.   *See* ANGLO-SAXON.

older than baseball.   An American expression meaning very, very old, as indeed baseball is, especially if one traces it back to the British bat-and-ball game of rounders, which is ancient in origin. *Old* also figures in baseball's most famous song, "Take Me Out to the Ball Game": "For it's one, two, three strikes, you're out, at the old ball game."

old field pine.   Various pine trees, including the loblolly, sand and yellow pines, are called "old field pines" because they grow best on the exposed mineral soil of old farms. The term is an expression often heard in the South but has some currency in other regions as well.

old fogey.   Originally a Scottish term, dating back at least to the late 18th century, *old fogey* means an old person far behind the times. Its derivation is unclear, but the *fogey* here may come from an old use of the word *fog*, for "moss-grown."

old fuddy-duddy.   A stuffy, fussy, old-fashioned person, either old or young, who often fusses over minor details. The expression was first recorded in 1904 and was mainly confined to Maine and other parts of New England, but is now heard nationally. The term's origin is not certain, but some suggest that it derives from the English dialect word *fud* for buttocks, *old fuddy-duddy* (*duddy* added for rhyme) referring to someone who sits around on his duff doing very little, fussing with details, etc.

old geezer.   This expression is something of a redundancy, because *geezer* itself means an eccentric old man. *Geezer* is a British dialect word for a mummer or masquerader who wore a disguise and often acted eccentrically.

Old Glory.   The many paintings that show the Stars and Stripes flying at Valley Forge and in major battles of the Revolution are all in error, for no official stars-and-stripes flags were used by the Army until 1783. *Old Glory* was named by Captain William Driver of the brig *Charles Doggett* on August 10, 1831. Captain Driver had brought back the British mutineers of the H.M.S. *Bounty* from Tahiti to their home on Pitcairn Island, and some say that in recognition of this humane service a band of women presented him with a large American flag. Others claim that friends gave him the flag as a present. In any case, as he hoisted the flag to the masthead, he proclaimed, "I name thee Old Glory." His ship's flag became famous and by 1850 its name became common for the flag in general.

old goat.   The male goat has since before Shakespeare's time been noted for his lascivious nature and his name applied to men of a randy temperament. Recently, however, the comparison has mainly been used in the form of *old goat* for a lecher of advanced years.

old guard.   This term for the conservative wing of a political party, or anyone who opposes change, dates back to Napoleon's Imperial Guard, troops chosen in 1804 to be the élite of the French military. Devoted to Napoleon, they were treated better than the rest of the army and opposed any change in the status quo, the French calling them the *Vieille Garde*, or "old guard." In their bearskin hats and colorful uniforms they made the last charge at Waterloo.

old hat.   Today *old hat* means out of date or not new, and it has meant this for at least a century. But back as early as 1754 it was "used by the vulgar in no very honorable sense," as Fielding put it. It then meant, in Grose's punning definition from his 1785 *Classical Dictionary of the Vulgar Tongue:* "a woman's privities: because frequently felt."

Old Hickory; Old Mad Hickory.   *See* HERO OF NEW ORLEANS.

Old Ironsides.   Built six months after the *Constellation*, the *Constitution* is America's oldest warship still afloat and in commission. A national historic monument today, she is moored in Boston Harbor flying the flag of the commandant of the First Naval District. The high point of her illustrious career came on August 19, 1812, when she engaged and defeated the British frigate *Guerrière* off Nova Scotia. During the battle an American sailor, watching British shots fall into the sea, cried: "Huzza! Her sides are made of iron!" and *Old Ironsides* she has been since that day. In 1830 Oliver Wendell Holmes, hearing that she was to be sold by the Navy, wrote his famous poem "Old Ironsides" in protest and she was saved.

old lady in Dubuque.   Dubuque, Iowa, is named for its first settler, a French Canadian lead miner named Julien Dubuque. But what about that famous symbol of prudery, *the little old lady in Dubuque?* The phrase seems to have originated in this sense with Harold Ross, when he promised in a prospectus of the *New Yorker* that his magazine would *not* be edited for "the old lady in Dubuque." According to Brendan Gill, in his fascinating *Here at the New Yorker* (1975), Ross may have been inspired by "Boots" Mulgrew, a former Broadway musical comedy skit writer forced by drinking and financial problems to retreat from New York to his birthplace. Mulgrew soon after began contributing squibs to a widely read *Chicago Tribune* column called "A Line o' Type or Two." These pieces, describing "the provincial absurdities of Dubuque" were signed with the pseudonym "Old Lady in Dubuque" and Gill suggests that "Ross read them, admired them, and, whether consciously or not, got the old lady in Dubuque fixed in his mind as a natural antagonist."

Old Lady of Threadneedle Street.   The Bank of England, located on Threadneedle Street in London, is called *the Old Lady* because the institution has traditionally been fiscally conservative or overly cautious. The bank was first called *the Old Lady of Threadneedle Street* in the late 18th century. The street was originally known as "Three Needle Street," this name recorded in 1598.

Old Line State.   A nickname for Maryland recalling the Maryland Line of fine soldiers in the Continental Army. Maryland has also been called the Terrapin State, the Monumental State (Baltimore, Maryland, is the Monumental City), and the Oyster State.

Old Man of the Mountain.   A natural formation on a mountainside in New Hampshire's White Mountains that resembled the face of an old man and was a popular tourist attraction until its destruction by natural causes in 2003. The old man of the mountain is also a name for the founder of the Assassins cult, Hassan ben Sabah, an 11th-century terrorist who operated in the mountains of northern Persia.

Old Man of the Sea.   In the *Arabian Nights* tale of Sinbad the Sailor, an old man clung to Sinbad's shoulders for many days and nights until Sinbad got him drunk and threw him off. The old man stands for any tenacious person.

Old Muddy.   A nickname used for both the Missouri and the Mississippi rivers since the mid 19th century.

Old Ned.   The Americanism to *raise Old Ned* means "to raise hell or start a row," *Old Ned* being recorded as a name for the devil, along with *Old Splitfoot* and *Old Scratch* as early as 1859. *See* OLD NICK; OLD SCRATCH.

Old Nick; Old Harry; Old Gentleman; Old Serpent.   *See* SCRATCH.

Old Philadelphia Lady.   One of the most famous letters to an editor in newspaper history is one an anonymous "Old Philadelphia Lady" sent James Gordon Bennett, the publisher and editor of the *New York Herald:* "I am anxious to find out the way to figure the temperature from centigrade to Fahrenheit and vice versa. In other words, I want to know, whenever I see the temperature designated on the centigrade thermometer, how to find out what it would be on Fahrenheit's thermometer—Old Philadelphia Lady, Paris, December 24, 1899." The letter became famous after it was unintentionally reprinted the next day, a mishap that made the famously eccentric Bennett so mad that he published it every day until he died in 1918. Readers cancelled their subscriptions, even threatened to kill the old woman, but Bennett nevertheless ran her letter for the next 18 years and five months, for a total of 6,718 continuous days in all. *See* F; CELSIUS SCALE.

Old Probabilities.   Americans have been having fun with the weatherman for several centuries now. Knowing that weather forecasters always hedge their bets with a "probability" ("There is a probability of rain tomorrow"), they dubbed such prognosticators Old Probabilities in the late 19th century. The term is first recorded in 1873 for the superintendent of the weather bureau in Washington, D.C. *Old Probs* was the nickname of Cleveland Abbe (b. 1838), the first American to make daily weather predictions. Today, weather forecasters are even vaguer, generally saying "there is a possibility."

Old Rowley.   Originally *Old Rowley* was the name of a famous stallion in the British royal stables, a prodigious stud that sired many offspring. The name became even better known as the sobriquet of his master, Charles II (1630–85), the pleasure-loving English king who sired many illegitimate children. *See* CHARLEY.

old saw.   A hackneyed saying, one that may or may not be true but is often refuted. *Saw* here has no relation to the saw used for cutting trees or lumber. It is an English word deriving from the Old English *sagu*, which derives from the Icelandic word that gave us *saga* for a story or narrative.

Old Scratch.   This is a synonym for the devil and has been traced back to early-18th-century England, possibly deriving from the Old Norse *skratte* meaning a monster or devil. In the U.S. *Old Scratch* has been used mainly in New England and is the devil's name for himself in the region's best-known short story, Stephen Vincent Benét's "The Devil and Daniel Webster" (1937), which is the basis for both a movie and a 1939 one-act folk opera of the same name by Benét and American composer Douglas Moore.

Oldsmobile.   One of America's best-known cars will soon be taken out of production by General Motors. The Oldsmobile, famed in song and fable, was named after its designer, Ransom Eli Olds, who headed the Reo Motor Car (*Reo* after his initials), which introduced the Oldsmobile in 1901. After over 100 years all that will be left of the Olds will be memories and popular song lyrics: "Won't you come with me, Lucille / In my merry Oldsmobile . . ."

Old Splitfoot.   *See* OLD NED.

old stamping grounds.   An interesting theory connects this Americanism, used before the Revolution, with the mating behavior of male prairie chickens, who congregated in spring on hills and performed elaborate courtship dances, stamping the hills bare. Another guess is that the stamping of stallions while they covered mares suggested the phrase. All that's known is that *stamping grounds* were first referred to as places where horses or other animals customarily gathered. It wasn't too long (1836) before the term became a place where people customarily gathered. The British definition of *stamping ground* as "a place for amorous dalliance," like a lover's lane, gives some support to the prairie chicken or stallion theories. The expression is generally used by or about males.

old tar.   *See* JACK TAR.

oligopsony; duopsony; monopsony; monopoly.   The 10-dollar word *oligopsony* has no 10-cent synonym, as so many high-toned words do. It means a market condition where there are so few buyers and the actions of just one of them could drastically affect the market. Deriving from the Greek *oligos*, few, and *opsōnēs*, buyer, it is not to be confused with *duopsony*, a market condition that exists where there are two buyers only, or *monopsony*, a market condition where there is only one buyer (*monopoly* can also be used to express this last condition).

olios.   *See* VAUDEVILLE.

olive.   *Wine within, oil without*, was the Roman formula for a happy life, and the oil with which they anointed their bodies was, of course, olive oil. Olives themselves were believed to stimulate drinking by the Romans, whose word *oliva* for the fruit became our *olive*. So interwoven is the olive with history—Noah's biblical olive branch the symbol of peace; some of the ancient olive trees in the Garden of Gethsemane possibly growing there since the time of Christ's betrayal; Athens named for the goddess Athena after she gave the olive to man—that books have been written about the fruit. The olive tree, which has been known to live well over 1,000 years, was simply a staple of life, yielding both food and light (from lamp oil) and grown also for its symbolism of joy, happiness, and peace. Green olives are those picked early; the black ones are picked ripe. Both are very bitter indeed before they are soaked in a lye and salt solution and readied for market.

oliver; Oliver's skull.   Oliver Cromwell's name "fairly stank" to the Royalists, which is why they dubbed their chamber pots *Oliver's skulls*. The term was popular slang in England from 1690 to 1820 and puts Cromwell in the select company of the relatively small handful of people who have been discommoded by commodes. On the other hand, Cromwell's supporters so admired the way he hammered at the Royalists that the *oliver*, a small smith's hammer, was probably named after him. Whether the British underworld term *oliver*, for "the full moon," is a compliment or an insult is uncertain, but it definitely arises from the fact that Oliver Cromwell led the Roundheads. *See* CRAP; FURPHY; SACHEVERELL; TWISS; VESPASIENNE.

olla. A large earthenware crock used for water storage that made its way from Mexico to Texas and California, where it was used for centuries in the same way. The Spanish word comes from Latin *aula*, a pot or jar.

olla podrida; potpourri. *Olla podrida* is Spanish for "a putrid or rotten pot" but it refers to a stew made of many kinds of meat, fowl, vegetables, and spices boiled in a large pot. Like the French *pot-au-feu*, it is made of many scraps, the "rotten" in the term referring not to its smell or taste, which is delicious, but to the way everything is cooked "leisurely, til it be rotten (as we say) and ready to fall in pieces." Since the 16th century *olla podrida* and *olio*, another word for the stew, have also meant an incongruous mixture, a hodgepodge, a farrago. *Olla podrida* isn't always used disparagingly when applied to miscellaneous collections of any kind, such as literary pieces, drawings, and musical medley. Often it just means a medley or *potpourri*, which, in fact, is the French translation of *olla podrida*. Some samples of the expression's use: "His work is an *olla podrida* of error, confusion's masterpiece"; "This *olla podrida* of a brain of mine." The nonce word *ollapodridical* means heterogeneous.

olly, olly oxen free. If you've ever wondered about the origins of this chant—used to call in all players at the end of a game of hide-and-seek—be advised that the experts only have a partial answer to your lifelong puzzlement. Word sleuths are fairly certain that the *oxen* (or *octen*) in the call is simply a childish corruption of "all in." The rest remains a mystery.

omelets can't be made without breaking eggs. *See* YOU CAN'T MAKE AN OMELET WITHOUT BREAKING EGGS.

omerta. There may be nothing to *omerta*, the law of silence said to be sworn by members of the Mafia for over a thousand years in Sicily. According to Mario Puzo in *The Godfather* (1969): ". . . the Mafia cemented its power by originating the law of silence, the *omerta*. In the countryside of Sicily a stranger asking directions to the nearest town will not even receive the courtesy of an answer." In *The Last Don* (1996) Puzo adds: "As a philosophy *omerta* was quite simple. It was a mortal sin to talk to the police about anything that would harm the Mafia. If a rival Mafia clan murdered your father before your eyes, you were forbidden to inform the police . . . The authorities were the Great Satan a true Sicilian could never turn to." Richard Condon casts more light on the practice today in *Prizzi's Money* (1994): "It had almost appeared as though he had been about to violate *omerta*, the sacred oath of manhood of the Mafia with which, among other things, he had pledged in blood that he would never violate a woman of the family of a mafiosa. Everyone in the room knew that *omerta* was only a myth, something observed by the people who wrote newspaper stories and movies. But he was expected . . . to pay solemn lip-service to it."

onanism. "Then Judah said to Onan, 'Go in to your brother's wife, and perform the duty of a brother-in-law to her, and raise up offspring for your brother.' But Onan knew that the offspring would not be his; so when he went in to his brother's wife he spilled the semen on the ground, lest he should give off-spring to his brother. And what he did was displeasing in the sight of the Lord, and he slew him also." This passage from the Revised Standard Version of the Bible (Gen. 38:8–11) shows what scholars have long told us, that Onan was not a habitual masturbator as the word *onanism* suggests. It is not even clear from the biblical passage whether Onan's one such mentioned act was masturbation or coitus interruptus, and many biblical scholars tell us that his real sin was not *onanism* but his refusal to take the childless Tamar to bed, get her with child, and rear their offspring as the son of his dead brother in accordance with the law of the levirate marriage.

on a shoestring. *See* SHOESTRING.

once in a blue moon. Seldom, rarely, as in "We go to the movies once in a blue moon." The moon does rarely appear blue due to the actions of dust particles in the upper atmosphere. It is also said that the moon turned bluish for a time in 1883 when colored by volcanic ash from the eruption of Krakatoa in Java. Another meaning of *blue moon* is "The second full moon in the same calendar month," which comes to about one blue moon every three years.

on cloud nine. One explanation for this expression, which only dates back to about 1950, is that meteorologists classify clouds by number, number nine being the highest clouds (the cumulonimbus). Thus if one is on cloud nine, he or she is feeling very high, very good.

on deck; in the hole. A baseball player batting next in an inning is said to be *on deck*, this obviously an old nautical term put to use on land. So is *in the hole* for the man scheduled to bat third, this a corruption of *in the hold*—the reasoning being that the third batter is *in the hold*, or *hole*, since the second is *on deck*. No one knows just how these nautical words were transferred to baseball early in this century.

one degree under. *One degree under* is a relatively recent expression, dating back 50 years or so, which means "feeling a bit poorly, slightly unwell." The phrase may be modeled on UNDER THE WEATHER, but the reference is to body temperature, not the thermometer. Someone one degree under the normal body temperature would indeed be "feeling a bit poorly."

one fishball. The popular song "One Meatball," with its well-known line "You get no bread with one meatball," was adapted from a New England song called "The Lay of One Fishball," apparently written by Harvard professor George Martin Lane in 1857 or thereabouts. Lane's line was: "We don't give bread with one fishball!"

one foot in Charon's ferryboat. The ancient Greeks used this term long before *one foot in the grave* was current, Charon's ferryboat being the legendary ferryboat that transported the dead across the river Styx to the Elysian Fields. In fact, it has been suggested that the Roman emperor Julian knew the Greek phrase and used it as the basis for his coinage of *one foot in the grave* when in his old age he exclaimed "I will learn this subject even if I have one foot in the grave!" The austere Julian the Apostate (A.D. 351–363) may or may not be the speaker, but one hopes so for the story's sake. Another story has it that this pagan Roman emperor, who had renounced Christianity, uttered as his last words, *"Vicisti Galilaee"* ("You have won, Jesus").

See ONE FOOT IN THE GRAVE; ONE FOOT ON A BANANA PEEL AND THE OTHER IN THE GRAVE.

one foot in the grave.   Used by Richard Burton, Swift, and other great writers, this phrase meaning "to be close to death" dates back to at least the early 17th century. The brilliant British wit Samuel Foote has the following epitaph on his grave in Westminster Abbey:

> Here lies one Foote, whose death may thousands save,
> For death has now one foot within the grave.

Foote, called "The English Aristophanes," invented the term *grand panjandrum. See also* NO SOAP.

one foot on a banana peel and the other in the grave. Very old or very ill, on the brink of death, slipping away fast; or not in good health recently, though far from dying. The words are a 20th-century humorous extension of ONE FOOT IN THE GRAVE. *See* ONE FOOT IN CHARON'S FERRYBOAT.

one for Ripley.   Cartoonist Robert Leroy Ripley traveled widely from his California home to gather bits of odd information for his "Believe It or Not" newspaper series, books, and radio program, though much of the material he used was library researched. His name became as well known as "Believe It or Not" itself, the phrase *one for Ripley* used to describe any strange, almost unbelievable happening. Though he died in 1949, aged 56, Ripley's series still runs in newspapers throughout the world today, along with a host of imitators. There was a Ripley "Odditorium" at the Chicago World's Fair of 1933–34 and today seven "Believe It or Not" wax museums are doing a thriving business in the United States and England.

one good turn (deed) deserves another.   Petronius Arbiter (d. ca. A.D. 66) coined or first recorded this expression in his *Satyricon*, along with such others as *beware the dog, not worth his salt,* and *my heart was in my mouth.* In direct opposition to the first saying is the cynical expression *no good deed goes unpunished,* which sounds modern, probably of recent vintage.

one-handed shot.   Today one-handed shots are the rule in basketball, but in the 1930s controversy raged between those who favored the old-fashioned two-handed stationary "set shot" and the one-hander introduced by San Francisco's Galileo High School star Angelo Enrico "Hank" Luisetti (1916–2002) in the early years of the decade. The debate was especially lively between fathers whose coaches had taught them to use the set shot and sons who had picked up the Hank Luisetti one-hander on garage and schoolyard courts. As for Luisetti, who went on to star for Stanford University, he said of his history-making shot: "Shooting two-handed, I just couldn't reach the basket. I was lucky with my coaches in high school and college, I guess, because I made the baskets, they left me alone. . . ." The man who changed basketball forever was elected to the Basketball Hall of Fame in 1959.

one-horse outfit.   At first a *one-horse outfit* was a small ranch, but today the words are applied to any small business. The term dates back to the late 19th century.

one hundred percent American.   *See* ANANIAS.

one-man tango.   Someone supremely self-confident, who looks like he could dance the grand tango all alone. In his autobiography *One Man Tango* (1955), actor Anthony Quinn claims Orson Welles gave him this nickname. Whether Welles invented the words or not isn't established, but the expression does deserve to be recorded.

one meatball.   *See* ONE FISHBALL.

One never knows, do one?   A saying associated with legendary black musician and composer "Fats" (Thomas Wright) Waller (1904–43), who wrote "Ain't Misbehavin' " and "Honeysuckle Rose," among many songs. The phrase means that a person can never predict what will happen; the unlikely or unexpected often comes true.

one over the eight.   Heard more in England than in the U.S., this expression means to be drunk. It derives from the old superstition that one always becomes drunk after the eighth drink and not before!

One people, one country, one leader!   How many remember that this was the slogan and rallying cry of the Nazis (German National Socialists) under Hitler? *Ein Volk, ein Reich, ein Führer!* were the German words that led to so many horrors.

One perry and one porter were too much for John Bull to swallow!   A popular American slogan after the War of 1812, this punning expression refers to American naval hero Oliver Perry, whose last name means a hard cider made of pears, and David Porter, whose last name means a strong, dark beer. John Bull, of course, is the national nickname for England.

one picture is worth a thousand words.   The Chinese proverb that inspired this cliché goes to greater extremes: "One picture is worth more than 10,000 words." Pictures certainly aren't always, or mostly, 10,000 or a thousand times more versatile than words. "If you're not convinced," author William Childress wrote, "fall in a lake and start gulping water—and then, instead of screaming the word HELP, hold up a picture of yourself drowning. If someone pulls you out, I lose my argument."

one's name is mud.   *See* HIS NAME IS MUD.

one's own man.   Today this expression (*he's his own man; I'm my own man,* etc.) generally means to be one's own master, beholden to no one, but in the past it also meant to be fully in control of all one's faculties and powers. The expression dates back to the early 16th century.

[That's] one small step for a man, one giant leap for mankind.   These were the words of American astronaut Neil Armstrong when he became the first man to step on the moon on July 20, 1969. Unfortunately, in Armstrong's transmission of the words, the indefinite article *a* was inaudible and thus the words are often given incorrectly today as *That's one small step for man, one giant leap for mankind,* which makes little sense.

one swallow does not a summer make.   The proverb was first recorded in English as *It is not one swallow that bryngeth in* *somer. It is not one good qualitie that maketh a man good* (1539). However, Aristotle recorded the Greek proverb *One swallow does not make a spring* long before this. The migratory swallow is still regarded as a harbinger of summer. The nests of some species, formed from the spawn of fish and seaweed bound together by the bird's solidified saliva, are used for *bird's nest soup*, among the most recherché of exotic gourmet foods. They are the subject of many legends—*e.g.*, that they mate while in flight and that they bring good luck to any house they build a nest upon. Scandinavian tradition says that swallows hovered over the cross of Christ crying *Svala! svala!* ("Console! console!"), hence their name *svalow*, "the bird of consolation." *One swallow does not a summer make* means that all of one's troubles aren't over just because one difficulty is surmounted.

one to show, one to blow. Handkerchiefs became uniform in length after Marie Antoinette issued a royal decree declaring that they should be. They then became quite fashionable and men began to wear one in the breast pocket for show, while carrying another in the rear pocket to blow their noses with. This led to the now rare expression *one to show, one to blow*, implying that "all isn't what it seems, someone has something hidden in reserve."

one touch of nature . . . The complete phrase is *one touch of nature makes the whole world kin* and it has come to mean that any appeal to the basic emotions of people will reveal, by their sympathetic response, the common humanity, the basic kinship of all people. Shakespeare, however, meant something quite different when he invented the line for the cynical Ulysses in *Troilus and Cressida*. There are no eternal verities of the heart, Ulysses says to Achilles; the one natural trait we all share is our preference for what's *au courant*, or "in," latest, no matter how superficial it may be:

> One touch of nature makes the whole world kin,
> That all with one consent praise new-born gauds
> [gaudy novelties]
> Then marvel not, thou great and complete man,
> That all the Greeks begin to worship Ajax;
> Since things in motion sooner catch the eye
> Than what not stirs . . .

In a world where there is perpetual chasing of things in motion, Shakespeare's meaning is far from obsolete.

onion. *Onion* comes from the Latin word *unio*, "oneness" or "union," in reference to the many united layers in an onion; the Romans used the same word for the multilayered pearl; thus our pearl onion would have been a Roman *unio unio*. Onions were fed to the Egyptian laborers who built the great Cheops pyramid, dispensed by Alexander the Great to his troops to promote valor, and praised by General Grant, who once wired the War Department that he would not move his army farther without onions. The onion is believed by some to be an aphrodisiac as well as strength-giving, though as Shakespeare wrote, "Eat no onions or garlic, for we are to utter sweet breath."

the only good Indian is a dead Indian. General Phil Sheridan is credited by *Bartlett's Familiar Quotations* with this prejudicial remark so often quoted in old western movies. But Sheridan said, "The only good Indians I ever saw were dead," which is a condensation of the words of the originator of the slander, Montana congressman James Cavanaugh, who earlier said: "I have never in my life seen a good Indian . . . except when I have seen a dead Indian." Which kind of ruins the old story about Sheridan making the remark at Fort Cobb, Indian Territory, in 1869 after the Comanche chief Toch-a-way ("Turtle Dove") was presented to him. Chief Toch-a-way reportedly said: "Me Toch-a-way, me good Indian." Sheridan reportedly replied: "The only good Indians I ever saw were dead."

onomatopoeia. The Greek for "making of words" is the ancestor of *onomatopoeia*, which is the term for forming a word by imitating the sound associated with the object designated. Examples of such words are bang, buzz, cackle, clatter, crackle, cuckoo, hiss, murmur, pop, sizzle, tingle, twitter, whiz, whoosh, and zoom.

on one's high horse. *See* HIGH HORSE.

on one's uppers. *On one's uppers* refers to being impoverished, destitute, as in "He was on his uppers before he got that job." The Americanism is first recorded in 1891 and refers to someone walking in shoes with holes in the soles, *uppers* referring to bare feet above the shoe soles.

on the ball. Depending on how it is used, the expression has two different origins. *To be on the ball*, "to be alert, knowledgeable, on top of things," probably refers to close and clever following of the ball by players in British soccer or American basketball. The phrase may have arisen independently in each sport, or it may have originated in the 1940s with the "bop and cool" jazz musicians and fans as the *American Dictionary of Slang* suggests. There is no hard evidence for any theory, but the sports analogy seems more logical. *To have something on the ball*, "to be talented or effective in some way," is surely of American origin, a baseball term referring to the various "stuff"—curves, spin, etc.—a good pitcher can put on the ball to frustrate a batter. *See* KEEP YOUR EYE ON THE BALL.

on the beam. At first glance *to be right on the beam*, "to be on the right course, accurate, functioning well," might be mistaken for an old expression connected with carpentry. The familiar phrase, however, is modern and has nothing to do with beams of wood. It probably originated in the RAF around 1938 and refers to the directional radio beams that guided planes to airfields. When a pilot is on course, the beam's signal is loudest; when he strays off course, the signal-from the beacons along the route grows weaker.

on the boards; to walk the boards. In the theatrical profession, *boards* are the stage of a theater. "The Booths were on the boards for three generations." *To walk the boards* means to be an actor.

on the carpet. When carpets first were used as floor coverings they were walked on only by the master or mistress of the house, and servants usually stood on them only when they were called before the gentry to be reprimanded for some misdeed. From this practice, dating to the early 1800s, came the meaning of *on the carpet.*

on the cuff. *On the cuff* apparently arose at the turn of the century. Since bartenders commonly wore starched white cuffs at the time, the theory that our term for "on credit" derives from bartenders jotting down the debts of patrons on their cuffs during the rush of business is an appealing one. *On the arm* probably derives from *on the cuff,* while *off the cuff,* unrehearsed or extemporaneous, may come from impromptu notes early Hollywood directors jotted down on their cuffs while shooting a difficult scene in a movie. These ideas, not in the script, were conveyed to the actors when the scene was reshot.

on the fritz. No one seems to have discovered where the *fritz* comes from in *on the fritz,* which means out of working order, in disrepair, worthless, or ruined. Since *on the fritz* isn't recorded before the 1920s, it may have something to do with the derogatory term "Fritz," for a German soldier in World War I. Fritz is the nickname for the common German name Friederich, and was popularized in the nickname of Frederick the Great of Prussia—Old Fritz—long before World War I. Someone out of working order or ruined, could have been compared to the defeated Germans. Another wild guess is that *fritz* is a corruption of "frittered," in its old sense of broken or torn into pieces—as in "the sail frittered in a thousand pieces." Maybe the phrase even refers to little Fritz of the early comic strip "The Katzenjammer Kids," who along with his twin brother Hans put a lot of things on the fritz.

on the hind tit (teat). The words describe someone who isn't getting as much as all the others, as in "I'm always on the hind teat when it comes to getting overtime." The analogy is to a last pig feeding on a sow, though there is no proof that a mother pig's last teat offers less milk than any other.

on the hip. To have someone under one's control. Traced back to the 1500s by the *OED,* this expression derives from an even older wrestling term. Shakespeare used it in several plays, including *The Merchant of Venice* (1596), and Eugene O'Neill used it in *The Iceman Cometh* (1940): "That bastard, Hickey, has got Harry on the hip."

on the house. This phrase originated in English public houses, "tippling houses" as they were called in Elizabethan times. It used to be common for tavern keepers to dispense a free drink with every three or so bought, one that was on the house. Bartenders still give drinks on the house, where the law doesn't prohibit this practice, but normally after a lot more than three are paid for. The expression is now common for anything given away free.

on the level. The phrases *upon* or *on the level* and *by* or *on the square* probably originated with the Freemasons in the 14th century. Freemasons, before they accepted honorary members several centuries later, were exclusively a class of skilled workers in stone who traveled from place to place wherever buildings were being erected. From their use of the square, which drew a straight line and made you go straight, and their use of the level, which made sure a surface was true or even, came these expressions meaning honestly, truthfully, and on the up-and-up.

on the make. In mid-19th-century America, *on the make* meant only to be out for money, to be ruthlessly ambitious. During the Great Depression, interests shifted outwardly from money to sex, there being more of the latter around then than the former, and the expression acquired its second meaning of to be "out for love." The words probably are the source of to *make it with* someone, "succeed in having sexual intercourse"; *make time,* "have relations," *make out* and *make-out artist.* The earlier meaning remains primarily in *to make it,* "to succeed in any endeavor, to rise to the top."

on the nail. *See* PAY ON THE NAIL.

on the nose. To *win by a nose* is an old horse racing expression, but *on the nose,* "exactly on time, perfectly correct, right on the button," originated in the early days of radio. Directors in their soundproof control rooms signaled their assistants on stage that the various segments of a program were running exactly on time by touching their forefingers alongside their noses. If portions of the program were running behind schedule, the director would relay other signs, and whole pages of a script might have to be cut out. The signal to cut something entirely, for example, was to saw violently at the throat with one hand. When everything was really copacetic, the director held up his thumb and forefinger pressed tightly together.

on the pad. Since the late 19th century this Americanism has referred to policemen who accept bribes, the *pad* meaning the account book in which the bagman recorded the bribes paid and the officers sharing in the split.

on the pig's back. *On the pig's back* is a mainly Irish expression meaning "to live a prosperous life," the same as TO LIVE HIGH ON THE HOG.

on the qui vive. French sentries once shouted *"Qui vive?"* literally "who lives?" as a challenge to discover to which party the person challenged belonged—appropriate answers being [*vive*] "*le roi* [king]," "*la France,*" etc. Thus to be on the *qui vive* is to be watchful (like a sentry), to be on the alert for something. The expression is first recorded in English by Jonathan Swift in 1726.

on the rocks. The allusion here is to a ship grounded off a rocky coast, battered by waves and ready to sink, and the expression arose among seamen, as would be expected. The figurative use of rocks for a symbol of destruction or ruin dates back to at least the early 16th century, but it wasn't until 300 years later (1889) that the phrase *on the rocks* appeared or is first recorded. When we use the expression today we always refer to ruin or impending disaster. Someone *on the rocks* can be stone broke, or bereft of sanity. A marriage *on the rocks* is wrecked and about to be sunk unless it is saved at the last minute. *On the rocks* is also a drinking term, meaning a drink served with ice in the glass, the expression dating back to the 1920s.

on the ropes. The allusion here is to a weary, exhausted boxer who is pinned against the ropes in a prizefight and just a punch or two away from being knocked out. The expression dates back long before Muhammad Ali's "rope-a-doping," in which he used the ropes to his advantage, and figuratively means to be on the edge of ruin. It is first recorded in 1924 but may be much older, for boxing rings have officially been enclosed by ropes since about 1840.

on the same sheet of music with. In agreement with. U.S. Secretary of Defense Donald Rumsfeld recently used and defined the expression: "I know that the interim [Afghanistan] government is right on the same sheet of music with us. They want the Taliban caught. They agree with us. They want the Al Qaeda the dickens out of their country."

on the shady side of 40. As the sun sets, shadows lengthen. Thus the allusion in this 19th-century expression is to late life, when one has become part of the shadows.

on the side of the angels. The phrase has long been used for someone who takes a spiritual view of things, or for someone who is on "our" side. Benjamin Disraeli coined it in 1864, before he became Britain's prime minister, in a speech he made at the Oxford Diocesan Conference opposing the Darwinian theory of organic evolution proposed in *On The Origin of Species.* "The question is this," he asserted. "Is man an ape or an angel? I, my lord, am on the side of the angels." Two years later Disraeli gave us another famous quotation. "Ignorance," he told the House of Commons, "never settles a question."

on the spot. *See* PUT ON THE SPOT.

on the spree. *See* SPENDING SPREE.

on the square. *See* ON THE LEVEL.

on the town. "On the Town" has been the title of several society columns over the years, the expression meaning "in the swing of fashionable life, pleasure." Steele first recorded the phrase, in *The Spectator* in 1712.

on the wagon. The original version of this expression, *on the water wagon* or *water cart*, which isn't heard anymore, best explains the phrase. During the late 19th century, water carts drawn by horses wet down dusty roads in the summer. At the height of the Prohibition crusade in the 1890s men who vowed to stop drinking would say that they were thirsty indeed but would rather climb aboard the water cart to get a drink than break their pledges. From this sentiment came the expression *I'm on the water cart*, I'm trying to stop drinking, which is first recorded in, of all places, Alice Caldwell Rice's *Mrs. Wiggs of the Cabbage Patch* (1901), where the consumptive Mr. Dick says it to old Mrs. Wiggs. The more alliterative *wagon* soon replaced *cart* in the expression and it was eventually shortened to *on the wagon. Fall off the (water) wagon* made its entry into the language almost immediately after its abstinent sister.

on the wrong side of the door when brains were handed out. A brainless, stupid, or very dull person. Coined toward the beginning of the 19th century, the British phrase was originally *on the wrong side of the hedge.*

on tick. *Tick* here is just an abbreviation of *ticket.* First recorded as early as 1648, *on tick* originally meant a written I.O.U. or "ticket," then came to mean "on credit."

on velvet. In the game of faro, money won from the house was called *velvet* and any player who won a lot of money was said to be *on velvet.* From these early-19th-century beginnings *on velvet* passed into general use as a synonym for "an unusual, unexpected profit or gain."

on your own hook. In the 19th century, fishermen on boats fishing the Grand Banks were paid according to what they caught individually on their own hooks and lines. To this practice we owe the expression *to be on your own hook*, "to be on your own."

oo. Sometimes called Bishop's oo (*Moho bishopi*), this most unusually named bird is a member of the honey eater family, birds that can eat nectar and flowers as a part of their diet. The *Bishop* of the bird's name honors no churchman, but American Charles Reed Bishop (1822–1915), who married a Hawaiian princess and became powerful in the islands' business and political affairs. *Oo* is simply the Hawaiian word for unknown, perhaps because so little was known about the bird before it was named.

oof. A slang term that can mean money, or, in boxing circles, strength or power. Said to be an abbreviation of Yiddish *offtish*, which in turn comes from Yiddish *off tishe*, "on the table."

oomph. Movie actress Ann Sheridan (1915–67) was dubbed the "Oomph Girl" for publicity purposes in 1939, making this word for sex appeal familiar to millions of Americans. But *oomph* goes back at least 40 years, first recorded by poet Paul Laurence Dunbar in *Gideon* (1900). The word is an echoic coinage that, according to Dr. Robert Chapman, suggests "the gasp of someone hit hard by . . . a transport of desire."

op-ed page. *Op-ed page* means "opposite the editorial page." The term was coined by Herbert Bayard Swope, editor of *The New York World* in the 1920s, to describe the page in a newspaper opposite the editorial page, where columnists and other contributors can present their own views, often different from the newspaper's editorial policy.

open and shut. First recorded in 1848, *open and shut* probably didn't originate in a lawyer's office. A good bet is that it had its origins in some card game, probably either poker or faro. Simpler versions of these games didn't allow complicated betting but shut the pot after the ante was put in it. The term could have passed into general use from the card tables to take on the meaning of "easily decided or immediately obvious," as in an open-and-shut case of murder.

open sesame! Ali Baba, of course, overheard the robbers use these magic words to open the door of their cave of riches in the tale of "The Forty Thieves" from the *Arabian Nights.* Sesame is a common herb producing an oily seed long important in cooking and soapmaking in the lands of the *Arabian Nights*, so its use by the robbers is logical. If sesame is also a laxative, as several reference books say, then the thieves were also remarkable punsters.

opera. An Italian word that comes from Latin *opera* meaning "work." Opera has been with us since the end of the 16th century, the first opera house built in Venice in 1637. This combination of drama and music is sometimes melodramatic and may never seem sensible to some, for, as Auden said, "in sensible situations people do not sing."

Oprah. *Oprah* has almost become a synonym for a television talk show host, referring to Emmy Award–winning Oprah Winfrey (b. 1954), American talk show host, actress, and producer, whose show has become a most influential entertainment. The actress also received a best supporting actress Oscar nomination for her performance in the film *The Color Purple* (1985).

opsimath; opsigamy. A rare word that should make a comeback with recent interest in the aged and the problems of growing old. An *opsimath* is a person who begins to learn or study late in life, the word deriving from the Greek for "late in learning." Formerly, the word was often used in a derogatory sense, to suggest a laggard, but there is no reason why it shouldn't be applied to old people learning new things in new fields. *Opsigamy*, a rare related word, is marriage late in life, an act that the Spartans punished with flogging but which is common today judging by all the *opsigamists* around.

oral days. When old horse-racing buffs talk of the *oral days* they mean the good old days—before the time of totalizer machines—when bets were made by word of mouth. The expression seems to have almost passed out of use, but it is worth remembering.

orange. The Sanskrit word *narange* became the Latin *aurangia*, "golden apple," from which our *orange* derives. *Portugals* is a name still used for sweet oranges in Greece, Albania, Italy, and the Middle East, for bitter oranges were the only oranges known in Europe until Portuguese ships brought sweet oranges back from India in 1529. Later, in 1645, still-sweeter Chinese oranges reached Lisbon, and they are responsible for the scientific name for the modern sweet orange, *Citrus sinensis* (*sinensis* is Latin for "Chinese"). Sweet oranges were a luxury enjoyed mainly by royalty until the mid 19th century. Thousands of varieties of fruits are named after their developers, and in this regard the orange is no exception. The best-known eponymous orange variety is the *Temple*. Others include the *Murcott Honey* orange, named for Florida grower Charles Murcott Smith, and the *Parson Brown*, which honors Nathan L. Brown, a Florida clergyman. The United States is by far the largest grower of oranges, producing more than 25 billion a year. An orange's color, incidentally, has nothing to do with its ripeness. Oranges turn orange only as a result of cold weather, which breaks down a membrane protecting their green chlorophyll. This is why summer oranges are often dyed and stamped with the words "color added." Long the traditional decoration for a bride in England, the orange blossom is said to indicate purity because of its whiteness, and fruitfulness because the orange tree is so prolific.

orangutan. One story claims that this ape native to Borneo looked so much like a man to the natives there that they named it from the Malay *orang*, man, and *hutan*, forest or jungle. On the other hand, it may be that Europeans mistakenly applied the Malay word for wild man, *orangutan*, to the ape, the word actually describing a tribe of the Sundra Islands.

orchard. *Hortyard*, one of the old spellings of *orchard*, best explains its origins. The word originally meant "a garden yard," deriving from the Old English *geard*, "yard," and the Latin *hortus*, "garden."

orchid. *Orchids* were once called *ballocks stones*, dogstones, and similar names—all because their tubers resemble human testicles. Indeed, the name *orchid* derives from *orchis*, the Greek for "testicle." An *orchotomy* is, in fact, medical castration.

orchis. The identity of the prodigious true male orchis of the Greeks and Romans has never been established. Mystery still surrounds this magic plant whose root was dissolved in goat's milk by the ancients. One drink of this solution, wrote an incredulous historian, and a man could perform sex as many as 70 consecutive times. Orchis is supposed to have been the main ingredient of *satyrion*, the love food of those lecherous satyrs of Greek mythology. It is a Greek word meaning "testicle," supposedly used because of the root's resemblance to that male organ. The orchid, the Turkish *Orchis morio*, the truffle, the mandrake, and several other plants have been credited with being the male orchis of the ancients, but the true identity of satyrion is probably lost for all time. *See also* ORCHID.

ordeal of battle; ordeal of fire, etc. *Ordeal* here comes from the Anglo-Saxon *ordel*, "to judge." In these ancient practices, outlawed since the 13th century, guilt or innocence was supposed to be left to supernatural decision: God would defend the just, even by miracle if necessary. In *ordeal of battle* the accused (if a noble) was allowed to fight his accuser, with the winner presumed right. *Ordeal of the bier* consisted of the accused touching a corpse, whose blood would start to flow if he was guilty. In the *ordeal of the eucharist* the eucharist would choke a guilty person trying to swallow it. *Ordeal of fire* had the accused holding his hand over red-hot irons or walking barefooted and blindfolded among nine red-hot ploughshares, his innocence established if he emerged unharmed. *Ordeal of water* consisted of ordeal by hot water and ordeal by cold water. In the former the accused plunged his arms to the elbow in boiling water—if his skin wasn't injured, he was innocent. In the latter the accused was bound and thrown into a river—if he floated he was a witch; if he sank he was innocent and lived, that is if he survived the sinking. Nobles, incidentally, could use stand-ins for their ordeals! *See also* WHIPPING BOY.

Order of the Garter. *See* BLUE RIBBON.

Oregon. *Oregon* may come from the Spanish *oregones*, meaning "big-eared men" and referring to Indians who lived there. Other possibilities are the Algonquian *Wauregan*, "beautiful water," for the Colorado River, and an unclear Indian name possibly meaning "place of the beaver" that was misspelled on an early French map. The Beaver State was admitted to the Union in 1850 as our 33rd state.

Oregon Trail.   A 2,000-mile-long route from Missouri to Oregon much used during the 1840–60 westward migrations and called "the longest unpaved highway in the world." Over half a million pioneers used it.

organdy.   The silk dress fabric called organdy, first recorded in 1835, takes its name directly from the French *organdi*, meaning the same. But its roots are ultimately in the ancient town of *Urgendi* in Turkestan, a place renowned for its weaving.

organoleptic analysis.   Decomposition of shellfish is detected by *organoleptic analysis*, the federal Food and Drug Administration reported recently. Pressed for a definition the *FDA Consumer* explained that this meant "by smelling the product with the nose." *See* GOBBLEDYGOOK.

orgasm; climax.   The *OED* nicely defines *orgasm* as "the height of venereal excitement in coition" and traces this first use of the word in this jolly sense to 1771 as a "spasm of the vitals." But although *orgasm* was originally a scientific term, deriving from Greek *organ*, "to swell, be excited," it is probably more commonly used than its synonym, the more modern *climax*, which British eugenist and birth control advocate Marie Stepes first used in this sense in 1918. The slang expression *to come*, dating back to about 1600, is certainly used more than either of the two and is found in the work of many modern writers, including Joyce's *Selected Letters*.

Oreo.   *See* APPLE.

orgy.   Every orgy, or drunken, licentious feast, takes its name from the secret nocturnal festivals the ancient Greeks and Romans held in honor of Dionysus or Bacchus, the god of wine. These ceremonies, called the *orgia*, featured wild drinking, dancing, and sexual license.

oriflamme.   The early kings of France carried the red banner of the abbey of St. Denis, near Paris, as a military ensign. The flag, called the oriflamme, was crimson, cut into three pennants to represent tongues of fire, and carried on a gilded staff. Legend had it that men were blinded by merely looking on the oriflamme, but it was replaced by the *fleurs-de-lis* in the 15th century. It took its beautiful name from the Latin for "golden flame."

Orlando, Florida.   The site of Disney World in Florida has an interesting etymology. It was originally named for its first settler, Aaron Jernigan, but rechristened Orlando in 1857 in memory of Orlando Reeves, who had been killed in a skirmish with Indians.

orrery.   All planetariums can trace their ancestry to the first *orrery* invented in about 1700 by George Graham. This complicated mechanical device showed the movements of the planets and satellites around the sun by means of rotating and revolving balls. Graham sent his model to instrument maker John Rowley, who made a copy that he presented to his patron Charles Boyle (1676–1731), fourth earl of Orrery, the apparatus being named in the earl's honor. Orrery, who used the device to help educate his children, was a noted patron of science and a descendant of the physicist Robert Boyle.

orthodoxy; heterodoxy.   *Orthodoxy* refers to the quality or state of adhering to traditional or established faith, while *heterodoxy* is the condition or quality of being not in agreement with widely accepted beliefs. Wiser definitions, however, may be found in Bishop William Warburton's reply when Lord Sandwich asked him in a parliamentary debate to define the two words. Replied the bishop: "Orthodoxy is my doxy; heterodoxy is another man's doxy."

Osage.   The name of these Sioux Indians derives from their tribal name *Wazhazhe*, meaning "war people."

Osage orange.   *See* BODOCK.

Oscar.   Hollywood's gold-plated Oscars remained nameless for years after the Academy of Motion Picture Arts and Sciences first awarded them in 1927. Called simply the Statuette, the 10-inch-high trophy was designed by Cedric Gibbons, weighed about seven pounds, was bronze on the inside, and originally cost about $100. The statuette quickly became a symbol of film fame, but not until 1931 did it get a name. At that time Mrs. Margaret Herrick, librarian of the Academy, was shown one of the trophies and observed, "He reminds me of my uncle Oscar." As fate would have it, a newspaper columnist happened to be in the room and soon reported to his readers that "Employees of the Academy have affectionately dubbed their famous statuette 'Oscar.' " The name stuck. Mrs. Herrick's uncle Oscar was in reality Oscar Pierce, a wealthy Texan from a pioneer family who had made his fortune in wheat and fruit and migrated to California, where he could now bask in glory as well as the sunshine. Did any real Oscar ever *win* an Oscar? The answer is: Oskar Homolka, Oscar Brodney, Oscar Werner, and Oscar Hammerstein II were all nominated for Oscars, but the only Oscar ever to win an Oscar was Hammerstein. In fact, Oscar Hammerstein II won two Oscars for best song. In 1941 he and composer Jerome Kern won for "The Last Time I Saw Paris" from *Lady Be Good.* In 1945 he and composer Richard Rodgers won an Oscar for "It Might As Well Be Spring" from *State Fair.*

Oscar Asche.   Another famous OSCAR is the Australian Oscar Asche (1872–1936), a musical comedy star who made a tidy fortune on the stage and whose full name became Australian rhyming slang for cash. "*Oscar Asche* for cash" was eventually shortened to *Oscar,* making him the only man whose prenomen means money in a generic sense. *See* BLUNT.

oscillate.   To swing back and forth. The word derives from the custom Roman farmers had of hanging little masks representing Bacchus, the god of wine, from their vines. These little masks, called *oscilla*, would sway back and forth in the wind.

oslerize.   In a widely reported speech, Canadian-born physician Sir William Osler (1849–1919) opined that all business and professional men should retire at 60. He mentioned Anthony Trollope's novel *The Fixed Period*, the plot of which "hinges upon the admirable scheme . . . into which at 60 men retired for a year of contemplation before a peaceful departure by chloroform." Generally misinterpreted in the press, Osler's plan enraged more than half of the population when his plan was interpreted as meaning that all men over 60 should be put to death as useless. His scheme actually provided for retirement at 60 on a generous pension, but the misconception prevailed and from 1905 on *to oslerize* implied just the opposite of "life begins at 40." It is interesting to note that Dr. Osler made some of his most valuable scientific contributions *after* he turned 60, his proposed date for compulsory retirement.

osprey. The osprey, or fish hawk, takes its name from Latin *ossifraga*, "bone-breaker." However, this bird does not break bones and eat marrow from inside them as its name suggests. Somehow over the centuries the dining habits of this fish eater got confused with those of the lammergeier, a large vulture that does drop bones on rocks to open them (much as gulls break clams and mussels). Due to this confusion the fish hawk has since early Roman times been called the osprey.

os sacrum. The *os sacrum*, "the triangular bone situated at the lower part of the vertebral column," is said to be so named because it was the sacred part used in ancient sacrifices. In rabbinical lore (where it is also known as the *luz*) the *os sacrum* is said to be called sacred because it resists decay and "will be the germ of the 'new body' at the resurrection."

ostracism. *Ostracism*, "to banish socially," derives from *ostrakon*, the Greek word for oyster shell. It seems that a vote of banishment in ancient Athens had to be a written one, for it was, of course, a serious matter to send a person into exile for crimes against the state. Because paper was scarce, the banishment ballot was written on pieces of tile called *ostrakon*, this name having first been applied to the shell of the oyster, which the tile resembled. It followed that the name *ostrakismos* was bestowed upon the act of banishment itself, which gives us our word for "to banish socially"—to *ostracize* or "oyster shell."

ostrich stomach. *Ostrich stomach* was the name for vitriol in medieval alchemy, because people believed at the time that the ostrich had vitriolic stomach juices that digested all the many things it was thought to swallow. The ostrich was considered a monstrous bird that could eat anything, often so insatiable that it plucked the iron shoes off horses. In heraldry it was represented chewing a horseshoe.

otaku. One of the latest Japanese words to enter into English, *otaku* literally means "your house" and is used to describe young people so obsessed with computers that they seldom leave their homes or offices where their computers are based. Since about 1990 the word has had the same meaning in the U.S. *See* JAPANESE WORDS IN ENGLISH.

other fish to fry. To have other, often more important, things to do. A variation is to have bigger fish to fry. The first recorded use of the expression is in British author John Evelyn's *Memoirs* (1660): "I fear he hath other fish to fry."

otorhinolaryngologist. Here you have an ear (*oto*), nose (*rhino*), and throat (*largngo*) medical specialist, an ear, nose, and throat physician. The word, all 21 letters of it, is made of Greek components. *See* MÉNIÈRE'S DISEASE.

ottoman. Osman I (1259–1326) would not appreciate the fact that many readers are resting their feet on him, or his namesake, while reading this. But the ottoman, a stuffed footstool more often called a hassock, its Old English designation, is definitely named for him. Osman, sometimes called Othman, led his Muslim followers farther west from Asia Minor in the late 13th century to found the Ottoman Empire, principally what we know as Turkey today. Tales of this great empire, which lasted until its dissolution in 1918, excited the imagination of Europeans and toward the end of the 18th century merchants saw that there was a ready market in Europe for items of Eastern luxury, for the carpets, pillows, and divans that people imagined sultans lounged upon in their luxurious harems. These included a small, backless couch for two that the French called the *ottoman* because they imported it from the Ottoman Empire, ignoring its Turkish name. The couch or divan eventually became both the overstuffed English ottoman sofa, acquiring a back in the process, and, in a much smaller form, the ottoman footstool.

Ouch! Critic Wolcott Gibbs is often credited with the shortest dramatic criticism in theatrical history. Reviewing the Broadway farce *Wham!*, he wrote only "Ouch!"

ought to be bored for the hollow horn. Said of a seemingly feeble-minded person. This Americanism was suggested by the hollow horn disease in cattle, which made cattle ill and feeble and was supposedly cured by drilling a hole in the horns.

ought to be bored for the simples. An old-fashioned phrase said, often fondly or humorously, of a dimwitted person whose mind might be improved by boring a hole in his or her head to let some of the stupidity drain out. "Old Johnson ought to be bored for the simples; he's seen better days." The expression dates back to the late 19th-century or earlier.

ouija board. The ouija board (pronounced "wee-jee board") was apparently intended to answer most questions put to it in the affirmative. Its name is simply a combination of the French *oui*, "yes," and the German *ja*, "yes." Obviously its inventor intended to stress the positive, to stress hope, whether the player be of French or Teutonic background.

an ounce of prevention is worth a pound of cure. *See* SNUG AS A BUG IN A RUG.

our cake is dough. This expression, for "miscarried plans and disappointments," goes back before Shakespeare, who used it in *The Taming of the Shrew*. It is first recorded in Thomas Beacon's *Prayers* (1559): "Or else your cake is dough, and all your fat lie in the fire."

our country right or wrong. At an 1816 dinner honoring him in Virginia, U.S. naval hero Stephen Decatur gave the toast: "Our Country! In her intercourse with foreign nations may she always be in the right; but our country, right or wrong." This seems to be the origin of the saying *our country right or wrong*, which is also heard as *my country right or wrong*. U.S. Senator Carl Schurz paraphrased the expression in an 1872 speech: "Our country right or wrong! When right, to be kept right; when wrong, to be put right."

our Lord's candle. Margaret Armstrong and John Thornbec describe this striking American plant in their *Field Book of Wild Flowers* (1915): "The flowers of Yucca Whipplei, one of the most beautiful of all Yuccas, are of a lovely golden hue, glowing in the bright sunlight like lighted candles before the altar, and known as 'Our Lord's candle' . . . After they have blossomed the tall, white stalks remain standing for some time, so that the hills look like they have been planted with numbers of white wands."

Our Perry and our Porter were too much for John Bull to swallow! A popular Yankee slogan after the War of 1812, this punning expression refers to American naval heroes Oliver Perry, whose last name means a hard cider made of pears, and David Porter, whose last name means a strong, dark beer. John Bull, of course, is the national nickname for England.

out at the elbows. *See* ELBOW.

out-Herod Herod. Shakespeare used this in *Hamlet:* "It out-Herods Herod: pray you avoid it," Hamlet says to the actors. The reference is to a king infamous for his barbaric cruelty. Herodes or Herod, King of Judea in 4 B.C., ordered all Bethlehem's infants to be killed (Matt. 2:16). The expression means, of course, to outdo the worst tyrant in wickedness and violence.

outlaw. A badman or desperado. *Outlaw* did not originate in the wild and wooly West, though it had much use there. It derives ultimately from an Old Norse word meaning "outlawed or banished." The Old Norse word became *utlaga* in Old English and was applied to criminals in general, *utlaga* eventually becoming *outlaw*.

out of kilter. Many have tried to explain the origins of *kilter* in this expression meaning to be out of order, out of whack, but no one has succeeded. The best suggestions, I think, are the *kilter*, meaning a "useless hand in cards," the dialect *kilt*, "to make neat," and the Dutch *keelter*, "stomach," because stomachs are often "out of order" with digestion problems. We only know that the expression is first recorded in 1643, as *kelter*.

out of left field. Since left field is not any more odd or less active a position than right or center field in baseball, it is hard to understand why it is featured in this common slang expression meaning "very unorthodox and wrong, weirdly unconventional, even crazy." In fact, anyone who has ever played sandlot baseball knows that the most inept (and therefore a little odd, to kids) fielders were relegated to *right* field, because there were fewer left-handed hitters to pull the ball to right field. It has been suggested that the phrase refers to the left field seats in Yankee Stadium that are far away from the coveted seats near Babe Ruth's right field position. Another suggestion links the phrase to the Neuropsychiatric Institute flanking left field in Chicago's 19th-century West Side Park, though there are no references to the expression at that time. I would suspect that the words simply refer to the relative remoteness of left field compared to all other positions except center field and that left field is used instead of center field in the expression because *center* by definition means in the middle (of things) and *left* has long had negative associations of clumsiness, awkwardness, and radical or eccentric behavior. The expression *from out of left field*,

meaning from out of nowhere unexpectedly, lends credence to this remoteness theory. The term *left field* itself was in use by the mid-1860s, along with the names for the other outfield positions, following by 20 years the first recordings of the names for the infield positions.

out of sight, out of mind. *See* ABSENCE MAKES THE HEART GROW FONDER.

out of sorts. Not feeling well, not feeling one's usual self. The expression may derive from the sorts or kinds of type printers work with. A printer who ran out of sorts in the midst of a job would certainly not feel good about it.

out of the ballpark. *See* BALLPARK FIGURE.

out of touch. Military drills of the late 18th century employed tight formations where every soldier in the ranks had to be close enough to the man on the left and right of him so that his swinging elbows brushed against his companions'. A soldier who failed to do this and caused a gap in the line was said to be *out of touch* and the military use of this expression yielded the civilian saying, meaning "to lose contact with a situation."

Outta sight! Often regarded as original college slang of the 1960s, *outta sight*, for "something remarkable or wonderful," has been part of the language since the 1840s, in the Bowery expression *out of sight*. Stephen Crane used it in his first novel *Maggie: A Girl of the Streets* (1896): "I'm stuck on her shape. It's outa sight . . ."

outten the light. An American expression meaning turn off the light, or put out the light, that is still heard in such places as South Carolina.

out to lunch. Used since the early 1950s to describe someone so stupid or inattentive that he or she isn't even there for all intents and purposes. This can be a temporary condition, however, the person being out to lunch, for example, only in the course of a conversation.

ovarimony. *See* TESTICLES.

over a barrel. Here the person over the barrel is in the other person's power or at his mercy. In the days before mouth-to-mouth resuscitation and other modern methods of lifesaving, lifeguards placed drowning victims over a barrel, which was rolled back and forth while the lifeguard tried to revive them. Victims were certainly in the lifeguard's power, and the process is probably the origin of the Americanism *to have someone over a barrel*.

Over-sexed Weekly. A nickname for the U.S. military newspaper the *Oversea's Weekly*, alluding to its pinups and lively, lurid stories. It was not published during World War II and thus has no connection with the anonymous British saying about Yank servicemen: "They're overfed, oversexed, overpaid and over here." The paper began publication in the 1960s.

overshoot the mark. *Overshoot the mark* is an old phrase dating from the late 16th century even in its figurative sense of exceeding limits, being irrelevant or inappropriate. Its source is probably archery, which was a popular sport for a thousand years in England. *See* WIDE OF THE MARK.

over-the-counter stocks. In the days before stock exchanges, banks used to sell securities over the counter. It is from this practice that we derive the term *over-the-counter* stocks. Today over-the-counter stocks are those not sold on the New York and other major stock exchanges, usually being those of smaller companies.

over the top. A very popular expression in the U.S. lately, when reality itself often seems over the top. It means "excessive, exaggerated, even gross," and may come from the name of the British television series *Over the Top*, which premiered in 1982. It apparently has no connection with the World War I expression *over the top*, meaning "to climb out of trenches and attack the enemy." Rather, it seems to refer to a container that is filled to overflowing.

overwhelm. Overwhelm means essentially the same thing as *whelm*, "to be completely overcome by something," but *overwhelm* is a more emphatic term. *Whelm* has its roots in the Middle English *whelven*, meaning to capsize or turn a vessel upside down. The English *whelm* was first recorded in the 13th century and soon took on the sense of turning a vessel upside down "so as to cover it" with water, which led to its modern meaning.

oxygen. French chemist Antoine-Laurent Lavoisier coined the word *oxygene*, which became our *oxygen*, in the late 18th century. At the time, the element was mistakenly thought to be a component of an acid and Lavoisier misnamed it, forming *oxygen* from Greek words meaning "acid producing." His misnaming has endured for over two centuries, however, and *oxygen* will always go by the wrong name.

oxymoron. Deriving from the Greek for "pointedly foolish," an *oxymoron* is a figure of speech in which incongruous and apparently contradictory words are combined for a special rhetorical effect by paradoxical means. A well-known example is Tennyson's "Lancelot and Elaine":

> The shackles of an old love straiten'd him
> His honour rooted in dishonour stood,
> and faith unfaithful kept him falsely true.

Many famous English writers have used this device. Other *oxymora* include the phrase *an eloquent silence* and the word *sophomore*, which derives from two Greek words meaning "wise" and "foolish."

Oy! A Yiddish expression that is uttered by Americans of dozens of religions, races, and former nationalities. "*Oy* is not a word," Leo Rosten writes in *The Joys of Yiddish* (1968). "It is a vocabulary. It is uttered in as many ways as the utterer's histrionic ability permits. It is a lament, a protest, a cry of dismay, a reflex of delight. But however sighed, cried, howled or moaned, *oy!* is the most expressive and ubiquitous exclamation in Yiddish." *Oy vay!*, a shortening of *oy vay iz mir*, is also used as an "all-purpose ejaculation," Rosten notes. He doesn't list *oy gevald*, which Henry Roth used as "a cry of alarm, concern or amazement" in *From Bondage* (1996). However, he does list *gevalt* or *gevald* alone as the same kind of cry and cites the folk proverb, "Man comes into the world with an Oy!—and leaves with a gevalt."

Oyez! Oyez! Oyez! This call made by a court officer is the French second-person plural imperative of *oyer*, "to hear," meaning "hear ye! hear ye! hear ye!" and was introduced to England by the Normans. It was formerly used by town criers, and Shakespeare rendered it as *O yes!*

Oy! Oy! Oy! A common cheer or cry heard at the 2000 Olympics in Sydney, Australia. No relation to Yiddish oy!

oyster "r" myth. *See* R MONTHS.

oysters Kirkpatrick. Oysters Kirkpatrick was named in honor of James C. Kirkpatrick, manager of San Francisco's Palace Hotel in the late 19th century. The Palace Hotel, born during the gold rush of 1849, destroyed in the earthquake of 1906 and rebuilt to become one of America's greatest eating places, offers the following simple original recipe for the delectable dish: "Open oysters on deep shell, put in oven for about 3 or 4 minutes until oysters shrink. Pour off the liquor, then add small strip of bacon and cover with catsup and place in very hot oven for about 5 to 6 minutes until glazed to a nice golden brown."

Oysters Rockefeller. Oysters broiled with a puree of spinach and seasonings on a bed of rock salt probably originated in 1899 at Antoine's, the famous New Orleans restaurant still in business. The first customer to taste the fabulous dish is supposed to have said, "It's as rich as Rockefeller," the name appearing on the menu shortly afterward. *See* RICH AS ROCKEFELLER.

Oy vay! A common Yiddish expression. Albert Einstein is said to have cried "Oy vay!" when told that the first atomic bomb, which he did not know was being built, had obliterated Hiroshima on August 6, 1945. Literally, the words mean "oh, pain," *vay* deriving from German *Weh*, meaning "woe." Leo Rosten in *The Joys of Yiddish* (1968) goes on to list fully 29 uses of the workhorse exclamation. *See* OY!

Ozarks. The Ozark Mountains in Missouri, Arkansas, and Oklahoma, ranging up to 2,300 feet high, cover an area of 50,000 square miles, and are noted more for their beautiful scenery and mineral springs, which make them a resort area, than their rich deposits of lead and zinc. The Ozarks are named for a local band of Quapaw Indians who lived in the Missouri and Arkansas region of the mountains. "The French were in the habit of shortening the long Indian names by using only their first syllables," an article in the *St. Louis Globe-Democrat* explains. "There are frequent references in their records to hunting or trading expeditions 'aux Kans,' or 'aux Os,' or 'aux Arcs,' meaning 'up into' the territory of the Kansas, Osage, or Arkansas tribes." This *aux Arcs* seems to be the more likely explanation for *Ozarks*, although the local Arkansas band may have been named from the French *aux Arcs*, meaning "with bows," which could also have been corrupted to *Ozarks* and later applied to the mountains where the Indians lived.

ozone. Although *ozone* means "fresh, pure air" in everyday speech (the reason for place-names like Ozone Park, New York), it translates as "stinking air," deriving from the Greek *ozein*, "to stink." German chemist Christian Friedrich Schonbein coined the name of this stable, pale bluish gas in 1840. Schonbein wrote that he named this most reactive form of oxygen (O_3) "ozone because of its strong smell," which he thought was similar to chlorine.

P

P. The ancient Phoenicians and Hebrews called our 16th letter *pe*, "mouth." *P.* in music means "piano," while *the five P's* is Englishman William Oxberry (1784–1824) who was for his all too brief 40 years a printer, poet, publisher, publican, and player (actor). The 16th-century Dominican monk Placentius wrote a poem of 253 verses called *Pugna Porcorum* in which every word begins with a *p*, the first line translating as "Praise Paul's prize pig's prolific progeny."

pablum. *Pablum* was a trademark name for a specific infant's cereal, although the word has become generic and is used to mean childish or insipid ideas. The trademark was coined from the Latin *pabulum*, food or fodder, early in this century.

Pacific Ocean. Portuguese explorer Ferdinand Magellan gave this great ocean its name in 1520, because of the calm, peaceful weather he enjoyed on it after a stormy passage in adjoining straits.

package-goods store. Liquor stores are so named not because liquor is sold in packages in such stores, but because of the quest for euphemisms after Prohibition was repealed. State legislatures did not want to offend "drys" at the time, or wanted to offend them as little as possible, and, in making liquor stores and saloons legal again, referred to them by such names as package-goods stores and taverns.

pack rat; trade rat. A *pack rat* is a person who compulsively saves things, almost everything. He or she takes this name from the eastern pack rat (*Neotoma flordiana*), a plague carrier, which lives at virtually every altitude over a range from northern Canada to the Florida Keys. No other animal carries thievery to such extremes, and its name has also become a synonym for a kleptomaniac or junk-picking miser. The capacious nest of the pack rat is usually a large, globe-shaped "castle" made of sticks, leaves, and grasses up to six feet high, resembling a small beaver lodge, but the nest can also be built in hollow logs, caves, abandoned cabins, openings of trees, and even under cactus plants in the desert. In its museum or treasure-house nest are found every bright shiny thing one can imagine, as well as some not-at-all shiny objects, including (all these stolen objects have been documented) keys, eyeglasses, coins, currency, belt buckles, pens and pencils, lipsticks, watches, tinfoil, china, rags, socks, cartridge cases, bleached bones and skulls, sets of false teeth, and even mousetraps. The pack rat has been known to steal coins from the pockets of sleeping campers. A legend persists that it will leave something in return for what it takes, but less romantic observers theorize that the little creature probably is passing by with something in its mouth when it comes upon a brighter trinket and drops whatever it is carrying to claim the glittering prize that some strange compulsion commands it to possess. Nevertheless, the legend persists, which accounts for the pack rat also being called the "trade rat." *See* RAT PACK.

paddleball. A fast-growing amateur sport today, paddleball is played with the same basic rules as handball but with short-handled, perforated paddles, and a tennis-like ball. The sport was invented in 1930 by University of Michigan physical education teacher Earl Riskey. Riskey even invented the ball and paddle for the game, and along with James Naismith (of basketball fame), William Morgan (the inventor of volleyball), and the Reverend Frank P. Beal (who invented paddle tennis), is one of the four people who are known to have invented a popular sport.

paddle your own canoe. *See* CANOE.

paean; peony. The gods wounded in the Trojan War were cured by the physician Paeon, according to Greek mythology. Thus many plants once prized for their curative powers were named for Paeon, including the beautiful flower called the peony with its hundreds of varieties. The species of peony called the tree peony (*Paeonia suffruticosa*) is called the "king of flowers" by the Chinese and is widely regarded as one of the most beautiful of all garden plants. Because they believed the god Apollo often disguised himself as Paeon, the Greeks sang hymns of thanks and tribute to him that came to be called *paeans;* these are the source for our expression *paeans of praise. See also* MANDRAKE.

Paget's disease. *See* BRIGHT'S DISEASE.

Pago Pago. *Pango Pango* should be the name of this Pacific island, the chief harbor of American Samoa, and that, in fact, is the way the locals pronounce the name. An old story, which may be true, explains that the island is called Pago Pago because missionaries transliterating the local speech into the Latin alphabet found that there were many sounds that had to be "represented by *n* in combination with a following consonant." So many, in fact, that there weren't enough *n*'s in their type fonts to enable them to set all such words in type. So they quite arbitrarily eliminated the *n* from some words—leaving us with *Pago Pago* instead of *Pango Pango*.

pain in the ass. An Americanism of the 20th century which has several euphemisms that often have slightly different meanings. A *pain* is a person who is mildly annoying, while *a pain in the neck* is more so and *a pain in the ass* is someone really obnoxious.

paint the town red. If Indians burning down a town suggested this phrase meaning to go on wild sprees, to make "whoopee," no one has been able to find the actual culprits. More than one scholar does nominate the flames Indians on the warpath often left behind for the "red" in the phrase, and the expression did originate in the American West, where it was first applied to the wild partying of cowboys in about 1880. Another good guess suggests a link with the older expression *to paint*, meaning "to drink," which, coupled with the way a drunk's nose lights up red, may have resulted in the phrase. Or *red*, a color commonly associated with violence, could have derived from the way the "painters" did violence to the town or to themselves.

paipu katto. One of the most humorous of Japanized expressions comes from the English words *pipe cut*. The Japanese use the expression to mean "vasectomy."

pajamas. Pajamas were first simply loose pants or trousers, as is shown by the word's roots—Hindi *pae*, "leg," and *jama*, "clothing." Muslims in India were the first to wear them, and in the early 19th century British men in India adopted the habit and added the jacket.

Pakistan. Pakistan is probably the only country whose name was constructed as an acronym, its letters standing for the the regions that make up the nation: *P* for *Punjab*; *A* for *Afghani* border tribes; *K* for *Kashmir*; *S* for *Sind*; and *tan* for Baluchi*stan*. A number of other place names are acronyms. Pawn, Oregon, for example, is composed of the first letters of the names of the men who founded it—Poole, Aberley, Worthington, and Nolen.

pal. Recorded in late 18th-century England for an "accomplice," *pal* came within 50 years or so to mean a chum or friend. Originally a Gypsy word, it derives from the Romany *pal*, "brother, or mate," which comes from the Turkish Gypsy *pral*, meaning the same.

palace. Augustus Caesar, the first Roman emperor, built his home on the most imposing of the seven hills of Rome, the Mons Palatinus, so named for the fence of stakes (Latin, *palus*) around it. His royal mansion was called a *palatium*, which became the French *palais* and finally the English *palace*, for the same.

palaver. The Portuguese *palavra* journeyed to Africa before it came to England in the form of *palaver*. Meaning "word," *palavra* was used to mean "talk" by Portuguese traders in East Africa when they bargained with natives in the area. By the early 18th century, English sailors had adopted the word and brought it back home in the form of *palaver*.

pale. The word *pale* for "stake" or "picket" comes from the Latin word *palus*, "stake," while the word *pale* for "colorless" or "whitish," lacking intensity of color, derives from the Latin word *palledus* meaning the same. One of the great uses of the latter *pale* came during the battle between the U.S.S. *Constitution* and the French frigate *Insurgente* in 1799. An officer on the victorious *Constitution* ran through a seaman who was fleeing his post. "We would put any man to death for looking pale on this ship," he said later.

paleface. Various American Indian tribes did use *paleface* as a general term for whites, but they also employed more specific insulting words, including *pale-colored-and-scrawny*, and *spirit-white-and-thin*, this last term comparing whites to ghosts. Some writers claim, however, that the word was invented by James Fenimore Cooper (1789–1851), who certainly did popularize the term in his novels. *Paleface* has also been applied to whites by blacks, and The Palefaces was an organization similar to the Ku Klux Klan that thrived during Reconstruction.

Palestine. An ancient designation from biblical days, the name *Palestine* derives ultimately from *Philistia*, meaning "land of the Philistines." The Romans borrowed *Philistia* as the basis for *Palestina*, the name of a Roman province. This word later became *Palestine*.

palindrome. So scurrilous in his satires was Sotades, a Greek poet of the third century B.C., that Ptolemy II had him sewn up in a sack and thrown into the sea. But his coarse, vile verses must have been clever, for Sotades is reputed to have invented palindromes, which are sometimes called Sotadics in his honor. Palindromes take their more common name from the Greek *palin dromo*, "running back again," and they are simply anagrams that read the same backward as forward. Making palindromes has been a favorite word game at least since early Grecian times, but English, with the largest and most varied vocabulary of all languages, offers the most fertile ground for the creator of palindromes. It's said that Sir Thomas Urquhart even invented a universal language based entirely on palindromes. Probably the longest common English palindromic word is *redivider*. The longest halfway sensible palindrome is one coined by an anonymous 19th-century English poet: *Dog as a devil deified/Deified lived as a god*. Another famous palindrome is the one English author Leigh Mercer wrote for Ferdinand de Lesseps, the man who began the Panama Canal: *A man, a plan, a canal: Panama! See* NAMBY-PAMBY; TATTARRATTAT.

palma Christi. The castor-oil plant (*Ricinus communis*) is called *palma Christi* because its leaf shape resembles the palm of the hand and in early times it brought to mind an image of Christ's hand nailed to the cross. The name is first recorded in a herbal published in 1548, but is certainly older.

Palmetto State. A nickname for South Carolina, after the palm tree called a palmetto that commonly grows there. South Carolina has also been called the Gamecock State (in honor of fiery Revolutionary War general Thomas "Gamecock" Sumter, after whom historic Fort Sumter is named), the Rice State, and the Swamp State. It is called the Sandlapper or Sand-hiller State after poor people in its sandy regions who ate aluminous earth to fill their stomachs. *See* CLAY-EATER.

palm of the hand; palm tree. Palm trees take their name from the Latin *palma*, "palm of the hand," because the tree's fronds resemble a spread hand. Palm Sunday, the Sunday before Easter, is named after Christ's triumphant entry into Jerusalem, when people strewed his way with palm branches and leaves. The palm was a symbol of victory in Roman times, and *to bear the palm* meant to be the best, after the Roman custom of awarding a palm branch to a victorious gladiator. This led to the expression *palmy days*, "prosperous" or "happy days," as those days were to a victorious gladiator when he received a palm branch. Incidentally, the palm of the hand had its own Old English word, *folm*, which was used until medieval times even while *palm* was used for the palm tree. It wasn't until then that the French *paume*, a derivative of the Latin *palma*, was borrowed, altered slightly to *palm*, and began to mean the palm of the hand in place of *folm*.

palomino. Palomino comes from the Spanish *paloma* (dove), the word first used to describe horses of a dovelike color. Palomino is the color of a horse, not a breed, and today describes a horse with a golden coat, white mane and tail and often white markings on the face and legs.

palooka. *See* HIGH HAT.

pamphlet. *Pamphilus, seu de Amore* was the title of an erotic love poem of the 12th century; nothing is known about its author Pamphilus except his name in the title. No more than a few pages in length, the Latin verses became very popular during the Middle Ages, the best-known love poem of their time. Just as the small book containing *Aesop's Fables* came to be familiarly called *Esopet* in French, the little poem became known as *Pamphilet*, the English spelling this *Pamflet*, and eventually *Pamphlet*. By the 14th century any small booklet was called a pamphlet and within another 300 years the word had acquired its sense of "a small polemical brochure," the transition completed from sensuous love poem to political tract. Generally, a pamphlet is defined as a paperbound or unbound booklet of less than 100 pages.

to pan. Apparently the parent of this is the expression *it didn't pan out*. American prospectors long before the California gold rush were expert at using metal mining pans to separate gold from the sand and gravel they scooped from a stream bed. When gold wasn't found after the pan was shaken, miners would say that it hadn't panned out. Similarly, when any effort, say a stage play, didn't pan out, it didn't succeed. After enough literary critics had said plays or books didn't pan out, to criticize

a production severely came to be known as panning it. Another suggestion is that *to pan* derives from the head, or "pan," of a tamping bar, which receives the blows of a sledgehammer, but the first recorded use of the word in this sense contains several allusions to mining processes, including panning.

Panacea. A daughter of Aesculapius, the Greek god of medicine, Panacea (her name formed from the Greek *pan*, "all," and *akeisthai*, "to heal") could cure any ailment. Over the years her name came to mean a cure-all, a panacea now being a remedy that will cure any problem, medical or otherwise.

panama hat. Made from plaited leaves of a palmlike plant *(Carludovica palmata)* of South America, the panama hat, or panama, is something of a misnomer. The hats originated in Ecuador, but have been called panama hats since they were first recorded in English in 1833—probably because Panama was the major distribution center for them.

panda. *See* POLO.

pandemonium. English poet John Milton gave us this word for wild lawlessness, tumult, or chaos when he dubbed the capital of hell *Pandaemonium* in *Paradise Lost*. He coined the word from the Greek for "all demons."

pander. Boccaccio, Chaucer, and Shakespeare all wrote about Pandarus, who in classical legend helped the Trojans in their war against the Greeks. In his poem *Il Filostrato* (1374) Boccaccio gives Pandarus the role of go-between for the lovers Troilus and Criseyde, a role that Chaucer and Shakespeare also presented in the former's long poem *Troilus and Criseyde* (1380?) and the latter's play *Troilus and Cressida* (1602). Shakespeare has Pandarus say: "Let all pitiful goers-between be called to the world's end after my name; call them all Pandars." So they are still called, with a slight change in spelling, but besides its meaning of a go-between in sexual intrigues, or procurer, *pander* has also come to mean to cater to the lower tastes and desires of others.

panetella. A long, slender cigar that takes its name from American Spanish *panatela*, a long slender bread or biscuit. The word can be spelled (correctly) three different ways: *panetella*, *panetela*, and *panatela*.

pangram. A pangram, from the Greek *pan*, all, plus *gramma*, something drawn, is a sentence containing all the letters of the alphabet. Many logolepts would take issue with *The Guinness Book of World Records*, which says that the shortest English sentence containing all twenty-six letters of the alphabet is: "Jackdaws love my big sphinx of quartz." That's 31 letters. "Frowsy things plumb vex'd Jack Q." has only 27 and there are certainly others just as short.

panhandler. *Panhandler* is said to derive from the Spanish *pan*, meaning both bread and money (just as the American slang *bread* does today). But though it is supposed to have been first recorded in 1890, the earliest quotation I am able to find for it is in humorist George Ade's *Doc Horne* (1899): "He had 'sized' the hustler for a 'panhandler' from the very start." However, the fact that Ade put the word in quotation marks probably indicates that he did not invent it, as has often been claimed. *See* TIGHTWAD; GLADHANDER.

Panhandle State. A nickname for West Virginia, after its long "panhandle" of land between Ohio and Pennsylvania. West Virginia is also called the Mountain State, the Switzerland of America (like four other states) and, by its proud residents, West by God Virginia.

panic. All panics can be linked with the great god Pan of the dark forests and fields—etymologically at least. The word *panic* derives from the name of Pan and the Greek term *panikon deima*, "the panic fear," a fear of the woods on a dark evening when eerie frightening sounds are heard.

panic button. *See* PUSH (HIT) THE PANIC BUTTON.

pansy. The French *pensée*, "thought," is the source of this flower's name, some poet in ancient times believing that the flower had a thoughtful, pensive face. The flower was called *pensee* in English during the early 16th century, but changed gradually in pronunciation and spelling to *pansy*. Other fanciful names for the *pansy (Viola tricolor hortensis)* have included hearts-ease, call-me-to-you, three-faces-under-a-hood, love-in-idleness, and kiss-me-at-the-garden-gate. *Pansy* has been a derogatory term for homosexuals since about 1930, this expression originating in England.

pantomime. Rome's only original contribution to Western theater was pantomime, a silent individual performance by a pantomimus, an actor who danced or acted in mask and cloak and did not speak a word, unlike the earlier Greek *mimi*, who spoke and sang while performing. This purely Roman creation was a favorite of audiences in Rome, who idolized the *pantomimi* and often made them rich. Just one *pantomimus* played each of the roles in a play, wearing a different mask for each character, while all the words were sung by a choir. Pantomime became so popular in Rome that it drove both tragedy and comedy from the stage. One of its most accomplished practitioners was Bathyllus, whose name came to be used for any pantomime actor. Paris was the name of two Roman pantomime performers. The first remained the emperor Nero's favorite until he was executed by Nero for beating him in an acting contest. The second took the first Paris's name and ironically met the same fate 20 years later in A.D. 87, when the emperor Domitian had him put to death.

pants; panties. *Panties* has become acceptable only in relatively recent years, despite the fact that the word has its roots in the name of a saint. St. Pantaleone, a Christian doctor who treated the poor without charge, was condemned to death by the Romans in A.D. 305, and miraculously survived six execution attempts before his persecutors finally beheaded him. The courageous saint (*Pantaleone* means "all lion") became patron saint of doctors and a martyr revered by the Venetians, his name all the more popular because so many boys were baptized in his honor. Probably for this reason, and because it was considered comical to call a foolish character "all lion," the saint's name attached itself to the buffoon in the 15th-century *commedia dell'arte*, in which an emaciated, bespectacled old man called Pantaloon wore slippers and one-piece, skintight breeches that bloused out above the knees and came to be known as *pantaloons*. Pantaloons later came to be a designation for trousers in general, the word introduced to America in the early 18th century and soon shortened to *pants*. *Pants* quickly replaced *trousers* in American speech and its diminutive form, *panties*, was used to describe women's underwear. In Britain, however, *pants* refers to men's underwear and is not a synonym for *trousers*.

paparazzi. This word is usually encountered in the plural, like the swarms of free-lance, celebrity-chasing photographers that it describes. Few people know that the Italian word comes directly from the name of Signore Paparazzo, a photographer in Federico Fellini's film *La Dolce Vita* (1960). The fictional character's name, in turn, came from an Italian dialect word for a particularly noisy, buzzing mosquito. Fellini had known a boy nicknamed Paparazzo (Mosquito) during his school days and the restless boy's fast, buzzing talk and constant movement put the director in mind of the photographer to whom he gave his name.

papaya. The versatile *papaya*, or tree melon, is a staple food in many parts of the world, and its enzyme *papain* aids in the digestion of food, one reason why its leaves are used as a meat tenderizer in some countries and the fruit is the basis for commercial tenderizers. Indians of Central America gorge themselves with *pawpaw* so that they can eat large quantities of food at their feasts without becoming ill. The word *papaya* is a corruption of the Carib Indian *ababai*. In Cuba and some other Spanish-speaking countries the large fruit (it sometimes weighs up to 20 pounds) is called *fruta bomba*, or "bomb fruit." *Papaya* itself has come to be slang for "the female fruit," or breasts, in Cuba, but isn't used in polite conversation.

paper. In ancient times paper was made from the pith and stem of the Egyptian papyrus plant soaked in water and pressed into sheets. The Latin *papyrus*, for the plant, came to mean paper and passed into French as *papier*, which gave us the English word *paper*.

paper bleeds little. A rare but useful Spanish proverb that speaks of the difference between written plans, especially military plans, and the consequences of carrying them out in reality. Hemingway used it in *For Whom the Bell Tolls* (1940): " 'Paper bleeds little,' Robert Jordan quoted the proverb."

paper chase. Thanks to a film and television series about the trials of Harvard Law School, *the paper chase* has since the late 1970s had currency as a synonym for the hectic, often self-defeating chase after good grades in school as a means for advancement in life. The phrase apparently derives from the ancient game of hares and hounds, also called the paper chase, in which some players (hares) start off in advance on a long run scattering pieces of paper called "the scent" behind them, with the other players (hounds) following the trail and trying to catch the hares before they reach a designated place.

paper tiger. Someone who appears much more ferocious and formidable than he or she is. The term was invented by communist Chinese leader Mao Tse-tung (1893–1976), who used it to describe the U.S. Mao is also remembered for the

Mao jacket, a plain, high-collared, shirtless jacket customarily worn by him and the many Chinese who emulated him.

papist.   Usually a hostile or opprobrious term, *papist* means an adherent of the pope, one who advocates papal supremacy; or, simply, a member of the Roman Catholic church. Appropriately enough, Martin Luther coined the word from the Latin *papa*, "pope," also coining the obsolete variants *papastres*, *papanos*, and *papenses*. Luther also invented the term *Romanist*, for a Roman Catholic. The words came from German into English, unchanged, in the early 16th century. *See* LUTHERAN.

papoose.   An Algonquian word for a child or baby that was used by colonists as early as 1633, long before the West was settled.

Pap test.   This simple test can detect cancer of the womb in its early stages, enabling it to be treated before it is too late. Best known as the *Pap test*, although the more accurate *Papanicolaou's stain* and *Pap smear* are also used, the procedure involves no more than the insertion of a small wooden spatula into the vagina to remove fluid mixed with uterine cells. This fluid is then dyed, spread on a glass slide and examined under the microscope. Few people know that Greek-born American physician George Nicholas Papanicolaou (1883–1962) invented the Pap test, his rather difficult name corrupted to the shortened form and obscuring the fame he so richly deserves. Pap smears can be taken of respiratory, digestive, and genitourinary secretions, too.

par.   *See* UP TO PAR.

Paracelsus.   A nervy name change. The Swiss physician and chemist Theophrastus Bombastus von Hohenhein (1493?–1541) believed that his work and learning were far superior to that of the first-century Greek physician Celsus. So much so, in fact, that he changed his name to Paracelsus, from Greek *para*, "beyond," and the name Celsus, making himself "beyond Celsus." His full new name was Philippus Aurealus Paracelsus. Famous in his day, he introduced opium, arsenic, mercury, and other early medicines, though his egotism and hot temper made him the enemy of many learned men of his time.

paradise.   The extensive parks and pleasure gardens of the Persian kings were the first *paradises*, for the word comes to us from the Greek *paradeisos*, meaning "park," "orchard," or "pleasure gardens," which the Greeks borrowed from a similar Persian word. Such gardens, and the word for them, were known more than 3,000 years ago in the Near East, where they were such prized retreats that they took on religious significance. The Septuagint translators of the Bible adopted the word as a name for the Garden of Eden, and later it was used by early Christian writers to mean heaven itself. *See also* GARDEN OF EDEN.

paradise shoots.   Legend has it that paradise shoots (genus *Burera*) is the only plant left from the Garden of Eden. When Adam left Paradise he took a shoot of this tree with him and it has since been prized for the pleasant aroma of its wood. It is also called the East Indian aloe tree and the legin aloes.

paraphernalia.   *Paraphernalia*, which comes from the Greek *para*, beside, and *pherne*, dowry, originally meant all that a woman could claim (beyond or besides her dowry) at the death of her husband. Since this included her jewelry, clothes, etc., the word came to mean personal belongings, and then equipment or furnishings used for a particular activity.

parasite.   In ancient Greece a parasite was a person who received free meals at someone's table in exchange for making brilliant conversation, or in any way entertaining and flattering his host; the word, in fact, derived from the Greek *parasitos*, one who eats at another's table, or at another's cost. No one really knows why over the centuries *parasite* took on the meaning of someone who contributed nothing to a relationship, just living off his host without "singing for his supper" or "dining out on a story." It may have had something to do with the flatterer attaching himself to his host like a leech, but by the 16th century we find the word used to describe "smelle-feastes" who feed themselves free at other people's tables. Today when a relationship is mutually beneficial, it is called *symbiotic* (Greek *sym*, "together" + *bios*, "life").

parchment.   Parchment, "animal skins prepared for writing," is said to have been developed at the great ancient library in Pergamum, Asia Minor, when Ptolemy, a rival book collector, refused to export Egyptian papyrus to Pergamum. The Romans called the writing material *pergamena charta*, "paper of Pergamum," which became the French *parchemin*, this yielding the English *parchment* in the early 14th century.

pardon my French.   This very common expression, usually prefacing a "bad" or "dirty" word, seems to have been invented a century ago by the British. It conveys the absurd idea that there are no "bad" or "dirty" words in English.

parentheses.   First recorded in 1568, *parenthesis* comes from a similar Latin word meaning the same. A parenthesis is a word, phrase, or clause inserted in a sentence that is grammatically complete without the insertion. The device goes back to at least the 16th century, when the parentheses, or "upright curves" themselves (the marks enclosing these words), were sometimes called "halfe circles" and "round brackets." Parenthetical remarks, however, can be made between dashes and commas as well as within parentheses. Mark Twain had the last word on parentheses. "Parentheses in literature and dentistry are in bad taste," he wrote, comparing parenthetical expressions "to dentists who grab a tooth and launch into a tedious anecdote before giving the painful jerk."

par for the course.   *Par* is an American golfing term dating back to 1898 and deriving from the Latin *par*, "equal." It means the score an expert is expected to make on a hole or course, playing in ordinary weather without errors. The expression *par for the course*, meaning just about normal or what one might have expected, owes its life to the golfing term and dates back to about 1920.

pariah.   The Indian class called the Paraiyar in Tamil are not outcasts at all. The Paraiyars were forced into menial positions with the Aryan invasion some 2,000 years before Christ and now form one of the lower castes in southern India, but, although they are regarded as "untouchables" by the Brahmins, they are not the lowest Hindu caste. Their name derives from *parai*, "a large drum," for their duty was to beat the drum at certain religious festivals. Eventually the Paraiyars became field workers in the Tamil country of Madras; however, when the British came to India they employed most of their household servants from that class, whose name they corrupted to *Pariah*. Believing that they were the lowest caste or had no caste at all, many British and other Europeans began to use *pariah* for the lowest of the low, an utter social outcast among his own kind—unjustly degrading the Paraiyars in language just as their countrymen degraded them in life.

Paris. The French still use the names *Lutetia* and *Lutece* for Paris, and though the words are considered poetic today, they actually serve to remind us that the beautiful city was once little more than a swamp. For *Paris* is simply a shortening of the Latin *Lutetia Parisianorum*, meaning "mud flats of the Parisi tribe," the longer name not dropped until after the Roman occupation.

parka. Another of the several words in English that derive from an Eskimo language. The parka, a long, warm jacket with a hood, takes its name from the Aleutian Eskimo *parka*, an outside garment made of skins; it came into the language in early 19th-century Alaska.

parking meter. This expression became common only after July 16, 1935, when the world's first parking meter was installed in Oklahoma City, Oklahoma. However, two Oklahoma State University professors developed the first Park-O-Meter in 1933 and it had been suggested by journalist Carl C. Magee a year or so before that. Park-O-Meter No. 1 is now on display in the Oklahoma Historical Society. It originally cost five cents for one hour's use and the first person to be arrested for a meter violation was a minister.

Parkinson's Law. Parkinson's Law (1957), formulated by and named after C. Northcote Parkinson, distinguished British author and scholar, puts down succinctly what employers have known for generations: "Work expands to fill the time allotted to it, or, conversely, the amount of work completed is in inverse proportion to the number of people employed."

parlay. *Parlay* is an Americanism first recorded in 1828, but probably used before then, that means to wager money on a horse race, cards or other sports event, and continue to bet the original stake plus all winnings on the next race, hand, or the like. The word derives from the Italian *paro*, meaning equal. It has since been extended to mean to use one's money, talent, or other assets to achieve a desired objective, such as spectacular wealth or success: "He parlayed his small inheritance into a great fortune."

Parliament. The British Parliament, where so many debates are heard, takes its name from the French *parler*, "to talk." In fact, the word came into Middle English as *parlement*. A *Parlement* under the old régime in France was the sovereign court of justice, a kind of Supreme Court that had some administrative powers.

parliamentary language. Language that is restrained, like the language generally heard in the British Parliament; a civil and courteous way of speaking or arguing. *Parliamentary language* is first recorded in 1818 and *unparliamentary language* probably made its appearance shortly afterward.

parlor. From the French *parler*, "to talk", "to converse." The parlor was traditionally the room in which general conversation took place. Such reception rooms were originally found in monasteries, where talking might be forbidden elsewhere on the premises.

Parmesan cheese. *Parmesan* is simply English for the Italian word *Parmigiano*, of Parma, and thus the latter word should be the name of the hard, often grated cheese. Parmigiano was once made mostly from milk from the old Italian duchy of Parma.

Parnassus; to climb Parnassus. The 8,000-foot-high Greek mountain Parnassos, called Parnassus by the Romans, had one of its summits consecrated to Apollo, the god of music, and thus the mountain near Delphi became associated with poetry and music in particular, and literature in general; all literary effort was connected with Parnassus—some in the foothills, some at the summit. *To climb Parnassus* means "to write poetry."

parrot. Parrots (their name believed to derive somehow from the French proper name *Perrot*, a diminutive of *Pierre*) reproduce human sounds with great accuracy and have been known to have "vocabularies" of over 100 words, but they of course speak by imitation, without understanding. Parrots have been called Pollys since the early 17th century, when Ben Jonson first recorded the word. Myna birds (from the Hindi *maina*) mimic human speech more precisely than parrots but have smaller vocabularies. *See* CHIMPANZEE; DOLPHIN.

parsley. "Parsley grows for the wicked, but not for the just," according to an old English proverb. Parsley takes its name ultimately from the Greek *petroselinon* for the herb. This member of the celery family began earning its shady reputation even before the Romans, who wore curly-leaved parsley garlands in their hair not only because they were attractive but because they believed that nibbling on parsley sprigs enabled one to drink more wine without becoming drunk. The Greeks crowned winning athletes with parsley at their Nemean and Isthmian games, and used the herb as a flavoring. The Romans fed it to their horses on the theory that it made them swift. The plant is described by Seneca, who notes that the tempting sorceress Medea gathered parsley and other forbidden herbs by moonlight.

parsnip. *Parsnip* derives from the Latin words *pastinare*, "to dig or trench the ground," and *napus*, "turnip," in reference to the fact that it was thought to be a kind of turnip that the ground had to be trenched for (so that it would grow straight). Incidentally, the Russian word for parsnip is *pasternak*, so the Nobel Prize–winning Russian poet's name translates as Boris Parsnip!

Parson Brown orange. *See* ORANGE.

parson's nose.   The walnut-size protuberance on the end of a turkey or other fowl that is actually the bird's tail (minus the feathers) and is also jocularly called "the part that went over the fence last."

Parsons table.   No old parson or any other clergyman invented the durable, easy-to-make Parsons table. It was an innovation of Manhattan's Parsons School of Design in the early 1930s.

Parthenon.   *See* PORNOGRAPHY.

Parthian shot; Parthian arrow, etc.   *See* PARTING SHOT.

parting shot.   The Parthian soldiers of antiquity were famed as deadly mounted archers. These mail-clad horsemen would ride furiously to the attack, pour a shower of arrows on their enemies and then evade any closer action by rapid flight, withdrawing according to plan and firing their shafts backwards from their horses while galloping away. Such tactics made Parthia, located in what is now northwest Iran, a world power that even defeated the Romans under Mark Antony when he attempted to invade their country in 36 B.C. *Parthian glance,* for a very keen backward glance, became proverbial, as did *Parthian arrow* or *shaft* or *shot,* the last by extension giving us the expression *parting shot.* Thus when you get in the last word in an argument, a *parting shot,* you are shooting a Parthian arrow.
See SAW.

partridge; partridge, always partridge.   Trace the roots of the word *partridge* back to the Greek *perdika,* "a partridge," and you'll find one of the oddest and most expurgated of bird name derivations. For the source for *perdika* is probably *perdesthai,* "to fart," the Greeks most likely naming the game bird for the sound the whirring wings of the rising bird made, which they thought resembled the breaking of wind. *Partridge, always partridge (perdrix, toujours perdrix)* means "too much of the same thing." It's said that the confessor of a French king admonished him for infidelity, and the king asked him what his favorite dish was. "Partridge," the priest said, and the king ordered him to eat only partridge every day. "How were your meals?" the king asked after a few weeks, and the priest replied, "Very good, but partridge, always partridge." "Ah, yes," said the amorous king, "and one wife is all very well, but not 'partridge, always partridge!' " Of the late brilliant lexicographer and etymologist Eric Partridge, an especially indefatigable worker who took on jobs few others would consider tackling, it was once said, "Partridge is always game." *See* SAW.

parts of speech.   An old anonymous poem nicely defines these:

> Three little words you often see
> Are ARTICLES, a, an and the.
> A NOUN'S the name of anything;
> As school or garden, hoop or swing.
> ADJECTIVES tell the kind of noun;
> As great, small, pretty, white, or brown.
> Instead of nouns the PRONOUNS stand;
> Her face, his face, our arms, your hand.
> VERBS tell of something being done;

> To read, count, sing, laugh, jump or run.
> How things are done the ADVERBS tell;
> As slowly, quickly, ill or well.
> CONJUNCTIONS join the words together;
> As men and women, wind or weather;
> The PREPOSITION stands before
> A noun, as in or through a door.
> The INTERJECTION shows surprise;
> As oh! how pretty! ah! how wise!
> The whole are called nine parts of speech,
> Which reading, writing, speaking teach.

part that went over the fence last.   *See* PARSON'S NOSE.

party crasher.   *See* CRASH.

party line.   *See* SPOILS SYSTEM.

party machinery.   *See* SPOILS SYSTEM.

pasquinade.   The first *pasquinades,* witty lampoons or satires, especially those posted in a public place, were hung upon an ancient statue unearthed in Rome in 1501 and reerected near the Piazza Navona by Cardinal Caraffa. The mutilated old statue, possibly a likeness of Ajax, Menelaus, or some unknown gladiator, was dubbed Pasquino—either because that had been the name of the Roman gladiator represented or more probably because it stood opposite quarters where a sharp-witted, scandal-loving old man named Pasquino had lived. Pasquino, variously described as a barber, tailor, cobbler, and schoolteacher, had died some years previously. But it became customary on St. Mark's Day to salute and mockingly ask advice from the statue named for the caustic old man, such requests being posted on the statue after a while. These written Latin verses soon took the form of barbed political, religious, and personal satires, often upon the Pope, which were called *pasquinate;* a book of such squibs was published in 1509.

passel.   *Parcel* has been pronounced "passel," without the *r,* since at least the late 15th century. But the use of *passel* as a collective noun indicating an indefinite number dates back to 19th-century America. Wrote Mark Twain in *Adventures of Huckleberry Finn* (1884): "[They] just kept a-smiling and bobbing their heads like a passel of sapheads."

passenger.   Originally *passenger* referred only to a passenger on a ship, deriving from the Old French *passager,* meaning the same, which came from the Latin *passare,* right of passage aboard a ship. The term came ashore in about the 14th century.

passion flower.   The passion flower was so named in medieval Spain because its parts are said to resemble Christ's instruments of passion, its corona being the crown of thorns, the five sepals and five petals representing the ten apostles (Peter and Judas not counted), etc. A list of these similarities follows:

Leaf—symbolizes the spear
Five anthers—the five wounds
Tendrils—the whips
Column of the ovary—pillar of the cross
Stamens—hammers
Three styles—three nails

Fleshy threads within flowers—crown of thorns
Calyx—the glory or nimbus
White tint—purity
Blue tint—heaven

passion for anonymity.   Not a man who liked to be upstaged by his staff, Franklin D. Roosevelt announced midway through his first term in office that he was going to appoint several new assistants "with a passion for anonymity." Possibly he was weary of all the newspaper coverage given his "brain trust." Anyway, he did manage to appoint several assistants so self-effacing that nobody remembers them today—and contributed a new phrase to the language as well.

passion gap.   Some South Africans swear by the "passion gap," the gap in the gums left when the four top middle teeth are missing. Believing this love gap, an alternative term, increases the erotic appeal of a kiss, they often have these teeth pulled by dentists.

passion killers.   During World War II, the British Wrens (Women's Royal Navy Service) were issued long, plain, unstylish black knickers (underwear) that they or other interested parties promptly dubbed "passion killers," at least getting even with the powers-that-were by way of the King's English. *See* WRENS.

passion play.   The world's longest-running play, an entirely amateur production, has been playing for more than three centuries, longer than any modern-day professional play. The record holder is the Oberammergau Passion Play, portraying Christ's last days, his suffering and death in Jerusalem. In 1633, the villagers of Oberammergau, in Germany's Bavarian Alps, vowed that if God would spare them from the terrible plague raging through Europe, they would enact Christ's last days on Earth every 10 years "until the end of time." Since then the Oberammergau Passion Play, performed 38 times out of its 354-year history, has become synonymous with *passion play* itself. More than half a million people visit Oberammergau every year the passion play is presented, watching from hard seats in a 5,200-seat theater whose stage is out in the open against an Alpine backdrop. Twice as many usually have to be turned away.

pass the buck.   *See* BUCK.

pass under the yoke.   After the Romans defeated an enemy they constructed a yoke of three long spears—two upright and one resting horizontally on them—making each vanquished soldier lay down his arms and pass under this archway. From this practice comes the expression *to pass under the yoke*, "to suffer a humility, or defeat, to be disgraced."

pasta.   There are some 500 Italian words describing various types of pasta. *Pasta* is simply Italian for dough and can be anything from CAPPELLETTI to ZITI. *See* SPAGHETTI.

pasta fazool.   There is no such Italian dish—not spelled this way. *Pasta fazool* is the Neapolitan-American pronunciation of *pasta e fagioli*, a soup containing beans (*fagioli*), other vegetables, and little *ditalini* pasta.

pasteboards.   *See* DEVIL'S PICTURE BOOK.

pastern.   This is the noted word that Dr. Johnson defined as the knee of a horse in his great dictionary. When a lady asked him why, he replied, "Ignorance, madam, sheer ignorance." *Pastern* actually means the part of a horse's foot between the fetlock and the hoof.

pasteurize.   We remember Louis Pasteur for the germ-free pasteurized milk that we drink in safety today, but we often forget that his well-known discovery arose out of experiments with France's national beverage—wine. In the 1850s the immortal French chemist first discovered that certain bacteria caused rapid "artificial" fermentation of wine, then that fermentation could be prevented if the wine was exposed to high temperatures—which led to the method whereby milk and other foods could be sterilized by heating and rapid cooling. A mediocre student in chemistry, just as Einstein was in math, Pasteur made many brilliant discoveries in his field. This compulsive worker—"I would feel that I had been stealing if I were to spend a single day without working"—proved that the spontaneous generation theory of disease was a myth, his most revolutionary scientific contribution. The Pasteur treatment honors his cure for rabies, which has reduced the death rate from hydrophobia to less than 1 percent.

Patagonian.   *Patagonian* generally refers to "a native of Patagonia," but the word was in frequent literary use to mean a gigantic specimen, a great soul, an immense figure in a field, up until the beginning of the 20th century. It is still effectively used that way today. Patagonia is a regional name applied to extreme southern South America, specifically the area south of the Colorado River in Argentina, which, incidentally, includes part of the Argentinian province Eva Perón (once La Pampa), named for the wife of the former dictator. The original inhabitants, now virtually extinct, were the Tehuelches, whom the Spanish called the Patagonian giants when they attempted settlements in southern South America in the 16th century. Early travelers had described these natives as being almost giants and they were named Patagonians from the Spanish *patagon*, "a large, clumsy foot."

pater.   Few, if any, of us have ever heard the word *pater* used for father, except in old movies about Britain over a century ago. *Pater* is Latin for father, used in English as early as the 14th century but heard only humorously today.

paternoster.   *See* PATTER.

pathfinder.   A person who makes a path for others to follow, one who finds a way. The word derives from the name of a fictional character created by American novelist James Fenimore Cooper, not the other way around. *Pathfinder* is the name Cooper coined for his colorful character Natty Bumppo in his novel *The Pathfinder* (1840), because of Bumppo's skill in finding his way through the wilderness. Before long the word was being used generally.

pathos; bathos.   *Pathos*, which derives directly from the Greek word for suffering, is the quality or power in any of the arts to evoke feelings of tender pity, compassion, or sadness, and gives us characters in literature like Ophelia in *Hamlet* or even Dickens's Little Nell. *Bathos* means quite the opposite and was coined by Alexander Pope from the Greek word *bathos*, "depth" (not related to our English word "bath"), to indicate a descent from the sublime to the depths of the ridiculous. Pope and other writers of the early 18th century, including Swift, Gay, and Arbuthnot, made a sport of parodying contemporary writers. Out of this game of wits came Pope's satire "Bathos, the Art of Sinking in Poetry" (1727), in which he invented the word because no similar one existed in English to express the idea.

paths of glory.   The antiwar film *Paths of Glory* (1957) has been named by the National Film Registry, administered by the Library of Congress, as one of the 200 or so films up to this date to be preserved in the National Library because of its "historical, cultural and aesthetic significance." The film's title, as well as the commonly used phrase, comes from a line in British poet Thomas Gray's "Elegy Written in a Country Churchyard" (1750): "The paths of glory lead but to the grave." Another line reads "Forbade to wade through slaughter to a throne." *See* FAR FROM THE MADDING CROWD.

patience of Job.   *See* JOB'S COMFORTER.

patio.   An open inner court or garden; the word, borrowed from the Spanish, was first used in California and the Southwest before becoming popular throughout the U.S.

patrol.   Infantrymen do a lot of slogging through the mud. French soldiers in the 17th century were no exception, as their slang word *patrouiller*, to paddle with the feet in the mud, clearly shows. The word was so commonly used that it came to mean "to pass around or through a specified area in order to maintain order and security."

patsy.   *Patsy*, American slang for a dupe or sucker since at least 1909, may derive from the Italian *pazzo*, "foolish or crazy," brought to America by Italian immigrants. *Pazzo*, in turn, could derive from the Italian expression *uno dei pazzi*, "one of the fools or crazies," which may come from the name of the much ridiculed Pazzi family of 15th-century Florence, who were foolish enough to oppose the powerful Medici and were slaughtered.

patter; paternoster.   Fast talk, often a salesman's or con man's spiel, is called *patter* after *paternoster*, the Lord's Prayer, so named from its first two words (*Pater Noster*, "Our Father") in Latin. When saying the Paternoster, priests recited it rapidly at the start of the prayer, giving us this synonym for rapid talk as early as the 14th century.

patza.   A casual, amateurish chess player, often one who plays chess in parks and other public places. The word, which has only been traced back to about 1955, derives ultimately from German *patzer*, "bungler."

Paul Bunyan.   A legendary giant lumberjack in many folk tales, an American folk hero of the Pacific Northwest. Originally, the tales described a French Canadian, Bon Jean. Among the prodigious feats credited to Paul Bunyan are the creation of the Grand Canyon, and the invention of the double-bitted ax. When his crews and his huge blue ox Babe logged winters on the Big Onion River it was "so cold that cuss words froze in the air, thawing out the next Fourth of July with a din." *See* SOCK SAUNDERS.

Paul Jones dance.   A popular square dance featuring promenades and numerous changes of partners that was named for American naval hero John Paul Jones during the Revolutionary War, one of the few honors awarded his name at the time.

Paul Pry.   A meddling idler with no business of his own except everybody else's is called a *Paul Pry*, after the character of that name in British playwright John Pool's comedy *Paul Pry* (1825).

Pavlovian response.   Another name for a conditioned reflex. Russian scientist Ivan Petrovich Pavlov (1849–1936) made the term famous with his experiments with dogs showing that their saliva can be stimulated not just by food, but by the sound of a bell that the dogs were conditioned to hearing before being served the food. Pavlov won the Nobel Prize in 1904, the first Russian to do so, but the award was given for his work on the nature of digestion. Today *Pavlovian response* or *reaction* generally means any response made without thinking, a knee-jerk reaction, one strongly influenced by others.

pawnbroker.   Long before their common name was coined in medieval days, pawnbrokers operated under the familiar three golden balls still hanging over many of their shops. It was the Medici family who contributed the symbol of their profession, for Charlemagne made this the family coat of arms long before the Medici family became moneylenders, as a reward to one of their forebears for using a weapon made of three golden balls to kill a fearsome giant who attacked him. *Pawnbroker* itself has a more prosaic origin, deriving from *pawn*, "a pledge," and *broker*, "agent," and was first recorded in 1678.

Pawn, Oregon.   *See* PAKISTAN.

payador.   *See* GAUCHO.

paydirt.   One authority traces this expression to the Chinese *pei* (to give) used by Chinese miners in California, *pay dirt* thus meaning "dirt that gives gold." However, it more likely derives from the fact that it is dirt containing enough gold dust to pay for working it. The expression is first recorded in 1856.

payoff.   *See* HIGH HAT.

payola.   Entering the American lexicon in 1960, when it was found that disc jockeys in New York, Chicago, and other cities accepted payments from record companies in return for airing their records, the coinage *payola* is a contraction of *pay* and Victro*la*. The word came into the news again in 1974 and 1985 with similar scandals in the record business, but *payola* is also used to mean bribes paid to anyone.

pay on the nail.   In medieval times a *nail* was a short pillar used as a counter in marketplaces. Accounts were settled at these nails, all money placed on them so that payment was quick and out in the open. This practice led to the expression *to pay on the nail*, for "prompt payment." *See* CASH ON THE BARRELHEAD.

pay the fiddler. This is an American expression that apparently arose in the early 19th century, based on the old English expression "to pay the piper," which dates back to 1681: "After all this Dance he has led the Nation, he must at least come to pay the Piper himself"—Thomas Flatman, *Heraclitus ridens.*

pay through the nose. Gamblers in the 17th century coined the expression *to bleed* a victim. "They will purposely lose some small sum at first, that they may engage him more freely to bleed as they call it," a contemporary writer on cardplaying noted. He also observed that these same gamblers would "always fix half a score packs of cards" beforehand whenever they intended to bleed a dupe. Once the "coll" had *paid through the nose*, lost all his blood through the nose, he was "bled white," weak and helpless, until he had nothing left to lose. These last expressions arose later but they clearly derive from the gambling term, which was used to describe extortion or blackmail at about the same time. The bloodletting that physicians and barbers commonly used to treat so many diverse illnesses certainly suggested the expression to the gamblers. Bleeding patients not only made them pale, weak, and helpless but often killed them, as it did Lord Byron.

PB & J; peanut butter; jelly. PB & J is recent shorthand, written and verbal, for a peanut butter and jelly sandwich. *Peanut butter* itself is first recorded in about 1890 as the health food invention of a St. Louis dentist, while the word *jelly* dates back to the 14th century. *See* PEANUT.

P.D.Q. *P.D.Q.* stands for "pretty damn quick," as in "you'd better get started P.D.Q." Its origin hasn't been established beyond doubt, though it has been attributed to Dan Maguinnis, a Boston comedian appearing about 1867–89.

pea. The word *pea* comes indirectly from the Latin *pisum*, "pea"; the early English singular for pea was *pease*, hence the old rhyme "pease-porridge hot, / Pease-porridge cold, / Pease-porridge in the pot, / Nine days old." Quite a mania for peas existed in 17th-century France. Madame de Maintenon, Louis XIV's mistress, called it "both a fashion and a madness," and it was at this time that the celebrated *petits pois à la française* was invented. Incidentally, it was quite proper at the time to lick green peas from their shells after dropping the whole pod in a sauce, so eating peas off a knife isn't so bad after all. Chinese sugar or snow peas, eaten pod and all, are sometimes properly called *mangetout* ("eat all"). *Till the last pea's out of the dish* is a southern Americanism meaning "till the end," or "a long time." Red Barber popularized the southern expression *tearing up the pea patch* for "going on a rampage" when he broadcast Brooklyn Dodger baseball games from 1945 to 1955, using it often to describe fights on the field between players. Barber came from the South, where the expression is an old one, referring to the prized patch of black-eyed peas, which stray animals sometimes ruined. "English peas" is a term used in the South for green peas to distinguish them from the black-eyed or brown-eyed varieties. *See* BLACKED-EYED PEAS.

peabody bird; peverly bird. This little sparrow is said to sound like it's singing, "Old Sam Peabody, Peabody, Peabody," hence *peabody bird*. As for *peverly bird*, an old story has it that a Mr. Peverly, a New England farmer, was walking in the fields one early spring day trying to decide whether he should plant his wheat yet. A little sparrow in the adjacent woods seemed to sing, "Sow wheat, Peverly, Peverly, Peverly!" so Mr. Peverly went ahead and did so, reaping an abundant harvest that fall. Ever after the little sparrow was called the *peverly bird*.

peace at any price. When British Quaker statesman John Bright (1811–89) opposed the Crimean War he was contemptuously called a *peace-at-any-price man* by Lord Palmerston. He resigned from public life in 1882 when British warships bombarded Egypt.

Peace Corps. A government organization formed in 1961 during the Kennedy administration under the Peace Corps Act. Initially about a thousand volunteers were chosen to teach their skills in 15 foreign countries, living like the people they help. Today Peace Corps volunteers work in about 100 countries.

peaceful coexistence. Lenin apparently coined the term *peaceful cohabitation* in February 1920, when he referred to "peaceful cohabitation with the workers and peasants of all nations." Two years later a resolution of the Ninth All-Russian Congress of Soviets used the term "peaceful and friendly coexistence [*sosushchestvovaniye*]" between nations. Unfortunately, the term has always been more a propaganda slogan than a sincere policy of any state.

peace in our time. British prime minister Neville Chamberlain used this expression after his return from Munich on September 30, 1938, after he had caved in to Hitler. He believed that his actions had averted war, but the Nazis saw them as a sign of weakness, war ensued, and Chamberlain's words became a symbol of the worst kind of appeasement.

Peacemaker. Swedish engineer John Ericsson was responsible for the first screw propeller warship, the *Princeton*, which embodied his ideas when built at the Philadelphia Navy Yard in 1843. A year later, another of Ericsson's ideas was incorporated in a big gun for the *Princeton*. It was called the Peacemaker, and its breech was strengthened with wrought iron. However, the Peacemaker, unlike the screw propeller, became one of the most famous guns in U.S. naval history because it was a failure. In February 1844 President John Tyler and some 200 prominent guests took a cruise down the Potomac aboard the *Princeton* to witness the highly touted gun being tested. When it was fired, the *Princeton* exploded its breech, killing the secretary of state, the secretary of the navy, and three others. President Tyler escaped only because he was dining below decks with his fiancée.

the peacemaker. This was the nickname of one of the most famous weapons in American history, the Colt Revolver Model 1873, the name being adopted because it helped lawmen keep the peace in the American West. As an extra benefit, its .44 ammunition could be used in the 1873 Winchester rifle.

peace with honor. The great British statesman Lord Beaconsfield (Disraeli) made this phrase popular in a speech he gave after returning from the Congress of Berlin in 1878, which Bismarck chaired as "the honest broker" (his own phrase). Said Disraeli: "Lord Salisbury [the foreign minister] and myself have brought you back peace—but a peace I hope with honour, which may satisfy our Sovereign and tend to the welfare of the country." Similar words, however, had been used by Shakespeare in *Coriolanus* almost 300 years earlier.

peach. Peaches were the "Persian apples" of the ancient Romans. Their name, *Persicum*, became *pessica* in Late Latin, *pêche* in French, and finally came into English as *peach*. The fruit, luscious to look at, touch, and taste, has described a pretty young girl at least since the ancient Chinese used it as slang for a young bride centuries ago. But the Chinese, and the Arabs, too, also regarded the peach's deep fur-edged cleft as a symbol of the female genitalia and used *peach* in a number of slang expressions referring to sexual love, such as *sharing the peach*, a euphemism for sodomy. In Europe the French have used their word *pêche* in similar sexual expressions and *a peach house* was once common in English slang as a house of prostitutes. "Venus owns this tree . . . the fruit provokes lust," English herbalist Nicholas Culpeper wrote in 1652 and language reflects that people around the world shared his opinion. The *Elberta peach*, the most widely sold of American peaches, was probably imported from Shanghai in 1850, but more than one source records a story that shows more imagination. According to this tale, Samuel Rumph of Marshallville, Georgia, received peachtree buddings from a friend in Delaware, planted them, and eventually harvested a good crop. His wife, Elberta, accidentally dropped a few pits from these peaches in her sewing basket and when their grandson wanted to start an orchard 10 years later, she dug them out and asked her husband to plant them. By 1870 trees from the pits were flourishing, and by an accidental cross-pollination a new golden variety resulted, which Rumph named for his spouse. Elbertas, however, aren't considered great eating peaches by those who know their peaches.

peach melba. *See* MELBA TOAST.

peach on someone. Once common in the jargon of criminals, *to peach on someone* means to inform or "rat" on him. The word is not related to the fruit, deriving instead from an obsolete English word *appeach*, "to accuse." The expression has been used at least since Shakespeare's time.

peacock. Although the word is now used for both male and female of the species, the peacock is strictly speaking the male of the peafowl, distinguished by the long, green iridescent tail that it spreads out like a fan. The name derives ultimately from the Latin *pavo* for the peafowl, plus the Old English *coc*, cock. The male peacock's beauty and bearing led to its name becoming a synonym for a vain, self-conscious person and to the expression *proud as a peacock*. Britain's George III, during one of his attacks of insanity, insisted on ending every sentence in all of his speeches with the word *peacock*. His ministers cured him of this by telling him that peacock was a beautiful word but a royal one that a king should whisper when speaking before his subjects so they couldn't hear it. As a result the speeches of George III were less absurd.

pea jacket. *Pea jacket* did not originally refer to a P.-jacket (an abbreviation of *pilot's jacket*), but derives from Dutch *pijjekker*, a short double-breasted coat very similar to the pea jacket of today, which was worn by Dutch sailors as early as the 15th century.

peanut; peanut gallery. Peanuts take their name from their resemblance to peas in a pod. They go by numerous descriptive aliases, including *monkey nuts* and *ground peas* or *nuts*, but their most common synonym, *goober*, is a corruption of *nguba*, a name plantation slaves gave to the peanut and one of the few African words still retained in English. Peanuts are used in hundreds of products. Peanut butter, for example, is an easily-digested, high-protein food that nutritionists say provides an adequate survival diet when combined with a citrus fruit like oranges. Four out of five American homes are said to stock a jar of it in the pantry. Americans aren't as partial to peanut butter soup, or to the dish called Young Monkey Stuffed with Peanuts invented by futurist chef Jules Maincave during World War I. The peanut gallery, usually the cheapest seats in the house, was the gallery, or "second balcony," high up in Gay Nineties theaters, so high up that the crowd seated there were sometimes called the gallery gods. Peanuts were the movie snack of the day and the occupants of these cheap seats often rained peanut shells on performers who displeased them. *See* PB&J.

Peanuts, Cracker Jack! Vendors have been crying "Peanuts, Cracker Jack!" in ballparks (and at circuses and carnivals) at least since the early 1900s. Cracker Jack, now a trademark of the Borden Co., was first sold, under another name, in 1893. The cry is often heard as "Peanuts, popcorn, Cracker Jax" [Jacks]!" The words have been inextricably linked with baseball since 1908, when the song "Take Me Out to the Ball Game" was published, its lyrics including the line "Buy me some peanuts and Cracker Jacks; I don't care if I never get back." Over 250 million boxes of Cracker Jacks are sold every year.

pear. One of the earliest cultivated fruits, pears are among the few fruits that ripen better after being picked, and the Chinese often ripened them in rooms filled with incense. The fruit, shaped like a Rubens nude, goes incomparably well with cheese desserts, Rabelais writing that: "There is no match you could compare/To Master Cheese and Mistress Pear." The old French *piere*, derived from the Latin *pirum*, gave us our word *pear*. Of the over 3,000 pear species, the Bartlett is perhaps the best known in America, representing 70 percent of this country's crop. It is a soft, late-ripening European-type, as opposed to earlier hard varieties like the Seckel, which is named for the Philadelphia farmer who first grew it, during the Revolution. The Bartlett wasn't, in fact, developed by Dorchester, Massachusetts merchant Enoch Bartlett, as is generally believed. Bartlett only promoted the fruit after Captain Thomas Brewer imported the trees from England and grew them in his Roxbury farm. The enterprising Yankee eventually purchased Brewer's farm and distributed the pears under his own name in the early 1800s. They had long been known in Europe as Williams, or William Bon Chrétien pears.

pease porridge. *See* PEA.

pea souper; pea soup fog. These terms originated in England toward the end of the 19th century. They describe a dense, yellowish fog or any very thick fog through which a fisherman can barely see the end of his outstretched arm.

peat. The word *peat* was first applied to the small bits of this substance used as fuel in peat fires. Keeping this in mind, it is easy to see the derivation of *peat*, from the English *piece*, which may come from the Latin *pecia*, "a bit." Peat, of course, is an organic material found in marshy ground, composed of partially decayed vegetable matter and is much used by gardeners in improving garden soil.

peckerwood. A poor Southern white (though its earliest meaning was "a redheaded woodpecker"). The derogatory term is often used in a joking way today.

pecking order. The famous study made by biologist W. C. Allee in the 1920s establishes that the pecking order among hens has a definite prestige pattern: hens, like many humans, freely peck at other hens below their rank and submit to pecking from those above them. Hens rarely peck at roosters in the barnyard, where the rooster is cock of the walk, but it was widely believed in the 17th century that they often pulled feathers from roosters below them in the pecking order. *See* HENPECKED.

Pecksniff. An arch hypocrite who cants moral homilies even while acting immorally, any *Pecksniff* takes his name from Mr. Pecksniff, the hypocritical architect in Charles Dickens's *Martin Chuzzlewitt* (1843–44). *See* GAMP.

Pecos Bill. A legendary folk hero of the Southwest, whose range-riding cowboy exploits rival the exploits of Paul Bunyan in the Northwest lumber camps.

pecuniary. *Pecu* is the Latin for cattle, and since cattle were once a common means of barter, the ancients often expressed an estate's value in terms of the number of cattle it was valued at, which gave them the word *pecunia*, for "money or property." *Pecunia*, in turn gave birth to numerous English words, such as *pecuniary*, "pertaining to money"; *impecunious*, "without money"; *peculate*, "to embezzle"; and *peculiar*, "pertaining to that which is one's own," that is, one's own cattle.

peddler. *Peddler* derives from the Old English *ped*, "a pack in which articles were stored to be hawked about the streets." In early America *Yankee peddlers* generally had a bad name, being "proverbial for their dishonesty," according to one early observer, and Northerners probably got the name *damn Yankee*, coined long before the Civil War, from Yankee peddlers who worked the rural South. There are nevertheless many notable exceptions. Among famous Americans who started as peddlers are Parson Weems, the biographer of Washington; Stephen Girard, the Philadelphia banker who helped America finance the War of 1812; Donald Alexander Smith, the Canadian fur trader who later headed the giant Hudson's Bay Company; William Rockefeller, John D.'s father; Abraham Lincoln's father; Bronson Alcott, father of Louisa May; and inventors John Fitch and Thomas Edison. Department stores vehemently oppose peddling today, but, ironically, at least 15 great department stores were started by former peddlers, including Gimbel's, Rich's, Saks, and Goldwaters. *See* YANKEE; EMPORIUM.

pedigree. A wavering three-line symbol used by medieval genealogists in denoting the line of descent of families they were tracing was thought by some observant scholar to resemble the imprint of the bony foot of a crane. In French, the court language in many kingdoms, "foot of the crane" was *pied de grue*, which came to be both the name for the genealogical symbol and the name for the line or genealogical table itself. Introduced into English in the 15th century, *pied de grue* became through distorted spelling *pee de grew*, *petiegrew*, and *peti degree*, among many other versions, before settling down here as *pedigree*.

peekaboo wave. Movie star Veronica Lake's famous "peekaboo wave," her hair partially covering one side of her face, was possibly the best-known hairstyle of the early 1940s. However, the peekaboo caused trouble when America went to war and women in large numbers began working in defense plants. Serious injuries became common because women often caught their long hair in the machines they were operating. The U.S. government asked Paramount to help by changing Lake's hairstyle, which the studio was glad to do for the war effort. It hasn't been popular since.

Peekskill. New York's city of Peekskill on the east bank of the Hudson is named for the nearby Peeks Kill Creek, which would strictly be Peeks Creek Creek if translated completely, as *kill* is from the Dutch *kil*, meaning "creek." The word *Peek* in Peeks Kill Creek is from the name of trader Jan Peek, who discovered the creek in 1685.

Peelers. *See* BOBBY.

Peel me a grape. This humorous request or command stems from an early Mae West movie in which the "Screen's Bad Girl" tells her maid (Louise Beavers) to do same: "Peel me a grape, Beulah." There is a 2002 song "Peel Me A Grape," a favorite of sexy singers. *See* MAE WEST.

Peeping Tom. According to a later version of the original story, Lady Godiva had but one admirer when she rode nude through the streets of Coventry. The earlier story has everyone in town feasting their eyes on Godiva, but here the plot thickens. Our later version says that a more cunning Lady Godiva issued a proclamation ordering all persons to stay indoors and shutter their windows, so that she could ride naked through Coventry, Lord Leofric would remit the town's oppressive taxes, and she could remain modest as well. But enter stage left Peeping Tom, the unfortunate town tailor, or butcher. We say "stage left" because Peeping Tom must have lived on the left-hand side of Hertfors Street—assuming that Lady Godiva rode sidesaddle. At any rate, Peeping Tom peeped, ruined Lady Godiva's plan, and was struck blind for his peeping—cruel and unusual punishment for merely being human and living in a strategic location. *See* LADY GODIVA.

peep of dawn. Although *at pype* was recorded in 1530, British poet Thomas Gray coined the term *peep of dawn* in his poem "Elegy Written in a Country Churchyard" (1750). It means the "first appearance of light at dawn," a tiny speck of light. *Peep o'day* is an Irish variation on the term, and the Peep O' Day Boys was an Irish faction of Protestants in the 1780s who raided their opponents' homes at dawn to catch them by surprise. *See* FAR FROM THE MADDING CROWD.

The Peg.   A popular nickname for Winnipeg, the capital of Manitoba, Canada. It is also called *Winterpeg.*

Pelé.   This is the nickname of retired Brazilian soccer star Edson Arantes do Nascimento, who is possibly the world's best-known athlete. In his homeland, Pelé, who was born in 1940, is known as the Black Pearl, *Perola Negra* in Portuguese, which is shortened to Pelé throughout most of the world. A popular Brazilian coffee is among the several things named after the colorful athlete. And on one occasion a daylong truce was declared in a war between Nigeria and Biafra so that everyone could see Pelé play in a scheduled game.

pelican.   The pelican is no woodpecker, but in his famous translation of the Bible, St. Jerome, thinking it pecked wood like a woodpecker, named the bird *pelican,* from the Greek word *pelekys,* or "ax beak." This name stuck, as did many legends about the bird, including one that it resurrected its dead young by feeding them its blood, which Shakespeare alludes to in *King Lear.* Wrote Dixon Lanier Merrith in his poem "The Pelican" (1910): "A wonderful bird is the/pelican/His bill will hold more than his/belican./He can take in his beak/Food enough for a week,/But I'm damned if I see how the/helican."

pelican in the wilderness.   A lonely person, a recluse. The term comes from the Bible: "I am like a pelican of the wilderness, / I am like an owl of the desert. / I watch and am / As a sparrow alone upon the housetop." (Ps. 102:6–7) It is used in the title of a recent book by Isabel Colegate: *A Pelican in the Wilderness: Hermits, Solitaires, and Recluses* (2002).

Pelican State.   A nickname of Louisiana, after the pelicans plentiful on its Gulf Coast and the pelican that appears on the state seal. Louisiana has also been called the Creole State.

pell-mell.   Pall-mall was an early 16th-century British game "wherein a round box ball is struck with a mallet through a high arch of iron, which he that can do it with the fewest blows, or at the number agreed upon, wins." Apparently pall-mall players thrashed about trying to strike the ball and tripping each other up, this resulting in the now obsolete game giving us the word *pell-mell,* meaning "headlong, in reckless confusion."

pemmican.   Dried buffalo meat pounded into a powder and sometimes mixed with berries was the staple winter diet of many Indian tribes in the American West. It was called *pemmican,* from the Konestino Indian words *pemis,* "fat," and *egan,* "substance."

P.E.N.   *P.E.N.* is the acronym for the International Association of Poets, Playwrights, Editors, Essayists, and Novelists, founded in 1921 by Catherine Dawson Scott and John Galsworthy, who set up a trust fund for the organization in 1932 with his Nobel Prize money. The organization was named P.E.N. when someone pointed out at the first meeting that the initial letters of *poet, essayist,* and *novelist* were the same in most European languages and could serve as the appellation.

pencil pusher; pencil-necked.   Both of these are Americanisms. The common *pencil pusher,* usually a contemptuous term for an office worker, is first recorded in 1890. *Pencil-necked* is of very recent origin, and recorded here because I have heard it several times and can find it listed in no dictionary of slang or standard English. *Pencil-necked* is a contemptuous reference to relatively genteel men made by the boisterous and bull-necked. I heard it last from a huge professional wrestler with bulging muscles in his neck who declared that only "pencil-necked geeks" don't like to watch professional wrestling. *See* LEAD PENCIL.

pendulum.   Prolific British scientist Robert Boyle—of whom it has been said, "the monotonous acres of his work are occasionally relieved by a colorful expression"—is said to have coined the word *pendulum* in 1660 from the Latin *pendulus,* a free-swinging body. But the word had been used before this in England and in 1637 Galileo used the Italian *pendolo* for the same thing.

Penelope.   Odysseus's wife, Penelope, in Greek mythology cunningly held off a horde of suitors while her husband was absent for 10 years. Her name has become synonymous for a faithful wife.

penguin.   Though the penguin has a black head, its name derives from Welsh words meaning "white head": *pen,* "head," and *gwyn,* "white." Welsh sailors were responsible for this odd christening when they gave the name *penguin* to the great auk, a flightless bird with white spots on its head that was common on North Atlantic islands in the 16th century. For some unknown reason sailors in other oceans later transferred the name *penguin* to the flightless bird so named today.

Penguinize.   In England *Penguinize* means "to publish or republish a book" in paperback. Penguin Books Limited, founded in 1935, specializes in paperbacks, which in days gone forever cost sixpence. No doubt the company hopes that *Penguinize,* or better yet, *penguinize,* will have currency in America, too. *Pocket book* is a term for a paperback book in America, taking its name from the firm Pocket Books, Inc., founded in 1939. There seems to be no verb equivalent to *Penguinize* here, although Penguin publishes books in the U.S. as well. Publishers speak of "bringing it out in paper" or "putting out a paperback edition," etc., but nobody "Pocketbookizes" a book. Here is one place where the English are clearly outdoing the American love of shortcuts in language. *Penguinize* might yet fill this American language gap, unless someone at Bantam Books comes up with "Bantamize" first.

penis.   Most dictionaries derive *penis* from the Latin word *penis* for the male sexual organ. The Latin *penis* probably derives from the Latin *penes,* "within." The word isn't recorded in English until 1693.

The pen is mightier than the sword.   It was Edward Bulwer-Lytton who coined *the pen is mightier than the sword*, in his play *Richelieu* (1839):

> Beneath the rule of men entirely great,
> The pen is mightier than the sword.

Long before, in his *Anatomy of Melancholy* (1621), Robert Burton had written: "The pen is worse than the sword." Cervantes, in *Don Quixote* (1605), expressed an entirely different point of view: "Let none presume to tell me that the pen is preferable to the sword." Curiously enough, two great writers, Sophocles and Demosthenes, were the sons of sword makers, the equivalent of munitions makers in our time.

penknife.   A penknife is a small pocket knife invented as far back as the 15th century. It was originally used for making and sharpening quill pens, hence its name. *See* JACKKNIFE.

Pennsylvania.   *Silvania* is the Latin for woodland, and *Pennsylvania*, formed on the analogy of Transylvania (that home of monsters and werewolves in fiction), means "Penn's woodland." The name does not honor the Quaker William Penn, as is generally believed, but his father, Admiral Sir William Penn (1621–70). Admiral Penn, a naval hero who helped frame the first code of tactics for the British navy, had been imprisoned in the Tower in 1655 for political reasons still unknown, and the author Samuel Pepys speaks bitingly of him in his diary. The crown, however, had become indebted to the admiral, Penn having loaned Charles II 16,000 pounds. On June 24, 1680, the younger Penn petitioned Charles for repayment of this debt, asking for a 300-by-160-mile "tract of land in America...." The tract was to become a colony for Protestant Quakers suffering religious persecution, and Charles repaid his debt with a charter. Penn's account tells us that he suggested the names Sylvania and New Wales. When Charles II added the "Penn" in honor of his father, he strongly objected since Quakers are opposed to such use of personal names.

penny.   *Penny* is probably from an Anglo-Saxon word related to the German *Pfenning*, though it may derive from the name of Penda, an early Mercian king. Pennies were originally called "coppers" in England, having been made of copper from 1797 to 1860 (before that they were made of silver).

penny-ante.   *Penny-ante* for anything or anyone of small importance is a figurative use of the poker term *penny-ante* meaning a poker game in which the ante, the first bet in the pot, is only a penny. The term dates back to mid-19th-century America.

penny dreadful.   The American equivalent of the British term *penny dreadful* is *dime novel*, which is purely a historical term today. However, the British still use *penny dreadful* for any thrilling or romantic novel that is considered trashy, even though such works sell for far more than the penny they cost in the 19th century. The original cheap penny dreadfuls and dime novels of yesteryear were replaced by pulp novels, which were themselves replaced by cheap paperbacks and television.

pennywise and pound foolish.   Known since at least the 16th century, this proverbial saying describes someone scrupulously thrifty in small financial transactions and exceedingly careless in larger ones. It has been traced back to Robert Burton's *Anatomy of Melancholy* (1621–51). Recently the old phrase was polished up by Jim Yardley, writing in the New York Times (2/18/02) of a Texas man who got the contract to clean up 7.6 million pennies ($76,000 worth, 20 tons) belonging to the U.S. Mint. The coins had spilled in a highway accident, resulting in a huge "pudding of mud and pennies." Mr. Yardley gave a new twist to an old chiché when writing of the Texan's "laundering" troubles: "Mr. Massengale is uncertain whether taking on the job was pennywise or 40,000 pounds of pennies foolish."

Pentagonese.   *See* GOBBLEDYGOOK.

penthouse.   Over the years folk etymology made *penthouse* out of *pentice*, the former word sounding more familiar to English ears even if *pentice* was correct. The *pentice* was a kind of "lean-to" attached to another building, usually a church, the word akin to "appendix." It took several centuries for *penthouse*, first recorded in early 1500s, to become the luxurious separate apartment or dwelling on a roof of a building that it generally is today.

peony.   *See* PAEAN.

People who live in glass houses shouldn't throw stones. This old proverb dates back to the 14th century. It means don't criticize others if you have faults yourself. English poet George Herbert used a variation on it in *Jacula Prudentum* (1640): "Whose house is of glass, must not throw stones at another."

Peoria.   *See* PODUNK.

pepper.   *Pepper* can be traced back to the Sanskrit *pippali*, for a type of condiment pepper that comes from the dried berries of a climbing shrub. Garden peppers are not related to this shrub, but received the same name when Columbus discovered hot varieties of the garden pepper in the West Indies and wrongly believed they were a new variety of the condiment pepper. *See also* CHILI PEPPER.

Pepsi generation.   The *Pepsi generation* is used, sometimes sarcastically, to mean the now, "with-it" generation. The term comes from the Pepsi-Cola slogan *Come alive, you're in the Pepsi generation*. Recently Pepsi-Cola moved into the Thailand soft drink market and had their slogan translated. It later developed that the Thai translation it was using said: "Pepsi brings back your ancestors from the dead." Incidentally, the word *Pepsi* in Pepsi-Cola is there because the drink's inventor, North Carolinian drugstore proprietor Caleb D. Bradham, first marketed his invention as an elixir to relieve dys*pepsi*a. *See* COKE.

period.   *See* COMMA.

peripeteia.   A peripeteia is a striking reversal in a play or in life, as Oedipus's discovery of his true identity. The same word with the same meaning was used by the ancient Greeks.

periscope.   *See* UP PERISCOPE!

Peritas and Bucephala. It is said that Alexander the Great, mourning his dog Peritas, renamed an ancient city Peritas in his honor. The tale isn't unlikely, considering that Alexander did name another city after his horse. Bucephalus was Alexander's favorite Thracian charger, a spirited stallion that only the conqueror could ride and who would kneel down to let his master mount. Alexander rode Bucephalus in his campaigns to conquer the world and "the bull-headed or bull-courage one" is said to have died of wounds or heart strain at the age of 20, after swimming the flooded Jhelum River and then carrying his master in full armor through a hard day's fighting on a hot June day. The emperor named the ancient city of Bucephala in northern India in his horse's honor, possibly even building it as the fabled charger's mausoleum, its site identified by a mound outside the modern Jhelum.

periwinkle. In Italy the periwinkle is called the *fiore di morto* because it used to be wreathed around dead infants. *Periwinkle* takes its name from the Latin *pervincire*, "to bind around," but whether it was so named because it was used in such burials is unknown.

perk. *Perk* is simply shorthand for *perquisite*, meaning a benefit received by an employee beyond his or her salary and standard fringe benefits. Perks range from a key to the executive washroom to a key to a company car. The expression probably dates from the 1960s.

pernod. ABSINTHE was generally made from species of wormwood, *Artemisia absinthium*, the plant so named because it had been dedicated to Artemesia, Greek goddess of the hunt and moon. Long prized for its reputed aphrodisiac powers by the French, the liqueur is 70–80 percent alcohol, but the oil of wormwood in it can cause blindness, insanity, and even death. For this reason absinthe was banned in Switzerland in 1908, in the United States four years later, and outlawed by France in 1915. Pernod, a greenish-colored, licorice-flavored liqueur named for its French manufacturer, quickly took its place. Pernod does not get a person drunk as quickly as absinthe, being 40–50 percent alcohol, but, except for the anise used to replace the banned oil of wormwood, it contains all the same ingredients.

perpetual peace. This expression was first used to describe the 1502 peace between England and Scotland, concluded when Henry VII married his daughter to Scotland's James IV. The perpetual peace ended two years later at the battle of Flodden Field, in which the British defeated the Scots. Other "perpetual peaces" since then, and WARS TO END ALL WARS, have ended just the same.

perp walk. *Perp walk*, short for the rarely heard term *perpetrator walk*, has been used for more than half a century by New York City police and the city's newspaper photographers, the words describing the moment when a criminal suspect is walked out of a police stationhouse on the way to jail or court. The exit was designed to allow the police to publicize their latest catch and to shame the suspect.

Persian words in English. Persian words that became English words, usually through other languages, are: tiger, para-
dise, pard, scarlet, chess, checkmate, checkers, azure, salamander, taffeta, arsenic, roc, mummy, spinach, jasmine, lilac, seersucker, khaki, scimitar, bazaar, shawl, lemon, divan, and van (from caravan).

persiflage. "Upon these delicate occasions you must practice the ministerial shrugs and persiflage," Lord Chesterfield wrote in one of his famous *Letters* (1774) to his natural son Philip Stanhope. This is the first recorded use of *persiflage*, "light frivolous talk or banter," which Chesterfield may have coined from the French *persifler*, "to banter."

persimmon. *See* EATIN' A GREEN 'SIMMON.

persneckity. All that's known about this word, originally spelled *pernicity*, is that it's from Scotland and was first recorded in 1885. It means "overly concerned about small details, fastidious, fussy."

person. The word *person* derives from the Latin *persona*, which was the term for the mask that actors in Greek and Roman dramas wore to portray the various characters. The word came to mean the part anyone played in this world, his or her individuality, coming into English as *person*. In his article "Language Liberated" in *The University Bookman* (Spring 1976), Robert Beum considers some alternatives for sexist "man" terms in the language. Believing, as someone has said, that "the proper study of personkind is person," I've recorded a number of Mr. Baum's tongue-in-cheek suggestions below. Note his advice that "the key rule is that the root 'man,' even when it is derived etymologically from the Latin 'manus' (hand), bears the degrading connotations of sexist tradition and is to be dropped":

> personners (manners)
> personslaughter (manslaughter)
> personhandle (manhandle)
> personnuscript (manuscript)

Person overboard! Person the oars! *See* POLITICAL CORRECTNESS.

personal names. The most common English surname is SMITH, while the longest English personal name is the 1,055–letter first and middle names given by Mr. and Mrs. James Williams of Beaumont, Texas, to their daughter, who was born on October 5, 1984. The most poetic long personal name may be the 102-letter-long Hawaiian first name given to Miss Dawne E. Lee of Honolulu, which translates as "the abundant, beautiful blossoms of the mountain begin to fill the air with their fragrance throughout the length and breadth of Hawaii."

pervert. Deriving from the Latin word for to turn, *pervert* originally meant to turn upside down. Three hundred years later, by the 17th century, it had come to be a noun meaning "one who practices sexual perversion." An old anecdote has Voltaire participating in an orgy with a group of dissolute Parisians. Invited to participate again, he replied, "No thank you, my friends. Once: a philosopher. Twice: a pervert!"

pesky. Troublesome or annoying. The word, first recorded about 1765, may come from England's Essex dialect, which also gives us *scrimp* and *snicker*. However, Ernest Weekley's *An*

Etymological Dictionary of Modern English (1921) says *pesky* is an Americanism based on "pest."

pest. At first *pest* was used to describe any *pestilence* or epidemic, such as the Black Death. But by the 17th century it was being employed to describe people who are a nuisance.

pestle. *See* PISTIL.

Pétain. Henri-Philippe Pétain, at a cost of 250,000 dead, halted the German advance at Verdun in World War I under the famous slogan "They shall not pass!" Acclaimed a hero and made commander in chief of the French armies, "the savior of Verdun" became associated with extreme rightist political elements in later years. In World War II, when 84, Marshal Pétain was appointed chief of staff of the Vichy government, collaborating with the Nazis and turning France into an authoritarian state. After the war he was found guilty of treason and sentenced to death, but President de Gaulle, his former aide, commuted his sentence to life imprisonment. Pétain, his name long a synonym for traitor, died in 1951, aged 95.

peter. A widespread euphemism for *penis* due to its association with the word *pee* and the first syllable of *penis*. Noted etymologist Vance Randolph wrote, "Very few natives of the Ozarks will consider naming a boy Peter" because of this significance. "An evangelist from the North shouted something about the Church being founded on the rock of St. Peter," Randolph noted, "and he was puzzled by the flushed cheeks of the young woman and the ill-suppressed amusement of the ungodly. Mountain folk don't even like to pronounce names like Hitchcock or Cock." (A dislike, it should be added, that is found among some people in many areas.)

peter boat. Every Peter ever born derives his given name from St. Peter, Peter being the name Christ gave the "Prince of the Apostles," this apparently the first time the name was ever used. Peter was a fisherman of Galilee, who denied knowing Christ three times during His trial, but later repented. Tradition tells us that he was crucified in A.D. 67, head down at his request because he said he was not worthy to suffer the same death as Jesus, and his tomb is under the high altar of St. Peter's in Rome. Many words and expressions derive from Peter's name: Eric Partridge devotes a page or so to them in his *Dictionary of Slang*. The Patron saint of fishermen and many other occupations connected with the sea gives us the standard English *peterman* for a fisherman and *peter boat* for a fishing boat with stem and stern alike. Stormy petrels also bear Peter's name, because the birds seem to be patting the waves with one foot and then the other in stormy weather, as though they were walking on water. Actually they are flying close to the waves in search of surface-swimming food like small shrimp, but the birds reminded sailors of St. Peter walking upon the Lake of Gennersareth to join Jesus (Matt. 14:29). They were thus named *peterels*, a diminutive of the English Peter, in honor of the apostle and this came to be *petrel* in time. All petrels are regarded as the protectors of sailors and the harbingers of approaching storms. It is considered bad luck to kill one, for the birds were long thought to be the souls of drowned men; whenever one died, sailors believed a crew member would soon die to take its place.

peter out. It seems unlikely that disappointed American miners during the '49 gold rush derived the expression *to peter out*, "to taper off or come to an end," from the French *peter*, "to break wind." This would indeed have been an expression of their disappointment when a mine failed to yield more gold, but there were ample American words available to express the same sentiment. Another guess is that the *peter* here refers to the apostle Peter, who first rushed to Christ's defense in the Garden of Gethsemane, sword in hand, and then before the cock crowed thrice denied that he even knew Him. Most likely the expression springs from the fact that veins of ore in mines frequently petered out, or turned to stone. The gunpowder mixture of saltpeter, sulfur, and charcoal, commonly called *peter* by miners, was used as an explosive in mining operations and when a vein of gold was exhausted it was said to have been petered out.

Peter Pan. Peter Pan, the boy who refused to grow up, has been familiar to readers and theatergoers for several generations and we now use his name to describe a person who retains in mature years the naturalness of spirit and charm associated with childhood, or one who absolutely refuses to escape from the comfortable irresponsibility of childhood. British dramatist and novelist Sir James M. Barrie introduced his immortal character on the stage in the play *Peter Pan* (1904), although the fantastic world of Peter Pan had previously been presented in his *The Little White Bird* (1902). *Peter Pan*, a poetical pantomime, as it has been called, charmed audiences from the night it first appeared. Peter has since been played by many great stars, ranging from Maude Adams to Mary Martin, and a statue of him stands in Kensington Gardens, London. Barrie, who described his business as "playing hide and seek with angels," named Peter for one of his nephews, for whom he wrote the story, giving the character his last name from the god Pan, "goat-footed," god of forests, meadows, flocks, and shepherds. Wendy, Peter's girl friend, also borrowed her name from a real person. This was Barrie's own nickname, bestowed upon him by the daughter of his friend, poet W. E. Henley. Little Margaret Henley called him Friendly, then Friendly-wendy, and this ultimately became Wendy, the name he dubbed his character.

the Peter Principle. Dr. Laurence Peter and Raymond Hull's book *The Peter Principle* (1969) became famous for its premise that "In a hierarchy, every employee tends to rise to the level of his incompetence."

Peter's Pence. For some 800 years, until Henry VIII abolished the practice in 1534, every English household paid a tax to the pope of a penny a year. The tax was called (Saint) Peter's penny, Peterpenny, and Peter's Pence, and several monarchs tried to withhold it from Rome before Henry VIII succeeded, after the pope refused to sanction his divorce from Catherine of Aragon so that he could marry Anne Boleyn.

Pete's sake! The *Pete* here is a euphemism for St. Peter, an expression of annoyance ("For Pete's sake, stop fooling around!") probably dating back at least to late 19th-century America.

Peter-see-me.   Partridge states that this Spanish white wine, known since the 17th century, is named after Cardinal Peter Ximenes, surely the only Catholic churchman so honored, if this is true. Other authorities say the sweet wine bears the corrupted name of grape grower Pedro Ximenes, who developed the special grape that makes the wine. Peter-see-me is called Peter for short.

petit pois.   *See* PEA.

petrel.   *See* PETER BOAT.

petri dish.   German scientist Julius Richard Petri invented this thin glass or plastic dish with a loose cover commonly used in laboratories today. The shallow dish named for the bacteriologist, who died in 1921, is generally employed in making bacteria cultures. Petri was an assistant of the great German scientist Robert Koch when he devised his dishes in 1887. Koch—the first scientist to introduce a rationalized system of bacteria culturing—had previously grown bacteria in a gel on flat glass slides, his assistant substituting the shallow glass dishes with covers that have been used ever since.

pettifogger.   A real family of financiers may have given its name to the word *pettifogger*, for "an attorney or anyone who argues over petty details with little meaning." The Fugger family, which can be traced back to Bavarian Swabia in the 15th century and who were descended from an Augsburg weaver, made their great fortune lending money to royalty, but became noted, justly or unjustly, for their petty ways. According to one theory, in time a "petty Fugger" became a pettifogger, the designation soon applied to people besides the Fuggers.

petunia.   This popular, funnel-shaped flower is botanically related to the tobacco plant, hence its name from the Portuguese word *petum*, meaning "tobacco." The Portuguese had taken the word from the Tupi-Guarani South America Indian word *petyn*. *Petum* became the French *petin*, which passed into English as *petun*, an archaic word for tobacco. Toward the end of the 19th century, the name of the genus *Petunia* was formed in New Latin by botanists from the French *petun* because it was so closely related to tobacco. It wasn't long before the flower of the genus was being called the petunia.

Phaedo.   It's said that the philosopher Cleombrotus killed himself after reading Plato's *Phaedo* "so that he might enjoy the happiness of the future life so enchantingly described." The *Phaedo* is a dialogue narrating the discussion that took place between Socrates and his friends during the last hour of his life. This work also influenced the Roman Stoic philosopher Cato, Caesar's chief political rival, when he committed suicide by falling on his sword after realizing that his cause against the Caesarians was hopeless. Cato had spent all of the last night of his life reading Plato's *Phaedo*. Eighteenth-century English poet Eustace Budgell was indirectly influenced by the *Phaedo* when he committed suicide by drowning himself, for he left behind a note reading: "What Cato did and Addison approved cannot be wrong."

phaeton.   Rooted in Greek mythology, this light horse-drawn four-wheel carriage takes its name from Zeus's son Phaeton, who took his father's chariot for a ride to the sun one day and drove so wildly that he nearly set the world on fire, before Zeus stopped him with a thunderbolt.

phallus.   *See* BULL.

phantasmagoria.   The word is defined as "a shifting series of phantasms, illusions, or deceptive appearances, as in a dream or created by the imagination," but it can also mean "a changing scene made up of many elements." It was apparently coined in 1802 by a London showman named Philipstal to describe his magic-lantern exhibition of optical illusions. The word may be based on *phantasm* or *phantom*, but "the inventor of the term probably only wanted a mouth-filling and startling term . . ." and no clear etymology is known.

pharaoh.   Egyptian pharaohs took their name from the palaces or big houses, *per-o*, where they resided. The title is first recorded in English in about 843.

pharisee.   *See* A THORN IN ONE'S SIDE.

pharos.   *Pharos* has become a synonym for "light-house," but it was originally one of the Seven Wonders of the World, a lighthouse built by Ptolemy II on the island of Pharos off Alexandria, Egypt, that was 200 to 600 feet high and could be seen 42 miles away. *See* PHARAOH.

phatic speech.   A term coined in 1923 by anthropologist Bronislaw Malinowski meaning speech employed to express good will or sociability rather than give information. The author and critic Anatole Broyard called phatic speech "a friendly noise." The word *phatic* comes from Greek *phatos*, "spoken." Malinowski's exact coinage was *phatic communion*.

Ph.D.   The abbreviation of the Latin term *Philosophiae Doctor*, doctor of philosophy. According to Mitford Mathews's *Dictionary of Americanisms*, "Ph.D. was known in British academic circles before it made its appearance in American use. British holders of the degree secured it from Germany. It was probably from Germany that the practice of granting such degrees came to be an established procedure in American education, and the use of *Ph.D.* appears to have a German rather than a British background." Yale probably granted the first U.S. Ph.D., and the first mention of *Ph.D.* in print seems to have been in 1869.

pheasant.   The bird's name came into English from the Old French, *faisant*, but it goes back to the Greek *phasianos ornis*, "the Phasian bird," because the Greeks first found the bird in the region of the Phasis river where it flows into the Black Sea.

phenom.   *Phenom* is short for any exceptionally gifted (or phenomenal) person. The expression first came into use in baseball in the late 19th century, when excellent players were called phenoms. Soon after it crossed over into general use to mean any gifted person.

Phi Beta Kappa.   A U.S. national honor society whose lifetime members, both college undergraduates and graduates, are chosen on the basis of high academic achievement. The letters constituting the society's name are from Greek *philosophia biou kubernetes*: philosophy the guide of life. Founded in 1776 at the College of William and Mary in Virginia, Phi Beta Kappa is the oldest Greek-letter society. It was originally a secret social society at the college but soon became a scholarship honorary society.

Philadelphia lawyer. Folklore has it that when Andrew Hamilton successfully defended New York printer John Peter Zenger against libel charges in 1735, establishing the right of freedom of the press in America, observers noted that it took a *Philadelphia lawyer* to get the printer off. But the term is first recorded more than 50 years later, in 1788, in the form of "It would puzzle a Philadelphia lawyer." Another theory claims the words come from the New England saying "any three Philadelphia lawyers are a match for the devil." Philadelphia at the time was the intellectual and literary center of America, and it was only fitting that a very clever lawyer, versed in the fine points of the law, should be named for the city.

philander. Our word for a male flirt who makes love without serious intentions comes from the name given to lovers in various medieval romances, but certain marsupial animals also bear the name *Philander* and these are named for the Dutch naturalist Kornelius Philader de Bruyn. Philanders, whose males may or may not be philanderers, include the small wallaby (*Macopus brunnii*), first described by de Bruyn in about 1700, the Australian bandicoot (*Perameles lagotes*), and the South American opossum (*Didelphys philander*). The name Philander comes from the Greek *philandros*, "one who loves."

philanthropy. *Philanthropy* clearly has its roots in the Greek *philos*, "love," and *anthropos*, "mankind," and means a love for mankind, especially as manifested in donations of money, property, or work to needy persons or socially useful purposes. It is first recorded by Bacon in 1607 and he refers to it as an ancient Greek term.

philippic. Incomparable orator that he was, Demosthenes' eloquent words could not triumph over the military might of Philip of Macedon (382–336 B.C.). Eventually, Philip II, father of Alexander the Great, defeated the Athenians, imposing a very generous peace settlement on them so that he could employ them as allies in his future plans for conquest. But Demosthenes had made such brilliant denunciatory orations against Philip over a period of seven years that these speeches are still known in history as *philippics*. The philippics were specifically a series of three passionate invectives against the Macedonian monarch's plan to weld Athens into his kingdom and they comprised a great defense of Athenian liberty, taking their name from the target of their fire.

the Philippines. The Spanish took control of these islands in 1571 and named them for Philip II of Spain.

Philistine. The original Philistines made their home in Philistia on the southwest coast of Palestine. These peoples were Israel's worst enemy, even capturing the sacred ark at one time, until Saul and David, the first Israelite kings, decisively defeated them in battle. They were considered a crude, avaricious people but their name did not come into the language until centuries later, in 1689. At that time a town-and-gown battle in the German university city of Jena had resulted in the death of several people, and a local preacher gave a sermon on the values of education to the ignorant townspeople, choosing as his text "The Philistines be upon thee..." from Judges 16. The German word for *Philistine* was *Philister* and students began calling ignorant townspeople opposed to education by this name. Almost two centuries later, in 1869, English poet and critic Matthew Arnold used the German slang in his book *Culture and Anarchy*, translating it from *Philister* to *Philistine* and giving the word its present meaning. Wrote Arnold: "The people who believe most that our greatness and welfare are proved by our being very rich, are just the very people whom we call Philistines." Since then *Philistine* has meant a materialistic, uncultured person.

philodendron. In its tropic homes our common houseplant the *philodendron* is a tree-climbing plant. Noticing this, the first botanists to observe the plant named it after the Greek *philos*, "loving," and *dendron*, "tree."

Philomela. After Procne discovered that her husband, Tereus, had cut out her sister Philomela's tongue and imprisoned her for years, Procne chose a terrible revenge. She killed their infant son Itys and served him to her husband for dinner. Tereus went into shock when told what kind of stew he had eaten, enabling Procne to escape with her sister, but Tereus eventually caught them. He was about to dispatch the sisters when the gods intervened and turned Philomela into a swallow because she had no tongue and swallows cannot really sing, while Procne was turned into a nightingale because the nightingale sings the saddest of songs and Procne was condemned to always sing sadly of the son she had killed so cruelly. Nevertheless, since Roman times poets have confused the Greek myth and made *Philomela* or *Philomel* a universal poetic name for "nightingale," when clearly the word should be *Procne*—though one must admit that *a procne* sounds prosaic at best and asinine at worst. T. S. Eliot is the latest great poet to make this mistake, in *The Waste Land*.

philosopher. The Greek Pythagoras is said to have coined the word *philosopher* from the Greek words for love and wisdom. Up until this time philosophers were called sophists, "wise men." Said Pythagoras: "No man, but only God is wise. Call me rather, a philosopher, a lover of wisdom."

phlogiston. From the 17th to the 19th century scientists searched for *phlogiston* (from the Greek word for "inflammable"), which was supposed to be the substance within all materials that burned. Great scientific investigators believed in the substance. Joseph Priestley, in fact, named oxygen *dephlogisticated air* when he isolated it in 1774. But by 1800 belief in *phlogiston* was largely abandoned and the word deleted from the lexicon of science, if not fable.

pho. A new word, unrecorded in any dictionary, that entered the language with Vietnamese immigrants to the U.S., pho is a noodle soup with beef that is becoming more popular every year. It is said that along Garden Grove Boulevard in Orange County, California, "it is easier to lunch on pho... than on a hamburger."

phoebe. Named in imitation of the bird's cry—a long-held "phee-bee pheebe" that strongly resembles the female name Phoebe—this flycatcher (*Sayornis phoebe*) has been known since colonial times. Theodore Dreiser's "The Lost Phoebe," (1929), about the love and loneliness of a bereaved old farmer, is among the most beautiful of American short stories.

phoenix. This fabulous bird of great beauty was said to live some 600 years in the Arabian wilderness, then burn itself on a funeral pyre and rise again from its ashes, becoming a symbol of immortality. It was named, indirectly, after the ancient Phoenicians, its color being purple-red, which the Greeks called *phoenix* because the Phoenicians had invented a dye of this color. *See* PHOENIX TREE.

phoenix tree. *Phoenix dactylifera*, the date palm, is called the *phoenix tree* because of the ancient belief, mentioned in Shakespeare's *The Tempest*, that if it burns down or falls from old age it will spring up fresher than ever from its ruins.

phony. Mencken suggested that a mendacious maker of fake jewelry named Forney is the eponym behind this word, but no one else seems to agree with him. The majority opinion is that *phony* is an alteration of *fawney*, British slang for a worthless ring, which itself derives from an Irish Gaelic word. The word, first recorded in 1890 or so, probably comes specifically from the *fawney rig*, a confidence game in which a worthless ring is planted, and when someone "finds" it he is persuaded by a "bystander" that he should pay the bystander for his share in the "find."

phooey. *Phooey*, as an expression of disgust, is first attested to as recently as 1929 in America and derives from the German-Yiddish *phui*, which seems to be an imitation of the sound of spitting. Most languages have similar throat-clearing sounds for words expressing disgust, these foreign *phooey* synonyms including the Italian *uffa*, the French *pfutt*, or *fi*, and the Spanish *bay*. For some reason the ancient Romans employed *pro*.

photography. *See* DIORAMA.

photo-op. White House press secretary Ronald L. Ziegler (1940–2003) coined this common term when serving as President Richard Nixon's press secretary, first using it as *photography-opportunity*. It means "a news event staged to produce flattering photographs," as the *New York Times* (2/12/03) put it. Ziegler was also noted, wordwise, for his description of the Watergate break-in as a "third-rate burglary."

Photostat. Surprising to many, *Photostat* is a proprietary name and must be capitalized. The photography machine that makes Photostats has been a U.S. registered trademark since 1911, its name, from Greek, literally meaning "making light stationary." *See* XEROX.

Phryne. *Phryne* is a synonym for a prostitute, and a rather complimentary one considering its source. It refers to the Athenian courtesan Phryne, who lived and loved memorably in the fourth century B.C. There was a gold statue of Phryne at Delphi dedicated by her admirers. Her real name was Mnesarite, but the hetaera was commonly called Phryne, "toad," because of her smooth complexion. Born in Boeotia, the country girl made good at her trade in Athens, where her beauty earned her a fortune so great that she once offered to rebuild the walls of Thebes if the words "Destroyed by Alexander, restored by Phryne the courtesan" were inscribed upon them. (There were no takers.) That her body was the most beautiful of her time, or perhaps any other, is illustrated by Praxiteles' statue called *Aphrodite of Cnidus*, which she is said to have posed for. During a festival of Poseidon at Eleusis, Phryne took off her clothes, let down her hair, and in full view of the crowd stepped into the sea, inspiring Apelles to paint his great *Aphrodite Anadyomene*, for which she modeled. But there is no better story about Phryne than that of her trial for impurity. One of her lovers, the great orator Hyperides, defended her. Just when it seemed that she would lose her case—and her life was at stake—Hyperides pulled the courtroom stunt of all time. Ripping open her robe, he exposed her breasts to the jury, who agreed with him that something so good could not be all bad and let Phryne go free.

Phudnick. *See* NUDNIK.

picaresque. A picaresque novel is a novel that deals with rogues and knaves, often satirizing society through their experiences. The word *picaresque*, in fact, derives from the Spanish *picaro*, "rogue." Alain René Lesage's *Gil Blas* (1715), Daniel Defoe's *Moll Flanders* (1722), and Thomas Mann's *Confessions of Felix Krull* (1954) are good examples of this type of novel, which is called *Räuberroman* in German.

picayune. In early 18th-century Louisiana both an old French copper coin and the Spanish half-real were called picayunes. *Picayune* itself probably derives from the Spanish *Pequeña*, "little," and the coin influenced the popularity of the contemptuous use of *picayune* for anything small, mean, or insignificant.

pickaninny. An old, offensive word for a black child that appears to have derived from African slaves' pronunciation of the Portuguese *pequenino* (small child).

picked too soon (early). Some fruits (pears, peaches, strawberries, etc.) ripen after they are picked, but not if they are picked before a certain time—if they are so picked they will never ripen. This may well be the origin of the old expression *picked too soon* or *early*, referring to a child who is forced to excel at something he or she may be good at but isn't ready to pursue, unable at the time to be anything but a child. *See* PRECOCIOUS; PRODIGY.

Picketwire. James Michener explains this river's colorful name in *Centennial* (1974):

> "At the end of the first full day in Colorado they came to the Picketwire, the western river with the most delicate name. It was properly El Rio de Las Animas Perdido en Purgatorio. In Coronado's time three difficult and greedy Spanish soldiers had revolted and struck out on their own to find the cities of gold. Sometime later the main body of explorers came upon them, naked and riddled with arrows, and one of the priests explained solemnly, 'God struck them down, using Indians as his agents, and

for their disobedience their souls remain in purgatory.' The River of the Souls Lost in Purgatory! French trappers had shortened it to Purgatoire, and practical men from Indiana and Tennessee, adapting the sound to their own tongue, called it Picketwire."

pickle.   *See* IN A PRETTY PICKLE.

Pickle Factory.   A little-known nickname of the CIA, among its members, in the Central Intelligence Agency's early days of the late 1940s and 1950s. The CIA is also called the Company.

picnic.   First recorded in Lord Chesterfield's *Letters* (1748), the word *picnic* comes to us from the French *pique-nique*, which is a century or so older. *Pique-nique* itself is a reduplication on *piquer*, "to pick."

Picts.   These ancient people who settled in Ireland and Scotland in about 100 B.C. were so named by the Romans, who called them *Picti*, from the Latin *pictor*, "painter," because they tattooed and painted their bodies.

a picture is worth a thousand words.   *See* ONE PICTURE IS WORTH A THOUSAND WORDS.

pidgin English.   Pidgin English, originally developed by British traders in China, takes its name from the way the Chinese pronounced "business"—"bijin." It combines English and Portuguese, as well as German, Bengali, French, and Malayan. There is even a magazine, *Frend Belong Me* ("My Friend"), published in pidgin by the Catholic Mission in New Guinea. *See* PIDGIN LANGUAGE; GUBMINT CATCHUM FELLA.

pidgin language.   A *pidgin language* has no native speakers, is a *second* language, that is, a language developed as a means of communication among speakers of various languages. A creole language, on the other hand, does have native speakers. It is simply defined as a pidgin language that has been passed on to succeeding generations as a native tongue. In the U.S. Gullah is an example, as is, of course, the creolized French language of the descendants of the original settlers of Louisiana, which is often called Creole or Cajun. Creole derives from the Portuguese *criollo*, "native," while *pidgin* is probably from the Chinese pronunciation of "business." *See also* PIDGIN ENGLISH.

pie.   *Pie* is an old English word of obscure origin, first recorded in 1275. Wrote Harriet Beecher Stowe in *Old Town Folks* (1869): "The pie is an English institution, which, planted on American soil, forthwith ran rampant and burst forth into an untold variety of genera and species. Not merely the old traditional mince pie, but a thousand strictly American seedlings from the main stock, evinced the power of American housewives to adapt old institutions to new uses. Pumpkin pies, cranberry pies, huckleberry pies, peach, pear and plum pies, custard pies, apple pies, Marlborough-pudding pies—pies with top crusts and without—pies adorned with all sorts of fanciful flutings and architectural strips laid across and around, and otherwise varied, attested the boundless fertility of the feminine mind, when let loose in a given direction."

piece.   *Piece*, for "a woman," especially in a sexual sense, has been used since the early 14th century, when it was standard English. Grose defines the word as: "A wench. A damned good or bad piece, a girl who is more or less active and skillful in the amorous congress. Hence the Cambridge toast, 'May we never have a *piece* (peace) that will injure the Constitution.'" The sense of *piece* today is generally "a sexually attractive woman," though the term is considered a sexist one by many. *Hunk* is its male counterpart, this a relatively recent coinage dating back only to the 1940s.

pieces of eight.   Famous as pirate booty, pieces of eight were Spanish silver coins worth about a dollar, though they were frequently cut into *bits* to make smaller coins. Other famous Spanish coins were half doubloons, quarter doubloons (pistols), one-eighth doubloons, and cobs, silver coins of various worth irregularly cut from a silver bar, which were heated and stamped with the royal arms.

Piedmont rice.   An old story holds that Thomas Jefferson stole seeds of Piedmont rice while traveling in the Piedmont region of Italy and smuggled them home in his pockets, despite the fact that Italy wanted to continue its monopoly on this type of rice and had made the crime of stealing the seeds punishable by death. Jefferson's introduction of the rice was important because Piedmont rice can be grown without irrigation. *See* CAROLINA RICE; WILD RICE.

pie in the sky.   An empty wish or promise. The expression may have originated with a song written by IWW (International Workers of the World) organizer Joe Hill, whose real name was Joseph Hilstrom, in the years before World War I. Called "The Preacher and the Slave" four of its lines went:

> "You will eat, by and by,
> In that glorious land above the sky (way up high!);
> Work and pray, live on hay,
> You'll get pie in the sky when you die." (That's a lie!)

Pierian Spring.   A spring in Greek mythology that the MUSES were said to hold sacred. The spring conferred inspiration and learning on anyone who drank of it.

piffle; piffling.   Piffle is twaddle, nonsense, idle talk. There have been many suggestions concerning the term's origins, including the words *puff*, *pitiful*, and a combination of *piddle* and *trifle*. The word is first recorded in this sense in 1890.

pig.   Partridge notes that *pig* was slang for "a British policeman" in 1811, while Farmer advises that it was American criminal slang for "a policeman" in 1848. But the designation died out in both England and America by the 20th century. It didn't surface again until American student demonstrations of the 1960s, which suggests a second, independent coinage of the term at that time.

pig and whistle.   All taverns called the Pig and Whistle take their name from an old English tavern that originally had the Norse name Piga Waes Hael. This name, meaning "Hail to the Virgin" was corrupted in speech to *Pig and Whistle*.

pigboy. "Before there were ever cowboys in America, there were pigboys, herding up pigs on horseback and setting them loose to forage," states Dr. Frederick V. Hebard of the American Chestnut Association, speaking of pigs that once fed on the huge crops of chestnuts that the now extinct American chestnut tree used to produce. I've been unable to find the term recorded anywhere outside the *New York Times* article (2/5/02) quoting Dr. Hebard, but even if it isn't in print, *pigboy* is a good coinage.

pigeonhole. In the mid or late 19th century side-by-side compartments in old-fashioned rolltop desks were called *pigeonholes* because of their resemblance to the holes in dovecotes or pigeon houses, which were made to enable pigeons to walk in and out. Since papers were filed in these compartments, *to pigeonhole* became a way of saying "to file away for future reference." But papers filed away in pigeonholes were often ignored because they presented a problem or the prospect of too much work, so the term *to pigeonhole* was humorously extended to mean filing something away with the intention of forgetting about it or doing nothing about it.

piggyback. The correct word is *pickaback*, but virtually no one calls it that. *Pickaback* dates back at least to the late 16th century, when it is first recorded to mean carrying a person, especially a child, on one's back. The term may have its origins in a *pack* that is *picked* (pitched, thrown) on someone's shoulders, but no one knows for sure. The term wasn't corrupted to *piggyback*, or *pigback*, until the late 18th century.

piggy bank. Though *piggy bank's* popularity over the years probably has something to do with the relation between hoarding or saving money and the pig's supposed greediness, the main reason the child's bank is called a piggy bank is simply because so many of the banks are made in the shape of pigs. They have been made in such shapes since at least 1909, though the first recorded use of the term *piggy bank* is in 1945.

pig in a blanket. A small cocktail frank wrapped and baked in dough, often served as hors d'oeuvres. Sometimes called *dog* (or *frank*) *in a blanket*, a description first recorded in the late 19th century. *See* HOT DOG.

pig latin; hog latin; dog latin. *Ixnay* ("nix"), *amscray* ("scram"), and several other slang words come to us directly from pig Latin. First known as *dog Latin*, the little language commonly used by schoolchildren can be traced back to at least mid-18th-century England, when there was a *dog Greek* as well as a *dog Latin*. The *dog* in the term means the same as it does in *doggerel*, something bad, spurious, bastard, mongrel. *Dog Latin* probably came to be called *pig Latin* and *hog Latin* because its sound resembles the grunting of hogs. The lopped language was at first a combination of Latin and English. Today it is basically formed by taking the first letter of a word, putting it as the rear of the word and adding to it an *ay*. For example, "you can talk pig Latin" is "Ouyay ankay alktay igpay Atinlay." One of the most interesting pig Latin words is *ofay*, a derogatory term among blacks for a white person, which is said to be pig Latin for the word *foe*.

pigs get slaughtered. This is an old Wall Street adage that I've never seen recorded anywhere. It probably dates back to

the 19th century and describes speculators who hold onto a stock after they have seen a good profit on it, hoping to make more and often losing their shirts when the stock drops sharply. A longer variation is *bulls make money, bears make money, but pigs get slaughtered* (or *die broke*)

pigskin. Though animal bladders were once kicked around in various games of football, pigskin was never used to make a football. Nevertheless, *pigskin* has been a word for a football since at least 1894, when the term was used by Amos Stagg's University of Chicago Maroons, the great football team of that era. Footballs are made of a rubber bladder covered with a casing of leather.

pigtail. The word *pigtail* did not appear first in English as the name for a twisted plait of hair. *Pigtail* was first used in the 16th century to describe tobacco twisted into a thin string like a pig's tail.

Pig War. According to the San Juan Island National Historical website: "On June 15, 1859, an American farmer named Lyman Cutler shot and killed a Hudson Bay Company pig rooting in his San Juan Island potato patch. By so doing he nearly started a war between the United States and Britain. Cutler's act drew the ire of the Hudson Bay Company, which then compelled U.S. Army Department of Oregon commander Brigadier General William S. Harney to dispatch a company of the 9th U.S. Infantry, under Captain George E. Pickett, to San Juan on July 27. British Columbia Governor James Douglas responded by sending a warship under Royal Navy Captain Geoffrey Phipps Homby to dislodge Pickett, but to avoid an armed clash if possible. The two sides faced off on the Cattle Point peninsula for more than two months with the opposing forces growing to nearly 500 U.S. soldiers, plus artillery, and three British warships. When the home governments learned of the crisis, leaders on both sides took positive steps to maintain the peace. The joint occupation ended 12 years later when, on October 21, 1872, Kaiser Wilhelm I of Germany, acting as arbitrator, settled the dispute by awarding the San Juan Islands to the United States. So ended the so-called war in which the only casualty was a pig." *See* WAR OF THE STRAY DOG.

pike. The *pike* takes its name from its *pike*, or pointed head. After Christ's crucifixion all fishes but the pike were supposed to have dived under the water in terror. Out of curiosity the pike lifted its head from the water and observed the whole scene. Thus parts of the crucifixion are said to be recognizable on a pike's head, especially the cross, three nails, and a sword.

piker. *Pikers*, or *Pikies*, were settlers who migrated to California from Missouri's Pike County during the 1849 gold rush. Like the "Okies" of the 20th century, the *pikers'* nickname, justly or not, became a synonym for poor, lazy good-for-nothings because they created such an unfavorable impression. Their name seems to have combined with the older English word *piker*, meaning a tramp or vagrant, to give us *piker* in its present sense of cheapskate, which was first recorded in 1901. The English word derives from *turnpike*, because many tramps traveled by foot along turnpikes, toll roads that took their name from the rotating barriers made of pikes, or sharpened rods, at their entrances. *See* PIKES PEAK OR BUST.

Pikes Peak or bust.   Long a Colorado landmark, Pikes Peak became a guidepost for traders in the early 19th century, and by the time of the California gold rush of 1849 Indians in the area had begun to tell of gold deposits on the mountain. Thousands of people headed West to answer the call "Pikes Peak or Bust." However, gold wasn't found high in the hills until 1860, a year after the height of the Colorado gold rush. The fortunes made from the pockets of gold deposits found in the soft quartz and sandy fillings of what was called PAYDIRT established Colorado as the successor to California in gold mining, but crime, violence, hardship, and death proved to be the common lot of the prospector, and most headed back home bitterly disappointed—having experienced elation going up and grim desolation coming down the mountain. In fact, many of the '59ers returned home with the words "Busted, By Gosh!" scrawled on their wagons. Pikes Peak was discovered in 1806 by Zebulon Montgomery Pike, who had been chosen to map the northern part of the Louisiana Purchase, but his badly equipped party failed to reach its summit. The explorer and army officer seems to be irrevocably associated with rocks. During the War of 1812, he was killed while leading a charge against the British garrison at York (Toronto), Canada. The retreating British set fire to their powder magazine, which exploded and loosed a piece of rock that fell on his head. *See* PIKER.

pilcrow.   *Pilcrow* is an old name for a paragraph mark or drawing of a hand pointing, which are printing marks used to attract attention—a paragraph sign in the first case and a direction in the other. The word is apparently a corruption of the word *paragraph*. *Webster's* gives *pilcrow* as an obsolete name for a paragraph mark. But since there are no other names for the two signs above, *pilcrow* ought to be rehired.

pile Pelion on Ossa.   Homer writes in the *Odyssey* of how when the giants Otus and Ephialtes attempted to climb to heaven and overthrow the gods they tried to pile Mount Pelion on Mount Olympus and Mount Ossa on Mount Pelion for a ladder. The giants were destroyed by Zeus, but their plan became synonymous for piling one difficulty on another until a whole plan becomes ridiculous. The two wooded mountains near the coast of Thessaly are now known as Mount Zagora and Mount Kissavo, but no one says "to pile Zagora on Kissavo."

pilgrim.   As a name for the early settlers in America, *Pilgrims* is little more than a century and a half old, having come into common usage in about 1840. According to George Williams's *Saints and Strangers* (1945): "The Pilgrims had no name for themselves as a group. For generations they were known to their descendants merely as the Forefathers, a name preserved in the only holiday officially dedicated to this memory, Forefathers' Day, tardily instituted in Massachusetts in 1895 . . ." Williams adds that the name "Pilgrims" for the "Forefathers" or "First Comers" was first employed by Governor William Bradford in 1630 when he used the phrase "they knew they were pilgrims" in his manuscript chronicle *Of Plimoth Plantation*, which wasn't widely available for more than two centuries. The story of the 102 Pilgrims who founded Plymouth Colony is too well known to bear repeating here, except to say that these Pilgrim Fathers landed on Plymouth Rock instead of in Virginia, as planned, because bad weather had kept them too long

at sea and they had run out of beer, among other supplies. The word *pilgrim* means a wanderer, a traveler, a person who journeys a long distance to a sacred place. It has an interesting history, coming from the Latin *peregrinus*, meaning a stranger. This came into English as *pelegrin* in about 1200, but dissimilation and slothful pronunciation over the years eventually made *pilgrim* out of *pelegrin*. Thus, the Pilgrim Fathers, a proverbially industrious group, take their name from a lazy man's word.

pill.   *See* BITTER PILL TO SWALLOW.

pillarbox.   *See* MAILBOX.

pillar to post.   At first this expression was *from post to pillar*, a figure of speech drawn from the old game of court tennis in the 14th century or earlier. Court tennis, played indoors, differed in many ways from today's lawn tennis, but volleys were even then crucial to the game. One popular volley was from post to pillar, from a post supporting the net or rope to one of the rear pillars supporting the tennis gallery. Apparently players commonly sustained long volleys between these two points, for by the early 15th century Englishmen were regularly using the expression *from post to pillar tossed* outside the game of tennis. In another century the phrase had been reversed to *from pillar to post*, but it still meant the same: "to and fro, hither and thither, from one thing to another without any definite purpose." Modern use of the expression in the sense of going monotonously or fruitlessly from one thing to another is just a logical extension.

pill-pusher.   *See* BITTER PILL TO SWALLOW.

pilot weed.   *See* COMPASS PLANT.

Pimm's.   The gin-based British drink was named for London bartender James Pimm after he invented it in 1840. There are now several variations on the original, which is called Pimm's No. 1. All are often mixed with ginger ale or lemonade and served with ice.

pimp.   Samuel Pepys (pronounced *Peeps*) was the first to record *pimp*, for "a procurer," in his famous *Diary* (1666). The word possibly derives from the French *pimpant*, "seductive," which may come from the Latin *papare*, "to chirp." For the unlikely connection between procuring and chirping, *see* CHIPPY.

pinch a loaf.   A euphemism for the euphemism *to have a bowel movement*. It is used in the film *The Shawshank Redemption* (1994), based on Stephen King's story of the same name, but I haven't seen it recorded elsewhere in any slang dictionary.

pinch an inch.   A term used by American runners since the beginning of the running craze, starting in about 1975, for the amount of flesh that should be on a runner's frame. Anyone who can pinch more than an inch of flesh in any one place on his/her body, according to this extreme formula, is not in good condition.

pinchbeck.   Watch and toy maker Christopher Pinchbeck (1670–1732) died the same year that he introduced the pinchbeck alloy of 15 percent zinc and 85 percent copper, a gold-colored alloy for the imitation gold watches and jewelry he sold in his shop on London's Fleet Street. Pinchbeck did not live to see pinchbeck become another word for "false or counterfeit, a cheap imitation." The term caught on probably because its first syllable suggests "cheap," which the alloy was, compared with gold, but whatever the reason, the word has survived. Anything spurious but resembling the genuine article is still called pinchbeck.

pinch hitter.   An old story has the 1905 New York Giants manager John J. McGraw using one Sammy Strang as baseball's first *pinch hitter* and apparently inventing the term himself. However, this phrase—for a player who bats in a pinch for someone else—had been recorded three years earlier. The expression has wide general use for any substitute or understudy in any endeavor.

pineapple.   The Spanish conquistadores named this fruit *piña* because of its pine-cone shape and the English translated *pina* to *pineapple*, which they also called the cones of the pine tree.

Pine State.   A nickname for Georgia first recorded in 1843. Georgia has also been called the Cracker State (*see* CRACKER), the Buzzard State, the Goober State (after its peanut crop), the Peach State, and the Empire State of the South. *See* EMPIRE STATE.

pine-tree shilling.   One of the earliest coinages in America, a Massachusetts coin with a pine tree as an emblem first issued in 1652. In his story "The Great Carbuncle" (1837) Nathaniel Hawthorne wrote of "a weighty merchant and selectman . . . Master ("Ichabod") Pigsnort [who] was accustomed to spend a whole hour after prayer time, every morning and evening, in wallowing naked among an immense quantity of pine-tree shillings."

Pine Tree State.   A nickname for Maine dating back beyond its first recorded use in 1860. Maine, also called the Lumber State, has a pine tree on its state seal.

Ping-Pong.   Ping-Pong is a trademark name used for table tennis, and was probably derived from the sound of the ball being hit during the game. *Ping-pong* also means "to move back and forth rapidly from one thing to another," as in "He was ping-ponged from one doctor to another," this suggested by the rapid volleys in the game.

pink.   Several plants of the *Dianthus* genus, including the carnation, are popularly called pinks, because the edges of the flower petals are pinked or notched, as if clipped by pinking shears. The designation has nothing to do with color. *See* CARNATION.

Pinkerton.   When he came to America from Glasgow in 1842, Allan Pinkerton opened a cooper's shop in West Dundee, Illinois, his shop becoming a station in the underground railroad smuggling slaves north. Later he captured a ring of counterfeiters, this leading to his appointment in 1850 as the first city detective on Chicago's police force—a one-man detective squad. In Chicago Pinkerton also organized a detective agency to capture railway thieves, which became Pinkerton's National Detective Agency in 1852. But he achieved national prominence in February 1861, upon foiling a plot to assassinate President-elect Lincoln when his train stopped in Baltimore on the way to his inauguration in Washington. Pinkerton died in 1884, aged 65, but his sons Robert and William continued the agency. It is from this period on that Pinkerton's was chiefly engaged by industry as spies and strikebreakers, earning the bitter condemnation of labor, especially for its role in suppressing the Homestead Strike in 1892. A *Pinkerton* or *Pinkerton man* came to mean either a private detective or, in the opinion of many working men, something lower than a fink. In 1937 the agency was subjected to congressional investigation during industrial disputes over the redecognition of unions. *See* FINK; PRIVATE EYE.

pink slip.   No one knows why *pink slip* is synonymous with the discharge notice a worker gets when he is fired. The best guess is that the term originated in the late 19th to early 20th century when some unknown company issued pink slips to discharge employees; perhaps the practice then spread to other companies.

pinky; pinkie.   We find this word for the smallest and last finger on the human hand first recorded in 1808, when it was defined as a term used by children that derives from the Dutch *pink*, small. It is also called the *little finger* and was once called the *little man*. *See* THUMB.

pin money.   Metal pins, invented in about the 14th century and later manufactured by a monopoly under grants from the British Crown, were so costly and scarce at first that there was a law forbidding their sale except on the first two days of January in every year. About that time of year husbands customarily gave their wives pin money to buy all the pins they would need for the months ahead. When pins became less expensive, the expression *pin money* was still used for this annual stipend and came to mean a personal allowance given to a wife by her husband. These were not the pins with solid heads that we know today (which were first called Poughkeepsie pins because they were invented in that New York city in 1839), nor safety pins, which were the brainchild of another American 10 years later.

pinnace.   This little, light, usually two-masted sailing vessel takes its name from the Latin *pinus*, "pine tree," which it was generally made of in days past. The word is recorded as early as 1521.

pinstriper.   There is no truth to the old story that the New York Yankees adopted their pinstriped uniform because it made the big-bellied Babe Ruth look thinner. The team was actually wearing pinstripes years before Ruth had his problems with hot dogs, soda pop, and beer. The Yankees are sometimes referred to as the Pinstripers, though nowhere nearly so often as they are called the Yankees, Yanks, Bronx Bombers, and even the Bronx Zoo. In baseball's early days they were first called the Highlanders and then the Hilltoppers.

pinto. A spotted horse or pony. The word, first recorded in 1860, is from the Spanish for "spotted" or "painted." A cowboy who rides such a horse often calls it "Paint."

pinup girl. During World War II, U.S. servicemen commonly decorated barracks walls with pictures of scantily clad film stars, the most popular of which showed Betty Grable wearing a one-piece bathing suit (*see also* GRABLE-BODIED SEAMEN). This practice led to the term *pinup girl*, which is still occasionally used for any attractive woman, while *pinup* alone can refer to an attractive woman or man.

pip. *Pip* is a shortening of *pippin*, which is used for an apple of good quality, hence the phrase *It's a pip!* The English word has its immediate roots in the French *pepin*, which probably comes from the French *petit*, "small." Sometimes pip is used as a nickname for a small boy, as it was for the cabin boy in Herman Melville's *Moby Dick*. See also APPLE.

pipe-burial. An unusual custom practiced in England by the Romans that was intended to bring one of the joys of life to the dead. As the *OED* defines it, *pipe-burial* refers to "a burial in which a pipe (usually of lead) passes from the coffin or tomb to the surface of the ground to permit the pouring of libations."

pipe down. *Pipe down* began life as a dismissal command given a ship's crew to go below decks after a task was completed or a formation had ended. This command was transmitted by the bos'n's pipe or whistle, on which the bos'n could sound notes representing many orders. *Pipe down* came in the late 19th century to mean "shut up," because it got much quieter on deck when the crew obeyed the order to go below and because the phrase *pipe down* itself suggested someone piping down or making less noise.

pipe dream. The opium pipe is the source of this phrase, for "a fantastic notion or story, an illusion." First recorded in Wallace Irvin's *Love Sonnets of a Hoodlum* (1901), the term probably dates back to the 1890s. The expression *pipe*, used by O. Henry, among others, once meant the same.

pipeline. The first pipelines to convey oil were conceived in about 1862 and with them came the obvious word describing them, which has over the years also become slang for a rich source of anything valuable. The best-known oil pipeline of the millions of miles of them in America is The Big Inch, which is actually a 24-inch pipe that conveys oil 1,341 miles from eastern Texas to New Jersey.

pipsqueak. By 1900 American hoboes were contemptuously calling young punk hoboes pip-squeaks, perhaps from the little pips on playing cards, or the pips that were small seeds, and *squeak* for their squeaky adolescent voices. Although these derivations are only guesses, *pipsqueak* did mean a little, worthless, insignificant person in hobo talk, whence it passed into general use. The term passed into British English by 1910, and during World War I, British soldiers called a small, high-velocity German artillery shell a pipsqueak. Use of *pipsqueak* for the shell reinforced the earlier meaning, which became a common expression on both sides of "the big pond," as the Atlantic still was called at the time.

piranha. The piranha takes its name from a Tupi Guarani Indian word meaning "tooth fish," and it couldn't be more aptly named. Piranha teeth are formidable indeed—razor sharp, triangular affairs that with each bite can sever a chunk of flesh the size of a quarter as cleanly as a scalpel. In 1976, when 38 Brazilians were skeletonized by a school of piranhas after a bus overturned in the Urubu River, the world knew without a doubt that these vicious little fish were indeed man-eaters. Americans had suspected as much since 1914, when Teddy Roosevelt came home from a hunt with an incredible tale about a man and his mule stripped to bones in moments while fording a Brazilian stream. Ever since that time, the piranha has been featured as the villain in as many jungle films as the crocodile or the boa constrictor.

pirates. Pirates, who have been so called since the 14th century, take their name from the Latin *pirata*, meaning "to attack." They are sea raiders who operate without any authorization except that of their own greed. See BUCCANEER; PITTSBURGH PIRATES; PRIVATEER; SWASH-BUCKLER; WALK THE PLANK.

pirogue. The Caribs, a fierce Caribbean tribe, called their dugout canoe *piraguas*, a word that French explorers changed slightly to *piroque* in the 17th century and passed on to the English, who called the canoe a *pirogue*.

piss. *Piss* is a fine old echoic word, echoing the sound of a bladder being voided, and is similar to several foreign words etymologically unrelated but meaning the same, including the Hungarian *pisalni*. The English word derives from the Latin *pissiare*, "to piss," just as does the Italian *pisciare* and the French *pisser*. "Urinate" derives from the Latin *urinare*, which is what the cultured Romans called the same thing that the common man called *pissiare*.

pissabed. Dandelions were called *pissabeds* because of the old folk belief that they made people urinate, a belief perhaps associated as much with their golden color as their diuretic property. Gerade recorded the word first, in his 1597 *Herbal*.

pistil. Apothecaries in ancient times used a club-shaped instrument called the *pistillum* to pound herbs and drugs in their mortars. Eventually, the name of this instrument was abbreviated to pestle, but when botanists named the similar-shaped female organs of flowers after it, they more carefully followed the old Latin name and called the female organs *pistils*.

pistol. The *pistolet* was originally a 15th-century dagger made in Pistoia, Italy, from which it took its name. Later small guns were made in that metalwork and gun-making center and were given the name *pistolet*, too, this subsequently shortened to *pistol*. The word has several meanings besides its use as a synonym for a hand gun. Among waiters and countermen in New York delis, *pistol* can mean pastrami, as when a waiter shouts to the cook, "One pistol on rye." Among Maine lobstermen *pistol* means a lobster with only one claw or none at all.

pistol-whip. This was not originally a gangster expression. *Pistol-whip* is first recorded in the western U.S., where it meant to beat someone with the barrel, not the butt, of a gun—it took too long to get a grip on the barrel in a fight.

pit. As the term for the stone of a fruit, *pit* isn't of ancient origin, as one would suppose. It is an Americanism that came into the language midway into the 19th century from the Dutch *pit*, meaning the same, though it may have been in New York State use long before this.

pit bull. Dogs of several different breeds—all crosses of bulldogs and terriers—are called pit bulls. So is a mongrel-type dog conforming to these general types. All were originally bred for the "sport" of bull-baiting (*see* BULLDOG) and are now used in the cruel blood "sport" of dogfighting. In a small pit or arena, the dogs are paired against each other in a fight to the death while spectators bet on the contest. Such vicious and fearless dogs, noted for their powerful, tenacious bites, have also been used as personal guard dogs in recent times and caused much trouble. One study shows that of 29 people killed by dogs in the U.S. over a four-year period, 21 were victims of pit bulls. Lately, the term *pit bull* has been extended to mean any very aggressive, mean person who is looking for a fight.

pitch. Every sales pitch, or presentation, harks back to the spiel of a carnival pitchman in the early years of this century. The pitchman, in turn, got his name from the pitch, or stand, that he worked from. And *pitch* itself originally meant land selected by a settler in colonial America, the expression recorded as early as 1699. Long before *to make one's pitch* meant to give a sales talk, it meant to settle down on one's land.

pitched battle. Pitched battles were first carefully planned, even gentlemanly, battles where the battleground was chosen beforehand and tents were pitched near it by the opposing armies at least several days before any fighting took place. They were called such as early as 1549, in contrast to skirmishes or chance encounters, but this term for a planned battle, where complete preparations have been made, came to mean a battle in which the opposing forces are completely and intensely engaged, this latter meaning far more common today.

Pitman. Sir Isaac Pitman devised his shorthand system in 1837, basing his simpler phonetic shorthand on an earlier method. The former clerk and schoolteacher lived to see almost universal acceptance of his invention, which his brother Benn helped popularize on the other side of the Atlantic when he immigrated to the United States in 1852 and established the Phonographic Institute in Cincinnati. The phonographer died in 1897, aged 84, when the even simpler GREGG SYSTEM was replacing Pitman.

the pits. *See* IT'S THE PITS.

pittance. During medieval times pittances were rather large bequests to the church, usually to religious orders, their name deriving ultimately from the Latin *pietas*, "piety." Over the years, however, these traditional bequests became smaller and smaller, a pittance finally becoming synonymous with a meager amount.

Pittsburgh, Pennsylvania; Pittsfield, Massachusetts; Pitt's pictures. The great English statesman William Pitt, the Elder (1708–78), is one of the few people to have two U.S. cities named after him. (Pittsburgh, however, was named after Fort Pitt, which had been named in his honor.) Pitt, the Younger (1759–1806), is remembered for the historical Pitt's pictures, blind windows that were blocked up because as prime minister he augmented England's "window tax" in 1784 and 1797. Rather than pay the tax, people boarded up their windows.

Pittsburgh Pirates. The baseball team takes its name from the nickname of its first president, J. Palmer "Pirate" O'Neill, who was so called because he signed a player from another club, pirating him away rather unscrupulously. *See* PIRATE.

Pity the poor sailor on a night like this! A saying *à propos* of a stormy night, this expression dates back to late-19th-century England and is still heard today.

pixilated. Although the British have used the term *pixy-led* for "enchanted by a pixie or fairy," *pixilated* is an Americanism dating back to about the mid-19th century. A combination of *pix(ie)* and *(tit)illated*, it means slightly eccentric, or amusingly whimsical, silly. The word also has the meaning of "drunk" in American slang.

pizza. One of America's favorite foods, pizza is also one of its most recent treats, the word pizza not recorded in the U.S. until 1935. *Pizza's* ultimate origins are unknown. One theory holds it comes from Italian *pizza* (or *pitta*) for the same, with the Italian word deriving from an unknown Greek word. Another theory has *pizza* coming from Italian *pizzicare*, "to pinch or pluck," in reference to the making of a pizza pie. The term *pizzeria* was first recorded in 1943, while *pizza parlor* appeared in print about five years later. In some regions, including New York, *slice* is the word to use when ordering a piece of pizza. Other places use *piece* exclusively. A *Neopolitan* pizza is the classic thin-sliced pizza, while a Sicilian pizza is a square, thick pie.

pizzaz. Energy, zest, power, and vitality are suggested by this invented word whose inventor is unknown and whose origins are unclear. *Pizzaz*, first recorded in 1937, is still heard today. Some word detectives say it was coined to capture the feeling of zestfulness, while others derive it from the older expression *piss and vinegar*, as in "He's full of piss and vinegar."

A plague on both your houses! Shakespeare probably coined this curse in *Romeo and Juliet* (1595) when Romeo's friend Mercutio is killed by Tybalt of Juliet's Capulet family. As he lays dying, he cries out, "A plague o' both your houses!" referring to both the Capulets and Romeo's Montague family. Today the words are often said by voters of America's two major political parties.

plain as the nose on your face. Shakespeare used the gist of this expression in *Two Gentlemen of Verona* (1591), but the full phrase wasn't recorded until 1655 in a work by British author Henry More: "As plain as the nose on a man's face." This phrase has been commonly used to describe anything that is perfectly obvious, the nose standing out farther than any other feature of the face.

plain brown wrapper. The designation *plain brown wrapper*, often used to describe how sexually explicit material will be sent through the mail, has its origins in the mail-order wars of the 1890s and at first had nothing at all to do with sex. Mail-order companies like Montgomery Ward (the beloved "Monkey Ward" of rural dwellers) and Sears, Roebuck sent their catalogs and goods in unmarked "plain brown wrappers" to protect customers from the wrath of local merchants and their allies, who wanted to see the mail-order firms go out of business from the time Aaron Montgomery Ward founded the first great national mail-order company in 1872.

plain sailing. In technical nautical language *plane sailing* means determining a ship's position on the assumption that the earth is flat and the ship is on a plane; this is a simple, straightforward method of computing distance. But in the 19th century, the words entered general use as an expression meaning "perfectly straightforward action, a course of action that there need be no hesitation about." The word *plane* came to be spelled *plain* and has remained that way ever since.

planet-struck. This medical term for "a tree struck by blight" stems from the old belief that malignant aspects of the planets caused death and suffering on earth. When plants and animals died or fell ill inexplicably they were said to be planet-struck. The term is first recorded in 1600.

plankton; plankter; nekton. Because it is the ocean's basic food, plankton is often called the pasture or grass of the sea. The word derives from Greek *planktus*, meaning "wandering or drifting." The term *plankton* collectively describes all the one-celled drifting life of the oceans, as opposed to *nekton*, which refers to strong swimmers such as fish, crabs, and whales (and even man in some cases). Possibly the most ingenious planktonic creature is the little animal called *Oikopleura*, which builds itself an underwater "glasshouse." The *Oikopleura* creates an envelope around itself, inflating it with a flow of water by moving its tail. This razor-thin jelly house traps the creature's food, water flowing through openings at both ends and being filtered through mesh nets that filter out minute plankton for *Oikopleura* to eat. Each resourceful *Oikopleura* plankter (the name for individual planktonic organism) has an emergency escape hatch at the rear of the house that is used when the fine-meshed nets become clogged and it has to leave home to build a dwelling elsewhere.

plant; plantation. Seeds and saplings were tucked into the soil and then stamped down into the ground with the sole of the foot by early Roman farmers, just as they are by gardeners today. From this process grew the word *plant*, which derives from the Latin *planta*, for "sole of the foot." The Latin word *plantatio*, "propagation of a plant, as from cuttings," is the source of our word *plantation*, used to describe a large estate or farm, or any area under cultivation. *Plantation* used in the sense of the early American "Plimoth Plantation" extended the word to mean the planting of a colony in a new land or country. *See also* PLANTAIN; PILGRIM.

plantain. One of our worst lawn and garden weeds, plantain takes its name from its leaves, which resemble the sole of the foot (the Latin word for "sole of the foot" is *planta*). The banana-like fruit called plantain doesn't share this derivation; its name is a corruption of the native West Indian word for the fruit. The eastern plane tree, however, does have broad leaves and takes its name from the Greek *plantanos*, "broad." *See* PLANT.

planter's wart. A good example of folk etymology (popular etymology as it is sometimes called) which, as Tom McArthur states in *The Concise Oxford Companion to the English Language* (1996) is the thoughts of "non-academic people about the origins, forms and meanings of words, sometimes resulting in changes to the words in question." Thus, the term *plantar wart*, a wart on the sole of the foot (*plantar*, Latin for sole of the foot) was changed by folk etymology into *planter's wart*.

plantocracy. A historical name, based on *aristocracy*, for the class of wealthy Southern planters before the Civil War, especially in South Carolina, where their huge plantations grew cotton, indigo, and rice as their major crops. Many of the "plantocracy" or "planting aristocracy" made their money on rice, a packet of which Captain John Thurber, a Yankee shipmaster, had presented to one of the early settlers on putting into Charleston Harbor late in the 1680s. The settler planted this Madagascar rice rather than dining on it, and after it sprouted, he gave seeds to his friends, who in turn raised rice on their fertile land. Charleston and the Carolina Low Country soon became the "Rice Coast," rice fortunes building Charleston and marking the beginning of a plantocracy considered by many at the time to be the New World aristocracy.

plaster of Paris. Calcined gypsum has had this name since the 14th century, when English artisans imported what they thought was the best quality gypsum from Montmartre, then outside Paris. Today the name is used no matter where the plaster of Paris comes from.

platonic love. Such love, devoid of anything sexual, was first described by Plato in his *Symposium*, where he tells of the pure love of Socrates for young men, a love unusual in its day. Later, in about 1626 in England, the Latin *amor Platonicus* was translated and applied to similar love between man and woman, the words often heard today in phrases like *platonic love*, a *platonic relationship*, and the like. The rare *platonics* is simply talk between *platonic lovers*.

play a hunch. Gamblers once believed that rubbing a hunchback's hump brought good luck. Although the superstition is fortunately all but dead, the expression *to play a hunch*, "to have a lucky notion or premonition," is still frequently heard. The belief that deformed people have special powers or links with the devil is an ancient one. Hunchbacks in particular were believed to share with the devil the ability to see into the future.

play ball. *Play ball* has come to mean to cooperate or collaborate, and also to begin. The words are from baseball, where *Play ball!* has been the plate umpire's command to begin play since at least 1901, when the term first appears in print.

play both ends against the middle. In faro, America's favorite game after poker in the 19th century, *playing both ends against the middle* described the way the dealer provided for a double bet by a player. The phrase came into general use soon after, meaning to use each of two sides for your own purpose.

playboy. A man, usually rich, devoted to the pursuit of pleasure. The term was not invented by Hugh Hefner with his magazine of that name. *Playboy* actually dates back to about 1620 in England. The word fell into disuse for a long period of time and was revived in New York City in about 1900 as a synonym for a bon vivant, a man about town.

play-by-play account. A detailed, sequential account of any event is called a play-by-play account or just a play-by-play. The term has been traced back to 1912 in baseball where it originated; radio play-by-play broadcasts of baseball games popularized the phrase.

play catch-up ball. *Play catch-up ball* means to play desperately toward the end of the game when one is losing. Common in the last 30 years or so, the phrase was suggested by the last-minute efforts of college football teams to pull victory from the jaws of defeat, to catch up with their opponents by throwing long, desperate passes (often called "Hail Marys"). The phrase has wide general use, especially when companies approach the end of each fiscal year.

play close to the vest. A cautious cardplayer often holds the cards close to the vest or chest to conceal them from possible cheaters. This old practice suggested the expression *play close to the vest* or *chest*, meaning "to be secretive or uncommunicative about something."

play fast and loose. This expression for "not being trustworthy or honest, promising one thing and doing another," probably derives from an old con game played by sharpsters at country fairs. In this obsolete game, its exact details long lost, the operator arranged a belt so that a spectator believed he could insert a skewer through its intricate folds and fasten the belt to the table. But the operator had cleverly coiled the belt so that it only appeared to have a loop in its center and he always pulled it loose from the table after the dupe thought he had skewered it. Metaphorical use of the phrase *play fast and loose* has been traced back to 1547, so the con game was probably being played before the 16th century.

play footsie. Since at least World War II, *play footsie* referred to expressing amorous interest in someone by furtively rubbing a bare foot against that person's body. It can also mean to pass signals under a card table to a partner and to cooperate or curry favor with someone in a sly, devious way. "Whatsa matter with ya, playin' footsie with the Commies," Thelma Ritter says in the movie *Lo* (1946).

play for fun. This term meaning to play for the enjoyment of a game, not for money or with the goal of winning, was originally *to play for love*. It first referred to games of cards played without stakes, the words probably British in origin and dating back to the 19th century. *See also* AMATEUR; PLAY FOR THE LOVE OF IT.

play for keeps. No one really knows the age of this expression, from the game of marbles. It refers to a marbles game in which players keep the marbles they win; they don't give them back to the loser. In general slang, *to play for keeps* has come to mean to be intent and serious to the point of callousness or to play rough. *See* PLAY HARDBALL.

play for the love of it. There's nothing new about this expression, meaning to play a game without stakes, for the pleasure of playing. It has its origins in Samuel Butler's satire *Hudibras* (1678), which tells of those who "play for love and money, too."

play hardball. Baseball was popularly called hardball in the early days of the game. A change in the rules—so that runners were tagged to be declared out rather than being hit with the ball—prompted a change from the soft ball formerly used to a hard one. There was never an official game called hardball, but, at least from the 1930s to 1960s, the term was common among kids in the Northeast and other areas to distinguish baseball from the game called softball. Softball is played with a larger ball (not nearly as hard on the hands for kids catching barehanded) that can't be hit as far; it is also officially played on a smaller field and the ball is pitched underhanded. Perhaps the term *hardball* we now use was born in the sandlots, but that is not certain. In any case, it gave birth in about 1944 to the expression *play hardball*, which means to act or work aggressively, competitively, or ruthlessly, to PLAY FOR KEEPS. Demeaning as it is to softball players, who can be just as serious and competitive as their "hardball" compatriots, the phrase lives on.

play hooky. There is no widely accepted explanation for the word *hookey*, or *hooky*. An Americanism that arose in the late 19th century, when compulsory attendance laws became the rule in public schools, *hooky* may be a compression of the older expression *hook it*, "to escape or make off," formed by dropping the *t* in the phrase. Or it could be related to the old slang word *hook*, meaning "to steal": kids stealing a day off from school. *Hooky* has so often been associated with going fishing that it may even owe its life to *getting off the hook* the way a fish can; anyway, school is often as insufferable as a hook to schoolchildren and many kids squirming in their seats all day look like they are on a hook.

playing chicken. *See* CHICKEN.

playing the air guitar. Miming the joyous playing of an imaginary guitar while listening to rock music. The first print use of the phrase appeared in the June 6, 1982, *Washington Post*, but it is certainly older. In the movie *Risky Business*, according to *Newsweek* (6/9/86), Tom Cruise famously "played air guitar in his underwear to 'Old Time Rock & Roll.' "

playing to the haircuts. An expression used by performers for the closing act of a vaudeville bill. Such an act would still be playing as the audience was leaving—with the backs of their heads facing the performers.

play penny pool. Anyone who deals in petty, trivial matters can be said to play penny pool, like a pool player who gambles for pennies on the outcome of the game or on a shot in the game. The expression is an Americanism dating back 50 years or so.

play possum. *Opossum* is one of the earliest of Americanisms. Borrowed from Indian language, it made its first appearance as *appossoun* in 1610, was changed to *opassom* a few years later and within a century was being written as *opossum* and its abbreviated form *possum*. The animal, which Captain John Smith described as having "an head like a swine, a taile like a rat, and is of the bigness of a cat," was known from the earliest days for the way it feigned death when threatened with capture. Trapped possums close their eyes and lay completely insufferable limp and no matter how much abuse they are subjected to, will only become active when thrown into water. Hunters knew this from the earliest days and so although the expression *play possum*, "pretend or deceive," was first recorded in 1822 the phrase is probably much older.

play the dozens. To insult one another in a rapid exchange of insults, a phrase used by both whites and blacks, though it seems to have originated with blacks in the American South toward the end of the 19th century.

play the field. *Play the field* means to have many sweethearts, many dates, with no serious attachment. It was originally a 19th-century British racing term meaning to bet on every horse in a race except the favorite.

play the market. This expression originated in the Roaring Twenties, or the Golden Twenties as they were known on Wall Street. Other expressions that were born in the 1920s include *moneybags* for a rich person, *good times*, and finally *Black Thursday*, October 29, 1929, the day of the stock market crash, and the start of the Great Depression.

play the sedulous ape. Robert Louis Stevenson originated the phrase in a charming essay in which he wrote: "I have played the sedulous ape to Hazlitt, to Lamb, to Wordsworth, to Sir Thomas Browne, to Defoe, to Hawthorne, to Montaigne, to Baudelaire, and to Obermann. . . . That, like it or not, is the way to learn to write." *Sedulous*, from the Latin *sedulus*, "careful," means diligent and persevering in application or attention, so the phrase describes anyone who slavishly imitates somebody.

play to the gallery. Like PLAY TO THE GRANDSTAND, this saying means "show off." It is the older phrase, having its origins in the 18th-century English theater, where actors overacted their roles and raised their voices in order to be appreciated by the larger audience up in the gallery beyond the orchestra.

play to the grandstand; grandstanding. *Play to the grandstand* is a baseball term first recorded in 1888 and describing a show-off player who tries to make difficult catches, or make easy catches look difficult. Within a few years such players were called grandstanders, and the term was soon applied to a show-off in any endeavor.

play with loaded dice. Play with loaded dice and nothing is left to chance. Dice can be loaded with lead or other weights

in such a way that a certain number will always or frequently come up. A gambler can then use them to his advantage by slipping them into a game and throwing all sevens, or by weighting them so that another player will shoot "craps" ("snake-eyes": two ones; or "boxcars": two sixes) on each roll. The practice is as old as the game of dice, but the expression seems to be a 20th-century Americanism.

play without a full deck. This expression, and its variant *playing with half a deck*, dates back to the 1960s, when it was first used to mean someone lacking in intelligence; that is, not having the usual allotment of brains. Besides having the obvious connection with a deck of cards, the phrase owes something to the earlier term *not all there*, for "stupid," or mentally defective, attested to as early as 1821. *Two sandwiches short of a picnic* is a synonym, as is *two bricks shy of a load*. See also NOBODY HOME.

plaza. A word widely used throughout the United States for a public square or open space; first recorded in the Southwest, it is an American borrowing of a Spanish word meaning the same.

pleach. An ancient, useful word that lives on mainly to describe a gardening method of pruning and training trees or bushes to make a hedgelike wall. Pleached alleys, rows of pleached (or plashed) trees on each side of a path, are among the most imposing garden features, one of the finest examples being the alley made of pleached London plane trees at Vienna's Schonbrunn Palace. But *pleach*, which means fold or intertwine, was mainly a poetic word in the past, used by Tennyson and Swinburne, among others. Shakespeare wrote in *Antony and Cleopatra*:

> Would'st thou be window'd in great Rome and see
> Thy master thus with pleach'd arms, bending down . . .

pleased as a basketful of possum heads. Why does this Southern expression mean "very pleased indeed"? Apparently the words capitalize on the possum's proverbial grin, or what seems to us a grin—a basketful of which would seem exceedingly pleased.

plentiful as blackberries. *See* BLACKBERRY.

plimp. In the early 1980s *Time* magazine predicted a new verb *to plimp*, meaning "the participatory journalism . . . in which the amateur ventures lamblike among the wolves of professional sport—and then writes about how to be a lamb chop." Said verb is based on the name of American author George A. Plimpton, who wrote a number of books about his adventures playing with professionals in various sports. The eponymous word isn't yet included in any major dictionary, but it has entered the language, having been noted in several books besides this one.

Plimsoll mark; plimsolls. The *Plimsoll mark* or *line*, adopted in 1876, was named in honor of maritime reformer Samuel Plimsoll's suggestion that every vessel have a load line, a mark that indicates the limit to which a ship may be loaded. Located amidships on both sides of the vessel, it is a circle with a horizontal line drawn through it showing the water level at maximum permitted loading. This innovation reformed shipping all over the globe, making Plimsoll's name world famous. His name is also remembered by *plimsolls*, rubber-soled cloth shoes or sneakers with the rubber extending about halfway up the shoe, the line between cloth and rubber somewhat resembling a Plimsoll mark.

Plot hound. For over a century the Plotts of western North Carolina bred this bear-hunting dog named after their family. The courageous, fierce dog is said "to have bear blood in him."

plow. Plowing, or turning over the soil for planting with an agricultural implement, is one of the world's oldest farming operations and the English word *plow*, in the form of *plough*, is recorded before A.D. 1000. To *plow back* is a recent term meaning to reinvest profits into a business or enterprise, while *to clean one's plow* means to beat someone up thoroughly, badly, in a fight. The last expression originated among Ozark farmers and is used throughout the United States today, especially in the South. It probably derives from the practice of farmers cleaning their plows by running them through coarse gravel, scratching the plows up badly in the process. *See also* BALK; DELIRIUM.

plow the sands. To undertake an impossible endless job, to waste time and energy on such a project. Farmers have long known that crops will not grow on beach and desert sands, and the expression itself goes back several centuries, first recorded in Robert Greene's play *Never Too Late* (1590). Greene, now best known as a detractor of Shakespeare, wrote: "With sweaty brows I long have ploughed the sands . . . Repent hath sent me home with empty hands."

plug; not worth a plugged nickel. Since at least 1860 *an old plug*, or simply a *plug*, has meant an inferior horse, one with defects. No one knows whether this expression came from the term *plug* for a counterfeit coin, that is, a coin with defects, or one that had been hollowed out and filled with an inferior metal, which is responsible for the still common saying *not worth a plugged nickel*. In any case, *plug* for a debased coin dates from the late 17th century. *Nickel* itself fits nicely in the phrase from an etymological point of view. Once the chief constituent of the U.S. five-cent piece, nickel was christened by German miners who often found it when mining for more expensive copper. In their disappointment they named nickel after a goblin called Nicholas, whom they blamed for such small mishaps.

plug ugly. *Plug ugly* describes "a city ruffian or rowdy" or any such disreputable character. First recorded as an Americanism in 1856, the word is of unknown origin, although one early source says "it derived in Baltimore . . . from a short spike fastened in the toe of [such rowdies'] boots, with which they kicked their opponents in a dense crowd, or as they elegantly expressed it, 'plugged them ugly.' "

plum. The Old English *plume*, derived from the Greek *proumnon* for the fruit, gives us the English word *plum*. Burbank plums are probably the most famous in America, and take their name from the noted plant breeder Luther Burbank, who developed some 60 varieties of plums besides the Burbank. The Damson plum, another favorite, is named for the place where it originated; according to tradition, Alexander the Great first brought it to Greece from Damascus, Syria; the Romans called it the plum of Damascus, *prunum damas cenum*, which became *damascene plum* and finally *damson plum* in English. The renowned Greengage plum, which is actually yellow with a tinge of green, was brought from Italy to France in about 1500, where it was named the *Reine-Claude* after Claudia, *la bonne reine*, queen to Francis I. About 1725, Sir William Gage, an amateur English botanist, imported a number of plum trees from a monastery in France, all of which were labeled except the Reine-Claude. A gardener named the unknown variety after his employer, and the Reine-Claude has been the greengage in England and America ever since. *See* POLITICAL PLUM.

plumb; plumber; plumb crazy, etc. A carpenter's plumb line is a lead weight on a string used to mark a true perpendicular, so that a house or floor, etc., is not "out of plumb," but corresponds to the perpendicular. *Plumb* (here pronounced "plum") derives from the Latin *plumbun*, "lead," the same word that *plumber* derives from, because a plumber works (or used to) with lead pipes. Since a plumb line is completely or absolutely perpendicular, the word *plumb* became an adverb meaning "completely or absolutely" in phrases like *plumb crazy, plumb mad*, and *plumb tired*. Its use is confined to informal or colloquial speech, but the expression is heard frequently. *Plumb* also means "very, completely, quite," as in "I plumb forgot about it." An old joke claims "There's a town [near Bluefield, West Virginia] called Plumnearly—plumb down in West Virginia and nearly in Virginia."

plumb the depths. Echo-sounders are now used to determine the depth of water, but in the past a piece of lead on a string (called a *plumb*) was dropped into the water to measure how deep it was. From this practice came the expression *to plumb the depths*, "to sink as low as possible in misfortune or unhappiness." The expression is first recorded in a figurative sense toward the end of the 16th century.

plum pudding dog. This was once a common name for the Dalmatian, or spotted coach dog, breed. The Dalmatian pointer was called the plum pudding dog because of its mottled appearance, its spots being like the plums or raisins in a pudding; the term was first recorded in 1897.

plunder. Raiders who plundered a town or country often carried off everything, down to the last rags of a place. Thus the German word *plunderen*, to plunder, comes from the German noun *Plunder*, rags, the verb passing directly into English in the late 17th century.

plus fours. These are long baggy knickers (not the women's short underpants knickers of the British) that were once commonly worn by golfers and other sportsmen and are still occasionally seen. Introduced in about 1912, they were so named because four more inches of material were added to the length of ordinary knickers to give them their comfortable looseness.

plushed to the scuppers. A character in Woody Allen's movie *The Purple Rose of Cairo* (1985) gets "plushed to the scuppers" (drunk) but the expression is recorded in no slang dictionary. It apparently derives from the British slang *plushed*, for "drunk," first recorded in the late 19th century, and *plushed* here coming from *flush* in its sense of "level with, full to the top" (with booze in this case). Perhaps the phrase is a nautical one. *Scupper* is a nautical word for a drain at the edge of the deck that allows accumulated water to run off into the sea or the bilge. So anyone *plushed to the scuppers* would be drunk to overflowing.

plutocrat. The Greek word for wealth is *ploutos*, which yielded the name Plutus for the god of riches in Greek mythology and our English word *plutocrat* for a very rich person. Plutus's female counterpart is Irene, who is also the goddess of peace.

P.M. *See* A.M.

P.M.; spiffs. For many years, perhaps since before 1900, the first term has been common among American retailers, especially in department stores. It means "a reward paid to a salesperson for selling a particular piece of merchandise, usually a slow-moving item." The initials may stand for *p*articular *m*erchandise, or *p*ush *m*erchandise, but no one seems to be sure and no one seems to know exactly where, when, and why the term originated. I would be glad to hear from any reader who can solve one or all of these minor mysteries. *Spiffs*, origin also unknown, means the same.

pneumonoultramicroscopicsilicovolcanoconiosis. The longest word listed in a general English dictionary (*Webster's*), this 45-letter giant means "a pneumoconiosis caused by the inhalation of very fine silicate or quartz dust, a miner's lung disease." But there are many specialized words longer than this. *See* DNA.

Pocahontas. Everyone knows one or another story about Pocahontas, among the most famous Native American women in history. But few know that Pocahontas was not her real name. Some American Indians at the time believed that knowing a person's real name gave one great power over that person. Therefore, her father Powhatan told the white settlers in Jamestown that his daughter's name was Pocahontas, when her real name was Matoaka, her parents having named her so from a word meaning "to play" because of her playful nature as a little girl. Powhatan himself was really named Wahunsonacock.

pocket book. *See* PENGUINIZE.

pocket borough. *See* BEAT THE BAND.

pocket veto. *See* VETO.

Podsnappery. Mr. Podsnap in Dickens's *Our Mutual Friend* (1864) is a self-important, self-satisfied man who wears blinders. His name has become a synonym for someone who refuses to admit the existence of a disagreeable situation.

Podunk. *Podunk* means "a neck or corner of land" in the Mohegan dialect of Algonquian. Originally an Indian place name used by settlers in Connecticut and Massachusetts, it came to be a derisive name for any small or insignificant, out-of-the-way place. (Peoria and Hooterville are other names generations of comedians have used for the home of the rube and the boob.)

Poes of Princeton. Edgar Allan Poe is arguably America's best-known poet. Few are aware, however, that he was an excellent athlete as well. Poe, who would hardly suggest anything but an emaciated aesthete today, long jumped 21 feet while at West Point. He was as good a swimmer as Lord Byron (who swam the Hellespont), and once swam 7½ miles from Richmond to Warwick, Virginia, "against a tide running two to three miles an hour." Another time he boxed the ears of and horsewhipped a scurrilous critic. He is also remembered for the *Poes of Princeton*, football players famous in their time if now all but forgotten. They were six members of the 1899 Princeton College football team, each named Poe and each a great-nephew of the poet. All of them apparently inherited Uncle Edgar's athletic prowess, but none his poetic genius off the field. *See* BALTIMORE RAVENS

poetaster. Erasmus coined this word for an inferior poet in a 1521 letter to a friend. Nineteenth-century Scottish poet William McGonagall is probably the only poetaster to actually have his work collected because it is so bad. In his introduction to McGonagall's selected poems, published by Stephen Greene Press, James L. Smith writes that the poet is "unquestionably the great master of Il-literature in the language." McGonagall, who never lost faith in his greatness and actually outsells Browning and Tennyson in Great Britain today, attracted audiences to his poetry readings because people who had read his poems wanted to pelt him with rotten tomatoes and eggplant. Others have produced poems with more mechanical regularity than McGonagall; present-day Indian poet Sri Chinmoy composed 843 poems within a day in 1975, and another time turned out 16,031 paintings in a day. However, no one's poetry has been so consistently bad as the Scottish bard's, which has been called "the worst poetry ever written, in any language, at any time." A sample of his work from "The Battle of Abu Klea":

> Oh, it was an exciting and terrible sight,
> To see Colonel Burnably engaged in fight;
> With sword in hand, fighting with might and main
> Until killed by a spear thrust in the jugular vain.

poet but don't know it. *See* HE'S A POET.

poetic justice. The first printed reference to the term, most often meaning just deserts or a fitting punishment for a crime, is found in Alexander Pope's *The Dunciad* (1742): "Poetic Justice with her lifted scale, / When in nice balance, truth with gold she weighs. . . ." At the time of Pope's invention it meant the ideal justice poets dispensed. Novelist Henry Fielding, also a British justice of the peace, wrote an article for a satirical journal demanding that there be a kind of poetic justice for the poet laureate Colley Cibber (1671–1757)—that he be tried for murder of the English language. Fielding was apparently getting even with Cibber for calling him a "broken wit."

poetic license. John Dryden called poetic license "the liberty which poets have assumed to themselves in all ages, of speaking things in verse, which are beyond the severity of prose." Poetic license is the liberty taken by any writer, especially a poet, to fit the language to his needs, to deviate from conventional form, fact, and even logic to create a desired effect. Everything depends on the end justifying the means, that is, whether the poem (or other piece of writing) "works." Luckily, Tennyson presented his poetic license after he wrote the line, "Every moment dies a man/ Every moment one is born." The literal-minded mathematician Charles Babbage had written him that "if this were true, the population of the world would be at a standstill" and urged him to change the line to: "Every moment dies a man/ Every moment $1\frac{1}{16}$ is born."

poet laureate.   In Greek legend Apollo fell in love with and tried to seize Daphne, the daughter of a river, and at her own request she was turned into a bay laurel tree, which became sacred to Apollo. The god ordered that laurel be the prize for poets and victors, this leading to the belief that laurel leaves communicated the spirit of poetry (the ancients put laurel leaves under their pillows to acquire inspiration while they slept) and the tradition of laurel symbolizing excellence in literature. The first laureates were university graduates in poetry and rhetoric who were presented laurel wreaths and called "doctors laureate" and "bachelors laureate." Before the title *poet laureate* was conferred upon any poet in England there were a number of court poets: King Henry I (1068–1135) had a Versificator Regis (King's versifier) named Wale. Ben Jonson was granted a pension by James I in 1616 and was a poet laureate in the modern sense, and Chaucer, Skelton, and Spenser had been called laureates before him; but it wasn't until John Dryden was appointed poet laureate by Charles II in 1668 that the position became official. Currently the poet laureate is chosen by the sovereign from a list of names submitted by the prime minister when the position falls vacant. Appointments are for life, and by custom the poet laureate composes odes for the sovereign's birthday and New Year's odes. Dryden was awarded a pension of 300 pounds and a tierce of canary wine as laureate, but today the annual pension is 70 pounds with 27 pounds more given instead of the wine.

poets are born, not made.   True, untrue, or partly true, this is an ancient belief, for it is a translation of the Latin *Poeta nascitur, non fit.* In his "To the Memory of . . . Shakespeare" (1623), in which he gave us the immortal lines "Sweet Swan of Avon!" and "He was not of an age but for all time," Ben Jonson wrote: "For a good poet's made, as well as born."

Poet's Corner.   Part of the south transept of Westminster Abbey, where many great authors are buried, the Poet's Corner was so named by Oliver Goldsmith, later buried there himself; it had been called "the poetical Quarter" before then. In the corner are, among others, the tombs of or monuments to Chaucer, Spenser, Ben Jonson, Shakespeare, Samuel Butler, Drayton, Milton, Davenant, Cowley, Prior, Gay, Addison, Thomson, Goldsmith, Dryden, Dr. Johnson, Sheridan, Burns, Southey, Coleridge, Campbell, Macaulay, Longfellow, Dickens, Thackeray, Tennyson, Browning, and Hardy. In the case of Hardy, his heart is buried in his native Dorset. One of the oddest stories about the Poet's Corner concerns Thackeray's bust there. The novelist's daughter had always "deplored the length of the whiskers on each side of the face of her father's bust," believing that the Italian sculptor Marachetti had made

them far too long. Finally, as an old woman, she managed to persuade officials to let another sculptor move the bust into a secluded alcove and chip away at the sideburns until they were the right length. This accomplished, an appropriately bewhiskered Thackeray was restored to his proper niche in the nave.

Poet's Poet.   A title first given in history to English poet Edmund Spenser (1552?–99), best known for his poem *The Faerie Queen*, which was written in the Spenserian stanza he invented. Spenser served many years as secretary to the lord deputy of Ireland, until in 1598 his castle was burned down during an Irish uprising and one of his children perished in the fire. He died the following year, in London, never recovering from the tragedy.

pogonip.   An icy winter fog that forms in mountain valleys, especially in Nevada, the heavy fog often blocking the sun for days and appearing like a fine snow; the Shoshonean word *pogonip* has been translated as "white death," the fog thought to cause pneumonia.

poikilothermia.   A rare ailment that makes one extremely sensitive to cold, unable to maintain a constant body temperature. The popular fantasy and science-fiction author H. P. (Howard Phillips) Lovecraft (1890–1937) suffered from this disorder, which takes its name from Greek. Lovecraft had to wear many layers of warm clothing on the hottest days and even on moving to Florida wore a heavy overcoat during the summer.

poinciana.   The tropical *royal poinciana* with its brilliant, long-clawed scarlet or yellow-striped flowers is probably the most striking of all cultivated trees. Popular in Florida and California as well as its native Madagascar, the broadheaded tree grows from 20 to 40 feet high and is sometimes called the *Delonix* (Greek for long claw) and the *peacock flower. Poinciana regia*, as well as the entire *Poinciana* genus, containing several showy plants of the pea family, was named by Linnaeus in honor of M. de Poinci, a 17th-century governor of the French West Indies, where the tree is also widely grown and admired. Another, more descriptive name for the tree is *flame-of-the-forest.*

poinsettia.   This bright red flower, a symbol of Yuletide, could not have been named for a more fiery personality. Joel Roberts Poinsett (1779–1851) had much of the Christmas spirit in him, too, at least a great love for the oppressed and a romantic revolutionary desire to better their lives. Poinsett served as a member of the South Carolina legislature and as a congressman for a number of years, but found himself more in his own element when appointed the first American minister to Mexico in 1825. Here his revolutionary ardor was so excessive that he lasted only four years, his recall demanded first by the regime that he helped overthrow and then by the republican regime that replaced it. By this time Poinsett was a familiar public figure and when he sent specimens of the large, fiery flowers that we know so well back to this country, they were named after him. Poinsett hadn't discovered the plant, of course, and it had even been introduced to the United States before him; his popularity alone accounted for the honor. The ousted ambassador went on to become Van Buren's secretary of war, and a Union leader during the Civil War, despite his southern origins. The *Poinsettia* genus commemorating him is now considered part of the genus *Euphorbia*, but the gorgeously colored Mexican species, its tapering scarlet bracts so much a part of Christmas, is still called the poinsettia. In England it is known as the *Mexican flame-leaf.*

point-blank.   A point-blank shot made by archers in 16th-century England was one in which the arrow was aimed or pointed directly at the small white, or blank, bull's-eye in the center of the target. With the advent of firearms a shot was said to be point-blank when it remained approximately straight over a certain distance. Because close-range point-blank firing in gunnery led to brutal destruction, the term became a synonym for direct, uncompromising rejection or blunt, brutal frankness in such terms as *point-blank refusal* and *point-blank denial.*

point the finger.   This expression is first recorded in Shakespeare's *Othello* (1604): "To make me the fixed Figure for the time of Scorne to point his slow, and moving finger at." It came to mean "to single out a guilty person" and ultimately gave us the expression *finger man* for a criminal who singles out a victim for a murder, robbery, or other crime, and *to finger,* the act of singling out a victim for a crime.

poke.   Poke or pokeweed (*Phytolacca americana*), also called "inkberry," has highly poisonous, even deadly, roots that cause trouble because they resemble horseradish. It is a handsome plant admired for its blackish-red berries (the seeds are also poisonous) whose young foliage is eaten by some after boiling. Poke played a minor role in American politics that few are familiar with. In the presidential campaign of 1844, supporters of James Polk proclaimed their allegiance by carrying tall stalks from the pokeweed plant through the streets (because *poke* sounded something like *Polk*). Ox drivers who favored Henry Clay covered the horns of their oxen with clay, and the Polk supporters gathered poke berries and stained the horns of their own oxen with these. Polk won, of course, thanks in a small part to poke.

poke fun at; poke.   *To poke fun at* has meant to ridicule since at least 1837, when it is first recorded in Barham's *Ingoldsby Legends:* "Poking your fun at us plain-dealing folk." A *poke* in this case isn't a bag (as in *a pig in a poke*), of course, but a thrust or dig with the fingers.

poker; poker face.   *Poker* takes its name from the French *poque,* for a similar card game, though the rules of the Persian game *As Nas* (played with five cards) and *poque* (played with three cards) were combined to make America's characteristic gambling game. The game is mentioned as early as 1834 and probably dates back at least 10 years earlier. *A poker face,* a face that conceals all emotions, also comes from the card game, in which bluffing is an important tactic.

pokey.   Someone going to jail, or the *pokey,* is doubtless often poked along by an officer with a nightstick. But while such pokes may have influenced the popularity of the word pokey, it probably has its roots in the French *poche,* "a small enclosure," or the older *pogy,* "a workhouse or poorhouse."

pokies.   Australian English for slot machines. According to Bill Bryson's *In A Sunburned Country* (2000), Australia, with less than 1 percent of the world's population, has over 20 percent of the world's "pokies."

polar plant.   *See* COMPASS PLANT.

polecat; polecat trail; wildcat trail.   Though a polecat is a kind of weasel (*Mustela putorius*) in Europe, the word is a synonym for a skunk in the U.S. Its name comes from Latin *pullus,* "chicken," plus *cat,* apparently due to the polecat's taste for chicken. In skiing, *polecat trail* refers to an easy trail for beginners, without sharp turns or pitches, the opposite of *wildcat trail.*

polecat weed.   *See* SKUNK CABBAGE.

police action.   Though 75,000 U.N. soldiers were killed in it and a quarter of a million wounded, the Korean war cannot officially be called a war because Congress never officially declared it one. It is officially known in history as the Korean police action, the Korean emergency and the Korean conflict. President Truman approved the coinage *police action,* after an anonymous reporter asked him if repelling a raid "by a bunch of bandits," as Truman called the North Koreans, could be termed a "police action." The reporter, however, probably got the term from a speech by Senator William F. Knowland. *See* FORGOTTEN WAR.

political correctness.   A philosophy advocating the rejection of expressions or actions that could be considered offensive to a race, sex, class, religion, etc. American in origin, the term was first recorded in this sense in 1970 and probably dates to the 1960s. The term is often intended derisively today, due in part to extremist use of the doctrine. *Political correctness* is often abbreviated PC, first recorded in 1986. *See* PERSON.

political infighting.   We have used this term in America since the late 1940s to mean fighting within a political party or any group. The word *infighting* dates back to 1790s England, where it originated as a method of fighting at close quarters, one generally used by lighter boxers to lessen the force of blows from heavier, stronger opponents.

political plum.   When a delighted Matthew S. Quay was elected U.S. senator from Pennsylvania in 1887, he assured his supporters that he would "shake the plum tree" for them. From this promise came our expression *a political plum,* an excellent or desirable thing, a fine job. The Little Jack Horner who pulled out a plum from the pie may have contributed to the term's popularity.

political slogans.   Even before "Tippecanoe and Tyler Too" swept William Henry Harrison and John Tyler into office (*see* CIDER), slogans played an important part in politics. Like all slogans, good political slogans are usually short and simple, with rhyme or rhythm, and say what the electorate feels but is unable to express. Yet some great slogans have had few or none of these qualities. For example, Herbert Hoover's backers used the negative scare slogan "Rum, Romanism and Rebellion" to defeat Al Smith in 1928. The Democrats' slogan against Grover

Cleveland's opponent in 1884 was: "James G. Blaine, James G. Blaine / Continental liar from the State of Maine!" Humorous slogans have also been effective, such as the Democrats' gem: "In Hoover we trusted, now we are busted." There is no space here for a complete accounting of political slogans, but below are some famous ones that may or may not have succeeded:

> "We Polked You in '44; "We Shall Pierce You in '52!"— Franklin Pierce (1852)
> "A Square Deal"—Theodore Roosevelt (1912)
> "He Kept Us Out Of War"—Woodrow Wilson (1916)
> "A Chicken in Every Pot"—Herbert Hoover (1928)
> "A New Deal"—Franklin Roosevelt (1932)
> "A Fair Deal"—Harry Truman (1948)
> "I Like Ike"—Dwight Eisenhower (1956)
> "The New Frontier"—John F. Kennedy (1960)
> "All the Way with L.B.J."—Lyndon Johnson (1964)
> "In Your Heart You Know He's Right—Barry Goldwater (1964)
> "Nixon's the One"—Richard Nixon (1968)
> "We Can't Stand Pat"—Pat Paulsen (1972)

See SLOGAN.

politician who is poor is a poor politician. In his obituary (*New York Times* 12/13/01) veteran Mexican politician Carlos Hank González (1928–2001) is cited as "famous for coining the phrase *a politician who is poor is a poor politician.*" These memorable cynical words were uttered by a man who "used his fame as a politician to enhance his private ventures" and was "the most powerful figure in Mexican politics for thirty years."

polka; polka dot. At least four dances have been named for the Poles by other countries, and the most popular of them, the polka, is not even Polish in origin. *Polka* simply means a Polish woman, just as *Polak*, which gives us the slang derogatory expression *Polock*, means a Polish man. Either the Czechs called the Bohemian dance *pulka* ("half") because of its short half-steps and this word became corrupted to *polka*, or they named it as a tribute to Polish womankind. At any rate, the lively dance—three steps and a hop in double time—took Europe and America by storm after it was introduced about 1830. The polka craze resulted in many fashionable garments and designs being named after the dance, including a close-fitting knitted jacket called the polka, and even the American dress fabric with a polka-dot pattern, introduced in 1880 or so. *Polka dot* may have been inspired by the hopping around characteristic of the polka. Its use was originally confined to the uniform, evenly spaced dots in the material, but the words *polka dot* or *polka dotted* are widely applied today.

polliwog. *See* TADPOLE.

Pollyanna. Pollyanna Whittier, the child hero of Eleanor M. Porter's eponymous novel *Pollyanna* (1913), was noted for playing "the glad game," in which she tried to find the bright side of even the darkest, most dire situations. She is given no credit for this trait, however, for her name has ever since been used to describe a foolish optimist, woman or man.

polo. One of the relatively few Tibetan words in English, *polo* derives from the Tibetan *pulu*, for the name of the ball hit with the mallet used in the game played on horseback. Polo probably originated in Tibet, was adopted by the Indians, and borrowed from them by British soldiers serving in India during the mid 18th century. Other English words whose ultimate ancestry is Tibetan include "panda" and "yak."

polonium. Marie and Pierre Curie named this element in 1898 after they discovered it in their work on radioactivity. The radioactive element polonium was named by the wife and husband team after Madame Curie's homeland, Polonia being medieval Latin for Poland. *See* CURIE.

poltroon. An abject coward. The word, heard infrequently, occasionally pops up in a historical romance or biography. It comes ultimately from Latin *pullus*, "young animal," such creatures often being easily frightened.

polyandry. The practice of having more than one legal husband at a time, the word deriving from the Greek words for "many" and "male." Kahina, an ancient queen of the Berbers, is said to be the record holder here with 400 legal husbands at her disposal at a time. *See also* POLYANDRY.

polygyny. The practice of having more than one legal wife at a time, the word deriving from the Greek words for "many" and "female." King Mongut of Siam (Thailand) (hero of *The King and I*) is said to be the record holder here with 9,000 wives, 8,600 more than his female counterpart, Berber Queen Kahina, had husbands. A Mormon arguing with Mark Twain defied him to cite any biblical passage expressly forbidding polygyny. "Easy," Twain replied: "No man can serve two masters!" *See* POLYANDRY.

pomato. *Pomato* was first used by Luther Burbank in 1905 for the fruit of a hybrid potato, but his creation didn't catch on, and *pomato* later became the name of the potato-tomato plant, with the potatoes growing underground on the roots of the plant and the tomatoes growing above the ground on the plant branches or vines. The chief drawback for this novelty is that potatoes can transfer several diseases to tomatoes and vice-versa, which is the reason potato fields on farms are generally widely separated from tomato fields. One of the earliest experiments with tomatoes, in 1910, produced a tomato-eggplant chimera having characteristics of each parent on the same branch. Many such experiments have been made. At North Carolina State University, for example, tomatoes were grafted on tobacco plant roots. The result was a tomato with a high nicotine content. *See* TIGON.

pomegranate; garnet; grenade. Commonly called "Chinese apples" in America, *pomegranates*, "the fruit of the ancients," take their name from the Latin for "many-seeded apple." The thick-skinned red fruit, about the size of an orange, is divided into numerous cells inside, each containing many seeds encased in a crimson, juicy pulp. When the fruit is eaten raw, it is broken open and the red flesh is sucked out. Today in the Orient when a newly married couple reaches their new home, pomegranates are broken at the doorway, their crimson-coated seeds signifying both the loss of virginity and an omen that many offspring will come of the marriage. A number of other words derive from the pomegranate with its red skin and seeds. Our *grenade*, a weapon first used in the late 16th century, comes from the French *grenade*, a shortening of French *pomegrenade*, for pomegranate. It was originally filled with grains or "seeds" of powder and thus facetiously named after the many-seeded fruit. Today the word is used in *hand grenade*, which isn't filled with grains of powder anymore, but can create a scene of carnage as bloody as any shattered pomegranate where it explodes. The military *grenadier*, originally for a soldier who threw grenades, evolved in much the same way from the French shortening, as did the term *grenadine* for the drink made from the fruit. But the garnet stone, its color similar to the flesh of the fruit, was given its name by the Romans, the Latin *granatum* (from *Punic granatum* or Punic apple: the pomegranate) becoming *grenat* in Old French and shifting by metathesis to *garnet* in English over the years.

Pomeranian.   One of the smallest dogs, the Pomeranian surprisingly counts among its ancestors the strong Spitz sled dogs of the north. The toy breed is named for Pomerania, once a German province, where it was first bred.

pommel.   This saddle knob takes its name from the apple, specifically from the Latin *pomum*, apple, because of its similar shape. *Pommel*, in turn, gives us *pummel*, which originally meant to hit someone with a knob-shaped weapon, to *pommel* or *pummel* him. Today, of course, *pummel* means to hit someone with anything.

pomology.   Pomona was a Roman goddess of fruit from whose name *pomology*, the science of fruits and fruit growing, derives. She was the wife of Vortumnus, a Roman god of orchards and fruit who presided over seasonal changes. Vortumnus, also called Vertumnus, courted Pomona in a variety of forms (as a reaper, ploughsman, pruner of vines, etc.). His name may derive from the Latin *vertere*, "to turn," as the god who changes his shape, or for the god of the turning or changing year. Flora, the old Roman deity of flowers and fertility was another agricultural goddess. Flora had a temple erected to her near the Circus Maximus, where a special priest was in attendance. The public games at Rome called the *Ludi Florales* were held in her honor in the Circus from April 28 to May 3. Men decked themselves with flowers and women wore colorful dresses during this time of public merriment.

pompadour.   Madame de Pompadour, born Jeanne-Antoinette Poisson, is probably history's most famous courtesan. In fact, La Pompadour, who became *maîtresse en titre* to Louis XV when 27 years old, had been educated at great expense to be a royal mistress. Raised from an early age by her mother's lover, a wealthy financier who took her from her poor parents, her future had been prophesied when she was only nine by an old fortune-teller, whom Pompadour later pensioned for the accuracy of her prediction. An extremely beautiful girl, she proved to be a kind, generous, and talented woman once she had entrenched herself with the monarch. Surrounding herself with beautiful objects was her passion and she was the undisputed leader of Parisian fashions, causing many styles and costumes to be attributed to her. The most famous, historically, is the pompadour hairstyle, which was at first worn in loose rolls around the face but swept upward high above the forehead in the next century and came to be a style worn by men as well as women. The woman's dress called a pompadour, cut square and low in the neck, is also named for her. However, her name is best known as a synonym for mistress. Even on her deathbed she painted her face for the king.

pompano.   A few fish of the genus *Trachinotus* bear this name, but *pompani* usually refers to *Trachinotus carolinus*, noted for its yellowish breast. Mark Twain called pompano "as delicious as the less conventional forms of sin."

pom-pom girl; pompon girl.   *Pom-pom girl* is a synonym for a prostitute, having its origins in the automatic pom-pom guns that Chicago gangsters used in the 1920s. Pompon girls or pom poms are cheerleaders, so named because they originally waved pompons, a variety of chrysanthemum.

poncho.   Both the blanket-like coat with the hole in the middle for one's head and *poncho*, the name for it, come from the Chilean Arucan Indians. Mexican *vaqueros* copied the coat from them and Americans adopted it early in the 19th century.

pone.   The *pone* of the famous southern pone bread and corn pone is from the Powhatan Indian word *apan* (something baked). Corn pone is baked in large, flat, oval, hand-shaped cakes. A variation of the word *pone* is recorded by Captain John Smith as early as 1612.

pongo.   The legendary pongo was "a cross between a tiger and a sea-shark," a huge monster that devastated Sicily before it was slain by the three sons of St. George. For centuries the name was applied not only to the terrible sea monster but also to a gorilla, of all things, probably because by some strange coincidence *pongo* is the name in Bantu dialect for a large ape.

Pontiac.   The one American car named after an Indian, in this case Chief Pontiac of the Ottawa tribe, who waged Pontiac's War against the British in 1763. Though his tribe lost the war, Pontiac's name became legend in Michigan, and two centuries later Detroit's General Motors Corporation gave his name to the car and mounted his head on the hood. *See* SEQUOIA.

ponticello.   Deriving from the Latin *pons*, "bridge," *ponticello* is an Italian word taken intact into English that means the bridge of a stringed instrument such as a violin. *Ponticello* is also used to describe an adolescent boy's changing voice, which is a little bridge connecting puberty and manhood.

pontiff.   How the title of the pope derives from the Latin word *pons* for a bridge is not completely clear. The word came into the language in the late 17th century, via French, from the Latin *pontifex*, meaning a "high priest" of Rome, and was applied to bishops as well as the pope. Some scholars believe *pontifex* is of Etruscan origin, but most derive it from Latin *pontifex*, meaning "bridge builder," the Tiber bridges of ancient Rome said to be the responsibility of its priests.

pontoon.   The Greek god of the sea, Pontus, gives his name to the pontoon bridge, a floating structure, as well as to the pontoons on seaplanes and the pontoon lifeboat, a lifeboat dependent for buoyancy on a watertight double bottom. *Pontoon* is first recorded in 1591.

pony; Pony Express. The pony is related to the young chicken, though only in language. Both words have their roots in the Latin word *pullus*, "a young animal," yielding the French *poulet*, "a young fowl," this becoming the English *pullet* and the French *poulenet*, "a young horse," which became the Scottish *powney* and then the English *pony*. The Pony Express, more often called simply the Pony at the time, was the common designation for the Central Overland Pony Express Company, which lasted only from April 3, 1860 to October 24, 1861, but is still operating in Western novels and films. It had 190 stations along its route between Missouri and California, riders, including "Buffalo Bill" Cody, changing swift Indian ponies at each station and riding on with the mail—often through bad weather and Indian ambushes. The record for its 2,000-mile run was seven days, 17 hours, but it couldn't beat the telegraph that connected East and West in 1861, and the Pony Express went out of business that year.

pony up. Since the early 1800s *pony up*, or *poney up*, has been American slang for "to pay up." These words may derive from the German *poniren*, "to pay," but *pony* was British slang for a small amount of money in the early 19th century, probably because a pony is a small horse (not over 14 hands high), and the term to *pony up* probably derived from this expression. Other uses of *pony* to indicate smallness include the *pony* that is a small glass or bottle of alcoholic beverage and the *pony* meaning a trot or crib—a translation used by students.

poo-bah. A politician who holds several offices, or a pompous self-important person, is called a poo-bah. In Gilbert and Sullivan's operetta *The Mikado* (1885) Pooh-Bah is the personal name of the arrogant Lord High Everything Else, this being the source of the word.

poodle. *Poodle*, first recorded in 1825, is short for the German *Puddlehund*. This extremely intelligent dog, bred for over 2,000 years, was widely valued for retrieving, as is shown by the components of its name: *pudeln*, "splash in the water," and *Hund*, "hound or dog." Female poodles (and toy or miniature poodles as well) are among the smartest of dogs. Standard poodles attained their greatest popularity as pets in France, which led to them being called French poodles, although the Germans probably developed them. They were one of the 25 or so breeds selected for training by the U.S. Army K-9 Corps during World War II.

poogye. A usual word for an unusual thing, *poogye*, or *poogyee*, a Hindi term that has come into English unchanged, stands for the Hindu nose flute, "the tubes of which are inserted into a gourd and are blown with the nose instead of the mouth."

pooh-pooh. *Pooh-pooh* is a reduplication of *pooh*, which is probably "a vocal gesture expressing the action of puffing or blowing anything away" and is first recorded in *Hamlet*, as "puh" ("Affection, puh. You speak like a greene girl.") By the early 19th century we find *pooh-pooh* being used to mean "to express contempt or disdain for, to make light of." So common

was the interjection *pooh-pooh* in the 19th century that a pooh-pooh meant "one addicted to using this expression."

poontang. Thomas Wolfe used this word for the vagina or "a piece" in *Look Homeward, Angel*, and Calder Willingham used it more graphically in *End As a Man*. The black and southern white expression, first referring to black women and now to both blacks and whites, might be expected to have a diverting story behind it, as unusual as *poontang* sounds. But it probably comes from the French *putain*, "prostitute," by way of New Orleans.

pooped out. Anyone *pooped out* or *all pooped* feels something like the 19th-century seamen who used the expression *pooped* to indicate what happened when they were caught on the poop or aft deck of a ship when a wave crashed down and washed over them.

poor as a church mouse. This saying, meaning poor indeed, goes back to 17th-century England, but probably was taken from similar German and French expressions that are much older. Church mice in centuries past had lean pickings, if they had any pickings at all. Churches then had no recreational facilities with well-stocked kitchens as do some of their modern-day counterparts. They were used only for religious services and prayer, and a mouse living in one would be hard put to find a crumb.

poor as Job's turkey. Though the Book of Job doesn't mention his having any turkeys, Job certainly was poor and miserable, which inspired 19th-century Canadian humorist Thomas Haliburton to coin this expression. Haliburton, whose contributions to American English were considerable, wrote in one of his Sam Slick tales about Job's turkey, which had but one feather and was so weak with hunger that it had to support itself against the barn when it wanted to gobble.

poor boy sandwich. *See* HERO SANDWICH.

poor Joe. The poor Joe or po' Joe, as it is called, is another name for the great blue heron, especially in the American South. No "Joe" is honored by the name. It is from the Vai language of Liberia and Sierra Leone, where *pojo* means "heron," and was introduced to America by Vai-speaking slaves.

poor man's manure. Snow that falls in early spring; it is thought to provide the soil with nutrients and to be a better source of moisture because it doesn't cause erosion by running off. The old expression has its counterparts in several languages.

poormouth. Poormouthing describes the talk of a person always pleading poverty or complaining about having no money or material things. This isn't a modern expression or practice—the practice is as old as mankind and the expression, apparently a Scottish one (*to make a poor mouth*), dates back to at least the early 19th century.

Poor Richard's Almanac. *See* ALMANAC.

a poor thing but mine own. Often heard as a disparagement of the speaker's own work, whatever it might be. The phrase is from Shakespeare's *As You Like It* (1599) and is actually "An ill-favored thing, sir, but mine own."

poor white. According to W. T. Couch, in *Culture in the South* (1941): "In discriminating Southern speech, it [*poor white*] was not used to include all white persons who were poor. . . . The 'poor whites' were those who were both poor and conspicuously lacking in the common social virtues and especially fell short of the standard in certain economic qualities." An old black southern rhyme goes:

> My name is Sam,
> I don't give a damn.
> I'd rather be black
> Than a poor white man.

poor white trash. Lower-class white people; similar in meaning to *poor white*, but a stronger term. The offensive term goes back at least to the early 19th century, when we find it in Francis Kimble's *Journal* (1833): "The slaves themselves entertain the very highest contempt for white servants, whom they designate as 'poor white trash.' " Terms like POOR WHITE, RED NECK and PECKERWOOD are often slur names.

Pooterish. *The Diary of a Nobody* (1892) has long been a favorite novel of many readers and has been called "immortal." Written by the brothers George and Weedon Grossmith, it recounts the life of Charles Pooter and his wife, Carrie, in early 1890s England. Pooter can be called many things, but when someone is described as "Pooterish" it usually means he is a trivial, over-sensitive person who reveres the wealthy.

pop. *See* ONOMATOPOEIA.

popcorn. Certainly known to the Aztecs, popcorn was so named by American settlers on the frontier in the early 19th century. It is a variety of small-eared corn (*Zea mays everta*), the kernels of which pop open when subjected to dry heat and has also been called "parching corn," "popped corn," "pot corn," "cup corn," "dry corn," and "buckshot" over the years. The great quantities of it sold in movie theaters prompted some early movie house corporations to grow thousands of acres of popcorn.

pope. As Gary Wills points out in *Why I Am a Catholic* (2002), the title "*pope* was not reserved for the bishop of Rome until the 5th century," though it applied to any bishop before then. The word *pope* comes ultimately from Greek *pappas*, father, or daddy, an infant's word for father. There have been 263 popes of the Catholic Church.

Popemobile. In this time of assassins even the pope needs a bullet-proof vehicle to transport him from place to place. This has been the case since 1979, when Pope John Paul II became the first pope to ride in the popularly named Popemobile, with its bulletproof glass and raised viewing platform. The vehicle's official name is Special Papal Transport, or SPT.

pop goes the weasel. The children's song "Pop Goes The Weasel" (ca. 1853) by W. R. Mandale is the source for this phrase. The refrain goes: "Up and down the City Road, / In and out the Eagle, / That's the way the money goes—/Pop goes the Weasel." The Eagle was a popular London pub or music hall of the day, while *weasel* referred to a hatter's tool, and *pop* was a contemporary term meaning "to pawn or hock."

poplar. After destroying the monster Kakos in a cavern of Aventine, the legendary hero Hercules took a branch from one of many poplar trees growing there and bound it around his head. When Hercules descended to Hades to return Cerberus, the three-headed watchdog of the infernal regions, the heat there caused a perspiration that blanched the underside of the leaves on the poplar branch, while the smoke of the eternal flames blackened their upper surface. And that is why, according to fable, the leaves of the poplar are dark on one side and white on the other. The poplar takes its name from *populus*, the Latin name for the tree.

poplin. This finely corded material is named, indirectly, after the Roman Catholic papacy. Avignon, the French city where it was first made in the 14th century, was a papal city and a seat of the Catholic church, and the cloth was named after the pope.

poppie. *Poppie* or *poppy* is American slang for a father or a grandfather. In South African English it is a slang term for a woman of any age.

poppy. *Opium* derives from the Greek *opion*, meaning simply "poppy juice" and reflecting the fact that the drug is made from the milky juice of the unripe pods of the opium poppy (*Papaver somniferum*). The poppy and its narcotic properties have been known since prehistoric times, however, and the Egyptians used it medicinally long before the ancient Greeks. There are some 100 other species of poppies besides the opium poppy, many of these beautiful flowers grown in the home garden. In England, the artificial red flowers sold on Remembrance Day for the benefit of war veterans are called "Flanders poppies." A 1915 poem by John McCrae seems to have been the first to connect this flower with the dead of World War I:

> In Flanders fields the poppies grow
> Between the crosses, row on row
> That mark our place; and in the sky
> The larks, still bravely singing, fly
> Scarce heard among the guns below.
>
> We are the Dead. Short days ago
> We lived, felt Dawn, saw sunset glow,
> Loved and were loved, and now we lie
> In Flanders field . . .

poppycock. *Poppycock* means nonsense, the Americanism first recorded in 1865 and deriving from the Dutch *pappekak*, which means "soft dung" and owes its life, in turn, to the Latin *pappa*, "soft food," and *cacare*, "to defecate."

popsicle. The popsicle might still be an "Epsicle" if Frank W. Epperson (1894–1983) hadn't gone broke in 1929 and sold his patent for his "handled, frozen confection or ice lollipop" to a small company, which changed its name from *Epsicle* to *Popsicle*. Epperson had dubbed his successful product the Epsicle some 19 years after he accidentally invented it one cold San Francisco night in 1905, when as an 11-year-old he left a glass of lemonade on his porch and "awoke the next morning to find the drink frozen solid around a spoon that was in it."

popskull. The word has nothing to do with pop music. *Popskull* refers to cheap, potent MOONSHINE, so named because enough of it seems to pop things inside your skull.

porcelain. Why is porcelain named for a pig? The earthenware takes its name from the Latin *porcella*, "little sow," because the Romans believed its finish resembled a cowrie shell, which in turn they thought resembled a sow's vulva.

porcupine. The porcupine (*Erethigon dorsatium*) of North America takes its name from Middle French *porc d'espine*, "thorny pig," the medieval French apparently considering the animal a kind of pig. The spiny rodent is actually of the same family as the guinea pig. The porcupine, well known in antiquity, was the subject of an ode by the Roman poet Claudius; its sharp quills (a mature porcupine has 30,000 of them) were once used as arrow tips and made into magic bundles and fetishes. Porklike porcupine meat, especially that of the crested porcupine, the largest species, is still eaten in Italy, Tunisia, Lebanon, Asia Minor, and South Africa, among other places. The cornered porcupine does throw its quills at enemies, though involuntarily. But the "terrible porcupine" of Shakespeare does not shoot hundreds of quills at dogs and hunters, as Aristotle and scores of cartoonists have portrayed it from early times. Many a zookeeper has been shot by a loose quill, and one farmer reported that a trapped porcupine had thrown several quills with such force that they became embedded in tree branches high above it. Despite its menacing barbed quills, large wild cats and trained dogs can overcome the porcupine. Still, the legendary animal lives longer than any rodent; a crested porcupine in India holds the record of 22 years. There has been much speculation and joking about how porcupines mate ("Carefully!"), but in reality the female simply flattens her tail against her back, and the male mounts her with his forefeet.

pore over. People often write *pour over* when they mean to think deeply about something or study something carefully, but the correct term is *pore over*. *Pore* means to read or study with steady attention, to gaze steadily, to ponder intently. Etymologists have only been able to trace the word back to the Middle English *pouren*, the same word that is the basis for *pour*, so the difference between the two words is something of a mystery.

pork barrel. Government appropriations used to supply funds for local improvements that are designed to ingratiate congressmen with their constituents have been called *pork barrel* since shortly before the Civil War. Before that the expression simply meant the total contributions to a congressman's campaign fund. In this case *pork* is synonymous with fat, which has always signified abundance or plenty.

pornography; Porneius. *Pornography* is Greek for "writing of harlots," the term probably deriving from the signs hung outside Greek brothels. Such writing can be divided into *erotica*, which generally centers on "normal" heterosexual love, describing it in detail, and *exotica*, centering on so-called abnormal sex, including sadism, masochism, and fetishism. Pornography can be found in elements of the Old Testament and the plays of Aristophanes and probably goes back far beyond them. The first masterpiece of English pornography is probably John Cleland's *Memoirs of the Life of Fanny Hill* (1749). Pornography has thrived only since the late 18th century, the English word itself first recorded in 1860, and authors of it since have been as varied as de Sade (*see* SADISM), Swinburne, and Mark Twain. An excellent reference giving details and titles is R. S. Reade's *Register Librorum Eroticorum* (1936). *Porneius* is a character in Greek legend who has been called "fornication personified," a good description, as his name comes from the Greek *porneia*, "fornication." He was the son of Anagnus (inchastity), two of his brothers being Maechus (adultery), and Aselges (lasciviousness). Porneius tried to rape Athena (maidenly chastity), after whom the Parthenon (Temple of the Maiden) was named, but the "martial maid" killed him with her spear.

port. Over 300 years ago *port* began to replace *larboard* as the word for the left-hand side of a ship (probably because *larboard* was too easily confused in speech with *starboard*, the right-hand side). The word *port* here probably derives from port, "a harbor." In the days when the steering gear was on the starboard (that is, steerboard) side, a vessel almost always had to tie up at the dock with her left side toward the port.

porter ale. *See* PORTERHOUSE STEAK.

porterhouse steak. Martin Morrison's Porterhouse in New York City introduced the porterhouse steak in about 1814, according to the *Dictionary of Americanisms*. The tender steak taken from the loin next to the sirloin is an even more succulent cut than its neighbor, but has a lot of waste. In England, there is generally no distinction between it and sirloin. A porterhouse was a tavern serving the dark brown beer or ale called porter, once favored by porters and other laborers.

portholes. Half of a ship's windows are on the starboard side. Yet all windows on a ship are called portholes. This is because in early times the only windows on a ship were the port holes for guns. When windows were later added for the comfort of sailors sleeping below, on both sides of a ship, they too were called portholes.

portmanteau word. A portmanteau traveling bag is a leather suitcase that opens flat into two parts. It gave its name to words made up of two parts like *brunch*, composed of *breakfast* and *lunch*, and *smog*, composed of *smoke* and *fog*. The traveling bag was so named from the French word *portmanteau* in the late 16th century, but *portmanteau word* was coined by Lewis Carroll in *Through the Looking-Glass* (1872), when Humpty Dumpty, who could be called the etymologist of the story, explains the meanings of some of its words: "Well, 'slithy' means 'lithe and slimy.' . . . You see it's like a portmanteau—there are two meanings packed into one word." *See* MOTEL.

Portuguese man-of-war. This is the common name of *Physalia pelagica*, derisively named the Portuguese man-of-war by the English in the 18th century, when the once powerful Portuguese navy had gone into a state of decline. The designation is a strange one, for small as it is, the Portuguese man-of-war can be deadly. Actually not an individual animal but a colony of highly specialized polyps, it has tentacles up to 50 feet long that discharge a toxic substance that has painfully stung, paralyzed, and even killed swimmers coming into contact with them.

Portuguese words in English.   Portuguese words that came into English, often through Spanish, include: apricot, molasses, marmalade, verandah, junk (via Japanese), and cuspidor (possibly through Dutch).

port wine.   This sweet red dessert wine is named port, the word first recorded in 1591, because it was first shipped to England from the town of Oporto in northern Portugal. Its types include vintage port, tawny port, ruby port, and white port (made from white grapes).

posey.   *See* NOSEGAY.

posh.   The old story says that *posh* is an acronym for "*p*ort *o*utward, *s*tarboard *h*ome." British civil servants traveling to India on the Peninsular and Oriental Steam Navigation Company line supposedly liked to have their accommodations on the port side of the ship leaving home and on the starboard side coming back, as these locations were shady and away from the weather. According to the tale, such first-class, or *posh*, staterooms became a synonym for anything elegant or sophisticated. But unfortunately, the famous P & O line has no record of such an expression ever being used. This doesn't prove that the ingenious story isn't true, but the term is just as likely a contraction of "polished" or "polish." *Posh* is first recorded in 1897 as meaning "a dandy" and so may also be a corruption of the slang term *pot* ("big"), a person of importance. A corruption of the Scottish *tosh*, "neat and trim" isn't out of the question, either.

postage stamp.   *See* CHRISTMAS CARD.

post-haste.   Used in England as early as the 16th century, *post-haste* refers to the post-horse system of delivering mail in those days. Much like the American Pony Express, this earlier system stationed men with fresh horses at intervals along the road, the letters taken relay-fashion at each post and delivered to the next post in haste.

Post Toasties.   Charles William Post was good at choosing names for the many food products he invented, which included *Postum* and *Grape-Nuts*. However, he made a big mistake when he marketed the breakfast cereal Elija's Manna in 1904. This biblical name appealed to few, and the cereal didn't sell until he renamed it Post Toasties.

potato.   The white potato is one of the most important vegetables in the world, yet it bears the wrong name. *Potato* derives from the Haitian word *batata*, for "sweet potato," which the Spanish found in the West Indies in 1526 and introduced to Europe. *Batata* was corrupted to *patata* in Spanish, and this altered to *potato* when first used in England. But then the Spaniards discovered the Peruvian white potato, an unrelated plant, and mistook it for just another variety of the West Indian plant. Ignoring the native name for the white potato, *papas*, they gave it the same name as the earlier tuber, and so it too became known as the *potato* in England. The only distinction between the two unrelated vegetables was that one came to be called the *sweet potato* and the other the *Virginia* or *white potato*. The white potato is called "apple of the earth," *pomme de terre* in French, and "earth-apple," *Erdapfel* in German. It acquired the name *Irish potato* when it was first brought to this country in 1719 by a group of Irish Presbyterians and planted in Londonderry, New Hampshire. The colloquial American name *spud* for it derives from the spade-like tool used in digging potatoes. The humorous *Murphy* derives from the wide consumption of potatoes in Ireland—where there are of course many Murphys—at a time when other European countries rarely used the tuber for anything but fodder.

potato chip.   George Crum, a Saratoga, New York cook of partial American Indian descent, is said to have invented potato chips in 1853 when a patron in the restaurant where he worked complained that the potatoes he had been served were too thick and undercooked. Crum sliced some potatoes paper thin, soaked them in ice-water and fried them in a kettle of boiling oil. According to the old story, the customer raved about them, they became a specialty of the restaurant and were soon dubbed potato chips.

pot-au-feu.   *See* POT LUCK.

potbelly.   Men, and rarely women, have been afflicted with potbellies since time immemorial, but the protruding stomachs have been so named only since about 1657, when the term was first recorded, in the form of *pot-bellied*. Later, in 1714, Alexander Pope was the first to use *potbelly*, writing of "an Animal" with "bandy legs" . . . "a short neck and a pot belly." *Potbelly* may refer to the shape of the protruding belly of a pot, or a love of food from the cooking pot, or both—no one knows for sure.

potboiler.   "All men who have to live by their labour have their pot-boilers," Hazlitt wrote, and an obscure English poet lamented: "No far'ving patrons have I got,/But just enough to boil the pot." A potboiler is of course a literary work written to make a living, a task performed to keep the pot boiling, or to eat. Financial gain is the only object in writing one, but sometimes genius transcends the immediate object and the result is a work of art. Dr. Johnson's "philosophical romance" *Rasselas* (1759), for example, was written over the nights of one week to meet the cost of his mother's funeral and pay off her debts. Coleridge's *Ancient Mariner* has been called "the most sublime of pot-boilers to be found in all literature," but I suspect there are even greater ones. In telling of the birth of *Sanctuary* (1931), William Faulkner observed that he was hungry. "[I began] to think of books in terms of possible money," he recollected. "I took a little time out, and speculated what a person in Mississippi would believe to be current trends, chose what I thought was the right answer and invented the most horrific tale I could imagine and wrote it in about three weeks."

pot calling the kettle black.   Dating back to the 17th century, this expression describes someone who faults another for faults conspicuously his own. In ancient times, pots as well as kettles would likely be blackened over the open cooking fires of the day.

Potemkin village. Russian army officer Gregory Potemkin helped his lover Catherine the Great try to improve the country's economy. He tried to make many reforms in the Ukraine, but corrupt administrators spoiled his plans, and when Catherine wanted to see good results, he decided to trick her. Whether the allegations are true or not, it was said that Potemkin led Catherine on tours to places where conditions were best and even constructed false-front villages, transporting "contented peasants" from one of these sham villages to another just ahead of the Russian empress. As a result *Potemkin village* has become the synonym for something that looks good on the outside but really isn't, or a government plan to fool the people.

potlatch. A ceremonial festival of American Indians of the Pacific Coast at which gifts are bestowed on the guests in a show of wealth that the guests later try to outdo.

pot likker. The rich liquid left after boiling vegetables like turnip greens with fatty meat, especially ham or fatback. Southern U.S. tradition insists it should be eaten with CORN PONE dipped or crumbled in it.

pot luck. No sirloins or barons of beef for peasants in the Middle Ages. Mostly their dinners came from the great iron pots simmering over their fires into which leftovers were tossed from day to day. Often they didn't know exactly what they were having for dinner, so when they asked a visitor to take pot luck with them they weren't trying to put him off. It *was* a matter of luck—what was in the pot and whether there would be enough of it to go around. The expression is first recorded in 1592 and came to mean "plain fare," nothing fancy, what we usually have, like the French *pot-au-feu* ("fire pot"), the ordinary family dinner. In Ireland the pot of hospitality always hung over the open fire ready to be dipped into by any unexpected visitor. People who offer visitors pot luck today, however, often wind up preparing an impromptu banquet for their guests.

pot of gold. *See* RAINBOW CHASER.

potshot. A *potshot* was originally "a shot for the pot," that is, a shot taken at an animal in order to fill the dinner pot, without any regard for rules and from any distance, no matter how close. The earlier *pothunter*, first recorded in 1781, suggested the word, which came to mean, in both military and civilian use, a shot aimed at somebody within easy reach, without giving the person any chance to defend himself, as in an ambush. An abbreviation is *to pot* somebody.

potter's field. The first cemetery known to be used as a potter's field, "a burial place for paupers, criminals and unknown persons," was Aceldama, or "field of blood," a barren piece of land near Jerusalem. The Bible tells us that it was originally used by potters and called Aceldama because it was bought with the blood money paid Judas. Believing he had sinned and betrayed innocent blood, Judas returned the 30 pieces of silver paid him for his treachery and went out and hanged himself, the elder he chose becoming known as the Judas tree. When the priests of the temple decided it was unlawful to return Judas's silver to the treasury, since it was "the price of blood," they used it to buy a field to bury strangers in. There are other versions of the origins of the first potter's field. Since the

seventh century an area called Hakked-Dumm, "price of blood," on a cliff southwest of Siloam, has been regarded as Aceldama, although the absence of clay in the area makes it an unlikely location for a potter's field.

Pott's disease. *See* BRIGHT'S DISEASE.

pot valor. *Pot valor* is an older name for *Dutch courage* or "whiskey courage," meaning valor or courage inspired by alcohol. *Pot valor* goes back to at least 1623, while Dutch courage dates to the troubles between the Dutch and British in the 17th century. *Whiskey courage* is a fairly recent Americanism.

pounamu. Greenstone or nephrite. A native Maori word recorded by the British explorer Captain James Cook in 1769 that is used by all New Zealanders today. Nephrite is a form of jade.

pound of flesh. Shakespeare apparently invented this term for vengeance in the *Merchant of Venice* where he has Shylock lend money to Antonio on the condition that if he doesn't repay it in time Shylock will take a pound of his flesh. If the Bard didn't invent the expression, he certainly was the first to popularize it.

pound sterling. *See* STERLING.

pour oil on troubled waters. To soothe or calm a situation by tact and diplomacy is the figurative meaning of the above phrase. The ancients, Pliny and Plutarch among them, believed that oil poured on stormy waters reduced the waves to a calm and allowed a vessel to ride through a storm. The Venerable Bede says in his *Historia Ecclesiastica Gentis Anglorum* (731) that Bishop Aidan, an Irish monk, gave a priest, who was to deliver King Oswy's bride to him, holy oil to pour on the sea if the waves became threatening; his miraculous oil would stop the wind from blowing. A storm did blow up and the priest saved the ship and the future queen by following this advice. Later, Benjamin Franklin mentioned the practice of pouring oil on troubled waters in a letter and it said that the captains of American whaling vessels sometimes ordered oil poured on stormy waters.

Powder River! Let 'er buck! A slogan of encouragement used since about 1893, when it was said to have originated as a joke by a cowboy who drove horses across the almost dry Powder River near Casper, Wyoming. It later became a battle cry among Wyoming volunteers and then all troops in the Argonne during World War I. There is controversy about the phrase, some contending that it first applied to the Platte River, not the Powder River. As a character notes in James A. Michener's *Centennial* (1974):

> "The full challenge was 'Powder River, let 'er buck. A mile wide and an inch deep. Too thin to plow, too thick to drink. Runs uphill all the way from Texas.' Today, wherever rodeos are held, the cowboy who draws the toughest bronco shouts as he leaves the chute, 'Powder River! Let 'er buck!' So do drunks entering strange bars . . . Wyoming is divided across the middle on this one. Those in the north are sure that the phrase belongs to the Powder; those in the south claim it for their Platte,

and each side is ready to fight. My own guess is that the words go far back in history and were probably applied to the Platte years before the Powder was discovered. But I am not brave enough to say so in print."

power lunch. A lunch attended by at least two powerful people, often movers and shakers of society, people who can get things done. The power lunch is said to have been born in the Grill Room of the Four Seasons restaurant in New York City, or at least to have been so named there. The Four Seasons, designed by Philip Johnson, opened in 1959 and is considered an "interior landmark" of New York City.

powwow. American Indians called the medicine man a pow-wow, ultimately from an Algonquian word meaning "dreamer." Early settlers used the word in the same way but were soon applying it to a ceremony or meeting where the medicine man performed his magic. It wasn't until the early 19th century that *powwow* was extended to mean any meeting or conference at all.

a pox on you. Smallpox has been wiped out in the world today thanks to universal vaccination with cowpox virus, a method introduced by Edward Jenner in 1796. But in days past the contagious disease killed thousands every year. *Pox* is an altered spelling of *pocks*, eruptive pustules on the skin that characterize smallpox and other less serious diseases such as chicken pox. *A pox on you!* was often a serious oath in the past, but the expression seems always to have been used humorously, too, as it is today. Shakespeare first recorded it as an exclamation of irritation or impatience in *All's Well That Ends Well* (1601): "A pox on him, he's a Cat [a spiteful backbiter] still."

P.P.C. Hardly anyone leaves calling cards anymore and fewer still leave calling cards with the initials *P.P.C.* on them. The practice was fairly common once, however, and should you receive one from the two or three people in the world who keep up the practice you'll be glad to know that the letters *don't* stand for "paying private call." They stand for the French *pour prendre congé*, "for taking leave," which means that the party called to say goodbye and found no one home.

practice what you preach. The King James Version of the Bible translates the idea behind this phrase as "they say and do not" (Matt. 23:3). Over the centuries these words inspired writers to devise poetic improvements upon them and in 1876 or so Rowland Howard came up with *practice what you preach.* The translators of the new Revised Standard Version of the Bible liked this so much that they changed Matt. 23:3 to "they preach but do not practice" and the phrase was in the Bible at last.

pragmatism. Though William James was the great popu-larizer of the philosophical doctrine of pragmatism, the word was coined in the 1870s by another philosopher, C. S. Pierce, from the Greek *pragma*, "a fact, a deed, a thing done." Stressing the practical as opposed to the theoretical, pragmatism tests the truth and value of something by its utility and workability.

prairie dog. *Prairie dog* was one of some 1,528 names given to animals, plants, and places observed on the Lewis and Clark Expedition into the Louisiana Territory in 1803—this said to be a record in vocabulary making. Captain Meriwether Lewis had first called the animal a barking squirrel, but this probably more accurate description was changed to *prairie dog* by his friend William Clark.

prairie oysters; mountain oysters. In a country where the prudish have called the bull "a cow's father," "a cow creature," "a male cow," "a Jonathan," and "a gentleman cow," it is no wonder that there are so many euphemisms for bulls' testicles. In French and Spanish restaurants bulls' balls are sometimes called just that on the menus, but in America, when they are offered, they're invariably labeled either "prairie oysters," "mountain oysters," "Rocky Mountain oysters," or "Spanish kidneys." Believed to be an elevating aphrodisiac dish despite their low origins, bulls' balls are probably no more than a psychological aphrodisiac. But French neurologist Charles Brown-Dequard, who founded the much disputed "science" of organotherapy in 1889, thought differently. He claimed that both he and his patients had greatly enhanced their sexual prowess by eating bulls' testicles. The 70-year-old scientist went so far as to transplant bulls' testicles under the abdominal walls of patients, but it has since been established that testicles cannot store sex hormones such as testosterone and that when transplanted they wither and die.

prairie schooner. A type of covered wagon, similar to but smaller than the Conestoga wagon, used by settlers on the way West. Also called a fore-and-after.

Prairie State. A nickaname for Illinois first recorded in 1842. Illinois has also been called the Garden of the West, the Corn State and the Sucker State (probably because land speculators often cheated the early settlers, but possibly after the catfish of the genus *Catostomus* common in the state's rivers).

prairie strawberries. *See* ARIZONA STRAWBERRIES.

Praise the Lord and pass the ammunition! These words, later made into a popular song by Frank Loesser, may have been spoken by Navy chaplain Lt. Commander Howell Maurice Forgy (1908–83) aboard the cruiser *New Orleans* during the Japanese attack on Pearl Harbor on December 7, 1941. Some authorities claim they were spoken by Captain William Maguire of the *New Orleans*. Still others say the words were first used in the Civil War. Whoever said them spoke to a chain of men passing ammunition to a ship's guns.

praline. César Du Plessis-Praslin, marshal of France and, later, duc de Choiseul, got heartburn from eating almonds but couldn't resist them, one story goes. So his servant suggested that he have his chef brown the almonds in boiling sugar to make them more digestible and *voila!*—the *praline*. But another story says that sugar-coated praline candy was named for Praslin when he had his cook prepare something special for King Louis XIV, the field marshal's dinner guest one night. More likely, pralines were invented by Praslin's man as one of the many culinary triumphs that all chefs vied with each other to produce in the 17th century. At first they were called *praslins* and in time the spelling was altered to *pralines*. The comte Du Plessis-Praslin, who put down a revolt of the nobles in 1649 and may have served Louis pralines, became Louis XIV's minister of state in 1652 and was later rewarded with the title of duke for which he had politicked so long. He died in 1675, aged 77, a silver tray of pralines, or praslins, no doubt at his side.

pratfall. A pratfall is old show business slang for a fall on the buttocks taken by a comedian to obtain laughs. *Pratts*, or *prats* is simply rogues' cant for the buttocks. No one knows the origin of the term, which dates back to the 16th century, and there seems to be no connection between it and the older *prat*, for "a trick or prank."

Pravda. *Pravda*, once one of the two most influential Soviet newspapers, means "truth" in Russian. The other important journal was *Izvestia*, meaning "news." A wry Russian witticism advises "There's no news in the Truth and no truth in the News."

praying mantis. The English were calling *Mantis religiosa* the praying mantis since at least 1706, when this name for the green or brown predatory insect is first recorded. Also called the praying locust, it is so named because of the position in which it holds its forelegs, as if in prayer. It is a beneficial insect in the garden, as it eats many bugs destructive to plants.

prebuttal. A new coinage deriving from *rebuttal*, which means giving a rebuttal *before* one's opponent has even presented his or her case—that is, anticipating that opponent's case and responding to it. The word may have been coined by someone in the Bush 2000 presidential campaign.

precocious. Trees and fruits that flowered or ripened early were called precocious by the English in the early 17th century, the word deriving from the Latin *prae*, "before," and *coquere*, "to cook," which formed *praecoquere*, "to cook beforehand." By the end of the century writers were applying this botanical word to people, especially children who are especially mature or learned for their ages, who are "cooked before their time."

prepone. A recent coinage from India, where English (along with Hindi) is the official language. *Prepone* is the opposite of *postpone* and means to move up a meeting, not put it off.

preposition. Although etymologically the word *preposition* itself means "placed before," prepositions need not always be placed before their objects in a sentence. Most times they are, but in some instances, a preposition must come *after* its object and in others the preposition can be placed either before or after the object. There are governing rules, but it is best to rely on the ear in this matter. For example, "What are you sitting on?" sounds a lot better than "On what are you sitting?" The record for the most prepositions strung together at the end of a sentence is the protest of a child against an Australian bedtime story book: "Mommy, what did you bring that book which I didn't want to be read to out of from about 'Down Under' up for?" Angry at a critic who corrected one of his sentences on the basis of the old bromide that a preposition should not end a sentence, Winston Churchill wrote to him: "This is the kind of nonsense up with which I will not put." British author Joseph Addison liked to end sentences with prepositions—at least he wrote a good many of them that

way—and sentences ending with prepositions are therefore said to have Addisonian terminations. Interestingly, Richard Hurd, the testy critic who coined that term, is heard of no more today, while Joseph Addison, dangling prepositions and all, remains a much-read author.

preposterous. *See* PUT THE CART BEFORE THE HORSE.

Presa Canario. A large breed of dog, up to 150 pounds, said to be trained to track and kill pit bull dogs. This breed was largely unheard of until, in 2002, the California owner of a Presa Canario was convicted on counts of second-degree murder and involuntary manslaughter when her dog got loose from its leash and killed a neighbor in her apartment house hallway. There are only a handful of such murder convictions in U.S. legal history.

president. The first Senate of the United States selected "His Highness" as the title of the president of the U.S., the full title decided upon being "His Highness the President of the United States of America and the Protector of the Rights of the Same." However, the House of Representatives voted the title down and the president was referred to as the more democratic *Mr. President.* The first president's wife, however, was called Lady Washington during his terms in office. President Washington himself objected to terms like "Your Majesty." The word *president*, also deriving from the Latin *praesidere*, to preside, govern, was used as the title of the highest officer in an American colony, a practice that began in Jamestown. William Howard Taft, a president handpicked for the position by his predecessor Theodore Roosevelt, once said that whenever he heard someone say "Mr. President" while he was in office, he looked around for Teddy. *See* PRIME MINISTER.

press gangs. *Impressment* became prominent in American vocabularies before the War of 1812, when British sailors forcibly removed British seamen from American vessels, claiming this was their right, and impressed American seamen into British service at the same time, always explaining later that they took the Americans by mistake. Press gangs were the hired thugs who impressed seamen for service aboard British ships during the War of 1812 and had indeed done so since the late 17th century.

press notice. *Press notice*, meaning praise in the newspapers for an actor's performance, a writer's book, etc., dates back to about 1885, when the term *press agent* is first recorded, and is still heard in good advice such as "Don't believe your press notices." It may have been coined by Mark Twain, who first used the term. A prolific word inventor, Twain is said to have coined or popularized barbed wire, billiard parlor, cussword, dust storm, ex-convict, Wild West, forty-niner, hayride, and race prejudice, among other words and phrases. But Twain also coined a number of losers, words that are rarely if ever used today, including: disenthuse, human-beingship, jumbulacious, mental telegraphy, perhapser, psychologizes, Shakesperiod, type girl, uncledom, and vinegarishly.

pretty-by-night. One Victorian horticulturist said that *pretty-by-night* and other flower names beginning with *pretty* were "used only by the vulgar," but folks knew better, and all are still in use, although sometimes little known. *Pretty-by-night* is an alias of the common "four-o'clock," also known as marvel-of-Peru, which lives up to its name when its handsome tubelike flowers open very late in the afternoon. The botanist who first classified the species thought it wonderful, too, for he christened it *Mirabilis jalapa*. It signifies "timidity" in the language of flowers. Pretty Face is a showy salmon or salmon-yellow flower streaked with dark purple that is common in southern California. A lily with slender grasslike leaves, it is known botanically as *Brodiaea ixiodes*, the group named for Scottish botanist James Brodie.

pretzel.   There is no proof that pretzels are twisted to represent "the folded arms of praying children," as is often claimed, and they certainly don't take their name from the Latin *pretiola*, "little reward," because they were given by monks to religiously faithful children. Why they are twisted no one really knows, and the word *pretzel*, first recorded here in 1824, in a reference to pretzels eaten by the Dutch, derives from the German word for "branch," in reference to the branches of a tree that the "arms" of the pretzels resemble.

prevarication.   Roman farmers who ploughed crooked ridges in Rome were called praevaricors, their name deriving from the Latin verb for "to go zigzag or crooked." The next step was to apply the word to men who deviated from the straight line and gave crooked answers in courts of law, which gave us our word *prevarication*, or "lie." *See also* DELIRIUM.

priapus.   The name of the Greek and Roman god Priapus has come to mean a representation of a phallus, and the adjective *priapic* means "relating to or overly concerned with masculinity." Originally, however, Priapus, said to be the son of Aphrodite and Dionysus, was a fertility god of gardeners whose statue was often placed in home gardens. Represented as a grotesque, deformed creature with a huge penis, he was thought by the Roman poet Virgil to be "little more than a venerable scarecrow" used to keep birds and thieves away from the fruits and vegetables.

prick song.   In ancient times prick songs were songs whose notes were pricked, or written down, unlike common songs, which weren't recorded and were preserved by memory. The expression is first recorded in 1463, in the form of *pricked song*.

pride goeth before a fall.   Since the early 16th century the saying has usually been something similar to *pride goeth before a fall* in English. But the biblical proverb (Prov. 16:18) this is based upon uses the words "Pride goeth before destruction, and a haughty spirit before a fall."

prime minister.   The term is recorded as early as 1646, but the first English prime minister generally recognized as such was Sir Robert Walpole (1676–1745). Walpole rejected the title because he considered it an abusive term; indeed, as the *OED* notes, quoting a 1733 magazine: "In Countries where Royal Prerogative is limited by Laws, the name of prime Minister has always been odious." In any case, *prime minister* was at first only a descriptive designation; it did not become an official title in England until 1910. A masterful politician with great influence over George II and Queen Caroline, Walpole is said

to have spent over 50,000 pounds annually in subsidizing newspapers and magazines that supported his political beliefs. He was also the first chief minister to reside at NO. 10 DOWNING STREET. *See* PRESIDENT.

primrose; primrose path.   The primrose path is the path of pleasure, the path strewn with flowers, the lazy, self-indulgent way. The expression is first recorded in *Hamlet*: "Shew me the steepe and thorny way to Heaven; Whilst like a puft and recklesse Libertine Himselfe the Primrose path of dalliance treads." The flower called a primrose is not a rose and not one of the first flowers of spring, as its name implies. It is said to be so named due to "a popular blunder."

Prince Albert coat; Albert chain, etc.   Queen Victoria married Albert Francis Charles Augustus Emmanuel, prince of Saxe-Coburg-Gotha in 1840, despite many objections, loved him deeply, and mourned him in seclusion many years after his untimely death in 1861, aged 42. A man of great character and culture, the royal consort was much loved by the British people, one token of their esteem shown by the heavy gold watch chain presented to him by the jewelers of Birmingham in 1849. The prince consort wore this watch chain from one pocket to a button of the waistcoat, setting a fashion named the *Albert chain* or *albert* in his honor. Also named for Albert are Lake Albert, or Lake Albert Nyanza, in central Africa, discovered by Samuel Baker in 1864, and, oddly enough, the alberts or rags that Australian tramps wear in place of socks. The Prince Albert, a long double-breasted frock coat, is named for the royal consort's eldest son, Albert Edward, Prince of Wales (1841–1910), who became Edward VII in 1901.

prince of physicians.   *See* GALENICAL.

Prince Rupert; Prince Rupert's drops, etc.   General of the Royalist armies against Cromwell during the Civil War, and admiral of the British navy in the Dutch Wars, Prince Rupert (1619–82), grandson of England's James I, was a multitalented military man also strongly interested in art and science. One of the earliest mezzotinters, his *Head of St. John the Baptist* is justly famous, and he experimented with guns, shot, and gunpowder. Prince Rupert invented the modified brass called Prince Rupert's metal, the alloy resembling gold and consisting of 60 to 80 percent copper and 15 to 40 percent zinc. Prince Rupert's drops, which he also devised, are toys made by dropping molten glass into water, the glass forming small tadpoles which explode into dust if their tails are nipped off. The port of Prince Rupert in British Columbia bears the prince's name also, as does Rupert's Land, once the name for all the land in Canada that drained into Hudson Bay, Prince Rupert having been the first governor of the Hudson's Bay Company when it was formed in 1670.

privateer.   Privateers operate with the consent of a government, usually their own. Privateers were privately owned vessels that in England were licensed under Letter of Marque and Reprisal to capture enemy ships in time of war. A captain who had such authorization would not be charged with piracy. Perhaps the most famous privateer in history was the British Sir Francis Drake, who preyed on Spanish shipping in the 16th century as captain of the *Golden Hind*. *See* CORSAIR.

private eye. Mystery writer Raymond Chandler popularized this term, for "a private investigator," but it has its origins in the "We Never Sleep" motto of the Pinkerton Detective Agency, which was printed over an open eye. *See* PINKERTON.

pro. One dictionary says the short form *pro* for a professional is first recorded in about 1850, so it could have originated in baseball, though there is no proof of this nor of any other origin. The first recorded mention of professional players in baseball is in 1867, when the Rockford, Illinois team began paying salaries to expert players, prompting amateur "gentlemen players" all over to complain about the practice. But by 1869 baseball's first professional team, the Cincinnati Red Stockings, was touring the country and a new age in the sport had begun. *See also* AMATEUR.

Proctophilus winchilli. While they were fishing in the Gulf of California, Nobel Prize winner John Steinbeck and his friend Doc Ricketts noticed a little fish that lived in the cloaca of the sea cucumber and that kept darting in and out of the creature's anus. They named the hitherto unrecorded fish *Proctophilus winchilli*, after gossip columnist Walter Winchell.

prodigy. The Roman word *prodigium* was used to denote an incident of an extraordinary nature to be taken as a prophetic sign, bad or good, by the entire nation. When adopted in English as *prodigy*, the term at first meant the same, but later became applied to an extraordinary person or animal, one with great intelligence or talent, and then to a child possessing these qualities. Since the early 16th century, society has known thousands of child prodigies.

profane. From the Latin *pro*, "before" and *fanum*, "temple." Those within the Roman temple were considered holy, while those outside the temple, *pro fanum*, were unholy, or *profane*.

Promethean. Anyone resembling Prometheus in spirit or action, or anyone creative or boldly inventive can be called Promethean. Prometheus of Greek mythology was put to work by Zeus to create men from mud and water. But Prometheus stole Olympian fire for his miserable creations and an angry Zeus chained him to a rock in the Caucasus, exposing him to the fierce vultures there, until Hercules released him.

Promised Land. *See* CANAAN.

promnesia. *Promnesia* is a little-known but useful word from the Greek, meaning roughly "memory of the future." It was apparently coined by a psychologist in 1903 and defined as "the paradoxical sensation of recollecting a scene which is only now occurring for the first time; the sense of the *déjà vu*." Science fiction is usually cited as the literary genre where near-perfect examples of promnesia are most often found. But it would be hard to find a better example of fiction's becoming reality than popular novelist Morgan Robertson's novel *Futility* (1898). Published 14 years before the *Titanic* sank in history's most famous marine disaster, it told of a great "unsinkable" luxury liner named the *Titan* that sank on its maiden voyage after hitting an iceberg, with the loss of almost all passengers because there weren't enough lifeboats aboard. There were at least 10 other similarities in the novel to the real tragedy.

pronghorn. The pronghorn (*Antilocapra americana*) of the western plains is of a separate family that differs widely from the Old World antelope; nevertheless, it has been called an antelope since it was so named in the journals of the Lewis and Clark expedition in 1804.

propaganda. Pope Gregory XVIII organized a *congregatio de propaganda fide*, a congregation for propagating the Christian faith, in 1622, and over the years this organization became the basis for the word *propaganda*, meaning deliberately to spread rumors, lies, or information to harm or help a cause.

prose . . . poetry. *See* MOTIVE-HUNTING.

proselytize. *Proselytize* means to convert someone to a religion or point of view. The word derives from the Greek *proselutos*, "one who has come to a place, or a convert." The first proselytes were apparently Greek converts to Judaism, some of whom accepted the religion wholly and some of whom only agreed to refrain from working on the Sabbath and making sacrifices to heathen gods. *Proselyte* is first recorded by John Wycliffe in 1382.

Prosit! The German *Prosit!* has been adopted as an English drinking toast. The German word (and the similar Dutch *Proost*) comes from the Latin *prosit*, "may it do good."

prospect. *Prospect*, as a synonym for a salesman's potential customer, is a term that became common only in the past half-century or so. *Prospect* has its roots in the Latin *prospecto*, "to look forward," which in the 15th century was altered to *prospect* and came to mean a landscape viewed from a distance. About 400 years later the word was finally extended to mean looking forward figuratively when it was applied to a possible customer.

prospector. Someone who explores an area for gold, silver, oil, or other valuables. Though *to prospect* for minerals is recorded as early as 1400 in England, *prospector* is an Americanism dating back to about 1846.

prostitute. *Prostitute* came into English early in the 16th century, but the word derives ultimately from the much older Latin *prostituere*, "to expose for sale." The best-known prostitute, at least of repentant prostitutes, is St. Mary Magdaline, who is also the patron saint of reformed prostitutes. She was cured of evil spirits by Jesus (Luke 8:2) and later was the first to see Jesus rise from the tomb after his crucifixion (John 20:1–18). For some unfathomable reason *prostitute* is regarded by some people as an obscene word. According to William Safire's *Coming to Terms* (1991), the U.S. State Department euphemisticaly refers to these ladies of the night as "available casual indigenous female companions."

protean. *Protean*, for "something that is constantly changing, or someone who assumes many roles," derives from the name of Proteus, herdsman of Neptune, Greek god of the sea. Wise old Proteus lived in a huge cave tending his herd of sea calves, and no one was able to catch the great prophet because he could rapidly change himself into different shapes.

protest; protestant. *See* TESTICLES.

protoplasm. Czech physiologist Jan Evangelista Purkinje first gave the name *protoplasm* to the living material within the cell, in 1839. He referred specifically to the gelatinous embryonic material in an egg, this first-formed material reminding him of the word *protoplasm* used to describe Adam, the first formed man, in the Bible.

proud as a peacock. *See* PEACOCK.

proud as Punch. The Punch-and-Judy show originated in early-17th-century Italy, where the main character's name was Pulcinello, a vain, pompous character with a shrewish wife, Judy. When the shows came to England Pulcinello's name was corrupted to Punchinello and then shortened to Punch, but his personality remained the same, as is reflected in the old saying *proud as Punch*, being proud over a victory, as Punch was when he bested Judy.

proud as sin. *As proud as sin*, probably originating in the 19th century, can be traced back to similar *proud as . . .* phrases close to 500 years old. The earliest appears to be *as proud as Nebuchadnezzar*, recorded in 1526. Since then the *devil*, *Beelzebub*, *Scratch*, *Satan* and even the *Prince of Darkness* have also been used in this phrase equating pride with evil.

proud below the navel. "Whenever I see her I grow proud below the navel," William D'avenant wrote in his first play *The Tragedy of Albovine* (1629). D'avenant, rumored to be Shakespeare's natural son and England's unofficial poet laureate, may have invented the phrase, which means "amorously aroused," to put it euphemistically. Nevertheless, Partridge says the expression "borders on Standard English." *See* CONTEMPLATE ONE'S NAVEL.

Provo. French *provocateur*, "one who provokes action," is the ancestor of *Provo*, for a member of the Provisional I.R.A. However, the Provos, who favored terrorist action, breaking from the I.R.A. in 1971, seem to have borrowed the shortened French word from a Dutch political group using it at the time.

Prussian; Prussian blue; prussiate; prussic acid. Since the Franco-Prussian War of 1870, when Prussia's militarism came into full flower, *Prussian* has been a synonym for arrogant, overbearing, cruel, and excessively military. *Prussian blue*, however, has nothing to do with the military, merely having been discovered by the Prussian chemist Diesbach in 1704. It is a color ranging from moderate to deep greenish blue used in painting and fabric printing. A prussiate is a ferricyanide or ferrocyanide, which the color was made from, while prussic acid (hydrocyanic acid) is made from Prussian blue. Prussian blue is sometimes called Berlin blue, after its place of discovery.

P.S. *P.S.*, first recorded in 1757, is an abbreviation always used in place of the Latin *post scriptum* (Latin *post* "after" plus *scribere*, "to write"), meaning postscript, an afterthought added after the signature in a letter. One family is said to have named its 14th child *Finis*. A problem arose when another child came along, but it was solved by naming the 15th *P.S.*

Psalmanazar hoax. George Psalmanazar (1679?–1763) was a pseudonymous literary faker whose real name still isn't known.

Psalmanazar, a Frenchman, fashioned his pseudonym from that of the biblical character Shalmaneser. Claiming to be a native of Formosa (Taiwan) and even inventing a complete "Formosan" language that he spoke, he attracted the attention of Scottish army chaplain William Innes, who saw through his imposture but became his confederate. Innes "converted" him in order to get credit for a "conversion" and in 1703 Psalmanazar went to London, where credulous authorities hired him to teach "Formosan" at Oxford and write a dictionary of "Formosan." The following year the impostor wrote *The Historical and Geographical Description of Formosa*, which described the odd customs of the "Formosans"—that they ate only raw meat, including the flesh of executed criminals, and they annually offered as a sacrifice to the gods 18,000 hearts cut from the breasts of boys under the age of nine. In 1706 Catholic missionaries to Formosa exposed Psalmanazar and after a time he confessed his fraud, renouncing his past life in 1728 and going on to become an accomplished scholar. But there remained something of the impostor in this friend of Dr. Johnson. The title of his autobiography, published posthumously in 1764, was *Memoirs of——commonly known by the Name George Psalmanazar*.

pshaw. Used since the 16th century and called "a natural expression of rejection" by the *O.E.D.*, this exclamation of impatience or contempt is usually pronounced *shaw*, though I often heard it spoken as *shah* when people still employed it. Oscar Wilde once asked George Bernard Shaw what title he'd give to a magazine he proposed starting. "I'd want to impress my own personality on the public," Shaw replied, banging his fist on the table. "I'd call it *Shaw's Magazine*: Shaw-Shaw-Shaw!" "Yes," Wilde said, "and how would you spell it?"

PT boat. PT boats were prompted by Prohibition rather than war. The little boats were originally used by rumrunners because they could outspeed the Coast Guard cutters of the day. Their inventor submitted their design to the Navy during World War II and they were introduced as *Patrol Torpedo* boats, although their size and annoyance to the enemy caused them to be dubbed *mosquito boats* as well.

Ptolemaic system. Before Copernicus scientists believed that the earth was the stationary center of the universe, a philosophy espousing the snug, smug little world where the sun, planets, and stars moved benignly around us. This theory, the Ptolemaic system, was essentially that of Ptolemy, an Alexandrine astronomer who lived from about A.D. 100 to 170. Claudius Ptolemaeus took his name from the Ptolemaic dynasty of Egypt, which reigned from the late fourth to the first century B.C. His famous work the *Almagest*, 13 books compiling his own and other astronomical findings, set forth the Ptolemaic theory. Nothing reliable is known about the great astronomer, geographer, and mathematician aside from his work, which included his famous *Geography*. His Ptolemaic system remained virtually unchanged and unchallenged until the heliocentric system advocated by Copernicus and Kepler replaced it in the 16th century. *See* COPERNICAN.

pub crawling. A mostly British term meaning "to frequent one pub after another," drinking as you go, for at least a night, until you are reduced to stumbling if not crawling or worse.

Partridge in his *Dictionary of Slang and Unconventional English* (1961) calls a *pub-crawl* "a liquorish peregrination from bar to bar" and traces its first appearance in print to about 1910.

public; pub. *Public* for people generally and collectively comes from the Latin *publicus*, meaning the same, which in turn derived from the Latin *populus*, the people. The term *pub* for a bar or tavern, used in England and much less frequently in America, is an abbreviation of *public house*. *Pub* is for some reason still called "low colloquial" by the *O.E.D.* The word isn't recorded until 1865, *public* being the contraction used before it.

public be damned. In 1882 a reporter asked William Henry Vanderbilt why the New York Central Railroad had continued to run a high-speed train from New York City to Chicago despite the fact that it was losing money. Commodore Vanderbilt told him he did it to compete with a similar Pennsylvania Railroad train. Wouldn't you run it just for the benefit of the public, competition aside, the reporter continued, and Vanderbilt roared the classic reply that has unfortunately become associated with big business ever since: "The public be damned! Railroads are not run on sentiment but on business principles."

public enemy number one. People have the mistaken notion that there is always a "public enemy number one" wanted by the Federal Bureau of Investigation. But there was only one American criminal so designated: John Dillinger (1903–34), so named by U.S. Attorney General Homer Cummings in 1933. After Dillinger was shot dead by F.B.I. agents the F.B.I. did maintain a "ten-most-wanted" list, but it did not rank those listed.

public intellectual. A writer or thinker who "addresses a general audience on matters of broad public concern," according to Rick Perlstein, writing in the *New York Times* (1/22/02). The term was coined by Russell Jacoby in his book *The Last Intellectuals: American Culture in the Age of Academe* (1987) but doesn't seem to have made the dictionaries yet. As examples of public intellectuals Mr. Perlstein names George Orwell, Lewis Mumford, and Hannah Arendt, among others.

public relations. American publicity writer Eddie Bernays (1891–1960), a nephew of Sigmund Freud, is said to have coined the name *public relations* in May 1920 as a respectable way to describe his profession—in the wedding announcements heralding his marriage. Bernays had previously established the first firm doing such work, though the term *public relations* had been recorded as far back as the early 19th century. Since about 1942 PR has been used as an abbreviation of *public relations*.

publisher. The first recorded use of *publisher* for "one whose business is the issuing of books, magazines, etc." dates back to 1740 in England. The first publishers, however, may have been Egyptian undertakers, who put into each burial place a *Book of the Dead*, which was a guide to the afterlife. About 550 publishers in the United States bring out over 50,000 new titles every year, but a nonprofit publisher, the U.S. Government Printing Office, is the largest publisher in the country, and in the world for that matter, mailing out more than 150 million items every year and publishing 6,000 new titles annually. Publishers have

of course been the butt of many writers' jokes. Said James M. Barrie in an 1896 speech: "Times have changed since a certain author was executed for murdering his publisher. They say that when the author was on the scaffold he said goodbye to the minister and to the reporters, and then he saw some publishers sitting in the front row below, and to them he did not say goodbye. He said instead, 'I'll see you again.'" In his *Memoirs of a Publisher*, F. N. Doubleday, dubbed Effendi by Kipling, relates Mark Twain's "perfect recipe" for making a modern publisher: "Take an idiot man from a lunatic asylum and marry him to an idiot woman, and the fourth generation of this connection should be a good publisher from the American point of view." Mark Twain, of course, later became a publisher himself.

publishing patron saints. The saints that watch over the publishing trade include: publishers, St. John the Apostle; editors, St. John Bosco; authors, St. Francis de Sales, St. John the Evangelist; poets, St. David, St. Cecilia, St. Columba, and St. John of the Cross. Publishers admit that even television has its patron saint—St. Clare of Assisi (1194–1253). All saints take their title ultimately from Latin *sanctus*, "holy."

puckish. The mischievous or impish are called puckish after the sprite in Shakespeare's *A Midsummer Night's Dream*, Shakespeare coining the proper name Puck from *puck*, for "a malicious demon," but creating a character far more merry and attractive. It is Puck who speaks Shakespeare's immortal line: "Lord, what fools these mortals be!"

pudder. *See* GOBBLEDYGOOK.

puffery. In his play *The Critic* (1779) English dramatist Richard Sheridan created a cast of characters including the bogus, verbose critic and author Mr. Puff. Sheridan named Mr. Puff after the English word *puff*, meaning inflated, which is suggestive of the sound made by puffing wind from the mouth and was commonly applied to exaggerated newspaper ads at the time. But Mr. Puff added a new dimension to the word in Sheridan's satire of the malignant literary criticism of the day. Puff talks with the spiteful critics Dangle and Sneer about the absurd, bombastic "tragedy" he has written called *The Spanish Armada*, pushing his play all the while, for he has reduced the art of puffery to a science. At one time he even catalogs the puff: "Yes, the puff preliminary, the puff collateral, the puff collusive and the puff oblique, or puff by implication. These all assume, as circumstances require, the various forms of letter to the editor, occasional anecdote, impartial critique, observation from correspondent, or advertisement from the party." So absurdly does Mr. Puff overpraise or blow up his work that his name entered the language in the form of *puffery* as a word for the kind of criticism produced by literary cliques, the mutual back-scratching or logrolling that is usually subtler, but still as common today among the Sneers and Smears of literature as it was in Sheridan's time. Thanks to Mr. Puff we also have a synonym for a BLURB.

Puget Sound. *See* VANCOUVER.

pug-nosed. People with short snub noses are called pugnosed because their proboscises resemble those of apes or a breed of dogs. In the 17th century, *pug*, which derives from *puck*, a term of endearment, was a pet name for both apes and a popular type of short-haired dog. Both apes and the pug dog have blunt noses with wide bases that slope upward, which inspired some wag to dub similar human noses pug noses. Students of physiognomy believed that a pug nose was an indication of weakness; even Emerson wrote that "a squint, a pug-nose, mats of hair . . . betray character." In fact, Charles Darwin had a snub nose and Captain Fitzhugh of the *Beagle*, a devotee of the "science," almost didn't hire him as the ship's naturalist because a snub nose was supposed to indicate a lack of energy or determination.

puke.   *Puke* for to vomit is probably an onomatopoetic word and is first recorded in Shakespeare's *As You Like It* (1599): "At first the infant, mewling and puking in his nurse's arms." *Puke* is also an old nickname, still used occasionally, for an inhabitant of Missouri. No one seems to be sure why the name was bestowed upon Missourians, though several explanations have been given. One of the earliest references claims that the first settlers in St. Louis ate poisonous wild greens that caused a virtual epidemic of puking. *See also* SHOW-ME STATE.

pukka.   Also spelled *pucka*, and rhyming with luck-a, *pukka* derives from the Hindu word *pokka*, meaning "cooked, ripe, mature." The English brought it home from India in the late 17th century and the word has since become a workhorse adjective meaning genuine, good, substantial, permanent, reliable, and conventional.

Pulitzer Prize.   Hungarian-born Joseph Pulitzer was persuaded to immigrate to America by an agent who recruited him for the Union Army in 1864. After serving until his discharge a year later, he settled in St. Louis, where he founded the *St. Louis Post-Dispatch* in 1878. But when his chief editorial aide, Col. John A. Cockerell, shot and killed Col. Alonzo Slayback during a bitter political quarrel, Pulitzer left his paper and moved to New York, where he founded the *New York World* in 1883. He proceeded to become a congressman and make his paper among the best in the world, despite the fact that he went blind at age 40. A liberal, crusading newspaper, the *World* did much to raise the standards of American journalism, employing many of the greatest reporters and columnists of the day. Absorbed by the Scripps-Howard chain in 1931, it was eventually merged out of existence. When Pulitzer died in 1911, aged 64, his will provided a fund to Columbia University, where he had established and endowed the school of journalism, which has been used since 1917 to give annual monetary awards for writing. Prizes in journalism for local, national, and international reporting; editorial writing; news photography; cartooning; and meritorious public service performed by an individual newspaper. There are also prizes for music and theater, and four traveling scholarships. *See* BOOKER PRIZE.

pull a boner.   "Mistah Bones" in American minstrel shows was the end man in the line who rhythmically played a pair of bones, originally polished rib bones from an animal. It is said that "Mistah Interlocutor," the middle man in the line, fired questions at him designed to evoke ridiculous or stupid answers, which became known as *pulling boners*. This is possible, or *to pull a boner* may simply derive from the older American term

"a bonehead," a stupid error, slang since about 1860. There is no connection between the Americanism of about 60 years' duration and the British expression *a boner*, a sharp blow on the spine that dates back about a century and a half, or *boner*, slang for an erection.

pull a fast one.   *Pull* has been slang for "to engineer a deception" for well over a century, but the expression *pull a fast one*, "to put over a trick or clever swindle," goes back to only about 1938. Baseball seems the obvious source—a pitcher coming in hard with a fast ball after throwing a lot of "junk." But the nod has to go to "fast-bowling at cricket," since the expression is first recorded in England. *See* CRICKET.

pulled teeth.   One's power decreases when teeth are pulled or drawn, according to ancient belief. This may well have been literally true among primitive people when teeth were a weapon (as they were in the recent Tyson-Holyfield fight when Tyson bit off a piece of his opponent's ear). The belief is said to come from a fable about a love-struck lion who agreed to have his teeth pulled and claws clipped if a fair lady would wed him. After Leo did this, the damsel's father slew the King of Beasts.

pullet.   *See* PONY.

Pullman car.   Abraham Lincoln's assassination made the Pullman sleeping car a reality. George Mortimer Pullman (1831–97), a cabinetmaker, had experimented in building much-needed railway sleeping cars just before the Civil War but couldn't sell his idea, even though he had made a successful test run with two converted coaches. In 1863 he invested $20,000, every penny he had, in a luxurious sleeping car called the Pioneer that he and his friend Ben Field built on the site of the present-day Chicago Union Station. But the Pioneer, unfortunately, was too wide to pass through existing stations and too high to pass under bridges. For two years it lay on a siding, a well-appointed waste, until President Lincoln was assassinated in 1865. Every area through which Lincoln's black-creped funeral train passed brought out its finest equipment, and Illinois, the Rail Splitter's birthplace, could be no exception. The Pullman Pioneer was the best that the state had, and Illinois spared no expense in promptly cutting down station platforms and raising bridges so that the luxurious car could join the presidential funeral train in its run from Chicago to Springfield. The funeral party traveling in the Pioneer was greatly impressed by the car. As a result, the Michigan Central cleared the line for the big car and other railroads around the country began to follow suit. Pullman soon went into partnership with Andrew Carnegie in the Pullman Palace Car Company and his sleeping cars, or Pullmans, eventually made him a millionaire many times over.

pull one's leg.   *See* YOU'RE PULLING MY LEG.

pull out all the stops.   An organist who pulled out all the stops—levers used to change the sound of the instrument—would be giving his all, the meaning of this phrase. Though the organ, or its rude prototype, originated in Greece, the expression deriving from it dates back to 19th-century England.

pull strings.   This expression was inspired by puppet masters of days past, who manipulated strings or wires on their marionettes from behind a curtain. Unseen, they completely controlled the actions of their puppets, so in the mid-19th century *pulling the strings* or *wires* came to mean controlling the affairs of humans from a distance as if they were puppets.

pull the string.   To pull the string is to pitch a change-of-pace ball to a baseball batter to put him off balance. The pitcher usually throws a fast ball first; his next pitch is often a slow ball, which to the off-balance batter appears to be "attached to and pulled back by a string." Quoting Burt Dunne's pamphlet collection *The Folger Dictionary of Baseball* (1958), in *The Dickson Baseball Dictionary* Paul Dickson tells a good story about another possible, if unlikely, derivation: "Burt Dunne says this is derived from a trick featuring 'a trapped badger' in a box overhead. The rookie releases the 'badger' by pulling the string, and says Dunne, 'down come refuse—and worse.' "

pull the wool over one's eyes.   Most investigations of this expression trace it to the huge wigs that were the fashion in the early 19th century, when *wool* was a joking term for hair. Judges often wore these poor-fitting wigs, which frequently slipped over the eyes, and it may have been that a clever lawyer who tricked a judge bragged about his deception by saying that he pulled the wool over his eyes. Or purse-snatchers may have pulled down the wigs of gentlemen to make it easier to snatch their purses while they stumbled about. The actual source is really unknown and although the expression is first recorded in America (1839), it is thought to be of older, English origin.

pull up stakes.   These stakes are boundary stakes, not the circus tent stakes that are pulled up when a circus moves to another town. The expression goes back at least to 1640 in America, where settlers who wanted better land than had been given them simply pulled up their boundary stakes and moved on to another location, resetting the stakes there.

pulse.   The word *pulse* in gardening terminology usually means the edible seeds of leguminous plants such as peas, beans, and lentils, or these legumes themselves. Sometimes the word is used to characterize any herbaceous plant of the pea family, such as alfalfa, clover, and vetch. The harvest festival of the ancient Greeks called the *Pyanepsia* took its name from the cooked pulse that was offered at the festival to the god Apollo as the first fruits of the harvest and eaten by all members of the household.

puma.   *Puma* is the Inca name for the American feline *Felis concolor*, also called the cougar, the jaguar, and even, rarely, the South American lion. This word for the big cat was brought back from the Andes by the Spanish conquistador Pizarro in the 1530s.

pumice.   Pumice is a porous, spongy form of volcanic glass used as an abrasive or polish; there is an entire mountain of it on the island of Lipari. In 1645 one writer reported that "Italians to this day have the habit of pumicing their skin to get off the hair." *Pumice* comes from the Latin *Pumex*, for the substance, while *pounce*, "a fine powder formerly used to blot ink on paper," comes from the same source.

pummel.   *See* POMMEL.

pumpernickel.   When in Germany, Napoleon's groom was supposedly offered a slice of coarse, dark rye bread and indignantly refused it, saying that it was fit only for the Emperor's horse, Nickel. "*C'est du pain pour Nickel*," the gourmet groom protested ("It is bread for Nickel"), and *pain pour Nickel* stuck as the name for the bread. But scholars don't appreciate this ingenious story that has the German bread named after a horse, though for once they do offer an interesting tale in exchange. *Webster's* and other authorities derive *pumpernickel* from the German *pumpern* ("to break wind") and *Nickel* ("a goblin or the devil"), implying that *pumpernickel* is so named because it made people who eat it "break wind like the devil."

pumping iron.   Lifting weights. The expression, dating back only to the 1970s, became a household term mainly due to the efforts and example of weight lifter and movie star Arnold Schwarzenegger.

pumpkin.   This member of the squash family originated in the Americas, where pumpkins were so ubiquitous among the Pilgrims that some wit wrote the following: "We have pumpkins at morning and pumpkins at noon, / If it were not for pumpkins we would soon be undoon." The pumpkin didn't get its name because it looks "pumped up" into a balloon shape. *Pumpkin* probably comes from the Greek *pepon*, a kind of melon, literally, "a fruit cooked by the sun." *Pepon* became the Middle French *ponon*, which became the English *pompion*, to which the diminutive suffix-*kin* was finally added. It is just another example of the many English words formed from mispronunciations of foreign words. Seneca is said to have written a satire on the deification of the Roman emperor Claudius Caesar, which he called *Apocolocyntosis*, coined from the Greek word for pumpkin and meaning "pumpkinification." *Pumpkinification*, suggesting a swollen head the size of a pumpkin and "pumped up," has meant pompous behavior or absurd glorification since at least the mid-19th century, when a British writer called attention to Seneca's satire.

pumpkin head.   *See* SAP.

pun.   No one has yet found the origin of the word *pun* for a play on words, and perhaps no one ever will. English author John Dryden appears to be the first to have used the word in 1662, and that is about the extent of our knowledge of it. Punning, however, goes back to Homer's time or earlier and great English writers from Shakespeare to Joyce have used puns, though others have called them the lowest form of art. There are many synonyms for *pun*, some dating back to the 15th century. These include bull, carriwitchet, clench, crotchet, figary, flam, jerk, liripoop, quartorquibble, quibbin, quiddity, quirk, and whim.

punch.   Legend has it that our beverage *punch* derives from the Hindi *panch*, "five," because it originally had five ingredients: arrack, tea, lemon, sugar, and water. More likely the word comes from the *puncheon*, or large cask, from which GROG was served to sailors in the East India trade. In any event, the Indian beverage was a great favorite with sailors and was brought back to England in the late 1600s.

Punch and Judy.   *See* PROUD AS PUNCH.

punch-drunk. Brain damage in boxers resulting from repeated blows to the head produces many symptoms, the most common being poor coordination, slurred speech, mental deterioration, and a broad-based gait. Old, very impaired fighters suffering this combination of effects were called punch-drunk by Dr. Harrison S. Martland in a 1928 article in the *Journal of the American Medical Association.* However, Dr. Martland probably did not coin the term, as *punch-drunk* is recorded in America as early as 1915. In the early 1940s *punchy* began to supplant *punch-drunk.*

punching bag. Someone who takes much abuse and punishment is said to be a punching bag. The term is American and comes from boxing; it is first recorded in 1897, although boxers practiced on heavy bags filled with sand long before then.

Punch it! "Punch it, baby!" Steve McQueen shouts several times to Ali McGraw as they escape from the law in *The Getaway* (1968). The classic film isn't the origin of this phrase, which dates back at least to the 1950s, years before Ms. McGraw was punching the gas pedal with her foot to accelerate the old getaway car in the film.

Punch's advice. *Punch's advice* derives from the most famous joke of the British humor magazine *Punch.* The magazine announced that it would send advice to those about to marry, the advice turned out to be: "Don't."

punchy. *See* PUNCH-DRUNK.

punctuation. The word comes from Latin *punction,* "with the point." Gertrude Stein was one of many writers who hated punctuation, especially commas, and would have rid the world of them. However, the lack of punctuation can lead to great trouble. In one instance a district attorney introduced an unpunctuated confession taken down by a policeman that read: "Mangan said that he never robbed but twice said it was Crawford." The prosecution contended this should have been punctuated: "Mangan said he never robbed but twice. Said it was Crawford." The defense said the sentence should read: "Mangan said he never robbed, but twice said it was Crawford." The last introduced a reasonable doubt, and the accused went free. Every written language has a system of punctuation, though they are not identical. In German, for example, nouns are capitalized, and in Spanish an inverted question mark goes at the beginning of a question. According to an old typesetter's maxim for punctuation: "Set type as long as you can hold your breath without getting blue in the face, then put in a comma; when you yawn, put in a semicolon; and when you want to sneeze, that's the time for a paragraph." *See* COMMA.

punk. *Punk* was originally 16th-century slang for a prostitute or harlot, the word of unknown origin. It has since come to mean a number of things, depending on the context it is used in, and usually refers to a male. These meanings include: a male, usually young, who has been or is said to have been sodomized; a young inexperienced boy; a petty criminal; and any insignificant person. *Punk style* of dress seems to come ultimately from the dress of young hoodlums in the 1950s, while *punk* in the sense of inferior or bad is said to be of 18th-

century British origin, deriving from "rotting wood" called punk.

punter. *Punter* has been slang for "a gambler or a bettor" since the early 18th century. This word has its origins in the French *punter,* meaning to place a bet against the bank in the game of faro. The football *punter,* or kicker, is of different yet uncertain ancestry, perhaps being of echoic origin from the sound of the ball when kicked.

puny. The British borrowed this word from the French in the mid-15th century, misspelling their *puisne* as *puny,* but retaining its meaning of "late born," that is, junior or subordinate. Over the years, however, *puny* took on the meaning of less than normal size or strength; weak; unimportant; insignificant; petty.

pupa. The great naturalist Linnaeus coined this technical term for "an insect in the third and usually quiescent state preceding that of the perfect insect." *Pupa* comes from the Latin *pupa,* "little girl or doll." The coinage has been called "a stroke of poetic genius," one writer noting: "If you look at the underside of a moth's pupa [you will] see the shape of its face, eyes and embryonic wings like little arms, all wrapped as if in swaddling clothes which emphasize its likeness to a doll." *See* LARVA.

pupil. The smallness of the mirror images seen on the pupil of the eye led to the pupil being named after the Latin *pupilla,* "little girl." Our word *pupil,* for "a student," comes from the Latin *pupulus,* or "little boy," most pupils in days past having been little boys.

puppy. Lapdogs were treated like dressed dolls or playthings by French ladies in the late 15th century, and so a lapdog was called *poupée,* "doll." When the word came into English years later, its spelling changed to *puppy,* and it lost its associations with lapdogs, applied instead only to young dogs, especially those less than a year old.

purdah. *Purdah* (which derives from the Hindu *pardah,* "curtain") is the Islamic custom of secluding women from the sight of all men except close relatives. It is still practiced by many Muslim women, who conceal themselves completely from onlookers when they go out into the street by wearing the *burga,* an ankle-length garment with slits for eyes.

puritan. The Puritans were originally members of a mid-16th-century Protestant reformation group that wanted to rid the English Church of all traces of Roman Catholicism. Their name means "pure of heart" and a Puritan was first defined as "an advanced reformer in the Anglican Church." In time their theology became CALVINISM, however, and many of them were driven into exile with the accession of James I in England. Immigrating to America, they composed the bulk of the population of Plymouth Colony, Massachusetts and Connecticut. Noted for industry and intellectual intensity, among other fine qualities, they were even more noticeable for their strict morality and absolute reliance on Scripture. It was these latter qualities, often carried to fantastic extremes, that made *puritan* a synonym for a narrow-minded, excessively religious person blind to the beauty around him.

Purple Heart.   George Washington originated the medal called the Purple Heart during the Revolutionary War. His order in 1782 explained that "the General, ever desirous to cherish virtuous ambition in his soldiers, as well as to foster and encourage every species of military merit, directs that whenever any singularly meritorious action is performed, the author of it shall be permitted to wear over the left breast, the figure of a heart in purple cloth, or silk, edged with narrow lace or binding." Originally given for "meritorious action," and awarded to three or four Revolutionary War soldiers, it is now granted for battle wounds.

purple prose.   This term for ornate, exaggerated writing has a long history. The Roman poet Horace said that all purple patches (*purpureus pannus*) should be deleted from literary works and put away for eight years before being reedited and published—for they could never again be recalled.

pursuit of happiness.   The Declaration of Independence (1776) famously holds that all men are entitled to the "pursuit of happiness," but this stirring phrase wasn't coined by the declaration's principal author, Thomas Jefferson. British philosopher John Locke coined the words nearly a century earlier in a treatise on government, and the phrase has been used frequently since.

pushover.   *See* HIGH HAT.

push (hit) the panic button.   Of the many panic buttons that could be the source of this expression, meaning "to act in unnecessary haste or panic," the original appears to be the bell system used for bailouts and ditchings in World War II bombers such as the B-17 and B-24. Often extensive damage to a plane was hard to determine and pilots sometimes pushed the button activating the bell system too soon, causing their crews to bail out unnecessarily when there was only minor damage to the aircraft. The expression is sometimes used today to demand that a job be completed rapidly and well.

puss.   Irish immigrants apparently introduced *puss* to America in the early 1880s, the slang word deriving from the Gaelic *pus*, "mouth." Not long after the expression *to make a puss*, "to pout," became part of our vocabulary. So did *sour puss*.

pussyfoot.   Teddy Roosevelt seems to have either coined or popularized *pussyfoot* in about 1905. Meaning crafty, cunning, or moving in a cautious manner, it refers to the way cats can walk stealthily by drawing in their claws and walking on the pads of their feet. It's very unlikely that the redoubtable William Eugene "Pussyfoot" Johnson, a crusading American do-gooder, has anything to do with the expression. Johnson was nicknamed "Pussyfoot" because "of his catlike policies in pursuing lawbreakers" when he served as chief special officer in the Indian Territory. Later his nickname, in the form of *pussyfooters*, was applied to all advocates of Prohibition. While crusading in England, fresh from his triumph of securing the passing of Prohibition in the U.S., Johnson was blinded by a stone thrown by a crusading drunk.

put all your eggs in one basket.   *See* EGG PHRASES.

put a sock in it.   Seldom heard anymore, this phrase goes back to the days of early phonographs, first invented by Thomas Edison in 1877. The first phonographs had no form of volume control and in order to hold the volume down, teenagers were told to put a sock in the horn to mute the sound. *To put a sock in it* came generally to mean "to stop anyone from talking too much or too loudly."

putative.   The fictional author of a work, a character to which the author assigns its authorship, a *putative author* almost always narrates the story and pretends to have written it. *Putative* comes from the Latin for "to think," because the narrator character and his readers really think he wrote the book. *Putative marriage*, for an illegal marriage but one made in good faith, is first recorded early in the 19th century.

put in a good word for someone.   To say something favorable about someone, often to help that person obtain a job or some other benefit. *Good word* in this sense is hardly modern slang, dating back to the late 12th century.

put in one's two cents' worth.   The oldest recorded use I can find for this American phrase, which means to interfere or meddle, to butt into a conversation, dates back to only 1945, but it must be much older. The similar British saying, "to put one's oar in another's boat," dates to at least 1500, and the similar but little-known COME IN WITH ONE'S FIVE EGGS is two or three centuries old.

put it all in the first paragraph.   This maxim urging conciseness and pungency in the lead of a newspaper story has its origin in advice to a young reporter given by editor Samuel Bowles (1826–78). Bowles was the founder of *The Springfield Republic*, a liberal Republican paper.

put one's best foot forward.   The *best foot* in the common phrase is the right foot, it having been considered unlucky by the ancients to begin any journey or enterprise with the left foot; many English brides, for example, still put the right foot forward first when they enter the church.

put (lay) one's finger upon.   Sherlock Holmes *seems* to be the first person to have used *to lay one's finger upon*, "to indicate with precision," in Sir Arthur Conan Doyle's *The Memoirs of Sherlock Holmes* (1895): "You lay your finger upon the one point . . ." But a little sleuthing reveals that the expression had been used at least five years earlier as *to put one's finger upon*, in reference to a physician (not Dr. Watson) discovering the cause of an illness.

put one's foot in one's mouth.   *Every time he opens his mouth he puts his foot in it* is first recorded in the 1770s, when it was said of Dublin politician Sir Boyle Roche, who made remarks in his speeches like: "Half the lies our opponents tell about me are not true!" The expression was probably suggested by the earlier *to put one's foot in it. See also* PUT YOUR FOOT IN IT.

put one's oar in another's boat.   *See* PUT IN ONE'S TWO CENTS' WORTH.

put on nothing but the radio. To be naked. When a reporter asked Marilyn Monroe what she wore when she went to bed, she supposedly replied, "I put on nothing but the radio." Another version of the tale has her answering that she put on nothing but Chanel No. 5.

put on the dog. Lap dogs were all the rage among the new rich in America shortly after the Civil War, especially King Charles and Blenheim spaniels, rather imperious-looking dogs to the common man and certainly very distant relatives sociologically of the average American mutt, who had to work or scrounge for his supper. These snooty dogs being pampered by their snooty owners probably inspired the expression *putting on the dog,* "showing off," which apparently arose in the 1860s as college slang at Yale University. Attempts to derive *put on the dog* from the older *put on side* all seem strained. The reasoning behind the latter is that dogs "show off" by arching out one side while moving their feet in intricate maneuvers.

put on the gloves. Since about 1847 to *put on the gloves* has meant to fight, in a ring or elsewhere, although boxing gloves only became mandatory under the Queensberry rules. Boxing gloves were used in England as early as 1734 but weren't commonly called by that name until about 1875; prior to that, they were called *mufflers, gloves,* and *padded mittens. See* BELOW THE BELT.

put on the spot. The ace of spades is a symbol of death to the superstitious in many lands; in recent times Vietcong soldiers were so afraid of it that American planes "bombed" their strongholds with thousands of the cards to demoralize them. The expression *put on the spot* has its origins in this superstition, which probably derives from the old practice among pirates of sending the ace of spades, which has one printed "spot" in the middle, as a death threat to an informer or coward they intended to kill. Anyone who was sent the ace of spades was put on the spot, "in a dangerous position, slated to die." American criminals perpetuated the expression, giving it wide currency, and early in the 20th century it took on a less sinister meaning—though someone on the spot is still someone in danger of great failure or embarrassment if he doesn't produce successful results within a short time.

putt. According to most sports historians, *putt* is simply a Scottish pronunciation and spelling of *put,* which was first recorded in 1743. Thus to *putt* a golf ball into the hole is to put it in the hole. Those who trace the origin of golf to Holland, however, believe that *putt* derives from the Dutch word for the hole itself.

put that in your pipe and smoke it. This expression of British origin is commonly heard in the U.S. First recorded in an 1884 novel, it means, in the words of the *OED,* "digest it or put up with it if you can," usually said by a person who has put someone else down in an argument.

put the cart before the horse; preposterous. When Cicero said these words in 61 B.C. they were already proverbial. Actually, their Latin version, literally translated, means "the plow draws the ox in reversed position," but it conveys the same idea, that is, to get things in the reverse order. The Roman proverb was first translated into English in 1279, and over the years the ox became a horse and the plow a cart. The proverb is ancient in French, German, and Italian as well as English. *Preposterous* conveys a similar idea. It is from the Latin *prae,* "before," and *posterus,* "after," and freely translated means "the before coming after," which suggests its meaning of "nonsensical or absurd." By the way, sometimes carts *were* legitimately put before horses, as when horses pushed empty carts into coal mines. American author Heywood Broun liked to tell a joke based on the old proverb: "If a philosopher lectured on Descartes in a bordello what would I say?—I would say the philosopher was putting Descartes before de whores."

put the toothpaste back in the tube. A recent saying meaning "to perform a very difficult, almost impossible task," as in "A lot of damage has been done; it's going to be hard to correct it, to put the toothpaste back in the tube." Robert Baer, author of *See No Evil* (2002), used the phrase on a Fox TV interview (2/2/02).

put the kibosh on. *See* KIBOSH.

put through the mill. Someone *put through the mill* gets rough treatment like the grain that is ground under millstones in a water mill. This is one of numerous old expressions deriving from the milling of grain. Another is the term MILL. Still another is the proverb *much water runs by the mill that the miller knows not of:* many things happen right before us about which we know nothing.

put to the pale. *See* BEYOND THE PALE.

put up your dukes. *Dukes,* for "fists," probably honors the duke of York, Frederick Augustus (1763–1820), the second son of England's George III. A total loss as commander-in-chief of the Army, Frederick was nevertheless popular among his subjects. As he had once dueled in public with the future duke of Richmond, his name was associated with fighting, and being an ardent sportsman, he was often seen at the racetrack and prize ring. Possibly this led boxers to nickname their fists *Dukes of York,* the phrase finally shortened to *dukes* and expressions like *put up your dukes,* "let's fight," becoming common. Or else *Duke of Yorks,* Cockney rhyming slang for "forks," was associated with fingers, then hands, and finally fists, or *dukes*—with the Duke of York somewhere in mind. Another even more ingenious explanation has it that noses were called *Dukes* because the Duke of Wellington's nose was big—fists therefore being dubbed *Duke busters,* which ultimately became *dukes.* The Duke may have been immortalized in the language, but he ended his career in disgrace when his mistress admitted to taking bribes with his permission. To save face, he had to pension her off so that she wouldn't publish his love letters.

put your foot in it. The old proverb "The Bishop hath put his foot in it" led to the common expression, *Now you've put your foot in it.* Bishop is, of course, usually an honorific, but the original proverb, used when soup was scorched, may have arisen because of the reputation of a certain bishop or bishops for burning heretics. An alternate explanation is that the saying arose when an anonymous cook stood at the window watching a procession headed by a noted bishop and blamed him for the port soup she burned. Or it may simply have been suggested by someone stepping in cow flops.

put your shoulder to the wheel. This expression refers to someone literally putting his shoulder to the wheel and pushing a cart out of the mud, as was so common on roads everywhere in the days before macadam. The expression goes back at least to Elizabethan times, when it probably was proverbial in the form of *Lay your shoulder to the wheel and push the oxen.*

Pygmalion. *See* HENRY HIGGINS.

Pyrrhic victory. After he defeated the Romans at the battle of Asculum in 279 B.C., losing the flower of his army in the action, King Pyrrhus remarked, "One more such victory and we are lost." Other versions of his immortal words are, "One more victory and I am undone," and "Another such victory and I must return to Epirus alone." Pyrrhus had come to Italy with 25,000 troops two years before when Tarentum asked him to help organize resistance against the Romans, but after Asculum and several other battles he returned to the kingdom of Epirus in northwest Greece with only 8,000 men. The great warrior, a second cousin of Alexander the Great, never did live to revive the conqueror's empire as he had hoped. He died in 272 B.C., aged 46, during a night skirmish in a street in Argos—

fatally struck by a tile that fell from a roof—his name only commemorated by the phrase *Pyrrhic victory*, a victory in which the losses are so ruinous that it is no victory at all.

Pyrrhonist. A Pyrrhonist is the ultimate skeptic, one who like the Greek philosopher Pyrrho (ca. 365–ca. 275 B.C.) believes that we have no certain knowledge of anything at all. It is said that a contemporary wrote the following mock epitaph on the philosopher:

> 'And oh, dear Pyrrho.'
> Pyrrho, are you dead?'
> 'Alas, I cannot tell,'
> Dear Pyrrho said.

pyrzqxgl. *Pyrzqxgl* plays a rather important role in American fantasy, being the magic word coined by Frank L. Baum in *The Wizard of Oz* (1900).

python. *Python* derives from the Greek verb meaning "to rot," not a likely source for the name of the largest living snake next to the anaconda. The first python was a huge serpent slain near Delphi by Apollo, and the monster rotted in the sun after it died. The name of the mythological serpent wasn't given to real snakes until 1836, though it had been applied in English to other mythical monsters two centuries before this.

Q. *Q*, developed from Latin, never appears at the end of an English word and is almost always followed by *u* in English, though there are transliterated Arabic words offering exceptions: the Arabian sheikdom Qatar, for example, and *qaf*, the 21st letter of the Arabic alphabet. Another exception is *Qvoens*, "queens," which early Finns called themselves, leading some ancient European geographers to believe that a race of Amazons lived in northern Europe. Contractions like Q-BOATS and abbreviations like *q.v.* don't count. *See also* CUE.

al-Qaeda. The name of the terrorist organization headed by Saudi-born terrorist Osama bin Laden, which is thought by many to have destroyed the World Trade Center in New York City on September 11, 2001, by hijacking two planes and crashing them into the Twin Towers. Another plane hijacked by al-Qaeda terrorists crashed in Pennsylvania, apparently before it could accomplish the terrorists' aim of destroying the White House, and a fourth plane struck the Pentagon, causing many deaths and much damage. *Al-Qaeda* is Arabic for "the base," or "military headquarters." *See* SUICIDE BOMBER.

Qatar. The name of this country on a peninsula in the Persian Gulf is usually pronounced "cutter" by radio and TV newscasters. Most dictionaries, however, pronounce it "cah-tar." Qatar has been an ally of the U.S. in the Mideast.

Q-boats. These British warships disguised as merchant ships destroyed many a German U-boat during World War II. "Panic parties," men who abandoned ship when fired upon, were launched by these decoys, tempting the U-boats to come closer so that concealed guns manned by hidden crews could blast them out of the water. They took their name from an abbreviation of the Latin *quaere* "inquire" (which the U-boats did). Q-boats were also called hush-hush ships and mystery ships.

QE 2. Short for *Queen Elizabeth 2*, the Cunard Line cruise ship that replaced the *Queen Elizabeth* in 1967, two years after that great ship was retired. The 1,791-passenger ocean liner offers a six-continent, 108-day world cruise ranging in price from $24,195 to $374,515 (yes, one suite costs $374,515). The *QE2* is not so large as her predecessor in tonnage or length, but is the world's largest operating luxury liner today.

Q rating. *See* NIELSEN RATING.

Q.T. A British broadside ballad (1870) contained the line "Whatever I tell you is on the Q.T." This is the first record of *Q.T.* for "on the quiet, in confidence" recorded in English, but no one has established whether the broad-side's anonymous author was the first person to use the initials *Q.T.* to stand for quiet. *On the Q.T.* gained more popularity when it appeared in an 1891 minstrel show number called "Ta-ra-ra-boom-de-ay." London "went stark mad over the refrain," which was written by Henry J. Sayers and sung by Lottie Collins. The first stanza follows:

> A sweet Tuxedo girl you see,
> Queen of swell society,
> Fond of fun as fun can be
> When it's on the strict Q.T.
> I'm not too young, I'm not too old,
> Not too timid, not too bold,
> Just the kind of sport I'm told—
> Ta-ra-ra-boom-de-ay . . .

If you or your children grew up with "Howdy Doody," you'll notice the similarity between "Ta-ra-ra-boom-de-ay" and Howdy's theme song.

Quaalude. This sedative drug, a former trademark, takes its name from a contraction of the words *qu*iet inter*lude*. The *aa* in the word, however, was taken from the well-known antacid drug Maalox, which the William H. Rorer, Inc., the manufacturer of both drugs, thought would lend prestige to the new product. Quaaludes, developed in the 1960s, are also called *ludes* and *downs*.

quack; medicine man. *Quack* is an abbreviation of the 16th-century word *quacksalver*, which meant an ignorant charlatan who peddled nostrums and cure-all medicines in the street, the word deriving from the *quack* sound a duck makes and *salve*, medicine or ointment. In America quacks were called medicine men, after the Indian medicine men, as early as 1830. It might be said that the most famous of American fortunes began with a medicine man, or a quack, as John D. Rockefeller's father, William, would be called today. "Dr." Rockefeller was one of the traveling medicine men who put on minstrel shows featuring "Negroes in black face" to sell their wares. He called himself "Dr. William A. Rockefeller, the Celebrated Cancer Specialist," claiming he could cure all cases of cancer ("unless too far gone") with patent medicines. He once bragged, "I cheat my sons every chance I get" in order to "make 'em sharp."

quack grass. *Agropyron repens* and the other weedy grasses called *quack grass* are not so named because ducks like them or because they are used by quacks like medicine men. *Quack grass*, an Americanism first recorded in 1817, derives from the older British word, *quitchgrass*, *quitch* being an old form of "quick" and *quitchgrass* being a very quick grower and insidious spreader into places where it is not wanted. Other names for *quackgrass* include quatchgrass, twitchgrass, couchgrass, couch, and quitch.

quadrant. Used in astronomy and navigation since its development centuries ago, the quadrant is an instrument properly having the form of a graduated quarter circle that is used for making angular measurements, especially for taking latitudes in navigation. It takes its name from the Latin *quadrant*, "fourth part," or quarter.

quadrille. This five-part square dance for four couples is of French origin, but takes its name from the Spanish *cuadrilla*, "company or troop of soldiers," which is a diminutive of the Latin *quadra*, "square." *Quadrille* was first applied to one of four groups of horsemen taking part in a tournament, but by 1773 was being used to describe the four-couple dance that became so popular in the American South.

quaff. The obsolete German word *quassen*, meaning the same, probably gives us our *quaff*, "to drink heartily." The word is spelled wrong (*quaff* instead of *quass*) because "the long *s*'s—in print exactly like *f*'s without the cross-stroke—were mistaken for *f*'s" at some unknown date.

quagmired. Hopelessly entangled in a terrible mess, bogged down. A *quagmire*, the word first recorded in 1579, is ground that appears firm but is really jellylike and swallows anyone who steps upon it. The *quag* in the word is a variant of *quake*, "to shake," while *mire* means "muddy land."

quahaug. *Venus mercenaria*, the edible hardshell clam. Indians introduced this name and the clams themselves to the first European settlers in New England. Quahaugs are usually divided into chowders, as large as four inches at the widest point; cherrystones, half-grown quahaugs; and littlenecks, the most tender and smallest of quahaugs, at two inches or so.

Quai d'Orsay. *See* D'ORSAY PUMP.

quail. *To quail*, "to cower, to lose heart in danger or difficulty," is of no relation etymologically to the bird called a quail. Of uncertain origin, it may come from the Middle English *fael*,

meaning the same, or from the Latin *coagulare*, "to curdle," which also gives us *coagulate*. *Quail* has been American slang for a sexually attractive girl since the mid-19th century and may derive from the Celtic *caile*, "a girl." However, *quail* meant a harlot or courtesan in the 16th and 17th centuries, because of the bird's supposed "inordinately amorous disposition." The term was used by Shakespeare in *Troilus and Cressida*. The Bard would have liked the alliterative *San Quentin quail*: a U.S. slang term of the 1930s meaning a sexually attractive but underage girl, one who is jailbait for any man who consorts with her, who can put a man in San Quentin prison. The bird's name *quail* is probably of Teutonic derivation and imitative origin.

quail fight. Few if any Americans had heard of the term *quail fight* before the war in Afghanistan. Men there gather at village markets to bet on such fights, which feature fighting quail that cost their owners up to $300 for a fierce competitor, a huge sum in an impoverished land. The contests are similar to cock fights, but the little quail are only the size of a large baby chick. A photo of them can be found in the *New York Times*, 12/4/01.

Quaker. The religious Quaker group was founded by George Fox in 1650 as the Society of Friends, but readily accepted the name Quakers, derisively bestowed upon them because they bade people to "quake and tremble at the word of the Lord." George Fox claimed that he had spoken these words when being arraigned before Justice Bennet of Derby in 1650 and that the judge sneeringly called him a quaker, but there are earlier references to the term. In one London letter dated October 14, 1647, for example, the writer observes, "I hear of a secte of woemen (they are at Southworke) come from beyond sea, called Quakers, and these swell, shiver and shake. . . ." It could well be, then, that the name derives from the trembling of Friends under the stress of religious emotion, which once caused them to "quake, and howl, and foam with their mouths." Despite intense persecution, the beliefs of the Quakers persisted and spread throughout England and America. The Quakers, incidentally, forsook the use of *you* because it was at the time the second-person pronoun employed when addressing superiors. The *thou* they chose in preference to *you* was used in the 17th century to address familiars or inferiors, affirming to them the equality of mankind.

Quaker guns. Fake or dummy guns on ships have long been called Quaker guns in allusion to the Quakers' opposition to war and killing. In 1830 an American naval officer wrote: "Our six iron six-pounders and six quakers (wooden guns), were, like millennial lion and lamb, lying down together in the hold."

quandary. Etymologists have long been in a quandary about the origins of *quandary*, "a state of perplexity, the difficulty causing it." The word is at least four centuries old. The French phrase *qu'en dirai-je?*, "What shall I say of it?," and Middle English *wandreth* have been considered as ancestors and rejected by the experts. Grose suggests "an Italian word signifying a conjurer's circle," without giving the word. The *O.E.D.* suggests "a corruption of a scholastic Latin phrase," perhaps *quam dare?* or *quando dare?*

quandong tree. *Quandong* is an Australian Aborigine word that has come intact into English, making it one of our most ancient words. The quandong tree is a sandalwood bearing blue berries the size of cherries whose kernel, or "nut," is edible. It is also called the native peach tree.

Quantrill. Any fabled gunfighter or guerrilla; after William Clark Quantrill (1837–65), who formed a pro-Confederate guerrilla band during the Civil War, more to serve his penchant for cruel bush whacking, bloodletting, and looting than out of any sympathy for the Confederacy. In 1863 he led 448 men into Lawrence, Kansas, where they slaughtered 142 Jayhawkers, or pro-Union, citizens. Quantrill died two years later after being shot in the back while trying to escape from a detachment of Union soldiers.

quantum leap (jump). A quantum leap, or jump, is a sudden, dramatic change or increase. The term is borrowed from the physicist's field of quantum mechanics, where it refers to an abrupt transition from one energy state to another. *Quantum,* derives from the Latin *quantus,* "how much."

quarantine. People have been quarantined in the United States for every disease from measles to the dread bubonic plague. *Quarantine* itself ultimately derives from the Italian *quaranta,* "forty," in reference to the 40 days that travelers from other countries were isolated during the Middle Ages if they had come from a plague-stricken country.

quark. Some scientists believe that quarks, three types of elementary particles, form the basis of all the matter in the universe. The word *quark* was applied to the particles by physicist W. Gell-Man, but he took it from a James Joyce coinage in *Finnegans Wake.* However, unlike Joyce's *quark,* which rhymes with *dark,* Gell-Man's *quark* is pronounced *quork.* There is no argument, as the coiner made this clear in a 1978 letter to the editor of the *O.E.D. Supplement, Volume III.*

quarry. The quarry is now the object of any chase—the deer in hunting, the bird flown at in falconry—but it once meant something entirely different. In the Middle Ages the quarry, the word deriving from the Latin *corium,* "skin," was the entrails of the deer placed on the animal's skin as a reward for the hounds after a hunt. Finally it came to mean what the hounds went after. The *quarry* in *stone quarry* derives from the Latin *quadraia,* "the place where stone is squared," or cut into blocks.

quarterback. Football's *quarterback,* the backfield player who directs the offensive play of a team on the field, suggested this general verb meaning "to lead, direct, or manage anything." The term has been in use for a good 70 years. *See also* MONDAY-MORNING QUARTERBACK.

quarterdeck. Historically, on sailing ships, a vessel's quarterdeck is that part of a full-rigged ship abaft the mainmast on the spar deck. Today the quarterdeck is usually the part of the main deck adjacent to the starboard gangway, where distinguished visitors are received on any ship.

quarter horses. Quarter horses are named for their ability to run well in quarter-mile races, not because of their size or lineage. The term is an Americanism, first recorded in 1834, though quarter races are mentioned a good 50 years earlier as being very popular in the South. Quarter horses, usually smaller than Thoroughbred racehorses, were also called quarter nags.

quarter section. The Americanism *quarter section* of land was popularized by the Homestead Act of 1862, which said that any settler on the frontier could have 160 acres of public land free if he could raise a crop on at least 40 acres of it for five years. The 160 acres equaled a quarter of a square mile and was commonly called a *quarter section* or *quarter.* The former term, however, had been used as early as 1804, and the latter as early as 1640.

quasar. An acronym composed of letters from "*quasi*-stellar object," *quasar* was coined by scientists in the 1960s to describe any of some 40 million celestial objects, up to 10 billion light years distant from earth, which are powerful emitters of radio waves. Quasars are also called *quasi-stellar radio sources.*

quassia; quassin. The black slave Graman Quassi gives his name to this genus of small trees. Quassi discovered the medicinal value of the bark and heartwood of a group of tropical trees common to the Dutch colony of Surinam in the South American Guianas. Using the drug he extracted to treat his fellow natives, he "came to be almost worshipped by some" and when his discovery was communicated to Linnaeus by C. G. Dahlberg in 1730, the botanist named the genus of trees in the slave's honor. (Quassia's name probably comes from the Ashanti dialect word *Kwasida.*) The drug he discovered is known as *Surinam quassi* today, and is effective against intestinal worms, as a tonic, and as an insecticide. The drug's chief constituent is the bitter *quassin,* which is extracted from the nearly white wood in minute quantities.

The Queen! *The Queen, God Bless her!*, frequently abbreviated to *the Queen,* is the Loyal Toast to Her Majesty's health often made in British naval wardrooms. It is customarily drunk while seated because King William IV, "the Sailor King," is said to have hit his head on a wardroom beam while rising to make the toast.

Queen Anne's fan. Since the beginning of the 18th century, this term has stood for putting the thumb to the top of the nose and spreading out and wiggling the fingers. It is said to be named after England's Queen Anne (1665–1714), who often hid her face behind a fan. The rude gesture is also called "Anne's fan," "Spanish fan," "cock a snook," and "thumb one's nose."

Queen Anne's lace. According to folklore, the beautiful wild carrot (*Daucus carota*) is named for the rather homely Anne of Bohemia, who married England's Richard II in 1382. One story tells of a ward of the queen who chose this herb's delicate flower as a tatting pattern. This little girl came to Anne's attention when she was found innocent of a childish prank and the queen discovered her pattern, which she liked so much that she gave the child permission to name it after her. Another story has it that Queen Anne challenged her ladies in waiting to a contest to see who could made embroidery most similar to the pretty flower. The queen, of course, won. In any case, the name *Queen Anne's lace* was later transferred to the wild carrot's flower and then to the herb itself. Still another tale has Queen Anne's lace named for Saint Anne, "Queen of Heaven," the mother of Mary and grandmother of Jesus. Appropriately this Anne is the patron saint of lacemakers. Tradition has it that she and her husband, Joachim, were unable to have children, and only divine intervention enabled her to conceive, which would explain why the plant named after her was long believed to have aphrodisiac properties. No matter which of these stories is correct, Queen Anne's lace will remain as beautiful as ever. It blooms as an escape on roadsides throughout America and England in late summer and is sometimes cultivated in the garden, as it well deserves to be; in fact, it was first brought to America by Virginia colonists for use in their formal gardens.

Queen Camilla.   *See* FAST AS LADAS.

Queen cities.   A good number of American cities have the nickname "Queen City," These include: Queen City of the Hills (Houston, Texas); Queen City of the Mountains (Helena, Montana, also called Queen City of Montana); Queen City of the Plains (Denver, Colorado); Queen City of the Rio Grande (Albuquerque, New Mexico); and Queen City of the West (Cincinnati, Ohio, from a time when Cincinnati was considered far west.) Perhaps the most famous of Queen cities is the Queen City of the Mississippi (St. Louis, Missouri).

Queen Dick; queer as Dick's hatband.   Oliver Cromwell's son Richard (1626–1712), who ineffectually ruled England as Protector after his father, had such effeminate ways that he was widely called Queen Dick. Whether he was a homosexual isn't known, but homosexuality certainly isn't alluded to in the expression *as queer as Dick's hatband*. This means as strange as Dick's crown, a crown on the head of such a weak, ineffectual person seeming incongruous or ridiculous to most of his subjects. Though several writers have associated "queer" with homosexual in the phrase, the slang *queer* for homosexual isn't recorded until the 1920s. *See* TIGHT AS DICK'S HATBAND.

Queen Mary's thistle.   The national flower of Scotland was supposedly named for Mary, Queen of Scots, after attendants presented her a basket of the flowers while she was imprisoned in Fotheringay Castle by England's Queen Elizabeth. Also called the cotton thistle, *Onopordum ancanthium* has a purple top and is covered with little threadlike white hairs.

Queen of Floods.   An old name for the Mississippi River. "Through a vast uncultivated territory coursed the Queen of Floods and her many tributaries" began a newspaper article in 1832.

Queen of the Hill Bill.   I've heard this expression just once, but I'm sure it must be common in the U.S. House of Representatives, because it was used as if it were an everyday phrase there by Congressman Harold Ford during a Fox News interview (7/1/01). The Tennessee Democrat defined a Queen of the Hill Bill as the favorite bill among many on a subject, the one bill that should be discussed and voted upon. The Hill, of course, is a synonym for the U.S. Congress.

queen of the prairie.   This tall plant of the rose family, *Filipendula rubra*, with branching clusters of pink flowers, was so named by American pioneers in the mid-18th century when they saw the plant growing in meadows and prairies and admired its graceful beauty. *Filipendula* is Latin for "hanging thread," alluding to the root fibers of the plant hanging together by threads.

Queensberry rules.   *See* BELOW THE BELT.

Queens County, N.Y.   *See* KINGS COUNTY.

queen's (or king's) peace.   The queen's peace is the peace or protection of all law-abiding British subjects, though in past times it applied only to those in the royal employ. The term is used in *Blackstone's Commentaries*.

queen's taste.   *To the queen's taste* means completely, thoroughly, utterly. The queen's taste, the most discriminating in the land, would demand the best, something completely or thoroughly done. No one has been able to connect any specific queen with this phrase, which is, oddly, an Americanism and not British in origin, dating back to the late 19th century.

queen's tears.   An English term used in South Africa for any strong, powerful drink, especially gin. One story contends that the words derive from Queen Victoria's crying after the Zulus defeated the British at Isandhelwana.

queen's weather.   Queen Victoria was fortunate in having good weather most of the times she appeared in public. Her good luck led to the British expression *queen's weather,* for "a fine day for a public occasion, an outing, a party, etc." First recorded in 1899, the phrase is probably 20 years or so older.

queer.   The German *Quere*, "oblique, adverse, perverse, wrongheaded," may be the source of *queer,* but the word is of uncertain origin. *Queer* is first recorded in 1508 with the meaning of strange, odd, or eccentric in appearance or character, taking on many other meanings over the years both in standard English and slang. *See* QUEER DICK.

queer as a three-dollar bill.   *Queer* has meant counterfeit money since at least 1810, but *queer as a three-dollar bill* is obviously an Americanism, there never having been an American three-dollar bill. The expression dates back to the 1920s and usually means anything strange, unusual, or suspicious, though it can also mean a homosexual.

queer as Dick's hatband.   *See* QUEER DICK.

queer plunger.   *Queer plungers* were men who faked drowning in order to be "rescued" by their accomplices, who "carried them to the Humane Society, where they are rewarded by the society with a guinea each." The expression is first recorded in 1758. W. C. Fields did the same as a young man; he was hired by concessionaires to pretend that he was drowning so that crowds would gather and they would sell more food. He called himself a drowner.

Queer Street. The *queer* in this phrase, meaning to be in financial trouble, comes from the word *query*, not from any real city street. The expression arose two centuries ago, when merchants commonly put a query, or question mark next to the names of customers whose financial solvency was dubious.

quell. *Quell*, from the Anglo-Saxon *cwellan*, originally meant to kill or slaughter an enemy. But by about the early 1700s it had taken on the sense of to subdue or quiet, possibly to some extent because of its resemblance to *quiet*. It is heard mostly today in the expression *to quell a riot*, to subdue or suppress it, not necessarily with any violence.

querencia. Texans in the 19th century often used *querencia* to mean the place where a Longhorn calf was born, and there are tales of Longhorns persistently returning to such spots. But *querencia* also meant the place where anyone was born. The word derives from the Spanish *querer*, "to love."

question mark. The question mark, interrogation mark, or interrogation point, one tradition has it, was formed from the first and last letters of the Latin *quaestio* ("a seeking") which was first contracted to *Q* and finally became ?. Some authorities claim, however, that it originated as the Greek semicolon—upside down. Another kind of question mark is a butterfly (*Polygonia interrogationis*) with two silver spots shaped like question marks under each wing. When Victor Hugo wanted to know how his publishers liked *Les Misérables* (1862), he wrote them simply: "?" His publishers shortly responded with a brief "!" completing the briefest correspondence in history. *See* EXCLAMATION MARK.

queue up. People "standing in (or on) line" in America are *queuing up* in Great Britain. The latter term is little heard in the U.S. and derives from the French word *queue*, for "pigtail or tail," which in turn comes from the Latin *cauda*, "tail."

quey calves are dear veal. A quey is a female calf, that is, a valuable calf that will one day give milk. To kill such a calf for veal would be foolish, which gives us this old saying similar to *killing the goose that lays the golden egg*.

quibble. The obsolete English word *quib* probably derived from the Latin *quibus* "who, which," which appeared on many legal documents and came to be associated with odd quirks of the law. In any case, *quib* came to mean an ambiguous or petty argument and may be the source of *quibble*, meaning the same, as well as petty carping criticism. *Quibble* is first recorded in the 17th century.

quiche. A quiche is a pielike dish made of custard flavored with cheese, onion, bacon, or other ingredients that are baked in an unsweetened pastry shell. The word came into French from the German *Kuche*, "little cake," and seems to have been first recorded in English late in the 19th century.

Quichua. *See* NAHUATL.

quick. *Quick*, spelled *cqicu* or *cwic*, originally meant "the presence of life," or "living" in Old English. Therefore, livestock was once called *quickstock*, "living stock," *quicksilver* was so named because it seemed alive, a *quick fence* was a living hedge of plants, the sensitive flesh under a fingernail was known as the *quick*, and a *quick wine* was a lively, sparkling one. The old use of the word also figures in several common phrases. A woman *quick with child* is carrying a baby that has begun to show signs of life, that is "kicking." *The quick and the dead* just meant the living and the dead before it acquired its present double meaning. As for *stung to the quick*, this simply means that a person is stung deeply in living tissue where it really hurts. Today's use of *quick* as "swift" probably derives from early train conductors telling people to "be quick" or "step lively." *See also* CUT TO THE QUICK.

quick and the dead. *See* CUT TO THE QUICK.

quick as a dog can lick a dish. Rapidly, very quickly. Erskine Caldwell wrote in *Jenny by Nature* (1961): "There's not a female alive who can be trusted when they've got man fever—they'll take a man away from you quick as a dog can lick a dish."

quick as a wink. Very quick, almost like the blink of an eye. The phrase goes back to the early 19th century, first recorded in 1836. *See* FORTY WINKS.

quick as greased lightning. *Quick as greased lightning* is an Americanism dating from about the 1840s, but is a typical western exaggeration of the British *quick as lightning*, first recorded 100 years earlier. *Quicker than hell can scorch a feather* is a similar Americanism from the mid-19th century.

quick as (or before) you can say Jack Robinson. Jackie Robinson, the major leagues' first black player, was one of the quickest base runners in baseball history, but he has nothing to do with the old expression *as quick as you can say Jack Robinson*. The phrase goes back to 18th-century England, where there may have been, as Francis Grose suggested in *A Classical Dictionary of the Vulgar Tongue* (1795), a certain Jack Robinson who was in the habit of paying extraordinarily quick visits to his friends—and leaving even before his name could be announced by the butler. *Jack Robinson* was much more likely used in the phrase because it is easy to pronounce and is a very common name in England.

quick-change artist. Someone good at changing from one thing to another, from changing a topic to changing a costume during a performance. The term probably derives from the latter use and was first recorded in print about 1885.

quicker than hell can scorch a feather. Davy Crockett is given credit for this Americanism, as well as for *singing psalms to a dead horse, ripsnorter, sockdollager*, and *fine as silk*. He did not of course coin *a Crockett*, for "a violent person," or *a sin to Davy Crockett*, "anything extraordinary."

quicker than you can cook asparagus. Some old-timers still call asparagus *grass*, from the homely expression *sparrowgrass* commonly used as a name for the vegetable over the last three centuries. Asparagus is a Latin word formed from the Greek for sprout or shoot. The Romans cultivated it as early as 200 B.C., growing some stalks at Ravenna that weighed a full three pounds and gathering stems in the Getulia plains of Africa that were actually 12 feet tall. The most flavorful "grass," however, is thin and tender and should be cooked in as little water and as rapidly as possible. Even the Romans knew this, and their Emperor Augustus originated the old saying, *quicker than you can cook asparagus*, for anything he wanted done within a few moments. Asparagus has been regarded as a phallic symbol since earliest times, but this certainly isn't why perennial patches of it are called *beds*, which is just a common garden term. There is an interesting true story about blanched white asparagus, however. Reported a *New York Times* correspondent at a recent Bonn dinner party: "A certain guest complimented the elegant German hostess and said, 'This white asparagus is as beautiful as an undressed woman,' thereby probably becoming the first asparagus eater to have noted a resemblance between asparagus and the attributes of the *female* sex."

quickie. *Quickie* was originally late 1920s Hollywood slang for a Grade B movie, a film comparatively cheap and quick to produce. By the 1930s the term was being used to mean a quick act of sexual intercourse. *Quickie* is also slang for a full-length book, usually based on fast-breaking news events and written, edited, and printed within a matter of days or hours. *Miracle on Ice*, the story of the U.S. Olympic hockey upset victory, was written by a team of *New York Times* reporters and "was received, printed and on its way to distribution in 46 hours and fifteen minutes." Since then 2,000 bound copies of another book have been printed in 5 hours and 23 minutes, the world record.

quicksand. *Quicksand*, first recorded in 1275, may not be so named because it quickly sucks down anyone stepping on it. In fact, people caught in the treacherous sands can last for hours if they don't panic. Quick action may account for its name, but *quicksand* could just as well derive from the "lively" meaning of *quick*, because the loose wet sand shifts in its place as if it were alive. It is dangerous because it yields easily to any presence upon it.

quicksilver. The Romans called this metallic element, mercury, by the name *argentum vivum*, "living silver," because of its liquid mobile form at ordinary temperatures. "Living silver" was translated as *quick silver* (*quick* meaning "living") into a number of languages, coming into English as *cuiceolfor* by about the year 1000.

Quick time, march! A familiar U.S. Army command dating from the 19th century. It specifically means marching 120 paces of 30 inches per minute, but has come to mean any fast march in general use.

Quick, Watson, the needle. *See* SHERLOCK HOLMES.

quick with child. *See* CUT TO THE QUICK.

quid. British slang today for a one-pound note and formerly meaning a sovereign or a guinea, *quid* is of uncertain origin. First recorded in Thomas Shadevell's *Squire of Alsatia* (1688) it may come from the Latin *quid*, "what," for "the wherewithal."

quiddity. *Quiddity* can mean the "essence of a thing, its essential nature," or be a "trifling subtle distinction in an argument." It was probably first used (though not recorded) in the former sense, deriving ultimately from the Latin *quid*, "what." But scholastics in the 16th century argued so much and so subtly about the *quiddity*, or essence, of things that *quiddity* came to mean a quibble as well.

quidnunc. A quidnunc is a busybody, a prying gossip who wants to know everything that's going on. The word is quite appropriately formed from the Latin *quid nunc?* "what now?"—because such people constantly ask "What now?" "What's the news?" "What's happening?" Steele first records the term in a 1709 issue of the *Tatler*.

quid of tobacco. Most authorities say that *quid*, for "a plug of tobacco," comes from the Old English *cuidu*, "cud," which makes sense except for the late date when it is first recorded (1727). One old story traces the word to 19th-century Dublin plug manufacturer and tobacconist Lundy Foot, who had the Latin *Quid rides?* ("What are you laughing at?") inscribed on his carriage. Most people who saw the inscription had no Latin and read the "witticism" as English: *Quid rides*. They figured that since Quid was riding, his product might as well be known by his name as well.

quid pro quo. *Quid pro quo*, Latin meaning "something for something," means in English "one thing in return for another, an equivalent, tit for tat, a Roland for an Oliver." Shakespeare used a similar expression in *Henry VI* (1591): "I cry you mercy, 'tis but Quid for Quo."

quietus. *Quietus* derives from the Latin *quietus est*, "he is quiet." The word originally applied only to the discharge of any financial account, or the settlement of obligation. But *quietus* came to apply to the discharge of life itself, as Shakespeare used it in Hamlet:

> Who would fardels [burdens] bear . . .
> When he himself might his quietus make
> With a bare bodkin [dagger]?

See BODKIN.

qui-hy. The Hindi *Koi hai*, meaning "is anyone there?," is a cry used in India to summon a servant. These words, in the form of *qui-hy*, were used by the British when they occupied India to mean an Anglo-Indian, especially one living in Bengal. It also had some British military use in the sense of a summons to a servant.

quillet. A quillet is an evasion, the word probably deriving from the Latin *quidlibet*, "anything you choose." Wrote Shakespeare in *Love's Labour's Lost*: "Oh, some authority how to proceed;/Some tricks, some quillets, how to cheat the devil."

quim. Henry Miller uses *quim* for "the female pudend, a woman's private parts" in several of his books. The term is first recorded in 1785 by Grose, who suggests that it may derive from the Spanish *quemar*, "to burn."

Quinapalus. In Shakespeare's *Twelfth Night* the clown invents a character called *Quinapalus* as the authority for a saying of his own. The name can thus be used for an apocryphal source, just as BEN TROVATO is.

quince. *Quince* may come from the Greek *kydonion* ("melon"), named for Cydonia in Crete. *Kydonion* became *cydoneum* in Latin, this becoming *coin* in Old French, then *quoyne* in Middle English, with *quince* deriving from the plural of the Middle English *quoyne*, which is *quine*.

quincunx. An old Roman coin of little value called the *quincunx* had five dots or dashes on its face (one in each corner and one in the center), indicating that it was worth five-twelfths of an *as*. Any like arrangement of five objects, especially trees in a square or rectangle, is also called a quincunx, after the markings on the ancient coin.

quinsy. *Quinsy*, a suppurating (pus-producing) inflammation of the tonsils, or suppurative tonsilitis, comes to us from the Latin *quinancia*, which, in turn, derives from the Greek *kunanche*—which means, simply, "a sore throat." The Greek *kunanche* comes from *kuon anche*, "dog strangulation," because people suffering from the malady "throw open the mouth like dogs, especially mad dogs."

quintessence. Pythagorean alchemists, like everyone before and since, failed in their efforts to find a fifth element other than earth, air, fire, and water. But they *thought* that they had found this *quinta essentia*, or "fifth essence," in the form of ether, which they believed was the rarest and most pervasive of all the elements and formed the substance of the heavenly bodies. Since in a figurative sense fifth essences have been discovered, however, the word *quintessence* (from the Latin *quinta essentia*) means the most essential part or principle of a substance, the rarest distillation of a perfume or an idea.

quinzhee. Minnesotans commonly use this Ojibwa word for a round snow shelter. Trekkers in snow country often built the igloo-like quinzhees for shelter through the night.

quip. The best anyone can come up with for the origin of *quip* is that the word is a variant of *quippy*, also meaning a sharp, biting, or clever remark, and that *quippy* may come from the Latin *quippe* meaning "indeed, forsooth (with sarcastic force)." Both words are first attested early in the 16th century.

the quip modest. Shakespeare seems to have invented this expression, which Touchstone defines in *As You Like It*, as "it was done to please myself." If a person was told that his beard was cut badly and he replied that he cut it to please himself, Touchstone says, this would be *the quip modest*, "six removes from the lie direct."

quiring. An archaic word for choiring, used beautifully by William Faulkner in "Barn Burning" (1939): "He went on down the hill, toward the dark woods within which the liquid silver voices of the birds called unceasing—the rapid and urgent beating of the urgent and quiring heart of the late spring night."

quirk of fate. A sudden twist or turn of fate, as in "He lost his fortune by a quirk of fate." The word *quirk* is of uncertain origin, but may have originally been an English western dialect word for a sudden flourish or curve in drawing or writing. It also came to mean a peculiarity in action or behavior (Shakespeare used it in this sense), and an evasion or quibble.

quirly. This odd Americanism had some currency into the early 20th century. It was originally a cigarette rolled in a corn shuck instead of paper, but came to be a cowboy word for any cigarette. Its origins are unknown.

quisling; quisle. Of the men and women whose names have become synonyms for traitor only Vidkun Quisling's has shed its capital letter in the dictionaries. A *quisling* is universal for "a traitorous puppet of the enemy" and was one of the most quickly adopted of modern additions to the language, even inspiring the little-used verb *quisle*, which means "to betray one's country." Maj. Vidkun Quisling (1887–1945) earned his rank in the Norwegian army, having served as military attaché in Russia and Finland. An ardent fascist, he formed the National Unity Party shortly after Hitler came to power in 1933, but never attracted more than a minuscule following, most Norwegians considering him mentally unbalanced. Then the Nazis invaded Norway on April 8–9, 1940, and the ridiculous lunatic of the right came into power. Brutally suppressing all opposition, he assumed King Haakon's throne in the palace and drove around in a bulletproof limousine presented to him by Hitler. A megalomaniac who ordered pictures of himself hung everywhere and refused to eat off anything but gold dishes, he was so paranoid that 150 bodyguards accompanied him at all times and every scrap of food he ate was sampled by someone else first. After the war, he was tried for treason, murder, and theft, found guilty on all counts, and shot by a firing squad, Norway changing its law against capital punishment for this purpose.

Quisqualis. Like MAHERNIA, the name of the plant genus *Quisqualis* is another joke played by the pioneer botanist Linnaeus. *Quisqualis*, the genus containing a few woody vines from Malaya and the Philippines, is grown today in southern Florida for its showy pink or red flowers. When Linnaeus examined the plant, he did not know how to classify it or for whom he could name it. He therefore called the genus *Quisqualis*, which in Latin means, literally, "who or what for." Although *Quisqualis* (kwis-kwal-is) is not eponymous, it clearly shows that the naming process is not always so serious a matter; it might even be called an anonymous eponymous word, or a word in want of an eponym. *See* MHO.

quixotic. Don Quixote de la Mancha, the lofty-minded but impractical hero of Cervantes's novel of the same name (1605–15), gives us this adjective embodying his characteristics. One of the great characters of literature, Don Quixote wanders the world with his squire Sancho Panza and his horse Rosinante searching for adventures in which he can be chivalrous. When he tilted with his lance at windmills, imagining them to be enemies, he added still another expression of frustration to the languages of many nations. *See* TILT AT WINDMILLS.

quiz. A short test. The tale may be apocryphal, but it's said that in the late 18th century Dublin theater manager James Daly bet that he could invent and introduce a new meaningless word into the language almost overnight. He proceeded to pay Dublin urchins to chalk the word *quiz* on every wall in town.

By morning almost all Dubliners had seen the word, and because no one knew what it meant, the meaningless *quiz* became the word for "a test of knowledge."

quoddy boat.   Quoddy boats, double-ended keelboats with a gaff mainsail and sometimes a jib set on a detachable bowsprit, take their name from the Pasama*quoddy* Bay between New Brunswick, Canada and Maine, where they first were built. They were long used for lobstering and fishing along the Maine coast.

quonset hut.   The quonset or quonset hut is a prefabricated corrugated metal building shaped like a tunnel that is named for its first place of manufacture, Quonset Point, Rhode Island, during World War II. Virtually the same thing by another name is the Nissen hut, designed by British engineer Lt. Col. Peter Nissen in 1930.

quotes; quotation; quotation mark; quote.   The word *quotation* comes from the Latin *quotation*, meaning the same, and dates back to about 1525, while the term *quotation mark* was first recorded in 1880. *Quote* as the statement of the current price for a commodity or stock was not recorded until about 1810. In the past few years speakers have increasingly used a sign made with the first two fingers of each hand to indicate that a word or phrase they have spoken should be in quotation marks or quotes (as the word or phrase would be written). The speaker usually holds up his or her fingers near each side of the head.

quotidian.   Meaning "daily, or everyday, ordinary" *quotidian* is first recorded by John Wycliffe in about 1380. It came into English intact from Latin and can also mean, as a medical term, a certain fever that recurs daily.

R

R. Since Roman times *R* has been thought of as the "dog's letter," or the snarling letter, because its sound resembles the snarling of a dog—*r-r-r-r*. Ben Jonson, in his *English Grammar Made for the Benefit of All Strangers* (1636), put it this way: "R is the dog's letter, and hurreth in the sound; the tongue striking the inner palate, with a trembling about the teeth." Shakespeare has Juliet's nurse in *Romeo and Juliet* call *R* the "dog-name," when she tells Romeo that his name and rosemary, an herb associated with weddings, both begin with an *R*. In parts of America, especially the Midwest, *R* is still pronounced as the dog letter, while in other regions, particularly parts of New England and the South, it is pronounced as *ah*.

rabage. This unfortunate vegetable is quite real but won't be found in any gardening books or seed catalogs. The rabage (*Raphanobrassica*) is a cross between a radish and a cabbage developed by a Soviet geneticist named Alexi Karpenchinko in 1924. What was expected was a plump head of cabbage on an edible round root of radish. Sadly, what developed was a head of scraggly radish leaves and the thin, useless roots of a cabbage. *See* RADISH.

rabbi. Meaning "my lord" or "master" in Hebrew, *rabbi* of course refers to a teacher and scholar of Jewish law who usually heads a synagogue or temple. In police jargon one's rabbi is a person who can help further one's career, the person so called because he has influence with higher-ups—just as a rabbi has influence with the ultimate higher-up.

rabbit. Some animal names incorporate human names, as in *jackass* and *jackdaw*. An excellent and little known example of this is *rabbit*, which comes ultimately from the Dutch name *Robert*, Robert.

rabbiteye blueberry. The rabbiteye blueberry is a blueberry bush native to the southern U.S. and widely grown there. It is so called because to some the berries on the tall (up to 20-foot-high) plants resemble rabbit eyes.

rabbit tobacco. *Rabbit tobacco*, or "rabbit terbarker," as Uncle Remus called it, is balsamweed, a plant used as a tobacco substitute by youngsters and others, despite its bad taste. It takes the name "rabbit" because it grows wild, often in fields where rabbits run.

Rabelaisian. *See* GARGANTUAN.

raccoon; raccoon-eyed. An Algonquian Indian dialect word is the basis for *raccoon*, which dates back to the first settlers in America. Dr. Johnson said of the clever creature: "The rackoon is a New England animal, like a badger, having a tail like a fox, being clothed with a thick and deep furr: it sleeps in the day time in a hollow tree, and goes out a-nights, when the moon shines, to feed on the sea side, where it is hunted by dogs." *Racoon-eyed* means someone with deep rings under his or her eyes from illness or lack of sleep, the face resembling the "masked" raccoon's. *See* COON'S AGE.

the race is not to the swift. "The race is not to the swift, nor the battle to the strong," according to Ecclesiastes 9:11. The biblical phrase has become proverbial over the past 400 years and has several humorous variations, including American humorist Franklin Pierce Adams's much-quoted "The race is not the swift, nor the battle to the strong; but the betting is best that way."

rachel. Discovered singing for pennies in the streets by the famous voice teacher Alexandre Choron, Élisa Félix, the daughter of poor Parisian peddlers, was trained for the stage and made her debut at the Comédie Française just before her 17th birthday. Élisa took the stage name Rachel, and her genius as a tragic actress, especially in the plays of Racine and Corneille, was acclaimed throughout Europe. "Rachel the immortal" ranks second only to Sarah Bernhardt among French actresses. While at the height of her fame in such roles as Phèdre in Racine's play of that name, the fawn-colored Rachel face powder, sometimes called rachel for short, was named in her honor by a Parisian cosmetic specialist. On a visit to America Rachel contracted tuberculosis, which led to her death three years later, in 1858. She was only 38, her tragic last illness and death the theme of a poem by Matthew Arnold.

Rachmanism.   The practice of driving out low-paying tenants by harassment in the manner of London landlord Peter Rachman (1920–62), a Polish immigrant whose ruthless practices included the use of strong-arm thugs. This slum lord became notorious in the late 1950s and early 1960s before his death from a heart attack.

rack and ruin.   A person gone to rack and ruin, "to destruction, utter destitution," may feel as though he's being stretched on the infamous rack, but the word *rack* in this centuries-old expression is only a misspelling of the word *wrack*. Even before Elizabethan times *wrack* was a variant form of *wreck*, and since the *w* in it is almost silent, writers took to spelling it *rack*. And so we have the phrase *rack and ruin*, which should really be *wreck and ruin*.

racket; racketeer.   English pickpockets, once the best of the breed, invented the ploy of creating disturbances in the streets to distract their victims while they emptied their pockets. This practice was so common that a law was passed in 1697 forbidding the throwing of firecrackers and other devices causing a racket on the city streets. From the common pickpocket ploy the old onomatopoeic English word *racket*, imitative like *crack* or *bang* and meaning a disturbance or loud noise, took on its additional meaning of a scheme, a dodge, illicit criminal activity. Before 1810, when it first appeared in print, the word had acquired this slang meaning in England, though it was later forgotten and the word *racket* for a criminal activity wasn't used again there until it was reintroduced from America along with the American Prohibition invention from it, *racketeer.* The only other, improbable, explanation given for the word is that it was originally the name of an ancient, crooked dice game. In tennis and similar games, the ball was originally hit with the palm of the hand, which was called *raquette* in Old French, deriving ultimately from the Arabic *rahah* meaning the same. In the evolution of tennis, various gloves were used next, then boards, then a short paddle, and finally the long-handled instrument employed today. All were called by the name *raquette*, which became the English word *racket*. The French still call tennis *le jeu de paume*, the palm game.

rack one's brains.   This phrase does have its origins in the *rack*, that old instrument of torture introduced into the Tower of London by the duke of Exeter in 1470 and often called "Exeter's Daughter" at the time. The machine was called the *rack*, or *reck*, from the German *recken*, "to stretch or draw out," and was usually a wooden frame (adapted from those used in leather factories), with rollers at each end. The victim was fastened to the rollers by the wrists and ankles and the joints of his limbs were stretched by their rotation, sometimes until they were torn from their sockets. The rack was abolished in England by 1640, but its memory lived on in many vivid uses of the name. The powerful image of someone racking—stretching or staining—his brains or wits to find the answer to a question is found in the language as far back as 1583, at a time when the real rack was still being used.

radar; laser.   These are among the most widely used and lasting of scientific acronyms. *Radar* was coined from *r*adio *d*etecting *a*nd *r*anging during World War II, while *laser* came after the war, from *l*ight *a*mplification by *s*timulated *e*mission of *r*adiation. The English alphabet can produce 456,976 acronyms composed of four letters and hundreds of thousands more if either additional or fewer letters are used. *See* QUASAR.

radio.   *Radio* is an Americanism that came into the language in about 1910, as a shortening of *radiotelegraph*. The *radio* in radiotelegraph derives from the Latin *radius*, beam, ray. *See* TELEGRAPH; TELEPHONE; TELEVISION; WIRELESS.

radish.   The easy-to-grow radish (*Raphanus sativus*) takes its scientific name from its Greek name, *raphanes*, "easily reared." *Radish* itself comes from the Latin *radix*, "root." The Greeks so valued the radish that they made small replicas of radishes in gold, while creating images of their other vegetables in lead or silver. The French call the radish by the poetic name *roses d'hiver*, "roses of winter." *See* RABAGE.

Raffles; Raffles Hotel; Rafflesia.   Naming the genus *Rafflesia* after English administrator Sir Thomas Stamford Bingley Raffles (1781–1826) could be interpreted as either a compliment or an insult. On the one hand, the species *Rafflesia arnoldi* has the largest single flower known to man—its bloom measuring up to six feet in diameter, three-quarters of an inch thick and attaining a weight of 15 pounds. On the other hand this same bowl-shaped, mottled orange-brown-and-white flower is commonly called the stinking corpse lily. A parasite that grows on the roots of vines in its Malaysian habitat, only the plant's bloom is visible above ground, the rest being a fungus growing beneath it, and its smell of decaying flesh attracts the carrion flies that pollinate it. On balance it seems that Sir Stamford would have been better off if he had only had the world-famous Raffles Hotel in Singapore named for him, but since he discovered the plant genus, he really had no one to blame but himself; he should have kept quiet about it. Raffles gained no gratitude from the British powers that were, either. An able colonial administrator in the East Indies, he did much to suppress the slave trade, was conspicuous for his liberal treatment of his subjects, zealously collected much historical and zoological information, and secured the transfer of Singapore to the East India Company in 1819. But he was censured for freeing slaves, and after his death his wife had to pay the costs of his mission to found Singapore. *Raffles* for "a gentleman burglar" comes from the name of a suave character created by Australian writer Ernest W. Hornung in a collection of stories published in 1899.

ragamuffin.   Until recently *ragamuffin* for a shabby, dirty child was thought to derive from the name of a demon in the 14th-century allegorical poem *Piers Plowman*. Recent research, however, has found that the word was used as a real person's last name before this and probably derives ultimately from the Middle English *raggi*, ragged, and the Middle Dutch *muffe*, mitten.

ragged robin.   This is the colorful name for *Lychnis flos-cuculi*, also called the cuckooflower. Tennyson compares the flower to a pretty maid in ragged clothes in *Idylls of the King*.

The genus name *Lychnis* comes from the Greek *lychnos*, "a lamp," in reference to the glowing flowers.

raglan sleeve. "I say, bring back my arm—the ring my wife gave me is on the finger!" Lord Raglan is supposed to have said something to this effect immediately after field surgery when surgeons cut off his badly wounded sword arm at the Battle of Waterloo. In any case, Fitzroy James Henry Somerset (1788–1855), first Baron Raglan, was renowned for his courage. Raglan served as aide-de-camp and secretary to the duke of Wellington, whose niece he married, succeeding him on his death as commander of all British forces. During the Crimean War, Raglan was a familiar figure on the battlefields, dressed in his raglan overcoat, a loose-fitting coat with sleeves extending to the neck. The raglan had been named for him at about this time, and today the loose raglan sleeve is still a popular fashion. He died soon after the siege of Sevastopol, in which 1,500 British troops were lost, and his men blamed him for the rout. Raglan's doctors claimed he died of a broken heart; the official report cited cholera.

to railroad. Americans built railroads in a hurry in the 19th century, and the mountains, rivers, and forests that stood in their way as they crisscrossed the continent were unfortunately regarded as mere obstacles blocking the right of way. The speed with which lines were built and the railroad builders' disregard for anything that stood in the way of "progress" inspired the term *to railroad* by the 1870s. At first it meant to send a person speedily to jail without a fair trial, or by framing him, and then it took on the additional meaning of rushing important legislation through Congress without regard for opposition to it and in disregard of regular procedures.

rainbow chaser. Ancient legend, its source unknown, had it that a pot brimming with gold was waiting to be found if a person dug at the exact spot where a rainbow touched the ground. Anyone who daydreams, who is a visionary, who puts nothing aside for a rainy day, who chases that pot of gold at the end of the rainbow is called a "rainbow chaser." The term, in turn, inspired the song "Over the Rainbow" by Harold Arlen and E. Y. Harburg that Judy Garland immortalized in *The Wizard of Oz* (1932), as well as the song "I'm Always Chasing Rainbows," whose title has become a popular phrase itself.

rain check. An old story says the rain check—the detachable part of a ticket that a spectator uses to gain admission to a future baseball game if the current game is postponed because of rain—was invented by Abner Powell of the minor league New Orleans Pelicans in 1888. Powell conceived the idea, according to the tale, because when his club's games were rained out, people who hadn't attended the cancelled game lined up to get replacement tickets for the next game, costing him a lot of money. The story sounds good, but the term *rain check* is first recorded four years earlier in St. Louis. Rain checks aren't common these days, as tickets usually list the rain date. The term is widely used today to mean an offered or requested postponement of an invitation until another time. When sale items (groceries, etc.) scheduled for a certain day are sold out on that day, customers are often gives rain checks to buy them when they are back in stock.

raining cats and dogs. A literal explanation for *raining cats and dogs* is that during heavy rains in 17th-century England some city streets became raging rivers of filth carrying many dead cats and dogs. The first printed use of the phrase does date to the 17th century, when English playwright Richard Brome wrote in *The City Witt* (1652): "It shall rain dogs and polecats." His use of "polecats" certainly suggests a less literal explanation, but no better theory has been offered. Other conjectures are that the hyperbole comes from a Greek saying, similar in sound, meaning "an unlikely occurrence," and that the phrase derives from a rare French word, *catadoupe* ("a waterfall"), which sounds a little like *cats and dogs*. It could also be that the expression was inspired by the fact that cats and dogs were closely associated with the rain and wind in Northern mythology, dogs often being pictured as the attendants of Odin, the storm god, while cats were believed to cause storms. Similar colloquial expressions include *it's raining pitchforks*, *darning needles*, *hammer handles*, and *chicken coops*. *See* FISHFALL.

raise cain. *Raising cain*, "to cause much trouble or a loud disturbance," is probably a synonym for "to raise the devil," for whom the biblical *Cain* was an early euphemism. The first recorded use of the expression, in a joke printed in the *St. Louis Pennant* in 1840, shows that it was well-known at the time: "Why have we every reason to believe that Adam and Eve were both rowdies? Because . . . they both raised Cain."

raise hob. *Hob* was the nickname of Robin Goodfellow, the mischievous household spirit of English folklore. *To raise hob* has for centuries meant to act devilishly like him, to be mischievous.

raise Old Ned. *See* OLD NED.

rally 'round the flag, boys. Andrew Jackson is said to have coined this phrase during the Battle of New Orleans in 1812. General Jackson, or Old Hickory, as he was called, may be the inventor, but the expression only gained widespread use during the Civil War after the publication of George Root's song "The Battle Cry of Freedom":

> Rally 'round the flag, boys,
> Rally once again,
> Shouting the battle-cry of freedom.

RAM. *See* ROM AND RAM.

Ramayana. *See* MAHABHARATA.

ramrod rolls. Margaret Mitchell described this military ration in *Gone With the Wind* (1936). "The men added as dessert some 'ramrod rolls' from their knapsacks, and this was the first time Scarlett had ever seen this Confederate article of diet about which there were almost as many jokes as about lice. They were charred spirals of what appeared to be wood. The men dared her to take a bite and, when she did, she discovered that beneath the smoke-blackened surface was unsalted corn bread. The soldiers mixed their ration of corn meal with water, and salt too when they could get it, wrapped the thick paste about their ramrods and roasted the mess over camp fires. It was as hard as rock candy and tasteless as sawdust . . ."

ramshackle. *Ramshackle* is one of the relatively few words Icelandic has contributed to English, if it does come from that language, as some scholars believe. *Ramskakkr*, "very twisted," is the possible Icelandic source for our word meaning "loosely made or held together, rickety, shaky," but there are other suspects, including *ranshacle*, "to wreck or destroy by plundering"—which would make something *ramshackled* "wrecked or destroyed by plundering." The word is first recorded in 1675.

R & R. In World War II, and during the Korean conflict, R & R meant a *r*est and *r*ecuperation leave, though in Korea it was extended to rear-echelon units as well as front-line outfits and the initials were generally thought to mean *r*est and *r*ecreation.

rankle. *Rankle* derives from Latin *dracunculus*, "little snake or dragon." It came to mean "festering sore" in French, perhaps because such sores sometimes resemble a little snake, or a coiled little snake, or the bite of a snake. In any case, *raoncler*, an alternative form of French *draoncles*, "to fester," passed into English about 1200 and over the years changed in spelling to *rankle*. *Rankle* held on to its literal meaning of "to fester" but also came to mean "to cause persistent irritation or resentment."

rap. *The New Dictionary of American Slang* (1986) suggests that *rap*, "to converse," dates from the 1960s, but it seems from the context of Damon Runyon's "Madame La Gimp" (1920) to have been used about a half century before then: "I got to the Marberry . . . and who opens the door of Madame La Gimp's apartment for me but Moosh, the door man. . . . I wish Moosh a hello and he never raps to me but only bows, and takes my hat." If this example of *rap* means "talks," then it may be the first use of the word *rap* in this sense, a theory that apparently hasn't been proposed before. *Rap* could have entered black English as "impromptu repartee or discussion," a meaning first recorded in 1965, and may have finally become the name of the rap style of popular music developed by blacks, a term first recorded in 1979. *See* RAP MUSIC.

rapeseed. The name of seed of rape (*Brassica napus*) of the mustard family derives from the Latin *rapum* for "turnip." It is used to make rape oil, a brownish yellow oil used chiefly as a lubricant and illuminant, and in the manufacture of rubber substitutes. In 1981 more than 600 Spaniards died in the largest recorded accidental mass poisoning in history from using a commercial cooking oil made with "denatured" industrial oil from rapeseed. Rape is used as a cover crop in the United States. *See* MUSTARD.

rap music; flyting. *Rap music* refers to popular music dating from the 1970s in which the beat provides the background for rapid, boasting, rhyming patter intoned by a singer. Though the music was mainly developed by black youths in the ghetto, one aspect of it—the insult rhymes the vocalists direct at one another—dates back at least five centuries. In times past these poetic insults were called *flytings*, a word meaning "word fighting." Flytings (from Old English *flyte*, "to contend or jeer") were contests held principally by 16th-century Scottish poets in which two persons "assailed each other alternately with tirades of abusive verse." Following is one of fully 32 stanzas directed at Scotland's James V by his former tutor, poet Sir David Lindsy (1490–1555). Bear in mind that this vitriolic diatribe *lost* the flyting contest:

> Purse-peeler, hen stealer, cat-killer, no I qyell thee;
> Rubiator, fornicator by nature, foul befal thee.
> Tyke-sticker, poisoner Vicar, Pot-licker, I mon pay thee.
> Jock blunt, dead Runt, I shall punt when I slay thee.

See RAP

rara avis; rare bird. A rare person or thing, someone out of the ordinary, *rara avis* is the Latin for "a rare bird" and the expression was first used figuratively by the Roman satirist Juvenal. "A bird rarely seen on earth, and very like a black swan," Juvenal called one of his fellow Romans ("*Rara avis in terris nigroque simillima cygne*"). He chose a black swan for his comparison because black swans, native to Australia, were unknown at the time.

rasher of bacon. The *rasher* in this British term, sometimes heard in America, means a slice and probably didn't get its name because it is cooked *rashly* or "quickly." *Rasher* here is more likely a corruption of *rasure*, "a thin slice or shaving."

Rasmussen's laugh. In Icelandic legend the story is told of a clergyman named Paul Rasmussen, whose son was kidnapped by English raiders. Acting impulsively, Rasmussen picked up three shells from the beach, each representing an English ship, and made black magic with them. When the shells sank in the water, so did the real ships out on the horizon. Rasmussen only realized that his son had been on one of the ships when the boy's body washed up at his feet, delivered by a huge breaker. He began laughing a horrible ironic laugh that did not stop even after he died, a laugh that superstitious sailors say is really what you hear when you think sea birds are calling in the distance.

raspberry. Known to the Romans as the "Red Berry of Mount Ida" (hence the name of the British species *Rubus idaeus*) for Mount Ida in Greece, the raspberry takes its name from the English *rasp*, "to scrape roughly," in reference to the thorned canes bearing the berries. Raspberries have not been cultivated for nearly as long as fruits like apples, peaches, and pears. Called a brambleberry or hindberry and considered a nuisance in England, it was not until about 1830 that the delicate, delicious fruit began to be developed in America. The *Fanny Heath* variety is a tribute to a determined pioneer woman who immigrated to North Dakota in 1881. This young bride had been told that she could never grow anything on the barren alkaline soil surrounding her house, but 40 years later her homestead was an Eden of flowers, fruits, and vegetables. After her death in 1931, the black raspberry she developed was named in her honor. A red raspberry variety honoring a famous person is the *Lloyd George*, named after British prime minister David Lloyd George (1863–1945), who led Britain to victory in World War I and dominated British politics in the first quarter of the 20th century. *Raspberry* meaning a BRONX CHEER, a rude vibrating of the lower lip, derives from British rhyming slang *raspberry tart*, which means "fart" and is at least a century old.

Rastafarian. Long, plaited hair known as dreadlocks mark the outward identity of Rastafarians, who are members of a religious and political group called the Ras Tafari, which in turn takes is name from a title (*Ras* "King," "Royal Prince," or "Duke") and a family name (*Tafari*) of Ethiopian emperor Haile Selassie (1892–1975). Originating in Jamaica during the 1920s, the group immigrated mainly to the U.S. and Europe. They believe that they are the chosen people, that Haile Selassie was their messiah, and that in time they will return to Africa.

Rat Catcher. A little-known nickname of Winston Churchill during World War I, because he said of the German fleet: "If they do not come out to fight, they will be dug out like rats from a hole." Churchill was first lord of the Admiralty at the time the war broke out but lost his cabinet post after the failure of the Dardanelles campaign, which he had supported.

ratfink. *See* FINK.

Ratkiller. The ancient Greeks placed great faith in their god Apollo Smintheus as a ratcatcher, calling him Ratkiller. He earned this sobriquet when he sent a swarm of rats against his priest Crenis because Crenis had neglected his duties. When the priest repented, seeing the rodent invaders coming, Apollo forgave him and with his far-reaching arrows killed the swarm of rats he had sent. Some authorities, however, say that Apollo should be called Mousekiller (his name Smintheus meaning a mouse) and was the god who protected Greek farmers against mice.

rat king. The famous *Rattenkonig*, or "rat king," occurs when young rats close to one another in the nest get their tails entangled and become a living Gordian knot glued together by dirt-encrusted wounds and the like. When they try to pull apart, the tails are pulled tight, and the knots strengthen, knitting the rats together. As many as 32 rats have been trapped in these knots and have died as a result of being unable to forage for themselves. However, they are often unselfishly fed for life by other family members. There is no doubt that rat kings exist; 60 or so have been reported in Europe since 1564 and about 40 (most of them found alive) have been authenticated, the latest in 1963. Rat kings have frequently been preserved, painted, and photographed, and in 1774 a 16–rat king was examined by a Leipzig court in connection with a charge that a miller's apprentice had cheated his master by stealing the king from him and pocketing a tidy sum by exhibiting it. The name *rat king* may come from the old superstition that an aged wise rat sat on the entangled tails of rats and was treated as royalty by the pack.

Rat Man. Sigmund Freud's famous Rat Man, readers will remember, didn't resemble a rat in any way; he, rather more simply, had an obsessional neurosis about rats. This Rat Man consulted with Dr. Freud sometime after he had been told by a fellow army officer of a Chinese torture in which a pot filled with rats was strapped onto a criminal's buttocks and the trapped rats bored their way into his body through the anus. Overwhelmed with the story, the patient began imagining the torture applied to two people very close to him. Freud discovered why he did this in an attempt to cure the man.

rat pack. The term *rat pack*, referring to humans, was first applied to singer Frank Sinatra (1915–98) and his close friends (Dean Martin, Peter Lawford, Sammy Davis, Jr., etc.) by Republicans angry at Sinatra for the help he gave John F. Kennedy in the 1960 presidential campaign. Later, angry at Kennedy, Sinatra supported Nixon, Reagan, and the Republicans. Sinatra ("Chairman of the Board," "The Voice," "Frankie Boy," "Old Blue Eyes") was a legend in his own time. The singer won an Oscar for his portrayal of Maggio in *From Here to Eternity*. Sinatra himself called the rat pack his "pallies." *See* PACK RAT.

rat race. *Rat race* originated in the 1930s among jazz musicians and fans as the name of a certain fast dance. It came to mean any difficult, tiring, often meaningless activity in which one struggles to keep up with or ahead of the competition. Today it also means the everyday world of work.

rats desert a sinking ship. That rats are the first to desert a sinking ship can be explained by the fact that water begins entering a sinking ship belowdecks, where they make their homes. An old American proverb instructed "When the water reaches the upper deck, follow the rats." In both America and England, *to rat* has long meant "to forsake a losing side for the stronger party" (a "ratfink" would do this today), or to desert one's party, an allusion to rats forsaking unseaworthy ships. Jonathan Swift wrote in "Epistle to Mr. Nugent": "They fly like rats from sinking ships."

the Rat, the Cat, and Lovell the dog. Probably the author who got in the most trouble for the slightest trifle was English poet William Collingham, who wrote:

> The Rat, the Cat and Lovell the Dog
> Rule all England under the Hog.

In this couplet the "Rat" was royal adviser Sir Richard Ratcliff, the "Cat" Sir John Catesby, the "Dog" Viscount Francis Lovell, and the "Hog" Richard III, whose crest was a boar. Collingham was executed for his witty rhyme.

Rattlesnake Buttes. A landmark in Colorado infested with myriad poisonous snakes. "Rattlesnake Buttes!" James Michener wrote in *Centennial* (1974): "A thousand westward travelers would remark about them in their diaries: 'Yesterday from a grate distance we seen the Rattlesnake Butes they was like everybody said tall like castels in Yurope and you could see them all day and wundered who will be bit by the snakes like them folks from Missuri?' "

raven. The best-known bird in American literature takes its name from Old Norse *hrafn* for this member of the crow family (*Corvus corax*). We are all familiar with the bird in Edgar Allan Poe's "The Raven" (1845) who visits a student in his room and can speak only the single word "Nevermore." This poem was recognized as a work of genius when it first appeared. Nevertheless, Poe looked so bad when he personally submitted the manuscript to *Graham's Magazine* that although the editors rejected it they took up a collection of $15 to give him; he eventually got $10 for "The Raven" but had to wait a year and a half for payment from the *Daily Mirror*. Ravens have been taught words since earliest times. They have generally been considered a bird of ill-omen, however, as in the old saying

"The croaking raven bades misfortune." But ravens have also been helpful to humankind. While they were sailing west, Viking navigators released ravens into the air. If the birds flew back on the same course, the Viking boats continued their westward course, but if the birds flew in any other direction, the Vikings followed them to new lands and new conquests.

ravine. *Ravine* is Middle English for "torrent of water," dating back to the 14th or 15th century. It was first used in America to mean a deep gorge or a narrow valley frequently eroded by running water. George Washington first employed it in this sense in a 1781 entry in his diary.

ravishing. In the "Winners & Sinners" bulletin he distributed to the *New York Times* staff, Theodore Bernstein (1904–79) criticized a *Times* headline that read ELM BEETLE INFESTATION RAVISHING THOUSANDS OF TREES IN GREENWICH. "Keep your mind on your work, buster," the editor wrote. "The word you want is 'ravaging'." He titled the piece "Insex."

rayon. A committee chose the name for this fabric, which was once known as *artificial silk*. The National Retail Drygoods Association committee coined *rayon* in 1924 from *ray*, as in a ray of light, and possibly from *on* in cotton. Never a trademark, *rayon* doesn't have to be capitalized. *See* NYLON.

razorback. A wild hog common in the southern U.S. that people often tamed and let roam free to forage for its food. The Americanism, traced back to about 1815, was inspired by the hog's ridge-like back. It was an argument over the ownership of a razorback hog that initiated the bloody Hatfield-McCoy feud that lasted from about 1873 to 1890 in the mountains of Kentucky and West Virginia. A *Hatfield-McCoy feud* itself became a synonym still occasionally used for any feud between families or neighbors. In fact, the Hatfields and McCoys are still feuding, though in a less violent way. A recent news item (12/23/01) advises that "In Pikesville, Ky., descendants of the Hatfield and McCoy clans, which battled each other in a famous, bloody feud from 1878 to 1890, are apparently still sore. In a lawsuit, the McCoys claim the Hatfields control access to a cemetery and won't let them get in." Like many Americans, they're getting more litigious.

read between the lines. Cryptographers commonly used a code whereby the secret message in a letter or other document could be discerned only by reading its alternate lines. This practice, and possibly the use of invisible ink to write messages between the lines of a letter, suggested to *read between the lines*, which by 1865 meant to discern the underlying fact or intention in any document or action.

read 'em and weep. A common cry of a cardplayer or crap shooter after a good hand or roll of the dice. The American expression is now used generally to mean "here's some very unwelcome information for you, information that will benefit me."

read the riot act. If you were actually reading the Riot Act to someone, here's what you'd proclaim: "Our Sovereign Lord the King chargeth and commandeth all persons being assembled immediately to disperse themselves, and peaceably to depart to their habitations or to their lawful business, upon the pains contained in the act made in the first year of King George for preventing tumultuous and riotous assemblies. God save the King." This is the opening section of the Riot Act of 1714, which a justice of the peace or other authorized persons was required by the Riot Act itself to read to rioters. The "pains" or penalty, provided by the act was death, later changed to terms in prison ranging up to life. These were certainly severe penalties, much more severe than those a parent has in mind when threatening a child with punishment if he doesn't cease and desist from a certain activity. But our expression *to read the riot act*, "to severely scold or warn someone," is nonetheless an allusion to the real Riot Act of 1714, designed to control the English middle class and prevent sedition.

real McCoy. Kid McCoy happened to hear a barroom braggart claim that he could lick any of the McCoys around—any time, any place. The Kid, then at the top of his boxing division, promptly delivered his Sunday punch in person. When the challenger came to, he qualified his statement by saying that he had only meant that he could beat any of the other fighters around who were using the Kid's name, not the real McCoy himself. In another version of the story, which also takes place in a saloon, a heckler sneers that if the Kid was the real McCoy, he'd put up his dukes and prove it. McCoy does so and the heckler, rubbing his jaw from his seat in the sawdust, exclaims, "That's the real McCoy, all right." But there have been numerous, unproved explanations for the origin of *the real McCoy* for "the genuine, the real thing." Still another is that advertisements of Kid McCoy's fights proclaimed that the real McCoy, and not some imitation, would appear. The fabulous Kid McCoy won the welterweight title in 1896, but outgrew his class; he was once ranked by *Ring Magazine* as the greatest light heavyweight of all time, though he never held this title. It is possible that the cachet of his name may have been strengthened by the ring exploits of Al McCoy, who held the middleweight title from 1917 to 1919. Certainly there were a lot of McCoys around in the early days of boxing, among the myriad Mysterious Billy Smiths, Dixie Kids, Honey Melodys and Philadelphia Jack O'Briens. But which McCoy is the real McCoy remains open to debate; he may not even have been a boxer. For example, another tale has it that the real McCoy was African-American inventor Elijah McCoy, whose machine for lubricating the parts of a steam train engine was widely popular and inspired many inferior knock-offs.

ream. Meaning a standard of paper, usually 500 sheets, *ream* comes from the Arabic *risma*, "a bundle of clothes." The explanation for this seemingly odd derivation stems from the fact that the Arabs learned from the Chinese how to make paper out of rags instead of papyrus and passed the technique and the word on to Europe.

Reaumur scale. René-Antoine Ferchault de Réaumur (1683–1757) invented the Réaumur thermometer and the thermal scale (0°–80°) on which it is based. Like the CELSIUS SCALE it was considered by some to be an improvement on Fahrenheit's invention 17 years earlier, in 1714. Réaumur has been called "the Pliny of the 18th century." Both a physicist and naturalist, his versatility involved him in researches ranging from the expansion of fluids and gases to an exhaustive study of insects.

The fluid under glass in his thermometer, unlike Fahrenheit's, was four-fifths alcohol and one-fifth water.

rebate.   A merchant who makes a rebate gives back part of the buyer's money. But *rebate* has taken a long, circuitous route to the meaning it has today. Once a sporting term, from falconry of all things, *rebate* meant "to bring back a bating hawk," that is, a hawk that has left its perch without being commanded to do so.

rebel yell; Texas yell.   A leading expert believes that the *rebel yell*, or *yalo*, originally used in combat in the Civil War and intended to strike terror into the hearts of the enemy, came from the Creek Indians, loosely combining "the turkey gobbler's cry with a series of yelps." The high-pitched, blood-chilling yell was borrowed by Texans and adopted for their *Texas yell*. But others say the Texans got their yell from the Comanche Indians. In any case, everyone agrees that the "Yah-hoo" or "Yaaaaahee" of fiction writers sounds nothing like the rebel yell. Several experts believe it is a corruption of the old English foxhunting cry *tallyho!*

received pronunciation.   Variously called *R.P.*, *BBC English*, the *King's English*, *London English*, the *Oxford accent* and *Southern Educational Standard*, this is a pronunciation of British English reflecting the past cultural and social predominance of the speech of southern England. It was once the characteristic speech of the English public (private) schools and Oxford and Cambridge Universities, which led to its being adopted as the pronunciation used in broadcasting. It is of course no better or worse than any other pronunciation. There is no similar standard of speech in American English, though at one time the so-called Harvard accent and the General American dialect (used by American broadcasters) were touted as such. Broadcasters do, however, avoid using regional accents.

reciprocity.   *Reciprocity* refers to a mutual interchange of favors or privileges, the word deriving from the Latin *reciprocus*, "alternating." In the *Analects of Confucius*, the Chinese sage rated reciprocity highly. "Tsze-king asked, 'Is there one word which may serve as a rule of practice for all one's life.' The master said, 'Is not *reciprocity* such a word? What you do not want done to yourself, do not do to others.'" *See* GOLDEN RULE.

record.   *See* LEARN BY HEART.

record album.   *See* ALBUM.

Red Baron.   His name still comes up, by way of comparison, when the exploits of any combat pilot or daring flier are discussed. He was Baron Manfred von Richthofen (1892–1918), the top German ace who shot down 80 Allied planes in World War I until he was killed in combat. He was called The Red Baron (and the Red Knight and the Bloody Red Baron) not because of his red hair, or because he was a bloody killer, but because he flew a bright red Fokker Triplane. *See* IMMELMAN.

Red Cross Banner.   The Confederate battle flag is the most familiar symbol of the American South but was not the official flag of the Confederacy, an honor that goes to the STARS AND BARS. The familiar Red Cross Banner was designed by General

P.G.T. Beauregard following the first battle of Bull Run, after Southern troops in the confusion of battle mistook the Stars and Bars for the Union flag, which it resembled. The flag that most southerners fly today is this Red Cross Banner or battle flag, not the Stars and Bars.

red dog.   Linebackers "hound" or "dog" the passer in a football red dog, crashing through the line to try to break up a play. When the tactic was invented in the 1960s, "red dog" was the signal if one linebacker was to try cracking the line, "blue dog" if two were to be used, and "green dog" if all three linebackers were to charge. Football fans, however, misused the terms and applied *red dog* to any rush through the offensive line, made by linebackers or linemen, and that is what the term means today. I've also heard it used outside of football for any rush on one person by a group of men.

red-eye.   Cheap but potent, often dangerous, whiskey has been called "red-eye" since the early days of Prohibition because its high alcohol content and questionable ingredients caused dilation of the eye's blood vessels.

red-haired villain.   As Rosalind says in *As You Like It*, "His very hair is of the dissembling color." Villains have frequently been depicted in fiction as redheads, perhaps due to the tradition that Judas Iscariot had red hair. Redheads were once thought to be so deceitful that the fat of dead red-haired men was used as an ingredient in poisons and fish baits. Actually it's hard to think of many murderous, lying, or unreliable real redheads aside from Judas, unless you include Salomé, Lizzie Borden, Nero, Napoleon, Henry VIII, and General Custer. Good old redheads in history include William the Conqueror, Shakespeare, Queen Elizabeth I, American Presidents Washington, Jefferson, and Van Buren (who was, however, called "the Little Magician" and worse), Emily Dickinson, Mark Twain, Sarah Bernhardt, George Bernard Shaw, Winston Churchill, Sinclair Lewis, football great Harold "Red" Grange, and Little Red Riding Hood.

red (bloody) hand of Ulster.   The badge of Ulster, called the red (or bloody) hand of Ulster, is a sinister, or left, hand, erect, open and couped at the wrist. According to legend, during an ancient expedition to Ireland it had been decided that he who touched land first would own the land he touched. The future prince O'Neill saw another boat edging ahead of his toward shore and seemed to be beaten. But he hacked off his left hand and threw it up on land ahead of his rival, claiming all of Ulster for his own.

red herring.   Red herring are herring that have been cured and become red in color. Escaping criminals in the 17th century would drag strong-smelling red herring across a trail to make pursuing bloodhounds lose the scent. This practice inspired the popular expression *to drag a red herring across the trail* and the more recent, shortened term *red herring*, which means confusing an issue by dragging in something irrelevant to the matter.

Red Indian.   An offensive name for Native Americans, but a historical term applied by the British to North American Indians, apparently because of "their copper-colored skin" and to distinguish them semantically from the Indians of India. From *Red Indian* came the derogatory word *redskin*.

red ink; red numbers.   *See* INK.

red-letter day.   Holidays, festivals, and saints' days have been marked in red ink on calendars since the 15th century. Red-letter days were memorable and usually happy ones, so the expression *red-letter day* eventually came to mean, more broadly, any pleasantly memorable day, a lucky day more important than most. Incidentally, since purple ink was also used to indicate special days in medieval times, the phrase could just as easily have been "purple-letter day."

red-light district.   Brothels once advertised their presence by burning electric lights covered with red shades or glass in their windows. This led to the Americanism *red-light district* for an area known for its houses of prostitution, the term first recorded in the late 19th century. *See* BABYLON OF THE WEST.

redneck.   A poor, white, often rowdy southerner, usually one from a rural area. The word, which is sometimes derogatory, has its origins in the sunburned necks of farmers and outdoor laborers, and originally meant a poor farmer. "A redneck is by no means to be confused with 'po' whites," wrote Jonathan Daniels in *A Southerner Discusses the South* (1938): "Poor white men in the South are by no means all po' white even in the hills. Lincoln and Jackson came from a southern folk the back of whose necks were ridged and red from labor in the sun." Another source claims that in the 1930s striking West Virginia coal miners wore red bandanas around their necks and were called "The Redneck Army." *See* POOR WHITE.

the Red One.   Also *Big Red One*. The name given to the famous American Army First Division. One story says that the Germans gave the name to the division after the red "I" on its shoulder patch. Another claims it is so named because it was the first American division in France during World War I.

red rain.   An alarm shouted in marine combat artillery units when radar operators detect incoming fire from enemy mortar or artillery. This cry of *Red rain! Red rain!* was often heard in the second Iraq War (Operation Iraqi Freedom) in 2003.

Reds; Red Square.   Communists are called Reds because the red flag was the national flag of the Soviet Union and was the banner of international communism before the Russian Revolution. The red flag has been a signal for battle since Roman times, and the color red in national flags usually represents the blood of the people. Before the communists used it as a symbol of revolution, red was associated with the Jacobins of the French Revolution, the "red republicans" who reportedly dipped their hands in the blood of their royal victims and triumphantly waved them aloft, and with the red-shirted followers of Garibaldi in Italy. Red Square, adjoining the Kremlin in Moscow, is *not* named after the communists, as many people believe. Red Square was so named long before the Russian Revolution. Its name may have something to do with the color of buildings formerly in the area, or the fact that Russians believe red to be the most beautiful of colors.

Red Sea.   The Romans named the Red Sea (*Mare rubrum*), but they took the designation from an old Semitic name whose meaning is not certain, so no one knows the real reason why the sea is called Red.

redskin.   A term invented by white men, who are not really white, for all Indians, who are not really red, in about 1699, long before whites went West. *Red man* is first recorded in 1725 and the derogatory *red devil* in 1834, all before the West was "won." *See also* RED INDIAN.

red tape.   In the early 1900s, when the term arose, lawyers and government officials often tied their papers together with red ribbons. Because excessive formality and time-consuming, rigid adherence to rules and regulations often characterized lawyers and governmental agencies, *red tape* became a synonym for these failings. The words were popularized mainly by Thomas Carlyle, who castigated government officials for *red tapism*.

reduplicated words.   Also called ricochet words, these are words containing a reduplicated or doubled element, which usually gives them an intensifying force. There are hundreds of them in English, some covered in these pages. They include chitchat, click-clack, dillydally, dingdong, drip-drop, flimflam, fiddle-faddle, flip-flop, hanky-panky, harum-scarum, helter-skelter, hobnob, hodgepodge, hoity-toity, hugger-mugger, hurly-burly, mishmash, namby-pamby, niminy-piminy, pell-mell, ping-pong, pitter-patter, razzle-dazzle, riffraff, roly-poly, shilly-shally, and wishy-washy.

reek.   One meaning of the Old English word *recan*, the ancestor of *reek* meant to expose to smoke. Since smoke can smell bad, *reek* came to mean "to give off an offensive odor, to stink."

Reflipe W. Thanuz.   Early in the 19th century William Randolph Hearst's *New York Journal* editors, suspecting that the *New York World* was ransacking its obituary columns, faked an obituary for one Reflipe W. Thanuz. The *World* promptly stole it, only to have their rival point out that Reflipe W. was "we pilfer" spelled backward and that Thanuz was a phonetic spelling of "the news." When enough time had passed, the *World* avenged itself by planting the name Lister A. Raah in a news story. After printing it, the *Journal* learned that this was an anagram of "Hearst is a liar."

reformatory.   *Reformatory* is an old English word dating back to at least the 16th century, but it wasn't applied to what is in effect a prison for juveniles until the Elmira, New York Reformatory was established early in the 19th century.

refrigerator.   The first refrigerator was named by its inventor, Maryland farmer Thomas Moore, in 1803. Moore coined the word from the Latin *re-*, "thoroughly," plus *frigerare*, "to cool." His invention was actually an icebox and such devices were usually called that until the first electric refrigerator was invented in 1916. It wasn't until the 1930s that refrigerators became inexpensive enough to begin replacing iceboxes in American homes.

refugee. French Protestants called Huguenots, who fled to England in 1685 after the revocation of the Edict of Nantes, were the first people to be called refugees. The word derives from the French *refugier*, "to take refuge."

regatta. A regatta was initially, back in the 17th century, a race between gondolas on the Grand Canal in Venice. This Venetian dialect word translates as "a strife or contention or struggling for mastery." The first English *regatta*, or yacht race, was held on the River Thames on June 23, 1775.

regeneration. In its biological sense of to replace or renew an organ by formation of new tissue, *regeneration* (from the Latin *regenerare*, "to replace") is limited in humans, restricted primarily to the healing of wounds, the regrowth of tissue in internal organs, and the regrowth of hair and nails. However, among simpler animals the ability can be more extensive. The starfish is highly developed in this respect, thanks to a nervous system that one investigator has described as more complicated than the London telephone exchange. A starfish wounded in a fight has the ability to cast off its arm at any point. Not only can it grow a new arm when it loses one, but an entire new body will be regenerated if the ray cut from the old body contains a portion of the central disk. A marine biologist applied a strong electric current to a laboratory specimen and found to his amazement that all five arms walked away from the body. About 12 of 100 starfish collected will show one or more rays in the process of regeneration. *See* STARFISH.

reggae. This style of Jamaican music, combining blues, calypso, and rock 'n' roll was named in 1968 after Frederick "Toots" Hibbert's song "Do the Reggay." The word *reggay* in the song comes from the Jamaican *rege* or *strege* for a raggedy or dowdy fellow.

a regular Trojan. Inhabitants of Troia, or Troy, an ancient city in what is now Turkey that came to be called *Troja* in Medieval Latin, the Trojans were a courageous, industrious people. Legend tells us they labored energetically and cheerfully at even the most arduous tasks. Hence the expressions *to work like a Trojan* and *a regular Trojan*, for hard work done without complaint and a high-spirited industrious worker.

rehash. Englishmen have been using the expression *hash* to mean "old matter served up in a different form" almost as long as they have used *hash* for meat cut up into small pieces, a word that derives from the French word *hache*, "hatchet." In 1672, for instance, Andrew Marvell complained about writers serving "the Reader continually the cold Hashes of plain repetition." It was another two centuries, however, before some wit coined the word *rehash*, meaning the same. More effective, the term suggests a hash made from leftovers that is served once, then warmed over and served at least once again.

rehoboam. *See* JEROBOAM.

reichstag; Third Reich. *Reichstag* is German for parliament. Ernest Weekley, in *An Etymological Dictionary of Modern English*, quotes a historian who regards Prussian minister Otto von Bismarck as "a man of infinite humor, who called his hound *Reichstag*." *Third Reich* refers to Germany under the rule of the

Nazis, 1933–45, one of the most vicious regimes in history. The term was coined by Arthur Moeller von der Bruck in his book *Das Dritte Reich* (*The Third Empire*, 1923).

Reign of Terror. *See* TERRORIST.

reimburse. Reimburse someone and you are putting money back into his purse, *reimburse* deriving from the Latin *re*, "back," *im*, "in," and *bursa*, "purse." The word is first recorded in 1611, probably coming into English via the French.

reindeer. One might think, and many do, that reindeer are so named because they are a kind of deer which Santa Claus and others have equipped with reins so that they can pull sleds. But the word *reindeer* has nothing to do with reins. The first part of the word is simply a borrowing of a Scandinavian word for the "creature," which derives ultimately from the Old Icelandic word *hreinn*. *Deer* derives from the Old English *deor* for beast or animal.

Reine-Claude plum. *See* PLUM.

relay. Today's track relay races have their etymological origin in hunting, where packs of fresh hounds were held at strategic points along a hunting route so that they could relieve the hounds that tired. In fact, the word *relay* derives ultimately from the obsolete French verb *relayer*, meaning "to loose the hounds."

relocation centers. Places to which U.S. Japanese-American citizens on the West Coast were unjustly removed by the U.S. government during World War II because they were thought at the time to be security risks, a charge totally unfounded.

remacadamized. *See* MACADAM for the meaning of this word. *Remacadamized* is given here because it is a memorable example of the many languages that have made contributions to English. Even though *macadam* is eponymous in origin, the one word *remacadamized* is composed of Latin, Celtic, Hebrew, Greek, and English elements: *Re* = Latin prefix; *mac* = Celtic "son"; *adam* = Hebrew "man"; *iz* = Greek suffix forming verbs; *ed* = Old English suffix.

Remember Goliard! This old war cry commemorates the battle of Goliard, three weeks after the ALAMO, when 330 Texan prisoners of war were ordered shot by Mexican General Santa Anna. *See* LET'S ROLL.

Remember Pearl Harbor! Sixteen ships were sunk, 2,400 American servicemen were killed, and virtually all American planes supporting the fleet were destroyed on December 7, 1941, when the Japanese launched a surprise attack from six aircraft carriers against Pearl Harbor in the Hawaiian Islands. This action at Oahu led to the expression DAY OF INFAMY and the battle cry *Remember Pearl Harbor!* that America carried into World War II. American intelligence evidently decoded a secret Japanese diplomatic note announcing the attack and sent a warning to Hawaii an hour and 25 minutes before the first enemy bombs hit. The special military communication lines to Hawaii were not working, and Washington intelligence sent the warning as a regular telegram via Western Union, which took 10½ hours to reach Honolulu. Had the warning arrived in time, the Pacific fleet might have been saved and the war provoked by Japan's attack concluded much sooner. *See* LET'S ROLL.

Remember the Alamo!   *See* ALAMO.

Remember the Maine!   Relations with Spain were already strained when the U.S.S. *Maine* docked at Havana, Cuba, on a courtesy call, although no trouble was expected. Then, at 9:58 P.M. on February 15, 1898, the ship suddenly exploded, killing 258 crew members. Spanish boats in the harbor helped rescue many of the survivors, and the dead were buried in a Havana cemetery. The cause of the explosion is not clear, and while Spanish authorities attributed it to an internal malfunction, an American panel announced that it was caused by a mine. "Remember the Maine" became a rallying cry in jingoist newspapers, helping to ignite the Spanish-American War some two months later. *See* LET'S ROLL.

Remember the River Raisin!   Kentucky soldiers cried this little-known slogan during the War of 1812 against the British. They were remembering their wounded compatriots who were scalped by Britain's Indian allies after they were defeated trying to capture Detroit. *See* LET'S ROLL.

Remembrance Sunday; Veteran's Day.   *Remembrance Sunday* is the British equivalent of the U.S. Veteran's Day, honoring those who died and served in all Great Britain's wars. It falls on the Sunday nearest November 11th. Originally the national holiday was called Armistice Day in both countries and honored only the dead of World War I. The British also call Remembrance Sunday Remembrance Day and Poppy Day, after the artificial poppies sold that day to help needy former soldiers. Veteran's Day, which replaced the U.S. Armistice Day in 1954, always falls on November 11th.

remora.   In ancient times Roman sailors believed that the little remora (*Remora remora*) fastened itself to their sailing vessels and slowed them down, delaying them, so they named the fish *remora*, or "delayer." In nature the remora attached itself to the undersides of sharks, whales, swordfish, and even tuna by means of its highly efficient suction disk, which is actually a greatly modified first and spiny dorsal fin. Not only does it hitch a free ride, but it also eats pieces of food dropped by the host fish. The remora does do some good, however, by acting as a cleaner fish and removing parasites from its host's hide.

remove (take) the scales from your eyes.   Realize the truth, wake up, stop being deceived about someone or something. This ancient expression is from the Bible (Acts 9:18): "And immediately there fell from his eyes as it had been scales; and he [Saul, later St. Paul] received sight forthwith, and was baptized."

reports of my death are greatly exaggerated.   A traditional story has it that in 1897 an American newspaper bannered Mark Twain's death. When another paper sent a reporter to check the story Twain came to the door of his Connecticut home and gave him the following statement: "James Ross Clemens, a cousin of mine, was seriously ill two or three weeks ago, but is well now. The reports of my illness grew out of his illness. The reports of my death are greatly exaggerated." Nothing any scholar says will change this tale, which is by now part of American folklore, but the true story is that a reporter from the *New York Journal* called on Twain while the author was staying in England—to check out a rumor that Twain was either dead or dying in poverty. Twain explained to the reporter that his cousin had been seriously ill in London and that reports of his own illness grew out of his cousin's illness, that "the report of my death was an exaggeration." But then maybe Twain had the facts wrong. "When I was younger," he confided toward the end of his life, "I could remember anything, whether it had happened or not; but my faculties are decaying now and soon I shall be so I cannot remember any but the things that never happened. It is sad to go to pieces like this, but we all have to do it."

requiem shark.   Tropical sharks of the family Carcharhinidae, especially tiger sharks, are often called *requiem sharks*, their name coming from the French word *requin*, for "shark." The pseudonymous sailor Sinbad explained the derivation of the French word in an 1887 book he wrote about sharks: "The French name for shark is *requin*. This word is probably derived from the Latin *requiem*, and signifies that if a man fall into the sea among sharks, his comrades may repeat for him the usual prayers for the dead. It is seldom, if ever, that a man who is so luckless as to fall amongst sharks appears again; a shriek is heard, a moving mass is seen under the surface and a fin above it; the next wave that breaks against the shipside is crimsoned, and the horror-stricken seamen know that their messmate has gone to that place from which no traveler returns."

Restaurant Into Which You Would Not Take a Dog.   This is the name of a Shanghai restaurant, in a country far removed from hype, where eating establishments often vie with one another in coining self-deprecating names for themselves. Other examples include The Second-Class Establishment of Mr. Hsiang and Enter Here If Your Must.

retail.   *See* WHOLESALE.

retire.   The etymology of this word does not paint a pretty picture of retirement. *Retire* comes from the Old French *retirer*, to draw back, and was first used in the military sense of drawing back; it wasn't until the mid 17th century that we find *retire* used in the sense of retiring from a job. Nothing to alarm one so far, but when we look to the origins of the Old French *tirer*, "to draw out, endure," we find that it probably comes from the Old French *martir*, "a martyr," possibly because martyrs were often drawn out on the rack almost beyond the limits of human endurance.

retiring a number.   Track competitors were the first athletes to wear numbers identifying them. Washington and Jefferson University had the first football team to do so, in 1908, and the 1929 New York Yankees were the first baseball team to adopt the practice (their numbers originally noted the player's place in the batting order). Soon the numbers of great players were "retired" when they retired from a sport, this being among the greatest honors a player could receive. The first player to have a number retired in any sport seems to have been football's Harold "Red" Grange, when he was at the University of Illinois. Grange, also known as "77" and most famously as the Galloping Ghost, later became a professional football star and a television sportscaster. Sportswriter Grantland Rice coined "Galloping Ghost" on the same weekend (October 18–19, 1920) that he coined the memorable "Four Horsemen." *See also* FOUR HORSEMEN.

Retreat, hell!   A remark made by Major General Oliver Prince Smith, 1st Marine Division commander during the Korean conflict when his division was retreating from North Korea. The full quote is: "Retreat, hell! We're not retreating, we're just advancing in a different direction." Said a U.S. reconnaissance pilot looking down on the same bloody retreat: "This hurts. It hurts where I can't scratch." *See* DEVIL DOGS.

Reuben.   No one is sure who invented this grilled sandwich of corned beef, Swiss cheese, sauerkraut, and Russian dressing on rye bread. The best guess is that it was first concocted at Reuben's Delicatessen in Manhattan during the early 1900s.

re-up.   A military term for "re-enlist," as in "They told him he'd make sergeant if he re-upped for three years." The word was being used as far back as 1905. Today it also means to sign any renewed employment contract.

Revenge is a dish that tastes best when it is cold.   An old Italian proverb that is a favorite of the Godfather, Don Corleone, in Mario Puzo's novel *The Godfather* (1969). A pithier variation is *Revenge is a dish best served cold.*

Rh disease.   People with Rh positive blood have any of several substances on their red blood cell surfaces, while Rh negative individuals, a much smaller group, lack these substances and are incompatible with Rh positive blood. Erythroblastosas (the destruction of red blood cells) is a disease of newborn infants associated with incompatible Rh blood factors of mother and child. It is often called "Rh disease" and is so named because it was first found in the blood of laboratory (Rh)esus monkeys.

rhinoceros.   As with HIPPOPOTAMUS and many other animals, the Greeks named the rhinoceros. They thought the huge horn on its head very formidable and called it *rhinokeros* after the Greek words *rhinos*, "nose," and *keras*, "horn." The rhino's horn, sometimes over four feet long, is an excellent defensive weapon, but it has plagued the animal through the ages, driving it at times to the shores of the Dead Sea of extinction. One old canard had it that a rhino horn used as a goblet could detect the presence of poison; other superstitions claimed that powdered rhino horn could cure many ailments, including epilepsy and bubonic plague, as well as ease the pain of childbirth. Yet what caused the rhino the most trouble was the belief that its horn, similar to the legendary unicorn's, was a sex stimulant. The ancient Chinese, Babylonians, Greeks, and Romans were among many people who believed this. Today at least three species of rhino are becoming extinct because the Chinese value their powdered horn (*hsi chio*) as an aphrodisiac—a large horn brings at least $1,000 in what is definitely a seller's market.

Rhode Island.   One story has Verrazzano, in 1524, observing the island now called Aquidneck in Narragansett Bay and naming it Rhodes Island because it reminded him of the island of Rhodes in the Mediterranean. Later, the island gave its name to the state. Most scholars contend that Rhode Island takes its name from the Dutch *Roodt Eylandt*, "red island," for its red clay.

Rhodesia; Rhodes scholarship.   Poor health, which plagued him all his life, forced empire builder John Rhodes to leave England and Oxford for Africa in 1870. There he joined the rush to the Kimberley diamond fields, and by 1888 he had established De Beers Consolidated Mines, dominating both the diamond mine area and later the Transvaal gold mines. His huge fortune facilitated his entrance into politics, and he served as prime minister of Cape Colony, 1890–96. It was Rhodes's desire from his youth that the British should rule the world. When the British government failed to take action he formed a private company to occupy and develop the territory of what became Rhodesia, which was named for him five years later, in 1899. (The British protectorate, Northern Rhodesia, became the republic of Zambia in 1964, and Southern Rhodesia later became Zimbabwe.) The "Empire Builder" had returned to Oxford several times in the course of his brief life—once being sent back to Africa under a virtual death sentence, the doctor noting privately that he had only six months to live. Rhodes finally earned his degree at the university, and his will left an endowment of 6 million pounds for the famed Rhodes scholarship that bears his name.

rhododendron.   This large genus of shrubs with very large, showy flowers takes its name from the Greek for rose (*rhodo*) and tree (*dendron*). The name was given by the Greeks to the oleander, an unrelated species, but Linnaeus applied it to the shrubs we now know as rhododendruns when classifying them. *See also* AZALEA; LINNAEAN SYSTEM.

rhubarb.   Speculation has been rife for years about how the slang term *rhubarb*, "a heated argument," arose from the name of a popular vegetable. Since the word is often associated with baseball, many writers say it has its origins there. But probably the best explanation, advanced about 25 years ago by a veteran actor familiar with theatrical traditions, is that actors simulating angry talk in crowd scenes for "the noise without" gathered backstage and "intoned the sonorous word 'rhubarb.'" The actor-etymologist Alexander McQueen advised that the word produces such an effect "only if two or three work at it," and claimed that this theatrical tradition went back to Shakespearean times, but the slang *rhubarb* for an argument arose only in the late 19th century. It therefore came to mean a "rumpus" or a "row" at about the time baseball was fast becoming America's national pastime. It is easy to see how the stage term could have been applied to an argument on the diamond, especially a mass argument that involved both teams, though there is no solid proof of this. *Rhubarb* itself has an interesting derivation, taking its name from the Latin *rha barbarum*. The Romans called it this because the plant was native to the river Rha (the Volga), a foreign, "barbarian" territory—the plant's name, thus meaning "from the barbarian (foreign) Rha." The first rhubarb planted in America was sent to the great naturalist John Bartram from Siberia in 1770. Americans long called the fruit pieplant because it made such delicious pies, especially when combined with strawberries.

rhyming slang. *See* BRISTOLS.

rice Christian. Used as early as 1816 in China and India, *a rice Christian* refers to someone converted to Christianity to improve his economic lot, for material rather than spiritual reasons.

Rice Coast. *See* CAROLINA RICE.

the rich are different from you and me. Ernest Hemingway's remark about the rich, the rest of us, and money has its roots in a remark critic Mary Colum made to Hemingway at lunch one day. "I am getting to know the rich," he told her. Replied Colum: "The only difference between the rich and other people is that the rich have more money." Hemingway later put the remark to good use in his short story "The Snows of Kilimanjaro"—at the expense of his friend F. Scott Fitzgerald—having the story's central character recall "poor Scott Fitzgerald and his romantic awe [of the rich] and how he had started a story once that began, 'The rich are different from you and me.' And how someone had said to Scott, yes, they have more money." The only truth to this is that Fitzgerald's story "The Rich Boy" begins: "Let me tell you about the very rich. They are different from you and me." Fitzgerald soon complained to Hemingway, advising him that "Riches have never fascinated me, unless combined with the greatest charm or distinction." Later, Maxwell Perkins, editor to both Hemingway and Fitzgerald at Scribner's, on Fitzgerald's request changed "poor Scott Fitzgerald" in the story to "poor Julian." But mistakes by biographers have made "the famous Hemingway-Fitzgerald exchange" a part of literary history that will probably be repeated as long as the two great authors are read.

rich as Croesus. *See* CROESUS.

rich as Rockefeller. *Rich as Rockefeller* refers to the family fortune amassed by John Davison Rockefeller (1839–1937). The oil refinery that became the Standard Oil Company made Rockefeller a billionaire before it was dissolved by the Supreme Court in 1911. Variations on the phrase above include *he's a regular Rockefeller*, and *Rockefeller* itself is the American equivalent of *Croesus*. John D. may have given only dimes to beggars, but his philanthropies included the founding of the University of Chicago, the Rockefeller Institute for Medical Research (1901), and the Rockefeller Foundation (1913) for worldwide humanitarian purposes, in all worth about half a billion dollars. John D. Rockefeller, Jr., built New York's Rockefeller Center, with Radio City completed in 1940. There is no popular saying "as rich as Bill Gates," despite a 2002 study by *New York Times* business editor Allen R. Myerson that concluded that Gates's fortune amounted to $46 billion compared with Rockefeller's $25.6 billion when both fortunes were adjusted for inflation.

Richmond, N.Y. *See* KINGS COUNTY.

Richter scale. A 0 to 9 open-ended logarithmic scale that indicates the intensity (the amount of energy released) of an earthquake. The scale is named for U.S. geologist and seismologist Charles Francis Richter (1900–85), who devised it in 1938 at the California Institute of Technology. The most destructive earthquakes register over 5.5 on the scale, every difference, from 1 to 2, for example, representing about a 32 fold difference in magnitude. According to the *Guiness Book of World Records* (1998), "The largest reported magnitudes on the Richter scale, are about 8.9, but the scale does not properly represent the size of the very largest earthquakes . . ." For these another rating system should be used. The deadliest earthquake known to history occurred in three Chinese provinces in 1556, claiming 830,000 lives. In 1976 another Chinese earthquake killed 750,000 people. Actually, the Richter scale should honor both Richter and his colleague Dr. Beno Gutenberg (1887–1960), who worked with him in developing it. But the term Guttenberg-Richter scale is rarely heard today.

rickey. *See* GIN RICKEY.

rickshaw. The name of this hooded, two-wheeled, mandrawn vehicle of Asian countries derives from the Japanese *jinricksha*. The Japanese word itself is an amalgam of the Japanese *jin*, "man or person," *riki*, "power or strength," and *sha*, "carriage," and would strictly be translated "man power carriage." A rickshaw powered by a driver peddling a tricycle is properly called a "trishaw."

ride. To kid, to ridicule or harass. Both this word and the American underworld phrase *take someone for a ride* are first recorded at about the same time, around 1915. It has been suggested that the facetious *ride* derives from the sinister gangster expression meaning to force or entice someone into a car, take him to a lonely place, kill him, and dump him. To ride a person is of course not nearly so brutal as to take someone for a ride, but it isn't especially pleasant, either.

ride backwards up Holburn Hill. To go to one's own hanging. Up until 1784, the year of the last execution at Tyburn in London, condemned men would go to the gallows riding backwards on a horse all the way up Holburn Hill, which rose steeply from Newgate Prison to the gallows at Tyburn. According to one account, "Some conceive the practice to increase the ignominy, but it is more probably to prevent the condemned from being shocked with a distant view of the gallows, as in amputations surgeons conceal the instruments with which they are going to operate."

ride close herd on. To *close herd* literally means to keep cattle close together, compact; thus *to ride close herd on something* is to pay close attention to it, not to let it get far out of your sight or out of hand, as in "He rode close herd on that plan from the start." The expression dates back to the 19th century.

ride herd on. *See* LIKE HERDING CATS.

ride out on a rail. *See* TARRED AND FEATHERED.

ride roughshod over someone. A roughshod horse had nail-heads projecting from its horseshoes to keep it from slipping, and it's said that similar shoes with projecting points were designed by blacksmiths in the 17th century for use by the cavalry on the battlefield. The gory spectacle of chargers with benailed hooves stomping over men in battle, or even the sight of a roughshod horse accidentally trampling a pedestrian on a city street, suggested the expression *to ride roughshod over someone*, "to treat someone brutally, without the least consideration."

ride shotgun. To act as a guard, or to ride in the front seat of a car. The expression was suggested by the armed guard with a shotgun who often rode beside the driver on stagecoaches in the old American West.

riffraff. *Riffraff* has a complicated history for a little word. It is apparently based on the French phrase *rif et raf*, meaning "one and all." When first used in English *rif and raf* meant just that, but by the 15th century *riffraff* had been compressed from the phrase and meant something entirely different—the dregs of humanity, trash, worthless people. This radical change has been explained in several ways. It may be that another sense of the French phrase *rif et raf*, "a collection of people who steal," is responsible. Or *raf*, may have become confused with the Swedish word *rafs*, meaning rubbish, *riffraff* coming to mean "refuse and rubbish." Another possibility is that the present meaning derives from the French verbs *rifler*, "to ransack," and *raffler*, "to snatch away," anyone who ransacked or snatched something away being considered *riffraff*. Or the opposite of the phrase *riff* and *raff* may have something to do with the coinage. *Riff* nor *raff* meant "nothing whatsoever" and someone who had *riff nor raff* might have become *riffraff*, worthless.

rigadoon. There is no Señor Mambo or Mademoiselle Twist, but there apparently once lived a Monsieur Rigadoon—a M. Rigaud, anyway. *Rigadoon* does sound Scottish, but the lively dance—which resembles the twist in that the two dancers do their pirouetting at a distance from one another—is decidedly Provençal in origin. It is named for Marseilles dancing master Rigaud, who invented it in the late 17th century; the English *rigadoon* is *rigaudon* in French.

Rigg's pyorrhea. *See* BRIGHT'S DISEASE.

right; adroit, etc. *Right* is of honorable origin, deriving from the Anglo-Saxon *riht*, "straight, just." As for *adroit*, "cleverly skillful," it is just the French *à droit*, "with the right hand." Similarly, *dextrous*, meaning skillful with the hands, body, or mind, derives from the Latin word *dexter* "right-handed"—to call a left-hander *dextrous*, then, is something of a contradiction. *Ambidextrous*, "able to use both hands well," combines the Latin *ambi*, "both," with *dextrous*, literally meaning someone who has two right (two good) hands! Unlike *left*, the word *right* usually has the connotation of cleverness and grace in English words and phrases. A *right-hand man* is an invaluable, trusted aide; the *right* side was the place of honor in political assemblies and gave its name to royal or conservative parties of the right; and *right foot foremost* means putting your best foot forward. *See* GET UP ON THE WRONG SIDE OF THE BED; LEFT-HANDED COMPLIMENT.

right as a trivet. Excellent, perfect. An old tale says *trivet* is a pronunciation of Truefit, the name of a London wigmaker whose wigs were perfect. But the facts do not bear this out.

Originally, the phrase was *steady as a trivet* and referred to the fact that three-legged trivets or tripods stand firm on almost any surface. Today a trivet is a small metal plate with short legs often put under a hot dish to protect a table.

right bower. *Right bower* used to be more frequently employed for someone's "right-hand man," like Sherlock Holmes's Dr. Watson. The expression is from the card game euchre, seldom played anymore, in which the right bower is the jack of trumps, among the most powerful cards in the deck.

right off the bat. The sound of a baseball hit sharply on the meat of a bat inspired the Americanism *right off the bat*, meaning at once, immediately, very quickly, the first thing. It is first recorded in 1910.

right on your drag. Edna Ferber explains the expression in her novel *Giant* (1952): " 'The two men at [the rear end of the herd], they're the drag . . . You know we've got a saying here in Texas if you owe money or somebody is after you hot on your trail we say, 'He's on your drag.' "

right stuff. The British were using this phrase a century ago to describe good soldiers, mainly in the form of "the right sort of stuff." American author Tom Wolfe made it popular again with his book *The Right Stuff* (1979), which described the character, intelligence, etc., needed by U.S. astronauts.

right up my alley. An inside-the-park home run in baseball is often hit *right down the alley*, between two fielders, but I doubt that this is the source of the above phrase, which is sometimes *right down my alley*. The expression, meaning "very familiar and appealing to me," probably has nothing to do with a bowling alley, either. *My alley* here seems to be a synonym for my street, the place where I live and where I'm most at home.

rigmarole. Often spelled and pronounced "rig-amorole," this word means confused, incoherent, foolish or meaningless talk, or any complicated procedure. It derives from a roll of names called the *rageman*, which originated in the 14th century. The name of this roll was altered through mispronunciation to *ragman role* and finally to *rigmarole* in the 18th century. Because the names and addresses on it were often changed or deleted, the rigmarole came to represent any confused or disconnected, incoherent statement.

rigor mortis. *Rigor mortis* refers to the muscular stiffening after death. The term, which came into English about 1830, derives from the Latin words meaning "stiffness of death." The American slang word *stiff* for a corpse also comes from this source.

rile. *Rile*, "to anger," derives from the word *roil*, meaning the same, and is one of the few English pronunciation spellings that became a standard word. Others like it, including *biled* for "boiled," *jine* for "join," *pint* for "point," and *pizen* for "poison," didn't make it.

ringer. For a fabled example of a ringer see DARK HORSE. A ringer is a counterfeit, especially a superior horse passed off as an unknown, or a professional athlete posing as an amateur. The word may derive, as *Webster's* says, from the old bell ringer's expression *ring in*, working a certain bell into a performance. But there seems to be very little evidence linking bell ringers with horseracing, sports, and gamblers. Perhaps a better explanation is that *ringer* was once a slang term for "counterfeit," which derived from the sale of brass rings for gold at country fairs. *Dead ringer* has no sinister connotations. It simply means a perfect imitation, a person with an uncanny resemblance to someone else. It derives from *ringer*, with *dead* in this case meaning "absolute," "complete."

ring finger. This name for the fourth finger of the human hand (including the thumb as a finger) has been traced back to about the year 1000. Today it most commonly is given to the fourth finger of the left hand, on which wedding rings are worn (because the left hand is closer to the heart than the right). It was in the past called the leech finger because doctors (a doctor was once called a leech) often used it for testing. One old superstition held that the ring finger could cure any wound it touched. *See* THUMB.

ring hollow; ring true. In the past, counterfeit coins could be detected by the dull, flat tone they produced when dropped on stone, in contrast to the clear ring of true coins. The test was called *ringing* or *sounding* a coin, a very old method that one writer dismissed as unreliable in 1796. Nevertheless, the practice was so common that it inspired the saying *to ring true*, to impress one as being genuine or good, as well as its opposite, *to ring false* or *to ring hollow*, the last a phrase that Ben Jonson used. Today real post-1963 U.S. "silver" coins don't give off a clear ring anymore.

ringing the changes. A *change* in the ancient art of bell ringing is the order in which a series of bells are rung. Theoretically it would be possible to ring 479,001,600 changes with 12 church bells without repeating their ringing order—although it would take nearly 38 years to do so. *Ringing the changes* has long been a competitive sport among bell ringers, and the present champions are eight English ringers and their conductor who rang a peal, all the possible changes on a series of bells—on eight bells in 1963. The peal consisted of 40,320 changes and took two minutes short of 18 hours. Past feats like this inspired the expression to *ring the changes*, to try every possible way of doing something, to state something again and again in different ways, or even to work something to death. The expression is also the name of a con game in which the swindler completely confuses his mark by continually changing money so that the victim loses track of what he gives out.

ring the bell; ring a bell. *To ring the bell*, "to succeed at something," is an Americanism that has its origins in either amusement park shooting galleries, where the marksman rings a bell when he hits the target, or in those familiar carnival strength-testing machines, where a person tries to sledgehammer a wooden ball hard and high enough up a board to ring a bell. *Ring the bell* is common in the spiels, or pitches, for both games. *To ring a bell*—"to strike a familiar chord, to evoke a memory"—on the other hand, may refer to memories evoked by ringing church bells or school bells.

ringtum ditty. A western U.S. dish whose name origins are unknown and whose ingredients vary. It usually consists of cheese cooked with bacon, onions, tomatoes, and corn, among other ingredients.

riot act. *See* READ THE RIOT ACT.

RIP. A long-used abbreviation for the Latin phrase *Requiescat in pace*, "May he (she) rest in peace," or *Requiescant in pace*, "May they rest in peace." The abbreviation is commonly found on tombstones and mourning cards. It is only a coincidence that the first letters of English *rest in peace* are the same as those of the Latin phrases.

rip-off. Since at least the 1960s *rip-off* has been a synonym for stealing or defrauding of any kind. It has been used to describe everything from pickpocketing to consumer fraud ("What a rip-off that store is.") No one is sure where the term comes from. One good possibility is a purse snatcher ripping a purse out of a woman's hands. Less likely is a burglar ripping the door off a house to get inside.

ripsnorter. *See* QUICKER THAN HELL CAN SCORCH A FEATHER.

rising beauties. Big, beautiful firm breasts, the expression made famous in American literature by this passage in Erskine Caldwell's *God's Little Acre* (1933): " 'I ain't ashamed of nothing,' Ty Ty said heatedly. 'I reckon Griselda is just about the prettiest girl I ever did see. There ain't a man alive who's ever seen a finer-looking pair of rising beauties as she's got . . . ' "

rising tide lifts all boats. This American proverbial saying may have originated in Cape Cod, as President Kennedy implied in a speech he made. The words seem to date back to the early 20th century and mean that in good times everybody prospers. A variation is *on a rising tide all boats are lifted*.

ritzy. César Ritz (1850–1918), Swiss restaurateur and hotel manager, built his first Ritz Hotel in Paris in 1898. By hiring the master chef George Auguste Escoffier and adopting such practices as sleeping in every room at least once in order to test the quality of its mattress, this perfectionist made his hotel the greatest of *la belle epoque* and himself the greatest hotelier in the history of the western world. Ritzes opened in London, New York, and other cities, and *ritzy* or *like the Ritz* quickly became American slang for anything lavish and costly. The word can mean vulgarly ostentatious, too; *putting on the ritz* means TO PUT ON THE DOG or showing off, and *to ritz* a person means to behave *ritzily* or superciliously toward him.

rival. The Latin word *rivalis* first meant "one who shares or uses the same river as another person." It then came to mean "a person or persons living on the opposite side or bank of a river." Once people live on opposite sides of a river, the river becomes a boundary, and the people often fight over it, becoming rivals or competitors.

river Styx; stygian. In Greek mythology the river Styx is the principal of the nine rivers of the underworld (Hades), over which Charon ferried the souls of the dead to Elysium for a small fee (the reason for the old custom of burying the dead with a coin called "Charon's toll" in their mouths). Styx is the name of an actual river that falls down a high cliff on Mount Aroanuis (modern Chelmos) in what was ancient Arcadia. Its waters were said to be poisonous, dissolving any ship trying to sail them. The name *Styx* comes from the Greek *Styx*, "the abhorrent," which derives from *stugnos*, "hateful, gloomy." Men swore solemn oaths on the supposedly poisonous waters of the actual Styx and believed that the gods themselves swore oaths on the legendary Styx; those who swore falsely were forced to drink of its waters, which made offenders speechless for a year. I can find no example of a phrase like *drink of the Styx* being applied to any liar, but the word *stygian*, "hellish, infernal, dark, gloomy," comes from the name of this river, called by poet John Milton "the flood of deadly hate."

R months.   Many people believe that oysters are safe to eat only during months containing the letter *R*. So common is this canard that it has been commemorated in the poem "The Man Who Dared" by Stoddard King: "Let's sing a song of glory to Themistocles O'Shea, / Who ate a dozen oysters on the second day of May." The U.S. Bureau of Commercial Fisheries has been trying to dispel this myth for years, but the rumor persistently finds its way into print. The truth is that American oysters can be eaten safely at any time of the year. In point of fact, American oysters reach the peak of perfection in May and June, months without an *R* between them, when they are fatter and taste better because they are beginning to store glycogen in preparation for summer spawning. During summer and early autumn, oyster flavor declines. Due to the expenditure of the glycogen, the meat becomes skimpier and the nectar watery. Ironically, the traditional oyster harvest time is still in the fall because the demand is seasonal and oyster prices highest at this time. The "R" myth derives partly from those days when poor refrigeration resulted in spoilage, but more important is the fact that the flat European oyster (*Ostrea edulis*), only one of a hundred oyster species, is definitely *not* desirable for human food during the "non-R" months. *Ostrea edulis* is unique in that its young are retained by the mother until tiny shells are developed, and the presence of those gritty shells makes the European oyster undesirable in the summer.

road.   *Road*, for "a rather narrow street or passage," came into English rather late, being first recorded in Shakespeare's *Henry IV, Part I* (1596). It may derive from the Old English word *rode*, for "a journey on horseback," but its origin is obscure.

roadhog.   Surprisingly, this term for a driver who doesn't keep to a lane, who takes more than a share of the road, was first applied to bicycle riders, not motorists. The term is an Americanism first recorded in 1891, according to the *OED*, but recorded two years later according to *A Dictionary of Americanisms*. At the time there were roughly 10 million bicycles on U.S. roads but no more than *two dozen* cars. See BICYCLE; CAR.

roadkill.   *Roadkill* is commonly heard for any animal vehicle-killed on the road, but it is not listed in any of the major dictionaries or even dictionaries of slang. It is hardly a new word anymore, first recorded in 1972, and for 10 years or so it has also meant a person dead or useless: "Smith has been roadkill up at the plate recently."

roadrunner.   *Geococcyx californianus* was dubbed the roadrunner by American cowboys in the mid-19th century because of its habit of running ahead of horsemen on trails. It is also called the ground cuckoo, lizard bird, paisano, cock of the desert, snake killer, and snake-eater, among other names. Mexicans used to capture young roadrunners and teach them to kill rats and mice.

road to Damascus.   *See* DAMASK ROSE.

roam.   No one has proved it, but several etymologists believe that *roam* derives from the city Rome, referring to the fact that English pilgrims took a roundabout course to the Eternal City. No better theory has been offered for the word's derivation.

Robert E. Lee.   Though it is rarely given in brief accounts of his life, the *E.* in the great Southern Civil War general's name stands for Edward. He is widely known as Robert E. Lee, but actually he was most often called R. E. Lee during the war, and sometimes the Gray Fox, Marse Robert, Uncle Robert, the King of Spades (for always urging his men to dig in deeper, deeper), the Great Entrencher, (the Southern "chivalry" were called the "shovelry"), and even Granny Lee (he was 57 and constantly fretted about his troops), but rarely Robert E. Lee or Robert Edward Lee, and never Bobby Lee to his face if one didn't want to provoke his famous temper. The more stately Robert E. Lee is the name found today in all the histories of the Brothers' War and on a myriad of statues throughout the South. *See* ULYSSES S. GRANT.

Robert's Rules.   *Robert's Rules of Order*, the last word in parliamentary procedure, was originally published as the *Pocket Manual of Rules of Order for Deliberative Assemblies*—a cumbersome title for a little book. Written in 1876, the manual has had surprisingly few revisions. Its author, Brig. Gen. Henry Martyn Robert (1837–1923), was an American military engineer responsible for the defenses of Washington, Philadelphia, and the New England coast.

robin; robin redbreast.   There are no true American robins; the bird we call a robin (*Turdus migratorius*) is actually a thrush. Our "robin" takes its name from *robin redbreast*, the British name for another bird species altogether. According to tradition, a robin pulled a thorn from Christ's crown on the way to Calvary, and the blood spurting from the wound dyed the robin's breast red forever.

Robin Hood.   Robin Hood, chivalrous defender of the poor and oppressed, may have been based on the earl of Huntington, Robert Fitz-Ooth, an outlawed 12th-century English nobleman (b. ca. 1160) who harassed England's Norman invaders. According to this popular theory, *Fitz* taken away from *Fitz-Ooth* leaves us with *ooth*, the *th* in this changing to *d* and yielding *Robert Ood*—not too far removed from *Robin Hood*. Both the bow and arrow of Robin Hood and the site of his grave are at Kirkless Hall in Yorkshire, where Robert Fitz-Ooth, legend says, was bled to death by a treacherous nun in 1247. But there are abundant theories and places claiming Robin Hood as their own. The legendary outlaw is likely a composite of numerous stories about many early English heroes.

Robin Hood's barn.   Places and plants named for Robin Hood abound all over Britain. To *go all around Robin Hood's barn* means to wander in a roundabout way, to arrive at the right conclusion in this manner. Robin Hood, of course, had no barn, living in Sherwood Forest, and trying to get around a barn that wasn't there was an apt description for early travelers lost in the woods.

Robinson Crusoe.   Daniel Defoe's novel was based on the true adventures of Alexander Selkirk (1676–1721), a seaman who in 1704 asked to be put ashore on the tiny island of Más a Tierra off South America because he objected to conditions aboard ship. Selkirk spent more than four years alone on the island before being rescued and returning to England, where he became a celebrity. Defoe, a journalist, certainly heard of Selkirk's story and possibly interviewed him. In any case, he wrote the immensely successful *The Life and Strange Adventures of Robinson Crusoe* in 1719, embellishing Selkirk's account and presenting it as a true story. In truth it was the first book to reveal Defoe's genius for vivid fiction and it was written when the author was almost 60. Selkirk never did go back to the Pacific island, as Defoe had Crusoe do in two sequels, which appeared the same year. His experiences had made him quite eccentric, however, and for a time he lived in a cave near his home in Largo, where it is said he taught alley cats how to do strange dances. A Robinson Crusoe is today anyone who lives alone like a hermit for a long time. *See* DOVER'S POWDER.

robot.   In Karel Capek's play *R.U.R.*, first produced in 1921, mechanical men manufactured by the Rossum Universal Robot Corporation revolt and threaten to take over the world. This play marked the first time mechanical men were called robots, a word which has since been extended to include people devoid of human feelings who act like mechanical men and any mechanism guided by automatic controls. Capek coined *robot* from the Czech word *robata*, "work," meaning "a slave." The world is saved in the play when the robots miraculously become human. The U.S. Census Bureau reported that 5,535 robots were made by American industry in 1984, after its first survey of such machines. The Robatics Industries Association estimates that tens of thousands of robots are now in use in the U.S. The Census Bureau defines a robot as "a reprogrammable multifunctional manipulator designed to move material, parts, tools, or specialized devices through variable programmed motions for the performance of a variety of tasks." We've all done work like that.

rob Peter to pay Paul.   The expression *rob Peter to pay Paul* goes back at least to John Wycliffe's *Select English Works*, written in about 1380. Equally old in French, the saying may derive from a 12th-century Latin expression referring to the Apostles: "As it were that one would crucify Paul in order to redeem Peter." The words usually mean take money for one thing and use it for another, especially in paying off debts.

The Rock.   *See* ALCATRAZ.

Rockefeller.   *See* RICH AS ROCKEFELLER.

rocking chair.   All that is certain about the rocking chair is that the name for it is first recorded in print in about 1760. It may have been invented at that time, perhaps based upon a rocking cradle, but some native genius may have come up with the idea much earlier. Several historians think that Benjamin Franklin may have been that inventor.

rock 'n' roll.   The best guess is that *rock 'n' roll* "reflects a sexual metaphor," as one writer puts it, quoting the lyrics "My baby rocks me with one steady roll." *Rock and roll* music, an outgrowth of black culture in America, of course dates back much earlier than the first recorded use of the term in the early 1950s, deriving from black "rhythm and blues." The first major film to use rock and roll music was *Blackboard Jungle* (1955). Director Richard Brooks bought the rights to use the song "Rock Around the Clock" in the film for $4,000. He could have bought the song outright for another $1,000, but the studio refused to pay. "Rock Around the Clock" went on to sell 1.5 million records that year, becoming one of the biggest hits of all time.

Rock of Gibraltar.   *See* GIBRALTAR.

Rocky Mountains.   North America's chief mountain system, ranging from central New Mexico to northern Alaska with its highest peak being Mount McKinley (Alaska) at 20,300 feet. Also called the Rockies. The Rocky Mountain states are those states in the Rocky Mountain region, traditionally Arizona, Colorado, Idaho, Montana, Nevada, New Mexico, Utah, and Wyoming. The Rocky Mountain goat is a long-haired, short-horned, white antelope-like animal (*Oreamnos montanus*) of mountainous regions, especially the Rocky Mountains, while the Rocky Mountain canary is a humorous term for a burro coined by early prospectors in the American West. Rocky Mountain spotted fever is an infectious disease transmitted by ticks that was first reported in the Rocky Mountain area.

rocky road.   The variety of ice cream, consisting of chunks of chocolate ice cream, marshmallows, and almonds, was originally the name of a candy bar in the Great Depression years. Both the candy and the ice cream that took its name were meant to symbolize the rocky road people had before them in hard times, making the hard times easier by joking about them.

rode hard and put up wet.   Someone who says he's been "rode hard and put up wet" feels he has been treated badly, abused. The analogy in this Americanism is to a horse that is sweaty from having been worked hard and is not properly cared for.

rodeo.   A rodeo, from the Spanish *rodear* (to surround), was originally a roundup of cattle held once a year on western ranches. Cowboys often challenged each other at these roundups to see who could throw a cow fastest, break a horse, etc., and *rodeo* came to mean a public contest or tournament of cowboy skills, the word first recorded in this sense in 1889.

rodomontade.   The braggart Moorish king Rodomonte in the Italian epic *Orlando Furioso* (1505–15) gave his name to this word for empty vainglorious boasting, which is sometimes incorrectly spelled *rhodomontade*. Thus Rodomonte's actual bravery has been forgotten in the language.

roentgen ray. The first Nobel Prize in physics was awarded to German scientist Wilhelm Konrad von Roentgen (Röntgen) in 1901 for his discovery of the X ray six years earlier. Roentgen called his largely accidental discovery the *X ray* because he was at first unable to fathom the nature of this shortwave ray; it was an unknown quantity to him and he borrowed the symbol from algebra for it. The physicist, a professor at Munich the last 20 or so years of his life, did much valuable work in thermology, mechanics, and electricity, most of it overshadowed by his great discovery. He died in 1923, aged 78. X rays are sometimes called roentgen rays in his honor today, and the fluoroscope the roentgenoscope. To roentgenize is to x-ray someone or something, which is done by roentgenologists, who take roentgenograms, or photographs made with X rays. But the use of Roentgen's name does not end here by any means. A roentgen is a measurement unit of radiation, and a roentgenometer is an instrument used for measuring X-ray intensity.

R.O.K. During the Korean conflict soldiers of the *R*epublic *of K*orea (South Korea) were called R.O.K.s, this acronym pronounced *rocks*. The *K*orean *N*ational *P*olice were called K.N.P.s, the letters pronounced individually. U.N. forces in Korea all used these U.S.-invented terms. *See* VIETCONG.

Roland for an Oliver. Roland and Oliver were two evenly matched knights of Charlemagne who once engaged in combat that lasted five full days on an island in the Rhine. Every time Roland got in a resounding whack, Oliver replied in kind and the contest to determine who was the better warrior ended in a draw. After the fight, Roland, Charlemagne's nephew, and the intrepid Oliver became devoted friends. Both brave knights were killed by the Arabs in A.D. 778, in an ambush at Roncevaux in the Pyrenees, though one legend tells us that Oliver accidentally killed Roland after himself receiving a fatal wound from the enemy. The long epic poem *Chanson de Roland* of the 11th century tells how Roland and Charlemagne's paladins died and how the king of the Franks avenged them. Many great deeds are credited to the two knights, so many that *a Roland for an Oliver* can mean an exchange of tall tales as well as blow for blow or tit for tat.

role. An actor's role in a play derives from the text an actor reads to learn his part. The Old French *rolle* meant a roll of manuscript. Actors learned their parts from plays written on such *rolles* and eventually their parts themselves became known as roles.

roller derby; roller disco. Famed author Damon Runyon invented the roller derby and named it in 1937 during the Great Depression. In brief, it is a rough body contact sport in which two roller-skating teams compete on an oval track in a race to complete as many laps as possible in a given time. A *roller disco*, invented in 1978, is a discotheque at which the dancers wear roller skates.

Rolling Stones; a rolling stone gathers no moss. In 1961 the British rock group called the Rolling Stones named themselves after the Muddy Waters classic blues song "Rollin' Stone." Muddy Waters, in turn, had been inspired by the anonymous ancient proverb, "a rolling stone gathers no moss," which dates back to at least the 14th century and means that

someone always moving won't ever accumulate a fortune (the moss on the rock).

Rolls-Royce. Regarded by many for many years as the best car in the world, the Rolls-Royce is named for Charles Stewart Rolls and Henry Royce, who first built it in 1904. Royce was the mechanical genius, a manufacturer of dynamos and electric cranes before Rolls, an auto dealer, heard of a new model auto Royce had built and sought him out.

roll with the punches. An expression from the boxing arena that probably dates to the 19th century, *roll with the punches* is based on the way a good, experienced boxer takes a punch. It means, of course, to take the blows of fate as they come, bending with them but springing back and moving on.

romaine lettuce. The French believed that this tall, upright lettuce with ribbed leaves was first cultivated by the Romans and named it *latique* (lettuce) *romaine*, soon shortening this to "romaine" alone. But the lettuce is also called Cos, after the Greek island where some botanists say the variety was first grown centuries ago.

roman à clef; livre à clef. *Roman à clef* translates from the French as "novel with a key" and is also known as a *livre à clef*, "book with a key," and in German as a *Schlüssel-roman*. In such novels thinly disguised portraits of actual well-known persons are presented under fictitious names. When the *roman à clef* originated in 17th-century France "keys" to the real persons involved were often published after the books appeared. Notable instances of "key novels" in England include Thomas Love Peacock's *Nightmare Abbey* (1818), which caricatured Byron, Shelley, and Coleridge; Benjamin Disraeli's *Venetia* (1837); Aldous Huxley's *Point Counter Point* (1928), featuring a disguised D. H. Lawrence, among others; and Somerset Maugham's *Cakes and Ale*, among others of his novels, in which the characters were often hardly disguised at all.

romance. *Romance* derives from the Latin *Romanice scribere*, "to write in the Roman vernacular," as distinguished from literary Latin. The Romance languages, French, Italian, Spanish, etc., are derived from this vernacular Latin. The old French adverb *romany*, for *Romanice*, became a noun meaning a tale told in verse about some hero of chivalry, this becoming *romance* in English.

ROM and RAM. These are acronyms for forms of computer memory. ROM stands for read-only memory, containing instructions for starting the computer that are permanent and cannot be modified. RAM means random-access memory, containing instructions for the particular task the operator wants the computer to perform; these instructions are temporary, entered from the keyboard or disc and lost when the power is turned off. One wonders if these will become general synonyms for "permanent" and "temporary."

Roman fever. *See* MALARIA.

Roman holiday. A holiday that is obtained at the expense of others, just as the Romans obtained their enjoyment at the expense of the doomed gladiators who fought in the arena.

Byron invented the expression in "Childe Harold" when writing of a captured Gaul forced to fight in the arena and "Butcher'd to make a Roman holiday." A Roman holiday is thus also BREAD AND CIRCUSES, a public spectacle marked by onlookers pleasuring in the brutal, barbaric display of anything, from an airplane crash to a violent hockey game.

roman noir; film noir; film.   *Roman noir,* from the French *roman,* "novel," and *noir,* "black," literally means a black novel, generally a whodunit that closely resembles a gothic novel in its atmosphere of doom and often gloom. Other *romans* include *roman policies,* a detective story; ROMAN À CLEF; *roman-feuilleton,* a novel published in installments; and *roman-fleuve,* a series of novels with the same character. *Film noir* literally means a black movie (dark subject matter and atmosphere), its name suggested by *roman noir.* The word *film* itself is not recorded until 1905. *See* MOVIE.

Roman nose.   A high-bridged nose, often thought of as regal because of its presence on surviving busts of Roman emperors. The old vaudville joke "He has a Roman nose—it's roamin' all over his face" has two eponymous words in it, for *roamin'* also derives from *Roman.*

Romany rye.   A Romany rye is to Gypsies a friendly gentleman who speaks their language. *Romany* (which rhymes with *hominy*) derives from the Gypsy *rom,* man or husband.

Romeo and Juliet.   Not much is known about Romeo and Juliet, but they were real lovers who lived in Verona, Italy, and died for each other in the year 1303. The Capulets and Montagues were among the inhabitants of the town at that time, and as in Shakespeare's play, Romeo and Juliet were victims of their parents' senseless rivalry. Their story was told in many versions before the Bard of Avon wrote of his "star-crossed lovers." The tale can be traced to Masuccio's *Novelle* (1476). Shakespeare found the tale in Arthur Brooke's poem "The Tragical Historye of Romeus and Juliet," containing "a rare example of love constancie . . ." (1562). *Romeo* alone means a male "lover" today and has a derisive ring, but *Romeo and Juliet* still means a pair of youthful, often helpless lovers.

rook.   Farmers in England called this member of the crow tribe (*Corvus frugilegus*) a *hrooc* as early as the eighth century, probably in imitation of its raucous cry. The bird has long been regarded as a pest and was distinguished from the crow, as this old seed-planting rhyme shows: "One for the rook / One for the crow / One for the weather / And one to grow." The chess piece called the *rook* has an entirely different origin, deriving from a Persian word whose original sense is unknown. The thieving bird, however, does give us the word *to rook,* or cheat, which has been used since Shakespeare's time, just as GULL has been.

rookie.   There is much dispute about *rookie's* origin. Some authorities trace the word to a shortening of *recruit,* a term first used in baseball at the end of the 19th century, and others suggest the rook from the game of chess as the source. Most etymologists, however, agree with Eric Partridge who claims *rookie* as British army slang for a raw recruit as well as a pun on *rooky,* British slang for a rascally person. It is possible, if not probable, that *rookie* had an independent coinage from *recruit* in American baseball and it is certain that the word achieved its popularity in the United States from its common use in baseball for "a player playing his first season in the major leagues." Now *rookie* can refer to a first-year player in any sport, as well as an army recruit, or any neophyte.

rooster story.   Both *cock* and *bull* are taboo words in the Ozark mountains, as is the word *tale* (a homophone for *tail*). Thus, a rare triple euphemism has arisen there for *cock and bull tale,* which many Ozarkians call a "rooster story."

root, hog, or die.   To get down to work and shift for oneself; originally a southern expression, first recorded by Davy Crockett and based on the hog's unfailing ability to provide for itself by rooting the ground with its snout, which yields it everything from trash to truffles.

rope-a-dope.   *See* ON THE ROPES.

rope of sand.   Expressing futility, ties that neither bind nor hold, *rope of sand* is an old English expression that is first recorded in 1624, but may well be proverbial. One early use: ". . . this rope of sand which Tradition is."

Roquefort.   "The King of the blue cheeses," pungent Roquefort is made in France's Roquefort district. Made from sheep's milk, it is marbled with blue-green mold.

roquelaure.   French marshal Antoine-Gaston, duc de Roquelaure (1656–1738), often wore and had named after him this hooded cloak or mantle reaching to the knees that was widely popular with men during the 18th and early 19th centuries.

Rorschach test.   Popularly known as the ink-blot test, this widely used psychological diagnostic technique was invented in 1921 by Swiss psychiatrist Hermann Rorschach (1884–1922). The Rorschach test consists of a series of 10 standardized ink-blot designs that the subject observes, relating what he sees by free association to a trained tester. The way the ambiguous, colored blots are perceived is thought to reflect the interpreter's personality and emotional conflicts. Though it has been used since 1921, the validity of the Rorschach is not universally accepted.

rosary.   The string of beads used by Roman Catholics to count repetitions of certain prayers is said to be so named because the first ones were made of rosewood, a hard, reddish, black-streaked wood that often has a roselike odor and comes from several tropical trees, including *Dalbergia nigra* and *Pterocarpus erinaceus,* the African rosewood, or molompi. Another theory is that it takes its name from the "Mystical Rose," one of the titles of the Virgin Mary.

Roscian.   Roman actor Quintus Gallus Roscius (ca. 126–62 B.C.) was born a slave but became the greatest performer of his time. Excelling in comedy roles, he was so esteemed that the golden-tongued orator Cicero took lessons from him and became his friend, the two often competing to see who could better express any idea or emotion. Roscius, in fact, wrote a treatise comparing acting and oratory. In an age when actors were held in contempt, his grace and eloquence were praised in poems, Sulla awarded him the gold ring signifying equestrian rank, and he amassed a great fortune, retiring from the stage when still a young man. Over 2,000 years have passed and his name is still a synonym for eminence or perfection in acting. *Roscian* means pertaining to or involving actors, and when we say someone gave a *Roscian performance*, we mean one of outstanding skill. *See* THESPIAN.

roscoe. A pistol or revolver. This old American slang word was first recorded at the end of the 19th century, but its origin is unknown. Maybe a criminal named Roscoe is involved, but I haven't found him. The male name Roscoe comes from the Germanic words meaning "swift horse." One Roscoe with something named after him is William Roscoe (1753–1831), a British philanthropist and historian who has the American bird *Roscoe's Yellowthroat* honoring his patronym.

rose. The rose may take its name from the Celtic word *rhod*, "red," in reference to its typical color. There are 100 to 4,000 species of roses, depending on which botanist you believe, not to mention the 8,000 or more rose cultivars. That great teller of tall tales Sir John Mandeville, who wrote of anthills of gold dust and fountains of youth, told the best story about the origin of the rose in his 14th-century *Voyage and Travels*. It seems that a beautiful Jewish maiden of Bethlehem rejected the brutish advances of a drunken lout named Hanauel. In revenge Hanauel falsely denounced her as a witch, and she was condemned to burn at the stake. But God answered her prayers and extinguished the flames; the stake itself budded and the fair maiden stood there unharmed under a rose tree of red and white blossoms, "the first on earth since Paradise was lost." Legends abound about the rose. One says that the white rose was turned red when Eve kissed one in the Garden of Eden; another tells of Cupid's blood shed upon it. Still another story holds that the rose bursts into bloom when a nightingale sings. Edward Phillips in *Sylva Florifera* tells this tale of the birth of the rose:

> Flora [the Roman goddess of flowers] having found the corpse of a favorite nymph, whose beauty of person was only surpassed by the purity of her heart . . . resolved to raise a plant from her precious remains . . . for which purpose she begged the assistance of Venus and the Graces, as well as of all the deities that preside over gardens, to assist in the transformation of the nymph into a flower, that was to be by them proclaimed queen of all the vegetable beauties. The ceremony was attended by the Zephyrs, who cleared the atmosphere in order that Apollo might bless the new-created progeny by his beams. Bacchus supplied rivers of nectar to nourish it; and Vertumnus [the Roman god of orchards] poured his choicest perfumes over the plant. When the metamorphosis was complete, Pomona [the Roman goddess of fruit] strewed her fruit over the young branches, which were then crowned by Flora with a diadem, that had been purposely prepared by the celestials, to distinguish this queen of flowers.

Since the beginning of time, it seems, roses have been the flowers of love, the true flowers of Venus. Cleopatra carpeted a room with red rose petals so that their scent would rise above Mark Antony as he walked toward her. Dionysius, the tyrant of Syracuse, filled his house with roses for the frequent compulsory orgies he held with the young women of his city; Nero used millions of the blooms to decorate a hall for a single banquet, and rose water–saturated pigeons fluttered overhead to sprinkle the guests with scent. In fact, roses were so popular in ancient times that they actually became a symbol of the degeneracy of later Roman emperors, and it took the Church, to which the rose became a symbol of purity, to rescue it from oblivion during the Dark Ages. According to one ancient story, a number of noble Romans were suffocated under tons of rose petals dropped on them during one of Emperor Heliogabalus's orgies. The Romans so loved the flower that they imported bargefuls of rose petals and hips from Egypt, where the growing season was longer, and they believed in the flower's powers so fervently that they used rose water in their fountains. Long before this the Greek physician Galen had used a full pound of rose oil in a facial cosmetic he invented, and "attar of roses" remains a much-valued cosmetic ingredient to this day. For centuries the rose has been employed to invoke love in some rather strange ways. Persian women thought that rose water was a philter that would bring back straying lovers; one old Chinese love recipe drunk during the fourth-month rose festivals consisted of prunes, sugar, olives, and rose petals; and colonial ladies made "rose wine" to stimulate their lovers by marinating rose petals in brandy. Finally we have Napoleon's empress Josephine, who, when her teeth turned bad, always carried a rose in her hand with which to cover her mouth when she laughed. *See also* SUB ROSA.

Rosebud Senator. Among the most unusual nicknames of U.S. senators, the Rosebud Senator was the cognomen of Senator Henry Anthony (1815–84). According to the *Congressional Record* of January 21, 1885, he was so called because of "the healthful glow that mantled his cheek, or as a tribute to the fact that he constantly wore a rose bud or other flower."

rose-colored glasses. Some unfortunate people never take their rose-colored glasses off, but everybody wears these spectacles occasionally. This attitude of cheerful optimism, of seeing everything in an attractive, pleasant light, has always been with us, while the expression itself goes back to at least 1861, when it is first recorded in *Tom Brown at Oxford:* "Oxford was a sort of Utopia to the Captain . . . He continued to behold towers, and quadrangles, and chapels, through rose-colored spectacles."

a rose is a rose is a rose. What Gertrude Stein really wrote in her poem "Sacred Emily" was "Rose is a rose is a rose, is a rose," but her words have been misquoted as the above so often that she might as well have written "a rose is a rose is a rose." In her prose Gertrude Stein had no use for nouns: "Things once they are named the name does not go on doing anything to them and so why write in nouns." But in poetry, she felt: "You can love a name and if you love a name then saying that name any number of times only makes you love it more." And poetry is "really loving the name of anything."

rosemary. The homely herb rosemary was originally called by the Latin name *ros marinus*, "sea dew," because it was often found on the sea cliffs in southern France. But over the years *ros* sounded more like "rose" to English ears, and *marinus* suggested the common name "Mary." The herb was thus dedicated to the Virgin Mary, and the word *rosemary* was recorded as early as 1440. This flowering shrub has contributed its dried leaves and stems to many recipes, and oils from its leaves and flowers figure in numerous potions and perfumes. Bouquets of rosemary, "emblematical of manly virtues," were once presented to bridegrooms on their wedding mornings, and bridal beds are still bedecked with the flowers in certain European countries to ensure conjugal bliss. Rosemary symbolizes remembrance, and Shakespeare's Ophelia presented a bunch to Hamlet, perhaps to remind him of their meeting on Saint Valentine's Day when the melancholy Dane "Let in the maid, that out a maid / Never departed more."

rose of Jericho.   Native to the deserts of Arabia, the rose of Jericho (*Anastatica hierochuntica*) or "resurrection plant" is, when dry, a tight ball the size of an orange that is driven across the sands by the winds. It can be kept like this for many years but will often continue to grow, unfolding and revealing small leaves and minute white flowers when exposed to water. It is also called "the rose of the virgin."

rose of Sharon.   There are at least 25 species of flowers and shrubs named after the rose, usually because of some physical resemblance. The rose of Sharon is one of them, taking its last name not from any woman named Sharon, but from the Hebrew place name Sharon, for the fertile level tract along the coast of Palestine, where the flower mentioned in the Bible was said to grow. The identity of the true rose of Sharon is uncertain and today the name is applied to several plants in America, generally to the showy late shrub *Hibiscus syriacus* (also called althea).

Rotokas.   Rotokas is a language spoken in the central part of Bougainville Island in the South Pacific. It has the distinction of having the shortest alphabet of any living language, composed of just 11 letters (*a, b, e, g, i, k, o, p, r, t,* and *u*), with six consonants (also the least of any language) and five vowels. The language with the most letters is Cambodian, with 72.

Rotten Row.   The London street, originally a royal route, may have originally been called La Route du Roi, the Royal Road, with the French expression corrupted into *Rotten Row*. But its name could also derive from *rotteran,* "to muster," for soldiers once mustered there, or from the Anglo-Saxon *rot,* "pleasant, cheerful," or even from *rotten,* referring to the soft material the road was made of. Another of many possibilities is the Norman *Rattan Row,* or "roundabout way," the route over which corpses were carried in olden times to avoid main streets and traffic.

Rottweiler.   A large, stocky, powerful dog with a black coat that was originally bred in the city of Rottweil, Germany, about 1910. *See* GERMAN MEASLES; DOBERMAN.

roué.   *Roué* was first used to describe the debauched rakes in the duc d'Orléan's crowd toward the beginning of the 18th century. These roués, who weren't really old at all (even though the old cliché makes all roués old), took their name from the French word *rouer,* meaning to torture on the wheel. The reason: the duc and his cronies were so dissolute that many people thought they deserved to be broken on the torture wheel.

rough and ready.   This was not only the nickname of General (later President) Zachary Taylor, but the name of a town in California. Applied to a person, *rough and ready* means someone who takes things as they come, who works in a rough but prompt and effective way; referring to things, it means something unelaborate, just good enough to serve the purpose. The term arose at the beginning of the 19th century, some time before the duke of Wellington could have invented it at Waterloo by instructing a Colonel Rough there, "Rough and ready, colonel!" as the old story goes.

rough it out.   *See* TOUGH IT OUT.

Rough Riders.   Teddy Roosevelt named his Spanish-American War cavalry unit the Rough Riders, after the American cowboy broncobusters called roughriders, many of whom were part of his regiment.

Roundheads.   Cromwell's soldiers and all Puritans of England's Civil War period were called Roundheads and *crops* because, in contrast to the Royalists, who had long flowing hair, their hair was "trimmed close to a bowl-dish, placed as a guide on their heads."

roundheels.   *Roundheels* has been slang for a prostitute or a promiscuous woman since at least the early 1940s. The expression derives from the 1920s boxing term *roundheels* for an inferior boxer who is more often on his back than on his feet.

round robin.   The round robin was originally a petition, its signatures arranged in a circular form to disguise the order of signing. Most probably it takes its name from the *ruban rond,* "round ribbon," in 17th-century France, where government officials devised a method of signing their petitions of grievances on ribbons that were attached to the documents in a circular form. In that way no signer could be accused of signing the document first and risk having his head chopped off for instigating trouble. *Ruban rond* later became *round robin* in English and the custom continued in the British navy, where petitions of grievances were signed as if the signatures were spokes of a wheel radiating from its hub. Today *round robin* usually means a sports tournament where all of the contestants play each other at least once and losing a match doesn't result in immediate elimination.

rove.   In Medieval English the archery term *roven* meant "to shoot randomly." Arrows shot randomly at distant targets, floating through the air, suggested comparison with a person strolling off to distant places, somewhat lazily, randomly, with no apparent purpose, and gave us our expression *to rove.*

row; oar.   The word *row* meaning to propel a boat of any size by oars has been used since the 14th century. It comes ultimately from Old Norse *roa,* meaning the same. The word *oar* also can be traced to Viking days, deriving from Old Norse *ar.*

rowanberry. The European mountain ash, as the rowanberry (*Sorbus aucuparia edulis*) is also called, has an interesting history. It takes the name *rowanberry* from the Danish *rune*, "magic," being so called because it was supposed to have magical powers to ward off evil.

Rowley poems. *See* ITS.

royalties. *Royalties*, in the sense of an agreed portion of the income of a work paid to an author, or a portion of the proceeds paid to the owner of a right (mineral, oil, etc.), is of course connected with the granting of royal rights. *Royalty* in this financial sense seems to have first been used to describe a duty of one shilling a ton on all coal exported from the Tyne for use in England, which England's Charles II granted in 1676 to his illegitimate son the duke of Richmond as part of a perpetual pension. In the sense of a payment to authors, *royalty* is first recorded in 1880 in *Scribner's Magazine*. But book royalties are of such tenuous value today that one author has suggested a name change to *peasantries*.

royal we. Two centuries ago, the critic Edward Copelstan wrote: "There is a mysterious authority in the plural *we* which no single name, whatever its reputation, can acquire." *Royal we* has been used by kings and queens since at least the reign of Richard I (1189–99) in England, and one old story claims that the practice was initiated by two Roman rulers who reigned in different capitals and issued identical joint decrees. Using *we* reflected the fact that sovereigns represented their many subjects, not just themselves, in addition to making the monarchs seem more authoritative. While the term *royal we* is fast dying among royalty today, it is often used by writers and editors because it seems both more authoritative and less egotistical than *I*.

Roystonea. It isn't often that someone's entire name, first and last, is taken for a word, but that is just what happened with General Roy Stone, a 19th-century American engineer in Puerto Rico who had the *Roystonea*, or royal palm, named after him. The genus *Roystonea* is well known, including six species of palms. Often used as an ornamental to line avenues in tropical America, its beautiful crest dominates every landscape where it grows, and every portion from its roots to its crown serves some useful purpose. Some of these feather palm species grow to over 100 feet high and the *Roystonea regia* species is widely planted in southern Florida. Florida's Palm Beach, the wealthy resort where over 25,000 millionaires are said to be resident in season, became a palm-fringed paradise when a cargo of coconuts washed ashore from a shipwreck in 1879, and early residents planted the nuts along the once desolate beach.

rubber chicken. An unappetizing dish invariably on the menu at dinners, banquets, and other large gatherings in the U.S. The British equivalent is *function fish*.

rubber; mackintosh. Rubber was not even named until 1770, when chemist Joseph Priestley accidentally discovered that the hardened substance could "rub" out pencil marks, and progress in waterproofing did not come until half a century after that. Young James Syme, later to become a famous surgeon, first invented the process for making waterproof fabrics while a student at Edinburgh University in 1823, but the fabric itself was patented a few months later by Scottish chemist Charles Macintosh, who exploited the idea and was really the first person to produce a practical waterproof cloth. Macintosh (1766–1843), a Fellow of the Royal Society, had already invented an effective bleaching powder and improved a number of dyes. Finding that rubber could be dissolved by naphtha, he spread the resulting solution on cotton cloth, cementing another layer of cloth to it. Raincoats made from such double-thick fabrics with a middle layer of rubber won popularity overnight, as did numerous waterproof items that Macintosh manufactured at his plant in Glasgow. But the man who revolutionized outdoor living somehow became associated with his raincoat alone, and even this was spelled wrong from the very beginning. Properly, *mackintosh* or the *mac*, as it is sometimes called, should be *macintosh*, although the incorrect spelling prevails.

rubber match. A *rubber match* or *rubber game* or simply *rubber* in any sport means a deciding contest between two tied opponents. The term dates back to the late 16th century but no one seems certain of its etymology or in what sport it originated. The expression was not used in card games until the mid 18th century and the earliest recorded use of it appears to be a 1599 reference, cited in the *Oxford English Dictionary*, to the game of bowls. The word *rubber* in the term seems to derive from a word of unknown origin, not the resilient substance called "rubber" or the verb "to rub."

rubberneck. Who invented *rubberneck* for a gawking tourist is unknown, but the Americanism dates back to the 1890s in New York City. In the words of H. L. Mencken (*The American Language*, 1948) *rubberneck* "is almost a complete treatise on American psychology . . . one of the best words ever coined . . . It may be homely, but it is nevertheless superb, and whoever invented it, if he could be discovered, would be worthy of a Harvard LL.D., but also the thanks of both Rotary and Congress, half a bushel of medals, and 30 days as the husband of Miss America."

rubber stamp. People have been making rubber stamps since the 19th century, but the first recorded use of the term figuratively to describe someone who approves things automatically and uncritically, a YES-MAN, dates back to a 1919 description of former president William Howard Taft by author William R. Thayer: "He may have heard the exhortation, 'Be your own President; don't be anybody's man or rubber stamp.' " The way Thayer uses the phrase suggests that it was current at least 30 or so years before.

rube. *See* CLODHOPPER.

Rube Goldberg contraption. Cartoonist Rube Goldberg, as the preposterously "logical" machinery in his comic strips showed, never wanted to disappoint anyone. His complicated diagrammed panels never did, either; the machinery in them performed childishly simple tasks that could have been done far easier by hand. A parody of this mechanized world, these wild and wonderful contraptions made his name synonymous with any complicated, wildly impractical invention or scheme and won him lasting fame as well as exhibitions in the most conservative museums. Goldberg died in 1970, aged 87, and some of his obituaries failed to mention the fact that he had won two Pulitzer Prizes for his political cartoons.

rub out. To *rub someone out*, "to kill him," isn't gangster talk from the Prohibition era, as is so often assumed. The term dates back to the early 19th-century American Far West and has its origins in Plains Indian sign language, which expresses *to kill* with a rubbing motion. The term is first recorded in George Ruxton's *Life in the Far West* (1848) and it is he who gives the sign language source.

rub the wrong way. An ingenious theory links this expression with the wet-rubbing of unfinished floors in Elizabethan homes. Oak floors that servants mopped against the grain became streaked, such carelessness giving rise to these words for the inept handling of people as well as floors. However, evidence is lacking; the phrase is first recorded in 1862 and must be marked "origin unknown."

Rudbeckia. Under ADAM'S APPLE we mentioned the Swedish professor who tried to prove that the site of the Garden of Eden was located in the Land of the Midnight Sun. The professor, Olaf Rudbeck (1630–1702), also claimed in his book *Atlantikan* that Sweden had been the locale of Plato's Atlantis. But he was otherwise a fine scientist, discovering the lymphatic system and making various botanical contributions. Linnaeus so admired the Rudbeck family that he named the North American coneflower after both Professor Rudbeck and his son, the junior Professor Rudbeck being a contemporary of Linnaeus. The *Rudbeckia* genus, some 25 species, includes the popular black-eyed Susan and golden glow. Plants in the genus are herbs, usually having yellow rays, and can be annual or perennial.

rudderless. Since the early 19th century *rudderless*, in reference to the absence of a ship's rudder, has figuratively meant "without guidance or control."

rugby. In 1823 at a football game at the Rugby School in England, a young player named William Ellis picked up the ball and ran down field with it, an unsportsmanlike maneuver at the time for which Ellis profusely apologized. But his play caught on and began to be imitated by other players, which of course inspired the defense to stop the ball carriers by tackling them, another practice unthinkable under the old rules of the game. This type of football began to be called rugby football or simply rugby and another rule of the new game allowed a player to run with the ball if it was caught on the fly or on the first bounce. Players who preferred the old, no-ball-carrying football formed the London Football Association in 1863 and published their own rules. Their brand of football was called association football, which became assoc football. *Assoc football* was shortened to *soc*, to which an *er* ending was added, giving us the word *soccer* for the game. *See* FOOTBALL.

rugger. *See* SOCCER.

rule of thumb. There are two good choices here. Brewmasters of old often tested the temperature of a batch of beer by dipping a thumb in the brew, their long experience telling them how well the beer was brewing. One theory has it that our expression for a rough, guesswork estimate derives from this practice. More likely it stems from the ancient use of the last joint of the thumb as a measuring device for roughly one inch. I can find no proof for the common claim that the term *rule of thumb* relates to wife beating, specifically that it was originally a rule permitting a husband to beat his wife with a stick no wider than his thumb. The *OED*'s first reference to the phrase is from 1692 and refers to an artless fencer. The other nine or so references also have no relation to wife beating or any assault upon anyone. See as well Cecil Adams's discussion of the term at www.straightdope.com.

rule the roost. There's no doubt that this expression is well over four centuries old, but there is controversy about whether it was originally *rule the roost* or *rule the roast*. To *rule the roost* would of course refer to the cock who rules the chicken coop and *to rule the roast* refers to the lord of the manor who presided over the carving and dishing out of roast meat at the table and was thus master of the house. Americans still prefer the former expression and the British use the latter. Since early references are found for both versions, the truth will probably never be known. What complicates matters impossibly is that *roost* was formerly pronounced as we now pronounce *roast*, and thus spelled "roast" erroneously, while *roast* was sometimes pronounced *roost* and spelled that way. In any case, the expression means the same—to rule the house or whatever, usually while making a display of power.

rum. Called *Kill-Devil*, a West Indian name, by early colonists, and the basic liquor that they made (from molasses and sugar), *rum* possibly takes its name from the English *rumbullion*, first recorded in the 1640s, which may have been named for the town of Rambouillet. Another possibility is that it derives from the canting term *rum*, for "good, excellent," which is recorded as early as 1567.

Rumford stove. Before Benjamin Thompson, Count Rumford (1753–1814), invented his "kitchen range" most housewives prepared meals in open fireplaces. But the Rumford stove was among the least of the count's accomplishments. Rumford led a remarkable life. The Massachusetts-born philanthropist fought for the British during the Revolution, leaving his wife, a wealthy widow 14 years his senior, and a baby daughter in New Hampshire. After serving as British undersecretary of state and being elected to the Royal Society, he entered the Bavarian civil and military service in 1783. Here he effected numerous reforms, including a reorganization of the army and the education of the poor. It is said that in one day he had 2,600 beggars arrested and sent to a Munich workhouse he had planned, where they were taught to support themselves. It was in this workhouse that the Rumford stove was invented, the wood- or coal-burning range proving so efficient that Rumford was commissioned to build similar cast-iron models for many aristocrats of the day.

rummage sale. As early as the 14th century the French word *arrimage*, related to our word "arrange," meant "loading a cargo ship." Sometimes cargo from the *arrimage* was damaged during the voyage and warehouses held special sales of these damaged items, sales that were at first called *arrimage* sales and then *rummage* sales. *Rummage* thus came to mean any damaged goods and finally any goods low in quality, including the used clothing and other items sold at charity rummage sales.

rum, Romanism, and rebellion.   This political slogan is usually attributed to the supporters of Herbert Hoover, who used it to defeat Catholic Democratic candidate Al Smith for the presidency in 1928, calling the Democrats the party of rum, Romanism, and rebellion. But the words were first used in 1884 by New York Presbyterian minister Samuel D. Burchard, who spoke, in presidential candidate James Blaine's presence, of the Democrats as "the party whose antecedents are rum, Romanism, and rebellion," this offending the large Irish Catholic vote in New York, causing Blaine to lose the state by a scant 1,000 votes and thus lose the election to Grover Cleveland. Blaine's political reputation didn't help him either. The Democrat's slogan for that election was "James G. Blaine, James G. Blaine,/ Continental liar from the state of Maine."

Rum Row.   During Prohibition, Rum Row was a line of ships anchored off New York City outside the three-mile coastal limit, waiting for smaller boats to speed out to buy their contraband liquor and bring the bootleg booze ashore. Fully one-third of all the illegal liquor that came into the country came in via this Rum Row.

rum, sodomy, and the lash.   While Winston Churchill was First Lord of the Admiralty (1911–15), he remarked acidly, in answer to a protest about British naval traditions being violated, that the traditions of the navy were "rum, sodomy, and the lash."

run amok (or amuck).   In 1516 an Englishman translated an Italian work that said of the Javanese, "There are some of them [under the influence of opium] who . . . go out into the streets and kill as many people as they meet. . . . These are called *Amuco*." Within a century, *to run amok* was common in English for "running viciously mad and frenzied for blood." The word *amok* comes ultimately from the Malay *amoq*, meaning attacking desperately, or murdering in a state of frenzy, and was originally applied to an animal in a state of rage.

run around like a chicken with its head cut off.   When chickens are slaughtered by decapitation, they run around for a moment before falling down dead. This unpleasant reference hasn't prevented the term above from being used to describe any person who behaves hectically, who seems to have no control, as in "Don't run around like a chicken with its head cut off." The expression doesn't seem to be recorded anywhere, but it was certainly common 60 years ago—about when I first heard it—and it is probably an Americanism dating back to at least the mid-19th century. In fact, that the term has international use today is demonstrated by advice the Afghanistan Taliban leader Mullah Omar gave to his scattered troops on 11/14/01. "Any person who goes hither and thither is like a slaughtered chicken that falls and dies."

run a taut ship.   To be a thoroughly efficient employer or supervisor. The saying dates back to the age of sailing ships, and captains who ran neat, perfectly maintained vessels with no slack in the rigging anywhere. The opposite expression is *to run a slack ship.*

runcible spoon.   A forklike utensil with two broad prongs and one sharp curved prong used for serving hors d'oeuvres. The word was coined in 1871 by English author Edward Lear. The spoon seems to have been invented after Lear described it thusly in "The Owl and the Pussycat":

> They dined on mince and slices of quince
> Which they ate with a runcible spoon.

run for your life.   According to one old tale, a fast runner of the duke of Monmouth was captured during the Battle of Sedgemoor in 1685 and told that he could run for his life, that is, his life would be spared if he could outrun a horse. The contest was held, the horse losing the long race, and the runner was freed. This is supposed to be the origin of *run for your life,* though it was probably common long before any such race— if indeed there was one. It is, however, possible for a good runner to beat a horse in a long race like a marathon.

run hot and cold.   There are many traditional stories about the semilegendary fabulist Aesop. He is said to have lived in the middle of the sixth century B.C. and been the black slave of a Thracian named Iadmon. Supposedly deformed and ugly, he won his freedom by telling fables. At any rate, many tales about animals, adapted to moral or satirical ends, circulated under his name, though some of them really date back a thousand years before his birth. One of Aesop's fables is about a satyr who finds a winter traveler blowing on his fingers to keep them warm. When the satyr gives the man a bowl of hot pottage and he blows on that, too, the satyr asks him why. "I am trying to cool it," the man says. The satyr thereupon orders the man out of his cave, declaring "I will have no dealings with one who can blow hot and cold from the same mouth!" Though the traveler wasn't inconsistent—his breath was first warmer and then colder than the object he blew upon—this fable became the basis for the saying *to blow hot and cold,* "to be inconsistent or vacillate." Today the expression is often heard in the form *to run hot and cold,* reinforced in modern times, perhaps, by plumbing that gives us alternately hot water and cold.

run into the ground.   To overdo something, as in, "You've already told us twice, don't run it into the ground." The phrase seems to have been first used by cowboys in the late 19th century.

runners famous in history.   *See* FAST AS LADAS; MARATHON.

run riot.   *The Master of Game,* a hunting manual published in 1410, explains in part that *to run riot* was originally a term describing a hunting dog who lost the scent of the animal he was chasing and began acting unruly and undisciplined—running after other animals instead of the intended quarry. Over the next century the phrase came to be used figuratively for anyone acting without constraint or control.

runt.   *Runt,* for "a small, weak person," came into the language as slang in about 1700. It derives from the name of the small breeds of oxen and cattle called "runts" in Wales and the Scottish Highlands as early as the 16th century.

run the gamut of emotions from A to B. Sometimes said of unaccomplished actors and actresses, this expression has its origin in a witticism of American author Dorothy Parker. "Kate's wonderful, isn't she?" a friend said of Katharine Hepburn's Broadway performance in *The Lake*, between acts at the Martin Beck Theater. "Oh, yes," Miss Parker agreed. "She runs the gamut of emotions all the way from A to B." These words became as celebrated as any of her ripostes, but years later Miss Parker told Garson Kanin that she didn't think there was a finer actress anywhere than Katharine Hepburn; she had made the remark for the same reason she said many things—because it was funny, a joke. Miss Hepburn, however, agreed with her assessment of *The Lake*.

run the gauntlet. The *gauntlet* in this expression was first spelled *gantlope*, deriving from the Swedish word *gattloppe*, from *gat*, "a narrow path," and *loppe*, "run" (akin to our "lope," "elope," and "gallop"), which literally meant "a running of the narrow path." *Gatloppe* was the name of a punishment that originated in the Swedish army. A soldier found guilty of a serious offense was forced to strip naked and run between two rows of his comrades, each of whom struck him with a whip, switch, or even sword as he ran. The length of the rows depended on the severity of his offense. The English observed the use of this punishment by the Germans during the Thirty Years' War (1618–48) and saw American Indians inflict a similar punishment on captives with war clubs. They first called the torture, which often resulted in maiming, *running the gantlope*, nasalizing the Swedish word *gatloppe*, but later further corrupted the key word in the phrase to *gauntlet*, probably because of its resemblance to the English *gauntlet*, for "glove." Today the expression means to encounter trouble on all sides, to be severely attacked or criticized. The confusion between this *gauntlet* and the *gauntlet* that is a glove has led some writers to spell the punishment "gantlet." In any case, both words are pronounced the same way. *See* THROW DOWN THE GAUNTLET.

run the table. In a *Times Magazine* William Safire column (*On Language* 11/4/01) Tom Shaw, managing editor of *Pool and Billiard Magazine*, advised that this term comes from the game of pool and means "to clear the table of all the balls and thereby to win the game." He also dates the term back about 40 years. Memories of my misspent youth at Dapper Dan's, the local pool emporium, assure me that the expression dates back at least 60 years, maybe 70, although the expression wasn't much used outside the pool room at the time.

runway. *Runway*, for "a landing strip at an airport," probably has its origins in the *runway* of burlesque, the narrow ramp extending from the stage into an aisle in theaters or nightclubs, on which women dance within reach of the audience. The Americanism *runway* is, however, recorded as early as 1835 as the path for a deer, and also means the bed or channel of a stream.

run wild as outhouse rats. Kansas wheat farmers appear to have coined this Americanism a century or so ago. It was often used to describe unsupervised, unruly kids.

Ruritanian. A humorous term for any country that appears to resemble the small, remote backward central European kingdom of Ruritania in Anthony Hope's very popular novels *The Prisoner of Zenda* (1894) and *Rupert of Hentzau* (1898). Anthony Hope was the pseudonym of Sir Anthony Hope Hawkins (1863–1933), an English barrister and author.

rush hour. The term *rush hour* came into the language long before the first cars clogged American streets. It dates back to 1883, when the Brooklyn Bridge was completed, releasing more traffic into Manhattan and Brooklyn. The subway expression *rush hour express* was first recorded in 1928. In Japan rush hour workers called "fanny pushers" (a euphemistic translation) are employed to pack people into rush hour trains.

Russia. *Russia* derives from the Russian word for the country, *Rossiya*, named after the Vikings who invaded it from the north to establish a kingdom in Russia and who called themselves *rothsmen*, "rowers."

Russian, Polish, and Slavic words in English. Russian and Slavic words are the basis for a number of English ones, including: ruble, czar, kvass, sable, mammoth, knout, cravat, ukase, vodka, droshky, astrakhan, samovar, mazurka, polka, troika, steppe, pogrom, bolshevik, commissar, soviet, intelligentsia, kulak, robot, sputnik, babushka.

Russian roulette. Sad to say, *Russian roulette* refers to a game played throughout the world, as harrowing scenes in the movie *The Deers Hunter* (1978) reveal. It is, to say the least, a game of high risk in which each player spins the cylinder of a revolver containing one bullet, points the muzzle at the temple, and pulls the trigger. The word *roulette* is from the gambling game of roulette, French for "little wheel." *Russian* may be used because czarist Russian officers played the game, but there is no solid evidence of this, and the term hasn't been traced back before 1935.

Russians (Rooshians). In the Great Smoky Mountains wild boars are named after the Russians (pronounced "Rooshians") on the theory that the boars were first imported to America from Russia. Domestic pigs are descended from these tusked wild pigs.

rustler. A cattle thief. This usage is first recorded in the American West in 1882. At first *rustler* meant an energetic person, one who rustled up stray cattle for his boss. The word appears to have evolved from "hustler," as this quote from Owen Wister's *The Virginian* (1902) indicates: "It [*rustler*] was not in any dictionary, and current translations of it were inconsistent. A man at Hossie Falls said that he had passed through Cheyenne, and heard the term applied in a complimentary way to people who were alive and pushing. Another man had always supposed it meant some kind of horse. But the most alarming version of all was that a rustler was a cattle thief. Now the truth is that all these meanings were right. The word ran a sort of progress in the cattle country, gathering many meanings as it went." Of course, the common meaning of the word came to be "a cattle or horse thief." As a matter of fact, a Texas state legislator was convicted of cattle rustling as recently as 1983.

rutabaga; Swedish turnip. Commonly called the Swedish turnip, the rutabaga derives its name from the Swedish dialect *rotabagge*, for the plant; this relatively new vegetable, first recorded in 1620, is extensively grown in Sweden. It is also called Swede.

rutherfordium. The first person to split the atom was New Zealand–born Ernest Rutherford (1871–1937). Baron Rutherford had won the Nobel Prize in chemistry in 1908. After another three years he proposed his new atomic theory, which led to his splitting of the atom in 1919 and the naming after him of the unit of radioactive disintegration called "rutherfordium." Strangely enough, Rutherford didn't believe that atomic power could ever be harnessed.

Rx. The Latin *recipe*, "take," provides the *R* in the symbol *Rx* used by pharmacists for centuries, while the slant across the *R*'s leg is the sign of the Roman god Jupiter, patron of medicine. The symbol looks like *RX* and is pronounced that way.

S

S. Our 19th letter can be traced back to the ancient Phoenician and Hebrew alphabets, where it was called *shin*. It did not acquire its present form until it came into Latin.

'S. Oaths like 'Sblood, 'Slife, and 'Sdeath are common in the works of Elizabethan writers like Ben Jonson. The *'S* is a euphemistic abbreviation of *God's*, always written continuously with the following word.

sabotage. The root of *sabotage* is the French *sabot*, "wooden shoe," but that is as much as anybody really knows about the word, which came into English during World War II from the French *saboter* meaning "to do work badly" or "to destroy machines or a plant in order to win a strike." Why the French made the verb *saboter* out of *sabot*, "shoe," isn't really known, though one persistent old story claims that wooden-shoed peasants trampled down a landowner's crops to win better wages and working conditions. Another story says the term was coined after the great French railway strike of 1912, when "strikers cut the shoes *(sabots)* holding the railway lines." Or it could be that French factory workers threw their shoes into machinery to disable and disrupt a plant.

Sacher torte. History's most famous chocolate cake is named for 19th-century Austrian confectioner Edward Sacher. Sacher, whose cigar-smoking mother served her son's creation to Prince Metternich, actually won a lawsuit from a rival confectioner over who could legally call the cake his own. The cake is made of chocolate torte batter, apricot jam, and chocolate frosting.

sacheverell. Not many preachers or politicians have been put down as properly as Dr. Henry Sacheverell (ca. 1674–1724). "Famous for blowing the coals of dissension," the English clergyman had both "the blower of a stove" and a chamber pot named *sacheverells* after him. The naming was undoubtedly done by Whigs, whom Sacheverell had violently attacked in 1709 in two sermons, especially lashing out against the government's toleration of dissenters. Charged with seditious libel, the fervent Tory was suspended from preaching for three years. But his trial brought about the downfall of the Whigs and he was rewarded with the important rectory of St. Andrew's immediately after his suspension expired. It remained for the dictionaries to take revenge for the Whigs. *See* TWISS.

sack; get the sack. *Sack*, according to legend, was the last word spoken at the Tower of Babel before the world's languages were scrambled, and for this reason it retains a strikingly similar form in over a dozen languages. As for *get the sack*, here etymologists have outdone themselves, with inventions worthy of Rabelais. By far the best tale is that Turkish sultans who grew tired of a wife or found her troublesome, had her taken from the harem, sewed up in a sack, and dumped into the Bosporus. As outrageous as the story seems, it could well be the origin of the old expression, which dates back to the Middle Ages, for such "sacking" was widespread among the Turks, and the Romans similarly sewed up condemned criminals in sacks and tossed them in the Tiber. Most authorities, however, seem to accept with some reservations the explanation linking the phrase to the tools of medieval artisans and mechanics. Workmen generally carried their tools in a sack and for convenience's sake left them in a safe place on the job overnight. When an unsatisfactory worker was fired, at the end of his last day on the job, his employer would hand him his pay and the sack containing his tools.

sackcloth and ashes. People used to show grief and sorrow by wearing sackcloth, a coarse material used for making sacks, and throwing ashes on their heads. From this custom came the expression *sackcloth and ashes*, meaning sorrow for something one has done or failed to do (*e.g.*, "He came to me in sackcloth and ashes saying he'd found the book he had insisted I'd taken"). The phrase is an ancient one that is found in the Bible (Matt. 11:21).

sacred cod. *See* COD.

sacred cow. The Hindu hero Prithu changed himself into a cow to encourage his countrymen to be vegetarians. This and the doctrine of Ahimsa, "harmlessness to all living things," preached by Buddha accounts for the fact that cows are still sacred in India, roaming the streets at will. Our fairly recent term *a sacred cow*, "any person or group so highly regarded as to be exempt from even justified criticism," appears to stem from the Hindu belief. It probably came into the language when Mahatma Gandhi's passive resistance movement brought worldwide attention to India. Gandhi himself was a confirmed vegetarian. In his youth he did try eating meat, but gave it up when he had recurring nightmares of animals bleeding in his stomach.

saddler of Bawtry. "Like the saddler of Bawtry, who was hanged for leaving his liquor." This Yorkshire proverb describes someone too much in a hurry. It seems that the real saddler of Bawtry was on his way to the gallows and adamantly refused to stop with his guards for a last drink, as was the custom in York in the 18th century. Passing the tavern by, he hurried to the gallows, where Jack Ketch quickly accommodated him. His pardon from the king arrived only a few minutes later.

Sadie Hawkins Day. In 1939 cartoonist Al Capp's comic strip *Li'l Abner* featured a race held on "Sadie Hawkins Day," in which single women chased bachelors, trying to win their love. The fictional day soon inspired real Sadie Hawkins Days all over America. Usually held in November, these Sadie Hawkins Days are days on which girls escort boys to dances and parties, or ask boys to escort them.

sadism. Marquis Donatien Alphonse François de Sade (1740–1814) seems to have emerged a full-blown "fanatic of vice," the "philosopher of vice," and *professeur de crime* that Michelet and Taine called him. When it happened, how it happened, would stymie a panel composed of Freud, Jung, Job, and the living Buddha. De Sade's upbringing was a factor, as were the licentious times in which he lived, his long years in prison, and perhaps there was even an organic problem. There is simply not enough reliable information available about de Sade—all his voluminous diaries were burned—and to try to make biography from a writer's fiction is fruitless. Sometimes his insights were deep and remarkable, but his was in the main a disordered, deranged mind reflected in his life and licentious work. Sadism, the derivation of satisfaction or pleasure from the infliction of pain on others, can be sexual in nature or stem from a variety of motives, including frustration or feelings of inferiority. De Sade's life indicates that many such causes molded his twisted personality. His final testament read in part: "The ground over my grave should be sprinkled with acorns so that all traces of my grave shall disappear so that, as I hope, this reminder of my existence may be wiped from the memory of mankind." *See also* MASOCHISM.

sad sack. The term *sad sack*, for "a maladjusted, blundering, unlucky soldier," likable but always in trouble, was widely popularized by George Baker's comic strip "Sad Sack," which appeared in several World War II military publications and later appeared in many newspapers. However, the words were American collegiate slang during the 1930s, their origin unknown.

safari. Safaris are getting back to the original meaning of the word. Once exclusively hunting trips into the African jungle complete with guns, they are now often sight-seeing excursions for camera-toting tourists more in keeping with the Arabic word *safara*, "travel," that is the root of *safari*.

safety bumps. *See* SLEEPING POLICEMEN.

saffron. Saffron costs about $400 a pound, making it one of the world's most expensive spices. This is primarily because it takes 4,000 blossoms of the autumn crocus (*Crocus sativus*), or 225,000 of its handpicked stigmas, to make one ounce of saffron. But luckily a little goes a long way, for the spice has been coveted by gourmets and lovers since the Arabs introduced it to Spain in the eighth century A.D. Even before then saffron was used by the Phoenicians to flavor the moon-shaped love cakes dedicated to Astoreth, their goddess of fertility. Today the spice is often called "vegetable gold." The old expression *he hath slept in a bed of saffron* refers to the supposed exhilarating effects of saffron, meaning "he has a very light heart." As an old poem puts it:

> With genial joy to warm his soul,
> Helen mixed saffron in the bowl.

See CROCUS.

sage (plant). *See* SALVIA.

sagebrush. *Artemisia tridentata* and several similar *Artemisia* species that grow wild on the plains and deserts and are a symbol of the American West. In *Roughing It* (1872), Mark Twain wrote, "... if the reader can imagine a gnarled and venerable live oak tree reduced to a little scrub two feet high, with its rough bark, its foliage, its twisted boughs, all complete, he can picture the 'sage-brush' exactly."

Sagebrush State. A popular nickname for Nevada, along with the Silver State. Nevada is called the Battle-Born State because it came into the Union during the Civil War, and, jocularly, the Divorce State because of Reno and Las Vegas, famous for quickie divorces.

Sahara. *Sahara* has become a synonym for any barren, lifeless place. The desert in northern Africa takes its name from the Arabic *cahra*, "desert," as if that is all that could be said about it.

sahib. *See* MEMSAHIB.

Sailor King; Clarence; Silly Billy. Because he served as a youth in the British navy, entering in 1779 as a midshipman when 15 and made lord high admiral 48 years later, William IV of England became known as the Sailor King. William had the Clarence, a closed four-wheel carriage, named after him when he was the duke of Clarence. Sad to say he was also known as Silly Billy during his reign (1830–37) because he often didn't take his duties seriously.

sail too close to the wind. An old nautical saying with a metaphoric extension, in this case meaning "to be reckless, take too many chances, risk losing everything."

sail under false colors. Pretending to be something you aren't, to be a hypocrite. These words have their roots in those pirate ships that at the moment of attack lowered their friendly or neutral flag and hoisted the deadly skull and crossbones. The unwritten law of the sea, of course, required that all ships display their true flags or colors so that they could be recognized as friend or foe, but the Jolly Roger was by its nature exempt.

sainfoin.   This perennial herb of the pea family is also called "holy clover" and has long been used as fodder, although it is sometimes planted in flower garden borders. It has among the most unusual of scientific names, *Onobrychis viciaefolia;* the genus name *Onobrychis* derives from the Greek for "food for asses," alluding to the plant's use for forage. Sainfoin, sometimes erroneously called "saintfoin," takes its name from the Latin *sanus,* "healthy," plus *foin,* "hay."

St. Barbara.   The ancients held that persons struck dead by lightning were incorruptible and honored them. However, many used charms to protect themselves against lightning. The Romans believed that the eagle, sea calf, and laurel warded off lightning, while people in medieval times grew houseleek on the roofs of houses to ward it off, Charlemagne ordering all his subjects to do so. People still invoke St. Barbara to protect themselves against lightning. She is the patron saint of those besieged by lightning because a lightning flash killed her father after he had tortured her and was about to lop off her head with a sword. *See* LIGHTNING NEVER STRIKES TWICE.

St. Bernard.   Men crossed the Alps between Switzerland and Italy centuries before St. Bernard de Menthon (923–1008) founded the shelter now called the Hospice of Great St. Bernard. But the house of refuge he built in 982 made it much easier for travelers to make pilgrimages to Rome through the Mons Jovis Pass, 8,098 feet above sea level and covered with snow 10 months of the year. St. Bernard, a wealthy French nobleman who renounced his fortune to become a man of God, was canonized in 1681. Perhaps 200 years before this the monks at this hospice had begun breeding the great dogs that are named after him and training them to track down and rescue travelers lost in blizzards and avalanches. The breed is said to be a cross between a bulldog and a Pyrenean shepherd dog or a Molossian hound, and it once had long hair believed to result from matings with the Newfoundland dog. The long hair was found to be a handicap in the snow, however, and a smooth-haired variety has been developed in relatively recent times. St. Bernards are still trained by the monks of the Alpine hospice. Measuring up to about six feet long, they are capable of carrying a man and are bred for intelligence and docility as well as strength. The breed is the world's heaviest dog, one specimen having reached a weight of 246 pounds. Numerous individual dogs have been honored as heroes, including the famous Barry, whose statue is in the St. Bernard Hospice. St. Bernards do not carry little kegs of brandy around their necks; this myth was the result of an early 1900s cartoon.

St. Boniface's cup.   Anyone who wants an excuse for an extra drink from time to time might do well to revive the custom of St. Boniface's cup. The expression derives from an indulgence granted by Pope Boniface VI or Pope Boniface I to anyone who drank to his good health. A St. Boniface's cup was long an excuse for another one of the same. The phrase is not related to *boniface,* for "an innkeeper," which we owe to the convivial

landlord of that name in the comedy *The Beaux' Strategem* (1707) by Irish playwright George Farquhar.

St. Elizabeth's flowers.   According to tradition, St. Elizabeth of Hungary gave so much food to the poor that her own household didn't eat well. Her husband suspected this and when he saw her leaving the house one day with her apron full of something, he demanded to know what she carried. "Only flowers, my lord," Elizabeth said, and God saved her lie by changing the loaves of bread in her apron to roses.

St. Elmo's fire.   Corposants are luminous discharges of electricity that extend into the atmosphere from projecting objects, their name deriving from the Portuguese *corpo santo,* "holy body." They are better known as St. Elmo's fire, and were believed by sailors to be a portent of bad weather. St. Erasmus, the patron saint of Neapolitan sailors, was a fourth-century Italian bishop whose name became corrupted to St. Elmo. An Italian legend tells us that he was rescued from drowning by a sailor and as a reward promised to ever after display a warning light for mariners whenever a storm was approaching. St. Elmo's fire does not involve enough discharge of electricity to be considered dangerous. The jets of fire are also seen on wings of aircraft, mountaintops, church steeples, on the horns of cattle, and blades of grass, and even around the heads of people, where it is said that they merely cause a tingling sensation. In ancient times St. Elmo's fire was called Castor and Pollux, for the twin sons of Zeus and Leda in Roman mythology, and a single burst of fire was called a Helen, for the twins' sister. A Helen was said to be a warning that the worst of a storm was yet to come, while two lights, Castor and Pollux, supposedly meant that the worst had passed. This has given rise to the theory that *St. Elmo* might be a corruption of *Helen* instead of *St. Erasmus.* Still another suggestion is that *St. Elmo* is a corruption of *St. Anselm* of Lucca.

St. Ignatius's bean.   The seed or bean of the woody vine *Strychnos ignatii* yields the deadly poison strychnine, which does have curative medical properties as well. All that is known about the bean's namesake is that he is one of seven saints named Ignatius, perhaps the Portuguese-born Jesuit Azevedo (1528–70), who may have come upon the plant in his travels. *Strychnine* itself is an old Greek name for a kind of nightshade, applied by Linnaeus to the 220 species of this genus because so many of them are poisonous. In the United States only one poisonous *Strychnos* species is found, the *Strychnos nux-vomica* or "strychnine tree" of extreme southern Florida, whose seeds yielded poisons for the arrows of Indians native to the area. A large strychnine tree specimen grows in New York's Brooklyn Botanic Garden.

St. Martin's Day; St. Martin's goose, etc.   After he became the patron saint of France, St. Martin's name formed the basis for a number of words. His feast day, Martinmas (Nov. 11) replaced the Roman Feast of Bacchus, retaining some of its customs, which probably accounts for the fact that he is regarded as the patron saint of bartenders, drunkards, and reformed drunkards as well. The phrase *Martin drunk,* "very drunk," also comes from St. Martin's association with the old pagan festival of *vinalia,* which noted the time when wines had reached their prime. St. Martin's goose was, according to legend, a bothersome goose that the saint ordered to be killed and served for dinner. Because he died while eating the meal, a St. Martin's bird was traditionally sacrificed every Martinmas. *St. Martin's summer*, like *St. Luke's summer* and *All Saints* (or All Hallow's) *summer*, is a European term for our *Indian summer*, the weather around November 11 often providing an unseasonable spell of warmth and pleasantness that was called *été de la Saint-Martin* by the French. The halcyon days of St. Martin's summer combine with St. Martin's goose in a strange way to give us the word *gossamer*. Due to its association with both the geese eaten on St. Martin's Day and throughout the season. St. Martin's summer came to be called "goose summer" in days past. At this time of the year fine, filmy cobwebs are often found floating lazily in the still air and these delicate "goose-summer webs" are the direct ancestors of *gossamer*, which can either be the webs themselves or fabrics like them.

St. Nicholas. *See* SANTA CLAUS.

St. Patrick's cabbage. Though native to Spain, Saint Patrick's cabbage (*Saxifrage umbrosa*) is found in the mountains of west Ireland as well, for which reason it is named for St. Patrick, archbishop of Armagh, the apostle of Ireland. This ornamental with crimson-spotted petals is also known as London Pride. St. Patrick is said to be responsible for the shamrock being the Irish national emblem. When captured by a pagan ruler while preaching in the country he plucked a shamrock and explained that its three leaves were distinct and separate on the plant, "just as the Trinity is the union of three distinct persons in One Deity."

Saintpaulia. The very popular African violet houseplant species are members of this genus of beautiful tropical African flowers. The genus is not named for a saint, however. It honors the German baron Walter von Saint Paul, who discovered one of the African violet species.

St. Peter's cock. *See* JOHN DORY.

St. Swithin's Day.

> St. Swithin's day if thou doest rain—
> For forty days it will remain;
> St. Swithin's day if thou be fair
> For forty days twill rain na mair—

These doggerel lines contain a well-known weather myth popular as early as the 12th century. The legend claims that St. Swithin, or Swithun, a ninth-century bishop of Winchester and counselor to King Egbert, had been buried in the churchyard outside the north wall of Winchester minster, where the "sweet rains of heaven might fall upon him as he wished and he be trodden under foot by those who entered the church." A century after his death it was decided that he should be canonized for miraculous cures he performed and his remains were to be reburied within the cathedral. The day was set, but as a miraculous sign of Bishop Swithin's displeasure, it began to rain on that day and rained for 40 days and 40 nights, causing the monks to abandon their plans. The date selected for his reinterment was July 15, 971, and July 15 has ever since been generally regarded as St. Swithin's Day.

St. Uncumber. St. Wilgefortes, who might be called the patron saint of unhappily married women, is a mythical saint, who, tradition says, prayed to grow a beard so that she could live her life "uncumbered with men." The prayer was granted and the ruse worked well until one of her enraged former lovers had her crucified. According to Sir Thomas More "women [later] changed her name [to St. Uncumber] because they reken that for a pecke of oats she will not faile to uncumber them of their husbondys."

St. Vitus's dance. *St. Vitus's dance*, or chorea, is named for the Roman St. Vitus, who became a martyr during the persecution of Christians by the Emperor Diocletian. In the 15th century it became customary for young people to dance frenetic dances around statues of St. Vitus to insure good health for the coming year. Soon, because of the nature of the wild dance, St. Vitus's aid was invoked against the nervous affliction most common among children and adolescents and the disease became popularly known as *St. Vitus's dance*.

salaam. The Arabs use this word, related to the Hebrew "peace," SHALOM, as a greeting, accompanying it with a low bow with the right palm held on the forehead. Thus in English to *salaam* someone came to mean to pay homage to someone.

salad days. Cleopatra, kidded by Charmian about her old love for Julius Caesar, joked that those were her *salad days* when she was "green in judgement, cold in blood." In other words she loved Caesar unskillfully and without much passion compared to the way she loved Mark Antony. Thus our expression for naive and inexperienced youth comes to us from Shakespeare's *Antony and Cleopatra*. The real Cleopatra was actually a flaming youth, a trained and artful lover before her adolescence, and the *salad days* that Shakespeare has her admit to were distant memories long before she married her brother at 17.

salad potatoes. *See* NEW POTATOES.

salary. *See* SALT.

Salem. The nine or 10 places around the world called Salem, including Salem, Massachusetts, might be called "Peace," for all take their name, ultimately, from the Hebrew *shalom*, or the Arabic *salaam*, both meaning "peace," or "wholeness," "welfare."

Salisbury steak; hamburger. *Hamburger* literally signifies an inhabitant of Hamburg, the great German seaport, the *Hamburg steak* originating there, but *Salisbury steak*, a hamburger without a bun, derives from the name of a 19th-century English physician, Dr. James H. Salisbury. Salisbury steak, as every Army veteran knows, is really something more, or less, than a hamburger. The "steak" part makes it look good on menus, but today it is usually either a well-done hamburger, or a combination of ground beef, eggs, milk and bread crumbs cooked in patties and drowned in a gooey gravy.

Salisbury steak started out as well-done hamburger alone. In 1888 Dr. Salisbury advised his patients to eat well-cooked ground beef three times a day, with hot water before and after each feast. This diet, the health faddist claimed over the laughter of his colleagues, would either cure or relieve pulmonary tuberculosis, hardening of the arteries, gout, colitis, asthma, bronchitis, rheumatism, and pernicious anemia.

During World War I and again in World War II, efforts were made to drive German loan words like *hamburger* out of the language, a *hamburger steak* becoming a *Salisbury steak* and a *hamburger* a *liberty sandwich*. These efforts by superpatriots didn't succeed. One suspects that *Salisbury steak* only survived because it made an excellent euphemism for hamburger. Certainly no one eats ground beef and hot water for health reasons anymore. *See also* GRAHAM CRACKERS; TARTAR SAUCE.

Salk vaccine; Sabin vaccine. The Salk vaccine is a vaccine composed of inactivated polio viruses used to immunize against polio (poliomyelitis). It was named after American virologist Jonas Edward Salk (1914–95), who developed this first effective killed-virus vaccine against the terrible viral disease (also called infantile paralysis) in 1954. American virologist Albert Sabin developed an oral vaccine, consisting of live polio viruses, at about the same time. Salk, a professor at the University of Pittsburgh, first tested his vaccine on a member of his own family. The Salk Institute for Biological Studies in San Diego is named in his honor.

sally a ship. A ship is sallied, or rolled, by assembling the crew all on one side, then signaling them to rush together to the other side. When the signal is repeated at certain intervals, the ship can be made to roll. In the age of sail, *sally* was also a common expression for the continuous rising and falling or the swinging or bounding motion of a ship at sea. The word derives from the Middle French *saillir*, "to rush forward," which comes from the Latin *salire*, "to leap."

Sally Bee. *See* SARAH BERNHARDT.

Sally Lunn. Sally Lunn used to cry out her wares in the streets of the then fashionable English resort city of Bath toward the end of the 18th century. Her basket was filled with slightly sweetened tea biscuits, which are still called Sally Lunns, although a number of cakes and breads also bear the name today. It took an enterprising baker and musician by the name of Dalmer to make Sally Lunn's buns universally known. Dalmer bought her recipe, built some portable ovens mounted on wheelbarrows to deliver Sally Lunns fresh, and even wrote a song about them. The song made the name a catchword that was still popular when nearly a century later a Gilbert and Sullivan character in *The Sorcerer* sang about "the gay Sally Lunn."

Sally Mae. *See* GINNIE MAE.

salmagundi. The origin of the word is really unknown. A *salmagundi*, "any mixture or miscellany," began as a mishmash of minced veal, chicken, or turkey, anchovies or pickled herring, and onions served with lemon juice and oil. One theory has it that the word comes from *salame condite*, Italian for "pickled meat"; another that it derives from the name of a lady-in-waiting to Marie de' Medici, wife of France's Henri IV. Marie is supposed to have invented the eclectic dish, or made it de rigueur at least, and named it after Madame or Mademoiselle Salmagundi, her lady-in-waiting. Later the word was used by Washington Irving for a series of 20 periodical pamphlets that

he and two other writers published (1807–08). *Salmagundi; or the Whim-Whams and Opinions of Launcelot Langstaff, Esq. and others*, consisted of satirical essays and poems on New York society and politics, generally satirizing "mobocratic" and "Logocratic" Jeffersonian democracy.

salmon. The often pink-fleshed fish (from the Latin *salmon*) gives its name to the color salmon, but the salmon's flesh doesn't have to be pink—in fact, it is frequently white. Nevertheless, many Americans believe that salmon should be pink to be good. Over half a century ago the legendary advertising genius Elmer Wheeler (he coined the slogan "Don't sell the steak—sell the sizzle") was hired by a West Coast salmon cannery to get people to eat the white variety and learn that it is just as tasty. Wheeler had new labels pasted on every can of the company's huge stock, each of them bearing the slogan: this salmon guaranteed not to turn pink in the can.

Salmonella. Salmon have no connection with *Salmonella* or *salmonellosis*. The latter is a form of food poisoning that can result in death and is caused by bacteria of the *Salmonella* genus, comprising some 1,500 species. The *Salmonella* genus was first identified by 19th-century American pathologist and veterinarian Daniel Elmer Salmon, who died in 1914. There are often outbreaks of salmonellosis, which is usually caused by infected and insufficiently cooked beef, pork, poultry, and eggs, as well as food, drink, or equipment contaminated by the excreta of infected animals. Nearly all animals are hospitable to the rod-shaped bacteria causing the acute gastroenteritis in humans, and food poisoning caused by them are almost as common as those caused by staphylococci. Incidentally, there is a "salmon disease" dogs and other animals get from eating salmon infested with cysts of flukes, but it has nothing to do with salmonellosis.

salt. In ancient times salt was highly valued, so much so that spilling salt became an unlucky omen among the Romans. Roman soldiers were in fact paid in salt, (*sal*) at one time, the origin of our word *salary*. Through the centuries a number of expressions reflected the importance of the precious seasoning and preservative. "Not worth his salt" referred to the salary the Romans paid their soldiers; "to eat a man's salt" meant to partake of his hospitality; and "to sit above the salt" was to sit in a place of distinction, above the saler, or saltcellar, at a medieval table. "The salt of the earth" is an even older saying, dating back to biblical times. In Matt. 5:13 the meek, the poor in spirit, the merciful, those persecuted for the sake of righteousness, the peacemakers, the pure of heart are told by Jesus that "Ye are the salt of the earth . . . Ye are the light of the world." The words are still a supreme compliment given to those we most admire as human beings.

salt a mine. To secretly stock a gold, silver, or diamond mine with ore or precious stones to make it appear valuable. The expression is said to derive from the practice of dishonest miners scattering a handful of salt, which is the color of gold dust, through mines they wished to sell to unwary investors.

salt horse. Beef or pork pickled in brine was often called *salt horse* on the New England coast and elsewhere. An old rhyme went:

"Old horse! old horse! what brought you here?"
"From Sacarap to Portland Pier
I've carted stone for many a year;
Till, killed by blows and sore abuse,
They salted me down for sailor's use.
The sailors they do me despise,
They turn me over and damn my eyes;
Cut off my meat and scrape my bones
And heave the rest to Davy Jones."

The "Sacarap" in the verse was a part of Westbrook, Maine, near Portland Pier, but the term *salt horse* is probably English in origin.

saltimbocca.   This Italian veal and ham dish looks so delicious that some poetic gastronome several centuries ago named it *saltimbocca:* "leaps into the mouth."

salt of the earth.   *See* SALT.

saluki.   Similar to the greyhound in appearance, the saluki is the oldest known breed of domesticated dog, excavations of the Sumerian empire finding its remains. The name of this hunting dog shows its place of origin, deriving from the Arabic *saluqiy,* meaning "of Saluq," an ancient city in southern Arabia.

salvia.   Some species of salvia have medical properties, causing the Romans to name the genus from the Latin *salveo,* "to save or heal." The flowers are also known as *sage,* which is a corruption of the French word *sauge,* for *salvia,* and *sage tea* has long been thought to have healing powers.

samarskite; samarium.   Russian engineer Col. M. von Samarski became one of the few men to have an element named after him, through an unusual set of circumstances. In 1857 a glasslike, velvet-black mineral was discovered in Russia and named samarskite in honor of this mine official. Twenty-two years later the scientist Lecoq de Boisbaudran found by means of the spectroscope that samarskite contained a new element. He named this samarium, after the mineral in which he discovered it. Thus the little-known engineer was commemorated, indirectly, in a way usually reserved for the famous. Samarium belongs to the rare-earth group and has little commercial importance, though it is used as a catalyst and in the ceramics industry. In about 1901 another element was discovered in samarskite, this called europium, after the continent.

sambo.   Blacks have probably been vilified with more slur names than any other group in history. All are, of course, disparaging and offensive, and this includes *sambo.* Ironically, the Little Black Sambo of the children's story who helped give the term widespread currency is really an East Indian, but *sambo* was with us long before the boy who melted the tiger to butter. Possibly of American origin, the term was introduced via the slave trade. The word, some believe, derives from the Kongo *nzambu,* "monkey," which became *zambo,* "bowlegged," in Spanish. Alternate choices are the Foulah *sambo,* "uncle," or the Hausan *sambo,* "second son." It may be that sambo simply comes from the name of a West African tribe called the Samboses, mentioned in European literature as early as 1564.

Sam Browne belt.   Born in India, Sir Samuel Browne, V.C. (1824–1901), served most of his military career there with the British army. Awarded the Victoria Cross and knighted for putting down the Indian Mutiny, a rebellion among native troops, he was promoted to general in 1888. Sometime during his long military career Browne invented the belt that bears his name. Designed originally as a sword belt that would support the weight of a sword smartly without sagging from the hips, it consisted of a belt with two auxiliary straps crossing over each shoulder. Later modified to one strap crossing from the left hip over the right shoulder—swords were worn on the left side—the Sam Browne belt became compulsory dress for all British officers and was widely adopted by armies throughout the world. It was declared optional in 1939, but is still seen today, especially as part of drill, band, and cadet uniforms.

the same dog bit me.   I feel the same way about it as you do. "Now you know," one of Marjorie Kinnan Rawlings's Floridian characters says in *The Yearling* (1938). "The same dog bit me." The author won the Pulitzer Prize for her novel in 1939.

Sam Hill.   If someone could locate any historical record of a Col. Samuel Hill of Guilford, Connecticut, we might find the origin of the phrase *go like Sam Hill* or *run like Sam Hill.* Edwin V. Mitchell makes mention of the man in the *Encyclopedia of American Politics* (1946). It seems that Colonel Hill perpetually ran for office—but no other evidence of his existence can be found. Since no one knows *who in the Sam Hill* he was, Sam Hill must remain "a personified euphemism our Puritan ancestors used for 'hell.' "

Samian letter.   *See* Y.

samoyed.   Samoyeds are working dogs resembling the chow, but their gentleness and intelligence make them highly valued pets. The dog takes its name from the Samoyed people, a nomadic race of Mongols only 7,000 or so in number living in northwest Siberia and gradually becoming extinct. The strong, heavy-coated samoyeds, usually white or cream colored, were developed for pulling sleds, hunting, and herding reindeer. Their masters are an interesting people who domesticate the reindeer and use it for riding as well as milking. The samoyed husky happens to be the most widely traveled of all dogs, one having gone along for the space ride in 1957 aboard the Russian *Sputnik II,* which attained an altitude of 1,050 miles. In Russian the breed is called *laika.*

samphire.   The seacoast plants were originally called *l'herbe de Saint Pierre* (the herb of St. Peter) in French, but over the centuries English tongues corrupted this to *samphire.*

Samson.   Just as Delilah's name symbolized treachery, Samson's symbolizes strength. The biblical Samson slew a thousand men with the jawbone of an ass and performed various other prodigious feats as recorded in Judges 13–17. Samson's Achilles' heel was not so much his hair as his weakness for Philistine women, and he met his match in Delilah, who cut off his long locks, in which his strength or soul resided. After his betrayal by Delilah to the Philistines, Samson's eyes were gouged out and he was brought down to Gaza. Eyeless in Gaza, he performed his last heroic deed when the Philistines tried making sport of him; he pulled down the temple of Dagon on his tormentors and himself. Samson's name has been used for weight lifters and strongmen since at least May 28, 1741, when Thomas Topham was called the British Samson.

sand. The old term *sand*, for "grit or courage," probably comes from the expression *sand in his craw*, used by Mark Twain in *Huckleberry Finn* (1884). "Sand in his craw" refers to the belief that a chicken that eats a little sand has more endurance than a chicken that doesn't.

Sandbox. A name used to describe the Middle East at the time of the 9/11 war, though the term may date back to the Gulf War of 1991, or perhaps earlier.

sand carpet. A carpet made of sand, with unusual colors such as blue and black, that was used in early American parlors. Housewives often drew designs and pictures in the sand, which were renewed again after company called and left.

sand in my shoes. Said by or of people who have spent their lives in a seaside community. The expression dates back to at least the late 19th century in the U.S. and is usually heard as *I've got sand in my shoes*.

sandlot baseball. Since the early 20th century, *sandlot baseball* has meant unorganized baseball games played by youngsters or loosely organized leagues of semiprofessional players. The term *sandlot* was made popular in 1880 by San Francisco's Sand-lot Party of workingmen, who held their meetings in vacant sand lots. *Sandlot* is also used as a synonym for anything amateur, though not so often as *bush league* or *bush*.

sandman. The U.S. personification of sleepiness, especially for children, a mythical man who puts sand in the eyes of youngsters to make them sleepy. Often parents tell kids, "The sandman is coming." The term originated in the mid-19th century; counterparts in other countries include Olaf Shuteye, Scandanavian, and Wee Willie Winkie, Scottish.

sandstorm. A phenomenon of the southwestern desert. Wrote J. Frank Dobie in *Coronado's Children* (1930): "A man caught in a sandstorm cannot see his hand . . . The yarn goes that a cowboy awoke one morning to find his horse standing on top of a mesquite tree instead of under it where he had staked him."

sandwich. At 5 A.M. on August 6, 1762, John Montagu, fourth earl of Sandwich, looked up from the gaming table and decided that he was hungry. The earl, an inveterate gambler in the midst of one of his famous round-the-clock sessions, didn't dare leave his cards for a meal and ordered his man to bring him some cold, thick-sliced roast beef between two pieces of toasted bread. Thus the first sandwich was born. The Romans had a similar repast called *offula* before this, and it is said that the refreshment was first invented when in about 100 B.C. Hillel ate bitter herb and unleavened bread as part of the Jewish Passover meal, symbolizing man's triumph over life's ills. But the modern sandwich, our convenient quick lunch or snack and an important source of nourishment in this frenetic age, defi-

nitely evolves from those mighty gambling sessions, some lasting 48 hours and more, in which the dissolute earl passionately participated. Gambling was one of John Montagu's lesser vices, but the earl has as many words honoring him as any politician, another example being the beautiful Sandwich Islands (Hawaii) that Captain James Cook named after him because the earl headed the British admiralty during the American Revolution and outfitted the great explorer's ship.

sandwich generation. A term coined about 2001 meaning the generation that is presently sandwiched between the responsibilities of raising their children and caring for their elderly parents.

Sanforize. The patented process of sanforizing cotton and other fabrics to resist shrinkage by mechanical compression of the fibers was developed by the Troy, New York shirt manufacturing firm George B. Cluett Brothers & Co. and named in honor of Sandford L. Cluett (1874–1968), the firm's longtime director of research. The term is a trademark.

sanguine. This word's actual meaning is "bloody," or the color of blood, from the Latin *sanguis*, blood, but it came to be applied to any ruddy-cheeked person, whose cheeks were red with good health. By extension it finally took on the meaning of someone vital, full of life, confident, and hopeful.

San Jose; San Juan; San Antonio; San Francisco. These, of course, are the names of three cities in the United States and one (San Juan) in Puerto Rico. They also have the distinction of being the four leaders in North and South America among places named after saints: San Jose is the name of 429 places, San Juan 365, San Antonio 337, and San Francisco 275. Sometimes these cities aren't named for the same saint, however. One apocryphal story has a construction worker falling from the 10th floor of a building. "San Antonio!" he cries as he passes the seventh floor and, miraculously, he remains suspended in air a few instants. "Which San Antonio?" a sepulchral voice asks. "San Antonio de Padua!" the worker cries. "That's not me," the voice says, and the worker plummets toward the ground below.

Sanka. Sanka, a brand of decaffeinated coffee, is a trademark, and must be capitalized. The name of the product, first marketed in 1903, was coined from the French *san*(s) *ca*(ffeine), "without caffeine."

San Marino. Reputedly the world's oldest republic, San Marino, located on the Italian peninsula, is said to have been founded in the fourth century A.D. by Marinus, a Christian stonecutter. Marinus was later canonized as Saint Marinus, or San Marino, and the republic was named after him.

sannup. A young married Indian male, the term deriving from a Maine Abnaki Indian word for a young man. *Sannup* can also mean a mischievous boy always getting into trouble. The word dates back to 17th-century America.

sans-culottes. French supporters of the French Revolution in 1789 were called *sans-culottes*, which literally translates as "without breeches." But the term has nothing to do with nudity.

The revolutionaries went without the knee breeches that the royalists wore. These *sans-coulettes* wore trousers or long pants, which soon became popular everywhere. Many held out, however. In America George Washington, John Adams, and Thomas Jefferson all wore knee breeches, despite their revolutionary faith. James Madison was the first U.S. president to wear trousers.

Santa Ana. Strong, hot, dusty winds that descend from inland desert regions to the Pacific Coast in the area of Los Angeles. Sometimes said to be named for Mexican general Antonio López de Santa Anna (or Ana) (1795–1876) who commanded Mexican forces at the Alamo and who, legend has it, later introduced chewing gum to the United States when he brought chicle here from Central America. More likely, the winds are named for the Santa Ana Canyon of Southern California.

Santa Claus. Yes, Virginia, there was a Santa Claus, a real one—probably. The custom of giving presents at Christmas is based on the legend that St. Nicholas—a bishop of Myra in Asia Minor during the fourth century—gave secret dowries to three sisters who could not have been married otherwise and would have been sold into prostitution if it hadn't been for his generosity. Nicholas, the story goes, was out walking one night when he heard the three sisters crying behind their curtained window. On being told that their poor father could find no husbands for them and had to sell them to a brothel, our Santa Claus dug into his coat and threw three bags of gold to them, disappearing into the night before their father could thank him. A twist on the tale has the bishop turning three brass balls into bags of gold, which is appropriate for the patron saint of pawnbrokers. St. Nicholas is also the patron saint of the Russian Orthodox church, Greece, Sicily, Aberdeen, scholars, travelers, sailors, thieves, and children, among other groups. Despite the lack of historical facts about him, he is no doubt the basis for our Santa Claus. The eve of his feast day, December 6, is a children's holiday when gifts are given in the Netherlands and elsewhere, the custom calling for someone to dress up as St. Nicholas and present the gifts. The English who settled in New York borrowed both the saint and this custom from the earlier Dutch settlers, moving his day to Christmas, their own gift-giving day, and corrupting his name from the Dutch dialect *Sint Klaas* to *Santa Claus. See* FATHER CHRISTMAS.

sap. Green, unseasoned wood is often full of sap, and so young, inexperienced foolish people have been called sapheads or sapskulls since the 17th century. By 1815, its first recorded usage, *sap* had succeeded *saphead* for a *cabbagehead* (1622). *Calabash* (1838), *pumpkin head* (1841) and *chump* (1883) are all similar agriculture-related words for "jingle-brained nincompoops."

Sapphism. *See* LESBIAN.

Sappho. The original Sappho was a great woman poet of ancient Greece as well as a LESBIAN. Other poets honored with the name include:

- *The English Sappho*—Mary Wortley Montagu (1689–1762, so named by Alexander Pope)
- *The English Sappho*—Mary D. Robinson (1758–1800)
- *The French Sappho*—Mlle. Scudéry (1607–1701)
- *The Scotch Sappho*—Catherine Cockburn (1679–1749)
- *Sappho of Toulouse*—Clémence Isaure (ca. 1450–1510)

Sarah Bernhardt. "The divine Sarah," as Oscar Wilde called her, is regarded by many as the greatest actress of all time. Born Henriette Rosine Bernard, the daughter of Jewish parents who converted to Catholicism, she was brought up in a convent until she entered the Paris Conservatoire at 13. After making her debut at the Comédie-Française in 1862, she played internationally, winning her great fame in tragic roles largely because of her "voice of gold" and magnetic personality. Probably the tallest, thinnest woman ever to star on the stage (Arthur "Bugs" Baer once wrote, "An empty cab drove up, and Sarah Bernhardt got out"), her nickname Sally Bee became the nickname for any tall thin woman, just as her name is a synonym for a great actress.

sarcasm. Thomas Carlyle noted in *Sartor Resartus: The Life and Opinions of Herr Teufelsdrockh* (1833–34) that he saw sarcasm to generally be "the language of the devil." The word came to us in the late 16th century from Greek *sarkázein*, "to rent or tear flesh, to sneer," the Greeks equating biting a person with speaking harshly, bitterly, or derisively. *See* SARDONIC, CYNIC.

sarcophagus. A coffin made of stone that rests above ground and is often decorated with sculpture. The word derives from the Greek *sarkophagos*, "eating flesh," especially in the term *lithos sarkophagos*, which described a limestone the Greeks believed decomposed the corpses laid in it. The Greek word later was used for any stone coffin and took this meaning after it passed into English via Latin in the 17th century. *See* TATTOO.

Sardanapalian; Sardanaplan. The dissolute Assyrian king Ashurbanipal was probably the prototype of Sardanapalus, the semilegendary king of Greek fable whose name has become a synonym for effeminate luxury. King Ashurbanipal lived in the seventh century B.C., the Greeks calling him Sardanapalus because his real name was a difficult one for them to pronounce. It is hard to separate fable from fact concerning Sardanapalus, but he does not deserve the designation "effeminate." Rather he appears to have been a shrewd military strategist and bloodthirsty tyrant who reigned for over 40 years, beginning in 658 B.C., and conquered Babylon, parts of Egypt, the Medes and Persians. But as he grew older, Sardanapalus surrounded himself with luxuries, his philosophy, it is said, summed up in a monument he had erected in the city of Anchiale. Its inscription read: "Sardanapalus the king . . . In one day built Anchiale and Tarsus. Eat, drink and love, the rest's not worth this!" The epicure retired to his magnificent palace filled with tempera paintings, woven carpets, and furniture inlaid with gold. Locked up with his wives and concubines, he devoted himself to sensual pleasure. So the legend goes anyway. We only know for certain that the virile king, last of the great Assyrian monarchs, was depicted as effeminately hedonistic by Greek writers under the name Sardanapalus and that he became famous for living in great luxury. Lord Byron helped this misconception along with his poem "Sardanapalus" (1821) in which he wrote: "And femininely meanth furiously. Because all passions in excess are female."

sardonic. A sardonic person might be called a dead one, inside and out. The ancient Greeks believed that the *sardone* (*herba Sardonia* in Latin), a poisonous plant native to Sardinia that gave the island its name, was so deadly that anyone unlucky or foolish enough to eat it would immediately succumb to its effects. Victims were said to literally die laughing, going into convulsions, their final contorted expressions after these death throes resembling bitter, scornful grins. The Greeks called their last bitter appearance of laughter *Sardonios gelos*, "Sardinian laughter," *Sardo* being their name for the island. *Sardonios gelos* became the French *rire sardonique*, this resulting in our *sardonic laughter* and *sardonic*, laughter or humor characterized by bitter or scornful derision.

Sardoodledum. French playwright Victorien Sardou (1831–1908) was born to great wealth, but when his family lost its fortune, he descended into poverty he could not have imagined. Sardou was found near death of typhoid fever in a garret, covered only by a pile of rejected play manuscripts. The woman who found him nursed him back to health, and he later married her. He became one of the most successful playwrights of his day, writing many vehicles for Sara Bernhardt, but his well-made, often contrived, shallow plays led George Bernard Shaw to coin the word *Sardoodledum* for such dramas.

Sargasso Sea. The relatively calm sea in the North Atlantic is named for the seaweed in it, not the other way around. *Sargasso* is the Portuguese name for the weed and the incredible tales of Sargasso weed choking the sea and holding ships captive forever were probably invented by the ancient Phoenecians to keep Greek ships away. The seaweed is also called gulfweed. *See* SEAWEED.

sarsaparilla. True sarsaparilla (*Smilac officinalis*) is related to the asparagus but isn't widely cultivated in the United States. The same legends surround its roots as surround asparagus; Mexican Indians, for example, have long used the roots of the vine in a concoction they believe cures impotence. In 1939 it was discovered that the sarsaparilla root contains large amounts of testosterone, and today much of the male sex hormone manufactured commercially comes from the plant. *See* ASPARAGUS.

Sartoris. An old-order family of southern aristocrats featured in William Faulkner's *Sartoris* (1929) and other novels. Throughout Faulkner's work, the Sartoris clan, whose name has become a synonym for southern aristocracy, tries to withstand the rise of the venal Snopeses, who have little history and are "just Snopeses, like colonies of rats or termites are just rats and termites." *See* SNOPESISM; WALL STREET PANIC.

sartorius. The longest muscle of the human anatomy, the thigh muscle called the *sartorius* takes its name from the Latin *sartor*, tailor. It is so called because the muscle is important in making possible the traditional cross-legged position of the tailor.

sashimi. Another Japanese word that has recently come intact into the English vocabulary. *Sashimi* means thinly sliced raw fish, which is eaten that way, often with sauces and seasonings.

saskatoon. Another Native American word that passed into English. The berry-bearing North American shrub (*Amelanchier alnifolia*) takes its name from the Cree Indian *misaaskwatoomin* for the fruit of the plant.

sass. The word *sass* is still used to refer to stewed fruit or fresh vegetables in sections of the United States, as is "garden sass." The word, first recorded around 1760, originally meant garden vegetables: "Short sass" was potatoes, onions, or turnips; "long sass" was carrots, parsnips, and other vegetables. *Sass*, which is probably an American alteration of "sauce," didn't acquire its more common meaning of "backtalk" until about the middle of the 19th century. This meaning possibly has something to do with the "freshness" of both long and short sass.

sassafrass. Folklore holds that the genus of small plants called *Saxifrage* (from the Latin *saxum*, "rock," and *frangere*, "to break") is so named because the plant was valued by the ancients as a medicine to break up kidney stones. However, the genus probably got its name because the plants grow naturally in the clefts of rocks and could be imagined to have broken them. A plant that definitely was helpful in the fight against kidney stones is *sassafras*. The Romans drank a concoction made of sassafras tree bark (*Sassafras albidum*) to break up stones in the bladder, which is why its name means "stonebreaker." Sassafras tea, a stimulant and diuretic, is also made from the tree's bark, and sassafras oil, used in flavoring, perfume, and medicine, is made from its roots.

satan. The Hebrew word *satan*, meaning "adversary," in the Old Testament usually denotes a human adversary, but in places (*e.g.*, Job 1:6–12) it designates an angelic being who torments man with the knowledge or direct authority of Jehovah. *Satan* has been the English proper name of the supreme evil spirit, the devil, since at least the year 900. *See also* OLD NICK.

Satchel Paige's rules. *See* DON'T LOOK BACK, SOMETHING MIGHT BE GAINING ON YOU.

satin. One might expect this smooth, glossy fabric to have a glamorous story behind its name, but it was apparently a place name originally. Arab traders named it *zaituni*, "cloth from Zaitun," this last word their name for the Chinese city of Zayton (now called Chuanzhou).

Saturday. Saturn was the Roman god of time and planting, the Romans naming the seventh day of the week *Saturni dies*, the day of Saturn, after him. This became the Anglo-Saxon *saterdaeg*, and finally our *Saturday*.

Saturday's child. *See* MONDAY'S CHILD.

satyagraha. Literally meaning "a grasping for truth" in Hindi, this Indian word has come to stand for the nonviolent "passive resistance" of Mohandas Gandhi, which the Mahatma practiced until his assassination in 1948 and which has been emulated by many other great leaders since then.

satyr. Alexander the Great had a dream about this word at the time when he was trying in vain to capture the city of Tyre and was about to abandon his campaign. Alexander dreamed he had captured a satyr. His advisers told him that the word *satyros* (satyr in Greek) in his dream was really *Sa Tyros*, "Tyre is his!" and he attacked and captured the city. In any case, our word *satyr* derives from the Greek word for the mythical woodland gods or demons who were the companions of Bacchus. First recorded in English by Chaucer, *satyr* came to mean a lascivious man. *Satyress* is a little-used word for "a female satyr," first recorded in 1840.

sauce Mornay. *See* MORNAY SAUCE.

sauce Robert. This mouth-watering French sauce, which took hours to prepare in its original form, has been credited to Robert Vinot, an early-17th-century sauce maker of whom nothing else is known. But Rabelais described the sauce earlier and it could not have been invented by Vinot, although he may have improved it and given it his name. Still in use today, the ancient sauce is made with white wine, beef gravy, onion, mustard, butter, and salt.

Saudi Arabia. In 1926, Ibn Saud, 46, became the first king of the territory later named Saudi Arabia. Ibn Saud had helped his father and the Saudi family, of the Wahabis sect of Islam, drive rivals from the city of Riyadh and capture the holy city of Mecca. His father was so impressed that he abdicated in favor of his imposing six-foot, four-inch, 240-lb. son. In 1932, Ibn Saud, a wise benevolent monarch who began modernizing the country, named the new nation after his family.

sausage. *Sausage* comes ultimately from the Latin word *salus*, meaning salted or preserved. This meat treat was invented centuries ago by the Chinese, but the planetary record for the biggest sausage ever made was long held by bakers in Scunthorpe, England. Some years ago they reportedly made the Great Scunthorpe Sausage from this recipe: "Take up 738 pounds of ground pork and work in cereal to extend the mixture to 896 pounds. Take salt, pepper and sage and season to taste. Blend into mixture and force into 3,124 feet of sausage casing (pig intestines). Will serve 6,248." However, today *The Guinness Book of World Records* (1998) gives the title to a Canadian butcher shop that in 1995 made a "continuous sausage" 28.77 *miles* long.

sauterne. This sweet white wine was first recorded in English (1711) as *sauternes*, coming from the Sauternes district near Bordeaux. But since the late 18th century it has commonly been spelled *sauterne* in both England and the U.S.

savage. The Latin *silvaticus* (from *silva*, "forest" or "man of the forest") became the Old French *sauvage*, which came into English as *savage* early in the 14th century.

savarin. *See* BRILLAT-SAVARIN.

Save a sailor! According to an 18th-century superstition, when a glass "rings" in a bar or at a table, a sailor will be drowned—unless a finger is placed on the glass to stop the ringing and someone cries out, "Save a sailor!"

saved by the bell. An expression first used in boxing, *saved by the bell* means to be rescued from something at the last moment. It originally described a fighter about to be counted out when the bell rings ending the round, saving him at least for another round. This practice became mandatory under the Queensberry rules, introduced in 1867.

saving face. *See* LOSING FACE.

savings bank. Although the term *savings bank* is now used to identify a bank that receives primarily the savings of individuals, as opposed to a commercial bank that caters to businesses, the words were first used to describe a child's bank made to save coins. These became popular in the United States after the Civil War, when small coins became popular; before then merchant tokens, certificates, and stamps had been more commonly used. The savings banks were fashioned in many shapes, including the ubiquitous PIGGY BANK.

saw. The name for this tool perhaps derives ultimately from the Latin *secare*, "to cut," its first use in England occurring before A.D. 1000. Legend has it that the saw was invented when Perdix, the nephew of Daedalus, picked up the spine of a fish while walking on the seashore and imitated it by notching a long piece of iron on its edge. According to legend, Perdix also invented the compass. The jealous Daedalus tried to push him off a high tower, but the goddess Minerva, favoring ingenuity, changed him into a bird as he fell, and that bird was called the partridge after his name. *See* PARTRIDGE.

sawbuck. Our word *sawbuck* for a sawhorse ("in which two supports at each end cross each other and so form a rack for holding that which is sawed") derives from either the Dutch *zaagbok* or the German *Sägebock*, both meaning the same. *Sawbuck* is also slang for a 10-dollar bill. First attested in 1850, it is so named because the Roman numeral X for 10 resembles the x-shapes on each end of the sawbuck.

sawed-off shotgun. A shotgun with its barrels sawed off short; the gun was first used by express messengers in the West.

saxophone. While working in his father's renowned musical instrument workshop in Brussels, 1840–44, Antoine-Joseph Sax invented a series of valved brass wind instruments with a new tone quality. These he named the *sax-horn* (which his father Charles actually invented and he improved upon); the *saxophone*; the *saxtromba*; and the *sax-tuba*. Antoine-Joseph, often called Adolphe, left his 10 brothers and sister in Brussels and journeyed to Paris to make his fortune with his inventions. Sax made many influential friends among musicians, including Hector Berlioz, and they helped him to borrow money for a workshop and to promote his innovative instruments. The most lasting of his inventions proved to be the saxophone, although he thought of it as merely a bass instrument, unaware of its true potential. The inventor received many awards in his lifetime, but a poor business sense prevented him from making the fortune he set out to make. He died in 1894, aged 80, just before the *saxophone*, or *sax*, achieved a major role in modern bands.

say it ain't so, Joe. They said "Shoeless Joe" Jackson, a poor boy from South Carolina, played ball without shoes down home, but he put on spikes when he made the majors and became a great star, his lifetime average of .356 the third highest in the history of baseball. Shoeless Joe never made Cooperstown's Hall of Fame, though, and never will. Jackson was one of the eight Chicago White Sox players who conspired with gamblers to throw the 1919 World Series, after which he was banished from baseball for life. After confessing his role in the affair on September 28, 1920, Jackson walked down the steps of the Cook County Courthouse through a crowd of reporters and a ragged little boy grabbed his sleeve and said "Say it ain't so, Joe." The phrase is still used in reference to any hero who has betrayed his trust, though Jackson denied that the boy said it. *See* BLACK BETSY.

say it with flowers. *See* FLOWER.

sayonara. *Sayonara* has become part of America's vocabulary since after World War II, when thousands of G.I.'s were stationed in Japan. But few knew that this is one of the most poignant words for good-bye, its literal translation from the Japanese being "If it must be so."

Say's Law. Says Say's Law: In a capitalist economy "the demand for products is equal to the sum of the products." Formulated by the French economist Jean-Baptiste Say (1767–1832) in his *Traité d'économie politique* (1803), the theory holds that "a nation always has the means of buying all it produces," and a "general glut" of products on the market is impossible, though there can be overproduction of one or more commodities.

scabiosa. Not a very nice name for a pretty flower, *scabiosa* derives from the Latin word *scabies*, for "itch." The plant was used by the ancients as a cure for certain skin diseases.

scalawag. Undersized, lean, undeveloped cattle that were of little use were called scalawags by American ranchers and farmers in the West toward the middle of the 18th century. The term then came to be applied to disreputable people, rogues, scoundrels, rascals, those who refused to work, and had a special use in the South after the Civil War to describe anyone willing to accept Reconstruction. As for *scalawag* itself, the word remains something of a mystery. It may derive from the Gaelic *sgalag*, for "a lowly servant or rustic," but more likely comes from *Scalloway*, one of the Shetland Islands that is known for its dwarf ponies and cattle, which could have been considered worthless. Other suggestions are the Scottish *scurryvaig*, "a vagabond"; the Latin *scurra vagas*, "a wandering buffoon"; and the English dialect *scall*, "skin-disease." No one seems to know why the word, with so many possible British derivations, is first recorded in America.

scallion. Crusaders returning from the Holy Land probably introduced the word *scallion* to Europe. These small onions were raised in the Palestinian seaport of Ascalon, now just ancient ruins, and had been named *Ascalonia caepa*, "Ascalonion onion," by the Romans. This was shortened to *scalonia* in the common speech of the Romans and passed into English as *scalyon*, which finally became *scallion*. *See also* ONION.

scalp. To remove the scalp of the head, along with the accompanying hair, from the heads of enemies as a sign of victory, a practice of some Indians and whites during the colonial and frontier periods of U.S. history.

scam. *Scam*, for "a scheme to swindle, rob, or deceive," seems to have originated as carnival talk late in the 19th century. Possibly a variant of "scheme," it may also derive from the British slang *scamp*, meaning to rob a person on the highway, which dates back to the 18th century, or to the British slang *scamp*, meaning a cheat or swindler, recorded in the early 19th century and obsolete by about the time *scam* was born.

Scandahoovian. A humorous, mildly derogatory name for a Scandinavian. It is first recorded over a century ago in the American Midwest. *See* NORSKIE.

Scandinavian words in English. The Vikings, who conquered nearly half of England, the Danelagh, and were later absorbed into the population, contributed thousands of words to the English language—at least 1,500 places in England have Scandinavian names. Words that we owe to their northern Germanic language include: steak, knife, law, gain, birth, dirt, fellow, guess, leg, loan, seat, sister, slaughter, thrift, trust, want, window, flat, ill, loose, low, odd, tight, weak, call, die, egg, get, lift, rid, same, scare, though, till, both, husband, skin, hit, happy, rotten, ugly, wrong, and fell.

a Scarborough warning. To strike someone first and warn him about his behavior afterward. The expression dates back to 1557, when Thomas Stafford captured Scarborough Castle in Yorkshire and *then* ordered all the inhabitants to leave the town.

scarcer than hen's teeth. Nothing is scarcer because not even Ripley has found a hen with even a single tooth. The Americanism, which also means nonexistent, probably goes back to Colonial days, though it was first recorded in 1862.

scarecrow. *See* CROWHERD.

scarlet Indian. John Josselyn explained this term in his *Account of Two Voyages to New England* (1674): "[Any woman] suffering an Indian to have carnal knowledge of her [was forced to] wear the figure of an Indian cut out of red cloth." *See also* SCARLET LETTER.

scarlet letter. The first mention of people being forced to wear a scarlet capital letter *A* that branded one as an adulterer is reported in the *Plymouth Colonial Records* (1639): "The Bench doth therefore censure the said Mary . . . to wear a badge upon her left sleeve." The letter *I* was used for those found guilty of incest. *See also* SCARLET INDIAN.

scatology. *Scatology* derives from a Greek word meaning "dung knowledge" and is used in pathology to mean "diagnosis by a study of feces." It is commonly applied today to obscene or bawdy literature, films, and dramatic performances.

scavenger's daughter. Like the earlier EXETER'S DAUGHTER, this vicious instrument of torture was introduced by an officer of the Tower of London. It consisted of wide iron manacles on which screws were tightened until the victim's head was clamped so tightly to his knees that blood was forced from his nose and ears, and sometimes from his hands and feet. Invented by Sir William Skeffington, lieutenant of the Tower during the reign of Henry VIII, it was first called *Skeffington's gyres*, or *irons*, and came to be called jocularly the *scavenger's daughter*, which both insulted the inventor and was more descriptive.

the scene opens.   These words have been used to mark the beginning of a play or a scene in a play since at least 1673, when they were recorded in Elkanah Settle's melodrama *The Empress of Morocco*. It is also written as "the scene is opened."

scenery-chewing.   Acting melodramatically, overacting, a term dating back in the theater to the 18th century, as in "Caspar W. Weinberger is played by the always superb Colin Feore . . . with an understated realism that stands out among much scenery-chewing."

Schadenfreude.   A German word that is part of many English vocabularies, *Schadenfreude* means "joy gotten from someone else's misfortune." Deriving from German *Schaden*, "harm," plus *Freude*, "joy," the word came into English about 1890, apparently filling a need.

schedule.   This word is often pronounced "shedyule" or something similar by the British and "skedule" or something similar by Americans. One story has an affected American actor entertaining a circle of admirers at a party that included the inimitable American wit Dorothy Parker. The actor kept advising his sycophants of how busy he was, continually referring to his crowded schedule, which he pronounced "shedyule" in the British manner. "If you don't mind my saying so," an annoyed Miss Parker finally said, "I think you are full of skit."

Schenectady.   An old joke has it that the town of Schenectady, New York, was so named after a raiding party of French colonials and Iroquois Indians massacred 60 English residents of the town in February 1690. The town's name, according to the story, comes from an Indian word meaning "skin neck today." The massacre did occur, but there is no such Indian word and the origin of *Schenectady* is unknown.

Schicklgruber.   *See* FÜHRER.

Schick test.   While a professor of pediatrics at the University of Vienna in 1913, Dr. Bela Schick devised the famed *Schick test*, a skin test to determine susceptibility to diphtheria. His test consists of injecting diphtheria toxin into a person's skin, the skin becoming red and swollen if the person is not immune. Dr. Schick, born in Hungary, immigrated to the United States in 1923, becoming a naturalized citizen six years later. A pediatrician for many years at New York's Mount Sinai Hospital, he did important work on allergies, wrote several books on child care, and helped found the American Academy of Pediatrics. He died in 1967, aged 90.

Schillerlocken.   *Schillerlocken*, a German fish dish named after the hair of a poet, is curled chips of smoked fish commemorating the curly locks of the poet Johann Christoph Friedrich von Schiller. Schiller (1759–1805) was one of the founders of modern German literature; only Johann von Goethe overshadowed him in his time. Schiller was a great favorite of the German people, and the wide popularity of his works led to the affectionate word made from his surname and *Locken* ("curl").

Schindler.   Oskar Schindler's name has come to mean someone who risked his life to save Jews from the Nazi concentration camps. Schindler (1908–74) was a German manufacturer who in 1944 employed Jews in his Cracow enamelware factory and his armaments factory in Czechoslovakia, saving the lives of over 1,200. Later, the movie *Schindler's List* (1993) made him famous. His name has wide currency. For instance, the Japanese diplomat Chiune Sugihara, who risked his life to save more than 10,000 Jews fleeing Germany, has been called the Japanese Schindler.

schipperke.   The breed of small dogs with thick black coat and erect ears takes its name from the Dutch word for "little boatman" or "skipper." The dogs were once commonly used as watchdogs aboard ships in the Netherlands and Belgium.

schizocarp.   The "wings" or "helicopters" on maple trees that spin like pinwheels when you toss them into the wind, and which you may have attached to your nose when you were a kid, are technically called schizocarps. *Schizo* means "split," and the scientific definition for a schizocarp is "a dry dehiscent fruit that at maturity splits into two or more one-seeded carpels." "Wings," or "helicopters," is better.

schlemiehl; schlemihl.   Nothing ever turns out right for the awkward and unlucky *schlemiehl*. The word, by now common American slang, comes from the Yiddish *shelumiel*, "one who is worthless," which is said to derive from the name of the first Shelumiel mentioned in the Bible. Shelumiel appears four times in the Book of Numbers as the son of Zurishaddai and the leader of the tribe of Simeon. Nothing is said about him except that he is the leader of 59,300 people and makes an appropriate offering for the dedication of the altar at the Lord's command, but it has been suggested that Shelumiel lost in battle all the time while the other tribal leaders were victorious. Be that as it may, the word *schlemiehl* got a boost from the allegorical tale *Peter Schlemihls Wunderbare Geschichte* (The wonderful story of Peter Schlemihl), written by the German botanist and poet Adelbert von Chamisso in 1814. In the story the impecunious Peter Schlemihl makes a foolish bargain with the devil, selling his shadow for a never-empty purse and finding himself an outcast from human society because he has no shadow. Through this story, which was translated into many languages and virtually became legend, *schlemihl* came to mean anyone making a foolish bargain, both living a life of its own and reinforcing the meaning of the earlier *schlemiehl*.

schlep.   This Yiddish word has become part of the American vocabulary, meaning either "to lug around" (He schlepped the package all the way from Jersey), or "to move in a slow, awkward, or tedious manner."

schmaltz. In Yiddish *schmaltz*, from the German *smaltz*, is chicken fat, a common, sticky, and greasy substance that gives its name to anything common and stickily sentimental.

schmo; shmoo. Though some authorities mark its origins unknown, this word for a stupid, foolish, or boring person, first recorded in about 1945, may be a shortened euphemism for the stronger, obscene Yiddish word *shmuck*, which can mean either a jerk or a detestable man. The word became popular at about the time cartoonist Al Capp created an egg-shaped, much-abused creature called a *shmoo* for his comic strip *L'il Abner*.

schmuck. One wouldn't think *schmuck* is an obscene word, judging by its common use in America. *Schmuck* is Yiddish for "penis," deriving somehow from a German word meaning "ornament," and has come to mean a stupid, obnoxious person, of whom there are apparently enough to make *schmuck* one of the best-known Yiddish expressions.

schnauzer. Bred for over five centuries in Germany, this breed of dog takes its name from the German word for "growler."

schneider; Schneiderian membrane. The only Schneider I can find whose name became a word is the German C. V. Schneider (1610–80), for whom, as a result of his anatomical researches, the Schneiderian membrane, or mucous membrane of the nose is named. But there may be a case for the gin rummy *schneider*: one *schneiders*, or *schneids*, an opponent in gin rummy by winning before one's opponent has scored any points. Did some gin champion named Schneider do this so often that the feat came to be named after him? Or does the word derive from the German *Schneider*, "tailor," as most scholars believe? The term is apparently an Americanism, in use only since about 1940. Perhaps the term derives from "tailor" because tailors cut clothes down and schneiders cut down the size of the loser's bankroll!

schnook. A person timid and ineffectual, someone usually pitied rather than disliked. In fact, a schnook can be quite likeable. The Yiddish expression comes from German *schnucke*, "little sheep."

schnorrer. Take your choice from an impudent beggar, a moocher, a sponger who acts as if it's one's duty to give him money, a haggler, a habitual bargain hunter, a cheapskate, or a chisler. *Schnorrer* can mean all these things and more. The word is Yiddish, probably from the German verb for "to beg."

schnozzola. This word for the nose, especially a large nose, was popularized by American comedian Jimmy Durante, who was called the Schnozzola or the Schnoz after his considerable proboscis, the most famous nose on the stage since that of CYRANO DE BERGERAC. The word comes from Yiddish *shnoz*, which derives from the German word for "snout."

schooner. "Oh, how she scoons!" an admirer is supposed to have exclaimed when Captain Andrew Robinson of Gloucester, Massachusetts, launched the first vessel of this kind back in 1713 as she glided gracefully over the water. Robinson, overhearing the remark, called his ship a *scooner*, which came to be misspelled *schooner* within a year. *Scoon* itself probably derives from the Scottish *scon*, "to skip a flat stone over the water," as in the game ducks and drakes.

schwa. The schwa was a Hebrew letter, or Masoretic point, expressing an obscure vowel, such as the vowel in the second syllable of the English *linen* or *button*. It became the name of such a vowel in modern languages, as well as the phonetic symbol (ə) for such a vowel.

sciamachy. *See* SQUIRREL.

scientist. The word *science*, from the Latin *scientia*, "knowledge," is recorded in English as early as 1340, but the word *scientist* didn't make its appearance until five centuries later, in 1840, when it was invented by William Whewell in his book *The Philosophy of the Inductive Sciences*. Wrote the English scholar: "We need very much a name to describe a cultivator of science in general. I should incline to call him a Scientist."

sciolist. *See* JACK OF ALL TRADES AND MASTER OF NONE.

scold. The best that word detectives have been able to do with this word is to trace it to the Old Icelandic *skald* for a poet. The guess here is that the *skalds* or poets in question were often poets who wrote biting, scolding verse.

scoots; scootberry. *Scoots* was 19th-century American slang for diarrhea (which sent one scooting to the outhouse), and because the sweetish red berries on the shrub *Streptopus roseus* almost always acted as a physic on youngsters who eagerly ate them, the plant was named the *scootberry*.

scorch; scorched-earth policy. The practice of invaded countries retreating before the enemy and burning all the land in his path, leaving nothing for his troops is as old as war itself, but it was first called the scorched-earth policy at the time when the Japanese invaded China in 1937. It became more familiar when the Nazis invaded Russia in World War II. *Scorch* as a cooking term, by the way, derives from the Old English *scorkle*, which at first meant to skin meat by searing.

score. *See* ACCORDING TO HOYLE.

scotch. "If a body could just find oot the exac' proper proportion and quantity that ought to be drunk every day, and keep to that, I verily vow that he might leeve forever, without dying at a', and that doctors and kirkyards would go oot of fashion." These were the words of a pioneer sage of Dufftown, Scotland on the benefits of Scotch whiskey, which has a base of malted barley and was first made in Scotland. The national name *Scotch* is used to describe many things, often referring to the penuriousness traditionally attributed to the Scottish, *scotch* itself sometimes meaning tight-fisted.

scotch a rumor. The people of Scotland weren't particularly noted for *scotching* or suppressing rumors—no more than anyone else. The expression is actually rooted in the Old French word *escocher*, "to cut."

Scotch Tape. *Scotch* in the trademarked adhesive tape's name refers to the supposed fugality of Scottish people. It seems that 3M (the *M*innisota *M*ining and *M*anufacturing Company) supplied masking tape to garages where cars were custom painted. To save money the company limited the adhesive coating to just a slight area on each side of the tape. This caused the tape to fall off and led to at least one garage owner telling 3M salesmen in no uncertain terms never to bring him that cheap Scotch tape anymore. The company mended its ways, and fully coated Scotch Tape became famous.

scot-free. Like *hopscotch*, this term for "absolutely free" has no connection with frugal Scotsmen. A *scot* or *sceot* was a municipal tax in 12th-century England and someone who went *scot-free* was one who succeeded in dodging these taxes. Later the term was given wider currency when *scot* was used to mean the amount that one owed for entertainment, including drinks, in a tavern—anyone who had a drink on the house went *scot-free*. The *scot* in the expression here was reinforced by the fact that all drinks ordered in taverns were *scotched*, or marked on a slate, enabling the landlord to make a reckoning of how much a person owed.

Scotland Yard. Scotland Yard, famous in the annals of crime and crime fiction, stands on the site of, and was named for, an ancient palace used by the Scottish kings when they came to London once a year to pay homage to the English sovereign.

Scottish Play. For some reason lost to history, actors consider it unlucky to mention the title *Macbeth*. Instead, they call Shakespeare's tragedy "the Scottish Play."

Scouse. Someone from Liverpool, England. From *lobscouse*, a word referring to a stew often served to sailors, many of whom come from the port of Liverpool.

scow. *Scow* is another word born in America; its parent is the Dutch *schouw*, "a large flat-bottomed pole boat or river boat," which, through a mispronunciation, became *scow*. Usually serving as a ferryboat or lighter in the beginning, the scow first entered the language in the mid 17th century and is first recorded in 1669. *To scow* meant to cross a river by scow and America has since known cattle, dumping, ferry, mud, oyster, snag, sand, steam, stone-trading, and garbage scows.

Scrabble. The word game's name was coined by unemployed architect Alfred Mosher Butts when he invented the game in 1931. *Scrabble* he said, stood for players "digging" for letters, part of game strategy. Two to four players in this popular game use counters of letters with various point value to build words on a playing board. The highest competition score in the game is 1,049, a record set in 1989.

scram. *Scram*, which gives us the pig Latin *amscray*, meaning the same—BEAT IT!, "get out of here!"—is thought by some semantic Sherlocks to be a shortening of *scramble*, but more likely it comes from the similar German slang *schrammen*. It is first recorded as underworld and circus slang at the turn of the century.

Scratch; Old Scratch. Although the name is featured in Stephen Vincent Benét's "The Devil and Daniel Webster" (1937) as a name for the devil, *Scratch* or *Old Scratch* is a much older term, deriving from Scandanavian *skratta*, "monster" or "goblin." Other "Old" names for the devil include Old Nick, Old Harry, Old Gentleman, and Old Serpent, but the origin of these cognomens is unknown.

screw. The screw used in woodworking takes its name from a pig, of all things, deriving from the Latin *scrofa*, "sow." The threads on a screw coil resemble a sow's tail; hence the word. Additionally, according to one theory, *screw*, for sexual intercourse, comes from the Latin *scrofa*, which was melded with another Latin word, *scrobis*, meaning "ditch" but also used as Latin slang for the vulva—these two words yielding our word *screw*, for "to copulate." Partridge and others believe that *screw*, first recorded in the early 19th century, is associated with the idea of stealing sex from a woman, giving the word's probable ancestor as the earlier British slang *screw*, for "a robbery effected with a skeleton key." Lastly, as underworld slang for a prison guard dating back to the mid-19th century, *screw* was suggested by someone harsh and brutal, one who used thumbscrews on prisoners.

screwball; screw loose. "King Carl!" Hubbell's famous screwball, which he introduced in the early 1930s, is probably responsible for this expression meaning an eccentric person. The New York Giant pitcher used his screwball in winning 24 games in a row, pitching 46 consecutive scoreless innings, and, most amazing of all, striking out in order the greatest concentration of slugging power ever assembled—Babe Ruth, Lou Gehrig, and Jimmy Foxx—in the 1934 All-Star game. Hubbell's erratic pitch obviously got a lot of publicity in the sports pages. Since it corkscrewed crazily as it approached the batter and you never knew how it was going to break, it was inevitably compared with an unpredictable, erratic, eccentric person, helped by the expression *he has a screw loose* ("is a little unhinged"), common since the 1860s.

The Screw Plot. According to the traditional story, in 1708 conspirators tried to kill England's Queen Anne by removing the screw-bolts from certain huge beams in St. Paul's Cathedral so that the roof would fall in on the queen and her party and kill them while they worshiped. Apparently, not enough screw-bolts were removed and the roof didn't cave in.

scrimmage. The football term *scrimmage* for the action that takes place between two teams from the moment the ball is snapped until it is declared dead is related to the military *skirmish*, for a brief fight. *Scrimmage* is a variation of the latter word, which originally referred to a medieval sword fight. A *scrimmage* can also be a practice game played by two teams.

scrimshaw. Up until relatively recent times sailors on long voyages would often spend their spare time carefully carving whalebone, shells, or ivory into decorative and useful objects, ranging from clothespins to elaborate canes and jewelry boxes. This intricate work was called scrimshaw, a word whose origins are rather vague. *Webster's* traces *scrimshaw* to the French *escrimer*, "to fight with a sword," in the sense of "to make flourishes," while other dictionaries suggest *scrimshank*, English military slang for "to evade duty, be a shirker." Just as many authorities believe the word comes from the proper name Scrimshaw, referring to some once-illustrious sailor-carver noted for his craftsmanship. But Scrimshaw, if he did exist, hasn't been identified. *Scrimshaw* work was also called *skrimshander* and today it can mean any good piece of mechanical work.

scriptorium. The ancient Greeks had commercial scriptoriums that copied texts for a price and sold texts, but these "publishing houses" were not called *scriptoriums*. This word from Latin *scribere*, "to write," wasn't recorded until medieval times, when it described a room in a monastery where manuscripts were stored, read, or copied. When the *Oxford English Dictionary* was being compiled, its editor, Sir James Murray (1837–1915), called an iron outbuilding in his Oxford garden the Scriptorium. He used it as a study, and in it were stored millions of reference slips for that great work.

scrod. Deriving from the Middle Dutch *schrode*, *scrod* means a strip or shred. New England scrod is immature cod or haddock weighing one and a half to two and a half pounds. Sometimes the term is applied to cusk of about the same weight, or to pollack weighing one and a half to four pounds. When fishermen use the word, they are usually referring to gutted small haddock.

Scrooge. Old Scrooge in Dickens's *A Christmas Carol* (1843) is not given any credit in the language for eventually becoming a genial old chap at the tale's end; his name still means a miserly, mean old man (and, sometimes, woman). Incidentally, Scrooge may well be a real English name. Dickens, like Balzac, was in the habit of collecting real names to use in his stories. As Joseph Shipley has pointed out, Scrooge is an apt name for the character, suggesting someone always ready "to put the screws on."

scrub team. The English word *scrub*, dating back to at least the 16th century, meant small stunted trees or cattle. In America, by the early 19th century, *scrub* commonly meant "inferior" as well as "dwarf" and by the end of the century was being applied to second-rate college football teams, these *scrub teams* usually "second teams" that couldn't compare with a school's "first teams." *Scrub* for "to wash vigorously" derives from the Middle English *scrobbe* meaning the same.

scuba. *Scuba* is simply an acronym standing for "*s*elf-*c*ontained *u*nderwater *b*reathing *a*pparatus." Popular since World War II, *scuba diving* has enabled millions to see underwater sights previously the province of a few thousand professional divers.

Scum. Certainly one of the most unusual names of nicknames. Nobody would expect anything from someone nicknamed Scum, and leading British actor Cardonnell "Scum" Goodman (1649–99) provided nothing. Nicknamed Scum since his schooldays, when he was kicked out of Cambridge, Cardonnell, the son of a clergyman, probably had the most reprehensible manners of any actor who ever trod the boards. Once he fatally stabbed a fellow actor in an argument over a shirt the two men shared—Goodman wanted to wear it out of turn. On another occasion he was fined for trying to poison the two older sons of his mistress, the duchess of Cleveland, by whom he had a son of his own—apparently to get the two boys out of the way so that his own son could inherit her fortune. Later, he turned highwayman but was soon caught. James II pardoned him, and Scum returned the royal favor by becoming involved in a plot to kill William II. Scum Goodman finally fled to Paris; a British syndicate paid the scoundrel an annual pension to remain there for the rest of his life.

scunner. A deep dislike, an aversion; originally a Scottish dialect word. "I took a scunner to him right off."

scuppernong. *Scuppernong* is the popular name for the muscadine grape (*Vitus rotundifolia*). Grown in the southern United States, it has large sweet fruit often used to make scuppernong wine. The name derives from the Scuppernong river and lake in Tyrell County, North Carolina, where the grape was discovered in the 18th century.

scuttlebutt. Corrupted to *scuttle* in English, the Old French word *escoutilles* first meant the hatch on a ship, then meant the hole or hatchway in the hatch, and finally was used as a verb meaning to open a hole in a ship in order to sink, or *scuttle*, her. The cask, or *butt*, for drinking water on ships was called a *scuttlebutt* because it was a *butt* with a square hole cut in it, and since sailors exchanged gossip when they gathered at the scuttlebutt for a drink of water, *scuttlebutt* became navy slang for gossip or rumors, in about 1935.

scuzzy; scuz. *Disgusting* gives us this relatively recent adjective, which was first recorded in 1969 and means "dirty, grimy, disgusting, awful." A scuz is simply someone who is scuzzy. Another theory states this Americanism is a blend of *scummy* and *fuzzy*.

sea. The Old English poets used over 30 words for sea (and 27 for ship), as befits bards of an island nation. *Sea*, however, has lasted in the language. *Sea* is an earlier English word than OCEAN and is first recorded in *Beowulf* in the 10th century, its origins doubtful, though it may derive ultimately from the Greek *huei*, "it rains." Today it often represents any large expanse of water more or less enclosed, but it originally had the same meaning as *ocean*.

Seabees. In World War II special navy construction battalions built airstrips or runways on many Pacific islands, among other duties. Their name, *Seabees*, is a phonetic acronym from the initials CB, Construction Battalion. The *C* was spelled "sea" because they were navy men.

seacoasts in Bohemia. The expression is used in referring to errors made by authors, deriving from *The Winter's Tale*, where Shakespeare writes of a vessel "driven by a storm on the coast of Bohemia," although Bohemia has no seacoast. Shakespeare made a number of such errors, as have many writers. In *Robinson Crusoe* Defoe has his hero swim naked to a wrecked ship and then put biscuits he finds there into his pockets.

seagoing bellhops. *Seagoing bellhops*, a contemptuous name given to marines by sailors in reference to their colorful uniforms, is an expression still heard among Navy men. It probably originated in England during the late 19th century.

sea horse. The little sea horse, or *Hippocampus*, as it is known scientifically, swims upright and has a head and an arched, very horselike neck. Sea horses are also unusual in their breeding habits. During mating, the female's eggs are fertilized by the male as they are shed, but the female deposits them in the male's abdomen. The male's pelvic fins are converted into a large incubating pouch that holds the eggs and he carries them about until they are ready to hatch, appearing as if *he* were pregnant.

sea lawyer. Back in 1867 one crusty old salt defined *sea lawyer* as "an idle litigious long-shorer, more given to questioning orders than to obeying them, one of the pests of the navy as well as the mercantile marine." This term for an argumentative seaman or nautical nuisance given to questioning regulations is still used, and the type is still with us for better or worse. A good example is the officer responsible for the mutiny against Captain Queeg in Herman Wouk's *The Caine Mutiny*. Because it is so clever and cunning, the tiger shark is also called the sea lawyer, as is the gray, or mangrove, snapper.

seamy side of life. The worst, most degraded side of life. This expression appears to have been suggested by the underside of clothing, where the crude seams, rough edges, and coarseness of the material shows, but another theory holds that the inspiration comes from carpets and tapestries, where the seams or threads of the pattern are visible on the underside. Shakespeare was the first to record the phrase, in *Othello*, where Iago's wife Emilia says that her husband's wit has been turned "the seam side without" by someone who has made him suspect her of adultery with the Moor. *See* COMING APART AT THE SEAMS.

séance. There is nothing mysterious about the etymology of the word *séance*. It derives from the French *séance*, "seat" or "session," which was used to describe many different kinds of meetings. In about 1845 *séance* was applied for the first time to meetings of people attempting to contact the spirits of the dead.

season. *Season* derives ultimately from a Latin word meaning time of sowing, or seedtime. The word was long used for the time of the year when seed was sown, and the division of the year into four separate seasons only dates back to around the 12th century.

season ticket. We often associate this term with modern-day sports events, the season ticket entitling the buyer to attend all that season's games, usually at a reduced rate. But the practice and its name are much older, first recorded in the early 19th century and offered for cultural events, transportation, etc.

seat belt. The designation *seat belt* was originally used on airplanes, the term coined in the early 1930s. However, the seat belt as we know it in cars was originally called a *safety belt*, though its design wasn't very safe. It wasn't until 1959, when Swedish inventor Nils Bohlin designed a safe device, that *safety belt* became *seat belt*. One estimate (*New York Times*, 9/26/02) calculates that Bohlin's "seat belt has saved more than one million lives in the last 40 years." Nils Bohlin died at the age of 82 on September 21, 2002, the same day he was inducted into the Inventor's Hall of Fame in Akron, Ohio, joining Orville and Wilbur Wright, Eli Whitney, and 168 other great inventors.

Seattle. Seathl, a chief of the Duwamish and Suquamish Indians, is remembered by Seattle, Washington, which was named for him in 1853, two years after it was founded as a lumber settlement. Actually, he sold his name to the whites for one dollar, believing that if your name is stolen after you die, you'll roll over in your grave and since the name no longer belonged to him he'd be able to rest in peace.

sea urchin. *See* URCHIN.

seaweed. *Seaweed* takes its name from Old English *sae*, "sea," and *weod*, "weed." It is generally divided into four groups: blue-green, green, brown, and red, with about 10,000 species in all. Kelps growing along the Pacific coast are the largest and most commercially important of the brown seaweeds, many growing to more than 100 feet long and the giant kelp (*Macro cystis pyrifera*) growing over 150 feet.

secateurs. The British, great gardeners that they are, use this name for what Americans call garden pruning shears. It is pronounced "sek-ah-tours" and derives ultimately from the Latin *secāre*, to cut.

secede. In the sense of "to secede from the United States," *secede* appears to have first been used by Thomas Jefferson in 1825: "Possibly their colonies might secede from the Union."

Seckel pear. *See* BARTLETT PEAR.

second Adam. *See* ADAM.

second childhood. When one says somebody is going through his or her *second childhood*, one echoes the words of the Athenian comic playwright Aristophanes (ca. 448 B.C.–ca. 380 B.C.), who coined the term in his play *The Clouds* (423). Aristophanes also coined *plenty of irons in the fire* (*The Frogs*); *I laughed till I cried*; and *throw fear* (caution) *to the wind* (clouds).

second fiddle. This expression arose in the mid-18th century, meaning to occupy a secondary position and alluding to the second violinist of symphony orchestras, who follows the lead of the first violinist.

second rate. *See* FIRST RATE.

secret; secretary. Advisers who handled confidential matters in medieval Europe were called *secretarii*, their name itself deriving from the Latin *secretum*, "secret." By 1400, we find the word being written as *secretary*, but it is not until Queen Elizabeth I's time that *secretary* was used as a synonym for a minister or cabinet member of the government. *Secretary* first began to be used in its modern sense of a private assistant to an individual in the early 19th century.

secretary bird. Standing four feet high and a relative of the eagle and hawk, the African secretary bird can kill the most venomous snakes with its taloned feet, striking and then jumping back to avoid being bitten. One would think this powerful wild bird of prey would have a less domestic name, but it was apparently so named because the erectile tuft of long black feathers hanging from the back of its head and nape seemed to resemble the quill pens that secretaries once used.

Secret Service.   *See* c.

secret weapon.   A weapon, usually one of great destructive force, often nuclear or biochemical, that a government has classified as secret, sometimes even denying its existence. The term was coined by British suspense and spy novelist Eric Ambler in *The Dark Frontier* (1936).

securities.   Though they sometimes aren't, *securities* should always be safe investments, judging by the derivation of the word from the Latin *se* and *cura*, which literally translate as "without care."

sedulous ape.   *See* PLAY THE SEDULOUS APE.

see eye to eye.   A biblical phrase that is still widely used. This one, meaning "to agree completely," comes from Isa. 52:8: "For they shall see eye to eye, when the Lord shall bring again Zion."

Seeing Eye dog.   Dogs used to guide blind people are called *Seeing Eye dogs*, after the Seeing Eye organization in Morristown, New Jersey, where such dogs have been trained for over half a century.

seeing stars.   This expression was probably used much earlier (there is a 1609 quotation that seems to imply its use), but it is first recorded in the 1891 *Century Dictionary*: "*To see stars*, to have a sensation as of flashes of light, produced by a sudden jarring of the head, as by a direct blow." The phenomenon results from a change in blood flow to the brain. According to neurologist Dr. C. Boyd Campbell: "Blood supplies nerve cells with oxygen, sugar, and other vital nutrients. Any loss of blood to the brain—easily caused by standing up, an action that forces blood away from the head—deprives the nerve cells of these nutrients. This causes a brief, random firing of neurons, which is interpreted by the brain's visual cortex as quick flashes of light, or 'stars.' The phenomenon is also produced by a blow to the head or by stimulating the eye electrically, both of which alter the normal state of nerve cells."

see no evil, hear no evil, speak no evil.   Typically, three wise monkeys illustrate this proverb, their hands respectively covering their eyes, ears, and mouth. The common saying only dates back to the late 19th or early 20th century.

see red.   *To see red*, "to be roused to violent anger," comes from the older saying "to wave a red flag at a bull." The expression became popular in America during this century, deriving of course from the waving of a red cape to rouse the bull in bullfights. No matter that bulls are color blind. The misconception is so widespread and red is so universally associated with violence that the words will be with us long after bullfighting is banned.

seersucker.   No "seer" or "sucker" is behind this one. The Persian *shīr o shakkar*, literally "milk and sugar," is the ultimate source for the name of this crimped linen, cotton, or rayon fabric that was first made in India, whence the British began to import it in the early 18th century for summer seersucker suits. *Shīr o shakkar* became the Hindu *sirsakar*, which was corrupted to *seersucker* in English.

See Spot run!   Many millions of Americans read this and similar memorable lines as their first effort at reading. The words are from the Dick and Jane elementary textbooks that were written by Zerna Sharp, a first grade teacher in Las Porte, Indiana, and were used from the 1940s through the 1970s. The characters in the stories included Mother, Father, Dick, Jane, Spot the dog, and Puff the cat.

see the elephant and hear the owl hoot.   To have a good time deep into the night. A variation on the older *see the elephant*, which referred to seeing the elephant at the circus, the elephant not being a common sight to Americans in the 19th century.

see you later.   This widespread good-bye is an Americanism first recorded in the early 1870s. There have since been a number of variations on it, such as SEE YOU LATER, ALLIGATOR.

see you later, alligator.   British rhyming slang spread to California in the 1850s, and one result was the word *alligator*, which rhymed with and meant "see you later." Rhyming slang never really caught on in America, and *alligator* in this sense didn't last long, but the full expression *see you later, alligator* remains with us.

seiche.   A *seiche* is a long wave that sloshes rhythmically back and forth as if in a bathtub as it reflects off opposite ends of an enclosed body of water (usually a bay) when it is disturbed by storms, winds, or tsunami. In Los Angeles harbor, one of the few major harbors that have seiching or surging problems, seiches cause big ships to move as much as 10 feet, to strain at or snap their mooring lines, and cause damage to piles and to the ships themselves. *Seiche*, a French word, is generally pronounced *saysh*, though people in some regions pronounce it to rhyme with "beach." The term seems to have been coined by a Swiss scientist and is first recorded in English in 1839.

seize the day.   *See* CARPE DIEM.

seize the moment.   To act immediately on one's impulse, not to delay or procrastinate, take the opportunity while it's available or you may lose it. *See* CARPE DIEM.

sekando waifu.   A Japanese expression for a mistress or kept woman. The words are a Japanization of English *second wife*. There is no term for *second husband*, but there is the polite *sekkusu furendo*, a Japanization of the English *sex friend*, which means a "lover" and can apply to a man as well as to a woman.

self-help.   British author Thomas Carlyle coined the term *self-help*, "the action or faculty of providing for oneself without assistance from others," in his book *Sartor Resartus* (1833): "In the destitution of the wild desert does our young Ishmael acquire for himself the highest of all possessions, that of Self-help."

self-made man.   This expression seems like it would be an Americanism, and it is, the *O.E.D* tracing it back to an 1832 speech by a Kentucky congressman. One time a politician collared American editor Horace Greeley at a convention and proudly confided to him that he was a "self-made man." "That, sir," Greeley replied, "relieves the Almighty of a terrible responsibility." But then author Henry Class said Greeley himself "was a self-made man who worshipped his creator."

self-starter.   *Self-starter* has come to mean "someone who doesn't need much help in performing a task," who has a remarkable amount of initiative. It is an Americanism dating back to 1894 and originally referred to an attachment for starting a car's engine without hand cranking.

sell down the river.   A universal phrase that has as its source the punishment of a slave by his owner by selling him to a sugarcane plantation on the lower Mississippi, where work conditions were at their worst. The expression appears to have been first recorded in Harriet Beecher Stowe's *Uncle Tom's Cabin* (1852).

sell like hot cakes.   Hot cakes cooked in bear grease or pork lard were popular from earliest times in America. First made of cornmeal, the griddle cakes or pancakes were of course best when served piping hot and were often sold at church benefits, fairs, and other functions. So popular were they that by the beginning of the 19th century *to sell like hot cakes* was a familiar expression for anything that sold very quickly, effortlessly, and in quantity.

sell the pass.   Irish legend holds that when a regiment of Crotha, Lord of Atha, was holding a pass against the invading army of Trathal, "King of Cael," one of Crotha's soldiers betrayed the pass for money, the invaders were victorious, and Trathal became King of Ireland. This inspired the ancient Irish expression *selling the pass*, "betraying one's own for money or other gain," which became common enough in English, both the expression and the practice.

seltzer.   The German *Wasser selterser*, "water of Selters," gives us the word *seltzer water*, or *seltzer*. Selters, a town in Hesse-Nassau, has long been famous for its effervescent mineral spring.

Semitic.   German historian August Ludwig von Schloyer gave this language group its name in 1781, taking it from the name of Shem, a son of Noah described in the Bible as the common ancestor of various ancient peoples who spoke this group of related languages. The principal languages in the group were Hebrew, Aramaean, Arabic, Ethiopic, and ancient Assyrian. Later (ca. 1825) the word was applied to the people who spoke or speak these languages and it has most recently (ca. 1875) been used to refer primarily to Jewish people.

senate.   The legislature in ancient Rome consisted of the popular assembly and another group of wise men who were always in their advanced years, because only old men were considered to be truly wise. The latter group was called the *senatus*, or "council of old men," in Latin, this word yielding our word *senate*.

send to Coventry.   The historic city of Coventry in England may have been built near and taken its name from *Cofa's tree*, in which case the otherwise anonymous Cofa family name is remembered in at least three words or phrases. The most common of these means boycotting a person by refusing to associate or have dealings with him, which is called *sending him to Coventry*. This phrase is of uncertain origin, arising either because Royalist prisoners were sent to the staunchly Puritan town during the Great Rebellion, or due to the fact that Coventry was at one time so antimilitary that any soldier posted there found himself cut off from all social intercourse, the townspeople even refusing to talk to the troops. The Germans with their devastating bombings laid waste to much of Coventry in World War II, destroying 70,000 homes, all but the great spire of the 14th-century Cathedral of St. Michael, and many other historic sites, which led to the term *to coventrate*—to attempt to bomb a city out of existence. *See also* TRUE BLUE.

send to the showers.   This phrase, meaning "to dismiss or reject someone," is from baseball, where it is first recorded in 1931. In baseball it means to take a failing pitcher out of a game and send in a relief pitcher. Since the pitcher can't play again in that game, he often takes a shower in the clubhouse and changes to street clothes.

se'nnight.   The Celts, like the Greeks, Babylonians, Persians, and Jews before them, customarily began each day at sunset, this practice giving us the term *se'nnight* for a week, or seven nights. In Genesis, for example, we find the evening coming before the morning in "The evening and the morning were the first day . . ." The same idea gives us *fortnight* (14 nights) for two weeks.

the sensation is momentary and the position ridiculous.   A comment on copulation by waspish Professor Charles Townsend Copeland (1860–1952), who taught English at Harvard for many years beginning in 1893, influencing numerous authors (including John Reed and John Dos Passos). Copeland was noted for his beautiful reading voice and brilliant wit. On the subject of a career in journalism for a writer he commented: "Get in, get wise, get out."

sensitive plant.   *Mimosa pudica*, the hairy sensitive plant, is so called because its leaves will fold together with sufficient irritation or cloudy weather—this representing one of the most remarkable cases of physiological response in the plant kingdom. It is also known by the terms *humble plant* and *touch me not*.

sentence.   A sentence is defined as "a grammatical unit that is syntactically independent and has a subject that is expressed (or, as in imperative sentences, understood) and a predicate that contains at least one finite verb." *Gates of Paradise* by George Andrzeyevski (Panther, 1957) is a book with no punctuation and technically might be said to be one long sentence. The 1942–43 Report of the President of Columbia University contained a sentence of 4,284 words. Sylvester Hassell's *History of the Church of God* (ca. 1884) has a sentence of 3,153 words (with

360 commas and 86 semicolons) that is regarded as the longest legitimate sentence in a book. James Joyce, William Faulkner, and many other writers have written long "sentences" with no punctuation, but the longest legitimate sentence in a highly regarded literary work is a 958-word monster in Marcel Proust's *Cities of the Plain.*

sent off with a flea in his ear. To be dismissed peremptorily, with no chance for denial or refusal. Someone so dismissed is distressed and restless—and can do nothing about it—like a dog with a flea in its ear. The expression dates back to the 15th century in England and a century earlier in France.

sent up the river. To be sent to prison. First recorded in the 1930s, this term must be much older. *The river* referred to is the Hudson in New York City and *up* it, at Ossining, is Sing Sing Penitentiary, which was founded in 1830.

separate the sheep from the goats. An old expression that has its origins in the New Testament, Matt. 25:32–33, reading: "And before him shall be gathered all nations; and he shall separate them one from another, as a shepherd divideth his sheep from the goats." It means to divide the good from the bad, the worthy from the unworthy.

sepia. This rich brown color is so named from the cuttlefish, which several centuries ago was widely known as the sepia (from the Latin *sepia,* "cuttlefish"). The inky fluid secreted by the sepia was first used to make a dye of this color.

September; October; November; December. When the Romans introduced the JULIAN CALENDAR, they retained several month names from their old Roman calendar, despite the fact that these months no longer had the same position on the calendar. Thus September, once the Roman seventh month of the year, deriving from the Latin *septem,* "seven," remained as the ninth month of the year. The same happened with October, deriving from *octo,* "eight," which became the 10th month; November, deriving from *novem,* "nine," became the 11th month; and December, deriving from *decem,* "10," became the 12th month.

Septuagint. Seventy-two men give their "name" to this word. Tradition has it that Ptolemy II, who reigned from 285 to 247 B.C., had the laws of the Jews translated into Greek by 72 scholars, six from each of the 12 Jewish tribes, in a period of 72 days on the island of Pharos. The translation became the earliest Greek version of the Old Testament, later erroneously named the Septuagint from the Latin *septuaginta,* which means 70, not 72. Scholars believe that the translation was made in Alexandria at this time, but not at Ptolemy's request, not by 72 Jewish scholars, and not in 72 days. Nevertheless, the fable about "the 70" is responsible for the word. The tradition, however, applies only to the Pentateuch; the other books of the Old Testament were translated later. *Septuagint* is often printed as the Roman numeral LXX.

sequin. The Italian gold coin called the *sequin* (based on a Turkish gold coin called a *sequin,* from the Arabic *sikkah,* "coin") had been known in England since at least the early 17th century. Some authorities say that in the late 1870s the word was transferred to the bright spangles on clothes, but others claim that *sequin* in the latter sense has nothing to do with gold coins and derives from "shining artificial flowers invented by a chemist named Sequin in 1802."

sequoia. The largest and tallest living things on earth, the giant sequoias of California and Oregon are named for the exalted Indian leader Sequoyah, who invented the Cherokee syllabary, which not only made a whole people literate practically overnight but formed the basis for many Indian languages. Sequoyah (also Sequoya, or Silwayi) was born about 1770, the son of a white trader named Nathaniel Gist; his mother was related to the great king Oconostota. Though he used the name George Guess, Sequoyah had few contacts with whites, working as a silversmith and trader in Georgia's Cherokee country until a hunting accident left him lame. With more time on his hands, Sequoyah turned his attention to the "talking leaves" or written pages of the white man and set out to discover this secret for his own people. Over a period of 12 years, withstanding ridicule by family and friends, he listened to the speech of those around him, finally completing a table of characters representing all 86 sounds in the Cherokee spoken language. Sequoyah's system was adopted by the Cherokee council in 1821; one story claims that his little daughter won over the council chiefs by reading aloud a message that they had secretly instructed her father to write down. Thousands of Indians would learn to read and write thanks to Sequoyah's "catching a wild animal and taming it." He joined the Arkansas Cherokee the following year, and in 1828 moved with them to Oklahoma after helping to negotiate in Washington, D.C., for more extensive lands. For the rest of his life he devoted himself to his alphabet and the study of common elements in Indian language, translating parts of the Bible into Cherokee and starting a weekly newspaper. Sequoyah was also instrumental in avoiding bloodshed and forming the Cherokee Nation when in 1839 the federal government heartlessly drove other Cherokee to Oklahoma from their ancestral homes in Alabama and Tennessee. He is believed to have died somewhere in Mexico around 1843 while searching for a lost band of Cherokee who were rumored to have moved there at about the time of his birth. It is said that he and his party of horsemen did ultimately find their lost brothers and taught them to read and write. Sequoyah, legendary in his own time among Indians and whites, is one of a few men to invent an entire alphabet adopted by a people.

In 1847, not long after Sequoyah's death, the Hungarian botanist Stephan Endlicher gave the name *Sequoia sempervirens* to the redwood tree, and it is generally assumed, though not definitely known, that he had the great Cherokee leader in mind. There are three types of sequoias, all conifers. The redwood species mentioned, native to the coast of California and a few miles into Oregon, includes probably the tallest tree currently standing in the world: a sequoia in California's Redwood National Park that stands 373 feet tall. (The tallest recorded tree of all time is probably an Australian eucalyptus that measured 470 feet before it fell in 1885.)

Another sequoia type is *Sequoiadendron giganteum,* which grows on the western slopes of California's Sierra Nevada. These are generally called giant sequoias or "big trees," not redwoods. They are not as tall as their relatives but are the largest plants on earth. Greatest among them, at 274.9 feet tall, is the General Sherman sequoia in California's Sequoia National

Park. This largest of all living things is popularly named for Union Civil War general William Tecumseh Sherman (1820–1891). It would take at least 17 adults with outstretched arms to encircle this tree, which contains enough timber to make 5 billion matches. From its beginnings as a minuscule seed nearly 30 centuries ago, the massive General Sherman increased in weight more than 125,000 millionfold and in combined height and girth dwarfs any other plant. The General Sherman, 3,000 years old, is also one of the oldest of living things, but a bristlecone pine in California's Inyo National Forest holds the age record: "Methuselah" has endured for more than 4,600 years on the windswept slopes of the White Mountains—since 2600 B.C.

The third sequoia type is the "dawn redwood" or "living fossil," *Metasequoia glyptostroboides*. Discovered growing in China in 1946, these trees are reputedly the ancestors of all sequoias, and their fossil remains date back 30 million to 50 million years. The dawn redwood is now grown in the United States. Incidentally, it is little known that some sequoias have been grown successfully in the East; one grown in Rochester, New York reached a height of more than 50 feet. Adrian Le Corbeau's *The Forest Giant*, translated by T. E. Lawrence (Lawrence of Arabia), is a beautifully written appreciation of the giant sequoia.

serendipity.   A desirable discovery made by accident. English novelist Horace Walpole coined the word in 1754, basing it upon a lucky faculty enjoyed by the three heroes of the old Persian fairy tale "The Three Princes of Serendip." Serendip is an old Arabic name for Ceylon (*Sindhalawipa*, "Lion Island").

a serpent in one's bosom.   According to legend, a kind Greek shepherd found a frozen serpent and put it under his shirt. The snake revived but bit its benefactor, which gives us this saying for an ungrateful person.

serpent-licked ears.   Anyone with serpent-licked ears is said to have the power of seeing into the future. The ancient Greeks believed that both Cassandra and Helenus had the power of prophecy because serpents licked their ears while they slept in the temple of Apollo.

serviceberry.   "The blueberry of the northern plains," or "juneberry," was dubbed the *serviceberry* as far back as the 18th century. This name has a touching story behind it. Since its white blossoms appeared almost as soon as the ground thawed in spring, American pioneer families that had kept a body through the winter to bury in workable ground used these first flowers to cover the grave. Covering such graves was the "service" this bush performed.

sesame seeds.   *Sesamum indicum* is said to be the oldest herbaceous plant cultivated for its seeds. *Benne*, as these sesame seeds are called in Africa and the South, or *sim sim*, another African name for them, were brought to America on the first slave ships. They have been used for everything from ink to cattle feed to flour to oil, and are a popular ingredient in cookies, crackers, and candies. *Sesamum* is the Greek version of the Arabic word for sesame.

set one's cap at.   This phrase most likely goes back to the 18th century, a time when ladies wore light muslin caps indoors as well as out. When a suitor came to call, a young woman would naturally put on her best cap and wear it at the most fetching angle in order to impress her man and win a husband. This was called *setting one's cap at* or *for* a man, an expression still occasionally heard today.

set the Thames on fire.   England's Thames River, that cradle of so many far-flung sea expeditions, is usually pronounced to rhyme with *hems*, not *James*. The name is first recorded as *Tamesis*, circa A.D. 893. To *set the Thames on fire* is an old expression, said of the Rhine and other rivers as well, meaning to do something marvelous, to work wonders, to almost set the world on fire. However, one persistent story claims that the *Thames* in the phrase is not the famous river, but a misspelling of *temse*, a word for a corn sieve in the 18th century. According to this theory, a joke about a farm laborer who worked his temse so hard that it caught fire probably led to this expression for "to do something remarkable." As with so many word derivations, the truth will probably never be known.

Seven Cities.   Ancient towns in New Mexico that inspired the Spaniards to explore the Southwest because of their reputed wealth; now thought to be Zuni pueblos, they are also known as the Seven Cities of Cibola.

Seven Deadly Sins; seven virtues.   The Seven Deadly (or Capital) Sins are pride, wrath, envy, lust, gluttony, avarice, and sloth, while the seven virtues are faith, hope, charity, prudence, justice, fortitude, and temperance. The latter expression is recorded in English as early as 1320, the former a hundred years before this.

Seven Dwarfs.   In the old German fairy tale "Snow White" collected by the Grimm Brothers, the seven dwarfs who help the eponymous heroine have no names. But in Walt Disney's cartoon film *Snow White and the Seven Dwarfs* (1937) they were immortalized and became known to billions as Happy, Sleepy, Doc, Bashful, Sneezey, Grumpy, and Dopey.

Seven Last Words.   The Seven Last Words are the last utterance of Christ on the cross. This was also the title of a musical composition by Haydn, written in 1785. The words are "My God, why hast thou forsaken me?" (more strictly, "My God, my God, why hast thou forsaken me?"), recorded in Mark 15:34, and Matt. 27:46, which gives the Hebrew as "Eloi, Eloi, lama sabachthani?" But the *seven last words of Christ* are also considered to be the seven expressions given in the Bible (including this) that are Christ's last words.

seven names of God.   Of the many names the ancient Hebrews had for the deity, the seven names of God were those over which their scribes had to take particular care, the names being: El, Elohim, Adonai, YHWH (Jehovah), Ehyeh-Asher-Ehyeh, Shaddai, and Zebaot.

Seven Sages of Greece.   These seven men of great practical wisdom lived in the sixth century B.C. and were philosophers, law-givers, and statesmen. The list of them varies from writer to writer but always includes SOLON, Thales, Bias of Priene, and Pittacus of Mitylene. Among the aphorisms they originated are "Know thyself," "Know thy opportunity," and "Nothing in excess."

Seven Seas. The Seven Seas (the designation became popular when a collection of Rudyard Kipling's poems was so entitled) are today generally regarded as the Arctic Ocean, Antarctic Ocean, North Pacific Ocean, South Pacific Ocean, North Atlantic Ocean, South Atlantic Ocean, and Indian Ocean. In olden times they were the Mediterranean Sea, the Red Sea, the China Sea, the West and East African Seas, the Indian Ocean, and the Persian Gulf. Someone who has sailed the seven seas has traveled widely.

seven-sided animal; seven-sided son of a bitch. A one-eyed man or woman: "each having a right side and a left side, a fore side and a back side, an inside and an outside, and a blind side." The expression originated in the late 17th century and lasted until the early 20th. A western U.S. variant was *seven-sided son of a bitch.*

seven sleepers. *See* DORMOUSE.

seven stages of drunkenness. This wise 19th-century expression defines the stages as verbose, grandiose, amicose, bellicose, morose, stuperose, and comatose.

Seventh-Day Adventists. In 1831 New York farmer and preacher William Miller (1782–1849) founded the Protestant sect of Second Adventists, often called Millerites. Convinced from his reading of the Bible that the second coming of Christ would occur 12 years later in 1843, he spread his belief throughout America, attracting many followers who prepared for the end of the world and Judgment Day. When 1843 and then 1844 passed without his prophecy coming true, Miller founded the Adventist Church, whose name was changed to the Seventh-Day Adventists 15 years later. Numbering well over a million members today, their church observes Saturday as the Sabbath (as do Seventh-Day Baptists) and forbids the use of alcohol and tobacco.

Seventh Heaven. The Muhammadan Seventh Heaven, is said to be "beyond the power of description." There each inhabitant is bigger than the whole earth and has 70,000 tongues that speak 70,000 languages—all forever chanting the praises of Allah. In the Islamic graded concept of Heaven, which also prevailed among the Jews, one goes after death to the Heaven he has earned on earth, and the Seventh Heaven, ruled by Abraham, is the ultimate one, a region of pure light lying above the other six, the Heaven of Heavens. Anyone in Seventh Heaven is thus in a state of ineffable bliss, having the greatest pleasure possible.

seventh-inning stretch. These words have become synonymous for a brief break from any long period of sitting. They derive of course from baseball's traditional seventh-inning stretch, which dates back to the late 19th century. One theory credits the ritual to President William Howard Taft, who is said to have stood up to stretch in the seventh inning of a Washington Senator game, prompting the rest of the crowd to follow suit. Better documented is the theory that the tradition originated at a game in 1882 at Manhattan College in New York City. Manhattan College baseball coach Brother Jasper, also the prefect of discipline, instructed restless students in the stands to rise and stretch for a minute in the seventh inning before the game continued. This seventh-inning stretch became a ritual at all Manhattan College games and spread to the major leagues during the 1880s when the college team played exhibition games against the New York Giants in the Polo Grounds.

seven virtues. *See* SEVEN DEADLY SINS.

seven wonders of the world. The ancient list of the seven greatest man-made structures of the world dates back at least to the second century B.C. They are:

- Hanging Gardens of Babylon
- Colossus of Rhodes
- Egyptian Pyramids
- Pharos of Egypt
- Temple of Artemis at Ephesus
- Mausoleum of Mausolus (Halicarnassus)
- Statue of Zeus at Olympia

See MAUSOLEUM; ISLE OF RHODES.

seven-year itch. Used to describe a husband's or wife's urge to stray from his or her mate after seven years of marriage, this expression appears to have been invented by American playwright George Axelrod in his play *The Seven Year Itch* (1952) and further popularized by the film version starring Marilyn Monroe (1955). Word and phrase hunters haven't been able to turn up any earlier use of the words in a sexual context, although *seven-year itch* had been used to describe a poison ivy itch that supposedly recurred once every seven years.

Seward's folly; Seward's icebox. After having been wounded by John Wilkes Booth's fellow conspirator Lewis Powell at the same time that Abraham Lincoln was assassinated, William Henry Seward recovered and remained in the cabinet of Lincoln's successor Andrew Johnson as secretary of state. A vigorous opponent of slavery, he had originated the well-known phrases *there is a higher law than our constitution* and *irrepressible conflict*, the last expressing the state of the nation until it became all slave or all free. Seward's most important work in Johnson's administration was the purchase of Alaska from Russia in 1867. Very few had the foresight to appreciate his $7 million acquisition at the time and because Alaska was purchased almost solely due to his determination, although others had made overtures toward buying it before the Civil War, it was widely called *Seward's folly*, or *Seward's icebox.* William Henry Seward died in 1872, aged 71, but the famous nicknames were used long after his death, even when fortunes were being made in Alaskan gold and fur. *Alaska*, from the Aleut *A-la-as-ka*, "the great country," became the 49th American state in 1959. The Seward Peninsula in West Alaska on the Bering Strait also bears the statesman's name, and Bering Strait and Bering Sea honor Captain Vitus Bering, a Dane who, in exploring for Russia in 1741, is believed to have been the first white man to visit Alaska.

sex for the students, athletics for the alumni, and parking for the faculty. These, according to President Clark Kerr of the University of California, in a speech delivered at another university in 1958, are "the three major administrative problems on U.S. college campuses."

sexist.   A relative newcomer, based on *racist* and coined in an 11/18/65 speech by Paulette M. Leet, director of special programs at Franklin and Marshall College. *Sexist* refers to a person whose attitude or behavior is based on traditional stereotypes of sexual roles. Said Ms. Leet in her speech: "When you argue . . . that since fewer women write good poetry this justifies their total exclusion [from taking English courses], you are taking a position analogous to that of the racist—I might call you in this case a 'sexist.' . . ."

sex-up.   An expression I've heard but haven't yet seen collected. It means "to liven up, energize," as in "Sex-up that speech or they'll fall asleep." Of recent origin, the term sounds like a Hollywood or Washington invention. In her book *Start With a Laugh* (2001), Liz Carpenter tells how to write a political speech: "Start with a laugh, put the meat in the middle, and wave a flag at the end."

sgnik sdneirf.   Early Americans liked to spell backwards things that they detested, as in the case of o-grab-me. This was also the case with the expression *king's friends*, which the Tories called themselves, contemptuous patriots calling them by the derogatory name *sgnik sdneirf*. As for the Loyalists, they called the patriots "rabble."

shack.   The Aztec *xacalli*, "wooden hut," gives us our word for a miserable hut or shanty. *Shack* came into English in the 1870s, in the American Southwest, via the Mexican *xacal*, or *jacal*, which is pronounced as though written "shacal."

shaddock.   The ancestor of the grapefruit, the shaddock, or pomelo, reached Europe in about the middle of the 12th century from the Malay archipelago. It was called the Adam's apple at first and didn't receive its common name until a Captain Shaddock, a 17th-century English voyager, brought its seed from the East Indies to Barbados, where it was grown extensively. The grapefruit (*Citrus paradisi*) is neither a mutation of the thicker-skinned shaddock (*C. grandis*) nor a cross between the shaddock and sweet orange. It was developed in the West Indies and was given its name because it often grows in clusters like grapes. To further complicate matters, the shaddock is sometimes called the forbidden fruit and the grapefruit is called the pomelo in different parts of the world. The pink grapefruit was developed in Florida, as was the seedless variety.

shag.   Mainly British and Australian English slang for "to copulate, have sex with," probably deriving, as Partridge notes, from *shag* meaning "to shake or toss about," and first recorded in the late 1700s. The title of the film *The Spy Who Shagged Me* (2000) caused little concern in the United States, where few people know what it means, but the expression is heard more frequently here today. *Shagged out*, slang for very tired, hasn't yet made it to America. In baseball lingo *shag* means to catch a fly ball hit to the outfield in practice.

shag; a shag on a rock.   A shag is a large seabird related to the cormorant, and one sitting alone on a rock in the ocean inspired the Australian saying *like a shag on a rock*, "someone who looks utterly alone, even in a crowd." The bird possibly takes its name from its shaggy crest.

shah.   *See* KAISER.

shahid.   Heard during the 9/11 war as an Islamic name for an Al Qaeda fighter or terrorist who dies in action and is granted immediate entrance to heaven as a martyr. *See* JIHAD.

shake a leg.   *See* SHOW A LEG.

shake like an aspen leaf.   As the *Canterbury Tales* (1386) attest, Chaucer knew this expression and it was probably used long before him, ever since people first noticed that the delicate aspen leaf trembles in the slightest wind.

Shakespeare.   As it now stands, no one really knows how William Shakespeare spelled his name. The seven unquestionably genuine signatures of Shakespeare are very difficult to decipher. The name is spelled *Shakspeare* on the Bard's own monument, but *Shakespeare* on the tombs of his wife and daughter. Other early variations are *Shakspere* and *Shagspere* (on his marriage license). In 1869 a Philadelphian named J. R. Wise published *Autograph of William Shakespeare . . . Together With 4,000 Ways of Spelling the Name*. If one of the seven known signatures of William Shakespeare came on the market today or a new one was discovered, it would sell for about $1.5 million—second only to a "Julius Caesar," which would be worth $2 million, according to experts.

Shakespearean.   *Shakespearean* means much more than "pertaining to the work of English writer William Shakespeare." The word has come to represent profound universal magistry and vision in writing, among a veritable dictionary of superlatives. Little is really known about the personal life of the world's greatest poet and dramatist. Shakespeare was born in 1564 at Stratford-on-Avon of substantial middle-class parents, his father being an alderman, and received a solid grammar school education, well above the standards for the times. There is evidence that the Sweet Swan of Avon, as Ben Jonson called him, left Stratford for London to avoid a charge of poaching. He probably acted in the earl of Leicester's company and by 1592 had achieved fame as a dramatist and actor. By this time Shakespeare had acquired property and lived like a gentleman with his wife, Anne Hathaway, whom he had married 10 years previously, and with their children, Susanna and the twins Hammet and Judith. Shakespeare was one of the few writers in his day to win fame and wealth. The Bard of Avon died on his own birthday in 1616, aged 52, in Stratford, where he had retired five years before. Countless stories and speculations surround the dramatist's life, ranging from the spelling of his name—the plentiful variations including Shakspeare, Shakspear, and Shakspeare—to the alleged infidelity of his wife, the identity of the "dark lady" of the sonnets, and the fantastic theory that Bacon actually wrote his plays. Most of these theories are familiar, but none has been proved.

Shakespearean words.   The *OED* credits over 500 invented words to Shakespeare. A small sample of these were cleverly arranged in the *New York Times* (11/10/02):

From the "spectacled" "pedant" to the "schoolboy," all "gentlefolk" recognize Shakespeare as a "fathomless" "fount" of coinages. The "honey-tongued" Bard had no "rival," nor could he "sate" his "never-ending" "addiction" to "madcap," "flowery" (or "foul-mouthed"!) neologisms. Even "time-honored" "exposure" cannot "besmirch" our "amazement" at the "countless" and "useful" words that lend "radiance" to our "lackluster" lives. All in a "day's work!"

Many other such coinages can be found throughout this book and in the index.

shako. A military cap in the form of a cylinder or truncated cone, with a visor and a plume or pompom, the *shako* is also worn in a similar version by members of marching bands. It is another of the few words of Hungarian origin in English, deriving from the Hungarian *ozako*, "a peaked cap," the original peak on the cap flattened off over the years.

Shall we tap the admiral? Shall we have another drink? According to legend, on the way home from the naval battle of Trafalgar, in which he was killed, Admiral Horatio Nelson's body was preserved in rum, and sailors repeatedly tapped the cask containing his body. *See* NELSON'S BLOOD.

shalom. *Shalom*, from a Hebrew root meaning "peace," is an Israeli greeting for both hello and good-bye, Leo Rosten noting that Israelis say they use it so "because we have so many problems that half the time we don't know whether we're coming or going." *See* SALAAM; SALEM.

sham. There is a good story about *sham* that merits repeating. One writer in 1734 claimed that "a Town Lady of Diversion [a prostitute] in Country Maid's Cloaths . . . to further her Disguise, pretends to be so *sham'd*." But her clients discovered after sleeping with her that she wasn't shamed, innocent, or healthy and "it became proverbial, when a maim'd lover [one with venereal disease] was laid up, or looked meagre, to say he had met with a *sham*." It may be true that *sham*, first recorded in the 1670s, derives from the tactics of some prostitute, but there is no absolute proof of it, though the word almost certainly has some connection with the word "shame."

shaman. The medicine man or priest called a *shaman* takes his name in a roundabout way from the Sanskrit *sram*, "to exhaust, fatigue," perhaps in reference to the exhausting epileptic seizures such medicine men often exhibit when working their magic. The English word *shaman* comes from a Greek modification of the Russian modification of the Tungusic *saman*. *Saman* derives from the Prakrit *samana*, "a Buddhist monk," which comes from the Sanskrit *sram*.

shambles. The Latin *scamellum*, "little bench," became *scamel* in Old English, changing to *shamel* in Middle English and meaning a butcher's block. *Shamel* became *shambles*, for "a slaughterhouse," in the 16th century and soon the word was being used to describe any scene of bloody disorder resembling a slaughterhouse, though in recent times *shambles* has come to mean any scene of disorder, not necessarily a bloody one.

shampoo. The thousands of ads plugging various shampoo formulas never mention that the word is one brought back from India, deriving from the Hindi word *champo*, "massage."

shamrock. A word representing the Irish from the Irish language. *Shamrock* simply means "little clover," deriving from the Irish *seamrog*, the diminutive of *seamar*, "clover." The three-leaved plant was used by St. Patrick to illustrate the trinity, which is why *to drown the shamrock* came to mean a drinking celebration on St. Patrick's Day.

shamus. A word for a private detective that probably came into the language of the underworld from Yiddish, in which a shammos is the paid caretaker of a synagogue, just as a shamus is often a paid caretaker of his clients. Partridge, however, believes that the word derives from the Irish name Seamus, because so many Irish immigrants in America became policemen.

shanghai. The old expression *to ship a man to Shanghai* is the original version of this term. Sailors first used the words to describe how press gangs got them drunk, drugged them, or blackjacked them and forced them in service aboard a ship in need of a crew. Shanghai, a long way from America, was a leading Chinese shipping port, and many a shanghaied sailor did wind up there. *Shanghai* became so common in the 19th century that it was applied to anyone seized or forced to work unwillingly.

Shangri-la. This word, for "a paradise on earth," came into the language in 1933, when English novelist James Hilton published his novel *Lost Horizon*, which described a hidden paradise named Shangri-la. The name was used during World War II for the secret base from which U.S. planes flew to bomb Hiroshima and Nagasaki. The secret base was Tinian Island in the Mariannas.

shank's mare. *See* GOING BY SHANK'S MARE.

shanty; shantytown. *Shanty*, for "shack or rough cabin," is an Americanism first recorded in 1820 that probably derives from the Gaelic *sean tig*, "old house," though the French Canadian *chantier*, "log hut," is also a strong possibility. *Shantytown*, recorded in 1845, first meant a cluster of shacks near a railyard where railroad construction workers lived. Because many Irish lived in such shantytowns the term soon meant a poor Irish district, *shanty Irish* (1925) coming to mean poor Irish people who lived in such districts.

sharecropper. A tenant farmer who in exchange for his labor receives certain necessities, such as lodging, and a share of the crop he raises. The sharecrop system dates back to the end of the Civil War in the South; the first sharecroppers were freed slaves.

Shariah. Islamic law, seen as deriving from the Koran. The word comes from Arabic *Shariah*, also *Sharia*.

shark. Sea sharks take their name from land sharks, rather than the other way around. The German *Schurke*, meaning "a greedy parasite," gives us the word *shark*, and German sailors applied this term to the sea creature with the voracious land shark in mind. English sailors brought the word home in 1569, the same year that John Hawkins, the first English mariner engaged in the African slave trade, exhibited a huge shark in London. Quickly adopted to describe the killer fish, the word is first recorded some 30 years earlier in English to describe its human counterpart. *See also* SHRIMP.

Sharps rifle. The Sharps rifle "could be fired today and kill tomorrow," said quipsters, in reference to the story that one model could hit a target at five miles. This probably wasn't true, but the rifle—40 different models were made by the Sharps Company between 1840 and 1880—did have remarkable range, power, and accuracy. Hunters called it the "Old Poison Slinger" and it was used extensively in slaughtering the buffalo of America.

shavetail. U.S. Army second lieutenants are called shavetails because they are often untrained and untested, like the mules and horses in the old cavalry whose tails were customarily shaven as a warning to handlers and riders.

Shavian wit. George Bernard Shaw contributed his own name to the language in a characteristically clever way. Not liking the way "Shawian" sounded, he Latinized his name to Shavius and coined the adjective *Shavian* from it, leaving us with a sample of his *Shavian wit.* Shaw died in 1950, aged 94, his wit Shavian till the end. However, even he could be bested occasionally. "Isn't it true, my dear, that male judgment is superior to female judgment?" Shaw once asked his wife. "Of course, dear," she replied, pausing briefly. "After all, you married me and I you." *See also* SUPERMAN.

Shawinigan handshake. To give someone a Shawinigan handshake means "to strangle him." The term comes from the mill town of Shawinigan in Quebec, Canadian prime minister Jean Chrétien's hometown. It seems that the prime minister once "literally wrung the neck of a protester who got close to him at a Flag Day rally in Ottawa" (*New York Times* October 28, 1998), and Canadians took to calling any such throttling a "Shawinigan handshake."

Shay's Rebellion. *See* LEFT HOLDING THE BAG.

Shazam! A magic word used by newsboy Billy Batson to change himself into the comic book hero Captain Marvel. Probably the best-known of contemporary magic words, *Shazam!* was the name of a wizard coined from the initial letters of *S*olomon's wisdom, *H*ercules' strength, *A*tlas's stamina, *Z*eus's power, *A*chilles' courage, and *M*ercury's speed. Both Billy and *Shazam!* were introduced in a 1940 Whiz Comics. *See* ABRACADABRA.

she. *She* for a ship has several explanations, none of them capable of proof. The oldest explanation is that the Romans called all ships she because the Roman goddess of navigation was Minerva. Another theory says the feminine is used because a ship was "as near and dear as one's wife or mother," while a third has it that a ship is "as capricious, demanding, and absorbing as a woman." Perhaps not so incidentally, *another* ship spotted from the bridge is often referred to as *he*, this

possibly referring to the captain of the other vessel, who is usually a man.

shebang. *See* WHOLE SHEBANG.

sheep-dipping. In military slang sheep-dipping has nothing to do with real sheep. A character defines the term in Tess Gerritsen's novel *The Apprentice* (2002): "It refers to the CIA's practice of occasionally borrowing the military's operations soldiers for certain missions. It happened in Nicaragua and Afghanistan, when the CIA's own special operations group—their SOG—needed additional manpower. In Nicaragua, navy SEALS were sheep-dipped to mine the harbors. In Afghanistan, the Green Berets were sheep-dipped to train the mujahideen. While working for the CIA, these soldiers become, essentially, CIA case officers. They go off the Pentagon's books. The military has no record of their activities." In days past *sheep-dipper* was a contemptuous name rustlers gave to a cowboy loyal to his employer, the reference to dipping sheep in sheep dip vats filled with disinfectants. Today *sheepdip* can also mean "cheap rotgut whiskey."

sheet anchor. This name for an emergency anchor has confused etymologists for many years. The best bet is that the word *sheet* here derives from *shoot*. According to this theory, the device was first called a *shoot anchor* because when an emergency came, it had to be "shot" out, that is, dropped quickly. In any event, no lines, or sails, were involved.

sheet anchor to windward. A nautical term that came ashore, this expression has come to mean "to take precautions." People have a sheet anchor to windward, for example, if they save money for retirement or make sure their house has ample smoke alarms. On sailing ships, the heaviest and best anchor was the amidships sheet anchor. Putting it out to windward often saved ships from being blown onto a lee shore. Making sure one's ship had a good one was an excellent precaution.

sheik. *Sheik* must be added to the number of terms such as CASANOVA, LOTHARIO, DON JUAN, and VALENTINO that we've treated in these pages. This word for a great lover or lady-killer derives from the name of the Arabian lover played by Rudolph Valentino in *The Sheik* (1921), a film based on E. M. Hull's novel *The Sheik* (1919).

sheila. One of the best-known Australianisms, *sheila* means "any girl or young woman." The term dates back to the late 19th century and is also used for a female kangaroo. The word derives from the personal name Sheila, but no one knows if any particular Sheila was the eponym. The name Sheila derives from Irish *Síle*.

shekels. *See* GELT.

Shell. An old story tells of a Shell gas station on a busy highway where a man has been pulled unconscious from a car wreck. When the man finally comes to that night, the first thing he sees are lights flickering about him and a huge sign in red letters reading HELL. It takes him a moment to realize that he's still alive and the sign is just a SHELL sign with a malfunctioning letter *S*. I don't know a better Shell story, but there is a tale about the British founder of the oil company, Marcus Samuel, naming his London curio shop the Shell Shop after his grandchildren brought him pretty seashells from a seaside vacation. In 1897, when Samuel's son took over and added bottled kerosene to the shells and other curios sold there, the business expanded greatly, but it retained part of its old name, and the Shell Oil Company, complete with its scallop shell logo, was born.

shell out.   From the actual "shelling out" of peas and corn—removing the first from their pods and removing corn from the cob—came the figurative use of *to shell out,* "to pay out." Removing a seed from the pod, etc., is like taking money out of a purse or pocket and, furthermore, dried shelled peas and "shelled corn," as it was called in America, were often a medium of exchange in the past. The phrase is first recorded in 1825.

shenango.   *See* LONGSHOREMAN.

shenanigans.   Though now it is always used in the plural, this Americanism for "mischief" or "trickery" was first recorded as *shenanigan* in 1855, in California. There have been several suggestions as to its ancestors, including the Spanish *chanada,* "trick," and the argot German *schinaglen,* meaning the same. More likely it comes from the Irish *sionnachuighim,* "I play the fox," or "I play tricks."

shepherd's sundial.   Shepherds used to tell time by the scarlet pimpernel (*Anagallis arvensis*), which opens a bit after 7:00 A.M., closes at a little past 2:00 P.M., and never opens at all if bad weather is imminent. Its genus name is from a Greek word meaning "delightful," though it is not a delight to one garden writer, who classifies the low prostrate annual herb with tiny, red bell-shaped flowers as one of the 50 worst garden weeds. *Poor man's weatherglass* is another name for it.

Sheraton style.   Only Thomas Chippendale has been more widely acclaimed than Thomas Sheraton (1751–1806) as a furniture designer. Unlike many of his predecessors, Sheraton was not a cabinetmaker and there is no record that he ever had a shop of his own or worked with his own hands building furniture. In fact, only one piece—a glass-fronted bookcase stamped with his initials—is known to have belonged to him. Sheraton's fame comes principally from his *The Cabinet-Maker and Upholsterer's Drawing Book* (1791), which introduced designs noted for simplicity and grace combined with utility. This book, followed by a cabinetmaking dictionary (1802) and an unfinished encyclopedia (1804), was intended for London cabinetmakers and the chairs and other pieces drawn in its pages strongly influenced many designers to adopt the Sheraton style, which was based on rectangular shapes, preferring straight lines to curves.

Sheridan's Ride.   General "Little Phil" Sheridan's jet black gelding Rienzi stands stuffed in the Smithsonian Institution today, having won fame comparable to General Robert E. Lee's mount Traveler. Rienzi was ridden by Sheridan in their famous ride to rally Union troops to victory at Cedar Creek in 1864, a breakneck ride of over 19 miles that rivaled Paul Revere's and became one of the most dramatic in military history thanks largely to poet and artist Thomas Buchanan Read, whose romantic (often singsong) narrative poem "Sheridan's Ride" and painting of the same subject glamorized both man and horse. In urging his men to cease retreating and face the enemy, Sheridan is said to have cried: "Boys turn back, face the other way—I am going to sleep in their camp tonight or in hell!" Sheridan always denied he uttered such "profane" words, but he did his denying in puritanical times.

Sherlock Holmes.   A. Conan Doyle probably named his detective after sage American author Oliver Wendell Holmes (1809–94), who was also a professor of anatomy and physiology at Harvard. Sherlock Holmes, however, was modeled in large part on Dr. Joseph Bell (1837–1911), an eminent Edinburgh surgeon under whom Doyle studied medicine and who, like Holmes, often deduced the life and habits of a stranger just by looking at him. Doyle once admitted: "I used and amplified his methods when I tried to build up a scientific detective who solved cases on his own merits." It is said that Dr. John H. Watson, Holmes's Boswell, was intended as a parody of Doyle. In any event, working out of their rooms at 221B Baker Street, Holmes and Watson collaborated on some 60 cases, beginning with *A Study in Scarlet* (1887). In none of these stories did Holmes ever say, "Elementary, my dear Watson," and although he was addicted to cocaine, the great detective never once cried, "Quick, Watson, the needle!" Today the word *Sherlock* has come to mean a detective.

Sherman's bummers; Sherman's hairpins; Sherman's monuments; Sherman's sentinels.   Civil War Union soldiers, often deserters, who looted and burned civilian property, among other offenses, were called "bummers" by Southerners. Many of them rode on the flanks of Union general William Tecumseh Sherman and were known as "Sherman's bummers." Sherman's name also became hated in the form of *Sherman's hairpins,* the 265 miles of mutilated railroad tracks that General Sherman's troops in their famous March to the Sea heated with fires of railroad ties and twisted into grotesque shapes so that they could not be repaired. These were also called "Jeff Davis neckties" or "Lincoln gimlets." The general's name was anathema, too, in *Sherman's monuments,* which referred to the many civilian homes his troops burned to the ground in their march through the South. Often chimneys were the only part of these houses left standing, and Southerners bitterly dubbed them "Sherman's monuments" as well as "Sherman's sentinels." The process of destroying the railroad tracks was described by an engineer on the scene: "The method of destruction is simple, but very effective. Two ingenious instruments have been made for this purpose. One of them is a clasp, which locks under the rail. It has a ring in the top, into which is inserted a long lever, and the rail is then ripped from the sleepers [ties]. The sleepers are then piled in a heap and set on fire, the rails roasting in the flames until they bend of their own weight. When sufficiently heated, each rail is taken off by wrenches fitting closely over the ends, and, by turning in opposite directions, it is so twisted that even a rolling machine could not bring it back into shape." *See* WAR IS HELL.

sherry.   Via an indirect route, *sherry* is still another word that derives from Caesar's name. Sherry is made in Jerez de la Frontera, Spain, for which it was named, and *Jerez* in turn, commemorates Julius Caesar, having originally been called

Xeres, this an adaptation of the Latin *urbs Caesaris*, "the town of Caesar." Sixteenth-century Spaniards pronounced Jerez something like *sherris*, which the English adopted and changed to *sherry* because they believed *sherris* was a plural form. Shakespeare wrote "a good sherris-sack hath a twofold operation in it" in *Henry IV, Part II*, but today the false singular is always used. It is said that when Sir Francis Drake burned the port of Cádiz in 1587, he seized 2,500 butts of sherry from nearby Jerez. Drake called the wine *sack*, according to the old folk story, but the dockers unloading the barrels noted the letters XERES (for Jerez) on them and became the first to use the word *zherry*, or *sherry*.

she-wolf.   *See* HONEST ABE.

shibboleth.   Perhaps only racial, religious, and national slurs have killed as many men as this word. *Shibboleth* has been extended to signify a catchphrase, especially one used so often that it has lost its effectiveness. But it still means a "password," which was its original biblical meaning. The word, deriving from the Hebrew *shibboleth*, for "stream in flood" or "ear of corn," is first recorded in Judges 12:1–16, where the Gileadites used it to pick out the sons of Ephraim from the members of other tribes. Jephthah's men slew 42,000 Ephraimites, who couldn't pronounce the *sh* in the password *shibboleth* and had to say "sibboleth." *See* HULA-HULA.

shill; shillibeer.   London's first buses were introduced from Paris by George Shillibeer (1797–1866) on July 4, 1829. His omnibuses, coaches carrying 22 passengers and pulled by three horses, immediately caught on in London and were being called "buses" within three years. Apparently, Shillibeer later went into the undertaking business, or at least a combined hearse and mourning coach was named the *shillibeer* after him. The word *shill*, for "a swindler's assistant," a "booster" hired to entice customers, may also derive from his name, especially considering that shills were and are still used to pack tourist buses in order to lure customers aboard. Shillibeer's connection with buses makes him a likely candidate, but there have been other suggestions. One is some notorious shill, probably a circus or carnival employee, surnamed Shillibeer. Another possibility is the American humorist Benjamin Penhallow Shillaber (1814–90), who printed Mark Twain's first work in his *Carpet Bag*, a weekly important in developing the new school of American humor. In 1847 Shillaber created the character Mrs. Partington, which he used in a number of books, beginning with his *Life and Sayings of Mrs. Partington* (1854). Critics charged Shillaber with lifting his character from English politician and author Sydney Smith. The American admitted that he took the name from Smith's allusion to the legendary Dame Partington, who had tried to sweep the flooding Atlantic Ocean out of her cottage and whom Smith had compared in an 1831 speech with the opposition of the House of Lords to reform. Although Shillaber denied using anything more than the Partington name for his gossiping Yankee Mrs. Malaprop, his own name came into some disrepute and may have become the basis for *shillaber* and then *shill*.

shillelagh.   The knobby wooden club, or cudgel, called a shillelagh and used as both weapon and walking stick takes its name from the stout oaks of Shillelagh, a town in southwestern Ireland. Once made only of oak or blackthorn, a shillelagh can now be any thick knarled stick. The name is first recorded in the 17th century.

shilly-shally.   A common expression in the 19th century, *shilly-shally* means "to vacillate, to act indecisively, or to hang about doing nothing:" "Stop your shilly-shallying around." The expression is a variation of "Shall I, shall I?"

shim.   A transvestite is called a "shim" in Singapore, the word a conflation of English *she* and *him*. This meaning is not widely known, but a *shim* in American and British English means a thin wedge of wood or metal used in carpentry.

shimose.   What word did Masashika Shimonose Kogakubachi give us? Masashika Shimonose Kogakubachi got his name into the dictionaries when he invented an explosive made of picric acid. Shimose powder, or shimose, was used against the Russians in the Russo-Japanese war of 1904–05 and proved highly effective. In France a powder to fill shells was made from it in 1886 and called melenite, while in England experiments in the town of Lydd two years later resulted in the explosive lyddite. All were names for essentially the same explosive, but shimose was the first to be extensively tested in war. Under whatever name you choose to call it, the first modern shell powder—it replaced black powder—has probably caused as much death and destruction internationally as any invention, still being one of the most common military explosives. Perhaps Masashika Shimonose Kogakubachi would rather have had it called by its scientific name of trinitrotoluene.

shindig; shindy.   *Shin-dig* is first recorded, in 1859, as a southernism for "a kick in the shins." It came to mean a loud, lively party within 10 years or so and most authorities believe that the party *shindig* derives from the word meaning a kick in the shins. Another possibility is that the party name comes from the Scottish *shinty*, for "a wild form of field hockey played in Scotland" and, later, in America, *shindy* here possibly suggested by players being kicked in the shins. According to this theory, *shinty* (first recorded in 1771) became *shindy* (1821), a sailor's word for "a spree, merrymaking" and *shindy* by mispronunciation later became *shindig*. There was, in fact, a U.S. expression *to kick up a shindy*, "to cause a row or commotion," at about the time *shindig* was born. I would guess that both *shin-dig* and *shindig* derive from *shinty—shindy*.

shinplaster.   During the Civil War, beginning in 1862, the North issued paper currency of from 3-cent to 50-cent denominations that were humorously called *shinplasters*. The old story that they were so named because an anonymous soldier plastered his shin wound with them probably isn't true, because paper money had been called shinplasters as early as 1824. More likely they were dubbed shinplasters because such paper money often became valueless and was good for nothing but plastering the shins.

ship.   *Ship* can be traced back to the Old English *scip* or "shape," evidence that the word *ship* arose when a ship was "no more than a trunk of a tree scooped out and *shaped* to enable it to glide safely and smoothly through the water," according to one authority.

ship names.   There has never been any universal system for naming ships. While the British preferred frightening names such as *Invincible, Devastation, Shark,* and *Hyena* for their warships, the Japanese have always liked romantic names such as *Siranui* (Phosphorescent Foam) and *Kasumi* (Mist of Flowers). No rigid logic seems ever to have been at work here, although the U.S. Navy did institute a comprehensive system during World War II, prescribing that the classes of ships be named in a certain manner (battleship after states, cruisers after cities, etc). Many ship names have been used scores of times. The revolutionary British DREADNOUGHT of 1906, for example, was the eighth ship in English naval history to bear that name, and others have used it since. Sailors on even the most strictly disciplined ships often called them by entirely different names; the great *Missouri,* for example, was sometimes jokingly called the *Misery;* the *Brooklyn* was called the *Teakettle;* while the *Salt Lake City* was often called the *Swayback Marie!* In 1982 the U.S. Navy broke an old tradition by naming a ship after a living person, Admiral Hyman G. Rickover, who pioneered the nuclear submarine fleet. As for small pleasure boats, the Boat Owners Association of America reports that the five most popular boat names, in order, are *Security, Irish Eyes, Island Time, Sea Spirit,* and *Obsession.* Some humorous samples of the over half a million boat names are: *A Loan Again, Beeracuda, Codfather, Freudian Sloop, Out to Launch, Prozac, Sloop Du Jour, Victoria's Sea-Cratem,* and *Wet Debt.*

ship of fools.   Sebastian Brandt's famous *Narrenschiff,* or *Ship of Fools,* published in 1494, had as its theme the shipping of fools of all kinds from their native land of Swabia to the fictional Land of Fools. The various fools were introduced in the book by classes and reproved for their folly. In fact, in 15th-century Germany there were real *Narrenschiffs.* These most unusual ships were riverboats used to imprison the insane and thus clear city streets of them. Real ships of fools plied up and down the Rhine carrying their cargoes of madmen, who were thought to have lost their souls and were supposed to sail back and forth until they became sane again. However, most of them died aboard these hell ships, which had no destination save death.

Ship of State.   *See* HANGING BREATHLESS ON; TEREDO

shipping lanes.   In his book *Sailing Directions* (1855) U.S. Navy Lt. Matthew Fontaine Maury recommended "lanes," or "strips," for ships traveling westbound in the Atlantic after the U.S. mail steamer *Arctic* collided with the French steamer *Vesta* in 1854. These lanes became the building blocks for today's complex, internationally approved seasonal routes.

Shiprock.   An interesting New Mexico landmark described by Willa Cather in *Death Comes to the Archbishop* (1927): "And north of the canyon de Chelly was the Shiprock, a slender crag rising to a dizzy height, all alone out on a flat desert. Seen at a distance of fifty miles or so, that crag presents the figure of a one-masted fishing boat under full sail, and the white man named it accordingly. But the Indian has another name; he believes the rock was once a ship of the air. Ages ago . . . that crag had moved through the air, bearing upon its summit the parents of the Navaho race from the place in the far north where all peoples were made—and wherever it sank to earth was to be their land."

ships that pass in the night.   People who meet by chance and aren't likely to meet again are sometimes compared to *ships that pass in the night.* The expression dates back to the 19th century and seems to have originated in Henry Wadsworth Longfellow's poem *Tales of a Wayside Inn* (1863): "Ships that pass in the night, and speak to each other in passing . . ."

shipworm.   *See* GRIBBLE; TEREDO

shiri oshi.   There is not yet a job classification corresponding to that of the *shiri oshi* in any American subway system, crowded as those systems may be. *Shiri oshi* translates, euphemistically, as "tushy pusher." These Japanese train attendants, wearing neat blue uniforms and white gloves, stand in front of subway train doors during rush hours helping to pack passengers into the trains.

shirtsleeves to shirtsleeves in three generations.   "There's no' but three generations atween clog and clog," says the old Lancashire proverb that is probably the ancestor of this expression, but American multimillionaire Andrew Carnegie (1835–1919) is credited with the exact words *shirtsleeves to shirtsleeves in three generations,* meaning that family wealth is not long-lasting. The words don't apply to the Rockefeller, Du Pont, Rothschild, and Ford families, to name but a few that come quickly to mind.

shit.   From the Indo-European root *skei,* "to divide," comes the Old English *scitan,* "to defecate," that is the ancestor of our word *shit. To shit* thus means strictly to divide or cut (wastes) from the body. *Shit,* as slang for nonsense or lies, is an Americanism probably first used by soldiers during the Civil War as a shortening of *bullshit,* another Americanism that probably goes back 30 years or more earlier, though it is first recorded, in the form of its euphemism *bull,* in about 1850.

shit belong-um fire.   This apt bit of pidgin English was used by Lascar seamen employed as stokers on 19th-century British steamers. It means ashes.

shitepoke; crazy as a shitepoke.   When flushed out by hunters, the small green heron (*Ardea virescens*) discharges its bowels and runs crazily to and fro. This led to American pioneers calling it the "shitepoke" (*shite* "excrement," plus *poke,* "bag"), which also became a name for any vile person. *Crazy as a shitepoke,* "very crazy," was first recorded in 1943 but must be much older. Wrote Laura Wood in *Walter Reed* (1943): "He'd be all right with a little rest, but sometimes, after a more severe ordeal by snow and silence, a man would come out crazy as—they had a word for it here—as a shitepoke, the awkward heron that seems to have no sense at all."

shitkicker.   Shitkicker is a Texas culture all to itself, according to Molly Ivins in *Molly Ivins Can't Say That, Can She?* (1991): "Shitkicker is pickup trucks with guns slung across the racks on the back and chicken-fried steaks and machismo . . . and cheap, pink nylon slips, and gettin' drunk on Saturday night and goin' to church on Sunday morning, and drivin' down the highway throwin' beer cans out the window, and Rastus-an'-Liza jokes and high school football, and family reunions where the in-laws of your second cousins show up. . . ." And much more and, with a few minor changes, a culture in many places. *Shitkicker* has also been used to mean a cowboy and as a synonym for cowboy boots.

shit or get off the pot.   Although Partridge gives this as World War II Canadian army slang "directed at a dice player unable to 'crap out,' " it has been traced to the early 1900s in America, its maiden aunt ancestor probably *fish or cut bait*, "do something now or give up."

" 'Shit!' said the Queen. . . ."   An old story, unproved one way or the other, has it that those good friends Rudyard Kipling and Mark Twain had a contest between them to see who could write the bawdiest, most offensive story. An effort of Kipling's beginning " 'Shit!' said the Queen . . ." was brought to an unamused Queen Victoria's attention, which is why Kipling was never knighted and never became poet laureate.

Shit! The Guard never surrenders!   *See* THE GUARD DIES BUT NEVER SURRENDERS.

shittimwood.   The bark of this American tree is a powerful cathartic; hence its name, first recorded in 1884. *Rhamnus purshiana* is also called "bearberry" and "bear-wood." Other trees called "shittimwood" were so named because their wood was worthless for lumber. Finally, there is the shittimwood (probably an acacia) that is said to have been used to make the ark of the covenant (Ex. 25–26), its name deriving from Hebrew *shittim*, "wood."

shiv.   *Shiv*, for "a dagger or knife," is centuries older than its first mention in 18th-century England. For it was taken into underworld English intact from the Romany *shiv*, meaning the same, long used by the Gypsies.

shivaree.   A noisy wedding reception or celebration usually held late at night at the home of the bride and groom, complete with a mock serenade with pots, pans, and other noisemakers and good-natured pranks on the newlyweds; from the French *charivari*, meaning the same, though the French word, appropriately, comes from a Medieval Latin word meaning "headache."

shiver me timbers.   Although this is a cricket expression referring to the scattering of wickets, for which timber is a slang substitute, it goes back much further. Originally, *timbers!* was an 18th-century nautical slang exclamation with no real meaning to it: "My timbers! what lingo he'd coil and belay." Novelist Capt. Frederick Marryat then embroidered the oath, making it *Shiver my timbers!* in *Jacob Faithful* (1834), an ejaculation you can be sure no one used before this.

shlock.   This Yiddish expression, for "shoddy, cheaply made, defective articles," derives from the German *Schlog*, "a blow" suggesting that the goods have been knocked around and damaged. Pronounced to rhyme with "stock," *shlock* is sometimes spelled *schlock*.

Shoah.   A widely heard term from Hebrew for the HOLOCAUST. Literally, the word means "catastrophe."

shock.   The French *choc*, a noun of action for "a military encounter," came into English early in the 16th century as *shocke*, with the meaning of the first charge in a battle, or two jousters charging each other and smashing together. By the early 18th century *shock* had come to mean a sudden disturbing impact on the mind as well as the body.

shoddy.   Civil War suppliers cheated the Union Army with a cheap uniform cloth called "shoddy," which literally unraveled on the wearer's back—and added a new adjective to the language.

shoeicide bomber.   This play on *suicide bomber* was applied to that alleged terrorist who was found to have explosives in his shoes during an international airline flight and was subdued by crew members and passengers. The expression is said to have been coined by talk-show host Jay Leno.

shoestring.   The expression may have come from faro, but it isn't recorded until 1904, although *shoestring gambler*, for a "petty, tinhorn gambler," is recorded 10 years or so earlier. *On a shoestring* suggests that one's resources are limited to the laces of one's shoes.

sholom aleichem.   A traditional greeting of Jews meaning "hello, how are you?" the response being the reverse order, *aleichem sholom*, "and unto you, peace." The Russian-born Yiddish-writing author Solomon Rabinowitz (1859–1916) took his pen name, Sholom Aleichem, from these words. According to one tale, Aleichem, called "the Jewish Mark Twain," claimed to have met Mark Twain in New York City. "I am the American Sholom Aleichem," Twain modestly told him. *See* TRISKAIDEKAPHOBIA.

shoofly plant.   There is only one garden species of the *Nicandra* genus, named after Nicander of Colophon, a Greek physician, poet, and botanist of the second century A.D. And this annual species, *Nicandra physalodes*, seems to have but one distinction: It is a repellent to the white fly if grown next to other plants troubled by this pest. It is also called *apple-of-Peru*, because it is plentiful in that country.

shoot deer in the balcony (theater).   This old show biz phrase, dating back a century or so, refers to the empty theaters that result due to a flop or bad business of any kind: "You could shoot deer in the balcony."

shoot down.   *To shoot down* someone's argument or *to shoot it down in flames* means to show that it is wrong or totally worthless, impossible. The expression originated during World War II, when so many planes were shot down and destroyed by the enemy.

shootin' iron.   A handgun. This term dates back to 18th-century America and did not originate in the West, despite its constant use in Hollywood westerns.

shoot one's bolt.   The *bolt* in this phrase, *he's shot his bolt*, meaning he's finished with his efforts, is not a door bolt, but an arrow—a bolt being an arrow with a bulletlike knob. Among other words and phrases owing their origin to the arrow are *thunderbolt, a bolt from the blue,* "a complete surprise," and *to bolt upright.*

shoot the cat; shoot one's cookies; shoot the moon; shoot one's cuffs.   *Shoot the cat* is British slang meaning "to vomit, throw up, be sick to one's stomach." The expression, similar to the American *shoot* (or *toss*) *one's cookies,* has been traced to the early 19th century, but the use of *cat* has never been satisfactorily explained. *Shoot the moon* means "to move out of a residence at night without paying the rent," while *shoot the crow* means "to suddenly leave a place (skip town, as Americans say), and *shoot one's cuffs* means "to display a large amount of shirt cuff when wearing a jacket."

shop.   The word *shop* derives from a Saxon term meaning the porch or lean-to of a house. Such "open rooms or stalls" eventually developed into enclosed stores.

shopping cart.   The first of America's 30 million shopping carts were invented and named by Sylman Goldman in 1936 for his Standard Supermarkets in Oklahoma, making him a millionaire in the process.

shopping days until Christmas.   *See* CUSTOMER IS ALWAYS RIGHT.

shopping mall.   In the 16th century the popular Italian game *pallamaglio* (from *palla,* "ball," and *maglio,* "mallet") spread to France, where it became known as *palemail,* which was called *pall mall* when the game was adopted by the English. A large playing area for the game called The Mall in London's St. James Park during the reign of Charles II later became a broad public walk, or promenade, called Pall Mall. It is this public walk where people promenaded that is the basis for our outdoor and indoor shopping malls (also called shopping centers), where people promenade along a broad walk lined with shops. Shopping malls, or malls, as we know them today, are a relatively recent American innovation dating back only to the years after World War II. But rude examples of their kind can be found further back in American history, and they have their deepest roots in many age-old institutions, including the bazaars of Persia, the agoras of ancient Greece, the forums of Rome, and the fairs and marketplaces of medieval Europe. They have been called "the quintessential American place of today," malls being the places where people spend more time than anywhere else except at home or work.

Shoreditch.

> I could not get one bit of bread
> Whereby my hunger might be fed . . .
> So weary of my life at length
> I yielded up my vital strength
> Within a ditch . . . which since that day
> Is Shoreditch called, as writers say—

Shoreditch in London is so named because Jane Shore, Edward IV's cast-off mistress, died there in a ditch, her tale told in the old ballad above.

short arms and deep pockets.   *See* DICK SMITH.

short bit.   In the old West, the *short bit* was a dime, being 2½ cents short of a bit (12½ cents). According to *A Dictionary of Americanisms,* "In the West, when small coins, except the dime and the quarter (2 bits), were scarce, a dime was accepted in payment for anything priced at one bit. A *long* bit was the equivalent of 15 cents, being the price paid when a dime was returned as change from a quarter tendered for a purchase priced at one bit."

short fuse.   *He has a short fuse,* we say of short-tempered people whose anger explodes at the slightest provocation. The expression originated during World War II, based upon short fuses in bombs and shells.

short hairs.   *See* GET BY THE SHORT HAIRS.

shorthand.   *See* STENOGRAPHY.

Shortia.   *Shortia* is definitely a "low-growing" genus of evergreen herbs, comprising only two species, but that is not the reason for its name. The genus honors Dr. Charles W. Short (1794–1863), a Kentucky botanist. Native to the mountains of the Carolinas and Japan, the flowers are well adapted for use in a rock garden. The American species is sometimes advertised as Oconee Bells and the Japanese, Nippon Bells. The plants have beautiful white bell- or heart-shaped flowers, solitary and nodding on long stalks. They are more often called *Shortia,* or coltsfoot, than by their "Bell" names.

short-list.   To be put on a list of people most likely to be chosen for something, a list that has been winnowed from a longer one. For example, several novels are short-listed each year for Britain's prestigious Booker Prize and from this short list a winner is selected. The expression is not a new one, dating back about 75 years.

short shrift.   So many crimes were punishable by execution in Elizabethan times that condemned persons were often given only a few minutes for last rites on the crowded scaffold. Roman Catholic prisoners were allowed the sacrament of *shriving,* commonly called *shrift,* during which sins were confessed and absolution granted, but their callous executioners frequently permitted only a short version of the customary ceremony. This became known as *to give short shrift,* which from its literal sense has come to mean to cut short, to make quick work of, or to give very little attention to. *Shriving* and *shrift* derive from the Anglo-Saxon *scrifan,* "to make a confession."

short story.   The name, though not the form, was invented in the U.S., its first mention in *Harper's Magazine* in 1887 in the form of "short story writing." A short story, briefly, is usually a prose work of fiction under 10,000 words, "differing from a novel in being shorter and less elaborate," according to the *O.E.D.* A short short story is even more condensed, perhaps of up to 1,200 words. Edgar Allan Poe is regarded as the originator of the modern short story, which Americans have excelled in. An old joke has an English teacher telling a class that the five requisites to a good short story are "brevity, a religious reference, a sexual reference, some association with society and an illustration of modesty." The next day a student handed in a story that read in full: "My God!" said the duchess. 'Take your hand off my knee!'"

shotgun wedding. Any wedding where the father or other member of the family, pointing a gun at his head, forces the groom to marry the bride, who has been made pregnant by or lost her virginity to the man. It is doubtful that many real shotguns were used in such weddings, but since 1925 or so, when first recorded, the Americanism has meant "a wedding made by pregnancy."

shot heard round the world. Baseball fans ascribe a different meaning to this Ralph Waldo Emerson line describing the opening of the American Revolution. For half a century now they have remembered the words as a name for the home run New York Giant slugger Bobby Thomson hit in the ninth inning of the last game of the 1951 playoffs against the Dodgers to win the National League pennant. The "Jints" victory was dubbed "The Miracle of Coogan's Bluff," after the hill behind the Giant's Polo Grounds stadium.

shot in the arm. Anything that gives a person renewed vitality, enthusiasm, determination, confidence, or hope. However, if the expression's origins were taken into account it would mean short-lived vitality and false hope, for the words derive not from a shot administered by a doctor but from hypodermic injections of narcotics by drug addicts. Some anonymous drug user coined *a shot in the arm* back in the 1920s, basing it on the medical *shot*, for medicine injected into the body, which had been invented shortly before it. The phrase has nothing whatsoever to do with "Quick, Watson, the needle!," a saying often attributed to Sherlock Holmes. *See also* SHERLOCK HOLMES.

shot in the dark. A random conjecture, a wild guess, and most likely a guess that will fail. This Americanism refers to a gun shot in the dark at a target or anything else, a shot that would rarely succeed.

shotten herring. Since Shakespeare's time worthless or spiritless persons have been called *shotten herring* because they resemble such fish. Shotten herring are herring that have "shot off," or ejected, their spawn and are weak, tired, and worthless.

shoulder candy. *Candy*, or *eye candy*, for a sexy young woman is documented as dating back to about 1968, but I haven't seen *shoulder candy* in any dictionary. The term is defined in a *New York Times Magazine* column (11/24/96) by John Tierney: "Models are visual bait," says David Jones, a gossip reporter at the *Daily News*. . . . "Even the serious playboys, the rich guys who live to chase models, often aren't that interested in sex. They mainly want their fellow wolves to see them walk in with a model. The term they use is 'shoulder candy.'"

shout. *Shout*, of course, means "to call out loudly." It possibly derives from Old Norse *skuta*, "a (loud) taunt," and has given birth since to such expressions as *it's all over but the shouting*, the allusion being to the end of a boxing match whose outcome the crowd in the arena is protesting, and *within shouting distance*, a short distance away. In Australia *shout* refers to a round of beers bought in a pub, "It's your shout, mate" being the Aussie equivalent of "It's your turn to buy the drinks, friend."

shout it from the housetops. Let everybody know. The old expression is from the Bible (Luke 12:3): ". . . and that which ye have spoken in the ear shall be proclaimed upon the housetops."

show a leg; shake a leg. *Show a leg* means to get up from bed, to hurry, or be alert. One version of its birth says that when the bos'n's mate on early 19th-century sailing ships woke up the crew in the morning, he cried, "Show a leg, show a leg or a stocking!" At that time, according to the story, women were allowed to be on board ship, ostensibly as sailors' wives, and a "leg in a stocking put over the side of a hammock indicated that the occupant was a woman, who was allowed to remain until the men had cleared out." A more prosaic and reasonable account says the bos'n cried, "Come on, all you sleepers! Hey! Show a leg and put a stocking on it." *Shake a leg*, meaning "hurry," may derive from this earlier phrase, for both are nautical expressions and no better explanation has been given.

Show-Me State. A nickname for Missouri (*see* I'M FROM MISSOURI). It has also been called the Ozark State, the Lead State, the Bullion State, (after Senator Thomas Hart Benton, "Old Bullion," an advocate of metallic currency), and the Pennsylvania of the West. Obsolete is the nickname the Puke State, possibly so named as a misprint for Pike County, Missouri, or after a word describing a backward yokel. *See also* PUKE.

show the white feather. A cock with any white feathers was believed to be poorly bred and too cowardly for cockfighting in days past. This led to the old expression *to show the white feather*, "to exhibit cowardice."

shrapnel. Shrapnel's shell, or shrapnel's shot, as it was first called, was the brainchild of Henry Shrapnel, a British artillery officer who held the rank of second lieutenant and had only turned 23 when he began work on his deadly contrivance in 1783. Shrapnel had joined the army at the age of 18 and served in Gibraltar, the West Indies, and Flanders under the duke of York. He devoted all his spare time and money to developing his invention, the shrapnel shell, which consisted of a spherical projectile filled with lead musket balls and a small charge of black powder that was set off by a time fuse, exploding the shell in midair and scattering the shot in an ever-widening circle over a large area. This antipersonnel weapon, which laid low everyone in its path, was finally adopted in 1803 due to Shrapnel's persistent efforts and he was promoted to regimental lieutenant colonel the following year. Although the shell itself wasn't used during World War II, the term *shrapnel* is still applied loosely to shell fragments from any high explosive, whether artillery, bomb, or mine. Henry Shrapnel, who had been promoted to lieutenant general in 1837, died five years later, aged 89. He had never been paid a cent for his important invention and the government refused even to compensate him for the several thousand pounds of his own money that he had spent in developing the weapon.

shrewd. *Shrewd* most likely comes from the name of the shrew, a small, mouselike animal with a long snout, common in England's forests. Extremely truculent animals, shrews will often fight to the death over a bit of food, the victor eating the loser in the bargain. Thus a shrew became an evil, vicious person, especially a woman who scolded or nagged, as in Shakespeare's *The Taming of the Shrew*, and the verb *to shrew* formed from this noun gave us the word *shrewd* in its past participle. Over the centuries *shrewd* lost its meaning of evil but retained the qualities of sharpness and cleverness that made the little shrew formidably wicked, so that today shrewd means keen-witted, clever, sharp in practical affairs.

shrimp.   Short people are *not* called shrimps because they resemble the shellfish in size. As with SHARKS, it is the other way around. The common little European species *Crago vulgaris* was named *shrimp* from the Middle English word *shrimpe*, which meant a puny person.

a shrimp short of a barbie.   Used by Australians to describe someone who isn't too smart, isn't quite normal. *Barbie*, of course, is the word Australians prefer for a barbecue or barbecue grill.

shrink.   *Shrink*, and *headshrinker*, from which it derives, are Hollywood terms, the latter dating back to the late 1940s and the former coming on the scene some 20 years later. Both, of course, mean a psychiatrist and may be a comparison to the medicine men of primitive tribes who literally shrunk heads to work magic; *headshrink* may refer to the *shrinking*, or lessening, of problems in a patient's head.

shtick.   Deriving ultimately from the German *Stuck*, "piece," *shtick* (or *shtik*) has a number of meanings in Yiddish, but its most recent meaning is best-known in English today. Since about 1955, it has been heard most as the term for a comic acting routine or piece of business inserted to get a laugh, to draw attention to oneself. Thus it also means one's special interest or talent, one's "thing," as in "That's his shtick."

shucks.   The expression *shucks* may derive from worthless "shucks" or husks of corn, but the interjection, used to express mild disgust or regret, first recorded in 1847, is thought by some to be simply a euphemism for "shit," as its oldest quotation in *A Dictionary of Americanisms* would seem to indicate: "And Mr. Bagley was there to [shoot] any gentleman who might say 'shucks.' "

shufti.   A term heard among the British but rarely in American English. First recorded during World War II, it derives from Arabic *saffa*, "try to see," and means "look or glimpse," as in "Have a shufti at this one."

shutmouth.   An old-fashioned word, not much used anymore, that describes someone who is closemouthed, keeps his real feelings to himself. "Lincoln was the most shutmouth man I ever met," said his law partner of 16 years.

Shut my mouth!   A southern expression of surprise that has become a national cliché because it has been used so often in comic routines. Another similar expression is "*Hush my mouth!*"

shut out.   Though the term is most commonly heard in baseball for a game in which the losing team doesn't score, *shut out* probably has its origins in horse racing. First recorded in 1855, *shut out* has long referred to a bettor who arrives at a track window when it is too late to bet, thus being shut out by the closed window. Today someone who fails to make any headway in an endeavor is said to be shut out.

shut up, he explained.   Perhaps the most famous of American author Ring Lardner's quips was inspired by the writer's move with his family from Chicago to New York, where he began his syndicated column. Somehow the Lardners went astray in the Bronx. The famous exchange came when the author's son asked him if they were lost, Lardner later re-creating the scene in his short story "The Young Immigrants," told from a child's viewpoint: "Are you lost, Daddy?" I asked tenderly. "Shut up," he explained.

shut your face.   Stop talking. This Americanism is first recorded by Upton Sinclair in *King Coal* (1917): "The marshall bade him 'shut his face,' and emphasized the command by a twist at his coat collar."

shyster.   *Shyster*, an American slang term for a shady, disreputable lawyer, is first recorded in 1846. Various authorities list a real New York advocate as a possible source, but this theory has been disproved by Professor Gerald L. Cohen of the University of Missouri-Rolla, whose long paper on the etymology I had the pleasure of reading. Shakespeare's money-lender Shylock has also been suggested, as has a racetrack form of the word *shy*, i.e., to be shy money when betting. Some authorities trace *shyster* to the German *Scheisse*, "excrement," possibly through the word *shicir*, "a worthless person," but there is no absolute proof for any theory.

Siamese twins.   Chang and Eng Bunker were born in Bangesau, Siam (now Thailand) on April 15, 1811, and were discovered at Mekong when they were 16. Their bodies were joined by a ligament between the xiphoid cartilages, a short tubular band uniting them at the chest through which their circulatory systems communicated. After P. T. Barnum brought the world-renowned "Chinese Double-Boys" to America, he had considerable trouble with them, claiming that they were the only show business people he couldn't get along with. But then Chang and Eng hated everybody, even each other, Barnum said. At any rate, the two often quarreled with the impresario over his methods and only exhibited when they needed the money. In April 1864 they married two English sisters, Sarah and Adelaide Yates, fathering 22 children between them—Chang, 10, and Eng, 12—according to the records. They finally settled with their families on a farm in New Hampshire, where they died on January 17, 1874, within two or three hours of each other. But the surviving twin did not die of a broken heart, as the story goes; fatal illness in one Siamese twin dooms the other unless they can be separated, which was impossible in Chang and Eng's case. The Siamese Twins, as they were billed, gave their name to all others so born after them and the term is also used to describe inseparable friends. Doubles of many kinds are called Siamese, such as the Siamese pipes with two openings almost at ground level outside some buildings, which fire engines use to pump water into a building for its standpipes and sprinkler system.

sic. Pronounced "sik," this little word is simply the Latin for "thus", "so." It is used in brackets by writers after a word or phrase to indicate that the word or phrase is being reproduced by the writer exactly as it is in the original, even though it is wrong in some way.

Sicilian vespers. In 1282, the Sicilians massacred their French oppressors throughout the country, the signal to begin the massacres in each city being the bell for evening church services, or vespers. Within a few days Sicilian wits were calling the massacres the Sicilian Vespers.

Sicily. *See* ISLAND OF THE SUN.

Sic semper tyrannis! John Wilkes Booth's infamous words after he assassinated Abraham Lincoln, which are Latin for "Thus always to tyrants!" The rest of Booth's words were "The South is avenged!" "Sic semper tyrannis" is the state motto of Virginia.

sideburns. General Ambrose Everett Burnside had a flair for doing the daring, innovative thing in war as well as fashion. Despite his many failures as a general he went on to be elected governor of Rhode Island for three terms, 1866–69, and United States senator for two terms, from 1875 until his death in 1881, at age 57. From the constant publicity given him, the flamboyant Burnside hat that he wore in the field came to be called after the big bluff and hearty general, as were the burnside whiskers, or *burnsides*, he affected. Innovative as ever, he had chosen to wear the hair on his face in a new way, shaving his chin smooth below a full mustache and big muttonchops, or sidebar whiskers. Thousands imitated him and his burnsides, because they were on only the sides of the face, were soon called sideburns, this reversal of Burnside's name having nothing to do with his military reversals, though that might have been appropriate.

sidekick. Side pants pockets are the hardest pockets for pickpockets to pick because they are closer to the hands of a victim and are constantly moving with the motions of the legs. About 1900, according to one story, men wise to the ways of pickpockets began keeping their wallets in their side pockets or side-kicks (*kick* being slang for a pants pocket since the 17th century). *Side-kickers* then became a slang synonym for a faithful buddy (usually male), a partner always at one's side. O. Henry first recorded the term in a 1904 story, and about 10 years later *side-kick* was shortened to *sidekick*.

sidewalk. Americans have been calling the part of a street reserved for pedestrians a sidewalk since at least 1851, when the word was first recorded, describing a cement walk at the side of a road. In fact, *side passage* was used as early as 1790. Today Americans rarely say anything but "sidewalk," except as regionalisms, while Australians use *footpath* and the British prefer *footway* and *pavement*.

sidewinder. A rattlesnake, or, figuratively, a dangerous, treacherous person. The word was suggested to American pioneers by the sidewinder rattlesnake, so called for its lateral locomotion.

Siegfried Line. A zone of heavy fortifications in Germany facing the French MAGINOT LINE that was built in the years before World War II. On March 7, 1945, the Western Allies smashed through the line and crossed the Rhine, the war in Europe ending for all intents and purposes about six weeks later. Siegfried, the line's eponym, is a great hero of German mythology. The line is also remembered by the old British song "We're gonna hang our washing on the Siegfried Line."

Sieg Heil! Heil Hitler! "Hail to victory!" is the translation of *Sieg Heil!*, a salute invented by German Nazis and used at their political meetings and rallies. *Heil Hitler!* was used by the Nazis as a greeting honoring Hitler. Both expressions date back to the early 1930s, when the Nazis came to power.

sienna. The Italian city of Siena lends its name to the red color sienna, while Venice gives its own to Venetian red. The colors were apparently invented by artists in those cities. *See also* MAGENTA; TITIAN.

Sierra Leone. Portuguese sailors off Africa thought they spied a great mountain chain along the west coast and were convinced they heard the roaring of lions coming from those mountains. They thus named the area Sierra Leone, "mountain range of the lions," a name that the African country Sierra Leone still bears today, even if the Portuguese seafarers did eventually discover that the "mountain range" they saw were great cumulus clouds in the sky and the roaring they heard was the surf breaking on the beach. *See also* NOME; GUINEA.

sign language. Sign language is any method of communication employing manual gestures, especially as used by deaf people. The term dates back to about 1840. *Signing* is the process of employing sign language. When ill in the South Pacific and unable to hold his pen or even speak, Tusitala, or "the Tale Teller," as the natives called Robert Louis Stevenson, dictated his stories with his fingers by the signing alphabet.

Silent League. A society organized in 1903 (in the U.S. Navy of all places), of men who "solemnly agree to discourage Profanity and Obscenity everywhere so long as they live," in the words of its founder, Chaplain Carroll Q. Wright. As Gary Jennings notes in his delightful *Personalities of Language* (1965): "I know of no sailor today who ever heard of the Silent League, but I know several who are walking evidence that Profanity and Obscenity have outlived it."

silent—like the p in swimming. British in origin and mostly British in use, this punning catchphrase (the obvious pun is on "pee," to urinate) dates back to the early 1900s and, as Partridge notes, is sometimes employed jokingly in explaining difficult pronunciations; *e.g.*, "Her name is Fenwick, where the *w* is silent—like the *p* in swimming."

silent majority. President Richard M. Nixon used this term in a November 3, 1969, speech to describe the majority of Americans, those who didn't protest against the Vietnam War. His vice president, Spiro Agnew, employed the phrase six months before that. Soon the term came to mean the "average American," all those who aren't outspoken and are considered to constitute a majority of the electorate, usually conservative in their opinions. Long before, the ancient Greeks used *silent majority* to mean "the dead."

silhouette. Madame de Pompadour had her friend Étienne de Silhouette appointed France's controller general in 1759, but was probably disappointed with the results. Silhouette, then 50, proceeded to try to get France back on her feet after the bankruptcy brought about by the Seven Years' War, not to mention the luxury-loving court where La Pompadour set the style and spent more than anyone else. The new minister started out well enough, raising a 72 million-livre loan, but he soon placed restrictions on the spending of Louis XV himself, proposed a land tax on the estates of nobles, and ordered a cut in government pensions. This naturally angered the nobles, who often found ways to circumvent Silhouette's reforms, and the minister trotted out plans to levy an income tax, triple the poll tax on bachelors, institute a luxury tax, and levy a stringent sales tax. People generally thought such reforms cheap, capricious, and petty, resenting the sacrifices demanded, and when financiers boycotted his treasury operations, Silhouette was forced to resign less than nine months after he took office. In the meantime, his parsimonious regulations had inspired the phrase *á la silhouette*, "according to Silhouette," or "on the cheap." Pants without pockets—and who needed pockets with such confiscatory taxes—were said to be made *á la silhouette*, as were snuffboxes constructed with wood, and coats that were required to be fashioned without folds. The term was also applied to shadow portraits made by tracing the outline of a profile and filling it in with black, or cutting the outline out of black paper. These were called portraits *á la silhouette*, cheap portraits in the fashion of Silhouette, and soon became known simply as *silhouettes*.

silicon; Silicon Valley. Silicon is a nonmetallic element occurring in minerals and rocks and constituting over one-fourth of the Earth's crust. It has been used most recently in manufacturing computer chips. *Silicon Valley*, the name first recorded in 1974, is an area in northern California, southwest of San Francisco in the Santa Clara valley. It is so named because the many microelectronic firms based there make it the world capital of computer technology. Regarding silicon, it's said that artist and wit James Whistler (1834–1903) was dismissed from West Point because he failed chemistry. "Had silicon been a gas," he later quipped, "I would have been a major-general." *See* GOD BLESS AMERICA.

silk purse out of a sow's ear. *See* YOU CAN'T MAKE A SILK PURSE OUT OF A SOW'S EAR.

Silly Billy. *See* SAILOR KING.

silo drippings. This synonym for homemade liquor dates back to the late 19th century when it was made on farms in the American Midwest, where Prohibition was often in effect. Silos held corn for the winter feeding of stock and the corn packed in a full silo slowly fermented, forming a potent brew that dripped out of holes drilled in the bottom of the silos and was collected by thirsty farmers.

Silver Knight of the West. William Jennings Bryan of Nebraska, who fought for the silver standard and was famous for his Cross of Gold speech at the 1897 Democratic National Convention.

silver or lead. The classic choice offered by mobsters to someone they want to bribe: either take the money or a bullet. This offer that can't be refused probably dates back to the 1930s in America.

silver spoon. The earliest spoons were made of wood, the word *spoon*, in fact, deriving from the Anglo-Saxon *spon*, "a chip of wood." Until the 19th century most people used pewter spoons, but traditionally, especially among the wealthy, godparents have given the gift of a silver spoon to their godchildren at christening ceremonies. The custom is centuries old throughout Europe and inspired the saying "born with a silver spoon in one's mouth," *i.e.*, born to hereditary wealth that doesn't have to be earned. This expression is not of American origin as the *O.E.D.* implies; the great dictionary only traces the phrase back to 1800 here, but it is much older, for Cervantes used it in *Don Quixote* (1605–1615): "Every man was not born with a silver spoon in his mouth." The duke of Bedford gave a nice twist to the phrase in the title of his biography, *A Silver-Plated Spoon*. The *silver shoon* in Walter de la Mare's poem "Silver" are "silver shoes," *shoon* being an old plural of *shoe*:

> Slowly, silently, now the moon
> Walks the night in her silver shoon.

Silver State. A nickname for Nevada, after the silver mined there. The state was once called Silverland.

silvertip. *See* GRIZZLY BEAR.

simba. This word, famous in animal tales, is Swahili for lion. Less well known Swahili animal names are *nyanyi* (baboon) and *tembo* (elephant).

Simenon. A Simenon is a serious psychological novel of about 50,000 words written by author Georges Simenon—and written in a rather unique way. Simenon gets a complete medical examination before he begins one of these critically praised short novels. He then literally locks himself in a room and, working from the barest of notes, allows himself seven days to write each book and three days to revise. Simenons are distinct from the author's popular Inspector Maigret stories, which are highly respected in the mystery field. Born in Liège, Belgium on February 13, 1903, the prolific but not prolix Simenon has authored some 500 novels since he began writing at the age of 19, many of these admittedly POTBOILERS turned out under a score of pseudonyms.

simoleon. Our slang for "one dollar," common since the late 19th century, may derive from the British slang *simon*, for "sixpence," which can be traced back to about 1700. First the British *simon* became our *simon* for a dollar (ca. 1859 but now obsolete) and then for some reason it became *simoleon*—though this leaves unexplained the shift in accent from the first syllable in *simon* to the second in *simoleon*. *Simon* is said to have been used by the British for "sixpence" because it is alliterative with "six," but Simon Magus (*see* SIMONY) has been suggested as an eponym.

Simon Legree. *See* UNCLE TOM.

Simon Pure. English dramatist and actress Susan Centlivre (1669–1723) created a host of APTRONYMS in her comedy *A Bold Stroke for a Wife* (1717). The most lasting proved to be one Simon Pure, a Pennsylvania Quaker who tries to win the heart of the heiress Ann Lovely. But Simon Pure's letter of introduction to her guardian, Obadiah Prim, is stolen by Colonel Feignwell, who pretends to be Simon Pure and convinces Ann Lovely's guardian to let her marry him. At the last minute Simon Pure shows up, proves that he is "the real Simon Pure," and provides a happy ending. As a result of the play, Simon Pure became an eponym, his name proverbial for anything authentic, true, the real and genuine article, "the real McCoy," as we say more often today. Mrs. Centlivre, married to Queen Anne's chef, turned to writing for a living when her husband died, and she became one of the few women of her time to earn her livelihood as a playwright.

simony. There is a legend that Simon Magus the magician tried to prove his divinity in a dispute with Peter and Paul before the emperor Nero. He attempted to fly up to heaven after jumping out a high window, succeeded in defying the laws of gravity for a few moments, and then found himself cast down to earth by the prayers of the disciples. Simon Magus, who lived in the first century in Samaria, was a skilled magician, his last name, in fact, meaning sorcerer. The story of his conversion to Christianity is told in the Bible (Acts 8:9–24), but the passage instructs us that Simon's conversion was made only so that he could obtain the new powers of sorcery that he thought the apostles possessed. Simon's name, in the form of *simony*, has since been a synonym for traffic in sacred things, such as the buying and selling of church offices, a *simoniac* being one who practices simony. Not much is known of Simon after he was reproached by Peter, but it is believed that he founded a rival religion, a Gnostic sect combining elements of Christianity and paganism, traveling with a former prostitute named Helen and winning a number of disciples called Simonians. The traditional belief is that the wily magician died trying to prove his divinity when he attempted to imitate the resurrection of Christ. Simon, it seems, allowed himself to be buried alive, mistakenly believing that he would rise on the third day.

simples. *Simples* is an old word for medicinal herbs. In days past, the market gardeners of Battersea in England used to grow simples, and London apothecaries went to the town to select or cut the herbs they wanted. The similarity of the word *simpleton* and the *simples* of this common practice led to the use of "you must go to Battersea to get your simples cut" as a reproof to a simpleton or someone who made a very foolish observation.

sincere. According to an old story, *sincere* has its roots in the quarries where Michelangelo worked before he became an immortal sculptor and an accomplished poet. Roman quarrymen often rubbed wax on marble blocks to conceal their imperfections temporarily. Then the Roman Senate decreed that all marble be "without wax," or *sine cera*, this eventually becoming our word *sincere*, "without deception." Most authorities, however, trace *sincere* to the Latin *sincerus*, "clean, pure, sound."

since the hogs et grandma. This humorous expression from the U.S. Ozark mountains means a long time ago, as in "I haven't had so much good fun since the hogs et grandma." A variation is *since the hogs et little brother.*

since time immemorial. We have used this phrase for at least eight centuries to mean "ancient beyond man's memory or records." But in English law *time immemorial*, according to a 1275 statute, is any time prior to 1189, the year Richard I came to power in England.

since when. Jamaicans condensed this expression meaning "a newly rich man or woman" from the phrase "Since when did he (she) get money?" commonly said of such a person.

sin-eater. Old, poor people called sin-eaters were hired at funerals in ancient times to eat beside the corpse and thus take on all the sins of the dead person, who was then thought to be freed from purgatory. Usually, all they got for taking on these often myriad sins was a small coin, a crust of bread, and a bowl of ale—small payment, though a living, for what amounted to a pawned soul.

sine die. A Latin expression used to mean "without fixing a day for future action or meeting," as in "The assembly adjourned sine die." *Sine* is the Latin for "without," *die* the Latin for "day." Italian author Carlo Guidi is said to have "died of shock" when he translated a religious work into Latin, presented a copy to the pope, and it was brought to his attention that the Latin word *sine* had been printed as *sin* throughout the book.

sine qua non. That which is indispensable, an indispensable condition, something essential. Although the words translate as "without which nothing," the original Latin phrase from which they were taken is *Sine qua non potest esse*, "Without which it is not possible to exist." Dating back in English use to the 16th century, the words have their origins in Aristotelian expressions. The term is also used attributively ("Publication is a *sine qua non* condition for the generation of literature"—Thomas De Quincey, *Works*, 1860) and can be used to mean "somebody indispensable." The little-known plural, *sine quibus non*, is not used in the humorous expression for men's trousers—"these indispensables" being called *sine qua nons*.

sing a different tune. Possibly the wandering minstrels of medieval Europe suggested this expression because they changed the words of their songs from court to court in order to praise the exploits of different lords. They could have, for the phrase is recorded as early as 1390. It now means to act or speak in a different manner, and usually to humble oneself in the process. Generally it's heard in the form of *to make someone sing another tune*, to make him change his behavior or recant what he's said.

Singapore. Owned originally by the sultan of Johore, who ceded it to the British in 1824, Singapore is a corruption of the sultan's name.

sing for one's supper. A proverbial phrase, immortalized in the nursery rhyme about little Tommy Tucker, *to sing for one's* *supper* has its origins in the troubadours who literally sang for their suppers in English taverns.

sing Indian. American Indians under torture or in great peril often courageously defied death by singing or chanting; this inspired the now historical expression *to sing Indian*, to act courageously in the face of death.

singing psalms to a dead horse. *See* QUICKER THAN HELL CAN SCORCH A FEATHER.

Sinhalese words in English. Sinhalese, spoken in Sri Lanka, has contributed several words to English, including beriberi and tourmaline.

sink one's teeth into. *To sink one's teeth into something* means to eat it, usually with great enjoyment, or to get into the spirit of anything. The Americanism was first recorded in 1892 as *sink tooth into:* "Only a favored few of the millions of feasters on Thanksgiving Day will sink tooth into genuine wild turkey meat."

sink or swim. An old saying that can be traced back at least to Chaucer about 1368. Chaucer, who may have coined the expression, wrote: "Ye rekke [reckon] not whethyr I flete [obsolete for swim] or sink." Since then, most writers give the phrase as *sink or swim*, not Chaucer's *swim or sink*, and it is often used to mean "no matter what happens," as in Byron's famous lines in *Don Juan* (1819) regarding the writing life: "And what I write I cast upon the stream / To sink or swim—I have had at least my dream."

Sinningia. Not named for any sinner, *Sinningia* is an eponymous plant genus that honors German horticulturist Wilhelm Sinning (1794–1874). It includes many tropical plants cultivated as houseplants, the popular gloxinia among them.

sin to Davy Crockett. A historical expression meaning something exceptional or extraordinary, as in "The way we used 'em up [killed them] was a sin to Davy Crockett." It refers, of course, to Davy Crockett (1786–1836), legendary frontiersman and hero at the Alamo.

si nummi immunis. *Si nummi immunis* has been called the lawyer's palindrome (reading the same backward as forward). The Latin can be translated as "Pay me your fee and you go scot-free." *See also* PALINDROME.

Sioux. These Indians called themselves *Dakotah*, "the allies." However, rival tribes called them the *Nadowessioux*, "little snakes, the enemy," and white explorers in the area mistakenly dubbed them the *Sioux*, from the last syllable of this slur upon them.

Sioux State. A nickname of North Dakota, where the Sioux Indians once ruled. North Dakota has also been called the Land of the Dakotas and the Great Central State. It is called the Flickertailed State after a ground squirrel called the flickertail found only in the state.

sippin' whiskey. An old name in the South and elsewhere for the best quality BOURBON.

Sir, I have not yet begun to fight! During the famous battle between the *Bon Homme Richard* and the *Serapis* it seems that some of John Paul Jones's men cried for surrender, but the captain laid one of them low with the side of his pistol, fracturing his skull. Captain Richard Pearson of the *Serapis* then shouted to Jones, asking if he had had enough. Jones uttered the immortal words: "Sir, I have not yet begun to fight!" So Lieutenant Richard Dale later recalled. Jones himself claimed that he answered Pearson's challenge with the far less colorful words "I have not yet thought of it, but am determined to make you strike."

sirens. Represented in mythology as birds with the heads of women, the Sirens were the three daughters of the Greek sea god Phorcu (Achelous). Perched on their pleasant island, they lured mariners to death, the sailors enchanted by the Sirens' song crashing their ships against the rocks. In rare instances they could be defeated, as when Orpheus, the legendary poet, outwitted the Sirens by playing his spellbinding lyre over the sound of their song. The name *siren* is now applied to any sexy, wilful woman.

Sir Galahad. The prototype of the chivalrous male, the original Sir Galahad may have been added to the Arthurian legends by Welsh author and clergyman Walter Map in about 1200. The son of Lancelot and himself a Knight of the Round Table, he is the hero of the Quest for the Holy Grail. His name is still synonymous with a courteous gentleman, mostly used in the same lighthearted, even humorous ways that it has been for a century or so.

sirloin. Sirloin, strictly speaking, is meat from the steer's hip, but today it is sold without the prized filet and often goes by the name of shell hip or rump steak. The widely accepted Sir Loin story about its origins shows how highly esteemed in the past was this aristocrat of steaks. The tale is told about numerous British monarchs, including the lusty Henry VIII, James I (on whom Jonathan Swift bestowed credit), and lastly, Charles II, who ruled England from 1660 to 1685. In each case the king in question was supposed to have been so pleased with the succulent slice of pink meat served him that he unsheathed his sword, laid it on the brown-crusted sirloin and knighted it, solemnly declaring, "Hereafter thou shalt be dubbed 'Sir Loin.' " The only bothersome fact is that *sirloin* really derives from an Old English word *surloin* (from *sur,* "above" or "over"), which simply meant the cut above the loin and came to be misspelled *sirloin* in about 1600. This, however, did not prevent writers like Scott from using terms like *the knightly sirloin* and *the noble baron of beef.* The last, practically unheard of today, was a double sirloin, a huge joint weighing up to 100 pounds and comprising both sides of the back. *See also* PORTERHOUSE.

sirocco. *See* MONSOON; WINDS.

sissy. In the mid 19th century *sissy* was merely a synonym for *sister* and it is still used as a nickname for girls, as is *Sis.* But by about 1890 the Americanism took on the meaning of a boy who acts like a girl, a coward or weakling. The word, as demeaning to women as it is to men, finally came to include among its derogatory definitions "a male homosexual," especially in the form *sissy-boy*.

Sisyphean. Endless heartbreaking toil is the lot of anyone engaged in Sisyphean labors. The term comes to us from the legend of Sisyphus, an ancient king of Corinth, who was sent to Hades for crimes against his subjects and condemned forever to roll a huge stone up a steep hill, only to have it roll downhill when he reached the top, so that he must roll it uphill again in an unending cycle.

sit-down strike; sit-in. Sit-down strikes, common in the 1930s, involved workers sitting down at their machines and refusing to let other workers take their places until a strike was settled. Sit-ins, a tool of civil-rights and other protest groups in the 1960s, employed the same technique, these passive protests originally being used only against racial segregation.

Sitting Bull. Sitting Bull (1834–90) was the great American Indian warrior and chief of the Hunkpapa who defeated Custer at Little Big Horn in 1876. In America, the buffalo (as our bison is commonly called) is responsible for all the bull names (Sitting Bull, White Bull, etc.) of the great plains Indian chiefs and warriors.

siwash. To travel lightly, without equipment. A Chinook jargon word *not* deriving from the name of an Indian tribe that traveled that way (there is or was no Siwash tribe) but from a corruption of the French word *sauvage*, "savage, wild," as if to insultingly say Indian "savages" traveled that way.

sixes and sevens. I'm at sixes and sevens, in a state of confusion, trying to explain this expression, which dates back to 1340. One theory is that it comes from the biblical phrase (Job 5:19): "He shall deliver thee in six troubles: yea in seven there shall no evil touch thee." More likely the term evolved from the old dice game of hazard. *Sinque* and *sice* ("five" and "six") were the most risky bets to make in the old game, and anyone who tried to throw these numbers was considered careless and confused. Later, *sinque* and *sice* became "six" and "seven." Perhaps the change simply occurred because the terms looked and sounded somewhat alike. But it is possible that six and seven (an impossible throw in dice and two numbers that add up to the unlucky 13) represents a joking shift. Only about a century and a half ago did *set on six and seven* take on its plural forms and become (set) at *sixes and sevens*. The phrase is still widely used today. A similar, older Italian expression, *a tredici*, "at 13," may be the source of the expression.

six of one and a half-dozen of another. Captain Frederick Marryat may have invented this phrase in *The Pirates and the Three Cutters* (1836), or else it was old sea slang that the author recorded. It apparently arose from no specific situation and means "nothing to choose between," "one and the same," simply because "six" and "a half dozen" are identical. ARCADES AMBO a similar phrase, means two persons having the same tastes or habits in common. It comes from Virgil's seventh eclogue: "*Ambo florentes aetabibus, Arcades ambo*" ("Both in the flower of youth, Arcadians both").

six-shooter. A popular name for the Colt revolver, patented by Samuel Colt in 1835 and also known as the *Colt* or *six-gun*. The revolver held six cartridges.

$64 question. On the radio quiz program "Take It or Leave It," which premiered in 1941 and was emceed by Bob Hawk, topics were chosen by contestants from the studio audience and questions on these topics answered by each contestant on seven levels. The easiest question was worth two dollars and the questions progressed in difficulty until the ultimate $64 Question was reached. The popularity of the show added to the language the expression *the $64 question*, "any question difficult to answer," and inspired a slew of similar quiz shows. A decade later came television's "$64,000 Question" with its plateaus instead of levels, its isolation booth, and its scandals involving prominent contestants who cheated in cahoots with the producers. Then, after a long hiatus, there was the "$128,000 Question," but despite these programs with their inflated prizes, *$64 question* retains its place in the national vocabulary.

sizzle. *See* ONOMATOPOEIA.

Sjambok rule. *Sjambok*, for "a rhino-hide whip," is said to come from Malay and ultimately from Urdu. The word, however, is associated with the Boers of South Africa, *sjambok rule* meaning a repressive tyrannical rule of whips and violence. The word is an international one, recorded in the dictionaries of many languages. It seems to have come into English in the first quarter of the 19th century.

skate on thin ice. The allusion here is to skating over ice so thin that it hardly bears the skater's weight. This was actually once a sport called tickledybendo in New England. The metaphor *skating on thin ice* means that someone is taking chances, or behaving in a questionable, dangerous, or indelicate manner.

skedaddle. *Skedaddle* is often thought of as an Americanism for "to retreat, flee, clear out, depart hurriedly." But the expression probably comes from Scottish and English dialect, possibly deriving from the Greek *skedannunai*, "to split up." First used in America during the 1820s it became popular among Northern troops during the Civil War as a word describing Rebels fleeing the battlefield after a loss.

skeeziks. A good-for-nothing, but more often the affectionate name for a mischievous young boy or teenager. The word, its origin unknown, dates back to about 1850 and has been kept alive in recent times by the character named Skeeziks in the *Gasoline Alley* comic strip, though it isn't used much anymore.

skeleton at the feast. The Egyptians, according to Herodotus and Plutarch, liked to sit a skeleton or "image of a corpse" at their feasts in order to remind guests of their mortality. Whether this inspired an "eat, drink and be merry, tomorrow you die" atmosphere or assured their hosts that their guests would leave early, isn't known, but the *skeleton at the feast*, now serves as a humorous term for a deadhead, a party pooper, a wet blanket, someone who won't be invited to the next feast.

skeleton in the closet. It took years to find what seemed to be "the perfect lady," one without "a single care or trouble," but, alack and alas, the lady proved to have her dark secret, too. She admitted this and took the investigators to her bedroom closet, where a skeleton hung from the ceiling. After explaining that the skeleton was once her husband's rival, whom he had killed in a duel, she cried: "I try to keep my trouble to myself, but every night my husband forces me to kiss that skeleton!" Certainly this would be one of the most interesting of phrase derivations if the old horror story could be proved. But it can't. No one knows the origin of a *skeleton in the closet*, a shameful secret which a family tries to hide. There have also been attempts to link the words with actual skeletons that doctors hid in their homes or offices when dissection was forbidden by law, none very convincing. We only know that William Makepeace Thackeray first used the expression in print in an 1855 story he contributed to *Punch* and that it was probably in use at least 10 years before that.

ski. The noun *ski* derives from the Old Norse *skith*, "snow-shoe." Over the centuries *ski* became a verb as well as a noun, so that we now go *skiing* on our *skis*.

skidoo. *See* 23 SKIDOO.

skin alive. *I'll skin you alive*, someone might say to another person in anger, meaning he will severely beat that person. The expression seems to have been recorded first in 1869, in a reference to a shady "skin-em-alive place." But it must be much older and is probably based upon the actual practice of skinning animals alive. According to Edward Hoagland in *The Tugman's Passage* (1982) "the more brutal [American] pioneers" skinned wolves alive "and turned them loose to scare the rest of the pack."

skinflint. A cheap, mean penny-pincher, a Scrooge. The term, first recorded in 1690, is said to derive from the medieval saying *to skin a flint*, to be very exacting in making a bargain. A flint is a hard stone and would be exceedingly difficult if not impossible to skin.

skin game. In the early 1800s *to skin* made its debut as a verb meaning "to strip one of his money." After another 50 years *skin game* was being used for a card game or any other game or scheme in which a person has absolutely no chance to win.

skinny dipping. *Dipping* has been used by Americans for swimming since early Colonial days, and *skinny dipping*, "swimming naked," has been popular just as long. While *dipping* is not much used by itself anymore, it is still found in the expression *let's take a dip*.

skipper. As *scip* meant SHIP in Old English, *scipper* meant a ship's captain. By 1830 the English were pronouncing the latter word *skipper* and using it for the captain of a small merchant vessel, though it now refers to the captain of any ship.

the skipper swallows the anchor. This expression originally meant that the captain or skipper of a ship has retired. *The skipper swallows the anchor* dates back to the late 19th-century steamship lines, and is now sometimes used to indicate that death has come as well.

skit. No one really knows the origin of the word *skit*, for "a short comical act in a variety show." A good guess is the Swedish *skjuta*, one of whose meanings is "full of frisks or capers." The word, first recorded in 1820, may also be a back-formation from *skittish*, in its sense of lively, humorous.

skivvies. *Skivvies*, slang for men's shorts, may derive from the Japanese *sukebei*, "lewdness." In the British navy *skivvy* is a greeting said to have been first encountered as a salutation of Japanese prostitutes, and "Skivvy-skivvy, G.I.?" or "Skibby-skibby, G.I.?" was indeed the way Japanese and Korean street prostitutes and pimps solicited Americans during both World War II and the Korean conflict.

skoshi; skosh. Little, little bit, few, a word from the time of the Korean conflict that probably derives from Japanese *sukoshi* meaning the same. *Skosh* (rhymes with *gauche*) and *skoshi* were both used frequently by G.I.s in Korea, the Koreans having borrowed it from the Japanese during their long occupation of Korea. *Skosh* is the form mostly used in American English today.

skulduggery. *Skulduggery*, for "dishonesty or trickery," has no connection with heads or skulls. It does have something to do with adultery. *Skulduggery* is the American variant of the Scottish *skulduddery*, which means illicit sexual intercourse or obscenity, the Scottish word originally coined as a euphemism for *adultery* (*duddery*, "adultery"). Thus the word is doubly euphemistic: *skulduddery* itself and the American *skulduggery* fashioned from it that is first recorded in 1856. In America the word has never suggested any sexual hijinks, usually meaning political trickery.

skull. When the English poet Lord Byron drank from a skull he was hardly being original. Human skulls used as drinking cups have been traced back before 7000 B.C. Herodotus, for example, mentions that the Scythians made drinking vessels out of skulls of their enemies by sawing off the skull below the eyebrows, covering the outside with leather and gilding the inside with silver or gold. He also notes that people near the River Don in southern Russia boiled the flesh of a dead parent with that of sheep and ate it, preserving the parent's skull as a keepsake cup. An old story, "The Lay of Weyland the Smith," tells how the eponymous hero slew his opponent's sons, making golden cups out of their brainpans and gems out of their eyes, which he sent to their mother, and fashioning broaches from their teeth, which he sent to their sisters. Skulls were also used as drinking cups by the Vikings and the skulls of saints were used as drinking cups in medieval monasteries. Such customs have led some etymologists to suggest that the word *skull* itself meant a drinking cup before it acquired its present meaning. No proof of the derivation has been established, but there is a strong connection between the Old Norse *skal*, "a bowl," and *skull*. Another possibility is that *skull* derived from the Old Norse *skel*, "a seashell."

skunk. The little striped mammal can squirt his foul yellow spray up to 12 feet, so American Indians called him *segankw*, or *segonku*, the Algonquian dialect word meaning simply "he who squirts." Pioneers corrupted the hard-to-pronounce Algonquian word to *skunk*, and it has remained so since. We know the skunk's foul spray as m-butyl mercaptain, or $CH_3C_2CH_2CH_2SH$, but it smells as bad under any name. The skunk was called *enfant du diable*, "child of the devil," by French Canadian trappers, but is also called the wood polecat and the wood pussy. The most common species is the striped skunk, *Mephitis mephitis*, which might be loosely translated as "double stinky," though *mephitis* means a noxious exhalation from the ground.

skunk cabbage. The much-maligned marshland *skunk cabbage (Symplocarpus foetidus)* bears little relation or resemblance to the cabbage (*Brassica capitata*). The plant takes its name from its fetid smell and its leaves' supposed resemblance to cabbage leaves. Actually the skunk cabbage's large, nearly round leaves are far more handsome and its sheath-like spathe is beautifully colored. But the plant's foul smell has caused it to be called pole-cat weed as well as skunk cabbage.

skunk in the churchhouse. *See* HAIR IN THE BUTTER.

Skutnik. Lenny Skutnik, the young hero of a 1982 Washington plane crash, was introduced by President Reagan during his State of the Union address. When such introductions became common in political speeches, the word *Skutnik* began to be used not as an eponymous synonym for heroism, as might be expected, but for "a human prop, used by a speaker to make a political point," as Jeff Greenfield defined it in his book *Oh, Waiter! One Order of Crow!* (2001). The word has no relation to SPUTNIK.

skyscraper. The world's first skyscraper office building was the 10-story Chicago office of the Home Insurance Company built in 1883 by architect William Le Baron Jenney. The fitting name *skyscraper* was given to this first building to employ steel skeleton construction, a building much higher than any other building of its time, but journalists had borrowed the word from the triangular sails that had long been used high on the masts of sailing vessels, scraping against the sky. Novelist Henry James wrote that Manhattan skyscrapers looked "like extravagant pins in a cushion already overplanted, and stuck in as in the dark, anywhere and anyhow."

Slainte! A drinking toast familiar to Irishmen everywhere, *slainte!* (pronounced *s-lawn-cheh*) is simply Gaelic for "cheers!"

slam dunk. *Dunk* simply meant to shoot a basketball through the goal in the 1930s when the term is first recorded. But in the mid-1960s tall players developed what is known as the dunk shot by leaping above the basket and stuffing the ball in. The slam dunk came soon after, this a more theatrical version of the dunk shot in which the ball is slammed down through the hoop. *See also* BASKETBALL.

slammer. *Slammer* had been slang for "a door" before it became a slang synonym for "prison" in the 1930s. Both terms, of course, refer to the slamming of doors, in the last case the slamming shut of all the metal doors in a cellblock at the same time. *See also* HOOSEGOW-JUG.

slang. The fabled "Dutch General Slangeuberg noted for his abusive and exaggerated epithets when he reproved the men under his command" is *not* the source for the word *slang*. Neither is the Italian *s-lingua—s*, the negative, and *lingua*, "language," equaling *slingua* (slang), or "bad language." No one is sure, but some prominent etymologists, including Ernest Weekley, believe that *slang* may come from the Norwegian *slengjakeften*, "to sling the jaw," "to abuse." The word dates back to the late 18th century.

slap-happy. The internal rhyme of this word has insured its long life, which dates back at least to the late 1920s. It means to be very confused, dazed, or PUNCH-DRUNK, and comes from the sport of boxing, which has produced too many men who act like this because they've taken too many blows to the head. Despite his nickname, clowning boxer Slapsy Maxie Rosenbloom was *not* one of them.

slapstick. The slapstick used in early low comedies was "a large paddling implement consisting of two boards hinged at one end but loose at the other." Clowns in late 19th-century American variety shows used this slapstick to give other performers laugh-getting light but loud whacks on the rear end. The slapsticks were so widely used that they gave their name to any broad, loud knock-about comedy.

slave; Slav. The word *slave* has nothing to do with Athens in the Periclean Age, when there were twice as many people in bondage as free, or with the "African trade" that created four centuries of suffering. *Slave* came into the language long after the former and long before the latter inhumanity, deriving from the name of a tribe living in what is now Poland and other areas of Eastern Europe. The name of these people meant "noble" or "illustrious" in their own tongue, but in about 6 A.D. they were conquered by German tribes from the west and forced to serve their conquerors or sold into bondage to the Romans. The Romans called them *Sclavus*, which became the Medieval Latin *sclavus*, "a Slav captive," this term of contempt applied to any bondsman or servile person. *Sclavus* became *esclave* in French and came into English as *sclave*, retaining the *c* until about the 16th century, when *slave* was first used. The word *Slav*, for the race of people in Eastern Europe, comes from the same source, the proud "noble" tribe whose name underwent a complete metamorphosis.

sleazy. Several respected sources mark the origin of *sleaze* "unknown." But this word meaning contemptibly low, mean, or disreputable may have originally been a derogatory reference to shoddy fabrics made in Siberia. At least folk etymology has it so. When first recorded in about 1635, *sleazy* did refer to cheap flimsy fabric.

sleep at the bottom of the ocean; sleep with the fishes. Dead, killed, assassinated. In the Academy Award–winning movie *The Godfather* (1972), the acting Corleone boss, Santino, or Sonny, is sent a large dead fish wrapped in the bulletproof vest of his Mafia family's chief enforcer, Luca Brasi. "It's a Sicilian message," one of his capos tells him. "It means Luca Brasi sleeps with the fishes." In Mario Puzo's novel *The Godfather* (1969) the expression varies some: "When he came back he was holding Luca Brasi's bulletproof vest in his hands.

Wrapped in the vest was a huge dead fish . . . 'The fish means that Luca Brasi is sleeping at the bottom of the ocean,' he said. 'It's an old Sicilian message.' " A humorous play on the words is *sleeps with the gefilte fishes.*

sleeper.   A *sleeper,* for "any unexpected success," dates to the 1930s. One speculation has the word deriving from *sleeper,* for "an unbranded steer," a late 19th-century term that came to mean, in one sense, "something taken for something else." Another vague possibility is *sleeper* for "a bet in faro when the owner has forgotten it, when it becomes public property, anyone having a right to take it." By this reasoning the *sleeper,* or bet, could turn out to be a good one.

sleeping.   A tender euphemism for "buried" used mainly by old-timers, as in: "My older boy went to war in '14. He's sleeping over in France . . ."

sleeping policemen.   In Trinidad these are humps in the road to slow traffic. In the U.S. they would be called, less colorfully, *speed bumps, road bumps,* or *safety bumps.*

sleep like a top.   A top spinning at high speed is so poised and steady that it hardly seems to move. Writers first compared sound sleepers to spinning tops over 350 years ago, and even though we now know that no one sleeps so soundly the whole night through, the comparison remains a good one—for a spinning top begins to wobble after a while, is rewound, and resumes its steady spinning. Some authorities have tried to trace the phrase back beyond its first recorded use in English (1616), to the French word *taupe,* a "mole," the implication being that one sleeps as peacefully as a mole. But the French saying is also to "sleep like a top," *dormir comme un sabot,* not *dormir comme une taupe,* "to sleep like a mole." Tops, like yo-yos, are in fact said to be "sleeping" when they are spinning perfectly. William Congreve played on both meanings when he wrote in his comedy *The Old Bachelor* (1693): "I can ensure his anger dormant, or should be seen to rouse, 'tis but well lashing him and he will sleep like a top." Congreve's play, which brought him sudden fame, has a cast of aptronyms second to few. There is Heartwell, the kind old bachelor; Vainlove, who forsakes his mistress; Fondlewife, the uxorious old banker; and even a cowardly bully named Captain Bluffe.

sleep on a clothesline.   The expression "I'm so tired I could sleep on a clothesline," with much more British than American use today, dates back to 18th-century England, when people unable to afford a bed in boardinghouses were charged two pennies to sit on a communal bench through the night, leaning on a clothesline stretched tight in front of them. The taut "two-penny rope" was cut in the morning, the sleepers jolted into reality again.

sleeps.   "It was many sleeps away." Among some American Indian tribes a *sleep* was one day, "the measure of time between one sleeping period and the next." The term is recorded as early as 1670 in South Carolina and was adopted by settlers.

sleeps with the gefilte fishes.   *See* SLEEP AT THE BOTTOM OF THE OCEAN.

sleuth.   The first sleuth was a *sleuthhound,* the name for a bloodhound which gave us our word *sleuth* for a human detective in about 1872. The *sleuthhound,* in turn, took the first part of its name from the Middle English *sleuth* meaning "track or trail."

slick as a peeled onion.   An onion peeled of several layers is indeed slick and glistening, which is why this old Americanism is used to describe a slick and slippery person, someone often dishonest.

slide; Kelly, slide.   As Dizzy Dean would have put it, when Kelly "slud," he "slud" hard. Michael Joseph "King" Kelly, who played ball for Chicago and Boston, was a talented hustling player called "the Ten Thousand Dollar Beauty" because he signed for that sum one year, an incredible amount of money for a ballplayer at the time. In 1889 a song was written about Kelly by his friend monologuist John W. Kelly exhorting him to *slide, Kelly, slide,* an expression which has become proverbial. Kelly innovated a number of techniques besides the "hook" or "fadeaway" slide. As a catcher he invented the dirty trick of throwing his mask up the first-base line in order to trip a batter trying to beat out a hit. Kelly played to win. As Boston's manager, he looked up from the bench one day to see a foul ball drifting toward him. At the time, baseball rules specified that substitutions could be made at any point in the game, and seeing that the Boston catcher could not possibly reach the foul, Kelly jumped up off the bench, shouted "Kelly now catching for Boston," and caught the ball for an out. His maneuver led to the rule now on the books that substitutions can only be made when the ball isn't in play.

sliding pond.   Is it pronounced "sliding pond" or "sliding pon?" That depends on where you come from in America. Many experts believe that the slides found in most playgrounds were first named *sliding ponds* because they reminded people of how they used to slide on the ice of ponds before playground slides were invented sometime in the 19th century. By this reasoning *sliding pon* is simply a shortening of *sliding pond.* But some *sliding pon* advocates claim that *pon* here is the corruption of any of a number of foreign words that could be applicable. Still another guess is that *sliding pon* comes from "sliding upon." More American terms for *sliding pond* include *sliding board, slide, sliding pot,* and even *chutey-chute* (from the British *chute,* and probably obsolete today). Strangely enough, no major American dictionary lists *sliding pond,* or *sliding pon,* including *A Dictionary of Americanisms* and *The Dictionary of American Slang*—though the terms have been commonly used in some areas since early in this century and must have spread throughout the country by now in both speech and literature.

Slim.   Over the past 20 years this has been a name given to the AIDS disease by English-speaking East Africans, because the disease has ravaged the African continent and often reduces those it attacks to living skeletons.

slim pickins; Slim.   *Picking* can refer to the harvesting of a crop, this sense of the word first recorded in 1828 and often used in the Americanism *picking bee. Pickings,* however, can mean "gleanings or scraps," and prefaced by *slim* (probably from German *schlimm,* "bad, small)," means "very little to be had, unprofitable." Charlotte Bronte coined *scanty pickings*, a synonym for *slim pickings*, in her novel *Jane Eyre* (1847). In the late 1930s a tall, slender actor in cowboy movies took the name Slim Pickins at the beginning of a long career, *Slim* even then having been a century-old cowboy nickname for a thin person.

slip.   *Slip*, as in "She's a mere slip of a girl," that is, she's small and thin, may derive from *sliver*, which comes from Middle English *slivere*. Or it may derive from the Middle Dutch *slippe*, which also gives us the word for any long, narrow strip; a small piece of paper; a scion or plant cutting.

slip of the tongue.   This phrase, first recorded in the work of English poet John Dryden in 1667, is a translation of the Latin *lapsus linguae*. The similar term *slip of the pen* isn't heard much anymore, but FREUDIAN SLIP remains popular. *See* GOLDWYNISMS; MALAPROPISM; SPOONERISM.

slippery slope.   A recent term with much currency in political circles. It means "a tricky, precarious situation," a slope on which it is an easy, smooth ride to your injury or destruction below.

slipshod.   The first slipshod people were men in the 16th century who walked the streets in slipshoes, a kind of loose slipper. Such men, slopping along shod in their slipshoes, were considered uncouth by respectable people, who soon coined the word *slipshod* for them, *slipshod* ultimately applying to anything done in a slovenly way.

slipslop.   A *slipslop* is a MALAPROPISM. In this case the synonym for the misuse of words comes from the name of Mrs. Slipslop, the chambermaid in Henry Fielding's novel *Joseph Andrews* (1742). Mrs. Slipslop utters a few words nobody has been able to translate yet, including "ragmaticellest mophrodites." *See* GOLDWYNISM.

slithy.   " 'Twas brillig and the slithy toves did gyre and gimble in the wabe." Author Lewis Carroll concocted this blend, or portmanteau, word from *lithe* and *slimy* in *Through the Looking Glass* as part of his "Jabberwocky" language.

slogan; campaign slogan.   Probably the most successful slogan ever written, or at least the most profitable one, is the "Think Mink" button invented by Jack Gasnick, which was conceived in 1929 and has sold 50 million copies since 1950 alone. Gasnick also invented the ubiquitous "Cross at the Green . . . Not in Between" slogan. All slogans, whether they be catchy advertising phrases or the rallying cries of political parties, are direct descendants of Gaelic battle cries, the word itself deriving from the *sluagh-ghairm* (battle cry) of the Gaels. Gaelic soldiers repeated these cries, usually the name of their clan or clan leader, in unison as they advanced against the enemy. Over the years the word came to describe any catchy phrase inducing people to support a cause (the LIBERTY, EQUALITY, FRATERNITY! of the French Revolution) or a commercial product (the 99 $^{44}/_{100}$% Pure of Ivory Soap). Sometimes *watchword* is used loosely for slogan, as is *catchword*, though this last is more often employed in a contemptuous sense (as in "advertising catchwords"). Advertising slogans were with us long before 1841, when the first advertising agency opened in Philadelphia (it

was called an *advertising brokerage*). Over the years, from the first tavern signs in the colonies to the first electric signs of the 1890s, there have been thousands of memorable slogans, but here are some of the best known:

> *Pink Pills for Pale People*—Dr. William's Pink Pills, ca. 1870
> *99 44/100% Pure*—Ivory Soap, 1879
> *More Than One Million Copies Sold!*—The Science of Life or Self Preservation, published in 1882
> *You Push the Button We Do the Rest*—Kodak, 1888
> *The Beer that Made Milwaukee Famous*—Schlitz, 1895
> *The Strength of Gibraltar* (the Rock)—Prudential Insurance, 1896
> *Good to the Last Drop*—Maxwell House Coffee, 1907
> *The Breakfast of Champions*—Wheaties Cereal, 1922
> *The Skin You Love to Touch*—Woodbury Soap, 1922
> *They Laughed When I Sat Down, but When I Started to Play* . . . —U.S. School of Music, 1925
> *Call for Philip Morris*—Philip Morris Cigarettes, 1933
> *There's a Ford in Your Future*—Ford Motor Co., 1944
> *Lifebuoy Stops B.O.* (Body Odor)—Lifebuoy Soap, 1948
> *Does She or Doesn't She?*—Miss Clairol, 1955

Another interesting one was *Don't Talk Chum, Chew Topp's Gum*, a variation on or the inspiration for the popular World War II slogan *Loose Lips Sink Ships. See* POLITICAL SLOGANS; CIDER.

slothful.   *Sloth*, deriving from the Middle English *slou*, "slow," dates back to at least 1175 as a word for laziness, and the adjective *slothful* is recorded as early as 1390. The arboreal mammal of South America called the sloth didn't get its name until the early 19th century. The sloth does virtually nothing for weeks on end, not breathing for long periods, taking at least two weeks to digest its food, and not even springing up if it falls out of its tree. It was named by explorers who observed it, one describing how a sloth took "three or four days at least, in climbing up and down a tree," and another observing that one took "a whole day in going fifty paces."

slow and steady wins the race.   When Charles Darwin measured the speed of a Galapagos turtle by walking beside it, he found that it "walked at the rate of sixty yards in ten minutes, that is 360 yards in an hour, or four miles a day—allowing a little time for it to eat on the road." That is certainly slow enough for an expression *slow as a tortoise*, but the creature, unlike the snail, has been noted for his reliability rather than his lack of speed. The expression *slow and steady wins the race* is from the poem "The Hare and the Tortoise" by Robert Lloyd (1733–64) but can be traced back in all but its exact form to Aesop's fable "The Hare and the Tortoise," in which the hare awakens to see the tortoise crossing the finish line in a race the hare was sure he would win.

slow bear.   A humorous Civil War term that foragers used for farmers' pigs that they stole, killed, and ate. Humorous, that is, so long as you weren't the farmer.

slug.   It is hard to find anything good to say about the slimey slug, which is technically a snail-like terrestrial gastropod with no shell that feeds on leafy garden crops. Interestingly, the slug takes its name from the Scandinavian *sluggje*, a heavy, slow person. In fact, in English the word *slug* meant a fat person before it was applied to the garden pest. Like the shark and the shrimp, the slug is named for a person sharing its characteristics, not the other way around. *See* SNAIL.

slugger. The term *to slug*, "to hit hard," has been used in baseball since the 1860s, and *slugger* for a hard or heavy hitter is recorded as early as 1883. But *slugger* was used in reference to a hard-hitting boxer before this, as well as to a cricket batter. Possibly the word derives from the early expression *to hit with a slug*, that is, a piece of lead fired from a gun.

slum; slumber. *Slum*, for "a squalid area of a city or town," is a relatively new word first recorded in 1812. The *O.E.D.* won't venture a guess at its origins, simply labeling it "cant," but it has been suggested that *slum* may derive from *slumber*—perhaps because *slum* first meant the squalid room where a poor person slept, or perhaps because slum areas were erroneously thought to be sleepy, quiet places! *Slumber* comes from the Middle English *slumeren*, "to doze."

slumgullion. By the end of the 19th century *slumgullion* meant a meat and vegetable stew in America, but the word started out meaning "slime." *Slum*, a mispronunciation of slime, had first meant the scummy liquid left over in the tryworks after blubber was processed aboard whaling ships. By mid-century *slum* came to mean a stew. Then miners in the 1849 gold rush borrowed *slum*, for "soup," added *gullion*, an English dialect word meaning "mud," and used *slumgullion* to mean the soupy liquid resulting from sluicing. *Slumgullions*, in turn, seemed to make a funny word for soup to some miners and this became its primary meaning.

slush fund. *Slush fund* originally referred to the surplus fat or grease from fried salt pork, a standard food on 19th-century ships. This slush was usually sold in port, the money raised from it put into a general fund that was used to purchase luxuries for the crew. By 1866 the nautical term had been applied to a contingency fund set aside from an operating budget by Congress, and in later years it took on its current meaning of a secret fund used for bribes or other corrupt practices.

slut's wool. *See* DUST BUNNY.

small fry. In her epochal *Uncle Tom's Cabin* Harriet Beecher Stowe introduced *small fry* ("smaller fry") to describe children, but *fry* had been used in this sense as early as 1697. Both expressions refer to the *fry*, "or young, of salmon, herring and other fish." The word derives from the Norse *frae* "seed," meaning the berry or seedlike masses of eggs these fish produce.

small potatoes. A favorite expression of the character based on big-time crook Meyer Lansky in *The Godfather* (1970), *small potatoes* means "something or someone trivial or insignificant." The term is an Americanism dating back to about 1831, when it was first recorded, and is frequently used in the form *small potatoes and few in a hill*, a favorite Davy Crockett expression. Small potatoes are often called new potatoes and SALAD POTA-

TOES in the U.S.. They are usually considered tastier than larger specimens.

small solace. *Solace*, meaning "comfort, consolation," came into the language about 1300, but no dictionary seems to have recorded the common phrase *small solace*, "consolation that doesn't help much," as in "You'll find small solace in the bottle." All my search turned up was *great solace* (*grat solas*), first recorded in 1400. *Solace* derives ultimately from the Latin *solari*, "to console."

smart aleck. If there ever lived a real "smart Aleck," an Alexander so much of an obnoxiously conceited know-it-all that his name became proverbial, no record of him exists. The term can be traced back to about the 1860s and is still frequently used for a wise guy today. The original *smart aleck* may have been at least clever enough to cover up all traces of his identity.

smart apple. A wise guy or smart aleck is a *smart apple* today, but when it originated in the early 1920s the term meant an intelligent person. An *apple* had simply been a "guy" before this.

smart as a steel trap; smart as a whip. Very smart and alert. The first expression dates back at least to humorist Seba Smith's *The Life and Writings of Major Jack Downing* (1833). Similar old terms are *smart as a whip* and (to have) *a mind* (or *memory*) *like a steel trap*.

smellefeastes. *See* PARASITE.

smellfungus. A discontented person, a grumbler and fault-finder. The first *smellfungus* was British novelist Tobias Smollett (1721–71), who was once imprisoned for libel. Smollett's book *Travels in France and Italy* (1766) was entertaining but ill-tempered and novelist Laurence Sterne parodied the author as "Smellfungus" in his *Sentimental Journey through France and Italy* (1768). Within a short time *smellfungus* was being applied to any ill-tempered grumbler.

Smell-O-Vision. Smell-O-Vision, "the first movies that stink on purpose," was invented in about 1955 by Hans Laube, who called himself an "osmologist" and believed that his process would make people desert their home television sets and come stampeding back into the empty movie theaters of the era. Unlike its rival process, Aroma-Rama, which released a variety of confusing scents one after another through a theater's ventilation system, Smell-O-Vision's scents were discharged at the proper time from 50 tiny "scent vents" attached to the back of every seat. The scents were often overwhelming and even gross, as when the bulls were running in the Festival of Pamplona. But a *New York Times* critic wrote of one movie, "The odor squirters are mildly and randomly used, and patrons sit there sniffing and snuffling like a bunch of bird dogs trying to catch the scent." Needless to say, the process never caught on.

smellsmock. Licentious priests were called smellsmocks in the early 16th century because people thought their sexual affairs made their smocks smelly and because they knew how to "smell a smock," how to recognize an easy conquest. *Smellsmock* soon came to cover any licentious man, but it survives today only as the popular name of several plants such as the cuckooflower and the woodsorrel.

smelt.   These small fish are said to take their name from the words *smell it*, because when first caught they smell like freshly cut cucumbers. More conservative etymologists smell a rat here and derive *smelt* from the Anglo-Saxon *smelt*, smooth and shiny, like fish itself. *Smeltania*, on Lake Charlevoix, Michigan, has long been a principal center for smelt fishing, and one of the few places named after a fish.

smile.   The Middle English word *smilen* is the direct ancestor of *smile*, but nobody knows where *smilen* came from—probably from a Scandinavian language. *Smiles* is said to be the longest word in English, according to an old riddle: "There's a mile between the first and the last letter."

smiley.   *Smiley*, or *smilie*, is an unusual word for a cut made by a club on the face of a golf ball, which somewhat resembles a smile. The term only dates back to the 1970s. *See also* DIMPLES.

smiley face.   Unaccountably absent from most dictionaries today, *smiley face* was first recorded in print in 1972. The ubiquitous cartoon-style picture of a smiling face—usually in black and yellow, always with mouth turned up and dots for eyes—was invented by some anonymous artist in the late 1960s. It has since been a symbol for peace and happiness, among other causes. Seen and heard occasionally as *happy face.*

smite someone hip and thigh.   *Smite someone hip and thigh* and you smite him all over his body violently. The old phrase is from the Bible, Judg. 15:8: "He smote them hip and thigh with a great slaughter . . ."

Smith.   If your name is Smith, you sport the most frequent family name among English-speaking nations. In the U.S. alone there are an estimated 2,382,500 Smiths, and that's not even counting Smythes. The first of the Smiths in the U.S. was the English explorer and colonist John Smith (1580?–1631).

smithereens.   *Smithereens*, as in the expression *blasted to smithereens*, derives from the Irish *smidirin*, "small fragment." It is first recorded in English in the 19th century.

Smithfield ham.   Famous Virginia hams made for over a century at Smithfield, Virginia, from hogs originally grown on a peanut diet and cured with the smoke of the burning shells.

Smithsonian Institution; smithsonite.   Despite the fact that he neither had visited nor known anyone living in America, British chemist James Smithson (1765–1829) left over $508,000, the whole of his estate, "to the United States of America to found at Washington under the name of the Smithsonian Institution an establishment for the increase and diffusion of knowledge among men." The money was actually willed to his nephew with the stipulation that the above condition apply if the nephew died without children—which he did in 1835. Smithson, the illegitimate son of Sir Hugh Smithson and Elizabeth Macie, made many valuable analyses of minerals, and smithsonite, an important zinc ore, is also named in his honor. Congress took 10 years debating whether or not to accept his

bequest, finally accepting largely through the efforts of John Quincy Adams. The museum was founded in 1846.

smoke-filled room.   Associated Press reporter Kirke Simpson first recorded the expression *smoke-filled room*, in a newspaper story describing the behind-the-scenes political manipulation used to secure Warren Harding's nomination for president in 1920. However, Harry Daughtery, a friend of Harding, probably coined the phrase.

smoking gun.   The term has been used so much over a relatively short period that it is almost a cliché. It means "indisputable proof or evidence of a crime," proof comparable to someone with a smoking gun in hand being guilty of a shooting. It was first recorded about 1970 and became a prominent expression during the Watergate political scandal that led to President Richard M. Nixon's resignation in 1974. *Smoking gun* referred to a Nixon tape on which he said he wanted minimal FBI participation in the Watergate investigation. *See* DEEP THROAT.

Smokin' Joe.   Fighter Smokin' Joe Frazier, and any boxer dubbed *Smokin'*, isn't so called because he smokes a lot of cigarettes or cigars. Smokin' Joe Frazier and all like him came "smokin' " into the center of the ring as soon as the bell rang.

smooch; smouch.   *Smooch*, "to kiss or pet, to make love," may oddly enough be another example of ethnic prejudice in language. Nobody has proved its origins, but it may derive from *smouch*, a favorite word of Mark Twain's, which in its original sense meant to obtain illicitly by cheating or swindling. In all probability it comes from the derogatory Dutch *Smous*, "a German Jew," this word possibly formed from the proper name Moses.

smooth-shaven.   English poet John Milton, not a copywriter for razor blades, coined *smooth-shaven*, in about 1635. Milton had as precedents the earlier *smooth-skinned* and *smooth-faced*. *See* LOVELORN.

s'mores.   A southern U.S. treat made of toasted marshmallows and chocolate sandwiched between graham crackers and sometimes wrapped in tin foil, then heated over a campfire; so named because they are so delicious you always want "s'more." Now packaged nationally as a sandwich cookie to be heated in a microwave oven.

snack.   Snacks, so named, probably, because they are quickly "snatched," have meant "mere bites or morsels of food, as contrasted with regular meals" since the 17th century. Wrote the first writer known to use the word: "When once a man has got a snack . . . he too often retains a hankering . . ."

snafu.   *See* FUBAR.

snail.   Since at least 1592 a *snail's pace* has meant "exceedingly slow," but until recently no one knew just how exceedingly slow that was. Recent studies have shown that garden snails travel at about two feet an hour, or one mile every three months or so. In the expression DRAW IN ONE'S HORNS, *horns* refers to the horns of the snail, because the garden pest draws in its horns and remains in its shell when threatened with danger, or when weather conditions aren't favorable. The snail's actions do suggest someone who draws away from a situation and takes no action while reconsidering the matter. The expression is first recorded in the early 1300s and clearly indicates that the garden snail is its source. *See also* SLUG.

snail mail. A humorous synonym for postal mail coined in the early 1980s by some anonymous e-mail user. Electronic e-mail is of course much faster than regular mail. The expression was born in the U.S. but is widely used today.

snake dance. An American Indian ceremonial dance in which snakes or representations of snakes are handled or imitated by the dancers; the Hopi Indians use it as a dance in which they pray for rain. The dance is often performed with poisonous snakes.

snake eyes. *See* WITHIN AN ACE OF.

snake in the grass. *Latet anguis in herbe* ("a snake lurks in the grass"), the Roman poet Virgil wrote in the third *Eclogue*, and from this ancient source comes our common expression for a hidden or hypocritical enemy. Proving that times don't change much, the Latin proverb first appears in English as a line in a political song of about 1290: "Though all appears clean, a snake lurks in the grass."

snake pit; cuckoo nest. M. J. Ward's bestselling novel *The Snake Pit* (1947), which was made into a movie nominated for an Academy Award in 1948, gave us the expression *snake pit* for a mental hospital where deplorable conditions prevail. Similarly, Ken Kesey's novel *One Flew Over the Cuckoo's Nest* (1962), also made into an award-winning film, helped popularize the term *cuckoo nest* for a psychiatric hospital. However, *cuckoo nest* was recorded as "a crazy place" two years before Kesey's title, in an episode of the TV series *The Many Lives of Dobie Gillis*, and the term *cuckoo house* for an insane asylum dates back to at least 1930. *Cuckoo* for an insane person is a British coinage of the late 19th century, though it first meant a stupid person. *See* CUCKOO.

snap beans. *See* STRING BEAN.

snapshot. *Snapshot* was originally a hunting term for a hurried shot taken without deliberate aim, especially at rapidly moving game. It was first recorded in an 1808 entry in the diary of a British Colonel Hawke, who wrote: "Almost every pheasant I fired at was a snapshot among the high cover." It wasn't for over 50 years that the term was used in photography to mean "a quick photo" taken with a hand camera, this meaning the only one heard today.

snark. An imaginary animal that is the subject of Lewis Carroll's poem *The Hunting of the Snark* (1876). The elusive troublesome snark when finally tracked down turned out to be only a Boojum and hence the name *snark* (a combination Carroll made of *snake* and *shark*) has come to be applied to the quests of dreamers. It is said that the poet Dante Gabriel Rossetti suffered from the delusion that Carroll caricatured him as the snark.

snath. Another unusual word whose use will make you look knowledgeable—or foolish. A snath is the handle of a scythe. "Do you carry scythe snaths?" you can ask your much-impressed, or perplexed, garden supply store owner. *See also* BERM.

snawfus. This unusual imaginary creature of the U.S. southern mountains is said to resemble a winged white deer with flowering branches as antlers. It figures in much southern folklore.

sneak. Though *sneak* sounds like *snake*, it doesn't derive from the latter word. It does, however, come from the Old English *snican*, to creep or crawl, just as a snake would do.

sneakers. The first sneakers were made in 1868 but the athletic shoes weren't called *sneakers* until about 1895. Once worn in many sports, the fabric and rubber shoes may have been so named because baseball players "stealing" bases favored them, or because thieves found them useful in their line of work. The word is an Americanism made, of course, from the word *sneak*. The British call these shoes *plimsolls*. *See also* PLIMSOLL MARKS.

snicker. A snide, slightly stifled, disrespectful laugh. Also *snigger*. The word originally came from England's Essex dialect. Snickers is the name of a long-popular American candy bar.

snipe hunting. *See* HUNT ELEVETRICH.

sniper. The snipe is a wary, quick bird that hunters had no success with in England until the bow and arrow was replaced with the gun in the 16th century. Even then the bird was difficult to bag unless the hunter concealed himself and patiently waited for a good shot. Snipe shooting became a favorite sport because of its difficulty, and because of the snipe hunter's *modus operandi*, the word *sniper* came to mean any marksman firing from a concealed position.

snitch. *Snitch* for an informer is not an Americanism from early days in the West, as some people believe. The term goes back at least to 18th-century England and is recorded in Francis Grose's *Classical Dictionary of the Vulgar Tongue* (1785). Originally *snitch* was a synonym for a nose. Since *nose* came to mean an informer in early English slang, so did *snitch*.

snobare. The Italians have adopted many English words over the past century. In this case they borrowed the word *snob* and made out of it the verb *snobare*, "to snub."

snollygoster. One very rarely hears this word today, but in the 19th century it was a common Americanism for "a pretentious boaster." The word is probably a fanciful formation coined by some folk poet who liked its appropriate sound; it is first recorded in 1862. A Georgia editor defined a snollygoster as a "fellow who wants office regardless of party, platform or principles, and who, whenever he wins, gets there by the sheer force of monumental talknophical assumacy." The type is still common, even if the word isn't.

snood.

> When thou hast heard his name upon
>   The bugles of the cherubim
> Begin thou softly to unzone
>   Thy girlish bosom unto him
> And softly to undo the snood
>   That is the sign of maidenhood.

One wouldn't think James Joyce wrote this, but it is from his early poem "Bid Adieu to Maidenhood." *Snood* is mostly a crossword puzzle word today; the silk ribbon with which Scottish and Irish maidens tied their hair isn't used much anymore. The headband was worn only by virgins and by custom had to be replaced with another hair covering if a girl married or lost her virginity before marriage. *Snood* is a very old word, dating back to the eighth century and probably derives from Swedish *sno*, "twine, string." In more recent times it has meant a woman's hair net.

snoop. The verb *snoop* derives from something Americans still do, but which we have no good word for—the Dutch *snoepen*, "to eat sweets secretively." *Snoepen* came to mean the prying and spying that the Dutch in early New York did on their neighbors, and passed into English as *snoop* in the late 18th century.

Snopesism. A word coined by William Faulkner for the taking over of the world by a grasping, greedy, money-grubbing middle class without any real culture, the word of course deriving from the Snopes family depicted in his novels of fictitious Yoknapatawpha County, Mississippi. Wrote Faulkner in *The Mansion* (1959): "He had to be the sole one masculine feller . . . not just to recognize she had a soul still capable of being saved from what he called Snopesism . . ." See SARTORIS; WALL STREET PANIC.

snorkel. The *snorkel*, introduced during World War II, was at first only a retractable tube that ventilated a sub cruising slightly below the surface. It took its name from the German *Schnorchel*, "air intake." After the war, *snorkel* became better known as a tube one breathes through while swimming facedown in the water or slightly below the surface.

snow. The word *snow* is first recorded in about A.D. 825 in the form of *snaw*. Though we have terms like *red snow*, *green snow*, *black snow*, and *golden snow* for snow tinged by algae or foreign substances, we basically make do with the one word *snow* to describe the crystalline white stuff. (The *powder* made for skiers is an exception to the rule.) On the other hand linguist Benjamin Lee Whorf once reported on an Eskimo tribe that distinguishes 100 different types of snow—and has 100 synonyms (including *tipsiq* and *tuva*) to match them. The walrus also has many synonyms in Eskimo language "In Yupik there are forty-seven words for a walrus, depending on what he's doing," writes Clay Hardy of the U.S. Fish and Wildlife Service. "There is no word for *time*. You tell me who's got the proper values." See WALRUS.

snowbirds. Southwesterners use this term today for northerners who come south for the winter, but it originated in the U.S. Army in the late 19th century as a name for men who enlisted for food and quarters during the winter and deserted in the spring.

snows of yesteryear. *See* YESTERYEAR.

snuffing the candle. It hasn't been depicted in a western film, but snuffing the candle was a genuine entertainment on the American frontier. The term is recorded as early as 1838 and referred to a frontier amusement in which incredibly accurate riflemen snuffed candles with bullets as a test of marksmanship. Some (using either rifles or pistols) were said to be so good that they could shoot through the flames *without* putting the candle out.

snuff out. *Snuff out*, "to kill," is best known as U.S. underworld slang from the 1920s, but it originated in World War I and is British in origin, deriving from the British slang *snuff out*, meaning "to die," which is first attested in 1864 and was probably suggested by the snuffing out of a candle, the flame of the candle compared to the flame of life. Sadistic *snuff movies* of the 1980s and earlier reputedly depict the actual killing of "actors" on the screen.

snug. This was originally a nautical term meaning neat, trim, compact, deriving from the Danish *snyg* meaning the same. It apparently came into maritime use in the 17th century or earlier and soon after came ashore.

snug as a bug in a rug. One would guess that this is a folk saying of untraceable origins, but it apparently is the invention of Benjamin Franklin, who jotted it off in a letter in 1772. It means "the utmost in contentment." Franklin is of course responsible for many maxims that are part of our speech today, including *a word to the wise*; *time is money*; *death and taxes*; *an ounce of prevention*; and *early to bed, early to rise*.

soapberry. The scientific name (*Sapindus*) for this tree explains the berry's use: *Sapindus* is a combination of the Latin for "soap" (*sappo*) and "Indus" (Indian). American Indians used the berries for soap. The pulp of soapberries contains saponin, so they lather up easily and were valued as shampoo, although the soap made from them does damage some materials. *Saponin*, the lather-producing agent in soapberries, can be poisonous if taken internally; in fact, American Indians caught fish by stupefying them with bits of the fruit thrown into pools.

soap opera. *Newsweek* seems to have used *soap opera* first in an 11/13/39 article, putting the expression in quotes as if it were new. Earlier a writer in the *Christian Century* (8/24/39) came very close to coining the term, however: "These fifteen minute tragedies . . . I call the 'soap tragedies' . . . because it is by the grace of soap I am allowed to shed tears for these characters who suffer so much from life." He was referring, of course, to the soap manufacturers who sponsored many of the early radio serials characterized by melodrama and sentimentality that are now called *soap operas*, or simply *soaps* (an abbreviated form that is 20 years or so old).

Soapy Sam. The first Soapy Sam, Samuel Wilberforce, bishop of Oxford and later Winchester, was a nonconformist and controversial clergyman if ever there was one. Wilberforce, son of the great antislavery leader William Wilberforce, tried to steer a middle course between High Church and Low Church factions in England. Although a devout man in his personal life, this position forced him to develop a suave, unctuous manner of speaking, persuasive but versatile and expedient almost to a fault. By 1860 he had earned the nickname Soapy Sam, which has since been applied to any slippery, unctuous speaker who can talk his way out of anything. The coining was perhaps given an assist by the initials "S.O.A.P." on the floral decorations above the stall where he preached—these standing for the names Sam Oxon and Alfred Port. Once someone asked him about the nickname and he assured his questioner that he was called Soapy Sam "Because I am often in hot water and always come out with clean hands." Bishop Wilberforce died in 1873, aged 68.

sober as a judge.   In the play *Don Quixote in England* (1734) one of Henry Fielding's characters says: "I am as sober as a judge." Perhaps it was simply Fielding's observation that judges are almost always sober on the bench, but the phrase may have its source in the saying AN APPEAL FROM PHILIP DRUNK TO PHILIP SOBER. *Sober* is the exact opposite of the Latin word for "in his cups," deriving from *so*, "apart from," and *bria*, "cup."

soccer; rugger.   Partridge tells us that *soccer* is a "perversion" of association football, formed in the late 19th century by adding what he calls "the Oxford-*er*" to as*soc*iation football. *Rugger*, a synonym for rugby, was formed in much the same way.

social butterfly.   The expression and the species are as common today as in the 15th or 16th century when *social butterfly* was coined, mainly because it aptly describes a pretty or well-dressed person of little substance flitting from one party or other social function to the next.

sociology.   French philospher Auguste Comte, the father of the discipline of sociology, invented the word *sociologie* for "the science or study of the origin, history and constitution of human society." The word was first anglicized in 1843.

sockdollager.   *See* QUICKER THAN HELL CAN SCORCH A FEATHER.

Sock Saunders.   A mythical American character of the woods more human than PAUL BUNYAN. Louise Dickenson Rich in *We Took to the Woods* (1942) explains Sock this way: "If I a man . . . slips on a log, but catches himself in time, he says, 'Foxed you that time, Sock Saunders.' If he cuts his foot, he explains, 'Sock Saunders got me.' There are no stories about Sock Saunders. He's just the guy who hangs around and makes life complicated."

so cold the wolves ate the sheep just for the wool.   A colorful old Ozark Mountains saying describing bitter, way below zero temperatures.

Socratic irony; Socratic method.   By feigning ignorance, Socrates led his audience into traps, easily defeating them in argument, and this pretended ignorance has since been known as Socratic irony. The great Greek philosopher also developed the inductive Socratic method, conducting a cross-examination by questions and answers carefully designed to impart knowledge, or to evoke knowledge from those who may have believed they were unknowing. Socrates was born about 470 B.C., the child of a sculptor and a midwife. After receiving a good

education and completing a tour of military service in which he was distinguished for his bravery, he devoted his life to the investigation of virtue, justice, and purity. His profound spiritual influence led him to be called the philosopher who "brought down philosophy from the heavens to earth" and he liked to call himself "the midwife of men's thoughts," but he left behind no writings and his work is known primarily through the *Dialogues* of Plato. Condemned to death by the Athenian government in 399 B.C. for neglecting the old gods, introducing new ones, and corrupting youth, Socrates was forced to commit suicide by drinking hemlock. "The hour of departure has arrived," he said at the last, "and we go our separate ways—I to die, and you to live. Which is the better, God only knows."

sod.   The mostly British slang word *sod* has gained some respectability over the years. It was first recorded in the early 19th century as short for SODOMITE. It then came to mean any obnoxious person, and finally was and is used to describe any fellow, as in "The poor sod lost his job last week." Partridge says the last two meanings are "often used in ignorance of the word's origin."

soda pop.   At the beginning of the 19th century soda water consisted of nothing but water, a little soda, and sometimes a bit of flavoring. Soon someone thought to force gas into the water and to keep it there under pressure, the soda water sparkling and foaming when the pressure is removed and the gas escapes. The soda was kept under pressure in cylinders that came to be called *soda fountains* and were often quite unsafe, for when dropped the pressure inside them could cause a tremendous explosion, which happened once in a while, according to newspapers of the day. At any rate, the sparkling, popping soda that came out of the fountains probably was responsible for the name *pop*, for "soda," long before soda was bottled. *Soda pop* or *pop*, is not recorded in the language, however, until the early 20th century.

soddy.   A prairie sodhouse of farmers or sodbusters. Wrote Lucia St. Clair Robson in *Ride the Wind* (1982): "The [collapsed] soddy had been dug into a hillside . . . The other three sides were made of large sod bricks laid in double rows. Grass and flowers grew thickly on the partially caved-in roof . . . The canvas door still hung askew from the broken cottonwood pole that served as a lintel. With charcoal someone had written on the stained, grey canvas:

> 250 miles to post office.
> 100 miles to wood.
> 20 miles to water.
> 6 inches to hell."

sodomite; sodomy.   Sodom and Gomorrah, the twin sin Cities of the Plain in the Bible, have long represented male and female vice respectively—a *Gomorrhean*, in fact, meaning a lesbian in 16th-century England. A sodomite is one who practices sodomy, "unnatural intercourse with a human or animal," such practices being attributed to Sodom's male inhabitants. The story of Sodom and Gomorrah is told in Genesis 18:19. Old Testament scholars believe the story is a mythological attempt to account for the destruction of a city once located near the Dead Sea. *See* SOD.

sofa. The Arabic word *suffah*, "cushion or long bench," gives us our word *sofa*, for "a couch." The word came into English early in the 17th century.

so far back in jail you can't shoot peas to him. A saying that became news when Georgia governor Marvin Griffin addressed civil rights protestors in the late 1960s: "We'll put him so far back in jail you can't shoot peas to him."

soft berm. A soft shoulder on the road. It could be argued that *berm* is a word dating back to the days of knightly chivalry, when in Norman times it meant "the ridge between the edge of the moat around a castle" and the castle.

soft sawder. To flatter someone, talk a lot of blarney; an old term that is still heard occasionally, though it isn't recorded in most dictionaries. The derivation is unclear, apparently having something to do with "soldier," but it is first recorded in Thomas C. Haliburton's *The Clockmaker* (1836): "If she goes to act ugly, I'll give her a dose of 'soft sawder.' "

soft soap. A relatively soft, semiliquid soap containing potash, introduced early in the 19th century, inspired the Americanism to *soft-soap* someone, which dates to about 1830. The soap was oily, as unctuous as a wheedling flatterer.

Soho. London's noted Soho area probably takes its name from the old hunting cry *Soho*, used centuries ago when there were hunting fields in the vicinity. This cosmopolitan area, however, noted for its nightclubs, striptease clubs, and restaurants, did not give its name to New York City's SoHo district in Manhattan, which is a shortening of *South of Houston* (Street) by which it is bordered on the north. The area, revitalized in the 1970s and 1980s, is a fashionable neighborhood, among the most vibrant in the city. In the early 19th century it was known as Hell's Hundred Acres. *See* TALLYHO.

soland. *See* MONSOON.

solar plexus. This term was first used as a synonym for the pit of the stomach in the 1890s by American fighters. Before this it had meant the network of nerves behind the stomach. Gentleman Jim Corbett lost the heavyweight championship in 1897 when Bob "Fitz" Fitzsimmons knocked him out with a blow to the solar plexus.

soldier's breeze or wind. A sailor's contemptuous regard for landlubbers is reflected in this 19th-century term for a wind that is equally forcible going or coming. In other words, when the wind is about abeam going out and coming back, it takes little ability to sail—even a soldier could do it.

solecism. An error in grammar, or in the use of words, or a breach of etiquette is called a *solecism*. Soli, or Soloi, was an ancient Greek colony in the province of Cilicia, Asia Minor, far removed from Athens. Colonists who settled there developed a dialect of their own that Athenian purists considered barbarous and uncouth, leading them to coin the word *soloikos* as a slang term for ignorant speech. From *soloikos* came the Greek noun *soloikismos*, "speaking incorrectly," like an inhabitant of Soloi, which eventually, through the Latin *soloecismus*, made its entrance into English as *solecism*. In years to come, Yankee colonists would be criticized in much the same way by Englishmen, but the label *Americanism* has always been accepted with pride by Americans. Soli, located in what is now Turkey, was an important, prosperous port in the time of Alexander the Great. When Pompey rebuilt the city after it was destroyed by Tigranes in the Third Mithridatic War, he named it Pompeiopolis. Few of Soli's ruins remain today, but *solecism*, originally slang itself, endures in all modern European languages as a remembrance of the way its citizens "ruined" Greek.

solicitor. In England solicitors handle the preliminaries of law cases, while BARRISTERS alone are members of the bar and can take cases to court. Barristers are composed of two classes: junior counsels called barristers and a higher class of king's (or queen's) counsels, who wear silk gowns, as opposed to the formers' gowns of common cloth. In times past a solicitor was "one who solicits in Courts of Equity through counsel," while ATTORNEYS (from the French *atourner*, to turn over to another) belonged to other courts.

Solid South. A political term much used from the Civil War to the late 1950s, when the South's electoral votes could be counted upon by the Democratic party. Political realignments have made the term purely historical today.

solitaire. *See* CANFIELD.

solitary as an oyster. No single Faulknerian sentence could contain all the miseries of the oyster's life, from the *Crepidula fornicata*, or slipper limpet, that multiplies as fast as its Latin name suggests and suffocates whole beds of oysters, to the starfish that grotesquely stick their whole stomachs out of their mouths and into open oyster shells to digest some soft meat. No wonder the oyster tries to keep to itself. No wonder we have the expression *as solitary as an oyster*, first recorded by Dickens in *A Christmas Carol*.

solitary confinement. Solitary confinement in "the hole," a cell removed from all others and often below ground, was a punishment originated by the state of Pennsylvania in the late 18th century. Suggested by the Quakers, "solitary" was considered a reform measure at the time, replacing brutal floggings for incorrigible prisoners.

Solomon; Solomon's ring. Solomon, the son of David and Bath-sheba, ruled over Israel for some 40 years, and was noted for his wisdom and wealth. The latter and perhaps the former are witnessed by the 700 wives and 300 concubines he kept in great splendor. His wisdom is shown by the tale of the baby he proposed to divide in two. By suggesting this, Solomon determined the child's rightful mother—the false claimant accepting his proposal and the real mother asking that the child be given to her rival rather than be killed. His reign was a great one marked by peace and economic and literary development, Solomon himself having the "Song of Songs" and the books of *Ecclesiastes* and *Proverbs* attributed to him. Yet there was a religious decline and increasing social injustice in the king's time, and the northern tribes revolted upon his death in about 933 B.C. Solomon left Israel saddled with taxes and dissension, but his name remains a synonym for wisdom, the

Bible referring to him as "wiser than all men . . . his fame . . . in all nations round about." The wisdom of Solomon is sometimes expressed by the phrase *to have Solomon's ring*, referring to a legendary ring he wore that told him all he wanted to know.

Solomon Grundy existence.   Life according to the old, anonymous rhyme *Solomon Grundy.*

> Solomon Grundy,
> Born on a Monday,
> Christened on Tuesday,
> Married on Wednesday,
> Took ill on Thursday,
> Worse on Friday,
> Died on Saturday,
> Buried on Sunday.
> This is the end
> Of Solomon Grundy.

Solomon's seal.   Some say that Solomon's seal (*Polygonatum multiflorum*) is so named because as the flower's stem decays the rootstalk of the plant becomes marked with scars that have some resemblance to official seals such as the seal of Solomon, king of Israel in about 900 B.C. Others hold that the root has medicinal value in sealing up and closing wounds.

solon.   "I grow old ever learning many things," wrote the sage Solon in the often quoted line. The wise statesman and lawgiver lived some 82 years before he left Athens in about 590 B.C. and died, according to tradition, while wandering somewhere in the East. One of the Seven Sages of Greece, his motto was "Know thyself." Solon initiated many legal and social reforms, including a new constitution for Athens that revived the popular assembly at a time when tension between the rich and poor had reached the breaking point. His love poems and patriotic verse were well known, but the proverbial remark "Call no man happy till he is dead" was probably not his, though attributed to him. Elected archon, officer of the state, in 594 B.C., Solon instituted reforms that laid the foundation for Athenian democracy. His name has come to mean any lawmaker, not necessarily a wise one, *solon* sometimes being used because it takes up less space in headlines and newspaper stories than representative or congressman.

So long!   *So long!*, for "good-bye," may not be an Americanism. The *O.E.D.* gives 1834 as its first recorded date, and the source is probably British, since *So long!* isn't recorded in the U.S. until the late 1850s. Other possibilities are that it comes from the Hebrew SHALOM, the German *so lange*, or the Arabic SALAAM. Another theory, contributed by linguist Howard Marblestone as "perhaps plausible," suggests that "British soldiers posted to Malaya in the 19th century heard there among the Muslims the Arabic *salaam* with native nasalization, thus: *salaang*. As this sounded to them like the English 'so long', they brought it back to England, greetings often being borrowed into other languages."

solwara he stret olgeta.   Literally "salt water he straight altogether," which means "the ocean very calm" in the Pidgin English spoken in New Guinea, which is called Tok (talk) Pisen (pidgin). Another example is *mi no manki bilong you*, "me no monkey belong you": "I'm not your slave or servant." *See* PIDGIN ENGLISH; PIDGIN LANGUAGE.

sombrero.   The great broad-brimmed hat long associated with Mexico takes its name from the shade (in Spanish, *sombra*) that it provides its wearer.

someone stole his rudder.   We find this expression, for "a helpless drunk," first recorded in the American West during the 19th century, but it is obviously a borrowing from nautical language, of the sea or the inland waterways of America.

something on the ball.   A baseball pitcher with *something on the ball* has the ability to throw a variety of pitches that are usually effective. Since the early 1900s the phrase has been extended to mean anyone with skill or ability. *See* NOTHING ON THE BALL; ON THE BALL.

something is rotten in Denmark.   Marcellus's suspicion about the kingdom of course proved to be well founded, but what Shakespeare had him say was *something is rotten in the state of Denmark*, not the persistent misquotation from *Hamlet* above.

something up one's sleeve; laugh up one's sleeve.   Garments in medieval times had few if any pockets, so men often carried whatever couldn't be hung from their belts in their full sleeves. Probably from this source, rather than from magicians with rabbits up their sleeves, comes our expression for having something in reserve or an alternative plan, although the phrase, in its sense of a scheme or trick, was most likely influenced by magicians concealing in their sleeves the means by which they do a trick. A second expression deriving from the same source is *to laugh up (or on) one's sleeve*, "to ridicule a person secretly." Someone wearing a garment with capacious sleeves was quite literally able to conceal a laugh by hiding his face in his sleeve.

son of a bitch.   *See* LES SOMMOBICHES.

son of a bitch stew.   You use everything but "the hair, horns and holler," according to one recipe for son of a bitch stew, commonly made on chuck wagons in the old West. All the innards of a steer, including heart, brains, and kidneys, had to be included in the stew, but the most indispensable ingredient was gut (tripe). This inspired the old saying: "A son of a bitch might not have any brains and no heart, but if he ain't got guts he ain't a son of a bitch."

son of a gun.   *Son of a gun* is now a euphemism for the much stronger *son of a bitch*, or even a term of affectionate regard between friends ("You old son of a gun!"), but this expression did not start out that way. It dates back to the early 1800s and was just a little less perjorative than *son of a bitch*, or *son of a whore*, which came into the language at about the same time. In the early 19th century, *son of a gun* meant "a sailor's bastard," but it proceeded to become more innocuous with the passing of time. *The Sailor's Wordbook* (1867), written by British navy adm. William Henry Smyth, attempts to explain the expression's origins, but bear in mind that the book was written a long time after the term was born: "An epithet conveying contempt in a slight degree, and originally applied to boys born afloat, when women were permitted to accompany their husbands to sea;

one admiral declared he literally was thus cradled, under the breast of a gun-carriage."

son of a sea cook. *Son of a sea cook*, which can mean either a "good guy" or a "mean SOB," depending on the context, really has little to do with the sea. No sea cook had any hand in it. It seems that the earliest American settlers appropriated the word *s'quenk*, for "skunk," from the Indians around the Massachusetts Bay Colony, pronouncing it *see-konk*. Thus, a *son of a see-konk* was first a stinking son of a skunk. Because *see-konk* sounded something like "sea cook" it came to be pronounced "sea cook" long after the Indian word was forgotten. The fact that sea cooks were often cantankerous old men probably reinforced the term's present ambivalent meaning.

Sooner; sooner. *Sooner*, capitalized, refers to a native of Oklahoma, the Sooner State. Uncapitalized, the word has several meanings: 1) someone who settles on government land before it's opened to settlers; 2) any person who unfairly gets ahead of another; and, most interesting of all 3) a child born fewer than nine months after his or her parents were married, one who came out sooner than he or she should have. The last is an expression used mainly in the Appalachian Mountains.

Sooner State. A nickname for Oklahoma, after the "sooners" who "jumped the gun sooner" and sneaked over the border before the lands there were thrown open to settlement by U.S. citizens at noontime on April 22, 1889. Many of the 20,000 people who came to claim land on that day found that "sooners" had gotten there before them. Indians, of course, were there sooner than anyone, for all the good it did them. Today residents of Oklahoma are called Sooners.

sop. See GIVE A SOP TO CERBERUS.

sophistry; sophomore. The Sophists were not really a school of philosophers but individual teachers who toured the cities of Greece in the mid-fifth century B.C. teaching rhetoric and other subjects. They did, however, share common beliefs. Far less idealistic than the Socratic school, they prepared their pupils for public life, placing little store in truth for truth's sake and accepting money for their teaching, being what might be called pragmatists today. Although their name derived from *sophos*, the Greek word for wise, it was a contemptuous term among their contemporaries. Because they taught the art of persuasion to young men eager for political careers and the methods they taught were often unscrupulous and over-ingenious, *sophist* came to meet someone who tries to mislead people with clever arguments, one who tries to "make the worse seem the better reason." *Sophism* is now used to mean a plausible but fallacious argument, and false, specious reasoning is called *sophistry*. The word has thus had almost a complete reversal in meaning since the time when the wise men of Greece were called sophists—before the Sophists came on the scene. The word *sophomore*, a second-year college or high school student, probably comes from *sophom*, an obsolete form of *sophism*.

SOS. SOS doesn't stand for "Save Our Ship," "Save Our Souls," or "Stop Other Signals." The letters, adopted in 1908 by international agreement, actually mean nothing at all and were chosen only because they are so simple for a wireless operator to remember and transmit in Morse code—three dits (dots), three dahs (dashes) and three dits (. . . - - - . . .). The doctrine of resemblances suggested this term to hungry G.I.'s during World War II. It is the abbreviation of *shit on a shingle*, the creamed chipped beef on toast so often served in messhalls. See CQD.

Sotadic. See PALINDROME.

sotto voce. This term, taken directly from Italian about 1730, means "to speak in a low, soft voice, an undertone," so that you are not overheard. The Italian words literally mean "under (the) voice." In music the term means "in very soft tones."

soubise. Charles de Rohan, prince de Soubise, may have created the superbly simple sauce that bears his name, but it's more likely that it was created and named in his honor by his majordomo, the great chef Marin. Soubise (1715–87), a famous gourmet who was the grandson of the princesse de Soubise, one of Louis XIV's mistresses, became marshal of France in 1758 through the influence of Madame de Pompadour, Louis XV's mistress. The prince liked to cook as much as he liked making love and war, and his chef Marin was among the greatest of 18th-century culinary artists, his cookbook, *Les Dons de Comus* (Gifts from the kitchen), appearing in 1739 and intended to brighten the tables of the bourgeoisie, enabling "even third-class persons to dine with grace." A soubise is a brown or white sauce containing strained or pureed onions and served with meat: it is made by blending onions simmered tender in butter with a creamy bechamel sauce and rubbing this through a fine sieve.

so ugly that when he was a little boy momma had to tie a pork chop around his neck so the dog would play with him. A saying heard in Texas, probably of recent origin.

soul brother, etc. As a term for blacks used by blacks, *soul brothers* has been around since at least the 1950s. Today it is often abbreviated, by blacks, as *the brothers* (or *sisters*) and further shortened to *bro* when used in a greeting. The meaning here is that blacks are alike in the soul, but in earlier combinations *soul* is used in many ways. *Soul sharks* were rapacious preachers, black or white, usually without a pulpit, and *soul butter* was a term for moralizing drivel, black or white, that Mark Twain popularized. *Soul mate* can be someone much loved, or even a mistress. *Soul music* and *soul food* (food like collard greens, black-eyed peas, hog maw, etc., associated with southern blacks) are also black terms dating back at least to the 1950s.

soul driver. A person who took slaves to market to sell them; an overseer. The expression is recorded as early as 1774 and came into the vocabulary of abolitionists.

soul kiss. Actress Olga Nethersole's long passionate onstage kiss in Dandot's *Sapho* in the late 1880s led to her prosecution for obscenity. It is said that her "intraoral and interlingual" kiss, or French kiss, as it is also called, inspired the term *soul kiss*, from a shortening of the name Nether*sole*. A good theory, but nothing more, for the expression *soul kiss* isn't recorded until the 1930s.

soul ships. Until the late 19th century, soul ships were believed to sail to Brittany's Bay of Souls near Point du Ray and collect recently deceased sailors for the journey to the fabled "Isles of the Blessed" somewhere to the west. Soul ships were sighted by many a mariner, just as mermaids and sea serpents were.

sound; sounding. The *sounding* that determines the depth of the water by means of a line and lead is of no relation to the word *sound*, meaning something audible, which derives from the Latin *sonus*. *Sounding* comes from the Old English word *sund*, for "water, sea, or swimming." The *sound* that is an inlet of the sea has the same roots.

soup. Nitroglycerin was dubbed *soup* by safecrackers because the liquid can be obtained by *very very very* gently simmering dynamite in water. The Americanism is first recorded in about 1905.

soup and fish. Dating back to 19th-century America, this term for formal white-tie dinner clothes probably derives from the obsolete American term *soup and fish*, for a lavish dinner of many courses. *Soup and fish* for an elaborate dinner, in turn, is apparently related to the still common expression *from soup to nuts*, but this last term seems to have been first recorded in the 1920s.

soupbone. Baseball pitching great Christy Mathewson appears to have first recorded this term for one's throwing or pitching arm, in his book *Pitching in a Pinch* (1912): "My old soupbone . . . was so weak that I couldn't break a pane of glass at fifty feet."

soup to nuts. *See* FROM SOUP TO NUTS.

sourdough bread. Now known in commercial forms throughout the United States, sourdough bread, made from sour or fermented dough, was first a mainstay of miners in the early West, who were in fact *sourdoughs* because they carried some of the fermented dough with them from place to place to start new batches of bread.

sour grapes. In Aesop's fable "The Fox and the Grapes," a fox spies luscious-looking grapes hanging from a vine. He leaps a number of times trying to get them, failing by a few inches with each leap, and gives up after rationalizing that they are probably sour and inedible anyway. La Fontaine, another great fabulist, later regarded the fox as admirable, remarking that his words were "better than complaining," but the fox's *sour grapes* have come to mean any belittling, envious remark.

sousaphone. "The Stars and Stripes Forever," "The Washington Post," "Semper Fidelis," "Hands Across the Sea," "Liberty Bell," "High School Cadets"—John Philip Sousa composed over 100 such popular marches, inspiring an English magazine to dub him the March King, a title that remained with the bandmaster throughout his long career. Sousa, the son of Portuguese refugees, began conducting theater orchestras when only 19. He became bandmaster of the U.S. Marine Corps band in 1882, his father having played there before him, and formed his famous Sousa's Band 10 years later. His band toured the world, bringing him great renown, and he composed numerous comic operas, suites, songs, and orchestral music in addition to his marches. Sousa died in 1932 aged 78. Besides greatly improving the quality of band music, he invented the sousaphone, a large circular tuba standing 52 inches high and weighing some 26 pounds, with a flaring adjustable bell, adjustable mouthpiece, and a full, rich sonorous tone.

South Carolina. *See* NORTH CAROLINA.

South Dakota. *See* NORTH DAKOTA.

Southern chivalry. Though rarely, if ever, heard today, this historical term was common up until the end of the Civil War. According to the *Magazine of American History* (vol. 3, 1885), "It was claimed as a proud title by Southerners and their friends, but has always been heard and used by the North with a shade of contempt."

southerner. Often capitalized, this common word for a resident of the American South may have been coined between 1820 and 1830. The term first appeared in *Western Monthly Magazine* in 1828. *Southern gentleman* was recorded about half a century earlier.

southern fried chicken. Originally chicken fried in bacon grease, southern fried chicken has been popular in the American South since before 1711, when the term *fried chicken* is first recorded there. It became popular throughout the country in the 1930s, when it was first widely sold at roadside restaurants. *See* GOSPEL BIRD.

southern gentleman. This term for a courtly, well-bred southerner dates back at least to the late 18th century. Clare Booth Luce, in *Kiss the Boys Goodbye*, offered this definition: "If you can shoot like a South Carolinian, ride like a Virginian, make love like a Georgian, and be proud of it like an Episcopalian, you're a Southern gentleman." But an anonymous infidel Yankee defined the chivalrous species as "one who rises to his feet when his wife comes in bearing the firewood."

southern hospitality. The words *southern hospitality*, the hospitality characteristic of southern people and sometimes considered the epitome of sectional hospitality, have been traced back to 1819, when a traveler from the North wrote in his journal, "The mistress . . . treated us to milk in the true spirit of Southern hospitality." But the South was famous for its hospitality long before this, as it still is today, and the much-used phrase is surely older.

south of the border. To Americans *south of the border* has long meant "down Mexico way," across the Rio Grande. In Scotland the expression refers to England, the border being the one between Scotland and England.

southpaw. Humorist Finley Peter Dunne, then a sportswriter, coined this word for a left-handed baseball pitcher while covering sports in Chicago in the 1880s. Home plate in the Chicago ball park was then to the west, so that a left-handed pitcher released the ball from the "paw," or hand, on his south side. The word soon came to describe any left-hander.

sowbread. *See* CYCLAMEN.

sow one's wild oats. The wild oat (*Avena fatua*) is a common tall plant that looks like its relative the cereal plant oat, but is really a pernicious weed that infests the planting fields of Europe and is difficult to eradicate. About all wild oats, or oat grass, have ever been used for is in making hygrometers, instruments that measure the humidity in the air, the plant's long twisted awn, or beard, readily absorbing moisture. The wild oat's uselessness has been known since ancient times and for almost as long we have had the expression to *sow wild oats,* "to conduct oneself foolishly," to sow weedseed instead of good grain. The expression has been traced back to the Roman comic Plautus in 194 B.C. and was probably used before him. It usually refers to a young man frittering his time away in fruitless dissipation, or to the prolific sexual activities of a young man, and is almost always said indulgently of the young. Rarely, the expression is used in the singular, with a prudish young man who sows "his one wild oat." In the 16th and 17th centuries dissolute or wild young men were called *wild oats.*

sow the wind and reap the whirlwind. To do something wrong, the results of which are even worse for the perpetrator. The expression is from the Bible, (Hos. 8:7): "For they [Israel] have sown the wind and they shall reap the whirlwind."

soybean. The ancient Chinese made a sauce called *shiyu* (*shi,* "salted food," + *yu,* "oil") from this bean, which they apparently named after the sauce; *shi-yu* became *shoyu* and then *shoy* in Japanese, which ultimately became *soy* and *soybean* (*soy* + *bean*) in English. The Japanese valued soy sauce so highly that it was part of the salary of Japanese imperial court officers in the fifth century.

spa. The town of Spa in eastern Belgium, famous since the 16th century as a health resort for its mineral springs, long ago gave its name to any similar resort. Spa, Belgium, was especially popular in the late 18th century, when royalty often came there "to take the waters."

spaghetti; macaroni. Italian for "little strings, strands, or cords," *spaghetti* was brought to Italy by Marco Polo in the early 14th century and so named at that time, though it is apparently not recorded in English until 1888, the editors of the O.E.D. much preferring *macaroni* (first recorded by Ben Jonson in 1599) and not including spaghetti until the first supplement to that masterful work. *Macaroni,* an Italian word of obscure origins, has had its derogatory uses. As early as 1764 *macaroni* meant a fop or a dandy (as in the "Yankee Doodle" lyric), referring to London's Macaroni Club, where the members enjoyed foreign foods like macaroni. Then there is *macaroni boats,* a mostly British term for ocean liners carrying Italian immigrants to America in the early 20th century. *See* MACARONIC VERSE; SPIC.

spaghetti western. A cheap western movie, first made in Italy in the 1960s, usually featuring bloody violence more prominently than plot or character.

Spalding; Spaldeen. Alfred Goodwill Spalding (1850–1915) deserves his place in baseball's Hall of Fame as much as any man. He may not be "the Father of Baseball," but is certainly "Father of the Baseball," and it was only when he came upon the scene with his uniform manufacturing methods that what had been a chaotic minor sport was fashioned into the national pastime. Lively balls were once so rubbery that baseball scores like 201–11 were not uncommon, and others so dead that the phrase "fell with a dull thud" found its way into the language. The former Chicago White Sox manager did not invent the hard ball when he founded his company in 1880, but the rigid manufacturing standards he maintained made it possible for the newly formed National League of Professional Baseball to survive. Such careful preparations over the years have made the Spalding trademark synonymous for a baseball. Other sporting equipment manufactured by the firm includes a red rubber ball called the Spaldeen (spelled *Spalding*), which has been known by that name to several generations of American youngsters.

Spam. People all over the world have eaten some 5 billion cans of Spam since the Hormel Foods Corporation began selling it under this name. At first Hormel sold the mixture of pork shoulder, ham, salt, sugar, and sodium nitrate as *special ham.* When other meatpackers began selling the same product, the company in 1936 sponsored a nationwide contest to create a memorable brand name. Actor Kenneth Daigneau, the brother of a Hormel executive, won a mere $100 for *Spam,* which Judith Stone in an exhaustive July 3, 1994, article in the *New York Times Magazine* ("Five Million Cans And Counting") called "arguably the planet's most recognizable portmanteau word" (a combination of the *s* from *shoulder,* the *p* from *pork* and the *am* from *ham*). However, *chortle* (from *chuckle* and *snort*) may be better known.

Spanglish. Many Hispanic people speak this combination of Spanish and English. The hybrid language features words such as *fafu* for "fast food", *tensen* for a "10-cent store," such as the late Woolworth's; *chopping* for "shopping", and *chileando* for "chilling out." Its combination of Spanish and English might result in a sentence like "Vamos a lonchar, or what?" ("Are we going to have lunch or not?")

spaniel; cocker spaniel. Shakespeare has Antony speak of the "hearts that spaniel'd me at heels, to whom I have their wishes." *Spaniel* can be a verb or adjective, signifying affectionate humility, as well as a noun. The dog's name simply means "Spanish dog," deriving from the old French *chien espagneul,* which was shortened to *espagnol,* "Spanish," and then *spaniel* in English. Either the spaniel was a breed developed in Spain or the dog reminded Europeans of the Spaniards, who were regarded as submissive and fawning during the Middle Ages. Neither the Spaniards nor the dogs are servile, but the breed's silky hair and soft, soulful eyes may have suggested the appearance of the Spaniards. There is no hard evidence for this, however. The cocker spaniel gets its first name either from the way it cocks its long drooping ears or because it was trained to retrieve woodcocks.

Spanish fly. The blister beetles, *Lytta vesicatoria,* used to make the dangerous reputed aphrodisiac Spanish fly are abundant in Spain. Cantharides, or Spanish fly, is medicinally a diuretic and skin irritant.

Spanish moss.   The familiar Spanish or long moss (*Tillandsia usneoides*), which drapes live oaks, cypresses, and other trees from Virginia southward, is not a moss but an epiphytic (tree-perching) nonparasitic plant that takes its own nourishment from the air and does not kill any supporting plant, as many believe. Contrary to what the great Linnaeus thought, it does best in moist locations. The Swedish botanist was so sure the plant disliked moisture that he named the genus after his countryman Elias Tillands, a physician and botanist traveler who so feared water that he once walked *1,000 miles* out of his way to avoid crossing the narrow Gulf of Bothnia. Why the plant is popularly called *Spanish moss* has not been determined.

Spanish words in English.   There are probably 500 words in American English alone that are borrowed from Spanish. Some of the more common ones include: cork, cask, anchovy, sherry, spade (cards), galleon, grenade, armada, comrade, sombrero, cannibal, Negro, iguana, alligator, armadillo, sassafras, sarsaparilla, mosquito, banana, cargo, desperado, matador, lime, embargo, parade, guitar, siesta, peon, chinchilla, cockroach, vanilla, barracuda, avocado, barbecue, tortilla, plaza, 10-gallon hat, chaps, serape, poncho, adobe, cafeteria, patio, plaza, pueblo, breeze, buckaroo, chaparral, cinch, corral, hacienda, lariat, lasso, machete, ranch, reata, rodeo, stampede, wrangler, alfalfa, marijuana, mesquite, yucca, bronco, buffalo, burro, barracuda, bonito, pompano, coyote, mustang, palomino, pinto, chili con carne, enchilada, frijole, jerky, mescal, pinon nuts, taco, tamale, tequilla, calaboose, hoosegow, vigilante, incommunicado, arroyo, canyon, mesa, sierra, couch, coon, creole, junta, mulatto, fiesta, filibuster, hombre, loco, marina, mosey, pronto, rumba, samba, savvy, stevedore, tornado, vamoose. Some of these are covered in this book.

spare the rod and spoil the child.   An old if widely ignored saying that goes back a thousand years and is found in Proverbs 13:24: "He that spareth his rod hateth his son."

spark.   Americans were "sparking" at least as far back as 1787, when the expression was first recorded. *To spark*, an old-fashioned term meaning "to make love, to court," especially by a young woman's sweetheart or "feller," may be of Scandinavian origin.

sparrow.   No bird is better known everywhere in Great Britain than the little sparrow, whose name, in the form of the Old English *spearwa*, is first recorded in the seventh century. The small brownish gray bird of the family Fringillidae, also native to the U.S., gives us the term "sparrow-legged," for a person with a big belly and skinny legs. The bird was even used in sparrow-pie, a dish that supposedly made the eater sharp-witted.

sparrow-fart.   Toward the beginning of the century British slang for "at dawn" was *at sparrow-fart*, the expression popularized by soldiers in World War I. A polite variant is *at sparrow's cough*.

Spars.   *See* WRENS.

Spartan.   "Either come back with it or on it," the proverbial Spartan mother tells her only son when she hands him the shield he is to carry into battle. The inhabitants of ancient Sparta, the Greek city-state noted for its military excellence, were forced to be courageous, frugal, and sternly disciplined almost to a fault. Life there seems to have been equal to one long term of military service without leave from the barracks and battlefields, for women as well as men. Weak children were discarded and the survivors subjected to an ascetic discipline without luxuries or even comforts. Spartan virtues, which can easily become vices, give us the terms *Spartan fare*, "a frugal diet," *Spartan courage*, "that of one who can unflinchingly bear pain or face danger," and *Spartan simplicity*, "the barest necessities of life."

Spasmodic School of Poetry.   A humorous term applied in the 1850s to a school of poetry devoted to violent wordy dramatic poems characterized by obscurity and wild imagery. The English poet Sydney Dobell's long, unfinished *Balder* (1854) is considered perhaps the most extreme example of the Spasmodic School. Two of its lines went: "Ah! Ah! Ah! / Ah! Ah! Ah! Ah! Ah! Ah! Ah! Ah! Ah!" When he wrote his poem *The Roman* (1850), Dobell inverted his first name to form the pseudonym Sydney Yendys.

spat.   A little, petty fight; *tiff* the English would say. This Americanism was first recorded in 1804, but no one has established its origin. Perhaps, if I may guess, it is from the sound made by a slap in a fight.

speakeasy.   The word goes back 30 years or more before its use during Prohibition, to at least the 1880s. Samuel Hudson, a newspaperman of the day, said he first heard it in Pittsburgh, used by an old Irish woman who sold liquor without a license and told her clients to "spake asy" when they came to buy it. Over a century before this there were Irish *spake-aisy* shops or smugglers' dens. Speakeasies were also called speaks during Prohibition. The original "spake-aisy" places may have been so named because patrons had to speak quietly when entering them to avoid alerting police and neighbors.

speak for yourself, John.   The famous words of the maid Priscilla to John Alden, who, in Henry Wadsworth Longfellow's poem "The Courtship of Miles Standish" (1858), courts her for his friend Miles Standish even though he, too, loves her. The full quote is "Why don't you speak for yourself, John?" Alden does finally marry Priscilla without losing the friendship of Miles. The poem, incidentally, sold 15,000 copies on the first day of publication, an incredible number for that time.

speak of the devil.   A common saying often heard when two people are talking about somebody and that somebody appears. Originally the phrase was *speak of the devil and he will appear*, and it was first recorded in a 1672 poem in this sense: "Talk of the devil and see his horns." Jonathan Swift, however, first recorded the term in its modern sense in *Polite Conversations* (1738). The French use the similar expression *When you speak of the wolf, you see his tail*, while an Arabic speaker often uses *Thinking of the cat, it comes leaping*, and for Germans it's *When you speak of the donkey, he comes running*.

speak softly and carry a big stick.   Apparently, this well-known proverb isn't an American invention, but is African in origin. Bartlett's *Familiar Quotations* should note that Theodore

Roosevelt's biographer, H. F. Pringle, in his *Theodore Roosevelt* (1931), quotes Teddy as saying in the first recorded use of the expression: "I have always been fond of the West African proverb 'Speak softly and carry a big stick; you will go far.'" Pringle has T. R. saying this in 1900; in the 1901 speech Bartlett's quotes, Roosevelt prefaces the proverb with "There is a homely adage that runs. . . ."

Special Forces. *See* GREEN BERETS.

speculator. The first speculators in the U.S. to be called speculators did business during the Revolutionary War boom, though there was no formal stock exchange at the time and wheeling and dealing was done in coffeehouses along Wall Street in downtown Manhattan, or outside. The word *speculator* has its roots in the Latin *speculatus*, observed, watched.

spencer. This repeating rifle, made by Christopher Spencer's Spencer Repeating Rifle Company, served the Confederates well in the Civil War and went West after that. Said boys in gray of the reliable carbine: "You can load it on Sunday and shoot all week." The rifle was light and ideal for mounted soldiers.

Spencerian. Spencerian refers to the thought of English philosopher Herbert Spencer (1820–1903), especially his attempt to unify all knowledge through the single principle of evolution, his "synthetic philosophy."

Spencerian script. Even as recently as 25 years ago penmanship remained an important subject in American grammar schools, but the increased use of the typewriter and computer has made penmanship exercises almost obsolete. In those days of yesteryear, when a fine hand was a great social asset and absolutely essential in conducting a business, one of the first American styles of calligraphy was that developed by Platt Rogers Spencer (1800–64), a system based on precise slanted strokes marked with flourishes at the ends of words. Spencer taught classes in a log cabin on his Geneva, New York farm and lectured at various business schools and academies. His Spencerian style, popularized by a series of textbooks he wrote, greatly influenced early-19th-century American calligraphy, so much so that today the term *Spencerian script* is used by collectors to describe the handwriting of his period and beyond.

spencer jacket, etc. First Lord of the British Admiralty George John, the second earl Spencer, who recognized Lord Nelson's potential early, created this short wool jacket. Another Spencer, possibly related, invented the spencer sail, and still another, the cork-filled Spencer life belt.

spend a penny. An interesting British expression that is a euphemism for "go to the bathroom." A penny used to be the nominal fee to use a public bathroom.

spending spree. Apparently British novelist Aldous Huxley coined the term *spending spree* in 1956 (according to the May 1993 *Atlantic*). However, he got help from the older British expression *on the spree*, meaning "out partying, out on the town," etc. The origin of *on the spree* is unknown.

spic. Before it was applied to Hispanic Americans this offensive derogatory name was given to Italian Americans. First recorded in 1915, it is thought to be a shortening of "spaghetti." *See* SPAGHETTI; MACARONIC VERSE.

Spice Islands. Punning on the Spice Islands, the Moluccas in Indonesia, this expression was 19th-century slang for a privy or any foul-smelling place.

Spider. Robert Frost described someone with the nickname Spider in his poem "The Code" (1914): "He was one of the kind sports call a spider, / All wiry arms and legs that spread out wary / From a humped body nigh as big's a biscuit. . . ." I remember a runner nicknamed Spider who leaped from the stands into a mile race and proceeded to win the race—wearing a raincoat and wing-tip shoes.

spiel. This Americanism, for "sales talk or a line," has been used at least since 1870. It derives from the German *spielen*, "to play a musical instrument." In its American usage the word meant "to talk in a high-flown, grandiloquent manner" before it was used to describe the voluble talk of the carnival barker and then the salesman.

spill the beans. A fanciful story, widely printed, holds that members of Greek secret societies voted on the admission of new members by dropping beans into jars or helmets. White beans signified an affirmative vote and black beans a negative ballot. Occasionally, the story says, voters would accidentally knock over the jar or helmet, revealing the secret vote, spilling the beans. However, the phrase is an American one that entered the language only around the beginning of this century. No one knows how it made its entrance, unless it was on the heels of an older expression, as an extension of KNOW BEANS, "to know what is what."

spinach. Popeye did so much for this vegetable with the young set that spinach growers in one Texas town erected a large statue to him. Some authorities claim *spinach* derives from the Latin *hispanicus olus*, "the Spanish herb." The word does come to us from Spain, but probably not directly. Apparently the Persian and Arabian *isfanakh* became the Old Spanish *espinaca*, which eventually changed into the Middle French *espinache*, which resulted in our word *spinach*. At any rate, the Arabs did introduce the vegetable into Spain, and then it spread to the rest of Europe. Dr. Johnson, for one, enjoyed it, according to Boswell. Napoleon did almost as much for spinach's fame as Popeye by decorating the golden epaulettes of his colonels with what looked like gold spinach leaves and were thus referred to as *spinach*—a term that lingers to this day. The phrase *gammon and spinach*, meaning "nonsense," or "humbug," is not as familiar today as it was in Dickens's time, when he wrote in *David Copperfield*, "What a world of gammon and spinnage it is; though, ain't it!" The phrase, most likely an elaboration of the slang word *gammon*, which meant "nonsense" or "ridiculous story," is probably patterned on the older phrase "gammon and patter," the language of London underworld thieves. The nonsense part of it was possibly reinforced by the old nursery rhyme "A Frog He Would A-Wooing Go" (1600), which was heard by millions: "With a rowley powley gammon and spinach / Heigh ho! says Anthony Rowley." E. B. White wrote the caption that became the catchphrase "I say it's spinach, and I say the hell with it" for the Carl Rose cartoon that appeared in the December 8, 1928, issue of *The New Yorker*. It shows a spoiled little girl who rejects her indulgent mother's offer of broccoli with words that have come to mean, "When I'm indulging my prejudices I don't want to be confused with facts." The phrase's abbreviated form, *spinach*, means "baloney," "malarkey," "bull." In 1991 President George Bush joined the ranks of broccoliphobes when he told the press that he hates the stuff. President Clinton has gone on record that he likes it.

spin doctor.   A *spin doctor* is an adviser of a politician who interprets or slants stories to the media in his or her client's favor. *Spin* here is probably from the spin a pitcher puts on a baseball to make it curve; thus the spin doctor is throwing the media a curve. The term is a new one only frequently heard in the last few years. *See also* THROW SOMEONE A CURVE.

spineless as a jellyfish.   *Jellyfish* for "a person of flabby character" was first recorded in 1883, and *spineless as a jellyfish* probably appeared soon after, though the exact date isn't known. This Americanism is based on the common sea creature jellyfish, which is 99 percent water, composed of a gelatinous substance called mesoglea, with no backbone. Considering its construction, however, the jellyfish, like man, is hardly spineless and does the best it can. *See* MEDUSA.

spinet.   Only in this century has *spinet* been used in the U.S. to describe a small, upright piano. Invented in about 1500 by Venetian musical instrument manufacturer Giovanni Spinetti, the spinet was at first similar to the clavichord. Having one keyboard, one string to each note, and until the middle of the 18th century no attached legs, the small instrument had often been called the virginal. In England today *spinet* still designates all small keyboard instruments with one string to a note that are plucked by a quill or plectrum of leather. The spinet may also be named from the Italian *spina*, "a thorn," in reference to the quill points on the instrument, the naming probably influenced by both *Spinetti* and *spina*. At any rate, the historical information available on the etymology is scanty. In fact, the only reference to the inventor is found in a rare old book entitled *Conclusione nel suona dell'organo, di Adriano Banchieri*, published in Bologna in 1608. Its author states that: "Spinetta [the spinet] was thus named from the inventor of that oblong form, who was one Maestro Giovanni Spinetti, a Venetian; and I have seen one of those instruments . . . within which was the inscription—Joannes Spinetvs Venetvs fecit, A.D. 1503."

spinnaker.   The most probable explanation we have for this word is that back in the 1860s an unknown yacht owner invented a sail rigged at right angles from his racing vessel's side, a sail that extended from masthead to deck and ballooned far out to take advantage of the slightest breeze. The racing vessel was named *Sphinx*, but its crew had difficulty in pronouncing its name, calling it *Spinnicks*. Thus, the new sail was referred to as *Spinnicker's sail* and finally became known as a *spinnaker*.

spirit away.   Originally, in 17th-century England, this expression referred to the kidnapping of boys to work on the West Indian plantations. The children were taken as quickly and quietly as possible, to give people the impression that they had been "supernaturally removed."

spit and polish.   Military in origin, this term goes back to Victorian times, probably to the middle of the 19th century, although it isn't recorded before 1895. Meticulous cleaning and smartness of appearance were demanded of sailors in the British navy, which became known as the "Spit and Polish Navy." Enlisted men liked it then no more than they do now and *spit and polish*—the application of one's spittle as a polishing agent and much elbow grease to make an object shine—came to be a perjorative term for finicky, wasteful work in general.

spitball.   *Spitball* is now used outside of baseball as the synonym for a deception or a dirty trick, and, as William Safire notes in *On Language:* "Because an old-time baseball pitcher never knew which way his spitball would break, the verb *to spitball* now means 'to speculate.' " The term's baseball origin probably goes back to 1902, when a pitcher named Frank Corridon accidentally discovered that a ball wet with saliva twisted and turned weirdly as it traveled to the plate. Corridon apparently told Chicago White Sox teammate Elmer Stricklett about his discovery and Stricklett perfected the pitch, even naming it when another teammate asked him what he called it: "Don't know. I suppose 'spitball' explains it as well as anything." Although other sources claim the spitball was invented by New Bedford pitcher Tom Dond in 1876, when he rubbed glycerine on the ball, the term is first recorded in 1904 and the Stricklett story seems more likely. Outlawed since 1920, the spitball was once a perfectly legal pitch in baseball. Many pitchers used it in its heyday and its unpredictable behavior made batters dread the pitch. Some modern-day pitchers have been charged with using the "spitter"—not usually by spitting on the ball anymore, but by more devious methods such as moistening the hands and scratching the ball. Schoolboys' *spitball* is even older than the baseball variety, as the word is first recorded in this sense in 1846. *See* THROW SOMEONE A CURVE.

spit curl.   The spit curl was a new and daring fashion in 1831: a short curl of a woman's hair plastered to her forehead with a little spit. In 1883 Henry Wadsworth Longfellow dubbed such curls "spite curls," a designation not much heard anymore, after he wrote the still popular poem "There Was a Little Girl" for Blanche Roosevelt and she refused to learn how to pronounce the word "forehead" mentioned in the poem. The "little curl" in the poem is a spit curl Blanche Roosevelt wore:

> There was a little girl
> Who had a little curl
> Right in the middle of her forehead,
> When she was good
> She was very, very good,
> But when she was bad,
> She was horrid.

spittin' image of.   The germ of the idea behind this phrase has been traced back to 1400 by Partridge, who cites the early example "He's . . . as like these as th' hads't spit him." Similarly, in England and the southern U.S., the expression "he's the very spit of his father" is commonly heard. This may mean "he's as like his father as if he had been spit out of his mouth," but could also be a corruption of "spirit and image." If the last is true, it would explain the use of "and image" in the expression since the middle of the 19th century. *Spittin' image* would then be derived from "he's the very spirit and image of his father," that is, the child is identical to his parent in both spirit and looks. It's possible that both sources combined to give us our phrase for "exactly alike," which is also written *spit and image*, *spitting image*, *spitten image*, and *spit n' image*.

spittlebug.   These small sucking insects produce a white frothy material in which they live and which is often called "frog spittle" (because gardeners once believed that such white masses on plants were made by frogs). Despite its looks, however, the froth or foam isn't spittle and does little harm to garden plants. It just forms a protective blob of foam under which the busy spittlebug larva, safe from predators, can happily feed.

spizorinkum.   Born on the American frontier, *spizorinkum* was originally used during the 1850s as the term for "good" hard money, as opposed to greenbacks or paper currency, but soon came to have many diverse meanings, including "tireless energy." It was possibly used so much because people liked the sound of the word! In any case, *spizorinkum* is "an impossible combination" of the Latin *specie* ("kind") and *rectum* ("right"), "the right kind." The word is sometimes spelled with two z's.

splash.   *Splash* seems an innocent word, evoking pleasant days at the beach or pool, but it is also a term for a wave generated by a landslip. One such wave was bigger than any ever recorded. On July 9, 1958, an earthquake caused nearly 100 million tons of rock and glacial ice from the Fairweather Range of the Saint Elias Mountains to fall into Lituya Bay, Alaska. A wave of almost 1,800 feet—a third of a mile high—splashed up the mountain on the opposite shore, stripping it of all vegetation to a height of 1,740 feet—which is taller than the Sears Tower in Chicago, America's tallest building. One trawler was lifted from anchor by the splash and carried unharmed from the bay to the ocean behind, its crew looking down at trees far below. *See* TSUNAMI.

splendid little war.   A name President William McKinley's secretary of state, John Hay, invented for the U.S. war against Spain, best known as the Spanish-American War (1898). The war only lasted from late April until mid-August, and the U.S. was victorious.

spliced.   This nautical expression, for "the joining together of two pieces of rope," eventually became nautical and then general slang for "to join together in matrimony." It is not modern slang in this sense, dating back to the 18th century, when it is first recorded in Tobias Smollett's *The Adventures of Peregrine Pickle* (1751), which contains characters like the old sea dog Commodore Howser Trunnion and boatswain Tom Pipes.

splice the main brace.   There is some doubt as to why *splice the main brace* has come to mean taking a strong, intoxicating drink. The main brace on a ship is the line secured to the main yard, from which the mainsail flies. The implication might be that a good drink braces a body. But one authority says the

term derives from the days of sail, when the main brace was the most difficult to splice, being in a highly dangerous position, and that the crew received a double tot of rum after finishing the job on it.

split hairs.   One Englishman has actually split a human hair 13 times into 14 parts, the world record, and there are drills so fine today that minute holes can be bored in a single hair. However, when the expression *to split hairs* was coined over three centuries ago (in the original form *to cut a hair*), it was thought to be impossible to really split a hair and the phrase described any argument making overrefined, caviling distinctions; a *hair-splitter* was one who quibbled over trifles. A politician, Machiavelli, was the first to have the word applied to him.

split infinitive.   The late Bergen Evans once compiled a list of writers who commonly split infinitives (that is, placed a word between *to* and the simple form of a verb, as in "to quickly walk away") to show that it has been the practice of our best writers. Over a relatively short period he came up with Sir Philip Sidney, Sir Thomas Browne, Donne, Pepys, Defoe, Samuel Johnson, Burns, Wordsworth, Coleridge, Lamb, Byron, De Quincey, Macaulay, Holmes, Whittier, George Eliot, Carlyle, Browning, Arnold, Pater, Ruskin, Hardy, Meredith, Galsworthy, Conan Doyle, Kipling, Shaw, Benjamin Franklin, Abraham Lincoln, Theodore Roosevelt, Woodrow Wilson, and even Henry James. One theory intended to justify the split infinitive holds that in Latin the infinitive form of a verb is only one word and thereby unsplittable, whereas in English the two-word infinitive need not be governed by any such classical rule.

split the log.   According to Everett Dick in *The Dixie Frontier* (1948), a peculiar way of "banking" gold and silver on the frontier was "to bore holes in large blocks of wood, fill the holes with coins, and drive tightly fitting pegs in them. Then the pegs were sawed off short. This left no way to remove the money except by splitting the log."

Spode.   "Josiah Spode produced a better porcelain than any that had yet been made in England," wrote Alexandre Brogniart, director of the French plant producing the famous Sèvres ware. "He endeavoured to equal the soft porcelain of Sèvres, which his paste closely resembled. He introduced, or at any rate perfected, the use of calcined bones in the body of the ware." Brogniart was referring to English potter Josiah Spode (1754–1827), who developed his formula of bone ash and feldspar at Stoke-on-Trent in 1799. England's leading chinaware manufacturers all adopted Spode's formula to produce the durable, fine bone china much esteemed ever since as Spodeware, or Spode.

spoiled priest.   *Spoiled priest* has been used so often in modern literature to mean someone who has failed to live up to the standard expected of him that it probably does mean that by now. But the 19th-century term originally meant a priesthood candidate who failed to take his vows.

spoils of the conquered ocean.   When he impulsively decided to become conqueror of Britain in A.D. 40, the mad

Roman emperor Caligula, who had made his horse Incitatus a priest and a consul of Rome, started to move his legions across the Channel from Gaul. Then he just as suddenly changed his mind and took his men on a march up and down the beach hunting for seashells! The Roman historian Suetonius says that when Caligula's legions gathered enough shells, the emperor marched them home in self-acclaimed triumph carrying "the spoils of the conquered ocean." It was Caligula who angrily exclaimed: "Would that the Roman people had but one neck!" His name means "little boots" in Latin, and he was so called because of the army sandals (*caligae*) he wore when a boy in the army. He was only 29 when he was assassinated in A.D. 41

spoils of war.   The spoils here are valuable goods, not ruined things, and take their name from the Latin *spolium*, "the hide stripped from an animal." Thus anything stripped or taken from a country after it lost a war became known as "spoils." The word was employed in this sense as far back as 1300 and Dryden used the expression *spoils-of-war* in 1697. *Spoil* in the sense of ruined, useless, takes its meaning from the remains of animal carcasses that have been left to rot after being stripped of their skin.

spoils system.   Often attributed to Andrew Jackson, this phrase did arise during his presidency, when the practice of giving appointive offices to loyal members of the party in power was first adopted on a large scale. However, the phrase was suggested by New York senator William Learned Marcy, who defended Jackson's 1829 policy in a speech a year later. Marcy, a member of the Albany Regency, a political group controlled by "The Little Fox," Martin Van Buren, rose in the Senate to defend the appointment of Van Buren as minister to England, his public defense of this political patronage being "the rule that to the victor belong the spoils of war." This remark led to the anonymous coining of *spoils system*, the phrase first recorded in 1838. The political atmosphere of an era can often be seen in the expressions born in that period and during the Jackson and Van Buren administrations we find the following first used in a political sense: *dyed in the wool* (1830), *party line* (1834), *picayune* (1837), *party machinery* (1829), *wirepuller* (1832), and even *exposé* (1830), among others. *See also* O.K.

spondee.   The Greeks often made drink-offerings called *sponde* ("libation") to the gods on solemn occasions. A slow meter used in poetry read on such occasions also came to be called *sponde* and it was this word that gave us our word *spondee*, for a "metrical foot of two stressed or long syllables." The spondee is often used to slow the rhythm of a line.

spondulix.   Where this old American word for money came from is anybody's guess, but *spondulix* is recorded as early as 1856. It's another word that can only be guessed to be of fanciful origin, a funny word that caught on because people liked its sound. Mark Twain used it in *Huckleberry Finn*.

sponge.   *To sponge* (from Greek *spongos*) means "to live like a parasite off someone," to suck up someone else's goods and goodness as a sponge sucks up water. Shakespeare used the word in this sense, and our term *sponger* was recorded as far back as 1677. As their Latin name *Porifera* ("porebearing") implies, all live sponges are covered with minute openings through which water is drawn by the beating of flagellated cells called lashers, the water passing through a complex system of canals before it is expelled from several larger exit holes or vents. The sponge's single purpose in life is to pass water through itself, the water yielding food, minerals, and oxygen to the animal and carrying away waste products. Everyone who is familiar with the natural commercial sponge has noticed the numerous canals opening into still larger tubes, which perforate the mass. In life these canals were lined with active cells formed within the skeleton, the whole resembling a gelatinous mass not unlike a piece of liver in consistency. *See* THROW IN THE TOWEL.

spoof.   This word for "a mocking imitation," was coined by British comedian Arthur Roberts, who invented a game called "Spoof" in the late 19th century. What he coined the word from no one knows.

spoonerism.   The Reverend William Archibald Spooner, dean and later warden of New College, Oxford, was a learned man, but not spell woken—well spoken, that is. "We all know what it is, to have a half-warmed fish inside us," he once told an audience, meaning to say "half-formed wish." On another occasion he advised his congregation that the next hymn would be "Kingering Congs Their Titles Take," instead of "Conquering Kings Their Titles Take," and he is said to have explained to listeners one time that "the Lord is a shoving leopard." Spooner's slips occurred both in church, where he once remarked to a lady, "Mardon me Padom, this pie is occupewed, allow me to sew you to another sheet," and told a nervous bridegroom that "it is kisstomery to cuss the bride," and in his classes, where he chided one student with, "You hissed my mystery lecture," and dismissed another with, "You have deliberately tasted two worms and can leave Oxford by the town drain!" Nobody knows how many of these spoonerisms were really made by Spooner, but they were among the many attributed to him. Spooner was an albino, and his metathetical troubles were probably due to nervousness and poor eyesight resulting from his condition. The scientific name for his speech affliction is metathesis, the accidental transposition of letters or syllables in the words of a sentence, the process known long before Spooner made it so popular that his slips of the tongue and eye were widely imitated. Spooner, who lived to the ripe old age of 86, once called Queen Victoria "our queer old dean" when trying to say "our dear old queen." *See* MARROWSKY.

spoor.   The track or footprint of a man or animal, including snakes, and extended to mean the track of a wagon or a motorized vehicle. Originally used in South Africa (from Dutch *spoor* meaning the same), but now widely used wherever English is spoken, even in such literary phrases as "the bulldozers barren spoor." First recorded in 1837.

sport.   *Sport* is simply an abbreviation of the English word *disport*, "to amuse oneself," and is first recorded in about 1350. *Disport* itself is composed of the Latin *des*, "away," and *porto*, "carry," *disport* originally meaning to carry away, especially to carry away from work, which is what one does by amusing oneself playing a sport.

spot. To spot someone something is to give him or her a handicap or concession. The expression is from billiards at a time in the early 19th century when the standard game consisted of knocking a red ball into a pocket with the cue ball from a white spot on the table, leaving the cue ball in position to make another shot. Some players spot shots: In order to equalize games with those less skillful, these experts granted their opponents a certain number of spot shots (as if they had made them). This became known as *spotting* an opponent points and added a new expression to the language.

a spot of tay. When an Irishman says he'll have *a spot of tay* he's being more British than the British. *Tay* is not an ignorant Irish pronunciation of *tea*. The Portuguese introduced the drink we now know as tea into Europe as *cha*, and that was the first English name it went by. But as far back as 1650 Englishmen were using the name the Dutch got from the Malayans for tea, *te*. This was pronounced *tay* in English long before it was pronounced *tea* and was often spelled *tay* to indicate its pronunciation. The pronunciation was common up until the end of the 18th century. In his "Rape of the Lock," for example, Pope spells the word *tea* three times, but rhymes it with "obey," "stay," and "away." *See* TEA.

sprain one's ankle. A euphemism meaning "to have been seduced." Rarely, if ever, heard today, it was coined in the late 18th century and was a popular euphemism in Victorian times. The French have a similar term.

spring chicken. We find the expression *now past a chicken*, meaning "no longer young," recorded as early as 1711 by Steele in *The Spectator:* "You ought to consider you are now past a chicken; this Humour, which was well enough in a Girl, is insufferable in one of your Motherly Character." *No spring chicken*, an exaggeration of the phrase, is first recorded in America in 1906.

sprout-kale month. Because cabbages began to sprout in February, the Anglo-Saxons called that month *sprote-Kalemonath*, or *sprout-kale month*.

spruce. Courtiers in the reign of England's Henry VIII affected the dress of Prussian noblemen, those *hautest* of the *haut* who wore such fashionable attire as broad-brimmed hats with bright feathers, silver chains around their necks, satin cloaks, and red velvet doublets. Anything from Prussia had been called *Pruce* during the Middle Ages, but by the 16th century an *s* had somehow been added to the word and courtiers who dressed as elegantly as the Prussian nobleman were said to be appareled in *spruce* fashion. *Spruce* soon meant a smart, neat, or dapper appearance, as is reflected in the phrase *to spruce up*. The neat, trim form of the *spruce tree* may have suggested its name, too, but it more likely derives from the belief that the spruce was first grown in Prussia.

spruce gum. Spruce gum was the first American chewing gum. All types of *Picea* produce an abundance of resin, this genus name for the spruce deriving from the Latin word for "pitch." Here in America a number of cultivated spruce species—as well as other native trees like the sweet gum and juniper—have been valued from colonial days for their chewy resins. But the black or bog spruce (*Picea mariana*) and the red spruce (*Picea rubens*) are the principal producers of resin gum. The Indians introduced us to chewing gum from these trees and they, in turn, may have emulated a bear or other animal "gumming up" on spruce resin in prehistoric times. Hunters say that bears customarily "gum up" before they hibernate by swallowing quantities of spruce gum as large as a man's fist. Chewing gum is today mainly made from synthetics and from chicle, the thick creamy latex of the sapodilla tree (*Achras zapota*), native to Central America. The Mayans chewed chicle, wrapping it in banana plant leaves to make an edible package.

Spruce gum is still collected in Maine and New England, sometimes as a small business, but in nothing like the 150-ton-a-year quantities collected in the early 1900s. This natural chewing gum (see my *The Great American Chewing Gum Book*, 1976) is collected in winter and comes from punctures made on the trunks of both black and red spruces the previous spring. Hayden Pearson recalled in *New England Flavor* (1961): "I knocked down a couple of good big chunks and took them back to the house. It was a good idea to trim the pieces of gum before I put them away in a shoebox. . . . I got rid of the bits of bark that clung, and trimmed the rough edges and any soft spots. Then from time to time I'd cut off a chunk and chew it into a pleasant purplish magenta ball. If it was first-quality gum it was chewable a considerable number of times."

spud. *Spud*, for "a potato," is a Scottish term dating back at least to the 19th century, when a *spud* meant a raw potato and a roasted spud was a *mickey*, cooked jacket and all in the cinders. The word derives from the sharp spade called a *spud* used to dig potatoes, which, in turn, dates back several centuries earlier and is of unknown origin, possibly deriving from the Middle English *spuddle*, a kind of knife. *Spud* definitely is *not* an acronym for the *Society* for the *Prevention* of *Unwholesome Diets*!

spunky. *Spunky* means "courageous, spirited, plucky." Among early American colonists *spunk* (from Scottish Gaelic *spong*) meant "tinder" and to *spunk up a fire* meant "to kindle it up, throw more wood on it." Soon *getting one's spunk up* meant "to become fired with courage," the term first recorded in 1834, *spunky* coming along a few years later.

Sputnik. The first Soviet satellite sent into earth orbit, launched on October 4, 1957, is so named from the Russian *sputnik*, meaning "fellow traveler [of Earth]." *See* FELLOW TRAVELER.

Squanto. The Pawtuxet Indian who lived with and befriended the Plymouth colonists from 1621 until he died in 1622, showing them the best fishing and hunting places and teaching them how to plant corn, among other things. Squanto, also called Tisquantum, may have visited England two times before meeting the Pilgrims. It is certain that British Captain Thomas Hunt kidnapped him in 1615 and that he lived in England for four years before being returned to America. The names of other Indians who helped the colonists include Samoset, who introduced Squanto to them, and Chief Massasoit, who made a peace pact with them.

square the circle. It is mathematically impossible to square the circle, as mathematicians discovered centuries ago.

Therefore, just as long ago, people began to use the expression figuratively to describe someone undertaking any futile, impossible task.

squaric acid. *See* CUBANE.

squash. *Asquutasquash*, meaning "that which is eaten raw," was the Narraganset Indian word for a kind of melon. No wonder that early colonists abbreviated the word to *squash*. Later, they somehow transferred the word *squash* to what we know now as squash, which of course is not usually eaten raw, but which resembles a melon.

squaw; squawman. The offensive term *squaw* for a Native American woman, or any wife or woman, derives from Algonquian *squa*, "young woman or wife." This is innocent enough, but *squaw* has had an insulting, degrading connotation almost from the first time it was recorded in 1634. The same can be said about the offensive word *squawman*, a white man who marries an Indian woman, which was first printed two centuries later in 1866.

the squeaky wheel gets the most grease. The expression is often heard as above, but what American humorist "Josh Billings" (Henry Wheeler Shaw, 1818–85) said exactly in his poem "The Kicker" was:

> The wheel that squeaks the loudest
> Is the one that gets the grease.

Josh Billings is also responsible for "It is better to know nothing than to know what ain't so" ("Proverbs," 1874), which, strangely enough, the German philosopher Nietzsche reiterated in *Thus Spake Zarathustra* (1883–91), though I'm sure Nietzsche never read him: "Better know nothing than half-know many things."

squeeze play. The squeeze play, or squeeze play bunt, or suicide squeeze, is said to have been invented by two Yale University baseball players in 1897, but wasn't consciously used much or widely known until the 1905 major league season. It consists of a batter trying to "squeeze in" a run by laying down a bunt in a no-out or one-out situation when there is a runner on third base. The runner breaks toward home plate with the pitch and the batter tries to place the bunt in a spot from which the fielder can't throw the runner out at the plate. *Squeeze play* in American English also means to apply pressure on a person in order to gain an advantage or force compliance; this expression is possibly influenced by the baseball term. *See also* BUNT.

squib. A word of uncertain provenance that was first recorded in the early 16th century, *squib* first meant "a short, witty, or sarcastic saying or writing." Since then it has come to mean a variety of things, including a short news story or film; a type of small firecracker; and an electric device for firing a rocket engine igniter. In Australia *squib* means "coward." Another interesting use of the word is the little-known movie term *squib*, meaning the vials or capsules containing a red liquid resembling blood that are wired to an actor's body and exploded when the actor is violently killed or wounded in a film. For the machine-gun killing in *The Godfather* (1972), for example, actor James Caan ("Sonny") was wired with 147 vials. Surpris-

ingly, Hollywood hasn't yet come up with a movie "vial rating system" for advertising purposes, as in: "A THREE-THOUSAND VIAL FILM!"

squirrel. The Greeks were impressed not so much by this bright-eyed rodent's acrobatic performances in trees as by its bushy tail, which they believed the animal wrapped around it like a parasol when the sun was too strong. So they named the animal *skiouros*, "shadow-tail," from their words for shade, *skia*, and tail, *oura*, meaning shadytail, the animal that makes shade with its tail. The allusion was pleasant, poetic, but the road to our word *squirrel* proved difficult. *Skiouros* became *sciurus* in Latin and then *escureul* in France before going through nearly a score of English spellings and becoming the *squirrel* that we know today. Another word from the Greek root *skia*, is *sciamachy*, which means a sham fight or shadow boxing, and comes directly from a Greek word meaning "fighting in the shade, fighting with shadows." The term isn't heard in the gym, but political or even CIA *sciamachy* is not unknown. *See* DRAY.

SS. SS stands for *Schutzstaffel*, meaning "protective echelon or elite guard." Growing out of a small group of thugs who were recruited in 1923 to protect Hitler and became the security arm of the Nazi Party, it was expanded under Heinrich Himmler in 1929 and about 1 million men had passed through its ranks by the end of World War II. The *Waffen* (weapons) SS were crack, cruel combat units. The *Totenkopf* (Death Head) SS served as guards, executioners, and torturers in concentration camps, taking their name from their black caps and the skull-and-crossbone insignia on their collars.

stack the deck. Stacking the deck against someone is dishonestly prearranging something against that person. The expression has its origins in the age-old gambling practice of stacking a deck of cards, that is, prearranging them in order to cheat the other players.

stag dance. A dance that apparently originated on the frontier in forts of mining camps, where there were few women, in which only men participated. The terms *stag dinner, stag smoker,* and *stag film* probably all derive from this term.

Stage Door Canteen. Probably the only "nightclub" celebrated in a song—Irving Berlin's "I Left My Heart at the Stage Door Canteen"—is the Stage Door Canteen that the United Service Organization (USO) and American Theater Wing ran during World War II in the basement of Broadway's 44th Street Theater. This was the first USO canteen in the country. Admission was free to all armed forces personnel, and Broadway players performed there gratis, danced with the GIs, and even waited on tables. The New York Stage Door Canteen was featured in several movies, as was its counterpart in Hollywood.

stage mother. Stage mothers (and fathers) have too often supported their own bank accounts and egos rather than the child actors they dragged by the collar to stardom. The term apparently dates back to early movie days. "My mother was the stage mother of all time," Judy Garland said in one of her last television interviews. "She really was a witch. If I had a stomachache and didn't want to go on, she'd say, 'Get out on that stage or I'll wrap you around a bedpost!'" There were many stage mothers even worse. Jackie Coogan's mother, Lillian, was the most historically important among them, along with his stage father, Arthur Bernstein. Jackie was one of the most popular child stars of all time—best known for his starring role in Charlie Chaplin's *The Kid* (1921) when he was only seven. He earned as much as $1 million a picture (making him the youngest self-made millionaire in history). But he was never given more than a $6.50 weekly allowance before he legally came of age. In 1935, Coogan sued his parents for the millions he had earned, but though he won in court, there was apparently only about $125,000 left for him to retrieve—barely enough to pay his legal expenses. Coogan died in 1984. His outrageous fleecing resulted in the passage of the 1939 Coogan Act, which protects child performers by empowering the courts to put in trust a large percentage of their earnings while they are minors.

stag party; bachelor party; stag films; stag movies. The British expression *stag party* would be termed *bachelor party* in Australia and the U.S. Americans use *stag* in the term *stag films*, because pornographic films were once shown only at male gatherings. A euphemism is *adult movies*. See PORNOGRAPHY.

stake a claim. Surveyors still use wooden stakes to mark property lines, as they have done since colonial times in America. Beginning in the 1830s, U.S. gold prospectors marked with "claim stakes" property they had claimed where they would dig for gold, hoping to find a bonanza. Those who staked a claim, however, often never hit pay dirt. See PIKES PEAK OR BUST.

Stakhanovite. Soviet authorities reported that coal miner Aleksei Stakhanov vastly increased his production in 1935 by the use of more rational working techniques and teamwork. This voluntary efficiency system, called Stakhanovism, or the Stakhanovite Movement, in the miner's honor, was strongly encouraged by the Soviet government to speed up completion of the then current five-year plan, and it did much to accomplish this national objective. Stakhanovite workers were rewarded with higher pay, bonuses, and other incentives, and while the idea behind Stakhanovism was nothing new, its success in the Soviet Union made the word widely known throughout the world. Aleksei Grigorievich Stakhanov, born in 1905, eventually worked for the U.S.S.R. Ministry of Coal Industries, having made the great leap forward from worker to commissar. He won many awards, including the Order of Lenin, before his death in 1977.

Stalag. During World War II the Germans called their prison camps for allied enlisted men *Stalags*, the word a shortening of *Stammlager*, "base camp," which comes from German *Stamm*, "base," and *Lager*, "camp." After the war the popular American play *Stalag 17* ran on Broadway for several years and was made into a movie.

Stalinism; Stalingrad, etc. Iosif Vissarionovich Dzhugashvili (1879–1953) took the name Joseph Stalin after joining the Russian revolutionary movement in 1896. Stalin, which means "man of steel," instituted what became known as Stalinism, a synonym for ruthless dictatorship rarely equaled in any other time or place. There is no doubt that the Soviet leader transformed his country into a great modern military and industrial power after succeeding Lenin. But no nation ever paid a higher

price for such "progress." Ten million or more Kulaks, wealthy peasants, were exterminated in order to make Stalin's collective farms a success; another 10 million people were eliminated in the Great Purge that lasted from 1934 to 1938; no one knows how many more millions were killed in the continual vengeful, fearful purge that seemed at times to be this paranoid's sole reason for living. De-Stalinization began in Russia in 1956 when Nikita Khrushchev exposed Stalin's crimes. By 1961 Stalin's body had been removed from the mausoleum in Red Square and every factory, mountain, street, and city named after him had been renamed—even the city of *Stalingrad* (now Volgograd), which had been dedicated to him in 1925 because forces under his command drove out the White Armies during the Revolution. Stalingrad will always be known historically for the great battle that proved to be the turning point in World War II, and Stalin's name is best remembered in *Stalinism*.

stalker. *Stalk*, according to Weekley, derives from Anglo Saxon *stealcian*, "to walk stealthily," but the word has only recently taken on the meaning of following a person (often prominent, such as a movie star) and harassing or persecuting her or him. The stalker is always an obsessed person and can be violent. The word isn't recorded before the late 1980s, but the practice is an old one.

stalking horse. Hunters of old sometimes trained their horses to walk toward their quarry while the hunters remained hidden behind them until the game was within shooting range. Such horses were called stalking horses in the 16th century; it wasn't long before a *stalking horse* came to mean a sham political candidate used to conceal the candidacy of a more important figure in order to draw votes from a rival, or anything put forth to mask plans, a pretext.

stampede. Cowboys borrowed the Spanish word for a sudden frenzied flight of a herd of animals. It derives from the Spanish *estampida* (stamp, rush, uproar) and is first recorded in 1843, though it was probably used 20 years earlier. A stampede is also an annual celebration combining a rodeo, contests, and exhibitions.

standing dead. A colorful name given by firefighters to trees left standing in a forest fire. Wrote Richard Ford in *Wildlife* (1990): " 'Do you know what they call the trees that're left up when the fire goes by?' 'No,' I said. 'The standing dead,' my mother said. 'Don't they have an interesting terminology for things?' "

Standing Fishes Bible. Various editions of the Bible have over the years earned popular names because of printers' errors. In the *Standing Fishes Bible* (1806) Ezekiel 48:10, reads: "And it shall come to pass that the fishes [instead of "fishers"] shall stand upon it. . . ."

stand pat. American poker players in the late 19th century invented this expression to indicate that a player was satisfied with the original hand dealt to him and would draw no more cards. Where did the *pat* come from? One theory is that because the word meant "in a manner that fits or agrees with the purpose or occasion" or "incapable of being improved" it was a natural for the poker expression. Another holds that *stand pat* is a corruption of *stand pad*, an older English expression meaning "to sell from a stationary position" and originally referring to peddlers who remained in a fixed location. *To stand pad* was to remain fixed or firm, like a poker player who didn't move to take any more cards. From poker, in any case, the expression passed into general use as a term for taking a firm, fixed position on something.

stand the gaff.   The *gaff* here is the sharp metal spur attached to the legs of cocks in cockfighting. A bird has to stand the slashes of such gaffs or lose the fight, which gave us the century-old expression *to stand the gaff*, meaning to weather hardship or strain, to endure patiently.

Stanislavski method.   The Russian actor and stage director Konstantin Stanislavski (1863–1938) taught his actors to identify closely with the characters they played and to use latent powers of self-expression, among other practices. By the early 1920s, people were calling such instruction the *Stanislavski method.* It took another 30 years before *method* alone began to be used and such terms as *method acting* and *method actor* were heard.

Stapelia.   Dutch physician J. B. Stapel (d. 1636) is remembered by a carrion flower; the large flowers of the cactuslike *Stapelia* genus, containing some hundred species and having a very unpleasant, fetid odor. Native to South Africa, a few of these curiously marked species—variously colored and sometimes marbled or barred—are grown in the greenhouse for their flowers. There is no record of whether the naming was meant as a compliment or insult.

star.   *Star*, for an actor of exceptional popularity or talent, or both, isn't some press agent's invention as many believe. The term is first recorded in a 1779 book on the theater in an appraisal of the great English actor David Garrick: "The little stars, who hid their diminished rays in his [Garrick's] presence, began to abuse him." *Star*, as a verb, wasn't used until about 1825. *Stardom* seems to have been coined by O. Henry in a 1911 short story. *See* MATINEE IDOL.

starboard; larboard.   Old English ships were steered (*steor*, "steer") by a paddle or board (*bord*) over the right side. This *steorbord* became *starboard* and starboard later became the name for the right side of the ship itself. *Larboard*, the left side of a ship, derives from the earlier *lureboard* (from the Anglo-Saxon *laere*, "empty"), in reference to the fact that the left side was usually empty because the steersman stood on the right, or steering-board (starboard), side.

star chamber proceedings.   A star chamber is any committee or tribunal that proceeds by arbitrary or unfair oppressive methods. The term dates to the reigns of British monarchs James I and Charles I when a civil and criminal court called the *star-chamber*, abolished in 1641, notoriously abused its powers and from which there was no appeal. The court, its judges the king's own counselors, was probably so named because it was held in a room, or chamber, in the royal palace at Westminster where the ceiling was decorated with gilt stars. However, Blackstone's *Commentaries* has it that the *star* here derives

from the *starra*, or "contracts and obligations of Jews," that were stored in the room.

starfish.   Crammedtogethercloserthanthis, each no bigger than the period ending this sentence, more than 1,000 tiny globules cling tenaciously to a handful of seaweed as they begin assuming their star shapes. Vaguely, the living, changing "nurse" eggs begin to resemble small asterisks, and then a few weeks later the five points of their stars suddenly become clearly visible. From a smattering of stardust, hundreds of sea stars, or starfish, that can be so many varied colors—orange, yellow, red, purple—are finally born to human eyes. Though the word *starfish* was first recorded about 1530, the sea creatures were known to earliest man, less for their beauty than for their destructive raids against oysters, clams, and coral reefs (including Australia's Great Barrier Reef). Another name for them is *the walking stomach of the sea*, because they actually eat with their stomachs, which they can push out through the mouth centrally located beneath their bodies and digest food on the spot. After dining, this amazing stomach proceeds to double as an excretory system. *See* REGENERATION.

stark naked.   Although *stark* was a common Middle English word meaning "strong" and is sometimes used to intensify other words, as in *stark raving mad*, it has nothing to do with *stark naked*. The original form of *stark naked* was *start naked*, *start* here being a corruption of the Anglo-Saxon *steort*, meaning "tail or rump." Someone *stark naked* is therefore literally "naked even to the rump."

starling.   This bird, whose name is akin to the Old English for tern, *stearn*, was brought across the Atlantic in 1890 and released in Central Park by literary enthusiasts seeking to introduce to America all the birds mentioned in Shakespeare. It has since become a pest, reminding some gardeners of the Englishman back in 1886 who said, "Few people are aware of how good the starling is to eat." The starling (*Sturnus vulgaris*) constitutes more of the 100 billion birds in the world than any other species, and has long been noted for its ability to speak and whistle.

Stars and Bars.   The official flag of the Confederacy during the Civil War. It had two broad red stripes commonly called the bars and a blue field in the upper left-hand corner bearing a circle of stars (one for each of the seceded states). The Stars and Bars is often erroneously depicted as the RED CROSS BANNER, or battle flag, in Civil War illustrations.

Stars and Stripes; Star-Spangled Banner.   Though the Continental Congress resolved in 1777 that the U.S. flag be composed of 13 stripes and 13 stars, the term *Stars and Stripes* for the flag isn't recorded until five years later. *Star-Spangled Banner*, for the flag, was of course inspired by the national anthem, whose lyrics Francis Scott Key wrote in 1814, but the song didn't become our official national anthem until 1931 (though it had for almost a century been called our "national ballad"). *See* OLD GLORY.

start from scratch.   Unlike COME UP TO SCRATCH, which probably derives from prize-fighting, this was originally a horse-racing expression. A scratch in England was the starting line in a horse race and horses started there with no advantage besides their own ability, like anyone who starts from scratch in any undertaking. In this sense a scratch race is a race without restrictions as to the age, weight, and winnings of the horses entered.

starvation. On March 6, 1775, Henry Dundas, first viscount Melville (1742–1811), made a Parliamentary speech speculating whether famine would result in America because of a 1775 British bill restricting trade with Britain's New England colonies. Dundas said he was "afraid" famine "would not be produced from the Act." This hard-hearted remark inspired author Horace Walpole and others to later nickname him "Starvation Dundas" and "Starvation," names he would be remembered by through the rest of his days and through history. The *OED* says that despite the absence of confirmation it is "not improbable" that Dundas used *starvation* before anyone else, and he may even have coined the word, but an examination of the records reveals that he did not employ *starvation* in his Parliament speech, as some sources claim.

State of Franklin. *See* TENNESSEE.

stateroom. One persistent old story has the term *stateroom* coined by an early owner of steamboats named Shreve, for whom the city of Shreveport, Louisiana was named. Shreve, according to this account, named luxurious cabins on his boats after states (*e.g.*, the Texas Room) and they came to be known as *staterooms*. *Stateroom* is first recorded for the "sleeping apartment on a U.S. passenger steamer" in 1837 by Harriet Martineau, but there is no evidence yet of any Shreve with his finger in the pie. More likely this *stateroom* evolved from the *stateroom* meaning "a captain's or officer's quarters on board ship," which is first recorded in Pepys's *Diary* in 1660.

stateside. *Stateside* may have been invented by G.I.'s in World War II for "to, toward or in the continental U.S." At least the word is first recorded at about that time when many soldiers were far from home. In the U.S. itself today the term is only used by Alaskans (it is rare in Hawaii) for the mainland. Alaskans also call the 48 contiguous states the Lower 48, the lower states, the Outside, and even the South!

States'-Rights Democrat. A designation, not frequently heard anymore, for southern Democrats espousing the doctrine of states' rights. It was apparently coined just after the Civil War.

Statue of Liberty. The statue of Liberty Enlightening the World, better known as the Statue of Liberty, is, of course, as much a symbol of the United States as Uncle Sam. The colossal 152-foot statue of a woman with uplifted arm holding a burning torch stands at the entrance to New York Harbor. It was a gift from France to the United States, designed by French sculptor Frédéric Auguste Barthold; its steel framework was designed by Gustav Eiffel, designer of the Eiffel Tower. French citizens contributed the $250,000 for the statue itself, and Americans gave $250,000 for its pedestal on Bedloes Island, whose name was changed in 1956 to Liberty Island. Dedicated in 1886, the statue is now under the protection of the National Park Service, which administrates it along with Ellis Island, a former deten-

tion center for immigrants entering America, as part of the Statue of Liberty National Memorial. In the statue's left arm is a tablet with the date July 4, 1776, engraved upon it. At its feet are the broken shackles of tyranny.

Statue of Liberty play. Named for its resemblance to the uplifted arm of the Statue of Liberty, this football play has a passer faking a pass, and another back coming behind him, taking the ball from his upraised hand and either passing it himself or running toward the goal with it. Outdated today, it was the pride of every kid's sandlot team a generation ago.

stave off. A stave is a stick of wood, the word a back formation from the plural of staff, *staves*. In the early 17th century staves were used in the "sport" of bullbaiting, where dogs were set against bulls. Too often these contests were badly matched, for the bulls frequently had the tips of their horns cut off, and when the dogs got a bull down, the bull's owner often tried to save him for another fight by driving the dogs off with a stave or stick. Because the owner actually "postponed" the bull's death until another day, the expression *to stave off* acquired its present figurative meaning of "to forestall." This is at least a possible explanation for *stave off*, which we know is associated in some way with beating off dogs.

Stavin Chain. *Stavin Chain* isn't heard much anymore, but since about 1910 it has meant a sexually powerful man very attractive to women, after the hero of a popular American southwestern folk song.

Steadi Cam. Short for *steady camera*, a traditional device that holds a camera steady to the cameraman's body, enabling him to take smooth shots without any jerking or shaking. The first Steadi Cams were used in the Oscar-winning film *Rocky* (1976).

steak. *Steak*, an old English word, takes its name from the way such meat was first cooked; on a thin *stake*, from the Old English *staca*, akin to stick. The word is first recorded as *styke* in the early 15th century.

steak tartare. Bloodthirsty about their meals as well as their conquests, the nomadic Tartars liked their meat raw, or almost always so—sometimes they placed a hunk of meat under the saddle and cooked it by friction during hours of riding. At any rate, in medieval times traveling Hamburg merchants learned about a recipe for scraped raw meat seasoned with salt, pepper, and onion juice and named it *tartar steak* or *steak tartare* in their honor. This was the first HAMBURGER, remaining so until some anonymous Hamburger shaped *steak tartare* into patties and cooked them. Tartar sauce, a mayonnaise containing diced pickles, onions, olives, capers, and green herbs, takes its name from tartar steak, which was often seasoned with similar ingredients.

steal a march on someone. Here the *march* is the distance armed troops can cover in a day. In medieval times enemies could easily figure this distance and, by marching at night, be waiting to surprise their opponents when they arrived at their destination. This was known as *stealing a march* on someone and came to mean "to anticipate someone's moves and thus gain an advantage over him."

steal my thunder. "Our author, for the advantage of this play, had invented a new species of thunder . . . the very sort that is presently used in the theatre. The tragedy itself was coldly received, notwithstanding such assistance, and was acted but a short time. Some nights after, Mr. Dennis, being in the pit at the representation of *Macbeth*, heard his own thunder made use of; upon which he rose in a violent passion and exclaimed, 'See how the rascals use me! They will not let my play run, and yet they steal my thunder.' " This early account of the origin of the expression *steal my thunder*, from the *Biographia Britannica*, is accurate in all respects, according to most authorities. Restoration playwright John Dennis (1657–1734) had invented a new and more effective way of simulating thunder on the stage (by shaking a sheet of tin) for his play *Appius and Virginia* (1709). The play soon closed, but a rival company stole his thunder, inspiring his outburst and giving us the expression *steal my thunder*.

steamboat. *Steamboat* is an Americanism dating back to at least 1785, when John Fitch invented the first workable one. Fitch was not able to secure the financial aid necessary to promote his invention after his fourth ship was destroyed, and he died a broken man, leaving a request that he be buried on the banks of the Ohio River so that he might rest "where the song of the boatman would enliven the stillness of my resting place and the music of the steam engine soothe my spirit." His dream became a reality in 1807, nine years after he died, when Robert Fulton's steamboat *Clermont*, which had been called "Fulton's Folly," proved a great success.

steatopygous. "With many Hottentot women," Darwin wrote, "the posterior part of the body projects in a wonderful manner; they are steatopygous." Darwin clearly appreciated this way that some women extend in his *Descent of Man*, but the word *steatopygous*, when applied to Hottentot Bushmen (especially the Bongos) or anyone else, clearly isn't nearly as complimentary as CALLIPYGIAN. Deriving from the Greek for "fat rumped," its dictionary definition is "a protuberance of the buttocks, due to an abnormal accumulation of fat in and behind the hips and thighs."

steeplechase. According to one tradition, *steeplechase* originated with a race from church steeple to church steeple in Irish horse country. Another tale credits a group of British riders returning home from a foxhunt with inventing the sport and the word—these foxless riders decided to run a race in a direct line, regardless of obstacles, to the steeple of the village church, the winner the rider "who first touched the stones of the steeple with his whip." In any case, the original horseback races called steeplechase races had a church steeple in view as the goal, the riders having to clear all intervening obstacles. The word is first recorded in the British *Sporting Magazine*, in 1805.

steerage. The ancestors of millions of Americans came to America in steerage, which literally was the noisy, crowded section of a ship below deck. Passage was $10 to $15 for such quarters, compared with about $40 for regular tickets. Later, the term came to mean any area on a ship where the passage was cheapest. *See* ELLIS ISLAND.

stem to stern. Loosely speaking, the stem is the bow of a ship and the stern is the rear. Thus *from stem to stern* means "throughout" as in "We turned the place over from stem to stern." The expression is an old one, dating back to at least the early 16th century.

Sten gun. This British light machine gun of World War II is an unusual blend of the first initials of its two inventors' names, *S*heppard and *T*urpin, plus the first two letters of the name of their country, *En*gland. The Sten gun, or Sten, is not extremely accurate, but is easy to operate, can be fired from the shoulder, weighing only eight pounds, and fires rapidly at the rate of 550 rounds per minute, making it an effective short-range weapon. Mass-produced mainly from stamped parts, the inexpensive *Sten* should really be classed as a submachine gun, like the American Thompson, or Tommy gun, and the German Schmeisser, or burp gun.

stenography. Though its practice dates back to the ancient Greeks, the word *stenography* is first recorded in the early 17th century. The word derives from the Greek *stenos*, "narrow," and *graphein*, "to write," literally meaning "narrow writing." Other synonyms are the rare *brachygraphy*, "short writing," and *shorthand*, which dates back to 1636 and is the most common term today.

stentorian. Under freak acoustical conditions the human voice has carried over 10 miles across water, but its average range is about 200 yards in still air. Stentor, Homer's Grecian herald of the Trojan War, who may have been based on some top sergeant of old, probably had a range far exceeding this. In the *Iliad* Homer tells how the herald faced the enemy to dictate terms in "a voice of bronze . . . as loud as 50 men together." Greek legend claims that Stentor finally met his match in Hermes, herald of the Gods, dying as the result of a vocal contest with him. But his name lived on as the Greek for loud-voiced and gave us the English word *stentorian*, "extremely loud." A howling monkey, a trumpet-shaped protozoan, and an electric magnifying speaker called the stentorphone also do him homage. *See* HECTOR; NESTOR.

Stepin Fetchit. American vaudevillian Lincoln Theodore Monroe Andrew Perry took his stage name, Stepin Fetchit, from a racehorse he had won money on, hoping that the nag's name would continue bringing him good luck. It didn't, in the long run. *Stepin Fetchit* instead became the synonym for a servile, silly black man when Hollywood typecast the talented actor in such roles throughout the 1940s. By the time of the civil rights movement, the actor was completely out of favor and out of work.

step on it. Speed it up. The expression is obviously a shortening of *step on the gas*, which of course means to push down harder on a car's gas pedal to make it go faster. The phrase dates back to the early days of the automobile.

stepping the mast. When a mast is about to be stepped, all those on board the new ship contribute good-luck coins to be placed under it. This old maritime tradition is said to have its origins in the ancient Roman custom of placing coins in the mouths of men killed in battle. The coins were supposed to pay Charon, the mythical ferryman, for transporting the dead men across the River Styx. Today the coins are often placed in corrosion-proof receptacles at the base of the mast, and the mast is stepped, put in place, immediately afterward.

sterling. In medieval England a starling was a coin worth about a penny and took its name from the star (*steorra*) embossed upon it. The pound sterling began life as 100 of the smaller sterlings, and its value, of course, has risen and fallen over the years.

stet. *Stet* is Latin for "let it stand," the printing term being used as a direction to the printer to reinstate a word or words that had been marked for deletion in a proof or manuscript. The term is a fairly recent one, first recorded in 1821.

Stetson. After poor health forced John Batterson Stetson (1830–1906) to travel west at the time of the Civil War, it occurred to him that no one was manufacturing hats suited to the practical needs of the western cowboy, and on his return to Philadelphia in 1865 he went into the hat business, specializing in western-style headgear. The wide-brimmed, 10-gallon felt hats he manufactured immediately became popular with cowboys and have been called Stetsons, or John B's, ever since.

stevedore. *See* LONGSHOREMAN.

stew. Now the synonym for a brothel or a prostitute, a stew was in medieval times the town bathhouse. Toward the end of the Middle Ages the town bathhouse became the gathering place for loose men and women, *stew* taking on its present meaning. Our word *stew* for meat and vegetables slowly boiled together comes from the same source, the verb meaning to bathe in a hot bath or stew.

stewed as a fresh boiled owl. Very drunk. The origin of the expression is anybody's guess, and I'd appreciate hearing any facts or theories. Maybe someone desperate did shoot and stew an owl whole for food and noticed its stewed resemblance to someone deep in his cups.

stick in one's craw. When you can't swallow something, when it won't go down, or you are loath to accept it, it sticks in your craw. The craw is the crop or preliminary stomach of a fowl, where food is predigested. Hunters centuries ago noticed that some birds swallowed bits of stone that were too large to pass through the craw and into the digestive tract. These stones, unlike the sand and pebbles needed by birds to help grind food in the pouch, literally stuck in the craw, couldn't go down any farther. This oddity became part of the language of hunters and the phrase was soon used figuratively.

stick it in your ear. This rude insult may have its origins in baseball, where *stick it in his ear* is often the cry of bench jockeys to a pitcher on their team who is facing a batter crowding the plate. Literally, it means "to hit the batter in the ear with the ball," but it usually means "to throw the ball very close to the hitter, to dust him off." No one has determined exactly when this phrase came into the language, but it was around in the 1950s. It may simply be a variation of much ruder phrases like *stick it up your ass* and *shove it up your ass.*

stickler. The earliest sticklers were umpires or moderators at wrestling or fencing matches and tournaments in the 16th century. Within another hundred years the word was being used figuratively, followed by *for*, to describe anybody who unyieldingly insists on something. *Stickler* derives from the Anglo-Saxon *stihtan*, "to arrange or regulate."

the sticks. *The sticks* is an Americanism for the country, or the backwoods. First recorded in 1905, it derives from the use of *sticks* by lumbermen for "timberlands."

stick to one's guns. It seems sure that this expression was born with some fort or ship being attacked, but though it may be military in origin it is first recorded, as late as 1839, in a popular novel called *Ten Thousand a Year*, the words put in the mouth of a civilian named Mr. Titmouse.

stick your neck out. *See* DON'T STICK YOUR NECK OUT.

sticky wicket. A sticky wicket is a difficult or awkward situation that calls for delicate handling, and this 1920s British expression still has some currency in the U.S. as a humorous term. It comes from the phrase *bat at a sticky wicket*, meaning to contend with great difficulties, which has its origins in cricket. In cricket a sticky wicket (goal) literally means that the ground around a wicket is soggy because of recent, heavy rain. This condition doesn't allow the ball to bounce well, making things difficult for the players trying to field it.

stiff; stiffing the world. In its sense of cheating someone of something he or she deserves—as in purposely failing to leave a worthy waiter a tip—the word *stiff* has frequently been in the news recently. It was first used in this sense, though as a noun, in *The Massarenes* (1897), a novel by Ouida, the pen name of Louise De la Ramée (Ouida is a childish pronunciation of Louise). Ouida used *stiff* to describe a passenger on board a ship who failed to tip, probably comparing that person to a corpse (an earlier meaning of *stiff*) in his spending habits. Over the years *stiff* came to be a verb, which was finally used by President George W. Bush when he charged that Iraqui leader Saddam Hussein "is stiffing the world."

stiff-necked. Obstinate, stubborn. The allusion here is to a horse that refuses to respond to the reins. The expression is recorded in the Bible (Jer. 17:23): "They obeyed not, but made their necks stiff." This refers to Jerusalemites dishonoring the Sabbath, but, according to Professor Howard Marblestone, "The better-known use appears in Exodus 32:9 (and other places) when God condemns the Israelites for being 'a stiff-necked people' of little faith, who followed Aaron in making the golden calf."

stiff upper lip. Since it is the lower lip that quivers when someone is afraid or on the verge of crying, keeping a stiff upper lip seems to be a rather meaningless expression. Probably there is no logic behind this admonition to be firm in times of trouble, but at least one attempt has been made at an explanation. Young British officers who adopted mustaches tried to keep them trim so that they didn't make their upper lips twitch, such twitching being a sign of lack of control and emotional immaturity to their superiors. The main problem here is that all recorded evidence shows this phrase to be of American origin, from New England in about 1830. Possibly it is just the reverse of the American expression "down in the mouth."

still as a stone.   Just as he probably originated BUSY AS A BEE. Chaucer probably coined the classic alliterative phrase *still as a stone*, which later became the Shakespearian *stone still:* "I will not struggle; I will stand stone-still"—*King John*. At least both expressions are first recorded in his work.

still have some snap left in one's garters.   An expression dating back to the late 19th century and meaning "still energetic, not yet worn out." "I really think," Senator Russell B. Long of Louisiana told the press on March 17, 1985, "that it's better to retire on Uncle Earl's terms, when you still have some snap left in your garters." Mr. Long was referring to his legendary uncle, former Louisiana governor Earl Long, who may have used the expression too.

still waters run deep.   Someone quiet on the outside is more worthwhile or even dangerous than any bigmouth. The germ of the idea behind this saying goes all the way back to the Roman poet Quintus Curtius of the first century A.D., who wrote: "The deepest rivers flow with the least sound." Later, in 1580, the British writer John Lyly (*see* EUPHUISM) wrote: "Where the streame runneth smoothest, the water is deepest." Finally, in *Henry VI* (1591) Shakespeare borrowed and improved a bit upon both with "Smooth runs the water where the brook is deep."

stink chariot.   *Stink chariot* for an automobile was invented by Australian author and editor John Norton, who published a weekly paper called *John Norton's Truth* earlier in this century. It is obsolescent if not obsolete but worth remembering.

stinker; stink on ice; stink out loud.   *Stinker*, one writer suggests, may derive from the unskilled hands among American buffalo hunters who skinned the freshly killed animals and stank from the blood and intestines that clung to them. Partridge, however, states that *stinker* has meant a disgusting contemptible person in British slang since the 17th century. *Stink on ice* and *stink out loud* are definitely 19th-century Americanisms.

stinkin' Benjamin.   This flower of the genus *Trillium* looks nice where it grows; it's only when picked for a bouquet that its fetid odor is noticed. It is also called purple trillium.

stinking iris.   The bruised evergreen foliage of the "stinking iris" (*Iris foetidissima*), also called "stinking gladium," makes up for its unpleasant smell by its medicinal uses. In fact, some gardeners must have *liked* its smell, for it went by the common name "roast beef plant" in days past. *See also* IRIS.

stinkpots.   Stinkpots, favorite weapons of pirates, were malodorous concoctions made from saltpeter (potassium nitrate), limestone (calcium carbonate), asafetida (a vile-smelling gum resin), and decayed fish that were packed into earthenware jugs, ignited, and hurled onto an enemy ship. Nauseating smoke spread over the deck and through the hold, often discouraging the enemy from fighting, or at least weakening his resistance. Pirates also hung stinkpots from the yardarms and cut them off when they projected over the vessel under attack.

stinky billy.   *See* SWEET WILLIAM.

stirrup cup.   A farewell drink of wine or liquor given to a mounted rider, feet in the stirrups and ready to depart. *Stirrup*, referring to an ancient device, derives ultimately from the obsolete German word *sty*, "climb," plus *rope*. This indicates that the first stirrups were looped ropes. The rider put his or her foot in one of the loops and climbed up on the horse's back. *See* DEOCH-AN-DORIS.

stitch.   *See* THROW INTO STITCHES.

Stix Nix Hix Pix.   This is among the most famous of the colorful headlines that have appeared in the show business newspaper *Variety*. It referred to a survey indicating that residents of small towns don't like movies about small town life.

Stockholm syndrome.   A condition in which hostages or kidnapped people bond with and help their captors. It is named after a 1973 bank robbery in Stockholm, Sweden, when the hostages showed hostility toward the authorities even though such actions might have been harmful to themselves. There have been many similar cases. In the bizarre 1974 Patty Hearst kidnapping case, for example, Patty changed her name to Tania and joined the Symbionese Liberation Army that kidnapped her.

stocking cap.   *See* TOQUE.

stocks and bonds; stock market.   Both *stocks* and *bonds* have their etymological roots in substantial things. No one knows exactly how the words came to be applied to securities, but *stocks* comes ultimately from the Old English word *stocc*, for "tree trunk," and *bonds* from the early English *band*, meaning "fastening." *Stock market*, and ultimately *stocks*, may come from the name of a London meat and fish market called the Stock Exchange near the site of the Mansion House in the 15th century. An ancient source says this market was so named because it was built on a site where "had stoode a payre of stocks for a punishment of offenders."

stogy.   *See* CONESTOGA WAGONS.

Stoksosaurus clevelandi.   This dinosaur species is included because it honors the person with the most dinosaur fossil species named after him, geologist William Lee Stokes (1915–94). Dr. Stokes was so honored eight times and a number of rock formations in Utah were named after him as well.

stone.   In Britain, Ireland, Australia, and New Zealand, but not in the U.S., *stone* refers to a weight measure equal to 14 pounds, or 6.35 kilograms, although the term has been used less frequently since the introduction of the metric system.

stone melons.   There are melon-shaped stones on Mount Carmel, said to have fallen there from the cart of a peasant.

According to Muslim tradition, Elijah saw the peasant carrying melons and asked him for one. The peasant lied that they were stones and Elijah promptly changed them into stones.

stone still.   *See* STILL AS A STONE.

stonewaller.   One who obstructs or blocks anything with stubborn, stonewall-like resistance. The term may come from the nickname of Civil War Confederate general Thomas Jonathan Jackson (1824–63), who got the name Stonewall at the first battle of Bull Run when a fellow officer told of seeing Jackson "standing like a stone wall." Stonewall Jackson was accidentally killed by his own troops at the battle of Chancellorsville. "I have lost my right arm," Robert E. Lee, commander of the Confederate armies, said on hearing of his death.

stone walls do not a prison make.   These famous words by the Cavalier poet Richard Lovelace are from his "To Althea, from Prison," which he wrote in 1642 while serving seven weeks in the Gatehouse prison at Westminster for presenting a petition to the House of Commons on behalf of King Charles I. The poem also contains words praising Charles ("The sweetness, mercy, majesty / And glories of my King"), yet Lovelace was freed not by any action of the monarch but on a large bail of 4,000 to 40,000 pounds that he posted. In 1648 Lovelace was again imprisoned, by the Commonwealth, and while in prison prepared for press another famous poem "To Lucasta, Going to the Wars," which contains the famous lyric "I could not love thee, Dear, so much / Loved I not Honour more." Lovelace named "Lucasta" for his beloved Lucy Sacheverell, who married another man when it was reported that the Cavalier poet was killed fighting for the French king in France. By the time Lovelace finished his second jail term, his great fortune had been exhausted supporting the monarchy. It is said that he died in a cellar, without money to buy food, before his 40th birthday in 1658.

stoning ground.   This phrase puts one in mind of Shirley Jackson's short story "The Lottery" (1949), but the practice of stoning was all too real under the Taliban in Afghanistan. According to a *New York Times* story (12/28/01): "At the direction of the religious police—mostly young thugs . . . couples caught in adultery were led out to the 'stoning ground' before a mosque, the woman buried in a pit up to her head, the man tied hand and foot beside her, their children required to cast the first rocks."

stool pigeon.   Fowlers in the past used live decoy birds to lure pigeons and other birds into range of their nets or guns, which helped them to wipe out several species. These live decoys, their eyes sometimes stitched closed, were called stool pigeons, stool-crows, or the like, probably because they were tied by a long string to small stools that the hunters could move up and down while waiting hidden for their prey (although their name may derive from the Old English word *stale*, meaning "a living bird used to catch others of the same species"). At any rate, in about 1830 the term *stool pigeon* became American slang for a criminal decoy used by the police to catch other criminals, and by the end of the century it meant a police informer. The last meaning was probably influenced by the use of the slang *carrier pigeon* for "an informer" at the time, a carrier pigeon carrying information to the police the way the bird carries messages. *Stoolie*, an abbreviated form of the term, is of relatively recent usage.

stop one's ears.   *See* TURN A DEAF EAR.

store; stoic.   *Store* derives from the roofed colonnades called *stoas* that housed the small shops of merchants in the ancient Athenian agora, that same marketplace where Socrates and his followers gathered, where Solon the wise lawgiver made his fortune as a merchant. In this marketplace the philosopher Zeno taught that "what will be will be," that man must accept his fate calmly in this world. He and his pupils came to be called Stoics because they met in a stoa. Thus the Greek word *stoa*, for "a shop," yielded both the words *store* and *stoic*, this last something many a storekeeper has been forced to be by economic and other calamities over the centuries.

storm door.   I had assumed that this term was an Americanism invented in relatively recent times. But lexicographers trace it back to the Dutch *storm deur*, meaning the same, used here in the 17th century, when New York was called New Amsterdam.

stormonter.   *Stormonter* is obsolete except in a historical sense and never made the dictionaries, but it tells an amusing story about Benjamin Franklin, who had among his many gifts a genius for coining words. Lord Stormont, the British ambassador in Paris during the Revolution, was the most assiduous spreader of tales about America's defeats at the hands of Great Britain, his aim of course to color the facts and discourage European nations from supporting the American cause. One time a French friend came to Franklin with Stormont's story that six battalions of Americans had laid down their arms. The Frenchman wanted to know if this was true. "Oh, no," Franklin replied gravely, "it is not the truth, it is only a Stormont." Within a day his witticism swept Paris and *stormonter* became a new French synonym for lying. Franklin is also responsible for *harmonica*, the musical instrument he invented in a rude form and named from the Italian *armonica*, "harmonious."

stovaine.   The anesthetic stovaine was named in an irregular way for its 20th-century French discoverer, Ernest Fourneau. The anesthetic has *cocaine* in it, accounting for the last syllable and the "Four" of *Four*neau's name translates into English as *stove*; hence, *stovaine*.

stove.   The first *stoves* were saunas, not kitchen appliances. *Stove* comes to us from the Old English *stofa* "a hot air bath," or sauna, the hot steam baths brought to England from Scandinavia. *Stofa* didn't change in spelling to *stove* until the 15th century and it wasn't until the 16th century that *stove* was used to mean a furnace.

Stradivarius.   When the Lady Blunt Stradivarius (1721) was auctioned off at Sotheby's in London for $200,000, it was the highest price ever paid for a musical instrument. Yet this violin is not considered to be the finest one made by Antonio Stradivari, that honor usually accorded to the Messiah, or the Alard Stradivarius. Amazingly, some 600 of the 1,100 or so violins, violas, and cellos made by Stradivari from 1666 to 1737 still survive today, half of them in the United States—a tribute to the master craftsman's genius. Only the barest essentials are known about the supreme Italian violin maker. Born at Cremona in northern Italy in 1644, he was an apprentice of the distinguished craftsman Niccolò Amati, but he soon developed his own methods, in 1684 opening a shop where his sons Francesco and Omobono worked with him. Stradivari was famous in his own time, his commissions including instruments for England's James II and Spain's Charles III. He died in 1737, aged 93, and to this day his secrets of success have not been discovered.

strafe. *Strafe* means "to attack enemy ground troops or fortifications, etc., by aircraft with machine-gun fire." The word is a joking one that the British coined from German *strafe* (punish) during the early years of World War I. In 1914 German author Alfred Funke had coined the popular catchphrase and salutation *Gott strafe England* (May God punish England). The British borrowed *strafe* and changed its meaning, using it to mean machine-gun fire that punished the Germans.

straight arrow. A decent, upstanding person; after an archetypical upright Indian brave. A variation on the 19th-century term is *straight shooter.*

straight from the horse's mouth. By examining a horse's teeth an expert can make a good estimation of its age; a horse's first permanent teeth, for example, don't appear until it is about two and a half years old. So despite what any crooked horse trader might have wished them to believe, informed horsemen in England stood little chance of being cheated about a horse's age—they had it on good authority, *straight from the horse's mouth.* The expression may have been used as far back as the Napoleonic Wars, according to one source, but there is no evidence to support this theory, and the phrase was first recorded in Great Britain in 1917.

straight from the shoulder. The expression means honestly, frankly, and to the point and derives from a boxing term of the mid 19th century. A punch straight from the shoulder was once made by bringing the fist to the shoulder and sending it forward straight and fast. Such undeceptive blows are quick, effective, and often to the point of the chin.

strait; straitlaced. Though used several hundred years earlier, *straitlaced* emerged as a popular figure of speech only in the early 17th century when girdles became fashionable. Wrote one arbiter of taste at the time: "No Maid here's handsome thought, unless she can with her short Palms her straight-lac'd body span." This of course required a lot of tugging on the laces of a bodice or corset, but a woman's body did become very *strait* or "tight and narrow" at the waist. Thus the term *straitlaced* derives not from the word "straight" but from the Middle English *strait*, the same word that gives us the tight and narrow geographical *straits. Strait*, in turn, comes from the Latin *strictus*, "to tighten, bind tightly," which also gives us *constriction.* The term *straitlaced* early became related to excessive prudishness because a straitlaced person supposedly drew moral bonds as tight as those on a girdle, while an unlaced, loose, woman was thought to be more voluptuous and less repressed.

the Strand. "The business belonged to Thomas Boller of the Strand." On reading a sentence like that, Americans often wonder just what the British mean by "the Strand." The name refers to a well-known London street that connects the area called the City of London to Westminster. Since the street runs along the shore (or strand) of the Thames River, it is called the Strand.

strata; Strata Smith. Geologically *stratum* refers to a horizontal layer of material, such as rock, often one of several parallel layers (strata) on top of one another. In 1815 William Smith (1769–1839) published 15 huge drawings illustrating his finding that strata regularly slant eastward in a slight ascending grade until they end at the Earth's surface. For his discovery he was pensioned off by the British government and earned the sobriquent "Strata Smith."

strawberry. Several theories have been proposed about the origin of *strawberry*, but none is convincing. Some say the straw mulch often used in its cultivation inspired the name, others that the dried berries were once strung on straw for decorations, still others that the long runners of the mother plant (strawlike when dry) gave the fruit its name. The word was used as early as A.D. 100 in England and doesn't derive from any other language. It may be that the *straw* in *strawberry* is a corruption of the word *strew.* Certainly the mother plant strews, or scatters, new plants all over a patch when it propagates itself by sending out runners. There's always been an air of mystery surrounding the strawberry. The early Greeks, in fact, had a taboo against eating them, as they did against any red food, and pregnant women in the Middle Ages avoided them because they believed their children would be born with *strawberry marks* (small, slightly raised birthmarks resembling strawberries) if they did. A *strawberry roan* is a reddish-coated horse flecked with white hair.

strawberry friend. This oldtime rural Americanism describes people who visit from the city when strawberries are in season to get free berries (and other produce) from their rural friends or relatives.

straw boss. A writer discussing hobo lingo in *American Speech* almost half a century ago traced this term to the late-19th-century American farm. "The (real) boss attended to the grain going into the thresher," he explained; "the secondman (or straw boss) watched the straw coming out and hence had little to do." Thus the term *straw boss* has come to mean anyone, especially a foreman, who gives orders but has no real authority to enforce them.

strawfoot. Union Army slang for a raw rural recruit during the Civil War, *strawfoot* may have been coined by the drill sergeants who taught these men to march. According to one story, many such men didn't know their left foot from their right and the instructors tied hay to their left foot and straw to the right, shouting the marching cadence "Hayfoot! Strawfoot!" rather than "Left foot! Right foot!" But, alas, *strawfoot* is more likely a description of recruits who still had straw from the farm in their shoes.

straw man. *See* MAN OF STRAW.

straw that broke the camel's back; last straw.   Charles Dickens probably invented these expressions in *Dombey and Son*, where he wrote: "As the last straw breaks the laden camel's back." But Dickens got the idea from an old English proverb: *'Tis the last feather that breaks the horse's back*. Both phrases refer to someone's limit or breaking point. The strongest camel can carry about 1,200 pounds—a straw more might literally break its back.

streak.   To run naked in a public place, outdoors or indoors, where a large number of people can see you. The word *streaking* was first recorded in 1973, but the practice of streaking probably began among college students a year or two earlier on campuses in California. In the most famous example of streaking, a nude man streaked across the stage during the televised 1974 Academy Awards ceremony.

stream of consciousness.   William James coined this now common term in *Principles of Psychology* (1890), and it has come to mean a literary technique that tries to express the multitude of thoughts and feelings that flow through the mind. James Joyce developed the technique in *Ulysses* (1922), but it had been used long before him by Aretino, Sterne, Diderot, Carlyle, and French novelist Edouard Dujardin, whose work Joyce is believed to have known.

street numbers and letters.   The numbering and lettering (*e.g.*, Fifth Avenue and 23rd, or Avenue C and 40th) of streets is an American custom probably invented by Major Pierre-Charles L'Enfant when he laid out the plan of Washington, D.C. in 1791. At first condemned by the English as unimaginative, the practice has by now won some acceptance in England.

streetwalker.   The use of this term for "a prostitute who works the streets," is an ancient one—older than the use of *streetwalker* for a pedestrian. It is first recorded by Shakespeare's detractor, dramatist Robert Greene, the same Bohemian who died of a surfeit of pickled herrings and Rhenish wine. In a tract on "Conny-catching" written in 1592, in which he describes London's lowlife, Greene wrote of "street walkers . . . in rich garded [attention-getting] gowns." It wasn't until almost three decades later that *streetwalkers* was applied to anyone who walks in the street.

the strenuous life.   *See* ANANIAS.

strike.   Though workers had certainly refused to work on occasion before 1768, the word *strike* is first recorded in that year, when British seamen threatened to strike (take down) the sails on their ships and cease all work until what they called their grievances were settled. This they did, and a new word entered the language. In reference to a sudden stroke of luck or success, the term strike is first recorded during the California gold rush to mean a find of gold, and was often called a lucky strike or a big strike by those who struck it rich.

strikeout.   In the American lexicon, *to strike out* means to fail completely; it is one of the most widely used baseball-derived terms. The baseball *strikeout*, a combination of three strikes, has been used in the sport since the 1840s. At first *strike* meant just a missed swing at the ball or a fouled-off ball. There were no called strikes by the umpire until 1863; a strike is called when a ball is pitched within the strike zone (which is the area above home plate between the batter's knees and his armpits) and the batter doesn't take a swing at it. *See also* TWO STRIKES AGAINST YOU.

strike sail.   *See* STRIKE.

strike while the iron is hot.   A blacksmith has to wield his hammer while the metal on the anvil is red-hot or he loses his opportunity and must heat the iron all over again. Which is the idea behind this phrase meaning to act at the most propitious moment, an expression that goes back at least to Chaucer, who in the *Canterbury Tales* wrote that while the "Iren is hoot men sholden smyte."

string along with someone.   To accept someone's decision or advice, to follow someone as a leader, to go along with someone. In 1799 a political observer speaks of "the sycophantic circle that surrounds the President in stringing to his quarters." *Stringing along* probably comes from the same source as this earlier phrase, which suggests docile pack animals tied together in single file and led by their masters. The phrase isn't recorded until the 1920s.

string bean.   *String beans* is an Americanism for green beans, first recorded in 1759 and so named for the stringlike fibers along the vegetable sutures. When Burpee & Co. seedsmen developed the Beautiful Burpee, "the stringless string bean," in 1894 the term *string bean* began to take a back seat to *green bean*. It is still heard, however, along with other synonyms like *snap beans* (named for the sound the pods make when broken), *wax beans* (yellow varieties), *kidney beans*, and *haricot*.

stringer.   A stringer is a part-time newspaper correspondent, often in an out-of-the-way place. Such reporters used to be paid by the column inch. After pasting together all their contributions for a certain period of time, they'd send their editor their string of clippings. The editor would then measure the length of the string and send the stringer his check.

strip poker.   Noticing our entry on POKER, a reader asked about the origins of *strip poker*, a usually coeducational variation on the game in which the losing players in every hand have to remove an article of clothing. I can only add that the *strip* in the term is of obvious derivation and that mention of the delightful game apparently hasn't been found before 1915, almost a century after *poker* is first recorded. The game's rules vary. "Beauty is Nature's brag and must be shown," wrote Milton.

stripteaser.   *See* ECDYSIAST.

strong-arm.   A term used in America for physical violence since about 1850. The words are first recorded as a verb meaning "to use physical force" some 50 years later. *Strong-arm tactics* is a common variant.

strontium 90.   This radioactive isotope of the element strontium, found in nuclear fallout, is named for the village of Strontium in Scotland—not because of any fallout in the beautiful country, but because strontium was first discovered there in 1764.

Strulbrug. Another word coined by Jonathan Swift in *Gulliver's Travels* (1726). The *Strulbrug* therein are people who never die, always remaining mentally and physically useless, hopeless wards of the state. *See also* BROBDINGNAGIAN; LILLIPUTIAN.

strung-out. From its early use as a term for out-of-tune musical instruments—that is, harps or other stringed instruments with their strings removed or relaxed—*strung-out* came to be applied to a human body weakened and unnerved, a strung-out person being someone, usually a drug user, whose nerves and muscles have lost their natural tension and have no tone. The figurative use is an old one, too, dating back to at least the late 17th century.

stubborn as a mule. *See* BUILD A FIRE UNDER.

studied felicity. *See* GREAT MAJORITY.

stuffed as a goose. *See* FOIE GRAS.

stuffed shirt. It may be that the ladies' shirtwaists stuffed with tissue paper displayed in many department store windows at the turn of the century suggested this term for a pompous, pretentious bore who insists on formalities. Though flimsy, the shirtwaists looked imposing and inflated when stuffed with paper. Comparing a man to a lady's shirtwaist would have been an insult in itself, but we only know that the first literary use of the term is by Willa Cather in *O Pioneers!* (1913). Another possibility is that the term simply derived from similar earlier "stuffed" expressions such as *stuffed ballot*, a fraudulent ballot; *stuffed monkey*, a conceited person; and *Stuffed Prophet*, an epithet the *New York Sun* hung on Grover Cleveland when he ran for president in 1892.

stumbling block. William Tyndale apparently coined this expression when he translated Rom. 14:13 into English for his Bible in 1534, the version that fixed the tone and style of the English Bible. In Romans, Paul of Tarsus had written that a good Christian should not put a *skandalon* in his brother's path. Since the *skandalon*, a kind of hunting trap, was unfamiliar to Englishmen of the time, Tyndale changed the word to *stumbling block*, making Paul's phrase "that no man putt a stomblinge blocke . . . in his brother's way." The translator may have invented the term, or it may have been suggested to him by the earlier (1450) phrase *to stumble at a block* (a tree stump), but in any case *stumbling block* quickly became an expression for an obstacle of any kind.

stumped. *To be stumped* for "to be baffled" has its origins in the stumps that American settlers had to pull from the earth after felling trees—some stumps were so big and deep-rooted that they perplexed the pioneers. The expression is first recorded in 1812: "John Bull was a little stumped when he saw [Brother] Jonathan's challenge."

stupid water. A Comanche name for whiskey, because it made people act stupidly. Wrote Lucia St. Clair Robson in *Ride The Wind* (1982): ". . . the men of God [on the reservation] stripped the warriors of their very reason for living, war. They no longer had any way to attain status within their tribe. Whiskey, the 'stupid water' that the People had always scorned, became their solace."

Sturm und Drang. The German phrase, pronounced "stoorm und drang," means storm and stress. First applied to the revolutionary literary movement that was awakening Germany under the inspiration of Goethe and Schiller in the late 18th century, the name was suggested by the play *Wirrwarr, oder, Sturm und Drang,* (1776), a romantic drama by Friedrich Maximilian von Klinger. Its adherents, extremely nationalistic, preferred inspiration to reason and were also characterized by opposition to established forms of society. The expression is now often used to mean a time of trouble and stress in the life of a nation or individual.

style is the man. The great French naturalist author Comte de Buffon (1707–88) did not say this upon his 1753 induction into the Académie Française. What he said in his *Discourse sur le style* address was *"Le style, c'este l'homme meme"*: *Style is the man himself*. Yet "style is the man" is the way his observation is usually heard in English today.

stymie. *Stymie*, meaning to block or prevent, first recorded in 1902, had been a golfing term meaning to block the hole on the green with your ball (thus stopping an opponent from holing his ball) since at least the mid 19th century. The golfing term, in turn, may derive from the Scottish expression *not to see a stymie*, "not to see at all," recorded in the 14th century, or the Dutch *stuit mij*, "it stops."

sub rosa. According to legend, the Greek god of silence, Harpocrates, stumbled upon Venus while she was making love and Cupid, the goddess of love's son, bribed him to keep quiet about the affair by giving him the first rose ever created. This story made the rose the emblem of silence and since the fifth century B.C. a rose carved on the ceilings of dining and drawing rooms where European diplomats gathered enjoined all present to observe secrecy about any matter discussed *sub rosa*, or "under the rose." A similar phrase used at such gatherings was *sub vino sub rosa est*, "What is said under the influence of wine is secret," a reminder that things revealed by tongues made loose with wine weren't to be repeated beyond these walls. The rose was also carved over the Roman Catholic confessional as a symbol of silence and the phrase *sub rosa*, became well known in German as *unter der Rose*, in French as *sous la rose*, and in English as *under the rose* as a term for strict confidence, complete secrecy, absolute privacy. Incidentally, the ancient legend of Harpocrates was inspired by what the Greeks thought was a picture of the Egyptian god of silence, Horus, seated under a rose with a finger at his lips. Actually, the rose in the picture was a lotus and the infant god Horus was merely sucking his finger.

suburbio. A good example of an English word borrowed for another language but given a completely opposite meaning. A suburbio (from *suburb*) in Spain is a slum quarter or shantytown in a city.

succotash. The first succotash was made by American Indians, who cooked corn and beans together in bear grease. Colonists used the word in the early 18th century, if not before then, and it apparently derives from the Narraganset Indian *misickquatash*, meaning "an ear of corn," or the Narraganset *manusqussedash*, "beans."

succubus. *See* NIGHTMARE.

suck eggs. *See* TEACH YOUR GRANDMOTHER TO SUCK EGGS.

sucker. The origin of the word *sucker*, for "a dupe or easily tricked person," is a mystery. One theory holds that the slang word comes from the name of one of the many American freshwater fishes called *suckers* because they have lips that suggest that they feed by suction. Several of these fish are easily caught and might have suggested an easily hooked or hoodwinked person. But the word, first recorded in 1831, could just as well derive from *sucker* in the sense of a not-yet-weaned animal, with the *sucker's* naïveté reminiscent of the innocence of a child still sucking at its mother's breast.

sucks. *See* COOL.

suck the hind tit. The runt of a pig litter feeding on the last teat of a sow suggested this old rural term meaning "to get the worst of something, have the worst position."

Sudan. Sudan's name translates as "land of the blacks," in reference to the dark-skinned people who live there.

sudden death. *Sudden death* is sometimes used today to mean a fight to the finish (but not death) of any kind. It is mainly confined to football, where it indicates an overtime period in which a tied game is won by the team that scores first. There are sudden death periods in hockey and soccer, too, but in basketball, the sport where the practice probably originated, overtime periods of a certain time duration are now played instead.

suede. *Gants de Suède*, or "gloves from Sweden," is what the French called the rough-surfaced gloves made in Sweden that were popular in Paris during the 19th century. The English abbreviated the name to *suede* and used it to describe similar leather made anywhere.

Suffrage State. *See* EQUALITY STATE.

sugar. The sweetener sugar, made mainly from sugarcane and beet sugar, takes its name from Persian *sukkar* for the same. First recorded as *zuker* in 1299, it has since the 1850s meant "money" and can be a welcome or unwelcome form of address from a man to a woman. *Sugar coat* means "to make something more palatable or acceptable." "Did you know that *sugar* and *sumac* are the only two words in English that begin with *su* and are pronounced *shu*?" historian B. H. Liddell Hart said to George Bernard Shaw. "Sure," replied Shaw.

Sugar Bowl. A college football end-of-season game held in New Orleans since 1936 and so named because the annual trophy is an antique sugar bowl. Also a nickname for Louisiana, famous for its output of sugar.

sugar daddy. A wealthy man, usually middle-aged or older, who supports and spends money freely on a young woman in the hope of sexual favors in return. The expression is American in origin, first recorded about 1915. Also called a "daddy," which can mean a prostitute's lover, or a sweetheart, as well.

sugared. *See* AIR BALL.

Sugar Loaf. The name of various hills and mountains in the U. S. The term derives from the cone-shaped loaves of sugar people used in olden times. A ski resort in Maine also shares the name, as does a mountain in Rio de Janeiro. *Sugar Hill* is a wealthy black neighborhood in New York City's Harlem.

suicide; suicide bomber; suicide squad; suicide charge; suicide mission; bomber. The word *suicide* derives from Latin *sui*, "of oneself," plus *cide*, "killer," but *suicide bomber* refers to a killer of far more than oneself. Though *suicide bomber* refers to terrorists like those who destroyed the World Trade Center on September 11, 2001, and killed thousands of civilians, the name was first recorded in 1981 when it was used to describe a terrorist who drove a car bomb into the Iraqi Embassy in Lebanon. Before this, in Vietnam, groups of Vietcong who raided behind American lines with little or no chance of getting back were called suicide squads. In World War II Japanese soldiers were sent on suicide charges, and Japanese kamikaze pilots were described as going on suicide missions. In World War I *suicide club* was a "humorous term for various specialist formations such as bombers, machine gunners, etc., whose work was exceptionally dangerous," according to the *O.E.D. Bomber* in the *suicide club* quote refers to a soldier who throws bombs; as the example from the *O.E.D.* explains: "The bombers . . . seizing one of these rocket-like bombs from their belts . . . hurl them high above the parapet [of the trench]." *Bomber* in the sense of a terrorist using bombs to kill was first recorded in 1927, *bomb* being from Greek *bombos*, of imitative origin. *See* WHAT CATO DID . . . ; TERRORIST.

suicide by cop. A recent phenomenon in which one commits some violent act or acts, expecting and hoping that a policeman or other law enforcement officer will kill one in responding to the violence.

suicide gun. Cowboys early in this century called the Colt .32 (and similar guns) a suicide gun because it lacked the power to stop an assailant dead in his tracks and thus often led to the death of the man who fired it.

suicide pact; the Constitution is not a suicide pact. The phrase *suicide pact*, an agreement between two or more people to commit suicide together, dates back to about 1910. The second phrase is much younger. According to Linda Greenhouse, writing in the *New York Times* (9/22/02): "Supreme Court cognoscenti usually attribute the phrase [*the Constitution is not a suicide pact*] to Justice Robert H. Jackson's dissent in a 1949 free-speech case, *Terminiello v. Chicago*. The court's majority opinion, by Justice William O. Douglas, had overturned the disorderly conduct conviction of a right-wing priest whose anti-

Semitic, pro-Nazi rantings at a rally had incited a riot. Chicago's breach-of-the-peace ordinance violated the First Amendment, the court held. Where his colleagues saw free speech, Jackson, after serving as a judge at the Nuremburg war crimes trial, saw the dangers of the mob. He countered the four-page ruling with a 24-page dissent ending: "The choice is not between order and liberty. It is between liberty with order and anarchy without either. There is danger that, if the court does not temper its doctrinaire logic with a little practical wisdom, it will convert the constitutional Bill of Rights into a suicide pact."

suits.   An often derogatory term, first used in Hollywood for studio executives, that is now used to describe all business executives. It derives of course from the wearing of a suit, skirt, tie, etc., especially at work.

suits you to a "T."   Most dictionaries attribute the expression to the accuracy of the draftsman's T-square, but this is impossible, according to the *O.E.D.*—for the phrase was around many years before the T-square got its name. The expression has been used to indicate exactness or perfection since at least the early 17th century and is probably an abbreviation of the older expression, *to a tittle. Tittle* or *titil* was the English name for small strokes or points made in writing the letters of the alphabet, a corruption of the word seen today in the Spanish *tilde.* Thus *to a tittle* meant to a dot, precisely, and was used this way more than a century before someone shortened it to *to a T.*

sulky.   The sulky carriage takes its name from sulky people. The light, two-wheeled carriage, which is principally used in harness racing today, seats only one person. Those who drove them in the 19th century were presumed to be aloof, and the carriage was named for these "sulky" people who preferred to be alone. The first quote using the word (1756) tells of "a formal female seated in a Sulky, foolishly pleased with having the whole vehicle to herself." The word *sulky* itself may come from the Old Frisian word *sultig* meaning the same, and *sulk* is a back-formation of sulky.

Sultan of Swat.   Baseball's Babe Ruth, whose name itself is of course a synonym for a great slugger, was called the *Sultan of Swat*—but not only because he swatted the ball. There was a real Sultan of Swat (a small country now part of Pakistan) whose name was well known thanks to a poem by Edward Lear: "Who, or why, or which, or what/ Is the Akhoond [Sultan] of Swat?" The alliterative name probably appealed to some sportswriter in the early 1920s as a natural for the "Bambino" (which Ruth was dubbed when he joined the Boston Red Sox as a pitcher in 1914 when only 19).

Sumerian words in English.   *See* HAMAL.

summer soldier and sunshine patriot; times that try men's souls.   Thomas Paine's famous words first appeared in *The American Crisis*, December 23, 1776: "These are the times that try men's souls. The summer soldier and the sunshine patriot will, in this crisis, shrink from the service of their country; but he that stands it now, deserves the love and thanks of man and woman." Paine was writing of men who supported the Revolution only when things were going well, some of whom served short summer enlistments when soldiering was comfortable. The great sloganeer also coined the expressions *the rights of man, the government is best which governs least, the age of reason,* and many other stirring phrases. His revolutionary book *Common Sense* is said to have been read on average by one in seven Americans at the time. *See* UNITED STATES OF AMERICA.

sunbeam.   A ray or rays of sunlight. The term would have been *column of light,* but the ninth-century translator of the Venerable Bede's *Historia Ecclesiastica Gentis Anglorum (The Ecclesiastical History of the English People),* written in Latin in 731, could not translate the Latin phrase *columna lucis,* "column of light," having no word for *column* in his Old English vocabulary. Instead, he used *sunne* for *lucis* and *beam,* which meant "a building post," for *columna,* making the new word *sunnebeam,* this eventually becoming *sunbeam.*

sundae.   Wisconsin ice-cream-parlor owner George Giffy probably first called this concoction, which he did not invent, a *Sunday* back in the early 1890s because he regarded it as a special dish only to be sold on Sundays. No one knows exactly why or when *Sunday* was changed to *sundae.*

Sunday.   The first day of the week, the *sunnendaeg,* "Sunday," of the Anglo-Saxons, was so called because the day was dedicated to the sun in ancient times.

Sunday best; Sunday-go-to-meeting clothes; Sunday face. *Sunday best* refers to a person's best clothes, those reserved for going to church. The term is still common over a century after it was first recorded in 1849. A humorous version of the phrase is *Sunday-go-to-meeting clothes,* first recorded in 1831. *Sunday face* means "a sanctimonious expression," the term, if not the expression, all but obsolete.

Sunday driver.   A poor driver, one who drives only on Sundays and often stops or slows down to "see the sights." The term was common before the 1920s and continues to be used today.

Sunday punch.   A fighter's best punch, often a knockout blow. The expression is patterned on SUNDAY BEST and was first recorded in 1931. In baseball a Sunday punch is a pitcher's strong, overpowering fastball.

Sunday's child.   *See* MONDAY'S CHILD.

The sun don't shine on the same dog's ass each day.   A saying, probably from the Midwest, meaning "we all have our day in the sun, don't assume the sun will always shine on you and not your opponent."

sunflower.   Sunflowers are so named because they resemble the full sun, not because they follow the direction of the sun during the day. *Helianthus* actually turns in every direction whether the sun is out or not. The word sunflower was coined toward the middle of the 17th century.

suni.   A rare word for a rare little antelope that is only about a foot high and weighs about 10 pounds. *Suni* is the only word from the Chaga language of Tanzania that has come into

English. Also called a bushbuck, the little antelope is quite a pest to Tanzanian farmers. The animals can be viewed in several U.S. zoos.

The sun never sets on the British Empire. Contrary to popular notion, this saying, which used to describe the world-wide empire of the British, originated with the Spanish. Long before the first British use of the term, in 1829 by Christopher North (a pen name of John Wilson) in *Blackwood's Magazine*, Giovanni Guarini, in *Il Pastor Fido* (1590) celebrated Spain's Philip II as "that proud monarch to whom when it grows dark [elsewhere], the sun never sets." It was also used by the English explorer John Smith in 1631, in the form of "the sun never sets in the Spanish dominions."

sunshine patriot. *See* SUMMER SOLDIER AND SUNSHINE PATRIOT.

Sunshine State. This is Florida's official nickname (at least it is on state license plates), but its nicknames the Everglade State and the Peninsula State are a century older. New Mexico shares the nickname the Sunshine State with Florida and adopted it in 1926. New Mexico has also been called the Cactus State, the Land of the Cactus, the Spanish State, the Land of the Montezumas, the Land of the Delight Makers, the Land of Opportunity, the Land of Enchantment, and the Land of Heart's Desire.

supercalifragilisticexpialidocious. This word, from a song in the film *Mary Poppins*, may be the longest (34 letters) commonly used word of all time. It means the greatest, the best of all. There are many far, far longer words, but no longer word has been spoken or sung by so many people. In fact, the only rival that comes even close is *antidisestablishmentarianism*, which many people think (falsely) is the longest English word.

supercilious. *See* HIGHBROW.

superman. George Bernard Shaw, not Friedrich Nietzsche, coined *superman*, never expecting a movie to be made of him. The German philosopher's word for a dominant man above good or evil, introduced in *Thus Spake Zarathustra* (1883–91), was *Übermensch*, "overman" or "beyondman." Shaw didn't like the sound of Nietzsche's word and so translated its German prefix *über* into the Latin *super-* then added to it the English *man*, translated from the German *Mensch*. Shaw used the new word for the first time in his play *Man and Superman* (1903). The term was widely popularized by an American comic book character of the same name who made his debut in the 1930s. *See* KAL-EL.

supermarket. The world's first supermarket was the A & P, the Great Atlantic and Pacific Tea Co., which was founded by tea merchant George Huntington Hartford in 1859 in New York City and had stores across the country by 1917. But the word *supermarket* didn't come into the language until the early 1920s in California. It was probably first applied to one of the stores in the Piggly-Wiggly self-service chain.

supermodel; model; superstar. The term *supermodel* for an internationally famous model wasn't coined in 1977 to describe

Margaux Hemingway, as several sources report. According to word hunter Barry Popik, the word first described Naomi Sims in a 1972 number of *Vogue* magazine. *Model*, in its present sense of one who models clothes (not an artist's model), dates back to at least 1904. Popik has also traced the term *superstar* to the sports world, not motion pictures, claiming it was first used by hockey commentator Stan Fischler in the mid-1960s. *See* STAR.

Supreme Example of Allied Confusion. This World War II American and British term, originating with American soldiers and sailors, was a sarcastic play on the initials SEAC, which stood for the *South East Asia Command.*

sure. Ultimately from Latin *securus*, "secure," and first recorded about 1300. *See* SUGAR.

sure as eggs is eggs. This 17th-century expression, for "a certainty," almost certainly has no connection with eggs. *Eggs* here is probably a corruption of X in a mathematical formula, the expression originally being *as sure as X is X.*

sure as God made little green apples. Though a very popular song includes this line in its lyrics, the phrase is an Americanism dating back to at least 1909, when it first appeared in print. It means, of course, something positive, a sure thing.

sure as shootin'. An Americanism meaning "for certain" that is first recorded in the mid-19th century, possibly as a euphemism for *sure as shit.*

surfing; surfboarding. *Surfing* is a recent term for using a television remote control to switch from channel to channel to see what is playing or to escape relentless unimaginative commercials. The term is apparently based on surfing with *a surfboard*, a word that dates back to about 1826.

surly. In medieval times a man who conducted himself admirably, like a knight, was called *sirly*, that is, "like a sir," even if he wasn't strictly speaking a *sir*, a title reserved for knights and baronets. The spelling changed to "surly" over the years and the meaning of *surly* changed from "knightly" to "arrogant" and finally "rude" as knighthood and its emulators faded out of flower and fashion.

surname. A family name (from the prefix *sur*, "over, above" plus name) as distinguished from a given, first, or Christian (to Christians) name. The term dates back to the 16th century in England. The English seem to have been the first to use surnames as given names, two of the best-known examples being *Rudyard* Kipling and *Aldous* Huxley.

surrey. The two-seated, four-wheeled carriage, still well-known in America from the popular old song "The Surrey with the Fringe on Top," takes its name from the county of Surrey in England, where it first was made in Victorian days.

surround. *Surround* derives not from *round*, but from the Latin *unda*, "a wave." *Unda* yielded the Latin *undare*, "to move in waves," which produced *superundare*, "to overflow." *Superundare* yielded the Medieval French *suronder*, "to overflow," a word with which English speakers associated the English word *round* and gave it its present meaning.

survival of the fittest. The term was coined not by Charles Darwin but by British philosopher Herbert Spencer. "This survival of the fittest which I have here sought to express in mechanical terms, is that which Mr. Darwin has called 'natural selection, or the preservation of favored races in the struggle for life,' " Spencer wrote in his *Principles of Biology* (1864–67). Darwin approved of Spencer's coinage in his epochal *On the Origin of the Species by Means of Natural Selection* (1859), which sold out on the day it was printed. Spencer was the founder of evolutionary philosophy, his ideal being the unification of all knowledge on the basis of the single all-providing principle of evolution.

sushi. Japanese sushi bars have found great popularity in America within the last 30 years, and the word *sushi* has become familiar to many Americans. *Sushi* means "it is sour," referring to the vinegar and other ingredients used in making it. It is often composed of cold rice molded into small pieces and topped with raw seafood (*sashimi*). In sushi bars diners enjoy raw fish like *maguro* (tuna); jellyfish cut into strips like spaghetti; and a kind of shrimp (*ebi*) that is eaten whole still alive and wiggling. Of the *ebi* the Japanese particularly relish a squirming delicacy called *ebi odori*, which is made by shelling, gutting, and splitting a shrimp down the middle—the creature's nerves are still functioning when it is pressed into a small ball of rice that doesn't stop trembling until it is popped into the mouth.

Susie stroke. The backstroke in swimming. The stroke is named after Susie O'Neill, the popular Australian swimmer who perfected and help popularize it. *See* TRUGEN STROKE; AUSTRALIAN CRAWL.

suttee. *Suttee* is the old Hindu custom of burning the widow on the funeral pyre of her husband, a custom also found in other cultures around the world. The word *suttee* derives from the Sanskrit *sati*, "a virtuous wife." The practice was practically obligatory by custom for 2,000 years but was outlawed in British India in 1829. Its purpose was purportedly to help the souls of both husband and wife in the next world, but its use is not supported by the Vedic texts that its adherents cited to condone the practice.

Svengali. *Svengali*, a common word unaccountably omitted from many dictionaries, means someone who controls other people and forces them to do as he wishes. The word comes from the assumed name of a Hungarian musician in George Louis Du Maurier's *Trilby* (1894) who hypnotizes the heroine, gaining complete control over her. *See* TRILBY HAT.

swab. Some 300 years ago a *swab* meant a merchant seaman, probably deriving from the Dutch *swabbe*, "mop," in reference to sailors swabbing or mopping the decks. Before that, as far back as 1592, sailors who cleaned the decks were called *swabbers*. *Swabbie*, related to both these terms, came into use in the late 19th century.

Swahili. *Swahili* is not spoken by more Africans than any other language, as is widely believed. This record is held by Hausa, spoken in Nigeria and other parts of West Africa, with some 25 million speakers in all, many of its words borrowed from Arabic. But Swahili, more correctly called *Kiswahili*, with more than 10 million speakers, is the most important language of East Africa, being the official language of Kenya and Tanzania, while spoken fluently in many other countries as a second language. Basically its vocabulary is Bantu but there are many Arabic borrowings. *Swahili* itself derives from an Arabic word meaning coastal, the language having developed in the seventh century among Arabic-speaking settlers of the African coast.

swallow. *See* ONE SWALLOW DOES NOT A SUMMER MAKE.

swallow the anchor. Some old salt coined this expression meaning "to retire from the sea," but it is now used for retirement in general. The phrase is thought to have originated among British liner officers.

Swamp Fox. General Francis Marion (ca. 1732–95), one of America's first war heroes, hid with his men in the South Carolina swamps whenever he encountered formidable British forces during the American Revolution. There he continued practicing the guerrilla warfare for which he became famous and earned the name *Swamp Fox* history remembers him by.

Swanee River. The first line in Stephen Foster's famous song "The Old Folks at Home" should go "Way down upon the Suwannee River," for there is no Swanee River. The American composer first considered the Pedee and Zazoo Rivers, but settled on the Suwannee for his song after consulting an atlas. Needing a two-syllable name, he changed *Suwanee* to *Swanee*. Had he seen the Suwannee, he might not have immortalized it. Running through swamps for most of its course in Georgia and Florida, the Suwannee's water is coffee black. Originally it was called the San Juan, which was corrupted into Suwannee by constant mispronunciation.

swan song; Swan of Avon; Swan of Meander, etc. The swan makes no sound other than a hiss when it is angry, but the ancient Greeks thought that the mute bird broke its lifelong silence with one last melodious song just before it died. This *swan song*, according to Socrates, was a happy one, for the dying bird, sacred to Apollo, knew that it would soon be joining its master. The superstition, embraced by poets through the ages, led to the use of swan song to mean a person's last, eloquent words or performance. Shakespeare was called the Swan of Avon; Homer was called the Swan of Meander, and Virgil the Mantuan Swan because Apollo, the god of poetry and song, was fabled to have been changed into a swan and the souls of all poets were at one time thought to pass into the bodies of swans after death. Still other "swans" of literature include: the Swan of Padua, Francesco Algarotti; the Swan of the Thames, John Taylor; the Swan of Usk, Henry Vaughn; and the Swan of Lichfield, Anna Vaughan. *See* BARDS.

Swartwout. Samuel Swartwout (1783–1856), collector of the port of New York in Andrew Jackson's administration, stole more than $1 million of public funds and fled to England. Thus *Swartwout* came to mean an embezzler and *to Swartwout* to embezzle or abscond.

swashbuckler.   Today's swashbucklers are action-packed, romantic films or novels featuring much sword-play. The word, in its oldest sense, means a swaggering show-off and was used this way in Elizabethan times. A buckler was a small shield used to catch the sword blows of an opponent and to *swash* meant to dash against. But swashbucklers weren't always good swordsmen and often ran when the going got tough. *See* PIRATES; WALK THE PLANK.

swear like a trooper.   The theatrical profession has been chastised for its vigorous swearing in times past, but this phrase *wasn't* originally *swear like a trouper*. It dates back almost two centuries, to a time when British cavalrymen were noted for their profanity. English soldiers, or troopers, had in fact been famous for their blasphemy since long before Shakespeare's soldier, the fourth of his seven ages of man, "Full of strange oaths and bearded like the bard."

sweaters.   The first garments called sweaters were heavy blankets fashioned to fit around a racehorse's body that trainers in the early 19th century used to induce profuse sweating during a workout on the track. The word is first recorded in this sense in 1828 and it was another 30 years before *sweater* was used to mean flannel underclothing that athletes wore when trying to work off weight. Finally, in 1882, the word *sweater* was applied to a woolen vest or jersey worn in rowing or other athletic activities, the direct ancestor of the sweater we know today.

sweatshop.   *Sweatshop*, for "clothing factories where people work long hours for little pay," is first recorded in 1892 in America, but the seed of the expression can be found in Henry Mayhew's *London Labour and the London Poor* (1851–61): "I have many a time heard both husband and wife . . . who were sweating for a gorgeous clothes' emporium, say that they had not time to clean."

Swede.   *Swede*, or *dumb Swede*, is American slang for a dope or a blunderer, a stupid person. Swedish-Americans have not fared well in the American-English language, also being called by such endearing terms as *square heads*, *box-heads*, and SCANDAHOOVIANS. Notre Dame football coach Knute Rockne, born in Norway, famously, or infamously, said of Swedes: "What's dumber than a dumb Irishman? A smart Swede." *See* RUTABAGA.

Sweden.   Sweden is named for the Suiones, a native tribe that became dominant in the country by the sixth century A.D.

sweepstakes.   *Sweepstake* is recorded as the name of a ship a century before its first mention as a gambling term in 1593, but no one has been able to connect the ship with the word in any way (or even explain the name of the ship!). *Sweepstakes* originally meant "winner take all," as if the winner *swept* all the *stakes* into his pocket after winning a game or race, but later a number of winners in sweepstakes, such as the Irish Sweepstakes have had to divide the stakes among them.

Sweet Adeline.   The "Sweet Adeline" in the song of the same name was originally "Sweet Rosalie." Songwriters Richard Gerard and Henry Armstrong wrote "You're the Flower of My Heart, Sweet Rosalie" in 1903, tried to sell it, and couldn't. When they decided to name the song's heroine in honor of popular prima donna Adelina Patti and shortened the title to "Sweet Adeline," it sold and eventually became the barbershop quartet hit of all time.

the sweet death.   Dating back to the 19th century, this expression refers to death while having sexual intercourse. The first person recorded to die the sweet death is Attila the Hun. Attila, said to be a dwarf, died in the arms of a Brunhildean blonde.

sweeten the kitty.   In the game of faro the "tiger" was the bank of the house, possibly because the tiger was once used on signs marking the entrance to Chinese gambling houses. Gamblers called the tiger a kitty, and it also became the name for the "pot" in poker and other card games. By the late 19th century *sweeten* or *fatten the kitty* had become a common expression for adding chips to the pot in a poker game or for increasing the payment in any business deal.

sweet Fanny Adams.   Fanny Adams was murdered and mutilated in 1812, her body cut into pieces and thrown into the River Wey at Alton in Hampshire. Her murderer, one Fred Baker, was publicly hanged in Winchester. Young Fanny Adams's name, given wide currency, was adopted by sailors to indicate a particularly distasteful meal, since Fanny Adams had been disposed of in a kettle. In fact, when kettles came into use in the British navy they were dubbed *Fannys* as were tins or cans of meat. There is no doubt that Fanny Adams is the basis for the military expression *sweet Fanny Adams*, meaning something worthless or nothing at all.

sweetheart contract.   Sweetheart contracts are contracts made with favored employers by labor unions in return for similar favors. This term first came into use in about 1900, when it was applied to favoritism by public officials in awarding contracts without open bidding, those who received the contracts making kickbacks and supporting the political machine.

sweetness and light.   Jonathan Swift invented this perennial phrase in his preface to *The Battle of the Books* (1697). Swift took the figure from the beehive when comparing the merits of the bee (the ancients) with the spider (the moderns): "The difference is that instead of dirt and poison, we have chosen to fill our hives with honey and wax, thus furnishing mankind with the two noblest things, which are sweetness and light." Later, Matthew Arnold, in *Culture and Anarchy* (1869), regarded these as the basic contribution of the artist and the basis of culture itself: "He who works for sweetness and light united, works to make reason and the will of God prevail."

sweet talk; sweet mouth.   Sweet talk is smooth, unctuous flattery designed to win over a person. There is no proof of it, but this southern Americanism possibly comes from Krio, an English-based Creole of Sierra Leone, specifically from the expression *swit mot*, sweet mouth, for "flattery." To *sweet mouth* someone is the opposite of to *bad-mouth* him.

sweet william.   The English named this flower sweet william after William, duke of Cumberland, who in 1746 defeated the Scots at the Battle of Culloden. The Scots of course feel quite different about the man and call the same flower the stinky billy.

Swiftian. Merciless, bitter, biting satire is called Swiftian after Johathan Swift (1667–1745), British author of *Gulliver's Travels* (1726) and many other trenchant satires.

swim fins. Benjamin Franklin was America's first great swimmer and he even taught the sport in his early years. It was then that he invented and named swim fins, not the least of his myriad inventions, considering the fun these flippers have brought to millions.

swindle. *Swindler*, deriving from the German *Schwindler*, "a giddy person," first meant a merchant who took "dizzy risks" that often led to the loss of money. *Swindler* soon came to mean "someone who made money disappear," hence a cheat.

Swiss chard. Chard is a variety of beet that is cultivated for its leaves and stalks. It apparently takes its name from the French *chardon*, "thistle," a word closely related to the Latin word for thistle. *Swiss chard* is the most famous variety.

switchel. *Switchel* is old sailor's slang for a very thirst-quenching drink of molasses and water seasoned with vinegar and ginger. However, the word has been used in contexts referring to alcoholic drinks as in Jeremiah N. Reynold's 1835 account of a whale hunt for Mocha Dick, the prototype of Herman Melville's Moby-Dick. Therefore, switchel almost surely was commonly seasoned with rum, as several writers suggest. Unfortunately, the origin of the word, first recorded in a 1700 poem by Philip Freneau, is unknown, but there is a spiritless recipe: Mix together one gallon water, two cups sugar, one cup molasses, one cup vinegar, one teaspoon ginger, and "hang in the well to cool." Add what you want to make it spiritous.

switch-hitter. There have been switch-hitters (hitters who can bat left-handed or right-handed) in professional baseball since at least 1870 when Robert V. Ferguson of the Brooklyn Atlanters batted this way. But the term switch-hitter may not have been coined until the 1920s. The word is now used generally to mean a versatile person and is also slang for a bisexual person.

swive. *Swive* or *swyve*, related to *swerve* and used by Chaucer and many English writers, was an early synonym for sexual congress. There was no shame attached to the expression; in fact, a 17th-century Scottish translation of the Book of Genesis, with all its "begots," was called the *Buke of Swiving*. The *O.E.D.* tells us of an old ballad about Richard of Alemaigne, a legendary king of Germany who "spend al is treasour opon swyving."

sword of Damocles. "Uneasy lies the head that wears a crown." Both Cicero and Horace tell the story of the flatterer Damocles, a fifth-century court follower of Dionysius I (405–367 B.C.), the Elder of Syracuse. Damocles annoyed Dionysius with his constant references to the ruler's great power and consequent happiness. Deciding to teach the sycophant the real perils of power, he invited Damocles to a magnificent banquet, surrounding him with luxuries that only a king could afford. Damocles enjoyed the feast until he happened to glance up and see a sharp sword suspended by a single hair pointing directly at his head, after which he lay there cowering, afraid to eat, speak, or move. The lesson was that there are always threats of danger, fears, and worries that prevent the powerful from fully enjoying their power, and the expression *sword of Damocles* has come to symbolize these fears. The phrase also gives us our expression *to* HANG BY A THIN THREAD, to be subject to imminent danger.

sybarite. One ancient Sybarite, legend says, complained to his host that he could not sleep at night because there was a rose petal under his body. Inhabitants of the Greek colony of Sybaris on the Gulf of Tarantum in southern Italy, the Sybarites were noted among the Greeks for their love of luxury and sensuousness, and to some extent for their effeminacy and wantonness, all qualities associated with the word *sybarite* today. The fertile land of Sybaris, founded in the sixth century B.C., made luxurious living possible, but too many pleasures weakened the people. The neighboring Crotons, assisting the Troezenians, whom the Greeks had earlier ejected from the city, destroyed Sybaris in 510 B.C., diverting the river Crathis to cover its ruins. It is said that the Sybarites had trained their horses to dance to pipes and that Crotons played pipes as they marched upon them, creating such disorder among their rivals that they easily won the battle. The city of Thurii was later built on or near the site of Sybaris.

sycophant. The old story, incapable of proof but widely accepted, is that this word for an APPLE-POLISHER originated in ancient Greece from the Greek *sukophantes* (*sukon*, "fig," and *phainen*, "to show"), which meant an informer on those who exported figs. At one time it was supposedly against the law to export figs from Athens, and *sukophantes*, or *sycophants*, often turned in violators of the unpopular law for their own personal gain, these toadies being widely despised.

syllabus. *Syllabus* began life as a printer's error in a 15th-century edition of Cicero's *Epistles to the Atticans*. In this work Cicero had written *indices . . . quos vos Graeci . . . sittubas appelatis*, meaning "indexes, which were called *sittubas* by the Greeks." The printer misprinted *syllabos* for *sittubas* and *syllabos*, later slightly changed to *syllabus* (instead of *sittubas*), became a synonym for index. Its meaning of index or table of contents was later expanded to mean "an outline or other brief statement of a discourse, the contents of a curriculum, etc."

synagogue. The Hebrew *keneseth*, "assembly," from *kanas*, "to collect or assemble," was translated into Greek in ancient times as *synagoge*, which eventually became the Latin *synagoga*. The Latin yielded the English *synagogue* for "a Jewish house of worship."

syphilis. "MRS. GRUNDY's disease" is on the increase in America and throughout the world. Over the ages it has claimed millions, often due to ignorance and superstition, its victims including Herod, Julius Caesar, three popes, Magellan, Columbus, Capt. James Cook, Louis XIV, Henry VIII, Keats, Baudelaire, Schubert, Schumann, Goya, Nietzsche, de Sade, Goethe,

Beethoven, Ivan the Terrible, Napoleon, and Lord Randolph Churchill. The disease has gone by many names through history and *wasn't* first contracted among natives in the New World; in fact, it may have been described by Thucydides as far back as 430 B.C. as "the plague of Pireaus." The word *syphilis* itself derives from the name of a character in Girolamo Fracastro's poem *Syphilis sive Morbus Gallicus*, "Syphilis, or the French Disease" (1530). This New World fable tells of the blasphemous shepherd Syphilis who so enraged the Sun God that he struck him with a "new" disease: "He first wore buboes dreadful to the sight,/First felt strange pains and sleepless past the night;/From him the malady received its name."

syringa. In days past, the stems of this plant were used in making pipes. Because the stems resembled hollow reeds, the attractive, fragrant, ornamental bush was named from the Greek *syringos*, "reed." The syringa (*Philadelphus coronarius*) is also called the "mock orange." Linnaeus named the genus *Philadelphus* after King Ptolemy Philadelphus, who ruled Egypt in the third century B.C.

T

T. Today's *T* is a modification of the earlier form *X* for the letter. In Hebrew it is called *taw*, and in Greek, *tau*. *T* or *tau* was in ancient times the last letter of the Greek alphabet (as it remains in Hebrew) and thus in medieval times the common expression *alpha to omega*, "including everything," was often rendered as *alpha to tau*.

Tabasco. The condiment sauce's name, which is a trademark, was apparently first applied to a potent liquor once popular in the American Southwest. The liquor, in turn, took its name from the state of Tabasco in Mexico.

tabby cat. Prince Attab, famed in Arab legend, lived in a quarter of old Baghdad named Attabiya in his honor. Here a striped silk taffeta material was woven, the streaked fabric called *attabi* by the Arabs after the quarter, *attabi* eventually being transformed to *tabis* in French during the Middle Ages and translated in English as *tabby cloth*. *Tabby* became a verb for "to stripe" soon after, and by 1695 the word was used to describe a brownish dark-striped or brindled tabby cat whose markings resembled the material. Old maids were also called tabbies, and this may have been because they often kept tabby cats and shared their careful habits, but the word for a spinster is more likely a pet form of Tabitha.

table d'hôte. This French term was borrowed by the English almost four centuries ago. Literally, it means "table of the host" and it originally meant a common table from which guests ate at a hotel. From this it came to mean the complete meal served at a hotel or restaurant.

tabloid. *Tabloid* was originally a trademark for a pill compressing several medicines into one tablet made by Great Britain's Burroughs, Wellcome and Company. The *Westminster Gazette* used the word for the title of a new newspaper it published in 1902 and won a court case in which the pharmaceutical company claimed that the word was private property. Though the first paper called a tabloid appeared in 1902, all of the journalistic practices associated with tabloids are much older.

taboo. The Friendly Islands (now Tonga) were visited by the great English explorer Captain James Cook in 1777. It is in Cook's journals that we find the first recorded use of *taboo* for something banned or prohibited. Cook had taken it, altering the spelling a little, from the Tongan *tabu*, meaning the same. He later lost his life for violating a taboo, being murdered by natives in Hawaii. Etymologist Alfred Holt reported seeing a dead-end street in Honolulu in 1920 that, instead of reading Dead End, bore the sign TAPU.

Tad. A good number of references are found in these pages to T(homas) A(loysius) D(organ) (1877–1929), the great American cartoonist better known as "Tad" to millions of newspaper readers early in the 20th century. Dorgan, born in a San Francisco tenement, taught himself to draw with his left hand when at the age of 13 an accident deprived him of the use of his right hand. He worked for a time on San Francisco newspapers, but his great fame came when William Randolph Hearst hired him away to New York. "Judge Rummy," "Silk Hat Harry," and many of Tad's characters, all dogs in human dress, became household words in America, and Dorgan was recognized as the country's most prolific and original coiner of words and catchphrases. If there is a writer anywhere who invented more lasting words and expressions than Dorgan, I've missed him. Just for the record, here are some of the most memorable ones, a good number of which are described at length in these pages. Many were listed by humorist S. J. Perelman, a student and early admirer of Tad, in a *New York Times Magazine* article: HOT DOG; YES-MAN; dumbhead; APPLESAUCE (for insincere flattery); *drugstore cowboy; lounge-lizard; chin music* (pointless talk); *the once-over; the cat's meow;* PRESS NOTICE; 23-SKIDDOO; *flat tire;* FOR CRYING OUT LOUD; *Officer, call a cop;* YES, WE HAVE NO BANANAS; *the first hundred years are the hardest* (sometimes credited to Wilson Mizner); *see what the boys in the back room will have; the only place you'll find sympathy is in the dictionary; half the world are squirrels and the other half are nuts; as busy as a one-armed paperhanger with the hives* (sometimes attributed to O. Henry, who in a 1908 story wrote: "Busy as a one-armed man with the nettle rash pasting on wallpaper").

tadpole. *Tade* was an early spelling for "toad," and *pol* meant "head" in 17th-century speech. Therefore, *tadpole* means toad head, an appropriate name for the early stage of a frog when it is little more than a big head with a small tail. The synonym *polliwog* comes from *pol*, "head," and "*wiglen*," "to wiggle," meaning "wiggle head."

tail between the legs. *See* WITH TAIL BETWEEN LEGS.

Taj Mahal. Shah Jahan built the magnificent Taj Mahal to commemorate his favorite wife, Mumtaz Mahal, whose title was Taj Mahal, Crown of the Palace. The mausoleum near Agra, India was begun by the Turkish or Persian architect Ustad Isa three years after Mumtaz died in 1632 and completed by about 1650, nearly 20 years later. The royal lovers are buried in a vault beneath the floor in the octagonal tomb chamber, surrounded by what many consider to be the finest example of romantic architecture in the world. If any structure proves that beauty can be the sole function of a building, it is this spectacular edifice, which is actually more a sculpture than architecture. The great tomb, the luxurious gardens, even the four 133-foot-high minarets at the great tomb's corners, were all built for beauty alone, at a cost of some $15 million.

take a bath. American slang meaning "to take a great financial loss," to lose everything or close to everything in a business venture. Someone who takes a bath financially is stripped of everything, as a person taking a bath is stripped of his clothes. The expression dates back only to the 1930s, when someone who took such a bath was said to be "in the tub." More recently, *take a bath* has come to be applied to any complete failure. The older phrase TAKE TO THE CLEANERS is similar but has the sense of fraudulent means being used to effect the loss.

take a leaf out of one's book. These words are never used literally for "plagiarism," to my knowledge. *To take a leaf out of one's book* is simply a figurative expression meaning to imitate another person. It is usually highly complimentary to the person aped, for it means he is a model for whatever you wish to do, that he succeeds at it so well that it is best to do it his way. The expression is first recorded in 1809, but the saying it appears to derive from, *to turn over a new leaf*, "to reform," goes all the way back to Holinshed's *Chronicle of England, Scotland and Ireland* (1577). In the earlier phrase the leaves or pages are from a book of lessons or precepts.

take a powder. Nobody agrees about the origins of this slang phrase but there are some wonderful explanations. To *take a powder* means to leave quickly, flee, take off, beat it, dust off, take it on the lam. *Powder* has been used in the sense of "to rush" since the early 17th century, deriving its meaning from the rapid explosiveness of gun-powder ("Cacheus climb'd the Tree: But O how fast . . . he powder'd down agen," 1632). But the phrase seems to date back only to the 1920s, when it was first *take a run-out powder*. One possibility is that it was suggested by the dust (or powder) of a person fleeing down the road, another that "flee" suggested "flea" and thus "flea powder." The most ingenious theory is that the *powder* in the expression represents the "moving" powers of a laxative powder.

take a walk up ladder lane and down hawser street. A humorous old nautical term for to be executed by hanging, a hawser being a thick nautical rope.

take down a peg. A ship's colors in Elizabethan times were raised and lowered by a system of pegs—the higher the peg, the higher the honor. Colors taken down a peg, therefore, reduced the esteem in which the ship was held, even by its crew. This practice probably suggested the expression *to take down a peg*, "to humble someone, lower him in his own or everyone else's eyes," which dates back to about the same time.

take it easy. This expression is an Americanism first recorded in 1927, but it is thought to derive from the British expression *easy does it*, which dates back to the early 17th century.

take it on the chin. To endure anything, especially pain, is the meaning of to *take it*, an American expression from boxing, where someone who can take it can endure anything an opponent can dish out. The same thought is behind the expression *take it on the chin*, also from boxing. Both of the phrases now generally mean to take punishment or adversity with courage and not let it defeat you.

take lying down. To take a beating or any attack with abject submission. The picture suggested by this expression is so basic to the idea of spineless surrender that you'd think the phrase went back a long way. But it is modern, first recorded in 1888, in an English journal deploring Englishmen who "take lying down any and every inconvenience that the victorious Irish may inflict."

taken aback. To be caught off guard, as in sailing when the wind is caught on the wrong side of the sails. The expression is at least a century old.

take one's wife to Paris. This is the German equivalent of "bringing coals to Newcastle," meaning any pointless action, the expression dating back to the late 19th century. *See* CARRY COALS TO NEWCASTLE.

take out. In the sense of to kill or destroy, to *take out* was first recorded in Raymond Chandler's detective novel *The Big Sleep* (1939): "I'll take him out. He'll think a bridge fell on him." Chandler may have coined the term, which has nothing to do, of course, with taking out food or taking out a date.

take the bull by the horns. Since the earliest quotation yet found for this expression is 1873, it seems unlikely that it has its roots in bull-running, a brutal English sport popular from the day of King John until it was outlawed in the mid-19th century. Bull-running consisted of a mob with clubs and dogs chasing a bull loosed in the streets and eventually beating it to death, a favorite trick for the braver bull chasers being to grab the poor beast by the horns and wrestle it to the ground. More likely the expression originated in Spain or America. In bull-fights Spanish banderilleros plant darts in the neck of the bull and tire him more by waving cloaks in his face and seizing him by the horns, trying to hold his head down. Rawboned early ranchers in the American Southwest also wrestled bulls, or steers, in a popular sport called bulldogging that is still seen in rodeos—the object being to grab the animal's horns and throw him. Either of these practices could have prompted the saying *take the bull by the horns*, "screw up your courage and cope with a dangerous or unpleasant situation decisively, head on."

take the cake; cakewalk. Cakes have been awarded as prizes since classical times, so when slaves on southern plantations held dance contests to help a needy neighbor, or just for the fun of it, giving a cake to the winning couple was no innovation. But the cakewalk inspired by these contests was definitely another black contribution to American culture. Dancers tried to outdo each other with fancy steps, struts, and ways of walking while the fiddler played and chanted, "Make your steps, and show your style!" By 1840 *cakewalk* was recorded as the name of these steps, which became the basis of many top dance routines still seen today. Whether the expression *that takes the cake*, "that wins the highest prize," comes from the cakewalk is another matter. Though the phrase is recorded a century earlier elsewhere, it almost certainly originated with the cakewalk in America. Today it has taken on a different meaning and is said of something (or someone) that is so unusual as to be unbelievable. What we know as *cakes*, however, are a comparatively recent innovation. *Fishcakes*, *pancakes*, and other round comestibles were known long before English cooks began experimenting with the sweet cakes that bear the name today.

take the long count. A boxer knocked out *takes the long count*, that is he stays down at least until the referee counts to 10. The American expression has also long been used in the past tense as a synonym or euphemism for death.

take the rag off the bush. *See* WELL, IF THAT DON'T TAKE THE RAG OFF THE BUSH!

take the scales from your eyes. *See* REMOVE (TAKE) THE SCALES FROM YOUR EYES.

take the stone out of my shoe. Apparently this is an old Italian proverb used by the Mafia meaning "to eliminate someone," remove him from my life so that he won't bother me anymore. In Richard Condon's *Prizzi's Honor* (1992) the godfather, Don Corrado, says with finality "After you take the stone out of my shoe, leave her in a rent-a-car at the airport."

take the wind out of one's sails. To stop or slow somebody down. Pirate ships often sailed to the windward of a merchant ship, cutting off the wind blowing on its sails and slowing the ship down so that they could board. Later, the same technique came to be used in yacht racing and soon the term was being used figuratively.

take the waters. *See* SPA.

take to journalism and strong drink. It is said of English author John Mitford (1782–1859) that he "took to journalism and strong drink." Mitford was paid a shilling a day by his Grub Street publisher, "of which he expended tenpence on gin and twopence on bread, cheese and an onion." Rent he had not, as he "lived in a gravel pit, with pen, ink and paper" for the last 43 days of his life.

take to the cleaners. A person defrauded or bilked in a business deal or a confidence game is said to have been *taken to the cleaners*. A relatively recent phrase, probably dating back no later than the early 1900s, the words are related to *to be cleaned out*, an early 19th-century saying that sometimes meant "to be duped of all one's money" (usually in a card game), but today always means to lose all one's money.

take to the hustings. A politician who takes to the hustings takes his campaign to the voters. Hustings were 18th-century platforms upon which candidates for Parliament made campaign speeches, named for a similar raised platform called the hustings where officials sat at the Court of Hustings, the supreme court of the city of London. The Court of Hustings, which met at the Guildhall, took its name from the English *husting*, for "a council or court of law," *husting* deriving from the Old Norse *hust-thing* (from the Old Norse *hus*, "royal house," and *thing*, "council"), a royal council, as opposed to a general assembly.

take to the tall timber. Meaning to depart suddenly and unceremoniously, *to take to the tall timber* is a variation on the early 19th-century *to break for the high timber*, which meant to escape into the high woods at the edge of civilization in order to make pursuit by the law difficult.

take under one's wing. A very old expression that was originally in the plural and alludes of course to a hen protecting her chicks under her wings. The source of the phrase is biblical, the famous passage from Matt. 23:37: "O Jerusalem, Jerusalem, thou that killest the prophets, and stonest them which are sent unto thee, how often would I have gathered my children together, even as a hen gathereth her chickens under her wings, and ye would not!"

take with a grain of salt. Pliny the Elder, who of all ancient historians should most often be taken with a *cellar* of salt, writes that when Pompey seized Mithridates' palace he found the king of Pontus's fabled secret antidote against poisons that had protected him from assassins all his life. It contained 72 ingredients, none of them given by the historian, but the last line of the famous formula supposedly read to "be taken fasting, plus a grain of salt *[addito salis granito]*." The incredulous Pliny isn't known for his subtlety, so it is doubtful that he meant the phrase in any but its literal sense. Nevertheless, the story arose in modern times that Pliny's remark was skeptical and was the origin of the expression *to take with a grain of salt*, "to accept something with reservations, to avoid swallowing it whole." People quoted Pliny's Latin phrase incorrectly and *cum grano salis* was widely accepted as the ancestor of the expression. Actually, the term is little more than three centuries old. Its origin is unknown, and it obviously stems from the idea that salt makes food more palatable and easier to swallow. The Romans knew this, and even sprinkled salt on food they thought might contain poison, but there is no record that they ever used the phrase to indicate skepticism. *See* MITHRIDATIZE.

taking a first. Americans often wonder just what the term *taking a first* means in relation to British universities. *First* simply stands for *first-class honors* in the university honors examinations, roughly the equivalent of *summa cum laude* in the U.S. There are "seconds" and "thirds" as well.

talent does what it can.   Toward the end of his days Edward Robert Bulwer, first earl of Lytton (1831–91), grew to regard his life as a failure, despite the many volumes of poetry he wrote and his diplomatic service as viceroy of India. In his "Last Words of a Sensitive Second-Rate Poet" (1868) he gave us the now proverbial:

> Talk not of genius baffled. Genius is master of man.
> Genius does what it must, and Talent does what it can.

talk a blue streak.   This American expressions refers to lightning bolts and has been traced back to about the middle of the 19th century, though it is probably much older. Similarly, *a bolt from the blue*, "something unexpected and startling," draws the picture of a lightning bolt striking from a cloudless blue sky, without any warning at all. *Blue streak* refers to a blue streak of lightning flashing through the sky and was used to describe the rapidity of horses and coaches that "left blue streaks behind them" before it became part of the expression *talk a blue streak*, "to talk rapidly and interminably, to talk someone's ear off."

talk dollars.   To have a command of English often determines one's fate in other countries. That is why to *talk dollars* means "to speak English" in the Philippines, where English is the language of government, education, and business and is spoken by 65 million Filipinos.

talkie.   A synonym for a motion picture with sound that was first recorded in 1910 (at least *talking motion picture* was). Movie myth insists that Al Jolson's *The Jazz Singer* (1927) was the first sound film ever made, but in truth sound had been used in movies long before this, ever since Edison's first Kinetoscopes in the late 19th century. Many short sound films at the time featured great actors and actresses speaking their parts, as when Sarah Bernhardt spoke in the dueling scene from a 1900 version of *Hamlet*. What held back talking pictures was the huge investment needed to convert Hollywood studios and movie theaters across the country to sound systems. Toward the middle of the 1920s Warner Bros. realized that they had fallen far behind the other major studios and decided as a last-chance gamble to produce synchronized sound movies. Warners built its own huge Hollywood theater, bought the old Vitagraph company with its 15 houses, and converted its studio stages to sound. On August 6, 1926, it premiered its first synchronized sound film, a lavish Vitaphone production of *Don Juan* starring John Barrymore. A year later, it had its first big hit with *The Jazz Singer*. *See* YOU AIN'T HEARD NOTHIN' YET.

Talking Water River.   Lucia St. Clair Robson defined this name in *Ride the Wind* (1982): "The Comanche called the Colorado Talking Water River for good reason. The racing, leaping rapids tumbling over its rock-strewn bed drowned out conversation."

talk through one's hat.   Since the phrase arose at about the time Benjamin Harrison was campaigning for the presidency in his tall handsome beaver hat, it has been suggested that his Democratic opponents coined the expression to help convince voters that Harrison was spouting nonsense in his speeches around the country. There isn't any proof that Harrison's trademark inspired the words, although cartoonists often caricatured him in a big beaver hat. Like another Americanism of about the same time, *keep this under your hat*, "keep it secret or confidential," the origins of the phrase are really unknown. The expression *to eat one's hat*, appears to have been invented by Dickens in *The Pickwick Papers*.

talk turkey.   According to an old story, back in Colonial days a white hunter unevenly divided the spoils of a day's hunt with his Indian companion. Of the four crows and four wild turkeys they had bagged, the hunter handed a crow to the Indian, took a turkey for himself, then handed a second crow to the Indian and put still another turkey in his own bag. All the while he kept saying, "You may take this crow and I will take this turkey," or something similar, but the Indian wasn't as gullible as the hunter thought. When he had finished dividing the kill, the Indian protested: "You talk all turkey for you. You never once talk turkey for me! Now I talk turkey to you." He then proceeded to take his fair share. Most scholars agree that from this probably apocryphal tale, first printed in 1830, comes the expression *let's talk turkey*, "let's get down to real business."

tall, dark, and handsome.   As the description of an attractive man, this cliché can be traced to newspaper descriptions of movie idol Rudolph Valentino in the late 1920s, though Valentino was only of average height. Mae West undoubtedly popularized the expression in her 1933 film *She Done Him Wrong*, in which Cary Grant is the object of her desire.

tall oil.   "An Americanized Swedish-German hybrid," this term illustrates the complicated ways some words are formed. As the magazine *Progress Through Research* (summer, 1948) put it: "The name *tall oil* is an Americanized Swedish-German hybrid. The Swedes, who were active in first developing tall oil, called it *tallolja* (meaning pine oil) because it is an oily material obtained from pine wood during the manufacture of paper. At the time, however, the term *pine oil* was already used in Europe and America to describe a different oil obtained from pine trees. To avoid confusion, the Germans, who were among the first to use tall oil extensively, coined the word *Tallol*, from the Swedish 'tall' for pine and the German 'ol' for oil. In the United States this became *tall oil*, the name by which the product is known today."

tally.   *Tallies*, or wooden sticks, were used to keep accounts in the British Royal Exchequer in medieval times. To make a tally, a notched stick of wood (the number of notches equaling the amount of money owed) was split down the center, each half stick retaining half of the notches—one half being given to the party owed money and the other being retained by the Exchequer. No money would be paid by the Exchequer unless a tally, or match of the sticks, was made. This cumbersome system, often involving notched sticks six feet or more long, wasn't abandoned until 1834, when all the remaining sticks were burned in the furnace of the House of Lords, which overheated the flues and caused the House of Parliament to burn down in the process! But the tallies did contribute the word *tally*, which today means count, to the language. *See* JUST IN THE NICK OF TIME.

tallyho. The cry *tallyho* originated on British fox hunts in the 19th century, where it was and still is, as far as I know, the cry of a hunter on first sighting the fox. The term is said to have its roots in the French hunter's cry of *tayau*, which dates back to about 1750. *See* IN AT THE KILL. *See* FOXHOUND.

tam; tam-o'shanter. The eponymous hero of Robert Burns's poem "Tam o'Shanter's Ride" (1791) wore a cap similar to the traditional woolen cap with the pompon that is worn by the Scots and called a *tam*, or *tam-o'shanter*.

tamale. A dish made of minced, seasoned meat stuffed in cornmeal dough, wrapped in corn husks and steamed; from the Nahuatl *tamalli* for the same.

Tammany; Tweed Ring. Tammany Hall hasn't the power it once did, but for over 150 years the machine held sway over New York City politics under such bosses as William Tweed, Richard Croker, and Carmine DeSapio. Tammany's unsavory association with machine politics dates back to the late 18th century, but Tammany clubs thrived in this country long before that, mostly as patriotic Revolutionary War organizations that ridiculed Tory groups like the Society of St. George. The clubs were named for Tammanend or Tammenund, a Delaware Indian chief said to have welcomed William Penn and signed with him the Treaty of Shakamaxon calling for friendly relations. Tammanend (sometimes his name is given as *Taminy* or *Tammany*) may have negotiated with Penn for the land that became Pennsylvania and may have been George Washington's friend. The colonists jocularly canonized this friendly Indian chieftain as St. Tammany and adopted his name for their patriotic societies. These gradually died out, but not before one William Mooney had formed a Tammany Society in New York in 1789. By the Jacksonian era the club became one of the strongest Democratic political organizations in America. Thomas Nast created the famous symbol of the Tammany tiger in his cartoons attacking the machine in the 1870s, when the corrupt TWEED RING was fleecing the city of over $100 million.

tandem. *Tandem* is a humorous coinage, first recorded in 1785. Some anonymous wit took the Latin *tandem*, "at length of time," and punningly applied it to a carriage drawn by two or more horses harnessed not side by side, but one before the other—strung out in a line or at length. *In tandem* has come to mean "in association or partnership" as well as "one following the other."

tangerine. This fruit is called the "kid-glove orange" because its loose skin can be peeled off as easily as soft kid gloves can be peeled off the hands. But it is far better known as the *tangerine* after the seaport Tangier in Morocco, where the small deep-orange fruit was extensively cultivated and first called the "tangerine orange." Tangerines belong to the mandarin group of oranges, which were first cultivated in southeast Asia. Residents of Tangier are called Tangerines.

tank. The motorized tank wasn't invented until World War I. Winston Churchill, who advocated its use, gave it the name *tank* as a "cover name" to help conceal the new weapon from enemy intelligence agents. Before this, *tank* had absolutely no connection with war. Possibly deriving from the Indian *tankh*, it had for centuries meant an irrigation pond and then a cistern holding water. The British brought the word back from India, using it exclusively as the term for any large metal container holding any liquid (such as gas and oil tanks) until Churchill appropriated the word.

tantalize. Tantalus, the son of Zeus in Greek mythology, divulged the secrets of the gods to humans. The Lydian king was punished by being submerged in a pool of water in Hades, a tree laden with fruit above his head. Whenever he attempted to drink the water or eat the fruit they moved just beyond him—the water receding and the fruit tree wind-tossed—causing him agonizing thirst and hunger. This punishment gives us the word *tantalize*.

Tantony pig. The smallest pig in every litter, one that is traditionally believed to follow its master anywhere, is called a Tantony pig after St. Anthony, long the patron saint of swineherds. St. Anthony probably had nothing to do with pigs, other than citing an "unclean demon" as one of the temptations he resisted, but he is often represented in art with a pig by his side. In the Middle Ages, when the pig began to lose its reputation as an unclean demon, it was popularly supposed that the animal was dedicated to the saint. St. Anthony, born about the year 250 in middle Egypt, defeated many "assaults by the devil," including temptations such as "gross and obscene imagings" of beautiful, naked women that Lucifer sent to "harass him night and day."

taper off. A taper, or candle, gradually diminishes in thickness from the base to the tip. This image suggested the term to *taper off* to Englishmen of the early 19th century. Like the candle growing smaller by degrees, anything becoming gradually less in intensity was said to taper off. The words were especially applied to shedding an established habit by degrees, usually to tapering off from the habit of hard drinking.

taps. The military bugle call taps may simply derive from the sound of a drum tap, but it could be a corruption of the British drum call tattoo, as the recorded first use of the latter word (in 1644) indicates: "If anyone shall be found tiplinge or drinkinge in any Taverne, Inne, or Alehouse after the houre of nyne of the clock at night, when the tap-too beates, hee shall pay 2S.6d." In fact, *tap-too* was still being used for *tattoo* in 1833, 11 years after the Americanism *taps* is first recorded. *Tattoo* itself may derive from the Dutch *tap toe*, "to close or turn off the tap," which 17th-century Dutch tavern owners were required to do by military authorities at a certain time every evening, so that soldiers wouldn't be tempted to stay out too late. In any case *taps* was first a drumroll in the American army, meaning "put out the lights and go to bed." The haunting tune we now know as *taps* was written by Union general Daniel Butterfield with the aid of his bugler, Lt. Oliver Wilcox Norton. Now also used at the end of a soldier's burial, its words are: Put out the lights,/ Go to sleep,/ Go to sleep, Go to sleep, Go to sleep./ Put out the lights,/ Go to sleep,/ Go to sleep." *See* TATTOO.

tar. *See* JACK TAR.

tarantula. This much-feared, hairy, venomous spider takes its name from the Italian seaport of Taranto, where it was thought to abound in medieval times. From the 15th to the 17th century the bite of tarantulas was believed to cause a dancing mania called *tarantism*, which was actually a hysterical disease epidemic to southern Europe at the time.

ta-ra-ra-boom-de-ay.   *See* Q.T.

Tarheel; Tarheel State.   A nickname for a North Carolinian. According to the *Overland Monthly* (V.3, 1869): "A brigade of North Carolinians . . . failed to hold a certain hill [in a Civil War battle] and were laughed at by Mississippians for having forgotten to tar their heels that morning. Hence originated their cant name, 'Tar heels.' " The state of North Carolina has been called the Tar and Turpentine State. Other North Carolina nicknames have included the Old North State and the Land of the Sky, in reference to its beautiful western mountain country. In putting down their older, once more sophisticated neighbors Virginia and South Carolina, North Carolinians have called their state the Valley of Humility Between Two Mountains of Conceit.

tariff.   According to one old tale, the island of Tarifa off the coast of Spain, where the Moors formerly levied taxes upon all who passed, is the source of our word *tariff*. A diverting story, but *tariff* has its ultimate roots in the Arabic *tarif*, "information," which became the Old French *tariffe*, "arithmetic."

tarmac.   *See* MACADAM.

tarnation.   The interjection *tarnation!*, a euphemism for damnation! or *damn!*, has been used in New England since colonial times and is familiar to millions of Americans from its use in books, movies, radio, and television. The best guess is that it derives from the English *tarnal!*, which itself derives from the mild interjection *eternal!*

tarot.   *Tarot* is the French name of the popular central European card game called *tarok*, which the *Encyclopaedia Britannica* says is the world's oldest surviving card game. The game is named after Tar, the Egyptian god of the underworld, whom the Greeks called Tartarus. It has many features borrowed by other card games, including competitive bidding and the wild joker, and is now played with 54 cards, 22 of them trump card tarots bearing allegorical representations. These 22 illustrated cards, depicting vices, virtues, and elemental forces, are the only ones used in the fortune-telling game called tarot that most people are familiar with.

tarred and feathered.   At Salem, on September 7, 1768, an informer named Robert Wood "was stripped, tarred and feathered and placed on a hogshead under the Tree of Liberty on the Common." This is the first record of the term *tarred and feathered* in America. Tarring and feathering was a cruel punishment where hot pine tar was applied from head to toe on a person and goose feathers were stuck into the tar. The person was then ignited and ridden out of town on a rail (tied to a splintery rail), beaten with sticks and stoned all the while. A man's skin often came off when he removed the tar. It was a common practice to tar and feather Tories who refused to join the revolutionary cause, one much associated with the Liberty Boys, but the practice was known here long before the Revolution. In fact, it dates back even before the first English record of tarring and feathering, an 1189 statute made under Richard the Lionhearted directing that any convicted thief voyaging with the Crusaders "shal have his head shorne and boyling pitch powred upon his head, and feathers or downe strewn upon the same, whereby he may be known, and so at the first landing place they shal come to, there to be cast up." Though few have been tarred and feathered or ridden out of town on a rail in recent years, the expression remains to describe anyone subjected to indignity and infamy.

tarred with the same brush.   Someone who shares the sins or faults of another, though possibly to a lesser degree, is tarred with the same brush. The saying may have something to do with tarred-and-feathered criminals, but the reference is probably to the tarring of sheep. Owners of a flock of sheep, which can't be branded, used to mark their wool all in the same place with a brush dipped in tar to distinguish them from sheep of another flock. It is said that red ochre was used to make the mark and that brushing sheep with tar served to protect them against ticks.

tart.   Another example of words that change in meaning. The fruit pie dessert called a tart derives from the Latin *tarta* meaning the same. By at least the 1860s *tart* was being used as a term of endearment for a girl or woman, but after another 20 years, for reasons unknown, it took on its present sense of an immoral woman or prostitute, never to be used endearingly again.

tartar.   Contrary to popular belief, Swiss physician, alchemist, and writer Paracelsus (Philippppus Theophrastus Bombastus von Hohenhein, 1493?–1541) did not invent the word *tartar*, which apparently derives from an Arabic word and was recorded before Paracelsus. Paracelsus did write that "All diseases can be traced to a coagulation of undigested matter in the bowels." He called these acids of putrefaction "tartar" because their deposits in joints, muscles, and other parts of the body "burn like hell, and Tartarus is hell." He went on to say that "Doctors boast of their [knowledge of] anatomy, but they fail to see the tartar sticking to their teeth." Thus, though not the inventor of *tartar*, he may have been the first to use the word as it is used in all the toothpaste ads.

tartar sauce.   *See* STEAK TARTARE.

Tarzan.   A Tarzan is any well-built outdoors man with great agility, strength, and valor. The word comes from American author Edgar Rice Burroughs's novels about Tarzan, the son of a British aristocrat orphaned in the jungle as a baby and raised by apes, his adventures beginning with *Tarzan of the Apes* (1914). The novelist's opinions may have been inspired by William Milden, earl of Streaham, who was shipwrecked off Africa in 1869 when barely 11 years old and supposedly lived with apes for 15 years before being found and returned home to England. *Tarzan* is the only eponymous word constructed from an invented language, in this case the "monkey language" Burroughs devised in his first book, in which the hero's foster mother, Kala the ape, names him from *tar*, "white," and *zan*, "skin," *Tarzan* literally meaning "white skin." The much-quoted humorous line "Me Tarzan, you Jane" wasn't invented by

Burroughs, coming from one of the many films or comics made of the author's 24 Tarzan books. Tarzan's cry, his chest pounding, his swinging on vines, and his high dives into the water have long been imitated by children of all ages.

taste. *To taste* meant to touch before it meant to taste. In *Merlin, or the Early History of King Arthur* (ca. 1450) we find the following: "Merlin leide his heed in the damesels lappe, and she began to taste softly till he fell on slepe." *Taste* is recorded in this sense as early as 1290, 50 years or so before the word began to take its present meaning—which may have been suggested by feeling food (tasting it) with the tongue.

tater. *Tater* is baseball slang for a base hit or a home run. It possibly derives from the admiring expression *that's some potatoes* that fans early in the game's history would shout out after a player got a good hit.

tattarrattat. This is at 12 letters the longest one-word palindrome (a word that reads the same backward or forward) in English. It is recorded in the *Oxford English Dictionary*. *See* PALINDROME.

tattletale. An informer, one who carries tales. *Tattletale*, which is still commonly heard, is an Americanism patterned on the much earlier British *tell-tale* (as in Tell tale tit / Your tongue shall be split . . .) meaning the same. It wasn't used by school children here until the 18th century, perhaps 300 years after its ancestor. American children increasingly use the gangster movie term *rat* for a tattletale today, calling tattling *ratting*.

tattoo. As far as is known, Capt. James Cook was the first European to record the practice of tattooing, when he sailed the *Endeavor* on his historic exploration of the South Seas in 1769. Noting that the Tahitians cut their skin and injected a black dye that left a permanent mark when the wound healed, he called the practice *tattowing* in his diary. This was a fair approximation of the native word *tatau* for the operation. Within a short time the word was being spelled *tattoo*. *See* TAPS.

taunt. *See* TIT FOR TAT.

tawdry. Anglo-Saxon princess Aethelthryth seems to have spent her married life trying to preserve her chastity. Daughter of the king of East Anglia, she protected her virginity through two unwanted marriages that her father had arranged for political reasons, keeping the promise she made as a girl that she would dedicate her life to God. The pious princess carried but one sin on her conscience: in her youth she had loved wearing golden chains and necklaces, and she believed that the cancer of the throat that she died of in 679 had been caused by this worldly vanity. In Norman times Aethelthryth's name was shortened to Audrey and she was finally canonized as St. Audrey. It became the custom to hold fairs on the Isle of Ely on St. Audrey's Day, October 17, and the souvenirs sold at these fairs included lace scarves and golden necklaces that were called St. Audrey's laces. This merchandise, at first treasured articles, declined in quality until it became known as cheap and showy. Shouted by hucksters as St. Audrey's lace, it was soon clipped in speech to "Sin t'Audrey lace" and eventually to *tawdry lace*. All the gaudy, worthless objects like it were sold as *tawdry*, too, and by the 18th century the word had come to mean anything cheap and tasteless, showy tinsel.

taxi. Incensed about the high fares horse cabs were charging in 1907, Harry N. Allen introduced taximeter cabs in Manhattan, naming the 4-cylinder, 16-horsepower cabs he imported from France from the Greek *taxa*, "charge," and the word *cab*, the common short form of the French *cabriolet*. Allen's coinage became shortened to *taxicab* and finally *taxi* long before taxi fares far surpassed those of the horse-driven cabs.

taxi squad. In the late 1940s Art McBride, the original owner of the Cleveland Browns football team, had a number of players under contract to him who weren't on the active player list and could only play if one of his active players was injured and deactivated. Since this seemed like a waste of his money, he put these extra players to work as drivers in his taxicab company. Soon all such players in the pro leagues were being called members of the taxi squad. Later, when the rules changed, the term was applied to the four extra players on a professional football team who aren't allowed to suit up for an official game but who are ready to join the team to replace injured or unsuccessful players.

tea. British slang for a cup of tea is "cuppa char." *Char* is a corruption of *cha*, which means tea in England, deriving from the Mandarin *ch'a* for the same. *Tea* comes to us from the Chinese Amoy dialect *t'e*. The scientific name of the tea plant, *Thea sinensis*, sometimes grown in the United States, is the Latinized version of the Amoy name. Tea bags weren't invented until the turn of the century, when an American tea wholesaler named Sullivan began mailing prospective customers one-cup samples of his tea contained in little silk bags. The idea didn't catch on because the cloth changed the flavor of the tea, but during World War II chemists developed a tasteless paper tea bag that became extremely popular and accounts for most of the tea sold in America today. *See also* ALL THE TEA IN CHINA; SPOT OF TAY; TEMPEST IN A TEAPOT.

tea caddy. No relation to the golf CADDY, the tea caddy, a small box for storing tea, takes its name from the Malayan *kati*, "a weight of about 21 ounces," perhaps because tea used to be packed in 21-ounce boxes. *See* TEA.

teach your grandmother to suck eggs. Someone who says "Trying to teach him how to swim is like trying to teach your grandmother to suck eggs" is saying that the whole idea is ridiculous because he knew how to swim well long before you were born. Most country grandmothers knew how to suck eggs in days past—poking two small holes in the shell and sucking out the contents through a straw while leaving the shell intact. Today not many grandmothers suck eggs, but people still use the expression, first recorded in the early 18th century.

teapoy. Because it is used for serving tea, this small, often three-legged table takes its name from the drink. But the table's name has nothing to do with tea. Brought back from India by the British, the little table is named from the Hindi *teen*, three, and the Persian *pae*, foot(ed).

tearing up the pea patch. Red Barber popularized this southern U.S. expression for "going on a rampage" when he broadcast Brooklyn Dodger baseball games from 1945–55, using it often to describe fights on the field between players. Barber hails from the South, where the expression is an old one, referring to the prized patch of black-eyed peas, which stray animals sometimes ruined. *See also* CATBIRD.

tears of Eos (Ē-os). A poetic name for the dewdrops of morning that is rarely used anymore but has a charming story. Maemmon, a handsome black prince, was slain by Achilles in the Trojan War. His mother Eos (the Dawn) was inconsolable and cries for him every morning, early morning dew said to be *the tears of Eos.*

tears of the sun. An old Apache Indian term for gold, which the Apaches held sacred and not to be touched.

teasel. There are scores of tiny hooks on the dried seed pods of the teasel plant (*Dipsacus fullonum*). These hooked seed pods have long been grown for use in mills to raise or tease up the nap on woolen cloth. From this practice we get the hairdressing expression "teasing," as well as the "teasing" that irritates somebody, just as drawing a teasel pod across someone's skin would do.

Technicolor. A trademark name used to describe a method of making movies in color. The word is often lowercased, however wrongly, in figurative contexts such as "The leaves were a technicolor spectacle of crimson and gold." The Technicolor process was developed in 1917, but the first feature film made in it was *Becky Sharp* (1935). The word is a combination of *techni*cal and *color.*

techy. Not an ignorant "hick" pronunciation of *touchy*, as many people believe. The word (meaning "irritable," or "peevish") is not related to *touch*, but derives from Middle English *tecche*, a bad habit, which in turn comes from Old French *teche* (a blemish).

teddy bear. Brooklyn candy store owner Morris Michtom fashioned the first teddy bear out of brown plush in 1902 and named it after President Theodore Roosevelt. Michtom's inspiration was a cartoon by *Washington Post* cartoonist Clifford K. Berryman called "Drawing the Line in Mississippi" that had been reprinted throughout the country. Based on a news story about an expedition Teddy Roosevelt made to hunt bears near the Little Sunflower River in Mississippi, it showed the old Rough Rider with his back turned to a helpless bear cub. Gallant Teddy, it had been reported, refused to kill and even set free the small brown bear that his obliging hosts had stunned and tied to a tree for him to shoot. Apocryphal or not, the story enhanced Roosevelt's reputation as a conservationist and made Michtom rich.

Teddy boys; Teddy girls. London's rebellious Teddy boys and Teddy girls in the 1960s took their name from the Edwardian styles they preferred, especially the boys' tightly fitted trousers and jackets. *Edwardian* in this case refers to the styles popular in the reign of England's Edward VII, Queen Victoria's son, who ruled from 1901–1910. The opulent styles of the period reflect the self-satisfaction prevalent before World War I and perhaps indicated a rebellious desire on the part of the Teddy boys to return to better days.

tee. The first tees were just small handfuls of sand or dirt off which golf balls were hit. The Scottish word was first recorded in 1673 as *teaz*, but people thought this was the plural of *tee* and over the years *tee* became the singular form. The little wooden pegs we call *tees* today were invented by New Jersey dentist William Lowell in the 1920s.

teeny-weeny. An Americanism that combines *teeny*, a variant of *tiny*, and *wee*, "small," *teeny-weeny* is first recorded in the 1890s as a word describing someone or something very little. Still used today and immortalized in the popular song "Itsy Bitsy Teenie Weenie Yellow Polka Dot Bikini" (1960), it was helped along by the "Teenie Weenies" comic strip that appeared in many U.S. newspapers from the 1920s up until the 1960s.

teetotal. The only invented word I know of that is recorded on the gravestone of its author. Some people believe this word for total abstinence from alcoholic beverages has something to do with tea: one drinks tea totally, nothing stronger. Perhaps this is one reason the word caught on when it was coined in 1833 by Dick Turner, an artisan in Preston, England. But Turner formed the word as a reduplicated variation of *total*, in a speech he made advocating total abstinence from intoxicating drink. The inscription on the reformer's gravestone reads: "Beneath this stone are deposited the remains of Richard Turner, author of the word *Teetotal* as applied to abstinence from all intoxicating liquors, who departed this life on the 27th day of October, 1846, aged 56 years."

Teflon; Teflon Don. *Teflon* is the trademark name for a chemical substance used to make nonstick cooking pans that Dupont introduced in 1945. Metaphorical use of the word didn't come until the 1980s, when it was used to describe Ronald Reagan as the "Teflon President" because no scandal or criticism seemed to stick to him. Said Representative Patricia Schroeder during a 1983 speech, in which she may have coined the new term: "Ronald Reagan . . . has been perfecting the Teflon-coated Presidency. He sees to it that nothing sticks to him." The term has since been applied to several politicians, including former President Clinton, but is best known as the nickname of John "the Teflon Don" Gotti, a New York Mafia crime boss. Before he was finally sentenced to life in prison, Gotti and his lawyers had managed to beat every charge brought against him.

telegram. *See* CABLEGRAM.

telegraph. Simple telegraphic devices have been known since ancient times, but the first to be called a *telegraph* was the one invented by Claude Chappe in 1792. The inventor wanted to call his device the *tachygraphe*, but was advised that this name was inappropriate and should be *telegraphe*, from the Greek words for "afar" and "to write"—"to write from afar." *See* WHAT GOD HATH WROUGHT.

telegraphese.   The clipped, concise language of telegraph messages. In a humorous, apocryphal example of it a fan wants to know actor Cary Grant's age and sends him a telegram reading: HOW OLD CARY GRANT. Grant replies: OLD CARY GRANT FINE. HOW YOU.

telemark.   A skiing turn in which the skier puts one ski far ahead of the other and angles the tip of that forward ski in the direction in which he wants to turn. It is named for Telemark, Norway, where it is said to have been invented in about 1905. Skiing is said to have began as a sport in Telemark in about 1860.

telepathy.   Psychologist and poet Frederick W. H. Myers coined this word for thought transference in an 1882 scientific paper. Later, in his book *Human Personality* (1903), he defined *telepathy* as "the communication of impressions of any kind from one mind to another independently of the recognized channels of sense."

telephone.   *Telephone*, from the Greek roots for "far" and "sound," was a term first used to describe any device for conveying sounds to a distant point. In 1667, for example, Robert Hooke invented a device in which vibrations in a diaphragm caused by voice or sound waves are transmitted mechanically along a string or wire to a similar diaphragm that reproduces the sound. He called this device a *string telephone.* Another inventor, in 1796, called his megaphone a *telephone*, as did the inventor of a speaking tube not much later. Alexander Graham Bell used the old name for his invention as soon as he invented it in 1876. *See* TELEGRAPH; "MR. WATSON COME HERE . . ."; NUMBER PLEASE.

telephone Hitler.   *See* I AM GOING TO TELEPHONE HITLER.

TelePrompTer; Laff Box.   The trademarked TelePromTer hidden from the audience, provides television performers with a magnified script he or she can read line by line. Its counterpart in the theater is its ancestor, the human prompter. The Tele-PromTer was introduced in 1951. In Britain it is called the "autocue." Another device invented for television is the trademarked Laff Box, or laugh track, which supplies recorded audience reactions for TV shows, reproducing "giggles, guffaws, cries, moans, jeers, ohs and ahs," etc., when needed. It was invented by Charles (Charlie) Rolland Douglass (1910–2003) in the early 1950s.

telescope.   The great Galileo did not at first use the word *telescope* for the famous instrument that he invented, calling it instead a *perspicillum* and sometimes an *organum*, or *instrumentum*, or *occidale*. In about 1610, a rival and lesser claimant to the discovery, Prince Cesi, head of the Italian Academy, named the instrument the *telescope*, from the Greek word for "far seeing." Only then did Galileo employ the word, and he, in fact, is the first person known to record *telescope*, in a letter of September 1, 1611. *See* MICROSCOPE.

telestitch.   *See* ACROSTIC.

television.   Like TELEPHONE, *television* seems to have been an old coinage, in this case from the Greek *tele*, far, and the Greek *vision*, vision. The word is not recorded until about 1910 and seems to have been applied to another device, not the television we know today. The first television set was demonstrated at Chicago's 1933 Century of Progress Exposition, but it wasn't until the 1940s that programming became common. *See* RADIO; TELEGRAPH; TV DINNER.

teller.   The bank teller takes his or her appellation from the Middle English *tellen* "to count." The term had much wider use in days past, when anyone who counted anything, money or merchandise, was called a teller. *Teller* is recorded in this sense as early as 1480.

tell him (her) where to get off.   Apparently a trolley-car conductor or the like has nothing to do with this expression meaning "to admonish someone for his or her audacity or arrogance." The phrase was first recorded by American author George Ade, often noted for his use of vernacular, in his *More Fables in Slang* (1879): "He said he was a gentleman and that no cheap skate in a plug hat could tell him where to get off." The expression may come from the old expression *to get up on one's high horse.* What is implied is "from what high horse does he think he can give me orders from; I'll tell him where to get off it." The phrase is also heard as *show him (her) where to get off. See* HIGH HORSE.

tell it to the marines.   Not the U.S. Marine Corps, but the British Royal Marines, formed in the 18th century, are the gullible ones here. The Royal Marines, quartered aboard ships and responsible for discipline, weren't well liked by sailors, who considered them stupid and gullible about the seafaring life and made them the butt of many jokes. Seamen even called empty bottles marines. Any tall tale told to a sailor was likely to be met with the response "Tell it to the marines—sailors won't believe it"; that is, sailors, unlike marines, were too intelligent to be gulled. The saying soon passed into popular use and was first recorded by Lord Byron in *The Island* (1823), the poet noting that it was an old saying even then.

Tell's apple.   *See* WILLIAM TELL'S APPLE.

tell the truth and shame the devil.   An English proverb from the 16th century that means "to be honest."

tempest in a teapot.   This saying for "making a big fuss over a trifle," was first *a tempest in a teacup.* It has been traced back only to 1857, but is probably older. Similar early English sayings were "storm in a wash basin" and "a storm in a cream bowl" (1678). For that matter Cicero, as far back as 400 B.C., referred to a contemporary who "stirred up waves in a wine ladle," and he indicated that the expression was ancient *See also* TEA.

Temple orange.   *See* ORANGE.

tempura.   In Japanese cookery tempura is seafood or vegetables dipped in batter and deep-fried. The word, however, is of Portuguese, not Japanese, origin. On Ember Days, which the Portuguese called by the Latin name *Quatuor Tempora*, "the four times of the year," most people in Portugal eschewed meat and ate deep-fried shrimp or other seafood, which came to be called tempura after the holy days. By the early 1540s Portuguese sailors had introduced tempura to Japan.

tempus fugit.   *See* TIME FLIES.

10 (ten).   Ten, more often written as 10, means anything perfect—from a perfect woman or man to a perfect situation. The expression dates back to the early 1970s and may come from the sport of gymnastics, in which a 10 is a perfect score on the scale of zero to 10.

tenderfoot.   As early as the 17th century the British applied this word to horses that needed breaking in before they could handle heavy loads. Next they used *tenderfoot* as a derogatory term for a vagrant. It wasn't until the California gold rush of 1849 that Americans applied the word to footsore people unused to the hardships of pioneer life as they traveled in search of gold. Soon *tenderfoot* was a term for any greenhorn, not only one with sore feet. "In my tenderfoot ignorance," Owen Wister wrote in *The Virginian* (1902), "I was looking indoors for the washing arrangements."

the tenderloin.   In New York City, where the expression originated, *the tenderloin* meant the area from 23rd to 42nd Streets west of Broadway. Gambling and prostitution flourished in this district, giving police officers "luscious opportunities" for graft. In fact, one cop named Williams was so happy to be assigned to the old 29th precinct covering the area in about 1890 that he said he had always eaten chuck steak but from now on he'd "be eating tenderloin." His remark led to the area being dubbed *the tenderloin*, that name eventually transferred to similar places throughout the country.

tenements.   American city tenements are bad enough today, but toward the end of the 19th century they were horrors, always without heat, water, or bathrooms, often with names like the Dirty Spoon or Bandit's Roost and located on streets actually named Poverty Gap, Bottle Alley, Penitentiary Row, etc. Often they were boardinghouses with signs advertising "Five Cents a Spot," "Hallway Space 3 cents" and "Standing Room Only."

10-foot pole.   *See* WOULDN'T TOUCH IT WITH A 10-FOOT POLE.

1040 form.   According to one story, U.S. personal income tax forms are called 1040s because in sma.D 1040 Lady Godiva rode naked through the streets of Coventry, England, protesting taxes. Another yarn has it that the infamous forms are so named because in 1040 B.C., Samuel, the last of the prophets, gave in to his people's demands that he give them a king, yet warned them that a king would require them to pay taxes. But though these tales are as ingenious as some tax deductions, the I.R.S. says "the mundane truth is that the four-digit number happened to be the next available in the forms numbering system when the 1040 was devised in 1913."

10-gallon hat.   Although the hat's name is usually thought to be an indication of its liquid holding capacity, the Americanism *10-gallon hat* has its origins in the Spanish word for braid, *galón*. The wide-brimmed hats worn by cowboys were originally decorated with a number of braids at the base of the crown.. Actually, a ten-gallon hat holds about a gallon of liquid. *See* STETSON

Tennessee.   Admitted to the Union in 1796 as our 16th state, Tennessee's name derives from the name of a Cherokee settlement in the area that is of unknown origin. It had been called Tenaqui by the Spanish in the 16th century and went by the name State of Franklin, after Ben Franklin, from 1784–88. *See* VOLUNTEER STATE.

Tennis, anyone?   *Tennis, anyone?* began life as *Who's for tennis?* in England about 80 years ago, also serving as a conversation opener or an ironic comment on the pastimes of the leisured classes. Partridge believes it may have arisen "as a good-natured comment upon lawn tennis as an adjunct of tea parties in the vicarage garden or at country-house weekends," but it has also been suggested that the catchphrase comes from some turn-of-the century English comedy of manners in which "an actor sprang through French windows calling, 'Anyone for tennis?' "

tennis racket.   *See* RACKET.

Tennyson bindings.   The 19th-century expression *Tennyson bindings* is used to indicate affectation of culture. According to Willard Espy, in *O Thou Improper, Thou Uncommon Noun:* "A *nouveau-riche* matron was showing a friend of similar stripe her library, which had been stocked by interior decorators 'and here,' she said, 'is my Tennyson,' 'No, no, darling,' corrected her friend. 'Those are green. Tennyson is blue.' " Chewing gum millionaire William Wrigley bought books by the yard. "Measure those bookshelves with a yardstick and buy enough books to fill 'em," he told his secretary while furnishing his Chicago apartment on Lake Shore Drive. "Get plenty of snappy red and green books with plenty of gilt lettering. I want a swell showing." At least more original is the advice *Lady Gough's Book of Etiquette* gave library owners in Victorian times: "Don't place books by married male authors next to those by female authors and vice versa."

tent.   *See* TENTERHOOKS.

tenterhooks.   Tenters were frameworks used to stretch woven cloth in the days before modern manufacture (as early as the 15th century) and tenterhooks were the pins or hooks that held the cloth in place. Tenterhooks was later applied to the hooks meat is suspended from in butcher shop windows and it is probably from this use of the word that we get the figurative *on tenterhooks*, to be in a state of "painful" or anxious suspense, your curiosity "torturously stretched" to its limits. The dreaded rack, an instrument of torture that literally stretched people, was also called the tenter and no doubt reinforced the meaning of the phrase, first recorded in the 17th century. *Tenter* probably derives from the same Latin word (*tentus*, "stretched") as *tent*, a tent being stretched canvas.

the 10th muse.   In Greek mythology there are commonly nine MUSES, the nine daughters of Zeus and Mnemosyne, each of them identified with individual arts and sciences. *The 10th muse* is a name traditionally given to Sappho, a Greek poet of Lesbos in about 600 B.C., who is thus the only real person to be accorded the status of a Muse. *See* LESBIAN.

tepee on wheels.   American Indians gave this American name to the covered wagons of settlers on the Oregon Trail.

teredo; shipworm.   From time immemorial the sharp-toothed teredo, or shipworm, which eats its life away, has been gnawing gluttonously at ships, piers, jetties, and every other wooden object man has dared to leave in the water for any appreciable period. This masticating mollusk of the genus *Teredo* has in the process caused damage amounting to billions of dollars. In San Francisco Bay, from 1917 to 1921, to cite just one example, shipworms damaged wharves and piers to the cash register tune of over $25 million, taking their rightful place beside the termite, the furniture beetle, and the death-watch beetle as one of nature's finest demolition experts. In 1733 the British scientist Godfrey Sellers proved that the teredo is a bivalve mollusk, although it differs widely from clams, oysters, and other members of that group. Since then scientists have preferred to call the shipworm by its Latin generic name, *Teredo*, which comes from the Greek for "to rub hard, wear away, bore." The reputation of these teredos can be seen in the many mentions of their name in England, that great maritime nation. One English politician called the opposition "teredos of every plank in the Ship of State." *See* GRIBBLE.

termagant.   Trivegant or Tervagent was a violent, noisy, overbearing character in old morality plays, in which he was erroneously called "a Mohammedan deity." Careless pronunciation changed the name to *termagant*, which became our word for a violent, turbulent, or brawling woman, as well as an adjective for "violent; turbulent; brawling; and shrewish." The term applied to men until about the 17th century, when it was applied to both men and women.

termination with extreme prejudice.   This is a CIA euphemism for assassination, which apparently originated in the 1960s. The CIA reportedly had (maybe still has) a special assassination unit called the Health Alternative Committee.

terminological inexactitude.   A euphemism invented by Winston Churchill. It means a lie.

terra firma.   This Latin term for "firm land," dating back at least to the 19th century, was first applied to the firm land of the continents, originally the Italian mainland territories controlled by Venice. Later *terra firma* came to mean any dry land as distinct from sea or air.

a terrible beauty is born.   The words are from W. B. Yeats' poem "Easter 1916," in which they appear at the end of three stanzas. Yeats wrote the poem on September 25, 1916, five months after the Easter Rising, in which Irish nationalists rose up against the British and proclaimed Irish independence. The event actually took place on Easter Monday, 1916.

terrier.   *See* AIREDALE TERRIER.

terrorist.   During the French Revolution period called the Reign of Terror, as many as 17,000 people may have been put to death for opposing the regime before the bloodshed ended in 1794 with the bloody-minded Robespierre's guillotine execution. Certainly thousands were killed in Paris alone by what

the French called *terroristes*, agents or partisans of the revolutionary tribunal who practiced terrorism. Soon the new word, shortened to *terrorist* in English, came to describe any such "hell hounds . . . let loose on the people," as Edward Burke called them. *See* GUILLOTINE; SUICIDE BOMBER.

testicles.   *Testicles* is from the Latin *testiculi* meaning "little witnesses." Apparently, in this case the witnesses testify to their owner's masculinity. From this come our words *testify*, *testimony*, and *testicles*, all deriving from the Latin. All such *test* words—including *protest*, *protestant*, and *attest*—have this *testicle* connection. Some time ago *Ms.* magazine published a letter stating: "I protest the use of the word 'testimony' when referring to a woman's statements, because its root is 'testes' which has nothing to do with being a female. Why not use 'ovarimony'?"

test tube baby.   *See* FALLOPIAN TUBES.

tetched.   *Tetched* isn't an American dialect term. This word for "slightly mad, touched" derives from the late Middle English *techyd*, meaning "marked or blemished." *Techyd* was confused in sense with *touched*, also coming to mean "a little crazy."

tête à tête.   *Tête* is the French word for "head," familiar to us in expressions like *tête à tête*, literally "head to head," which means a private conversation between two people. Interestingly, this important French word came into French from Latin slang. Few people would guess that the French word for head was originally the Latin slang for "pot."

Teton Range.   A mountain range in northwestern Wyoming that takes its name from the French *téton* (breast) because the mountains somewhat resemble women's breasts.

Tetragrammaton.   *See* FOUR-LETTER WORD.

Texas.   Texas takes its name from a Caddo Indian word meaning "friends or allies" (written "texas," "texios," "tejas," "teyas") applied to the Caddos by the Spanish in eastern Texas, who regarded them as friends and allies against the Apaches. *See also* NORTH DAKOTA.

Texas leaguer.   A cheap hit that falls between the infield and the outfield in baseball is called a Texas leaguer because back in 1886 three players who had been traded up to the majors from a Texas league team enabled Toledo to beat Syracuse by repeatedly getting such hits. After the game, the disgusted Syracuse pitcher described the hits as just "little old dinky Texas leaguers," and the name stuck.

Texas longhorn.   A once-common breed of southwestern beef cattle developed from cattle introduced from Spain and noted for their fecundity and resistance to disease. Also called coasters, these cattle have horns that can measure over 77 inches.

Texas mouse.   A euphemism for a rat, or rather a failed euphemism. Back in February 1983, American Airlines captain Karl Burrell reported a big rat foraging aboard his plane in the first-class cabin as he prepared for takeoff to New York from Dallas. "The stewardesses prevailed on the captain to turn the plane around, and we sat on the ground for 45 minutes," said an eyewitness. "Finally, Captain Burrell polled all the first-class passengers and they decided we should go on with the rat. It was at least six inches long. We heard the captain say to the control tower, 'Let them take care of the problem in New York.'" The airline's public relations director euphemistically called the rodent a "Texas mouse," but a local exterminator said, "Smells like a rat to me—we don't get six-inch mice even in Texas." The rat was killed once the plane landed at La Guardia.

Texas T-shirt. William Safire's "On Language" column in the *New York Times* (March 27, 1991) defined this as a humorous derogatory term for "one of those disposable [toilet] seat bibs that are found in interstate roadside bathrooms."

Texas turkey. *See* ARMADILLO.

Texas wedge. A humorous golfing term, not for a wedge club but for a putter "when it can be used for a short approach shot over very flat rather bare ground, as might be found in Texas," according to Stuart Berg Flexner in *Listening to America* (1982).

Texas yell. *See* REBEL YELL.

Tex-Mex. This word, dating back to about 1945, means of or pertaining to aspects of culture developed in Texas but based on or strongly influenced by Mexican elements, such as Tex-Mex cooking.

Thaïs. Like ASPASIA the proper name *Thaïs* has become a literary euphemism for a courtesan. Thais was a Greek courtesan with whom Alexander the Great consorted in 330. One night she suggested that he set fire to the palace of Xerxes in Persepolis. This Alexander did, burning it to the ground.

Thames. *See* SET THE THAMES ON FIRE.

thanks for nothing. One might think this is a sarcastic contemporary rejoinder to someone who has made an unacceptable offer. Its ancestor, however, is a line from Cervantes's *Don Quixote* (1605–15): "Thank you for nothing." Others of the several hundred phrases first recorded in that great novel include *the sunset of my brows; in a pickle; without a wink of sleep; no limits but the sky (the sky's the limit); a finger in every pie; every dog has its day; you may go whistle; I give up the ghost; let every man mind his own business; within a stone's throw; naked I came into this world, and naked must I go out; thou has seen nothing yet; give the devil his due; wild-goose chase; I shall cry my heart out; split his sides with laughter; think before thou speakest; let us forget and forgive injuries (forgive and forget); I must speak the truth and nothing but the truth; I begin to smell a rat; birds of a feather flock together; the proof of the pudding is in the eating; the fair sex; neither will I make myself anybody's laughingstock; forewarned forearmed; turn over a new leaf; honesty's the best policy; he would not budge an inch; with a grain of salt; mum's the word; the pot calls the kettle black; there were but two families in the world, Have-much and Have-little (haves and have-nots).*

thank you. In Kenya *thank you* is the customary English reply when someone says "good-bye."

thank your lucky stars. The idea that the stars sway human destiny is as old as mankind. The phrase *thank your stars* goes back at least to Ben Jonson, who used it in *Every Man Out of His Humour* (1599): "I thanke my Starres for it." *Thank your good stars* is next recorded in 1706, and the variation *thank your lucky stars* is a relatively modern development of the 19th century or so.

that damned cowboy. Vice President Theodore Roosevelt, who had been a North Dakota rancher from 1884 to 1886 and formed a cowboy "Rough Riders" unit during the Spanish-American War, became president of the United States in 1901 when William McKinley was assassinated. Political boss Senator Mark Hanna's comment was "Now look, that damned cowboy is president."

that dog don't hunt. That idea or theory isn't logical, doesn't wash; popularized in the movie *J.F.K.* (1991), set in New Orleans and Texas.

that gets me. *Get one's dander up, get one's Irish up, get one's Indian up,* and even *get one's Ebenezer* (Ebenezer was a nickname for the devil) *up,* were only a few of the many *get me . . .* terms meaning "to become angry" that were common in 19th-century America. So common were such terms that *that gets me* came to mean "that angers or annoys me."

that rings the bell. That's perfect, just what we wanted. This Americanism, first recorded in 1904, is almost certainly from the carnival game where one tests his strength by driving a weight up a pole with a mallet and wins if he rings the bell at the top.

that's a good one. That's a great joke or story, although it can also mean "that's quite a lie." It is in the first sense that the expression was first recorded, in William Wycherley's *The Country Wife* (1672). There Alithea tells Sparkish he ought to hate his rival for courting her. "That's a good one!" Sparkish says. "I hate a man for loving you! If he did love you, 'tis but what he can't help; and 'tis your fault, not his, if he admires you."

that's a hell of a note. *Note* in this expression probably refers to a badly tuned note on a musical instrument, not a counterfeit banknote. The words mean "something disagreeably or unpleasantly surprising"—"What a revoltin' development!" as one TV comedian of old put it. The expression is an Americanism first recorded in 1871.

That's all, folks! These are the concluding words of many *Merry Melodies* cartoons produced by Warner Brothers since about 1930. It is said that Mel Blanc (1908–89), the voice of Bugs Bunny and other Merry Melodies cartoon characters, chose the words for his epitaph. I've read that others have done so too. *See also* WHAT'S UP, DOC.

that's all she wrote. Meaning that's the end of it, it's finished, that's all there is, *that's all she wrote* is first recorded in 1948 as college slang, but probably dates back before World War II. It may have derived from the Dear John letters breaking up a relationship that some soldiers received from wives and sweethearts while away from home. This seems to be indicated by its use in James Jones's novel *From Here to Eternity*, which takes place just before World War II: "All she'd have to do, if she got caught with you, would be to holler rape and it would be Dear John, that's all she wrote."

that's a no-no; no-no.   *No-no* is baby talk first recorded in 1942 that means "something is forbidden, must not be done," as in "that's a no-no," a phrase frequently heard today. Television's *Rowan & Martin's Laugh In*, which premiered in 1968, featured the expression, making it a national catchphrase.

that's George.   Some anonymous eponymous George may have inspired the coining of *that's George*, or *that's real George*, but no one has ever revealed a real George behind the words. *That's George*, meaning "excellent, great, or fine" ("That's a real George car he's got there") was first recorded in 1930, far too late for George Washington or George III to be responsible, as someone has suggested.

that's how the cow ate the cabbage.   An expression to indicate the speaker is laying it on the line, telling it like it is, getting down to brass tacks—with the connotation of telling someone what he or she needs to know but probably doesn't want to hear. According to Little Rock attorney Alston Jennings, who submitted this southernism to Richard Allen's February 2, 1991, "Our Town" column in the *Arkansas Gazette*, the expression has its roots in a story about an elephant that escaped from the zoo and wandered into a woman's cabbage patch. The woman observed the elephant pulling up her cabbages with its trunk and eating them. She called the police to report that there was a cow in her cabbage patch pulling up cabbages with its tail. When the surprised police officer inquired as to what the cow was doing with the cabbages, the woman replied, "You wouldn't believe me if I told you!"

that's life; that's the way it goes; that's the way the ball bounces.   *That's life*, meaning "that's fate, that's the fortunes of life, the way things happen," probably dates back at least to the turn of the century. It is thought to be a loan translation of the French *c'est la vie*. The American expression *That's the way the ball bounces*, meaning the same, appears to have originated with U.S. forces in Korea, while the synonymous *that's the way it goes* came into the language a little later.

that's really gross.   In Australia this expression means "that's really great, very good," just the opposite of what it means in American English.

that's show biz!   That's how things are and you'd better accept it, there's nothing else to do. Though it sounds like a modern expression, the words date back to the mid-19th century. *That's life* is a similar phrase, as is *That's the way the world whirls*.

that's that.   Common in both the U.S. and England for "that's the end of it," *that's that!* probably dates back to World War I,

though it isn't recorded until the late 1920s. Variants are *and that's that* and *and that is that!*

that's the ball game.   One would suspect that phrases like this, meaning that's the end of anything from a sports contest to an election, have been used since the first baseball game was played. So were expressions like *it's a whole new ball game*, "it's a new beginning," and *it's the only ball game in town*, "it's the only choice available."

that's where the West begins.   An expression from Arthur Chapman's poem "Out Where the West Begins," the refrain of which goes: "Out where the handclasp's a little stronger, / Out where the smile dwells a little longer, / That's where the West begins."

that was no lady—that was my wife.   The vaudeville comedian's answer to the question "Who was that lady I saw you with last night?" The joke was old when it was used it British music halls over a century ago.

that won't wash.   That (usually exaggerated) excuse, story, or alibi won't do. Though it seems like a recent coinage this expression dates back to about the early 1840s in England. It was originally said of poor fabrics that wouldn't hold up to washing. "That willn't wash, miss," is said by a character in Charlotte Bronte's *Shirley* (1849), set in the time of the Luddite riots when the Yorkshire wool industry suffered great losses. "He won't wash," the didactic British novelist and poet Charles Kingsley (1819–75) said about the poet Robert Browning's literary reputation in a letter to a friend.

the.   The definite article *the* is, according to at least three major studies, the most frequently used word in English. *I*, surprisingly enough, only ranks among the top 10 in two of the three surveys.

theater.   The word *theater* or *theatre* comes from the Greek *theatron*, a place for seeing. No theater existed in this sense of the word before the planned theaters of the ancient Greeks; all previous plays were performed in such places as temple courts and terraces. The very first theater, so far as is known, was the theater of Dionysus at Athens, the ruins of which can be seen today. It was patterned on "natural theaters" at the foot of hillsides on which spectators stood or sat. Rome's Colosseum, built in A.D. 180 and covering five acres, was the largest of the classical theaters or amphitheaters measured by its dimensions and seating capacity, with a total of 87,000 seats. According to *The Guiness Book of World Record* (1998), Australia's Perth Entertainment Centre (1976) is the world's largest indoor theater, with 8,003 seats. *See* COLOSSEUM; YOUNG FOLK OF THE PEAR GARDEN.

theater of the absurd.   *See* ABSURD.

Theon's tooth.   A bitter, biting critic is sometimes said to have Theon's tooth. The expression commemorates the ancient Roman poet Theon, noted for his sharp satires.

Theophrastus.   No one knows the real name of the Greek philosopher Theophrastus (ca. 37–ca. 287 B.C.). So eloquent was this pupil of Aristotle's that he is remembered only by the name his master gave him: Theophrastus—meaning that he spoke like a god. Another godlike philosopher was the French visionary preacher and pamphleteer Catherine Theot (1725–94), who believed that she was the mother of God and changed her name (*Theot*) to *Theos,* "God." Chilean poet Vicente Huidobro (1893–1948) often signed himself "The God of Poetry." *Godlike* was a nickname of American statesman Daniel Webster.

therblig. A term used in time and motion study, meaning "any of the basic elements involved in completing a given manual task that can be subjected to analysis," *therblig* is an anagram of the name of American engineer Frank B. Gilbreth (1868–1924) of *Cheaper by the Dozen* fame.

there ain't no horse that can't be rode / there ain't no man that can't be throwed. An old saying common among American cowboys.

there, but for the grace of God, goes God. Winston Churchill is credited with coining this phrase. Noticing the pompous Sir Stafford Cripps pass by him one day, he turned to a friend and observed, "There, but for the grace of God, goes God."

there but for the grace of God go I. On seeing several criminals being led to the scaffold in the 16th century, English Protestant martyr John Bradford remarked: "There, but for the grace of God, goes John Bradford." His words, without his name, are still very common ones today for expressing one's blessings compared to the fate of another. Bradford was later burned at the stake as a heretic.

there's a one-eyed man in the game. Watch out for a cheat. The expression had its origins in poker, from an old superstition that it was unlucky to play cards with a one-eyed gambler.

there's as good fish in the sea as ever came out of it. Don't be discouraged if you lose one chance; there will be another just as good. A proverbial English saying since the late 16th century.

there's a sucker born every minute. Showman P. T. Barnum lived by this principle, but he probably didn't invent the phrase so often attributed to him. Since there is no recorded instance of Barnum uttering the words, they must be credited to "Anonymous," like another famous American cynicism, *Never give a sucker an even break,* which was the title of a W. C. Fields movie. Terms that Barnum did coin or help popularize include JUMBO, BANDWAGON, SIAMESE TWINS, the Bearded Lady, the Wild Man of Borneo, Swedish Nightingale, Tom Thumb, Three-Ring Circus, and the Greatest Show on Earth.

there's many a slip twixt (between) cup and lip. This ancient expression, which means that no plan is sure until it is accomplished, is supposed to have originated with a slave of the legendary Ancaeus, the son of Poseidon. The abused slave told his cruel master that he would not live to drink the wine from his treasured vineyards. Spiting him, Ancaeus took a cup of new wine and prepared to drink it. "There's many a slip

betwixt cup and lip," the slave quipped and just then another slave entered the room with news that a wild boar was rooting up vines in the vineyard. Putting down his untasted cup, Ancaeus ran out to deal with the wild boar, which proceeded to kill him.

there's nothing in the middle of the road but yellow stripes and dead armadillos. An admonition against excessive moderation attributed to Texas politician Jim Hightower.

there's nothing new under the sun. This old saying goes back to the 16th century and derives from the biblical "There is no new thing under the sun," found in Ecclesiastes 1:9.

"There Was a Little Girl." The well-known poem by Henry Wadsworth Longfellow was written just after he had witnessed his little daughter Edith strongly protesting her mother's attempts to curl her hair:

> There was a little girl
> Who had a little curl
> Right in the middle of her forehead;
> And when she was good
> She was very very good
> But when she was bad she was horrid.

there were giants in the earth in those days. There seems always to be a feeling, among older people at least, that the present generation is a degeneration of generations past. The notion is an ancient one, the above expression, for example, recorded in the book of Genesis.

thermos. *See* DEWAR FLASK.

thersitical. Among the loudest, most foulmouthed men of all time was Thersites, an officer in the Greek army at the siege of Troy. The ugly, deformed Thersites, whose name means "the Audacious," liked nothing better than arguing, we are told in the *Iliad,* his mean temper sparing no one, be he humble or great. Greek legend tells us that he reviled even Achilles—laughing at his grief over the death of Penthesilea, the queen of the Amazons—and that Achilles promptly kayoed him permanently with one blow to the jaw. Thanks largely to Shakespeare's treatment of the scurrilous Thersites in *Troilus and Cressida,* we have the adjective *thersitical,* "loudmouthed and foulmouthed." *See* HECTOR; NESTOR; STENTORIAN.

thesaurus. First recorded as the word for a collection of synonyms in 1852, with the publication of Peter Mark Roget's *Thesaurus of English Words and Phrases* (often called simply *Roget's* today), our word *thesaurus* can be traced all the way back to the Greek *thesauros,* treasury. It was used in this sense of treasury in English long before it was applied to a collection of synonyms, dictionaries, for example, being called *thesauruses.*

thespian. A *thespian* is an actor, and as an adjective the word means "pertaining to tragedy or dramatic art." Both words pay tribute to the first professional actor. According to legend, Thespis was a Greek poet of the late sixth century B.C., who recited his poems at festivals of the gods around the country; he is even said to have invented tragedy and to have created the first dialogue spoken on the stage in the form of exchanges between himself as an actor reading his poems and responses by a chorus. Thespis is probably a semilegendary figure, his name possibly an assumed one. The popular story that he went around Attica in a cart in which his plays were acted is of doubtful authenticity, but may be partly true. *See* ROSCIAN. In recent times *thesping* has become theatrical slang for acting.

they never go back to Pocatello.   An old political saying meaning that legislators who lose elections don't usually return home, but remain in Washington, D.C., in some other occupation. Pocatello is a city of some 50,000 inhabitants in southeast Idaho.

they shall not pass!   The French rallying cry in World War I when on February 20, 1916, the Germans tried to break the deadlock in the Great War by launching a huge assault on the town of Verdun. The French did hold fast, though they suffered enormous losses, a total of over 1 million men eventually killed on both sides in the nine-month battle for the city, which was the war's longest and bloodiest battle. Verdun had to be almost completely rebuilt after the war. The words *They shall not pass (Ils ne passeront pas!)* are attributed by some to MARSHAL PÉTAIN, the great French hero of World War I, whose name became synonymous for *traitor* in World War II.

thick as Jesse.   Very thick-skinned, unreasonably resistant to arguments. Another reference (like Jumbo) to the name of an elephant—in this case the London Zoo's pachyderm Jesse, who was very popular in the late 19th century.

thimblerig.   Thimblerig is a sleight-of-hand swindling game in which the operator palms a pea while appearing to cover it with one of three thimblelike cups, and offers to bet that no one can tell under which cup the pea lies. The name is first recorded in about 1815 and is still heard, but is mainly known as the shell game today after the walnut shells it is played with.

thin air.   *See* VANISH INTO THIN AIR.

thingamabob; thingamajig.   *See* DINGBAT.

A thing of beauty is a joy forever.   Not a proverb but from John Keats's poem "Endymion," which the poet based upon the legend of Endymion, the handsome shepherd of Greek mythology who was loved by the moon goddess Selena. The full line from the long poem, dedicated to poet Thomas Chatterton, goes:

> A thing of beauty is a joy for ever:
> Its loveliness increases; it will never
> Pass into nothingness; but still will keep
> A bower quiet for us, and a sleep
> Full of sweet dreams, and health, and quiet breathing.

The poem was written in September 1818, the beginning of a year ending in September 1819 that became known as "The Great Year," when Keats, only 24, wrote over a dozen masterpieces, including "La Belle Dame sans Merci," "Ode to a Nightingale," and "ODE ON A GRECIAN URN". Yet for all this, he would later write to Fanny Brawne (Feb. 1820): " 'If I should die,' said I to myself, 'I have left no immortal work behind me—nothing to make my friends proud of my memory—but

I have loved the principle of beauty in all things, and if I *had* time I would have made myself remembered.' " *See* DEATH'S HEAD MOTH.

thin ice.   *See* CAT ICE; SKATE ON THIN ICE.

thinking cap.   This expressions seems to have originated in the 17th century as *put on your considering cap*, that is, "take time to think something over." At the time square-cut, tight-fitting caps were worn by scholars, clergymen, and jurists, who were all regarded as intelligent "thinking men" by the masses. Any or all of these professional men could have suggested the phrase, the common man believing that their caps helped them to think. But *considering cap* is most likely a reference to the fact that English judges once put on their caps before passing sentences in all cases, just as they still do before passing the death sentence.

think out of the box.   Here's another one that may not be recorded anywhere else. *Think out of the box* means "to find unconventional solutions to problems, to be unbound by traditional thinking." Its origins are unclear, but the expression has been common in business circles for a few years.

thinks one hung the moon and stars.   Someone who loves somebody madly, and blindly, as if that person were a god. According to Professor Frederick Cassidy, who is in the process of compiling a monumental study of American regionalisms, this expression is a southernism. It has been around since at least early in this century and by now, deservedly, has spread to other regions of the country.

thin red line of heroes.   "The Russians dashed on toward that thin-red line streak tipped with a line of steel," wrote W. H. Russell, the greatest war correspondent of his day, in reporting the Battle of Balaclava for the *London Times*. He was describing the 93rd Highland Infantry which hadn't formed in a defensive square. Rudyard Kipling scoffed at this romantic notion in his poem "Tommy," where his British soldier remarks about a *thin red line of 'eroes* and later adds "We aren't no thin red 'eroes."

third degree.   As a term for "prolonged questioning and rough handling of a person by the police in order to obtain information or a confession of guilt," *to get the third degree* dates back only to about the 1890s in America. The phrase has no connection with "murder in the third degree" or any language of criminal law. The third degree is the highest degree, that of Master Mason, in Freemasonry. Any Mason must undergo very difficult tests of proficiency before he qualifies for the third degree and it is probably from these "tests" that the exhaustive questioning of criminals came to be called the *third degree*, though there is no brutality, physical or mental, involved in the Masonic exam.

third rate.   *See* FIRST RATE.

Third Reich.   *See* REICHSTAG.

30 (thirty).   For over a century the symbol *30* has been used by reporters to mark the end of a typewritten newspaper story.

It comes either from the old telegraphy symbol indicating the end of a day's transmission, a kind of "Goodnight, I'm closing up the office," or from old printers' jargon. The maximum line on Linotype composing machines is 30 picas, about five inches, and when an operator reaches 30 picas, he can go no farther.

38th parallel.   *See* FORGOTTEN WAR.

30-something.   Used to describe someone between 30 and 40 years old, *30-something* was popularized by the U.S. T.V. show of the same name in the late 1980s. Unlike the earlier term *29-plus*, which people once used to hide their age, *30-something* is not an attempt at such concealment.

this great stage of fools.   This world. The full line, from Shakespeare's *King Lear* (1604–5), is "When we are born, we cry, that we are come / To this great stage of fools." Lear's words (act IV, scene 6) are preceded by his lines "Thou know'st the first time that we smell the air / We waul [wail] and cry. . . ."

this is a hell of a way to run a railway.   An example (*see* MUTT AND JEFF) of a cartoon contributing an expression to the language. In this case the common saying describing something in a state of confusion possibly originated in a cartoon published in a 1932 issue of *Ballyhoo Magazine*. The cartoon shows two trains coming at each other on the same track and about to crash. "This is a hell of a way to run a railway," a railway signalman says. But the expression may date back to the turn of the century, according to the recollections of several word enthusiasts who remember hearing it that far back.

this is the sort of nonsense up with which I will not put.   Winston Churchill made the above comment when told that a sentence can never be ended with a preposition.

thistle.   The thistle became the heraldic emblem of Scotland in the eighth century or earlier in commemoration of the role it played in an attack by the Danes on Stirling Castle. Barefooted Dane scouts stepped on thistles during that night attack, alarming the Scots and enabling them to defeat the raiders. All thistles are members of the *Compositae*, one of the largest families of plants in the world, including among its relatives such fine garden flowers as marigolds, asters, cosmos, dahlias, and chrysanthemums. But thistles are generally thought of as a prickly weed that is little valued. Abraham Lincoln's lowest estimate of a man was to call him a thistle. The word dates back in English to at least A.D. 752 and its origins are unknown.

Thomism.   The philosophy of St. Thomas Aquinas (ca. 1225–74), who has been called, among many more titles, the "Angelic Doctor," the "Father of Moral Philosophy," and the "Prince of Scholastics." His name, Thomas of Aquino, comes from his birthplace in southern Italy, from where he set out as a Dominican friar on pilgrimages in search of truth and knowledge, against the wishes of his father, the count of Aquino. His system of philosophy has greatly influenced Roman Catholic doctrines.

thorn in one's side.   The Talmud describes 10 classes of Pharisees, members of a strict, ascetic Jewish sect arising in the second century whose name in Hebrew means "apart" (from the crowd), "separated" (from the rest of mankind). These classes include the "Immovables," who stood like statues for hours while praying; the "Mortars," who wore mortars, or caps, which covered their eyes so that their meditations wouldn't be disturbed by the sight of passersby; and the "Bleeders," who put thorns in their trousers so that their legs would be pricked as they walked. The Pharisees' tendency to look upon themselves as holier than others gives us our modern definition of a Pharisee as "a self-righteous hypocritical person," and the "Bleeders" among the sect possibly inspired the saying *a thorn in one's side*. At least St. Paul may have had them in mind when he described a source of constant irritation or personal vexation as *a thorn in the flesh* in 2 Cor. 12:7. Then again, he may have simply taken the image from native plants like the buckthorn and acadia, whose thorns made travel difficult in the Holy Land. Over the years Paul's biblical phrase was altered to *a thorn in my side*, although the original is still used as well.

thorn in the flesh.   *See* THORN IN ONE'S SIDE.

thou.   *See* QUAKER.

three blind mice.   Only "Hickory, dickery, dock" rivals the jingle "Three Blind Mice" as a popular rhyme: "Three blind mice, three blind mice, / See how they run, see how they run! / They all run after the farmer's wife, / Who cut off their tails with a carving knife, / Did you ever see such a sight in you life / As three blind mice?" Several historians have linked these words with three men whom England's Queen Mary I put to death during her reign, the farmer's wife being "Bloody Mary" herself. In the U.S. today *three blind mice* is often a taunt shouted at baseball umpires.

three bricks shy of a load.   An Americanism dating back to the 1960s, which is also heard as "a few bricks shy of a load." It describes someone simple-minded, or a little crazy or eccentric. The Australian version is *a few snags* (sausages) *shy of a Barbie* (barbecue).

three cheers.   Much has been written about the REBEL YELL Confederate soldiers often gave when going into battle. The *Union* forces in the Civil War gave what was called three cheers when they attacked.

three-fifths compromise.   Under the U.S. Constitution, slaves were considered property and had no vote, but in order to redress the imbalance of representation between the populous North and the sparsely settled South, the southern states were allowed by the Founding Fathers to count each slave as three-fifths of a person for their congressional apportionment. This meant in practice that the more slaves there were, the less power they had and the more power the slaveholders enjoyed.

360-degree son of a bitch.   Cormac McCarthy explains the term in his novel *Child of God* (1974), set in the Kentucky backwoods: "No, those were sorry people all the way around, every man jack a three hundred and sixty degree son of a bitch, which my daddy said meant they was a son of a bitch any way you looked at them."

three-martini lunch.   A business lunch with martinis or other potables that is used as a tax write-off. Who invented the term is unknown, but pundit William Safire, in his *Safire's Political Dictionary* (1978), says South Dakota senator George McGovern popularized the expression when he ran for president in 1972, attacking the three-martini (or "martoonie") lunch as a common example of unnecessary business expense footed by the taxpayer. *See* MARTINI.

three-mile limit.   This is usually the limit of territorial waters—that is, waters on their coasts—claimed by maritime nations. It is the limit claimed by the law of the U.S., Britain, and most other nations, but, as recent disputes have shown, some nations claim much wider jurisdiction over their waters.

threepeat.   A relatively new word, based on *repeat* and meaning to do something three times in a row, this expression may have been coined by New York Knicks coach Pat Riley in 1993, when the Chicago Bulls won the National Basketball Association title for the third straight year. There is already some controversy about the word's first use. After the previous edition of this book was published, San Francisco running back Roger Craig claimed he used the word in 1990.

three-ring circus.   *See* THERE'S A SUCKER BORN EVERY MINUTE.

three R's.   The three R's are of course reading, writing and arithmetic. One persistent old story has it that they are so called because an early Lord Mayor of London, Sir William Curtis, a man with good intentions if not learned, once proposed a toast: "To Reading, Riting, and Rithmetic!"

three score and ten.   The phrase is biblical, from Psalm 90: 10, which advises that "The days of our years [our lifespan] are three score years and ten [seventy years]." The passage goes on to say, however, that "if by reason of strength they [our years] be fourscore [80] years, yet is their strength labor and sorrow, for it is soon cut off, and we fly away." *See* FOURSCORE AND SEVEN.

3-7-77.   The numerals 3-7-77, accompanied by a skull and crossbones, were first used by vigilantes to warn a man to leave the county; the measurement three feet wide, seven feet long and 77 inches deep is roughly that of a grave.

three sheets to the wind.   "Sheets" aren't sails in nautical use; neither are they bed coverings. A sheet is the rope or chain attached to the lower corner of a sail that is used for shortening and extending it. When all three sheets on a three-sailed vessel (such as a ketch) are loosened, allowed to run free, the sails flap and flutter in the wind. Thus sailors would say a person slightly drunk had *one sheet to the wind* and that someone who could barely navigate had *three sheets to the wind*. The expression is first recorded in Richard Henry Dana's *Two Years Before the Mast* (1840). Professor Albert Huetteman of the University of Massachusetts advised me of another possible derivation of *three sheets to the wind*: "On Nantucket Island . . . we took the local tour bus, which stopped at the Nantucket windmill. The elderly gentleman tour guide told us a story of how the windmill keeper's job was to install the canvas sheets on the four arms of the windmill when the wind conditions were right. If he drank too much, however, he might only install three sheets, thus giving rise to the phrase, 'three sheets to the wind.' "

three sisters.   The Iroquois Indian name for corn, pole beans, and squash, the staples of their diet before the Europeans came. The beans were planted next to the hills of corn and climbed the corn stalks, enriching the soil with nitrogen at the same time, while the broad-leaved squash plants that were planted shaded the soil, inhibiting weed growth.

three-tailed bashaw.   Hardly heard anymore, this old phrase is worth reviving. A *bashaw* is an important Turkish official, now more often called a *pasha. Three-tailed* refers to the horse tails attached to this official's standard, three being the most any bashaw boasted. The expression dates back to the 17th century.

threshold.   Farmers originally threshed wheat, separated the grain from the chaff, by trodding on piles of it. According to one theory, this trodding seemed similar to wiping one's feet at the doorway of a house, which took the name *threshold* from such threshing. In any case, the word is first recorded in about A.D. 1000.

thrice.   *Thrice,* "three times," isn't used much today in British or American English, but is still commonly heard in India, as in "She saw him thrice in one day."

Throgmorton Street.   Throgmorton Street is to England what Wall Street is to America—the center of the financial or business world. The Stock Exchange is located on this narrow London Street, which was named for Sir Nicholas Throgmorton (1515–71), who served Queen Elizabeth I as a soldier and ambassador to France and Scotland. The diplomat was given to intrigue, however, and also served two stretches in the Tower, though not stretched on the rack there.

through the mill.   *See* PUT THROUGH THE MILL.

throw.   When we say "These tickets are a dollar a throw," we mean they are a dollar apiece. The expression possibly derives from those carnival games where players throw balls, hoops, or rings, trying to win a prize. *Throw* meaning to deliberately lose a fight or game is an American sports and gambling term from the mid-19th century.

throw cold water on (something).   To cold-pie or cold-pig someone, to wake him up by throwing cold water on him, was a practice well known and despised in Elizabethan times. Perhaps *cold-pigging* suggested the expression to *throw cold water on* (something), "to discourage a plan or practice," for it surely ruined many a good dream. But a lot of guesses are possible here. The expression is at least 200 years old and could also have been suggested by hydrotherapy, the so-called ocean cold-water cures with which many a physical and mental illness was treated by dousing a patient with cold seawater. Anyway, the treatment was said to reduce the "mental heat" of extremely nervous persons and make them apathetic.

throw down the gauntlet. The English language contains two wholly different words spelled and pronounced *gauntlet*. The *gauntlet* in this expression means glove and derives from the medieval French *gantelet*, "a little glove." Knights of the age of chivalry, though not so noble as they seem in romances, did play by certain rules. When one knight wanted to cross swords with another, he issued a challenge by throwing down his mailed glove, or gauntlet, and his challenge was accepted if the other knight picked up the metal-plated leather glove. This custom gave us the expression *to throw down the gauntlet*, "to make a serious challenge." *See* RUN THE GAUNTLET.

throw dust in the eyes of. To mislead or deceive. Throwing dust or sand in the air to conceal their movements from their enemies on the field of battle was an ancient Arab trick in desert warfare. This is probably the origin of the expression, which Quintillian used figuratively as early as A.D. 80 to describe the great Roman orator Cicero: "He threw dust in the eyes of the jury."

throw fear (caution) to the wind. *See* SECOND CHILDHOOD.

throw in the towel. *Throw in the towel* and *throw in the sponge*—both meaning to give up, quit, or admit one has been defeated—have been around at least since the 1860s and probably date back to 18th-century England. The expression comes from boxing, where a fighter's corner man throws a towel into the ring to stop the fight when he determines that his fighter has taken enough punishment and has no chance of winning. Figuratively, the colorful phrase came to mean the admission of defeat by anyone from a politician to a saint. Possibly the color of a white towel, suggesting a white flag of surrender, has helped the first variation endure.

throw into stitches. Here stabbing became a joking matter. The Old English *stice*, from the same Teutonic root that gives us "stick," meant a prick, stab, or puncture inflicted by a pointed object, especially pain caused by acute spasms of the rib muscles after prolonged or violent exercise such as running. These stitches in the side are more painful but similar to pains from excessive laughter, when one "laughs so much that it hurts." Thus anyone who told a funny story that convulsed his audience was said to *throw them into stitches*. Shakespeare seems to have first suggested the expression in *Twelfth Night* (1601) when he wrote, "If you . . . will laugh yourselves into stitches, follow me," but when the exact words were coined is unknown. A *stitch* in sewing comes from the same root word.

thrown for a loss. Born as a football expression, *thrown for a loss* refers to a ball carrier who is thrown back for a loss by the opposing line on trying to penetrate its defense and gain yardage. Common in football, the words began to be used in post–World War II years to describe someone's loss in any endeavor.

throw someone a curve. If you surprise someone in a negative way, deceive or mislead or ask a tricky question, you are throwing someone a curve. The expression has its roots in the curve pitch of baseball, which comes directly toward the batter and then breaks away, often surprising or tricking him. The first recorded mention of a *curveball* in baseball is 1874,

but the pitch was introduced by Hall of Famer William Arthur "Candy" Cummings.

throw the book at. Sorry, but I can find no record of a judge literally throwing a law book at a convicted criminal. However, during the Prohibition gangster era many judges did figuratively throw the *contents* of law books at criminals when sentencing them, imposing every penalty found in books of law for their particular crimes. In underworld argot *the book* came to mean the maximum penalty that could be imposed for a crime, especially life imprisonment. Although its original meaning is still common, the metaphor has come to stand for penalties much less severe as well, sometimes nothing more serious than a parent taking away the car keys from a child as a punishment for coming in too late.

throw to the dogs. *See* GO TO THE DOGS.

throw to the wolves. In a grisly Russian folk tale a family pursued by a wolf pack throws infants from their sleigh at intervals to keep the wolves busy until they reach their house. This, or some story like it, may be the origin of the expression *to throw to the wolves*, which means of course to adandon someone or turn someone in in order to benefit oneself.

thug. An Indian sect of religious fanatics called the P'hanisigars, "noose operators," whom the British euphemistically called Thugs, from a Sanskrit word (sthaga) meaning "rogue or cheater," dated back to at least the 13th century. The thugs supposedly honored Kali the Hindu goddess of destruction with their murders and thievery. They would worm their way into the confidence of travelers, or would follow a wealthy victim for weeks sometimes before finding him in a lonely place and slipping a rope or cloth noose around his neck. The group was as well organized as the Syndicate today, even speaking a secret language, Ramasi, and bribing government officials for protection. The British eliminated the Thugs in India in the 1830s when they hanged 412 of them and sentenced another 2,844 to life imprisonment, but the name of the band lives on after them. *Thug*, an ugly word, is still used for ugly criminal types from tough guys to assassins, and *thuggee* is sometimes heard for the crime of strangulation that the Thugs perfected.

thumb. The thumb is of course the thickest of the five fingers on the human hand, unless one takes the view that we do not have five fingers but four fingers and a thumb. In any case, the thumb, so important to the development of the human race, was thought to be a thick digit by our ancestors and it takes its name from the Old English *thumba*, thick or swollen. *See also* INDEX FINGER; MIDDLE FINGER; PINKY; RING FINGER.

thumbs down. First, we have the traditional story: *Habet!* or "He's had it," Roman spectators shouted when they wanted a defeated gladiator to be killed. Their shouts were accompanied by a thumbs-down gesture that is believed to be the ancestor of the same gesture we use today and of our expression *thumbs down* for "no!" Some Latinists, however, say that *thumbs down* is a mistranslation of the Latin phrase *pollice verso*, which means "thumbs turned." According to this theory, spectators made the gesture *pollice primo*, "thumbs in front," when a gladiator fought a good fight, and made the gesture *pollice verso* if he fought poorly and they wanted him killed. The idea that *pollice verso* meant "thumbs down," this story holds, seems to have been first suggested by a painting of 19th-century French artist Jean Léon Gérôme that depicted scowling Roman spectators holding their thumbs down at the end of a gladiatorial contest.

thunderbolt.   *See* SHOOT ONE'S BOLT.

Thursday.   Thor was considered the god of thunder in ancient times, and it was thought that it thundered when his great chariot was drawn across the sky. His day was *thuresdaeg* in Anglo-Saxon times, this becoming our *Thursday*.

Thursday's child.   *See* MONDAY'S CHILD.

thyme.   We pronounce the *th* in *thyme* (time) as a *t* because it passed into English from the French with that pronunciation at an early date. Thyme ultimately comes from the Greek *thuo*, "perfume," in reference to the herb's sweet smell.

thyroid.   The thyroid cartilage, or ADAM'S APPLE, which protects the throat, was named for its resemblance to the shields of Homeric warriors, deriving from the Greek word for "shield" or "shield-shaped." It gave its name to the thyroid gland that straddles the windpipe. The term is first recorded in 1693.

tick.   Ticks, a species of which spreads Lyme disease, are insects to be avoided. Though only pinhead size in most cases, they attach themselves to the skin, gorging themselves on blood until they swell to twice their size or larger. This led to the expression "full as a tick" to describe someone who has had much too much to drink.

ticker tape.   The tape emanating from the first stock ticker installed in the New York Stock Exchange in 1867 was called ribbon. Ticker tape didn't come into use until the turn of the century.

tick-tock.   Journalists use this recent U.S. term to mean "the time sequence of events," as in "What's the tick-tock on this?" when does it happen, how long will it last?, etc.

tiddly; tiddlywinks.   In British Cockney rhyming slang a *tiddlywink* meant a drink. From this expression comes *tiddly*, for "a little drunk," first recorded in the late 19th century. The game *tiddlywinks* is first recorded in 1870 and may be so named because of the little counters used in playing it, *tiddly* here perhaps being baby talk for "little."

tide.   Though a sea tide is usually thought to be high or low water, anything between ebb and flood, *tide* really means "the fixed time of flood and ebb." *Tide* was originally a synonym for *time* (as in eventide), so the expression "Time and tide wait for no man" is something of a tautology. The Greek navigator Pytheas observed and explored ocean tides in the third century B.C., but it wasn't until Isaac Newton's time that scientists widely believed that the Moon had any effect on ocean tides. The greatest tides occur in the Bay of Fundy, Nova Scotia, where there is an extreme range of 57 feet between high and low tides and 100 million tons of water are carried out of the bay twice each day.

tidy.   Since TIDE was originally a synonym for *time*, *tidy* came to mean "in tide, in time, timely." Something timely or tidy later became something methodical or neat, the word's meaning today.

tied to one's mother's apron strings.   "Apron-string hold" or "apron-string tenure" was a law about four centuries ago under which a husband could hold title to property passed on to his wife by her family only while his wife lived—provided that she had not divorced him. Many wives therefore controlled the purse strings and made all important family decisions, in which their husbands didn't have much to say. Such men, who often did just as they were told, were said to be *tied to their wives' apron strings*, a phrase suggested by "apron-string hold." Because male children in such a family tended to be dominated by their mothers as well, even when they were fully grown, the now more common expression *tied to his mother's apron strings* arose. French writer Gérard de Nerval (1808–55) actually hanged himself from a lamppost with an apron string. *Apron* is a corruption of *napron*, from the French *naperon*, "a little table-cloth," a *napron* corrupted to *an apron* in English.

tie the knot.   In ancient times the marriage ceremony in many parts of the world consisted only of a priest or the family patriarch knotting together the garments of the bride and groom to symbolize a permanent union. The practice, still a custom in some countries today, is the basis for the universal saying *to tie the knot*, meaning to get married, for which *tying the knot* has been a symbol in England since at least 1275. The Greeks followed the custom of *untying* a knot to declare a marriage. Brides used the Herculean knot, a representation of the snakes entwined on the rod of Mercury, to fasten their woolen girdles. Only the bridegroom was allowed to untie this knot, praying as he did so that the gods would make his marriage as fruitful as that of Hercules—that is, very fruitful indeed, for Hercules once married the 50 daughters of Thestius, all of whom gave birth to his children on the same night. This last was *not* one of the legendary 12 labors of Hercules.

Tiffany glass, etc.   Tiffany and Company, the famous jewelry firm in New York City, was founded by Charles Lewis Tiffany (1812–1902). During the Civil War the firm turned out swords and other war supplies, but was noted for its manufacture of gold and silver jewelry, the improvement of silverware design, and the importation of historic gems and jewelry from Europe. Branches were soon opened in London and Geneva, Charles Tiffany winning fame as the inventor of the *Tiffany setting*, as in a ring where prongs hold the stone in place. His son, Louis Comfort Tiffany (1848–1933), became an artist and art patron, remembered chiefly for his invention of *Tiffany glass* in 1890. Trademarked as *Favrile glass*, the iridescent art glass was made by the Tiffany Furnaces, which Louis established at Corona, New York. There glass for mosaics and windows, vases, and Tiffany lampshades was manufactured.

tiger lily.   This ubiquitous flower, often found on roadsides and in woods in the northeastern United States, originated in Japan or China. It takes its name from its orange and black colors. According to a Korean legend, *Lilium tigrinum* was named when a magician-hermit changed his pet tiger into a flower he could keep in his garden. After the magician died, the tiger lily left the garden and journeyed all over the world searching for his friend, which is why tiger lilies are so widespread. There is no reason why tiger lilies should talk more than other flowers, except that Lewis Carroll made them so inclined in *Through the Looking Glass*. The tiger lilies there tell Alice that they talk all the time "when there's anybody worth talking to." They also offer a tip to people who'd like to hear their flowers talk. When Alice wants to know why she's never heard flowers talk in other gardens, they explain, "In most gardens, they make the beds too soft—so that the flowers are always asleep."

tigers of the desert. A name for the Apache Indians among U.S. soldiers and settlers in the 19th century, when they were looked upon with fear and awe.

tiggerty-boo. *See* EVERYTHING'S ALL TIGGERTY-BOO.

tight as Dick's hatband. This phrase refers to the fact that the crown was too tight or dangerous to be worn by a certain king of England. The particular king's identity is unknown, but one popular theory suggests Oliver Cromwell's son Richard, often called Tumbledown Dick, who was nominated by his father to succeed him but served for only seven months beginning in September, 1658 because he received no support from the army. Another candidate is King Richard III, who assumed the throne in 1483, denouncing the rightful claims of his two young nephews. Long regarded as an evil king who ordered the "accidental deaths" of his nephews, Richard is said to have been uncomfortable wearing a crown bought with blood. He was killed by the earl of Richmond at the Battle of Bosworth Field in 1485. In recent times his historical reputation has improved considerably. *See also* QUEEN DICK.

tightwad. *Tightwad*, for a cheapskate who won't part with his money, has its origins in a tightly folded wad of money, *wad* having meant a large roll of money since 1814 or so and *tight* having meant "stingy" since about the same time. *Tightwad* is said to have been invented by Indiana humorist George Ade in his *More Fables* (1900), which first records the term: "Henry was undoubtedly the Tightest Wad in town." *See* GLADHANDER; PANHANDLER.

tigon; liger. *Tigon* refers to the offspring of a male tiger and a female lion, the name of the cross first recorded in 1927. About 10 years later, in 1938, a male lion and female tiger were mated, and their offspring was called a "liger." *See* POMATO.

Tijuana. The Mexican city doesn't take its name from the Spanish *Tia Juana*, "Aunt Jane," as is sometimes claimed. *Tijuana* is a corruption of the Amerindian name *tiwana*, meaning roughly "by the sea."

Tillandsia. *See* SPANISH MOSS.

till death or distance do us part. The marriage vow among American slaves contained this change in the traditional words *till death do us part* because families were often broken up when slaves were sold down the river.

till the cows come home. Relatively modern amplifications of this one include *Till the cows come home in the morning* and *Till hell freezes over and the cows come skating home over the ice*. The expression has meant "a long, long time" for a long, long time, since about 1600, and the idea behind it is that cows take their own good time about coming home if they aren't driven—often until the next morning, when, with udders painfully swollen, they come home to be milked.

till the last dog is hung. Until the very end or resolution of something. The earliest mention of the phrase is in a history of the Civil War published in 1865: "I stayed until the last dog was hung and had to laugh to see how mad the Col (Colonel) got."

tilt at windmills. Advising his squire Sancho Panza that 30 or 40 windmills were "monstrous giants," Don Quixote spurred his steed Rosinante forward, his lance extended to "do good service" and "sweep so evil a breed off the face of the earth." Attacking a windmill, his lance got caught in one of its sails, which lifted the valiant knight into the air and smashed him to the ground, leaving him with nothing but injuries for his effort. This was perhaps the most absurd of the QUIXOTIC adventures of Don Quixote, hero of Cervantes's great satirical novel *Don Quixote* (1605–15). The book was meant to satirize the age's romantic tales of chivalry that filled its hero's mind, and this particular episode is among its most memorable. Almost as soon as *Don Quixote* was published it inspired the expression *to fight with* or *tilt at windmills*, "to combat imaginary foes or ward off nonexistent dangers," and the phrase *to have windmills in your head*, "to be full of fanciful notions or visionary schemes."

time flies. An old workhorse of a phrase that goes back at least to the Latin *tempus fugit*, meaning the same, which in turn was suggested by a phrase in the Roman poet Virgil's *Georgics* that translates: "Irretrievable time is flying."

Time, gentlemen, please! A British barman's reminder that the pub will soon close, in keeping with the legal closing hours, so please finish your drink. It can be abbreviated to Time!

time heals all wounds; time wounds all heels. "Healing is a matter of time, but it is sometimes also a matter of opportunity," the Greek physician Hippocrates (460 B.C.–377 B.C.) wrote in his *Precepts*. This is the first suggestion of the common saying *time heals all wounds*. The clever twist on the words *time wounds all heels* is attributed to Frank Case (1870–1946), the owner of New York City's Algonquin Hotel, where the famed Round Table of wits (Dorothy Parker, Robert Benchley, etc.) held sway in the 1920s. Apparently some of the wit rubbed off on Case. *See* HIPPOCRATIC OATH.

time is money. *See* SNUG AS A BUG IN A RUG.

time is of the essence. No eminent philosopher or statesman said this. It was originally a legal term, first recorded in 1873, applied to a contract where time was essential, indeed indispensable to that contract's fulfillment. If, for example, the contract required a manufacturer to deliver goods within three months, he had to deliver them within that time or suffer the consequences.

times that try men's souls.   *See* SUMMER SOLDIER AND SUN-SHINE PATRIOT.

times, ver' quiet, ver' soft, like summer night, but when she mad she blaze.   A poetic term said to be "the Indian equivalent for firefly" by Mark Twain in his short story "A Horse's Tale" (1906).

time to whistle up the dogs and piss on the fire.   A saying among old cowboys that means "it's time to leave," "light a rag," "hit the grit," "VAMOOSE".

timothy grass; herd's grass.   *Timothy* is another, more popular name for *herd's grass*, both designations referring to meadow cat's-tail grass, *Phleum pratense*, which is native to Eurasia and is widely cultivated for hay in the United States, where it was probably brought by early settlers. Then, in about 1770, one John Herd supposedly found the perennial grass with its spiked or panicled head growing wild near his New Hampshire farm, the grass receiving his name when he began cultivating it shortly thereafter. Timothy Hanson or Hanso gave his prenomen to the same grass when he quit his New York farm in 1720 and moved to Maryland, or possibly Carolina, introducing *Phleum pratense* seed there. *Timothy's seed* became *timothy grass* when it grew and this was finally shortened to timothy.

tin cans (naval destroyers).   During World War II American destroyers were called tin cans because they were the smallest, thinnest-armored fleet vessels. Destroyers were also called rust buckets at the time, though *rust bucket* more often meant any old ship.

tin ear.   A person who has a tin ear is tone deaf and thus doesn't appreciate good music, especially jazz. He can also be deaf to the rhythm of words. The term, dating back to the 1930s, was probably suggested to jazz musicians by the adjective *tinny*, "cheap and poorly made," and the earlier term *tin ear* from boxing, which meant about the same as *cauliflower ear*.

tingle.   *See* ONOMATOPOEIA.

tinhorn gambler.   In chuck-a-luck, an ancient dice game very popular during the Gold Rush, gamblers bet against the house that all three dice used would read the same when rolled, or that the sum of all three dice would equal a certain number, or that one of the three dice would turn up a specified number. It is a monotonous game and was looked down upon by players of faro, a more complicated and costly pastime. Faro operators coined the name *tinhorn gamblers* for *chuck-a-luck* players, giving us the expression for any cheap gambler. Pulitzer Prize winner George Williston explained how in his book *Here They Found Gold* (1931): "Chuck-a-luck operators shake their dice in a 'small churn-like affair of metal'—hence the expression 'tinhorn gambler,' for the game is rather looked down upon as one for 'chubbers' [fools] and chuck-a-luck gamblers are never admitted within the aristocratic circles of faro dealers."

tinker.   *See* NOT WORTH A TINKER'S DAMN.

Tinkers to Evers to Chance.   This synonym for a routine double play in baseball should really be *Tinker to Evers to Chance*, referring as it does to the Chicago Cub infield combination of Joe Tinker, shortstop, Johnny Evers at second base, and Frank Chance at first. All three are enshrined in Baseball's Hall of Fame at Cooperstown, New York, but aren't there for the double plays they executed. Actually, the vaunted trio only averaged 14 twin killings a year from 1906–09, the peak of their careers, very low for a double-play combo. Their fame is due principally to a famous Franklin P. Adams poem heralding them.

Tin Lizzie.   *See* FORD.

Tin Pan Alley.   The original Tin Pan Alley was and is located between 48th and 52nd Streets on Seventh Avenue in New York City, an area where many music publishers, recording studios, composers, and arrangers have offices. The place was probably named for the tinny sound of the cheap, much-abused pianos in music publishers' offices there, or for the constant noise emanating from the area, which sounded like the banging of tin pans to some. *Tin Pan Alley*, the term first recorded in 1914, today means any place where popular music is published, and can even stand for popular music itself.

Tinseltown.   "Strip the phony tinsel off Hollywood," musician and wit Oscar Levant said in the early 1940s, "and you'll find the real tinsel underneath." This sardonic remark allegedly led to the cynical name "Tinseltown" for Hollywood.

tip.   A persistent unsubstantiated story has the word *tip*, for "gratuity," originating with the initials, *t. i. p.*, "to insure promptness (or promptitude)," which was supposed to be inscribed on offering boxes in 18th-century English coffeehouses. More likely the word comes from the 16th-century slang *to tip*, meaning "to hand over," which possibly derives from the verb *tip* in its meaning of "to touch lightly." A *tip* as "secret information" probably derives from the same slang source.

Tippecanoe and Tyler too.   *See* CIDER.

Tironian notes.   Marcus Tullius Tiro, the man who invented the ampersand (&), introduced it as part of the first system of shorthand of which there is any record. A learned Roman freedman and amanuensis to Cicero, Tiro invented Tironian notes about 63 B.C. in order to take down his friend's fluent dictation. Though a rudimentary system, Tiro's shorthand saw wide use in Europe for almost a thousand years, outlasting the Roman Empire. The ampersand, sometimes called the Tironian sign in Tiro's honor, was a symbol for the Latin *et*, or "and." Taught in Roman schools and used to record speeches made in the Senate, Tiro's system was based on the orthographical principle and made abundant use of initials. *Ampersand*, first recorded in 1837 by Canadian humorist Thomas Haliburton, is a contraction of *and per se and*.

'tis better to have loved and lost, than never to have loved at all.   Alfred, Lord Tennyson wrote these lines in his famous poem *In Memoriam A.H.H.* (1850), which was written for his close friend and sister's fiancé, Arthur Henry Hallam, a scholar of great promise who died suddenly at the age of 22. Tennyson wrote the long elegy, if it can be called that, between Hallam's death in 1833 and 1850.

tit; titman. This word has no vulgar connotation among farmers in New England, who often refer to the runt in a litter of pigs as a *titman* or *tit. Tit* here derives from an old Germanic word meaning "small," whereas *tit* as slang for a woman's breast comes from the Old English *titt*. A century ago, *titman* meant a small or stunted person, as when Thoreau called his generation "a race of titmen." *Titman* or *tit man*, is of course in American slang a male who prefers breasts to any other part of a woman's anatomy.

Titania. *See* URANUS.

Titanic; titanium. *See* URANIUM; URANUS.

tit for tat. Probably the French phrase *tant pour tant*, "so much for so much," influenced the formation of *tit for tat*, and possibly the Dutch *dit vor dat*, "this for that," helped as well. But the expression derives directly from the six-century-old English phrase *tip for tap*, a "tip" at the time meaning the same as a "tap"—a light blow. As for the idea of tit for tat, a blow for a blow, the Latin *quid pro quo* itself has been around for over four centuries. The French phrase *tant pour tant*, with its sense of paying back, also gave us our word *taunt*, "a sharp or clever rejoinder."

Titian. Tiziano Vecellio, or Vecelli, whose name is anglicized as Titian, began his training as an artist in 1486 when nine years old and did not stop painting until his death of the plague 90 years later, when he was approaching one hundred. The greatest artist of the Venetian school, Titian produced hundreds of paintings during his unusually long and prolific career, including portraits and religious and mythological works, all noted for their magnificent use of color and design rather than for his drawing. In his many paintings the artist often depicted a model with shades of bright golden-auburn hair, and rendered the color so beautifully that the lustrous bronze has since been called Titian hair, or simply Titian. One tradition claims that Titian's auburn-haired model was his daughter Lavinia, whom he did paint several times.

tittle. *Tittle* is another word for the dot above an *i*, and can also mean an accent, a vowel mark, or any diacritical mark. The word is found in Matt. 5:18: ". . . one jot or one tittle shall in no wise pass from the law, till all be fulfilled." *See* I.

ti yi yee, ti yi yi yay. A cowboy cry, as in this old folk song stanza quoted by Kerry Newcomb in *Morning Star* (1983):

> So come on you dogies
> It's late in the day
> Sing ti yi yee
> Ti yi yi yay.

T.L.C. As an abbreviation for *tender loving care, T.L.C.* is first recorded as the title of a 1960 song. The expression *tender loving care*, however, goes all the way back to Shakespeare, who used it in *King Henry VI, Part II* (1592).

toady. The toady was in the 17th century a toad-eater, a conjuror's assistant who would eat a toad (said to be poisonous) so that his master could demonstrate his magic healing powers. Anyone who would eat a toad was considered so low that the word became a contemptible term for a sycophant. By the early 18th century *toad-eater* had been replaced by the shorter *toady*.

tobacco. The common name for the tobacco plant is the result of a mistake and seems to have first been recorded in Christopher Columbus's journal for November 6, 1492: "My messengers reported that after a march of about twelve miles they had discovered a village with about 1,000 inhabitants. The natives had received them ceremoniously, and had lodged them in the most beautiful houses. They encountered many men and women carrying some sort of cylinder in which sweetly smelling herbs were glowing. The people sucked the other end of the cylinder and, as it were, drank in the smoke. Natives said they called these cylinders tabacos." Clearly then, the Carib word *tabaco* meant the reed pipes in which the natives smoked the dried leaves, but over the years *tabaco*, the ancestor of our *tobacco*, came to designate the leaves themselves and then the tobacco plant.

tobacco road. Erskine Caldwell explained the term in his famous novel *Tobacco Road* (1932): "The road on which Jeeter lived was the original tobacco road his grandfather had made. . . . The road had been used for the rolling of tobacco casks, large hogsheads in which the leaf had been packed after being cured and seasoned in the clay-chinked barns; thousands of hogsheads had been rolled along the crest of the ridge which connected the chain of sand hills, and they had made a smooth firm road the entire distance of fifteen miles. . . . There were scores of tobacco roads on the western side of the Savannah Valley, some only a mile or so long, others extending as far back as twenty-five or thirty miles into the foothills of the Piedmont. Anyone walking cross-country would more than likely find as many as six or eight in a day's hike. The region, topographically, was like a palm leaf; the Savannah was the stem, large at the bottom and gradually spreading out into the veins at the top. On the side of the valley the creeks ran down like the depressions in the palm leaf, while between them lay the ridges of sand hills, like seams, and on the crests of the ridges were the tobacco roads."

Tobit's fish. The principal character in the Book of Tobit, included in the Old Testament Apocrypha, was blinded by the dung of sparrows while he slept in a courtyard. The angel Raphael bid Tobit's son to catch a huge fish in the Tigris and apply its gall to Tobit's eyes, thus curing him of his blindness.

toddy. *See* TOT.

toe the line. Before the Queensberry rules were devised, English prizefights were long and bloody. There was no footwork, and no tactics aside from dirty ones. No attempt was made to evade blows from an opponent. Their bare fists often hardened from soaking in walnut juice, fighters firmly placed their toes on a line officials marked in the center of the ring and slugged it out until one man fell, thus ending the round. The fighters then staggered or were dragged back to their corners for 30 seconds and the match continued until one man couldn't come out to toe the line when the bell rang for the next round. One of these bouts, the Burke-Byrne fight in 1833, lasted 99 rounds, and poor Byrne—who never gave up—died from the beating he took. The sight of lurching, leaden-armed, broken-handed fighters toeing the line for hours at a time, and doing their job of battering each other bloody and senseless with superhuman willpower, inspired the saying *to toe the line*, "to do one's job, to live up to what is expected of you or conform to the rules." That the expression was an early one used in track events, meaning that all contestants must place their forward foot on the starting line ("Get ready, get on your mark . . .") also contributed to the popularity of this phrase.

tohu-bohu.   I like the sound of this unusual old word, which derives from the Hebrew lamentation *Thohu-wa-bhōhū*. It means emptiness and despair, confusion, formlessness, chaos itself, and unusual as it is, great writers such as Rabelais, Voltaire, Purchas, Browning, and Gladstone have employed it. The original Hebrew words are translated in the Bible in the second verse of the first chapter of Genesis: "And the earth was without form, and void; and darkness was upon the earth." Wrote one 19th-century author: "The world is a *tohu-bohu* of confusion and folly."

toilet.   In America, the term refers to what the British call the water closet. The word comes from the French *toilette*, which originally meant a "little cloth." This became the British name for the cloth used to cover a dressing table, then meant the table itself, and was finally used for the dressing room in which the dressing table was located. It took over four centuries, but Americans ultimately used *toilet* for the *john* in the room most often used for dressing or making one's toilet. *See also* CRAP; JOHN THOMAS.

toilet paper.   *Toilet paper*, or lavatory paper, which Nancy Mitford says is the "U" term for it, isn't recorded until the 1880s. The first commercial toilet paper had been marketed, however, in 1857, when Joseph C. Gayetty of New York City began selling an unbleached, pearl-colored pure manila hemp product at 300 sheets for 50 cents. "Gayetty's Medicated Paper—a perfectly pure article for the toilet and for the prevention of piles" had Gayetty's name watermarked on each sheet. Before this the Ward and Sears's mail-order catalogs were indispensable in the outhouses of America, and regretfully, many other books have served this purpose. Wrote Lord Chesterfield to his son in the 18th century: "I know a gentleman who was such a good manager of his time that he would not even lose the small portion of it which the calls of nature obliged him to pass in the necessary-house; but gradually went through all the Latin poets in those moments. He bought, for example, a common edition of Horace, off which he tore gradually a couple of pages, carried them with him to that necessary place, read them first, and then sent them down as a sacrifice to Cloacina: this was so much time fairly gained, and I recommend you to follow his example . . ." A *New York Times* critic related an anecdote about a famous musician's reply to a critic who had panned his performance the night before: the riposte began, "As I sit here in the bathroom, your review in hand . . ."

toilet paper capital of the world.   Green Bay, Wisconsin, is the home of football's Green Bay Packers. It has been known as the Toilet Paper Capital of the World (an appellation the local chamber of commerce won't acknowledge, even though paper manufacture is a big industry in Green Bay) ever since the late great sportswriter Red Smith, a native son, affectionately named it so.

Tokay wine.   Produced near Tokay (Tokaj) in the Carpathian Mountains near the Ukranian border, Tokay is a long-lasting Hungarian white wine with a strong grape flavor.

Tokyo Rose.   AXIS SALLY, LORD HAWHAW, and Tokyo Rose were the best known Axis radio propagandists of World War II. Of the triumvirate only Tokyo Rose worked for the Japanese and she was actually a number of women, her name bestowed upon her by American G.I.'s in the Pacific. Iva Toguri d'Aquino and Ruth Hayakawa, both Americans of Japanese descent, were mainly responsible for the radio programs beamed from Tokyo. Their sweet, seductive voices and the sentimental music they played were designed to promote homesickness, but more often than not were good for a laugh. Mrs. d'Aquino was sentenced to 10 years in prison for treason in 1949 and was paroled in 1956. Mildred E. (Axis Sally) Gillars was convicted of treason by a federal jury the same year and received a 10- to-30-year sentence but won a parole in 1961. d'Aquino was pardoned by President Gerald Ford in 1977.

Tom and Jerry.   The sweet spicy rum drink is named for Tom and Jerry Hawthorne, men-about-town who lived the good life in Pierce Egan the elder's *Life in London* (1821). Egan's books threw light on the manners and slang of London in his day, while his son and sometime collaborator Pierce Egan the younger was known as "a pioneer of cheap literature."

tomato.   Those "affected" people who pronounce it "toe-mah-toe" are historically correct. The plant was first called *tomate* in Spain when introduced there from the New World, and even in the early 16th century it was pronounced in three syllables. The *o* incidentally has no place at all in "tomato," apparently being there because mid-18th-century Englishmen erroneously believed that it should have this common Spanish ending. *Lycopersicon esculentum* has also been called the *wolf apple*, the *wolf peach*, and the *love apple*. The first two designations arose because most Americans thought that tomatoes were poisonous and didn't eat them until about 1830—the tomato *vine* is, in fact, poisonous, the plant a member of the deadly nightshade family. "You say toe-may-toe and I say toe-mah-toe," Cole Porter wrote, and he might have added if he had the space that Americans also pronounce the fruit's name ta-mater, termater, mater, tomarters, and tomaties, among other variations. Regional pronunciations of the plural *tomatoes* are even stranger, including tomatoeses, tomatussis, and martisses,. *See also* LOVE APPLES.

Tom Collins.   Many sources tell us that the Tom Collins—that refreshing, tall drink made with gin (or vermouth), lemon (or lime), sugar, and soda water—honors its bartender-creator. Yet no one has been able to establish who Tom Collins was, where he came from, or when he first mixed the drink. Variations on the Tom Collins include the John Collins (whiskey) and the Marimba Collins (rum). The Tom Collins is claimed by many, but the lack of evidence indicates that its real creator didn't mix well, at least socially. The best prospect is probably John Collins, a 19th-century bartender at London's Limmer Hotel who did not devise but was famous for his gin sling—a tall gin and lemon drink that resembles the Tom Collins.

Tom, Dick, and Harry. All of these are very common names, reason enough for them to represent "everybody" or an indiscriminate, unnoteworthy collection of men in the phrase. However, one ingenious theory tried to link the expression with nicknames of the devil. The trouble is that while Old Harry and Dick (the dickens) or Nick have long been nicknames for Olde Horney, he has never been known intimately as Tom. Also, every *Tom, Dick, and Harry* is an American expression of the late 19th century, before the British used *Dick, Tom, and Jack* for the same purpose. *Browns, Jones, and Robinson* was used by the British in Victorian times to mean "the vulgar rich."

Tom Fuller. The Choctaw Indians' national dish was a fermented hominy called *tahfula*. To the ears of early settlers in the West this sounded like "Tom Fuller" and by 1848 they had Anglicized the name.

Tommy Atkins. The British army account or record books in the 19th century had a fictitious sample entry in the name of "Private Thomas Atkins" to help soldiers fill in details about themselves. So ubiquitous was Thomas Atkins that he became affectionately known as *Tommy Atkins* and became a nickname for all British soldiers, similar to the American G.I. Joe. British soldiers were frequently referred to simply as Tommies.

tommygun. The infamous *chopper* so often hidden in violin cases in gangster movies, takes its name from the patronym of one of its inventors, American army officer John T. Thompson (1860–1940). Thompson and Navy Comm. John N. Blish invented the .45 caliber portable automatic weapon during World War I and much improved it in later years. Gangsters and reporters popularized the nickname *tommygun* in the Prohibition era along with colorful expressions like *torpedo, triggerman, bathtub gin, hideout, hijacker, to muscle in,* and *to take for a ride.* Although *tommygun* originally identified the Thompson machine gun, with its pistol grip and shoulder stock, the term is now used to describe any similar lightweight weapon with a drum-type magazine. *See* UZI.

tommyrot. Partridge says that the *tommy* in *tommyrot,* "nonsense, bosh," may be a euphemism for the strong British expression *bloody*—British soldiers, called Tommies, once wore scarlet (bloody) uniforms. More likely, as he seems to agree, it comes from the British expression *tommy,* meaning "goods supplied instead of wages" by employers who ran stores on the side, something like the more infamous American company stores (first recorded in 1872). According to Edwin Radford's *Unusual Words* (1946): "Employees of labour not infrequently owned shops to which the worker had to go to draw money; and there he was compelled to spend a portion of his wages on the purchase of the goods he must consume during the week in order to leave. To the working man, these shops were known as 'Tommy-shops'—the shops where he purchased his 'tommy', or food. The viciousness of this system will be realized when it is stated that the employer could charge pretty well

what he liked in the way of high prices for the most inferior food, and the workingman had no chance but to take it, or lose his job." Workers, incensed at the poor stuff bundled onto them at high prices, referred to the goods of the Tommy-shop as "Tommy-rot." The workers' only possible revenge was with words. *See* TOMMY ATKINS.

Tom Thumb. This term, often applied to a "little person," as many "dwarfs" prefer to be called, and to little children as well, has its origins in fairy tales of old, in which Tom Thumb was the size of a man's thumb. However, its modern use is due in great part to "General Tom Thumb" (Charles Sherwood Stratton, 1838–83), whom American showman P. T. Barnum exhibited in the mid-19th century.

Tom Thumb golf. *Tom Thumb* golf is a synonym for *miniature golf* (also known as *midget golf*), which is a game played with a putter and golf ball on a very short course that has many wooden and concrete obstacles. The game was invented around 1910. One of the first courses was built in Pinehurst, North Carolina, by landscape architect E. H. Wiswell and named "Thistle Dhu"—supposedly because Wiswell tired of the job and pronounced it finished, saying "This'll do."

tom-tom. American Indians did not call their drums tom-toms. They were so named by the British, who, in the late 17th century, had brought the word *tom-tom* back to England from the East Indies, where such a drum was called a *tam-tam,* this Hindustani word imitative of the sound a drum makes.

tone down. *To tone down,* "to soften or make less emphatic," may be an expression that originated among artists, rather than among musicians as might be suspected. It could have arisen along with the reaction against the varied and vivid colors used by Turner and his school. Many artists in the early 19th century, when the expression is first recorded, did return to the use of more subdued tones in their paintings, and bright canvases at the time were sometimes coated with varnish to soften them.

tongue; tongue-tied; wondrous tongue. *Tongue* comes to us from the Old English *tunge,* meaning the same. To be tongue-tied is to be unable to speak from shyness or embarrassment, the expression dating back to the early 16th century. There is a medical condition called tongue-tied: impeded motion of the tongue caused by shortness of the frenum, which binds it to the floor of the mouth. At the other extreme we have the great actor Richard Burbage, Shakespeare's friend, whose elegy when he died on May 13, 1617, included the famous words "He's gone, and with him what a world is dead." Burbage's death brought on such grief in London that people forgot the death of Queen Anne, wife of James I, a few weeks before. Still another dirge claimed that if Burbage with his "enchanting tongue" had been able to speak to Death he would with his "all-charming art" have convinced the Grim Reaper to let him remain alive, but Death knew this and seized his wondrous tongue first. According to the elegy, this explained Burbage's dying of paralysis that began with his tongue and gradually extended to his entire body:

Death first made seizure on thy wondrous tongue,
Then on the rest, 'twas easy; by degrees
The slender ivy twines the hugest trees.

tongue in cheek.   Before Richard Barham invented this phrase in his *The Ingoldsby Legends* (1845) nobody stuck tongue in cheek as a humorous warning that something just said was insincere, so Barham could be credited with inventing the custom as well as the expression. Why he chose *with tongue in cheek* to describe someone engaging in insincerity or irony is a mystery. Especially as anyone actually speaking with tongue in cheek—the tongue tip lodged against the inside of the cheek—wouldn't be understood at all.

tongue oil.   In my continuing quest for synonyms for whiskey and other strong drink I've come upon *tongue oil* several times. It's a western U.S. expression dating back perhaps to the mid-19th century and obviously refers to the way spirits loosen one's tongue.

tongue twister.   The name tongue twister for a sequence of words difficult to pronounce is first recorded in 1898, long after some of the classic tongue twisters were invented. Probably the oldest or best-known is "Sally" (or "she") "sells seashells at the seashore." But experts hold that "the sixth sick shiek's sixth sheep's sick" is the worst tongue twister in English, especially if spoken rapidly. The 72 muscles we use in speaking one word seem to rebel against pronouncing all of these together. Almost as famous as Sally and her seashells is "Peter Piper picked a peck of pickled peppers" etc. Try also: "The skunk sat on a stump; the skunk thunk the stump stunk, but the stump thunk the skunk stunk." Or say "Toy boat" fast five times. More great old tongue twisters like "How much wood would a woodchuck chuck if a woodchuck could chuck wood?" can be found in *Peter Piper's Practical Principles of Plain and Perfect Pronunciation* (1834). In the meantime, try those 72 muscles on Carolyn Wells's:

> A tutor who tutored the flute
> Tried to tutor two tutors to toot
>   Said the two to the tutor,
>   "Is it harder to toot, or
> To tutor two tutors to toot?"

and on the vowelless Czech words for "stick a finger in the throat":

> *Strch prst skrz krk.*

ton of bricks.   *See* COME DOWN LIKE A TON OF BRICKS ON SOMEONE.

ton of cobblestone.   A large quantity of anything ordinary or commonplace. American radio comedian Fred Allen (1894–1956) coined the expression. He bound all the scripts for his long-running radio show—39 a year—and stacked them on 10 feet of shelves beside a one-volume copy of Shakespeare's collected works, which occupied a mere 3½ inches of space. "I did that as a corrective," he explained, "just in case I start thinking a ton of cobblestone is worth as much as a few diamonds."

tontine.   The tontine was an early form of life insurance devised by Italian banker Lorenzo Tonti (1635–90) and introduced by him into France in 1653. Under the system a number of people subscribe to the tontine, the annuity increasing in value to the survivors as each subscriber dies. Finally, the last surviving member takes all. When the tontine was first introduced, any money from the fund that hadn't been spent by the "winner" reverted to the state after the death of that last subscriber.

Tonto.   Tonto, the name of the fabled Lone Ranger's sidekick, was a name indiscriminately given by the Spanish to several Indian tribes, including the Tonto Apaches. Tonto is a Spanish word meaning "fool." It also came to be a term for Indians who have broken with traditions and are looked down upon by their tribes.

Tonton Macoutes.   The Tonton Macoutes were the secret police thugs who terrorized "enemies of the state" under the dictatorial Duvalier regimes in Haiti from 1957–86. After the Duvaliers were deposed, the name was applied to any thug who terrorized poor people in that country. The Tonton Macoutes were named for Tonton Macoute (Uncle Knapsack), a giant bogeyman who roamed the Haitian countryside stuffing children in his sack. The mythical character became all too real.

Tony.   This award presented annually for outstanding performances in the theater honors Antoinette (Tony) Perry (1884–1946), an American actress and producer who served as chairman of the American Theater Council. *See also* OSCAR.

too big for one's breeches.   Describing someone obsessed with his own importance, *too big for one's breeches* is first recorded in the work of Davy Crockett—born on a mountaintop in Tennessee (1786), died at the Alamo (1836)—congressman and frontier hero, whose life was a tall tale.

too high for picking cotton.   An old term describing someone who is a little drunk; first recorded in Parson Weem's *The Drunkard's Looking Glass* (1818).

too lazy to work and too nervous to steal.   An Americanism describing any person regarded as a totally useless no-account.

too many cooks spoil the broth.   A proverb from the late 16th century. There are counterparts in many languages, including: *Too many chefs ruin the sauce* (French); *A ship directed by many pilots soon sinks* (Spanish); and *With too many rowers the ship will crash into a mountain* (Japanese).

too many irons in the fire.   "They that have many irons in the fires, some must burne," Captain John Smith wrote in *The General Historie of Virginia, New England and the Summer Isles* (1624), and almost a century before another writer warned, "Put no more so many yrons in the fyre at ones." Then there is the old Scottish proverb "Many Irons in the Fire, some must cool." All of these admonitions illustrate the meaning of the phrase: to be engaged in more activities than one can manage at one time, to bite off more than you can chew. What is alluded to is another matter. Blacksmiths might be the source; no doubt some blacksmiths weren't skilled enough to handle many pieces of steel in the forge and work over them in rapid order. But the "cool" in the Scottish proverb suggests that old laundry flatirons, which had to be heated in hot coals, may have been the source. Leave too many laundry irons in the fire at once and those at the edge of the fire might not be hot enough to use.

too much of a good thing.   This old proverb, dating back to the 15th century, is found in Cervantes's *Don Quixote* as "Can we ever have too much of a good thing?"

too old to cut the mustard.   *See* CUT THE MUSTARD.

too poor to paint and too proud to whitewash.   A term describing any impoverished southern gentleman or lady. Whitewash is much cheaper than paint.

toothache tree.   American pioneers called the prickly ash (*Zanthophylum americanum*) the toothache tree or toothache bush, because the white-spined ash-leafed tree's fruit has pungent properties when applied to an aching tooth. The term is first recorded early in the 19th century.

tooth and nail.   The Latin equivalent for this ancient phrase was *toto corpore atque omnibus ungulis*, "with all the body and every nail." The French have a similar saying, too: *bec et ongles*, "beak and talons." All mean the same: to fight with tooth and nails, biting and scratching, with weapons, with all the powers at one's command. Figurative use of the expression in England brings us back to the early 16th century, and it was listed as a proverb then.

too thick to drink and too thin to plow.   Muddy, unpalatable water, the expression probably first said by American pioneers over a century ago.

tooth-jumping.   An aptly described practice from early pioneer days that few people would suffer today. Tooth-jumping, once a common toothache remedy, was the extraction of a tooth by holding a nail at an angle against it and striking the nail with a hammer so that the tooth jumped out.

toothwalker.   A name for the WALRUS, which sometimes uses its huge tusks, up to three feet long, as a means of locomotion, digging them into the earth or ice and pulling themselves along. *Toothwalker* is the translation of the Inuit name for the animal.

Tootle-oo!   Good-bye, see you later. The saying is British, dating back to about 1905. Partridge suggests that it may derive from a Cockney corruption of French *à tout à l'heure*, "see you soon." The word has some American humorous usage and is sometimes heard as "toodleoo."

Tootsie Roll; Chunky.   The still popular Tootsie Roll was invented by American candy maker Leo Hirschfield in 1896. He named the chewy chocolate for his daughter Clara, whose nickname was Tootsie. Another similar named candy is the square hunk of chocolate, cashews, brazil nuts, and raisins called the Chunky. Candy maker Philip Silverstein invented the confection and named it after his daughter, nicknamed Chunky.

top banana.   A comic or comedian in American burlesque or vaudeville. The expression derives from an old turn-of-the-century burlesque skit that involved the sharing of bananas.

top brass.   *See* BRASS.

top dollar.   This expression, meaning "full value," probably arose from the game of poker, from the image of the highest stack of poker chips on the table, the pile whose top chip or dollar is higher than all the rest.

top-drawer.   Of the best or highest quality. This American term comes from the early 1900s British expression *out of the top drawer*, meaning "well-bred, gentlemanly, upper class, aristocratic." *Drawer* refers to a chest of drawers, one's valuables usually kept in the top drawer.

topiary.   Topiary is the clipping and training of plants like yew and arborvitae into fantastic shapes such as peacocks, elephants, foxes, birds, and grotesque geometrical figures. The word itself comes to us from the Latin word *topia*, akin to "artificial landscape." The Romans were expert at the art or craft, as were the English in Tudor times, and topiary is still far more common in England than in America. Alexander Pope denounced topiary, inventing a mock garden catalog description of: "Adam and Eve in Yew, Adam a little shattered by the fall of the tree of knowledge in the great storm: Eve and the Serpent very flourishing . . . Divers eminent modern poets, in bays, somewhat blighted, to be disposed of, a pennyworth." But topiary can be used effectively. Examples often cited are the topiary at the Alhambra in Granada and Italian gardens at Florence and Rome.

top of the heap.   The biggest, or best, an American expression that goes back at least to the 1930s. *Heap* itself can mean a pile or large amount of money, that meaning a century older. I remember an old Mark Hellinger story about a gangster who vowed he'd wind up with more money and fame than anyone— on top of the heap. He was finally killed by rival gangsters and dumped on the top of a garbage heap.

top of the morning to you.   A well-known greeting that Irish English speakers use only humorously today. More common is *how's about you?* and *how's she cuttin'?* or *what's the crack?*

topping.   An old-fashioned British term meaning "excellent, the very best." "It was topping, absolutely topping." The word never had much currency in the U.S.

toque.   *Toque* refers to what Canadians call a woolen hat with a small ball of wool on top. Americans call this a "stocking cap," while the British call it a "bobble hat," and the Australians prefer "beanie."

tor.   *Tor* may be one of the first words spoken in England. Generally held to be a Celtic term used in place names, it may be a remnant of the prehistoric language of Bronze Age people on the island. These tribesmen lacked the writing to record their language but may have used *tor* as a place name that the Celts somehow adopted. *Tor* has come to mean "a high rock, a pile of rocks." *See also* TORPENHOW HILL.

tornado.   Dorothy, her dog, Toto, and her house were carried off to the land of Oz by a tornado or cyclone in Frank Baum's *The Wizard of Oz* (1900) and the movie made from it (1939). *Tornado* is used synonymously for a cyclone, a violent funnel-shaped wind located in a small area. *Tornado* derives from Spanish *tronado*, "thunderstorm," and *tornar*, "turn." It was so named by Spanish navigators in tropical seas. *See* HURRICANE.

torpedo.   *Torpedo* can mean several things. The electric ray, or torpedo fish, was the first "torpedo," taking its name from the Latin *torpere*, "to be stiff or numb," in reference to the ray's numbing sting. In World War I, naval men named the self-propelled mines called torpedoes after the fish because the mines resembled the actions of the electric ray, stunning all that came into contact with them. Yet torpedo meant a percussion shell before this, in 1786, and described a stationary explosive mine, the kind Admiral Farragut spoke of when he said, "Damn the torpedoes, full speed ahead!" The torpedoes Farragut disdained, were in fact, beer kegs filled with powder.

torpedo juice.   Thirsty sailors in World War II sometimes made a potent drink called torpedo juice from alcohol drained from Navy torpedoes. This deadly brew soon lent its name to any raw homemade whiskey with killing power.

Torpenhow Hill.   *Torpenhow Hill*, a ridge near Plymouth in England, literally means Hillhillhill Hill. The Saxons called it *tor*, "hill"; the Celts, not knowing the meaning of *tor*, added *pen*, "hill," for the same reason. The Scandinavians added *haug* (how), "hill"; and finally Middle English speakers, not knowing that all the components of the word *Torpenhow* meant hill, added a second word *hill* to the place name. *See also* TOR.

Torquemada.   More than 100,000 cases were tried and 1,000 people executed under the administration of Tomás de Torquemada (ca. 1420–98) after the pope appointed him Spanish Grand Inquisitor in 1483. The harsh rules Torquemada devised and strictly enforced for the Inquisition, including the use of torture as a means of obtaining information, made the inquisitor-general's name a synonym for a cruel persecutor or torturer. Torquemada particularly distrusted the Maranos and Moriscos, Jewish and Moorish converts to Catholicism, many of whom he felt were insincere, and he was partly responsible for the royal decree in 1492 which expelled 200,000 unconverted Jews from Spain. One story, probably exaggerated, says that the hated grand inquisitor never traveled anywhere unless guarded by 250 armed retainers and 50 horsemen.

tortoni.   In one story a Signore Tortoni, an Italian restaurateur in Paris during the late 19th century, invented this rich ice cream studded with cherries and almonds or macaroons. Others claim that *tortoni* derives from the Italian *torta*, "tart."

Tory.   Dictionary makers were not always nonpartisan. In his great groundbreaking dictionary, Dr. Johnson, committed to the Tory party, defined a Tory as: "One who adheres to the ancient constitution of the state, and the apostolic hierarchy of the Church of England—opposed to a Whig." (*Whig* was dealt with as if by the ax-man: "The name of a faction.") *Tory* derives from the Irish *toraidhe*, a pursued person, the term first applied to Irish who were forced from their land by the English and took to the hills, becoming outlaws. It then became the name for Catholics fighting for James II and finally described those who supported the Stuarts as a political party. By the reign of George III, the party had lost its Stuart bias and vigorously supported the Crown, State, and Church as established by law. Since about 1830 the Tory Party has gradually become known as the Conservative Party and *Tory* has become a synonym for "conservative." *See* WHIG.

toss in a blanket.   Tossing someone, usually a girl, in a blanket has been an amusement among young people at beaches in relatively recent times, but the practice, at first a rough punishment, goes back at least five centuries. Shakespeare was the first to record blanket tossing, in *2 Henry IV* (1597): "I will toss the rogue in a blanket." Twelve years later Ben Jonson used *blanket* as a verb to describe the practice. *See* BLANKET; WET BLANKET.

tot.   A relatively recent word, first recorded in 1725, *tot*, for "a small child," may go back to the Old Norse *tuttr*, "dwarf," or the Danish *tommeltot*, for "Tom Thumb." It could also derive from *totterer*, or be connected somehow with the Anglo-Saxon *totrida*, "swing." And since *tot* means a small drink, too, the word could come from the earlier *toddy* (rum toddy, etc.), which derives from the Hindi *tari*, "a drink," and is first recorded in 1609. A lot of theories for a little word—and no proof for any of them.

tote.   *Tote* is of uncertain origin, but most likely comes from the African Konga and Kikonga language *tota*, meaning "to carry." The word may have passed into English through the Gullah dialect in the southern U.S.

totem.   A totem is an object toward which individuals or groups have a special mystical relationship. Often these people observe totemic taboos, such as the Buffalo people of Ruanda, who will not eat buffalo meat, explaining that they are descended from the animal for whom they are named. The word *totem*, appropriately, comes from the Algonquian Indian *ototema*, meaning "his relations."

To the babies!   A toast made at an 1879 Chicago banquet for General Ulysses S. Grant. Mark Twain answered it: "We haven't all had the good fortune to be ladies; we haven't all been generals, or poets, or statesmen; but when the toast works down to babies, we stand on common ground."

to the manor born; to the manner born.   Some people are to the manor born, but Shakespeare, who invented the phrase, has Hamlet say "to the manner born" when he is speaking to Horatio. When Horatio asks what means the flourish of trumpets, roll of drums, and discharge of cannon he hears at midnight, Hamlet replies that the king is having a drinking bout and that each time he drains a flagon he is hailed with this uproar. Horatio wants to know if this is an old Danish custom and Hamlet answers:

Ay, marry, it is;
But to my mind, though I am native here
And to the manner born, it is a custom
More honored in the breech than the observance.

The phrase therefore refers to a custom, not to aristocracy or high estate, as the word *manor* would imply.

touch all bases.   Not touching a base in baseball can result in big trouble (*see* BONEHEAD PLAY) and even a player who hits a home run must touch all the bases as he rounds them, which led to the common general expression *to touch all bases*, to be thorough and leave nothing undone. This phrase, in turn, is the source of the expression *to touch base with*, meaning to consult or inform someone concerning an impending matter.

touch and go.   Either coach driving or ship pilotage gave us this term for a narrow escape or a precarious situation in which the outcome is doubtful for a time. Coach drivers used the term *touch and go* for a narrow escape after the wheels of two coaches touched in a near accident, a favorite scene in many costume adventures. The *Sailor's Word Book* (1867) explains the term's possible nautical derivation: "Touch and go—said of anything within an ace of ruin; as in rounding a ship very narrowly to escape rocks, etc., or when, under sail, she rubs against the ground with her keel."

touch-me-not.   *See* NOLI ME TANGERE.

a touch of Caruso.   A great tenor and a lighthearted man of boyish charm, Enrico Caruso (1873–1921) was something of a cutup and once pinched a girl's derrière in a Paris park. Resulting publicity gave rise to the expression *a touch of Caruso* ("Give her a touch of Caruso, chief!"), meaning the turn of a ship's engines astern.

tougher than a 30-cent steak.   This humorous expression was used in the 1943 movie *Heaven Can Wait* to describe a tough guy. It must date back a century or so, for there were no 30-cent steaks (no matter how tough) available in 1943.

tough it out.   An Americanism meaning "to undergo hardship," as in "They toughed it out on that rocky soil for three years before they quit." The expression was first recorded in 1830 and is still heard today. *Rough it out* is also used.

tournedos; Tournedos à la Rossini.   Tournedos are small, round thick pieces of beef, served with a number of sauces and garnished. The Italian composer Gioacchino Antonio Rossini (1792–1868), best known for the *Barber of Seville* (1816), is said to have invented the cut of beef when he conceived Tournedos à la Rossini at the height of his popularity. According to the old tale, Rossini was dining at the Café Anglais in Paris. Tired of the beef dishes on the menu, he gave instructions for his meat to be prepared in a different way. "Never would I dare to offer such a thing—it is unpresentable!" the maître d'hôtel protested. "Well then, arrange not to let it be seen!" the composer countered. Ever after, we are told, *tournedos* were to be served not before the eyes, but behind the diner's back. Hence the name in French: *tourne le dos* ("turn the back"). There is no doubt, anyway, that Tournedos Rossini are named

in the composer's honor: succulent slices of fried fillet of beef set on fried bread, capped with foie gras, crowned with truffles, and coated with Périgueux sauce. One of the richest, most expensive dishes in the world.

towering rage, etc.   *Towering* in all such phrases derives from a term in falconry. Castle watchtowers were the tallest structures in the Middle Ages, so high-flying hawks were said "to tower." *Towering ambition* is thus, ambition that is beyond ordinary bounds, as high as the towering of a hawk. *Towering rage* or *passion* could both be explained in the same way, rage or passion mounting to its highest point, but there is an added dimension that strengthens the phrases. When a falcon "towers" she hovers at the height of her ascent searching for prey, is ready to swoop down on her victim.

toxic; toxin.   *See* INTOXICATED.

Toyota.   The very popular Japanese car would be called a *Toyoda* if its manufacturers in the early 1930s hadn't been superstitious. The Toyoda family wanted to name their car after the family, but *Toyoda* needs 10 characters in Japanese writing, while *Toyota* needs only eight. As eight is a lucky number in Japan, the family actually changed its name to Toyota, and the car's lucky name was born.

tradattore, traditore.   *Tradattore, traditore* translates literally from the Italian as "translator, traitor." It is an old Italian saying claiming that a great book or poem can never be translated into another language and retain all its original shades of meaning.

trademarks and generic terms.   Trademarks—"the name or symbol legally adopted and used by a manufacturer in order to distinguish the goods he manufactures or sells and to distinguish them from those manufactured or sold by others"—must always be capitalized. *Coca-Cola*, a trademark registered in 1887, has always been jealously protected by its owner. In 1930 the company went to the Supreme Court to obtain a ruling that the nickname *Coke* belonged exclusively to it and subsequently registered it too as a trademark. In the case of *cola*, however, the Supreme Court ruled in 1938 that any soft drink using the cola nut in its manufacture could call itself a cola, as cola is a generic word and therefore not the Coca-Cola Company's exclusive property. Trademarks are also known as brand names or brands, this term deriving from the practice of branding animals to indicate ownership. The U.S. Patent Office began to officially register trademarks in 1870 although they were used several centuries before this. The *Trade Name Dictionary* (1977) lists over 106,000 trade names. Trademarks that have entered into general use as generic terms include: typewriter, shredded wheat, corn flakes, raisin bran, cube steak, dry ice, kerosene, lanolin, yo-yo, heroin, trampoline, cellophane, celluloid, Ferris wheel, aspirin, hoover, windbreaker, escalator, linoleum, lanolin, thermos, razor, nylon, acetate, spandex, asbestos, pullman, mimeograph, milk of magnesia, malted milk, mason jar, photostat, diesel, polyester, vinyl, zeppelin, and zipper. These former trademarks most often lost their trademark status because they were not properly protected. Others that are often used erroneously as generic terms, though they are still legally trademarks, include B.V.D.s, Skivies, Band-Aid,

Frisbee, Ping-Pong, Ouija Board, Listerine, Frigidaire, Teflon, Victrola, Kotex, Kleenex, Latex, Plexiglass, Kodak, Muzak, Pyrex, Vaseline, Scotch Tape, Jello, Xerox and Technicolor.

trade rat. *See* PACK RAT.

trade winds. These are winds that regularly "blow trade" in one direction or another. In the northern hemisphere they blow from the northeast, and in the southern hemisphere from the southeast. In some places they blow six months of the year in one direction and six months in the opposite direction. *Trade winds* is first recorded in 1626, but the term *to blow trade* is first mentioned in Richard Hakluyt's *Diverse Voyages* (1582). *See* WINDS.

tragedy. "Goat singer," the Greek *tragodia*, is the earliest ancestor of the word *tragedy*. But we don't know exactly why R. C. Trench wrote in *On the Study of Words* (1888): "There is no question that tragedy is the song of the goat; but *why* the song of the goat, whether because a goat was the prize for the best performance of that song in which the germs of the future tragedy lay, or because the first actors were dressed, like satyrs, in goatskins, is a question which has stirred abundant discussion, and will remain unsettled to the end."

trailblazer. A trailblazer isn't someone who blazes new paths by "setting the world on fire." To *blaze a trail* means to indicate a new path by notching trees with an ax or knife. *Blaze* in this sense is the white mark in the notch when the bark is removed. It originally meant the white spot on the forehead of a horse before American pioneers *trailblazed* the new use of the word.

trailer trash. A trailer is a mobile home, and people who live in them permanently are often looked down upon for no good reason. The derogatory term was first recorded in 1993 and is very common, sometimes meaning "any poor people."

Trail of Tears. The term is explained by Edna Ferber in *Cimarron* (1930): "Tears came to his own eyes when he spoke of that blot on southern civilization, The Trail of Tears, in which the Cherokees, a peaceful and home-loving Indian tribe, were torn (1838–39) from the land which a government had given them by sworn treaty to be sent far away on a march which, from cold, hunger, exposure, and heartbreak, was marked by bleaching bones from Georgia to Oklahoma."

train. In the mid-19th century, people first gave the name *train* to railway carriages attached to locomotives, obviously because what was most impressive about the locomotive was the fact that it could pull a long train of carriages behind it. *Train*, which comes from the Latin *trahir*, "to drag," had previously been used for anything that trailed behind, but now it took on an entirely new meaning.

tramp. A tramp is so called because he or she tramps from place to place. The word has meant a wandering vagabond or beggar since the mid-16th century and has also become a term for a promiscuous woman. For more on these "knights of the road" *see* BUM, HOBO.

transatlantic. *See* CISATLANTIC.

trash. Shakespeare, in *Othello* (1604), is the first recorded author to use *trash* as a term for worthless or disreputable people. *Trash fish* and *trash duck* are old terms used by fishermen and hunters to mean various species of fish and ducks that are not edible. These latter terms date back to the Dutch in New York and are widely used today. *See* POOR WHITE TRASH.

trashing. During Vietnam War protests in the 1960s, student protestors emptied administration wastepaper baskets and garbage cans in what were the first incidents of "trashing" and the first uses of the word. Later, trashing involved breaking windows and writing on walls in administration buildings, often to protest war-related research by the colleges.

travelogue. A lecture, slide show, or motion picture describing travels. The word was coined in 1903 by writer Burton Holmes, who fashioned it from *travel* and mono*logue*. Some scholars objected that it was "irregularly formed" because its first half is French and its second Greek, but *travelogue* has stood the test of time.

T.R.D.J.S.D.O.P.I.I. Probably the most unusual or complicated pseudonym in English literary history. The initials conceal The Reverend Doctor Jonathan Swift, Dean of Patrick's in Ireland. Swift also used at least four other pen names: Isaac Bickerstaff (*see* BICKERSTAFF HOAX); A Person of Quality, A Person of Honor; M.B. Drapier; and A Dissenter.

Treacle Bill. *See* NO BALM IN GILEAD.

Treasure State. A nickname for Montana, which once was called the Bonanza State. It has been called the Stub-Toe State because of its steep hills and mountains.

tree. In his *Origins*, etymologist Eric Partridge traces the adjective *true* to the Old English *treow*, which means both "loyalty" and "tree." A true person is thus "as firm and straight as a tree." Trees figure in many other words and phrases. The Tree of Knowledge of Good and Evil is an unidentified tree in the Garden of Eden (Gen. 2:17, 3:6–24) bearing the forbidden fruit that Adam and Eve tasted. The Tree of Life is another name for this tree (Gen. 2:9, 3:22), while *the tree is known by its fruit* is an old biblical proverb (Matt. 12:33) meaning "one is judged by actions not by words." An expression common to several languages, *a tree must be bent while it's young* means essentially "you can't teach an old dog new tricks." A *Gregorian tree* is a synonym for the gallows. Obsolete in speech though not in literature, since the early 19th century, the expression derives from the names of two hangmen, Gregory Brandon, royal executioner in the time of England's James I, who was succeeded by his son Richard, often called "Young Gregory." In the United States poplars and other trees, called trees of liberty, were planted as symbols of growing freedom during the Revolutionary War. The custom was adopted by other countries, notably France during the French Revolution. First recorded in the early 1900s but probably older, *go climb a sour apple tree* means "go to blazes, go to hell." It is an Americanism that is still occasionally heard in its shortened form *go climb a tree*. To hang someone from a sour apple tree was to show the ultimate contempt for him, hence the Civil War's Union lyric

"We'll hang Jeff Davis [president of the Confederacy] from a sour apple tree." Tree Day is the exact translation of Arbor Day, *arbor* being the Latin word for "tree." Arbor Day was first celebrated in 1872, when Nebraskan J. Sterling Morton and his supporters persuaded their state to set aside April 10 for tree planting, to compensate for all the trees Americans had destroyed over the years in clearing the land for settlements. More than a million trees were planted on just the first Arbor Day alone and today the holiday is celebrated in every state.

tree of heaven.   Though never named in Betty Smith's novel *A Tree Grows in Brooklyn* nor the movies made from it, the tree in the book is *Ailanthus altissima*, also called the "tree of heaven." No other tree withstands smoke and city conditions so well, and the ailanthus seeds easily everywhere, often growing out of cracks in deserted sidewalks. Only female trees should be planted, however, as the odor of the male flower is noxious to many, which is why the ailanthus, a native of China, is also called the "stink tree" or "stinkweed." The tree was brought to France by a missionary in 1751 and reached America 39 years later.

tree of sadness.   This pretty name describes the small Indian tree *Nyctanthes arbortristis* of the verbena family. It has very fragrant white and orange flowers that bloom at night. Also called the sad tree, it apparently suggested sadness to the unknown person who named it more than a century ago.

trek.   The *trek* we use to describe a long, slow, or difficult journey is an Afrikaans word adopted by British settlers in South Africa in about 1849. It originally meant a long, slow journey by ox wagon. Today it is familiar from the television science-fiction series *Star Trek*.

trembling poplar.   *See* ASPEN.

triangular trade.   In the triangular trade, ships carried New England rum to the African Gold Coast on the first passage, traded the rum for slaves and transported the shackled slaves to the West Indies on the middle passage, where the slaves were sold for molasses and sugar, which were brought back to New England to make more rum on the final passage. The middle passage was, of course, the worse and most inhuman of the three legs of the journey.

tribulations.   The Roman *tribulum* was a sledge consisting of a wooden block studded with sharp pieces of flint or iron teeth. It was used to bring force and pressure against wheat in grinding out grain. The machine suggested the way trouble grinds people down and oppresses them, *tribulations* becoming another word for troubles and afflictions. The word is first recorded in English in 1330.

Tricky Dick.   A sobriquet for former president Richard Nixon that may have its roots in an Irish-American nickname for another politician named Richard. My grandmother spoke of a New York ward heeler named Tricky Dick, but she may have meant Slippery Dick Connolly, comptroller for the Tweed Ring. In any case, James Joyce named a politician Tricky Dick Tierney in his short story "Ivy Day in the Committee Room" (1914), and it is not inconceivable that it was a felicitous Irish

turn of speech, one of so many that came to New York with Irish immigration.

trilby hat.   Trilby O'Ferrall, the heroine in British author, George Louis Du Maurier's novel *Trilby* (1894), was a beautiful artist's model who fell under the spell of SVENGALI and came to a tragic end. Many articles of clothing were named after Trilby while the novel was popular, including the soft felt hat with indented crown that the heroine wore in the stage version of the novel, a hat that remains fashionable today.

trillionaire.   It seems impossible that anyone will ever become a British *trillionaire* (a trillion is a million billions in Great Britain; that is 1 followed by 18 zeroes), but some oil-rich Arab might become an American *trillionaire* (a trillion is "only" a thousand billions in the U.S.). Needless to say, there are presently no trillionaires (from the French *trillion*) in the world, but there are a few dozen billionaires, thousands of millionaires, and, as John Jacob Astor 4th said: "A man who has a million dollars is as well off as if he were rich." *See also* BILLIONAIRE; MILLIONAIRE; MULTIMILLIONAIRE.

trim his sails.   A sailor who *trims his sails*, "adjusts them to take advantage of the prevailing winds," is a good one, but this 19th-century expression is now usually applied to an opportunist in everyday life, one who is skillful in shifting his principles with the prevailing winds, without regard for anyone or anything else.

trip the light fantastic.   Milton's poem "L'Allegro" (1632) gives us this expression, meaning "to dance":

> Haste the Nymph and bring with thee
> Jest and youthful Jollity . . .
> Come, and trip it as ye go
> On the light fantastick toe.

triskaidekaphobia.   Fear of the number 13. One of the most notable sufferers of this phobia was the author Sholom Aleichem (Solomon Rabinovitch), whose manuscripts never had a page 13. He died on May 13, 1916, aged 63, but the date on his stone in Mount Carmel Cemetery, Glendale, New York, reads May 12a, 1916.

trivet.   *See* RIGHT AS A TRIVET.

trivial.   Some trivia about the word *trivial*. One theory holds that *trivia* derives from the Roman *trivium*, or "crossroads," where people met to discuss small, insignificant things. Another, less favored, says that during the Middle Ages the seven liberal arts were divided into the *quadrivium* (consisting of arithmetic, geometry, astronomy, and music) and the *trivium* (consisting of rhetoric, logic, and grammar). Since the *trivium* was considered less substantial, its subjects more superficial, the word *trivium* eventually gave us the word *trivial*.

Trojan.   *See* REGULAR TROJAN.

Trojan horse.   Ancient Troy is believed to have been located where Hissarlik, Turkey now stands. Here the Greeks waged the Trojan War (about 1200 B.C.) in an effort to claim their

Queen Helen, who had been abducted by Paris, the son of the king of Troy. At least so the classical writers claim. The war, probably fought for the control of trade, lasted for some 10 years before Troy fell, the last year of the siege recorded by Homer in the *Iliad* and the burning of Troy described by Virgil in the *Aeneid*. Troy finally fell, Virgil writes, when the famous *Trojan horse* was left near the gates of the city overnight. The Trojans believed the giant horse to be a gift to the gods, but its hollow interior was filled with Greek soldiers, who slipped out in the dark and opened Troy's gates to their comrades. Since then the phrase *Trojan horse* has been used for any deceptive scheme.

trolling. The trolls, or dwarfs, of Scandinavian mythology have nothing to do with this word. Meaning in its nautical sense to angle with a running line (which may have originally run on a *troll*, or winch), or to trail a baited line behind a boat, the word *troll* has its beginnings in a hunting term, the Middle French *troller*, which meant "to go in quest of game," or "to ramble."

trompe l'oeil. A painting so realistic that it at first appears three-dimensional is a *trompe l'oeil*. The term is French for "trick the eye."

trophy. The Greeks and the Romans often collected the arms of a vanquished enemy army after a battle and hung these swords, helmets, and armor on the branches of trees, arranging the display as if the tree were an armed man. This monument was called a *trapaion*, "a turning point," because it was always situated at the place where the turning point of the battle occurred. It is to this monument of victory, the *tropaion*, that our word *trophy* owes its birth.

Trotskyite. A follower of Leon Trotsky, the pseudonym of Lev (or Leib) Davidovich Bronstein (1879–1940), the brilliant and prolific Russian revolutionary whose brand of communism advocated worldwide revolution, among other theories. Opposed by Stalin after the death of Lenin, Trotsky was sent into exile in 1929 and was assassinated, allegedly by a Stalinist agent, in Mexico 11 years later.

trouble goin' fall. This old Gullah proverb, once common among slaves on the South Carolina rice plantations, is part of what one scholar calls the slaves' "acceptance strategy of survival." As it was explained by a Gullah speaker: "Trouble made for man. Ain't goin' fall on the ground! Goin' fall on somebody!"

Troy weight. During the 13th century the fairs at Troyes, France, in the province of Champagne, were the most famous in Europe. The weights and measures among merchants there were strictly supervised to ensure honesty and *Troy weight* became a standard of excellence still used today to measure precious metals and drugs.

truck garden. *Truck*, deriving from the Old French *troquer*, "to exchange," was another word for COUNTRY PAY in earlier times. Since truck most often consisted of vegetables from gardens, the term *truck garden* came to refer to a vegetable garden.

true. *See* TREE.

true as Troilus. The phrase is a coinage of Shakespeare's in his play *Troilus and Cressida* (1602), Troilus standing for faithfulness, loyalty, and devotion in the tragedy.

true blue. Cloth made at Coventry in England in medieval times was noted for its permanent blue dye, which withstood many washings, not fading at the first washing like so many blue dyes of the day. Its constancy inspired the saying *as true as Coventry blue*, which meant dependable and faithful and was later shortened to *true blue*. The term's meaning was reinforced in the 17th century when the Scotch Presbyterians who fought for their religion called themselves Covenanters and selected blue as the color of their flag. Those unequivocally on their side were referred to as true blue.

true love never runs smooth. Strictly speaking, the saying is *the course of true love never did run smooth*, and it is from Shakespeare's *A Midsummer Night's Dream* (1595), in which (act I, scene I) Lysander consoles Hermia with the words. The young couple do finally overcome the resistance of Hermia's father and the Duke of Athens and are wed.

truffle. The "diamonds of gastronomy," as black truffles are called, and the "pearls of the kitchen," white truffles, are the world's most expensive food (save for a few rare spices), selling some years for more than $2,000 a pound. The underground fungi probably take their name from the Osco-Umbrian *tufer*, which is a variation of the Latin *tuber*, "truffle." According to this explanation *tufer* changed to the Vulgar Latin *tufera*, which became by metathesis (the transposing of letters) the Old Provençal *trufa*, which was the basis for the French *truffe* and the English *truffle*. So far, so good—black truffles, after all, are more plentiful in Italy's Umbria region than anywhere in the world. But why the *l* in truffle? Some authorities believe that it's there because the English *truffle* derives directly from the Swiss *trufla*, not from the French *truffe*. The Swiss word, they claim, comes from the French *truffe*, with the *l* added from another French word, *trufle*, which means "mockery" or "cheating," alluding to the hard-to-find fungi's habit of hiding underground. In any event, there was inevitable confusion between the French *truffe* and *trufle*, and it is easy to believe that people accidentally combined the two words, given the truffle's evasive qualities.

It's interesting to note that the eponymous hero of Molière's famous play *Tartuffe* was named for the Italian word for truffles. Tartuffe appears to have been drawn from the character of a bawdy French abbot of the period, and Molière is thought to have used *tartuffe* to symbolize the sensuous satisfaction displayed by certain religious brethren when contemplating truffles. It is said that the name came in a flash to the playwright "on seeing the sudden animation that lighted on the faces of certain monks when they heard that a seller of trufles awaited their orders."

People have always been excited by truffles, so much so that they have gone to the trouble of training many animals with keen senses of smell to sniff them out from under the earth—pigs, dogs, goats, ducks, and even bear cubs among them. No other food has been so eulogized. The "pearl of banquets" has been apostrophized by poets like Pope—"Thy truffles, Périgord!" Porphyrus called truffles "children of the gods"; they were "daughters of the earth conceived by the sun" to Cicero, and "*la pomme féerique*" (the fairylike apple) to George Sand. "Who says 'truffle'," wrote Brillat-Savarin of the reputed aphrodisiac, "pronounces a grand word charged with toothsome and amorous memories for the skirted sex, and in the bearded sex with memories amorous and toothsome." Perhaps the truffle's aphrodisiac reputation can be explained by the old French proverb, "If a man is rich enough to eat truffles, his loves will be plenty." But aside from this cynical saying, little can be found in any language derogatory of the truffle. About the only such expression is the French slang word *truffle*, which means a "peasant" or "boor," in reference to the peasants of the Périgord and elsewhere who dig for truffles. Truffles are found by gatherers throughout America, though they are inferior varieties and no dogs or pigs are employed to sniff them out. There have been recent successful efforts to farm truffles in Spain.

Trugen stroke. Outstanding British amateur swimmer John Arthur Trudgen (1852–1902), introduced the Trugen stroke to Europe in 1893, after seeing it used in South America. The stroke, employing a double overarm motion and a scissors kick, is regarded as the first successful above-water arm action used in swimming. Trudgen popularized the idea of minimizing water resistance by bringing both arms out of the water, which paved the way for the reception of the now common Australian crawl adopted from South Sea natives. His stroke was sometimes called the Trudgeon, another misspelling of the swimmer's name.

trump. *Trump* or *trumps*, meaning a suit in card games outranking all other suits for the duration of a hand, is an old alteration of the word *triumph*. The word was first recorded in 1529 and apparently first meant both the name of a card game called trump, and the term described above. Later the term spread to whist and then to bridge.

trumped-up charges. Groundless accusations that are fabricated, usually by a law enforcement agency. *Trump* derives from the Medieval French *tromper*, "to deceive," and has been used in this sense for over five centuries.

truth is stranger than fiction. Lord Byron is the author of the saying, in his poem *Don Juan* (1823): "'Tis strange,—but true; for truth is always strange; / Stranger than fiction. . . ."

truth lay at the bottom of the well. An expression British poet Percy Bysshe Shelley (1792–1822) may have coined after he leaped into the Arno River and his friend Edward Trelawny, a strong swimmer, saved him. Shelley protested, saying, "The truth always lay at the bottom of the well and in another minute I should have found it." Despite several such close calls Shelley never learned to swim and did indeed drown when his schooner, the *Ariel*, sank in the Gulf of Spezia.

try it out on the dog. A late 19th-century theatrical expression meaning to try out a play or a vaudeville act in a small city, making improvements before bringing it to New York. The small towns involved came to be called "dog towns."

tsunami. *Tsunami* means "storm wave" in Japanese. Tsunami (soo-nam-ee) waves have killed tens of thousands. Starting as the result of an undersea volcanic eruption or earthquake, tsunamis gather force and can travel at over 400 miles an hour, rising to heights of over 100 feet before they crash into shore. Tsunamis have been traced back almost to the beginning of recorded history, but the word itself did not come into English until the 20th century. *See* SPLASH.

tuba. A straight war trumpet was called a *tuba* by the ancient Romans, after the Latin word for "arouser or exciter." Over the centuries this word for a war trumpet became attached to an entirely different musical instrument that hadn't even been invented in Roman times.

tuberose. This plant is no relation to the rose and, in fact, was first pronounced in three syllables, "tu-ber-ose." However, people so often mistakenly associated the flower with the rose that its name came to be pronounced in two syllables, "tube rose." The tuberose is the only cultivated species of the genus *Polianthus* and has many fragrant waxy-white flowers that are used in making perfume.

Tucson bed. A humorous expression from the western range that probably dates back to the late 19th century, a Tucson bed, after Tucson, Arizona, means "lying on your stomach and covering that with your back." Early cowboys apparently didn't think much of Tucson's accommodations.

Tuesday. *Tuesday* is named for the Germanic god of war, Tiw, deriving from the Anglo-Saxon *tiewesdaeg*, "the day of Tiw."

Tuesday's child. *See* MONDAY'S CHILD.

tug of war. Lord Byron used the phrase *tug of war* in *Don Juan* (1819–24), but not to describe the popular game of that name. In the game two teams pull on opposite sides of a thick rope, each trying to pull (tug) the other side over the dividing line between them. The words in this sense were first recorded in an 1876 British magazine article: "The tug of war was the most popular item in Saturday's entertainment." At "The Pull," held annually in Michigan's Hope College since 1898, two teams pulled for three hours and 51 minutes before one team was tugged over the line—a record for the event there.

tuk-tuk. A South African three-wheeled six-seater taxi that is powered by a motorcycle. The name is said to derive from the "tuk-tuk" sound its motor makes.

tulip. Of all the foolish investment schemes the world has known, the 17th-century tulipomania was certainly one of the most reckless. Starting in Holland, the mania for the purchase of tulip bulbs spread throughout Europe and rose to its height from 1634 to 1637, when investors purchased bulbs for more than $10,000 each and people lost fortunes on speculations in unusual bulbs that often came to nothing. The tulip takes its name from a Latinized version of an Arabic word for "turban," an allusion to the shape of the flower. Tulips were first grown in Turkey and brought with the Turks to Europe when they invaded the Continent. They have since become one of the most popular flowers in the world, with thousands of varieties available. *See also* MULBERRY.

tumbleweed. Any of several plants, including the *Amaranthus* genus and the Russian thistle (*Salsola kali*), whose branching upper parts come loose from the roots and are driven by the wind across the prairie. The plant, like sagebrush, has become a symbol of the West, as in song lyrics such as "drifting along with the tumbling tumbleweed." One old belief has it that God put tumbleweed here to show cowboys which way the wind is blowing. The plant was originally imported to the U.S. as a border hedge!

tuna. An Americanism first recorded in 1884, *tuna* appears to be an anagram of the Spanish *atun*, for the fish, which had been called the tunny (from the Latin *thunis*) in English since at least the 16th century.

tundra. One of the few words contributed to English by the Laplanders in Europe's far north is the word *tundra*, for the bleak, nearly level barrens these people inhabit. The Lapp *tundra* passed into Russian before being recorded in English during the mid-19th century.

tunnel. In Medieval English a *tonel* was a net with a wide mouth used to trap birds. From this word derived *tunnell*, for "the shaft of a chimney or any pipe or tube," which gave us the word *tunnel*, for "an underground passage."

tunny. *See* TUNA.

tupelo. The native American tupelo tree genus (*Nyssa*), which includes the black or sour gum tree, means "tree of the swamp" in Creek Indian language. *Tupelo*, recorded in 1730, is a good example of the mess Americans made of some Indian words. It was *ito opilwa* in Creek.

Tupperware. Plastic bowls and food containers named after American engineer Earl Tupper, who invented them in the 1940s and set up a company manufacturing them. The airtight containers are primarily used for storing food in the refrigerator. Tupperware parties held in housewive's homes proved very successful for direct sales.

Turing machine; Turing test. In 1937 British mathematician Alan Mathison Turing (1912–54) described what many regard as the theoretical forerunner of the modern computer. This "Turing machine," however, was not an object but a mathematical model. Another eponymous term from Turing's name is the "Turing test," which no computer has yet passed— that is, no computer has been able "to impersonate a human well enough to fool a human judge," according to Mitchell Kapor, the founder of Lotus Development, quoted in the *New York Times* of 9/1/01. A brilliant codebreaker during World War II, Turing committed suicide after being prosecuted and persecuted as a homosexual.

Turk. A cruel, brutal, and domineering man is sometimes called a Turk or an unspeakable Turk, such qualities ascribed to the Turks from early times. The word *Turk* itself is Arabic or Persian for a native of Turkey. *Turk*, uncapitalized, can also mean one of a breed of Turkish horses similar to the Arabian horse, the distinctive plum curculio insect, or a scimitar. *See* YOUNG TURK.

turkey. The domesticated turkey hardly knows what to eat and has to be attracted to food by colorful marbles placed in its feed; it often catches cold by getting its feet wet and frequently panics and suffocates itself when the flock presses together in fear. For such reasons *turkey* has been slang for any stupid, worthless, useless, unsuitable thing since before 1930. *Turkey* for a poor, third-rate play, movie, or book is said to be an invention of humorist S. J. Perelman, who in the 1920s called himself a "Pennsylvania farmer of prized turkeys, which he displays on Broadway once a year." The word is also used for a socially incompetent, awkward person, a fake drug capsule, easy money (because turkeys are comparatively easy to catch), an easy task (a *turkey shoot*), a valise, a 50-cent piece (from the eagle on the coin), and a hobo's suitcase. *Turkey* comes from *turkey hen*, native to Turkey, which was confused with the American bird. *See* ELEPHANT BIRD.

Turkish words in English. Turkish words that have enriched the English language include the ancestors of: turban, tulip, yogurt, caviar, horde, fez, and vampire.

turmeric. The powdered root of the East Indian turmeric plant is often the chief ingredient in a flavorful curry dish. This led the French to name it *terre merite*, roughly "worthy earth," which gives us its English name, *turmeric*. The plant is botanically called *Curcuma domestica*.

turn a blind eye. To deliberately ignore something when you know it is going on. The expression is said to have been inspired by a famous incident at the Battle of Copenhagen. Admiral Nelson had been ordered by flag signal from his superior to halt the bombardment of enemy ships. He deliberately placed his telescope to his blind eye, ignored the order as if he had not seen it, and proceeded to win the day for England.

turn a deaf ear. People have been *turning* or *giving deaf ears* to others, "refusing to listen," since at least the 14th century. A similar expression is to close or stop one's ears, the latter used by Shakespeare in *A Winter's Tale*.

Turnera aphrodisiaca. As its name implies, this Mexican and African plant, commonly known as *damiana* and scientifically named by Linnaeus in honor of William Turner, author of the *New Herball* (1551), has been widely used as an aphrodisiac. Distributed throughout tropical America, the plant is believed to be effective in treating impotence and is supposed to have a tonic effect on the genitals and nervous system. Long ago, the Aztecs used the leaves of damiana to make an aphrodisiac tea. A commercial liqueur made from damiana, called "Liquor for Lovers," can be purchased in the United States. The plant's scientific name is sometimes given as *Turnera diffusa*.

turnip. *Turnip* comes from the early English *turnepe*, that word blending the noun *turn* (with reference to the vegetable's neatly round shape) and the earlier English word *nepe*, for turnip.

turn of the century. The expression has been around since the turn of the 19th century, which was midnight December 31, 1900. Contrary to popular belief, the last turn of the century did not fall on midnight, December 31, 1999. The next turn of the century was midnight, December 31, 2000. Midnight December 31, 1999 was only the beginning of the last year of the old century.

turn over a new leaf. The leaf turned over is one from a book not a tree. People have been using the expression, for "reforming or amending one's conduct" for almost 500 years and it refers to turning to a blank page in an exercise book where one can begin work afresh, or to a new lesson in a book of precepts. A page of a book is called a *leaf*, however, because the leaves of certain plants were used as manuscript pages before the invention of paper. Many ancient manuscripts written on palm leaves still survive.

turn over gravel. Down deep in the holler, or hollow (valley), mountain folk say this of a man in good health, indicated by his ability to urinate so vigorously he can turn over gravel on the ground.

turnpike. *See* PIKER.

turn the tables. Collecting antique tables was a fad among wealthy men in ancient Rome, we're told. When these collectors chided their wives about expensive purchases, the women turned them toward these antique tables and reminded their husbands of their own extravagances, "turning the tables on them." A good story, but there is no evidence that it is true. The expression *to turn the tables* doesn't date from Roman times, is only about 400 years old, and possibly derives from the game of backgammon. In backgammon, formerly called "tables" in England, the board is usually divided into two "tables." One rule of the complicated game allows a player to double the stakes in certain situations and literally turn the tables. Another possibility is that the phrase comes from the old custom of reversing the table or board in chess, which enabled a player at a disadvantage to shift the disadvantage to his opponent.

turn turtle. British sailors in the Caribbean during the 17th century noticed that natives would capture huge sea turtles by turning them over, thereby rendering them helpless, when the creatures came ashore to bury their eggs. Later they used this image when they said that a capsized ship *turned turtle*, and soon the expression came to mean anything upside down.

turn up one's nose. *Turn up one's nose* means "to show contempt or disdain." Lord Byron may have coined this phrase in *Don Juan* (1819), writing of "Antonia . . . turning up her nose, with looks abused her master." But a century or so earlier, *hold up one's nose* had been recorded as meaning "to be proud and haughty."

turpinite. Used in making shells, *turpinite* was for a short time the most powerful explosive in the world, and like the atom bomb inspired the false hope that its terrible effects would end war for all time. The French inventor Turpin concocted *turpinite* about 1894, about six years after he had invented the explosive *lyddite*, which is named for Lydd, England, the town where its preliminary tests were made. Turpinite, said to have been tested among sheep with devastating results, inspired fear even among French troops.

turquoise. This blue or green gem was mined in Persia in medieval times and shipped through Turkey to Europe. Europeans, however, believed it to be mined in Turkey and the French called it *la pierre turquoise* ("the Turkish stone"), which soon became simply *turquoise*.

turtledove. No turtles involved here. The mourning dove takes its name from the Latin *turtur*, echoic for the sound that the bird makes, and *dove*, for "a diver." *Turtur* became the Dutch *tortelduyf*, the German *Turteltaube*, and finally the English *turtledove*. The *Song of Solomon*'s "The voice of the turtle is heard in the land," refers to the turtledove.

Tusitala. *See* SIGN LANGUAGE.

tussie mussie. *See* NOSEGAY.

tutania. British manufacturer William Tutin, who had a plant in Birmingham in about 1770, may have been as patriotic as the inventors of the *sten gun*, who named their invention from their initials plus the *En* of England. Tutin manufactured a silvery white alloy of tin, antimony, and copper, which he probably named after himself and four letters from Brit*annia*. Possibly someone else fashioned the odd word, however, and the coining of *tutania* was probably influenced by *tutenag*, "a crude zinc."

tuxedo. What do Indians have to do with tuxedos? In 1890, dress requirements at the local country club in Tuxedo Park, New York, 40 miles or so from Manhattan, called for men to wear a tailless dinner jacket at most nightly affairs. This was known as a *tuxedo coat* until matching pants were added to the outfit and it became known as a *tuxedo*, which inevitably was shortened to *tux*. The word *tuxedo* itself derives from the white settlers' pronunciation of the name of the Ptuksit Indians, a subtribe of Delaware Indians who lived in what is now Tuxedo Park. *Ptuksit* meant "roundfoot" or "wolf tribe" in allusion to the wolf, "he of the roundfoot."

tuzzy-muzzy. *See* NOSEGAY.

TV dinner. Few people realize that the ubiquitous frozen TV dinner is a trademark name of the C. A. Swanson Company. It was coined in 1953, during the early days of television, when people first began to sit around their TV sets and eat prepared dinners that were easily heated in the oven. *See* TELEVISION.

tweed. "Twill" would have been the name of the coarse woolen cloth named "tweed" if the Scotch weavers who wove it in the mid-19th century had had their way. *Twill* referred to the weaving style used to make the cloth, but English merchants at the time dubbed it *tweed* both because *twill* was pronounced *tweal* in Scottish dialect and because the Tweed River passes through the southern part of Scotland where the cloth is made.

Tweedledum and Tweedledee. A 1725 epigram about the relative merits of the composers Handel and Giovanni Battista

Bononcini, or Tweedledum and Tweedledee as the poet called them, went as follows:

> Some say compared to Bononcini
> That mynheer Handel's but a ninny;
> Others aver that he to Handel
> Is scarcely fit to hold a candle.
> Strange all this difference should be
> Twixt Tweedledum and Tweedledee.

The epigram, variously attributed to John Byrom, Pope, and Swift, first used the words Tweedledum and Tweedledee, which has since described two people, groups, or things identical in looks, opinions, or certain characteristics. The nicknames, which suggested the contrast between high- and low-pitched musical instruments, were given to German-born English musician George Handel and the musician G. B. Bononcini when a rivalry sprang up between the two while Handel served as director of the Royal Academy of Music. English aristocrats mainly sided with Bononcini, who is little-known today and left no work nearly as popular as Handel's *Messiah*. Tweedledum and Tweedledee were made more famous as the twins in Lewis Carroll's *Through the Looking Glass* (1872).

Tweed Ring. *See* TAMMANY.

12 (twelve). Twelve is first recorded in English at about the time the Danish Vikings began invading England in 789 and it may derive from the Old Frisian *twelf*. In any case the victorious Vikings did transmit their duodecimal system to the English. They counted in twelves instead of tens and our 12 inches to a foot, 12 men to a jury and marketing unit of a dozen all evolved from their system.

21-gun salute. Guns were fired as salutes in early times, but a 21-gun salute is an American expression. According to an official U.S. Navy publication: "Guns could not be loaded quickly then, so the act of firing one in a salute indicated that the saluter had disarmed himself in deference to the person being saluted. The larger the number of guns fired the greater degree of disarmament . . ." Since 21 guns was the greatest number found on one side of one of the larger ships of the line, firing all of them became the highest mark of respect, reserved for heads of state. Fewer numbers of guns were fired in salutes to people of lesser importance. But for any salute only odd numbers are used, reflecting the old seagoing superstition against even numbers. This form of saluting was first recognized in the U.S. in 1875. As commander in chief, the president is accorded the highest salute of 21 guns.

20 tailors around a buttonhole. An old American variation on the older 16th-century TOO MANY COOKS SPOIL THE BROTH

23 skiddoo. For well over half a century no one has used this expression seriously, but it is still remembered today—mainly as a phrase representative of the Roaring Twenties, which it is *not*. Twenty-three skiddoo is important, too. It goes back to about 1900 and for 10 years enjoyed great popularity as America's first national fad expression, paving the way for thousands of other dispensables such as *Yes, we have no bananas, Shoo-fly, Hey, Abbott!, Coming, mother!* and *I dood it!* Twenty-three skiddoo practically lost its meaning of "scram" or "beat it" and just became the thing to say, anytime. As for its derivation, it is said to have been invented or popularized by that innovative early comic-strip artist "Tad" Dorgan, encountered frequently in these pages under *hot dog, yes man,* and other of his coinages. Regarding its composition, *skiddoo* may be a shortening of the earlier "skedaddle." *Twenty-three* is a mystery. Perhaps it was a code number used by telegraphers. There is even a theory that it "owes its existence to the fact that the most gripping and thrilling word in *A Tale of Two Cities* is twenty-three": Sydney Carton, the 23rd man to be executed on the 23rd of the month. Finally, there is the story that *twenty-three* referred to the address of New York City's Flatiron Building, on whose windy corner men liked to watch women's skirts blow upward, until cops told them to scram—"Twenty-three skiddo!"

twepping. Homicide was called by the acronym *twep*, "terminate *with* extreme *p*rejudice," in C.I.A. circles during the Vietnam War, and may still be used today. *Twep* was used so frequently that it gave rise to the euphemistic verb *twepping*.

twerp. This word for an insignificant objectionable little person may well be an eponym. The Englishman in question, according to several authors, is T. W. Erp, who attended Oxford in about 1911. Author J. R. R. Tolkein has called this T. W. Erp "the original twerp," while author Roy Campbell shares his opinion and suggests that T. W. Erp was first called a *twerp* by "rugger-playing stalwarts" who were jealous of his charm and intellectual gifts. Both these authors are referring to Thomas W. Earp (1892–1958), whose last name is pronounced *Erp*, making the eponymous word just as likely. Earp, an art critic and author, criticized D. H. Lawrence's paintings in the *New Statesman* (Aug. 17, 1929) and Lawrence replied with a poem that began: "I heard a little chicken chirp:/ My name is Thomas, Thomas Earp!/ And I can neither paint nor write,/ I only can set other people right." It is said that Earp really did have a curious high-pitched voice similar to a "chirp," making Lawrence's putdown all the more effective. Another theory has *twerp* deriving from the Danish *tver,* perverse; still another that it is a variant of *twit*.

Twin Towers. Until their tragic destruction by terrorists on September 11, 2001, the Twin Towers of the World Trade Center complex in downtown Manhattan were New York's tallest office buildings, surpassed only by the Petronas Towers in Malaysia and the Sears Tower in Chicago. Over 50,000 people worked in the World Trade Center complex, thousands of whom were killed in the terrorist attack on the Twin Towers. *See* EMPIRE STATE BUILDING.

Twiss. Here the Irish had the last word, as is often the case. Author Richard Twiss (1747–1821) may have thought he had put the natives down when he published his uncomplimentary *Tour in Ireland* in 1775, but he hadn't counted on the Irish wit. They promptly began to manufacture a chamber pot called the *Twiss,* but didn't let it go at that. On the bottom of the chamber pot was a portrait of *Richard Twiss,* the picture captioned thus:

> Let everyone———
> On lying Dick Twiss.

See also CRAPPER; FURPHY; OLIVER; SACHEVERELL; VESPASIENNE.

twist slowly, slowly in the wind.   President Richard Nixon's assistant for domestic affairs, John D. Ehrlichman, coined this expression on March 8, 1973, while on the phone with presidential counsel John Dean discussing the withdrawal of Patrick Gray's nomination for director of the F. B. I. Gray had not been told about the withdrawal and was waiting for his appointment. "I think we ought to let him hang there," Ehrlichman said. "Let him twist slowly, slowly in the wind."

twist (turn) someone around one's little finger.   "[She] had already turned that functionary around her finger," historian John Motely wrote in *The Rise of the Dutch Republic* (1855). This is the first recorded mention of anything like the more embellished expression *to twist someone around one's little finger*, though Motely makes no claim to having coined the phrase.

twitter.   *See* ONOMATOPOEIA.

two bits.   *Bit* was British slang for money or any small coin (a threepenny bit, etc.) as far back as the early 16th century. In U.S. regions bordering on Mexico the term was applied to the Mexican *real*, worth 12½ cents and called a shilling in many eastern states. By 1730 the expression *two bits*, two Mexican reales, or 25 cents, was being used in the American Southwest and for many years *quarter* was practically unknown there. *Two bits* became popular throughout the country, as did the expression *not worth two bits*, "practically worthless," but *four bits* and *six bits* never caught on nationally.

two comma kid.   Recent clever, unrecorded black slang for a millionaire, especially a young one, like a rap star. Million written in numbers (1,000,000) has two commas.

two down, one to go.   When something is close to being accomplished, when the finish is near, one might say *two down, one to go*. The common expression is from baseball, where *down* is a synonym for "out" and has been used that way for over a century. There are of course three outs an inning allowed to a team at bat before the opposing team gets a chance to bat.

twofers.   *Twofers* has meant "two theater tickets for the price of one" since about 1948 in America. Previously, since as early as 1890, *twofers* had referred to "two-for-a-nickel" cigars.

two lamps burning and no ship at sea.   A foolishly extravagant person. Someone with ships at sea in the days of sail was rich and could afford to burn two expensive oil lamps. Anyone else who burned two lamps was likely a fool.

two percent to glory.   Albert Einstein was a dedicated pacifist and in 1930 made a speech declaring that "If only two percent of those assigned to military service would announce their refusal to fight . . . governments would be powerless. They would not dare to send such a large number of people to jail." He was soon affectionately dubbed "Two percent Einstein" by a pacifist group, which made its slogan "Two Per Cent to Glory." *See* EINSTEIN.

two strikes against you.   When you have two strikes against you, you are close to striking out in baseball, a game in which a batter has three missed chances before his turn at bat is over.

Thus we have the widely used phrase *to have two strikes against you*—borrowed from baseball, no one knows exactly when—meaning perilously close to losing, or, in another sense, starting out with an unfair disadvantage. *See also* STRIKEOUT.

two strings to one's bow.   To be prepared for anything, to have an alternate plan. This expression is probably much older than its first recorded use, by Cardinal Wolsey in 1524, having its roots in the archer of ancient times who always carried at least two bowstrings when he went into battle.

two-time loser.   In some states a third conviction for a major crime results in an automatic term of life imprisonment for the offender. Thus a criminal who has two such convictions and remains a criminal is a desperate man, a two-time loser.

two whoops and a holler.   In western U.S. parlance *two whoops and a holler* means a short distance, not far, "within spitting range." The phrase probably dates back to the late 19th century.

tycoon.   *Tycoon* is just an American phonetic spelling of the Japanese *taikun*, for "great prince." The Japanese word, in turn, comes from the Chinese *ta*, "great," and *chun*, "prince." Americans encountered the *taikun*, whose military title was *shogun*, during Commodore Perry's expedition to Japan of 1852–54 and brought the word home, where it was applied to any powerful man, especially a wealthy businessman.

Tyler grippe.   John Tyler (1790–1863) has the dubious honor of being the only U.S. President for whom an epidemic is named. The Tyler grippe was a virulent influenza that swept the country at the time he became President in 1841. In fact, Tyler, elected vice-president, assumed office when his running mate, old William Henry Harrison, died a month after being inaugurated as President. Harrison died of pneumonia or the Tyler grippe, or a combination of both.

typefaces named for printers.   Numerous typefaces for printing have been named for their designers. Several of the most famous are: 1) Baskerville, after Englishman John Baskerville, who died in 1775. He is said to have made all the tools of his trade, including his own inks. 2) Bodoni (1740–1813), the son of a printer, who produced many works over his long career that are considered classics today. 3) Caslon, after Englishman William Caslon (1692–1766), one of London's leading printers. 4) Gill, for British sculptor and type designer Eric Gill (1882–1940). 5) Plantin, after Christiphe Plantin, who died in 1549 when only 35. Famous for his excellent craftsmanship in his own lifetime, he is now honored by the Musee Plantin in Antwerp, which was the site of his famous printing house.

typewriter.   The word *typewriter* was coined by American Christopher Latham Sholes, who patented the first practical commercial typewriter in 1868 (slow, difficult machines, intended primarily for the blind, had been invented as early as 1714). Sholes's "type-writer" had only capital letters. Manufactured by Remington, it was owned by Henry James, Mark Twain, and Sigmund Freud, among other famous early experimenters. Mark Twain, in fact, typed *The Adventures of Tom Sawyer* on Sholes's machine in 1875, this being the first typewritten book manuscript (a fact that Twain kept secret in his lifetime because he didn't want to write testimonials or show the uninitiated how to use the machine).

typhoon. There is some doubt about the origin of this term for a violent tropical storm in the area of the China Seas, but it probably derives from Chinese *tai fung*, "big wind," influenced by Greek *tuphon*, "whirlwind," and Arabic *tufan*, "storm." Typhon, the giant Greek father of the winds, also influenced the coinage. Joseph Conrad's short story "Typhoon" (1903) deals with typhoons so violent that even the imperturbably obtuse captain of a tramp steamer doubts his ship's survival. *See* HURRICANE.

typo. *Typo*, short for typographical error, is an Americanism dating back to the 1890s. Newspapers and magazines regularly run features pointing out the best or worst typographical errors in other newspapers and magazines. For example, a Clive Barnes review in the *New York Times* of *A Midsummer Night's Dream* found "David Waller's virile bottom (instead of 'Bottom') particularly splendid." Possibly the worst modern-day slip appeared in the *Washington Post* in 1915, where it was noted that President Wilson had taken his fiancée, Edith Galt, to the theater and rather than watching the play "spent most of his time entering Mrs. Galt," instead of "entertaining Mrs. Galt."

tyro. A green recruit was called a *tiro* by the Romans, to distinguish him from an experienced ordinary soldier, called a *miles*. In Medieval Latin *tiro* was often spelled *tyro*, which became our term for a novice or greenhorn in any field.

U

U. The letters *U* and v were at first interchangeable in English, the letters not separated in dictionaries until the early 19th century (*upon*, for example, was often spelled *vpon*). *U* in recent times has become a humorous term for "upper class" or "correct," *non-u* or *un-u* being its opposite.

U-boat. The German *unterseeboot*, "undersea boat," gives us this universal abbreviation, which became popular during World War I.

UFO. *UFO*, as a term, has been in use since the 1950s or earlier, but the first *u*nidentified *f*lying *o*bjects were reported in America in 1896. UFOs are often called flying saucers, but they have been reported in many different shapes. The first were said to resemble "cigar-shaped airships."

ugh! There is no record of an American Indian ever uttering the sound "ugh" when he or she meant "yes" or "hello." The term can be traced to dime romances about the American West popular at the turn of the century, its use perpetuated by early American motion pictures. As a sound of contempt and disgust *ugh* is first recorded in 1837 but is probably much older.

ugli fruit. *Ugli* here is simply a spelling variation of *ugly* and is used to describe a large sweet variety of tangelo with rough, wrinkled yellowish skin that originated in Jamaica. A tangelo is a cross between a tangerine and grapefruit. *See* GRAPE; TANGERINE.

ugly as a mud fence. American pioneers often made fences of sod and dirt when stone and wood were in short supply on the prairie. These homely fences served their purpose but were eyesores, leading to the expression *ugly as a mud fence* for someone or something extremely ugly.

ugly as sin. One can't be much uglier than this, even if some sins seem lovely. The expression, though possibly much older, is first recorded in Sir Walter Scott's novel *Kenilworth* (1821) with its many glimpses into the court of Queen Elizabeth.

ugly duckling. Hans Christian Andersen's tale "The Ugly Duckling" tells of a sad "ugly duckling" that was actually a cygnet and, to its mother's surprise, grew up into a magnificent swan. Soon after the story was translated into English in 1846 the expression *ugly duckling* became part of the language, usually meaning an unpromising child who grows into an admirable adult.

Ugly Valley. One of many New Zealand place names translated into English from Maori words. In this case the original was *Awakino*, which means "valley ugly." About 60 percent of New Zealand place names are of Maori origin.

uh, oh; uh-huh; uh, uh; huh. Humorist H. Allen Smith thought *uh, oh* was the most terrifying phrase in English, "as when a doctor looks at your X-rays and says 'uh, oh.' " It is not to be confused with *uh-huh* and *um*, "yes"; *uh-uh*, "no"; or *huh?*, "what?" All of these expressions or grunts have been traced back to at least the 1830s. Stuart Berg Flexner in *I Hear America Talking* has described *uh-uh*, *huh?*, and *um* as "among the most common 'words' heard in America . . . truly native earmarks of an American," and points out that perceptive English author Captain Frederick Marryat properly identified them as Americanisms over a century ago. Flexner doesn't mention it but *y'know* is replacing *uh* as a surrogate crutch today, y'know; I mean, uh, *y'know* is a form of "inarticulatese," that is, uh, y'know . . .

ukulele. *Ukulele* is the Hawaiian word for "flea." Apparently, it was transferred to the musical instrument that the Portuguese brought to Hawaii in 1879, either because one's fingers hop like fleas from string to string when playing the instrument, or because British army officer Edward Purvis, a member of King Kalakaua's court, nicknamed "the flea" because of his small stature, was a skilled ukulele player who helped make the instrument popular in Hawaii.

Ultima Thule. A distant territory or a remote goal or ideal. The original Thule was the northernmost region of the habitable world to ancient Greek geographers, from the time the fourth century Greek navigator Pytheas visited a northern island he called Thule, which has variously been identified as Iceland, Norway, or the Shetland Islands. The words *Ultima Thule*, sometimes used in the lower case, are from the Latin *ultima*, "farthest," plus *Thule*. There is a real town called *Thule* in northwest Greenland.

ultracrepedarian. *See* COBBLER SHOULD STICK TO HIS LAST.

ululate. Meaning to howl or wail, to lament loudly, *ululate* is a word of imitative origin, possibly going back to the Sanskrit *ulukas*, a name for the screech owl.

Ulysses. *See* ODYSSEY

Ulysses S. Grant. Most people believe this was the name of Union Civil War general U. S. Grant, but his real name was Hiram Ulysses Grant—a clerical mistake at West Point had listed him as Ulysses Simpson Grant, and he accepted the error until the end of his life, even in the title of his *Memoirs*. He was called Sam at the Point, however; the old story was that an upperclassman spied his name given as U. S. Grant on a bulletin board listing of new cadets and joked that this stood for United States Grant, or better yet, Uncle Sam Grant. "That's what he is," another joker supposedly chimed in: "Uncle Sam Grant—the grandson of our good old Uncle Sam." The awkward little soldier was glad to be called Sam, too, throughout his career. He liked it better than the strange Ulysses and far better, of course, than the Useless of his childhood playmates. It was also clearly preferable to his other nickname, "Little Beauty," given to the good-looking soldier by the officers of his regiment before the Mexican War. During the Civil War he would be called *Unconditional Surrender* Grant and also the Butcher for his unsparing sacrifice of Union troops. *See* ROBERT E. LEE.

umber. The color *umber*, dark dusty brown or dark reddish brown, is named for the earth called umber that makes such pigments. *Umber earth* comes from the Italian *terra d'Umbria*, "earth of Umbria," referring to the soil in Umbria, east of Tuscany in northern Italy. Umbria is named for the *Umbri*, a tribe that once inhabited the region. It is a great TRUFFLE producing region.

umbrage. *Umbrage* derives from the Latin *umbra*, "shadow or shade," the same root that gives us UMBRELLA. The expression means to take offense, suggesting someone "shadowed in offended pride, retreating into the darkness of proud indignation." There is a story about the editor of a small newspaper who quickly read a wire service story during World War II stating that the Russians had *taken umbrage* at something, as they often did. Not knowing what the phrase meant, he headlined the story: "Russians Capture Umbrage."

umbrella. The umbrella is named for the benefit it provides in hot, sunny countries. It derives from the Latin *umbra* "shade," its diminutive ending making the word mean "a little shade." (*Sombrero* similarly comes from the Spanish *sombra*, "shade.") The umbrella has been known in England since Anglo-Saxon times, but is said to have first been used there as a protection against rain by the world traveler Jonas Hanway in 1760. His

innovation caused a riot among sedan chairmen and coachmen, whose vehicles up to then had been the pedestrian's only protection from downpours. *See also* GAMP; UMBRAGE; UNDER THE UMBRELLA OF.

umlaut. In German the umlaut is used to indicate an internal vowel change in a word or to show that a letter is pronounced differently than it ordinarily would be. It is also called a *diaeresis* in English, when it is used above the second of two coupled vowels to show separate pronunciation, as in *coöperate*. The only English or American authors, and perhaps the only English or American family, with an umlaut in their name are the Brontë sisters—Charlotte, Emily, and Anne. Their father, Patrick Brunty, trying to distinguish himself at Cambridge, changed the family name to Brontë soon after Lord Nelson was created duke of Bronte; he added the German umlaut for even more éclat.

ummern; dummern. Words often take on almost unrecognizable forms in remote places. A century ago, for example, the scholar Horace Kephart found that "the word *woman* has suffered some strange sea-changes" in the North Carolina Appalachians. There, in Mitchell County, he heard "the extraordinary forms *ummern* and *dummern*" for *woman*.

umpire. *Umpire* is a later form of *noumpere*, which meant the same: "one who decides disputes between parties." *Noumpere*, in turn, ultimately derives from the Old French *nonper* (*non*, "not" plus *per*, "equal"). Thus, the idea behind the word is that the umpire is not equal to either party in a dispute, is the impartial third person. *Noumpere*, the accepted form up until the 15th century, began to be pronounced *umpire* because people transferred the *n* in the word to the indefinite article: *noumpere* becoming an *oumpere* and finally an *umpire*. In the same way a *napron* became an *apron*, a *nadder* became an *adder*, and an *ewt* became a *newt*.

umpteen, umpty. These are words meaning a large number, as in "She has umpteen pairs of shoes." Of World War I origin, both words may have been coined by army telegraphers. *Umpty* was slang for a dash in Morse Code, and a great many dashes or umptys may have become *umpteen* (patterned on thir*teen*, four*teen*, etc.)

un-American. *Un-American* is a very American word, dating back to at least 1817, when it is first recorded, and not at all of recent vintage. It means contrary to U.S. values, even traitorous, and was most prominent recently in the name of the House [of Representatives] Un-American Activities Committee, active from 1938 to 1975, which critics claim was more un-American than many of the people it investigated. In 1945 HUAC's name became the Committee on Un-American Activities; in 1969 it was renamed the Committee on Internal Security; and it was finally abolished in 1975.

uncial. An *uncial* is a majuscule script, often used in ancient manuscripts, that takes its name from the Latin *uncia*, "inch," because the letters in it are about an inch high.

uncle! *To say* or *cry uncle* has since the beginning of this century meant "to give up, to surrender, to say you've had enough." Apparently it is of schoolboy origin, at least it is most used by schoolboys when fighting, especially when one has another pinned helplessly on the ground. For about 30 years the cry *give!* has been more common in the New York City area, but one still hears the earlier expression. Why *uncle* was chosen by kids is anybody's guess; there probably is no good reason unless a defeated boy originally had to curse his uncle, just as bullies often make their victims curse their mothers and sisters before letting them go. Which is no more than a guess. *Cavy!* a similar expression not heard anymore, is said to date back to Tudor times, a corruption of the Latin *peccavi*, meaning "I have sinned, I am wrong."

Uncle Miltie. *See* I'LL TELL YOU WHAT I'M GONNA DO.

Uncle Remus. Joel Chandler Harris's Uncle Remus tales, collected in *Uncle Remus: His Songs and His Sayings* (1880) and many other books, were among the first and remain the greatest of black folk literature. In the books, Uncle Remus, a former slave, entertains the young son of his employer with traditional "Negro tales" that in St. Augustine's words "spare the lowly and strike down the proud," including the "Tar-Baby" stories and other tales of Brer Rabbit (always the hero), Brer Fox, and Brer Wolf. Harris, born a "poor white" or "redneck," a piney-woods "Georgia cracker," collected the authentic tales from numerous former slaves. One who helped him a great deal was an old gardener in Forsyth, Georgia called Uncle Remus, and Harris named his narrator after him. The tales, however, probably go back to Africa, where they were born among people who spoke the Bantu language and of course no Uncle Remus is in them. Uncle Remus is considered "a servile groveling 'Uncle Tom' " by some blacks today. Versions of the Brer Rabbit tales without him have been told by Arna Bontemps and Langston Hughes.

Uncle Sam. The original *Uncle Sam* was Samuel Wilson, the nephew of army contractor Elbert Anderson, who owned a store or slaughterhouse in Troy, New York and had a contract to supply the army with salt pork and beef during the War of 1812. Wilson and his uncle Ebenezer, Elbert's brother, worked as army inspectors and frequently inspected the meat Elbert Anderson packed in barrels with the initials "E.A.—U.S." stamped on them. According to a popular version of the story, one soldier asked another what the initials E.A.—U.S. (Elbert Anderson United States) meant and his companion quipped that they stood for "*E*lbert *A*nderson's *U*ncle *S*am." Some scholars dispute this story, which was widely accepted during Wilson's lifetime, but no better explanation has been given. The term's first recorded use was in the *Troy Post* of September 7, 1813, which speaks well for the Samuel Wilson theory except that the article only says the words derive from the initials on government wagons. The name *Uncle Sam* caught on quickly as a symbol of the army and then as a national nickname to counteract that of England's John Bull.

Uncle Tom. Everyone knows that *Uncle Tom* comes from the character in Harriet Beecher's Stowe's *Uncle Tom's Cabin* (1852), the immensely popular American antislavery novel that caused President Lincoln to say on meeting Mrs. Stowe, "Is this the little woman whose book made such a great war?" Mrs. Stowe depicted Uncle Tom as simple, easygoing, and servile,

willing to put up with anything, though it should be remembered that she intended him as a noble, high-minded, devout Christian and that he is flogged to death by the brutal overseer Simon Legree at the end of the book for bravely refusing to reveal the hiding place of Cassie and Emmaline, two female slaves. Few people know that Mrs. Stowe's model for Uncle Tom was a real-life slave named Josiah Henson, born in Maryland in 1789, who wrote a widely read autobiographical pamphlet. Henson was far from an *Uncle Tom* in the term's recent sense. Like many slaves, he served as the overseer, or manager, of a plantation before he escaped to Canada. Once free, he started a prosperous sawmill, founded a trade school for blacks, whites, and Indians and helped over 100 slaves escape to Canada. When he journeyed to England on business, the archbishop of Canterbury was so impressed with his speech and learning that he asked him what university he had studied at. "The University of Adversity," Henson replied.

Uncle Tomahawk. Recent slang for an American Indian who is accused of being servile to whites by other Indians; patterned on the older familiar term "Uncle Tom." Also *Uncle Taco (Tio Taco)*.

unconditional surrender. "Unconditional Surrender" was the nickname of Union General U. S. (Ulysses Simpson) Grant, who would give "no terms but unconditional surrender" to the Confederates in 1862 when his forces captured Fort Donelson in Tennessee, the first major Union victory of the war. The term has been used in every war since, but got its start with "Old Unconditional." *See* ULYSSES S. GRANT

uncouth. *Couth*, originally meaning "known or familiar," dates back before Chaucer's day. Its antonym *uncouth* is just as old, the word being used in *Beowulf* for "unknown or unfamiliar." The dislike of the unfamiliar, of strangers, foreigners, is probably responsible for the change in the word's meaning over the years to unseemly, awkward, uncultured, etc.

underdog. *Underdog* appears to have originated in a popular 19th century song by David Barker called "The Under-Dog in the Fight," two stanzas of which follow:

> I know that the world, that the great big world
>   Will never a moment stop
> To see which dog may be in the fault,
>   But will shout for the dog on top.
>
> But for me, I shall never pause to ask
>   Which dog may be in the right,
> For my heart will beat, while it beats at all,
>   For the under dog in the fight.

underhanded. We know that four centuries ago card sharks were as proficient at palming cards, holding extra cards under their hands, as sharpsters are today. Such cheating, widespread as it has always been, may have suggested the expression *underhanded*, "in a secret or stealthy manner," though the first writer to use the word in this sense (1545) refers to a plain thief "stealing under hande or craftily."

undertaker. *Undertaker* has been used since at least 1698 for what is in the U.S. euphemistically called a mortician. Perhaps the term originated as a joke (for an undertaker does *take* someone *under* the ground), but there is no proof of this. *Undertaker* is recorded three centuries earlier in the sense of "one who undertakes a task or enterprise," and an *undertaker* meant "a publisher," and, to be fair, "an author," before it came to mean one who arranged funerals.

under the counter.   During World War II, dishonest merchants often stored rationed or hard-to-get items under the counter and sold them at inflated prices to dishonest customers. Before the war ended, this practice led to expressions like *under the counter* for any illegal or shady transaction.

under the doctor.   To say someone is "under the doctor" in the U.S. would be a bit risqué. Here we say someone is "under the doctor's care," but the British prefer the shortcut.

under the hammer.   The Romans used to stick a spear into the ground on consummating a sale, which led to their expression *under the spear*, for something sold or about to be sold. By the 18th century the English, having fewer spears around, were using the expression *under the hammer* for something on the auction block, anything from a painting to an entire estate. The *hammer* in the phrase is of course in reference to the small wooden hammer or gavel that an auctioneer brings down when a bid on an item has been accepted.

under the rose.   *See* SUB ROSA.

under the table.   An odd New York character named George Washington "Chuck" Connors, the so-called Bowery Philosopher from the late 1890s into the early years of the 20th century, is said to have coined the expression *under the table* for dead drunk. He is also thought to be responsible for the catchphrases *oh, forget it* and *the real thing*. For another use of *under the table see* ABOVEBOARD.

under the umbrella of.   This phrase means under the protection, dominion, or influence of someone. In various Asian and African countries the umbrella was a symbol of rank or state, an emblem of sovereignty, and the expression may be an allusion to this. As far back as the early 17th century, English writers were commenting on the practice of servants carrying umbrellas to shade sultans from the sun. But the expression could be home-grown, too; just as early, there were figurative references in English to umbrellas as a means of protection. Perhaps the phrase is simply an extension of the earlier *under the aegis of*, which means the same. The *aegis* was the storm and thundercloud of the Greek god Zeus, who sometimes put it between a favorite and his enemies to protect his favorite. A bright, blazing shield fringed with gold tassels, it had at its center the head of Medusa, a glimpse of which could turn men to stone.

under the weather.   Ik Marvel, a pseudonym that resulted from a misprinting of J. K. Marvel, was the pen name of American author Donald Grant Mitchell. In his *Reveries of a Bachelor* (1850) Ik Marvel is the first to record *under the weather*, which has been a synonym for everything from "ill and indisposed" to "financially embarassed" and "drunk," and has even been a synonym for "the discomfort accompanying menstruation."

under the wire.   *See* JUST UNDER THE WIRE.

underworld.   Since about 1608, when the term is first recorded, *underworld* had meant hell, or the nether world of the dead beneath the earth. But in the 18th century the word was applied to the world of criminals, who were considered "beneath" proper society. By the 1920s *underworld* was being used in this second sense only to describe organized crime, which the word generally means today.

under your hat.   *See* TALK THROUGH ONE'S HAT.

under your own nose.   Right in front of someone, as in "He cheated you here, right under your own nose." The expression dates back to at least 1548 and usually refers to "an action that is done in defiance of a person without his perceiving it," in the words of the *OED*. Variations on the phrase are *right under your nose* and *under your very nose*.

undine.   An *undine* is a female water spirit, one of the elemental spirits, the spirit of the waters. The word was coined by Paracelsus from the neo-Latin *unda*, "a wave." *Undine*, in the 1811 tale of the same name by German author Friedrich de la Motte Fouqué, obtains a soul by marrying a mortal and bearing him a child.

Uneasy lies the head that wears a crown.   *See* HANG BY A THIN THREAD.

unicorn.   Medieval writers represented this mythical animal as having "the legs of a buck, the tail of a lion, the head and body of a horse and a single horn—white at the base, black in the middle and red at the tip—its body white, head red, and eyes blue." It takes its name, of course, from the most distinctive of its features, the single horn in the center of its forehead, from the Latin *unum cornu*, "one horn." Described as early as 400 B.C., the mythical beast was thought to be the only animal able to defeat an elephant—by ripping the elephant's belly with its sharp hooves. It could be caught only by "placing a young virgin in its haunts"—the unicorn would lie down placidly at her feet.

Union Jack.   *Jack* has meant a small flag used as a mark of distinction on a ship since the early 17th century. It may be that the Union Jack, the national flag of Great Britain, takes its last name from this *jack* flown aboard ships. Other possibilities are the French *Jacques*; James, for King James I introduced the Union flag; or a leather surcoat called the *jack* that was often "emblazoned with the cross of St. George."

union suit.   Still heard occasionally, as a comic or euphemistic term for men's underwear, the union suit was probably so named because top and bottom were "united" in one piece. However, some authorities say the underwear, dating back to the early 19th century, got its name because it was made of a "united" mixture of flax and cotton called "union."

United Nations. Before Winston Churchill suggested the name *United Nations* to President Roosevelt the world body was called the *Associated Powers*. Churchill took the name from a poem by Lord Byron, which he quoted to FDR:

> Millions of tongues record thee, and anew
> Their children's lips shall echo them and say—
> "Here, where the sword united nations drew,
> Our countrymen were warring on that day!"
> And this is much, and all which will not pass away.

United States of America. Thomas Paine, the author of *Common Sense*, a popular tract that attracted many to the side of the American Revolution in 1776, coined the name *United States of America* for his adopted country. The name was first used in the subtitle of the Declaration of Independence: "The Unanimous Declaration of the Thirteen United States of America." However, before the Articles of Confederation was ratified in 1781 the nation was known as The Congress. Under the Articles it was called The United States in Congress Assembled and under the Constitution was finally called Paine's United States of America. It should be added that from as early as 1617 to as late as 1769 the kingdom or republic of Holland was called the United States. *See* SUMMER SOLDIER AND SUNSHINE PATRIOT.

united we stand, divided we fall. The commonly-quoted words are originally from "The Liberty Song," by John Dickman, first published in the *Boston Gazette*, July 18, 1768: "Then join hand in hand, have Americans all! / By uniting we stand, by dividing we fall."

Univac. *Univac* is an acronym for *univ*ersal *a*utomatic computer system. This early computer gave its name to its manufacturer, which was taken over by another company in the early 1950s and became a division of the Sperry Rand Corporation.

University of Adversity. *See* UNCLE TOM.

Unknown Child. Canadian sailors buried an unidentified infant who died in the sinking of the *Titanic* (1912) in a Halifax graveyard, where his grave became known over the years as the Grave of the Unknown Child. In 2002, DNA tests identified the child as Eino Panula, 13 month old, whose mother and four brothers and sisters also died in the tragedy. The grave has since been visited by other members of his family. *See* UNKNOWN SOLDIER.

Unknown Soldier; Unknown Warrior. The Unknown Soldier is the body of an unidentified American soldier killed in France during World War I and buried in the National Cemetery at Arlington, Virginia, his grave a national shrine. The *Unknown Warrior* is his British counterpart, "buried among the kings" in Westminster Abbey. There are similar shrines in Paris and Berlin for French and German unknown soldiers, all from that bloody war. Since 1958 unknown soldiers who died in World War II, Korea, and Vietnam have been buried in the Tomb of the Unknown Soldier at Arlington. *See* UNKNOWN CHILD.

unmentionables. Few if any people would use this expression today, but it was a humorous term for both trousers and underwear in Victorian times. *Inexpressibles*, *unutterables*, and *unwhisperables* were other such terms.

unmuzzled. British prime minister Gladstone used *unmuzzled* in 1865 to describe a former government officeholder no longer restrained from speech by his position. Shakespeare was the first to use the word figuratively (it had been used previously of dogs) in *As You Like It* (1599): "Ay, marry, now unmuzzle your wisdom."

unreconstructed southerner. A term applied to a southerner not reconciled to the results of the Civil War; first recorded in 1867, it is still used today. *Unreconstructed rebel* is a later variation. For a stanza of "A Good Old Rebel (Unreconstructed)" by Innes Randolph (1837–87), *see* GOOD OLE BOY.

until the last dog is hung. This colorful Americanism was appropriately first recorded in an old-fashioned western, Stuart Edward White's *The Blazed Trail* (1902), in which the hanged dogs referred to hanged men. Today the words are usually heard in reference to someone staying at a party, bar, event, etc., until the very last, as in "We were there until the last dog was hung."

unvarnished truth. An unembellished account without any evasions. This is a variation on *unvarnished tale*, meaning the same, which is said to have been invented by Shakespeare in *Othello* (1602): "Yet, by your gracious patience, / I will a round unvarnished tale deliver."

upas. According to fable a foul vapor rises from the Javanese upas tree (*Antiaris toxicaria*) and "not a tree, nor blade of grass is to be found in the valley or surrounding mountains near it, not a beast or bird, reptile or living thing lives in the vicinity." A Dutch physician noted in 1783 that "on one occasion 1,600 refugees encamped within fourteen miles of it and but 300 died within two months." Such legends inspired the use of the word *upas*, for "a corrupting or evil influence." Legends aside, the milky juice of the upas contains a virulent poison that is used for tipping arrows.

upblown; unupblown. Regarding a rumor that a British nurse had been killed in an Italian air raid on Ethiopia, author Evelyn Waugh's newspaper editor cabled him "Send two hundred words upblown nurse." Finding that the story had no basis in fact, Waugh cabled back, "Nurse unupblown."

up Green River. When American mountain men killed a man a century ago they sent him *up Green River*, this referring not directly to Wyoming's Green River but to the common Green River knives used in many a fight. They were called that because they were made at the Green River works and stamped with that designation.

upholsterer. An upholsterer was originally a worker hired by a merchant to "hold up the goods" so that they could be seen by prospective buyers—he was a "holder upper" and was, in fact, first called an *upholder*. Over the years, this same worker came to repair the goods he had held up. By the 17th century he was being called an *upholsterer*, his work consisting of repairing, finishing, or making articles of furniture.

up in the paints. "She is up in the paints as regards age," Damon Runyon wrote in a short story. The expression means "high up." I've been unable to find the origin of this phrase but guess it derives from the slang *paints* for playing cards, *up in the paints* referring to the higher valued cards in the deck.

up one's alley. Very suitable to someone's likes or abilities, as in, "Let me play, this game is right up my alley." Eugene O'Neill must have known the expression was common about 1924, when he put it in quotes in a letter. It is infrequently heard as "down one's alley."

up one's sleeve; laugh up one's sleeve. Fifteenth-century garments had few if any pockets, so men often carried whatever things couldn't be hung from their belts in their full sleeves. It is probably from this source, rather than magicians with rabbits up their sleeves, that we derive our expression for having an alternative plan or something in reserve, although the phrase in its sense of a scheme or trick was most likely influenced by magicians concealing their professional paraphernalia. Another expression deriving from the same source is to laugh up (or in) one's sleeve, "to ridicule a person secretly." A man wearing a garment with capacious sleeves was quite literally able to conceal a laugh by hiding his face in his sleeve.

upper class. *Class* was used as early as the mid-17th century in England for a division of society, *higher* and *lower orders* being previously used. The term *lower class* was employed as early as 1772, while *upper class* is recorded about half a century later in 1826 and *middle class* in 1830. *Upper* and *upper ranks* (1825) are also first recorded in England, while little-used *upper 10* or *upper 10,000* (1844) originated in the U.S., as did the UPPER CRUST (1850) for the upper classes or aristocracy. Often these terms do not indicate wealth but social status, as when Maupassant writes in his story "How He Got The Legion of Honor": "They lived in Paris, like many rich middle-class people."

upper crust. "Kutt the upper crust [of the loaf] for your souerayne [sovereign]," an arbiter of good manners wrote in about 1460. He was referring to the old custom, or proper etiquette, of slicing the choice top crust off a loaf of bread and presenting it to the king or the ranking noble at the table. This practice led to the expression *upper crust*, for "rich or important people," those who ate the upper crust, though this meaning isn't recorded until the mid-19th century. *See also* UPPER CLASS.

uppercut. An uppercut can be both a blow directed upward to an opponent's chin in boxing and a play in bridge of a higher trump than necessary. The boxing term, recorded in 1840, probably came first.

upper hand. *See* GETTING THE UPPER HAND.

Up periscope! Originally used by the English on land to see over hills and bushes, its use recorded as early as 1822, the periscope became forever linked with submarines during World War I. At the time, *up periscope!* became a familiar command, and "feather" became the word for a periscope's wake. The word *periscope* itself is a learned coinage from the Greek *peri*, "near," and *scope*, "an instrument for observing."

upper 10. *See* UPPER CLASS.

upset the apple cart. Just as Shakespeare improved the ancient curse *son of a bitch* by making it *son and heir of a mongrel bitch*, some anonymous English wit in the late 18th century transformed an old Roman phrase into *upset the apple cart*. The Roman expression *Perii, plaustrum perculi* ("I am undone, I have upset my cart") meant the same thing, "to ruin carefully laid plans," and might have been changed by some schoolboy who translated the line from Plautus's *Epidicus*. Why the Romans didn't think of using a specific fruit in the expression to make it more graphic is a mystery. They certainly knew all about apples; in fact, the famous French *api* variety of apple (our "Red Lady") is named after the legendary Roman gourmet Apicius, who is said to have produced it by grafting.

upshot. As far back as the early 16th century, an *upshot* meant the last shot in an archery contest, the shot that often determined the outcome of a match by forcing one archer to drop out and another to raise himself up in the standings. By the end of the century the now obsolete archery term had wider currency and came to mean any result or conclusion. Shakespeare, in fact, was one of the first to use the new word, in *Hamlet:* "So shall you hear . . . of accidental judgements . . . and in this upshot, purposes mistook."

upstage. *Upstage*, in theatrical talk, refers to the back of the stage, while *downstage* refers to the part of the stage nearest the audience. The expression *to upstage*, "to divert attention or praise from," comes from the practice of an actor overshadowing another actor by moving upstage and forcing him to play with his back to the audience. The expression dates back to the early 20th century.

up the creek, etc. *Up the creek* means in a bad predicament, on the spot, behind the eight ball. Sometimes the expression is *up Salt Creek*, or even *up Shit Creek*—often *without a paddle*. The expression goes back about 100 years and was probably first *up Salt Creek*, if we are to judge by the popular 1884 political campaign song "Blaine up Salt Creek." A salt creek is a creek leading through the salt marsh or marshland to the ocean and best explains the phrase, for it is very easy to get stuck in one and, without a paddle, a boatman would have no way to get out. The excremental version conveys the same idea, but makes the situation even worse.

up the river. *See* SENT UP THE RIVER.

up the spout. *Spout* in this sense is a 19th-century slang word for an elevator on which pawnbrokers lifted hocked goods upstairs to be stored. Pawned articles thus went up the spout and were often never seen by the customer again. In time, the expression came to mean something gone forever.

uptick. Though it has more complicated technical meanings on Wall Street, *uptick* has come to mean an upsurge or a pickup, especially when referring to the state of the economy. A 1980s term, it of course has its roots in the Street's stock ticker or ticker tape machine.

up to par.   Someone performing or feeling *up to par* is performing or feeling much like he always does. But *par* is a U.S. golf term, from the Latin *par*, "equal," dating to about 1898 and meaning "the score an expert is expected to make on a hole or course, playing without errors, without flukes, under ordinary weather conditions."

uranium; Uranus.   English astronomer Sir William Herschel first named the planet Uranus Georgium Sidus after England's absurd King George III, this name later changed, more appropriately, to Uranus by German astronomer Johann Bode, so it would be in conformity with other planetary names from classical mythology. *Uranus* is the Latin name of the Greek god of heaven, who was both son and husband of Gaea, goddess of the earth, whose name gives us *geography*, *geology*, and other words relating to the earth. The children of Uranus and Gaea, 12 male and female giants called Titans, have their name honored in *titanic*, "anything of great size or force," and the element *titanium*, discovered in 1795. The element uranium, so important in today's world, is also in the family, named for Uranus in 1789.

urbi et orbi.   *Urbi et orbi* is the traditional solemn blessing given by popes from the balcony of St. Peter on special occasions such as the election of a pope, though in modern times the custom has fallen into disuse. The words mean "To the city [Rome] and to the world."

urchin.   Englishmen have often been poor at spelling French words and stumbled badly over the synonym for "hedgehog" that the Normans brought to England, spelling *hurcheon* a number of ways before finally settling on *urchin*. They called the hedgehog an *urchin* for a time and also applied the name *urchin* to a mischievous child, because the urchin, or hedgehog, was popularly believed to be a mischievous elf in disguise. People eventually stopped using *urchin* as a synonym for "hedgehog," but not for an impish child. Neither was the name *sea urchin* abandoned. This spiny creature was originally named for its resemblance to the urchin, or hedgehog, and once was called the *sea hedgehog*.

Urginea.   Ben Urgin, not a man but an Arabian tribe in Algeria, gives its name to the genus *Urginea*, comprising about 75 species belonging to the lily family and native to the Mediterranean, the East Indies, and South Africa. The bulbs of *U. maritenia*, the only species found in the Mediterranean, are known in medicine as *squills*. Generally gathered for their drug properties, they are used in Sicily for making whiskey. These bulbs often weigh up to four pounds and yield a fluid once considered valuable medically as an expectorant, a diuretic, and for its digitalis-like action on the heart. The first specimen of *Urginea* was found in the territory of the Ben Urgin tribe and named by the German botanist Steinheil.

Uriah Heep.   Uriah Heep, the name of the smooth, deceptive law clerk in Dickens's *David Copperfield* (1849), has become over the years a synonym for any "sanctimonious hypocrite, full of sharp practices."

urinate.   *See* PISS.

Uruguay.   Coming from the native Guaraní language, the name of this South American country means "river that makes the sea."

uscuse-me.   *See* EXCUSE-ME-PEOPLE.

used up; wasted.   *Wasted*, for "killed," is a slang of recent times, dating back to about 1955, at least in the sense of "to completely destroy," *to lay waste to*. Far older is *used up*, also meaning "killed," which originated in 1740 at the battle of Cartagena when General John Guise sent a message to his commander in chief asking him to send more grenadiers, for those he had were all "used up." All of the 1,200 men Guise had sent to attack the castle of St. Lazar had been killed or badly wounded within a couple of hours.

use him as though you loved him.   It's not true that Izaak Walton said of the worm, as bait for fish: "Use him as though you loved him, that is harm him as little as you may possibly, that he may live the longer." He was referring to the frog when he wrote this in his classic *The Compleat Angler, or the Contemplative Man's Recreation* (1653), but his words became misinterpreted over the years, probably because fishermen use worms more than frogs.

Useless Parliament.   A name given to the Parliament convened by Charles I in June 1625, which was dissolved early in August after "having done nothing but offend the king." In the U.S. various Congresses have been given derogatory names; Harry Truman, in an election year, called one Republican-dominated Congress the Do-Nothing Congress.

U.S. Navy.   America had a Colonial Navy until the Revolution, this replaced by the 53-ship Continental Navy in 1776 after the break with Great Britain. Commodore Esek Hopkins was appointed its commander in chief (the only time a navy head has held that title except for presidents). The Continental Navy became the United States Navy in 1794.

Utah.   Utah takes its name from the fierce proud tribe called the Utes that resided there and whose name meant "hill dwellers." In 1850 the area encompassing present-day Utah was constituted the Utah Territory, the colorful Mormon name for it, *Deseret*, or "honeybee," being rejected by Congress.

utopia.   Sir Thomas More's utopia, described in his 1516 book of that name, is probably the most famous of all utopias. More invented the name of his fictional island where everything is perfect, using the Greek for "nowhere" (*ou*, "not," and *topos*, "a place"). His book, translated from English into all the chief European languages, gave us the name for any ideal, visionary place. But "Utopia" is only one of a great many utopias invented by writers over the centuries. Among the first of them was Plato's "Republic," which he described in *The Republic*. Other famous utopias include Tommaso Campanella's City of the Sun; James Harrington's Oceana; Thomas Spencer's Spenconia; Edward Bellamy's Boston (in the year 2000); H. G. Wells's Utopia;

Aldous Huxley's Pala; James Hilton's Shangri-la; B. F. Skinner's Walden II; Ernest Callenbach's Ectopia; Austin Tappan Wright's Islandia; and Samuel R. Delany's Triton.

Utopian Turtletop; Edsel.   The esteemed poet Marianne Moore in 1955 was commissioned by Henry Ford to create a name for a new Ford car. Moore came up with *Utopian Turtletop*, which, of course, Ford didn't use, though he thoughtfully sent the poet a dozen roses. It soon became apparent that Moore was lucky not to have become linked with the car, which as the Edsel (named after Ford's son Edsel) is unfairly remembered due to its supposed defects as the most laughable car in automotive history. See EDSEL.

Uzi.   This widely used, highly reliable submachine gun bears the nickname of its inventor, Israeli arms expert Uziel Gal (1923–2002). An employee of the government-owned Israeli military industries, Gal invented the 9-millimeter, 9-pound weapon but received no royalties on the estimated 1½ million Uzis sold around the world. It is said that he protested when the state agency named the machine gun for him. *See* TOMMYGUN.

V

V. *V*, along with *j*, is one of the two youngest letters in the English alphabet, not coming into the language until after Shakespeare's time, in about 1630. It previously shared its form with *u*. In Roman numerals it represents five.

"V" (for victory sign). In *The Do's and Taboos of Body Language Around the World* (1991) Roger E. Axtell advises that this common gesture could get you into trouble in England, where it means "up yours!" if the palm and fingers face inward. "There may be a connection between the two meanings dating back 500 years," he writes, "when the French used to cut off the middle finger and forefinger of the English archers they captured in battle. After the battles of Agincourt and Crécy, so the story goes, where the French were heavily defeated by the expert English archers, the surviving French were marched off the battlefield to the taunts of the victorious English. The English added further insult to the French by holding up their hands, forefinger and middle finger stiffly upright, palms inward, to show both fingers fully intact."

vade mecum. A vade mecum is generally a manual or handbook someone carries for ready reference, such as a travel guide, but can be anything a person carries for frequent use. The term, first recorded in 1629 as the title of a book of theological essays, is from the Latin *vade mecum* "go with me."

vagina. *Vagina*, for "the female sexual organ," the word first recorded in 1682, comes from the Latin *vagina*, "a sheath, a scabbard." Vanilla, the plant that produces the vanilla bean, derives from the same source, being a scientific Latin reshaping of the Spanish *vainilla* (from the Latin *vagina*), meaning "little sheath," in reference to the bean's pod. *See* VANILLA.

valance. Some authorities believe that the short curtain or drapery called a valance takes its name from the Old French *avalant*, "hanging down." But the word more likely comes from the Old French town of Valence, once famed for its manufacturers, including curtain makers.

valentine. There were at least two St. Valentines, legend tells us, both Christian martyrs who were put to death on the same day, one an Italian priest and physician and the other the bishop of Terni. Butler's *Lives of the Saints* recounts the priest's story, which is almost identical to the bishop's: "Valentine was a holy priest in Rome, who . . . assisted the martyrs in the persecution under Claudius the Goth. He was apprehended and sent by the emperor to the prefect of Rome who, on finding all his promises to make him renounce his faith ineffectual, commanded him to be beaten with clubs, and afterwards to be beheaded, which was executed on February 14, about the year 270." February 14 had been associated with the mating of birds in ancient times, making St. Valentine's Day, which accidentally fell on this date, an excellent choice for a day for lovers, the day also being fairly close to spring, when as Tennyson wrote, "a young man's fancy lightly turns to thoughts of love." It became the custom to draw lots for sweethearts, or *valentines*, for the ensuing year on St. Valentine's Day, this practice probably deriving from a similar Roman custom said to be taken from either the feast of Lupercalia, the feast of Februata, or the day honoring the goddess Juno, all of which fell around St. Valentine's Day. By the end of the 18th century, the exchange of gloves and other gifts that accompanied the drawing of lots became the exchange of letters, which were sometimes secret and often humorous or insulting. These letters evolved into the valentines that we know today.

Valentino. To say silent screen star Rudolph Valentino was a sex symbol is to put it mildly. Italian born Rodolpho Alfonzo Raffaelo Pierre Filibert Guglielmo di Valentina d'Antonguolla came to the United States in 1913, and after working as a gardener, a cabaret dancer-gigolo, and then a bit player in Hollywood, he zoomed to stardom under his stage name in *The Four Horsemen of the Apocalypse* (1921), which was followed by hits like *The Sheik*. Valentino became the embodiment of romance and sex to women all over the world, his name still a synonym for a handsome lover. Yet despite his dark good looks, this star of stars was a timorous lover, a superstitious man who tried to bolster his sexual powers with aphrodisiacs and magic amulets, who always preferred food to women and found his neurotic, clamorous admirers completely undesirable. Valentino died of peritonitis caused by a bleeding ulcer when only 31 years old. Over 50,000 people, overwhelmingly women, attended his funeral in New York in 1926, and even today admirers come to mourn at his crypt in the Los Angeles cemetery where he is buried. Some 250 women have claimed publicly that "The Sheik" fathered their love children, many of whom were born years after Valentino's death. *See* MATINEE IDOL; STAR.

valerian.   The small fragrant white and lavender flowers of valerian (*Valeriana officinalis*) were common in the Roman province of Valeria, for which the plant may have been named (most sources say it was named for the Roman emperor Valerian). At one time a drug called "Valerian" made from its root was used as a nerve sedative and antispasmodic.

Valhalla.   In Norse mythology, the souls of heroes slain in battle spend eternity feasting and rollicking in the celestial hall of Valhalla. *Valhalla* comes from the Old Norse *valholl*, "the hall of the slain," and is sometimes applied to buildings such as Westminster Abbey, where a nation's great men are buried. *See* VALKYRIES.

Valium; Librium.   These brand names have become synonymous with *tranquilizer* since 1960, when Librium was introduced, and the year after, when Valium came on the scene. Neither name, both arbitrary coinages by Roche Laboratories, is Latin, even though they both sound as if they were. *Librium* may have been suggested by *liberating*, and *Valium* could have been inspired by *value*, but there is no proof for any derivation.

Valkyries.   The ancient Norse believed that the 12 nymphs of VALHALLA rode into battle with them and chose those heroes destined to die, escorting them back to their honored place in Valhalla. These nymphs were called the *Valkyries*, taking their name from the Old Norse for "choosers of the slain."

vamoose.   Leave quickly, as in "He vamoosed out of there." From the Spanish *vamos* (let's go).

vamp.   The name of a bookseller in Samuel Foote's play *The Author* (1757) became synonymous with an avaricious publisher, because the character Vamp held that binding was more important than the contents of a book: "Books are like women; to strike they must be well-dressed. Fine feathers make fine birds. A good paper, and elegant type, a handsome motto, and a catching title, have driven many a dull treatise through three editions." *Vamp* was later used as the name of a critic in Thomas Peacock's novel *Melincourt* (1817) and is supposed to be a caricature of the bitter author, editor, and critic William Gifford. Peacock also satirized Gifford, Coleridge (Mr. Mystic), Malthus (Mr. Fox), and Wordsworth (Mr. Paperstamp) in his book. *Vamp* is more commonly used today to mean an unscrupulous woman of seductive charm. Both terms are probably short for VAMPIRE.

vampire.   Vampire is one of the few English words of Hungarian origin. It comes from the Magyar *vampir* and is infrequently spelled that way, although its ultimate source may be the Turkish *uber*, "witch." This word for a creature of the living dead, "a reanimated corpse" that spends its nights searching for human blood to quaff, is first recorded in English in 1734, and is the same in Russian, Polish, Czechoslovakian, Serbian, and Bulgarian. The term vampire was popularized by Bram Stoker's *Dracula* (1897) and some 47 spinoffs on the novel.

vanadium.   The grayish metallic element vanadium, used in many alloys, is named for Freya, the fair Scandinavian goddess of love, one of her other names being Vanadis. *See also* FRIDAY.

Van Allen Belt.   The Van Allen Belt, or Van Allen Radiation Belt is "a zone of high intensity radiation surrounding the earth," beginning at altitudes of about 621.4 miles. It was discovered by James A. Van Allen (b. 1915).

Vancouver.   Vancouver, the largest city and chief port in British Columbia, Vancouver Island, the largest island off the west coast of North America, and the city of Vancouver, Washington, are all named for English navigator and explorer George Vancouver (1757–98). Capt. Vancouver, who sailed with Capt. James Cook on his second and third voyages, explored and surveyed the northwest coast of America aboard *Discovery* in 1792. Puget Sound is named for Vancouver's Lt. Peter Puget, who helped the captain's brother finish his book *A Voyage of Discovery to the North Pacific Ocean and Round the World* (1798).

vandalism.   In the year 455 A.D. the Vandals, all 80,000 of them, were led by their King Genseric into Rome, which they captured easily and sacked thoroughly, loading their ships with plunder and sailing off to new conquests. The savage Teutonic tribe finished off the Roman Empire before falling from power almost a century later, after persecuting Christians and extorting their sacred treasures. The Vandals destroyed many precious cultural objects when they sacked Rome and it is probably from their later behavior that the word *vandalism* derives, meaning as it does wanton destruction of property, especially works of art. It is interesting to note that a French churchman first used the word *vandalisme* in this sense at the end of the 18th century. The name Vandal literally means "the wanderers." Before they sacked Rome the tribes had wandered across the Rhine to France, Spain, and Africa, making conquests all the while.

vandyke.   When only 19, Flemish artist Sir Anthony Van Dyck became Rubens's assistant and pupil. One of 12 children of a wealthy silk merchant, the artist had shown great talent from his early youth and learned much from his Flemish master. Later he went to England where he married a Scotswoman and was knighted by Charles I, becoming one of the most noted portrait and religious painters of his day. Vandyke, as his name was spelled by the English, lived a life of luxury, keeping numerous mistresses, and had to paint prolifically to maintain his lifestyle. He is known to have done at least 350 portraits in England alone and overwork is often cited as the reason for his early death—he died in 1641, 42 years old. Van Dyke turned out masterpieces on a kind of assembly-line basis. He trained assistants to paint a sitter's clothes, used special models for the hands (in the painting of which he excelled), and would never allot more than an hour at a time to a sitting. Van Dyck depicted noblemen attired in wide collars adorned with V-shaped points forming an edging or border, and his subjects often wore sharp V-shaped beards similar to his own. The large points on the *Vandyke capes* or *collars* were called *Vandykes*, the verb *to vandyke* meaning to adorn a collar with such points, and the characteristic beards were and are still known as *vandykes*.

Vanessa. A legendary English literary lover. Esther Vanhomrigh (pronounced "Vanummery") met Jonathan Swift in 1708, fell deeply in love with him, and followed him to Ireland, where she later proposed marriage to him. Dean Swift gently rejected her in his 1713 poem "Cademus and Vanessa." Vanessa was his pet name for Esther (composed of *Van* of her last name plus *Essa* for Esther), and Cademus is an anagram of *Decanus*, Latin for Dean: When in 1723 Swift broke off their relationship, due to her jealousy, she is said to have died of a broken heart. She had preserved his poem among her papers, and it was published three years later.

vanilla. Vanilla was thought to be wickedly aphrodisiac in Elizabethan England because the pod of the plant resembled the vagina. In fact, the word *vanilla* comes from the Spanish for "little vagina." Queen Elizabeth I used vanilla to flavor her marzipan, making it a favorite flavoring for candy ever since, and Thomas Jefferson was the first to introduce it as a flavoring in America. Today, however, natural vanilla is in short supply and we generally use a synthetic; there isn't enough natural vanilla in the world to flavor the vanilla ice cream made in America alone. Needless to say, natural vanilla is much more flavorsome than the synthetic product. *See* AVOCADO; VAGINA.

vanish into thin air. When Shakespeare used this phrase in *The Tempest* to describe ghosts "Melted into air, into thin air," it was already in common use. All air was considered thin at the time, nothing being known about its varying density, and *thin air* was simply employed as an intensive. Other similar phrases of the day were *vanished* (or *melted*) *into smoke, wind* and even into *liquid tears*—all meaning the same, "to disappear."

vaquero. A direct borrowing of the Spanish word for a ranch hand or cowboy that westerners were using as early as 1800. *Buckaroo*, meaning the same, is an English corruption of *vaquero* also used in the West, though in Texas the buckaroo is a roaming bachelor cowboy and in California a buckaroo is a cowboy born or raised on a ranch and living there with his family.

Vardon grip. Harry Vardon (1870–1937), who won the British Open a record six times as well as the U, S, Open, is one of the outstanding golfers of all time. Born on the Channel Island of Jersey, Vardon also won eponymous fame for the *Vardon grip*, the overlapping grip used by most golf players today. The *Vardon trophy*, named in his honor, is awarded to the golfer with the lowest yearly average for the pro tour.

variety is the spice of life. William Cowper's poem "The Task" (1785) is the source of this well-known expression: "Variety is the very spice of life,/ That gives it all its flavors."

varmint. *Varmint* is not an American word, as one would think from scores of westerns. The word for an animal pest or a despicable person is a corruption of *vermin* and of British origin. *Vermin* comes from the Latin *vermis*, "worm."

varnish. *See* COMA BERENICES.

varsity. *Varsity*, for the first-string team of a U.S. college or any school, is simply a shortened form of "university," the *varsity team* initially meaning the university team. In England, where the word is first recorded in 1846, *varsity* (formerly *versity*) means Oxford University or Cambridge University.

Vaseline. Among those flocking to America's first oil strike near Titusville, Pennsylvania in 1858, was Robert A. Chesebrough, a Brooklyn chemist, who noticed that workmen with cuts, bruises, and burns used as a soothing ointment a waxy substance from the pump rods bringing up the oil. Gathering some of the oily residue, Chesebrough took it back to Brooklyn and made a jelly-like product from it. This he patented at once, giving it the trademark *Vaseline*, a word he formed from the German *Wasser* (pronounced "vasser") "water" and the Greek *elaion*, "olive oil."

vaudeville. In its heyday from 1885 to 1928, there were as many as 20,000 acts playing American vaudeville. *Vaudeville* derives from the village of Vire in 15th-century Normandy, where a group of performers was called the Compagnons du Vau de Vire (the Companions of the Vire Valley). Their popularity spread, and soon the word *ville* (town) was substituted for Vire, the name of the original village. *Vaudeville* came to mean "valley town songs" and then the acts that featured them. Much later, in the mid-19th century, Americans borrowed the French word to describe variety shows offering musical and comedy acts on the same bill—also called "olios." Such shows, often coarse at first, initially played in saloons and honky-tonks around the country but did not become tremendously popular until the establishment of the B. F. Keith national circuit in 1883. Vaudeville featured many famous stars of musical comedy and the legitimate theater, including the Barrymores and Sarah Bernhardt, but relied mainly on its own star comics and song-and-dance acts, such as Weber and Fields, Gallagher and Shean, Harry Lauder, Harrigan and Hart, the Marx Brothers, Will Rogers, the Seven Little Foys, Fanny Brice, Al Jolson, Eddie Cantor, and Jimmy Durante, many of whom later left vaudeville for the theater or movies. The most prestigious theater a vaudevillian could play was New York's Palace Theater, built by Martin Beck on Broadway between 46th and 47th Streets in 1913; "playing the Palace" became the dream of every "two-a-dayer." The Palace was converted to a movie theater and later a legitimate theater after vaudeville's demise, which came in the early 1930s with the perfection of radio and sound films. *See* BURLESQUE.

Vauxhall. It is very rare for an English word to be adopted in Russian as anything more than a slang expression. But that is just what happened with the Vauxhall railroad depot in London, which became the Russian *voksal*, their generic word for railroad station. The London depot was named for the Vauxhall district in London, which contained the famous Vauxhall gardens, a popular pleasure resort from 1661 to 1859. The gardens, in turn, took their name from Falkes or Fulkes de Breante, who was lord of a manor called Falkes Hall on the site in the early 13th century. Pepys mentions the public gardens, which soon came to be called Vauxhall, and Thackeray described them later before the gardens were closed and the site built over. From manor to garden to district to depot to Russian word—many stops along the line, but so it is that the communists, who would not consciously pay homage to royalty, honored an early Norman knight.

vaya con Dios. Go with God. A Spanish term commonly heard in the Southwest for over a century now.

VE Day; VJ Day. Both these designations were coined by U.S. director of war mobilization James F. Byrnes in the same 1944 speech. He called the eventual date of Germany's surrender "VE Day," Victory in Europe Day; and designated Japan's eventual surrender as "VJ Day," Victory over Japan Day. VE Day came the next year on May 8, 1945, and VJ Day, the end of World War II, came on September 2, 1945.

veep. From the common abbreviation V.P. for the vice president of the United States came the informal word *veep*, which was coined about 1949. The first person to be called a *veep* was Harry S Truman's vice president Allen William Barkley (1877–1956), who hold office from 1949–53. A variation on it is *vee-pee*.

veg. Like VEGGIES, *veg* (or *vedge*) is a relatively new word; in fact, it probably isn't even 21 yet. It means to loaf, relax, do nothing strenuous, and is apparently an abbreviation of *vegetate:* "Let's order some drinks and veg around the pool for a while." A variation is *veg out.*

vegan. A strict VEGETARIAN who doesn't eat any food of animal origin, including fish, cheese, and eggs. The word wasn't coined until 1944, in Britain, some 105 years after *vegetarian.*

vegetable. Vegetables have usually been highly prized, right from the beginning, too, the word *vegetable* itself deriving from the Latin *vegetabilis*, which meant animating or life-giving. The Greeks venerated vegetables, making small gold and silver replicas of the most prized ones. The Roman Fabii, who took their name from the *faba*, or bean; the Piso clan, who derived theirs from the *pisa*, or pea; the *Lentuli*, who named themselves after the *lente*, or lentil; and the great house of Cicero, which took its name from the *cicer*, or chickpea—these are only a few noble Roman families whose patronyms honored widely hailed vegetables.

vegetable lamb. In medieval times the Far Eastern fern *Dicksonia barometz* was thought to be a hybrid animal and vegetable, mainly because of its woolly rootstalk. The down of the plant is used in India to staunch wounds. It is called the *Tartarian* or *Scythian lamb*, as well as the *vegetable lamb.*

vegetarian. *Vegetarianism* (which is a relatively recent word, used in 1895 by a British health magazine in describing the eating habits of a Chinese sect and modelled after *unitarianism*, etc.) may or may not be the thing for you, though it certainly was for Pythagoras, Aristotle, Epicurus, Diogenes, Cicero, Plato, Socrates, Buddha, Montaigne, Wesley, Pope, Wagner, Swedenborg, Shelley, Tolstoy, Shaw, Gandhi, Mussolini, Hitler, and many other famous, infamous, and obscure people who only ate vegetables.

veggies. This "cute" word for vegetables apparently arose in the early 1960s, for it is first recorded in 1966. Obviously a shortening and rearrangement of *vegetables*, it is used by young and old alike.

veil. *See* YASHMAK.

vein of my heart. *See* CUSHLAMACHREE.

velaric ingressive bilabial stop; kiss. A sound from the southern Bushman language that has been called the rarest speech sound in any language. This sound, written *!xo* and described by the term above is a click articulated with both lips, essentially a kiss.

Velcro. Swiss inventor Georges de Mestral, the inventor of Velcro, is said to have been inspired by the way the burrs of the weed burdock stuck to people's clothing. He invented the trademark fabric "touch and close" fastener in 1957 and named it from French vel*ours*, "velvet," and cro*che*, "hooked." The fastener is actually two nylon strips, one made up of little hooks and the other consisting of small loops. When the two nylon strips are pressed together, the hooks grasp the loops, fastening the strips. The material is used on hundreds of products and made Georges de Mestral a fortune.

vendetta. *Vendetta* is used loosely to describe the sworn vengeance of anyone against another person, but the word, which comes from Latin *vindicta*, "vengeance," and dates back at least two centuries, strictly means vengeance against the murderer of a person in one's family, requiring the murder of that murderer. This blood vengeance and feuds based on it are common in Sicily and Corsica.

vending machine. The term *vending machine* seems to have been introduced either by the Adams' Gum Company (now part of American Chicle) in the 1880s to describe the machine the company used to sell tutti-fruitti gumballs on New York City elevated train platforms, or at about the same time by the Frank H. Fleer Gum Company. At that time Fleer's founder agreed to an experiment proposed by a young vending machine salesman. The salesman argued that vending machines were so great a sales gimmick that people would actually drop a penny in them for nothing. Frank Fleer agreed to buy several machines if the young man's pitch proved true, and the experiment was conducted at New York's Flatiron Building. The salesman set up a vending machine there, with printed instructions to "drop a penny in the slot and listen to the wind blow." He got Fleer's order when hundreds of people contributed their pennies and continued to do so until New York's Finest hauled the machine away.

venerable monosyllable. *The monosyllable* has been used since about 1715 as slang for the "female pudend," as Partridge puts it, or "a woman's commodity," as it is defined in the 1811 edition (called *Lexicon Balatronicum*) of Captain Francis Grose's *Classical Dictionary of the Vulgar Tongue. The Venerable Monosyllable*, dating to about 1785, means the same, Grose defining it here as "the pudendum muliebre." Both terms are practically obsolete except as encountered in literature.

venetian blinds. The slatted window shades called venetian blinds are named after the early Venetian traders who introduced them to Europe, but they were invented by the Persians, from whom the Venetians bought them. They are, in fact, called *persiani* by Italians.

Venezuela. Spanish explorers in the area of this country found the inhabitants living along canals that reminded them of Venice, Italy. They accordingly named the area *Venezuela*, "little Venice."

Vengeance is mine, saith the Lord. This biblical saying, from Rom. 12:19, doesn't bless or condone human vengeance, as is often thought. This is made abundantly clear by the pertinent passage: "Dearly beloved, avenge not yourselves, but rather give place unto wrath: for it is written, Vengeance is mine; I will repay, saith the Lord." Not only does the whole passage advise against human revenge, it goes on to say: "Therefore if thine enemy hunger, feed him; if he thirst, give him drink: for in so doing thou shalt heap coals of fire on his head. Be not overcome of evil, but overcome evil with good."

venial sin. A venial sin, in the Catholic church, is one that doesn't forfeit grace, a sin that may be pardoned, hence its name from the Latin *venia*, "grace, pardon." Its opposite, a mortal sin, is a sin that deserves everlasting punishment, a deadly sin, hence its name from the Latin *mort*, "death."

Venice glass. Long considered to be perfection among glassware, Venice glass has been known since the Middle Ages, when it was frequently used for drinking glasses—because poisonings were common at the time and it was widely believed the Venice glass was so sensitive that it would break into slivers if poison touched it.

venison. *Venison* comes from the Latin *venatio*, "hunting," and was formerly applied to the flesh of any animal killed in the hunt and used as food. The word is first recorded in the early 14th century and gradually came to mean only the meat of deer. The venison mentioned in Genesis is wild goat.

veni, vidi, vici. The laconic words of Julius Caesar when he told his friend Amintius of his victory over Pompey's ally Pharnaces at Zela in 47 B.C., the phrase is Latin for "I came, I saw, I conquered." So Plutarch says, but Suetonius doesn't ascribe the words to Caesar, noting only that they were displayed before his title after his victories at Pontus.

venom. Though it means "poison," *venom* began life as the love potion, *venenum*, that the Roman goddess Venus used to infect human hearts. The Latin *venenum* eventually became the basis of words meaning poison in several languages, our English *venom* being first recorded in 1220 as *venim*.

vent one's spleen. When a person vents his or her spleen, he is feeling low or acting spitefully. The expression is first recorded in 1641 and derives from the ancient belief that the human gland called the spleen caused low spirits or melancholy.

Venus de Milo, etc. The Venus de Milo, now in the Louvre and possibly the finest example of ancient art extant, dates from about 400 B.C., but was discovered in 1820 on the Greek island of Milo, or Milos. Other famous statues of the goddess of love are the Venus de' Medici, so called because it was once kept in Rome's Medici Palace; the Venus Genetrix, a symbol of fecundity, its last name meaning "she that produces"; and the lost nude Venus of Cnidus, purchased from Praxiteles by the Cnidians, an ancient copy of which is in the Vatican. The Venus Callipyge is a late Greek statue standing in the Museo Nazionale at Naples. There is no good reason for connecting this statue with Venus and its last name translates as "beautiful buttocks," to use a euphemism.

Venus mercenaria. Like many seafoods, clams are often regarded as a potent aphrodisiac, especially the common hard-shell clam *Venus mercenaria*. This quahog gets its last name from the Indian wampum beads used in commerce. It probably boasts its suggestive first name because Venus has often been depicted standing in a large seashell. A good example is Sandro Botticelli's famed *The Birth of Venus*, sometimes jocularly called "Venus on the Half Shell."

Venus's-flytrap. This odd plant is said to have been discovered by the governor of North Carolina, Arthur Dobbs, in 1760 and named Fly Trap Sensitive. One of the few plants that wreak revenge on insects, the Venus's-flytrap was officially named *Dionaea muscipula* by English naturalist John Ellis in 1770. This translates as "Aphrodite's mousetrap," indicating sensual love. However, shortly afterward Ellis also coined the common name *Venus's-flytrap* for the plant, this being very similar, as Venus is simply the Roman version of Aphrodite or Dionaea. *Mousetrap* or *flytrap* is understandable, but why was the vegetable animal-eater named after Venus or Aphrodite when it is not particularly beautiful? Though neither etymological nor entymological reference books make any mention of it, John Ellis clearly referred to the similarity of the plant's leaves to the human vagina when he named it for the goddess of love. The *Venus's-flytrap*, a perennial native only to North and South Carolina, is widely grown indoors by gardeners.

Venus's looking-glass, etc. Their strikingly beautiful purple flowers are responsible for all species of the blue-bell family (*Specularia*), especially the bellflower, or *Campanula*, being named for Venus, the Roman goddess of beauty. Other plants named after Venus include Venus basin bath, the wild teasel; Venus's-comb, the shepherd's needle; Venus's-golden apple (*Atlantia monphylla*); Venushair, the maidenhair; Venus's-lover; Venus-navel; Venus's-pear; Venus's pride, blue houstonia; and Venus's-slipper, the lady slipper.

verbicide. *Verbicide*, "word murder," the act of destroying the sense or value of words, or the perversion of a word from its proper meaning, has been applied in our time to political speechmaking and government gobbledygook or officialese. But the word seems to have been coined by Oliver Wendell Holmes, who patterned it on *homicide*, and applied it to punning in his *The Autocrat of the Breakfast-Table* (1858).

verb. sap. *See* A WORD TO THE WISE.

verdigris. This greenish or blueish patina, formed on copper and other surfaces when they are exposed to the atmosphere for long periods, takes its name from Old French *vert de grece*, "green of Greece." The reason for the name is not known, nor is the reason why people later called the patina the "Spanish green." The word *verdigris* can be traced to the 14th century in Europe.

Verdi! Verdi!   The Austrians occupying northern Italy in the 19th century couldn't understand why the chant *Verdi! Verdi!* at the end of operas written by Italian composer Giuseppe Verdi frequently inspired anti-Austrian riots. They finally learned that *Verdi* was also an acronym for the name of the man Garibaldi was advocating as head of a united Italy: *Vittorio Emanuele, Re d'Italia* ("Victor Emmanuel, King of Italy"). After the Austrians were expelled in 1857 Victor Emmanuel was crowned king.

verme.   The *verme* is a legendary fish of the Ganges, which was said to be able to reach up out of the Indian river, seize *elephants* in its jaws and destroy them. The fish was named for the Latin *vermes*, "worm," perhaps by error, perhaps because the fish was thought to be eellike. The word is first recorded in 1572.

vermicelli.   Few diners would want to dwell on the etymology of this word for a very thin pasta. For *vermicelli* means "little worms" in Italian, deriving from the Latin *vermis*, "worm, maggot, or crawling insect."

vermilion.   Why does this bright red take its name from the Latin *vermis*, for "worm, maggot, or crawling insect"? It seems that in days past *vermilion* dye was made from scarlet body fluid of cochineal insects.

vermin.   *See* VARMINT.

Vermont.   *Vermont* had been called New Connecticut before being named from the French *vert*, "green," plus *mont*, "mountain." The Green Mountain State was admitted to the Union in 1791 as our 14th state.

Vermont charity.   According to Hugh Rawlins in *Wicked Words* (1989), this is "a symbol of cheapness . . . what hoboes call sympathy which is accompanied by nothing else." The same source gives *Vermont kindling* as "rolled-up newspapers used in place of wood."

Vermont psalm.   Psalm 121 from the Bible, a psalm often used to start funeral services in Vermont: "I lift my eyes unto the hills." This was noted in a *New York Times* news story on May 2, 1994, from Woodstock, Vermont: "Psalm 121 . . . They call it the Vermont Psalm here."

vernacular.   The vernacular is the everyday or native language of a country, as opposed to the formal language of its learned people. The Latin *vernaculus*, "native" or "domestic," is the basis for the word, this in turn deriving from the Latin *verna*, "a native slave, a slave born in a country."

vernier; vernier caliper, etc.   A vernier is any small, auxiliary movable scale attached to another graduated instrument. It is often attached to the transit, sextant, quadrant, and barometer for very accurate measurements. French mathematician Pierre Vernier (1580–1637) invented the scale, describing it in a treatise he wrote in 1631. Vernier was commandant of the castle in his native town of Ornans in Burgundy and later served the king of Spain as a counselor. His invention estimates the nearest 10th of the smallest division on the scale it is attached to. It was originally an improvement on a scale called the nonius, invented by the Portuguese scientist Nunez, and proved to be a milestone in the techniques of precise measurement. The vernier caliper, the vernier compass, both incorporating verniers, and the vernier engine, a small rocket engine that corrects the heading and velocity of a long-range missile, also bear the French inventor's name.

vernis Martin.   *See* COMA BERENICES.

veronica.   The classic Spanish bullfighting cape movement called the *veronica* takes its name from St. Veronica, who in ancient legend was the woman who wiped the face of Christ as He carried the cross, her handkerchief retaining an imprint of Christ's face. The cape movement is swung so slowly and near to the face of the bull that it suggested St. Veronica using her handkerchief.

vers de société.   The French expression translates literally as "society verse," which is a type of light, often satirical verse dealing with contemporary fashions and foibles. Many poets have written such verse, including the English Alexander Pope, W. S. Gilbert, and Hilaire Belloc, and the Americans Ogden Nash, Phyllis McGinley, and Richard Armour.

verse.   Poems are of course almost always written in straight lines across a page, each line turning at the end into a new line. This suggested the synonym for "poem," *verse*, which comes from the Latin *versus*, a form of the Latin *vertere*, "to turn." *Verse* is recorded in English as far back as 1200 and today often means light pieces of poetry.

vertically challenged.   Among the latest of politically correct terms, *vertically challenged* describes a person who is short. Used mainly in a humorous sense.

very.   *Very*, which ultimately derives from the stem of the Latin *verus*, "true," is not one of the 10 most frequently used English words (these are *I, the, and, to, of, in, we, for, you,* and *a,* in that order). But *very,* first recorded 10 centuries ago, bears the distinction of being the only foreign (not Anglo-Saxon) word, as well as the only word of more than one syllable, to have any rank at all in the "highest-frequency" category of words used, ranking within the top-50 according to one expert.

very close veins.   Heard in the southern U.S. for *varicose veins,* this folk etymology has some sense to it. Not only does *varicose veins* sound like *very close veins,* the location of these blood vessels is just under the skin!

Very light: Very pistol.   American naval officer Edward Wilson Very (1847–1910) was an admiral by the time he retired in 1885. The rank came mainly as a reward for his invention of the Very light, the important illuminating flare signal that was fired from the Very pistol, which he also invented.

vespasienne. Roman emperor Vespasian (A.D. 9–79) taxed his people inordinately to build public urinals, improving the *pissoirs* even more by selling the urine collected in them to launderers, who used it for bleaching clothing. His obsession with public urinals led the witty French to name them *vespasiennes* after him. *See* CRAPPER; FONTAGE; FURPHY; MONEY DOESN'T STINK; OLIVER; SACHEVERELL; TWISS.

Veteran's Day. *See* REMEMBRANCE SUNDAY.

veterinarian. This word, for "an animal doctor," derives from the Latin *veterinarius*, "belonging or pertaining to beasts of burden," which in turn comes from *veterina animalia*, "beasts of burden"—showing that the veterinarians originally cared exclusively for farm animals. Several rare names for a veterinary used through history are *emplastrist* (for the plasters they used), *unguentarian* (for their ointments), and *hippologist* (though this strictly means anyone well versed in the study of horses). Other names that are rarely if ever used anymore are horse doctor and horse leech. In the 17th century *veterinarian* was also the name for a man who rented out horses or mules, like Hobson of HOBSON'S CHOICE. Vet, a synonym for *veterinarian* today, has in recent years become a verb meaning to treat or cure as a veterinary does, as, for example, an editor who vets a manuscript.

veto. *Veto*, for "a head of state's power to annul a law passed by a lower body," is the Latin for "I forbid," and was the word used by the Roman tribunes to oppose measures of the Roman Senate. *Pocket veto* is a U.S. term, meaning the veto of a bill by the President or a state's governor in the closing days of a legislative session by retaining it unsigned, by "pocketing" it; it was first employed by Andrew Jackson. France's Louis XVI and Marie Antoinette were called Monsieur and Madame Veto because they vetoed so many decrees of the Constituent Assembly in 1791.

V for victory sign. The V sign made by two fingers, palm outward, seems to have first been used during the early years of World War II. The British prime minister used it often, making it famous, but he did not invent it, that rare genius as of yet unknown. When the V sign is made palm inward by a Briton it means "fuck you." Said Winston Churchill in 1941: "The V sign is the symbol of the unconquerable will of the occupied territories, and portent of the fate awaiting the Nazi tyranny."

Via Dolorosa. The Via Dolorosa, "the Dolorous, or Anguished Way, the Way of the Cross," is the mile-long road in Jerusalem over which Christ carried the cross to Golgotha. It has also come to mean any painful path.

Viagra. The trademarked name of a Pfizer Company drug used primarily to treat male impotence by stimulating blood flow to the penis but said to be effective on women as well. Introduced in 1998, it soon became famous worldwide, resulting in a rash of jokes by late-night talk show hosts and the happiness of millions.

vials of wrath. In Revelation 15:7 seven angels pour upon the earth "seven golden vials full of the wrath of God." This later became the expression *vials of wrath* for stored-up anger, vengeance, or the execution of wrath upon the wicked.

Vicar of Bray. A *Vicar of Bray* is someone who holds onto his office or position no matter who is in power and will go to any length to do so. The term refers to a semi-legendary Vicar of Bray, Berkshire, in England who became twice a Roman Catholic and twice a Protestant under four different monarchs between 1520 and 1560, in the words of one contemporary writer "being resolved, whoever was king, to die Vicar of Bray."

Vicar of Hell. Henry VIII playfully gave this title to his "poet laureate," John Skelton, the term being a pun on Skelton being the rector of Diss in Norfolk. *Dis* is a Roman name for Pluto, the mythological ruler of the infernal regions.

vichyssoise. The soup has a French name but was created by a chef at New York's Ritz-Carlton hotel in 1917. *Vichyssoise* means "cream soup" in French. It is specifically a cream soup of potatoes and leeks, usually served cold and garnished with chives.

Vichy water. Originally *Vichy* was natural mineral water from springs at Vichy in central France. The term came into use in about 1855 but lost its capital over the years when the name was applied to other natural and artificial mineral waters. Such waters are mostly called *vichy water* or *mineral water* today. The city of Vichy was also the capital of unoccupied France during World War II and all of unoccupied France was frequently called *Vichy*.

Victorian. Myriad things have been named after Britain's Queen Victoria, who reigned an amazing 63 years, from 1837–1901. A plum, a cloth, a large water lily, and a pigeon all bear the name *victoria*, as does the low carriage for two with a folding top and an elevated driver's seat that was designed in France and named in her honor. Victoria is also the capital of both British Columbia and Hong Kong and a state in Australia; there is a Lake Victoria in East Africa; the Great Victoria Desert in Australia; a Mount Victoria in New Guinea; a Victoria Falls between Zambia and Zimbabwe; a Victoria Island in the Arctic Ocean; and Victoria Land, a region in Antarctica. Then we have Victoria Day, a Canadian national holiday in late May; the Victorian box, a tree; the victorine, a ladies' fur tippet; and the Victoria Cross, a military decoration first awarded "for valor" by Victoria in 1856. And that isn't nearly a complete list. *Victorian* means of, or pertaining to, the queen or the period of her reign and adds a score of terms, such as Victorian sideboard, to the total. *Victorian* alone often refers to the smugness and prudery characteristic of the period, especially concerning sex.

victory garden. The victory garden was a home vegetable garden popular in the United States during World War II; such gardens were encouraged by the government to increase food production during a time of shortages. The idea helped revive the idea of home vegetable gardens, once known as kitchen gardens, among many Americans who had lost touch with the land.

video. *Video*, the Latin for "I see," has been used as a term for television or TV since the 1950s. In addition to serving as shorthand for *videocassette*, another recent coinage, dating to the early 1960s, is the videophone, or picturephone, a telephone with a small TV screen on which callers can see each other. The system has so far proved too expensive to put into general use, but promises to be commonplace in the future.

vie. In the 16th century, *envy* meant to challenge someone to a gambling contest. The word's contraction, *vie*, became popular in gambling houses, meaning to back up one's hand with a bet. One *vied* at cards in this way, that is, "contended or strived against others," and the term later came to mean contending or striving in any sense.

Vietcong; Charlie. This name of the Communist guerrillas in Vietnam was first recorded when the French were fighting there in 1957 but probably dates back to the early 1950s. *Vietcong* translates roughly as "Vietnamese Communist." U.S. forces called them "Charlie" or "Mr. Charlie" (among other appellations), a name they gave to North Vietnamese soldiers as well. *Charlie* may derive from *Victor Charlie*, the radio code for *VC* (Vietcong). Or it may come from the World War II derogatory military slang *Charlie* for a Japanese soldier, whose origins are unknown, though the movie detective Charlie Chan has been nominated as the source. *See* R.O.K.

vigorish. Many people have paid usurious rates of interest to loan sharks. The margin of profit in such transactions, 20 percent or more a week, late payment penalties, and other fees, is called vigorish, which also means the percentage set by a bookmaker in his own favor. *Vigorish* is one of the few English words with Russian roots, deriving from the Russian *vyigrysh*, "gambling gains or profit," which first passed into Yiddish early in 20th-century America as *vigorish* and was reinforced by its similarity to *vigor*.

Viking. These Scandinavian pirates and explorers may derive their name from the Old English *vicing*, "pirate," although this etymology is disputed and some experts hold that Viking comes from the Old English *wic*, "camp," because these Scandinavians set up temporary camps while carrying out raiding expeditions. Today *viking*, with a small *v*, can mean any sea-roving pirate or bandit.

villain. *Villain* derives from the Latin *villanus*, "a serf," and the first *villains*, the word recorded early in the 14th century, were serfs in feudal England. From its meaning of a poor lowborn rustic, *villain* within half a century came to mean a base person disposed to criminal acts. The word was first applied to a play's antagonist by Charles Lamb in 1822.

vim. *Vim* is an Americanism first recorded in 1843 and usually regarded as the accusative singular of the Latin *vis*, "strength or energy," though it may possibly be, judging by some of its earliest uses, of imitative or interjectional origin ("He drove his spurs . . . *vim* in the hoss's flank," 1850). The word is usually heard in the alliterative expression *vim and vigor*.

Vincent's infection. *See* BRIGHT'S DISEASE.

a vintage year. *A vintage year* is a year notable for anything. The phrase originated with and still mainly refers to the year in which a good *vintage*, "gathering," of grapes was made into an excellent wine. *Vin ordinaire* is a cheap wine that can be good but is rarely excellent, while *vin de goutte* is an inferior wine made from the last pressing of the grapes.

violet. The word *violet* derives from the classical Latin name for this flower, *viola*. There are blue, white, reddish-purple, lilac, yellow, and gold violets. In 1324, a golden violet was offered as a prize for the best poem written in the Provençal language:

> And in that golden vase was set
> The Prize—the golden violet.

See also CORPORAL VIOLET.

VIP. This commonly used acronym for a *very* *i*mportant *p*erson only dates back to World War II, when it was coined in England by a British officer in charge of arranging flights for important military leaders. He used the acronym in order to conceal the identity of these very important people from spies.

virago. *Virago* meant a "man-like or heroic woman, a female warrior" when first attested to in about 1000, deriving from the Latin *virago*, meaning the same. Such a woman was likely to be bold and strong-willed, which led to the derogatory use of *virago* for "a bold impudent woman, a shrew, a termagant, a scold," this later use first recorded by Chaucer in 1386.

Virgilian. Virgil (70–19 B.C.), called the Mantuan Swan because he was born near Mantua, Italy, is considered the greatest poet of ancient Rome and in medieval times was regarded as the wisest of poets, a magician and enchanter. His name lives on, however, mainly as a synonym for the simple, pastoral beauty described in his poetry, which is Virgilian, or has a Virgilian charm. *See* SWAN.

Virgil's fly; Virgil's gnat. According to an old legend the Roman poet Virgil's (70–19 B.C.) "pet housefly" was given a funeral that cost over $100,000. Musicians, mourners, and eulogists were hired and Virgil's mansion was declared the fly's mausoleum. Later it was discovered that Virgil buried the fly so that he could prevent the state from confiscating his estate and distributing it to war veterans as payment for service—all family cemetery plots and mausoleums being exempt from such confiscations. History confirms that Virgil's property was confiscated and that he got it back, but tells us nothing about his pet housefly. Many medieval legends arose about Virgil, and though this story may be partly true, it probably is an exaggerated version of Virgil's real troubles with his property, plus a tale that he allegedly wrote called the "Culex." Spencer wrote a poem called "Virgil's Gnat," based on the "Culex," in which a sleeping shepherd is stung by a gnat, which has bitten him only to warn him that he is about to be attacked by a serpent. The shepherd kills that gnat and then slays the serpent, but the next night the gnat reproaches him for his cruelty and the remorseful shepherd builds a monument honoring the gnat.

Virginia. That gallant of gallants, Sir Walter Raleigh, suggested that what became Virginia be named after England's Elizabeth I, the Virgin Queen, when in 1584 he founded his colony there, probably on what is now Roanoke Island. (The island, which is in North Carolina, was originally part of the great area from Florida to Newfoundland that Virginia encompassed.) Virginia, the Old Dominion state, was the site of the first permanent English settlement, at Jamestown in 1607, and the scene of the British surrender in the American Revolution at Yorktown. Called the Mother of Presidents, the state sent Washington, Jefferson, Monroe, Madison, Tyler, William Henry Harrison, Taylor, and Wilson to the White House, and is renowned for many historic shrines. As to the state's exact naming, one writer tells us that "Queen Elizabeth graciously accorded the privileges proposed by Raleigh, giving to this new land a name in honour of her maiden state, and it was called Virginia. Raleigh was knighted for his service and given the title of 'Lord and Governor of Virginia.' "

Virgin Queen. *See* ELIZABETHAN AGE.

visa. A visa is an endorsement of a person's passport by an agent of another country testifying that his passport has been examined and he is permitted entry into that country. *Visa* is short for the Latin *carta visa*, "the document [has been] examined." It was originally a French term that came into English early in the 19th century.

visiting fireman. A distinguished visitor from out-of-town. Here *fireman* is not related to a firefighter but to a Native American dignitary responsible for lighting his tribe's fires.

vitamin. American biochemist Casimir Funk coined the word *vitamin* (or, rather, *vitamine*) in 1912, at which time he was credited with the discovery of the existence of vitamins, organic substances necessary for normal health. Funk constructed the word from the Latin *vita*, "life," and *amine*, from the Greek *ammoniakon*, because he believed that an amino acid was present in vitamins. *Vitamine* was stripped of its *e* when it was found that amino acids were not involved.

vitex. A family of ornamental shrubs and trees often planted to attract bees, vitex is named from the Latin *vieo*, "to bind with twigs," in reference to the flexible nature of its twigs. One vitex, *Agnus castus*, is called the chaste tree because the Romans considered it an anaphrodisiac that calmed the body, and Athenian maidens who wished to remain chaste often strewed their couches with its leaves.

vittles. Victuals, food. This back-country southern word is actually a very old, proper English one, and *victuals* is a pedantic misspelling of it.

vixen. Why should a female fox be a *vixen?* The word arose as a corruption in southern English dialects, with their predilection for *v*, of the Old English *fyxen*, "female fox." First recorded in the early 15th century, it took almost 200 years before the word was applied to an ill-tempered woman or shrew, Shakespeare using it thus in *A Midsummer Night's Dream*.

viz. *Viz*, meaning "namely," represents the Latin word *videlicit*. It needs no period after it. The abbreviation was being used by writers as early as 1540.

vocabulary. *Vocabulary* comes from the Latin *vocabularius*, meaning the same, and is first recorded in the early 16th century. As for the English vocabulary, there are well over a million scientific names for animals, a million for insects, well over 7.4 million for chemical compounds alone; more than 350,000 names are registered as trademarks in the U.S. Patent Office; and one general dictionary lists over 650,000 entries. That alone totals over 10 million English words and with scientific words from many other disciplines, jargons of professions and trades, and slang expressions from England and America, the total must come to at least between 15 and 20 million. But of the millions of English words the average person uses only about 2,800 in everyday conversation, the most extensive individual vocabulary being about 60,000 words. Here are some other word counts:

> *Webster's Second International Dictionary*—650,000 words
> *Oxford English Dictionary*—450,000
> Shakespeare's Complete Works—19,000–25,000
> *New York Times* (Sunday edition)—ca. 25,000
> Chaucer's Works—8,000
> Milton's Works—8,000
> King James Version of the Bible—6,000

vodka. This alcoholic drink, made from rye, barley, and even potatoes, among other fruits and vegetables, takes its name from the Russian *voda*, meaning "water." The unaged, colorless drink does look something like water, but is so named because such spirits were once thought to be as essential to life as water—*whiskey* and the Scandinavian *aquavit* also derive from words meaning "water." *Vodka* is first recorded in English in 1801, though the drink is of course many centuries older. *See* MARTINI; SCOTCH; WHISKEY.

voice mail. *Voice mail*, first recorded in 1980, was coined by American inventor and entrepreneur Gordon Matthews (1937–2002). According to his *New York Times* obituary (2/26/02), Matthews was inspired to invent the system when "he was stuck in heavy rain and noticed in a nearby dump a large bunch of pink 'While You Were Out' message slips. This gave him the idea that an apparatus permitting callers to record substantial messages in their own voices could help do away with the multitudes of message slips . . . that were burdening modern communications, notably in corporations." Today, over 8 percent of American corporations use voice mail.

volcano. The Roman god of fire and blacksmiths Vulcan was believed to live and work at his forge inside Mount Etna, which was said to belch his fire and flame periodically. Over the ages all mountains that erupted like Etna came to be called volcanoes after Vulcan. Vulcan is also honored in the *vulcanization* process for making rubber more useful, invented by American Charles Goodyear in 1839. In 1845 the astronomer Leverrier gave the name Vulcan to a planet he believed was even closer to the sun than Mercury. Astronomers, however, never located the new planet, and in 1915 Albert Einstein proved that it did not exist.

Volkswagen.   Hitler himself drove (or had himself driven) in a Mercedes, but he ordered this little car, costing about $250, built for the little man. The first Volkswagen, "people's car" in German, with its air-cooled rear engine, was made in 1936. The VW has become one of the best-selling cars around the world, but some people refuse to buy it because of its history.

volleyball.   When William Morgan, the YMCA director in Holyoke, Massachusetts, invented the game we call volleyball in 1895, for some unknown reason he called the new sport *mintonette*, Morgan, a Springfield College student himself, encouraged young people to play the sport and, as the volleying of the ball seemed the most exciting part of the game, its name was changed to volleyball. But a far better story anyway is playwright Arthur Kopit's apocryphal origin of the game, noted in Willard Espy's *Thou Improper, Thou Uncommon Noun* (1978): ". . . every evening in King Louis XV's prison compound a court official named Jacques de Vollet supervised eight nude chambermaids as they, four to a side, batted a loaf of sour bread hither and thither across a line draped with their underclothing. The bouncy play of the young ladies greatly agitated the manacled prisoners looking on. When the bread had been beaten into morsels too small to bat, the chambermaids tossed the remnants to the inmates for supper. Hence, logically, *volleyball*."

Volstead Act.   Minnesota congressman Andrew Joseph Volstead drafted and introduced the *Volstead Act* (1919), which provided for the enforcement of the 18th Amendment to the U.S. Constitution forbidding the manufacture, sale, and import or export of liquor. In spite of the strict law, enforcement proved impossible and there followed a period of unparalleled drinking and lawbreaking that some commentators claim marked the beginning of a moral breakdown in society. In 1933 the 21st Amendment, repealing Prohibition, was ratified. Under the Volstead Act an intoxicating beverage was defined as one that contains more than .5 percent of alcohol by volume.

volt; voltaic pile.   Count Alessandro Giuseppe Antonio Anastasio Volta invented Volta's pile or the voltaic pile in 1800, this the first electric battery or device for producing a continuous electric current. Volta, the son of an Italian Jesuit priest who left the order to marry, was something of a prodigy as a child. His voltaic pile consisted of zinc and silver plates stacked alternately with moist pads and touched with a conductor to produce an electric force. He also invented an electric condenser and devised the electrochemical series. Before his death in 1827, aged 82, the scientist had reaped honors in almost every country in Europe, had statues erected to him and kings contending for his presence. Napoleon, who once visited his classroom to praise him, made Volta a member of France's National Institute and a count and senator from the Kingdom of Lombardy in 1801. It is said that Bonaparte so admired the great pioneer that he once crossed out the last three letters from the phrase "*Au grand Voltaire*" inscribed on a wall of the National Institute library. Today the unit of electrical force called the *volt* sings electrically of his fame.

volume.   Early books consisted of parchment rolled on sticks, just as religious books sometimes are today. Thus the Latin *volumen*, "a coil or roll," from the Latin, *volvere*, "to roll," became the French and English *volume*, for "a book."

voluminous.   Sufficient to fill a large volume (book) or many volumes. First recorded in 1611, *voluminous* derives directly from the English word VOLUME. That the word sometimes has a derogatory connotation is witnessed by a story about the British historian Edward Gibbon. Gibbon noted that author and politician Richard Brinsley Sheridan had complimented him. "Sheridan said," he exulted, "that if you search the history of the world . . . read all the past histories, peruse the annals of Tacitus, read the *luminous pages of Gibbon* . . ." Gibbon, however, was not so happy when he heard Sheridan's reply to his exultations. "I did not say *luminous*," he told a fellow parlimentarian, "I said *vol*uminous."

volunteer plant.   A volunteer plant is any plant that grows without being seeded, planted, or cultivated by a person; it is one that springs up spontaneously. The expression goes back at least to the turn of the century. Among mountain folk it is also a euphemism for an illegitimate child.

Volunteer State.   A nickname for Tennessee since the Mexican War in 1847, when 30,000 men from the state enlisted. It has also been called the Lion's Den (possibly after border ruffians nicknamed lions), the Hog and Hominy State, from the Tennesseans' reputed liking for fatback and cornmeal (grits), and the Big Bend State, after the big bends in the Tennessee River. At the time of the Scopes "Monkey Trial" there in 1925 Tennessee was called the Monkey State.

V-1, V-2.   Toward the end of World War II the Nazis as a desperation measure unleashed their newly developed *Vergeltungswaffe* ("reprisal weapon") against Britain. Between June 1944 and March 1945 the pilotless jet rocket with explosive warhead killed more than 5,500 people, mostly London civilians. The V-2 was an improved version that became the basis for postwar rocket design. Both were also called "buzz bomb" (for their buzzing noise on approach), "robot bomb," "doodlebug," and "flying bomb."

voodoo.   The *Waldensians*, followers of Peter Waldo or Valdo (d. 1217), were accused of sorcery and given the name *Vaudois* by the French. French missionaries later remembered these "heretics" when they encountered the witch doctors who preached black magic in the West Indies. They called the native witch doctors Vaudois and the name was soon applied to any witchcraft similar to the magic spells they cast, *Vaudois* eventually being corrupted to *voodoo*. This is the view of Ernest Weekly and some other respected etymologists on the origin of *voodoo;* however, the *Oxford English Dictionary* and a majority of authorities believe the word derives from the African *vodun*, a form of the Ashanti *obosum*, "a guardian spirit or fetish." Today the West African religion is practiced in its best-integrated form in the villages of Haiti, voodoo having been brought to the New World by slaves as early as the 1600s.

Vote for Boyle, a son of the soil.   Hal Boyle, a columnist for the Associated Press, drove into Tunis soon after it fell to the Allies in World War II shouting: "Vote for Boyle, a son of the soil: Honest Hal, the Arab's Pal." Arabs picked up the former part of the phrase, without having any idea what it meant, and kept repeating it as a greeting to puzzled new troops from 1943 through 1944.

à votre santé! *À votre santé* is the most familiar, and one of the oldest, of French drinking toasts. Dating back to the 18th century or earlier, it means simply "To your health!"

vowel. Our word *vowel* comes ultimately from the Latin *vocalis* and is first recorded in the late 13th century. The most common vowel sound in English is the upside down *e* (ə) of the International Phonetic Alphabet, the unaccented syllable that is found in so many English words—as in the first syllable of *attend, observer,* and *alleviate;* in the last syllable of words like *custom* and *sofa;* and in most pronunciations of the indefinite article, such as *a man.* Alistair Cooke makes this point in discussing the lack of phonetic training in England and America, venturing that 99 scholars in 100 wouldn't know it. Few would know, either, that *w* and *y* are also letters that can represent vowel sounds, of which there are as many as 23 in English. Fewer still would know that the English word with the most consecutive vowel sounds is *queueing,* lining up, which has five. The word with the most consonants in a row? Maybe the six in *latchstring.* In order of use, the seven most frequent vowel sounds are ə, a, ai, o, u, w, and y. When a certain Dr. Vowel died in the early 19th century, a certain Dr. Barton Warren commented to a friend: "Thank Heaven it was neither *you* nor *I!*"

voyageur. An expert boatsman, woodsman, and guide, often French-Canadian, who transported people or goods in the early Northwest. The word is a borrowing from the French.

Vulcan; vulcanization. *See* VOLCANO.

vum. An old-fashioned word that means vow, or swear, as in the expression of surprise, "Well, I vum!" The old term derives from the verb *vum,* dating back to the 18th century.

W

W. *W* takes its name from "double *U*." The 23rd letter of the alphabet is simply two *V*'s (*VV*) joined together. *V* in centuries past was the symbol of both *V* and *U*, being pronounced as a *U* whenever it represented that letter.

W. Several presidents have been called by their initials, including F.D.R. (Franklin Delano Roosvelt) and J.F.K. (John Fitzgerald Kennedy), but only one has been called by *one* initial: President George W. Bush (the *W* stands for Walker), who was dubbed W (pronounced Dubya) by the press.

Waa hoo! A cowboy yell that the prolific western writer Zane Grey (1872–1939) explained in *The Last of the Plainsmen:* "We'll use a signal I have tried and found far-reaching and easy to yell. Waa hoo!"

wabenzi people. Rich people, that is, people who own Mercedes-Benz cars. The term is a combination of Swahili and English used in West Africa.

waffle. The waffle takes its name from the Dutch *wafel* for the crisp batter cake baked in a waffle iron. But folklore holds that it was created by a knight who had returned to England from the Crusades in 1204. Sir Giles, it is said, came into the kitchen where his wife was baking cakes and accidentally sat on one while wearing his full suit of chain armor. He smashed the cake flat as a pancake but with rows of little indentations—the imprint of his armor. These proved excellent for holding butter and syrup and the waffle was born. According to this tongue-in-cheek story, the delectable dish was called the waffle "because waffle is a word that is easy to pronounce when one's mouth is full!"

wag. *Waghalters* were mischievous young men, merry rogues, who were so called in medieval times because it was facetiously said that all such jokers would wind up wagging in a halter on the gallows instead of wagging their tongues. The word was shortened to *wagge*, then *wag*, and came to mean a humorist, most *wags* today being unaware that their name means "a gallows bird."

wailing like a banshee. A wailing banshee is in Irish folklore a spirit in the form of a woman—often beautiful, but sometimes an old hag—who appears to or is heard by members of a family as a warning that one of them will soon die. *Banshee* is from the Gaelic *bean sidhe*, "woman of the fairies," and *wailing like a banshee* has come to mean someone, especially a woman, screaming shrilly.

wake me up when Kirby dies. Theater buffs will be interested in this old catchphrase not heard anymore but whose story is well worth hearing. The tale is told in Charles Hemstreet's *When Old New York Was Young* (1902): "Something more than sixty years ago [in about 1840] the attention of theatergoers was directed to a young actor who appeared at intervals in the Chatham Theatre. He was J. Hudson Kirby. His acting had not much merit, but he persisted in a theory that made him famous. It was his idea that an actor should reserve all his strength for scenes of carnage and death. The earlier acts of a play he passed through carelessly, but when he came to death scenes he threw himself into them with such force and fury that they came to be the talk of the town. Some of the spectators found the earlier acts so dull and tiresome that they went asleep, taking the precaution, however, to nudge their neighbor, with the request to wake them up for the death scene. And for long years after Kirby's time, the catch-phrase applied to any supreme effort was 'Wake me up when Kirby dies.' "

wake-up call. An expression that originated in U.S. hotels about 1835, long before the telephone. At the time clerks from the front desk would knock at your door, calling you whenever you wanted to be awakened in the morning. Over the years the telephone ring replaced the knock on the door, and the expression also took on the figurative meaning of waking a person or people up from lethargy or unpreparedness.

Wales. *See* WELSH.

walk down the aisle. Americans have been using *walk down the aisle* as a synonym for "getting married" for almost a century now. A bride who literally "walked down the aisle," however, would be walking along either side of the church and might confuse everyone. The passageway the bride walks "down" to the altar is actually called the nave, though there is no chance that this will alter the expression in the slightest.

walking off with the persimmons.   *See* EATIN' A GREEN SIMMON.

walk like Agag.   The phrase, meaning to walk softly, remembers the biblical King Agag (I Samuel 15:32), of whom the Bible says, "And Agag came to him [Samuel] delicately," which did him no good, for Samuel hewed him to pieces anyway. Agag, an Amelekite king, had previously been captured and spared by Saul.

walk on water.   This expression refers in a humorous way to Christ walking on the sea, in Matthew 14:15, Mark 6:48–51, and John 6:19–21. "He thinks he can walk on water" and similar phrases are usually said of someone who thinks he is divine. One time the powerful newspaper publisher Lord Beaverbrook (William Maxwell Aitken) was called upon by British statesman David Lloyd George. "Is the lord at home?" Lloyd George asked the butler. "No, sir, the lord is out walking." "Ah," replied Lloyd George. "On the water, I presume."

walk softly and carry a big stick.   *See* ANANIAS.

walk the chalk.   As far back as the 17th century it was customary in the American navy for a straight line to be drawn along the deck of a ship as a test for drunkenness. Any sailor who couldn't walk the whole line, placing each foot on it in turn, was adjudged drunk and punished accordingly—often by flogging. Thus, to *walk the chalk*, first recorded in 1823, came to mean to walk a line of sobriety, to obey the rules.

walk the plank.   Probably no pirate ever forced anyone to walk the plank into the ocean—except in swash-buckling books and movies. The expression most likely originated in the yarn of an old salt or from the pen of a 19th-century magazine writer. Pirates did feed captives to the fishes or told them they were free to "walk home" while far out at sea, but no planks were used. The common practice was to maroon prisoners and pirate offenders on a desert island. The offenders were simply put ashore without clothes or provisions. *See* SWASHBUCKLER; PIRATES.

wall-eyed.   A wall-eyed person has an eye or eyes with unusually large white areas, making for defective sight. Shakespeare uses the old term, which dates back to the 14th century and is a corruption of the Icelandic *vald eysthr*, "having a beam in the eye," and has nothing to do with walls, though no one really knows what the "beam" in the Icelandic word means.

wallflower.   The prosaic explanation for this word, describing a girl who sits to the side at a dance or party because she is shy or without a partner, is simply that it originated with some poor girl who sat against the wall during a party. But the romantic story is nicer. This holds that such girls are named after the common wallflower of Europe (*Cheiranthus cheiri*), a sweet-scented, yellow spring flower that grows wild on walls and cliffs. Indeed, the English poet Robert Herrick (1591–

1674) claimed that the flower itself is named after such a girl, his delightful derivation telling of a fair damsel who was long kept from her lover and finally tried to escape to him:

> Up she got upon a wall
> 'Tempting down to slide withal;
> But the silken twist untied,
> So she fell, and, bruised, she died.
> Love in pity of the deed,
> And her loving luckless speed
> Turned her to this plant we call
> Now the "Flower of the wall."

walls have ears.   Some walls really did have ears. Dionysius, the Greek tyrant of Syracuse (430–367 B.C.), had a narrow tube inserted from his palace room to the walls of the prison below so that he could overhear the prisoners—and the listening post that he put his ear to in his wall was even shaped like a human ear. In the 16th century Catherine de Médicis, queen of France's Henry II, is said to have had several rooms in the Louvre constructed similarly, so she could overhear any plots against her. In any event, the expression *the walls have ears*, meaning "you'd better take care, there are spies everywhere," is an old one, first recorded in English in 1620 and probably dating back much further. The *ears have walls* is a recent twist on the old phrase, meaning that some people, especially those in authority, are incapable of listening. It was coined in the late 1960s.

Wall Street.   Wall Street, which is both a street and a term symbolizing the American financial world in general, is located in downtown Manhattan at the southern end of the island and takes its name from the wall that extended along the street in Dutch times. The principal financial institutions of the city have been located there since the early 19th century. *Wall Streeter*, *Wall Street broker*, *Wall Street plunger*, and *Wall Street shark* are among terms to which the street gave birth. We find *Wall Street broker* first used as early as 1836, and Wall Street being called *The Street* by 1863.

Wallstreet Panic.   Among the most humorous names in American fiction. William Faulkner created or recorded the unusual name in his novel *The Hamlet* (1940). As Ech Snopes explains therein: ". . . [We] figured if we named him Wallstreet Panic it might make him get rich like the folks that run that Wall Street panic [in 1928]." Other humorously named Faulkner characters, all from his Snopes family, include Admiral Dewey and Montgomery Ward. *See* SNOPESIAN; SARTORIS.

walnut.   *See* WELSH.

walrus.   Walrus comes to us from the Dutch *walrus*, for the animal, which may have been suggested by the Dutch *wolvisch*, "whale." The word is first recorded in about 893. The walrus was often called the sea horse and morse in ancient times. The Eskimos, closer to nature, have at least six words for *walrus*, ranging from *nutara*, "baby walrus," to *timartik*, "large male walrus," and *naktivilik*, "mature walrus." *See* SNOW; TOOTH WALKER.

Walrussia.   *See* ALASKA.

Walter Mitty. An ordinary person who has vivid dreams and daydreams of exciting adventures in which he is a hero, like the main character of the short story and film "The Secret Life of Walter Mitty" by American author James Thurber (1894–1961).

Waltzing Matilda. *Matilda* in this century-old Australian song refers to the pack a tramp carries, but no one seems to know the origin of the term. *Waltzing* describes the way a tramp ambles along, his pack flopping up and down.

wampum. *Wampumpeak* was a name American Indians in New England gave to shell money. Like most Indian names—including the longer forebears of *squash, hickory,* and *raccoon*—the colonists found *wampumpeak* too long and shortened it to *wampum,* which it remains today. All Indians didn't have the same name for shell money. Virginia Indians called wampum *roanoke;* the Mohave Indians called it *pook;* in northern California it was called *ali-qua-chick;* and in the Northwest it was *hiaqua.* But only *wampum* remains well known today.

wan. This Chinese family name, whose Chinese character means "10,000," has an apocryphal story attached to it. It's said that when soothsayers advised the emperor Ch'in-Shih-Huang-Ti that he would not be able to finish the Great Wall of China until 10,000 more men were buried in it, the tyrannical emperor found a man named Wan, had him buried in the Wall, and went on about his work. *Wan* for sad comes from the Old English *wann,* dark, gloomy.

war. *War* is an Old High German word, long used (at least since 1154) instead of the Latin *bellum. Bellum* is a poor word for war because of its similarity to *belle,* "beautiful."

war correspondent. "Since the first gun discharged at Fort Sumter awoke the American world to arms, War Correspondence on this side of the Atlantic has been as much an avocation as practicing law or selling dry goods . . . The War Correspondent is the outgrowth of a very modern civilization." So wrote the first observer to record *war correspondent,* in 1861, when the term, if not the profession, came into being.

ward heeler. A *ward heeler* is a political hanger-on of a ward boss in American politics, the *heeler,* coming from the comparison of such a man to a dog that "heels" for its master, that is, follows behind submissively in its master's footsteps. The term is first recorded in 1888.

warfarin. A chemical compound that is used both to kill rats and medically to thin the blood. It derives from the initials of the research foundation where it was discovered, the *Wisconsin Alumni Research Foundation,* plus *arin.* The letters *arin* are from *coumarin,* a substance extracted from the tonka bean that is used in making the chemical compound.

War for the Blacks. *See* ABE LINCOLN WAR.

war game. A simulation of a military operation done physically or electronically. It was perfected from his father's invention in 1824 by a Lieutenant von Reiswitz of the Prussian army under its German name *Kriegsspiel.*

war horse. The original *war horse,* which has been used to describe an experienced veteran of anything from military operations to peace negotiations (!), was Confederate general James Longstreet, whose men nicknamed him War Horse. Since the 17th century, the term has been used for a horse by the military. It is often heard as *old war horse.*

war is cruelty and you cannot refine it. *See* WAR IS HELL.

war is hell. Union general William Tecumseh Sherman said this in an 1880 Columbus, Ohio, speech after the Civil War: "There is many a boy here who looks on war as all glory, but, boys, it is all hell." "Red" Sherman (red-haired and red-bearded) had however said the equivalent throughout the war. "War is cruelty and you cannot refine it," he said of his destruction of Atlanta, and "You might as well appeal against the thunderstorm as against these terrible hardships of war." "Cump" or "Uncle Billy," as his "Yankee Bummers" often called him, was called the "Hun," the "Burner," the "Killer," and "Human Fungus" by Southerners as he marched through Georgia to the sea. For more Sherman coinages see HOLD THE FORT and SHERMAN'S HAIRPINS.

warmonger. In the Latin dialect spoken by Roman soldiers in western Europe *mangones* were conniving dealers or traders in anything. This word passed into English as *monger* and was used for many compound words, including *fishmonger.* As early as 1590 one who traffics in war (for one reason or another) was called a *warmonger,* by Edmund Spenser in *The Faerie Queene.*

warm the cockles of one's heart. The most popular explanation for the *cockles* here says that late-17th-century anatomists noticed the resemblance of the shape of cockleshells, the valves of a scallop-like mollusk, to the ventricles of the heart and referred to the latter as *cockles.* Whether this is the case or not, *cockles* isn't used much anymore except in the expression *to warm the cockles of one's heart,* "to please someone immensely, to evoke a flow of pleasure or a feeling of affection." Behind the expression is the old poetical belief that the heart is the seat of affection.

Warning: The Surgeon General Has Determined That Cigarette Smoking Is Dangerous To Your Health. Since 1973 this well-known warning has by law appeared on the side panel of all cigarette packs. From 1971 up until 1973 the words were somewhat different, advising that cigarette smoking ". . . May Be Dangerous To Your Health."

War of Jenkins' Ear. Carrying his left ear back to London in a leather case, master mariner Robert Jenkins claimed that Spanish sailors boarded his brig, the *Rebecca,* which had been peacefully trading in the West Indies, rifled her, and that their commander had lopped off the ear as a further humiliation. Jenkins sent his ear to the king and brought the matter before Parliament, which decided that this was one cutting Spanish insult too many. Jenkins' ear became the major cause of the war between England and Spain that led the War of the Austrian Succession. The conflict (1739–41) was popularly called *the War of Jenkins' Ear,* which is definitely the oddest name of all wars and surely the only one ever initiated by an ear. Admiral

Sir Edward Vernon put down the Spaniards at Portobelo and "One-Eared" Jenkins was given command of another ship in the East India Company's service. He later rose to company supervisor.

War of the Giants.   The War of the Giants was a mythological one in which the giants revolted against Zeus and were put down by the gods with the help of Hercules. The Battle of the Giants took place on September 13, 1515, when the French under Francis I defeated the Swiss mercenaries defending the city of Milan at Mulagnano.

War of the Roses.   In 1551 the red and white variety of the damask rose (*Rosa damascena versicolor*) was popularly named "York and Lancaster" to memorialize the English Wars of the Roses between the houses of York and Lancaster. This 30-year struggle for the throne of England began in 1455; the house of York adopted a white rose for its emblem and the house of Lancaster chose a red rose. The war ended only when the two houses were united through marriage.

War of the Stray Dog.   The War of the Stray Dog in 1925, a conflict not much more stupid than most wars, took place when a Greek soldier ran after his dog, which had strayed across the border in Macedonia. A Bulgarian sentry shot the soldier and Greek troops invaded Bulgaria in retaliation. Before the League of Nations intervened over 50 men were killed. Almost as foolish was the Emu War. This took place in 1935 when west Australian farmers, enraged at ostrichlike emus trampling their wheat fields, demanded government help. The government sent troops with machine guns after the birds, which led the soldiers on a wild chase through the back country for over a month. Twelve emus were killed and several soldiers injured.

war paint; war dance; on the warpath.   These are all well-known expressions that originally referred to Native Americans but are used figuratively today. *War council* and *war cry* did not originate with any Indian tribe. *See* WAR GAME.

warren.   Just as George Bernard Shaw's play *Mrs. Warren's Profession* resulted in the coining of COMSTOCKERY, it also gave rise to the word *warren*, for "a prostitute," after the title character in the play. The earlier *warren*, for "a brothel," origin unknown but dating back to the late 17th century, may have reinforced the usage.

war to end all wars.   World War I. The expression is not from Woodrow Wilson's address to Congress calling for a declaration of war against Germany in 1917, as many people believe. What Wilson said then was: "The world must be made safe for democracy." *The war to end all wars* was suggested by H. G. Wells's book *The War That Will End War* (1914). In announcing the end of World War I, Britain's prime minister Lloyd George told the House of Commons: "I hope we may say that thus . . . came to end all wars."

War to Free the Slaves.   *See* ABE LINCOLN WAR.

war to make the world safe for democracy.   *See* WAR TO END ALL WARS.

warts and all.   The roots of *warts and all* reach way back to a remark Oliver Cromwell (1599–1658) made to an artist painting his portrait: "Mr. Lely, I desire you would use all your skill to paint my picture truly like me, and not flatter me at all; but remark all these roughnesses, pimples, warts, and everything as you see me, otherwise I will never pay a farthing for it." The story may be apocryphal, though it does sound like Cromwell, and historians believe that the Lord Protector, if he did say this, was speaking to Samuel Cooper rather than Sir Peter Lely, who painted less realistic full-length portraits of Cromwell from a miniature Cooper had done.

war will be over by Christmas.   An expression—which always comes in the form of a rumor around Christmas time—that has been heard by U.S. troops in every war from the Civil War (1861–65) to the present. In no war have the words ever been true.

Washington.   *Washington* is the most popular place name in the United States, recorded in the nation's capital, Washington, D.C., the state of Washington, at least 29 counties, and numerous towns. Washington State, the only state named for an American, was admitted to the union on February 22, 1889, appropriately on George Washington's birthday. Other terms honoring the "Father of his country," first in war, first in peace, first in the hearts of his countrymen, are *the bird of Washington* (the American eagle), *the American Fabius* (*see* FABIAN TACTICS), *Washingtonia* (a California palm tree), the *Washington thorn*, the *Washington lily*, and *Washington pie*. A *George Washington*, for an honest person, derives from the famous cherry-tree story apparently invented by M. L. (Parson) Weems in his biography of the first president written in about 1800. *See* I CANNOT TELL A LIE.

Washoe.   The former name of the territory that became Nevada; from the name of the Washoe Indians of the region.

wash one's hands of a matter.   Pontius Pilate's washing his hands at the trial of Jesus was a favorite scene in biblical dramas presented by strolling players in medieval times. Pilate was portrayed washing his hands in a basin (although the passage in Matt. 27:24 just says, "He took water and washed his hands") while denying any responsibility for Christ's death sentence. From these dramas and the biblical story of the Crucifixion, *to wash one's hands of a matter* came into popular use as an expression for abandoning something entirely after having been concerned in the matter, for a public disavowal disclaiming all accountability for something, or for disowning all associations with someone.

washout.   Not all word derivations are CUT AND DRIED. Sometimes the same expression arises in two or more places from different sources, which may be the case with *washout*, both British and American slang for "a failure." British usage of this term derives from military slang on the rifle range. After one squad had finished shooting at an iron target, the bullet marks in the bull's-eye were painted over with black paint and the rest of the target whitewashed to prepare it for practice by the next squad. A shot completely off the target was called a *washout*, because it went off into the air, washed itself out, so to speak, and the military slang for a missed shot, common in about

1850, became slang for a failure some 50 years later during the Boer War. However, before this, probably as early as the 1860s, *wash out* was an American term for the washing away by heavy rains of part of a road or railway. Some writers claim that this term independently suggested American usage of the expression *washout* for a failure, but there are no recorded instances of the figurative usage here until the 1920s. By that time British and American forces had come in close contact during World War I. It seems likely that American soldiers borrowed the term for a failure from British slang without even realizing it, the wash-out of roads and railways being so familiar to them!

Was it Eliot's toilet I saw?   This famous but possibly apocryphal palindrome is said to have been uttered in mock awe by an American publisher on visiting the London office of Faber and Faber, where the renowned poet T. S. Eliot worked.

WASP.   A disparaging acronym for *White Anglo-Saxon Protestant*, WASP has been commonly used in America since the early 1960s to describe the nation's "ruling class," who are supposed to be white, of British descent, Protestant, and wasp-ish, too. During World War II, WASP was also an acronym for *Women's Auxilliary Service Pilot. See* DAGO; HARP; KIWI; WELSH.

Wasserman test.   Many medical tests, including the Pap test for cancer and the Schick test for diphtheria, are named for the physicians who devised them. The Wasserman test was invented in 1906 by August von Wasserman (1866–1925), a German physician and bacteriologist. This laboratory blood test for the diagnosis of syphilis, also known as the cardiolipin test, has been perfected to the point where it is 99 percent effective on normal persons. The test is based on the presence of antibodies in the blood. In most cases a positive Wasserman reveals that the patient has syphilis, although vaccination procedures and several diseases, such as leprosy, also produce a positive Wasserman. August von Wasserman, who began his career as a physician in Strasbourg, won international fame for his discovery. He became director of Berlin's Kaiser Wilhelm Institute in 1913.

watercress.   Both watercress and land cress are herbs of the mustard group. Cress takes its name from the German *kresse*, for the salad green, this word perhaps deriving from an older German word that meant "to creep or crawl" and described the plant's way of growing.

watered stock.   To water a stock is to increase its number of shares without increasing the value of its assets; it is thus diluted or watered down. According to one old story, the expression originated with Wall Street speculator Daniel Drew, who was a cattle dealer after the Civil War. Drew sold his cattle by weight, of course, and did so immediately after they finished drinking a large quantity of water.

Watergate.   *See* DEEP THROAT.

Waterloo.   One who *meets his Waterloo* suffers a complete and final defeat, just as Napoleon did in 1815 at the Battle of Waterloo, about nine miles from Brussels in Belgium. The battle was actually fought a few miles south of Waterloo, between Mont-Saint-Jean and Bellenoon.

watermelon.   Originating in Africa, watermelon has been cultivated for thousands of years, but seems to have been so named only since 1605. There were many old names for the melon, including names in Arabic and Sanskrit. The watermelon is an important water source in many arid regions but considered a fruit dessert in most places. Mark Twain considered it "chief of the world's luxuries . . . When one has tasted it, he knows what angels eat." The Chinese call the watermelon the *west-melon* (shih-quah).

water of jealousy.   Under Mosaic law a woman who had committed adultery was to be stoned to death. But if a husband only suspected his wife of adultery she was given the water of jealousy to drink (Deut. 22:22) before the Sanhedrin. The dust from the sanctuary was mixed with the water and the priest said: "If thou hast gone aside may Jehovah make this water bitter to thee, and bring on thee all the curses written in this law." He then wrote down the curses, sprinkled the water on this writing, and gave the woman the rest of the water of jealousy to drink.

Water Poet; waterman.   Eccentric British poet John Taylor (1580–1653) was known as the Water Poet because of the nature of many of his rollicking poems and because he was a river waterman, a boatman who transported passengers along the River Thames. He claimed that he knew no grammar, though he had written over 80 books. One time he set out from London to Queensborough in a cardboard boat, using two cured fish tied to canes for oars, and nearly drowned when the boat sank moments after he launched it.

watt.   There is probably no truth in the charming old tale that James Watt watched his mother's teakettle boiling as a child, and later invented the steam engine as a result. Watt, born in Scotland of poor parents, did, however, get off to an early start in his scientific endeavors. In 1765 the inquisitive Scotsman launched into a study of steam when a model of Thomas Neucomen's steam engine was brought to him to repair. He soon invented the first economical steam engine, which was initially used only for pumps in mines but eventually brought steam power to industry on a large scale. Watt devoted his life to perfecting and producing his new engine, manufacturing it with Matthew Boulton of Birmingham. He died in 1819, aged 83. Toward the end of the century the International Electrical Congress named the watt, the unit of electrical power—736 watts equal to about one horsepower—in the inventor's honor. His name is also remembered by the kilowatt, one thousand watts; the kilowatt hour, a measurement by which electricity is sold; the watt-hour meter, which measures kilowatts; the watt-meter, an instrument for measuring a power load; and the watt-second, a unit of work. Wattage is power measured in watts, and "wattless" is an electrical term meaning without watts or power.

wave a red flag at a bull.   Though the bullfight matador waves his traditional red-lined cape to make the bull charge, it is the motion of the cape, not the color, that irritates the animal, as bulls are colorblind. Nevertheless, the image of the red cape long ago inspired the expression *to wave a red flag at a bull*, meaning to provoke or enrage someone. *Cloth* or *rag* are sometimes substituted for *flag* in the phrase.

Waves.   *See* WRENS.

wave the bloody shirt.   Used in both the North and the South from after the Civil War until the present to indicate any means employed to stir up hostility between the North and the South. "The G.A.R. [Grand Army of the Republic] waved the Bloody Shirt in many a political campaign, advising its boys in blue to 'vote as you shoot!'," wrote Jerome Kerwin, *Civil Military Relationships in American Life*, 1948.

the way of all flesh.   Death, as in the first recorded use of the phrase, English playwright John Webster's *Westward Ho* (1607): "I saw him now going the way of all flesh." Three hundred years later, in 1903, British author Samuel Butler made the words famous again with the posthumous publication of his novel *The Way of All Flesh*, which he had actually finished writing in 1886. Originally called *Ernest Pontifex*, after its main character, the book is in some respects autobiographical.

we.   *See* THE ROYAL WE.

we-all.   Early during World War II, Thomas J. Watson, the president of I.B.M., borrowed this expression from southern mountain talk to use in full-page newspaper advertisements throughout the country. He proclaimed: " 'I' represents only one person. 'We' may mean only two or a few persons. Our slogan now is WE ALL. . . . President Roosevelt, our Commander-in-Chief, can be certain that WE-ALL are back of him."

wear a two-inch belt and Big Jim suspenders.   To be very cautious. This cowboy variation is more colorful than the more common American expression *wear a belt and suspenders*, which means the same.

we are not amused.   It has been said that this reproof often attributed to Queen Victoria is "not in keeping with Queen Victoria's conversation or character" and that she never used the royal "we" save in official proclamations. However, J. A. Fuller-Maitland wrote about an 1884 concert in *A Doorkeeper of Music:* "Alick Yorke sang comic songs, one of them in a flannel petticoat bestowed upon him by the Queen after she had insisted on his giving his famous impersonation of herself in her own presence, as a *douceur* [kindness] after the reproof she felt bound to utter in words that have often been quoted." Another story, one of many more, has the queen saying "we are not amused" upon seeing an imitation of herself by the Honorable Alexander Granthan Yorke, her groom-in-waiting. Richard the Lion-Hearted, incidentally, was the first king to use the royal *we* in place of *I*.

wearing calluses on his elbows.   *Western Words* (1961) by Ramon F. Adams defines *wearing calluses on his elbows* as "spending time in a saloon." Similarly, an *elbow bender*, another term from the Old West, means a "drinking man," because he bends his elbow to convey his glass to his lips.

wear one's heart on one's sleeve.   To make one's feelings obvious. Shakespeare probably coined the phrase in *Othello* (1604): "I will wear my heart upon my sleeve / For daws [crows] to peck at . . ." But it may have originated in medieval tournaments when contestants sported knots of ribbon ladies they loved gave them to wear on their sleeves in competitions.

wear the willow.   *See* WILLOW.

weasel words.   "Weasel words are words that suck all of the life out of the words next to them just as a weasel sucks an egg and leaves the shell," a writer explained in the June 1900 issue of the *Century Magazine*. The writer then gives an example: " 'The public should be protected.' 'Duly protected,' said Gamage, 'that's always a good weasel word.' " The term was applied to politicians in this first recorded use and has often been associated with politicians since then.

weber; Weberian apparatus; Weber's law.   The *weber* is the practical unit of magnetic flux, named after German physicist Wilhelm Eduard Weber (1804–91). While a professor at the University of Göttingen, Weber worked with Karl Gauss on terrestrial magnetism, devised an electromagnetic telegraph, and did valuable research on electrical measurements—the *coulomb*, in fact, being once known as the *weber*. A politically committed teacher, he was dismissed from the university for protesting the king's suspension of the constitution. Weber's two brothers were also noted scientists. Wilhelm Eduard collaborated with his younger brother Eduard in 1833 on a study of human locomotion. With his elder brother Ernst he wrote a well-known book on wave motion published in 1825. This same Ernst Heinrich Weber (1795–1878), a physiologist and early psychophysical investigator, is the author of Weber's law, a mathematical formulation showing that the increase in stimulus necessary in producing an increased sensation depends on the strength of the preceding stimulus. The Weberian apparatus, small bones connecting the inner ear with the air bladder in certain fishes, honors Ernst too.

webfoot.   *See* BEAVER STATE.

webfooter.   *See* BEAVER STATE.

the web of life.   Meaning the destiny of a person from birth to death, *the web of life* is an old expression that alludes to the three Fates of Roman mythology. These Fates are supposed to spin the thread of life, that is, the pattern in which events will occur.

Webster's.   Noah Webster's name has become a synonym for a dictionary since he published his *Compendious Dictionary of the English Language* in 1806 and his larger *An American Dictionary of the English Language* 22 years later. But the "father of American lexicography" was a man of widespread interests, publishing many diverse books over his long career. These included his famous *Sketches of American Policy* (1785), on history and politics; *Dissertations on the English Language* (1789), advocating spelling reform; and *A Brief History of Epidemic and Pestilential Diseases* (1799). Webster also found time to edit *The American Magazine* and the newspaper *The Minerva*. Beginning in 1806, he lived on the income from his speller—which sold at the rate of over 1 million copies a year—while he took the 22 years needed to complete his monumental dictionary. *Webster's*, as it came to be called (it is now published as *Webster's Dictionary* by Merriam) helped standardize American spelling and pronunciation and recorded many Americanisms.

Wedgwood. *See* ODE ON A GRECIAN URN.

wedlock. *See* DEADLOCK.

Wednesday. Traditionally a good day for planting crops in ancient times, *Wednesday* is named for Woden, the Old English name of Wotan, the Scandinavian god of agriculture, war, wisdom, and poetry. The Old English *Wodensdaeg*, or *Woden's day*, became our Wednesday.

Wednesday's child. *See* MONDAY'S CHILD.

weed. "What is a weed? A plant whose virtues have not yet been discovered," Ralph Waldo Emerson wrote in *Fortune of the Republic* (1878). But James Russell Lowell seems to have expressed the same sentiment 30 years earlier in *A Fable for Critics* (1848): "A weed is no more than a flower in disguise." Later, Ella Wheeler Wilcox wrote in her poem "The Weed" (1872): "A weed is but an unloved flower." In any case, these sentiments are the ancestors of our current expression *a weed is just an uncultivated plant*. Poet Mildred Howells spoke less admiringly of weeds in her poem "The Difficult Seed" (1910):

> And so it criticized each flower
> This supercilious seed
> Until it woke one summer hour,
> And found itself a weed.

While a weed is really only an uncultivated plant, weeds are generally regarded as unwanted pervasive plants to be rooted out from gardens. The word *weed*, recorded in one form or another since the ninth century, comes from the Old English *wiod*, a variant of an early Saxon term for "wild." Nevertheless, plants regarded as weeds change from century to century. The tomato was considered a pernicious weed in cornfields until the Mayans began cultivating it. Similarly, rye and oats were once known as weeds in wheat fields. Today, experts regard the world's worst land weeds as purple nutsedge, Bermuda grass, Cogan grass, and lantana. Some weeds aren't plants but simply clothing of any kind, deriving from the Anglo-Saxon word *waede*, "garment." *Widow's weeds* are mourning garments, the black often worn by widows. The expression contributes the only use of the word *weeds* for clothing remaining in English, but *weeds* was used by Spenser, Shakespeare, and many other writers to mean everyday clothing for both men and women.

weekend. A relatively recent word, first recorded in England in 1879 and rarely used in America until the mid-1930s. Until that time the great majority of Americans didn't know what a weekend was. For the most part they worked long six-day, 60-hour weeks, steelworkers (1923) and then Ford employees (1926) being the first five-day, 40-hour workers.

weekend warrior. The term was originally, and still is, a nickname for a National Guardsman who serves weekends in the military for a certain time. Now the words are also used to describe professionals who work nine to five during the week and then go wild on the weekend, either with partying or by playing sports.

Weeping Philosopher. The Greek Heraclitus (d. ca. 475 B.C.) was called the Weeping Philosopher, this AGELAST so labeled because he grieved at the folly of mankind. His opposite was Democritus of Abdera (fifth century B.C.), called the *Laughing Philosopher* because he laughed contemptuously at mankind's feeble powers.

Weeping Saint. St. Swithin of ST. SWITHIN'S DAY fame is called *the Weeping Saint* because of the tradition of 40 days' rain if it rains on his day, July 15.

weeping water. A colorful term for a waterfall that is a translation of Maori *waitangi* and has become part of New Zealand English.

weevil. *See* BOLL WEEVIL.

we fly away. *See* THREE SCORE AND TEN.

we have met the enemy and he is us. Another way of saying we (humankind) are our own worst enemies. Cartoonist Walt Kelly invented the expression for his *Pogo* comic strip. Centuries before him, poet John Milton wrote in *Religio Medici* (1642) "yet is every man his greatest enemy, and, as it were, his own executioner."

We have the receipt of fern seed, we walk invisible. These words, from Shakespeare's *Henry IV, Part I, iv, 4*, were widely believed in medieval times. Because the seed of some fern species was invisible to the naked eye, it was thought to confer invisibility on anyone who carried it.

weigela. The long-popular *Weigela* genus of the honeysuckle family, containing some 12 species, is named for German physician C. E. Weigel (1748–1831). *Weigela*, sometimes spelled *weigelia*, is often grouped with the *Diervilla* genus, the bush honeysuckle, but its bushes have larger, much showier flowers than the latter. *Diervilla* itself is named for a Dr. Dierville, a French surgeon in Canada. Native to Asia, the weigela bush is easily cultivated in America and Europe. Its funnel-shaped flowers are usually rose-pink but vary in color from white to dark crimson.

weigh anchor. *Weigh* in this phrase derives from the Old English *wegan*, "to carry or move," which later came to mean "lift" as well. Thus the expression means to lift or haul up the anchor. It is more correct, however, to say *under way* than *under weigh* to describe a ship in motion.

welfare. *Welfare*, in the sense of financial assistance for the poor and needy, goes back only about 90 years. It seems to have first been used in this sense in Dayton, Ohio, in 1904, according to the *Westminster Gazette* (January 28, 1905) and Ernest Weekley's *Something About Words* (1935).

well, back to the old drawing board. Few would suppose that this very common expression for a resigned unruffled reaction to the failure of plans of any kind derives from a cartoon caption. It almost certainly does: from a 1941 Peter Arno cartoon in *The New Yorker* which shows an airplane crash, the plane mangled, rescue squads working frantically, and the plane's designer, plans under his arm, musing aloud, "Well, back to the old drawing board." Partridge says it's used "when one has to make an agonizing re-appraisal" and traces it "probably" to World War II aircraft designers.

well-heeled.   Before *well-heeled* meant "well provided with money" in American slang, it meant "well provided with weapons." Back in frontier days men who went "heeled" carried a gun, the expression apparently deriving from a cockfighting term meaning to provide a fighting cock with an artificial spur before he went into the pit. *Well-heeled* is recorded in this sense as early as 1867 and it wasn't until over a decade later that it took on the meaning it has today, perhaps because men found that it was easier and safer to protect themselves with money than with guns. In any case, *well-heeled* is not simply the opposite of *down at the heels*, someone so hard pressed for money that his shoes are run down at the heels. *Down at the heels* may even be traced back to Shakespeare, who wrote in *King Lear* (1600): "A good man's fortune may grow out at the heels."

Well, I declare!   This expression is hardly used today, but was common among our grandparents, who also used *I declare to goodness!*, which was considered a rather strong term! Both expressions probably date back to 16th-century England, or earlier.

Well, if that don't take the rag off the bush!   A southern Americanism originating in the late 19th century, this expression refers to outrageous behavior, as lowdown as stealing the rags or clothes someone in the swimmin' hole has left spread out on a bush.

Wellington.   Napoleon's greatest adversary fares as well in the dictionaries as he did on the battlefield. Arthur Wellesley, the first duke of Wellington, who began his army career in India and was knighted for his victories there, drove the French from Spain during the Peninsular War and completely crushed Napoleon at Waterloo in 1815. One of England's greatest soldiers, "the Iron Duke" served as prime minister from 1828–30 and in 1842 was made commander in chief of the British armed forces for life. About the only blemish on his record was his aristocratic opposition to parliamentary reform, which caused his ministry to fall. Wellington died in 1852, an idolized old man of 83, and it is said that even death "came to him in its gentlest form." A number of hats, coats, and trousers were named after the great soldier, as were two types of boots: the full Wellington riding boots, which were tight-fitting and came up slightly over the knee, and the half-Wellington, which came half-way up the calf, having a boot made of patent leather and a top of softer material. One apocryphal story has it that Queen Victoria once asked the duke the name of the boots he was wearing. When he replied that they were called *Wellington's*, she remarked, "Impossible! There could not be a *pair* of Wellington's!" The capital of New Zealand is also named for Wellington, as well as the *Wellingtonia*, a New Zealand sequoia. The duke took his title from the town of Wellington in England, where a statue of him stands today. *See* BEEF STROGANOFF; BEEF WELLINGTON.

well-made play.   Apparently this expression, for "an entertaining, carefully constructed play with more attention given to plot than characters," is a literal translation of the French *pièce bien faite*, which was applied to the well-made plays of Scribe and Sardou in the 19th century.

Welsh.   England's native Celts were called *wealhs*, "foreigners"—by the invading Saxons, of all people—and driven off into the western hills. *Wealhs* became Welsh in time and these inhabitants of Wales suffered almost as much abuse at the hands and tongues of the English as did the Scots or Irish. Their traditional enemies used *Welsh* to signify anything poor, such as a *Welsh comb*, the fingers, a *Welsh carpet*, a painted floor, and *Welsh rabbit*, melted seasoned cheese poured over buttered toast. To *welsh*, or renege, on a bet is another contemptuous English reference to the Welsh. The most common explanation is that there were thought to be a great many crooked Welsh bookmakers at the racetracks in the 19th century, *Welshers* or *welshers*, who did not pay when they lost. Names of individual bookmakers, such as a Mr. Bob Welch, have also been suggested, but with no positive proof or identification. *Walnut*, an ancient word, comes from the Anglo-Saxon *wealhhnutu*, meaning "the foreign or Welsh nut." Kinder terms using the Welsh prefix include three breeds of dogs—the *Welsh corgi*, *springer spaniel*, and *terrier*; the *Welsh poppy*, with its pale yellow flowers; and the small sturdy *Welsh pony*, originally raised in Wales. *See* WELSH RABBIT.

Welsh rarebit; Welsh rabbit.   *Welsh rarebit* is entirely wrong as the name for melted seasoned cheese poured over buttered toast. But rather than being an affected, mannered corruption of the correct Welsh rabbit, it is a well-meaning, if misdirected, attempt to remove a slur on Welshmen from the language. The term *Welsh rabbit*, an example of country humor dating back to Shakespeare's time, conveys the idea that only people as poor and stupid as the Welsh would eat cheese and call it *rabbit*, while the much later *Welsh rarebit* of restaurant menus makes the Welsh dish a rare and tasty bit. *Rarebit*, therefore, is an artificial, invented word used in no other connection. *See* WELSH.

We Polked you in '44; we shall Pierce you in '52!   This is my favorite of the interesting political slogans interspersed throughout this book. It was the slogan of the Democratic Party in 1852, when dark horse Franklin Pierce did indeed "pierce" the Whigs to become the 14th President of the U.S., just as James Polk had beaten them in 1844.

werewolf.   *See* WOLFMAN.

"We Shall Overcome."   This anthem of the Civil Rights movement was written by folk singer Pete Seeger and set to the music of an old Baptist hymn. Its first line is not "We shall overcome," but "We shall end Jim Crow some day, . . ."

West.   Generally used in the United States today to mean the region west of the Mississippi River. The term *westerner* for someone who lives in the region west of the Mississippi is first recorded in 1835.

West-by-God-Virginia. This humorous name for West Virginia is said to have been coined by an irate native when it was said that he came from Virginia. Replied the man: "Not Virginia, but *West* by God!, Virginia!" *See* WEST VIRGINIA.

westering. American pioneers in the 19th century coined this term meaning to travel West, but it had been used in England six centuries before.

western sandwich. A sandwich made of an omelet with onions, green peppers, and chopped ham between slices of bread or toast; also called a *Denver sandwich*.

Westinghoused. To be put to death in the electric chair. Thomas Edison championed DC (direct current) over the AC (alternating current) that his competitors preferred to use in converting the world to electricity. AC eventually triumphed, but not before Edison campaigned stubbornly against it over the years. The Wizard of Menlo Park even went so far as to coin *Westinghoused* (after the name of his rival the Westinghouse Company) as a replacement for the word *electrocuted*, in reference to criminals put to death in the (AC) electric chair. The coinage didn't live long but did have some currency. *See* ELECTROCUTE.

West Virginia. West Virginia is composed of 40 western mountain counties that seceded from Virginia at the outbreak of the Civil War, these counties voting not to secede from the Union and forming their own state government. After rejecting New Virginia, Kanawha, and Alleghany, the new state settled on West Virginia for a name, an ironic choice since Virginia extends 95 miles farther west than it does. West Virginia had considered seceding from Virginia several times, due to unequal taxation and representation, and the Civil War provided an excellent excuse. Its constitution was amended to abolish slavery and President Lincoln proclaimed *West Virginia* the 35th state in 1862, justifying his action as a war measure. Called the Panhandle State, it has an odd outline, leading to the saying that it's "a good state for the shape it's in." *See* VIRGINIA.

wetback. A disparaging term for an illegal Mexican immigrant or worker who crosses the Rio Grande into the United States, sometimes swimming to get across. The term is a relatively recent one, first recorded in 1948.

wet behind the ears. *He's still wet behind the ears* would refer to someone as innocent in the ways of the world as a newborn baby. The American expression goes back at least a century and refers to the traditional belief, which may be true, that the last place to dry on newborn animals such as calves and colts is the small indentation behind each ear.

wet blanket. *Wet blanket* in reality probably refers to a water-soaked blanket used to smother a fire. Figuratively, the term is a name for someone who throws a damper over anything, who depresses others at a gathering because of a depressed lack of enthusiasm, a real "party pooper." The expression is British in

origin and was first recorded in 1830. *See* BLANKET; TOSS IN A BLANKET.

wet hen. *See* MAD AS A WET HEN.

We the people of the United States, in order to form a more perfect Union. . . . These words that begin the preamble of the U.S. Constitution were, appropriately enough, taken from a Native American document, a 1520 treaty that established the Iroquois Confederacy, which begins, "We, the people, to form a union . . ."

wet one; wet ship. *Wet one* in sailor's talk refers to a vessel liable to ship water over the bow or gunwale. Wrote Captain Frederick Marryat in *Newton Fortes or the Naval Service* (1832): "She was what sailors term rather a *wet one*, and the sea broke continually over her bows." *Wet ship* is British naval slang for a ship that has a reputation for heavy drinking aboard.

wet one's beak. The Roman historian Suetonius mentions a boy whose nickname was Beak. For untold centuries *beak* (of an animal) has been a humorous synonym for the human nose. Even the expression *to dip one's beak*, "to take a drink," is over 150 years old. The expression *to wet one's beak*, "to partake of an enterprise," usually a criminal activity, was not recorded in English until Mario Puzo's *The Godfather* (1970): " 'After all, this is my neighborhood [he said] and you should let me wet my beak.' He used the Sicilian phrase of the Mafia, *'Fari vagnavie a pizzu.'* *Pizzu* means the beak of any small bird such as a canary. The phrase itself was a demand for part of the loot."

wetting a commission. *Wetting a commission* was an old naval custom, dating back over a century, which consisted of giving a party to a naval officer who had just received his commission. The parchment commission was formed into a cornucopia, filled with champagne, and drunk from as it was passed from hand to hand.

wet your whistle. *Whistle* has been slang for the mouth (because we whistle with it) since Chaucer's time—"So was her jolly whistle wely-wet," he wrote in "Reeve's Tale" (ca. 1386). This explains the phrase *wet your whistle*, "have a drink," very simply, but although the derivation is certain, people keep inventing stories for the expression—all very interesting, all untrue. One old theory makes "wet" a corruption of "whet," while another conjures up an imaginary tankard that whistled for more liquor when it was empty—to *wet your whistle*, according to this yarn, deriving from the pouring of more liquor into the tankard to stop its damn whistling.

we wuz robbed. When Jack Sharkey won a decision over Max Schmeling in 1932 to take the world heavyweight championship, Schmeling's manager Joe Jacobs grabbed the radio fight announcer's mike and shouted "We wuz robbed!" to a million Americans, his words still a comic protest heard from losers in any endeavor. Jacobs's *I should of stood in bed* is even more commonly used in fun. He said it after leaving his sickbed to watch the 1935 World Series in Detroit. According to John Lardner's *Strong Cigars and Lovely Women* (1951), *Bartlett's* is wrong in saying Jacobs made the remark to sportswriters in

New York after returning from Detroit, and it had nothing to do with his losing a bet that Detroit would win the Series. Jacobs made the remark, Lardner says, in the press box during the opening game of the Series, when "an icy wind was curdling his blood" at the coldest ball game anyone could remember.

whaling. Two centuries ago a *whaling*, "a terrible beating," was one given with a whalebone whip. Or possibly, both the whalebone whip and the wales it raised on the skin contributed to the phrase, making it more vivid. Riding whips were commonly made of whalebone in the 18th and 19th centuries and were used to beat more than horses. *Whalebone*, incidentally, is a misnomer: It's not made from the bone of a whale but from a substance found in the whale's upper jaw.

wham bam (thank-ye-ma'am). *Thank-ye-ma'am* is an American courtship term that dates back to the 19th century. Roads at the time had diagonal earthen ridges running across them that channeled off rainwater from the high to the low side and prevented washouts. Rural Casanovas driving their carriages along these rude roads made sure that they hit these ridges hard so that their female companions would bounce up in the air and bump into them. With the head of his sweetheart so close, the gentleman could steal a kiss and usually express his gratitude with a *Thank-ye-ma'am*, that expression becoming synonymous for a quick kiss or for any hole in the road that caused riders to bump up and down. It wasn't long before some wit took this innocent phrase to bed, or to the side of the road somewhere, and elaborated on it, for in 1895 we find recorded the related expression *wham bam (thank-ye-ma'am)* for quick coitus. As a matter of fact, the first recorded use of both expressions occurs in that year.

What am I, chopped liver? A half-humorous complaint that a person is being regarded as trivial or unimportant. The phrase was first recorded in a routine of American comedian Jimmy Durante.

What are you, a man or a mouse? There are similar phrases in German and many other languages, and this expression, in a rudimentary form, dates back at least to 1541, when it came from the mouth of a woman, as it often still does today: "Fear not, she saith unto her spouse, a man or a Mouse whether ye be."

What Cato did, and Addison approved, cannot be wrong. This old saying has an interesting story behind it. A prolific man of letters who contributed to the *Spectator*, the *Tatler*, and the *Guardian* and later published and edited his own weekly, the *Bee*, Eustace Budgell was a confidant of Joseph Addison, who was his mother's cousin, as well as other English literary notables. Budgell, however, was an extravagant eccentric who lost over 20,000 pounds in the infamous South Sea stock scheme and spent huge amounts of money to get elected to Parliament. When his friend and fellow deist Dr. Matthew Tindal died, it seemed that Budgell's financial worries were over, for a legacy of some 2,000 pounds was left him in Tindal's will. But Tindal's nephew charged that Budgell had inserted the bequest in the will, and the courts agreed. Budgell was ridiculed in Pope's satire *Epistle to Dr. Arbuthnot* (1735): "Let Budgell charge low Grub Street in his quill, / And write whate'er he pleased—

except his will." Scandal plagued him for two years as he vainly tried to prove his innocence in various lawsuits. Finally, on May 4, 1737, after filling his pockets with rocks from the beach, he hired a boat at Somerset-Stairs and, while the waterman rowed them under the bridge there, threw himself overboard. Budgell had tried to persuade his daughter, the actress Anne Eustace, to kill herself with him, but she had refused. Found on his desk was a slip of paper on which he had written of his act of suicide: "What Cato did, and Addison approved, cannot be wrong." *See* PHAEDO; SUICIDE BOMBER

whatchamacallit. *See* DINGBAT.

What do you know about that? An Americanism meaning "isn't that amazing, I would never have believed it," etc. Sometimes heard as "Well, what do you know," or "How about that!" The earliest appearance of the expression in print was the 1914 novel *Perch of the Devil* by American author Gertrude Atherton.

What fools these mortals be. *See* PUCKISH.

What hath God wrought? These words constitute the first public telegram, sent by Samuel F. B. Morse over an experimental 40-mile line constructed between Washington, D.C. and Baltimore, Maryland on May 24, 1844. There had been telegraphs before Morse's but his was the first electromagnetic telegraph. *See* TELEGRAPH.

what's good for General Motors is good for the country. Former head of General Motors Charles E. Wilson didn't say this when testifying before a Senate committee in 1953 when nominated for secretary of defense. The words have become proverbial, but what Wilson said was less arrogant: "I thought that what was good for our country was good for General Motors, and vice versa."

What's new?; What's with you? The greeting *What's new?* has been traced back to 1880s New York. It is thought to be a translation of the *was ist los?* ("what's the matter?") of German immigrants, as is the similar expression *what's with you?*

What's the good word? John Kendrick Bangs used the catchphrase in his poem "The Answer" (1913):

> What's the good word
> Now that's a phrase I truly love to hear,
>   Ane when tis heard,
> I always smile and promptly answer 'CHEER' . . .

Bangs apparently did not coin the American expression, meaning "what's the news?" which is first recorded about three years earlier. Other similar American greetings include *What's up?* and *What do you say?* (both from about the 1800s) and *What's cooking?* (the 1940s).

What's up, Doc? Bugs Bunny first said this to Elmer Fudd in his famous cartoon series launched in 1937, though it may be an old western expression suggested by Tex Avery, one of the cartoon's animators. It is said that when Mel Blanc, the voice of Bugs Bunny in the cartoons, emerged from a coma in 1983, he looked at his physician and asked, "Er, what's up, Doc?" *See also* THAT'S ALL, FOLKS!; WILEY E. COYOTE.

what's what. *See* KNOW WHAT'S WHAT.

what the dickens. See DICKENS.

what the hey. *See* I'LL TELL YOU WHAT I'M GONNA DO.

What time does the next swan leave? According to the old story, a boat drawn by a swan used in a performance of Wagner's *Lohengrin* was pushed onto the stage before the actor playing Lohengrin could get into it. The perfectly composed tenor quipped: "What time does the next swan leave?" This famous remark has been attributed to a number of famous singers over the years, but it actually goes back to the first tenor to sing the role, over a century ago.

what we gave, we have. These wise old words are a loose translation of lines by the Roman poet Martial, which seem to have first appeared as an epitaph on "the good Earl of Courtenay" in the 17th century:

> What wee gave, wee have;
> What wee spent, wee had;
> What wee left, wee lost.

what we have here is failure to communicate. The "Cap'n" in the film *Cool Hand Luke* (1967) famously says this to the incorrigible Luke, played by Paul Newman.

what will be will be. *See* STORE.

wheatear. The name of this Old World thrush originally had nothing to do with "wheat" or "ears." First recorded in 1591, *wheatear* comes from the Anglo-Saxon *hwitt*, "white," and *eeres*, "ass," in reference to its white rump. *Wheat* later replaced *hwett* in its name because the bird "came when the wheat was yearly reaped."

wheat germ. *See* GERM.

wheel. I remember my father telling me to get my wheel out and we'd go for a ride. This synonym for a bicycle isn't heard much any more—at least I haven't heard it in years—but it is recorded as far back as 1880, probably suggested by the large front wheel of early bicycles, or, less likely, by unicycles, which date back 20 years or so earlier. There was, in fact, a bicycle manufacturer called the Chicopee Overman Wheel Company, which is also remembered in sports history for making the first basketballs at a time (about 1894) when soccer balls were being used in the infant game. *See* BASKETBALL.

wheeler dealer. In gaming houses of the 18th-century American West a big wheeler and dealer was a heavy bettor at cards and the roulette wheels. Through this tradition, and the association of a *big wheel* as the man (or wheel) who makes the vehicle (things) run, the expression came to mean a big-time operator by the early 1940s, usually with an unsavory connotation, the *wheeler dealer* being the type who runs over anything in his path with no regard for rules of the road.

when a dog bites a man . . . Crusty old *New York Sun* editor John B. Bogart (1845–1921) is said to have originated in conversation the old saw "When a dog bites a man, that is not news, because it happens so often; but if a man bites a dog, that is news." However, the adage may be based on an old story.

when chickens have teeth. A 19th century Americanism meaning "never, it won't happen," as in "She'll be on time when chickens have teeth." Chickens, of course, have no teeth.

when hemp is spun, England's done. Francis Bacon, despite his scientific training, gave the following interpretation of the above prophecy, which he had heard as a child. *Hempe*, he explained, is an acrostic, a word formed from the first letters of the names of five of England's rulers: *H*enry, *E*dward, *M*ary with *P*hilip, and *E*lizabeth. When the last one of them, Elizabeth, died in 1603—when Hempe was spun, or finished—England was done, for the new king, James, was not called king of England, but the king of Great Britain and Ireland.

when in doubt win the trick. *See* ACCORDING TO HOYLE.

when in Rome do as the Romans do. This was St. Ambrose's advice to St. Augustine when the latter consulted him as to the proper day of the week to fast. He and his mother were confused because in Rome Italians fasted on Saturday, whereas in Milan they chose another day, and St. Ambrose said: "When I am in Milan, I do as they do in Milan; but when I go to Rome, I do as Rome does!"

when it hits the fan. This expression "indicative of grave consequences" is of course an expurgated version of *when the shit hits the fan*. Common in the U.S. since about 1930, it is traced by some to the punch line of an old joke. Partridge, however, says the original reference is to "an agricultural muckspreader," without further elaboration.

when my ship comes in. *When my ship comes in* dates from several centuries ago, when shipping completely dominated commerce. Many merchants made great profits selling cargo for which they had traded in distant parts of the world and from which they were assured of fortunes if their ships made it back into home port.

when the cat's away the mice will play. *See* CHINESE LANGUAGE CONTRIBUTIONS TO ENGLISH.

when the Cocqcigrues come. In French legend the *Cocqcigrues* (kok-se-groo) are fantastic creatures unlike animals anybody has ever seen. Thus when the French say *A la venece des Cocqcigrues* ("at the coming of the Cocqcigrues") they mean "never." The same meaning is conveyed in English with *When the Cocqcigrues come*. The word is sometimes spelled *Cocquecigrue*.

when the rubber hits the road. When things get started, when action begins. Apparently a relatively new expression, heard on the political discussion program *Evans, Novak and Shields* (9/22/01). It refers to a car starting out on a trip or journey.

when the shit hits the fan. A common expression meaning "when big trouble breaks out." The saying apparently derives from the old story, dating to the 1930s, about a man who hurried upstairs to the bathroom in a bar and found no toilet. After using a hole in the floor, he went back downstairs and found the crowded bar almost empty. "Why isn't anybody here?" he asked. Replied the bartender: "Where were you when the shit hit the fan?"

when the world grows honest. In other words, never. An expression dating back to at least late 19th-century England. *Not in a month of Sundays* says the same.

when two people ride a horse, one must ride behind. A late 16th-century saying advising that when two people are working on a project, one of them must take a secondary position.

when you call me that, smile! A famous now-national expression often heard as *Smile when you call me that* (or *say that*). It has its origins in one of the most famous scenes in American literature, in Owen Wister's *The Virginian* (1902), whose eponymous cowboy hero became the basis for American heroes like John Wayne. When called a "son-of-a———" by the saddlebum Trampas, "the Virginian's pistol came out, and his hand lay on the table, holding it unaimed. And with a voice as gentle as ever, the voice that sounded almost like a caress, but drawling a little more than usual, so that there was almost a space between each word, he issued his orders to the man Trampas: 'When you call me that, smile!' And he looked at Trampas across the table. Yes the voice was gentle. But in my ears it seemed as if somewhere the bell of death was ringing." Trampas, of course, backs down, "failing to draw his steel."

when you seek revenge, dig two graves—one for your enemy, one for yourself. A Mideast proverb heard during the Palestinian-Israeli conflict in 2002. Quoted by Laura Blumenfeld, author of *Revenge: A Story of Hope* (2002).

Where's the beef? Actress Clara Peller delivered this line hundreds of times in a 1984 television ad campaign for the Wendy's hamburger chain comparing the beef content of its burgers with that of its competitors. The words soon became a catchphrase meaning "where's the real substance of a plan, or an idea, or an issue." It is still heard, often in political circles, as when Walter Mondale used it in his unsuccessful run for president in 1984.

Where's the fire? "What's your rush?" this phrase inquires when directed at a rather busy person or someone hurrying along. The Americanism is first recorded in the 1920s, but must have been in use before this. *Where's the fire?* may even date back before the invention of the gasoline fire engine in the 1890s, to the days of horse-drawn "fire engines."

where the hoot owl hollers at noon. A faraway place, so distant and deep in the dark southern woods that even the nocturnal owl can't tell day from night. The expression is from the late 19th century.

wherewithal. Money or the necessary (financial) means, as in "I don't have the wherewithal to compete with his TV ads." The term dates back at least to the early 16th century.

whig. England's Whig political party, supplanted by the Liberal Party in the late 19th century, was the party opposed to the TORIES, being generally a less conservative group in favor of more democratic government. Its name derives from the obsolete *whiggamore*, a nickname for Scots who drove wagons to Leith to purchase corn, *whiggamore* deriving from *whiggam*, a Scottish expression meaning "Git up!," addressed to horses. Bishop Burnet explained the origin of the term in *Our Times* (1723): "The south-west counties of Scotland have seldom corn enough to serve them all the year round, and, the northern parts producing more than they used, those in the west went in summer to buy at Leith the stores that came from the north. From the word *whiggam* used in driving their horses, all that drove were called the *whiggamores*, contracted into *whigs*. Now, in the year before the news came down of Duke Hamilton's defeat, the ministers animated their people to rise up and march to Edinburgh; and they came up, marching to the head of their parishes with an unheard of fury, praying and preaching all the way as they came. . . . This was called the 'Whiggamor's Inroad'; and ever after that, all who opposed the court came in contempt to be called *whigs*. From Scotland the word was brought into England, where it is now one of our unhappy terms of dissension." There was also a Whig Party in the U.S. from 1824–54, headed by Henry Clay and Daniel Webster.

whip of God. Charles O. Locke describes the term in *The Hell Bent Kid* (1957): "With the men and the horses and the steers mingling and the ground near shaking with the rush, and the dust rising, a strange thing happened. This was that a red scut of blood like a hell-red rainbow came up from the center, shooting to the sky, then bending over and fanning away south. Some horn had slashed a big artery in a cow or horse. Times later I told a Mex about it, and he rolled his eyes and said it was the Whip of God. Said he had seen similar. It is possible he had."

whipping boy. Because royalty was considered sacred, or possibly because he was born frail and sickly, the son of England's Henry VIII, the young prince who became King Edward VI when only nine years old, had a whipping boy to take all his punishments for him. Barnaby Fitzpatrick, a sturdy lad, was flogged every time Edward deserved chastisement, whether it be for botching his Greek lessons or insulting an archbishop. Despite this early form of national health insurance, Edward died of consumption in 1553 at the age of 16, the commoner Fitzpatrick surviving all his floggings and living to a comparatively old age. Anyway, the practice of princelings employing commoner whipping boys wasn't unusual in Europe four or five centuries ago; Fitzpatrick is only England's first recorded one. When the common practice ceased in more democratic times, it left us with the expression *whipping boy* for a scapegoat, someone punished for mistakes committed by another—especially an official or worker punished for the wrongs of his superior.

Whiskers. *See* G-MEN.

whiskey. *Whiskey*, first recorded in 1715, is the spelling used by the Irish, Americans, and French, while the English spell the stuff *whisky*, as do the Germans. Call for whiskey in almost any country in the world and you'll get what you want—a truly universal word that is an Anglicized version of the Gaelic *uisce beathadh*, "water of life." *See* MARTINI; SCOTCH; VODKA.

whiskey courage. *See* POT VALOR.

the whiskey is all right but the meat is weak. Computers will never take the place of human translators, as the above illustrates. It is said to have been produced recently by an electronic translator as a translation of *the spirit is willing but the flesh is weak*!

whistle for it. *See* GO WHISTLE FOR IT.

whistling up the wind. Talking wishfully. The expression has its origins in the superstitious practice of sailors in the days of sail whistling for a wind during a calm.

white bread. Relatively recent slang, *white-bread* means "bland," or "white middle-class values." It goes back to the 1970s, first recorded in 1977, when *Newsweek* reported that a top black comedian walked off a Las Vegas stage "fed up with doing white bread humor." The expression may have black origins, but this is not certain. It may also be partly a pun of *white-bred*, but it mostly refers to the synthetic white bread of the supermarket, without flavor or character.

white cliffs of Dover. The white cliffs of Dover on the Kent coast of England only became white when a huge white ship the size of a mountain tried to pass through the Strait of Dover and scraped the cliffs that color in its passage, according to ancient legend. Scientists have ruined a good story by establishing that the formation and color of the famous cliffs are due to Foraminifera plankton. The chalk cliffs have been a British patriotic symbol at least since the World War II song by Nat Burton: "There'll be bluebirds over the white cliffs of Dover . . ."

white-collar worker; blue-collar worker. *White-collar worker*, dating back to about 1920, means anyone who performs nonmanual labor; it especially indicates salaried office workers and lesser executives who haven't been unionized. His or her opposite in America is the *blue-collar worker*, anyone who works with his or her hands, is usually unionized, and often works for an hourly wage. The *white-collar worker's* counterpart in Britain is called a "black coat." All of these designations were obviously suggested by working attire, just as a "hard-hat," a construction worker, takes his or her name from the protective helmets such workers wear.

whited (painted) sepulchre. Someone who pretends to be morally better than he really is. The expression is from the Bible (Matt. 23:27): "Woe unto you, scribes and Pharisees, hypocrites! for ye are unto whited sepulchres, which indeed appear beautiful outward, but are within full of dead men's bones, and of all uncleanness."

white elephant. The king of Siam, who held the title Lord of the White Elephants, was once considered the owner of all the rare albino elephants in his kingdom, and since they were sacred to him, only he could ride or work one of them. When he wanted to punish a courtier he simply gave a white elephant to him—the beast eating his luckless victim out of house and home. This story is thought to be the source of our expression *a white elephant*—any possession, especially a big house, that is useless, eats up money, and can't be gotten rid of—even though no one has ever found any firm evidence of a king of Siam indulging in any such maleficent munificence.

White Fleet. In 1907 the United States decided to show the world we were a great naval power by sending 16 battleships and four destroyers on a world cruise. Because all these ships were painted white, they were popularly called the White Fleet, or Great White Fleet.

white-glove inspection. *See* G.I. PARTY.

White Graveyard of the Atlantic. This poetic name belongs to the famous shifting shoals of Race Point, Nauset, and Monomoy on Cape Cod, where so many sailing ships were wrecked over the past three centuries.

white hats and black hats. Early western silent movies dressed the hero in a white hat and the villain in a black hat to make it easier for the audience to follow the plot. Observed Louis L'Amour in a 1982 interview: "They joke about the black hats and the white hats, but there were very few grays in the West . . . There were a few men who shifted from one side of the law to the other, but by and large that was not true, they were just what they seemed to be."

White House. Designated the Palace by its architect, the Washington, D.C. residence of U.S. presidents was painted white after being gutted by a fire that darkened its gray Virginia limestone. The designation *White House* is first recorded in 1811, but Teddy Roosevelt made the term an official title by using it on his stationery. Today, of course, it is also a synonym for the Presidency and the U.S. executive branch.

white lie. A harmless lie, often one that is told to spare someone's feelings. The term, dating back several centuries, has its roots in the traditional belief that white is the color of purity. *Little white lies* is a frequent variation.

white list. *See* BLACKLIST.

white-livered. *See* LILY-LIVERED.

white man's burden. Rudyard Kipling (1865–1936), the first English writer to receive the Nobel Prize, was often accused of jingoism and prejudice. Kipling contributed many expressions to the language in his novels, poems, and stories, including the well-known *white man's burden*, which depicts black, brown, and yellow people in Great Britain's colonies at the time as backward children the white man must take care of. The derogatory term is rarely heard anymore.

white meat. A Victorian term still often used in America for the breast meat of a chicken or turkey, which the British call breast. "May I have some breast?" Winston Churchill once asked his American hostess at a buffet luncheon. "In this country, Mr. Churchill, we say *white meat* or *dark meat*," his hostess replied, a little prissily. Churchill apologized and the next day sent her an orchid along with a card reading, "I would be most obliged if you would pin this on your white meat." *White meat* and *dark meat* are also derogatory slang terms applied to white or black men and women, usually in a sexual sense.

The White Queen. This designation has nothing to do with Mary Queen of Scots' complexion. She is called *The White Queen* because she wore white mourning clothes after the death of her French husband Francis II.

white rhinoceros. The white rhinoceros of Africa is misnamed, for it is slate gray in color. The white rhino takes its first name from the Dutch *wijd*, "wide," for its wide upper lip and muzzle, this corrupted to *white* over the years. *See also* RHINOCEROS.

white slavery. *The White Slave*, an 1882 play by Barley Campbell, popularized the term *white slavery* for prostitution. The term is also used as a synonym for the widespread indentured servitude (a form of slavery) of whites in Colonial America.

whitey. A derogatory term for a white man that doesn't appear to have been much used by blacks before the early 1960s, when Black Muslims began preaching about *white devils*. The first recorded use of the term, however, dates back to 1828, when an Australian writer employed the terms *blacky* and *whitey* in referring to Australian aborigines and white men. *See also* HONKIE; OFAY; PALEFACE; PECKERWOOD; REDNECK; WASP.

whiz. *See* ONOMATOPOEIA.

whodunit. Two writers for the show business paper *Variety* are usually proposed as the coiners of the word *whodunit*, for "a mystery story": Sime Silverman, in 1936, or Wolfe Kaufman in 1935. But the term wasn't invented by either of them. Daniel Gordon used whodunit in the July 1930 *American News of Books* and probably used it first.

Who he? Writers often find these traditional words scribbled on manuscript pages next to names unknown to their editors. The first editor to do this seems to have been Harold Ross of *The New Yorker*. On one of Robert Benchley's manuscripts Ross, who had a "profound ignorance," according to Dorothy Parker, wrote "Who he?" in the margin opposite a rather obscure name. Benchley wrote below: "You keep out of this."

whole ball of wax. Everything sticks to wax and leaves an impression on touching it. Therefore, *whole ball of wax* (sometimes *ball of wax*) has come to mean "everything, the whole lot, the whole kit and caboodle." That is possibly the origin of this common Americanism, first recorded in 1953 and still common on Madison Avenue, although several more complicated explanations have been suggested by word and phrase Hawkshaws.

One such guess involves wax balls used in a complicated drawing for the distribution of estates; another claims *whole ball of wax* is a corruption of *whole bailiwick*. No one is sure.

whole enchilada. *See* BIG ENCHILADA.

whole hog. *See* GO WHOLE HOG.

whole kit and caboodle. The *caboodle* in this American expression meaning "the whole lot," is the same as the word *boodle*, for "a pile of money," deriving from the Dutch *boedal*, "property." The *whole kit*, of course, means entire outfit. The phrase doesn't read "the whole kit and boodle" because Americans like alliteration in speech and added a "k" sound before *boodle* in the phrase.

whole megillah. *See* MEGILLAH.

whole nine yards. For at least 45 years this expression has meant "all of it, everything," as in "Give me the whole nine yards." It did not arise in the garment business but possibly among construction workers, the *nine yards* referring to the maximum capacity a cement-mixer truck can carry—nine cubic yards of cement. There is no firm proof of this or any other derivation, however.

wholesale; retail. Both of these terms have their origins in the cloth trade. *Wholesale* initially meant to sell whole pieces of cloth, while *retail* derives from a French word meaning to cut up (*tailor*, similarly, means "a cutter"), *retailer* coming to mean anyone who sold anything in small, cut-up lots. According to the real estate brokers Cushman and Wakefield, the world's most expensive location for a retail store is Manhattan's 57th St. from Fifth Avenue to Park Avenue, with rents averaging $700 a square foot annually. New York's Fifth Avenue between 49th and 59th St. is in second place ($650 a square foot), and third place goes to Causeway Bay in Hong Kong ($523 a square foot).

whole shebang. The earliest recorded use of *shebang* is by Walt Whitman in *Specimen Days* (1862), and Mark Twain used it several times as well. Meaning a poor, temporary dwelling, a shack, this Americanism possibly derives from the Anglo-Irish *shebeen*, "a low illegal drinking establishment," older than it by a century or so. In the expression *the whole shebang*, first recorded in 1879, *shebang* means not just a shack but anything at all, that is, any present concern, thing, business—as in "You can take the whole shebang," you can take all of it.

whole shooting match. Large crowds gathered at frontier shooting matches in America to watch marksmen compete in hitting targets, snuffing out candles, etc. *The whole shooting match* thus came to mean "the whole crowd in attendance" and, by extension, "the totality, everything, the whole thing." An earlier British phrase *the whole shoot*, meaning the same but with a different origin, may have strengthened the usage.

Whoops! Traced only to 1925 by the *O.E.D.* (Volume IV, Supplement, 1986), *whoops* may be considerably older, though there is no proof of this. It is, of course, an exclamation of dismay or surprise when one stumbles or recognizes a mistake one has made. The expression first appeared in a *New Yorker* cartoon, in the form of *whoops-a-daisy*; it isn't recorded as *whoops* until 1937, in one of Ezra Pound's letters, of all places.

whoop ti do.   A cowboy cry, as in this old cowboy song quoted by Edna Ferber in *Cimarron* (1930):

> Hi rickety whoop ti do,
> How I love to sing to you.
> Oh, I could sing an' dance with glee,
> If I was as young as I used to be.

whoosh.   *Whoosh*, as an exclamation evocative of a sudden explosive rush of sound (it is used by one television sportscaster presently to indicate a basketball shot going through the hoop), is first recorded in 1899 and is probably older. The term is an Americanism with limited British usage and is an example of ONOMATOPOEIA.

whore.   *Hore*, the first English spelling of *whore*, was recorded at the beginning of the 12th century, deriving from Norse *horr* and Gothic *hors*, meaning "adulterer," the word *hore*, strangely enough, related to Latin *carus*, "dear," which gives us terms of endearment such as *caress* and *cherish*. *Whore* is still regarded as a terrible insult to a woman, more so even than *prostitute*, HARLOT, and TRAMP, not to mention many "softer" terms such as *courtesan*, HOOKER, *hustler, call girl, sporting girl, painted woman, lady of the night*, and *streetwalker*. Obsolete U.S. synonyms include *soiled doves* and *calico queens*. In extended use *whore* is applied to anyone who sells out his or her principles for personal gain.

"Who reads an American book?"   British author Sydney Smith almost set off a full-scale literary war when he asked this famous sardonic rhetorical question in a book review he wrote for the *Edinburgh Review* in 1820. Smith, however, had been reviewing the *Statistical Annals of the United States* by Adam Seybert and was on his way toward making an ironic point that has little to do with literature, as the last paragraph of his essay shows: "In the four corners of the globe, who reads an American book? or goes to an American play? or looks at an American picture or statue? What does the world yet owe to American physicians or surgeons? What new substances have their chemists discovered? or what old ones have they analyzed? What new constellations have been discovered by the telescopes of Americans? What have they done in mathematics? Who drinks out of American glasses? or eats from American plates? or wears American coats or gowns? or sleeps in American blankets? Finally, under which of the tyrannical governments of Europe is every sixth man a slave, whom his fellow creatures may buy, and sell, and torture?"

whortleberry.   *Whortleberry* originated as the dialect form of *hurtleberry* in southwestern England. *Hurtleberry*, however, remains a mystery etymologically speaking, though there have been attempts to link the *hurt* in the word to the fact that the blue berry could resemble a small black and blue mark or "hurt," on a person's body. Both words refer to the berry *Vaccinium myrtillus* of the blueberry family, and our word *huckleberry* probably derives from *hurtleberry*—which makes Mark Twain's famous character, perhaps aptly, "Hurt" Finn.

Who's Afraid of Virginia Woolf?   Playwright Edward Albee (1928–) has said that he got the title of his famous 1962 play from a line of graffiti he saw in Manhattan. A leading figure of the new drama of the absurd, Albee won a Pulitzer Prize for his play *Three Tall Women* (1994).

who watches the watchdogs?   These ancient words take many forms, but derive from the Roman saying *Quis custodiet custodes?*, which means "the shepherd watches over the sheep, but who keeps watch over the shepherds?" The expression is used to indicate doubt about the integrity of someone in a position of trust.

who won't be ruled by the rudder must be ruled by the rock.   This nautical saying isn't found in the *Oxford English Dictionary*, *Bartlett's Familiar Quotations*, or any other major collection of quotations. Dating back at least a century in the U.S., it means "those who won't listen to reason must suffer the consequences," like a ship that runs upon a rock if it doesn't answer the helm.

Why did the chicken cross the road?   Among the oldest of jokes still told (by children), the answer being "to get to the other side." The words date back at least to mid-19th-century England. They are also used by adults as a reply to what seems to be an unanswerable question. A recent gangster film, *Heist* (2001), has the lines: "Why did the chicken cross the road?" "Because the road crossed the chicken."

Why should the devil have all the good tunes?   English composer Charles Wesley (1707–88) reputedly said this. The author of over 6,500 hymns, Wesley put the words of them to popular tunes of the day to insure their popular appeal. Many of these hymns, including the famous "Hark! the Herald Angels Sing," and "Christ, the Lord, is Risen Today," are still great church favorites.

Wichita.   The Wichita Indians, and thus Wichita, Kansas, which is named for the tribe, may take their name from the tribe's word *wichita* (waist-deep). One old story, which I can't verify, says that these Indians pushed their squaws out into rivers to see how deep they were. If a place was safe for crossing, the squaws would cry out "wichita" to the relatively timid braves on shore, who proceeded to ford the river. If they sank, presumably, the river wasn't safe to cross.

wickiup.   Indians in Colorado and California sometimes lived in crudely constructed huts called *wickiups*, improvised structures made of brush, saplings, or both. Cowboys often used the word in referring humorously to their own homes.

wide-awakes.   *Wide-awakes* were young Republicans, some 400,000 in number throughout the country, who avidly supported Abraham Lincoln for president in 1860. The group originated in Hartford, Connecticut, and was named for the hat members wore. The hat was made of a fabric that contained no "nap"—hence the pun *wide-awake*.

wide of the mark.   An ancient expression dating at least to the 1600s, this phrase means "inaccurate or erroneous, irrelevant." It probably comes from the sport of archery, referring to an archer's unsuccessful shot at the mark or target.

wide place in the road.   Truckers popularized this synonym for a very small town. But the phrase was born over a century ago in the American West, where there were many towns so small they were not even on the map.

Widow.   *The Widow* is often encountered in literature as slang for champagne, the words a translation of the name of the excellent Veuve Cliquot brand. This usage dates back to Victorian times, when the *widow* was also slang for "the gallows." A real Widow Cliquot may have run the brand's vineyard.

widow and orphan makers.   A name given to the famed Pennsylvania rifles that American backwoodsmen used in the Battle of New Orleans (1815) in the War of 1812. The accurate rifle and these sharpshooters were a lethal combination.

widow maker.   Rudyard Kipling is the first writer to record *widow maker* as a synonym for the sea, in *Puck of Pook's Hill* (1906): "What is a woman that you forsake her . . . To go with the old grey Widow-maker?" *Widow maker* was used by Shakespeare for a killer in general, however, and it seems likely that the term was used before Kipling to describe the great elementary force that made widows of so many sailors' wives. *Widow maker* can also describe trees or limbs that fall on people.

widow's peak.   A point formed by the hair growing down and meeting in the middle of the forehead is called a widow's peak. The term, which dates back at least to the 19th century, derives from the earlier *peak*, for "the point of a beard," and possibly from the pointed or peaked hoods that old women sometimes wore. Superstition had it that women with widow's peaks would become widows at an early age.

widow's walk.   A widow's walk is an elevated observatory on a dwelling, usually with a railing and affording a good view of the ocean. These watchtowers, often seen on the roofs of old houses, date back to Colonial times and were so named because many women walked in vain on them, waiting for incoming ships that never returned. Taking the form of a cupola, railed-in deck, or balcony, they have also been called, less poetically, the walk, the captain's walk, the observatory, and the lookout.

widow's weeds.   *See* WEED.

wigging.   To be dressed down, reprimanded by a superior. The phrase dates back to the 18th century, when most important people wore wigs. Scoldings from such people were, of course, commonplace.

wild and wooly West.   First came *wild West*, recorded in 1851 and so called because the American West was relatively lawless compared with the "civilized" East. Some 30 years passed before the more alliterative *wild and wooly West* was invented by some unknown poet, the *wooly* in the phrase perhaps referring to uncurried wild horses or the sheepskin chaps some cowboys wore, or perhaps to the bragging of cowboys in a popular song:

I'm a wooly wolf and full of fleas,
I never been curried below the knees—
And this is my night to howl!

The first use of the expression, in an 1885 book called *Texas Cow Boy*, has *wild and wooly* referring to a herd of steers.

Wild Bill Hickok.   Any fabled gunfighter; after James Butler "Wild Bill" Hickok (1837–76), army scout, gambler, and town marshall of Abilene, Kansas. Though a handsome dandy, with long blond hair hanging over his shoulders, Hickok was first called "Duck Bill" after his long nose and protruding lip. He met his violent end at the hands of a paranoid rival who shot him in the back of the head while he was playing poker. *See* DEADMAN'S HAND.

wild card.   The term *wild card* has been known in card games since the early 16th century, meaning "a card whose value is determined by the players in a particular game." Since then it has taken on special meanings in several sports, including tennis and football, and has come to mean generally anything outside of the normal rules or categories, an unpredictable person, thing, or event.

wildcat.   A wildcat venture, such as a wildcat oil well, is generally a speculative one. The word *wildcat* here comes from the term *wildcat bank*, which originally referred to a Michigan bank that went bankrupt in the 1830s and had on its banknotes a prominent picture of a panther or wildcat.

Wildean.   For the British writer and wit Oscar Wilde (1854–1900). His much publicized affairs and trial made his first name a British slang expression for a homosexual, *to Oscar*, *Oscarizing*, and *Oscar-Wilding*, in fact, meaning active homosexuality. Wilde is also represented by *Wildean*, referring to his razor-sharp wit. In this respect he was probably even greater than George Bernard Shaw. Once Wilde told a customs inspector that he had nothing to declare but his genius; another time he remarked to some proud chamber of commerce types that Niagara Falls "would be more spectacular if it flowed the other way."

wild-goose chase.   Englishmen in the late 16th century invented a kind of horse race called the wild-goose chase in which the lead horse could go off in any direction and the succeeding horses had to follow accurately the course of the leader at precise intervals, like wild geese following the leader in formation. At first the phrase *wild-goose chase* figuratively meant an erratic course taken by one person and followed by another; Shakespeare used it in this sense. But later the common term's origins were forgotten and a *wild-goose chase* came to mean "a pursuit of anything as unlikely to be caught as a wild goose," any foolish, fruitless, or hopeless quest.

wild man of Borneo.   *See* THERE'S A SUCKER BORN EVERY MINUTE.

wild oats.   *See* SOW ONE'S WILD OATS.

wild rice.   The seed of an aquatic grass rather than a true rice, wild rice was grown and eaten by American Indians. The words were first recorded in 1778. Wild rice was earlier called water oats and water rice and has also been known as Indian rice and Meneninee, after a Chippewa subtribe that grew it. *See also* CAROLINA RICE; PIEDMONT RICE.

Wild West show. A circus of cowboys and Indians performing various feats ranging from riding to shooting, the words first applied to William F. (Buffalo Bill) Cody's Wild West Show, which opened at Omaha, Nebraska May 17, 1883.

Wiley E. Coyote. The name of this famous cartoon character, who has become synonymous with ineptitude and humiliation for his futile efforts to get Roadrunner, was coined by cartoonist and director Chuck Jones (Charles Martin Jones, 1912–2002) when he invented the Coyote-Roadrunner series in 1949. There is no dialogue except "beep beep" in the cartoon. The animator claimed Mark Twain's *Roughing It* inspired his invention. Mr. Jones also solely created the skunk Pepe Le Pew, sketched Bugs Bunny for more than 50 years, and helped create Daffy Duck, Elmer Fudd, and Porky Pig, among other beloved cartoon characters. His autobiography is entitled *Chuck Amuck: The Life and Times of an Animated Cartoonist* (1989). *See* WHAT'S UP DOC?

Williamson. "The terrible Williamsons" have fleeced so many people in recent years that their name has become a generic term for itinerant hustlers. An inbred clan of gyp artists numbering about 2,000, the family descends from Robert Logan Williamson, who emigrated from Scotland to Brooklyn in the 1890s and soon imported his relatives. Today the wandering clan makes its headquarters and major burial grounds in Cincinnati, a crossroads city, or at least they meet there once a year in the spring to bury their dead, exchange notes, and renew friendships. There is not a nonviolent hustler's trick unknown to the Williamsons, from resurfacing a homeowner's driveway with crankcase oil—and departing across the county line with the payment before the next rain washes the "blacktop" away—to an attractive Williamson woman selling her "dead mother's valuable Irish linen" door to door in order to "buy milk" for a baby conveniently bawling in her arms. The family still does well, despite many newspaper and magazine exposés of their cons.

William Tell's apple. According to fable, William Tell was a famous marksman and the champion of Swiss independence when Switzerland was ruled by Austria in the 13th century. Tell refused to salute the imperial governor and was sentenced to shoot an apple from his son's head. After doing this, another arrow fell from his coat and the governor demanded to know what it had been intended for. "To shoot you with, had I failed in the task imposed upon me," Tell told him and he was cast in prison, from which he was rescued and went on to lead his country to freedom. There are at least 10 earlier versions of the tale involving other countries and heroes, the oldest found in the Old Norse *Vilkinia Saga*.

William the Conqueror was [came] before Richard the Third. With the passing of time there have been many variations, one more risqué than the other, on the old joke about Shakespeare, actor Richard Burbage, and their lady friend. The incident may or may not have occurred, but here is the original story from the diary of 17th-century English author John Manningham:

> Upon a time when Burbage played Richard the Third there was a citizen grew so far on liking him, that before she went from the play she appointed him to come that night unto her by the name of Richard the Third. Shakespeare, overhearing their conversation, went before, was entertained and at his game ere Burbage came. Then, message being brought that Richard the Third was at the door, Shakespeare caused return to be made that William the Conqueror was before Richard the Third.

willow. The willow is a lovely tree with a lovely name full of *l*'s and *w*'s. As Ivor Brown wrote in *A Word in Your Ear* (1945): "The willow has ever been as much the poet's joy as a symbol of mourning and melancholy. It both weeps and bewitches. 'Sing, willow, willow, willow,' Always it sings . . . so lovely is the tree, in all its forms, not least *Salix babylonica*, the weeping willow." To wax prosaic, a few species of the *Salix* genus yield the drug *salicin*, used in making aspirin. *Wearing a willow* means to be in mourning, especially for a wife or sweetheart, the weeping willow from earliest times having been a symbol of sorrow. In the Book of Psalms the Jews in captivity are said to hang their harps on willow branches as a sign of mourning. Shakespeare's famous song in *Othello* has the refrain "Sing willow, willow, willow":

> The fresh streams ran by her, and murmur'd her moans;
>   Sing willow, willow, willow
> Her salt tears fell from her and softened the stones;
>   Sing willow, willow, willow.

To wear the green willow means to be sad or disappointed in love.

willy-willy; willywaw. A willy-willy is a severe tropical cyclone common to Australia that can be seen approaching in a high column of dust from a great distance. The word is probably an Australian Aboriginal term for the phenomenon, but Partridge suggests that *whirlwind* became *whirl*, which became *wil*, which became *willy!* Willywaw are squalls in the Straits of Magellan, but light, variable winds elsewhere at sea, the word either deriving from *willy-willy* above or as a corruption of *whirl-whirly*.

Wilson's petrel. Alexander Wilson (1766–1813) was a Scottish-born American ornithologist whose *American Ornithology* (1808–14) is a classic in its field. Not only Wilson's petrel, but Wilson's phalarope, plover, snipe and thrush are named in his honor.

wimp. Weak, unmanly, indecisive men have been called wimps since the 1970s and the term is still frequently used. Although the *Popeye* cartoon character Wimpy (of hamburger fame) may have influenced the coinage, it more likely comes from *whimper*.

Wimpy. J. Wellington Wimpy, a hamburger-loving character in the Popeye comic strip, gave the Wimpy hamburger chain its name about 1939. J. Wellington Wimpy could eat scores of burgers at a sitting; it was the only thing he could do better than Popeye, who specialized in SPINACH.

Winchester. The Model 73 Winchester rifle, made in 1873, is the prototype for all the famous Winchester models now extensively used for hunting. The first Winchester, however, was made in 1866. Oliver F. Winchester (1810–80) manufactured the rifle at his plant in New Haven, Connecticut, the weapon based on a number of patents the industrialist had acquired from different inventors. This early repeater became generic for any repeating rifle and was widely used on the frontier. Its design, a lever-action rifle with a tubular magazine in the forestock, became the standard repeating rifle mechanism; the Winchester Arms Company, which still operates today, has been eminent in its field for many years.

Winchester geese. In the 16th century prostitution and geese raising were two major Winchester industries and British prostitutes were called Winchester geese, probably because they seemed almost as ubiquitous in the area as the birds. The first part of their name may honor the bishop of Winchester, however, as the brothels in Southwark were under his jurisdiction, and the Church received rent from many establishments based in houses he owned. These revenues, incidentally, helped found and maintain a number of esteemed Oxford colleges. A Winchester goose also came to mean a venereal bubo (sore), or anyone infected with venereal disease.

windfall. Unexpected good fortune has been called a windfall since the early 16th century. The expression has its origins in the medieval English law that forbade commoners from cutting down trees but allowed them to keep any trees or branches that the wind blew down.

windfucker. An old name for the kestrel that is recorded as early as 1599 by English author Thomas Nashe: "The Kestrelles or windfuckers that filling themselves with winds, fly against the winde euermore." The kestrel (*Falco tinnunculus*) is a small falcon noted for hovering, its head facing into the wind. Exactly why its name also came to mean a worthless or disgraceful person is not known—probably because of the name "windfucker" itself.

windjammer. *Windjammer* meant a "horn player," then came to mean a "talkative person or windbag," and finally, at the end of the 19th century, was the name for any ship with sails. It seems that windy defenders of sailing vessels at the beginning of the age of steamships boasted so much about the superiority of sail that they were called *windjammers* and their name soon became attached to the sailing ships they bragged about.

windmills in one's head. *See* TILT AT WINDMILLS.

window. "An eye of the wind" is the meaning of the Old Norse *vindauga* (*vinde*, "wind," plus *auga*, "eye"), which gave us our word *window*. The poetic word appropriately suggests a window's function of letting in both air and light. Shakespeare made *window* a verb in *Antony and Cleopatra* when he had Antony ask: "Wouldn'st thou be windowed [put in a window] in great Rome?" The Old English for *window* was *eyethirl*, "eye hole."

window-shopping. A. T. Stewart's cast-iron palace, built in 1862, was the first store encountered when walking north along New York's Ladies Mile. At the top of this stretch of Broadway and Sixth Avenue between Ninth and 23rd Streets was Stern Brothers. Many early American department stores, such as R. H. Macy's, Lord and Taylor, and B. Altman, lined the elegant, cobblestoned streets of this shopping district, which played host daily to exquisitely clad ladies in flowing gowns and feathered bonnets who alighted from their horse-drawn carriages and floated toward the grand emporiums or came on the Sixth Avenue El. Women promenaded in their best here up until the end of the century, when the shopping district began to move uptown, but many of the old buildings that housed the stores still remain. So does the term *window-shopping*, which may have been inspired by the women who strolled by the displays these great stores designed for them. The Ladies Mile Historic District extends from Union Square at 23rd Street. For early photographs of the stores see my *The Grand Emporiums* (1978).

Windsor knot. The neat triangular knot in a tie is named for England's fashionable duke of Windsor (1894–1972), who became the Edward VIII in 1936 and abdicated the throne later that year so that he could marry American divorcée Mrs. Wallis Simpson: "I have found it impossible to carry the heavy burden of responsibility and to discharge my duties as King as I would wish to do, without the help and support of the woman I love."

Windy Cap. Laplanders of yore and many other ancient peoples made a profitable trade in selling favorable winds to mariners, as did individuals like Bessie Millie of the Orkney Islands, who sold winds to sailors for sixpence as late as 1814. These people undoubtedly had knowledge of the weather that others didn't have at the time, but the belief persisted that they could actually influence the winds. It is said that King Eric of Sweden was so familiar with the "evil spirits" that controlled the winds that wherever he turned his cap, the wind would blow. Olaus Magnus, a Swedish historian, says he was commonly known as *Windy Cap*.

Windy City. A nickname for Chicago that was first recorded in the late 19th century. It is said to have been coined by a *New York Sun* reporter who was put off by Chicagoans' windy bragging during the 1896 World's Fair. Chicago is not an especially windy city, so the blustering theory seems tenable.

wine book. According to an October 31, 1989 article in the *New York Times*, a wine book is a ledger in which the crew leaders or bosses of migrant workers "record the claims that they make on the worker's wages, beyond the $40 or $50 per week that they charge for their meals. The name of a worker is written at the top of each page, which, except for the occasional date and odd notation is nothing but a list of numbers showing dollars and cents. But the crew leaders know what transaction each charge represents." Transactions often include wine, of course, and also cocaine and crack, the crew leaders rarely telling a worker the high price of the drugs until the money is deducted from his salary. Such are the more subtle ways of debt servitude today. The expression *wine book* has been around at least two or three decades but is not often recorded.

wine of ape. Surly or obnoxious drunkenness. Brewer tells us: "There is a Talmud parable which says that Satan came one day to drink with Noah, and slew a lamb, a lion, a pig, and an ape, to teach Noah that man before wine is in him is a lamb, when he drinks moderately he is a lion, when like a sot he is a swine, but after that any further excess makes him an ape that senselessly chatters and jabbers." Other sources say Satan killed and buried the animals near vines Noah was planting. Why Satan would give Noah any advice is not explained.

wine, women, and song. Despite Thackeray's tongue-in-cheek attribution, this famous phrase, and the couplet of advice to men that it comes from wasn't written by Martin Luther! German poet Johann Heinrich Voss wrote the little poem in about 1775:

> Who does not love wine, women and song
> Remains a fool his whole life long.

And Byron wrote:

> Let us have wine and women
> mirth and laughter
> sermons and soda-water the day after.

wing it. To do something without preparation or without much preparation. This was first a 19th-century theater expression that originated with actors who went on stage without knowing their lines, usually in taking the place of an absent actor. They depended on prompters in the wings to get them through the performance.

win hands down. A jockey who wins a race *hands down* is so far ahead of the field that he doesn't have to flick the reins to urge his horse forward and crosses the finish line with his hands down, letting up on the reins. From racetrack slang toward the end of the 19th century the metaphor *to win hands down* passed into general use for any easy, effortless victory, a walkover.

winning isn't everything, it's the only thing. The cynical remark is almost always attributed to Green Bay Packers coach Vince Lombardi in the 1960s. It should be credited to a Hollywood scriptwriter, having first been uttered by John Wayne when playing a football coach in *Trouble Along the Way* (1953)

win one for the Gipper. This one is so well known, of course, because President Ronald Reagan played George Gipp, or the Gipper, in a movie about Knute Rockne and his football team at Notre Dame (*Knute Rockne, All American*, 1940). Rockne urged his team to go out and "win this game for the Gipper," who on his deathbed had requested that the team win a game in his honor—and Notre Dame proceeded to do it. Actually, Gipp had made this request of Rockne in 1920 when dying of pneumonia and the coach had used the same appeal several other times before the 1928 game with heavily favored Army that is depicted in the film.

win one's spurs. The allusion here is not to cowboys of the American West but to those days four centuries before when knighthood was in flower and young men dubbed knights by their lords were presented with a gilded pair of spurs. Since then the expression *to win one's spurs* has been extended from the idea of a knight performing a valorous act and winning honor to anyone performing any deed and gaining honor among his peers—from a doctor delivering his first baby to an author publishing his first book.

win, place, and show. Terms for horses that finish first, second, and third in a race. *Win, place, and show* originated at early United States racetracks where small boards were used to record the names of the first three finishers of every race. These boards were so small that only the names of the first two finishers were "placed" on the first board, *place* thus designating the number two horse. A second board was used to "show" the name of the third finisher, and *show* became the term for third place.

winter bloom. *See* WITCH HAZEL.

winter golf. Thousands of golfers don't let northern winters interfere with their outdoor golf games, braving the severest weather to play on the links. *Winter golf* is said to have been invented by British author Rudyard Kipling, a devoted golfer who painted his golf balls red so that he could play in the snow, but there were probably others who went to such extreme lengths before him.

wireless. This is an old British name for the radio that never really caught on in the U.S., although it has had limited use here. The word derives directly from the name of the Marconi Wireless Telegraph Company. Guglielmo Marconi (1874–1937) was an Italian inventor in the field of wireless telegraphy and his company tried to establish a monopoly in the North Atlantic. Eventually the British applied the name for his wireless telegraph to the wireless radio, though now they too generally say *radio*. Marconi is remembered more directly for the marconigram, a radiogram, and the Marconi mast, once used for the mast for a radio antenna and now any elaborately rigged mast on a ship. *See also* RADIO; TELEGRAPH; TELEPHONE; TELEVISION.

wirepuller. *See* SPOILS SYSTEM.

Wisconsin. Wisconsin takes its name from the Algonquian name for a river within its boundaries that translates as either "place of the beaver" or "grassy place." The Badger State was admitted to the Union in 1848 as our 30th state.

wisdom teeth. *See* CUT ONE'S EYETEETH.

wiseacre. *See* ACRE.

wisecrack. A witty, often caustic remark, the word possibly coined in the early 20th century by vaudvillian CHIC SALES. *Wisecrack* is sometimes heard today as *crack wise*.

wiseguy. Originally, since the early 1900s, *wiseguy* meant "a smug know-it-all, a shrewd person." It has since become another name for a member of the Mafia, made famous in Nicholas Pileggi and Henry Hill's book *Wiseguys* (1985), which became the movie *Goodfellas* (1990).

wisest man of Greece. Socrates was declared the wisest man of Greece by the Delphic oracle. He said he deserved the honor "because I alone of all the Greeks know that I know nothing." His remark may be the basis of many similar sayings, such as the commonly heard *The longer I live the more I realize how little I know.*

wisteria. A spelling error made by Thomas Nuttal, curator of Harvard's Botanical Garden, led to the accepted misspelling of this beautiful flowering plant—*wisteria* being the common spelling today even though *wistaria* is correct. Nuttal, who named the plant after Dr. Caspar Wistar, had meant to write "wistaria," but his slip of the pen was perpetuated by later writers, and *wisteria* has become accepted. All attempts to remedy the situation have failed, even Joshua Logan's play *The Wistaria Trees,* in which the author purposely spelled the word with an *a.* A Philadelphia Quaker, Caspar Wistar (1761–1818) taught "anatomy, mid-wifery, and surgery" at what was then the College of Pennsylvania. The son of a noted colonial glassmaker, Dr. Wistar wrote America's first anatomy textbook, succeeded Jefferson as head of the American Philosophical Society, and his home became the Sunday afternoon meeting place of many notable Philadelphians. Anyone in the vicinity of Sierra Madre, California in the late springtime should see the giant Chinese wisteria near the Los Angeles State and County Arboretum. During its five-week blooming period this giant species becomes a vast field filled with over one and a half million blossoms, the largest flowering plant in the world. Planted in 1892 the fabulous vine covers almost an acre, has branches surpassing 500 feet in length, and weighs over 252 tons.

Witch City. A nickname for Salem, Massachusetts, where in 1692 a wave of hysterical witch-hunting led to the hanging of 19 innocent people. This was the beginning of witch-hunting in America, but the practice had been common elsewhere since ancient times. Thousands were executed worldwide from 1450 to 1650. In England "Witch-Finder General" Matthew Hopkins (1621–47), as he named himself, hanged more than 100 people in one year. Since about 1920 *witch-hunting* has been applied to any effort to expose subversion or disloyalty, usually based on little evidence.

witches weigh less than a Bible. When Jane Wenham was tried as a witch in 1712 she was set free because people at her trial insisted that she be weighed. A true witch always weighed less than a Bible, according to British superstition, and Jane weighed considerably more than the 12 pound church Bible of the day.

witch hazel. Witch hazel solution is extracted from the leaves and bark of the witch hazel shrub. This plant, in turn, might take its first name from the fact that its branches were often used as divining or dousing rods to locate water. The *O.E.D.* however, believes that the *witch* here comes from the Anglo-Saxon *sych,* meaning a tree with pliant branches. Witch hazels (*Hamamelis*) are not true hazel trees. They are also called winter bloom because they bloom from October to April when their twigs are bare. The cuckold hazel, also called the beaked hazel, is a true hazel of the genus *Corylus,* and takes its name not because wives betrayed their husbands under it but because of its long hornlike fruits, which someone centuries ago compared to a cuckold's horns.

witch-hunting. *See* WITCH CITY.

with a heart and a half. A lovely old Irish expression of thanks, first recorded in 1636. "Once more to you with a heart and a half," wrote the first man to record this expression, in ending a letter to his sweetheart.

with all deliberate speed. Chief Justice Earl Warren used these words in the historic *Brown* v. *Board of Education* decision of May 17, 1954, when the Supreme Court ruled that all public schools be integrated and racial discrimination be ended in them "with all deliberate speed." Oliver Wendell Holmes, however, recorded the words first, in 1912.

wither on the vine. Anyone who has seen grapes shrivel and dry up on the vine when left unpicked has a good picture of the source of this phrase. It means "neglected and wasted" and has been used in this figurative sense for several centuries.

within an ace of. Dice, not cards, gave us this expression for "coming as close as one can get," the "ace" in the phrase referring to the ace, or small point, on a single die. Originally the expression was *within ambsace of,* "ambsace" being a mispronunciation of the Old French for the lowest possible throw in dice—*ambes as* ("both aces"). But by the 17th century "ambsace" was further corrupted to "an ace" and the phrase became *within an ace of. Ambsace* itself was long a figurative term for bad luck. Today *snake eyes* is better known as the lowest throw in dice.

without a pot to piss in. Having not a thing to one's name, not even a chamber pot. *Piss pot* for a chamber pot dates back to the early 15th century and PISS itself goes back a few centuries earlier, deriving from the Latin *pissiare.*

without rhyme or reason. Francis Bacon wrote that Sir Thomas More, chancellor to Henry VIII, once told a friend who had versified a rather poor book he had written: "That's better! It's rhyme now, anyway. Before it was neither rhyme nor reason." But More's witty remark isn't the basis for our expression meaning lacking in sense or any other justification, fit for neither amusement nor instruction. Used in English since the early 16th century, the phrase is simply a translation of the medieval French saying, *na rhyme ne raison.*

with tail between legs. When the expression was figuratively applied no one knows, but it must have been long ago, for as early as 1400 writers have described frightened dogs with their tails between their legs. The attitude of scared, cowardly dogs was transferred to any thoroughly cowed and abased person who stands back *with tail between legs.* The word *coward* is ultimately from the Latin *cauda,* "tail"; it may be an allusion to an animal cowering with its tail between its legs or "turning tail" and running.

witticism. John Dryden coined *witticism* in his play *The State of Innocence, and Fall of Man* (1677), a dramatic version in rhymed couplets of *Paradise Lost* said to be written with Milton's permission, but which was never performed, though the immoderate Dryden considered it "undoubtedly one of the greatest, most noble and most sublime poems which either this age or nation has produced." The first official poet laureate and royal "historiographer" was immoderate in his wit, too—but he did not pen the acid remarks about John Wilmot, the second earl of Rochester, that Wilmot thought Dryden had written in 1679. Thinking he had, however, the furious Wilmot hired a band of masked thugs who severely cudgeled the poet. The prolific Dryden based *witticism* on the earlier *criticism*, writing: "A mighty Wittycism (if you will pardon a new word!) but there is some difference between a Laughter and a Critique."

woe-begone. Woe-begone people, those oppressed with misfortune, distress, or sorrow, have been so called since before Chaucer's time. The word is a combination of *woe* and *bigon*, "beat," as is illustrated by the Old English sentence "Me is woe bigon" ("I am beset with woe").

woe is me. *Woe*, first recorded in about 725, has been called "a truly international exclamation of sorrow." The world has always been full of woes, including the Latin *vae* (*vae victus*, "woe unto the conquered!"), the Welsh *gwoe*, the Gothic *wai*, the Armenian *vae*, and the Old Persian *avoi*, among many, many others. The still common expression *woe is me!* is first recorded in 1205 and is probably much older.

wog. Arabs, Indians, and Orientals were called *wogs* by the British during the heyday of their empire, or at least since about 1830, the derogatory appellation *wog* said to be a word formed from the first letters of *wily* (or *westernized*) *Oriental gentleman*. Another *O.E.D.* suggestion is *gollywog*, "with reference to frizzy or curly hair," *wog* "indeed being a nursery shortening of *golliwog*."

wolffia. Said to be the smallest flowering plant in the world, wolffia, of the genus *Wolffia*, is named in honor of German physician and botanist Dr. J. F. Wolff, who over a short lifetime—he died in 1806 when only 28—made many valuable botanical contributions. *See* ZINNIA.

wolf in sheep's clothing. One of the oldest of expressions, still used in many languages, *a wolf in sheep's clothing* dates back to biblical times, being recorded in Matt. 7:15: "Beware of false prophets, which come to you in sheep's clothing, but inwardly they are ravaging wolves."

wolf man. Werewolves have been the subject of legend throughout the world for centuries, but the most memorable film portrayal of one was by Lon Chaney, Jr., in *The Wolf Man* (1941). Chaney played a lycanthrope who turned into the beast after being bitten by a real wolf (played by Bela Lugosi) and could be killed only by a silver bullet. He thought it was the best performance of his career, calling it "My Baby," and it contributed the term *wolf man*, in this popularized sense, to the language. *Wolf man*, however, dates back to the 16th century, while *lycanthrope*, which comes from Greek *lukos*, "wolf," and *anthropos*, "man," goes back to ancient times. The word *werewolf* derives from Old English *were*, "man," and *wolf*.

wolfsbane. This species of poisonous aconite, *Aconitum vulparia*, may have been called wolfsbane because meat soaked in its juices is poisonous to wolves. But it could have arisen through an involved etymological error, as explained by a 19th-century writer: "Bane is a common term for poisonous plants, and some early botanist translated it into the Greek *kuamos*, meaning bean. The plant has a pale yellow flower and was thus called the white-bane to distinguish it from the blue aconite. The Greek for white is *leukos*, hence *leukos-kuamos*, but *lukos* is the Greek for wolf, and by mistake got changed to *lukos-kuamos* (wolf bean). Botanists, seeing the absurdity of calling an aconite a bean, restored the original word bane but retained the corrupt word *lukos* (a wolf) and hence we get the name wolf's bane for white aconite." *See also* ACONITE.

Wolverine State. A nickname for Michigan since the 1830s, though no one knows why since there were no wolverines in what was Michigan at the time. Michigan has also been called the Lake State because it borders on the Great Lakes.

woman. Etymologically, *woman* has no connection with *man*. The word *woman* derives not from *man*, but from the Old English *wif-man*, *wif* meaning "female" and *man* meaning "human being." *Man* derives from the Old English *mannian* meaning the same. *See* UMMERN.

woman of Babylon. *See* BABBLE.

a woman's place is in the home. Perhaps the Greek dramatist Euripides (484–406 B.C.) foreshadowed this proverbial Victorian saying when he wrote in a fragment of the *Meleager*: "A woman should be good for everything at home, but abroad good for nothing." But *a woman's place is in the home* found its way into print for the first time in the mid-19th century. When she ran for Congress in 1970, women's rights activist Bella Abzug campaigned under the slogan "This woman's place is in the House—the House of Representatives!" She won, serving three terms.

woman's work is never done. The old saying, author unknown, is properly "Man may work from sun to sun, but woman's work is never done." It comes from a time when the great majority of people lived on farms, dating back perhaps to the 16th century.

women and children first. For more than a century this saying has been part of the unwritten law of the sea—women and children shall be saved before anyone else in the event of a disaster—and in the vast majority of cases, the words have been gallantly honored. The saying seems to have arisen, anonymously, after H.M.S. *Birkenhead* went down off the Cape of Good Hope in 1852 and 491 men were lost while all the women and children aboard were saved, and a great tradition was born.

Wonder State. A nickname for Arkansas officially adopted by the state in 1923. Arkansas is sometimes called the Bear State and the Hot Water State (after Hot Springs, Arkansas). Residents of Arkansas are called *Arkansawyers*. *See also* BOWIE KNIFE.

won't hold water. Said of an argument that is wrong, that is like a boat with leaks, that won't bear close inspection. The expression dates back to the 19th century or further.

wong. *Wong* here is not a Chinese word, as might be expected, but an Old English word meaning meadowland, often used as a commons, that derives from the German *wang*, "mountain slope." First recorded in *Beowulf*, the word's only use today is in British place names and designations of certain fields and common lands.

woodchuck. A New England name for the groundhog (*Marmota monax*), *woodchuck* probably derives from a New England Algonquian Indian word meaning the same. "A boy always had woodchuck holes to explore after the leaves were down in the fall . . . ," Mayden Pearson wrote in *New England Flavor*, 1961. *See also* GROUNDHOG.

wooden nickels. *See* DON'T TAKE ANY WOODEN NICKELS.

Wooden O. Shakespeare described London's famous Globe Theatre as the "wooden O," and his playhouse did have a doughnut shape. The Globe was built from timbers used in the construction of London's first theater, which was built in 1576 on the north side of the Thames by actor James Burbage and torn down when Burbage's sons decided in 1599 to build the Globe on Bankside in Southwark. Shakespeare had a share in the Globe and performed there. The auditorium of the Globe was an old inn yard. Shilling patrons sat onstage near the actors, three-penny patrons rated stools in the balcony, while one-penny customers stood in the yard. Because the huge stage jutted into the yard, the actors found themselves with an audience pressing on three sides. The balconies and stage were roofed, but the center inn yard was open to the sky. The original Globe burned to the ground in 1613. There are replicas today in London; Stratford, Ontario, Canada; Stratford, Connecticut; San Diego, California; Berlin, Maryland; and Odessa College, Odessa, Texas.

wooden walls. *Wooden walls* is an old term for England's warships, which protected the country from invasion like a great wooden wall in the water that the enemy could not get by. The term, however, had been used long before the English first recorded it in 1598, for Themistocles called the ships of ancient Athens "wooden walls." *Our watery and wooden walls* was an English variation on the phrase.

woodman, spare that tree.

> Here on my trunk's surviving frame,
> Carved many a long-forgotten name . . .
> As love's own altar, honor me:
> Spare woodman, spare the beechen tree.
>
> —Thomas Campbell,
> "Beech Tree's Petition" (1807)

Smooth-skinned beech trees, as the old poem above shows, have always been the favorite of lovers carving their names or initials inside a heart. The beech tree lines quoted above are the real source of the familiar proverb "Woodman, spare that tree," *not* the following more famous poem by George Pope Morris written in 1830, 23 years later:

> Woodman, spare that tree!
> Touch not a single bough!

> In youth it sheltered me,
> And I'll protect it now.

See also BOOK.

woolgathering. In the past, and perhaps even today, people wandered the countryside gathering bits of wool from hedges and bushes that sheep had brushed against. These actual "woolgatherers," often children, went about their work aimlessly, often frolicking in the fields, never able to do their job systematically because the sheep were scattered all over. There wasn't much money to be gained in such an occupation, either. So as far back as the 16th century this literal woolgathering suggested our expression *woolgathering*, meaning unprofitable or trivial employment, absentminded inattention, purposeless thinking, or aimless reverie.

Woolworth's. *See* FIVE-AND-TEN.

wop. *See* DAGO.

word association test. *See* JUNGIAN.

word for word. As one would expect, this is a very old expression for "exactly" or "precisely," Chaucer first recording it in about 1385: "I could folwe word for word Virgile."

word of honor. One might think that this phrase, for "a solemn promise," goes back to those days when knighthood was in flower. But so far as is known it only dates to 1814, when it is recorded in Donat H. O'Brien's *Narrative Containing an Account of His Shipwreck, Captivity and Escape from France:* "They suspected we were deserters . . . We assured them upon our word of honour, they were very much mistaken.

word processor. A term that came into the language about 1975 for a computer system specifically designed for or capable of word processing (the creation, input, editing, and production of texts by means of computer systems). For surely the most beautiful tribute ever written to a word processor, read the Prologue to Henry Roth's *From Bondage* (1996), which was written on a word processor.

word to the wise. So old is this expression that it probably goes back beyond the Latin *verbum sapienti* that it is a translation of. *Verbum sapienti* is so well known in British university usage that it is commonly rendered as *verb. sap.* there. *A word to the wise (is enough)* is recorded in English as early as the 15th century. An old variant is *a word to the wise suffices*.

workaholic. American pastoral counselor Wayne Oates coined the word *workaholic* for "an uncontrollable need to work incessantly," in 1971, from *work* and *alcoholic*. Himself a workaholic who discovered his sickness only when his "five-year-old son asked for an appointment to see him," Oates published his *Confessions of a Workaholic* in 1972. There have since been many similar but less popular constructions, including *bookaholic* (1977), *wordaholic* (1978), and *hashaholic* (1973), someone who uses a lot of marijuana or hashish.

Workers of the world, unite! The communist slogan has its counterpart in every language of the world. It comes from the first page of *The Communist Manifesto* (1848) by Karl Marx and Friedrich Engels.

work into a lather. When we tell someone "Don't work yourself into a lather" over something, we mean don't get hot and bothered, don't get angry or worried. *Lather* derives from the Anglo-Saxon word for washing soda or foam and has long been used to describe the flecks of foam on a heavily perspiring horse. From the notion of a horse worked into a hot and bothered state came our expression, probably in the mid-19th century.

work like a navvy. To work hard at physical labor. The word is *navvy* here, not *navy*, and means laborer. A *navvy* was a man who worked on the many canals that were excavated in England starting in the mid-18th century. These canals were called "navigations" and a laborer working on one was dubbed a "navigator," this soon being shortened to *navvy*.

work like a Trojan. *See* A REGULAR TROJAN.

world-class. An athlete who competes in the Olympics or holds world records or approaches world records in a sport is said to be world-class. In recent times the term has been applied to people outstanding in anything, even negatively, as in "He's a world-class liar."

the world is my oyster. All the pleasures and opportunities of life are open to someone because he is young, rich, handsome, successful, etc. Shakespeare invented or popularized this expression in *The Merry Wives of Windsor* (1600): *Falstaff:* I will not lend thee a penny. *Pistol:* Why, then, the world's mine oyster which I with sword will open.

World Series. This term is, of course, still used in baseball and has been extended to cover any highest-level contest, from the *world series* of poker to the *world series* of go-cart racing. The first World Series in baseball called the *World Series* was held in 1889, the term a shortening of the World Championship Series. This was a series of post-season games held each year between the pennant winners of the National League and the American Association beginning in 1884. But the first World Series between two major league teams came in 1903, when the American League was recognized as a bona fide major league. The American League's Boston Pilgrims (later the Boston Red Sox) beat the National League's Pittsburgh Pirates in this best-of-nine game series, which fans paid one dollar a game to see. *See also* MAJOR LEAGUE.

World's Largest Store. The slogan of New York's Macy's, and it is no hype. Macy's Herald Square store covers a full 55.5 acres, containing 2.2 million square feet of floor space. A good-size house has 2,000 square feet, so you could put 10,000 houses in Macy's. The store opened in 1902 on a site that had been occupied by, among other enterprises, a few quality brothels and a music hall where Thomas Edison first projected a movie. Harrods, the largest store in the United Kingdom, is only half as big as Macy's.

World Trade Center. *See* TWIN TOWERS.

World War I. No one *knew* that World War I was only the first world war until 1939, when World War II started, but wise men and cynics began using the term even before World War I was over, the phrase being coined in 1918 before the armistice! World War I had another common name: THE WAR TO END ALL WARS. Over 10 million killed and 20 million wounded in *The Great War*, as it was also called, is a conservative estimate, yet this was less than half of those to be killed in World War II. Before the U.S. entered World War I in 1917 it was called The Great European War.

worm. The lowly worm's name has a grand history. *Worm* derives from the Latin *vermis*, which first meant "dragon" or "serpent." In time, however, it came to include the garden worm as well. Today worms are often raised on worm farms and sold to fishermen and to gardeners who use them to help aerate the soil.

wormwood. Since there is nothing wormy about it, why is the herb so named? The best theory is that the "worm" in the word is from the Teutonic *wer*, for "man" and the "wood" from *mod*, the Teutonic for "courage." By this account the word was originally *wermod*, meaning "man's courage," in reference to the herb's supposed aphrodisiacal and healing properties. Absinthium, the classical wormwood, is an ingredient of absinthe, which has probably killed more people than it has sexually inspired. Tarragon is also one of the wormwoods.

worry. *Worry* derives from the Old English *wyrgan*, "to strangle," which became the Middle English *worien*. In Middle English the word came to describe the way dogs or wolves kill prey by grasping it with their teeth and shaking it. By the 16th century, *worry* had evolved and meant to harass. By the time another century had passed, *worry* was being used for bother or distress.

worship the golden calf. One who worships the golden calf sacrifices his or her principles for money or personal gain. The expression is biblical in origin, referring to the golden calf made by Aaron that the Israelites worshipped while Moses was absent on Mount Sinai (Exodus 23), a sin for which they paid dearly.

worth his weight in gold. At present gold prices a person weighing 150 pounds who was literally worth his weight in gold would be worth nearly $1 million. To say someone is *worth his weight in gold* is to say he is an extremely valuable person to the enterprise at hand. The phrase has been traced back to at least 1705, when Joseph Addison, writing about a statue in Italy, said: "It is esteemed worth its weight in gold."

would God I had died for you. Part of the famous biblical lament for an erring, beloved son uttered by David over his son Absalom, widely praised for his brilliance and beauty ("without blemish"), who had marched against his father's army and was killed. David's commander, Joab, sent a messenger to David telling of his victory and his son's death, David then crying out his anguished words: "O my son Absalom, my son, my son Absalom! Would God I had died for thee, O Absalom, my son, my son!" (Sam. 28:33). *Absalom! Absalom!* (1936) is the title of a novel by William Faulkner.

wouldn't touch it with a 10-foot pole. This expression may have been suggested by the 10-foot poles that river boatmen used to pole their boats along in shallow waters. Possibly the expression was first something like *I wouldn't touch that with the 10-foot pole of a riverman* and that this shortened with the passing of pole boats from the American scene. However, the image first appears in the Nantucketism *can't touch him with a 10-foot*, meaning "he is distant, proud, reserved." In the sense of not wanting to get involved in a project or having a strong distaste for something, the words aren't recorded until the late 19th century.

Wow! As an exclamation of surprise, admiration, etc., *wow* derives from Scottish *wow!* meaning the same, an exclamation that dates back to the early 16th century. For some 10 years *a wow* has meant "something excellent," and *to wow* has meant "to gain great approval," especially from an audience.

wowser. There has been much speculation over the years about the origin of this term for a puritanical person, a bluenose, or a fanatic. The word appears to have been coined in 1890s Australia to describe fanatic prohibitionists, perhaps even from the initials of a reform organization's slogan: "*We Only Want Social Evils Righted.*" The *O.E.D.* quotes *The Nation's* (5/11/12) definition of *wowser*: ". . . one who wants to compel everybody else . . . to do whatever he thinks right, and abstain from everything he thinks wrong." To all of which I'll only add that D. H. Lawrence wrote a satirical poem entitled "The Little Wowser," probably learning of the word on a visit to Australia in 1922. The little wowser is in this case the penis. Lawrence's poem begins:

> There is a little wowser
> John Thomas by name
> and for every bloomin', mortal thing
> that little blighter's to blame . . .

And ends four stanzas later with:

> I think of all the little brutes
> as ever was invented
> that little cod's the holy worst,
> I've chucked him, I've repented.

See also JOHN THOMAS.

Wreck of the Hesperus. A huge submerged rock off the coast of Gloucester, Massachusetts caused so many shipwrecks in the 18th century that it was called Norman's Woe. Wrote Henry Wadsworth Longfellow in his diary for December 17, 1837: "News of shipwrecks horrible on the coast. 20 bodies washed ashore near Gloucester, one lashed to a piece of wreck. There is a reef called Norman's Woe where many of these took place; among others the schooner *Hesperus* . . . I must write a ballad upon this." The ballad proved to be "The Wreck of the Hesperus," which became so well known that "wreck of the *Hesperus*" also became an expression for any battered or disheveled thing, as in "You look like the wreck of the Hesperus."

Wrens; Waves; Spars. An acronym for the *Women's Royal Naval Service, Wrens* was coined in Great Britain during World War I and is the first acronym invented for a woman's naval unit. The *Waves, Women Accepted for Voluntary Service*, seems more labored but worked during World War II. The most ingenious of such inventions is *Spar*, an acronym for the Woman's reserve of the U.S. Coast Guard Reserve (World War II), which was constructed from the Coast Guard motto: *Semper Paratus, Always Ready. See* PASSION KILLERS.

wrestling; Pancration. *Wrestling* was recorded before 1100 in English, but the sport goes back to prehistoric times though differing widely in its rules and regulations. In the Olympian Games, for example, the Pancration, a brutal rough-and-tumble form of wrestling combined with boxing, allowed almost any way of defeating an opponent. This later became known as the "catch-as-catch-can" style. Today we have a variety of wrestling styles that might be called "TV wrestling" or "entertainment wrestling," which many people take seriously. Purer forms of the sport are still widely practiced in schools and colleges, including the Greco-Roman style of ancient Rome, in which the wrestlers can't trip, tackle, or use holds beneath the waist. The Greek philosopher Plato, whose name means "broad-shouldered" in Greek, wrestled for sport, as did Abraham Lincoln (in some 300 matches) and George Washington, among many other notables.

Wright Flyer. *See* FLYING MACHINE.

write like an angel. Isaac D'Israeli in his *Curiosities of Literature* (1791–93) says that the phrase *to write like an angel* originally had nothing to do with literary style, but referred to fine penmanship. According to D'Israeli (Prime Minister Disraeli's father) a "learned Greek" named Angelo Vergecie immigrated to Italy and then to France, where his beautiful handwriting attracted attention; Francis I, in fact, modeled a Greek typeface on it. *To write like an Angelo* became synonymous with exquisite calligraphy, and *Angelo* was shortened to *Angel* at which point the meaning was expanded to include literary style. A good story even if it can't be confirmed.

writ in water. Said of somebody whose work has come to naught, is ephemeral, inconsequential. Still heard because the phrase was carved on the gravestone of the great English poet John Keats. His grave is at the Protestant Cemetery in Rome. Here is his epitaph:

> This Grave
> Contains all that was Mortal
> of a
> YOUNG ENGLISH POET
> Who
> on his Death Bed
> in the Bitterness of his Heart
> at the Malicious Power of his Enemies
> Desired
> these words to be engraven on his Tomb Stone
>
> HERE LIES ONE
> WHOSE NAME WAS WRIT IN WATER
> Feb. 24th 1821

wrong side of the bed.   *See* GET UP ON THE WRONG SIDE OF THE BED.

wrong side of the tracks.   This American expression arose in the 19th century when railroad tracks, which sometimes split a town in two, provided a clear social demarcation—well-to-do people living on the right side of the tracks and the poor living on the wrong side, in the slums or seedy area of town. Today the expression *to be born on the wrong side of the tracks*, "to be born poor and disadvantaged," hangs on despite the fact that the physical distance between rich and poor has increased and that they now tend to live in different towns or counties altogether.

Wrong-Way Corrigan.   Douglas "Wrong-Way" Corrigan *may* have gone the wrong way unintentionally. The 31-year-old pilot flew from California to New York in a record time of less than 28 hours and took off the next day in his battered plane to return to California. His plane had no radio, beam finder, or safety devices, and had failed safety inspections, which would indicate that he had no plans for a publicity stunt. But even though extra gas tanks blocked his view, it is hard to explain how, after he took off in a westerly direction over Jamaica Bay, near the present Kennedy International Airport in New York, he swung his plane in a wide arc and crossed the Rockaway Peninsula, heading out over the Atlantic Ocean. Presumably, he flew through a thick fog, convinced he was California-bound until the fog lifted that fine morning of July 18, 1938, and he looked down at the grass roofs and cobble-stoned streets of Ireland! Corrigan told officials at Dublin's Baldonnel Airport that he had accidentally flown the wrong way, and he promptly became known as *Wrong-Way Corrigan.* As a result he became a hero, made close to $100,000, and even played himself in *The Flying Irishman*, a movie based on his "mistake." When asked recently if he had really meant to fly to California, Corrigan replied, "Sure . . . well, at least I've told that story so many times that I believe it myself now."

Wrong-Way Riegels.   Like WRONG-WAY CORRIGAN, Roy Riegels (1909–93) won fame by going the wrong way. Riegels, playing center for the University of California in the 1929 Rose Bowl, took off in the right direction on recovering a Georgia Tech fumble, but after spinning away from tacklers, he turned and ran 67 yards toward his own goal line before an alert teammate stopped him and Georgia Tech players tackled him on the one-yard line. California tried to punt out from that terrible field position, but Georgia Tech blocked the punt for a safety and edged ahead 2–0. Both teams went on to score a touchdown (California scoring an extra point as well), but Georgia Tech's two-point safety proved to be their margin of victory.

wuzzy.   A good example of how the English have fractured French over the centuries is the London teenage slang *wuzzy*, for "a girl." It was coined in the 1960s from the French word for bird (*bird* being English slang for "girl"), which is *oiseau.*

Wyatt Earp.   A fabled gunfighter; after Wyatt Barry Stapp Earp (1848–1929), most famous for his part in the 1879 gunfight at the O.K. Corral in Tombstone, Arizona. Considered quick on the draw (from a leather-lined, waxed coat pocket), Earp was never bested and died quietly in his sleep, one of the two legendary western gunfighters who definitely didn't meet a violent end (Bat Masterson was the other).

Wyoming.   *Wyoming* comes from the Algonquian *Macheweaming*, meaning "place of the big flats," actually a west Pennsylvania valley where a pre-Revolutionary Indian massacre had occurred that was celebrated in the popular sentimental poem "Gertrude of Wyoming." It became the name of several U.S. counties and in 1890 that great name-giver Congressman James M. Ashlet bestowed it upon our 44th state ("The Equality State") because it was "a beautiful name," never thinking that "place of the big flats" hardly suited this mountainous western state.

X

X. The 24th letter in our alphabet represents the 14th letter of the Greek alphabet, *xi*. The Romans used *X* to denote the number 10 and *x* in mathematics generally means "an unknown quantity." One theory holds that the *X* stands for a kiss because it originally represented a highly stylized picture of two mouths touching—*x*. Furthermore, in early times illiterates often signed documents with a St. Andrew's cross of *X* and kissed that *X* to show their good faith (as they did with any cross or the Bible), which reinforced the association. But these explanations may be folk etymology, as may the story that mathematically the *X* is a "multiplier"—in this case of love and delight.

Xanthippe. Legend paints Socrates' wife Xanthippe as the classic shrew and her name has become proverbial for a quarrelsome, nagging, shrewish woman. In *The Taming of the Shrew* Shakespeare writes: "Be she as foul as was Florentius' love,/ As old as Sibyl, and as curst and shrewd/ As Socrates' Xanthippe, or a worse,/ She moves me not." The gossips in Athens talked much of Xanthippe's terrible temper and she may have literally driven Socrates out into the open and his marketplace discussions. But then Socrates may have been a difficult husband, and by most accounts is said to have been unusually ugly and uncouth in appearance. Xenophon writes that Xanthippe's sterling qualities were recognized by the philosopher, and various historians, including Zeller in his *Vortrage and Abhandlungen* (1875), argue that she has been much maligned, that Socrates was so unconventional as to tax the patience of any woman, as indeed would any man convinced that he has a religious mission on earth. *See* HENPECKED.

Xanthos. Xanthos or Xanthus of Lydia was one of the *logographi*, the early Greek chroniclers who were the predecessors of true historians. The name takes on a different meaning in Henry Miller's *Tropic of Capricorn* (1939), when he writes: ". . . I felt alone in the world . . . When I say that I was at Far Rockaway [a popular beach resort town at the time in New York City's Queens County] I mean that I was standing at the end of the earth, at a place called Xanthos, if there be such a place, and surely there ought to be a word like this to express no place at all . . . I used the word Xanthos before. I don't know whether there is a Xanthos or not, and I really don't care one way or another, but there must be a place in the world, perhaps in the Grecian islands, where you come to the end of the known world and you are thoroughly alone and yet you are not frightened of it but rejoice, because at this dropping off place you can feel the old ancestral world which is eternally young and new and fecundating. You stand there, wherever the place is, like a newly hatched chick beside its eggshell. This place is Xanthos, or as it happened in my case, Far Rockaway." Miller's coinages (new meanings for both *Xanthos* and *Far Rockaway*) are recorded here for the first time in any dictionary; it seems likely that he had read of the Greek chronicler Xanthos and forgotten him, but there is no absolute proof of this.

Xanthus. In the *Iliad*, Achilles' immortal horse Xanthus, who takes his name from the Greek for "reddish gold," weeps when Achilles' gentle friend Patroclus, who had taken Achilles' place on the battlefield, is killed by Hector while leading the Myrmidons into battle. When Achilles reprimands him for leaving Patroclus on the field of battle, Xanthus reproachfully tells his master that he will soon die, through no fault of his horse but by the decree of inexorable destiny. It is not likely that Xanthus gave his name to the Xanthus River, the ancient name of the Scamander. The river was probably called Xanthus because legend held that it colored the fleece of sheep washed in its waters a reddish gold. *See* PERITAS AND BUCEPHELA.

***x* as a baseball symbol.** The letter *x* is used as an English language symbol in many ways, including baseball scoring. When an unusual or extraordinary play occurs in a baseball game, the scorer marks it on his scorecard with an *x*.

xat. This familiar crossword puzzle and Scrabble word hails from the northwestern U.S. It is a Haida Indian word for the carved totem pole of many North American Indian tribes.

x-chaser. British naval slang since about 1910 for an officer with high qualifications, especially as to his scientific education. The *x* in the phrase is "the x which figures so disturbingly in mathematics," according to one slang authority.

xebec. Xebec is a small three-masted vessel once used by pirates on the Mediterranean. Also called zebec, or chebec, and deriving ultimately from the Arabic word *shabbak*, the vessel is today used to a small extent in commerce.

xeme. The xeme (pronounced "zem") is the fork-tailed arctic gull familiar to maritime explorers and adventurers. It was first observed in Greenland by a British mariner in 1832.

xenia. Xenia were the gifts, usually delicacies from the table, that subjects in the Middle Ages presented to their prince when he passed through their estates. The Romans and Greeks had a similar custom, offering xenia to guests and strangers passing by, and the word, in fact, derives from the Greek for "guest or stranger." The singular is *xenium*.

Xenocratic. The Greek philosopher Xenocrates (396–314 B.C.) was not a great thinker, but this disciple of Plato was of a noble character and led an ascetic life, his Xenocratic ways an example to all. It is said that even the famed courtesan Lais could not tempt him.

xenophobia. Meaning an unreasonable fear or hatred of anyone or anything foreign or strange, *xenophobia* derives from *xeno*, a learned borrowing from Greek meaning "alien" or "strange," and *phobia*, fear. The word is a relatively new word, first recorded in 1912.

xenotine. When this mineral was discovered it was thought to be a new metal, but that thought proved to be in vain. Thus it was named, a short time later in 1832, from the Greek word for "empty, vain," in reference to the dashed hopes of its discoverer.

Xer. *See* GENERATION X.

Xerox. U.S. inventor Chester Carlson invented the Xerox machine in 1938 and *Xerox* remains a trademark of the company that makes it, its name deriving from *xero*, a learned borrowing from the Greek for "dry," and *graph*, an element from the Greek meaning "drawn, written." Inventor Carlson became a multimillionaire from royalties on his dry copier, the rights to which he sold to what is now the Xerox Corporation in 1947. *See* PHOTOSTAT.

Xerxes' tears. The Persian conqueror Xerxes I was a despot with a great heart, according to one legend. When he was about to invade Greece he is said to have reviewed his huge army and wept at the thought of the slaughter about to take place, saying sadly, "Of all this multitude who knows how many will return?" *Xerxes' tears* came to mean a commander's concern for the lives of his troops.

Xipe. Here in the Americas gardeners might do better to erect shrines to Xipe than to Saint Fiacre. Xipe (pronounced *she-pay*) was the Aztec god of sowing and planting. Another name for this patron saint of gardeners is *Xipe Totec*. *See also* ADAM'S PROFESSION.

X marks the spot. Now a catchphrase applied to any triviality, *X marks the spot* began life as a common caption under crime photographs in newspapers indicating the exact spot where the murder, etc., occurred. The expression dates back to England early in this century.

Xmas. *Xmas* is neither an abbreviation nor a "vulgar commercial invention" of recent vintage. *X* has been used to symbolize the syllable "Christ" in English since at least 1100, when it was recorded in *Xianity*, for "Christianity." The Old English word for Christian recorded in the 12th-century *Anglo-Saxon Chronicle* begins with an *X*, and the word *Xmas* itself was used as early as 1551. The Greek word that gives us the English word Christ begins with the letter *chi*, or *X*, leading some writers to believe that the *X* in *Xmas* symbolized the cross.

X rated. In 1968 the Motion Picture Association of America began to rate films as a guide for moviegoers. Their system ranged from *G*, "general, all ages permitted," to *X*, "restricted, no one under 17 admitted." The *X* rating referred to explicit sex and violence in a movie and became so common that *x-rated* almost immediately became a term for anything pornographic or sexy, from a film to a book or even a person!

X ray. *See* ROENTGEN RAY.

XX. *XX* was slang for a twenty-dollar bill back in the 19th century. The term seems to have originated in about 1850, a variation on it being the *double X*.

XXX. Bottles marked with *X*s, for "booze in cartoons," have their basis in reality. Nineteenth-century British breweries marked bottles *X*, *XX*, or *XXX* to indicate alcoholic content— the more *X*s, the more kick. *See* x for *XXX*s used for kisses. Another use of three *x*'s that isn't noted in any dictionary, William A. Strockbine writes that he was "told years ago by the redoubtable Ronald W. Siegal, formerly of the State University of New York at Stony Brook, that XXX (thirty) was used by telegraphers to indicate the end of a transmission because that combination of letters could not be found in any word and was easily recognized for its symmetry. It could be interspersed in the transmission of a string of messages that might not otherwise be so clearly separated."

xylophage. Any *xylophage*, which takes its name from the Greek *xylo*, "wood," and *phagein*, "to eat," is a wood-eating insect, such as a termite. The adjective *xylophagous* means "feeding on wood" and usually refers to the teredo worm and other crustaceans, mollusks, and fungi that perforate or destroy timber.

xylophone. *Xylophone*, the word first recorded in 1866, is composed of the Greek *xylo*, "wooden," plus *phone*, "voice or sound," the "wood," of course, referring to its flat wooden bars, which are played by a small mallet. When tubular resonators are attached to these bars the instrument is called a marimba.

xyst. A xyst (pronounced *zist*) is a garden walk planted with trees, or a covered portico in a garden used as a promenade.

Both were common in Roman villas and take their name from the Latin *xystus,* "garden terrace."

XYZ affair. In 1797 President John Adams sent three representatives to France to negotiate a maritime treaty that would prevent French pirates from attacking American ships. But three of Talleyrand's agents (identified only as X, Y, and Z) intercepted them and demanded a $1-million "loan" for France before they would be received by the French government. The agents refused to negotiate on these terms and returned home. One of them, Charles Cotesworth Pinckney, allegedly uttered the slogan "Millions for defense, sir, but not one cent for tribute." Pinckney, however, always claimed he only said: "No, no, no! Not a single sixpence!"

Y

Y. Our letter *y* can be traced back to the Greek alphabet, the Greeks having added it to the Phoenician alphabet. It is called the Samian letter after Pythagoras (the Samian Sage, born at Samos in the sixth century B.C.) because the Greek philosopher employed the letter (also called the Letter of Pythagoras) as his emblem of the straight and narrow of virtue, "which is one, but, if once deviated from, the farther the lines are extended the wider becomes the breach."

yacht. Yachts were originally pirate ships. This pleasure craft takes its name from a type of speedy German pirate ship of the 16th century called the *Jacht* that was common on the North Sea. British royalty found that this type of vessel made excellent pleasure boats a century later, spelling the German word *Yaught*, which finally became *yacht*.

yackety yack. The British used the imitative word *yack* for "a snapping sound" as early as 1861 and were soon after using it to mean "to talk about." It took almost a century before Americans began to use *yack* and then *yackety yack* as terms for incessant talk or laughter.

yahoo. Bestial or brutish people are called yahoos, after the Yahoos in Jonathan Swift's satire *Gulliver's Travels*, nauseating hateful beasts in human form who prefer "nastiness and dirt." Eric Partridge suggested that Swift may have coined the word after *yah!* and *who?*—"*yah!* being typical of coarse ignorance and brutality, and *who?* of defiance." Other possibilities are (1) the name of "the Cariban tribe the Yahos, on the coast near the borderline of Brazil and French Guiana"; (2) "the name of a degraded East African tribe often mentioned by early travelers"; and (3) "a learned pun by Swift on a Greek word sounding like *yahoo* that meant sleepy or dopey."

yak. *See* POLO.

yakka. Only a handful of Australian Aboriginal words have come into the English language. One such word is *yakka*, meaning "work," a term frequently used in Australia. *Hard yakka* means hard manual labor. Other Aboriginal words heard in the Land Down Under include: *yabber*, "to talk"; *cooee*, "within calling distance in the bush"; *woomera*, "a wooden stick or club"; *dingo*, "a wild dog domesticated by the Aborigines"; and many place names, including *Canberra*, the capital's name, which is said to mean "Women's Breasts," after two local hills.

Yale blue; Yale lock. Yale blue, a reddish blue, takes its name from the Yale University colors. It is the royal blue of the Egyptian Rameses dynasty, also called Rameses. *Yale lock* has no connection with the school. American inventor Linnus Yale (1821–68) invented numerous locks, including the trademarked key type with a revolving barrel that bears his name. Linnus founded a company to manufacture locks at Stamford, Connecticut the same year that he died.

Yale University. Yale University, ranking after Harvard and William and Mary as the third oldest institution of higher education in the United States, is named for English merchant Elihu Yale (1649–1721). Founded in 1701 as the Collegiate School of Saybrook, Connecticut, the school was named Yale College at its 1718 Commencement, held in the first college building at New Haven. It became a university in 1887. Yale might have been called Mather University, for Cotton Mather suggested naming it so in return for his financial support, but Elihu Yale won out when he donated a cargo of gifts, books, and various goods that brought about 562 pounds when sold. Yale had been born in Boston in 1649, but returned with his family to England three years later. He served with the British East India Company, and as governor of Fort St. George in India until scandals in his administration led to his removal in 1692.

y'all. *See* YOU-ALL.

yam. *Yam* can be traced back to the Senegal *nyami*, meaning "to eat," and was introduced to America via the Gullah dialect *njam*, meaning the same, in 1676. The word, however, had come into European use long before this. *See also* DIOSCOREA.

yank. *Yank*, to pull abruptly or vigorously, is of uncertain origin. A U.S. invention, probably originating in New England early in the 19th century and much used since then, it has nothing to do with the word YANKEE for a New Englander. It may be akin to the English dialect word *yerk*, a variant of *jerk*, but there is no proof of this.

yank. Bird watchers named this Carolinian bird (*Sitta carolineusis*) the yank because its blue coat suggested the Yankee (Union) Civil War uniform. It is also known as the nuthatch.

Yankee. The source of *Yankee* has long been disputed and its origin is still uncertain, despite all the research devoted to it. Candidates, among many, have included a slave named Yankee offered for sale in 1725, a Dutch sea captain named Yanky, the Yankos Indians, the Dutch name Janke ("Johnny"), which the Dutch applied to the English, and an Indian mispronunciation (*Yengees*) of the word *English*. The most popular explanation, also unproved, is that Yankee comes from *Jan Kees*, a contemptuous Flemish and German nickname for the Dutch that the English first applied to the Dutch in the New World. In any case, *Yankee* seems to have been first applied to Americans by British soldiers serving under General James Wolfe in the French and Indian War prior to 1758. A letter written by Wolfe himself in that year uses the word as a contemptuous nickname for Americans: "My posts are not so fortified that I can afford you two companies of Yankees, and the more as they are better for ranging and scouting than either work or vigilance . . . [they] are in general the dirtiest most contemptible cowardly dogs that you can conceive. There is no depending on them in action. They fall down dead in their own dirt and desert by battalions, officers and all. Such rascals as those are rather an encumberance than any real strength to an army." Wolfe's low opinion of the Americans and further contemptuous use of *Yankee* is seen in a 1775 chronicle, which is also notable as an early description of the practice of "mooning": "They [British soldiers] abused the watch-men on duty, and the young children of Boston by the wayside, making mouths at them, calling them Yankeys, shewing their posteriors, and clapping their hands thereon."

It wasn't until the Battle of Lexington, the first battle of the Revolution in 1775, that Americans began applying the nickname *Yankee* to themselves and making it respectable. Soon after, the process of dignification began and the story about the Yankos Indians was invented. In this tale a mythical tribe of Massachusetts Indians are said to have been defeated by a band of valorous New Englanders, the defeated Yankos so admiring the bravery of their victorious adversaries that they gave them their name, *Yankos*, which meant "Invincibles" and was soon corrupted to *Yankees! Yankee* has been an admirable or contemptuous nickname for Americans ever since, depending by whom and in what context it is used. At any rate, *Yankee* described a New Englander by the middle 18th century and was used by the British to designate any American during the Revolution, the most notable example found in the derisive song *Yankee Doodle*. Nowadays the British still use the word for an American, southerners use it for northerners (*see* DAMN YANKEE) and northerners use it for New Englanders, who, despite its early history, remain proud of the designation.

Yankee cheesebox on a raft. A widespread derisive description of the U.S. armored warship the *Monitor*, which fought the famous Civil War battle against the Confederate *Merrimac*. The *Monitor* was also called a cheesebox upon a plank.

Yankee Clipper. One of sport's best-known nicknames, *Yankee Clipper* honors New York Yankee centerfielder Joe DiMaggio, one of baseball's greatest players, who hit safely in 56 consecutive games, a record that still stands. The popular song "Joltin' Joe DiMaggio" was written in his honor. DiMaggio was also called the Yankee Clipper both for the way he "clipped" the ball and for his grace as a fielder, moving as effortlessly as a clipper ship (or possibly the popular Yankee Clipper plane of the 1930s) across the field to make even the hard catches seem easy.

Yankee Doodle. Legend has it that during the French and Indian War, the shabbily dressed troops of Colonel Thomas Fitch of Norfolk, Connecticut, inspired a British army surgeon with musical talents, a Dr. Sheckburgh or Shackburg, to write the derisive song "Yankee Doodle." The story is recounted in the *Federal Writer's Project Connecticut* (1938): "According to local tradition, Elizabeth Fitch, on leaving the house to bid goodbye to her brother [Colonel Fitch], was dismayed by the ill-sorted costumes of the 'cavalry.' Exclaiming, 'You must have uniforms of some kind,' she ran into the chicken yard, and returned with a handful of feathers announcing, 'Soldiers should wear plumes,' and directed each soldier to put a feather in his cap. When Sheckburgh saw Fitch's men arriving at Fort Crailo, Rensselaer, New York, he is reputed to have exclaimed, 'Now stab my vitals, they're macaronis!' sarcastically applying the slang of the day for fop, or dandy, and proceeded to write the song, which instantly caught popular fancy." There is no firm proof of this theory about the origin of the song, which ironically came to be a popular song of patriot troops during the Revolutionary War. There are said to be hundreds of verses to the song. Before the Civil War, the tune, identified with New England, was often hissed off the stage in the South. *See* FROZEN YANKEE DOODLE.

"Yankee Doodle Dandy"; "Over There." These patriotic songs were both written by George M. Cohan (1878–1942) to support America and her allies in World War I. Both the "Over There" lyrics ("The Yanks are coming, the Yanks are coming") and "Yankee Doodle Dandy" lyrics ("a real live nephew of my Uncle Sam, born on the Fourth of July . . .") have been used as titles for novels and movies, most recently the film *Born on the Fourth of July*. Enrico Caruso lent his great tenor voice to an early recording of "Over There." For more patriotic songs *see* GOD BLESS AMERICA.

Yankee peddler. "The whole race of Yankee Peddlers," wrote a British observer of American character in 1833, "are proverbial for dishonesty. They go forth annually in the thousands to lie, cog, cheat, swindle; in short to get possession of their neighbor's property in any manner it can be done with impunity." In fact, the name "damn Yankee," coined long before the Civil War, probably came from Yankee peddlers who worked the rural South. Yankee peddlers were known as far away as Europe for their trickery and sharpness, especially for their wooden nutmegs (it took an expert wood carver a full day to make just *one* in a recent experiment) when these kernals of an evergreen tree cultivated in the Spice Islands sold for less than a penny apiece. But whether carved wooden nutmegs ever existed (no one has yet turned up an authentic one), many country people did believe that Yankee peddlers sold them, along with carved wooden hams painted pink ("Basswood Hams"), carved cigars, and wooden pumpkin seeds. Connecticut is still called the Nutmeg State for this reason, and the warning *don't take any wooden nutmegs* probably influenced the coining of the still current phrase DON'T TAKE ANY WOODEN NICKELS. An old rhyme went: "There is in Yankeeland / a class of men called tin-peddlers, / A shrewd, sarcastic band / Of busy meddlers." And an old joke went: "Know how to revive a Yankee peddler when he drowns?" "Just turn out his pockets!" But though they were well-versed in chicanery and the Yankee art of giving people "a steer in the wrong direction," as P. T. Barnum put it, Yankee peddlers helped settle America, carrying the materials of civilization to sparsely inhabited regions. Wherever a man swung an ax in the wilderness, an old saying went, a Yankee peddler would show up in the clearing the next day.

yap. *Yap* is an echoic word that first meant only the barking of a small dog. The word is first recorded in this sense in 1603, and it apparently took over two centuries before *yapping* was applied to a person who yaps as well as a dog that yaps. In the process *yap* also became American slang for the mouth, as in *shut your yap*, recorded in about 1900, and American slang for a stupid person. The Yap Islands in the West Pacific, noted for the stone money long used by the Micronesians there, are not named from the English *yap*, taking their name instead from a native language.

yapp. A book binding featuring a cover with soft edges that project beyond and fold over the edges of the pages to protect them. Invented by London bookseller William Yapp about 1880 for Bibles and prayer books, it also goes by the terms *circuit binding*, *divinity circuit binding*, and *yapp binding*. *Yapp* has lost its capital over the years.

Yarborough. Little is known about Charles Anderson Worsley, the second earl of Yarborough, aside from the fact that he was a knowledgeable card player and made himself a small fortune, giving 1,000 to 1 odds that his bridge-playing companions held no cards higher than a nine. The odds were with the English lord, for the chances of drawing such a 13-card hand are actually 1,827 to 1 against. Yarborough, born in the early 19th century, died in 1897, an old and probably rich man. Since his wagers, a *Yarborough* has been any hand in whist or bridge with no card higher than a nine, although the term also means a hand in which there are no trumps.

yardarm. A ship's yard (from the Anglo-Saxon *givid*) is a long, thin spar hung crosswise to the mast to support a square sail. The yardarm is simply one arm or part of this yard.

yare. Properly pronounced to rhyme with *care* (though one often hears it pronounced to rhyme with *car*), *yare* is usually applied to a sailing vessel and means shipshape, ready, deriving from the Old English *gearu* meaning the same. "Our ship is tyte and yare," wrote Shakespeare in *The Tempest*. Katharine Hepburn pronounced it to rhyme with *car* in *Philadelphia Story*.

yarmulke. *Yarmulke*, the skullcap worn by Jewish males, is said by most dictionaries to be a Yiddish word that derives from a Tartar word, which in turn comes from the Polish word for skullcap. However, in an article published in the *Hebrew Union College Annual* (V.26, 1955) Dr. W. Gunther Plaut concludes that *yarmulke* derives ultimately "from the Latin *almucia* or *armucella*, the amice (vestment) worn by the priest." The theory that *yarmulke* derives from a Hebrew word meaning "awe of the king" is a nice story but only folklore. The skullcap is worn, of course, as a sign of respect before God, this a custom not only among Jews but practiced by many people of the East. Hebrew scholar Professor Howard Marblestone advises me that the *yarmulke* etymology he finds most convincing is found in a Hebrew book, *The Origin of Hebrew Words* by Abraham Stahl (Tel Aviv, 1999), which he translates here: "The word originates in the Turkish *yagmurluk*, 'rain coat,' from *yagmur*, "rain," with the suffix *luk*, indicating pertaining to. It passed via the Balkans to the Slavic and Romance languages in various senses, such as coat or hat. The Jews took it over, apparently from Ukrainian or White Russian, and applied it to the covering they wear on their heads."

yarn. To *spin a yarn* was originally naval slang dating back to the early 19th century for "to tell a long, often incredible story." Its obvious source is the yarn lofts ashore where yarn was spun to supply ships with rope, work that took a long time and in which the threads of a rope were interwoven like the elements of a good story. Eventually *yarn* became a synonym for a story or tale itself.

yarrow. A plant with whitish flowers, yarrow has often been used as a medicine and love tonic. According to one old superstition, the drinking of such potions insured "seven years love for wedded couples." Strictly speaking, *Achillea millefolium* is an herb, named for the legendary Achilles, who is supposed to have used one species to heal his wounds. It is sometimes called "Old Man's Pepper," to which family it does not belong, although it may make old men peppery. American folklore gives us the following advice concerning the plant: "Pick a sprig of yarrow, put the stem up your nose and say: *Yarrow, yarrow, if he loves me and I love he, / A drop of blood I'd wish to see.* If blood appears, it shows that you are loved." Yarrow is called the carpenter's herb in France, because it was once widely used there to heal cuts made by carpenters' tools.

yashmak. In case you've been looking for the word for the white or black double veil used to cover the whole face of Muslim women in public, or to hang just below their eyes, this is that word. *Yashmak*, from the Arabic *yashmaq*, for the same, isn't attested to in English until 1844. The first English writer to record the word noted that "the yashmak . . . is not a mere semi-transparent veil, but rather a good substantial petticoat applied to the face." *Veil*, first recorded in 1276, comes ultimately from the Latin *velum* for "covering."

Yat. A dialect heard in sections of New Orleans, Louisiana, said to take its name from the pronunciation of the greeting

"What are you?": *What y'at.* *Yat* has some similarities with Brooklynese, or New Yorkese.

yawp. Walt Whitman famously wrote that he would "sound my barbaric yawp over the roofs of the world." *Yawp* refers to a sharp cry, a bark, a yelp; or loud, coarse talk. *Yawp* is sometimes used as the cry of a gull lifting its head and letting loose, sqwarking at the universe. Gulls often make a cacophony of sounds while floating in the water or flying high: yawping, barking, yelping, mewling, even cawing like crows.

Yazoo fraud; Yazoo claims; Yazoo purchase. Expressions pertaining to Georgia's 1795 sale of lands near the Yazoo River to four crooked companies who profited immensely from their resale to the U.S. government.

yclept. *Yclept* is the only survivor, and a weary one at that, of many words formed with the prefix *y* in Middle English. *Y* was simply used to make past participles, and so *yclest* was blessed, *yclad* was clothed, etc. *Yclept,* the last of these irregular English verb forms is just *y* attached to the old verb *clepe,* "call" and means "called (so-and-so), named, styled." It is abundant in the works of many Elizabethan poets and is occasionally still used humorously, when the writer knows he is affecting a literary archaism. John Taylor the Water Poet has a poem on birds *yclept* "Wheat ears" (1653):

> The name of Wheat ears on them is yclep'd
> Because they come when wheat is yearly reaped.

ye; ye olde gift shoppe. *Ye* served in the past as both the plural of "you" and as a mark of respect when talking to a single person, but has never meant "your" in English. The "Ye's" on those signs adorning half-timbered Tudor-style establishments that read *Ye Olde Gifte Shoppe, Ye Olde Hot Dogge House,* etc., should actually be pronounced "the," not "ye," for that was what they meant in Ye Olde Englishe times. The letter *Y* in "ye" really is not a *Y* but a "thorn," the Anglo-Saxon symbol for "th." This Anglo-Saxon diphthong was originally written something like a *P,* but careless writers and sign painters in later years left it partially open at the side so that it came to resemble a *Y,* and early printers printed it as such. The "ye" in old manuscripts and signs was never pronounced as anything but "the" until modern times.

yeah. *Yeah* is not a modern corruption of "yes" as many people believe. It is an old form of the affirmative still used in England's East Anglia dialect.

yeah, yeah. It is said that about 30 years ago English philosopher Stuart Hampshire observed that "in all languages a double negative made a positive, but not the reverse," and American philosopher Sidney Morganbesser was heard to reply "Yeah, yeah." Another good reply would have been the current sarcasm, "*Yeah, right.*" A *no-no,* something impermissible, is also an exception to Professor Hampshire's rule.

yegg. *Yegg* can mean a safecracker, an itinerant burglar, a thief, or an insignificant criminal. The most common explanation has the word deriving from the surname of John Yegg, a late 19th-century American safe-blower whose life remains a blank. The word first appeared in print as *yeggmen,* "tramps," in 1901. Other suggestions for its source are the German *Jager,* meaning "hunter"; *yekk,* a Chinese dialect word once used in San Francisco's Chinatown that means beggar; and the Scottish and English dialect *yark* or *yek,* "to break."

yellowbacks. *See* GREENBACKS.

yellow-dog contract. The yellow dog, generally considered to be a cowardly common cur or mongrel, has long been a symbol of utter worthlessness in America. The term *yellow dog* has been used in expressions of contempt since at least 1833, when it is first so recorded, and toward the late 19th century it began to be heard in the term *yellow-dog contract,* a contract in which company employees do not or cannot join the union. Though outlawed by the Wagner Act in 1935, yellow-dog contracts still persist.

yellow-dog Democrat. A term applied to loyal Democrats, so named, according to the old story, because they would vote for a yellow dog before voting for any Republican. The designation dates back to post-Civil War days.

yellowhammer. This bird is named not for any hammer but from the earlier *yellow-ham* (Old English *geolu,* "yellow" plus *hama* "covering"), in reference to its bright yellow markings. The European yellow bunting, as it is also called, was once believed to be cursed because it fluttered about the Cross and was stained by Christ's blood, which colored its plumage and marked its eggs with red forever after. In times past children were encouraged to destroy its "cursed eggs."

yellow journalism. *Yellow* has been used to describe sensational books and newspapers in the U.S. since 1846, the "yellow" referring to the cheap yellow covers some sensational books were wrapped in. *Yellow journalism* was first used in 1898, when the phrase was applied to the sensational stories that appeared in Hearst's *New York Evening Journal* and Pulitzer's *New York World* about Spanish atrocities in Cuba. Hearst's cartoon character the "Yellow Kid" could also have figured in the coining.

yellow pages. The classified ad sections in telephone books which are printed on yellow paper in contrast to the white pages of the rest of the phone book, have been so called since 1906 when the Michigan State Telephone Company of Detroit first included such pages in its directory. *Yellow pages* has led to such recent coinages as the *Silver Pages,* telephone numbers of particular interest to older people or "senior citizens." *Yellow pages* used to be a trademark of the Bell Companies.

Yellow Peril. Late in the 19th century fears arose in Germany that China and Japan would vastly increase in population within a few decades and would invade nations all over the globe, massacring the inhabitants. These irrational fears spread throughout Europe and America during the 1890s under the name *Yellow Peril.*

yellow rose of Texas. The yellow rose of Texas, which is part of the state's folklore and even has a famous song written about it, actually originated in the 1830s on a farm in New York City near the present-day Pennsylvania Station. There a lawyer named George Harrison found it as a seedling growing among other roses on his property and began cultivating it. Settlers soon took the yellow rose west with them, and legend has it that Texans finally claimed it as their own when Mexican general Santa Anna, the villain of the Alamo, "was distracted by a beautiful woman with yellow roses in her hair." We have this nice story on the authority of Stephen Scanniello, rosarian of the Crawford Rose Garden in the New York Botanical Garden, who told it to the *New York Times* (6/19/92). *See also* BLUSHING THIGH OF AN AROUSED NYMPH.

Yellowstone National Park.   The *Yellowstone* here is an anglicization of the French *roche jaune*, "yellow rock," which was probably a translation of the Minnataree Indian name *Mitsiadazi*, meaning the same.

Yemen.   This republic in southwest Arabia takes its name from the Arabic for "to the right," that is, to the right of Mecca, the holy city in Arabia that is the birthplace of Muhammad. In ancient times it was called *Arabia Felix*, due to a mistranslation of *Yemen* by Ptolemy.

yen.   The *yen* meaning an intense craving and the *yen* that is a Japanese monetary unit could both derive from Chinese words. The *yen* for a craving possibly comes from the Pekinese *yen*, "opium" (though it may be an alteration of the noun *yearn* or *yearning*), and is first recorded in America toward the beginning of the 20th century. The *yen* that has been the Japanese monetary unit since 1875 derives from the Chinese *yuan*, "a circle or round object," hence a coin.

yenta.   Yiddish for a gossipy woman who talks too much, who talks nonstop relentlessly and can't keep a secret, *yenta* may derive from the name of some unknown blabbermouth called Yenta. The proper name Yenta for a woman probably derives from the Italian *gentile*. A talkative character named Yenta Talabenta in a play by Sholom Aleichem popularized this term.

Yerba Buena.   An old name for San Francisco; so named from the Spanish for "good grass" because the area had excellent pasturage for animals.

Yersinia pestis.   The ferocious *Yersinia pestis* bacillus, which causes bubonic plague or the Black Death, as it is known throughout history, is among the oldest living things on Earth, dating back three thousand billion years, 30 times older than the oldest mammal. Dr. Alexandre Emile Jean Yersin, a brilliant if unconventional Swiss-born French bacteriologist investigating a plague epidemic in Hong Kong, discovered the rod-shaped plague organism in the swellings of victims and named it *Bacillus pestis*. At about the same time in the same place the Japanese microbiologist Dr. Shibasaburo Kitasato also isolated the plague agent, and he named it *Pastuerella pestis* after Louis Pasteur, which it was called until 1970, when it was officially named *Yersinia pestis* after Dr. Yersin. Yersin's discovery, it was determined, preceded Kitasato's by several months but had been published in a French research journal less widely read than the English journal in which Kitasato had published his findings. Unfortunately, he did not live to see the bacillus officially named in his honor, dying in 1943 at the age of 80.

yes-man.   In a 1913 cartoon the great sports cartoonist T. A. Dorgan depicted a newspaper editor and his assistants looking over sheets fresh from the press. The assistants, all praising the edition, are labeled *yes-men*, leading many authorities to credit TAD with the coinage. The expression quickly became a name for assistant directors in Hollywood (Wilson Mizner's "land where nobody noes"), *Variety* labeling one unfortunate director "super-yes-man," and was well known enough in general speech for *Yes-Man's Land* to be used as the title for a book in 1929. Another theory is that *yes-man* may be of German origin, a translation of *Jaherr*, "a compliant person, one unable to say no," which was used by a German author who wrote about America in 1877. In any case, Dorgan certainly popularized the expression.

yesteryear.   The *OED* advises that *yesteryear*, "last year," or "time past," was coined in 1870 by British painter and poet Dante Gabriel Rossetti (1828–82) as an English equivalent for the French word *antan* (from Latin *ante annum*) in a poem of François Villon's. This resulted in the famous translated line in Villon's poem "But where are the snows of yesteryear?" However, *yesterday, yestereven, yestermorning,* and *yesternight* were all recorded long before Rossetti's *yesteryear*. It is said that Rossetti practiced his poetic craft by playing the once popular versifying game bouts-rimes (rhymes without lines) in which lines are composed for certain given rhymes. He could write a sonnet from such lines in five to eight minutes.

yes, we have no bananas.   Originally, this was the title of a song written by Americans Frank Silver and Irving Cohen in 1923. One story has the team borrowing the first line from wordsmith Tad Dorgan and creating the song with the refrain "Yes, we have no bananas, / We have no bananas today." Another more dramatic account has Silver getting the idea for the song when he heard a Greek fruit peddler yell up to a woman at a New York City tenement window, "Yes, we have no bananas!" Whatever the case, the song became immensely popular, and, according to H. L. Mencken, *yes, we have no bananas* became the most widely used catchphrase of the 1920s, even spreading across the sea to England. In his book *The Illiterate Digest* (1924) Will Rogers wrote, "I would rather have been the Author of that Banana Masterpiece than the author of the Constitution of the United States."

yet I am learning.   Two centuries ago Isaac D'Israeli wrote of the artist Michelangelo's outlook on life: "Michelangelo preserved his creative genius even in extreme old age; there is a device said to be invented by him, of an old man represented in a go-cart, with an hourglass upon it: the inscription *Ancora imparo*—YET I AM LEARNING!"

yet is this strength labor and sorrow.   *See* THREE SCORE AND TEN.

yggdrasil.   In Scandinavian mythology the *yggdrasil* is the *world tree*, an ash whose roots and branches bind together in heaven, hell, and earth. Sitting in this fabulous tree from which honey drips, are an eagle, a squirrel, and four stags; at its base is a fountain of wonders.

Yiddish; Yinglish.   Yiddish, which has contributed many words and expressions to English, is an entirely separate language from Hebrew. The word *Yiddish* is an Anglicized form of the German word *judisch*, "Jewish," referring to a Jewish-German language. Yiddish therefore is an Indo-European language like German and English. Hebrew belongs to the Semitic language family, as does Arabic. *Yinglish* is a blending of *Yiddish* and *English* to make a word.

Yiddish words in English.   Among the Yiddish words that have become part of American English are the common kosher, kibitzer, chutzpah, schlemiel, schnook, schmuck, pastrami, matzo, lox, borscht, bagel, blintz, knish, nosh, gelt, mavin, mazeltov, mazuma, megillah, mensch, meshuga, nebbish, schlock, schmaltz, schnozzola, shamus, shekel, yenta, zaftig and many, many more, some of which are treated at length in these pages. *See* HEBREW WORDS IN ENGLISH.

yippie-ki-yi-yay.   A cry of cowboys, perhaps in part suggested by the cry of a coyote. *Yip* for a short high-pitched human cry is first recorded in the West, while *yip* for a dog's bark is recorded as early as 1400 in England.

y'know.   *See* UH, OH.

Yo.   Often used to indicate someone is "present" or "here," especially in answer to a roll call. This widely used U.S. expression is often considered to be recent slang, but it can be traced back to 14th-century England. *Yo* can also be used like *hey*, to get someone's attention, as in "Yo, John." Other times it means "Here I am!" In this last case someone might call "John!" and John would call back, "Yo!"

yob.   A young person who is a rude, offensive, and often violent lout is sometimes called a "yob" in Britain and Australia. The term's origin is the word *boy* spelled backward. This process is called back slang. It has produced hundreds of slang words but very few that are commonly spoken. Another more complicated one is *ecilop*, "police," which is often modified to *slop* ("Here come the slop!")

yoked.   *Yoked* is today a synonym for "mugged." It arose with 19th-century "Jumper Jacks," or muggers, who preyed on seamen, who *yoked* a sailor by grabbing him from behind by the yoke of his tight collar and twisting his neckerchief.

yokel.   The English green woodpecker was named the yokel because its call sounds like "yo-KEL, yo-KEL." Toward the beginning of the 19th century, people in England began calling country bumpkins *yokels* because they lived where the yokels sang.

Yoknapatawpha County.   Certainly the most famous sustained fictional setting in American literature, this county was created by William Faulkner and based on Lafayette County in Mississippi. It appears in 14 Faulkner novels and many stories, beginning with *Sartoris* in 1929. The fictional county, according to Don Doyle's excellent *Faulkner's Country: The Historical Roots of Yoknapatawpha County* (2002), takes its name from the Chickasaw Indian word meaning "divided or split apart land." The name *Yoknapatawpha*, in abbreviated form, also survives as the name of a real local river. Faulkner actually drew a map of the county for one of his books on which he indicated that it covered 2,400 square miles, had 6,298 whites and 9,313 blacks, and had as its capital Jefferson (based on Oxford, Miss.). Ernest Hemingway caustically called Faulkner the creator of ONOMATOPOEIA COUNTY.

yonks.   A word that may derive from DONKEY'S YEARS, also meaning a very long time, as in "I haven't seen him in yonks." The term was first recorded in the late 1960s and is mainly used by the British.

Yooper; Yoopanese.   Someone who lives on the Upper Peninsula of Michigan. The name was born in 1962 when residents there formed the U.P. (Upper Penninsula) Independence Association, their aim to give the Upper Peninsula statehood, and lower Michiganders dubbed them *Yuppes*, which soon became *Yoopers. Yoopanese* is the dialect of the Yoopers, which is based somewhat on Finnish, both in phrases like "let's go store" instead of "let's go to the store," and in the substitution of "da" for "the" or "dat" for "that."

York.   NEW YORK is named for a duke of York who ruled over York in England. The name *York* itself comes from the Celtic *Eburacon*, "the place of the yew trees." This became the Latin *Eburacum*, but to the Anglo-Saxons who ruled England after the Romans *Eburacum* sounded like *Eoforwic*, their "boar town," and to the Vikings who invaded after them *Eoforwic* sounded like *Iorwik*. Over the years *Iorwik* was shortened to *Iork*, which was finally transliterated into *York*.

Yorkshire pudding.   Not a dessert pudding, but an unsweetened baked batter made of flour, salt, eggs, and milk that is often put under roasting meat to catch its drippings. *Yorkshire pudding* honors the county in northern England where it was invented or perfected, its name being first recorded in a 1747 cookbook.

Yosemite.   Yosemite Valley and Yosemite National Park are said to take their name from a distortion of the Miwok Indian *uzamaiti* (grizzly bear), a word the Indians never used for the area.

you.   *See* QUAKER.

You ain't heard (seen) nothin' yet!   No one has had much luck finding the source of this phrase still commonly used today. It is an Americanism and the title of a 1919 popular song; but probably dates back 50 years or more before that. It was popularized in Al Jolson's movie *The Jazz Singer* (1927) and again in the 1940s in two film biographies of Jolson's life.

you ain't nothin' but a hound dog.   *See* HOUND DOG.

you-all.   The plural of "you" in American southern dialect. *You-all* (often pronounced *y'all*) is widely considered the *ne plus ultra* of southern dialect, but this expression, used throughout the South, is much misunderstood. Mainly applied to two or more people, *you-all* can be used when the speaker is addressing one person, but only when the sentence implies plurality. Except for some speakers in the Ozarks and rural Texas, only a ham of a stage southerner would use *you-all* so undiscriminately as to say "That's a pretty dress you-all are wearing." But a southerner might well say "How you-all?"—the question intended to inquire of the health of you and your entire family or group. Further, the inflection of the phrase is all important. When the *you* in *you-all* is accented, as in "*You*-all must come," this means that the group near the speaker is invited. The contraction of *you-all*, *y'all*, is always used in this plural sense. Recently the American southernism *y'all* (or *yawl*) has been explained, though hardly to the satisfaction of everyone, as a calque (a filling in of an African structure with English material) from the West African second person plural *unu*, which is also used in the American black Gullah dialect. This interesting theory is advanced in a study by Jay Edwards in Hancock's and Decamp's *Pidgins and Creoles* (1972): "In the white plantation English of Louisiana the form *y'all* (semantically *unu*) was probably learned by white children from black mammies and children in familiar domestic situations." In any case, the closest thing that has been found in English to the collective second person plurals *you-all* and *you-uns* is the collective second person *you-together* that is sometimes heard in England's East Anglia dialect today.

You bet!; You betcha!, etc.   *You bet!* means "surely, without a doubt, certainly" and has been a popular-American expression of affirmation since the mid-19th century, the variants *you betcha!*, *bet your sweet ass!* and *you bet your sweet life!* being not much younger. The expression arose with the gambling-pioneering spirit in 19th-century America. Wrote Mark Twain in "Buck Fanshaw's Funeral" (1872): "Slang was the language of Nevada . . . Such phrases as 'You bet!' . . . and a hundred others, became so common as to fall from the lips of a speaker unconsciously." *You bet your bippy!* is a comical play on the expression dating back to the 1960s, with the nonsense word "bippy" probably a euphemism for "ass." I believe the expression was invented for, or popularized by, Rowan and Martin's *Laugh In*—a television comedy show.

you better believe.   Surprisingly enough, this popular phrase was first recorded in the *Yale Literary Magazine* about a century and a half ago. Oliver Wendell Holmes is among the literary greats who used it.

you can bet your bottom dollar.   Originating out West in about 1857, these words, meaning to bet one's last dollar or money, referred originally to the last silver dollar in a stack or hoard of coins and came eventually to mean to bet the last of one's resources.

you can play with my dog, you can play with my wife, but you'd better leave my gun alone.   A humorous Texas saying, possibly of recent vintage.

you can run but you can't hide.   Rated by many as the greatest fighter of all time, Joe Louis didn't talk as much as many fighters (he let his fists do the talking, as someone said), but he does have the distinction of being one of the few boxers to have coined a phrase. When Louis was preparing for his championship fight with Billy Conn in 1946, he was asked how he would deal with the challenger's fancy footwork. "He can run, but he can't hide," the champion said. *See* JOE LOUIS; THE REAL MCCOY.

You can say that again!   An emphatic agreement with what a previous speaker has said. Originally a U.S. expression probably originating in the early 20th century, it is now heard in Britain, Australia, and New Zealand as well, In *Strong Cigars and Lovely Women* (1951), John Lardner wrote: "This year's drought has got real significance, and don't tell me I can say that again. I know I can. It has got real significance."

you can't cheat an honest man.   W. C. Fields is responsible for this by now proverbial expression, not P. T. Barnum, as is sometimes reported. Fields did manage to cheat an honest man once in a while.

you can't con me.   *See* CON.

you can't judge a book by its cover.   An early 1900s American saying meaning "not to judge things from surface appearances." In writing a review of Stephen King's *Everything's Eventual: 14 Dark Tales* (2002), *New York Times* critic Janet Maslin praised the jacket illustration by artist Mark Stutzman and turned the old saying around: ". . . a tranquil restaurant scene on the front cover with just a wee trace of blood in one water glass. But turn to the back, and all hell has broken loose. You *can* tell the book by its cover."

you can't make an omelet without breaking eggs.   The end justifies the means; sometimes evil must be done to accomplish good. Russian communist leader V. I. Lenin is said to have originated the saying, though this is far from certain.

you can't make a silk purse out of a sow's ear.   By painstakingly using both silk fibers and the skin or hair of a sow's ear, a man actually did make a silk purse out of a sow's ear a few years back. But the expression means you can't make something good out of something naturally inferior in quality. George Herbert was the first to record an approximation of the old saying in his *Jacula Predentum or Outlandish Proverbs* (1633), but Jonathan Swift first recorded it fully in *Polite Conversations* (1768). The French variation on the saying is "There's no way to turn a buzzard into a hawk," while the Russians say "If you're born to crawl, you won't fly," and the Spanish instruct "You can't find pears on an elm tree."

you can't win 'em all.   Baseball legend attributes the saying *you can't win 'em all* to Boston pitcher Clifton G. Curtis—who is a good choice, having lost 23 games in a row during the 1910–1911 seasons—but it probably goes back further. It is often used as a rueful expression said after one has failed at anything, or as a consoling remark to someone who has failed.

you can whistle for it.   *See* GO WHISTLE FOR IT.

you could have heard a pin drop.   An expression synonymous with complete silence. The saying probably dates back to at least the late 18th century. *Pin-drop silence* is a synonym. "A pin-drop silence strikes o'er the place" Leigh Hunt wrote in *The Story of Rimini* (1816).

you couldn't detect my interest with a high-powered telescope.   Sometimes used to indicate that the speaker couldn't care less about something, that one has no interest in it at all.

I've found no proof of this, but the expression may derive from Algonquin wit George S. Kaufman's reply to popular singer Eddie Fisher on a TV show when Fisher asked him what he could do about women refusing to date him because he looked so young. "Mr. Fisher," Kaufman said, "on Mount Wilson there is a telescope that can magnify the most distant stars up to twenty-four times the magnification of any previous telescope. This remarkable instrument was unsurpassed until the construction of the Mount Palomar telescope, an even more remarkable instrument of magnification. Owing to advances and improvements in optical technology, it is capable of magnifying the stars to four times the magnification and resolution of the Mount Wilson telescope—Mr. Fisher, if you could somehow put the Mount Wilson telescope *inside* the Mount Palomar telescope, you *still* wouldn't be able to detect my interest in your problem."

you have money, give money; you don't have money, give yourself (volunteer).   Heard in New York's Chinatown, said to be an old Chinese saying.

you have the words, but you don't have the music.   You don't have the essence of something. The phrase can be traced back to Mark Twain. In a foul mood one morning and unable to find a clean shirt fit to wear, he unleashed a string of expletives only he could have strung together. His wife, Livy, standing in the doorway, decided to teach him a lesson and slowly repeated each curse he had uttered. But when she was done, Twain simply sighed and said, "My dear, you have the words, but you don't have the music."

you know it makes one feel rather good deciding not to be a bitch.   *See* BUNG-O!

you might as well appeal against the thunderstorm.   *See* WAR IS HELL.

youngberry.   The youngberry is generally considered to be a hybrid variety of dewberry, which, in turn, is simply an early-ripening prostrate form of blackberry. The large, dark purple sweet fruit has the high aroma and flavor of the LOGANBERRY and native blackberry. The youngberry was developed by Louisiana horticulturist B. M. Young about 1900 by crossing a southern dewberry and trailing blackberry, or several varieties of blackberries. Its long, trailing canes are generally trained on wires. Popular in the home garden, the berry is extensively planted in the American Southwest, South, Pacific Northwest, and California.

Young Folk of the Pear Garden.   An ancient name for any Chinese actor. About A.D. 720 Chinese emperor Ming Huang visited the Moon, according to Chinese legend, and was royally entertained there by plays and players. This inspired the emperor to establish a lavish theater and the world's first school of acting in the Pear Garden of the Imperial Park. Perhaps Ming Huang visited the Moon in his dreams—no astronaut has reported resident actors there—but he did build his theater and dramatic academy. His actors were called "Disciples (or Young Folk, or Students) of the Pear Garden," and, indeed, all Chinese actors were so called up until the mid-20th century.

The term is still heard occasionally today, but the theater no longer exists. *See* THEATER.

young in (at) heart.   This expression, meaning those emotionally and spiritually youthful, only dates back to the 1920s and is probably American in origin, but no more is known about it. A movie so entitled popularized the phrase in 1939.

Young Turk.   A *Young Turk* is an insurgent within any group, such as a political party, supporting progressive policies. The phrase derives from the Turkish reform party that dominated Turkish politics from 1908–18. Many modern European methods were introduced by these Young Turks, who succeeded in making Turkey a republic.

you pays your money and you take your choice.   This expression meaning "to proceed in a regular or orthodox manner" sounds as if it originated with a carnival show where one paid an admission price to see one of several shows offered. It may have, but the first recorded American use of the phrase is in the *Sacramento Union* (January 5, 1864): "The reader 'pays his money and can take his own choice.' " Note the quote marks, however, as if the phrase was commonly used at the time. Possibly it derived from a line in a short poem published in the British magazine *Punch* in 1846.

your all's.   A Texan variation of *you all's.* "I'll get your all's bread," says a waitress in Cormac McCarthy's *All the Pretty Horses* (1992). It is also found in the same author's *Blood Meridian, or, The Evening Redness in the West* (1985): " 'Where's your all's horses?' said Glanton."

"You're a Grand Old Flag."   The title of a 1906 song by actor, singer, and playwright George M. Cohan (1878–1942). Originally, the popular patriotic song was entitled "You're a Grand Old Rag," but the song-and-dance man changed the title when critics protested that he was profaning the Stars and Stripes. *See* GOD BLESS AMERICA.

you're not the only pebble on the beach.   You're not the only woman or man available. This 19th-century expression became a common one with Harry Braistel's 1896 song of the same title.

you're pulling my leg.   Early English hangmen were so inept that friends or relatives were permitted to pull on a victim's dangling body to end his suffering. This gruesome practice was once thought to be the origin of the humorous phrase *you're pulling my leg,* meaning you're fooling me, making fun of me, putting me on. Several word detectives worked overtime to establish the round-about explanation for this, to no avail in the end, for it turned out that the phrase didn't go back to the days of blundering English hangmen at all; that misconception had been fostered by the misdating of the first quotation using the phrase, which appears now to have originated no earlier than the mid-19th century. Instead of being real gallows humor, the phrase seems to be connected somehow with tripping a person up. One theory is that British footpads or muggers worked in pairs, including a specialist known as a "tripper up." Using a cane with a curved handle or piece of wire, this tripper up would trip his victim so that his accomplice could pounce on him and relieve him of his wallet. Since this was a ruse and a leg was actually being pulled, it gave rise to the expression *you're pulling my leg*. This, too, is only a theory, however. The most we can say is that the phrase probably has some relation to somebody being tripped up or fooled.

Your Majesty.   All English kings and queens are called Your Majesty, but the custom did not begin until the reign of Henry VIII. Previously, titles such as His Grace, His Excellent Grace, His Highness, and High and Mighty Prince had been used.

youse.   A very common word used primarily in New York but heard in other eastern cities and even in the Midwest. *Youse*—the so-called generous plural—is usually employed when a speaker is referring to the second person plural, helping the speaker differentiate between one person in the group and the group as a whole. It is the New York counterpart of the southern *y'all. Youse* is also a feature of Irish speech, as is *yis* ("Is he in there with yis?")

you should see the other guy.   A response by someone teased because he has been badly roughed up or wounded in a fight. The expression, implying that the other participant got the worst of it, probably dates back to the late 19th century. In Britain the words are usually *you should see the other fellow* (or *chap*).

you-uns.   *See* YOU-ALL.

yo-yo.   Yo-yo, for the child's toy that spins up and down on a string, was once a trademark. In 1929 a Chicago toymaker patented the toy and was granted the trademark Yo-Yo. The manufacturer had noticed a Filipino youth playing with such a toy on the streets of San Francisco and purchased it from him. In his application for the trademark he claimed that he had coined the word *Yo-Yo* after noticing that children often shout "You! You!" to each other when playing some games. All he had done was to strike the *u* from these words, he explained. In any case, the novelty sold millions, until a competitor marketed the same product under the same name. The Chicago manufacturer quickly brought suit for infringement of his trademark, but after hearing the evidence the court ruled against him. It seems that his competitor offered incontrovertible proof that he had been raised in the Philippines and as a boy had often played with a toy called a yo-yo. There was no doubt that the toy was of ancient Oriental origin and that it was long called by the Philippine name *yo-yo*. The court ruled that the trademark should never have been issued and today any manufacturer can use the term *yo-yo*.

Ypres.   Poison gas was first used in the World War I battle of Ypres in 1915. The first bitter battle of Ypres was fought in 1914, and in 1917 the final battle, or slaughter, of Ypres took place. Ypres is a town in Belgium, bordering France. Its name is pronounced *e* (as in *be*), *pr* (as in *proof*), and *a* (as in *about*).

Yttria.   *See* GADOLINITE.

Yucatán.   Though not proven, *Yucatán*, meaning "I don't understand you," is supposed to be the answer the Spanish explorer Francisco Fernández de Córdoba received and recorded as a place name in 1517 when he asked a native the name of the area we know today as Yucátan. *See* INDRI; KANGAROO; LLAMA; LUZON; NOME.

yucca.   Any plant of the genus *Yucca* native to the Southwest. Yucca, the state flower of New Mexico, has pointed sword-shaped leaves and bears clusters of white waxy flowers on tall stalks.

yuen.   A Chinese borrowing meaning a vegetable garden, the word is sometimes heard on the West Coast but is unrecorded in the rest of the country.

yule.   *Yule*, which is akin to *jolly*, meant December or January in English before it meant Christmas, the word first recorded in 1726. In this sense it derives from an Old Norse word meaning one of the winter months. As a word for Christmas it probably derives from the Old Norse *jol*, the name of a heathen festival at the winter solstice.

yuppie.   A slang term that has been around for over a decade and threatens to stay longer. It is generally a disparaging term meaning Young Urban Professional, especially one who puts getting ahead ahead of everything, and was first recorded in 1983 by syndicated columnist Bob Greene, who overheard it in a bar. As Green explained the word's origin: "While [Gerry Rubin] and Abbie Hoffman once led the Yippies—the Youth International Party—one social commentator has ventured that Rubin is now attempting to become the leader of the Yuppies—Young Urban Professionals."

Z

Z. Z has been called "izzard," "zed," and "zee" in English. It has been considered useless by many writers, including Shakespeare, who wrote: "Thou whoreson Zed! Thou unnecessary letter!" It is the last letter in the Roman as well as the English alphabet.

zaftig. Said of a woman who is full-bodied, well-proportioned, pleasantly plump. Deriving from the German word for "juicy" and first recorded in about 1935 in America, the word is pronounced, and sometimes spelled, *zoftig*.

Zaluzania; Zaluzianskya. Polish physician Adam Zaluziansky von Zaluzian probably never dreamed that his long tongue twister of a name would be given to anything, yet it became the scientific designation for not one but two plant genera. *Zaluzianskya* (often spelled with an "ie" ending) is the beautifully fragrant night-blooming phlox, the genus embracing about 40 South African species. While all such nocturnal flowers may bloom in the daytime, on overcast days, or toward evening, their finest flowering and greatest fragrance comes long after sunset. The Prague doctor, who published an important herbal, *Methodus Herbariae* (1602) has his last name honored by the genus *Zaluzania*, comprising about seven species of small shrubs with white or yellow flowers that are mainly grown in the greenhouse outside their native Mexico. Strangely enough, despite their long, scientific designations, neither genus seems to be known by any popular common name.

Zamzummin. Zamzummin is a synonym for giant ignored by American dictionaries, though the word has been used allusively and figuratively by writers like Sir Thomas More and Richard Burton for centuries. The original Zamzummins were a race of giants, "a people great, and many, and tall" mentioned in Deuteronomy.

zanella. Antonio Zanelli was a great Italian authority on fabrics who published *Le Lone Italiane* (The Italian fabrics) in 1878. This fabric of cotton and worsted often used for linings and umbrellas is named in his honor.

zanja. A ditch or trench. The Spanish word is used in the American West and Southwest. Louis L'Amour wrote in *The Lonesome Gods* (1983): "I led my horse to the zanja for water. . . ."

zany. *Zanni* in Italian is the pet form of the proper name Giovanni (John). As early as the 16th century *zanni* meant a silly fool in Italian, perhaps for some Giovanni no longer remembered. In any case, the word *zanni* came into English, corrupted to *zany*, and became our word for the same and for anything ludicrously or whimsically funny.

zap. The exact origin of *zap* is unknown, but the term possibly arose during World War II, as an onomatopoetic word imitating the sound of a rifle shot hitting someone. According to the *New Dictionary of American Slang* (1986), the word began life as an exclamation deriving from "the sound of a ray gun in the old comic strip Buck Rogers in the Twenty-fifth Century." Since then the word has taken on wider meanings. As slang for "to kill or strike violently," *zap* probably dates back to the Vietnam War. It is also used for "to cook" when food is being prepared in a microwave oven (a common synonym of this is *to nuke*).

Za vasheh! This Russian drinking toast has some currency in the U.S. and England. *Za vasheh!* translates as "To yours."

zealot. The Jewish sect called the Zealots fiercely resisted the Romans until the fall of Jerusalem in A.D. 70. Their name thus came to describe a fanatical person who immoderately pursues his goals with great passion, the word *zealot* recorded in this sense as early as 1638. *Zealot* is ultimately from the Greek *zeloun*, to be zealous.

zebra. The African cross between a horse and ass could be named for the wind god Zephyrus, because of the animal's swiftness, but *zebra* most likely comes from the Abyssinian word *zebra*, for "the striped beast." Referees in several sports, including football and basketball, wear black-and-white striped shirts while officiating games. Because of these colors, fans have been calling them zebras since about 1975. In medical jargon *zebra* means an unlikely or obscure diagnosis, a shortening of the old advice to doctors: "If you hear horses' hoofbeats going by, don't look for zebras."

zed.   During World War II, American and Canadian men evading the draft often blended in on opposite sides of the border. However, immigration agents from both countries found one way to tell where they came from, even though they generally looked, dressed, and talked alike. Agents made the suspects recite the alphabet, because Americans had been taught to recite the last letter of the alphabet as "zee," while Canadians had learned to say "zed." *See* z.

zenadia bird.   *See* BONAPARTE'S GULL.

zenith.   In some obscure way unknown to scholars the Arabic *samt* in the term *samt ar-rar*, "way or path over the head," became the Greek *zenith*, which ultimately became the English term for the point of sky directly overhead, or, figuratively, "the highest point, the acme, the culmination or climax." The word is first recorded in 1387.

zep.   Short for *zeppelin* and one of the many names for the Italian hero sandwich or hero in America. These names include *hoagies* (in Philadelphia), *submarines* or *subs* (in Pittsburgh and elsewhere), *torpedos* (Los Angeles), *wedgies* (Rhode Island), *Garibaldis* (Wisconsin), *bomber* (upstate New York), *wedge* (downstate New York), *Cuban sandwich* (Miami), *Italian sandwich* (Maine), *an Italian* (Midwest), *grinder* (New England), *rocket* (New York State), and *poor boy* (New Orleans), though this last one is made with French instead of Italian bread. *Blimpie*, though it's a tradename and is on a shorter roll, might also qualify, as might *Dagwood sandwich*, for any large sandwich—after *Blondie* comic strip character Dagwood Bumstead's midnight snack creations. That's 20 in all—and there must be more. Is the *Italian hero* possibly the most numerous-named thing in English? *See* HERO.

zephyr.   A *zephyr* is a soft, gentle breeze, taking its name from Zephyrus, the Greek god of the west wind. Shakespeare makes the first recorded mention of the word in this sense in 1611: "They are as gentle as zephires blowing below the violet, / Not wagging his sweet head."

zeppelin.   After a career as a soldier that included a volunteer stint with the Union army during the Civil War, the intrepid German adventurer Count Ferdinand von Zeppelin retired from the German army with the rank of general and devoted himself to the development of dirigible airships. Zeppelin, inspired by a balloon ascent he made in St. Paul, Minnesota, built and flew his first rigid airship in 1900 when 62 years old, the initial flight lasting 20 minutes. But he had to build and test four Luftschiff Zeppelins in all before convincing the German government that his invention was militarily sound. Zeppelins came to be used extensively by the Germans in World War I, some 88 of them constructed by their inventor at his factory in Friedrichshafen. Nevertheless, they didn't work out. Although they attained speeds of up to 36 miles per hour and were used to bomb Paris and London, the airships ultimately proved too unwieldly in combat. Count Zeppelin died in 1917, aged 79, the term *zeppelin* being used by then to mean any dirigible.

zero.   *Zero* derives from the Arabic *cifr*, meaning the same, which passed into Italian as *zefiro*, finally becoming *zero* in French and English. The word wasn't used in English for the arithmetical figure 0 until the early 17th century. The Arabic *cifr*, in turn, came from a Sanskrit word meaning "empty, nothing." Our word *cipher*, which meant "zero" before it meant a code, also derives from *cifr*.

zero hour.   In World War I, *zero hour* among the Allied forces meant the time chosen for the commencement of an assault on the enemy lines. Brought home by veterans, the term soon came to mean any deadline.

zest.   In the 17th century the French called a piece of lemon or orange peel added to a drink to give it flavor a *zest*, a term that may have derived from the Latin *scistus*, "cut." *Zest* passed into English and came to mean anything agreeable or piquant in flavor and, finally, hearty enjoyment or gusto.

zeugma.   *Zeugma* is the Greek word for "yoking" or "joining" and in English means a figure of speech in which a verb is used with two subjects or two objects, or an adjective is used to modify two nouns—although the verb or adjective is appropriate to only one noun. *Zeugma* is often unintentional, as in "She caught a cold and a husband" but it is a common satrical device. An example often quoted is Dickens's phrase in the *Pickwick Papers*: "Miss Bobo . . . went straight home, in a flood of tears, and a sedan chair."

Z-gram.   Chief of U.S. Naval Operations Admiral Elmo Zumwalt issued terse, direct memos that were models of conciseness and clarity. These were dubbed *Z-grams* in the 1960s and became naval slang for such model memos, a thing rare in the armed services.

zhlub.   *Zhlub* has during the past 15 years or so been slang for an insensitive, boorish person. It derives from the Yiddish *zhlub*, meaning the same, which, in turn, comes from a Slavic word. A variation is *zhlob*.

zigged when I should have zagged.   This expression entered the language on April 17, 1939, when Jack Roper was knocked out in the first round of his fight with Joe Louis in Los Angeles. Roper, an unknown fighter in one of Louis's "bum of the month" bouts, had zigged and zagged, trying to dodge Louis's punches. When he came to, the fight's radio announcer asked him how he got tagged. "*I zigged when I should have zagged*," he explained.

zigzag.   To *zigzag*, to make frequent sharp turns from side to side, probably comes from the German *Zickzack*, which is an echoic word possibly formed of the elements *ziche*, "to dodge about" and *zacke*, "a serrated edge." The word came into English, from the French *zigzag*, in the early 18th century.

zigzag course.   This term probably arose during World War I. A *zigzag course* is a ship's course first to the right of the base course and then to the left. It was originally used in avoiding enemy submarines, but the term is now applied to any devious action.

zilch. *Zilch,* "nothing," is an Americanism that has been traced back to the 1920s when a *Joe Zilch* meant a good for nothing college boy. Other sources, however, trace the expression to a character called Mr. Zilch in a *Ballyhoo* magazine cartoon series of the 1930s, in which Mr. Zilch was never seen but scantily clad, wide-eyed girls, reacting to things he had obviously done, cried "Oh, Mr. Zilch!" Since Mr. Zilch wasn't depicted, according to this theory, he came to represent nothing, or *zilch.*

zillionaire. *Zillionaire,* for someone with wealth of mythical proportions, is an Americanism that appears to date back only to the late 1940s or early 1950s. *See* MILLIONAIRE.

zinc. The German *Zinc* is the direct ancestor of our metal *zinc,* first attested to in 1651, but the origin of the German word is obscure—though it may be linked with the German *Zin,* for "tin."

zing. *Zing,* in the sense of "to cause to move with a sharp, singing noise," may derive from baseball, where a pitcher often zings a fastball over the plate. There's no firm proof of this, though. The word, first recorded in 1910, might also derive from the sound of an arrow shot in archery, or even that of a rifle shot.

zinnia. *Youth and old age,* the *zinnia* species *elegans* is called, and anyone who has seen how profusely the annual flower blooms and how quickly it succumbs to the first frost will appreciate the folk name. The same applies to all the zinnia genus, which Linnaeus named for Johann Gottfried Zinn, whose life was as bright and brief as his namesake's. Zinn, a German botanist and physician who was a professor of medicine at Gottingen, died in 1759 when barely 32. In 1753 he had published what is said to be the first book of the anatomy of the eye. There are about 15 species of the zinnia, which is the state flower of Indiana. Most modern tall forms, with flowers in many colors, come from the Mexican *Zinnia elegans* introduced in 1886 and growing to heights of about three feet. Another explanation for *elegans's* youth-and-old-age nickname may be the stiff hairs on the stem or the coarse plant itself, in contrast to the soft flowers, or the plant's tendency to develop the powdery mildew disease when poorly cultivated. But the spring frost analogy is nicer.

Zionist. A Zionist is a supporter of the policy of Zionism, that is, the settlement of Jews from all over the world in Palestine. *Zion* is the name of a hill in Jerusalem of great historic religious significance to Jews as the home of David and his successors.

zip; zipper. *Zip* is common American slang for zero, nothing, and probably derives in part from the *z* sound in *zero.* The story that American soldiers in Vietnam named Vietnamese Zips from an acronym for Zero Intelligence Potential is unlikely—it probably derived from the earlier *zip. Zip* for zero is not related to *zipper;* this slide device for fastening clothing, once a trademark, takes its name from *zip* for fast, which is

first recorded in about 1855 and is imitative of the sound *zip.* The zipper was invented in 1893 by Whitman L. Judson, who called it the Universal Fastener. An anonymous executive at the B.F. Goodrich Company changed the name to Zipper, but Goodrich did not protect its trademark and the word is not capitalized today.

zip code; zip. The *zip* in *zip-code* is an acronym for zone *improvement plan,* an acronym that was invented to convey the idea of speed—zip! The system and name for it were introduced by the U.S. Post Office in 1963. The actual inventor of the code was postal employee Robert A. Moon (1918–2000), who first submitted his idea in 1944 but waited almost 20 years to see it accepted. Mr. Moon's contribution consisted of the first three digits of the zip code—those referring to the general regions of the U.S. The last two digits—identifying smaller delivery areas—are credited to others. At the time of his death Mr. Moon was said to be working on a zip code plan for interplanetary mail.

Zippity-do-dah. In January 2002 an Englishman legally changed his name to Zippity-do-dah, because he thought his previous name was too difficult to pronounce. Mr. Zippity-do-dah had to obtain permission from the Disney Corporation, for "Zippity-do-dah" is the title of a popular Disney song, whose lyrics begin "Zippity-do-dah, zippity-a, my oh my what a wonderful day. . . ." *Zippity-do-dah* is also used sarcastically in conversations after someone has said something quite obvious that doesn't need saying: "Well, zippity-do-dah." *See* NORFORK HOWARD; THE OFFICIAL MONSTER RAVING LOONY PARTY.

ziti. Familiar to Americans in the form of the tasty Italian dish baked ziti, the word *ziti* is the name of a tubular pasta that derives from the obsolete Italian word *ziti,* meaning "boys." The phallic shape of the pasta may have suggested the "boys" appellation.

zizzer. Since at least 1930, *zizz* has meant "to sleep" in the British navy because the word is suggestive of snoring. From this came the naval slang *zizzer,* for "bed," mainly confined to British English.

zob. Zob is the name of an old game played among officers in the British Navy to decide which of two people will pay for drinks, but the game is now common outside England, where it's often known as "Rock, paper, scissors." The players face each other, repeating the word *zob* three times. Each then makes a closed fist, an open palm, or two fingers extended like a pair of scissors. The game is decided on this basis: "Scissors can cut paper, stone can blunt scissors, and paper can wrap up a stone." Thus, a player who holds out two fingers (a scissors) beats a player who holds out an open palm (a piece of paper); a player who holds out a closed fist (a stone) beats a player who holds out two fingers (a scissors), etc. The player who loses two out of three zobs pays for the drinks.

zodiac. Many people know the signs of the zodiac: Taurus, the bull; Pisces, the fishes, etc. But few know the origin of the word *zodiac* itself. *Zodiac* derives from the Greek *zoon,* "animal," being so named, of course, because most of the signs were named for animals.

Zoilost.   Not many authors would want the fourth-century-B.C. Greek philosopher Zoilus as a critic. The cynical Zoilus was nicknamed "Homeromastix," "the scourge of Homer" for his severe criticism of the poet, though he was just as scathing about Plato and Isocrates, too. The spiteful but witty Zoilus called the companions of Homer's Odysseus "weeping porkers" (Circe turned them into swine). So scathing were his words that his name is still used for a spiteful, envious, malignant, carping critic.

zombie.   Zombie was originally the snake god worshipped in West Indian voodoo ceremonies based upon the worship of the python god in West Africa. Since dead people were said to be brought to life in these ceremonies, such imagined corpses shuffling along half dead and half alive were called zombies. By the 1920s this word naturally became applied to any oafish "dummy" without much intelligence or spirit. It is also the name of a cocktail that makes one feel like a zombie.

Zonta Club.   Zonta Club is one of many service clubs composed of businesswomen. Its members are devoted to promoting world peace and fellowship. The club, founded in 1919, takes its name from the American Sioux Indian word *zonta*, meaning "to be trusted."

zoom.   *See* ONOMATOPOEIA.

zoopraxiscope.   One of the earliest motion picture projectors, the zoopraxiscope was built by photographer Eadweard Muybridge in about 1880 to project sequential pictures he had taken a few years earlier of a running horse—the pictures taken for railroad tycoon Leland Stanford, who had bet (correctly) $25,000 that a running horse sometimes had all four feet off the ground at the same time. Muybridge coined the word from the Greek elements *zoi*, "living" plus praxis, "action" plus *skopein*, "viewing instrument." He seems to have first called the instrument the zoogyroscope.

zoot suit.   A men's clothing style of the 1930s and early 1940s featuring peg trousers, jacket with padded shoulders, wide-brimmed hat and wide tie, among other flamboyant items of apparel, all in bright colors. A good example of the style can be seen in the film *Malcolm X* (1993). *Zoot suit* is probably a rhyming phrase, *zoot* an alteration (!) of suit.

Zoot Suit Riots.   A name for the Los Angeles rioting in 1943 primarily between U.S. sailors and soldiers and Mexican-American youths who wore the ZOOT SUITS. Twenty-three of the zoot-suiters were arrested, though their side seems to have been subjected to the most violence, servicemen even stripping them of their clothing and burning it. The trial was a travesty, but the guilty verdict was overturned on appeal.

Zoroastrianism.   A religion founded by the Persian prophet Zoroaster (also called Zarathustra) in the sixth century B.C. Zoroastrianism was one of the world's great religions for over 13 centuries but is largely confined to India today. Its founder was called the prophet of light and good triumphing over evil and darkness. Some scholars believe that his name means "old camel," but no one knows if this is true or why he would be so named. The German philosopher Friedrich Nietzsche's greatest work was *Thus Spake Zarathustra*.

zotz.   Apparently first used among college students, *zotz* means "nothing, zero, zip, zilch," as in "He's completely zotz as a teacher." The word seems, like *zip* and *zilch*, to be based on the z in *zero*, though it may have been suggested by *squat*, which it sounds like and which also has a meaning of nothing or zero. *Zotz* has recently come to mean "kill" or "hit" in underworld talk; since *zotz* means "nothing or zero," *to zotz* refers to making a person nothing, to kill that person.

Zoysia grass.   For some odd reason few of the major dictionaries include *Zoysia grass*, which is commonly planted today, especially for play areas and for lawns in the deep South. The popular grass, generally planted from bits of rootstock called Zoysia plugs, is named for Austrian botanist Karl von Zois. There are only four species of the creeping grass. Zoysia takes a lot of wear and tear, forming a dense, tough turf, but has one major drawback—it turns a haylike color in the late fall and is among the slowest of grasses to green up again in the spring. Some zealous Zoysia lawn keepers give nature a tender, loving hand by painting their grass with green latex and other preparations in the off-seasons. Yet another reason why anyone reincarnated in suburbia wouldn't do badly if he came back as a lawn.

z's.   *Z's* is American slang for sleep. Originating within the last 35 years or so, the term probably derives from the *Z's* indicating snoring in comic strip and cartoon captions, which themselves represent the sound of snoring.

Zulu.   *See* INDABA.

zwieback.   Zwieback is a hard dry toast popular with adults and even made specifically for babies. The word, first recorded here in 1894, is a German one meaning "twice baked."

Zwinglian.   Pertaining to Huldrych Zwingli or his doctrines. Huldrych or Ulrich Zwingli (1484–1531), a Swiss Protestant reformer, served as chaplain and standard bearer to troops fighting against Catholic sections of Switzerland that did not accept the official recognition of the Reformation. He was killed at the battle of Kappel. Zwingli's views were close to Martin Luther's, except for his purely symbolic interpretation of the Lord's Supper, which estranged the two men and made a united Protestantism impossible.

zyzzyva.   Often destructive to plants, the *zyzzyva* (pronounced ziz-ih-vuh) weevil is a leaf-hopping insect of tropical America that provides one of the best examples of onomatopoeia at work in the creation of words. Although most dictionaries give its origin as "obscure," if they give it at all, the word probably derives from the Spanish *ziz, zas!*, which is "echoic of the impact of a blow," the reference being, of course, to the noise made by these cicada-like insects.

ZZZ. ZZZ has been used by cartoonists to represent the sound of snoring for 50 years or so. It can also represent the sound of locusts or an electric saw. In any case, the last possible word with which to end an alphabetically arranged word book is ZZZ, unless there is somewhere an unrecorded ZZZZ . . .

Index

A

Aaron (biblical figure) 1–2, 690, 783
Aaron, Hank 46
Aasen, Iva Andreas 269
Abas II (king of Persia) 2
Abbe, Cleveland 530
Abbott, Carlisle S. 375
Abbott, E. C. 376
Abdullah, Mohammed bin 457
Abel (biblical figure) 189, 424, 468
Abel, Clarke 2
Abernathy, John 213
Abert, J. W. 3
Abigail (biblical figure) 3
Abraham (biblical figure) 4, 382
Absalom (biblical figure) 783
Absorbine Jr. 37
Abu Bakr (first Muslim caliph) 9
Abzug, Bella 781
Academus (mythological figure) 321–322
Acestes (mythological figure) 34
Achelous (mythological figure) 663
Achilles (mythological figure) 6, 501, 710, 716, 787
Achises (mythological figure) 29
Actaeon (mythological figure) 461
Acts (New Testament) 24, 152, 435, 612, 662
Adam (biblical figure) 7–8, 189, 218, 259, 260, 468, 501, 528, 547, 586
Adams, Caswell 386
Adams, Cecil 624
Adams, Fanny 700
Adams, Franklin P. (F. P. A.) 31, 477, 510, 603, 723
Adams, James Truslow 402
Adams, John 8, 361, 392, 636, 789
Adams, John Quincy 109, 303, 378, 670
Adams, Maude 558
Adams, Rámon 232, 766
Adams, Samuel 465
Addison, Joseph 170, 195, 215, 234, 364, 380, 414, 499, 559, 583, 770, 783
Addison, Thomas 9
Ade, George 113–114, 299, 483, 545, 711
Adelman, Enrico 84
Adian, Bishop 581
Adonis (mythological figure) 9, 26, 29, 501
Ady, Thomas 351
AE (George William Russell) 10
Aeacus (mythological figure) 501
Aegeus (mythological figure) 10
Aeneas (mythological figure) 177, 298
Aeneid 25

Aeolus (mythological figure) 328
Aeschylus (Greek dramatist) 48, 205, 317
Aesculapius (mythological figure) 366
Aesop (Greek fabulist) 8, 217, 433, 442, 625, 668, 677
Aethelthryth (Anglo-Saxon ruler) 709
Afghana (biblical figure) 10
Agag (biblical figure) 762
Agave (mythological figure) 11
Agnew, Spiro 660
Agricultural Adjustment Administration (AAA) 1
Agrippa (Roman general and statesman) 508
Agrippina (Roman aristocrat) 165
A. G. Spalding & Co. 78
Ahab (biblical figure) 503
Aharoni, I. 330
Ahasuerus (biblical figure) 331
Ahern, Michael 495
Ahura Mazda (mythological figure) 474
Aitken, William Maxwell 762
Akers, Elizabeth Chase 461
Alabama 178
Alaska 426
Albee, Edward 775
Albert (Austrian archduke) 189, 382
Albert (prince of Saxe-Coburg-Gotha) 584
Albert Edward (prince of Wales) 584
Albertus Magnus 26
Alcinous (mythological figure) 14
Alcott, Bronson 307, 554
Alcott, Bronson, Mrs. 49
Alcott, Louisa May 49, 307, 393
Alcyone (mythological figure) 328
Alden, John 679
Aleichem, Sholom 656, 732, 795
Alemaigne, Richard of 701
Alençon, duc d' 101
Alexander, Charles 392
Alexander (duke of Gordon) 310
Alexander VI (pope) 95, 300, 507
Alexander the Great 15, 33, 128, 178, 191, 209–210, 254, 317, 346, 406, 422, 448, 483, 533, 557, 560, 571, 593, 637–638, 714
Alfonso (king of Spain) 189, 380
Algarotti, Francesco 699
Alger, Horatio, Jr. 358
Ali, Muhammad 266, 466, 535
Ali Baba (fictional character) 535
Alice the Goon 308
Alithea (fictional character) 714
Allainville, Abbé d' 239
Allee, W. C. 342, 554
Allen, Ethan 379

Allen, Fred 353, 727
Allen, Harry N. 709
Allen, Richard 715
Allen, Woody 571
Alley Oop (fictional character) 16
Allie (cat) 140
Allison, Clay 376
Allman, Sherman 359
Alzheimer, Alois 21
Aman, Reinheld 189
Amaryllis (fictional character) 66
Amati, Nicolò 693
Ambler, Eric 645
Amboise, Georges d' 291, 434
Ameche, Don 22
America 22–23
American Sign Language (ASL) 23
American Telephone and Telegraph (AT&T) 37
Amman, Jakob 23
Ammon (mythological figure) 23
Ampère, André-Marie 491
Amphitrite (mythological figure) 70, 507
Anacreon (Greek poet) 24
Anagnus (mythological figure) 579
Ananias (biblical figure) 24
Anastasia, Albert 498
Anburey, Thomas 109
Ancaeus (mythological figure) 716
Ancient Society of Cogers 163
Andersen, Hans Christian 240, 741
Anderson, Elbert 743
Anderson, Maxwell 334
Anderson, Sherwood 162
André, John 67
Andromeda (mythological figure) 25
Andrzeyevski, George 646
Angstrom, Ander Jonas 26
Anne (empress of Russia) 63
Anne (queen of Bohemia) 597
Anne (queen of England) 139, 413, 506, 597, 642, 726
Anstie, Edward 27
Anthony, Henry 621
Antichrist 60, 259, 508
Antiochus I (Seleucid ruler) 425
Antiphanes (Greek playwright) 279
Antisthenes (Athenian philosopher) 192
Antony. *See* Mark Antony
Apache Indians 29
Apelles (Greek artist) 160
Aphrodite (mythological figure) 9, 26, 29, 30, 257, 344, 584
Apicius, Marcus Gavius 29, 435, 746
Apollo (mythological figure) 59, 136, 192, 305, 341, 348, 366, 382, 513, 548, 573, 593, 621, 699

Apollo Smintheus (mythological figure) 607
Appleton, Edward 31
Appleton, Thomas Gold 279, 500
A. P. Watt and Sons 11
Arabian Nights 55
Arachne (mythological figure) 32
Arbuthnot, John 57, 188, 398, 551
Archimedes (Greek mathematician) 32, 247
Archy (fictional character) 162
Arden Enoch (fictional character) 242
Arendt, Hannah 587
Aretino, Pietro 32–33, 294
Argall, Samuel 202
Argus (mythological beast) 33
Argyll, duke of 33, 478
Aristarchus of Samonthrace 33
Aristocles 31
Aristophanes 160, 317, 579, 644
Aristotle 33, 40, 116, 167, 246, 301, 436, 483, 533, 579, 752
Arizona 44
Arkansas 33, 781
Arlen, Harold 605
Arlette (mother of William the Conqueror) 334
Arlington, Henry Bennet, earl of 123
Armour, Richard 34, 754
Armstrong, Henry 700
Armstrong, Jack 387
Armstrong, Margaret 539
Armstrong, Neil 532
Armstrong, Robert 179
Arnold, Benedict 67
Arnold, Kenneth 268
Arnold, Matthew 560, 604, 700
d'Artagnan (fictional character) 288
d'Artagnan, Charles de Batz-Castelmore 196–197
Artemis (mythological figure) 4, 133, 461, 557
Artemisia (queen of Caria) 472
Arthur (king of England) 127
Arthur Guinness, Son & Co., Ltd. 5
Asbury, Elise 86
Asbury, Herbert 115, 152, 175
Ascham, Roger 35
Asche, Oscar 537
Aselges (mythological figure) 579
Ashfield, Farmer and Dame (fictional characters) 495
Ashlet, James M. 785
Ashley, Lady Brett (fictional character) 167
Ashurbanipal (king of Assyria) 243, 636. *See also* Sardanapalus
Aspasia of Miletus 35

Astor, John Jacob 482, 497, 732
Astor, Mrs. 274
Astoreth (mythological figure) 630
Athena (mythological figure) 30, 32, 37, 458, 477, 530, 579
Athenaeus (Greek writer) 242
Athenaios of Naucratis 202
Athens 38
Atherton, Gertrude 770
Atkins, Thomas 726
Atlantic Ocean 73
Atlas (mythological figure) 133
Atropos (mythological figure) 38
Attab (legendary figure) 703
Atticus (Roman man of letters) 195
Attila the Hun 364, 700
d'Aubigné, Françoise. *See* Maintenon, Françoise Aubigné, marquise de
Aubrey, John 183, 521
Aubriet, Claude 38
Aubry of Montdidier 38
Auden, W. H. (Wystan Hugh) 11, 524, 536
Augeus (mythological figure) 157
Augin, Emile 518
Augustus Caesar 38–39, 108, 125, 158, 192, 256, 294, 505, 544, 600
Aurora (mythological figure) 39, 314
Austen, Jane 9, 27, 56, 519
Australia 39
Autry, Gene 290
Avalon, Frankie 362
Avery, Tex 770
Avogadro, Amedeo 40
Axelrod, George 649
Axolotl VIII (Aztec ruler) 162
Axtell, Roger E. 749
Azevedo, Ignatius 631

B

Babbage, Charles 573
Babbitt (fictional character) 43, 94
Babbitt, Isaac 43
Babcock, Stephen Moulton 43
Babel, Isaac 168
Bacall, Lauren 371
Bacchus (mythological figure) 67, 308, 537, 621
Bacon, Francis 186, 238, 245, 356, 359, 486, 519, 560, 650, 771, 780
Baedeker, Karl 47
Baekeland, Leo Hendrik 48
Baer, Robert 592
Bagot, Robert 460
Baha Allah 47
Bailey, Donald Coleman 48
Bailey, Frankie 276
Bailey, L. H. 440
Bailey, Roy F. 495
Baily, Francis 255
Baker, Fred 700
Baker, George 630
Baker, Samuel 584
Balboa, Vasco Núñez de 189
Baldwin, Loammi 49
Baldwin, Stanley 190, 501
Baldwin, William 220
Bales, Peter 126
Balfour, Arthur J. 88–89, 138
Ball, Lucille 280
Ballantyne, James 317
Baltimore 50
Balzac, Honoré de 117
Banco, Mark 51
Bandello, Matteo 495
Bang, Bernhard L. F. 52
Bangs, John Kendrick 770
Banks, Joseph 170
Bannister, Roger 274
Banting, William 52
Baptiste, Jean 57
Bara, Theda 383
Barani, Robert 53
Barber, Red 137, 185, 552, 710
Barbier, Charles 101
Barca, Hamilcar 54
Barclay, Florence 461
Barebones, Praise-God 54

Barham, Richard Harris 281, 574, 727
Barker, David 743
Barley Mow Tavern 163
Barlow, Joel 335
Barlow, Russel 54
Barming asylum 50
Barnes, Clive 739
Barnum, P. T. 357, 364, 393, 402, 659, 716, 726, 793, 797
Barrie, James M. 9, 509, 558, 587
Barron, Walker 222
Barrymore, John 270, 315, 317, 706
Barrymore family 751
Bartas, Guillaume de Salluste du 391
Barter, Robert 55
Bartholdi, Frédéric Auguste 236, 688
Bartholomew Fair 55
Bartleby (fictional character) 199
Bartlett, Enoch 55, 553
Bartlett, John 11, 55–56, 285, 335, 436
Barton, William 27
Bartram, John 276, 406
Basedow, Karl von 104, 315
Baskerville, John 738
Bass, Thomas A. 246
Bates, Katherine Lee 23
Bates, William 517
Bath-sheba 674
Batista, Fulgencio 466
Bator 304
Batson, Billy (fictional character) 652
Battos 58
Batu Khan 35
Baudelaire, Charles 246, 570
Baum, L. Frank 498, 593, 729
Bayer Aspirin Company 36
Bayly, Thomas Haynes 4
Beacon, Thomas 538
Beaconsfield, Lord. *See* Disraeli, Benjamin
Beal, Frank P. 543
Beamer, Todd 434
Beardsley, Charles A. 432
Beaufort, duke of 47
Beaufort, Sir Francis 62
Beauharnais, Alexandre de 425
Beaulier, Monsieur 99
Beaumont, Francis 3, 160, 174, 343, 521
Beauregard, A. Toutant de 473
Beauregard, Pierre Gustave Toutant 58, 465, 609
Beavers, Louise 554
Bechamel, Louis de 62
Beck, Martin 751
Becker, May Lamberton 477
Becket, Thomas A. 166
Beckett, Samuel 223
Beckford, William 373
Bede, the Venerable 581, 697
Bedford, duke of 661
Beebee, William 57
Beecher, Henry Ward 63
Beer, Thomas 473
Beerbohm, Max 300
Beers, E. L. 18
Begon, Michel 65
Belcher, Jim 66
Belides (mythological figure) 194
Bell, Alexander Graham 12, 202, 495, 711
Bell, Joseph 653
Bellamy, Edward 747
Bellarmino, Roberto Francesco Romolo 66
Belloc, Hilaire 754
Bellow, Saul 133
Bell Telephone Company 202
Benchley, Peter 344
Benchley, Robert 11, 435, 477, 722, 774
Benedict, Le Grand, Mrs. 236
Benedict, Samuel 236
Benét, Stephen Vincent 78, 270, 302, 530, 642
Benjamin (biblical figure) 68
Benjamin, Judah Philip 68
Bennet, Justice 596

Bennett, Arnold 147
Bennett, James Gordon 310, 530
Bentham, Jeremy 40
Bentley, Edmund Clerihew 158–159, 291
Bentley, Nicholas 24
Benzedrine 68
Berenice (Ptolemaic queen) 167, 372
Berg, Moe 306
Bergen, Edgar 226
Bergerac, Cyrano de 192, 216
Bergman, Ingrid 344
Bering, Vitus 649
Berkeley, Lord 509
Berkman, Alexander 370
Berkow, Ira 273, 290
Berle, Milton 278, 372
Berlin, Irving 301, 685
Berlioz, Hector 638
Berlitz, Charles 385
Bermúdez, Juan de 68
Bernard, Henriette Rosine. *See* Bernhardt, Sarah
Bernard, John 117
Bernays, Eddie 587
Bernhardt, Sarah 103, 256, 603, 636, 637, 706, 751
Bernstein, Arthur 686
Bernstein, Carl 202
Bernstein, Theodore 608
Berra, Yogi 302
Berryman, Clifford K. 710
Berthelot, Marcellin 467
Berthollet, Claude-Louis, Comte 470
Bertillon, Alphonse 75
Bertini 465
Berwanger, Jay 341
Bessemer, Henry 69
Beste, Henry Digsby 20
Beukel, William 374
Beum, Robert 557
Bevin, Ernest 70
Bharata (Hindu king) 459
Bialystok 47
Bias of Priene 648
Bibb, John B. 71
Bible. *See specific books*
Bich, Marcel 71
Bickerstaff, Isaac 71, 731
Biilg, Gottfried Johannes (fictional character) 373
Billings, Josh 400, 685
Billing's Gate 75
Billington, Ray Allen 417
Binet, Alfred 75
bin Laden, Osama 248, 595
Bird, Edward 333
Bird, Robert 185
Biro, Ladislas 71
Bishop, Charles Reed 535
Bishop, Henry 354
Bishop, Mr. 76
Bismarck, Otto von 611
Black Ball Steamer Line 78
Blackburne, Lena "Slats" 433
Blackstone, William 233
Blackwell, Henry Brown 453
Blaine, James 44, 496, 575, 625
Blair, Robert 258
Blake, 437
Blake, William 304
Blanc, Mel 714, 770
Blanket, Thomas 81
Blazer, H.M.S. 82
Blenker, Louis 82
Bligh, William 131, 388
Blish, John N. 726
Bloody Mary. *See* Mary I
Bloomer, Amelia Jenks 84
Blücher, Gebhard Leberecht von 85
Bluffe, Captain (fictional character) 667
Blumenfeld, Laura 772
Blunt, John 87
Bly, Nelly 507
Bobadill, Captain (fictional character) 88

Bobbitt, John Wayne 88
Boccaccio, Giovanni 54, 56, 89, 545
Bode, Johann 747
Bodley, Thomas 89
Bodoni 738
Bogart, Humphrey 217, 344, 371
Bogart, John B. 771
Bogey, Colonel (fictional character) 90
Bohlin, Celestine 226
Bohlin, Nils 644
Bohn, Henry George 91
Boisbaudran, Lecoq de 634
Boleyn, Anne 238, 517, 558
Bolívar, Simon 90, 189
Bolo, Paul 90
Bona Dea (mythological figure) 473
Bonaparte, Charles-Lucien 91
Bonaparte, Louis-Napoleon. *See* Napoleon III
Bonaparte, Napoleon. *See* Napoleon
Bond, James 284
Bondone, Giotto di 297
Bonds, Barry 519
Boniface I (pope) 631
Boniface VI (pope) 631
Bonnie Prince Charlie. *See* Charles Edward Stuart
Bononcini, Giovanni Battista 736–737
Bontemps, Arna 743
Booker McConnell firm 93
Boone, Daniel 94, 195
Booth, John Wilkes 204, 349, 440, 649, 660
Booze, E. G. (or E. S.) 95
Borah, William E. 514
Borde, Andrew 478
Borges, Jorge Luis 54, 373
Borgia, Cesare 95, 300, 507
Borgia, Giovanni 507
Borgia, Lucrezia 95, 300
Borgia, Roderigo. *See* Alexander VI
Bork, Robert H. 95
Borkenstein, Robert F. 103
Borrow, George 247
Boruwlaski, Joseph 468
Bosanquet, B. J. T. 96
Bosquet, Maréchal 132
Bossuet, Jacques 14
Boston Common 168
Boswell, James 96–97, 136
Botticelli, Sandro 753
Bottomley, Horace 97
Bougainville, Louis-Antoine de 97
Boulanger, Georges-Ernest-Jean-Marie 97
Boulton, Matthew 765
Bow, Clara 383
Bowditch, Nathaniel 98
Bowdler, Thomas 98
Bowen, Charles, Baron 384
Bowie, James 98–99
Bowie, Rezin Pleasant 98
Bowles, Samuel 591
Boycott, Charles Cunningham 100
Boyle, Charles 537
Boyle, Hal 758
Boyle, Robert 186, 537, 555
Boysen, Rudolf 100
Bradbury, John 101
Braddock, General 195
Braddock, Jim 397
Bradford, John 716
Bradford, William 564
Bradham, Caleb D. 556
Bradley, Voorhies, and Day 121
Brady, James 206
Brahma 96
Braille, Louis 54, 101
Brainerd, J. G. 170
Braistel, Harry 798
Brandon, Gregory 319, 731
Brandt, Jackie 264
Brandt, Sebastian 655
Brassière, Phillippe de 100
Brawne, Fanny 717
Brecht, Bertholt 205
Breslin, Jimmy 130
Brevoort, J. C. 103

Brewer, Ebenezer 20, 298, 438, 474
Brewer, Thomas 55, 553
Brewster, William 103
Briad, James 367
Briand, Aristide 508
Briareus (mythological figure) 103
Brice, Fanny 294
Bright, John 267, 552
Bright, Richard 104
Brillat-Savarin, Anthelme 104, 144, 734
Brinell, Johann August 105
Brinker, Hans 228
Bristed, John 60
Britannicus 508
Brocard, Henri 106
Broderick, Johnny "The Boffer" 106
Brodie, James 584
Brodie, Steve 212
Brodie, William 212
Brogniart, Alexandre 682
Brokaw, Claire Booth 11
Brome, Richard 605
Bronck, Jonas 106
Bronstein, Lev Davidovich 733
Brontë, Charlotte 54, 668, 715
Brontë family 742
Brooke, Arthur 620
Brooklyn 107
Brooks, Richard 618
Brooks, Van Wyck 500
Brougham, Henry Peter 107
Broughton, Lord 514–515
Broughton, Philip 120
Broun, Heywood 477, 592
Brown, Bundini 266
Brown, Claude 400
Brown, Dee 316
Brown, Ivor 777
Brown, Joe E. 315
Brown, John 334, 378
Brown, Lancelot "Capability" 130
Brown, Nathan L. 536
Brown, Thomas 212
Brown, Wiley 346
Brown-Dequard, Charles 582
Browne, Samuel 634
Browne, Thomas 127, 501–502, 570
Brownell, Charles 108
Browning, Elizabeth Barrett 200, 214, 362
Browning, John M. 53
Browning, Robert 18, 252, 362, 434, 572, 715, 725
Browning automatic rifle (BAR) 53
Broyard, Anatole 559
Bruce, David 52
Bruce, James 108
Bruce, Robert 460
Brudenell, James Thomas 132
Brumby, William 108
Brummell, George Bryan "Beau" 61, 441
Brunelleschi, Filippo 166
Brutus, Marcus Junius 108, 173
Bryan, William Jennings 186, 316, 357
Bryant, William Cullen 77, 216, 290
Bryson, Bill 254, 299, 492, 522, 574
Bucephalus 359, 557
Buchalter, Louis "Lepke" 349
Buchanan, Robert 266
Bucket, Edward 109
Buckingham 123
Buddha 260, 464, 629, 752
Budding, Edwin 429
Budgell, Eustace 215, 559, 770
Buffalo Bill (William Frederick Cody) 27, 111, 115
Buffon, George-Louis Leclerc, comte de 295, 695
Bug, Joshua 516
Bugs Bunny (fictional character) 512, 770, 777
Bull, John (fictional character). See John Bull
Bull, John (musician) 302
Bull Durahm Tobacco 113
Bulwer-Lytton, Edward George 98, 136, 556, 706

Bumppo, Natty (fictional character) 337, 550
Bumstead, Dagwood (fictional character) 344, 802
Buncombe County 115
Bunker, Archie (fictional character) 32, 209
Bunker, Chang and Eng 659
Bunn, Austin 463
Bunsen, Robert Wilhelm 115
Buntline, Ned 115
Bunyan, John 31, 448
Bunyan, Paul 551, 554
Burbage, James 782
Burbage, Richard 726, 777
Burbank, Luther 115–116, 571, 575
Burchard, Bishop 106
Burchard, Samuel 625
Burgess, Anthony 214, 228, 235
Burgess, Gelett 87, 308, 380
Burgoyne, John "Gentleman Johnny" 116, 204, 237, 512
Buridan, Jean 116
Burke, Edmund 210, 238, 274
Burke, Edward 713
Burke, John 117
Burke, Martha Jane Canary (Calamity Jane) 125
Burke, Patrick 304
Burke, William 116–117
Burmann, Gottlob 442
Burnet, Gilbert 426, 772
Burnett, Frances Hodgson 443
Burnham, George 292
Burns, Bob 59
Burns, Robert 39, 54, 69, 157, 160, 185, 192, 320, 511, 707
Burns, Tommy 388
Burnside, Ambrose Everett 660
Burr, Aaron 359, 456
Burrell, Karl 713
Burros, Marian 108
Burroughs, Edgar Rice 708
Burton, Montague 280
Burton, Nat 773
Burton, Richard 8, 214, 532, 801
Burton, Robert 65, 512, 556
Busby, Richard 118
Bush, George 681, 761
Bush, George W. 41, 248, 435, 690
Butler, Alban 142, 749
Butler, Benjamin 44
Butler, James D. 379
Butler, Rhett (fictional character) 298
Butler, Samuel 24, 67, 417, 448, 456, 569, 766
Butterfield, Daniel 707
Butts, Alfred Mosher 642
Buzzell, Charles 235
Byerly, Captain 121
Byng of Vimy 75
Bynner, Harold Witter 416
Byrd, William 267
Byrnes, James F. 752
Byrom, John 737
Byron, George Gordon, Lord 95, 104, 122, 199, 216, 219, 342, 443, 482, 513, 514, 520, 552, 619, 620, 636, 663, 665, 711, 734, 736, 779

C

Caan, James 685
Cabell, J. H. 480
Cabell, James Brand 373
Cabot, John 421
Cadillac, Antoine de la Mothe 124
Cadman, S. Parker 137
Cadmus (mythological figure) 11, 124–125
Caen, Herb 61
Caepio 305
Caesar, Julius. See Julius Caesar
Caesarion 158
Cagney, Jimmy 210
Cain (biblical figure) 189, 424, 468
Calabash, Mrs. 372
Calchas 208

Caldwell, Erskine 98, 302, 599, 616, 724
Calepino, Ambrosio 126
Calhoun, John C. 126
California 305
Caligula 359, 683
Calista (fictional character) 289
Callenbach, Ernest 748
Callimachus 4–5, 167, 317
Calliope (mythological figure) 499
Callisto (mythological figure) 380
Calloway, Cab 489
Calloway, Elvy E. 287
Calvert, George 50, 470
Calvert family 471
Calvin, John 127
Cambronne, Pierre 323
Camellus 127
Cameron, Simon 17–18
Camilla (queen of the Volsci) 254
Camoëns, Luis de 8
Camp, Walter Chauncey 16, 254, 313, 320
campaign slogans 668
Campanella, Tommaso 747
Campbell, Barley 774
Campbell, Boyd 645
Campbell, Roy 737
Campbell, Thomas 258, 520, 782
Canaris, Walther Wilhelm 472
Canfield, Richard C. 129
Cant, Andrew 129
Cantor, Eddie 213
Capek, Karel 618
Caplin, Hymie 221
Capone, Al 14
Capote, Truman 164
Capp, Al 410, 630, 641
Captain Marvel 652
Captiva, Joseph 302
Caraffa, Cardinal 549
Carême, Marie-Antoine 132–133, 144
Carew, George 81
Carey, Henry 153, 504
Carlson, Chester 788
Carlson, Evans F. 324
Carlyle, Jane Welsh "Jenny" 393
Carlyle, Thomas 242, 610, 636, 645, 694
Carmer, Carl 334
Carmichael, Hoagy 372
Carnegie, Andrew 133, 655
Carney, Julia A. Fletcher 442
Caro, Robert 120
Caroline (queen of England) 584
Caroline of Brunswick 206
Carpenter, Liz 650
Carpentier, Georges 410
Carroll, Lewis 15, 93, 124, 152, 294, 320, 387, 456, 457, 579, 668, 671, 722, 737
Carter, Billy 307
Carter, Howard 413
Carter, Jimmy 95
Carter, Robert "King" 482
Carteret, George 509
Cartier, Jacques 128
Carton, Sydney (fictional character) 737
Cartwright, Alexander 255
Caruso, Enrico 730, 792
Carvalas, Thomas Andreas 133
Carver, John 133
Casanova de Seingalt, Giovanni Jacopo 135, 196, 216
Case, Frank 722
Casey, Daniel Maurice 135
Casey, Patrick 411
Casey, Phil 330
Caslon, William 738
Cassandra (mythological figure) 136, 648
Cassidy, Frederick 717
Cassini (naturalist) 426
Cassius 108, 173
Casson, Lionel 102
Castelbajac, Jean-Charles de 289
Castilly y Lopez, Juan 136
Castlemaine, Madame 517

Castor and Pollux (mythological figures) 321, 631
Castro, Fidel 148, 466
Catesby, John 607
Cather, Willa 1, 352, 655, 695
Catherine of Aragon (queen of England) 558
Catherine of Braganza (queen consort of England) 413, 517
Catherine the Great (czarina of Russia) 581
Catiline, Lucius Sergius 138
Catlin, George 138, 285
Catnach, James 137
Cato 133, 559, 770
Catt, Christopher (Kit) 414
Cattley, William 139
Catullus 40, 64, 255
Caudell, Harry M. 45, 77
Caulfield, Joan 352
Cavanaugh, James 533
Cavanilles, Professor 194
Caxton, William 375, 513
Cecil, William (Lord Burleigh) 19, 140–141
Cecrops (mythological figure) 37
Celsius, Anders 141
Centlivre, Susan 662
Cerberus (mythological figure) 6, 141, 214, 298, 578
Ceres (mythological figure) 11, 31, 67, 141
Cerf, Bennett 27
Cervantes, Miguel de 18, 76, 169, 187, 236, 238, 244, 247, 289, 306, 337, 521, 556, 601, 661, 714, 722, 728
Cesi, Prince 711
Chadwick, Henry 254–255, 405
Chalkenteros 102
Chamberlain, Neville 552
Chamberlain, Wilton 514
Chambers, John Graham 67
Chamisso, Adelbert von 640
Champlain, Samuel de 142
Champney, John 515
Chan, Charlie (fictional character) 756
Chance, Frank 723
Chandler, Raymond 74, 334, 585, 704
Chaney, Lon, Jr. 781
Chapanis, Alphonse 243
Chapin, Charles E. 384
Chaplin, Charlie 267, 276, 686
Chaplin, Henry 344
Chapman, Arthur 715
Chapman, Robert 535
Chappe, Claude 710
Chargoggagoggmanchaugagoggchaubunagungamaug (Lake Webster) 424
Charlemagne (Charles the Great) 143, 361, 484, 551, 619, 631
Charles I (king of England) 65, 80, 143, 185, 319, 470, 517, 687, 692, 747, 750
Charles II (king of England) 80, 123, 143, 171, 222, 312, 408, 413, 416, 468, 509, 510, 517, 523, 530, 556, 573, 623, 663
Charles II (king of Spain) 39
Charles III (king of Spain) 693
Charles V (Holy Roman Emperor, and, as Charles I, king of Spain) 39
Charles V (king of France) 275
Charles V (king of Spain) 17
Charles IX (king of France) 518
Charles X (king of France) 213
Charles XI (king of France) 517
Charles Edward Stuart (Bonnie Prince Charlie) 223, 389
Charles, Ezzard 397
Charles the Bald 17, 48
Charles the Simple 74
Charlevoix, Pierre de 422
Charlotte, Princess 144
Charon (mythological figure) 531, 616–617, 690

Charpentier, Henri 183
Charybdis (mythological figure) 70
Chase, Stuart 485
Chase, William R. 56
Chateaubriand, François-Auguste-René de 144
Chatterton, Thomas 384, 717
Chaucer, Geoffrey 12, 18, 29, 77, 108, 119, 145, 168, 174, 187, 200, 241, 245, 331, 336, 341, 413, 431, 434, 437, 449, 457, 498, 499, 519, 545, 573, 638, 650, 663, 691, 694, 701, 756, 769, 782
Chauvin, Nicolas 144–145
Cheri, Rose 146
Chesebrough, Robert A. 751
Chesterfield, Philip Dormer Stanhope, earl of 146, 201, 203, 557, 725
Chesterton, G. K. 159, 207
Chevrolet, Louis 147
Cheyne, William 147
Childe, Francis James 149
Childress, William 532
Chinchon, Ana de 77, 155
Chinmoy, Sri 572
Ch'in-Shih-Huang-Ti 763
Chippendale, Thomas 151, 653
Chisholm, Jesse 151
Chiune Sugihara 640
Choate, Rufus 300, 303
Choiseul, César, comte Du Plessis-Pralin, duc de (marshal of France) 582
Chopin, Frédéric 139
Choppin, Gregory 476
Choron, Alexandre 603
Chrétien, Jean 652
Christian II (king of Denmark) 508
Christy, Edwin 153
1 Chronicles (Old Testament) 68
Chrysanthemum-Blossom (mythological figure) 153
Chun, Ellery 19
Churchill, Winston 78, 83, 154, 214, 290, 381–382, 391, 583, 607, 625, 707, 713, 716, 718, 745, 755, 774
Churriguera, José 154
Ciardi, John 86, 215, 259, 360
Cibber, Colley 412, 498, 572
Cicero, Marcus Tullius 23, 138, 154, 178, 203, 255, 331, 374, 423, 592, 620, 701, 711, 720, 723, 734, 752
Cimabue, Giovanni 297
Cincinnatus, Lucius Quinctius 155
Cinyras (mythological figure) 501
Circe (mythological figure) 155–156, 486
Clapin, Sylva 17
Clarence, duke of 630
Clark, George Roy 156
Clark, Palmer 112
Clark, William 156–157, 582. See also Lewis and Clark
Clarke, Charles Langston 413
Clarke, Richard W. 200
Class, Henry 646
Claudia (queen of France) 318, 571
Claudius I (emperor of Rome) 165, 479, 579, 589
Claudius the Goth 749
Clausius, Rudolf 242
Clay, Cassius 266. See also Ali, Muhammad.
Clay, Henry 316, 574, 772
Cleaveland, Moses 159
Cleghorn, Sarah N. 441
Cleland, John 253, 579
Clemens, Samuel. See Twain, Mark
Clement VII (pope) 475
Clement X (pope) 468
Cleombrotus (Greek philosopher) 559
Cleopatra 36, 158, 159, 211, 436, 454, 468, 500, 621, 632
Cleveland, Daryl 346
Cleveland, duchess of 643
Cleveland, Grover 44, 159, 378, 496, 574–575, 625, 695
Cleveland, Ruth 44

Clinton, George 140
Clinton, William Jefferson 109, 214, 681, 710
Clio (mythological figure) 499
Clive, Robert 79
Clough, Arthur Hugh 4
Cluett, Sandford L. 635
Clytie (mythological figure) 341
Cobb, Irvin S. 384
Cobden, Richard 34
Cockburn, Catherine 636
Cockburn, George 123
Cocker, Edward 5
Cockerell, John A. 588
Codd, Hiram 163
Cody, William Frederick (Buffalo Bill) 27, 111, 115, 577, 777
Coe, Sebastian 274
Cofa family 646
Coffin, Robert P. Tristan 369
Cogniard, Charles and Jean 145
Cohan, George M. 278, 313, 792, 798
Cohen, Gerald 395, 659
Cohen, Irving 795
Cohen, Randy 362
Cohen, Stephen Philip 147
Coke, Arthur 351
Coke, Edward 121, 164, 492
Coke, William 99
Cole, Henry 153
Colegate, Isabel 555
Coleridge, Samuel Taylor 122, 268, 372, 493, 580, 619, 750
Coles, Jack 185
Colet, Louise 456
Collier's Magazine 6
Collingham, William 607
Collings, John 726
Collings, Tom 725
Collins, Lottie 595
Colorado 141
Colt, Samuel 166, 664
Colum, Mary 614
Colum, Padraic 262
Columbus, Christopher 22, 129, 136, 166, 369, 375, 471, 505, 556, 724
Compton, Henry 169–170
Comstock, Anthony 170
Comstock, Henry Tompkins Paige 170
Comte, Auguste 673
Conaway, Frank 73
Condon, Richard 531, 705
Conduit, Mrs. 510
Condum, Colonel 171
Confucius 172, 304
Congreve, William 31, 98, 120, 172, 414, 667
Conn, Billy 797
Connecticut 521
Connolly, Slippery Dick 732
Connors, George Washington "Chuck" 744
Conon of Samos 167
Conrad, Joseph 739
Considine, Tim 264
Constantine (emperor of Rome) 142, 412, 468
Conton, Dr. 171
Conway, Jack 347
Coogan, Jackie 686
Cook, James 94, 97, 131, 170, 406, 581, 635, 703, 709, 750
Cook, Joe 294
Cook, Thomas 174
Cooke, Alistair 759
Coolidge, Calvin 15, 370
Cooper, James Fenimore 96, 337, 427, 544, 550
Cooper, Kenneth 175, 397
Cooper, Pastor 623
Cooper, Samuel 764
Copeland, Charles Townsend 646
Copelstan, Edward 623
Copernicus 175, 265, 586
Corbett, "Gentleman Jim" 73, 212, 316, 338, 674

Corbin, John 140
Córdoba, Fernández de 189, 799
Corinthians (New Testament) 718
Corneille, Pierre 603
Cornelessin 128
Corridon, Frank 681
Corrigan, Douglas "Wrong-Way" 785
Corse, Montgomery 353
Cortés, Hernán 40, 111, 450
Cosby, Bill 302
Costello, Frank 498
Cotterel, James 178
Couch, W. T. 578
Coué, Emile 179
Coulomb, Charles-Augustin de 179
Coupland, Douglas 290
Courrèges, André 483
Courtenay, earl of 771
Cousteau, Jacques 31
Coville, Frederick V. 85
Coward, Noël 43, 373, 510
Cowboy Bob (fictional character) 180
Cowper, William 77, 312, 374, 396, 465, 751
Cox, Palmer 108
Coxe, William 247
Coxey, Jacob Sechler 180
Craig, Roger 719
Crane, Stephen 539
Crapaud, Johnny 181–182
Crapper, Thomas 181
Crassus, Marcus Licinius 182
Crawford, Robert 34
Creech 506
Crenis (mythological figure) 607
Cressida (mythological figure) 29, 545
Crichton, James 9, 348
Crichton, Michael 25, 402
Crillon, Louis Balbis de Berton de 183–184
Crippen, Hawley Harvey 184
Cripps, Stafford 716
Criseyde (mythological figure) 29, 545
Crisparkle, Mr. (fictional character) 499
Crockett, Davy 197–198, 279, 293, 342, 356, 385, 447, 460, 519, 599, 620, 663, 669, 727
Croesus (king of Lydia) 185
Croly, David Goodman 484
Cromwell, Oliver 54, 70, 185, 222, 270, 342, 411, 530, 622, 764
Cromwell, Richard 598, 722
Cronos (mythological figure) 29
Crook, C. J. 516
Crotha, Lord of Atha (mythological figure) 646
Crow, Jim 395
Cruden, Alexander 15
Cruikshank, George 415
Cruise, Tom 569
Crusoe, Robinson (fictional character) 221, 225, 464, 618
Cuffey, Paul 72
Cullinan, Thomas Major 188
Culpeper, Nicholas 553
Cumberland, William Augustus, duke of 20, 700
Cumming, John 123
Cummings, Homer 587
Cummings, William Arthur "Candy" 511
Cunningham, Lt. 82
Cupid (mythological figure) 188, 244, 621, 695
Curie, Marie 188, 575
Curie, Pierre 188, 575
Curll, Edmund 188
Curtis, Clifton G. 797
Curtis, William 719
Curzon (of Kedleston), George Nathaniel, marquess 189
Cush (biblical figure) 512
Cushing, Harvey William 190
Custer, George Armstrong 190, 288, 664
Cutler, Lyman 563

Cyparissus (mythological figure) 192
Cyrus the Great (king of Persia) 185
Cytherean (mythological figure) 29

D

Daedalus (mythological figure) 421, 638
Daffy Duck 777
Da Gama, Vasco 8, 126, 131, 160
Dahl, Anders 194
Dahlberg, C. G. 597
Daigneau, Kenneth 678
Dale, Richard 663
Daley, Bill 75
Dall, Horace 127
Dall, William Healey 194
Dalmer 633
Dalton, John 194
Daly, James 601
Damastes 63
Damien, Robert-François 194
Damocles 331, 701
Damon 195
Dampier, William 323
Dana, Richard Henry 64, 417, 719
Dangle (fictional character) 587
Daniel (biblical figure) 195, 256
Daniel (Old Testament) 256
Daniels, Jonathan 610
D'Annunzio, Gabriele 195–196
Daphne (mythological figure) 59, 573
D'Aquino, Iva Toguri 725
Darb, Ruby 196
Darby, John and Joan 196
Dardin, Amy 23
D'Arezzo, Guido 219, 421
Darius (king of Persia) 195, 345, 466
Darley, Richard 121
Darlington, William 196
Darsy, Emile 29
Darwin, Charles 197, 328, 463, 588, 668, 689, 699
Dassler, Adi 9
Datis (Persian general) 466
Daughtery, Harry 670
D'Avenant, William 289, 586
Davenport, Captain 197
Davenport, Fanny 256
David (biblical figure) 3, 60, 305, 560, 674, 783, 803
David (king of Ireland) 334
Davies, John 499
Davis, Charles 293
Davis, Dwight Filley 197
Davis, James Bolton 101
Davis, Jefferson 68, 440, 732
Davis, Owen 369
Davis, Sammy, Jr. 607
Davison, Francis 4
Davy, Humphrey 20, 198, 439–440
Day, Benjamin 67
Dean, Dizzy 667
Dean, James 147
Dean, John 738
DeBeck, Billie 340
Debrett, John 201
De Bruyn, Kornelius Philader 560
Debussy, Claude 195
De Camp, L. Sprague 249
Decatur, Stephen 86, 538
Defoe, Daniel 78, 172, 191, 203, 221, 464, 561, 570, 618, 643
De Groat, John 398–399
De la Mare, Walter 251, 661
Delany, Samuel R. 748
De la Pole, William 387
De la Ramée, Louise 690
Delaware 86
De La Warr, Baron (Thomas West) 202
Del Giocondo, Zanobi 487
Delilah (biblical figure) 634
Della Cruscan school 58
Dellinger, David 55
Delmonico's restaurant 48, 148, 445
Demeter (mythological figure) 141
Democratic Party 55
Democritus 2, 348, 427, 767

Demosthenes 7, 203, 218, 345, 556, 560
Dempsey, Jack 388, 397, 410
Dennis, John 689
De Quincey, Thomas 171, 662
Derby, Edward Stanley, earl of 204
Deringer, Henry 204
Derrick, Godfrey 204, 207
De Sade, Donatien-Alphonse-François de 630
De Sade, Hugues 428, 579
Descartes, René 133, 245, 592
De Soto, Hernando 29, 146, 291
Deuteronomy (Old Testament) 30, 84, 339, 463, 479, 518, 765, 801
Devereux, Robert. See Essex, Robert Devereaux, earl of
Deverson, Jane 290
De Veuster, Joseph 254
Deviene, Catherine 357
Devoe, Alan 36
De Vries, Hugo 476
Dewar, James 206
Dewey, Melvil 206
Dewey, Thomas E. 284
Diana (mythological figure) 207, 513
Di Bascio, Matteo 132
Dick, Everett 317, 682
Dick, George Frederick and Gladys H. 207
Dickens, Charles 28, 29, 31, 44, 54, 70, 87, 174, 207, 223, 247, 285, 286, 298, 339, 346, 364, 410, 438, 480, 494, 499, 512, 525, 551, 554, 572, 643, 674, 680, 694, 706, 747, 802
Dickman, John 745
Dickson, Paul 107, 264, 490, 589
Diddler, Jeremy (fictional character) 207–208
Diderot, Denis 694
Dido (mythological figure) 191
Didymus of Alexandria 102
Diefenbach, J. F. 493
Dierville, Dr. 767
Diesbach 586
Diesel, Rudolph 208
Dietrich, Marlene 370
Dietz, Howard 34
Dillinger, John 270, 587
Dilsey (fictional character) 466
DiMaggio, Joe 55, 792
Dimond, William 528
Dinkens, David 271
Diocletian (emperor of Rome) 60, 632
Diogenes (Greek philosopher) 45, 178, 192, 209–210, 346, 752
Dionysius (Sicilian ruler) 15, 195
Dionysius the Elder 331, 701, 762
Dionysius the Younger 621
Dionysus (mythological figure) 29, 480, 537, 584, 715
Dioscorides 290, 471
Dirty Harry (fictional character) 461
Dis (mythological figure) 755
Discord (mythological figure) 30
Dismal Jimmy 300
Disney, Walt 211, 395, 480, 648
Disraeli, Benjamin 196, 333, 535, 552–553, 619
D'Israeli, Isaac 280, 784, 795
Dixon, Jeremiah 471
Dobbs, Arthur 753
Dobell, Sydney 679
Dobermann, Louis 212
Dobie, J. Frank 635
Dodd, John Bruce, Mrs. 255
Dodgson, Charles Lutwidge. See Carroll, Lewis
Dole, Sanford 216
Dolly (sheep) 140, 216
Domingo, Placido 30
Domitian (emperor of Rome) 546
Dond, Tom 681
Don Juan 216–217
Donne, John 118, 169, 170, 231–232, 243
Donnelly, Daniel 217

Don Quixote (fictional character) 601, 722. See also Cervantes, Miguel
Doolittle, Eliza (fictional character) 343
Doolittle, Hilda. See H. D.
Doolittle, James "Jimmy" 219
Dopey (fictional character) 219
Dorgan, Thomas Aloysius "Tad" 31, 119, 150, 226, 263, 270, 273, 308, 360, 462, 703, 737, 795
Doris (mythological figure) 507
Dorman-Smith, E. E. 122
Dortmann 444
Dos Passos, John 189, 646
Doubleday, Abner 255
Doubleday, F. N. 587
Douglas, David 221
Douglas, James 563
Douglas, John Sholto. See Queensberry, eighth marquis of
Douglas, Paul 113
Douglas, William O. 696
Douglass, Charles Rolland 711
Doulton, Henry 221
Doulton, John 221
Dover, Thomas 221
Dow, Charles Henry 222
Dow, Lorenzo 195
Down, John L. H. 222
Downing, George 222
Downing, Jack (fictional character) 182
Dowson, Ernest 306
Doyle, Arthur Conan 11, 591, 653
Doyle, Don 796
Draco 30, 223, 410
Dracula (fictional character) 276
Dragon (dog) 38
Drake, Francis 14, 238, 304, 584, 654
Drapier, M. B. 731
Dreiser, Theodore 334, 561
Drennan, William 239
Dresser, Paul 344
Drew, Daniel 765
Driver, William 529
Drummond, Edmund 474
Drummond, Thomas 439
Drunkometer 103
Drury, William 226
Drusus 106
Dryden, John 18, 24, 65, 148, 191, 243, 298, 329, 342, 352, 403, 498, 572, 573, 589, 668, 780
Du Bartas, Guillaume de Salluste 18
Dubuque, Julien 529
Duchamp, Marcel 526
Dudley 387
Duff, James 390
Dugsdale, Richard L. 401
Dujardin, Edouard 694
Duke, James 195
Dulles, John Foster 12
Dumas, Alexandre 16
Dumas, Alexandre (Jr.) 128
Dumas, Alexandre (Sr.) 16, 196–197, 295, 374
Du Maurier, George Louis 699, 732
Dumpos 222
Dun, Joe 227
Dunbar, Paul Laurence 535
Dundas, Henry (viscount Melville) 688
Dundreary, Lord (fictional character) 227
Dunmow Flitch 105
Dunn, Charlie 144
Dunn, Jack 44
Dunne, Burt 589
Dunne, Finley Peter 677
Duplessis, Marie 128
Du Pont family 655
Durant, William 147
Durante, Jimmy 20, 315, 360, 371–372, 641, 770
Durham, earl of 68
Durocher, Leo 510
Duryea, Oscar 275
Dus (mythological figure) 205

Duse, Eleanora 196, 219
Dusky Pete 196
Dutch 228–229
Duvalier, François "Papa Doc" 80
Dzhugashvili, Iosif Vissarionovich. See Stalin, Joseph

E

Earp, Thomas W. 737
Earp, Wyatt 364, 785
Eastman, George 108, 418
Eastre (mythological figure) 232
Eastwood, Clint 362, 461
Eaton, Charles "Charlie" 75
Ecclesiastes (Old Testament) 233, 268, 674, 716
Echo (mythological figure) 234, 504
Eckert, J. Presper, Jr. 170
l'Ecorcheur, Jean 144
Eddy, Mary Baker 234
Eden, Richard 461
Edgar (king of England) 26
Edinburgh 39
Edison, Charles 235
Edison, Thomas 32, 234–235, 238, 266, 521, 554, 591, 769, 783
Edward I (king of England) 6, 143, 303, 329
Edward II (king of England) 354
Edward III (king of England) 87
Edward IV (king of England) 657
Edward VI (king of England) 772
Edward VII (king of England) 584, 710
Edward VIII (king of England) 501, 778
Edward the Confessor (king of England) 423
Edwards, James Gardiner 337
Edwards, Jay 797
Edwards, Richard 195
Egan, Pierce 725
Egbert (king of England) 632
egg 235–236
Ehrlichman, John 73, 738
Eiffel, Alexandre Gustave 236, 688
Einstein, Albert 32, 237, 540, 738, 757
Eisenhower, Dwight D. 128, 235, 237, 293, 341, 346, 357, 575
Eishiro Abe 412
Eleanor (queen of England) 143
Elijah (biblical figure) 692
Eliot, T. S. 226, 560, 765
Elizabeth (queen of Belgium) 381
Elizabeth I (queen of England) 3, 19, 127, 238, 288, 296, 302, 450, 451, 521, 598, 719, 751, 757, 771
Ellery, William 509
Ellicott, Andrew 454
Ellis, Frederick 304
Ellis, John 753
Ellis, William 624
Elmer, Ebenezer and Jonathan 239
Elyot, Thomas 241
Emerson, Ralph Waldo 22, 112, 132, 173, 191, 300, 349, 477, 500, 588, 658, 767
Emmett, David D. 41
Empson 387
"Endicott and the Red Cross" (Hawthorne) 1
Endlicher, Stephan 647
Endymion (mythological figure) 717
Engelbrecht, H. C. 477
Engels, Friedrich 470, 783
ENIAC (Electronic Numerical Integrator and Analyzer and Computer) 170
Enobarbus (fictional character) 211
Enoch (biblical figure) 528
Eos (mythological figure) 710
Ephialtes 564
Epicurus 242, 752
Epilogue 30
Epimenides 183
Epperson, Frank W. 578
Erasmus 126, 457, 461, 572
Erato (mythological figure) 499

Eric (king of Sweden) 778
Eric XIV (king of Sweden) 174
Ericsson, John 552
Erie Canal 73
Eriksson, Leif 469
Eris (mythological figure) 30
Erlenmeyer, Emil 244
Eros (mythological figure) 29, 244
Esau (biblical figure) 244, 433
Eschscholtz, J. F. von 244
Escoffier, Georges Auguste 244, 616
Espy, Willard 414, 712, 758
Essex, Robert Devereaux, earl of 204, 238
Esslesiatstes (Old Testament) 476
Esther (biblical figure) 331
Esther (Old Testament) 327, 476
Estienne, Henri 303
Estrées, Maréchel d' 144
Euclid 246
Eugene the Jeep 392
Eugénie (empress of the French) 240
Euhemerus 246
Euripides 125, 205, 317, 781
Europa (mythological figure) 380
Eurysteus (mythological figure) 157
Eustace, Anne 770
eusystolisms 2
Euterpe (mythological figure) 499
Evans, Bergen 682
Eve (biblical figure) 8, 189, 248, 259, 260, 468, 621
Evelyn, John 126–127, 237, 538
Everest, George 494
Evers, Johnny 91, 723
Exeter, duke of 604
Exodus (Old Testament) 2, 128, 266, 460, 492, 520, 656, 690, 783
Ezekiel (Old Testament) 686

F

Faber, Geoffrey 251
Fabius Cunctator 251
Fadia 454
Fadiman, Clifton 146
Fahrenheit, Daniel 251
Fairbanks, Douglas, Jr. 252
Falbert of Falaise 334
Falk, John H. 429
Falstaff (fictional character) 55, 435
Faraday, Michael 253, 343
Farina, Johann Maria 165
Fariña, Richard 64
FARK (Folklore Article Reconstruction Kit) 121
Farmer, John S. 456, 524
Farnum, Joseph 361
Farquhar, George 36, 92, 422, 631
Farragut, David 205, 729
Farrell, Frank X. 15
Farrell, James T. 281
Fates (mythological figures) 38
Fat Man 3
Fatman, Thomas 552
Faulkner, William 13, 88, 165, 232, 244, 255, 466, 499, 508, 513, 580, 601, 637, 647, 672, 762, 784, 796
Fauvel (fictional character) 189
Fawkes, Guy 325
Feignwell, Colonel (fictional character) 662
Feinagle, Gregor von 261
Félix, Élisa 603
Fell, John 212
Fellini, Federico 546
Ferber, Edna 130–131, 139, 180, 191, 379, 417, 615, 731, 775
Ferdinand II (king of the Two Sicilies) 412
Ferguson, Robert V. 701
Fermi, Enrico 257
Ferrari, Andrea dei 25
Ferris, George Washington Gale 257
Fetchit, Stepin 689
Feuchtwanger, Antoine 276
Feydeau, Georges 105, 258
Feynman, Richard Phillips 258
Field, Ben 588

Fielding, Henry 77, 266, 366, 498, 529, 572, 668, 673
Fielding, Temple Hornaday 47
Fields, W. C. 28, 119, 353, 598, 716, 797
Fillmore, Millard 417
Fink, Albert 262
Fink, Mike 481
Finn, Huckleberry (fictional character) 363
Finn, Mickey 480
Firpo, Luis 410
Fischler, Stan 698
Fisher, Eddie 798
Fisher, Henry Conway "Bud" 500
Fisk, Jim 79
Fiske, A. D. 416
Fitch, Elizabeth 792
Fitch, John 554, 689
Fitch, Thomas 792
FitzGerald, Edward 518
Fitzgerald, F. Scott 392, 435, 443, 614
Fitz-Ooth, Robert. See Huntington, earl of
Fitzpatrick, Barnaby 772
Fitzroy, Robert 588
Fitzsimmons, Robert "Bob" 73, 674
Flagg, James Montgomery 386
Flaubert, Gustave 456
Fleer, Frank 752
Fleet, Thomas 492
Fleischmann, Lewis 103
Fleming, Ian 123, 284
Fletcher, Bob 217
Fletcher, Horace 266
Fletcher, John 3, 160, 174, 343, 521
Flexner, Stuart Berg 87, 92, 169, 264, 354, 521, 714, 741
Flibbertigibbet 266
Flinders, Matthew 39
Flora (mythological figure) 458, 576, 621
Florida 267, 698
Florio, John 279, 354
Flyn, Sam 196
Flynn, "Boss" 377
Focke, Henrich K. I. 341
Folengo, Teofilo 455
Foley, Larry 333
Folger, Timothy 323
Folliard, Edward 269
Fondlewife (fictional character) 667
Foote, Samuel 460, 518, 532, 750
Fontages, Marie-Angélique de Scorraille de Rousilles, duchesse de 269–276
Foote, Shelby 333
Ford, Edsel 235, 748
Ford, Gerald 130, 725
Ford, Harold 598
Ford, Henry 36, 124, 237, 270, 748, 767
Ford, John 266
Ford, John Thompson 270
Ford, Richard 686
Ford, Robert 394
Ford family 655
Foreman, Grant 313
Forgy, Howell Maurice 582
Forman, Grand 294
Forster, E. M. 409
Forsyth, Frederick 110
Forsyth, William 272
Fortescue, John 169
Fortune, Robert 272
Fosbury, Dick 272–273
Foster, Stephen 396, 507, 699
Fouquet, Nicolas 197
Fourdrinier, Henry and Sealy 273
Fourier, François-Marie-Charles 274
Fourneau, Ernest 692
Fowler, F. G. 5
Fowler, Henry Watson 5
Fox, Charles James 143
Fox, George 596
Fox, Gilbert 327
Fox, Harry 275
Foxe, John 162, 460
Foxx, Jimmy 642

Fracastro, Girolamo 702
France, Anatole 71
Francis I (king of France) 17, 318, 486, 571, 764, 784
Francis II (king of France) 774
Francis II (king of the Two Sicilies) 287
Francis (Franz) Ferdinand (archduke of Austria) 79, 432
Franco, Francisco 259
Frangipani, Muzio 275
Frankenstein (fictional character) 275–276
Frankenstein, Victor (fictional character) 275–276
Franklin, Benjamin 19, 41, 71, 125, 157, 276, 302, 323, 436, 445, 478, 496, 581, 672, 692, 701, 712
Franklin, John 276
Franks, Tommy R. 139, 155
Frazee, Harry 189
Frazier, Joe 267, 670
Frederick the Great 500, 534
Freese, F. H. T. 276
Frémont, John C. 126, 298
French, Richard 330
French words 277
Freneau, Philip 701
Freud, Sigmund 11, 277, 355, 402, 587, 607, 738
Freya (mythological figure) 278, 750
Friedman, Bruce Jay 79
Fries, E. M. 276
Fries, John 361
Frietchie, Barbara 53
Froebel, Friedrich Wilhelm August 411
Frome, Michael 146, 493
Frost, Robert 306, 680
Frum, David 41
Fuchs, I. L. 279
Fuchs, Leonhard 279
Fudd, Elmer (fictional character) 512, 770, 777
Fudge, Captain 280
Fulbright, James William 280
Fuller, Alfred C. 280
Fuller, William 280
Fuller-Maitland, J. A. 766
Fulton, Robert 689
Fulvia 454
Funakoshi Gichin 406
Funicello, Annette 362
Funk, Casimir 757
Funk, Charles Earle 339
Funkia, C. H. 281
Furphy & Co. 281
Fust, Johann 325

G

Gabriel (biblical figure) 259, 283
Gadolin, Johann 283
Gaea (mythological figure) 291, 747
Gage, William 318, 571
Gainsborough, Thomas 284
Gaius Julius Caesar. See Julius Caesar
Gaius Laelius 423
Gaius Silius 479
Gal, Uziel 748
Galahad (legendary figure) 284, 663
Galatea (mythological figure) 284
Galatians (New Testament) 416
Galbraith, John Kenneth 10, 130
Gale, Sammy 387
Galen, Claudius 284, 621
Galileo 251, 380, 480, 711
Gall, Franz Joseph 346
Gallup, George Horace 284
Galore, Pussy (fictional character) 284
Galsworthy, John 555
Galt, Edith 242, 739
Galvani, Luigi 284
Gamp, Sara (fictional character) 174, 286, 495
Gandhi, Mohandas K. 630, 637, 752
Gandy Manufacturing Co. 286
Ganymede (mythological figure) 380
Garand, John Cantius 286
Garbo, Greta 385

García, Calixto 479
Garden, Alexander 286
Gardiner, Charles A. 291
Gardini, Caesar 125
Gardner, Martin 373
Gargantua (fictional character) 287, 354
Garibaldi, Giuseppe 74, 287, 610, 754
Garland, Judy 605, 685
Garrick, David 289, 687
Garrison, Edward H. "Snapper" 287
Gasnick, Jack 668
Gates, Bill 614
Gatling, Richard Jordan 288
Gauguin, Paul 283
Gaulle, Charles de 146, 288, 558
Gauss, Karl Friedrich 289, 766
Gautama Buddha 110
Gautier, Marguerite 128
Gay, John 57, 551
Gaye, Marvin 493
Gayetty, Joseph C. 725
Gay-Lussac, Joseph-Louis 363
Geber (Arab alchemist) 295
Gehrig, Lou 449, 642
Geiger, Hans 290
Geiger, Robert 228
Geisel, Theodor Seuss 320, 507
Gellius, Aulus 157
Gell-Man, W. 597
Geman, Gershon 121
Genesis (Old Testament) 8, 43, 68, 84, 177, 189, 244, 260, 287, 290, 342, 382, 389, 400, 424, 443, 468, 512, 528, 542, 646, 673, 701, 716, 725, 731, 753
Genghis Khan 120
Genseric (king of the Vandals) 750
Gentius 290
Geoffrey of Monmouth 412
George I (king of England) 416
George II (king of England) 222, 291, 584
George III (king of England) 20, 291, 422, 553, 592, 715, 729
George IV (king of England) 61, 441
George V (king of England) 516
George, Edwin 429
George John. See Spencer, George John, Earl
Georges, Ferdinand 459
Georgia 565
Gerade, 359, 566
Gerard, John 9
Gerard, Richard 700
Gerarde, 444
German words 292
Gérôme, Jean Léon 721
Geronimo 292
Gerritsen, Tess 652
Gerry, Elbridge 292
Gerson, Mike 41
Gertner's restaurant 195
Gesner, Konrad von 255
Ghiorso, Albert 237, 257, 429
Gianni, Francisco 374
Gibbon, Edward 20, 98, 758
Gibbons, Cedric 537
Gibbs, Wolcott 538
Gibson, Charles Dana 295
Gibus, Antoine 295
Gideon (biblical figure) 295
Gifford, William 58, 160, 750
Giffy, George 697
Gilbert, William (scientist) 238, 296
Gilbert, William Schwenck 4, 296, 577, 633, 754. See also Sullivan, Arthur
Gilbreth, Frank B. 716
Giles, Sir 761
Gill, Brendan 103, 529
Gill, Eric 738
Gillars, Mildred E. 725
Gilman, George 1
Gimbel, Adam 265
Gimbels department store 213, 265, 554

Gimlette, T. O. 296
Ginsberg, Allen 61
Giocondo, Francesco 486
Gioja, Flavio 266
Gipp, George 779
Girard, John 450–451
Girard, Stephen 554
Gissing, George 93
Gist, Nathaniel 647
Gitlow, Benjamin 158
Giuliani, Rudolph 131
Gladstone, William Ewart 266, 299, 309, 725, 745
Glasse, Hannah 263
Gloomy Gus 300
Gloucester, duke of 20
Gloucester, duke of (Humphrey) 209
Gluck, Christoph William 300
Glyn, Elinor 383
Godden, Rumer 23
Godet, Charles H. 253
The Godfather 48, 83, 173, 178, 256, 302, 461, 531, 613, 666, 669, 685, 769
Godgifu 423
Godiva, Lady 422–423, 554, 712
Goebbels, Joseph 93, 381
Goethe, Johann von 32, 242, 289, 640, 695
gold 38
Goldberg, Rube 339, 623–624
"Golden Horde" 35
Goldman, Emma 370
Goldman, Sylman 657
Goldschmidt, Otto 393
Goldsmith, Oliver 130, 370, 372, 443, 463, 573
Goldwater, Barry 575
Goldwyn, Samuel 200, 305
Goliath (biblical figure) 60, 305
Gongora y Argote, Luis de 306
Gonzales, Miguel "Mike" 306
González, Carlos Hank 575
Goodall, Jane 149
Goodfellow, Robin (fictional character) 605
Goodman, Cardonnell "Scum" 643
Goodnight, Charles 153, 307
Goodyear, Charles 757
Goodyear Company 82
Google, Barney (fictional character) 308
Goose, Elizabeth 492
Gordius (mythological figure) 191, 480
Gordon, Charles George 174
Gordon, Daniel 774
Gordon, George. See Byron, Lord
Gordon, Maurice B. 475
Göring, Hermann 292
Gosnold, Bartholomew 469
Gotti, John 710
Gould, Chester 94
Gould, Jay 79
Gould, John 473
Gower, John 445
Gowers, Ernest 415
Goyeneche, Don Juan de 154
Grable, Betty 276, 312, 315, 566
Gracchus, Tiberius 145
Graces (mythological figures) 621
Graham, George 537
Graham, Sylvester 312
Grange, Harold "Red" 274, 613
Granger, James 313
Grant, Cary 167, 362, 706, 711
Grant, Ulysses S. 295, 528, 533, 729, 742, 743
Grateau, Marcel 467
Graves, Robert 15, 171, 315
Gray, Patrick 738
Gray, Thomas 214, 253, 371, 551, 554
Great Atlantic and Pacific Tea Company 1
Greeley, Horace 312, 646
Green, Matthew 198
Greenacre, James 318

Greene, Bob 799
Greene, Charles Gordon 527
Greene, Robert 457, 527, 571, 694
Greenfield, Jeff 666
Greenhouse, Linda 696
Gregg, John Robert 319
Gregory X (pope) 171
Gregory XIII (pope) 319
Gregory XVIII (pope) 585
Gresham, Thomas 319
Greville, Charles 464
Griffi, Francesco 383
Griffin, Marvin 674
Griffin, Mary M. 425
Griffith, D. W. 290
Grimaldi, Joseph 397
Grimm, Jacob 181, 320, 648
Grimm, William 320, 648
Grimthorpe, Edmund 72
Grocey, Leo 199
Grolier, Jean 321
Grose, Francis 77, 114, 198, 222, 268,
  279, 256, 269, 293, 295, 331, 388, 436, 529, 562,
  596, 599, 600, 752
Grossmith, George and Weedon 578
Grothe, Mardy 147
Grugno, Cardinal 516
Grundy, Mrs. (fictional character)
  302, 495
Guarini, Giovanni 698
Guess, George 647
Guevara, Antonio de 323
Guidi, Carlo 662
Guillotin, Joseph Ignace 323
Guinan, Texas 72
Guinness brewery 5
Guise, John 747
Guiterman, Arthur 415
Gum, Colin 324
Gump, Andy (fictional character) 324
Gunhilda 324
Gunter, Edward 5
Gunther, John 183
Guppy, R. J. Lechmere 325
Gustavus I 508
Gutenberg, Beno 614
Gutenberg, Johannes 325
Guthinger, Charles 294
Guthrie, A. B., Jr. 191
Guyot, Arnold 326
Gybbon family 295

H

Haakon (king of Norway) 601
Haas, Robert 93
Habirshaw, W. M. 512
Hagner, Helen Ray 318
Haig, Alexander 327, 355
Haile Selassie 607
Haines, Jackson 388
Hakluyt, Richard 731
Hale, Edward Everett 466
Hale, Nathan 380
Hale, Sara Josepha 245, 470
Haliburton, Thomas 73, 93, 167, 187,
  191, 256, 269, 293, 426, 445, 456,
  577, 674, 723
Hall, Benjamin 72
Hall, E. Beatrice 370
Hall, Huntz 199
Hallam, Adam 319
Hallam, Arthur Henry 723
Halleck, Henry Wager 528
Halley, Edmund 329
Halsey, Eric 62, 436, 465
Haman (biblical figure) 331
Hamblett, Charles 290
Hamilton, Alexander 15, 80, 329,
  359, 560
Hamilton, Anthony 312
Hamilton, Duke 772
Hamilton, Elizabeth 312
Hamilton, John 314
Hamilton, William 525
Hamlet (fictional character) 140, 293,
  294, 317, 457, 622
Hammerstein, Oscar, II 537

Hammonneau, Maurice 455
Hammurabi 249
Hampshire, Stuart 794
Hanauel (fictional character) 621
Hancock, John 398
Handel, George 81, 736–737
Handler, Ruth 53
Hanighan, F. D. 477
Hanna, Mark 714
Hanrahan, May 39
Hansard, Luke 332
Hansen, Armauer, Gerhard Henrik 333
Hansom, Joseph Aloysius 333
Hanson, Timothy 723
Hanway, Jonas 742
Harburg, E. Y. 605
Hardcastle, Squire (fictional character)
  372
Harder, D.S. 40
Hardin, John Wesley 399
Harding, Warren G. 35, 285, 670
Hardouin-Mansart, Jules 465
Hardy, Clay 672
Hardy, Thomas 11, 253, 339
Hardy, Thomas (Captain) 413
Hare, William 116–117
Harmon, Tom 341
Harney, William S. 563
Harper, James 175
Harper, Robert 334
Harpocrates (mythological figure) 695
Harrigan, Ed 313
Harrington, James 747
Harrington, Robert 44
Harris, Frank 183
Harris, Israel 379
Harris, Joel Chandler 55, 92, 743
Harris, Mrs. (fictional character) 495
Harrison, Benjamin 706
Harrison, George 795
Harrison, William Henry 154, 351,
  376, 407, 527, 574, 738, 757
Hart, B. H. Liddell 696
Harte, Bret 511
Hartford, George Huntington 1, 698
Harvard, John 335
Harvey, Bernard 476
Harvey, Gabriel 400
Harvey, William 462
Hasbruck, Jonathan 400
Hassell, Sylvester 646
Hastings, marquis of 344
Hastings, Zeb 59
Hatfield family 608
Hathaway, Anne 381, 650
Hauptmann, Bruno Richard 441
Haussman, Georges Eugène 336
Hauy, Valentin 101
Havelock Henry 336
Hawaii 19
Hawk, Bob 664
Hawke, Colonel 671
Hawking, Stephen 374
Hawkins, Anthony Hope 626
Hawkins, John 103, 652
Hawthorne, Julian 331
Hawthorne, Nathaniel 8, 38, 316,
  330, 456, 565, 570
Hawthorne, Tom and Jerry (fictional
  characters) 725
Hay, John 682
Hay, William Howard 338
Hayakawa, Ruth 725
Haydn, Joseph 648
Hayes, Helen 15
Hayes, Keith and Cathy 149
Hayes, Rutherford B. 257
Hays, Constance L. 83
Hays, Will Harrison 338
Hazlitt, William Carew 149, 160, 169,
  570, 580
H. D. 373
Head, Richard 493
Headrick, Ed 278
Hearne, Thomas 478
Hearst, Patty 691
Hearst, William Randolph 336, 610,
  794

Heartwell (fictional character) 667
Heath, Robert 517
Heaviside, Oliver 339
Hebard, Frederick V. 563
Hebrew words 340
Hector (mythological figure) 340, 787
Heep, Uriah (fictional character) 747
Hefner, Hugh 569
Heimlich, Henry J. 340
Heinlein, Robert A. 437
Heisman, John W. 341
Held, John 392
Helen (mythological figure) 321, 631,
  733
Helenus (mythological figure) 648
Heliogabalus (emperor of Rome) 621
Helius (mythological figure) 382
Heller, Joseph 137
Hellinger, Mark 728
Hemingway, Ernest 10, 77, 113, 115,
  122, 167, 231, 244, 259, 312, 334,
  434, 449, 520, 546, 614, 796
Hemingway, Margaux 698
Hemstreet, Charles 761
Hench, Philip S. 178
Henderson, Harry 353
Henley, Margaret 558
Henrietta Maria 470
Henry I (king of England) 573
Henry III (king of France) 455
Henry IV (king of England) 360
Henry IV (king of France) 148, 183,
  191, 230, 470, 491, 633
Henry VI (king of England) 387
Henry VII (king of England) 27, 557
Henry VIII (king of England) 78, 99,
  238, 387, 388, 478, 517, 558, 663,
  684, 755, 772, 799
Henry, Benjamin Tyler 343
Henry, John 398, 472
Henry, Joseph 342
Henry, O. 119, 123–124, 129, 130,
  274, 284, 367, 395, 526–527, 566,
  660, 687, 703
Henry, Patrick 299
Henry of Prussia 459
Henson, Josiah 743
Hep, Joe 348
Hepburn, Katharine 626, 793
Hepplewhite, George 343
Hera (mythological figure) 30, 234
Heraclitus (Greek philosopher) 427,
  767
Herbert (English botanist) 454
Herbert, A. P. 199
Herbert, George 303, 556, 797
Herbert, George E. S. M. 413
Herbert, William 495
Hercules (mythological figure) 6, 141,
  157, 343, 578, 585, 721, 764
Herd, John 723
Herken, Greg 385
Herleva 470
Hermann, Paul 459
Hermaphroditus (mythological figure)
  344
Hermes (mythological figure) 254,
  344, 486, 689
Hermes Trismegistus (mythological fig-
  ure) 344
Hermia (fictional character) 344
Herod (king of Judea) 372, 539
Herodotus 58, 73, 155, 185, 664, 665
Herrick, Margaret 537
Herrick, Robert 64, 163, 193, 243,
  286, 762
Herschel, John 231, 489
Herschel, William 36, 747
Hertz, Heinrich 344
Hertzberg, Hendrik 168
Hervey, John 424
Hesiod (Greek poet) 254
Heyerdahl, Thor 50
Heyn, H. H. 204
Heywood, John 19, 120, 328, 417,
  461
Heywood, Thomas 410
Hibbert, Frederick "Toots" 611

Hickok, James Butler "Wild Bill" 200,
  359, 776
Hiero 247
Hieronymus, Karl Friedrich (Freiherr
  von Munchausen) 497–498
Higgins, Andrew 346
Higgins, George V. 470
Higgins, Henry (fictional character)
  343
Hightower, Jim 716
Hill, Abigail 3
Hill, Henry 779
Hill, Joe 562
Hill, Mildred J. 333
Hill, Patty Smith 333
Hill, Samuel 634
Hill, Thomas 361
Hillary, Edmund 62, 494
Hillegass, Clifton Keith 159
Hilstrom, Joseph 562
Hilton, James 128, 651, 748
Himmler, Heinrich 292, 685
Hinckley, John W. 355
Hindley, Charles 493
Hippocrates 125, 184, 249, 348, 437,
  722
Hippolytus (mythological figure) 501
Hirschfield, Leo 728
Hitchcock, Alfred 139, 349, 456
Hitchcock, Lambert H. 349
Hitler, Adolf 81, 280, 506, 512, 532,
  552, 601, 660, 752, 758
Hoagland, Edward 665
Hoare, Samuel 516
Hobart, George V. 232
Hobbes, Thomas 349
Hobson, 755
Hobson, Richmond Pearson 349, 414
Hobson, Thomas (Tobias) 351
Ho Chi Minh 351
Hodgkin, Thomas 104
Hofer, Johannes 518
Hoffman, Abbie 799
Hoffmann, Friedrich 292
Hogan, William 352
Hogarth, William 352
Hogg, Ima 373
Hohenheim, Theophrastus Bombastus
  von 16, 91, 547
Holbein, Hans 455
Holden, William 352
Holinshed, Raphael 704
Holland, George 442
Holland, Josiah G. 507
Hollingshead, Richard M., Jr. 224
Holmes, John Clellon 61
Holmes, Oliver Wendall 26, 35, 69,
  96, 153, 158, 262, 332, 336, 362,
  426, 500, 529, 653, 753, 780, 797
Holmes, Sherlock (fictional character)
  125, 380, 525, 591, 615, 653, 658
Holofernes 354
Holt, Alfred 703
Holt, David 109
Holt, V. M. 195
Holyfield, Evander 588
Homby, Geoffrey Phipps 563
Homer 33, 54, 77, 89, 141, 155, 340,
  354, 372, 374, 449, 477, 486, 508,
  525, 564, 699, 733, 804
Hone, William 3
Honoratus Maurus Servius 452
Hood, Thomas 374
Hooke, Robert 711
Hooker, Joseph 356
Hooligan, Patrick 357
Hoover, Herbert 148, 355, 357, 377,
  514, 574, 575, 625
Hope, Anthony 626
Hope, Bob 356
Hope, Harry (fictional character)
  437
Hopkins, Mr. 218
Hopkins, Esek 174, 747
Hopkins, John 498
Hopkins, Matthew 780
Hopkinson, Joseph 327
Hopper, De Wolf 135

Horace 58, 69, 125, 140, 331, 348, 354, 452, 504, 591, 701, 725
Hore-Belisha, Leslie 358
Horlick, James and William 463
Horner, Jack 388, 574
Hornung, Ernest W. 604
Hornung, Paul 341
Horsley, John 153
Horus (mythological figure) 695
Hosack, David 359
Hosea (Old Testament) 678
Host, Nicholaus and Joseph 281
Houdini, Harry 361
Housman, A. E. 147, 304, 446
Houston, Sam 361
Howard, Norfolk 516–517
Howard, Rowland 582
Howard, Thomas 394
Howard, W. L. 115–116
Howdy Doody (fictional character) 595
Howe, Julia Ward 58, 314, 493
Howells, Mildred 767
Hoyle, Edmond 5
Hoyle, Fred 72
Hubbard, Elbert 479
Hubbard, Elyabeth 363
Hubbell, "King Carl" 642
Hubble, Edwin Powell 363
Hubbs, Carl L. 424
Huchbald 17
Hudson, Henry 363, 412
Hudson, Samuel 679
Huebsch, B. W. 87
Hughes, Langston 80, 743
Hughes, Richard 188–189
Hugo, Victor 599
Huidobro, Vicente 716
Hull, E. M. 652
Hull, Raymond 558
Humboldt, Alexander von 194, 210
Hume, Joseph 397
Humphrey, duke of Gloucester 209
Hunt, Leigh 393
Hunt, Thomas 684
Huntington, earl of 617
Hurd, Richard 583
Huss, John 366
Hussein, Saddam 690
Huxley, Aldous 54, 456, 517, 619, 680, 698, 704
Huxley, Thomas H. 12
Huysmans, Joris Karl 373
Hyacinthus (mythological figure) 366, 504
Hygeia (mythological figure) 366
Hyman (mythological figure) 366
Hypatia 366–367
Hyperbolus 367
Hyperides 561
Hypnos (mythological figure) 367, 491

I

Iacino, Tom 179
Iadmon (Thracian master of Aesop) 625
Iago (fictional character) 60
Ibarruri, Dolores 426
Ibn Saud 638
Ibrahim, Izzat 500
Icarus (mythological figure) 421
Idaho 290
Ida May 103
Idhunn (mythological figure) 31
I-Ho-Chuan 99
Illinois 582
Immelmann, Max 373
Indian words 376, 505
Ingermarsson, Nils 440
Inglis, William 208
Ingraham, Joseph 183
Innes, William 586
Innocent X (pope) 71
Innocent XII (pope) 462
Io (mythological figure) 33, 380
Iowa 337
Iphicles (Greek runner) 254
Ireland, William Henry 381

Irene (mythological figure) 572
Iris (mythological figure) 266, 381
Irish words 381
Irvin, Wallace 566
Irvin, Will 346
Irving, Washington 19, 30, 87, 104, 114, 166, 219, 310, 333, 415, 438, 633
Irwin, Wallace 163
Isabella II (queen of Spain) 380
Isabella of Austria 382
Isaiah (Old Testament) 70, 106, 225, 240, 430, 645
Isaure, Clémence 636
Ishmael (biblical figure) 382
Isocrates 804
Italian words 383
Itys (mythological figure) 560
Ivan the Terrible (czar of Russia) 192
Ivins, Molly 109, 328, 370, 655

J

Jabir ibn Hazyan 14–15, 295
Jack, David 488
Jackson, Andrew 198, 344, 389, 440, 457, 476, 605, 610, 683, 699, 755
Jackson, Carlton 439
Jackson, John Hughlings 104
Jackson, Robert H. 696
Jackson, Shirley 692
Jackson, Shoeless Joe 78
Jackson, Thomas Jonathan "Stonewall" 692
Jacob (biblical figure) 35, 244, 394
Jacobs, Joe 382, 769–770
Jacobs, Mary Phelps 100
Jacoby, Russell 587
Jacquard, Joseph Marie 389
Jacuzzi, Candito 390
Jaeger, Gustav 390
Jagger, Joseph Hobson 466
James (biblical figure) 88
James I (king of England). See James VI and I
James II (king of England) 364, 389, 643, 693, 729
James IV (king of Scotland) 557
James V (king of Scotland) 446, 606
James VI and I (king of Scotland and England) 111, 389, 444, 496, 516, 573, 584, 590, 687, 726, 744, 771
James, duke of York 413, 509, 510
James, Frank 394
James, Henry 462, 666, 738
James, Jesse 394
James, William 266, 582, 694
James Francis Edward Stuart (The Old Pretender) 223, 389
Jane, Fred T. 390
Janus (mythological figure) 390
Japanese words 390
Jason (mythological figure) 33
Jasper, Brother 649
Jefferson, Joseph 442
Jefferson, Thomas 8, 66, 242, 263, 316, 337, 392, 432, 436, 440, 450, 457, 494, 517, 562, 591, 636, 644, 751, 757, 780
Jeffries, James "Jim" 73, 388, 500
Jehoshaphat (biblical figure) 395
Jehu (biblical figure) 394
Jellinik, Emil 477
Jenkins, Robert 763
Jenner, Edward 582
Jenney, William Le Baron 666
Jennings, Alston 715
Jennings, Gary 101, 660
Jennison, "Doc" 391
Jephthah (biblical figure) 654
Jeremiah (biblical figure) 393, 394, 514
Jeremiah (Old Testament) 116, 433, 514, 690
Jernigan, Aaron 537
Jerry, Mr. 394
Jespersen, Otto 245, 365
Jesse (biblical figure) 394

Jessel, Georgie 278
Jesus Christ 24, 60, 82, 88, 95, 127, 152, 162, 184, 186, 211, 221, 233, 234, 238, 240, 245, 260, 278, 304, 305, 307, 329, 345, 353, 372, 392, 401, 414, 416, 430, 435, 464, 469, 472, 515, 530, 545, 558, 563, 585, 633, 762, 764
Jezebel (biblical figure) 394
Joab (biblical figure) 783
Joachim (biblical figure) 598
Job (Old Testament) 122, 299, 396, 461, 499, 528, 577, 637
John (biblical figure) 88
John (king of England) 217, 296, 310, 458, 704
John II (king of France) 275
John II (king of Portugal) 131
John XXII (pope) 524
John, Gospel of (New Testament) 95, 98, 221, 233, 305, 472, 520, 585, 762
John Bull (fictional character) 398, 532, 539, 743
John of Gaunt 491
John Paul II (pope) 578
Johnson, Andrew 14, 349, 649
Johnson, Charles J. 265
Johnson, Claudia Taylor 422
Johnson, Esther 247
Johnson, Frank H. 399
Johnson, Gerald 373
Johnson, John Arthur "Jack" 388, 500
Johnson, Lyndon 120, 130, 575
Johnson, Robert W. 51
Johnson, Samuel 28, 78, 87, 92, 96–97, 110, 124, 146, 147, 156, 179, 187, 188, 248, 278, 289, 295, 322, 327, 399, 403, 413, 436, 504, 505, 512, 518, 550, 580, 586, 603, 680, 729
Johnson, William Eugene "Pussyfoot" 591
Johnson & Johnson 51
Joliot-Curie, Irène 188
Jolson, Al 315, 706, 796
Jonah (biblical figure) 298, 399
Jones, Chuck 777
Jones, David (phonetician) 343
Jones, David (reporter) 658
Jones, Davy 198
Jones, Edward D. 222
Jones, George 457
Jones, James 22, 340, 715
Jones, John Luther 135
Jones, John Paul 551, 663
Jonson, Ben 6–7, 19, 45, 61, 72, 88, 94, 121, 164, 168, 214, 243, 252, 254, 277, 289, 451, 463, 548, 573, 603, 629, 650, 678, 714, 729
Jordan, Robert 546
Jordan family 369
Joseph (biblical figure) 400
Joseph, Monsieur 183
Josephine (empress of the French) 425, 621
Joshua (biblical figure) 400
Joshua (Old Testament) 345
Josselyn, John 15, 639
Joule, James Prescott 400
Joyce, James 11, 23, 54, 84, 113, 190, 195, 246, 262, 279, 290, 525, 537, 589, 597, 647, 672, 694, 732
Joyce, John A. 427
Joyce, William 449
Joynson-Hicks, William 396
Juba 128
Judah (biblical figure) 394, 531
Judas Iscariot (biblical figure) 401, 414, 468, 549, 581
Judges (Old Testament) 35, 203, 278, 295, 303, 391, 560, 634, 654, 670
Judith (Apocrypha) 354
Judson, Edward Z. C. 115
Judson, Whitman L. 803
Judy 586
Jukes family 401
Julian the Apostate 531

Juliet (fictional character) 620
Julius Caesar 7, 38–39, 108, 118, 125, 132, 138, 158, 182, 186, 192, 207, 256, 295, 401, 402, 405, 559, 632, 653–654, 753
Jung, Carl 376, 402
Jung, David 272
Junia 173
Juno (mythological figure) 30, 256, 402, 458, 487, 749
Jupiter (mythological figure) 380, 412, 487, 627
Jupiter Optimas Maximus 131
Justin, Joseph 403
Justinian I (Byzantine emperor) 25, 138
Juvenal 102, 403, 427, 606

K

Kafka, Franz 405
Kahina (Berber queen) 575
Kakos (mythological figure) 578
Kalakaua (king of Hawaii) 741
Kalashnikov, Mikhail 405
Kal-El (Superman; comic book hero) 405
Kali (mythological figure) 720
Kamel, George Joseph 127
Kane, James 146
Kanin, Garson 626
Kanka, Megan 476
Kano, Jigoro 401
Kansas 391, 406
Kant, Immanuel 12
Kapor, Mitchell 735
Karenga, Maulana Ron 419
Karloff, Boris 276
Karno, Fred 276
Karpenchinko, Alexi 603
Kasner, Edward 308
Katzenjammer Kids (fictional characters) 534
Kaufman, George S. 72, 302, 477, 798
Kaufman, Murray 82
Kaufman, Wolfe 774
Kaye, Danny 357
Kean, Edmund 442
Keats, Edgar 81
Keats, John 160, 176, 201, 343, 525, 717, 784
Keeler, Wee Willie 349
Keene, Foxhall 21, 148
Keene, J. R. 148
Keene, Mary 112
Keith, B. F. 751
Keller, Helen 54
Kelley, Sydney "Buster" 408
Kellogg, Frank Billings 508
Kelly, Alice Douglas 302
Kelly, John "Smelly" 383
Kelly, John W. 667
Kelly, Machine Gun 14
Kelly, Michael Joseph "King" 667
Kelly, Ned 285
Kelly, Walt 767
Kelly, William 69
Kelvin, Baron (William Thomson) 408, 479
Kemble, William 408
Kemmler, William 238
Kendall, Edward C. 178
Kendall, Henry 184
Kennedy, Jacqueline 263
Kennedy, John F. 9, 35, 73, 148, 260, 312, 337, 575, 607, 616, 761
Kennedy, Randall 511
Kennelly, Arthur Edwin 339
Kenny, James 207
Kent, Frank R. 254
Kentucky 86, 409
Kephart, Horace 742
Kepler, Johannes 269, 586
Kern, Jerome 537
Kerouac, Jack 61
Kerr, Clark 649
Kerwin, Jerome 766
Kesey, Ken 671
Ketch, Jack 388, 630

Ketcham, Hank 203
Key, Francis Scott 172, 687
Keynes, John Maynard 409
Keys, Ancel 418
Keyserling, Count 370
Khomeini, Ayatollah 255
Khrushchev, Nikita 486, 686
Kidd, Captain 261, 304
Kieran, James M. 101
Killikaks family 401
Kilrain, Jack 316
Kilroy, James J. 411
Kimble, Francis 578
King, Billie Jean 100
King, Doris E. 492
King, Edward 426
King, Richard 413
King, Stephen 564, 797
King, Stoddard 36, 617
Kings (Old Testament) 221, 393, 394, 503
Kingsley, Charles 367, 498–499, 715
Kinkaid, Moses 413
Kipling, Rudyard 8, 11, 71, 268, 341, 383, 403, 411, 448, 482, 587, 649, 656, 698, 717, 773, 776, 779
Kirby, J. Hudson 761
Kirby, Norvel E. 413
Kirchhoff, Gustav 115
Kirk, James T. (fictional character) 59
Kirkpatrick, James C. 540
Kirks, Edmund 172
Kitasato, Shibasaburo 795
Kittel, R. 330
Klatt, Professor 276
Klem, Bill 376
Kliegl, John H. and Anton T. 415
Klinger, Friedrich Maximilian von 695
Kneller, Godfrey 414
Knickerbocker, Diedrich 415, 438
Knickerbocker, Harmon 415
Knopf, Alfred 305–306, 344
Knowland, William F. 574
Knox, John 126
Knox, Robert 117
Koch, Ed 217
Koch, Frederick 164
Koch, Robert 559
Koch, W. D. J. 147
Kookie (fictional character) 418
Kopit, Arthur 758
Koufax, Sandy 55
Krafft-Ebing, Richard 471
Kraft, Joseph 480
Kray, Ronnie and Reggie 154
Kremer, Gerhard. See Mercator, Gerhardus
Kreutzer, Rodolphe 418
Kreuzberg, Georg 29
Kristke, Anke 270
Kroc, Ray 474
Kruck, William E. 171
Krupp von Bohlen und Halbach, Bertha 72
Ktesias (Greek physician) 465
Kublai Khan 467
Kundera, Milan 414
Kunz, George Frederick 419
Kuru (legendary figure) 459

L

Laban, Rudolph 421
La Baume Le Blanc, Françoise-Louise de 428
Ladas (Greek courier) 254
Lady Margaret 82
La Fontaine, Jean de 677
Lagasse, Emeril 410
La Guardia, Fiorello 516
Lajoie, Napoleon 159
Lake, Veronica 554
Laman (Hebrew prohet) 424
Lamarck, chevalier de (Jean-Baptiste-Pierre-Antoine de Monet) 424
Lamb, Charles 71, 108, 349, 570, 756
Lamb, William. See Melbourne, William Lamb, Viscount
Lambert, Johann Heinrich 424

Lambert le Begue 64–65
Lamentations (Old Testament) 476
La Motte Fouqué, Friedrich de 744
L'Amour, Louis 111, 773, 801
Lancelot (fictional character) 663
Landers, Ann 51
Landon, Alfred M. 333
Landru, Henri Desire 85
Lane, Alan 359
Lane, George Martin 531
Lang, Fritz 179
Langerhans, Paul 383
Langland, William "Long Will" 66
Langley, Samuel Pierpont 425
Langtry, Lillie 425
Lansky, Meyer 498, 669
Laodice 422, 425
La Plante, Georgette de 291
Lapostolle, Marnier 313
Lardner, John 769–770, 797
Lardner, Ring 15, 526, 659
Larousse, Pierre Athanase 426
La Salle, René-Robert-Cavalier de 450
Lash, Almon 429
Lasthenia (pupil of Plato) 426
Lasus (Greek lyric poet) 442
Latan, A. M. 143
Latimer, Robert 429
Latta, Lorenzo 361
Laube, Hans 669
Lauderdale, John, first earl and duke of 123
Laughlin, James 503
Laurel, Stan 276
Laurence, James 218
Laurence, William L. 499
Laval, Pierre 428
La Vallière, Françoise-Louise de la Baume Le Blanc de 488
Lavoisier, Antoine-Laurent 540
La Voison (French sorceress) 489
Lawford, Peter 607
Lawlor, Charles B. 437
Lawrence, D. H. 197, 210, 279, 398, 619, 737, 784
Lawrence, Ernest Orlando 429
Lawrence, Mary Wells 372
Lawrence, T. E. 648
Lawson, Isaac 429
Lawson, John 429
Lazarus (biblical figure) 4, 430, 469
Lear, Edward 440, 625, 697
Leblang, Joseph 431
Le Carré, John 486
Le Clerc du Tremblay, François (Père Joseph) 239–240
Lecoq de Boisbaudran, Paul-Emil 284
Le Corbeau, Adrian 648
Leda (mythological figure) 631
Lee, Annie (fictional character) 242
Lee, C. 28
Lee, Dawne E. 557
Lee, Gypsy Rose 117, 234
Lee, Henry 263
Lee, Maria 80
Lee, Robert E. 31, 151, 263, 359, 617, 653, 692
Leet, Paulette M. 650
Leeuwenhoek, Antonie van 432
Legman, Gershon 308
Le Grand, Alexandre 68
Legree, Simon (fictional character) 743
Lehár, Franz 478
Leicester, Robert Dudley, earl of 650
Leigh, Augustus, Mrs. 122
Leip, Hans 439
Lely, Peter 764
Lemkin, Raphael 290
Lemmon, Jack 403
Lempira (Honduran chief) 189
L'Enfant, Pierre-Charles 694
Lenin, Vladimir Ilyich 91, 433, 686, 733, 797
Lennon, John 452
Leno, Jay 656
Leo III (Byzantine emperor) 370
Leo X (pope) 475

Leo XI (pope) 475
Leo XIII (pope) 171
Leofric, earl of Mercia 423, 554
Leonard, Helen Louise 439
Leonardo da Vinci 341, 486
Leopold (duke of Austria) 413
Léotard, Jules 433
Lepine, Jules 273
Lerner, Max 474
Leroy, Louis 373
Lesage, Alain René 561
Lesseps, Ferdinand de 544
Leto (mythological figure) 513
Levant, Oscar 723
Leverrier, Urbain-Jean-Joseph 757
Lewis, Meriwether 157, 582. See also Lewis and Clark
Lewis, Paul 275
Lewis, Sinclair 43, 94
Lewis, Ted 382
Lewis, Wyndham 28
Lewis and Clark 76, 89, 156, 169, 316, 582, 585
Li Chung-yun 273
Liddell, Alice 15
Liddell, Henry George 15
Lieber, Charles S. 27
Liechtenstein family 436
Liège, Jacques de 388
Lifebuoy Health Soap 88
Life magazine 76, 94
Ligowsky, George 157
Liliuokalani (queen of Hawaii) 19
Lille, Alain de 18
Lillie, Beatrice 357
Lincoln, Abraham 3, 4, 129, 217, 236, 239, 270–271, 274, 349, 355, 372, 387, 440, 457, 494, 501, 565, 588, 610, 649, 659, 660, 718, 769, 775, 784
Lind, Jenny 393
Lindau, Arvid 104
Lindbergh, Charles 344, 440–441
Lindley, John 423
Lindsay, David 446, 606
Lindsay, John V. 281
Link, Robert 94
Linnaeus, Carolus (Carl von Linné) 25, 50, 51, 127, 142, 210, 255, 286, 354, 426, 429, 433, 440, 441, 444, 458, 459, 511, 573, 590, 597, 613, 631, 679, 735, 803
Lippmann, Walter 165
Lister, Joseph 442
Little Black Sambo (fictional character) 634
Little Boy 3
Little Egypt 357
Little Nell (fictional character) 57, 551
The Little Pretty Pocket Book 56
Littleton, Thomas 164
Livingstone, David 213
Llano, Queipo de 259
Lloyd, David 225
Lloyd, Edward 28–29
Lloyd, Robert 668
Lloyd George, David 36–37, 253, 606, 762, 764
Lloyd's of London 28–29, 312
L'Obel, Matthias de 444, 458
Locke, Charles O. 772
Locke, John 241, 591
Locke, Richard Adams 489
Locker-Lampson, Frederick 495
Loesser, Frank 582
Logan, James Harvey 445
Logan, John A. 80
Logan, Joshua 780
Lombardi, Vince 779
Lombard Street 29
London, Jack 145, 293, 316
Lone Ranger (fictional character) 359, 727
Long, Earl 691
Long, Russell B. 691
Longabaugh, Harry 119
Longacre, Sara 375

Longfellow, Henry Wadsworth 118, 169, 271, 332, 379, 423, 481, 500, 655, 679, 681, 716, 784
Longinus (Roman soldier) 450
Longstreet, James 763
Longworth, Alice Roosevelt 15–16
Lonitzer, Adam 355
Looney, John Don 264
Loos, Anita 290
Lope de Vega y Carpio, Félix 244
Loren, Sophia 362
Lothario (fictional character) 216, 289
Loudon, John C. 8, 215
Louis IX (king of France) 413
Louis XII (king of France) 434
Louis XIII (king of France) 239, 450, 491
Louis XIV (king of France) 62, 74, 208, 269, 275, 312, 398, 428, 435, 449, 450, 460, 469, 488, 552, 582
Louis XV (king of France) 194, 450, 505, 576, 661, 758
Louis XVI (king of France) 450, 478, 755
Louis, Antoine 323
Louis, Joe 107, 397, 500, 797, 802
Louisiana 555
Louis-Napoleon. See Napoleon III
Lovecraft, H. P. (Howard Phillips) 573
Lovelace, Linda 202
Lovelace, Richard 692
Lovelace, Robert 451
Lovell, Francis 607
Lovely, Ann (fictional character) 662
Lover, Samuel 331
Low, David 211
Lowell, James Russell 198, 234, 303, 324, 500, 767
Lowell, William 710
Lowther, Hugh Cecil 448
Lucas, George 208
Luce, Claire Booth 11, 677
Lucian (Greek satirist) 126, 460
Luciano, Lucky 498
Lucifer (biblical figure) 8, 707
Lucius Furius 487
Lucretius (Roman poet and philosopher) 506
Lucullus, Lucius Licinius 452
Ludd, Ned 453
Ludlam, Mrs. 430
Lugosi, Bela 781
Luisetti, Angel Enrico "Hank" 532
Luke (New Testament) 4, 88, 106, 211, 307, 411, 463, 528, 585, 658
Lumpking, Katherine 272
Lunn, Sally 633
Luther, Martin 60, 366, 454, 547, 779, 804
Lutz, Alois 454
Lycoris (Roman actress) 454
Lycurgus (king of Sparta) 104
Lydgate, John 169
Lyly, John 323, 451, 691
Lyman, Tommy 133
Lynch, Thomas 411
Lynch, William 454
Lysimachus (Greek general) 448

M

Macabees (Apocrypha) 455
Macadam, John 455
MacArthur, Douglas 237
Macarthy, Harry 92
Macaulay, Thomas Babington 35, 39, 93, 123, 348, 384, 388, 413
MacFadden, Bernard 172
MacGregor, Patrick 365
Mach, Ernst 456
Machiavelli, Niccolò 456, 682
Macie, Elizabeth 670
Macintosh, Charles 623
Mackenzie, Frederick 380
Mackinnon, John 223
Macklin, Charles 319, 518
MacLeish, Archibald 295
MacLeod, H. D. 319

Macrobius, Ambrosius Theodosius 148
Macy's (department store) 47, 169, 213, 377, 783
Madison, Dolley 263
Madison, James 440, 457, 636, 757
Maechus (mythological figure) 579
Maemmon (mythological figure) 710
Magee, Carl C. 548
Magellan, Ferdinand 454, 543
Maginot, André 458
Magnol, Pierre 458
Maguinnis, Dan 2
Maguire, William 582
Maine 565
Maintenon, Françoise Aubigné, marquise de 460, 489, 552
Maitland, Thomas 266
Major League Baseball 73
Malaprop, Mrs. (fictional character) 462
Malay words 462
Malcolm X (Malcolm Little) 148
Malinowski, Bronislaw 559
Mallery, Richard E. 224
Mallory, George Leigh 62
Malone, Edmund 381
Malpighi, Marcello 462
Malthus, Thomas Robert 463, 750
Mama Dyumbo (mythological figure) 497
Mamet, David 302
Mammon, Epicure (fictional character) 463
Manchly, John W. 170
Mandale, W. R. 578
Mandeville, John 621
Mandrake the Magician (fictional character) 464
Manes (Persian prophet) 464
Mann, Thomas 561
Mannin, Ethel 430
Manningham, John 777
Mansart, Nicolas-François 465
Manutius, Aldus 166, 383
Mao Zedong (Tse-tung) 51, 297, 466, 546
Map, Walter 663
Marachetti (Italian sculptor) 573
Marblestone, Howard 10, 675, 690, 793
Marciano, Rocky 397
Marconi, Guglielmo 779
Marcus Aurelius 284
Marcy, William Learned 683
Maria Louisa (queen of Spain) 154
Marie Antoinette (queen of France) 133, 435, 533, 755
Marie Louise of Austria 426
Marie-Thérèse (queen of France) 460, 488
Marignac, J. C. G. de 283
Marigny, Bernard 181–182
Marin (French chef) 676
Marino, Giambattista 467
Marinus (sonecutter; later, saint) 635
Marion, Francis 699
Marivaux, Pierre Carlet de Chamblain de 468
Mark (New Testament) 88, 648, 762
Mark I (tank) 74
Mark Antony 108, 158, 211, 402, 436, 454, 468, 492, 549, 621, 632
Marlowe, Christopher 105, 168, 413, 465, 517
Marlowe, Julia 478
Marquis, Don 162
Marryat, Frederick 113, 129, 139, 194, 439, 656, 664, 741, 769
Mars (mythological figure) 257, 458, 467
Marshall, George Catlett 469
Martha (biblical figure) 430, 469
Martial (Roman poet) 771
Martin, Betty 17
Martin, Dean 364, 607
Martin, Mary 558
Martineau, Harriet 21, 688

Martinet, Jean 469
Martini, Frederic de 343
Martland, Harrison S. 590
Marvel, Ik 744
Marvell, Andrew 243, 611
Marx, Chico 470
Marx, Groucho 133–134, 276, 470, 484
Marx, Gummo 470
Marx, Karl 470, 783
Marx, Zeppo 470
Mary (mother of Jesus) 467, 470, 620, 622
Mary (sister of Lazarus and Martha) 430, 469
Mary I (queen of England) 84, 718
Mary Queen of Scots 124, 189, 238, 598, 774
Maryland 529
Mary Magdalene 472, 515, 585. See also Mary (sister of Lazarus and Martha)
Marzip, Franz 470
Masashika Shimonose Kogakubachi 654
Maslin, Janet 797
Mason, Charles 471
Mason, John 459, 471, 509
Massachusetts 59, 181
Massasoit (grand sachem of Wampanoag Confederacy) 684
Massinger and Field 289
Masterson, William Barclay "Bat" 57, 785
Masuccio (Italian writer) 620
Mather, Cotton 22, 791
Mathew, Father 254
Mathews, Mitford 87, 223, 251, 342, 559
Mathewson, Christy 395, 677
Matisse, Henri 165
Matoaka. See Pocahontas
Matthew (New Testament) 82, 84, 106, 136, 186, 194, 234, 238, 240, 304, 310, 345, 353, 380, 384, 435, 443, 463, 539, 558, 582, 629, 633, 647, 648, 705, 724, 731, 762, 764, 773, 781
Matthews, Chris 219
Matthews, Gordon 757
Maugham, Somerset 96, 125, 619
Maundeville, John 184
Maupassant, Guy de 746
Maury, Matthew Fontaine 655
Mauser, Peter Paul and Wilhelm 472
Mausolus (king of Caria) 472
Maverick, Maury 301
Maverick, Samuel Augustus 473
Maxim, Hiram Percy 473
Maxim, Hiram Stevens 473
Maximian (emperor of Rome) 184
Maximinus (emperor of Rome) 138
Maximus, Quintus Fabius 251
Maxwell, James Clerk 473
Mayhew, Henry 700
Mazarin, Jules, Cardinal 206
Mazza, Angelo 374
McAdam, John Loudon 455
McAllister, Ward 274
McArthur, Tom 271, 568
McAuliffe, Anthony 521
McBride, Art 709
McCall, Jack 200
McCarthy, Cormac 81, 718, 798
McCarthy, Joseph 474
McCarthy, Mary 322
McClain, James L. 74
McClellan, George 18
McCormick, Moose 91
McCoy, Al 608
McCoy, Elijah 608
McCoy, Kid 608
McCoy family 608
McCracken, Herb 363
McCrae, John 265, 578
McCutcheon, George Barr 291
McDonald, James 163
McDougal, Mary 117

McGinley, Phyllis 754
McGonagall, William 572
McGovern, George 719
McGraw, Ali 590
McGraw, John 349, 565
McGuane, Thomas 371
McGuffey, William Holmes 474
McGwire, Mark 332
McIntosh, John 474
McKenzie, Kenneth 164
McKinley, William 682, 714
McMurtry, Larry 442
McNaughton, Daniel 474
McPaul, William 223
McQueen, Alexander 613
McQueen, Steve 590
Meader, Nick 516
Medea (mythological figure) 548
Medici, Catherine de' 275, 322, 475, 511, 762
Medici, Giovanni di Bicci de' 475
Medici, Lorenzo d' 22
Medici, Marie de' 230, 475, 633
Medici family 551
Medusa (mythological figure) 310, 475, 744
Meet the Press 260
Megiddo 34
Mehitabel (fictional character) 162
Meigs, Return J. 81
Melba, Nellie 476
Melbourne, William Lamb, Viscount 431
Melpomene (mythological figure) 499
Melville, Herman 21, 199, 284, 382, 485, 504, 566, 701
Melville, Thomas 426
Melville, Henry Dundas, Viscount 688
Menander 317–318
Menches, Charles and Frank 329
Mencken, H. L. 24, 41, 49, 71, 82, 85, 162, 171, 193, 201, 202, 233–234, 285, 290, 291, 297, 333, 340, 410, 437, 446, 450, 470, 527, 561, 623, 795
Mendel, Gregor Johann 476
Mendeleyev, Dmitri Ivanovich 476
Mendoza, Cardinal (Pedro Gonzales de Mendoza) 166
Mendoza, Daniel 61
Mendoza, David 376
Ménière, Prosper 477
Menke, Arnold 12
Mentor (mythological figure) 477
Menzies, Archibald 483
Mercator, Gerhardus 22, 37, 477
Mercer, John 477
Mercer, Leigh 544
Mercury (mythological figure) 477–478, 721
Meriwell, Frank 387
Merkle, Fred 91
Merlin (legendary figure) 709
Merrith, Dixon Lanier 555
Mesmer, Franz Anton 478
Messalina (empress of Rome) 479
Messerschmitt, Wilhelm 479
Mestral, Georges de 752
Methuselah (biblical figure) 528
Metis (mythological figure) 458
Metz, Theodore 361
Mezzofanti, Giuseppe Caspar 103–104
Micawber, Wilkins (fictional character) 480, 494
Michael (archangel) 527
Michaux, André 434
Michel, Dan 11
Michelangelo 795
Michelet, Jules 630
Michener, James 490, 561, 581, 607
Michigan 781, 796
Michtom, Morris 710
Mickey Mouse (fictional character) 211, 214, 315, 480
Midas (mythological figure) 191, 480
Middleton, Dean 319
Middleton, Thomas 28

Milden, William. See Streaham, William Milden, earl of
Miles, Alfred H. 25
Miles Laboratory 16
Millay, Edna St. Vincent 26, 118, 235
Miller, Mr. 286
Miller, Andrew 25
Miller, Elizabeth Smith 84
Miller, Henry 279, 600, 787
Miller, Joseph (Josiah) 397
Miller, William 649
Miller, William Bancroft 379
Millie, Bessie 778
Miltiades (Greek commander) 467
Milton, John 8, 16, 21, 54, 64, 159, 248, 253, 267, 322, 426, 446, 451, 499, 501, 512, 524, 545, 617, 670, 694, 732, 767
Miner, Charles 41
Miner, Tom 294
Minerva (mythological figure) 30, 638, 652
Ming Huang 798
Minié, Claude Étienne 483
Minnesota 309–310, 483
Minoso, Minnie 302
Minotaur (mythological figure) 421
Minthe (mythological figure) 483
Miranda, Ernesto A. 483
Mississippi 458, 484
Mississippi River 73
Missouri 658
Missouri River 73
"Mistah Bones" (fictional character) 588
"Mistah Interlocutor" (fictional character) 588
Mr. Ed (fictional character) 359
Mitchell, Donald Grant 744
Mitchell, Edwin V. 634
Mitchell, Helen Porter 476
Mitchell, John 73
Mitchell, Margaret 172, 259, 302, 306, 605
Mitchell, Samuel Latham 276
Mitford, John 705
Mitford, Nancy 725
Mithridates VI (king of Pontus) 452, 484–485, 705
Mitty, Walter (fictional character) 763
Mizner, Wilson 20, 263, 353, 795
Mnemosyne (mythological figure) 499, 712
Modjeska, Helena 478
Moeller von der Bruck, Arthur 611
Mohorovičić, Andrija 485
Mola, Emilio 259
Moley, Raymond 1, 509
Molière (Jean-Baptiste Poquelin) 491, 733
Mollien, François N. 486
Molotov, Vyacheslav Mikhailovich 486
Momand, Arthur R. "Pop" 407
Momus (mythological figure) 486
Moncke, Charles 488
Mondale, Walter 772
Mondriaan, Pieter Cornelis (Piet Mondrian) 487
Moneke (fictional character) 488
Monet, Claude 38, 373
Money, E. E. 233
Mongut (king of Siam) 575
Monmouth, Geoffrey, duke of 412, 625
Monroe, Earl "the Pearl" 114, 592
Monroe, James 8, 488, 757
Monroe, Marilyn 403, 649
Montagu, Elizabeth 87
Montagu, John. See Sandwich, John Montagu, earl of
Montagu, Lady Mary Wortley 636
Montaigne, Michel Eyquem de 436, 519, 570, 752
Montana 74, 488, 731
Montespan, Françoise Rochechouart de Mortemart, marquise de 460, 488–489

Montessori, Maria 489
Montezuma (Aztec emperor) 40, 41, 489
Montgomery, Bernard, viscount Montgomery of Alamein 48, 280
Montgomery, Tim 274
Moody, Joseph 330
Moog, Robert 489
Moon, Robert A. 803
Mooney, William 707
Moore, Douglas 530
Moore, Marianna 748
Moore, Thomas 427, 610
Moose, Chief 226
Mor, McCarthy 81
Morceli, Noureddine 274
Mordecai (biblical figure) 331
More, Charley 143
More, George 243
More, Henry 567
More, Thomas 432, 489, 632, 747, 780, 801
Morgan, J. P. 182
Morgan, Justin 490
Morgan, William 306, 543, 758
Morganbesser, Sidney 794
Morgan le Fay (legendary figure) 254
Morier, James 96
Morison, Samuel Eliot 527
Morley, Christopher 377
Mornay, Philippe de 491
Morpheus (mythological figure) 491
Morris, George Pope 782
Morris, Gouverneur 141
Morris, Lewis 173
Morris, William 266, 491
Morrison, Herbert S. 491
Morrison, Marion. See Wayne, John
Morrison, Martin 579
Morrison, William 278
Morse, Samuel Finley Breese 491, 770
Mortemart, duc de. See Rochechouart, Gabriel de, duc de Mortemart
Morton, J. Sterling 32, 732
Morton, John Maddison 99
Morton, Thomas 302, 495
Morton, William Thomas Green 26
Moses (Hebrew prophet and lawgiver) 492, 520, 783
Moss, Howard 59
Mostel, Zero 47
Motely, John 738
Motteux, Peter 514
Mottley, John 397
Mountbatten, Louis, first earl Mountbatten of Burma 248
Mozart, Wolfgang Amadeus 216
Mozee, Phoebe Annie Oakley 27
Mudd, Samuel 349
Muhammad 9, 60, 371, 496, 795
Mulford, Samuel 336
Mulgrew, "Boots" 529
Mullah Omar 625
Muller, Mr. 496
Mulligan, David 497
Mumford, Lewis 587
Mumtaz Mahal (Mughal empress) 704
Munchausen, Freiherr von (Karl Friedrick Hieronymus) 497–498
Munster, Ernst F. 4
Murger, Henri 90
Murphy, William Lawrence 498
Murray, James 643
Murray, William H. "Alfalfa Bill" 314
Murray the K (radio personality) 82
Murrell, K. F. H. 243
Musa, Antonio 51
Muses (mythological figures) 499, 562, 712
Mussolini, Benito 205, 290, 752
Mutt, Augustus (fictional character) 500
Muybridge, Eadweard 804
Myers, Frederick W. H. 711
Myerson, Allen R. 614
Myrray, John 520
Myrrha (mythological figure) 9, 501

N

Nabal (biblical figure) 3
Nabokov, Vladimir 446, 503
Naboth (biblical figure) 503
Naismith, James 56, 543
Napoleon 60, 77, 97, 177, 196, 208, 323, 425–426, 436, 445, 450, 458, 486, 504, 519, 520, 529, 589, 680, 758, 765, 768
Napoleon III 53, 373
Narcissus (mythological figure) 234, 504
Narcissus (Roman informer) 479
Narian, Nanddo 273
Nascimento, Edson Arantes do. See Pelé
Nash, Beau 62
Nash, Ogden 431, 754
Nashe, Thomas 60, 400, 472, 778
Nast, Thomas 707
Nathan, George Jean 353
Nation, Carry 133
Native American words 376, 505
Nattier, Jean-Marie 505
Neal, John 269, 461
Neander, Joachim C. 506
Nearchos (Greek tyrant) 77
Nebraska 177, 506
Nebuchadnezzar (king of Babylon) 256, 332, 354, 586
Negus, Francis 506
Neisser, A. L. S. 376
Neleus (mythological figure) 508
Nelson, "Baby Face" 255
Nelson, Horatio, Viscount 224, 241, 280, 301, 389, 413, 452, 507, 651, 735, 742
Nemesis (mythological figure) 507
Neptune (mythological figure) 14, 190, 507, 585
Nereus (mythological figure) 478, 507
Nero Caesar 60, 165, 166, 259, 295, 432, 507–508, 546, 621, 662
Nerval, Gérard de 721
Nesselrode, Count Karl Robert 508
Nestor (mythological figure) 508
Nethersole, Olga 676
Neucomen, Thomas 765
Nevada 630, 661
Newberry, John 443
Newcomb, Kerry 724
New Hampshire 314
New Jersey 287
Newle, John 270
Newman, Paul 771
New Mexico 698
Newton, Charles 472–473
Newton, Isaac 214, 329, 510, 526
New York 240
New York Yankees 107
Nicander of Colophon 656
Nicaro 510
Nicholls, Richard 510
Nicodemus (Apocrypha) 450
Nicot, Jean, lord of Villemain 511
Nietzsche, Friedrich Wilhelm 511, 685, 804
Nightingale, Florence 423, 432
Nimrod (biblical figure) 512
Niobe (mythological figure) 513
Nissen, Peter 602
Nixon, Richard 214, 248, 285, 403, 513, 561, 575, 607, 660, 670, 732, 738
Noah (biblical figure) 27, 513, 528, 530, 778–779
Noah, Captain 513–514
Nobel, Alfred 230, 514
Noble, C. J. 516
Noble, Charles 143
Noda, Uichi 177
Noisette, Philippe 515
Nolan, Philip 466
Norbury, Lord 206
Norgay, Tenzing 62, 494
Norris, Frank 316
North, Christopher 698
North Carolina 708

North Dakota 266, 517, 663
Norton, John 691
Norton, Oliver Wilcox 707
Nostredame, Michel de (Nostradamus) 518
Noyes, Audibert de 428
Numbers (Old Testament) 2, 263, 346, 640
Nunez, Peter 754
Nuttal, Thomas 780

O

Oakley, Annie 27
Oates, Titus 408
Oates, Wayne 782
O'Brien, Donat H. 782
O'Brien, Tim 315
O'Brien, Willis H. 412
O'Briens, Esse F. 113
Obsius 524
Occam, William of 524
Oceanus (mythological figure) 507
Ochs, Adolph S. 18
Ochus Bochus 351
O'Connor, William Douglas 307
Oconostota 647
Octavia (wife of Antony) 454
Octavia (wife of Nero) 508
Octavius Augustus. See Augustus Caesar
Odin (mythological figure) 278, 767
Odysseus (mythological figure) 14, 70, 155–156, 213, 477, 486, 525, 555
Oedipus (mythological figure) 556
Oersted, Hans Christian 525
O'Ferrall, Trilby (fictional character) 699, 732
Ogden, C. K. 245
O'Hara, Scarlett (fictional character) 298, 302, 605
Ohio 109–110, 527
Ohm, Georg Simon 479, 527
Ojeda, Alonso de 22
O'Keefe, Patrick F. 267
O-Kiku (mythological figure) 153
Oklahoma 354, 528, 676
Olafsen, Swanhilda 100
Old Berserkr (mythological figure) 68–69
Old Blind Tom 83
Olds, Ransom Eli 530
Olds Motor Vehicle Company 36
O'Leary, Patrick, Mrs. 495
Oliver (knight) 619
Oliver, Raymond 63, 97
Onan (biblical figure) 531
Onassis, Jacqueline Bouvier Kennedy. See Kennedy, Jacqueline
O'Neill, Eugene 150–151, 299, 325, 334, 437, 467, 534, 746
O'Neill, Hugh 609
O'Neill, J. Palmer "Pirate" 567
O'Neill, James 150–151
O'Neill, Rose Cecil 409
O'Neill, Susie 699
Onions, C. T. 417
Ophelia (fictional character) 57, 293, 551, 622
Ophelia, Aunt (fictional character) 322
Oppenheimer, Robert 385
Opper, Frank 300
Orchan, Sultan 390
Oregon 62, 536
Orelland, Francisco de 21
Orléans, duc de 622
Orpheus (mythological figure) 141, 663
d'Orsay, Alfred Guillaume Gabriel, Count 220
Orwell, George 72, 221, 222, 301, 587
Oscar (maitre'd) 236
Osler, William 190, 537
Osman I (Ottoman sultan) 538
O'Sullivan, John L. 464
Oswy (king of Ireland) 581

Ott, Mel 510
Otus (mythological figure) 564
Otway, Thomas 234
Ouida (Louise de la Ramée) 690
Ouija board 40
Overbrook, (William Maxwell Aitken), Lord 762
Overbury, Thomas 62
Ovid 40, 234, 491, 496
Owen, Richard 209
Owen, Wilfred 515
Owens, R. C. 16
Oxberry, William 543
Oxon, Sam 673

P

Pacific Ocean 73
Pacino, Al 346
Paeon 543
Paget, James 104
Pahlavi, Reza Shah 189
Paige, Leroy "Satchel" 218
Paine, Albert Bigelow 317
Paine, Thomas 12, 279, 697, 745
Pal, Johann 520
Palmer, Arnold 276
Palmer, Joseph 477
Palmerston, Henry John Temple, Lord 552
Pamphilus (Greek grammarian) 545
Pan (mythological figure) 200, 546, 558
Panacea (mythological figure) 545
Pandarus (mythological figure) 545
Pandu (legendary figure) 459
Pantagruel (fictional character) 287
Panula, Eino 745
Papanicolaou, George Nicholas 547
Paparazzo, Signore (fictional character) 546
Paracelsus 16, 91, 547, 708, 744
Pardaillan, Françoise Athénaïs de 488
Paris (mythological figure) 6, 29, 30, 321, 733
Park, Mungo 497
Parker, Dorothy 11, 147, 186, 382, 477, 626, 640, 722, 774
Parker, F. M. 228
Parker, George LeRoy 119
Parker, Matthew 517
Parker, Richard 517–518
Parker, Robert E. 168
Parkinson, C. Northcote 548
Parkinson, John 275
Parnell, Charles Stewart 100
Parson, George 398
Partington, Dame 194, 654
Partington, Mrs. (fictional character) 654
Partridge, Eric 18, 84, 92, 114, 140, 146, 164, 172, 175, 188, 207, 227, 253, 254, 322, 332, 349, 356, 382, 413, 414, 422, 449, 463, 484, 549, 558, 559, 562, 586, 587, 620, 642, 650, 651, 656, 660, 673, 681, 691, 712, 726, 728, 731, 752, 768, 771, 777, 791
Partridge, John 71
Pascal, Blaise 158
Pasco, Captain 241
Pasquino 549
Pasternak, Boris 548
Pasteur, Louis 442, 550
Patroclus (mythological figure) 787
Patti, Adelina 700
Paul (biblical figure). See St. Paul
Paul III (pope) 175
Paul VI (pope) 375
Paulding, James K. 513
Paulmier, Madeleine 457
Paulsen, Axel 41
Paulsen, Pat 575
Pavarotti, Luciano 30, 412
Pavlov, Ivan Petrovich 551
Payne, John Howard 354
Pazzi family 551
Peacock, Thomas Love 268, 619, 750
Peale, Norman Vincent 370–371

Pearce (baseball player) 115
Pearlroth, Norbert 66
Pearson, Hayden 684, 782
Pearson, Richard 663
Peattie, Roderick 29
Pecksniff, Mr. (fictional character) 554
Pecos Bill 554
Pedanius Dioscurides 210
Peek, Jan 554
Peel, Robert 88, 474
Pei, Mario 462, 503, 504
Peirce, William 19
Pelé (Edson Arantes do Nascimento) 555
Peleus (mythological figure) 30
Pell, John 211, 379
Pemberton, John S. 164, 219
Pembroke, earl of 495
Penda (king of Mercia) 556
Pendergast, Mark 396
Penelope (mythological figure) 555
Peneos (mythological figure) 59
Penn, William 556, 707
Penn family 471
Pennsylvania 409, 556
Penthesilea (mythological figure) 716
Pepe Le Pew (fictional character) 777
Pepys, Samuel 78, 185, 335, 359, 416–417, 517, 556, 564, 688, 751
Percy, Henry 360
Perdix (mythological figure) 638
Père Joseph. See Le Clerc du Tremblay, François
Perelman, S. J. 346, 703, 735
Pericles (Athenian statesman) 35
Pérignon, Pierre 142, 216
Peritas (dog) 557
Perkin, William 473
Perkins, Dorothy 220
Perkins, Maxwell 614
Perlez, Jane 500
Perlstein, Rick 587
Pernollet, Monsieur 449
Perrault, Charles 85, 300, 526
Perry, Antoinette 727
Perry, Lincoln Theodore Monroe Andrew (Stepin Fetchit) 689
Perry, Matthew (Commodore) 738
Perry, Oliver 532, 539
Persephone (mythological figure) 11, 190. See also Persephone; Proserpina
Perseus (mythological figure) 25, 359, 501
Pershing, John J. 80, 373
Persian words 557
Peruzzi, Vincenzo 105
Pétain, Henri-Philippe 558, 717
Peter (biblical figure). See St. Peter
Peter, Laurence 558
Peter Pan (fictional character) 558
Peters, Samuel 85
Peter the Venerable 18
Petrarch (Italian poet) 383, 428
Petri, Julius Richard 559
Petronius Arbiter 70, 316, 501, 532
Peverly, Mr. 552
Pforzheimer, Walter L. 486
Phaedra (mythological figure) 501
Phaeton (mythological figure) 559
Phaon (Greek youth) 434
Pharnaces (king of Pontus) 753
Pheidippides 466
Philip (king of Macedon) 30, 126, 203, 317, 422, 560
Philip II (king of Spain) 382, 398, 560, 698
Philips, Ambrose 504
Philipstal (English showman) 559
Phillies Blunt 87
Phillips, Edward 621
Philomela (mythological figure) 560
Phinotias (Pythias) 195
Phorcu (mythological figure) 663
Phryne (Athenian courtesan) 561
Phyfe, Duncan 227
Piccini, Niccolò 300
Pickett, Bill 113
Pickett, George E. 563

Pickins, Slim 668
Piddington, Henry 192
Pierce, C . S. 582
Pierce, Franklin 575, 768
Pierce, Oscar 537
Pigsnort, Ichabod (fictional character) 565
Pike, Zebulon Montgomery 564
Pileggi, Nicholas 779
Pimm, James 564
Pinchback, Christopher 564
Pinckney, Charles Cotesworth 789
Pindar (Greek poet) 73, 442, 499
Pindar, Peter 320
Pink (English tailor) 365
Pinkerton, Allan 565
Pinocchio (fictional character) 395
Pipes, Tom (fictional character) 682
Pisistratus (Athenian tyrant) 436
Pitman, Isaac 567
Pitt, William 567
Pittacus of Mitylene 40, 648
Pius IV (pope) 174
Pizarro, Francisco 285, 589
Placentius 543
Plantin, Christophe 738
Plato 31, 33, 37, 246, 279, 322, 326, 426, 436, 499, 559, 568, 624, 673, 747, 752, 784, 788, 804
Plaut, W. Gunther 793
Plautus (Roman playwright) 30, 465, 678, 746
Plimpton, George A. 570
Plimsoll, Samuel 570
Plinge, Walter 291
Pliny the Elder 106, 125, 161, 214, 290, 436, 485, 505, 521, 524, 581, 705
Pliny the Younger 71
Plotts family 571
Plumier, Charles 279
Plutarch (Greek biographer) 76, 126, 223, 247, 452, 581, 664, 753
Pluto (mythological figure) 192, 483, 494, 755
Plutus (mythological figure) 572
Pocahontas (Powhatan princess) 572
Podsnap, Mr. (fictional character) 572
Poe, Edgar Allan 50, 234, 304, 454, 489, 508, 572, 607, 657
Poinci, Monsieur de 573
Poinsett, Joel Roberts 573
Poisson, Jeanne-Antoinette. See Pompadour, Jeanne-Antoinette Poisson, marquise de
Polish words 626
political slogans 574–575
Polk, James 4, 196, 260, 355, 395, 574, 768
Polo, Marco 467, 678
Polonius (fictional character) 103, 160
Pol Pot 411
Polybius 479
Polycrates 431
Polydorus (mythological figure) 177
Polyhymnia (mythological figure) 499
Polypemon 63
Pomona (mythological figure) 576, 621
Pompadour, Jeanne-Antoinette Poisson, marquise de 468, 576, 661, 676
Pompey (Roman statesman) 182, 452, 674, 705, 753
Ponce de León, Juan 267
Pontiac (Ottowa chief) 576
Pontius Pilate 24, 127, 233, 764
Pontus (mythological figure) 576
Pool, John 551
Poor Richard's Almanac 19
Pooter, Charles and Carrie (fictional characters) 578
Pope, Alexander 28, 54, 57, 77, 188, 195, 244, 281, 403, 412, 424, 444, 451, 504, 512, 514, 551, 572, 580, 684, 728, 733–734, 737, 752, 754, 770
Popik, Barry 698
Poppaea (empress of Rome) 508

Porky Pig (fictional character) 777
Porneius (mythological figure) 579
Port, Alfred 673
Porter, Cole 217, 410, 725
Porter, David 532, 539
Porter, Eleanor M. 575
Porter, William Syndey. See Henry, O.
Portunus (mythological figure) 507
Poseidon (mythological figure) 37, 70, 507, 716
Post, Charles William 580
Potemkin, Gregory 581
Potiphar's wife (biblical figure) 400
Pott, Percivall 104
Potter, Beatrix 398
Potter, Stephen 285
Poulter, B. 17
Pound, Ezra 113, 373, 775
Powell, Abner 605
Powell, Lewis 649
Power, Eileen 270
Powers, "Shorty" 28
Powhatan (chief of Powhatan confederacy) 572
Prassell, Frank Richard 46–47, 217
Praxiteles (Athenian sculptor) 472, 561, 753
Prescott, William Hickling 54
Presley, Elvis 18, 361, 476
Priapus (mythological figure) 29, 501, 584
Priestley, Joseph 560, 623
Prim, Obadiah (fictional character) 662
Pringle, H. F. 680
Priscilla (fictional character) 679
Prithu (legendary figure) 629
Procne (mythological figure) 560
Procopius (Byzantine historian) 25
Procrustes (mythological figure) 63
Prometheus (mythological figure) 458, 585
Proserpina (mythological figure) 31
Protagoras (Greek philosopher) 2
Proteus (mythological figure) 585
Proust, Marcel 457, 647
Proverbs (Old Testament) 77, 297, 465, 519, 584, 674, 679
Pry, Paul (fictional character) 551
Psalmanazar, George 586
Psalms (Old Testament) 2, 68, 200, 210, 385, 498, 555, 719, 754, 777
Ptolemy 246, 547, 586
Ptolemy II (king of Egypt) 544, 559, 647
Ptolemy III (king of Egypt) 167
Ptolemy XIII (king of Egypt) 158
Ptolemy Philadelphus (king of Egypt) 702
Puccini, Giacomo 90
Puff, Mr. (fictional character) 587
Puffwater, Jabey 373
Puget, Peter 750
Pulcinello (fictional character) 586
Pulitzer, Joseph 54, 588, 794
Pullman, George Mortimer 588
Purchas, Samuel 725
Pure, Simon (fictional character) 662
Purkinje, Jan Evangelista 586
Purkiss (English charcoal burner) 121–122
Purvis, Edward 741
Puzo, Mario 48, 173, 178, 256, 302, 461, 531, 613, 666, 769
Pye, Josephy 397
Pygmalion (mythological figure) 343
Pyle, Ernie 392
Pyramus (mythological figure) 496
Pyrrho (Greek philosopher) 593
Pyrrhus (king of Epirus) 593
Pythagoras (Greek philosopher and mathematician) 499, 560, 752, 791
Pytheas (Greek navigator) 721, 742

Q

Quantrell, Mary 53
Quantrill, William Clark 597
Quarles, Francis 117
Quassi, Graman 597

Quay, Matthew S. 574
Queeg, Captain (fictional character) 644
Queensberry, John Sholto Douglas, marquis of 67
Quimby, Phineas P. 234
Quinault, Mademoiselle 173
Quinn, Anthony 532
Quint, Captain (fictional character) 344
Quintillian 720
Quintus Curtius 691
Quisling, Vidkun 601
Quixote, Don (fictional character). See Don Quixote

R

Raah, Lister A. 610
Rabelais, François 11, 17, 133, 287, 354, 373, 489, 490, 500, 513, 553, 638, 725
Rabinowitz, Solomon 656, 732
Rachman, Peter 604
Racine, Jean 603
Radford, Edwin 726
Rafferty (fighter) 5
Raffles, Thomas Stamford Bingley 604
Raglan, Fitzroy James Henry Somerset, baron 605
Rainbow (cat) 140
Raine, Marie 272
Raleigh, Sir Walter 184, 238, 450, 757
Rama (mythological figure) 459
Ramus, Charles Meade 366
Randolph, Innes 307, 745
Randolph, Vance 558
Raphael (biblical figure) 26, 724
Rasmussen, Paul 606
Raspe, Rudolph Erich 497
Ratcliff, Richard 607
Rattigan, Terence 39
Raver, Anne 195
Rawlings, Marjorie Kinnan 634
Rawlins, Hugh 754
Rawson, Hugh 161
Ray, Philip (fictional character) 242
Razz, Mr. 392
Read, Allen Walker 527
Read, Thomas Buchanan 653
Reade, R. S. 579
Reagan, Nancy 355, 447
Reagan, Ronald 81, 316, 355, 448, 607, 666, 710, 779
Réard, Louis 74
Réaumur, René-Antoine Ferchault de 608
Réaux, Gédéon Tallemant des 191
Rebekah (biblical figure) 244
Reculet, Monsieur 444
Red Thunder Cloud 136
Reed, John 646
Reeves, Orlando 537
Rehoboam (biblical figure) 393
Reichenbach, Baron von 525
Reichenberg, Suzanne 183
Reichler, Joseph L. 405
Reles, Abe 498
Remarque, Erich Maria 18
Rembrandt 233
Retz, Gilles de 85
Revelation (New Testament) 20, 34, 43, 60, 259, 755
Revere, Paul 481
Reynard the Fox (fictional character) 487–488
Reynolds, Jeremiah N. 485, 701
Rhodes, John 613
Rice, Alice Caldwell 535
Rice, Dan 156
Rice, Grantland 273, 385, 613
Rice, Thomas D. 395
Rich, Louise Dickenson 673
Richard I, the Lion-Hearted (king of England) 413, 623, 662, 708, 766
Richard II (king of England) 389, 597
Richard III (king of England) 607, 722
Richard of Macaire 38
Richards, I. A. 245
Richardson, 349

Richardson, Samuel 451
Richelieu, Armand-Jean du Plessis, Cardinal 239–240
Richelieu, Armand-Emmanuel du Plessis, duc de 473–474
Richler, Mordecai 441
Richmond, duke of 413, 444
Richmond, earl of 722
Richmond Public Guard 82
Richter, Charles Francis 614
Richthofen, Manfred von 609
Rickenbacker, Eddie 373
Rickerts, Doc 585
Rickey, Colonel 297
Rickey, Branch 253
Rickles, Don 351
Rickover, Hyman G. 655
Rider, Edward 512
Riegels, Roy 785
Rigaud, Monsieur 615
Riggs, John M. 104
Riis, Jacob 362
Riley, James Whitcomb 357, 437
Riley, Pat 719
Rinehart, James Brice Gordon 527
Ringgold, Samuel 320
Ripley, Robert 66, 532
Riskey, Earl 543
Ritter, Thelma 569
Ritty, James J. 135
Ritz, César 244, 300, 313, 616
Rizzo, Ratso (fictional character) 255
Robert, Henry Martyn 617
Robert le Diable, duke of Normandy 334, 343
Roberts, Barbara Millicent 53
Roberts, John 399
Robertson, Morgan 585
Robespierre 389
Robinson, Andrew 641
Robinson, Edward G. 409
Robinson, Frank M. 164
Robinson, Jackie 388, 599
Robinson, Mary D. 636
Robinson, William Heath 339
Robsinson, Luther Bill "Bojangles" 175
Robson, Lucia St. Clair 673, 695, 706
Roche, Boyle 591
Rochechouart, Gabriel de, duc de Mortemart 488
Rochester, Lord 498
Rockefeller, John D. 75, 246, 266, 596, 614
Rockefeller, William 554, 596
Rockefeller family 655
Rockne, Knute 700, 779
Rodack, A. A. 246
Rodger, Walter 512
Rodgers, Richard 537
Rodomonte (fictional character) 618
Roe, F. M. A. 111
Röntgen, Wilhelm Conrad von 619
Rogers, Roy 217, 315, 333, 359
Rogers, Will 17, 795
Roger of Wendover 423
Roget, Peter Mark 716
Roland (knight) 619
Rolle, Richard 246
Rolls, Charles Stewart 619
Romanoff, Fedora (fictional character) 256
Romans (New Testament) 695, 753
Romeo (fictional character) 216, 620
Rood, Micah 480
Rook, Clarence 356
Rooney, Pat 437
Roosevelt, Blanche 681
Roosevelt, Eleanor 237–238, 266
Roosevelt, Franklin Delano 1, 52, 101, 128, 180, 198, 214, 237–238, 271, 295, 333, 336, 377, 501, 509, 519, 550, 575, 745, 761, 766
Roosevelt, Theodore 24, 324, 361, 401, 439, 494, 495, 509, 566, 575, 583, 622, 679–680, 710, 714, 773
Root, George 605
Roper, Jack 802

Roquelaure, Antoine-Gaston, duc de 620
Rorer, William H. 595
Rorschach, Hermann 620
Rosalind (fictional character) 609
Roscius, Quintus Gallus 620–621
Roscoe, Henry 115
Roscoe, William 621
Rose, Carl 382, 681
Rosefield, Harry 44
Rosenbloom, Slapsy Maxie 666
Rosenfeld, Morris 520
Rosenman, Samuel 1, 509
Ross, Betsy 339
Ross, Harold 529, 774
Ross, Robert 343
Rossetti, Dante Gabriel 266, 671, 795
Rossini, Gioacchino Antonio 730
Rostand, Edmund 192
Rosten, Leo 28, 312, 353, 356, 416, 418, 484, 520, 540, 651
Rostow, Eugene V. 521
Roth, Henry 106, 540, 782
Rothschild family 655
Rothstein, Edward 518
Rouget de Lisle, Claude Joseph 469
Rough, Colonel 622
Rousseau, Jean-Jacques 12, 87, 97, 435, 455
Rowan, Andrew Summers 479
Rowe, Nicholas 289
Rowlands, John 213
Rowley, John 537
Rowley, Thomas 384
Roxana 15
Royall, Anne 378
Royce, Henry 619
Royer-Collard, Pierre Paul 213
Rubens, Pieter Paul 750
Rudbeck, Olaf 624
Rudofsky, Bernard 163
Ruggle, George 371
Rumford, Benjamin Thompson, Count 624
Rumph, Samuel 553
Rumsfeld, Donald 535
Runyon, Damon 106, 255, 360, 365, 606, 619, 746
Rupert, Prince 584
Rushdie, Salman 255
Rushmore, Charles 494
Ruskin, John 127
Russell, Benjamin 292
Russell, Charles T. 392
Russell, Geroge William. See AE
Russell, John 388
Russell, Lillian 206, 439
Russell, M. 440
Russell, W. H. 717
Russell, William 263
Russian words 626
Russo, Richard 471
Ruth (fictional character) 176
Ruth (Old Testament) 476
Ruth, George Herman "Babe" 18, 44, 50, 55, 78, 189, 361, 565, 642, 697
Rutherford, Ernest 290, 627
Ruxton, George 624

S
Sabah, Hassan ben 529
al-Sabah, Muhammed Salah al-Salem 500
Sabatini, Rafael 95
Sabin, Albert 633
Sacagawea 76
Sacher, Edward 629
Sacher-Masoch, Leopold von 471
Sacheverell, Henry 629
Sacheverell, Lucy 692
Safire, William 12, 44, 73, 163, 199, 216, 275, 293, 302, 336, 374, 409, 496, 585, 626, 714, 719
St. Ambrose 771
St. Anne 598
St. Anselm of Lucca 631
St. Anthony 487, 707
St. Athanasius 37, 264

St. Audrey 709
St. Augustine 303, 771
St. Barbara 631
St. Bartholomew 50, 55
St. Benedict 67
St. Bernard 451
St. Bernard de Menthon 451, 631
St. Bruno of Cologne 144
St. Catherine of Alexandria 138
St. Cecilia 587
St. Clare of Assisi 587
St. Columba 587
St. Crispin 184
St. Crispinian 184
St. Cuthbert 353
St. Cyril of Alexandria 367
St. David 198, 587
St. Diego 193
St. Dunstan 452
Sainte-Beuve, Charles-Augustin 385
St. Elizabeth of Hungary 267, 631
St. Erasmus 631
St. Expeditus 248
St. Fiacre 258, 788
St. Filbert 260
St. Francis de Sales 587
St. George 121, 576
St. Gregory the Great 301
St. Hilarion 383
St. Ignatius 631
St. Isadore of Seville 124
St. James 171
St. Jerome 218, 555
St. Joachim 216
St. John the Apostle 587
St. John the Baptist 245
St. John Bosco 587
St. John of the Cross 587
St. John the Evangelist 587
St. Lawrence 587
St. Marinus 635
St. Martha 469
St. Martin 470, 631–632
St. Martin of Tours 142–143
St. Nicholas 636
St. Pantaleone 546
St. Patrick 632, 651
St. Paul 194, 261, 487, 612, 618, 662, 695, 718
Saint Paul, Walter von 632
St. Peter 24, 549, 558, 618, 662
St. Philibert 260
St. Robert 343
St. Swithun 632, 767
St. Tammany 707
St. Thomas 221
St. Thomas Aquinas 26, 227, 718
St. Uncumber 632
St. Undecemilla 459
St. Valentine 749
St. Veronica 754
St. Vitus 632
St. Wilgefortes 632
Sale, Chick 149
Salinger, J. D. 352, 487
Salisbury, Countess of 87
Salisbury, James H. 632
Salk, Jonas 633
Salmacis (mythological figure) 344
Salmagundi, Madame 633
Salmon, Daniel Elmer 633
Samarski, M. von 634
Samos 436
Samoset (Pemaquid leader) 684
Samson (biblical figure) 203, 634
Samuel (biblical figure) 712, 762
Samuel (Old Testament) 3, 305, 393, 762, 784
Samuel, Marcus 653
Sancho Panza (fictional character) 187, 337, 601, 722. See also Cervantes, Miguel
Sand, George (Amandine-Aurore-Lucille Dupin, baronne Dudevant) 734
Sandburg, Carl 31, 246
Sanders, George 95
Sanderson, James 328

Sandwich, John Montagu, earl of 537, 635
Santa Ana, Antonio López de 636
Santa Claus 418, 636
Santayana, George 290
Sapphira (biblical figure) 24
Sappho (Greek poet) 434, 636, 712
Sardanapalus (Assyrian king) 636. See also Ashurbanipal
Sardou, Victor 256, 445, 637
Sasquatch (mythological figure) 73
Saturn (mythological figure) 637
Saul (king of Israel) 10, 60, 560, 762
Saunders, Sock (legendary figure) 673
Savage, Thomas S. 310
Sawyer, Mary 470
Sax, Antoine-Joseph 638
Say, Jean-Baptiste 639
Sayers, Henry J. 595
Scaliger, Joseph 401
Scandinavian words 639
Scanniello, Stephen 88, 795
The Scarlet Letter (Hawthorne) 1
Scarron, Paul 460
Schapp, Dick 281
Schele de Vere, Maximilian 49, 85, 459
Schelling, Friedrich von 32
Scherman, Harry 93
Scherwin von Krosigk, Count Lutz 381–382
Schiaparelli, Giovanni Virginio 469
Schick, Bela 640
Schicklgruber, Alois 280
Schiller, Johann Christoph Friedrich 640, 695
Schindler, Oskar 640
Schloyer, August Ludwig von 646
Schmeling, Max 397, 769
Schmidt, Mike 490
Schneider, C. V. 641
Schonbein, Christian Friedrich 541
Schouten, Captain 34
Schult, Minnie 385
Schultze, Norbert 439
Schumann, Karl 2–3
Schurz, Carl 538
Schwarzenegger, Arnold 335, 589
Scipio Africanus Major 423
Scipio Africanus Minor 423
Scopas 472
Scorraille de Roussilles, Marie-Angélique de. See Fontanges, Marie-Angélique de Scorraille de Rousilles, duchesse de
Scott, Catherine Dawn 555
Scott, Mary Relief Niles 467
Scott, Peter 445, 508
Scott, "Scotty" (fictional character) 59
Scott, Sir Walter 31, 33, 60, 140, 165, 233, 276, 317, 328, 347, 663, 741
Scott, Winfield 162, 281, 317, 337
Scotus, John Duns 227, 524
Scrooge (fictional character) 643, 665
Scudéry, Madeleine de 636
Scylla (mythological figure) 70
Seaborg, Glenn 188, 476
Seabury, George J. 51
Seaman, Elizabeth Cochrane 507
Seeder, James 156
Seeger, Pete 768
Segar, Elzie Crisler 308, 392
Selby, Harry 291
Selena (mythological figure) 717
Seleucus (Seleucid king) 422
Selfridge, H. Gordon 190
Selkirk, Alexander 221, 618
Sellers, Godfrey 713
Seneca (Roman orator) 295, 548, 589
Sequoyah (inventor of the Cherokee alphabet) 647
Sergius IV (duke of Naples) 516
Seth (biblical figure) 528
Settle, Elkanah 640
Seuss, Dr. 320, 507
Severn, Joseph 343
Severus Sammonicus, Quintus 3

Sewall, Samuel 118
Seward, William Henry 14, 382, 649
Sexby, Edward 411
Seybert, Adam 775
Shaddock, Captain 650
Shah, Zahis 238
Shah Jahan (emperor of India) 704
Shakespeare, William 10, 13, 18–19, 53, 54, 55, 61, 98, 146, 149, 160, 162, 168, 169, 190, 191, 206, 216, 232, 238, 243, 252, 256, 272, 293, 316, 331, 342, 348, 372, 381, 412, 422, 435, 436, 439, 442, 457, 465, 490, 491, 497, 499, 519, 521, 533, 571, 579, 589, 650, 678, 699, 746, 762, 776, 777, 782, 801
  All's Well That Ends Well 582
  Antony and Cleopatra 24, 75, 161, 211, 570, 632, 778
  Comedy of Errors 381
  Coriolanus 83, 303, 447, 553
  Cymbeline 108, 247
  Hamlet 8, 14, 89, 103, 127, 140, 147, 160, 241, 293, 330, 374, 417, 457, 479, 539, 622, 675, 729, 746
  Julius Caesar 384, 492, 501
  King Henry IV, Part I 24, 78, 211, 360, 462, 617, 767
  King Henry IV, Part II 354, 410, 462, 654, 729
  King Henry V 361
  King Henry VI, Part I 160, 507, 600
  King Henry VI, Part II 183, 691, 724
  King Henry VI, Part III 8
  King John 10, 19, 24, 273, 296, 360
  King Lear 156, 186, 202, 247, 266, 269, 270, 383, 555, 718, 768
  King Richard II 59, 343, 524
  King Richard III 19, 27, 92, 174
  Love's Labour's Lost 184, 354, 356, 600
  Macbeth 37, 46, 315, 416, 481
  Measure for Measure 237, 242
  The Merchant of Venice 318, 451, 534, 581
  The Merry Wives of Windsor 74, 360, 413, 783
  A Midsummer Night's Dream 54, 344, 453, 587, 733, 757
  Much Ado About Nothing 67, 169, 462, 495
  Othello 60, 241, 318, 483, 493, 574, 644, 731, 745, 766, 777
  The Rape of Lucrece 495
  Romeo and Juliet 19, 114, 374, 402, 567, 620
  The Taming of the Shrew 208, 410, 538, 659, 787
  The Tempest 126, 374, 561, 751, 793
  Titus Andronicus 451
  Troilus and Cressida 533, 545, 596, 733
  Twelfth Night 19, 101, 125, 391, 481, 720
  Two Gentlemen of Verona 310, 374, 450
  Venus and Adonis 495
  The Winter's Tale 63, 235, 248, 363, 643, 735
  As You Like It 18, 25, 588, 601, 609, 745
Shakespearean words 650–651
Shalmaneser (biblical figure) 586
Shank, Mr. 303
Sharkey, Jack 769
Sharp, Becky (fictional character) 90
Sharp, Zerna 645
Sharps repeater rifle 63
Shaw, Artie 452
Shaw, David T. 166
Shaw, George Bernard 170, 267, 304, 343, 511, 586, 637, 652, 696, 698, 752, 764, 776

Shaw, Henry Wheeler 400, 685
Shaw, Samuel 297
Shaw, Tom 626
Shawquaathquat 397. See also Josephy Pye
Shchastny, Aleksie 341
Sheba, queen of 468, 500
Sheckburgh, Dr. 792
Shelley, Mary 275–276
Shelley, Percy Bysshe 127, 160, 619, 734, 752
Shelumiel (biblical figure) 640
Shepard, Alan 28
Sheppard and Turpin 689
Sheraton, Thomas 653
Sheridan, Ann 535
Sheridan, Phil 533, 653
Sheridan, Richard Brinsley 19, 48, 199, 381, 427, 462, 523, 587, 758
Sherk, William 108
Sherman, John 257
Sherman, William Tecumseh 114, 353, 648, 653, 763
Sherrill, Patrick Henry 303
Sherwood, Robert 295, 336
Shi Huang Ti (emperor of China) 93
Shillaber, Benjamin Penhallow 654
Shillibeer, George 654
Shipley, Joseph T. 407, 524, 643
Shipton, Ursula 493
Shirley, James 423
Shirley, Robert 152
Sholes, Christopher Latham 738
Shore, Jane 657
Short, Charles W. 657
Shoumatoff, Alex 241
Shrapnel, Henry 658
Siddhartha 110
Sides, Hampton 140, 279
Sidney, Philip 69
Siegal, Ronald W. 788
Siegfried (mythological figure) 223, 660
Sikorsky, Igor I. 341
Silentiarius, Paulus 168
Silenus (mythological figure) 480
Silhouette, Étienne de 661
Silva, J Feigo da 257
Silver, Frank 795
Silverman, Sime 774
Silverstein, Phil 728
Simenon, Georges 370, 661
Simms, William Gilmore 157
Simon, André 457
Simon, Theodore 75
Simon Magus 661, 662
Simon Marius 380
Simons, Menno 23
Simpson, Bart (fictional character) 180
Simpson, Kirk 670
Simpson, O. J. 341, 511
Simpson, Wallis, Mrs. 778
Sims, Naomi 698
Sinatra, Frank 278, 349, 362, 607
Sinbad (fictional character) 529, 612
Sinclair, Upton 659
Sinhalese words 663
Sinning, Wilhelm 663
Siraj Uddaula 79
Sirens (mythological figures) 663
Sisyphus (mythological figure) 664
Sitting Bull 664
Sixtus II (pope) 430
Skeat, Walter William 295
Skeffington, William 640
Skelton, John 315, 349, 573, 755
Skelton, Red 219, 280
Skinner, B. F. 748
Sklodowska, Manya. See Curie, Marie
Skutnik, Lenny 666
Slade, J. A. 278
Slade, Larry (fictional character) 437
Slangeuberg, General 666
Slavic words 666
Slayback, Alonzo 588
Slick, Sam (fictional character) 187, 191, 256, 269, 426, 445, 577

Slipslop, Mrs. (fictional character) 668
Smith, Adam 421, 505
Smith, Alfred E. "Al" 90, 333, 377, 574, 625
Smith, Betty 732
Smith, Charles Murcott 536
Smith, Derek 346
Smith, Dick 207
Smith, Donald Alexander 554
Smith, George 446
Smith, Gerrit 84, 378
Smith, H. Allen 28, 741
Smith, Harvey 335
Smith, Helene Huntington 376
Smith, Hiram 337
Smith, Horace 243
Smith, J. L. B. 163
Smith, James L. 572
Smith, John 54, 110, 161, 390, 509, 570, 576, 670, 698, 727
Smith, Joseph 304, 490
Smith, Joshua T. 16
Smith, Kate 301
Smith, Logan Pearsall 99
Smith, Oliver Prince 613
Smith, Red 725
Smith, Richard Penn 207
Smith, Samuel Francis 23
Smith, Seba 182, 293, 669
Smith, Snuffy (fictional character) 89
Smith, Solomon Franklin 515
Smith, Sydney 177, 194, 654, 775
Smith, Thorne 390
Smith, Tim 243
Smith, William (publisher) 693
Smith, William "Bill" (antiques dealer) 75
Smith, Winchell 291
Smithee, Alan 13
Smithson, Hugh 670
Smithson, James 670
Smollett, Tobias 10, 12, 67, 198, 459, 460, 669, 682
Smuts, Jan C. 353
Smyth, William Henry 675
Sneer (fictional character) 587
Snerd, Mortimer (fictional character) 226
Snopes family (fictional character) 672, 762
Snow, C. P. 177
Snow, J. T. 519
Snurge, E. Maxwell 373
Sockalexis, Louis 159
Socrates (Greek philosopher) 178, 342, 378, 430, 568, 673, 752, 787
Sodom and Gomorrah 31
Soichirio Honda 355
Solomon (king of Israel) 10, 393, 468, 500, 674–675
Solon (Athenian ruler) 185, 223, 648, 675, 692
Solzhenitsyn, Aleksandr I. 341
Song of Solomon (Old Testament) 79, 168, 243, 385, 476, 501, 674, 736
Sophocles 205, 244, 317, 556
Sotades 544
Sothern, Georgia 233
Soubise, Charles de Rohan, prince de 676
Soukhanov, Anne H. 275, 303
Soule, John Babsone Lane 312
Sousa, John Philip 677
Southampton, earl of 381, 495
South Carolina 545
South Dakota 517
Southey, Robert 148
Southworth, E. D. E. N., Mrs. 53
Spalding, Alfred Goodwill 678
Spanish Inquisition 40
Spanish words 679
Sparkish (fictional character) 714
Spartacus 182
Spears, Britney 299
Spelvin, George 13, 291
Spencer, Christopher 680
Spencer, George John, earl 680
Spencer, Herbert 197, 680, 699

Spencer, Platt Rogers 680
Spencer, Thomas 747
Spenser, Edmund 19, 31, 101, 188, 216, 238, 243, 248, 355, 573, 756, 763
Spinetti, Giovanni 681
Spinola, Ambrogio 382
Spode, Josiah 682
Spooner, William Archibald 468, 683
SPQR (Senatus Populusque Romanus) 2
Spruijt, Jon 229
Squanto 176, 684
Squire, J. C. 344
Stafford, Thomas 639
Stagg, Amos 145, 274, 313, 363, 435, 563
Stahl, Abraham 793
Stair, earl of 189
Stakhanov, Aleksei 686
Stalin, Joseph 686
Stanberry, William 361
Standford, Leland 804
Standish, Miles 679
Stanislavski, Konstantin 687
Stanley, Alessandra 83
Stanley, Edward. See Derby, Edward Stanley, earl of
Stanley, Henry Morton 121, 213
Stapel, J. B. 687
Star Trek 59
Stassen, J. I. 72
Steele, Richard 71, 243, 342, 414, 485, 600
Steffe, William 58
Steffens, Lincoln 495
Stein, Gertrude 449, 590, 621
Steinbeck, John 314, 528, 585
Stelluti, Francisco 480
Stengel, Casey 130
Stentor (mythological figure) 689
Stepes, Marie 537
Stephanson, George 291
Sterling, E. H. 358
Stern, Philip Van Doren 27
Sterne, Laurence 161, 197, 303, 421, 669, 694
Sternhold, Thomas 498
Stetson, John Batterson 690
Stevens, Harry 360
Stevens, Thaddeus 316
Stevens, Wallace 375
Stevens, Walter B. 373
Stevenson, Adlai 235, 403
Stevenson, Robert Louis 78–79, 212, 322, 570, 660
Stewart, A. T. 778
Stewart, George 311, 459
Stillingfleet, Benjamin 87
Stimpson, George 431
Stoddard, R. H. 412
Stoeckl, Baron 14
Stoker, Bram 750
Stokes, William 147, 691
Stone, Judith 678
Stone, Lucy 453
Stone, Phil 513
Stone, Roy 623
Stone, Sid 372
Stormont, Lord 692
Stover, Russell 245
Stowe, Harriet Beecher 30, 54, 63, 322, 562, 646, 669, 743
Strachey, Lytton 171, 432
Stradivari, Antonio 692–693
Strang, Sammy 565
Stratton, Charles Sherwood 726
Strauss, Levi 435
Strauss, Phil 498
Straw, Jack 389
Streaham, William Milden, earl of 708
Strickler, George 273
Stricklett, Elmer 681
Stritch, Elaine 43
Strockbine, William A. 788
Stroganoff, Paul 63
Stuart, George R. 433
Stuart, Gilbert 292

Stubbs, John 302
Stutzman, Mark 797
suan pan 2
Subramanya (mythological figure) 464
Suckling, John 183
Suetonius 259, 372, 683, 753
Sulla (Lucius Cornelius Sulla; Roman dictator) 182, 621
Sullivan, Arthur 4, 296, 577, 633. *See also* Gilbert, William Schwenck
Sullivan, John L. 73, 212, 316, 448
Sumner, William G. 271
Sun Myung Moon 489
The Superfriends 114
Superman 405
The Supremes 493
Sutch, Screaming Lord 526
Sutoku 333
Sutton, Thomas 144
Swartwout, Samuel 699
Swedenborg, Emanuel 525, 752
Sweet, Henry 343
Swift, Jonathan 35, 51, 57, 60, 71, 73, 106, 169, 188, 190, 191, 194, 247, 248, 260, 316, 330, 338, 362, 381, 403, 409, 424, 439, 442, 443, 477, 485, 519, 526, 532, 534, 551, 607, 679, 695, 700, 701, 731, 737, 751, 791, 797
Swinburne, James 23, 103, 266, 445, 579
Swope, Herbert Bayard 535
Syme, James 623
Systematic Buzz Phrase Projector 120–121

T

Tabernaemontanus, J. T. 8
Tacitus (Roman historian) 173, 259, 758
Taft, William Howard 583, 623, 649
Taine, Hippolyte 630
Tallentyre, S. G. 370
Talmadge, Norma 315
Tamar (biblical figure) 531
Tamil words 462
Tammany Hall 96, 159, 456, 707
Tantalus (mythological figure) 707
Tappan, Austin 748
Tar (mythological figure) 708
Tarleton, Richard 14
Tasmania 30
Tattnall, Josiah 84
Taylor, Ann 475
Taylor, Deems 26
Taylor, John 699, 765, 794
Taylor, Tom 227
Taylor, William 209
Taylor, Zachary 298, 622, 757
Tearsheet, Doll (fictional character) 216
Teeter, Carl 136
Telegonus (mythological figure) 155–156
Telegue words 462
Telemachus (mythological figure) 477
Tell, William (legendary figure) 777
Tennessee 352, 712, 758
Tennyson, Alfred, Lord 9, 28, 45, 132, 185, 242, 489–490, 524, 540, 570, 572, 573, 604, 723, 749
Terence (Roman poet) 285, 318, 423
Tereus (mythological figure) 560
Terpsichore (mythological figure) 499
Tertullian (Roman writer) 177
Tetrazzini, Luisa 148–149
Thackeray, William Makepeace 90, 93, 120, 263, 456, 472, 477, 573, 665, 751, 779
Thais (Greek courtesan) 714
Thales (Greek philosopher and scientist) 648
Thalia (mythological figure) 499
Thanuz, Reflipe W. (fictional character) 610
Thatcher, Margaret 330, 526
Thayer, Ernest Laurence 135
Thayer, William Roscoe 439, 623
Theagenes of Thasos 142

Theimer, Walter 516
Theobald, Lewis 412
Theocritus 66
Theophrastus (Greek philosopher) 715
Theot, Catherine 716
Thersites (mythological figure) 716
Theseus (mythological figure) 10, 321, 501
Thespis (legendary figure) 716
Thessalonians 421
Thetis (mythological figure) 30
Thisbe (mythological figure) 496
Thomas, John 397
Thomas Aquinas. *See* St. Thomas Aquinas
Thompson, Benjamin (Count Rumford) 624
Thompson, Howard 362
Thompson, J. W. 521
Thompson, John T. 726
Thompson, S. G. 476
Thompson, William 67
Thoms, William John 269
Thomson, Bobby 658
Thomson, William (Baron Kelvin) 408, 479
Thor (mythological figure) 721
Thoreau, Henry David 205, 339, 471, 519
Thornbec, John 539
Thorpe, Thomas 495
Thoth (mythological figure) 344
Three Musketeers (fictional characters) 16
Throgmorton, Nicholas 719
Thucydides (Greek historian) 702
Thurber, James 47, 54, 116, 137, 384, 442, 568, 763
Thurber, John 133
Thutmos III (king of Egypt) 158
Tiberius (emperor of Rome) 174
Tierney, John 658
Tiffany, Charles Lewis 721
Tiffany, Louis Comfort 721
Tigranes (king of Armenia) 674
Tillands, Elias 679
Time magazine 94
Timothy (biblical figure) 261
Timothy (New Testament) 407, 487
Tindal, Matthew 770
Tinker, Joe 723
Tiro, Marcus Tullius 23, 723
Tisquantum 684
Titantic, R.M.S. 29
Titcomb, Timothy 507
Tithonus (mythological figure) 314
Titian (Tiziano Vicelli; Venetian painter) 233, 724
Tjton, William 370
Tittle, Y. A. 16
Titus (biblical figure) 261
Titus (Roman emperor) 372
Titzling, Otto 100
Tiw (mythological figure) 734
Tobit (Apocrypha) 724
Toch-a-way 533
Tocqueville, Alexis de 22
Tofana, Mrs. 6
Tolkein, J. R. R. 737
Tolstoy, Leo 752
Tomerlin, Oscar T. 492
Tonti, Lorenzo 727
Tonto (fictional character) 727
Tooke, Horne 335
Topham, Thomas 635
Topper, Cosmo (fictional character) 390
Topsy (fictional character) 322
Torquemada, Tomás de 729
Torrey, John 196
Touchstone (fictional character) 601
Toulouse-Lautrec, Henri de 151
Tournefort, J. P. de 73
Town-Mouse, Johnny (fictional character) 398
Townsend, Lyman A. 243–244
Toyotomi Hideyoshi 74
Tracy, Dick (fictional character) 94
Tracy, Margaret 45

Trampas (fictional character) 772
Trathal, king of Cael (mythological figure) 646
Trelawny, Edward 734
Trench, R. C. 731
Trevelyan, RC 427
Triana, Rodrigo de 166
Trimalchio (Roman merchant) 288
Triton (mythological figure) 507
Tritton, William 74
Trivegant (fictional character) 713
Troilus (mythological figure) 545
Trollope, Anthony 16, 164, 219, 459, 537
Trotsky, Leon 257, 415, 733
Troubridge, St. Vincent 382
Trovato, Ben 68
Trudgen, John Arthur 734
Truman, Harry S 44, 271, 284, 298, 335, 357, 371, 574, 575, 752
Trumbull, Jonathan 107
Trunnion, Howser (fictional character) 682
Tucker, Josiah 505
Tucker, Tommy (fictional character) 662
Tupper, Earl 735
Turing, Alan Mathison 735
Turner, Dick 710
Turner, William 735
Turpin, Dick 359, 736
Tutankhamen (king of Egypt) 413
Tutin, William 754
Tuttle, John Donald 95–96
Tutu, Desmond 506
Twain, Mark 20, 28, 29, 54–55, 140, 145, 236, 278, 295, 317, 329, 334, 340, 363, 380, 437, 451, 468, 509, 511, 525, 547, 549, 575, 576, 579, 583, 587, 612, 630, 635, 654, 656, 670, 676, 723, 729, 738–739, 765, 774, 775, 777, 797, 798
Tweed, William "Boss" 497, 707
Twiss, Richard 737
Tyler, John 351, 376, 407, 527, 552, 574, 738, 757
Tyler, Royall 432
Tyler, Wat 389
Tynan, Kenneth 526
Tyndale, William 106, 261, 695
Typhon (mythological figure) 739
Tyrwitt, Thomas 384
Tyson, Mike 588
Tzara, Tristan 193

U

Udall, John 528
Udall, Nicholas 461
Ulyanov, Vladimir Ilyich. See Lenin, Vladimir Ilyich
Ulysses (mythological figure). *See* Odysseus
Urania (mythological figure) 499
Uranus (mythological figure) 29, 747
Urban II (pope) 303
Urdang, Laurence 260
Uris, Leon 137
Urquhart, Thomas 348, 544
Ustad Isa (Persian architect) 704
Utah 56, 747

V

V-52 Stratofortress 110
Vainlove (fictional character) 667
Valdo, Peter 80
Valentine, Jimmy 395
Valentino, Rudolph 216, 273, 472, 652, 706, 749
Valerian (emperor of Rome) 430, 750
Valerianus 341
Valeria Messalina. *See* Messalina
Valerius Maximus 30
Valkyries (mythological figure) 750
Van Brugh, John 45
Van Buren, Martin 154, 376, 385, 407, 412, 519, 527, 573, 683
Vancouver, George 750

Vanderbilt, William Henry 587
Van der Buerse family 98
Van Dyck, Anthony 233, 750
Van Helmont, Jean Baptiste 288
Vanhomrigh, Esther 751
Van Laar, Pieter 50
Vanzetti, Bartolomeo 465
Vardon, Harry 751
Varenne, François Pierre de la 230
Vatel 208
Vaughan, Anna 699
Vaughan, Robert A. 173
Vaughn, Harry 371
Vaughn, Henry 699
Vecellio, Tiziano 724
Venables, Richard 454
Venus (mythological figure) 30, 67, 127, 133, 188, 244, 257, 501, 621, 695, 753
Verdi, Giuseppe 28, 754
Vergecie, Angelo 784
Verity, William S. 312
Vermont 319, 754
Vernier, Pierre 754
Vernon, Edward 321, 764
Verrazano, Giovanni da 363
Vertov, Dziga 155
Very, Edward Wilson 754
Vespasian (emperor of Rome) 487, 755
Vespucci, Amerigo 22
Victor Emmanuel II (king of Italy) 287, 754
Victoria (queen of England) 401, 473, 493, 584, 598, 656, 683, 755, 766, 768
Villon, François 795
Vincelli, Bernardo (Don) 68
Vincent, Jean Hyacinthe 104
Vincente (Don) 71
Vinot, Robert 638
Virgil 27, 58–59, 66, 141, 177, 191, 243, 317, 584, 664, 671, 699, 722, 733, 756
Virginia 528
Visconti, Bernabo 233
Vollet, Jacques de (legendary figure) 758
Volstead, Andrew Joseph 758
Volta, Count Alessandro Giuseppe Antonio 758
Voltaire (François-Marie Arouet) 11–12, 173–174, 213, 468, 506, 510, 557, 725
Vortumnus (mythological figure) 194, 576, 621
Voss, Johann Heinrich 779
Vowel, Dr. 759
Vreeland, Diana 62
Vulcan (mythological figure) 757

W

Wagner, Richard 752, 771
Wahunsonacock 572
Wait, Mary 393
Wait, Pearl B. 393
Waksman, Selman 27–28
Waldo, Peter 80, 758
Waldseemüller, Martin 22
Walker, Felix 115
Walker, John 356
Walker, Stanley 384
Wallace, De Witt 261
Waller, David 739
Waller, "Fats" (Thomas Wright) 532
Walles, Edmund 229
Walpole, Horace 77, 370, 414, 481, 506, 648, 688
Walpole, Robert 88, 110, 222, 247, 584
Walsh, Adam 273
Walsh, William 20
Walton, Izaak 254
Warburton, William 537
Ward, Aaron Montgomery 568
Ward, Arch 18
Ward, M. J. 671
Ware, Eugene F. 440

Ware, J. Redding 146
Warner, Jack 135
Warren, Barton 759
Warren, Earl 780
Warren, William, Jr. 528
Washington 247, 465
Washington, Charles "Chaz" 392
Washington, George 24, 107, 155, 186, 216, 240, 242, 255, 256, 263, 275, 291, 369, 445, 494, 583, 591, 608, 636, 707, 715, 757, 764, 784
Washington, Laurence 321
Wasserman, August von 765
Watch and Ward Society 52, 170
Waters, Muddy 619
Watson, Dr. John H. (fictional character) 615, 653
Watson, Thomas A. 495
Watson, Thomas J. 766
Watt, Alexander Pollock 11
Watt, James 359, 765
Watts, Isaac 304–305
Waugh, Evelyn 745
Wayne, John 46–47, 399, 772, 779
Weber, Eduard 766
Weber, Wilhelm Eduard 766
Webster, Daniel 78, 302, 716, 772
Webster, H. T. 482
Webster, John 766
Webster, Noah 66, 272, 766
Wedgwood, Josiah 525
Weekley, Ernest 21, 24, 27, 37, 61, 64, 76, 78, 149, 214, 283, 341, 346, 492, 557, 611, 758, 767
Weems, Mason L. 8, 166, 369, 374, 554, 727, 764
Weigel, C. E. 767
Weiss, Ehrich 361
Welch, Bob 768
Welch, Edward 333
Weller, Sam 28
Welles, Orson 532
Wellesley, Arthur 64, 768
Wellington, Arthur Wellesley, duke of 64, 359, 456, 519, 622, 768
Wells, Carolyn 83, 727
Wells, H. G. 37, 54, 249, 381, 747, 764
Wells, Madolin Johnson 307
Wen-Amon (mythological figure) 71
Wenberg, Benjamin J. 444–445
Wenham, Jane 780
Werner, Zacharias 353
Wernik, Robert 373
Wescott, Edward Noyes 304
Wesley, Charles 479, 775
Wesley, John 12, 157, 479, 752
Wesson, Daniel B. 243
West, Mae 167–168, 458, 554, 706
West, Nathaniel 484
West, Rebecca 23, 449
Weston, Colly 416
West Virginia 546, 769
Wham-O Manufacturing Company 278, 363
Wheeler, Edward L. 200

Wheeler, Elmer 633
Wheeler, John 79
Whewell, William 523, 641
Whistler, James 661
White, E. B. 382, 680–681
White, Elizabeth C. 85
White, George 294
White, Stuart Edward 745
Whitefield, George 479
Whitman, Walt 54, 269, 307, 505, 528, 774, 794
Whitney, Caspar 16
Whitney, Eli 241
Whittier, John Greenleaf 53, 78, 384, 415
Whittier, Pollyanna (fictional character) 575
Whittke, Carl 365
Whorf, Benjamin Lee 672
Wiel, Gustav 168
Wiggins, Kate Douglas 114
Wilberforce, Samuel 672–673
Wilce, John W. 378
Wilcox, Ella Wheeler 427, 767
Wilcox family 353
Wilde, Oscar 173, 275, 374, 388, 391, 425, 495, 500, 586, 636, 776
Wilder, Thornton 122, 361
Wilhelm I (emperor of Germany) 563
Wilhelm II (emperor of Germany) 364, 459
Wilkes, John 25, 327, 370
Willard, Jess 388, 410
William II (king of England) 643
William III (king of England) 408
William III (king of the Netherlands) 206
William IV (king of England) 597, 630
William the Conqueror (duke of Normandy; king of England) 233, 334, 447
William Rufus (king of England) 121–122
Williams, George 564
Williams, James, Mr. and Mrs. 557
Williams, Lloyd 205
Williams, Tennessee 72, 138
Williamson, Robert Logan 777
Willingham, Calder 311, 577
Willis, Bruce 333
Williston, George 723
Wills, Gary 578
Willson, Meredith 307
Wilmot, John 781
Wilmut, Ian 216
Wilson, Alexander 777
Wilson, Charles E. 293, 770
Wilson, John 698
Wilson, Robert (fictional character) 122
Wilson, Samuel 743
Wilson, Sloan 464
Wilson, W. G. 74
Wilson, Woodrow 242, 341, 364, 493, 509, 575, 739, 757, 764

Wimpy, J. Wellington (fictional character) 777
Winchell, Walter 106, 347, 462, 585
Winchester, Oliver E. 778
Winfrey, Oprah 536
Winner, Septimus 306
Winstanley, Robert and William 19
Winthrop, John 222
Wirt, William 299
Wisconsin 46
Wise, J. R. 650
Wiseman, Nicholas 174
Wistar, Caspar 359, 780
Wister, Owen 56, 626, 712, 772
Wiswell, E. H. 726
Witherspoon, John 22
Witthauer, Charles 36
Woden (mythological figure) 278, 767
Wolcot, John 320
Wolcott, Imogene 30, 483
Wolfe, James 792
Wolfe, Thomas 577
Wolfe, Tom 615
Wolff, J. F. 781
Wolkomir, Richard 429
Wolsey, Thomas, Cardinal 738
Wonder, Stevie 493
Wood, Alphonso 103
Wood, Laura 655
Wood, Robert 708
Woodfall, Henry 196
Woodward, Robert 202
Woodward, William 201
Woolf, Virginia 207, 409
Woollcott, Alexander 11, 15, 477
Woolley, Monty 315
Woolworth, Frank 138, 264
Wordsworth, William 193, 490, 499, 570, 750
Work, Henry Clay 313
World Trade Center 76, 240, 248, 321, 512, 595, 696, 737
Wotan (mythological figure) 278
Wouk, Herman 644
Wray, Fay 412
Wren, Christopher 465
Wright, Carroll Q. 660
Wright, Ernest Vincent 442
Wright, Orville and Wilbur 268
Wright, Thomas 47
Wrigley, William 712
Wriothesley, Henry 495
Wycherley, William 714
Wycliffe, John 121, 136, 263, 264, 339, 366, 376, 514, 585, 602, 618
Wyoming 785

X
Xanthippe (Socrates' wife) 787
Xanthus (mythological figure) 787
Xavier, Captain (fictional character) 528
Xenocrates (Greek philosopher) 788

Wimpy, J. Wellington (fictional character) 777
Xerxes (king of Persia) 260, 714, 788
Ximenès, Augustin-Louis, marquis de 14
Ximenes, Pedro 559
Ximenes, Peter 559
Xipe (mythological figure) 788
Xochitl (Aztec princess) 162

Y
Yair, Phinehas ben 157
Yale, Elihu 791
Yale, Linnus 791
Yapp, William 793
Yarborough, Charles Anderson Worsley, earl of 793
Yardley, Jim 556
Yates, Sarah and Adelaide 659
Yatimer, Marjorie Courtney 163
Yeager, Charles 456
Yeats, William Butler 234, 524, 713
Yegg, John 794
Yersin, Alexandre Emile Jean 795
Yiddish words 796
York, Frederick Augustus, duke of 592
York, James, duke of 413, 509, 510
Yorke, Alexander Granthan 766
Yorker, Gay 391
Young, B. M. 798
Young, Brigham 40, 204
Young, Edward 316
Yule, Sarah S. B. 112

Z
Zaluziansky von Zaluzian, Adam 801
Zamenhof, Lazarus 245
Zamzummins (biblical figures) 801
Zanelli, Antonio 801
Zangwill, Israel 476
Zelle, Margaretha Geertruida 471–472
Zénaïde, Princess (wife of Charles-Lucien Bonaparte) 91
Zenger, John Peter 560
Zeno of Citium 17, 77, 692
Zenodorus (sculptor) 508
Zephyrus (mythological figure) 366, 621, 801, 802
Zeppelin, Ferdinand von 802
Zespedes, V. M. de 434
Zeus (mythological figure) 33, 234, 244, 314, 458, 486, 499, 501, 559, 564, 585, 631, 707, 712, 744, 764
Ziegler, Ronald L. 561
Zilch, Mr. (fictional character) 803
Zimmerman, Charles A. 25
Zinn, Johann Gottfried 803
Zoilus (Greek philosopher) 804
Zois, Karl von 804
Zoroaster (Persian religious leader) 464
Zumwalt, Elmo 802
Zuppke, Bob 363
Zurishaddai (biblical figure) 640
Zwingli, Huldrych 804